NOBEL PRIZE WINNERS

Biographical Dictionaries from The H. W. Wilson Company

Greek and Latin Authors 800 B.C.–A.D. 1000
European Authors 1000–1900
British Authors Before 1800
British Authors of the Nineteenth Century
American Authors 1600–1900
Twentieth Century Authors
Twentieth Century Authors: First Supplement
World Authors 1950–1970
World Authors 1970–1975
World Authors 1975–1980

The Junior Book of Authors
More Junior Authors
Third Book of Junior Authors
Fourth Book of Junior Authors and Illustrators
Fifth Book of Junior Authors and Illustrators

Great Composers: 1300–1900
Composers Since 1900
Composers Since 1900: First Supplement
Musicians Since 1900
Popular American Composers
Popular American Composers: First Supplement
American Songwriters

World Artists 1950–1980

American Reformers

World Film Directors

NOBEL PRIZE WINNERS

An H. W. Wilson Biographical Dictionary

Editor

Tyler Wasson

Consultants

Gert H. Brieger, M.D.
William H. Welch Professor of the History of Medicine
The Johns Hopkins University School of Medicine

Erwin H. Hiebert
Professor of the History of Science
Harvard University

Martin J. Klein
Eugene Higgins Professor of the History of Physics
Yale University

Erik F. Lundberg
Professor Emeritus
Stockholm School of Economics

William McGuire
Former Editorial Manager, Bollingen Series
Bollingen Foundation and Princeton University Press

Alden Whitman
Former Chief Obituary Writer
New York Times

The H. W. Wilson Company
New York
1987

Library of Congress Cataloging-in-Publication Data

Nobel prize winners: an H. W. Wilson biographical dictionary / editor, Tyler Wasson: consultants, Gert H. Brieger . . . [et al.].
    p.   cm.
  "Editorial development and production by Visual Education Corporation, Princeton, N.J."—T.p. verso.
  ISBN 0-8242-0756-4
  1. Nobel prizes. 2. Biography—20th century—Dictionaries.
I. Wasson, Tyler. II. Brieger, Gert H. III. Visual Education Corporation.
AS911.N9N59 1987
001.4′4′0922—dc 19
[B]   87-16468
                                               CIP

Editorial development and production by
Visual Education Corporation, Princeton, N.J.

All photographs courtesy of the
Nobel Foundation unless otherwise noted.

PRINTED IN THE UNITED STATES OF AMERICA

CONTENTS

LIST OF NOBEL PRIZE WINNERS

LIST OF NOBEL PRIZE WINNERS

LIST OF NOBEL PRIZE WINNERS

LIST OF NOBEL PRIZE WINNERS

NOBEL PRIZE WINNERS BY PRIZE CATEGORY AND YEAR

Nobel Prize for Chemistry

1901	Jacobus van't Hoff
1902	Emil Fischer
1903	Svante Arrhenius
1904	William Ramsay
1905	Adolf von Baeyer
1906	Henri Moissan
1907	Eduard Buchner
1908	Ernest Rutherford
1909	Wilhelm Ostwald
1910	Otto Wallach
1911	Marie Curie
1912	Victor Grignard
	Paul Sabatier
1913	Alfred Werner
1914	Theodore W. Richards
1915	Richard Willstätter
1916	Not awarded
1917	Not awarded
1918	Fritz Haber
1919	Not awarded
1920	Walther Nernst
1921	Frederick Soddy
1922	Francis W. Aston
1923	Fritz Pregl
1924	Not awarded
1925	Richard Zsigmondy
1926	Teodor Svedberg
1927	Heinrich Wieland
1928	Adolf Windaus
1929	Hans von Euler-Chelpin
	Arthur Harden
1930	Hans Fischer
1931	Friedrich Bergius
	Carl Bosch
1932	Irving Langmuir
1933	Not awarded
1934	Harold C. Urey
1935	Frédéric Joliot
	Irène Joliot-Curie
1936	Peter Debye
1937	Walter N. Haworth
	Paul Karrer
1938	Richard Kuhn
1939	Adolf Butenandt
	Leopold Ružička
1940	Not awarded
1941	Not awarded
1942	Not awarded
1943	George de Hevesy
1944	Otto Hahn
1945	Artturi Virtanen
1946	John H. Northrop
	Wendell M. Stanley
	James B. Sumner
1947	Robert Robinson
1948	Arne Tiselius
1949	William F. Giauque
1950	Kurt Alder
	Otto Diels
1951	Edwin M. McMillan
	Glenn T. Seaborg
1952	Archer Martin
	Richard Synge
1953	Hermann Staudinger
1954	Linus C. Pauling
1955	Vincent du Vigneaud
1956	Cyril N. Hinshelwood
	Nikolay N. Semenov
1957	Alexander Todd
1958	Frederick Sanger
1959	Jaroslav Heyrovský
1960	Willard F. Libby
1961	Melvin Calvin
1962	John C. Kendrew
	Max Perutz
1963	Giulio Natta
	Karl Ziegler
1964	Dorothy C. Hodgkin
1965	R. B. Woodward
1966	Robert S. Mulliken
1967	Manfred Eigen
	Ronald Norrish
	George Porter
1968	Lars Onsager
1969	Derek Barton
	Odd Hassel
1970	Luis F. Leloir

NOBEL PRIZE WINNERS BY PRIZE CATEGORY AND YEAR

Nobel Prize for Chemistry

1971	Gerhard Herzberg
1972	Christian Anfinsen
	Stanford Moore
	William H. Stein
1973	Ernst Fischer
	Geoffrey Wilkinson
1974	Paul J. Flory
1975	John W. Cornforth
	Vladimir Prelog
1976	William N. Lipscomb
1977	Ilya Prigogine
1978	Peter D. Mitchell
1979	Herbert C. Brown
	Georg Wittig
1980	Paul Berg
	Walter Gilbert
	Frederick Sanger
1981	Kenichi Fukui
	Roald Hoffmann
1982	Aaron Klug
1983	Henry Taube
1984	R. Bruce Merrifield
1985	Herbert A. Hauptman
	Jerome Karle
1986	Dudley R. Herschbach
	Yuan T. Lee
	John C. Polanyi

Nobel Memorial Prize in Economic Sciences

1969	Ragnar Frisch
	Jan Tinbergen
1970	Paul Samuelson
1971	Simon Kuznets
1972	Kenneth Arrow
	John Hicks
1973	Wassily Leontief
1974	Friedrich A. von Hayek
	Gunnar Myrdal
1975	Leonid Kantorovich
	Tjalling C. Koopmans
1976	Milton Friedman
1977	James Meade
	Bertil Ohlin
1978	Herbert Simon
1979	W. Arthur Lewis
	Theodore Schultz
1980	Lawrence Klein
1981	James Tobin
1982	George Stigler
1983	Gerard Debreu
1984	Richard Stone
1985	Franco Modigliani
1986	James M. Buchanan

Nobel Prize for Literature

1901	René Sully-Prudhomme
1902	Theodor Mommsen
1903	Bjørnstjerne Bjørnson
1904	José Echegaray
	Frédéric Mistral
1905	Henryk Sienkiewicz
1906	Giosuè Carducci
1907	Rudyard Kipling
1908	Rudolf Eucken
1909	Selma Lagerlöf
1910	Paul Heyse
1911	Maurice Maeterlinck
1912	Gerhart Hauptmann
1913	Rabindranath Tagore
1914	Not awarded
1915	Romain Rolland
1916	Verner von Heidenstam
1917	Karl Gjellerup
	Henrik Pontoppidan
1918	Not awarded
1919	Carl Spitteler
1920	Knut Hamsun
1921	Anatole France
1922	Jacinto Benavente y Martinez
1923	William Butler Yeats
1924	Władyslaw Reymont
1925	George Bernard Shaw
1926	Grazia Deledda
1927	Henri Bergson
1928	Sigrid Undset
1929	Thomas Mann
1930	Sinclair Lewis
1931	Erik Karlfeldt
1932	John Galsworthy
1933	Ivan Bunin
1934	Luigi Pirandello
1935	Not awarded
1936	Eugene O'Neill
1937	Roger Martin du Gard
1938	Pearl S. Buck
1939	Frans Sillanpää
1940	Not awarded
1941	Not awarded
1942	Not awarded
1943	Not awarded
1944	Johannes Jensen
1945	Gabriela Mistral
1946	Hermann Hesse
1947	André Gide
1948	T. S. Eliot
1949	William Faulkner
1950	Bertrand Russell
1951	Pär Lagerkvist

1952	François Mauriac	1910	International Peace Bureau
1953	Winston Churchill	1911	Tobias Asser
1954	Ernest Hemingway		Alfred Fried
1955	Halldór Laxness	1912	Elihu Root
1956	Juan Jiménez	1913	Henri La Fontaine
1957	Albert Camus	1914	Not awarded
1958	Boris Pasternak	1915	Not awarded
1959	Salvatore Quasimodo	1916	Not awarded
1960	Saint-John Perse	1917	International Committee of the
1961	Ivo Andrić		Red Cross
1962	John Steinbeck	1918	Not awarded
1963	George Seferis	1919	Woodrow Wilson
1964	Jean-Paul Sartre	1920	Léon Bourgeois
1965	Mikhail Sholokhov	1921	Karl Branting
1966	S. Y. Agnon		Christian Lange
	Nelly Sachs	1922	Fridtjof Nansen
1967	Miguel Asturias	1923	Not awarded
1968	Yasunari Kawabata	1924	Not awarded
1969	Samuel Beckett	1925	J. Austen Chamberlain
1970	Aleksandr Solzhenitsyn		Charles Dawes
1971	Pablo Neruda	1926	Aristide Briand
1972	Heinrich Böll		Gustav Stresemann
1973	Patrick White	1927	Ferdinand Buisson
1974	Eyvind Johnson		Ludwig Quidde
	Harry Martinson	1928	Not awarded
1975	Eugenio Montale	1929	Frank Kellogg
1976	Saul Bellow	1930	Nathan Söderblom
1977	Vicente Aleixandre	1931	Jane Addams
1978	Isaac Bashevis Singer		Nicholas Murray Butler
1979	Odysseus Elytis	1932	Not awarded
1980	Czesław Miłosz	1933	Norman Angell
1981	Elias Canetti	1934	Arthur Henderson
1982	Gabriel García Márquez	1935	Carl von Ossietzky
1983	William Golding	1936	Carlos Saavedra Lamas
1984	Jaroslav Seifert	1937	Robert Cecil
1985	Claude Simon	1938	Nansen International Office for
1986	Wole Soyinka		Refugees
		1939	Not awarded
		1940	Not awarded
Nobel Prize for Peace		1941	Not awarded
1901	Henri Dunant	1942	Not awarded
	Frédéric Passy	1943	Not awarded
1902	Élie Ducommun	1944	International Committee of the
	Albert Gobat		Red Cross
1903	William Cremer	1945	Cordell Hull
1904	Institute of International Law	1946	Emily Greene Balch
1905	Bertha von Suttner		John Mott
1906	Theodore Roosevelt	1947	American Friends Service
1907	Ernesto Moneta		Committee
	Louis Renault		Friends Service Council
1908	Klas Arnoldson	1948	Not awarded
	Fredrik Bajer	1949	John Boyd Orr
1909	Auguste Beernaert	1950	Ralph Bunche
	Paul d'Estournelles de Constant	1951	Léon Jouhaux

NOBEL PRIZE WINNERS BY PRIZE CATEGORY AND YEAR

Nobel Prize for Peace

1952	Albert Schweitzer
1953	George C. Marshall
1954	Office of the United Nations High Commissioner for Refugees
1955	Not awarded
1956	Not awarded
1957	Lester Pearson
1958	Georges Pire
1959	Philip Noel-Baker
1960	Albert Luthuli
1961	Dag Hammarskjöld
1962	Linus C. Pauling
1963	International Committee of the Red Cross
	League of Red Cross Societies
1964	Martin Luther King Jr.
1965	United Nations Children's Fund
1966	Not awarded
1967	Not awarded
1968	René Cassin
1969	International Labour Organisation
1970	Norman Borlaug
1971	Willy Brandt
1972	Not awarded
1973	Henry Kissinger
	Le Duc Tho
1974	Sean MacBride
	Eisaku Sato
1975	Andrei Sakharov
1976	Mairead Corrigan
	Betty Williams
1977	Amnesty International
1978	Menachem Begin
	Anwar Sadat
1979	Mother Teresa
1980	Adolfo Pérez Esquivel
1981	Office of the United Nations High Commissioner for Refugees
1982	Alfonso García Robles
	Alva Myrdal
1983	Lech Wałesa
1984	Desmond Tutu
1985	International Physicians for the Prevention of Nuclear War
1986	Elie Wiesel

Nobel Prize for Physics

1901	Wilhelm Röntgen
1902	Hendrick Lorentz
	Pieter Zeeman
1903	Henri Becquerel
	Marie Curie
	Pierre Curie
1904	J. W. Strutt
1905	Philipp von Lenard
1906	J. J. Thomson
1907	Albert A. Michelson
1908	Gabriel Lippmann
1909	Ferdinand Braun
	Guglielmo Marconi
1910	Johannes van der Waals
1911	Wilhelm Wien
1912	Nils Dalén
1913	Heike Kamerlingh Onnes
1914	Max von Laue
1915	W. H. Bragg
	W. L. Bragg
1916	Not awarded
1917	Charles G. Barkla
1918	Max Planck
1919	Johannes Stark
1920	Charles Guillaume
1921	Albert Einstein
1922	Niels Bohr
1923	Robert A. Millikan
1924	Manne Siegbahn
1925	James Franck
	Gustav Hertz
1926	Jean Perrin
1927	Arthur H. Compton
	C. T. R. Wilson
1928	Owen W. Richardson
1929	Louis de Broglie
1930	Venkata Raman
1931	Not awarded
1932	Werner Heisenberg
1933	P. A. M. Dirac
	Erwin Schrödinger
1934	Not awarded
1935	James Chadwick
1936	Carl D. Anderson
	Victor F. Hess
1937	Clinton J. Davisson
	G. P. Thomson
1938	Enrico Fermi
1939	Ernest O. Lawrence
1940	Not awarded
1941	Not awarded
1942	Not awarded
1943	Otto Stern
1944	I. I. Rabi
1945	Wolfgang Pauli
1946	P. W. Bridgman
1947	Edward Appleton
1948	P. M. S. Blackett
1949	Hideki Yukawa
1950	Cecil F. Powell

1951	John Cockcroft		John H. Van Vleck
	Ernest Walton	1978	Pyotr Kapitza
1952	Felix Bloch		Arno A. Penzias
	Edward M. Purcell		Robert W. Wilson
1953	Frits Zernike	1979	Sheldon L. Glashow
1954	Max Born		Abdus Salam
	Walther Bothe		Steven Weinberg
1955	Polykarp Kusch	1980	James W. Cronin
	Willis E. Lamb Jr.		Val L. Fitch
1956	John Bardeen	1981	Nicolaas Bloembergen
	Walter H. Brattain		Arthur L. Schawlow
	William Shockley		Kai Siegbahn
1957	Tsung-Dao Lee	1982	Kenneth G. Wilson
	Chen Ning Yang	1983	Subrahmanyan Chandrasekhar
1958	Pavel Cherenkov		William A. Fowler
	Ilya Frank	1984	Simon van der Meer
	Igor Tamm		Carlo Rubbia
1959	Owen Chamberlain	1985	Klaus von Klitzing
	Emilio Segrè	1986	Gerd Binnig
1960	Donald A. Glaser		Heinrich Rohrer
1961	Robert Hofstadter		Ernst Ruska
	Rudolf L. Mössbauer		

Nobel Prize for Physiology or Medicine

1962	Lev Landau	1901	Emil von Behring
1963	J. Hans D. Jensen	1902	Ronald Ross
	Maria Goeppert Mayer	1903	Niels Finsen
	Eugene P. Wigner	1904	Ivan Pavlov
1964	Nikolai Basov	1905	Robert Koch
	Aleksandr Prokhorov	1906	Camillo Golgi
	Charles H. Townes		Santiago Ramón y Cajal
1965	Richard P. Feynman	1907	Charles Laveran
	Julian S. Schwinger	1908	Paul Ehrlich
	Sin-itiro Tomonaga		Ilya Metchnikoff
1966	Alfred Kastler	1909	Theodor Kocher
1967	Hans A. Bethe	1910	Albrecht Kossel
1968	Luis W. Alvarez	1911	Allvar Gullstrand
1969	Murray Gell-Mann	1912	Alexis Carrel
1970	Hannes Alfvén	1913	Charles Richet
	Louis Néel	1914	Robert Bárány
1971	Dennis Gabor	1915	Not awarded
1972	John Bardeen	1916	Not awarded
	Leon N Cooper	1917	Not awarded
	J. Robert Schrieffer	1918	Not awarded
1973	Leo Esaki	1919	Jules Bordet
	Ivar Giaever	1920	August Krogh
	Brian D. Josephson	1921	Not awarded
1974	Antony Hewish	1922	Archibald V. Hill
	Martin Ryle		Otto Meyerhof
1975	Aage Bohr	1923	Frederick G. Banting
	Ben R. Mottelson		John J. R. MacLeod
	James Rainwater	1924	Willem Einthoven
1976	Burton Richter	1925	Not awarded
	Samuel C. C. Ting	1926	Johannes Fibiger
1977	Philip W. Anderson	1927	Julius Wagner von Jauregg
	Nevill Mott		

NOBEL PRIZE WINNERS BY PRIZE CATEGORY AND YEAR

Nobel Prize for Physiology or Medicine

			Severo Ochoa
1928	Charles Nicolle	1960	Macfarlane Burnet
1929	Christiaan Eijkman		P. B. Medawar
	Frederick Gowland Hopkins	1961	Georg von Békésy
1930	Karl Landsteiner	1962	Francis Crick
1931	Otto Warburg		James D. Watson
1932	Edgar D. Adrian		Maurice H. F. Wilkins
	Charles S. Sherrington	1963	John C. Eccles
1933	Thomas Hunt Morgan		Alan Hodgkin
1934	George R. Minot		Andrew Huxley
	William P. Murphy	1964	Konrad Bloch
	George H. Whipple		Feodor Lynen
1935	Hans Spemann	1965	François Jacob
1936	Henry H. Dale		André Lwoff
	Otto Loewi		Jacques Monod
1937	Albert Szent-Györgyi	1966	Charles B. Huggins
1938	Corneille Heymans		Peyton Rous
1939	Gerhard Domagk	1967	Ragnar Granit
1940	Not awarded		H. Keffer Hartline
1941	Not awarded		George Wald
1942	Not awarded	1968	Robert W. Holley
1943	Henrik Dam		Har Gobind Khorana
	Edward A. Doisy		Marshall W. Nirenberg
1944	Joseph Erlanger	1969	Max Delbrück
	Herbert S. Gasser		Alfred Hershey
1945	Ernst B. Chain		Salvador Luria
	Alexander Fleming	1970	Julius Axelrod
	Howard W. Florey		Ulf von Euler
1946	Hermann J. Muller		Bernard Katz
1947	Carl F. Cori	1971	Earl W. Sutherland Jr.
	Gerty T. Cori	1972	Gerald M. Edelman
	Bernardo Houssay		Rodney R. Porter
1948	Paul Müller	1973	Karl von Frisch
1949	Walter R. Hess		Konrad Lorenz
	Egas Moniz		Niko Tinbergen
1950	Philip S. Hench	1974	Albert Claude
	Edward C. Kendall		Christian de Duve
	Tadeus Reichstein		George E. Palade
1951	Max Theiler	1975	David Baltimore
1952	Selman A. Waksman		Renato Dulbecco
1953	Hans Krebs		Howard M. Temin
	Fritz Lipmann	1976	Baruch S. Blumberg
1954	John F. Enders		D. Carleton Gajdusek
	Frederick C. Robbins	1977	Roger Guillemin
	Thomas H. Weller		Andrew V. Schalley
1955	Hugo Theorell		Rosalyn S. Yalow
1956	André Cournand	1978	Werner Arber
	Werner Forssmann		Daniel Nathans
	Dickinson W. Richards		Hamilton O. Smith
1957	Daniel Bovet	1979	Allan Cormack
1958	George W. Beadle		Godfrey Hounsfield
	Joshua Lederberg	1980	Baruj Benacerraf
	Edward L. Tatum		Jean Dausset
1959	Arthur Kornberg		George D. Snell

NOBEL PRIZE WINNERS BY PRIZE CATEGORY AND YEAR

1981 David H. Hubel
   Roger W. Sperry
   Torsten Wiesel

1982 Sune Bergström
   Bengt Samuelsson
   John R. Vane

1983 Barbara McClintock

1984 Niels K. Jerne
   Georges Köhler
   César Milstein

1985 Michael S. Brown
   Joseph L. Goldstein

1986 Stanley Cohen
   Rita Levi-Montalcini

CONTRIBUTORS TO *NOBEL PRIZE WINNERS*

Mark W. Andrews
Ruth Hogue Angeletti
Ken R. Arnold
I. Tipler Blount
Michael J. Boersma
David Marshall Borkenhagen, M.D.
Robert McAfee Brown
Deborah C. Brunton
Fred Cohn
David L. Cooke Jr.
Mary Ellen Curtin
Laura A. Curtis
Alice Delman
Patrick L. Doddy
Ron Doel
John Drexel
Judith Egan
Frederick H. Fellows
James R. Flemming
Gerald Friedman
Henry Louis Gates Jr.
Joan Stevenson Graf
Mary Lee Grisante
Joel D. Howell, M.D.
Eileen L. Hughes
Frank J. Ieva
Tony Kaye
Nelson R. Kellogg
Geraldine A. Kenney-Wallace
Lloyd E. King Jr., M.D.
Carol Krugman
George H. Kwei
Jeffrey D. LaPlante

Susan Dye Lee
Judith S. Levey
Robert J. Mackay
Phyllis Manner
Anthony Manousos
Joseph C. Marchese
Robert A. Margo
Margaret Marynowski
Dale McAdoo
Paula McGuire
Gregg D. Merksamer
David C. Michener
John R. Michener
Steven D. Mirsky
Peter J. T. Morris
Paul Mulshine
Frederik Nebeker
Steven O'Brien
Tom O'Grady
Donna J. Palomäki
Linda Pearlstein
Carol Potera
Karen Little Pressman
Richard E. Rice
Alan J. Rocke
Norman Rudnick
Henry F. Schaefer III
Philip L. Taylor
Genevieve Veith
Craig B. Waff
Robert F. Waterhouse
Michele Whitney

Preface

NOBEL PRIZE WINNERS is a biographical reference work containing profiles of all 566 men, women, and institutions that have received the Nobel Prize between 1901 and 1986. Intended for students and the general reader, it introduces the lives and achievements of the laureates, placing special emphasis on the body of work for which they were awarded the Nobel Prize.

The Nobel Prize owes its unique prestige in part to a rigorous and painstaking selection process, in part to the size of its monetary award, and not least to the character of the man who conceived and endowed it. In his introductory essay, "Alfred Nobel," Alden Whitman, author, journalist, and historian, sketches Nobel's early years, the rise of his vast industrial empire, and the diverse, often contradictory facets of his personality. The essay concludes by relating the singular circumstances in which Nobel dissolved his corporate holdings and, in an unwitnessed, handwritten document, bequeathed the bulk of his fortune to the prize that bears his name.

How Nobel's controversial will was executed through the establishment of an administrative foundation and three prize-awarding institutions is the subject of a second introductory article, "The Nobel Prizes and Nobel Institutions," by Carl Gustaf Bernhard, president emeritus of the Royal Swedish Academy of Sciences and a former professor at the Karolinska Institute. Dr. Bernhard, who also served on the Nobel committee for the physiology or medicine prize, describes the structure of the Nobel Foundation and the function of the organizations that nominate and select the laureates. He discusses the constraints Nobel placed on the awards as well as the controversies the prizes have provoked over the years. Together, these essays explain the origin of the Nobel Prize, the criteria governing the selection of laureates, and the significance of the awards.

The main body of *Nobel Prize Winners* is composed of the biographical profiles themselves, arranged alphabetically. Each sketch offers a narrative overview of a laureate's life and career, while focusing on the individual's prizewinning work and attempting to assess its significance.

Because this work is often highly technical in nature and has not always been discussed in detail in secondary sources, factual accuracy has been a particular concern. To assure both correctness and clarity, a board of expert advisers was assembled. The members of the board played a guiding role in the development of *Nobel Prize Winners* by reviewing each sketch and by offering their critiques, suggestions, and corrections.

The Advisory Board consisted of, for *physiology or medicine,* Gert H. Brieger, M.D., William H. Welch Professor of the History of Medicine at the Johns Hopkins University School of Medicine; for *chemistry,* Erwin N. Hiebert, professor of the history of science at Harvard University; for *physics,* Martin J. Klein, Eugene Higgins Professor of the History of Physics at Yale University; for *economics,* Erik F. Lundberg, professor emeritus, Stockholm School of Economics and former president of the Royal Swedish Academy of Sciences; for *literature,* William McGuire, former editorial manager, Bollingen Series, Bollingen Foundation and Princeton University Press; and for *peace,* Alden Whitman, journalist, historian, and former chief obituary writer for the *New York Times.*

Each laureate has been given a separate profile, even when a prize has been awarded jointly to two or three persons, as is often the case with the science prizes. Although this decision results in a certain amount of repetition in descriptions of joint work, it permits the reader to find in one place a unified account of an individual laureate's work. As leading members of the literary, scientific, and political community, the Nobel Prize winners shared in a wide network of mutual influence. To assist the reader in following these connections, the names

PREFACE

of other laureates appear in small-capital letters when first mentioned in a profile other than their own. This cross-referencing device encourages the reader to explore related profiles, thereby making it possible to trace developments in such fields as, for example, international arbitration, modern genetic theory, national income accounts, high-energy physics, and polymer chemistry.

Since it is not possible to portray the full scope of a person's life in an article some 1,500 words in length, readers may pursue their interest in greater depth by consulting the bibliographies that follow each profile. The bibliographies, which supplement titles cited in the sketches, are selective listings that include only works available in English. Works written by the subject appear chronologically by date of first publication in English; those about the subject are listed alphabetically by author or source.

In the text of sketches, foreign titles are followed in parentheses by both an English translation of the title and a date. The English translation appears in italics if the book has been published under that title; in quotation marks if it is a poem, story, or essay published under that title; and in roman type if the editors have supplied the translation. The date is that of first publication of the original work.

By consulting the finding tables on pages xiii–xix, the reader can locate subjects by prize category and by year of award.

The efforts of many people brought this book to fruition, above all, those of the contributors, most of them specialists in their fields, who are gratefully acknowledged on page xx.

Special thanks are owed to Stig Ramel, executive director of the Nobel Foundation, and to the members of his staff, especially Margaretha Ehrén and Birgitta Lemmel, for their generous assistance in providing information and photographs.

For their abundant contributions to research, both in the United States and abroad, the editor is indebted to the British Government Information Services, New York City; the Center for the History of Chemistry, Philadelphia, Pennsylvania; Larilyn Congdon, the Embassy of Sweden, Washington, D.C.; the German Information Center, New York City; Leon Gordenker; Eliane Hecht; Ilona Kasler; Angelika Kolb-Fichtler; Dimitri Nicolaidis; Scotia MacRae; and the staff of the Van Pelt Library, University of Pennsylvania.

The editor notes with special thanks the help of Yelena Bonner's son-in-law, Efrem Yankelevich, who was kind enough to review the profile of Andrei Sakharov and who corrected a number of errors and distortions while also providing valuable new information.

The editor is particularly grateful to his colleagues at Visual Education Corporation: Susan J. Garver, for copyediting; Marc Epstein, for coordinating research; Darryl Kestler and Paula McGuire, for translating foreign titles and source materials; Cindy Feldner and Sharon Lucas, for patiently typing and retyping the manuscript; Meredyth Carrick for her administrative support; John Drexel and Ann M. Harvey for their editorial contributions; Robin A. Buckingham for coordinating production; and Richard Lidz, William J. West, and Dale Anderson for their support and encouragement.

The editor extends his deepest appreciation to The H. W. Wilson Company, which commissioned this work, and to Bruce R. Carrick and Annemarie Erena for editorial suggestions that have been an indispensable source of guidance.

—Tyler Wasson
Princeton, N.J., 1987

ALFRED NOBEL
by Alden Whitman

Alfred Nobel, the Swedish chemical experimenter and businessman who invented dynamite and other explosive compounds and whose will established the prizes that have brought him lasting fame, was a person of many paradoxes and contradictions. His contemporaries in the last half of the nineteenth century often found him perplexing because he did not quite fit the mold of the successful capitalist of his expansionist era. For one thing, Nobel was fonder of seclusion and tranquility than of ostentation and urban life, although he lived in cities most of his life and traveled widely. Unlike many contemporary barons of business, Nobel was spartan in his habits; he neither smoked nor drank, and he eschewed cards and other games. While his heritage was Swedish, he was a cosmopolitan European, comfortable with the French, German, Russian, and English languages as well as with his native tongue. Despite the heavy demands of his business and industrial affairs, he managed to build a well-stocked library and was well acquainted with the works of such authors as Herbert Spencer, the British philosopher and exponent of social Darwinism; Voltaire; and Shakespeare. Of nineteenth-century men of letters, he most admired a number of French writers: the Romantic novelist and poet Victor Hugo; Guy de Maupassant, the short story craftsman; Honoré de Balzac, the novelist whose keen eye pierced the human comedy; and the poet Alphonse de Lamartine. He also liked to read the works of the Russian novelist Ivan Turgenev and the Norwegian playwright and poet Henrik Ibsen. The naturalism of the French novelist Émile Zola, however, left him cold. Above all, he loved the poetry of Percy Bysshe Shelley, whose works inspired in him an early resolve to embark on a literary career. To that end, he wrote a considerable number of plays, novels, and poems, only one of which was published. He then turned instead to a career in chemistry.

ALFRED NOBEL

Likewise puzzling to his fellow entrepreneurs was Nobel's reputation for holding advanced social views. The notion that he was a socialist was, in fact, quite undeserved, for he was actually an economic and political conservative who opposed suffrage for women and expressed grave doubts about democracy. Nevertheless, as much as Nobel lacked confidence in the political wisdom of the masses, he despised despotism. As an employer of many hundreds of workers, he took a paternalistic interest in their welfare, without wishing to establish any personal contact. Shrewdly, he realized that a work force with high morale is more productive than a crudely exploited one, which may well have been the basis for Nobel's reputation as a socialist.

Nobel was quite unassuming and even reticent about himself. He had few confidants and never kept a diary. Yet at dinner parties and among friends, he was an attentive listener, always courteous and considerate. The dinners given at his home in one of the most fashionable neighborhoods of Paris were convivial and elegant, for he was a well-informed host able to call upon a fund of small talk. He could strike off words of incisive wit when the occasion arose, for instance once remarking, "All Frenchmen are under the blissful impression that the *brain* is a French organ."

He was a person of medium height, dark and slender, with deep-set blue eyes and a bearded face. In the custom of the time, he wore a pair of pince-nez (for nearsightedness) attached to a black cord.

Largely because his health was not robust, Nobel was sometimes capricious, lonely, and depressed. He would work intensely; then, finding it difficult to relax, he would often travel in search of the curative powers of various spas, at that time a popular and accepted part of a healthy regimen. One of Nobel's favorites was the spa at Ischl, Austria, where he kept a small yacht on a nearby lake. He was also fond of Baden bei Wien, not far from Vienna, where he met Sophie Hess. At their introduction in 1876, she was twenty years old, petite, and good-looking; he was forty-three. There appears to be no doubt that Nobel fell in love with "Sophieschen," a clerk in a flower shop, for he took her to Paris with him and provided her with an apartment. The young woman called herself Madame Nobel, but with time she is said to have become financially demanding. The relationship ended around 1891, only a few years before Nobel's death.

Despite his physical frailty, Nobel was capable of bursts of concentrated work. He had an excellent scientific mind and loved to tackle problems in his chemistry laboratory. Nobel managed his decentralized industrial empire through the board of directors of his many companies, which operated independently of one another and in which Nobel typically owned a 20 to 30 percent interest. Despite his limited financial interest, Nobel personally oversaw many of the details of decision making in the companies that bore his name. According to one of his biographers, "Apart from his scientific and business activities, much of Nobel's time was taken up by voluminous correspondence and paperwork, every detail of which he coped with entirely alone, from duplicating to keeping his private accounts."

In early 1876 he attempted to engage a housekeeper and part-time secretary by advertising in an Austrian newspaper: "A wealthy and highly educated old gentleman living in Paris seeks to engage a mature lady with language proficiency as secretary and housekeeper." One respondent was thirty-three-year-old Bertha Kinsky, then working in Vienna as a governess. Daringly, she came to Paris for an interview and impressed Nobel by her personality and language fluency, but after a week or so, homesickness overtook her and she returned to Vienna to marry Baron Arthur von Suttner, the son of her former employer in Vienna. She and Nobel met again, and in his last ten years they corresponded about her projects for peace. Bertha von Suttner became a leading figure in the European peace movement and through her friendship with Nobel was able to gain from him substantial financial support for the cause. She received the 1905 Nobel Prize for Peace.

In his final three years, Nobel worked with a private assistant, Ragnar Sohlman, a Swedish chemist in his twenties and a person of great tact and patience. Sohlman functioned as both a secretary and a laboratory aide. Nobel liked and trusted the young man enough to name him chief executor of his will. "It was not always easy to be his assistant," Sohlman recalled. "He was exacting in demands, plainspoken, and always seemingly in a hurry. One had to be wide awake to follow his swiftly leaping thought and often amazing whims when he suddenly appeared and vanished as quickly."

During his lifetime, Nobel often exhibited uncommon generosity toward Sohlman and other employees. When the assistant got married, Nobel impulsively doubled his salary; and, earlier, when his French cook married, he gave her a gift of 40,000 francs, a large sum in those days. Nobel's generosity also often went beyond the realm of personal and professional contacts. For instance, although he was not a churchgoer, Nobel frequently gave money for the parish work of the Swedish church in Paris, whose pastor in the early 1890s was Nathan Söderblom, later the Lutheran archbishop of Sweden and the recipient of the 1930 Nobel Prize for Peace.

Although he was often called the Lord of Dynamite, Nobel strongly opposed the military uses to which his inventions were frequently put. "For my part," he said three years before his death, "I wish all guns with their belongings and everything could be sent to hell, which is the proper place for their exhibition and use." On another occasion, he stated that war was "the horror of horrors and the greatest of crimes" and added, "I should like to invent a substance or a machine with such terrible power of mass destruction that war would thereby be impossible forever."

Alfred Nobel's distinguished career is all the more remarkable considering his humble origins. The Nobel family came of peasant stock, emerging from obscurity with the surname of Nobelius only late in the seventeenth century. Alfred's grandfather, a barber-surgeon, shortened it to Nobel in 1775. His eldest son, Immanuel (1801–1872), was Alfred's father. Immanuel, an architect, builder, and inventor, had a precarious business life for several years until the family began to make its fortune in the oil fields of Baku, Russia. He married Caroline Andriette Ahlsell (1803–1879) in 1827; the couple had eight children, only three of whom survived to adulthood: Robert, Ludvig, and Alfred.

Born October 21, 1833, in Stockholm, Alfred Bernhard Nobel was the couple's fourth child. From his first days, he was weak and sickly, and his childhood was marked by chronic illness. Both as a young man and as an adult, Alfred enjoyed an especially close and warm relationship with his mother. No matter how busy he was as an older man, he managed a yearly visit and kept in frequent touch by letter.

After trying his hand at a business making elastic cloth, Immanuel fell on hard times and in 1837, leaving his family in Sweden, moved first to Finland and then to St. Petersburg (now Leningrad), where he manufactured powder-charged explosive mines, lathes, and machine tools. In October 1842, when Alfred was nine, he and the rest of the family joined his father in Russia, where his now prosperous family was able to engage private tutors for him. He proved to be a diligent pupil, apt and eager to learn, with a special interest in chemistry.

In 1850, when he was seventeen years old, Alfred took an extended trip, traveling in Europe, where he visited Germany, France, and Italy, and the United States. He pursued his chemical studies in Paris, and in the United States he met John Ericsson, the Swedish inventor of the caloric engine who later designed the ironclad warship, the *Monitor*.

Returning to St. Petersburg three years later, Nobel was employed in his father's growing business, by then called Fonderies & Ateliers Mécaniques Nobel & Fils (Founderies and Machine Shops of Nobel and Sons), which was producing material for the Crimean War (1853–1856). At the end of the war, the company shifted to the manufacture of machinery for steamboats plying the Volga River and the Caspian Sea. Its peacetime production, however, was not enough to offset the loss of military orders, and by 1858 the company fell into financial trouble. Alfred and his parents returned to Stockholm while Robert and Ludvig remained in Russia to salvage what they could. Back in Sweden, Alfred became engrossed in mechanical and chemical experiments, obtaining three patents. This work sharpened his interest in further experimentation, which he conducted in a small laboratory his father had established on his estate near the capital.

At that time, the only usable explosive for powder-charged mines—either for military or for peaceful uses—was black gunpowder. It was known, though, that the substance nitroglycerin was an extraordinarily powerful explosive compound, which posed extraordinary risks because of its volatility. No one had yet figured out how to control its detonation. After several small experiments with nitroglycerin, Immanuel Nobel sent Alfred to Paris in search of financing in

1861; he succeeded in raising a 100,000-franc loan. Despite some initial failures by Immanuel, Alfred became actively involved in the project. In 1863 he invented a practical detonator, which used gunpowder to set off the nitroglycerin. This invention was one of the primary foundations of his reputation and his fortune.

One of Nobel's biographers, Erik Bergengren, has described the device in this fashion:

> In its first form, . . . [the detonator] is so constructed that initiation of the liquid nitro-glycerin explosive charge, which is contained in a metal cap by itself or in a blocked-up borehole, is brought about by the explosion of a smaller charge let down into this, the smaller charge consisting of gunpowder in a wooden cap by itself, with a plug, into which a fuse has been inserted.
>
> In order to increase the effect, the inventor altered various details of this construction several times, and as a final improvement in 1865 he replaced the original cap with a metal cap charged with detonating mercury. . . . With the inventions of this so-called blasting cap, the Initial Ignition Principle was introduced into the technique of explosives, and this was fundamental to all later developments in this field. It was this principle which made possible the effective use of nitroglycerin and later other violent explosives as independent explosives; it also made it possible to study their explosive properties.

In the process of perfecting the invention, Immanuel Nobel's laboratory was blown up, an explosion that resulted in the loss of eight lives, including Immanuel's twenty-one-year-old son Emil. Shortly thereafter, the father suffered a stroke, and remained bedridden until his death eight years later in 1872.

Despite the setback caused by the explosion and the resulting public hostility to the manufacture and use of nitroglycerin, Nobel persevered, and in October 1864 he persuaded the Swedish State Railways to adopt his substance for the blasting of tunnels. In order to manufacture it, he won the financial backing of a Stockholm merchant; a company, Nitroglycerin, Ltd., was set up and a factory built in the Swedish countryside. In its first years, Nobel was the company's managing director, works' engineer, correspondent, advertising manager, and treasurer. He also traveled extensively to demonstrate his blasting procedure. Among the company's customers was the Central Pacific Railroad in the American West, which used Nobel's nitroglycerin in blasting the line's way through the Sierra Nevadas. After obtaining patents in other countries for his device, Nobel established the first of his foreign companies—Alfred Nobel & Co. in Hamburg—in 1865.

Although Nobel was able to solve the major problems of manufacture, his explosives were sometimes carelessly handled by their purchasers. There were accidental explosions and deaths and even a ban or two on imports. Nonetheless, Nobel continued to expand his business. He won a United States patent in 1866 and spent three months there raising money for his Hamburg plant and demonstrating his blasting oil. Nobel also decided to found an American company that, after some maneuvering, became the Atlantic Giant Powder Company; following Nobel's death, it was acquired by E. I. du Pont de Nemours and Company. The inventor felt badly treated by American businessmen who were eager to float shares in his blasting oil companies. "In the long run I found life in America anything but agreeable," he later wrote. "The exaggerated chase after money is a pedantry which spoils much of the pleasure of meeting people and destroys a sense of honor in favor of imagined needs."

Although blasting oil, correctly used, was an effective explosive, it was nevertheless so often involved in accidents (including one that leveled the Hamburg plant) that Nobel sought some way to stabilize nitroglycerin. He hit upon the idea of mixing the liquid nitroglycerin with a chemically inert and porous substance. His first practical choice was kieselguhr, a chalklike, absorbent material. Mixed with nitroglycerin, it could be fashioned into sticks and placed into boreholes. Patented in 1867, it was called "Dynamite, or Nobel's safety blasting powder."

The new explosive not only established Alfred Nobel's lasting fame, but it also found such spectacular uses as in the blasting of the Alpine tunnel on the St. Gotthard rail line, the removal of underwater rocks at Hell Gate in New York City's East River, the clearing of the Danube River at the Iron Gate, and the cutting of the Corinth Canal in Greece. Dynamite was also a factor in oil drilling in the Baku fields of Russia, an enterprise in which Nobel's two brothers were so active and became so wealthy that they were known as the Russian Rockefellers. Alfred was the largest single stockholder in his brothers' companies.

Although Nobel held patent rights to dynamite and its later refinements in all the world's major countries, in the 1870s he was constantly harassed by competitors who stole his processes. In these years he refused to hire a secretary or a full-time lawyer, and he was forced to spend much time in patent litigation as his factories steadily increased production.

In the 1870s and 1880s, Nobel expanded his network of factories into the chief European countries, either besting his rivals or forming cartels with them to control prices and markets. Eventually, he established a worldwide web of corporations for the manufacture and sale of his explosives, which, in addition to an improved dynamite, by then included a blasting gelatin. The military uses of these substances began in the Franco-Prussian War of 1870–1871, but during his lifetime, the investments Nobel made in military inventions lost considerable amounts of money. The profits from his industrial ventures came from the use of dynamite in the construction of tunnels, canals, railways, and roads.

Describing the consequences to Nobel of the discovery of dynamite, Bergengren has written:

Not a day passed without his having to face vital problems: the financing and formation of companies; the procuring of trustworthy partners and assistants for managerial posts, and suitable foremen and skilled laborers for a manufacturing process that was extremely sensitive and contained very dangerous ingredients; the erection of new buildings on remote sites, with intricate security measures in accordance with the differing laws of each country. The inventor took part eagerly in the planning and starting of a new project, but he seldom lent his personal assistance to the detailed working of the various companies.

The biographer characterized Nobel's life in the ten years after the invention of dynamite as "restless and nerve-racking." After his move from Hamburg to Paris in 1873, he was some-times able to escape to his private laboratories, one a part of his house. To help him there, he employed Georges D. Fehrenbach, a young French chemist, who remained with him for eight-een years.

Given a choice, Nobel would have preferred his laboratory to his business, but his companies always seemed to claim a priority as the trade in explosives increased and new factories were established to meet the demands. Indeed, at Nobel's death in 1896, some ninety-three factories were in operation producing 66,500 tons of explosives, including ammunition of all kinds as well as ballistite, a smokeless blasting powder that Nobel patented between 1887 and 1891. The new substance could be used as a substitute for black gunpowder and was relatively inexpensive to manufacture.

In marketing ballistite, Nobel sold his Italian patent to the government, an action that aroused the anger of the French. He was accused of stealing the idea for the substance from the French government's monopoly, and his laboratory was ransacked and shut down; his factory was also forbidden to make ballistite. Under these circumstances, in 1891, Nobel decided to close his

Paris home and to leave France for a new residence in San Remo on the Italian Riviera. Apart from the uproar over ballistite, Nobel's last Paris years were not totally happy; his mother died in 1889, a year following the death of his older brother Ludvig. Moreover, his French business associate had involved his enterprises in dubious speculations in connection with an unsuccessful venture to build a Panama canal.

At his San Remo villa, which was set in an orange grove overlooking the Mediterranean, Nobel built a small chemical laboratory, where he worked as time permitted. Among other things, he experimented in the production of synthetic rubber and silk. However much he liked San Remo for its climate, Nobel had warm thoughts of his homeland, and in 1894 he bought the Bofors ironworks in Värmland, where he fitted out a nearby manor house for private quarters and built a new laboratory. He spent the last two summers of his life at the Värmland manor house. During the second summer, his brother Robert died, and Nobel himself began to feel unwell.

Examined by specialists in Paris, he was warned that he had angina pectoris, a lack of oxygen supply to the heart, and was advised to rest. He then returned to San Remo, where he worked on a play he hoped to complete and where he drew up a remarkable will in his own hand. Shortly after midnight on December 10, 1896, he suffered a cerebral hemorrhage and died. Except for Italian servants who could not understand him, Nobel was alone at his death, and his final words went unrecorded.

The origins of Nobel's will, with its provisions for awards in a number of fields of human endeavor, are imprecise. The final document is a revision of earlier testaments. Its bequests for science and literature awards, it is generally agreed, are extensions of Nobel's lifelong concern with those fields—physics, physiology, chemistry, and the elevation of the art of writing. Evidence suggests that the award for peace may well have been the fruition of the inventor's long-standing aversion to violence. Early in 1886, for example, he told a British acquaintance that he had "a more and more earnest wish to see a rose red peace sprout in this explosive world."

As an inventor with a fertile imagination and as a businessman with a robust eagerness to exploit the industrial and commercial aspects of his brainchildren, Alfred Nobel was typical of his times. Paradoxically, he was a reclusive and lonely person whose worldly success failed to bring him the consolations of life for which he so avidly yearned.

THE NOBEL PRIZES AND NOBEL INSTITUTIONS
by Carl Gustaf Bernhard

Alfred Nobel died on December 10, 1896. In his remarkable will, written in Paris on November 27, 1895, Nobel stated:

The whole of my remaining realizable estate shall be dealt with in the following way:

The capital shall be invested by my executors in safe securities and shall constitute a fund, the interest on which shall be annually distributed in the form of prizes to those who, during the preceding year, shall have conferred the greatest benefit on mankind. The said interest shall be divided into five equal parts, which shall be apportioned as follows: one part to the person who shall have made the most important discovery or invention within the field of physics; one part to the person who shall have made the most important chemical discovery or improvement; one part to the person who shall have made the most important discovery within the domain of physiology or medicine; one part to the person who shall have produced in the field of literature the most outstanding work of an idealistic tendency; and one part to the person who shall have done the most or the best work for fraternity among nations, for the abolition or reduction of standing armies, and for the holding and promotion of peace congresses.

The prizes for physics and chemistry shall be awarded by the [Royal] Swedish Academy of Sciences; that for physiological or medical works by the Karolinska Institute in Stockholm; that for literature by the [Swedish] Academy in Stockholm; and that for champions of peace by a committee of five persons to be elected by the Norwegian Storting [Parliament]. It is my express wish that in awarding the prizes no consideration whatever shall be given to the nationality of the candidates, so that the most worthy shall receive the prize, whether he be a Scandinavian or not.

The invitation to assume the responsibility of selecting laureates was accepted by the awarding bodies designated in Nobel's will only after considerable discussion. Several members of these organizations were doubtful and, referring to the vague formulation of the will, claimed that it would be difficult to implement. In spite of these reservations, in 1900 the Nobel Foundation was established and statutes were worked out by a special committee on the basis of the will's stipulations.

The foundation, an independent, nongovernment organization has the responsibility of administering the funds in a manner "destined to safeguard the financial basis for the prizes, and for the activities associated with the selection of prizewinners." The foundation also protects the common interests of the prize-awarding institutions and represents the Nobel institutions externally. In this capacity the foundation arranges the annual Nobel Prize ceremonies on behalf of the awarding institutions. The Nobel Foundation itself is not involved in proposing candidates, in the evaluation process, or in the final selections. These functions are all performed independently by the prize-awarding assemblies. Today, the Nobel Foundation also administers the Nobel Symposia, which since 1966 have been supported mainly through grants to the foundation from the Bank of Sweden's Tercentenary Foundation.

The statutes for the Nobel Foundation and the special regulations of the awarding institutions were promulgated by the King in Council on June 29, 1900. The first Nobel Prizes were awarded on December 10, 1901. The political union between Norway and Sweden came to a peaceful end in 1905. As a result, the current special regulations for the body awarding the peace prize, the Norwegian Nobel Committee, are dated April 10, 1905.

THE NOBEL PRIZES AND NOBEL INSTITUTIONS

In 1968 the Bank of Sweden at its tercentenary made a donation for a prize in the economic sciences. After some hesitation, the Royal Swedish Academy of Sciences accepted the role of prize-awarding institution in this field, in accordance with the same rules and principles that apply to the original Nobel Prizes. This prize, which was established in memory of Alfred Nobel, is also awarded on December 10, following the presentation of the other Nobel Prizes. Officially known as the Prize in Economic Sciences in Memory of Alfred Nobel, it was awarded for the first time in 1969.

Today, the Nobel Prize—independent of the monetary award which at present exceeds 2 million Swedish kronor ($225,000)—is widely regarded as the highest recognition of intellect that can be bestowed on a man or woman. It is also one of the few prizes known by name to a great part of the nonscientific public, and probably the only prize about which almost every scientist knows. According to the statutes, the Nobel Prize cannot be given jointly to more than three persons. As a consequence, relatively few, however distinguished, can hope to receive the award.

The prestige of the Nobel Prizes depends on the serious work devoted to the selection of the prizewinners and on the effective mechanisms for this procedure, which were instituted from the very outset. It was felt desirable to obtain properly documented proposals from qualified experts in different countries, thereby also emphasizing the international character of the prizes.

For each prize there is a Nobel committee. The Royal Swedish Academy of Sciences appoints three committees, one each for physics, chemistry, and the economic sciences. The Karolinska Institute names a committee for physiology or medicine, and the Swedish Academy chooses a committee for literature. In addition, the Norwegian Parliament, the Storting, appoints a peace prize committee. The Nobel committees play a central role in the selection process. Each consists of five members but may also request temporary assistance from additional specialists in relevant fields.

Nominations of candidates for the prizes can be made only upon invitation, and these invitations are distributed in the fall of the year preceding the award. The recipients are invited to submit a written proposal stating the reasons for their choice. For each prize, more than 1,000 individuals in different parts of the world are invited to submit nominations. Invitations for the science prizes are sent out to active scholars at universities and research institutions. For the literature prize, submissions are invited from academic representatives in the fields of literature and languages as well as from members of distinguished academies and societies of the same character as the Swedish Academy. In order to obtain proposals for the peace prize, representatives from the fields of philosophy, history, and the legal and political sciences, as well as those active in various peace activities, are contacted. Some individuals always receive invitations to submit nominations; among them are previous Nobel laureates and members of the Royal Swedish Academy of Sciences, the Nobel Assembly of the Karolinska Institute, and the Swedish Academy, as well as permanent and active professors in the respective fields from all the Scandinavian countries. Invitations to propose names are confidential, as are the nominations.

Nominations must be received by February 1 of the award year. At that date, the work of the Nobel committees begins, and from then until September committee members and consultants evaluate the qualifications of the nominees. Committees meet several times, with proposals assigned to different committee members as well as to outside experts, all of whom attempt to determine the originality and significance of the nominee's contributions. Several committee members or outside experts may report on various aspects of a single proposal. Every year several thousand persons are involved in the preparatory work. After this work is completed, the committees submit their secret reports and recommendations to the respective prize-awarding bodies, which have the sole right to make the final decisions.

By September or the beginning of October, the Nobel committees are ready with their work. In physics, chemistry, and the economic sciences, they submit their reports to the respective "classes" of the Royal Swedish Academy of Sciences, each of which has about twenty-five members. The classes then send their recommendations to the academy for the final decision. The procedure for the prize in physiology or medicine is similar, except that the recommendation of the Nobel committee goes directly to the fifty-member Nobel Assembly of the Karolinska Institute. In deciding the literature prize, the eighteen members of the Swedish Academy make the decision on the basis of the proposal from the Nobel committee. The decision for the peace prize is made by the Norwegian Nobel Committee itself.

In October, final votes are cast in the various assemblies. The laureates are immediately notified of the decisions, which are then announced internationally at a press conference held in Stockholm and attended by representatives of the international news media. The messages contain the names of the laureates and a short statement describing the reasons for the awards. At this occasion, specialists in the various fields are also present to give a more comprehensive explanation of the winners' achievements and their significance.

Subsequently, the Nobel Foundation invites the laureates and their families to the Nobel ceremonies held in Stockholm and Oslo on December 10. In Stockholm the prize ceremony takes place in the Concert Hall and is attended by about 1,200 persons. The prizes in physics, chemistry, physiology or medicine, literature, and the economic sciences are presented by the King of Sweden following a short résumé of the laureates' achievements presented by representatives of the prize-awarding assemblies. The celebration continues at a foundation banquet in the Town Hall.

In Oslo the peace prize ceremony takes place in the Assembly Hall of the University of Oslo in the presence of the King of Norway and the royal family. The laureate receives the prize from the chairman of the Norwegian Nobel Committee. In connection with the ceremonies in Stockholm and Oslo, the laureates present their Nobel lectures, which are later published in the volume *Les Prix Nobel*.

Obviously, a considerable amount of work is devoted to the sifting process by which laureates are selected. In the sciences, the distribution of more than 1,000 invitations for each prize results in 200 to 250 nominations. Since the same scientists are often proposed by several nominators, the number of actual candidates is somewhat less. In literature the Swedish Academy makes the choice from 100 to 150 candidates. Generally, most of the strong candidates are proposed over several years, and very rarely is a laureate selected after having been proposed only once.

The Nobel selections have often been criticized in the international press, as has the secrecy of the selection procedure. As to the complaints about the secrecy, suffice it to say that the statutes mandate that the deliberations, opinions, and proposals of the Nobel committees in connection with the awarding of prizes may not be made public or otherwise revealed. They direct that no protest shall be laid against the award of an adjudicating body and that if conflicts of opinion have arisen, they shall not be recorded in the minutes or otherwise revealed.

As to the singularity of the prizes, it is certainly true that there are many more worthy candidates than prizes. The 1948 Swedish Nobel laureate in chemistry, Arne Tiselius, who served as chairman of the Nobel Foundation for several years, described the situation in the following way: "You cannot in practice apply the principle that the Nobel Prize should be given to the person who is best; you cannot define who is best. Therefore, you are left with the only alternative: to try to find a particularly worthy candidate."

THE NOBEL PRIZES AND NOBEL INSTITUTIONS

Naturally, the handling of the prizes is based on the principles delineated in the will of Alfred Nobel. In physics, chemistry, and physiology or medicine, the will speaks of an important discovery, improvement, or invention within these fields. Thus, the science prizes are awarded not for the work of a lifetime, but for a specific achievement or a particular discovery. As an experimenter and inventor, Nobel knew very well what a discovery was. Concepts are extremely useful, but concepts change; what remains are the experimental facts—the discoveries. The contributions of some scientists may be of great importance in the development of their fields, but they may not fulfill the specific requirements stipulated by the Nobel Prize rules.

The performance of scientific work and the conditions under which scientists now labor are quite different from those in effect during Alfred Nobel's lifetime, a fact that complicates the selection of laureates. Today, teamwork is common and often results in significant discoveries. The prizes, however, are meant for individuals and not for large groups. This contemporary situation has resulted in a dilemma with which the prize-awarding juries have had to deal in their efforts to fulfill Nobel's intentions.

In his will, Nobel declares that "an idealistic tendency" should be an essential qualification for the prize in literature. This vague expression has caused endless arguments. In *Nobel, The Man and His Prizes* (1962), Anders Österling, a past secretary of the Swedish Academy, writes: "What he really meant by this term was probably works of a humanitarian and constructive character which, like scientific discoveries, could be regarded as of benefit to mankind." Today the Swedish Academy by and large refrains from trying to find guidance from this expression.

To appraise achievements in widely different fields with reference to the phrase "for the benefit of mankind" is, of course, extremely difficult. A glance at the lengthy list of Nobel Prize winners in all fields shows, however, that serious efforts have been made to pay respect to a great variety of claims. For instance, the science prizes have been given for discoveries in pure sciences as well as for advances in applied fields. Lars Gyllensten, a former secretary of the Swedish Academy, has noted, "One has to adopt some sort of pragmatic procedure and take into consideration the basic view in Alfred Nobel's will to promote science and poetry and to distribute prizes in an international perspective to the benefit of mankind, not to distribute empty status awards."

At an early point, it became clear that the stipulation that the prizes be awarded for literary or scientific achievements made during the preceding year could not be observed in practice while at the same time maintaining a high standard. To resolve this difficulty, the following rule was inserted in the regulations: "The provision in the will that the annual award of prizes shall refer to works during the preceding year shall be understood in the sense that the award shall be made for the most recent achievements and for older works only if their significance has not become apparent until recently." The discovery of penicillin, for instance, took place in 1928, but the prize was not given until 1945 when the drug's value had been established by practical use. Likewise, the importance of literary contributions may not be fully appreciated until they can be seen in the context of an entire body of work. Therefore, many laureates in literature have received their prizes late in their careers.

That the choice of laureates for the peace and literature prizes often arouses controversy is self-evident; that there are some unfortunate mistakes in the list of the science prizes must also be admitted. These circumstances reflect the difficulties that the prize juries encounter. It is, however, surprising that criticism is so relatively scarce in the extensive literature that has been written about the Nobel Prizes and the Nobel work.

Very often the Nobel Foundation is criticized for not awarding prizes in other fields. The reason is simply that it was Nobel's wish that only the five specific areas he designated be taken into account. The single exception is the Nobel Prize in Economic Sciences, also administered by the foundation. Nonetheless, contemporary juries are in fact acting within successively widening frameworks. In 1973, for instance, the medicine prize was given to three ethologists for their discoveries concerning organization and elicitation of individual and social behavior patterns, and in 1974 pioneering research in radio astrophysics was honored. The physics prize in 1978, given for the discovery of cosmic microwave background radiation, also provides an example of the increasingly liberal interpretation of the prize field.

For twenty-five years, while a professor of physiology at the Karolinska Institute, I served as a member and chairman of its Nobel committee. Subsequently, as president and later secretary-general of the Royal Swedish Academy of Sciences, I also had the pleasure of taking part in the Nobel work in physics, chemistry, and the economic sciences for ten years. During this thirty-five-year period, I saw firsthand the diligence with which the members of the science prize juries fulfilled their delicate mission and witnessed the painstaking work of the specialists in various fields when adjudicating the prize proposals.

While engaged in work relating to the Nobel Prizes, I was often asked by representatives of organizations around the world to discuss the Nobel selection process when some new international prize was going to be created. I usually gave three pieces of advice. First, define the topics carefully so that a proper assessment can be made. We know how extremely difficult it is to make a selection, even in a "hard science" like physics. Second, allow enough time for the selection process. Third, ask for sufficient funds to cover the costs of the selection process, one which may involve a great many specialists and consist of several steps. Actually, the magnitude of the costs of selecting the Nobel laureates and of organizing and conducting the prize ceremonies is more or less the same as that of the Nobel Prizes themselves.

The Nobel Prizes are unique and carry with them considerable prestige. It is frequently wondered why the prizes attract more attention than any other twentieth-century award. One reason may be that they were created at the right time and that they epitomize some of the principal historical transformations of the age. Alfred Nobel was a true internationalist, and from the very beginning, the international character of the prizes made an important impression on society. The strict rules of the selection process, which were implemented from the outset, have also been crucial in establishing the importance of the awards. As soon as the prizes are awarded in December, the task of selecting of the next year's Nobel laureates begin. This year-round activity, in which so many of the world's intellectuals are engaged, plays a decisive role in directing the interest of society to the importance of the work that is proceeding in the various fields covered by the prizes, for "the benefit of mankind."

KEY TO PRONUNCIATION

ā	āle	ō	ōld	ü	Pronounced approximately as ē, with rounded lips: French u, as in *vu* (vü); German ü, as in *Gefühl* (gə fül′)
â	câre	ô	ôrb		
a	add	o	odd		
ä	ärm	oi	oil		
		o͞o	o͞oze		
ē	ēve	o͝o	fo͝ot		
e	end	ou	out	ə	the schwa, an unstressed vowel representing the sound that is spelled
g	go				
		th	*th*en		a as in sofa
ī	īce	th	thin		e as in fitted
i	ill				i as in edible
		ū	cūbe		o as in melon
ʀ	German ch as in *ich* (iʀ)	û	ûrn; French eu, as in *jeu* (zhû), German ö, oe, as in *schön* (shûn), *Goethe* (gû′tə)		u as in circus
				zh	azure
ɴ	Not pronounced, but indicates the nasal tone of the preceding vowel, as in the French *bon* (bôɴ)	u	tub	′	= main accent

ADDAMS, JANE

(September 6, 1860–May 21, 1935)
Nobel Prize for Peace, 1931
(shared with Nicholas Murray Butler)

Laura Jane Addams, pioneer American social reformer, peace activist, and founder of Hull House, was born in Cedarville, Illinois, the eighth of nine children. Her parents—John Huy Addams, a prosperous banker, Republican state senator, and ardent abolitionist, and the former Sarah Weber—were of English and German descent. When Addams was two years old, her mother died. A somewhat withdrawn and shy child, she became deeply attached to her broad-minded Quaker father, who remained her principal role model throughout her life.

In 1877 Addams entered the Rockford Female Seminary, an institution that trained women for missionary work. She graduated valedictorian of her class of seventeen in 1881 and received her B.A. when Rockford became a degree-granting institution a year later. Choosing not to pursue missionary work, Addams entered the Women's Medical College in Philadelphia in the fall of 1881, but poor health forced her to withdraw after only a few months. The death of her father that same year triggered a depression that lasted eight years, a period marked by illness, unhappiness, and uncertainty about her future.

In 1883 Addams and a friend, Ellen Gates Starr, toured Europe. They visited Toynbee Hall, a settlement house in London's destitute East End, run by a group of Oxford University students. Moved by this work, Addams and Starr returned to the United States determined to find a house in the slums where they "might learn of life from life itself." Their search led to Chicago's Nineteenth Ward, a poor district populated by a variety of immigrant groups. In September 1889 the two women moved into the decaying Charles Hull mansion and began an experiment in settlement work that was to attract some of the ablest reformers of the Progressive Era.

Within a few years, Hull House was serving a wide range of community needs. It included a day nursery, bookbindery, library, gymnasium, community kitchen, art studio, labor museum, and cooperative boarding house for young working women. There were dozens of clubs—an art group, a music school, even a troupe of actors. Newcomers could study English or take classes in cooking, sewing, or literature. Thousands of slum-dwellers, from James Petrillo to Benny Goodman, crossed its

JANE ADDAMS

threshold. With financial assistance from wealthy Chicago philanthropists, Hull House grew to include thirteen buildings devoted to the educational, social, and recreational needs of the working class.

Nevertheless, Addams's political efforts to improve social conditions in the neighborhood sometimes alienated contributors and cost Hull House financial support. The institution lobbied successfully for passage of Illinois's first factory inspection act in 1893, and two years later it published *Hull-House, Maps and Papers,* a path-breaking sociological survey of sweatshops, tenement housing, and other harsh conditions in the Nineteenth Ward. That summer, after residents complained about inadequate trash collection, Addams got herself appointed garbage inspector for the ward and rose each morning at dawn to make sure the job was done. Pressure from Hull House helped establish the nation's first juvenile court in 1889. Moreover, Addams used her influence to support child labor laws, legislation protecting female factory workers, compulsory school attendance, and industrial safety regulations. Assisted by educated women like herself, she became practiced in lobbying, collecting evidence, marshaling statistics, and mobilizing public support.

Believing that the "moral energy of women" should be expressed through the vote, Addams participated in the Chicago suffrage campaign of 1907, served as vice president of the National American Woman Suffrage Association from 1911 to 1914, and attended the International Woman Suffrage Alliance in Bu-

1

dapest. Her rationale for suffrage stemmed from her belief that women by nature possessed special civilizing qualities that were needed in the civic realm. If women were given the vote, Addams felt, they would be able to attack social problems more effectively. At the 1912 Progressive party convention, she seconded the nomination of THEODORE ROOSEVELT and campaigned actively for his election.

The outbreak of World War I drew Addams actively into the peace movement. In January 1915 she was elected chairwoman of the newly formed Woman's Peace party. Several months later, she attended the International Congress of Women at The Hague with EMILY GREENE BALCH and others. Addams was elected president of the congress. Among the group's efforts was the unsuccessful attempt to persuade neutral nations to mediate a truce between the belligerents in the war.

When the United States entered the war in 1917, Addams did not modify her pacifist stance. She opposed the draft and defended German immigrants who were persecuted for their nationality during the war hysteria. Few colleagues shared her position. The press vilified her; Roosevelt called her a Bull Mouse; and the Department of Justice kept her under surveillance. Undaunted, she worked with Herbert Hoover's Food Administration to feed "enemy women and children." In 1920 she became a founding member of the American Civil Liberties Union. Called subversive and a traitor, she was expelled from the Daughters of the American Revolution for alleged Communist views.

Addams's dedication to peace did not end with the European armistice. In 1919 she was elected president of the Women's International League for Peace and Freedom, an outgrowth of the congress held in The Hague five years earlier. The league stood for "the solution of conflicts by the recognition of human solidarity, by conciliation and arbitration, by world cooperation, and by the establishment of social, political, and economic justice for all, without distinction of sex, race, class, or creed."

Addams believed that Mohandas Gandhi's practice of passive resistance could not by itself ensure peace: peace could be preserved only if organizations put pressure on governments. Under her direction, the Women's International League sought to eliminate the causes of war by supporting revision of peace treaties, elimination of conscription, worldwide disarmament, and an end to war reparations. With Emily Greene Balch, the league's

secretary-treasurer, Addams attempted to influence the development of the League of Nations, urging that it be made more democratic through recognition of minority rights. Ill health forced her to resign from the league in 1929.

In 1931, after repeated nominations, Addams became the first American woman to be awarded the Nobel Prize for Peace, as "the right spokesman for all the peace-loving women of the world." She shared the prize with NICHOLAS MURRAY BUTLER. Because of continued ill health, Addams could not attend the award ceremonies.

Privately, Addams lived in a world of women. Unable to have children because of spinal surgery, she resisted a match with a stepbrother and never married. Her acquaintances found Addams warm and sympathetic but also impersonal and aloof, yet she enjoyed deep and abiding friendships with Ellen Gates Starr and Mary Rozet Smith. Near the end of her life, Addams made her home with Smith rather than at Hull House. She died of cancer on May 21, 1935, and is buried in a small cemetery in Cedarville.

Addams's humanitarian efforts were wideranging and enduring. Her work at Hull House not only alleviated immigrant alienation and poverty but also furnished an example for settlement workers elsewhere. Through her efforts to improve urban social conditions, she created the profession of social worker. In her efforts to eradicate war, she remained a pacifist despite strong pressure to join the supporters of World War I. In a climate of war hysteria and red-baiting, she stood resolutely for the protection of individual civil liberties. At the international level, she sought to influence government leaders on behalf of mediation and disarmament.

For Jane Addams, peace was not simply the absence of war but the "nurturing of human life." Women, with their special sensibilities, she believed, were ideally suited to this nurturing. Addams cared deeply about women's "long historical role of ministration to basic human needs," and by acting in this role, she made enduring contributions to America's reform tradition.

SELECTED WORKS: Democracy and Social Ethics, 1902; Newer Ideals of Peace, 1907; The Spirit of Youth and the City Streets, 1909; Twenty Years at Hull-House, 1910; A New Conscience and an Ancient Evil, 1912; Women at The Hague, 1915, with Emily Greene Balch and Alice Hamilton; The Long Road of Woman's Memory, 1916; Peace and Bread in Time of War, 1922; The Second Twenty Years at Hull-House, 1930; The Excellent Becomes the Permanent, 1932; A Centennial Reader, 1960.

ABOUT: Davis, A. F. American Heroine: The Life and Legend of Jane Addams, 1973; Deegan, M. J. Jane Addams and the Men of the Chicago School, 1986; Farrell, J. C. Beloved Lady: A History of Jane Addams's Ideas on Reform and Peace, 1967; Fishwick, M. W. Jane Addams, 1968; Johnson, A. D., and Pileggi, S. The Value of Friendship: The Story of Jane Addams, 1979; Lasch, C. The Social Thought of Jane Addams, 1982; Levine, D. Jane Addams and the Liberal Tradition, 1971; Linn, J. W. Jane Addams: A Biography, 1935; Lubove, R. The Professional Altruist, 1972; Mooney, E. C. Jane Addams, 1968; Peterson, H. S. Jane Addams: Pioneer of Hull House, 1965; Tims, M. Jane Addams of Hull House, 1961; Wise, W. E. Jane Addams of Hull House, 1935; Woods, R. A., and Kennedy, A. J. The Settlement Horizon, 1922.

ADRIAN, EDGAR D.

(November 30, 1889–August 4, 1977)
Nobel Prize for Physiology or Medicine, 1932
(shared with Charles S. Sherrington)

EDGAR D. ADRIAN

Edgar Douglas Adrian, an English physiologist, was born in London, the second of three sons of Alfred Douglas Adrian, a legal adviser to the local government board, and the former Flora Lavinia Barton. After receiving his secondary schooling at a prestigious public school of Westminster, Adrian entered Trinity College, Cambridge, in 1908 to study the natural sciences. There his studies were directed by the physiologist Keith Lucas, who was investigating the reactions of nerves and muscles to electrical stimulation; soon, Adrian became involved in the research.

It had been established in 1871 that heart muscle responds to an electrical impulse by an "all-or-none" reaction; that is, either the muscle responds with full force or it does not respond. In 1905 Lucas had shown that not only the heart but all muscles exhibit smooth muscular activity, as such responses are known. Smooth muscle activity is produced by altering the number of active fibers and the frequency with which they contract. Although Lucas's subsequent experiments strongly suggested that nerves also exhibit such all-or-none responses, there was no direct proof, since there was as yet no way to detect the activity in a single nerve cell.

In their research Adrian and Lucas examined whether the energy for the nerve impulse (the action potential) is derived from the energy of the stimulus, as in the flight of a bullet, or is a self-propagating reaction, like the movement of a spark along a fuse. Their evidence suggested the latter, although it was not until the 1940s that ALAN HODGKIN and ANDREW HUXLEY explained the mechanism by which the action potential operates.

Two years after graduating from Cambridge in 1911, Adrian was elected a fellow of Trinity College. Then, having decided that a medical degree would enhance his research career, he began working at St. Bartholomew's Hospital in London just before the outbreak of World War I. Upon completing clinical training in the record-breaking time of little more than a year, he spent the rest of the war in England, studying and treating shell shock and neurological injuries while trying strenuously to get posted to France.

Before Lucas's death in an airplane crash in 1916, he and Adrian had discussed possible ways of recording the electrical impulses in single nerve fibers. The impulses were known to be only a few thousandths of a second in duration and to have the strength of only a few microvolts—too brief and too weak to be measured by available instruments. Lucas had suggested the use of thermionic valves, such as those invented by GUGLIELMO MARCONI and FERDINAND BRAUN, to amplify the electrical signal from the nerve before they tried to detect the impulses.

This idea lay dormant for several years, however, since the influx of students after the war greatly increased Adrian's teaching responsibilities. Although his research was hindered, he made important observations on the refractory period (the span of time directly after an electrical impulse, when the tissue cannot be excited) of nerves and muscles, and in 1922, working with the American neurobiologist Alexander Forbes, he obtained convincing evidence that sensory nerves, as well

3

as those controlling actions, obey the all-or-none law. This observation was unexpected; at the time, many scientists believed that the information conveyed by the sensory nerves was too complex to be the result of such simple impulses.

In 1925 Adrian began employing electrical methods, particularly valve amplifiers, in his experiments. HERBERT S. GASSER and his colleagues at the Johns Hopkins School of Medicine had constructed an amplifier for recording action potentials in bundles of motor nerve fibers. Adrian built his own amplifier to Gasser's specifications and tested it on nerves taken from frog muscle. Earlier, CHARLES S. SHERRINGTON had postulated that the muscle contains sensory nerves that signal how much it is stretching; Adrian found that he could reduce the muscle until it contained only one sense organ, which became stimulated when the muscle was stretched. Each impulse in the sensory nerve has exactly the same strength and duration; however, as Adrian later said, "the frequency [of the impulses] depends on the extent and the rapidity of the stretch; it depends, that is to say, on the intensity of excitation in the sense organ, and in this way the impulse message can signal far more than the mere fact that excitation has occurred."

For the next several years Adrian and his colleagues investigated impulses in various sensory and motor nerves, and their experiments produced the information necessary to formulate a general theory of sensation. According to Adrian, human sensory receptors react only to changes in the environment; after the change has occurred, the receptors adapt to the new state of affairs. The intensity with which the receptors react determines the rate at which impulses in the sensory nerves are produced.

Later, Adrian described the path between this excitation and the mind: "The excitatory process in the receptor declines gradually, and as it declines, the intervals between the impulses in the sensory fiber become longer and longer. The impulses are integrated by some central process, and the rise and decline of the sensation is a fairly close copy of the rise and decline of the excitatory process in the receptor. The quality of the sensation seems to depend on the path which the impulses must travel." In other words, all sensory impulses are alike. Therefore, light is sensed as light, and sound as sound, not because of a fundamental difference between sensations perceived by the ear and the eye, but because the brain interprets any stimulation of the optic

nerve as light and any stimulation of the auditory nerve as sound.

The studies conducted by Adrian on motor nerves revealed that "the messages which pass down the motor fibers to the muscles have . . . the same limitations as the sensory messages, and again we find that the effect is graded by changes in the frequency of the impulse discharge and in the number of units in action." His discoveries concerning adaptation and the coding of nerve impulses enabled researchers to study sensations objectively and directly.

Adrian shared the 1932 Nobel Prize for Physiology or Medicine with Sherrington "for their discoveries concerning the functions of neurons." "Adrian's investigations have given us a highly important insight into the question of the nerve principle and the adaptability of the sense organs," said Göran Liljestrand of the Karolinska Institute in his presentation speech.

At this time Adrian's interest shifted from the peripheral sense organs to the brain. Through his research on brain waves in the early 1930s, he contributed to the development of the electroencephalograph for measuring brain activity.

The next twenty years of Adrian's work as an experimental scientist involved a variety of subjects, including hearing, the sensory cortex (those areas of the brain involved in processing complex sensory data), the cerebellum, the vestibular apparatus, and the sense of smell—all perhaps part of an effort to survey the entire central nervous system. Renowned for his skills as an experimenter, he often used himself as a subject and once injected a long needle into his arm, keeping it there for two hours while he recorded the workings of the muscle.

In 1951 Adrian relinquished his duties as professor of physiology at Cambridge to become master of Trinity College, after which much of his time was taken up with administration, lecturing, and politics. From 1950 to 1955 he served as president of the Royal Society of London, to which he had been elected in 1923. During his tenure as president of the society, he was also president of the British Association for the Advancement of Science for one year and was only the third person in history to head both organizations concurrently.

He was vice-chancellor of Cambridge from 1957 to 1959 and chancellor from 1968 through December of 1975. Alan Hodgkin recalls that "when he became chancellor, some Trinity rowing men called on Adrian and asked if they might have the honor of rowing him upriver from Trinity to the University Centre. In spite of his seventy-eight years Adrian accepted and, dressed in formal clothes, he coxed the boat successfully through a succession of upriver bridges."

The culminating honor in a life rich with honors occurred in 1955 when Queen Elizabeth II made him a baron. As Baron Adrian of Cambridge, one of the last hereditary peers created in England, he attended the House of Lords as regularly as possible and spoke on a variety of subjects ranging from foot-and-mouth disease to nuclear disarmament.

In 1923 Adrian married Hester Pinsent, a descendant of the Scottish philosopher David Hume; they had a son and two daughters. Hester Adrian was noted for her work in the fields of mental health and juvenile delinquency. A high-spirited person who enjoyed driving fast cars and climbing mountains when he was young, Lord Adrian lived in his rooms in Neville's Court in Trinity College until shortly before his death in 1977.

Adrian was a member of more than forty scientific and professional organizations. His many awards included the Royal Medal (1934) and Copley Medal (1946) of the Royal Society, the Albert Gold Medal of the Royal Society of Arts (1953), the Medal for Distinguished Merit of the British Medical Association (1958), and the Jephcott Medal and Lecture of the Royal Society of Medicine (1963).

SELECTED WORKS: The Action of Light on the Eye, 1927, with Rachel Mathews; The Basis of Sensation, 1928; The Mechanism of Nerve Action, 1932; The Physical Background of Perception, 1947; Sensory Integration, 1949; The Responsibilities of the Brain, 1951.

ABOUT: Biographical Memoirs of Fellows of the Royal Society, volume 25, 1979; New York Times August 6, 1977; Oxbury, H. (ed.) Great Britons, 1985.

S. Y. AGNON

AGNON, S. Y.
(July 17, 1888–February 17, 1970)
Nobel Prize for Literature, 1966
(shared with Nelly Sachs)

The Israeli novelist and short story writer S. Y. Agnon (ug non') was born Shmuel Yosef Halevi Czaczkes in the small town of Buczacz, in Galicia, a region of the Austro-Hungarian Empire, now part of Poland. His father, Shalom Mordecai Halevi Czaczkes, had received rabbinical training but was a fur trader by profession. His mother, the former Esther Farb, was a well-read woman, and his maternal grandfather, Yehuda Farb, was a merchant whose prodigious knowledge strongly influenced the young Agnon.

Agnon's boyhood education and upbringing provided the basic themes and subject matter for much of his subsequent writing. In addition to attending the traditional heder (elementary school), Agnon studied the Talmud under the tutelage of his father and the local rabbi. In the local *beth hamidrash* (house of learning), he read the works of ancient and medieval Jewish sages and the lore of the Hasidim (followers of a mystical Jewish sect that arose in eighteenth-century Poland), as well as contemporary Hebrew literature. When Agnon was a teenager, he became an active Zionist. His first poetry, published in a local newspaper when he was fifteen, was written in Hebrew and Yiddish. When he was eighteen, he went to Lvov to work on a Hebrew newspaper. In 1907, he journeyed to Jaffa, in Palestine (then part of the Turkish Ottoman Empire), and a year later he moved to Jerusalem. At the time, he was a secretary of the Jewish court and served on several Jewish councils. In 1909 he published the short novel *Agunot* (*Forsaken Wives*). From this title he derived his pen name, Agnon (which means "cut off" in Hebrew). He adopted Agnon as his legal last name in 1924. Like all Agnon's subsequent work, *Agunot* was written in Hebrew. The characteristics of his writing—its use of folklore and fantasy and its religious overtones—were already present in this early work. Agnon's writing, thoroughly rooted in traditional Jewish village culture, represented a break with the cosmopolitanism of the secular Hebrew writers, such as Shalom Aleichem, Shelomo Rubin, and Reuven Broides, who preceded him.

In 1912 Agnon returned to Europe and settled in Berlin, where he continued his studies of literature, lectured on Hebrew literature, tutored private students in Hebrew, and served as a research assistant to scholars. With the theologian and philosopher Martin Buber, he set about collecting stories of the Hasidim. He and Buber also founded the journal *Der Jude* (*The Jew*). During this time, Agnon became friendly with the German-Jewish businessman Salman Schocken, who in 1916 gave Agnon a five-year stipend so that he could devote himself to his writing; the only condition attached to the stipend was that Agnon edit an anthology of Hebrew literature for Schocken. Schocken eventually established his own publishing house in Berlin, mainly to publish Agnon's works. During Agnon's twelve-year stay in Berlin, a local Jewish firm published several of his short novels and collections of short stories.

To ensure that he would be exempted from military service in World War I, Agnon deliberately smoked heavily, took pills, and slept as little as possible for several weeks before taking an army physical examination in 1916. His efforts resulted in his being hospitalized for a kidney disease, but he succeeded in not being conscripted. In 1919 Agnon married Esther Marx, with whom he had a daughter and a son.

The war and its aftermath prevented Agnon from returning to Jerusalem until 1924, by which time Palestine had become a British mandate. In 1927 he moved to the Talpiyot section of the city. After his home was pillaged in the Arab riots of 1929, he built the house he was to live in for the rest of his life.

It was in the late 1920s that Agnon wrote his most substantial work up to that time, the two-volume novel *Hachnasat Kalah* (*The Bridal Canopy*), which was published in 1931. This picaresque novel describes the adventures of a poor Hasid as he travels through Eastern Europe in search of husbands and dowries for his three daughters. In its method of combining humor and irony with compassion, *The Bridal Canopy* typifies Agnon's writing.

In 1930 Agnon again returned to Europe, where he supervised Schocken's publication in Berlin of his *Kol Sippurav* (*Complete Stories*, 1931). Before returning to Jerusalem in 1932, he toured the Jewish communities he had known in Poland and found them greatly changed from the days of his childhood. This experience is reflected in his third full-length novel, *Oreach Natah Lalun* (*A Guest for the Night*, 1937), in which the hero returns to his native village and finds it physically and culturally devastated by the effects of World War I. In his second published novel, *Sippur Pashut* (*A Simple Story*, 1935), Agnon drew on techniques perfected by Gustave Flaubert and THOMAS MANN to contrast the hero's romantic longing with the interests of bourgeois society in a Galician town of the early twentieth century.

During the early 1930s, Agnon's work was widely published in German-language editions. After completing *A Guest for the Night*, he increasingly used Palestine as the setting for his fiction. When the Nazis closed the Schocken publishing operation in 1938, the firm moved to Tel Aviv, where it continued to publish Agnon's work. At the end of World War II, Schocken opened a branch in New York and began to publish English translations of Agnon's books, thus bringing his work to wider attention. (The earliest appearance of Agnon's work in English had been in 1931, with a short story published in the *Canadian Jewish Chronicle*.)

One influential American reader who became familiar with Agnon's work was the critic Edmund Wilson, who formally proposed in the late 1950s that Agnon receive the Nobel Prize for Literature. However, it was not until a third nomination that Agnon received the award in 1966 "for his profoundly characteristic narrative art with motifs from the life of the Jewish people." He shared the prize with NELLY SACHS. The citation made special mention of *The Bridal Canopy* and *A Guest for the Night*. Agnon did not deliver a Nobel lecture, but in his brief acceptance speech, he stressed the influence of the Talmud and other traditional Hebrew writings on his own work.

In his later years, Agnon came to be regarded as an Israeli national institution. When construction threatened to disturb the peace of the Talpiyot sector of Jerusalem, the mayor, Teddy Kollek, ordered that a sign be erected near Agnon's house reading, "Quiet. Agnon is writing." Nevertheless, although he continued to write, Agnon believed that his readership was dwindling. The Holocaust had annihilated a huge number of the people for whom he was writing, and he felt that the younger generation had little interest in the traditional cultural values his work embodied. Agnon died of a heart attack in 1970. He is buried on the Mount of Olives.

In addition to the Nobel Prize, Agnon received a number of honors, including the prestigious Bialik Prize of Tel Aviv (1935 and 1951), the Ussishkin Prize (1950), and the Israel Prize (1950 and 1958). He also held honorary degrees from the Jewish Theological Seminary of America, Hebrew University in Jerusalem, and Yeshiva and Columbia universities. The city of Jerusalem made him an honorary citizen in 1962.

Largely unknown outside Jewish circles when he won the Nobel Prize, Agnon today is considered one of the most outstanding writers of Hebrew fiction. He has been compared to James Joyce, Marcel Proust, and WILLIAM FAULKNER, among others, but perhaps most often to Franz Kafka, whose fiction Agnon's resembles in its ambiguity and eeriness. Criticism of his writing is made difficult by his custom of often reworking published material and by the peculiarly archaic syntax of his language, which resists translation. Yet, even in translation, his prose retains much of its characteristic power. Assessing Agnon's achievement in *Commentary* (1961), American critic Robert Alter noted that "Agnon has in his varied literary enterprise confronted some of the most disturbing aspects of the contemporary world. . . . Yet, by remaining constantly in touch . . . with the spiritual wholeness of the past, he has preserved the conviction that such wholeness of spirit is both indispensable and still possible to achieve."

KURT ALDER

ADDITIONAL WORKS IN ENGLISH TRANSLATION: In the Heart of the Seas, 1948; Days of Awe, 1948; Two Tales, 1966; Twenty-One Stories, 1970; Selected Stories of S. Y. Agnon, 1970; A Dwelling Place of My People, 1983.

ABOUT: Aberbach, D. At the Handles of the Lock, 1984; Alter, R. After the Tradition, 1969; Band, A. J. Nostalgia and Nightmare, 1968; Fisch, H. S. Y. Agnon, 1975; Fleck, J. Character and Context, 1984; Hochman, B. The Fiction of S. Y. Agnon, 1970; Kaspi, J. A Study in the Evolution of S. Y. Agnon's Style, 1972; New York Times February 18, 1970; Rosenberg, I. Shay Agnon's World of Mystery and Allegory, 1978.

ALDER, KURT

(July 10, 1902–June 20, 1958)
Nobel Prize for Chemistry, 1950
(shared with Otto Diels)

The German chemist Kurt Alder was born in Königshütte, Germany (now Chorzów, Poland), near Kattowitz (now Katowice), where his father, Joseph Alder, was a teacher. The boy received his early education in the local schools. At the end of World War I, shortly before Poland regained its independence, the family moved to Kiel, Germany, in order to retain their German citizenship. In 1922, after completing his secondary education at the *Oberrealschule* in Berlin, Alder entered the University of Berlin to study chemistry.

Continuing his studies at the Christian Albrecht University (now the University of Kiel), Alder worked under OTTO DIELS, a professor of organic chemistry and director of the university's chemical institute. In 1926, upon completing a dissertation, "On the Causes of the Azoester Reaction," Alder received his Ph.D. and became Diels's assistant.

The following year he and Diels began to investigate diene synthesis. A diene is a molecule with a base structure consisting of a four-carbon chain in which two double bonds are separated by a single bond. The chemists discovered that at room temperature a diene will combine with a philodiene (literally, a diene lover) molecule to form a new, stable six-carbon ring molecule. This form of reaction, they found, occurs readily between many different dienes and philodienes that are present in living systems, and the combination produces a potentially immense variety of molecules. The principle of diene synthesis, which Alder and Diels first announced in 1928, subsequently became a basic chemical tool which enabled chemists to study many previously inaccessible types of organic reactions and which laid the foundations of polymer chemistry. The Diels-Alder reaction has been used in the commercial production of pharmaceutical drugs, dyes, lubricating oils, insecticides, synthetic rubber, and plastics.

During the next eight years, Alder and Diels further clarified the nature of diene synthesis. In 1930 Alder was appointed a reader in organic chemistry at Kiel, and in 1934 he became extraordinary professor of organic chemistry. His growing expertise in diene synthesis led to an invitation to become director of scientific research at the Interessen-Gemeinschaft Farbenindustrie Aktiengesellschaft (I. G. Farben) plant in Leverkusen, which Alder accepted in 1936. At Leverkusen, Alder investigated the effects of joining butadiene (a form of diene) to various philodienes, notably styrene, to form synthetic rubber. He also studied the molecular structure of the syntheses he produced.

Returning to academic life in 1940, Alder, who was not involved in Germany's wartime research, was appointed to the chair for experimental chemistry and chemical technology at the University of Cologne. Concurrently he served as director of the university's Chemistry Institute. In this capacity he applied diene synthesis to unravel the chemical constitutions of complex natural products such as the terpenes (isomeric hydrocarbons found in the oil of conifers), the vitamin D precursor ergosterol, and the D vitamins. An exceptionally able stereochemist, Alder was also interested in learning why, when several possible structures for the resulting molecule seemed equally likely, a particular reaction took place.

In 1949, the same year that he was named dean of the Faculty of Philosophy at Cologne, Alder shared the Nobel Prize for Chemistry with Diels "for their discovery and development of the synthesis of dienes." In his Nobel lecture Alder reviewed the research leading to this discovery and described the structural determinants governing the selection of a particular configuration over others. He noted that this pronounced steric selective property of the diene synthesis is "one of the decisive factors determining the value of the diene synthesis as a method. The fact that it can be used as a means of isolating and separating substances from mixtures, and that it is uniquely suitable as a means of determining the character of specific types of substances," he continued, "could otherwise never have been known."

After receiving the Nobel Prize, Alder continued to teach and to conduct research into further potential commercial applications of the diene synthesis. In 1955 he joined seventeen other Nobel laureates in signing a declaration calling upon all nations to renounce war as an instrument of foreign policy. An intensely dedicated worker, Alder, who remained unmarried, succumbed to exhaustion in 1957 and was advised by his doctor to take a complete rest. He died the following year at the age of fifty-five.

In addition to the Nobel Prize, Alder also received the Emil Fischer Medal from the German Chemical Society (1938) and honorary degrees from the Medical Faculty of the University of Cologne (1950) and the University of Salamanca (1954). He held membership in the Leopoldina German Academy of Researchers in Natural Sciences.

ABOUT: Dictionary of Scientific Biography, volume 1, 1970; New York Times November 25, 1950.

ALEIXANDRE, VICENTE
(April 26, 1898–December 14, 1984)
Nobel Prize for Literature, 1977

The Spanish poet Vicente Aleixandre (ä läx än′ drä) y Merlo was born in Seville to Cirilo Aleixandre Ballester, a civil engineer with the Andalusian Railways, and Elvira Merlo García de Pruneda, daughter of the district military superintendent. Aleixandre was the elder surviving child in his family; an older sister had died in infancy, and a younger sister, Conchita, was born in 1899. When the boy was still an infant, his father was transferred to Málaga, where Aleixandre grew up surrounded by the sunny beauty of the Mediterranean coast, images of which appear throughout his poetry. While attending the local elementary school, he became familiar with the tales of Hans Christian Andersen and the brothers Grimm.

After the family moved to Madrid in 1909, Aleixandre attended the Colegio Teresiano, a secular school, from which he received his *bachillerato* degree (the equivalent of a high school diploma for academic students) in 1913. During these years his maternal grandfather encouraged him to use the library, and there Aleixandre encountered the works of Arthur Conan Doyle and Fedor Dostoevsky, as well as Homer's *Iliad* and the plays of Friedrich Schiller.

Entering the University of Madrid in 1914, Aleixandre studied law and took occasional classes in Spanish literature. While vacationing in the province of Ávila during the summer of 1917, he met Dámaso Alonso, a student his own age (later the president of the Royal Spanish Academy), who introduced him to the work of the Nicaraguan modernist poet Rubén Darío and awakened his interest in poetry.

Upon graduation in 1920 with degrees in law and in business management, Aleixandre became an assistant professor at the School of Mercantile Management in Madrid. Two years later he took a job with the Andalusian Railways and began writing articles on railway economics for a business weekly. Although he was also writing poetry during this time, he kept his literary work secret for several years.

In 1922 he suffered an attack of infectious arthritis, the first in a series of illnesses that kept him a semi-invalid for the remainder of his life. When he contracted tuberculosis of the kidney in 1925, he resigned from the railroad and retired to a house his father had taken in the countryside near Madrid. There, for the next two years, he concentrated his efforts on writing. The poems he produced during this period of convalescence, eventually published as *Ambito* (Scope) in 1928, reflect his sexual yearnings and the overpowering fear of death that illness had instilled in him. Filled with sensual imagery, these poems are written in traditional ballad form.

Discovering that Aleixandre had been writing, several friends persuaded him to submit his work to the review *Revista de Occidente* (Journal of the West), which, in 1926, became the first journal to publish his poems. In May 1927 he and his family moved into a small villa on the northern outskirts of Madrid, where he spent the rest of his life. That year marked the tercentenary of the death of the great Spanish poet Luis de Góngora. A group of young writers who paid homage on the occasion became known as the Generation of 1927. Its members, which included Aleixandre, Jorge Guillén, Dámaso Alonso, Rafael Alberti, Luis Cernuda, and Federico García Lorca, among others, embraced surrealism in a form that was termed *superrealismo*.

Around the time that *Ambito* appeared, Aleixandre began reading the works of Sigmund Freud, which he used to interpret the morbid daydreams he experienced during his illness. The strains of surrealism and Freudianism can be seen in *Pasión de la tierra* (Passion of the Earth), in which the ballad form gives way to cadenced prose poems that consist of seemingly disordered images. Composed between 1928 and 1929, *Pasión de la tierra* was not published until 1935. Meanwhile, Aleixandre wrote *Espadas como labios* (Swords Like Lips, 1932) and the intensely erotic volume *La destrucción o el amor* (Destruction or Love, 1933). For the latter work, which is widely considered

VICENTE ALEIXANDRE

his masterpiece, he received the National Prize for Literature in 1933.

With the outbreak of the Spanish Civil War in 1936, hard times befell the Generation of 1927. Most of its members fled Spain; García Lorca was executed by the troops of Francisco Franco. Because of his illness, Aleixandre remained in Spain, though his house, located at the Madrid front, was destroyed near the end of the war. After their father's death in 1940, Aleixandre and his sister rebuilt the house. Aleixandre continued to write even though his poems were banned for a time. "My task was not too easy in the early postwar years," he later recalled.

Mundo a solas (World Alone), written on the eve of the Civil War but not published until 1950, served as a prelude to *Sombra del paraíso* (Shadow of Paradise, 1944), an evocation of a utopia of beauty and happiness perceived from the distant perspective of a poet troubled by intimations of death. *Historia del corazón* (The Story of the Heart, 1954) marked a shift from the sadness of his earlier work to a kind of humanistic and spiritual affirmation. According to Aleixandre's translator Lewis Hyde, "[Aleixandre] is one of the few pessimistic poets of the century who managed to emerge and find something above the darkness." Aleixandre's later volumes of poetry include *En un vasto dominio* (In a Vast Dominion, 1962), *Poemas de la consumación* (Poems of Consummation, 1968), and *Diálogos del conocimiento* (Dialogues of Knowledge, 1974). In 1958 he published *Los Encuentros* (Encoun-

9

ters), affectionate prose portraits of his fellow writers.

Aleixandre received the 1977 Nobel Prize for Literature "for a creative poetic writing which illuminates man's condition in the cosmos and in present-day society, at the same time representing the great renewal of the traditions of Spanish poetry between the wars." "He never submitted" to the Franco regime, said Karl Ragnar Gierow of the Swedish Academy in his presentation speech, "and went on with his writing, frail but unbroken, thereby becoming the rallying point and source of power in Spain's spiritual life." Too ill to attend the ceremonies, Aleixandre was represented by his friend Justo Jorge Padron, a young Spanish poet and the translator of Aleixandre's work into Swedish. Shortly after the prize was awarded, King Juan Carlos of Spain visited Aleixandre to bestow upon him the Grand Cross of the Order of Charles III.

A bachelor all his life, Aleixandre died in Madrid on December 14, 1984, at the age of eighty-six.

Although not widely translated into English, Aleixandre's work nevertheless has received favorable comment outside Spain. "He is a poet of intellectual vigor, spiritual depth, and tenacity," wrote Lewis Hyde. "He did the work, he went far down into the soul and brought back pieces of life as a gift for the rest of us."

ADDITIONAL WORKS IN ENGLISH TRANSLATION: Poems, 1969; Vicente Aleixandre and Luis Cernuda, 1974; The Cave of Night, 1976; Twenty Poems, 1977; Poems/Poema, 1978; A Bird of Paper, 1979; A Longing for the Light, 1982.

ABOUT: Cabrera, V., and Boyer, H. Critical Views on Vicente Aleixandre, 1979; Cohen, J. M. Poetry of This Age, 1966; Current Biography March 1978; Daydi-Tolson, S. Vicente Aleixandre: A Critical Appraisal, 1981; Ilie, P. The Surrealistic Mode in Spanish Literature, 1968; Ley, C. D. Spanish Poetry Since 1939, 1962; Morris, C. B. A Generation of Spanish Poets, 1969; Schwartz, K. Vicente Aleixandre, 1970.

ALEPOUDELIS, ODYSSEUS
See ELYTIS, ODYSSEUS

ALFVÉN, HANNES
(May 30, 1908–   )
Nobel Prize for Physics, 1970
(shared with Louis Néel)

The Swedish physicist Hannes Olof Gösta Alfvén (älf vān′) was born in Norrköping to

HANNES ALFVÉN

Johannes and Anna-Clara (Romanus) Alfvén, both practicing physicians. After receiving his early education in Norrköping, Alfvén entered the University of Uppsala in 1926, received his Ph.D. in 1934, and remained at the university as a lecturer in physics until 1937, when he became a research physicist at the Nobel Institute for Physics in Stockholm. He was appointed professor of the theory of electricity at the Royal Institute of Technology in Stockholm in 1940, professor of electronics in 1945, and professor of plasma physics in 1963. Four years later, he left Sweden, partly due to disputes with the government over questions ranging from education policy to nuclear reactor design, and accepted a professorship at the University of California, San Diego.

Alfvén's early work concerned the nature of sunspots and the aurora borealis. Because the sun is extremely hot, it consists of a special form of matter called plasma, a gaslike mixture of electrons, stripped from atoms and molecules by high-energy collisions, and the charged ions the collisions produce. Stars and most of the matter in the universe are composed of plasmas, as is the solar wind, the stream of particles ejected from the sun. When these particles enter the earth's magnetic field, they are diverted toward the poles, and their collisions with the ionosphere produce the auroral display. Alfvén made many prophetic discoveries about plasmas that were unappreciated, or even rejected, at the time. For example, he showed that a plasma was associated with a magnetic field, related to the flow of charged particles (electric currents) in the plasma, and that under certain conditions the magnetic field could become "frozen" in the plasma; that is, if such a plasma moves, the field moves with it. For the conditions to be met, the electrical conductivity, in combination with other characteristics, must be sufficiently high; and the particles must be close enough together to ensure that the likelihood of collisions with neighbors will prevent electrons from escaping.

In considering the complex motion of a charged particle in a magnetic field, Alfvén introduced the simplifying approximation of circular rotation about a "guiding center," which was itself drifting along magnetic field lines (a field line indicates the direction of the field at each point; the closeness of field lines indicates field strength). He applied this principle to the study of magnetic storms and auroras, finding that particles in the earth's magnetic field should bounce back and forth along the field lines, reflected from regions of increasing field strength. This concept of a magnetic mirror became important in work on controlled thermonuclear fusion requiring the confinement of hot plasmas whose contact would destroy the walls of any container. Alfvén's ideas, not always acknowledged, were later useful in interpreting such phenomena as the Van Allen radiation belt (doughnut-shaped currents of electrons circulating in the earth's magnetic field) and the reduction in the earth's magnetic field during magnetic storms. Another of Alfvén's early suggestions that proved to be valid was the existence of large-scale weak magnetic fields throughout the galaxy due to the presence of even small amounts of plasma, fields that influenced the motions of cosmic rays.

In 1942 Alfvén predicted that magnetic field lines in a plasma acted like stretched rubber bands and could transmit a disturbance he called a hydromagnetic wave, much like the plucking of a violin string. This notion ran counter to the prevailing view, which was based on the accepted inability of electromagnetic waves to penetrate deeply into an electrical conductor. In fact, metal sheets were routinely used as shields against such penetration. Although Alfvén's theory seemed experimentally unverifiable, it began to gain acceptance and was endorsed by ENRICO FERMI, who heard Alfvén lecture at the University of Chicago in 1948. Contrary to general expectations, the waves, which became known as Alfvén waves, were observed in liquid metal in 1949 and in plasmas in 1959. Alfvén waves have helped explain small variations in the earth's magnetic field and the close relation between magnetic disturbances separated by large distances but linked by geomagnetic field lines.

Alfvén also showed in 1942 how the evolution of the solar system from a plasma accounted for the fact that almost all its momentum (mass times velocity) is possessed by the planets rather than the sun. Many of Alfvén's ideas had come from his consideration of sunspots, and he had concluded that the spots were regions of intense magnetic fields embedded in the body of the sun. In 1943 he used the association between plasmas and their magnetic fields to explain why the spots, known to be cooler (and therefore denser) than their surroundings because they are darker, did not sink. The reason was a magnetic pressure that counteracted the gravitational forces.

The new field of physics Alfvén established, called magnetohydrodynamics, has proved essential not only to thermonuclear fusion research but also to such developments as hypersonic flight, rocket propulsion, and the braking of reentering space vehicles. However, Alfvén's own interest in plasmas has centered on their behavior in stars and in interplanetary and interstellar space. His collection of early papers, Cosmical Electrodynamics (1950), has greatly influenced space and plasma physicists. Alfvén's later important works have dealt with the formation of the solar system.

Belated recognition came when Alfvén received the 1970 Nobel Prize for Physics "for fundamental work and discoveries in magnetohydrodynamics with fruitful applications in different parts of plasma physics." He shared the prize with LOUIS NÉEL, honored for his contributions to the theory of magnetization. In the presentation speech, Torsten Gustafsson of the Royal Swedish Academy of Sciences said that Alfvén's ideas "have found widespread application in astrophysical problems, particularly in studying that phase of the development of the solar system in which the planets and satellites were created." Alfvén said in his Nobel lecture that clarifying how the solar system was formed "is indeed one of the fundamental problems of science," adding that from a philosophical point of view "this is just as important as the structure of matter, which has absorbed most of the interest during the first two-thirds of this century."

Concerned with keeping theory firmly related to physical observations, Alfvén has long championed the use of spacecraft for scientific exploration. In particular, he has advocated sending spacecraft to asteroids and comets rather than planets and moons, believing that information about primordial conditions has almost entirely been lost on the larger bodies due to internal mixing and surface erosion.

An early advocate of nuclear power, Alfvén later warned of the risks posed by nuclear generating plants. As a result of his concern over the nuclear arms race, he became active in the Pugwash Movement on Science and World Affairs.

Alfvén married Kerstin Maria Erikson in 1935; they have five children. In addition to his scientific papers, he has written popular science books, sometimes with his wife. *Worlds-Antiworlds: Antimatter in Cosmology* (1966) suggests that the universe may consist of equal amounts of matter and antimatter, a controversial subject in conflict with many modern theories. Under the pen name Olaf Johannesson, he wrote a science fiction novel, *The Great Computer: A Vision* (1968), which describes how increasingly sophisticated computers gain control over governments first and then the earth.

The first space scientist to have received the Nobel Prize, Alfvén has also been awarded the Gold Medal of the Royal Astronomical Society in London (1967) and the Lomonosov Gold Medal of the Soviet Academy of Sciences (1971). He is a member of the Royal Swedish Academy of Sciences, the American National Academy of Sciences, the Royal Society of London, and other scientific academies.

SELECTED WORKS: Investigations on the Ultrashort Electromagnetic Waves, 1934; A Theory of Magnetic Storms and of Aurorae (2 vols.) 1939–1940; On the Origin of the Solar System, 1954; Cosmical Electrodynamics: Fundamental Principles, 1963, with Carl-Gunne Falthammer; Atom, Man, and the Universe: A Long Chain of Complications, 1969; Living on the Third Planet, 1972, with Kerstin Alfvén; Structure and Evolutionary History of the Solar System, 1975, with Gustav Arrhenius; Cosmic Plasma, 1981.

ABOUT: New York Times October 28, 1970; Science November 6, 1970.

ALVAREZ, LUIS W.
(June 13, 1911–   )
Nobel Prize for Physics, 1968

The American physicist Luis Walter Alvarez (al' vä rez) was born in San Francisco, California, to the former Harriet Skidmore Smythe and Walter Clement Alvarez, a physician, a professor at the University of Cali-

LUIS W. ALVAREZ

fornia, and a medical journalist. In 1926, when Alvarez's father took a position at the Mayo Clinic, the family moved to Rochester, Minnesota. Alvarez, one of four children, graduated from Rochester High School in 1928 and entered the University of Chicago. Initially, he majored in chemistry but, with encouragement from one of his teachers, he switched to physics. After earning a B.S. with highest honors in 1932, he remained at Chicago for graduate study and received his M.S. in 1934 and his Ph.D. in 1936. An aviation enthusiast, Alvarez took flying lessons while attending the university; he was so proficient that he made his first solo flight after only three hours and fifteen minutes of instruction.

Returning to California, Alvarez became a research assistant in nuclear physics at the University of California at Berkeley, where he was appointed an instructor in 1938. In the late 1930s Alvarez and Jacob H. Wiens used the cyclotron at Berkeley to create the artificial isotope mercury 198; the wavelength of light emitted by a mercury-vapor lamp filled with this isotope was later adopted by the United States Bureau of Standards as a standard of length. In further research, Alvarez demonstrated experimentally in 1937 that nuclei can capture some of the innermost electrons that orbit an atom. His development of a method for producing beams of very slow neutrons opened the way to fundamental studies of neutron scattering and led to the first measurement of the magnetic moment of the neutron. Shortly before the outbreak of World War II, Alvarez and a colleague discovered tritium, the radioactive isotope of hydrogen, and helium 3, an isotope important in low-temperature research.

In 1940 Alvarez took a leave of absence from Berkeley to conduct military research at the newly established Radiation Laboratory at the Massachusetts Institute of Technology (MIT). There, in collaboration with Lawrence H. Johnston, Alvarez developed three important radar systems. He perfected a microwave radar system that could locate planes lost in foul weather over airports and guide them to a safe landing. This ground-control approach technology was soon put into wide use, first by the armed services and later at civilian airports. In 1946 it earned Alvarez the Collier Trophy, the highest aviation award in the United States, from the National Aeronautical Society. During his wartime research at MIT, Alvarez also developed both the Eagle, a high-altitude radar device that facilitated pinpoint bombing of Japanese oil refineries, and the microwave early-warning set, which transmitted images of aerial combat.

Alvarez left MIT in 1943 for Los Alamos, New Mexico, where, as a member of the Manhattan Project, he worked with ENRICO FERMI, J. Robert Oppenheimer, Edward Teller, and other scientists on the development of the atomic bomb. It was Alvarez who suggested the method by which one version of the bomb was detonated. After observing the first nuclear explosion at Alamogordo, New Mexico, in 1945, he was sent to a military base in the Pacific and flew in a B-29 to witness the detonation of the atomic bomb over Hiroshima. Some years later, Alvarez was among the scientists who, in opposition to Oppenheimer and many other members of the Atomic Energy Commission's Scientific Advisory Committee, persuaded President Harry S Truman to proceed with the development of the hydrogen bomb.

Returning to Berkeley after the war, Alvarez supervised the construction of a radiation laboratory for the advanced study of atomic energy, including a 40-foot-long linear accelerator for protons, the first of its kind.

In order to study the many subatomic particles produced by the new accelerators, it was necessary to record their paths, or tracks. The first device for making such recordings was the cloud chamber, invented in 1911 by C. T. R. WILSON. When Wilson expanded and thereby cooled a supersaturated vapor in the chamber, atomic particles crossing the chamber left paths of liquid drops that could be photographed. Further advances in particle detection came in

the 1940s through CECIL F. POWELL's development of photographic emulsions that could record particle tracks directly. The advent of new, more powerful accelerators in the early 1950s rendered these methods inadequate, however, because the high-energy particles they produced had such short lives and track lengths. A breakthrough occurred in 1952 when DONALD A. GLASER devised the bubble chamber, in which particles passing through a superheated fluid—a liquid heated beyond its boiling point—create a trail of gas bubbles.

After learning of Glaser's work at a conference in 1953, Alvarez developed the bubble chamber into a far larger device, using liquid hydrogen as the superheated fluid. The following year Alvarez and his group observed particle tracks in liquid hydrogen. Over the next five years they built a series of chambers that increased in size from 1 inch in diameter to a 72-inch chamber in 1959. By 1960 the first of many new elementary particles had been observed at Berkeley.

To photograph the tracks of these particles, Alvarez's colleague Jack Franck designed a revolutionary stereophotography system. Nicknamed the "Franckenstein," it became operational in 1957 and was subsequently widely copied in the high-energy physics community. To analyze the millions of photographs they produced each year, Alvarez and his colleagues employed high-speed computers. In the late 1950s they developed sophisticated computer programs capable of manipulating and analyzing data with unprecedented speed and precision. As a result of these studies, by the early 1960s the number of known particles had risen from around 30 to more than 100. Many of them were short-lived "resonance states," which could not be observed directly but whose existence was indicated by a sudden increase in the number of other particles appearing at a certain energy. Nearly all of the resonance states were discovered either by Alvarez and his colleagues or by others using his bubble chambers and his analytic techniques.

Alvarez received the 1968 Nobel Prize for Physics "for his decisive contributions to elementary particle physics, in particular the discovery of a large number of resonance states, made possible through his development of the technique of using hydrogen bubble chamber and data analysis." In his presentation speech, Sten von Friesen of the Royal Swedish Academy of Sciences said: "With the establishment of the hydrogen bubble chamber, entirely new possibilities for research into high-energy physics present themselves. Results have already been apparent in the form of newly discovered elementary particles. Practically all the discoveries that have been made in this important field have been possible only through the use of methods originated by Professor Alvarez."

A scientist of wide-ranging interests, Alvarez led a 1965 joint American-Egyptian expedition that used cosmic rays to learn whether there were hidden chambers in King Kefren's Pyramid at Giza (none were found). Moving further from elementary particles, in 1979 he and his son Walter, a professor of geology at Berkeley, proposed a radical theory to explain the extinction of dinosaurs and other forms of life 65 million years ago. They suggested that an asteroid struck the earth with such force that the resulting dust and smoke blocked sunlight, killing the vegetation on which dinosaurs fed. Their idea gained support in 1985 with the reported discovery of widely distributed soot particles dating from 65 million years ago and possibly caused by a global fire ignited by a meteor's impact. The theory, however, remains controversial.

In other work, Alvarez has produced nuclear chain reactions without uranium, invented a novel color television system, and discovered a radioactive isotope of helium. He once devised an electric indoor golf-training system that was used by President Dwight D. Eisenhower. For the extraordinary variety of his work, Alvarez has been called the "wild idea man" of physics.

In 1936 Alvarez married Geraldine Smithwick; they had a son and a daughter. The marriage ended in divorce, and in 1958 Alvarez married Janet Landis, with whom he has a son and a daughter.

Alvarez's other awards include the John Scott Award of the city of Philadelphia (1953), the Albert Einstein Award of the Lewis and Rosa Strauss Memorial Fund (1961), the Pioneer Award of the Institute of Electrical and Electronics Engineers (1963), and the National Medal of Science of the National Science Foundation (1964). He served as president of the American Physical Society in 1969 and is a member of the National Academy of Sciences and the National Academy of Engineering. He has received honorary degrees from the University of Chicago, Carnegie Mellon University, Kenyon College, and the University of Notre Dame.

SELECTED WORKS: Adventures of a Physicist, 1987.

ABOUT: Current Biography May 1947; Libby, L. M. The Uranium People, 1979; New York Times Magazine March 24, 1985; Science November 8, 1968; Stuewer, R. H. (ed.) Nuclear Physics in Retrospect, 1979.

AMERICAN FRIENDS SERVICE COMMITTEE

(founded June 4, 1917)
Nobel Prize for Peace, 1947
(shared with the Friends Service Council)

The American Friends Service Committee was founded in Philadelphia, Pennsylvania, as an outgrowth of Quaker opposition to World War I. Its origins and the rationale for its subsequent work were rooted in Quaker religious beliefs, especially the conviction that the spirit of God inheres within each person. This teaching began with George Fox, an English shoemaker, who in 1643 set out to preach a doctrine that would unite daily conduct with Christian precept. In 1668 Fox established the Religious Society of Friends, known popularly as the Quakers. Among its teachings was the belief that each individual could experience a divine illumination that would guide his or her behavior in accordance with divine principles.

Part of the radical wing of the Puritan movement, the Quakers won numerous converts in the British Isles, parts of the European continent, and North America. Especially controversial was their literal adherence to principles of brotherhood, for the Quaker belief in humankind's shared divinity led the Friends to treat all people equally, without regard to social distinctions, race, or sex. Moreover, convinced that war was contrary to the will of God, the Quakers renounced violence in favor of such spiritual weapons as love, compassion, and understanding.

During the 1750s, Quaker missionaries settled along the eastern seaboard of North America, where William Penn and other influential Friends established a foothold in New Jersey and Delaware and founded the colony of Pennsylvania. American Quakers pioneered not only in religious toleration but also in social reform. By the end of the American Revolution, most Friends had renounced slavery. Working to end the slave trade, they founded the new nation's earliest abolition societies. Throughout the nineteenth century, Quakers assumed leadership positions in such progressive causes as temperance, humane care for imprisoned criminals and the insane, women's suffrage, and the abolition of capital punishment. As early advocates of pacifism, American Quakers were listed in the membership rolls of the American Peace Society, founded in 1828.

When the United States entered World War I in April 1917, the Quakers placed an advertisement in national newspapers affirming their belief in the "constructive power of goodwill" as an alternative to armed combat. Later that month, a small group of Philadelphia Friends offered their services to the government "in any constructive work in which we can conscientiously serve humanity." By June they had established permanent headquarters, proposed various avenues of alternative service, and adopted their official name: the American Friends Service Committee (AFSC). Rufus M. Jones, a philosophy professor at Haverford College and a prolific writer on Quaker theology, agreed to serve as the group's chairman.

One of the most pressing problems the AFSC faced was conscription. Although the Selective Service Act offered noncombatant military service to those with religious objections to war, many Friends rejected this option. Appealing to President WOODROW WILSON, Jones won approval for voluntary civilian work in France instead. Joining the English Friends War Victims Relief Committee and the American Red Cross Commission, a unit of about 100 AFSC volunteers arrived in France. In the words of J. Henry Scattergood, a founding member of the group, they were "ready to do the hardest and lowliest kind of work."

Some volunteers served at a maternity hospital at Châlons, east of Paris, and at factories in Dôle and Ornes. Others made prefabricated housing for refugees. Still others built a children's tuberculosis sanitarium at Troyes. The main Quaker field base, however, was located at Sermaize, a railhead and farming center in the Marne River valley. There, American Quakers set up a surgical hospital and, during the winter of 1917–1918, moved from farm to farm, plowing, sowing, and reaping grain to prevent starvation. At the Second Battle of the Marne in April 1918, Quakers repeatedly came under fire as they helped evacuate the old, the sick, the orphaned, and the wounded.

After the war, the Friends distributed food and clothing in Germany. Then Herbert Hoover, who had administered massive relief programs during the war and now headed the American Relief Administration, asked the Friends to assume specific responsibility for raising funds for food and distributing it to German children. Accepting Hoover's proposal, the organization formed a unit under Scattergood that was sent to Berlin in early 1920. Within six months, the AFSC was feeding more than one million youngsters—in many cases providing their only daily meal. Similar assistance was furnished to refugees in Poland, Serbia, and Austria.

After touring Eastern Europe the following year, Rufus Jones alerted Hoover to an impending famine in the Soviet Union. Millions of people faced starvation in the Volga River valley because of crop failures and the dislocation produced by civil war. In October 1921 a team of Quakers reached what they described as "the desolate frontiers of death," and by the end of the year they were feeding 50,000 people daily, a program that continued until April 1923.

The years between the world wars saw the AFSC broaden its scope by reorganizing into four sections: Foreign, Interracial, Peace, and Home Service. The Interracial section, for example, sponsored visits by Japanese students to the United States in 1927 in opposition to restrictive immigration quotas. When the Spanish Civil War broke out in 1936, the Quakers provided relief to women and children on both the Nationalist and the Loyalist sides. Immediately after the *Kristallnacht* (Night of Broken Glass) in 1938, when the Nazis vandalized Jewish temples and shops and put 35,000 German Jews into concentration camps, Jones and two other leading Quakers went to Berlin, where they obtained permission to provide relief to these Jews. In the United States, Friends such as EMILY GREENE BALCH filled out dozens of affidavits that enabled at least a handful of persecuted Jews to emigrate safely.

When the United States declared war in 1941, conscientious objectors were barred by law from foreign service. Instead, the AFSC administered public service camps where war objectors worked in forestry, fire fighting, and soil conservation jobs. They also assisted Japanese-Americans who had been forcibly relocated to internment camps after the Japanese attack on Pearl Harbor. Although most countries occupied by Axis forces were closed to AFSC ministrations, the group undertook relief efforts in China, unoccupied France, London, and other areas. In the aftermath of the war, the AFSC distributed food, clothing, medical supplies, and other relief to refugees around the globe.

In recognition of its long history of humanitarian service, the AFSC shared the 1947 Nobel Peace Prize with the British FRIENDS SERVICE COUNCIL as representatives of the Society of Friends. In his presentation speech, Gunnar Jahn of the Norwegian Nobel Committee said of the Quakers: "It is not in the extent of their work or in its practical form that the Quakers have given most to the people they have met. It is in the spirit in which this work is performed." He elaborated, "The Quakers have shown us that it is possible to translate into action what lies deep in the hearts of many: compassion for others and the desire to help them."

Representing the AFSC, Henry J. Cadbury, its chairman from 1928 to 1934 and again from 1944 to 1960, accepted the prize and delivered a Nobel lecture entitled "Quakers and Peace." Here he emphasized that the committee's "international service is not mere humanitarianism; it is not merely mopping up, cleaning up the world after war. It is aimed at creating peace by setting an example of a different way of international service. So our foreign relief is a means of rehabilitation, and it is intended not merely to help the body but to help the spirit and to give men hope that there can be a peaceful world." He also expressed the hope "that our service will help to cool the passions of hate and fear and give faith to man . . . and thus promote the cause of peace."

Since receiving the Peace Prize, the AFSC has ministered to the victims of war, terrorism, injustice, and oppression—as well as to those who suffer from drought, famine, and natural disasters—in Southeast Asia, Africa, and Central America. It has also initiated programs—such as rural development, public health, and technical assistance—that are intended to reduce the conflicts from which violence may spring. In Central America, for example, Friends have supported orphanages and have provided legal aid to political prisoners and their families. In 1984 the AFSC began distributing tons of medicine, clothing, shoes, blankets, and other supplies to fulfill the human needs of the people of Nicaragua. In 1985 similar aid was given to the victims of the Mexico City earthquake. The organization has furnished aid to African nations devastated by drought and famine. In the summer of 1985, AFSC representatives visited South Africa when the South African government refused to meet with DESMOND TUTU to discuss racial tensions and black demands for equality. "African officials," declared Avel Gordly, a member of the delegation, "must themselves renounce the violence of armed repression and the violence of apartheid before they can call on others to give up their reactive violence."

The AFSC has also made commitments to address the problems of poverty, human rights, hunger, and public health in the United States. It has supported peace movements and peace education by sponsoring conferences and informal meetings where people from various countries could discuss their differences.

Through these and many other efforts, the AFSC continues to uphold the beliefs expressed three centuries ago by William Penn: "A good end cannot sanctify evil means; nor must we ever do evil, that good may come of it. . . . Let us then try what love can do." The AFSC adopted as its motto in 1967, "To See What Love Can Do."

SELECTED PUBLICATIONS: Pacifist Handbook, 1939; Some Quaker Approaches to the Race Problem, 1946; Steps to Peace: A Quaker View of U.S. Foreign Policy, 1951; Toward Security Through Disarmament, 1952; Minds in Movement, 1953; Meeting the Russians, 1956; Race and Conscience in America, 1959; A New China Policy, 1965; Peace in Vietnam, 1966; In Place of War, 1967; The Draft? 1968; Anatomy of Anti-Communism, 1969; Who Shall Live? 1970; Uncommon Controversy, 1970; Struggle for Justice, 1971; Almost as Fairly, 1977; The Police Threat to Political Liberty, 1979; A Compassionate Peace, 1982; South Africa, Challenge and Hope, 1982; Taking Charge of Our Lives, 1984; Treaties on Trial, 1986.

PERIODICALS: (annual) Annual Report. (three a year) Quaker Service Bulletin.

ABOUT: Bowden, J. The History of the Society of Friends in America, 1954; Drake, T. Quakers and Slavery in America, 1950; Forbes, J. The Quaker Star Under Seven Flags, 1962; Fry, A. R. A Quaker Adventure, 1926; Hall, W. H. Quaker International Work in Europe Since 1914, 1938; Hinshaw, D. An Experiment in Friendship, 1947; Jonas, G. On Doing Good, 1971; Jones, M. H. Swords Into Ploughshares, 1937; Jones, R. M. A Service of Love in Wartime, 1920; Milligan, E. H. The Past Is Prologue: 100 Years of Quaker Service Overseas, 1968; Pickett, C. E. For More Than Bread, 1953; Trueblood, D. E. The People Called Quakers, 1966; Weisbord, M. R. Some Form of Peace, 1968; Wilson, R. C. Quaker Relief, 1952; Yarrow, C. H. M. Quaker Experiences in International Conciliation, 1978.

AMNESTY INTERNATIONAL
(founded 1961)
Nobel Prize for Peace, 1977

Amnesty International, a nongovernmental human rights organization, was founded in London, England, by Peter Benenson, a lawyer. Benenson had participated in political trials in Cyprus, Hungary, South Africa, and Spain during the 1950s. Outraged by a newspaper account in November 1960 of two Portuguese students sentenced to seven years in prison for drinking a toast to freedom, Benenson resolved to protest to the Portuguese authorities. Realizing that he could accomplish nothing alone, he initiated a massive letter-writing campaign to Antonio Salazar, Portugal's dictator. He quickly expanded the idea into a plan for a yearlong crusade to publicize the plight of political and religious prisoners throughout the world.

Benenson discussed his ideas with Eric Baker, a prominent Quaker, and Louis Blom-Cooper, an internationally known defense lawyer. Together they drew up plans for "Appeal for Amnesty, 1961," a campaign aimed not only at obtaining the release of prisoners jailed for political or religious beliefs but also at helping them gain fair trials and political asylum. They launched the campaign on May 28 with an article in the *Observer,* a liberal London newspaper where one of Benenson's friends was an editor. "Open your newspapers any day of the week," the article began, "and you will find a report from somewhere in the world of someone being imprisoned, tortured, or executed because his opinions or religion are unacceptable to his government." In the article, which described eight "forgotten prisoners," Benenson proposed that groups of concerned citizens adopt one prisoner each from the Western nations, the Soviet bloc, and the Third World.

The article was reported by newspapers around the world, and contributions, inquiries, and reports of other political prisoners began pouring into Benenson's office. Groups were established in several nations. Within two months, representatives from Great Britain, the United States, Ireland, Belgium, France, and Switzerland met in Luxembourg to discuss the movement's future. Agreeing that a one-year effort would not accomplish enough, they founded Amnesty International as a permanent organization to be directed by Benenson and responsible for assigning cases to various national groups for action. As its symbol, Amnesty International adopted a candle enclosed in a strand of barbed wire, an image inspired by the proverb, "It is better to light one candle than to curse the darkness."

One of the first cases the new organization took up was that of Josef Beran, a Czechoslovakian priest. Imprisoned first by the Nazis, he was later jailed by the Communists when, as archbishop of Prague, he delivered a sermon defying the regime. SEAN MACBRIDE, a lawyer and human rights activist who had joined Amnesty International, went to Prague in an effort to free Beran. The only person to have won both the Nobel Prize for Peace and the Lenin Peace Prize, MacBride managed to ob-

tain an interview with the foreign minister of Czechoslovakia; eighteen months later, Beran and four other bishops were released. In this as in all subsequent cases, Amnesty International claimed no credit for the releases, reasoning that no government wishes to admit it holds political prisoners and that any publicity by the organization might endanger the outcome of its actions.

Many other apparent successes followed. After a visit to Ghana by Blom-Cooper in 1962, 152 political prisoners were freed. The following year, a West German trade union leader who had been kidnapped by the East German government was released. In 1964 the organization saw the release of 38 prisoners in Ireland and thousands of others in Burma, Egypt, Greece, and Romania. MacBride credited such victories to the flood of mail on behalf of the prisoners. "Soon the issue is being raised at cabinet level," he explained, "and everyone is wondering whether the guy is worth the trouble. The answer frequently is no."

Although Amnesty International continued to expand, its leadership was plunged into controversy in 1966. Benenson charged that an Amnesty International report alleging inhumane treatment of Arab prisoners held by the British in Aden (now part of the People's Democratic Republic of Yemen) had been suppressed by members of the Amnesty organization because of pressure from the British Foreign Office. Benenson was in turn accused by members of Amnesty International of having links to the British government. In the ensuing crisis of leadership, Benenson resigned, and Eric Baker, one of the group's founding members, was appointed to succeed him as director-general.

During his one-year tenure, Baker rallied the faltering organization. The number of participating groups, which stood at 410 in June 1967, rose to 550 within the year. At that point, Baker was replaced by Martin Ennals, a former leader of the British National Council for Civil Liberties, who guided Amnesty International through the next twelve years. During this period, it consolidated its reputation as the most credible proponent of human rights around the world.

Amnesty International departed from its customary practice of dealing with human rights abuses on a case-by-case basis in 1972, when it initiated a campaign to abolish torture and ensure humane treatment for political prisoners. As part of this effort, the group collected more than one million signatures on a petition "to outlaw immediately the torture of

17

prisoners throughout the world." This document was submitted to the United Nations General Assembly the following year.

Much of the work of Amnesty International has focused on prisoners of conscience, those men and women imprisoned for their beliefs, ethnic origin, language, or religion. Amnesty International declared a "Prisoners of Conscience Year" in 1977. That year the group was awarded the 1977 Nobel Prize for Peace. In her presentation speech, Aase Lionæs of the Norwegian Nobel Committee reviewed progress in the field of human rights since the founding of the organization. "In deciding to honor Amnesty International," she said, "the Nobel committee does so in the conviction that the defense of human dignity against torture, violence, and degradation constitutes a very real contribution to the peace of this world."

The group's acceptance speech was delivered by Mumtaz Soysal, an Amnesty International representative from Ankara, Turkey. "Peace," he declared, "is not to be measured by the absence of conventional war, but constructed upon foundations of justice. Where there is injustice, there is the seed of conflict. Where human rights are violated, there are threats to peace." While noting recent advances in the cause of human rights, Soysal nevertheless pointed out "an alarming increase in disappearances, and the use of summary execution without benefit of fair or even of any trial." He took the occasion to announce a new "program of work aimed at the total and global abolition of the death penalty."

Shortly after the award ceremonies, Amnesty International convened a conference on capital punishment in Stockholm, which concluded with a statement denouncing government-ordered executions. *The Death Penalty,* its report based on the conference, was published in 1979 and attracted widespread support. For example, ANDREI SAKHAROV wrote, "The abolition of the death penalty is especially important in [the Soviet Union], with its unrestricted dominance of state power . . . and its widespread contempt for law and moral values."

Other special campaigns have included a 1978 endeavor to publicize the fate of children abused by political regimes in order to silence their parents. The organization uncovered thousands of instances of brutality against children in Haiti, Ethiopia, South Africa, the Soviet Union, East Germany, Paraguay, and Central America. In 1979 Amnesty International adopted a statement opposing international arms traffic, specifically the sale of weapons to governments that use them to suppress political dissent. For this effort, the organization chose three principal targets: West Germany for its arms sales to Guatemala, the United States for supplying arms to El Salvador, and Great Britain for its arms trade with the government of Idi Amin in Uganda. In ceremonies in London in 1981, Peter Benenson lighted the original Amnesty International candle in observance of the organization's twentieth anniversary. On that occasion, he proposed the slogan Against Oblivion for the campaign that year "to expose and halt the use by governments of 'disappearances' as a means of eliminating suspected opponents."

At the heart of Amnesty International's activities are its adoption groups, small circles of concerned individuals who select a prisoner, write to the prisoner, and write to the government asking for the prisoner's immediate release. More than 3,400 local groups are active in about fifty-five nations. Additional individual members, supporters, and subscribers bring the ranks of Amnesty International to over half a million. The work of the adoption groups and local chapters is coordinated by a central administration in London, whose research department investigates the cases of individual prisoners. After the facts are meticulously verified, the results are disseminated to local groups for action. To maintain objectivity, groups do not work on behalf of prisoners in their own countries.

In 1984 Amnesty International launched "a worldwide campaign to expose and end the use of torture as a tool of state policy." Its report *Torture in the Eighties* (1984) analyzed conditions under which torture is used, cited allegations of torture or ill-treatment in ninety-eight countries, and proposed a series of steps by which governments could prevent the torture of prisoners.

In addition to direct intervention, Amnesty International conducts a vigorous publicity campaign through newsletters, press conferences, and publications and supports a variety of educational programs intended to increase public awareness of human rights issues.

SELECTED PUBLICATIONS: Rights and Wrongs: Some Essays on Human Rights, 1969; Report on Torture, 1973; Amnesty International and the Use of Violence, 1976; Evidence of Torture, 1977; Impartiality and the Defense of Human Rights, 1978; Children, 1979; Prisoners of Conscience, 1981; Political Killings by Governments, 1983; Against Torture, 1984.

PERIODICALS: (annual) Amnesty International Report.

(monthly) Amnesty International Report. (irregular) Country Mission Reports.

ABOUT: Intellect September-October 1976; Lang, O. F. If You Are Silenced, I Will Speak for You, 1978; Larsen, E. A. Flame in Barbed Wire, 1978; New Republic December 18, 1976; Power, J. Amnesty International: The Human Rights Story, 1981.

CARL D. ANDERSON

ANDERSON, CARL D.
(September 3, 1905–)
Nobel Prize for Physics, 1936
(shared with Victor F. Hess)

The American physicist Carl David Anderson was born in New York City, the only son of Emma Adolfina (Ajaxson) and Carl David Anderson. After the family moved to California, he attended the Los Angeles Polytechnic High School, graduating in 1924 and entering the California Institute of Technology (Caltech) in nearby Pasadena.

After receiving a B.S. in physics and engineering from Caltech in 1927, Anderson began graduate studies in physics under ROBERT A. MILLIKAN. He received a Ph.D. magna cum laude in 1930 for a doctoral dissertation on the spatial distribution of electrons ejected from gases by the action of X rays. Anderson then continued to work as a research fellow with Millikan, who encouraged him to study cosmic radiation (electromagnetic radiation and atomic particles of extraterrestrial origin). Within a year Millikan decided to entrust Anderson with the daily operation of a project to identify and measure the energy of different kinds of cosmic radiation, and together they designed a more effective variant of the cloud chamber, a device developed by C. T. R. WILSON that is used to detect charged particles. The cloud chamber is a closed vessel filled with a gas (usually air) that is supersaturated with water vapor; the vessel is placed between the poles of an electromagnet. As charged particles pass through the vessel, they ionize gas molecules in their path, and the ionized molecules serve as condensation centers for the water vapor. Each kind of particle leaves a characteristic condensation trail that can be photographed, and under the influence of the magnet, positively charged and negatively charged particles curve in opposite directions.

Studying thousands of photographs of condensation trails caused by high-energy particles from outer space, Anderson noticed a few paths that differed in only one respect from those caused by electrons: they curved in the opposite direction. Other researchers had noticed similar paths from time to time, but since there was no theoretical basis for the existence of a positively charged electronlike particle, they had dismissed them as experimental artifacts. However, in 1928 P. A. M. DIRAC had predicted the existence of an entire family of antiparticles—particles corresponding to the known ones, but with opposite charges and magnetic moments. Physicists were skeptical of this prediction at first, and Anderson was not searching for antiparticles when he noticed the peculiar tracks—the discovery for which he won the Nobel Prize, he said later, was quite accidental. Instead of dismissing his finding, however, he set out to determine whether the tracks might be those of "antielectrons." After eliminating other possible explanations experimentally, Anderson concluded that his observations could be explained only in terms of a positively charged particle with about the mass of an electron. In September 1932 he announced his discovery of the particle, which he named positron.

Anderson's discovery confirmed the existence of antimatter and led to intensive investigation of matter-antimatter interactions. Anderson and others observed that when an electron meets a positron, the two are annihilated, producing a burst of gamma rays (high-energy electromagnetic radiation). Conversely, if gamma rays of high enough energy are stopped, they vanish, leaving in their place a newly created electron-positron pair. These transformations are dramatic confirmations of the equivalence of mass and energy according to ALBERT EINSTEIN's formula $E = mc^2$. Additional antiparticles (antiprotons and antineutrons) were not found until the 1950s, but by then physicists were convinced that every particle has a corresponding antiparticle. Antiparticles reaching the earth as cosmic radiation or created from gamma rays in the laboratory are quickly destroyed by interaction with ordinary particles. However, physicists speculate that there may be antimatter galaxies, in which atomic nuclei contain antiprotons and are surrounded by positrons, reversing the charge relationship found in our "local" atoms.

"For his discovery of the positron," Anderson received the 1936 Nobel Prize for Physics. He shared the prize with VICTOR F. HESS, who had discovered cosmic rays in 1912 and demonstrated their extraterrestrial origin. In his presentation speech Hans Pleijel of the Royal Swedish Academy of Sciences told Anderson that "by utilizing ingenious devices, you have succeeded in finding one of the building stones of the universe, the positive electron."

Anderson was appointed assistant professor of physics at Caltech in 1933, associate professor in 1937, and full professor in 1939. Two years after his discovery of the positron, he and S. H. Neddermeyer observed another previously undetected particle in cosmic radiation. However, they waited until 1937, patiently gathering additional evidence from cloud-chamber photographs, before announcing their discovery of the particle now known as the muon. This particle is approximately 200 times more massive than the electron.

During World War II, Anderson worked on military projects involving rockets for the National Defense Research Committee and the Office of Scientific Research and Development. In 1944 he spent a month on the Normandy beachhead to observe the functioning of aircraft rockets under combat conditions. After the war, Anderson returned to Caltech where he taught and did research, especially on cosmic radiation and fundamental particles, until his retirement in 1976.

Anderson married Lorraine Elvira Bergman in 1946, and they have two sons. He enjoys playing tennis in his leisure time.

In addition to the Nobel Prize, Anderson has received numerous awards and honors, including the Elliott Cresson Medal of the Franklin Institute (1937) and the John Ericsson Medal of the American Society of Swedish Engineers (1960). He holds honorary degrees from Colgate and Temple universities. Anderson is a member of the National Academy of Sciences, the American Academy of Arts and Sciences, the American Physical Society, and the American Philosophical Society.

ABOUT: Current Biography January 1951; Kevles, D. J. The Physicists, 1978; National Cyclopedia of American Biography, volume F, 1942.

ANDERSON, PHILIP W.
(December 13, 1923–   )
Nobel Prize for Physics, 1977
(shared with Nevill Mott and John H. Van
  Vleck)

The American physicist Philip Warren Anderson was born in Indianapolis, Indiana, and grew up in Urbana, Illinois, where his father, Harry Warren Anderson, was a professor of plant pathology at the University of Illinois. His mother, Elsie (Osborne) Anderson, was the daughter of a mathematics professor; his uncles and many family friends were teachers. "At Illinois," Anderson wrote later, "my parents belonged to a group of warm, settled friends, whose life centered on the outdoors . . . , and my happiest hours as a child and adolescent were spent hiking, canoeing, vacationing, picnicking, and singing around the campfire with this group."

After attending University High School, Anderson entered Harvard University and graduated summa cum laude with a B.S. in electronic physics in 1943. Because of World War II, he delayed his graduate studies to serve as a chief petty officer in the United States Navy. He worked for the next two years at the Naval Research Laboratory in Washington, D.C., as a radio engineer, building antennas. At the end of the war he returned to Harvard, where his graduate thesis adviser was JOHN H. VAN VLECK.

In his master's and doctoral research, Anderson advanced the applications of quantum theory by mathematical modeling to explain the broadening of lines in spectra. Although usually taken to be a single frequency, each line in a substance's spectrum (the particular frequencies of light or other electromagnetic radiation absorbed or emitted by the substance) in fact consists of a small range of frequencies. The breadth of a spectral line depends partly on intermolecular interactions. Anderson found that the advanced mathematical techniques of modern quantum field theory, which he had studied under JULIAN S. SCHWINGER and others, could be used to explain how line broadening in the spectrum of

PHILIP W. ANDERSON

a gas depends on the pressure of the gas. His were among the first quantitative results obtained for line breadths as a function of intermolecular interactions. Some of his methodology has become established modern usage.

For this work, Anderson was awarded an M.S. in 1947 and a Ph.D. in 1949. He then took a position on the technical staff of the Bell Telephone Laboratories, which was one of the foremost research centers for solid-state physics at the time; among the theorists then working in solid-state physics at Bell Labs were JOHN BARDEEN, LEON N COOPER, Charles Kittel, and WILLIAM SHOCKLEY. While continuing to work on line-broadening problems, Anderson also began investigating the magnetic properties of solids, guided by Charles Kittel. He succeeded in explaining certain properties of insulating magnetic materials such as ferrites and antiferromagnetic oxides. Later, in 1961, by means of another quantum model, Anderson explained the magnetic behavior of isolated magnetic ions in a nonmagnetic material (for example, iron atoms in aluminum).

This work intensified Anderson's interest in the phenomenon of superconductivity, the complete absence of electrical resistance in certain substances at very low temperatures. In 1957 Bardeen, Cooper, and J. ROBERT SCHRIEFFER had presented the first satisfactory theory of superconductivity (named the BCS theory after the scientists' last initials). In collaboration with others at Bell Labs, Anderson extended the investigation both theoretically and experimentally and succeeded in relating superconductivity to other properties of the superconducting substances.

The effects of impurities in superconductors had long been puzzling; sometimes the effects were small, sometimes large. Anderson worked out what he called a "theory of dirty superconductors" that did much to clarify the issue. Working with Pierre Morel, he predicted in 1960 that superconducting liquid helium has an anisotropic phase, a form of the liquid exhibiting unequal properties along different axes. Twelve years later, this phenomenon was confirmed experimentally by Douglas Osheroff and his co-workers at Bell Labs.

Anderson thus contributed to the understanding of superfluidity, a frictionless flow that has been observed in liquid helium. In 1962, working with J. M. Rowell, Anderson achieved a laboratory demonstration of the Josephson effects (the "tunneling" of electrons through a thin insulating barrier, predicted in 1962 by BRIAN D. JOSEPHSON). Anderson's resulting paper on spontaneous symmetry breaking has been much cited by elementary particle physicists.

While serving as a visiting lecturer at the University of Tokyo in 1953–1954, Anderson acquired a lasting admiration for Japanese culture and a passion for the Japanese board game called go. That year, at the Kyōto International Theoretical Physics Conference, he met the English physicist NEVILL MOTT, who invited him to spend 1961–1962 at the Cavendish Laboratory, Cambridge University, where Anderson and Mott had many discussions about the behavior of electrons in amorphous (noncrystalline) solids, a topic on which Anderson had published a paper in 1958.

Almost all previous theoretical work in solid-state physics had concerned crystalline solids, because the regular (lattice) arrangement of atoms in a crystal facilitates the mathematical analysis required by quantum theory. Anderson showed that under certain conditions the so-called free electrons of an amorphous solid are tied to specific positions, a phenomenon now known as Anderson localization. Although few scientists appreciated the importance of this work, Mott recognized that amorphous materials can perform as efficiently as more perfectly ordered systems that cost more to produce. Anderson's investigations into conductivity helped establish the foundation for the development of amorphous semiconductors that are used today in such devices as solar cells and photocopying machines.

From 1967 to 1975, after Mott arranged a

unique tenured visiting professorship, Anderson spent half of each year at Cambridge, the other half at Bell Labs. He became assistant director at Bell Labs in 1974, and the following year he gave up his Cambridge position to accept a half-time appointment at Princeton University as Joseph Henry Professor of Physics.

Anderson, Mott, and Van Vleck shared the 1977 Nobel Prize for Physics "for their fundamental theoretical investigations of the electronic structure of magnetic and disordered systems." In his presentation speech, Per-Olov Löwdin of the Royal Swedish Academy of Sciences described the activity of atomic particles as an "electron dance that is essentially responsible for the electric, magnetic, and chemical properties of matter. . . . Through their work, Anderson, Mott, and Van Vleck have shown that the understanding of the electronic choreography is not only remarkably beautiful from the point of view of science but also of essential importance for the development of the technology of our everyday life."

In 1976 Anderson was appointed consulting director at Bell Labs' Physical Research Laboratory in Murray Hill, New Jersey, a position he held until 1984, when he retired. In 1987, when several major breakthroughs occurred in the field of superconductivity, Anderson became the first physicist to publish a theory explaining how certain new materials can achieve the transition to superconductivity at temperatures much higher than those previously attained. According to Anderson, there is no theoretical reason why superconductivity could not occur at room temperature.

Anderson continues to teach at Princeton, where he lives with his wife, the former Joyce Gothwaite. The Andersons, who married in 1947, have one daughter. Anderson's leisure-time interests include gardening, hiking, studying the biological sciences, and Romanesque architecture.

In addition to the Nobel Prize, Anderson has received the Oliver E. Buckley Solid-State Physics Prize of the American Physical Society (1964), the Dannie Heineman Prize of the Göttingen Academy of Sciences (1975), the Guthrie Medal of the Institute of Physics in London (1978), and the National Medal of Science of the National Science Foundation (1982). He is a member of the National Academy of Sciences, the American Academy of Arts and Sciences, the Japanese Physical Society, the American Physical Society, and the American Association for the Advancement of Science.

SELECTED WORKS: Concepts on Solids, 1963; Basic Notions of Condensed Matter Physics, 1984.

ABOUT: New Scientist October 20, 1977; New York Times October 12, 1977; Science November 18, 1977.

ANDRIĆ, IVO
(October 10, 1892–March 13, 1975)
Nobel Prize for Literature, 1961

The Yugoslav poet, novelist, and short story writer Ivo Andrić (an' drĕch) was born in the village of Dolac in Bosnia, now part of Yugoslavia. His father, an artisan, died when Andrić was three years old; his mother subsequently took him to live with an aunt near the town of Višegrad, where he received a strict Roman Catholic upbringing.

From an early age Andrić was keenly aware of the disparate peoples that inhabited the Balkans and of the region's lively, but often uneasy, mix of cultures. Ruled successively by the Eastern Orthodox Byzantines, the Muslim Turks, and minor Slavic nobility, Bosnia had long been isolated from the European mainstream. Nevertheless, during the nineteenth century the region had increasingly become the object of the imperial designs of both Russia and Austria-Hungary. In 1908, following the fate of several of its Balkan neighbors, Bosnia was formally annexed by Austria-Hungary.

Shortly after the annexation, while attending secondary school in Sarajevo, Andrić joined the revolutionary nationalist student organization Mlada Bosna (Young Bosna), which opposed the Austro-Hungarian Hapsburg rule and sought unity and independence for the southern Slavs. When Gavrilo Princip, a fellow member of the group, assassinated Archduke Francis Ferdinand of Austria on June 28, 1914, Andrić was among those arrested. Imprisoned for three years, he devoted his time to reading the works of the Russian novelist Fedor Dostoevsky and the Danish philosopher Søren Kierkegaard. Strongly influenced by the somber, pessimistic attitude of these two authors, Andrić wrote two volumes of poetry, Ex Ponto (From the Sea, 1918) and Nemiri (Anxieties, 1920). "There is no truth but pain," he wrote in one poem, "there is no other reality but suffering."

After the war Andrić traveled and completed his studies of philology, philosophy, and history at the universities of Zagreb, Vienna, Kraków, and Graz, where he earned his doctorate in 1923 with a thesis on Bosnian culture.

IVO ANDRIĆ

Soon afterward, he began a diplomatic career representing the Kingdom of the Serbs, Croats, and Slovenes, the nation which was formed in the aftermath of the war and which became Yugoslavia in 1929. By this time Andrić had given up poetry for fiction; his first short story was published in 1920. Posted to a number of European capitals during the 1920s and 1930s, Andrić found little time for literary pursuits. Nevertheless, between 1924 and 1936 he published three collections of stories—each titled *Pripovetke* (Stories)—in which he drew upon the history and folklore of Bosnia's diverse population. These stories also reflected his view of human existence as essentially a sinister and futile endeavor.

In 1939 Andrić was appointed minister to Germany, and he remained in Berlin until the eve of the German invasion of Yugoslavia in April 1941. When he received word that invasion was imminent, he hurriedly returned to his homeland, arriving in Belgrade only hours before the first German bombers struck the city.

During the German occupation, Andrić remained under virtual house arrest in his Belgrade apartment. Unable to participate in the partisan resistance, he began writing again. Between 1941 and 1945 he produced the trilogy of novels that would ultimately stand as his most important work: *Na Drini ćuprija* (*The Bridge on the Drina*), *Travnička chronika* (translated as *Bosnian Chronicle*), and *Gospodjica* (translated as *The Woman From Sarajevo*). Each of these works was published in 1945.

Of these books, known collectively as the Bosnian Trilogy, *The Bridge on the Drina* is the most widely translated and admired. The novel depicts the struggle of Jews, Muslims, and Catholics through three and a half centuries of Bosnian history. The bridge mentioned in the title, a sixteenth-century span built by the Turks over the Drina River in Višegrad, symbolizes Andrić's conviction that "life is an incomprehensible marvel, since it is incessantly spent and wasted, but nonetheless . . . lasts and stands firmly." In Andrić's fictional world, individual acts and characters are consumed in the larger rhythms of history.

In the second book of the trilogy, *Bosnian Chronicle* (U.K. *Bosnian Story,* 1959), Andrić describes the intrigue and moral drama that develop when a French consul and his Austrian counterpart vie for influence over the Turkish vizier (high executive officer) of Bosnia at the beginning of the nineteenth century. In *The Woman From Sarajevo,* Andrić delves into the human soul to present a psychological study of a miserly and miserable woman. Set in the period between the two world wars and much narrower in its focus than the two chronicles that preceded it, *The Woman From Sarajevo* marked a notable shift in Andrić's style and concerns. The contrasts among all three books of the trilogy demonstrate the author's technical mastery and thematic versatility.

During the postwar period, Andrić's reputation grew steadily within Yugoslavia, and he came to be recognized not as a provincial colorist writing in Serbian but as a major creative figure who had tapped the core of Yugoslavia's complex history and society. A supporter of Premier Tito, who had recognized Bosnia as one of six integral republics within the Yugoslav federation, Andrić joined the Communist party after the war and later served as president of the Union of Yugoslav Writers. His significant works of this period include *Nove pripovetke* (New Stories, 1948), a collection of short stories that deal with events of World War II and the immediate postwar period, and *Prokleta avlija* (*The Devil's Yard,* 1954), a novella that explores the desperate lives of prison inmates through the eyes of a Bosnian imprisoned during the Ottoman Turkish rule.

In 1959 Andrić married Milica Babic, a painter and designer for the Belgrade National Theater. At about this time, he was also elected to Yugoslavia's federal assembly as a representative for Bosnia, a position he held for a number of years.

Andrić was awarded the 1961 Nobel Prize

for Literature "for the epic force with which he has traced themes and depicted human destinies from his country's history." Noting Andrić's use of Bosnian folk legends as a guide to greater truths, Anders Österling of the Swedish Academy remarked in his presentation address that "the study of history and philosophy has inevitably led [Andrić] to ask what forces, in the blows and bitterness of antagonisms and conflicts, act to fashion a people and a nation." In his acceptance speech, Andrić addressed himself to the role of "the story and the storyteller" throughout human history. In all the tales that have ever been told from the beginning of time, he asserted, "it is the story of the human condition that is being spun. . . . The manner of telling and the form of the story vary according to periods and circumstances, but the taste for telling and retelling a story remains the same." Refuting those who charge that the writer of histories ignores the present, Andrić declared that "past and present confront us with similar phenomena and with the same problems." The question that all true storytellers attempt to answer, he told his audience, is what it means to be alive at a particular point in history, what it means to be human.

The remainder of Andrić's life was spent quietly in Yugoslavia, where he became the first creative artist honored with the Prize for Life Work, an annual national award usually reserved for politicians or scientists. Upon the announcement of Andrić's death following a stroke, Tito declared his passing "a great loss for our culture and for the whole country."

Although Andrić's work has received little critical attention in the West, those familiar with his writing have made substantial claims on his behalf. In *The Bridge on the Drina,* according to the Yugoslav critic Peter Džadžić, Andrić has taken on "the task of interpreting the meaning of the human adventure. The historical myth redeems the individual." The Czech poet and literary critic E. D. Goy noted that "despite the considerable difference between his early and later works, his writings present a unity." And, in the view of the literary scholar Thomas Eekman, Andrić's writing plumbs "the wondrous, fascinating, and infinitely rich domains of the human spirit that are hidden from normal logic and tangibility. . . . By the description of those uncommon fateful moments, Andrić marks . . . the highest and the lowest points, the accelerations and the rifts in life, in human fate, which are indeed momentous and decisive for human existence."

"Although Andrić's work frequently betrays his profound sadness over the misery and waste inherent in the passing of time," commented the Yugoslav-American scholar Nicholas Moravcevich, "it still contains some heartening messages of faith in man's struggle against evil as well as sympathy for his pains." Moravcevich continued, "The plasticity of his narrative, the depth of his psychological insight, and the universality of his symbolism remain unsurpassed in all of Serbian literature."

ADDITIONAL WORKS IN ENGLISH TRANSLATION: The Vizier's Elephant, 1962; Lavrin, J. (ed.) An Anthology of Modern Yugoslav Poetry, 1963; Lenski, B. (ed.) Death of a Simple Giant, 1965; Koljević, S. (ed.) Yugoslav Short Stories, 1966; The Pasha's Concubine and Other Tales, 1968.

ABOUT: Alvarez, A. Under Pressure, 1965; Current Biography February 1962; Džadžić, P. Ivo Andrić, 1960; Eekman, T. Thirty Years of Yugoslav Literature, 1978; Hawkesworth, C. Ivo Andrić: Bridge Between East and West, 1984; Juričić, Z. B. The Man and the Artist: Essays on Ivo Andrić, 1986; Kadić, A. Contemporary Serbian Literature, 1964.

ANFINSEN, CHRISTIAN

(March 26, 1916–   )
Nobel Prize for Chemistry, 1972
(shared with Stanford Moore and
    William H. Stein)

The American biochemist Christian Boehmer Anfinsen was born in Monessen, Pennsylvania, a small industrial town outside Pittsburgh. His father, after whom he was named, had immigrated to the United States from Norway; his mother, the former Sophie Rasmussen, was of Norwegian descent. After attending the local schools, Anfinsen entered Swarthmore College, where he received his B.A. in 1937. He then studied organic chemistry at the University of Pennsylvania while serving as an assistant instructor in the same subject. He received his M.S. in 1939 and spent the following year at the Carlsberg Laboratory in Copenhagen, Denmark, as a fellow of the American Scandinavian Foundation.

Returning to the United States in 1940, Anfinsen became a fellow at Harvard University. Three years later he received his Ph.D. in biochemistry from Harvard and became an instructor in the Department of Biological Chemistry at Harvard Medical School in Boston. Between 1944 and 1946 he served in a civilian capacity with the United States Office of Scientific Research and Development. Dur-

CHRISTIAN ANFINSEN

ing the 1947–1948 academic year, he was an American Cancer Society senior fellow in the biochemical division of the Medical Nobel Institute in Sweden, where he worked under HUGO THEORELL. After returning to the United States, Anfinsen was appointed an associate professor at Harvard but left at the end of the year to become chief of the Laboratory of Cellular Physiology at the National Heart Institute of the National Institutes of Health (NIH) in Bethesda, Maryland.

Anfinsen's doctoral dissertation described his investigations into methods for measuring enzymes present in the retina of the eye. Enzymes are chains of amino acids that direct chemical reactions within living organisms. Because they are catalytic rather than structural proteins (such as muscle tissues), enzymes regulate reactions without being used up. At the time Anfinsen began his work, it was known that the amino acid chain folds into a globular three-dimensional form. Each kind of protein was believed to fold, by an unknown means, into a characteristic shape that was related to its function. No one, however, had yet worked out the actual amino acid sequence in an enzyme, and virtually nothing was known about how enzymes control the immense variety of known biochemical reactions.

Anfinsen believed that to understand the structure and function of enzymes, it was necessary to study how they are assembled in living organisms. In the mid-1940s he and a colleague, David Steinberg, began to examine how radioactively labeled amino acids are incorporated into proteins. FREDERICK SANGER

at Cambridge University in England had recently elucidated the sequence of the fifty-one amino acids in the protein insulin (also an enzyme). Applying Sanger's methods to his own research, Anfinsen reasoned that if he synthesized a duplicate chain of amino acids one by one and checked its function after each addition, he would be able to determine how many properties of an enzyme are determined solely by its amino acid sequence. For his investigations, Anfinsen selected bovine ribonuclease, an enzyme of 124 amino acids, produced in the pancreas. By breaking down the amino acid chain of the ribonucleic acid (RNA) in food, ribonuclease makes the components of the chain available for reuse in the body.

Around the same time, a research team at the Rockefeller Institute (now Rockefeller University), led by STANFORD MOORE and WILLIAM H. STEIN, began working on the same problem. It soon became apparent to Anfinsen that their massive effort would determine the enzyme's amino acid sequence before he was able to do so himself.

A Rockefeller Public Service Award enabled Anfinsen to take a leave of absence from the NIH and spend the academic year 1954–1955 at the Carlsberg Laboratory, under Kai Linderstrøm-Lang. As a physical chemist, Linderstrøm-Lang helped Anfinsen study enzymes as "organic chemicals, stripped of their classical mystique as large, amorphous macromolecules," Anfinsen said later. Rather than building the enzyme, as he had initially attempted, he began with a complete ribonuclease molecule and observed it under a variety of conditions.

It had been known for some time that proteins denature (lose their function) under various chemical conditions. Denaturation occurs when the forces that hold the chain of amino acids (the primary structure) in a specific, tightly coiled configuration (the tertiary structure) are altered, turning the protein into a random coil. One of the forces believed to be responsible for maintaining the tertiary structure was disulfide bonding—bridges that form between sulfur-containing cystine amino acids. Anfinsen partially unfolded ribonuclease by denaturing it and chemically severing its four disulfide bonds to obtain a single, randomly folded (and therefore inactive) chain of amino acids. He then observed that when this random structure was placed in a chemical environment similar to the one ribonuclease occupies in the body, the original, active tertiary structure gradually reappeared.

By 1962 Anfinsen had performed physical-

25

chemical studies that demonstrated his "thermodynamic hypothesis." According to this view, the tertiary structure of active ribonuclease arises because it is the most energy-efficient, and hence the most stable, arrangement of its amino acids under normal physiological conditions. The amino acid sequence alone is sufficient to determine not only the enzyme's tertiary structure but also its function.

Anfinsen left the NIH in 1962 to become a professor of biological chemistry at Harvard Medical School, but he returned the following year to direct the Laboratory of Chemical Biology at the National Institute of Arthritis, Metabolism, and Digestive Diseases. There, during the late 1960s, he studied the structure-function relationship of many proteins. Realizing that he could simplify his work by using an enzyme in which there are no disulfide bonds, he investigated the nuclease molecule of the bacterium *Staphylococcus aureus*. By 1970 the enzyme was finally synthesized by researchers at Rockefeller University.

"For his work on ribonuclease, especially concerning the connection between the amino acid sequence and the biologically active conformation," Anfinsen received half of the 1972 Nobel Prize for Chemistry. Moore and Stein shared the other half of the prize for related work. In his presentation speech, Bo G. Malmström of the Royal Swedish Academy of Sciences hailed the three laureates for having enabled other researchers "to approach the problem of enzymatic activity on a molecular basis." Malmström noted that Anfinsen's particular interest had been in the mechanism responsible for the configuration of the peptide chain. "In a series of elegant experiments, he showed that the necessary information is inherent in the linear sequence of amino acids in the peptide chain, so that no further genetic information than that found in DNA is necessary."

After receiving the Nobel Prize, Anfinsen became interested in interferon, a protein that plays a central role in the body's defense against viruses and cancer. After isolating the substance, he launched a series of investigations into its structure and properties. In 1982 he was appointed professor of biology at Johns Hopkins University.

In 1941 Anfinsen married Florence Bernice Kenenger, with whom he had two daughters and one son. They were divorced in 1978. The following year Anfinsen married Libby Esther Schulman Ely. In his leisure time he enjoys sailing and listening to music.

Anfinsen is a member of the Board of Governors of the Weizmann Institute of Science in Rehovot, Israel, and holds membership in the American Society of Biological Chemists, the National Academy of Sciences, and the Royal Danish Academy. He received the Public Service Award of the Rockefeller Foundation in 1954. He has received honorary degrees from Swarthmore College, Georgetown University, New York Medical College, the University of Pennsylvania, Brandeis University, and Providence College.

SELECTED WORKS: The Molecular Basis of Evolution, 1959.

ABOUT: New York Times October 21, 1972; Science November 3, 1972.

ANGELL, NORMAN
(December 26, 1873–October 7, 1967)
Nobel Prize for Peace, 1933

Ralph Norman Angell (ān′ jel), English author and peace activist, was born in Holbeach, Lincolnshire. The seventh and youngest child of Thomas Angell Lane, a well-to-do landowner and tradesman, and the former Mary Ann Brittain, Angell later dropped his father's last name, changing his name legally. After preparatory schooling in England, he was sent to board at the Lycée de St. Omer in northern France. There, at the age of twelve, he first read John Stuart Mill's *Essay on Liberty* and was deeply impressed by its eloquent defense of liberty on pragmatic as well as rational grounds.

Regarding himself as a radical, Angell at the age of fifteen went to Geneva, whose international community included many revolutionaries and political émigrés. There he edited a biweekly English-language newspaper and also attended lectures at the University of Geneva. In 1891, at the age of eighteen, he left Switzerland without taking a degree. After a brief period in England, he accepted a gift of fifty pounds from his father and departed for the United States.

For the next seven years, Angell worked at various jobs: cowboy, ditchdigger, prospector, and mail carrier. He staked a homestead claim in California, but it was denied. He then took up journalism, writing for the *St. Louis Globe-Democrat*, the *San Francisco Chronicle*, and other newspapers.

In 1898 Angell married Beatrice Cuvellier

NORMAN ANGELL

also marked the first time Angell used the shortened version of his name. In *The Great Illusion,* Angell argued that the supposed economic benefits of war are a mirage. War is no longer profitable in an age of economic interdependence, he asserted; rather than enriching the aggressor, war harms both victor and vanquished by destroying international trade and credit. Furthermore, he argued, imposing reparation payments on defeated nations only plants the seeds for future conflict.

Angell resigned from the *Daily Mail* in 1912, although he contributed to it frequently, despite ideological differences with the conservative Northcliffe. The following year, several of Angell's friends established the periodical *War and Peace* as a forum for his views. Angell also wrote extensively for American journals, especially the *New Republic.*

When World War I broke out in August 1914, Angell joined Ramsey MacDonald, Charles Trevelyan, and several others in founding the Union of Democratic Control, an organization that advocated greater public control over the government's foreign policy. During the war, Angell proposed a permanent association of nations to protect international peace and security. He publicized this proposal through lectures in England and the United States, his ideas contributing to President WOODROW WILSON's vision of a League of Nations.

Angell attended the Paris Peace Conference in 1919 and was disappointed by the terms of the Treaty of Versailles, which ran counter to the beliefs he had expressed in *The Great Illusion.* He served as vice-chairman of the Fight the Famine Council, an organization that urged the Allied governments to draw up a more equitable treaty. He also founded the Fight the Famine movement to provide food, medicine, and clothing for the children of Central Europe, a region that suffered terrible deprivations in the aftermath of the war. Meanwhile, through his articles and books, he maintained a continual commentary on world affairs. In *The Fruits of Victory* (1921), he argued that the outcome of World War I confirmed the propositions he had outlined earlier in *The Great Illusion.* In *The Unseen Assassins* (1933), he discussed the adverse effects of imperialism, nationalism, and patriotism. He also devised "The Money Game," a card game intended to teach the principles of economics and credit.

In 1920 Angell stood for Parliament as a Labour party candidate in Nottinghamshire, the first of three unsuccessful bids to enter

of New Orleans. Throughout his life he remained highly secretive and sensitive about his wife, apparently a highly unstable woman. He had separated from her by 1914, but she remained a financial and emotional burden on him until her death in 1955. The couple had no children.

Angell returned briefly to England in 1898 to attend to family matters. He then moved to Paris, where he managed to support himself by contributing articles on the Alfred Dreyfus treason case to American newspapers. The following year, he became editor of the Paris *Daily Messenger,* an English-language newspaper. His observations on the Spanish-American War, the Dreyfus case, and the Boer War inspired his first book, *Patriotism Under Three Flags: A Plea for Rationalism in Politics,* which appeared in 1903. A year later, he accepted an offer by the English newspaper magnate Lord Northcliffe (Alfred C. W. Harmsworth) to edit the Paris edition of the *Daily Mail.* This position greatly expanded Angell's perspective on international affairs.

During this period, Angell wrote *Europe's Optical Illusion,* a small book that examined the economic basis of war, which he published at his own expense in 1909. The book impressed Lord Esher (Reginald Brett), an influential English government official and historian, who brought it to public attention by distributing copies to 200 prominent Europeans. Expanded and reprinted the following year as *The Great Illusion,* it eventually sold almost two million copies and was translated into more than twenty-five languages. It

politics. In 1929 he won a seat in the House of Commons as Labour member for North Bradford but gave it up in 1931, convinced that he could accomplish more as a writer and speaker. That year he was knighted in recognition of his public service.

In 1934 Angell received the 1933 Nobel Peace Prize, which had been reserved in the absence of a suitable candidate. In his presentation speech, CHRISTIAN LANGE of the Norwegian Nobel Committee described Angell as "one of the educators . . . who pave the way for reforms which the statesmen attempt to carry out." Lange noted that "few people have done as much as Sir Norman . . . to clear away the mists which prevent us from seeing the road we should travel." Cecil Dormer, British minister to Norway, accepted the prize for Angell, who was ill. In his Nobel lecture, given in Oslo the following year, Angell discussed some of the reasons that lead nations to wage war, including isolationism, propaganda, fear, and public acquiescence. "The obstacles to peace are not obstacles . . . in inanimate nature," he concluded. "The obstacles to peace are in the minds and hearts of men."

Although opposed to war, Angell did not consider himself a pacifist. Armed force is a reality, he said. "The real issue . . . is its organization and employment, and by whom." He believed that a collective security system open to all nations, including fascist Germany, could help avert another war. He disagreed with British socialists who held that war would disappear with the abolition of private property.

When Italy invaded Ethiopia in 1935, Angell chastized the British government for refusing to intervene or impose sanctions. He became an outspoken critic of Prime Minister Neville Chamberlain's policies of appeasement toward Nazi Germany. These, he said, conveyed but one lesson: "Kill quickly and kill often and you get away with it." Increasingly fearful "that Europe will certainly pass under Hitler's dominion," he urged Great Britain to open its doors to Jewish refugees and sheltered a refugee family himself at his home at Northey Island on the Essex coast.

When Great Britain declared war on Germany in September 1939, Angell volunteered his services to the Ministry of Information, which dispatched him to the United States the following year to seek support for the British war effort. He took an apartment in New York City, where he remained until 1951, writing, lecturing, and meeting with American political leaders.

After the war, Angell advocated a gradual move toward world government under the United Nations, even though he believed it to be a less effective organization than the League of Nations had been. He was dismayed by the Korean War and by the repressive climate that prevailed in the United States during the anti-Communist crusade of Senator Joseph McCarthy in the 1950s.

Returning to England in 1951, Angell took up residence in Fern Hill, Haslemere, Surrey. From there he continued to issue a steady stream of books and articles. Many expressed his concern over anticolonialism and the growing influence of Third World nations, whose separatism and frequent recourse to violence would, he feared, preclude the goal of international cooperation to which he had dedicated his life. He grew increasingly critical of Israel, particularly for such acts of terrorism as the assassination of Count Folke Bernadotte, a United Nations mediator in the Palestine dispute. Seeking to assist Palestinian refugees, Angell approached Arab groups in the United States but was rebuffed.

As his health began to fail, Angell made fewer lecture appearances. In 1958 he fell and shattered his leg. Two years later, he was hospitalized with a broken hip but still managed to lecture at the Conference on Reduction of World Tension at the University of Chicago. In 1961 he accepted an invitation to donate his papers to Ball State Teachers College (now Ball State University) in Muncie, Indiana. He made his last trip to the United States in 1966 to present the papers officially and receive an honorary law degree from Ball State.

Angell died in a nursing home in Croydon, Surrey, on October 7, 1967.

ADDITIONAL WORKS: Peace Theories and the Balkan War, 1912; War and the Essential Realities, 1913; Arms and Industry, 1914; Prussianism and Its Destruction, 1914; The World's Highway, 1915; America and the New World-State, 1915; Why Freedom Matters, 1916; War Aims, 1917; The Political Conditions of Allied Success, 1918; The Peace Treaty and the Economic Chaos of Europe, 1919; If Britain Is to Live, 1923; Foreign Policy and Our Daily Bread, 1925; The Public Mind: Its Disorders, Its Exploitation, 1926; Must Britain Travel the Moscow Road? 1926; The Story of Money, 1930; Can Governments Cure Unemployment? 1931; The Foreigner's Turn to Disarm, 1931; The Great Illusion: 1933, 1933; We Can Abolish War, 1933; What Causes War? 1933; The Menace to Our National Defense, 1934; Preface to Peace, 1935; This Have and Have-Not Business, 1936; The Defense of the Empire, 1937; Peace With Dictators? 1938; For What Do We Fight? 1939; What Kind of Peace? 1941; Let the People Know, 1943; The Steep Places, 1947; After All: The Autobiography of Norman Angell, 1951; Defense of the English-Speaking Role, 1958.

ABOUT: Bisceglia, L. Norman Angell and Liberal Internationalism in Britain, 1982; Ceadel, M. Pacifism in Britain, 1914–1945, 1980; Hamilton, M. A. Remembering My Good Friends, 1944; Historical Journal September 1974; Marrin, A. Sir Norman Angell, 1979; Miller, J. D. B. Norman Angell and the Futility of War, 1986.

APPLETON, EDWARD
(September 6, 1892–April 21, 1965)
Nobel Prize for Physics, 1947

EDWARD APPLETON

The English physicist Edward Victor Appleton was born in Bradford, Yorkshire, the son of Peter Appleton, a mill worker, and the former Mary Wilcock. From his parents the boy acquired an avid interest in music, but around the age of sixteen he suddenly turned his attention to physics and mathematics. A brilliant student, he won scholarships to the Hanson Secondary School, where he studied from 1903 to 1911, and to St. John's College, Cambridge. At Cambridge he studied under ERNEST RUTHERFORD and J. J. THOMSON, won prizes in mineralogy and physics, and received his bachelor's degree with highest honors in 1913.

A scholarship enabled him to remain at Cambridge to conduct graduate research under W. H. BRAGG on the crystallographic structure of metals and minerals. When World War I broke out in 1914, however, Appleton joined an infantry battalion. He was soon transferred to the Royal Engineers, where as a signal officer, he worked with radio communications and investigated the problem of fading radio signals. His wartime work on vacuum tubes and their application to radio communications stimulated his curiosity about this field. Returning to Cambridge at the end of the war, Appleton continued his studies on the applications of vacuum tubes.

Appleton was elected a fellow of St. John's in 1919, followed the next year by an appointment as assistant demonstrator in physics at Cambridge's Cavendish Laboratory. Together with C. T. R. WILSON, Appleton began to investigate the emission of radio waves by electrical storms.

In 1924, at the age of thirty-two, Appleton became Wheatstone Professor of Physics at the University of London. That year, with Miles Barnett, his first graduate student, he began to study how radio waves are propagated in the atmosphere. In 1902 the British physicist Oliver Heaviside had proposed that the upper atmosphere contains an ionized electrical layer capable of reflecting the long-distance radio waves that GUGLIELMO MARCONI had successfully bounced across the Atlantic Ocean the preceding year. Appleton wondered if radio waves reflecting off this Heaviside-Kennelly layer, as it has become known, might interfere with radio waves traveling straight across the ground, thus causing the nighttime fading of signals that he had observed.

With assistance from the British Broadcasting Corporation, Appleton and Barnett bounced radio waves of differing frequencies off the Heaviside layer on December 11, 1924. Their technique, now known as frequency modulation radar, provided the first experimental proof of the existence of the ionosphere, established its height at 60 miles above ground, led to the development of radio research, and paved the way for the invention of radar.

Two years after his measurement of the ionosphere, Appleton discovered a second nonconducting layer some 150 miles above the surface of the earth. Now called the Appleton layer, its greater strength enables it to reflect shortwave radio signals. By this second discovery Appleton established the feasibility of direct, worldwide radio broadcasts.

Using the interference of the reflected and ground radio waves, Appleton continued to investigate the detailed structure and properties of these high layers for the rest of his life. By observing the effect of a total solar eclipse in 1927, Appleton established that sunlight is responsible for forming and controlling the ionosphere. Shifting from the radio interference technique to a pulsed radio height measurement technique used in the United States, Appleton and his colleagues measured the height and structure of the ionosphere in the polar region as well as at lower latitudes. Moreover, they found that the ionosphere is affected by particles emitted by the sun (the solar wind) as well as by solar ultraviolet emission. Finally, they determined that the height of the ionosphere is subject to lunar tides.

Two years after C. T. R. Wilson's resignation in 1934, Appleton was appointed to the Jacksonian Chair of Natural Philosophy at Cambridge University. An important member of the international radio community, he served as president of the International Union of Scientific Radio from 1934 to 1952.

With the outbreak of World War II in 1939, Appleton was appointed secretary of the Department of Scientific and Industrial Research, Britain's primary scientific research office. In this capacity he directed not only research into military radio communications but also the British effort to develop the atomic bomb. The team of researchers he had assembled in the early 1930s applied its knowledge to the radiolocation of aircraft, a technology that ultimately made it possible for the Royal Air Force to defeat Germany's superior air offensive early in the war. According to Robert Watson-Watt, who perfected radar as Britain's secret weapon, if it were not for Appleton's early research, radar would have come too late to be decisive in the 1940 Battle of Britain. For his services, Appleton was knighted in 1941. As the war progressed, Appleton began to formulate an agenda for postwar recovery in which he proposed that the Department of Scientific and Industrial Research, and scientists in general, play an important role in restoring civilian food supplies, transportation, housing, and other services.

Appleton was awarded the 1947 Nobel Prize for Physics "for his investigations of the physics of the upper atmosphere, especially for the discovery of the so-called Appleton layer." In his presentation speech, Erik Hulthén of the Royal Swedish Academy of Sciences outlined the theoretical aspects of Appleton's research and then went on to describe some of its practical benefits. He noted that "the echo methods which were developed by Appleton and his co-workers . . . must be looked upon as precursors of the radar methods which were so successfully employed by the Allies" during World War II. This technology, Hulthén added, also found important applications in meteorology and commercial radio broadcasts.

In 1949 Appleton was named vice-chancellor of the University of Edinburgh. An outstanding leader who devoted much time to administrative duties, he also maintained an active interest in the behavior of the atmosphere and stayed in close contact with scientists working in this field. During the International Geophysical Year 1957–1958, he played an active role in planning worldwide radio experiments.

In 1916 Appleton married Jessie Longson, with whom he had two daughters. In 1965, a year after his first wife died from the effects of a stroke, Appleton married Helen Allison. A month later, he died at his home. A short man endowed with abundant energy, Appleton was known for his warmth and great kindness. Like his father, who for many years served as choirmaster in a Bradford church, Appleton possessed a ringing tenor voice that enhanced his effectiveness as a public speaker.

Appleton's many awards included the Hughes Medal (1933) and the Royal Medal (1950), both of the Royal Society, and the Albert Medal of the Royal Society of Arts (1950). He was presented with honorary degrees by the University of Aberdeen, London University, the University of Glasgow, Oxford University, Cambridge University, the University of Cincinnati, and other institutions. He was decorated by the governments of the United States, Norway, France, and Iceland and held membership in the Royal Society in addition to foreign membership in the American Academy of Arts and Sciences, the Royal Swedish Academy of Sciences, the American Meteorological Society, the American Academy of Arts and Sciences, the Pontifical Academy of Sciences, and many other professional societies.

SELECTED WORKS: Thermionic Vacuum Tubes and Their Applications, 1931; Empire Communication, 1933; The Application of Ionospheric Data to Radio Communication, 1948, with W. J. G. Beynon; Science and the Nation, 1957.

ABOUT: Biographical Memoirs of Fellows of the Royal Society, volume 12, 1966; Clark, R. W. Sir Edward Appleton, 1971; Current Biography September 1945; Dictionary of Scientific Biography, volume 1, 1970.

ARBER, WERNER
(June 3, 1929–)
Nobel Prize for Physiology or Medicine, 1978
(shared with Daniel Nathans and Hamilton O. Smith)

The Swiss molecular biologist Werner Arber was born in Gränichen, Aargau canton, where he received his early education in the public schools. Entering the Swiss Polytechnical School in Zurich in 1949 to study natural science, he received his first exposure to experimental research. His early research efforts involved the isolation and characterization of a radioactive isotope of chlorine.

In 1953 Arber enrolled as a graduate student at the University of Geneva and was appointed research assistant in the biophysics department. There he helped develop techniques for preparing bacteriophages (viruses that attack bacteria) for electron microscopy, a technique that permits examination of the fine microscopic structure of cells or other tissue by means of electron beams. As a graduate student, Arber presented an analysis of the JAMES D. WATSON–FRANCIS CRICK model of deoxyribonucleic acid (DNA) to a journal club of the biophysics department, a discussion group in which new discoveries published in journals are presented by members. These activities marked the beginning of a lifelong interest in bacteriophage physiology and genetics.

Among the simplest forms of life, bacteriophages (virus particles that infect bacterial cells) consist of an inner core of nucleic acid and an outer coat of protein. After it infects a bacterial cell, there are three possible fates for a bacteriophage. First, it may take over the biochemical apparatus of the cell and multiply, causing destruction of the cell by releasing new phage particles. Second, it may be incorporated into the DNA of the bacterial cell (in which case it is called a prophage) and then be transmitted to daughter cells during cell division, as if it were a bacterial-cell gene. Finally, the bacteriophage may be broken down into its constituent parts by bacterial enzymes in a phenomenon now known as host-controlled modification.

In the early 1950s, while Arber was still a graduate student, the first electron micrographs of bacteriophages were produced in the biophysics department of the University of Geneva. Arber received a Ph.D. from the University of Geneva in 1958 (for a dissertation on deficiencies of a mutant strain of bacteriophage lambda) and for the next two years was a postdoctoral fellow and research associate in the microbiology department at the University of Southern California. Before returning to the University of Geneva in 1960, he spent a few weeks in the United States visiting several laboratories where bacteriophage research was being done. In addition to gaining considerable skill in the techniques of bacterial genetics and bacteriophage research

WERNER ARBER

while abroad, Arber developed an interest in the phenomenon of host-cell-induced variation, or restriction. Upon his return to the University of Geneva, he was made a member of the faculty. With assistance from the Swiss National Science Foundation, Arber turned his attention to the molecular basis of bacteriophage restriction.

It was in collaboration with a doctoral student in 1962 that Arber discovered the mechanism of host-cell-induced variation, or host-controlled restriction-modification as it is now known, a process in which the bacteriophage DNA is cleaved, or cut, into its component parts by the action of a restriction endonuclease enzyme, acting in concert with a methylase enzyme. The bacterial cell's restriction endonuclease recognizes a certain nucleotide sequence on the bacteriophage DNA and cleaves the DNA molecule at several sites, rendering it inactive. Meanwhile, the methylase enzyme recognizes the identical nucleotide sequence in the DNA of the bacterial, or host, cell, methylates it, and thus protects it from enzymatic cleavage by its own endonuclease. (Methylation involves the addition of a methyl group—a carbon atom and three hydrogen atoms—to the DNA molecule.)

Arber called this two-enzyme system a restriction-modification system. In addition to isolating and purifying the endonuclease and methylase enzymes (which restrict the replication of bacteriophage DNA and modify the host-cell DNA, respectively), Arber and his colleagues found bacterial mutants that were defective in both endonuclease and methylase enzymes. Arber called this restriction endonuclease (isolated from the colon bacillus *Escherichia coli*) a type I endonuclease. Although type I endonuclease recognizes specific nucleotides on bacteriophage DNA, it cleaves the DNA at random sites. Arber predicted that another type of endonuclease (type II) that was specific for the cleavage site would eventually be found, that endonuclease enzymes would permit precise analysis of the genetic structure of DNA, and that gene splicing would someday be commonplace—all of which proved to be accurate.

A year after his appointment as associate professor of molecular biology at the University of Geneva in 1965, Arber married; he and his wife Antonia have two daughters. Later in that decade, lamenting the decline of student interest in research and what he considered to be an increasingly political atmosphere in academic life, he accepted the offer of a professorship with ample research facilities at the Biocentrum, a new research institute under construction at the University of Basel. While its facilities were being completed, Arber spent 1970–1971 as visiting investigator in the Department of Molecular Biology at the University of California at Berkeley. Returning to Switzerland, he was appointed professor of molecular biology at the University of Basel.

For "the discovery of restriction enzymes and their application to problems of molecular genetics," Arber shared the 1978 Nobel Prize for Physiology or Medicine with DANIEL NATHANS and HAMILTON O. SMITH. In his presentation speech, Peter Reichard of the Karolinska Institute hailed Arber for his discovery of restriction enzymes. "In a series of simple but elegant experiments, Arber showed that [host-controlled modification] was caused by a change in DNA and apparently served to protect the host from foreign genes," Reichard said. "The application of restriction enzymes has revolutionized the genetics of higher organisms and completely changed our ideas of the organization of their genes," he went on. "In contrast to the DNA of bacteria, the DNA of higher organisms is not a contiguous structure coding for one protein. Instead, genes contain 'quiet' regions alternating with regions containing the genetic code."

Continuing his research at the University of Basel, Arber has become interested in the different types of genetic systems, genetic recombination, and genetic diversification. It is now known that genetic elements and genes can be mobile and that genes can be exchanged between different genetic systems. For example, they can be inserted in recombinant DNA technologies, and they can be transposed from one molecule of DNA to another. Arber has speculated that genetic exchange may explain the diversification of bacterial genetic codes in the course of evolution.

A devoted family man, Arber considers himself fortunate in having the support and encouragement of his wife and two daughters. "In response to their interest and understanding for my scientific activities," he says, "I have tried to give them my personal affection needed for a harmonious life."

ABOUT: New York Times October 13, 1978; Science December 8, 1978.

ARNOLDSON, KLAS
(October 27, 1844–February 20, 1916)
Nobel Prize for Peace, 1908
(shared with Fredrik Bajer)

The Swedish journalist Klas Pontus Arnoldson was born in the port city of Göteborg to Olof Andersson Arnoldson, a musician, and the former Inga Hagbom von Seth. His father died when the boy was sixteen, and he was compelled to leave school. He took a job as a railway clerk and worked twenty-one years for the railways, becoming stationmaster midway through his career.

During this time he studied on his own, reading widely in philosophy, history, and religion. Influenced by nineteenth-century liberal theology, especially the humanistic beliefs of Unitarianism, Arnoldson developed a strong aversion to religious dogmatism. He became convinced that individual conscience and freedom of thought could improve human life, an idea he began to promote in articles written for newspapers and periodicals during the 1870s.

To international issues, Arnoldson brought the same faith in the power of human reason. He was appalled by the bloodshed caused by the 1864 war in which Prussian and Austrian troops seized the Danish duchies of Schleswig and Holstein and by the Franco-Prussian War of 1870–1871. Arnoldson felt that Otto von Bismarck's use of these wars to unite Germany was not worth the casualties they had cost.

Increasingly alarmed by the arms buildup among the major European powers, he quit his job in 1881 to devote full time to journalism and the cause of peace. Although he had little formal education, Arnoldson was a highly successful writer. His articles appeared frequently

KLAS ARNOLDSON

in Swedish periodicals and newspapers, where they attracted wide interest. By 1882 he had gained sufficient recognition as a writer and speaker to win a seat in the lower chamber of the Swedish Parliament. In this capacity he pursued his commitment to individualism and democracy, introducing legislation to ensure religious tolerance, reduce militarism, and extend suffrage to all adult male citizens (passed in 1909). He was a founding member of the Swedish Peace and Arbitration Union, established in 1883. That year he persuaded his colleagues in the Parliament to adopt a resolution urging Sweden to become neutral, a position it eventually adopted in 1914. To Arnoldson, it seemed clear that small nations could not hope to compete with the military might of such European powers as Germany and Great Britain. He urged all the Scandinavian nations to join in a union pledged to neutrality, but his efforts failed.

While serving in the Parliament, he continued to write. From 1883 to 1885 he edited *Tiden* (The Times), a compendium of views on peace and progressive ideas. He also edited *Fredsvännen* (The Friend of Peace) from 1885 to 1888 and *Nordsvenska Dagbladet* (North Sweden Daily) from 1892 to 1894. He wrote several novels and books on the subjects of peace and religion.

Believing that he could exert more influence by speaking and writing, Arnoldson declined to run for reelection to the Swedish Parliament in 1887. His talent for expressing abstract concepts in language that large numbers of people could understand made him one of the most

successful and most popular voices in the early years of the European peace movement. On a speaking tour of Sweden and Norway in 1889–1890, he lectured on the need for international arbitration as a means of preventing armed conflict. His speeches won a following in the Norwegian Parliament, which in 1890 became the world's first national assembly to endorse arbitration as a national policy.

Since 1815, Norway had been united with Sweden under a single monarch, but in 1895 Norway's demands for self-rule threatened to dissolve the union. At first, Sweden refused to consider separation. Arnoldson's visits to Norway had made him sympathetic to the Norwegian cause, however, and he saw the issue as a chance to test the value of arbitration. Although the dispute did not go to arbitration, Arnoldson was instrumental in convincing Swedish politicians to accept the separation peacefully when the Norwegian Parliament voted for independence in 1905.

Arnoldson and the Danish pacifist FREDRIK BAJER shared the 1908 Nobel Prize for Peace. The award provoked outrage among those militant Swedes who considered Arnoldson a traitor because of his attitude toward Norway's independence. Nevertheless, his nomination had been supported unanimously by the Swedish Group of the Interparliamentary Union and by thirty-four members of the Swedish Parliament.

In his Nobel lecture, "World Referendum," Arnoldson observed, "Nowadays it is probable that no subject of international disagreement would lead to war if it were first submitted to a panel of experts." Then he discussed a resolution of The Hague Peace Conference of 1907 that governments should resume "serious examination" of the topic of limitation of military expenditure, which was first proposed by The Hague Peace Conference of 1899. "If the whole of humanity is now weary of the burdens of war," he said, "something more effective than a mere 'serious examination' is required if we are to lighten these burdens and perhaps finally eradicate them. If this is regarded as impossible, it is not so much because of certain technical difficulties as it is because we lack strong moral fiber."

He then proposed his idea for an international referendum whereby adult citizens of all nations would be asked to sign a declaration stating: "If all other nations will abolish their armed forces and be content with a joint police force for the whole world, then I, the undersigned, wish my own nation to do the same." He argued that such a referendum would encourage governments to agree on general disarmament and peaceful resolution of their disputes. Pacifism, he said, was the necessary next step if the world was to progress from barbarism to civilization.

Although he was not wealthy, Arnoldson contributed his prize money to various peace organizations with which he was affiliated. Even after the outbreak of World War I, he continued to promote his plan for a referendum and to support the cause of world peace.

In 1869 Arnoldson married Ava Bernhardina Wahlgren, whom he divorced in 1903, the same year he married Edit Viktoria Blomsköld. He died of a heart attack in Stockholm at the age of seventy-one.

WORKS IN ENGLISH TRANSLATION: Pax Mundi, 1892.

ABOUT: New York Times February 21, 1916.

SVANTE ARRHENIUS

ARRHENIUS, SVANTE
(February 19, 1859–October 2, 1927)
Nobel Prize for Chemistry, 1903

The Swedish chemist and physicist Svante August Arrhenius (ə rā′ nē əs) was born on the Vik estate, near Uppsala, the second son of Carolina Christina (Thunberg) and Svante Gustav Arrhenius. Arrhenius's ancestors were farmers; his father was a surveyor and the administrator of the estate. A year after Arrhenius was born, his family moved to Uppsala, where his father became a supervisor at the university. Even as a small child Arrhenius enjoyed adding the numbers in his father's reports. He received his early education at the cathedral school in Uppsala and showed exceptional ability in biology, physics, and mathematics.

Entering the University of Uppsala in 1876, Arrhenius studied physics, chemistry, and mathematics and was awarded a B.S. in 1878. For the next three years he pursued graduate studies in physics at Uppsala but transferred to the Swedish Academy of Sciences in Stockholm in 1881 to conduct research in the field of electrical theory under Erik Edlund.

At the time, the physics of electricity was not fully understood. It was known, however, that neither pure water nor dry salts could by themselves transmit an electrical current, whereas in aqueous solution salts could. Arrhenius studied the passage of electricity through many types of solutions. He hypothesized that molecules of some substances dissociate, or split, into two or more particles (which he later called ions) when they are dissolved in a liquid. Although each intact molecule is electrically balanced, the particles carry a small electrical charge, either positive or negative depending on the nature of the particle. For example, sodium chloride (salt) molecules break into charged atoms of sodium and oppositely charged atoms of chlorine when dissolved in water. These charged atoms, the active components of the molecule, form only in solution and permit the passage of electricity. The electrical current, in turn, directs the active components toward electrodes of opposite charge.

This hypothesis was the subject of Arrhenius's doctoral dissertation, which he submitted to the University of Uppsala in 1884. At the time, however, most scientists doubted that oppositely charged particles could coexist in solution, and the faculty rated his dissertation fourth class, too low for him to qualify as a lecturer.

Undaunted, Arrhenius not only published his theories but sent copies of his thesis to a number of leading European scientists, including the prominent German chemist WILHELM OSTWALD. Ostwald was so interested in the work that he visited Arrhenius in Uppsala and invited him to join the faculty at the technical college in Riga. Arrhenius declined the invitation, but Ostwald's support encouraged the Uppsala faculty to appoint Arrhenius a lecturer, a post he held for two years.

In 1886 Arrhenius received a fellowship from the Swedish Academy of Sciences that enabled him to work and study abroad. During the next five years he worked with Ostwald in Riga, with Friedrich Kohlrausch at the University of Würzburg (where he met WALTHER NERNST), with Ludwig Boltzmann at the University of Graz, and with JACOBUS VAN'T HOFF at the University of Amsterdam. Returning to Stockholm in 1891, he became a lecturer in physics at Stockholms Högskola (the equivalent of an engineering college), where he was appointed physics professor in 1895 and rector in 1897.

Throughout this time Arrhenius continued his work on electrolytic dissociation and osmotic pressure. (Osmotic pressure is a measure of the effort of two different solutions to equalize their concentrations when separated by a semipermeable membrane.) Van't Hoff had expressed osmotic pressure as $PV = iRT$, where P stands for the osmotic pressure of a substance dissolved in a liquid; V, the volume; R, the pressure of any gas present; T, the temperature; and i, a coefficient that often equals 1 in gases but that is greater than 1 for solutions containing salts. Van't Hoff was unable to explain why the value of i varied, but Arrhenius's work enabled him to show that i could be correlated with the number of types of ions in the solutions.

Arrhenius was awarded the 1903 Nobel Prize for Chemistry "in recognition of the extraordinary services he has rendered to the advancement of chemistry by his electrolytic theory of dissociation." In his presentation speech, H. R. Törnebladh of the Royal Swedish Academy of Sciences pointed out that Arrhenius's theory of ions had given a quantitative basis to electrochemistry, "thus allowing it to be treated mathematically. One of the most important consequences of Arrhenius's theory," Törnebladh said, "was the completion of the great generalization for which the first Nobel Prize for Chemistry was awarded to van't Hoff."

A scientist of wide-ranging interests, Arrhenius investigated many aspects of physics. In 1883 he published a paper on ball lightning. He worked on the effects of solar radiation on the atmosphere. He attempted to explain such climatic changes as the glacial eras and to apply physicochemical theories of volcanic action. In 1901 he and several colleagues confirmed James Clerk Maxwell's hypothesis that cosmic radiation exerts pressure on particles. Arrhenius went on to use this phenomenon in an effort to explain the aurora borealis and solar corona. He also suggested that radiation pressure could carry spores and other living seeds through space. In 1902 he proposed a theory of immunology, a subject that continued to interest him for many years.

After retiring from Stockholms Högskola in 1905, Arrhenius was named director of the physical chemistry department of the Nobel Institute in Stockholm. He remained in this position for the rest of his life.

Arrhenius was married in 1894 to Sofia Rudbeck; they had one son. The marriage ended two years later. In 1905 he married Maria Johansson, with whom he had one son and two daughters. He died in Stockholm on October 2, 1927, after a brief illness.

Arrhenius was the recipient of many honors and awards, including the Davy Medal of the Royal Society of London (1902), the first Willard Gibbs Medal of the American Chemical Society (1911), and the Faraday Medal of the British Chemical Society (1914). He was a member of the Swedish Academy of Sciences and a foreign member of the Royal Society of London and the German Chemical Society. He received honorary degrees from the universities of Birmingham, Edinburgh, Heidelberg, and Leipzig and from Oxford and Cambridge universities, among others.

SELECTED WORKS: Textbook of Electrochemistry, 1902; The Development of the Theory of Electrolytic Dissociation, 1904; Theories of Chemistry, 1907; Immunochemistry, 1907; Worlds in the Making: The Evolution of the Universe, 1908; The Life of the Universe, 1909; Theories of Solutions, 1912; Quantitative Laws in Biological Chemistry, 1915; The Destinies of the Stars, 1918; Chemistry in Modern Life, 1925.

ABOUT: Dictionary of Scientific Biography, volume 1, 1970; Farber, E. (ed.) Great Chemists, 1961; Harrow, B. Eminent Chemists, 1927; Jaffe, B. Crucibles: The Story of Chemistry, 1930; Lindroth, S. (ed.) Swedish Men of Science, 1952.

ARROW, KENNETH

(August 23, 1921–)
Nobel Memorial Prize in Economic
Sciences, 1972
(shared with John Hicks)

The American economist Kenneth Joseph Arrow was born in New York City to Harry Arrow and the former Lillian Greenberg. He attended the City College of New York (CCNY), graduating in 1940 with a degree in social science and a major in mathematics. His college education, he said later, "was made possible only by the existence of that excellent free institution [CCNY] and the financial sacrifices of my parents."

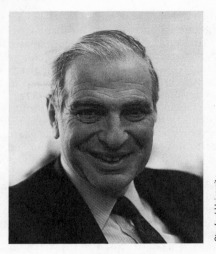

Stanford University

KENNETH ARROW

Entering Columbia University in 1940, Arrow began his graduate studies in mathematics and received an M.S. the following year. He then switched to economics, on the advice of the statistician and mathematical economist Harold Hotelling. Arrow's graduate studies were interrupted by World War II: from 1942 to 1946 he did research as a weather officer in the United States Army Air Corps and was eventually promoted to captain. He continued his graduate studies at Columbia from 1946 to 1949, while also serving as a research associate and assistant professor with the Cowles Commission for Research in Economics at the University of Chicago. There (and for many years at the Rand Corporation), Arrow pursued his interests in general equilibrium theory, mathematical programming, and welfare economics while working with TJALLING C. KOOPMANS and many other mathematically inclined economists.

In 1949 Arrow became acting assistant professor of economics at Stanford University. He remained at Stanford, where he rose to professor of economics, statistics, and operations research, until 1968, when he joined the faculty of Harvard University. From 1974 to 1979 he was James Bryant Conant University Professor at Harvard. Since 1980 he has been professor of economics and professor of operations research at Stanford.

Arrow's doctoral dissertation was published in 1951 as *Social Choice and Individual Values*. In it, building on earlier work by PAUL SAMUELSON and the Harvard economist Abram Bergson, Arrow sought to establish the con-

ditions, if any, under which group decisions could be rationally and democratically derived from individual preferences. For Arrow, a democratic "social welfare function"—that is, one relating individual preferences to social choices—had to satisfy four conditions: transitivity (if social choice A is preferred to B, and B to C, then A is preferred to C); Pareto efficiency (an alternative is never chosen such that there is another feasible alternative that makes some members of society better off and no one worse off); nondictatorship (social choices are not made by a single person); and independence of irrelevant alternatives (the choice between A and B is unchanged if a third, logically possible but unfeasible alternative, C, is introduced). Arrow proved that the four conditions are contradictory; hence, it was impossible for any social welfare scheme to satisfy all of them simultaneously.

The simplest example of Arrow's "impossibility theorem" is known as Condorcet's paradox after the noted eighteenth-century French mathematician. It relates to majority-rule voting, a widely used method of social choice in democratic societies and small groups. Suppose there are three candidates for public office, Adams (A), Smith (S), and Jones (J). One-third of the voters rank them A, S, J; one-third rank them S, J, A; and the remainder, J, A, S. A majority, then, favors A to S, S to J, and—seemingly irrationally—J to A. But this violates transitivity, the first of Arrow's conditions. Arrow thus appeared to prove—or rediscover—that democratic decision making as traditionally understood was, in principle, impossible.

Few economics dissertations have spurred such an outpouring of comment by economists, philosophers, and political scientists as Arrow's did. Some critics claimed that the independence-of-irrelevant-alternatives assumption was too restrictive; others, including the political economist Gordon Tullock, argued against transitivity. Although much progress has been made in extending Arrow's original analysis, the implications of the impossibility theorem are not yet fully understood.

In the early 1950s, Arrow made several other fundamental contributions to economic theory. His paper "An Extension of the Basic Theorems of Classical Welfare Economics" (1951) showed not only that a competitive market equilibrium was Pareto-efficient but that any Pareto-efficient allocation could be obtained by market forces. The policy implication was clear: governments wishing to redistribute income should not interfere directly (for example, through price controls) with the market mechanism. Rather, they should use other means (specifically, lump-sum taxes and transfers) and then allow market forces to operate freely.

Continuing in this direction, Arrow collaborated three years later with GERARD DEBREU on a celebrated proof of the existence of competitive equilibrium in an abstract, multimarket model of the economy. Aside from filling an important gap in general equilibrium theory, their paper was the first to apply mathematical set theory and topology to economic analysis. In related work the two economists showed how their model could be extended to an uncertain world by introducing futures markets and insurance. Other papers by Arrow made significant contributions to optimal inventory theory, the stability analysis of market models, mathematical programming, and statistical decision theory.

Continuing to work on general equilibrium problems, Arrow summarized his results in *General Competitive Analysis* (1971), written with the English economist Frank Hahn. Much of his research during these decades, however, concerned economic growth and distribution, the economics of uncertainty, and policy issues. In a 1961 paper, "Capital-Labor Substitution and Economic Efficiency," Arrow (with others) showed how to measure JOHN HICKS's "elasticity of substitution" between capital and labor. In "The Economic Implications of Learning by Doing" (1962), Arrow suggested that production becomes more efficient as total output rises, because the labor force gains experience. A related paper argued that market economies tend to underinvest in research and development because of the public goods nature of innovation. His *Essays on the Theory of Risk Bearing* (1963), comprising the Yrjo Johnassen lectures, is still considered one of the best introductions to the economics of uncertainty. By means of such work, Arrow has significantly enlarged our understanding of the virtues and limitations of the market mechanism.

Appropriate criteria for public investment in the face of uncertainty were the subject of Arrow's 1970 book *Public Investment, the Rate of Return, and Optimal Fiscal Policy,* written with the economist Mordecai Kurz. His other efforts have focused on such diverse topics as economic development and the urban crisis, the problems of management science, and the economics of discrimination.

Arrow shared the 1972 Nobel Memorial Prize in Economic Sciences with John Hicks for "pioneering contributions to general economic equilibrium theory and welfare theory."

The technical nature of Arrow's work has made it forbidding even to economists. Many, including SIMON KUZNETS, WASSILY LEONTIEF, and GUNNAR MYRDAL, have publicly decried the advanced mathematics favored by Arrow, Debreu, Samuelson, and most other economic theorists since World War II. Yet Arrow's work typically stems from a concern for basic economic issues and pressing social problems. His interest in modeling competitive equilibrium processes arises, as his Nobel lecture made clear, not from a penchant for advanced mathematics but from a desire to understand how a balance is struck between the amounts of goods and services that some individuals want to supply and the amounts that others want to buy. "This experience of balance is indeed so widespread," he noted, "that it raises no intellectual disquiet among laymen. . . . The paradoxical result is that they have no idea of the system's strength and are unwilling to trust it in any considerable departure from normal conditions."

Arrow's great gift has been the application of deep theoretical insights to matters of social and political relevance. He is one of the most influential teachers of economics and has written a number of lucid and comprehensive works on economic theory.

In 1947 Arrow married Selma Schweitzer; they have two sons.

In addition to the Nobel Prize, Arrow has received many honors and awards, including fellowships from the Center for Advanced Study in the Behavioral Sciences, the Social Science Research Council, and the Guggenheim Foundation. He is a member of the National Academy of Sciences, the American Philosophical Society, the Finnish Academy of Sciences, and the British Academy and a fellow of the American Academy of Arts and Sciences and the Econometric Society.

ADDITIONAL WORKS: Studies in the Mathematical Theory of Inventory and Production, 1958; Studies in Linear and Nonlinear Programming, 1958; The Economic Implications of Learning by Doing, 1961; Information and Economic Behavior, 1973; The Limits of Organization, 1974; The Crisis in Economic Theory, 1980; Collected Papers (6 vols.) 1983–1985; Applied Economics, 1985.

ABOUT: Breit, W., and Spencer, R. W. (eds.) Lives of the Laureates, 1986; New York Times October 26, 1972; Science November 3, 1972; Swedish Journal of Economics, number 4, 1972.

ASSER, TOBIAS
(April 28, 1838–July 29, 1913)
Nobel Prize for Peace, 1911
(shared with Alfred Fried)

TOBIAS ASSER

Tobias Michael Carel Asser, Dutch states-man and jurist, was born in Amsterdam, one of three children and the only son of Rosette Henry Godefroi-Asser and Carl Daniel Asser. Both of Asser's parents came from Jewish families with backgrounds of distinguished service in the legal profession in the Nether-lands. Both his father and paternal grand-father were lawyers, and one of his uncles served as Dutch minister of justice. An outstanding student, Asser won a competition in 1857 with a thesis on the economic concept of value. Although he considered a career in business, he decided instead to follow his family's ex-ample and entered the Amsterdam. Athe-naeum (later the University of Amsterdam) to study law. After receiving his doctorate in law in 1860, he accepted an appointment to an international commission to negotiate the ab-olition of shipping fees on the Rhine River, which gave him his first practical exposure to international law.

After practicing law briefly, Asser took a position as professor of international and com-mercial law at the athenaeum in 1862, when he was twenty-four years old. His numerous papers and books on international law soon earned him a prominent reputation in legal circles. With two colleagues, Gustave Rolin-Jaequemyns of Belgium and John Westlake of England, he founded the *Revue de Droit In-ternational et de Législation Comparée* (Jour-nal of International Law and Comparative Legislation) in 1869. One of the first publi-cations in its field, the journal quickly acquired a wide readership thanks to the high standards set by its articles, many of which were con-tributed by Asser.

Four years later, Asser joined Rolin-Jae-quemyns and other jurists to found the IN-STITUTE OF INTERNATIONAL LAW at Ghent, Belgium. Over the next several years, the in-stitute drafted international legal codes for cit-izenship rights, extradition of criminals, and various aspects of private law. It also estab-lished guidelines for international judicial pro-ceedings and wartime conduct and sought legal means for the establishment of neutral zones during times of war.

While continuing to teach and write, Asser also served as legal adviser to the Dutch min-ister of foreign affairs beginning in 1875. This was the first of a series of government posts

he held. Fluent in German, French, and Eng-lish as well as Dutch, Asser became a noted negotiator and participated in nearly every treaty his government signed over the next thirty-eight years. One of his most outstanding achievements in this capacity occurred during an international conference that met in Con-stantinople (now Istanbul) in 1888 to discuss the neutrality of the Suez Canal. In the course of the negotiations, Asser persuaded the del-egates to include Holland and Spain on the Suez Canal Commission, thus securing rep-resentation of the lesser European powers in the canal's administration. In October of that year, the delegates signed the Suez Canal Con-vention, which provided that the waterway would "always be free and open in time of war as in time of peace" to vessels of all nations.

Asser resigned his post at the University of Amsterdam in 1893 when he was asked to join the Dutch Council of State, the central ad-ministrative body of the Netherlands. He played a prominent role in the Dutch government's decision to convene international law confer-ences at The Hague in 1893, 1894, 1900, and 1904. He also presided over all four meetings. At the first two meetings, the delegates drew up a uniform international procedure for con-ducting civil trials. The third and fourth con-ferences produced uniform codes of international family law, including matters re-lated to marriage, separation, divorce, and guardianship of minors.

As the chief delegate from the Netherlands to The Hague Peace Conferences of 1899 and 1907, Asser promoted the principle of compulsory arbitration as an alternative to armed conflict between nations. During the first conference, he helped plan and organize The Hague Permanent Court of Arbitration, to which he was appointed in 1900. Two years later, while sitting on the court, he heard its first case, a dispute between the United States and Mexico involving the Pious Fund. This fund had been set up by Mexican Catholics in the eighteenth century to finance the Catholic church in California, then part of the Spanish empire in the Americas. After Mexico lost California to the United States in the Mexican-American War, Mexico refused to pay Catholic clergy in California out of the Pious Fund. Asser and the other arbitrators at The Hague ruled in favor of the California churches. Among his other important cases was the conflict between Russia and the United States over fishing rights in the Bering Straits. In 1904 he became his country's minister of state, the highest government position open to a Dutch commoner at that time.

In recognition of his work on behalf of international arbitration, Asser was awarded the 1911 Nobel Prize for Peace, an honor he shared with ALFRED FRIED. "Asser has above all been a practical legal statesman," said Jørgen Løvland of the Norwegian Nobel Committee. "As a pioneer in the field of international legal relations, he has earned a reputation as one of the leaders in modern jurisprudence." Neither Asser nor Fried attended the award ceremonies, and no acceptance speeches were given.

Asser's marriage in 1864 to Johanna Ernestina Asser, his first cousin, produced three sons and a daughter. Asser died on July 29, 1913, at The Hague, shortly after being chosen honorary president of the Institute of International Law.

Widely esteemed for his scholarship, Asser received honorary degrees from the universities of Cambridge, Edinburgh, Bologna, and Berlin. He was the author of standard works on the codification of private international law and on Dutch commercial law. His library of international legal works, which he donated to the Peace Palace at The Hague, still bears the name "The Asser Collection."

ABOUT: American Journal of International Law April 1914; Hull, W. I. The Two Hague Conferences and Their Contributions to International Law, 1908; Institute of International Law. Livre du Centenaire, 1973; Review of Politics July 1957; Scott, J. B. The Hague Peace Conferences (2 vols.) 1909.

ASTON, FRANCIS W.
(September 1, 1877–November 20, 1945)
Nobel Prize for Chemistry, 1922

The English chemist Francis William Aston was born in Harborne, Birmingham, the third of seven children of William Aston, a metal merchant and farmer, and Fanny Charlotte (Hollis) Aston, the daughter of a successful Birmingham gunmaker. Growing up on the family farm, young Aston showed an early interest in science and conducted his own scientific experiments in an improvised laboratory. He was educated at Harborne Vicarage School from 1889 to 1891 and at Malvern College from 1891 to 1893, graduating from Malvern at the head of his class.

In 1893 Aston entered Mason College in Birmingham (now the University of Birmingham), where he studied chemistry with W. A. Tilden and P. F. Frankland and physics with J. H. Poynting. He won the Forster Scholarship in 1898, which enabled him to return to Mason College and work with Frankland on the optical properties of tartaric acid derivatives. He published the results of his research in 1901. Since his scholarship funds were inadequate, Aston studied fermentation chemistry to prepare himself for a position as chemist in a brewery, which he held from 1900 to 1903. During this time, he built a laboratory in his father's house and constructed the necessary apparatus for measuring electrical discharges in vacuum tubes. On the basis of this work he was awarded a scholarship to the newly established University of Birmingham, where from 1903 to 1908 he again worked with Poynting. There he investigated the phenomenon known as Crookes dark space (named for the English chemist William Crookes), an area that appears between the cathode and the negative glow produced when electricity is passed through a tube containing gas at low pressure. He discovered that the size of this dark space was proportional to the pressure and the electrical current and that there was a new primary dark space (now called the Aston space) next to the cathode.

After making a world tour in 1909, Aston became an assistant to J. J. THOMSON both at the Cavendish Laboratory at Cambridge University and at the Royal Institution in London. Although he had been trained as a chemist, Aston's familiarity with cathode rays and positive rays enabled him to conduct experiments that lay on the boundary between physics and chemistry. Thomson soon gave him the task of improving an apparatus called the spherical

FRANCIS W. ASTON

discharge tube, which measured charge-mass ratios for a beam of positively charged particles. Thomson was also interested in FREDERICK SODDY's isotope idea and attempted the separation of neon isotopes. To this end, he invented an apparatus for the fractional distillation of neon and a slightly heavier component, which Thomson called meta-neon. To weigh the products of distillation, Aston developed a quartz microbalance sensitive to one-billionth of a gram.

While suggestive but inconclusive results were being obtained by Aston, World War I interrupted his work and forced him to redirect his research. During the war, Aston worked at the Royal Aircraft Establishment at Farnborough, studying the effect of atmospheric conditions on airplane fabrics and their coatings. Nevertheless he managed to find the resources and time to design a new apparatus for attacking the neon problem. Constructed in 1919 and called the mass spectrograph, this instrument accelerates positively charged ions through an electric field and uses a strong magnetic field to focus them onto a photographic plate. Because heavy atoms are deflected somewhat less than light atoms, particles of different mass are separated to produce a mass spectrum. The patterns formed as particles strike the photographic plate enabled Aston to deduce their masses and relative quantity. In this way, he discovered that almost all the elements were mixtures of isotopes.

Aston went on to formulate the whole-number rule, which states that the weights of atoms are always whole numbers. Observations had shown, however, that some atomic weights were not exact whole numbers. These fractional atomic weights were due, Aston reasoned, to the presence of isotopic constituents. For example, he found that neon contains ten isotopes of mass 20 for every isotope of mass 22, resulting in an atomic weight for ordinary neon of 20.2. The chemical properties of neon are not affected by this mix of isotopes; they depend only on neon's atomic number, its place in the periodic table. English chemist William Prout's 1815 hypothesis that all atoms might be built of common constituents finally appeared to have a measure of experimental support. However, later research showed that this view presented a picture of the structure of matter that was much too simplistic.

Aston received the 1922 Nobel Prize for Chemistry "for his discovery, by means of his mass spectrograph, of isotopes in a large number of nonradioactive elements and for his enunciation of the whole-number rule." The award was presented by H. G. Söderbaum of the Royal Swedish Academy of Sciences. "By this discovery," Söderbaum said, "a riddle which for over a hundred years has engaged chemical research has attained its solution, and a surmise which for thousands of years has floated before the human mind has thereby been confirmed."

Following his personal motto, "Make more, more, and yet more measurements," Aston developed larger and more powerful mass spectrographs (in 1927 and 1935), with which he could measure very small deviations from the whole-number rule. He explained these deviations as the loss of mass as it was converted to binding energy between particles within the nucleus. Thus, the more closely packed the nuclear charges are, the more their mass deviates from the sum of their individual masses. Aston measured these deviations, called packing fractions, and plotted them against atomic mass numbers for many elements. The results provided fundamental information about the abundance and stability of the elements and were later incorporated into an explanation for the release of atomic energy from the nucleus of the atom.

While Aston excelled in outdoor sports such as skiing, swimming, rock climbing, bicycling, tennis, and golf, he was also fond of sea travel. He was a skilled photographer and an accomplished amateur musician. He died on November 20, 1945, at Cambridge. At his death Aston, who never married, left his large estate to Trinity College, Cambridge.

Aston was a fellow of Trinity College (where

he taught until his death) and the Royal Society; he was also a foreign member of the Italian and Russian academies of science. Among his many honors were the John Scott Award given by the city of Philadelphia (1923), the Hughes Medal (1920) and Royal Medal (1938) of the Royal Society, and the Duddell Medal and Prize of the Institute of Physics (1941). From 1936 to 1945, he served as chairman of the Committee on Atoms of the International Union of Chemistry.

SELECTED WORKS: Isotopes, 1922; The Structural Units of the Material Universe, 1925; Mass Spectra and Isotopes, 1933.

ABOUT: Dictionary of National Biography, 1941–1950, 1959; Dictionary of Scientific Biography, volume 1, 1970; Farber, E. (ed.) Great Chemists, 1961; Obituary Notices of Fellows of the Royal Society, volume 5, 1945; Thomson, G. The Inspiration of Science, 1961.

MIGUEL ASTURIAS

ASTURIAS, MIGUEL
(October 19, 1899–June 9, 1974)
Nobel Prize for Literature, 1967

Miguel Angel Asturias (ä stōō' rē äs), Guatemalan novelist, poet, and journalist, was born in Guatemala City, the eldest of two sons of Ernesto Asturias, a magistrate, and the former María Rosales, a teacher. As a result of their political differences with the Guatemalan dictator Estrada Cabrera, who came to power in 1898, his parents were stripped of their jobs. The family, forced to move to the town of Salamá to live with relatives, did not return to Guatemala City until 1907.

As a student at the Universidad de San Carlos de Guatemala, Asturias took part in the successful 1920 uprising against Cabrera. Shortly thereafter, he helped found the Universidad Popular de Guatemala, a free evening school for workers that was staffed by volunteer teachers. He received a law degree from the Universidad de San Carlos in 1923, winning the Gálvez Prize for his thesis, "The Social Problem of the Indian."

Although Cabrera had been overthrown, political turmoil continued to plague Guatemala as various military factions fought for control of the country. After a friend of Asturias's was severely beaten for expressing his political views, Asturias's parents, fearing for their son's safety, sent him to Europe to continue his education. Although he had originally planned to study economics in London, Asturias enrolled instead at the Sorbonne in Paris, where he was profoundly influenced by Georges Raynaud, a specialist in Mayan myth and culture. Asturias studied with Raynaud for five years, translating a number of his major works into Spanish. Stirred by the work of the French surrealists, whose vision of the world Asturias found closer to Latin American reality than that of traditional Western rationalism, he also began to write poetry and fiction at this time.

While in Europe, Asturias wrote *Leyendas de Guatemala* (Legends of Guatemala), a poetic exploration of Mayan myth, which was published in Madrid in 1930 and received the Sylla Monsegur Prize for its French translation in 1932. He also wrote his first novel, *El Señor Presidente* (*The President*), a savage, surrealistic account of life in a Latin American dictatorship based on his experiences under the Cabrera regime. Because of its controversial political content, this book did not appear until 1946, and then was only privately published in Mexico. It appeared in an English translation under its Spanish title in 1964.

In 1928 Asturias visited Guatemala and Cuba, giving a series of lectures, which were published that year as *La Arquitectura de la Vida Nueva* (*The Building of a New Life*). Five years later he returned to live in Guatemala, which was then under the dictatorship of Jorge Ubico. He wrote poetry, worked as a journalist, and made broadcasts for *El Diaro del Aire* (The Newspaper of the Air). When Ubico was overthrown in 1944 and replaced by the relatively democratic Juan José Arévalo, Asturias entered the diplomatic service and later served as cultural attaché in Mexico and Argentina and as ambassador to El Salvador. While working in Buenos Aires, Asturias wrote the novel *Hombres de Maíz* (*Men of Maize*, 1949), considered by some critics to be his masterpiece. In this dreamlike work written in an incantatory prose, Asturias evokes the magical world of the Mayan Indians and contrasts their reality with that of the Latins against whom they rebel.

Men of Maize was followed by three novels sometimes called the Banana Trilogy: *Viento Fuerte* (1950, translated in different English editions as *The Cyclone* and *Strong Wind*); *El Papa Verde* (*The Green Pope*, 1954); and *Los Ojos de los Enterrados* (*The Eyes of the Interred*, 1960). In these novels of protest, which inveigh against the outrages committed in Central America by United States interests (the United Fruit Company, in particular), Asturias was seen by many critics to have sacrificed art to polemics. In reaction to such charges, Asturias told an interviewer: "I think that the function of our literature up until now has been to expose the suffering of our people. I think it's difficult for this type of literature to be purely literary, to be concerned merely with what is beautiful or pleasing."

When the American-backed colonel Castillo Armas took power from Arévalo's successor, Colonel Jacobo Arbenz, in 1954, Asturias was stripped of his citizenship and exiled to South America. His collection of stories, *Week-end en Guatemala* (*Weekend in Guatemala*), dealing with the treachery of Armas's invasion, was published in Buenos Aires in 1956. During his exile, he lived with the poet PABLO NERUDA in Chile, and later in Buenos Aires, where he worked as a correspondent for the Venezuelan newspaper *El Nacional* (The National) and as an adviser to an Argentine publisher. He was married to an Argentine woman, Blanca Mora y Aruajo, with whom he had two children. His first wife was Clemencia Amado. In 1962 Argentinian politics forced him into exile again, and he moved to Genoa, Italy. There he wrote two novels that describe the historical clash between the Indian and European (Catholic) cultures, *Mulata de tal* (*Mulata*, 1963) and *Maladrón* (Bad Thief, 1969). His cycle of poems on Mayan themes, *Clarivigilia primaveral* (Spring Light Vigil), probably his best-known work in verse, was published in 1965. In 1966, after Asturias was awarded the Lenin Peace Prize, the new president of Guatemala, Julio César Méndez Montenegro, named him ambassador to France.

"For his vivid achievement, deep-rooted in the national traits and traditions of Indian peoples of Latin America," Asturias received the 1967 Nobel Prize for Literature. On accepting the award, Asturias remarked: "My work will continue to reflect the voice of the peoples, gathering their myths and popular beliefs and at the same time seeking to give birth to a universal consciousness of Latin American problems." In his brief acceptance speech, Asturias described the contrast between Europe's literary tradition and the kind of writing that was evolving in Latin America. "Our novels appear to Europeans as illogical or aberrant," he told the Swedish Academy. "They are not shocking for the sake of shock effects. It is just that what happened to us was shocking," he explained.

In 1970 Asturias resigned his diplomatic post in Paris in order to devote his full time to writing. Before his death in Madrid on June 9, 1974, he published several other books, including collections of essays and stories.

As Asturias's critic and biographer, Richard Callan, has said, "Recent criticism no longer judges him by established literary criteria, but in terms of his own objective: that of dealing with the coexistence in Guatemala (as elsewhere in the Third World) of all the different stages through which societies have passed." In Callan's opinion, "Asturias's work marks the beginning of the mature phase of Latin American fiction."

ADDITIONAL WORKS IN ENGLISH TRANSLATION: The Bejeweled Boy, 1971; The Talking Machine, 1971.

ABOUT: Anderson-Imbert, E. Spanish-American Literature: A History, 1963; Brotherston, G. The Emergence of the Latin American Novel, 1977; Callan, R. J. Miguel Angel Asturias, 1970; Dohmann, B., and Harss, L. Into the Mainstream, 1967; Guibert, R. Seven Voices, 1973; Jaksic, I., and Rogachevesky, J. R. Politics and the Novel in Latin America, 1977.

AXELROD, JULIUS

(May 30, 1912–)
Nobel Prize for Physiology or Medicine, 1970
(shared with Bernard Katz and Ulf von Euler)

The American biochemical pharmacologist Julius Axelrod was born in New York City to Molly (Leichtling) and Isadore Axelrod. Axelrod attended the College of the City of New York, which was free to city residents, and obtained a B.S. in 1933. Unable to enter medical school because of quota limitations (he was Jewish), he worked as a laboratory assistant in the New York University School of Medicine Department of Bacteriology for two years before taking a position as chemist at the Laboratory of Industrial Hygiene in 1935. While working full-time at the laboratory, Axelrod continued his graduate studies and received his M.S. from New York University in 1941.

While working at the laboratory—where an accident cost him the sight of one eye—Axelrod became acquainted with Bernard Brodie, a professor at New York University. Brodie's studies of the breakdown and modification of drugs in the body profoundly influenced modern pharmaceutical design and testing. In 1946 Axelrod moved to the Third New York University Research Division at Goldwater Memorial Hospital to work with Brodie. After three years the two colleagues moved to the National Heart Institute in Bethesda, Maryland. By this time Axelrod's research in drug biochemistry, especially metabolism, was well developed, but he lacked a doctorate, which would be necessary for him to progress as a research scientist. Paul K. Smith, professor of pharmacology at George Washington University, knew of Axelrod's abilities and was instrumental in his being granted a Ph.D. in chemical pharmacology in 1955. Axelrod obtained his doctorate just after he had accepted an offer to become chief of the Section on Pharmacology, Laboratory of Clinical Science, at the newly established National Institute of Mental Health (NIMH).

During the early 1950s Axelrod and Brodie investigated amphetamines, drugs with powerful stimulant effects that bear a strong chemical resemblance to a group of natural compounds called catecholamines. The first catecholamine to be discovered was adrenaline (also called epinephrine). In 1946 ULF VON EULER had shown that adrenaline's precursor, noradrenaline (or norepinephrine), is a neurotransmitter, a chemical released by a nerve cell to stimulate or inhibit adjacent neurons or other excitable cells. Neurotransmitters are the most important vehicles for communication among cells in the nervous system. Adrenaline, noradrenaline, and dopamine (a precursor of noradrenaline) are the catecholamine neurotransmitters; other neurotransmitters include acetylcholine (the first neurotransmitter to be identified, through the work of OTTO LOEWI and HENRY H. DALE), serotonin, and several amino acids.

National Academy of Sciences

JULIUS AXELROD

Axelrod's studies of amphetamine pharmacology revealed much about the degradation and metabolism of amphetamines in the body. Yet in the course of this work, he later said, "I was surprised to learn that very little was known about the metabolism of noradrenaline and adrenaline." It was this topic that Axelrod began to investigate shortly after he joined NIMH. Within a few years, Axelrod and his co-workers had isolated catechol-O-methyltransferase (COMT), one of the two most important enzymes that break down catecholamines in the body, the other being monoamine oxidase (MAO). Although these enzymes are important for the long-term maintenance of appropriate catecholamine levels, research by Axelrod's team in the early 1960s showed that the degradation of COMT or MAO is not the factor that terminates a given catecholamine-mediated nerve impulse.

This was an unexpected finding, for Dale had shown that acetylcholine-mediated impulses are terminated when the neurotransmitter is broken down by enzymes in the synapse—the region of communication between neurons, in which an impulse passes from one presynaptic nerve cell to another postsynaptic cell. Axelrod's research, however, showed that catecholamine-based impulses end when the neurotransmitter is reabsorbed by the presynaptic nerve terminal. BERNARD KATZ's studies of other neurons indicated that acetylcholine is released from presynaptic cells in discrete packets, or quanta; Axelrod and his colleagues found that noradrenaline release is also quantized. It is now generally assumed that this quantization is observed because neurotransmitters are packaged into the small vesicles, or storage granules, found in presynaptic cells, with each vesicle containing a certain amount of neurotransmitter, which is released as a unit.

One of the most important aspects of Axelrod's research was the light it cast on psychoactive drugs, first discovered in the 1950s, which can control symptoms of the major mental illnesses: schizophrenia, mania, and depression. Even though these drugs revolutionized the treatment of mental illness, their use raised a number of questions. Despite their efficacy, little was known about how they worked, how they were broken down in the body, or how other similar drugs might be produced.

While conducting his initial studies of noradrenaline metabolism in the involuntary nerves (where Euler had originally found the neurotransmitter), Axelrod discovered that drugs such as cocaine or reserpine (used to control high blood pressure) act by modifying the normal recycling of catecholamines. They alter the amount of transmitter packed into a vesicle, the rate of vesicle release, or the uptake of neurotransmitters by the presynaptic cell.

At first, Axelrod's investigations of catecholamine activity had to be conducted in the test tube or in the autonomic (involuntary) nervous system. His studies involved injecting laboratory animals with artificial radioactive noradrenaline and adrenaline, the movements of which could be easily tracked. The brain, however, is not directly exposed to the bloodstream because it is protected by a blood-brain barrier, through which catecholamines (as well as many other substances) cannot pass. In 1964 one of Axelrod's colleagues, Jacques Glowinski, developed a method for bypassing the barrier by injecting radioactive catecholamines into the ventricles of the brain. This technique was subsequently used at NIMH and elsewhere to conduct studies of brain neurotransmitters and the pharmacology of psychoactive drugs.

Hormones and neurotransmitters are closely related—both are classes of biochemicals that are released by one cell to affect another—as can be seen from the fact that adrenaline and noradrenaline perform two functions: They can act as either neurotransmitters or hormones, depending on the circumstances. Later in the 1960s Axelrod concentrated his research on hormone-neurotransmitter relationships and conducted many studies of the effects of neurotransmitters on hormone production (for ex-

ample, in the pineal gland) and of the effects of hormones on neurotransmitter release (for example, in the adrenal gland).

The 1970 Nobel Prize for Physiology or Medicine was shared by Axelrod, Katz, and Euler "for their discoveries concerning the humoral transmitters in the nerve terminals and the mechanism for their storage, release, and inactivation." In concluding his Nobel lecture, Axelrod pointed out that "drugs therapeutically effective in the treatment of affective disorders and neurological and cardiovascular diseases have also been shown to influence the uptake, storage, release, formation, and metabolism of catecholamines. These findings, implicating the peripheral and central sympathetic nervous system, have provided insight into the causes and treatment of mental depression, Parkinson's disease, and hypertension."

Among Axelrod's awards and honors are the Gairdner Foundation International Award (1967), the Distinguished Achievement Award of George Washington University (1968), the Claude Bernard Medal of the University of Montreal (1969), the Albert Einstein Achievement Award of Yeshiva University (1971), the Torald Sollman Award in Pharmacology given by the American Society for Pharmacology and Experimental Therapeutics (1973), and the Paul H. Hoch Memorial Lecture and Award of the American Psychopathological Association (1975). He is a member of the Royal Society of London, the American Academy of Arts and Sciences, the American Chemical Society, and the National Academy of Sciences. He has been awarded honorary doctorate degrees from the University of Chicago, the Medical College of Wisconsin, New York University, the Medical College of Pennsylvania, and George Washington University.

SELECTED WORKS: Biochemical Actions of Hormones, 1970, with Gerald Litwack.

ABOUT: New York Times October 16, 1970; Science October 23, 1970.

BAEYER, ADOLF VON
(October 31, 1835–August 20, 1917)
Nobel Prize for Chemistry, 1905

The German chemist Johann Friedrich Wilhelm Adolf von Baeyer (bā′ yər) was born in Berlin, the first of five children of Johann Jakob Baeyer and Eugenie (Hitzig) Baeyer. His father was a Prussian army officer who published works on geography and the atmospheric refraction of light, and his mother was the daughter of the noted jurist and historian Julius Eduard Hitzig. The boy displayed an early interest in chemistry, and at the age of twelve he discovered a new double salt of copper and sodium. After attending the Friedrich-Wilhelms Gymnasium, he entered the University of Berlin in 1853 and for the next two years devoted himself to the study of mathematics and physics.

After a year of military service, Baeyer attended the University of Heidelberg to study chemistry under Robert Bunsen, who had recently developed the laboratory burner that bears his name. At Heidelberg Baeyer concentrated on physical chemistry, but after publishing a paper on chloromethane and methyl chloride in 1857, his interest shifted to organic chemistry, and the following year he joined the structural chemist Friedrich August Kekulé at his private laboratory in Heidelberg. There Baeyer conducted research on organic arsenic compounds, for which he received his Ph.D. Later in 1858 he accompanied Kekulé to the University of Ghent, in Belgium, but he returned to Berlin two years later to become a lecturer in chemistry at a technical academy.

Stimulated by Kekulé's interest in the structure of organic compounds, Baeyer first investigated uric acid and then, beginning in 1865, the structural composition of indigo, a commercially valuable blue dye obtained from the plant of the same name. As early as 1841 the French chemist August Laurent had examined the complex structure of this substance and in the course of his research had isolated isatin, a water-soluble crystalline compound. Extending Laurent's efforts, Baeyer in 1866 prepared isatin by the novel technique of reducing indigo by heating it with finely divided zinc, a method that permitted a more profound structural analysis than did Laurent's oxidation process.

Reversing his conversion of indigo by oxidizing isatin, Baeyer in 1870 was able to synthesize indigo for the first time, thus making feasible its commercial production. After moving to Strasbourg in 1872 to accept the position of professor of chemistry at the University of Strasbourg, Baeyer began to study condensation reactions in which water is released. While investigating the condensation reactions of the chemical groups known as the aldehydes and the phenols, he and his colleagues isolated several important dye sub-

ADOLF VON BAEYER

stances, particularly eosin pigments, which he subsequently synthesized.

In 1875, after the death of Justus von Liebig, Baeyer succeeded the noted organic chemist as professor of chemistry at the University of Munich. There, over the next four decades, Baeyer attracted many brilliant students, more than fifty of whom went on to become university teachers.

Turning to an analysis of the precise chemical structure of indigo, Baeyer announced his findings in 1883. The compound, he said, was composed of two linked "kernel" molecules (which he called indole), a model that remained unchanged for forty years, until it was revised with the help of techniques far more sophisticated than those available to Baeyer.

The researches into dyes led Baeyer to study benzene, a hydrocarbon molecule in which the six carbon atoms are arranged in a ring. There were competing theories about the nature of the bonds between the carbons and about the location of the hydrogen atoms within the molecule's ring. More an empirical than a theoretical chemist, Baeyer disagreed with all current prevailing theories. Instead, he developed his "strain" theory, which states that the bonds between the carbon atoms are stressed (strained) by the presence of other atoms in the molecule and that this stressing determines not only the shape of the molecule but its stability as well. The theory in revised form has proved to be essentially correct. His benzene investigations also led Baeyer to realize that the structure of a group of aromatic benzene compounds called the hydroaromatics was transitional between the ring-based types and aliphatic hydrocarbons (those without the ring structure). This discovery indicated a relationship between the three types of molecules and opened new possibilities for their study.

In 1885, on his fiftieth birthday, Baeyer was granted a hereditary patent of nobility in recognition of his importance to Germany, an honor that enabled him to add *von* to his name. He was awarded the 1905 Nobel Prize for Chemistry "for the services he has rendered to the development of organic chemistry and the chemical industry through his work concerning organic dyes and hydrocarbon hydroaromatic compounds." Too ill to attend the presentation ceremony, Baeyer was represented by the German ambassador. Although Baeyer did not deliver a Nobel lecture, in 1900 he noted in an article on the history of indigo synthesis, "I finally had in my hands the mother substance of indigo, and I rejoiced the way EMIL FISCHER may have done when he found purine, the mother substance of uric acid, after fifteen years' work."

After receiving the Nobel Prize, Baeyer continued his study of molecular structure. His work on oxygen compounds led to discoveries about the role of quadrivalent and basic oxygen. He also investigated the relationship between molecular structure and optical properties, particularly color.

In 1868 Baeyer married Adelheid Bendemann; they had one daughter and two sons. Highly respected for his experimental skills and intellectual persistence, Baeyer remained an enthusiastic researcher until his retirement in 1913. Although he received many attractive offers from chemical firms, Baeyer refused to become involved in the commercial applications of his discoveries and received no profits from his work. "His appearance was imposing and pleasing," RICHARD WILLSTÄTTER recalled in a biographical sketch; "his face expressed clarity, repose, and mental strength; the blue eyes were expressive, penetrating, brilliant." After suffering a stroke, Baeyer died at his country house at Lake Starnberg near Munich on August 20, 1917.

Baeyer's other awards included the Davy Medal of the Royal Society of London. He held membership in the Berlin Academy of Sciences and the German Chemical Society.

ABOUT: Dictionary of Scientific Biography, volume 1, 1970; Farber, E. (ed.) Great Chemists, 1961; Journal of Chemical Education June 1930.

BAJER, FREDRIK

(April 21, 1837–January 22, 1922)
Nobel Prize for Peace, 1908
(shared with Klas Arnoldson)

Fredrik Bajer (bī′ ər), Danish author, pacifist, and politician, was born in Vester Egede, the son of Alfred Beyer, a clergyman; Bajer altered the spelling of his name in 1865. At the age of eleven, he entered Sorø Academy, Denmark's premier boarding school. As he would later recount in his memoirs, he was an indifferent student and resisted subjects he considered obscure, such as classical languages. At the same time, he became fascinated with military subjects and idolized Napoleon Bonaparte, whom he often emulated by composing imaginary proclamations to soldiers. In 1854 Bajer entered the National Cadet Academy in Copenhagen, graduating two years later with a commission as a cavalry lieutenant.

From 1856 to 1864 Bajer served in the Danish army, interrupting his career in 1860 to study for two years at another military school. Becoming interested in social problems, he published a number of articles about education. He also studied French, Norwegian, and Swedish. During the war that erupted in 1864 over possession of the duchies of Schleswig and Holstein, the numerically superior Prussian forces overwhelmed the Danes and seized the duchies. Bajer served with honor and was promoted to first lieutenant during the conflict, but this firsthand experience of the horrors of war demolished his romantic notion of soldiering and awakened his interest in pacifism.

When Denmark reduced the size of its army in 1865, Bajer lost his commission and was forced to delay for two years his marriage to Mathilde Schlüter, to whom he had recently become engaged. To support himself, he began teaching and writing newspaper articles. During this time he also developed his pacifist ideas. In 1867, stimulated by FRÉDÉRIC PASSY's writing, he attempted to found a peace society in Denmark but was rebuffed by his compatriots, who were still stung by their defeat at the hands of Germany. Broadening the scope of his peace campaign, Bajer then endorsed the idea that replacing monarchies with republican governments would further the cause of peace in Scandinavia. In 1870 he established the Association of Scandinavian Free States, which aimed to unite the Scandinavian nations into a federation that might eventually provide the model for a union of all nations. The next

FREDRIK BAJER

Parliament derided him for participating in this gathering, but the following year he persuaded one other member to attend the meetings with him. In 1891, after speaking privately to every member of the lower house, he succeeded in forming a Danish Interparliamentary Group. In 1893 Bajer won election to the Council of the Interparliamentary Union, representing Norway, Sweden, and Denmark.

Bajer also perceived the need to broaden and coordinate international peace efforts. At the International Peace Congress in London in 1890, he proposed the formation of an international bureau to serve as a clearinghouse for information and to promote the peaceful resolution of international conflicts. Meeting in Rome the following year, the delegates to the Third International Peace Congress adopted his proposal and established the INTERNATIONAL PEACE BUREAU in Bern, Switzerland, under the leadership of ÉLIE DUCOMMUN. Bajer was named the first chairman of the bureau's governing board, a position he held until 1907.

Meanwhile, his pacifist efforts continued to gather support in Denmark. In 1893 the Danish Peace Society collected the signatures of more than 240,000 citizens, which it submitted to the government with a plea for peace. Bajer's advocacy of arbitration treaties to settle conflicts between nations met with some success in 1904 and 1905, when Denmark signed such treaties with Portugal, Italy, and the Netherlands.

Bajer's goal of establishing a Scandinavian Interparliamentary Union to encourage regional cooperation became a reality in 1908. That year, he received the 1908 Nobel Prize for Peace. Too ill to attend the award ceremony, he delivered his Nobel lecture at the Norwegian Nobel Institute the following May. Emphasizing the need for international law as a means of settling disputes, he noted, "It is quite usual to maintain that treaties become just so much wastepaper when war breaks out. . . . This is a military concept that pacifists should not tolerate. We should do everything within our power to ensure that the idea of law conquers."

In a series of publications during his long career, Bajer urged Denmark to adopt a policy of permanent neutrality. His efforts were seen as a major contribution to the government's decision to declare neutrality when World War I broke out in 1914. Despite the fighting that engulfed much of Europe, Bajer remained optimistic. "There is now more need for work in the cause of peace than ever before," he said.

year, in keeping with their belief that political emancipation of women could lead to a healthier society, Bajer and his wife founded the Danish Women's Association, which became instrumental in winning political equality for Danish women.

Bajer's activities soon drew him into politics, and in 1872 he won election to the lower house of the Danish Parliament as a member of the Liberal party. He held his seat until 1895, working for many progressive goals, including women's rights, reduced military spending, and peace.

In 1875 Bajer wrote an article pointing out the perils Scandinavians might face in any future European wars. He argued that because the Scandinavian countries border the waterways connecting the North Sea with the Baltic Sea, control of their territory could be vital to the belligerents in any northern European conflict. The danger could be averted, he said, by an international treaty guaranteeing permanent Scandinavian neutrality. To promote this goal, Bajer founded the Association for the Neutralization of Denmark (later the Danish Peace Society) in 1882. The group not only provided a forum for Bajer's views but also became a permanent fixture in efforts for international peace.

Bajer was the sole Danish representative at the founding session in 1889 of the Interparliamentary Union. Established by WILLIAM CREMER and Passy, the union sought to promote world peace by bringing members of European parliaments together for discussion and cooperation. Bajer's colleagues in the Danish

BAKER

Crippled by a painful illness, Bajer nevertheless worked to maintain contact between international pacifists during and after the war. After he died on January 22, 1922, his wife continued his work for many years.

WORKS IN ENGLISH TRANSLATION: Tactics for the Friends of Peace, 1891; A Serious Drama of Modern History: How Danish Slesvig Was Lost, 1897.

ABOUT: Interparliamentary Union. The Interparliamentary Union From 1889–1939, 1939.

BAKER, PHILIP NOEL
See NOEL-BAKER, PHILIP

BALCH, EMILY GREENE
(January 8, 1867–January 9, 1961)
Nobel Prize for Peace, 1946
(shared with John Mott)

EMILY GREENE BALCH

Emily Greene Balch (bolch), American social reformer, economist, and peace activist, was born of old New England stock in Jamaica Plain, Massachusetts, near Boston. The second daughter of Francis Vergnies Balch and the former Ellen Maria Noyes, Balch grew up in a Unitarian household that valued intellectual rigor, self-discipline, and high moral standards. Her father was a prosperous lawyer and former aide to the abolitionist and pacifist Charles Sumner.

Balch's education reflected the widening opportunities for higher learning available to women in the late 1800s. In 1886 she entered the newly founded Bryn Mawr College for women and completed the requirements for a B.A. in three years, graduating in 1889 with the first class. Upon recommendation of the faculty, who described Balch as a woman "of extraordinary beauty of moral character," Bryn Mawr awarded her a fellowship for further study abroad. She attended the Sorbonne in Paris for two years, studying the French system of relief for the poor.

When she returned from Europe in 1891, Balch became a social worker with the Boston Children's Aid Society. The following year, she and several other pioneers in the settlement house movement founded Denison House in Boston. During this time, Balch also became involved in the trade union movement and in 1893 joined the Federal Labor Union. Despite her desire to be "of use," Balch became dissatisfied with these activities and re-

jected full-time social work to pursue an academic career. Feeling that she would be able to exert greater influence by awakening "the desire of women students to work for social betterment," she decided to become a teacher. To that end, she studied economics at the Harvard Annex (later named Radcliffe College) and at the University of Chicago, completing her training at the University of Berlin in 1896.

That year she began teaching economics at Wellesley College, joining such faculty members as Katherine Coman, Vida Scudder, and Ellen Hayes. Innovative in topic and content, Balch's courses included offerings in socialism, labor issues, immigration, the theory of consumption, and the role of women in the economy. One of her students, Mary A. Wyman, later described Balch as a woman of vision who "emphasized in her teaching the necessity of clearing one's mind of class and race prejudice."

In addition to her academic career, Balch retained an active interest in reform, and her social stance placed her among the faculty radicals. She often supported unpopular strikes, and in 1902 she was cofounder of the Boston branch of the Women's Trade Union League, an organization that sought better wages and safer working conditions for women. Declaring herself a socialist in 1906, Balch served on numerous state and municipal bodies. In 1913 she chaired the Massachusetts Minimum Wage Commission, which drafted the nation's first minimum wage law.

Balch's involvement in social causes not only

infused her teaching with practical knowledge but also influenced her scholarly work. From 1904 to 1906 she studied immigration and racism by visiting Slavic communities throughout the United States as well as by traveling to the regions of Austria-Hungary from which many Slavic immigrants had come. Her research culminated in the publication of *Our Slavic Fellow Citizens* (1910), a major study that refuted assumptions of racial superiority then popular among Americans who sought to limit Slavic immigration. Despite her controversial ideas, Balch was promoted in 1913 to a professorship at Wellesley and began a five-year tenure as chairwoman of the economics and sociology departments.

After the outbreak of World War I, Balch, JANE ADDAMS, and forty other women joined the United States delegation to the International Congress of Women at The Hague in 1915 in an effort to draft a peace plan that would halt the war. Balch discovered that international pacifism provided the most integrated framework for the expression of her beliefs. The following two years, spent on leave writing for the *Nation*, a liberal magazine, drew Balch back into public life as a committed and outspoken pacifist opposed to the war, the draft, and espionage legislation. Through membership in the Committee Against Militarism (predecessor of the American Civil Liberties Union), she defended conscientious objectors and participated in demonstrations. As a result of "her outspoken views on pacifism and economics," the Wellesley trustees dismissed Balch in 1918.

Over the next forty years, she poured her energies into promoting world peace. In 1919 she attended the second International Congress of Women, which established itself as the Women's International League for Peace and Freedom. As its first secretary-treasurer, Balch—who converted to the Quaker faith in 1921—made the elimination of war a goal of the league's efforts. Her work for the Women's League brought Balch into close contact with the newly formed League of Nations. Her correspondence with officials of the League of Nations during this period indicates the breadth of her concerns, among them Albania's admission to the league, international disarmament, narcotics control, and protection of persecuted minorities.

Balch worked for the Women's League for the rest of her life, serving in a wide range of capacities. In 1926 she represented the league on a committee investigating conditions in occupied Haiti; the committee's report, written primarily by Balch, recommended the withdrawal of American troops and Haitian self-government. She also helped initiate international summer schools to promote peace. In addition to serving on committees, holding a variety of offices, and drafting resolutions, Balch exerted influence in unofficial capacities. Her ability to reconcile divergent opinions and forge a working consensus, for example, was widely acknowledged and helped unite the diverse international constituency of the Women's League. In her work, Balch manifested qualities of cooperation and reconciliation that she believed would bring peace if practiced internationally.

During the 1930s, deeply disturbed by Adolf Hitler's treatment of German Jews, she helped dozens of European refugees resettle in the United States. The outbreak of World War II confronted Balch with bitter choices about pacifism that she never satisfactorily resolved. After the December 7, 1941, attack on Pearl Harbor by Japan, she departed from absolute pacifism by supporting America's entry into the war. Through the Women's League, she helped relocate Japanese-Americans who had been forcibly interned in concentration camps. Balch opposed the government's policy that demanded unconditional surrender, on the grounds that it would lengthen the war; and in 1944, acting through the league, she submitted to President Franklin D. Roosevelt proposals aimed at postwar reconciliation.

In 1946 Balch became the second American woman to receive the Nobel Peace Prize. It was awarded "for her lifelong, indefatigable work for the cause of peace." She shared the prize with JOHN MOTT. Ill health prevented Balch from attending the award ceremonies; she belatedly delivered her Nobel lecture, "Toward Human Unity or Beyond Nationalism," during a trip to Norway in April 1948.

Looking beyond the different histories and cultural traditions that divided nations, Balch considered herself at home "wherever I pass upon the earth." She described herself as "an impersonal person," able to live on what was offered through books, nature, and religion. "We are not asked to subscribe to any utopia or to believe in a perfect world," she said in her Nobel acceptance speech. "We are asked to equip ourselves with courage, hope, readiness for hard work, and to cherish large and generous ideals."

In 1956 Balch, who never married, moved into a Cambridge, Massachusetts, nursing home, where she died in 1961.

ADDITIONAL WORKS: Public Assistance of the Poor in France, 1893; Women at The Hague, 1915, with Jane Addams and Alice Hamilton; Approaches to the Great Settlement, 1918; Occupied Haiti, 1927, with others; The Miracle of Living, 1941; Vignettes in Prose, 1952.

ABOUT: Dictionary of American Biography, supplement 7, 1981; New York Times January 11, 1961; Randall, J. H. Emily Greene Balch of New England, 1946; Randall, M. M. Improper Bostonian: Emily Greene Balch, 1964; Randall, M. M. (ed.) Beyond Nationalism: The Social Thought of Emily Greene Balch, 1971; Solomon, B. M. Ancestors and Immigrants, 1956; Whitman, A. (ed.) American Reformers, 1985.

BALTIMORE, DAVID
(March 7, 1938–)
Nobel Prize for Physiology or Medicine, 1975
(shared with Renato Dulbecco and Howard M. Temin)

DAVID BALTIMORE

The American molecular biologist David Baltimore was born in New York City to Gertrude (Lipschitz) and Richard I. Baltimore. He received his early education in the public schools, where he demonstrated a particular aptitude for biology and mathematics. Under a program for gifted high school students, he spent a summer at the Jackson Laboratory for the study of mammalian genetics in Bar Harbor, Maine. There he became acquainted with HOWARD M. TEMIN, a biology student who had recently graduated from Swarthmore College in Pennsylvania.

After graduating from high school in 1956, Baltimore enrolled in Swarthmore College and majored in chemistry. He received his B.A. with honors in 1960 and began graduate studies at the Massachusetts Institute of Technology (MIT) in Cambridge. After a year at MIT he transferred to Rockefeller University in New York City to work under Richard Franklin, an authority on animal viruses. Baltimore was especially interested in how viruses replicate in animal cells. When he received his Ph.D. from Rockefeller University in 1964, one of his professors remarked, "David's teachers and associates have all been impressed with his broad grasp of concepts and the integrative quality of his mind."

Baltimore pursued his research as a postdoctoral fellow in the MIT Department of Biology during the 1963–1964 academic year. During the following year he was a fellow in molecular biology at the Albert Einstein College of Medicine in New York City. His studies there were followed by further work as a research associate in virology at the Salk Insti-

tute for Biological Studies in La Jolla, California, during the period from 1965 to 1968. At the Salk Institute he worked with RENATO DULBECCO, who had developed quantitative methods for experimental study of viral genetics and had classified the differences between normal cells and those that have been transformed into tumor cells by viruses. Through these studies Dulbecco had shown that although normal cells are governed by physiological restriction on cell growth, tumor cells divide indefinitely.

In 1968 Baltimore was appointed associate professor of microbiology at MIT, and in 1969 he became editor of the Journal of Virology. In an attempt to clarify how the genetic system replicates in animal cells, he pursued his initial interest in the genetics of poliovirus, assuming that by this means he would be able to form a general hypothesis about all viral replication systems. By the late 1960s, however, it appeared that there was more than one system of replication. Temin, who had joined the University of Wisconsin, had postulated that certain viruses (for example, the Rous sarcoma virus, named for PEYTON ROUS) possess an enzyme in their protein coat that facilitates the duplication of viral genes into the deoxyribonucleic acid (DNA) of the animal cell. Temin called this hypothetical gene a proviral gene. Since the nucleic acid of the Rous sarcoma virus consists of ribonucleic acid (RNA), Temin's proviral theory indicated that genetic information was conveyed from RNA to DNA in the host cell. The idea that RNA viruses could make DNA copies of themselves was derided by many other scientists, who held to the orthodox view that genetic information was transmitted from DNA to RNA protein but never in the reverse order.

The proof of Temin's provirus hypothesis depended on the existence of an enzyme that incorporated viral genes into cellular DNA. Working independently, Baltimore and Temin isolated such an enzyme in 1970 and called it RNA-directed DNA polymerase. After Temin announced his findings in May at the tenth International Congress of the International Union Against Cancer, Baltimore presented his at a symposium at the Cold Spring Harbor Laboratory on Long Island. Both scientists published the results of their work in the British journal *Nature* in June 1970. Not long afterward, their findings were confirmed by Solomon Spiegelman, director of the Institute of Cancer Research at Columbia University, who had been one of Temin's chief critics. During the rest of the decade, the process of reverse transcription became a central research problem in microbiology.

Two years after publishing his findings on reverse transcriptase, Baltimore was appointed professor of biology at MIT. That year he and his colleagues partially synthesized the gene responsible for the biosynthesis of mammalian hemoglobin, the molecule in red blood cells that carries oxygen to the tissues. Their achievement constituted a major step toward the possibility of manipulating and recombining genes artificially.

Baltimore, like many other biologists, feared the adverse consequences that might stem from the misuse of genetic-engineering techniques, and he joined a group of molecular biologists who drafted a proposal for a moratorium on certain aspects of DNA research. In 1973 he was appointed American Cancer Society Professor of Microbiology at MIT, a lifetime appointment that provides sustained financial support for his research. While continuing his search for the reverse transcriptase enzyme in other tumor-causing viruses, he discovered eight viruses that possess this enzyme. Known now as retroviruses, they have subsequently been implicated in such diseases as hepatitis, certain forms of human cancer, and acquired immune deficiency syndrome (AIDS).

The significance of Baltimore's work was recognized in 1975 when he shared the Nobel Prize for Physiology or Medicine with Dulbecco and Temin "for their discoveries concerning the interaction between tumor viruses and the genetic material of the cell." In summarizing his research in his Nobel lecture, Bal-

timore explained that each virus "directs synthesis of two critical classes of proteins: proteins for replication and proteins for constructing the virus particle. By encoding the reverse transcriptase, retroviruses have evolved the ability to integrate themselves into the cell chromosome as a provirus."

The year after he received the Nobel Prize, Baltimore was instrumental in the founding of the Recombinant DNA Advisory Committee of the National Institutes of Health, a group, supported by federal funds, that has formulated guidelines to restrict genetic-engineering research. After reconsidering his position, however, Baltimore suggested in 1981 that the guidelines be made voluntary, but his proposal was defeated by the committee.

In addition to his responsibilities at MIT, Baltimore is a consultant in medicine and pediatric oncology (the study of tumors in children) at the Children's Hospital Medical Center and at the Sidney Farber Cancer Institute in Boston, Massachusetts. In 1986 he served as chairman of a National Academy of Sciences committee that conducted an extensive study of AIDS, warning that the government's measures had not been adequate to deal with the epidemic.

In 1968 Baltimore married Alice Huang, a microbiologist; they have a daughter. He holds membership in several professional societies, including the American Association for the Advancement of Science, the American Academy of Arts and Sciences, and the National Academy of Sciences. In addition to the Nobel Prize, he has received the Eli Lilly and Company Research Award in Microbiology and Immunology of the American Society for Microbiology (1971), the Gairdner Foundation International Prize (1974), and the United States Steel Foundation Award in Molecular Biology of the National Academy of Sciences (1974).

SELECTED WORKS: Animal Virology, 1976, with others; Molecular Cell Biology, 1986, with others.

ABOUT: Current Biography July 1983; Levy, H. B. (ed.) The Biochemistry of Viruses, 1969; New Scientist October 23, 1975; New York Times October 17, 1975; August 26, 1980; May 31, 1983; Science November 14, 1975.

BANTING, FREDERICK G.
(November 14, 1891–February 21, 1941)
Nobel Prize for Physiology or Medicine, 1923
(shared with John J. R. MacLeod)

The Canadian physiologist Frederick Grant Banting, the youngest of five children, was

FREDERICK G. BANTING

born on a farm near Alliston, Ontario, to William Thompson Banting and Margaret (Grant) Banting. Educated in the local public schools, he participated in athletics and enjoyed drawing and painting. In an effort to fulfill his parents' wish that he become a minister, he entered the divinity school of the University of Toronto in 1912. At the end of a year, after realizing that his true interest lay in medicine, he transferred to the university's medical school.

When it appeared that his medical studies were to be interrupted by World War I, Banting enlisted in the Royal Canadian Army Medical Corps in 1915. He was sent back to medical school, however, and he obtained a bachelor of medicine degree the following year. For the next two years he served as a military surgeon, first in England and then in France, where at Cambrai he sustained severe shrapnel wounds to his right forearm. Aware that an amputation would mean the end of his surgical career, he persuaded the attending physician not to proceed with the operation; eventually the arm was saved.

After the war Banting returned to Toronto and served for two years as resident surgeon at the Hospital for Sick Children. In the summer of 1920 he moved to London, Ontario, and opened a general surgical practice. When his practice proved unsatisfactory from a financial standpoint, he accepted an appointment as demonstrator at the University of Western Ontario Medical School in the same city. There he also conducted research under F. R. Miller, a neurophysiologist.

A childhood friend had died of the disease now called diabetes mellitus, and the incident helped stimulate Banting's interest in finding a cure for the disease. Diabetes mellitus was described in the first century A.D. by the Roman physicians Celsus and Araeteus, who noticed copious urine, excessive thirst, and weight loss in certain patients. In the seventeenth century, the English physician Thomas Willis observed that the urine of patients with those same symptoms tasted sweet. Later, in the nineteenth century, it was discovered that starch carbohydrate is converted into glucose (sugar) in the small intestine, and that glucose is then absorbed from the bloodstream by the liver, where it is stored in the form of glycogen (a starchlike substance made of glucose molecules linked together in chains).

The pancreas was suspected of being involved in diabetes mellitus because pancreatic tissue from patients who had died from the disease appeared to be diseased. In 1889 the German physiologists Joseph von Mering and Oscar Minkowski surgically removed the pancreas from dogs and observed that the experimental animals developed abnormally high blood and urine glucose levels, as well as symptoms resembling those of clinical diabetes mellitus.

The pancreas is a gland with two basic types of cells: Acinar cells synthesize and secrete digestive enzymes into the pancreatic ducts; the enzymes are carried to the small intestine, where they participate in the digestion of food. Islet cells (found in the islets of Langerhans, irregular structures in the pancreas) synthesize and discharge insulin directly into the bloodstream, a process that promotes the uptake of glucose into cells, where it is utilized as a source of energy. When glucose is not available to cells, fat (in the form of fatty acids) is utilized instead, and its biochemical degradation results in diabetic acidosis, or abnormally high acid levels in the blood and tissues. Before the availability of insulin, this disorder was usually fatal.

Digestion of insulin from the islet cells by trypsin, an enzyme from the acinar cells, had doomed earlier attempts to isolate insulin. One evening in October 1920, Banting read an article by Moses Barron that described how blockage of the pancreatic duct by gallstones results in atrophy of the acinar cells. Later that night Banting awoke and jotted down a note to himself: "Tie off pancreas ducts of dogs. Wait six or eight weeks. Remove and extract." It was his hope that "by ligating [tying off] the duct and allowing time for the degeneration of the acinus cells, a means might be provided for obtaining an extract of the islet cells free from the destroying influence of trypsin and other pancreatic enzymes."

Miller suggested that Banting present his idea to JOHN J. R. MACLEOD, a professor of physiology at the University of Toronto, who was in a position to provide Banting with research facilities. According to Banting, MacLeod scoffed at his proposed project, and it was only after several visits to MacLeod's office that he finally received support for his research. Eventually, MacLeod provided laboratory space, ten dogs, and a research assistant, Charles Best, an undergraduate medical student who was skilled at determining the glucose content of blood and urine. Banting resigned from the University of Western Ontario and returned to Toronto.

In May 1921 Banting and Best began a series of experiments at the University of Toronto, while MacLeod left for a holiday in Scotland. By the time he returned in August, Banting and Best had managed to extract insulin from the islet cells of the pancreas of dogs. They had also removed the pancreas of a dog and, as the animal lay dying of diabetic acidosis, injected it with their extract of pancreas. The dog recovered; its blood glucose fell to within normal range, and its urine became free of glucose.

Later in the same year Banting and Best reported their findings to the Physiological Journal Club at the University of Toronto, and in December 1921 they presented their results to members of the American Physiological Society in New Haven, Connecticut. There, MacLeod also participated in the presentation, and he subsequently made available all the resources of his department for the task of isolating more insulin and purifying it; he enlisted the aid of J. B. Collip, a biochemist, in the effort. At the Hospital for Sick Children in Toronto, in January 1922 the first patient— a fourteen-year-old boy with severe juvenile diabetes mellitus—was successfully treated with insulin. A series of clinical studies followed that defined the biological effects of insulin and established guidelines for its clinical use. Further investigation of dosage levels in human beings was carried out by Banting, who administered various amounts of insulin extracted from beef pancreas to Dr. Joe Gilchrist, a former classmate and a diabetic, who offered himself as a "human rabbit."

Later that year MacLeod announced the discovery in a press release issued at a meeting of the Association of American Physicians. According to one of Banting's biographers, who was present at the time of the announcement, MacLeod conveyed the impression that it was he who had made the discovery of insulin, with assistance from his colleagues. The incident so enraged Banting that later, while working with Collip, whom he regarded as one of MacLeod's allies, he "suddenly and unexpectedly knocked [Collip] cold." It was an uncharacteristic episode, for Banting was known as a gentle man who went to great lengths to avoid subjecting his laboratory animals to pain.

Instead of taking out a patent on insulin, which would have made him immensely wealthy, Banting turned over his rights to the University of Toronto. The patent rights for the manufacture of insulin were then assigned to the Medical Research Council of Canada, and the substance was commercially available by late 1922.

That year Banting wrote a doctoral dissertation based on his research and received a medical degree from the University of Toronto. He had become an international celebrity. In 1923 the Ontario Provincial Legislature created the Banting and Best Department of Medical Research at the University of Toronto; Banting was granted an annuity for life by an act of the Canadian Parliament. In his honor, the Banting Research Foundation, the Banting Institute, and the Banting Memorial Lectureship were also established in Toronto.

Banting and MacLeod shared the 1923 Nobel Prize for Physiology or Medicine "for the discovery of insulin." Outraged that Best had not been included in the honor, Banting threatened to refuse the award but was persuaded to accept it. He did, however, give half of his share of the prize money to Best, publicly acknowledging Best's contribution to the discovery of insulin. (Members of the Nobel committee later privately admitted that Best should have been awarded a share of the prize.)

In 1924 Banting married Marion Robertson; they had a son. Banting's first marriage ended in divorce in 1932; later, in 1939, he married Henrietta Bell.

Shortly before World War II, Banting became involved in aviation medicine, concentrating on the biological effects of high-altitude flying. In 1940 he volunteered to serve as a liaison officer for the Canadian air force, conveying important messages from Canada to England by air. In 1941, a military plane in which he was flying crashed in a remote area of Newfoundland; Banting died before the rescue team arrived.

In addition to being knighted by King George V, Banting was elected a fellow of the Royal

Society of London and an honorary member of the Royal College of Surgeons and the Royal College of Physicians. He received the Reeve Prize from the University of Toronto (1922), the Cameron Prize and Lectureship of the University of Edinburgh (1927), and the Flavelle Medal of the Royal Society of Canada (1931), as well as honorary degrees from Queens College and the University of Toronto.

SELECTED WORKS: Preliminary Studies on the Physiological Effects of Insulin, 1922, with others; The Internal Secretion of the Pancreas, 1922, with C. H. Best; The Effect Produced on Diabetes by Extracts of Pancreas, 1923, with others.

ABOUT: Bliss, M. Banting: A Biography, 1984; Dictionary of Scientific Biography, volume 1, 1970; Harris, S. Banting's Miracle, 1946; Jackson, A. Y. Banting as an Artist, 1943; Levine, I. E. The Discoverer of Insulin, 1959; Rowland, J. The Insulin Man, 1966; Shaw, M. M. He Conquered Death, 1946; Stevenson, L. G. Sir Frederick Banting, 1947.

ROBERT BÁRÁNY

BÁRÁNY, ROBERT
(April 22, 1876–April 8, 1936)
Nobel Prize for Physiology or Medicine, 1914

Robert Bárány (bär′ än yə), Austrian physiologist and otologist, was born in Vienna, the eldest of six children, to the former Maria Hock, the daughter of a scientist, and Ignaz Bárány, a Hungarian Jew who was a bank official and estate manager. Encouraged by his mother in intellectual and scientific pursuits, Bárány became interested in medicine after recovering from a childhood attack of tuberculosis. An exceptional student both in high school and at the University of Vienna, from which he received a medical degree in 1900, he went on to specialize in internal medicine at Frankfurt am Main for a year. He continued his studies at the universities of Heidelberg and Freiburg for two years, investigating disorders of the nervous system, and trained as a surgeon for a year on his return to Vienna.

In 1903 Bárány was appointed demonstrator at the University of Vienna ear clinic. At the clinic, ear infections were routinely treated by irrigating the ear canal with warm water, a procedure that occasionally caused dizziness. Bárány observed that during such an attack of vertigo, the patient's eyes oscillated unevenly in a characteristic pattern known as nystagmus.

As early as 1825 the Czech physiologist Jan Purkyně (also known as Purkinje) had shown that nystagmus is an involuntary reaction associated with vertigo. Near the end of the nineteenth century, it was established that vertigo arises from overstimulation of the vestibular apparatus, which consists of three tiny perpendicular loops of fluid-filled tissue in the inner ear and which serves as the organ of balance. Endolymph, the fluid in these semicircular canals, does not move in exact synchronization with the body but sloshes slightly, like water in a bucket. Cells within the vestibular apparatus sense the sloshing action, and this information is coordinated with visual sensations to produce a sense of relationship with the outside world.

Vertigo occurs when the eyes and the vestibular apparatus disagree about the body's movement. Either the endolymph in the semicircular canals is moving and the picture of the world is not (as happens when stepping off a merry-go-round), or the world seems to be moving but the endolymph is not (as would happen if one were standing still in a room with moving walls). The eye movement of nystagmus is a reflex attempt to force into agreement the information from the visual and vestibular systems.

These facts alone, however, did not explain why syringing the ear caused Bárány's patients to become dizzy. A clue came when Bárány happened to treat a patient first with water that was too cold and then with water that was too warm. On both occasions the patient complained of vertigo; Bárány later said he "noticed that the nystagmus [provoked by warm water] was in an exactly opposite direction from the previous one when cold water had been used. It came to me in a flash that obviously the temperature of the water was responsible for the nystagmus." Syringing the ear with cold water cools the endolymph nearest the ear canal. Because the cool endolymph is heavier than normal, it sinks and is replaced by the warm endolymph, which in turn cools and sinks. As a result, the fluid in the semicircular canal moves while the body and the visual field remain stationary, thus producing the sensation of vertigo. Treating the ear with warm water has the opposite effect of cold water, so the nystagmus—the reflex attempt at compensation—also occurs in the opposite direction.

Like most sense organs, the vestibular apparatus occurs in a pair, one on each side of the head. Bárány's discovery of the caloric (or heat-related) reaction was a milestone in research of the vestibular apparatus, because for the first time it enabled the activities of each set of semicircular canals to be studied separately. The caloric reaction remains the favored method of testing the function of the semicircular canals in healthy people. It is also valuable in diagnosing patients suspected of having inner-ear disease, because the caloric test does not produce nystagmus when there is a disturbance in the vestibular apparatus itself.

A quiet, dedicated researcher, Bárány published the first reports of his studies on the vestibular apparatus in 1906. Three years later he was appointed docent (teacher) at the University of Vienna. When World War I began in 1914, Bárány volunteered for the Austrian Army Medical Service and was stationed at the fortress of Przemyśl in Galicia (now Poland), where he developed a new surgical method of treating bullet wounds to the brain. His procedure is now so nearly universal that it is taken for granted: cutting away damaged tissue, removing foreign material, disinfecting the wound, and closing immediately.

When Przemyśl fell to the Russian army in April 1915, Bárány was captured and interned in a prison camp in Turkestan. It was there, while serving as physician to the Russians as well as to the Austrian prisoners, that Bárány learned he had been awarded the 1914 Nobel Prize "for his work on the physiology and pathology of the vestibular apparatus." In his presentation speech, Professor Gunnar Holmgren of the Karolinska Institute said that after Bárány reported his observation, "there followed during the next ten years a tremendous, almost revolutionary development of otology, in which Bárány's work was both the foun-

dation and the central theme." Despite efforts by Prince Carl of Sweden to convince the czar to release Bárány, his freedom was not granted until two years later, when he went to Sweden to receive the Nobel Prize, returning to Vienna later that year.

Bárány's triumph was short-lived. Soon after his return, members of the medical faculty accused him of failing to acknowledge the work of other researchers in some of his publications. Although most of the charges were shown to be unwarranted, Bárány left Vienna to take a position as principal and professor of the Otological Institute at the University of Uppsala, Sweden, where he continued his research on the vestibular apparatus. Through this work he demonstrated the important connections between the equilibrium apparatus and the nervous system that are necessary to maintain the body's balance and coordination.

In 1909 Bárány married Ida Felicitas Berger, with whom he had two sons and a daughter—all of whom became physicians. After suffering a series of strokes, Bárány died in Sweden, only a few weeks before his sixtieth birthday. A gold medal, coined in his memory, is awarded at five-year intervals to the vestibular scientist considered most worthy by the University of Uppsala. The Bárány Society was also set up in his honor, its membership confined to outstanding scientists in his field. An accomplished pianist with a fondness for the music of Robert Schumann, Bárány was also a mountain climber and tennis player.

In addition to the Nobel Prize, Bárány's other awards included the ERB Medal of the German Neurological Society (1913) and the Jubilee Medal of the Swedish Medical Society (1925).

SELECTED WORKS: Physiology and Pathology of the Semicircular Canals, 1910.

ABOUT: Archives of Otolaryngology September 1965; Dictionary of Scientific Biography, volume 1, 1970; Haymaker, W., and Schiller, W. Founders of Neurology, 1970.

BARDEEN, JOHN
(May 23, 1908–)
Nobel Prize for Physics, 1956
(shared with Walter H. Brattain and
William Shockley)
Nobel Prize for Physics, 1972
(shared with Leon N Cooper and J. Robert
Schrieffer)

The American physicist and electrical engineer John Bardeen was born in Madison,

JOHN BARDEEN

Wisconsin, to Charles R. Bardeen, professor of anatomy and dean of the medical school at the University of Wisconsin, and Althea (Harmer) Bardeen. After the boy's mother died in 1920, his father married Ruth Hames. Bardeen has two brothers, a sister, and a half-sister.

Bardeen attended an experimental elementary school in Madison, skipping the fourth, fifth, and sixth grades. He entered University High School, then transferred to Madison Central High School, from which he graduated in 1923. Despite having a congenital condition that produced a tremor of the hand, he was in his youth a champion swimmer and proficient billiards player.

At the University of Wisconsin, Bardeen earned a B.S. in electrical engineering in 1928, minoring in physics and mathematics. While still an undergraduate, he worked in the engineering department of the Western Electric Company (the department later became Bell Telephone Laboratories). In 1929 he was awarded an M.S. in electrical engineering by Wisconsin, having conducted research on applied geophysics and radiation from antennas. The next year he followed one of his research advisers, American geophysicist Leo J. Peters, to the Gulf Research and Development Corporation in Pittsburgh, Pennsylvania, where they developed new techniques for analyzing maps of magnetic and gravitational field strengths to determine likely locations of petroleum deposits.

In 1933 Bardeen entered Princeton University to study mathematical physics under EU-

GENE P. WIGNER. He concentrated on the quantum theory as applied to solids. By then quantum mechanics had evolved into a highly successful description of individual atoms and of the particles within the atom. Solids obey the same quantum-mechanical laws, but because a macroscopic solid is made up of vast numbers of atoms, the task of analysis is formidable. For his Ph.D. from Princeton in 1936, Bardeen wrote a thesis on the attractive forces that hold electrons within metals. A year before completing his dissertation, he accepted a postdoctoral research fellowship at Harvard University, which he held until 1938. At Harvard, Bardeen worked with JOHN H. VAN VLECK and P. W. BRIDGMAN on problems in cohesion and electrical conduction in metals.

When the fellowship ended, Bardeen became an assistant professor of physics at the University of Minnesota, where he continued his research on the behavior of electrons in metals. Between 1941 and 1945, he served as a civilian physicist for the Naval Ordnance Laboratory in Washington, D.C., studying the magnetic fields of ships (a matter of importance to underwater ordnance and minesweeping).

Bardeen went to Bell Telephone Laboratories in 1945, joining WILLIAM SHOCKLEY and WALTER H. BRATTAIN in their quest for semiconductor devices that could both rectify and amplify electric signals. Semiconductors, such as silicon and germanium, are materials whose electrical resistance is intermediate between that of a metal and that of an insulator.

Shockley was trying to develop what is now called a field-effect transistor. In such a device an electric field, induced by a voltage imposed from outside the semiconductor, influences the motion of electrons within the material. Shockley hoped to use the electric field to control the supply of mobile electrons in one region of the semiconductor and thus modulate a current flowing through the device. Also, the transistor had the potential to be an amplifier because a small signal (the applied voltage) should cause large changes in the current flowing through the semiconductor.

All attempts to build a device according to this plan failed. Bardeen then suggested that the external voltage was prevented from creating the desired electric field within the semiconductor by a layer of electrons trapped at its surface. Successive studies then tested the response of a semiconductor surface to light, heat, cold, liquids, and the deposit of metallic films. In 1947, once the group had achieved an adequate understanding of the surface properties of semiconductors, Bardeen and Brattain constructed the first working transistors.

One of the early designs was a point-contact transistor built from a block of germanium. The point contacts were two fine metal "cat's whiskers," called the emitter and collector, attached to the top of the block; a third electrical contact, called the base, was made through the bottom of the block. Instead of an externally applied voltage and associated electric field, the point-contact transistor used a small current flowing between the emitter and the base to control a larger current flowing from the emitter to the collector. In a later design, called the junction transistor, the point contacts were eliminated, and the emitter and collector were formed out of semiconductor materials "doped" with small amounts of specific impurities. Field-effect transistors did not become practical until silicon replaced germanium as the favored base material.

Like the vacuum tube, the transistor permits a very small signal (voltage for the tube, current for the transistor) in one circuit to control a relatively large current in another circuit. Because of their small size, rugged structure, low energy requirements, and reduced cost, transistors rapidly replaced vacuum tubes in all applications except those requiring the control of very large amounts of power, for example, in broadcasting and in industrial radio-frequency heating. Today bipolar transistors are routinely used when very high speed is needed, as well as in many high-frequency power applications which are not so demanding that they require vacuum tubes. Improvements in technology made it possible to form many transistors on a single silicon chip that could perform more complex functions. The number of transistors per chip has increased from 10 to about 1 million, in part by the reduction of the dimensions of wires and devices to a range from one-half to several microns (1 micron equals 0.00004 inch). These chips permit the construction of modern computers, communications equipment, and controllers, and the technology is still developing rapidly.

Bardeen shared the 1956 Nobel Prize for Physics with Shockley and Brattain "for their researches on semiconductors and their discovery of the transistor effect." "A transistor functions much like a radio valve," noted E. G. Rudberg of the Royal Swedish Academy of Sciences in his presentation speech. Pointing out that transistors are smaller than vacuum tubes and, unlike the latter, do not require an electric current to heat a filament, Rudberg added that "hearing aids, computing machines, telephone stations, and many others are in need of just such a device."

In 1951 Bardeen left Bell Labs to accept a dual appointment as professor of electrical engineering and professor of physics at the University of Illinois. There he resumed in earnest a research interest he had developed as a graduate student, set aside during World War II, and returned to in 1950—superconductivity and the properties of matter at very low temperatures.

Superconductivity had been discovered in 1911 by the Dutch physicist HEIKE KAMERLINGH ONNES, who found that some metals lose all resistance to the flow of electric current at temperatures a few degrees above absolute zero. An electric current consists of electrons moving in a particular direction. In metals, many electrons are so loosely bound to their atoms that the force of an electric field, set up by an applied voltage, causes them to migrate in the direction of the field. However, the electrons also vibrate in random directions due to their heat content. This scattered movement results in opposition (resistance) to directed flow under the influence of the field. When thermal motion is reduced by cooling, resistance normally decreases. At absolute zero, where thermal motion ceases, resistance is also expected to cease. However, absolute zero is practically unattainable. The surprise of superconductivity was that the resistance vanished at temperatures above absolute zero despite the persistence of thermal vibrations. No satisfactory explanation was then available.

Superconductors proved to have another unusual characteristic, discovered in 1933 by the German physicist Walther Meissner. He found them to be perfectly diamagnetic; that is, they prevented the penetration of a magnetic field to their interior. Paramagnetic materials, which include common magnetic metals such as iron, are more or less susceptible to being magnetized by a nearby magnet. Since the magnetic field of the magnet induces a field of opposite polarity in a paramagnetic body, the body is attracted to the magnet. Since a diamagnetic body rejects the magnetic field, the body and the magnet mutually repel each other, regardless of which pole of the magnet is presented. A magnetic material placed above a superconductor will hover on a cushion of magnetic repulsion. If the applied magnetic field is sufficiently strong, however, a superconductor will lose its superconductivity and behave like an ordinary metal. In 1935 the

German physicist Fritz London suggested that diamagnetism was the fundamental property of superconductors and that superconductivity might be a quantum effect somehow manifested by an entire body of material.

A clue that London was on the right track appeared in 1950. Several American physicists discovered that different isotopes of a given metal became superconducting at different temperatures and that the critical temperature was inversely proportional to the atomic mass. Isotopes are forms of an element that have the same number of protons in their nuclei (hence the same number of surrounding electrons) and are chemically similar, but their nuclei contain different numbers of neutrons and therefore have different masses. Bardeen knew that the only effect of different atomic masses on the properties of a solid body manifested itself as variations in propagation of vibrational motions within the body. He therefore suggested that the superconductivity of a metal involved an interaction between conduction electrons (those relatively free to move as an electric current) and the vibrations of atoms in the metal body, and that their link to atomic vibrations also coupled the electrons to each other.

Bardeen was later joined in his investigation by two of his students at the University of Illinois, LEON N COOPER, a postdoctoral research associate, and J. ROBERT SCHRIEFFER, a graduate student. In 1956 Cooper showed that an electron (which carries a negative charge) moving through the regular structure (lattice) of a metal crystal attracts nearby positively charged atoms, slightly deforming the lattice and creating a momentary increase in the concentration of positive charge. The concentration of positive charge then attracts a second electron, and the two electrons become paired, indirectly bound together through the local distortion of the crystal lattice. In this way, many electrons throughout the metal become joined two by two, called Cooper pairs.

Bardeen and Schrieffer tried to apply Cooper's insight to the behavior of a large portion of the population of free electrons in a superconducting metal, with a frustrating lack of success. When Bardeen left for Stockholm to receive his 1956 Nobel Prize, Schrieffer was ready to concede failure, but he persisted at Bardeen's urging and succeeded in developing the necessary statistical methods for solving the problem.

Bardeen, Cooper, and Schrieffer were then able to show that Cooper pairs interact to compel many of the free electrons in a supercon-ductor to flow in unison. As London had guessed, the superconducting electrons form a single quantum state that encompasses the entire metal body. The critical temperature at which superconductivity appears represents the degree of reduction of thermal vibrations required to allow the influence of Cooper pairs to predominate in coordinating the movement of free electrons. Since the introduction of resistance by the deviation of even one electron from the common stream would necessarily affect all others participating in superconduction, and thus destroy the integrity of the quantum state, such a disturbance is highly unlikely. The superconducting electrons therefore drift collectively without loss of energy.

The achievement of Bardeen, Cooper, and Schrieffer has been called one of the most important in theoretical physics since the development of quantum theory. In 1958 they used their theory to predict superfluidity (the absence of viscosity and surface tension) in liquid helium 3 (an isotope whose nucleus contains two protons and one neutron) near absolute zero, which was confirmed experimentally in 1962. Superfluidity had been observed previously in helium 4 (the most common isotope, with an additional neutron) and had been considered impossible in isotopes with an odd number of nuclear particles.

Bardeen, Cooper, and Schrieffer shared the 1972 Nobel Prize for Physics "for their jointly developed theory of superconductivity, usually called the BCS theory." Stig Lundqvist of the Royal Swedish Academy of Sciences, in his presentation speech, noted the completeness of the explanation of superconductivity and added, "Your theory has also predicted new effects and stimulated an intensive activity in theoretical and experimental research." He also pointed out that "further developments . . . confirmed the great range and validity of the concepts and ideas in your fundamental paper from 1957."

The BCS theory has had far-reaching effects on technology and theory. The development of materials that become superconducting at higher temperatures or withstand strong magnetic fields has made possible the construction of exceptionally powerful electromagnets of relatively small size and energy consumption. The magnetic field produced by an electromagnet is directly related to the current in its windings. In ordinary wire, the presence of resistance is a severe limitation because heat is produced in proportion to the resistance and to the amount of the current squared. Not only is heat wasted energy, which is costly, but it also causes deterioration of materials. Superconducting magnets are used in the study of nuclear fusion; in magnetohydrodynamics; in high-energy particle accelerators; in frictionless trains lifted magnetically above their rails; in biological and physical research on the interactions of atoms and electrons with strong magnetic fields; and in the construction of compact, powerful electric generators. The Welsh physicist BRIAN D. JOSEPHSON discovered that, under appropriate conditions, junctions between superconductors give rise to so-called supercurrents (Josephson effects) sensitive to magnetic fields. Sensors based on the Josephson effects can detect minute amounts of magnetic activity in living organisms and help locate ore and petroleum deposits by their magnetic properties.

In 1959 Bardeen joined the Center for Advanced Study at the University of Illinois and continued his research in solid-state and low-temperature physics. In 1975 he became professor emeritus.

Bardeen married Jane Maxwell in 1938; they have two sons and a daughter. During his leisure time Bardeen travels and plays golf.

Bardeen's many awards include the Stuart Ballantine Medal of the Franklin Institute (1952), the John Scott Award of the city of Philadelphia (1955), the Oliver E. Buckley Solid-State Physics Prize of the American Physical Society (1954), the National Medal of Science of the National Science Foundation (1965), the Medal of Honor of the Institute of Electrical and Electronics Engineers (1971), and the Presidential Medal of Freedom of the United States government (1977). For many years Bardeen was associate editor of the *Physical Review*. He is a member of the National Academy of Sciences and the American Academy of Arts and Sciences and was elected a fellow of the American Physical Society.

SELECTED WORKS: Understanding Superconductivity, 1964; The Collected Works of John Bardeen From 1930–1967 (2 vols.) 1968; Impact of Basic Technology, 1973, with others; Scientific Research and Industrial Development, 1977; "To a Solid State," Science 84 November 1984.

ABOUT: Current Biography September 1957; National Geographic Society. Those Inventive Americans, 1971; Saturday Review of Science March 1973; Science November 3, 1972.

BARKLA, CHARLES G.
(June 27, 1877–October 23, 1944)
Nobel Prize for Physics, 1917

The English physicist Charles Glover Barkla was born in Widnes, Lancashire, to John Martin Barkla, an executive in a chemical company, and Sarah (Glover) Barkla. He attended secondary school at the Liverpool Institute and, in 1895, entered University College in Liverpool on scholarship, to study mathematics and experimental physics. In 1898 he received a B.S. with first-class honors in physics. The following year he was awarded an M.S.

On scholarship at Trinity College, Cambridge, in 1899, Barkla studied physics with George Stokes and did research in the Cavendish Laboratory under J. J. THOMSON. A year and a half later, he moved over to King's College so that he could sing in its famous choir; an excellent baritone, he often performed as a soloist. In 1902 Barkla refused a choral scholarship at Cambridge and returned to Liverpool as an Oliver Lodge Fellow, obtaining his doctorate two years later. He remained at Liverpool until 1909, first as a demonstrator, then as an assistant lecturer, and finally as a special lecturer. During these years Barkla continued his researches on X rays, a subject that he had taken up in 1901 during his third year at Cambridge. In 1909 he left Liverpool to become Wheatstone Professor of Physics at King's College, London.

The discovery of X rays by WILHELM RÖNTGEN in 1895 had caused great controversy among physicists. Some believed them to be a form of electromagnetic radiation such as light, whereas others maintained that they consisted of particles. An experiment Barkla performed in 1904 supported the idea that X rays are pulses of electromagnetic waves, resulting from the deceleration of electrons striking the anode of a cathode-ray tube. Classical electromagnetism predicted—and Barkla's experiment showed—that such pulses are partially polarized; that is, radiation emitted in a plane perpendicular to the motion of the electrons has a stronger electric field perpendicular to the plane than in it.

It had been observed in 1897 that whenever X rays fall upon a substance—whether solid, liquid, or gas—a secondary radiation emerges. In 1903 Barkla published his first results on secondary radiation, which he assumed was due entirely to the scattering of the primary beam. His finding that the scattering increased proportionally to the presumed atomic weight of the scattering substance lent support to the

CHARLES G. BARKLA

electron theory of matter, which had not yet been fully accepted.

Barkla's later observations of X radiation of the heavier elements showed that the secondary radiation actually has two components: unchanged X rays scattered from the primary beam and a less penetrating, or "softer," radiation produced by and characteristic of the scattering substance. This softer radiation, which came to be called characteristic radiation, increases in penetrating power according to the position of the X-radiated element in the periodic table. H. G. J. Moseley later used this information to establish the meaning of atomic number (the number of units of nuclear charge), an important step toward understanding the structure of the atomic nucleus.

By 1911 Barkla had shown that the characteristic radiation of heavy elements is of two types: a more penetrating radiation, which he called K radiation, and a less penetrating type, which he called L radiation. Later it would be shown that K and L radiation arise from transitions of the innermost electrons (after they have been excited by the primary X ray) in the quantum atomic model proposed by NIELS BOHR and Arnold Sommerfeld to explain the emission of visible light.

Barkla's findings gained him international recognition, and in 1918 he was awarded the 1917 Nobel Prize for Physics "for his discovery of the characteristic Röntgen radiation of the elements." (Moseley, who might have shared the Nobel Prize with Barkla, had been killed in World War I at Gallipoli.) "Barkla's discovery of the characteristic X radiation has

proved to be a phenomenon of extraordinary importance as regards physical research," wrote G. D. Granqvist of the Royal Swedish Academy of Sciences in an essay written in 1918. "The discovery of the diffraction of X rays in crystals gave a means of measuring their wavelengths, and since then the further investigation of the K-series and the L-series has yielded results of fundamental importance as regards our conception of the inner structure of atoms." Wartime restrictions on travel caused the cancellation of the awards ceremonies, and it was not until 1920 that Barkla delivered his Nobel lecture, "Characteristic Röntgen Radiation."

From 1913 on, Barkla was professor of natural philosophy at the University of Edinburgh in Scotland, where he remained until his death. By the time he received the Nobel Prize, however, Barkla's eminence as a physicist was beginning to wane, and he isolated himself from the physics community. Although respected as a strong experimentalist, he failed to realize his weakness as a theorist. He tended to ignore the experimental work of others and increasingly referred only to problems that he himself had investigated. In 1916 he rejected the quantum theory developed by MAX PLANCK, ALBERT EINSTEIN, and Niels Bohr. By this time, Barkla's conclusion that energy was not quantized was hardly tenable in the face of available evidence. He refused to accept the existence of the Compton effect, discovered by ARTHUR H. COMPTON in 1923, which was extremely important to the development of quantum theory in the 1920s. (In the Compton effect, incident X ray ejects an atomic electron and is scattered, showing that X rays, like light, sometimes act like particles.) After 1916 Barkla devoted himself to searching for what he called the "J phenomenon," involving radiation more penetrating than the K type. However, no such phenomenon has ever been demonstrated.

In 1907 Barkla married Mary Esther Cowell, daughter of the receiver-general of the Isle of Man. They had three sons and one daughter. Shortly after his youngest son was killed in World War II, Barkla's health failed. He died at his home in Edinburgh on October 23, 1944.

Known as a friendly man with a charming manner, Barkla was a deeply religious member of the Methodist church. Serving for many years on the examination committees of the British universities, he acquired a reputation as knowledgeable and fair. In addition to singing, he enjoyed playing golf and driving in the Scottish highlands.

Barkla was a fellow of the Royal Society of London and the recipient of its Hughes Medal (1917). He held an honorary degree from the University of Liverpool and several other institutions.

SELECTED WORKS: Radiation and Matter, 1920.

ABOUT: American Journal of Physics February 1967; Dictionary of Scientific Biography, volume 1, 1970; Obituary Notices of Fellows of the Royal Society, volume 5, 1947.

BARTON, DEREK
(September 8, 1918–   )
Nobel Prize for Chemistry, 1969
(shared with Odd Hassel)

DEREK BARTON

The English chemist Derek Harold Richard Barton was born in Gravesend, on the Thames River near London, to William Thomas Barton and Maude (Henrietta) Barton. After receiving his early education at the Tonbridge School, he attended Gillingham Technical College but transferred in 1938 to the Imperial College of Science and Technology, University of London, where he received his B.S. with honors (1940) and his Ph.D. in organic chemistry (1942). For the next two years he performed wartime chemical research, after which he worked briefly as an industrial research chemist for the Birmingham firm of Albright and Wilson.

At the end of the war in 1945, Barton became an assistant lecturer in the chemistry department at the Imperial College. There, between 1946 and 1949, a research fellowship enabled him to pursue investigations into organic molecules, for which he received a second doctorate in 1949. The following year, while serving as a visiting lecturer in the chemistry of natural products at Harvard University, Barton became interested in how to determine the precise configuration of organic (carbon-based) molecules.

At the time Barton began his studies, chemists were able to classify molecules in two fundamental ways: by their constitution (the identity of the component atoms) and by their configuration (the arrangement of the molecules into patterns that were either symmetrical along the major axis or asymmetrical in left- or right-handed patterns). The three-dimensional structure of molecules was not clearly understood, however. It was anticipated that the ability to determine the form of a given molecule would provide vital information about its chemical behavior and the nature of its reactions with other molecules. Knowledge of the structure of organic molecules appeared particularly promising, because these carbon-based molecules, which bond readily with other atoms, are the chemical building blocks of living systems.

During his year at Harvard, Barton became curious about the different reaction rates of various forms of steroids, an important group of organic compounds prevalent in bile acids, hormones, and other physiological compounds. Barton wondered if these differences might be explained by the physical structure of the molecules. In such molecules, the basic carbon atoms are joined to one another in a closed pattern called a ring. It was known that six-carbon rings can assume a boat-shaped configuration when they are twisted at certain bonding locations. Twisted in the same direction, mirror-image six-carbon rings assumed a chair-shaped configuration. In earlier but little-known work, the Norwegian chemist ODD HASSEL had shown that the chair configuration is preferred by six-carbon rings at rest, because it is the more energy-efficient of the two possible shapes.

Barton was aware of Hassel's findings and developed them into a method for analyzing the structure of highly complex organic molecules. This method, now known as conformational analysis, not only made it possible to understand and predict how such biologically important molecules as steroids and carbohydrates would behave under various conditions; it also enabled chemists to study the

61

structure of large molecules in three dimensions.

On his return to England in 1951, Barton joined the faculty of Birkbeck College, University of London, where he became professor of organic chemistry two years later. In 1955 he accepted a position as Regius Professor of Chemistry at the University of Glasgow. There he applied the techniques of conformational analysis to investigate many types of organic chemicals, among them the alkaloids, a class of complex molecules that includes nicotine and morphine.

Barton was professor of organic chemistry at the Imperial College of Science and Technology, University of London, from 1957 to 1970 and Hoffmann Professor of Organic Chemistry from 1970 to 1978. During these years he also lectured extensively in the United States. While visiting the Research Institute for Medicine and Chemistry in Cambridge, Massachusetts, in 1960, he devised a method of producing chemical reactions by the use of light, which became known as the Barton process. This process led to the synthesis of aldosterone, a hormone that helps to regulate sodium and potassium readsorption in the kidney.

Barton and Hassel shared the 1969 Nobel Prize for Chemistry "for their contributions to the development of the concept of conformation and its application in chemistry." In his Nobel lecture, Barton traced the development of conformational analysis and described its implications for the fields of chemistry and biology. "It is interesting to observe," he concluded, "how an acorn of hypothesis can become a tree of knowledge."

Upon his retirement from the Imperial College in 1978, Barton became director of the Institute for the Chemistry of Natural Substances in Gif-sur-Yvette, France. Since 1960 his interest has turned from conformational analysis to such topics as photochemistry and biosynthesis.

In 1944 Barton married Jeanne Kate Wilkins, with whom he had one son. After they were divorced, he married Christiane Cognet, a professor at the Lycée Français de Londres.

Known as a dedicated researcher, Barton has also devoted much of his time to sharing his knowledge through lectures delivered throughout the United States and in Canada. His many awards include the Corday-Morgan Medal of the British Chemical Society (1951); the Fritzsche Award (1956) and the Roger Adams Award (1959) of the American Chemical Society; and the Davy Medal (1961), the Royal

Medal (1972), and the Copley Medal (1980) of the Royal Society. He is a fellow of the Royal Society and the Royal Society of Edinburgh and a foreign member of the American Academy of Arts and Sciences. He holds honorary degrees from Columbia and Oxford universities and from the University of Manchester, among others.

SELECTED WORKS: Some Modern Trends in Organic Chemistry, 1958; Specific Fluorination in the Synthesis of Biologically Active Compounds, 1969.

ABOUT: New York Times October 31, 1969; Science November 7, 1969.

BASOV, NIKOLAI
(December 14, 1922–)
Nobel Prize for Physics, 1964
(shared with Aleksandr Prokhorov and
   Charles H. Townes)

The Russian physicist Nikolai Gennadiyevich Basov was born in the village of Usman, near the city of Voronezh, to Gennadiy Fyodorovich Basov and Zinaida Andreyevna Molchanova. His father, a professor at the Voronezh Forest Institute, specialized in the effects of forest belts on underground water and surface drainage. Graduated from high school in Voronezh in 1941, young Basov then entered the Soviet army. During World War II, he was trained as a doctor's assistant at the Kuibyshev Military Medical Academy and served near the Ukrainian front.

After his discharge in December 1945, Basov studied theoretical and experimental physics at the Moscow Institute of Physical Engineers. In 1948, two years before graduation, he joined the P. N. Lebedev Physical Institute of the Soviet Academy of Sciences in Moscow as a laboratory assistant. After graduation he went on to receive a candidate's degree (similar to a master's degree) in 1953 under the direction of M. A. Leontovich and ALEKSANDR PROKHOROV. Three years later he received a doctorate in physical and mathematical sciences in recognition of his theoretical and experimental work with molecular oscillators using ammonia as the active medium.

The underlying principle of a molecular oscillator—now known as a maser, an acronym for *m*icrowave *a*mplification by *s*timulated *e*mission of *r*adiation—was first elucidated by ALBERT EINSTEIN in 1917. While investigating the interaction between electromagnetic

NIKOLAI BASOV

radiation and a group of molecules in a confined space, Einstein developed an equation with three terms that contained a surprise. The terms described the absorption and emission of radiation by the molecules. Quantum physics had shown that electromagnetic radiation is composed of discrete units of energy, called photons, and that the energy in each photon is proportional to the frequency of the radiation. Also, the energy of atoms and molecules, related to the configurations and motions of their electrons, is restricted to certain discrete values, or energy levels. The set of allowed energy levels is unique to a particular atom or molecule. Photons whose energy equals the difference between two energy levels can be absorbed, and the atom or molecule jumps from the lower to the higher level. A very short time later, it spontaneously falls back to a lower level (not necessarily the one it started from) and gives up energy equal to the difference between its previous and new levels in the form of a photon of radiation.

The first two terms in Einstein's equation related to the already known processes of absorption and spontaneous emission. The third term, Einstein discovered, represented a then unknown kind of emission. It was a transition from an upper to a lower energy level due merely to the presence of radiation of a suitable frequency whose photons had an energy equal to the difference between those two levels. Since this emission did not occur spontaneously, but was instigated by the special circumstances, it was called stimulated emission. Although it was an interesting phenom-

enon, stimulated emission was not necessarily useful. A physical law derived by the Austrian physicist Ludwig Boltzmann indicated that at equilibrium, higher energy levels would be occupied by fewer electrons than would lower levels. Thus, the stimulated emission would involve relatively few participants.

Basov conceived a way of using stimulated emission to amplify incoming radiation and to create a molecular oscillator. To do so, he had to invert the equilibrium condition by increasing the number of excited molecules relative to the number in the ground state. This was possible through segregation of the excited molecules by means of nonhomogeneous electric or magnetic fields. Incoming radiation of the correct frequency, whose photons had an energy equal to the difference between the excited and ground states of the molecules, would then trigger stimulated emission of radiation of the same frequency, thus amplifying the original signals. He could then create an oscillator by feeding back some of the radiation energy to excite more molecules and produce more stimulated emission. The device would then be not merely an amplifier but a generator of radiation at a frequency precisely determined by the energy levels of the molecule.

At the All-Union Conference on Radio Spectroscopy in May 1952, Basov and Prokhorov proposed the construction of a molecular oscillator based on population inversion, an idea they did not publish, however, until October 1954. The following year Basov and Prokhorov published a note on the "three-level method." According to this scheme, if atoms are raised from the lowest to the highest of three energy levels, then the intermediate level attains a greater population than the lowest level, and stimulated emission can occur at the frequency corresponding to the energy difference between the two lower levels.

CHARLES H. TOWNES, an American physicist working independently along similar lines at Columbia University, produced a working maser (he and his colleagues coined the term) in 1953, just ten months before Basov and Prokhorov published their first paper on molecular oscillators. Townes used a resonant chamber filled with excited ammonia molecules and achieved enormous amplification of microwaves at 24,000 megahertz. In 1960 the American physicist Theodore H. Maiman, working at the Hughes Aircraft Company, constructed a device based on the three-level principle to amplify and generate red light. Maiman's resonant chamber was a long crystal of synthetic ruby with mirrored ends; the exciting radiation was supplied by flashes from a spiral tube filled with xenon gas (similar to a neon tube), which encircled the ruby. The Maiman device became known as the laser, an acronym for *l*ight *a*mplification by *s*timulated *e*mission of *r*adiation.

"For fundamental work in the field of quantum electronics, which has led to the construction of oscillators and amplifiers based on the maser-laser principle," Basov shared the 1964 Nobel Prize for Physics with Prokhorov and Townes. The two Soviet physicists had already received the Soviet government's Lenin Prize for their work in 1959.

Basov has written or co-written several hundred articles on masers and lasers. His work on lasers goes back to 1957, when he and his colleagues began laser design and construction. They have subsequently devised numerous lasers based on crystals, semiconductors, gases, and various combinations of chemicals, as well as multichannel and powerful short-pulse types. Basov was also the first to demonstrate laser action in the ultraviolet region of the electromagnetic spectrum. In addition to his fundamental research on population inversion in semiconductors and on transition processes in various molecular systems, he has devoted considerable attention to practical laser applications, particularly to thermonuclear fusion.

From 1958 to 1972 Basov was deputy director of the Lebedev Institute; since 1973 he has been its director. At Lebedev, he has also headed the Laboratory of Quantum Radio Physics since its inception in 1963. Since that year, he has also been a professor at the Moscow Institute of Physical Engineers.

In 1950 Basov married Kseniya Tikhonovna Nazarova, a physicist at the Moscow Institute. They have two sons.

In addition to the Nobel Prize, Basov has received the Soviet Government's Hero of Socialist Labor citation (1969 and 1982) and the Gold Medal of the Czechoslovak Academy of Sciences (1975). He was elected a corresponding member of the Soviet Academy of Sciences in 1962, a full member in 1966, and a member of its Presidium in 1967. He also belongs to many other scientific academies, including those of East Germany, Poland, Czechoslovakia, Bulgaria, and France; and he is a member of the Leopoldina German Academy of Researchers in Natural Sciences, the Royal Swedish Academy of Engineering Sciences, and the Optical Society of America. Basov has been vice-chairman of the executive council of the World Federation of Research Workers and president of the All-Union Learned Society. He is a member of the Soviet Committee of Defense of Peace and of the World Peace Council and serves as editor in chief of the popular science magazine *Priroda* (Nature) and the *Soviet Journal of Quantum Electronics*. A member of the Communist party since 1951, he was elected to the Supreme Soviet (Soviet parliament) in 1974 and to its Presidium in 1982.

SELECTED WORKS: Lasers and Their Applications, 1976; Optical Properties of Semiconductors, 1976; Research in Molecular Laser Plasmas, 1976; Superconductivity, 1977; Synchrotron Radiation, 1977; Cosmic Rays in the Stratosphere and in Near Space, 1978; High-Power Lasers and Laser Plasmas, 1978; Problems in the General Theory of Relativity, 1978; Pulsed Neutron Research, 1979; Lasers and Holographic Data Processing, 1984.

ABOUT: New York Times October 30, 1964; Science November 7, 1964.

BEADLE, GEORGE W.
(October 22, 1903–)
Nobel Prize for Physiology or Medicine, 1958
(shared with Joshua Lederberg and Edward L. Tatum)

The American geneticist George Wells Beadle was born in Wahoo, Nebraska, the second of three children of Chauncy Elmer Beadle, a farmer, and the former Hattie Albro, who died when the boy was four years old. When George's older brother was killed in an accident, his father assumed that Beadle would eventually take over the family's 40-acre farm, but a young high school physics teacher had kindled the boy's interest in science and persuaded him to go to college. Beadle enrolled in the College of Agriculture at the University of Nebraska in 1922 and spent his second summer vacation studying the genetics of hybrid wheat in the university's agronomy department.

After receiving his B.S. in 1926 and his M.S. the following year, he began graduate studies in biology at Cornell University. There he worked under R. A. Emerson, a well-known plant geneticist whose students included BARBARA McCLINTOCK. Emerson gave Beadle a part-time assistantship, reviewing all published research on the genetics of maize, and Beadle wrote his dissertation on the process of meiosis in maize.

GEORGE W. BEADLE

Chromosomes, strands of genetic material in the nucleus of plant and animal cells, are composed of genes. Genes are molecules of deoxyribonucleic acid (DNA) that carry the genetic code that directs and controls the biochemical processes of the cell. Meiosis, a process of cell division, leads to the formation of germ, or sex, cells, which have half the number of chromosomes of somatic, or tissue, cells. During fertilization, the number of chromosomes returns to normal as the pairs re-form. Beadle discovered that the inheritance of genetic defects in maize pollen is related to abnormal behavior of the chromosomes during meiosis.

In 1931 Beadle received his Ph.D. in genetics from Cornell, and for the next two years was a National Research Council Fellow in the division of biology at the California Institute of Technology (Caltech) in Pasadena. There he worked under THOMAS HUNT MORGAN, a leading geneticist who specialized in the genetics of the fruit fly, *Drosophila melanogaster*. Beadle's research concerned the phenomenon of chromosomal crossover, a process that occurs during meiosis and involves the exchange of genetic material from one chromosomal strand to another. Beadle discovered that crossover and recombination of genetic material during meiosis occur randomly.

As an instructor in the division of biology at Caltech from 1933 to 1935, Beadle collaborated with Boris Ephrussi, an embryologist from the University of Paris who was working temporarily in Morgan's department. The two scientists became interested in the inheritance of eye color in the fruit fly. Beadle and Ephrussi were interested in the biochemical processes that produce a particular phenotype (physical traits, such as eye color) from a specific genotype (a set of genetic instructions). Beadle spent 1935 in Ephrussi's laboratory at the Institute of Physicochemical Biology in Paris. There they demonstrated that the amino acid tryptophan is the biochemical precursor of one of the eye pigments of the fruit fly; that is, it is the substance from which the pigment is formed.

When he returned to the United States in 1936, Beadle became assistant professor of genetics at Harvard University, but the following year he moved to Stanford University as professor of biology. At the time, biochemical genetics, the discipline that seeks to determine the biochemical processes involved in the development of phenotype from genotype, was in its infancy. The modern study of genetics itself began in 1856, when Gregor Mendel, a Dominican monk living in Czechoslovakia, published his theory of the laws of inheritance. Mendel postulated that "elements," now called genes, govern the inheritance of physical traits, such as flower color. Mendel's plant studies demonstrated that some genes are dominant, others recessive. A dominant gene can be expressed as a physical trait even when it is carried by only one of a pair of chromosomes; a recessive gene must be carried by both chromosomes of a pair in order to be expressed. Mendel's paper and his laws of inheritance, forgotten for half a century, were rediscovered at the turn of the century by a new generation of scientists.

Studies during the first three decades of the twentieth century had determined that genes reside on chromosomes. Archibald Garrod, an English physician and biochemist, had discovered in 1902 that certain enzyme deficiencies in his patients were inherited (enzymes are proteins that are necessary for a wide variety of chemical changes in the body). Garrod's studies wondered whether specific genes direct and control the synthesis of specific enzymes, a question that intrigued Beadle. Then in 1926 HERMANN J. MULLER, working with fruit flies, showed that X rays produce mutations in genetic material and the mutations result in physical abnormalities and deformities.

In 1937 Beadle was joined at Stanford by EDWARD L. TATUM, who had studied microbiology and biochemistry at the University of Wisconsin. Beadle was searching for a more suitable organism than the fruit fly for his own genetic studies. As a graduate student at Cornell and later at Caltech, he had heard about the genetics of *Neurospora crassa,* the pink mold that forms on bread. Because it grows and reproduces rapidly, it is possible to study several generations of *Neurospora* within a short time. The genetics of this organism had been partly described by other investigators, and Tatum, who had studied its nutritional requirements, decided to begin experiments with it in 1941.

Beadle and Tatum correctly assumed that gene function could be studied by making some of the genes defective. From Muller's work it was known that although genes undergo spontaneous mutation, the mutation rate could be increased about 100 times by exposing the genetic material to X rays. Accordingly, they grew colonies of *Neurospora* on a culture medium that contained only the few nutrients essential to growth of the organism and then irradiated the colony with X rays. After irradiation, some of the colonies reproduced normally, some died, and some grew but failed to thrive. Beadle and Tatum focused their attention on this third group. They replanted its members on 1,000 different culture media, adding to each some substance that the organism normally was able to synthesize (reproduce) for itself. On the 299th medium, to which vitamin B_6 had been added, the irradiated culture grew normally, suggesting that irradiation had produced a mutation in the gene responsible for the synthesis of vitamin B_6. To determine whether this was in fact a genetic defect, Beadle and Tatum mated the organisms deficient for vitamin B_6 with normal organisms and found that the defect was inherited in a pattern that showed it to be a Mendelian recessive gene. The experiment proved that specific genes control the synthesis of specific cellular substances. The laboratory methods that Tatum and Beadle developed during this work at Stanford proved useful in increasing the pharmaceutical production of penicillin, which was discovered by ALEXANDER FLEMING and is synthesized by a fungus, when it was in great demand during World War II.

Beadle remained at Stanford until 1946, when he was appointed professor of biology at Caltech and chairman of the department Morgan had formerly headed. In 1953, as president-elect of the American Association for the Advancement of Science (AAAS), Beadle urged a review of government security procedures, arguing for a more open society, less secrecy in scientific research, and admission of qualified investigators to classified research information. Under his leadership the AAAS voted in 1955 to hold no professional meetings in cities that practiced segregation.

Beadle and Tatum shared half of the 1958 Nobel Prize for Physiology or Medicine "for their discovery that genes act by regulating definite chemical events." The other half of the prize was awarded to JOSHUA LEDERBERG for related work in genetics. Beadle concluded his Nobel lecture by commenting, "In the beginning botanists and zoologists were often indifferent and sometimes hostile toward [genetics]. '[Genetics] deals only with superficial characters,' it was often said . . . [yet today] our rapidly growing knowledge of the architecture of proteins and nucleic acids is making it possible, for the first time in the history of science, for geneticists, biochemists, and biophysicists to discuss basic problems of biology in the common language of molecular structure."

Beadle left Caltech in 1961 to become professor of biology and president of the University of Chicago. He retired from administrative work in 1968 and resumed his research into the genetics and evolution of maize, returning to California in 1970 when he became a trustee of Caltech. The following year he became an honorary trustee of the University of Chicago.

Beadle married Marion Cecil Hill in 1928; they had one son. The marriage ended in divorce in 1953; later that year, Beadle married Muriel McClure Burnett, a writer and mother of a son by a previous marriage. No children were born of the latter marriage. An amiable man with an air of intellectual excitement, Beadle enjoys skiing, rock climbing, and gardening, and he is particularly fond of Siamese cats.

He has received many honors and awards other than the Nobel Prize, among them the Lasker Award of the American Public Health Association (1950), the Emil Christian Hansen Foundation for Microbiology Research Award given by the Danish Carlsberg Laboratory (1953), the Albert Einstein Commemorative Award of Yeshiva University (1958), and the Kimber Genetics Award of the National Academy of Sciences (1960). He is a member of several learned societies, including the Genetics Society of America (president, 1946), the American Association for the Advancement of Science (president, 1955), the Royal Society of London, and the Danish Royal Academy of Science. He has served on the Committee on Genetic Effects of Atomic Radiation (National Academy of Sciences) and on the Advisory Committee on Biology and Medicine of the Atomic Energy Commission.

SELECTED WORKS: An Introduction to Genetics, 1939, with A. H. Sturtevant; The Physical and Chemical Basis of Inheritance, 1957; Science and Resources, 1959, with others; The Place of Genetics in Modern Biology, 1959; The Language of the Gene, 1961; Genetics and Modern Biology, 1963; The Language of Life, 1966, with Muriel Beadle.

ABOUT: Current Biography April 1956; The Excitement and Fascination of Science, volume 2, 1978; Madden, C. F. (ed.) Talks With Scientists, 1968; Moulton, F. R., and Schrifferes, J. J. Autobiography of Science, 1945; Time July 14, 1958.

SAMUEL BECKETT

BECKETT, SAMUEL
(April 13, 1906–)
Nobel Prize for Literature, 1969

Samuel Barclay Beckett, Irish playwright, novelist, and poet, was born in Dublin, the younger of two sons of William Beckett, a surveyor, and the former Mary May, the daughter of a prosperous family from Kildare. Raised in a Protestant household, Beckett received his early education first at a private academy and then at Earlsfort House School. At the Portora Royal School in Northern Ireland, which he attended between 1920 and 1923, he displayed a keen interest in cricket, rugby, boxing, and swimming.

Entering Trinity College, Dublin, Beckett studied modern languages and first discovered the works of LUIGI PIRANDELLO and Sean O'Casey. After receiving his B.A. with first-class honors in 1927, he taught for a year in Belfast, then moved to Paris and lectured in English at the École Normale Supérieure. In Paris he became acquainted with James Joyce, who remained a close friend until Joyce's death in 1941.

While teaching in Paris, Beckett wrote *Proust* (1931), a critical monologue, and *Whoroscope* (1930), a cryptic dramatic monologue spoken by René Descartes, a philosopher whose works Beckett was studying at the time. Returning to Trinity later in 1930, he received his M.A. in 1931, and then taught French for a year. Like Joyce before him, Beckett increasingly felt his creativity hampered by what he regarded as "the repressive aspects of Irish life," and he resolved to move abroad permanently. After his father died of a heart attack in 1933, Beckett received an annuity that enabled him to settle in London, where he underwent psychoanalysis; published *More Kicks Than Pricks*

(1934), a collection of ten short stories; and began writing *Murphy,* a novel that appeared in 1938, the year after Beckett returned to Paris. Though not a commercial success, *Murphy* drew favorable comment from Joyce and established Beckett as a writer of note.

Around this time Beckett met Suzanne Dechevaux-Dumesnil, whom he married in 1961. While he was in Ireland visiting his mother in 1939, World War II began, and Beckett hastened to Paris where he and Dechevaux-Dumesnil joined a Resistance network. Narrowly escaping arrest by the Gestapo in 1942, they fled to Roussillon in southern France. For the next two years, while employed as a laborer, Beckett worked on *Watt* (1953), the last novel he wrote in English. Its title—and the name of its protagonist—is intended as a pun on the word *what;* its theme is Watt's futile quest for a rational life in an irrational world.

When the war ended, Beckett worked briefly with the Irish Red Cross in Paris; for his wartime services, he was awarded the War Cross and the Medal of the Resistance by the French government. It was at this point that he began writing in French, producing the novel *Mercier et Camier* (*Mercier and Camier,* 1970) and the trilogy that consists of *Molloy* (1951), *Malone meurt* (Malone Dies, 1951), and *L'Innommable* (The Unnamable, 1953). These last three works were published in English as *The Trilogy* in 1955.

Despite the importance of this trilogy, it was the play *En Attendant Godot,* written in 1949 and published in English in 1954 as *Waiting for Godot,* that brought Beckett international acclaim and established him as a central playwright of the theater of the absurd. Beckett worked closely with the director Roger Blin in the play's first production in Paris in 1953. *Waiting for Godot* is static and circular; Act II repeats Act I with only minor variations. Its two hobo protagonists, Vladimir and Estragon, wait in an indeterminate place on an open road for the mysterious Godot to arrive and give meaning to the ennui and isolation they suffer; Godot never appears, however. The play includes two other figures, a master-slave pair named Pozzo and Lucky. Beckett draws on elements of music-hall comedy to leaven the pervasive atmosphere of pessimism and intersperses lyrical passages amid the generally spare prose of the play. *Waiting for Godot* "forced me to reexamine the rules which have hitherto governed the drama," wrote the British critic Kenneth Tynan, "and, having done so, to pronounce them not elastic enough."

Fin de partie (1957), a one-act play written between 1954 and 1956 and translated by Beckett into English as *Endgame* (1958), is even more static and claustrophobic than *Waiting for Godot.* Confined to a bleak room, its four characters—the blind, paralyzed Hamm; his servant; and his two parents—wait in vain and without hope for the end of the world. Hamm, Beckett explained, "is a king in the chess game lost from the start." In chess, the endgame is the final phase of the game, during which the king is cornered, but in *Endgame,* as in *Waiting for Godot,* the final event never occurs; there is no checkmate, only stalemate.

For his next major play, *Krapp's Last Tape* (1959), Beckett returned to his native language. Its only character, the aged Krapp, spends his final days listening to tape recordings of his own monologues, which he had made thirty years earlier. Although he plans to record one last monologue, Krapp allows the old tape to play out in silence as the play concludes. In this dialogue between youth and old age, the themes of futility and unfulfillment recur. First produced in London in 1958, *Krapp's Last Tape* had its American premiere in New York City in 1960 in a production directed by Alan Schneider. The British critic A. Alvarez detected in this work "a new tone and a new direction for Beckett's writing." Unlike the earlier plays, wrote Alvarez, "its subject is not depression, but grief, and . . . it shows, poignantly and with great beauty, precisely what has been lost."

After completing a series of sketches and radio plays, Beckett wrote *Happy Days* (1961). Produced at the Cherry Lane Theater in New York in 1961, this almost unbearably ironic two-act play features Winnie, who, half-buried in a pile of earth, optimistically awaits the ring of a bell that will permit her to fall asleep until death arrives.

Throughout the 1960s, as Beckett continued to write for radio, theater, and television, he was increasingly troubled by glaucoma, for which he underwent eye surgery in 1969. That year Beckett was awarded the Nobel Prize for Literature "for a body of work that, in new forms of fiction and the theater, has transmuted the destitution of modern man into his exaltation." In his presentation speech, Karl Ragnar Gierow of the Swedish Academy noted that Beckett's fundamental pessimism nevertheless "houses a love of mankind that grows in understanding as it plumbs further into the depths of abhorrence, a despair that has to reach the utmost bounds of suffering to discover that compassion has no bounds."

The reclusive Beckett, who had agreed to accept the prize with the understanding that he would not attend the ceremonies, isolated himself in Tunis to escape publicity. In his absence, the prize was accepted by his French publisher, Jérôme Lindon.

For the next ten years, Beckett wrote short plays, several of which he directed in Germany and London. His seventieth birthday was celebrated with a series of productions at the Royal Court Theater in London. In 1978 he published *Mirlitonnades,* a collection of short poems, followed the next year by *Company,* a text that was later adapted for performance by British Broadcasting Corporation (BBC) radio and for the stage in London and New York. It was, wrote Christopher Ricks in the London *Times,* Beckett's "latest view of what it is to be interned and then interred." *All Strange Away* (1979), written in 1976 and performed in New York in 1984, begins with the words: "Imagination dead. Imagine!"

Although Beckett has maintained an almost unbroken silence about his own work, he has been the subject of countless books, articles, reviews, and monographs. In 1971, saying that he would "neither help nor hinder" her, he allowed Deirdre Bair, an American graduate student, to begin work on a biography whose purpose Bair said was "to concentrate on the life of Samuel Beckett's mind, to find out as much as I could about the circumstances that led to the writing of each work."

Some critics have focused on what they perceive to be Beckett's nihilism. "Beckett settles us in the world of the Nothing," writes the French critic Maurice Nadeau, "where some nothings which are men move about for nothing." Others, such as the British critic Richard Roud, have commented on Beckett's use of language. "I do not think," Roud said, "there is anyone alive who writes English (and French) as well as Samuel Beckett." In the opinion of the American scholar Sanford Sternlicht, "Beckett is the most influential living playwright, the seminal figure in contemporary drama."

ADDITIONAL WORKS: Dante . . . Bruno . . . Vico . . . Joyce, 1929; Return to the Vestry, 1931; Home Olga, 1934; Echo's Bones, 1935; Cascando, 1936; Three Dialogues With Georges Duthuit, 1949; All That Fall, 1957; From an Abandoned Work, 1958; Embers, 1959; Henri Hayden, 1959; Act Without Words, 1960; Words and Music, 1962; How It Is, 1964; Collected Shorter Prose, 1945–66, 1967; Come and Go, 1967; Eh Joe and Other Writings, 1967; Enough, 1967; Film, 1967; No's Knife, 1967; Stories and Texts for Nothing, 1967; Lessness, 1970; Breath and Other Stories, 1971; The Lost Ones, 1972; First Love and Other Shorts, 1973; Not I, 1973; Ghost Trio, 1975; But the Clouds, 1976; Ends and Odds, 1976; Footfalls, 1976; For to End Again and Other Fizzles, 1976; I Can't Go On, I'll Go On, 1976; That Time, 1976; The Museum, 1977; A Piece of Monologue, 1979; One Evening, 1980; Ohio Impromptu, 1981; Rockaby and Other Short Pieces, 1981; Castastrophe, 1983; Disjecta, 1983; Worstward Ho, 1983; Collected Poems, 1930–78, 1984; Quad, 1984; What Where, 1984.

ABOUT: Alvarez, A. Samuel Beckett, 1973; Bair, D. Samuel Beckett: A Biography, 1978; Ben-Zvi, L. Samuel Beckett, 1986; Bishop, T., and Federman, R. (eds.) Samuel Beckett, 1977; Brater, E. Beckett at 80: Beckett in Context, 1986; Calder, J. (ed.) Beckett at 60: A Festschrift, 1967; Coe, R. N. Beckett, 1964; Cohn, R. Samuel Beckett: The Comic Gamut, 1962; Dearlove, J. E. Accommodating the Chaos, 1982; Esslin, M. (ed.) Samuel Beckett: A Collection of Critical Essays, 1965; Fletcher, J. Samuel Beckett's Art, 1967; Friedman, M. J. (ed.) Samuel Beckett Now, 1970; Gluck, B. Beckett and Joyce: Friendship and Fiction, 1979; Gontarski, S. E. Samuel Beckett: Thirty-Five Years of Criticism, 1986; Hamilton, A., and Hamilton, K. Condemned to Life: The World of Samuel Beckett, 1976; Hoffman, F. J. Samuel Beckett: The Man and His Works, 1969; Knowlson, J., and Pilling, J. Frescoes of the Skull: The Later Prose and Drama of Samuel Beckett, 1977; Lyons, C. R. Samuel Beckett, 1983; Mercier, V. Beckett-Beckett: The Truth of Contradictions, 1977; Murray, P. The Tragic Comedian, 1970; Rabinovitz, R. The Development of Samuel Beckett's Fiction, 1984; Rosen, S. J. Samuel Beckett and the Pessimistic Tradition, 1976; Simpson, A. Beckett and Behan, 1962; Tindall, W. Y. Samuel Beckett, 1964; Webb, E. Samuel Beckett: A Study of His Novels, 1970; Worth, R. (ed.) Beckett the Shape Changer, 1975; Zilliacus, C. Beckett and Broadcasting, 1976.

BECQUEREL, HENRI

(December 15, 1852–August 25, 1908)
Nobel Prize for Physics, 1903
(shared with Marie Curie and Pierre Curie)

The French physicist Antoine-Henri Becquerel (bek ə rel′) was born in Paris. Both his father, Alexandre-Edmond, and his grandfather, Antoine-César, were distinguished scientists, professors of physics at the Museum of Natural History in Paris, and members of the French Academy of Sciences. Becquerel received his early education at the Lycée Louis-le-Grand and began his advanced education at the École Polytechnique in Paris in 1872. Two years later he transferred to the École des Ponts et Chaussées (School of Bridges and Highways), where he studied engineering, taught, and did independent research. In 1875 he started a study of the effect of magnetism on linearly polarized light, and the following year he began a teaching career as lecturer at the École Polytechnique. He received his engineering degree from the École des Ponts et Chaussées in 1877 and obtained a position with the National Administration of Bridges and Highways. A year later Becquerel became his father's assistant at the Museum of Natural History, while continuing to work at the École Polytechnique and at the Administration of Bridges and Highways.

Becquerel collaborated with his father for four years on a series of articles on the temperature of the earth. Completing his own research on linearly polarized light in 1882, Becquerel extended his father's studies on luminescence, the nonthermal emission of light. During the mid-1880s Becquerel also developed a new method of analyzing spectra, displays of the various wavelengths emitted by light sources. In 1888 he received his doctoral degree from the Faculty of Sciences at the University of Paris with a dissertation on the absorption of light in crystals.

In 1892, a year after his father's death, Becquerel succeeded to his father's chairs of physics at the National Conservatory of Arts and Trades and at the Museum of Natural History in Paris. Two years later Becquerel became chief engineer with the Administration of Bridges and Highways, and in 1895 he succeeded to his third chair of physics, at the École Polytechnique.

In 1895 the German physicist WILHELM RÖNTGEN discovered highly energetic and penetrating radiation, known today as X rays, generated when cathode rays (electrons) emitted by the negative electrode (cathode) of a vacuum tube strike another portion of the tube during a high-voltage electric discharge. Since the incident cathode rays also produce luminescence when they strike the tube, it was wrongly suspected that luminescence and X rays were both produced by the same mechanism and that all luminescence might be ac-

HENRI BECQUEREL

companied by X rays. Intrigued, Becquerel decided to see whether luminescent material activated by light rather than cathode rays also emits X rays. He placed photographic plates wrapped in thick black paper against a luminescent material he had on hand, potassium uranylsulfate (a uranium salt), and exposed the assembly to sunlight for several hours. He then found that radiation had penetrated the paper and affected the photographic plate, apparently indicating that the uranium salt emitted X rays as well as light after excitation by sunlight. To Becquerel's amazement, however, the same thing happened when the assembly was stored in the dark, with no exposure to sunlight. He seemed to be observing the effect, not of X rays, but of a new type of penetrating radiation emitted without external excitation of the source.

Over the next few months Becquerel repeated his experiment with other known luminescent materials and found that only uranium compounds emitted the spontaneous radiation he had discovered. Furthermore, nonluminescent uranium compounds produced the same emissions, so the radiation was not linked to luminescence. In May 1896 Becquerel tested pure uranium and found that the photographic plates indicated exposure to radiation three to four times as intense as that from the original uranium salt. The mysterious radiation, which clearly was an intrinsic property of uranium, became known as Becquerel rays.

During the next few years of investigation by Becquerel and other researchers, it was found that, among other things, the radiation did not seem to diminish with time. In 1900 Becquerel determined that the rays consisted in part of electrons, discovered in 1897 by J. J. THOMSON as the constituents of cathode rays. Becquerel's student MARIE CURIE discovered that thorium also emitted Becquerel rays and renamed them radioactivity. She and her husband, PIERRE CURIE, after an extensive search, discovered two new radioactive elements, which they named polonium (after Marie Curie's homeland, Poland) and radium.

Becquerel and the Curies shared the 1903 Nobel Prize for Physics. Becquerel was personally cited "in recognition of the extraordinary services he has rendered by his discovery of spontaneous radioactivity." In the presentation speech by H. R. Törnebladh of the Royal Swedish Academy of Sciences, the three laureates were hailed for having shown "that special forms of radiation that were only known hitherto by electric discharges through rarefied gas are natural phenomena of wide occurrence." Törnebladh added that as a result "we have gained new methods . . . to examine under certain conditions the existence of matter in nature. Finally, we have found a new source of energy, for which the full explanation is not yet forthcoming."

Becquerel married Lucie-Zoé-Marie Jamin, the daughter of a professor of physics, in 1874. She died four years later after giving birth to their son and only child, Jean, who became a physicist. In 1890 Becquerel married Louise-Désirée Lorieux. After receiving the Nobel Prize, he continued to teach and do research. He died in 1908 at Le Croisic, in Brittany, during a trip with his wife to her ancestral home.

Becquerel received many honors in addition to the Nobel Prize, including the Rumford Medal of the Royal Society of London (1900), the Helmholtz Medal of the Royal Academy of Sciences of Berlin (1901), and the Barnard Medal of the American National Academy of Sciences (1905). He was elected to membership in the French Academy of Sciences in 1889 and was elected as one of its permanent secretaries in 1908. He was also a member of the French Physical Society, the National Academy of Sciences of Italy, the Royal Academy of Sciences of Berlin, the American National Academy of Sciences, and the Royal Institution in London.

SELECTED WORKS: On the Radioactivity of Matter, 1902.

ABOUT: Dictionary of Scientific Biography, volume 1, 1970; Nature September 3, 1903; Romer, A. (ed.) The Discovery of Radioactivity and Transmutation, 1964.

BEERNAERT, AUGUSTE
(July 26, 1829–October 6, 1912)
Nobel Prize for Peace, 1909
(shared with Paul d'Estournelles de
    Constant)

AUGUSTE BEERNAERT

The Belgian statesman Auguste Marie François Beernaert (bâr nar′) was born in Oostende to a middle-class Flemish family of Catholic descent. His father, Bernard Beernaert, was a civil servant in the Revenue Department. Shortly after Beernaert's birth, his father was transferred to Namur, becoming one of the town's leading citizens. Beernaert and his sister, Euphrosine, grew up in a comfortable home staffed with servants.

Because the public schools of Namur could not provide the training Beernaert needed for admission to a university, he received much of his education from tutors and from his mother, Euphrosine-Josepha (Royon) Beernaert. Under her guidance, he developed a zeal for learning as well as a mature appreciation of the value of hard work and perseverance. He entered the University of Louvain in 1846 and received his doctorate in law five years later. Assisted by a grant, he spent the next two years visiting universities in France and Germany, where he studied the system of legal education. He summarized his findings in a report submitted to the Belgian minister of the interior in 1853. Titled "De l'État de l'enseignement du droit en France et en Allemagne" (State of the Teaching of Law in France and in Germany), the report earned Beernaert much praise for its remarkable maturity.

Admitted to the Court of Appeal of Brussels, Beernaert was enrolled in the Order of Barristers in 1853. He served his legal internship under Hubert Dolez, a prominent business attorney who exerted a major influence over Beernaert's subsequent career. After completing his internship, Beernaert quickly established a successful practice, specializing in fiscal law. A massive man with dark, piercing eyes, he made an imposing figure in the courtroom, where he overwhelmed his opponents with his lucid arguments and formidable logic.

For the next twenty years, Beernaert maintained a flourishing law practice. Then in 1873 Prime Minister Jules Malou, leader of the rightist Catholic party, named Beernaert minister of public works. The appointment of a lawyer rather than an engineer drew criticism from liberal quarters and inspired little enthusiasm among the members of Malou's party. Under the Belgian parliamentary system, it was necessary for Beernaert to be elected to the national legislature before assuming his cabinet position. After an unsuccessful try in Soignies, he was elected in 1874 by the West Flanders district of Thielt; from this time until his death in 1912 he remained a member of Parliament. As minister of public works, Beernaert worked diligently to improve the nation's road, rail, and canal systems. He established new port facilities at Oostende and Antwerp, beautified the capital, and sought to end child labor in the mines.

The Catholic party was defeated by the liberals in the elections of 1878, but when Malou was returned to office as prime minister in 1884, Beernaert was made head of the Department of Agriculture, Industry, and Public Works. Four months later, King Leopold II asked Malou to resign, and out of solidarity Beernaert stepped down also. Within three days, however, the king chose Beernaert as prime minister and minister of finance. Beernaert accepted both positions with Malou's approval.

Beernaert soon showed himself to be one of Belgium's most capable political leaders. In 1885 he played a considerable role in convincing Parliament to allow King Leopold II to rule the Congo Free State as autonomous sovereign. In domestic matters, Beernaert's tenure witnessed enactment of labor reform laws, a balanced budget, and extension of suffrage to every citizen over the age of twenty-five. After failing to convince the majority in the Chamber of Deputies to support his proportional representation bill, Beernaert resigned in 1894. In recognition of his service to the nation, he was named an honorary minister of state, and in 1895 his colleagues elected him chairman of the Assembly. He remained a member of the Chamber of Deputies until his death. Nevertheless, his effectiveness in domestic affairs had ended.

During his years in public office, Beernaert grew increasingly concerned about international problems, especially the issue of peace. In 1896 he became an active member of the Interparliamentary Union, founded in 1889 by WILLIAM CREMER and FRÉDÉRIC PASSY to promote mandatory arbitration as an alternative to war. Beernaert presided over the union's conferences in Brussels in 1897, 1905, and 1910. When the Interparliamentary Council was created in 1899, he was chosen to be its president and, in that capacity, he directed the union's executive committee and bureau until his death.

Beernaert spent the final years of his life trying to halt the international arms race and to persuade nations to settle disputes through arbitration. He considered it absurd that nations were wasting valuable resources on weapons instead of using them to eliminate poverty and suffering. Still, he felt certain that national leaders would eventually realize the importance of compulsory arbitration and arms reduction.

At The Hague Peace Conference of 1899, Beernaert presided over the first Commission on Arms Limitation. Appointed a member of the Permanent Court of Arbitration at The Hague, he represented Mexico in a dispute with the United States in 1902 and worked to standardize codes of international maritime law. Beernaert's efforts on behalf of disarmament brought him into conflict with King Leopold II, who favored increased military defenses to protect Belgian neutrality. Beernaert was undaunted. "The first among political virtues," he said, "and the first condition for success, is perseverance."

In recognition of his tireless efforts to promote arbitration and halt the arms race, Beernaert received the 1909 Nobel Prize for Peace, which he shared with PAUL D'ESTOURNELLES DE CONSTANT. Neither laureate was present at the ceremony, and no acceptance speeches were delivered.

Beernaert was particularly concerned about the development of military aviation, and at the Interparliamentary Union conference in Geneva in 1912, he presented proposals to ban air warfare. Although the proposals were received coolly, he eventually persuaded the delegates to adopt them. As a member of the second Commission on Arms Limitation, he argued brilliantly for measures to ensure humane treatment for prisoners of war. Illness forced him to return to Belgium, however, and on the way he was hospitalized in Lucerne, where he died of pneumonia on October 6. He was buried at Boitsfort, near Brussels.

In 1870 Beernaert married Mathilde Wilhelmine Marie Borel, daughter of the Swiss counsel in Brussels. From an early age, Beernaert had shown a marked talent for painting, and he remained interested in the arts throughout his life, serving as president of the Belgian Superior Council of Fine Arts and of the Commission on the Royal Museum.

Regarded by some of his political adversaries as utopian, Beernaert nevertheless sought to implement his ideals through legislative and legal channels. "At an age when many live in the past," wrote Count Carlton de Wiart, Belgian minister of state, "[Beernaert] remained not only alert to the evolution of ideas, customs, and institutions . . . [but] . . . insisted on taking his part in that evolution."

ABOUT: Hull, W. I. The Two Hague Conferences and Their Contributions to International Law, 1908; Interparliamentary Union. The Interparliamentary Union From 1889–1939, 1939; Scott, J. B. The Hague Peace Conferences (2 vols.) 1909.

BEGIN, MENACHEM
(August 16, 1913–)
Nobel Prize for Peace, 1978
(shared with Anwar Sadat)

The Israeli statesman Menachem Begin (bā' gin) was born in the Polish city of Brest Litovsk (now part of the Soviet Union). He was the son of Wolf (Ze'ev Dov) Begin, secretary of the local Jewish communal organization, and the former Hassia Kossovsky. Taught by his father that the Jews were destined to return to the land of Israel, Begin at the age of ten joined a Zionist scouting organization that trained its members for kibbutz life. By the age of sixteen he had become a member of Betar, a militant youth organization associated with the Revisionist party of the World Zionist Organization. Founded by the Zionist leader Vladimir Jabotinsky, the party called for immediate and direct action to establish a Jewish state.

Begin attended Mizrachi Hebrew School and a Polish high school in his home city. In 1931 he entered the law school of the University of Warsaw, graduating with a doctor of jurisprudence degree in 1935. Becoming increasingly active in Betar, he served for two years as general secretary of its Czechoslovakian branch. In 1939 he was named commander of Polish Betar. The same year he married Aliza Arnold, with whom he had a son and two daughters.

As Betar commander, Begin ordered mass demonstrations in May 1939 outside the British embassy in Warsaw to protest British restrictions on Jewish immigration to Palestine, then a British-mandated territory. As a result, he was arrested and spent several months in prison. Released as invading German forces were closing in on Warsaw, Begin fled with his family to Lithuania, hoping to reach Palestine. When Lithuania was annexed by the Soviet Union in 1940, Begin was arrested for his political activities and sentenced to eight years in Siberia. With the German attack on the Soviet Union in 1941, however, he and thousands of other Polish prisoners were freed to join a new Polish army. Begin's unit was sent to British-mandated Transjordan (now Jordan), and in May 1942 he entered Palestine. There he resumed active membership in Betar as head of a local group in Jerusalem. In these years Begin's parents and only brother died in the Nazi Holocaust.

Demobilized from the Polish army in exile, Begin became commander of another group, the Irgun Zvai Leumi (National Fighting Organization), a paramilitary force whose campaign of sabotage against the British administration of Palestine had been suspended because of the war. Led by Begin, the Irgun demanded that Jews fleeing Nazi-occupied Europe be free to come to a politically independent Jewish state in Palestine. Until 1947 Begin and his wife and children lived in hiding; he himself was often in disguise and used an assumed name while he waged a guerrilla war against the British authorities, who in turn offered a $30,000 reward for his capture. Two events of the guerrilla war made Begin extremely controversial. In 1946 members of Irgun bombed British headquarters in the King David Hotel in Jerusalem, killing 91 people. Two years later the group took part in attacking the Palestinian village of Deir Yassin, where 200 Arab men, women, and

MENACHEM BEGIN

children were killed. Begin maintained that in both incidents advance warnings of attack were ignored. Nevertheless, his paramilitary career caused his critics to label him a terrorist.

With the founding of Israel as an independent state in 1948, the paramilitary Irgun became the right-wing Herut (Freedom) movement, with Begin at its head. For the next thirty years, Begin was a member of the Knesset (Parliament), often expressing fierce opposition to the policies of the Mapai (Labor) government of David Ben-Gurion. In 1977 Begin's Herut faction led the Likud (Unity) party, a right-center bloc, to election victory. Begin became Israel's sixth prime minister, at the head of a coalition government.

In his first months in office, Begin took a hard line on foreign policy. He encouraged new Jewish settlements on the occupied West Bank and resumed military strikes against Palestinian positions in Lebanon. Then, in November 1977, ANWAR SADAT, the president of Egypt, made an unexpected peace initiative. Despite the long history of conflict between Arabs and Jews, he offered to visit Jerusalem. Begin matched Sadat's offer by welcoming Israel's former enemy. "After all," he later stated, "we were welcoming a man who only four years ago had feigned routine autumn maneuvers and then deliberately attacked us at the precise moment that he knew we would all be in the synagogue."

In the coming months the long series of negotiations begun by Sadat's visit faltered. Finally, in August 1978 American President Jimmy Carter intervened, inviting both men to visit the United States for a conference at Camp David in the Maryland mountains. The difficult thirteen-day conference ended with a ceremony at which the antagonists signed two agreements: "A Framework for Peace in the Middle East" and "A Framework for the Conclusion of a Peace Treaty Between Egypt and Israel."

To the surprise of many observers who had expected the summit meeting to fail, Israel agreed to return most of the Sinai region to Egypt in exchange for a full peace. The agreements left many questions about the Middle East open to future negotiations, including the disposition of Israel's controversial settlements on the West Bank of the Jordan River and its occupation of the West Bank and the Gaza Strip.

For their efforts in concluding the two peace agreements, Begin and Sadat were jointly awarded the 1978 Nobel Prize for Peace. While acknowledging that problems still remained to be solved, Aase Lionæs of the Norwegian Nobel Committee stated in her presentation speech that "for the first time since the reestablishment of the state of Israel in 1948, an agreement has successfully been reached which, on a long-term basis, provides a genuine opportunity for peace in an area over which the shadow of war had hovered so long." The two laureates, she added, "have played key roles in the quest for peace between two former enemies, which today is such a source of gratification to true friends of peace the world over."

In his Nobel lecture on December 10 in Oslo, Begin spoke of the quest for peace in the nuclear age. "Perhaps that very capability of total destruction of our little planet—achieved for the first time in the annals of mankind—will one day, God willing, become the origin, the cause, and the prime mover for the elimination of all instruments of destruction from the face of the earth; and ultimate peace, prayed for and yearned for by previous generations, will become the portion of all nations. Despite the tragedies and disappointments of the past, we must never forsake that vision, that human dream, that unshakable faith."

In the years following the awarding of the Nobel Peace Prize, Begin found peace an elusive goal. He once told an interviewer that he wished history to record him as "the man who set the borders of Eretz Israel for all eternity." Such a wish may have been behind his controversial decision to invade Lebanon on June 6, 1982. Begin's stated goal was to destroy strongholds of the Palestine Liberation Organization (PLO) there. In little more than a week, Israeli forces encircled Beirut and began massive bombing that quickly led to the PLO's evacuation of the city. But Israel found itself bogged down in Lebanon; its troops did not leave until 1985.

After the death of his wife in 1982, Begin became withdrawn and took on a gaunt, frail appearance. His decline was attributed to his depression over the failure of the Lebanon invasion, with its enormous casualties, and an abiding guilt over not being with his wife when she died. In September 1983, telling colleagues of his decision to resign, he was quoted as saying, "I cannot continue."

At the time he assumed office as prime minister, Begin was described by a *New York Times* correspondent as "a slight, baldish figure in horn-rimmed glasses, pale and hollow cheeked after a recent heart attack. He kisses women on the hand or cheek on introduction. He is particular about his attire. In Israel's shirt-sleeved Parliament, he is never seen without jacket and tie." Begin, who has a grasp of nine languages, was considered an astute politician and a firebrand orator during his long career.

WORKS IN ENGLISH TRANSLATION: The Revolt: The Story of the Irgun, 1951; White Nights: The Story of a Prisoner in Russia, 1957.

ABOUT: Brenner, L. The Iron Wall, 1984; Caspi, D., et al. (eds.) The Root of Begin's Success, 1984; Eckman, L., and Hirschler, G. Menachem Begin, 1979; Freedman, R. O. Israel in the Begin Era, 1982; Friedlander, M. A. Sadat and Begin, 1983; Garron, D. Israel After Begin, 1984; Gervasi, F. H. The Life and Times of Menachem Begin, 1979; Haber, E. Menachem Begin: The Legend and the Man, 1978; Heydemann, S. (ed.) The Begin Era, 1984; Hurwitz, H. Menachem Begin, 1977; New York Times Magazine July 17, 1977; Rowland, R. C. The Rhetoric of Menachem Begin, 1985; Schweitzer, A. Israel: The Changing National Agenda, 1986.

BEHRING, EMIL VON

(March 15, 1854–March 31, 1917)
Nobel Prize for Physiology or Medicine, 1901

The German bacteriologist Emil Adolf von Behring (ber' ing) was born in Hansdorf (now part of Poland), the oldest of twelve children of August Georg Behring, a schoolmaster, and his second wife, Augustine (Zech) Behring. The boy's father expected him to enter one of the family's traditional professions, theology or teaching, and consequently, Behring was enrolled in the gymnasium at Hohenstein in

EMIL VON BEHRING

his discharge from the army in 1889, he joined the institute as a full-time researcher.

By that time, Behring's research was focused on tetanus and diphtheria, two symptomatically different diseases that shared one outstanding feature: victims of both diseases died while infected with relatively few bacteria. Furthermore, important symptoms (neurological in the case of tetanus and cardiological for diphtheria) were not confined to the actual sites of infection. The bacteria of tetanus and diphtheria were dangerous because of the toxins they produced, a fact established by Pierre Roux at the Pasteur Institute and by Friedrich Loeffler in Germany. Behring proposed that a treatment for diphtheria could be developed by neutralizing the toxin excreted by the diphtheria bacilli, thus allowing the natural prophylactic power of the human body to take over.

At the Institute of Hygiene, Behring worked with the Japanese scientist Shibasaburo Kitasato, and in 1890 they showed that the immunity of rabbits and mice which have been immunized against tetanus depends, as Behring said, "on the ability of the cell-free blood fluid to render harmless the toxic substance which the tetanus bacillus produces." Extending this finding to diphtheria, Behring demonstrated that nonimmune animals could be protected against the toxin from the diphtheria bacillus by an injection of antitoxin from immune animals. He stated that with his serum therapy, the "possibility for the cure of very acute diseases can therefore no longer be denied." Nevertheless, Behring and his colleagues at the institute encountered major difficulties in producing diphtheria antitoxin in quantities that were medically significant. At the time, PAUL EHRLICH, who was also working at the institute, was responsible for several important innovations, among them the large-scale production of antitoxin in horses and the standardization of serum samples. Until 1892, when a commercial firm began funding his work, Behring supported his own research. As the use of the serum increased, however, so did Behring's wealth and reputation.

East Prussia in 1865. There he developed an interest in medicine; however, realizing that his family could not afford to send him to medical school, he planned to enter the University of Königsberg as a theology student. Instead, one of his gymnasium teachers arranged for him to attend Friedrich Wilhelm Institute—the Army Medical College—in Berlin, where prospective army surgeons received free training. Behring enrolled there in 1874 and obtained his medical degree in 1878; two years later he passed the state board examination and in 1881 was posted to Posen (now Poznań, Poland) as an assistant surgeon.

In return for his medical training, Behring was required to serve in the Prussian army until 1889. While serving in a cavalry regiment in Posen and as a physician to a battalion stationed in Wohlau, Behring became interested in the use of disinfectants in fighting infectious diseases. He was especially interested in iodoform (a yellow, crystalline substance that has a strong odor and contains about 96 percent iodine), a compound that had recently been introduced as a dressing for wounds and syphilitic ulcers. His initial investigations of iodoform led him to conclude that the compound was an effective antiseptic because it neutralized bacterial toxins.

In 1883 Behring was transferred to Winzig, Silesia; four years later he was sent to the Pharmacological Institute in Bonn, where he continued his investigation of disinfectants. Later, in 1888, he became a part-time researcher at the Institute of Hygiene in Berlin, which was directed by ROBERT KOCH. After

In 1894 Behring left the Institute of Hygiene for a university position, first at Halle and the following year at Marburg. Although he was now hailed as the Savior of Children because his diphtheria antitoxin had become the treatment of choice for the deadly children's disease, the use of the antitoxin posed a serious problem that had not been immediately apparent: The antitoxin worked in accordance with the principle of passive immunity; that is, the antibodies it contained had been formed by an animal, not by the patient's cells. As a result, the antitoxin conveyed only short-term immunity and had to be administered as close to the time of infection as possible. By the time diphtheria symptoms were observed, it was often too late for the antitoxin to work, resulting in the patient's death. Undaunted, Behring continued his research on diphtheria for the next several decades, and in 1913 he produced a vaccine that provided lasting protection against the disease.

Behring was awarded the first Nobel Prize for Physiology or Medicine in 1901 "for his work on serum therapy, especially its application against diphtheria, by which he has opened a new road in the domain of medical science and thereby placed in the hands of the physician a victorious weapon against illness and deaths." In his Nobel lecture, Behring acknowledged that his serum therapy was based on the theory held by "Loeffler in Germany and by Roux in France, that the parasites causing diphtheria, the Loeffler diphtheria bacilli, do not themselves cause diphtheria, but that they produce poisons which cause the disease to develop." He added that "without this preliminary work by Loeffler and Roux, there would be no serum treatment for diphtheria."

By the time he received the Nobel Prize, Behring had shifted the focus of his research from tetanus and diphtheria to the study of tuberculosis. At that time, tuberculosis was responsible for one out of seven deaths worldwide; therefore, many bacteriologists—including Robert Koch—sought to produce a vaccine for this widespread disease. For several years, Behring attempted to develop a tuberculosis antitoxin but finally admitted defeat. A good deal of his research concerned the relationship between tuberculosis in human beings and the disease in cattle. He believed that the two diseases were identical, a view that brought him into direct conflict with Koch. Although today human and bovine tuberculosis are not considered the same disease, the cattle form can be transmitted to human beings; thus, Behring's recommendations for reducing the disease in animals and for disinfecting milk were important public health measures.

During World War I, the tetanus vaccine developed by Behring helped save the lives of so many German soldiers that he was awarded the German government's Iron Cross, a rare honor for a noncombatant. An authoritative and solitary man, Behring had few close friends

and attracted few followers. Throughout most of his life, he was subject to severe depression, which occasionally required treatment in a sanatorium.

In 1896 Behring married Else Spinola, the daughter of one of the directors of a Berlin hospital; the couple had six sons. Behring later suffered a fractured thigh, which led to the development of pseudarthrosis, a condition affecting his joints, which limited his mobility. After contracting pneumonia, he died in Marburg on March 31, 1917.

Behring was named an officer in the Legion of Honor of France and a privy councillor to the German state of Prussia. He was a member of numerous European academies of science.

SELECTED WORKS: The Suppression of Tuberculosis, 1904; The Extermination of Tuberculosis, 1905.

ABOUT: British Medical Journal March 20, 1954; Brock, J. D. Milestones in Microbiology, 1961; De Kruif, P. Microbe Hunters, 1926; Dictionary of Scientific Biography, volume 1, 1970; Nature April 9, 1955; Snyder, E. E. Biology in the Making, 1940.

BÉKÉSY, GEORG VON
(June 3, 1899–June 13, 1972)
Nobel Prize for Physiology or Medicine, 1961

Georg von Békésy (bā′ ke shē), Hungarian-American physicist, was born in Budapest to Alexander von Békésy, a diplomat, and Paula (Mazaly) Békésy. His father's career provided young Békésy with a cosmopolitan upbringing not only in Budapest but also in Munich, Constantinople, and Zurich. Békésy, who displayed an early aptitude for science and music, considered a career as a concert pianist but chose science instead. He entered the University of Bern, Switzerland, in 1916, and after debating the merits of mathematics, astronomy, and chemistry, he decided to concentrate on physics. The end of World War I and the Hungarian revolution of 1918 threw Hungary—and Békésy's family finances—into turmoil, and he returned home to "reconstruct Hungary," as he said later. After a brief period of military service, he entered the University of Budapest, where he completed his Ph.D. in physics in 1923 with a thesis on fluid dynamics. He was then hired by the research laboratory of the Hungarian post office, which was in charge of the newly installed Hungarian telephone system.

Because several European telephone con-

GEORG VON BÉKÉSY

generally assumed . . . that the mechanical properties of the tissues of the ear changed rapidly after death and that there was virtually no possibility of determining the mechanical properties of the inner ear of man." One of Békésy's first advances was to show that this alteration is largely due to dehydration and that ears from cadavers may be gainfully studied, provided they are kept as moist as they were in life. Because many of Békésy's experiments had to be performed on small laboratory animals, such as guinea pigs, whose cochleas are even smaller than those of human beings, he had to devise new microsurgical tools and procedures for opening, examining, manipulating, and recording from the various components of the middle and inner ear.

These techniques enabled Békésy to investigate the movement of the basilar membrane. Four competing theories had been proposed to account for the ear's ability to distinguish different pitches of sound: a tone might cause only one portion of the membrane to resonate; it might send a traveling wave down the length of the membrane; it might be reflected back from the end to make a standing wave; or it might move the membrane as a unit. "Although the handbooks . . . were much occupied with pointing out the differences among the four theories," Békésy later wrote, "I reversed the question and tried to find their common features." He devised a model membrane made of rubber and demonstrated that the vibration pattern proposed by each of the four theories could be produced simply by varying the thickness of the membrane. From this finding he deduced that the way to determine which theory correctly described the workings of the inner ear was to measure volume elasticity. His measurements showed that the vibrations in the basilar membrane are traveling waves.

The basilar membrane is not uniform throughout. It is thin and tightly stretched at the base of the cochlea (near the middle ear) but wider and floppier at the apex of the cochlea. Although a traveling wave in the cochlea moves the entire basilar membrane, one section moves more than the rest. The location of this peak depends on the frequency of the stimulating vibration; for high sounds it is closer to the middle ear, and for low sounds it is closer to the apex. The brain receives information about the location of the peaks from nerve fibers in the cochlea and uses this message to differentiate high- and low-pitched sounds.

All Békésy's research was performed at the telephone research laboratory of the Hungar-

nections ran through Hungary, failures in the national system brought international complaints. Early in his career, Békésy was asked to determine which of three components—the receiving microphones, the transmitting line, or the sending earphones—was most in need of improvement. His preliminary studies indicated that the problem lay with the membranes of the earphones, which produced greater distortions of vibration than those of the eardrum. This finding led him to investigate the mechanical properties of the ear in greater detail.

When sound waves enter the human ear, they strike the eardrum, causing it to vibrate. These vibrations are passed along the leverlike bones of the middle ear and transmitted to the cochlea, a long, coiled tube in the fluid-filled inner ear. The cochlea is divided lengthwise by the basilar membrane; specialized hair cells in an area known as the organ of Corti respond to the vibration of this membrane by exciting nerve fibers leading to the auditory nerve. By the mid-1920s the anatomy of the inner ear was known in considerable detail; as Békésy later said, "the problem of how we hear was reduced largely to a mechanical question: How does the basilar membrane vibrate when the eardrum is exposed to . . . sound pressure?"

If it was easy to decide which property of the ear to investigate, performing the actual experiments proved difficult. The human cochlea is very small—less than a centimeter across at its widest point—and is encased in the thickest part of the skull. Furthermore, Békésy recalled later, "in those days it was

ian post office, where he was employed throughout the 1930s. In 1939 he was named professor of experimental physics at the University of Budapest but continued to work for the post office. Budapest was heavily bombed by the Allies near the end of World War II, and the city was almost destroyed during its occupation by the Soviet army in 1945. The following year Békésy was invited to move to the Karolinska Institute in Sweden to continue his research. After working there for a year, he immigrated to the United States to work at Harvard University's Psycho-Acoustic Laboratory.

At Harvard, Békésy continued measuring the essential biomechanical properties of the inner ear until he had gathered enough information to construct an enlarged model of the cochlea. The model consisted of a water-filled plastic tube containing a membrane 30 centimeters long; when the water was vibrated by a piston at one end, traveling waves moved along the membrane. Békésy simulated the organ of Corti (the terminal acoustic apparatus within the scala media, the spiral membrane in the bony canal of the cochlea) by simply placing his arm on the tube. "Although the traveling waves ran along the whole length of the membrane with almost the same amplitude," he reported, "I had the impression that only a section of the membrane, 2 to 3 centimeters long, was vibrating." He could feel only the peak of the traveling waves, which moved up and down the cochlea when the input frequency was changed. "The simple fact that on the model the whole arm vibrates . . . but only a very small section is recognized as vibrating proves that nervous inhibition must play an important role in the way sound is perceived," Békésy concluded. This statement supported his earlier view of how the ear analyzes the frequency of sound. A similar phenomenon may occur within the organ of Corti, for, as DAVID H. HUBEL and TORSTEN WIESEL later showed for the eye, inhibition around the area of peak sensation is common in the human nervous system.

By the late 1950s Békésy had developed a complete picture of the biomechanics of the cochlea, work that led to significant advances in the diagnosis and treatment of hearing disorders. Thanks to the research conducted by Békésy, ear surgeons can now construct new eardrums of skin or vein tissue and can even replace small bones of the ear with plastic facsimiles.

"For his discoveries of the physical mechanism of stimulation within the cochlea" Bé-

késy received the 1961 Nobel Prize for Physiology or Medicine. "Békésy has provided us with the knowledge of the physical events at all strategically important points in the transmission system of the ear," said Carl Gustaf Bernhard of the Karolinska Institute on presenting the award. Moreover, Bernhard added, Békésy's "discoveries contribute most significantly to the analysis of the relation between the mechanical and the electrical phenomena in the receptors which are involved in the transformation of sound into nerve impulses."

In 1966 Békésy became professor of sensory sciences at the University of Hawaii. Through his work with the ear he developed an interest in similarities among all the senses, especially touch and taste. Békésy, who never married, remained at the University of Hawaii until his death in 1972. A devoted art collector with a special interest in Oriental art, he bequeathed his entire collection to the Nobel Foundation. He was a naturalized American citizen.

In addition to the Nobel Prize, Békésy received the Leibniz Medal of the German Academy of Sciences (1937), the Academy Award of the Hungarian Academy of Science (1946), and the Howard Crosby Warren Medal of the American Society of Experimental Psychologists (1955). He was a member of the National Academy of Sciences and was awarded honorary degrees by Wilhelm University and the University of Bern.

SELECTED WORKS: Experiments in Hearing, 1960; Sensory Inhibition, 1967.

ABOUT: Current Biography December 1962; The Excitement and Fascination of Science, volume 2, 1978; New York Times October 20, 1961; Stevens, S. S., and Davis, H. (eds.) Hearing: Its Psychology and Physiology, 1938.

BELLOW, SAUL
(June 10, 1915–)
Nobel Prize for Literature, 1976

The American novelist Saul Bellow was born Solomon Bellows in Lachine, Quebec, a suburb of Montreal, the youngest of four children of Abraham Bellows and Liza (Gordon) Bellows, Russian Jews who had immigrated to Canada from Leningrad in 1913. During his early childhood—which he has described as "partly frontier, partly the Polish ghetto, partly the Middle Ages"—he read Shakespeare and nineteenth-century novelists, learned to speak four languages fluently, and was steeped in the traditions of the Old Testament. His father, a bootlegger for American rumrunners, became a coal dealer after the family moved to Chicago in 1924.

The move transplanted Bellow from an Orthodox shtetl in Lachine to a bustling metropolitan center. "I grew up there and consider myself a Chicagoan, out and out," Bellow wrote later. The family settled in Humboldt Park, a polyglot neighborhood where Bellow and his Tuley High School friends gathered weekly at the Mission House to share their writing. "Where I grew up," he said, "we dreamed of the literary life—we were mad for it." After graduating from Tuley, Bellow entered the University of Chicago in 1933; but finding its "dense atmosphere of learning" oppressive, he transferred two years later to Northwestern University, where he studied with the anthropologist Melville J. Herskovits. In 1937 Bellow was awarded a B.S. with honors in sociology and anthropology. After a few months of graduate school at the University of Wisconsin, he returned to Chicago to write, supporting himself with a variety of jobs: biographer for the federal Works Progress Administration (WPA) Writers Project, teacher at the Pestalozzi-Froebel Teachers College, and editor at the Encyclopædia Britannica. During World War II, he served in the United States Merchant Marine and completed his first novel, *Dangling Man,* which was published in 1944 and written in the form of a journal. The novel's protagonist—a civilian awaiting a draft summons—is a man with no foothold, no grip, on life. The American critic Edmund Wilson praised *Dangling Man* as "one of the most honest pieces of testimony on the psychology of a whole generation who have grown up during the Depression and the war."

While teaching at the University of Minnesota from 1946 to 1948, Bellow wrote essays, short stories, and a second novel, *The Victim* (1947), which explores the domestic and religious conflicts of a New York journalist. Although this work did not receive the wide critical acclaim that had greeted his first effort, Bellow was awarded a Guggenheim Fellowship that enabled him to work on a third novel while living in Paris and Rome from 1948 to 1949. Published in 1953, this book, *The Adventures of Augie March,* won Bellow the National Book Award the following year. Describing the exuberant, picaresque hero's search for "a worthwhile fate," the novel traces Augie's life from boyhood in Chicago to maturity as a black marketer in postwar Europe.

SAUL BELLOW

Augie March represented a breakthrough for Bellow. Eschewing the conventional chronological narrative, Bellow brought his characters into existence by using such devices as debates between the protagonist and an internal commentator, lengthy philosophical monologues, and colloquial dialogue spoken by a varied cast that struggles with life against a richly evoked urban setting. "The open and comically pretentious style in which Augie talks . . . is a tour de force," remarked the American literary critic Alfred Kazin. "Both the stunning wit and the emotional range are new here to Bellow," noted the American poet John Berryman.

While teaching English, first at Princeton University and then at Bard College, Bellow wrote *Seize the Day* (1956), which consists of three short stories; a one-act play; and the title piece, a novella. The novella, which has mid-twentieth-century alienation as its theme, recounts the downfall of Tommy Wilhelm, who, believing that easy riches will enable him to transcend "the anxious and narrow life of the average," attempts to "seize the day" by making ill-fated investments in lard futures. After a losing day, Wilhelm finds himself at a stranger's funeral, weeping at the realization that "the end of all distractions" is not consolation but oblivion. Writing for the *New York Times Book Review,* Kazin called the novella Bellow's "most moving single piece of fiction"; and the British writer V. S. Pritchett considered it "a small, gray masterpiece." *Seize the Day* was followed three years later by *Henderson the Rain King,* the story of a millionaire's spiritual safari into Africa, in quest of what Bellow later called "a remedy to the anxiety of death."

Discouraged by what he considered to be the highly political and parochial nature of New York's literary community, Bellow returned to Chicago—"the undiluted U.S.A."—where he settled permanently in 1962. He soon joined the faculty at the University of Chicago as a member of the Committee on Social Thought, an interdisciplinary department. With the publication of *Herzog* two years later, Bellow received his second National Book Award and became the first American to be awarded the French International Literature Prize. *Herzog* examines a university professor's struggle to come to terms with his alienation from self and society. The erudite Moses Herzog, an expert on the plagues and misfortunes of modern humanity, forces himself to confront the reality of an unjust world, an effort that leads him to accept the human condition and choose life. Writing about *Herzog,* the American critic Philip Rahv said: "Saul Bellow emerges not only as the most intelligent novelist of his generation but also as the most consistently interesting in point of growth and development. To my mind, too, he is the finest stylist at present writing in America." Acclaimed by critical and popular audiences, *Herzog* quickly reached the top of the best-seller lists in the United States.

Bellow has not restricted himself to the novel. In 1964 his play *The Last Analysis* had a brief run on Broadway. Three years later Bellow covered the 1967 Arab-Israeli conflict as a correspondent for the newspaper *Newsday.* Although *Mosby's Memoirs* (1968), a collection of six short stories, and *Mr. Sammler's Planet* (1970), his seventh novel, were greeted with mixed reviews, Bellow received his third National Book Award in 1971 for the latter work.

With the publication of *Humboldt's Gift* in 1975, Bellow achieved international recognition. Juxtaposing the careers of two American writers—the successful and worldly Charles Citrine and the late poet Von Humboldt Fleisher, said to be modeled after the American poet and critic Delmore Schwartz—the novel explores the spiritual authority of artists in a contemporary society that values success, fame, and money above all else. Although *Humboldt's Gift* "shows no flagging of Bellow's intelligence and stylistic powers, . . . the fictional impulse is out of adjustment," said the American critic Roger Shattuck in the *New York Review of Books.* "Charlie Citrine is too close to Bellow to fill out a fully extruded

novel." "The only real trouble with *Humboldt's Gift,*" wrote the American novelist and critic John Updike in the *New Yorker,* "is that the problems that engage the author do not engage the gears of the story." For this novel, Bellow received the 1975 Pulitzer Prize.

Bellow was awarded the 1976 Nobel Prize for Literature "for the human understanding and subtle analysis of contemporary culture that are combined in his work." In making the presentation, Karl Ragnar Gierow of the Swedish Academy pointed to Bellow's pivotal role in the development that led away from "the so-called hard-boiled style" of American fiction toward "the antihero of the present." Gierow continued, "The result was something quite new, Bellow's own mixture of rich picaresque novel and subtle analysis of our culture, of entertaining adventure, . . . interspersed with philosophical conversation with the reader . . . all developed by a commentator with a witty tongue and penetrating insight into the outer and inner complications that drive us to act or prevent us from acting." Moreover, he added, that by "giving value a place side by side with palpable facts," Bellow "gives man freedom, thereby responsibility, thereby a desire for action and a faith in the future."

In his Nobel lecture, Bellow spoke of the erosion of character in modern fiction but scoffed at those intellectual authorities who presume to "run the arts." "It amuses me that these serious essayists should be allowed to sign the death notices of literary forms," he asserted, noting that "the imagination must find its own path." In an age when literary, philosophical, and political systems have failed human beings, Bellow continued, "the essence of our real condition, the complexity, the confusion, the pain of it is shown to us in glimpses, in what Proust and Tolstoy thought of as 'true impressions.' . . . A novel moves back and forth between the world of objects, of actions, of appearances, and that other world from which these 'true impressions' come and which moves us to believe that the good we hang onto so tenaciously—in the face of evil, so obstinately—is no illusion."

The same year that he received the Nobel Prize, Bellow published *To Jerusalem and Back: A Personal Account,* based on diaries he kept while visiting Israel the previous year. *The Dean's December,* a novel set in Communist Romania and in the American academic environment, appeared in 1982 to generally unfavorable reviews. It was followed two years later by *Him With His Foot in His Mouth and*

Other Stories, in which, according to several critics, Bellow regained his literary stride.

In 1937 Bellow married Anita Goshkin, with whom he had a son, Gregory. After their divorce, he married Alexandra Tschacbosov in 1956; they had a son, Adam. By his marriage to Susan A. Glassman, in 1961, he had a third son, Daniel. He is now married to Alexandra Bagdasar, a Romanian-born mathematician who teaches at Northwestern University. White-haired under a jaunty fedora, Bellow, like so many of his fictional creations, has been described as witty, urbane, intellectual, and passionately serious about life.

Despite high praise from critics and the public, Bellow has his detractors. His penchant for presenting moral dilemmas has led some critics to fault his novels for poor characterization, especially of women; weak plot development; and an excessively essayistic style. Although Bellow pursues compelling ideas, "at times his novels veer too close to monologue," according to the American writer Stephen Miller. The American critic Hugh Kenner has remarked that the result of this technique is "the Novel as First Draft Dissertation."

Despite such judgments, Bellow is widely considered to be one of the most perceptive contemporary American writers, one who has articulated such universal themes as the human struggle for self-mastery, the individual's search for balance between self and society, the difficulty of recognizing reality in a world of illusion, and the conflict between hope and despair. "The best living American novelist," wrote the distinguished American author and literary critic Irving Howe, "is also a man of brains."

ADDITIONAL WORKS: More Die of Heartbreak, 1987.

ABOUT: Bloom, M. Saul Bellow, 1986; Bradbury, M. Saul Bellow, 1982; Braham, J. A Sort of Columbus, 1984; Clayton, J. J. Saul Bellow: In Defense of Man, 1968; Cohen, S. B. Saul Bellow's Enigmatic Laughter, 1974; Detweiler, R. Saul Bellow: A Critical Essay, 1967; Dutton, R. R. Saul Bellow, 1971; Fuchs, D. Saul Bellow: Vision and Revision, 1984; Goldman, L. H. Saul Bellow's Moral Vision, 1983; Harris, M. Saul Bellow, Drumlin Woodchuck, 1980; Howe, I. (ed.) Saul Bellow: Herzog, 1976; Malin, I. Saul Bellow's Fiction, 1969; Newman, J. Saul Bellow and History, 1984; Opdahl, K. M. Saul Bellow: An Introduction, 1967; Plimpton, G. (ed.) Writers at Work, volume 3, 1967; Porter, M. G. Whence the Power? 1974; Rodrigues, E. L. Quest for the Human, 1981; Rovit, E. Saul Bellow, 1967; Rovit, E. (ed.) Saul Bellow: A Collection of Critical Essays, 1975; Sheer-Schatzler, B. Saul Bellow, 1972; Tanner, T. Saul Bellow, 1965; Trachtenberg, S. Critical Essays on Saul Bellow, 1979; Wilson, J. On Bellow's Planet, 1985.

BENACERRAF, BARUJ

(October 29, 1920–   )

Nobel Prize for Physiology or Medicine, 1980

(shared with Jean Dausset and George D. Snell)

Baruj Benacerraf, a Venezuelan-American geneticist, was born in Caracas, Venezuela, to a wealthy Spanish-Jewish textile merchant and a French-Algerian mother. In 1925 the family moved to Paris, where they remained until the outbreak of World War II in 1939, at which time they returned to Venezuela. A year later, the Benacerrafs moved to New York so that Baruj could complete his education in the United States. After graduating from Columbia University's School of General Studies in 1942, Benacerraf entered the Medical College of Virginia. Although he was subsequently drafted into the United States Army, he was allowed to continue with his medical training. In 1943 he was made a naturalized citizen, and two years later he received his medical degree and commission as a first lieutenant in the United States Army Medical Corps. After a two-year tour of duty in Nancy, France, he was discharged from the army.

Having suffered from asthma as a child, Benacerraf became interested in the mechanism of immune hypersensitivity, an abnormal response of the body to foreign agents. Several scientists from whom he sought advice recommended that he work with Elvin Kabat, an immunochemist, at the Neurological Institute, Columbia University School of Physicians and Surgeons. Upon receiving a fellowship from Kabat, Benacerraf began allergy research in 1948. The next year he accepted a research position at the Broussais Hospital in Paris, where he continued his immunological studies.

Although his investigation of white blood cell function was productive, Benacerraf was unable to establish his own laboratory and thus advance his scientific career in France. He believed that his status as a foreign scientist was impeding his progress in the European scientific community. At the invitation of Lewis Thomas, Benacerraf returned to the United States in 1956 to become assistant professor of pathology at the New York University School of Medicine. There he established his own laboratory, resumed his study of hypersensitivity mechanisms, and developed an interest in cellular hypersensitivity. He was appointed professor of pathology in 1960.

At New York University, Benacerraf concentrated his research on the cells involved in

BARUJ BENACERRAF

immune responses, the body's defense against foreign substances or antigens. In the early 1960s he worked with GERALD M. EDELMAN, who was investigating the structure of antibodies, which the immune system produces in response to an invasion of antigens. Edelman's research was hampered by the fact that animals normally produce mixtures of different antibodies in response to a single antigen. Benacerraf wondered if immunizing animals (guinea pigs were the initial subjects) with very simple synthetic antigens might result in a more uniform set of antibodies. "What I found," he later explained, "is that some animals responded by making antibodies [to the antigen] and others did not."

It was this finding that enabled Benacerraf to show that the ability to respond to certain antigens is determined genetically. He called the involved factors the Ir (for immune-response) genes. In 1965 Hugh McDevitt and his colleagues observed similar genes in mice and determined that the genes were located inside the major histocompatibility complex (MHC). The MHC is a set of closely linked genes first described in the late 1940s by GEORGE D. SNELL, which are called transplantation genes because differences between donor and host antigens lead to rejection of transplanted organs. Human MHC, known as HLA, was discovered mainly by the efforts of JEAN DAUSSET. In 1968 Benacerraf and several of his co-workers moved to the National Institutes of Health, where he was appointed chief of the laboratory of immunology. There Benacerraf and his colleagues confirmed

McDevitt's findings using inbred strains of guinea pigs maintained at the National Institute of Allergy and Infectious Diseases.

Simultaneous appointments as Fabyan Professor of Comparative Pathology and chairman of the department of pathology at Harvard Medical School were accepted by Benacerraf in 1970. Two years later he and his Harvard colleagues—working independently of Donald Shreffler and his associates, who were engaged in similar research—discovered Ir-region restriction, a phenomenon involving two types of white blood cells designated B and T cells. These cells play central roles in the ability of the immune system to recognize and respond to specific substances of invading organisms. B cells produce antibodies to attack foreign antigens, whereas T cells respond directly to other cells. Different groups of T cells can kill cancerous or virus-infected cells, destroy bacteria, and enhance or inhibit the activity of specific B cells. Interactions between T cells and B cells are MHC-restricted; that is, a T cell affects antibody production by a B cell only if both cells carry the same Ir genes. By 1976 other researchers had discovered that T cells can kill virus-infected cells when both cells carry the same transplantation antigens (the products of the MHC genes originally discovered by Snell and Dausset).

It soon became clear that although the products of Ir genes and transplantation genes differ chemically, their functions are related; both should be considered MHC products. Transplantation gene products, found on the surfaces of most body cells, are known as class I molecules, while Ir gene products, which are found in the immune system, are class II MHC molecules.

"The evolutionary significance of [MHC] restrictions," wrote Benacerraf, "and of the role played by MHC antigens becomes readily apparent when we consider that T-cell immune responses are primarily responsible for monitoring self and nonself on cell surfaces. T cells need to determine when a cell becomes malignant or virally infected and must be destroyed." He proposed that, for some unknown reason, class I MHC products are altered on diseased cells; thus, T cells are specialized for sensitivity to small variations in class I molecules, in particular to combinations of the body's normal class I products and virus or tumor antigens.

Benacerraf suggested that this phenomenon might explain why transplants of foreign tissues are usually so quickly rejected: The host's T cells respond to the donor's class I MHC antigens (which are normally slightly different from the host's) by killing the cells, just as they destroy cells whose class I antigens are altered by viruses or cancer.

As in the case of T-cell detection of diseased cells, the capacity of T cells to regulate B-cell activity depends on the recognition of slight variations in MHC products. B cells are thought to inform T cells of the antigen to which their antibodies will react by presenting the antigen together with a class II molecule. The role of these Ir gene products (in humans, HLA-D antigens) in T cell–B cell interactions suggests how Ir acts in the immune response. If a person has no T cells that recognize a particular combination of HLA-D and antigen, the antigen will be "invisible," and there will be no immunological response.

A growing appreciation of the central role of MHC in immune interactions was sufficient to gain Benacerraf, Dausset, and Snell the 1980 Nobel Prize for Physiology or Medicine "for their discoveries concerning genetically determined structures on the cell surface that regulate immunological reactions." Georg Klein of the Karolinska Institute stated in his presentation speech that Benacerraf, Dausset, and Snell "have been responsible for turning what at first appeared as an esoteric area of basic research on inbred mice into a major biological system of the greatest significance for the understanding of cell recognition, immune responses, and graft rejection."

At Harvard, Benacerraf continues his research on the genetics and biochemistry of the MHC and its importance to T-cell function.

In 1943 Benacerraf married Annette Dreyfus (a niece of JACQUES MONOD), whom he met at Columbia University. Their daughter Beryl is a radiologist. His students and colleagues know him as a man with a "dry, sharp wit." Lewis Thomas, with whom he was associated at New York University, has referred to him as an "absolutely magnificent scientist."

Benacerraf is the recipient of the Rabbi Shai Shacknai Prize in Immunology and Cancer Research of Hebrew University of Jerusalem (1974) and the T. Duckett Jones Memorial Award of the Helen Hay Whitney Foundation (1976) as well as an honorary degree from the University of Geneva. He is a member of the National Academy of Sciences, the American Association of Immunologists, the American Society for Experimental Pathology, the Society for Experimental Biology and Medicine, the British Association for Immunology, the French Society of Biological Chemistry, and

the American Academy of Arts and Sciences. He has served as associate editor of the *American Journal of Pathology* and the *Journal of Experimental Medicine* and as a member of the Board of Governors of the Weizmann Institute of Science, an adviser to the World Health Organization, and president of the Sidney Farber Cancer Institute, as well as numerous other professional activities.

SELECTED WORKS: Immunogenetics and Immunodeficiency, 1975; Textbook of Immunology, 1979, with Emil R. Unanue.

ABOUT: New Scientist October 16, 1980; New York Times October 11, 1980; Science November 7, 1980.

BENAVENTE Y MARTINEZ, JACINTO
(August 12, 1866–July 14, 1954)
Nobel Prize for Literature, 1922

The Spanish dramatist Jacinto Benavente y Martinez (bā′ nä vān′ tā ē mär tē′ nāth) was born in Madrid, the youngest of three children of a noted and well-to-do pediatrician. Raised in an atmosphere of culture and learning, he began to attend the theater at an early age and staged puppet plays for his neighbors. In 1882 he enrolled in the University of Madrid to study law. However, he proved to be a reluctant student, and after his father's death in 1885, he left school and devoted himself to writing and reading. After spending several years as a fashionable man-about-town, he joined a theater company as an actor.

Benavente's first published work was *Teatro Fantástico* (Fantasy Plays, 1892), a group of short dramatic dialogues. The following year he published a volume of poetry, *Versos* (Poems), and a fiction collection, *Cartas de mujeres* (Letters From Women), which foreshadowed his lifelong interest in feminine psychology. His first full-length play, *El nido ajeno* (Another's Nest), which was produced in 1894, was not a success. But in 1896 his second play, *Gente conocida* (Well-known People), established his reputation as a playwright.

He soon became known as a leader of a group of Spanish writers known as the Generation of '98, who sought to revive Spain's prestige after its defeat in the Spanish-American War. In 1899 he was named editor of the journal *Vida literaria* (Literary Life), which served as a voice for that group.

In his early plays, Benavente made a deliberate break with the melodramatic theater of

BENAVENTE Y MARTINEZ

JACINTO BENAVENTE Y MARTINEZ

JOSÉ ECHEGARAY, Spain's leading playwright of the previous generation. He substituted satire and irony for Echegaray's romantic declamation. Benavente's plays generally contain little action; instead, they concentrate on verbal wit, subtle social commentary, and the psychology of character. Among his early successes were such dramas as *La gobernadora* (*The Governor's Wife,* 1901), a satirical study of political corruption in a provincial Spanish city; *La noche del Sábado* (*Saturday Night,* 1903), an allegorical play concerning decadents at a Riviera resort; and *La Princesa Bebé* (*Princess Bebé,* 1906), a gentle satire that contrasts aristocratic and democratic ideals.

Benavente never limited himself to one genre. His prolific output includes comedies, peasant dramas, tragedies, short dialogues, operetta librettos, children's plays, fairy tales, and pieces in the style of Oriental theater. In 1907 he wrote *Los intereses creados* (*The Bonds of Interest*), his fifty-third play, in the manner of the Italian masked commedia del l'arte. In this, probably Benavente's most important play, a wily servant, Crispín, contrives to win the heart and hand of a wealthy girl for his master and acts the role of puppet master for a group of self-absorbed human puppets. In later years, Benavente himself often played the role of Crispín on stage.

Between 1908 and 1912, Benavente's prodigious theatrical output abated slightly. During these years, he wrote a weekly column for the Madrid newspaper *El Imparcial* (The Impartial) on whatever subject happened to interest him, and these essays established him as Spain's leading literary critic. His most popularly successful play, *La malquerida* (*The Passion Flower*), was produced in 1913. This naturalistic and psychological tragedy of peasant life was the only one of Benavente's plays to achieve popularity in the United States, where it ran for two years in New York and on tour.

In 1920 Benavente was named director of the Teatro Español, Spain's national theater. That year he also campaigned unsuccessfully for election to the Chamber of Deputies. In the early 1920s the quality of his writing began to decline, and a new generation of critics disparaged his work. In response, Benavente wrote no plays for a period of four years.

It was during this time, in 1922, that Benavente received the Nobel Prize for Literature "for the happy manner in which he has continued the illustrious traditions of the Spanish drama." Per Hallström of the Swedish Academy stated in his presentation speech that Benavente "has observed his world with extremely clear and keen eyes, and what he has seen he has measured and weighed with an alert and flexible intelligence." Hallström continued, "To reproduce the wealth and mobility of life, the play of characters, and the struggle between wills, in a way that comes as near truth as possible—that is his chief aim." Benavente declined to attend the ceremonies, and in his absence the prize was accepted by the Spanish ambassador to Sweden.

When Benavente was awarded the Great Cross of Alfonso el Sabio, a prestigious national literary prize, and named favorite son of the city of Madrid in 1924, he was moved to resume his writing for the stage. That year his *Lecciones de buen amor* (Lessons in Good Love) was produced. In the following years, Benavente's prodigious dramatic output continued, and he ultimately wrote over 170 plays. However, the dramas written after he received the Nobel Prize are universally regarded as inferior to his earlier work.

During the Spanish Civil War, Benavente sympathized with the Republicans. His whereabouts became uncertain; according to one report he had been killed by the Nationalist forces of Generalissimo Francisco Franco. However, reliable sources indicate that he fled to Valencia, where he was captured by the Nationalists, brought back to Madrid, and placed under house arrest. After the war, he disappointed his liberal friends and admirers by endorsing the Franco government.

In 1944, on the fiftieth anniversary of his first theatrical production, Benavente was feted with honors from all over Spain and with revivals of his most celebrated plays. Four years later he won the Mariano Cavia Prize for the best newspaper article published in the Spanish press that year.

Benavente, who never married, continued writing for the theater until his death from a heart condition in Madrid in 1954.

At the height of his career, Benavente's work was highly esteemed, not only in Spain but elsewhere in Europe and in the United States. Writing in 1920, the English novelist Storm Jameson ranked Benavente's writing "in the highest tradition of the Spanish drama. . . . His comedies have exquisite fantasy, poetic grace, technical perfection, and intellectual distinction." In his 1929 study of the literature of modern Spain, the British critic Leslie A. Warren hailed Benavente as "the leading Spanish dramatist"; and as late as 1947, the American scholar Horatio Smith remarked that Benavente's work "entitles him to a place among the great modern satirists." "Many of [Benavente's] characters will survive him," said the Ecuadoran writer Luis Jaramillo in a 1971 article, "because they are not phantoms, but real men and women integrated into daily life. And they preserve that poetic aura with which Benavente surrounded them by virtue of his secret and magic power."

Since Benavente's death, however, his critical reputation has declined considerably. "His plays cannot stand close analysis," wrote American scholar Roberto G. Sánchez in 1955, "and yet he was clever enough to deceive many intelligent people." Although Spanish critic Alfredo Marquerie found "Benavente's theater . . . devoid of ideological conceptions or philosophical observations," he pointed out that "Benavente . . . had much in common with Oscar Wilde and [GEORGE] BERNARD SHAW, particularly in the game of dialects and irony . . . in which the characters disclose their thoughts in a newly justified monologue."

ADDITIONAL WORKS IN ENGLISH TRANSLATION: The Smile of Mona Lisa, 1915; Plays, 1917; Plays: Second Series, 1919; Plays: Third Series, 1923; Plays: Fourth Series, 1924; Brute Force, 1936; At Close Range, 1936; Don Juan's Servant, 1957; The Secret of the Keyhole, 1957.

ABOUT: Boyd, E. Studies From Ten Literatures, 1925; Clark, B. H. A Study of the Modern Drama, 1925; Current Biography June 1953; Diaz, J. A. Jacinto Benavente and His Theatre, 1972; Dos Passos, J. Rosinante to the Road Again, 1922; Goldberg, I. The Drama of Transition, 1922; Jameson, S. Modern Drama in Europe, 1920; Peñuelas, M. C. Jacinto Benavente, 1968; Sheehan, R. L. Benavente and the Spanish Panorama, 1976; Starkie, W. Jacinto Benavente, 1925; Warren, L. A. Modern Spanish Literature, 1929.

BERG, PAUL
(June 30, 1926–   )
Nobel Prize for Chemistry, 1980
(shared with Walter Gilbert and Frederick Sanger)

The American biochemist Paul Berg was born in Brooklyn, New York, one of three sons of Harry Berg and the former Sarah Brodsky. After graduating from Abraham Lincoln High School in 1943, Berg entered Pennsylvania State College to study biochemistry, but his education was interrupted for service in the United States Navy from 1944 to 1946. He returned to Penn State in 1946 and graduated with a B.S. in biochemistry in 1948. Berg did his graduate work at Western Reserve (now Case Western Reserve) University in Cleveland, Ohio, where he received his Ph.D. in 1952. In 1952–1953 he conducted postdoctoral research at the Institute of Cytophysiology in Copenhagen, followed by a year of further study with ARTHUR KORNBERG at Washington University in St. Louis. In 1955 he became assistant professor of microbiology at Washington University. In 1959 he accepted a position at Stanford University, first as associate professor and later, in 1969, as chairman of the biochemistry department.

While working under Kornberg, Berg became familiar with the chemistry of deoxyribonucleic acid (DNA) and ribonucleic acid (RNA). A section of DNA consists of a linear sequence of linked molecules called nucleotides. In turn each nucleotide is composed of chemical substances called bases, which are attached to a supporting structure. This structure is linked to other nucleotides to form a polypeptide chain. Blueprints are carried in specific codons, three-base sequences in the DNA chain, which also include instructions for the assembly of proteins from amino acids. The various types of RNA perform specific functions that translate the blueprint into proteins. Among the proteins are enzymes, catalysts that perform such functions as restricting the chain at a particular base or causing some of the pieces to unite.

At Stanford, Berg became especially interested in the role of transfer RNA (tRNA). This substance delivers amino acids to the proper position during protein assembly. In this process, one end of a tRNA molecule corresponds to a piece of the blueprint sequence,

PAUL BERG

while the other carries a special instructional amino acid codon. Each type of amino acid has its own tRNA molecules, whose structures were first described in 1965 by ROBERT W. HOLLEY, HAR GOBIND KHORANA, and MARSHALL W. NIRENBERG. Berg elucidated the role of tRNA in protein assembly by purifying many of the different tRNAs and the enzymes that link them to the correct amino acids.

By the mid-1960s the genes of prokaryotic organisms (microbes, such as bacteria, that have no defined cell nucleus), were understood in great detail. Much of this knowledge was possible because several varieties of virus can enter the cell of the bacterium *Escherichia coli* and, once there, can replace some of the bacterium's DNA with its own, thereby forcing the bacterium to produce viral proteins. Moreover, because each type of virus affects specific proteins, they became important for the extraction and chemical manipulation of genes present in *E. coli*. Berg wanted to know whether a similar method could be devised to examine and manipulate the far more complicated genes of multicellular organisms, including those of the human body.

To pursue this line of inquiry Berg took a year's sabbatical leave from the Salk Institute, where he worked with RENATO DULBECCO. Dulbecco had been investigating a newly discovered virus called polyoma, which causes tumors in rodents. Polyoma was of particular interest to Berg not only because it could move between mammalian cells in a laboratory dish but also because its DNA could move in and out of the DNA of its host cells. Polyoma

therefore acted much like the well-studied bacterial viruses but could be used to examine mammalian cells.

Returning to Stanford in 1968, Berg began research on the genes of simian virus 40 (SV40), a monkey tumor virus closely related to polyoma. He soon realized, however, that the virus would best serve as a vector if it was altered to incorporate any segment of the mammalian DNA that the experimenter chose. DNA that carries material from more than one type of organism is called recombinant DNA. Although recombinant DNA occurs naturally in living organisms, Berg believed that it could be controlled more precisely if it could be produced in the laboratory.

Berg began his first recombinant DNA experiments around 1970, using SV40 and a well-studied *E. coli* virus called bacteriophage lambda. By adding specific enzymes to these normally noninteracting organisms, he was able to cleave their DNA at points that allowed them to be recombined. The technique provoked much controversy, however. Many scientists feared that synthetic viruses might produce new, cancer-causing bacteria, and for this reason Berg discontinued his recombinant DNA experiments. For the next several years he concentrated on devising more efficient and precise techniques for manipulating SV40.

Concerned about the potential hazards of recombinant DNA research, Berg helped to organize a year-long moratorium on such work in 1974. The following year he was chairman of an international conference at which guidelines for such research were drafted. As scientists realized that recombinant DNA techniques were less risky than they had initially believed, the guidelines were relaxed. The techniques that Berg and his colleagues developed enabled researchers not only to manipulate genes to create new pharmaceuticals, such as interferon and growth hormones, but also to study the molecular biology of higher organisms in unprecedented detail.

Berg was awarded half of the 1980 Nobel Prize for Chemistry "for his fundamental studies of the biochemistry of nucleic acids, with particular regard to recombinant DNA." The other half of the prize was divided between WALTER GILBERT and FREDERICK SANGER. In his Nobel lecture Berg reviewed his research, noting the continuing need to confront the inherent ethical questions posed by recombinant DNA experiments. Nevertheless, he concluded, "the recombinant DNA breakthrough has provided us with a new and powerful approach to the questions that have intrigued and plagued man for centuries. I, for one, would not shrink from that challenge."

Since receiving the Nobel Prize, Berg has continued his research at Stanford, refining his methods for molecular studies of the genes of higher animals. Since 1970 he has been the Wilson Professor of Biochemistry at the Stanford University Medical Center.

In 1947 Berg married Mildred Levy. They have one son.

In addition to the Nobel Prize, Berg has received the Eli Lilly Prize of the American Chemical Society (1959), the V. D. Mattia Award of the Roche Institute for Molecular Biology (1974), the Gairdner Foundation Annual Award (1980), the Albert Lasker Basic Medical Research Award (1980), and the New York Academy of Sciences Award (1980). He is a member of the National Academy of Sciences, the American Association for the Advancement of Science, the American Academy of Arts and Sciences, the American Society of Biological Chemists, and the American Chemical Society. He holds honorary degrees from the University of Rochester and Yale University.

SELECTED WORKS: Computers in Schools, 1985, with others.

ABOUT: Chemical Engineering News August 13, 1984; New York Times October 15, 1980; Science November 21, 1980.

BERGIUS, FRIEDRICH
(October 11, 1884–March 30, 1949)
Nobel Prize for Chemistry, 1931
(shared with Carl Bosch)

The German chemist Friedrich Karl Rudolf Bergius (ber′ gē əs) was born in Goldschmieden (now part of Poland) to Heinrich and Marie (Haase) Bergius. He attended primary and secondary schools in nearby Breslau (now Wrocław, Poland), where he avidly observed the industrial processes at his father's chemical factory. Following secondary school, Bergius was sent by his father to study the operation of a large metallurgical plant in the Ruhr Valley for six months.

In 1903 Bergius studied chemistry at the University of Breslau under Albert Ladenburg and Richard Abegg. He spent the following year in the military before entering the University of Leipzig, where he conducted doc-

toral research under Arthur Hantzsch on concentrated sulfuric acid as a solvent. He completed his dissertation under Abegg and received a doctoral degree from Breslau in 1907.

For the next two years Bergius assisted WALTHER NERNST in Berlin and then FRITZ HABER in Karlsruhe with research on high-pressure methods for synthesizing ammonia from hydrogen and atmospheric nitrogen. In 1909 he joined Ernest Bodenstein's physical-chemical laboratory at the technical university in Hannover, where he investigated the dissociation of calcium peroxides, using pressures as high as 300 atmospheres. During these years Bergius began developing leakproof high-pressure apparatus.

When his need for space quickly outstripped that allotted him in Bodenstein's facilities, Bergius used his family's personal wealth to establish a private laboratory in Hannover. There his research focused on two topics: the transformation of heavy oils and oil residues into lighter oils (and ultimately into gasoline) and the effects of high pressure and high temperature on wood and peat in the formation of coal. In the course of this work Bergius became convinced that more viscous types of petroleum possessed less hydrogen than lighter types. Therefore, the addition of hydrogen to petroleum to replace hydrogen lost during refining (which breaks down petroleum into simpler, lighter molecules) would increase the gasoline yield. Applying this procedure, he achieved a greater yield of gasoline. He subsequently filed a patent for the high-pressure hydrogenation of oils.

During the early years of the twentieth century, increasing use of the internal combustion engine intensified the demand for petroleum. Convinced by the studies he had conducted on coal formation that hydrogen is present in coal, Bergius wondered if it might be possible to produce a petroleumlike hydrocarbon from this abundant fuel. By late 1913 he had produced a liquid hydrocarbon by forcing hydrogen into lignitic coal. His method consisted of injecting hydrogen gas into a slurry of ground coal and tar at high temperatures and at pressures of more than 50 atmospheres.

Using his personal fortune and with support from two German petroleum refining companies, Bergius built a plant in 1915 at Rheinau near Mannheim to expedite large-scale development of the coal-hydrogenation process. After World War I, however, the demand for petroleum temporarily slackened, and Bergius's project languished until 1921, when he

FRIEDRICH BERGIUS

raised additional funds by selling his patent rights to German and foreign companies.

At Rheinau, Bergius and his assistants developed industrial apparatus for the coal-hydrogenation process. Pumps forced the gases, liquids, and solids involved into a vessel, where they reacted while being mixed and heated under extremely high pressure. Until this time, commercially successful high-pressure equipment could accommodate only gaseous reactions.

Between 1922 and 1925 Bergius made his process continuous, mastered control of the reaction temperature, and provided an effective hydrogen source by igniting a mixture of methane and oxygen. Despite these and many other improvements, the process never became economically feasible. After Bergius sold his patents to the Badische Anilin- und Sodafabrik (BASF), a large German chemical company, in 1925, his work was continued under CARL BOSCH. BASF had successfully commercialized Haber's ammonia synthesis and the high-pressure hydrogenation of carbon monoxide to produce methanol. In January 1925 BASF developed a sulfur-resistant molybdenum catalyst that facilitated the coal-hydrogenation process and improved its efficiency.

Later in 1925 BASF and six other German chemical companies joined to form the Interessen-Gemeinschaft Farbenindustrie Aktiengesellschaft (I. G. Farben). Under the new organization, hydrogenation development was expanded. In 1926 Matthias Pier, one of Nernst's former students and director of research at BASF, improved Bergius's process and increased the yield of gasoline. Two years later, I. G. Farben constructed a large plant at Leuna for the production of oil from coal.

The 1931 Nobel Prize for Chemistry was awarded jointly to Bergius and Bosch "in recognition of their contributions to the invention and development of chemical high-pressure methods." In his presentation speech K. W. Palmær of the Royal Swedish Academy of Sciences discussed the technical hurdles Bergius had overcome in perfecting his high-pressure techniques. He added that "the introduction of the chemical high-pressure methods represented an epoch-making improvement in the field of chemical technology."

By the time he received the Nobel Prize, Bergius had turned to research on the hydrolysis of cellulose, the chief component of wood, using highly concentrated hydrochloric acid. The process, dubbed "food from wood," yielded sugar, which in turn could be transformed into alcohol or a nutrient form of yeast. Through the 1930s and 1940s Bergius continued his wood hydrolysis research, and in 1943 he established an industrial plant at Rheinau. Both the coal-hydrogenation and the cellulose conversion processes provided Germany with crucial resources during World War II.

Unable to find suitable work after the war, Bergius lived briefly in Austria before moving to Spain, where he founded a chemical company. In 1947, at the invitation of the government, he settled in Argentina and served as a science consultant to the Ministry of Industries.

Bergius was married to the former Ottilie Krazert, with whom he had two sons and a daughter. He died in Buenos Aires in 1949.

In addition to the Nobel Prize, Bergius received several awards and honors during his life, including the prestigious Liebig Medal of the German Chemical Society, as well as honorary degrees from the universities of Heidelberg and Hannover.

ABOUT: Dictionary of Scientific Biography, volume 2, 1970; Isis December 1984.

BERGSON, HENRI
(October 18, 1859–January 4, 1941)
Nobel Prize for Literature, 1927

The French philosopher Henri Louis Bergson was born in Paris to a cosmopolitan Jewish family. Bergson's father, Michel, an accomplished musician who was said to have studied with Chopin, left his native Warsaw, toured Europe, and eventually reached England. There he became a British citizen and married Katherine Levinson, a woman of Irish-Jewish descent. Bergson spent his early years in London, where he learned English and became acquainted with British culture. When he was eight years old, the family returned to France; at the age of twenty-one, he became a naturalized French citizen.

From 1868 to 1878 Bergson attended the Lycée Condorcet in Paris, showing promise in both the humanities and mathematics. At nineteen, his prizewinning solution to a mathematical problem was published in the journal *Annales de Mathématiques* (Annals of Mathematics). Although encouraged to specialize in the sciences, he chose instead to study philosophy at the École Normale Supérieure, where he displayed a keen interest in the seemingly irreconcilable ideas of John Stuart Mill and Herbert Spencer.

After earning his degree in 1881, Bergson taught at the Lycée d'Angers. Two years later he accepted a post at the Lycée Blaise Pascal in Clermont-Ferrand. While living and lecturing in the Auvergne region, Bergson wrote his first major work, *Essai sur les données immédiates de la conscience,* in 1889; it was translated into English as *Time and Free Will.* This work, along with a short Latin thesis on Aristotle, earned him a Ph.D. from the University of Paris in 1889.

In *Time and Free Will,* Bergson introduced a concept central to his metaphysics: the dynamic nature of time. Scientists influenced by Newtonian physics had conceived of time as a constant, a series of discrete moments like points on a line or ticks of a clock. Bergson argued, instead, that time as experienced by living organisms is dynamic, variable, and qualitative. Lived time, which Bergson referred to as duration, can be comprehended only intuitively, and its effects are too subtle and far-ranging to be measured by the analytic methods of positivism. Moreover, he believed, deterministic philosophers like Herbert Spencer had failed to take into account the unpredictable, novel, and creative elements in decision making, which are the products of lived time and personal history. In Bergson's view, free will and deliberation—which, like temporality, can be grasped only intuitively—are rare but crucial elements in the development of human consciousness.

In 1891 Bergson returned to Paris. The fol-

HENRI BERGSON

lowing year he married Louise Neuberger, with whom he had one daughter. For eight years he taught at the Lycée Henri IV, where he wrote his second important work, *Matière et mémoire (Matter and Memory),* which was published in 1896. Analyzing the way in which brain physiology is related to consciousness, Bergson concluded that the mind does more than simply provide a correlation between mental images and physical stimuli. The brain functions not just as a passive recording instrument but as a highly selective screening device whose purpose is to direct attention to life. Neurophysiology can offer explanations only for rote or habitual memory; psychological insight is necessary to understand the process of recollection as it is modified and directed by the life principle.

In 1900 Bergson accepted the chair of Greek philosophy at the Collège de France, an institution second only to the Sorbonne in intellectual prestige. His next publication was *Le Rire (Laughter,* 1900), a short but provocative essay that examines the nature of comedy. What is laughable, Bergson argued, is any mechanical habit of mind or body that impedes the flow of life. By exposing such automatism, comedy, like all art, facilitates the ongoing evolution of society and individuals.

In 1903 Bergson published *Introduction à la métaphysique (Introduction to Metaphysics).* Distinguishing sharply between science and philosophy, he noted that the scientific mind attempts to dominate nature by "freezing the flux" of time and reducing wholeness into discrete, analyzable elements. Philosophy, on the other hand, enables the mind to perceive the dynamic reality of things by insight and empathy. Both methods, Bergson believed, are necessary for human growth, but only the latter is truly creative and life-enhancing.

When Bergson's third and epoch-making book, *L'Évolution créatrice* (*Creative Evolution*), appeared in 1907, it had an enormous impact not only in academic circles but also upon the general reading public. "Old-fashioned professors, whom his ideas quite fail to satisfy, nevertheless speak of his talent almost with bated breath," wrote the American philosopher William James, an ardent admirer, "while youngsters flock to him as to a master." James noted that style, as well as substance, accounted for Bergson's appeal. "The lucidity of Bergson's way of putting things is what all readers are first struck by," he went on. "It seduces you and bribes you in advance to become his disciple. It is a miracle, and he a real magician."

For those who found neo-Darwinian and positivistic thought dull and oppressive, Bergson offered a lively and inspiring alternative. In Bergson's view, evolution is not simply the passive and mechanical adaptation of organisms to the physical environment but a purposeful and creative process. Life cannot be understood by intellectual analysis alone, he argued, because it consists of movements and change, a "stream of consciousness" at odds with inert matter. Skeptical philosophers such as BERTRAND RUSSELL were less enthusiastic about the poetic intensity of Bergson's style. "As a rule," said Russell, Bergson "does not give reasons for his opinions, but relies on their inherent attractiveness, and on the charm of an excellent style."

Nevertheless, writers and artists as diverse as Claude Debussy, Claude Monet, Marcel Proust, Paul Valéry, André Maurois, Charles-Pierre Péguy, and Nikos Kazantzakis turned to Bergson for inspiration and intellectual stimulation. His work also profoundly influenced such philosophers as John Dewey, Samuel Alexander, and Alfred North Whitehead. Bergsonian concepts of time and consciousness figure prominently in the fiction of Proust and Virginia Woolf, as well as in THOMAS MANN's novel *The Magic Mountain* (1922).

During the buoyant era before World War I, Bergson's popularity soared, and he was invited to lecture throughout Europe and the United States. He was elected to the French Academy in 1914, the same year he became president of the Academy of Moral and Political Sciences. His views became so voguish

that both liberal Catholics and Syndicalists (a socialist group) tried to appropriate his philosophy for their own ends.

Bergson was invited to deliver the 1914 Gifford Lecture at the University of Edinburgh in Scotland; he completed the spring series, "The Problem of Personality," but the outbreak of World War I prevented him from giving the autumn series. Instead, he wrote two provocative essays, "The Meaning of War" and "The Evolution of German Imperialism," in which he argued that war was essentially a conflict between a self-impelling life force (represented by those advocating spiritual and political freedom, such as the French) and a self-defeating mechanism (represented by those who would deify the masses, such as the Germans and Hegelians). Hoping that the Great War would lead to "the rejuvenation of France and the moral regeneration of Europe," Bergson represented his country on diplomatic missions to Spain and the United States. He later became active in the League of Nations serving as president of the Commission on Intellectual Cooperation.

Bergson was stricken with severe arthritis in 1920; at about the same time, the optimism that his philosophy had inspired in prewar years began to wane. Nevertheless, in 1928 he was awarded the 1927 Nobel Prize for Literature "in recognition of his rich and vitalizing ideas and the brilliant skill with which they have been presented." In his presentation lecture, Per Hallström of the Swedish Academy described Bergson's principal achievement: "By a passage he has forced through the gates of rationalism, he has released a creative impulse of inestimable value, opening a large access to the waters of living time, to that atmosphere in which the human mind will be able to rediscover its freedom and thus be born anew." Although he was unable to attend the awards ceremony in Stockholm, Bergson sent a message of acceptance to the Swedish Academy in which he warned that historical "experience has proved that the technological development of a society does not automatically result in the moral perfection of the men living in it, and . . . an increase in the material means at the disposal of humanity may even present dangers unless it is accompanied by a corresponding spiritual effort."

The religious tendency of Bergson's thought is ambitiously expressed in his final work, *Les Deux Sources de la morale et de la religion* (*The Two Sources of Morality and Religion*), published in 1932. Challenging the rationalistic assumptions of German philosophy, Bergson argues that vital morality, like vital religion, has an emotional, not a logical, basis. Most institutionalized religions try to freeze the life-affirming insight of their great teachers in order to perpetuate a "closed society" intent on protecting itself against the hostile world. Dynamic religion, in Bergson's view, springs from the mystically grounded activism of those who, accepting the life force, devote their lives to breaking down the barriers between individuals and between nations. God, Bergson insisted, is manifested as a process, not as a timeless entity. "The function of the universe," Bergson concluded, is to be "a machine for the making of gods."

Christian mysticism exerted a strong influence on Bergson in his later years, and he was tempted to join the Roman Catholic church. But with the outbreak of World War II and Nazi persecution of the Jews, Bergson resolved to be true to his heritage and suffer the consequences. When the Vichy government offered to excuse him from the restrictions it had imposed upon its Jewish population, Bergson refused to accept a privileged status. Even though he was eighty-two and ailing, he waited in line to register as a Jew. According to E. W. F. Tomlin, "That last silent protest in inclement weather, unnoticed and almost anonymous in its humble dignity, hastened the end." Bergson died not long afterward of pulmonary congestion. His funeral oration was given by his friend Paul Valéry.

In *The Bergsonian Heritage* (1962), Thomas Hanna observed that "if the traditions of philosophy remain largely unaffected by 'Bergsonism,' they do not . . . remain impervious to Henri Bergson himself, for the man Bergson brought to philosophy an eloquence, an imagination, an expansiveness, and a concern for the value and uniqueness of men that is as rare as it is irreplaceable."

ADDITIONAL WORKS IN ENGLISH TRANSLATION: Dreams, 1914; The Meaning of War, Life, and Matter in Conflict, 1915; Mind-Energy, 1920; The Creative Mind, 1946; Duration and Simultaneity, 1965.

ABOUT: Alexander, I. W. Bergson: Philosopher of Reflection, 1957; Capek, M. Bergson and Modern Physics, 1971; Carr, H. W. Henri Bergson: The Philosophy of Change, 1912; Chevalier, J. Henri Bergson, 1928; Gallagher, I. J. Morality in Evolution: The Philosophy of Change, 1912; Hanna, T. (ed.) The Bergsonian Heritage, 1962; Herman, D. J. The Philosophy of Henri Bergson, 1980; Kolakowski, L. Bergson, 1985; Lindsay, A. D. The Philosophy of Bergson, 1968; Pilkington, A. E. Bergson and His Influence, 1976; Russell, B. The Philosophy of Bergson, 1914; Scharfstein, B. Roots of Bergson's Philosophy, 1943; Solomon, J. Bergson, 1970.

BERGSTRÖM, SUNE

(January 10, 1916–   )
Nobel Prize for Physiology or Medicine, 1982
(shared with Bengt Samuelsson and John R. Vane)

The Swedish biochemist Sune Karl Bergström was born in Stockholm, the son of Sverker and Wera (Wistrand) Bergström. After completing his secondary school education in 1934, he began working with Erik Jorpes at the Karolinska Institute in Stockholm. Jorpes was researching the clinical uses of heparin, a drug that interferes with the clotting of blood, and encouraged Bergström, who had become his assistant, to do research on the biochemistry of lipids (fats) and steroids (a group of compounds with a particular carbon-ring configuration that includes a number of hormones and bile acid). In 1938, under Jorpes's sponsorship, Bergström spent a year as a research fellow at the University of London investigating the biochemistry of bile acids. Bile acids are secreted by the cells of the liver and are transported via the bile ducts to the small intestine, where they prepare cholesterol and other lipids for digestion and absorption.

The following year Bergström received a fellowship from the British Council to continue his research in Edinburgh, but World War II intervened and the fellowship was canceled. After obtaining a Swedish-American Fellowship in 1940 for study in the United States, he spent the next two years as a research fellow at Columbia University in New York City and at the Squibb Institute for Medical Research in New Jersey, where he worked with Oscar Wintersteiner, an authority on the auto-oxidation of cholesterol. (Auto-oxidation is the chemical process by which a substance combines with oxygen at room air pressure and temperature.)

At the conclusion of his fellowship, he returned to Sweden in 1942. Bergström received his medical degree from the Karolinska Institute in 1944 and was appointed assistant in the Department of Biochemistry at the Medical Nobel Institute of the Karolinska, a position he held for three years. During that period, he did research on the auto-oxidation of linoleic acid, a constituent of certain vegetable oils and an essential fatty acid in the human diet. After discovering that an enzyme of the

SUNE BERGSTRÖM

soybean called lipoxygenase is necessary for the oxidation of linoleic acid, he participated in an effort to purify this enzyme in the laboratory of HUGO THEORELL at the Karolinska Institute and presented the results of this research at a meeting of the Physiological Society of the Karolinska Institute in 1945.

ULF VON EULER, who also attended that meeting, later spoke to Bergström about some research he had done on prostaglandins before World War II. (Prostaglandins are active substances obtained from the prostate gland and seminal vesicles.) The prostaglandins were first described by gynecologists at Columbia University's College of Physicians and Surgeons in 1930. During the course of artificial inseminations, the gynecologists observed that the seminal fluid caused the smooth muscle of the uterus to contract and relax. Later, Euler extracted a substance from the seminal fluid of sheep that also stimulated contractions of uterine muscle. He observed that this substance relaxed smooth muscle in the walls of blood vessels and lowered blood pressure. He called it prostaglandin because it was first found in the secretions of the prostate gland. Euler preserved these extracts and in 1945 gave them to Bergström, who had acquired a new extraction device in the United States that enabled him to purify the extracts to a high degree. Bergström followed the progress of his extraction procedures on a test strip of rabbit smooth muscle and reported that "after purification essentially to weightlessness," the prostaglandins "retained extraordinary activity."

After spending the year 1946 as a research fellow at the University of Basel in Switzerland, Bergström was offered an appointment as professor of physiological chemistry at the University of Lund in Sweden. Assisted by the Swedish Medical Research Council and the American National Institutes of Health Program for International Biomedical Research, he restored and improved the university's research facilities, which had been abandoned during the war. He also undertook the training of graduate students, including BENGT SAMUELSSON, and resumed his research on the prostaglandins. During the 1950s and the 1960s, he and his staff collected and organized a large number of sheep seminal glands to obtain enough seminal fluid for the isolation and further study of the prostaglandins. By 1957 Bergström and his colleagues had isolated and purified small amounts of two prostaglandin compounds. Their molecular weights and chemical formulas were determined with the help of Ragnar Ryhage at the Karolinska Institute and other collaborators in Stockholm and Uppsala. That joint effort produced the first descriptions of the chemical structure of the prostaglandins.

Appointed professor of chemistry at the Karolinska Institute in 1958, Bergström was soon joined there by Samuelsson. Within four years Bergström and his colleagues managed to isolate a total of six prostaglandins, each of which contained twenty carbon atoms and displayed a structure similar to that of certain fatty acids. This discovery in turn led to the question of whether prostaglandins are formed from fatty acids. In 1964, proceeding on this assumption, Samuelsson demonstrated that arachidonic acid—an unsaturated fatty acid found in certain meats and vegetables—is the precursor, or initial stage, in the development of prostaglandin. During the next several years, he determined just how prostaglandins are formed. In the course of their research, Bergström and Samuelsson learned that arachidonic acid and the enzymes needed to convert it into prostaglandins are present in all nucleated animal cells. Different tissues synthesize different prostaglandins, with the various prostaglandins performing different biological functions. Those prostaglandins that have undergone the most study are known as the E and F series.

Bergström served as dean of the Faculty of Medicine at the Karolinska Institute from 1963 until 1966, and from 1969 until 1977, was the institute's rector. During those years, a series of investigations into the biological functions of the prostaglandins were performed at the institute. Prostaglandins of the E series were found to be vasodilators, which relax smooth muscle in the walls of blood vessels, lower blood pressure, and may also be useful in treating patients with peripheral vascular disease (blockage of blood vessels) and certain congenital abnormalities of the circulatory system. In addition, E-series prostaglandins protect the lining of the stomach from the formation of ulcers and from the toxic side effects of aspirin and indomethacin, an anti-inflammatory drug. Prostaglandins of the F series are vasoconstrictors; that is, they stimulate contraction of smooth muscle in the walls of blood vessels, thereby raising blood pressure. They also stimulate the contraction of the muscle of the uterus and may be used to induce abortions.

Bergström shared the 1982 Nobel Prize for Physiology or Medicine with Samuelsson and JOHN R. VANE "for their discoveries concerning prostaglandin and related biologically active substances." Upon learning that his protégé, Samuelsson, would share the prize with him and Vane, Bergström remarked that there is "no greater satisfaction than seeing your students successful."

In his Nobel lecture, "The Prostaglandins: From the Laboratory to the Clinic," Bergström discussed the background of the early research on prostaglandins, as well as the more recent clinical developments with which he has been associated. The clarification of the nature of prostaglandins and their biological importance has been a valuable contribution to many areas of medicine, providing a basis for the acquisition of new knowledge and the development of therapy.

In 1943 Bergström married Maj Gernandt. They have one son.

In addition to the Nobel Prize, Bergström received the Anders Jahre Prize in Medicine given by Oslo University (1970), the Louisa Gross Horwitz Prize of Columbia University (1975), the Albert Lasker Basic Medical Research Award (1977), and the Bar Holberg Medal of the Swedish Chemical Society. In 1975 he was appointed chairman of the Board of Directors of the Nobel Foundation. From 1977 until 1982 he served as chairman of the World Health Organization Advisory Committee on Medical Research. According to Bergström, in that capacity he spent about a third of his time "traveling around the world, helping to build research facilities."

A tall, reserved man, Bergström is a former member of the Swedish Medical Research Council and the Swedish Natural Science Research Council. He is currently a member of the Royal Swedish Academy of Science, the Academy of Science of the Soviet Union, and the American Academy of Arts and Sciences.

SELECTED WORKS: Prostacyclin, 1979, with John Vane.

ABOUT: New York Times October 12, 1982; Science November 19, 1982.

BETHE, HANS A.
(July 2, 1906–   )
Nobel Prize for Physics, 1967

The German-American physicist Hans Albrecht Bethe (bā′ te) was born in Strasbourg, Alsace-Lorraine (then part of Germany), the only child of Albrecht Theodore Julius Bethe, an eminent physiologist and professor of medicine, and Anna (Kuhn) Bethe, the daughter of a professor. From 1915 to 1924 Bethe attended the Goethe Gymnasium in Frankfurt am Main, followed by two years at the University of Frankfurt. After another two and a half years of graduate study at the University of Munich, he received a Ph.D. in theoretical physics in 1928 under Arnold Sommerfeld, an important contributor to modern physics.

While still a graduate student, Bethe became interested in quantum mechanics, a mathematical theory dealing with interactions between matter and radiation. Formulated in the mid-1920s by WERNER HEISENBERG, ERWIN SCHRÖDINGER, and P. A. M. DIRAC, it was an outgrowth of early developments in quantum theory: MAX PLANCK's discovery that radiation was not seamless but consisted of discrete bits of energy later called quanta; ALBERT EINSTEIN's demonstration that photons, the quanta of light (electromagnetic radiation), acted like particles in the photoelectric effect; NIELS BOHR's application of quantum theory to a description of atomic energy levels that accounted for characteristic spectra of emitted radiation; and LOUIS DE BROGLIE's bold suggestion that if radiation (light) could behave like a particle, then a particle could behave like a wave. Broglie's idea was experimentally verified by CLINTON J. DAVISSON, who observed the wave behavior of electrons. In 1927 Bethe wrote a scientific paper on electron diffraction by crystals, in which he used quantum mechanics, still little understood at the time by most physicists, to explain Davisson's observations. Bethe was one of the first scientists to make such a cogent appli-

93

HANS A. BETHE

cation of the new principles, an initiative he was to demonstrate frequently in his career as new theories appeared.

After earning his doctorate, Bethe spent 1928–1929 as a physics instructor at the universities of Frankfurt and Stuttgart. He was appointed a lecturer at the University of Munich in 1929, but spent much of the next three years in Cambridge, England, where he met ERNEST RUTHERFORD, and in Rome, where he worked with ENRICO FERMI. He also came in contact with Niels Bohr. During this time, Bethe pioneered the use of the mathematical techniques known as group theory to elucidate the quantum-mechanical behavior of crystals. After making significant contributions to the theory of atomic structure, Bethe, in the early 1930s, began a theoretical study of how fast particles lose energy when passing through matter, a subject to which he has repeatedly returned throughout his scientific career.

Appointed assistant professor at the University of Tübingen in 1932, Bethe, whose mother was Jewish, lost his position the following year, after Adolf Hitler imposed anti-Semitic edicts upon becoming chancellor of Germany. Bethe left Germany in 1933, lectured for a year at the University of Manchester in England and then spent 1934–1935 as a fellow at the University of Bristol. In 1935 he accepted a post as assistant professor at Cornell University in Ithaca, New York, where he became a full professor in 1937.

After emigrating, Bethe turned to the study of nuclear physics. In 1936, collaborating with the American physicists Robert F. Bacher and

M. S. Livingston, Bethe wrote several comprehensive journal articles summarizing current knowledge in the then-infant field. The three journal issues were immediately recognized as classics and subsequently used widely as a basic nuclear physics textbook for over twenty years.

In 1938, while attending a conference on theoretical physics in Washington, D.C., Bethe's attention was drawn to the unsolved question of the mechanism that supplies the energy of the sun and other stars. Astronomers had accumulated much information about the extremely high temperatures and other stellar characteristics and had concluded that the energy source must be thermonuclear. However, they had not been able to determine the reactions that could account quantitatively for the observed radiation, size, age, and other properties. Quickly acquiring the necessary familiarity with astronomical data and applying his encyclopedic knowledge of nuclear physics, Bethe solved the problem in six weeks.

The simplest reaction, first suggested by the German astronomer Carl Friedrich von Weizsäcker, was the fusion of two protons (hydrogen nuclei, abundant in the sun) to form deuterium (also called heavy hydrogen, with a proton and a neutron in its nucleus), causing the release of energy in the form of a positron (positive electron) and a neutrino (uncharged particle). Protons are positively charged, and the number of protons in the nucleus identifies the element (a hydrogen nucleus contains a single proton, but may also contain neutrons, which have almost the same mass as a proton but no charge). In the fusion of two protons, the emission of a positive charge (positron) converts one of the protons into a neutron. Bethe considered such solar conditions as temperature, density, and composition, together with expected reaction rates, and calculated that the fusion reaction proceeded at the correct rate to fit the sun's observed energy production. However, his calculations suggested that stars more massive than the sun must also involve the reaction of heavier nuclei.

For more massive stars, Bethe proposed a six-step carbon-nitrogen cycle. In the first step, carbon 12 (the most common and stable form of carbon, with 6 protons and 6 neutrons in its nucleus) captures a proton to form nitrogen 13 (7 protons, 6 neutrons), emitting energy in the form of a gamma ray. Unstable nitrogen 13 decays by emitting a positron (which converts a proton into a neutron) and a neutrino to form carbon 13 (6 protons, 7 neutrons). Carbon 13 then captures one of the ever-present protons to create nitrogen 14 (7 protons, 7 neutrons), with the emission of another gamma ray. Nitrogen 14, in turn, captures a proton to become oxygen 15 (8 protons, 7 neutrons), emitting still another gamma ray. Unstable oxygen 15 emits a positron (changing a proton to a neutron) and a neutrino, producing nitrogen 15 (7 protons, 8 neutrons). In the final step, nitrogen 15 captures a proton, but the product is not a heavier nucleus containing 8 protons and 8 neutrons, which would be oxygen 16. Instead, two nuclei result: carbon 12 and helium 4 (2 protons and 2 neutrons). The carbon 12 can then repeat the cycle, while the helium 4 enters the star's store of that gas. The various emissions at each step in the cycle supply the energy that gives the star its luminosity. Bethe's analysis provided a deeper understanding of the behavior and evolution of stars.

During the late 1930s, Bethe continued his theoretical studies of atomic nuclei. Among his many contributions was the first mathematical demonstration that the newly discovered meson might be linked to the force that holds nuclei together. He also investigated the highly complex shock waves generated by explosives, a study that proved to be useful in his later work on the Manhattan Project to develop the atomic bomb.

In 1941, shortly before the United States entered World War II, Bethe became a naturalized American citizen. For a short time he worked on microwaves and their application to radar at the Massachusetts Institute of Technology's Radiation Laboratory before joining the Manhattan Project at Los Alamos, New Mexico, in 1943. There, as director of the Theoretical Physics Division, he was responsible for calculating how the atomic bomb might behave. His comprehensive understanding of nuclear physics, shock waves, and electromagnetic theory played a major role in the program's success.

After returning to Cornell in 1946, Bethe continued his many research interests, for example, making fundamental contributions to the field of modern quantum electrodynamics. He also joined forces with other scientists to publicize the dangers posed by nuclear weapons. He has remained a prominent advocate of arms control measures while continuing to support the civilian use of nuclear power. From 1956 to 1959 Bethe served on the President's Science Advisory Committee.

Bethe was awarded the 1967 Nobel Prize for Physics "for his contributions to the theory of nuclear reactions, especially his discoveries concerning the energy production in stars."

On presenting the prize, Oskar Klein of the Royal Swedish Academy of Sciences acknowledged Bethe's extraordinary breadth of knowledge and noted that several of his contributions to physics were individually worthy of the Nobel Prize. Bethe's work on the energy sources of stars, Klein said, "is one of the most important applications of fundamental physics in our days, having led to a deep-going evolution of our knowledge of the universe around us."

In subsequent work, Bethe has studied the distribution of matter in neutron stars as well as the behavior of collapsing giant stars. His research into the effects of high-velocity reentry into the earth's atmosphere contributed to the design of both military and civilian space vehicles. Although he recalls his experience at Los Alamos as "terribly exciting," he opposes government-sponsored efforts to develop an antimissile defense shield, regarding it as technically unfeasible.

In 1939 Bethe married Rose Ewald, the daughter of a noted German physicist who had fled Nazi Germany. They have two children. Known as a modest and thoughtful man, Bethe, who once enjoyed skiing and mountain climbing, is said to like economics. His colleagues express a high regard for his mental ability and painstaking scientific methods.

In addition to the Nobel Prize, Bethe has received the Medal of Merit of the United States government (1946), the Henry Draper Medal of the National Academy of Sciences (1947), the Max Planck Medal of the German Physical Society (1955), the Enrico Fermi Medal of the United States Atomic Energy Commission (1961), the Eddington Medal of the Royal Astronomical Society in London (1963), and the Vannevar Bush Award of the National Academy of Sciences (1985). He is a member of the American Philosophical Society, the National Academy of Sciences, the American Physical Society, and the American Astronomical Society, as well as a foreign member of the Royal Society of London. He has received honorary degrees from the universities of Birmingham and Manchester.

SELECTED WORKS: Elementary Nuclear Theory, 1947; Mesons and Fields, 1955, with others; Quantum Mechanics of One- and Two-Electron Atoms, 1957, with Edward Salpeter; The Future of Nuclear Tests, 1961, with Edward Teller; Intermediate Quantum Mechanics, 1964, with Roman Jackiw; Theory of the Fireball, 1964; Reducing the Risk of Nuclear War, 1985, with Robert S. MacNamara; Basic Bethe: Seminal Articles on Nuclear Physics, 1936–37, 1986.

ABOUT: Bernstein, J. Hans Bethe, Prophet of Energy,

...aphy April 1950; Marshak, R. E. Per-
... Modern Physics, 1966; National Cyclopedia of
...erican Biography, supplement I, 1960; Weintraub, P.
(ed.) The Omni Interviews, 1984.

BINNIG, GERD
(July 20, 1947–   )
Nobel Prize for Physics, 1986
(shared with Heinrich Rohrer and Ernst
   Ruska)

GERD BINNIG

The German physicist Gerd Karl Binnig was
born in Frankfurt am Main to Karl Franz Binnig, a machine engineer, and Ruth (Bracke)
Binnig, a drafter. After receiving his secondary education at the Rudolf Koch School, he
earned a doctorate in physics for work on superconductivity from the University of Frankfurt in 1978.

Immediately after receiving his degree, Binnig became a research staff member at the
research laboratory of the International Business Machines Corporation (IBM) in Zurich,
Switzerland. There he began collaborating with
HEINRICH ROHRER on research on the surfaces of materials. The two investigators were
drawn to the topic because of the challenging
problems it poses; a thorough understanding
of the surfaces of materials has proved virtually impossible to obtain. The source of the
difficulty lies in the fact that the arrangement
of atoms in the surface of a solid is so different
from the arrangement of atoms in the bulk that
known methods for exploring the latter are
useless where surfaces are concerned. Surfaces
are of considerable interest, however, because
it is there that most interactions among materials take place.

In their attempt to probe the surfaces of
materials, Binnig and Rohrer decided to try a
variant of an effect of quantum mechanics
known as tunneling. The effect, which was first
verified experimentally by IVAR GIAEVER in
1960, is one of the many ways in which the so-
called Heisenberg uncertainty principle makes
itself felt. According to that principle, named
for the German physicist WERNER HEISEN-
BERG, it is impossible to measure the position
and velocity of a subatomic particle simultaneously. As a consequence, the position of a
particle such as an electron becomes "smeared
out" over space: the particle behaves as a diffuse cloud of matter. Such a cloud of matter
can "tunnel," or diffuse, between two surfaces, even if they are not touching, in much
the same way that water can seep through the
ground from one puddle to another.

The tunneling effect was well known at the
time Binnig and Rohrer began their collaboration and had been used to explore—albeit
somewhat crudely—the nature of interfaces
in "sandwiches" of materials. What Binnig and
Rohrer set out to accomplish was to get electrons to tunnel through a vacuum, an idea that
proved unexpectedly feasible. Their approach
ultimately led to the development of a new
instrument called the scanning tunneling microscope. The basic principle underlying this
device involves scanning the surface of a solid
in a vacuum with a sharp needle tip. A voltage
is applied between the sample and the tip, and
the distance between the two is kept small
enough that electrons will tunnel from one to
the other. The resulting flow of electrons is
called a tunneling current. The amount of tunneling current has an exponential relationship
with the distance between the sample and tip.
Therefore, by sweeping the tip over the sample and measuring the current, a map of the
surface can be produced at the atomic scale.

Binnig and Rohrer made their first successful test of the scanning tunneling microscope
in the spring of 1981. Collaborating with two
other IBM workers, Christoph Gerber and
Edmund Weibel, they resolved features only
1 atom high on the surface of calcium-iridium-
tin ($CaIrSn_4$) crystals. A similar device had
been built earlier, and independently, by the
American physicist Russell Young at the United
States National Bureau of Standards, using a
somewhat different principle that yielded substantially lower resolution.

In developing the scanning tunneling microscope, the IBM team faced a formidable obstacle: they first had to eliminate all sources of vibrational noise. The vertical position of the scanning tip must be controllable to within a fraction of the diameter of an atom, owing to the sensitive dependence of the tunneling current on the distance between the sample surface and the tip. Street noises and even footsteps can jar the delicate operation of the instrument. Binnig and Rohrer initially attacked the problem by suspending the microscope with permanent magnets over a bowl of superconducting lead placed on a heavy stone table. They isolated the table itself from the laboratory building with inflated rubber tires. Piezoelectric materials, which contract or expand upon the application of voltages, were used to move the tip with great precision. Because of subsequent refinements, the scanning tunneling microscope can now resolve vertical features as small as 0.1 angstrom (1 hundred-billionth of a meter), or roughly one-tenth the diameter of a hydrogen atom. Lateral resolutions of 2 angstroms have resulted from scanning tips only a few atoms wide, and tips only 1 atom wide are being developed. Since its perfection, the scanning tunneling microscope has become a standard tool in many research laboratories. The instrument is effective in a variety of environments besides the vacuum, including air, water, and cryogenic fluids. It has been employed to study a variety of materials other than inorganic substances, including virus particles.

Binnig and Rohrer shared half of the 1986 Nobel Prize for Physics "for their design of the scanning tunneling microscope." The other half was awarded to ERNST RUSKA for his work on the electron microscope. In awarding the prize to Binnig and Rohrer, the Royal Swedish Academy of Sciences declared: "It is evident that this technique is one of exceptional promise, and that we have so far seen only the beginning of its development. Many research groups in different areas of science are now using the scanning tunneling microscope. The study of surfaces is an important part of physics, with particular applications in semiconductor physics and microelectronics. In chemistry, also, surface reactions play an important part, for example, in connection with catalysis. It is also possible to fixate organic molecules on a surface and study their structures. Among other applications, this technique has been used in the study of DNA molecules." In recalling his emotions upon learning about the award, Binnig remarked, "It was beautiful and terrible at the same time,"

because while it signaled a great success, it also concluded "an exciting story of discovery."

In 1969 Binnig married Lore Wagler, a psychologist; they have a daughter and a son.

Apart from research, Binnig's interests include skiing, soccer, tennis, golf, and sailing. A talented musician, he composes music, plays the violin and the guitar, and sings. Since 1986 he has been an IBM Fellow, the corporation's highest research position.

Binnig and Rohrer have shared other honors for their work in addition to the Nobel Prize. In 1984 they received the Hewlett-Packard Prize of the European Physical Society and the King Faisal International Prize in Science of the Saudi Arabian government for their efforts in scanning tunneling microscopy. Binnig is also the recipient of the Physics Prize of the German Physical Society (1982).

SELECTED WORKS: "The Scanning Tunneling Microscope," Scientific American August 1985, with Heinrich Rohrer.

ABOUT: New York Times October 16, 1986; Science November 14, 1986; Science News October 25, 1986.

BJØRNSON, BJØRNSTJERNE
(December 8, 1832–April 26, 1910)
Nobel Prize for Literature, 1903

The Norwegian poet, dramatist, novelist, and journalist Bjørnstjerne Martinius Bjørnson (byûrn' son) was the first of six sons born to Peder Bjørnson, a Lutheran pastor, and Elise (Nordraak) Bjørnson, a merchant's daughter. When Bjørnson was five years old, his family moved from their small mountain parish of Kvikne to the picturesque Romsdal district of western Norway, where he attended grammar school in the coastal city of Molde. A precocious child, he wrote poetry, edited a handwritten newspaper, and displayed an avid interest in politics.

In 1849 Bjørnson went to Christiania (now Oslo) to prepare for the university's entrance exams. There he met Henrik Ibsen and other Norwegian literary figures. Bjørnson entered the University of Oslo in 1852. However, upon coming of age the following year, he abandoned his formal studies and plunged into the city's political, theatrical, and literary life. Within two years his theater reviews and literary criticism were appearing in various newspapers, and he had mounted a campaign to develop a distinctive Norwegian theater.

BJØRNSTJERNE BJØRNSON

These activities brought him prominence as a leader in cultural affairs.

Bjørnson became the theater critic for *Morgenbladet,* the Oslo morning newspaper, in 1854. Two years later he began editing *Illustreret Folkeblad,* the periodical in which his folktales were first published. According to the critic Harald Larson, Bjørnson attended a student gathering in Sweden during the summer of 1856, where he "was overwhelmed by memories of the past and the sight of the garments, weapons, and tombs of the Swedish kings." Inspired to recreate his own country's history, he wrote "How I Became a Poet," an essay in which he pledged to create a Norwegian "ancestors' gallery" of historical dramas in order to encourage a sense of national pride.

Pursuing his commitment to theater, Bjørnson became director of the new Norske Theater in Bergen in 1857. The following year he married Karoline Reimers, an actress, with whom he had several children. One son, Bjørn, became a distinguished actor and director; and a daughter, Bergljot, married Ibsen's son Sigurd. While working in the theater, Bjørnson continued to write poetry, plays, and novellas; edited a Bergen newspaper; and took part in liberal politics. His lyric poem "Ja, vi elsker dette Landet" (Yes, We Love This Land), written in 1859, was later set to music as Norway's national anthem.

Returning to Oslo in 1859, Bjørnson edited *Aftenbladet,* a daily afternoon newspaper that he transformed into an organ of the new Liberal party. However, his liberal and reformist editorials proved so unpopular that he soon resigned. Between 1860 and 1863 he lived abroad, mostly in Italy. After his return to Oslo, he was appointed director of the Christiania Theater (1865–1867).

Until 1873 Bjørnson devoted most of his creative work to poetry, songs, folktales, novellas, and historical saga dramas. Like Ibsen's early work, these writings mainly concern the peasantry and medieval saga heroes of Norway. The lyrical novellas *Synnøve Solbakken* (1857, translated as *Sunny Hill*), *Arne* (*Arne,* 1859), and *En Glad Gut* (*A Happy Boy,* 1860), with their stylistic resemblance to Norwegian folktales of the oral tradition, depict the assimilation of the peasantry into modern society and conclude on a positive note. The influential Danish critic Georg Brandes commented in an 1886 essay that *A Happy Boy* was "like a refreshing breeze bringing deliverance from the brooding melancholy that oppresses the Norwegian mind." Nevertheless, rather than romanticizing the lives of these apparently joyous rural folk, Bjørnson sought to show that through their stoicism and love of adventure, they were the spiritual successors to the often-doomed heroes of his historic tragedies who struggled to reconcile paganism with Christianity.

Bjørnson withdrew his first play, *Valborg,* from production because he thought it trivial; instead, he launched his career as a playwright with *Mellem Slagene* (Between the Battles, 1857), a drama set in twelfth-century Norway. It was followed by the historical plays *Halte Hulda* (*Lame Hulda,* 1858), *Kong Sverre* (*King Sverre,* 1861), *Sigurd Slembe* (*Sigurd the Bad,* 1863), and *Maria Stuart i Skotland* (*Mary Stuart in Scotland,* 1864). *Sigurd the Bad,* a trilogy about an obscure pretender to the medieval throne, is considered the best of Bjørnson's saga plays and has been compared with Ibsen's *The Pretenders,* also written in 1863.

During the late 1860s Bjørnson's poetic powers reached their peak; he wrote little poetry after 1870. In that year, he published *Digte og Sange* (*Poems and Songs*), a collection of lyrics, many of which were later set to music. The short epic poem *Arnljot Gelline,* fifteen cantos in length, was also published in 1870. This work, which was published in English under the same title, was praised by the critic Georg Brandes as "unsurpassed for the beauty of its description of nature." Yet it was Brandes, fired by the new social concepts of Charles Darwin, John Stuart Mill, Charles Augustin Sainte-Beuve, and Hippolyte Taine, who persuaded Bjørnson to change his course. In a series of lectures delivered at Copenhagen in 1871, Brandes exhorted Scandinavian writers to put aside romantic and nationalistic notions in favor of a realistic treatment of human problems, and Bjørnson soon heeded his call.

While living in Rome between 1873 and 1876, Bjørnson turned from folk themes to social criticism. An ardent advocate of Norway's cultural and political independence from Sweden, he moved toward pan-Scandinavianism and campaigned for international civil rights and world peace. Although Bjørnson viewed Christianity as a positive and life-affirming religion, he ultimately rejected the divinity of Christ and openly criticized the Lutheran church for its creationist view of evolution and its stress on sin and damnation. Bjørnson's views caused pious Norwegians to condemn him as a heretic. Largely as a result of this condemnation, he spent long periods abroad, including a visit to the United States in 1881. In 1893 Bjørnson settled on a farm in Norway, from which he frequently traveled to Denmark, France, Germany, and Italy.

Bjørnson was the first Norwegian to write plays that addressed serious social problems, a genre that Ibsen was to develop further. *En fallit* (*A Bankruptcy,* 1875) dramatized the effects of dishonest business practices, a subject previously considered taboo for serious drama. *Redaktøren* (*The Editor,* 1875) dealt with the repercussions of sensational journalism. The dramatic poem *Kongen* (*The King,* 1877), an odd mixture of comedy and melodrama, attacked the monarchy and church dogma.

In the 1880s Bjørnson produced the best of his then controversial "problem" plays, beginning with *En handske* (*The Gauntlet,* 1883), which challenges the double standard of sexual morality for men and women. *Over Ævne, I* (*Beyond Our Power, Part I,* 1886), a poignant study of a faith-healing pastor who may have deliberately failed to save his own wife, proposes that morality and common decency outweigh formal religious observance. This popular drama was produced throughout Europe and presented in New York, where it starred Mrs. Patrick Campbell. Bjørnson satirizes his own crusading preoccupations in *Geografi og kjærlighed* (*Love and Geography,* 1885).

In 1884 Bjørnson wrote the realistic novel *Det Flager i Byen og på havnen* (*Flags Are Flying in Town and Port*), which was published as *The Heritage of the Kurts* in 1892. This novel presents an uneven account of sex education in a girls' school. Another realistic novel, *På Guds Veje* (*In God's Way,* 1889), is a trenchant analysis of the conflict between science and religion. These works, according to the English critic Edmund Gosse, are "well executed in detail and full of valuable and exact observation of human life."

Bjørnson was awarded the 1903 Nobel Prize for Literature "as a tribute to his noble, magnificent, and versatile poetry, which has always been distinguished by both the freshness of its inspiration and the rare purity of its spirit" and as a reward for his achievements as "a great epic and dramatic writer." In his acceptance speech he discussed the writer's responsibility to delineate between good and evil: "The old ideas of right and wrong . . . have played their part in every field of our life; they are part of our search for knowledge and our thirst for life itself. . . . It is the purpose of all art to disseminate these ideas."

In 1910, a year after the production and publication of his last drama, *Nar den ny vin blomstrer* (*When the New Wine Blooms*), Bjørnson died in Paris at the age of seventy-seven. His collected works were published in a nine-volume edition in 1919.

According to the Norwegian-born American critic Hjalmar Hjorth Boyesen, writing in 1873, Bjørnson "saw in the rugged Norwegian peasant the true type of the national greatness, and pressing his ear close to the nation's heart, he heard the throbs of its hidden emotions. And when he raised his voice and sang, every Norseman felt as if the voice were his own." Although in his own time he was regarded as an equal of Ibsen, today Bjørnson is better known and more highly regarded for his poetry and folktales than for his plays. The power of his poems, wrote the twentieth-century British critic James Walter McFarlane, lies "in the directness and forcefulness of their altruism, in the simple and moving enunciation of the homelier emotions" as well as in their lyricism and patriotic appeal. Comparing Bjørnson with Ibsen (who never received a Nobel Prize), the British critic Brian W. Downs remarked that "posterity, on the whole, has come down on the side of Ibsen . . . [who] . . . remains a great power in the whole Republic of Letters. The same cannot be said of Bjørnson . . . [even though] . . . Bjørnson's work almost always commands attention."

ADDITIONAL WORKS IN ENGLISH TRANSLATION: The Fisher-Maiden, 1869; The Newly Married Couple, 1870; Life by the Fells and Fjords, 1879; The Bridal March and Other Stories, 1882; Captain Mansana and Other Stories, 1882; Pastor Sang, 1893; Magnhild and Dust, 1897; Absalom's Hair and a Painful Memory, 1898; Paul Lange and Tora Parsberg, 1899; Laboremus, 1901; Wise-Knut,

BLACKETT

1909; Mary, 1909; Leonarda, 1911; Three Dramas, 1914; Land of the Free, 1978.

ABOUT: Beyer, H. A History of Norwegian Literature, 1956; Brandes, G. Henrik Ibsen, Bjørnstjerne Bjørnson: Critical Studies, 1899; Brandes, G. Creative Spirits of the Nineteenth Century, 1923; Downs, B. Modern Norwegian Literature 1860–1918, 1966; Gosse, E. The Novels of Bjørnstjerne Bjørnson, 1894; Koht, H., and Skard, S. The Voice of Norway, 1944; Larson, H. Bjørnstjerne Bjørnson, 1944; McFarlane, J. W. Ibsen and the Temper of Norwegian Literature, 1960; Payne, W. M. Bjørnstjerne Bjørnson, 1832–1910, 1910; Phelps, W. L. Essays on Modern Novelists, 1910; Scandinavica May 1965.

P. M. S. BLACKETT

BLACKETT, P. M. S.

(November 18, 1897–July 13, 1974)
Nobel Prize for Physics, 1948

The English physicist Patrick Maynard Stuart Blackett was born in London, the only son among the three children of Arthur Stuart Blackett, a stockbroker, and the former Caroline Frances Maynard. At the age of nine, Blackett began attending a small preparatory school in London. Then, in anticipation of a naval career, he entered Osborne Royal Naval College in 1910 and Dartmouth Royal Naval College in 1912, where he was ranked at the top of his class.

With the outbreak of World War I in 1914, Blackett began active naval duty as a midshipman on H.M.S. *Carnarvon*. He took part in the battles of the Falkland Islands and Jutland, and was appointed lieutenant a few months before the armistice in 1918. After the war, under naval orders, he began a six-month course of general studies at Magdalene College, Cambridge. He resigned his commission in 1919 and enrolled at Cambridge to study physics, graduating in 1921 with a B.A.

A fellowship enabled him to remain at Cambridge to work under ERNEST RUTHERFORD in the university's Cavendish Laboratory, a leading center for the study of radioactivity and atomic structure. There he used the cloud chamber invented by C. T. R. WILSON to investigate the bombardment of nitrogen atoms with alpha particles (helium nuclei). The cloud chamber is a transparent-walled cylinder filled with a supersaturated vapor and placed between the poles of an electromagnet. Charged particles passing through the vessel create ions on which vapor condenses, producing visible vapor trails that can be photographed. Blackett sought to discover the nature of the end products of the alpha particle–nitrogen atom interaction. In 1924, after he had examined more than 25,000 photographic plates, Black-

ett showed that the collision of an alpha particle with a nitrogen atom results in a hydrogen nucleus (a proton) and an isotope of oxygen, thus confirming Rutherford's expectation that one element can be artificially transmuted into another.

Blackett took a leave of absence from Cambridge in 1924–1925 to study quantum physics and spectral analysis under JAMES FRANCK at the University of Göttingen in Germany. On his return, he continued to do research at the Cavendish, and in 1930 he became a lecturer.

In 1932 Blackett and the Italian physicist Giuseppe P. S. Occhialini began to investigate cosmic rays. To construct a countercontrolled cloud chamber, they placed a pair of Geiger counters (one above the chamber and one below), with an electrical relay that triggered the photographing of the track produced by any charged particle passing through the chamber. This system replaced one of photographing at discrete intervals, which was much less efficient in recording particle tracks in the chamber. Within a year, Blackett and Occhialini observed the vapor trails of the positron, a positively charged particle with a mass equal to that of the electron, thus confirming the discovery of the positron several months earlier by the American physicist CARL D. ANDERSON. Furthermore, they were the first to observe that positrons and electrons usually occur as pairs, in "showers."

In their study of the emissions produced by radioactive substances, Blackett and Occhialini noted that showers of positron-electron pairs apparently arose from gamma rays (radiation of short wavelength emanating from the nucleus). Since positrons do not normally exist on earth, they reasoned that the transformation of gamma radiation into positron-electron pairs must satisfy ALBERT EINSTEIN's relationship equating mass and energy ($E = mc^2$). In this way, Blackett and Occhialini offered the first experimental confirmation of Einstein's equation, in the instance in which energy is transformed into matter.

After leaving Cambridge in 1933 to become professor of physics at Birkbeck College, the evening college of the University of London, Blackett continued his cosmic-ray research. In 1935–1936 he served on the Tizard Committee, created by the Air Ministry to improve Great Britain's air defense against the growing menace of the German Luftwaffe. In 1937 Blackett succeeded W. L. BRAGG as Langworthy Professor of Physics at the University of Manchester. Within a year, he replaced most of the staff and faculty in the physics department, which had worked on Bragg's specialty of X-ray crystallography, with staff and faculty from Birkbeck College, because he wanted their help on further cosmic-ray research.

World War II took Blackett out of the university laboratory. As principal scientific officer in the instrument section of the Royal Aircraft Establishment, he worked to improve bombsights. Later, as scientific adviser to the Anti-Aircraft Command, he helped coordinate radar systems and antiaircraft guns. Both as scientific adviser to the British Coastal Command and, subsequently, as director of naval operational research at the Admiralty, Blackett's main task was to improve British antisubmarine warfare. Blackett's international reputation as a physicist led to his appointment to a subcommittee of the Committee for the Scientific Study of Air Warfare, under G. P. THOMSON. When the subcommittee (later called the Maud Committee) submitted a report to the government in 1941 urging Great Britain to produce an atomic bomb, Blackett was the only member who dissented. Convinced that the government lacked the means to complete the project quickly, he recommended that England join with the United States, which it did.

After the war, Blackett criticized the decision of the United States to drop atomic bombs on the Japanese cities of Hiroshima and Nagasaki, arguing that it was motivated by political rather than military reasons and was intended "as the first act of the cold diplomatic war with Russia now in progress." He expressed these views in his book *Military and Political Consequences of Atomic Energy,* which

appeared in 1948. After its publication, Blackett's role as a government adviser was sharply curtailed for many years.

Returning to Manchester, Blackett resumed his research on cosmic radiation. He also proposed a new theory linking the magnetic properties of the earth, sun, and stars, but declared the theory untenable several years later. He subsequently turned to a related topic, rock magnetism, the study of the magnetized material found in ancient rock formations. From measurements in this field, Blackett concluded that polar wandering and continental drift had occurred.

Blackett was awarded the 1948 Nobel Prize for Physics "for his development of the Wilson cloud-chamber method and his discoveries therewith in the fields of nuclear physics and cosmic radiation." On presenting the award, G. A. Ising of the Royal Swedish Academy of Sciences pointed out that "the immense value of the Wilson method for research purposes did not become really apparent until the early twenties, and the credit for this changed attitude was largely due to the work of Blackett."

Blackett resigned from Manchester in 1953 to succeed G. P. Thomson as head of the physics department of the Imperial College of Science and Technology in London. Two years later he also became dean of the Royal College of Sciences of the Imperial College, a position he held until 1960. In 1963 Blackett resigned to serve as adviser to the Labour party on science and technology. When the party won the general election of 1964, Blackett became chairman of the Advisory Council on Technology. He resigned from that post in 1965 to become president of the Royal Society.

During his later years, Blackett, who described himself as a Fabian Socialist, devoted much of his time and energies to political issues. Elected president of the Association of Scientific Workers, a component of the British Trades Union Council, in 1943, he declared that "the way [scientists] can best help in changing [society] is to throw in their lot with the organized working class, for it is they who, in the long run, stand to gain most from the widest possible application of science." He lectured extensively on science and its relation to society and served on numerous organizations, including the Council of the Overseas Development Institute, the 1963 United Nations Conference on the uses of science and technology for economic development, and the Council for Scientific Policy. After attending the Indian Science Congress Association in

1947, Blackett developed a keen interest in India's scientific efforts as well as its political and economic problems.

In 1924 Blackett married Costanza Bayon, with whom he had a son and a daughter. Tall, vigorous in manner and speech, Blackett was known for the enthusiasm he brought to a remarkable range of interests that included not only science but also political, social, and economic issues. He died in London on July 13, 1974.

Among his many awards and honors, Blackett received the Royal Medal (1940) and the Copley Medal (1956) of the Royal Society, the Medal for Merit of the United States government (1946), the Dalton Medal of the Manchester Literary and Philosophical Society (1949), and the Mexican government's Order of the Eagle of Aztec (1970). He was a member of ten foreign scientific societies and held twenty honorary degrees. In 1965 he was awarded the Order of Merit, and in 1969 he was made a life peer, Baron Blackett of Chelsea.

SELECTED WORKS: Cosmic Rays, 1936; Lectures on Rock Magnetism, 1956; Atomic Weapons and East-West Relations, 1956; Studies of War, Nuclear and Conventional, 1962; The Gap Widens, 1970; Reflections on Science and Technology in Developing Countries, 1970.

ABOUT: Biographical Memoirs of Fellows of the Royal Society, volume 21, 1975; Current Biography February 1949; Oxbury, H. (ed.) Great Britons, 1985.

BLOCH, FELIX

(October 23, 1905–September 10, 1983)
Nobel Prize for Physics, 1952
(shared with Edward M. Purcell)

The Swiss-American physicist Felix Bloch was born in Zurich to Gustav Bloch, a wholesale grain dealer, and Agnes (Mayer) Bloch. He attended the gymnasium of the canton of Zurich, graduating in 1924. Because of Bloch's interest in mathematics and astronomy, his father enrolled him at the Federal Institute of Technology in Zurich as an engineering student. However, after his first course in physics, Bloch decided to become a physicist rather than an engineer. From 1924 to 1927 he studied at the Federal Institute, where his teachers included PETER DEBYE and ERWIN SCHRÖDINGER. Bloch then went to the University of Leipzig to study with WERNER HEISENBERG. He was awarded a Ph.D. from Leipzig in 1928 for a thesis on the conduction of electrons in metals. In this thesis, which is recognized as the basis of the modern theory of solids, he

FELIX BLOCH

presented a theorem that specified the forms that electron wave functions take in metals (Bloch functions).

After completing his Ph.D., Bloch held numerous fellowships that allowed him to work with Heisenberg, NIELS BOHR, ENRICO FERMI, and WOLFGANG PAULI, and during this period he made major contributions to theoretical physics. Bloch theoretically derived the empirical law of the German physicist Eduard Grüneisen concerning the temperature dependence of the electrical conductivity of metals, now known as the Bloch-Grüneisen relationship. As a result of his contributions to the theory of superconductivity and to the theoretical understanding of magnetic systems, a number of other theorems and effects were named after him: the Bloch theory on superconductivity, the Bloch law concerning the temperature dependence of magnetization in a ferromagnetic material (a material whose atomic structure makes it highly magnetized, such as iron), and Bloch walls (the transition regions between areas of a ferromagnetic material with different magnetic orientations). In 1932 Bloch advanced the work of Bohr and HANS A. BETHE on the slowing down of moving charged particles in matter, determining the Bethe-Bloch expression for this effect.

When Hitler came to power in 1933, Bloch, who was Jewish, left Germany and settled in the United States. He became an associate professor at Stanford University in 1934, and two years later he was named a full professor there. During this period he made contributions to the quantum theory of the electromagnetic field. He then investigated the properties of the recently discovered neutron, predicting that its magnetic moment (a measure of magnetic strength) could be observed by scattering slow neutrons in iron and that the neutron beam would be polarized after scattering off an iron target. These predictions were confirmed the following year. Bloch then turned to experimental research. In 1939 he and LUIS W. ALVAREZ measured the magnetic moment of a neutron using the cyclotron at the University of California at Berkeley as a neutron source. During World War II, as a member of the Manhattan Project to develop an atomic bomb, Bloch investigated the properties of uranium isotopes. He later became an associate group leader in war-related counter-radar research at the Harvard University Radio Research Laboratory.

After the war Bloch returned to Stanford University. There he applied the radio-wave techniques he had learned during his wartime work on radar to the study of nuclear magnetic moments. Physicists who were attempting to understand the behavior of the atomic nucleus needed to know the relative magnetic moments of various kinds of nuclei to a very high degree of precision. In the 1930s I. I. RABI had developed a technique for measuring nuclear magnetic moments, but his method, which required vaporizing the sample, was not very precise. In 1946 Bloch described a method of measurement that was both highly precise and completely nondestructive. Although Bloch is known among physicists for his many other achievements, it was the development of this technique that won him the Nobel Prize.

When an atom is in a magnetic field, the magnetic moment of its nucleus causes the nucleus to precess, an effect analogous to that of gravity when it causes a spinning top to wobble. The frequency, or rate, of nuclear precession depends on the strength of the magnetic field and on the magnetic moment of the nucleus. Thus, if the strength of the field is known and the precession frequency can be determined, the magnetic moment can be calculated. To determine the precession frequency, Bloch placed a sample of the material to be studied within the magnetic field of a powerful electromagnet, causing the nuclei in the sample to precess at a fixed rate. He then excited the sample with a much weaker magnetic field controlled by radio signals; this second field fluctuated (turned on and off) with a frequency corresponding to the frequency of the controlling radio waves. When the fluctuation frequency of the exciting field was equal to the precession frequency of the nuclei, the spin

orientation of the nuclei suddenly reversed, an easily detected effect called nuclear magnetic resonance (NMR). The known frequency of the radio signals corresponding to this resonance is the frequency of the nuclear precession. Knowing the exact precessional frequency of a given nucleus in a field of a given strength makes it possible to determine the nuclear magnetic moment of that nucleus with extraordinary precision. Bloch's technique provided precise and much-needed information to nuclear physicists, and it did so without affecting the sample in any perceptible way. Moreover, it provided a new and simple method for measuring magnetism: once the magnetic moment of a given nucleus was known, it could be used to determine the strength of any magnetic field.

At the same time, EDWARD M. PURCELL (who had also been involved with radar during the war) was investigating the same problem. Simultaneously and independently, he developed a technique for measuring nuclear magnetic moments that was nearly identical to Bloch's. Using NMR techniques, Purcell then found that hydrogen emits a radio-frequency signal, a discovery that led to the development of radio astronomy.

Researchers using NMR measurements found that the resultant magnetic moment of an atomic nucleus in a molecule is altered by the magnetic fields of surrounding electrons. Since these alterations are clues to molecular structure, NMR rapidly became one of the great analytic tools of chemistry. Furthermore, NMR measurement is so nondestructive that it can be used to study living organisms without damaging them. The techniques and computational approaches used for computer-assisted tomography (CAT) scanners (developed by ALLAN CORMACK and GODFREY HOUNSFIELD) were applied to NMR observation techniques in the 1970s, resulting in the development of NMR scanners that can image specific chemical reactions within the human body. Immediately recognized as extraordinary research tools, these scanners were also found to be powerful instruments for medical diagnostics. NMR diagnostic scanning equipment became commercially available to the medical community in the mid-1980s.

Bloch and Purcell were awarded the 1952 Nobel Prize for Physics "for their development of new methods for nuclear magnetic precision measurements and discoveries in connection therewith." In his presentation speech, Erik Hulthén of the Royal Swedish Academy of Sciences remarked that "the methods of Pur-

BLOCH

cell and Bloch imply a great simplification and generalization" of I. I. Rabi's molecular-ray method, "which enables their application to solid, liquid, and gaseous substances." Hulthén continued, "Since each kind of atom and its isotopes have a sharply defined and characteristic nuclear frequency, we can, in any object placed between the poles of an electromagnet, seek out and examine with radio waves all the various kinds of atoms and isotopes present in the object in question . . . without in any perceptible way affecting the sample." The application of their research in physics to developments in astronomy, chemistry, and medicine is an outstanding example of basic research having effects that go far beyond the field in which it was conducted.

Most of Bloch's research after 1946 was devoted to investigations utilizing NMR or, as he originally called it, "nuclear induction." In 1954–1955 Bloch took a two-year leave of absence from Stanford to serve as director-general of CERN (the European Organization for Nuclear Research) in Geneva, Switzerland. He was named Max H. Stein Professor of Physics at Stanford in 1963. After retiring in 1971, Bloch returned to Zurich, where he died on September 10, 1983.

In 1940 Bloch married Lore C. Misch, a physicist and a refugee from Germany, with whom he had three sons and a daughter. He became a United States citizen in 1939.

Bloch was a member of the National Academy of Sciences; the American Academy of Arts and Sciences; the Swiss Academy of Natural Science; and the American Physical Society, of which he was president in 1965.

ABOUT: Chodorow, M., et al. (eds.) Felix Bloch and Twentieth-Century Physics, 1980; Current Biography September 1954; National Cyclopedia of American Biography, supplement I, 1960.

BLOCH, KONRAD
(January 21, 1912–   )
Nobel Prize for Physiology or Medicine, 1964
(shared with Feodor Lynen)

The German-American biochemist Konrad Emil Bloch was born in Neisse, Germany (now Nysa, Poland), to Hedwig (Striemer) and Fritz Bloch. After receiving his early education in the local schools, he enrolled in 1930 in the technical university in Munich. While there, he studied chemistry under HANS FISCHER and attended lectures by ADOLF WINDAUS and

KONRAD BLOCH

HEINRICH WIELAND at the Chemical Society of Munich. Bloch received the equivalent of a B.S. in chemical engineering from the technical university in 1934, a year after Adolf Hitler became German chancellor. Bloch, who was Jewish, moved to Switzerland and found a position at the Swiss Research Institute in Davos. There he studied the biochemistry of phospholipids in tubercle bacilli, the bacteria that cause tuberculosis.

Bloch immigrated to the United States in 1936. With financial support from the Wallerstein Foundation, he began graduate studies in biochemistry at the College of Physicians and Surgeons at Columbia University in New York City. After receiving a Ph.D. in biochemistry from Columbia in 1938, Bloch joined the research group at the College of Physicians and Surgeons headed by Rudolf Schoenheimer. In Schoenheimer's laboratory, Bloch acquired experience in the use of radioisotopes and, as he said later, a "lasting interest in intermediary metabolism and the problems of biosynthesis." Radioisotopes are radioactive forms of atoms used experimentally to trace the course of specific molecules in cells and organisms. Intermediary metabolism involves the biochemical degradation of glucose (sugar) and fat molecules and the generation of cellular energy in the form of high-energy phosphate molecules, adenosine triphosphate (ATP), which drive other biochemical processes of the cell.

After Schoenheimer's death in 1941, his associate David Rittenberg and Bloch continued working on the biosynthesis of cholesterol.

104

Cholesterol is a lipid composed of twenty-seven carbon molecules arranged in four rings, with an eight-carbon side chain. Present in all animal cells, cholesterol stabilizes cell membrane structures and is the biochemical precursor of steroid hormones and bile acids. It is ingested in the diet and is also synthesized by liver and intestinal cells. Plaques, or deposits, that line blood vessels in association with some cardiovascular diseases such as atherosclerosis, contain cholesterol deposits. Using acetic acid labeled with hydrogen and carbon radioisotopes, Bloch and Rittenberg showed that acetate, a compound containing two carbon atoms, is the major biochemical building block of cholesterol.

In 1946 Bloch became assistant professor of biochemistry at the University of Chicago. He was subsequently appointed associate professor in 1948 and professor of biochemistry in 1950. At Chicago he continued his efforts to establish the origin of all carbon atoms of the cholesterol skeleton. Bloch and his colleagues used a mutant strain of the bread mold fungus *Neurospora crassa,* which depends on an outside source of acetate for its growth. By growing the fungus on a culture medium containing radioisotope-labeled acetate, Bloch showed that all carbon atoms of cholesterol originate in the two-carbon molecule of acetate. Bloch and his colleagues confirmed that in the intermediate steps the acetate molecules combine to form squalene, a thirty-carbon hydrocarbon. Squalene is then cyclized to lanosterol, a sterol found in wool fat, which in turn is converted to the twenty-seven-carbon cholesterol. The overall conversion of acetic acid to cholesterol occurs in thirty-six separate steps.

In other research, Bloch studied the biosynthesis of glutathione, a tripeptide important in protein metabolism. A tripeptide is a product formed by the union of three amino acids and contains two peptide groups. After a year as a Guggenheim Fellow at the Institute of Organic Chemistry in Zurich, Switzerland, Bloch was appointed Higgins Professor of Biochemistry in the Department of Chemistry at Harvard University in 1954.

FEODOR LYNEN at the University of Munich had discovered that the chemically active form of acetate is acetyl coenzyme A. (A coenzyme is a heat-stabilized, water-soluble portion of an enzyme.) Bloch and others then determined that acetyl coenzyme A, in a series of combinations, is converted in an irreversible step to mevalonic acid. Working independently, Bloch and Lynen proved that mevalonic acid is transformed into chemically active iso-prene (a hydrocarbon), from which the unsaturated hydrocarbon squalene and, finally, cholesterol are formed.

Prior to the investigations of Bloch and Lynen, little was known about the formation of cholesterol and fatty acids or about their interrelationships. There had been considerable speculation, however, about the correlation between atherosclerosis (a condition in which large- and medium-sized arteries are lined with deposits of lipids and cholesterol) and the amount of cholesterol and other fats in the diet and in blood. The research of Bloch and Lynen clarified the role of acetic acid as a building block for cholesterol and fatty acids. Bloch's discovery that cholesterol is a necessary constituent of all body cells—that it is a precursor of bile acids and one of the female sex hormones—was of fundamental importance. As a result of their work, it is now known that all substances of a steroid nature in the human body are formed from cholesterol.

Bloch was awarded the 1964 Nobel Prize for Physiology or Medicine, which he shared with Lynen "for their discoveries concerning the mechanisms and regulation of cholesterol and fatty acid metabolism." SUNE BERGSTRÖM of the Karolinska Institute said in his presentation speech, "The importance of the work of Bloch and Lynen lies in the fact that we now know the reactions that have to be studied in relation to inherited and other factors. We can now predict that through further research in this field . . . we can expect to be able to do individual specific therapy against the diseases that in the developed countries are the most common cause of death."

Bloch's marriage in 1941 to Lore Teutsch produced two children.

The recipient of the Fritzsche Award of the American Chemical Society (1964) and the Distinguished Service Award of the University of Chicago Medical Alumni Association (1964), Bloch is a member of the National Academy of Sciences, the American Academy of Arts and Sciences, the American Chemical Society, the American Society of Biological Chemists, and the American Philosophical Society.

SELECTED WORKS: Membranes, Molecules, Toxins, and Cells, 1981, with others.

ABOUT: New York Times October 16, 1964; Science March 6, 1964; October 23, 1964.

BLOEMBERGEN

BLOEMBERGEN, NICOLAAS
(March 11, 1920–   )
Nobel Prize for Physics, 1981
(shared with Arthur L. Schawlow and Kai
   Siegbahn)

NICOLAAS BLOEMBERGEN

The Dutch-American physicist Nicolaas
Bloembergen (blüm' bər gən) was born in
Dordrecht, the Netherlands, the second of six
children of Auke Bloembergen and the former
Sophia Maria Quint. His father had a degree
in chemical engineering and was an executive
with a Dutch fertilizer company. His mother,
the daughter of a school principal who had a
Ph.D. in mathematical physics, had an advanced degree to teach French but gave up a
career to rear her family. Raised in a conservative, disciplined, and intellectually stimulating atmosphere, the boy was encouraged
to read as well as to participate in outdoor
activities such as swimming, sailing, and ice
skating.

Shortly after the family moved to Bilthoven,
a suburb of Utrecht, Nicolaas began elementary school. At the age of twelve, he entered
the municipal gymnasium in Utrecht, a secondary school that emphasized the humanities
and prepared students for the university. Almost all his teachers held Ph.D. degrees. His
preference for science became apparent only
in the last few years when the basics of physics
and chemistry were taught.

In 1938 Bloembergen entered the University of Utrecht to study physics. "The choice
of physics," he wrote later, "was probably based
on the fact that I found it the most difficult
and challenging subject." After the German
occupation of the Netherlands in 1940, many
faculty members were dismissed or seized by
the Gestapo. Nevertheless, Bloembergen received the equivalent of an M.S. in 1943, just
before the Nazis closed the university. For the
next two years he eluded the Nazis, studying
quantum theory while in hiding. At the end
of the war, Europe had been devastated, so
Bloembergen applied to American universities and was accepted by the Harvard University graduate school in 1945. Supported by
his family, he continued his studies there, attending lectures by such leading physicists as
JULIAN S. SCHWINGER and JOHN H. VAN
VLECK.

Only six weeks before Bloembergen's arrival, EDWARD M. PURCELL and two colleagues had detected nuclear magnetic
resonance (NMR), the absorption and emission by the atomic nucleus of electromagnetic
energy at a high frequency related to the nu-

clear spin. The nucleus behaves as if it were
spinning like a top. Since it has a positive electric charge, its motion is equivalent to an electric current, which generates a magnetic field
similar to that created by the current in the
windings of an electromagnet. Nuclear magnetism, like all magnetism, has both strength
and direction, and interacts with electromagnetic fields from an outside source.

As Purcell's graduate assistant, Bloembergen helped develop early NMR instruments,
and in 1948 he, Purcell, and R. V. Pound published an influential paper on relaxation effects
in NMR, the return of nuclear magnetic orientations to their original condition after excitation by fields from an external source. This
return is affected by the surrounding structure
and reveals structural details. Much of the same
material appears in Bloembergen's doctoral
dissertation, which he submitted to the University of Leiden later that year, having gone
there in 1947 as a research fellow at the laboratory named for the Dutch physicist HEIKE
KAMERLINGH ONNES.

Returning to the United States in 1949,
Bloembergen was chosen to be a member of
the highly select Society of Fellows at Harvard. He became an associate professor there
in 1951 and a full professor in 1957. He was
named Rumford Professor of Physics at Harvard in 1974 and Gerhard Gade University
Professor in 1980.

In 1953 CHARLES H. TOWNES and two colleagues at Columbia University demonstrated
the first maser (*m*icrowave *a*mplification by
*s*timulated *e*mission of *r*adiation), a device that

produces intense, highly directional, monochromatic microwaves. Stimulated emission had been predicted by ALBERT EINSTEIN in 1917 on the basis of quantum theory and the NIELS BOHR model of the atom, as electrically negative electrons circling about a positively charged dense central nucleus. The electron motion was restricted to certain orbits (or energy levels) and could be excited from a lower level to a higher level by absorbing electromagnetic radiation. MAX PLANCK had shown that such radiation consisted of discrete bits, now called photons, and that the frequency was proportional to the energy in the photon. A photon absorbed by the atom had an energy equal to the difference between two of the atom's characteristic energy levels. An excited electron soon fell back to a lower level, emitting a photon of energy (and associated frequency) equal to the difference between the two levels. Normally, photons were emitted at random times and in random assortments. Einstein showed that, if atoms (or molecules, which also have energy levels but are more complicated than atoms) could be raised to a particular energy level and held there, radiation of appropriate photon energy (frequency) would then trigger their simultaneous fall to the lower level. The correct frequency and photon energy would correspond to the difference between the two energy levels. The result would be a cascade of photons all at the same time, the same frequency, and the same phase (point in a frequency cycle), producing a strong, coherent (all-in-phase) emission. Since a relatively small electromagnetic signal triggered a relatively large output of the same frequency, stimulated emission caused amplification.

Townes's maser used ammonia gas with two particular energy levels whose difference corresponded to photons of a microwave frequency. Drawing on his magnetic resonance work, Bloembergen, in 1956, proposed a three-level design principle that would allow the use of a solid material, such as a crystal. In his scheme, the crystal would be stimulated by radiation of an appropriate frequency to the highest of three particular energy levels. Natural relaxation would cause a drop to the next level, which would be the source of stimulated emission. Radiation of a frequency corresponding to the difference between the two lowest levels would then stimulate the emission of the desired radiation. ARTHUR L. SCHAWLOW later called Bloembergen's design the first really useful maser.

The first device to produce stimulated emission of visible light was constructed in 1960 by the American physicist Theodore H. Maiman and was called the laser (l for $l$ight). In the same year, Schawlow and others also built lasers. Both the maser and laser were developed independently during this period by NIKOLAI BASOV and ALEKSANDR PROKHOROV. In 1965 ARNO A. PENZIAS and ROBERT W. WILSON used a solid-state maser, a crystal of ruby, to detect cosmic background radiation, the remnant from the hypothetical big bang that gave birth to the universe.

Bloembergen is known as one of the founders of nonlinear optics, a field theory of the interaction of electromagnetic radiation and matter more general than that formulated in the nineteenth century by James Clerk Maxwell. According to Maxwell's theory, the effects on matter of visible light, or of any form of electromagnetic radiation, are straight-line functions of the intensity of the radiation.

In 1962 Bloembergen and three colleagues published a general theory of nonlinear optics, which Bloembergen subsequently enlarged. He made a significant contribution to laser design by showing that nonlinear optical behavior could give rise to harmonics, multiples of the fundamental frequency like overtones in sound, thus producing higher-frequency beams. By suggesting how three laser beams could interact to produce a fourth whose frequency can be controlled with great precision, Bloembergen also provided a theoretical basis for the tunable laser. Using tunable lasers, other researchers, notably Schawlow, developed sophisticated techniques of laser spectroscopy that revealed new, highly detailed information about the structure of atoms and molecules. In spectroscopy, laser beams excite atoms or molecules to higher energy levels than the lowest (ground) state. By noting which frequencies are preferentially absorbed or emitted, the spectroscopist can determine the characteristic energy levels, or structure, of the material under study. A precise knowledge of beam frequency, provided by the monochromatic (single-frequency) nature of laser light, and the ability to adjust the frequency to explore different levels permit a more accurate and detailed analysis.

"For their contribution to the development of laser spectroscopy" Bloembergen and Schawlow shared half of the 1981 Nobel Prize for Physics. The other half was awarded to KAI SIEGBAHN for electron spectroscopy using X rays. At the conclusion of his Nobel lecture, Bloembergen pointed out a few of the applications of nonlinear optical processes, including the development of "optical communications systems, . . . time and length metrology, . . . and information processing."

While attending a physics meeting in the Netherlands in 1948, Bloembergen met Huberta Deliana Brink, a premedical student who was a native of Indonesia. She followed him to the United States the following year as an exchange student, and Bloembergen "proposed to her the day she arrived." They were married in 1950 and have one son and two daughters. He became an American citizen in 1958. Described by one of his colleagues as "a sweet old Dutch gentleman," Bloembergen enjoys tennis, hiking, and skiing. The Bloembergens live in Lexington, Massachusetts.

In addition to the Nobel Prize, Bloembergen has received the Oliver Buckley Prize of the American Physical Society (1958), the Morris E. Liebmann Award of the Institute of Radio Engineers (1959), the Stuart Ballantine Medal of the Franklin Institute (1961), the National Medal of Science of the National Science Foundation (1974), and the Frederic Ives Medal of the Optical Society of America (1979). He is a member of the American Academy of Arts and Sciences, the National Academy of Sciences, and the Royal Dutch Academy of Sciences.

SELECTED WORKS: Nuclear Magnetic Relaxation, 1948; Nonlinear Optics, 1965; Nonlinear Spectroscopy, 1977.

ABOUT: New York Times October 20, 1981; Physics Today December 1981; Science November 6, 1981.

BLUMBERG, BARUCH S.

(July 28, 1925–   )
Nobel Prize for Physiology or Medicine, 1976
(shared with D. Carleton Gajdusek)

Baruch Samuel Blumberg, American physician and medical researcher, was born in New York City, the second of three children of Meyer Blumberg, a lawyer, and the former Ida Simonoff. After attending Far Rockaway High School in Brooklyn, he joined the United States Navy in 1943 and served on landing craft before he was assigned to study physics at Union College in Schenectady, New York. Having reached the rank of lieutenant, Blumberg received his naval discharge in 1946, the same year he obtained his B.S. from Union College and enrolled in the graduate mathematics program at Columbia University. On his father's

BARUCH S. BLUMBERG

advice, he switched to Columbia's College of Physicians and Surgeons the following year to study medicine.

After receiving his medical degree in 1951, Blumberg became an intern and assistant resident at Bellevue Hospital in Manhattan. He then worked for two years in the Arthritis Division at Columbia-Presbyterian Medical Center, where he researched the chemistry of hyaluronic acid, a major component of connective tissue, which holds together and supports structures in the body. From 1955 to 1957, Blumberg continued his study of hyaluronic acid, as a graduate student in biochemistry at Balliol College, Oxford. While there, he also began investigating human protein variation.

After receiving a Ph.D. in biochemistry from Oxford, Blumberg moved to the United States National Institutes of Health (NIH) in Bethesda, Maryland. There, as chief of the Section on Geographic Medicine and Genetics, he studied protein polymorphisms in human populations from all over the world. The British medical scientist Anthony C. Allison, a colleague of Blumberg's from Oxford, joined him at the NIH in 1960.

Blumberg had been interested in physiological differences among human populations since traveling to Suriname in 1957, when he had been struck by the variation in disease susceptibility among people from different ethnic groups. While finishing his research on hyaluronic acid at Oxford, he had learned up-to-date methods—most notably gel electrophoresis—for purifying and distinguishing proteins on the basis of minute chemical differences. He decided to use these techniques to discover differences (or polymorphisms) in the proteins of people of different genetic backgrounds.

The human immune system produces antibodies in response to the presence of foreign compounds, or antigens. Antibodies are much more sensitive to differences among proteins than were the chemical methods Blumberg and Allison had been using previously. The two scientists realized, however, that they could exploit the body's own machinery to detect polymorphisms they might have overlooked before. As Blumberg later recalled, "We decided to test the hypothesis that patients who received large numbers of transfusions might develop antibodies against one or more of the polymorphic serum proteins (either known or unknown) which they themselves had not inherited, but which the blood donors had."

For the study, Blumberg and Allison tested blood samples from patients with such blood diseases as hemophilia, anemia, or leukemia, which often require blood transfusions from dozens of different donors each year. Their goal was to determine whether antibodies in the blood would precipitate antigens from a variety of serums (the watery portion of blood that has clotted), representing blood samples from people of many different ethnic groups. Through these methods they were able to isolate variants of important serum proteins.

In 1963 they made an unexpected discovery. From the blood of a hemophilic patient in New York they isolated antibodies that reacted against only one serum in the panel—a specimen from an Australian aborigine. Although Blumberg and his colleagues were not surprised that the Australian, who was a member of a distinctive and isolated race, differed from their other test subjects, they could not explain how a New York hemophiliac had encountered the so-called Australia antigen, which had been assumed to be unique to aborigines.

After moving to the Institute for Cancer Research in Philadelphia in 1964, Blumberg continued his efforts to trace the distribution of the Australia antigen. He and his associates discovered that the occurrence of the antigen did not follow ethnic lines as closely as they had originally expected. If the Australia antigen was a polymorphism (or variant form) of a normal human protein, those who contracted it would retain it all their lives. Thus, when an antigen-negative patient at the institute became antigen-positive following an attack of liver disease, Blumberg realized he was dealing with a disease rather than a polymorphic protein. By 1967 Blumberg and his colleagues were sure that the Australia antigen was associated with the hepatitis B virus, which produces inflammation of the liver.

An epidemic of hepatitis B has been spreading in the United States since the 1960s, but the disease is even more common in other areas and infects approximately 100 million people worldwide. The hepatitis B virus, however, had never before been isolated. It does not grow in cultured cells, such as those developed by JOHN ENDERS for studying polio, nor does it infect any species other than the human being and the chimpanzee. Although it had been determined that hepatitis B could be spread by blood transfusion, before Blumberg's discovery there had been no way to tell whether a particular sample of blood was contaminated. Once Blumberg proved that Australia antigen and hepatitis B were linked, programs were established to screen blood banks for the virus, thus reducing one of the major risks associated with blood transfusions.

Preventing transfusion hepatitis was only the first important consequence of Blumberg's discovery. He and his associates had originally supposed that the Australia antigen was a human genetic polymorphism because people who were once antigen-positive remained antigen-positive. Most people who are infected with hepatitis B develop antibodies that protect against the outer protein coat of the virus (the surface antigen HBsAg) and thus overcome the disease. About 1 out of every 100 patients, however, becomes a carrier. Although carriers appear to be healthy, they produce the virus and HBsAg for decades after their original infection.

"It occurred to us that the existence of the carrier state provided an unusual method for the production of a vaccine," Blumberg later said, by making it possible to obtain "the immunizing antigen directly from the blood of human carriers of the virus." The HBsAg, without the virus, was subsequently purified from hepatitis B carriers, and it proved to be a safe, effective vaccine. This natural hepatitis vaccine, which was first sold in 1982, is extremely expensive because the raw materials come only from a small subset of all hepatitis patients. Blumberg's success, however, inspired the development of hepatitis vaccines based on HBsAg and produced by genetically engineered bacteria.

Blumberg shared the 1976 Nobel Prize for Physiology or Medicine with D. CARLETON GAJDUSEK "for their discoveries concerning new mechanisms for the origin and dissemination of infectious diseases." In addition to his research on hepatitis carriers, Blumberg has gathered evidence that hepatitis B infection may lead to liver cancer. Throughout his career, Blumberg has drawn on many disciplines, and he typifies an era of biomedical science in which the fields of immunology, virology, genetics, biochemistry, and molecular biology overlap to provide answers to research problems. Since 1964, Blumberg has been associate director for clinical research at the Institute for Cancer Research in Philadelphia. In 1977 he was also named professor of medicine and anthropology at the University of Pennsylvania, and during 1983–1984 he was George Eastman Visiting Professor at Oxford.

Blumberg married Jean Liebesman, an artist, in 1954; they have four children.

In addition to the Nobel Prize, he has received numerous awards for his work, including the Eppinger Prize from the University of Freiburg (1973) and the Passano Award in Medical Science of the Passano Foundation (1974).

SELECTED WORKS: Australia Antigen and the Biology of Hepatitis B, 1977.

ABOUT: Current Biography November 1977; New Scientist October 21, 1976; New York Times October 19, 1969; October 15, 1976; Science November 26, 1976.

AAGE BOHR

BOHR, AAGE

(June 19, 1922–)
Nobel Prize for Physics, 1975
(shared with Ben R. Mottelson and James Rainwater)

The Danish physicist Aage Niels Bohr (bōr) was born in Copenhagen, the fourth of six sons of Margrethe (Nørlund) and NIELS BOHR. Growing up at the Institute for Theoretical Physics (now the Niels Bohr Institute) in Copenhagen, which his father directed, the boy met many of the world's leading physicists. After attending the Sortedam Gymnasium, he began studying physics at the University of Copenhagen in 1940, the same year that German forces occupied Denmark. Faced with imminent arrest by the Gestapo in 1943, Niels Bohr fled to Sweden, where he was joined by the rest of the family. Aage then accompanied his father to England and later to the United States, where the elder Bohr played a major role in the Manhattan Project to develop the

atomic bomb. At the Los Alamos Scientific Laboratory in New Mexico, Aage Bohr served as his father's secretary and general assistant.

When World War II ended, the Bohrs returned to Denmark. After completing his M.S. at the University of Copenhagen in 1946, Aage Bohr became a research assistant at the Institute for Theoretical Physics. He returned to the United States in 1949 to work at the Institute for Advanced Study in Princeton, New Jersey, and to conduct research at Columbia University. At Columbia, I. I. RABI stimulated Bohr's interest in the hyperfine structure of deuterium (a splitting in the lines of the atomic spectrum), and Bohr remained there until 1950 to pursue theoretical research. During this time he shared an office with JAMES RAINWATER, with whom he discussed the fundamental structure of the atomic nucleus.

Bohr and Rainwater were dissatisfied with the two prevailing models of the atomic nucleus. One of them, the liquid-drop model, had been put forward in 1936 by Bohr's father. It proposed that protons and neutrons (collectively called nucleons) are held together by nuclear forces in much the same way that water molecules are held together in a raindrop. The liquid-drop theory offered a satisfactory explanation for such phenomena as fission, but it could not account for certain other properties of the nucleus, most notably its spectrum of excited states.

The second model was proposed in 1949 by MARIA GOEPPERT MAYER and J. HANS D. JENSEN. Called the shell model, it described the movement of nucleons in independent concentric orbits, or shells, within the nucleus, by analogy with the shells of electrons in an atom. According to the shell model, it is the sum of all forces exerted by the nucleons that governs the behavior of each individual nucleon. The result is a so-called force field, which Mayer and Jensen believed to be spherical. The validity of this model was challenged by experimental evidence showing that the distribution of electric charge surrounding some nuclei is not spherical.

After hearing a lecture by CHARLES H. TOWNES in 1949, Rainwater realized that the orbiting shells might be subject to distortions caused by centrifugal forces. Similar ideas had occurred to Bohr, and upon his return to Copenhagen in 1950 Bohr and BEN R. MOTTELSON began collaborating in an effort to arrive at a new description of nuclear matter. Drawing on Rainwater's insight, they forged a synthesis uniting the liquidlike properties of the nucleus with its shell structure. The result was called the collective model.

In the collective model, the surface of the nucleus behaves like that of a liquid drop, but the shell structure is subject to deformations that appear on the surface as oscillations and rotations. With a full outer shell of nucleons, Bohr and Mottelson said, the nucleus is spherical; with an incomplete outer shell, it is distorted into a shape resembling a football. In such distorted nuclei, they predicted, new modes of vibration and rotation would be observed, including surface waves and "breathing" oscillations in nuclear size.

The collective model enabled Bohr and Mottelson not only to calculate the likely properties of deformed nuclei but also to confirm Rainwater's hypothesis. They reported their results in 1953. The following year, Bohr received his Ph.D. from the University of Copenhagen, and in 1956 he was appointed professor of physics.

After his father's death in 1962, Bohr was named director of the Institute for Theoretical Physics, a position he retained until he resigned in 1970 to resume active research. He became director of the Nordic Institute for Theoretical Atomic Physics (Nordita) in 1975.

Bohr, Mottelson, and Rainwater shared the 1975 Nobel Prize for Physics "for the discovery of the connection between collective motion and particle motion in atomic nuclei and the development of the theory of the structure of the atomic nucleus based on this connection." In his Nobel lecture Bohr called his work with Mottelson "an important testing ground for many of the general ideas on nuclear dynamics." Response to these ideas, he said, "has played a prominent role in the development of dynamic concepts ranging from celestial mechanics to the spectra of elementary particles."

After receiving the Nobel Prize, Bohr continued theoretical research at Nordita until his retirement in 1981. He married Marietta Bettina Soffer in 1950; they had two sons and one daughter. Three years after the death of his first wife in 1978, Bohr married Bente Meyer. Bohr, who enjoys listening to classical music, has advocated international cooperation in scientific research, calling it "a vital factor in the development of science itself" as well as "a means to strengthen the mutual knowledge and understanding between nations."

Bohr's other awards include the Dannie Heineman Prize of the American Physical Society (1960), the Atoms for Peace Award established by the Ford Motor Company Fund (1969), the Rutherford Medal of the Institute of Physics in London (1972), and the John Price Wetherill Medal of the Franklin Institute (1974). He has received honorary degrees from the universities of Oslo, Heidelberg, Trondheim, Manchester, and Uppsala. He is a member of the science academies of Denmark, Norway, Sweden, Poland, Finland, and Yugoslavia and holds membership in the American Academy of Arts and Sciences, the American Philosophical Society, and the American National Academy of Sciences, as well as other professional societies.

SELECTED WORKS: Collective and Individual Particle Aspects of Nuclear Structure, 1953, with Ben R. Mottelson; Rotational States of Atomic Nuclei, 1954; Nuclear Structure (2 vols.) 1969–1975, with Ben R. Mottelson.

ABOUT: New York Times October 18, 1975; Physics Today December 1975; Science November 28, 1975.

BOHR, NIELS

(October 7, 1885–November 18, 1962)
Nobel Prize for Physics, 1922

The Danish physicist Niels Henrik David Bohr (bōr) was born in Copenhagen, the second of three children of Christian and Ellen (Adler) Bohr. His father was an eminent professor of physiology at the University of Copenhagen; his mother came from a Jewish family well known in banking, political, and intellectual circles. Their home was the center of much lively discussion of the scientific and philosophical issues of the day, and throughout his life Bohr concerned himself with the philosophical implications of his work. He attended the Gammelholm Grammar School in Copenhagen and graduated in 1903. He and his brother, Harald, who became a noted mathematician, were enthusiastic soccer players during their school years; later Niels took up skiing and sailing.

As a physics student at the University of Copenhagen, from which he received a B.S. in 1907, Bohr was recognized as an unusually perceptive investigator. His undergraduate project, in which he determined the surface tension of water from the vibration of a water jet, won him a gold medal from the Royal Danish Academy of Sciences. He received an M.S. from Copenhagen in 1909. His doctoral dissertation on the theory of electrons in metals was judged to be a masterful theoretical study. Among other things, it revealed the inability of the classical theory of electrodynamics to account for magnetism in metals. This study made Bohr aware at an early stage in his research that classical theory could not fully describe the behavior of electrons.

After receiving his Ph.D. in 1911, Bohr went to Cambridge University in England to study with J. J. THOMSON, who had discovered the electron in 1897. Thomson's attention had since turned to other topics, however, and he showed little interest in Bohr's dissertation and its implications. In the meantime, Bohr had become interested in the work of ERNEST RUTHERFORD at the University of Manchester. Rutherford and his colleagues were studying radioactive elements and the problem of atomic structure. Bohr moved to Manchester for a few months early in 1912 and threw himself energetically into this research. He worked out many of the implications of Rutherford's nuclear model of the atom, which had not yet gained wide acceptance. In his discussions with Rutherford and others, Bohr explored ideas that led to his own future model of atomic structure.

In the summer of 1912 Bohr returned to Copenhagen and was appointed assistant professor of physics at the University of Copenhagen. That year he married Margrethe Nørlund. They subsequently had six sons, one of whom, AAGE BOHR, also became a noted physicist.

Over the next two years Bohr continued to work on the problems raised by the nuclear model of the atom. Rutherford had proposed in 1911 that an atom consists of a positively

NIELS BOHR

charged nucleus orbited by negatively charged electrons. The model was based on solid experimental evidence, but it presented a troubling paradox. According to the principles of classical electrodynamics, an orbiting electron should continuously lose energy by giving off light or some other form of electromagnetic radiation. As the electron's energy was dissipated, it would be expected to spiral into the nucleus, and the atom would collapse. Actually, atoms are quite stable, and so there must be some flaw in the classical theory. Bohr was especially interested in this apparent failure of classical physics because it so closely resembled the difficulties he had encountered in his thesis research. A possible resolution of the paradox, he believed, might lie in a quantum theory.

In 1900 MAX PLANCK had proposed that the electromagnetic radiation given off by hot matter is not emitted in a continuous stream, but in discrete chunks of well-defined energy. Naming these units quanta in 1905, ALBERT EINSTEIN had extended the theory to account for the emission of electrons, when light is absorbed by some metals (photoelectric effect). Applying the new quantum theory to the problem of atomic structure, Bohr suggested that electrons have certain allowed stable orbits in which they do not radiate energy. It is only when an electron jumps from one orbit to another that it gains or loses energy, and then the gain or loss is always precisely equal to the energy difference between the two orbits. The idea that a particle could have only certain orbits was revolutionary, since according to classical theory it should be able to orbit at any distance from the nucleus, just as a planet could, in principle, have any orbit around the sun.

Although Bohr's model seemed strange and somewhat mysterious, it suggested solutions to problems that had long puzzled physicists. In particular, it offered a clue to the baffling spectra of the elements. When light from a glowing element (such as a heated gas of hydrogen atoms) is passed through a prism, it does not produce a continuous spectrum including all colors, but rather a sequence of discrete bright lines separated by wider dark regions. According to Bohr's theory, each bright line of color (that is, each distinct wavelength) represents light emitted by electrons as they jump from a specific allowed orbit to another orbit of lower energy. Bohr derived a formula for the frequencies of the lines in the hydrogen spectrum, obtaining an expression that involved Planck's constant. The frequency times Planck's constant is equal to the energy difference between the initial and final orbits, between which the electrons make a transition. Bohr's theory, published in 1913, established his reputation; his atomic model became known as the Bohr atom.

Immediately recognizing the importance of Bohr's work, Rutherford offered him a lectureship at the University of Manchester, a position Bohr held from 1914 to 1916. In 1916 Bohr accepted a professorship created for him at the University of Copenhagen, where he continued to work on atomic structure. In 1920 he founded the Institute for Theoretical Physics in Copenhagen; except for his absence from Denmark during World War II, he directed the institute for the rest of his life. Under Bohr's leadership, the institute played a major role in the development of quantum mechanics (the mathematical description of the wave and particle aspects of matter and energy). During the 1920s Bohr's model of the atom was superseded by a more complex quantum-mechanical model based largely on the work of his students and colleagues. Nevertheless, the Bohr atom had provided the essential bridge between the world of atomic structure and the world of quantum theory.

Bohr was awarded the 1922 Nobel Prize for Physics "for his services in the investigation of the structure of atoms and of the radiation emanating from them." In his presentation speech SVANTE ARRHENIUS of the Royal Swedish Academy of Sciences noted that Bohr's discoveries had "compelled him to make use of theoretical ideas that substantially diverge from those which are based on the classical doctrines of [James Clerk] Maxwell." Arrhenius added that the principles Bohr established "promise abundant fruit for the work of the future."

Bohr wrote extensively on the problems of epistemology raised by modern physics. During the 1920s he made pivotal contributions to what was later called the Copenhagen interpretation of quantum mechanics. Based on WERNER HEISENBERG's uncertainty principle, the Copenhagen interpretation holds that rigid laws of cause and effect familiar in the everyday, macroscopic world do not apply to subatomic phenomena, which can be understood only in terms of probability. For example, the path of an electron cannot be predicted in advance, even in principle; instead, probabilities must be assigned to all possible paths.

Bohr also formulated two of the fundamental principles that guided the development of quantum mechanics: the correspondence principle and the complementarity principle. The correspondence principle states that quantum-mechanical descriptions of the macroscopic world must correspond to the descriptions of classical mechanics. The complementarity principle states that the wavelike and the particlelike character of matter and radiation are mutually exclusive properties, although both descriptions are necessary components of an understanding of nature. Either wavelike or particlelike behavior may be exhibited in an experiment of a given type, but mixtures of the two behaviors are never observed. Accepting the coexistence of two apparently conflicting descriptions requires dispensing with visual models, an idea Bohr expressed in his Nobel lecture. In dealing with the subatomic world, he said, "we must be modest in our demands and content ourselves with concepts that are formal in the sense that they do not provide a visual picture of the sort one is accustomed to require."

During the 1930s Bohr turned to nuclear physics. ENRICO FERMI and his collaborators were studying the effects of bombarding atomic nuclei with neutrons. Bohr and others proposed a liquid-drop model of the nucleus that accounted for many of the observed reactions. This model, in which the behavior of an unstable heavy atomic nucleus is compared to a rupturing drop of liquid, provided the theoretical basis for understanding nuclear fission, identified in late 1938 by Otto R. Frisch and Lise Meitner. The discovery of fission on the eve of World War II led to immediate speculation about its potential for releasing massive amounts of energy. During a visit to Princeton in early 1939, Bohr determined that one of the two common isotopes of uranium, uranium 235, is a fissile material, a finding that was essential to the development of the atomic bomb.

During the early years of the war, Bohr continued to work on the theoretical details of fission in Copenhagen, despite the Nazi occupation of Denmark. In 1943, however, warned of his impending arrest, Bohr and his family fled to Sweden. From there, Bohr and his son Aage were flown to England in the empty bomb rack of a British military plane. Although Bohr had regarded an atomic bomb as technologically unfeasible, work on such a bomb was already underway in the United States, and the Allied powers sought his help. In late 1943 Niels and Aage Bohr went to Los Alamos to work on the Manhattan Project. The senior Bohr made technical contributions to the development of the bomb, and he served as an elder statesman to the many scientists there; however, his main concern during the last years of the war was the implications of the atomic bomb for the future. He met with President Franklin D. Roosevelt and Prime Minister WINSTON CHURCHILL in an effort to persuade them to be open with the Soviets about the new weapon, and he urged the establishment of a system of arms control after the war. His efforts were not successful, however.

After the war, Bohr returned to the Institute for Theoretical Physics, which expanded under his leadership. He helped found CERN (the European Organization for Nuclear Research) and was active in its research program throughout the 1950s. He also participated in the establishment of the Nordic Institute for Theoretical Atomic Physics (Nordita) in Copenhagen, a joint program of the Scandinavian governments. During these years Bohr continued to press for peaceful uses of nuclear energy and to warn against the dangers of nuclear weapons. In 1950 he sent an open letter to the United Nations repeating his wartime plea for an "open world" and international arms control. For his efforts he received the first Atoms for Peace Award from the Ford Motor Company Fund in 1957.

Upon reaching the mandatory retirement age of seventy in 1955, Bohr retired as a professor at the University of Copenhagen but remained as head of the Institute for Theoretical Physics. In his later years he continued to contribute to developments in quantum physics, and he took great interest in the new field of molecular biology.

A tall man with a keen sense of humor, Bohr was known for his great personal warmth and hospitality. "Bohr's kind interests in people made the personal relations in his institute very much like those in a family," JOHN COCKCROFT recalled in a biographical memoir of Bohr. "What is so marvelously attractive about Bohr as a scientific thinker," Einstein once said, "is his rare blend of boldness and caution; seldom has anyone possessed such an intuitive grasp of hidden things combined with such a strong critical sense. He is unquestionably one of the greatest discoverers in our age in the scientific field." Bohr died November 18, 1962, at his home in Copenhagen, following a stroke.

Bohr was a member of more than twenty major scientific societies, and he served as president of the Royal Danish Academy of Sciences from 1939 until his death. In addition to the Nobel Prize, he received the highest honors of many of the world's major scientific societies, including the Max Planck Medal of the German Physical Society (1930) and the Copley Medal of the Royal Society of London (1938). He was the recipient of many honorary degrees from major universities, including Cambridge, Manchester, Oxford, Edinburgh, the Sorbonne, Princeton, McGill, Harvard, and Rockefeller.

SELECTED WORKS: On the Quantum Theory of Line Spectra (3 vols.) 1918–1922; The Effect of Electric and Magnetic Fields on Spectral Lines, 1922; The Theory of Spectra and Atomic Constitution, 1922; Atomic Theory and the Description of Nature, 1934; On the Transmutation of Atomic Nuclei by Impact of Material Particles, 1937, with Fritz Kalckar; The Penetration of Atomic Particles Through Matter, 1948; The Unity of Knowledge, 1955; Atomic Physics and Human Knowledge, 1958; On the Constitution of Atoms and Molecules, 1963; Essays, 1958–1962, on Atomic Physics and Human Knowledge, 1963; Collected Works (7 vols.) 1972–1987.

ABOUT: Biographical Memoirs of Fellows of the Royal Society, volume 9, 1963; Folse, H. J. The Philosophy of Niels Bohr, 1985; French, A. P., and Kennedy, P. J. (eds.) Niels Bohr: A Centenary Volume, 1987; Hendry, J. The Creation of Quantum Mechanics and the Bohr-Pauli Dialogue, 1984; Moore, R. Niels Bohr: The Man, His Science and the World They Changed, 1966; Pauli, W. (ed.) Niels Bohr and the Development of Physics, 1955; Rosenfeld, L. Niels Bohr, 1945; Rozental, S. (ed.) Niels Bohr: His Life and Work as Seen by His Friends and Colleagues, 1967.

BÖLL, HEINRICH
(December 21, 1917–July 16, 1985)
Nobel Prize for Literature, 1972

Heinrich Theodor Böll (bûl), the German novelist and short story writer, was born in

Cologne, a major port city in the Rhine Valley, the eighth child of Viktor and Maria (Hermanns) Böll. His father was a cabinetmaker and sculptor whose shipbuilding ancestors had emigrated from England during the reign of Henry VIII. They fled to escape the persecution suffered by Roman Catholics after the establishment of the Church of England, and the Böll family remained staunchly Catholic.

After receiving his early education in the public schools of Cologne, Böll, who wrote poetry and short stories during his teens, was one of the few boys in his class who did not join the Hitler Youth movement. However, one year after graduation he was drafted into the compulsory work program, and in 1939 he was conscripted for military service. Serving as a corporal on both the Soviet and the Western fronts, he was wounded several times before being captured by the American army in 1945. Thereafter, he was interned for several months in a prisoner-of-war camp in eastern France.

After returning to his native city, Böll studied briefly at the University of Cologne. He then worked for a short time in the family workshop and later at the city's Bureau of Vital Statistics. Meanwhile, he continued to write, and in 1949 his first published novel, *Der Zug war pünktlich* (*The Train Was on Time*), appeared to favorable notices. This terse account of a young soldier's final days before returning to the front and his death was followed by a series of books that depict the senselessness of war and the bleak hardships of the postwar years. Among these works are *Wanderer, kommst du nach Spa* (*Traveler, If You Come to Spa*, 1950), a collection of short stories; the novel *Wo warst du, Adam?* (*Adam, Where Art Thou?* 1951); and *Das Brot der frühen Jahre* (*The Bread of Our Early Years*, 1955). Writing in a sober, terse, and understated style, Böll sought to renew the German language after the inflated rhetoric of the Nazi era.

Moving away from the mode of *Trümmerliteratur* (rubble literature) with his first major novel, *Billiard um halbzehn* (*Billiards at Half Past Nine*, 1959), Böll tells the story of a prominent family of Cologne architects. Although it takes place in a single day, flashbacks and reminiscences cover three generations, from the final years of Kaiser Wilhelm's reign to the prosperity of the "new" Germany of the 1950s. *Billiards at Half Past Nine* differs significantly from Böll's earlier work not only in its broader scope but in its structural complexity. "Most of all," wrote the German critic Henry Plard, "it offers consolation to the reader by showing

HEINRICH BÖLL

what healing power is contained in human love."

Throughout the 1960s Böll continued to develop greater technical complexity in his writing. *Ansichten eines Clowns* (*The Clown*, 1963) also takes place in one day, but the plot is developed through a series of telephone calls by its first-person narrator, a young man who prefers to earn his livelihood by playing the fool than by embracing the hypocrisies of postwar society. "Again the focus is on Böll's central themes," said the German critic Diether Haenicke: "the National Socialist past of the new authorities, and the political influence of the Catholic church on the development of postwar Germany."

Resistance to established authority is also the theme of *Entfernung von der Truppe* (*Absent Without Leave*, 1964) and *Das Ende einer Dienstfahrt* (*End of a Mission*, 1966). Longer and of still greater complexity than his earlier works, the novel *Gruppenbild mit Dame* (*Group Portrait With Lady*, 1971) takes the form of a report comprising interviews and documents about the protagonist, Leni Pfeiffer, through whom the lives of some sixty other characters are viewed. "By tracing Leni Pfeiffer's life through half a century of German history," said the American reviewer Richard Locke, "Böll has written a novel celebrating common humanity."

Group Portrait With Lady was cited by the Swedish Academy the following year when it awarded Böll the 1972 Nobel Prize for Literature "for his writing, which through its combination of a broad perspective on his time and a sensitive skill in characterization has contributed to a renewal of German literature." This renewal, said Karl Ragnar Gierow of the Swedish Academy in his presentation address, "is a rebirth out of annihilation, a resurrection, a culture which, ravaged by icy nights and condemned to extinction, sends up new shoots . . . to the joy and benefit of us all."

By the time Böll received the Nobel Prize, his work had become immensely popular not only in West Germany but also in East Germany and even the Soviet Union, where several million copies of his books have been sold. Nonetheless, Böll took an active role in the PEN (Poets, Essayists, Novelists) Club, an international writers' organization, through which he supported the rights of authors who suffered repression under Communist governments. After ALEXSANDR SOLZHENITSYN was expelled from the Soviet Union in 1974, he stayed with Böll before moving to Paris.

The same year that he aided Solzhenitsyn, Böll published the political novella *Die verlorene Ehre der Katharina Blum* (*The Lost Honor of Katharina Blum*), which attacks sensational journalism by telling the story of an unjustly accused woman who at last murders the reporter who has hounded her. The 1972 press coverage of the Baader-Meinhof terrorist group inspired the novel *Fürsorgliche Belagerung* (*Safety Net,* 1979), which depicts the socially destructive consequences that arise from the necessity of excessive security measures in a time of public violence.

In 1942 Böll married Annemarie Cech; they had two sons. The couple frequently collaborated on German translations of such American writers as Bernard Malamud and J. D. Salinger. It was while visiting one of his sons near Bonn in 1985 that Böll died, at the age of sixty-seven. The same year, his earliest novel, *Das Vermächtnis* (*A Soldier's Legacy*), appeared. Written in 1947 but not previously published, it is a wartime murder story set on the Atlantic Wall and on the Eastern front. Though flawed, wrote the American author William Boyd, *A Soldier's Legacy* "was born out of a hard-won maturity, and the clear-eyed wisdom that emerges from it makes it a remarkable achievement."

In nearly forty volumes of novels, short stories, plays, and essays, Böll portrayed—and often satirized—the Germany he knew during and after World War II. Yet according to the British critic and scholar W. E. Yuill, "Böll has always been more than a local writer: he is concerned with the fate and experience of a whole generation of Germans and of the individual in the great materialistic urban societies of the modern world." Not all critics agree on Böll's success, however. "That sentimentalism and idealism dominate his work and that he cannot always adequately execute his intentions are the charges most often heard," wrote the American scholar Robert C. Conard.

In Böll's attack on the materialism of modern society, the American critic Peter Demetz perceived an underlying naivete. Böll's "moral commitment," Demetz wrote, "actually masks a fundamental disgust with the inevitable politics of small, daily, pragmatic steps. It is all or nothing once again." To the American scholar Theodore Ziolkowski, "Böll is one of the very few postwar German novelists who have created what can properly be called . . . a unified fictional world informed by a consistent moral vision." Comparing Böll's Cologne to WILLIAM FAULKNER's Yoknapatawpha County, Ziolkowski added: "Böll has not only added to the literary map of Germany a province that is unmistakably his own; he has also established himself as the leading fictional historian of Germany at mid-century."

ADDITIONAL WORKS IN ENGLISH TRANSLATION: Acquainted With the Night, 1954; Tomorrow and Yesterday, 1957; Dr. Murke's Collection of Silences, 1961; When the War Ended, 1964; Eighteen Stories, 1966; Irish Journal, 1967; Adam and the Train, 1970; Children Are Civilians Too, 1970; Missing Persons, and Other Essays, 1977; And Never Said a Word, 1978; What's to Become of the Boy? 1985; The Stories of Heinrich Böll, 1986; The Casualty, 1987.

ABOUT: Conard, R. C. Heinrich Böll, 1981; Current Biography July 1972; Demetz, P. Postwar German Literature, 1970; Ghurye, C. W. The Writer and Society, 1976; Keith-Smith, B. Essays on Contemporary German Literature, 1966; Prodaniuk, I. The Imagery in Heinrich Böll's Novels, 1979; Reed, D. The Novel and the Nazi Past, 1985; Reid, J. H. Heinrich Böll: Withdrawal and Re-Emergence, 1973; Schwartz, W. J. Heinrich Böll, Teller of Tales, 1968; Thomas, R. H. The German Novel and the Affluent Society, 1968; White, R. L. Heinrich Böll in America, 1979.

BORDET, JULES
(June 13, 1870–April 6, 1961)
Nobel Prize for Physiology or Medicine, 1919

The Belgian bacteriologist and immunologist Jules Jean Baptiste Vincent Bordet (bôr dā') was born in Soignies, the second son of Charles Bordet, a schoolteacher, and Celestine (Vandenabeele) Bordet. At the age of sixteen he moved with his family to Brussels, where he entered the Free University and completed the seven-year medical course in only six years. During this time Bordet studied how bacteria are protected from being engulfed by other cells. His findings were published in 1892, the same year he received his medical degree, and attracted the interest of ILYA METCHNIKOFF. The Belgian government subsequently awarded Bordet a scholarship that enabled him to work in Metchnikoff's laboratory at the Pasteur Institute in Paris in 1894.

That same year, the bacteriologists Richard Pfeiffer and B. Issaeff had discovered that cholera bacteria die when injected into cholera-immune animals, a phenomenon known as bacteriolysis. They had also observed that bacteriolysis occurred when the bacteria, together with serum from immune animals, were injected into nonimmune animals, but it did not occur in test tubes. Metchnikoff had explained the findings of Pfeiffer and Issaeff by proposing that phagocytes (cells that ingest microorganisms and other cells) from either immune or nonimmune animals were necessary for bacteriolysis to take place. Bordet proved otherwise, reporting that "cholera serum, when it is fresh, contains two substances: a bactericidal substance and a preventive substance. In serum that has been kept for a long time, or better yet, in serum that has been heated to 55°C, the bacteriological material no longer exists." Today, the bactericidal substance, at that time called "alexine," is now known as complement; the preventive substance called "sensibilizer" is known today as the antibody.

These were pioneering discoveries in immunology—the study of how the body resists infection. It is now known that when a foreign body, whether protein, bacterium, or toxin (antigen), enters an organism, antibodies are produced. Each different antigen stimulates the formation of a specific antibody. When antibody and antigen combine and react with complement, a protein substance in the blood, the antigen is rendered harmless.

Continuing his work at the Pasteur Institute, Bordet established that hemagglutination and hemolysis (clumping and destruction of transfused red blood cells) are caused by the same process as bacteriolysis. He explained these phenomena by introducing the concept of antigenic specificity. According to this idea, different organisms are made of a variety of proteins (antigens) that can be distinguished by using specific antiserums (blood serums containing specific antibodies). Bordet was the

JULES BORDET

first to realize that the specificity of antibody-antigen complexes, and the fact that they react with complement and precipitate out of a solution, could be used to detect the presence of any substance to which an antibody can be produced. Such immunological reactions are the basis for thousands of modern medical and laboratory techniques.

In 1899 Bordet married Marthe Levoz; they had two daughters and one son. Two years later he left Paris to become director of a newly established antirabies and bacteriological institute in Brussels, which became the Pasteur Institute of Brussels in 1903. The methods he developed over the next decade laid the foundations for immunological research and diagnosis.

Bordet showed that complement will combine with an antigen only if the antigen is bound to an antibody. This complement binding causes red blood cells or bacteria to agglutinate, a reaction that can be observed with the naked eye. Bordet and his colleague and brother-in-law Octave Gengou realized that this property could be exploited for diagnosis by a complement-fixation reaction. In this process the antibody to be tested is added to a known antigen and a small amount of complement. If the antibody and antigen match, the antigen-antibody complex binds the complement; if they do not match, complement remains. If complement remains, the cells agglutinate and the test is negative; if the complement has been fixed, the cells do not agglutinate and the test is positive. Bordet and Gengou also developed the indirect hemagglutination test, in which

117

red blood cells are used as "carriers" for foreign antigens and are agglutinated by complement and the appropriate antibody.

Bordet differed with PAUL EHRLICH over the nature of the reaction between antigens and antibodies. Ehrlich maintained that the reaction is purely chemical and should therefore always occur in strict proportions. Bordet claimed that the reaction resembles adsorption, in which the components unite in variable proportions. Bordet's view prevailed for several decades, supported by the fact that antigens and antibodies react in variable proportions. It was later demonstrated that the reaction between a particular antigenic site (several of which usually occur on a given protein) and either of the antibody's two binding sites is chemical.

Bordet devised complement-fixation tests, the most famous of which—the Wassermann reaction for the diagnosis of syphilis—was put into practice by August von Wassermann, Albert Neisser, and Carl Bruck in 1906. During the same year, Bordet and Gengou employed these new methods to isolate the bacterium *Bordetella pertussis,* which causes whooping cough (pertussis). The following year, Bordet was appointed professor of bacteriology at the University of Brussels, a position he held for twenty-eight years.

Bordet's further investigations of whooping cough led in 1910 to the first report of antigenic variation in bacteria. This phenomenon is medically significant because disease organisms (notably, the influenza virus) that can change their antigens may be able to resist antibodies or vaccines.

The Nobel Prize for Physiology or Medicine was reserved in 1919 but awarded the following year to Bordet "for his discoveries relating to immunity." According to Alfred Petterson of the Karolinska Institute in his presentation speech, "Bordet's discovery, showing that the introduction of red corpuscles into an animal brings about the formation of a specific antibody . . . was of great importance, especially as it proved that this reaction of the animal organism is a general biological phenomenon." Petterson added that Bordet's finding "was of further fundamental importance as it paved the way to other research work on immunity." Bordet, who was lecturing in the United States, did not attend the award ceremonies; the prize was accepted by the Belgian ambassador to Sweden.

While studying immunological hemagglutination, Bordet also investigated the natural coagulation of blood. His most important contribution in this field was the clarification of the roles of calcium ions and the enzyme thrombin in the early stages of coagulation.

After World War I, Bordet became interested in the interactions between bacteria and bacteriophages, the viruses that destroy them. His experiments on bacterial inheritance of lysogeny (the ability to cause the destruction of cells) helped establish the foundations for the successes of molecular genetics during the mid-1900s.

On his retirement as director of the Pasteur Institute of Brussels in 1940, Bordet was succeeded by his son, Paul. He maintained an active interest in science until his death at his home in Ixelles on April 6, 1961.

Among Bordet's many honors were the Prize of the City of Paris (1911) and the Hansen Prize and Pasteur Medal of the Swedish Medical Society (1913). He was a member of the Belgian Royal Academy and an honorary member of the Royal Society of London, the Royal Society of Edinburgh, the French Academy of Medicine, and the American National Academy of Sciences. He was awarded honorary degrees by the universities of Cambridge, Paris, Strasbourg, Toulouse, Edinburgh, Nancy, and Quebec, as well as other institutions.

SELECTED WORKS: Studies in Immunity, 1909.

ABOUT: Biographical Memoirs of Fellows of the Royal Society, volume 8, 1962; De Kruif, P. Men Against Death, 1932; Dictionary of Scientific Biography, volume 2, 1970; Journal of General Microbiology September 12, 1962.

BORLAUG, NORMAN
(March 25, 1914–   )
Nobel Prize for Peace, 1970

The American plant pathologist and geneticist Norman Ernest Borlaug was born in Iowa to Henry and Clara (Vaala) Borlaug, immigrant farmers from Norway. Borlaug and his two younger sisters were raised on a farm near Cresco, where he attended grade school and high school. Harry Shroeder, who taught agriculture at Cresco High School, later remarked that he had "sensed Borlaug's innate curiosity about the processes of plant growth and the nature of soils." Noting this interest, Shroeder began tutoring Borlaug in various fields of agriculture.

Graduating from high school in 1932, Borlaug entered the University of Minnesota to study forestry. Elvin Charles Stakman, a leading crop researcher, was then head of the plant pathology department at the university. Borlaug attended one of Stakman's lectures in his freshman year and was so impressed that he decided to study with the eminent plant pathologist. When Borlaug obtained a B.S. in forestry in 1937, Stakman urged him to do graduate work in plant pathology. Following Stakman's advice, Borlaug remained at the University of Minnesota for postgraduate work, supporting himself as a part-time forester. He received an M.S. in 1939 and a Ph.D. in plant pathology in 1942. His dissertation dealt with a fungal disease of the flax plant.

In 1937, the year he graduated from college, Borlaug married Margaret G. Gibson. They have one son and one daughter.

Widespread use of chemical pesticides had begun when PAUL MÜLLER developed DDT (dichloro-diphenyl-trichloro-ethane) for use on farm crops. The insecticide was first used successfully in 1939 against Colorado potato beetles threatening the potato crop in Switzerland. During World War II, the development of herbicides, fungicides, and preservatives received top United States–government priority in agricultural and chemical research. DDT was employed extensively on American farms and by the military services, especially in tropical regions where ticks and other disease-bearing insects posed serious health problems. From 1942 to 1944 Borlaug was employed as a microbiologist by E. I. du Pont de Nemours and Company in Wilmington, Delaware, where he was placed in charge of research on industrial and agricultural bactericides, fungicides, and preservatives.

During this period, Mexico was experiencing severe crop failures. Concerned about Mexico's lack of strong, disease-resistant strains of wheat, the Mexican Ministry of Agriculture appealed to the Rockefeller Foundation for technical assistance. In 1944 the foundation sent George Harrar, a plant pathologist and later president of the foundation, to Mexico. The team of agricultural scientists that Harrar took with him included Borlaug, who was assigned to organize and direct the Cooperative Wheat Research and Production Program in Mexico.

This task involved research in genetics, plant breeding, plant pathology, entomology (the study of insects), agronomy (crop production), soil science, and cereal technology. Working with Mexican agricultural scientists, Borlaug and his assistants developed high-yield, disease-free strains of wheat that would be suit-

NORMAN BORLAUG

able for local conditions. "We never waited for perfection," Borlaug said. "Research from the outset was production-oriented." To accelerate crop production, Borlaug grew two generations of plants each year, one during the short autumn days in Sonora, close to sea level, the other during the longer summer days in the mountains near Mexico City. The resultant strains of wheat proved adaptable to a wide range of growing conditions and resistant to most plant diseases.

By 1948 Mexican wheat yields had increased dramatically and the country that previously had imported more than 50 percent of its wheat became self-supporting. In the 1950s, however, wheat yields leveled off, mainly because liberal use of fertilizers made the plants grow too tall; consequently, the stalks fell over, or "lodged," and much wheat was lost. In 1954 Borlaug and his colleagues crossed Mexican wheat with a dwarf strain from Japan. The resulting dwarf wheat plant had yields twice as high as the improved Mexican parent strain and ten times as high as the original, unimproved Mexican wheat. The Mexican dwarf wheat strains used fertilizers more efficiently, concentrating their growth in the grain rather than the stem.

In 1961 seeds from the improved dwarf strains were distributed to Mexican farmers. The remarkable achievements of Borlaug's research group, now called the International Center for Maize and Wheat Improvement, then came to the attention of other countries experiencing crop production difficulties. Borlaug visited Pakistan in 1959 and India in 1963, but administrative and political barriers slowed his efforts to improve crop production in both nations.

Borlaug's so-called Green Revolution programs were introduced in the mid-1960s. His policy of a "yield blast-off" gave the programs both economic and psychological impact. "I am impatient," he said, "and do not accept the need for slow change and evolution to improve the agriculture and food production of the emerging countries." His stated goal for each program was to double wheat yields in any needy country in the first year of implementation.

Scientists at the International Rice Research Institute, established in the Philippines in the 1960s, developed semidwarf rice strains modeled on Borlaug's Mexican dwarf wheat strains. The new dwarf rice strains provided the impetus for the Green Revolution in Southeast Asia. Altogether, six Latin American countries, eight in the Middle East, and two in Asia have benefited from Borlaug's Green Revolution programs.

Borlaug once said, "One of the greatest threats to mankind today is that the world may be choked by an explosively pervading but well-camouflaged bureaucracy." To achieve the results he desired, Borlaug found it necessary, as he put it, to "move governments."

The 1970 Nobel Prize for Peace was awarded to Borlaug for his achievements in the fields of agriculture and nutrition, particularly for his leadership of the Green Revolution. In her presentation speech, Aase Lionæs of the Norwegian Nobel Committee said of Borlaug, "More than any other single person of this age, he has helped to provide bread for a hungry world. . . . Dr. Borlaug has introduced a dynamic factor into our assessment of the future and its potential."

In his Nobel lecture, Borlaug stated his belief that "the first essential component of social justice is adequate food for all mankind. . . . If you desire peace, cultivate justice, but at the same time cultivate the fields to produce more bread; otherwise there will be no peace." He continued that people must nevertheless "recognize the fact that adequate food is only the first requisite for life. For a decent and humane life we must also provide an opportunity for good education, remunerative employment, comfortable housing, good clothing, and effective and compassionate medical care. Since man is potentially a rational being, I am confident that within the next two decades he will recognize the self-destructive course he steers along the road of irresponsible population growth and will adjust the growth rate to levels which will permit a decent standard of living for all mankind."

During the early 1970s, he became involved in an often acrimonious dispute with environmentalists who attacked his agricultural programs and practices because they emphasized tillage machinery, chemical fertilizers, and controversial pesticides such as DDT. Although opposed to environmental pollution, Borlaug refuted these attacks, calling them irrational and alarmist.

As he indicated in his Nobel lecture, Borlaug shared with many environmentalists the belief that a real effort must be made to curb "the frightening power of human reproduction." The Green Revolution, according to Borlaug, "has won a temporary success in man's war against hunger and deprivation; it has given man a breathing space." He conceded that the Green Revolution has not solved all the problems of food production and distribution. Nevertheless, "it is far better for mankind to be struggling with new problems caused by abundance rather than with the old problem of famine."

Borlaug retired in 1979 as director of the International Wheat Research and Production Program at the International Center for Maize and Wheat Improvement in Mexico City, but he retains links with his work there as associate director of the Rockefeller Foundation, a post he has held since 1964. The foundation continues to cosponsor agricultural research with the Mexican Ministry of Agriculture.

Since 1984 Borlaug has been Distinguished Professor of International Agriculture at Texas A&M University. In addition, he has served as a member of the United States Citizen's Commission on Science, Law, and Food Supply and the Commission on Critical Choices for America. He has served on the advisory council of the Renewable Resources Foundation and has been a consultant to the Foundation for Population Studies in Mexico. He is the author of several books and over seventy scientific and semipopular articles.

In 1977 Borlaug was awarded the United States Medal of Freedom, and he has received numerous honors from foreign governments and scientific societies around the world.

SELECTED WORKS: The Composite Wheat Variety, 1958, with William C. Cobb; Wheat Breeding and Its Impact on World Food Supply, 1968; Mankind and Civilization at Another Crossroad, 1971; The Green Revolution, Peace and Humanity, 1971; The World Food Problem, Present and Future, 1972; Food Production in a Fertile, Unstable World,

1978; Wheat in the Third World, 1982, with Haldore Hanson; Land Use, Food, Energy and Recreation, 1983, with Paul F. Bente Jr.

ABOUT: Atlantic Monthly February 1973; Bickel, L. Facing Starvation, 1974; Brown, L. R. Seeds of Change, 1970; Current Biography July 1971; Foreign Affairs July 1968; Freeman, O. World Without Hunger, 1968; Hardin, C. M. (ed.) Overcoming World Hunger, 1969; Johnson, D. G. The Struggle Against World Hunger, 1967; Myrdal, G. The Challenge of World Poverty, 1970; Paarlberg, D. Norman Borlaug: Hunger Fighter, 1970.

BORN, MAX
(December 11, 1882–January 5, 1970)
Nobel Prize for Physics, 1954
(shared with Walther Bothe)

MAX BORN

The German physicist Max Born was born in Breslau, (now Wrocław, Poland), the elder of two children of Gustav Born, an anatomy professor at the University of Breslau, and Margarethe (Kauffmann) Born, a talented pianist who came from a prominent family of Silesian industrialists. Max was four years old when his mother died, and four years later his father married Bertha Lipstein, with whom he had a son. Through his family's association with the leading intellectual and artistic circles of Breslau, Born grew up in a stimulating environment. He received his early education at the Kaiser Wilhelm Gymnasium in Breslau.

Although Born considered an engineering career, his father encouraged him to take a broad range of courses at the University of Breslau, which Born entered in 1901, shortly after his father's death. At Breslau, Born took many subjects but concentrated on mathematics and physics. He spent two summer semesters at the universities of Heidelberg and Zurich. In 1904 he entered the University of Göttingen, where he studied under the renowned mathematicians David Hilbert and Felix Klein and the mathematical physicist Hermann Minkowski. Hilbert, impressed with Born's intellectual gifts, made Born his assistant in 1905. Born also studied astronomy at Göttingen. By the time he received his Ph.D. in 1907, for a dissertation on the theory of elastic stability, his interests had turned to the study of electrodynamics and relativity.

Upon graduation, Born was called up for a year of compulsory military service and joined a cavalry unit in Berlin, but he was discharged a few months later, after suffering asthma attacks. This brief military experience strengthened the dislike of war and militarism that Born already felt and was to retain all his life.

For the next six months Born attended Cambridge University, where he attended lectures by J. J. THOMSON. Returning to Breslau, he conducted experimental research before beginning theoretical work on ALBERT EINSTEIN's special theory of relativity, which had been published in 1905. Combining Einstein's ideas with Minkowski's mathematical approach, Born discovered a new and simplified method for calculating the mass of an electron. Impressed with this work, Minkowski invited Born to return to Göttingen as his assistant. However, Born worked with him for only a few weeks before Minkowski's untimely death in early 1909.

After completing a theoretical study on relativity later that year, Born became a lecturer at Göttingen, where he studied how the properties of crystals depend on the arrangement of their atoms. With the applied mathematician Theodore von Karman, Born created an exact theory of the heat capacity of crystals as a function of temperature, a theory that remains fundamental to the study of crystals. Crystal structure remained Born's chief field of research until the mid-1920s.

In 1915 Born became assistant professor of theoretical physics under MAX PLANCK at the University of Berlin. During World War I, despite his aversion to war, Born conducted military research on sound ranging and evaluated new artillery inventions. It was during the war years that he began his friendship with Einstein. In addition to physics, the two men shared a love of music and enjoyed playing

121

sonatas together, Einstein on the violin and Born on the piano.

After the war, Born continued his work on the theory of crystals, collaborating with FRITZ HABER on the relation between the physical properties of crystals and the chemical energies of the compounds of which the crystals were composed. Their efforts culminated in an analytic technique now known as the Born-Haber cycle.

When MAX VON LAUE expressed a wish to work with Planck, Born agreed to exchange positions with him temporarily and moved to the University of Frankfurt in 1919 as professor of physics and director of the Institute of Theoretical Physics. After returning to Göttingen two years later, he became director of the university's Physical Institute, on the condition that his old friend and colleague JAMES FRANCK be appointed to direct the institute's experimental work. Under Born's leadership, the Physical Institute became a leading center in theoretical physics and mathematics.

Initially, Born continued his crystal research at Göttingen, but he soon began working to establish a mathematical basis for quantum theory. Although his work on crystals was extremely important and helped lay the foundations of modern solid-state physics, it was Born's contributions to quantum theory that eventually earned him the Nobel Prize.

Quantum theory, which deals with the behavior of atomic and subatomic systems, originated with Max Planck's proposal in 1900 that the energy of vibrating systems interacting with radiation can take on only certain discrete values. Einstein, expanding this idea of quantized energy, described light as consisting of energy particles, which he named quanta. NIELS BOHR later used the quantum theory to elucidate atomic structure and explain the spectra of some of the elements. By the 1920s most physicists were convinced that all energy is quantized, but early quantum theory left many important problems unsolved. Born sought a general theory to account for all quantum effects.

In 1925 Born's assistant WERNER HEISENBERG solved a critical aspect of the problem by proposing that certain mathematical rules govern atomic phenomena. Although Heisenberg himself failed to recognize the mathematical foundations of the relations he had discovered, Born perceived that Heisenberg had used matrix operations (mathematical operations that are performed on arrays of numbers or variables). With a student, Pascual Jordan, Born formalized Heisenberg's insight

and published the results later that year in a paper titled "Zur Quantenmechanik" (On Quantum Mechanics). The term *quantum mechanics,* which Born coined, came to designate the new, highly mathematical quantum theory that developed in the late 1920s. During the winter of 1925–1926, Born was a visiting lecturer at the Massachusetts Institute of Technology.

In 1926 ERWIN SCHRÖDINGER developed wave mechanics, an alternate formulation of quantum mechanics that he showed was equivalent to the matrix mechanics formulation. In a return to some of the methods of classical physics, wave mechanics treated subatomic particles as waves described by a wave function. Applying the principles of wave mechanics and matrix mechanics to the theory of atomic scattering (the deflection of one particle by another, due to collision or close approach), Born argued that the square of the wave function evaluated at some point in space expresses the probability that the particle being described is at that specific location. For this reason, he maintained, quantum mechanics gives only a statistical description of a particle's location. Born's description of particle scattering, which became known as the Born approximation, proved extremely important to the calculations used later in high-energy physics. Shortly after the publication of the Born approximation, Heisenberg published his influential uncertainty principle, which states that one cannot simultaneously determine the exact location and momentum of a particle. Again, only a statistical prediction is possible.

The statistical interpretation of quantum mechanics was developed further by Born, Heisenberg, and Bohr; because Bohr, who was in Copenhagen, did extensive work on this interpretation, it became known as the Copenhagen interpretation. Although some of the founders of quantum theory, including Planck, Einstein, and Schrödinger, objected to this approach on the grounds that it rejected causality, most physicists accepted the Copenhagen interpretation as the most useful one. Born and Einstein conducted a lengthy debate on this question by correspondence, although their fundamental scientific disagreement never clouded their friendship. Born's prominence in the development of quantum mechanics—which lay in the creation of a new picture of atomic structure and the consequent transformation of physics and chemistry—led many gifted young physicists to Göttingen to work with him.

After attending a physics conference in Leningrad in 1928, Born succumbed to poor health and physical exhaustion and was forced to spend a year in a sanatorium. There he spent his time writing a textbook on optics, which was later suppressed by the Nazis but which was widely used in English translation. This was one of several textbooks and popular works that Born wrote on various physics topics, in addition to his more technical publications.

Born was appointed dean of the Faculty of Science at Göttingen in 1932, but with the advent of Hitler's government the following year and the promulgation of anti-Semitic civil service laws, he was expelled from his post. Born left Germany for Great Britain, where for the next three years he was Stokes Lecturer at Cambridge. After spending six months at the Indian Institute of Physics in Bangalore, where he worked with the Indian physicist VENKATA RAMAN, Born was appointed Tait Professor of Natural Philosophy at the University of Edinburgh in 1936. There he taught and conducted research until his retirement in 1953, when he became emeritus professor at Edinburgh.

Although several of Born's students and colleagues had received the Nobel Prize for their work on quantum theory, Born's contributions were not so honored until 1954, when he was awarded the Nobel Prize for Physics "for his fundamental research in quantum mechanics, especially for his statistical interpretation of the wave function." He shared the prize with WALTHER BOTHE, who was honored for his experimental work with subatomic particles. In his Nobel lecture Born described the origins of quantum mechanics and its statistical interpretation, concluding by asking, "Can we call something with which the concepts of position and motion cannot be associated in the usual way a thing or a particle? The answer to this," he said, "is no longer physics, but philosophy."

Born married Hedwig Ehrenberg, the daughter of a Göttingen law professor, in 1913. They had one son, who became head of the pharmacology department at Cambridge, and two daughters.

Shortly after his retirement, Born and his wife settled in Bad Pyrmont, a small town near Göttingen, their pension rights and confiscated property having been restored by the postwar government. There Born continued his scientific work, brought out new editions of his publications, and wrote and lectured on the social responsibilities of scientists, particularly with respect to nuclear weapons. In 1955 he was one of sixteen Nobel laureates who gathered on Mainau Island in Lake Constance, Switzerland, to draft a statement condemning the further development and use of nuclear weapons. Fifty-one Nobel Prize winners eventually signed this declaration. Two years later Born was one of the Göttingen Eighteen, a group of leading West German physicists who vowed not to work on weapons production or development and who campaigned against nuclear arms for West Germany.

Born died in a Göttingen hospital on January 5, 1970.

Although Born is remembered best for his work in quantum mechanics, his research and writings were noteworthy for the variety of fields they encompassed. "I never liked being a specialist," he wrote in his autobiography. "I would not fit into the ways of science today, done by teams of specialists. The philosophical background of science always interested me more than its special results."

Born's many awards in addition to the Nobel Prize included the Stokes Medal of Cambridge University (1936), the Max Planck Medal of the German Physical Society (1948), and the Hughes Medal of the Royal Society of London (1950). He received nine honorary doctorates and was a member of scientific academies in several countries, including the Royal Society of London and the American National Academy of Sciences.

SELECTED WORKS: The Constitution of Matter: Modern Atomic and Electron Theories, 1923; Einstein's Theory of Relativity, 1924; Problems of Atomic Dynamics, 1926; The Mechanics of the Atom, 1927; Atomic Physics, 1935; The Restless Universe, 1935; Experiment and Theory in Physics, 1943; Atomic Energy and Its Use in War and Peace, 1947; Natural Philosophy of Cause and Chance, 1949; A General Kinetic Theory of Liquids, 1949, with H. S. Green; Dynamical Theory of Crystal Lattices, 1954, with Hun Huang; Physics in My Generation, 1956; Principles of Optics, 1959; Diffraction, 1959, with Emil Wolf; Physics and Politics, 1962; My Life and My Views, 1968; The Born-Einstein Letters, 1971, with Albert Einstein; My Life: Recollections of a Nobel Prize Winner, 1978.

ABOUT: Biographical Memoirs of Fellows of the Royal Society, volume 17, 1971; Current Biography May 1955; Dictionary of Scientific Biography, volume 15, 1978; Nachmanson, D. German-Jewish Pioneers in Science 1900–1933, 1979.

BOSCH, CARL
(August 27, 1874–April 26, 1940)
Nobel Prize for Chemistry, 1931
(shared with Friedrich Bergius)

The German chemist Carl Bosch was born in Cologne, the eldest child of Carl Bosch and

Paula (Liebst) Bosch. His father was a prosperous entrepreneur who sold gas and plumbing equipment. From an early age he was an excellent student of natural sciences and technology and wanted to become a chemist. Deferring to his father's wishes, however, he worked for a year in several machine shops, and from 1894 to 1896 he studied metallurgy and mechanical engineering at the technical university in Charlottenburg (now part of West Berlin). After completing technical school, Bosch began graduate studies in chemistry at the University of Leipzig and received his doctorate in 1898 for a dissertation on pure organic chemistry.

The following year Bosch took a position in Ludwigshafen am Rhein at Badische Anilin- und Sodafabrik (BASF), a large chemical company that specialized in the production of coal-tar dyes. Initially, he worked under Rudolf Knietsch, helping develop a process for the production of synthetic indigo in commercial quantities. Turning his attention to nitrogen fixation (the formation of nitrogenous chemical compounds through the use of atmospheric nitrogen), he experimented with metal cyanides and nitrides. Impressed with Bosch's technical expertise, sound judgment, and leadership, BASF entrusted him in 1907 with the development and operation of a pilot plant designed to test the effectiveness of the company's method for producing barium cyanide.

A great advance in nitrogen fixation was made in 1909 when FRITZ HABER, a professor of chemistry at the technical university in Karlsruhe, synthesized ammonia from atmospheric nitrogen and hydrogen. This accomplishment had great commercial implications, since ammonia could serve as the basis for producing sodium nitrate, an important constituent of explosives. Moreover, when absorbed into sulfuric acid, ammonia yielded ammonium sulfate, an excellent fertilizer. In his method Haber employed not only unusually high pressure and temperature but also two rare and expensive catalysts, osmium and uranium.

BASF acquired the synthesis process from Haber in 1909 and put Bosch in charge of transforming it into a commercial method. This formidable task called for massive quantities of pure and relatively inexpensive hydrogen gas; cheap, effective, and abundant catalysts; and equipment capable of withstanding both extremely high temperatures and high pressures. Bosch and his staff came up with the needed amounts of hydrogen by separating it

CARL BOSCH

from water gas (a mixture of hydrogen and carbon monoxide produced when coal is alternately heated and then sprayed with water). They went on to develop inexpensive catalysts to replace Haber's costly osmium and uranium. Finally, Bosch oversaw the design and construction of equipment capable of withstanding the high pressures and temperatures that Haber's process required.

The greatest challenge, however, lay in the construction of a reaction chamber. After several failed attempts, Bosch observed that under high pressure and temperature, hydrogen gas penetrated the iron walls of the chamber, turning the iron into a brittle alloy that subsequently ruptured. Bosch's solution was to separate the effects of temperature and pressure by building a double-walled container with a thin annular space between the two walls. The inner cylinder allowed hydrogen gas to diffuse through it, whereas the outer cylinder did not. BASF metallurgists developed a soft, low-carbon chrome steel for the inner cylinder and a sturdy carbon steel for the outer one. While hydrogen and nitrogen reacted within the inner cylinder at 200 atmospheres pressure and at a temperature of 500°C, a mixture of cold hydrogen gas and nitrogen gas was forced into the annular region under a pressure of 200 atmospheres. In this way the inner wall was protected from severe imbalances of pressure, while the outer wall was exposed to high pressure but not high temperature.

In 1913 BASF constructed the first commercial ammonia synthesis plant at Oppau, near Ludwigshafen am Rhein. There Bosch installed a laboratory where researchers investigated such topics as catalytic methods, phase relationships of saline manures, photochemistry, and polymerization. He also established a biological research laboratory at Oppau and an experimental agriculture station at Limburgerhof in 1914. With his appointment as managing director of BASF in 1919, he began work on an inorganic method for the synthesis of methanol.

At the time, methanol—a highly volatile solvent—was used chiefly to produce formaldehyde, a feedstock for many organic compounds, especially resins and fertilizers. Manufactured as a by-product of charcoal production, methanol had become more costly as wood became scarcer. Bosch and his staff synthesized methanol in 1923 by reacting carbon monoxide and hydrogen under high pressure in the presence of a catalyst. Soon afterward they found optimum operating conditions for commercial production.

In 1925 FRIEDRICH BERGIUS sold BASF the patent rights to his coal-hydrogenation process. This method transformed lignitic coals (those with relatively high hydrogen content) into liquid fuel during the forced mixing of hydrogen gas and coal at elevated temperature and pressure. Later that year, when BASF and six other chemical companies merged to form the Interessen-Gemeinschaft Farbenindustrie Aktiengesellschaft (I. G. Farben), Bosch was named president of the mammoth new chemical company. Employing Farben's expertise in catalysis, hydrogen production, and high-pressure equipment, Bosch encouraged the staff to demonstrate the technological feasibility of converting lignitic coals to liquid fuel. The project never became commercially successful, however.

In 1931 Bosch and Bergius received the Nobel Prize for Chemistry "in recognition of their contributions to the invention and development of chemical high-pressure methods." In his presentation speech K. W. Palmær of the Royal Swedish Academy of Sciences summarized the methods the two laureates had devised and described some of their practical benefits. In particular, he pointed out that ammonia synthesis prevented a worldwide shortage of fertilizers as supplies of Chilean sodium nitrate dwindled. By 1931 the long-term importance of this work for the chemical industry had become apparent. In addition to its effect on the production of methanol, urea, and other chemicals, it profoundly influenced the design and construction of reactors and compressors, the instrumentation of process monitors and regulators, and the use of catalysts. Perhaps even more significant were the myriad topics in pure research that Bosch stimulated and supported.

In 1902 Bosch married Else Schilbach, with whom he had a son and a daughter. Even in his private life Bosch enjoyed scientific pursuits, such as collecting butterflies, beetles, plants, and minerals. A regular financial contributor to ALBERT EINSTEIN's astrophysical observatory in Potsdam, he spent many hours in his own observatory at Heidelberg. He was named chairman of I. G. Farben's board of directors in 1935. Two years later he succeeded MAX PLANCK as president of the Kaiser Wilhelm Society (now the Max Planck Society), a position he held concurrently with his I. G. Farben post. He died on April 26, 1940, in Heidelberg.

In addition to the Nobel Prize, Bosch received the Liebig Medal of the German Chemical Society and the Carl Lueg Memorial Medal of the Association of German Metallurgists, as well as honorary degrees from technical universities in Karlsruhe, Munich, and Darmstadt and from Halle University.

ABOUT: Dictionary of Scientific Biography, volume 2, 1970; Farber, E. (ed.) Great Chemists, 1961.

BOTHE, WALTHER
(June 8, 1891–February 8, 1957)
Nobel Prize for Physics, 1954
(shared with Max Born)

The German physicist Walther Wilhelm Georg Bothe (bō' te) was born in Oranienburg, the son of Friedrich Bothe, a merchant. In 1908 Bothe entered the University of Berlin, where he studied physics, mathematics, and chemistry. He obtained his Ph.D. in 1914 under MAX PLANCK, for theoretical research on the interaction of light with molecules.

During World War I, Bothe served in the German army. In 1915 he was captured by the Russians and sent to Siberia, where, as a prisoner of war, he studied Russian and managed to continue his theoretical work in physics. Returning to Germany in 1920, he took a position under Hans Geiger (inventor of the Geiger counter) at the radioactivity laboratory at the State Physical-Technical Institute in Berlin, where he had worked briefly in 1913. (He later credited Geiger with having turned his research efforts toward physics.) At the same time, Bothe taught physics at the University of Berlin.

125

WALTHER BOTHE

During the early 1920s Bothe conducted experimental and theoretical research into the deflection of alpha and beta particles by matter. Most of the work that had been performed on this topic had concerned single interactions of particles with isolated atoms. Bothe, however, analyzed the far more difficult instance in which a fast particle enters a block of matter and has small interactions with many of its atoms, each interaction deflecting the particle by an amount proportional to the interaction's strength. Since it is far more common for a particle to experience many small interactions than a single large one, the statistical techniques that Bothe developed to treat this problem were important for understanding the interaction of particles with thick materials.

During the first two decades of the twentieth century, Max Planck, ALBERT EINSTEIN, NIELS BOHR, and others had developed the quantum theory, a radical approach to the study of atomic and subatomic systems. This theory, based on the idea that energy is transmitted in discrete amounts, or quanta, resolved some of the dilemmas of classical physics, although in turn it presented difficulties of its own. Quantum theory seemed to show that light and other electromagnetic energy have characteristics of both waves and particles, a duality many physicists were reluctant to accept. A number of experiments performed in the early 1920s supported the idea that things long-considered to be waves (such as light) could behave as particles, while things long-considered particles (such as electrons) could behave as waves. One of the most impressive pieces of evidence was

ARTHUR H. COMPTON's discovery in 1923 (now known as the Compton effect) in which X rays (previously shown to be waves) are scattered by the electrons in matter as though they were particles.

In 1924 Niels Bohr, Hendrik Kramers, and John Slater attempted to resolve the wave-particle problem by proposing a reformulation of the quantum theory that challenged some of the most basic tenets of classical physics. According to the well-established conservation laws, energy and momentum are conserved—that is, in any interaction the total energy and momentum of the objects before the interaction must be equal to their total energy and momentum afterward. Bohr, Kramers, and Slater suggested that at the atomic level the interactions of individual particles do not have to conserve either energy or momentum. Instead, they proposed, energy and momentum are conserved only in the sum of many individual interactions. Existing techniques for studying subatomic particles, however, were inadequate for testing the statistical interpretation of the conservation laws suggested by Bohr and his colleagues. After reading their paper, Bothe set out to devise a technique for testing their proposal.

Compton's 1923 experiments had demonstrated that when X-ray quanta are scattered by colliding with electrons, they lose some of their energy and momentum. Compton had predicted and C. T. R. WILSON had confirmed that the electrons involved in such collisions recoil—that is, they are knocked away from their atoms. Bothe realized that if the classical conservation laws applied at the atomic level, each collision must produce both a scatter quantum and a recoil electron: the energy and momentum lost by the quantum must be gained by the electron. On the other hand, if the proposed statistical interpretation of conservation were correct, there would be only a chance relationship between the scattering of a quantum and the recoil of an electron in any given collision. Bothe therefore decided to apply the Compton effect to test Bohr's hypothesis.

Geiger's original particle counter, which he invented in 1913, could detect only heavy charged particles; but by 1924 he had developed a modified counter, called a needle counter, capable of detecting electrons. Working with Geiger, Bothe devised a way of using such counters that came to be called the coincidence method. Two needle counters, each with a hydrogen-filled cylinder, were connected in such a way that when an X-ray beam was directed at them, the collision between X-ray quanta and hydrogen atom electrons occurred in the first counter. The recoil electrons were detected by the first counter, but the scatter quanta passed into the second counter, where they caused a much smaller number of electrons to recoil and be detected, thus demonstrating the presence of the scatter quanta. The particle-indicating electric pulses from each counter were recorded side by side on a graph, enabling the researchers to see whether they coincided in time.

Bothe and Geiger found that the simultaneous recording of a scatter quantum and a recoil electron occurred far more often than was possible on the basis of chance, and their statistical calculations indicated that the two particles always resulted from a single collision. From this observation they concluded that Bohr's statistical proposal was incorrect. Their research showed that the classical conservation laws are valid for individual events at the subatomic level. This conclusion, which Bohr and other physicists accepted, influenced the development of quantum mechanics, the complex mathematical treatment of quantum theory that was developed in the 1920s.

Bothe's coincidence technique, for which he eventually won the Nobel Prize for Physics, provided a significant tool for modern particle detection and measurement systems, although physicists now use greatly improved counters that record only coincident events. In order to observe the particles released during a nuclear reaction, for example, researchers can set their instruments to process only those data that satisfy simultaneously a number of predetermined criteria. They can then statistically analyze their data to discriminate between coincidences due to the desired reactions and those due to chance.

From 1926 on, Bothe investigated the transmutation of elements that occurs when their atomic nuclei are bombarded by alpha particles, and in 1930 he and a colleague discovered a new, highly penetrating radiation, produced when they used alpha particles to bombard beryllium. This work led to the discovery of the neutron by JAMES CHADWICK in 1932. Working with Werner Kolhörster in 1929, Bothe used the coincidence method to detect cosmic rays. These investigations established that cosmic rays are high-energy particles rather than gamma rays as had been generally believed.

Bothe became director of the Institute of Physics at the University of Giessen in 1930. Two years later he was appointed director of the Institute of Physics at the University of Heidelberg, and in 1934 he became director of the Institute of Physics at the Max Planck Institute for Medical Research in Heidelberg. At the Max Planck Institute he oversaw the construction of a cyclotron, a particle accelerator used in nuclear research, which was completed in 1943.

During World War II, Bothe was a leading member of a nuclear energy project directed by WERNER HEISENBERG. He worked on the nuclear properties of uranium and on neutron transport theory, which describes how neutrons are scattered, absorbed, and emitted in systems containing fissionable elements such as uranium. After the war, Bothe returned to the problems of electron scattering and cosmic-ray physics; he contributed as well to the theoretical understanding of electron and gamma-ray emission from nuclei.

Bothe was awarded the 1954 Nobel Prize for Physics "for the coincidence method and his discoveries made therewith." He shared the prize with MAX BORN, who was honored for his contributions to quantum mechanics. Suffering from a serious circulatory disorder and confined to his bed, Bothe was unable to attend the ceremonies but sent his daughter to receive the prize on his behalf. "I think the main lesson that I have learned from Geiger," Bothe wrote in his Nobel lecture, "is to select from a large number of possible and perhaps useful experiments that which appears the most urgent at the moment, and to do this experiment with the simplest possible apparatus."

Despite his illness, Bothe continued to direct the institute in Heidelberg from his bed. His illness caused him much suffering and diminished the pleasure he was able to derive from the honors bestowed upon him.

Bothe married Barbara Below of Moscow in 1920, and they had two children. Known for his intense concentration and rapid work, Bothe was strict in the laboratory, although warm and hospitable at home. He was a gifted artist in both oils and watercolors, and an avid pianist who particularly enjoyed playing Bach and Beethoven. He died in Heidelberg on February 8, 1957.

In addition to the Nobel Prize, Bothe was awarded the Max Planck Medal of the German Physical Society and the Grand Cross of the Order for Federal Services from the German government. In 1952 he was made a knight of the government's Order of Merit for Science and the Arts. He was a member of the academies of sciences of Heidelberg and Göttingen and of the Saxon Academy of Sciences in Leipzig.

SELECTED WORKS: Nuclear Physics and Cosmic Rays (2 vols.) 1948, with others; An Atlas of Typical Expansion Chamber Photographs, 1954, with others.

ABOUT: Current Biography May 1955; Dictionary of Scientific Biography, volume 2, 1970; Rossi, B. Cosmic Rays, 1964.

BOURGEOIS, LÉON

(May 29, 1851–September 29, 1925)
Nobel Prize for Peace, 1920

LÉON BOURGEOIS

The French statesman and jurist Léon Victor Auguste Bourgeois (bŏŏr zhwä′) was born in Paris, the son of Marie Victor Bourgeois, a poor clockmaker, and Augustine Elise (Hinoult) Bourgeois. He displayed an early appetite for knowledge, and while attending first the Institut Massin and then the Lycée Charlemagne, he learned Hindi and Sanskrit, became proficient in music, and exhibited a talent for sculpture and drafting. After serving in an artillery regiment during the Franco-Prussian War, Bourgeois entered the University of Paris, where he received a doctor of law degree. In 1876, following several years of law practice, he became deputy head of the Claims Department of the Ministry of Public Works.

Thus, Bourgeois entered civil service in the early years of the Third Republic, which had been formed after the surrender of Emperor Napoleon III to Prussia in 1870. This period marked the end of monarchical government in France, the ascendancy of middle-class rule, and the introduction of social legislation for workers. At the age of thirty-six, Bourgeois was named prefect of the Paris police. An effective spokesman for France's growing left wing, he resigned his position three months later to stand as deputy from the working-class district of Châlons-sur-Marne. In February 1888 he was elected over his opponent, General Georges Boulanger, the popular and politically ambitious minister of war.

Although politically a Socialist-Radical, Bourgeois did not espouse doctrinaire Socialist principles but favored social reform within the existing system. In addition to his seat in the Chamber of Deputies, he held a series of positions in successive French cabinets. These included under secretary of state for the interior (1888–1889), minister of the interior (1890), minister of public instruction (1890–1892), and minister of justice (1892–1893). During these years, he won public support for his reforms in education. As minister of justice, he prosecuted the parties involved in the

Panama Canal scandal. The French effort to construct a canal across the Isthmus of Panama, begun in 1883 under the direction of Ferdinand de Lesseps, designer of the Suez Canal, ran into serious technical and financial difficulties. In 1888 the canal company declared bankruptcy, and de Lesseps returned to France to stand trial for bribery and mismanagement of funds. He was found guilty and sentenced to prison, but the conviction was later reversed.

Named prime minister in November 1895, Bourgeois formed the Third Republic's first government to be composed exclusively of members from the left wing of the Chamber of Deputies. His administration proposed unprecedented social and economic reforms, including progressive income and inheritance taxes, the extension of existing pension plans to cover more workers, compulsory insurance programs, and comprehensive social security benefits, a program that exhibited deep concern for the underprivileged.

During this time, Bourgeois wrote a series of articles, later published collectively under the title *Solidarité* (Solidarity, 1896), in which he expounded his view that society should provide all its members with the opportunity to develop their capacities. To realize these ideals, he argued, the state is obliged to guarantee employment opportunities; a minimum standard of living; free access to the educational system; and protection in the event of unemployment, illness, accident, and old age. His program was overwhelmingly opposed by conservatives in the French Senate, and in April

128

1896 Bourgeois chose to resign rather than face a constitutional battle over finances. Two years later he reentered the government as minister of public instruction in the cabinet of Eugène Henri Brisson.

Bourgeois's work in international affairs began with his appointment as chairman of the French delegation to The Hague Peace Conference of 1899. Convened largely at the urging of the Interparliamentary Union founded by WILLIAM CREMER and FRÉDÉRIC PASSY, it was attended by 100 delegates representing twenty-six nations. The conference addressed such issues as arms limitation, the peaceful settlement of disputes, and conventions for the humane conduct of war.

Presiding over the conference's Commission on Arbitration, Bourgeois proposed a plan to establish compulsory arbitration of "disputes . . . which imperil peace." This proposal was strongly supported by his colleague and compatriot PAUL D'ESTOURNELLES DE CONSTANT and by TOBIAS ASSER, also members of the commission. An international court of arbitration, declared Bourgeois, would be "the guarantee of the weak against the strong." The arbitration proposal was adopted at the conference's plenary session, although no provision was made for its enforcement. Nevertheless, the commission's work led to establishment of the Permanent Court of Arbitration, known also as The Hague Tribunal, to which Bourgeois was appointed in 1903. As a principle of international law, arbitration remained strictly a voluntary method by which nations could settle disputes, and many countries lacked confidence that the court's panel of jurists would act impartially.

Elected to the French Senate in 1905, Bourgeois served as minister of foreign affairs in the cabinet of Jean Marie Ferdinand Sarrien. As leader of the French delegation to the Algeciras Conference in January 1906, he won substantial commercial and administrative rights for France in Morocco, despite German opposition. The following year he attended a second peace conference in The Hague, proposed by THEODORE ROOSEVELT and attended by 256 delegates from forty four nations. There Bourgeois served as president of a commission that considered peaceable solutions to international conflict. As in the previous conference, Germany led the opposition to a general treaty of arbitration. Moreover, the commission rejected a recommendation to establish a court of arbitral justice composed of elected, salaried judges who would serve for a fixed period—improvements also suggested by a

United States delegate, ELIHU ROOT. Nevertheless, Bourgeois felt confident, that a foundation had been laid for a juridical organ of peace. "The League of Nations is created," he declared in a 1908 speech. "It is very much alive."

During World War I, Bourgeois was minister-without-portfolio in the war cabinet of ARISTIDE BRIAND. Not even the magnitude of the war shook his fundamental faith in the need for a cooperative international organization. "There will be no policy of justice if the League of Nations is not set up," he wrote in 1916. The next year he was appointed chairman of a French commission to study the possibility of forming a League of Nations. Drawing on many of Bourgeois's ideas, the commission proposed an organization whose sole function was the preservation of peace. Authorized to function only in time of crisis, the body would enforce compulsory arbitration on disputing parties and would have at its disposal an international armed force to carry out sanctions.

As a delegate to the Paris Peace Conference of 1919, Bourgeois advocated an international armed force to maintain world peace, as well as inspection and verification of any disarmament agreements—proposals that were overwhelmingly rejected by the other Allied powers. Bourgeois's insistence upon these points sorely tried the patience of WOODROW WILSON. "Without military backing in some force, and always ready to act," Bourgeois told the American president, "our league and our covenant will be filed away, not as a solemn treaty but simply as a rather ornate piece of literature."

In 1920, when the League of Nations began operating, Bourgeois became the principal representative of France at its Geneva headquarters, serving not only in the Assembly but also as first president of the Council.

Bourgeois received the 1920 Nobel Prize for Peace in recognition of his efforts to establish world peace through arbitration. Unable to attend the award ceremonies, he submitted a formal paper, "The Reasons for the League of Nations," to the Norwegian Nobel Committee. Illness prevented his traveling to Oslo to deliver the lecture himself. Addressing the question of whether international law was sufficient to overcome the instincts that lead nations to war, Bourgeois asserted: "Man has a sensitivity which can either be selfish or altruistic; but it is *reason* which is his essence." He envisioned the League of Nations not as "a 'superstate' whose will could be imposed on the governing bodies of each nation," but as a mutual contract among nations that would preserve and protect the rights of each member.

Bourgeois served as president of the French Senate from 1920 until 1923, when approaching blindness forced him to resign from French politics as well as from international affairs. He died at the age of seventy-four at the Château d'Oger near Épernay and was honored with a state funeral.

In the view of many historians, Bourgeois's notions of international law and his concept of a League of Nations were at once more visionary and more realistic than those of his contemporaries. Fifty years before LESTER PEARSON called for an international force to keep peace, Bourgeois made the same appeal. Bourgeois recognized that international law was still in its infancy. Nevertheless, he believed its impartiality would in time "appease passions, disarm ill will, discourage illusory ambitions, and create that climate of confidence and calm in which the delicate flower of peace can live and grow." Optimistic about the future and convinced that world justice could be achieved, Bourgeois believed that "if the road toward the final goal is clearly marked, if an organization like the League of Nations realizes its potential and achieves its purpose, the potent benefits of peace and of human solidarity will triumph over evil."

ABOUT: American Journal of International Law October 1925; Bonsal, S. Unfinished Business, 1944; Chapman, G. The Third Republic of France, 1962; Earle, E. M. (ed.) Modern France: Problems of the Third and Fourth Republic, 1951; Hull, W. I. The Two Hague Conferences and Their Contributions to International Law, 1980; New York Times September 30, 1925; Times (London) September 30, 1925.

BOVET, DANIEL

(March 23, 1907–   )
Nobel Prize for Physiology or Medicine, 1957

The Swiss-Italian pharmacologist Daniel Bovet (bō vā′) was born in Neuchâtel, the only son of the four children of Amy (Babut) and Pierre Bovet, a professor of experimental education at the University of Geneva. "We children were guinea pigs for testing Father's educational theories," Bovet recalled in later years. "It was wonderful." Among the experiments his parents encouraged their children to conduct was the cultivation of molds in fruit jars and mushrooms in the cellar. After completing his early education under his father's tutelage, Bovet entered the University of Geneva to study zoology and comparative anatomy. He received his *licence* (equivalent to a master's degree) in 1927, and after two years, during which time he worked as an assistant in physiology on the Faculty of Medicine, he obtained a doctor of science degree.

At the invitation of the Pasteur Institute in Paris, Bovet became assistant to Ernest Forneau, chief of the Laboratory of Therapeutic Chemistry, who exerted a major influence on Bovet's subsequent career. In 1935, while still at the Pasteur Institute, Bovet learned the results of experiments conducted by the German biochemist GERHARD DOMAGK, who discovered that an orange-red dye (sulfamyldiaminobenzene) destroyed streptococci, infectious organisms that cause many diseases. Although the large molecules of the dye were effective in the human body, Bovet was not able to achieve the same results in laboratory cultures. This observation led him to theorize that the effective element must be only part of the molecule, specifically, the part released as the molecule is broken down within the body. In collaboration with A. M. Staub, Bovet set out to discover the structure of that specific part, and, after months of intensive work, he isolated sulfanilamide (a white powder consisting of para-amino-benzene-sulfonamide), which destroys streptococcal bacteria both in the body and in cultures. Their work led to the production of the first "wonder drug," one that would act directly against the cause of a disease. Bovet then synthesized various derivatives of the sulfanilamide molecule, searching for a substance with the proper combination of potent antibacterial action and few side effects. He found that the most promising derivatives consisted of a complex carbon-based group in place of the hydrogen atoms in the sulfonamide group. Bovet eventually synthesized many sulfanilamide derivatives and ultimately created an entire family of sulfa drugs.

In 1939 Bovet succeeded Forneau as director of the Laboratory of Therapeutic Chemistry, where he focused his research on the damaging inflammation caused by the action of histamine, a hormone that occurs naturally in all body tissue. When an irritant, such as pollen grains or a bee sting, triggers a local overproduction of histamine, the swelling that results can cause more damage than the irritant itself. Bovet was intrigued by the fact that, unlike other natural hormones he had studied, histamine has no naturally occurring antidote. He knew, however, that structurally it resembles the two hormones adrenaline and acetyl-

DANIEL BOVET

from the sap of various species of jungle plants and used originally as an arrow poison by South American Indians. To gain firsthand knowledge of the substance, Bovet spent some time with the Indians of Brazil. Curare paralyzes the motor end plates of nerves. It is used for the reduction of spasms in tetanus, in shock treatments, in the treatment of muscular rigidity, and as an adjunct to general anesthesia. Before the use of curare, it was necessary to administer large doses of anesthetic to ensure against muscle spasm during surgery, a condition that posed a danger to the patient.

Ten years before Bovet began his investigation of curare, the active agent in the extract had been discovered by Harold King, and a chemically pure form had been introduced by Thomas Cullen and a co-worker. Since the effects of curare are unpredictable, Bovet sought to develop a simpler synthetic form that would be more predictable than natural curare, while at the same time retaining its original properties; he achieved his goal in 1946 with the creation of gallamine. Over the next eight years, Bovet's search for even simpler curare synthetics led to the creation of more than 400 forms, including the widely used drug succinylcholine.

Bovet received the 1957 Nobel Prize for Physiology or Medicine "for his discoveries relating to synthetic compounds that inhibit the action of certain body substances, and especially their action on the vascular system and the skeletal muscles." In his Nobel lecture he reviewed his work during the previous two decades; in concluding he said, "The future of pharmacodynamics is . . . so rich and promising, it still allows so many theoretical and practical possibilities, that I still have the hope of justifying, by my future work, not only the wonderful distinction paid me today but also the trust and friendship of my masters and colleagues whose work could not be separated from that which I now pursue with confidence, enthusiasm, and love."

In the 1960s Bovet intensified his research on the interaction between chemicals and the brain in the belief that "the key to mental illness lies in chemistry." In 1964 he became professor of pharmacology at the University of Sassari, and from 1969 to 1975 he served as director of the Laboratory of Psychobiology and Psychopharmacology at the Consiglio Nazionale delle Richerche in Rome. He has been a professor of psychobiology at the University of Rome since 1971.

In addition to the Nobel Prize, Bovet has received the Martin Damourette Prize of the

choline, for which antagonists do occur naturally. He also knew that histamine is highly toxic except when absorbed through the intestine. With these clues, he reasoned that, as in sulfanilamide, only part of the histamine molecule is active; its action is normally blocked by its "carrier" substance. The goal, therefore, was to find a substance that could reliably counter the effects of free histamine. Bovet began by studying two groups of substances, the sympatholytics and the parasympatholytics, which block the effects of adrenaline and acetylcholine, respectively. Within a year he had synthesized the first antihistamine, thymoxydiethylamine. The substance proved too toxic for practical use, however; therefore, in the period between 1937 and 1941 he performed 3,000 experiments, seeking a less toxic form of the substance. It was through this work that Bovet discovered the structural bases of most of the antihistamines available today.

Moving to Rome in 1947, Bovet became director of the Laboratories of Therapeutical Chemistry at the state-owned Istituto Superiore di Sanità. He was encouraged to settle in Rome not only because his wife, the former Filomena Nitti, whom he married in 1939, was Italian, but also because the laboratory provided better research facilities than those available at the Pasteur Institute. The Bovets, who have one son, have collaborated closely on scientific research since their marriage. Bovet became an Italian citizen in 1947.

At the Istituto Superiore, Bovet became interested in the muscle-relaxant properties of curare, a highly toxic alkaloid extract derived

131

BOYD ORR

French Academy of Sciences (1936), the General Muteau Prize of the Italian Academy of Science (1941), the Burgi Prize of the University of Bern (1949), and the Addingham Gold Medal of the University of Leeds (1952). He was made a chevalier of the Legion of Honor of France (1946) and a Grand Official of the Order of Merit of the Italian Republic (1959). He is a member of learned societies in several countries, including the Chemical Society of France, the National Academy of Sciences of Italy, the American Academy of Arts and Sciences, and the Royal Society of London.

SELECTED WORKS: Curare and Curarelike Agents, 1959, with others; Controlling Drugs, 1974, with others.

ABOUT: Current Biography January 1958; New York Times October 25, 1957; Time November 4, 1957.

JOHN BOYD ORR

BOYD ORR, JOHN
(September 23, 1880–June 25, 1971)
Nobel Prize for Peace, 1949

The Scottish nutritionist and educator John Boyd Orr was born in Kilmaurs, the fourth of seven children of Robert Clark Orr, owner of a small quarry, and the former Annie Boyd. Given a strict religious upbringing in the fundamentalist Free Church of Scotland, he was also exposed to the intellectual discussions that his father, elder brothers, and family friends enjoyed. When the boy was five years old, some of his father's investments failed, and the family was forced to move from its comfortable home in Kilmaurs to more humble accommodations in the rural village of West Kilbride, near the Firth of Clyde.

Boyd Orr received his early education at home from his mother and paternal grandmother. At the age of thirteen he won a scholarship to the nearby Kilmarnock Academy, but he showed so little interest in his studies that he was sent home. There he worked for his father and attended a village school while reading widely on his own. At the age of nineteen, he won a Queen's Scholarship and entered Glasgow University to study theology. Out of curiosity, he attended a zoology class one day and was so struck by the Darwinian theories he encountered that he took up the study of science and eventually abandoned his plans for the ministry.

Upon graduation in 1902, Boyd Orr fulfilled the terms of his scholarship by teaching for

four years, first in the slums of Glasgow and then in Saltcoats, a depressed area near the city. Appalled by the wretched poverty, malnutrition, and disease that he saw among his pupils, Boyd Orr returned to the university to study medicine. He completed his medical degree with honors in 1914 and practiced medicine briefly. He then accepted a position as director of animal nutrition at the University of Aberdeen's newly founded Animal Nutrition Research Laboratory. Arriving there in the spring and finding that the entire facility was housed in a cellar, he started raising funds for an ambitious construction program that began just as World War I broke out.

Requesting a leave of absence from Aberdeen, Boyd Orr volunteered for military service. After eighteen months in England, he became medical officer for the First Sherwood Foresters, an infantry unit that saw combat at the battles of the Somme, Ypres, and Passchendaele. His courage under fire earned him the Military Cross and the Distinguished Service Order. Convinced he could better keep in touch with nutritional and medical advances in the navy, he arranged for a transfer but was soon recalled to work on army food requirements, thus acquiring a dual status in the two services.

After the armistice, Boyd Orr returned to Aberdeen, finished building a laboratory, and gathered a small staff. In the years that followed, he created the Rowett Research Institute, a research center and clearinghouse for nutritional studies; the Walter Reid Library; the John Duthie Webster Experimental Farm;

132

and the Strathcona House Nutrition Center, a meeting place for nutritionists from all over the world.

During his early years at Rowett, Boyd Orr investigated the role of protein and mineral metabolism in farm and dairy animals, work that quickly established his reputation. While conducting surveys in Africa in 1925, he compared the diet and health of the Masai—a herding tribe that lived on meat, milk, and blood—with that of the maize-eating Kikuyu. This and other studies persuaded Boyd Orr that the institute's findings on animal nutrition could also be used to improve human health. An early step in this direction was Boyd Orr's 1927 investigation into the nutritional properties of cow's milk.

Despite Great Britain's substantial dairy industry, the nutritional value of milk—particularly for growing children—was unappreciated by the public, and in order to maintain price levels, producers regularly discarded what they considered to be surpluses. In their first study, Boyd Orr and his colleagues selected three groups of schoolchildren in Scotland and Ireland. To one group, they gave half a pint of whole milk daily, to the second a pint of skim milk, and to the third a biscuit with equivalent caloric value. Within seven months, the children who had received milk showed marked improvement in their health and rate of growth. Similar results were demonstrated among mothers and children in the Lanarkshire mining district. Based on these findings, the British Parliament passed a bill providing inexpensive or free milk in government schools.

During the 1930s, Boyd Orr continued to pour his energies and the institute's resources into the study of human nutrition. He became convinced that Great Britain needed a coordinated, scientifically based national food policy but was unable to win government support for his proposals. The publication in 1936 of his *Food, Health, and Income* provoked widespread debate by showing that less than half the British population could afford an adequate diet, while at least a tenth was badly undernourished. Meanwhile, as a member of the League of Nations Technical Commission on Nutrition, Boyd Orr helped to draft a statement of dietary standards and to lay plans for what he called "the marriage of health and agriculture" on a worldwide scale.

International political tensions during the late 1930s, however, forced these plans to be set aside. In 1938, alarmed by the prospect of war, the British government sent Boyd Orr to assess food supplies in Hitler's Germany. On his return, he reported high levels of health and nutrition among young Germans and the existence of a carefully managed agricultural program. When hostilities began the next year, Boyd Orr turned his attention to wartime food policies. His book *Feeding the People in War Time,* written with David Lubbock and published in 1940, outlined an inexpensive diet utilizing home-produced foods that could sustain the British public throughout the conflict. This influential book also proposed measures for rationing, controlling prices, and regulating agricultural production, many of which were subsequently adopted.

In 1942 Boyd Orr accepted an invitation from the Milbank Memorial Fund to visit the United States, where he met with American Vice President Henry Wallace and other officials to discuss a world food policy. In 1943 President Franklin D. Roosevelt invited delegates from the Allied nations to Hot Springs, Virginia, to begin implementing plans for one of his four Atlantic Charter pledges, "Freedom From Want." The British government did not appoint Boyd Orr to the British delegation, however, in part because he advocated international measures that might infringe upon Great Britain's ability to compete in the free market.

In 1945 Boyd Orr retired from the Rowett Research Institute and was elected an independent member of Parliament for the Scottish universities. He was also elected rector by the students of the University of Glasgow.

As a direct outgrowth of the Hot Springs conference, a meeting of the United Nations Food and Agriculture Organization (FAO) was convened in Quebec in the fall of 1945. Again excluded from the British delegation, Boyd Orr was asked by its leader, PHILIP NOEL-BAKER, to join in an unofficial capacity. When invited to address the delegates by LESTER PEARSON, then Canadian ambassador to the United States, Boyd Orr urged them to give the agency not only advisory but broad executive powers. Discouraged and frustrated, he was packing his bags to return to England when he received word that he had been chosen unanimously to serve as the FAO's director-general.

Accepting the post for a two-year term, Boyd Orr quickly organized a staff whose survey of postwar food supplies revealed that as many as 75 million Europeans faced an imminent crisis. To avert the threat of famine, Boyd Orr called a special meeting of the FAO and set up an International Emergency Food Council to coordinate food distribution and impose temporary rationing. At an FAO conference in Copenhagen in 1947, Boyd Orr proposed that the United Nations establish a world food board to cope with the world's rapidly expanding population. The plan was defeated by the United States and Great Britain, who viewed it as a threat to national sovereignty.

When his term at the FAO expired in 1948, Boyd Orr continued to promote his views through articles and speeches. He urged the technologically advanced nations to abolish world hunger and advocated a world government capable of eliminating war. He also traveled widely in Europe and in 1949 accepted an invitation to visit India, where he advised the government on agricultural development and food distribution.

Boyd Orr was awarded the 1949 Nobel Prize for Peace in recognition of his efforts "not only . . . to free mankind from want, but also to create a basis for peaceful cooperation between classes, nations, and races," said Gunnar Jahn of the Norwegian Nobel Committee in his presentation speech. He continued, "Few can claim to have planned and carried through a work as important to the human race as his, a work which clearly paves the way for peace."

In his Nobel lecture, "Science and Peace," Boyd Orr addressed the "possibility of eliminating the causes of war and bringing in a new era of world unity and peace by the intelligent application of the new knowledge and new powers over the forces of nature which modern science has given mankind." Proposing that "some form of world government, with agreed international law and means of enforcing the law, is inevitable," he added a necessary corollary: "There can be no peace in the world so long as a large proportion of the population lack the necessities of life and believe that a change of the political and economic system will make them available. World peace must be based on world plenty."

Boyd Orr remained active in national and international affairs after receiving the Nobel Prize. He visited Pakistan in 1951 to establish a program of food distribution, joined a British delegation to an economic conference in Moscow in 1952, and participated in scientific and economic exchanges with various Eastern European nations. He also toured China in 1956 and Cuba in 1962. In 1971, at the age of ninety, he died at his home near Brechin, Angus, Scotland.

Throughout his professional life, Boyd Orr was assisted by his wife, the former Elizabeth Pearson Callum, whom he had married in 1915. The couple had two daughters and a son who was killed during World War II. Known as a hard worker, Boyd Orr customarily devoted six days a week to his duties. Tall and lean, with bushy eyebrows and mild, blue eyes, Boyd Orr's plainspoken manner belied great powers of persuasion. In his leisure time, he enjoyed long, solitary walks in the Scottish hills, traditional Scottish dances, and curling.

The recipient of more than a dozen honorary degrees from universities at home and abroad, Boyd Orr was knighted in 1935 and elevated to the peerage in 1948. He was a member of the Royal Society and an honorary member of the American Public Health Association and the New York Academy of Sciences. He served as president of the National Peace Council in 1945. His other honors included the Harben Medal of the Royal Institute of Public Health, the Lasker Award of the American Public Health Association, and membership in the Legion of Honor of France.

ADDITIONAL WORKS: The National Food Supply and Its Influence on National Health, 1934; Nutrition in War, 1940; Fighting for What? 1942; Food and the People, 1943; Welfare and Peace, 1945; The New World Food Proposals, 1947; Food: The Foundation of World Unity, 1948; International Liaison Committee of Organizations for Peace, 1950; Economic and Political Problems of the Atomic Age, 1953; The White Man's Dilemma: Food and the Future, 1953, with David Lubbock; Feast and Famine, 1957; The Wonderful World of Food, 1958; As I Recall, 1966; The Rising Tide, 1967.

ABOUT: Biographical Memoirs of the Fellows of the Royal Society, volume 18, 1972; Hambridge, G. The Story of FAO, 1955; Kenworthy, L. S. Lord Orr Speaks, 1952; New York Times Magazine May 19, 1946; Oxbury, H. F. Great Britons, 1985; Survey Graphic March 1948; Times (London) June 26, 1971; de Vries, E. Life and Work of Sir John Boyd Orr, 1948.

BRAGG, W. H.
(July 2, 1862–March 12, 1942)
Nobel Prize for Physics, 1915
(shared with W. L. Bragg)

The English physicist William Henry Bragg was born on a farm near Wigton, Cumberland, to Robert John Bragg, a former merchant marine officer, and Mary (Wood) Bragg, the daughter of the vicar of the parish of Westward. Bragg's mother died when he was seven years old, and thereafter he lived with his uncle, who saw to his education. When the boy was thirteen, his father sent him to King William College, a secondary school on the Isle of Man, where he excelled in all subjects except church history and Greek.

In 1881 Bragg entered Trinity College,

W. H. BRAGG

are emitted from all radioactive atoms as they decay, that is, as their nuclei disintegrate into nuclei of other atoms. He found that the alpha particles emitted by a given radioactive substance can be divided into well-defined groups, with all the particles in one group traveling the same distance before being absorbed by a substance placed in their path. The discovery of these groups, which was quite unexpected, showed that alpha particles are emitted with only certain initial velocities. It further suggested that a radioactive parent nucleus disintegrates in stages, each intermediate daughter nucleus emitting an alpha particle with a different initial velocity. The distance an alpha particle traveled could therefore be used to identify the type of nucleus from which the particle came. This discovery, along with experimental work on other radioactive emissions, secured Bragg international renown.

In 1908 Bragg became Cavendish Professor of Physics at the University of Leeds, returning to England with his family in 1909. Over the next several years, Bragg made extensive investigations of the properties of X rays and gamma rays, concluding that both were particulate, rather than wavelike, in character. During this period he and CHARLES G. BARKLA engaged in an extensive debate over the nature of X rays. In 1912, however, MAX VON LAUE observed that X rays are diffracted (bent) by crystals, producing interference patterns like those made by light. Since these patterns can be produced only by waves, Bragg abandoned his defense of the particle theory, saying that "theories were no more . . . than familiar and useful tools." The problem, he declared, was "not to decide between two theories of X rays, but to find . . . one theory that possesses the capacity of both." Quantum theory, as developed during the first quarter of the twentieth century by MAX PLANCK, ALBERT EINSTEIN, and NIELS BOHR, eventually provided a view of electromagnetic radiation (such as light and X rays) as having properties of both waves and particles.

Cambridge, where he was a brilliant student of mathematics. During his final year he attended lectures in physics by J. J. THOMSON, who mentioned to Bragg an opening at the University of Adelaide in Australia. Bragg applied and was appointed professor of mathematics and physics, a position he held for eighteen years. Because his background in physics was weak compared to his grasp of mathematics, he spent much of the long sea voyage studying the physics textbooks he had brought with him.

Bragg arrived in Adelaide in 1885. Although he wrote a few minor papers, he devoted himself mainly to teaching, university affairs, and the Australian Association for the Advancement of Science; he did not attempt any original research for nearly twenty years. In 1889 he married Gwendoline Todd, daughter of Sir Charles Todd, postmaster general and government astronomer of South Australia. They had two sons, the younger of whom was killed in World War I, and a daughter. During these years Bragg became prominent in South Australian society but published only a few minor papers.

In 1904, when he was forty-two years old, Bragg became deeply interested in the results of recent studies of radioactivity, including the work of ERNEST RUTHERFORD and of MARIE and PIERRE CURIE. Convinced that this new field was in a state of confusion, he undertook his first original research to help elucidate radioactive phenomena. Over the next three years Bragg investigated the penetrating power of alpha particles (helium atom nuclei), which

Bragg's elder son, W. L. BRAGG, who had entered Cambridge to study physics when the family moved to England, began research under J. J. Thomson in 1912. After discussing X-ray diffraction with his father, W. L. Bragg became convinced that Laue's wave picture of X rays was correct, but he felt that Laue's explanation of the details of X-ray diffraction was needlessly complicated. The younger Bragg proposed that the atoms of a crystal are arranged in planes and that X rays are reflected off the planes in patterns determined by the specific arrangement of the atoms. This theory suggested that X-ray diffraction patterns could be used to determine the atomic structure of crystals. In 1913 W. L. Bragg published a formula, now called Bragg's law, describing the angle at which X rays should be aimed at a crystal in order to determine its structure from diffraction patterns.

While his son was working on the theoretical aspects of X-ray diffraction, W. H. Bragg was inventing an instrument called the X-ray spectrometer for detecting and measuring the wavelengths of diffracted X rays. Working together, the Braggs used the X-ray spectrometer to determine the structure of various crystals, and by 1914 they had reduced the analysis of simple crystals to a standard procedure.

In their initial diffraction analyses of simple alkaline halides such as sodium chloride (table salt), the Braggs noted that these compounds are composed not of molecules, but of arrays of sodium ions and chloride ions (an ion is a charged atom). Previously, it had been supposed that all compounds were molecular—that table salt, for example, was made up of individual molecules consisting of sodium atoms and chlorine atoms. The Braggs' discovery that some compounds are ionic—that there is no such thing, for example, as a sodium chloride molecule—was of fundamental importance to chemists. The Dutch chemist PETER DEBYE utilized these results in his fundamental studies of the behavior of ions in solution.

Bragg's invention of the X-ray spectrometer and his work with his son on crystal analysis laid the foundations of the modern science of X-ray crystallography. X-ray diffraction techniques are used by materials scientists, mineralogists, ceramists, and biologists and have solved problems ranging from the determination of the internal stresses in metal machine components to the structure of biological molecules such as deoxyribonucleic acid (DNA). Although modern X-ray spectrometers are highly automated, the basic device and analytic techniques are those developed by the Braggs.

The Braggs were awarded the 1915 Nobel Prize for Physics "for their services in the analysis of crystal structure by means of X rays." World War I had broken out the year before, and the awards ceremony was canceled. In an essay written in 1919, G. D. Granqvist of the Royal Swedish Academy of Sciences described the Braggs' work. Thanks to their methods, he said, "an entirely new world has been opened and has already in part been explored with marvelous exactitude." W. H. Bragg did not deliver a Nobel lecture.

The year he won the Nobel Prize, W. H. Bragg became Quain Professor of Physics at University College, London. The outbreak of World War I slowed research on crystal structure, and during the war Bragg headed a group of scientists who investigated marine acoustics and underwater acoustic sensors. After the war he assembled a large research group that pioneered X-ray analysis of organic crystals, a field that gave rise to the modern science of molecular biology. Bragg himself succeeded in identifying the structures of naphthalene and its derivatives, while others in the group investigated different classes of organic compounds and did theoretical work on X-ray diffraction in complex crystals.

In 1923 Bragg became director of the Royal Institution in London, and his group continued organic crystal research there. An extremely effective speaker, Bragg was much in demand throughout England as a lecturer to students as well as to professional colleagues. During World War II, Bragg served actively on several scientific advisory committees to the government, so that his time for research was limited. Nevertheless, he maintained a lively interest in the work of the Royal Institution, and he continued to write papers on new developments in X-ray crystallography until shortly before his death in London on March 12, 1942.

Known as a warm, generous, and unpretentious man, Bragg was an admirer of tradition and of craftsmanship. Deeply religious, he was interested in the relationship of science and faith and wrote a book on the subject. His family was his greatest pleasure, and his wife's death in 1929 was a great blow to him. Bragg was an avid golfer as well as a talented amateur painter and flute player.

In addition to the Nobel Prize, Bragg's many awards included the Rumford Medal (1916) and Copley Medal (1930) of the Royal Society. He was knighted in 1920 and received the Order of Merit in 1931. President of the Royal Society from 1935 to 1940, Bragg was also a member of the leading scientific academies of other countries. He held sixteen honorary doctorates from British and foreign universities.

SELECTED WORKS: Studies in Radioactivity, 1912; X Rays and Crystal Structure, 1915, with W. L. Bragg; The World of Sound, 1920; Electrons and Their Waves, 1921;

State, 1925; Creative Knowledge: Old Trades and New Science, 1927; An Introduction to Crystal Analysis, 1928; Craftsmanship and Science, 1928; The Universe of Light, 1933; Science and Faith, 1941; The Story of Electromagnetism, 1941.

ABOUT: Caroe, G. M. William Henry Bragg 1862–1942: Man and Scientist, 1978; Dictionary of Scientific Biography, volume 2, 1970; Grant, K. The Life and Works of Sir William Bragg, 1952; Obituary Notices of Fellows of the Royal Society, volume 4, 1943.

BRAGG, W. L.
(March 31, 1890–July 1, 1971)
Nobel Prize for Physics, 1915
(shared with W. H. Bragg)

W. L. BRAGG

The English physicist William Lawrence Bragg was born in Adelaide, Australia, to W. H. BRAGG, then professor of mathematics and physics at the University of Adelaide, and Gwendoline (Todd) Bragg, daughter of Sir Charles Todd, postmaster general and government astronomer of South Australia. Young Bragg first encountered X rays at the age of five, only a few weeks after their discovery by WILHELM RÖNTGEN. Upon learning of the rays, the elder Bragg constructed a crude X-ray apparatus, which was ready just when the boy happened to fracture his elbow. Young Bragg's uncle, a physician, used the device to determine the extent of the damage, the first recorded medical use of X rays in Australia.

Bragg spent his childhood in Adelaide, except for a year in France and England with his parents. He attended St. Peters College, a secondary school in Adelaide, and in 1905 he entered the University of Adelaide, graduating three years later with first-class honors in mathematics. During Bragg's years at the university, his father was conducting research on radioactivity and X rays, and the two often engaged in lively discussions of physics.

When Bragg's father was offered the Cavendish Professorship of Physics at the University of Leeds in 1908, the family moved to England, arriving there early the following year. Bragg studied physics at Trinity College, Cambridge, and passed the natural science examinations with first-class honors in 1912. He then began doing research under J. J. THOMSON at Cambridge while collaborating with his father in the investigation of the X-ray diffraction patterns discovered by MAX VON LAUE earlier that year. In his early work the elder Bragg had supported the idea that X rays were beams of particles, but he was impressed by Laue's

discovery that X rays are diffracted (bent) by crystals, producing interference patterns like those made by light. Such patterns can be made only by waves.

After discussing X-ray diffraction with his father, Bragg became convinced that Laue's wave interpretation was correct, but that Laue's explanation of the details of diffraction was unnecessarily complicated. Atoms in crystals are arranged in planes, and Bragg proposed that specific diffraction patterns are due to the specific arrangements of the atoms in different kinds of crystals. If so, X-ray diffraction could be used to determine the structures of crystals. In 1913 he published an equation, later called Bragg's law, that described the angles at which an X-ray beam should be aimed in order to determine the structure of a crystal from the diffraction of X rays reflected off the crystal's planes. Bragg then used his equation to analyze various crystals. The X-ray spectrometer invented by his father in the same year proved invaluable, because its sensitive measurements allowed the analysis of more complex crystals than was possible with earlier methods.

The first substances the Braggs investigated by means of X-ray diffraction were the alkaline halides, which include sodium chloride, or common table salt. By 1913 the atomic theory of matter was well established, and it was generally held that a chemical compound was made up of molecules composed of atoms of different elements. Sodium chloride, for example, was thought to consist of molecules, each containing a sodium atom and a chlorine atom. Bragg's investigations showed that a sodium chloride crystal is made up not of molecules, but of arrays of sodium ions and chloride ions (an ion is a charged atom). Molecules of sodium chloride do not exist in the crystal. The distinction thus established between molecular compounds (where crystals are made up of molecules) and ionic compounds (where crystals are made up of arrays of ions) was of enormous importance and enabled scientists to achieve a much greater understanding of the behavior of solutions. Working jointly, the Braggs reduced X-ray analysis of simple materials to a standard procedure by 1914. That year the younger Bragg was elected fellow and lecturer at Trinity College.

The work done by Bragg and his father between 1912 and 1914 established the basis of the modern science of X-ray crystallography. The analysis of X-ray diffraction patterns is a powerful tool for mineralogists, metallurgists, ceramists, and other researchers concerned with the atomic structure of materials. This method has also allowed scientists to determine the structure of highly complex molecules, giving rise to the field of molecular biology.

The 1915 Nobel Prize for Physics was awarded jointly to Bragg and his father "for their services in the analysis of crystal structure by means of X rays." Because of the disruption caused by World War I, the awards ceremony was canceled. In an essay written in 1919, G. D. Granqvist of the Royal Swedish Academy of Sciences pointed out that through their work, the Braggs had made it possible not only to treat X-ray diffraction mathematically but also to "attack the problem of crystal structures" experimentally. "Thanks to the methods that the Braggs . . . have devised," Granqvist went on, "an entirely new world has been opened and has already in part been explored with marvelous exactitude."

In his Nobel lecture, delivered in Stockholm in 1922, Bragg summarized the work for which he had been awarded the prize. He concluded by reminding his listeners that "there is a still deeper application of the X-ray analysis" than determining crystalline structure, namely "the structure of the atom itself. Since the wavelength of the X rays is less than the 'atomic diameter,' as it is somewhat vaguely termed, and since the rays are presumably diffracted by the electrons in the atom, we ought to be able to get some idea of the distribution of those electrons in the same way that we draw conclusions as to the groupings of the atoms."

During World War I, Bragg served as a technical adviser on sound ranging (locating the enemy from the sound of artillery fire), rising to the rank of major. After the war he returned to Trinity College as a lecturer. In 1919 he succeeded ERNEST RUTHERFORD as Langworthy Professor of Physics at the University of Manchester, where Bragg returned to his investigations of crystal structures by means of X rays. For many years he devoted himself to the study of the complex structures exhibited by the silicate family of minerals, work that revolutionized the science of mineralogy and placed it on a sound scientific basis. Subsequently, the results of Bragg's studies were of great value to LINUS C. PAULING.

After completing his mineral analysis around 1930, Bragg supervised and participated in studies of metals and metal alloys. In 1937 he became the director of the National Physical Laboratory, and the following year he accepted a concurrent appointment as Cavendish Professor of Physics at Cambridge, a position he held until 1953. At the end of World War II, Bragg helped organize the International Union of Crystallography and served as its first president in 1949.

In the late 1930s MAX PERUTZ had interested Bragg in the crystallographic analysis of the complex globular proteins. World War II interrupted this research, but after the war it was resumed. Bragg organized the research effort, found support for the project, and assembled a resourceful team to tackle the problem. By the time Bragg left Cambridge, his group had made significant advances and developed powerful analytic tools. Within two years Perutz and JOHN C. KENDREW succeeded in analyzing globular proteins, particularly hemoglobin. In the same period, FRANCIS CRICK, JAMES D. WATSON, and MAURICE H. F. WILKINS analyzed the structure of deoxyribonucleic acid (DNA). Bragg's support of these research efforts and the tools and techniques developed under his guidance made an invaluable contribution to these achievements.

The field of physics changed to such an extent during Bragg's lifetime that, except for the early work for which he won the Nobel Prize, virtually all of his research lay outside the main areas of interest of the physics community. He is known as much for his contributions to chemistry, mineralogy, metallurgy, and molecular biology as for his work in experimental physics. Although some of his contributions were directly his own, those of the scientific groups he organized and guided were at least as important. Bragg was highly regarded as an outstanding scientific organizer with great energy, tact, vision, and leadership abilities.

From 1954 until his retirement in 1966, Bragg was director of the Royal Institution in London (a position held earlier by his father). During this time he was very concerned with science education, and he frequently addressed lay audiences, particularly of schoolchildren, on the beauty and excitement of scientific discovery. A popular and effective speaker, he was asked to deliver a series of lectures on television. He continued lecturing after his retirement, and he also wrote on scientific topics, completing a history of X-ray crystallography shortly before his death on July 1, 1971.

Bragg married Alice Hopkinson in 1921; they had two sons and two daughters. Bragg, who was an amateur painter, also enjoyed literature and gardening.

In addition to the Nobel Prize, Bragg's many honors included the Roebling Medal of the Mineralogical Society of America (1948) and the Hughes (1931), the Royal (1946), and the Copley (1966) medals of the Royal Society. He was knighted in 1941, and in 1967 he was made a Companion of Honour. A fellow of the Royal Society, Bragg was also a member of the scientific academies of the United States, France, Sweden, China, Netherlands, and Belgium and of the French Society of Mineralogy and Crystallography.

SELECTED WORKS: X Rays and Crystal Structure, 1915, with W. H. Bragg; The Structure of Silicates, 1930; The Crystalline State: A General Survey, 1934; Electricity, 1936; Atomic Structure of Minerals, 1937; The Structure of Alloys, 1938; The History of X-Ray Analysis, 1943; The Crystal Structures of Minerals, 1965, with G. F. Claringbull; Ideas and Discoveries in Physics, 1970; The Development of X-Ray Analysis, 1975.

ABOUT: Biographical Memoirs of Fellows of the Royal Society, volume 25, 1979; Dictionary of Scientific Biography, volume 2, 1970; Ewald, P. P. (ed.) Fifty Years of X-Ray Diffraction, 1962.

BRANDT, WILLY
(December 18, 1913–   )
Nobel Prize for Peace, 1971

Willy Brandt, German chancellor and diplomat, was born Herbert Ernst Karl Frahm in the Baltic seaport of Lübeck, the son of an unknown father and Martha Frahm, an unmarried salesclerk. Under the tutelage of his working-class grandfather, he became a socialist in the European democratic tradition. With a scholarship, he attended the Lübeck

WILLY BRANDT

Johanneum, and while still at the gymnasium, he began contributing articles to the socialist newspaper *Volksbote* (People's Herald) under the pseudonym Willy Brandt, a name he later adopted. At the age of sixteen he was admitted to full membership in the Social Democratic party. As Hitler and the National Socialists increasingly undermined the Weimar Republic, Brandt often brawled with Nazi brownshirts in the streets. Convinced that the Social Democrats were too weak and ineffectual to resist Nazism, he switched his allegiance to the more radical Socialist Workers party in 1931. Graduating from the Johanneum the following year, he supported himself as a clerk for a shipping company while continuing to contribute articles to socialist publications.

When Hitler became chancellor of Germany in 1933, Brandt, like many other socialists, found himself in jeopardy. Ordered by his party to establish a center for exiled socialists, he fled Germany for Oslo, Norway, two months before Hitler banned leftist opposition parties and began imprisoning and executing their leaders. In Oslo, Brandt headed the Refugee Federation and began writing for the Norwegian Labor party newspaper *Arbeiterbladet* (Worker's News). With the aid of a scholarship, he studied history and philosophy at Oslo University and became imbued with the reformist tenets of Scandinavian social democracy.

In subsequent prewar travels throughout Western Europe (including several months in Berlin incognito), Brandt helped organize anti-Nazi movements. While reporting from Spain on the Civil War in 1937, he developed a firm opposition to Soviet Communism even though he supported the leftist Loyalists. Returning to Norway, Brandt acquired Norwegian citizenship in 1940, the same year Germany invaded Norway. Imprisoned briefly as a Norwegian soldier, Brandt escaped to neutral Sweden, where he practiced journalism and stayed in touch with Resistance leaders for the remainder of the war.

As an accredited Norwegian correspondent, Brandt covered the Nuremberg war-crimes trials in 1946. The following year he was appointed Norwegian press attaché to Berlin. However, Brandt resigned this position after resuming relations with the Social Democratic party in Germany, and again he became a German citizen. In 1948–1949, as an aide to Ernst Reuter, mayor of West Berlin, Brandt worked with British and American authorities during the Soviet blockade of the city.

After the Federal Republic of Germany was established in 1949, Brandt was elected to the Bundestag, the lower house of the legislature, where he represented Berlin until 1957. Also elected to the Berlin municipal legislature in 1950, he steadily built a political reputation that led to his election as mayor of Berlin in 1957. The following year Nikita Khrushchev, the Soviet premier, demanded that Berlin sever its political ties with West Germany and become "an independent political entity." When Brandt rejected the ultimatum, East Germany began erecting a wall to seal off access to West Berlin. Expecting that the United States would act to halt further construction, Brandt became disillusioned when President John F. Kennedy indicated in a letter that no such effort would be made. Some historians have suggested that this incident, which represented the acceptance of two Germanys by the United States, encouraged Brandt to seek rapprochement with the East.

During the early postwar years, Brandt was instrumental in moderating the leftist views of his party, thereby giving the Social Democrats broader national appeal. In 1959, for example, party leaders meeting at Bad Godesberg decided to break with traditional Marxist ideology. Brandt, who played a leading role at this conference, supported a policy that endorsed private property, a free-market economy, and religious observance.

By 1961, Brandt had become the dominant figure in the Social Democratic party. Although defeated in his attempt to become chancellor in that year's general election, he became the party's deputy chairman in 1962 and its chairman two years later.

During the early 1960s the Christian Democrats maintained their majority, but under Brandt's leadership the Social Democrats gradually gained strength. With the formation of a coalition government under the Christian Democratic chancellor Kurt Kiesinger in 1966, Brandt became vice-chancellor and minister of foreign affairs. As such, he pursued policies intended to achieve what he called a "European peace order." Believing in the necessity of a unified Western Europe, he advocated economic and military cooperation with Germany's former enemies. At the same time, he initiated his *Ostpolitik*, or Eastern policy, in pursuit of détente with West Germany's neighbors to the east. In keeping with this policy, West Germany exchanged ambassadors with Romania in 1967 and reestablished diplomatic relations with Yugoslavia the following year.

In the general election held on September 28, 1969, the Social Democrats won enough seats in the Bundestag to give them control of the house with the backing of the Free Democrats. On October 21, 1969, the Bundestag elected Brandt chancellor by a vote of 251 to 235. "I will not be the chancellor of a conquered Germany but of a liberated Germany," he told reporters. He added that West Germany would remain America's ally but would take a more independent course.

As the fourth chancellor of the Federal Republic, Brandt continued to work for peaceful coexistence with the Eastern-bloc nations while strengthening economic agreements with Western Europe. He strongly urged that Britain be admitted to the European Economic Community, signed the multilateral nuclear nonproliferation treaty of 1969, and began negotiations with Poland and the Soviet Union over such issues as territorial claims, diplomatic and cultural ties, and military force.

In March 1970 Brandt traveled to East Germany for talks with the nation's Communist leader, Willi Stoph. Although their discussions proved inconclusive, they served to ease tensions between the two Germanys. Several months later, extended negotiations between Brandt and Soviet Premier Aleksei Kosygin produced a nonaggression pact between the two nations. In the Bonn-Moscow Treaty, signed on August 12, 1970, West Germany recognized the de facto existence of East Germany, and both sides renounced the use of force. The Bonn-Warsaw Treaty, signed during Brandt's historic visit to Warsaw in December 1970, normalized relations between West Germany and Poland.

The following year, with Brandt's support, the four powers that had divided Germany, and Berlin, after the war (Great Britain, France, the United States, and the Soviet Union) signed an accord permitting free travel between West Berlin and West Germany across East Germany. The agreement also allowed West Berliners to visit their relatives in the eastern part of the city.

In recognition of his "concrete initiatives leading to the relaxation of tension" between East and West, Brandt was awarded the 1971 Nobel Prize for Peace. In his Nobel lecture Brandt discussed the importance of European unity. "Ideological contrasts create and have created frontiers," he said, "but it is a big step forward when more importance is attached to mutual interests than differing ideologies."

Brandt was reelected chancellor in 1972, when the Social Democrats won their first plurality in the Bundestag. However, his campaign promises to reform education, taxation, and the representation of labor in factories were blocked by the Free Democrats in his ruling coalition. Continuing domestic inflation and a series of strikes also undermined the effectiveness of his government. Brandt's unprecedented visit to Israel in 1973 and West Germany's admission to the United Nations helped Brandt maintain his popularity, but the arrest in 1974 of one of his personal aides on charges of espionage created a political scandal that forced him to resign.

In retirement, Brandt has again come full circle to the radicalism of his youth. As chairman since 1976 of the Socialist International, an organization of forty-nine Social Democratic parties around the world, he has attracted leftist members by his support of revolutionary causes in the Third World. Many socialist leaders, including François Mitterrand of France, have criticized Brandt's activities as detrimental to more pragmatic efforts, however. Other critics have charged that, as chancellor, Brandt's attitude toward the Soviet Union was tantamount to appeasement. Despite his image abroad as a man of decisive action and courage, Brandt has often been criticized in Germany for periods of apathy and depression. In 1987 he resigned as chairman of the Social Democratic party when his choice of a controversial spokesman aroused protests among party leaders.

While living in Norway, Brandt married Carlota Thorkildsen in 1940, and they had a daughter. They later divorced, and in 1948 he married Rut Hansen, a Norwegian journalist, with whom he had three sons, Peter, Lars, and Mathias.

"No people can escape from their history," Brandt has said. As leader of postwar West Germany, he helped his nation face its recent past. As mayor of West Berlin, he steered a moderate course between the extremes of appeasement and bloodshed. As architect of West Germany's foreign relations, he supported close ties with the West, articulated a vision of a unified Europe, and worked for reconciliation with Germany's neighbors. In 1985 Brandt was awarded the Einstein Peace Prize, established to honor ALBERT EINSTEIN's commitment to world peace.

WORKS IN ENGLISH TRANSLATION: My Road to Berlin, 1960; The Ordeal of Co-existence, 1963; A Peace Policy for Europe, 1969; Peace: Writings and Speeches, 1971; In Exile: Essays, Reflections, Letters, 1971; People and Politics: The Years 1960–1975, 1978; Dangers and Options: The Matter of World Survival, 1982; Arms and Hunger, 1986.

ABOUT: Binder, D. The Other German, 1975; Bolesch, H. O., and Leicht, H. D. Willy Brandt: A Portrait of the German Chancellor, 1971; Commentary July 1983; Current Biography December 1973; Görgey, L. Bonn's Eastern Policy: 1964–1971, 1972; Harpprecht, K. Willy Brandt: Portrait and Self-Portrait, 1972; Hynd, J. B. Willy Brandt: A Pictorial Biography, 1966; Prittie, T. Willy Brandt: Portrait of a Statesman, 1974; Whetten, L. L. Germany's Ostpolitik, 1971.

BRANTING, KARL
(November 23, 1860–February 24, 1925)
Noble Prize for Peace, 1921
(shared with Christian Lange)

Karl Hjalmar Branting, Swedish journalist and politician, was born in Stockholm, the only child of Lars Gabriel and Emerentia (af Georgii) Branting. His father was director of the Stockholm High School of Gymnastics and a developer of the Swedish system of gymnastics. As a boy, Branting attended Stockholm's exclusive Beskow School, where one of his classmates was the future king Gustav V.

Entering the University of Uppsala in 1877 with the intention of becoming an astronomer, Branting majored in mathematics and natural science. During his university years, however, he became attracted to liberal political philosophy when he discovered such social issues as unemployment, public health, and poverty. In 1881 he acted upon his liberal convictions by contributing his own money to help the

KARL BRANTING

financially threatened Stockholm Workers Institute continue its program of lectures and study courses.

Upon graduating from the university in 1882, Branting became assistant to the director of the Stockholm Astronomical Society. Two years later, the same year he married Anna Jaderin, he left the society to write for the radical newspaper *Tiden* (The Times), which was edited by fellow countryman KLAS ARNOLDSON. As foreign editor, Branting traveled in France, Switzerland, Germany, and Russia, talking with workers and socialist thinkers. As a result, he became convinced that socialism offered the best solution to the problems of the day. In 1885 he succeeded Arnoldson as editor in chief of the newspaper.

During the 1880s liberal political and social ideas were beginning to take hold in Sweden. For the previous two centuries, political power had been held by a rigid class of conservative bureaucrats and by the landed nobility. But in 1884 the Liberal party won a majority for the first time in the general elections, while the embryonic trade union movement began to advocate socialist measures. During this period playwrights such as August Strindberg, Henrik Ibsen, and BJØRNSTJERNE BØRNSON attacked what they perceived as the stultifying social and political attitudes that had long dominated Scandinavian life.

When *Tiden* failed in 1886, the Swedish Socialist party asked Branting to establish and edit its first newspaper, the *Social Demokraten* (Social Democrat). During his thirty-one years with the paper, Branting shaped it into an im-

portant educational and political organ of socialist opinion. Moreover, the experience he gained while covering sessions of the Swedish Parliament gave him a detailed knowledge of the political process.

As an active member of the Socialist party, Branting made speeches, settled disputes, formed clubs for workers, organized unions, and supported strikes. He helped found the Social Democratic Labor party in 1889, and he was chosen to be its president in 1907, a position he held until his death. Under Branting's leadership the party quickly became a strong force in Swedish politics. Meanwhile, in 1896 Branting became the first Social Democrat to win a seat in the Parliament; in 1902 three more Social Democrats were elected, and their numbers grew steadily during the following years.

For twenty-nine years as a legislator, Branting championed universal suffrage and an improved standard of living for all citizens, drawing on working-class support without alienating the progressive middle class. An early anti-militarist, he opposed arms allocations at the expense of social services. "If in the hour of danger," he said, "we could only muster an army . . . which nourished a doubt as to what they really had to defend in this native land, in which all they can hope for is work and toil in days of good health and the poorhouse in their old age, then our fate would be sealed whether we had ninety days' military training or not."

Branting's pacifism was much in evidence during the dispute over Norway's desire for independence from Sweden. Although many Swedes called for war to prevent Norway's secession, Branting, like Arnoldson, urged arbitration rather than force to settle the issue. When Norway voted for independence in 1905, Branting's and Arnoldson's influence helped obtain a peaceful separation of the two countries.

During World War I, Branting, again with Arnoldson, strongly supported Swedish neutrality, opposing those who wanted Sweden to side with the Central Powers, led by Germany. Although favoring neutrality, Branting's sympathies lay with the Allies, led by Great Britain and France and later the United States, because of their commitment to liberal political institutions. As a long-standing advocate of international peace based on justice, Branting was elected to preside over preliminary meetings to prepare for the 1919 Paris Peace Conference, which he attended as Sweden's representative. He became an early supporter of the League of Nations and led the movement to bring Sweden into the league.

In 1917, as a member of the Swedish Parliament, Branting helped bring to power a Liberal–Social Democratic coalition government, in which he served as minister of finance. This government succeeded in achieving a reform of the constitution that helped spread social democracy throughout Sweden and that extended the franchise to all male citizens. When in March 1920 the Liberals refused to support Social Democratic measures such as tax reform and unemployment insurance, the coalition was dissolved. Branting then established his own government and became Sweden's first socialist prime minister. In October Branting called elections to try to increase the Social Democrats' power in Parliament over the Liberals. When the effort failed, Branting resigned as prime minister but retained his seat in Parliament.

At the same time, Branting continued his work in the League of Nations, representing Sweden at the first league Assembly in 1920. As a leader of the disarmament faction, he opposed the use of military force to uphold league decisions. Arbitration, he believed, offered the best hope for peaceful resolution of international conflict.

In part for his efforts toward the peaceful separation of Sweden and Norway but primarily for his work with the league, Branting was awarded the 1921 Nobel Peace Prize, which he shared with CHRISTIAN LANGE of Norway. In his Nobel lecture, delivered in Oslo the following year, he expressed his view that World War I represented "the birthpangs of a new Europe," and that from the darkness of the war years came a great benefit: "the beginning development of a *League of Nations* in which disputes between members are to be solved by legal methods and not by the military superiority of the stronger." He took the opportunity to urge support of "the demand which we small, so-called neutral countries should make at Geneva and everywhere: the demand that the League of Nations become *universal* in order truly to fulfill its task."

Furthermore, he said, "If we all do our best to work for that real peace and reconciliation between peoples which it is our first duty to promote within the League of Nations, then the power to command attention will be available to us, even though, as small nations, we are so isolated and powerless that individually we can exert little influence on the great powers in world politics."

In 1921 Branting again became head of a Socialist government in Sweden, serving as both prime minister and minister of foreign affairs. Under this government, which remained in office for two years, women received the right to vote. In 1923 he joined the Council of the League of Nations and took part in settling the dispute between Greece and Italy over control of the Dodecanese Islands, which Greece subsequently ceded to Italy. The following year he became a member of the Council's Committee on Disarmament, in which he helped draft the Geneva Protocol, a document that outlined an international security system based on arbitration. He also acted as mediator in the dispute between Great Britain and Turkey over the stationing of British troops in Istanbul in 1924. The mediation resulted in withdrawal of the troops and British recognition of the independent Republic of Turkey.

Branting became Sweden's prime minister for the third time in 1924. In January 1925 illness forced him to retire, and he died in Stockholm shortly thereafter.

ABOUT: Fortnightly Review July 1917; Jones, S. S. The Scandinavian States and the League of Nations, 1939; Living Age June 6, 1925; New York Times February 25, 1925; Nordstrom, B. J. (ed.) Dictionary of Scandinavian History, 1986; Scott, F. D. Sweden: The Nation's History, 1977; Tingsten, H. The Swedish Social Democrats, 1973; Verney, D. Parliamentary Reform in Sweden, 1957.

BRATTAIN, WALTER H.

(February 10, 1902–)
Nobel Prize for Physics, 1956
(shared with John Bardeen and William Shockley)

The American physicist Walter Houser Brattain was born in Amoy in southeastern China. The son of Ross R. Brattain, a teacher at a private school for Chinese boys, and Ottilie (Houser) Brattain, he was the oldest of five children. Early in Brattain's childhood, the family returned to the state of Washington, where the elder Brattains had grown up, and settled in Tonasket. His father became a homesteader, cattle rancher, and flour miller. The boy attended public school in Tonasket before entering Whitman College in Walla Walla, majoring in physics and mathematics. He earned a B.S. in 1924, an M.A. in physics at the University of Oregon in 1926, and a Ph.D. in physics at the University of Minnesota in 1929. Although he loved ranching and outdoor life, he loathed farming. "Following three horses and a harrow in the dust was what made a physicist out of me," he said later.

While completing his doctoral program, Brattain spent the academic year 1928–1929 at the United States National Bureau of Standards, where he worked on improving the accuracy of time and vibration-frequency measurements and helped design a portable temperature-controlled oscillator. In 1929 he joined the Bell Telephone Laboratories as a research physicist, remaining there until he reached mandatory retirement age in 1967, when he returned to Whitman College to teach physics and to study the surface of living cells.

In his first seven years at Bell Labs, Brattain investigated the effect of adsorbed films on electron emission from hot surfaces, electron collisions in mercury vapor, magnetometers, infrared phenomena, and frequency standards. At the time, the primary electronic amplifying device was a three-electrode (triode) vacuum tube, invented by Lee De Forest in 1907. Thomas A. Edison had discovered in the late nineteenth century, while developing his electric light, that a current would flow between a hot filament and a second electrode sealed into an evacuated bulb if a battery was connected between them, with the electrode positive. This was the birth of the two-electrode (diode) tube. Physicists later showed that the filament emitted electrons, which carry a negative electric charge and are attracted to the positive electrode. Since diodes conduct electricity in only one direction, they came to be used as rectifiers for converting alternating current into unidirectional direct current. De Forest inserted a wire mesh (grid) between the electron emitter (cathode) and the positive electrode (anode). A small variation in grid voltage produced a large variation in the current flowing through the grid from cathode to anode, thus permitting amplification of a signal applied to the grid. The high temperature needed to produce electron emission also shortened the life of the cathode and harmed the vacuum tube. Brattain found that certain thin cathode coatings provided satisfactory emission at reduced temperatures, improving amplifier action and prolonging life.

When WILLIAM SHOCKLEY came to Bell Labs in 1936, he soon became involved in research on the properties of a class of materials called semiconductors. His aim was to replace vacuum tubes with solid-state devices that would be smaller, less fragile, and more energy-efficient. The electrical conductivity of semiconductors lies between that of good conductors (mostly metals) and that of insulators and is sensitive to the presence of minute amounts of impurities. Early crystal radios used a con-

WALTER H. BRATTAIN

tact between a curl of wire (cat's whisker) and a piece of the mineral galena (a semiconductor) to rectify the small signals antennas picked up from radio waves. Investigating semiconductors, Brattain and Shockley sought a material that could amplify as well as rectify. Their research was interrupted from 1942 to 1945 by a wartime assignment to the Division of War Research at Columbia University, where they were engaged in the application of scientific methods to antisubmarine warfare. (Shockley's efforts were diverted even earlier to work on radar.)

Returning to Bell Labs after the war, Brattain and Shockley were joined by JOHN BARDEEN, a theoretical physicist. In this collaboration, Brattain served as the experimentalist who determined the properties and behavior of the materials and devices under investigation. Shockley theorized that the current flowing through a semiconductor could be affected by an electric field established by a voltage applied from the outside, creating a field-effect amplifier. The field would be like that supplied by the grid in a triode vacuum tube amplifier. The group built many devices to test Shockley's theory, but all failed.

At this point Bardeen suggested that the electric field was prevented from entering the body of the semiconductor by a layer of electrons trapped on its surface. This led to an extensive study of surface effects. Semiconductor surfaces were subjected to light, heat, cold, and the application of liquids (insulating and conducting) and metallic films. In 1947, when the group had achieved a greater understanding of surface behavior, Brattain and Bardeen constructed a device that displayed for the first time what came to be known as the transistor effect. The device, called a point-contact transistor, consisted of two closely spaced gold film contacts on one face of a block of germanium crystal containing a small concentration of impurities, and a third terminal on the opposite face. A positive bias voltage was placed between one gold contact (emitter) and the third terminal (base) and a negative bias between the second gold contact (collector) and the base. A signal applied to the emitter influenced the current flowing in the collector-base circuit. Although the device amplified the signal, as desired, its principle of operation turned out to be unanticipated and stimulated another round of research to find a satisfactory explanation.

Although much semiconductor theory had already been developed with the application of quantum mechanics, predictions had not yet received adequately quantitative confirmation by experiment. Atoms in crystals are held together by interaction between the electrons most loosely bound to their nuclei. In a perfect crystal, the bonds are said to be "filled" or "satisfied." The electrons are difficult to detach, do not flow readily, and manifest a very high electrical resistance. The crystal is an insulator. However, imperfections, introduced by alien atoms that do not quite fit into the regular crystal structure, can either make some of the electrons surplus, and therefore available to participate in a current, or produce a deficiency of electrons, known as "holes." In a mathematical description, holes move as if they were positively charged electrons, although at a different rate. In fact, they are spaces left by missing electrons and therefore appear to move backward as neighboring electrons move forward to fill previously emptied spaces and leave other holes in their wake. The explanation of transistor action proved to involve a complex interplay of the kinds and concentrations of impurities, the local character of contacts between dissimilar materials, and contributions to the current by both electrons and holes. The important role of holes had not before been sufficiently appreciated.

Shockley then predicted that the device could be improved by replacing the metal semiconductor contacts with rectifying contacts between different kinds of semiconductors, one in which excess electrons predominated (N type) and one in which holes predominated (P type). A successful model, called the junction transistor, was made in 1950. Consisting of a thin P-type region sandwiched between two N-type regions, with metallic contacts to each region, it performed as Shockley had predicted. Junction transistors largely replaced point-contact types because they are easier to make and superior in performance. Shockley's early idea, the field-effect transistor, turned out to have been thwarted by the inadequacies of available material. A practical field-effect transistor was made with silicon crystals when growing and purifying techniques were sufficiently advanced.

Like the vacuum tube, the transistor permits a very small current in one circuit to control a much larger current in another circuit. Transistors rapidly replaced vacuum tubes in all applications except those requiring the control of very large amounts of power, such as broadcasting and industrial radio-frequency heating. Bipolar transistors are routinely used where high speed is needed, as well as in many high-frequency power applications not so demanding as to require vacuum tubes. The field-effect transistor is the basic design used in the vast majority of electronic devices. It is easier to fabricate and consumes even less power than similar bipolar devices. Although some transistors are still made of germanium, most are fabricated from silicon, which is more resistant to high temperatures. With subsequent advances in technology, up to a million transistors are able to be incorporated in a single silicon chip, and the number is still rising. These chips are the basis for the rapid development of modern computers, communications equipment, and controllers.

Brattain shared the 1956 Nobel Prize for Physics with Bardeen and Shockley. It was awarded "for their researches on semiconductors and their discovery of the transistor effect." In his Nobel lecture, "Surface Properties of Semiconductors," Brattain emphasized the importance of surfaces, "where many of our most interesting and useful phenomena occur. In electronics, most if not all active circuit elements involve nonequilibrium phenomena occurring at surfaces."

Brattain's subsequent research into the properties of semiconductors and their surfaces has been of great importance for field-effect transistors, which are critically susceptible to surface defects, and to solar cells, which are sensitive to surface electrical behavior.

In 1935 Brattain married Keren Gilmore, a physical chemist; they had a son. A year after his first wife's death in 1957, he married Emma Jane Kirsch Miller. Known for his blunt, outspoken manner, Brattain enjoys golf, fishing, and reading.

Brattain's other awards include the Stuart Ballantine Medal of the Franklin Institute (1952), the John Scott Award of the city of Philadelphia (1955), and the University of Oregon Distinguished Alumnus Award (1976). He is the recipient of five honorary doctorates, a member of the National Academy of Sciences and the Inventors Hall of Fame, and a fellow of the American Academy of Arts and Sciences, the American Association for the Advancement of Science, and the American Physical Society.

ABOUT: Current Biography September 1957; National Cyclopedia of American Biography, supplement I, 1960; National Geographic Society. Those Inventive Americans, 1971; Science 84 November 1984.

FERDINAND BRAUN

BRAUN, FERDINAND
(June 6, 1850–April 20, 1918)
Nobel Prize for Physics, 1909
(shared with Guglielmo Marconi)

The German physicist and inventor Karl Ferdinand Braun was born in the town of Fulda to Konrad and Franziska (Gohring) Braun. After attending the local gymnasium, he studied at the University of Marburg and then pursued doctoral studies in physics at the University of Berlin. There, under the guidance of the German physicist Georg Quincke, he wrote a dissertation on the vibration of elastic rods and strings and was awarded a Ph.D. in 1872. When Quincke accepted a position at the University of Würzburg that year, Braun followed to serve as his assistant. In 1874 Braun became headmaster of the Thomas Gymnasium in Leipzig. He also published his discovery that crystals of mineral metal sulfides, such as galena and pyrite, conduct electric currents in only one direction. Five decades later, the principles Braun discovered were employed in the receivers of crystal radios.

In 1876 Braun returned to Marburg as professor of theoretical physics, remaining there four years. He served as professor of theoretical physics at the University of Strasbourg from 1880 to 1883, then as professor of physics at the technical university in Karlsruhe until 1885. For the next ten years he served as professor of experimental physics at the University of Tübingen and directed the creation of its Physics Institute. In 1895 Braun came back to the University of Strasbourg as professor of physics and director of the Strasbourg Physics

Institute, where most of his best-known research took place.

In 1897 Braun invented the oscilloscope, in which an alternating voltage is used to move a beam of electrons within an evacuated cathode-ray tube. The trace made by this beam on the fluorescent surface of the tube could be graphed by means of a rotating mirror, thus making the controlled flow of voltage visible. Because television tubes operate on the same principle, the Braun tube laid the foundation for television engineering.

Around this time, Braun began research in wireless telegraphy. The Italian electrical engineer GUGLIELMO MARCONI had just transmitted wireless messages through the air for a distance of 9 miles. Braun was puzzled by Marconi's difficulties in increasing the range of the transmitter simply by increasing its power. The Marconi transmitter used an electric sparking apparatus to generate so-called Hertzian waves (periodic oscillations) that travel through the air. Up to a point, increasing the size of the "spark gap" increased the range of transmission. Braun observed that when the spark gap exceeded a certain size, waves were produced that interfered with one another and weakened transmission. Within a year, he had developed the Braun transmitter, which employed a sparkless antenna circuit.

Power from the Braun transmitter, generated in an oscillatory circuit, was coupled magnetically to the antenna circuit by a transformer effect instead of including the antenna directly in the power circuit. An essential feature of Braun's system was the inclusion of a condenser in the circuit containing the spark gap, a principle that is now employed in all radio, radar, and television transmission. Moreover, the insulation difficulties that plagued Marconi's transmitter were practically nonexistent in Braun's sparkless telegraphy. At the receiver, Braun used direct coupling between the condenser circuit and the aerial; through resonance, the oscillations from the transmitting station produced the maximum effect at the receiving station, with the added advantage that the waves at the receiving station were of the same period as those emitted by the transmitter—in other words, they were tuned to the same frequency. As a result, it was possible to select the frequency to which the receiver responded so that it was not affected by signals of different frequency from other transmitters.

Braun took out a patent for his sparkless invention in 1899 and founded a company, Professor Braun's Telegraph Company, through which he introduced his subsequent inventions. Among them was the crystal detector (a forerunner of the transistor), which marked a great advance over the coherer used by Marconi. In 1901 he published his papers on wireless telegraphy in a booklet titled *Wireless Telegraphy Through Water and Air*. The following year he demonstrated the first functional transmission and reception of directional wireless communication, using both a directional transmitter and a directional receiver.

In his last important scientific contribution, made in 1904, Braun was able to demonstrate identical reflection and absorption of both light and electricity by minute striations set at various angles to the incident radiation. This evidence that light is a manifestation of electrical oscillations provided additional confirmation of the theoretical formulations made in the 1860s by the Scottish physicist James Clerk Maxwell.

Braun and Marconi shared the 1909 Nobel Prize for Physics, which was awarded "in recognition of their contributions to the development of wireless telegraphy." In his Nobel lecture, Braun quoted a lecture he had given in 1900. "Sometimes, wireless telegraphy has been described as spark telegraphy, and so far a spark in one place or another has been unavoidable. Here, however, it has been made as harmless as possible. This is *important*. For the spark which produces the waves also destroys them again. . . . What was pursued here could be truthfully described as *sparkless telegraphy*. . . . I feel happy to think," he went on, "that . . . we have come appreciably nearer

to this target, and have thereby made the coupled transmitter still more effective."

In 1886 Braun married Amelie Büchler, with whom he had two sons and two daughters. Known as a man of pleasant and cheerful disposition, Braun was considered by his colleagues and assistants to be without arrogance or self-importance. He enjoyed painting, sketching, travel, and writing stories for children.

In 1914 Braun traveled to New York to testify in a patent dispute. Numerous legal delays and intermittent periods of ill health kept him in New York through 1917. When the United States entered World War I that year, Braun was not allowed to return to Germany. Falling ill at the home of his son, he died on April 20, 1918, at a hospital in Brooklyn.

ABOUT: Dictionary of Scientific Biography, volume 2, 1970; Kurylo, F., and Susskind, C. Ferdinand Braun, 1981.

BRIAND, ARISTIDE
(March 28, 1862–March 7, 1932)
Nobel Prize for Peace, 1926
(shared with Gustav Stresemann)

The French statesman Aristide Briand was born in the town of Nantes in Brittany. The son of a successful innkeeper and his wife, Briand attended school first in the nearby port town of St.-Nazaire and then at the Nantes Lycée, where for a time the novelist Jules Verne became his mentor. Despite a keen intelligence manifested in his quick wit, verbal facility, and impressive memory, Briand was a mediocre student who preferred to drink, play cards, and indulge his gift for mimicry.

After obtaining a degree in law, Briand opened a practice in St.-Nazaire, where he also briefly edited his own newspaper. As his practice was slow to develop, Briand grew increasingly interested in journalism and politics. Joining the Socialist party, he became a spokesman for trade unionism and a leading advocate of militant action—particularly the general strike—as a method for achieving workers' goals. In 1894, after a workers' congress at Nantes endorsed his proposal for a general strike, Briand was named secretary-general of the Socialist party, abandoned his law practice, and embarked on a full-time political career.

In 1902, after several unsuccessful attempts, Briand won election to the Chamber of Deputies, where he soon earned a reputation as

ARISTIDE BRIAND

an accomplished debator. There he was instrumental in drafting legislation that effected the separation of church and state in France. Consequently, in March 1906 he was appointed minister of public instruction and worship in the centrist government of Jean Marie Ferdinand Sarrien, with responsibility for implementing the laws he had helped create. However, Briand's own Socialist party, adamantly opposed to any cooperation with Sarrien, expelled him. In his defense, Briand argued that his cabinet post would give the Socialists a voice in the government and that they would be better served by cooperating with other parties than by taking a rigid, all-or-nothing stance in the expectation of eventually forming their own majority government.

The Third Republic saw a succession of short-lived and often ineffectual governments as the various French political factions shifted their alliances in attempts to push through their own programs. In this unstable environment, Briand managed over a period of some twenty years to occupy important seats in a number of diverse cabinets. As prime minister, he was able to form his own cabinet on ten separate occasions.

The first government of Georges Clemenceau, formed in October 1906, kept Briand in his post as minister of public instruction and worship. Two years later, he was given the additional portfolio of minister of justice. When Clemenceau's government fell in July 1909, Briand was named prime minister.

Despite his proclaimed intention of promoting tranquility and national understanding, Briand faced a crisis in October 1910 when French railway workers called a general strike. Although he supported the principle of the general strike, Briand believed that rail transport was so vital to the nation's economy and security that the strike must be broken. He called up all eligible railway workers for active military duty, fired those remaining who refused to work, and had the strike leaders arrested. In the ensuing political uproar, he reshuffled his cabinet but was unable to maintain a majority coalition and was forced to resign in February 1911.

The following January, Briand was named minister of justice in the cabinet of Raymond Poincaré, whom he succeeded as prime minister when Poincaré was elected president a year later. This government lasted only two months, however, and Briand remained out of high office until the outbreak of World War I. Then, in an effort to broaden the government, Prime Minister René Viviani appointed him minister of justice again. When Viviani's government fell in October 1915, Briand became head of a new government of national conciliation, composed of representatives from all French political factions. Holding both the position of prime minister and that of minister of foreign affairs, Briand favored a negotiated peace with Germany. This policy was opposed by many in the government who charged that he was not prosecuting the war with sufficient vigor. Following the resignation of his minister of war, Briand lost considerable support and resigned in March 1917, to be succeeded in turn by Paul Painlevé and Georges Clemenceau.

Out of office for the next four years, Briand took no official role in the 1919 Paris Peace Conference but publicly registered his disapproval of the resultant Treaty of Versailles, calling it too harsh on Germany and therefore unlikely to bring about a lasting reconciliation. In January 1921 Briand was again named prime minister. He tendered his resignation a year later when the Chamber of Deputies failed to ratify the Anglo-French defense pact that he had negotiated with British Prime Minister Lloyd George. Nevertheless, he reentered the cabinet in April 1925 as minister of foreign affairs, a post he would hold in succeeding French governments over the next five and a half years.

In the years immediately following the Paris Peace Conference, it became clear to many concerned parties that the terms of the treaty were not adequate to assure future peace. To correct these oversights, the Dawes Plan (named for CHARLES DAWES) for restructuring Germany's reparation payments was put into effect in September 1924. Then on February 9, 1925, GUSTAV STRESEMANN, the German foreign minister, sent a note to the French government suggesting that Britain, France, and Germany sign a mutual nonaggression pact to guarantee the Franco-German border. Briand regarded such a pact as compatible with France's foreign policy goals. Moreover, such a pact would bind Britain to the protection of France and might also persuade the United States, which had developed considerable European interests, to become a guarantor of French security. Therefore, Briand entered into secret negotiations with Stresemann, British Foreign Secretary J. AUSTEN CHAMBERLAIN, and representatives of other former enemies of Germany. Briand's goal was to ensure French security while redressing the inequities of the Treaty of Versailles.

The results were announced in a series of public meetings attended by the foreign ministers of seven European nations at Locarno, Switzerland, in October 1925. The agreements announced at these sessions became known collectively as the Locarno Pact. Among its provisions, of particular significance to France were the perpetual demilitarization of the Rhineland; a mutual pledge of military support among France, Poland, and Czechoslovakia in the event of an attack upon any of them; and international recognition of the postwar border between Germany and France. In addition, the pact committed Britain to aid France in the event of a German attack.

The terms of the Locarno Pact were received favorably in France, greatly enhancing Briand's domestic political reputation. One month after the pact was signed, he was again named prime minister. Although this government lasted less than four months, Briand remained a significant figure in French political life and, as prime minister and foreign minister in succeeding governments, exerted great influence over Europe's postwar recovery.

For his role in securing the Locarno Pact and establishing an amicable dialogue between France and Germany after years of distrust, Briand was awarded the 1926 Nobel Prize for Peace, which he shared with his German counterpart at Locarno, Gustav Stresemann. He did not attend the award ceremonies, nor did he deliver a Nobel lecture.

Briand still envisioned a permanent alliance with the United States as the ultimate guarantor of French security and European peace in general. During 1926 he was approached by NICHOLAS MURRAY BUTLER and James T. Shotwell of the Carnegie Endowment for Peace, who suggested that the United States might respond positively to French overtures for such an alliance. On April 6, 1927, the tenth anniversary of the entry of the United States into World War I, Briand sent a formal note to American Secretary of State FRANK KELLOGG, proposing that the two nations negotiate a treaty of mutual friendship. Wary of any agreement that might bind the United States to French security, Kellogg withheld the American reply until the end of the year. At that time, he sent a message to Briand suggesting that, rather than forming a bilateral alliance, the two nations work together to bring all nations into a pact "renouncing war as an instrument of national policy." Over the next few months, Briand and Kellogg exchanged polite diplomatic counterproposals. Although Briand rightly suspected that a multilateral treaty outlawing war would prove unenforceable, he could scarcely reject Kellogg's idea. The result of these transatlantic exchanges was the Pact of Paris, better known as the Kellogg-Briand Pact, which was signed in the French capital on August 17, 1928, by representatives of fifteen nations. A total of sixty-five nations ultimately became signatories. Although all fifteen original parties to the pact have since violated it, none has ever formally denounced or abrogated it.

Despite the considerable credit Briand received in France for both the Locarno Pact and the Kellogg-Briand Pact, as well as the additional prestige that came with the Nobel Peace Prize, his political power had waned by the end of the 1920s. A 1930 memorandum he wrote and submitted to twenty-six nations, outlining a plan for a United States of Europe, was never seriously considered by the League of Nations or by the heads of government to which it was addressed. In the election of May 1931, Briand lost his bid to become president of France. He died suddenly in Paris less than a year later, on March 7, 1932.

WORKS IN ENGLISH TRANSLATION: The Locarno Treaties, Their Importance, Scope, and Possible Consequences, 1926, with others.

ABOUT: Baumont, M. Aristide Briand: Diplomat and Idealist, 1966; Bryant, A. The Man and the Hour, 1972; Chamberlain, A. Down the Years, 1935; Ferrell, R. H. Peace in Their Time, 1952; Foreign Affairs October 1932; de Madariaga, S. Morning Without Noon: Memoirs, 1974; Miller, D. H. The Peace Pact of Paris, 1928; Sontag, R. A Broken

BRIDGMAN

World, 1971; Stern-Rubarth, E. Three Men Tried, 1939;
Thomson, V. Briand: Man of Peace, 1930.

BRIDGMAN, P. W.
(April 21, 1882–August 20, 1961)
Nobel Prize for Physics, 1946

P. W. BRIDGMAN

The American physicist Percy Williams
Bridgman was born in Cambridge, Massachusetts, the only child of Raymond Landon
Bridgman, a newspaper reporter, a writer on
public affairs, and an early advocate of a world
state, and the former Mary Ann Maria Williams. Shortly after his birth, the family moved
to the town of Newton, where Bridgman grew
up attending the Congregational church, playing chess, and participating in sports. Attending the public schools in Newton, he was
inspired by a high school teacher to make science his career.

In 1900 he entered Harvard University, beginning a lifelong association with the school.
He concentrated on chemistry, mathematics,
and physics, receiving his B.A. summa cum
laude in 1904. He was awarded an M.S. the
following year and a Ph.D. in 1908 with a thesis on the effect of pressure on the electrical
resistance of mercury. Appointed a research
fellow in 1908, he became an instructor in 1910,
assistant professor in 1913, professor in 1919,
Hollis Professor of Mathematics and Natural
Philosophy in 1926, Higgins University Professor in 1950, and professor emeritus in 1954.

Bridgman's enormous lifetime scientific
output of 260 papers and 13 books was linked
to his successful avoidance of all institutional
obligations: he was never seen at a faculty
meeting and rarely served on a university committee. The statement "I am not interested in
your college, I want to do research," which
he made to the university's president, Abbott
Lawrence Lowell, marked him as an individualist, a characteristic expressed also by his
reluctance to do joint research or to accept
more than a few thesis students.

In 1905 Bridgman invented a leakproof
method for sealing pressure vessels. In principle, the construction of the Bridgman seal
ensures that the sealing gasket, made of rubber or soft metal, is always compressed to a
higher pressure than the pressure to be confined. The packing plug automatically becomes tighter as pressure is increased and can
never leak, no matter how high the pressure,
provided that the wall of the containing vessel
does not break.

The development of high-strength, heat-
treated alloy steels, such as cobalt-bonded
tungsten carbide (Carboloy), enabled Bridgman to use his ever-improving apparatus to
measure the compressibility, density, and
melting point of hundreds of materials as a
function of applied pressure and temperature.
Through this work he discovered that many
materials are polymorphic under high pressure, their crystal structure changing to allow
tighter packing of the atoms in the crystal. His
studies of pressure-induced polymorphism revealed two new forms of phosphorus and "hot
ice," ice that is stable at 180°F under a pressure
of 290,000 pounds per square inch. In later
years, other researchers made synthetic diamonds, cubic boron nitride crystals, and high-
quality quartz crystals under high pressure.
Bridgman found that high pressure could affect even the electronic structure of atoms, as
shown by the atomic volume contraction of
elemental cesium under 45,000 atmospheres
(675,000 pounds per square inch) of pressure.
His investigations proved that drastic alterations in the physical properties and crystal
structure of rock materials must occur under
the high pressures that prevail in the earth's
interior.

By using double high-pressure equipment,
in which one high-pressure press acts within
another high-pressure vessel, Bridgman routinely obtained pressures of 100,000 atmospheres (1.5 million pounds per square inch) in
small volumes. He occasionally studied the effects on matter of pressures as high as that
exerted by 400,000 atmospheres.

Bridgman was awarded the 1946 Nobel Prize

for Physics "for the invention of an apparatus to provide extremely high pressures and for the discoveries he made therewith in the field of high-pressure physics." In his presentation speech, A. E. Lindh of the Royal Swedish Academy of Sciences hailed Bridgman's "outstanding pioneer work in the field of high-pressure physics. By means of your ingenious apparatus, combined with a brilliant experimental technique, you have . . . very greatly enriched our knowledge of the properties of matter at high pressures."

During World War I, Bridgman, working in New London, Connecticut, developed sound-detection systems for antisubmarine warfare. During World War II, he measured the compressibility of uranium and plutonium as part of the development of the first atomic bomb.

In 1912 Bridgman married Olive Ware, daughter of Edmund A. Ware, founder of Atlanta University. The couple had a son and a daughter. Their family life, divided between Cambridge and a summer home in Randolph, New Hampshire, gave Peter, as he had been called since college days, ample time for gardening, mountaineering, photography, piano, chess, handball, and reading detective stories. For his daughter's wedding, Bridgman composed the marriage service and, as a temporary justice of the peace, performed the ceremony.

At the age of seventy-nine, seven years after his retirement, Bridgman learned that he had bone cancer and would die within months. Rapidly losing the use of his legs and unable to find a doctor who was willing to help end his life, Bridgman committed suicide on August 20, 1961. He left a note that read, "It isn't decent for Society to make a man do this thing himself. Probably this is the last day that I will be able to do it myself. P.W.B."

Bridgman was a member of the National Academy of Sciences, the American Philosophical Society, the American Academy of Arts and Sciences, the American Association for the Advancement of Science, and the American Physical Society. He held foreign membership in the Royal Society of London, the National Academy of Sciences of Mexico, and the Indian Academy of Sciences. His many honors included the Rumford Medal of the American Academy of Arts and Sciences (1917), the Elliott Cresson Medal of the Franklin Institute (1932), the Comstock Prize of the National Academy of Sciences (1933), and the Science Award of the Research Corporation of America (1937). He received honorary degrees from Brooklyn Polytechnic Institute, Harvard University, Princeton University, Yale University, and Stevens Institute of Technology.

SELECTED WORKS: Dimensional Analysis, 1922; The Logic of Modern Physics, 1927; The Physics of High Pressure, 1931; The Thermodynamics of Electrical Phenomena in Metals, 1934; The Nature of Physical Theory, 1936; The Intelligent Individual and Society, 1938; The Nature of Thermodynamics, 1941; Reflections of a Physicist, 1950; The Nature of Some of Our Physical Concepts, 1952; The Way Things Are, 1961; A Sophisticate's Primer of Relativity, 1962; Collected Experimental Papers (7 vols.) 1964; Philosophical Writings of Percy Williams Bridgman, 1980.

ABOUT: Biographical Memoirs of Fellows of the Royal Society, volume 8, 1962; Biographical Memoirs of the National Academy of Sciences, volume 41, 1970; Current Biography April 1955; Dictionary of Scientific Biography, volume 2, 1970; Frank, P. The Validation of Scientific Theories, 1956.

BROGLIE, LOUIS DE
(August 15, 1892–March 19, 1987)
Nobel Prize for Physics, 1929

The French physicist Louis Victor Pierre Raymond de Broglie (də brô gle′) was born in Dieppe, the youngest of the three children of Victor de Broglie and the former Pauline de la Forest d'Armaillé. As the male head of this aristocratic family, his father held the title *Duc*. The Broglies had long served their nation in military and diplomatic positions, but Louis and his older brother, Maurice, broke from the family tradition by becoming physicists.

Raised in the cultivated and privileged atmosphere of the French aristocracy, Broglie was exposed to a broad range of intellectual stimuli even before attending the Lycée Janson-de-Sailly in Paris. His chief interest was history, a subject he pursued after entering the Sorbonne, the center of the University of Paris Arts and Letters Faculty, where he earned his bachelor's degree in 1910. Broglie found himself increasingly drawn to science and scientific philosophy, he later said, "by philosophy, by generalizations, and by the books of [Henri] Poincaré," a prominent French mathematician. The example of his brother, Maurice, also played a part. After a period of intensive study, he received a degree in science in 1913 from the university's Faculty of Sciences.

That year, Broglie was called up for military service and assigned to the French Engineering Corps. After World War I began in 1914, he served in the radiotelegraph division, spending most of the war years at a wireless

151

station in the Eiffel Tower. A year after the 1918 armistice, he resumed his study of physics in his brother's private research laboratory, investigating the behavior of electrons, atoms, and X rays.

It was an exciting and perplexing time for physicists. In the nineteenth century, classical physicists had been so successful that some wondered if any major new scientific questions remained to be answered, only to be confronted with such challenging discoveries as X rays, radioactivity, and the electron in the last years of the century. Then, in 1900, MAX PLANCK presented his radical quantum theory to explain the relationship between the temperature of a body and the radiations it emitted. Contrary to centuries of evidence that light traveled in continuous waves, Planck proposed that electromagnetic radiation (light was shown to be electromagnetic only a few decades earlier) was composed of indivisible units, each proportional to the frequency of the radiation. The new theory worked for Planck's immediate purpose but was too startling to be universally accepted. In 1905 ALBERT EINSTEIN showed that Planck's theory was not just a mathematical trick. He used the quantum theory in a remarkable explanation of the photoelectric effect, the emission of electrons from a metal surface exposed to radiation. It was known that the emitted electricity increased with intensity of irradiation, but that the velocity of the ejected electrons never exceeded a certain maximum. According to Einstein, each quantum gave its energy to a single electron, enabling it to break free; more intense radiation contributed more photons, which liberated more electrons; but the energy of each photon was fixed by the frequency and set a limit on the electron's escaping velocity. Einstein's achievement not only extended the quantum theory but also supported its validity. Light, which undoubtedly had wave properties, also behaved like particles.

More support for the theory came in 1913, when NIELS BOHR proposed a model of the atom that combined ERNEST RUTHERFORD's conception of a dense central nucleus orbited by electrons with quantum theoretical restrictions on the electron orbits. The restrictions enabled Bohr to account for atomic line spectra. Line spectra arise when the light emitted by substances energized by burning or by an electric discharge is passed through a slit and when its component frequencies or wavelengths (which correspond to colors) are separated by an optical device called a spectroscope. The result is a series of colored

LOUIS DE BROGLIE

lines (images of the slit), or a spectrum; the positions of these spectral lines indicate their different frequencies. The spectrum is characteristic of the atoms or molecules that produce it. Bohr attributed the spectral lines to "jumps" of atomic electrons from one "allowed" orbit to another of lower energy. The energy difference between the two orbits, lost by the electron in transit, is emitted as a quantum, or photon, of radiation whose frequency is proportional to the energy difference. Thus, the spectrum is a coded display of the electron energy states. Bohr's model also solidified the dual nature of light as both a wave and a congregation of particles.

Despite the mounting evidence, many physicists remained uncomfortable with the double character of electromagnetic radiation. The new theory also had some loopholes. For example, the Bohr model assigned allowed orbits to the electrons on the basis of observed spectral lines; the orbits did not follow naturally from the theory, but were chosen to fit the data.

Broglie arrived at the insight that if waves could act like particles, particles might be able to act like waves. He was extending to matter the Einstein-Bohr idea of wave-particle duality. Waves and matter are different. Matter has a rest mass; in principle, it can either be motionless or move at various velocities. Light, however, has no rest mass; it must move at only one velocity (which may change with the medium) or cease to exist. In parallel with the link between the wavelength of light and the energy in a photon, Broglie proposed that a matter wavelength is related to momentum (mass multiplied by velocity). Momentum is directly related to kinetic energy. Thus, a fast electron would be associated with a wave of higher frequency (shorter wavelength) than a slow electron would. Whether matter and radiation appear as particles or waves depends on the circumstances of observation.

With considerable daring, Broglie applied his concept of Bohr's model of the atom. A negative electron is attracted to the positive nucleus. To circle the nucleus at a particular distance, the electron must be traveling at a particular speed. If the speed is changed, the orbit must change to remain compatible. The centrifugal force is said to balance the centripetal force. A particular electron speed, associated with a particular orbit at a certain distance from the nucleus, corresponds to a particular momentum (speed multiplied by electron mass) and therefore, by Broglie's supposition, to a particular electron wavelength. Broglie then said that allowed orbits were those whose circumference equaled an integral number of electron wavelengths. Only in these orbits would electron waves be in phase (at the same point in a frequency cycle) and not interfere destructively with themselves.

In 1924 Broglie presented this analysis, "Researches on the Quantum Theory," in his doctoral thesis at the Faculty of Sciences of the University of Paris. His doctoral examiners were astonished but also deeply skeptical, viewing Broglie's ideas as a theoretical leap without experimental basis. Nevertheless, with some urging by Einstein, they awarded Broglie his doctorate. The following year Broglie published his work in a major article that received respectful attention. He became a lecturer in physics at the University of Paris in 1926 and two years later was appointed professor of theoretical physics at the university's Henri Poincaré Institute.

Impressed by Broglie's work, Einstein advised many physicists to study it carefully. ERWIN SCHRÖDINGER took Einstein's advice and found in Broglie's ideas the foundation for the development of wave mechanics, an extension of quantum theory. The wavelike behavior of matter was experimentally confirmed in 1927 by CLINTON J. DAVISSON and Lester H. Germer working with low-energy electrons in the United States and by G. P. THOMSON working with high-energy electrons in England. The fact that electrons proved to be associated with waves that could be bent and focused led in 1933 to the design of electron microscopes by ERNST RUSKA. Waves asso-ciated with material particles are now called de Broglie waves.

"For his discovery of the wave nature of electrons," Broglie received the 1929 Nobel Prize for Physics. By proposing that "light is at once a wave motion and a stream of corpuscles [particles]," said C. W. Oseen of the Royal Swedish Academy of Sciences in his presentation speech, Broglie had revealed "an aspect of the nature of matter that is completely new and previously quite unsuspected." Broglie's insight, Oseen went on, resolved a long-standing conflict by establishing that "there are not two worlds, one of light and waves, one of matter and corpuscles. There is only a single universe."

Broglie continued his research into the nature of electrons and photons. Together with Einstein and Schrödinger, he spent many years trying to find a formulation of quantum mechanics that obeyed ordinary rules of cause and effect. However, they all failed at this endeavor, and it has been demonstrated experimentally that such theories are not correct. The prevailing viewpoint in quantum mechanics is the statistical interpretation based on the work of Bohr, MAX BORN, and WERNER HEISENBERG. This concept is frequently referred to as the Copenhagen interpretation because Bohr, who did extensive work on it, was in Copenhagen.

In 1933 Broglie was elected a member of the French Academy of Sciences, becoming its permanent secretary in 1942. The following year he founded the Center for Studies in Applied Mathematics at the Henri Poincaré Institute in order to strengthen the bonds between physics and applied mathematics. In 1945, after the end of World War II, Broglie and his brother, Maurice, were named counselors to the French High Commission on Atomic Energy.

Broglie, who never married, enjoyed walking, reading, quiet contemplation, and playing chess. He assumed the title *Duc* on the death of his brother in 1960. Broglie died at a hospital in Paris on March 19, 1987; he was ninety-four years old.

In addition to the Nobel Prize, Broglie was awarded the first Henri Poincaré Medal of the French Academy of Sciences (1929), the Albert I Grand Prize of Monaco (1932), the first Kalinga Prize of the UNESCO (1952), and the Grand Prize of the Society of Engineers of France (1953). He held honorary degrees from many universities and was a member of many scientific organizations, including the Royal Society of London, the American National

Academy of Sciences, and the American Academy of Arts and Sciences. In 1945 he was inducted into the French Academy by his brother Maurice, in recognition of his literary achievements.

SELECTED WORKS: An Introduction to the Study of Wave Mechanics, 1928; Selected Papers on Wave Mechanics, 1928, with Léon Brillouin; Matter and Light: The New Physics, 1939; The Revolution in Physics, 1953; Physics and Microphysics, 1955; Non-Linear Wave Mechanics, 1960; New Perspectives in Physics, 1962; Introduction to the Vigier Theory of Elementary Particles, 1963; The Current Interpretation of Wave Mechanics, 1964; Einstein, 1979, with others.

ABOUT: Barut, A. O., et al. (eds.) Quantum, Space, and Time: The Quest Continues, 1984; Current Biography September 1955; Diner, S. (ed.) The Wave-Particle Dualism, 1984; Flato, M., et al. (eds.) Quantum Mechanics, Determinism, Causality, and Particles, 1976.

HERBERT C. BROWN

BROWN, HERBERT C.
(May 22, 1912–)
Nobel Prize for Chemistry, 1979
(shared with Georg Wittig)

The American organic chemist Herbert Charles Brown was born in London, England, the only son and second of four children of Pearl (Gorinstein) and Charles Brovarnik. His parents were Ukrainian Jews who immigrated to London in 1908 and moved on to Chicago six years later. His paternal grandparents had already settled in Chicago and anglicized their surname to Brown, a name his parents also adopted. Brown attended Haven School and Englewood High School on the South Side of Chicago, graduating in 1930. After his father died of an infection in 1926, Brown also managed the family hardware store. Continuing to work at a succession of odd jobs, he managed to graduate from Wright Junior College in 1935. He then received a partial scholarship to attend the University of Chicago, where he completed his B.S. in one year.

At that time the University of Chicago was one of the leading American centers for the study of chemistry, and Brown's mentors included two highly regarded scientists, Morris Kharasch and Julius Stieglitz. Upon graduation Brown planned to find a job, but Stieglitz persuaded him to consider a career as a research chemist and to enter graduate school. Continuing his studies at Chicago under the direction of the noted chemist H. I. Schlesinger, Brown received his Ph.D. in 1938.

Unable to find an industrial position, Brown

accepted a one-year postdoctoral fellowship with Kharasch and then became research assistant to Schlesinger, with the rank of instructor. He moved to Wayne (later Wayne State) University in Detroit in 1943, first as assistant professor and three years later as associate professor. In 1947 he was appointed full professor of chemistry at Purdue University in West Lafayette, Indiana, where he has spent the rest of his career. He was named R. B. Wetherill Distinguished Professor in 1959 and emeritus professor in 1978. In addition to his academic responsibilities, he has also served as a consultant to the Exxon Corporation.

Brown has made a number of fundamental contributions to physical organic and synthetic organic chemistry, most of which involve the chemistry and synthetic utility of boron derivatives. In 1936, in collaboration with Schlesinger, he investigated diborane, at that time an exceedingly rare and expensive substance. For his doctoral research, he studied the reactions of diborane with organic carbonyl compounds (molecules containing a carbon-oxygen double bond, such as aldehydes, ketones, and esters). After mastering the difficult high-vacuum techniques required for this work, Brown found that diborane was an excellent reducing (hydrogenation) agent; upon hydrolysis, the carbonyl groups were reduced smoothly and completely to alcohols, under exceedingly mild conditions. Despite the advantages it offered organic chemists, however, Brown's method was severely limited because of the expense and difficulty of working with diborane.

In the fall of 1940 Brown and Schlesinger were asked to join the Manhattan Project, which eventually developed the atomic bomb. To prepare isotopically pure uranium for an atomic weapon, it was necessary to find volatile compounds of uranium for use in a gaseous diffusion process. Since the newly synthesized borohydrides of aluminum and beryllium were volatile, Schlesinger and Brown used diborane to synthesize uranium borohydride, which fortuitously shared this characteristic. However, the slow and difficult preparation of diborane proved to be a critical roadblock, and they began to seek new methods of producing boron hydrides. Their search resulted in an inexpensive and rapid route to diborane, using lithium or sodium hydride, and the discovery later of a new reducing agent, sodium borohydride. Meanwhile, a method for handling uranium hexafluoride in the gaseous diffusion process was developed by others.

Although the work of Schlesinger and Brown contributed little to the bomb project, it had enormous impact on organic chemistry by revolutionizing methods of reduction, one of the two most basic chemical processes. Reductions carried out with diborane or sodium borohydride provided new synthetic routes to scientifically and technologically interesting compounds. In further research at Wayne and Purdue universities, Brown produced a number of new borohydrides and metal hydrides that provided organic chemists with a full spectrum of reducing agents suitable for a wide range of specific applications. This work also opened up fundamental lines of research in physical organic chemistry. For instance, Brown made important contributions to the study of the quantitative relationship between molecular structure and reactivity, and he advanced the study of steric effects (mechanical interactions of the parts of reacting molecules) in organic reactions.

In 1955 Brown discovered that adding diborane to carbon-carbon double bonds produced organoboranes, through a process called hydroboration. The organoboranes in turn underwent a number of further reactions, thus providing a flexible series of novel or improved synthetic routes. This reaction is now often used to convert olefins to alcohols or to saturated compounds. Additional advantages of hydroboration include the smoothness and selectivity of the reactions, which often provide convenient paths to highly pure products, and the rarity of intramolecular rearrangements. Brown found that organoboranes could also serve as intermediates for the creation of new carbon-carbon bonds, in reactions he refers to jocularly as "riveting and stitching" of pieces of molecules. The work of Brown and his co-workers during the last thirty years has transformed organoboranes into one of the most versatile chemical intermediates in the armamentarium of the synthetic organic chemist. There have also been important technical applications; for example, in the synthesis of pheromones for use as pest control agents.

Brown shared the 1979 Nobel Prize for Chemistry with GEORG WITTIG "for their development of boron- and phosphorus-containing compounds, respectively, into important reagents in organic synthesis." In his Nobel lecture Brown compared his research to the preliminary surveying of a newly discovered continent. "We have been moving rapidly over that continent, scouting out the major mountain ranges, river valleys, lakes, and coasts," he said. "But it is evident that we have only scratched the surface. It will require another generation of chemists to settle that continent and to utilize it for the good of mankind."

In 1937 Brown married Sarah Baylen, a fellow chemistry student. Their son Charles is also a chemist. An indefatigable worker, Brown remains active, working with a large group of postdoctoral students and continuing to publish regularly.

Brown's many honors include the Nichols Medal of the American Chemical Society (1959), the National Medal for Science of the National Science Foundation (1969), the Charles Frederick Chandler Medal of Columbia University (1973), the Elliott Cresson Medal of the Franklin Institute (1978), the Christopher Ingold Medal of the British Chemical Society (1978), and the Priestley Medal of the American Chemical Society (1981). He is a member of the National Academy of Sciences and the American Academy of Arts and Sciences, an honorary fellow of the British Chemical Society, and a foreign member of the Indian National Academy of Sciences.

SELECTED WORKS: Hydroboration, 1962; Boranes in Organic Chemistry, 1972; Organic Syntheses via Boranes, 1975; The Nonclassical Ion Problem, 1977, with Paul Schleyer.

ABOUT: Brewster, J. H. (ed.) Aspects of Mechanism and Organometallic Chemistry, 1978; New Scientist October 18, 1979; New York Times October 16, 1979; Science January 1980.

BROWN, MICHAEL S.
(April 13, 1941–   )
Nobel Prize for Physiology or Medicine,
  1985
(shared with Joseph L. Goldstein)

The American geneticist Michael Stuart Brown was born in New York City to Harvey Brown and Evelyn (Katz) Brown. As an undergraduate he attended the University of Pennsylvania, where he majored in chemistry but spent most of his time writing sports and feature stories for the university newspaper. He received his B.A. in 1962 and his M.D., also from the University of Pennsylvania, in 1966. For the next two years, Brown was an intern and resident in internal medicine at the Massachusetts General Hospital in Boston, where he met JOSEPH L. GOLDSTEIN, also a medical house officer.

After completing his residency in 1968, Brown joined the National Institute of Arthritis and Metabolic Diseases as a clinical associate in the Digestive and Hereditary Disease Branch. There he worked on glutamine metabolism in the Laboratory of Biochemistry. In 1971 he was appointed assistant professor of medicine at the University of Texas Southwestern Medical School in Dallas. When Goldstein came to Southwestern the next year, the two scientists began to investigate cholesterol metabolism in general and the disease familial hypercholesterolemia in particular.

Cholesterol is a lipid (fat) molecule present in membranes of all animal cells. It is also a precursor of bile acids and steroid hormones. Cholesterol, which is both synthesized within the body and absorbed from food, is transported through blood and lymphatic fluid by low-density lipoproteins (LDLs), large spherical particles with a core of cholesterol esters enclosed by a surface coat of phospholipids and free cholesterol. This hydrophilic (that is, capable of combining with water) coating allows the particles to be dissolved in blood. Embedded in the outer layer is one large protein called apoprotein B-100. When excessive cholesterol accumulates in the walls of blood vessels, it can block blood flow, causing heart attacks and strokes.

Characterized by extremely high blood levels of cholesterol and LDL, and by deposits of cholesterol in the body, the genetic disease familial hypercholesterolemia is inherited as a dominant trait. Heterozygous patients—with only one gene for the disease—develop coronary heart disease between the ages of thirty-five and fifty, particularly males. This form of

MICHAEL S. BROWN

the disease occurs in 1 of 500 Americans and Europeans, and 85 percent of those afflicted suffer a heart attack by the age of sixty. The more severe homozygous form of the disorder, resulting from inheritance of two mutant genes, appears in 1 of 1 million individuals, and members of this group usually have heart attacks beginning in childhood.

Using tissue culture techniques, Brown and Goldstein grew skin cells taken from individuals with familial hypercholesterolemia. In these cells they found an unusually high level of the enzyme that controls the rate at which cholesterol is synthesized. Because the enzyme was so active, the result was an oversupply of cholesterol. They also found that cells from familial hypercholesterolemic patients exhibited defective binding of LDL. This led to the discovery of receptors for the LDL molecule on cell surfaces.

In normal cells, as the level of LDL in the blood rises, the LDL molecules bind to cell-surface receptors and turn off cholesterol synthesis by a negative feedback loop. Since the cells from patients with familial hypercholesterolemia do not bind the LDL, the cells keep on making cholesterol as though more were needed.

Studying the mechanism by which the LDL receptor governs the synthesis of cholesterol, Brown and Goldstein, with their colleague Richard G. Anderson, described how the apoprotein portion of the LDL is bound to a specific receptor on the cell surface. By a process called receptor-mediated endocytosis, the LDL-cholesterol binding occurs in coated pits on the cell membrane that are subsequently folded into vesicles that pinch off and carry the LDL-cholesterol into the interior of the cell. This mechanism of receptor-mediated endocytosis has since become a model for the cellular uptake of other large molecules such as insulin, iron, vitamin B_{12}, growth factors, transferrin, and immune complexes.

Within the cell, LDL is broken down to release cholesterol, which then reduces the levels of the enzyme responsible for making more cholesterol, and increases the activity of an enzyme involved in cholesterol storage. Increased amounts of cholesterol within the cell also inhibit production of more LDL receptors. Thus, normal cells can balance cholesterol absorption from the diet with cellular synthesis.

In 1984, by molecular cloning techniques, Brown and Goldstein determined the nucleotide sequence of the gene controlling the LDL receptor. They described several genetic mutations that lead to familial hypercholesterolemia. Some mutations cause defective synthesis of the receptor, others render the LDL receptor unable to bind LDL, and still others result in bound LDL that cannot deliver the proper signal.

The work by Brown and Goldstein has already produced tangible clinical benefits. In heterozygous patients, who have one functional gene for the LDL receptor, treatment with drugs such as compactin, mevinolin, or resin therapy can increase the number of LDL receptors made by the single functioning gene and thus reduce the blood levels of LDL and cholesterol. This therapy, however, cannot work for patients homozygous for familial hypercholesterolemia, who have no functioning gene for the LDL receptor. In 1984 experimental liver transplantation was performed in a six-year-old child with homozygous familial hypercholesterolemia, and, as Brown and Goldstein's theories had predicted, the presence of normal LDL receptors on the transplanted liver produced a dramatic lowering of the blood cholesterol levels.

Brown and Goldstein were awarded the 1985 Nobel Prize for Physiology or Medicine for their revolutionary discoveries about the regulation of cholesterol metabolism and treatment for disorders of blood cholesterol levels.

Brown is currently professor of medicine and genetics and director of the Center for Genetic Disease at the University of Texas Southwestern Medical School. He is also a member of the Board of Scientific Advisors of the Jane Coffin Clinical Fund, and consultant to the Lucille Markey Trust. He is on the editorial boards of *Arteriosclerosis* and *Science*. Author of over 200 scientific articles and textbook chapters, Brown co-edited *The Metabolic Basis of Inherited Disease*.

In 1964 Brown married Alice Lapin; they have two daughters. A sailing enthusiast, he also enjoys listening to popular music.

With Goldstein, Brown also shared the Pfizer Award for Enzyme Chemistry of the American Chemical Society (1976), the Lounsbery Award of the National Academy of Sciences (1979), the Gairdner Foundation International Award (1981), the V. D. Mattia Award of the Roche Institute of Molecular Biology (1984), and the Louisa Gross Horwitz Prize of Columbia University (1984). He is a member of the National Academy of Sciences, the American Academy of Arts and Sciences, the American Society of Biological Chemists, and the Association of American Physicians.

ABOUT: New York Times October 15, 1985; Science January 10, 1986.

BUCHANAN, JAMES M.
(October 2, 1919–   )
Nobel Memorial Prize in Economic Sciences, 1986

The American economist James McGill Buchanan was born in Murfreesboro, Tennessee. His father and namesake was a farmer, and his mother, Lila (Scott) Buchanan, was a former schoolteacher; both were active in local politics. His grandfather, John P. Buchanan, had served one term as governor of Tennessee as the Farmers' Alliance nominee of the Populist party. His parents urged Buchanan to follow in his grandfather's path, but the Great Depression thwarted his plans to study law at Vanderbilt University. Instead, he attended Middle Tennessee State Teacher's College in Murfreesboro while living at home and milking cows to pay for fees and books.

Graduating at the top of his class with majors in mathematics, English literature, and social science, Buchanan won a fellowship to do graduate work in economics at the University of Tennessee, from which he received an M.A. in 1941. In August of that year, he was drafted into the military and attended naval officer training in New York, followed by a period at the Naval War College. After the United States entered World War II, he was assigned to the operations staff of Admiral

JAMES M. BUCHANAN

Virginia Tech

Chester W. Nimitz, commander in chief of the Pacific Fleet. For the duration of the war, Buchanan served at fleet headquarters at Pearl Harbor and on Guam.

After the war, Buchanan resumed graduate study, this time at the University of Chicago, where he came under the influence of Frank H. Knight, one of his economics professors. Although Buchanan arrived at Chicago a self-described "libertarian socialist," he later recalled that "within six weeks after enrollment in Frank Knight's course in price theory, I had been converted into a zealous advocate of the market order." The other major influence on Buchanan's subsequent work was Knut Wicksell's 1896 dissertation on taxation, which he happened upon in the stacks of the library and later translated from the German. Wicksell, a Swedish economist, viewed politics as a process of complex, yet mutually advantageous, exchange between citizens and the structures they create to organize society. Wicksell also argued that reform in economic policy requires changing the rules under which politicians act. The concepts of both Knight and Wicksell had a major impact on Buchanan's development of public choice and constitutional economics.

After receiving a Ph.D. in economics from Chicago in 1948, Buchanan became an associate professor of economics at the University of Tennessee, rising to full professor in 1950. The following year he moved to Florida State University and was named chairman of the economics department in 1954. With the aid of a Fulbright grant, Buchanan spent the academic year 1955–1956 in Rome and Perugia

studying the classical Italian works in public finance theory and developing his own ideas on the relationship between political structures and economic policies.

Returning to the United States, Buchanan was appointed professor and chairman of the James Wilson Department of Economics at the University of Virginia in Charlottesville. In 1957 he and the American economist G. Warren Nutter founded the Thomas Jefferson Center for Studies in Political Economy. Their purpose, according to Buchanan, was to establish "a community of scholars who wished to preserve a social order based on individual liberty," as well as "to counter the increasing technical specialization of economics." Buchanan served as director of the center from 1957 to 1969. In 1963 Buchanan and Gordon Tullock, who had done postdoctoral work at the center shortly after its founding, organized the Committee on Non-Market Decision Making, the predecessor to the Public Choice Society.

After spending the academic year 1968–1969 as a visiting professor at the University of California at Los Angeles, Buchanan moved to the Virginia Polytechnic Institute and State University in Blacksburg as University Distinguished Professor. There he was joined by Tullock, with whom he founded the Center for Study of Public Choice, with Buchanan as its general director. The purpose of the new center was to apply and extend economic methods and ways of thinking to the study of political processes. When Buchanan was appointed Holbert L. Harris University Professor at George Mason University in 1983, the center was relocated to the university's campus in Fairfax, Virginia.

As a result of his scholarly contributions over the last forty years, Buchanan is internationally recognized as the leading researcher in what is called public choice theory, which applies methods of economics to subjects that have traditionally fallen within the scope of political science. The basic units of analysis are individuals, capable of making rational choices to benefit the whole of society, rather than organic units such as the nation, the state, or the party. Public choice theory seeks to predict how the behavior of individuals in their political roles—whether as voters, taxpayers, lobbyists, political candidates, elected representatives, political party members, bureaucrats, government regulators, or judges—can affect the political community as a whole. Economic theory, in comparison, attempts to relate the behavior of individuals in their economic roles—whether as buyers, sellers, producers, workers, investors, or entrepreneurs—to the results that emerge for the whole economy.

In analyzing political exchange, Buchanan emphasizes two conceptually different levels of public choice—an initial constitutional level of choice and a postconstitutional level. Study of the first level involves the economic theory of constitutions, whereas the second involves the economic theory of political institutions. The distinction between the two levels of choice can be viewed as an analogy to the choices made by people playing a game. First, rules by which the game is to be played are chosen; then strategies are conceived for playing the game within those rules. Broadly described, a constitution is a set of rules for playing a political game. Day-to-day politics is the playing out of the game within the constitutional rules.

As Buchanan has pointed out, several important insights follow from this analogy. Just as the rules of a game shape its likely results, so political outcomes are shaped and constrained by constitutional rules. Improvements in the results of policy or in the outcomes of legislative and regulatory decision making may, therefore, require changes in or reform of a constitution. Underlying the search for better rules for any game is an analysis of how play is likely to proceed under different rules. Similarly, an approach to constitutional reform must be guided by positive, predictive analysis of the likely workings of alternative political policies and processes.

The distinction between constitutional and postconstitutional choice was originally presented in *The Calculus of Consent* (1962), which Buchanan wrote with Gordon Tullock. Drawing on the Wicksellian view of politics as a complex, yet mutually advantageous, exchange, Buchanan and Tullock asked how these exchanges could be organized so that all participants might expect to receive positive net benefits—the level of constitutional choice. Specifically, what political rules and procedures should govern the making of collective or governmental policy choices? They addressed this question from the perspective of individual members of the public faced with choices among alternative decision rules and procedures, when the individuals will later be subject to decisions made under these rules and procedures. Numerous decision rules and procedures were examined, including, among others, the unanimity rule, the qualified majority rule, the simple majority rule, vote trading or logrolling, the basis of representation, and bicameral versus unicameral legislatures.

Buchanan developed different applications of these themes in *Public Finance in Democratic Process* (1967) and in *Demand and Supply of Public Goods* (1968).

In *The Limits to Liberty: Between Anarchy and Leviathan* (1975), Buchanan distinguished between the protective state and the productive state. In his view, constitutional contract (or set of rules and procedures for political organization) leads to the establishment of the protective state. This legally constituted structure defines individuals' rights of ownership and control over resources, enforces private contracts, and limits government power. The emergence of the protective state represents the leap from anarchy to political organization. Within this organized structure, orderly trade and exchange of private goods and services can take place to the mutual advantage of the parties involved.

In Buchanan's opinion, the productive state would, ideally, embody a postconstitutional contract among citizens with regard to their demands for jointly shared goods and services. However, the self-interested behavior of individuals charged with operating the political structure—politicians, regulators, and bureaucrats—leads to governmental excess at the postconstitutional stage. Therein lies the threat of Leviathan, Thomas Hobbes's famous political symbol for an authoritarian state. For Buchanan, the challenge is to use modern theories of politics, regulation, and bureaucracy to design institutions and rules that will limit self- and special-interest political behavior.

In his later works, Buchanan has further analyzed and developed the need for constitutional reform. *Democracy in Deficit* (1977), written with Richard E. Wagner, derives a constitutional requirement for a balanced budget from analyzing a model of postconstitutional political behavior in which deficit finance allows politicians to gain political support from a variety of public segments by increasing government spending for special interests while deferring the tax increases necessary to pay for them. *The Power to Tax* (1980), written with Geoffrey Brennan, derives constitutional limits on the taxing authority of the government from a model of postconstitutional politics in which the government is viewed as a body that maximizes revenue. Buchanan has supported, directly and indirectly, controversial proposals for a constitutional amendment that would require a balanced federal budget.

Buchanan was awarded the 1986 Nobel Memorial Prize in Economic Sciences for "his development of the contractual and constitu-

159

tional bases for the theory of economic and political decision making." According to the Royal Swedish Academy of Sciences, "Buchanan's foremost achievement is that he has consistently and tenaciously emphasized the significance of fundamental rules and applied the concept of the political system as an exchange process for the achievement of mutual advantages."

In 1945 Buchanan married Anne Bakke, whom he met during the war. The Buchanans, who have no children, divide their time between their home in Fairfax and their farm in southwestern Virginia. Buchanan has maintained a lifelong interest in the study of languages and has translated numerous important economic works from German and Italian.

In addition to the Nobel Prize, Buchanan has received many awards and honors, including the Frank E. Seidman Distinguished Award in Political Economy of the University of Tennessee (1984) and honorary degrees from the University of Zurich in Switzerland and from the University of Giessen in Germany. He is a distinguished fellow of the American Economic Association and a fellow of the American Academy of Arts and Sciences. He served as president of the Southern Economic Association (1963), vice president of the American Economic Association (1971), vice president (1981–1982) and president (1983–1984) of the Western Economic Association, and vice president (1982–1984) and president (1984–1986) of the Mt. Pelerin Society.

ADDITIONAL WORKS: Public Principles of Public Debt, 1958; Fiscal Theory and Political Economy, 1960; Fiscal Choice Through Time, 1964; Cost and Choice, 1969; Freedom in Constitutional Contract, 1978; The Economics of Politics, 1978; What Should Economists Do? 1979; Uncertainty, Subjective Probabilities, and Choice, 1979, with Alberto DiPierro; The Public Finances, 1980, with Marilyn Flowers; Monopoly in Money and Inflation, 1981, with Geoffrey Brennan; Political Economy, 1957–1982, 1983; The Reason of Rules, 1985, with Geoffrey Brennan; Liberty, Market, and State, 1985; The Political Economy of Budget Deficits, 1986, with others.

ABOUT: Forbes November 17, 1986; New York Times October 17, 1986; Regulation January–February 1987; Shackleton, J. R., and Locksley, G. Twelve Contemporary Economists, 1981.

BUCHNER, EDUARD

(May 20, 1860–August 13, 1917)
Nobel Prize for Chemistry, 1907

The German chemist Eduard Buchner (būk′ nər) was born in Munich to Ernst Buch-ner, a professor of forensic medicine and obstetrics at the University of Munich, and Friederike (Martin) Buchner, the daughter of a clerk in the royal treasury. After his father died in 1872, Buchner's older brother, Hans, oversaw Eduard's education. Graduating from the Realgymnasium in Munich in 1877, Buchner served briefly in a field artillery unit of the German army before entering the Munich Technical University to study chemistry. However, financial hardship forced him to withdraw from school and work for four years in canning factories in Munich and in Mombach. Although this work interrupted his studies, it acquainted him with the process of alcoholic fermentation, whereby sugar is broken down into alcohol and carbon dioxide by the action of yeast.

Support from his brother Hans enabled Buchner to resume his studies in 1884. Soon afterward, he received a three-year scholarship. He studied chemistry under ADOLF VON BAEYER at the University of Munich and botany under Carl von Nägeli at the Botanic Institute. Hans Buchner, who later became a noted hygienist and bacteriologist, was a member of the institute, and under his guidance Eduard Buchner began investigating alcoholic fermentation. In 1885 the latter published his first paper, on the influence of oxygen on fermentation. Buchner's research led him to depart from the prevailing view held by Louis Pasteur that fermentation could not occur in the presence of oxygen.

Buchner received his Ph.D. in 1888 and two years later, following a brief period in Erlangen, became Baeyer's assistant. In 1891 he was appointed a privatdocent (unsalaried lecturer) at the University of Munich. With private funds from Baeyer, he set up a small laboratory where he continued his research into the chemistry of fermentation. Buchner left Munich in 1893 to become head of the section for analytical chemistry at the University of Kiel; in 1895 he became full professor. The following year he joined the faculty of the University of Tübingen, where he taught analytical and pharmaceutical chemistry. In 1898 he was named professor of general chemistry at the College of Agriculture in Berlin and director of the Institute for the Fermentation Industry.

In 1893, when Buchner began to seek the active agent of fermentation, two competing theories of fermentation prevailed. The mechanistic theory held that yeast, by continually decomposing in a liquid, set up chemical stresses that broke down sugar molecules. According to this view, alcoholic fermentation was a com-

EDUARD BUCHNER

both within and outside of the yeast cell, not by a so-called vital force.

The publication in 1897 of Buchner's paper "On Alcoholic Fermentation Without Yeast Cells" stirred controversy among his fellow scientists, and Buchner spent much of the following years consolidating the evidence for his theories. By 1902 he had published an additional fifteen papers explaining and defending his work, as well as several others setting forth the results of investigations he had made into the chemical effects of yeast on milk sugar.

Buchner received the 1907 Nobel Prize for Chemistry "for his biochemical researches and his discovery of cell-free fermentation." Because of the death of Sweden's King Oscar II, the award ceremonies were canceled, but in a written presentation K. A. H. Mörner of the Royal Swedish Academy of Sciences summarized the competing views of fermentation that Buchner had resolved. "So long as fermentation was regarded as an 'expression of life,' " Mörner said, "there was little hope of being able to penetrate more deeply into the question of its course." Therefore, he continued, "a great sensation was created when Buchner . . . succeeded in showing that alcoholic fermentation could be produced from the juices expressed from yeast cells, free from live cells. . . . Hitherto inaccessible territories have now been brought into the field of chemical research, and vast new prospects have now been opened up to chemical science."

In his Nobel lecture Buchner described his findings and paid tribute to his predecessors and colleagues. "We are seeing the cells of plants and animals more and more clearly as chemical factories," he said, "where the various products are manufactured in separate workshops. The enzymes act as the overseers. Our acquaintance with these most important agents of living things is constantly increasing. Even though we may still be a long way from our goal, we are approaching it step by step."

Two years after receiving the Nobel Prize, Buchner transferred to the University of Breslau (now Wrocław, Poland), where he held the chair of physiological chemistry. His last academic appointment was at the University of Würzburg in 1911.

With the outbreak of World War I, Buchner volunteered for military service. While serving as a major in a field hospital in Romania in 1917, he sustained shrapnel wounds and died in Focşani on August 13. He was survived by his wife, the former Lotte Stahl, the daughter of a Tübingen mathematician.

plex but otherwise normal chemical reaction. This theory was opposed by the vitalists, who, like Louis Pasteur, believed that living cells contained a "vital substance" that was responsible for fermentation. In their opinion, without some vital but unidentified component of the living cell, chemicals alone could not produce fermentation. Although the mechanists had shown that substances found in living cells could be synthesized, no one had yet isolated the agent of fermentation or produced the process from nonliving substances.

Encouraged by his brother, Buchner set out to find the active agent by obtaining pure samples of the inner fluid of yeast cells. Using a method suggested by his brother's assistant, Martin Hahn, Buchner pulverized yeast cells in a pestle with a mixture of sand and diatomaceous earth, thus avoiding the destructive high temperatures and solvents that had foiled previous investigators. When squeezed through canvas under pressure, the cellular material yielded its fluid contents. Buchner assumed that the fluid was incapable of causing fermentation. Later, however, when he and Hahn tried to preserve the fluid by adding a concentrated solution of sucrose, carbon dioxide was released. The implication was startling, for even though the yeast cells were dead, it was clear that something in their fluid produced fermentation. Buchner hypothesized that the active agent was an enzyme, which he called zymase. His findings implied that fermentation works by the chemical activity of enzymes

They were married in 1900; they had two sons and a daughter.

ABOUT: Dictionary of Scientific Biography, volume 2, 1970.

BUCK, PEARL S.
(June 26, 1892–March 6, 1973)
Nobel Prize for Literature, 1938

PEARL S. BUCK

The American novelist Pearl Comfort Sydenstricker Buck was the daughter of Presbyterian missionaries to China, the only one of six children in the family to be born in the United States, at Hillsboro, West Virginia. Her father, Absalom Sydenstricker, was an austere, scholarly man who spent years translating the Bible from Greek to Chinese. Her mother, the former Caroline Stulting, was a cultivated woman who had traveled widely in her youth and who had a fondness for literature.

When Buck was still an infant, her parents returned to China. Settling in the interior city of Chinkiang, they chose to live among the Chinese rather than in the compound designated for foreigners. As a result, Pearl learned to speak Chinese before she learned English. She was so well accepted by her Chinese peers that she remained unaware of her foreignness until the age of nine. When the Boxer Rebellion broke out and the empress decreed that all whites were to be executed, the Sydenstrickers fled to Shanghai but moved back to Chinkiang after peace was restored.

After being educated by her mother and by a Chinese tutor who was a Confucian scholar, Buck was sent to boarding school in Shanghai at the age of fifteen. In 1910 she returned to the United States and attended Randolph-Macon Woman's College in Virginia, where she studied psychology and won two literature prizes. Upon graduating in 1914, she went back to China as a teacher for the Presbyterian Board of Missions. Three years later she married John Lossing Buck, an agricultural expert who was also serving as a missionary in China. The couple settled in a village in the north, where Buck continued to teach and to serve as an interpreter for her husband as they traveled through the countryside. In 1921 their daughter Carol was born. Later that year her mother died, and in tribute, Buck decided to write her biography. By this time the Bucks had moved to Nanking, where, at the university, John taught agriculture and Pearl taught English and American literature.

Buck's first literary efforts had appeared during her childhood in the *Shanghai Mercury,* an English-language newspaper that ran a weekly edition for children. After finishing her mother's biography (which she did not attempt to publish until many years later), Buck began a novel and produced articles on aspects of Chinese life that were published during the early 1920s in the *Atlantic Monthly* and other American magazines.

Returning to the United States for a year in 1925, the Bucks did postgraduate work at Cornell University, where Pearl Buck earned an M.A. in literature. By this time the couple had learned that their daughter was severely retarded, a discovery that prompted them to adopt an infant girl, Janice, in an attempt to overcome their grief.

When the Bucks went back to China in 1927, the country was in the throes of civil war. They found that their house in Nanking had been overrun and that the manuscript of Buck's first novel was missing. Later that year they were evacuated, first to Shanghai and then to Japan. By this time Buck had completed a second novel, *East Wind: West Wind,* which she had begun aboard ship during their voyage from the United States. Published in 1930, this realistic, conventional love story involves a conflict between generations. Its setting is the China of Buck's upbringing, its characters the simple Chinese people she knew from her earliest life. Though initially turned down for publication because of a presumed lack of reader interest in its Chinese setting, *East Wind: West Wind* quickly went through three printings. It was followed in 1931 by *The Good Earth,* for which Buck received the Pulitzer Prize. Still considered her premier work, *The Good Earth* describes the struggle of an impoverished Chinese peasant family to gain wealth and to establish a family dynasty. Its straightforward story is told in the simple style that became Buck's hallmark, one often described as biblical in tone. *The Good Earth* became a phenomenal best-seller and was described by one critic as "a parable of the life of man." Indeed, the novel derives from the tradition of Chinese vernacular literature, whose cyclical form reflects a belief in the continuity of life, and which is conceived as an entertainment for the common people. *The Good Earth* was followed by two sequels, *Sons* (1932) and *A House Divided* (1935). The three novels were published in one volume in 1935 as *The House of Earth.*

During these early years of her writing career, Buck's output was unceasing. She brought out the novel *Mother* in 1934; biographies of her mother (*The Exile*) and her father (*Fighting Angel*) in 1936; and *The Proud Heart,* her first novel with an American setting, in 1938. A two-volume translation of the classic Chinese novel *Shui-hu Chuan,* translated as *All Men Are Brothers,* appeared in 1933.

In 1938 Pearl Buck became the first American woman to receive the Nobel Prize for Literature, "for her rich and truly epic descriptions of peasant life in China and for her biographical masterpieces." In his presentation address, Per Hallström of the Swedish Academy summarized the themes of Buck's most notable books, "which," he concluded, "pave the way to a human sympathy passing over widely separated racial boundaries" and which offer "studies of human ideals which are a great and living art of portraiture."

"This award, given to an American, strengthens not only one, but the whole body of American writers," Buck said upon accepting the award. "And I should like to say, too, that in my country it is important that this award has been given to a woman." She also acknowledged her debt to "the people of China, whose life has for so many years been my life also."

The award stirred controversy, especially among critics who believed that although Buck was a capable popular novelist, she lacked the stature the Nobel Prize was intended to confirm. Despite critical dissent, Buck's work continued to be remarkably popular, and Buck produced at a prodigious rate. During a professional life spanning forty years, she wrote eighty works, including novels, biographies, an autobiography, radio plays, and children's books.

The critical praise she won for *The Good Earth* was not to be repeated, however; and after receiving the Nobel Prize, Buck's reputation began to decline. In particular, her work was perceived as didactic in its intention and too sentimental in its tone. Pearl Buck the humanitarian was declared by some critics to be less interested in the development of her art than in hammering out a message about the need for "one world." The controversy over her contribution has continued, with critics such as Kenneth Tynan defending the quality of her work, while others, such as George Steiner, remain equally persuasive in disparaging it.

In 1935 Pearl Buck divorced her first husband and married her publisher, Richard Walsh. Their large family included a number of adopted children. Buck and Walsh were active in humanitarian causes through the East and West Association, which was established to promulgate intercultural understanding, and through Welcome House, which sponsored the adoption of children of Asian-American ancestry. The Pearl Buck Foundation became the recipient of Buck's sizable earnings from her work, which were dispensed among a variety of charitable and educational causes.

Pearl Buck died at the age of eighty in Danby, Vermont, outliving Walsh by some thirteen years. Her many other awards included the William Dean Howells Medal of the American Academy of Arts and Letters (1935); numerous humanitarian awards; and honorary degrees from Yale, the University of West Virginia, Howard University, the Women's Medical College of Philadelphia, and other institutions. Pearl Buck was elected to membership in the American Academy of Arts and Letters in 1951.

ADDITIONAL WORKS: The Young Revolutionist, 1931; The Spirit and the Flesh, 1937; The Patriot, 1938; Today and Forever, 1941; Other Gods, 1941; China Sky, 1942; Dragon Seed, 1942; The Promise, 1943; China Flight, 1945; The Townsman, 1945; Pavilion of Women, 1946; Far and Near, 1947; The Angry Wife, 1947; Kinfolk, 1949; The Child Who Never Grew, 1950; The Man Who Changed China, 1953; My Several Worlds, 1954; Imperial Woman, 1956; Letter From Peking, 1957; American Triptych, 1958; A Desert Incident, 1959; Command the Morning, 1959; A Bridge for Passing, 1962; Stories of China, 1964; Death in the Castle; 1965; The Time Is Noon, 1967; The People of Japan, 1968; The Three Daughters of Madame Liang, 1969; Mandala, 1970; The Kennedy Women, 1970; China As I See It, 1970; The Chinese Story Teller, 1971; Pearl Buck's America, 1971; China Past and Present, 1972; The Rainbow, 1974; East and West, 1975; The Woman Who Was Changed, 1979.

ABOUT: Block, I. The Lives of Pearl Buck: A Tale of China and America, 1973; Doyle, P. A. Pearl S. Buck, 1965; Gray, J. On Second Thought, 1946; Harris, T. F. Pearl S. Buck: A Biography, 1969; Myers, E., and Fiorentino, A. Pearl S. Buck, 1974; Schoen, C. V. Pearl Buck, 1972; Spencer, C. The Exile's Daughter, 1944; Stirling, N. B. Pearl Buck: A Woman in Conflict, 1983.

BUISSON, FERDINAND
(December 20, 1841–February 16, 1932)
Nobel Prize for Peace, 1927
(shared with Ludwig Quidde)

The French educator and peace advocate Ferdinand Édouard Buisson (büē sôN') was born in Paris to Protestant parents; his mother was Adèle Aurélie (de Aibeaucourt) Buisson and his father was Pierre Buisson, a judge of the St.-Étienne Tribunal. He attended the Collège d'Argentan and Lycée de St.-Étienne, but when his father died in 1857, he took a teaching job to help support his mother and younger brothers. He later completed his secondary education at the Lycée Condorcet and studied philosophy at the University of Paris (Sorbonne), where he received his degree. Although Buisson passed the state teachers' examination in philosophy, he refused to swear allegiance to Emperor Napoleon III, whom he regarded as a dictator, and consequently was unable to find a teaching position in France. Moving to Switzerland, he taught philosophy at the Académie de Neuchâtel from 1866 to 1870.

In 1867 Buisson took part in the first Congress for Peace and Liberty in Geneva and, with FRÉDÉRIC PASSY and Giuseppe Garibaldi, the Italian patriot, helped found the International League of Peace and Freedom. During the years of his exile in Switzerland, Buisson wrote numerous articles on the subject of peace and education. He also revised an earlier work, Le Christianisme libéral (Liberal Christianity, 1865), in which he advocated supplanting organized religion by a code of personal morality. In these works Buisson expressed two ideas that were characteristic of his radical humanism: that the way to world peace lay in changing human attitudes by reaching people at the onset of their education and that church and state had to be formally separated.

With the defeat of France in the Franco-Prussian War and the subsequent abdication of Napoleon III, Buisson returned to Paris in

FERDINAND BUISSON

1870. One of his first actions there was to establish an asylum for war orphans. Later that year, the Third Republic's new minister of public instruction appointed him inspector of primary education in Paris. Controversy soon developed in the French National Assembly over Buisson's demand that the Catholic church end its domination of the French educational system, and Buisson was forced to resign. Nevertheless, support for his views grew over the decade, and in 1879 he was named director of primary education, an influential post he held for seventeen years. During his tenure, Buisson helped draft national laws that ensured free, compulsory, nondenominational primary education throughout France. He also published the four-volume Dictionnaire de pédagogie et d'instruction primaire (Dictionary of Pedagogy and Primary Instruction, 1878–1887), and edited a progressive education journal. In 1896 he resigned his government post to become a professor of education at the Sorbonne.

Buisson was drawn into politics by the infamous Dreyfus affair, which began in 1894 when Captain Alfred Dreyfus, a Jewish officer in the French army, was falsely convicted of treason on the basis of perjured evidence. Outraged by the anti-Semitism that made Dreyfus a scapegoat while high-ranking military officers tried to cover up the actual crime, Buisson helped form the League of the Rights of Man in 1898. The league's purpose was not only to exonerate Dreyfus but also to expose injustice anywhere and in any form. In 1902 Buisson was elected to the Chamber of Deputies as a member of the Radical-Socialist party, a seat he held until 1914 and again from 1919 to 1924.

At the outbreak of World War I, believing that a German victory would be a victory for militarism and a defeat for humanitarian ideals, Buisson declared his full support for the French war effort. In 1916 he defended WOODROW WILSON's proposal for forming the League of Nations. Bitterly disappointed by the terms of the 1919 Versailles treaty, which he felt would perpetuate the enmity between victor and vanquished, Buisson continued to support the league as the most effective political instrument for maintaining peace. At the same time, he put into practice his conviction that education held the key to long-term peace. When French and Belgian troops occupied the Ruhr Valley, Germany's industrial heartland, after Germany defaulted on its reparations payments in 1923, Buisson worked to promote understanding between the French and German people. He invited German peace activists to speak in Paris and undertook his own speaking tour in Germany. Although his efforts met with hostility from both French and German nationalists, French and Belgian forces were later withdrawn from the Ruhr and Germany's debt restructured under the 1925 Dawes Plan, named for the American statesman CHARLES DAWES.

Buisson shared the 1927 Nobel Prize for Peace with LUDWIG QUIDDE, then president of the German Peace Society. In presenting the award, Fredrik Stang of the Norwegian Nobel Committee stated, "Governments and their policies are not the only potential menace to peace. A constant and real threat of war also lies in the mentality of men, in the psychology of the masses. Therefore, the great organized work for peace must be preceded by the education of the people, by a campaign to turn mass thinking away from war as a recognized means of settling disputes, and to substitute another and much higher ideal: peaceful cooperation between nations, with an international court of justice to resolve any disagreements which might arise between them. It is in the task of reorienting public opinion that [the recipients] have played such prominent roles."

Buisson attended the award ceremonies, and although he did not deliver a Nobel lecture, he submitted an essay to the Nobel committee the following year: "Changes in Concepts of War and Peace." Noting that war was no longer restricted to professional soldiers, he warned that submarine, aerial, and chemical warfare meant that war "has put itself in the position of executioner of the whole earth." He expressed his hope that the proposals to outlaw war recently put forth by French Foreign Minister ARISTIDE BRIAND and United States Secretary of State FRANK KELLOGG would lead the world powers "to reject warfare as a tool of national policy." Enlarging on the theme of peace through education, he declared that, while diplomats may seek negotiated resolutions between governments, the "foremost moral obligation" of educators "is to bring influence to bear, not on governments, but on the people themselves."

A long life of public service to education strengthened Buisson's view that education must be the agent of change in human attitudes about war and peace. To this end, in the years after he received the Nobel Prize, he promoted the formation of international contacts between professional associations of teachers.

Buisson donated his Nobel Prize money to pacifist organizations. In 1924 he was named a grand officer of the French Legion of Honor. A widower with two sons and a daughter, he died of heart disease at the age of ninety in the town of Thieuloy-St.-Antoine, north of Paris.

ABOUT: Talbott, J. E. The Politics of Educational Reform in France 1918–1940, 1969.

BUNCHE, RALPH
(August 7, 1904–December 9, 1971)
Nobel Prize for Peace, 1950

Ralph Johnson Bunche, American statesman and United Nations official, was born in Detroit, Michigan. The grandson of a slave and the elder child and only son of Fred Bunche, a barber, and the former Olive Agnes Johnson, his childhood was one of poverty. Orphaned at the age of twelve, he was raised by his grandmother, Nana Johnson, who moved him and his sister, Grace, to Los Angeles in 1916.

Education took Bunche out of the ghetto. Valedictorian of his class at Jefferson High School, he was described by a teacher as someone who "seemed completely at ease with the world and always looked up." With an athletic scholarship and a job as a janitor, he worked his way through the University of California at Los Angeles, graduating at the head of his class in 1927 with a B.A. in international relations. In 1928 he received an M.A. from

RALPH BUNCHE

Harvard University, where he continued his studies in political science. In 1932–1933 Bunche traveled to Africa to complete research for a doctoral dissertation about French colonial rule in Togoland (now the independent nations of Togo and Ghana) and in Dahomey (now Benin). When Harvard awarded him a Ph.D. in 1934, he became the first black American to receive a doctorate in political science.

While completing his graduate studies, Bunche began a career in college teaching. Rejecting offers from white institutions, he joined the faculty of Howard University in 1928 as a political science instructor and was named head of the department a year later. In June 1930 he married Ruth Ethel Harris, an elementary school teacher,with whom he had three children.

In 1936 Bunche became codirector of the Institute of Race Relations at Swarthmore College and published *A World View of Race*. Continuing to develop his expertise in colonial policy and race relations, he did postdoctoral work in anthropology from 1936 to 1938 at Northwestern University, the London School of Economics, and Capetown University in South Africa. He collaborated with the Swedish sociologist GUNNAR MYRDAL from 1938 to 1940 in conducting field studies, the results of which were published in *An American Dilemma* (1944), an influential study of racial prejudice.

Bunche's career in public service began in 1941 when he joined the Office of the Coordinator of Information, National Defense Program. As senior social science analyst for Africa

and the Far East, he wrote intelligence reports on colonial areas of strategic military importance to the United States. He remained with the bureau when it became the Office of Strategic Services (OSS) the following year. "The man's a walking colonial institute!" one of his OSS chiefs boasted. With such recommendations, Bunche transferred in 1944 to the Department of State, where he became a specialist on Africa in the Division of Territorial Studies. In that position, he drew on his vast knowledge of the Third World to combat long-entrenched misconceptions about the peoples of Africa, Asia, and the Middle East.

As a member of the United States delegation to the Dumbarton Oaks Conference in 1944, Bunche drafted most of the trusteeship section of the United Nations Charter. This section provided the framework for administering former colonies of nations defeated in World War II, dealing with such issues as government, health and welfare, education, economics, and individual rights. So adept was Bunche at balancing the interests of Western powers and colonized peoples that delegates to the 1945 San Francisco Conference accepted the trusteeship chapters virtually as written. At the conference, Bunche acted as an adviser to the United States delegation.

From that time on, Bunche became, in his words, an "international servant." In January 1946 he served as a member of the United States delegation to the First General Assembly of the United Nations. During that year, Trygve Lie, the first secretary-general of the United Nations, requested Bunche's services "on loan." In 1947 Bunche assumed the directorship of the United Nations Department of Trusteeship and Information From Non-Self-Governing Territories, where he remained a firm, if realistic, advocate of decolonization.

During the Arab-Israeli War of 1948, Bunche's mediating abilities came to the fore. The Arab states protested Israel's declaration of statehood and warred with the new nation throughout the year over the occupation of Palestine. As Lie's special representative, Bunche was assigned to accompany United Nations–appointed mediator Count Folke Bernadotte of Sweden to the Middle East. When Bernadotte was assassinated by Israeli terrorists in September 1948, the United Nations Security Council put Bunche in charge of negotiations.

Bunche's skill at resolving conflicts produced an armistice despite circumstances that seemed almost hopeless. Since Arab representatives refused to sit at the same table with the Israelis, Bunche set up committees to meet in small rooms, each to consider one issue at a time. Point by point, day by day, Bunche poured his energy, objectivity, and patience into creating an atmosphere of trust and compromise. He joked. He cajoled. He threatened. In 1949 his "unfailing sense of optimism" paid off when Israel, Egypt, Lebanon, Jordan, and Syria hammered out four separate armistice agreements.

Bunche received the 1950 Nobel Prize for Peace, the first black to receive the prize. In his presentation speech, Gunnar Jahn of the Norwegian Nobel Committee described Bunche's long public career and his "infinite patience" during the Arab-Israeli negotiations. "The outcome was a victory for the ideas of the United Nations," he said, "but . . . it was one individual's efforts that made victory possible."

In his Nobel lecture, "Some Reflections on Peace in Our Time," Bunche discussed the paradox of a world desperately desiring peace yet continually engaging in war. Describing "mankind's great dilemma" in the nuclear age, Bunche noted that "some values—freedom, honor, self-respect—are higher than peace or life itself. . . . Many would hold that the loss of human dignity and self-respect, the chains of enslavement, are too high a price even for peace. But the horrible realities of modern warfare scarcely afford even this fatal choice. There is only suicidal escape, not freedom, in the death and destruction of atomic war." The reason for this dilemma, Bunche suggested, is that "the values [man] has created have been predominantly materialistic; his spiritual values have lagged far behind." Calling the United Nations "the greatest peace effort in human history," Bunche acknowledged the organization's weaknesses but declared that "the United Nations strives to be realistic. . . . The world and its peoples being as they are, there is no easy or quick or infallible approach to a secure peace. It is only by patient, persistent, undismayed effort, by trial and error, that peace can be won."

Bunche dedicated the remainder of his career to making the United Nations an effective peacekeeping organization. In 1955 he became under secretary for special political affairs, and from 1967 until his retirement in 1971, he served as under secretary–general. His primary role in these positions was that of peacemaker. During the 1956 Suez crisis, for example, Bunche directed the United Nations Emergency Force in Egypt. In 1960 Secretary-General DAG HAMMARSKJÖLD, Trygve Lie's successor, sent Bunche to the Congo (now Zaire), newly independent of Belgian rule. When political conditions there deteriorated, Bunche found himself at the head of the improvised United Nations military and civilian operation that temporarily ran the country. He was also instrumental in establishing the United Nations Peacekeeping Force in Cyprus in 1964, and the following year he directed monitoring of the India-Pakistan cease-fire.

Although he did not make civil rights the focus of his career, Bunche worked actively for black equality in American life. His philosophy as a minority citizen was that of his grandmother: "to stand up for our rights, to suffer no indignity, but to harbor no bitterness toward anyone." In that spirit, he refused the job of assistant secretary of state offered in 1949 by President Harry S Truman, because segregated housing still existed in the nation's capital. In 1965 he helped lead the civil rights march organized by MARTIN LUTHER KING JR. in Montgomery, Alabama. Like King, Bunche argued that money spent on the Vietnam War should instead be used to combat racism by eliminating inner-city ghettos.

Until his retirement from the United Nations in 1971, Bunche served as an adviser to Secretary-General U Thant. He died in New York City on December 9, 1971.

ADDITIONAL WORKS: Native Morale in the Netherlands Antilles, 1941; "The United Nations Is the Only Bridge: How Peace Came to Palestine," Common Sense August 1949; Peace and the United Nations, 1952; The Political Status of the Negro in the Age of FDR, 1973.

ABOUT: Cornell, J. G. Ralph Bunche, Champion of Peace, 1976; Finger, S. M. Your Man at the UN, 1980; Haskins, J. Ralph Bunche, A Most Reluctant Hero, 1974; Hughes, L. Famous American Negroes, 1954; Johnson, A. D. The Value of Responsibility: The Story of Ralph Bunche, 1978; Kugelmass, J. A. Ralph J. Bunche: Fighter for Peace, 1952; Mann, P. Ralph Bunche, UN Peacekeeper, 1975; New Yorker January 1, 1972.

BUNIN, IVAN

(October 22, 1870–November 8, 1953)
Nobel Prize for Literature, 1933

Ivan Alexeyevich Bunin (boo' nyin), Russian poet and novelist, was born on his parents' estate near Voronezh, in the Orel Province of central Russia (now part of the Russian Soviet Federated Socialist Republic), the region that was also home to such eminent literary figures as Leo Tolstoy, Ivan Turgenev, and Ivan Goncharov. Bunin's father, Alexey Nikolaevich Bunin, came from a line of landed gentry that can be traced back to a fifteenth-century Lithuanian knight; his mother, the former Ljudmila Alexsandrovna Chubarova, was also of noble descent. Acute mismanagement and the emancipation of the serfs in 1861 severely depleted the Bunin and Chubarova estates, and by the turn of the century the family fortune was nearly exhausted.

Until he was eleven years old, Bunin was tutored at home. In 1881 he entered the public school in Yelets, but after a few years the family's financial troubles forced him to return home. There his education was entrusted to his brilliant and politically rebellious elder brother, Yuliy, who was under house arrest for distributing pamphlets for the revolutionary populist movement. An aristocrat at heart, Bunin did not share his brother's passion for radical politics. Nevertheless, Yuliy, recognizing his brother's affinity for literature, introduced him to the Russian classics and encouraged him to write. Bunin avidly read the works of Aleksandr Pushkin, Nikolay Gogol, and Mikhail Lermontov and, at the age of seventeen, began to write poetry himself.

Aware of his family's impending penury, Bunin took a job in 1889 as assistant editor of the newspaper *Orlovskiy Vestnik* (Orel Herald) and soon fell in love with Varvara Pashchenko, a junior member of the staff. Although her parents would not permit them to marry, Bunin and Pashchenko moved to Poltava in the Ukraine in 1892. Their relationship lasted until 1894 when Pashchenko married Bunin's friend, the writer A. N. Bibikov.

In 1891 Bunin's first volume of poetry was published as a supplement to a literary journal. Classical in style, his verses are imbued with images of nature, a quality that remained constant in most of his poetic output. He also began to write short stories, which appeared in various literary magazines, and started a correspondence with Anton Chekhov. Four years later, in 1895, the two writers met and became close friends. Despite some similarities between them, their themes and styles are markedly different. Bunin's traditional approach to storytelling, with its emphasis on narrative and description, differs from Chekhov's innovative brevity. Like the pianist-composer Sergei Rachmaninoff and the basso Fyodor Chaliapin, two of his conservative friends, Bunin remained skeptical of modern artistic movements.

For a time in the early 1890s, Bunin was profoundly affected by Tolstoy's philosophical

IVAN BUNIN

tenets, especially his fraternity with nature, his apparent dedication to the virtues of manual labor, and his advocacy of nonviolence in the face of oppression. When he met Tolstoy in 1894, however, Bunin was disappointed by his mentor's utopian outlook. Nevertheless, he continued to admire Tolstoy's naturalism and to believe that Tolstoy was the supreme statesman of Russian letters.

In 1895 Bunin began dividing his time between St. Petersburg (now Leningrad) and Moscow. In both cities he achieved literary recognition through the publication of a number of short stories. These included "Na chutore" ("On the Farm"), "Vesti s rodiny" ("The News From Home"), and "Na krayu sveta" ("To the Edge of the World"), which dealt with contemporary events such as the 1891 famine, the 1892 cholera epidemic, the peasant migration to Siberia, and the gentry's decay and impoverishment. *To the Edge of the World* was chosen as the title story for Bunin's first collection of short fiction, which appeared in 1897. The following year he published a collection of poetry, *Pod otkrytym nebom* (Under the Open Sky), as well as a highly regarded translation of Henry Wadsworth Longfellow's *The Song of Hiawatha*, for which he was awarded the first of three Pushkin prizes. Later that year he married Anna Nikolaevna Cakni, the daughter of a Greek revolutionary, whom he met while visiting Odessa. The couple separated after a brief and troubled marriage; their only child, a son born in 1900, died of scarlet fever at the age of five.

In early 1899 Bunin met Maxim Gorky, who

introduced him to the coterie of liberal writers known as Znaniye (Knowledge). Although Gorky's stylistic realism and progressive ideals did not appeal to the nostalgic Bunin, he dedicated *Listopad* (Falling Leaves, 1901), a collection of poetry, to Gorky, and remained associated with Znaniye until the 1917 Russian Revolution.

An active translator of English and French poets, Bunin wrote Russian versions of Alfred Lord Tennyson's "Lady Godiva" and Lord Byron's *Manfred,* as well as works by Alfred de Musset and François Coppée. From 1900 to 1909 he published dozens of short stories, including "Antonovskie yabloki" ("Antonov Apples") and "Sosny" (The Pines). These works reflected his concerns with the decadence of the Russian landowning classes as well as the dislocation of the urban and rural populations.

In late 1906 Bunin fell in love with Vera Nikolaevna Muromceva, the daughter of a Moscow city councilman, who became his common-law wife and who accompanied him on several trips abroad in the decade before the 1917 revolution. During this period, Bunin produced some of his finest fiction. The prose poem *Derevnia* (The Village, 1910), his first full-length work, is a somber portrayal of the Russian peasantry after the revolution of 1905. Although this work disturbed the sensibilities of liberal writers, Bunin's literary reputation was growing, and in 1911 Gorky lauded him as "the best contemporary writer." *The Village* was followed in 1912 by the novella *Sukhodol* (*Dry Valley*), an unsparing portrait of the degeneration of a family of landed gentry and their servants. In a volume of his mature stories published in 1917, he included what is probably the best-known of all his works, "Gospodin iz San Francisko" ("The Gentleman From San Francisco"), a symbolically rich account of the death of an American millionaire on vacation in Capri.

Although the revolution in October 1917 came as no surprise to Bunin, he feared that the impact of a Bolshevik Communist victory would be catastrophic. Leaving Moscow in 1918, he resided in Odessa for two years while the city was controlled by reactionary Whites and, after a period of stateless wandering, eventually emigrated to France with Muromceva in 1920. They settled first in Paris and then in Grasse on the Riviera; they eventually married in 1922. Bunin expressed his bitter hatred for the Bolshevik regime in his diary, *Okayannye dni* (*The Accursed Days,* 1925–1926). Of the stories published in the 1920s, perhaps the most

memorable are the novella *Mitina lubov* (*Mitya's Love,* 1925), with its themes of romance, exile, and death, and the tales in *Roza Ierixona* (*Jericho Rose,* 1924) and *Solnechny udar* (A Sunstroke, 1927). The highly regarded autobiographical novel *Zhizn Arsen'eva: U istoka dnej* (*The Life of Arsenyev: The Well of Days,* 1933) contains a panoply of characters, real and imagined, from prerevolutionary Russia.

Bunin was awarded the 1933 Nobel Prize for Literature "for the strict artistry with which he has carried on the classical Russian traditions in prose writing." In his presentation address, Per Hallström of the Swedish Academy, while acknowledging Bunin's gift as a lyric poet, praised his "concentration and richness of expression—of a description of real life based on an almost unique precision of observation." In his acceptance speech Bunin modestly commended the academy's courage for honoring an émigré writer.

To satisfy international demand for his collected works, Bunin prepared an eleven-volume edition from 1934 to 1936, with the help of the Berlin publishing firm Petropolis. Although he also received overdue acclaim from the Soviet public, the thought of returning to his homeland under Joseph Stalin appalled him. Despite the belated recognition, life in exile remained difficult. His last volume of fiction, *Tyomnyye allei* (*Shadowed Paths,* 1946), written during the dark days of the Nazi occupation of France, went unheralded. Toward the end of his life, he wrote more fiction and the singularly caustic *Vospominaniya* (*Memories and Portraits,* 1950), in which he scathingly criticized Soviet culture. The year after this volume appeared, Bunin was elected as the first honorary member of the PEN (Poets, Essayists, Novelists) Center for Writers in Exile. In his last years Bunin also began his reminiscences of Chekhov, a project he had pledged to undertake upon his friend's death in 1904. The Chekhov portrait remained unfinished at the time of Bunin's death in Paris from a debilitating respiratory ailment.

Bunin is best remembered as a writer of prose, although some modern critics reserve greater praise for his poetry. The renowned Russian émigré writer Vladimir Nabokov, for instance, preferred Bunin's poetry to his fiction. The Italian scholar Renato Poggioli surmised that Nabokov may have felt that way because Bunin's "verse is far more direct and laconic, far less heavy and ornamental than his prose."

Although he was widely considered to be the leading Russian émigré writer during the

1930s, Bunin never developed a reputation that matched those of Tolstoy and Chekhov. While he is largely neglected by today's general readers, he is held in relatively high esteem by contemporary scholars and critics. *The Life of Arsenyev* is generally regarded as his masterpiece. However, the American critic Mark Van Doren found that in this work "Bunin has been too conscious of the autobiography as literary form." Scholars such as Poggioli believe that "in spite of its quality, it is not *The Life of Arsenyev,* but the far shorter *Dry Valley* (along with "The Gentleman From San Francisco") which must be considered the high point of Bunin's work."

ADDITIONAL WORKS IN ENGLISH TRANSLATION: Fifteen Tales, 1923; Grammar of Love, 1934; The Elaghin Affair, 1935; Dark Avenues, and Other Stories, 1949; Velga, 1970; In a Far Distant Land, 1983; Long Ago: Fourteen Stories, 1984.

ABOUT: Connolly, J. W. Ivan Bunin, 1982; Kryzytski, S. The Works of Ivan Bunin, 1971; Poggioli, R. The Phoenix and the Spider, 1957; Woodward, J. Ivan Bunin, 1980.

BURNET, MACFARLANE
(September 3, 1899–August 31, 1985)
Nobel Prize for Physiology or Medicine, 1960
(shared with P. B. Medawar)

The Australian immunologist Frank Macfarlane Burnet (bər net′) was born in Traralgon, a country town in the province of Victoria, the second of six children of Frank Burnet, a branch manager of the Colonial Bank, and Hadassah Pollock (MacKay) Burnet. As a child, Burnet enjoyed natural history and was especially fond of collecting beetles. After attending Geelong College, he entered Ormond College, University of Melbourne, as a medical student in 1917. He took a B.S. in 1922 and a medical degree in 1923, whereupon he was appointed a resident pathologist at Melbourne Hospital. While remaining affiliated with the hospital for the rest of his career, he also worked for many years at the University of Melbourne's Walter and Eliza Hall Institute for Medical Research.

About the time he joined the institute in 1924, Burnet read Felix d'Herelle's classic work on bacteriophages, *Le Bacteriophage: son rôle dans l'immunité* (The Bacteriophage: Its Role in Immunity, 1921). Bacteriophages are viruses that infect bacteria; Burnet became especially interested in the ecological and genetic

MACFARLANE BURNET

relationships between these organisms and their hosts. In 1926 a Beit Fellowship for Medical Research enabled him to work at the Lister Institute in London, where he also received a Ph.D. from the University of London in 1927.

After Burnet returned to Melbourne in 1928, his career was influenced by the death of twelve children who had received diphtheria vaccinations. During the investigation that ensued, Burnet found that the deaths had been due to contamination of a vaccine sample by *Staphylococcus* bacteria. The discovery stimulated his interest in how the body defends itself against such invasions.

Pursuing the study of animal viruses, Burnet spent 1932–1933 at the National Institute for Medical Research in Hampstead, England, under a special fellowship in virus disease research. In the course of his work, he refined techniques for cultivating viruses in chicken eggs. Viruses are parasites, incapable of growing outside of living cells; mammalian cells, however, are difficult to grow in laboratory dishes. Burnet's methods for inducing viruses to reproduce in the self-contained environment of eggs were among the most useful techniques in virology until JOHN F. ENDERS and his colleagues developed improved cell-culture methods in 1947.

Burnet's egg cultures succeeded because the embryonic chickens, unable to resist virus infections, produced no antibodies to the virus. Antibodies were discovered in 1890 by EMIL VON BEHRING, who, with PAUL EHRLICH and other collaborators, demonstrated that blood can develop immunological responses to a variety of substances, or antigens. Antibody responses are highly specific; antibodies to one strain of bacteria often do not react to related strains. Immunity to measles, for example, confers no protection against rubella.

In Burnet's view, theories to explain the production of antibodies could be divided into two groups. "In a *selective* theory," he wrote later, "it is assumed that the function of the antigen is to stimulate a preexistent pattern into activity; in an *instructive* theory, the antigen is assumed to impress a new pattern on the cell concerned." According to Ehrlich, who developed the first important immunological theory (a selective one), antibodies are receptors on the surface of cells; when antigens bind to the antibodies, the cell overproduces antibodies in response.

Selective theories such as Ehrlich's fell out of favor during the 1930s after KARL LANDSTEINER found that mice could produce antibodies to a wide variety of chemicals not present in nature. Because it seemed unlikely that animals could contain specific preformed receptors for so many unusual compounds, most immunologists came to favor instructive theories. The most important such theory was proposed by LINUS C. PAULING, who suggested that antigens were taken inside cells, where antibody molecules were folded around them to obtain a tight, specific fit.

Burnet believed that instructive theories failed to account for what he called "the basic problem of immunology," namely, "how can an immunized animal recognize the difference between an injected material . . . from another species and its own corresponding substance?" Self-recognition (the capacity of a body to recognize its own proteins) could not be easily explained by instructive theories, Burnet pointed out. Drawing upon his observation that chickens do not develop antibodies to viruses they encounter as embryos, he proposed that animals do not produce antibodies to any substance they encounter at an early stage of life, and that this early exposure is the key to self-recognition and self-tolerance.

Burnet and his colleagues at the Hall Institute tried to produce artificial tolerance in chickens by briefly exposing them to synthetic antigens. They failed because, it was later realized, contact with the antigen must continue for a relatively long time in order for a long-lasting tolerance to develop. In 1953 P. B. MEDAWAR and his co-workers produced acquired tolerance using organ transplants and thus confirmed Burnet's theory.

Burnet and Medawar shared the 1960 Nobel Prize for Physiology or Medicine "for discovery of acquired immunological tolerance." Their work, which disproved instructive theories, marked the beginning of modern selective immunology theories. In his Nobel lecture, "Immunological Recognition of Self," Burnet dealt with "a single problem. How does the vertebrate organism recognize self from not-self—in the immunological sense—and how did this capacity evolve?" He concluded that "the only possible type of approach [to this problem] is by a 'selective' theory of immunity, which must be developed on a cellular and probably on a clonal basis."

"Clonal selection theories," developed in the late 1950s by Burnet, David Talmage, NIELS K. JERNE, and JOSHUA LEDERBERG, state that the embryo contains examples of all the tens or hundreds of millions of antibodies an adult animal can produce. Each antibody-producing cell can make only one type of antibody. During a critical period in fetal development and early life, any cell that encounters an antigen corresponding to its specific antibody (which would normally be a "self" antigen) is killed or inactivated. Therefore, by the end of the critical period all "antiself" cells have been eliminated from the set of antibody-producing cells.

After retiring from the Hall Institute in 1965, Burnet continued to conduct major research in immunology, especially on aging, autoimmune diseases (in which self-tolerance breaks down), and cancer. He also wrote a number of books for the general public on issues in biology, medicine, and human nature and an autobiography, *Changing Patterns* (1968).

In 1928 Burnet married Edith Linda Druce, a fellow Australian; they had a son and two daughters. Three years after the death of his first wife in 1973, Burnet married Hazel Jenkin. He died of cancer in Melbourne on August 31, 1985.

Burnet received the Royal Medal (1947) and the Copley Medal (1959) of the Royal Society of London. He was elected a fellow of the Royal Society of London in 1947. He was knighted in 1951, received the Order of Merit in 1958, and was named a fellow of the Royal College of Surgeons of England in 1953.

SELECTED WORKS: Biological Aspects of Infectious Disease, 1940; Production of Antibodies, 1949; Viruses and Man, 1955; Principles of Animal Virology, 1955; Enzyme, Antigen and Virus, 1956; Clonal Selection Theory of Immunity, 1959; Integrity of the Body, 1962; Auto-Immune Diseases, 1963, with I. R. Mackay; Biology and the Appreciation of Life, 1966; Cellular Immunology, 1969; Self and Not-Self, 1969; Immunological Surveillance, 1970;

BUTENANDT

Dominant Mammal, 1970; Genes, Dreams and Realities, 1971; Auto-Immunity and Auto-Immune Disease, 1972; Natural History of Infectious Disease, 1972; Immunology, 1976; Immunology, Aging and Cancer, 1976; Endurance of Life, 1978; Credo and Comment, 1979; Biological Foundations and Human Nature, 1983.

ABOUT: Current Biography May 1954; New Scientist October 3, 1974; New York Times September 2, 1985; Norry, R. Virus Hunter in Australia, 1966; Wolstenholme, G., and Porter, R. (eds.) The Thymus, 1966.

BUTENANDT, ADOLF
(March 24, 1903–   )
Nobel Prize for Chemistry, 1939
(shared with Leopold Ružička)

ADOLF BUTENANDT

The German physiological chemist Adolf Friedrich Johann Butenandt (büt′ ən änt) was born in Bremerhaven-Lehe to Wilhelmine (Thomfohrde) and Otto Butenandt, a businessman. After receiving his early education in the *Oberrealschule* in Bremerhaven, he entered the University of Marburg in 1921 and began studying chemistry and biology. Continuing his studies at the University of Göttingen, he worked under of ADOLF WINDAUS.

A lecture on the biochemistry of cholesterol, given by Windaus in 1924, concerned the way variants of the basic cholesterol molecule are used for numerous biological purposes by different species of animals. Windaus's remarks had a decisive effect on Butenandt, who later recalled, "Both the form and the content of the lecture . . . appealed to my own, hitherto vainly sought, path in scientific research in the borderline between chemistry and biology." Having written a dissertation on the chemistry of rotenone, a compound used in insecticides, he received his Ph.D. in chemistry from Göttingen in 1927 and was appointed an assistant in the university's Institute of Chemistry.

It was around this time that Walter Schoeller, director of research for Schering Corporation, a pharmaceutical firm, asked Windaus for help in an investigation of the chemical structure of the female sex hormones. Windaus recommended Butenandt. Schering then provided Butenandt with concentrated extracts of a biologically active hormonal substance obtained from the urine of pregnant women. From this substance Butenandt isolated a female sex hormone in pure crystalline form in 1929. Because it was synthesized and secreted by cells lining the follicles of the ovary, he called the substance folliculin. Later renamed estrone, the hormone is an estrogen that feminizes the

human body, stimulates closure of long-bone epiphyses, and promotes growth of the lining of the uterus. Independently of Butenandt, the American biochemist EDWARD A. DOISY isolated crystalline estrone at about the same time. In 1931 Butenandt and his colleagues confirmed the discovery by G. F. Merrian in London of a second female sex hormone, an estrogen called estriol.

Butenandt then turned his attention to the isolation and chemical identification of a particular male sex hormone synthesized and secreted by the Leydig cells of the testes. In 1931 he and his colleagues reported the isolation and purification in crystalline form of this hormone, which they called androsterone. It was later shown to be related biochemically to the principal male sex hormone, testosterone.

In 1931 Butenandt was appointed privatdocent (unsalaried lecturer) in the Department of Biological Chemistry and acting chairman of the Laboratories of Inorganic and Organic Chemistry at the University of Göttingen. Two years later he was named professor of chemistry and director of the Institute for Organic Chemistry at the Danzig Institute of Technology, where he remained for three years.

Having isolated and purified the estrogens and androsterone, Butenandt began to analyze the precise chemical structure of the estrogenic hormones estrone and estriol. Earlier X-ray crystallographic studies had suggested a structural relationship between estrone and estriol and the sterols, which are complex organic alcohols containing four fused rings (cholesterol being an example). In 1932 Butenandt and his colleagues showed by spectrographic and chemical methods that the biological activity of estrone and estriol is related to double carbon bonds in the cyclic structure of the sterol molecule. By examining the chemical structure of estrone and estriol, molecule by molecule, they also demonstrated that the core of each hormone was a phenanthrene ring system containing two methyl groups. This discovery was particularly important because it proved that the female sex hormones and the sterols (specifically, cholesterol and the bile acids) were closely related chemically. Cholesterol was later shown to be a biochemical precursor of the male and female sex hormones.

In 1934 Butenandt and his colleagues isolated crystalline progesterone, a hormone that prepares the lining of the uterus for implantation of the fertilized ovum. They demonstrated that progesterone and its derivative pregnanediol, obtained from the urine of pregnant women, were closely related. Five years later Butenandt synthesized progesterone from its cholesterol precursor.

Butenandt and his colleagues also elucidated the structure of androsterone, finding that it has one more carbon atom than the estrogens and eight more hydrogen atoms than estrone. They also found that, like the estrogens, androsterone is a four-ring sterol but with an additional methyl group and five additional hydrogen atoms projecting from the sterol nucleus. The principal male sex hormone, testosterone, was isolated from extracts of testicular tissue by other investigators. In 1935 Butenandt and LEOPOLD RUŽIČKA, working independently, synthesized testosterone from its biochemical precursor. Butenandt also discovered biochemical pathways of interconversion of the male and female sex hormones, which are chemically related by their common sterol nucleus. The two researchers discovered that male sex hormonal activity is determined by a double bond between the fourth and fifth carbon atoms of the four-ring sterol nucleus. If this double bond occurs between the first and second carbon atoms of the sterol nucleus, the molecule has female estrogenic effects. The discovery of these specific chemical sites of biological activity was one of the most important aspects of Butenandt's research on the mammalian sex hormones.

In 1936 MAX PLANCK, president of the Kaiser Wilhelm Society, an organization that oversaw all scientific research in Germany, asked Butenandt to become director of the Kaiser Wilhelm (now the Max Planck) Institute of Biochemistry in Berlin.

Butenandt was awarded the 1939 Nobel Prize for Chemistry "for his work on the mammalian sex hormones." He shared the award with Ružička. The onset of World War II intervened, however, and it was not until 1949 that Butenandt was able to receive the award in Stockholm. During the war years Butenandt remained at the Institute of Biochemistry in Berlin, where he and the zoologist Alfred Kühn studied the genetic regulation of eye pigment biosynthesis in insects. They were able to demonstrate that specific genes govern the synthesis of specific enzymes, which catalyze the formation of eye pigments from the amino acid tryptophan. The eye pigments, called ommochromes, constituted a new class of biological compounds, natural pigments later shown to occur in many animals. Butenandt's research on the one-gene–one-enzyme hypothesis was concurrent with that of two other American researchers, GEORGE W. BEADLE and EDWARD L. TATUM.

After the war, the Kaiser Wilhelm Institute of Biochemistry moved to Tübingen, where Butenandt was appointed professor of physiological chemistry. In 1953 he and a colleague, Peter Karlson, isolated the first crystalline insect hormone. Called ecdysone, this substance stimulates the formation of the chrysalis of the caterpillar. Karlson later demonstrated that ecdysone is a derivative of cholesterol and related chemically to the mammalian sex hormones.

With the relocation of the Kaiser Wilhelm Institute of Biochemistry to Munich in 1956, Butenandt was appointed professor of physiological chemistry at the University of Munich. There he isolated and identified bombykol, a member of another new class of biological compounds called pheromones. Synthesized by female silkworms, bombykol has the biological function of attracting a male.

From 1960 until 1972, Butenandt served as president of the Max Planck Society for the Advancement of Science. After retiring from the University of Munich in 1971, he became professor emeritus.

In 1931 Butenandt married Erika von Ziegner; they have two sons and five daughters. He lives in Munich.

Butenandt's many awards and honors include the Grand Cross for Federal Services of the West German government (1959), commander of the Legion of Honor of France (1969), and the Adolf von Harnack Medal of the Max Planck Society (1973). He has received honorary degrees from the universities of Graz, Leeds, Munich, Madrid, and Tübingen. He holds honorary membership in the New York Academy of Sciences, the Japanese Biochemical Society, the Austrian Academy of Sciences, the French Academy of Sciences, and the Royal Society of London.

ABOUT: Journal of Chemical Education February 1949.

BUTLER, NICHOLAS MURRAY
(April 2, 1862–December 7, 1947)
Nobel Prize for Peace, 1931
(shared with Jane Addams)

The American educator Nicholas Murray Butler was born in Elizabeth, New Jersey, the eldest of five children of Henry Leny Butler, a textile importer and manufacturer, and the former Mary Jones Murray.

After attending private and public schools in Paterson, New Jersey, Butler entered Columbia College in 1878 to study law. Under the influence of Frederick A. P. Barnard, however, he decided to devote his life to education. Graduating with honors in 1882, he continued his studies in philosophy at Columbia, earning an M.A. in 1883 and a Ph.D. the following year. A fellowship enabled him to spend an additional year studying at the universities of Berlin and Paris.

Butler returned to Columbia in 1885 as an assistant professor of philosophy. Two years later, while maintaining his teaching responsibilities at Columbia, he became president of the Industrial Education Association, a philanthropic organization that advocated domestic and manual arts training in public schools. Under his direction, the organization established the New York College for the Training of Teachers, which was chartered in 1889 and renamed Teachers College in 1892. In 1901 Butler succeeded in affiliating Teachers College with Columbia.

Butler became professor of philosophy, ethics, and psychology at Columbia in 1890. That year the faculty and trustees adopted his plan for creating parallel philosophy and natural science faculties to provide graduate training for Columbia seniors as well as for graduate students. In addition, he introduced education as an academic discipline at the university.

During these years, Butler also worked to establish a more centralized administration for public schools and to promote acceptance of education as a profession. While serving on the New Jersey State Board of Education from

NICHOLAS MURRAY BUTLER

1887 to 1895, he headed the Committee on Education. He instituted such reforms as the transfer of teacher certification from local to state officials and the introduction of manual training courses into the curriculum.

After moving to New York City in 1894, Butler helped persuade the state legislature to abolish the city's ward-based school boards, long an instrument for political patronage. He also advocated the Greater New York Charter of 1897, which created a city superintendent of schools, further diminishing the power of local school boards. Moreover, his organizational abilities were instrumental in unifying the New York State educational system and establishing a commission on education.

Butler shared the Progressive movement's goal of institutionalizing nationwide performance standards in professional life. To publicize this goal, in 1890 he founded and edited the *Educational Review*, a scholarly journal for the dissemination of "serious educational thought." As a member of the National Education Association and its head in 1894–1895, he helped create the Committee of Ten (founded to bring educators together "to consider the problems of secondary and higher education") and the Committee on College Entrance Requirements. In 1900 he took a leading role in founding the College Entrance Examination Board, serving as its first secretary and from 1901 to 1914 as its chairman.

When Columbia's president resigned in 1901, Butler was named acting president. The following year he was installed as the university's twelfth president. In this position, which he held until 1945, Butler continued to emphasize specialization and graduate study, establishing the schools of journalism and dentistry and expanding the professional curriculum. Columbia's growing cultural influence and scientific reputation attracted to its staff such noted scholars as the philosopher John Dewey, the historian Charles Beard, and the zoologist Thomas Hunt Morgan. By 1914, largely through Butler's initiative, Columbia had become one of the world's largest and most heavily endowed universities.

The increased need for administrative control that accompanied this growth encouraged Butler's autocratic tendencies. Citing efficiency, in 1905 Butler began appointing deans rather than allowing faculty to elect them. Dubbed "Czar Nicholas" by his detractors, he dismissed a number of faculty members during the years preceding World War I and in 1917 removed two professors who spoke out against the Conscription Act. Several members of the faculty, including Beard, subsequently resigned in protest. Butler defended his actions by arguing that academic freedom did not include the right to violate moral and social standards.

A conservative Republican, Butler participated actively in politics. He attended national party conventions, helped draft party platforms, campaigned for candidates, and advised national leaders, including President THEODORE ROOSEVELT. In 1920 he sought the Republican presidential nomination but garnered only favorite-son support on the first ballot and withdrew.

During several trips to Europe during the 1880s and 1890s, Butler was drawn into the peace movement, associating with French senator PAUL D'ESTOURNELLES DE CONSTANT, among other statesmen. As president of the Lake Mohonk Conference on International Arbitration in 1907 and again from 1909 to 1912, he lectured on the need for arms limitation and for an international world court. His lectures were published in 1912 as *The International Mind*, a phrase quickly taken up by internationalists.

In 1910 Butler helped persuade Andrew Carnegie to contribute $10 million to establish the Carnegie Endowment for International Peace. Butler directed the organization's Division of Education until 1925, when he succeeded ELIHU ROOT as president. Under Butler's direction, the endowment rebuilt European libraries after World War I, sponsored cultural exchanges, and funded college courses on international relations.

Butler was also largely responsible for mobilizing public opinion in favor of the Kellogg-Briand Pact, named after its principal negotiators, FRANK KELLOGG and ARISTIDE BRIAND. Fifteen nations met in Paris in 1928 to sign the pact, which renounced war as an instrument of national policy but included no provisions to ensure enforcement.

Butler was awarded the 1931 Nobel Prize for Peace, which he shared with JANE ADDAMS, for "tireless energy and a zeal almost without parallel" in his work for peace. Unable to attend the presentation ceremony, he delivered a lengthy radio address two days later in which he outlined a series of proposals for establishing permanent world peace; there is, apparently, no extant transcript of this address. Throughout the 1930s, Butler continued to argue that economic nationalism threatened peace, to propose European economic unity, and to criticize the neutrality laws of the United States.

In 1887 Butler married Susanna Edwards Schuyler, daughter of a munitions manufacturer; she died in 1903. Their only child, Sarah, born in 1893, also predeceased Butler. His second marriage, to Kate La Montagne in 1907, was marked by turmoil and acrimony.

A controversial figure throughout his long public career, Butler's beliefs and actions won him both powerful friends and powerful enemies. His admirers included the French philosopher HENRI BERGSON, the British novelist H. G. Wells, the American social critic H. L. Mencken, and Supreme Court Justice Benjamin Cardozo. On the other hand, such Progressive leaders as Robert M. La Follette, Justice Harlan Fiske Stone, and writer Upton Sinclair attacked Butler as an opportunist and a champion of the upper class. He was also much criticized for his close relationships with Germany's Kaiser Wilhelm II and the Italian dictator Benito Mussolini. Yet, at the outbreak of World War II in Europe, Butler became one of the first important public figures in the United States to urge that America side with the Allies against the Axis powers.

At the age of seventy-five, Butler announced his intention to "die on the job," but failing eyesight and near deafness forced him to resign from Columbia in 1945. He contracted pneumonia and died two years later in New York.

ADDITIONAL WORKS: The Meaning of Education, 1898; True and False Democracy, 1907; The American as He Is, 1908; Philosophy, 1911; Why Should We Change Our Form of Government? 1912; The Basis of Durable Peace, 1917; A World in Ferment, 1918; Is America Worth Saving? 1920;

Scholarship and Service, 1921; Building the American Nation, 1923; The Faith of a Liberal, 1924; The Path to Peace, 1930; Looking Forward: What Will the American People Do About It? 1932; Between Two Worlds, 1934; The Family of Nations, 1938; Across the Busy Years: Recollections and Reflections (2 vols.) 1939–1940; Why War? Essays and Addresses on War and Peace, 1940; Liberty-Equality-Fraternity, 1942; The World Today: Essays and Addresses, 1946.

ABOUT: Burgess, J. W. Reminiscences of an American Scholar, 1934; Coon, H. Columbia: Colossus on the Hudson, 1947; De Benedetti, C. Origins of the Modern American Peace Movement, 1978; Erksine, J. The Memory of Certain Persons, 1947; Herman, S. R. Eleven Against War, 1969; Israel, J. (ed.) Building the Organizational Society, 1972; Kuehl, W. F. Seeking World Order, 1969; Martin, A. Nicholas Murray Butler, 1976; Summerscales, W. Affirmation and Dissent, 1970; Whittemore, R. Nicholas Murray Butler and Public Education, 1970.

MELVIN CALVIN

CALVIN, MELVIN

(April 8, 1911–   )
Nobel Prize for Chemistry, 1961

The American organic chemist Melvin Calvin was born in St. Paul, Minnesota, the son of Rose I. (Hervitz) and Elias Calvin, both of whom had immigrated from Russia. As a child, he showed great curiosity and an enthusiasm for learning, and by the eleventh grade he had decided to become a chemist. The family had moved to Detroit, Michigan, where Calvin attended the local high school. Because he was often too eager to reach conclusions, his physics teacher predicted that "this student will never be a scientist." Calvin won a full scholarship to the Michigan College of Mining and Technology, where he received a B.S. in 1931. Four years later, with a thesis on the electron affinity of iodine and bromine, he was awarded a Ph.D. in chemistry from the University of Minnesota.

A Rockefeller grant enabled him to conduct postdoctoral studies in England at the University of Manchester under Michael Polanyi, a professor of physical chemistry and the father of JOHN C. POLANYI. There Calvin studied hydrogen paramagnetic conversion and the catalytic action of metalloporphyrins, complex organic molecules containing metal atoms, of which hemoglobin and chlorophyll are derivatives. Returning to the United States in 1937, Calvin was appointed an instructor in chemistry at the University of California at Berkeley, where he investigated the electronic nature of colored organic compounds under the chemist Gilbert N. Lewis.

During World War II, Calvin worked with the National Defense Research Council from 1941 to 1944 and the Manhattan Project from 1944 to 1945. During this time he developed a method for obtaining pure oxygen from the atmosphere for use in industrial processes such as welding at sites where bottled oxygen was not available.

He returned to Berkeley as an associate professor in 1945 and became a full professor of chemistry two years later. In 1946 he was also appointed director of the Bio-organic Chemistry Group at the Lawrence Radiation Laboratory, a post he held until 1980. His research interests were in photosynthesis, the complex process by which green plants use energy from sunlight to produce carbohydrates and oxygen from carbon dioxide and water. Although the conditions required for photosynthesis, as well as its end products, had been known in their nascent form since their discovery in 1772 by Joseph Priestley, the intermediate reactions in this process were not understood.

Two new analytical techniques were available to Calvin. The first was the use of carbon 14, a radioactive isotope of carbon that, when assimilated by plants, can be readily detected in organic compounds. Calvin introduced carbon dioxide containing carbon 14 into a thin, round flask (called the lollipop because of its shape) filled with the green alga *Chlorella pyrenoidosa* in suspension. The apparatus was illuminated, allowing the algae to incorporate the labeled carbon dioxide into compounds involved in photosynthesis.

To identify the radioactive tracers, Calvin employed the second technique, paper chromatography. In this method, developed by

ARCHER MARTIN and RICHARD SYNGE, a mixture is separated into its component substances by allowing them to be carried by solvents along a piece of filter paper. Each component forms a spot in a characteristic position on the paper, which can then be compared to the distribution of spots produced by known chemicals. To distinguish spots containing the labeled carbon, the chromatograph is placed in contact with X-ray film, which darkens in the presence of any radioactivity. "The paper ordinarily does not print out the names of these compounds, unfortunately," Calvin later commented, "and our principal chore for the succeeding ten years was to properly label those blackened areas on the film."

Through this work Calvin and his associates determined that carbon dioxide first reacts with ribulose diphosphate, a five-carbon compound, to form phosphoglyceric acid, which, in a series of reactions, becomes fructose-6-phosphate and glucose-6-phosphate. The steps in the conversion of carbon dioxide to carbohydrates, called the Calvin cycle, take place in chloroplasts, highly organized subcellular bodies in plant and algal cells. The Calvin cycle, containing the "dark" reactions of photosynthesis, is driven by the high-energy compounds ATP (adenosine triphosphate) and NADPH (reduced nicotinamide adenine dinucleotide phosphate) generated in "light" reactions, in which light is absorbed by chlorophyll molecules. Using radioactive isotopes, Calvin also traced the path of oxygen in photosynthesis.

Calvin was awarded the 1961 Nobel Prize for Chemistry for "his research on the carbon dioxide assimilation in plants." Although Calvin received the Nobel Prize for Chemistry, his work has been characterized by an interdisciplinary approach to chemistry, biology, and physics, and he stressed its importance in his Nobel lecture. "Chemical biodynamics, involving as it does the fusion of many scientific disciplines, will play a role in this problem [how chlorophyll passes on light energy], as it has in the elucidation of the carbon cycle. It can be expected to take an increasingly important place in the understanding of the dynamics of living organisms on a molecular level."

Calvin was appointed professor of molecular biology at the University of California at Berkeley in 1963 and university professor of chemistry eight years later. From 1960 to 1980 he also served as director of the Laboratory of Chemical Biodynamics, where research has been done on such topics as photosynthesis and solar energy conversion, radiation chemistry, brain chemistry, the molecular basis of learning, and the origin of life on earth. Using the cyclotron, Calvin irradiated carbon dioxide and hydrogen atoms, which were rearranged into molecules of amino acids and adenine, one of the components of nucleic acid. Finding traces of organic substances within meteorites, he suggested the possibility of life elsewhere in the solar system.

Calvin has served on many national and international committees concerning peaceful uses of atomic energy, molecular biophysics, science and public policy, and bioastronautics; in the latter area, he served as adviser to the National Aeronautics and Space Administration (NASA).

In 1942 Calvin married Marie Genevieve Jemtegaard, a social worker; they have two daughters and one son. He holds numerous honorary degrees and has received the Davy Medal of the Royal Society of London (1964), the Priestley Medal of the American Chemical Society (1978), the Gold Medal of the American Institute of Chemists (1978), and the Oesper Prize of the American Chemical Society (1981). He is a member of the Royal Society of London, the Royal Netherlands Academy of Sciences, the American Philosophical Society, the National Academy of Sciences, and the American Chemical Society (of which he was president in 1971).

SELECTED WORKS: The Theory of Organic Chemistry: An Advanced Course, 1941, with Gerald E. K. Branch; Chemistry of the Chelate Compounds, 1949; The Path of Carbon in Photosynthesis, 1949; Isotopic Carbon, Techniques in Its Measurement and Chemical Manipulation, 1949, with others; Chemistry of Metal Chelate Compounds, 1952, with others; Origin of Life on Earth and Elsewhere, 1959; Chemical Evolution, 1961; The Photosynthesis of Carbon Compounds, 1962, with James Bassham.

ABOUT: Current Biography April 1962; Dictionary of Scientific Biography, volume 3, 1973; National Cyclopedia of American Biography, volume I, 1960; Thomas, S. Men of Space, volume 6, 1963.

CAMUS, ALBERT
(November 7, 1913–January 4, 1960)
Nobel Prize for Literature, 1957

The French novelist, essayist, and playwright Albert Camus (ka mü') was born in Mondovi, Algeria, the younger of two sons in a working-class family. His father, Lucien Camus, an agricultural laborer of Alsatian origin, was killed in World War I at the First Battle of the Marne, when Albert was less than a

ALBERT CAMUS

year old. Shortly thereafter, his mother, the former Catherine Sintes, an illiterate woman of Spanish descent, suffered a stroke that left her a near-mute. The family then moved into the home of Madame Camus's mother and invalid brother in Algiers, where Madame Camus took work as a housemaid in order to support Albert and his brother, Lucien. Although the circumstances of his early life were unusually harsh, Camus did not experience a corresponding impoverishment of the spirit. As a child he was keenly aware of the natural beauty of the North African coast—a beauty, he realized, that transcended the handicaps of his deprived background. As a man and an artist, he was to celebrate this legacy throughout his life.

Entering primary school in 1918, Camus came under the influence of Louis Germain, a teacher who recognized and encouraged the boy's intellectual gifts. Under Germain's tutelage, Camus in 1923 won a scholarship to the lycée in Algiers, where his intellectual awakening was matched by a deep love of sports, particularly boxing. In 1930 incipient tuberculosis—a disease that was to trouble Camus for the rest of his life—put an end to his athletic activities. Nevertheless, for the next several years, Camus was able to support himself at various jobs while studying philosophy at the University of Algiers. In 1934 Camus entered into an unhappy marriage with Simone Hie, a morphine addict. They separated the following year and were divorced in 1939.

Completing his dissertation on the works of

Saint Augustine and the Roman philosopher Plotinus, Camus received his *diplôme d'études supérieures* (the equivalent of an M.A.) in philosophy in 1936. Although he hoped to remain at the university to prepare for an academic career, another attack of tuberculosis curtailed his postgraduate education.

To recover his health, Camus traveled to the French Alps—his first visit to Europe. He recorded the impressions of his subsequent European tour (which included travel in Italy, Spain, Czechoslovakia, and other parts of France) in his first published work, *L'Envers et l'endroit* (*Betwixt and Between,* 1937), a collection of essays that also includes portraits of his mother, grandmother, and uncle. In 1936 he also began work on his first novel, *La Mort heureuse* (translated as *A Happy Death*), which was not published until 1971.

By this time Camus's reputation in Algeria as a leading writer and intellectual was established and growing. Active in the theater as a writer, actor, and director, he also served as a political reporter, book reviewer, and editorial writer on the staff of the newspaper *Alger Républicain* (Republican Algiers). A year after the publication of his second book of essays, *Noces* (*Nuptials*), in 1938, Camus moved to France, where he settled permanently.

During the German occupation of France in World War II, Camus was active in the Resistance movement and served as the editor of the Paris-based underground newspaper *Combat.*

In the midst of these dangerous activities, Camus completed his second novel, *L'Étranger* (1942), which he had begun in Algeria before the war and which was to make him internationally famous. Published as *The Stranger* in the United States and as *The Outsider* in Great Britain, the novel is a study of alienation and the apparent meaninglessness of human existence. *The Stranger* tells the story of Meursault, a fictional character who has come to be the prototypical existential antihero. Indifferent to bourgeois morality, Meursault refuses to abide by its conventions. When he commits an "absurd" murder—that is, one without explicit reason or motivation—Meursault is condemned to die as much for his refusal to conform to conventional standards of behavior as for the crime itself. The detached, understated tone of the novel (which, some critics have noted, resembles the taut prose style of ERNEST HEMINGWAY) only serves to heighten the horror of the action.

This immediately successful novel was followed in the same year by the philosophical essay *Le Mythe de Sisyphe* (*The Myth of Sisyphus,* 1942), an analysis of nihilism in which Camus compares the absurdity of the existence of humanity to the labors of the mythical character Sisyphus, who is fated to wage a perpetual struggle against forces he cannot overcome. Rejecting the Christian ideas of salvation and an afterlife that might give meaning to the struggle, Camus paradoxically finds meaning in the struggle itself. Salvation, for Camus, resides in the ordinary labors of living; meaning inheres in doing.

When the war ended, Camus for a time continued his journalistic activities for *Combat,* by then an established daily. However, political disagreements with hardening factions on both the Left and the Right led Camus, who considered himself an independent leftist, to resign his post in 1947. The same year, he published his third novel, *La Peste* (*The Plague*). On the literal level, the novel recounts the course of an epidemic in the Algerian city of Oran; on the symbolic level, *The Plague* has been called an allegory of the Nazi occupation of France, in which the disease is seen as an emblem of death and evil. Camus's interest in the problem of evil was also reflected in *Caligula* (1945), generally considered the most influential of his plays, if not the most successful as drama. Drawn from Suetonius's history of the Roman emperors, *Caligula,* which was published in English under the same title, is regarded by many critics as a landmark in the theater of the absurd.

A leading literary figure in France, Camus at this time was closely associated—both intellectually and personally—with his contemporary JEAN-PAUL SARTRE. However, in his determination to find a positive mode of existence in the face of life's absurdity, Camus differed markedly from Sartre. In the early 1950s a complex ideological disagreement ended their friendship, and Camus dissociated himself from the philosophical school of existentialism championed by Sartre. In *L'Homme révolté* (*The Rebel,* 1951), Camus explores the theories and forms of humanity's revolt against authority through the centuries, refuting the rigid ideologies (including communism and other forms of totalitarianism) that deny freedom and, therefore, dignity. Though as early as 1945 Camus had said, "I have little liking for the too famous existential philosophy . . . and . . . I think its conclusions are false," it was his condemnation of Marxism that sealed his break with the pro-Marxist Sartre.

During the 1950s Camus continued to work on essays, drama, and fiction. In 1956 he brought out *La Chute* (*The Fall*), an ironic novel in which the penitent judge Jean-Baptiste Clamence confesses his own moral crimes. Focusing on the theme of guilt and repentance, Camus makes notable use of Christian symbolism in *The Fall.*

Camus was awarded the 1957 Nobel Prize for Literature "for his important literary production, which with clearsighted earnestness illuminates the problems of the human conscience in our times." On presenting the awards, Anders Österling of the Swedish Academy remarked that "Camus reveals a spiritual attitude that was born of the sharp contradictions within him between the awareness of earthly life and the gripping consciousness of the reality of death." In his acceptance speech, Camus stated that his writing was "rooted in two commitments . . . : the refusal to lie about what one knows and the resistance to oppression."

Only forty-four years old at the time of his Nobel Prize and, in his own view, just reaching artistic maturity, Camus planned many future works, which he described in his notebooks and in conversations with friends. However, when at the beginning of 1960 he was killed in an automobile accident in the south of France, most of these projects remained uncompleted.

Although the significance of Camus's work has been debated since his death, many critics regard him as a seminal figure of his generation. He articulated the alienation and disillusionment of the postwar period, yet he never ceased to search for a valid solution to the problems posed by the absurdity of modern life. Although he came under attack for his repudiation of both Marxism and Christianity, his influence on contemporary letters is undisputed. In his obituary in the Milan newspaper *Corriere della sera* (The Evening Courier), the Italian poet EUGENIO MONTALE wrote that Camus's "nihilism does not exclude hope, does not exempt man from the difficult task of living and dying with dignity."

In the opinion of the American critic Susan Sontag, "Camus's fiction is not so much about its characters . . . as it is about the problems of innocence and guilt, responsibility and nihilistic indifference." Although she believes that "neither art nor thought of the highest quality is to be found in Camus," Sontag declared that "what accounts for the extraordinary appeal of his work is beauty of another order, moral beauty." The British critic A. Alvarez agrees, calling Camus "a moralist who managed to make a persuasive system out of his novelist's preoccupation with conduct."

CANETTI

ADDITIONAL WORKS IN ENGLISH TRANSLA-
TION: Cross Purpose, 1947; State of Siege, 1958; Neither
Victims nor Executioners, 1960; The Possessed, 1960; Let-
ters to a German Friend, 1961; Resistance, Rebellion, and
Death, 1961; Notebooks (3 vols.) 1963–1969; Lyrical and
Critical, 1967; Summer, 1968; Youthful Writings of Albert
Camus, 1976; American Journals, 1987.

ABOUT: Anderson, D. The Tragic Protest, 1969; Brée,
G. Albert Camus, 1962; Brée, G. (ed.) Camus: A Collection of Critical Essays, 1962; Cruickshank, J. Albert Camus
and the Literature of Revolt, 1959; Freeman, E. The Thea-
ter of Albert Camus, 1971; Hanna, T. The Thought and
Art of Albert Camus, 1968; King, A. Albert Camus, 1965;
Lazare, D. The Unique Creation of Albert Camus, 1973;
Lebesque, M. Portrait of Camus, 1971; Lottman, H. R.
Albert Camus, 1979; McCarthey, P. Camus: A Critical Bi-
ography, 1982; Melancon, M. Albert Camus: An Analysis
of His Thought, 1983; Parker, E. Camus: The Artist in the
Arena, 1965; Pollman, L. Sartre and Camus, 1970; Rhein,
P. H. Albert Camus, 1969; Roeming, R. R. Camus: A
Biography, 1968; Tarrow, S. Exile From the Kingdom, 1985;
Thody, P. Albert Camus, 1930–1961, 1961; Trundle, R.
C., and Puligandla, R. Beyond Absurdity, 1986; Ungar, C.
P. Albert Camus, 1969.

ELIAS CANETTI

CANETTI, ELIAS
(July 25, 1905–   )
Nobel Prize for Literature, 1981

The Bulgarian-born English novelist, essayist, and dramatist Elias Canetti, eldest of three
sons, was born into a Sephardic Jewish family
in Ruse, Bulgaria, a port city on the lower
Danube with a mixed ethnic population. The
Canetti family were well-to-do merchants whose
native tongue was Ladino, a dialect of Spanish
spoken by the Sephardic people. Canetti's paternal grandfather knew seventeen languages;
his parents, Mathilde (Arditti) and Jacques
Canetti, who had been educated in Vienna,
spoke only German at home, and it is in German that Canetti writes.

When Canetti was six years old, his family
moved to Manchester, England, where he attended school, learned English, and was encouraged to read the classics by his father,
whose own youthful artistic inclinations had
been stifled when he was forced to follow a
career in the family cotton business. According to Canetti, his father told him, "You will
be what you want to be." After little more
than a year in England, Canetti's father died
suddenly, and his mother took the family back
to the Continent, where she prepared Canetti
for school in Vienna by helping him master
the German language. Canetti attributes his
passionate attachment to that language to his
mother's influence. He later wrote that without his mother and the German language, which
were closely associated in his mind, "the fur-

ther course of my life would have been senseless and incomprehensible."

After attending school for three years in Vienna, Canetti studied from 1916 to 1921 in
Zurich, which he later called "the paradise of
my youth." During those years, he produced
his first literary work, *Junius Brutus,* a verse
play. In 1921 Canetti's mother, deeply concerned about her son's development and fearing that life in Zurich was too sheltered, took
him to Frankfurt in the hope that the harsh
conditions in Germany after World War I would
give him a keener sense of reality. There he
completed his secondary education in three
years. Then he returned to Vienna, where, in
deference to his mother's desire that he prepare himself to lead a useful professional life,
he entered the University of Vienna as a chemistry student, receiving his doctorate in 1929.
However, because he had long wished to be
a writer and had no real interest in a chemistry
career, he thereafter devoted himself exclusively to literature. While in Vienna, Canetti
attended lectures by the celebrated Austrian
satirist Karl Kraus, whose influence, according
to Canetti, included the creation of an awareness of "the combination . . . of language and
person" in the young would-be writer. Later
Canetti also credited Kraus with teaching him
how to truly hear: "Since hearing him, it has
not been possible for me not to do my own
hearing."

Following a visit to Berlin in 1928, during
which he met Bertolt Brecht, Isaak Babel, and
Georg Grosz, Canetti planned a series of novels on the subject of human madness, in which

each of several monomaniacal types would figure as the hero of a separate volume. While this ambitious plan has not yet been fully realized, one such effort, his novel *Die Blendung* (1935), resulted. The German word *Blendung* implies both "dazzling" and "blinding"; although first translated in the United States as *The Tower of Babel* (1947), it was the 1964 translation by Veronica Wedgwood titled *Auto-da-Fé* that ultimately resulted in the novel's international fame. *Auto-da-Fé* (the phrase literally means "act of faith" and refers to the burning of convicted heretics during the Inquisition) recounts the story of Kien, a recluse and an obsessive scholar who lives in the Vienna apartment that houses his vast library. Kien's gradual disintegration begins with a rash marriage to his housekeeper, who drives him out to face the ravages of a corrupt society, which, in turn, hastens his derangement and leads to his self-immolation. Considered by critics writing after World War II to have been ahead of its time in its implicit dissection of the fascist mentality, *Auto-da-Fé* was well received by THOMAS MANN and other influential literary figures at the time of its publication. A few years later, the novel was officially banned in Nazi Germany. More recently, *Auto-da-Fé* has been hailed as "one of the few great novels of the century," in the words of the British novelist Iris Murdoch. Murdoch dedicated her novel *The Flight From the Enchanter* (1956) to Canetti and may have used him as the basis of the character of the powerful philosopher in that work.

In the 1930s Canetti wrote two plays—*Die Hochzeit* (The Wedding, 1932) and *Die Komödie der Eitelkeit* (The Comedy of Vanity, 1934)—that are satirical treatments of human depravity and forerunners of the theater of the absurd. A later drama, *Die Befristeten* (Those Whose Days Are Numbered, 1952), produced in England in 1956, is a philosophical work concerning a society in which everyone knows the precise moment of his own death; like the earlier plays, it utilizes absurdist elements.

The rise of Nazism and the systematic persecution of the Jews caused Canetti to flee Vienna for Paris in 1938. As the Nazi grip on Europe became tighter and more murderous, he again moved the following year, this time to London, where he has lived since. There he devoted himself to years of research that led to his masterwork, *Masse und Macht* (*Crowds and Power,* 1960), a multidisciplinary study that draws on folklore, myth, literature, and history in its analysis of mass movements. The work was inspired by the events of what

Canetti described as "the most crucial day" in his life: July 15, 1927, when he witnessed the burning of the Palace of Justice in Vienna by a group of protesting workers. Profoundly disturbed by the incident, Canetti set out on his obsessive search for an understanding of the crowd mentality.

Canetti received the 1981 Nobel Prize for Literature "for writings marked by a broad outlook, a wealth of ideas, and artistic power." In his presentation speech, Johannes Edfelt of the Swedish Academy praised "the great novel *Die Blendung*" as Canetti's "foremost purely fictional achievement," adding, "The book has such fantastic and demoniac elements that associations with Russian nineteenth-century writers like Gogol and Dostoevsky are apparent." Edfelt further cited *Crowds and Power* as "a magisterial work" that aims "to expose and attack . . . the religion of power." Although he attended the award ceremonies, Canetti did not deliver a Nobel lecture.

Following the publication of his masterwork, Canetti continued to produce insightful examples of literary reflection and analysis, such as *Der andere Prozess: Kafkas Briefe an Felice* (*Kafka's Other Trial: The Letters to Felice,* 1969), which explores the connection between Franz Kafka's life and his writing. He also published two autobiographical works— *Die gerettete Zunge* (*The Tongue Set Free: Remembrance of a European Childhood,* 1980) and *Die Fackel im Ohr* (*The Torch in My Ear,* 1982).

At the time Canetti received the Nobel Prize, his work was best known among the German-speaking people of Western Europe, by whom he was highly regarded for his mastery of style and his pure, lapidary German in the tradition exemplified by Goethe. One of his translators, Joachim Neugroschel, has defined Canetti's style as twofold: "His early work has a very complex syntax. But his memoirs are lucid, straightforward, and animated. Even though he writes in German, it is still an acquired language for him, which possibly gives his writing a greater accuracy, variety, and richness."

Like many major European writers of his generation, Canetti has experienced exile both immediately, in his personal experience, and historically, in the uprooting of his forebears. "The language of my intellect will remain German—because I am Jewish," he has said, "but I bring along a universal human legacy." Indeed, Canetti the exile, as the Swedish Academy noted, has "one native land, and that is the German language."

Auto-da-Fé won Canetti a significant place

in the tradition of Central European letters represented by Kafka, and with its translation his gifts were acclaimed as well in Western literary and academic circles, where his reputation has continued to grow. Because of the cosmopolitan, universal qualities of his work, he has been described as an "eighteenth-century writer living in the twentieth century." As the critic George Steiner wrote, Canetti's "exacting presence honors literature."

Iris Murdoch remarked that "Canetti has done what philosophers ought to do, and what they used to do. . . . He has also shown . . . the interaction of 'the mythical' with the ordinary stuff of human life." The American critic Susan Sontag described Canetti as "someone who has felt in a profound way the responsibility of words; and much of his work makes the effort to communicate something of what he has learned about how to pay attention to the world. There is no doctrine," she concluded, "but there is a great deal of scorn, urgency, grief, and euphoria. The message of the mind's passion is passion."

In 1934 Canetti married Venetia Toubner-Calderon, whom he had first met at a lecture by Karl Kraus in 1924. She died in 1963, and in 1971 Canetti remarried. He and his second wife, Hera Buschor, have one child and live part of the time in Zurich and part in London. Canetti has been a British citizen since 1952.

In addition to winning the Nobel Prize (as the first Bulgarian to be so honored), Canetti has received many other literary awards, including the International Prize of Paris (1949); the Author's Prize of the city of Vienna (1966); the Georg Büchner Prize of Munich (1972); the NELLY SACHS Prize of the city of Dortmund (1976); and the Kafka Prize (1981), one of Austria's major literary awards.

ADDITIONAL WORKS IN ENGLISH TRANSLATION: Fritz Wotruba, 1955; The Human Province, 1978; The Voices of Marrakesh, 1978; The Conscience of Words, 1979; Earwitness: Fifty Characters, 1979; The Play of the Eyes, 1986.

ABOUT: Best, A., and Wolfschütz, H. Modern Austrian Writing, 1980; Current Biography January 1983; New Yorker November 22, 1982; Norman, F. (ed.) Essays in German Literature I, 1965; Sontag, S. Under the Sign of Saturn, 1980.

CARDUCCI, GIOSUÈ

(July 27, 1835–February 16, 1907)
Nobel Prize for Literature, 1906

The Italian poet and critic Giosuè Carducci (kär dōōt′ chē) was born in Val di Castello in the northwestern corner of Tuscany, the eldest of three children. His father, Michele Carducci, a doctor, belonged to the Carbonari, a secret organization dedicated to Italian nationalism in the era that preceded the unification of Italy. Because Dr. Carducci's political beliefs, cantankerous nature, and outspoken anticlericalism made him unpopular in the conservative Tuscan villages in which he practiced, the family was forced to move frequently during Carducci's childhood. However, the Carduccis managed to stay in Bolgheri, south of Livorno, for a nine-year period. They moved three times during 1848 and 1849 because of political tensions caused by the continuing revolutionary struggle in Italy and the elder Carducci's hot temper.

In 1849 the family settled in Florence. There Carducci, who previously had been taught by his father, entered a secondary school run by the Piarist religious order. His ad hoc education seems to have served him well, for he performed ably on his first examinations. A voracious reader, Carducci devoured the classics and such nineteenth-century Italian works as Alessandro Manzoni's popular novel *I promessi sposi* (*The Betrothed*), as well as the poetry of Lord Byron and Friedrich Schiller. During this time he began to write historical poetry. He translated book 9 of Homer's *Iliad,* dashed off satirical poems mocking his classmates and teachers, and wrote tender verses such as "A mia madre" (To My Mother).

Carducci's father accepted a post as medical officer in Celle in 1851. The provincial atmosphere of the town offered little stimulation to a budding intellectual, and the young Carducci spent some of his time teaching patriotic songs to the village boys. Under the influence of his father, who had recently modified his political views and again embraced Catholicism, he wrote odes to Saint Elizabeth and Saint John the Baptist.

In 1853 Carducci was granted a scholarship to the prestigious Scuola Normale Superiore in Pisa. After entering the school later that year, he found the teachers pedantic and the curriculum outmoded. The chief value of being a student, he felt, was the exposure it offered to a Pisan literary circle that included the historian Ercole Scaramucci. When Scaramucci died, Carducci delivered a funeral oration praising his friend as a patriot who avoided "the pitiful, worthless daydreams" of the proponents of Italian unity. His condemnation of the unity movement, an abrupt shift from his previous stance, typifies a series of mercurial

GIOSUÈ CARDUCCI

patriotic sentiments and their avoidance of the trappings of romanticism.

The years 1857 and 1858 were difficult for Carducci. Holding no official post, he was forced to live on little money and also faced severe emotional trauma. His brother Dante committed suicide in 1857, and his father died the following year. Shortly thereafter, however, Carducci's circumstances improved. In 1859 he married Elvira Menicucci, and the following year he was appointed to the high school faculty at Pistoia, where he taught Greek. Later that year Carducci was named professor of Italian literature at the University of Bologna, a position that provided financial security and allowed him to devote himself to his family, which included three daughters and a son. He remained at the university for almost the rest of his life.

In the early 1860s Carducci strongly realigned himself with the republican cause, a political stance that brought about a brief suspension from the university in 1863 and a threatened transfer in 1867. Controversy was also sparked by the publication of his most notorious poem, *Inno a Satana* (*Hymn to Satan*), in 1865. This pantheistic and vehemently anticlerical work celebrates the triumph of rationalism, rebellion, and progress over the repressive force of Christian theology. A year after its publication, Carducci was elected a republican member of Parliament, but was prevented from assuming his seat by a technicality.

In 1878 Carducci published the first of three volumes of *Odi barbare* (*Barbarian Odes*, 1878–1889), verses that attempted to capture the spirit of the classical world by emulating the rhythmic structure of ancient Greek and Latin poetry. Generally historical in theme, these poems, together with the more personal verses of *Rime nuove* (*The New Lyrics*, 1861–1887), are generally considered Carducci's finest and most distinctive poetry. Carducci's verse collections also include *Levia gravia* (Light and Serious Poems, 1861–1871); *Giambi ed epodi* (Iambics and Epodes, 1867–1879); and *Rime e ritmi* (Rhymes and Rhythms, 1899), his last book of poems, in which his poetic powers are considered to have waned. At its best, Carducci's verse displays a deep, although almost always distanced, emotionality and a sweeping vision that stresses the continuity of human experience. Whether following the forms of ancient poetry or the traditional meters of Italian verse, his poems eschew the excesses of romanticism in favor of a restrained and classical mode of expression.

changes in political viewpoints that occurred throughout his life.

The elder Carducci again found himself in disrepute in 1854 when he argued violently with Celle's mayor. He was subsequently convicted of assault and forced to resign from his position and assume a low-paying job as surgeon in the nearby commune of Piancastagnaio. Finding himself with no funds, the young Carducci supported himself by compiling *L'arpa del popolo, scelta di poemi religiosi, morali e patriotici* (*The People's Harp: A Selection of Religious, Moral and Patriotic Poems*, 1855), an anthology of Italian verse intended to stir the moral and patriotic sentiments of its readers. He also wrote articles for *L'appendice* (The Appendix), a journal edited by his friend Pietro Thouar. He soon became a leading figure in the coterie of writers associated with *L'appendice,* which strove to protect the classicism of Italian verse from what they considered to be the corrupting influence of romanticism.

After graduating from the Scuola Normale Superiore in 1856, Carducci became a teacher at the *ginnasio* (high school) in the little town of San Miniato al Tedesco, but his tenure was not happy. Quarrelsome and aggressively anticlerical, he was soon censured by the minister of education, thereby losing a position in Arezzo that he had been anticipating. Carducci moved to Florence in 1857 and published his first volume of poetry, *Rime* (*Rhymes*), later revised and included in *Juvenilia* (Juvenile Poems, 1880). Although conventional in form, these sonnets and ballads are notable for their

183

Although Carducci's reputation always rested primarily on his poetry, which he felt served an almost priestly function, his poetic output was relatively modest. In fact, it occupies only four of the thirty volumes that constitute his collected works. The remaining prose works consist of monographs and essays, by turn learned and polemical, that discuss various figures from literature and criticize contemporary literary and political matters.

In his later years Carducci, who was also a powerful and influential orator, was widely celebrated for his scholarship and generally regarded as Italy's unofficial poet laureate. He was appointed a senator in 1890, partly as a tribute to his literary reputation but also in recognition of the change in his political attitudes, which by then included support for the monarchy and for Italy's imperialist aims in Africa.

Carducci was an uncontroversial choice for the 1906 Nobel Prize for Literature, having been mentioned as a candidate for the award since 1902. He was cited "not only in consideration of his deep learning and critical research, but above all as a tribute to the creative energy, freshness of style, and lyrical force which characterizes his poetic masterpieces." In his presentation speech, C. D. af Wirsén of the Swedish Academy discussed Carducci's career in the light of Italian political activity. He explained Carducci's "paganism" as a reaction to the excesses of the Catholic church rather than as a condemnation of all Christianity. "Carducci is a learned literary historian who has been nurtured by ancient literature and by Dante and Petrarch," Wirsén noted. "He is . . . devoted . . . to the classical ideal and Petrarchan humanism." Wirsén added that "the irrefutable truth remains that a poet who is always moved by patriotism and a love of liberty . . . is a soul inspired by the highest ideals." Carducci was unable to attend the ceremony because of ill health, and he died the following year. Now read largely by scholars and specialists, he is most often cited for the vitality and universality of his verse. Perhaps most of all, his work reflects the spirit that infused the Risorgimento, the nineteenth-century movement that advocated Italian political unity.

ADDITIONAL WORKS IN ENGLISH TRANSLATION: Poems of Giosuè Carducci, 1892; Carducci, 1913; A Selection of His Poems, 1913; From the Poems of Giosuè Carducci, 1929; Political and Satiric Verse of Giosuè Carducci, 1942; The Lyrics and Rhythms of Giosuè Carducci, 1942; Twenty-Four Sonnets, 1947.

ABOUT: Bailey, J. C. Carducci, 1926; Scalia, S. E. Carducci, 1937; Stade, G. (ed.) European Writers: The Romantic Century, 1985; Williams, O. Giosuè Carducci, 1914.

CARREL, ALEXIS
(June 28, 1873–November 5, 1944)
Nobel Prize for Physiology or Medicine, 1912

Alexis Carrel (ka' rel), French surgeon and biologist, was born in Lyons, the eldest of three children of Anne-Marie (Ricard) Carrel-Billiard and Alexis Carrel-Billiard, a silk manufacturer who died when the boy was five years old. Carrel received his early education from his devoutly religious mother and later attended St. Joseph's, a Jesuit day school and college near his home. Although Carrel was not a distinguished student, he showed an early interest in science by dissecting birds and conducting chemistry experiments under his uncle's guidance. By the age of twelve he had decided to become a doctor. However, before entering medical school, he earned two baccalaureate degrees, one in letters from the University of Lyons in 1890 and the other in science from the University of Dijon in 1891. From 1893 to 1900 he worked in various hospitals in Lyons, where his talent for dissection and surgery became apparent. After receiving a medical degree from Lyons, he served as prosector (preparer of dissections) at the University of Lyons from 1899 until 1902.

While Carrel was working in the hospitals of Lyons, President Marie François Carnot of France was struck by an assassin's bullet that severed a major artery; at that time there was no method for repairing such wounds, and Carnot bled to death. The incident stimulated Carrel's interest in devising a way to join severed blood vessels. To do so, he took lessons in embroidery. For suturing he used exceptionally fine needles and silk thread. Before he was thirty years old Carrel had perfected an ingenious technique in which he turned back the ends of the cut vessels and stitched them so that the only surface exposed to the flow of blood was their smooth lining. When he connected the ends of blood vessels, he used three retaining sutures that converted a round opening into a triangular one. He could then easily stitch along each of the three sides of the triangle. As a further measure against clotting, one of the major problems in vascular surgery, he coated his instruments and threads with paraffin jelly. He not only succeeded in suturing arteries and veins but was able to re-

ALEXIS CARREL

eons and engaging in philosophical discussions with some of his colleagues. During his initial years at Rockefeller, Carrel undertook experimental organ transplants and further perfected his surgical techniques to the point where he could transplant not only blood vessels and kidneys but entire limbs from one animal to another.

Carrel was awarded the 1912 Nobel Prize for Physiology or Medicine "in recognition of his work on vascular suture and the transplantation of blood vessels and organs." In his presentation speech, Jules Åkerman of the Karolinska Institute hailed Carrel's invention of a new suturing method. "By virtue of this method," Åkerman said, "you ensure a free flow at the site of the suture, and at the same time you prevent postoperative hemorrhage, thrombosis, and secondary stricture. Thanks to the same method, you are able to reconstruct the vascular pathway, to replace a segment removed from the patient with another segment taken from another part or from another person."

Although the surgical wounds in Carrel's recipient animals often healed and the organs seemed to become incorporated into their new hosts, the organs were eventually rejected. Carrel acknowledged that "while the problem of transplantation of organs has been solved from a surgical point of view, we see that this by no means suffices to render such operations of definite surgical practicability." It was not until fifty years later that JEAN DAUSSET demonstrated that the success of an organ transplant depends on genetic and immunological factors.

Carrel experienced far fewer problems in transplanting sections of blood vessels than in transplanting organs; he had no difficulty in replacing part of a damaged artery or vein with a less crucial vessel from a different area of the same animal. Such "autoplastic" vascular transplantation is the basis of many important operations commonly done today; coronary bypass surgery, for example, involves replacement of a clogged heart artery with a healthy vein from the patient's own leg. In Carrel's skilled hands operations of this sort succeeded. It was only after the 1940s, however, when antibiotics and anticoagulants became available, that vascular surgery became widespread.

In 1913 Carrel married Anne de la Motte de Meyrie, who had a son by a previous marriage; she and Carrel had no children of their own. Anne Carrel was a trained nurse who encouraged her husband in his research and

store the flow of blood through severed vessels, an accomplishment he first reported in 1902.

Despite these achievements, Carrel was unable to obtain a professorship at the University of Lyons. Opposition to his appointment may have arisen because of his shyness, which made him seem stiff in social situations, and because of his intellectual independence and critical attitude toward some of the traditions within the medical faculty. Discouraged by his rejection at Lyons, he moved to Paris in 1903 and spent a year in advanced medical study; after completing his medical studies, he immigrated to Canada with the intention of becoming a cattle rancher. Before he could change professions, however, the University of Chicago offered him an assistantship in the physiology department. During his stay in Chicago, which lasted from 1904 to 1906, he perfected his surgical technique and conducted his first experiments in organ transplantation, which would have been impossible without his suturing method and skill.

Soon Carrel's achievements came to the attention of Simon Flexner, who was recruiting talented researchers for the recently established Rockefeller Institute for Medical Research (now Rockefeller University) in New York City. In 1906 Carrel accepted an appointment as an associate member of the Rockefeller Institute, where, despite his characteristic aloofness, he found a more congenial group of co-workers than he had had in Lyons. He felt at home and was frequently observed wearing his white surgeon's cap at staff lunch-

often assisted in his surgical experiments. Carrel, who never became a citizen of the United States, was recalled to France in 1914 at the outbreak of World War I. As a major in the Medical Corps of the French army, he used his suturing techniques on wounded soldiers. For his war service he was awarded the Legion of Honor.

In collaboration with the biochemist Henry D. Dakin, Carrel developed a mild, nontoxic, nonirritating disinfectant, consisting of a buffered aqueous solution of sodium hypochlorite that was used effectively during surgical procedures and for the irrigation and dressing of wounds. Although at that time the Carrel-Dakin treatment greatly reduced the incidence of gangrene, it has since been superseded by the use of antibiotics.

A similar fate befell one of Carrel's most renowned achievements, the cultivation of living tissues in the laboratory. He and his assistants removed a bit of tissue from the heart of a chick embryo and managed to keep its cells alive and reproducing through successive transfers to fresh nutrient media. The culture attracted widespread interest, and the strain of connective tissue cells was maintained for thirty-four years, outliving even Carrel himself. Although his work helped establish a better understanding of normal cell life, as well as of malignant growths and viruses, tissue culture—like vascular surgery—did not become widely useful in Carrel's lifetime.

After World War I, Carrel returned to the Rockefeller Institute; in the early 1930s he attempted to cultivate entire organs in the laboratory. In these efforts he was aided by the American aviator Charles Lindbergh, who invented a perfusion pump with which nutrient fluid could be circulated through an excised organ in a moist chamber. This germproof pump was designed to keep separate vital organs alive in fluid; by changing the contents of the fluids, abnormalities could be developed for study. Even though the technique enabled Carrel to keep certain animal organs alive for days or even weeks, it was not long enough for practical use in surgery. These experiments, however, proved useful to those who later developed heart-lung machines and other vascular surgery aids. Lindbergh found Carrel to have "one of the most brilliant, penetrating, and versatile minds."

When Simon Flexner retired from the Rockefeller Institute in 1935, Carrel lost a mentor who not only encouraged his efforts but understood his temperament. By mutual agreement with Flexner's successor, Carrel retired in 1938 as member emeritus. After the fall of France in 1940, Carrel returned to Paris, where, having declined an offer to head the Ministry of Health, he established the Institute for the Study of Human Problems, under a charter from the Vichy government.

In his best-selling book *Man, the Unknown* (1935), Carrel presented a grandiose plan that he believed would safeguard humanity and improve the quality of the human population. He proposed the creation of a "High Council" that would rule the world for its own good; political leaders could seek advice from this council. According to Carrel, such an organization "would acquire enough knowledge to prevent the organic and mental deterioration of civilized nations."

Carrel's ideas seemed to parallel some of the tenets of Nazism, and his elitist theories—coupled with the fact that he had accepted the Vichy government's support and negotiated with the Germans on behalf of his institute—led to exaggerated charges of collaboration with the Nazis. Not long after the liberation of France in 1944, the institute was disbanded. Carrel's supporters contend that his ideas were those of a visionary bent on guiding postwar France to recovery along the philosophical and biological lines expounded in his book. The American anatomist and author George W. Corner wrote that "Carrel was at heart not disloyal either to France or to the America that had so long adopted him but sought only the welfare of France according to his own conscience." Although he was not arrested for collaboration, the controversy permanently clouded his reputation. Suffering from heart disease and with his health undermined by wartime deprivations, Carrel died in Paris on November 5, 1944.

Carrel held memberships in learned societies in the United States, Spain, Sweden, Russia, the Netherlands, Belgium, France, Vatican City, Germany, Italy, and Greece. He received honorary doctorates from the University of Belfast, from Princeton, Brown, New York, and Columbia universities, and from the University of California. He was made a commander in the Leopold Order of Belgium; he was also made a grand commander in the Swedish Order of the Polar Star and was decorated by Spain, Serbia, Great Britain, and the Vatican.

SELECTED WORKS: Latent Life of Arteries, 1910; The Treatment of Infected Wounds, 1917, with Georges Dehelly; The Culture of Organs, 1938, with C. A. Lindbergh; Prayer, 1948; Reflections on Life, 1952.

ABOUT: Dictionary of American Biography, supplement 3, 1973; Dictionary of Scientific Biography, volume 3, 1971; Durkin, J. T. Hope for Our Time: Alexis Carrel on Man and Society, 1965; Edwards, W. S. Alexis Carrel, Visionary Surgeon, 1974; Malinin, T. I. Surgery and Life: The Extraordinary Career of Alexis Carrel, 1979.

CASSIN, RENÉ

(October 5, 1887–February 20, 1976)
Nobel Prize for Peace, 1968

The French jurist René-Samuel Cassin (ka-saɴ′) was born in Bayonne, one of two children of Henri Cassin, a Jewish merchant, and the former Gabrielle Déborah Dreyfus. He attended the lycée in Nice and the University of Aix-en-Provence, from which he received degrees in humanities and law in 1908. He completed his education at the University of Paris, where he studied juridical, economic, and political sciences and was awarded a doctorate in 1914. After beginning his career as a lawyer in Paris, Cassin was drafted into the French army at the outset of World War I and commissioned as an infantry officer. In 1916 he survived a stomach wound by German shrapnel when his mother, who was serving as a nurse in the field hospital to which he was taken, insisted on immediate surgery. Nevertheless, he suffered intestinal pain for the rest of his life.

Following the war, he taught international law, first at Lille and then in Paris. He also served as a French delegate to the League of Nations and to various disarmament conferences in Geneva from 1924 to 1938.

In the meantime, as a result of his wartime experiences, he considered it vital to care for the disabled and to provide for war widows and orphans. He formed and directed the Federal Union of Associations of Disabled and Aged War Veterans and became vice president of the High Council for Wards of the Nation. In 1921 he organized conferences for war veterans in Italy, Poland, Germany, Czechoslovakia, and Austria. Through the INTERNATIONAL LABOUR ORGANISATION, he tried unsuccessfully to bring together war veterans who had formerly been enemies to demonstrate in support of the Disarmament Conference of 1932.

The invasion of France by the German army began in June 1940. Cassin was one of the first prominent Frenchmen to join General Charles de Gaulle's Free French government-in-exile in London. He was appointed secretary of the Council of Defense, which was responsible for the military activities of the Free French. Later,

RENÉ CASSIN

he held the position of commissioner for justice and public education.

After the liberation of France in 1944, Cassin became vice president of the Council of State, the administrative high court of France. He was also a member of the Constitutional Council, which rules on the constitutionality of French laws. In 1945 he was named president of the council of the National School of Administration.

Cassin was also selected to be a delegate to the Commission on Human Rights, which was established by the United Nations Charter in response to atrocities committed during World War II. Eleanor Roosevelt was chosen the commission's chairwoman, and Cassin became its vice-chairman. The commission's task was to draft a Universal Declaration of Human Rights that all nations could endorse. Roosevelt often noted that Cassin wrote the document the commission produced.

Writing the declaration proved difficult because it had to take into account the various religious traditions, political philosophies, laws, and economic systems of United Nations member nations. The commission met first in January 1947. The following year, when the General Assembly convened in Paris, Cassin's draft was submitted. After two months, ninety-seven meetings, and 1,200 ballots on proposed amendments, it was adopted on December 10, 1948. Since 1950 this date has been celebrated as Human Rights Day.

Not a binding agreement, the declaration, consisting of a preamble and thirty articles, was meant to set "a common standard of achievement for all peoples and all nations." Among the principles it proclaims are that all citizens are entitled to the following: the right to life, liberty, and personal security; equality before the law; freedom of conscience, religion, expression, and assembly; the right to work, equal compensation for equal work, and reasonable working hours; and a free education. Dozens of nations that have come into being since 1948 have incorporated these provisions into their constitutions.

However, it was not until 1966 that the declaration was drafted into the form of a treaty and adopted by the United Nations General Assembly. By that time, Cassin was chairman of the Commission on Human Rights. He had also written two covenants—one on civil and political rights and the other on economic, social, and cultural rights—in an effort to make the document more binding. Nevertheless, it was apparent that its goals would often not be implemented by signatory nations for many years.

Universal human rights and world peace continued to be the motivating interests of Cassin's later life. He was a founder of the United Nations Educational, Scientific, and Cultural Organization (UNESCO), whose constitution was adopted in 1945, and he served as French delegate to UNESCO from then until 1952. During this time, he was frequently critical of the organization's actions when he considered them to have political rather than humanitarian aims. From 1950 to 1960 Cassin was a member of the Court of Arbitration at The Hague, and from 1965 to 1968 he was president of the European Court of Rights.

On the twentieth anniversary of the adoption of the United Nations Declaration of Human Rights, Cassin was awarded the 1968 Nobel Prize for Peace. In her presentation speech, Aase Lionæs of the Norwegian Nobel Committee pointed out, "To be sure, the United Nations Charter does mention several times that it will promote human rights. But we do not find these rights defined anywhere in the charter. So the question was, what did human rights mean to people from these fifty or sixty nations, coming as they did from all parts of the world, and from different levels of cultural development, with diverse traditions, religions, ideologies." Thus Lionæs stressed the enormous difficulties facing Cassin and the commission when they took up the work of preparing the declaration.

In his acceptance speech, Cassin described the declaration as "the first document of an ethical sort that organized humanity has ever adopted, and precisely at a time when man's power over nature became vastly increased because of scientific discoveries and when it was essential to decide to what constructive ends these powers should be put." Acknowledging that the "jurisdiction of the states will always be a fundamental principle," he added that "it will no longer be exclusive." He saw adoption of the declaration as meaning "first, the permanent accession of every human being to the rank of human society—in legal parlance one would say to the rank of subject of international law; second . . . that the states consent to exercise their sovereignty under the authority of international law."

For many years Cassin served as president of the International Institute of Human Rights in Strasbourg. In this capacity he joined the American Jewish Committee in sponsoring a conference held in Uppsala, Sweden, in 1972 that influenced the human rights section of the Helsinki Declaration adopted by thirty-five countries in 1975. He was also a campaigner for Jewish rights and president of the Jewish Alliance in France.

Cassin married Simone Yzomard on March 29, 1917; she died in 1969. While hospitalized by a heart attack in November 1975, he married Ghislaine Bru. He died in Paris the following year. Before his death, France conferred on Cassin the Grand Cross of the Legion of Honor.

WORKS IN ENGLISH TRANSLATION: "How the Charter on Human Rights Was Born," UNESCO Courier January 1968.

ABOUT: Green, J. F. The United Nations and Human Rights, 1956; International Labour Review February 1969; Moskowitz, M. Human Rights and Work Order, 1958; New York Times February 21, 1976; Robinson, N. Universal Declaration of Human Rights: Its Origins, Significance, and Interpretations, 1950.

CECIL, ROBERT

(September 14, 1864–November 24, 1958)
Nobel Prize for Peace, 1937

The English statesman Edgar Algernon Robert Gascoyne Cecil (Viscount Cecil of Chelwood), was born in London, the third of five sons of Lord Robert Arthur Talbot Cecil, Marquess of Salisbury. Cecil's father, then a member of the House of Commons, later became prime minister. Surrounded by the wealth and privilege of the British aristocracy, Cecil was tutored at home until the age of thirteen.

He then followed his two older brothers first to Eton and then to University College, Oxford, where he read law and received his degree in 1886. The following year he was called to the bar and practiced law in London. He married Lady Eleanor Lambton in 1889; they had no children.

When he was elected to Parliament in 1906 as a Conservative member for East Marylebone, a London constituency, Cecil had already acquired a reputation for progressive views. An advocate of moderate free trade and of women's suffrage, he came into conflict with his party the following year. Breaking with the Conservatives, he then stood for Parliament as an independent and lost two elections before winning a seat from the Hitchin division of Hertfordshire, which he held for twelve years.

Cecil was fifty years old when Great Britain declared war in 1914. Too old for military service, he worked instead with the INTERNATIONAL COMMITTEE OF THE RED CROSS in the Department of the Wounded and Missing in Paris, Bologna, and London. The following year he was appointed under secretary of foreign affairs and in 1916 minister of blockade. His exposure to the horrors of war during his work with the Red Cross motivated Cecil to initiate a peace plan. In September 1916 he sent a memorandum to other British cabinet members proposing a commission to study the formation of a postwar tribunal where nations could attempt to settle disputes without recourse to war. Despite opposition from the British Foreign Office, his proposal was endorsed by the cabinet and incorporated in a memorandum that later became the British draft of the Covenant of the League of Nations.

Shortly after the armistice that ended World War I, Cecil was named chancellor of Birmingham University. He attended the Paris Peace Conference in 1919 as special adviser to the British delegation. After establishing contact with the American representatives, led by WOODROW WILSON, and the French delegates, headed by LÉON BOURGEOIS, Cecil formed a committee to advise the British team about the terms of the Covenant. Among his recommendations was a proposal to admit Germany and its allies to the League of Nations. The defeat of this measure, he wrote later, "was a great misfortune to the league. It helped to create the impression that the league was dominated by France and England and was . . . a mere continuance of their war alliance." Though defeated on this issue, Cecil, aided by FRIDTJOF NANSEN, strengthened the

ROBERT CECIL

league by convincing the neutral nations to join.

Shortly after the conference, Cecil resigned from the government in protest over the disestablishment of the Church of Wales. In 1920, 1921, and 1922 he participated in the Assembly of the League of Nations as a representative of South Africa appointed by Jan Smuts. In this capacity he joined a small group of delegates, including Nansen and KARL BRANTING, who worked diligently to place the league's sessions on a strictly parliamentary basis. With the formation of a new government in Britain in 1923, Cecil was created Viscount Cecil of Chelwood and named lord privy seal, a position that freed him to devote all his efforts to league work. The next year he was made chancellor of the duchy of Lancaster and assumed chief responsibility for Britain's role in the league.

Almost from the beginning, the league operated in a climate of increasing militarism. In 1923 Benito Mussolini dispatched warships to seize the Greek island of Corfu after an Italian citizen was shot on Greek territory. Cecil and Nansen led the effort to persuade the league Council to adopt a settlement proposal until the question could be put before the league's Permanent Court. Their efforts failed, and the dispute was settled outside the league.

Cecil suffered another setback the next year when the British government rejected the Geneva Protocol, which called for giving the Permanent Court jurisdiction over conflicts that could be decided according to international law. It also called for collective security agreements and international disarmament conferences. In 1927 Cecil represented Great Britain at a naval disarmament conference in Geneva, which was also attended by Japan and the United States. When the British cabinet would not agree to parity with the United States, the talks collapsed, and Cecil once again resigned. He remained active in league affairs as president of the International Federation of League of Nations Societies, a private organization.

In 1932 American President Herbert Hoover incorporated many of Cecil's ideas in a disarmament plan that won initial acceptance from Germany, Italy, the Soviet Union, and several other nations. But this plan also was frustrated by British opposition, and its failure seriously undermined the league's power and influence. Undaunted, Cecil helped organize the so-called Peace Ballot, a private plebiscite held in 1934–1935, in which more than 11 million Britons recorded their views on disarmament and international peace measures. More than 90 percent expressed support for the league, and over 80 percent favored the abolition of national air forces.

The league faced another crisis when Italian forces invaded Ethiopia in 1935. In Great Britain, public opinion overwhelmingly favored sanctions against Italy, but the government failed to take action, much to Cecil's disappointment. Nevertheless, in 1936 he founded the International Peace Campaign, a group that attempted to rally world support for disarmament and for the creation of mechanisms within the league to resolve conflicts.

In recognition of his efforts for the League of Nations, Cecil was awarded the 1937 Nobel Prize for Peace. In his presentation speech, CHRISTIAN LANGE of the Norwegian Nobel Committee praised "the unity and continuity" Cecil had displayed in his "lifelong work for peace." Previous commitments kept Cecil from attending the award ceremonies, but he delivered his Nobel lecture at the University of Oslo on June 1 the following year. Reviewing the events that had once more brought the world to the brink of war, Cecil warned his audience that "the horrors and dangers" of war "are enormously greater than they were before 1914." "Do not let us underrate the danger," he said; "it is now apparently part of the normal doctrine of those who advocate [nationalism] that no distinction can be made between combatants and noncombatants, and that a perfectly legitimate and indeed necessary method of warfare will be the wholesale destruction of unfortified cities and their inhabitants." He concluded with a fervent, last-minute plea that world leaders support the League of Nations "before Europe has been again plunged into a fresh bloodbath."

During World War II, Cecil published *A Great Experiment* (1941), an account of his years with the league. After the war, he attended the final meeting of the league in Geneva and was named honorary life president of the United Nations Association. His autobiography, *All the Way,* appeared in 1949.

Cecil died at age ninety-four at Tunbridge Wells in Kent, only a few months before the death of his wife.

ADDITIONAL WORKS: The Principles of Commercial Law, 1891, with Joseph Hurst; The New Outlook, 1919; The Moral Basis of the League of Nations, 1923; The Way of Peace: Essays and Addresses, 1928; International Arbitration, 1928; Woolf, L. (ed.) The Intelligent Man's Way to Prevent War, 1933; Peace and Pacifism, 1938; An Emergency Policy, 1948.

ABOUT: Birn, D. S. The League of Nations Union, 1981; Dictionary of National Biography 1951–1960, 1971; Disarmament and Arms Control Autumn 1965; Egerton, G. W. Great Britain and the Creation of the League of Nations, 1978; History Today February 1975; de Madariaga, S. Morning Without Noon: Memoirs, 1974; Times (London) November 25, 1958.

CHADWICK, JAMES
(October 20, 1891–July 24, 1974)
Nobel Prize for Physics, 1935

The English physicist James Chadwick was born in the town of Bollington, near Manchester, the eldest of four children of John Joseph Chadwick, who owned a laundry business, and Anne Mary (Knowles) Chadwick. After attending a local primary school, he went to Manchester Municipal Secondary School, where he excelled in mathematics. In 1908 Chadwick entered the University of Manchester intending to study mathematics, but he was inadvertently interviewed for consideration as a physics major. Too shy to rectify the error, Chadwick listened attentively to the interviewer and decided to change his field of interest. Three years later he graduated with honors in physics.

In 1911 Chadwick started graduate research under ERNEST RUTHERFORD in the Physical Laboratory at Manchester. It was during this time that experiments on the deflection of alpha particles (known to be charged helium atoms) by atoms in thin metal foils led Rutherford to propose that almost all the mass in an atom is concentrated in a dense, positively

JAMES CHADWICK

charged nucleus, which is surrounded by negatively charged electrons, known to have relatively little mass. Chadwick earned his M.S. in physics from Manchester in 1913 and in the same year was awarded an 1851 Exhibition Scholarship that enabled him to study radioactivity with Hans Geiger (a former Rutherford assistant) at the State Physical-Technical Institute in Berlin, Germany. When World War I began in 1914, Chadwick was interned as an enemy alien and confined for more than four years in a civilian prison camp in Ruhleben. Although he suffered severe privations that permanently undermined his health, he was able to participate in a scientific society created by some of his fellow prisoners. The group's activities were encouraged by several German scientists, including WALTHER NERNST, whom Chadwick met while he was interned.

Chadwick returned to Manchester in 1919, just after Rutherford had discovered that bombardment with alpha particles (now regarded as helium nuclei) could cause a nitrogen nucleus to disintegrate into the lighter nuclei of other elements. Rutherford was chosen a few months later to succeed J. J. THOMSON as director of the Cavendish Laboratory at Cambridge University and invited Chadwick to accompany him. Chadwick received the Wollaston Scholarship at Gonville and Caius College, Cambridge, and was able to work with Rutherford on a continuation of his alpha-particle experiments. They found that bombarded nuclei often expelled what appeared to be the nuclei of hydrogen, the lightest of the elements. The hydrogen nucleus carried a posi-

tive electric charge equal in magnitude to the negative charge of its surrounding electron but had about 2,000 times the electron mass. Rutherford later named it the proton. It became clear that an atom as a whole was electrically neutral because it had a number of protons in its nucleus equal to the number of surrounding electrons. However, such a number of protons did not account for all the mass of atoms, except in the simplest case of hydrogen. To reconcile the difference, Rutherford proposed in 1920 that nuclei might also contain electrically neutral particles he later named neutrons, formed by the union of an electron and a proton. An opposing view held that atoms had electrons inside as well as outside the nucleus, and that the negative charge on nuclear electrons simply canceled some of the positive charge of the protons. Nuclear protons could then contribute their full mass to the atom, but only enough charge to offset that of the extranuclear electrons. Although Rutherford's suggestion of a neutral particle was respected, no experimental evidence proved that the particle actually existed.

Chadwick received his Ph.D. in physics from Cambridge in 1921 and was named a fellow of Gonville and Caius College. Two years later he became assistant director of the Cavendish Laboratory. He spent the rest of the 1920s investigating atomic phenomena such as the artificial disintegration by alpha-particle bombardment of the nuclei of light elements and the spontaneous emission of beta particles (electrons). In the course of this work, he considered ways to demonstrate the existence of Rutherford's neutral particle, but it was research in Germany and France that provided the crucial clues.

In 1930 German physicists WALTHER BOTHE and Hans Becker found that some light elements bombarded with alpha particles emitted an especially penetrating radiation they assumed to be gamma rays. Gamma rays were first known as emanations from radioactive nuclei. They are more penetrating than X rays because they have shorter wavelengths. However, some results were puzzling, particularly when beryllium was used as the target of bombardment, in that forward emissions (in the direction of motion of the incoming alpha particles) were more penetrating than backward emissions. Chadwick suggested that the beryllium emissions might be neutral particles rather than gamma rays. In 1932 the French physicists FRÉDÉRIC JOLIOT and IRÈNE JOLIOT-CURIE, investigating the penetrating power of the beryllium emissions, placed various absorbing materials between the bombarded beryllium and an ionization chamber, a form of radiation detector. When they used paraffin (a hydrogen-rich substance) as an absorber, they detected an increase, rather than a decrease, in the radiation issuing from the far side. Their tests led them to conclude that the increase was due to protons (hydrogen nuclei) ejected from the paraffin by the penetrating radiation. They suggested that the protons were recoiling from collisions with quanta (discrete units of energy) of unusually powerful gamma rays, similar to the recoil of electrons from collisions with X rays (Compton effect) demonstrated by ARTHUR H. COMPTON.

Chadwick promptly repeated and extended the experiment by the Joliot-Curies. He found that a thick plate of lead had a negligible effect on the beryllium emissions, neither stopping them nor producing secondary radiations, thus demonstrating their great penetrating power. However, paraffin again gave rise to fast protons. Chadwick performed tests that positively identified the protons and measured their energy. He then showed that, by all available evidence, it was extremely unlikely that a beryllium–alpha-particle collision could produce a gamma ray with sufficient energy to eject protons at such speeds from paraffin. He abandoned the gamma-ray possibility and focused on the neutron hypothesis. Assuming the neutron's existence, he showed that the capture of an alpha particle by a beryllium nucleus could result in the formation of a nucleus of the element carbon and the release of a neutron. (He did the same for boron, another element that generated penetrating rays when bombarded by alpha particles. An alpha particle and a boron nucleus combine to form a nucleus of nitrogen and a neutron.) The high penetrating power of the neutron follows from its lack of charge, which enables it to pass through matter unaffected by the electric fields in atoms, interacting with nuclei only by direct hit. A neutron also requires less energy than a gamma ray to eject a proton from paraffin because a particle has more momentum than a quantum of electromagnetic radiation of the same energy. The fact that beryllium emissions in the forward direction are more penetrating can be attributed to the preferential emission of neutrons in that direction due to the momentum of the incoming alpha particles.

Chadwick also confirmed Rutherford's hypothesis that the neutron's mass would be similar to that of the proton by analyzing the exchange of energy between neutrons and ejected protons as if they were colliding billiard balls. The exchange is particularly effective because their masses are almost the same. He also analyzed the tracks of nitrogen atoms struck by neutrons in a cloud chamber, a device developed by C. T. R. WILSON. Vapor in the cloud chamber condenses along the path of electrification left by an ionizing particle in its interaction with vapor molecules. The path is visible although the particle itself is not. Since the neutron does not ionize directly, it leaves no path. Chadwick had to deduce the neutron properties from the track left by the recoil of the struck nitrogen atom. The neutron mass proved to be just over 0.1 percent greater than that of the proton.

Experiments and computations by other physicists confirmed Chadwick's findings, and the neutron's existence was quickly accepted. Shortly afterward, WERNER HEISENBERG showed that a neutron cannot be an amalgam of a proton and an electron, but is a unique, uncharged nuclear particle—the third subatomic, or elementary, particle to be discovered. Chadwick's demonstration of the neutron's existence in 1932 dramatically altered the picture of the atom and paved the way for further advances in physics. The neutron also had practical use as an atom smasher: unlike the positively charged proton, it is not repelled when it approaches a nucleus.

"For his discovery of the neutron," Chadwick was awarded the 1935 Nobel Prize for Physics. "The existence of the neutron having been fully established," said Hans Pleijel of the Royal Swedish Academy of Sciences in his presentation speech, "scientists have . . . come to a new conception of the structure of atoms that agrees better with the distribution of energy within the nuclei of atoms. It has proved obvious that the neutron forms one of the building stones of atoms and molecules and thus also of [the] material universe."

Chadwick moved to the University of Liverpool in 1935 to accept the Lyon Jones Chair of Physics and to establish a new center for nuclear physics research. At Liverpool he supervised the modernization of the university's facilities and oversaw the construction of a cyclotron, a device that accelerates charged particles to very high speeds.

When World War II began in 1939, the British government asked Chadwick if a nuclear chain reaction was possible, and he began using the Liverpool cyclotron to explore this possibility. The following year he joined the Maud Committee, a small, select group of eminent British scientists that submitted an optimistic report about Britain's ability to produce an atomic bomb, and he became coordinator of the experimental atomic weapons programs at Liverpool, Cambridge, and Bristol. Eventually, however, Britain decided to join the American nuclear weapons program and transferred its nuclear research scientists to the United States. From 1943 to 1945 Chadwick coordinated the efforts of the British scientists working on the Manhattan Project (the secret program to develop the atomic bomb) in its various locations.

Chadwick returned to the University of Liverpool in 1946. Two years later, he retired from active research to become master of Gonville and Caius College. In 1958 he retired to northern Wales with his wife, the former Aileen Stewart-Brown, whom he had married in 1925. They returned to Cambridge in 1969 to be near their twin daughters. Chadwick died five years later in Cambridge.

In addition to the Nobel Prize, Chadwick received the Hughes Medal (1932) and the Copley Medal (1950) of the Royal Society, the Medal for Merit of the United States government (1946), the Franklin Medal of the Franklin Institute (1951), and the Guthrie Medal of the Institute of Physics in London (1967). Knighted in 1945, he held honorary degrees from nine British universities and was a member of many scientific societies and academies in Europe and the United States.

SELECTED WORKS: Radioactivity and Radioactive Substances, 1921; Radiations From Radioactive Substances, 1930, with others.

ABOUT: Biographical Memoirs of Fellows of the Royal Society, volume 22, 1976; Current Biography November 1945; Oxbury, H. (ed.) Great Britons, 1985.

CHAIN, ERNST B.
(June 19, 1906–August 12, 1979)
Nobel Prize for Physiology or Medicine, 1945
(shared with Alexander Fleming and Howard W. Florey)

The German-English biochemist Ernst Boris Chain was born in Berlin of Jewish parents. His Russian-born father, Michael Chain, had emigrated to Berlin to study chemistry and established a prosperous chemical-manufacturing business. His mother, Margarete (Eisner) Chain, was born in Germany. Chain's father died in 1920, leaving him an inheritance

ERNST B. CHAIN

that was wiped out by the inflation of 1923–1924. Enough money remained, however, for him to attend Friedrich Wilhelm University, where he earned a degree in chemistry. Although Chain seriously considered a career as a concert pianist and frequently performed in public, he obtained his Ph.D. in chemistry in 1930 and began to study enzyme biochemistry at the Charité Hospital in Berlin.

Two years earlier Chain had become a naturalized German citizen, but as a part-Russian Jew of leftist political preferences, he decided to emigrate to England immediately after Adolf Hitler became chancellor of Germany in 1933. Six years later he became a British citizen. He was unable to arrange for his mother and sister to leave, however, and after 1942 his mother died in a concentration camp and his sister vanished.

Chain's first stop in England was the University College Hospital in London, where he found the laboratory facilities inadequate—a constant feature of his scientific experiences in England. Later that year he was able to transfer to Cambridge, where he worked under FREDERICK GOWLAND HOPKINS. Although the laboratory at Cambridge was no better equipped than the one in London, Chain was much happier, and he formed a great and lasting admiration for Hopkins.

Meanwhile, in 1935, HOWARD W. FLOREY was appointed professor of pathology at Oxford University. Florey, a pathologist and bacteriologist, was intent on reforming pathology teaching and research and urged closer cooperation between experimental pathologists

193

and chemists. Florey asked Hopkins to recommend someone to head biochemistry research at Oxford's William Dunn School of Pathology, and Hopkins suggested Chain.

After Chain's arrival at Oxford, one of the first projects Florey suggested was a study of antibacterial substances, including lysozyme, a compound discovered by ALEXANDER FLEMING in 1922. "Lysozyme had all the properties of an enzyme," Chain said later, "but the properties of its substrate in the bacterium on which it acted were unknown." Chain set out to isolate this substrate (the substance upon which the enzyme acted) and to study its interactions with lysozyme. Later in his life he said "this was the first time in my life that I was confronted with the necessity of obtaining large amounts of microbial biomass, and this problem has dominated my whole scientific career since then."

In the course of his research on the chemical properties of lysozyme, Chain read all the available papers on natural antimicrobial substances. "This seemed to me a large field, almost completely unstudied, which could bring to light new antibacterial structures of possible scientific and clinical interest," he later wrote. Among the papers he read was Fleming's original 1929 description of penicillin.

Fleming discovered penicillin in 1928, but by the early 1930s his research on the topic was essentially abandoned, primarily because penicillin is chemically unstable and difficult to produce in quantities sufficient for research purposes. The difficulties Fleming encountered in his effort to purify the substance, Chain said, "only increased my interest in Fleming's penicillin. I told Florey that we would certainly find a method for at least partially purifying penicillin despite lability [instability]. . . . So we started out work on the isolation and purification, not in the hope of finding some new antibacterial chemotherapeutic drug, but to isolate an enzyme which we hoped would hydrolyze a substrate common on the surface of many pathogenic bacteria."

At Chain's suggestion, Florey obtained funding from the Rockefeller Foundation for their penicillin research, which began in 1938. Chain and his colleague Norman G. Heatley quickly discovered that penicillin was not, in fact, an enzyme but a relatively small organic molecule. Its size was misleading, for they initially assumed that the molecular structure would be easy to determine and to synthesize; both assumptions were wrong.

Penicillin turned out to incorporate a tight combination of reactive groups (later called a beta-lactam structure) that had never before been found in nature and only rarely been found in the laboratory. Chain proposed the existence of such a structure in 1943, but he was not the only scientist to do so, nor was this structure the only one whose existence he proposed. It was not until 1949 that the debate was resolved by the X-ray crystallography work of DOROTHY C. HODGKIN. The beta-lactam ring proved difficult to synthesize; although the synthesis was accomplished in 1957, it still is not economically feasible.

Meanwhile, however, Chain and Heatley discovered that instead of synthesizing drugs, they could concentrate penicillin by the newly invented technique of freeze-drying, in which a solution of penicillin was frozen, after which water vapor was pumped away and condensed at a very low temperature. Heatley played a particularly important role in designing and constructing the laboratory equipment. By May 1940 Chain and Florey had obtained enough impure penicillin to test its effects on lethally infected mice. The results proved the drug's therapeutic value in cases of systematic infection. Florey began the first clinical trials in humans the following year.

Chain's volatile personality had a pugnacious streak. Initially, his relationship with Florey was warm; Florey provided guidance, while Chain gave Florey enthusiasm. Their friendship began to deteriorate in 1941, however, when Florey and Heatley visited the United States to encourage an American effort in penicillin research and production, leaving Chain behind. In 1944 Chain was upset by reports that Fleming alone, or Fleming and Florey together, might be awarded the Nobel Prize.

Nevertheless, it was Chain, Fleming, and Florey who shared the 1945 Nobel Prize for Physiology or Medicine "for the discovery of penicillin and its curative effects in various infectious diseases." In his presentation speech, Göran Liljestrand of the Karolinska Institute reminded his audience that "the extraordinarily good effects of penicillin have been established in a number of important infectious illnesses, such as general blood poisoning, cerebral meningitis, gas gangrene, pneumonia, syphilis, gonorrhea, and many others."

Despite the acclaim he and his colleagues received for their work, Chain grew increasingly dissatisfied. From the outset, he had wanted to take out a patent on the methods the team devised, and in 1948 he applied for a provisional patent. The British Medical Research Council, however, was opposed to the idea. When the war ended, Chain expected Oxford and the British government to show their appreciation for the development of penicillin by setting up a program in industrial microbiology and fermentation technology. When no funds were forthcoming, his hopes were further frustrated.

These dissatisfactions led Chain to accept an offer from the Italian State Institute Research Center for Chemical Microbiology, where he headed the first international center for research on antibiotics. Before moving to Rome in 1948, Chain married Anne Beloff, an Oxford biochemist. They had two sons and a daughter. In Italy, Chain continued to work on penicillin. Having played an important role in the debate during World War II over the structure of penicillin, in the late 1950s he helped direct British efforts to produce semisynthetic penicillins.

Chain was persuaded to return to England in the 1960s to become chairman of the Department of Biochemistry at the University of London's Imperial College of Science and Technology and director of the Wolfson Laboratories, newly established there. Always a complex and contentious man, he retired in 1973 after a tenure that was marked by running battles over administrative and financial issues. Chain became ill in 1978 and died at his country home in Ireland the following year.

Chain's many honors included the Berzelius Medal of the Swedish Medical Society (1946), the Pasteur Medal of the Pasteur Institute in Paris (1946), the Paul Ehrlich Centenary Prize of the Paul Ehrlich Foundation (1954), and the Marotta Medal of the Italian Chemical Society (1962). He served as chairman of the World Health Organization and was a member of the New York Academy of Medicine, the French Academy of Medicine, the Weizmann Institute of Science (Israel), the Chemical Society of Italy, and the Finnish Biochemical Society. In 1949 he was elected a fellow of the Royal Society.

SELECTED WORKS: Antibiotics (2 vols.) 1949, with others; Social Responsibility and the Scientist in Modern Western Society, 1970; Food Technology in the 1980s, 1975; Biologically Active Substances: Exploration and Exploitation, 1977.

ABOUT: Biographical Memoirs of Fellows of the Royal Society, volume 29, 1983; Clark, R. W. The Life of Ernst Chain, 1985; Hare, R. The Birth of Penicillin, 1970; Nachmanson, D. German-Jewish Pioneers in Science 1900–1933, 1979; Oxbury, H. (ed.) Great Britons, 1985; Parascandola, J. (ed.) The History of Antibiotics, 1980.

CHAMBERLAIN, J. AUSTEN
(October 16, 1863–March 16, 1937)
Nobel Prize for Peace, 1925
(shared with Charles Dawes)

The British politician Joseph Austen Chamberlain was born in Birmingham, England. His father was Joseph Chamberlain, a successful manufacturer and politician. His mother, the former Harriet Kenrick, died in childbirth. His father remarried and six years later had another son, Neville, later prime minister of Britain. Raised in an intensely political atmosphere, J. Austen Chamberlain received an early education in statesmanship at home. He attended Rugby School and later Trinity College, Cambridge, and received his degree in 1885.

During a nine-month stay in France, he attended lectures at the École des Sciences Politiques in Paris. He then studied for a year in Germany. Returning to England in 1888, he served as his father's personal secretary until 1892. In that year, he was elected to Parliament, unopposed, as a Liberal Unionist from East Worcestershire, near Birmingham, a seat he held for the next twenty-two years.

In a letter to Queen Victoria written after hearing Chamberlain's maiden speech in Parliament, William Gladstone described him "as a person of whom high political anticipations may reasonably be entertained." Chamberlain fulfilled Gladstone's expectations by rising rapidly through the political ranks. He was appointed junior whip for the Liberal Unionists in 1892, civil lord of the Admiralty in 1895, financial secretary of the Treasury in 1900, postmaster general with a cabinet seat in 1902, and chancellor of the Exchequer in 1903. During these years, he developed a reputation as a diligent politician and a formidable debater.

In 1906, the same year that his party was defeated by the Liberals, Chamberlain married Ivy Muriel; they had two sons and one daughter. During his years out of office, he continued to sit in Parliament, where he played a major role in persuading the government to support its French and Russian allies on the eve of World War I.

In the coalition government that was formed in 1915, Chamberlain served as secretary of state for India. Two years later, an official commission uncovered scandalous deficiencies in the medical care given during the British attack on Baghdad, in Mesopotamia. Although he was neither personally responsible nor officially blamed for the deficiencies, Chamberlain resigned from the government because his department was involved.

J. AUSTEN CHAMBERLAIN

In April 1918 Chamberlain became a member of Prime Minister David Lloyd George's coalition cabinet and was again appointed chancellor of the Exchequer. During his two years in this post, he bolstered British credit and imposed heavy domestic taxes to repay the government's war debt.

When Bonar Law temporarily withdrew from politics in 1921 owing to ill health, Chamberlain succeeded him as leader of the House of Commons, but his loyalty to Lloyd George increasingly alienated him from his fellow Conservatives. His decision to support the establishment of the Irish Free State further undermined Conservative confidence in him, and at a party conference in 1922 leadership passed back to Law. This move effectively foreclosed Chamberlain's prospects of becoming prime minister.

With his appointment as secretary of foreign affairs under Stanley Baldwin in 1924, Chamberlain entered the arena of international politics. It was a particularly difficult moment. The previous British government had endorsed the Geneva Protocol, a French proposal to the League of Nations requiring that signatories submit disputes to compulsory arbitration. The agreement empowered the league's Council to determine the steps member nations should take to enforce the league's authority. Therefore, the measure was widely opposed in Great Britain, and it fell to Chamberlain to reject the protocol in a speech before the Council. At the same time, however, he suggested that the Council deal with crises on an individual basis "by making special arrangements in order to meet special needs."

Such an opportunity arose that year when GUSTAV STRESEMANN, the German foreign minister, announced his government's willingness to guarantee the postwar boundaries along the Rhine. A long and intricate series of negotiations ensued among Chamberlain, Stresemann, ARISTIDE BRIAND (the French foreign minister), and representatives of Belgium, Italy, Poland, and Czechoslovakia. The meetings were held in Locarno, Switzerland, where the results were announced on October 5, 1925, and the documents signed on October 16, Chamberlain's sixty-second birthday.

According to the eight agreements, known collectively as the Locarno Pact, Germany was admitted to the League of Nations and the seven signatories guaranteed Germany's western borders, agreed to binding arbitration, and declared their intention "to seek the realization" of disarmament as members of the League of Nations. "It follows that one of the chief consequences of the Locarno treaties will be to accentuate the growth in prestige and authority of the League of Nations," ROBERT CECIL predicted. Chamberlain returned to England in triumph and was made knight of the Garter.

Throughout the world, the Locarno Pact was hailed as an unprecedented contribution to peace. By helping to dispel French animosity toward Germany and German anger over the vindictiveness of the Versailles Treaty, it made possible the international cooperation necessary for rebuilding Europe's political and economic systems. For his role in the Locarno negotiations, Chamberlain shared the 1925 Nobel Prize for Peace with CHARLES DAWES. The prize, which had been reserved in 1925, was bestowed the following year in Oslo. Chamberlain did not attend the ceremonies and gave no lecture, but his telegraphed message of acceptance was read by the British ambassador to Norway, Sir Francis Lindley.

During his remaining four years as foreign secretary, Chamberlain took strong measures to protect Shanghai against possible attack by Japan, drew up draft treaties in an unsuccessful effort to stabilize Great Britain's relations with Egypt, and threw his support behind the Kellogg-Briand Pact, named for the French foreign minister Aristide Briand and the American statesman FRANK KELLOGG.

After the fall of the Baldwin government in 1929, Chamberlain spent much of his time assisting the political career of his half brother, Neville. With the formation of the all-party government in 1931, he accepted the position of first lord of the Admiralty, despite his bitter disappointment at not being reappointed foreign secretary. At the Admiralty, he complained, "I appear . . . as an old party hack who might be dangerous outside and so must have his mouth stopped with office." A naval mutiny over pay cuts at Invergordon, Scotland, furnished an opportunity for Chamberlain to submit his resignation after the general elections in October 1931. "I hope," he wrote to Baldwin, "that my elimination will make Neville's accession to the chancellorship easier to secure."

As a member of Parliament, Chamberlain remained active in politics, warning against the threat posed by Adolf Hitler's Nazi government and favoring economic sanctions against Italy for its invasion of Ethiopia. He also served as chancellor of Reading University between 1935 and 1937 and sat on the board of the British Postgraduate Medical School. During his semiretirement, he wrote *Down the Years* (1935), character sketches of great men he had known, and *Politics From Inside* (1936), a collection of the letters he had written to keep his father informed about political affairs during the eight years before his father's death in 1914. Tall, immaculately attired, and elegant, Chamberlain's aristocratic appearance belied a personal warmth and sociability that earned him a wide circle of close friends.

After suffering a stroke, Chamberlain died in London on March 16, 1937, only two months before Neville became prime minister.

ADDITIONAL WORKS: The League of Nations, 1926; Peace in Our Time: Addresses on Europe and the Empire, 1928; Speeches on Germany, 1933; Seen in Passing, 1937.

ABOUT: Cecil, R., et al. The Locarno Treaties, 1926; Dictionary of National Biography 1931–1940, 1949; Glasgow, G. From Dawes to Locarno, 1925; Petrie, C. A. The Chamberlain Tradition, 1938; Petrie, C. A. The Life and Letters of the Right Hon. Sir Austen Chamberlain (2 vols.) 1939; Stern-Rubarth, E. Three Men Tried, 1939; Times (London) March 17, 1937; Toynbee, A. J., et al. Survey of International Affairs, 1926.

CHAMBERLAIN, OWEN
(July 10, 1920–   )
Nobel Prize for Physics, 1959
(shared with Emilio Segrè)

The American physicist Owen Chamberlain was born in San Francisco, California, to Edward Chamberlain, a radiologist at the Stanford University Hospital, and Genevieve Lucinda (Owen) Chamberlain. When the boy was ten years old, his family moved to Philadelphia, where he attended the Germantown Friends School. He earned a B.A. from Dartmouth College in 1941 and registered for graduate work in physics at the University of California at Berkeley. However, after the United States entered World War II, he interrupted his studies in 1942 to join the Manhattan Project, the secret program for the development of the atomic bomb. He investigated uranium isotopes at Berkeley, under the direction of ERNEST O. LAWRENCE, inventor of the cyclotron, and in 1943 was assigned to Los Alamos, where he continued his work and observed the first test of the bomb in 1945.

After the war, Chamberlain specialized in particle physics at the Argonne National Laboratory, Chicago, concentrating on slow-neutron diffraction in liquids. He simultaneously resumed his graduate studies at the University of Chicago under ENRICO FERMI, earning his Ph.D. in 1948. That year, he accepted an invitation to return to Berkeley as an instructor in physics, becoming an assistant professor in 1950, an associate professor in 1954, and a full professor in 1958.

At Berkeley, Chamberlain used the university's cyclotron, an advanced high-energy particle accelerator, to investigate the scattering of fast-moving protons and neutrons. In the early 1950s he began a collaboration with EMILIO SEGRÈ, a Berkeley colleague whom he had met during the war at Los Alamos, and a research team that included Clyde Weigand and Thomas Ypsilantis. Segrè had been a member of the celebrated Italian school of physics led by Fermi at the University of Rome in the 1930s. The collaboration led to the discovery of the antiproton, a theoretically predicted twin of the proton, but with opposite electric charge and reversal of certain other properties.

In 1928 the English physicist P. A. M. DIRAC had predicted the existence of antiparticles, somewhat like mirror images of familiar particles such as the electron and the proton, on the basis of equations he derived in combining ALBERT EINSTEIN's relativity theory with quantum theory. In the absence of experimental verification, the existence of antiparticles was not universally accepted. Confidence rose when CARL D. ANDERSON, four years later, discovered the positron, a twin of the negative electron but with positive electric charge (that is, an antielectron). The positron

197

Lawrence Radiation Laboratory, AIP Niels Bohr Library

OWEN CHAMBERLAIN

was observed in cosmic rays, high-energy radiation bombarding the earth from space. The discovery stimulated the search for other antiparticles, using newly available particle accelerators. Since antiparticles are created by the violent impact between an accelerated particle and the target material, large amounts of energy are required. A heavy particle such as the antiproton required more energy for its creation than available accelerators could deliver.

The situation changed with the construction at Berkeley of the bevatron, the most powerful particle accelerator of its day, able to propel particles to energies reaching billions of electron volts. Using this device, Chamberlain, Segrè, and their colleagues accelerated protons to an energy of 6.2 billion electron volts and bombarded a target of copper atoms. Although the energy was theoretically sufficient to produce antiprotons, they would be relatively few, very short-lived, and extremely difficult to detect in the debris left by the collision, which included large numbers of other subatomic particles.

The solution to the problem of detecting and identifying the antiprotons was the major achievement of Chamberlain, Segrè, and their research group. They devised an elaborate and sophisticated system that included magnets and magnetic focusing devices to single out particles of antiproton mass, charge, and velocity from others; electronic counters and timers to measure the velocity of the particles as they traversed a path of known length; a photographic emulsion that recorded proton-anti-

proton annihilations (as final confirmation of other indications); and other means to rule out possible errors. The emulsion showed the track of an incoming antiproton ending in an annihilation that produced a starlike cluster of tracks of annihilation products. The products proved to be about five mesons per annihilation.

In 1955, when they had seen a convincing number (forty) of confirmed detections (only 1 out of about 30,000 particles was an antiproton, and one antiproton was observed about every fifteen minutes), the scientists announced their discovery of the antiproton. "[The bevatron] is the only energy source high enough to produce the antiprotons," Chamberlain said later. "Even the stars are a million times too cool, while the hydrogen bomb, which is basically a star, is not in the same league." The experiment also demonstrated that antiprotons are produced only in proton-antiproton pairs, not by themselves, just as positrons are produced only in electron-positron pairs. This observation further verified Dirac's theory and fostered the general belief in the existence of other antiparticles, whether or not they could be observed.

In the months that followed the original experiments, Chamberlain and others carried out related studies using photographic techniques to produce more records of proton-antiproton annihilations. A Guggenheim Fellowship enabled him to spend 1957 at the physics department of the University of Rome, where he continued his investigations of the antiproton, partly in collaboration with Edoardo Amaldi, another physicist on Fermi's original team in the 1930s. On his return to Berkeley, Chamberlain was appointed full professor of physics and the following year was invited to serve for a semester as Loeb Lecturer in Physics at Harvard.

"For their discovery of the antiproton," Chamberlain and Segrè received the 1959 Nobel Prize for Physics. In making the presentation, Erik Hulthén of the Royal Swedish Academy of Sciences hailed Chamberlain's "ingenious methods for the detection and analysis of the new particle." In his Nobel lecture Chamberlain summarized the work he and his colleagues had performed. "Since the proton and neutron are close sisters," he said, "it was expected that the discovery of the antineutron would quickly follow that of the antiproton. In fact, it is natural to infer that antiparticles of all charged particles exist."

Remaining at Berkeley, Chamberlain has continued his work in particle physics, investigating the interaction of antiprotons with hydrogen and deuterium, the scattering of pi-mesons, and the possible production of anti-neutrons from antiprotons.

Chamberlain's marriage in 1943 to Beatrice Babette Cooper, with whom he had three daughters and a son, ended in divorce in 1978. He is a member of the American Physical Society, the National Academy of Sciences, and the American Association for the Advancement of Science, as well as a fellow of the American Academy of Arts and Sciences.

ABOUT: Current Biography March 1960; New York Times October 25, 1959; Physics Today December 1959.

CHANDRASEKHAR, SUBRAHMANYAN
(October 19, 1910–   )
Nobel Prize for Physics, 1983
(shared with William A. Fowler)

SUBRAHMANYAN CHANDRASEKHAR

The Indian-American astrophysicist Subrahmanyan Chandrasekhar (chun drä shä′ kar) was born in Lahore, India (now Pakistan), the first son and the third of ten children of Chandrasekhara Subrahmanya Ayyar, an Indian government official and musicologist, and the former Sita Balakrishnan, a literary scholar and linguist. Inspired by his uncle, the physicist VENKATA RAMAN, the boy decided to become a scientist. Chandra (as he has always been called) was educated at home by his parents and tutors until 1922, when he entered the Hindu High School in Madras, where the family had moved in 1918. Upon graduation from high school in 1925, he entered Presidency College of the University of Madras, where he majored in theoretical physics and followed with interest the latest developments in astrophysics. He earned a B.S. with honors in 1930. As an undergraduate in 1928, he published a paper analyzing the thermodynamics of the Compton effect (named for ARTHUR H. COMPTON) with reference to the interior of the stars.

Having won a Government of India Scholarship for graduate study at Cambridge University, Chandrasekhar set sail for England in 1930. On the long voyage he read a book he had received as a prize in a physics competition, Arthur Eddington's *The Internal Constitution of the Stars.* In the book, the eminent British astronomer maintained that all stars, once they exhaust the fuel sustaining their nuclear reactions, collapse under their own weight, radiating excess energy into space. A star such as the sun would shrink to an earth-sized, white-

hot ball, called a white dwarf, with a density of 10 tons per cubic centimeter, after which it would simply cool but remain otherwise unchanged forever. At Trinity College, Cambridge, Chandrasekhar investigated the behavior of dying stars under the physicist Ralph Howard Fowler, and within one year, at the age of twenty-one, he had published three papers: "The Highly Collapsed Configurations of a Stellar Mass," "The Maximum Mass of Ideal White Dwarfs," and "The Density of White Dwarf Stars." In these papers, Chandrasekhar contradicted Eddington. Fowler's own work supported Eddington's views to a large extent, indicating that stars would collapse to form objects of planetary size, becoming either white dwarfs that were hot and relatively bright or brown dwarfs that were cool and relatively dim.

On the advice of P. A. M. DIRAC, Chandrasekhar spent the final year of his doctoral studies with NIELS BOHR at the Institute for Theoretical Physics in Copenhagen. After receiving his Ph.D. in 1933, he remained at Cambridge as a fellow of Trinity College for four years. Meanwhile, he continued his investigation of stars.

In his earlier papers, Chandrasekhar had shown that large and small stars do not have the same fate once their nuclear fires have burned out. Using quantum mechanics and relativity theory, he analyzed the behavior of stellar matter, with special attention to electrons (a normal constituent of atoms), as a star becomes smaller and denser. If the mass of a star is small enough, the gravitational pressures promoting collapse eventually become balanced by outward pressures, and the star reaches equilibrium at the size of a white dwarf. This is true whether the outward pressures are calculated on the basis of classical physics, which attributed them primarily to the thermal energy of the electrons, or quantum mechanics, which involves a value called Fermi energy (named for ENRICO FERMI) that depends on how crowded the electrons become. However, if the stellar mass is above a certain magnitude, the electrons will eventually become so compressed that their velocities will approach that of light, a condition called relativistic degeneracy. As a consequence, gravitational contraction will overwhelm opposing forces, and the star will continue to shrink to an incredibly small size and enormous density. The critical stellar mass below which a star might become a white dwarf is now known as the Chandrasekhar limit. It is 1.4 times the mass of the sun.

Although Chandrasekhar, in his characteristic way, did not dramatize the consequences of his findings, it was already known from ALBERT EINSTEIN's general theory of relativity that a massive star whose size contracts below a certain radius would allow no radiation to escape. It would become invisible. Chandrasekhar's calculations predicted what are now known as black holes.

By 1934 these calculations had led Chandrasekhar to foresee another stellar event. A shrinking dead star of a mass two to three times that of the sun would develop so much energy in its outer layers that they would explode as a supernova. This thick shell would be blown out into space, and the remnant would shrink to a stable neutron star containing no electrically charged electrons and protons. Its density would be about 100 million tons per cubic centimeter.

In January of the following year, at the age of twenty-four, Chandrasekhar was invited to present his calculations at a meeting of the Royal Astronomical Society in London. He had learned only the day before, to his consternation, that Eddington also was to speak. He and Eddington, with whom he had become friends, had been discussing Chandrasekhar's figures for months, but Eddington had never hinted at his own work on the same topic, revealed his invitation to speak, or indicated what he intended to say. After Chandrasekhar finished his presentation, Eddington, fifty-two years old and the world's most eminent astronomer, delivered a deeply humiliating and derisive rebuttal. "There is no such thing as relativistic degeneracy," he said dismissing a black hole as "a *reductio ad absurdum*. I think there should be a law of nature to prevent a star from behaving in this absurd way."

Although Eddington did not support his condemnation with any substantive refutation, Chandrasekhar was distraught. No one came publicly to his defense, but such prominent physicists as Niels Bohr and WOLFGANG PAULI privately reassured him. He did not abandon his work, even remained friendly with Eddington, and was eventually completely vindicated. After Eddington's dismissal of his ideas, Chandrasekhar's prospects for a tenured faculty position in England were dim, and in 1937 he came to the United States as a research associate at the University of Chicago. He has remained at Chicago, becoming an associate professor the following year, a full professor in 1944, and Hull Distinguished Service Professor of Astrophysics in 1947.

After working on problems of stellar structure at Chicago, Chandrasekhar investigated stellar dynamics, especially dynamic friction, the slowing down of any star hurtling through a galaxy because of the gravity of surrounding stars. Between 1943 and 1950, he developed his theory of radiative transfer, important for an understanding of stellar atmospheres, stellar luminosity, and spectral line formation, as well as for planetary atmospheres and the illumination and polarization of the sunlit sky. During World War II, he served as a consultant to the United States War Department at the Aberdeen Proving Ground in Maryland. When the University of Chicago became involved in the Manhattan Project to develop the atomic bomb, Chandrasekhar participated, working with Fermi, JAMES FRANCK, and others.

In other research he has investigated hydrodynamics and hydromagnetic stability (1952–1961), the equilibrium and stability of ellipsoidal figures of revolution (1961–1968), and the general theory of relativity and relativistic astrophysics (1962–1971). His work on the mathematical theory of black holes, conducted between 1974 and 1983, helped confirm the very views that Eddington had attacked in 1935. In fact, no white dwarf has been found to have a mass greater than 1.4 times that of the sun, and the Chandrasekhar limit has become one of the foundations of modern astrophysics, leading to the recognition of neutron stars and black holes. The quasi-stellar object, or quasar, may be a black hole in the center of a galaxy. Black holes are detected by radiation emitted by matter accelerated to very high energy as it is drawn into the black hole.

Chandrasekhar was awarded the 1983 Nobel Prize for Physics "for his theoretical studies of the physical processes of importance to the structure and evolution of the stars." He shared the prize with WILLIAM A. FOWLER. In his acceptance speech, Chandrasekhar quoted some lines of poetry written by RABINDRA-NATH TAGORE: "Where the mind is without fear and the head is held high; / Where knowledge is free; / into that haven of freedom, Let me awake."

Throughout his career, Chandrasekhar has been both a theorist and a teacher. At the University of Chicago, his doctoral students have included TSUNG-DAO LEE and CHEN NING YANG. He was the sole editor of the *Astrophysical Journal* from 1951 to 1972. A slender, orderly man, Chandrasekhar listens to classical music or reads during his few leisure hours.

Chandrasekhar, during a trip to India in 1936, married Lalitha Doraiswamy, who had been a fellow student at Presidency College. He became an American citizen in 1953.

In addition to the Nobel Prize, Chandrasekhar has received the Bruce Gold Medal of the Astronomical Society of the Pacific (1952), the Gold Medal of the Royal Astronomical Society in London (1953), the Rumford Medal of the American Academy of Arts and Sciences (1957), the Royal Medal of the Royal Society of London (1962), the National Medal of Science of the National Science Foundation (1966), and the Dannie Heineman Prize of the American Physical Society (1974). He is a member of the National Academy of Sciences, the American Academy of Arts and Sciences, the American Astronomical Society, the Royal Astronomical Society in London, and the Royal Society of London.

SELECTED WORKS: An Introduction to the Study of Stellar Structure, 1939; Principles of Stellar Dynamics, 1942; Radiative Transfer, 1950; Plasma Physics, 1960; Hydrodynamic and Hydromagnetic Stability, 1961; Ellipsoidal Figures of Equilibrium, 1969; The Mathematical Theory of Black Holes, 1983.

ABOUT: Current Biography March 1986; Hammond, A. L. (ed.) A Passion to Know, 1984; New York Times October 20, 1983; Physics Today January 1984; Science November 25, 1983; Stibbs, D. W. N., and Woolley, R. R. The Outer Layers of a Star, 1953.

CHERENKOV, PAVEL

(July 28, 1904–   )
Nobel Prize for Physics, 1958
(shared with Ilya Frank and Igor Tamm)

The Russian physicist Pavel Alekseyevich Cherenkov (chə reng' kəf) was born in Novaya Chigla near the city of Voronezh. His father, Aleksey, and his mother, Mariya, were peasants. After earning a bachelor's degree in physics and mathematics at Voronezh State University in 1928, he spent two years as a schoolteacher in nearby Michurinsk. In 1930 he became a graduate student at the Institute of Physics and Mathematics of the Soviet Academy of Sciences in Leningrad and received the candidate's degree (roughly equivalent to a master's degree) in 1935. He then began scientific work at the recently formed P. N. Lebedev Physical Institute of the Soviet Academy of Sciences in Moscow, where he has remained throughout his scientific career.

In 1932, under the direction of academician S. I. Vavilov, Cherenkov began an investigation into the light produced when high-energy radiation, such as emissions from radioactive substances, is absorbed by liquid solutions. He was able to show that, in almost all cases, the light was attributable to already familiar causes such as fluorescence. In fluorescence, the incoming energy excites atoms or molecules to higher energy states (quantum theory restricts each atom or molecule to a characteristic set of discrete energy levels) from which they quickly return to various lower energy states. The energy difference between a higher and lower state is given off as a unit (quantum) of radiation whose frequency is proportional to the energy in the quantum. If the frequency is in the visible range, the radiation appears as light. Since the differences between the atomic or molecular energy levels through which the excited substances pass in returning toward their lowest energy levels (ground state) are generally not the same as the energy in a quantum of the incoming radiation, the emissions from the absorbing substances do not have the same frequency as the radiation that produced them. In general, their frequencies are lower.

However, Cherenkov found that the gamma rays (much higher in energy, and therefore frequency, than X rays) emitted by radium produced a faint blue glow in the liquid that could not easily be explained. The glow had been noticed by others, even decades before by MARIE and PIERRE CURIE in their pioneering discoveries of radioactive elements, but it

201

CHERENKOV

PAVEL CHERENKOV

was thought to be merely one of many known luminescence phenomena. Cherenkov painstakingly explored all possibilities. He used double-distilled water to eliminate impurities as a hidden source of fluorescence. He tried heat and the addition of chemicals such as potassium iodide and silver nitrate, which diminish the brightness and alter other characteristics of ordinary fluorescence, always applying the same treatment to control solutions. Light from the controls was affected as usual, but not the blue glow.

The work was especially difficult because Cherenkov lacked the high-energy radiation sources and sensitive detectors that later became commonplace. Instead, he had to use weakly radioactive natural materials to supply his gamma rays, which produced exceedingly faint blue light, and he had to rely on his eye as a detector, sensitized by long waiting periods in darkness. Nevertheless, he was able to show convincingly that the blue glow must be something extraordinary.

A significant finding was the glow's unusual polarization. Light consists of electric and magnetic fields that undergo repeated cycles of rise and fall in strength and reversal of direction in a plane perpendicular to the direction of travel. If the fields are restricted to particular lines in the plane, as happens in reflection from a flat surface, the light is said to be polarized, but the polarization is still perpendicular to the line of travel. When polarization occurs in fluorescence, light from the excited substance is polarized in a direction at right angles to the path of the exciting beam.

Cherenkov found that the polarization of the blue light was parallel, not perpendicular, to the path of the incoming gamma rays. Tests conducted in 1936 also showed that the blue light was not emitted in all directions, but traveled forward from the incoming gamma rays and formed a cone of illumination whose axis was the gamma-ray path. This decisive clue helped his colleagues ILYA FRANK and IGOR TAMM develop the theory that conclusively explained the nature of the blue light, now known as Cherenkov radiation (Vavilov-Cherenkov radiation in the Soviet Union).

According to this theory, the gamma ray strikes an electron in the liquid and ejects it from its parent atom. Such collisions were described by ARTHUR H. COMPTON and are called the Compton effect. The mathematical description is remarkably similar to the collisions of billiard balls. If the exciting ray is sufficiently energetic, the electron is propelled at a very high velocity. The dramatic insight of Frank and Tamm was that Cherenkov radiation arose when the electron traveled faster than light. Others may have been intimidated from making such a proposition because it is a fundamental assumption of ALBERT EINSTEIN's theory of relativity that no particle velocity could exceed that of light. However, this restriction applied only relatively to the velocity of light in a vacuum. Light travels more slowly in substances such as liquids and glass. In liquids, electrons ejected from atoms can move faster than light in the same medium if the striking gamma ray has sufficient energy. One of Cherenkov's confirming experiments proved that X rays, which can also strip electrons from their atoms, could not produce the blue radiation because they did not have enough energy.

The cone of Cherenkov radiation is analogous to the bow wave created by a boat moving faster than the speed with which waves travel through the water. It is also like the shock wave created when an airplane exceeds the speed of sound in air.

For this work, Cherenkov received the degree of doctor of physical and mathematical sciences in 1940. Together with Vavilov, Tamm, and Frank, he received the Soviet government's State Prize in 1946.

In 1958, with Tamm and Frank, Cherenkov was awarded the Nobel Prize for Physics "for the discovery and the interpretation of the Cherenkov effect." MANNE SIEGBAHN of the Royal Swedish Academy of Sciences, on presenting the award, noted that "the discovery of the phenomenon now known as the Cherenkov effect . . . is an interesting example of how a relatively simple physical observation, if followed through in the right way, can lead to important findings and open up new paths to research."

Commenting on this first award to Soviet scientists of the Nobel Prize for Physics, the *New York Times* observed that it offered "definitive international recognition to the high quality of experimental and theoretical research in physics being done in the Soviet Union." This recognition is ironic—at least in part—because at the time of Cherenkov's original experiments, his primitive methods left many physicists unconvinced of his results.

For a number of years the theory of Cherenkov radiation remained of fundamental importance but without practical application. Eventually, however, Cherenkov counters (based on the detection of Cherenkov radiation) were developed for counting and measuring the velocity of high-speed single particles such as those found in particle accelerators and in cosmic rays. The determination of velocity makes use of the fact that the angle of the Cherenkov cone becomes narrower the faster the particle moves. Because Cherenkov radiation has an energy threshold and a short decay time, the Cherenkov counter can discriminate against lower-speed particles and distinguish two particles entering almost simultaneously. Detection of the radiation also yields information about particle mass and energy. This type of detector was instrumental in the discovery of the antiproton (the negative hydrogen nucleus) by OWEN CHAMBERLAIN and EMILIO SEGRÈ in 1955; it was later employed in a cosmic-ray counter in the Soviet satellite *Sputnik III.*

For many years Cherenkov was a section leader at the Lebedev Institute and, after World War II, carried out studies on cosmic rays and assisted in the development of electron accelerators. For his work in designing and building the Lebedev Institute's synchrotron, he was awarded a second Stalin Prize in 1951. In 1959 Cherenkov became director of the institute's Laboratory of Photomeson Processes, where he led investigations of the photodisintegration of helium and other light nuclei and the photoproduction of subatomic particles.

In addition to his research activities, after 1944 Cherenkov taught physics for many years, first at the Moscow Power Engineering Institute and later at the Moscow Institute of Physical Engineers. He was named professor of experimental physics in 1953.

In 1930 Cherenkov married Maria Putin-tseva, the daughter of a professor of Russian literature. They have two children.

Cherenkov was elected a corresponding member of the Soviet Academy of Sciences in 1964 and a full academician in 1970. He has received the State Prize of the Soviet government three times, in addition to two Orders of Lenin, two Orders of the Red Banner of Labor, and other state decorations. He has been a member of the Communist Party of the Soviet Union since 1946.

ABOUT: Jelley, J. V. Cherenkov Radiation and Its Applications, 1958; New York Times October 29, 1958; Science November 14, 1958.

CHURCHILL, WINSTON
(November 30, 1874–January 24, 1965)
Nobel Prize for Literature, 1953

Winston Leonard Spencer Churchill, English statesman, historian, and biographer, was born at Blenheim Palace, Woodstock, Oxfordshire. He was the elder son of the former Jeanette ("Jennie") Jerome, the daughter of an American financier, and Lord Randolph Churchill, a descendant of John Churchill, first duke of Marlborough. A brilliant politician, the elder Churchill openly disagreed with his Conservative party. In 1886 he resigned as leader of the House of Commons and chancellor of the Exchequer in the mistaken expectation that he would be reinstated on his own terms. The abrupt end to his father's political career, wrote the British historian Hugh Trevor-Roper, was an injury that "Winston Churchill never forgot or forgave."

After preparatory schooling at Ascot and Brighton, Churchill entered Harrow in 1888 and then the Royal Military College at Sandhurst, from which he graduated twentieth in a class of 130. In 1895, shortly after his father's death, he was assigned to the Fourth Hussars. However, he soon obtained a leave to cover the Cuban war of independence from Spain for the London *Daily Graphic*. Later, while serving as a soldier and journalist on the northwest frontier in India in 1896–1897, he wrote dispatches that formed the basis for *The Story of the Malakand Field Force,* published in 1898. While in India, he began work on his first and only work of fiction, *Savrola, a Tale of the Revolution in Laurania* (1900). He then joined Lord Kitchener's Nile expedition in the Sudan in the dual role of soldier and correspondent for the London *Morning Post,* an experience he described in *The River War, an Account of*

WINSTON CHURCHILL

the Reconquest of the Sudan (1899). Churchill resigned his commission in 1899 and returned to England to stand for Parliament as a Conservative. He lost the election and soon returned to journalism, covering the Boer War for the London *Morning Post*. His sensational adventures—including capture by the Boers, a prison escape, and a trip across the border by coal train—made him a hero on his return to England in 1900. He stood for election again, this time successfully, and became Conservative member of Parliament from Oldham. Six years later, objecting to a government tariff proposal, he resigned from his party, crossed the floor of the House of Commons, and joined the Liberals.

With the Liberal victory in 1906, Churchill was appointed colonial under secretary, in which position he argued for conciliation with South Africa. Two years later he was promoted to the Board of Trade, where he supported such progressive measures as reduced working hours, a minimum wage, labor exchanges, and unemployment insurance. In 1908 he married Clementine Hozier, with whom he had one son and three daughters.

Promoted to the Home Office in 1910, Churchill initiated penal reforms but remained opposed to women's suffrage. The next year, after being appointed first lord of the Admiralty, he urged large increases in naval expenditures in preparation for what he saw as a probable war with Germany. Soon after Great Britain declared war in 1914, Churchill organized and accompanied a military expedition to defend the port of Antwerp, Belgium. Al-

though the city eventually fell to German forces, Churchill's action enabled the Belgian army to escape and saved several vital English Channel ports. The following year, however, he was blamed for the failure of the Dardanelles expedition, an ambitious land-sea operation against the Turks, intended to gain control of the straits and open a direct route to Russia. For this reason, he was forced to resign from the government.

Again rejoining the army, Churchill saw action with the Second Grenadier Guards, rose to the rank of colonel, and commanded a battalion of the Royal Scots Fusiliers. He returned to England in 1916. The following year he became minister of munitions in David Lloyd George's coalition cabinet, where he threw his efforts behind the development and production of a new weapon, the tank.

After the war Churchill was transferred to the War Office. There, even as he presided over demobilization and urged a reduction in the military budget, he expressed a deeply felt concern over the rise of the Bolsheviks, who had seized power in Russia in 1917. As colonial secretary, a post he assumed in 1921, Churchill lent his support to the new government of Ireland. However, his chief concern was for the mandated territories in the Middle East, assigned to Great Britain by the League of Nations. His 1922 white paper affirmed the eventual status of Palestine as a Jewish national homeland, while pledging recognition of Arab rights. Under Churchill's leadership Great Britain created the emirate of Transjordan. However, his aggressive attitude toward the Turks over the Dardanelles led to squabbling within the fragile coalition government. In elections to form a new cabinet, Churchill was defeated by more than 10,000 votes.

Out of office, Churchill began writing *The World Crisis* (1923–1929), "perhaps the greatest work of war memoirs ever written," in Trevor-Roper's opinion. Royalties from this four-volume book enabled Churchill to purchase Chartwell, his country home. Running as a Constitutionalist in 1924, he was elected to Parliament and, to his surprise, appointed chancellor of the Exchequer by Stanley Baldwin, the new Conservative prime minister. During Churchill's five-year tenure, the government restored the gold standard. This fiscal decision indirectly led to economic deflation, a rise in unemployment, and, in 1926, a general strike.

Two years after the Conservatives were defeated in the 1929 elections, Churchill, who had rejoined that party, once again found himself out of office. His absence from government lasted a decade, during which time he opposed greater freedom for India, sided with Edward VIII in the king's wish to marry a divorced American woman, and warned the nation against the growing menace of Hitler's Germany. During this period he also wrote a comprehensive four-volume biography of his distinguished ancestor, *Marlborough: His Life and Times* (1933–1938). After Prime Minister Neville Chamberlain returned from Munich in 1938 claiming that he had secured "peace in our time," Churchill uttered a prophetic warning: "All over Europe the lights are going out."

With the outbreak of World War II, Churchill was again appointed first lord of the Admiralty and took immediate steps to combat German submarine warfare. Six months later the German invasion of Norway brought down Chamberlain's government and led to a coalition government with Churchill as prime minister and minister of defense. As German and Italian forces overran the Continent, Great Britain battled for survival. Churchill's efforts were directed at staving off German air attacks, courting the United States for assistance, and rallying his nation's sagging morale through the force of his leadership and the power of his oratory. After the British evacuation of Dunkirk, Churchill roused his nation with a now-famous declaration: "We shall defend our island whatever the cost may be. We shall fight on the beaches. We shall fight on the landing grounds. We shall fight in the fields and in the streets. We shall fight in the hills. We shall never surrender."

Churchill's close relationship with President Franklin D. Roosevelt was instrumental in obtaining lend-lease aid in March 1941; after the United States entered the war later that year, the friendship between the two leaders grew stronger. Throughout the war Churchill endeavored to maintain Allied unity. Drawing on his remarkable grasp of military strategy, he also directed the British theaters of war in Europe, North Africa, and Asia. As the war neared an end, he pressed first Roosevelt and later Harry S Truman to "join hands with the Russian armies as far to the east as possible" to curb Soviet designs on central Europe, but his warnings were ignored.

Though cherished as a national hero after the defeat of Germany, Churchill was replaced as prime minister by the Labour party candidate, Clement R. Attlee, in the 1945 elections. However, he remained active as a political thinker. Speaking in Fulton, Missouri, the following year, Churchill added the phrase *iron curtain* to the world's political lexicon. At Zurich in 1946 he proposed a United States of Europe that would include Germany. During his six-year absence from office he wrote *The Second World War* (1948–1954), a magisterial six-volume account of the conflict that is at once personal and sweeping in scope.

Although Churchill was returned to office as prime minister in 1951, a stroke forced him to resign four years later. He was awarded the 1953 Nobel Prize for Literature "for his mastery of historical and biographical description as well as for brilliant oratory in defending exalted human values." "Churchill's political and literary achievements are of such magnitude," said P. S. Siwertz of the Swedish Academy in his presentation address, "that one is tempted to portray him as a Caesar who also has the gift of Cicero's pen." Churchill's magnificent speeches loom above all his written volumes. As his fellow Englishman WILLIAM GOLDING remarked three decades later, "He got [the Nobel Prize] for those passionate utterances which were the very stuff of human courage and defiance. . . . Churchill's poetry of the fact changed history." Called to an international conference in the Bermudas, Churchill was unable to attend the Nobel ceremonies. His wife, who accepted the award on his behalf, read a brief acceptance speech.

Churchill, who was a talented amateur painter and skilled brick mason as well as a political and literary figure, was showered with honors during his lifetime. These included the Order of the Garter (1953), the Charlemagne Prize (1956), honorary citizenship in the United States (1963), and honorary degrees from more than twenty universities. After his retirement from public life, he published his four-volume *A History of the English-Speaking Peoples* between 1956 and 1958. His death in London at the age of ninety, which was followed by a state funeral of great pageantry, marked the end of an era of British history.

ADDITIONAL WORKS: London to Ladysmith via Pretoria, 1900; In Hamilton's March, 1900; Mr. Brodrick's Army, 1903; Lord Randolph Churchill, 1906; My African Journey, 1908; Liberalism and the Social Problem, 1909; The People's Rights, 1909; Irish Home Rule, 1912; The Aftermath, 1929; My Early Life, 1930; India, 1931; The Unknown War, The Eastern Front, 1931; Amid These Storms, 1932; Great Contemporaries, 1937; While England Slept, 1938; Step by Step, 1939; Britain's Strength, 1940; Blood, Sweat, and Tears, 1941; On Human Rights, 1941; The Unrelenting Struggle, 1942; The End of the Beginning, 1943; Onwards to Victory, 1944; Foreign Policy, 1944; The Dawn of Liberation, 1945; Into Battle, 1945; Secret Session Speeches, 1946; Victory, 1946; Painting as a Pastime, 1948;

CLAUDE

The Sinews of Peace, 1948; Europe Unite, 1950; Into the Balance, 1951; Stemming the Tide, 1953; The Unwritten Alliance, 1961; Young Winston's Wars, 1972; Churchill and Roosevelt (3 vols.) 1984, with Franklin D. Roosevelt.

ABOUT: Arthur, G. Concerning Winston Spencer Churchill, 1940; Ashley, M. Churchill as Historian, 1968; Bonham-Carter, V. Winston Churchill: An Intimate Portrait, 1965; Broad, L. Winston Churchill, 1963; Churchill, R. S., and Gilbert, M. Winston S. Churchill (7 vols.) 1966–1986; Colville, J. R. Winston Churchill and His Inner Circle, 1981; Cowles, V. S. Winston Churchill: The Man and the Era, 1953; Davenport, J., and Murphy, C. J. V. The Lives of Winston Churchill, 1945; Eade, C. (ed.) Churchill by His Contemporaries, 1953; Fowler, M. Winston S. Churchill, Philosopher and Statesman, 1985; Gardner, B. Churchill in Power, 1968; Gibert, M. Churchill's Political Philosophy, 1981; Hughes, E. Winston Churchill in War and Peace, 1950; Humes, J. C. Churchill: Speaker of the Century, 1980; Lewin, R. Churchill as War Lord, 1973; Longford, E. Winston Churchill, 1974; Manchester, W. The Last Lion, 1983; Nielson, F. Churchill's War Memoirs, 1979; Pelling, H. Winston Churchill, 1974; Prior, R. Churchill's World Crisis as History, 1983; Rodgers, J. Churchill, 1985; Schoenfeld, M. P. Sir Winston Churchill, 1986; Taylor, A. J. P., et al. Churchill Revised: A Critical Assessment, 1969; Thompson, K. W. Winston Churchill's World View, 1983; Wheeler-Bennet, J. (ed.) Action This Day, 1968; Wiedhorn, M. Sir Winston Churchill, 1979.

CLAUDE, ALBERT
(August 23, 1899–May 22, 1983)
Nobel Prize for Physiology or Medicine, 1974
(shared with Christian de Duve and George E. Palade)

The Belgian-American biologist Albert Claude (klōd) was born in Longlier, a small village in the Ardennes Forest. His father, Florentin Joseph Claude, was a baker; his mother, the former Marie-Glaudicine Watriquant, died of cancer when the boy was seven. Claude received his early education in a one-room schoolhouse and in later years was largely self-taught. During a depression in the years before World War I, he moved with his father, sister, and two brothers to the manufacturing town of Athus, where he worked for a time in a steel mill, first as an apprentice and later as a draftsman.

When an uncle suffered a cerebral hemorrhage, Claude, at the age of thirteen, returned to Longlier to help his aging aunt take care of him. As a result, he became friendly with his uncle's physician, who made frequent house calls and who impressed Claude by his experience, common sense, and equanimity. During World War I, Claude volunteered for the British Intelligence Service and was later cited for his bravery by WINSTON CHURCHILL, then Britain's war minister.

ALBERT CLAUDE

After the war Claude wanted to study medicine, but he lacked a high school diploma, the customary prerequisite for entrance to a university. In 1921 he passed an examination that allowed him to study at the School of Mining in Liège. At that point the Belgian government decreed that war veterans could attend a university even if they had no high school diploma, and in 1922 Claude entered the School of Medicine at the University of Liège. He obtained his doctorate in medicine and surgery in 1928. Claude later recalled his preoccupation with the light microscope during his student years, when he would spend hours "turning endlessly the micrometric screw . . . gazing at the blurred boundary, which concealed the mysterious ground substance where the secret mechanisms of cell life might be found." Failing in an attempt to isolate the granules that were visible in the cytoplasm of the cell under the microscope lens, he instead wrote his thesis on the effects of grafting mouse tumor cells onto rats.

This work won him a government scholarship for postgraduate study at the Cancer Institute in Berlin, where he soon came into conflict with the director of the institute, who maintained that cancer was caused by bacteria. Claude pointed out that the bacterial samples injected into experimental animals by the director—which had produced cancers—had been contaminated with tumor cells. As a consequence of this audacious statement, Claude was forced to leave the institute prematurely. However, he finished his scholarship in 1929 at the Kaiser Wilhelm Institute in the laboratory of Albert Fischer, a pioneer in techniques of tissue culture.

That year Claude designed a research program and sent it to Simon Flexner, then director of the Rockefeller Institute for Medical Research (now Rockefeller University) in New York City. In his program Claude proposed to isolate and identify the tumor agent of the Rous sarcoma (a tumor that occurs in chickens and is named after its discoverer, PEYTON ROUS). The possibility that tumors were caused by viruses was a consideration, and Claude wanted to explore the possibility in a specific tumor. When Flexner accepted him, Claude received a government scholarship for the work, and in the summer of 1929 he sailed to New York; he spent the next twenty years at the Rockefeller Institute.

To separate the tumor agent from the rest of the cell, Claude developed the technique of cell fractionation (the separation of cells into their component parts), which utilized a high-powered centrifuge, a machine that causes particle separation by centrifugal force. In Claude's early experiments, tissue containing the cells in question was first broken down into small particles in a meat grinder (more sophisticated methods were developed later). The tissue was then placed in a centrifuge, where the fragments of the cells separated according to their size and shape, thus making them available for individual study.

By the mid-1930s, Claude had completed his project. Working in the laboratory of James Murphy, he isolated the tumor agent from the rest of the cancerous cell. He then injected the agent into experimental animals and compared the rate of tumor appearance in these animals with the rate in a control set of animals. In this way he proved that the agent he had isolated was in fact the cause of the tumor. He then identified the agent as ribonucleic acid (RNA), known to be a constituent of viruses. It was the first evidence of the association of tumors with viruses.

After isolating and testing the chicken tumor agent, Claude continued using cell fractionation to study the components of normal cells. In the course of his experiments, he discovered that he could separate the cell's nucleus (the structure within the cell that contains the chromosomes) from the cytoplasm (the rest of the living material in the cell). He could then separate the specialized parts of the cell, including organelles (specialized parts of a cell that function as organs) and mitochondria (small granules or rod-shaped structures found in the cytoplasm of cells), from the cytoplasm; each

part of the cell could then be analyzed individually. In 1943 Claude reported that normal cells also contain particles of ribonucleic acid, which he called microsomes (later called ribosomes). It was later shown that the microsomes or ribosomes are the sites within the cell where protein is formed.

Claude published his studies of the mitochondrial fraction of the cell in 1945. With the assistance of the biochemists George Hogeboom and Rollin Hotchkiss, he had established that the mitochondria are the sites of respiration and energy generation within the cell, that is, the sites where oxygen combines with other molecules and energy is released.

Meanwhile, in 1941, Claude had become an American citizen. In 1942 the director of research at Interchemical Corporation asked him to work with the company's microscopist. Interchemical Corporation had the only electron microscope in New York, and Claude had expressed interest in its biological applications. Previously, only physicists and metallurgists had used this instrument, which bombarded the material being examined with electrons. The great potential advantage of the use of the instrument in biological research was that it would allow scientists to see structures within cells that were much too small to be observed with light microscopes. However, no one knew whether cells could tolerate the electron bombardment.

In the mid-1940s Claude and Keith Porter obtained the first electron micrographs (photographs taken through an electron microscope) of layers of cultured cells, revealing for the first time a lacelike network, or reticulum, of strands and small sacs or pouches. Porter named the network the endoplasmic reticulum, and it was later shown to specialize in the formation and transport of fats and proteins. As Claude and Porter continued to study normal cells under the electron microscope, they discovered a "new world" of microscopic cellular anatomy. In 1946 Claude published two articles on the basic principles of cell fractionation and the structure of cells as seen through the electron microscope. In 1948 he delivered the annual lecture of the Harvey Society in New York, summarizing his research experiences at the Rockefeller Institute and reviewing the structural and functional organization of the cell.

Claude chose to regain his Belgian citizenship in 1949, and the following year he moved to Brussels to become director of the Jules Bordet Institute. After retiring in 1971 he joined the faculty at the Catholic University in Louvain, where he once again conducted research. He was named director of the university's Laboratory of Cellular Biology and Oncology in 1972.

The 1974 Nobel Prize for Physiology or Medicine was shared by Claude, GEORGE E. PALADE, and CHRISTIAN DE DUVE "for their discoveries concerning the structural and functional organization of the cell." In his Nobel lecture Claude reminded his audience, "It is hardly more than a century since we first learned of the existence of the cell." He went on to say that the cell is an "autonomous and self-contained unit of living matter, which has acquired the knowledge and the power to reproduce; the capacity to store, transform, and utilize energy; and the capacity to accomplish physical works and to manufacture practically unlimited kinds of products."

Claude's marriage to Joy Gilder in 1935 produced a daughter, Philippa Claude, who became a neurobiologist. The marriage ended in divorce. Known for his candor and common sense, Claude was respected by his colleagues for his open-mindedness, tolerance, and fierce individuality. He died in Brussels on May 22, 1983.

In addition to the Nobel Prize, Claude was awarded the Louisa Gross Horwitz Prize of Columbia University (1970). He was a member of the French and Belgian academies of medicine and an honorary member of the American Academy of Arts and Sciences. He received the Grand Cordon of the Order of Leopold II from Belgium. He was awarded honorary degrees by Rockefeller University, the University of Liège, and the Catholic University of Louvain, among others.

ABOUT: New Scientist October 24, 1974; New York Times October 12, 1974; May 24, 1983; Science November 8, 1974.

COCKCROFT, JOHN
(May 27, 1897–September 18, 1967)
Nobel Prize for Physics, 1951
(shared with Ernest Walton)

The English physicist John Douglas Cockcroft was born in Todmorden, Yorkshire, the eldest of five sons of John Arthur and Maude (Fielden) Cockcroft. His father owned a small cotton mill, and three of his brothers went into the business, which had belonged to the family for five generations. John, however, an outstanding student and athlete, won a scholarship to the University of Manchester in 1914.

At Manchester, Cockcroft began studies in mathematics and attended lectures by the physicist ERNEST RUTHERFORD. Rutherford, who was acclaimed for his work on radioactivity and the atom, had identified alpha particles as the nuclei of helium atoms. Moreover, he had shown that atoms consist of a positively charged nucleus orbited by negatively charged electrons. This was a challenging time to be in the fields of mathematics and physics. Radioactivity had been discovered by HENRI BECQUEREL less than twenty years before, in 1896; and ALBERT EINSTEIN's special theory of relativity, published in 1905, was beginning to be incorporated into scientific thinking. World War I had broken out, however, and in 1915, after only one year at the university, Cockcroft volunteered for war service with the YMCA. He was called up for military duty later that year. Before he was discharged in 1918, he served on the western front and was promoted from signaler to officer in the Royal Field Artillery.

Returning to Manchester, Cockcroft changed his field to electrical engineering, in which he earned an M.S. in 1922. He then received a scholarship to study mathematics at St. John's College, Cambridge, where he earned a distinguished bachelor's degree in 1924 before joining Cambridge's Cavendish Laboratory as a junior research assistant. Four years later he received his Ph.D. At Cambridge, Cockcroft lectured in physics and performed mathematical and engineering research. Collaborating with the Russian physicist PYOTR KAPITZA, he designed transformer coils for intense magnetic fields. He also investigated the surface films produced by atomic beams.

Rutherford had been director of the Cavendish Laboratory since 1919, after showing that the atomic nucleus could be split by bombarding it with subatomic particles. Rutherford's atom splitting, accomplished by using naturally emitted alpha particles (helium nuclei) to change atoms of nitrogen into oxygen, opened a new field of experimental investigation. The next primary goal was to transmute atoms in far greater amounts than could be achieved by Rutherford's methods. Some researchers thought that this could be done by developing a technique for accelerating atomic particles in large quantities. Because positively charged particles are strongly repulsed by the positively charged atomic nucleus, extremely high accelerations would be required.

Many scientists in both Europe and the United States were racing to improve particle acceleration, using two different approaches. In the so-called direct method, a single surge

JOHN COCKCROFT

of high-voltage electricity would be used to supply the energy. The indirect method would accelerate particles by cycling them through a lower-voltage field several times. Of the two methods, the indirect appeared more promising to most researchers. Although it required more sophisticated equipment, it also used a more manageable amount of electricity than the direct method, which demanded high voltages that were difficult to produce with the equipment of that time.

Inspired by the theories of the Russian-born physicist George Gamow, Cockcroft was encouraged to develop the direct method. Gamow had calculated from quantum mechanics that because subatomic particles have wave properties, they would occasionally penetrate the nuclear barrier even when they lacked the force to overcome it. Gamow's equations explained how alpha particles could escape the nuclei of radioactive materials; but Cockcroft's insight was to perceive that the same principles would allow other particles to penetrate a nucleus, using considerably less energy than previously thought necessary.

With ERNEST WALTON, his associate at the Cavendish, Cockcroft developed a direct-method device capable of applying only 600,000 volts of electricity to a tube containing hydrogen. (Overcoming the nuclear barrier would have required several million volts.) Using this device, Cockcroft and Walton bombarded lithium with hydrogen nuclei, or protons, in April 1932. "Almost at once," Cockcroft later recalled, "at an energy of 125 kilovolts, Dr. Walton saw the bright scintillations characteristic

of alpha particles." They had transmuted lithium and hydrogen into helium, thus becoming the first scientists to split the atom by artificial means. Their achievement also provided experimental confirmation of Gamow's theory and demonstrated that the amount of energy released by atomic transmutation is precisely that predicted in Einstein's basic equation of relativity: $E = mc^2$.

During the 1930s Cockcroft continued his experiments using a variety of bombarding particles and atomic nuclei, such as boron and fluorine. After the discovery of artificial radioactive elements by FRÉDÉRIC JOLIOT and IRÈNE JOLIOT-CURIE, Cockcroft and Walton showed that they could also produce such elements by irradiation of boron and carbon with hydrogen nuclei. In 1934 Cockcroft, an able administrator, was appointed director of the Royal Society's Mond Laboratory in Cambridge. A year later, he aided Rutherford in reequipping the Cavendish Laboratory, including the installation of a cyclotron, an accelerator that had been invented by ERNEST O. LAWRENCE. (Indirect methods had been quickly perfected and were now becoming standard, even though the Cockcroft-Walton generator continued to be used as a proton source on some of the later, larger machines.)

In 1939 Cockcroft was appointed Jacksonian Professor of Natural Philosophy at Cambridge, but with the outbreak of World War II later that year, he again joined the British war effort, this time as a member of the Ministry of Supply. He was given major responsibility for developing and deploying radar, a key factor in Britain's successful air war with Germany. In 1940 he was sent to the United States as vice-chairman of the Tizard Commission, which negotiated an exchange of technical military information with American scientists before the United States entered the war. After returning from the United States, Cockcroft was appointed chief superintendent of Britain's Air Defense Research and Development Establishment. In 1944 he went to Canada to head the Atomic Energy Division of the National Research Council of Canada; this group contributed to the Manhattan Project, which designed and produced the first atomic bomb.

Cockcroft returned to England in 1946 to become head of the new Atomic Energy Research Establishment, which was responsible for developing the world's first nuclear power station at Calder Hall in northern England. Active in a number of fields, he was a member of the British Atomic Energy Authority and

CERN (the European Organization for Nuclear Research in Geneva, Switzerland). He founded what is now the Rutherford High-Energy Laboratory, a nonclassified nuclear research facility open to Britain's university research community.

Cockcroft and Walton shared the 1951 Nobel Prize for Physics "for their pioneer work on the transmutation of atomic nuclei by artificially accelerated atomic particles." In his presentation speech Ivar Waller of the Royal Swedish Academy of Sciences pointed out that through Cockcroft's and Walton's work "a verification was provided . . . for Einstein's law concerning the equivalence of mass and energy. Energy is liberated in the transmutation of lithium, because the total kinetic energy of the helium nuclei produced is greater than that of the original nuclei. According to Einstein's law," Waller went on, "this gain in energy must be paid for by a corresponding loss in the mass of the atomic nuclei."

In 1959 Cockcroft was appointed master of Churchill College, Cambridge. At the time of his death in 1967, Cockcroft had been elected president of the Pugwash Conferences on Science and World Affairs, and he was about to become chairman of the Liberal party.

Cockcroft married Eunice Elizabeth Crabtree, daughter of a cotton manufacturer, in 1925. They had four daughters and a son.

In addition to the Nobel Prize, Cockcroft received the Royal Medal of the Royal Society (1954), the Faraday Medal of the Institution of Electrical Engineers (1955), the Niels Bohr International Gold Medal of the Danish Society of Civil, Electrical, and Mechanical Engineers (1958), and the Atoms for Peace Award established by the Ford Motor Company Fund (1961). He was a member of the Royal Society as well as an honorary fellow of the American Academy of Arts and Sciences and the Royal Swedish Academy of Sciences. Cockcroft, who was knighted in 1948, received honorary degrees from Oxford University, the University of London, the University of Toronto, and the University of Glasgow.

SELECTED WORKS: The Development and Future of Nuclear Energy, 1950; Problems of Disarmament, 1962; The Future of Nuclear Power, 1965; Technology for Developing Countries, 1966.

ABOUT: Biographical Memoirs of Fellows of the Royal Society, volume 14, 1968; Current Biography November 1948; Dictionary of Scientific Biography, volume 3, 1971; Hartcup, G., and Allibone, T. E. Cockcroft and the Atom, 1984; Oxbury, H. (ed.) Great Britons, 1985.

COHEN, STANLEY
(November 17, 1922–   )
Nobel Prize for Physiology or Medicine, 1986
(shared with Rita Levi-Montalcini)

The American biochemist and zoologist Stanley Cohen was born in the Flatbush section of Brooklyn in New York City, one of four children of Louis and Fannie (Feitel) Cohen, who were Russian Jewish immigrants. His father was a tailor. The family was financially distressed during the Depression, but Cohen's parents insisted that their children become well educated. When Cohen contracted polio in childhood, it not only left him with a permanent limp but also had a profound emotional impact. Turning increasingly to intellectual pursuits as a student at James Madison High School, he developed a lasting devotion to science and classical music, at the same time learning to play the clarinet. He later said that he knew as a youth that his "main driving force is trying to understand, within my capabilities and talents, the world around me."

After graduating from high school, Cohen studied chemistry and zoology at Brooklyn College and received his B.A. in 1943. His academic achievements earned a scholarship to Oberlin College in Ohio, from which he obtained an M.A. in zoology in 1945. He proceeded to Ann Arbor, became a teaching fellow in biochemistry at the University of Michigan, and received his Ph.D. there in 1948 with a dissertation on metabolic functions in the earthworm.

Cohen spent the next four years as an instructor in the Department of Biochemistry and Pediatrics at the University of Colorado School of Medicine in Denver, where he and the American pediatrician Harry H. Gordon performed highly regarded studies on the metabolism of creatinine—a substance found in urine, muscle tissue, and blood—in premature and newborn infants. In 1952 Cohen moved to St. Louis, where he was an American Cancer Society postdoctoral fellow in the Washington University radiology department for one year and then associate professor in the zoology department for the next six years. In St. Louis he continued his research on the biochemistry of growth processes, and it was there, in collaboration with Viktor Hamburger and RITA LEVI-MONTALCINI, that he made his first major contribution to the field.

At the time, it was known that the addition of certain extracts from body organs and serum (the clear liquid remaining when clotted blood

STANLEY COHEN

solids are removed) can prolong the growth of cells in glass plates (in vitro). However, the controlling factors were unknown and extremely difficult to study. The subject touched on one of life's fundamental mysteries: how the union of genetic material from one egg cell and one sperm cell eventually produces billions of body cells organized into many different tissues with specialized functions. In 1952 Levi-Montalcini had shown that substances taken from certain tumors in mice could induce dramatic growth in parts of the nervous system of chick embryos. The active agent in these substances was called nerve growth factor (NGF). In 1953 Cohen joined the Washington University research group in attacking the intricate task of purifying and identifying NGF. Three years later, he and his colleagues achieved a concentrated growth-promoting extract from a mouse tumor. Composed of protein and nucleic acids, the extract was highly gelatinous and difficult to separate. To isolate the active component, Cohen added snake venom containing a concentration of an enzyme that destroys nucleic acids. To his surprise, the snake venom showed more NGF activity than the tumor extract itself. The discovery stimulated the search for NGF in other tissues, and in 1958 a rich source was found in the salivary gland of adult male mice. Cohen was then able both to purify NGF and to produce NGF antibodies. The chemical structure of NGF was later analyzed and found to consist of a chain of 118 amino acids. Two such chains join together to become biologically active. Cohen's achievement was of great value

for neurobiological research since it provided a well-defined chemical agent for stimulating nerve growth and another to inhibit its activity.

Washington University was a productive research center for scientists like Cohen. There, in the laboratory of CARL F. CORI and GERTY T. CORI, many now-illustrious biochemists and physiologists, including SEVERO OCHOA, Herman Kalckar, EARL W. SUTHERLAND JR., and Sidney Colowick, received their training. Cohen and Colowick formed a lifelong friendship and in 1959 both joined the medical school faculty of Vanderbilt University in Nashville, Tennessee, which had a strong interest in endocrinology (the study of hormone-secreting glands and other tissues) and the action of hormones. At Vanderbilt, Cohen continued his research on growth factors as an assistant professor of biochemistry, rising to associate professor in 1962 and full professor in 1967. In 1976 he was appointed an American Cancer Society research professor of biochemistry.

During earlier studies of the effects of NGF, Cohen had observed that newborn mice injected with an extract from the salivary gland of adult mice opened their eyelids by the seventh day instead of the usual thirteenth or fourteenth day. Moreover, their teeth appeared surprisingly early. To Cohen, though to no one else at the time, it seemed clear that "the opening of the eyelids of newborn mice was offering some kind of clue to the mystery of biological timing." He felt that "since nature has spent so many millions of years perfecting her processes, it must be of interest to know how we change the normal program." The answer was the existence of a second agent in salivary gland extract, which Cohen called epidermal growth factor (EGF) because it stimulated the growth of epithelial cells in the skin and cornea (epithelial cells form the covering of internal organs and external body surfaces). At Vanderbilt, Cohen devised an ingeniously simple method for isolating and purifying mouse EGF in relatively large quantities, and by 1972 he and his colleagues had determined the sequence of its fifty-three amino acids as well as three points at which the chain doubles back on itself to form closed loops. He also produced EGF antibodies. In 1975 he managed to isolate human EGF from the urine of pregnant women and established its amino-acid sequence. EGF became an important tool for research into the biochemical signals that regulate cell division and differentiation.

EGF was found to stimulate the growth of many types of cells and to enhance a variety

211

of biological processes. Using a radioactive tracer technique to study the interaction of EGF with EGF receptors (chemical groupings with a special affinity for EGF) on cell surfaces, Cohen and his co-workers elucidated the mechanism by which EGF and its receptors combined and were taken into the cell. This process involved, among other elements, an enzyme activity that proved to be a general phenomenon applicable to the understanding of the action of other growth factors, hormones, and cancer-inducing viruses. The work played a major role in the subsequent discovery by others of previously unknown growth factors and led to greater insights into the action of viruses and cancers.

NGF promises to have therapeutic value in the repair of damaged nerve tissues. EGF has been shown to stimulate the healing of wounds in the skin and cornea of animals, and clinical trials with human EGF are in progress. EGF may also be useful in improving the effectiveness of skin transplantation and the treatment of tumors that involve EGF or EGF-receptor defects.

The 1986 Nobel Prize for Physiology or Medicine was awarded to Cohen and Levi-Montalcini "in recognition of their discoveries which are of fundamental importance for our understanding of the mechanisms which regulate cell and organ growth." Cohen was cited for his meticulous documentation of the series of molecular events initiated by the interaction of EGF with its receptor, which established new principles widely applicable to other hormone-cell interactions.

In 1951 Cohen married Olivia Barbara Larson, with whom he had three children. After they were divorced, he married Jan Jordan in 1981. In addition to his love of classical music, he enjoys playing tennis. A longtime colleague has remarked that Cohen "comes from a generation when science was personal, and he still has calluses on his fingers." He is known to spend much of his time in the laboratory or pacing the corridor wearing old pants with pockets burned by his corncob pipe.

In addition to the Nobel Prize, Cohen's many honors include the Earl Sutherland Prize for Achievement in Research of Vanderbilt University (1978), the H. P. Robertson Memorial Award of the National Academy of Sciences (1981), the Lewis S. Rosenstiel Award for Distinguished Work in Basic Medical Research of Brandeis University (1982), the Louisa Gross Horwitz Prize of Columbia University (1983), the Gairdner Foundation International Award (1985), the National Medal of Science of the National Science Foundation (1986), and the Albert Lasker Basic Medical Research Award (1986). He is a member of the American Society of Biological Chemists, the International Institute of Embryology, the National Academy of Sciences, and the American Academy of Arts and Sciences. Cohen was awarded an honorary degree by the University of Chicago.

ABOUT: Alberts, B., et al. (eds.) Molecular Biology of the Cell, 1983; New York Times October 14, 1986; Science October 31, 1986; Science News May 21, 1977.

COMPTON, ARTHUR H.
(September 10, 1892–March 15, 1962)
Nobel Prize for Physics, 1927
(shared with C. T. R. Wilson)

The American physicist Arthur Holly Compton was born in Wooster, Ohio. His parents were Elias Compton, a Presbyterian minister, professor of philosophy, and dean of the College of Wooster, and Otelia Catherine (Augspurger) Compton. One of four children of keenly intellectual parents, Arthur showed an early interest in the natural sciences, collecting butterflies, studying paleontology, and reading about astronomy. After graduating from the College of Wooster in 1913 with a B.S., he entered Princeton University for graduate work in physics and received his M.A. in 1914. Two years later Compton earned his Ph.D. for a dissertation on the interaction of X rays with matter.

After teaching physics for a year at the University of Minnesota, Compton served for two years as a research engineer at the Westinghouse Lamp Company in Pittsburgh. There he worked on the design and construction of sodium vapor lamps and, after the United States entered World War I, helped develop aircraft instruments for the Signal Corps. At Westinghouse he also continued his X-ray research, which eventually led to his discovery of the effect named for him.

Attracted by pure research, Compton accepted a fellowship from the National Research Council in 1919 and spent that year at the Cavendish Laboratory at Cambridge University. It was an exciting time at Cavendish: Compton witnessed ERNEST RUTHERFORD's early atom-splitting experiments, which he later cited as a crucial experience in his scientific life. Since the Cavendish Laboratory did not have high-voltage X-ray equipment, Compton studied the scattering and absorption of gamma rays, which are energetic X rays emitted by

ARTHUR H. COMPTON

radioactive nuclei. He observed that radiation which had been scattered by a target was more easily absorbed by matter than primary radiation (the radiation used to bombard the target), but neither he nor his Cambridge colleagues could find an explanation for this observation that was in accord with the laws of classical physics.

During the first two decades of the twentieth century, physicists had begun to realize that classical physics failed to explain events occurring on an atomic or subatomic scale. MAX PLANCK, ALBERT EINSTEIN, NIELS BOHR, and others had developed a new theory to account for some subatomic phenomena, based on the radical notion that energy is quantized—that is, that energy can be transferred only in discrete units, or quanta. The quantum theory proved to be very useful in explaining certain previously mysterious effects, and it enabled Bohr to develop the most convincing model of the atom that had yet been proposed. However, in its early form, the quantum theory did not lend itself to the analysis of more general problems, and most physicists were not convinced of its fundamental importance. Between 1910 and 1920, Compton and others who were investigating the interaction of matter and energy continued to seek classical explanations for their experimental results.

After returning to the United States in 1920, Compton became chairman of the physics department at Washington University in St. Louis, Missouri, where he performed his most famous experiments. Using W. H. BRAGG's X-ray spectrometer, he made precise measurements of the wavelength of X rays that had been scattered from a target. The scattered radiation, Compton found, was of two types, one with a wavelength the same as that of the primary rays, the other with a longer wavelength. The increase in wavelength, which became known as the Compton effect, was proportional to the angle of the scattering. Once again, Compton's results defied explanation in terms of classical physics, but now Compton took the bold step of applying quantum theory to them. He found that he could explain the increases in wavelength by viewing X rays as particles, with values of energy and momentum that were predicted by quantum theory. An X-ray "energy particle," or quantum, colliding with an electron in the target gives up some of its energy to the electron; consequently, the particle has a lower energy after the collision, corresponding to a lower frequency—or longer wavelength—of radiation. Compton's new finding was in accord with his earlier discovery that scattered gamma rays were more absorbable than primary gamma rays: lower-energy (or longer-wavelength) radiation is more absorbable than higher-energy (or shorter-wavelength) radiation.

Since light, like X rays, is a form of electromagnetic radiation, the Compton effect provided strong support for Einstein's 1905 proposal that light behaves like a particle as well as a wave. The particlelike aspect of electromagnetic radiation is demonstrated by the interaction of the primary X rays with the electrons, while its wavelike aspect is demonstrated by the method of detecting the scattered rays—the functioning of the spectrometer can be explained only by considering X rays to be waves.

Compton published his results in 1923, the same year he accepted a professorship at the University of Chicago. He suggested that as X-ray quanta are scattered, the electrons with which they have collided are ejected from atoms at high velocity. Such recoil electrons, as Compton called them, were discovered and experimentally verified later that year by C. T. R. WILSON, whose invention of the cloud chamber made it possible to observe the tracks of electrically charged particles.

Compton's results created a stir among physicists, but his quantum interpretation was not immediately accepted because it conflicted with the ideas of J. J. THOMSON. The American physicist William Duane opposed Compton's theory and tried to show that Compton's data could be explained by another effect. Compton, Duane, and others conducted additional experiments, and in 1924 Duane withdrew his objections after finding excellent agreement between his own measurements and Compton's theory. Recognition of the Compton effect was an important stimulus to the development of quantum mechanics, a complex mathematical treatment of quantum theory with profound and far-reaching applications in physics and chemistry.

During the 1920s Compton conducted other significant X-ray research. In 1922, for example, he showed that X rays can be totally reflected from a smooth surface such as glass or metal, demonstrating that light and X rays behave in similar ways. In 1925 Compton and a colleague demonstrated this effect using the diffraction grating of a spectrometer to scatter X rays into their component wavelengths for analysis. Their work established the study of X rays as a branch of optics, which by itself would have earned Compton a reputation as an outstanding scientist.

Compton received the 1927 Nobel Prize for Physics "for his discovery of the effect named after him." He shared the award with C. T. R. Wilson. In his presentation speech, KAI SIEGBAHN of the Royal Swedish Academy of Sciences noted that the Compton effect "is now so important that, in the future, no atomic theory can be accepted that does not explain it and lead to the laws established by its discoverer."

After his work on the Compton effect, Compton developed ways to determine experimentally the distribution of electrons in atoms. Together with the measurements of X-ray energies by Kai Siegbahn, this work laid the foundation for subsequent theories of atomic structure. Compton's experimental work also contributed to an understanding of the magnetism of ferromagnetic materials, such as iron.

In the early 1930s Compton became interested in cosmic rays (radiation that strikes the earth from space), because the interaction of gamma rays and electrons in cosmic rays offers an important example of the Compton effect. Between 1931 and 1933 he led expeditions to many parts of the world to obtain cosmic-ray data. On the basis of this information, he rediscovered the variation in intensity of cosmic rays with the earth's latitude, a phenomenon first observed in the 1920s by Jacob Clay. Compton correctly explained the variation by showing that, contrary to prevailing thought, cosmic rays are affected by the earth's magnetic field and consist, at least in part, of charged particles.

In 1941 Compton was appointed chairman of the physics department and dean of the physical sciences division at the University of Chicago. Later that year he headed a National Academy of Sciences committee that was convened to study the potential use of atomic energy for military purposes. The group's favorable recommendation led to the establishment of the Manhattan Project. From 1942 to 1945 Compton served as director of the branch of the project known as the Metallurgical Laboratory at the University of Chicago. There, under the guidance of ENRICO FERMI, the first nuclear reactor was constructed. Later, Compton oversaw construction of the Oak Ridge National Laboratory in Tennessee, which was devoted to the separation of uranium 235 from the more common uranium 238.

When Compton was offered the chancellorship of Washington University in 1945, he decided to accept and left Chicago, even though the new position brought an end to his research. After resigning as chancellor in 1954, he remained at Washington as Distinguished Service Professor of Natural Philosophy. He resigned from this position in 1961, planning to divide his time among Washington University, the College of Wooster, and the University of California at Berkeley.

In 1916 Compton married Betty Charity McCloskey, with whom he had two sons. For the rest of his professional life he maintained such a close partnership with his wife that, at his insistence, she received the same clearance he did during his World War II work. A man of distinguished appearance, Compton was regarded as an inspiring, enthusiastic teacher and researcher. Devoutly religious, he served as general chairman of the Laymen's Missionary Movement from 1934 until 1948 and participated actively in the National Conference of Christians and Jews. He died of a cerebral hemorrhage on March 15, 1962, in Berkeley, California.

Compton's many honors included the Rumford Medal of the American Academy of Arts and Sciences (1927), the Hughes Medal of the Royal Society of London (1940), the Franklin Medal of the Franklin Institute (1940), and the Medal for Merit of the United States government (1946). He received honorary degrees from many universities, including Yale, Princeton, and Harvard. Compton was a member of the American Association for the Advancement of Science, the American Philosophical Society, the American Physical Society, the National Academy of Sciences, and the New York Academy of Sciences, among others, as well as an honorary member of more than twenty foreign scientific societies.

SELECTED WORKS: The Freedom of Man, 1935; X Rays in Theory and Experiment, 1935, with S. K. Allison; The Human Meaning of Science, 1940; The Birth of Atomic Energy and Its Human Meaning, 1947; Man's Destiny in Eternity, 1949; Atomic Quest: A Personal Narrative, 1956; Scientific Papers of Arthur Holly Compton, 1973.

ABOUT: Biographical Memoirs of the National Academy of Sciences, volume 38, 1965; Blackwood, J. R. The House on College Avenue: The Comptons at Wooster, 1968; Dictionary of Scientific Biography, volume 3, 1971; Johnson, M. (ed.) The Cosmos of Arthur Holly Compton, 1967; Stuewer, R. H. The Compton Effect, 1975.

COOPER, LEON N
(February 28, 1930–   )
Nobel Prize for Physics, 1972
(shared with John Bardeen and J. Robert Schrieffer)

LEON N COOPER

The American physicist Leon N Cooper was born in New York City to Irving Cooper and the former Anna Zola. Growing up in New York, he attended the Bronx High School of Science and then entered Columbia University, where he majored in physics. He received his B.A. in 1951, his M.A. in 1953, and his Ph.D. in 1954. During his years at Columbia, Cooper's principal interest was quantum field theory, which describes the interaction of particles and fields in systems of atomic or subatomic size.

A National Science Foundation fellowship enabled Cooper to spend the academic year 1954–1955 at the Institute for Advanced Study in Princeton, New Jersey, followed by two years of postdoctoral work under JOHN BARDEEN at the University of Illinois. Bardeen was studying superconductivity and other properties of matter at temperatures only a few degrees above absolute zero ($-273°C$).

The Dutch physicist HEIKE KAMERLINGH ONNES had discovered in 1911 that when some metals are cooled to within a few degrees of absolute zero, they lose all resistance to the flow of electricity, a phenomenon known as superconductivity. His observations, highly puzzling at the time, were not fully understood for several decades.

As they cool, nearly all metals increase in conductivity because the thermal vibrations of their atoms create electrical resistance by scattering the electrons that carry an electric current. Cooling the metal reduces the amplitude of the vibrations and thus improves conduc-

tivity. As the temperature falls, this improvement takes place gradually in normal metals, whereas in a superconductor all electrical resistance disappears at some temperature above absolute zero. Although its atoms continue to vibrate, the current-carrying electrons seem to flow without impediment.

Around 1950 studies of superconductivity were undertaken in metals that have several isotopes (forms of the element with the same number of protons and electrons—and hence the same chemical properties—but different numbers of neutrons). It was found that the critical temperature at which an isotope becomes superconducting is inversely proportional to the isotope's atomic mass. Atomic mass alters the properties of a solid only through its effect on the propagation of vibrations in the crystalline structure of the substance. This observation led Bardeen to propose that superconductivity depends on the interaction of electrons with atomic vibrations. Bardeen and his colleagues had been studying these interactions for several years before Cooper joined them in 1956.

Within a short time, Cooper demonstrated that the interaction between electrons and the crystal lattice creates bound pairs of electrons. As it moves through the metallic crystal, one electron attracts the surrounding, positively charged atoms, producing a slight deformation of the crystal lattice. This deformation in turn creates a momentary concentration of positive charge which then attracts the second electron. In this way, the two electrons are bound together through the intermediate action of the crystal lattice, forming what is known as a Cooper pair.

Building on this discovery, J. ROBERT SCHREIFFER, a graduate student at Illinois who was also studying under Bardeen, discovered a method for analyzing the motions of large numbers of pairs of interacting electrons. Within a month, he, Bardeen, and Cooper had extended Schrieffer's model into a general theory of superconductivity. Called the BCS theory, after the initials of the three scientists, it states that the interaction between Cooper pairs allows a large fraction of the free electrons in the superconducting material to behave cooperatively. In the resulting coherent state, the electrons move in lockstep. Below the critical temperature, the pairing force that holds the electrons in their coordinated motion is stronger than the thermal vibrations of the metal atoms. A disturbance that would deflect an individual electron, and therefore give rise to electrical resistance, cannot do so in a superconductor without affecting all the electrons participating in the superconducting state. This event is unlikely, and so the paired electrons drift coherently without loss of energy. The BCS theory is widely regarded as one of the most important contributions to theoretical physics since the development of the quantum theory.

Cooper and his two colleagues shared the 1972 Nobel Prize for Physics "for their jointly developed theory of superconductivity, usually called the BCS theory." Cooper's Nobel lecture discussed microscopic quantum interference effects in the theory of superconductivity. While acknowledging the practical applications of his work, he noted that "a theory (though it may guide us in reaching them) does not produce the treasures the world holds. A theory is more. It is an ordering of experience that both makes experience meaningful and is a pleasure to regard in its own right."

From 1957 to 1958 Cooper was an assistant professor of physics at Ohio State University, followed by an appointment as an associate professor at Brown University. He served as Goddard University Professor at Brown from 1966 to 1974, when he became Watson Professor of Science with a concurrent appointment as codirector of Brown's Center for Neural Sciences. Much of his work has been an attempt to develop a theory of the central nervous system. He is especially interested in how neuronal modification leads to the organization of distributed memories. With a colleague, Charles Elbaum, Cooper developed a software system capable of recognizing and transforming handwritten letters into typed characters. The system was introduced by the International Business Machines Corporation (IBM) in 1987.

Cooper and his wife, the former Kay Anne Allard, were married in 1969 and have two daughters.

In addition to the Nobel Prize, Cooper has been awarded the Comstock Prize of the National Academy of Sciences (1968) and the Descartes Medal of René Descartes University (1977). He holds honorary degrees from Columbia University, the University of Sussex, the University of Illinois, Brown University, and Ohio State University. He is a member of the American Academy of Arts and Sciences, the American Physical Society, the National Academy of Sciences, the American Philosophical Society, and the Federation of American Scientists.

SELECTED WORKS: An Introduction to the Meaning and Structure of Physics, 1968; The Physics and Applications of Superconductivity, 1968, with Brian Schwartz.

ABOUT: New Scientist October 26, 1972; New York Times October 21, 1972; Parks, R. D. (ed.) Superconductivity, 1969; Science November 3, 1972.

CORI, CARL F.

(December 5, 1896–October 19, 1984)
Nobel Prize for Physiology or Medicine, 1947
(shared with Gerty T. Cori and Bernardo Houssay)

The Austrian-American biochemist Carl Ferdinand Cori (kôr′ i) was born in Prague, Czechoslovakia (then part of Austria-Hungary), the son of Maria (Lippich) Cori and Carl I. Cori, a professor of zoology at the University of Prague and director of the Marine Biology Station in Trieste. After receiving his early education in Prague and Trieste, Cori enrolled in the German University of Prague in 1914 to study medicine. His work was soon interrupted by the outbreak of World War I, during which he served in the Austrian army as a sanitation officer on the Italian front.

When he returned to the university to complete his medical studies, Cori met Gerty Theresa Radnitz, another medical student, whom he married in 1920. That year Cori received his medical degree from the University of Prague, and during the next two years, he served as assistant at the First Medical Clinic

CARL F. CORI

of Vienna and later as assistant in pharmacology at the University of Graz. Meanwhile, GERTY T. CORI worked as an assistant at the Karolinen Children's Hospital in Vienna.

Cori's work came to the attention of the New York State Institute for the Study of Malignant Diseases (later, the Roswell Park Memorial Institute) in Buffalo, New York; in 1922 the institute offered him a position as a staff biochemist. Leaving his wife temporarily in Europe, Cori sailed for the United States. Once in Buffalo, he found her a position as assistant pathologist at the institute, where she later became an assistant biochemist.

Since the Coris were especially interested in carbohydrate metabolism in normal and malignant tissue, during their early years in Buffalo they concentrated on the metabolism of carbohydrates in tumor cells. They also investigated the effects of ovariectomy (surgical removal of the ovaries) on tumor-cell growth.

In 1929, a year after he and his wife became American citizens, Cori was appointed assistant professor of physiology at the University of Buffalo. Two years later the Coris moved to Washington University School of Medicine in St. Louis, Missouri, where he was appointed professor of pharmacology and she was named a fellow and research associate in pharmacology and biochemistry. There they continued their research on carbohydrate metabolism, focusing on the biochemistry of glucose and glycogen.

Glycogen had been known since 1857, when the French physiologist Claude Bernard discovered large quantities of the starchlike substance in the liver cells of experimental animals. Composed of glucose molecules linked together in chains, glycogen is the biochemical form in which glucose is stored in liver and muscle cells. Glucose, the principal energy source for living cells, is a simple sugar molecule containing hydrogen, oxygen, and six carbon atoms.

Dietary starch (in the form of amylose and amylopectin) is converted into glucose in the small intestine by the pancreatic enzyme amylase. The glucose is then absorbed into the portal bloodstream and carried to the liver, where it is converted to glycogen and stored for future use. Normally, the liver stores approximately a three-day supply of glucose in this form. In the 1930s and 1940s, the Coris performed a series of experiments that clarified the biochemical reactions involved in the conversion both of glucose to glycogen and glycogen to glucose. The complete cycle of glucose-glycogen interconversion is known as the Cori cycle.

In 1936 the Coris discovered glucose-1-phosphate, later known as the Cori ester (a type of chemical bond). During this time the Coris also discovered the biochemical mechanism of the action of insulin, a hormone that is synthesized and secreted by the islet cells of the pancreas. (A deficiency of insulin is the cause of the disease diabetes mellitus, in which glucose cannot be normally taken up and utilized as an energy source by cells.)

In 1938 the Coris first described the conversion of glucose-1-phosphate to glucose-6-phosphate (and the reverse process) by the enzyme phosphoglucomutase. They isolated and purified phosphorylase in crystalline form in 1943, and, finding that the enzyme exists in both an active and an inactive form, they were able to establish the biochemical conditions under which the inactive form is activated.

The following year the Coris synthesized glycogen in a test tube, starting with a primer molecule of glycogen, glucose, phosphate, and three enzymes (hexose kinase, phosphoglucomutase, and phosphorylase), thereby verifying their hypothesis of a three-step biochemical pathway from glucose to glycogen. It was also in 1944 that Cori was appointed professor of biochemistry at Washington University School of Medicine. Two years later he became chairman of the biochemistry department.

Carl and Gerty Cori were awarded the 1947 Nobel Prize for Physiology or Medicine "for their discovery of the course of the catalytic conversion of glycogen." They shared the prize with the Argentine physiologist BERNARDO HOUSSAY. In his presentation address, HUGO THEORELL of the Karolinska Institute declared that the Coris' work had "elucidated in great detail the extremely complicated enzymatic mechanism involved in the reversible reactions between glucose and glycogen," a discovery he described as "one of the most brilliant achievements in modern biochemistry" and one responsible for "a new conception of how hormones and enzymes cooperate."

After retiring from Washington University in 1966, Cori was appointed visiting professor of biochemistry at Harvard University School of Medicine, where he continued his research until the final years of his life. He died in 1984 at his home in Cambridge, Massachusetts, at the age of eighty-seven.

In addition to their scientific collaboration, the Coris climbed mountains together, played tennis, ice-skated, and worked in their garden. They had one son. After Gerty Cori's death in 1957, Cori married Ann Fitz-Gerald Jones, a resident of St. Louis, who had two daughters and two sons by a previous marriage.

Cori was the recipient of the Lasker Award of the American Public Health Association (1946), the Squibb Award of the Society of Endocrinologists jointly with his wife (1947), and the Willard Gibbs Medal of the American Chemical Society (1948). He was a member of the National Academy of Sciences, the American Association for the Advancement of Science, the American Philosophical Society, the American Society of Biological Chemists, and the American Chemical Society. He was awarded honorary degrees by Western Reserve (now Case Western Reserve) University; Yale, Boston, Cambridge, St. Louis, Brandeis, and Washington universities; and Gustavus Adolphus College.

ABOUT: Current Biography, December 1947; National Cyclopedia of American Biography, volume H, 1952; New York Times October 22, 1984.

CORI, GERTY T.

(August 15, 1896–October 26, 1957)
Nobel Prize for Physiology or Medicine, 1947
(shared with Carl F. Cori and Bernardo Houssay)

The Austrian-American biochemist Gerty Theresa Radnitz Cori (kôr' i) was born in Prague, then part of Austria-Hungary and now the capital of Czechoslovakia. The eldest of three daughters of Martha (Neustadt) and Otto Radnitz, a businessman and manager of a sugar refinery, she received her early education from private tutors and at the *Realgymnasium* in Tetschen (now Děčín, Czechoslovakia), from which she graduated in 1914. That year, encouraged by her uncle, a professor of pediatrics, she enrolled in the German University of Prague to study medicine. At the university she met CARL F. CORI, another medical student, with whom she did research on serum complement, a set of biological compounds involved in immunological reactions. During 1917–1918 she served as a medical demonstrator at the German University, from which she received her medical degree in 1920, the same year that she married Carl Cori.

Shortly after their marriage, the Coris moved to Vienna. There, for the next two years, Gerty Cori worked as an assistant at the Karolinen Children's Hospital, investigating cretinism (congenital thyroid deficiency). In 1922 her husband obtained a position as staff biochemist at the New York State Institute for the Study of Malignant Diseases (later the Roswell Park Memorial Institute), in Buffalo, New York. Once in Buffalo, he found a position for her as assistant pathologist at the institute, where she later became an assistant biochemist. Soon the Coris were working together again. Since they were particularly interested in carbohydrate metabolism in normal and malignant tissue, during their early years in Buffalo they concentrated on the metabolism of carbohydrates in tumor cells. They also investigated the effects of ovariectomy (surgical removal of the ovaries) on tumor-cell growth.

In 1931, three years after becoming American citizens, the Coris moved to St. Louis, Missouri, where Cori was a fellow and research associate in pharmacology and biochemistry at the Washington University School of Medicine, and her husband was professor of pharmacology. Continuing their investigation of carbohydrate metabolism, the Coris paid particular attention to the biochemistry of glucose and glycogen. Glycogen was identified in 1857 by the French physiologist Claude Bernard, who discovered large amounts of the starchlike substance in the liver cells of experimental animals. Glycogen is composed of glucose molecules linked in chains and is the form in which glucose is stored in liver and muscle cells. Glucose, the principal energy source of cells, is a simple sugar molecule composed of hydrogen, oxygen, and carbon.

Dietary starch (in the form of amylose and amylopectin) is converted into glucose in the

GERTY T. CORI

small intestine by the pancreatic enzyme amylase. Absorbed into the portal bloodstream and carried to the liver, glucose is then converted to glycogen and stored for future use. In a series of experiments performed in the 1930s and 1940s, the Coris elucidated the biochemical reactions involved in the processes of glucose-glycogen and glycogen-glucose conversion. The complete cycle of this interconversion is known as the Cori cycle.

In 1936 the Coris discovered glucose-1-phosphate, which came to be known as the Cori ester (a type of chemical bond). Later in the 1930s the Coris discovered the biochemical mechanism of action of insulin, a hormone that is synthesized and secreted by the islet cells of the pancreas. A deficiency of insulin causes the disease diabetes mellitus, in which glucose cannot be taken up normally and utilized as an energy source by cells.

The Coris first described the transformation of glucose-6-phosphate into glucose-1-phosphate (and the reverse process) by the enzyme phosphoglucomutase in 1938. Five years later, when isolating and purifying the phosphorylase enzyme in crystalline form, they discovered that phosphorylase exists in both an active and an inactive form, which they called phosphorylase a and phosphorylase b, respectively. They subsequently were able to establish the biochemical conditions under which the inactive form is activated.

In 1944 the Coris synthesized glycogen in a test tube, starting with a primer molecule of glycogen, glucose, phosphate, and three enzymes (hexose kinase, phosphoglucomutase,

and phosphorylase). The synthesis confirmed their hypothesis of a three-step biochemical pathway from glucose to glycogen. Gerty Cori later discovered a fifth enzyme that is involved in the synthesis and degradation of a branched form of liver- and plant-cell glycogen. That year, she was appointed associate professor of biochemistry at the Washington University School of Medicine; three years later she became professor of biochemistry.

The Coris were awarded the 1947 Nobel Prize for Physiology or Medicine "for their discovery of the course of the catalytic conversion of glycogen." They shared the prize with the Argentine physiologist, BERNARDO HOUSSAY. On presenting the award, HUGO THEORELL of the Karolinska Institute pointed out that "for a chemist, synthesis is the definite proof of how a substance is built up. Professor and Doctor Cori have accomplished the astounding feat of synthesizing glycogen in a test tube, with the help of a number of enzymes, which they have prepared in a pure state and whose mode of action they have revealed. This would be impossible by methods of organic chemistry alone. . . . The Cori enzymes made this synthesis possible, because the enzymes favor certain modes of linkage." Theorell went on to describe the Coris' elucidation of the enzymatic mechanism responsible for reversible glucose reactions as "one of the most brilliant achievements in modern biochemistry."

In subsequent work Cori discovered the chemical structure of glycogen and, in the early 1950s, identified the biochemical defects that cause glycogen-storage disease. In this condition, abnormally high levels of glycogen accumulate in liver cells and other tissues. She went on to show that the disease is in fact a group of disorders that result from deficiencies of specific enzymes.

In the last years of her life Cori suffered from myelosclerosis, a long and painful illness in which normal bone marrow tissue is progressively replaced by fibrous tissue. After her death in 1957 in Glendale, Missouri, scientists from all over the United States attended a memorial service held in St. Louis. During the service, a tape recording that she had made for Edward R. Murrow's "This I Believe" television series was played. "For a research worker," she said, "the unforgotten moments of his life are those rare ones, which come after years of plodding work, when the veil over nature's secret seems suddenly to lift and when what is dark and chaotic appears in a clear and beautiful light and pattern." Houssay once described her life as "a noble example of dedication to an ideal . . . to the advancement of science for the benefit of humanity."

The Coris' close collaboration extended beyond the laboratory. They were both outdoor enthusiasts who enjoyed mountain climbing in the Austrian Alps and later in the American Rockies. Among their other interests were tennis, ice skating, and gardening. They had one son.

Cori was awarded the Squibb Award of the Society of Endocrinologists in 1947 (with her husband), the Garvan Medal of the American Chemical Society (1948), and the Borden Award in the Medical Sciences of the Association of American Medical Colleges (1951). She was a member of the American Society of Biological Chemists, the National Academy of Sciences, the American Chemical Society, and the American Philosophical Society, and she held honorary degrees from Boston University, Smith College, Yale University, Columbia University, and the University of Rochester.

ABOUT: Annual Review of Biochemistry, volume 38, 1969; Current Biography December 1947; Dictionary of American Biography, supplement 6, 1980; Dictionary of Scientific Biography, volume 3, 1971; Science July 4, 1958; Yost, E. Women of Modern Science, 1959.

CORMACK, ALLAN
(February 23, 1924–   )
Nobel Prize for Physiology or Medicine, 1979
(shared with Godfrey Hounsfield)

The American physicist Allan MacLeod Cormack was born in Johannesburg, South Africa, the youngest of three children of George Cormack, a civil service engineer, and Amelia (MacLeod) Cormack, a teacher. Both parents had emigrated to South Africa from Scotland before World War I. When the boy was twelve years old, his father died and the family moved to Cape Town. He attended the Rondebosch Boys High School, where he displayed a strong interest in astronomy, physics, and mathematics. He also enjoyed tennis, debating, and acting.

After graduating from high school, Cormack decided that "the prospects for making a living as an astronomer were not good" and enrolled in the University of Cape Town to study electrical engineering. Within two years his interest had shifted to physics, in which he received a B.S. in 1944, followed by an M.S. the next year. While in college, he became an

ALLAN CORMACK

avid mountaineer and developed a lasting love of music.

Later Cormack worked as a research student in the Cavendish Laboratory at Cambridge University, England, where he investigated radioactive helium under Otto Frisch and attended P. A. M. Dirac's lectures on quantum mechanics. After writing to the head of the physics department at the University of Cape Town, he received an appointment as lecturer in physics. In 1956 he also became a part-time medical physicist at the Groote Schuur Hospital.

Cape Town lacked the advanced laboratory facilities Cormack had enjoyed at Cambridge, and he also felt isolated from other nuclear physicists. According to Cormack, however, R. W. James, head of the physics department at the university, gave him sufficient freedom to study and to publish several scientific papers. In the radiology department of Groote Schuur Hospital, he supervised the use of radioisotopes and performed such tasks as calibrating film badges that indicated the amount of radiation received by hospital workers. It was his observations of radiation treatment of cancer patients that led to the work for which he received the Nobel Prize.

Cormack perceived the need for accurate information about the absorption of X rays by different body tissues to aid in planning radiation doses administered to tumors. In thinking about how to measure such absorption properties, he realized that they could also have diagnostic value, for example, in locating tumors more precisely. Conventional

X-ray images were not adequate for these purposes.

X-ray techniques originated in the late nineteenth century, when WILHELM RÖNTGEN discovered and named X rays and made the first X-ray pictures, of his wife's hand. In this technique, a relatively broad stream of X rays passes through the hand or other object onto a sensitive film. X-ray energy reaching different parts of the film varies because of differences in internal absorption along different paths through the object. Dense tissue such as bone is very absorptive and greatly weakens the beam passing through it; soft tissues and body fluids are far less absorptive; and air is even less so. Where the bones in Röntgen's wife's hand (and the ring on her finger) lay in the path of the beam, they cast shadows on the film, much as a tree in sunlight casts a shadow on a lawn. Since developing darkens the film according to the amount of X-ray energy it receives, the shadows of the bone and the ring appeared white.

The X-ray image represents only the effect of total absorption along each path. It cannot distinguish the contributions of different absorbing tissues in line along the same path. This presents special difficulties in X-ray images of the head, for example, where the bony skull is the dominant absorber and masks soft brain tissue. Cormack realized that a series of X-ray measurements in which the beam passed through the object at many different angles would supply the information needed to reveal absorptions by individual interior regions.

Although it was reasonable to suppose that multiple X-ray measurements would contain the desired information, there remained the mathematical problem of interpreting the mass of data to achieve a reconstruction of interior detail. The problem was somewhat simplified by assuming that the X-ray beam would always pass through the object in the same plane, in effect probing a thin slice of material and resulting in a two-dimensional cross section. By repeating the measurements in a series of closely spaced parallel planes, a three-dimensional reconstruction could be achieved.

Such a thin-slice X-ray image is now called a tomogram, from the Greek word *tomos,* meaning "section." The technique became known as computer-assisted (or computerized axial) tomography (CAT), or CAT scanning. It is also called simply computerized tomography (CT), or CT scanning. Cormack developed a mathematical procedure for analyzing the X-ray data and continued to refine it for several years, in his spare time.

In 1956 Cormack took a sabbatical leave to conduct research in the cyclotron laboratory at Harvard University in Cambridge, Massachusetts. (A cyclotron accelerates atomic particles to very high speeds; their high-energy collisions with targets, such as other particles, yield useful data about atomic structure and interactions.) There he studied the interactions of protons and neutrons and also formed a lasting friendship with Andreas Koehler, director of the laboratory. After a brief period back in Cape Town in 1957, Cormack returned to the United States to become an assistant professor of physics at Tufts University in Medford, Massachusetts.

While in Cape Town, and later in Medford, Cormack conducted experiments to test his mathematical method. His early trials involved the use of cobalt 60 gamma rays, for which the principle is the same as for X rays. He collimated the rays into a thin, pencillike beam in line, with a Geiger counter as a detector on the opposite side of a simulated body. At first, in Cape Town, the body consisted of a concentric arrangement of an aluminum cylinder surrounded by a ring of wood, thus providing two materials with different absorbing properties. The beam source and detector were fixed, while the aluminum-wood cylinder was mounted on a platform so that it could be moved to different positions relative to the beam for scanning. The method not only worked but also unexpectedly detected a core in the aluminum of different density from the main body. Cormack repeated the experiment later, in Medford, with a more complicated simulation: a ring of aluminum representing the skull, a plastic interior representing soft (brain) tissue, and two aluminum disks representing tumors. Again he was successful. In 1963 and 1964 he published two papers on his mathematical procedure and experimental results, hoping to excite interest among radiological physicists. The papers received no significant response. Cormack had, however, successfully proven the feasibility of his method for producing cross sections of a body, showing interior detail, on the basis of differences in X-ray absorptivity. At that time, it was only a laboratory demonstration using mechanical simulations, but computers had already been applied to speed the mathematical calculations. The results were displayed generally as graphs rather than as photographlike images.

Cormack then continued his research in particle physics at Tufts University, and he became an American citizen in 1966. He eventually rose to the academic rank of associate professor and then full professor of physics at Tufts, where he served as chairman of the physics department from 1968 to 1976.

In the late 1960s and early 1970s, GODFREY HOUNSFIELD, a research scientist at Electrical and Musical Instruments Limited (EMI), an English conglomerate, independently developed a similar but more practical method for performing CAT scans. He was greatly helped by the availability of modern computers. In 1971 the first clinical CAT scanner was installed at Atkinson Morley's Hospital in Wimbledon, England, and studies were performed on patients with brain tumors and other brain diseases. In April 1972, EMI announced the production of the first commercial CAT scanner, the EMI CT 1000. Clinical testing of the EMI CT 1000 scanner made it immediately clear that CAT scanning represented a significant advance over other techniques then available for obtaining radiological images of human tissues.

A commercial CAT scanner has four main components: an X-ray generator; a scanning unit (X-ray tube and detector); a computer to calculate X-ray attenuation due to absorption in the tissue being scanned; and an oscilloscope-and-printer unit for displaying the computed patterns of X-ray absorption. The patient is held still while the beam and scanning unit rotate around the patient's head, taking several hundred thousand measurements of brain-tissue X-ray attenuation, from which a two-dimensional cross section is constructed. By sliding the patient in steps along the axis of rotation, successive cross sections can be accumulated to produce a three-dimensional representation. (In some models, a large number of detectors are fixed in a circle, and only the X-ray source rotates.)

Hounsfield has said that the CAT scanner is 100 times as efficient as a conventional X ray, because it uses all the information it gathers, whereas the X ray records only about 1 percent. The scanner is also more sensitive and requires less energy per view than a conventional X ray, although the total exposure is about the same because of the large number of views required. More importantly, the scanner clearly differentiates soft tissues from their surroundings, in spite of only small differences in X-ray absorption. It is thus better able to distinguish between normal and abnormal tissue. Although initially used for brain scanning, the scanner is now applied to virtually all parts of the body.

Cormack was awarded the 1979 Nobel Prize for Physiology or Medicine "for the development of computer-assisted tomography," an honor he shared with Hounsfield. In his Nobel lecture Cormack explained the impetus for his research: "It occurred to me that in order to improve treatment planning, one had to know the distribution of the attenuation coefficient of tissues in the body, and that this distribution had to be found by measurements made external to the body. It soon occurred to me that this information would be useful for diagnostic purposes and would constitute a tomogram or series of tomograms, though I did not learn the word *tomogram* for many years."

In 1980 Cormack was appointed University Professor at Tufts University, the highest professorial rank at the university, and in 1980 he was awarded an honorary doctor of science degree.

In 1950 Cormack married Barbara Seavey; they have a son and two daughters. Cormack leads a rather sedentary life; he spends some time swimming and sailing and much of his time reading and listening to music.

He is currently an associate editor of the *Journal of Computed Tomography,* a member of the South African Institute of Physics, a fellow of the American Physical Society, and a fellow of the American Academy of Arts and Sciences.

ABOUT: New Scientist October 18, 1979; New York Times October 12, 1979; Physics Today December 1979; Science November 30, 1979.

CORNFORTH, JOHN W.
(September 7, 1917–)
Nobel Prize for Chemistry, 1975
(shared with Vladimir Prelog)

The Australian organic chemist John Warcup Cornforth was born in Sydney to J. W. Cornforth, an Englishman, and the former Hilda Eipper, a native Australian of German descent. During his childhood Cornforth lived in Sydney and in rural New South Wales. At the age of ten he developed the first signs of deafness from otosclerosis, a disease of the bones of the ear, and within a decade he was totally deaf. He attended Sydney Boys' High School, where one of his teachers encouraged him to take a serious interest in chemistry.

In 1933 Cornforth entered Sydney University and graduated four years later with first-class honors and a university medal. After a year of graduate work in chemistry, both he and Rita H. Harradence, an organic chemistry student at the university, won scholarships for

JOHN W. CORNFORTH

graduate study at Oxford University. While they were on their way to England in 1939, World War II began. At Oxford, in the laboratory of ROBERT ROBINSON, they studied the synthesis of steroids, organic molecules containing a fused four-ring structure with various side chains. Naturally occurring mammalian steroids include cholesterol, male and female sex hormones (androgens and estrogens), adrenocorticosteroids (such as cortisone), and bile acids. In 1941 Cornforth and Harradence were married, the same year each received a Ph.D. in chemistry from Oxford.

During the war years Cornforth continued to conduct research on steroid synthesis as well as on the chemical structure of penicillin, an antibiotic which had been discovered by ALEXANDER FLEMING and which was particularly effective in treating wound infections and pneumonia. In 1949 Cornforth contributed to *The Chemistry of Penicillin,* a record of the international effort to synthesize penicillin. The Cornforths worked in the laboratories of the Medical Research Council from 1946 until 1962.

Cholesterol, a naturally occurring steroid, is a component of biological membranes as well as a precursor of the steroid hormones and bile acids. Cholesterol contains twenty-seven carbon atoms arranged in a nineteen-carbon tetracyclic ring system and an eight-carbon side chain. In the 1940s KONRAD BLOCH demonstrated that the synthesis of cholesterol in biological systems begins with the two-carbon molecule acetyl coenzyme A (the activated form of acetic acid), from which all the carbon atoms of cholesterol are derived. Three molecules of acetyl coenzyme A combine to form the six-carbon molecule of 3-hydroxy-3-methylglutaryl coenzyme A, which is reduced to mevalonic acid, also a six-carbon molecule. Mevalonic acid is then converted to the five-carbon isopentenyl pyrophosphate, which, in a series of condensation steps, forms squalene. This thirty-carbon hydrocarbon cyclizes to lanosterol, and with the final loss of three carbon groups, cholesterol is formed.

Using radioactive carbon labeling techniques, Cornforth and his colleague George Popják demonstrated the structural position of each acetic acid precursor in cholesterol and also identified the fourteen intermediate steps between mevalonic acid and squalene. The labeled mevalonate precursors were synthesized by Rita Cornforth.

In 1962 Cornforth and Popják were appointed codirectors of the Milstead Laboratory of Chemical Enzymology of Shell Research Ltd. in Sittingbourne, Kent, near London. Between 1965 and 1971 Cornforth served concurrently as an associate professor at the School of Molecular Science of the University of Warwick.

Cornforth and Popják focused on the stereochemistry, or three-dimensional geometry, of the molecular interactions between enzymes and their substrates in the synthesis of squalene from mevalonic acid. They systematically labeled each of the six methylene hydrogens in mevalonic acid with deuterium or tritium (isotopes of hydrogen). By combining isotopic labeling, enzymology, synthetic methodology, chemical degradation techniques, and sensitive measurement of physical parameters, Cornforth and Popják eventually showed that all enzyme-substrate interactions between mevalonic acid and squalene are stereospecific; that is, their interactions produce a specific stereoisomer. Moreover, they discovered that enzyme-substrate interactions mediating the biosynthesis of terpenoid compounds are also stereospecific. Terpenoids are derivatives of terpenes, naturally occurring resins and oils. Terpenoids, like squalene, are formed from mevalonic acid.

Cornforth and Popják also identified the hydrogen atom of the coenzyme NADH (reduced nicotinamide adenine dinucleotide) that is transferred to molecular oxygen in biological oxidation-reduction reactions. When Popják accepted an appointment at the University of California at Los Angeles in 1968, his twenty-year collaboration with Cornforth came to an end.

The stereochemical phenomena of molecular symmetry and asymmetry may be illustrated by the following examples. A carbon atom has a valence, or chemical combining power, of 4 (it may combine with four other atoms or molecules). If a carbon atom combines with four normal hydrogen atoms (H), the resulting molecule, methane (CH_4 or CHHHH), has the geometric structure of a symmetrical tetrahedron, a central carbon atom surrounded by four hydrogen atoms, one at each corner of the tetrahedron. If deuterium, or heavy hydrogen (D), is substituted at the first hydrogen position of methane, CHHHH becomes CDHHH. The deuterated methane is said to be artificially asymmetrical around its carbon atom. Larger molecular groups may be substituted at one of the hydrogen positions of methane. The rules of symmetry and asymmetry also hold for larger organic molecules.

According to Cornforth, the object of this work "has been to detect hidden asymmetry, chirality, stereospecificity, in life processes by superimposing an asymmetry that we were able to perceive." Chirality is a stereochemical property describing the optical activity of organic compounds in solution. Beginning in 1967, Cornforth collaborated with the German chemist Hermann Eggerer on the problem of the chiral methyl group, a methyl group with normal, deuterated, and tritiated hydrogen atoms. Their synthesis and enzymatic assay of compounds bearing a chiral methyl group were difficult technical achievements. Cornforth and his colleagues then used chiral methyl-labeled acetic acid to study further the stereochemistry of enzyme-substrate reactions. They determined not only which hydrogen atom is transferred in the condensation of isopentenyl pyrophosphate molecules (an intermediate step in cholesterol biosynthesis), but also the origin of all fifty hydrogen atoms in squalene. Moreover, they demonstrated that stereospecificity is essential to enzyme action; that this stereospecificity may be hidden or inapparent except by stereochemical analysis; and that the stereospecificity of enzyme-substrate reactions is independent of the structural relation of substrate to product.

Cornforth was awarded the 1975 Nobel Prize for Chemistry "for his work on the stereochemistry of enzyme-catalyzed reactions." In accepting the Nobel Prize, which he shared with VLADIMIR PRELOG, Cornforth eloquently described the nature of scientific inquiry: "In a world where it is so easy to neglect, deny, corrupt, and suppress the truth, the scientist may find his discipline severe. For him, truth is so seldom the sudden light that shows new order and beauty; more often, truth is the uncharted rock that sinks his ship in the dark. He respects all the more those who can accept that condition . . . and make our load lighter by sharing it."

After retiring from the Milstead Laboratory in 1975, Cornforth was appointed Royal Society Professor at the University of Sussex, a position he held for the next seven years. The Cornforths, who over the years have collaborated in the chemistry laboratory, live in Saxon Down, East Sussex, and have one son and two daughters. Tennis, chess, and gardening are Cornforth's recreational interests.

Many other honors and awards have been bestowed on Cornforth, including the Corday-Morgan Medal (1953) and the Flintoff Medal (1966) of the British Chemical Society; the Ciba Medal of the British Biochemical Society (1966); the Davy Medal (1968), the Royal Medal (1976), and the Copley Medal (1982) of the Royal Society of London. He was elected to membership in the Royal Society in 1953 and has received honorary degrees from Oxford University and from the universities of Dublin, Liverpool, Warwick, Aberdeen, and Sydney.

ABOUT: New Scientist October 23, 1975; New York Times October 18, 1975; Science November 12, 1975.

CORRIGAN, MAIREAD

(January 27, 1944–)
Nobel Prize for Peace, 1976
(shared with Betty Williams)

The Irish pacifist Mairead Corrigan was born in the Falls Road section of western Belfast in Northern Ireland, the portion of Ireland that maintains political ties with Great Britain. The second of seven children of Andrew and Margaret Corrigan, she received a Catholic upbringing at home and in private schools in Belfast. Because her father, a window-washing contractor, could not continue to pay tuition fees, Corrigan left school at the age of fourteen and, using her earnings from babysitting, put herself through business school. Beginning as an assistant bookkeeper, she had become private secretary to the director of the Guinness brewery in Belfast by the age of twenty-one.

As a lay member of the Legion of Mary, a volunteer Catholic welfare organization she joined in her early teens, Corrigan was en-

MAIREAD CORRIGAN

couraged to serve others. When she moved with her parents to the poverty-stricken Andersontown section of Belfast, she helped to organize the construction of a community meeting hall, set up a nursery school, and arrange recreational activities for children and adolescents.

This was a time of increasing civil violence in Northern Ireland, where a Catholic minority was pitted against a predominantly Protestant population. In 1968 a group of Catholic students formed the Northern Ireland Civil Rights Association to protest discrimination in housing, government, and employment. A year later, when violence between Catholics and Protestants threatened public order, the government of Northern Ireland asked Great Britain to dispatch troops in an effort to maintain order. As the conflict grew more brutal, each faction formed its own paramilitary force. A militant wing of the Irish Republican Army (IRA) defended the Catholics, and the Ulster Defense League—later the Ulster Defense Association—policed Protestant neighborhoods. In 1972, amid further violence, the British government suspended the Protestant-dominated parliament of Northern Ireland and instituted direct rule from London.

Working in the heart of the conflict, Corrigan witnessed arson, bombings, tear-gas attacks, and other terrorist acts on both sides. Through her work with the Legion of Mary, she urged young people in Catholic Andersontown to refrain from rioting and provoking British soldiers. In 1971 the British authorities established an internment camp for convicted IRA terrorists at Long Kesh. Corrigan visited the inmates "to remind them that they were Christians," as she explained later, "and that violence was not the way of Christ."

The following year, she attended a meeting of the World Council of Churches in Bangkok, Thailand, with a Protestant minister from the Shankill section of Belfast. In 1973 she traveled to the Soviet Union to help produce a film for the Legion of Mary on religion under Communist rule.

In the violence that had now become routine, one event occurred that changed the direction of Corrigan's life. On August 10, 1976, British soldiers killed an escaping IRA member at the wheel of his car. Veering out of control, the vehicle struck Corrigan's sister, Anne Maguire, and killed three of her children. Another witness to the accident, BETTY WILLIAMS, at once began collecting signatures for a peace petition. The response was overwhelming. Three days later, after the children's funeral, Corrigan appeared on television and risked her life by condemning the IRA. Williams also appeared on television with the petition and announced plans for a peace march the next day. The event brought 10,000 Protestant and Catholic women into the streets, praying and singing hymns. Encouraged by this spontaneous reaction, Corrigan and Williams joined with Ciaran McKeown, a journalist, to found the Community of Peace People.

Under their leadership, the Peace People staged demonstrations throughout 1976. In August 35,000 marchers crossed from Falls Road into the Protestant Shankill section, where they were greeted warmly by the residents. More demonstrations took place in Dublin, Glasgow, London, and other cities; in December an international rally in Drogheda, in the Republic of Ireland, attracted delegations from Canada, Norway, Sweden, and the United States. The site of this demonstration, the Bridge of Peace over the Boyne River, was richly symbolic. It was here in 1690 that the armies of Protestant King William III defeated those of the deposed Catholic monarch James II—an event that still holds a prominent place in Northern Ireland's Protestant mythology.

From the beginning, Corrigan's spiritual fervor and magnetic personality inspired crowds and drew adherents to the Peace People movement. Small, green-eyed, and gentle, she was a favorite of the press and the public wherever she spoke. Late in October 1976, she and Williams visited the United States in an effort to persuade Irish-Americans not to contribute money to the IRA.

Many of Corrigan's and Williams's supporters were disappointed when they learned that the women's work had begun too late in the year to be considered for that year's Nobel Peace Prize. So popular were the peace activists' efforts, however, that the Norwegian press and several private groups in Norway raised $340,000, which was presented to Corrigan and Williams as a "People's Peace Prize" at the end of the year.

In addition, the following year, Corrigan and Williams were awarded the 1976 Nobel Prize for Peace, which had been reserved in the absence of suitable candidates. It was given, said Egil Aarvik of the Norwegian Nobel Committee in his presentation address, "for tackling so fearlessly the perilous task of leading the way into no-man's-land, in the cause of peace and reconciliation." The Nobel lecture was delivered by Betty Williams. "We are deeply, passionately dedicated to the cause of nonviolence," she declared. "To those who say we are naive, utopian idealists, we say that we are the only realists, and that those who continue to support militarism in our time are supporting the progress toward total self-destruction of the human race."

The prize money helped Corrigan and Williams finance the second phase of the Peace People movement, in which they worked to achieve nonsectarian cooperation through religiously integrated community programs. In 1977 Corrigan and Williams initiated a "demilitarization campaign" in which all terrorist groups were asked to surrender their weapons. The following year, both they and McKeown resigned their positions in the Community of Peace People so that others could exercise leadership.

Corrigan has remained active in the peace movement and in the effort to integrate Protestant and Catholic youths in volunteer work camps. In 1981 she married her brother-in-law, Jack Maguire; her sister, Anne Maguire, had committed suicide a few years after the incident that killed three of her children. The family, which now includes two girls and three boys, continues to live in Belfast.

SELECTED WORKS: "A Mother Pleads for Peace," Parade Magazine December 29, 1985.

ABOUT: Current Biography April 1978; Deutsch, R. Mairead Corrigan, Betty Williams, 1977; Family Circle March 27, 1978; Nation April 16, 1977; Newsweek March 27, 1978; New York Times October 11, 1977; October 21, 1984; New York Times Magazine, December 19, 1976; O'Donnell, D. The Peace People of Northern Ireland, 1977.

COURNAND, ANDRÉ
(September 24, 1895–   )
Nobel Prize for Physiology or Medicine, 1956
(shared with Werner Forssmann and Dickinson W. Richards)

André Frédéric Cournand (kōōr' nänd), a French-American physiologist, was born in Paris, the son of Jules Cournand, a physician, and Marguerite (Weber) Cournand. An excellent soccer player and mountain climber in his youth, Cournand had by the age of nine decided to become a surgeon. After receiving his early education at the Lycée Condorcet, he took his B.A. from the University of Paris (the Sorbonne) in 1913. The next year he received a certificate in physics, chemistry, and biology from the Faculté des Sciences and entered medical school; however, World War I interrupted his studies.

From 1915 through 1918 Cournand served in the French army as an infantryman and medical corpsman; he was awarded the War Cross with Three Bronze Stars. Immediately after the war he resumed his medical studies at the University of Paris. As a medical intern from 1926 until 1930, he studied with the distinguished neurologist Georges Guillain. Cournand's doctoral dissertation dealt with multiple sclerosis, a disorder of the nervous system. During his internship he also received extensive clinical training in internal medicine, pediatrics, and chest diseases.

After obtaining his medical degree from the University of Paris in May 1930, Cournand moved to the United States, where he secured a residency in the Columbia University Division of Bellevue Hospital in New York City. Over the next three years he became assistant resident, senior resident, and chief resident. In 1934 he was appointed instructor in medicine at the College of Physicians and Surgeons of Columbia University. The same year, in the Cardiopulmonary Laboratory at Bellevue Hospital, he started his research on respiration and, in 1935, began a twenty-five-year association with DICKINSON W. RICHARDS.

Cournand and Richards had read about the experiments of WERNER FORSSMANN at the Eberswalde Surgical Clinic in Germany. In 1929, in an attempt to develop a reliable method for monitoring conditions in a diseased human heart, Forssmann had inserted a catheter (a long, thin tube) into a vein in his own arm and advanced it approximately two feet into the right side of his heart. Cournand and Richards wanted to develop a similar method to meas-

ANDRÉ COURNAND

ure blood pressure in the heart and blood flow through the lungs. In the 1930s they began a series of experiments designed to develop Forssmann's technique of cardiac catheterization, and by 1936 they were performing the procedure on dogs and chimpanzees in the Cardiopulmonary Laboratory at Bellevue. Since the technique was new, the problems were unique. The first related to the catheter itself: it had to be stiff enough to reproduce accurately the pressure pulse through a 4-foot column of fluid, yet flexible enough to be manipulated safely through the vessels and the heart without damaging them. The first catheters, with an inner diameter of slightly more than a millimeter, were made of a woven material impregnated with plastic. The catheter was filled with a fluid such as physiological saline (salt water), and its external end was attached to a manometer, an instrument used to measure blood pressure.

In 1941 Cournand performed the first human cardiac catheterization since Forssmann's 1929 experiment, with the assistance of Dr. Hilmert Ranges of the New York University School of Medicine. Cournand and his colleagues found that catheters could be left in the human circulation system for up to seven hours without causing clots or other complications, thus demonstrating that cardiac catheterization was a safe procedure. The technique permitted the measurement of blood pressure within the heart and blood vessels, the oxygen content of blood samples extracted through the catheter, and the total amount of oxygen consumed by breathing. With this informa-

tion, physicians could calculate the rate of blood flow through the lungs. By the late 1940s cardiac catheterization became a standard diagnostic procedure in several academic medical centers.

Cournand became an American citizen in 1941, and the following year he was appointed assistant professor of medicine at the College of Physicians and Surgeons of Columbia University. During World War II he served on Richards's team at Bellevue Hospital, studying shock and its treatment for the Office of Scientific Research and Development of the United States government. He also worked for the Chemical Warfare Service. In 1945 Cournand was named associate professor of medicine at the College of Physicians and Surgeons; he rose to full professor in 1951.

Using the techniques of cardiac catheterization to further his research on the lungs, Cournand became the first person to advance a catheter through the right atrium and ventricle (two chambers of the heart) and into the pulmonary artery, the vessel that carries blood from the heart to the lungs. He also made the first measurements of pulmonary artery blood pressure, which necessitated that he first discover the relationship between the oxygen content of the blood and the blood pressure in the pulmonary artery. In the laboratory it became clear that emphysema and other chronic lung diseases resulted in oxygen deprivation, or hypoxia, and high blood pressure in the pulmonary circulation. Cournand wanted to know how the level of blood pressure in the pulmonary arteries and the level of oxygen in the blood were mediated. He also wished to determine whether hypoxia caused the volume of blood in the pulmonary vessels to increase, thereby increasing blood pressure, or if a hypoxic reflex in the nervous system sent messages to the pulmonary arteries to constrict, causing blood pressure to rise. In the course of his research, Cournand demonstrated that neither mechanism is involved. Instead, he proposed that the smaller arteries of the pulmonary circulation respond directly to the oxygen content of the blood in which they are bathed. When the oxygen content is low, the muscles in the walls of these arteries constrict and the blood pressure rises. Cournand's hypothesis appears to have been verified by subsequent research.

Cournand went on to perform cardiac catheterizations on infants and children with various types of congenital heart disease. In one such condition, an atrial septal defect, there is an abnormal opening between the right and left atria. Cournand was able to advance a catheter into the left atrium of patients with this condition and measure the blood pressure in that chamber.

In 1956 Cournand shared the Nobel Prize for Physiology or Medicine with Forssmann and Richards "for their discoveries concerning heart catheterization and pathological changes in the circulatory system." In his presentation speech, Gören Liljestrand of the Karolinska Institute described Forssmann's courageous experiments and the work Cournand and Richards had done to "set their seal of approval on the method, which then made its triumphant entry into the world of clinical medicine." Liljestrand went on to discuss Cournand's and Richards's findings on pulmonary changes and the factors responsible for them. Cournand's Nobel lecture discussed "Control of the Pulmonary Circulation in Man With Some Remarks on Methodology."

In 1924 Cournand married Sibylle Blumer, whose son by a previous marriage he adopted. The couple had three daughters. After the death of his first wife in 1959, Cournand married his former laboratory assistant, Ruth Fabian, in 1963. He retired from his post at Bellevue's Cardiopulmonary Laboratory the following year. Ruth Cournand died in 1973, and he married Beatrice B. Berle in 1975. The couple divide their time between New York City and Northampton, Massachusetts.

A professor emeritus since 1964, Cournand is the recipient of the Anders Retzius Silver Medal of the Swedish Society of Internal Medicine (1946), the Lasker Award of the American Public Health Association (1949), the John Phillips Memorial Award of the American College of Physicians (1952), and the Gold Medal of the Belgian Royal Academy of Medicine (1956). He holds honorary degrees from the universities of Strasbourg, Lyons, and Pisa; the Free University of Brussels; and Columbia University. He is a member of the National Academy of Sciences, the American Physiology Society, the Association of Thoracic Surgeons, and the American Thoracic Society, and he is an honorary fellow of the Royal Society of Medicine of London.

SELECTED WORKS: Cardiac Catheterization in Congenital Heart Disease, 1949, with others; From Roots to Late Budding: The Intellectual Adventures of a Medical Scientist, 1985.

ABOUT: Current Biography March 1957; National Cyclopedia of American Biography, volume I, 1960; New York Times October 19, 1956; Robinson, D. The Miracle Finders, 1976.

CREMER, WILLIAM
(March 13, 1828–July 22, 1908)
Nobel Prize for Peace, 1903

William Randal Cremer (krē' mər), English labor leader and pacifist, was born in Fareham, Hampshire, in the south of England, to George Cremer, a coach painter, and the former Harriet Tutte. Abandoned by his father shortly after birth, Cremer and his two sisters were raised in great poverty by their mother, who supported the family on the small salary she earned teaching village children to read and write. After briefly attending a church school, Cremer worked in a local shipyard and in 1852 became an apprentice to his uncle, a London carpenter. Bright and eager to learn, Cremer took classes at a workman's institute and became active in the trade union movement.

His interest in peace began in 1856 when he heard a speaker from the London Peace Society call on the nations of the world to renounce war and settle their disputes by negotiation. Although the lecture "sowed the seeds of international arbitration" in his mind, as Cremer later wrote, he concentrated his efforts on labor issues for the next twenty years.

The building trades stood in the vanguard of the British union movement at this time, and in 1858 Cremer, a gifted orator, was elected to a committee that spearheaded a drive to reduce the customary twelve-hour workday to nine hours. The campaign, met by an employers' lockout in 1859 that left 70,000 men unemployed, ended in 1860 with few concessions to labor. In June of that year, Cremer helped found the Amalgamated Society of Carpenters and Joiners and quickly established himself as a leading figure in trade unionism. In the same year, he married Charlotte Spaulding; they had no children.

During the American Civil War, Cremer played an active role in rallying working-class support for the North, an unpopular cause among British mill owners who depended upon cotton imported from the Confederate states. Even though the war created economic hardships in England—mainly from the Union blockade of the South—Cremer, like the majority of his fellow workers, staunchly opposed slavery.

When Giuseppe Garibaldi visited London in 1864, Cremer was among those who helped

WILLIAM CREMER

organize an enthusiastic reception for the charismatic Italian republican leader. That year Cremer also helped establish the International Workingmen's Association and was chosen secretary of the British section. At the association's conference in Geneva in 1866, he and the other members of the British delegation argued for moderate and gradual reforms. This position alienated them from the more radical, largely continental delegates, including Karl Marx, who advocated revolution.

With the outbreak of the Franco-Prussian War in 1870, Cremer and several close associates founded the Workingmen's Peace Association to organize opposition to British intervention in the conflict. As the association's secretary, a position he held for life, Cremer worked tirelessly to give the working class a voice in the nascent European peace movement, whose adherents were drawn chiefly from the middle and upper classes. Through the association, he opposed British intervention in the Russo-Turkish War; British annexation of the Transvaal, a region in South Africa; British occupation of Egypt; and the Boer War. He also promoted the cause of international arbitration through the association, which was renamed the International Arbitration League in 1875. After his wife died the following year, Cremer married Lucie Coombes; she died in 1884.

Passage of the Reform Act in 1867 had given urban working men the vote and entry to British politics. After several unsuccessful bids, Cremer won a seat in the House of Commons in 1885 as a representative of London's pre-

dominantly working-class Haggerston district. With his election, he was in a position to promote the cause of arbitration in Parliament.

Two years later, he met American industrialist Andrew Carnegie, who was vacationing in Great Britain. Carnegie, a philanthropist and advocate of world peace, contributed financial support to the International Arbitration League. He also suggested that Cremer draft a treaty calling on the United States and Great Britain to resolve any future disputes through arbitration. Cremer took up the suggestion and gathered signatures from 234 colleagues in the House of Commons. Carnegie also arranged a meeting in October 1887 between Cremer and President Grover Cleveland in the United States, at which Cleveland gave his support to the treaty. Although official action was delayed, Cremer's efforts laid the groundwork for a permanent Anglo-American arbitration treaty that was signed in 1914.

Encouraged by his visit to America and impressed by American expressions of goodwill toward the French, Cremer sailed from the United States directly to France, arriving in Paris in August 1888. There he and FRÉDÉRIC PASSY organized a meeting of thirty-four French and British legislators to discuss an arbitration agreement between their nations and the United States. The delegates decided to hold a second conference in Paris the following year.

On that occasion, in June 1889, 100 legislators from ten European nations and the United States met at a two-day conference during which the delegates adopted a resolution stating that "further interparliamentary reunions shall take place each year." Cremer was chosen British secretary of this newly formed Interparliamentary Union, a position he held until his death. At subsequent conferences, the union discussed various peace proposals, outlined arbitration measures, and drafted a plan that inspired the establishment in 1899 of the Permanent Court of Arbitration at The Hague.

Cremer received the 1903 Nobel Prize for Peace in recognition of his efforts to promote international peace through arbitration. Unable to attend the award ceremonies that year, he delivered his Nobel lecture two years later. In it, he described the tangible achievements of the peace movement and listed the many nations that had bound themselves by arbitration treaties. "There is still a great work before us," he reminded his listeners. "The advocates of peace are, however, no longer regarded as idle dreamers."

229

CRICK

After refusing a knighthood on the grounds that it would compromise his position as a spokesman for labor, Cremer accepted the honor in 1907 as a tribute to the working class. The following year, he planned to visit Berlin to present German workers with a declaration of fraternity signed by more than 3,000 officers of British workingmen's organizations, but his failing health precluded the trip. He contracted pneumonia and died on July 22, 1908, in London.

In the opinion of Andrew Carnegie, "Cremer was the ideal of the twentieth-century hero; the hero of civilization as contrasted with that of the barbarous past. . . . Truly, I know of no . . . more heroic life than that of Cremer."

SELECTED WORKS: "Parliamentary and Interparliamentary Experiences," The Independent August 30, 1906.

ABOUT: Dictionary of National Biography 1901–1911, 1912; Evans, H. Sir Randal Cremer: His Life and Work, 1909; Interparliamentary Union. The Interparliamentary Union From 1889–1939, 1939; Oswald, E. Reminiscences of a Busy Life, 1911; Ralston, J. H. International Arbitration: From Athens to Locarno, 1929; The Independent July 19, 1906; Times (London) July 23, 1908.

FRANCIS CRICK

CRICK, FRANCIS

(June 8, 1916–   )
Nobel Prize for Physiology or Medicine, 1962
(shared with James D. Watson and
    Maurice H. F. Wilkins)

The English molecular biologist Francis Harry Compton Crick was born in Northampton, the elder of two sons of Harry Compton Crick, a well-to-do boot and shoe manufacturer, and the former Annie Elizabeth Wilkins. Spending his early years in Northampton, he attended the Northampton Grammar School. In the economic slump that followed World War I, the family business failed, and his parents moved to London. As a student at the Mill Hill School, Crick showed a strong interest in physics, chemistry, and mathematics. In 1934 he entered University College in London to study physics and graduated three years later with a B.S. Remaining at University College for graduate studies, he conducted research on the viscosity of water at high temperatures, work that was interrupted in 1939 by the outbreak of World War II.

Crick joined the British Admiralty Research Laboratory and spent the war years working on the development of mines. After the war,

he remained at the Admiralty for two years, and it was during this time that he read ERWIN SCHRÖDINGER's influential book *What Is Life? The Physical Aspects of the Living Cell,* which was published in 1944. In this book Schrödinger asked, "How can the events of space and time which take place within the . . . living organism be accounted for by physics and chemistry?"

So stimulating were Schrödinger's ideas that Crick, who had been considering a career in particle physics, turned instead to biology. With the support of ARCHIBALD V. HILL, Crick obtained a Medical Research Council Studentship, and in 1947 he began working at the Strangeways Research Laboratory at Cambridge. There he learned biology, organic chemistry, and the techniques of X-ray diffraction, a method used to determine the three-dimensional structure of molecules. His knowledge of biology deepened in 1949 when he transferred to the Medical Research Council Unit for Molecular Biology at the Cavendish Laboratories at Cambridge. Working under MAX PERUTZ, he investigated the molecular structure of proteins and developed an interest in the genetic code for the amino acid sequence of protein molecules. Amino acids, of which there are twenty types, are the building blocks of proteins. Deeply interested in what he called "the division between the living and the nonliving," Crick sought the chemical basis of genetics, which he suspected could be found in deoxyribonucleic acid (DNA).

The science of genetics began in 1866, when

Gregor Mendel postulated that "elements," now called genes, govern the inheritance of physical traits. Three years later, the Swiss biochemist Friedrich Miescher discovered nucleic acid, compounds present in the nucleus of the cell. At the turn of the century scientists found that genes reside on chromosomes in the nucleus of the cell. During the first half of the twentieth century, biochemists gradually determined the chemical structure of the nucleic acids, and by the 1940s researchers had discovered that genes are made of one of these nucleic acids, DNA. They also proved that genes or DNA direct the biosynthesis, or production with living organisms, of cellular proteins called enzymes and thus control the biochemical processes of the cell.

By the time Crick began his doctoral work at Cambridge, scientists knew that nucleic acids consist of DNA and RNA (ribonucleic acid). Each is constructed of five-carbon sugar molecules (deoxyribose or ribose), phosphate, and four nitrogen-containing bases—adenine, thymine, guanine, and cytosine (in RNA, uracil replaces thymine). In 1950 Erwin Chargaff of Columbia University showed that DNA contains equal numbers of adenine and thymine and of guanine and cytosine. MAURICE H. F. WILKINS and his associate, Rosalind Franklin, of King's College, University of London, made X-ray diffraction studies of DNA molecules and demonstrated that DNA is shaped like a double helix, a structure resembling a ladder twisted into a spiral.

Crick was joined at the Cavendish Laboratories in 1951 by JAMES D. WATSON, a twenty-three-year-old American biologist with whom he soon formed a close working relationship. Drawing on the earlier work of Chargaff, Wilkins, and Franklin, Crick and Watson set out to determine the chemical structure of DNA. Within two years they proposed a three-dimensional structure for the DNA molecule, and a month later they constructed a model from beads, pieces of wire, and cardboard. According to their model, DNA is a double helix consisting of two strands of sugar and phosphate (deoxyribose phosphate) joined by pairs of bases inside the helix, one adenine paired with every thymine, and one guanine paired with every cytosine. The bases are attached to one another by hydrogen bonds.

The model enabled other researchers to visualize the replication of DNA. The two parts of the molecule separate at the points of hydrogen bonding, similar to the opening of a zipper. One new molecule is then synthesized opposite each half of the old one. The sequence of bases acts as a template, or mold, for the new molecule.

In 1953, the same year that he and Watson completed their DNA model, Crick received his Ph.D. from Cambridge for a dissertation on X-ray diffraction analysis of protein structure. During the following year he studied protein structure at the Brooklyn Polytechnic Institute in New York and lectured at several universities in the United States. Returning to Cambridge in 1954, he continued his research at the Medical Research Unit at the Cavendish, turning his attention to deciphering the genetic code. Although primarily a theoretician, Crick began experimental research with Sydney Brenner on genetic mutations in bacteriophage particles (viruses that infect bacterial cells).

By 1961 three types of RNA had been discovered: messenger RNA, ribosomal RNA, and transfer (or soluble) RNA. Crick and his colleagues suggested a way in which the genetic code could be read. According to Crick, messenger RNA receives genetic information from DNA in the nucleus of the cell and conveys it to ribosomes (the sites of protein synthesis) in the cytoplasm, or nonnuclear portion, of the cell. Transfer RNA carries amino acids to the ribosomes. Messenger and ribosomal RNA then cooperate to join amino acids in the correct sequence to form protein molecules. The genetic code consists of triplets of DNA and RNA bases for each of the twenty amino acids. Genes consist of many base triplets, which Crick called codons. The genetic code—that is, the codons—appears to be similar in different species.

Crick, Wilkins, and Watson shared the 1962 Nobel Prize for Physiology or Medicine "for their discoveries concerning the molecular structure of nuclear acids and its significance for information transfer in living material." A. V. Engström of the Karolinska Institute said on presenting the award, "The discovery of the three-dimensional molecular structure of . . . DNA is of great importance, because it outlines the possibilities for an understanding, in its finest details, of the molecular configuration, which dictates the general and individual properties of living matter." Engström went on to say that "the formulation of [the] double helical structure of the deoxyribonucleic acid, with the specific pairing of the organic bases, opens the most spectacular possibilities for the unraveling of the details of the control and transfer of genetic information."

The same year that he received the Nobel Prize, Crick became director of the Molecular

Biology Laboratory at Cambridge University and a nonresident fellow of the Salk Institute of Biology in San Diego, California. He moved to San Diego in 1977 when the institute appointed him Kieckhefer Distinguished Research Professor. At the Salk Institute, Crick has conducted research in the field of neurobiology, especially the mechanism of vision and the function of dreams. He and Graeme Mitchison, a British mathematician, proposed in 1983 that dreams are a side effect of a process through which the human brain discards redundant or useless associations made during waking hours. This form of "reverse learning" takes place, they suggested, to prevent an overloading of the neural circuits.

In *Life Itself: Its Origin and Nature* (1981), Crick pointed out the remarkable similarity found among all life forms. "With the exception of mitochondria," he wrote, the genetic "code is identical in all living things so far examined." Citing discoveries in molecular biology, paleontology, and cosmology, he hypothesized that life on earth may have originated from microorganisms that were disseminated through space from another planet, a theory he and his colleague Leslie Orgel named directed panspermia.

In 1940 Crick married Ruth Doreen Dodd, with whom he had a son. The marriage ended in divorce in 1947, and two years later he married Odile Speed. They have two daughters. A tall man with blue eyes, Crick is known for his incisive mind and blunt way of speaking.

Crick's numerous awards include the Charles Leopold Mayer Prize of the French Academy of Sciences (1961), the Science Award of the Research Corporation of America (1962), and the Royal Medal (1972) and Copley Medal (1976) of the Royal Society. He is a fellow of the Royal Society, the Royal Society of Edinburgh, and the Royal Irish Academy; an honorary fellow of the American Association for the Advancement of Science; and an honorary member of the American Academy of Arts and Sciences and the American National Academy of Sciences.

SELECTED WORKS: Of Molecules and Men, 1966.

ABOUT: Current Biography March 1963; Holton, G. (ed.) The Twentieth Century Sciences, 1972; Jevons, F. R. Winner Take All, 1979; Judson, H. F. The Eighth Day of Creation, 1979; Olby, R. The Path to the Double Helix, 1974; Watson, J. D. The Double Helix, 1968; Weintraub, P. (ed.) The Omni Interviews, 1984.

CRONIN, JAMES W.

(September 29, 1931–)
Nobel Prize for Physics, 1980
(shared with Val L. Fitch)

The American physicist James Watson Cronin was born in Chicago, Illinois, to James Farley Cronin, then a graduate student of classical languages at the University of Chicago, and Dorothy (Watson) Cronin. His parents had met while attending a Greek class at Northwestern University. In 1939, after living briefly in Alabama, the family moved to Dallas, Texas, where Cronin's father became a professor of Latin and Greek at Southern Methodist University. Cronin attended the local Highland Park public elementary and secondary schools and went on to obtain a B.S. in physics and mathematics from Southern Methodist University in 1951.

According to Cronin, his real education began in the fall of 1951 when he became a graduate student at the University of Chicago. There his teachers included ENRICO FERMI, MARIA GOEPPERT MAYER, Edward Teller, Val Telegdi, Marvin Goldberger, and MURRAY GELL-MANN. It was Gell-Mann, in particular, who stimulated Cronin's interest in the emerging field of particle physics. Cronin received his Ph.D. in 1955 with a thesis on experimental nuclear physics, written under the direction of Samuel K. Allison.

Cronin then joined a group led by Rodney Cool and Oreste Piccioni, research physicists at the Brookhaven National Laboratory on Long Island, who were working with the newly completed cosmotron, a particle accelerator capable of raising protons to an energy of 3 billion electron volts. At Brookhaven, Cronin met VAL L. FITCH, who invited him to move to Princeton University in the fall of 1958. While pursuing independent research programs, in 1963 the two scientists collaborated on a classic experiment that broke one of the seemingly inviolable rules of nature.

At one time scientists had thought that nature obeyed three fundamental rules of symmetry. According to the first rule, called symmetry of charge conjugation (C), the outcome of any physical experiment should be unchanged if every particle in the experiment is replaced by the corresponding antiparticle (a twin of the particle but with reversed electric charge and other properties). In other words, a world composed entirely of antimatter should obey the same physical laws as one composed entirely of matter. The second rule, parity (P), says that a particle reaction should

JAMES W. CRONIN

appear the same if all geometric quantities, such as position coordinates, are replaced by their mirror images. In effect, a reaction should give no clue to distinguish right from left. The third rule, time-reversal symmetry (T), states that any reaction between elementary particles should run equally well in either direction; for example, if two particles can coalesce to form a third particle, the third particle can break down to yield the original two.

In 1956 TSUNG-DAO LEE and CHEN NING YANG found that evidence was lacking for P conservation in certain weak reactions (reactions involving the force associated with some forms of radioactivity as opposed to the strong force, which holds nuclei together). They suggested experiments to explore the question, and soon thereafter Chien-Shiung Wu and her colleagues at Columbia University demonstrated that parity is not absolutely conserved in the beta decay (electron emission) of certain radioactive nuclei; the nuclei emit more "left-handed" than "right-handed" electrons. Other workers then discovered that C conservation is also imperfect. Some physical processes give preference to particles over antiparticles. Physicists were able to salvage a sense of order by joining C and P into a combined CP conservation rule obeyed by the experimental results. A violation of C was compensated for by a simultaneous violation of P, and vice versa. For example, if an excess of left-handed electrons violates parity conservation, then a simultaneous exchange of antiparticles for particles would convert left-handed electrons into right-handed positrons and keep the phys-

ical laws intact. It was the universal validity of CP combined symmetry, invoked to explain individual C and P symmetry violations, that was overturned by Cronin and Fitch in the summer of 1963.

Cronin and Fitch were working with beams of neutral K-mesons, now called kaons (particles about half as massive as the proton), generated by an accelerator at Brookhaven. They did not set out to overthrow CP symmetry; on the contrary, they expected to confirm it. Nevertheless, in a series of experiments done in collaboration with René Turlay, on leave from the Center for Nuclear Studies in France, and with James Christenson, a Princeton graduate student, they found unmistakable evidence of CP violation. When a certain subpopulation of neutral K-mesons decays, about 1 event in 500 fails the symmetry test. The first evidence of CP violation was indirect; later experiments made the effect obvious. The K-meson decays favor left-handed particles over right-handed ones (P violation) and matter over antimatter (C violation). Furthermore, the combined CP transformation also fails: the decay events favor left-handed matter over right-handed antimatter. This was revealed in the form of a forbidden mode of decay. In accordance with the CP symmetry rule, a short-lived neutral K-meson decays into two pi-mesons, but a long-lived neutral K-meson (it survives on average about 500 times as long as the short-lived type) is allowed to decay only into three pi-mesons. The experimental results, disbelieved at first and checked and scrutinized for six months before publication, conclusively showed some long-lived K-mesons decaying into two pi-mesons.

One very general symmetry remains above suspicion: CPT, the combination of all three symmetries applied simultaneously. If any given event is observed in nature, then the corresponding event, with left and right reversed, with matter and antimatter exchanged, and with time running backward, must be equally possible. This fact and the violation of CP led to a remarkable conclusion: time-reversal symmetry itself must be violated. If CP fails, then for CPT to hold, T must fail. The CP-violating decay of a K-meson cannot be reversed. These conclusions not only led physicists to rethink their explanations of physical phenomena but may also explain one theory of how the universe evolved. If, in the early moments of the big bang, matter and antimatter were formed in equal amounts, they would have annihilated each other. CP violation, however, would allow antiparticles to decay faster than particles and consequently disappear sooner, leaving an excess of particles as the substance of the universe. Particle-antiparticle annihilations would have contributed to the store of electromagnetic radiation.

Cronin became a full professor at Princeton in 1964; he spent that year in France at the Center for Nuclear Studies, working with Turlay. The following year he returned to Princeton, where he continued his work on CP violation in K-mesons. In 1971 he joined the faculty at the University of Chicago, doing experiments with the new accelerator at the Fermi National Accelerator Laboratory just outside the city.

Cronin and Fitch shared the 1980 Nobel Prize for Physics "for the discovery of violations of fundamental symmetry principles in the decay of neutral K-mesons." At the conclusion of his Nobel lecture Cronin said, "We must continually remind ourselves that the CP violation, however small, is a very real effect. . . . The effect is telling us that there is a fundamental asymmetry between matter and antimatter, and it is also telling us that at some tiny level interactions will show an asymmetry under the reversal of time. . . . We are hopeful," he went on, "that at some epoch, perhaps distant, this cryptic message from nature will be deciphered."

Since winning the Nobel Prize, Cronin has remained at the University of Chicago, where his work includes efforts to understand why CP violations sometimes occur.

In 1954 Cronin married Annette Martin, a fellow student at the University of Chicago, with whom he has three children. He relaxes on ski weekends at his cabin in Wisconsin.

Cronin's other honors include the Science Award of the Research Corporation of America (1968), the John Price Wetherill Medal of the Franklin Institute (1975), and the Ernest Orlando Lawrence Memorial Award for Physics of the United States Energy Research and Development Agency (1977). He is a member of the National Academy of Sciences, the American Physical Society, and the American Academy of Arts and Sciences.

SELECTED WORKS: Excitation Functions and Angular Distributions of Alpha Particles, 1955.

ABOUT: New York Times October 15, 1980; Physics Today December 1980; Science November 7, 1980.

CURIE, IRÈNE JOLIOT
See JOLIOT-CURIE, IRÈNE

CURIE, MARIE
(November 7, 1867–July 4, 1934)
Nobel Prize for Physics, 1903
(shared with Henri Becquerel and Pierre
 Curie)
Nobel Prize for Chemistry, 1911

The French physicist Marie Sklodowska Curie was born Maria Sklodowska in Warsaw, Poland, the youngest of five children of Wladyslaw Sklodowski and Bronislawa (Boguska) Sklodowska. Curie was reared in a family that valued academic achievement. Her father taught physics in high school, and her mother directed a girls' school until she contracted tuberculosis. Curie's mother died when the girl was eleven years old.

Curie distinguished herself both in primary school and in high school. Even as a child, she was fascinated by science, and she worked as an assistant in her cousin's chemistry laboratory. The prominent Russian chemist Dmitry Mendeleev, who devised the periodic table, was a friend of Curie's father; observing the girl at work in the laboratory, he predicted a great future for her if she stuck to her chemistry. Growing up under Russian rule (Poland was then partitioned among Russia, Germany, and Austria), Curie was also active in a clandestine movement of young intellectual and anticlerical Polish nationalists. Although she was to spend most of her life in France, she remained passionately dedicated to the cause of Polish independence.

In her quest for a higher education, Curie faced two obstacles: her family's poverty and the University of Warsaw's prohibition against the matriculation of women. She and her sister Bronya devised a scheme: Curie would work as a governess for five years to put Bronya through medical school, then Bronya would defray the cost of her sister's higher education. Bronya received her medical education in Paris, and when she became a doctor, she invited her sister to join her. Leaving Poland in 1891, Curie enrolled at the Faculty of Science of the University of Paris (Sorbonne). It was at this time that she began to use the name Marie Sklodowska. In 1893 she received a *licence* (equivalent to a master's degree) in physics from the Sorbonne, placing first in her class. A year later she earned a *licence* in mathematics, placing second.

It was also in 1894 that Marie met PIERRE

MARIE CURIE

CURIE at the home of a Polish émigré physicist. Director of laboratory work at the Municipal School of Industrial Physics and Chemistry, Pierre had done important research on crystals and on the magnetic properties of substances as a function of temperature. Marie was doing research on the magnetization of steel, and her Polish friend had hoped that Pierre could provide her a laboratory in which to work. Drawn together at first by their obsessive interest in physics, Marie and Pierre married the following year, soon after Pierre had defended his doctoral dissertation. Their daughter Irène (IRÈNE JOLIOT-CURIE) was born in September 1897. Three months later Marie Curie finished her research on magnetism and began seeking a topic for her own dissertation.

In 1896 HENRI BECQUEREL had discovered that uranium compounds emit strongly penetrating radiation. Unlike X radiation, discovered in 1895 by WILHELM RÖNTGEN, Becquerel radiation was not the result of excitation by an external energy source such as light; rather, it seemed to be an intrinsic property of uranium itself. Fascinated by this strange phenomenon and attracted by the prospect of initiating a new field of research, Curie decided to study Becquerel radiation, which she would later name radioactivity. Beginning in early 1898, Curie sought first to ascertain whether any substances other than uranium compounds emit Becquerel rays. Since Becquerel had observed that uranium compounds cause air to conduct electricity, Curie measured the conductivity of air around other compounds, using several precise laboratory

instruments that Pierre Curie and his brother, Jacques, had designed and built. She concluded that, of the known elements, only uranium, thorium, and their compounds were radioactive. Soon, however, she made a far more remarkable discovery: pitchblende, a mineral ore, emits more Becquerel radiation than the uranium and thorium compounds in it could possibly produce—at least four times as much, in fact, as pure uranium. Curie hypothesized that an undiscovered and highly radioactive element was present in pitchblende. In the spring of 1898 she reported her experimental findings and her hypothesis to the French Academy of Sciences.

The Curies next tried to isolate the new element, Pierre having put aside his own research on crystals in order to assist Marie. Using acids and hydrogen sulfide, they separated pitchblende into its known constituents. They then examined each of the portions they had obtained and determined that only two, those containing the elements bismuth and barium, were strongly radioactive. Since Becquerel radiation was uncharacteristic of bismuth and barium, they concluded that these portions also contained one or more previously undetected elements. In July and December 1898, respectively, the Curies announced the discovery of two elements they called polonium (after Marie's native country) and radium.

Because the Curies had not isolated either of these elements, they had not presented chemists with definitive proof of their existence. They therefore began the arduous task of extracting the two new elements from pitchblende. They had determined that the substances they were seeking constituted only about one-millionth part of pitchblende; in order to extract them in measurable quantities, they needed enormous amounts of the ore. Working under primitive and physically trying conditions, the Curies spent the next four years performing chemical separations in large vats in a drafty shed; they analyzed the products in the tiny, dilapidated laboratory of the Municipal School. During this difficult but exciting period, Pierre's salary was not adequate to support the Curies. Despite the overwhelming demands of conducting her research while raising a child, Marie began teaching physics at the École Normale Supérieure, a secondary teachers' training school in Sèvres, in 1900. Pierre's widowed father came to live with the Curies and helped care for Irène.

In September 1902 the Curies announced that they had isolated one-tenth of a gram of radium chloride from several tons of pitchblende. (They had been unable to isolate polonium, which turned out to be a disintegration product of radium.) Analyzing the compound, Marie found the atomic weight of radium to be 225. The radium salt glowed with a bluish light, and it emitted heat. This fantastic-seeming substance caught the world's attention; recognition and awards for the discovery came to the Curies almost at once.

Her doctoral research complete, Marie finally wrote her dissertation. Titled "Researches on Radioactive Substances" and presented to the Sorbonne in June 1903, it incorporated a wealth of important observations about radioactivity that she and Pierre had made during their search for polonium and radium. The committee that awarded her doctoral degree considered her work the greatest contribution to science ever made by a doctoral thesis.

In December 1903 the Royal Swedish Academy of Sciences awarded the Nobel Prize for Physics to Becquerel and the Curies. Marie and Pierre Curie received half the award, "in recognition of . . . their joint researches on the radiation phenomena discovered by Professor Henri Becquerel." Marie Curie was the first woman to receive a Nobel Prize. Both Marie and Pierre were in poor health and declined to travel to Stockholm for the awards ceremony; they collected the prize the following summer.

Even before the Curies' research was completed, it had stimulated other physicists to undertake work on radioactivity. In 1903 ERNEST RUTHERFORD and FREDERICK SODDY proposed that radioactive emissions are produced by the disintegration of atomic nuclei. By disintegrating (losing some of their constituent particles), radioactive nuclei undergo transmutation into the nuclei of other elements. Marie Curie was reluctant to accept this theory, since the disintegration of uranium, thorium, and radium is so slow that she had seen no evidence of it in the course of her experiments. (There was evidence for the disintegration of polonium, but she regarded the behavior of this element as an exception.) However, by 1906 she had accepted the Rutherford-Soddy theory as the most plausible explanation of radioactivity, and it was she who introduced the terms *disintegration* and *transmutation.*

The Curies had noticed that radium affects the human body (like Becquerel, they sustained radium burns before the danger of handling radioactive substances was understood), and they suggested that it might be used to treat tumors. The therapeutic value of radium was recognized almost at once, and the price of this scarce element soared. Nevertheless, the Curies refused to patent their extraction process or otherwise exploit the commercial possibilities of radium. To do so, they held, would be contrary to the spirit of science— that knowledge should be freely shared. Although they rejected a fortune, their life was made easier by the money from the Nobel Prize and other awards. In October 1904 Pierre was appointed professor of physics at the Sorbonne, and one month later Marie was named as the superintendent of his laboratory. In December, Marie gave birth to their second daughter, Eve, who became a concert pianist and her mother's biographer.

Invigorated by the success of her scientific achievements and sustained by work she loved and by the affection and support of Pierre, Marie had found "all I could have dreamed at the moment of our union and more." But in April 1906 Pierre was killed in a traffic accident. Bereft of her closest companion, she lost her warmth and retreated into herself; nonetheless, she carried on her work. In May, after she had refused a pension from the Ministry of Public Education because she wanted to continue working, the Faculty Council of the Sorbonne voted to appoint Marie to Pierre's chair of physics. When Curie delivered her first lecture six months later, she became the first woman to teach at that institution.

In her laboratory at the Sorbonne, Curie focused her efforts on trying to isolate metallic radium—the pure, uncombined element. With the assistance of André Debierne, she succeeded in preparing pure radium in 1910, completing the quest she had begun twelve years earlier and establishing, beyond all doubt, the status of radium as an element. Curie developed a method for measuring radioactive emanations, and she prepared the first international standard of radium—a pure sample of radium chloride to which all others could be compared—for the International Bureau of Weights and Measures.

Late in 1910 Curie was persuaded to stand for election to the nation's most prestigious scientific society, the French Academy of Sciences. Pierre Curie had been elected to this organization only a year before his death. No woman had ever been admitted to the academy, and Curie's candidacy led to a bitter faction fight that spilled over into the press. When the vote came in January 1911, after months of invective, Curie was rejected by a single vote.

A few months later, the Royal Swedish Academy of Sciences awarded Curie the 1911 Nobel Prize for Chemistry "for her services to the advancement of chemistry by the discovery of the elements radium and polonium, by the isolation of radium and the study of the nature and compounds of this remarkable element." Curie thus became the first person ever to be awarded a second Nobel Prize. In his presentation speech E. W. Dahlgren noted that "research on radium has led during recent years to the birth of a new branch of science, radiology, which already commands institutes and journals of its own."

Just before the outbreak of World War I, the University of Paris and the Pasteur Institute jointly established the Radium Institute, devoted to the study of radioactivity. Curie was appointed director of the division for basic research, while her colleague Claude Regaud directed the division for research into biological and medical applications of radioactivity. During the war, Curie taught the army medical staff the use of radiology, using X rays to find shrapnel, for example. Traveling in the war zone, she helped build radiological installations, and she was instrumental in equipping ambulances with portable X-ray equipment. Drawing upon these experiences, Curie wrote *La Radiologie et la guerre* (Radiology and War) in 1920.

After the war, Curie returned to the Radium Institute. For the rest of her life she guided students in their work and actively promoted the medical use of radiology. She wrote a biography of Pierre Curie that was published in 1923. Periodically, Curie traveled to Poland, which had gained its independence at the end of the war, to advise researchers there. In 1921, accompanied by her daughters, she traveled to the United States to receive the gift of a gram of radium for her research. On her second visit to the United States, in 1929, she accepted a donation with which to purchase a gram of radium for therapeutic use in a hospital in Warsaw. By this time her own health was seriously impaired due to the effects of radium.

Marie Curie died on July 4, 1934, of leukemia, at a small nursing home in Sancellemoz in the French Alps.

Marie Curie's great strength as a scientist was her enormous persistence in the face of difficulties: once she set her sights on a problem she would not be deterred from solving it. Known as a quiet, modest woman who was never comfortable with fame, Curie was intensely devoted to the things she believed in and the people she cared for. After her husband's death, when she grew distant from others, she remained a warm and devoted mother to her two daughters. She loved nature, and while Pierre was alive, they found time to take bicycle tours of the countryside. She also enjoyed swimming.

In addition to the two Nobel Prizes, Marie Curie received the Berthelot Medal of the French Academy of Sciences (1902), the Davy Medal of the Royal Society of London (1903), and the Elliott Cresson Medal of the Franklin Institute (1909). She was a member of eighty-five scientific societies throughout the world, including the French Academy of Medicine, and she received twenty honorary degrees. Curie participated in the prestigious Solvay Physics Conferences from 1911 until her death, and she served for twelve years on the League of Nation's International Commission on Intellectual Cooperation.

SELECTED WORKS: Radioactive Substances, 1904; Pierre Curie, 1923.

ABOUT: Cunningham, M. Madame Curie and the Story of Radium, 1918; Curie, E. Madame Curie, 1939; De-Leeuw, A. Marie Curie, Woman of Genius, 1970; Dictionary of Scientific Biography, volume 3, 1971; Feuerlicht, R. Marie Curie: A Concise Biography, 1965; Giround, F. Marie Curie: A Life, 1986; Ivimey, A. Marie Curie, Pioneer of the Atomic Age, 1969; Reid, R. W. Marie Curie, 1974; Rubin, E. The Curies and Radium, 1961.

CURIE, PIERRE
(May 15, 1859–April 19, 1906)
Nobel Prize for Physics, 1903
(shared with Henri Becquerel and Marie Curie)

The French physicist Pierre Curie was born in Paris, the younger of two sons of Eugène Curie and Sophie-Claire (Depoully) Curie. His father, a physician, decided to educate his independent and reflective son at home. He proved to be such a proficient student that he received a bachelor of science degree from the University of Paris (Sorbonne) in 1876 at the age of sixteen. Two years later he earned a *licence* (equivalent to a master's degree) in physical sciences from the Sorbonne.

In 1878 Curie became a demonstrator at the Sorbonne's physical laboratory, where he also undertook research on the nature of crystals. Together with his older brother, Jacques, who worked in the mineralogy laboratory at the

PIERRE CURIE

Sorbonne, Curie began four years of intensive experimental activity. During this period the Curie brothers discovered piezoelectricity, electricity caused by the exertion of force on the surface of certain crystals. They also discovered an inverse effect: the same crystals undergo compression under the influence of an electric field. When alternating currents are used, these crystals can be made to vibrate at ultrahigh frequencies, causing sound waves beyond the range of human hearing. Such crystals have become essential components of such equipment as microphones, amplifiers, and stereo systems. The brothers also designed and built an important laboratory instrument, the piezoelectric quartz balance. This apparatus, which produces electricity in amounts proportional to the force exerted on it, was the forerunner to the devices that govern modern quartz watches, clocks, and radio transmitters. In 1882, on the recommendation of the British physicist William Thomson, who had taken an interest in Pierre Curie's work, Pierre was appointed chief of the laboratory of the new Municipal School of Industrial Physics and Chemistry. Although the position paid very little, he remained at the Municipal School for twenty-two years. One year after Pierre's appointment, Jacques left Paris to become professor of mineralogy at the University of Montpellier, ending the brothers' period of collaboration.

Between 1883 and 1895 Pierre Curie conducted a notable series of researches, concentrating initially on crystals. His papers on the geometric symmetry of crystals still remain useful to crystallographers. Between 1890 and 1895 Curie elucidated the magnetic properties of substances at different temperatures. His doctoral dissertation presented an important summary of the relation between temperature and magnetization that became known as Curie's law.

While working on his dissertation in 1894, Curie met Marie Sklodowska (MARIE CURIE) a young Polish physics student at the Sorbonne. They married in July 1895, a few months after Curie received his doctorate from the Sorbonne. In 1897, shortly after the birth of their first child, Marie Curie began the study of radioactivity, which would soon involve Pierre as well and which would absorb his attention for the rest of his life.

In 1896, HENRI BECQUEREL had discovered that uranium compounds constantly emit radiation capable of exposing a photographic plate. Selecting this newly discovered phenomenon as the subject of her doctoral research, Marie began investigating other substances to determine whether anything other than uranium emitted "Becquerel rays." Since Becquerel had found that the radiation from uranium increases the electrical conductivity of the air around it, Marie used the Curie brothers' piezoelectric quartz balance to measure the conductivity of air around other substances. She soon concluded that only uranium, thorium, and compounds of these two elements emit Becquerel radiation, which she later named radioactivity. Then, however, she made a startling discovery: pitchblende, a mineral ore, produces much higher conductivity in the surrounding air than the uranium and thorium compounds present in it could possibly produce—more, in fact, than pure uranium. From this observation she deduced that an undiscovered and highly radioactive element must occur in pitchblende. In 1898 she communicated her experimental findings and her deduction to the French Academy of Sciences. Convinced that his wife's hypothesis was not only correct but highly significant, Pierre Curie put aside his own research to assist her in extracting the elusive element. From this time, their research interests merged so completely that their laboratory notes always used the pronoun we.

The Curies undertook the laborious task of separating the chemical constituents of pitchblende, until only the very tiny portion that was highly radioactive remained. This portion, it turned out, contained not one but two unknown radioactive elements. In July 1898 they published the paper "Sur une substance radioactive contenue dans la pechblende" (On a Radioactive Substance Contained in Pitchblende), in which they reported the discovery of one of the new elements, which they named polonium after Marie Curie's native country. In December they announced the discovery of the second element, which they called radium. Both elements are many times more radioactive than either uranium or thorium, and they constitute only one-millionth part of pitchblende ore. In order to extract enough radium from pitchblende to determine its atomic weight, the Curies worked with several tons of pitchblende over the following four years. Working under primitive and physically arduous conditions, they performed chemical separations in large vats in a drafty shed; they analyzed the products in the tiny, dilapidated laboratory of the Municipal School.

In September 1902 the Curies announced that they had recovered one-tenth of a gram of radium chloride and determined the atomic weight of radium to be 225. (They were unable to isolate polonium, which turned out to be a disintegration product of radium.) The radium salt glowed with a bluish light, and it emitted heat. This seemingly fantastic substance caught the world's attention; recognition and awards for the discovery came almost at once.

In addition to isolating radium, the Curies published a wealth of information about radioactivity that they gathered during their research—thirty-six papers between 1898 and 1904. Even before their research was completed, it had stimulated other physicists to begin work on radioactivity. In 1903 ERNEST RUTHERFORD and FREDERICK SODDY proposed that radioactive emissions are produced by the disintegration of atomic nuclei. By disintegrating (losing some of their constituent particles), radioactive nuclei undergo transmutation into other elements. The Curies were also responsible for the early recognition of the medical uses of radium. Observing that it affected living tissue, they suggested that it might be useful in the treatment of tumors.

The Royal Swedish Academy of Sciences awarded the Curies half the 1903 Nobel Prize for Physics "in recognition of . . . their joint researches on the radiation phenomena discovered by Professor Henri Becquerel," with whom they shared the prize. Both Curies were in poor health, and they did not attend the awards ceremony. In his Nobel lecture, delivered two years later, Pierre Curie acknowledged the potential dangers of radioactive substances in the wrong hands, but added that he was "one of those who believed with Nobel that mankind will derive more harm than good from the new discoveries."

Owing to the extreme scarcity and medical value of radium, its price quickly soared. The Curies had lived in poverty, their research hampered by inadequate facilities. Nevertheless, they refused to patent their extraction process or otherwise exploit the commercial possibilities of radium. To do so, they believed, would be contrary to the spirit of science—that knowledge should be freely shared. Although they rejected a fortune, their life was made easier by the money from the Nobel Prize and other awards.

In October 1904 Pierre Curie was named professor of physics at the Sorbonne and Marie Curie was appointed superintendent of his laboratory. Shortly afterward, their second child was born. Adequate income, increased funding, plans for a new laboratory, and the admiration of the world's scientific community promised to make the remaining years of the Curies' research highly productive. Like Becquerel, however, Pierre Curie died too soon to savor his triumphs or to win new ones. On a rainy day, April 19, 1906, he slipped while crossing a Paris street. The wheel of a horse-drawn cart crushed his skull, and he died instantly.

Marie Curie inherited Pierre's chair at the Sorbonne, where she carried on radium research. She succeeded in isolating elemental radium in 1910, and in 1911 she won the Nobel Prize for Chemistry. In 1923 she published a biography of Pierre Curie. The Curies' elder daughter, Irène (IRÈNE JOLIOT-CURIE), shared the Nobel Prize for Chemistry with her husband in 1935. Their younger daughter, Eve, became a concert pianist and her mother's biographer.

Known as a serious, reserved man who was devoted almost entirely to his work, Pierre Curie nevertheless had a kind and gentle disposition. He was a knowledgeable amateur naturalist, and one of the few diversions he enjoyed was walking or cycling in the country. Despite the pressures of their work and family life, he and Marie found time for bicycle trips together.

Pierre Curie received several awards and honors in addition to the Nobel Prize, including the Davy Medal of the Royal Society of London (1903), and the Matteucci Gold Medal of the National Academy of Sciences of Italy (1904). He was elected to the French Academy of Sciences in 1905.

SELECTED WORKS: Recent Research on Radioactivity, 1904.

DALE

ABOUT: Curie, M. Pierre Curie, 1923; Dictionary of Scientific Biography, volume 3, 1971; Riedman, S. R. Men and Women Behind the Atom, 1958; Romer, A. (ed.) The Discovery of Radioactivity and Transmutation, 1964; Rubin, E. The Curies and Radium, 1961.

DALE, HENRY H.
(June 9, 1875–July 23, 1968)
Nobel Prize for Physiology or Medicine, 1936
(shared with Otto Loewi)

HENRY H. DALE

The English physiologist and pharmacologist Henry Hallett Dale was born in London, the son of Charles Dale, a businessman, and the former Francis Hallett. He received his early education at Tollington Park College in London and at the Leys School in Cambridge. Dale later attributed his early interest in the natural sciences to what he called his good fortune in encountering teachers who had some special knowledge of those subjects and the gift for transmitting their own enthusiasm. In 1894 he entered Trinity College, Cambridge University, on a scholarship. Cambridge, a humanistic college with a centuries-old scientific tradition, was at the time one of the great European centers for research in physiology. There Dale attended advanced lectures given by the well-known physiologist W. H. Gaskell, and in 1898 he took high honors on his final examination in the natural sciences, zoology, and physiology. Awarded the Coutts-Trotter Studentship, he worked for the next two years in the physiology laboratories at Cambridge, doing experimental research.

While at Cambridge, Dale became acquainted with two other well-known physiologists, J. N. Langley and H. K. Anderson, who had recently described the two divisions of the autonomic, or involuntary, nervous system: the sympathetic and parasympathetic systems. The autonomic nervous system, first described in the seventeenth century, serves the internal organs of the body (for example, the heart, the blood vessels, and the intestinal and urinary tracts). By contrast, the voluntary nervous system, as the name implies, serves the muscles under conscious control, such as those that manipulate the arms and legs.

In the early years of the twentieth century, it was generally assumed that nerve impulses moved directly from one nerve cell to the next, or from a terminal nerve cell to the tissue it affected, in a chain reaction. It was also assumed that the rapid transmission of nerve impulses ruled out the possibility that they were transmitted by a chemical substance. Dale's colleague and lifelong friend T. R. Elliott, also at the physiology laboratories in Cambridge, was the first to propose the chemical-transmission hypothesis. He suggested in 1903 that nerve impulses in the sympathetic nervous system were transmitted by adrenaline.

Dale himself was not yet involved in the study of nerve transmission. He had continued his clinical training at St. Bartholomew's Hospital in London for two years until 1902, when, faced with the choice of further training in clinical medicine or in research, he chose research. For the next two years he did experimental work at University College, London, with the physiologists Ernest Starling and William Bayliss, who had recently discovered a hormone in the intestinal tract that caused the pancreas to release insulin. In his research Dale investigated the effects of this hormone, called secretin, on pancreatic tissue. Working in Starling's laboratory, he gained a better understanding of experimental methods and of the problems of interpreting experimental data. Near the end of his studentship, he spent several months at PAUL EHRLICH's institute in Frankfurt, Germany.

Dale rejected the advice of friends to remain in academic research and in 1904 accepted an offer from Henry Wellcome, the proprietor of Burroughs Wellcome and Company, a pharmaceutical firm. He subsequently became director of research at the company's Physiological Research Laboratories in London. Wellcome expressed a hope that Dale "might find it possible to do something about the pharmacology of ergot," a chemical product of a fungus that grows on rye and other grains. Extract of ergot had been used for years to produce contractions of the muscles of the uterus, especially after childbirth. Dale and George Barger, the laboratory's organic chemist, sought to identify the various chemical components of ergot and to determine their biological functions.

During his first two years at the Wellcome laboratories, where he remained as director for ten years, Dale made two important discoveries, both by chance. He noticed in the course of one experiment that ergot interfered with the effects of the hormone adrenaline on blood pressure. Usually, adrenaline causes the blood vessels to constrict and blood pressure to rise. Ergot caused what Dale called adrenaline reversal. His findings later became the basis for a diagnostic test for high blood pressure caused by tumors of the adrenal gland (pheochromocytomas). Dale also discovered the pituitary gland hormone oxytocin, which facilitates contractions of the uterus and stimulates lactation.

While attending a conference of physiologists in 1907 in Heidelberg, Germany, Dale witnessed a demonstration of the biological effects of an extract of ergot. He concluded that the effects produced by the demonstration were caused by a contaminant in the extract, and when he returned to London he began a series of experiments to prove his hypothesis. By 1910 he and Barger had identified the contaminant as histamine, a chemical found in many animal and vegetable tissues. Four years later Dale published an extensive review of the physiology of acetylcholine, another substance that he had isolated from a batch of ergot. He described a remarkable similarity between the biological effects of acetylcholine and those produced by electrical stimulation of parasympathetic nerve fibers.

With the outbreak of World War I in 1914, Dale was appointed to the staff of the National Institute of Medical Research, where he worked to standardize the dosages of certain drugs, including diphtheria antitoxin.

Resuming his research after the war, Dale demonstrated that histamine is the chemical mediator of "the weal and erythema reaction," that is, the red welt that forms when tissue is injured. He also proposed that histamine is the chemical mediator of anaphylactic shock, the hypersensitive reaction to certain foreign substances, such as that from a bee sting. Anaphylactic shock was later shown to be caused by other chemical substances in addition to histamine. In 1919 and again in 1927, Dale delivered lectures on the physiology of histamine before the Royal Society of London and the Royal Society of Physicians of England.

Meanwhile, he continued the work on the international standardization of drugs and antitoxins that he had begun during World War I. At conferences of the Health Committee of the League of Nations, which were convened in Copenhagen and Geneva in the 1920s, Dale was instrumental in obtaining agreements among nations for the standardization of dosage and quality of insulin, digitalis, vitamins, thyroid and pituitary gland extracts, and diphtheria antitoxin.

In 1921 OTTO LOEWI demonstrated that nerve impulses in the sympathetic and parasympathetic nervous systems are transmitted by chemical substances. Five years later, he proved that the parasympathetic neurotransmitter is acetylcholine. Between 1929 and 1936, Dale and his colleagues at the National Institute of Medical Research, where Dale had been appointed director of research in 1927, performed a series of notable experiments on acetylcholine. They observed that acetylcholine was also the neurotransmitter in the ganglia, or relay stations, of the autonomic nervous system and at the terminal nerve endings of the voluntary nervous system.

Dale and Loewi shared the 1936 Nobel Prize for Physiology or Medicine "for their discoveries relating to chemical transmission of nerve impulses." Based on Dale's and Loewi's research, an effective treatment for myasthenia gravis, a disease characterized by muscle weakness, was found the same year the pair won the Nobel Prize. In his presentation speech, Gören Liljestrand of the Karolinska Institute said, "You and your school have greatly extended the range of the new conception by later discoveries. Through these various discoveries . . . pharmacology has been very considerably influenced, and physiology or medicine enriched to a high degree."

Dale married his first cousin, Ellen Harriet Hallett; they eventually had one son and two daughters. Their eldest daughter, Alison Sarah, married ALEXANDER TODD. Dale served as president of the Royal Society of London from 1940 until 1945 and as resident director of the Royal Institute of Great Britain from 1942 until 1946. From 1942 until 1947, he was chairman of the Scientific Advisory Committee of the War Cabinet. He was also a trustee of the Wellcome Trust for Medical Research for many years; he retired in 1960. By his own count, Dale made eighteen visits to the United States

241

and Canada, often to deliver lectures. He died in Cambridge, England, on July 23, 1968, at the age of ninety-three.

Dale received numerous international awards and medals, including the Royal Medal and the Copley Medal of the Royal Society. He was awarded two dozen honorary degrees, including one from Princeton University, and was a foreign member of the American Academy of Arts and Sciences and the American National Academy of Sciences.

SELECTED WORKS: Biology and Civilization, 1931; Viruses and Heterogenesis, 1935; The Protection of Science and Learning, 1936; Methods and Aims of Scientific Research, 1945; Adventures in Physiology, 1953; An Autumn Gleaning, 1954.

ABOUT: Biographical Memoirs of Fellows of the Royal Society, volume 16, 1970; Dictionary of Scientific Biography, volume 15, 1978; The Excitement and Fascination of Science, 1965; Ingle, D. J. (ed.) A Dozen Doctors, 1963; Oxbury, H. (ed.) Great Britons, 1985.

DALÉN, NILS

(November 30, 1869–December 9, 1937)
Nobel Prize for Physics, 1912

The Swedish engineer and inventor Nils Gustaf Dalén (dä lān') was born in Stenstorp, in southern Sweden, to Anders Johansson Dalén, a farmer, and the former Lovisa Andersdotter. After completing his preliminary education, he studied agriculture, horticulture, and dairy farming in a school of agriculture. Endowed with a marked mechanical aptitude, Dalén, while still in school, designed and constructed several improved versions of farm equipment. His invention of a device for measuring the butterfat content of milk came to the attention of Gustav de Laval, owner of the de Laval Steam Turbine Company of Stockholm, who suggested that Dalén pursue a technical education.

To prepare himself for an engineering career, Dalén enrolled at the Chalmers Institute in Göteborg in 1892. Four years later he graduated with a degree in mechanical engineering, after which he studied for a year at the Federal Institute of Technology in Zurich, Switzerland. Returning to Sweden in 1897, Dalén established himself as a consulting engineer and began conducting research into hot-air turbines, compressors, and air pumps. In 1900 he and a colleague founded Dalén and Celsing, a small engineering firm.

Dalén joined the Swedish Carbide and

NILS DALÉN

Acetylene Company as technical chief in 1901, the same year that the company acquired the Scandinavian patent rights to a French invention called *Acétylène Dissous*. This product consisted of acetylene dissolved in acetone, the solution then being absorbed by a porous mass that was enclosed within a metallic container. Acetylene, a hydrocarbon gas, burns with an extremely bright white light. Acetone is a highly flammable organic liquid that is often used as a raw material in the manufacture of chemicals. The entire unit, comprising acetylene, acetone, porous mass, and container, is called a gas accumulator.

The Swedish Carbide and Acetylene Company hoped to improve the French version of the gas accumulator so that it could produce a safe and effective fuel for the illumination of lighthouses and buoys. Experience had shown that storing acetylene alone in a gas container was unsafe because of the danger of explosion. Moreover, although acetylene dissolved in acetone is not explosive, the slightest reduction in volume of the solution (from use or from shrinkage induced by low temperature) allows highly explosive acetylene gas to accumulate in the space above the surface of the liquid. Only by forcing the mixture of acetylene and acetone into a porous mass could the potential for explosion be sharply reduced. Not even the patent holders of *Acétylène Dissous* could produce a porous mass that would withstand the jolting and shaking that occur during shipment. The slightest crumbling of the porous material produced fine spaces in which explosive acetylene gas accumulated.

In 1901 Dalén undertook to design an improved gas accumulator and within a short time produced a substance that he called aga. By introducing aga into a steel container half-filled with acetone and then forcing acetylene into the container under pressure of 10 atmospheres, Dalén was able to produce a unit that, at 15°C, contained 100 times its own volume of acetylene and could be transported without danger of detonation from shock.

Subsequently, Dalén made two other improvements in the gas accumulator and the uses to which it could be put. First, he invented a regulator to control the pressure of the gas inside the container; then, in 1905, he designed a highly reliable device that greatly increased the number of extremely brief flashes emitted by a lighthouse to about several thousand per liter of acetylene. The most common arrangement produced a flash with a duration of three-tenths of a second every three seconds. As a reward for his innovative work, the Gas Accumulator Company, which had acquired the Swedish Carbide and Acetylene Company in 1906, promoted Dalén to chief engineer. In 1907 Dalén, in his most ingenious improvement of the gas accumulator, designed a valve that assured that the accumulator would provide gas only at night or in overcast weather, so that light issued from lighthouses and buoys only at those times. Called a sunvalve, the device consisted of four vertical metallic rods enclosed in a transparent glass tube and fixed at their upper ends. Three highly polished rods surround a fourth blackened one. When heated by sunlight reflected onto it by the polished rods, the blackened rod expanded in length and depressed a lever that closed the gas vent, thus extinguishing the light. At nightfall, now cut off from sunlight, the blackened rod cooled and contracted, which permitted the spring-activated lever to rise and open the vent, allowing the passage of gas that was then ignited by a bypass jet. The apparatus could be adjusted to light up at any degree of darkness. The reorganized Swedish Gas Accumulator Company named Dalén its managing director in 1909.

Three years later, while testing safety devices on cylinders of acetylene, Dalén was seriously injured by an explosion that left him permanently blinded. He was awarded the 1912 Nobel Prize for Physics "for his invention of automatic regulators for use in conjunction with gas accumulators for illuminating lighthouses and buoys." "Aga lighting makes it possible for lighthouses and buoys to be established in the most inaccessible spots," said H. G. Söder-

baum of the Royal Swedish Academy of Sciences on presenting the award. Söderbaum added that "the aga light has proved to be extremely useful . . . for the lighting of railway carriages, for railway track signals, for the headlights of cars, for welding, for smelting and cutting metals." Dalén did not deliver a Nobel lecture, and his brother accepted the award for him.

Dalén continued to conduct research despite his blindness. Among his other inventions was an extremely efficient stove. In 1901 he married Elma Persson, with whom he had two sons and two daughters. He was elected to membership in the Royal Swedish Academy of Sciences in 1913; five years later, he received an honorary degree from Lund University. In 1919 Dalén was elected to Sweden's Academy of Science and Engineering. He died in Lidingö, Sweden, on December 9, 1937.

ABOUT: New York Times December 10, 1937; Shipp, H. Lives That Moved the World, 1948.

DAM, HENRIK
(February 21, 1895–April 17, 1976)
Nobel Prize for Physiology or Medicine, 1943
(shared with Edward A. Doisy)

Carl Peter Henrik Dam, Danish biochemist, was born in Copenhagen to Emil Dam, a pharmaceutical chemist and writer of biographical and historical books, and the former Emilie Peterson, a teacher. He studied chemistry at the Polytechnic Institute in Copenhagen and received an M.S. in 1920. After serving as a chemistry instructor at the Royal School of Agriculture and Veterinary Medicine for three years, Dam became a biochemistry instructor at the physiology laboratory of the University of Copenhagen in 1923.

Dam spent the year 1925 at the University of Graz, in Austria, studying microchemical analysis (the microscopic investigation of chemical reactions) with FRITZ PREGL. Returning to Copenhagen, he was appointed assistant professor at the university's Institute of Biochemistry in 1928 and associate professor the following year. For a thesis on the biological importance of sterols, he was awarded a Ph.D. in biochemistry in 1934 from the same university.

It was between 1928 and 1930, while he was studying cholesterol metabolism in chickens, that Dam made his first discoveries about vi-

HENRIK DAM

tamin K. He noted that some of the newly hatched chicks on a sterol-free diet hemorrhaged under the skin, other organs, or in muscles; he also observed a delay in coagulation of blood taken from the chicks for examination. The phenomenon could not be explained by any known dietary factors. "It was therefore safe to announce," he wrote later, "that the new experimental disease was due to a lack of a hitherto unrecognized factor in the diet." Funded by a Rockefeller Fellowship, Dam pursued his studies with Rudolf Schoenheimer in Freiburg, Germany, in 1932–1933, and in Zurich, Switzerland, two years later. There, in collaboration with PAUL KARRER, Dam isolated the previously unrecognized dietary factor from the chlorophyll of green leaves and described it as a fat-soluble vitamin. He called the substance vitamin K, from the first letter of the Scandinavian and German word *koagulation,* thus symbolizing its ability to coagulate blood and prevent hemorrhage.

In his research on the role of the vitamin in blood clotting, Dam found that the synthesis of prothrombin, a protein necessary for initiation of the chain of events in the blood-clotting mechanism, is dependent on vitamin K. Analyzing the chemical structure of vitamin K, EDWARD A. DOISY at St. Louis University showed that its animal and plant forms differ slightly. A third synthetic form, menadione, is used clinically to prevent hemorrhage.

Dam learned that intestinal bacteria produce vitamin K in animals and human beings, and since sufficient amounts of the vitamin are therefore synthesized by most healthy people,

bleeding disorders caused by a diet lacking in the vitamin are rare. Before the discovery of vitamin K, bleeding during surgery and bleeding caused by hemorrhagic diseases, such as jaundice, often proved fatal. Patients with gallstones or similar obstructions were at high risk during surgery because of possible fatal bleeding. Other high-risk patients included those with intestinal disorders such as sprue, celiac disease, and ulcerative colitis; those undergoing antibiotic or anticoagulation treatment; and newborn babies, who are normally born with a low level of prothrombin. The administration of vitamin K, however, has been found to prevent fatal hemorrhaging; moreover, a routine dose of the vitamin given to pregnant women before delivery and to neonatal infants has significantly reduced the death rate among newborns.

Sponsored by the American-Scandinavian Foundation, Dam went on a lecture tour of Canada and the United States in 1940. When the Nazis occupied Denmark that year, he elected to remain in the United States, conducting research first at Woods Hole Marine Biology Laboratory in 1941, then for the next three years at the University of Rochester as a senior research associate. He joined the Rockefeller Institute of Medical Research (now Rockefeller University) in 1945 as an associate member.

For his vitamin K discoveries, Dam was awarded the 1943 Nobel Prize for Physiology or Medicine, which he shared with Doisy. Because of World War II, regular awards ceremonies were suspended. Instead, Dam and Doisy received the prize from the Swedish ambassador to the United States in special ceremonies held in New York under the aegis of the Swedish-American Foundation. Dam delivered a Nobel lecture on "The Discovery of Vitamin K, Its Biological Functions and Therapeutical Application" in 1946.

During his stay abroad, the Polytechnic Institute in Copenhagen named Dam professor of biochemistry in 1941. Assuming the post in 1946, he continued his research on vitamins K and E, fats, cholesterol, and gallstone formation, on which he published more than 100 papers. From 1956 until 1962 Dam served as head of the Biochemical Division of the Danish Fat Research Council.

In 1924 Dam married Inger Olsen of Esrom, Denmark; the couple had no children. He died in Copenhagen on April 17, 1976.

Dam was a member of the American Society of Biological Chemists, the American Institute of Nutrition, the American Botanical Society, the Royal Danish Academy of Sciences and Letters, the Danish Biological Society, the Swiss Chemical Society, and the American Society for Experimental Biology and Medicine.

SELECTED WORKS: Some Studies on Vitamin E, 1941.

ABOUT: Current Biography September 1949; National Cyclopedia of American Biography, volume 6, 1946; New York Times April 25, 1976.

DAUSSET, JEAN
(October 19, 1916–   )
Nobel Prize for Physiology or Medicine, 1980
(shared with Baruj Benacerraf and George D. Snell)

JEAN DAUSSET

The French biologist Jean Baptiste Gabriel Joachim Dausset (dō se′) was born in Toulouse, the fourth child of Henri Pierre Jules Dausset, a successful physician who specialized in radiology and rheumatism, and Elisabeth (Brullard) Dausset. After spending his early years in Biarritz, he moved with his family to Paris when he was eleven. There he attended the Lycée Michelet and graduated with a degree in mathematics. Having decided to follow his father and become a doctor, Dausset entered the University of Paris medical school in the late 1930s. At the outbreak of World War II in 1939, Dausset was drafted into the French medical corps, and the following year, after the German occupation of France, he joined the Free French army in North Africa.

First in Tunisia and later in France during the liberation, Dausset observed many blood transfusions that produced severe reactions in the patient, even when the patient's blood and the transfused blood were of the same type. He later described these adverse reactions as being caused by donors possessing strong anti-A antibodies in their plasma (blood from which blood cells have been removed). He found that these antibodies developed after vaccination with diphtheria and tetanus toxoids, which had a soluble component called substance A. KARL LANDSTEINER's discovery of the main types of human blood had made transfusions safe, for the most part, when blood types were matched. Human blood types are distinguished by the presence or absence of certain proteins (antigens) on the red blood cells. The reaction of antibodies against foreign antigens causes a given blood type to re-

ject another. The ABO antigen system Landsteiner discovered accounts for most reactions of this kind, although other blood antigens and antibodies also play a role.

After his discharge from the military in 1945, Dausset obtained his medical degree from the University of Paris in the same year. He was appointed director of laboratories at the French National Blood Transfusion Center the following year. Upon receiving a leave of absence from the transfusion center in 1948, he obtained a fellowship in hematology at Harvard University; he remained at Harvard for another year as a fellow in immunohematology. After returning to the transfusion center, he studied various aspects of transfusion biology during the late 1940s and early 1950s, concentrating on the problem of abnormal transfusion reactions.

Some patients who have received many transfusions or who have been treated with certain drugs develop reactions against white blood cells, in addition to the red blood cell reactions that Landsteiner had observed. In 1952 Dausset reported on a patient who produced antibodies to an antigen found on some other people's white blood cells but not on his own. In 1958, the year he joined the Faculty of Medicine at the University of Paris, Dausset discovered a number of variants of the white blood cell antigen in the French population. He called these variants MAC (the initials of the three donors in whose blood he had found them). Anti-MAC antibodies are formed when an MAC-negative person receives blood from a donor who is MAC positive.

245

Blood transfusion, Dausset pointed out, is a type of organ transplantation. Early in the twentieth century it was found that tissues transplanted from one person to another are almost certain to be rejected unless the donor and recipient are closely related, preferably as identical twins. Dausset hypothesized that the MAC antigen is one of the factors whereby the body can distinguish its own components from those of another.

Dausset was appointed associate professor of medicine at the University of Paris in 1962. The following year he became chief biologist in the Paris municipal hospital system and co-chairman of the Institute for Research Into Diseases of the Blood.

Following Dausset's discoveries of MAC variants, other researchers amassed a bewildering collection of data on newly found antigens. At a workshop convened in 1965 by Bernard Amos to coordinate research in histocompatibility (the lack of antagonism or toxicity between different tissues that allows a graft to survive and function), Dausset proposed that most of these antigens form part of a single system, a theory suggested by the work of GEORGE D. SNELL and his colleagues during the 1940s. Snell had shown that tissue rejection in mice is controlled by a few physically linked genes called the major histocompatibility complex (MHC). Dausset suggested that an MHC also exists in human beings. Transplantation antigens occur in great variety, he said, not because many different genes affect transplantation, but because many variant forms (or alleles) arise from a single set of genes. It had become clear that, as in mice, the human MHC consists of several genes called the human-lymphocyte-antigen group (HLA). Since each gene occurs in dozens of allelic forms, millions of different HLA combinations are possible.

In 1967 Dausset and a colleague, Felix T. Rapaport, began studies of skin grafts performed among members of the same family. Their results showed conclusively that grafts between family members that have the same HLA type are much more successful than when HLA types differ. The finding led Dausset to urge surgeons to choose organ donors on the basis of HLA type.

The technique of HLA matching makes a substantial difference in the survival of transplanted organs, but only when donor and recipient are also related, usually as siblings. Among unrelated people, genetic differences—other than those identified by Dausset—cause rejection in spite of HLA matching.

Some of these genetic differences are caused by other genes in the MHC. In 1967 Amos and his colleague Fritz Bach discovered another gene, called HLA-D (because it was the fourth HLA gene to be described), which is the human equivalent of the Ir (immune-response) genes in the MHC of the mouse. BARUJ BENACERRAF and other researchers found that Ir genes not only affect survival of transplanted organs but also play a major role in the body's ability to mount an immunological defense against a particular disease. By the early 1970s it was apparent that HLA-D genes were a significant factor in the connection between HLA types and certain diseases.

In 1967 Dausset searched for a link between HLA and disease—he was the first researcher to do so—and although his initial results were not conclusive, his efforts encouraged other researchers. Since then, certain HLA types have been shown to be associated with increased risks for particular diseases, such as joint diseases, diabetes, and autoimmune diseases. Dausset suggested that "each HLA haplotype [group of alleles contributed by either parent] . . . has its own gene configuration that confers on it a particular capacity for immune response, which may be favorable in certain environmental conditions and unfavorable in others."

Dausset became director of the French National Institute for Scientific Research in 1968. That year he also began to teach immunohematology—the study of antigen-antibody reactions in blood disorders—at the University of Paris. In addition, since 1978 he has been a professor of experimental medicine at the Collège de France. During the 1970s he also served as visiting professor at New York University and at the universities of Brussels and Geneva.

The function of the MHC gene products (antigens) has not been definitely established, but in the mid-1970s a number of scientists, including Benacerraf, discovered that cooperation among various cells, especially those in the immune system, is MHC-restricted; that is, both interacting cells must carry the same MHC antigens on the surfaces. Dausset has said that "the restriction phenomenon is probably the most direct proof of the role of the products of the HLA complex in the immune response of man." Although much remains to be learned about the structure of the MHC genes, their activities in the body, and ways to manipulate them for medical purposes, it is clear that the MHC holds a key to knowledge of the immune system in general.

Dausset shared the 1980 Nobel Prize for Physiology or Medicine with Benacerraf and Snell "for their discoveries concerning genetically determined structures on the cell surface that regulate immunological reactions." In his presentation speech, Georg Klein of the Karolinska Institute hailed the three laureates "for turning what at first appeared as an esoteric area of basic research on inbred mice into a major biological system of the greatest significance for the understanding of cell recognition, immune responses, and graft rejection."

Dausset remains at the University of Paris, where he continues his studies of HLA at the Hospital St.-Louis.

A collector of modern art, Dausset lives with his wife, the former Rosa Mayoral Lopez, whom he married in 1962; they have a son and a daughter. He still abides by the credo he adopted in his early days: "vouloir pour valoir," which, loosely translated, means "to reach a worthy goal, one must wish it hard enough."

In addition to the Nobel Prize, Dausset is the recipient of the Gairdner Foundation International Award (1977) and the Wolf Prize in Medicine of the Wolf Foundation in Israel (1978). He is a member of the French academies of science and medicine and of the Belgian Royal Academy of Medicine, an honorary member of the Yugoslavian Academy of Arts and Sciences, an honorary member of the American Academy of Arts and Sciences, and an officer in the Legion of Honor.

SELECTED WORKS: Histocompatibility, 1976, with others; A Modern Illustration of Experimental Medicine in Action, 1980, with Felix T. Rapaport.

ABOUT: Current Biography March 1981; New Scientist October 16, 1980; New York Times October 11, 1980; Science November 7, 1980.

DAVISSON, CLINTON J.

(October 22, 1881–February 1, 1958)
Nobel Prize for Physics, 1937
(shared with G. P. Thomson)

The American physicist Clinton Joseph Davisson was born in Bloomington, Illinois, one of two children and the only son of Joseph Davisson, a painting contractor, and Mary (Calvert) Davisson, a schoolteacher. Davisson graduated from Bloomington High School in 1902. On a scholarship to the University of Chicago, he proved to be such an outstanding physics student that one of his professors,

CLINTON J. DAVISSON

ROBERT A. MILLIKAN, recommended him as a temporary instructor to Purdue University in the middle of the 1903–1904 academic year, to replace a physics teacher who had died. Davisson returned to Chicago in 1904 and became a physics instructor at Princeton University the following year. During four summer sessions at the University of Chicago, he completed his B.S. in 1908. At Princeton, Davisson served as research assistant to the English physicist OWEN W. RICHARDSON, who was also his doctoral thesis adviser. He completed his Ph.D. in physics (with a minor in mathematics) in 1911. His thesis, "On the Thermal Emission of Positive Ions From Hot Bodies," was in the field of *thermionics,* a word Richardson had coined to describe the emission of electrically charged particles from hot bodies.

Throughout his college and graduate school years, Davisson was almost entirely self-supporting. In August 1911 he married Richardson's sister Charlotte Sara, with whom he had four children. When Davisson became an assistant professor of physics at the Carnegie Institute of Technology, the couple moved to Pittsburgh. His teaching load was so heavy that in six years he was able to carry only one research project to the point that he could publish it.

When the United States entered World War I in 1917, Davisson tried to enlist but was rejected. He was unusually slight of stature, and although his health was generally sound, he was forced to conserve his energy, which seemed limited.

Taking a leave from Carnegie Tech during

the war years, Davisson joined the engineering department of the Western Electric Company, where he worked on vacuum tubes for use in military telecommunications. These devices act as electronic valves to regulate the flow of electrons from a heated filament to a positively charged metal plate. The voltage on a metal mesh interposed between filament and plate modulates the flow of electrons. Despite the demands of wartime research, Davisson was able to work on fundamental physics propositions and soon established a reputation for his ability to solve problems. At the end of the war, Davisson remained at Western Electric's engineering department (which later became Bell Telephone Laboratories).

At Western Electric, Davisson investigated thermionics and the emission of electrons from metals under electron bombardment, seeking the mechanisms responsible for electron emission from the metallic filament of vacuum tubes. If the filament or its coating of metallic oxides (which increases the rate of electron emission) fails, the vacuum tube becomes useless. Davisson's research played a major role in making vacuum tubes into long-lived electronic devices.

In these newer, more complex vacuum tubes containing intermediate metal grids, when primary electrons traveling from the filament to the receiving plate were too energetic, they caused the grids to emit numerous secondary electrons that affected the performance of the tubes adversely. In 1919 Davisson set out to study the interaction of electrons with metal surfaces by directing an electron beam against such a surface and measuring the rate at which electrons left it, as well as their energies and angles. With a colleague, C. H. Kunsman, Davisson measured the scattering of electrons by polycrystalline metals (commercially available metals consist of many very small crystals) but was unable to explain the scatter patterns obtained. In 1925 the German physicist Walter Elsasser suggested that such patterns were caused by the wavelike nature of the electron. Indeed, the French physicist LOUIS DE BROGLIE had recently suggested that electrons had a wavelike nature, the wavelength of each electron being inversely proportional to its velocity. Elsasser argued that the voltages employed by Davisson had given the electrons a wavelength comparable to that of X rays, one that interacted effectively with the atomic spacing of the metal crystal. Because Elsasser was unable to confirm this hypothesis experimentally, however, Davisson did not accept it.

During an investigation of the scattering of electrons, also conducted in 1925, the nickel target being used by Davisson and Lester H. Germer became heavily oxidized after a vacuum failure. To remove the oxide, they heated the target first in hydrogen and then in a vacuum. Focusing a beam of high-speed electrons on different faces of the nickel crystal target, they measured the number of electrons reflected at different angles. Initially, the electrons wired reflected regularly, like rubber balls bouncing off a hard wall. After the heat-induced alteration in structure of the crystal target, the electron-scattering pattern showed a strong dependence on crystal direction. Davisson and Germer, attributing the altered distribution-in-angle to the diffraction of electrons by the target, which now consisted of a few large crystals instead of many tiny ones, undertook studies of electron scatter from single-crystal metal targets.

At the 1926 meeting of the British Association for the Advancement of Science, Davisson discussed his experimental results with MAX BORN, JAMES FRANCK, and P. M. S. BLACKETT. They convinced him that Elsasser's explanation was correct, and that his results were due to the effects of de Broglie waves. Returning to his laboratory, Davisson began a systematic search for some sort of interference phenomenon; in January 1927 he observed electron beams resulting from diffraction by a single crystal of nickel. The experimental results agreed closely with predictions based on Broglie's electron wave theory.

Davisson and G. P. THOMSON shared the 1937 Nobel Prize for Physics "for their experimental discovery of the diffraction of electrons by crystals." Both men had demonstrated the same phenomenon, although Thomson had worked independently and had employed different methods. On presenting the award, Hans Pleijel of the Royal Swedish Academy of Sciences pointed out that the achievement of Davisson and Thomson had not only "widened . . . our knowledge of the nature of electrons" but also "resulted in . . . the first positive, experimental evidence of the wave nature of matter."

Davisson turned next to the study of electron optics, particularly as applied to engineering problems. His work on the interaction of electron beams with electric and magnetic fields in space contributed to the development of the electron microscope by ERNST RUSKA in 1933.

Davisson's later application of electron beams to crystal physics led to tools for investigating surface structure and chemistry. Davisson's work was also applied to the design of microwave sources for radar applications as well as to the physics and design of quartz oscillators.

With their four children, the Davissons spent summers at their home in Brooklin, Maine, which Davy, as he was known to his friends, built with his own hands during these yearly visits. There he walked, read, played tennis, attended the theater, and worked on problems of theoretical physics. Davisson was one of the few industrial scientists with no desire for positions of management or leadership; his inner driving force was for complete and exact knowledge of the physical phenomena under study. Throughout his career in industry, associates came to Davisson to discuss fundamental problems in urgent need of solution; they rarely left him without having benefited.

After retiring from Bell Laboratories in 1946, Davisson became a visiting research professor at the University of Virginia, remaining there until 1954. He died in his sleep in Charlottesville, Virginia, on February 1, 1958.

Davisson belonged to many scientific societies, including the National Academy of Sciences and the National Research Council. He received the Comstock Prize of the National Academy of Sciences (1928), the Elliott Cresson Medal of the Franklin Institute (1931), the Hughes Medal of the Royal Society of London (1935), and the Alumni Medal of the University of Chicago (1941). He held honorary doctorates from Purdue University, Princeton University, the University of Lyons, and Colby College.

SELECTED WORKS: The Conception and Demonstration of Electron Waves, 1932.

ABOUT: Biographical Memoirs of the National Academy of Sciences, volume 36, 1962; Dictionary of American Biography, supplement 6, 1980; Dictionary of Scientific Biography, volume 3, 1971; Thomson, G. The Inspiration of Science, 1961.

DAWES, CHARLES
(August 27, 1865–April 23, 1951)
Nobel Prize for Peace, 1925
(shared with J. Austen Chamberlain)

Charles Gates Dawes, American diplomat, statesman, and vice president of the United States, was born in Marietta, Ohio, to Rufus R. Dawes and the former Mary Beman Gates. His father, the owner of a thriving local mill, had risen to the rank of general during the Civil War and had served one term in Congress. The Yankee flavor of Marietta, which had been founded by settlers from New England after the American Revolution, strongly influenced Dawes's character and personality. Dawes attended Marietta Academy and College before graduating from Cincinnati Law School in 1886.

At the age of nineteen, Dawes set out to make his fortune in the then-booming city of Lincoln, Nebraska, where he founded the law firm of Dawes, Coffroth & Cunningham in 1887. Two years later, he married Carol Blymyer of Cincinnati; they had one son and one daughter and adopted two more children. Dawes soon established a reputation as a strong advocate of farmers in their grievances against the railroads, which often charged arbitrary and discriminatory freight rates. His successful handling of one important case against the railroads made him a local hero. As his law practice flourished, Dawes formed close friendships with the populist politician William Jennings Bryan and Lieutenant (later General) John J. Pershing.

When the panic of 1893 drove him $200,000 in debt, Dawes moved to Chicago. He borrowed money to invest in gas and electric companies in La Crosse, Wisconsin, and Evanston, Illinois, and within a few years was once again on the road to prosperity. During this time, he remained active in local politics and successfully managed William McKinley's campaign for the Republican presidential nomination in Illinois. In 1897, after McKinley had been elected president, he appointed Dawes comptroller of the currency. During his four years in this capacity, Dawes helped reorganize many of the banks that had collapsed in the panic of 1893.

At McKinley's urging, Dawes resigned his federal post in 1901 to run for the United States Senate. However, McKinley's assassination cut short Dawes's political career for the time being. Defeated at the polls, Dawes gave up elective politics and instead used his knowledge of banking to found the Central Trust Company of Illinois. Under his leadership, the bank—often referred to as the Dawes Bank—became one of the largest in the Midwest.

When the United States entered World War I in 1917, Dawes volunteered to serve in the army. General Pershing obtained a commission for him as a major and assigned him to manage the army's acquisition and distribution of supplies. Arriving in France in July, Dawes joined the headquarters staff of the American Expeditionary Force. He was so successful in

CHARLES DAWES

his job that by the end of the war he had been promoted to brigadier general and was overseeing the supply needs of all the European Allied forces. He remained on active duty into 1919 to supervise the liquidation of surplus military equipment in France.

On his return to the United States, Dawes urged American involvement in the League of Nations. Also a strong advocate of a national budget, he was appointed first director of the Bureau of the Budget in 1921 after turning down the post of treasury secretary.

Shortly before becoming budget director, Dawes was called to testify before a congressional committee investigating wartime fraud and corruption. Angrily denouncing politicians who sought to gain headlines at the expense of the men who had fought in the war, Dawes won a national reputation for bluntness. He also acquired the nickname "Hell and Maria." When a member of the committee asked him if it were true that excessive prices had been paid for mules in France, he slammed his fist on the table and exclaimed in frustration, "Hell and Maria, I'd have paid horse prices for sheep if the sheep could have pulled artillery to the front! We were fighting a war. We did not have time for duplicate vouchers and double entry bookkeeping."

As part of the Treaty of Versailles signed at the end of the war, the victorious Allies forced Germany to accept the blame for the war and to pay them the massive sum of 20 billion marks in reparations. The war-ravaged German economy could not manage such a debt, and when Germany defaulted in 1923,

French and Belgian troops occupied the Ruhr Valley. The United States was drawn into the crisis because the French and English were counting on German reparations to repay their own war debts to the United States.

Secretary of State Charles Evans Hughes proposed in December 1922 that an international committee of financial experts be created to resolve the crisis. The Allied Reparations Commission accepted the American proposal a year later and invited two prominent citizens each from Italy, Belgium, Great Britain, France, and the United States to sit on the committee. Dawes was well qualified for the position, since his role as purchasing agent for the Allied forces had brought him into contact with many European leaders, who regarded him highly. Accompanied by the American businessman Owen D. Young and an industrious staff, Dawes sailed for Europe in December 1923.

The Committee of Experts, as it was known at that time, faced a seemingly insoluble dilemma. For the European economy to revive, Germany had to regain economic prosperity; yet the prospect of an economically strong Germany troubled the French and Belgians, who feared that Germany would then again pose a threat to European peace. In his first speech to the committee, Dawes, named chairman in January 1924, captured the public imagination. "This is no time to mince words. The house is afire," he declared. "We propose to find some water to put it out, without the further use of mathematics involving the fourth dimension."

The committee presented its report, which became known as the Dawes Plan, in April. It called for the evacuation of the Ruhr Valley by Allied occupation troops, a sliding scale of reparation payments that would start at 1 billion gold marks and rise over a period of four years to 2.5 billion marks per year, and reorganization of the German Reichsbank under Allied supervision. It also allowed for loans to be given to Germany by Allied nations. Moreover, it stipulated that excise and transportation taxes and custom duties should serve as sources for reparation funds. Responding to criticism that the scheme might make Germany too strong, Dawes replied: "It is clear that every program is attended by dangerous contingencies. The only course we can take is a plain one—to assume that peace, well guarded, and not war, is the normal state of modern man." After the provisions went into effect in September 1924, German currency and credit were reestablished.

Hailed as "the savior of Europe" on his return to the United States, Dawes was chosen as Calvin Coolidge's vice presidential running mate at the 1924 Republican National Convention. After assuming office the following year, Dawes took an active role in legislative matters. Among his efforts was a futile campaign to curtail the use of the filibuster in the Senate.

Largely in recognition of his contributions to the Dawes Plan, Dawes was awarded the 1925 Nobel Prize for Peace, which he shared with J. AUSTEN CHAMBERLAIN. Reserved in 1925, the prize was given the following year and accepted by Laurits Swenson, a member of the United States diplomatic mission in Oslo, in Dawes's absence. Although he delivered no lecture, Dawes sent a brief message expressing his gratitude to the Norwegian Nobel Committee and to the other members of the Reparations Commission.

During the two years it was in operation, the Dawes Plan enabled Germany to pay more than two billion marks in reparations and at the same time begin to rebuild its economy. As American banks and corporations lent money to Germany, the United States, with its own strong manufacturing capabilities, became a major economic force and captured a large part of the European market. The plan dissolved through the mutual neglect of both sides. France and other former Allies objected because part of Germany's payment was in goods rather than in gold, whereas Germany, as it recovered, felt it was sacrificing too much of its economic growth to satisfy the plan.

At the end of his vice presidential term in 1929, Dawes was appointed American ambassador to Great Britain, a post he held until 1932. He was then recalled by President Herbert Hoover to assume responsibility for the Reconstruction Finance Corporation (RFC). Created at the outset of the Great Depression, the RFC attempted to stimulate the economy through loans to banks, railroads, and other fundamental enterprises. After four months, however, Dawes resigned to head the board of Chicago's failing Central Republic Bank and Trust Company, the institution with which his bank (the Central Trust Company) had merged. In response to appeals by the bank's board members and the RFC directors, Dawes agreed to apply for a large government loan to avoid a general banking collapse. Even though he drew extensive criticism for accepting the loan, this move stabilized banking in Chicago, and his reorganized bank repaid the RFC in full.

Dawes never held public office again, devoting his time to diverse business and philanthropic interests. In memory of his son, who had drowned in 1912, Dawes founded two homes for indigent men in Chicago and Boston. An accomplished pianist and flutist, he composed a number of works for these instruments; his "Melody in A Major" achieved some popularity. Dawes also combined his love of music with his business skill to establish grand opera in Chicago. He died of a coronary thrombosis on April 23, 1951.

SELECTED WORKS: The Banking System of the United States, 1894; Essays and Speeches, 1915; Journal of the Great War (2 vols.) 1921; The First Year of the Budget of the United States, 1923; Notes as Vice President 1928–1929, 1935; How Long Prosperity? 1937; Journal as Ambassador to Great Britain, 1939; A Journal of Reparations, 1939; A Journal of the McKinley Years, 1950.

ABOUT: Ackerman, C. W. Dawes the Doer, 1924; Auld, G. P. The Dawes Plan and the New Economics, 1927; Dawes, R. C. The Dawes Plan in the Making, 1925; Dictionary of American Biography, supplement 5, 1977; Leach, L. R. That Man Dawes, 1930; Leffler, M. P. The Elusive Quest, 1979; National Cyclopedia of American Biography, volume A, 1930; New York Times April 24, 1951; Ostrower, G. B. Collective Insecurity, 1979; Timmon, B. N. Charles G. Dawes: Portrait of an American, 1953.

DEBREU, GERARD

(July 4, 1921–)
Nobel Memorial Prize in Economic
 Sciences, 1983

The French-American economist Gerard Debreu (də brû′) was born in Calais, the son of Camille and Fernande (Decharne) Debreu. Both of his grandfathers and his father owned small lace-making businesses in the area.

Debreu studied at the College of the City of Calais and received his baccalaureate in 1939. He intended to study mathematics in Paris, but because World War II had broken out, he instead attended two improvised preparatory schools, one in Ambert, the other in Grenoble, both in the Free Zone established after the German occupation of France. In the summer of 1941, he entered the École Normale Supérieure in Paris, where he found a "superheated intellectual atmosphere" heightened by the "dark outside world of Paris under German occupation." He remained there until the liberation of Paris in 1944, when he enlisted in the French army. He attended officers' training school in Algeria and then served in Germany with the French army until the summer of 1945.

GERARD DEBREU

Returning to the École Normale, he passed his *agrégation* in mathematics in 1946, which qualified him to teach. Since he had developed an interest in economics, he then went to the National Center for Scientific Research as an associate in economics. In the summer of 1948 he studied in Austria under the economist WASSILY LEONTIEF at the Salzburg Seminar in American Studies. He spent the following year and a half as a Rockefeller Fellow, visiting the economics departments of several leading universities in the United States and Scandinavia.

In the fall of 1949 Debreu accepted a position as research associate at the Cowles Commission for Research in Economics, then located at the University of Chicago. He remained with the commission for eleven years, except for a six-month leave in 1953 to work at the Electric Service of France in Paris. In 1956 he received a Ph.D. from the University of Paris. In 1962 he went to the University of California at Berkeley as a professor of economics, and in 1975 he was appointed professor of mathematics there.

Debreu's work has been concerned with the central issue in economics, the theory of general equilibrium, a topic whose basis lies in the writings of Adam Smith, the eighteenth-century Scottish economist. The interdependent nature of the market economy and its related laws of supply and demand were subsequently the focus of the work of Léon Walras, a French mathematician, who is credited with forming the theory of general equilibrium in the 1840s.

Debreu encountered the problem of general equilibrium at the École Normale through Maurice Allais, who in 1943 reformulated the theory in his book *A la recherche d'une discipline économique* (In Search of an Economic Discipline). In 1952, while at the Cowles Commission, Debreu published his first article on this subject. Two years later he collaborated with KENNETH ARROW on a classic article titled "Existence of an Equilibrium for a Competitive Economy," in which they proved the existence of nonnegative equilibrating prices under relatively unrestrictive conditions. In his 1959 book *The Theory of Value: An Axiomatic Analysis of Economic Equilibrium,* Debreu extended his "existence proofs" to more general cases, discussing many possible equilibrium solutions.

The Theory of Value, which contains Debreu's mathematical analysis of general equilibrium, is a classic work in twentieth-century economic theory, the culmination of a tradition reaching back to Adam Smith. Its expository elegance and mathematical rigor are unrivaled. This book and many of his other works show Debreu's great contributions to various fields of economics, such as welfare theory, utility theory, and the derivation of demand functions. Debreu has even used mathematical tools to approach such a "practical" problem as welfare loss from taxation policy. He has also considered problems of economic uncertainty, including future markets for commodities, and has investigated the conditions under which prices in the system converge toward their equilibrating values.

Many economists have difficulty grasping Debreu's highly abstract thinking and mathematical language. His assumptions about how markets and people function may seem unrealistic, and his results may appear impossible to apply to economic reality. There is a need, however, for pure theory as a basis for analyzing economic reality. Debreu and his followers have in this indirect way contributed immensely to the progress of economic science.

Debreu was awarded the 1983 Nobel Memorial Prize in Economic Sciences for his contributions "to our understanding of general equilibrium theory and the conditions under which there exists a general equilibrium in an abstract economy." According to Karl-Göran Mäler of the Royal Swedish Academy of Sciences, Debreu's work on general equilibrium theory "has not merely given us information about the price mechanism but also introduced new analytical techniques, new tools in the toolbox of economists." Moreover, Mäler continued, Debreu's "insightful analysis of models of abstract economies" has provided economists with a general theory that can be applied to a wide variety of situations.

In 1945 Debreu married Françoise Bled; they have two daughters. He became a United States citizen in 1975. Unlike many of his colleagues, Debreu has remained an academic, declining invitations to serve as a consultant to industry or government. He lives a quiet life in Berkeley. Gifted students and colleagues from all over the world have been drawn to Berkeley because of his work, and his well-attended lectures have been described as exceptional for their mathematical rigor and virtual lack of verbal explanation.

In addition to the Nobel Prize, Debreu was made a chevalier of the Legion of Honor of France in 1976. He has been a Guggenheim Fellow at the Center for Operations Research and Econometrics at the University of Louvain, Belgium (1968–1969); an Erskine Fellow at the University of Canterbury, Christchurch, New Zealand (summer of 1969); and an overseas fellow, Churchill College, Cambridge (spring of 1972). He is a member of the American Academy of Arts and Sciences, the National Academy of Sciences, the American Economic Association, and the American Association for the Advancement of Science. He has received honorary degrees from the universities of Bonn and Lausanne, Northwestern University, and the University of Social Sciences of Toulouse.

ADDITIONAL WORKS: Mathematical Economics, 1981.

ABOUT: Hildenbrand, W., and Mas-Colell, A. (eds.) Contributions to Mathematical Economics in Honor of Gerard Debreu, 1986; New York Times October 18, 1983; October 23, 1983; Scandinavian Journal of Economics, number 1, 1984; Science December 2, 1983.

DE BROGLIE, LOUIS
See BROGLIE, LOUIS DE

DEBYE, PETER
(March 24, 1884–November 2, 1966)
Nobel Prize for Chemistry, 1936

The Dutch-American physicist Peter Joseph William Debye (de bī′) was born Petrus Josephus Wilhelmus Debjie in Maastricht, the Netherlands, to Maria (Reumkens) Debjie and Wilhelmus Johannes Debjie, a supervisor at a metalware manufacturing firm. While attend-

ing the local primary and secondary schools, he studied languages, mathematics, and the natural sciences. Upon graduation in 1901 he entered the technical university in Aachen, Germany, to study electrical engineering.

At Aachen, Debye (as he later spelled his name) developed an interest in chemistry and physics. One of his teachers, the physicist Max Wien, gave Debye permission to conduct private experiments in the school's physics laboratory when it was not in use, which further whetted his appetite for scientific research. While still an undergraduate, he became an assistant to Arnold Sommerfeld, who was then a professor of technical mechanics.

In 1906, a year after receiving his degree in electrical engineering, Debye accompanied Sommerfeld to the University of Munich and served as his assistant for five years. Debye completed his dissertation on the effects of radiation pressure on spheres of arbitrary electrical properties and received his Ph.D. in physics in 1908. Two years later he qualified as a lecturer at Munich but left in 1911 to succeed ALBERT EINSTEIN as professor of theoretical physics at the University of Zurich in Switzerland.

At Zurich, Debye began investigating the structure of molecules. Although the chemical composition of complex molecules was generally understood at the time, little was known about the physical and structural connections between atoms. Within a year Debye had focused his attention on the distribution of electrical charges in atoms and molecules. He became particularly interested in polarity (the positive-to-negative orientation of such charges) and found that differences between the degree of polarity, or dipole moment, of a molecule and that of its component atoms can clarify their relative positions when chemically combined. Debye also revised Einstein's quantum theory of specific heat (the amount of energy needed to raise the temperature of a substance by one degree Celsius) and developed a formula for calculating the associated temperature, now called the Debye temperature.

In 1912 Debye transferred to the University of Utrecht in the Netherlands, and two years later he became professor of theoretical physics at the University of Göttingen, where he remained for the next six years. During this time Debye's molecular studies took a new direction, based on a recent discovery by MAX VON LAUE that X rays are diffracted, or bent in characteristic patterns, when passed through crystals. Aware that the wavelength of X rays was small enough to be useful in measuring

PETER DEBYE

the distances between atoms in a molecule, Debye demonstrated an association between the diffraction patterns and thermal movements of atoms in crystals. His major insight came in 1916 when, working with Paul Scherrer, he realized that, even in a powder of small or imperfect crystals, enough crystals would be so aligned that X-ray diffraction studies could elucidate molecular structure. The Debye-Scherrer method emerged as a powerful tool for determining the structure of highly symmetrical crystals.

Debye returned to the University of Zurich as a professor of physics in 1920, serving also as director of the physical institute of the prestigious Federal Institute of Technology. Over the next few years, he made fundamental contributions to the study of electrolytes, substances that break into positive and negative ions in solutions. The Debye-Hückel theory, published by Erich Hückel in 1923, mathematically calculates the ionic intensities of electrolytic solutions. It was also in 1923 that Debye developed a quantitative theory of the Compton effect (named for ARTHUR H. COMPTON), providing additional evidence for the wave-particle nature of light.

At the University of Leipzig between 1927 and 1934, Debye used X-ray diffraction to measure interatomic distances in gases and continued his studies on dipole moments and electrolytes. He then moved to the University of Berlin, where he supervised the founding of the Kaiser Wilhelm Institute of Physics (now the Max Planck Institute) and used electrons in his diffraction work on gases.

Debye was awarded the 1936 Nobel Prize for Chemistry "for his contributions to our knowledge of molecular structure through his investigations on dipole moments and on the diffraction of X rays and electrons in gases." In addition to the theoretical value of his findings, Debye's work later contributed to improved manufacturing techniques for explosives, pharmaceuticals, dyes, and other chemical products.

Although he had been assured he could retain his Dutch citizenship while working in Berlin, Debye found in 1939 that he was barred from his laboratory unless he became a German citizen. Refusing this option, Debye left to deliver the Baker lectures at Cornell University in Ithaca, New York. He remained there as chairman of the Cornell chemistry department. His work at Cornell and at Bell Laboratories yielded new ways of calculating the size of complex polymer molecules.

In 1946 Debye became a naturalized American citizen. After retiring from Cornell in 1952, he was made an emeritus professor and continued his investigations in the field of polymers. In addition to lecturing widely, he contributed much of his time helping to establish an institute of science and technology at the University of Michigan in 1960.

In 1914 Debye married Mathilda Alberer, with whom he had a son and a daughter. Admired by his students and colleagues as a friendly, highly accessible man and an excellent lecturer, Debye enjoyed fishing in his leisure time. He died of a heart attack in Ithaca on November 2, 1966.

Debye was the recipient of many honors and awards in addition to the Nobel Prize. He received the Rumford Medal of the Royal Society of London (1930), the Lorentz Medal of the Royal Netherlands Academy of Arts and Sciences (1935), the Franklin Medal of the Franklin Institute (1937), the Willard Gibbs Medal of the American Chemical Society (1949), and the Priestley Medal of the American Chemical Society (1963). He was awarded honorary degrees from Harvard University, Brooklyn Polytechnic Institute, St. Lawrence University, Colgate University, the Federal Institute of Technology of Zurich, Boston College, Oxford University, and the universities of Brussels, Liège, and Sophia. He held membership in numerous scientific societies, including the Royal Society of London, the American Physical Society, the American Chemical Society, the American Philosophical Society, the Franklin Institute, the Royal Netherlands Academy of Arts and Sciences, the Scientific Society of Brussels, the Göttingen Academy of Sciences, and the science academies of Munich, Leningrad, Berlin, Boston, and Washington.

SELECTED WORKS: Polar Molecules, 1929; The Structure of Matter, 1934; The Structure of Polymers, 1949; Collected Papers, 1954; Topics in Chemical Physics, 1962; Molecular Forces, 1967.

ABOUT: Current Biography July 1963; Dictionary of Scientific Biography, volume 3, 1971; Journal of Chemical Education July 1968; Physics Today January 1985.

DE CONSTANT, PAUL D'ESTOUR-
NELLES
See D'ESTOURNELLES, DE CONSTANT, PAUL

DE DUVE, CHRISTIAN
See DUVE, CHRISTIAN DE

DE HEVESY, GEORGE
See HEVESY, GEORGE DE

DELBRÜCK, MAX
(September 4, 1906–March 10, 1981)
Nobel Prize for Physiology or Medicine, 1969
(shared with Alfred Hershey and Salvador Luria)

The German-American molecular biologist Max Ludwig Henning Delbrück (del′ brük) was born in Berlin, the youngest of seven children of Hans Delbrück, a professor of history at the University of Berlin and editor of the journal *Prussian Yearbook*. His mother, Lina (Thiersch) Delbrück, was the daughter of a Leipzig surgery professor and the granddaughter of the chemist Justus von Liebig. Raised in the middle-class suburb of Grünewald, Delbrück showed an early interest in mathematics and astronomy.

After graduating from the Grünewald Gymnasium, he enrolled in the University of Tübingen in 1924 to study astronomy, but after one semester he transferred to the University of Berlin, where his tuition was free because his father was a faculty member. He made another move to the University of Bonn and then returned to the University of Berlin, settling eventually at the University of Göttingen for three years. At Göttingen, Delbrück began

MAX DELBRÜCK

California Institute of Technology

writing a dissertation on the origin of celestial novae, but, hampered by an inability to read the pertinent literature, which was in English, and an insufficient command of the mathematics of astrophysical theory, he abandoned the thesis. At the time, Göttingen was a leading center of quantum mechanics, and in the course of his work there, Delbrück encountered EUGENE P. WIGNER and MAX BORN, both of whom were on the faculty. Using one of Born's theorems as the basis for a second dissertation, Delbrück worked out mathematical proofs for the chemical bonding of lithium and received a Ph.D. in physics from Göttingen in 1930.

A research grant enabled Delbrück to conduct postgraduate studies at the University of Bristol in England for the next year and a half. During this time he shared rooms with CECIL F. POWELL and became friends with P. M. S. BLACKETT, P. A. M. DIRAC, and others who would soon make major contributions to twentieth-century physics. His work at Bristol, largely theoretical in nature, included two papers on quantum mechanics. A Rockefeller Foundation Fellowship permitted Delbrück to spend the next six months working under NIELS BOHR at the University of Copenhagen, followed by another six months with WOLFGANG PAULI at the University of Zurich. In Copenhagen, Delbrück developed lifelong friendships not only with Bohr but with the physicists George Gamow and Victor Weisskopf. Bohr's theory of complementarity profoundly influenced Delbrück's thinking about biology and genetics. According to complementarity, wave

255

theory and quantum theory represent different aspects of electromagnetic radiation and therefore express different aspects of physical reality. Bohr's suggestion that this paradox of physics would also be found in biological phenomena greatly influenced Delbrück's outlook.

After returning to Berlin in 1932, Delbrück became an assistant to Lise Meitner, who, with OTTO HAHN, was studying neutron irradiation of uranium. During these Berlin years, Delbrück met regularly with a group of physicists and biologists who shared an interest in genetics. HERMANN J. MULLER had recently demonstrated that ionizing radiation produces genetic mutations, a finding that bolstered the Berlin group's belief "that genes had a kind of stability similar to that of the molecules of chemistry," as Delbrück later said. In the mid-1930s, however, genes "were algebraic units of the combinatorial sciences of genetics and it was anything but clear that these units were molecules analyzable in terms of structural chemistry." In an influential 1937 paper Delbrück proposed that genes be viewed as molecules and "the replication of viruses as a particular form of a primitive replication of genes. . . . Such a view," he said, "would mean a great simplification of the question of the origin of the many highly complicated and specific molecules found in every organism . . . and indispensable for carrying out its most elementary metabolism."

In 1937 Delbrück received a second Rockefeller Foundation Fellowship, which he used to study biology and genetics at the California Institute of Technology in Pasadena (Caltech). There, working with THOMAS HUNT MORGAN, he investigated the genetics of the fruit fly (*Drosophila melanogaster*), an organism common in genetic research because it has a short life span and many progeny. Although Morgan and other geneticists were studying *Drosophila* to elucidate chromosomal behavior and abnormalities, Delbrück became interested in the genetics of the bacteriophage, a type of virus that infects bacterial cells. Bacteriophages (like all viruses) are the simplest form of life, consisting of an inner core of nucleic acid and an outer coat of protein. It is now known that there are three possible outcomes if a bacteriophage particle enters a bacterial cell. It may take over the biochemical apparatus of the cell, replicate, and cause destruction (lysis) of the cell, releasing new phage particles. Or the bacteriophage may be incorporated into the deoxyribonucleic acid (DNA) of the bacterial cell, in which case the resulting

prophage is transmitted to progeny cells during cell division, similar to that of a bacterial gene. If the prophage is activated (for example, by ultraviolet light), it may again behave as an autonomous bacteriophage and cause bacterial-cell lysis. The third alternative is that the bacteriophage may be destroyed by bacterial-cell enzymes. Delbrück and the biologist Emory Ellis developed experimental methods for investigating bacteriophages, as well as a mathematical system for analyzing the results of their experiments. In a pioneering paper written in 1939, they compared phage multiplication in individual cells in a one-step growth experiment; the work launched a new era of virus research.

When World War II broke out, Delbrück remained in the United States. Accepting a low-paying position as instructor of physics at Vanderbilt University in Nashville, Tennessee, he continued his bacteriophage research for the next seven years. During the war several members of Delbrück's family, including his brother and brother-in-law, were persecuted for their resistance to the Nazi regime.

At a meeting of the American Physical Society in Philadelphia in 1940, Delbrück met SALVADOR LURIA, who was conducting bacteriophage research at the College of Physicians and Surgeons of Columbia University in New York City. Finding that they shared common interests, Delbrück and Luria began sharing the results of their work and collaborating by correspondence and occasional meetings. Their experiments suggested that bacterial-cell DNA underwent spontaneous mutations, which conferred upon the cell an immunity, or resistance, to lysis by bacteriophages. Their observations, published in 1943, became a standard for the analysis and presentation of experimental results in genetics research. In presenting the first evidence that heredity in bacteria is mediated by genes, their paper overturned prevailing ideas about the acquisition of genetic traits and marked the beginning of the era of bacterial genetics and molecular biology.

It was in 1943 that Delbrück began to collaborate in bacteriophage research with ALFRED HERSHEY, a microbiologist at Washington University, St. Louis. Delbrück, Hershey, and Luria founded the so-called Phage Group and drafted guidelines for bacteriophage research. Through informal meetings, the members of the group encouraged other investigators in the field to concentrate on seven bacteriophages that infect the colon bacillus *Escherichia coli* strain B, so that experimental results from different laboratories could be readily compared. Two years later Delbrück organized the first of his summer bacteriophage courses at the Cold Spring Harbor Laboratory on Long Island, New York. These courses, which emphasized quantitative and statistical methods, were offered every summer through 1971 and were attended by biologists, geneticists, and physicists from all over the world. Delbrück was appointed professor of biology at Caltech in 1947 and was elected to the National Academy of Sciences two years later.

Working independently, Delbrück and Hershey discovered in 1946 that different strains of bacteriophage may exchange genetic material (genes) if more than one strain infects the same bacterial cell. The phenomenon, which they called genetic recombination, was the first experimental evidence of recombination of DNA in viruses. Later, in 1952, Hershey and Martha Chase, a colleague, confirmed that genes consist of DNA. The following year FRANCIS CRICK and JAMES D. WATSON determined the three-dimensional structure of DNA; Watson revealed the first details of the double helix structure of DNA in a letter to Delbrück. In the 1950s and 1960s, Delbrück's laboratory was a gathering place for numerous investigators—including Watson and FRANÇOIS JACOB—who discussed experimental design, the solution to the genetic code, and other current problems of genetic research.

Delbrück, Hershey, and Luria shared the 1969 Nobel Prize for Physiology or Medicine "for their discoveries concerning the replication mechanism and the genetic structure of viruses." "The honor in the first place goes to Delbrück, who transformed bacteriophage research from vague empiricism to an exact science," said Sven Gard of the Karolinska Institute on presenting the award. "He analyzed and defined the conditions for precise measurement of the biological effects. Together with Luria he elaborated the quantitative methods and established the statistical criteria for evaluation, which made the subsequent penetrating studies possible."

After World War II Delbrück was approached by several institutions, and at the end of 1946 he accepted the chair in biology at Caltech, which was offered to him by GEORGE W. BEADLE. Returning there in 1947, he remained at Caltech until his retirement in 1977, when he was appointed to the institute's board of trustees. During his later years he became interested in the molecular biology of sensory perception and investigated *Phycomyces,* a simple fungus that perceives and moves toward light. During a leave of absence from 1961 to 1963, he served as a guest professor at the University of Cologne in West Germany, where he helped to establish the university's Institute of Genetics.

In 1941 Delbrück married Mary Adeline Bruce, whom he had met at Caltech. They eventually had four children. His students and colleagues appreciated not only Delbrück's leadership but also his light wit and his disdain for stuffiness and protocol. On one occasion he held a party and invited half the guests to dress formally and the other half to wear tennis clothes; his own outfit combined both styles. In 1978 Delbrück developed cancer of the bone marrow, which, together with the side effects of chemotherapy, restricted his activities. He maintained an active interest in philosophy, music, and literature, and was invited to lecture on the German poet Rainer Maria Rilke at the Poetry Center in New York, but illness prevented him from appearing. He died in Pasadena on March 10, 1981.

Delbrück's awards and honors included honorary degrees from Copenhagen, Chicago, Heidelberg, Harvard, and Göttingen universities, as well as Gustavus Adolphus College and the University of Southern California. He was a recipient of the Kimber Genetics Award of the National Academy of Sciences (1964), the Gregor Mendel Award of the Leopoldina German Academy of Researchers in Natural Sciences (1967), and the Louisa Gross Horwitz Prize of Columbia University (1969). He held memberships in the National Academy of Sciences, the American Academy of Arts and Sciences, the Royal Danish Academy, the Royal Society of London, and the French Academy of Sciences.

SELECTED WORKS: Mind From Matter? 1985.

ABOUT: American Scholar Summer 1982; Biographical Memoirs of Fellows of the Royal Society, volume 28, 1982; Cairns, J. (ed.) Phage and the Origins of Molecular Biology, 1966; New York Times March 13, 1981; Physics Today June 1981.

DELEDDA, GRAZIA
(September 27, 1871–August 16, 1936)
Nobel Prize for Literature, 1926

The Italian novelist Grazia Deledda (dä led′ dä) was born in the Sardinian village of Nuoro, where her father, a modestly successful attorney, served three terms as mayor. Like many of the people of this small mountain community, Deledda's mother, the former Francesca Cambosa, was illiterate. Although the family owned an olive-oil press and a winery and was well off by local standards, life for young Deledda, her two brothers, and her four sisters was relatively primitive. She later described Nuoro, an isolated town in which life had changed little for centuries, as "a village of the Bronze Age." So remote was village life from that of the Italian mainland that the villagers spoke not Italian but Logudorese, a dialect closely related to Latin. Deledda's childhood was shaped by a strict traditional upbringing; she and her sisters were rarely allowed out of the house alone. Nevertheless, because the Deledda home was a focal point of the community, she came into contact with a cross section of the Sardinian population at an early age.

Until the age of ten, Deledda attended the local elementary school—her only formal education, although she was privately tutored in French and Italian. She also read extensively on her own, especially translations of nineteenth-century Russian fiction and the novels of Victor Hugo and Honoré de Balzac. Sardinian ballads and legends also influenced her; as early as the age of eight, she had begun to write poems and stories based on local folklore. Deledda was fifteen years old when her story "Sangue sardo" (Sardinian Blood) appeared in a Roman fashion magazine. Thereafter, her work was published frequently in Roman journals. In 1892 her first novel, *Fior di Sardegna* (Flower of Sardinia), was well received by critics. It was followed by *Anime oneste* (Honest Souls, 1895), with a preface by the Italian scholar Ruggero Bonghi.

During this time Deledda remained in Nuoro. After the death of her father, she directed the family winery and corresponded with a growing number of authors and critics. However, after receiving an unexpectedly large sum of money for the French translation of *Anime oneste,* she turned over the management of the winery to her brother Andrea. In 1899, at the invitation of Donna Maria Manca, the editor of the journal *Donna sarda* (Sardinian Lady), to which Deledda was a frequent contributor, she visited the Sardinian capital, Cagliari. There she met Palmiro Madesani, a civil servant in the Ministry of Finance, whom she married in 1900. Later that year, when Madesani was transferred to Rome to work in the War Ministry, Deledda made her first trip outside Sardinia. The couple sub-

GRAZIA DELEDDA

sequently settled in the Italian capital, where they raised their two sons.

For the remainder of her life, Deledda wrote novels at the rate of about one a year. Although she enjoyed life in Rome, in her writing she was preoccupied with Sardinia and its people. Her finest novels depict, with clarity and intensity, a simple and harsh way of life at odds with the modern world. "I know and love Sardinia," she remarked. "Its people are my people. Its mountains and valleys are part of me. Why should we search for subjects beyond the horizon when we have only to open our eyes upon all the drama of human life close at hand? . . . Sardinia *called* to be put into print."

Although Deledda's writing cannot be easily categorized, the fiction from the middle part of her career can be seen in the context of the naturalist movement. Naturalist writers such as Émile Zola and Theodore Dreiser were influenced by the theories of Charles Darwin, Herbert Spencer, and other scientists and philosophers. The naturalists believed that an individual's behavior was determined by heredity and environment—natural forces beyond human control. These writers typically concentrated their characterizations on people of the lower classes—previously considered unfit as literary subjects—who were kept from attaining happiness by the forces of society and by their own ungovernable instincts. Until the early 1920s Deledda's work exhibited many of these characteristics, although the lyrical, seamless quality of her writing is not typical of the naturalists. Also unlike the naturalists, who tended to support socialism, Deledda remained strictly apolitical.

The hero of her first major success, *Elias Portolu* (1903), becomes a priest in order to escape an impossible love and must learn to face his own inadequacy. Unable to resolve the conflict between his passions and the demands of society, he knows a destiny that is common among Deledda's characters: moving from innocence to sin and guilt, he ultimately finds redemption through suffering.

Over the next decade, Deledda's popularity in Italy grew steadily. *Cenere (Ashes,* 1904) is the story of a woman who sacrifices herself for her illegitimate child. In 1916 it was made into a film featuring the Italian actress Eleonora Duse in her only screen appearance. Deledda also collaborated on a stage adaptation of her novel *L'edera* (The Ivy, 1908), performed in 1909. The libretto of the opera *La grazia* (The Pardon), which was written and composed by Vincenzo Michetti and which had its premiere in 1923, was based on one of Deledda's short stories. Other notable works of this period include the novels *Colombi e sparvieri* (Doves and Sparrowhawks, 1912) and *Canne al vento* (Reeds in the Wind, 1913).

According to most critics, Deledda's naturalistic period reached its culmination in *La madre (The Mother,* 1920; published in the United Kingdom as *The Woman and the Priest*). It is her best-known novel in the English-speaking world, thanks largely to an introduction to the British edition by the English novelist D. H. Lawrence. Set in an isolated Sardinian village, the action of *The Mother* is compressed into two days. A priest has fallen in love; his mother, witnessing his anguish, suffers more than she can bear. Although the characters and plot are simple, they are presented with a clarity and integrity that raise the story to the level of classical tragedy.

After *The Mother,* Deledda's style changed noticeably. Her early pessimism was relieved by a new emphasis on the possibilities of redemption through love. The novels of this period are generally considered by critics as inferior to Deledda's earlier work. They lack the vivid portrayal of Sardinian life that was her chief strength as a writer and adhere less closely to physical and economic reality. Among these works are *Il segreto dell'uomo solitario* (The Secret of the Solitary Man, 1921) and *Il Dio dei viventi* (The God of the Living, 1922).

Deledda received the 1926 Nobel Prize for Literature in 1927 "for her idealistically inspired writings which with plastic clarity pic-ture the life on her native island and with depth and sympathy deal with human problems in general." Presenting the award, Henrik Schuck of the Swedish Academy remarked that "as a painter of nature [Deledda] has few equals in European literature." He noted that her work was marked by "a serious and profound vision with a religious cast . . . frequently sad, but never pessimistic." Deledda accepted the prize with only a few words of thanks and did not deliver a formal Nobel lecture.

Several months after Deledda received the Nobel Prize, a malignant tumor was found in her left breast. She was able to continue working steadily for nine more years before succumbing to cancer, in Rome, on August 16, 1936.

Deledda was a quiet, retiring woman who wrote from an inner compulsion and without intellectual pretensions. Although her most powerful works are set in Sardinia, the Italian critic Giuseppe Ravegnani considered her far more than a regional writer: "Life, in the art of Grazia Deledda, is searchingly explored, with an intensely feminine insight and sensitivity." He found her best works "rich in overtones of an almost biblical flavor, something of the primitive grandeur of the Old Testament." D. H. Lawrence compared Deledda with Thomas Hardy because of her masterful depiction of "an isolated populace." Lawrence acknowledged in his introduction to *The Woman and the Priest* that Deledda "does not penetrate, as a great genius does, the very sources of human passion and motive." However, he found that "she does . . . create the passionate complex of a primitive populace."

Reflecting a more contemporary view of Deledda, the American scholar Thomas G. Bergin noted in 1980 that "in recent years her prestige has declined somewhat." However, he continued, "If her world now seems archaic and her approach a little dated, the human situations she presents are still moving and her unpretentious manner still carries conviction."

ADDITIONAL WORKS IN ENGLISH TRANSLATION: After the Divorce, 1905.

ABOUT: Balducci, C. A. Self-Made Woman, 1975; Collison-Morley, L. Modern Italian Literature, 1911; Kennard, J. S. Italian Romance Writers, 1906; Picifici, S. The Modern Italian Novel, 1973; Vittorini, D. The Modern Italian Novel, 1930.

D'ESTOURNELLES DE CONSTANT

D'ESTOURNELLES DE CONSTANT, PAUL
(November 22, 1852–May 15, 1924)
Nobel Prize for Peace, 1909
(shared with Auguste Beernaert)

PAUL D'ESTOURNELLES DE CONSTANT

Paul Henri Benjamin Balluet d'Estournelles de Constant (des tŏŏr nel′ də kôn stän′), French diplomat and peace advocate, was a member of an aristocratic French family that traced its ancestry to the Crusaders. He was born in the Château de Clermont-Créans at La Flèche in the Sarthe district of the Loire Valley, the son of Léonce Balluet d'Estournelles de Constant de Rebecque. An exceptionally energetic and talented young man, the hereditary baron excelled in yachting, fencing, and painting and developed a strong interest in the possibilities of flight. He studied law at the Lycée Louis-le-Grand in Paris, receiving a law degree in 1874; he was awarded an advanced degree from the School of Oriental Languages in Paris, after which he toured in Asia.

Entering the French foreign service in 1876, d'Estournelles spent the next six years in Montenegro, Turkey, the Netherlands, England, and Tunis. On the basis of his experience in Turkey, he wrote *La Politique française en Tunisie* (French Politics in Tunisia, 1891), which won a prize from the French Academy. He was recalled to Paris in 1882 and made assistant director of the Near Eastern Bureau of the Ministry of Foreign Affairs.

Appointed chargé d'affaires of the French embassy in London in 1890, d'Estournelles played a significant role in resolving the crisis that broke out in 1893 between England and France over a French blockade of Siam (now Thailand). The Siam crisis confirmed his growing conviction that a diplomat could make only limited contributions to international peace. The substitution of law for war, he believed, was the only avenue to peace, and that was the task of a legislator rather than a diplomat. Therefore, he decided to abandon what he called the "gilded existence of the diplomatist in order to undertake the real struggle . . . against ignorance" by entering politics. As a legislator, he said, he hoped to remedy a situation in which "the silent majority allow themselves to be persuaded that they know nothing of 'foreign affairs.' "

In 1895 d'Estournelles was elected to the Chamber of Deputies as the representative for Sarthe, the same district that years earlier had elected his great-uncle, the author Benjamin Constant de Rebecque, to the Chamber. Nine years later, the same constituency elected d'Estournelles to the Senate, where he served as a Radical-Socialist until his death.

Although physically small of stature, d'Estournelles had a commanding personality and aristocratic bearing. He was an eloquent debater and a gifted writer. As a pacifist, he was totally convinced of the justice of his cause. He became a formidable force in French politics and a legislative spokesman for world peace.

D'Estournelles was chosen, along with LÉON BOURGEOIS, to represent France at The Hague Peace Conference of 1899. The conference produced only meager results because the delegates failed to reach agreement on measures to limit arms. D'Estournelles was nevertheless encouraged by the commitments that were made: to restrict the use of certain weapons in war, to codify international law with regard to war, and to establish an international court of arbitration at The Hague. After the conference, he was convinced more than ever that it was possible to end war. Consequently, he decided to devote his life to educating the people of Europe about the benefits of arbitration so that they could exert pressure on their leaders to resolve disputes peacefully.

To explain the work of the 1899 conference, d'Estournelles gave lectures throughout France, Austria, Scandinavia, England, and Italy. In 1902 he helped persuade American President THEODORE ROOSEVELT to submit a dispute with Mexico to the new Permanent Court of Arbitration at The Hague. His success in dealing with Roosevelt, his fluent command of

English, and his trips across the Atlantic all contributed to his growing fascination with the potential of the United States for playing a leading role in securing world peace. An additional link to the United States was his marriage in 1885 to an American, Daisy Sedgwick-Barant, with whom he had a son, Paul.

In addition to lecturing and writing pamphlets, d'Estournelles created organizations to help promote the cause of peace. In 1903 he founded a group composed of members of the French Chamber of Deputies and Senate and dedicated to the advancement of voluntary international arbitration. In a brilliant stroke for the advancement of international goodwill, he took the group to visit the British Parliament in 1903. That fall a similar group of British parliamentarians journeyed to Paris. These visits paved the way for the Franco-British Entente Cordiale of 1904. Also in 1903 d'Estournelles visited Munich, where he formed a Franco-German association dedicated to improving relations between the two countries. Subsequent visits to France by Danish, Norwegian, and Swedish legislators were returned by the French in 1909.

In Paris, d'Estournelles founded the Association for International Conciliation in 1905, along with a periodical, *International Conciliation,* to explain its purpose. Never financially successful, the magazine was eventually taken over by the Carnegie Endowment for International Peace. That link and his friendship with NICHOLAS MURRAY BUTLER, an associate of Andrew Carnegie, led to the appointment of d'Estournelles as head of the Carnegie Endowment in Europe.

At The Hague Peace Conference of 1907, d'Estournelles, again representing France, campaigned tirelessly for compulsory international arbitration. He was appointed to the Permanent Court of Arbitration. He also actively supported the efforts of the Interparliamentary Union, which was founded in 1889 by WILLIAM CREMER and FRÉDÉRIC PASSY to promote the principle of arbitration.

D'Estournelles believed that European political discord could be resolved only by a European union. Still, he was realistic enough to see that the prospects for such a union were remote. One barrier to unification was the deep-seated animosity of European nations like France and Germany. Ever since France's humiliating defeat in the Franco-Prussian War of 1870–1871, the desire for revenge had been a cornerstone of French foreign policy. It was, therefore, a courageous gesture when in 1909 d'Estournelles spoke before the Prussian House of Peers on the need for "Franco-German rapprochement as a basis for world peace." Although the past could not be forgotten, he declared, both nations must act on the principle that peace was an imperative, for "war drives republics into dictatorship, and monarchies into the grip of revolution."

D'Estournelles shared the 1909 Nobel Prize for Peace with AUGUSTE BEERNAERT, in recognition of his contributions to the cause of peace and arbitration. "A practical result of his efforts," said Jørgen Løvland of the Norwegian Nobel Committee in his presentation speech, "was the arbitration treaties between France and other countries, and he saw his policy adopted beyond the frontiers of France."

In the few years remaining before World War I, d'Estournelles continued to lecture and write on peace. His visits to the United States had made him a respected French authority on America, and his study of the country, *Les États-Unis d'Amérique* (*America and Her Problems*), was published in 1913.

During World War I, d'Estournelles set aside the issue of arbitration and supported his government by studying measures to counter German submarine warfare and by converting his chateau at La Flèche into a hospital. After the war, he resumed his efforts to foster international understanding, joining Léon Bourgeois in submitting a plan for a League of Nations to Prime Minister Georges Clemenceau in 1918.

A man of wide interests and learning, d'Estournelles translated classical Greek texts and wrote a book on ancient Greece as well as a play based on the myth of Pygmalion. In his later years, he devoted much of his energy to encouraging an expanded program of legislative exchange visits.

At the Interparliamentary Union conference in Stockholm in 1921, d'Estournelles was unable to effectively counter the delegates' animosity toward members from the German delegation. Frustrated by this failure, he gradually withdrew from public life in the years before his death. He died in Paris in 1924.

ADDITIONAL WORKS IN ENGLISH TRANSLATION: International Peace, 1906, with others; The Result of the Second Hague Conference, 1907, with David J. Hill; Women and the Cause of Peace, 1911.

ABOUT: Chickering, B. R. Imperial Germany and a World Without War, 1975; Davis, H. Among the World's Peacemakers, 1907; Hull, W. I. The Two Hague Conferences and Their Contributions to International Law, 1908; Scott, J. B. The Hague Peace Conferences (2 vols.) 1909.

DIELS, OTTO
(January 23, 1876–March 7, 1954)
Nobel Prize for Chemistry, 1950
(shared with Kurt Alder)

OTTO DIELS

The German chemist Otto Paul Hermann Diels (dēlz) was born in Hamburg, the second of three sons of Hermann Diels, a teacher and noted philologist, and Bertha (Dubell) Diels. When Otto was two years old, the family moved to Berlin, where his father had been appointed professor of classical philology at the University of Berlin. Four years later he entered the Joachimsthal Gymnasium in Berlin. Diels was twenty when he entered the University of Berlin to study chemistry. In 1900 he received his Ph.D., magna cum laude, under EMIL FISCHER and became Fischer's assistant at the university's Institute of Chemistry.

In 1904 Diels discovered an unusual compound containing three carbon atoms and two oxygen atoms, which he called carbon suboxide. In the same year he began to study the structure of cholesterol, a substance about which little was known. Through dehydration (the removal of hydrogen and oxygen), he converted cholesterol into cholesterone, a ketone.

Diels was named a lecturer in 1904 and professor of organic chemistry in 1906. During this time he turned his attention to other aspects of chemistry, and in 1907 he published a successful and highly influential textbook, *Einführungen in die organische Chemie* (Introduction to Organic Chemistry). He became head of the university's organic chemistry department in 1913.

After spending the year 1914 as an associate professor at the Chemical Institute of the Royal Friedrich Wilhelm (now Humboldt) University, Diels returned to the University of Berlin as a full professor. In 1916 he accepted an appointment as professor of chemistry and director of the Chemical Institute at Christian Albrecht University (later the University of Kiel). He became rector of the university in 1925.

Spurred by what he believed to be errors in the cholesterol-structure models proposed by other researchers, Diels returned to the study of cholesterol. After attempting to use traditional methods, he found that mixing selenium with cholesterol dehydrated the cholesterol without causing the destructive heat and agitation produced by other methods. Diels was the first researcher to use selenium to dehydrate any substance, and his method, developed in 1927, was eventually applied by other chemists to produce polyunsaturated oils. The

substance that Diels obtained proved to be the base molecule of many naturally occurring substances and was soon used by other researchers to elucidate the structure and nature of cortisone, sex hormones, steroids, and the D vitamins.

In 1928 Diels and one of his former students, KURT ALDER, published a paper in which they explained the diene synthesis. Diene synthesis occurs when a diene (a molecule containing two double carbon bonds) is united with a molecule called a philodiene (literally, a diene-lover), which possesses one double carbon bond. The product of this combination is a six-membered carbon-ring molecule called an adduct. Although the diene synthesis had already been observed by a few chemists, the phenomenon had never been adequately explained. In their paper Diels and Alder described how they had combined cyclopentadiene (the diene) with maleic anhydride (the philodiene) to form the highly stable adduct (3,6 endomethylene-4-tetrahydrophthalic anhydride) by a revision of the carbon bonds. Until this time, some organic reactions had been difficult to study because the temperatures and the force of available analytical methods tended to interfere with the results. Diels and Alder noted that many dienes are present in nature and that dienes and philodienes join readily at normal temperatures. From this observation they concluded that the diene synthesis might offer a new avenue for chemists to investigate many kinds of organic reactions. In the years that followed, diene synthesis did, in fact, become an indispensable tool for organic chemists, who used it to synthesize such substances as pharmaceuticals, vitamins, hormones, steroids, synthetic rubber, and plastics.

Diels continued his collaboration with Alder until 1936, when Alder joined the staff of the Interessen-Gemeinschaft Farbenindustrie Aktiengesellschaft (I. G. Farben) plant in Leverkusen. The privations and destruction caused by World War II increasingly hampered Diels's research. Allied bombing eventually destroyed not only the Chemical Institute and its library but also Diels's home. Two of his sons were killed on the eastern front, and in 1944 he submitted his resignation, which became effective the following year. After the war, however, at the age of seventy, he was persuaded to return to the institute, where he labored to rebuild its facilities before retiring permanently in 1948.

Diels and Alder were awarded the 1950 Nobel Prize for Chemistry "for their discovery and development of the synthesis of dienes." In his presentation address, Arne Fredga of the Royal Swedish Academy of Sciences described the chemistry of carbon compounds as "somewhat recondite and not easy to describe in words that everyone can understand." The Diels-Alder synthesis, Fredga said, "has now developed into one of the most important working methods in organic chemistry. By means of this method, a large number of compounds of complex structure can easily be produced—compounds which it would be quite impossible or very difficult to produce in any other way." Illness prevented Diels from attending the award ceremonies. In his Nobel lecture, published the following year, he discussed the importance of the aromatic basic skeleton of steroids.

Married in 1909 to the former Paula Geyer, Diels had three sons and two daughters. Known as a reserved man with a good sense of humor, he was highly respected for his bold and original scientific ideas. An avid mountain climber in his youth, Diels enjoyed painting in his leisure time. He died in Kiel on March 7, 1954, shortly after his seventy-eighth birthday.

In addition to the Nobel Prize, Diels was awarded the Adolf von Baeyer Medal of the German Chemical Society (1930) and received an honorary medical degree from the University of Kiel. He held membership in the academies of science of Göttingen, Halle, and Munich.

ABOUT: Dictionary of Scientific Biography, volume 4, 1971; Journal of Chemical Education September 1976.

DIRAC, P. A. M.
(August 8, 1902–October 20, 1984)
Nobel Prize for Physics, 1933
(shared with Erwin Schrödinger)

The English physicist Paul Adrien Maurice Dirac (di rak′) was born in Bristol to Charles Adrien Ladislas Dirac, a Swiss-born teacher of French at a private school in Bristol, and Florence Hannah (Holten) Dirac, an Englishwoman. He was educated at the Merchant Venturers Secondary School in Bristol before going on to study electrical engineering at the University of Bristol, where he obtained a B.S. in 1921. While attending the university, Dirac became interested in ALBERT EINSTEIN's theory of relativity and stayed two more years to study mathematics. He then went to St. John's College in Cambridge as a mathematics research student, obtaining his Ph.D. in 1926. The following year he became a fellow of the college.

While Dirac was studying at Cambridge, WERNER HEISENBERG and ERWIN SCHRÖDINGER developed their formulations of quantum mechanics, an application of quantum theory to the behavior of atomic and subatomic systems and the motions of particles such as the electron. Dirac began to study the Heisenberg and Schrödinger equations as soon as they were published in 1925, making some useful suggestions. One of the limitations of quantum mechanics was its restriction to low particle velocities, which allowed a neglect of Albert Einstein's relativity theory. Effects of relativity, such as the increase in particle mass with increasing velocity, become significant only when the velocities begin to approach the velocity of light. Schrödinger had first attempted to include all velocities but failed. One cause of the failure was the omission of the electron property called spin (toplike rotation), little known at the time and proposed hypothetically only to account for certain otherwise unexplainable details in line spectra. Dirac set out to incorporate relativity in the wave equation by introducing the relativistic expression for particle motion. The result, now called the Dirac equation, was published in 1928 and achieved agreement with experimental observations. In particular, electron spin, previously only a makeshift hypothesis, arose naturally from the equation, a major theoretical triumph. Moreover, the equation predicted the electron's magnetic properties (magnetic moment).

Other surprises were in store. Dirac's theory of the electron, expressed in his equation, in-

P. A. M. DIRAC

dicated possible negative energies, incomprehensible in the view of all existing theories. Tempted at first to ignore negative energy as a mathematical aberration, Dirac concluded that negative energy states did in fact exist. Considering the effect of an electromagnetic field on an electron in a negative energy state, he found that it caused motion equivalent to that of an electron of reversed electric charge, positive instead of negative. (It was first thought that the positive particle might be the proton.) Applying the WOLFGANG PAULI exclusion principle, which states that only one electron can occupy any state of motion, Dirac suggested that almost all of the negative states are already occupied so that the uniform background is not observable. However, an unoccupied energy state, like a hole in an otherwise featureless fabric, is observable. The hole behaves like a positive electron. Moreover, since it represents a shortage of negative energy, its energy is positive like that of all particles in the known world. In effect, he predicted the existence of an antielectron, a reversed twin. He also showed that an electron could fall into the vacant hole, equivalent to the meeting of an electron and an antielectron in which they annihilate each other, their energy reappearing as a photon of radiation. He also predicted that a photon of sufficient energy could produce an electron-antielectron pair. Dirac's predicted antielectron was discovered in 1932 by CARL D. ANDERSON and named the positron. His prediction of pair production was also later confirmed. He later predicted that other particles, such as the proton,

would have antimatter counterparts, but that a more complicated theory would be needed to encompass them. Existence of the antiproton was confirmed experimentally in 1955 by OWEN CHAMBERLAIN, and many other antiparticles are now known.

The Dirac equation helped clarify the scattering of X rays by matter. It had been found that the X rays emerging from collisions have longer wavelengths (less penetrating power) than before the collisions. This finding conflicted with earlier theory that predicted no change in wavelength. In 1923 ARTHUR H. COMPTON had discovered the Compton effect, which showed quantitatively that an X-ray photon interacts with a single electron. The electron is driven off, and its acquired kinetic energy is subtracted from the X-ray photon. The scattered photon thus has less energy than before and therefore corresponds to an X ray of lower frequency and longer wavelength. The interaction is mathematically much like a simple collision between billiard balls. It was further evidence for the dual wave-particle nature of radiation. The X ray enters as a wave, reacts with the electron as a particle (photon), and then emerges again as a wave. Dirac's theory characterized the interaction in full detail.

Dirac later discovered, as ENRICO FERMI did independently, the statistical distribution of energy in electron systems, now known as Fermi-Dirac statistics. This work is essential to the theoretical understanding of the electrical behavior of metals and semiconductors.

Other Dirac predictions included the existence of magnetic monopoles, single positive or negative magnetic particles similar to the individual positive and negative electric particles. Attempts to detect magnetic monopoles have so far been unsuccessful. (All known magnets have both positive and negative poles inseparable from each other.) He also predicted that the physical constants in nature (such as the force of gravity) may not be truly constant and may change very slowly with time. The weakening of gravity, if it is occurring, is so slow as to be extremely difficult to observe and is still conjectural.

Dirac and Schrödinger shared the 1933 Nobel Prize for Physics "for the discovery of new productive forms of atomic theory." "From general philosophical grounds," Dirac said in his brief Nobel lecture, "one would, at first sight, like to have as few kinds of elementary particles as possible, say only one kind, or at most two. . . . It appears from the experimental results, though, that there must be more than this. In fact, the number of kinds of elementary particles has shown a rather alarming tendency to increase during recent years." Dirac concluded by suggesting the possibility, based on the symmetry between positive and negative electric charges, of the existence of "stars . . . built up mainly of positrons and negative protons. In fact, there may be half the stars of each kind. The two kinds of stars would both show exactly the same spectra, and there would be no way of distinguishing them by present astronomical methods."

After completing his theory of relativistic quantum mechanics, Dirac traveled extensively, visiting universities in Japan, the Soviet Union, and the United States. From 1932 until his retirement in 1968, he was Lucasian Professor of Physics at Cambridge (a position once held by Isaac Newton). After retiring from Cambridge, Dirac became a professor at the University of Florida, remaining there until his death in Tallahassee in 1984.

In 1937 Dirac married Margit Wigner, sister of the physicist EUGENE P. WIGNER. They had two daughters. A quiet, solitary man known for his extreme economy of words, Dirac was a lone worker who accepted only a few students throughout his career. He enjoyed hiking and, while on sabbatical leave at the Institute for Advanced Study at Princeton, New Jersey, often worked at building trails in nearby woods.

In addition to the Nobel Prize, Dirac was awarded the Royal Medal (1939) and the Copley Medal (1952) from the Royal Society of London (to which he was elected a fellow in 1930). He was made a foreign associate of the American National Academy of Sciences in 1949 and a member of the Pontifical Academy of Sciences in 1961. In 1973 he was appointed to the Order of Merit of Great Britain.

SELECTED WORKS: The Principles of Quantum Mechanics, 1930; Theory of Electrons and Positrons, 1933; Quantum Electrodynamics, 1943; Developments in Quantum Electrodynamics, 1946; The Dynamical Theory of Fields, Classical and Quantum, 1949; Lectures on Quantum Mechanics and Relativistic Field Theory, 1955; Lectures on Quantum Mechanics, 1964; Lectures on Quantum Field Theory, 1966; Spinors in Hilbert Space, 1970; The Development of Quantum Theory, 1971; General Theory of Relativity, 1975; Directions in Physics, 1978; The Prediction of Antimatter, 1978.

ABOUT: Buckley, P., and Peat, F. O. (eds.) A Question of Physics, 1979; Kragh, K. Methodology and Philosophy of Science in Paul Dirac's Physics, 1979; New Yorker November 26, 1984; Salam, A., and Wigner, E. P. (eds.) Aspects of Quantum Theory, 1972.

DOISY, EDWARD A.

(November 13, 1893–October 23, 1986)
Nobel Prize for Physiology or Medicine, 1943
(shared with Henrik Dam)

The American biochemist Edward Adelbert Doisy (doi' zi) was born in Hume, Illinois, to Ada (Alley) Doisy and Edward Perez Doisy, a traveling salesman of French ancestry. At the University of Illinois at Champaign, he studied science, participated in team sports, and was elected to the scholastic and scientific societies Phi Beta Kappa and Sigma Xi. He received his B.A. in 1914 and his M.A. two years later from the same university.

From 1914 to 1917 Doisy was an assistant biochemistry instructor at Harvard Medical School. When the United States entered World War I in 1917, he took his Medical Corps training at Rockefeller Institute and then served for two years at Walter Reed Hospital, as a second lieutenant in the Sanitary Corps of the United States Army.

Upon discharge from military service, Doisy returned to Harvard for doctoral studies under the chemist Otto Folin; he received his Ph.D. in biochemistry in 1920, having joined the Washington University School of Medicine in 1919 as an instructor in biochemistry. He was appointed associate in 1920 and associate professor in 1922. The following year he became a full professor at the St. Louis University School of Medicine and director of the Department of Biochemistry. Appointed distinguished service professor in 1951, Doisy was named emeritus professor at St. Louis in 1965.

His early research consisted of a collaboration with Edgar Allen in the preparation of female sex hormones. Together, they developed the Allen-Doisy vaginal smear test of estrogen potency; they also succeeded in purifying the hormones estrone, estriol, and estradiol, which are used to treat gynecological disorders. His other research interests included blood buffers, carbon dioxide transport, lactic acid in muscles, nerve tissue, antibiotics, and the purification of insulin and chorionic gonadotropin (a substance found in human placenta).

When the discovery of vitamin K and its ability to prevent hemorrhage by clotting blood was reported in 1936 by the Danish biochemist HENRIK DAM, Doisy and his colleagues Sidney Thayer, Stephen Blinkley, Ralph McKee, and D. W. Corquodale began the study of the chemical structure of vitamin K. After two years of investigation, their almost-completed

EDWARD A. DOISY

findings were invalidated when exposure to light destroyed the activity of the vitamin. Another year of experiments, this time with precautions to protect the light-sensitive vitamin from photodestruction, resulted in the identification of two distinct active forms of the vitamin: K-1 from alfalfa and K-2 from fish meal. Doisy and his associates also synthesized vitamin K-3, called menadione, which is twice as potent as the natural vitamin and is used clinically. Although the vitamin had been simultaneously synthesized and purified in other American laboratories, St. Louis University was awarded a patent for menadione. The pharmaceutical firm Parke-Davis and Company funded Doisy's studies in a joint effort that was considered a model for industry-university research relationships.

Vitamin K is essential for the synthesis of prothrombin, a clotting factor in blood. Administration of the vitamin has saved the lives of many people, including patients with obstruction of the bile ducts, who often bled to death during surgery before the introduction of vitamin K. It has also been beneficial for infants, who are born with a natural deficiency of prothrombin and are therefore susceptible to possible fatal hemorrhages. At birth most babies now routinely receive a preventive dose of vitamin K.

"For his discovery of the chemical nature of vitamin K," Doisy received the 1943 Nobel Prize for Physiology or Medicine, which he shared with Henrik Dam. During World War II award ceremonies in Stockholm were suspended, and the prize was presented to Doisy

and Dam by the Swedish ambassador to the United States in special ceremonies held in New York City in 1944. Doisy did not deliver a Nobel lecture.

In 1918 Doisy married Alice Ackert, a teacher. They had four sons, one of whom, Richard Joseph Doisy, also became a biologist. In addition to his scientific research and academic responsibilities, Doisy served on the Standardization of Sex Hormones Committee of the League of Nations between 1932 and 1935 and was a member of the Biology and Medicine Committee of the Atomic Energy Commission. He died in St. Louis of heart disease on October 23, 1986.

Doisy received the Willard Gibbs Medal of the American Chemical Society (1941), the Squibb Award of the Infectious Diseases Society of America (1944), and the Barren Medal (1972), among many other honors. He was a member of the National Academy of Sciences, the American Association for the Advancement of Science, the American Society of Biological Chemists, the Endocrine Society, and the Society for Experimental Biology and Medicine. He held honorary degrees from Washington, Yale, and St. Louis universities, as well as from the universities of Chicago, Illinois, and Paris.

SELECTED WORKS: Sex Hormones, 1936; Sex and Internal Secretions, 1939, with others.

ABOUT: Current Biography March 1949; National Cyclopedia of American Biography, volume H, 1952; Olson, R. E. (ed.) Perspectives in Biological Chemistry, 1970.

DOMAGK, GERHARD
(October 30, 1895–April 24, 1964)
Nobel Prize for Physiology or Medicine, 1939

The German bacteriologist Gerhard Johannes Paul Domagk (dō′ mäk) was born to Paul Domagk and Martha (Reimer) Domagk in Lagow, a small town in Brandenburg. He received his early schooling in Sommerfeld, where his father was a teacher and assistant headmaster. After completing secondary school in Liegnitz, Domagk started medical training at the University of Kiel in 1914 just before the outbreak of World War I. He volunteered for combat service, was wounded on the eastern front, and after recovery served in the medical corps until the end of the war. He then resumed his studies at Kiel and received his med-

GERHARD DOMAGK

several microbic genera. Doses that could be tolerated by laboratory animals were then determined, and finally, their effect on the infections of animals and human beings was studied. In 1932 Domagk found that a red azo dye (synthesized by chemists Fritz Mietsch and Joseph Klarer, and commercially marketed by I. G. Farben as Prontosil as a fast dye for leather), when combined with a sulfonamide radical, showed protective power against streptococcal infections in mice.

The experimental findings on Prontosil as a therapeutic agent were not reported until February 1935 in a now classic article in the journal *Deutsche Medizinische Wochenschrift* (German Medical Weekly). One of the first patients to be treated with Prontosil was Domagk's daughter, Hildegard, who had a streptococcal infection that remained unresponsive to all other treatment. When she was near death, Domagk injected her with large quantities of Prontosil, which produced a dramatic recovery.

Surveys were made to discover the effect of Prontosil on human diseases caused by other bacteria. Doctors established that cerebrospinal meningitis, pneumonia, and gonorrhea could be quickly brought under control with Prontosil. The sulfonamide compounds were immediately introduced into surgical and dental practice. In France, DANIEL BOVET and other researchers found that a component of Prontosil, sulfanilamide, had similar action. Only one year after Prontosil was placed on the market, I. G. Farben announced that more than 1,000 derivatives of sulfanilamide had been made. Two of them, sulfapyridine and sulfathiazole, reduced mortality from pneumonia to a fraction of its former rate.

The discovery of the antibacterial effects of Prontosil, the first of the so-called sulfa drugs, was one of the greatest therapeutic advances in the history of medicine. René Dubos then observed that natural compounds produced by microorganisms could also serve as antibacterial agents; ALEXANDER FLEMING noted the actions of penicillin, and a new era of medicine was launched.

Domagk was awarded the 1939 Nobel Prize for Physiology or Medicine "for the discovery of the antibacterial effects of Prontosil." Three years earlier, however, Adolf Hitler, angry that the anti-Nazi CARL VON OSSIETZKY had been awarded the Nobel Prize for Peace, had decreed that no German could accept a Nobel Prize. After acknowledging the honor, Domagk was arrested, jailed briefly, and forced to decline the award. At the awards ceremonies Nanna Svartz of the Karolinska Institute

ical degree in 1921 with a thesis on creatinine precipitation in humans after exercise.

Remaining at Kiel, Domagk worked as an assistant in the chemistry and pathology departments and also studied the use of X rays in nephritis and cancer at the Pathological Institute in Greifswald, where he was named privatdocent (unsalaried lecturer) in general pathology and anatomy in 1924. The following year Domagk was appointed privatdocent at the University of Münster, and in 1928 he became professor of general pathology and pathological anatomy. It was at Greifswald and Münster that his studies on cancer began.

In 1927 the German chemical company Interessen-Gemeinschaft Farbenindustrie Aktiengesellschaft (I. G. Farben) appointed Domagk, at age thirty-two, to be director of its research laboratory for experimental pathology and bacteriology at Wuppertal-Elberfeld. He remained in the post for the rest of his active life.

When the pharmacologist and immunologist PAUL EHRLICH discovered the organic arsenic compound Salvarsan for the treatment of syphilis in 1910, research for other chemical agents to combat infection was stimulated. Although advances had been made in the use of chemotherapy for protozoan and tropical diseases, it was not until Domagk began testing potential antibacterial agents that research was pursued on bacterial infections, such as the pneumonias and tuberculosis.

Domagk began a systematic screening of new dyes for possible medical application. Compounds were first tested for their effect on

presented an account of Domagk's work. "The discovery of Prontosil opened up undreamed-of prospects for the treatment of infectious diseases," he said. "The foundations for this unprecedented expansion which chemotherapy has undergone in the brief span of less than five years were laid by Domagk and his co-workers." He went on to add that "thousands upon thousands of human lives are being saved each year by Prontosil and its derivatives." In 1947 Domagk traveled to Stockholm to receive his diploma and gold medal, but in accordance with regulations, the prize money had reverted to the Nobel Foundation's reserve fund, and he was unable to collect it.

During World War II, Domagk took up research on tuberculosis, and by 1946 he was able to report the antitubercular effects of sulfathiazole and sulfathiodiazole. Thiosemicarbazones and isonicotinic acid hydrazide were also found to be effective compounds against tubercular infections, even those resistant to streptomycin. During the last few years of his life, Domagk became increasingly interested in cancer and hoped to find a substance to destroy malignant tumor cells without destroying the animal or human host.

Domagk married Gertrude Strübe in 1925; they had one daughter and three sons. He died in Burberg, Baden-Württemberg, Germany, on April 24, 1964.

Domagk was the recipient of many honors, including the Emil Fischer Medal of the German Chemical Society (1937), the Cameron Prize and Lectureship of the University of Edinburgh (1938), the Paul Ehrlich Gold Medal of the University of Frankfurt (1956), and the Order of the Rising Sun given by the Japanese government (1960).

ABOUT: Biographical Memoirs of Fellows of the Royal Society, volume 10, 1964; Dictionary of Scientific Biography, volume 4, 1971; Journal of Chemical Education April 1954; Times (London) April 27, 1964.

DUCOMMUN, ÉLIE
(February 19, 1833–December 6, 1906)
Nobel Prize for Peace, 1902
(shared with Albert Gobat)

The Swiss journalist, educator, and peace advocate Élie Ducommun (dü ko maN') was born in Geneva, Switzerland, the youngest of three sons of Octavie (Mattey) Ducommun and Jules Ducommun, a clockmaker from Neuchâtel. Although his parents could not afford to send him to college, the boy's academic record was so outstanding that, after completing his secondary education at the age of seventeen, he was employed as a tutor by a prosperous family in Saxony. Living there for three years, he mastered German before returning to Geneva in 1853 to teach languages in the public schools.

Two years later Ducommun became editor of the *Revue de Genève* (Geneva Review), a political journal. This position made him prominent in local politics and led to his appointment as vice-chancellor of the canton of Geneva in 1857 and, five years later, as chancellor.

Returning to journalism in 1865, Ducommun was named editor of *Progrès* (Progress), a political newspaper, in the town of Delémont. It was around this time that he became involved in the peace movement then gathering adherents throughout Western Europe. His interest in the goals of the movement led him in 1868 to become coeditor of *Les États-Unis d'Europe* (The United States of Europe), with responsibility for the journal's French section. The journal was published in Paris by the International League of Peace and Freedom, a pacifist organization that had been established the previous year.

During this time, Ducommun participated in discussions among the members of various workers' groups and the Liberal Society of Bern. From these talks emerged the idea of a mutual credit organization to serve the needs of Swiss workers, a plan Ducommun put into effect in 1869 when he founded the Swiss Popular Bank. Starting with 93 members, it rose to over 40,000 by 1907.

In 1871, after a year of military service as secretary to General Hans Herzog, Ducommun and a colleague, Auguste Schneegans, established *L'Helvetia* (Switzerland), a lively and widely circulated newspaper. Ducommun's support of a federal Swiss constitution, however, cost the paper its French readers, and it ceased publication in 1872.

The following year, Ducommun was appointed secretary-general of the Jura-Bern (later the Jura-Simplon) railroad, a position he acquired through his contacts as a prominent journalist. Moving to Biel, he supervised the construction of the railroad while remaining active in the peace movement. Upon completion of the line in 1887, Ducommun returned to Bern. Despite the demands of his administrative duties at the railroad, he sat on the Grand Council of Geneva for nine years and on the Grand Council of Bern for ten years.

While attending the fourth conference of the

ÉLIE DUCOMMUN

Interparliamentary Union in Rome in 1891 with ALBERT GOBAT, Ducommun helped found the INTERNATIONAL PEACE BUREAU to coordinate the activities of the many peace societies scattered throughout Europe. Ducommun served, without salary, as secretary of the new organization, while continuing to support himself with his railroad job.

Devoting evenings, weekends, and vacations to his work for the bureau, Ducommun conducted an extensive correspondence, laid the ground for annual conferences, wrote and disseminated statements and brochures, and collected a massive library of documents on peace and disarmament. He also served as head of the bureau's Swiss delegation.

In recognition of these efforts, Ducommun shared the 1902 Nobel Prize for Peace with Gobat. Although the text of the presentation address has not been preserved, a toast offered by Jørgen Løvland of the Norwegian Nobel Committee, on the occasion of Ducommun's Nobel lecture in 1904, was recorded. Paying tribute to the people of Switzerland, who "have a special gift for taking ideas from the realm of dreams and turning them into realities," Løvland hailed Ducommun as "the head of the united work of all the peace societies of the world."

In his Nobel lecture, Ducommun examined "the annals of history" and found there a long record of violence. "I leave to the military the difficult task of trying to explain to us how these wars have served to shape character or to promote the progress of civilization or to achieve the reign of justice on earth," he said.

As an alternative, he suggested such measures as arbitration treaties and the strengthening of international conventions whereby nations could settle their disputes without recourse to arms.

Ducommun donated his prize money to the peace movement. In response, his colleagues presented him with a collection of funds donated by all the chapters of the bureau. When the Jura-Simplon railroad was purchased by the Swiss government in 1903, Ducommun resigned his position there, but he continued his peace work.

In 1857 Ducommun married his cousin, Adèle Ducommun. A man of wide-ranging interests, he enjoyed literature and theater and founded two cultural societies devoted to the French-speaking population of Switzerland. A volume of his poetry, *Derniers Sourires* (Last Smiles), was published in 1886. Ducommun died in Bern on December 6, 1906. Ducommun's life, wrote FRÉDÉRIC PASSY, one of his associates in the peace movement, was one "of incessant toil, of zeal, of scrupulous application and devotion to his tasks."

WORKS IN ENGLISH TRANSLATION: A Key to the Deliberations of the Annual Peace Congress, 1897; "The Permanent International Bureau of Peace," The Independent March 19, 1903; The Probable Consequences of a European War, 1906.

ABOUT: The Independent March 5, 1903.

DU GARD, ROGER MARTIN
See MARTIN DU GARD, ROGER

DULBECCO, RENATO
(February 22, 1914–)
Nobel Prize for Physiology or Medicine, 1975
(shared with David Baltimore and Howard M. Temin)

The Italian-American virologist Renato Dulbecco (dəl bek' ō) was born in the town of Catanzaro, in southern Italy. Shortly after his birth, his father, Leonardo Dulbecco, was called up to serve in the Italian army in World War I. The boy, his mother Maria (Virdia) Dulbecco, and his siblings spent the war years living in the northern Italian towns of Turin and Cuneo. After the war the family moved to Imperia in the province of Liguria, where Dulbecco received his early education in the public schools. In his youth he developed an

RENATO DULBECCO

interest in physics and built an electronic seismograph, one of the first of its kind.

After graduating from high school at the age of sixteen, Dulbecco entered the University of Turin to study medicine and biology. He soon realized that biology held a greater interest for him than medicine, and he began working in the laboratory of Giuseppe Levi, a professor of anatomy and histology. In Levi's laboratory, Dulbecco learned the techniques of cell culture; he also became acquainted with SALVADOR LURIA and RITA LEVI-MONTALCINI, fellow medical students at Turin, both of whose influence he later acknowledged.

After receiving his medical degree in 1936, Dulbecco was called up for military service as a medical officer in the Italian army. After his discharge two years later, he returned to Turin for postdoctoral work in pathology, but in 1939 his studies were again interrupted by military service. During the early years of World War II he served for a time in France and then on the Soviet front, where he was wounded in 1942 and spent several months recovering in a hospital. After the collapse of Mussolini's government—and during the subsequent German occupation—he worked in the Italian Resistance movement as a physician to the partisans.

After the war Dulbecco was appointed assistant professor of experimental embryology at Turin. In 1946 Luria, who had moved to the United States and became a professor at the University of Indiana, spent the summer at Turin. At his invitation, Dulbecco left Italy the following year and was named a research

associate in the bacteriology department at the University of Indiana in Bloomington. There, during the 1940s, Luria had been developing quantitative experimental methods for studying bacterial genetics and the bacteriophage, a virus that attacks bacteria. Using Luria's experimental procedures, Dulbecco began investigating phage viruses.

His research work at Bloomington soon attracted the interest of MAX DELBRÜCK, who in 1949 offered Dulbecco an appointment as senior research fellow at the California Institute of Technology (Caltech) in Pasadena. Driving from Indiana to Oregon and then down the Pacific coast, Dulbecco was "fascinated by the beauty and immensity" of the United States and by "the kindness of its people." At Caltech, he continued to study bacteriophages until the mid-1950s, when Delbrück asked him to conduct research on animal viruses, which resemble bacteriophages but infect animal cells. In this research Dulbecco applied the quantitative methods of Luria and Delbrück to the study of poliomyelitis virus and the Rous sarcoma virus (discovered by PEYTON ROUS), work that contributed to the development of polio vaccine.

Dulbecco was appointed associate professor of biology in 1952 and full professor in 1954, and he gradually shifted his interest to the tumor virus and the study of tumor cells. With HOWARD M. TEMIN, a graduate student, Dulbecco investigated the genetics of the Rous sarcoma virus. He also studied the polyoma virus, which causes multiple tumors in mice, and simian virus 40, which produces leukemia in monkeys.

After developing a method for determining the number of tumor cells in cell cultures, Dulbecco and his colleagues found that tumor cells are transformed by tumor viruses in such a way that they divide indefinitely, a process they termed cell transformation. In the course of classifying the biological properties of tumor cells, they discovered that when normal cells divide and begin to encroach on neighboring tissue, a cellular regulatory system signals to the cells to stop dividing. In tumor cells, however, this regulatory system is impaired. Temin proposed that cell transformation was caused by a viral gene that had become part of the cellular DNA. According to this so-called provirus hypothesis, the genetic code of certain RNA tumor viruses could be copied into cellular DNA by an enzyme in the protein coat of the virus, thus enabling the genes of the invading virus to take control of the genes of the host cell. The enzyme was, in fact, later discovered by Temin and DAVID BALTIMORE and called reverse transcriptase; the RNA viruses that possess a reverse transcriptase and form proviral genes are now called retroviruses. They are believed to be responsible for such diseases as hepatitis, acquired immune deficiency syndrome (AIDS), and some forms of cancer.

In 1963 Dulbecco was also appointed senior research fellow at the Salk Institute for Biological Studies in La Jolla, California, where he headed a research group to investigate the regulatory systems of tumor-cell growth. He remained at the Salk Institute until 1972, when he became assistant director of the Imperial Cancer Research Foundation Laboratories in London. There he focused his research on the clinical applications of his earlier findings on tumor viruses.

"For their discoveries concerning the interaction between tumor viruses and the genetic material of the cell," Dulbecco, Baltimore, and Temin shared the 1975 Nobel Prize for Physiology or Medicine. Their discoveries furnished scientists with a blueprint of the interaction between tumor viruses and genetic material of the cell, a tool that could make it possible to identify human cancers caused by tumor viruses. In his Nobel lecture Dulbecco pointed out that "in recent years . . . the separation between science and society has become excessive, and the consequences are felt especially by biologists. Thus, while we spend our life asking questions about the nature of cancer and ways to prevent or cure it, society merrily produces oncogenic [tumor causing] substances and permeates the environment with them."

Since 1977 Dulbecco has been distinguished resident professor at the Salk Institute. His marriage in 1940 to Giuseppina Salva produced a son and a daughter. After divorcing his first wife in 1963, Dulbecco married Maureen Muir in that year; they have a daughter. He is a naturalized American citizen.

Dulbecco's many honors include the Albert Lasker Basic Medical Research Award (1964), the Louisa Gross Horwitz Prize of Columbia University (1973), and the Selman A. Waksman Award in Microbiology of the National Academy of Sciences (1974). He is a member of the National Academy of Sciences, the American Association for the Advancement of Science, and the American Academy of Arts and Sciences, as well as a foreign member of the Royal Society of London and the National Academy of Sciences of Italy. He is the recipient of honorary degrees from Yale University, the University of Glasgow, and Vrije University in Belgium.

SELECTED WORKS: Virology, 1980, with Harold Ginsberg; "A Turning Point in Cancer Research," Science March 7, 1986.

ABOUT: New Scientist October 23, 1975; New York Times October 17, 1975; Science November 14, 1975.

DUNANT, HENRI
(May 8, 1828–October 30, 1910)
Nobel Prize for Peace, 1901
(shared with Frédéric Passy)

Jean Henri Dunant (dü nän′), Swiss humanitarian and founder of the INTERNATIONAL COMMITTEE OF THE RED CROSS (ICRC), was born into a pious, wealthy, and charitable family in Geneva. His father, Jean-Jacques Dunant, was a member of Geneva's governing council and the official responsible for supervision and protection of orphans. His grandfather directed a Geneva hospital and was mayor of nearby Avully. Dunant's mother, the former Anne-Antoinette Colladon, was the sister of the noted physicist Daniel Colladon.

Three interests—finance, religion, and public service—dominated Dunant's early years. He studied economics during the day and, as a representative of the League of Alms, visited the poor and the sick in the evenings. On Sundays, after attending church with his Calvinist family, he held services at the local prison. At eighteen years of age, Dunant joined the Réveil (Awakening), an evangelical movement then popular in Geneva. In 1853 he met the American writer Harriet Beecher Stowe, who convinced him to support the abolition of slavery, a cause he pursued for several decades. He was active as well in the newly formed Young Men's Christian Association (YMCA), whose first European branch opened in Paris in 1855.

Realizing that he would never be able to earn a living simply through good works, Dunant took a job at the age of twenty-six representing one of Geneva's largest banking houses in North Africa and Sicily. At the same time, he continued his charitable efforts, establishing a YMCA outpost in Algeria, where he was based. In 1858 he published *Notice sur la régence de Tunis* (An Account of the Regency in Tunis), mainly travel observations of North Africa. One long chapter was later pub-

HENRI DUNANT

lished as a separate volume, *L'Esclavage chez les musulmans et aux États-Unis d'Amérique* (Slavery Among the Mohammedans and in the United States of America, 1863).

Dunant decided to strike out on his own in 1859, buying a large tract of land in the French colony of Algeria on which to raise cattle and grain. To finance his venture, he organized a company in which he encouraged friends and family from Geneva to invest. He eventually raised 100 million Swiss francs. In order to develop the tract, Dunant needed water piped from government-owned land. After being shunted from one Algerian official to another, he decided to appeal personally to Emperor Napoleon III of France, who was in Solferino, Italy, directing the French army and its Italian allies against the invading Austrian army. On June 24, 1859, Dunant arrived in nearby Castiglione, where he watched one of Europe's bloodiest nineteenth-century encounters, the Battle of Solferino, which claimed 40,000 dead and wounded. "This was hand-to-hand fighting, indescribably hideous," he later recalled. "Austrian and allied troops trampled on one another, slaughtering one another over the bleeding corpses, felling their adversaries with rifle butts, smashing in their skulls, disemboweling them with saber or bayonet. There was no question of quarter; it was butchery, a battle of wild beasts, maddened with rage and drunk with blood."

After the battle, 6,000 people poured into Solferino to remove the wounded to Castiglione. Obtaining a pass from the French army,

Dunant joined the effort. Makeshift hospitals were set up in houses, army barracks, and the town church and cloister. Dunant happened upon a group of Italian soldiers preparing to throw some wounded Austrian soldiers down the steps of the Chiesa Maggiore, a church in Castiglione. "Stop," he cried. "You must not! They are brothers!" The soldiers released the Austrians, and *Sono fratelli* (They Are Brothers) became the motto of the relief effort.

Only two badly injured doctors were available to treat the wounded. Dunant directed the work at the Chiesa Maggiore, gathering food, organizing first-aid workers, and enlisting the efforts of tourists, priests, and journalists. The volunteers set up a bandaging room and found four doctors among the prisoners. After three sleepless days and nights, Dunant went to French army headquarters, where he obtained the release into his custody of all medically trained Austrian prisoners. He also asked charitable organizations in Geneva to send supplies. Later he organized relief efforts at battle sites in Brescia and Milan.

The memory of Solferino seemed to haunt Dunant. He dreamed of blood and of the moans and screams of the wounded and had a feeling of helplessness in the face of suffering. In *Un Souvenir de Solferino* (*A Memory of Solferino,* 1862), he described the "chaotic disorder, despair unspeakable, and misery of every kind" wrought by the battle, detailed the relief effort in Castiglione, and proposed that all nations form officially recognized cooperative war relief organizations. The book made Dunant famous. He was courted by Europe's high society and by journalists eager to publicize his plan.

In February of the following year, the Geneva Public Welfare Society, a private humanitarian organization of leading citizens, took up his suggestion for cooperative national war relief organizations. The society appointed a five-member committee that included Dunant, who called for a public campaign to generate support. "We must get up an agitation," he told his Swiss colleagues at their first meeting. "We must get our point of view recognized throughout the world among high and low; we must get the adherence of the sovereigns of Europe as well as the masses in all countries." Dunant called on governments and corresponded with such well-known public figures as Victor Hugo, Charles Dickens, and Florence Nightingale in an effort to organize an international conference that would help coordinate the work of national war relief groups.

On October 26, 1863, thirty-nine delegates

from sixteen countries met at Geneva. They drafted a treaty guaranteeing the neutrality of relief workers and adopting an emblem, a red cross on white—the Swiss flag with colors reversed. The delegates also agreed that the five-member committee should begin coordinating the work of the national relief groups, which in essence created the ICRC. The treaty, commonly known as the Geneva Convention, was signed in Paris the following year by representatives from twelve nations.

Pursuing his humanitarian efforts with zeal, Dunant neglected his business in Algeria and declared bankruptcy in 1867. Unimpressed by his good deeds or his good intentions, several investors accused him of fraud. Shunned by the Geneva society that had once celebrated him, he fell into poverty. Even so, he attended the 1867 general meeting of the Red Cross, held in Paris during the World Exhibition. There he proposed that prisoners of war be granted the same inviolable status as the sick and the wounded.

In 1871 during the Franco-Prussian War, Dunant founded the Provident Society. Its purpose was to promote the inviolability of war prisoners through branches in France, England, Belgium, Bavaria, and the United States. Renamed the World Alliance for Order and Civilization in 1872, its French and British chapters took up Dunant's call to extend official neutrality to prisoners. Czar Alexander II of Russia helped organize a conference in Brussels in 1874 to draw up a convention on the rules of war and the treatment of prisoners. Although the meeting bore no immediate results, it shaped later agreements on the rights of prisoners. For example, the United States, adhering strictly to the Monroe Doctrine, had not yet officially recognized the Red Cross. However, the American nurse and humanitarian Clara Barton worked for the Red Cross during the Franco-Prussian War and in 1881 established the first Red Cross chapter in the United States. In 1882 the United States Senate accepted the conditions outlined for the treatment of war prisoners in the Geneva Convention.

From 1871 to 1874, Dunant devoted much of his time to the World Alliance. Starting in 1874, he also initiated a campaign against the slave trade, which still flourished in parts of Africa, Egypt, Turkey, and Afghanistan. Although slavery was illegal in Europe, in 1875 the British Admiralty drafted regulations requiring British naval vessels to surrender runaway slaves who sought British protection when the ships called at the fugitives' home ports.

As a member of the Anti-Slavery Society in both Britain and France, Dunant organized such vocal opposition to the new orders that they were rescinded.

Dunant also supported the goal of European Jews who hoped to return to their homeland in Palestine. In 1864 he founded the International Society for the Revival of the Orient, which was dedicated to establishing a European colony in Palestine. To finance such a colony, he drafted a prospectus in 1876 for the Syrian and Palestine Colonization Society. The plan's success depended on land grants from the Turkish sultan, Abdul-Hamid; when war broke out between Turkey and Russia in 1876, Dunant's hopes were dashed.

Dunant lived as a recluse after 1876, venturing out only occasionally. To raise funds for the World Alliance, he lectured briefly in England. Scorned by family and forgotten by friends, Dunant retreated to a garret in southern England, although for a short time he returned to Paris to act as secretary for FRÉDÉRIC PASSY's French Society of the Friends of Peace.

In time, Dunant made his way back to Switzerland, wandering from village to village, often begging for bread. Despite his poverty, he remained well-groomed, blackening his coat with ink and using chalk to whiten his shirt. In 1892 he entered a hospice in the village of Heiden, where he remained for the rest of his life.

After these years of obscurity, Dunant was discovered in 1895 by Wilhelm Sondregger, a journalist, whose interview with Dunant was published in newspapers throughout Europe. Learning about his plight, the dowager empress of Russia granted Dunant a small pension. BERTHA VON SUTTNER visited him to offer her assistance in reestablishing his reputation. She wrote frequently about Dunant, and he began contributing regularly to the pacifist periodical she edited.

Dunant received the first Nobel Prize for Peace in 1901, an honor he shared with Frédéric Passy. Too ill to attend the award ceremony, Dunant remained in Heiden. His selection provoked controversy among those who believed that his work legitimized war by attempting to mitigate its effects. Yet the prize recognized Dunant's work as a great contribution to peaceful cooperation among nations.

Dunant never married. Upon his death in 1910, his will gave the proceeds of the prize, which he had never spent, to philanthropic organizations in Norway and Sweden. It also endowed a free bed for the poor in Heiden at the hospice that had sheltered him during the last eighteen years of his life. Above the legend on his tombstone is the figure of a man kneeling to offer water to a dying soldier.

ABOUT: Gagnebin, B., and Gazay, M. Encounter With Henri Dunant, 1963; Gigon, F. The Epic of the Red Cross, 1946; Gumpert, M. Dunant: The Story of the Red Cross, 1938; Hart, E. Man Born to Live: Life and Work of Henri Dunant, 1953; Rothkopf, C. Z. Jean Henri Dunant, Father of the Red Cross, 1969; Stoiber, R. M. Henri Dunant, Man in White, 1963.

DUVE, CHRISTIAN DE

(October 2, 1917–   )
Nobel Prize for Physiology or Medicine, 1974
(shared with Albert Claude and George E. Palade)

CHRISTIAN DE DUVE

The Belgian biochemist Christian René de Duve (dü' və) was born in Thames Ditton, near London, to Madeleine (Pungs) and Alphonse de Duve, Belgian citizens who had taken refuge in England during World War I. Returning to Belgium in 1920, the family settled in Antwerp, where Duve received his education in French and Flemish. In 1934 he entered the Catholic University of Louvain, a Jesuit school, where the curriculum emphasized the humanities. The appeal of a medical career, however, led him to undertake premedical and medical studies at Louvain, where he worked in the physiology laboratory of J. P. Bouckaert, studying the process of glucose (sugar) uptake by cells. By 1941, when he obtained his medical degree, Duve's goal was to elucidate the mechanism of action of insulin, a hormone that regulates the body's use of sugar.

During World War II, Duve served briefly in the Belgian army, was taken prisoner, escaped, and returned to Louvain. He then undertook a four-year course at the university, leading to a degree in the chemical sciences. He also performed clinical duties under Joseph Maisin, read the early insulin literature extensively, and did experimental work in the research laboratory. By 1945 he had written several research papers and a book, *Glucose, Insulin, and Diabetes*. He received an M.S. in chemistry in 1946. For the next eighteen months, Duve worked at the Medical Nobel Institute in Stockholm in the laboratory of HUGO THEORELL, followed by six months as a Rockefeller Foundation fellow at Washington University in St. Louis, where he met CARL F. and GERTY T. CORI. At Washington University, he also had the opportunity to collaborate with EARL W. SUTHERLAND JR.

Back in Belgium, he accepted a faculty appointment at the medical school of the Catholic University of Louvain, where he taught biochemistry and set up a research laboratory. Still interested in the action of insulin, Duve conducted a series of experiments designed to characterize the properties of a liver cell enzyme involved in the metabolism of glucose, the process by which this sugar is transformed into the basic elements that the body uses for energy. In order to perform biochemical studies on the cell, it was necessary to break up the cells into their components and spin the cell fragments in a centrifuge. Once the fragments settled out in different layers in the centrifuge tube—according to their size, shape, and density—they could be examined separately. Through these techniques, devised by ALBERT CLAUDE and called cell fractionation, several fractions of the cell could be isolated: the nuclei, which contain the chromosomes; the mitochondria, the energy plants of the cell; the microsomes (later called ribosomes), the site of cell manufacture of protein molecules; and the supernatant, the fluid portion. Duve and his colleagues in Louvain refined the method used to analyze the fractions that were separated. The new method, which they called analytical cell fractionation, enabled them to learn more about the enzyme activity of the fractions (enzymes are proteins that speed up the rate of chemical reactions), specifically that of the organelles, structures within the cells that perform specific functions for the cell as a whole.

Duve's first major discovery was the identification of a new organelle, the lysosome. In 1949 he and his team observed that the activity of the liver cell enzyme acid phosphatase, obtained from the mitochondrial fraction of the cell, was much greater on the fifth day after fractionation than on the first day. From this observation he deduced that a new cytoplasmic organelle was involved and that the delay in the enzyme's activity was caused by the aging of the membrane of the organelle in the laboratory. In the early 1950s Duve and his collaborators discovered another subcellular organelle that contained the enzyme urate oxidase; they called it the peroxisome.

Duve and his associates next set out to determine the functions of these two new organelles, a problem that had been investigated by many other researchers. Summarizing his findings in 1983, he reported that lysosomes are saclike membrane-bound particles. They contain several enzymes involved in the cell's digestion of nutrient molecules, foreign substances, and sometimes the cell itself and are prevalent in the liver and kidney cells of mammals. Peroxisomes, which occur widely in the plant and animal kingdoms, appear to have two metabolic functions: the conversion of a variety of intracellular molecules to hydrogen peroxide, which is then reduced to water, and the conversion of intracellular protein to glucose. Neither lysosomes nor peroxisomes are able to generate energy for use by the cell as do the mitochondria.

In 1951 Duve was appointed professor of physiological chemistry at Louvain. Later, in 1962, he was appointed Andrew W. Mellon Professor of Biological Cytology at the Rockefeller University in New York. These appointments enabled him to conduct research on the functions of the two new organelles. In 1962 he and several colleagues founded the International Institute of Cellular and Molecular Pathology (ICP) at the new Louvain Medical School in Brussels.

The 1974 Nobel Prize for Physiology or Medicine was shared by Duve, Albert Claude, and GEORGE E. PALADE "for their discoveries concerning the structural and functional organization of the cell." In his Nobel lecture Duve pointed out the goal of enzyme research by quoting Hugo Theorell: "The first stage is to investigate the entire steric constitution of all enzymes. In the second stage, it is a matter of deciding how the enzymes are arranged in the cell structures. This implies, as a matter of fact, the filling of a yawning gulf between biochemistry and morphology."

Since receiving the Nobel Prize, Duve has devoted his efforts to a variety of scientific studies whose impact may not be fully realized for some time. Among these studies are the properties and function of lysosomes and peroxisomes in both normal and diseased organisms. He and his colleagues have shown that deficiencies of lysosomal enzymes may contribute to twenty distinct clinical diseases involving the storage of glycogen (large molecules containing glucose) and the production of fat molecules and mucopolysaccharides (components of the intercellular connective tissue), and Duve has postulated that lysosomes and their enzymes may be involved in the process of aging and tissue breakdown. They have also studied the action of drugs, such as steroids, that suppress inflammatory reactions in tissue, and they have shown that such agents may affect the membranes of the lysosomal particles of the cell. In addition, the researchers have sought to develop drugs that can increase the effectiveness and reduce the harmful effects of chemotherapy in leukemia.

In 1943 Duve married Janine Herman, the daughter of a physician; they have two sons and two daughters. Duve maintains residences in New York and Brussels, dividing his time equally between his two laboratories. His hobbies are bridge, skiing, and tennis.

In addition to the Nobel Prize, Duve is the recipient of the Pfizer Prize of the Belgian Royal Academy of Medicine (1957), the Francqui Prize of the Francqui Foundation (1960), the Special Award of Merit of the Gairdner Foundation (1967), and the Dr. H. P. Heineken Prize of the Royal Netherlands Academy of Sciences (1973). He holds memberships in the Royal Academy of Belgium, the Royal Academy of Medicine of Belgium, the Pontifical Academy of Sciences, the American Academy of Arts and Sciences, and the American National Academy of Sciences. He has been awarded more than a dozen honorary degrees from American and European universities.

SELECTED WORKS: "Microbes in the Living Cell," Scientific American May 1983; A Guided Tour of the Living Cell, 1984, with Neil Hardy.

ABOUT: Dingle, J. T., and Fell, H. B. (eds.) Lysosomes in Biology and Pathology (2 vols.) 1969–1973; New York Times October 12, 1974; Science November 8, 1974.

DU VIGNEAUD, VINCENT
(May 18, 1901–December 11, 1978)
Nobel Prize for Chemistry, 1955

The American biochemist Vincent du Vigneaud (doō vēn' yō) was born in Chicago,

Illinois, to Alfred du Vigneaud, an inventor and designer of machines, and the former Mary Theresa O'Leary. He received his early education in the Chicago public school system. Showing an early interest in science, the boy performed chemistry and physiology experiments in a basement laboratory at home. In 1918 he entered the University of Illinois, where he majored in organic chemistry and received a B.S. in 1923 and an M.S. in chemistry the next year, with a thesis on his efforts to synthesize a drug having local anesthetic and vasopressor (blood-pressure-raising) effects. This early research gave him what he later called "a lasting interest in the relationship of organic chemical structure to biological activity."

Du Vigneaud's interest in insulin was aroused by a lecture given by W. C. Rose of the Department of Biochemistry at the University of Illinois, shortly after the discovery of insulin by FREDERICK G. BANTING and JOHN J. R. MACLEOD. Later, du Vigneaud recalled his "curiosity as to the chemical nature of a compound that could bring about the miracles [Rose] described. Little did I know at that time that insulin would eventually turn out to be a sulfur compound."

In 1924 du Vigneaud worked briefly at the Jackson Laboratories of E. I. du Pont de Nemours and Company in Wilmington, Delaware, before becoming an assistant biochemist at the Graduate School of Medicine of the University of Pennsylvania and at the Philadelphia General Hospital, where he worked in the clinical chemistry laboratory. In 1925 he joined the Department of Vital Economics (actually a department of endocrinology and metabolism) in the new School of Medicine at the University of Rochester.

At Rochester, du Vigneaud investigated the chemistry of insulin. Within two years he reported that insulin was probably a derivative of the amino acid cystine, that the sulfur found in insulin was in the form of disulfide linkages, and that insulin was probably a peptide (two or more amino acids linked together). Since there are twenty naturally occurring amino acids, the chemical structure of large peptides and proteins is often highly complex.

In 1927 du Vigneaud received a Ph.D. in chemistry from the University of Rochester. With the help of a National Research Council Fellowship, he went to the Johns Hopkins School of Medicine in the Department of Pharmacology, where he isolated the amino acid cystine from crystals of insulin. He also discovered that insulin consists only of amino

VINCENT DU VIGNEAUD

acids and ammonia, although ammonia was later shown to be a by-product.

Du Vigneaud spent the year 1928 in Dresden, Germany, the laboratory of Max Bergman, a former student of EMIL FISCHER and an authority on the chemistry of amino acids and peptides. Although Bergman offered him an assistantship, du Vigneaud went on to work with the biologists George Barger of the University of Edinburgh in Scotland and Charles Harrington of University College at the University of London, England.

Returning to the University of Illinois, du Vigneaud joined in the Department of Physiological Chemistry. In 1932 he became professor of biochemistry and chairman of the Department of Biochemistry at the George Washington University School of Medicine in Washington, D.C., where he organized a teaching program in biochemistry for medical students. In addition, he conducted research on the possibility that the hypoglycemic (or blood-sugar-lowering) effects of insulin are related to the disulfide bonds of cystine. In order to find out, he synthesized peptides containing cystine and tested them in physiological (bioassay) systems for insulin activity.

In 1936 he and his colleagues synthesized glutathione, a tripeptide containing the amino acids cysteine, glycine, and glutamic acid. Glutathione, present in all animal tissues, acts as a reducing agent (electron donor). In 1937 du Vigneaud published conclusive evidence that the amino acid cystine accounts for the entire sulfur content of insulin and that reduction of the disulfide bonds of insulin by glutathione or cysteine renders it physiologically inactive.

The following year du Vigneaud was appointed professor of biochemistry and chairman of the Department of Biochemistry at Cornell University Medical College in New York City. There he continued his efforts to isolate, purify, and synthesize the hormones oxytocin (which stimulates contraction of the uterus at the time of birth and causes ejection of milk from the female mammary glands) and vasopressin (which stimulates the constriction of peripheral blood vessels and promotes reabsorption of water by the kidney, thus reducing urine flow). While studying biological transmethylation (the transfer of methyl groups from one molecule to another), he and his colleagues determined that methyl groups are essential dietary factors. They also isolated biotin, a coenzyme involved in cellular respiration, from liver tissue and milk and proved that it is identical in structure and function to substances then known as vitamin H and coenzyme R.

During World War II, du Vigneaud worked on the synthesis of penicillin, a fungal antibiotic discovered in 1928 by ALEXANDER FLEMING. It was not until after the war, however, in 1946, that he and his colleagues completed the synthesis.

Du Vigneaud and his colleagues went on to isolate oxytocin from commercial extracts of pituitary glands and from bovine and porcine pituitary tissue. They found that, regardless of its source, oxytocin always contains the same eight amino acids and produces identical biological effects. The sulfur content of oxytocin is accounted for entirely by the amino acid cystine. In 1953 du Vigneaud determined that oxytocin is a cyclic polypeptide, consisting of a pentapeptide (five amino acids) ring structure and a tripeptide side chain. The pentapeptide ring system, a twenty-member structure closed by a disulfide bridge, had not previously been recognized as a naturally occurring chemical structure. Du Vigneaud and his colleagues prepared the first crystalline oxytocin, which was tested in women about to give birth and found to be clinically effective. It was the first in vitro synthesis of a polypeptide hormone.

Du Vigneaud was awarded the 1955 Nobel Prize for Chemistry "for his work on biochemically important sulfur compounds, and especially for the first synthesis of a polypeptide hormone." In his Nobel lecture he described the history of his research on sulfur-containing peptides: "One starts out on a trail of exploration in the laboratory not knowing where one is eventually going, starting out, to be sure, with some immediate objective in mind, but also having a vague sense of something beyond the immediate objective towards which one is striving."

Over the years du Vigneaud advocated close and equal cooperation between clinical specialists and basic scientists like himself. From 1967 until 1975 he was professor of chemistry at Cornell University in Ithaca. He became a trustee of the Rockefeller Institute for Medical Research, the National Institute for Arthritis and Metabolic Disease, and the Research Council of the Public Health Research Institute of the City of New York. He also served as president of the Harvey Society and the American Society of Biological Chemistry and as chairman of the board of the Federation of American Societies for Experimental Biology.

In 1924 du Vigneaud married Zella Zon Ford, with whom he had one son and one daughter. A tall man with a thin mustache, du Vigneaud enjoyed playing bridge and riding horses. He died on December 11, 1978, in Scarsdale, New York.

Du Vigneaud's other awards include the Nichols Medal of the American Chemical Society (1945), the Borden Award in the Medical Sciences given by the Association of American Medical Colleges (1947), the Lasker Award of the American Public Health Association (1948), the Osborne and Mendel Award of the American Institute of Nutrition (1953), the Charles Frederick Chandler Medal of Columbia University (1956), and the Willard Gibbs Medal of the American Chemical Society (1956). He was a member of the National Academy of Sciences, the American Academy of Arts and Sciences, the New York Academy of Sciences, and the American Philosophical Society.

SELECTED WORKS: A Trail of Research in Sulfur Chemistry and Metabolism and Related Fields, 1952.

ABOUT: Current Biography January 1956; National Cyclopedia of American Biography, volume I, 1960; New York Times December 12, 1978.

ECCLES, JOHN C.
(January 27, 1903–   )
Nobel Prize for Physiology or Medicine, 1963
(shared with Alan Hodgkin and Andrew Huxley)

The Australian physiologist John Carew Eccles was born in Melbourne, the oldest of two children of Mary (Carew) Eccles and William James Eccles, both of whom were teachers. He attended high school for three years in Warrnambool, Victoria, before returning to Melbourne, where he graduated in 1919. He entered the University of Melbourne to study medicine. He was also strongly attracted to philosophy, especially "the nature of the mind and consciousness in relation to brain activity," and resolved to study with the eminent neurophysiologist CHARLES S. SHERRINGTON. After graduating from the University of Melbourne in 1925 with first-class honors in medicine and a bachelor of medicine degree, he received a Victorian Rhodes Scholarship to Magdalen College, Oxford, where he took first-class honors in the natural sciences two years later and began working with Sherrington as a junior research fellow.

, Sherrington had established his reputation with careful, exhaustive studies of the way muscles and nerves act together in reflexes. On the basis of his research and that of SANTIAGO RAMÓN Y CAJAL, the founder of neuroanatomy, Sherrington devised the word *synapse* and defined it as the junction at which the electrical nerve impulse (the action potential) passes from one neuron, or nerve cell, to the next. He also discovered that although electrical excitability is the outstanding characteristic of nerve cells, not all nerve cells act to excite one another. Inhibition, he found, is as important a feature of nervous circuits as excitation. At the time, however, it was not known how action potentials move in individual nerves and in synapses between nerves, or how inhibitory and excitatory impulses differ.

Experiments conducted by OTTO LOEWI and HENRY H. DALE in the late 1920s and early 1930s suggested that chemical neurotransmitters (such as acetylcholine) carry nerve signals across synapses, a process fundamentally different from the normal, electrical action potential in the nerves themselves. Eccles, however, disagreed. Suspecting that the impulse in the synapse moved too rapidly to be caused by chemical diffusion, he advocated the electrical hypothesis of synaptic transmission.

Eccles received his M.A. and Ph.D. in 1929, and in 1932 he became a Staines Medical Fellow. Two years later he was appointed lecturer in physiology at Magdalen College. The likelihood of a European war was increasing, and in 1937 Eccles returned to Australia as director of the Kanematsu Memorial Institute of Pathology at Sydney Hospital. He built a research laboratory and soon attracted a number

JOHN C. ECCLES

of outstanding colleagues, including BERNARD KATZ and Stephen Kuffler.

Eccles, Katz, and Kuffler investigated the effect of chemicals on the transmission of impulses from nerve cells to muscles. (Similar research by DANIEL BOVET led to the development of modern muscle relaxants and anesthetics.) Eccles said later: "The action of anticholinesterases [substances that inhibit the action of certain enzymes] in increasing and prolonging the [electrical impulse in nerve-muscle synapses] finally convinced me in 1942 that acetylcholine was the sole transmitter." This conclusion forced him to relinquish the electrical hypothesis, at least for neuromuscular transmission.

The outbreak of World War II interrupted Eccles's research, and from 1941 until 1943 he worked on problems related to vision, airsickness, and blood processing for the Australian Armed Forces Commission.

In 1944 Eccles moved to New Zealand to become professor of physiology at the University of Otago Medical School, a position that brought him in contact with Karl Popper, one of the twentieth century's most prominent philosophers of science. Popper considered the disproving of hypotheses to have a central place in scientific progress. His views encouraged Eccles, who felt "concerned at the fate that seemed to be threatening my electrical hypothesis of synaptic transmission." Popper urged Eccles to try disproving his own hypothesis, assuring him that to do so would be as significant as finding evidence in its favor.

Challenged by Popper's advice, Eccles devised a method of monitoring and stimulating neurons in the spinal cords of live cats by inserting extremely fine electrodes into individual nerve cells. To measure electrical activity in several linked neurons in an individual reflex arc, he used a device known as an electrical stimulating and recording unit designed by Jack Coombs, one of his colleagues. A reflex arc is the path a nervous impulse takes from the nerve terminals that respond to stimuli to a nerve center, and then to a muscle or gland that acts as response.

In an inactive neuron, the interior side of the membrane is normally about 60 millivolts more electrically negative than the exterior; this difference is called its resting potential. In an active neuron, the interior becomes slightly electropositive in comparison with the exterior, and then quickly returns to normal. This phenomenon was established and explained in the 1940s and early 1950s by ALAN HODGKIN and ANDREW HUXLEY. Through his research, Eccles showed that firing of the stimulating (presynaptic) neuron at a synapse produces an excitatory postsynaptic potential (EPSP) in the stimulated neuron.

A typical EPSP changes the potential of the membrane from the normal -60 millivolts to about -50 millivolts. The postsynaptic cell approaches an action potential, but a single EPSP is usually insufficient to raise the postsynaptic neuron above the threshold (about -40 millivolts) at which an action potential begins. Eccles and his co-workers showed that action potentials are set off by combinations of EPSPs.

Some of the neural circuits Eccles studied were inhibitory rather than excitatory. In those cases, stimulation of the presynaptic cell produced an inhibitory postsynaptic potential (IPSP) that was greater than the resting potential by about 15 millivolts. Eccles announced his discovery in 1951, calling it the deathblow to his electrical neurotransmission hypothesis, which could not explain how a positive action potential in one cell is transformed to a more negative IPSP at the synapse.

That year Eccles left New Zealand, where a heavy teaching load interfered with his research, to lecture at Magdalen College for one year before moving to the newly established Australian National University of Canberra. Jack Coombs accompanied him to Canberra, and together they continued their investigations of excitation and inhibition. Their work proved that the firing of a neuron depends on the arithmetical sum of the incoming IPSPs and EPSPs. It also showed that the output of a given neuron is either inhibitory or excita-

tory, but not both; in short, a particular neuron produces only one kind of chemical neurotransmitter. Eccles next investigated different types of ion movements in excitatory or inhibitory synapses. (Ions are atoms or groups of atoms with a positive or negative electrical charge.)

Eccles shared the 1963 Nobel Prize for Physiology or Medicine with Alan Hodgkin and Andrew Huxley "for their discoveries concerning the ionic mechanisms involved in excitation and inhibition in the peripheral and central portions of the nerve cell membrane." At the conclusion of his presentation address, RAGNAR GRANIT of the Karolinska Institute congratulated the three laureates. "By elucidating the nature of the unitary electrical events in the peripheral and central nervous system," Granit said, "you have brought understanding of nervous action to a level of clarity which your contemporaries did not expect to witness in their lifetime."

By the time he received the Nobel Prize, Eccles had turned most of his attention to the cerebellum, the part of the brain that is responsible for muscular coordination. The basic cerebellar cells had been known since Ramón y Cajal's work at the beginning of the twentieth century. Eccles mapped out their connections, in which inhibition proved to play a particularly important role. Although he was nearing the mandatory retirement age at Canberra, Eccles had no wish to stop his research; in 1966 he retired and accepted a position as head of the American Medical Association's Institute for Biomedical Research in Chicago. When personality and administrative conflicts developed, he left Chicago in 1968 to become distinguished professor of physiology and medicine at the State University of New York in Buffalo. There he continued his research on the cerebellum until his retirement in 1975, whereupon he settled in Switzerland. Since then he has pursued his interest in the philosophical questions that intrigued him in his youth.

In 1928 Eccles married Irene Frances Miller, with whom he had four sons and five daughters. They were divorced in 1968, and that year Eccles married Helena Tabořiková, a medical researcher from Czechoslovakia who has collaborated with Eccles on much of his subsequent research.

Eccles is a foreign member of the American Academy of Arts and Sciences and the National Academy of Sciences of Italy. He is also a member of the Pontifical Academy of Sciences, the American Philosophical Society, the American National Academy of Sciences, the

ECHEGARAY

Indian National Science Academy, and the Royal Academy of Belgium. He was awarded the Royal Medal of the Royal Society of London (1962) and the Cothenius Medal of the Leopoldina German Academy of Researchers in Natural Sciences (1963).

SELECTED WORKS: Reflex Activity of the Spinal Cord, 1932, with others; Neurophysiological Basis of Mind, 1953; Physiology of Nerve Cells, 1957; Physiology of Synapses, 1964; The Cerebellum as a Neuronal Machine, 1967; Inhibitory Pathways of the Central Nervous Systems, 1969; Facing Reality, 1970; The Understanding of the Brain, 1973; The Self and Its Brain, 1977, with Karl Popper; Molecular Neurobiology of the Mammalian Brain, 1978; The Human Mystery, 1979; Sherrington: His Life and Thought, 1979, with W. C. Gibson; The Human Psyche, 1980; The Wonder of Being Human, 1984, with Daniel Robinson.

ABOUT: Buffalo Physician Spring 1972; Cousins, N. Nobel Prize Conversations, 1985; Curtis, D. R., and McIntyre, A. K. (eds.) Studies in Physiology, 1965; The Excitement and Fascination of Science, volume 2, 1978; Science October 25, 1963.

JOSÉ ECHEGARAY

ECHEGARAY, JOSÉ
(April 19, 1832–September 14, 1916)
Nobel Prize for Literature, 1904
(shared with Frédéric Mistral)

The Spanish dramatist José María Waldo Echegaray (ā chä gä rī') y Eizaguirre was born in Madrid to parents of Basque descent. When he was three years old, his family moved to Murcia, an old provincial city in what was once the Moorish kingdom of the same name on the Mediterranean coast.

Echegaray's father held a professorship in Greek at the Institute of Murcia, where his precocious son began to study at an early age. Concentrating on Latin, Greek, and natural history, Echegaray received a bachelor of philosophic science degree at the age of fourteen. He then returned to Madrid to study mathematics at the Escuela de Caminos (a school of engineering), where he continued to distinguish himself, graduating first in his class in 1853. After a few years as a practicing engineer, he was appointed to the faculty of the same institution as a professor of mathematics. Echegaray taught both theoretical and applied mathematics and published papers and treatises in his field, earning a reputation as the foremost Spanish mathematician of his time.

During this period Echegaray studied political economy, philosophy, and geology; becoming an avid playgoer, he also developed a deep interest in the theater. At this time Echegaray had no idea of becoming a writer himself, although he had read a great deal of European literature. Around 1864 Echegaray's younger brother, Miguel, who was only a boy at the time, wrote a one-act verse play, Cara o Cruz (Heads or Tails), which was given a simple staging. Evidently, the experience made an impression on Echegaray, who, according to one of his translators, James Graham, "immediately . . . composed his first play." The result of this effort apparently was never staged.

Before literary work would come to dominate his interests, however, Echegaray's career was to take yet another direction. After the overthrow of Queen Isabella II in the revolution of 1868, he entered politics and was appointed minister of public works. As a leading advocate of free trade, he was named minister of commerce the following year. He was elected to the Cortes, the Spanish parliament, in 1869, and then served in various official posts; as minister of finance, he founded the Bank of Spain.

When the Bourbon monarchy was restored in 1874, Echegaray went into temporary exile in Paris. There, unfettered by political and administrative concerns, he actively began to pursue his theatrical interests and to write drama. Upon his return to Madrid later that year, his first play, El libro talonario (The Checkbook), was produced under the pseudonym Jorge Hayaseca y Eizaguirre. Exchanging his mathematical and political professions for a full-time career in the theater, for the next three decades Echegaray wrote prolifically. He often completed two or three plays annually, and at least one of his works was produced each year. Thus, for an entire generation, Echegaray's work dominated the Spanish stage. His popularity can be attributed to several factors: a deep-rooted interest among the Spanish in the classical theater of Pedro Calderón de la Barca, whose stylized works of the golden age of Spanish drama served as prototypes; Echegaray's recognition of his audience's taste for high melodrama; and his introduction of contemporary settings in works dealing with the romantic themes of honor, duty, and love.

About half of Echegaray's sixty plays were written in verse, an example of which was his first popular success, *La esposa del vengador* (*The Avenger's Wife*, 1874). This romantic drama was followed by an even greater success the next year, *En el puño de la espada* (*At the Hilt of the Sword*, 1875). In 1877 *O locura o santidad* (*Folly or Saintliness*), which deals with the fate of Don Lorenzo, was produced. This character's integrity is so great and unyielding that he is considered insane. When *Folly or Saintliness* was eventually translated into English in 1895, it brought the playwright to international attention. GEORGE BERNARD SHAW considered Echegaray to be "of the school of [Friedrich] Schiller, Victor Hugo, and Verdi— picturesque, tragic to the death, showing us the beautiful and the heroic struggling either with blind destiny or with an implacable idealism which makes vengeance and jealousy points of honor."

Indeed, it was these very elements of Echegaray's work that had helped generate his initial popularity with Spanish audiences. Later in his career he adopted a more naturalistic style with the introduction of the thesis play *El hijo de Don Juan* (*The Son of Don Juan*, 1892). Inspired by Henrik Ibsen's *Ghosts*, the work deals with the effects of a father's profligacy upon the life of his son. While most critics at the time found fault with the play, Shaw contended in 1895 that Echegaray's "treatment of the *Ghosts* theme is perfectly original." Shaw noted further, "The fact that Mrs. Alving and Manders have no counterparts in the Spanish play, and that the dissipated father, who does not appear in *Ghosts* at all, is practically Echegaray's hero, will make it plain to anyone who had really comprehended *Ghosts* that the story has been taken on to new ground nationally, and back to old ground morally."

El gran Galeoto (*The Great Galeoto*, 1881), perhaps Echegaray's best-known work, concerns the destructive force of gossip on the lives of its innocent victims. According to the scholar Federico de Onís, these plays "revive in modern guise, coldly and with an eye to effect, the old themes and conflicts . . . which . . . are the very essence of drama."

When elected to the Royal Spanish Academy in 1894, Echegaray was at his peak of popularity. Soon afterward, a new generation of Spanish writers—known as the Generation of '98—began to react against what they considered sentimentality, an outmoded literary style, and a reliance upon the models of Ibsen and the French naturalists in the dramatist's work. His critics further charged that Echegaray was out of touch with the contemporary social concerns of the Spanish people.

"In recognition of the numerous and brilliant compositions which, in an individual and original manner, have revived the great traditions of the Spanish drama," Echegaray received the 1904 Nobel Prize for Literature, an honor he shared with FRÉDÉRIC MISTRAL. "Just as in the masters of the old Spanish drama, there is in him a striking union of the most lively imagination and the most refined artistic sense," said C. D. af Wirsén of the Swedish Academy in the presentation address. The laureate did not attend the award ceremony.

Although his selection provoked a storm of controversy among younger Spanish writers, more recent critical evaluations have pointed out Echegaray's historical significance as a link between the classical and modern periods of Spanish drama. While the critic Donald Shaw called Echegaray "the maximum representative of Spain's theatrical decadence in the late nineteenth century," other critics have singled out several of his works as forerunners of modern drama. Comparing Echegaray's work with that of LUIGI PIRANDELLO, the American scholar Wilma Newberry noted a "current in [Echegaray's] plays that goes beyond superficial romantic characteristics and puts forth several of the ideas with which Pirandello later would revolutionize twentieth-century theater." She observed further that both writers "question the nature of reality, have written theater-within-the-theater, use the problems connected with play production as conflict in drama, and have attempted to describe the creative process. Both . . . satirize romanticism, and they anticipate or answer the criticism they know they will receive or have received for the romantic characteristics of their own work."

Echegaray, who was also awarded the Order of the Golden Fleece by King Alfonso XII in

281

1912, died in 1916 in Madrid at the age of eighty-four.

ADDITIONAL WORKS IN ENGLISH TRANSLATION: Mariana, 1895; Shay, F. (ed.) Twenty-five Short Plays, 1925.

ABOUT: Chandler, F. W. Modern Continental Playwrights, 1931; Jameson, S. Modern Drama in Europe, 1920; Poet Lore May–June 1910; Shaw, G. B. Dramatic Opinions and Essays, 1906; Warren, L. A. Modern Spanish Literature, 1929.

EDELMAN, GERALD M.

(July 1, 1929–   )
Nobel Prize for Physiology or Medicine,
1972
(shared with Rodney R. Porter)

GERALD M. EDELMAN

The American biochemist Gerald Maurice Edelman was born in New York City, the son of Edward Edelman, a physician, and Anna (Freedman) Edelman. After attending public schools in New York, he entered Ursinus College in Pennsylvania, from which he received a B.S. in chemistry in 1950. Edelman then matriculated at the University of Pennsylvania Medical School, where he took his medical degree in 1954, followed by a year as medical house officer at Massachusetts General Hospital. In 1955 he joined the United States Army Medical Corps and practiced general medicine at a station hospital in Paris.

After his discharge in 1957, Edelman, who had decided to become a research biochemist rather than a physician, began graduate work at Rockefeller University under Henry Kunkel, a biochemist who was investigating the structure of antibodies. Discovered by EMIL VON BEHRING in 1890, antibodies are blood proteins known as immunoglobulins (Ig's). Because they can bind to and inactivate bacteria, viruses, and poisons, Ig molecules are a crucial part of the body's chemical defenses. Antibodies have an unusual combination of biochemical properties. KARL LANDSTEINER showed that the body can produce literally millions of different antibodies, each of which binds best to one particular substance, or antigen. All of these antibodies are so similar in chemical structure, however, that it is virtually impossible to isolate a single antibody from normal blood. Kunkel and his co-workers wanted to determine how Ig molecules could be at once structurally uniform and functionally diverse.

Research on antibody structure was hampered because Ig could not be purified and because Ig molecules are very large in comparison to others, far too large to be studied using the chemical methods available in the late 1950s. Edelman believed that antibody structure and function could be elucidated by breaking an Ig molecule into smaller pieces in the hope that the individual fragments would retain their ability to combine with antigens. In his doctoral dissertation, he examined various methods of splitting Ig molecules. After obtaining a Ph.D. in 1960, Edelman remained at Rockefeller as a researcher and faculty member.

Previous researchers—including RODNEY R. PORTER, who first split antibodies into functional subunits—had concluded that IgG molecules, the most important Ig variety in the blood, were made up of a single chain of 1,300 amino acids. Edelman thought this unlikely; even insulin, which has only 51 amino acids, is composed of two amino acid chains. Because the chemical bonds that link amino acid chains are different from and much weaker than those joining the individual amino acids within the chains, they can be broken with relative ease. In 1961 Edelman and a colleague, M. D. Poulik, reported that they had split IgG molecules into two components, which are now called light and heavy chains. After repeating Edelman's experiments under different conditions, Porter combined the results with his own studies of IgG functional units and, in 1962, announced that the basic structure of the IgG molecule had been determined. Although Porter's model was a general one, it nonetheless provided a crucial frame of reference for specific biochemical studies.

In the flurry of antibody research that ensued during the 1960s, Porter and Edelman encouraged an exchange of information among scientists through a series of informal "antibody workshops." In their own work they studied proteins of myelomas, cancers of the Ig-producing cells. One of the main difficulties in studying antibodies had always been that natural Ig preparations usually contain mixtures of many slightly different molecules. In the 1950s Kunkel had realized that since all of the myeloma cells in any given patient usually are descended from a single ancestor, they produce naturally homogeneous antibodies. (The monoclonal-antibody technology developed by GEORGES KÖHLER and CÉSAR MILSTEIN in 1975 exploited this capability to produce homogeneous qualities of preselected antibodies, in addition to those that occur randomly in cancers.)

During the early 1960s, Edelman, Porter, and their colleagues studied the sequences of amino acids in subsections of different myeloma proteins. In 1965 Edelman and his coworkers, "mad as we were," he later said, "started on the whole molecule, a ghastly big job." In their effort to determine how all of the parts of an antibody fit together, they established the precise amino acid sequence of an entire IgG molecule from a myeloma. The completion of the project in 1969 elucidated the order of all 1,300 amino acids in the protein, the longest amino acid sequence identified at that time.

Porter's Ig model was particularly important because it predicted that both heavy and light chains were involved in the active site (the portion of the antibody that actually binds the antigen). This discovery led to a fundamental reconsideration of the central question of antibody diversity: how the different antibodies are formed. This question had attracted increasing interest during the 1950s as more became known about the relationship between genes and proteins. The human body may produce at least 10 million different IgG proteins with as many as 10 million active sites. If antibodies, like other proteins, were produced according to the "one gene, one protein" theory of GEORGE W. BEADLE and EDWARD L. TATUM, the body would have to have 10 million IgG genes and would have no DNA left for other purposes. To resolve this dilemma, MACFARLANE BURNET had proposed in the late 1950s that antibodies are produced from genes that mutate in the Ig-producing cells.

However, if Ig active sites are made from parts of two different amino acid chains, as Porter's model indicated, 10 million antibody genes are not needed. A sufficient number could be made from all possible combinations of some 3,000 heavy- and 3,000 light-chain genes. Throughout the 1960s and the 1970s, a debate raged between those scientists who subscribed to a theory of separate genes for each heavy chain and each light chain and those who thought that only a few heavy- and light-chain genes mutated to produce the different proteins.

Edelman disagreed with both theories, and in 1967 he and an associate, Joseph Gally, proposed a new solution. By that time, it was known that each chain, whether heavy or light, is the product of two genes that move around and recombine while antibody-producing cells are developing. Edelman and Gally suggested that much antibody diversity arises from small errors that occur during the process of recombination. Although essentially correct, their theory was too far ahead of its time to win general acceptance until the late 1970s, when genetic-engineering techniques allowed antibody genes to be examined directly.

Edelman and Porter were awarded the 1972 Nobel Prize for Physiology or Medicine "for their discoveries concerning the chemical structure of antibodies." In his Nobel lecture, Edelman asserted that the field of immunology is a particularly fruitful one for the scientist because "it provokes unusual ideas, some of which are not easily come upon through other fields of study," and predicted that "for this reason, immunology will have a great impact on other branches of biology and medicine."

After receiving the Nobel Prize, Edelman investigated other substances that, like antibodies, can stimulate cells in the immune system. He also proposed in 1978 a radically new theory of the brain suggested by his experiences in immunology. In the body's immune response, an invading virus or bacterium was found not to teach the immune system how to construct an appropriate antibody, but rather to induce a selection of effective antibodies from among the available varieties, whereupon the body then clones the antibodies. Somewhat analogously, Edelman implied, a sensory stimulus does not trigger a reaction from a predetermined set of brain cells, but rather leads to a selection from among competing cell groups and interconnections. The principle of selection is consistent with Darwinian evolution. A primary requirement is variety, to allow selection a range of action, as opposed to relatively fixed biologic structures limited to inflexible responses to changing conditions. Edelman found the source of variety in the brain in embryonic development.

According to this view, genes oversee the formation of body tissues in the embryo but do not dictate every detail. Particular cells are not predestined for particular organs. Rather, certain genes direct the production of various types of cell cement (several of which were discovered by Edelman and his colleagues in the late 1970s), and cells carrying like cement adhere in groups. Cell groups send signals that turn cement-producing genes on and off, thus exercising some control over their own destiny. Different cell groups (with different cements) form borders between them, and Edelman and his colleagues have shown that groups on opposite sides of a border specialize into different kinds of cells. This process was dramatically demonstrated in Edelman's laboratory in experiments that followed the formation of a single feather on a chicken. Since a cell's future depends on where it happens to be, its past history, its present neighbors, and possibly other factors, no two embryos can be identical, even twins with apparently identical genetic endowments.

Edelman then showed how an intrinsically versatile structure and organization of brain cells could, after birth and the cessation of embryonic development, function as a system for learning by selection. His theory had three fundamental elements: in the embryo, the brain develops a highly variable and individual pattern of connections between brain cells; the pattern of connections is fixed after birth and different for each individual, but a stimulus can evoke a response involving certain combinations of connections; and groups of cells are connected in sheets (like road maps), which communicate with each other in the performance of various high-level brain activities. His theory accounts for much of the brain's enormously flexible capabilities to cope with unfamiliar scenes and events, as well as the many failures of researchers to pinpoint specific sites of such brain functions as memory.

Edelman served as associate dean of graduate studies at Rockefeller University from 1963 to 1966, when he became a full professor there. Since 1974 he has been Vincent Astor Distinguished Professor at Rockefeller. He is on the board of governors of the Weizmann Institute of Science and is a trustee of the Salk Institute for Biological Studies.

Edelman married Maxine Morrison in 1950; they have one daughter and two sons.

In addition to the Nobel Prize, he has received the Spencer Morris Award of the University of Pennsylvania (1954), the Eli Lilly Prize of the American Chemical Society (1965), the Albert Einstein Commemorative Award of Yeshiva University (1974), and the Buchman Memorial Award of the California Institute of Technology (1975). He is a member of the New York Academy of Sciences, the American Academy of Arts and Sciences, the National Academy of Sciences, the American Society of Cell Biologists, and the Genetics Society. He holds honorary degrees from the University of Pennsylvania, Ursinus College, Williams College, the University of Siena, and Gustavus Adolphus College.

SELECTED WORKS: The Mindful Brain, 1982, with Vernon Mountcastle; How We Know, 1985, with others.

ABOUT: New York Times October 13, 1972; New Yorker January 10, 1983; Science October 27, 1972.

EHRLICH, PAUL
(March 14, 1854–August 20, 1915)
Nobel Prize for Physiology or Medicine, 1908
(shared with Ilya Metchnikoff)

The German pharmacologist and immunologist Paul Ehrlich was born in Strehlen (now Strzelin, Poland), the son of Ismar Ehrlich, a prosperous Jewish innkeeper, and Rosa (Weigert) Ehrlich, both of whom came from families with a scientific background. Ehrlich's paternal grandfather, who lectured to his neighbors on physics and botany, was an early influence, but his career was decisively stimulated by his cousin, Carl Weigert.

Weigert, a bacteriologist, was among the first scientists to use aniline dyes (discovered in 1853) for staining microscopic preparations. These dyes make selective staining possible; that is, one element of a tissue is stained while others are stained only lightly or not at all. Under his cousin's tutelage, Ehrlich learned the binding properties of various dyes. In 1876 he read a book on the distribution of lead in the organs of poisoned animals, which stimulated what was to be a lifelong interest in what he later described as "the manner and the method of the distribution of substances within the body and its cells."

Ehrlich entered the University of Breslau (now Wrocław, Poland) in 1872. However, after one semester he transferred to the University

PAUL EHRLICH

of Strasbourg, where he exhibited an aptitude for chemistry, even though he took no formal courses in that field. Returning to Breslau two years later, he did most of the work for his medical degree there, before completing his requirements at Leipzig University in 1878.

During these years, Ehrlich, who possessed a remarkable faculty for three-dimensional chemical visualization, developed new dyes with specific affinities for different cell types. By this work, he was able to distinguish different types of white blood cells, a discovery that proved crucial for studies of hematology, leukemia, and immunology. After obtaining his medical degree, Ehrlich was appointed head physician in Friedrich von Frerichs's clinic at the Charité Hospital in Berlin, where he conducted many of his histological studies.

In Berlin, Ehrlich expanded his staining technique to include bacteria as well as animal tissues. When ROBERT KOCH announced the discovery of the tubercle bacillus in 1882, Ehrlich was able to offer him an improved staining method, essentially the same method that is used today. Three years later Ehrlich published "The Oxygen Need of Organisms," in which he outlined his side-chain theory of cell function. "The living protoplasm must represent a giant molecule, which bears the same relation to the ordinary chemical molecule as the sun does to the smallest meteorite," he wrote. "We can assume that in living protoplasm a nucleus of special structure is responsible for the specific function peculiar to the cell, and that to this nucleus are attached, as side chains, atoms and atom complexes."

Frerichs died in 1885, and his successor, Karl Gerhardt, was not sympathetic to Ehrlich's interests. After Ehrlich contracted tuberculosis in 1888, while performing a laboratory experiment, he and his family went to Egypt seeking a cure; they remained there for almost two years. Upon his return to Berlin, Ehrlich learned that he had lost his position at the Charité Hospital. For a time he worked in his own laboratory until Koch arranged successive appointments at the Moabit Municipal Hospital and at the Institute for Infectious Diseases. Working under Koch, Ehrlich continued to pursue his interest in immunology. He showed that antibodies can cross into the milk of a lactating mammal, thereby providing passive immunization to her offspring. At the Institute for Infectious Diseases he worked with EMIL VON BEHRING, the discoverer of antitoxins, who was having difficulty making useful quantities of diphtheria antitoxin. Ehrlich developed a method for repeatedly injecting horses with the toxin until a concentrated antitoxin was produced.

In 1896 Ehrlich was appointed director of the State Institute for Serum Research and Control at Steglitz, a suburb of Berlin. There he applied his expertise in chemistry to the setting up of standards for toxins, antitoxins, and serum samples. The system of international units he devised was widely adopted and remains in general use today.

After the State Institute was expanded and moved to Frankfurt am Main in 1899, Ehrlich published his definitive discourses on the side-chain theory as applied to immunology. Following the lines of thought set out in his original work on the oxygen needs of organisms, he emphasized that antibodies could be produced only by direct chemical interactions between toxins (or other antigens) and cells. Because they resemble some nutritive substances, antigens interact with cellular receptors. In response, the cell overproduces the receptors, which bind to the toxins in the bloodstream. Antibodies are therefore receptors—or, in Ehrlich's terminology, reactive side chains—of cells affected by the antigen.

The side-chain theory was highly influential, although few scientists agreed with it completely. Ehrlich's unique contribution was to conceptualize the interactions between cells, antibodies, and antigens as essentially chemical responses. This approach to the theory served to stimulate investigation because it was a testable, working hypothesis. His work also helped to establish the vocabulary of immunology.

Ehrlich shared the 1908 Nobel Prize for Physiology or Medicine with ILYA METCH-NIKOFF "for their work on the theory of immunity." In his Nobel lecture, Ehrlich expressed confidence that scientists had begun to obtain "an insight into the nature of action of therapeutic substance. . . . I also hope that if these aspects are followed up systematically, it will be easier than heretofore to develop a rational drug synthesis."

Two years before he received the Nobel Prize, Ehrlich was given funds for the construction of the Georg Speyer House, a laboratory for research on therapeutic agents. There, as head of the Research Institute for Chemotherapy, Ehrlich sought an arsenic derivative that would prove effective against trypanosomes (organisms that cause sleeping sickness and other diseases) and the spirochete that causes syphilis. In 1910, after testing 606 compounds, he announced the discovery of a complete cure for syphilis. The compound, which he named Salvarsan, was an arsenic molecule whose chemical makeup directed the poison to the spirochete rather than to the patient.

The introduction of Salvarsan was widely hailed, although it was later attacked by researchers who discovered that when the drug was administered in insufficient doses, the spirochete became immune to subsequent doses. After further research, in 1912 Ehrlich developed a modified compound, Neosalvarsan, which was soon recognized for its effectiveness and won great acclaim for Ehrlich.

In 1883 Ehrlich married Hedwig Pinkus, the daughter of a textile manufacturer. The couple had two daughters. For relaxation, Ehrlich enjoyed reading the detective stories of Sir Arthur Conan Doyle. A dedicated researcher who spent long hours in the laboratory and often neglected to eat, Ehrlich suffered from heart disease near the end of his life. Distressed by the furor over Salvarsan and by the war that raged in Europe, he died of a stroke on August 20, 1915, at Bad Homburg, where he had gone on vacation.

Ehrlich's many awards included the Prize of Honor of the International Congress of Medicine (1906), the Leibig Medal of the German Chemical Society (1911), and the Cameron Prize and Lectureship of the University of Edinburgh (1914). He was a member of eighty-one scientific societies and academies throughout the world and received honorary degrees from the universities of Chicago, Göttingen, Oxford, and Breslau, among others.

SELECTED WORKS: Histology of the Blood, 1900, with Adolf Lazarus; Anemia, 1905; Experimental Researches on Specific Therapeutics, 1908; Collected Studies on Immunity, 1910; Collected Papers of Paul Ehrlich (4 vols.) 1956–1958.

ABOUT: Bäumler, E. Paul Ehrlich, Scientist for Life, 1984; Brock, T. D. Milestones in Microbiology, 1961; De Kruif, P. Microbe Hunters, 1926; Dictionary of Scientific Biography, volume 7, 1973; Farber, E. (ed.) Great Chemists, 1961; Marquardt, M. Paul Ehrlich, 1949; New York Academy of Science. Paul Ehrlich Centennial, 1954; William, J. H. Between Life and Death, 1951.

EIGEN, MANFRED
(May 9, 1927–)
Nobel Prize for Chemistry, 1967
(shared with Ronald Norrish and George Porter)

The German chemist Manfred Eigen (ī' gən) was born in Bochum to Ernst Eigen, a chamber musician, and Hedwig (Feld) Eigen. After receiving his secondary education at the Bochum Gymnasium, he was drafted and served in an antiaircraft battery during the final months of World War II. After the war he studied physics and chemistry at the University of Göttingen, where he received his doctorate in natural sciences in 1951. His dissertation concerned the specific heat of heavy water and aqueous electrolyte solutions. After two years as an assistant lecturer in physical chemistry at Göttingen, Eigen joined the staff of the Max Planck Institute for Physical Chemistry in Göttingen. In 1964 he was named director of the institute.

Physicists conducting sonar research had found that sound waves are more readily absorbed by seawater than by pure water or sodium chloride (salt) solutions in water. Eigen found that this phenomenon was due to small amounts of magnesium sulfate dissolved in seawater. High-frequency sound waves disrupt the associated cluster of magnesium and sulfate ions (charged particles) in water, causing the loss of a small amount of energy from the sound wave.

Eigen thus saw high-frequency sound waves as a means of producing small disturbances in a chemical system. By observing the adjustment of the chemical system to a slight displacement from equilibrium, he could determine rates of chemical processes hitherto unmeasurable. He later used very rapid heat and electrical pulses to effect small changes in a chemical system's electrical conductivity or absorption of light. With these methods, called relaxation techniques because they measure the relaxation of a chemical system to a new

MANFRED EIGEN

state of equilibrium, Eigen studied chemical reactions a thousandth to a billionth of a second in duration.

Among Eigen's physicochemical investigations were studies of the dissociation and recombination of ions in pure water, diffusion-controlled proton transfer in liquids, sound absorption by electrolyte solutions, and the kinetics of keto-enol tautomerism (compounds with different arrangements of atoms existing in equilibrium). Applied to problems in molecular biology, relaxation techniques have been used to study enzyme-catalyzed reactions, the formation of polypeptides into helical coils, and the coding of biological information.

"For their studies of extremely fast chemical reactions, effected by disturbing the equilibrium by means of very short pulses of energy," Eigen, GEORGE PORTER, and RONALD NORRISH shared the 1967 Nobel Prize for Chemistry. "Although chemists have long been talking of instantaneous reactions, they had no way of determining the actual reaction rates," said H. A. Ölander of the Royal Swedish Academy of Sciences in his presentation speech. "There were many important reactions of this type, such as the neutralization of acids with alkalis. Thanks to you, chemists now have a whole range of methods that can be used to follow these rapid processes, so that this large gap in our chemical knowledge has now been filled."

In the 1970s Eigen's scientific interests turned to the origin of life. His recent studies have concerned hypercycles: the self-organization of individual nucleic acids into more complex structures, their interaction with proteins, and the development of primitive genes.

Eigen married Elfriede Mueller in 1952; they have a son and a daughter. A gifted pianist, Eigen also enjoys hiking, mountain climbing, and gathering wild mushrooms. He is known to his colleagues for his good nature, his inexhaustible appetite for work, and his readiness to assist others with scientific problems.

Eigen has written more than 100 scientific and technical papers. In addition to the Nobel Prize, he has received the Otto Hahn Prize for Chemistry and Physics of the German Chemical Society (1962); the Kirkwood Medal (1963), Harrison E. Howe Lectureship (1965), and Linus Pauling Medal (1967) of the American Chemical Society; the Carus Medal of the Leopoldina German Academy of Researchers in Natural Sciences (1967); and the Faraday Medal of the British Chemical Society (1977). He is a member of the Royal Society of London, the French Academy, the American National Academy of Sciences, the American Academy of Arts and Sciences, and the Göttingen Academy of Sciences. He holds numerous honorary doctorates from major universities.

SELECTED WORKS: The Hypercycle, a Principle of Natural Self-Organization, 1979, with Peter Schuster; Laws of the Game: How the Principles of Nature Govern Chance, 1981, with Ruthild Winkler.

ABOUT: New York Times October 31, 1967; Nova: Adventures in Science, 1983; Science November 10, 1967.

EIJKMAN, CHRISTIAAN
(August 11, 1858–November 5, 1930)
Nobel Prize for Physiology or Medicine, 1929
(shared with Frederick Gowland Hopkins)

The Dutch physician Christiaan Eijkman (āk′ män) was born in Nijkerk, the seventh child of Christiaan Eijkman, a schoolmaster, and Johanna Alida (Pool) Eijkman. One of his brothers became a chemist and another a linguist. At the age of seventeen, Eijkman received a scholarship to attend the Military Medical School of the University of Amsterdam in return for military service upon graduation. Because of his academic achievements, he was made an assistant to his physiology professor. He wrote a doctoral thesis entitled "On Polarization of Nerves" and graduated with honors as a medical doctor in 1883. That

EIJKMAN

CHRISTIAAN EIJKMAN

year he also married Aaltje Wigeri van Edema and began his military career.

He was posted as medical officer first at Semarang in the Dutch East Indies (now Indonesia) and then at Tjilatjap, on the southern coast of Java. Within two years his wife had died of malaria, and Eijkman himself was so severely debilitated by the disease that he returned to Amsterdam in 1885 to recover. After regaining his health, he went to Berlin to work with ROBERT KOCH and gain an expertise in bacteriology.

At the time, bacteriology (the study of microorganisms) was a challenging new science, an emerging discipline that offered a promising approach to the study and control of diseases. For example, all of the deficiency diseases (disorders caused by a serious vitamin deficiency), such as beriberi and pellagra, were at first thought to be infectious. In studying pellagra in humans, however, the American physician Joseph Goldberger had ruled out infection as the causative agent.

Koch had recently proven that tuberculosis is caused by a bacterium; therefore, it was proposed that many other diseases might also be caused by bacteria. At Koch's laboratory, Eijkman met two members of a Dutch medical commission, Cornelius A. Pekelharing and Clemens Winkler, who came to seek Koch's help in solving the problem of beriberi, a disease that was epidemic in the Dutch East Indies. Koch was too busy to join the commission but suggested that Eijkman be added to the team. Eijkman readily agreed and set out for Java in 1886.

Beriberi, neither a new disease nor unique to Java, had first been described by a Dutch physician in the early 1600s. For years it was as common a problem in the Japanese navy as scurvy had been among British sailors. Beriberi (named from a Sinhalese phrase that means "I cannot" and signifies that a person is too ill to do anything) causes paralysis and numbness of the feet and legs, as well as heart and lung disorders; the disease is often fatal. Those in regimented communities, such as prisons and military organizations, suffered the most. In fact, a jail sentence in Java was considered tantamount to a death sentence. At that time there were at least two theories that connected beriberi with a diet containing large amounts of rice. One held that rice contained a poison that brought on the symptoms of beriberi; the other suggested that the lack of fat and protein in a rice diet led to the disease.

The director of the Japanese navy, who had studied the problem himself, eradicated the disease by feeding his sailors meat, vegetables, and milk, rather than their standard fare of raw fish and polished rice. Other interested persons inferred from the report of the Japanese navy that the rice had been infected with germs, and most scientists, including the team with whom Eijkman worked, thought beriberi was caused by a bacterium. At one point Eijkman and his colleagues thought they had found the causative bacteria in the blood of beriberi patients, but when the standard disinfecting routine did little to eliminate the disease, they admitted their error and resumed the search. Pekelharing and Winkler returned home in 1887, leaving Eijkman in charge of the Laboratory for Bacteriology and Pathology, which consisted of two small rooms in the military hospital in Batavia on the island of Java. Eijkman also was appointed director of the Javanese Medical School.

Eijkman's group began using chickens as laboratory animals because they were cheap and abundant. To the team's surprise, the chickens developed a paralytic disease similar to beriberi. When autopsies were performed on the animals, the cause of the paralysis was found to be a simultaneous inflammation of many nerves, a condition Eijkman called "polyneuritis." Eijkman contended that polyneuritis must be caused by a type of bacterium, but he could not find one in the chickens.

Suddenly, in the midst of his experiments, all of the chickens recovered for no apparent reason. Baffled, Eijkman wondered whether the chickens' diet could be responsible. His suspicion proved correct. Eijkman later wrote that "the laboratory keeper—as I afterwards discovered—had for the sake of economy fed the chickens on cooked rice, which he had obtained from the hospital kitchen. Then the cook was replaced and his successor refused to allow military rice to be taken for civilian chickens."

Eijkman next experimented with different kinds of rice. The "military" rice was polished, whereas the rice that cured the chickens was "civilian," or unpolished rice. When he resumed feeding polished rice to half of the now-healthy chickens, they again developed polyneuritis. The other half, which were fed the unpolished rice, remained healthy. The birds that became ill while eating polished rice improved when they were fed unpolished rice once again.

Could polished and unpolished rice play a role in human beriberi as well? Eijkman found that in prisons where inmates were fed polished rice, the incidence of beriberi was 300 times greater than in prisons where unpolished rice was served. In 1890, in a paper titled "Polyneuritis in Chickens," Eijkman described the similarities between polyneuritis in chickens and beriberi in human beings, and he reported his experiments with rice. He reasoned that polished white rice must become poisoned during the milling process.

While in Java, Eijkman made several other medical contributions. Through a series of experiments, for example, Eijkman disproved the then-current theory that Europeans living in the tropics underwent changes in blood composition and metabolism in order to adapt to warmer climates.

In 1896 ill health once again forced Eijkman to return to the Netherlands, this time accompanied by his wife Berthe Julie Louise van der Kemp, whom he had married in 1888, and their son. Eijkman was appointed professor of public health and forensic medicine at the University of Utrecht in 1899. In addition to his academic work, he became involved in problems of city water supply, housing, education, alcoholism, and tuberculosis.

Gerrit Grijns, who had been Eijkman's assistant in Java, continued the studies on beriberi at the laboratory in Batavia. In 1901 Grijns proposed that the disease was caused by a nutritional deficiency, or the lack of a specific natural substance found in certain foods. For nearly two more decades, however, most medical authorities refused to accept that anything but a bacterium caused beriberi. In 1911 the Polish chemist Casimir Funk extracted the substance that protects against beriberi from the outer husk of rice grains. This substance, now called thiamine, or vitamin B_1, is not present in polished rice, from which the hulls are removed. Funk coined the term *vitamine,* a Latin hybrid of *vita* ("life") and *amine* ("nitrogen"). The final *e* was eventually dropped, and although new vitamins were found not to contain nitrogen, the term persisted.

Eijkman's work in Java had laid the groundwork for the discovery of deficiency diseases. FREDERICK GOWLAND HOPKINS called these indispensable nutrients "accessory factors." Eijkman and Hopkins shared the Nobel Prize for Physiology or Medicine in 1929 for their respective roles in the discovery of vitamins. Eijkman, who had retired in 1928, was too ill to accept the award in person. He died in Utrecht in 1930 after a prolonged illness.

Eijkman was a member of the Royal Netherlands Academy of Arts and Sciences, a foreign associate of the American National Academy of Sciences, and an honorary fellow of the Royal Sanitary Institute in London. He received several orders of knighthood, and an Eijkman Medal was established by the Dutch government in his honor.

ABOUT: Dictionary of Scientific Biography, volume 4, 1971.

EINSTEIN, ALBERT
(March 14, 1879–April 18, 1955)
Nobel Prize in Physics, 1921

The German-Swiss-American physicist Albert Einstein (īn′ stīn) was born in Ulm, a medieval city in the state of Württemberg, Germany, the son of Hermann and Pauline (Koch) Einstein. He grew up in Munich, where his father and uncle ran a small electrochemical plant. Einstein was a quiet, withdrawn child who was attracted to mathematics but otherwise disliked school because of its rote teaching and armylike discipline. During his undistinguished years at the Luitpold Gymnasium in Munich, he read philosophy, mathematics, and popular science on his own and was deeply impressed by the idea of an orderly universe. When his father's business failed in 1895 and the family moved to Milan, Italy, Einstein remained behind but soon quit school, without earning a diploma, and joined his family.

The sixteen-year-old Einstein was struck by the atmosphere of freedom and culture he found in Italy. Although he had superior, largely self-

ALBERT EINSTEIN

taught mathematical and scientific knowledge and was precociously independent in his thinking, he had not chosen a career. At his father's urging to study for a technical occupation, needed to bolster the family's meager finances, he took the examination for entrance to the Federal Institute of Technology in Zurich, which did not require a high school diploma. Because he was unprepared, he failed; but the school's principal, who recognized Einstein's mathematical ability, sent the boy to finish high school in Aarau, twenty miles west of Zurich. After a year's study, he passed the examination for the Federal Institute in the summer of 1896. Einstein flourished in Aarau, enjoying the close contact with teachers and the absence of militarism. He so resented his earlier experiences that he formally requested an end to his German citizenship, to which his father reluctantly assented.

In Zurich, Einstein studied physics, again paying more attention to his independent reading than to his courses. He had planned to teach, but after graduating in 1901 and becoming a Swiss citizen, he was unable to find a regular teaching post. In 1902 he went to work as a patent examiner in the Swiss Patent Office in Bern, a position he held seven years. This was a happy and productive time for him. He had already published one paper, on capillarity (the effect on liquid surfaces of confinement in narrow tubes). Although his salary was barely enough to support him, his patent work was sufficiently undemanding to allow him the time and energy to pursue theoretical scientific investigations. His early papers dealt with intermolecular forces and applications of statistical thermodynamics. One of them, "A New Determination of Molecular Dimensions," was accepted as a doctoral dissertation, and the University of Zurich awarded him a Ph.D. in 1905. It was also in 1905 that he published a small group of papers that not only established his powers as a theoretical physicist but also changed the face of physics.

One of these papers, related to his early work, explained Brownian motion, the chaotic zigzagging of particles suspended in a liquid. Einstein linked the particle motion observed with a microscope to collisions with unseen molecules; moreover, he predicted that such observations would permit the calculation of the masses and numbers of molecules in a given volume. His prediction was confirmed by JEAN PERRIN a few years later. Einstein's accomplishment was particularly significant because the existence of molecules as anything but a convenient invention was much in dispute at the time.

Another paper explained the photoelectric effect, the emission of electrons from a metal surface irradiated by ultraviolet rays or other electromagnetic radiation. PHILIPP VON LENARD had suggested that the electrons were knocked out by the impact of the light. He also predicted that electrons ejected by a brighter light should emerge at greater speeds. Experiments showed that this was not the case. Meanwhile, in 1900 MAX PLANCK was able to account for the radiation from hot bodies by making the radical proposal that energy was not emitted continuously but in discrete bits that came to be called quanta. The physical significance of a quantum was obscure, but its magnitude equaled a certain number (Planck's constant) multiplied by the frequency of the radiation.

Einstein's insight was to relate the photon, the name given to the quantum of electromagnetic energy, to the energy of the ejected electron. Each photon ejected one electron. The electron's kinetic energy (related to its velocity) equaled the energy from the photon left over after expenditure of the energy required to dislodge the electron from its attachment to the metal. A brighter light contained more photons and dislodged more, but not faster, electrons. Faster electrons could be produced by radiation of a higher frequency because its photons contain more energy. Einstein went on to make the far-reaching proposition that light must have a dual nature: it could behave like a wave, as demonstrated by centuries of optical experimentation, but it could also behave like a particle, as in the photoelectric effect. Einstein's view was to be confirmed experimentally many times, not only for light but for X rays and gamma rays. In 1924 Louis de Broglie proposed an additional step in the transformation of physics: that matter, such as electrons, also had wave properties. This idea, too, was experimentally confirmed and laid the groundwork for the field of quantum mechanics. Einstein's contributions to quantum theory also elucidated such phenomena as fluorescence and photoionization and explained puzzling variations of the specific heats of solids at different temperatures.

Einstein's third dramatic achievement in 1905 was his special theory of relativity, which gradually revolutionized all areas of physics. At the time, it was generally believed that light waves were propagated by the ether, a mysterious substance thought to fill the universe. Ether, however, eluded all experimental attempts to demonstrate it. An ingenious experiment in 1887 by Albert A. Michelson and Edward Morley failed to detect any difference between the velocity of light measured parallel to the motion of the earth through the supposed ether and its velocity measured at right angles to the motion. If ether carried the light as a disturbance, as air propagates sound waves, the ether velocity should add to or subtract from the apparent velocity of light, just as a river affects the velocity, relative to an observer on the shore, of a boat being rowed downstream or upstream. Although it is not certain whether Einstein was directly influenced by the Michelson-Morley results, his new theory was based on two universal assumptions that dispensed with the need for the ether: all laws of physics have equal validity for any two observers, regardless of their relative motion; and light always travels through free space at the same velocity, regardless of the motion of its source.

The consequences of these assumptions changed ideas of space and time. No material object can travel faster than light. As seen by a stationary observer, the dimension of a moving object shortens in the direction of motion, and the object's mass increases. To make the velocity of light the same for moving and stationary observers, moving clocks must run more slowly. Even the meaning of the word *stationary* must be carefully considered. Motion or stillness must always be relative to some reference observer; an observer riding on a moving object is stationary relative to the object but may be moving relative to some other observer. Since time becomes a relative variable, like the x, y, and z coordinates of geometry, simultaneity becomes relative. Two events that appear simultaneous to one observer may be separated in time to another. Among other consequences is the equivalence of mass and energy. A mass m is a kind of frozen energy E related by the equation $E = mc^2$, where c is the velocity of light. Thus, the emission of photons of light is paid for by a reduction in mass of the source.

Relativistic effects, which are generally negligible at ordinary velocities, become significant only at the great speeds characteristic of atomic and subatomic particles. Moreover, the loss of mass required to account for light emission is extremely small, generally undetectable by even the most sensitive chemical balance. However, relativity did provide the means for explaining otherwise incomprehensible features of atomic and nuclear physics. In the atomic bomb that was developed some forty years later, physicists were able to calculate the expected energy release on the basis of the mass lost in the splitting of uranium nuclei.

After the publication of his 1905 papers, Einstein began to receive academic recognition. He became an associate professor of physics at the University of Zurich in 1909 and a professor, first at the German University in Prague, Czechoslovakia, in 1911 and then at the Federal Institute of Technology in 1912. In 1914 he went to Germany as a professor at the University of Berlin and director of the Kaiser Wilhelm (now Max Planck) Institute for Physics. His German citizenship was restored, and he became a member of the Prussian Academy of Sciences. He did not support the German cause in World War I, however, advocating pacifism instead.

In 1915, after years of intensive effort, Einstein succeeded in developing his general theory of relativity, which went beyond the restrictions of the special theory of 1905 that motions be uniform and relative velocities constant. He now encompassed all kinds of motion and accelerations (varying velocities), and the previously prevailing theory of mechanics, founded by Isaac Newton in the 1600s, became only a special case useful at relatively slow speeds. Einstein also replaced many of Newton's concepts. He had been disturbed by such aspects of Newtonian mechanics as the coincidental equality of gravitational and inertial masses. According to Newton, bodies attracted each other across even enormous distances, and the force exerted itself instantaneously. Gravitational mass was a measure of the attractive force. The motion of a body in response to a force, however, was governed by its inertial mass, a measure of how much the body was accelerated by a given force. Einstein wondered why these two masses happened to be the same.

Einstein performed what he called a "thought experiment." If a man in a freely falling box, for example, an elevator, dropped his keys, the keys would not fall to the floor. Box, man, and keys would be falling at the same speeds and would retain their positions relative to each other. This would be true in an imaginary location in space far away from any gravitational source. As a friend of Einstein's described the situation, the man in the box could not "tell whether he was in a gravitational field or subject to uniform acceleration." Einstein's equivalence principle—gravitational and inertial effects are indistinguishable—explained the coincidence between Newton's gravitational and inertial masses. Einstein then extended the picture to light. If a light ray crossed the box "horizontally" while the box was falling, the ray would strike the far wall at a point farther from the floor than its point of entry because the box would have dropped a little during the interval. To the man in the box, the light ray would obviously have been bent upward. To Einstein this meant that light rays are bent by gravitation in the everyday world if they pass close enough to a sufficiently massive body.

Einstein's general theory replaced Newton's theory of gravitational attraction between bodies by a space-time mathematical description in which bodies influence the characteristics of space in their vicinity. According to this view, bodies do not attract each other; rather, each influences space-time geometry, which then guides the motion of bodies passing through. As Einstein's colleague, the American physicist J. A. Wheeler, explained, "Space tells matter how to move, and matter tells space how to curve."

Einstein's work in this period was not confined to relativity theory. For example, in 1916 he introduced into quantum theory the idea of stimulated emission of radiation. In 1913 NIELS BOHR had developed a model of the atom as a central nucleus (discovered some years earlier by ERNEST RUTHERFORD) surrounded by electrons restricted to certain orbits (energy levels) by quantum limitations. According to Bohr's model, atoms emitted radiation when the electrons were excited to higher energy levels and then fell back. The energy difference between levels equaled the energy in the photons absorbed or emitted. The return of excited electrons to lower energy levels was a random process. Einstein predicted that, under appropriate circumstances, electrons could be excited to a particular energy level and then triggered to cascade down simultaneously, a process that underlies the action of modern lasers.

Although the relativity theories were too radical to be greeted with immediate acceptance, they were supported by a series of confirmations. Among the first was an explanation of a peculiar wobble in the orbit of the planet Mercury that could not be fully accounted for by Newtonian mechanics. In 1919, during observations of an eclipse, a star that should have been hidden behind the rim of the sun was visible, indicating that its light had been bent by the sun's gravitation. Universal fame came to Einstein after World War I, when the findings of the 1919 eclipse team were reported throughout the world and relativity became a household word. In 1920 Einstein was appointed visiting professor at the University of Leiden. In Germany, however, Einstein also came under attack because of his opposition to the war and because his revolutionary theories were in disfavor with some German scientists, including a few who were anti-Semites. Some labeled Einstein's work "Jewish physics," calling it contrary to German standards. In the 1920s Einstein continued to espouse pacifism and actively supported the peace efforts of the League of Nations. He was also a spokesman for the Zionist cause and was instrumental in the establishment of the Hebrew University in Jerusalem in 1925.

In 1922 Einstein received the 1921 Nobel Prize for Physics "for his services to theoretical physics, and especially for his discovery of the law of the photoelectric effect." "Einstein's law has become the basis of quantitative photochemistry in the same way as [Michael] Faraday's law is the basis of electrochemistry," said SVANTE ARRHENIUS of the Royal Swedish Academy of Sciences on presenting the award. Prior commitments to lecture in Japan prevented Einstein from attending the ceremonies, and he did not deliver his Nobel lecture until a year later.

As physicists were moving toward acceptance of the quantum theory, Einstein seemed to be moving away from its implications. In 1927 he expressed his unhappiness with the statistical interpretation of quantum mechanics advocated by Bohr and MAX BORN, which held that the principle of cause and effect does not apply to subatomic phenomena. Only the probabilities of events could be calculated. Einstein was convinced that statistics was nothing more than a tool and that a fundamental theory could not be statistical. As he expressed it, "God doesn't play dice" with the universe. Whereas proponents of the statistical interpretation rejected physical models for unobservable phenomena, Einstein thought a theory incomplete unless it could give "the real state of a physical system, something that objectively exists, and which can, in principle, be described in physical terms." His lifelong goal became a unified field theory that could derive quantum phenomena from a relativistic description of nature. In this he was unsuccessful. He engaged in many arguments about quantum mechanics with Bohr, but these tended only to strengthen Bohr's position.

When Hitler came to power in 1933, Einstein was not in Germany, and he never returned. He became a professor of theoretical physics at the new Institute for Advanced Study in Princeton, New Jersey. In 1940 he became an American citizen. He lived in Princeton for the rest of his life, formally retiring from the institute in 1945. As World War II approached, he renounced his earlier pacifism, feeling that only military force could stop Nazi Germany's expansion. He concluded that it was necessary "even to face battle" in order to "safeguard law and human dignity." In 1939, at the urging of several other refugee physicists, he wrote a letter to President Franklin D. Roosevelt warning that Germany might be developing an atomic bomb and urging support for American nuclear fission research. Einstein himself played no part in the subsequent development, which led to the explosion of the world's first atomic bomb on July 16, 1945, in Alamogordo, New Mexico.

After World War II, horrified by the use of the atomic bomb against Japan and by the accelerating arms race, Einstein urged the abolition of war to ensure the survival of humanity. He was active in the movement for a world government. Shortly before he died, he signed what became known as the Russell Statement, drafted by BERTRAND RUSSELL, warning governments of the dangers of the hydrogen bomb and calling on them to renounce nuclear weapons. He championed the free expression of ideas and argued for the responsible use of science to make a better world.

Einstein's first wife was Mileva Maric, a fellow student at the Federal Institute of Technology in Zurich, whom he married in 1903, despite his parents' adamant opposition. They had two sons. The marriage ended in divorce in 1919, after a five-year separation. In the same year, he married his cousin Elsa Einstein, a widow with two daughters. She died in 1936. Einstein's two favorite pastimes were music and sailing. He began to study the violin when he was six years old and continued throughout his life, often playing music with other physicists, such as Max Planck, who was an accomplished pianist. Einstein found the serenity of sailing to be conducive to thinking about physics. In Princeton he became a local fixture, known as the world-famous scientist but also as the kindly, shy, gentle, and somewhat eccentric man down the street. He died in Princeton of an aortic aneurysm.

The most famous scientist of the twentieth century and one of the greatest of all time, Einstein brought unique insights and an unsurpassed creative imagination to physics. From an early age he had a sense of the world as a harmonious and understandable whole, "which stands before us like a great, eternal riddle." He believed, he said, "in Spinoza's God, who reveals himself in the harmony of all being." This "cosmic religious feeling" induced Einstein to try to describe nature with a mathematical system of great beauty and simplicity.

Among Einstein's many honors was an invitation in 1952 to become the president of Israel; he declined. He received numerous awards in addition to the Nobel Prize, including the Copley Medal of the Royal Society of London (1925) and the Franklin Medal of the Franklin Institute (1935). He held honorary doctorates from many universities and was a member of all the leading scientific academies of the world.

SELECTED WORKS: Relativity, the Special and the General Theory, 1920; The Meaning of Relativity, 1921; Sidelights on Relativity, 1922; Investigation on the Theory of Brownian Movement, 1926; The Unitary Field Theory, 1929; About Zionism, 1930; Cosmic Religion, 1931; Essays in Science, 1933; The Fight Against War, 1933; Why War? 1933, with Sigmund Freud; On the Method of Theoretical Physics, 1933; Origins of the General Theory of Relativity, 1933; The World as I See It, 1934; The Evolution of Physics, 1938, with Leopold Infeld; Test Case for Humanity, 1944; The Arabs and Palestine, 1944, with E. Kahler; Out of My Later Years, 1950; Essays in Humanism, 1950; Essays in Physics, 1950; H. A. Lorentz: His Creative Genius and His Personality, 1953; Ideas and Opinions, 1954; Einstein on Peace, 1960; Letters on Wave Mechanics, 1967, with others; The Born-Einstein Letters, 1971, with Max Born; Autobiographical Notes, 1979; Collected Papers of Albert Einstein, volume 1, 1987.

ABOUT: Aichelburg, P. C., and Sexl, R. U. (eds.) Albert Einstein: His Influence on Physics, Philosophy, and Politics, 1979; Armand, L., et al. Einstein, 1979; Bernstein, J. Einstein, 1973; Clark, R. W. Einstein: The Life and Times, 1971; Frank, P. Einstein, His Life and Times, 1947; Friedman, A. J. Einstein as Myth and Muse, 1985; Goldsmith, M., et al. (eds.) Einstein: The First Hundred Years, 1980; Hoffmann, B. Albert Einstein, Creator and Rebel, 1972; Infeld, L. Albert Einstein, His Work and Its Influence on Our World, 1950; Kuznetsov, B. Einstein, 1965; Moszkowski, A. Conversations With Einstein, 1971; Pais, A. Subtle Is the Lord: The Science and Life of Albert Einstein, 1982; Quasha, S. Albert Einstein: An Intimate Portrait, 1980; Reiser, A. Albert Einstein: A Biographical Portrait, 1930; Schilpp, P. A. (ed.) Albert Einstein, Philosopher-Scientist, 1949; Seelig, C. Albert Einstein: A Documentary Biography, 1956; Woolf, H. (ed.) Some Strangeness in the Proportion, 1980.

EINTHOVEN, WILLEM

(May 21, 1860–September 28, 1927)
Nobel Prize for Physiology or Medicine, 1924

WILLEM EINTHOVEN

The Dutch physiologist Willem Einthoven (ānt' hō fən) was born in Semarang, Java (then the Dutch East Indies, now Indonesia), the third of six children of Jacob Einthoven, a physician, and the former Louise M. M. C. de Vogel. Einthoven's father died when the boy was six years of age, and in 1870 the family returned to Utrecht in the Netherlands. There Einthoven completed his secondary education and entered the University of Utrecht as a medical student in 1879. A frequent participant in sports, he was president of the Gymnastics and Fencing Union and founded the Utrecht Student Rowing Club. While still an undergraduate, he published a study of the motion of the shoulder and elbow joints that was based on a sporting accident in which he had broken a wrist. For a thesis on stereoscopy through color differentiation, Einthoven received a Ph.D. in medicine in 1885. That year, at the age of twenty-five, he was appointed professor of physiology at the University of Leiden, a post he held until his death.

Although trained as a physician and physiologist, Einthoven was deeply interested in physics. As an assistant to the ophthalmologist Herman Snellen and the physiologist F. C. Donders, he studied the physical properties of light and their effects on the muscles of the eye. He became adept at designing highly technical instruments to measure physiological events.

Electrophysiology is the study of electrical phenomena occurring in the normal functions of the body. In the 1880s it was recognized that electrical changes are involved with the contracting heart, but the only method known for recording these cardiac currents was by direct contact with the exposed heart. In 1887 the English physiologist Augustus Waller discovered that potential changes associated with the heartbeat could be recorded by electrodes on the surface of an intact animal. These electrical currents were measured with a capillary electrometer, an instrument that consisted of a column of mercury that rose and fell with the changes in the electrical field. The resulting electrocardiogram (ECG or EKG) provided a highly inaccurate reading because of the lag before the action of the mercury. Einthoven found that precise EKGs using the capillary electrometer could be achieved by laborious mathematical corrections.

To avoid such long calculations, Einthoven designed an apparatus that could record small, fluctuating differences in potential accurately and directly. The result, after six years of work, was the string galvanometer, an instrument consisting of a fine quartz wire (so thin that it was disturbed by the motion of air particles) held under tension in a magnetic field. When subjected to an electrical current, the wire deflected according to the amount of the charge. This motion was then magnified and photographed on a moving reel of film. Since it was very light in weight, the wire responded almost instantaneously to any changes in the electrical field.

A normal EKG shows three waves, which Einthoven called P, QRS, and T. The small P wave reflects electrical activity of the atria (upper chambers of the heart), while the rapid, high-amplitude QRS and slower T waves are related to ventricular (lower cavities of the heart) currents. Einthoven also designated three points on the body where electrodes should be placed: lead I from the right and left hands, lead II from the right hand and left foot, and lead III from the left hand and left foot. The angle at which the heart lies in the chest can be calculated from the equilateral triangle formed by these three leads or placements. Einthoven's law states that the voltage in leads I and III equals the voltage in lead II. Therefore, only two standard leads need be recorded to determine cardiac function. The string galvanometer revolutionized the study of heart disease. With this device, physicians were able to record the action of the heart accurately and thus to discover abnormalities revealed by characteristic EKG tracings.

Einthoven was awarded the 1924 Nobel Prize for Physiology or Medicine for "his discovery of the mechanism of the electrocardiogram." In his Nobel lecture he cited many examples of EKGs showing rhythmical abnormalities and correlation with heart sounds. He concluded by acknowledging the work of others in his field: "A new chapter in the scientific knowledge of heart disease has been introduced, not through the work of a single person, but through the labor of many talented men who have carried out their investigation unlimited by any political boundaries."

The string galvanometer was later applied to the measurement of nerve potentials, and to the electrical changes associated with the movement of muscles. In one of his last experiments, carried out with his son Willem, an electrotechnical engineer, Einthoven used the string galvanometer to receive radiotelegraph signals broadcast from Java. This was achieved by synchronizing the tension of the string with the vibrations of the transmitting wave. The telegrams were then photographed on paper. His son later developed the vacuum string galvanometer used in wireless communication. Einthoven developed no school of followers, although many scientists visited his laboratory and later utilized his methods of enquiry.

In 1886 Einthoven married his cousin, Frédérique Jeanne Louise de Vogel; they had three daughters and a son.

Short and stocky in appearance, Einthoven was known for his love of good jokes, candor, and generosity to his friends and colleagues. His final work was a treatise on the action current of the heart, which appeared posthumously. He died in Leiden on September 28, 1927.

A regular participant in the Royal Dutch Academy of Sciences, Einthoven was widely respected and honored. He was elected a foreign member of the Royal Society of London. He was in demand as a lecturer and lectured extensively in Europe and the United States.

ABOUT: American Heart Journal June 1930; Archives of Internal Medicine March 1961; Barron, S. L. Willem Einthoven, 1952; Dictionary of Scientific Biography, volume 4, 1971; Snellen, H. A., et al. History and Perspectives of Cardiology, 1981; Willus, F. A., and Keys, T. E. Cardiac Classics, 1941.

ELIOT, T. S.
(September 26, 1888–January 4, 1965)
Nobel Prize for Literature, 1948

The American poet Thomas Stearns Eliot was born in St. Louis, Missouri, the seventh and youngest child of a distinguished family of New England origin. His forebears included the Reverend William Greenleaf Eliot, founder of Washington University in St. Louis, and, on his mother's side, Isaac Stearns, one of the original settlers of the Massachusetts Bay Colony. Eliot's father, Henry Ware Eliot, was a prosperous St. Louis industrialist; his mother, the former Charlotte Stearns, had broad intellectual interests and wrote a biography of William Greenleaf Eliot as well as a dramatic poem, *Savonarola*.

After graduating from the Smith Academy in St. Louis, Eliot spent a year at Milton Academy in Massachusetts in preparation for Harvard, which he entered in 1906. A gifted and outstanding student, Eliot completed his undergraduate work in three years and received an M.A. in philosophy in his fourth. During this time he contributed poetry to the *Harvard Advocate* and served as the magazine's editor in 1909–1910. Subsequently, he spent a year in Paris, where he attended lectures at the Sorbonne and pursued an interest in French literature, particularly symbolist poetry. At Harvard he had been introduced to symbolism—particularly the poems of Jules Laforgue—through *The Symbolist Movement in Literature* (1899), a work by Arthur Symons that profoundly influenced Eliot's development as a poet.

Returning to Harvard for graduate work in philosophy in 1911, Eliot completed a dissertation on the English idealist philosopher F. H. Bradley and studied Sanskrit and Buddhism. He was awarded a Sheldon Traveling Fellowship that took him first to Germany and then to England, where he continued his study of philosophy at Merton College, Oxford, where

T. S. ELIOT

sion and the difficulty of expression, particularly between man and woman. "Prufrock" proved to be a milestone of twentieth-century verse; many critics have noted its importance, and the American poet John Berryman felt that it marked the beginning of modern poetry.

While Eliot's reputation as a poet was growing quickly, his position as the most influential critic of his time was also beginning to emerge. From 1919 onward he was a regular contributor to the *Times Literary Supplement,* in which he published a series of articles on Elizabethan and Jacobean drama, collected with other critical essays and reviews in *The Sacred Wood* (1920). In these and other essays on William Shakespeare, John Dryden, Christopher Marlowe, John Donne, George Herbert, Andrew Marvell, and Dante, Eliot attempted "to bring back the poet to life—the great, the perennial task of criticism." The essays Eliot wrote in the 1920s (*Homage to John Dryden,* 1924) and 1930s (*Selected Essays,* 1932) formed the basis of the influential critical movement that came to be known as the Cambridge school, and later, in the United States, as New Criticism. Moreover, Eliot contributed to the literary lexicon two phrases that identified crucial approaches to critical interpretation over the next few decades: the *objective correlative,* the correspondence between an emotion and the "set of objects, . . . situation, [or] chain of events which shall be the formula for [evoking] that particular emotion"; and *dissociation of sensibility,* by which Eliot meant the loss of integrative or unifying "mind" in the poetry written after the seventeenth century. Many of Eliot's critical views were articulated in the *Criterion,* a highly influential British literary quarterly that he edited from 1922 until it ceased publication in 1939.

In 1922 Eliot published *The Waste Land,* described by his friend and mentor Ezra Pound as "the longest poem in the English langwidge [sic]." Pound's hyperbole (the poem consists of 434 lines) is a comment on its poetic concentration and allusive density (Pound helped shape the finished version by reducing it to two-thirds its original length). Considered by many critics to be Eliot's finest work, *The Waste Land* is generally regarded as his most influential because of the sheer force of its impact on the course of poetry thereafter. The poem consists of five sections or "movements" that find unity in the subsuming themes of sterility and the erosion of values. As a summation of the doubts and disillusionments of the post–World War I generation, *The Waste Land* gave expression to the intellectual temper of an era.

Bradley was a fellow. Uncertain about his future, and torn between an academic and a literary career, Eliot decided not to return to Harvard to defend his dissertation and thereby earn his degree, choosing instead to remain in England and write poetry. With the encouragement of Ezra Pound and Wyndham Lewis, he began circulating his work, some of which was published in 1915. To support himself, he taught for a year at Highgate Junior School in London, after which he worked as a clerk at Lloyds Bank. In 1925 he joined the publishing house of Faber and Gwyer (later Faber and Faber), first as a literary editor and eventually as one of the firm's directors.

In 1915 Eliot had married Vivienne Haigh-Wood. Although the marriage proved unhappy, the Eliots remained together for nineteen years. Following their separation, Vivienne Eliot was committed by her family to a mental institution, where she died in 1947.

Between 1917 and 1919 Eliot was assistant editor of the journal the *Egoist.* His early poems appeared in various periodicals, and some were included in Ezra Pound's *Catholic Anthology* in 1915. Two volumes of his poetry, *Prufrock and Other Observations* and *Poems,* were published by Virginia and Leonard Woolf at the Hogarth Press in 1917 and 1919, respectively. Reflecting the influence of Laforgue, the poems in both these volumes reveal Eliot's disillusionment with his times. "The Love Song of J. Alfred Prufrock," Eliot's first major poem, explores the consciousness of a character ("Deferential, glad to be of use, / Politic, cautious, and meticulous") tormented by indeci-

Eliot became a British subject in 1927, shortly after he was baptized and received into the Church of England. In his introduction to *For Lancelot Andrewes* (a collection of essays), he defined himself as "an Anglo-Catholic in religion, a classicist in literature, and a royalist in politics." Even in his days as a Harvard student, Eliot's predilection for the culture and country of his ancestors was well known. He was then archly described by his fellow students as "English in everything but accent and citizenship." If his taking British citizenship in some way fulfilled an earlier predisposition, his conversion to the Church of England marked a divergence from the tradition of his Unitarian family. Nevertheless, the conversion answered a need in Eliot for a moral fastidiousness and definition that was also characteristic of his Puritan heritage. The poem "Ash Wednesday" (1930) is foremost among several that reflect the anguish accompanying his conversion. It was in this time of intellectual and emotional ferment that Eliot published his translation of *Anabase* (1924, translated as *Anabasis,* 1930). This long poem, which symbolically explores humanity's spiritual history, introduced the work of SAINT-JOHN PERSE to the English-speaking world.

In the 1930s Eliot began to write poetic drama. *The Rock* (1934) and *Murder in the Cathedral* (1935) were written for religious performance. The latter play deals with the martyrdom of Saint Thomas à Becket and is considered Eliot's finest drama; it was a theatrical success in both Europe and the United States. The four plays of modern life written for the commercial theater—*The Family Reunion* (1939), *The Cocktail Party* (1950), *The Confidential Clerk* (1954), and *The Elder Statesman* (1959)—are thought to be less successful. They fail, to a large degree, in their attempts to employ themes from Greek drama in contemporary situations. *The Cocktail Party* was, however, successfully staged on both sides of the Atlantic.

The sequence of poems entitled *Four Quartets* (1943) (*Burnt Norton,* 1941; *East Coker,* 1940; *The Dry Salvages,* 1941; and *Little Gidding,* 1942) is regarded by many critics as the culmination of Eliot's poetic maturity. Each poem is a meditation occasioned by a different landscape, in which the poet interweaves his reflections on history, time, the nature of language, and the pattern of his own experience.

Eliot was awarded the 1948 Nobel Prize for Literature "for his outstanding, pioneer contribution to present-day poetry." In his presentation speech, Anders Österling of the Swedish Academy stated that Eliot's verse contains "a special accent, . . . a capacity to cut into the consciousness of our generation with the sharpness of a diamond." "I take the award of the Nobel Prize in Literature, when it is given to a poet, to be primarily an assertion of the supranational value of poetry," Eliot said in his acceptance speech. "To make that affirmation, it is necessary from time to time to designate a poet: I stand before you, not on my own merits, but as a symbol, for a time, of the significance of poetry."

In 1957 Eliot married Esmé Valerie Fletcher. He died in 1965 at the age of seventy-six and was buried in East Coker, the Somerset village from which Andrew Eliot set out for Boston in the mid-seventeenth century.

Eliot's many other awards include the Order of Merit from Great Britain (1948), the Legion of Honor from France (1954), and the Hanseatic-Goethe Prize (1954); sixteen honorary degrees from English, American, and European universities; and honorary fellowships at Magdalen College and Merton College, Oxford.

Through the years, Eliot made frequent trips to his native country to lecture, visit his family, and conduct his publishing business. He was the recipient of many American awards and was a fellow of the Institute for Advanced Study in Princeton, New Jersey in 1948 and a fellow in American letters of the Library of Congress from 1947 to 1954.

The body of critical and interpretive writing inspired by Eliot's work as a poet and a critic—already vast before his death—has continued to grow. For the American critic Irvin Ehrenpreis, "the strength of T. S. Eliot's poetry depends on insights that mediate between morality and psychology. Eliot understood the shifting, paradoxical nature of our deepest emotions and judgments, and tried to embody this quality in his style." This style, said Ehrenpreis, is marked by "disruptions of syntax and meaning that startle the reader into attention while forcing him to reconsider the purpose and value of literary experience."

"His double task," wrote the British critic M. C. Bradbrook, "was the interpretation of the age to itself, 'holding the Mirror up to Nature,' as the greatest poet of all proclaimed, and maintaining the standards of strict literary excellence."

ADDITIONAL WORKS: Andrew Marvell, 1922; Poems 1909–1925, 1925; Journey of the Magi, 1927; A Song for Simeon, 1928; Animula, 1929; Tradition and Experiment in Present-Day Literature, 1929; Marina, 1930; Charles

Whimbley, 1931; Triumphal March, 1931; Thoughts After Lambeth, 1931; Sweeney Agonistes, 1932; The Use of Poetry and the Use of Criticism, 1933; After Strange Gods, 1934; Elizabethan Essays, 1934; Essays Ancient and Modern, 1936; Collected Poems 1909–1935, 1939; Old Possum's Book of Practical Cats, 1939; The Idea of a Christian Society, 1940; Later Poems 1925–1935, 1941; The Classics and the Man of Letters, 1942; Notes Towards the Definition of Culture, 1949; The Aims of Poetic Drama, 1949; The Cultivation of Christmas Trees, 1954; Religious Drama, 1954; The Three Voices of Poetry, 1954; On Poetry and Poets, 1957; George Herbert, 1962; Collected Poems 1909–1962, 1963; To Criticize and Other Writings, 1965; The Waste Land: A Facsimile and Transcript, 1971.

ABOUT: Ackroyd, P. T. S. Eliot: A Life, 1984; Bergonzi, B. T. S. Eliot, 1972; Browne, E. M. The Making of T. S. Eliot's Plays, 1969; Chiari, J. T. S. Eliot: Poet and Dramatist, 1973; Drew, E. T. S. Eliot: The Design of His Poetry, 1949; Frye, N. T. S. Eliot, 1963; Gardner, H. The Art of T. S. Eliot, 1949; Gordon, L. Eliot's Early Years, 1977; Haskot, S. S. T. S. Eliot: His Mind and Personality, 1961; Howarth, H. Notes on Some Figures Behind T. S. Eliot, 1964; Jones, D. E. The Plays of T. S. Eliot, 1960; Kenner, H. The Invisible Poet, 1959; Litz, A. W. (ed.) Eliot in His Time, 1970; Lucy, S. T. S. Eliot and the Idea of Tradition, 1960; McGreevy, T. Thomas Stearns Eliot, 1931; March, R., and Tambimuttu, M. J. (eds.) T. S. Eliot: A Symposium, 1948; Martin, G. (ed.) Eliot in Perspective, 1970; Matthiessen, F. O. The Achievement of T. S. Eliot, 1958; Maxwell, D. E. S. The Poetry of T. S. Eliot, 1952; Oras, A. Critical Ideas of T. S. Eliot, 1932; Plimpton, G. (ed.) Writers at Work, volume 2, 1963; Rajan, B. The Overwhelming Question, 1976; Schneider, E. T. S. Eliot, 1975; Sencourt, R. T. S. Eliot: A Memoir, 1971; Smith, G. C. T. S. Eliot's Poetry and Plays, 1956; Spender, S. T. S. Eliot, 1975; Tate, A. (ed.) T. S. Eliot: The Man and His Work, 1967; Unzer, L. T. S. Eliot: Moments and Patterns, 1966; Williamson, G. (ed.) A Reader's Guide to T. S. Eliot, 1953; Wilson, F. A. C. Six Essays on the Development of T. S. Eliot, 1949.

ELYTIS, ODYSSEUS
(November 2, 1911–   )
Nobel Prize for Literature, 1979

Odysseus Elytis (e lē′ tis) is the pen name of the Greek poet Odysseus Alepoudelis, who was born in Iráklion, on the island of Crete. Both of his parents came from wealthy landowning families on the fabled Aegean island of Lesbos, but his father set out to make his own fortune and established a successful soap manufacturing business in Crete. When the boy was six years old, the family moved to Athens, where he attended primary and secondary schools. From 1930 to 1935 he studied law at the University of Athens but left without taking a degree.

In his late teens Elytis became interested in poetry. As he read the works of the French poet Paul Eluard, he became fascinated by the emergent surrealist movement. This interest was further intensified when, during his last

ODYSSEUS ELYTIS

year at the university, he heard a lecture by Andreas Embiricos, an exponent of surrealism. When he began to write poetry himself, he gave up the family surname because of its commercial associations and created the pen name of Elytis, a composite whose prefix is drawn from such words as *Ellas* (Greece), *elpida* (hope), *eleftheria* (freedom), and *Eleni* (Helen, the personification of beauty) and whose suffix indicates a citizenship in all of Greece. At the time he met Embiricos, who became a lifelong friend, Elytis was introduced to the literary group associated with *Ta Nea Grammata* (New Letters), a journal that published the work of the poets (notably GEORGE SEFERIS) who were to give shape to the new spirit of Greek letters. These writers rejected the stultifying influence of Katharevusa, the artificial literary language based on Attic Greek, in favor of the vitality of the demotic, or vernacular, Greek. Elytis's first poems were published in *Ta Nea Grammata* late in 1935.

Although the work of some of the surrealist writers associated with *Ta Nea Grammata* was met with ridicule, Elytis's poetry was well received from the start, for he successfully adapted certain techniques of the surrealist school (for example, free-associative comparisons) to his particular Greek sensibility. As Elytis later explained, "I was never an orthodox surrealist. . . . Surrealism was the only school of poetry . . . that aimed at spiritual health and reacted against the rationalist currents that had filled most Western minds."

For Elytis, being a Greek was not, as he put it, "a national or a local thing." It was a way of perceiving "certain values and elements that can enrich universal spirits everywhere." Moreover, by being a Greek poet, he was continuing a tradition that had endured for twenty-five centuries without interruption. In his early work Elytis rejected the tone of despair and desolation that he found in the verse of such poets as Seferis and T. S. ELIOT. He drew his imagery and joyful spirit from the Aegean world of his childhood. *Prosanatolismi* (Orientations, 1939) is replete with images of light, the sea, and the brilliant sun. *Ilios o protos* (Sun the First, 1943), which continues the exaltation of this sensuous world of radiance and youth, earned Elytis a reputation as the preeminent lyric poet of his time, the poet of joy and health. This was a poetic world "synonymous with the purest forms of Hellenic character," as Elytis's translator Kimon Friar has written. Its roots are deep in the tradition of classical Greece, which strove to present in its artistic expression the world as it should be, the Ideal.

After the invasion by Benito Mussolini's forces across the Albanian border, Elytis served as a second lieutenant in Albania in 1940–1941. The Greeks responded to the Fascist invasion with the full fervor of their heritage, despite overwhelming odds. For Elytis, the firsthand experience of war deepened his view that "poetry on a certain level of accomplishment is neither optimistic nor pessimistic. It represents rather a third state of the spirit where opposites cease to exist." The fruit of this perception was *Asma iroiko ke penthimo ghia ton hameno anthipolochago tis Alvanias* (Heroic and Elegiac Song for the Lost Second Lieutenant of the Albanian Campaign, 1943). In this long poem in symphonic form, Elytis used surrealist associations, as Kimon Friar noted, "to find national identification and thus speak not only for himself but also for his nation." This work became a sort of poetic talisman for the youth of wartime Greece.

After the liberation of Greece, Elytis served as director of programming for the National Broadcasting Institute in Athens from 1945 to 1946. During the following two years, he was a regular literary and art critic for the newspaper *Kathimerini* (Daily). In 1948 he moved to Paris, where he studied literature at the Sorbonne for four years. During the time he spent in Paris, Elytis became increasingly interested in art and art criticism. He contributed articles to the journal *Verve* and formed friendships with many of the modern artists about whom he wrote, including Pablo Picasso, Henri Matisse, Alberto Giacometti, and Giorgio de Chirico.

Following his return to Greece in 1953, Elytis resumed his post with the National Broadcasting Institute for a year and took an active role in cultural affairs. It was not until 1959 that his next literary work appeared. *To Axion Esti* (Worthy It Is), on which he had worked since 1948, is a spiritual autobiography that alternates prose and verse in a form patterned on the liturgy of the Greek Orthodox church. A work of intricate structure, *To Axion Esti* is written in demotic Greek, although it makes use of the entire range of the Greek linguistic tradition. (An English translation by Edmund Keeley and George Savidis, entitled *The Axion Esti of Odysseus Elytis,* appeared in 1974.) Elytis's next work, a collection of poems entitled *Exi kai mia typseis ghia ton ourano* (*Six and One Remorses for the Sky*), was published soon after, in 1960.

During a four-month period in 1961, Elytis toured the United States at the invitation of the Department of State; this trip was followed by a similar visit to the Soviet Union the next year. Between 1965 and 1968 Elytis served on the administrative board of the Greek National Theater; he then spent the next two years in voluntary exile in France in protest against the military coup that had overthrown the Greek government in 1967. His creative work from this period of exile includes *O ilios o iliatores* (*The Sovereign Sun,* 1971) and *To fotodendro ke i dekati tetarti omorfia* (*The Light Tree and the Fourteenth Beauty,* 1971).

During much of this time, Elytis was preoccupied with a long poetic work, *Maria Nefeli* (*Maria Nephele*), that he eventually published in 1978. In this poem, whose title means "Maria the Cloud," alternating monologues are spoken by a girl (a representative of a radical, liberated generation) and a poet (Elytis himself). Unlike Elytis's other works, *Maria Nephele* derives from an actual experience in the poet's life. Having finished *To Axion Esti,* Elytis explained that he met a young woman and that "suddenly I wanted to write something very different." Although some of Elytis's admirers were baffled by the new direction of *Maria Nephele,* it has achieved a wide popularity, especially among the generation whose point of view Maria represents. The critic Byron Raizis praised *Maria Nephele* for its "poetic wealth and contemporary thematic relevance. . . . This original, dynamic, and impressive poetic collage records and dramatizes the anguish and tragicomedy, the promise and vulgarity of our aggressive and incoherent decade."

Elytis received the 1979 Nobel Prize for Literature "for his poetry, which, against the background of Greek tradition, depicts with sensuous strength and intellectual clearsightedness modern man's struggle for freedom and creativeness." The poet accepted the Swedish Academy's tribute as "not only an honor for me but for Greece and its history through the ages, . . . the most ancient tradition in Europe."

The critic and translator Edmund Keeley noted Elytis's growth and the continuity of his concerns: "Though his focus and ambition have remained essentially as he described them early in his career, . . . he has continued to experiment with new modes for expressing his perennial themes." The British poet and novelist Lawrence Durrell wrote of Elytis, "He has a romantic and lyrical mind which deploys a metaphysic of complete intellectual sensuality. . . . His poems are spells, and they conjure up that eternal Greek world which has haunted and continues to haunt the European consciousness with its hints of a perfection that always remains a possibility."

Odysseus Elytis, also a painter and collagist, is a lifelong bachelor who resides in Athens. Besides the Nobel Prize, he has also received Greece's first National Poetry Prize (1960) and the Order of the Phoenix (1965).

ADDITIONAL WORKS IN ENGLISH TRANSLATION: Barnstone, W. (ed.) Modern European Poetry, 1966; Trypanis, C. A. (ed.) The Penguin Book of Greek Verse, 1971; Odysseus Elytis: Selected Poems, 1981; What I Love: Selected Poems, 1986.

ABOUT: Books Abroad Spring 1971, Autumn 1975; Current Biography September 1980; Ivask, I. Odysseus Elytis: Analogies of Light, 1981; Keeley, E. Modern Greek Poetry, 1983; Keeley, E., and Sherrard, P. (eds.) Six Poets of Modern Greece, 1961; World Authors, 1950–1970, 1975.

ENDERS, JOHN F.

(February 10, 1897–September 8, 1985)
Nobel Prize for Physiology or Medicine, 1954

(shared with Frederick C. Robbins and Thomas H. Weller)

The American bacteriologist John Franklin Enders was born in West Hartford, Connecticut, to John Ostrum Enders, a banker, and Harriet (Whitmore) Enders. He attended the prestigious St. Paul's School in New Hampshire and enrolled at Yale in 1915. When the United States entered World War I in 1917, Enders left Yale and joined the Navy Flying

JOHN F. ENDERS

Corps, qualifying as a pilot with the rank of ensign. At the end of the war, he returned to Yale and received his B.A. in 1920.

After graduation, Enders became a real estate agent in Hartford but soon decided he was unsuited for business. He entered Harvard University, earned an M.A. in English literature in 1922, and remained to continue his graduate studies. During that time he shared rooms with a Harvard Medical School student who introduced him to Hans Zinsser, a microbiologist and the head of Harvard's Department of Bacteriology and Immunology.

Zinsser was a man of wide-ranging intellect. Scientist, writer, and thinker, he was able to convey his enthusiasm for science to others. Zinsser persuaded Enders to take up the study of microbiology, and in 1927 Enders began working in Zinsser's laboratory.

Enders obtained his Ph.D. from Harvard in 1930; his thesis was on anaphylaxis, an allergylike disorder discovered by CHARLES RICHET. He accepted a teaching position at Harvard and continued working with Zinsser and conducting research on the immune system's resistance to bacterial invasion, especially that of pneumonia. Then, in 1937, as he later recalled, he "turned from the study of bacterial immunity to an investigation of the growth of herpes simplex virus. Experience with herpes virus served to establish an enduring preoccupation with pathogens of this class," that is, with mammalian viruses.

Viruses are parasites. Although they contain genes, they have none of the mechanisms needed for translating the genetic information into proteins. Thus, in order to live, they must invade a cell and use its genes and proteins to reproduce themselves.

Knowledge about viruses was limited in the 1930s. Scientists had learned that certain disease agents are too small to be trapped by filters used to isolate bacteria or to be seen with the best optical microscopes. It was also known that these disease agents cannot be grown in the lifeless media used to culture bacteria but must be cultivated in live creatures or in living tissue.

Early in the twentieth century, ALEXIS CARREL had developed a technique for cultivating living tissue in a laboratory dish, but it had never been widely used. The growth of mammalian cells in vitro, that is, in an artificial environment, is an extremely sensitive and slow process. Moreover, if bacteria invade a tissue culture, they grow so much faster than the mammalian cells that the experiment is quickly ruined. Even though Carrel had succeeded in avoiding contamination of his cultures, his methods were so complicated that the Nobel committee later likened them to secret rites and Carrel himself to a high priest.

When he first became interested in viruses, Enders was already familiar with many of the problems involved in tissue culture. One of Zinsser's main fields of research was the study of typhus, a disease caused by rickettsias, microorganisms that are similar to viruses in that they can reproduce only within other cells. Zinsser and Enders tried to produce a typhus vaccine by growing rickettsias in tissue culture. After Zinsser died in 1940, it was Herald R. Cox, a United States Public Service scientist, who eventually grew the microbe, using chicken eggs as a culture.

During his initial venture into virus research, Enders studied a variety of disease organisms. In 1940 he and his assistant, THOMAS H. WELLER, then a medical student at Harvard, were studying vaccinia virus, the strain of cowpox virus used to produce smallpox vaccine. Although Enders and his colleagues were unable to grow enough of any virus in culture to make vaccines, they developed a feline distemper vaccine from infected animals. Their work gave them a valuable education in tissue culture.

When the United States entered World War II in 1941, Enders abandoned his tissue culture work and returned to more conventional research, using live animals for research on mumps virus. From 1942 to 1946 he was a civilian consultant on epidemic diseases to the secretary of war. After the war Enders agreed

to set up a new Infectious Diseases Research Laboratory at the Boston Children's Hospital. He invited Weller to join his staff, and Weller in turn brought in FREDERICK C. ROBBINS, his former medical school roommate.

In early 1947, Enders and his colleagues resumed research on virus tissue culture, continuing their wartime efforts to grow mumps virus in cultured chicken cells. Their most important innovation was continuous culture. "Instead of transferring material from one culture to another after an interval of three or four days," they later wrote, "the tissues were preserved while the nutritive medium was removed." By adding new medium, they could maintain cells for up to a month, which gave the slow-growing mumps virus ample time to develop. They were able to dispense with Alexis Carrel's complicated methods for avoiding bacterial contamination, largely because penicillin (the work of ALEXANDER FLEMING, ERNST B. CHAIN, and HOWARD W. FLOREY) and streptomycin (discovered by SELMAN A. WAKSMAN) had become available. Because these two antibiotics effectively destroy bacteria without harming mammalian cells, using the two in combination virtually eliminated the possibility of bacterial contamination.

Once they had proved that their method worked for mumps, Enders and his associates sought to cultivate varicella (chicken pox) virus. For these experiments, Weller began growing tissue culture from human embryos. "In this way," the collaborators later said, "such cultures were made available while close at hand in the storage cabinet was the Lansing strain of poliomyelitis virus. Thereupon it suddenly occurred to us that everything had been prepared almost without conscious effort on our part for a new attempt to cultivate the agent in extraneural tissue."

In 1948, somewhat to their surprise, Enders, Robbins, and Weller succeeded in growing poliovirus in cultures of human tissues that were not nerve cells, then thought to be the only tissue in which the virus would grow. They also developed new methods for growing cells in a solid layer (rather than suspended in fluids as they had done for mumps virus), for keeping track of the multiplication of the virus, and for using virus-containing cell cultures to test poliomyelitis antibodies.

Enders, Weller, and Robbins were awarded the 1954 Nobel Prize for Physiology or Medicine for their "discovery of the ability of poliomyelitis virus to grow in cultures of various types of tissue." On presenting the award, Sven Gard of the Karolinska Institute pointed out

301

that "the use of cultures of human tissues has permitted attacks on many virus problems previously out of reach because of the lack of susceptible laboratory animals." These problems included not only polio, Gard said, but also measles and herpes zoster. In time, their methods were adopted by Jonas Salk, Albert Sabin, and others who produced the first polio vaccines.

Enders continued his research in virology at the Children's Hospital in Boston for the rest of his career. Having isolated the measles virus in 1954, he and his co-workers grew the virus in culture until they found a strain that produced immunity without causing the disease. This virus provided the basis for present-day measles vaccines. After retiring from Harvard in 1967, Enders was named emeritus professor of bacteriology and immunology at the Harvard Medical School. He retained an active interest in medical research, however, and during the last several years of his life studied the acquired immune deficiency syndrome (AIDS).

In 1927 Enders married Sarah Frances Bennett; they had a daughter and a son. Sarah Enders died in 1943, and in 1951 Enders married Carolyn Keane. In his leisure time he enjoyed playing the piano, gardening, and fishing. He died suddenly on September 8, 1985, at his summer home in Waterford, Connecticut.

In addition to the Nobel Prize, Enders was awarded the Passano Award in Medical Science of the Passano Foundation (1953), the Lasker Award of the American Public Health Association (1954), the Science Achievement Award of the American Medical Association (1963), and the Presidential Medal of Freedom (1963), among other honors. He received honorary degrees from various universities, including Yale, Harvard, Northwestern, Case Western Reserve, Tufts, Oxford, and Tulane, as well as from Trinity College. He was a member of the American Academy of Arts and Sciences, the National Academy of Sciences, the American Association for the Advancement of Science, and the American Association of Immunologists.

SELECTED WORKS: Immunity, 1939, with others; Viruses and Rickettsial Diseases, 1940, with others.

ABOUT: Current Biography June 1955; New York Times October 22, 1954; September 10, 1985; Williams, G. Virus Hunters, 1959.

ERLANGER, JOSEPH

(January 5, 1874–December 5, 1965)
Nobel Prize for Physiology or Medicine, 1944
(shared with Herbert S. Gasser)

The American physiologist Joseph Erlanger was born in San Francisco, California, where his father, Herman Erlanger, had settled after emigrating from Württemberg, Germany, in 1842. When the gold rush began in 1849, the elder Erlanger shipped from New Orleans to Panama, crossed the isthmus by mule, and sailed to California. He worked for a time at placer mining before starting a business and marrying his partner's sister, Sarah Galinger. Neither parent had more than an elementary school education, and Joseph, the sixth of their seven children, became the only member of the family to attend college. Greatly interested in animals and plants from the time he was very young, Erlanger decided on a medical career and entered the University of California at Berkeley after completing his secondary schooling at San Francisco Boys' High School in 1891.

On graduating from college in 1895, Erlanger entered the third class of the newly formed Johns Hopkins School of Medicine in Baltimore, Maryland. Johns Hopkins was the first American university to focus on research rather than undergraduate education; Erlanger's research on embryology, conducted in his senior year at Berkeley, demonstrated his aptitude for scientific investigation. While in medical school, he continued to conduct research on neurobiology and digestion. After obtaining his medical degree in 1899, Erlanger served as an intern for a year under William Osler, a Canadian physician and leading clinician of his time who was a professor of medicine at Johns Hopkins, and in 1900 he joined the Johns Hopkins physiology department.

As the lowest-ranking member of the department, Erlanger was responsible for preparing demonstrations for physiology lectures. He once broke a valuable sphygmomanometer, a glass instrument that recorded pulsations in the first two fingers of both hands. So that the lecture could proceed, Erlanger improvised a novel sphygmomanometer that recorded the arterial pressure in the upper arm. His device was later patented and sold, although eventually it was superseded by more sophisticated instruments using the same principle.

At Johns Hopkins, Erlanger conducted research on the regulation of blood pressure and

JOSEPH ERLANGER

the transmission of excitation from the auricles to the ventricles of the heart. By means of a clamp that he invented to control pressure, all degrees of auricular and ventricular blocking could be analyzed.

In 1906 Erlanger was asked to head the physiology department of the new medical school at the University of Wisconsin in Madison. Erlanger spent his first two years at Wisconsin organizing the department; once that was accomplished, he returned to his experiments on conduction of nerve impulses between sections of the heart.

Four years later Erlanger moved to St. Louis to become chairman of the Department of Physiology at Washington University School of Medicine. Erlanger spent the next four years as a full-time administrator of the department with which he was to be affiliated for thirty-five years. In 1915 he was able to resume his studies of blood pressure, concentrating on the production of Korotkov sounds (heard when listening to blood pressure and caused by sudden distention of an artery), which are routinely used when determining arterial pressure in the body. During World War I, he investigated the effects of blood loss and wound shock on cardiovascular function. One of the colleagues Erlanger attracted to the Washington University physiology department was HERBERT S. GASSER, who had been an undergraduate while Erlanger was at Wisconsin, and who had since become a pharmacology professor. He and Erlanger began collaborating on studies of the electrical impulses in nerves.

The research of the eighteenth-century Italian physician and physiologist Luigi Galvani had shown that the information carried in nerves is electrical. Subsequent research had been hampered by the extreme brevity of the action potential of nerves—that is, the electrical manifestation of the nerve impulse. "It is so brief," Erlanger wrote later, "that there were reasons for believing, in 1921, that the details of its configuration had never been accurately recorded." Most neuroelectrical studies utilized string galvanometers (instruments for measuring current by electromagnetic action), but these instruments were not sensitive enough to record action potentials, which have a strength of only a few microvolts; moreover, the instruments were prone to technical failure.

Gasser and his associate, H. Sidney Newcomer, had overcome some of these problems by combining a galvanometer with valve amplifiers (similar to those developed by GUGLIELMO MARCONI for use in radios), which increased the strength of the action potential to a point at which it could be studied. The amplifier-galvanometer combination, however, still had a rather slow response. Since action potentials are much less than a microsecond in duration, studying their various components required an instrument that could produce a permanent record of very rapid events.

In 1920 Gasser learned that the Western Electric Company had recently invented an especially sensitive cathode-ray oscilloscope. Unable to persuade the company to sell them a cathode-ray tube, the two scientists built their own out of a distillation flask. Linking the device to an amplifier, they were able to record the time course of action potentials in nerves for the first time.

The most important discoveries made by Erlanger and Gasser with the oscilloscope—many of which were achieved only after 1932, when a high level of amplification became possible—revealed that visible nerves are made up of nerve fibers (the axons of individual cells) with differing properties. The most significant differences between these fibers are their size. These studies confirmed the hypothesis (proposed in 1907 by the Swedish physiologist Gustaf Göthlin, but never testable before) that thick axons transmit nerve impulses more quickly than do thin axons. Their instruments were able to exhibit the shape of the action potential in detail, crucial data for the nerve conduction theory of ALAN HODGKIN and ANDREW HUXLEY.

Erlanger was awarded the 1944 Nobel Prize for Physiology or Medicine, which he shared with Gasser "for their discoveries concerning the multiple functional differences of specific nerve fibers." Awards ceremonies were suspended during World War II, but in a radio braodcast lecture, RAGNAR GRANIT of the Karolinska Institute summarized the work leading to Erlanger and Gasser's discoveries. "One of their most important discoveries was the demonstration that sensory nerves in many respects differed from motor nerves," Granit said. Erlanger delivered his Nobel lecture in Stockholm in 1947.

With the electrophysiologist Alexander Forbes, Erlanger was the center of "The Axonologists," an informal group of neurologists from various laboratories and institutions who exchanged information and findings during the late 1920s and early 1930s. Both through his research and as a teacher, Erlanger exerted a pervasive influence on the development of neurophysiology in the United States. After becoming emeritus professor of physiology at Washington University in 1946, Erlanger continued to conduct research and publish scientific papers.

In 1906 Erlanger married Aimee Hirstel of San Francisco; they had two daughters and a son. Highly devoted to his family, Erlanger took pleasure in photography, playing the flute, and mountain climbing. He died in St. Louis on December 5, 1965.

He was a member of the National Academy of Sciences, the American Philosophical Society, the American Physiological Society, the American Medical Association, the American Association for the Advancement of Science, the Association of American Physicians, and the Society for Experimental Biology and Medicine. He held honorary degrees from the universities of California, Wisconsin, Pennsylvania, and Michigan and from Washington University, the Johns Hopkins University, and the Free University of Brussels.

SELECTED WORKS: Electrical Signs of Nervous Activity, 1937, with Herbert Gasser.

ABOUT: Biographical Memoirs of the National Academy of Sciences, volume 41, 1970; Dictionary of Scientific Biography, volume 4, 1971; The Excitement and Fascination of Science, 1965; Haymaker, W., and Schiller, W. The Founders of Neurology, 1970; National Cyclopedia of American Biography, volume 51, 1969.

ESAKI, LEO

(March 12, 1925–   )
Nobel Prize for Physics, 1973
(shared with Ivar Giaever and Brian D.
   Josephson)

The Japanese physicist Leo Esaki (ə säk′ ē) was born in Ōsaka to Soichiro Esaki, an architect, and Niyoko Ito. He studied at the University of Tokyo and received an M.S. in physics in 1947. In 1956, after working for the Kobe Kogyo Corporation, he joined the Sony Corporation in Tokyo, where he led a small research group while continuing his graduate studies.

Classical physics predicts that no current will flow in an electrical circuit interrupted by an insulating barrier. Quantum mechanics predicts somewhat different behavior, namely, that if the barrier is narrow enough, it is possible for electrons to "tunnel" through it. Quantum-mechanical tunneling takes place because the position of an electron cannot be determined precisely, and hence there is always at least a small probability that an electron will appear on the far side of a barrier. The thinner the barrier, the higher the probability of tunneling. Although tunneling had been predicted in the early 1930s, by the mid-1950s no measurement had unambiguously demonstrated its occurrence.

During his doctoral research, Esaki decided to see whether his research group could observe this effect in semiconductors. Semiconductors are materials such as silicon and germanium that have relatively small numbers of current carriers, whose concentration can be adjusted by controlling the concentration of impurities in the semiconductor.

Esaki and his colleagues worked with junction diodes, in which adjacent regions in a semiconductor are "doped" with electrically active impurities of opposite polarity. The diode conducts current freely in one direction, but the junction presents a barrier to the flow of current in the opposite direction. The barrier forms when a region near the junction becomes depleted of charge carriers. The width of the depleted region becomes smaller as the impurity concentration is increased, and therefore Esaki's group fabricated diodes with very high doping levels. In this way he created devices with extremely thin junctions and increased the probability of tunneling. Esaki found that the diodes exhibited electrical behavior consistent with the predictions of quantum mechanics.

While testing the properties of these diodes,

LEO ESAKI

Esaki noted that in some of them the relation of current to voltage appeared to be "fuzzy." When the diodes had large tunneling currents, they appeared to have a negative resistance; over a limited range of current variation, the voltage across the device dropped as the current through it increased. (In an ordinary resistor, current is proportional to voltage.) A circuit incorporating such a negative resistance can generate high-frequency oscillations. Esaki then developed more heavily doped devices with greatly increased negative resistance. These tunnel (or Esaki) diodes, with junctions only 10 billionths of a meter (or roughly 30 atoms) wide, were recognized immediately after their discovery in 1957 as useful devices for generating and detecting high-frequency signals. The tunneling effect was found to be a powerful tool for understanding the properties and behavior of semiconductors and superconductors. For a doctoral thesis on tunneling phenomena in semiconductors, Esaki received a Ph.D. from the University of Tokyo in 1959.

The next year he joined the research laboratories of the International Business Machines Corporation (IBM) in the United States to work in semiconductor physics. In 1965 he was made an IBM Fellow, the highest research position at the company. At IBM, Esaki pioneered in the investigation of semiconductor superlattices, which are complex structures made by depositing extremely fine layers of different semiconductors in such a way that the entire structure is one crystal. Superlattices exhibit novel physical properties and are ideal tools for seeking to understand effects in solid-

state physics. They may also become important engineering materials and could permit the construction of computer circuitry that is much faster and consumes less power than the silicon circuitry now in common use. Superlattice materials are expected to be crucial components of high-speed computers by the 1990s.

Esaki shared half of the 1973 Nobel Prize for Physics with IVAR GIAEVER for "their experimental discoveries regarding tunneling phenomena in semiconductors and superconductors, respectively." (The other half of the prize was awarded to BRIAN D. JOSEPHSON, also for work on tunneling.) "In a series of brilliant experiments and calculations, you have explored different aspects of tunneling phenomena in solids," Stig Lundqvist of the Royal Swedish Academy of Sciences told the three physicists in his presentation address. "Your discoveries have opened up new fields of research and have given new fundamental insight about electrons in semiconductors and superconductors and about macroscopic quantum phenomena in superconductors." Lundqvist continued that the discoveries of Esaki, Giaever, and Josephson are closely related, "because the pioneering work by Esaki provided the foundation and direct impetus for Giaever's discovery, and Giaever's work . . . led to Josephson's theoretical predictions."

In his acceptance speech, Esaki said, "Brian Josephson, Ivar Giaever, and I come from very different cultures. . . . In some way we symbolize that there are *no* national or racial boundaries in physics and other sciences. . . . Basic knowledge about nature," he continued, "is one of man's greatest treasures . . . and belongs to all mankind. . . . Many high barriers exist in this world: barriers between nations, races, and creeds. Unfortunately, some barriers are thick and strong. But I hope, with determination, we will find a way to tunnel through these barriers easily and freely, to bring the world together."

Esaki, who has remained a Japanese citizen, married Masako Araki in 1959; they have two daughters and one son.

Esaki is a member of the Japan Academy, a fellow of the American Academy of Arts and Sciences, and a foreign associate of the American National Academy of Sciences. Since 1977 he has served as a director of IBM. He holds honorary degrees from Doshida School, Japan, and the Polytechnical University of Madrid. His other awards include the Morris N. Liebmann Award of the Institute of Radio Engineers (1961), the Stuart Ballantine Medal of the Franklin Institute (1961), and the Japanese government's Order of Culture (1974).

ABOUT: New York Times October 24, 1973; Physics Today December 1973; Science November 16, 1973.

ESQUIVEL, ADOLFO PÉREZ
See PÉREZ ESQUIVEL, ADOLFO

EUCKEN, RUDOLF
(January 5, 1846–September 15, 1926)
Nobel Prize for Literature, 1908

RUDOLF EUCKEN

The German philosopher Rudolf Christoph Eucken (oi' kən) was born in the small town of Aurich in the province of East Friesland, near the Dutch border. His father, Ammo Becker Eucken, worked in the postal service, although he was by inclination a mathematician. His mother, the former Ida Maria Gittermann, was a well-read and deeply religious woman whose father was a clergyman. Eucken's early childhood was marred by his own serious illnesses and the deaths of his father and his only sibling, a younger brother. To help support the family, his mother took in lodgers. She had lofty ambitions for her son and, despite hardships, enabled him to receive a good education.

As a student at the gymnasium at Aurich, Eucken was initially interested in mathematics and music, but under the influence of one of his teachers, the theologian Wilhelm Reuter, he also studied religion and philosophy. Eucken was still very young when he entered the University of Göttingen to study classical philosophy and ancient history. There, he also attended lectures by the philosopher Hermann Lotze, whose rationalist teachings left him dissatisfied. Later, during a period of study at the University of Berlin, he encountered the Aristotelian philosopher Adolf Trendelenburg. This great teacher impressed upon Eucken the interconnections between philosophy, history, and religion. Trendelenburg's idealism had a profound influence on Eucken's own work.

After receiving his Ph.D. in philosophy from Göttingen, Eucken spent the next five years as a high school teacher. In 1870 he published two pamphlets on Aristotle, and the following year he was appointed professor of philosophy at the University of Basel. His *Die Methode der aristotelischen Forschung* (The Method of Aristotelian Inquiry), a discussion of Aristotelian logic, was published in 1872.

Two years later, Eucken was named professor of philosophy at the University of Jena, a post he retained until 1920. When his book *Die Grundbegriffe der Gegenwart* (*The Fundamental Concepts of Modern Philosophic Thought*) was published in 1878, it aroused widespread interest among scholars. An outgrowth of his study of the history of philosophy, it discusses the historical origins of various philosophical concepts. Revising the work in 1908 as *Geistige Strömungen der Gegenwart* (*Main Currents of Modern Thought*), Eucken linked the historical development of philosophy with his own philosophical ideas. The volume brought Eucken to the attention of academic philosophers throughout the world.

Published in 1890 and extremely popular in his own time, *Die Lebensanschauungen der grossen Denker* (*The Problem of Human Life as Viewed by the Great Thinkers*) was a continuation of Eucken's historical interests in its emphasis on the relevance to modern life of the teachings of the great philosophers of the past. From the 1890s on, his writings moved away from the historical concerns of his previous work, and he began to articulate his own idealistic, religious, and ethical philosophical thinking in such works as *Der Kampf um einen geistigen Lebensinhalt* (The Struggle for a Spiritual Life, 1896), *Der Wahrheitsgehalt der Religion* (*The Truth of Religion*, 1901), and *Grundlinien einer neuen Lebensanschauung* (*Life's Basis and Life's Ideal*, 1907). Maintaining that eternal spiritual values lie behind everyday life, he stressed the importance of personal ethical efforts in daily life and exhorted humankind to strive toward the elevated spiritual level.

Eucken was awarded the 1908 Nobel Prize for Literature "in recognition of his earnest search for truth, his penetrating power of thought, his wide range of vision, and the warmth and strength in presentation with which in his numerous works he has vindicated and developed an idealistic philosophy of life." The bestowal of the literature prize upon a philosopher came as a surprise to some. In his presentation address, Harald Hjärne of the Swedish Academy explained that Alfred Nobel, who had intended the literature award to recognize "excellence in works of an idealistic tendency," would have approved of the choice. "For over thirty years," Hjärne said, "Professor Eucken has been publishing profound contributions in several areas of philosophy."

Eucken delivered his Nobel lecture, "Naturalism or Idealism," the following year. Naturalism, he declared, is "faith in man's relation to Nature." He stated that although the idealism he advocated encompasses this faith, it represents a higher level of understanding, one that raises "life above the mere transient culture, by the realization of something eternal."

In 1911 Eucken delivered a series of lectures in England, and the following year he spent six months as an exchange professor at Harvard University. While in the United States, he spoke at Smith College; the Lowell Institute in Boston; and Columbia University, where NICHOLAS MURRAY BUTLER, then president of Columbia, gave a banquet for Eucken and HENRI BERGSON. On this visit Eucken also met Andrew Carnegie and THEODORE ROOSEVELT, among other notables.

Eucken intended to visit Japan and China, but the outbreak of World War I forced him to cancel his plans. During the war he denounced England for what he called its "brutal egoism" and argued that Germany should not be blamed for the hostilities.

In 1882 Eucken married Irene Passow; they had a daughter and two sons. Eucken died at Jena in 1926.

Although Eucken was often criticized—especially in his native Germany—for failing to take into account the findings of modern science, he attracted many adherents, some of whom regarded him as a leading thinker and moralist of his age. In *Rudolf Eucken: His Life and Influence* (1913), Meyrick Booth pointed to Eucken's "rare combination of intellectual depth and keenness with emotional insight and sensitive sympathy." Although today Rudolf Eucken occupies little more than a footnote in the study of philosophy, contemporary philosophers occasionally refer to him. In 1970, for instance, Warren Steinkraus called Eucken an advocate "of the *spiritual life,* not a narrow, superficial morality but a life of nobility and dignity."

ADDITIONAL WORKS IN ENGLISH TRANSLATION: The Life of the Spirit, 1909; The Meaning and Value of Life, 1909; Christianity and the New Idealism, 1909; Religion and Life, 1911; Back to Religion, 1912; Ethics and Modern Thought, 1913; Rudolf Eucken, His Life, Work, and Travels, 1921; Socialism: An Analysis, 1921; The Spiritual Outlook of Europe Today, 1922; The Individual and Society, 1923.

ABOUT: Booth, M. Rudolf Eucken: His Life and Influence, 1913; Gibson, W. R. B. Eucken's Philosophy of Life, 1906; Gibson, W. R. B. God With Us, 1909; Hermann, E. Eucken and Bergson, 1912; Jones, T. An Interpretation of Rudolf Eucken's Philosophy, 1912.

EULER, ULF VON
(February 7, 1905–March 18, 1983)
Nobel Prize for Physiology or Medicine, 1970
(shared with Julius Axelrod and Bernard Katz)

The Swedish physiologist Ulf Svante von Euler was born in Stockholm, the second son of HANS VON EULER-CHELPIN, a biochemist, and the former Astrid Cleve, a botanist. Euler received his early education in Stockholm and Karlstad and entered the Karolinska Institute in 1922.

After winning a prize in 1925 for his study of the properties of the blood of fever patients, Euler was encouraged to pursue a research career. He began working in the Karolinska's pharmacology department under Göran Liljestrand. Euler received his medical degree in 1930, the same year he was appointed assistant professor in pharmacology at the Karolinska Institute. A Rockefeller Fellowship enabled him to study abroad during 1930–1931, partly in London, where he worked in the laboratory of HENRY H. DALE.

In the mid-1920s OTTO LOEWI had shown that impulses in the autonomic (involuntary) nervous system are conveyed from nerves to muscles by a chemical neurotransmitter, acetylcholine. Dale, an experienced pharmacologist and a leading figure in the study of acetylcholine's effects on different tissues and organs, assigned Euler to demonstrate the presence of acetylcholine in the intestine. While working with John Gaddum, one of Dale's

ULF VON EULER

which coordinates relaxation and digestion. Loewi's original studies of chemical neurotransmitters had shown that acetylcholine is the transmitter in the parasympathetic nervous system; Dale had proved that it also carries impulses from nerves to the voluntary muscles. During the 1930s scientists debated the identity of the neurotransmitter in the sympathetic nervous system. Although some researchers favored a hormone from the medulla of the adrenal gland, the evidence was inconclusive.

Realizing that the study of impulse transmission in the sympathetic nervous system offered "some chances of obtaining more information," Euler turned his attention to analysis of tissue and nerve extracts. "Such extracts," he wrote later, "clearly showed the presence of an adrenalinelike substance, but it became gradually clear that the activity pattern did not wholly agree with that of adrenaline. Could it be noradrenaline?" Noradrenaline (usually called norepinephrine in the United States) is a precursor of adrenaline; both are considered catecholamines because of their general structure and their sympathomimetic (simulating effects caused by stimulation of the sympathetic nervous system) action.

Euler was appointed professor of physiology at the Karolinska Institute in 1939; he held the position until his retirement in 1971. Since Sweden was neutral during World War II, Euler continued his research throughout the early 1940s, uninterrupted by military service. By 1946 he had completed the isolation and identification of noradrenaline as the neurotransmitter in the sympathetic nervous system.

Intensive research at several institutions during the 1950s and 1960s revealed that several catecholamines—including adrenaline, noradrenaline, and noradrenaline's precursor, dopamine—are important neurotransmitters in the central nervous system, including the brain itself. Such catecholamine-containing cells are called adrenergic neurons. Euler's students and co-workers at the Karolinska Institute played a leading role in these investigations; their development of fluorescent catecholamines, which are easily observed in tissues or extracts, marked a major advance in this field of research. Initially, Euler concentrated his personal research on measuring the distribution of noradrenaline in various tissues under varying degrees of emotional or physical stress; this work led to his involvement in aviation medicine, in which he developed considerable expertise.

In the late 1950s Euler and his colleague

principal assistants, Euler isolated a chemical that exhibited many of the muscle-activating properties of acetylcholine. What they had found, however, was not acetylcholine but a new compound, which they named substance P. A polypeptide, substance P was the first to be identified in a large group of peptides that are active in the brain and the intestines. These substances are now believed to function not as neurotransmitters but as modulators of muscle activity.

Supported by additional Rockefeller funds, Euler continued his research in Birmingham, England; in Frankfurt, Germany; and with CORNEILLE HEYMANS in Ghent, Belgium. His early experiments with substance P and other compounds, he later said, "not only whetted the appetite for finding more active substances in biological material but also provided the necessary 'know-how' for making such attempts successful." After returning to Stockholm in late 1931, he achieved another noteworthy success in 1935 when, using purification techniques developed by HUGO THEORELL, he isolated a substance from seminal fluid that lowers blood pressure and has other effects on smooth muscles. Euler named this substance prostaglandin but passed the problem of further purification and characterization on to a colleague, the biochemist SUNE BERGSTRÖM, who devoted his career to investigating it.

The autonomic nervous system is divided into two branches: the sympathetic, which coordinates the body's response to stress or strenuous activity, and the parasympathetic,

Nils-Åke Hillarp established that within adrenergic neurons, catecholamines are stored and transported by vesicles similar to those BERNARD KATZ proposed as crucial for acetylcholine storage and release. Euler's work during the following decade involved more detailed studies of the way catecholamines are produced, released, and recycled. In many respects, this research paralleled investigations in the United States by JULIUS AXELROD, but Axelrod and his collaborators focused their studies on the biochemical aspects of catecholamine production and on the relationships between catecholamines and various psychoactive drugs. Euler's discovery of prostaglandins, which are used in birth-control pills, may ultimately prove to be the achievement for which he is best known, however.

From 1953 to 1960 Euler was a member of the Nobel Committee for Physiology or Medicine and then served as its secretary from 1961 to 1965, at which time he was appointed chairman of the board of the Nobel Foundation.

Euler shared the 1970 Nobel Prize for Physiology or Medicine with Axelrod and Katz "for their discoveries concerning the humoral transmitters in the nerve terminals and the mechanism for their storage, release, and inactivation." This work, said Börje Uvnäs of the Karolinska Institute in his presentation speech, "has not only enriched our knowledge in theoretical medicine, it has also been of far-reaching importance for the understanding and treatment of nervous diseases of peripheral and central origin," such as high blood pressure and Parkinson's disease.

In 1930 Euler married Jane Sodenstierna; they had four children. After divorcing his first wife in 1957, Euler married Countess Dagmar Cronstedt in 1958. He died of arterial disease in 1983.

Among the awards bestowed on Euler were the Gairdner Foundation International Award (1961), the Anders Jahre Prize in Medicine from Oslo University (1965), the Stouffer Award of the American Sociological Association (1967), and the La Madonnina International Prize given by the city of Milan (1970). Euler received honorary doctorates from the universities of Umeå, Rio de Janeiro, Dijon, Ghent, Tübingen, Buenos Aires, Edinburgh, and Madrid and from Gustavus Adolphus College. He was elected to membership in the academies of science in Stockholm and Copenhagen and to the Leopoldina German Academy of Researchers in Natural Sciences. He was also made an honorary member of the American College of Physicians and a member of the Swedish College of Physicians, the Italian Pharmacological Society, the Swedish Endocrinological Society, and the Acromedical Society.

SELECTED WORKS: Noradrenaline, 1956; Prostaglandins, 1968, with R. Elasson.

ABOUT: Biographical Memoirs of Fellows of the Royal Society, volume 31, 1985; The Excitement and Fascination of Science, volume 2, 1978; Science October 23, 1970.

EULER-CHELPIN, HANS VON

(February 15, 1873–November 6, 1964)
Nobel Prize for Chemistry, 1929
(shared with Arthur Harden)

The German-Swedish biochemist Hans Karl August Simon von Euler-Chelpin (oi' lər kel' pən) was born in Augsburg, Germany, the son of Gabrielle (Furtner) and Rigas von Euler-Chelpin. Soon after the boy's birth, his father, a captain in the Royal Bavarian Regiment, was transferred to Munich, and young Hans was sent to live with his grandmother in Wasserburg. He received his early education in Munich, Würzburg, and Ulm before entering the Munich Academy of Painting in 1891. While studying art, he became preoccupied with problems of color, and his interest turned to science.

He was admitted to the University of Munich in 1893, where he studied physics under Emil Warburg and MAX PLANCK and organic chemistry under EMIL FISCHER. He received his doctorate from Munich in 1895. After a brief period of postdoctoral research in physical chemistry, he worked with WALTHER NERNST at the University of Göttingen from 1896 to 1897. The following year he became a laboratory assistant to SVANTE ARRHENIUS at the University of Stockholm, where in 1899 he was appointed a privatdocent (unsalaried lecturer). That summer he continued his studies under JACOBUS VAN'T HOFF and EDUARD BUCHNER in Berlin, remaining there until 1900.

Returning to Stockholm, Euler-Chelpin became a Swedish citizen in 1902. During this period his research focused on the action of catalysts in reactions involving inorganic substances, but his interest soon shifted to organic chemistry, particularly after he learned about Buchner's investigations into the chemistry of fermentation. In 1906 Euler-Chelpin was appointed professor of general and organic

HANS VON EULER-CHELPIN

chemistry at the University of Stockholm, where he continued to work for the rest of his professional life.

When World War I broke out, Euler-Chelpin arranged to teach at Stockholm for six months a year and serve as a volunteer pilot in the German army during the other six. In 1916 and 1917 he took part in a military mission assigned to increase the production of munitions for Turkey, one of Germany's wartime allies. During the final years of the war he commanded a bomber squadron.

After the armistice in 1918, Euler-Chelpin resumed his full-time faculty responsibilities while initiating research into the chemistry of enzymes, complex products of living cells that serve as catalysts for specific biochemical reactions. He was especially interested in the role that enzymes play in fermentation. In this process, sugar molecules split and recombine to produce water, alcohol, and carbon dioxide, thus furnishing energy and raw materials for the cell. At the time, little was known about this process except for some early, inconclusive findings by Buchner and the English chemist ARTHUR HARDEN.

In 1896 Buchner had shown that the fluid obtained from yeast cells could induce fermentation, even though it contained no living yeast cells. Buchner also discovered that one component of the fluid, an enzyme he called zymase, causes glucose molecules to split into fragments of hexose (a simple sugar). Building on Buchner's work, Harden determined that zymase consists of two components, each of which is essential to the fermentation process.

In the first step of the process, Harden learned, sugar combines with a phosphate molecule (consisting of one phosphorus atom and four oxygen atoms). Before the process of fermentation is complete, the phosphate breaks free. Harden hypothesized that only when two phosphate molecules interact with two hexose molecules can fermentation begin.

Euler-Chelpin reasoned that for an enzyme to perform its function, it first had to become attached to the molecule it would act upon (the substrate). To elucidate the chemistry of fermentation, then, it was necessary to identify each of these substrates at each step of the process. He did so by introducing metal atoms into the fermenting solutions, in this way arresting the process at selected stages and enabling him to investigate each step.

Harden had hypothesized that two molecules of hexose and two molecules of phosphate combined to form alcohol, carbon dioxide, water, and a phosphorus-containing compound that he called zymodiphosphate. Euler-Chelpin learned that the reaction was more complex than that. He showed that the two hexose fragments split from the sugar molecule are neither complete nor equal. One is more energy-rich than the other. Moreover, the phosphate is attached to the less energetic fragment, and it is this fragment that is subsequently destroyed with the production of zymodiphosphate.

In addition to tracing the path of the phosphate, Euler-Chelpin described the chemical nature of the nonprotein constituent of zymase, which he called cozymase, a task complicated by its extremely small size. Using a long series of purification processes with remarkable experimental skill, he obtained highly concentrated levels of cozymase and was able to determine its molecular weight. He established that cozymase contains fragments of sugar, phosphoric acid, and a crystalline chemical called purine. He also revealed that cozymase is a constituent of the enzymes that regulate the cell's hydrogen-transferring activity and thus affect respiration.

"For their investigations on the fermentation of sugar and fermentative enzymes," Euler-Chelpin and Harden were awarded the 1929 Nobel Prize for Chemistry. In his presentation speech, H. G. Söderbaum of the Royal Swedish Academy of Sciences called the elucidation of fermentation "one of the most complicated and difficult problems of chemical research." By solving it, said Söderbaum, Euler-Chelpin, Harden, and their co-workers made it possible "to draw important conclusions concerning carbohydrate metabolism in general in both the vegetable and the animal organism."

In other research, Euler-Chelpin collaborated with PAUL KARRER on studies of vitamins, whose chemical structure was only then being elucidated by such investigators as Karrer, WALTER N. HAWORTH, and RICHARD KUHN. For the duration of his career, Euler-Chelpin continued his biochemical research, with particular attention to enzymes. In 1935 he began investigating the biochemistry of tumors. In collaboration with GEORGE DE HEVESY, he devised a technique for labeling the nucleic acids present in tumors so that their behavior could be traced.

In 1902 Euler-Chelpin married Astrid Cleve, who for several years collaborated with him on scientific research. Among their five children was ULF VON EULER, who became a noted physiologist. Divorced in 1912, the following year Euler-Chelpin married Elisabeth, Baroness Uggla, with whom he had four children. Euler-Chelpin died in Stockholm on November 6, 1964.

In addition to the Nobel Prize, Euler-Chelpin received the Grand Cross for Federal Service of the German Federal Republic (1959) as well as honorary degrees from the universities of Stockholm, Zurich, Athens, Kiel, Bern, Turin, and New Brunswick. He was a member of the Swedish Academy of Sciences, the Swedish Academy of Engineering Sciences, and the Finnish Academy of Sciences and a foreign member of many other professional societies.

SELECTED WORKS: General Chemistry of the Enzymes, 1912; Studies on Experimental Rheumatism, 1951, with Leo Heller.

ABOUT: Dictionary of Scientific Biography, volume 4, 1971.

FAULKNER, WILLIAM
(September 25, 1897–July 6, 1962)
Nobel Prize for Literature, 1949

The American novelist and short story writer William Cuthbert Faulkner was born in New Albany, Mississippi, the oldest of four sons of Murry Charles Faulkner and Maud (Butler) Faulkner. His great-grandfather, William Clark Falkner (as the family sometimes spelled its name), had served in the Confederate army and published a novel, *The White Rose of Memphis,* which enjoyed a brief success. While Faulkner was still a child, the family moved to the town of Oxford in north-central Mississippi. Taught to read by his mother before he started school, Faulkner was shy and detached from his classmates. At about the age of thirteen, he began writing poetry, which he showed to his childhood sweetheart, Estelle Oldham. He dropped out of high school before graduating and worked briefly in his grandfather's bank.

Faulkner hoped to marry Estelle, but his financial prospects were poor. When she married someone else in April 1918, his "world went to pieces," according to his brother John. He tried to enlist in the army but was rejected because he was too short. While visiting a friend at Yale University, he decided to enlist in the Royal Canadian Air Force, was accepted, and began basic training in Toronto in July. When World War I ended a few months later, Faulkner returned to Oxford, where he attended classes at the University of Mississippi. His poem "L'Après-midi d'un faune" was published in the *New Republic* in 1919.

The following year Faulkner left the university without taking a degree. At the invitation of Stark Young, a Mississippi novelist and drama critic, he moved to New York City. He lived in Greenwich Village and worked as a clerk in a bookstore that was managed by Elizabeth Prall, but after a short time he again returned to Mississippi. Back in Oxford, he supported himself as postmaster at the University of Mississippi until he was fired for reading on the job. Drifting to New Orleans in 1925, he visited Prall, who in the meantime had married the writer Sherwood Anderson. Anderson took an interest in Faulkner's writing and urged him to concentrate on fiction rather than poetry. The failure of *The Marble Faun,* a collection of Faulkner's verse published the previous year, seemed to confirm Anderson's advice. Turning to fiction, Faulkner wrote the novel *Soldiers' Pay,* which Anderson submitted to his publisher.

While *Soldiers' Pay* was being considered for publication, Faulkner roamed Europe for a few months. The novel appeared in 1926, followed in 1927 by *Mosquitoes,* a satirical portrait of bohemian life in New Orleans' Vieux Carré. Neither book attracted many readers. Undaunted, Faulkner wrote *Sartoris* (1929), the first of fifteen novels set in Yoknapatawpha County, a fictional region of Mississippi, which he peopled with several generations of vivid characters. The original version of this novel, which was abridged by the publisher, was issued in 1973 as *Flags in the Dust.*

WILLIAM FAULKNER

Although *Sartoris* received encouraging notices, it was not until *The Sound and the Fury*, published later in 1929, that Faulkner achieved wide recognition as a writer. Using a complex narrative form that reveals the same events and characters from several perspectives, the novel traces the degeneration of the once wealthy and distinguished Compson family. Hailed by critics as "a great book" whose tragic theme was "worthy of the attention of a Euripides," *The Sound and the Fury* made less impact on a reading public that found Faulkner's innovative narrative technique difficult to comprehend.

During this time, Faulkner had continued to see Estelle; and after her divorce in 1927, they were married. They had two daughters, Alabama, who died in 1931, and Jill.

Faulkner wrote his next novel, *As I Lay Dying* (1930), in six weeks while working the night shift at an electrical power station. Consisting of fifty-nine interior monologues, the book recounts the journey of the Bundrens, a poor-white Southern family, as they carry the decaying body of Mrs. Bundren to her final resting place in the town of Jefferson. Along the way, they are overtaken by a series of accidents in which the macabre and the comic intermingle.

Even though the American writer Conrad Aiken called *As I Lay Dying* "a remarkable tour de force" when it was published, commercial success continued to elude Faulkner. In need of money to support his family, he set out to write "the most horrific tale I could imagine," as he put it later. The result, dashed

off in three weeks, was *Sanctuary* (1931), the story of a young woman who, after being raped by a murderer, finds ironic sanctuary in a Memphis brothel. It became Faulkner's best-selling work. Despite its sensational subject matter and frankly commercial intention, *Sanctuary* impressed many critics, including André Malraux, who declared that the book marked "the intrusion of Greek tragedy into the detective story."

The success of *Sanctuary* brought only temporary relief from Faulkner's financial pressures, however, as book sales slumped during the Depression years. Moreover, Faulkner's work afforded readers little comfort or escape during this era of economic hardships. In search of more lucrative work, Faulkner made the first of several trips to Hollywood in 1932—the same year in which *Light in August* appeared—to adapt one of his short stories to the screen. Over the next several years, he worked on screenplays for such popular films as *The Road to Glory* (1936), *Gunga Din* (1939), *To Have and Have Not* (1945), and *The Big Sleep* (1946).

Between screenwriting assignments, Faulkner found time to write *Pylon* (1934); *Absalom, Absalom!* (1936); *The Wild Palms* (1939); *The Hamlet* (1940); and *Go Down Moses, and Other Stories* (1942), which contains "The Bear," one of his most celebrated pieces of short fiction. Much of his work was translated into French and elicited enthusiastic comment from many European writers and critics. "Faulkner c'est un dieu (Faulkner is a god)," wrote JEAN-PAUL SARTRE to the American critic Malcolm Cowley. Yet at home, as Cowley later observed, "Faulkner's books were little read and often disparaged," and by 1945, all of his published work had gone out of print.

Determined to bring Faulkner before a larger public, Cowley edited *The Portable Faulkner* the next year, and its popularity stimulated a marked revival of interest in Faulkner's work. In his introduction, Cowley examined the Yoknapatawpha cycle as an American myth, calling it "a labor of imagination that has not been equaled in our time." During the same year, rumors began to circulate that Faulkner was under consideration for a Nobel Prize.

Unable to agree upon a suitable candidate in 1949, the Nobel committee reserved the Nobel Prize for Literature that year but awarded it to Faulkner in 1950 "for his powerful and artistically unique contribution to the modern American novel." At the time, it was a controversial decision. "He has been called a reactionary," Gustaf Hellström of the Swedish

Academy said in his presentation speech, referring to Faulkner's preoccupation with the hatred and violence of the racially segregated American South. "But even if this term is to some extent justified," Hellström continued, "it is balanced by the feeling of guilt" that pervades Faulkner's portrait of "a way of life which he himself, with his sense of justice and humanity, would never be able to stomach. It is this that makes his regionalism universal."

Faulkner's brief acceptance speech, revised for publication in *The Faulkner Reader* (1954), addressed the question of human survival and the writer's responsibility. Threatened with nuclear annihilation, he said, "the young man or woman writing today has forgotten the problems of the human heart in conflict with itself." Yet, Faulkner declared, "I believe that man will not merely endure, he will prevail. He is immortal . . . because he has a soul, a spirit capable of compassion and sacrifice and endurance."

The Nobel Prize came at a time when Faulkner was experiencing great difficulty as a writer. After another stint in Hollywood, he went back to Oxford and completed *Requiem for a Nun* (1951). He then sought to write his magnum opus in *A Fable* (1954), a World War I novel whose protagonist, the Corporal, bears a marked resemblance to Christ. The critics, however, were virtually unanimous in their disappointment.

His health seriously weakened by a life of hard drinking, Faulkner nevertheless accepted a State Department invitation to represent the United States at an international writers' conference held in Brazil in 1954. The following year he undertook a world tour on behalf of the government.

With *The Town* (1957) and *The Mansion* (1959), Faulkner resumed the story of the Snopes family, which he had begun in 1940 in *The Hamlet*. From 1957 until shortly before his death, he was writer-in-residence at the University of Virginia, a position that further enhanced his reputation and his financial security. Voted the most popular American author in a Venezuelan readers' poll, Faulkner was chosen by the State Department to take part in that nation's sesquicentennial celebrations in 1961. Although the trip was successful, Faulkner was increasingly worried by the declining health of his wife Estelle, and he was plagued by his own drinking problems.

The following year Faulkner began writing his last book, *The Reivers* (1962). On June 17, 1962, he was thrown from a horse; only a few weeks later, on July 6, after entering a sanatorium in Byhalia, Mississippi, he died of a coronary occlusion.

Faulkner's literary reputation has continued to grow since his death. According to Michael Millgate, critics have "increasingly revealed the intricate structural and imagistic patterns which operate within the novels, and shown that the elaboration of the style . . . possesses an organic relationship with the material of the novels and with their moral and emotional themes."

"Working alone down there in that seemingly impenetrable cultural wilderness of . . . Mississippi," wrote the American critic and novelist John W. Aldridge, Faulkner "managed to make a clearing for his mind and a garden for his art, one which he cultivated so lovingly and well that it has come in our day to feed the imagination of literate men throughout the civilized world."

ADDITIONAL WORKS: Sherwood Anderson, 1926, with William P. Spratling; These Thirteen, 1931; Idyll in the Desert, 1931; A Green Bough, 1933; Dr. Martino and Other Stories, 1934; The Unvanquished, 1938; A Rose for Emily and Other Stories, 1943; Intruder in the Dust, 1948; Knight's Gambit, 1949; Collected Stories, 1950; Notes on a Horsethief, 1950; Mirrors of Chartres Street, 1953; Big Woods, 1955; New Orleans Sketches, 1958; Early Prose and Poetry, 1962; Faulkner at West Point, 1964; Essays, Speeches, and Public Letters, 1965; The Faulkner-Cowley File, 1966, with Malcolm Cowley; The Wishing Tree, 1967; Selected Letters, 1977.

ABOUT: Aiken, C. Collected Criticism, 1968; Beck, W. William Faulkner, 1976; Blotner, J. Faulkner, A Biography (2 vols.) 1974; Brooks, C. William Faulkner: First Encounters, 1983; Campbell, H. M., and Foster, R. E. William Faulkner, 1952; Coindreau, M. E. The Time of William Faulkner, 1971; Coughlin, R. The Private World of William Faulkner, 1954; Cowley, M. (ed.) Writers at Work, volume 1, 1958; Faulkner, J. My Brother Bill, 1963; Fowler, D. Faulkner's Changing Vision, 1983; Friedman, A. W. William Faulkner, 1985; Hoffman, F. J. William Faulkner, 1961; Howe, I. William Faulkner: A Critical Study, 1952; Kreiswirth, M. William Faulkner: The Making of a Novelist, 1983; Longley, J. L. The Tragic Mask, 1957; Mathews, J. The Play of Faulkner's Language, 1982; Meriwether, J. Faulkner and the South, 1964; Millgate, M. The Achievement of William Faulkner, 1966; Miner, W. L. The World of William Faulkner, 1952; Minter, D. William Faulkner, His Life and Work, 1982; Oates, Stephen B. Wm. F.: The Man and the Artist, 1987; O'Connor, W. V. The Tangled Fire of William Faulkner, 1954; Richardson, H. E. William Faulkner: The Journey of Self-Discovery, 1969; Sensibar, J. L. The Origins of Faulkner's Art, 1984; Sundquist, E. Faulkner: The House Divided, 1983; Vickery, W. The Novels of William Faulkner, 1959; Wagner, L. W. (ed.) William Faulkner, Four Decades of Criticism, 1973; Warren, R. P. (ed.) Faulkner, A Collection of Critical Essays, 1966.

FERMI, ENRICO
(September 29, 1901–November 30, 1954)
Nobel Prize for Physics, 1938

The Italian-American physicist Enrico Fermi (fär' mē) was born in Rome, the youngest of three children of Alberto Fermi, a railroad official, and the former Ida de Gattis, a school-teacher. As a boy, Fermi showed an aptitude for mathematics and physics; his advanced knowledge of both fields, obtained largely through independent study as a teenager, won him a fellowship in 1918 to the Scuola Normale Superiore, a unit of the University of Pisa. After only four years at Pisa, Fermi received his doctoral degree in physics magna cum laude in 1922 for a thesis on experimental studies of X rays.

Fermi then returned to Rome, where a government fellowship allowed him to increase his knowledge of modern physics by studying in Germany under MAX BORN, who was head of the theoretical physics department at the University of Göttingen, and in the Netherlands with the physicist Paul Ehrenfest at the University of Leiden. Ehrenfest greatly encouraged the young Fermi.

In 1924 Fermi became lecturer of mathematical physics and mechanics at the University of Florence. His early research concerned ALBERT EINSTEIN's general theory of relativity, statistical mechanics, quantum theory, and the theoretical behavior of electrons in solids. In 1926 he developed a new form of statistical mechanics, suggested by WOLFGANG PAULI's exclusion principle, that successfully described the behavior of electrons and was later applied to protons and neutrons. It led to a greater understanding of the conduction of electricity in metals and to a useful statistical model of the atom.

When the University of Rome established its first chair of theoretical physics in 1927, Fermi, who had already acquired an international reputation, was elected to fill the new post. At Rome, he recruited a number of outstanding colleagues and founded Italy's first modern school of physics. They were to become internationally noted as Fermi's group. Two years later, Fermi was appointed by Benito Mussolini to an honorary membership in the newly founded Royal Academy of Italy.

In the early 1930s Fermi shifted his attention from the atom's outer electrons to its nucleus. In 1933 he proposed a theory of beta decay that explained how the nucleus spontaneously emits electrons and the important role played by neutrinos, which were undetected, electri-

ENRICO FERMI

cally uncharged particles postulated by Pauli and named by Fermi. (Neutrinos were eventually detected in 1956.) Fermi's beta-decay theory also included a new type of force called the weak interaction. The weak force, which acts between neutrons and protons of the nucleus and is responsible for beta emission, is far less powerful than the strong force that binds the nuclear particles together. His paper on beta decay was rejected as too novel by the English journal *Nature* and was published in an Italian journal and, to a wider readership, in a German journal. Fermi's insights inspired HIDEKI YUKAWA's prediction in 1935 of a new elementary particle (now known to be the pi-meson, or pion).

In the 1920s the atom was believed to contain two kinds of charged particles, negative electrons circling around a nucleus of positive protons. Physicists wondered whether the nucleus might not also contain a particle with no charge. Experiments to detect this particle culminated in 1932 with JAMES CHADWICK's discovery of the neutron, which was almost immediately accepted, particularly by WERNER HEISENBERG, as a nuclear companion of the proton. Fermi fully appreciated the significance of the neutron as a powerful tool for inciting nuclear reactions. Atoms had been bombarded with charged particles, but these required powerful and costly accelerators to overcome electric repulsion. Electron projectiles are repelled by atomic electrons, and protons and alpha particles are repelled by the nucleus, because electric charges of the same kind repel each other. Since the neutron has no electric charge, it eliminates the need for accelerators.

An important advance occurred in 1934 when FRÉDÉRIC JOLIOT and IRÈNE JOLIOT-CURIE discovered artificial radioactivity. By bombarding boron and aluminum nuclei with alpha particles, they were the first to create new radioactive isotopes of known chemical elements. Extending this work, Fermi and his colleagues in Rome bombarded each element on the periodic table with neutrons, hoping to produce new radioactive substances by the attachment of neutrons to nuclei. Their first success came with fluorine. As they methodically bombarded increasingly heavier elements, Fermi and his team produced hundreds of new radioactive substances. When he bombarded uranium, element 92, the heaviest naturally occurring element, a complex mixture resulted. Chemical analysis revealed formation of neither a uranium isotope nor a neighboring element (tests excluded the possibility of elements 86 to 91). He wondered whether he had created the first artificial element, with atomic number 93. The director of the laboratory, Orso Corbino, prematurely announced such an achievement publicly, to Fermi's chagrin. In fact, however, Fermi had not discovered a new element; rather, without realizing it, he had caused nuclear fission, the splitting of a heavy nucleus into the nuclei of two or more lighter elements and other fragments. The discovery of nuclear fission was made later, in 1938, by OTTO HAHN, Lise Meitner, and Fritz Strassman.

In 1935, several months after beginning their neutron bombardment experiments, Fermi and his colleagues discovered that neutrons were actually more effective in causing reactions if their speed was slowed down by passing them through water or paraffin. This was due to impacts of neutrons with hydrogen nuclei (protons) abundant in these substances. Much energy was lost in such impacts because neutrons and protons have almost exactly the same mass, similar to the large transfer of energy in collisions between billiard balls of identical mass.

Meanwhile, life in Italy was increasingly affected by Mussolini's Fascist dictatorship. Italy's attack on Ethiopia in 1935 led to economic sanctions by members of the League of Nations, and in 1936 Italy became allied with Nazi Germany. Fermi's colleagues at the University of Rome began to disperse. When the government enacted anti-Semitic civil service laws in September 1938, Fermi and his wife, who was Jewish, decided to immigrate with their family to the United States, which he had visited and liked. Accepting an offer from Columbia University to serve as a professor of physics, he informed Italian officials that he was going for a six-month visit. In November he learned of his award of the 1938 Nobel Prize for Physics.

Fermi was awarded the prize "for his demonstrations of the existence of new radioactive elements produced by neutron irradiation, and for his related discovery of nuclear reactions brought about by slow neutrons." "Along with Fermi's significant discoveries, and to a certain extent equivalent, can be placed his experimental skill, his brilliant inventiveness, and his intuition . . . which throw new light on the structure of atomic nuclei and which open up new horizons for the future development of atomic investigation," declared Hans Pleijel of the Royal Swedish Academy of Sciences on presenting the prize.

Immediately after the Stockholm presentation ceremony in December, during which Fermi shook hands with the Swedish king instead of giving a Fascist salute (an act for which he was severely criticized in the hostile Italian press), he went directly to the United States. Upon his arrival, Fermi, like all immigrants at that time, was required to take an aptitude test. The Nobel laureate was asked to add 15 and 27 and to divide 29 by 2.

Shortly after the Fermis reached New York, NIELS BOHR came from Copenhagen on his way to spend a few months in Princeton at the Institute for Advanced Study. Bohr reported the discovery by Hahn, Meitner, and Strassman of the splitting of uranium by neutron bombardment. Many scientists began to discuss the possibility of a chain reaction. If neutrons were emitted when one neutron split an atom of uranium, they could strike other atoms, produce more neutrons, and possibly start a self-sustaining chain reaction. Since the energy released with each fission is so large, the result would be a huge outpouring of power and an unprecedented explosive force, if the process could be harnessed. Fermi started designing experiments to determine the possibility of such a chain reaction and its controllability, with the purpose of then producing one.

In discussions with the United States Department of the Navy in 1939, Fermi first suggested the possibility of an atomic weapon using a powerful chain reaction. He received federal funds to continue his research, during which he and EMILIO SEGRÈ, a fellow Italian physicist and former student, raised the possibility of using the still undiscovered element plutonium as another fuel for an atomic bomb. Although plutonium, of mass number 239, did not then exist, the two scientists believed an element of that mass number should be fissionable and might be produced in a uranium reactor through the capture of a neutron by uranium 238.

In 1942, when the United States created the Manhattan Project to build an atomic bomb, Fermi, although technically an "enemy alien," was given responsibility for chain-reaction and plutonium research. The following year the research was moved from Columbia to the University of Chicago, where Fermi, as chairman of the Theoretical Aspects Subsection of the Uranium Committee, directed the construction of the world's first nuclear reactor, located on a squash court under the stands of Stagg Field, the university's football stadium.

The reactor was known as a pile because graphite (pure carbon) blocks were piled high on top of each other to moderate the chain reaction (slow down the neutrons). Uranium and uranium oxide were placed between the graphite blocks. On December 2, 1942, neutron-absorbing cadmium control rods were slowly withdrawn to initiate the world's first self-sustaining chain reaction. "It was clear," JOHN COCKCROFT wrote later, "that Fermi had unlocked the door to the atomic age." Fermi was later named chief of the advanced physics department of a new laboratory, headed by J. Robert Oppenheimer and created to build the bomb at a secret site in Los Alamos, New Mexico. Fermi and his family became naturalized United States citizens in July 1944, and in the following month moved to Los Alamos. He witnessed the first atomic bomb explosion on July 16, 1945, near Alamogordo, New Mexico. In August of that year, atomic bombs were dropped on the Japanese cities of Hiroshima and Nagasaki.

At the end of the war, Fermi returned to the University of Chicago to become the Swift Distinguished Service Professor of Physics and to join the university's newly created Institute for Nuclear Studies. He was an enthusiastic and popular lecturer whose graduate students included MURRAY GELL-MANN, CHEN NING YANG, TSUNG-DAO LEE, and OWEN CHAMBERLAIN. When the construction of a cyclotron (a particle accelerator) was completed at Chicago in 1951, Fermi began experiments on the interactions between the newly discovered pi-mesons and neutrons. He also formulated theories on the origin of cosmic rays and the source of their high energy.

In 1928 Fermi married Laura Capon, a member of a prominent Jewish family in Rome. They had a son and a daughter. A man of great intelligence and boundless energy, Fermi enjoyed mountaineering, winter sports, and tennis. He died of stomach cancer at his home in Chicago shortly after his fifty-third birthday. The following year, the newly discovered element 100 was named fermium in his honor.

Fermi was elected a member of the American National Academy of Sciences (1945), an honorary member of the Royal Society of Edinburgh (1949), and a foreign member of the Royal Society of London (1950). He served on the General Advisory Committee of the Atomic Energy Commission (1946–1950) by presidential appointment. He also served as vice president (1952) and president (1953) of the American Physical Society. In addition to the Nobel Prize, Fermi was awarded the Matteucci Gold Medal of the National Academy of Sciences of Italy (1926), the Hughes Medal of the Royal Society of London (1943), the Civilian Medal of Merit of the United States government (1946), the Franklin Medal of the Franklin Institute (1947), the Barnard Gold Medal for Meritorious Service to Science of Columbia University (1950), and the first Fermi Prize awarded by the United States Atomic Energy Commission (1954). He received honorary degrees from many institutions, including Washington University, Yale University, Rockford College, Harvard University, and the University of Rochester.

SELECTED WORKS: Thermodynamics, 1937; Nuclear Physics, 1950; Elementary Particles, 1951; Notes on Quantum Mechanics, 1961; Collected Papers (2 vols.) 1962–1965; Molecules, Crystals, and Quantum Statistics, 1966; Notes on Thermodynamics and Statistics, 1966.

ABOUT: Dictionary of Scientific Biography, volume 4, 1971; Fermi, L. Atoms in the Family, 1954; de Latil, P. Enrico Fermi: The Man and His Theories, 1966; MacPherson, M. C. Time Bomb: Fermi, Heisenberg, and the Race for the Atomic Bomb, 1986; Segrè, E. Enrico Fermi, Physicist, 1970.

FEYNMAN, RICHARD P.

(May 11, 1918–)
Nobel Prize for Physics, 1965
(shared with Julian S. Schwinger and Sinitiro Tomonaga)

The American physicist Richard Phillips Feynman (fin' man) was born in New York City, the son of Melville Arthur Feynman and the former Lucille Phillips. He and his younger sister were raised in Far Rockaway in the borough of Queens. His father, a sales manager for a uniform manufacturer, was deeply interested in the natural sciences and encouraged Richard to conduct experiments in an improvised laboratory at home. With a school friend, Feynman put on neighborhood magic shows using simple chemistry principles, and while attending Far Rockaway High School, he earned pocket money by repairing radios. He was especially fond of solving puzzles and, as head of the school's algebra team, developed an ability to solve mathematical problems quickly by visualizing them as a whole, dispensing with many computational steps.

After graduating from high school in 1935, Feynman entered the Massachusetts Institute of Technology (MIT) and earned a B.S. in physics in 1939. At MIT he realized, as he said later, that "the fundamental problem of the day was that the quantum theory of electricity and magnetism [quantum electrodynamics] was not completely satisfactory." Quantum electrodynamics is concerned with interactions between elementary particles and between particles and electromagnetic fields. Existing theory, as formulated by WERNER HEISENBERG, WOLFGANG PAULI, and P. A. M. DIRAC, was brilliantly successful in many predictions but also involved disturbing aspects in its structure, such as infinite electron charge and mass. Feynman began to formulate radically new theoretical approaches to resolve the difficulties. For example, he thought that the action of an electron on itself (the source of an infinity) seemed "silly," and he proposed that electrons affected only other electrons, the effect being delayed because of the intervening distance. This concept also eliminated the idea of fields, and thus another troublesome infinity. Although he was unable to reach a satisfactory conclusion, Feynman retained his unconventional way of thinking.

In 1939 Feynman began graduate studies at Princeton University as a Proctor Fellow working under John A. Wheeler. There he pursued his theoretical experimentation with different approaches to quantum electrodynamics, learned the faults in his early schemes, and tested many new ideas, some suggested by discussions with Wheeler. He tried to retain the principle of delayed action by one electron on another, assuming that the affected electron then exerted action on the first after an additional delay, like light being reflected back to its source. At Wheeler's suggestion, he supposed that the reflection consisted not only of

RICHARD P. FEYNMAN

an ordinary delayed wave but also of an "advanced" wave that arrived before the initiating action even started. This paradoxical running of time both backward and forward did not bother him, he said later. "I was enough of a physicist at that time not to say, 'Oh, no, how could that be?' " After many months of mathematical manipulations, false starts, and attempts in new directions, he became adept at modifying and reformulating concepts and equations from varying points of view. He found novel ways of incorporating quantum mechanics into classical electrodynamics and methods for arriving simply and quickly at conclusions that usually required lengthy mathematical labor. One clarifying insight was the application of the principle of least action, based on the assumption that nature chooses the most economic path to reach a particular goal. Although he was not satisfied with his achievements, Feynman knew he had made important advances and that his work was respected. He published his dissertation, "The Principle of Least Action in Quantum Mechanics," and received a Ph.D. in 1942.

Shortly before completing his dissertation, Feynman was invited to join a small group of Princeton scientists who were attempting to separate the uranium isotopes needed by the Manhattan Project to construct an atomic bomb. He later served as a group leader under HANS A. BETHE at the project's facilities at Los Alamos, New Mexico, from 1942 until 1945. During these years he found time, wandering "about on buses and so forth, with little pieces of paper," as he later put it, to further develop his theory of quantum electrodynamics. At Los Alamos, Feynman came in contact with NIELS BOHR, AAGE BOHR, ENRICO FERMI, J. Robert Oppenheimer, and other leading physicists, and was among those who observed the first test of a nuclear bomb at Alamogordo, New Mexico.

After the war, Feynman spent the summer of 1945 working for Bethe at the General Electric Company in Schenectady, New York, before accepting Bethe's offer to become an associate professor of theoretical physics at Cornell University. Quantum electrodynamics was facing new challenges. For example, in 1947 WILLIS E. LAMB JR., in precise experiments with hydrogen, showed that two energy levels predicted by the Dirac equation to have the same value actually differed significantly (the Lamb shift). In another discrepancy, measured by POLYKARP KUSCH, the intrinsic magnetic moment of the electron was found to exceed its orbital magnetic moment by more than 0.1 percent.

Aided by Bethe's pioneering work at Cornell, Feynman began to attack these fundamental problems, but soon entered a period of mental stagnation brought on, he felt, because he had ceased to enjoy physics as a form of intellectual play. Some time later, he was watching someone in the Cornell cafeteria tossing a plate into the air and, intrigued by the relationship between the plate's rate of spin and its wobble, he worked out equations to explain it. The exercise restored his spirits, and he resumed his work on quantum electrodynamics. "There was no importance to what I was doing," he wrote later, "but ultimately there was. The diagrams and the whole business that I got the Nobel Prize for came from that piddling around with the wobbling plate." "The whole business" was a modified theory that regarded quantum-electrodynamic interactions from a new point of view, that of a space-time path. A particle is said to propagate from the initial to the final point of a path; the possible interactions along the way are expressed in terms of their relative probabilities. The probabilities are summed into a sometimes complex series for which Feynman devised computational rules and a pictorial representation (Feynman diagram). The deceptively simple, yet profoundly beneficial, Feynman diagrams are widely used in many areas of physics. Feynman successfully accounted for the Lamb shift, the electron's magnetic moment, and other particle properties.

Independently of Feynman and of each other,

and by different theoretical approaches, JULIAN S. SCHWINGER and SIN-ITIRO TOMONAGA almost simultaneously reformulated quantum electrodynamics and were able to resolve the fundamental difficulties. Their work involved a mathematical procedure called renormalization. Awkward infinities were avoided by postulating positive and negative infinities that almost completely canceled each other, leaving a residue—for example, the electron charge—that corresponded to the conventionally measured values. The Feynman-Schwinger-Tomonaga quantum-electrodynamic theory is considered probably the most accurate physical theory known today, its validity having been proved experimentally over an enormous range of dimensions, from subatomic to astronomical.

Feynman shared the 1965 Nobel Prize for Physics with Schwinger and Tomonaga "for their fundamental work in quantum electrodynamics, with deep-ploughing consequences for the physics of elementary particles." In his presentation address, Ivar Waller of the Royal Swedish Academy of Sciences said that they had introduced new ideas and methods into an old theory and created a new and successful theory that now occupies a central position in physics. It not only explains previous discrepancies but increases the understanding of the behavior of the mu particle and other phenomena in nuclear physics, solid-state physics, and statistical mechanics.

Feynman remained at Cornell until 1950, when he moved to the California Institute of Technology as professor of theoretical physics; in 1959 he became Richard Chace Tolman Professor of Theoretical Physics. In addition to his work in quantum electrodynamics, Feynman provided an atomic explanation for the theory of liquid helium developed by the Russian physicist LEV LANDAU. Helium, which can be liquefied at an absolute temperature of about 4°K (−269°C), becomes superfluid at about 2°K, behaving in ways seemingly contrary to the laws governing ordinary fluids. It loses, rather than gains, heat when it flows; it flows freely through microscopically narrow tubes; and it appears to defy gravity by creeping up the walls of its containers. Feynman derived the "rotons," postulated by Landau to explain this unusual behavior. The explanation is based on very cold helium atoms aggregating in the roton form, collections shaped like smoke rings.

With his colleague MURRAY GELL-MANN, Feynman was also responsible for an important theory of weak interactions such as beta-particle emission by radioactive nuclei. This theory developed out of Feynman diagrams that graphically represent the interactions of elementary particles and their possible transformations. His recent work has been on the strong forces holding the atomic nucleus together and on the subnuclear particles, or "partons" (such as quarks), of which protons and neutrons are composed.

Feynman's originality and showmanship in the classroom have influenced an entire generation of physics students. His intuitive method of guessing at a formula and proving it later is imitated more often than it is criticized. The impact of his theories and his personality has been felt in every area of modern particle physics.

Feynman has been married three times. Arline H. Greenbaum, whom he married in 1941, died of tuberculosis in 1945 while Feynman was in Los Alamos. His marriage in 1952 to Mary Louise Bell ended in divorce. In 1960 he married Gweneth Howarth in England; they have a son and a daughter. Often described as outspoken and irreverent, Feynman served on the Presidential Commission that investigated the explosion of the *Challenger* space shuttle in 1986 and issued his own thirteen-page report criticizing the managers of the National Aeronautics and Space Administration (NASA) for having "fooled themselves" into overlooking flaws in the design of the spacecraft. A man of intense curiosity and diverse interests, he enjoys playing the drums and has learned Japanese, taught himself to draw and paint, decoded Mayan codices, and investigated the claims of parapsychologists.

In addition to the Nobel Prize, Feynman has received the Albert Einstein Award of the Lewis and Rosa Strauss Memorial Fund (1954), the Ernest Orlando Lawrence Memorial Award for Physics of the United States Atomic Energy Commission (1962), and the Niels Bohr International Gold Medal of the Danish Society of Civil, Electrical, and Mechanical Engineers (1973). Feynman is a member of the American Physical Society, the Brazilian Academy of Sciences, and the Royal Society of London. He was elected to the National Academy of Sciences, but later resigned.

SELECTED WORKS: Quantum Electrodynamics, 1961; Theory of Fundamental Processes, 1961; The Feynman Lectures on Physics (3 vols.) 1963–1965, with others; The Character of Physical Law, 1965; Quantum Mechanics and Path Integrals, 1965, with Albert R. Hibbs; Photon-Hadron Interactions, 1972; Statistical Mechanics: A Set of Lectures, 1972; Surely You're Joking, Mr. Feynman! 1984, with Ralph Leighton; QED: The Strange Theory of Light and Matter, 1985.

ABOUT: Current Biography October 1955; New York Times October 22, 1965; January 27, 1985; Science October 29, 1965; Strachan, C. The Theory of Beta Decay, 1969.

FIBIGER, JOHANNES

(April 23, 1867–January 30, 1928)
Nobel Prize for Physiology or Medicine, 1926

The Danish physician and medical researcher Johannes Andreas Grib Fibiger was born in Silkeborg, the son of C. E. A. Fibiger, a physician, and Elfride (Muller) Fibiger, a writer. Fibiger obtained his medical degree in 1890 and briefly studied bacteriology under ROBERT KOCH and EMIL VON BEHRING. He worked with Carl J. Salomonsen, one of the leading bacteriologists of his day, at the University of Copenhagen until 1894, and then became an army reserve doctor at Blegham Hospital in Copenhagen.

His doctoral dissertation, on the bacteriology of diphtheria, was completed in 1895, and in 1900 he was appointed to a professorship in pathological anatomy at the University of Copenhagen. Fibiger's early research centered on diphtheria—he promoted the use of Behring's serum therapy in Denmark—and on tuberculosis, especially the relationship between tuberculosis in cows and the disease in human beings.

With the emergence of the discipline of cell biology in the nineteenth century came the first scientific descriptions of cancerous growths. Although bacteriology and the first useful theories of disease were also developed during the same period, these advances were not applied to the study of cancer. One obstacle to cancer research was the lack of a reproducible animal model of cancer. Several theories of cancer were prevalent; however, since cancers could not be produced and studied at will, no theory could be definitely proved or disproved. As Fibiger later wrote, "The problem of inducing cancer would have to be solved before the disease could be made the subject of the kind of experimental work which has provided important results in the study of the pathology of other diseases."

In 1907, while performing postmortem examinations of tubercular rats, Fibiger noticed that some of the rats had stomach cancers and that within the cancers were nematodes (*Spiroptera neoplastica,* now called *Gongylonema*

JOHANNES FIBIGER

Prize for Medicine or Physiology, which was presented the following year. "By feeding healthy mice with cockroaches containing the larvae of the *Spiroptera,* Fibiger succeeded in producing cancerous growths in the stomachs of a large number of animals," said W. Wernstedt of the Karolinska Institute in his presentation speech. "It was therefore possible, for the first time, to change by experiment normal cells into cells having all the terrible properties of cancer. It was thus shown authoritatively not that cancer is always caused by a worm," Wernstedt continued, "but that it can be provoked by an external stimulus."

Through his work on *Spiroptera* and coal tar, Fibiger prompted renewed interest in cancer research, especially the effects of carcinogens. Nevertheless, his theories on the relationship between cancer and parasites proved to be fruitless. It was not until much later in the century—during the 1980s—that true cancer genes were isolated, an advance that depended on recombinant DNA techniques.

Fibiger was married in 1894 to Mathilde Fibiger. After developing cancer of the colon and suffering heart failure, he died at Copenhagen on January 30, 1928.

Fibiger was a member of the Danish Medical Association, the Royal Danish Academy of Sciences and Letters, and the Swedish Medical Association, and he was a foreign member of the Royal Academy of Medicine of Belgium and the Royal Society of Science of Uppsala (Sweden). He held honorary degrees from the universities of Paris and Louvain, among other institutions.

neoplasticum). His thoughts "naturally turned to the possibility of these parasites having been the cause of the neoplasms [tumors]." Setting out to learn if there was any connection between the nematodes and the stomach tumors in the rats, he found that the animals had come from a sugar refinery.

Following this lead, Fibiger went to the refinery and, after making an inspection, discovered nothing unusual, except that the refinery was well populated with cockroaches. Suspecting a possible link between the roaches, the rats, and the stomach tumors, he collected roaches from the refinery and fed them to rats that he obtained from other locations. When a rat died, Fibiger conducted an autopsy; in many of the rats that he examined, he found stomach cancers. In 1913 he published his first detailed studies of rodent cancers caused by the larvae of the parasite *S. neoplastica.*

During World War I two Japanese scientists produced skin cancer in rabbits by painting the ears of the rabbits with coal tar. After the war, Fibiger was the first European scientist to repeat the experiment. During the 1920s he made numerous studies of coal-tar cancers. Comparing them to cancers caused by *Spiroptera* and to the clinical disease, he concluded that cancer is caused by interactions between a variety of external influences and an inheritable (genetic) predisposition, the latter usually not a predisposition to cancer in general but a tendency to develop the disease in a particular organ if a stimulus is present.

"For his discovery of the *Spiroptera* carcinoma," Fibiger was awarded the 1926 Nobel

SELECTED WORKS: Investigations on Spiroptera Cancer, 1919; Experimental Production of Tar Cancer in White Mice, 1921, with Fridtjof Bang.

ABOUT: Dictionary of Scientific Biography, volume 7, 1973; Meisen, V. (ed.) Prominent Danish Scientists, 1932; Secher, K. The Danish Cancer Researcher, Johannes Fibiger, 1947.

FINSEN, NIELS

(December 15, 1860–September 24, 1904)
Nobel Prize for Physiology or Medicine, 1903

The Danish physician and medical researcher Niels Ryberg Finsen was born in Thorshavn in the Faroe Islands, a part of Denmark that lies some 200 miles north of the British Isles. Although both his parents—

Hannes Steingrim Finsen, a government official in the Faroes, and Johanne (Froman) Finsen—were Icelandic, Finsen grew up speaking Danish. After attending primary school in Thorshavn, Finsen enrolled in a preparatory school in Herlufsholm, Denmark. He disliked the school intensely, especially the hazing to which the younger students were subjected, and did poorly in his classes.

After he transferred to a school in Reykjavik, the boy's grades improved; he also showed himself to be a good marksman. Even during childhood, however, Finsen's activities were restricted by poor health. Living in Iceland, just below the Arctic Circle, Finsen became acutely aware of the effects produced by sunlight. He noticed that increased exposure to the sun's rays markedly improved his feeling of well-being. All living creatures, he noticed, seemed deeply affected by the sun. "Let [sunlight] break through suddenly on a cloudy day and see the change!" he wrote later. "Insects that were drowsy awaken and take wing; lizards and snakes come out to sun themselves; the birds burst into song. We ourselves feel as if a burden were lifted."

Entering the University of Copenhagen in 1882, Finsen began his medical studies at a time when the discoveries of Louis Pasteur and ROBERT KOCH were introducing the bacterial theory of disease. Within his first year at Copenhagen, Finsen developed symptoms that were incorrectly diagnosed as heart disease. In fact, as it was discovered later, he suffered from Pick's disease, a chronic, progressive condition that affects the liver and the lining around the heart. Although his health continued to deteriorate, Finsen completed his studies and received his medical degree from the University of Copenhagen in 1891. He was subsequently appointed a demonstrator in anatomy in the department of surgery. By that time, he had also developed ascites, a condition in which fluid accumulates in the abdominal cavity, and was confined to a wheelchair.

In 1892 Finsen married Ingeborg Balslev, the daughter of the Lutheran bishop of Ribe, Denmark; the couple had four children. It was around this time that Finsen began to study the therapeutic effects of light. From earlier investigations, he knew that light inhibits the growth of certain bacterial colonies and can also kill bacteria. In 1889 a Swedish researcher had discovered that ultraviolet light irritates biological tissue more than does infrared light.

Approaching the subject as a naturalist would, Finsen observed and recorded the effects of sunlight on insects, salamanders, tad-

NIELS FINSEN

poles, and amphibian embryos. From his findings he learned that sunlight falling on the tail of a tadpole can cause the tissue to become inflamed, and that the harmful effect of ultraviolet light on frog embryos is many times greater than that of infrared light. He concluded that light—or its absence—could have therapeutic value.

By 1893 Finsen had begun to advocate the use of red light in the treatment of smallpox lesions. He suggested that by filtering out the irritating high-frequency radiation of sunlight with red glass it might be possible to facilitate the healing of the lesions and thus prevent disfiguring scars. When a demonstration of his "red rooms" proved successful, Finsen resigned from the department of surgery at the university to devote himself to the medical applications of phototherapy. The papers he published on the topic in 1893 and 1894 established his international reputation in the field.

Extending his inquiries, Finsen began to experiment with sources of artificial light, especially light generated by electrical carbon arcs. He wanted to know if it would prove effective in treating lupus vulgaris, a particularly intractable skin disease caused by the tubercle bacillus that often disfigured its victims so severely that they became social outcasts. In 1895, after making arrangements to use the facilities of the Copenhagen Electric Light Works, Finsen began treating a lupus vulgaris patient for two hours each day with ultraviolet light from a 25-ampere direct-current carbon-arc lamp. After many months, the lesions began to shrink and the patient showed definite signs of improvement.

In 1896 the Finsen Institute for Phototherapy was established in Copenhagen, with Finsen as its director. Among the methods that were developed at the institute were the Finsen carbon-arc bath and techniques for increasing the therapeutic dose of ultraviolet rays while minimizing tissue damage. Over the next five years, 800 lupus vulgaris patients were treated at the Finsen Institute. Of these, 50 percent were completely cured and 45 percent improved significantly. Finsen correctly predicted that the disease would someday disappear from Denmark.

Finsen received the 1903 Nobel Prize for Physiology or Medicine "in recognition of his contributions to the treatment of diseases—especially lupus vulgaris—with concentrated light radiation, whereby he has opened a new avenue for medical science." "This method represents an immense step forward," said K. A. H. Mörner of the Karolinska Institute in his presentation address, "and . . . has led to developments in a field of medicine which can never be forgotten in the history of medicine." Finsen was too ill to attend the ceremonies or to deliver a Nobel lecture.

In an effort to improve his failing health, Finsen experimented with a variety of diets—high and low salt, high and low fluid—as his physical condition grew worse. The summer of 1904 was especially sunny in Denmark. Still seeking the benefits of sunlight, Finsen built a sun room on the roof of his home in Copenhagen, where he sunbathed. At the age of forty-three, he died in Copenhagen, in the arms of his wife, of Pick's disease.

In his short but productive career, Finsen garnered many awards and honors, including membership in scientific societies in Denmark, Iceland, Russia, and Germany, among others. He became a knight of the Order of Dannebrog in 1899 and was awarded the Cameron Prize and Lectureship of the University of Edinburgh in 1904.

SELECTED WORKS: Phototherapy, 1901.

ABOUT: De Kruif, P. Men Against Death, 1932; Dictionary of Scientific Biography, volume 4, 1971; Meisen, V. (ed.) Prominent Danish Scientists, 1932.

FISCHER, EMIL
(October 9, 1852–July 15, 1919)
Nobel Prize for Chemistry, 1902

The German organic chemist Hermann Emil Fischer was born in Euskirchen, a small town near Cologne, to Laurenz Fischer, a well-to-do merchant, and Julie (Poensgen) Fischer. He was tutored privately for three years before attending the local public school and the gymnasiums at Wetzlar and Bonn. In the spring of 1869 he graduated from the Bonn Gymnasium with high honors.

Although Fischer hoped for an academic career, he agreed to work in his father's lumber business for two years but showed so little interest or motivation that his father encouraged him to enroll in the University of Bonn in the spring of 1871. There he attended lectures by the influential chemist Friedrich August Kekulé, the physicist August Kundt, and the mineralogist Paul Groth. Largely because Kekulé showed little enthusiasm for laboratory instruction, Fischer's interest in chemistry waned, and he became absorbed in physics.

In 1872, urged by his cousin, the chemist Otto Fischer, he transferred to the University of Strasbourg in Alsace-Lorraine, a former French province annexed by Germany at the end of the Franco-Prussian War. At Strasbourg Fischer's interest in chemistry was revived by one of his professors, the young organic chemist ADOLF VON BAEYER. Soon Fischer was immersed in chemical research, and he achieved notice through his chance discovery of phenylhydrazine (an oily liquid used to test for the presence of dextrose), a substance that proved to be valuable in his later classification and synthesis of sugars. After obtaining his Ph.D. in 1874, he was appointed instructor at the University of Strasbourg.

When Baeyer accepted a post at the University of Munich the following year, Fischer agreed to join him as his assistant. Financially independent and unhampered by administrative or teaching duties, Fischer was able to concentrate on laboratory research. In collaboration with his cousin Otto, he used phenylhydrazine to study substances employed in the manufacture of synthetic dyes developed from coal. It was not until Fischer's research that the chemical structure of these substances was elucidated.

In 1878 Fischer became a privatdocent (an unsalaried lecturer) at the University of Munich and associate professor of analytical chemistry in 1879. He left Munich three years later to accept a position as full professor of chemistry at the University of Erlangen. There he investigated such compounds as caffeine, theobromine (an alkaloid), and the animal excrement components uric acid and guanine, which he found to be derived from a colorless crystalline substance he called purine. Uric acid

EMIL FISCHER

than forty types of proteins based on the number and types of amino acids yielded under hydrolysis (a chemical process of decomposition involving the splitting of a bond and the addition of the elements of water).

An active proponent of basic research, Fischer campaigned for such interdisciplinary projects as a solar eclipse expedition to test the theory of relativity. Impressed by the policies of the Rockefeller Foundation, which allowed American scientists to concentrate exclusively on research, Fischer raised funds for the establishment of the Kaiser Wilhelm Institute for Chemistry in Berlin in 1911. He was also instrumental in the founding of the Kaiser Wilhelm Institute for Coal Research in Mülheim in 1914.

The 1902 Nobel Prize for Chemistry was awarded to Fischer "in recognition of his special services in connection with his synthetic experiments in the sugar and purine groups of substances." Fischer's discovery of the hydrazine derivatives proved to be a brilliant solution to the problem of artificially reproducing sugars and other compounds. Furthermore, his method of synthesizing glucosides added to the knowledge of vegetable physiology. Speaking of his sugar studies in his Nobel lecture, Fischer stated that "progressively, the veil behind which Nature has so carefully concealed her secrets is being lifted where the carbohydrates are concerned. Nevertheless, the chemical enigma of Life will not be solved until organic chemistry has mastered another, even more difficult subject, the proteins."

In 1888 Fischer married Agnes Gerlach, daughter of a professor of anatomy at the University of Erlangen; they had three sons. His oldest son Hermann became a professor of biochemistry at the University of California at Berkeley. Fischer's wife died seven years after their marriage. After a lifelong exposure to phenylhydrazine in the laboratory, Fischer contracted chronic eczema and gastrointestinal disorders that contributed to his death in 1919. RICHARD WILLSTÄTTER considered him an "unmatched classicist, master of organic chemical investigation with regard to analysis and synthesis [and] as a personality a princely man." In his honor, the German Chemical Society established the Emil Fischer Medal.

had been discovered much earlier by Carl Wilhelm Scheele in 1776, and in 1820 Friedlieb Ferdinand Runge had isolated caffeine. However, Fischer showed that the two compounds were similar in structure and could be synthesized from each other. Pursuing this line of research until 1899, Fischer synthesized many members of the purine group, as well as purine itself. Purine is significant in the field of organic chemistry because it was later discovered to be an important component in cell nuclei and the nucleic acids.

After being appointed professor of chemistry at the University of Würzburg in 1885, Fischer continued his studies of the purine derivatives. He also investigated the stereochemistry (the spatial arrangement of atoms) of sugar molecules. By applying the principle of asymmetrical carbon atoms (published in 1874 by JACOBUS VAN'T HOFF), Fischer predicted all possible atomic structure transformations of compounds in the sugar group; by 1890 he was able to synthesize mannose, fructose, and glucose in the laboratory.

In 1892 Fischer became director of the Chemical Institute at the University of Berlin, a position he held until his death. Extending his sugar studies into the field of enzymes, he discovered that enzymes react only with substances with which they have a close chemical relationship. Through his research on proteins, he established the number of amino acids that form the basis of proteins, as well as the relationship between the different amino acids. He eventually synthesized peptides (combinations of amino acids) and classified more

Fischer's many awards and honors included the Davy Medal of the Royal Society of London, the Prussian Order of Merit, and the Maximilian Order for the Arts and Sciences. He was the recipient of honorary doctorates from the universities of Oslo, Manchester, and Brussels and from Cambridge University. He

FISCHER

was a member of the Prussian Academy of Sciences and served as president of the German Chemical Society.

SELECTED WORKS: Introduction to the Preparation of Organic Compounds, 1909.

ABOUT: Dictionary of Scientific Biography, volume 5, 1972; Farber, E. (ed.) Great Chemists, 1961; Harrow, B. Eminent Chemists, 1927.

FISCHER, ERNST
(November 10, 1918–   )
Nobel Prize for Chemistry, 1973
(shared with Geoffrey Wilkinson)

ERNST FISCHER

The German chemist Ernst Otto Fischer was born in Solln, a suburb of Munich, the youngest of three children. His parents were Karl Tobias Fischer, a professor at the Physics Institute of the Technical University of Munich, and Valentine (Danzer) Fischer. Fischer received his early education in the local schools before attending the Theresiengymnasium and Technical School in Munich. After graduating in 1937, he began a two-year period of compulsory military service in the German army, and when World War II began, he served in Poland, France, and the Soviet Union. He spent six months as an American prisoner of war and was released in 1945.

When the technical university at Munich was reopened in 1946, Fischer resumed his studies, working under the eminent chemist Walter Hieber, a pioneer in the study of metal carbonyls (metals chemically joined with molecules containing carbon and oxygen). In 1952 Fischer received his doctorate from Munich and remained there as an assistant researcher.

With his thesis work on metal carbonyls, Fischer had undertaken a detailed analysis of the structure of dicyclopentadienyl iron, or ferrocene, in 1951. Earlier that year the chemists T. J. Kealy and P. L. Pauson had discovered ferrocene and found that it consists of two five-sided rings of hydrogen and carbon atoms united with one atom of iron. Prevailing theories predicted that such molecules would be highly unstable, but this compound proved to be remarkable for its chemical and thermal stability. Fischer set out to explain the anomaly.

His initial research on the stability of ferrocene convinced him that Kealy and Pauson had erred in their belief that ferrocene's two carbon-hydrogen rings lay side by side, joined by a single, relatively weak link with the central atom of iron. Instead, Fischer described ferrocene as "an entirely new type of covalent complex." Using X-ray crystallography, Fischer determined that the two rings are parallel, forming a layered, or sandwich, structure with the iron atom positioned centrally between them. As a result, the central metal atom is bonded with each of the five carbon atoms in the upper and lower rings. This explained the molecule's remarkable stability and marked the discovery of a new class of compounds.

In further experiments Fischer confirmed that other molecules with this structure could exist. Aided by Walter Hafner, Fischer synthesized dibenzenechromium, which consists of two overlying rings of benzene centrally united by an atom of chromium. Many chemists had believed this molecule impossible to create. Fischer continued his studies of the transition metals (elements whose inner electron shell is incompletely filled and whose properties are intermediate between metals and nonmetals), focusing on metal complexes of arenes (aromatic hydrocarbons).

In 1954 Fischer was appointed assistant professor at the technical university in Munich. Three years later he became professor of inorganic chemistry at Munich University's Institute of Inorganic Chemistry. At that time he began traveling as a visiting professor, first to the universities of Jena and Marburg and later to the University of Wisconsin at Madison.

In 1964 Fischer succeeded Walter Hieber as director of the Institute for Inorganic Chemistry at the Technical University of Munich, where he acquired advanced facilities for X-ray and spectroscopic studies of molecular structure. His laboratory soon became a leading center for research in organometallic chemistry. Concerned with promoting effective scientific education and research, Fischer has often spoken on these issues. He has also continued to lecture abroad. He was visiting professor at the University of Florida in 1971 and Arthur D. Little Visiting Professor at the Massachusetts Institute of Technology in 1973.

Fischer shared the 1973 Nobel Prize for Chemistry with GEOFFREY WILKINSON "for their pioneering work, performed independently, on the chemistry of the organometallic, so-called sandwich compounds." Ingvar Lindqvist of the Royal Swedish Academy of Sciences, in his presentation speech, called "the discovery and confirmation of the new bonding and structural principles applying to sandwich compounds" a "notable achievement" whose practical applications it was still not possible to predict.

Fischer's work provided the foundation for the development of new catalysts used in a variety of industrial processes, including the manufacture of pharmaceuticals and low-lead fuels. He has since conducted research on carbyne–transitional-metal complexes that has led to the development of new classes of compounds.

Regarded by his colleagues and students as a warm, friendly person and an inspiring teacher, Fischer reads history in his leisure time. He has never married.

In addition to the Nobel Prize, Fischer has received the Chemistry Prize of the Göttingen Academy of Sciences (1957) and the Alfred Stock Memorial Prize of the German Chemical Society (1959). He is an honorary member of the American Academy of Arts and Sciences as well as many other scientific societies and holds honorary degrees from the universities of Munich, Erlangen, and Nuremberg.

SELECTED WORKS: Metal Complexes, 1966, with Helmut Werner.

ABOUT: New York Times October 24, 1973; Science November 16, 1973.

FISCHER, HANS

(July 27, 1881–March 31, 1945)
Nobel Prize for Chemistry, 1930

The German chemist Hans Fischer was born at Höchst-am-Main to Anna (Herdegen) and Eugen Fischer, a chemist and the director of the Kalle and Company dye works. After attending primary school in Stuttgart, Fischer received his secondary education in Wiesbaden and graduated in 1899. Entering the University of Lausanne, he studied chemistry and medicine. He continued his work at the University of Marburg, receiving his degree in chemistry in 1904 and his medical degree four years later.

After serving as a physician at the Second Medical Clinic in Munich, Fischer spent the year 1909 working in chemistry under EMIL FISCHER (no relation) at the First Berlin Chemical Institute. There, he investigated the complex structure of sugars and peptides (complexes, built in part of amino acids, that are fundamental to living organisms). Returning to Munich in 1910, he began research into the structure of bilirubin, a reddish yellow pigment found in bile and known to be chemically related to the blood pigment hemin. Although many other chemists had tried to elucidate the structure of both compounds, and thus the nature of their relationship, the problem had proved too complex.

In 1913 Fischer was appointed a lecturer in physiology at the Physiological Institute in Munich. Three years later he became professor of medical chemistry at the University of Innsbruck. The restrictions imposed by World War I made it difficult for him to pursue experimental research. His work was further interrupted in 1917 when complications from a bout with tuberculosis many years earlier required the removal of a kidney. At the end of the war, he went to the University of Vienna as a professor of organic chemistry and in 1921 assumed the same position at the technical university in Munich, where he remained for the duration of his career.

At Munich, Fischer organized a chemistry laboratory and initiated a research program to study naturally occurring pigments. Like all complex chemicals, these pigments consist of combinations of simpler compounds. One such compound, pyrrole, is made of four carbon atoms and one nitrogen atom arranged in a ring. When four pyrrole nuclei are linked in a ring structure, the result is called porphyrin. At the time, porphyrin was thought to be the basis for all naturally occurring pigments, including bilirubin and hemin. In fact, however, each pigment consists of particular replacements and additions to specific arrangements of porphyrin groups. A single hemin molecule, for example, contains seventy-six atoms. In the case of such a large molecule, the laws of

HANS FISCHER

chemical combination permit many structural variations (or isomers), each of which may exhibit widely differing chemical properties.

Despite the difficulties the topic posed, a significant amount of research had already been conducted on natural pigments. In his investigations, Fischer built and split the larger molecules in various ways in an effort to discover the characteristics of each combination. His ultimate goal was to elucidate the structure of hemin, bilirubin (which he believed to be produced by the breakdown of hemin), and the green plant pigment chlorophyll (which he believed to be similar to hemoglobin). In the course of this work, Fischer and his associates produced a vast amount of new information about thousands of pyrrole combinations, and in 1929 he synthesized hemin.

Fischer was awarded the 1930 Nobel Prize for Chemistry "for his researches into the constitution of hemin and chlorophyll and especially for his synthesis of hemin." In his presentation speech, H. G. Söderbaum of the Royal Swedish Academy of Sciences called Fischer's work on hemin and blood pigments "a scientific achievement which would scarcely have been considered possible even a generation ago." Fischer's research showed, Söderbaum continued, "that nature, in spite of her extravagant diversity, was sufficiently economical to use exactly the same building material when constructing . . . two substances which are so greatly different in appearance and occurrence" as chlorophyll and red blood pigment.

Known as a fiercely dedicated researcher,

Fischer was deeply distressed by the restrictions that World War II placed on his work. Distraught over the almost total destruction of his institute by Allied bombing, he took his life in 1945. After his death, several of his former colleagues continued his work on chlorophyll and eventually described its structure in 1960.

In 1935 Fischer married Wiltrud Haufe, who at the time was half his age. They had no children. Although chemical research was his chief passion, he also enjoyed mountain climbing and skiing. A demanding teacher, he felt a strong responsibility toward his students and assisted them generously.

In addition to the Nobel Prize, Fischer received the Liebig Medal of the German Chemical Society (1929) and the Davy Medal of the Royal Society of London (1937), among other honors. He held an honorary doctorate from Harvard University.

ABOUT: Dictionary of Scientific Biography, volume 15, 1978; Farber, E. (ed.) Great Chemists, 1961.

FITCH, VAL L.

(March 10, 1923–   )
Nobel Prize for Physics, 1980
(shared with James W. Cronin)

The American physicist Val Logsdon Fitch was born on a cattle ranch in Cherry County, Nebraska, near the South Dakota border, the youngest of three children of Frances M. (Logsdon) and Fred B. Fitch. Fitch was still a small child when his father was injured while riding a horse, and the family moved to the nearby town of Gordon. There the elder Fitch sold insurance, and Val attended the public schools.

After graduating from high school, Fitch joined the army and in 1943 was sent as an enlisted man to Los Alamos, New Mexico, to be a member of the Special Engineer Detachment working on the Manhattan Project, the secret program for developing the atomic bomb. Assigned as a laboratory technician to a group headed by the English physicist Ernest Titterton of the British mission to Los Alamos, Fitch learned the techniques of experimental physics and came in contact with such eminent scientists as ENRICO FERMI, I. I. RABI, J. Robert Oppenheimer, R. C. Tolman, NIELS BOHR, and JAMES CHADWICK. Their professional and personal integrity made a lasting impression on him. He also learned "not just to consider

VAL L. FITCH

at Brookhaven National Laboratory on Long Island, New York, to study neutral K-mesons (kaons). Kaons, noted for their odd behavior, are unstable particles with about half the mass of the proton and are produced in high-energy nuclear collisions. They had previously figured in work by TSUNG-DAO LEE and CHEN NING YANG in 1956 as unusual particles that, in certain reactions called "weak," might violate one of three basic symmetry relationships, or conservation rules, of physics, designated C, P, and T. C (charge conjugation) invariance requires that reactions between particles look the same if the particles are replaced by their antiparticles (twins of particles but with reversed electric charge), for example, electrons by positrons and protons by antiprotons. P (parity) conservation requires reactions to be the same if geometric characteristics are replaced by their mirror images, for example, left by right and clockwise rotation by counterclockwise rotation. T (time-reversal symmetry) invariance requires that a reaction run equally well backward and forward.

Lee and Yang suggested experiments to verify their theoretical finding, and Chien-Shiung Wu and her colleagues at Columbia University soon found that parity is not absolutely conserved in the beta decay (electron emission) of radioactive nuclei; the nuclei preferentially emit "left-handed" electrons. Other workers showed that C is imperfectly conserved, some reactions favoring particles over antiparticles. The theoretical difficulties were smoothed over by assuming that a combined CP conservation rule was obeyed. A violation of C was compensated for by a simultaneous violation of P, much as the product of two positive numbers in algebra remains positive if both numbers are made negative at the same time. Since overall CPT conservation seemed to be well supported by basic principles, and CP was at that time regarded as invariant, it followed that T by itself must be invariant. A T discrepancy could not be balanced by what seemed to be a highly improbable CP discrepancy.

In 1955 MURRAY GELL-MANN and Abraham Pais had proposed that a beam of kaons actually consisted of particle-antiparticle combinations, which appeared in experimental observations as two different electrically neutral kaons: K_S^0 (S for short-lived) and K_L^0 (L for long-lived). The K_L^0 survival time was only about a ten-millionth of a second, but this was over 500 times as long as that of K_S^0. CP conservation allowed K_S^0 to decay into two pi-mesons (pions), one electrically positive, the other negative (pions are associated with the

using existing apparatus" in making measurements "but to allow the mind to wander freely and invent new ways of doing the job," as he recalled later. Fitch was to witness the first atomic explosion in the New Mexico desert when his group laid the cable that transmitted the triggering signal.

After his discharge in 1946, Fitch earned a B.S. in electrical engineering at McGill University, Montreal, Canada, in 1948 and entered Columbia University in New York City for graduate studies. Under JAMES RAINWATER, he wrote a dissertation on mu-mesic atoms, a topic suggested to him by AAGE BOHR, who was then sharing an office with Rainwater. In a mu-mesic atom, ordinary orbital electrons are replaced by mu-mesons, particles originally discovered in cosmic rays. Mu-mesons appear to be identical to electrons except that they are about 200 times as heavy. Their extra mass is calculated to accentuate the differences between certain closely spaced energy levels and thus affect the spectrum of radiation emitted by the atom. Fitch served as a physics instructor at Columbia during his final year there and received his Ph.D. in 1954. He then became an instructor in the physics department at Princeton University, was appointed full professor in 1960, and in 1976 was named department chairman and Cyrus Fogg Brackett Professor of Physics.

In 1963 Fitch and JAMES W. CRONIN, together with James Christenson, one of Cronin's graduate students, and René Turlay, a physicist on leave from the Center for Nuclear Studies in France, performed an experiment

strong force that holds the atomic nucleus together). However, this was forbidden for K_L^0, which was allowed to decay only into three pions, positive, negative, and neutral. The theory received support in 1956 with the experimental observation of K_L^0 decay into three pions. The two kaons could be separated for observation of K_L^0 alone because in a typical experimental situation the short-lived particles traveled an average of only a few centimeters before decaying, whereas the long-lived particles traveled tens of meters.

Fitch, Cronin, and their colleagues began their study of kaons with improved equipment, particularly a spark chamber that permitted an especially precise determination of the tracks of decay products and the selection of particular reactions for observation. They produced the kaons by bombarding a beryllium target with high-energy protons from the Brookhaven alternating-gradient synchrotron, a particle accelerator capable of imparting energies up to billions of electron volts. Their detectors were placed more than 17 meters from the kaon origin, a distance long enough to ensure K_S^0 decay and leave a pure K_L^0 beam. However, one of the oddities of kaon behavior they were examining is that passage through a block of material absorbs K_L^0 in such a way that the emerging beam once again contains K_S^0 particles. The phenomenon is called regeneration. The research group used blocks of tungsten, copper, carbon, and liquid hydrogen to study regeneration and found agreement with theoretical expectations and no anomalies. From these data, they could show that regeneration contributed insignificantly to their later test results when they used a bag filled with helium as the K_L^0 decay region. Their results indicated, to their initial disbelief, that in 45 out of 23,000 photographed events in the spark chamber, a K_L^0 underwent the decay to two pions, forbidden by the CP conservation rule, rather than the expected decay to three pions. Because of the importance of the results, the group confirmed them by repetition and spent half a year searching unsuccessfully for alternative explanations before publishing the evidence for violation of CP conservation.

Violation of CP conservation was especially consequential because it meant that T invariance could also be violated, to maintain the overall integrity of CPT conservation. This meant that nature was not indifferent to forward and backward directions in time. Symmetry violations also allowed scientists to speculate on the reasons matter and antimatter, created according to the big-bang theory of the birth of the universe, had not totally annihilated each other. A slight favoritism toward matter in the form of a longer decay time could have left the present universe as the matter residue after mutual destruction by the unevenly matched rivals and more rapid decay had eliminated all antimatter. The destruction would also have been the origin of much of the electromagnetic energy that pervades the cosmos.

"For the discovery of violations of fundamental symmetry principles in the decay of neutral K-mesons," Fitch and Cronin were awarded the 1980 Nobel Prize for Physics. In his presentation speech, Gösta Ekspong of the Royal Swedish Academy of Sciences described the three symmetries as "guiding rules to help us discover the mathematical laws of nature." Citing the work of Gell-Mann on neutral K-mesons and the discoveries of Lee and Yang, Ekspong noted that Cronin and Fitch "interpreted the results of their experiment as a small but clear lack of symmetry." He added that "nobody, absolutely nobody, had anticipated anything like it."

CP violation may be explainable by recent theories that postulate the existence of fundamental particles, quarks, out of which other subatomic particles are made. Quarks were first postulated by Gell-Mann, and six have now been detected: up, down, strange, charm, bottom, and top (or truth).

In 1949 Fitch married Elise Cunningham, with whom he had two sons. Four years after her death in 1972, he married Daisy Harper, who had three children by a previous marriage. Fitch, who has been an avid outdoorsman since his youth, jogs, hikes, and camps out; he also enjoys listening to classical music and growing dwarf trees.

Fitch is a member of the American Physical Society, the American Academy of Arts and Sciences, and the National Academy of Sciences. He is a fellow of the American Association for the Advancement of Science and, from 1970 to 1973, served on the President's Science Advisory Committee. Among the awards he has received are the Science Award of the Research Corporation of America (1968), the Ernest Orlando Lawrence Award for Physics of the United States Atomic Energy Commission (1968), and the John Price Wetherill Medal of the Franklin Institute (1976).

ABOUT: New York Times October 15, 1980; Physics Today December 1980; Science November 7, 1980; Wilson, J. (ed.) All in Our Time, 1974.

328

FLEMING, ALEXANDER

(August 6, 1881–March 11, 1955)
Nobel Prize for Physiology or Medicine, 1945
(shared with Ernst B. Chain and Howard W. Florey)

ALEXANDER FLEMING

The Scottish bacteriologist Alexander Fleming was born in the county of Ayrshire to Hugh Fleming, a farmer, and his second wife, Grace (Morton) Fleming. He was his father's seventh child and his mother's third. When the boy was seven, his father died, and his mother was left to manage the farm with his oldest half brother, Thomas. Fleming attended the tiny moorland school nearby, and later, the Kilmarnock Academy. Although his education was hard-earned and primitive, he learned early to observe nature intimately.

At the age of thirteen he joined his older brothers in London, where he worked as a clerk, attended classes at Regent Street Polytechnic, and in 1900 joined the London Scottish Regiment. Fleming enjoyed life in the regiment and won the reputation as a first-class water polo player and a crack shot, but the Boer War ended, and he never got overseas.

A year later, he inherited 250 pounds (which was nearly $1,200, a substantial sum of money at the time) and at Thomas's suggestion, took the nationwide test to enter medical school. He passed with the highest marks in all of England and was awarded a scholarship to St. Mary's Hospital Medical School. Fleming studied surgery and in 1906 passed the examination to become a fellow of the Royal College of Surgeons. Remaining at St. Mary's to work in the laboratory of pathology professor Almroth Wright, he also earned an M.S. and a B.S. in 1908 from London University.

The most remarkable advances in the treatment of bacterial diseases at the turn of the century—the first vaccines, EMIL VON BEHRING's serum therapy, and ILYA METCHNIKOFF's studies of phagocytosis—were in the realm of immunotherapy and exploited the natural defensive capabilities of the body to fight disease. For this reason, physicians and bacteriologists expected that future progress would result from efforts to alter, amplify, or supplement the immune system.

PAUL EHRLICH's discovery of Salvarsan in 1910 reinforced those expectations. Ehrlich was looking for what he called a "magic bullet" that would kill invading bacteria without harming or even interacting with the patient's tissues. Salvarsan, the first modern drug, accomplished only half of this goal. Although it proved effective against the syphilis spirochete, it often produced toxic side effects. Wright's laboratory was among the first to receive Salvarsan samples for testing in 1908, and Fleming conducted experiments with the drug. He used it, too, in his private medical practice, in the treatment of syphilitics. While acknowledging the problems Salvarsan posed, he believed that chemotherapy could be useful. For several years, however, his research did little to support this belief.

When Britain entered World War I, Fleming served as a captain in the Royal Army Medical Corps and saw action in France. Working in a wound research laboratory, Wright and Fleming tried to determine whether antiseptics were of any use in treating infections. Fleming found that antiseptics such as carbolic acid, then commonly used for the treatment of open wounds, killed the white blood cells that constituted the body's own defense and allowed bacteria to survive in the tissues.

Quite by accident in 1922, while trying unsuccessfully to isolate the organism responsible for the common cold, Fleming discovered lysozyme, an enzyme that kills some bacteria without harming normal tissues. Unfortunately, lysozyme has relatively little medical use, being most effective against bacteria that do not cause illness and having no effect at all on disease-causing organisms. The discovery, however, put Fleming on the lookout for other antibacterial substances that were harmless to humans.

329

FLEMING

Fleming's discovery of penicillin in 1928—another fortunate happenstance—resulted from a combination of chance circumstances improbable almost beyond belief. Unlike his tidy colleagues who discarded culture plates when they were through with them, Fleming kept his cultures for two or three weeks until his bench was crowded with forty or fifty of them. Eventually he would discard the cultures, first looking at each one to see whether anything interesting had developed. In one dish, contaminated by mold, he noticed that the *Staphylococcus* bacteria seemed to be dissolving. Culturing the mold separately, he found that "the broth in which the mold had been grown . . . had acquired marked inhibitory, bacteriocidal, and bacteriolytic properties to many of the more common pathogenic bacteria."

Fleming's untidy habits and accidental observation were only two of the chance elements that led to his discovery. The mold that contaminated the culture was a very rare organism, *Penicillium*, ultimately traced to a laboratory on the floor below, where molds from the homes of asthma sufferers were being grown and extracts of them made for desensitization. Fleming left the now-famous dish on his bench and went on vacation. A cold spell in London created conditions in which the mold grew first, followed by the bacteria when the weather turned warm again. These were the only conditions, it was later found, under which the discovery could have been made.

Fleming's initial studies established a number of important facts about penicillin. It is, he wrote, "a powerful antibacterial substance. . . . The action is very marked on the pyogenic cocci [pus-inducing *Staphylococcus* and *Streptococcus*] and the diphtheria group of bacilli. . . . Penicillin is nontoxic to animals in enormous doses. . . . It is suggested that it may be an efficient antiseptic for application to, or injection into, areas infected with penicillin-sensitive microbes." Knowing this, Fleming unaccountably failed to take the obvious next step, the step that HOWARD W. FLOREY took twelve years later, namely, to find out whether an injection of his broth would protect mice from lethal infection. Fleming applied the broth externally to a few patients, with mixed results, and was discouraged. The substance was not only difficult to purify in any large quantity but unstable.

Like the Pasteur Institute in Paris, the inoculation department at St. Mary's where Fleming worked supported itself by the sale of vaccine. Fleming found that penicillin kept the cultures clear of staphylococci when he prepared vaccines. It was a minor technical advance, and Fleming ordered that batches of the broth be prepared weekly. He gave subcultures of his *Penicillium* to several colleagues in other laboratories but never mentioned penicillin in any of his twenty-seven papers and lectures published between 1930 and 1940, even when his subject was germicides.

Penicillin might have been forgotten but for Fleming's earlier discovery of lysozyme. It was this discovery that led Florey and ERNST B. CHAIN to investigate the therapeutic value of penicillin, and it was their work that led to the isolation of penicillin and to its clinical trials. The credit and the fame, however, went to Fleming. The accidental discovery of penicillin in a contaminated culture dish furnished the press with a dramatic story that captured the imagination of the world.

The 1945 Nobel Prize for Physiology or Medicine was awarded jointly to Fleming, Chain, and Florey "for the discovery of penicillin and its curative effect in various infectious diseases." Göran Liljestrand of the Karolinska Institute said in his presentation speech, "The story of penicillin is well known throughout the world. It affords a splendid example of different scientific methods cooperating for a great common purpose. Once again it has shown us the fundamental importance of basic research." In his Nobel lecture Fleming noted that "the phenomenal success of penicillin has led to an intensive research into antibacterial products produced by molds and other lowly members of the vegetable kingdom." Few, he said, have proved useful. "There is one, however, streptomycin, which was found by [SELMAN A.] WAKSMAN . . . which will certainly appear in practical therapeutics, and there are many others yet to be investigated."

Fleming spent the remaining ten years of his life collecting twenty-five honorary degrees, twenty-six medals, eighteen prizes, thirteen decorations, and honorary membership in eighty-nine scientific academies and societies. He was knighted in 1944.

He was married to Sarah Marion McElroy, an Irish nurse, in 1915; the couple had one son. After his wife's death in 1949, Fleming's health deteriorated. He married Amalia Coutsouris-Voureka, a bacteriologist and former student, in 1952. Three years later, at the age of seventy-three, he died of a heart attack.

SELECTED WORKS: Studies in Wound Infections, 1929,

with others; Recent Advances in Vaccine and Serum Therapy, 1934, with G. F. Petrie; Chemotherapy: Yesterday, Today, and Tomorrow, 1946.

ABOUT: Biographical Memoirs of Fellows of the Royal Society, volume 2, 1956; Dictionary of Scientific Biography, volume 5, 1972; Hare, R. The Birth of Penicillin, 1970; Hughes, W. H. Alexander Fleming and Penicillin, 1974; Ludovici, L. Fleming: Discoverer of Penicillin, 1952; MacFarlane, G. Alexander Fleming: The Man and His Myth, 1984; Maurois, A. The Life of Sir Alexander Fleming, 1959; Osserman, E. F., et al. (eds.) Lysozyme, 1974; Parascandola, J. (ed.) The History of Antibiotics, 1980.

HOWARD W. FLOREY

FLOREY, HOWARD W.

(September 24, 1898–February 21, 1968)
Nobel Prize for Physiology or Medicine,
  1945
(shared with Ernst B. Chain and Alexander
  Fleming)

Howard Walter Florey, an English pathologist and bacteriologist, was the third child and only son of Joseph Florey, a prosperous boot manufacturer in Adelaide, Australia, and his second wife, Bertha Mary (Wadham) Florey. Although his father suffered financial setbacks before World War I, scholarships enabled young Florey to attend St. Peter's Collegiate School and Adelaide University. Interested in scientific research from boyhood, Florey was initially attracted to chemistry but turned instead to medicine. He received a B.S. in 1921. His brilliant academic career and broad interest in athletics and politics won him a Rhodes Scholarship to Oxford University. Arriving in England in 1922, he enrolled at Magdalen College.

At Oxford, Florey's research concerned interactions between the nervous system and the muscles that line small blood vessels. Working under the great neurophysiologist CHARLES S. SHERRINGTON, Florey came to believe that the study of disease must be based on knowledge of the normal structure and function of the body.

Earning a B.Sc. and an M.A. at Oxford in 1925, Florey continued his studies at Cambridge as a John Lucas Waller Student and worked with FREDERICK GOWLAND HOPKINS, studying capillary action. Although Florey was not a chemist and did not follow in Hopkins's footsteps, he learned from the senior researcher the importance of biochemistry in studies of cell function and disease, an attitude that influenced his subsequent choice of research projects.

Florey was awarded a Rockefeller Traveling Scholarship in 1925, and his ten-month stay in the United States played an important part in his future career and in the history of science. He returned to England the following year and took up research fellowships at London Hospital and Cambridge. The same year Florey married Mary Ethel Reed, who had been a fellow medical student at Adelaide; the couple had a daughter and a son. Florey was awarded a Ph.D. from Cambridge in 1927 for his studies of circulation.

As a result of his work on mucus secretion in 1928, Florey became interested in the resistance of the digestive tract to infection by bacteria. Searching the literature, he learned of ALEXANDER FLEMING's 1921 discovery of the antibacterial enzyme lysozyme. After preliminary research on lysozyme's distribution and function in the body, Florey concluded that his efforts would not yield results unless he collaborated with a chemist. Although he was unable to secure funding for such a collaboration at the time, the idea stayed with him for the next several years and he kept in mind a remark made to him in 1929 by ALBERT SZENT-GYÖRGYI at Cambridge. "He said that biochemical methods were then sufficiently good to enable any naturally occurring substance to be extracted, provided there was a quick test for it," Florey later recalled.

In 1932 Florey moved to the University of Sheffield to accept the chair in pathology. Two years later he became professor of pathology in charge of Oxford's William Dunn School of Pathology. The post put him in a position to guide the study of pathology at Oxford along the lines Sherrington and Hopkins had suggested, emphasizing physiology and biochemistry. Florey asked Hopkins to recommend someone to head the department's biochemistry research, and Hopkins suggested one of his own graduate students, ERNST B. CHAIN, who joined Florey at Oxford in 1935.

Enthusiastic and hardworking, Chain was a skilled and original chemist. Since Florey had a talent for guiding other people's research in fruitful directions, the combination of his direction and Chain's energy resulted in an amicable and productive collaboration. Later, differences in their personalities brought them into conflict. Not long after Chain moved to Oxford, Florey suggested that he begin biochemical studies of lysozyme. As Chain was completing his work on lysozyme in 1938, he became interested in antimicrobial products in general. While reading everything he could find on the topic, he came across Fleming's original 1929 paper on penicillin.

After discovering penicillin by good luck and sharp observation, Fleming had turned to other work because the drug was chemically unstable and could be produced only in small quantities. Production of enough penicillin for substantial research would require a coordinated effort among scientists in a variety of disciplines—the sort of teamwork Florey was especially well suited to direct.

The penicillin project developed in three stages. The first stage was devoted to overcoming the major difficulty of obtaining enough penicillin to work with. Between 1939 and 1940 Florey, Chain, and their colleagues sought new methods for growing *Penicillium* mold in quantity, for getting the mold to produce penicillin, and for extracting and purifying the active antibiotic. The work of the biochemist Norman G. Heatley, who had a remarkable flair for designing and constructing laboratory equipment, was particularly crucial to their success.

The second stage of the project began in May 1940, when the team finally extracted enough crude penicillin to test its effects on infected mice. Although the scientists knew that the antibiotic worked against bacteria in culture dishes without destroying normal mammalian tissues, even Florey, who was known for his extremely laconic and even deflating personal style, was astonished at the results, remarking, "It looks like a miracle." The first clinical tests in humans in early 1941 confirmed the results of the animal experiments: penicillin was far more effective and nontoxic than any known antibiotic.

World War II, now well under way in Europe, made the need for penicillin crucial, but an adequate supply could not be produced in wartime England. Florey and Heatley left for the United States in June 1941 to begin the third stage of their work. In Washington, Florey discussed large-scale production of penicillin with the United States Department of Agriculture and several pharmaceutical firms. One factor in the American decision to press forward, however, was the recommendation of A. Newton Richards, with whom Florey had worked in Pennsylvania in 1926. Richards was now chairman of the Committee on Medical Research of the United States Office of Scientific Research and Development. He supported Florey's suggestion and helped persuade the American government to provide massive funding for the project. As a result, American pharmaceutical laboratories were able to produce enough penicillin to treat serious casualties by the time of the Normandy invasion in 1944.

With production of penicillin under way in the United States, Florey returned to England later in 1941. He and his wife conducted extensive trials to determine the best methods for testing the antibiotic. After publication of their second clinical trial, the *Times* of London carried an editorial about the Oxford work, without naming the researchers. Fleming's old mentor Almroth Wright, in a letter to the *Times,* said credit for the discovery was Fleming's. When interviews with Fleming appeared in the press, an Oxford professor informed the *Times* that Florey's group deserved credit. Florey refused to see reporters and forbade any of his staff to talk to the press. In Florey's opinion, publicity debased scientists and their work.

Florey shared the 1945 Nobel Prize for Physiology or Medicine with Chain and Fleming "for the discovery of penicillin and its curative effect in various infectious diseases." In his Nobel lecture Florey discussed new methods in the investigation of antibacterial substances and the research that they made possible. Pointing to the practical aspects of such research, he noted that "there are in addition many interesting theoretical points. For the chemist there is the investigation of the structure of substances which are often of quite novel types. From a still wider point of view," he went on, "the clear definition of these antibacterial substances may help us to understand the ceaseless struggle for existence which is being waged by microscopic organisms everywhere."

After the war Florey continued work on antibiotics, the most successful of which were the cephalosporins. He also returned to his early interest in the structure and function of the smaller blood vessels, using electron microscopy to extend his research beyond what was possible in the 1920s.

In 1960 Florey was elected president of the Royal Society, the highest office in British science. A colorful, eloquent, and forceful man, he continued to exercise his formidable organizational skills. During his five-year tenure the Royal Society was radically transformed; its membership was expanded and its headquarters moved. It took a more active role in government and in society at large. For his service to medicine, Florey was knighted in 1944 and received a life peerage and the Order of Merit in 1965.

Ethel Florey, who had experienced ill health since her youth, died in 1966. The following year Florey married Dr. Margaret Jennings, a physiologist with whom he had collaborated since 1936. He died of a heart attack on February 21, 1968.

The recipient of the Lister Memorial Medal of the Royal College of Surgeons (1945), the Copley Medal of the Royal Society (1957), and the Lomonosov Gold Medal of the Soviet Academy of Sciences (1965), Florey was awarded honorary degrees by many universities and held membership in numerous professional societies.

SELECTED WORKS: Antibiotics (2 vols.) 1949, with others; Lectures on General Pathology, 1954; Biological Technology, 1964; The Responsibilities of Medicine in the Modern World, 1967.

ABOUT: Bickel, L. Rise Up to Life, 1972; Biographical Memoirs of Fellows of the Royal Society, volume 17, 1971; Dictionary of Scientific Biography, volume 5, 1972; Hare, R. The Birth of Penicillin, 1970; MacFarlane, R. G. Howard Florey: The Making of a Great Scientist, 1979; Oxbury, H. (ed.) Great Britons, 1985; Williams, T. I. Howard Florey, Penicillin and After, 1984.

FLORY, PAUL J.
(June 19, 1910–September 8, 1985)
Nobel Prize for Chemistry, 1974

The American chemist Paul John Flory was born in Sterling, a small town in Illinois, to Ezra Flory, a clergyman-educator, and Martha (Brumbaugh) Flory, a teacher. After graduating from the local high school in Elgin, Illinois, in 1927, Paul entered his mother's alma mater, Manchester College in North Manchester, Indiana, where one of his professors,

PAUL J. FLORY

Carl W. Holl, encouraged him to major in chemistry. After receiving his B.S. in 1931, Flory began postgraduate work at Ohio State University and received an M.S. in organic chemistry. He then switched to physical chemistry to escape what he called "cookbook chemistry" (a reference to SINCLAIR LEWIS's novel Arrowsmith). His thesis concerned the photochemistry of nitrogen oxides, a topic with practical implications, since nitrogen oxides contribute to the formation of smog.

After obtaining his Ph.D. at Ohio State in 1934, Flory joined E. I. du Pont de Nemours and Company in Wilmington, Delaware, where he was assigned to a basic research group under Wallace H. Carothers at the Chemical Department Experimental Station. At the time, Carothers's group was developing synthetic polymers, molecules far larger than those previously encountered by chemists. Polymers are produced as a limited variety of smaller units (monomers) joined together in a process called polymerization. Vinyl chloride, for example, is polymerized to polyvinyl chloride (PVC), and natural rubber is a polymer of a hydrocarbon called isoprene. Most macromolecules (those containing more than a thousand or so atoms) are true polymers, although many biological macromolecules are not. Hemoglobin, for example, is a macromolecule but is nonpolymeric.

In the 1920s and early 1930s the idea that many compounds, especially such natural substances as cellulose, rubber, and proteins, are macromolecules was supported by the German chemist HERMANN STAUDINGER. Staudinger and his allies showed that polymers are true molecules existing as chains of various lengths and that the function of a polymer is determined by its three-dimensional shape (configuration), which is itself determined by the components. In this way they established conclusively the existence of macromolecules. Polymer chemists were then able to concentrate their research on the configuration of individual macromolecules. Although macromolecules are subject to the same natural laws as are smaller molecules, however, their great size required new methods of studying configuration. One of the most successful methods involved statistical mechanics, a mathematical tool developed in the nineteenth century to increase understanding of the mechanical property of gases. The first scientist to apply this technique to polymers was the Swiss chemical physicist Werner Kuhn, followed shortly by Herman Mark and Eugene Guth in Vienna.

Even though Carothers's systematic program of polymer synthesis had made Du Pont the leader in the study of the organic chemistry of polymers, he realized that much work remained to be done on their physical chemistry. Recognizing Flory's superior mathematical abilities, Carothers urged him to develop this aspect of the research. In the course of his work Flory became especially interested in the speed of polymerization reactions. Much to the surprise of other chemists, he showed that there was no significant difference between the chemical reactivity of a small molecule and that of a polymer with the same chemical group, although the polymer might be thousands of times larger. In 1936 he discovered that the end group of atoms on one polymer growing in solution was sometimes transferred to a neighboring polymer chain, thus ending the growth of the donor polymer.

Carothers committed suicide in 1937, and the following year Flory left Du Pont to become a research associate at the Basic Science Research Laboratory at the University of Cincinnati in Ohio. There he developed a theory to explain the rate at which some polymers develop a branched configuration that often forms meshlike networks. Such networks are characteristic of elastic polymers, such as vulcanized rubber and silicones. By 1940 World War II was raging, and fears had grown about a possible rubber shortage in America. In September, Flory joined the Standard Oil Development Company (now Exxon Research and Engineering Company) as senior chemist at the company's Esso Laboratories in Linden,

New Jersey. While helping to improve butyl rubber, a novel synthetic rubber made from refinery gases, he began research into an area of long-standing interest, the elasticity of rubber. Partly because of the wartime situation, however, there was only limited scope for basic research at Standard Oil. When the Goodyear Tire and Rubber Company invited him to head a small fundamental research group, Flory seized the opportunity and moved to Akron, Ohio, in October 1943. During his five years at Goodyear, Flory made many basic discoveries in polymer chemistry, among them the proof that the tensile strength of a rubber is related predictably to flaws in the network structure.

His work at Goodyear established Flory's international reputation, and as a result he was invited by PETER DEBYE, chairman of the chemistry department at Cornell University in Ithaca, New York, to give the university's prestigious George Fisher Baker lectures during the 1948 spring semester. These remarkable lectures laid the foundation for the still relatively young discipline of polymer chemistry. That fall Flory became a professor of chemistry at Cornell.

In his research at Cornell, Flory discovered that, although the configuration of small molecules in a solution can be accurately described by a random-walk statistical approach, the size of polymer molecules makes that approach unreliable unless the temperature of the solution is reduced to a particular point, which varies with each type of polymer. At that temperature the solution acts as an "ideal" solution (analogous to Boyle's "ideal gas" state used to study the properties of gases). Flory called the temperature at which a solution became ideal the theta point. Now known as the Flory temperature, it is fundamental to study of the shape of macromolecules.

Flory also found it possible to define a constant summarizing all the properties of a polymer solution. In 1930 Staudinger had suggested that there was a linear relationship between the viscosity of a polymer solution and the polymer's average molecular weight. His model was too simple, however, and by 1949 many chemists, including Debye, had concluded that several difficulties stood in the way of a proper interpretation of viscosity. Flory went on to show that viscosity is a reliable indicator of polymer length, since the increase in viscosity produced by each polymer molecule is proportional to the cube of its structural radius. The constant involved is essentially the same for all polymer solutions. On the basis of this new understanding, Flory was able to use a large body of existing data to study the configuration of polymer chains. He also studied the configuration of proteins and polypeptides, macromolecules that play a role in living processes.

Liquid crystals, familiar today through their use in digital watches and calculators, were almost unknown when Flory published his first paper on the theory of liquid crystals in 1956. Twelve years elapsed before the first synthetic liquid crystal was made. Flory maintained an interest in this field until the end of his life.

In 1956 Flory was appointed executive director of research at the Mellon Institute of Industrial Research in Pittsburgh, Pennsylvania. There he was asked to oversee a shift in the institute's research from applied research closely controlled by industrial sponsors to more pure and fundamental research. However, Flory found the administrative responsibilities irksome, and when it became clear that the board was reluctant to abandon its industrial connections, he accepted a professorship at Stanford University in California in 1961. Five years later he became its first J. G. Jackson–C. J. Wood Professor of Chemistry.

Flory was awarded the 1974 Nobel Prize for Chemistry "for his fundamental achievements, both theoretical and experimental, in the physical chemistry of the macromolecules." In his Nobel lecture Flory noted that one of Alfred Nobel's explosives, nitrocellulose, was a macromolecule. He added, "Acquisition of a thorough understanding of the subject [of macromolecules] must be regarded as indispensable to the comprehension of rational connections between chemical constitution and those properties that render polymers essential to living organisms and to the needs of man."

After retiring from Stanford in 1975, Flory remained an active researcher. He had become a consultant for the International Business Machines Corporation (IBM) in 1968 and after 1977 spent two days a week at the IBM polymer science and technology unit at San Jose, California. The new technique of neutron scattering provided unequivocal support for Flory's view, developed years before, that the configuration of polymers is random in the amorphous state. In collaboration with other researchers at San Jose, Flory played an important role in the development of this new field of polymer science. He maintained his interest in polymer solutions and liquid crystals and extended his work on elasticity to the study of fibrous proteins such as muscle.

Hitherto almost unknown outside the world of polymer science, Flory used his fame as a Nobel laureate to publicize two causes he passionately supported: human rights and polymer education. He sought to help oppressed scientists, especially those in Communist nations, and he supported a moratorium on scientific cooperation with the Soviet Union while it continued to oppress scientists, such as ANDREI SAKHAROV. He even offered himself as a hostage to the Soviet government if it would permit Sakharov's wife, Yelena Bonner, to come to the West for medical treatment. Although his offer was not accepted, Bonner was later permitted to visit hospitals in Rome and the United States.

Flory believed that polymer science was scandalously neglected in American universities, particularly at the undergraduate level. He warned that while this economically important subject was being virtually ignored in chemistry courses in United States schools, it was receiving much more attention in Japan and Europe.

In 1936 Flory married Emily Catherine Tabor. They had two daughters and one son. A tall, slender man, Flory was fond of swimming and golf and remained physically active until the end of his life. On September 8, 1985, he died of a heart attack while working at his weekend home in Big Sur, California.

In addition to the Nobel Prize, Flory received the American Chemical Society's Nichols Medal (1962), the Charles Goodyear Award (1968), the Peter Debye Award in Physical Chemistry (1969), the Willard Gibbs Medal (1973), and the Priestley Medal (1974), as well as the Charles Frederick Chandler Medal of Columbia University (1970) and the John G. Kirkwood Medal of Yale University (1971). He was a member of numerous scholarly societies, among them the National Academy of Sciences, the American Academy of Arts and Sciences, and the American Chemical Society and was a fellow of the American Physics Society and the American Association for the Advancement of Science. He held honorary degrees from several universities, including Manchester (England), Manchester College (Indiana), Ohio State University, and the University of Milan (Italy).

SELECTED WORKS: Principles of Polymer Chemistry, 1953; Statistical Mechanics of Chain Molecules, 1969; Selected Works of Paul J. Flory (3 vols.) 1985.

ABOUT: Chemistry January 1975; Current Biography March

1975; Markovitz, H., and Casassa, E. F. (eds.) Polymer Science, 1976; New York Times October 16, 1974; September 12, 1985; Science November 22, 1974.

FORSSMANN, WERNER
(August 29, 1904–June 1, 1979)
Nobel Prize for Physiology or Medicine, 1956
(shared with André Cournand and Dickinson W. Richards)

WERNER FORSSMANN

The German physician Werner Theodor Otto Forssmann (fôrs′ män) was born in Berlin to Julius Forssmann, an attorney, and Emmy (Hindenberg) Forssmann. He received his early education in the Askanisches Gymnasium in Berlin. In 1916, when Forssmann was twelve years old, his father, then serving as a captain in the German army, was killed in the Battle of Galicia. Forssmann entered the University of Berlin as a student at the Faculty of Medicine in 1922, at which time the postwar economic crisis made it necessary for Forssmann to work part-time in a bank. Nevertheless, he passed his preliminary medical examinations, and after a two-year internship, he passed the state medical examinations in 1928. The following year he received his medical degree from the University of Berlin for a dissertation on the effects of a liver diet on serum cholesterol and the red blood cell count.

In 1929 Forssmann joined the Eberswalde Surgical Clinic near Berlin, where he began a series of experiments designed to demonstrate the anatomy and physiology of the diseased human heart by the technique of cardiac catheterization, the passage of a tube into the heart through a vein. Until that time, little work had been done in this field. Two French physiologists had performed cardiac catheterizations on experimental animals in 1861. Later, in 1912, three German physicians had inserted catheters into the abdominal aorta (a large artery that carries blood from the heart to the trunk and legs) of women with childbed fever (an infection of the birth canal after delivery) in order to inject drugs more effectively. The women had experienced no ill effects from the procedure. In 1928 an Italian investigator had inserted catheters into the hearts of experimental animals and human cadavers. In 1929, after making similar probes into the right side of the hearts of human cadavers, Forssmann sought to prove that the procedure was safe. He persuaded a fellow resident at the Eberswalde Surgical Clinic to attempt the procedure

on him. His colleague was able to insert a catheter (a tube approximately 65 centimeters long and 1 millimeter in diameter) into the vein of Forssmann's arm. He advanced the catheter partway to the heart, but then, believing it was too dangerous to continue, he stopped the procedure.

A week later Forssmann performed a cardiac catheterization on himself, without the knowledge or approval of his supervisor. With a nurse observing, Forssmann applied an anesthetic to his arm, made an incision, exposed a vein, inserted a catheter, and advanced it approximately two feet until it entered the right side of his heart. He then walked to the radiology department and, while the nurse held a mirror, observed the tip of the catheter in his heart with a fluoroscope. Subsequently, he performed a total of nine similar experiments. In two he injected contrast media into the heart, allowing him to make X rays that outlined the anatomy of the heart in much greater detail than was possible with a standard X ray. Upon completing this series of experiments, Forssmann published a paper, "Probing the Right Heart," in which he described the technique of right heart catheterization and suggested that the procedure offered a potentially useful method for studying the anatomy and physiology of the normal and abnormal heart, and the circulation of blood. Hoping to develop the technique further, Forssmann began a series of experiments using laboratory animals, but a shortage of funds at the clinic forced him to discontinue the series.

Forssmann presented a summary of his research at the twenty-fifth meeting of the German Surgical Society in April 1931; the German medical establishment, however, refused to recognize the validity of his work in this field. Later that year he was appointed to the service of Ferdinand Sauerbruch at the Charity Clinic in Berlin. Shortly thereafter, however, when a Berlin newspaper published a sensational story about his research at the Eberswalde Clinic, Forssmann was widely criticized by his colleagues. Calling him a charlatan, Sauerbruch discharged Forssmann, who, after this rebuke, decided to do no further research on the cardiovascular system.

Meanwhile, in the United States, ANDRÉ COURNAND and DICKINSON W. RICHARDS at Columbia University's College of Physicians and Surgeons read about Forssmann's experiments at the Eberswalde Clinic. Their reaction was quite the opposite of the German doctors', and, undertaking a program of research in the 1930s, they eventually accomplished the goals that Forssmann had originally set for himself. In 1941 Cournand performed the first cardiac catheterization in the United States. By the late 1940s and early 1950s cardiac catheterization and the X-ray techniques that Forssmann had envisioned were becoming standard diagnostic and investigative procedures.

Having abandoned his cardiovascular research, Forssmann began training in 1932 in the surgical specialty of urology under Karl Heusch at the Rudolf Virchow Hospital in Berlin. The following year he married the urologist Elsbet Engel; the couple eventually had six children. Forssmann later became chief of the surgical clinic at the City Hospital in Dresden-Friedrichstadt and at the Robert Koch Hospital in Berlin, where he practiced surgery and urology until the outbreak of World War II. During the war Forssmann served as a health officer in the German army, operating on military and civilian casualties and rising to the rank of surgeon-major. Early in 1945, as Germany's defeat became imminent, Forssmann made his way across the country toward the American lines, evading both Nazi and Soviet troops, and surrendered to the Americans. Released at the end of the war, he worked briefly as a lumberjack in the Black Forest before going into general surgical practice with his wife.

In 1950 the Forssmanns moved their practice to the small Rhineland town of Bad Kreuznach; he later described his work there as "the slave labor of a health insurance doctor." He published an article on the historical development of cardiac catheterization, with special reference to diseases of the lungs, in 1954.

Forssmann, Cournand, and Richards were awarded the 1952 Nobel Prize for Physiology or Medicine "for their discoveries concerning heart catheterization and pathological changes in the circulatory system." In his Nobel lecture, "The Role of Heart Catheterization and Angiocardiography in the Development of Modern Medicine," Forssmann briefly reviewed the significant advances in heart research since the Renaissance. He also raised the issue of the potential risks of cardiac catheterization and urged that the procedure be limited to patients who require it for diagnosis.

Two years after he received the Nobel Prize, Forssmann was appointed chief of the Surgical Service at the Evangelical Hospital in Düsseldorf. From 1962 until his death he served on the executive board of the German Surgical Society. He retired from surgical practice in 1970 and died June 1, 1979, at a spa in the Black Forest, after suffering a heart attack.

The recipient of the Leibniz Medal of the German Academy of Sciences (1954) and the Gold Medal of the Society of Surgical Medicine of Ferrara, Italy (1968), Forssmann was a member of the American College of Chest Physicians, the German Society of Urology, and the German Child Welfare Association; he was an honorary member of the Swedish Society of Cardiology.

SELECTED WORKS: Experiments on Myself: Memoirs of a Surgeon in Germany, 1974.

ABOUT: Current Biography March 1957; New York Times October 29, 1956; June 7, 1979; Robinson, D. The Miracle Finders, 1976.

FOWLER, WILLIAM A.

(August 9, 1911–   )
Nobel Prize for Physics, 1983
(shared with Subrahmanyan Chandrasekhar)

The American physicist William Alfred Fowler was born in Pittsburgh, Pennsylvania, the first of three children of Jennie Summers (Watson) and John MacLeod Fowler, an accountant. When the boy was two years old, the family moved to Lima, Ohio, a major railroading center, where he acquired a lifelong love of steam trains. At both Horace Mann Grade School and Lima Central High School, the boy's teachers encouraged his interest in science and engineering. Entering Ohio State

WILLIAM A. FOWLER

University in 1929 to study ceramic engineering, he switched in his sophomore year to a newly offered major in engineering physics and graduated with high honors. To support himself, Fowler worked at many jobs at school and during summer vacations. As a senior, he wrote a thesis in experimental physics titled "Focusing of Electron Beams." He also worked after school hours in the electronics laboratory of the electrical engineering department. "It was the best of worlds," he later recalled, "making real measurements in physics along with practical training in engineering."

Moving on to the California Institute of Technology (Caltech) for graduate work, Fowler studied at the Kellogg Radiation Laboratory under the Danish physicist Charles C. Lauritsen, from whom he learned, as Fowler put it, "how to *do* physics and how to enjoy it." In 1936 he received his Ph.D. for his thesis "Radioactive Elements of Low Atomic Number." Since then, Fowler has been associated with the Kellogg Laboratory, where he became the first Institute Professor of Physics in 1970.

During World War II, the Kellogg Laboratory was engaged in military research, and Fowler, as a civilian, helped develop military proximity fuses, rocket and torpedo ordnance, and atomic weapons. For this work, he received the United States government's Medal for Merit in 1948. At the end of the war, Fowler, Lauritsen, and Lauritsen's son, Thomas, continued their nuclear research, concentrating especially on nuclear reactions in stars.

In 1939 the nuclear and theoretical physicist

HANS A. BETHE had discovered the source of energy of the stars, a sequence of nuclear reactions leading to the fusion of hydrogen nuclei into nuclei of helium. Hydrogen appears in several forms, or isotopes, each with one proton (carrying a positive electric charge) in its nucleus and therefore the atomic number 1. The most common form has only the one proton, so its mass number is also 1. A nucleus of heavy hydrogen, or deuterium, however, has one proton and one neutron and therefore mass number 2; and a tritium nucleus has one proton and two neutrons and mass number 3. Every helium nucleus contains two protons (atomic number 2), and the most common form also has two neutrons (mass number 4); but other helium isotopes have fewer than or more than two neutrons and therefore different mass numbers. Nuclear reactions may involve various isotopes, many of them unstable (radioactive). The isotopes found under ordinary conditions in nature are generally the most stable; others have decayed over time into more stable types by emitting radiation. To make his discovery about the energy source of stars, Bethe extrapolated laboratory measurements of the nuclear reactions to calculate probable reaction rates under the conditions believed to exist in the center of a star.

The cosmologist George Gamow, in his big-bang concept of the origin of the universe, had proposed that all atomic nuclei heavier than helium could be built by neutron addition, one mass unit at a time. However, Hans Staub and William Stephens established that no stable nucleus had mass 5, and Fowler and his colleagues confirmed that no stable nucleus had mass 8. These two gaps disproved Gamow's proposed scheme in two ways. First, the addition of one neutron to a helium nucleus of mass 4 cannot lead to atoms of heavier elements because the unstable nucleus of mass 5 would decay before additional neutrons could interact with it. Second, the fusing together of two helium nuclei of mass 4 (in the manner of two hydrogen nuclei) also cannot lead to atoms of heavier elements because the unstable nucleus of mass 8 would decay before nuclear reactions could add more neutrons. (Heavier elements also have more protons, but neutrons can transform into protons to supply them, so this presents no obstacle.)

When the physicist E. E. Salpeter joined the Kellogg Laboratory in 1951, he showed that three helium nuclei (each of mass 4) might be fused into one carbon nucleus (mass 12) under the conditions present in red giant stars (stars at an intermediate stage of evolution with large volumes and relatively low surface temperatures), but not under those present in the big bang. Two years later, the British astronomer Fred Hoyle induced Ward Whaling at Kellogg to perform an experiment that resulted in quantitative confirmation that helium could be burned to carbon under the conditions of temperature and density known to exist in red giants.

Working with Hoyle and Margaret and Geoffrey Burbidge in England during a 1954–1955 sabbatical as a Fulbright scholar at Cambridge University, Fowler formulated a comprehensive theory that summarized the nuclear reactions leading to the synthesis of all the naturally occurring elements and explained the relative abundances observed by astronomers. Their 1957 paper, "Synthesis of the Elements in Star," which appeared in *Reviews of Modern Physics,* showed that all the elements from carbon to uranium could be created by nuclear processing in stars, starting with the hydrogen and helium produced in the big bang, and would subsequently be expelled into space by a supernova explosion at the end of the evolution of a heavy star. The physicist A. G. W. Cameron independently published the same broad ideas at the same time.

By combining the data of nuclear astrophysics and the theory of stellar structure, Fowler played a major role in creating a basic model of star development. According to this model, a cloud of gas (mostly hydrogen and helium) contracts under its own gravitational attraction. When the cloud becomes sufficiently dense and hot, hydrogen fuses into helium, and the cloud becomes a star. When hydrogen at the star's center is exhausted, the star contracts further. If the star is sufficiently massive, the core again becomes sufficiently dense and hot to allow the fusion of helium into carbon. The star then expands greatly and becomes a red giant. If the star has enough mass, its core will undergo repeated cycles of nuclear fuel exhaustion, core contraction, and re-ignition of nuclear burning of the products of previous nuclear reactions, until the residual core consists mainly of iron (mass 56). When the iron core becomes too massive, it blows off the stellar atmosphere as a supernova and collapses to a density like that of the atomic nucleus. If the star is not massive enough to form an iron core, it will typically shed much of its atmosphere after it has become a red giant.

Fowler and his associates also proposed that elements heavier than iron are made by successive neutron capture by nuclei in heavy stars, either before or during a supernova. These processes scatter some of the synthesized heavy elements into space, where they can be incorporated into future stellar systems.

Fowler received the 1983 Nobel Prize for Physics "for the theoretical and experimental studies of the nuclear reactions of importance in the formation of the chemical elements of the universe." He shared the prize with the astrophysicist SUBRAHMANYAN CHANDRASEKHAR. In his presentation address, Sven Johansson of the Royal Swedish Academy of Sciences described Fowler's work as "a complete theory for the formation of the chemical elements of the universe. This theory is still the basis of our knowledge in this area." In his acceptance speech, Fowler remarked that he "came to Caltech as a new graduate student fifty years ago and I am now known as the oldest graduate student at Caltech," adding, "it is the great glory of the quest for human knowledge that, while making some small contribution to the quest, we can also continue to learn and to take pleasure in learning." At the conclusion of his Nobel lecture, in which he reviewed the experimental and theoretical aspects of his work on the origins of the elements, Fowler reminded his listeners that their bodies consisted mostly of the heavy elements in addition to hydrogen and oxygen. "Thus it is possible to say that you and your neighbor and I, each one of us and all of us, are truly and literally a little bit of stardust."

In 1940 Fowler married Ardiane Foy Olmsted; they have two daughters. "The most outstanding characteristic of Willy Fowler is that he loves people," Hans Bethe once wrote. "He is full of humor and cheerfulness, and his example is infectious." Fowler, who enjoys mountain climbing in the British Isles, is an enthusiastic supporter of Pittsburgh's professional baseball and football teams and has retained from his childhood a fondness for steam-powered trains.

Fowler is a member of the National Academy of Sciences, a Benjamin Franklin Fellow of the Royal Society of Arts in London, an associate of the Royal Astronomical Society in London, and a past president of the American Physical Society. He has also served on both the National Science Board and the Space Science Board. His other awards include the Apollo Achievement Award of the National Aeronautics and Space Administration (1969), the Tom W. Bonner Prize of the American Physical Society (1970), the National Medal of Science of the National Science Foundation (1974), the Eddington Medal of the Royal Astronomical Society in London (1978), and the Bruce Gold Medal of the Astronomical Society of the Pacific (1979). He holds honorary degrees from the universities of Chicago and Liège, Ohio State University, and Denison University, as well as from the Observatory of Paris.

SELECTED WORKS: The Origin of the Nuclear Species, 1958; Nucleosynthesis in Massive Stars and Supernovae, 1965, with Fred Hoyle; Nuclear Astrophysics, 1967.

ABOUT: Barnes, C. A., et al. (eds.) Essays in Nuclear Astrophysics, 1982; Current Biography September 1974; New York Times October 20, 1983; Physics Today January 1984; Science November 25, 1983.

FRANCE, ANATOLE
(April 16, 1844–October 13, 1924)
Nobel Prize for Literature, 1921

ANATOLE FRANCE

The French novelist and critic Anatole France was born Jacques Anatole François Thibault, in Paris, the only child of François Noël Thibault, a bookseller, and Antoinette (Gallas) Thibault. The boy's early years were spent rambling along the quays of the Seine, among the bookstalls—"a library three-quarters of a mile in length," as he later wrote—and listening to the conversations of the learned customers who frequented his father's bookstore.

France, who took his pseudonym, a diminutive of François, from his father's professional name, attended the Collège Stanislas, a Jesuit school in Paris. Although he enjoyed reading the Greek and Roman classics, he disliked the school otherwise and developed a lifelong aversion to institutionalized religion. A mediocre student who excelled only in literary composition, France was encouraged by his mother to become a writer. After failing his baccalaureate examination several times, he finally passed at the age of twenty.

When his father retired in 1866, France was obliged to make his own living, and he took a series of jobs as an editorial assistant. While working for the publisher Alphonse Lemerre, he made the acquaintance of a recently emerged literary group, the Parnassians. The publication in 1868 of his first book, a study of the poet Alfred de Vigny, made France a central figure in the Parnassian circle.

During the Franco-Prussian War, France served briefly in the military; after his discharge he continued to write and to perform a variety of editorial jobs. His first important journalistic opportunity came in 1875, when the Paris newspaper Le Temps (The Time) commissioned him to write a series of critical articles on contemporary writers. The next year, as the paper's chief literary critic, he began a weekly column called "La Vie littéraire," which he wrote for seven years; his columns were collected under the same title in four volumes published between 1889 and 1892. These volumes were translated as On Life and Letters in 1911–1914. In the preface to the collection, France declared his position on the subjectivity of literary criticism: "A good critic is he who relates the adventures of his soul among masterpieces."

In 1876 France was appointed assistant librarian for the French Senate, a post he held for the next fourteen years and one that helped support his literary efforts. He married Valérie Guerin de Sauville in 1877.

During this period, he began to distance himself from the Parnassians and arranged for his next two works to be brought out by the publishing firm of Calmann Levy. The first, which appeared in 1879, consisted of two novellas, Jocaste (Jocasta) and Le Chat maigre (The Famished Cat). The second, published in 1881, was Le Crime de Sylvestre Bonnard (The Crime of Sylvester Bonnard), the novel that made France famous and won him a prize from the French Academy. It remains the best loved of all his writings. Its protagonist, the charming, skeptical, and tolerant old scholar Sylvester Bonnard, was the first of a series of fictional characters who embody France's own personality and who represent the spirit of the age. As French literary critic Jules Lemaître explained, "Other ages have incarnated the best of themselves in the citizen, in the artist, in the knight, in the priest, in the man of the world; the nineteenth century in its decline . . . is an elderly scholar and bachelor, very intelligent, very meditative, very ironic, and very gentle."

The success of *Sylvester Bonnard* and his weekly newspaper column thrust France into Parisian society. He was introduced in 1883 to Léontine Arman de Caillavet, who held one of the city's most brilliant literary, political, and artistic salons. Five years later the two became lovers, and after France divorced his wife in 1893, they lived openly together until de Caillavet's death in 1910. She took care of the petty details of life for France (who was helpless in such matters), coached him in social behavior, and guided his career.

Other important works during this period include *Thaïs* (*Thaïs*, 1890), a novel about the ironic fates of a religious hermit and a courtesan, and *La Rôtisserie de la reine Pédauque* (1893, translated as *The Queen Pédauque*), a novel that introduced France's second important fictional persona, Jerome Coignard, an imaginary eighteenth-century Rabelaisian abbé. After giving up his literary column in *Le Temps* in 1893, France used Coignard as his vehicle for social criticism of contemporary French life in *Les Opinions de M. Jérôme Coignard* (*The Opinions of Mr. Jerome Coignard*, 1893). *Le Lys rouge* (*The Red Lily*, 1894) is a novel inspired by the love affair between France and Léontine de Caillavet and by their first trip to Italy. France's short story collection *L'Étui de nacre* (*The Mother-of-Pearl Box*, 1892) contains one of his two most celebrated stories, "Le Procurateur de Judée" ("The Procurator of Judea"). In 1896 France was elected to the French Academy.

France's interest began to shift to contemporary social and political matters, and in 1897 he began a series of four volumes collectively entitled *L'Histoire contemporaine* (*Contemporary History*). The first volume introduced another important France persona, Monsieur Bergeret, a provincial schoolteacher. In 1898 France became involved in the Dreyfus affair. Prompted by Marcel Proust, he was the first to sign Émile Zola's famous 1898 manifesto, *J'Accuse*, condemning the false indictment for treason of Alfred Dreyfus, a Jewish army captain, which had been made to protect high army officials from the scandal of exposed corruption. France discussed the affair in the fourth volume of *Contemporary History,* entitled *Monsieur Bergeret à Paris* (*Monsieur Bergeret*

in Paris, 1900). Through his political activities, France became a close friend of the socialist leader Jean Jaures and was soon the literary lion of the French Socialist party.

His next important work, the two-volume biography *Vie de Jeanne d'Arc* (*The Life of Joan of Arc,* 1908), inspired in part by the work of France's friend, the historian Ernest Renan, was poorly received. Catholics objected to its demystification of Joan, and historians objected to it as serious history. On the other hand, France's burlesque epic of French history, *L'Île de pingouins* (*Penguin Island*), also published in 1908, was received with great enthusiasm. In *Penguin Island,* the nearsighted Abbot Mael, by mistaking penguins for human beings and baptizing them, causes all sorts of complications in heaven and in the evolution of the human race. *Les Dieux ont soif* (*The Gods Are Athirst,* 1912) is a historical novel about the French Revolution, in which France put to good use the erudition he had gained from browsing in his father's bookshop.

After 1913 France returned to the autobiographical themes of his earlier work, writing sketches of his childhood that he later incorporated in the novels *Le Petit Pierre* (*Little Pierre,* 1918) and *La Vie en fleur* (*The Bloom of Life,* 1922).

In 1921 France received the Nobel Prize for Literature "in recognition of his brilliant literary achievements, characterized . . . by a nobility of style, a profound human sympathy, and a true Gallic temperament." In his presentation speech, ERIK KARLFELDT of the Swedish Academy stressed the purity of France's style and his role as the champion of civilization. "In our time Anatole France has been the most authoritative representative of [French] civilization," Karlfeldt said. "He is the last of the great classicists. He has even been called the last European." In his acceptance speech, France expressed his strong pacifist sentiments.

France died on October 13, 1924, in Tours, where he had moved ten years earlier. His funeral was attended by the highest ranking members of the French government. After his death, however, France's literary reputation suffered a precipitous decline. Members of the post–World War I generation tended to agree with the English novelist Arnold Bennett's earlier criticism of what he termed France's "spiritual anemia." Since then, appreciation of his work has been confined mainly to scholars trained in textual criticism. Wayne Booth, for example, has analyzed France's complex irony, and Murray Sachs has examined his contribution to the development of the short story in France. For Paul Valéry, France "demonstrated that it was still possible, in our language, to make patent the priceless value of a prolonged culture and to combine and sum up the heritage handed down by an uninterrupted series of admirable writers." Dushan Bresky, discussing the author whom Joseph Conrad once characterized as the Prince of Prose, concluded: "In spite of the vicissitudes of critical fashion, France will always rate with [GEORGE BERNARD] SHAW as the greatest satirist of his era, and with Rabelais, Molière, and Voltaire as one of the greatest French wits."

ADDITIONAL WORKS IN ENGLISH TRANSLATION: The Garden of Epicurus, 1908; A Mummer's Tale, 1908; The Well of Saint Clare, 1909; Balthasar, 1909; The Merrie Tales of Jacques Tournebroche, 1909; The Wickerwork Woman, 1910; The White Stone, 1910; The Elm-Tree on the Mall, 1910; Child Life in Town and Country, 1910; The Honey-Bee, 1911; The Aspirations of Jean Servien, 1912; My Friend's Book, 1913; The Revolt of the Angels, 1914; The Man Who Married a Dumb Wife, 1915; Crainquebille, 1915; The Path of Glory, 1916; Pierre Nozière, 1916; The Amethyst Ring, 1916; The Human Tragedy, 1917; The Bride of Corinth, 1920; The Seven Wives of Bluebeard, 1920; Marguerite, 1921; Clio, 1922; Count Morin, Deputy, 1924; The Latin Genius, 1924; Little Sea Dogs, 1925; One Can But Try, 1925; Under the Rose, 1926; Stendhal, 1926; The Unrisen Dawn, 1928; Rabelais, 1928; The Tale of Saint Mary of Egypt, 1933; Prefaces, Introductions, and Other Uncollected Papers, 1970.

ABOUT: Axelrad, J. Anatole France: A Life Without Illusions, 1944; Brandes, G. Anatole France, 1908; Bresky, D. The Art of Anatole France, 1969; Brousson, J. J. Anatole France Himself, 1925; Cerf, B. Anatole France, 1926; Chevalier, H. The Ironic Temper, 1932; Durant, W. Adventures in Genius, 1931; Gsell, P. Conversations With Anatole France, 1924; Jefferson, C. Anatole France: The Politics of Skepticism, 1965; Kemeri, S. Rambles With Anatole France, 1926; May, J. L. Anatole France: The Man and His Work, 1926; Pouquet, J. M. Last Salon, 1927; Sachs, M. Anatole France, 1974; Shanks, L. P. Anatole France: The Mind and the Man, 1932; Shishmanova, I. V. Philosophical Novels of Anatole France, 1926; Smith, H. B. The Skepticism of Anatole France, 1927; Stewart, H. L. Anatole France the Parisian, 1927; Tylden-Wright, D. Anatole France, 1967; Virtanen, R. Anatole France, 1969; Walton, L. B. Anatole France and the Greek World, 1950.

FRANCK, JAMES
(August 26, 1882–May 21, 1964)
Nobel Prize for Physics, 1925
(shared with Gustav Hertz)

The German-American physicist James Franck (frängk) was born in Hamburg, to Jacob Franck, a banker, and the former Rebecca Nachum Drucker, daughter of a noted rabbinic family. Franck's high school, the Hamburg Gymnasium, emphasized the classics and languages, subjects that did not interest him. Sent by his father to the University of Heidelberg in 1901, Franck was expected to learn law and economics before returning to join the family's banking business. At Heidelberg, however, he also studied geology and chemistry, and there he met his lifelong friend and colleague, MAX BORN, who encouraged him to pursue his interest in science. Eventually, Born helped persuade Franck's parents to support their son's scientific education.

In 1902 Franck moved to the University of Berlin, then the center of physics study and research in Germany. He received his Ph.D. in 1906 for research on the movement of ions in gas discharges. After a brief period as assistant instructor at the University of Frankfurt am Main, Franck returned to Berlin as an assistant in the physics laboratory, and he became a lecturer at Berlin in 1911.

Franck began his collaboration with GUSTAV HERTZ in 1913. In their first joint experiments Franck and Hertz examined how electrons interact with atoms in low-density noble gases. They found that at low energy, electrons collide with the atoms of noble gases without losing much energy; these are elastic collisions. In 1914 the two scientists repeated their experiments using mercury vapor and found that electrons interact strongly with mercury atoms, transferring a great deal of energy to them. It was this work on inelastic collisions that led Franck and Hertz to the discovery of quantized transfer of energy between atoms and electrons. Between 1900 and the time of Franck and Hertz's experiments, MAX PLANCK, ALBERT EINSTEIN, and NIELS BOHR had developed the quantum theory. This theory proposed that energy is not transferred continuously, but in discrete amounts that Einstein named quanta. The energy of a quantum is related to the frequency of the emitted or absorbed energy by a factor that came to be known as Planck's constant. In 1913 Bohr had proposed a quantum model of the atom, in which electrons moved around the nucleus only in allowed orbits corresponding to specific energy states; as electrons jumped from one orbit to another, they emitted or absorbed quanta. Bohr's model answered some of the then-current objections to a nuclear model of the atom, and it partially explained the spectra of the elements. When a gas is heated, it absorbs energy in the form of heat, then emits it in the form of light: each element gives off

JAMES FRANCK

Bohr's ideas, which had a profound impact on the development of quantum theory.

In 1926 the Royal Swedish Academy of Sciences awarded the 1925 Nobel Prize for Physics to Franck and Hertz "for their discovery of the laws governing the impact of an electron upon an atom." In his Nobel lecture Franck pointed out that "the first works of Niels Bohr on his atomic theory appeared half a year before the completion of this work. . . . Subsequently," he continued, "it appeared to me completely incomprehensible that we had failed to recognize the fundamental significance of Bohr's theory, so much so, that we never even mentioned it once in the relevant paper."

Franck's research was disrupted in 1914 by the outbreak of World War I. He served on the Russian front as an officer until a severe case of dysentery sent him home for a lengthy recovery. In 1917 Franck became a section head, under FRITZ HABER, of the Kaiser Wilhelm Institute for Physical Chemistry, where he continued his research on inelastic collisions of electrons with atoms and molecules. Franck and his colleagues discovered that they could excite an atom (cause it to absorb energy) in such a way that it could not dispose of the excitation energy by emitting light. Such atoms are in a "metastable state," a phrase coined by Franck and his associates, and can lose their excitation energy only by colliding with particles. Metastable states play an important role in chemistry and physics: in photosynthesis, for example, they are critical to the plant's ability to store energy. Franck later turned to the study of photosynthesis, which remained his primary research interest for the last thirty years of his life.

When Max Born was offered the chair of theoretical physics at the University of Göttingen in 1921, he accepted on the condition that Franck be offered the chair of experimental physics. For the next twelve years the two scientists worked closely, discussing every aspect of each other's research; as Born sought to develop a formal mathematical quantum theory, which he named quantum mechanics, he found Franck's physical insight invaluable. At Göttingen, Franck was primarily concerned with the interactions of atoms with electrons, light, and other atoms. His work on the formation and structure of molecules, using molecular spectra, allowed him to determine basic chemical properties from spectroscopic measurements. The approach that he developed with his associate Edward Condon is known as the Franck-Condon principle.

light of specific colors, or wavelengths, that can be separated to produce a series of lines called the element's spectrum. According to Bohr, each line of spectrum corresponds to a specific quantity of energy emitted as an electron jumps from a higher-energy orbit to a lower one. Although this theory aroused great interest among physicists and did much to persuade them of the validity of quantum theory, it had not been confirmed experimentally.

In their famous experiments of 1914, Franck and Hertz showed that electrons can impart energy to a mercury atom only in units that are integral multiples of 4.9 electron volts. (An electron volt is the amount of energy an electron gains when accelerated by a voltage difference of 1 volt.) They then theorized that the mercury atoms should emit energy equal to the amount they absorb, producing a spectral line of a predictable wavelength. Finding this line in the mercury spectrum, Franck and Hertz concluded that atoms bombarded by electrons both absorb and emit energy in indivisible units, or quanta. Work on the gases of other elements corroborated this finding.

Franck and Hertz's experiments not only demonstrated the existence of energy quanta more convincingly than any previous work, but also provided a new method for measuring Planck's constant. Moreover, their results gave experimental support to the Bohr model of the atom. Neither Franck nor Hertz realized this at first, having paid little attention to Bohr's proposal. However, Bohr and others soon used the results of Franck and Hertz to corroborate

Shortly after Adolf Hitler became chancellor in 1933, the German government began expelling Jews from academic positions. Although he was Jewish, Franck's service in World War I initially protected him from dismissal. He nonetheless resigned his professorship and—against the advice of colleagues who feared for his safety—publicly refused to dismiss his Jewish co-workers and students. Before leaving Germany, Franck managed to find positions abroad for every member of his laboratory, despite the depression.

After spending a year in Copenhagen at Bohr's research institute, Franck emigrated to the United States in 1935, accepting a professorship at the Johns Hopkins University. There he studied the impact of light on chemicals and began his effort to understand photosynthesis, the fundamental photochemical process in nature. In 1938 he was appointed professor of physical chemistry and director of the new photosynthesis laboratory at the University of Chicago. He became an American citizen three years later.

After the United States entered World War II, Franck directed the chemistry division of the Metallurgical Laboratory in Chicago—part of the Manhattan Project to develop an atomic bomb. Although he abhorred the prospect of nuclear weapons, he feared that Germany had a similar goal. After Germany's defeat, Franck headed a committee that considered the social and political implications of nuclear weapons. The committee's June 1945 report, known as the Franck Report, urged that nuclear weapons not be used militarily until they had been demonstrated in an uninhabited area to representatives of all nations, particularly the Japanese. The report also predicted a dangerous nuclear arms race. Its recommendations were ignored, and the Japanese cities of Hiroshima and Nagasaki were destroyed that August.

In 1907 Franck married Ingrid Josephson, with whom he had two daughters. Ingrid Franck died in 1942 after a long illness. In 1946 Franck married Hertha Sponer, a former student of his who had become professor of physics at Duke University in Durham, North Carolina. After World War II, Franck returned to his research at the University of Chicago, dividing his time between Chicago and the couple's home in Durham. In 1949 he became professor emeritus at Chicago and remained active in research, particularly in photosynthesis.

Franck died suddenly in 1964 while he and his wife were visiting friends in Göttingen.

His colleagues knew Franck as a warm, kind, unpretentious man, and many of them sought his scientific and personal advice throughout his life. They cite his public protest against the Nazis and his attempt to prevent the use of the atomic bomb on civilians as examples of his moral courage.

In addition to the Nobel Prize, Franck received the Max Planck Medal of the German Physical Society (1951) and the Rumford Medal of the American Academy of Arts and Sciences (1955). In 1953 he was made an honorary citizen of Göttingen. Franck was a member of many scientific organizations, including the American National Academy of Sciences, the Association for the Advancement of Science, the American Philosophical Society, the American Physical Society, the American Chemical Society, the American Botanical Society, and the Royal Society of London.

SELECTED WORKS: Some Fundamental Aspects of Photosynthesis, 1941; Photosynthesis in Plants, 1949.

ABOUT: Biographical Memoirs of Fellows of the Royal Society, volume 11, 1965; Current Biography May 1957; Dictionary of Scientific Biography, volume 5, 1972; Nachmanson, D. German-Jewish Pioneers in Science 1900–1933, 1979.

FRANK, ILYA
(October 23, 1908–   )
Nobel Prize for Physics, 1958
(shared with Pavel Cherenkov and Igor Tamm)

The Russian physicist Ilya Mikhailovich Frank was born in St. Petersburg (now Leningrad), the younger son of Mikhail Lyudigovich Frank, a mathematics professor, and the former Elizaveta Mikhailovna Gratsianova, a physician. In 1930 he graduated as a physics major from Moscow State University, where his teacher was S. I. Vavilov, later president of the Soviet Academy of Sciences, and under whom Frank experimented with luminescence and its quenching in solution. At the State Optical Institute in Leningrad, Frank studied photochemical reactions by optical means in the laboratory of A. V. Terenin; there his research was noted for its procedural elegance, originality, and thorough analysis of experimental data. His dissertation, based on this work, earned him the degree of doctor of physical and mathematical sciences in 1935.

At Vavilov's invitation, Frank joined the newly created P. N. Lebedev Physical Institute of the Soviet Academy of Sciences in Moscow

ILYA FRANK

in 1934, where he has worked ever since. Vavilov urged Frank to shift his research to atomic physics. Accordingly, with a colleague, L. V. Groshev, Frank performed a rigorous and comprehensive comparison of theory and experiment on the recently discovered phenomenon of electron-positron pair production by gamma radiation in krypton.

Around this time, PAVEL CHERENKOV, one of Vavilov's graduate students at the Lebedev Institute, began studying the blue glow (later termed Cherenkov radiation or Vavilov-Cherenkov radiation) from refractive media subjected to gamma rays. Cherenkov showed that this radiation was not simply another kind of luminescence, but he could not explain it theoretically. In 1936–1937 Frank and IGOR TAMM were able to calculate the properties of an electron moving uniformly through a medium faster than the speed of light in that medium (somewhat analogous to a boat moving through the water faster than the waves it creates). In such an instance, they found, energy is radiated and the angle of propagation of the emitted wave can be simply expressed in terms of the electron's velocity in the medium and the speed of light, both in the medium and in a vacuum.

One of the very first triumphs of Frank and Tamm's theory was its description of the polarization of Cherenkov radiation, which, unlike the case of luminescence, is parallel to the incident radiation rather than perpendicular to it. The theory appeared to be so successful that Frank, Tamm, and Cherenkov experimentally tested some of its other predictions, such as the need for a particular energy threshold of incident gamma radiation, the dependence of this threshold on the refractive index of the medium, and the form of the emitted radiation (a hollow cone with an axis along the path of the incoming radiation). All their predictions were borne out. In recognition of this work, Frank in 1946 was elected a corresponding member of the Soviet Academy of Sciences and, along with Tamm, Cherenkov, and Vavilov, was awarded the Soviet government's State Prize.

The three surviving members of this research team (Vavilov died in 1951) were awarded the 1958 Nobel Prize for Physics "for the discovery and the interpretation of the Cherenkov effect." In his Nobel lecture, Frank pointed out that the Cherenkov effect "has found numerous applications in the physics of high-energy particles. A connection between this phenomenon and many other problems has also been found," he added, "as, for example, the physics of plasma, astrophysics, the problem of radio-wave generation, [and] problem of acceleration of particles."

Frank's investigation of Cherenkov radiation marked the beginning of a long-term interest in the effects of a medium's optical properties on the radiation of a moving source; he published a paper on Cherenkov radiation as late as 1980. One of Frank's most important contributions to this field is the theory of transition radiation, which he formulated with the Soviet physicist V. L. Ginzburg in 1945. This form of radiation arises from the altered electric field of a uniformly moving particle as it crosses the interface between two media having different optical properties. Although the theory was subsequently verified experimentally, some of its fundamental consequences were not observed in the laboratory for more than a decade.

Besides optics, Frank's other interest, especially since World War II, has been nuclear physics. In the mid-1940s he did theoretical and experimental work on neutron propagation and multiplication in uranium-graphite systems in the Soviet effort to develop the atomic bomb. He also studied experimentally neutron production from reactions of low-weight atomic nuclei and interactions between high-speed neutrons and various nuclei.

In 1946 Frank organized and became director of the Lebedev Institute's Laboratory of the Atomic Nucleus, a post he still holds. After being named professor at Moscow State University in 1944, he also headed the Laboratory of Radioactive Radiation at the university's Institute of Scientific Research Physics from

1946 to 1956. A year later, the Laboratory of Neutron Physics at the Joint Institute of Nuclear Research at Dubna, north of Moscow, was established under Frank's direction. There, in 1960, a pulsed fast-neutron reactor was put into operation for spectroscopic neutron study. In 1977 a new and more powerful pulsed reactor was inaugurated.

Frank has been described by his colleagues as having the "depth and clarity of thought and ability to reveal the essence of a subject by the most elementary methods" as well as "special insight into the deepest aspects of experiment and theory." His scientific articles and lectures are widely respected for their lucidity and logical reasoning.

In 1937 Frank married Ella Abramovna Beilikhis, a noted historian. Their only child, Aleksandr, a physicist at the institute at Dubna, shares his father's interest in neutron physics.

Frank has received numerous awards from the Soviet government, including the Lenin Prize, two Orders of Lenin, the Order of the Red Banner of Labor, the Order of the October Revolution, and the Vavilov Gold Medal from the Soviet Academy of Sciences. He was elected to full membership as an academician in the Soviet Academy of Sciences in 1964.

ABOUT: Jelley, J. V. Cherenkov Radiation and Its Applications, 1958; New York Times October 29, 1958; Science November 14, 1958.

FRIED, ALFRED

(November 11, 1864–May 5, 1921)
Nobel Prize for Peace, 1911
(shared with Tobias Asser)

Alfred Hermann Fried (frēt), Austrian journalist and pacifist, was born in Vienna, the son of Bertha (Engel) and Samuel Fried. His maternal uncle, Moritz Engel, owned and edited the periodical *Wiener Salonblatt* (Journal of the Vienna Salon). Fried, whose family name translates as "peace" in English, attended school until the age of fifteen. He then became a bookseller in his native city. Later moving to Berlin, he founded his own publishing company in 1887.

About this time, Fried was attracted to the work of BERTHA VON SUTTNER, whose antiwar novel, *Die Waffen nieder* (*Lay Down Your Arms*), had gained a wide and receptive audience. In 1891 Suttner established the Austrian Peace Society. Inspired by her example, Fried created the German Peace Society the following year. Suttner agreed to edit a peace

ALFRED FRIED

journal to be published by Fried, and it first appeared in 1891 under the title *Die Waffen nieder,* the same as her popular novel. Three years later, it was superseded by *Die Friedenswarte* (The Peace Watch), which Fried edited and published until his death. This publication soon became, as NORMAN ANGELL called it, "the most efficient periodical of the pacifist movement in the world."

When Fried entered peace work, to which he devoted his life after 1891, the European nations were busily arming, while those in the peace movement, idealistic in concept, were supporting such measures as international arbitration and disarmament. In his peace efforts Fried maintained regular contact with pacifists throughout Europe, including the Polish economist and financier Ivan Bliokh. As a high-ranking adviser to Czar Nicholas II of Russia, Bliokh helped persuade the czar to convene the first Hague Peace Conference in 1899. This was a significant event in the development of Fried's ideology.

Previously, he had believed that arms limitation and international legal codes provided the best avenues to peace. After attending the conference, he began to emphasize economic and political internationalism in the belief that the way to peace lay in understanding the causes of war and anarchy and propagandizing about them. "War," he once wrote, "is not in itself a condition so much as the symptom of a condition, that of international anarchy. If we wish to substitute for war the settlement of disputes by justice, we must first substitute for the condition of international anarchy a condition of international order." The change in his attitude toward methods of achieving peace led Fried to break from the German Peace Society in 1903, after which he returned to Vienna.

From the time of the first Hague conference, Fried was angered by the negative public reaction to the peace movement, particularly by the press. He bitterly attacked "the priests of philistinism, the newspaper editors, who had the pleasant task of mocking and making ridiculous the work of the Hague conference." He also deplored what he considered inadequate newspaper coverage of international politics. "The events of an international bicycle race," he wrote, "are described in great detail and are eagerly swallowed by the public, just as the least significant comedian on the local stage is better known to the public than the people who make world history."

To promote the work of the Hague conference and the cause of internationalism, Fried began publication of the *Annuaire de la Vie Internationale* (Annual of International Life) in 1905. He also pressed his arguments for peace in several books, notably *Handbuch der Friedensbewegung* (Handbook of the Peace Movement, 1911). This volume contained a historical overview of the movement, biographies of leading pacifists, reports on peace conferences, and a directory of leading peace societies.

Fried was awarded the 1911 Nobel Prize for Peace, an honor he shared with TOBIAS ASSER. In the presentation address, Jørgen Løvland of the Norwegian Nobel Committee described Fried as "a self-educated man who, with true German persistence and application, worked his way up until he had mastered scholarly writing." Løvland saluted Fried as "the most industrious literary pacifist in the past twenty years." Fried did not attend the award ceremonies, nor did he deliver a Nobel lecture.

Although Fried was the author of seventy books and pamphlets and numerous newspaper articles, as well as the translator of works by foreign peace workers, he contributed more than writing and editing to the cause of peace. He was a founding member of the Society for International Understanding and held membership in the Bern Peace Bureau, the International Institute for Peace, and the International Conciliation for Central Europe, which he served as secretary. The University of Leiden awarded him an honorary doctoral degree in 1913.

At the start of World War I in 1914, Fried was in Vienna, where his peace activities and antigovernment articles brought accusations of high treason against him. Fleeing to Switzerland, he continued to publish *Die Friedenswarte* and worked to improve conditions for prisoners of war. He also edited yet another internationalist publication, *Blätter für internationale Verständigung und zwischenstaatliche Organisation* (Publications for International Understanding and Interstate Organization).

After the war Fried was drawn into the ideological battle over the terms of the peace. At an international workers' meeting in Bern, he helped draft a proposal for a negotiated peace. Although he wrote a series of articles blaming German leaders for causing the war, he nevertheless attacked the inequities of the Versailles Treaty. In *Mein Kriegstagebuch* (My War Journal) he recorded his wartime activities and sentiments.

During the postwar years Fried often argued that World War I had proved the need for internationalism and vindicated the pacifist analysis of world politics. A supporter of the League of Nations, he nevertheless opposed the concept of an international police force. The league's first task, he wrote in the *Neue Zürcher Zeitung* (New Zurich Daily), should be to "acquire a moral authority which will give prestige to its decisions and which will distinguish them completely from the anarchic enterprises of individual governments." The league, he believed, could establish its moral authority only by devoting its efforts to "building up a system of superstate law and justice."

Fried was married three times: in 1889 to Gertrud Gnadenfeld, later to Martha Holländer, and in 1908 to Therese Volandt.

In the collapse of Austria-Hungary at the end of World War I, Fried lost what little money he had managed to save. Returning to the capital of the defeated nation, he found little sympathy for his views on war and peace, and he sank into poverty and obscurity. He died of a lung infection in Vienna in 1921.

WORKS IN ENGLISH TRANSLATION: The German Emperor and the Peace of the World, 1912; The Restoration of Europe, 1916; International Cooperation, 1918.

ABOUT: Chickering, R. Imperial Germany and a World Without War, 1975; Peterson, H. F. Power and International Order, 1964.

FRIEDMAN, MILTON
(July 31, 1912–)
Nobel Memorial Prize in Economic
  Sciences, 1976

MILTON FRIEDMAN

The American economist Milton Friedman
was born in Brooklyn, New York. When he
was still an infant, his parents, Sarah Ethel
(Laundau) and Jeno Saul Friedman, both
Eastern European immigrants, moved to Rah-
way, New Jersey. His mother ran a retail dry-
goods store, and his father, Friedman recalled,
"engaged in a succession of mostly unsuccessful 'jobbing' ventures." He continued, "The
family income was small and highly uncertain;
financial crisis was a constant companion. Yet
there was always enough to eat, and the family
atmosphere was warm and supportive."

Entering Rutgers University at the age of
sixteen on a competitive partial scholarship,
Friedman obtained a B.A. in 1932 with the
equivalent of a double major in mathematics
and economics. At Rutgers he was strongly
influenced by two graduate teaching assistants: Arthur F. Burns, later chairman of the
Federal Reserve System, and Homer Jones,
who became an authority on interest rates.
Jones encouraged Friedman to do graduate
work in economics and recommended him to
the University of Chicago.

After receiving an M.A. from Chicago in
1933, Friedman went to Columbia University
in New York City on a fellowship. He then
returned to the University of Chicago as a research assistant in the fall of 1934. The following summer he helped design a large
consumer budget study for the United States
National Resources Committee in Washington, D.C. Friedman's association with the National Bureau of Economic Research (NBER)
began in 1937 when he became an assistant to
SIMON KUZNETS. Together they completed
*Incomes From Independent Professional Prac-
tices* in 1940. This work later served as Friedman's doctoral dissertation at Columbia, for
which he was awarded a Ph.D. in 1946. The
book's conclusion—that the medical profession had used restrictive monopoly practices
to raise doctors' incomes relative to those of
dentists—caused such controversy at the NBER
that publication was delayed until after World
War II.

The pattern of Friedman's career as an
economist is clear from these early beginnings.
His subsequent contributions to theoretical and
empirical economic analysis have been diverse
and often highly provocative; he has been a
prolific academic and popular writer on eco-

nomics; and he has engaged in important collaborative efforts with government and
academic colleagues, notably as the so-called
dean of the Chicago School of economics. While
many of his views on economic theory and
public policy remain controversial, he has, as
the English economist John Burton succinctly
said, "provided us with an agenda for the future of macroeconomic research."

During World War II, Friedman worked on
tax policy at the United States Treasury Department in Washington and on military statistical problems at Columbia University. He
taught economics at the University of Minnesota in 1945–1946. He then returned to the
University of Chicago as an assistant professor
of economics. Under the auspices of the NBER,
he also began a continuing research project on
monetary economics.

In 1950 Friedman visited Paris as a consultant to the Marshall Plan, created by GEORGE
C. MARSHALL to help rebuild Western Europe's fragmented postwar economies. In this
capacity, Friedman became a forceful advocate of floating exchange rates and predicted
that the fixed-exchange-rate system of curren-
cies established at the 1944 Bretton Woods
Conference would eventually collapse, as it
did in the early 1970s. His firsthand experience
of European theoretical and practical approaches to economic problems was enhanced
when he spent 1953 as a visiting Fulbright Professor at Cambridge University in England.

Building on his earlier work with Kuznets,
Friedman, working with the economists Dorothy Brady, Margaret Reid, and Rose Direc-

tor, formulated and empirically tested his "permanent income hypothesis" of consumption. In his book *A Theory of the Consumption Function,* published in 1957, Friedman argued that John Maynard Keynes's concept of consumption function, which relates current consumption to current income, was misleading. Instead, he maintained that consumers do not base their consumption decisions, except transitory ones, on current income but on their expected long-run, or "permanent," income. Although not directly observable, permanent income could be reliably calculated by a weighted average of the past values of income. This weighting he called distributed lag.

Surveying a wide range of empirical data on consumption, Friedman found that nearly all the evidence was consistent with his permanent-income hypothesis. (In the 1950s FRANCO MODIGLIANI presented an alternative, but related, approach to Friedman's theory of consumption: his life cycle hypothesis explains the same economic phenomena.) Permanent income played an important role in Friedman's influential reformulation of the quantity theory of money. He would later show that long-run shifts in the demand for money throughout American history were almost always determined by changes in permanent income.

The significance of Friedman's theory of permanent income is difficult to exaggerate. Much subsequent work on aggregate consumption recognizes its role, and the definition and measurement of expected future incomes has become a central concern of macroeconomists everywhere. Moreover, important advances in econometrics during the 1960s and 1970s owe much to the statistical methods Friedman used for estimating permanent income.

Publication in 1963 of the monumental *A Monetary History of the United States* by Friedman and the economic historian Anna J. Schwartz revealed the significance of his theories when applied empirically and in the field of monetary history. The two authors compiled monetary statistics dating back to the American Revolution and documented the pervasive role of changes in the nation's money supply on its inflationary episodes. Their chapter on the Great Depression laid much of the blame on the Federal Reserve for failing to keep an adequate level of liquidity in the United States banking system. "The Great Contraction [of money supply]," they wrote, "is tragic testimony to the power of monetary policy—not, as Keynes and so many of his contemporaries believed, evidence of impotence."

Continuing this argument, Friedman and the economist David Meiselman published in 1963 an article attacking a central idea in Keynesian economics by showing that nominal consumption expenditures are determined more closely by the money supply than by autonomous government expenditures. These arguments laid the foundation of the so-called supply-side economic theories of the 1980s.

In Friedman's words, "only money matters": changes in the growth rate of nominal income are caused primarily by changes in the growth rate of the money stock. The counterattack on Friedman and Meiselman by neo-Keynesians sparked the monetary-fiscal policy debates of the 1960s and 1970s, but Friedman's central propositions are generally acknowledged to have held up remarkably well.

Friedman's monetary economics also offers a good illustration of his economic methods. Economic models, he believes, should be judged by their ability to predict real economic occurrences, not by their assumptions. Also, simple, single-equation models of monetary phenomena are preferable to the multiequation models favored by Keynesians. Friedman's one-sided, forcefully argued monetarist doctrine has been a fruitful challenge to existing policy doctrines, even if his excessive emphasis on one causal factor, money supply, has encountered increasing skepticism.

Friedman's outstanding contributions remain his analysis of the failures of Keynesian theories and his effective criticism of the stability of the Phillips curve, which attempts to describe the so-called natural rate of unemployment. This criticism has had a lasting impact on policy theory as well as on the way economists look at the trade-offs between inflation and unemployment. Furthermore, his penetrating criticism of the meaning of stabilization policy and particularly his famous analysis of the lags in policymaking explain why and how stabilization measures can easily have destabilizing effects.

Friedman received the 1976 Nobel Memorial Prize in Economic Sciences for "his achievements in the fields of consumption analysis, monetary history and theory, and for his demonstration of the complexity of stabilization policy." In his Nobel lecture he returned to the theme he had introduced in his influential address to the American Economic Association in 1967: the rejection of the Keynesian notion of a stable trade-off between the rate of inflation and unemployment. In the long run, he asserted, the Phillips curve was vertical in conditions of a natural rate of unemployment. He went on to assert that the natural unemployment rate was "not a numerical constant" but could be a rising factor. In the short run, he explained, an inflationary monetary or fiscal policy might lower unemployment, but as workers and companies accustomed themselves to higher money growth, the price level (and eventually unemployment) would rise. Indeed, he showed that under certain conditions a positively inclined Phillips curve was possible, an explanation for the "stagflation" of the early 1970s. The social costs of variable inflation were so high that Friedman advocated "stable" over "discretionary" monetary policies. Not only would a stable rate of money growth dampen monetary fluctuations, it would also provide a predictable environment for the formation of expectation in the private sector.

Friedman became prominent as an adviser to President Richard M. Nixon, even though he disagreed when the president instituted wage and price controls in 1971. Friedman's laissez-faire views on social policy became widely known through his column in *Newsweek* magazine, beginning in 1966, and through the earlier publication of *Capitalism and Freedom* in 1962. His popular book *Free to Choose,* published in 1980, became the title for his television series on economics and social questions.

Many of Friedman's proposals—economic deregulation, a volunteer army, and a negative income tax—have been adopted. Other proposals—educational vouchers, and abolition of social security and the minimum wage—remain politically controversial.

Although he has often been labeled a conservative, or worse, by political opponents, Friedman is much closer to the classic liberalism of Adam Smith or John Stuart Mill than to traditional conservative economists. He believes that his goals do not, in fact, differ from modern liberal ones. "Differences in economic policy among disinterested citizens," he says, "derive predominantly from different predictions about the economic consequences of taking action . . . rather than from fundamental differences in basic values." Although the awarding of the Nobel Prize to Friedman drew protests from some economists and non-economists who objected to his policy recommendations, the importance of Friedman's contributions to economic theory and empirical research is widely recognized. PAUL SAMUELSON, for example, has called him "an economist's economist."

Since retiring in 1977 from the University of Chicago, where he held the Paul Snowden Russell Distinguished Services Professorship, Friedman has been a senior research associate at Stanford University's Hoover Institution. For three decades, he has been active in the American Economic Association, serving as its president in 1967.

Since 1938 Friedman has been married to the former Rose Director, an economist whom he met at the University of Chicago and with whom he often collaborates. They have a son and a daughter.

In addition to the Nobel Prize, Friedman has received the John Bates Clark Medal of the American Economic Association (1951) and honorary degrees from Rutgers, Lehigh, Loyola, Harvard, Brigham Young, Roosevelt, St. Paul's (Tokyo), and Hebrew (Jerusalem) universities; from the universities of New Hampshire and Rochester; and from Kalamazoo, Dartmouth, Rockford, and Bethany colleges.

ADDITIONAL WORKS: Essays in Positive Economics, 1953; A Program for Monetary Stability, 1959; Price Theory: A Provisional Text, 1962; Inflation: Causes and Consequences, 1963; Postwar Trends in Monetary Theory and Policy, 1963; Monetary vs. Fiscal Policy, 1969, with Walter W. Heller; The Optimum Quantity of Money and Other Essays, 1969; The Counterrevolution in Monetary Theory, 1970; An Economist's Protest: Columns in Political Economy, 1972; Money and Economic Development, 1973; Free Markets for Free Men, 1974; Unemployment Versus Inflation? 1975, with David Laidler; Inflation and Unemployment: The New Dimension of Politics, 1977; The Future of Capitalism, 1977; Milton Friedman Speaks, 1980; The Invisible Hand in Economics and Politics, 1981; Market Mechanisms and Central Economic Planning, 1981; Monetary Trends in the United States and the United Kingdom, 1981, with Anna Jacobson Schwartz; Bright Promises, Dismal Performance, 1983; Tyranny of the Status Quo, 1984, with Rose D. Friedman.

ABOUT: Breit, W., and Spencer, R. W. (eds.) Lives of the Laureates, 1986; Butler, E. Milton Friedman: A Guide to His Economic Thought, 1985; Current Biography October 1969; Gordon, R. J. (ed.) Milton Friedman's Monetary Framework, 1974; Scandinavian Journal of Economics, number 1, 1977; Selden, R. T. (ed.) Capitalism and Freedom: Problems and Prospects, 1975; Shackleton, J. R., and Locksley, G. Twelve Contemporary Economists, 1981.

FRIENDS SERVICE COUNCIL
(founded 1927)
Nobel Prize for Peace, 1947
(shared with American Friends Service
   Committee)

The Friends Service Council was established in London in 1927 as a standing committee to coordinate missionary and relief work conducted by the Religious Society of Friends, or

Quakers, as the group is commonly known. The Quaker belief that God's spirit dwells within each individual originated with the teachings of George Fox (1624–1691), an English shoemaker who became disillusioned with the disparity he observed between the teachings of Christianity and the daily conduct of those who professed those beliefs. At the age of nineteen, he began to preach that every person could experience divine illumination, the personal revelation of God's will that would guide human behavior along righteous paths.

As religious radicals in the Puritan movement, Fox's converts often suffered brutal persecution. Among their more controversial stands was a literal adherence to the principles of equality and brotherhood. Moreover, they renounced warfare and violence as contrary to the will of God, proclaiming in 1660: "We utterly deny all outward wars and strife and fightings with outward weapons, for any end and under any pretense whatsoever."

The application of these tenets to everyday life prompted the historian Auguste Jorns to call Quakers "pioneers in social work." In 1671, for example, while visiting banished Quakers in the West Indies, Fox exhorted them to free and provide for the future well-being of their slaves. A century later, Quakers were conducting a vigorous antislavery campaign through tracts, meetings, and memorials to Parliament, calling for an end to the slave trade in the British colonies.

In 1792 the Friends founded a retreat at York for the humane treatment of the insane. In the early 1800s, they worked to improve prison conditions through such reforms as separation of the sexes, classification of criminals, and the use of female guards for incarcerated women. Quakers also played an early role in the temperance movement, adopting a policy of total abstinence in 1839 and urging members to refrain from brewing or dispensing liquor. Carrying their service abroad, Quaker volunteers helped feed victims of the Irish famine of 1847–1848. During the Crimean War, when British ships shelled the coast of Finland (then part of Russia), a party of Friends brought medical supplies and tended the wounded.

These and other humanitarian efforts were conducted with little formal organization or planning, but as the Friends' overseas ministrations grew during the nineteenth century, so did the need for centralized administration. Therefore, in 1868 the Quakers formed the Friends Foreign Mission Association (FFMA) to organize and operate schools, hospitals, and Quaker societies abroad. Under the FFMA's auspices, Quakers were dispatched to India, Madagascar, China, Ceylon (now Sri Lanka), and elsewhere.

Another group, the Friends War Victims Relief Committee, was formed in 1870 when Quaker volunteers undertook relief and rehabilitation in towns ravaged by the Franco-Prussian War. This was the first time that the eight-pointed, red-and-black star was worn as a badge to identify Quaker relief workers. It was also the first time that the group provided assistance to both sides in a military conflict.

During World War I, Carl Heath, a recent Quaker convert, proposed that the Friends establish peace centers throughout the world, a suggestion that was adopted by the London Yearly Meeting and put into practice in 1919 with the formation of the Council for International Service (CIS). In cooperation with the AMERICAN FRIENDS SERVICE COMMITTEE (AFSC), the CIS founded Quaker International Centers, chiefly in Europe, to serve as bases for spreading goodwill and fostering peace. The center in Geneva, Switzerland, for example, lent support to the newly formed League of Nations through newspaper articles; by lobbying on behalf of refugees, minorities, and stateless persons; and by attempting to foster cooperation among the various organizations vying to influence league policies.

In 1927 the FFMA and the CIS merged to create the Friends Service Council (FSC), which was headed first by Harry T. Silcock and Carl Heath and after 1932 by Heath alone. The new body, with headquarters in London, gave most of its attention to what it called "the ministry of reconciliation." For example, Quaker International Centers in Berlin and Warsaw sponsored conferences to discuss conflicts arising from the terms of the Treaty of Versailles. Quakers continued to intercede with government authorities to relieve the suffering of persecuted minorities such as the Germans during the French occupation of the Ruhr; the Austrians in the South Tirol under the Italians; and German political prisoners in Memel, then under Lithuanian control.

During World War II, the Friends War Victims Relief Committee (after 1943 the Friends Relief Service) was activated for the fifth time since 1870. From 1940 to 1948 it operated in Great Britain, France, the Netherlands, Greece, Germany, Austria, and Poland. Friends drove ambulances, distributed food and clothing to war orphans, and established camps for refugees and displaced persons. This and other Friends relief committees were absorbed by the FSC after the war and contributed to the task of postwar reconstruction.

The 1947 Nobel Prize for Peace was awarded jointly to the Friends Service Council and the American Friends Service Committee in recognition of the Quakers' long tradition of humanitarian service. In his presentation speech, Gunnar Jahn of the Norwegian Nobel Committee noted that "the Quakers have shown us that it is possible to translate into action what lies deep in the hearts of many: compassion for others and the desire to help them— that rich expression of the sympathy between all men, regardless of nationality or race, which, transformed into deeds, must form the basis for lasting peace."

The prize was accepted by Margaret A. Backhouse, chairwoman of the Friends Service Council and vice-chairwoman of the Friends Relief Service. In her Nobel lecture, she outlined the principles underlying the Friends' activities. She also described the scope of their efforts over three centuries, giving many illustrations of their specific works. She concluded, "As I have picked out one example after another, I have been conscious that many of them reveal methods and motives shared by all people of goodwill, and the Society of Friends makes no claim to the monopoly of any of them; rather would we proclaim the universality of the truth that binds us together and pray that the day may quickly come when all men will seek first the kingdom of God."

Since receiving the Nobel Prize, the FSC has continued its humanitarian works in many parts of the world. For two years after the Arab-Israeli War of 1948, for example, it operated relief camps for 235,000 Arab refugees in the Gaza Strip. In 1961 the FSC joined with the AFSC to cosponsor the International Dialogue program in West Africa. This program organized seminars by students, journalists, educators, rural development planners, and government officials on problems confronting the newly independent nations of Africa south of the Sahara. Quaker relief efforts have also aided victims of riots in India; civilian victims of war in Korea and Vietnam; and starving people in Ethiopia, Chad, and other parts of Africa.

The Friends Service Council and Friends Peace and International Relations Committee merged in 1978 to form Quaker Peace and Service. Since that time, the organization has provided relief through medical clinics and agricultural stations in India and parts of Africa; schools and play centers in Lebanon and Jordan; and refugee aid in Zimbabwe, Somalia, and Pakistan. It has continued to maintain peace workers in Northern Ireland, to hold peace vigils in various British cities, and to press the British government to reduce its expenditures for armaments. More recently, Quaker Peace and Service has expanded its activities in the Republic of South Africa, where it has assisted the residents of squatters' camps in Cape Town, offered legal advice to blacks in Soweto, and reported on the plight of political prisoners.

Modest in their claims of achievement, Friends believe their service is a personal expression of each individual's peace witness. For the Quakers, "In every human soul there is a witness for God which can be appealed to and which, with God's grace, can be reached and made active."

SELECTED PUBLICATIONS: International Understanding: The Quaker Contribution, 1928; Friends Service East and West, 1928; Friends and World Crisis, 1931; Friends Travel "Hard": A Collection of Accounts, 1941; Quaker Service in the Middle East, 1975.

PERIODICALS: (annual) Annual Report of Quaker Peace and Service. (quarterly) QPS Reporter.

ABOUT: Forbes, J. V. G. The Quaker Star Under Seven Flags, 1962; Fry, A. R. A Quaker Adventure, 1926; Hall, W. H. Quaker International Work in Europe Since 1914, 1930; Hodgkin, H. T. Friends Beyond Seas, 1916; Howard, E. Across Barriers, 1942; Jonas, G. On Doing Good, 1971; Jones, R. M. A Service of Love in Wartime, 1920; Milligan, E. H. The Past Is Prologue: 100 Years of Quaker Service Overseas, 1968; Trueblood, D. E. The People Called Quakers, 1966; Wilson, R. C. Quaker Relief, 1952; Yarrow, C. H. M. Quaker Experiences in International Conciliation, 1978.

FRISCH, KARL VON

(November 20, 1886–June 12, 1982)
Nobel Prize for Physiology or Medicine, 1973
(shared with Konrad Lorenz and Niko Tinbergen)

The Austrian zoologist Karl von Frisch was born in Vienna, the youngest of four sons of Anton Ritter von Frisch, a surgeon and urologist, and the former Marie Exner. His family, which included scientists, physicians, and professors, stimulated the boy's curiosity and encouraged his intellectual development. At the family's summer home in Brunnwinkl on Lake Wolfgang, young Karl was able to explore his interest in nature, and he spent many hours observing animals, keeping careful records of

KARL VON FRISCH

his observations, and submitting papers to journals for amateur naturalists.

After receiving his secondary education at the Schottengymnasium, a Benedictine school in Vienna, Frisch hoped to join a scientific expedition. Instead, he bowed to his father's wishes and entered the medical school of the University of Vienna in 1905. There, under the guidance of his uncle, the distinguished physiologist Sigmund Exner, he immersed himself in a research project involving the distribution of pigments in the compound eyes of beetles, butterflies, and shrimp. Shortly afterward he abandoned his medical studies for ethology, the study of animal behavior, and transferred to the Zoological Institute of the University of Munich, a noted center for experimental biology. While studying under Richard von Hertwig, Frisch became interested in light perception and the color changes that occurred in certain fish. After returning to the University of Vienna, he continued this research, for which he received his Ph.D. in 1910.

At that time it was generally assumed that fish and all invertebrates were completely color-blind, a view championed by Karl von Hess, the director of the Munich Eye Clinic. Frisch disproved the theory through experiments in which minnows were trained to respond to colored objects. When Hess refused to accept the conclusion that Frisch drew from the minnow experiments, Frisch attacked the views of the older scientist, who Frisch believed was trying to discredit his work. In later years Frisch came to regard the incident philosophically, for the dispute served to bring his work to the attention of other scientists.

As a Darwinian, Frisch believed it was unlikely that insects were unable to perceive color. In fact, he considered it reasonable to assume that the striking color patterns of flowers evolved because the patterns acted as signals to attract insects seeking nectar and pollen, thus fertilizing the flowers and ensuring their propagation. After accepting a post at the University of Munich in 1912, he began experiments to confirm his assumption that honeybees have a color sense. He found that these insects could be trained to associate food with particular hues. Once trained to link food with a specific colored square, the bees alighted on that square even when food had been removed and the positions of various colored squares had been shifted.

World War I interrupted Frisch's research. Because of his poor eyesight, he was not conscripted into the army but worked in a military hospital near Vienna. In January 1919 Frisch returned to the Zoological Institute in Munich as an assistant professor. Two years later he became an assistant professor at the University of Rostock, and in 1923 he joined the faculty of the University of Breslau (now Wrocław, Poland) as a full professor. During these years he continued his work on bees. In the course of proving that bees were able to distinguish among dozens of odors, he noted that they invariably entered only one of several cardboard boxes—the box that had been baited with a dish of sugar water and a fragrant blossom. Once the food was consumed, the bees stopped entering the box. When a scout bee found another source of food, however, a large swarm of bees quickly gathered.

"It was clear to me," Frisch later wrote in his autobiography, "that the bee community possessed an excellent intelligence service, but how it functioned I did not know." In the spring of 1919, after marking a few forager bees with paint, he set out a dish of sugar water, watched a bee feed, and followed her back to the hive. There the scout bee performed a circular dance that aroused the other bees. "I could scarcely believe my eyes," Frisch wrote. "She performed a round dance on the honeycomb which greatly excited the marked foragers around her and caused them to fly back to the feeding place. . . . This I believe was the most far-reaching observation of my life," he declared. Over the next few years, he worked to discover the meaning of the dance of the honeybees.

In 1925 Frisch returned to the Zoological Institute of the University of Munich as the successor to Richard von Hertwig. Eight years later, he supervised the construction of a new zoological research building tailored to his specifications. After the institute was almost completely destroyed during World War II, Frisch retreated to Brunnwinkl to continue his research. In 1946 he accepted a position at the University of Graz, but he returned to Munich four years later to the rebuilt Zoological Institute, where he served as director until he was named emeritus professor in 1958.

Through the years, Frisch realized that the honeybee dance was far more complex than he had initially suspected. He discovered that bees inform each other of the approximate direction, distance, and quantity of a new food source using a series of elaborate dances whose components contain the relevant information. If the food is close at hand, for example, the informant bee performs a "round dance"; for sources more than 85 meters away, the bee uses a tail-wagging dance in the shape of a figure 8. Frisch also found that the angle at which the waggle dance is performed with respect to the vertical dimension of the honeycomb is equal to the angle of the food source with respect to the sun. He further learned that even when the sun is obscured by broken clouds, honeybees are able to find food by using the plane of polarization of light from patches of blue sky.

The 1973 Nobel Prize for Physiology or Medicine was awarded jointly to Frisch and two other ethologists, KONRAD LORENZ and NIKO TINBERGEN, "for their discoveries concerning organization and elicitation of individual and social behavior patterns." "The discoveries made by this year's Nobel Prize laureates . . . might . . . seem to be of only minor importance for human physiology or medicine," said Börje Cronholm of the Karolinska Institute in his presentation speech. "However, their discoveries have been a prerequisite for the comprehensive research that is now pursued also on mammals." Moreover, Cronholm added, the laureates' work may have important implications for the "effects of abnormal psychosocial situations on the individual"—effects, he said, that "may lead not only to abnormal behavior but also to serious somatic illnesses," such as high blood pressure and heart attack. Frisch, who was eighty-seven years old at the time, was represented at the award ceremonies by his son, Otto.

Frisch has been credited with revealing unsuspected "sensory windows" through which animals perceive the world—such as the honeybee's use of color or polarized light. According to the behavioral scientists Peter Marler and Donald R. Griffin, "the revolutionary discovery was that an insect sometimes communicates with fellow members of a closely integrated society by flexible, iconic, graded gestures about distant objects that are urgently needed by the social group as a whole. Behavioral continuity between animals and men extends even to fruitful comparisons between animal communication and human language."

In 1917 Frisch married Margarethe Mohr, a nurse and artist who subsequently illustrated the published collection of his lectures; they had three daughters and a son. Frisch died on June 12, 1982.

Frisch's awards included the Magellanic Premium Award of the American Philosophical Society (1956), the Kalinga Prize given by UNESCO (1959), and the Eugenio Balzan Prize for Biology of the Balzan Foundation (1963). He was a member of the scientific academies in Munich, Vienna, Göttingen, Uppsala, Stockholm, and Washington, D.C., and a foreign member of the Royal Society of London.

SELECTED WORKS: Bees: Their Vision, Chemical Sense, and Language, 1950; The Dancing Bees, 1954; Ten Little Housemates, 1960; Man and the Living World, 1963; Biology, 1965; A Biologist Remembers, 1967; The Dance Language and Orientation of Bees, 1967; Animal Architecture, 1974, with Otto von Frisch.

ABOUT: Biographical Memoirs of Fellows of the Royal Society, volume 29, 1983; Current Biography February 1974; New York Times October 12, 1973; Science November 2, 1973; Thorpe, W. H. The Origins and Rise of Ethology, 1979.

FRISCH, RAGNAR

(March 3, 1895–January 31, 1973)
Nobel Memorial Prize in Economic
    Sciences, 1969
(shared with Jan Tinbergen)

The Norwegian economist Ragnar Anton Kittil Frisch was born in Oslo, the son of Anton Frisch and Ragna Frederikke (Kittilsen) Frisch. For many generations, the Frisch family had been goldsmiths and silversmiths, and in that tradition, Ragnar was trained by the famous Oslo firm of David Andersen and certified as a goldsmith in 1920. At his mother's insistence, he also studied at the University of Oslo, selecting economics as his major because, he said, it was "the shortest and easiest study." He received his B.A. in 1919 and left Norway the following year for graduate stud-

RAGNAR FRISCH

ies, first in France, and then in Germany, Great Britain, Italy, and the United States.

In 1925 Frisch returned to Oslo as an assistant professor of economics at the university. On completion of his dissertation in mathematical statistics (on semi-invariants and moments used in the study of statistical distributions), he received his Ph.D. in 1926. He became an associate professor in 1928 and was appointed a full professor of social economy and statistics and director of research at the Economics Institute at the University of Oslo in 1931.

Frisch based his early teaching on the work of classical economists, preparing careful notes on the works of such prominent figures as David Ricardo, Knut Wicksell, and Alfred Marshall. Although some of these economists had a thorough grounding in mathematics, they employed "literary" rather than mathematical language in presenting their theories, a style of reasoning Frisch saw as "vague and obscure." He wished to give economics a "new start," to make it more like the natural sciences by creating a theory based on mathematical and axiomatic reasoning and combining it with empirical research supported by mathematical statistics.

Frisch sought to advance this new beginning in economics in his first major work, an article published in 1926 titled "Sur un problème d'économie pure" (On a Problem of Pure Economics), in which he reformulated consumer demand theory, the branch of economic theory concerned with the behavior of individuals. His theory derived its predictions mathematically from a small number of axioms that characterized the behavior of consumers trying to maximize their utility (that is, their capacity for satisfying their wants and needs). For example, he proposed that consumers do in fact maximize their utility and that the utility function has certain nice mathematical properties. Because the axioms Frisch developed were simple and comprehensible, they could be subjected to experimental verification; later economists were able to build on his work, refining the theory and showing additional implications.

Employing the same mathematical and axiomatic reasoning, Frisch reformulated production theory, which dealt with the behavior of producers and firms. Many of his ideas on the subject reached only a limited audience, however, partly because he did not publish a good deal of his major work and partly because the originality of his ideas and the mathematical style in which they were presented made them incomprehensible to most economists of the time.

Frisch's production theory work included the characterization of production functions by use of isoquants, or combinations of inputs yielding equal levels of output. In this work, as elsewhere, he aimed at quantitative applications and statistical testing of his hypotheses, insisting that these statistical methods of analysis must be based on stringent economic theory. He published some of these ideas on production theory and its applications in 1935 in his article "The Principle of Substitution: An Example of Its Application in the Chocolate Industry." His production theory concept provided the foundation upon which later neoclassical economists built.

In his first important quantitative study, "Correlation and Scatter in Statistical Variables" (1929), Frisch explored the difficulty of establishing causal relationships in economics when observed developments are generated by the complex operations of interrelated variables, such as the problems of supply and demand for goods and services. Frisch stressed the importance of time and of changes over time; a pioneer in creating dynamic models of analysis, he influenced later work in the field, such as PAUL SAMUELSON's *Foundations of Economic Analysis* (1947). Frisch's pioneering empirical study of consumer behavior, *New Methods of Measuring Marginal Utility*, published in 1932, was followed in 1934 by his *Statistical Confluence Analysis by Means of Complete Regression Systems*. In the latter work, Frisch discussed and refined the problem of interrelationships among variables, a problem he called multicollinearity and defined as the tendency of many variables to move together because of common trends, cycles, or other shared characteristics.

Frisch created the term *econometrics* for the application of mathematics in economic theory and in empirical research. In 1930 he was instrumental in establishing the Econometric Society, an international association of mathematical economists and statisticians. For over thirty years he served as editor of the society's journal, *Econometrica*.

During the Great Depression of the 1930s, Frisch devoted increasing attention to broad problems affecting the economic performances of nations. His new concerns were reflected in a classic article published in 1933, "Propagation Problems and Impulse Problems in Dynamic Economics." This article made several major contributions to the development of business cycle analysis, including the first use of the terms *microeconomics,* used to describe individual economic behavior, and *macroeconomics,* used to describe the behavior of the whole of a national economy. Frisch's article also contained one of the earliest systems of national-income accounting, work he developed further in a 1948 mimeographed paper titled "A System of Concepts Describing the Economic Circulation and Production Process".

In both the 1933 article and a 1936 article, "On the Notion of Equilibrium and Disequilibrium," Frisch made a profound contribution toward explaining business cycles. He elucidated the acceleration principle, explaining how changes in investment and income levels can be self-reinforcing; that is, higher investment levels produce higher income levels leading to further increases in investment. His dynamic macroeconomic model showed how economic fluctuations (business cycles) could be produced by unexpected events or so-called random shocks, such as a war, a stock market panic, or a large increase in the price of an imported raw material. The duration of such fluctuations in his model varied in ways similar to the short and long business cycles of the real world.

During the Depression, Frisch was among those who first introduced the new approach to macroeconomics associated with the Swedish economist Erik Lindahl and other members of the Stockholm School and with the work of the English economist John Maynard Keynes. In 1933 Frisch published *Sparing og Cirkulasjonsregulering* (Saving and Circulation Planning), a pamphlet that anticipated many of Keynes's views on the importance of government intervention in the economy to prevent prolonged economic depressions. Frisch addressed the problem of restarting production in a depressed economy where insufficient demand discourages individual entrepreneurs from investing for fear that the products of their investment will not sell. Although its unfamiliar mathematics limited interest at the time, *Sparing* was a pioneering work in macroeconomics. Moreover, it foreshadowed many of the elements of modern planning theory later associated with the work of WASSILY LEONTIEF, TJALLING C. KOOPMANS, and LEONID KANTOROVICH.

After the election of a Norwegian Labor Party government in 1936, Frisch devoted much of his time to problems of economic planning, a concern that he pursued both before and after World War II, creating complicated linear and nonlinear programming models. Although he was generally not fervid in political matters, Frisch was imprisoned during the Nazi occupation of Norway as an outspoken opponent of Nazism and as a Jew; he happened to share a cell with the Norwegian chemist ODD HASSEL.

After the war, Frisch consulted with various governments, in Norway and around the world, particularly in India and Egypt. He developed decision models to aid economic planners, first by identifying the effects of alternative economic policies on national income and its distribution, and then by helping to formulate preference functions for choosing among economic alternatives. Much of Frisch's work on this topic remains unpublished. Nevertheless, his work and teaching had a lasting impact on the development of the Oslo School of economists who have continued his work (two internationally known figures in this group are Trygve Haavelmo and Leif Johansen).

After retiring from the University of Oslo in 1965, he continued his study of economic theory and practice. Throughout his life, Frisch enjoyed mountain climbing and other outdoor activities, in addition to his scholarly fascination with and study of bees. Over a sixty-year period, he engaged in a statistical and genetic study to improve the quality of the bee, a pursuit he once described as less a "pleasant and entertaining" recreation than "an obsession which I shall never be able to get rid of."

In 1969 Frisch and JAN TINBERGEN were awarded the first Nobel Memorial Prize in Economic Sciences "for having developed and applied dynamic models for the analysis of economic processes." In his presentation speech, Erik Lundberg of the Royal Swedish Academy of Sciences noted that "Professor Frisch's pioneer work . . . involv[ed] a dynamic formulation of the theory of cycles." He continued that Frisch "was before his time in the building of mathematical models, and he has many successors. The same is true of his contribution to methods for the statistical testing of hypotheses."

Illness prevented Frisch from attending the presentation ceremonies, but on June 17, 1970, he delivered his Nobel lecture at the University of Oslo under the title "From Utopian Theory to Practical Applications: The Case of Econometrics."

Frisch and Marie Smedal were married in 1920, and they had one daughter. His first wife died in 1952, and the following year he married Astrid Johannessen. Frisch died in Oslo in 1973.

In addition to the Nobel Prize, Frisch received the Schumpeter Prize of Harvard University (1955) and the Antonio Feltrinelli Prize of the National Academy of Sciences of Italy (1961). He was a member of the Royal Statistics Society in London, the American Economic Association, and the American Academy of Arts and Sciences.

ADDITIONAL WORKS: Principles of Linear Programming, 1954; Macroeconomics and Linear Programming, 1956; Planning for India: Selected Explorations in Methodology, 1960; Theory of Production, 1965; Economic Planning Studies: A Collection of Essays, 1976.

ABOUT: Econometrica April 1960; Science November 7, 1969; Sills, D. (ed.) International Encyclopedia of the Social Sciences: Biographical Supplement, 1979; Swedish Journal of Economics December 1969.

FUKUI, KENICHI
(October 4, 1918–   )
Nobel Prize for Chemistry, 1981
(shared with Roald Hoffmann)

The Japanese chemist Kenichi Fukui (foo-koo′ ē) was born in the city of Nara on the island of Honshū, the eldest of three sons of Chie Fukui and Ryokichi Fukui, a foreign trade merchant and factory manager. As a student in high school, young Kenichi showed little interest in chemistry, but his father persuaded him to enroll in the Department of Industrial Chemistry at Kyōto Imperial University (now Kyōto University). "It was the most decisive occurrence in my educational career," Fukui recalled later. He completed his undergradu-

KENICHI FUKUI

ate studies in 1941, and for the next three years he worked on synthetic-fuel chemistry in the Army Fuel Laboratory. In 1948 he received a Ph.D. in engineering from Kyōto University, having been appointed assistant professor three years earlier. He became full professor of physical chemistry in 1951 and has been associated with Kyōto University ever since.

Fukui's early research was diverse, including work in such areas as reaction engineering, organic synthesis by inorganic salts, and polymerization kinetics and catalysts. In the course of this work, he developed an interest in the submolecular and mathematical levels of the gross macroscopic reactions under study.

Molecules are groups of atoms held together by electrons. In chemical reactions between two or more molecules, old electron bonds break and new ones form, thus creating new entities. Often, these new substances exhibit very different properties from those of the original materials. Electrons are constantly moving around the atomic nuclei in paths called orbitals. The best-understood reactions are those in which only one bond breaks or forms at a time. However, in many so-called concerted reactions, several bonds are formed or broken simultaneously and are subject to forces not previously recognized. Every molecule has many electrons, each with its orbital encompassing the entire molecule. As described by NIELS BOHR, each orbital has a specified energy level.

Inspired by ROBERT S. MULLIKEN's theory of donor-acceptor complexes, Fukui discovered in the early 1950s that only a few of these molecular orbitals, which he called frontier orbitals, are significant in a reaction. He perceived a chemical reaction as an interaction between the highest occupied molecular orbital (HOMO) of one compound with the lowest occupied molecular orbital (LOMO) of the other compound. One molecule shares its most loosely bound electrons with another which accepts them at a site able to bind them tightly, creating a new orbital with an intermediate energy level.

Within ten years, Fukui had determined that the geometric arrangement (or symmetry) of the frontier orbitals plays an important role in chemical reactions. At the same time, ROALD HOFFMANN and R. B. WOODWARD, working independently of Fukui, had developed a set of rules to predict whether reactions of organic molecules will proceed. Because Fukui reported his theories in complicated mathematical terms in Japanese journals, they did not attract much attention elsewhere. It was the publication in 1965 of the Woodward-Hoffmann rules, which are also based on the concept of orbital symmetry, that brought recognition of the usefulness of Fukui's ideas.

As a result, Fukui and Hoffmann received the 1981 Nobel Prize for Chemistry "for their theories, developed independently, concerning the course of chemical reactions." "By use of his theory, Fukui found the laws for many groups of organic-chemical reactions," said Inga Fischer-Hjalmars of the Royal Swedish Academy of Sciences. Fischer-Hjalmars went on to offer an illustration. "Naphthalene is an important initial material in the dyestuff industry," she said. "For a long time the puzzling fact had been known that hydrogen atoms at different positions in the naphthalene molecule are reacting most unequally. The explanation came first through Fukui's theory." Moreover, Fischer-Hjalmars added, the two laureates' contributions to stereochemistry have "radically changed the conditions for the design of chemical experiments."

In subsequent work Fukui has broadened the concept of frontier orbitals, with application to three or more reacting molecules.

Fukui's American colleagues describe him as low-key, modest, and pleasant. His favorite leisure activities are walks around Kyōto, fishing, and playing golf. He and Tomoe Horie, who were married in 1947, have one son and one daughter.

Fukui was elected a senior foreign scientist of the American National Science Foundation in 1970 and, since 1982, has been president of Kyōto University of Industrial Arts and Tex-

tile Fibers. He is a member of the International Academy of Quantum Molecular Science. In 1978–1979 he was vice president of the Chemical Society in Japan and served as its president from 1983 to 1984. In addition, he participated in the United States–Japan Eminent Scientist Exchange Program in 1973 and is a member of both the European Academy of Arts, Sciences, and Humanities and the American Academy of Arts and Sciences.

SELECTED WORKS: Orientation and Stereoselection, 1970.

ABOUT: New York Times October 20, 1981; Physics Today December 1981; Science November 6, 1981.

GABOR, DENNIS
(June 5, 1900–February 9, 1979)
Nobel Prize for Physics, 1971

The Hungarian-English physicist Dennis Gabor was born in Budapest as Dénes Gábor, the oldest of three sons of Adrienne (Kálmán) and Bertalan Gábor. His mother had been an actress before she married; his father, a grandson of Russian Jewish immigrants, eventually became the director of the Hungarian General Coal Mines, then the largest industrial enterprise in Hungary. Gabor's parents took an active interest in the education of their children and created an atmosphere at home in which intellectual achievement was admired and respected. After attending the local primary school, Gabor entered Miklós Toldi State School (a high school), where he learned modern languages, mathematics, and science, and displayed a precocious grasp of physics. In their homemade laboratory, he and his brother George repeated experiments they read about in scientific books and journals.

When he was called up for military service in the Austro-Hungarian army in 1918, during the final months of World War I, Gabor joined the Officers' Training Corps and trained in artillery and horsemanship. In the fall of that year he was assigned to the Italian front. He was sent home and demobilized in November, after the defeat of the Central Powers.

On his return to Hungary, Gabor entered the Budapest Technical University, where he registered for a four-year course in mechanical engineering, since so few professional positions in the field of physics existed in Hungary. In his third year, however, he received an order to register once again for military service.

DENNIS GABOR

Opposed to the monarchy that had been restored in Hungary in 1920, he fled to Berlin to complete his studies at the Berlin Technical University, earning a diploma in engineering in 1924. During his years in Berlin he often visited the University of Berlin, where he heard lectures by such eminent scientists as MAX PLANCK, WALTHER NERNST, and MAX VON LAUE, and attended a seminar conducted by ALBERT EINSTEIN.

After receiving his doctorate in electrical engineering in 1927, Gabor worked at the physics laboratory of the Siemens and Halske Company in Siemensstadt. His work there included the invention of the quartz mercury lamp. Shortly after Hitler came to power in 1933, Gabor's contract expired and he returned to Hungary. Working without salary, he developed a new kind of fluorescent lamp, called the plasma lamp, at the laboratory of the Tungsram Electron Tube Research Institute in Budapest. Unable to sell his patent in Hungary, he decided to emigrate and try to sell it in England. In England he found employment with the British Thomson-Houston Company (BTH), where he worked from 1934 until 1948. In 1946 he became a naturalized British citizen.

At BTH, Gabor attempted to develop his plasma lamp, but after two years the project was dropped because it posed insurmountable technological difficulties. From 1937 until 1948 Gabor worked chiefly in electron optics, a field that concerns the directing and focusing of beams of electrons. During World War II, his work in this field was temporarily sidetracked

as he attempted to aid the war effort. Because he was not a British citizen at the time, Gabor was at first barred from contributing directly to war-related research. When he applied for military service, he was rejected, although his name was subsequently placed on a list of aliens with special qualifications. As such, he could continue his research but had no access to classified information. Accordingly, he worked in a research hut outside the BTH high-security area. Unaware of the development of radar, he worked on a system that he hoped would be capable of detecting airplanes by the heat of their engines.

The outbreak of the war brought many changes in Gabor's personal life too. His brother André had come for a visit in December 1938, and Gabor convinced him to remain permanently in England. He also persuaded his parents to visit England, but they returned home shortly before Hitler invaded Poland. Gabor's father died in 1942; his mother survived the war and came to live with him in 1946.

Near the end of the war, Gabor returned to his research on electron optics and began the work that was eventually to lead to the development of holography. His initial aim was to perfect the electron lens, a device that focuses beams of electrons in much the same way that a glass lens focuses beams of light. The device's primary application was in the electron microscope, which had been invented in 1933 by ERNST RUSKA. The electron microscope is similar to a light microscope. It produces a highly magnified image by directing a beam of electrons at an object and then focusing the reflected electrons onto a specially treated plate. According to quantum mechanics, electrons, like light, have wavelike properties. Because the wavelengths of fast electrons are in general much shorter than those of light, an electron microscope is able to resolve images with much finer detail than a light microscope. In the 1930s the electron microscope's resolving power was limited by flaws inherent in the electron lens. Above certain levels of magnification, the lens distorted the image, causing some of the information to be lost.

Gabor wondered whether it was possible to "take a bad electron picture, but one which contains the whole information, and correct it by optical means." In other words, he would use light to magnify and "read" a "picture" taken with electron beams. He developed the theory underlying such a technique in 1947 and 1948 and coined the term *hologram* to describe it (from the Greek *holos,* meaning complete, and *gram,* meaning written). He demonstrated the technique using beams of light rather than electrons, and in fact it is now used mainly as an optical, not an electron-optical, technique.

By taking advantage of a property of waves that is known as relative phase, a hologram is able to capture information that is absent from a normal photograph—the distance from each part of the object scene to the film. Two intersecting waves traveling through space are said to be in phase at any point where the peaks and troughs of one wave always intersect with those of the other. At such points the two waves together create a wave with an amplitude greater than that of either original wave. At other points in space, the peaks of one wave meet the troughs of the other, thus canceling each other exactly. When two waves take different paths from a light source to a film emulsion, whether the two waves are in phase when they reach the emulsion depends on the difference between the distances they have traveled.

To produce a hologram of an object, a single beam of light is split into two beams. One "daughter" beam, called the reference beam, is allowed to pass straight to the film; the other beam is reflected off the object before it strikes the film. Because the two beams travel different distances to reach the same point, they produce an interference pattern: a pattern of dark and light fringes, representing points on the film where the intersecting waves are respectively in or out of phase. The interference pattern bears no resemblance to the object, but when a single beam of light, identical to the reference beam, is aimed through the pattern, it is split into two beams identical to those that originally struck the film. When looking at these two beams, an observer sees a three-dimensional image.

The holographic effect is most pronounced when all the light waves in the original unsplit beam are completely in phase with one another. Such light, called coherent light, can be produced only by lasers. As a result, the full potential of Gabor's invention was not appreciated until the invention of the laser in 1960. Holography has found a wide range of applications, including medical imaging, mapmaking, diagnosing faults in high-speed equipment, and, most recently, information storage and computing.

In 1949 Gabor left BTH to become a reader (associate professor) in electron physics at the Imperial College of Science and Technology of the University of London. In 1958 he was appointed professor of applied electron physics. He retired in 1967 and worked as a part-

time consultant for CBS Laboratories in Stamford, Connecticut, while retaining his office and some of his privileges at Imperial College.

Gabor received the 1971 Nobel Prize for Physics "for his invention and development of the holographic method." In his Nobel lecture he struck a theme that had first concerned him during his war research, the role of science and technology in society. "We have progressed by what one could call a whole day of creation beyond the basic technology which [Alfred Nobel] and his contemporaries have created," he said. "The social consequences of the new technology are immense. . . . Many of us strongly suspect that man's nature was admirably adapted for bringing us from the jungle and the cave to the present high stage of industrial civilization—but not for staying long and happily on this height."

In retirement Gabor lectured widely, continued his own research (including work on a system for projecting three-dimensional motion pictures), and wrote papers. Although in 1974 he suffered a stroke that left him unable to read or write, he remained in touch with his colleagues and followed their work. When the Museum of Holography was opened in New York City in 1977, Gabor visited as its first member.

In 1936 Gabor married Marjorie Butler, a colleague at BTH. The couple had no children. He died in a nursing home in London on February 9, 1979.

Gabor was a fellow of the Royal Society, an honorary member of the Hungarian Academy of Sciences, and a commander of the Most Excellent Order of the British Empire. He was honored with the Thomas Young Medal of the Physical Society in London (1967), the Rumford Medal of the Royal Society of London (1968), the Albert Michelson Medal of the Franklin Institute (1968), the Medal of Honor of the Institute of Electrical and Electronics Engineers (1970), and the Holweck Prize of the French Physical Society (1971). He held honorary degrees from the University of Southampton, Delft University of Technology, the University of Surrey, the City University of New York, Columbia University, and London University.

SELECTED WORKS: The Electron Microscope, 1946; Electronic Inventions and Their Impact on Civilization, 1959; Inventing the Future, 1963; Innovations: Scientific, Technological, and Social, 1970; The Mature Society, 1972; Beyond the Age of Waste: A Report to the Club of Rome, 1978, with others.

ABOUT: Biographical Memoirs of Fellows of the Royal Society, volume 26, 1980; Current Biography October 1972; Science November 12, 1971.

GAJDUSEK, D. CARLETON
(September 9, 1923–   )
Nobel Prize for Physiology or Medicine, 1976
(shared with Baruch Blumberg)

D. CARLETON GAJDUSEK

The American pediatrician and virologist Daniel Carleton Gajdusek (got' ə chek) was born in Yonkers, New York, the first of two sons of Karl Gajdusek, a prosperous butcher of Slovakian birth who had emigrated to the United States, and Ottilia (Dobrozscky) Gajdusek, the daughter of Hungarian immigrants. "Because of my mother's unquenchable interest in literature and folklore," he recalled, "my brother and I were reared listening to Homer, Hesiod, Sophocles, Plutarch, and Virgil long before we learned to read." But unlike his brother, who became a poet and critic, Gajdusek showed an early interest in mathematics and science. As a child he enjoyed spending hours at the Boyce Thompson Institute for Plant Research in Yonkers, where his aunt, Irene Dobrozscky, was employed as an entomologist. During his high school years, he spent summers working at the institute, and his experience there led him to study physics, biology, and mathematics at the University of Rochester, which he entered in 1940 at the age of sixteen. After graduating from Rochester with a B.S. in biophysics in 1943, he was accepted at accepted at Harvard Medical School, from which he received his medical degree three years later.

Although Gajdusek had planned since childhood to be a medical researcher, he found himself drawn instead to clinical pediatrics. "Children fascinated me," he later said, "and their medical problems . . . seemed to offer more challenge than adult medicine." He pursued this interest through residencies in Boston and New York, followed by a two-year fellowship in physical chemistry at the California Institute of Technology, where he worked with LINUS C. PAULING and was greatly influenced by GEORGE W. BEADLE and MAX DELBRÜCK, among others. He conducted virology research at JOHN F. ENDERS's laboratory at Harvard from 1949 to 1952, during which time he was also a senior fellow at the National Foundation for Infantile Paralysis.

In 1952 Gajdusek was drafted and served two years at the Walter Reed Army Medical Center. After being discharged, he spent the next two years at the Pasteur Institute in Tehran, Iran, investigating epidemic diseases such as rabies, plague, and scurvy. The work led him to Australia in 1954 to conduct virology research with MACFARLANE BURNET at the Walter and Eliza Hall Institute of Medical Research in Melbourne.

While studying child development and disease patterns among native Australian and New Guinean populations, he met Vincent Zigas, an Australian public health officer. Zigas told Gajdusek about the Fore, a Stone Age tribe in the highlands of eastern New Guinea. Many of the Fore people suffered from a fatal degenerative brain disease they called kuru, which had never been scientifically described. Visiting the Fore with Zigas, Gajdusek learned their language and remained with them for almost a year while he began his studies of kuru.

In 1958 he became laboratory chief of the National Institute of Neurological and Communicative Disorders and Stroke, National Institutes of Health (NIH), in Bethesda, Maryland, but he simultaneously continued his research into the kuru problem of New Guinea, returning there at least once a year.

Gajdusek and Zigas had originally assumed that kuru was caused by a virus, but they were unable to isolate the causative agent or to infect animals with the disease using conventional virological methods. Since kuru appeared to run in families, they next began to entertain the idea that it was a complex genetic disease.

In 1959, however, William Hadlow, a veterinary neuropathologist (one who studies diseases of nerve tissue) at the NIH's Rocky Mountain Laboratory, saw the results of the kuru research and pointed out that the symptoms of kuru were similar to those of scrapie, a degenerative neurological disease of sheep. Scrapie has an extremely long incubation period—usually, years pass between exposure to the disease and appearance of symptoms—and thus it is known as a slow virus. Although scrapie could be transmitted from one animal to another, no scrapie virus had been isolated.

Gajdusek realized that he could explain the method of kuru transmission if it was also caused by a slow virus. The Fore people practiced ritual cannibalism, honoring their dead relatives by eating their brains. Such a practice would provide a direct route for transmission of the virus. In 1963 Gajdusek began implanting material from the brains of kuru victims into apes; two years later the first of the experimental animals showed symptoms of the disease. Chimpanzees were used initially, and Gajdusek was eventually able to transmit kuru to monkeys as well.

The success of these studies prompted Gajdusek and his colleagues to look for possible slow-virus causes for other degenerative brain disorders. By 1971 they had discovered that Creutzfeldt-Jakob disease (CJD) could be transmitted to animals. This rare degenerative brain disease has symptoms similar to those of kuru and is found all over the world.

Gajdusek's studies of scrapie, kuru, and CJD indicated that slow-virus diseases share important characteristics in addition to their long incubation period. Whereas ordinary viral infections normally cause a pronounced immune response characterized by inflammation, fever, and the production of antibodies and interferon, slow viruses do not seem to induce any such response.

The most startling and controversial aspect of slow viruses is their composition. Other known viruses are made of a small amount of nucleic acid—deoxyribonucleic acid (DNA) or ribonucleic acid (RNA)—wrapped in a protein coat. The protein acts as a vehicle for transport of the nucleic acid into the host cell, where it can take over the cell's machinery to produce more viruses. Slow viruses, however, are not inactivated by such treatments as formaldehyde, ultraviolet light, or high temperature, which destroy nucleic acids and thus render most viruses noninfectious. Viruses can be extremely small, but they are not invisible to the electron microscope. In electron microscope studies of slow-virus diseases, however, no viruslike particle has been found.

These factors persuaded Gajdusek and other researchers that slow viruses may be representative of a fundamentally new agent of disease: the infectious protein. Certain small strands of protein found in slow-virus-infected brains are thought to cause the disease. It is not yet known, however, whether the deviation producing the abnormal form or quantity of these apparently normal cellular proteins is due to a cellular disturbance or to an unusual property of the protein (for instance, the ability of a cell to reproduce itself). The protein strands are remarkably similar to structures that form in the brain of individuals with Alzheimer's disease and senile dementia, disorders in which changes in the brain result in mental deterioration; these diseases may be caused by a slow virus or by a spontaneous defect that parallels the action of slow viruses.

Gajdusek shared the 1976 Nobel Prize for Physiology or Medicine with BARUCH S. BLUMBERG "for their discoveries concerning new mechanisms for the origin and dissemination of infectious dieases." Gajdusek was given the award not specifically for his discovery of the origin of kuru but because his research resulted "in the identification of a new class of human diseases caused by unique infectious agents," according to the presentation speech delivered by Erling Norrby of the Karolinska Institute.

Gajdusek continues to work at the NIH, alternating laboratory work on slow viruses with field trips to Micronesia, Melanesia, and New Guinea. A man of wide knowledge and interests, Gajdusek is also noted for his expertise in anthropology and child behavioral science. Although unmarried, he has adopted twenty-seven boys and one girl from various Pacific cultures, several of whose languages he speaks in addition to Russian, German, French, Spanish, and Slovak. He donated a large portion of his collection of primitive art to the Salem Peabody Museum in Massachusetts.

In addition to the Nobel Prize, Gajdusek has received the Mead Johnson Award of the American Academy of Pediatrics (1963). He is a member of the Society for Pediatric Research, the American Pediatric Society, the National Academy of Sciences, the American Academy of Arts and Sciences, the American Philosophical Society, and the American Academy of Neurology. He holds honorary memberships in the Colombia Academy of Medicine, the Slovak Academy of Medicine, and the Mexican Academy of Medicine.

SELECTED WORKS: Field Journals (35 vols.) 1954–1982; Studies on Kuru (6 vols.) 1961, with Vincent Zigas; Slow, Latent and Temperate Virus Infections, 1965; Kuru: Early Letters and Field Notes, 1981.

ABOUT: Current Biography June 1981; Hammond, A. (ed.) A Passion to Know, 1984; Nature October 1976; Omni March 1986; Science November 26, 1976.

GALSWORTHY, JOHN
(August 14, 1867–January 31, 1933)
Nobel Prize for Literature, 1932

The English novelist, dramatist, and poet John Galsworthy was born in Combe, Surrey, into a conventional upper-middle-class family. The only son of John Galsworthy, a wealthy solicitor and company director in London, and Blanche (Bartleet) Galsworthy, he was educated at Harrow and at Oxford University. Although called to the bar in 1890, he never settled into a practice, preferring the leisured pursuits of the well-to-do, including reading and travel. During a voyage around the world, which he undertook ostensibly to learn about maritime law, Galsworthy met Joseph Conrad, who became a lifelong friend.

At the age of twenty-eight, Galsworthy embarked on a writing career with the encouragement of Ada Galsworthy, who was unhappily married to his cousin, Arthur, and with whom Galsworthy began a liaison. Laboriously training himself to write, in 1897 he published his first work, *From the Four Winds,* a collection of short stories, under the pseudonym John Sinjohn. His first novel, *Jocelyn,* appeared the following year; his second, *Villa Rubein,* was published in 1900. Another collection of short stories, which was issued the next year, included members of the fictional Forsyte family he was to immortalize in later works. Influenced by the literary techniques of Ivan Turgenev, Guy de Maupassant, and Leo Tolstoy, Galsworthy spent three years writing and rewriting his fifth book, *The Island of Pharisees* (1904), the first work published under his own name.

With the death of his father in December 1904, Galsworthy became financially independent. He and Ada set up house, and when her divorce decree became final the next year, they were married. The relief of living openly together, after nine years of being ostracized by family and friends, inspired Galsworthy to finish *The Man of Property* (1906), in which he depicted Ada's unhappy marriage through the relationship of Soames and Irene Forsyte.

JOHN GALSWORTHY

The novel, which established Galsworthy's reputation as an important writer, became the most widely read and highly regarded of his works. According to Dudley Barker, Galsworthy claimed that "in these pages he had pickled the upper middle class." *The Man of Property* was the first volume in what was to become a trilogy known as *The Forsyte Saga.* Galsworthy did not return to the Forsytes until after World War I, but in the meantime, he published *The Country House* (1907), about the gentry; *The Fraternity* (1909), about the intelligentsia; and *The Patrician* (1911), about the aristocracy.

The production of his first completed play, *The Silver Box*, in September 1906, brought Galsworthy additional recognition as a dramatist. The most successful of the plays he wrote before World War I were *The Silver Box* and *Strife,* produced in 1909, and *Justice,* produced in 1910. All three were realistic plays attacking social abuses; the last, directed against solitary confinement of criminals, led WINSTON CHURCHILL, then home secretary, to assert that *Justice* had been an important influence on his program for prison reform.

Galsworthy gave away at least half of his income to humanitarian causes and worked actively for social reform, campaigning for revised censorship and divorce laws, a minimum wage, women's suffrage, and slum clearance. Even in his final illness he remembered to specify that his Nobel Prize money should be given to the PEN (Poets, Essayists, Novelists)

Club, the international writers' organization that he founded in October 1921.

Galsworthy refused a knighthood in 1917 in the belief that writers and social critics should not accept titles. Early the following year he published five short stories titled *Five Tales,* one of which, "The Indian Summer of a Forsyte," led him back to the history of the Forsyte family. *In Chancery,* the second volume of *The Forsyte Saga,* appeared in 1920, and *To Let,* the last of the trilogy, in 1921. The one-volume edition of *The Forsyte Saga,* published in 1922, sold widely and made Galsworthy a major literary figure in England and the United States.

Writing faithfully each morning, Galsworthy produced a sizable body of work that comprises 20 novels, 27 plays, 3 collections of poetry, 173 short stories, 5 collections of essays, at least 700 letters, and many sketches and miscellaneous works.

He completed a second trilogy dealing with the Forsytes, called *A Modern Comedy,* in 1928; it was published posthumously in one volume in 1929. His last trilogy, a study of the Charwell family, was collected by his wife and published in 1933 in a one-volume edition entitled *End of the Chapter.*

Galsworthy was awarded the Order of Merit of England in 1929. In 1932 he received the Nobel Prize for Literature "for his distinguished art of narration, which takes its highest form in *The Forsyte Saga.*" "The novelist has carried the history of his time through three generations," said Anders Österling of the Swedish Academy in making the presentation, "and his success in mastering so excellently his enormously difficult material, both in its scope and in its depth, remains an extremely memorable feat in English literature." Österling congratulated Galsworthy for revealing behind the stories of individual characters "the dark fabric of historical events," the "transformation and the dissolution of the Victorian age up to our days." Österling compared Galsworthy's charm as a narrator with that of Turgenev, praising him for a sense of irony that is "friendly to life, springing from warmth, interest, and humanity." Galsworthy was too ill from a brain tumor to attend the award ceremony; he died less than two months later.

After his death, Galsworthy's reputation declined sharply. Among his most devastating critics were D. H. Lawrence and Virginia Woolf. Accusing Galsworthy and his contemporaries Arnold Bennett and H. G. Wells of propagandizing, Woolf wrote, "In order to complete [their books], it seems necessary to do something—to join a society or more desperately, to write a check." Writing in *The Spectator* in 1963, the British critic Bernard Bergonzi observed that "defiance of convention had, perhaps, made [Galsworthy] a novelist, but once he was established he was entirely repossessed by all the fundamental assumptions of his class and upbringing. . . . He continued . . . to be an excellent storyteller-. . . . But once he ceased to be a satirist, his work lost all emotional coherence." British novelist Anthony Burgess, in a 1969 article in the *New York Times Magazine,* similarly viewed Galsworthy as a successful man of letters who was not possessed to write out of any passionate convictions. "He influenced giants like THOMAS MANN, was read in France and taken seriously in Russia," said Burgess, "but in his native England he ruled chiefly in the hearts of the middlebrows. The intellectuals spurned him." For Burgess, Galsworthy is one of the many British writers of the period "who cared less about words than what lay behind the words." Although Galsworthy's values and literary techniques may seem old-fashioned in an era in which alienation and social nihilism are dominant themes, he "will come to be recognized as the last important Victorian novelist," according to the American critic Earl E. Stevens.

During his lifetime Galsworthy received honorary degrees from Trinity College, Dublin University; St. Andrews, Cambridge, Oxford, and Princeton universities; and the universities of Manchester and Sheffield.

ADDITIONAL WORKS: A Man of Devon, 1901; A Commentary, 1908; Joy, 1909; A Motley, 1910; Moods, Songs, and Doggerels, 1912; The Inn of Tranquility, 1912; The Pigeon, 1912; The Eldest Son, 1912; The Little Man, 1913; The Dark Flower, 1913; The Fugitive, 1913; The Mob, 1914; The Freelands, 1915; A Bit o' Love, 1915; A Sheaf, 1916; Beyond, 1917; Another Sheaf, 1919; The Burning Spear, 1919; Saint's Progress, 1919; The Foundations, 1920; Tatterdemalion, 1920; The Skin Game, 1920; The Awakening, 1920; The Bells of Peace, 1921; Loyalties, 1922; Windows, 1922; Captures, 1923; Abracadabra, 1924; The Forest, 1924; The White Monkey, 1924; Old English, 1924; The Show, 1925; Verses Old and New, 1926; The Silver Spoon, 1926; Escape, 1926; Castles in Spain, 1927; Swan Song, 1928; Exiled, 1929; The Roof, 1929; On Forsyte Change, 1930; The Creation of Character in Literature, 1931; Maid in Waiting, 1931; Candelabra, 1932; Over the River, 1933; Collected Poems, 1934; Forsytes, Pendyces, and Others, 1935.

ABOUT: Barker, D. The Man of Principle: A View of John Galsworthy, 1963; Coats, R. H. John Galsworthy as a Dramatic Artist, 1926; Dupont, V. John Galsworthy: The Dramatic Artist, 1942; Dupre, C. John Galsworthy: A Biography, 1976; Frechet, A. John Galsworthy: A Reassessment, 1982; Galsworthy, A. Over the Hills and Far Away, 1938; Gindin, J. The English Climate, 1979; Gindin, J. John

Galsworthy's Life and Art, 1987; Huang, J. Shaw and Galsworthy, 1976; Hynes, S. The Edwardian Turn of Mind, 1968; Kaye-Smith, S. John Galsworthy, 1916; Marrot, H. V. The Life and Letters of John Galsworthy, 1935; Mottram, R. H. For Some We Loved, 1956; Ould, H. John Galsworthy, 1934; Reynolds, M. E. Memories of John Galsworthy, 1936; Sauter, R. Galsworthy the Man, 1967.

GARCÍA MÁRQUEZ, GABRIEL
(March 6, 1928–)
Nobel Prize for Literature, 1982

GABRIEL GARCÍA MÁRQUEZ

The Colombian novelist, short story writer, and journalist Gabriel José García Márquez (gär sē′ ä mär′ kes), the eldest of sixteen children, was born in Aracataca, a banana port on the Caribbean coast of Colombia. When he was an infant, his father, a low-paid telegraph operator, moved with his wife to another town, leaving the boy to be raised by his maternal grandparents until the age of eight. García Márquez was particularly close to his grandmother, the source of many of the legends and myths that later influenced the content and style of his fiction. His grandfather was a former colonel who, according to García Márquez, "told endless stories of the civil war of his youth, took me to the circus and the cinema, and was my umbilical cord with history and reality."

After his grandfather's death in 1936, García Márquez studied briefly in Barranquilla until he received a scholarship that enabled him to attend school in the town of Zipaquirá, near Bogotá, where he earned a *bachillerato,* roughly equivalent to a junior college degree in the United States. He entered the Colombian National University as a law student in 1947, the year his first story, "La tercera resignación" (The Third Resignation), was published in *El Espectador* (The Spectator), a Bogotá newspaper. Over the next six years, about a dozen of his short stories appeared in this paper. Moving to Cartagena in 1948, he continued his law studies, and two years later he became a reporter in Barranquilla for *El Heraldo* (The Herald), for which he wrote a regular column, "La jirafa" (The Giraffe). In 1954 he moved to Bogotá to take a full-time position with *El Espectador.*

It was in 1955 that García Márquez's career as a serious writer of fiction began, with the publication of the novella *La hojarasca.* This work was published in English as *Leaf Storm* in the volume *Leaf Storm and Other Stories* (1972). Meanwhile, *El Espectador* ran a series of fourteen articles he had written on the experiences of a young sailor, revealing that a Colombian naval ship had carried contraband. The revelation was so embarrassing to the government that it shut down the newspaper, leaving García Márquez temporarily stranded in Europe, where he had been sent as a correspondent.

In 1958 García Márquez married Mercedes Barcha; they have two sons, Rodrigo and Gonzales.

After working as a free-lance journalist in Europe for two years, García Márquez joined Prensa Latina, the official Cuban news agency. In 1961 he moved to Mexico City, where he supported himself by writing screenplays and magazine articles while composing fiction in his spare time. His novella *El coronel no tiene quien le escriba* appeared in 1961, followed the next year by a collection of short stories, *Los funerales de le Mamá Grande.* The title story of this collection, "Big Mama's Funeral," and the 1961 novella were published in English in 1968 under the title *No One Writes to the Colonel and Other Stories.*

It was the appearance in 1967 of *Cien años de soledad* (*One Hundred Years of Solitude*), however, that won García Márquez commercial success. Hailed by PABLO NERUDA as "perhaps the greatest revelation in the Spanish language since Cervantes's *Don Quixote,*" the novel's first edition sold out within a week and provoked what Mario Vargas Llosa, a leading Peruvian author, called "a literary earthquake throughout Latin America." In this novel, the fictional village of Macondo (modeled closely after García Márquez's childhood village of Aracataca) serves as a microcosm of Latin

America, and its founder and his descendants represent the history of the world. *One Hundred Years of Solitude* is "a vast jungle of a novel," wrote the American critic William McPherson, "at once so rich, so dense, and so extravagant as to be overwhelming; a fabulous creation of magic and metaphor and myth."

His next novel, *El otoño del patriarca* (*The Autumn of the Patriarch*, 1975), is a fictionalized portrait of a Latin American dictator, seen from shifting points of view and related in a deliberately hyperbolic style. *Crónica de una muerte anunciada* (*Chronicle of a Death Foretold*) appeared in 1981. Innovative in form, it recounts a murder through the varying and unreliable accounts of eyewitnesses.

The following year, García Márquez received the 1982 Nobel Prize for Literature "for his novels and short stories, in which the fantastic and the realistic are combined in a richly composed world of imagination, reflecting a continent's life and conflicts." "For a long time, Latin American literature has shown a vigor as in few other literary spheres," remarked Lars Gyllensten of the Swedish Academy in his presentation speech. In the fiction of García Márquez, Gyllensten said, "Folk culture, . . . currents from Spanish baroque . . . , influences from European surrealism and other modernism are blended into a spiced and life-giving brew." Gyllensten also pointed out that "García Márquez is strongly committed politically on the side of the poor and the weak against oppression and economic exploitation."

In his Nobel lecture, García Márquez underscored the theme of oppression and exploitation by reviewing political conditions in Central and South America. "I dare to think," he added, "that it is this . . . reality, and not just its literary expression, that has deserved the attention of the Swedish Academy." In conclusion, he affirmed the writer's responsibility to "engage in the creation" of a utopia "where no one will be able to decide for others how they die, where love will prove true and happiness be possible, and where the races condemned to 100 years of solitude on earth will have, at last and forever, a second opportunity on earth."

Although García Márquez continues to live in Mexico City, he also spends part of his time in Cartagena, near his birthplace. He is said to be a personal friend of Fidel Castro, despite his reservations about life in Cuba, where he is a frequent visitor.

His experiences as a child growing up on Colombia's Caribbean coast left an indelible mark on García Márquez's fiction. "It seems that the greatest force at work on the imagination of Márquez . . . is the memory of his grandmother," wrote the English novelist Salman Rushdie in the *London Review of Books*. Yet "many, more formal antecedents have been suggested for his art," Rushdie added. "He himself admitted the influence of [WILLIAM] FAULKNER, and the world of his fabulous Macondo is at least partly Yoknapatawpha County transported into the Colombian jungles." Other critics have cited as influences on García Márquez writers as diverse as John Dos Passos, Virginia Woolf, ALBERT CAMUS, and ERNEST HEMINGWAY.

A few critics, however, have questioned whether García Márquez deserves to be considered a great writer and whether his principal book, *One Hundred Years of Solitude*, will prove to be an enduring masterpiece. Writing in *Commentary*, the American critic Joseph Epstein praised the novelist's skill as a teller of tales but found that his "nonstop virtuosity tends to pall." "Outside of his politics," Epstein remarked, "García Márquez's stories and novels have no moral center; they inhabit no moral universe."

Reviewing *Chronicle of a Death Foretold* in the *Times Literary Supplement*, Bill Buford found it a "work that clearly established Márquez as one of the most accomplished and the most 'magical' of political novelists writing today." "His works are illumined by flashes of irony and the belief that human values are perennial," said George R. McMurray in *Gabriel García Márquez* (1977). His work, McMurray stated, "captures simultaneously the essence of both Latin American and universal man."

ADDITIONAL WORKS IN ENGLISH TRANSLATION: Innocent Erendira and Other Stories, 1978; In Evil Hour, 1979; Collected Stories, 1984; The Story of a Shipwrecked Sailor, 1986.

ABOUT: Brotherson, G. The Emergence of the Latin American Novel, 1979; Dohmann, B., and Harss, L. Into the Mainstream, 1967; Gallagher, D. P. Modern Latin American Literature, 1973; Guibert, R. Seven Voices, 1973; Jaksic, I., and Rogachevesky, J. R. Politics and the Novel in Latin America, 1980; Janes, R. Gabriel García Márquez, 1981; McMurray, G. R. Gabriel García Márquez, 1977; Plimpton, G. (ed.) Writers at Work, volume 6, 1984; Pritchett, V. S. The Myth Makers, 1979; Rodman, S. Tongues of Fallen Angels, 1974; Williams, R. L. Gabriel García Márquez, 1984.

GARCÍA ROBLES, ALFONSO
(March 20, 1911–)
Nobel Prize for Peace, 1982
(shared with Alva Myrdal)

The Mexican diplomat Alfonso García Robles (gär sē′ ä rôb′ les) was born in Zamora, the capital of the state of Michoacán, to Quirino and Theresa Robles García. Although he originally planned to become a priest, he decided instead to enroll in the law faculty of the National University of Mexico in Mexico City, graduating in 1933 with a degree in international law and international relations. He pursued postgraduate studies at the University of Paris from 1934 to 1937 and at the International Law Academy at The Hague in 1938. The following year, while still in Europe, he joined the Mexican foreign service and was posted to the Mexican embassy in Sweden for two years.

Returning to Mexico in 1941, García Robles was appointed head of the Department of International Organizations, later becoming director-general of Political Affairs and Diplomatic Service. In 1945 he served on the Mexican delegation to the San Francisco Conference, at which the United Nations was created. Granted a leave of absence the following year to join the United Nations Secretariat in New York City, he served until 1957 as director of the organization's Division of Political Affairs.

While leading a United Nations mission to the Middle East in 1949, García Robles met Juana Maria de Szyszlo, a Peruvian delegate, and they married the following year. They have two sons, Alfonso and Fernando.

Upon his return to Mexico in 1957, García Robles was named head of the Department for Europe, Asia, and Africa in the Ministry of Foreign Affairs. In this capacity, he played a major role in the international Law of the Sea conferences of 1958 and 1960. From 1962 to 1964 he was Mexico's ambassador to Brazil.

Alarmed by the Cuban missile crisis of 1962, García Robles conceived of a treaty that would establish Latin America as a nuclear-free zone. Its purpose would be twofold: "to avoid any possibility of a recurrence of the Cuban experience in some other country of Latin America," as he later said, and "to preclude even the relatively remote possibility of a nuclear arms race among the countries of the region." In April 1963 the presidents of Bolivia, Brazil, Chile, Ecuador, and Mexico signed a joint declaration endorsing his proposal, and in November the United Nations General Assembly

ALFONSO GARCÍA ROBLES

also adopted such a resolution. Despite these initial endorsements, however, the movement for the treaty began to lose momentum. Undeterred, García Robles, who in 1964 became Mexico's under secretary for foreign affairs, played a crucial role in convening a conference of Latin American diplomats in Mexico City to lay the groundwork for a treaty. From November 1964 to February 1967, a series of negotiations was held, involving representatives from twenty-one Latin American nations, to hammer out the details of the agreement. García Robles himself was coauthor of the final draft. The resulting Treaty for the Prohibition of Nuclear Weapons in Latin America—also known as the Treaty of Tlatelolco—was signed by representatives of fourteen nations on February 14, 1967, in Tlatelolco Plaza, the site of the Mexican Ministry of Foreign Affairs in Mexico City. Ten more Latin American nations have since signed, although three of the most powerful signatories—Argentina, Brazil, and Chile—have not officially recognized the treaty as being in force. Great Britain, the United States, the Soviet Union, the People's Republic of China, France, and the Netherlands have signed additional protocols to the treaty agreeing not to use nuclear weapons in the region and not to introduce them there.

Later in 1967, García Robles led the Mexican delegation to the United Nations Disarmament Conference in Geneva, where he worked closely with ALVA MYRDAL, among others. As an experienced negotiator with a reputation for fairness, patience, and persistence, García Robles was chosen to be coauthor of the 1968 Nuclear Nonproliferation Treaty, which has since been signed by more than 115 nations.

From 1970 to 1975 García Robles served as Mexico's ambassador to the United Nations. In December 1975 he was appointed his country's foreign minister by President Luis Echeverría Álvarez. At his own request, the following year he was named Mexico's permanent representative to the United Nations Disarmament Committee in Geneva by Echeverría's successor, President José López Portillo. García Robles continued his efforts to encourage the superpowers to compromise on disarmament issues. At a special United Nations General Assembly session in 1982, he introduced a motion calling for the United Nations to initiate a world disarmament crusade. Although the motion was not adopted, the idea of such a crusade received widespread support, and during the summer of 1982, massive antinuclear demonstrations were held throughout the United States and Europe.

García Robles and Alva Myrdal were jointly awarded the 1982 Nobel Prize for Peace in recognition of their work for international disarmament. In his presentation address, Egil Aarvik of the Norwegian Nobel Committee noted that "in international disarmament work García Robles bears a name that is truly illustrious." As "the driving force behind the [Treaty of Tlatelolco]," Aarvik continued, García Robles helped shape an agreement that took "a realistic view of the destructive power inherent in nuclear arms." In his Nobel lecture, García Robles recounted "the genesis and the provisions" of the Treaty of Tlatelolco, reminding his audience that "the Latin American nuclear-weapon–free zone has the privilege of being the only one in existence which covers densely inhabited territories."

In 1985 García Robles was elected chairman of the United Nations Disarmament Committee. A prolific writer, described by his friends as "obsessed" with the cause of nuclear disarmament, García Robles has, over the course of his long diplomatic career, written twenty books and more than 300 hundred articles on foreign affairs.

WORKS IN ENGLISH TRANSLATION: The Denuclearization of Latin America, 1967; The Latin America Nuclear-Weapon–Free Zone, 1979; Nuclear Disarmament: A Crucial Issue for the Survival of Mankind, 1984.

ABOUT: New York Times October 14, 1982; Time October 25, 1982; United States Arms Control and Disarmament Agency. Arms Control and Disarmament Agreements, 1984.

GARD, ROGER MARTIN DU
See MARTIN DU GARD, ROGER

GASSER, HERBERT S.
(July 5, 1888–May 11, 1963)
Nobel Prize for Physiology or Medicine, 1944
(shared with Joseph Erlanger)

The American physiologist Herbert Spencer Gasser was born in Platteville, Wisconsin, to Herman Gasser, a physician who had emigrated to the United States from the Austrian Tirol, and the former Jane Elizabeth Griswold, a native of Connecticut and a teacher in the Platteville Normal School, which young Gasser later attended. Gasser then entered the University of Wisconsin, where he majored in zoology; he received a B.A. in 1910 and an M.A. in 1911. Remaining at Wisconsin, he began graduate work in the university's physiology department, which had recently been reorganized and equipped by JOSEPH ERLANGER. To support himself Gasser worked as an assistant instructor in physiology, and during that period he published several scientific papers on the biochemical and neurological signals that regulate heart rate.

After completing the two-year medical course, Gasser transferred to the Johns Hopkins School of Medicine to complete his medical degree, which he received in 1915. He returned to Wisconsin and taught pharmacology for a year before joining Erlanger at Washington University School of Medicine in St. Louis, where Erlanger had become chairman of the physiology department. Gasser and Erlanger shared many research interests, including the study of the electrical properties of nerve signals.

The fact that nerve impulses (or action potentials) are electrical had been known since the late eighteenth century. The action potential of a single nerve cell is extremely brief, often only a few thousandths of a second in duration; it is also very weak, consisting of electrical potential changes of only a few microvolts. Therefore, instruments to study these impulses must be highly sensitive and responsive. While still at Johns Hopkins, Gasser and H. Sidney Newcomer, a colleague from Wisconsin, had begun to amplify the electrical signals from individual nerve fibers with vacuum

HERBERT S. GASSER

tubes similar to those used by GUGLIELMO MARCONI in the first radios.

Their research was interrupted by Gasser's move to St. Louis. During World War I, Gasser and Erlanger concentrated their research on the traumatic shock that follows loss of blood. Concurrently, Gasser performed pharmacological research in the Chemical Warfare Service in Washington, D.C. When the war ended, he and Newcomer published their results on amplified nerve impulses. These experiments had used a conventional string galvanometer (an instrument for measuring current by electromagnetic action) to record amplified electrical signals from individual nerve fibers. Although this system could be used to study the sequence of signals in a nerve—as EDGAR D. ADRIAN had done in his groundbreaking studies of the behavior of single nerve cells—string galvanometers were not sufficiently sensitive to record the action potential as much more than a spike (the main deflection of the oscillographic tracing of the action potential wave). An instrument that could analyze a rapid sequence of events was needed to resolve the action potential itself into distinct components.

By 1920 the Western Electric Company had invented an especially sensitive cathode-ray oscillograph, an instrument for recording vibrations or fluctuations. Because the company was reluctant to sell Gasser and Erlanger a cathode-ray tube (the sort of device now used in television sets), the physiologists built their own, using a collection of laboratory equipment and great effort and ingenuity. By linking the mechanism to an amplifier, they were able to record the time course of individual nerve impulses for the first time.

The recordings of action potentials from visible nerves did not produce as clear-cut a picture as Gasser and Erlanger had expected. Nevertheless, by careful experimentation they were able to demonstrate that what had previously appeared to be a single action potential was in fact a collection of impulses from different types of nerves bound together in a single fiber. Their studies of different nerves demonstrated that action potentials move faster in thick axons (the propagating fibers of nerve cells) than in thin ones, thus confirming a hypothesis proposed in 1907 by the Swedish physiologist Gustaf Göthlin but never before tested. Through their research, Gasser and his colleagues elucidated the action potential in unprecedented detail. They showed that different sensations tend to be transmitted by axons of different widths and therefore at different rates. Touch, for example, may be carried by thick, fast nerves, while pain is transmitted by thin, slow nerves. These differences are not entirely consistent, for a given sensation may be conducted at a variety of speeds, and a particular nerve fiber size may correspond to axons carrying different types of sensations. Their findings were later incorporated in the theory of nerve conduction developed by ALAN HODGKIN and ANDREW HUXLEY.

Gasser was appointed professor of pharmacology at Washington University in 1921. On academic leave in 1923–1925, Gasser studied in Europe, where he worked with a number of notable researchers, including ARCHIBALD V. HILL and HENRY H. DALE. In 1931 he became professor of physiology and head of the Cornell University Medical College. After four years at Cornell he was invited to become director of the Rockefeller Institute for Medical Research (now Rockefeller University). Although he was able to continue his work on the properties of nerve trunks, most of his time was devoted to administrative responsibilities during a time of economic depression that strained the institute's resources. With the outbreak of World War II, many research projects were interrupted by war-related work.

Gasser and Erlanger received the 1944 Nobel Prize for Physiology or Medicine "for their discoveries relating to the highly differentiated functions of single nerve fibers." Because of the war, there were no awards ceremonies in Stockholm that year. In a lecture broadcast by radio, however, RAGNAR GRANIT of the Karolinska Institute described the two scientists' achievements and the contributions they had made to the physiology of nerves. When ceremonies were resumed the following year, Gasser delivered a Nobel lecture entitled "Mammalian Nerve Fibers."

After his retirement from Rockefeller in 1953, Gasser pursued his research, making use of the electron microscope to delineate nerve differentiation in ever greater detail. Gasser, who remained unmarried, was known for his personal charm, his hospitality, and his warm interest in his friends. A stroke left him physically impaired during the final years of his life.

Between 1936 and 1937 Gasser served as editor of the *Journal of Experimental Medicine.* He was a member of the National Academy of Sciences, the American Association for the Advancement of Science, the American Physiological Society, the American Society for Pharmacology and Experimental Therapeutics, the Association of American Physicians, the American Philosophical Society, and the Harvey Society. He received honorary degrees from the universities of Rochester, Wisconsin, Pennsylvania, and Paris, among others.

SELECTED WORKS: Physical and Chemical Changes in Nerve During Activity, 1934, with others; Electrical Signs of Nervous Activity, 1937, with Joseph Erlanger; Symposium on the Synapse, 1939, with others.

ABOUT: Biographical Memoirs of Fellows of the Royal Society, volume 10, 1964; Dictionary of Scientific Biography, volume 5, 1972; Experimental Neurology, supplement 1, 1964; Haymaker, W., and Schiller, W. The Founders of Neurology, 1970; National Cyclopedia of American Biography, volume E, 1938; Scientific Monthly August 1935.

GELL-MANN, MURRAY
(September 15, 1929–)
Nobel Prize for Physics, 1969

The American physicist Murray Gell-Mann (gel' män) was born in New York City, the youngest son of Arthur and Pauline (Reichstein) Gell-Mann, both Austrian immigrants. He entered Yale University at the age of fifteen and, after receiving a B.S. there in 1948, went on to the Massachusetts Institute of Technology, where he obtained a Ph.D. in physics in 1951. Following a year at the Institute for Advanced Study in Princeton, New Jersey, he went to the University of Chicago, where he worked with ENRICO FERMI and was

MURRAY GELL-MANN

an instructor (1952–1953), an assistant professor (1953–1954), and an associate professor of physics (1954–1955).

In the 1950s subatomic physics, Gell-Mann's field of interest, was in a confusing state. The fundamental experimental tools of subatomic physics were particle accelerators, which fired beams of particles at stationary targets; the resulting collisions produced other particles. In this way, investigators had created many more kinds of subatomic particles than the protons, neutrons, and electrons with which they were familiar. Theoretical physicists were still struggling to devise an ordering framework into which the newly created particles could fit.

As the number of particles grew, several were found to exhibit what was called "strange" behavior. The rate at which they were created in certain collisions with other particles suggested that their behavior was governed by the strong nuclear force, which characteristically acts very rapidly. (The strong force, the weak nuclear force, electromagnetism, and gravity make up the four fundamental forces that are believed to underlie all phenomena.) The strange particles took a surprisingly long time to decay, however, which should not have been the case if they were governed by the strong force. The rate at which they decayed seemed to indicate that this process was governed by the much slower weak force.

It was to this puzzle that Gell-Mann turned his attention. His starting point was a concept called charge independence, a method of grouping certain particles in a way that emphasizes their similarities. For example, although the proton and the neutron differ in their electric charge (the proton has a charge of $+1$ and the neutron has a charge of 0), they are virtually identical in every other respect. Thus, they can be thought of as two varieties of a single kind of particle called the nucleon, which has an average charge, or charge center, of $+\frac{1}{2}$. The proton and the neutron are said to form a doublet. Other particles can be placed in similar doublets or in groups of three called triplets, or they can be said to stand alone in singlets. (The general term for a group of such particles is *multiplet*.)

Similar arrangements had been tried with the strange particles but none had been satisfactory. Devising his own scheme for grouping the strange particles, Gell-Mann found that the charge centers of multiplets of strange particles differed from $+\frac{1}{2}$, the charge center of the nucleon doublet. He thought that this displacement might represent a fundamental quality of the strange particles, and he proposed a new quantum property of particles called the strangeness number. For algebraic reasons, the strangeness of a particle is equal to twice the amount by which the charge center of that particle's multiplet differs from $+\frac{1}{2}$. Gell-Mann showed that strangeness is conserved in all interactions governed by the strong force; in other words, the total strangeness of all the particles that exist before a strong interaction must be exactly equal to the total strangeness of all the particles that exist after the interaction.

Conservation of strangeness explains why the decay of strange particles cannot be governed by the strong force. Strange particles are produced in pairs when certain other, nonstrange particles collide. They are created in such a way that the strangeness of one particle exactly cancels that of the other—for example, one particle will have a strangeness of $+1$ if the other has a strangeness of -1—and therefore the total strangeness before and after the collision of the initial, nonstrange particles is 0. After the strange particles are created, they move apart. An isolated strange particle cannot decay by means of the strong interaction if its decay would leave particles having no strangeness, because that would violate the conservation of strangeness. Gell-Mann showed that electromagnetic interactions (which have a characteristic time of action between that of the strong and weak interactions) also conserve strangeness; thus strange particles, once they have been created, survive until they decay by means of the weak interaction, which

does not conserve strangeness. Gell-Mann published his ideas in 1953.

In 1955 Gell-Mann joined the faculty of the California Institute of Technology as an associate professor; the following year he became a full professor, and in 1967 he was named Robert A. Millikan Professor of Physics.

In 1961 Gell-Mann found that the system of multiplets he had devised to describe the strange particles could be subsumed under a much more general theoretical framework that enabled him to group all the strongly interacting particles into "families." He called this scheme the eightfold way (a reference to the eight attributes of right living in the Buddhist faith) because some particles were grouped into families having eight members. The classification scheme is also known as $SU(3)$ symmetry. The Israeli physicist Yuval Ne'eman independently proposed a similar system a short time later.

Gell-Mann's construction of the eightfold way is often compared to Dmitry Mendeleev's construction of the periodic table of the elements, in which individual chemical elements are grouped into families of elements that have similar properties. Just as Mendeleev left certain spaces in the periodic table empty, predicting the specific properties of the new elements that would be found to fill those spaces, so Gell-Mann left spaces empty in some families of particles and predicted that particles would be discovered that had the correct ensemble of properties to fill the gaps. His theory was partially confirmed with the 1964 discovery of the so-called omega-minus particle, whose existence he had predicted.

In 1963, while a visiting professor at the Massachusetts Institute of Technology, Gell-Mann discovered that the particular structure of the eightfold way can be explained by assuming that every strongly interacting particle consists of some triplet of particles, each having a fraction of the proton's electric charge. The American physicist George Zweig, working independently at CERN (the European Organization for Nuclear Research), made the same discovery. Gell-Mann called these fractionally charged particles quarks, after a passage from James Joyce's novel *Finnegans Wake:* "Three quarks for Muster Mark!" Quarks can have the charge $+\frac{2}{3}$ or $-\frac{1}{3}$; there are also antiquarks, which have the charge $-\frac{2}{3}$ or $+\frac{1}{3}$. A neutron, which has no charge, is made up of one quark with a charge of $+\frac{2}{3}$ and two with charges of $-\frac{1}{3}$. A proton, which has a charge of $+1$, is made up of two quarks that have charges of $+\frac{2}{3}$ and one that has a charge of $-\frac{1}{3}$. Quarks that have the same charge may differ in other properties (that is, there are several types of quarks having the same charge), and different combinations of quarks account for all the strongly interacting particles.

Gell-Mann was awarded the 1969 Nobel Prize for Physics "for his contributions and discoveries concerning the classification of elementary particles and their interactions." In his presentation speech, Ivar Waller of the Royal Swedish Academy of Sciences declared that Gell-Mann "has during more than a decade been considered as the leading scientist in this field [the theory of elementary particles]." Waller added that the methods Gell-Mann introduced "are among the most powerful tools for further research in particle physics."

Gell-Mann's other contributions to theoretical physics include the introduction, with RICHARD P. FEYNMAN, of the notion of "currents" to weak interactions and the subsequent development of "current algebras."

In 1955 Gell-Mann married J. Margaret Dow, an archaeologist; they had a son and a daughter. His wife died in 1981. Gell-Mann enjoys bird-watching, hiking, camping, and wilderness trips, and in 1969 he helped organize an environmental study program sponsored by the National Academy of Sciences. His other outside interests include historical linguistics.

Gell-Mann is the recipient of the Dannie Heineman Prize of the American Physical Society (1959), the Ernest Orlando Lawrence Memorial Award for Physics of the United States Atomic Energy Commission (1966), the Franklin Medal of the Franklin Institute (1967), and the John J. Carty Medal of the National Academy of Sciences (1968). He is a member of the National Academy of Sciences, the American Physical Society, and the American Academy of Arts and Sciences and is a foreign member of the Royal Society of London. He was awarded an honorary degree by Yale University in 1959.

SELECTED WORKS: Lectures on Weak Interactions of Strongly Interacting Particles, 1961; The Eightfold Way, 1964, with Yuval Ne'eman; Broken Scale Variance and the Light Cone, 1971.

ABOUT: Berland, T. The Scientific Life, 1962; Current Biography February 1966; Nova: Adventures in Science, 1982; Science November 8, 1969; Strachan, C. The Theory of Beta Decay, 1969.

GIAEVER, IVAR

(April 5, 1929–   )
Nobel Prize for Physics, 1973
(shared with Leo Esaki and Brian D. Josephson)

The Norwegian-American physicist Ivar Giaever (yā' vər) was born in Bergen, Norway, the second of three children of John A. Giaever, a pharmacist, and the former Gudrun M. Skaarud. He attended elementary school in Toten and secondary school in Hamar. After graduating from high school in 1946, Giaever worked for a year at the Raufoss Munitions plant before entering the Norwegian Institute of Technology in Trondheim in 1948. He graduated in 1952 with a degree in mechanical engineering.

Giaever spent 1952 as a corporal in the Norwegian army, after which he took a job as a patent examiner in the Norwegian Patent Office. In 1954, prompted by the housing shortage in Norway, Giaever moved to Canada, where he spent a brief period as an architect's aide before joining the Advanced Engineering Program of the General Electric Company as a mechanical engineer. In 1956 he transferred to General Electric's Research and Development Center in Schenectady, New York, where he worked as an applied mathematician. It was in Schenectady that he became interested in physics, and in 1958 he joined a solid-state physics research group. At the same time, he returned to school as a part-time graduate student, pursuing a Ph.D. in physics at the Rensselaer Polytechnic Institute.

At General Electric, Giaever conducted research on the electrical behavior of junctions formed by metal contacts that are separated by very thin insulating layers. This work was of commercial interest because, for most electrical contacts between conductors, thin insulating layers of oxide and dirt lie between the metal contacts. In classical physics it would be expected that if the voltage between two contacts was not high enough to allow the electrons to surmount the electrical barrier created by the insulator, no current would flow, because there would be no electrons with enough energy to penetrate the insulator. Quantum mechanics, however, which describes the behavior of systems on an atomic or subatomic scale, predicts that if the insulating film is thin enough, it is possible for the electron to "tunnel" through and cross the barrier. The Japanese physicist LEO ESAKI had recently invented a diode (the tunnel, or Esaki, diode) in which the electrical junctions were so thin (10 bil-

IVAR GIAEVER

lionths of a meter) that electrons could tunnel through them, exhibiting unusual and useful electrical behavior.

While engaged in this research, Giaever was introduced at graduate school to the BCS theory of superconductivity, named for JOHN BARDEEN, LEON N COOPER, and J. ROBERT SCHRIEFFER. In superconductivity, a phenomenon exhibited by some metals and metallic compounds, materials lose all resistance to the flow of electrical current when they are cooled below critical temperatures close to absolute zero; the critical temperature of a material depends on its composition and structure. Bardeen, Cooper, and Schrieffer had found, in 1957, that superconductivity in a material is dependent on the interaction of pairs of electrons by way of their mutual exchange of atomic vibrations (phonons). This hypothesis led them to propose the BCS theory, the basic theory of superconductivity. According to this theory, the interaction of electrons with the atomic vibrations in the material creates so-called forbidden energies of electrons in the superconductor—that is, electrons in superconductors are not permitted to have these energies.

Giaever sought to determine whether the presence of forbidden energies in superconductors would affect the electrical behavior of an insulated junction between a normal metal and a superconductor. He found that the forbidden energies were easily observable and measurable with his technique, thus providing powerful support for the BCS theory. Further work with evaporated films of aluminum separated only by a layer of aluminum oxide re-

vealed that the electrical characteristics of these junctions provided large amounts of information about the atomic vibration characteristics and behavior of the superconductors, information that was difficult to obtain any other way. Giaever's tunneling technique rapidly became one of the most important ways to observe the behavior and determine the properties of superconductors.

In 1962 BRIAN D. JOSEPHSON extended Giaever's analysis to include the case of an insulated junction between two superconductors. Josephson correctly predicted that currents could flow between two superconductors even with no voltage difference between them and that a high-frequency alternating current would flow when a voltage was applied across the junction (the Josephson effects). Josephson's theory led to the construction of extremely sensitive detectors of change in magnetic field and electrical voltage. Devices based on the Josephson effects may be usable for high-speed, low-power logic circuitry in computers. Giaever received his Ph.D. in 1964 and became a naturalized United States citizen the same year.

Giaever and Leo Esaki shared half of the 1973 Nobel Prize for Physics "for their experimental discoveries regarding tunneling phenomena in semiconductors and superconductors." The other half of the prize was awarded to Josephson. In his presentation address, Stig Lundqvist of the Royal Swedish Academy of Sciences declared that the three scientists had "opened up new fields of research in physics. They are closely related because the pioneering work by Esaki provided the foundation and direct impetus for Giaever's discovery, and Giaever's work in turn provided the stimulus which led to Josephson's theoretical predictions." Their discoveries, Lundqvist pointed out, were quickly adopted in electronics, in detecting gravitational waves, "for ore prospecting, for communication through water and through mountains, [and] to study the electromagnetic field around the heart or brain."

In his acceptance speech, Giaever suggested that "the road to a scientific discovery is seldom direct and that it does not necessarily require great expertise. In fact, I am convinced that often a newcomer to a field has a great advantage because he is ignorant and does not know all the complicated reasons why a particular experiment should not be attempted. However," he added, "it is essential to be able to get advice and help from experts in the various sciences when you need it. . . . I was at the right place at the right time and . . . found so many friends . . . who unselfishly supported me."

After spending 1970 studying biophysics at Cambridge University on a Guggenheim Fellowship, Giaever returned to General Electric, where he was named a Coolidge Fellow in 1973. His subsequent research has involved the properties of cell membranes and the behavior of protein molecules at solid surfaces. His latest work in immunology is being conducted at General Electric and at the Albany Medical Center.

In 1952 Giaever married Inger Skramstad, with whom he has four children. Always an outdoorsman, he is fond of tennis, hiking, camping, skiing, sailing, and windsurfing.

A recipient of the Oliver E. Buckley Solid-State Physics Prize of the American Physical Society (1965), Giaever is a member of the American National Academy of Sciences, the Institute of Electrical and Electronics Engineers, the Norwegian Academy of Sciences, and the Biophysical Society, as well as a fellow of the American Physical Society.

ABOUT: New York Times October 24, 1973; Physics Today December 1973; Science November 16, 1973.

GIAUQUE, WILLIAM F.
(May 12, 1895–March 29, 1982)
Nobel Prize for Chemistry, 1949

The American chemist William Francis Giauque (jē ōk) was born in Niagara Falls, Ontario, Canada, the eldest of the three children of Isabella Jane (Duncan) and William Tecumseh Sherman Giauque, both United States citizens. The family lived in Michigan until the death of Giauque's father in 1908, when they returned to Canada. After graduating from the Niagara Falls Collegiate Institute, Giauque worked for two years in the laboratory of the Hooker Electro-Chemical Company in Niagara Falls. Intent on becoming a chemical engineer, he entered the University of California at Berkeley, where he earned his B.S. in chemistry with highest honors in 1920.

Remaining at Berkeley, Giauque continued fundamental research under the eminent chemists Gilbert N. Lewis and G. E. Gibson. For a thesis on the behavior of materials at very low temperatures, Giauque received a Ph.D. in chemistry with a minor in physics in 1922. He was immediately appointed an in-

WILLIAM F. GIAUQUE

structor in the chemistry department at Berkeley, where he remained for his entire career, becoming assistant professor in 1927, associate professor in 1930, full professor in 1934, and professor emeritus in 1962.

Giauque's chief interest was in the properties and behavior of matter at extremely low temperatures, a field that involves the principles of thermodynamics. Thermodynamics is concerned with the properties of systems at equilibrium and with the conversion of heat into mechanical, chemical, and electrical energy. This branch of physics developed from nineteenth-century efforts to construct efficient machines that would use expanding hot gases to perform work.

The first law of thermodynamics, that of the conservation of energy, states that energy may be transferred from one form to another but cannot be created or destroyed. The second law of thermodynamics predicts whether a chemical reaction or a physical change will occur spontaneously. It is expressed mathematically by the concept of entropy, a measure of the amount of disorder or randomness in a system. The tendency of natural processes is always toward an irreversible state of greater entropy, or disorder. The third law of thermodynamics, postulated by WALTHER NERNST, states that the entropy of a pure crystalline element is zero at a temperature of absolute zero (notated as 0°K). In this state, molecules of matter are arranged in a relatively orderly fashion, thus permitting the study of natural phenomena not usually observable.

In the first decade of the twentieth century,

temperatures of about 1°K were achieved in the laboratory. The technique, developed by the Dutch physicist HEIKE KAMERLINGH ONNES, consisted of evaporating liquid helium at a low temperature with a vacuum pump. In 1924 Giauque suggested a method that would permit the experimental observation of even lower temperatures based on a phenomenon known as adiabatic demagnetization.

An adiabatic system is one in which heat is neither gained nor lost. Paramagnetic substances, such as several rare earth and transition metal ions, contain weak magnetic dipoles due to the spin of unpaired electrons. As Giauque explained, "Their normal state is one of disorder, which corresponds to the presence of entropy. When a sufficiently powerful magnetic field is applied, the magnets line up and the entropy is removed." Because any process involving a change in entropy may be used to produce cooling or heating, it occurred to Giauque that adiabatic demagnetization might provide a method for producing lower temperatures than those obtainable with liquid helium.

For a period of eight years, Giauque and his research team at Berkeley constructed the equipment needed for adiabatic demagnetization. In 1933, using gadolinium sulfate, Giauque and a co-worker, Duncan MacDougall, finally achieved a temperature of 0.25°K. To measure temperatures below 1°K, Giauque devised a thermometer that employed the electrical-resistance properties of amorphous carbon. This method of magnetic cooling furnished additional proof of the validity of the third law of thermodynamics and has since had numerous industrial applications, including improved forms of rubber, gasoline, and glass.

Giauque compared the entropy values obtained by adiabatic demagnetization with spectroscopic data. Together with a Berkeley graduate student, Herrick Johnston, he spectroscopically identified the two hitherto unknown oxygen isotopes 17 and 18. The nuclei of most oxygen atoms contain eight protons and eight neutrons. These isotopes of oxygen have one or two additional neutrons, the presence of which results in minor but important changes in physical properties. Prior to Giauque's discovery, oxygen 16 had been used by chemists as a standard for atomic-weight determinations. Discovery of the oxygen isotopes led to the recalibration of atomic-weight scales. WERNER HEISENBERG had predicted that hydrogen molecules could exist in two different forms depending upon the relative orientation of the molecular nuclei. Giauque's

experimental observations verified this theoretical prediction.

During World War II, Giauque devoted his efforts to military research. In this capacity he designed high-field electromagnets and mobile units for producing liquid oxygen.

Giauque was awarded the 1949 Nobel Prize for Chemistry "for his contributions in the field of chemical thermodynamics, particularly concerning the behavior of substances at extremely low temperatures." According to ARNE TISELIUS of the Royal Swedish Academy of Sciences, who presented the award, "Giauque's achievements in the field of chemical thermodynamics and especially his work on the behavior of matter at low temperatures . . . comprise one of the most significant contributions to modern physical chemistry."

After receiving the Nobel Prize, Giauque remained active in low-temperature research at Berkeley until a year before his death.

In 1932 Giauque married Muriel Frances Ashley, a physicist who conducted botanical research. The couple had two sons. Described by a colleague as "a bear for work," Giauque enjoyed few pursuits outside the laboratory and classroom. "I am one of those fortunate people who get a kick out of their work," he once said. Giauque died in Oakland, California, on March 29, 1982.

In addition to the Nobel Prize, Giauque received the Charles Frederick Chandler Medal of Columbia University (1936), the Elliott Cresson Medal of the Franklin Institute (1937) and the American Chemical Society's Willard Gibbs Medal (1951) and Gilbert Newton Lewis Medal (1956). He was a member of the National Academy of Sciences, the American Philosophical Society, the American Chemical Society, the American Physical Society, and the American Academy of Arts and Sciences. He received honorary degrees from Columbia University and the University of California.

SELECTED WORKS:The Third Law of Thermodynamics, 1923; Low Temperature, Chemical, and Magneto Thermodynamics: The Scientific Papers of William F. Giauque, 1969.

ABOUT: Current Biography January 1950; New York Times November 4, 1959; April 1, 1982.

GIDE, ANDRÉ

(November 22, 1869–February 19, 1951)
Nobel Prize for Literature, 1947

André Paul Guillaume Gide (zhēd), French novelist, essayist, and critic, was born in Paris, the only child of Paul Gide, a professor of law at the University of Paris, and Juliette (Rondeaux) Gide, both of whom were of Huguenot stock. After his father died in 1880, Gide was raised (with the aid of a governess and an aunt) by his strict, Calvinist mother, who devoted her life to him.

Education for the young Gide was erratic because of his poor health; he attended several different schools and was also tutored at home. At the École Alsacienne, a Protestant secondary school in Paris, Gide developed a serious interest in literature and was especially impressed by the Greek poets. Encouraged by his mother, he also became deeply involved in the study of music. He passed his lycée examination in 1889 and subsequently decided to become a writer.

Since his father's bequest enabled him to live independently, Gide was able to devote himself to writing, and in 1891 he published his first book, *Les Cahiers d'André Walter* (*The Notebooks of André Walter*). The theme of this autobiographical work, written in verse and prose poetry, is the struggle between the flesh and the spirit, a struggle that ends with renunciation of the flesh. This theme was to recur in later works, but not always with the same conclusion. Gide's school friend, the writer Pierre Louÿs, introduced him into the salons of the symbolists, the reigning literary group of the time. There he met some of the era's most important men of letters, including the poet Stéphane Mallarmé. Between 1891 and 1893, Gide produced an essay and two tales written in the symbolist manner.

Rejected for army service because he had tuberculosis, Gide decided to accompany a painter friend, Paul Albert Laurens, on a trip to North Africa in October 1893. There, at Sousse, in Tunisia, he had his first homosexual experience. Upon his return to Europe, Gide found that the sensual pleasures he had experienced in North Africa made him feel alienated from the literary society he had so recently enjoyed. Consequently, he wrote a satirical portrait of the pretentious symbolist literary salons, *Les Paludes* (*Marshlands*, 1895). By this time he was cured of tuberculosis, and in January 1895 he returned to North Africa. There, in Algeria, he encountered Oscar Wilde and Lord Alfred Douglas at Biskra. Confronted by Wilde with the issue of his sexual preference, Gide was compelled to recognize and finally accept his homosexuality.

He returned to France later in 1895, to be with his dying mother. In October of that year, shortly after his mother's death, Gide married

ANDRÉ GIDE

his cousin Madeleine Rondeaux, to whom he had been chastely devoted for many years. Some critics have regarded his wife, because of her inflexible puritanism, as a substitute for Gide's mother. Although the marriage produced no children, Gide had a daughter, Catherine Gide, in 1923 as a result of his liaison with Elisabeth van Rysselberghe. A year after he married, Gide was elected mayor of La Roque. He continued to write, however, and shortly thereafter returned to Algeria.

Gide first expressed his new sense of personal liberation in *Les Nourritures terrestres* (*Fruits of the Earth*, 1897), a book of prose poems written mostly in Biskra. In this work, flesh and spirit become harmonized; conventions, habits, and principles are discarded in favor of the liberation of the self and its capacity for pleasure and joy. Unsuccessful commercially, the book caused a definitive break between Gide and his symbolist friends who, preferring to transcend reality, did not appreciate Gide's celebration of it. In the 1920s, however, *Fruits of the Earth* became Gide's most popular work and influenced a generation of younger writers, including the existentialists ALBERT CAMUS and JEAN-PAUL SARTRE.

After 1897 Gide's physical and emotional health suffered because of the continuing struggle between his spiritual aspirations and his physical desires. He was also deeply troubled by guilt over the neglect of his wife who, shocked by the revelation of her husband's homosexuality, had retreated to their estate at Cuverville, in Normandy. (From that time,

Gide spent frequent periods away from his wife, but he appears to have remained deeply, spiritually devoted to her until her death in 1938.) In February 1909, the work of launching the *Nouvelle Revue Française* (New French Revue), a periodical that rapidly became one of the most influential literary journals in the world, no doubt helped relieve his depression. The *Nouvelle Revue* and its offspring, the publishing firm of Gallimard, welcomed new talent and also, under Gide's influence, issued translations of foreign authors he admired, such as Fedor Dostoevsky, Joseph Conrad, Walt Whitman, and Herman Melville.

Between 1902 and 1919, Gide published four short psychological novels, which he called *récits,* or stories: *L'Immoraliste* (*The Immoralist*, 1902), *La Porte étroite* (*Strait Is the Gate,* 1909), *Isabelle* (*Isabelle*, 1911), and *La Symphonie pastorale* (*Pastoral Symphony*, 1919). (The latter two works were published together in English in 1931 as *Two Symphonies.*) *Strait Is the Gate,* an unexpected success, brought him a larger readership for his subsequent writings. Many critics consider this group of stories, all of which explore the struggle of the individual to determine and fulfill his or her own nature, to be among Gide's best works.

A new stage in his development as a novelist began in 1914 with the publication of *Les Caves du Vatican* (translated into English as *Lafcadio's Adventures*), which he called a *sotie,* after a medieval form of satiric farce whose characters are fools. Structurally and psychologically more complex than the *récits, Lafcadio's Adventures* is an irreverent hoax in which Gide examines the idea of a gratuitous act, a murder committed for no motive except to demonstrate the freedom of the murderer. Gide also satirizes bourgeois conformism among Catholics and Freemasons, and he caricatures the false sincerity of hypocritical Catholics. Raised in a strict Protestant household, Gide had gone through a religious crisis in 1906 and, like many important writers who were his friends, had been strongly attracted to Catholicism, particularly the zealously apostolic Catholicism of the poet and dramatist Paul Claudel. *Lafcadio's Adventures* cost Gide Claudel's friendship and precipitated violently personal attacks on his anticlericalism from a number of quarters.

The overwhelming success of the *Nouvelle Revue Française* (whose illustrious contributors included Marcel Proust and Paul Valéry, among others) and the growing popularity of his books gave Gide a degree of security he had never before known. During the 1920s,

however, he again came under attack, this time by several conservatives in the French establishment, who asserted that Gide's works corrupted the young. In 1924 he replied by distributing thousands of copies of *Corydon,* a defense of homosexuality in the form of Platonic dialogue, which he had begun writing in 1918. With the publication of *Corydon,* which was translated into English under the same title in 1950, Gide seemed to be courting the public condemnation of homosexuality that had humiliated and imprisoned his friend Oscar Wilde. Gide was shunned, even by former friends, and few voices were raised in his defense. His reputation as a major writer did not revive until the end of the 1920s, by which time public attitudes toward homosexuality had become more relaxed.

In July 1925 Gide set out for an extended trip to the Congo, accompanied by his friend Marc Allegret. During this time, several of his works were published. "Numquid et tu . . . ?" ("Art Thou Also of Galilee?"), published in 1926, was part of a journal he had begun a decade earlier, dealing with his personal religion. The result of a religious crisis, it chronicles Gide's search for a divine presence and seeks to justify his rejection of the concept of guilt. Also published that year was the intensely confessional autobiography *Si le Grain ne meurt* (*If It Die*), which he had begun in 1919. Condemned as shameless at the time, *If It Die* is now considered a great work of autobiographical literature, ranking with Jean Jacques Rousseau's *Confessions.*

Les Faux-Monnayeurs (*The Counterfeiters*), a novel Gide completed right before he left on his trip, was also published in 1926. Gide called this his only novel because it was bigger in scope and in scale than his other works of fiction. Its structural complexity, marked by unrelated stories that occur simultaneously, resides in its contrapuntal use of multiple plots, themes, characters, moods, and points of view. In explaining its significance in Gide's oeuvre, the French critic Jean Hytier observed, "There are only two books in which Gide has tried to put all of himself—prematurely in *André Walter;* at the peak of his maturity in *The Counterfeiters."* This work brought Gide international recognition as one of the major writers of the twentieth century.

Returning from the Congo in 1927, Gide published two travel diaries in which he criticized French colonial policies. For the next ten years he continued to involve himself actively in controversial social and political causes, including support for the Loyalists during the

Spanish Civil War. He scandalized many in 1932 by announcing his conversion to Communism; however, in 1937, in the second of two travel essays written after a disillusioning trip to the Soviet Union, he made a decisive break with Communism.

From 1942 until the end of World War II, Gide lived in North Africa, where he wrote the novella *Thésée* (1946), which was published in English in *Two Legends: Oedipus and Theseus* in 1950. Gide regarded this affirmation of faith in humanity's perfectibility and in the sufficient value of earthly existence as his literary testament.

In 1947 Gide received an honorary doctorate from Oxford University. Later that year he was awarded the 1947 Nobel Prize for Literature "for his comprehensive and artistically significant writings, in which human problems and conditions have been presented with a fearless love of truth and keen psychological insight." In his presentation address, Anders Österling of the Swedish Academy noted that "more than any of his contemporaries, Gide has been a man of contrasts. . . . This is why his work gives the appearance of an uninterrupted dialogue in which faith constantly struggles against doubt, asceticism against the love of life, discipline against the need for freedom." Poor health prevented Gide from attending the award ceremony in Stockholm; his acceptance speech was read by the French ambassador to Sweden, Gabriel Puaux. In thanking the Swedish Academy for the award, Gide wrote, "For many years I thought that I was crying in the wilderness, later that I was speaking only to a very small number; but you have proved to me today that I was right to believe in the virtue of the small number and that sooner or later it would prevail. . . . [Your] votes were cast not so much for my work as for the independent spirit that animates it, that spirit which in our time faces attacks from all possible quarters."

In 1950 Gide published the last volume of his *Journal*, covering the years 1939 to 1949. (These works are collected in English in four volumes as *The Journals of André Gide, 1889–1949*.) Many readers agree with FRANÇOIS MAURIAC in preferring Gide's journals and his autobiography to all his other works. The lifetime journal, begun in 1889 and consisting of more than a million words, was appraised by Enid Starkie, a distinguished British authority on French literature, as "a work unique in French literature—indeed in any literature; a treasure house of discussion on every artistic and intellectual movement, on every moral

problem, of more than sixty years." Paying tribute to Gide shortly after his death from pneumonia on February 19, 1951, Sartre wrote, "He taught or retaught us that *everything* could be said . . . but that it must be said according to specific rules of good expression." Gide's reputation has not eroded in the years since his death. In 1980, for example, the American scholar A. Leslie Willson wrote that Gide's "position as one of the major literary figures of the century . . . has grown with time."

Gide was buried beside his wife at Cuverville. *Et Nunc Manet in Te* (translated as *Madeleine*), his intimate portrait of his marriage, was published posthumously in 1951.

ADDITIONAL WORKS IN ENGLISH TRANSLATION: Oscar Wilde, 1905; Prometheus Illbound, 1919; Amyntas, 1925; Dostoevsky, 1925; Travels in the Congo, 1927; The Prodigal Son, 1928; Montaigne, 1929; The School for Wives, 1929; Afterthoughts, 1937; Return From the U.S.S.R., 1937; Recollections of the Assize Court, 1941; Imaginary Interviews, 1944; Notes on Chopin, 1949; Autumn Leaves, 1950; Genevieve, 1950; The Trial, 1950; Robert, 1950; My Theater, 1951; The Secret Drama of My Life, 1951; Persephone, 1952; Philoctetes, 1952; Urien's Travels, 1952; The Lover's Attempt, 1953; El Hadj, 1953; The Return of the Prodigal, 1953; Pretexts, 1959; So Be It, 1959; The White Notebook, 1965; Self-Portraits, 1966, with Paul Valéry.

ABOUT: Ames, V. M. André Gide, 1947; Bettinson, C. D. Gide: A Study, 1977; Brée, G. Gide, 1963; Cordle, T. André Gide, 1969; Fowlie, W. André Gide: His Life and Art, 1965; Guérard, A. J. André Gide, 1951; Hytier, J. André Gide, 1962; Ireland, G. W. André Gide, 1962; Ireland, G. W. André Gide: A Study of His Creative Writings, 1970; Littlejohn, D. (ed.) Gide: A Collection of Critical Essays, 1970; McLaren, J. C. The Theater of André Gide, 1953; Mann, K. André Gide and the Crisis of Modern Thought, 1943; March, H. Gide and the Hound of Heaven, 1952; Martin du Gard, R. Recollections of André Gide, 1953; Nersoyan, H. J. André Gide: The Theism of an Atheist, 1969; Painter, G. D. André Gide: A Critical and Biographical Study, 1951; Rossi, V. André Gide, 1968; Starkie, E. André Gide, 1953; Thomas, L. André Gide: The Ethic of an Artist, 1950; Vier, J. and Roberts R. P. André Gide, the Shameless Confessional, 1976.

GILBERT, WALTER
(March 21, 1932–   )
Nobel Prize for Chemistry, 1980
(shared with Paul Berg and Frederick Sanger)

The American molecular biologist Walter Gilbert was born in Boston, Massachusetts, to Richard V. Gilbert, a Keynesian economist who taught at Harvard University from 1924 to 1939, and Emma (Cohen) Gilbert, a child psychologist who gave her two children their early education at home. When the boy was seven, he and his family moved to Washington, D.C. During World War II his father worked for the Office of Price Administration. Educated in the public schools of Washington and later at Sidwell Friends High School, Gilbert displayed a deep interest in science and a voracious appetite for reading. After graduating from high school in 1949, he entered Harvard and majored in physics. He graduated summa cum laude in 1953, the same year that he married Celia Stone, a poet. They have two children. Gilbert remained at Harvard for graduate work in physics and received an M.S. in 1954. He then moved to Cambridge University, England, as a doctoral candidate, working under ABDUS SALAM on mathematical formulas designed to predict scattering of elementary particles.

At Cambridge, Gilbert became acquainted with JAMES D. WATSON and FRANCIS CRICK, both of whom were investigating the consequences of their 1953 discovery of the structure of deoxyribonucleic acid (DNA), the cell's master blueprint for the production of proteins. Proteins, which make up not only the cell itself but also the hormones and enzymes that regulate its functions, are composed of amino acids. According to the Watson-Crick model, a strand of DNA consists of a chain of structural units called nucleotides, each of which carries one of four bases—adenine (A), thymine (T), cytosine (C), and guanine (G). The blueprint, or genetic code, for each amino acid is coded by a particular three-base sequence, as are the instructions for combining amino acids to create a particular protein.

After receiving his Ph.D. in mathematics from Cambridge in 1957, Gilbert returned to Harvard for a year of postdoctoral study, followed by a year as a research assistant to the physicist JULIAN S. SCHWINGER. In 1959 he was appointed assistant professor in the physics department at Harvard.

By 1960, James Watson had joined the Harvard faculty and renewed his friendship with Gilbert. At the time, Watson was interested in the chain of events that link the DNA of a given nucleotide sequence to the synthesis of the protein that it encodes. Protein synthesis was known to occur in ribosomes, structures within the cell that were discovered in 1949 by ALBERT CLAUDE. Scientists suspected that genetic information was carried from DNA to the ribosomes by an unstable nucleic acid called messenger RNA (mRNA). Asked by Watson to assist him in the task of isolating mRNA, Gilbert found the experimental work compel-

WALTER GILBERT

ling and began a lifelong career in molecular biology.

In 1964 Gilbert transferred from the physics department to become an associate professor in the biophysics department, where he and a colleague, Benno Müller-Hill, became interested in a question raised by FRANÇOIS JACOB and JACQUES MONOD. Three years earlier, Jacob and Monod had pointed out that in genetics the issue is not how genes act but how they are prevented from acting—in other words, why it is that all DNA sequences do not constantly produce encoded proteins. The sequence of bases in DNA is copied (or transcribed) into mRNA as an enzyme called RNA polymerase moves along the strand of the DNA molecule. Jacob and Monod suggested that the transcription process might be inactivated when a repressor molecule binds to the DNA and prevents RNA polymerase from moving along it.

Using the bacterium *Escherichia coli*, Gilbert and Müller-Hill began to investigate the problem. *E. coli* produces a group of proteins that digest the milk sugar lactose. Production of the proteins is initiated by the so-called lac operon when lactose is present; in its absence, a repressor protein inhibits the lac operon. By 1966 the two scientists had isolated the repressor, and within another four years Gilbert had discovered the structure and location of the operator, the position on the DNA strand to which the repressor becomes attached.

It was now obvious that the pattern of nucleotides in the operator DNA plays a central role in the process by which the repressor recognizes and binds itself to the operator. Using methods devised by FREDERICK SANGER at Cambridge University, Gilbert and Allan Maxam elucidated the sequence of the lac operator in 1973. Two years later, at the suggestion of a visiting Soviet scientist, Andrei Mirzabekov, Gilbert set out to determine the specific nucleotides in the lac operator that are most important in the binding process. Mirzabekov and his colleagues had been studying interactions between DNA and antibiotics by using dimethyl sulfate, a substance that weakens the A and G nucleotides. Because methylated DNA breaks easily at specific sites, it could be used to break the DNA strand into fragments of varying but selected lengths.

Adapting Mirzabekov's method to study the lac operon, Gilbert and Maxam separated the DNA fragments according to length, using gel electrophoresis. In this technique the fragments pass through a thin gel in response to a weak electric current. Moving at characteristically differing rates and marked by radioactive tags, the fragments produce a dark band on photographic paper. So effective was this method that Gilbert and Maxam were able to resolve fragments that differed in length by only one base.

By 1977 Gilbert and his colleague had determined the entire sequence of bases for the protein. Another sequencing technique had meanwhile been devised by Sanger, and both methods quickly became fundamental tools in the expanding field of recombinant DNA, or gene splicing. Gilbert's expertise in this field led him to help found Biogen, Inc., in 1978, one of the first companies to specialize in genetic engineering. In 1982, a year after being appointed chairman of Biogen, he left Harvard, but he returned after resigning from the company at the end of 1984. At Harvard he resumed his research on gene structure and on the production of proteins from recombinant organisms.

Half of the 1980 Nobel Prize for Chemistry was awarded to Gilbert and Sanger "for their contributions concerning the determination of base sequences in nucleic acids." The other half of the prize was bestowed on PAUL BERG for related research. The work of the three scientists "has already given benefits to mankind," said Bo G. Malmström of the Royal Swedish Academy of Sciences in his presentation address, "not only in the form of new fundamental knowledge but also in the form of important technical applications [such as] the production of human hormones with the aid of bacteria."

In addition to the Nobel Prize, Gilbert's honors include the United States Steel Foundation Award in Molecular Biology of the National Academy of Sciences (1968), the V. D. Mattia Award of the Roche Institute for Molecular Biology (1976), the Louis and Bert Freedman Award of the New York Academy of Sciences (1977), the Louisa Gross Horwitz Prize of Columbia University (1979), the Gairdner Foundation Annual Award (1979), the Albert Lasker Basic Medical Research Award (1979), and the Herbert A. Sober Memorial Award of the American Society of Biological Chemists (1980). He has received honorary degrees from the University of Chicago, Columbia University, and the University of Rochester and holds membership in the American Academy of Arts and Sciences, the National Academy of Sciences, the American Society of Biological Chemists, and the American Physical Society.

SELECTED WORKS: Genetic Repressors, 1970, with Mark Ptashne; "Useful Proteins From Recombinant Bacteria," Scientific American April 1980.

ABOUT: New York Times October 16, 1980; December 18, 1984; Nova: Adventures in Science, 1983; Science November 21, 1980.

GJELLERUP, KARL
(June 2, 1857–October 13, 1919)
Nobel Prize for Literature, 1917
(shared with Henrik Pontoppidan)

The Danish novelist and playwright Karl Adolph Gjellerup (gel' ə ro͞op) was born in Roholte, the son of Anna (Fibiger) Gjellerup and Carl Adolph Gjellerup, a Lutheran minister who died when the boy was three years old. The young Gjellerup was brought up in Copenhagen by his mother's cousin, Johannes Fibiger, a minister, theological scholar, and poet, who exerted a formative influence on his intellectual development. While still a schoolboy, Gjellerup began to write, and soon after graduating from Hærslevs Grammar School in 1874, he composed a tragedy, Scipio Africanus, and a drama, Arminius, neither of which was published.

That year, Gjellerup entered the University of Copenhagen to study theology. There he embraced Charles Darwin's views on natural selection and fell under the sway of the radical literary theories of the prominent Danish critic and scholar Georg Brandes. It was a period

KARL GJELLERUP

of objective critical examination of the Bible, and the authenticity of the Fourth Gospel was being called into question. Gjellerup lost his faith during his university years, and although he took his degree in theology, by the time of his graduation in 1878 he had become an atheist. Among the chief influences of Gjellerup's student years were the giants of German literature: Goethe, Immanuel Kant, and especially Friedrich Schiller, upon whose model Gjellerup fashioned his own poetry.

En idealist (An Idealist, 1878), a short novel written immediately after his graduation, was Gjellerup's first published work. Published under the pseudonym Epigonos, it portrays a headstrong young intellectual who denounces theology and organized religion. A second novel, *Germanernes lærling* (The Apprentice of the Teutons, 1882), features a young hero who undergoes a crisis of faith much like that of Gjellerup.

Over the next few years, Gjellerup was influenced by the writing of Ivan Turgenev, as is particularly evident in two short stories of 1883: "G-Dur" (G-Major) and "Romulus." During this period, he traveled in Italy, Greece, Germany, Russia, Switzerland, and Sweden, recording his impressions in *En klassisk maaned* (A Classical Month, 1884) and *Vandreaaret* (The Wanderyear, 1885). The latter work marked his break from the cause of radicalism and from Brandes, whose naturalism Gjellerup rejected in favor of German classicism and the literature of antiquity. Gjellerup's most significant early work is the verse drama *Brynhild* (1884), inspired by Richard Wagner's op-

eratic cycle *Der Ring der Nibelungen* and influenced by Greek drama, Shakespearean blank verse, and the alliterative verse of the Scandinavian Eddas.

Between 1885 and 1887, Gjellerup lived in Dresden, Germany, where he completed his dramatic poem "Thamyris." In 1887 he married Eugenia Anna Caroline Heusinger, the divorced wife of the musician Felix Bendix and a cousin of Georg Brandes. On the strength of *Brynhild* and "Thamyris," Gjellerup was granted a state pension for life. He next wrote *Hagbard og Signe* (Hagbard and Signe, 1888), a tragedy in alternating prose and poetry, based on an ancient Danish folktale, and the novel *Minna* (*Minna,* 1889), a romance set in Dresden. He also published the poetry collection *Min kaerligheds bog* (The Book of My Love, 1889).

Turning away from heroic tragedy, Gjellerup began writing contemporary dramas in the style of Henrik Ibsen: *Herman Vandel* (1891), about the unhappy marriage and suicide of a young schoolmaster; *Wuthorn* (1893), the story of star-crossed lovers in a mountain community; and *Hans Excellence* (His Excellence, 1895), about a corrupt government official. *Wuthorn* was performed more than 100 times at Copenhagen's Dagmar Theater.

In 1892 Gjellerup settled permanently with his family in Dresden. Writing now in German, which he called his "true artistic medium," he produced the novels *Pastor Mors* (1894), a trenchant portrait of a Protestant minister, and *Møllen* (The Mill, 1896), which depicts the remorse and repentance of a murderer in rural Denmark. His later works, Gjellerup wrote, "belong chiefly to German literature and . . . have found their true understanding and appreciation almost exclusively in Germany."

Around the mid-1890s, Gjellerup, inspired by his study of Arthur Schopenhauer and Buddhist teachings, was drawn to the concept of the annihilation of the personality in nirvana. Out of his interest in Buddhism grew a series of works: *Die Opferfeuer* (The Sacrificial Fires, 1903), a play dealing with the religious instruction of a young disciple of Gautama Buddha; and the poetic novels *Der Pilger Kamanita* (The Pilgrim Kamanita, 1906), about a pair of lovers at the time of the Buddha, and *Die Weltwanderer* (The World Travelers, 1910), a tale of two lovers who realize they have led previous lives.

The award of the 1917 Nobel Prize for Literature was strongly influenced by political considerations. Although Sweden remained neutral during World War I, its proximity to Germany caused tensions with the Allies. Meetings between the kings of Denmark, Norway, and Sweden had strengthened unity among the Scandinavian nations. Partly to emphasize Sweden's neutrality and its fraternal ties with Denmark, the Swedish Academy awarded the prize jointly to two Danish writers: Gjellerup and HENRIK PONTOPPIDAN, another of Brandes's disciples. The award cited Gjellerup "for his varied and rich poetry, which is inspired by lofty ideals." Because of the war, there was no award ceremony that year. The news of Gjellerup's prize was received with little enthusiasm in Denmark, where he had long been regarded as essentially a German writer.

Gjellerup died in 1919 in Klotzsche, near Dresden. In his lifetime, he was admired for his use of literary forms to present his lofty philosophical ideas; but subsequently, his style of writing has fallen out of favor, and his posthumous reputation is severely diminished.

ADDITIONAL WORKS IN ENGLISH TRANSLATION: A Second Book of Danish Verse, 1947, with others.

ABOUT: American-Scandinavian Review March–April 1918; The Times (London) December 20, 1917.

GLASER, DONALD A.
(September 21, 1926–   )
Nobel Prize for Physics, 1960

The American physicist Donald Arthur Glaser was born in Cleveland, Ohio, to Lena and William J. Glaser, a sundries wholesaler. Both his parents had immigrated to the United States from Russia. As a child, he attended public schools in Cleveland Heights. A talented musician, he also studied violin, viola, and composition at the Cleveland Institute of Music and performed with a local symphony orchestra at the age of sixteen.

Glaser's early interest in mathematics prompted him to enter the Case Institute of Technology (now Case Western Reserve University), where he earned a B.S. in physics and mathematics in 1946. He then attended the California Institute of Technology (Caltech) for graduate studies under CARL D. ANDERSON. In 1950 Glaser received his Ph.D. in physics and mathematics for a thesis dealing with his experimental study of high-energy cosmic rays and mesons at sea level. The previous year, after completing his coursework at

DONALD A. GLASER

Caltech, he had become an instructor in physics at the University of Michigan. He was made assistant professor in 1953, associate professor in 1955, and full professor in 1957.

At Michigan, Glaser pursued his interest in the elementary particles found in cosmic radiation, which bombarded the earth at enormously high velocities. When they interact with matter, they often give rise to new particles, equally energetic and often very short-lived. Physicists first found a way to visualize the tracks of such particles in the second decade of the twentieth century, with the invention of the cloud chamber by C. T. R. WILSON. Wilson's chamber contained air supersaturated with water vapor. When an atomic or subatomic particle passed through the chamber, it caused tiny droplets of water to condense along its path. The tracks created in this way—minuscule versions of the condensation trails sometimes left by high-flying jets—could be photographed for subsequent study.

The new and powerful particle accelerators of the 1950s, however, made these tracking techniques inadequate. The particles they produced had energies 1,000 times greater than those of twenty years earlier. The low density of the gas in a cloud chamber meant that these fast-moving particles could travel relatively long distances before they decayed or dissipated their energy. To track such particles in a Wilson chamber would have required an instrument over 100 meters long—a practical impossibility. At the same time, the infrequency of collisions between incoming particles and atoms of the gas limited the number of interactions that could be observed and the number of exotic new particles that could be created. The amount of data that could be collected using a cloud chamber was also limited by its slowness; as much as thirty minutes might be required between the brief periods during which the apparatus was ready to record incoming particle tracks.

After building several conventional cloud chambers, Glaser began searching for alternative ways to detect high-energy particles, using denser substances in larger chambers. It occurred to him that pressurized, superheated liquid might provide a suitable medium. Glaser knew that a liquid can be maintained for some time in an unstable condition above its normal boiling point. It will not begin to boil spontaneously but must be triggered in some way. Curious about whether high-energy particles could provide such a trigger, Glaser first experimented with bottles of warm beer and soda to see whether their foaming was affected by the presence of a radioactive source. Eventually, after more sophisticated experiments and calculations, he found that under the proper conditions, radiation could indeed induce liquids to boil. When diethyl ether, for example, was superheated to 140°C (far above its normal boiling point), it boiled instantly when exposed to radiation from cosmic rays or other sources.

Using a series of small glass chambers of different shapes, each containing several cubic centimeters of superheated ether, Glaser attempted to record accurately the paths of ionizing radiation. When he heated the liquid under high pressure and then dropped the pressure abruptly, creating an extremely unstable condition, he was able to record well-defined tracks on high-speed film before the liquid came to a boil. Glaser had succeeded in devising a technique that was, in effect, the mirror image of Wilson's. Whereas Wilson's cloud chamber produced a track of liquid droplets in a gas, Glaser's bubble chamber, the first version of which was built in 1952, reversed the process to produce a track of gaseous bubbles in a liquid.

Glaser quickly realized that other liquids would be even more useful for high-energy physics experiments. He therefore constructed a bubble chamber utilizing liquid hydrogen at a temperature of −246°C. This instrument, completed at the University of Chicago in 1953, soon revealed subatomic events never before detected. By 1956 Glaser had experimented with chambers containing liquefied xenon gas. The high density of this medium enabled physicists to photograph the tracks of neutral as well as charged particles and permitted the observation of many more reactions. As Glaser hoped, it proved possible to construct large bubble chambers with very short cycling times. Such instruments have recorded the behavior of many atomic particles that could not be studied using the cloud chamber, yielding thousands of times more information.

In 1959 Glaser served as visiting professor of physics at the University of California at Berkeley, where he joined the faculty the following year. During 1959–1960, he collected nearly half a million photographs using Berkeley's new bubble chamber, built under the direction of LUIS W. ALVAREZ. Equipped with a refrigerating plant and a large magnet for deflecting the paths of charged particles, the Berkeley chamber was about the size of a minivan, in sharp contrast to the 3-cubic-centimeter flasks Glaser had used just seven years earlier.

Glaser received the 1960 Nobel Prize for Physics "for the invention of the bubble chamber." "Several other scientists also left important contributions to the practical shaping of different types of bubble chambers, but Glaser is the one who made the really fundamental contribution," said KAI SIEGBAHN of the Royal Swedish Academy of Sciences in his presentation speech.

After receiving the Nobel Prize, Glaser became interested in applying physics to molecular biology. In 1961 he spent a year studying microbiology as a fellow at the University of Copenhagen. Since then he has investigated such topics as bacterial evolution, the regulation of cell growth, and substances that cause cancer and genetic mutations. Adapting equipment used to analyze photographs taken in the bubble chamber, Glaser developed a computerized scanning system that automatically identifies bacterial species. Since 1964 he has been professor of biology, as well as physics, at Berkeley.

In 1960, shortly before traveling to Stockholm to accept the Nobel Prize, Glaser married Ruth Bonnie Thompson, a graduate student he had met at the Lawrence Radiation Laboratory at Berkeley. The couple, who had two children, were divorced in 1969. An athletic person who enjoys mountain climbing, skiing, tennis, and sailing, Glaser retains his lifelong interest in music by playing the viola with local chamber music groups.

In addition to the Nobel Prize, Glaser has been awarded the Henry Russel Award of the University of Michigan (1953), the Charles

Vernon Boys Prize of the Physical Society in London (1958), and the American Physical Society Prize (1959). He is a member of the National Academy of Sciences and a fellow of the American Physical Society.

ABOUT: Current Biography March 1961; National Cyclopedia of America Biography, volume N, 1984; New Yorker November 19, 1960; Science November 11, 1960.

GLASHOW, SHELDON L.
(December 5, 1932–)
Nobel Prize for Physics, 1979
(shared with Abdus Salam and Steven
    Weinberg)

SHELDON L. GLASHOW

The American physicist Sheldon Lee Glashow (glash' ō) was born in New York City, the youngest of three sons of Lewis Gluchovski and the former Bella Rubin, immigrants from Bobruisk, Russia. His father, who established a successful plumbing business in New York, changed the family name to Glashow. Glashow received his secondary education at the Bronx High School of Science. Among his classmates were STEVEN WEINBERG and Gerald Feinberg, who became a physicist at Columbia University. Glashow credits Weinberg and Feinberg with sparking his interest in physics.

After earning a B.S. at Cornell University in 1954, Glashow went on to get a Ph.D. from Harvard University in 1959. His thesis, "The Vector Meson in Elementary Particle Decays," was written under JULIAN S. SCHWINGER, who exerted a major influence on Glashow's career. From 1958 to 1960, Glashow was a postdoctoral fellow at the University of Copenhagen. He then spent a year as a research fellow at the California Institute of Technology and taught at Stanford University and at the University of California at Berkeley. In 1967 he returned to Harvard, where in 1979 he was appointed to the Eugene Higgins Chair of Physics, a post he still occupies.

Much of Glashow's work has focused on the problem of unifying all the forces observed in nature. To the physicists of the early nineteenth century, three separate and apparently independent forces were at work in the universe: gravitation, electricity, and magnetism. An important step toward simplifying this view of the world was completed in the 1860s by James Clerk Maxwell, a Scottish mathematician and physicist, who showed that electricity and magnetism are different manifestations of a single underlying entity known now as the

electromagnetic field. Maxwell's achievement explained much that had seemed mysterious—notably the nature of light—and predicted the existence of radio waves. It later inspired attempts to devise a still more comprehensive theory that would encompass all the forces of nature.

In the first three decades of the twentieth century, after the discovery of the atomic nucleus, two more forces were recognized: the strong force, which binds together the protons and the neutrons that compose the nucleus of an atom, and the weak force, which breaks the nucleus apart. For example, the radioactive decay of neutrons with the emission of beta particles (electrons) and neutrinos, a process that contributes to the energy output of the sun, is an effect of the weak force. Both the strong force and the weak force differ in an important way from the forces known earlier. Whereas gravitation and electromagnetism have an unlimited range, the strong force is effective only at distances no larger than the dimensions of an atomic nucleus, and the weak force acts only at even closer range.

The theoretical innovations for which Glashow, ABDUS SALAM, and Weinberg were awarded the Nobel Prize led to the unification of electromagnetism and the weak force. As with Maxwell's unification of electricity and magnetism, electromagnetism and the weak force came to be regarded as different aspects of a single "electroweak" force. Glashow's first attempt, in 1960, to link electromagnetism and the weak force was based on a concept called gauge symmetry. (Salam proposed a similar formulation about a year later.) In everyday usage, an object is said to be symmetrical if it is indistinguishable from its mirror image. Physicists, however, have introduced many other kinds of symmetry; for example, in charge symmetry in electromagnetism, the force between two particles remains unchanged if their electric charges are reversed. Gauge symmetry, introduced in the 1920s, refers to physical properties or relationships that remain invariant when the dimension scale or chosen reference point for relative measurements is changed. In 1954 CHEN NING YANG and Robert L. Mills, working at the Brookhaven National Laboratory, tried to extend the principle of gauge symmetry to the more complicated physics of the strong force. Although their investigation did not yield a workable theory, it paved the way for all subsequent accounts of the forces of nature, including the theories devised by Glashow, Weinberg, and Salam.

In a sense, Glashow's 1960 unification of electromagnetism and the weak force was too successful, for it not only unified the forces but also made them indistinguishable. The theory predicted the existence of four particles that would serve as carriers of the forces. One of the particles could be identified with the photon, the quantum of light, which was already known as the carrier of the electromagnetic force. The other three particles, since named W^+, W^-, and Z^0, would presumably mediate the weak interactions of matter. In the 1960 theory, all four particles were massless. In quantum mechanics the range of a force is inversely proportional to the mass of the carrier particle, so that a mass of zero corresponds to an infinite range. Thus, contrary to all experimental evidence, Glashow's theory predicted an unlimited range not only for electromagnetism but also for the weak force.

Glashow's proposed gauge symmetry led to another unconventional prediction. When two particles interact by means of the electromagnetic force, their electric charges are not altered. This is to be expected because the photon (the particle exchanged in electromagnetic events) carries no electric charge. In all weak interactions known at that time, however, a unit of electric charge was transferred; for example, a decaying neutron (with zero charge) might give rise to a proton (with a charge of $+1$) and an electron (with a charge of -1). Events of this kind could be explained by the exchange of W^+ and W^- particles, which have charges of $+1$ and -1 respectively. The introduction of the electrically neutral Z^0, how-

ever, implied that some weak interactions should proceed without charge transfer, as in electromagnetic exchanges. The prediction of such events, called weak neutral currents, later became a crucial experimental test of the unified theories.

Glashow tried to mend the major failing of his theory—the apparently unlimited range of the weak force—by simply postulating large masses for the W^+, W^-, and Z^0 particles. The strategy, however, was unsuccessful. When the masses were included, the theory gave impossible results, such as predicting that certain weak interactions would have an infinite strength. Similar problems, encountered two decades earlier, had been solved by a mathematical procedure called renormalization, but it, too, did not work in this case. The problem of massive W and Z particles was solved some years later when Weinberg, Salam, and others applied new methods.

Working independently in 1967 and 1968, Weinberg and Salam devised a unified theory of the weak and electromagnetic forces based on the same gauge symmetry employed by Glashow. Again, four carrier particles were predicted, but a new mechanism was introduced to give mass to the W^+, W^-, and Z^0 particles while leaving the photon massless. The idea for the mechanism, called spontaneous symmetry breaking, originated in solid-state physics. The W and Z particles were subsequently detected by CARLO RUBBIA in highly energetic collisions in a particle accelerator.

Glashow, Salam, and Weinberg shared the 1979 Nobel Prize for Physics "for their contributions to the theory of the unified weak and electromagnetic interaction between elementary particles, including, inter alia, the prediction of the weak neutral current." In his Nobel lecture Glashow reminisced about the days when Julian Schwinger had first encouraged him to work on the unification of forces. "In 1956, when I began doing theoretical physics, the study of elementary particles was like a patchwork quilt. Electrodynamics, weak interactions, and strong interactions were clearly separate disciplines, separately taught and separately studied. There was no coherent theory that described them all." He then commented, "Things have changed. . . . The theory we now have is an integral work of art: the patchwork quilt has become a tapestry."

In addition to his work on the weak and electromagnetic forces, Glashow has made important contributions to the understanding of the strong force. In the 1940s and 1950s, many short-lived particles related to the proton and the neutron were discovered in experiments with high-energy particle accelerators. By 1960 there were more than 100 known particles, all of which appeared to be equally elementary. Many physicists considered this situation unsatisfactory, and in 1963 MURRAY GELL-MANN and the American physicist George Zweig, working independently, suggested a way to reduce the number of fundamental entities needed in a theory of matter. They pointed out that the proton, the neutron, and all their known relatives might be composite objects, built up from a few, more basic particles that Gell-Mann named quarks. The quarks would interact with one another by means of the strong force.

Gell-Mann's original formulation had three species of quarks, given the names *up, down,* and *strange.* Just a year later, when the quark model was still highly speculative, Glashow, in collaboration with the physicist James D. Bjorken, proposed adding a fourth quark. He called it the charmed quark because it "worked like a charm" in suppressing certain events predicted by the three-quark theory but not, in fact, observed. In 1970 Glashow, with John Iliopoulos and Luciano Maiani, gave even stronger arguments for the existence of the charmed quark. Particles incorporating charmed quarks were discovered in 1974, confirming Glashow's prediction and supporting the quark hypothesis.

Since winning the Nobel Prize, Glashow has continued to teach and do research at Harvard. Recently, he has attempted to construct a theory (again based on gauge symmetry) that would unify the strong force with the electroweak force. In 1987, in collaboration with John N. Bahcall of the Institute for Advanced Study at Princeton, New Jersey, Glashow reported that the mass of neutrinos was lower than some previous estimates had predicted. These findings, based on studies of a supernova explosion, provide evidence that the combined mass of all neutrinos is not sufficient to reverse the expansion of the universe, as some scientists had predicted.

Glashow married Joan Shirley Alexander in 1972; they have three sons and a daughter. He is the recipient of the J. Robert Oppenheimer Memorial Medal of the University of Miami (1977) and the George Ledlie Prize of Harvard University (1978), as well as honorary degrees from Yeshiva University and the University of Aix-Marseilles. He is a member of the American Physical Society, the American Academy of Arts and Sciences, and the National Academy of Sciences.

SELECTED WORKS: "Quarks With Color and Flavor," Scientific American October 1975; "Toward a Unified Theory: Threads in a Tapestry," Science January 11, 1980.

ABOUT: Hammond, A. (ed.) `A Passion to Know, 1984; New Scientist October 18, 1979; Science December 14, 1979; Science 84 March 1984.

GOBAT, ALBERT
(May 21, 1843–March 16, 1914)
Nobel Prize for Peace, 1902
(shared with Élie Ducommun)

The Swiss politician and internationalist Charles Albert Gobat (gô bä') was born in the town of Tramelan in northwestern Switzerland, where his father was a Protestant minister. After completing his secondary education, he studied philosophy, history, and literature at the universities of Basel, Bern, and Heidelberg. Upon receiving a doctorate in law summa cum laude from Heidelberg in 1867, he began graduate studies in economics and international law at the Sorbonne and the Collège de France in Paris.

Returning to Switzerland in 1868, Gobat practiced law and lectured at the University of Bern before moving to the nearby town of Delémont, where he established a flourishing law practice. A large, powerfully built man, Gobat was said by one of his contemporaries to "attack his opponent's convictions as one would storm a fortress." Drawn into local politics, Gobat was elected to several minor public offices. In 1882 he won a seat in the Grand Council of Bern, the legislative body of the canton.

That year, Gobat was also appointed superintendent of Bern's Department of Public Education where, during his twenty-four-year tenure, he effected many progressive reforms. He introduced vocational education into the curriculum, obtained state funding for the study of the fine arts, and reduced the requirements for classical languages to permit increased study of modern languages and the natural sciences. Moreover, he persuaded the University of Bern to offer adult education courses and helped raise funds for the university's extensive building program.

As a scholar, Gobat wrote *République de Berne et la France pendant les guerres de religion* (The Republic of Bern and France During the Religious Wars, 1891) and the popular *Histoire de la Suisse racontée au peuple* (People's History of Switzerland, 1900).

Meanwhile, Gobat continued to be active

ALBERT GOBAT

lementaire (Joint Conference of Both Houses), and wrote a brief history of the organization.

Carrying his internationalist beliefs into the political sphere, in 1902 Gobat introduced a bill into the Swiss legislature that applied the principle of arbitration to commercial treaties. Under its terms, Switzerland agreed to insert into any such treaties it might sign a clause requiring the parties to submit all otherwise unresolvable disputes to the Permanent Court of Arbitration at The Hague.

For his work on behalf of international arbitration, Gobat shared the 1902 Nobel Prize for Peace with ÉLIE DUCOMMUN. No text of the presentation address remains. However, in a toast to Gobat given at an official banquet, Jørgen Løvland of the Norwegian Nobel Committee noted that under the laureate's leadership the Interparliamentary Union had become "one of the major factors in international politics." He lauded Gobat for his "eminently practical administration" of the organization. In his Nobel lecture, delivered four years later, Gobat began by summarizing the development of the peace conventions held at The Hague. "It is true," he said, "that I am not one of those who laugh at utopias. The utopia of today can become the reality of tomorrow." Nonetheless, he added, "I draw a distinction between aims which can be realized and those for which we are not yet ready. Today one thing is certain: thanks to the marvelous inventions and discoveries of our era, the human spirit has finally awakened a social order long dormant: the solidarity of nations. . . . May The Hague conference be its instrument!"

Two years after receiving the Nobel Prize, Gobat led the Swiss delegation to an Interparliamentary Union conference in St. Louis, Missouri. There he was chosen to deliver a petition to THEODORE ROOSEVELT, asking the president to urge all nations to participate in a second peace conference at The Hague, which ultimately took place in 1907.

After Ducommun's death in 1906, Gobat succeeded him as director of the INTERNATIONAL PEACE BUREAU, a center for the dissemination of information about the peace movement. Thus, between 1906 and 1909 Gobat was in charge of the world's two largest organizations devoted to peace. When the Interparliamentary Union moved to Brussels in 1909, Gobat resigned from his leadership post in the bureau. He withdrew from the government of the canton of Bern in 1911. He continued his peace work, however, and he wrote *Le Cauchemar de l'Europe* (The Nightmare of

in local and national politics, winning election to the Council of States of Switzerland in 1884 and the presidency of the canton of Bern two years later. In 1890 he became a member of the National Council, where he served until his death.

His interest in international law and politics brought Gobat into contact with members of the peace movement that was gathering momentum in Europe during the second half of the nineteenth century. In 1889 he attended the first major conference of the Interparliamentary Union, an organization founded the previous year by FRÉDÉRIC PASSY and WILLIAM CREMER. Its purpose was to encourage parliamentary representatives from all European nations to discuss their problems and differences, thus promoting international cooperation. Gobat was especially interested in the union's advocacy of international arbitration, for only by arbitration agreements, he believed, could modern nations coexist peacefully.

As head of the Swiss delegation to the third Interparliamentary Union conference in Rome in 1891, Gobat proved to be such an effective leader that he was asked to organize the union's next meeting in Bern the following year. There he was chosen director of the Interparliamentary Bureau, an administrative body responsible for coordinating activities of the union's member nations, recruiting new members, and organizing annual conferences. In addition, between 1893 and 1897 Gobat edited the union's monthly newsletter, *La Conférence Interpar-*

Europe), a widely read book that warned against the potentially disastrous consequences of the European arms race that was then taking place.

Gobat presided for the last time over a conference of the Interparliamentary Union in 1912 in Geneva. The following year he helped arrange a meeting in Bern between members of the French and German parliaments to seek arms reductions, but little came of these talks. Gobat did not live to see World War I. At a meeting of the International Peace Bureau in Bern on March 16, 1914, he suffered a stroke and died.

At Gobat's funeral, the Belgian statesman HENRI LA FONTAINE described him as one whose "fighting temperament did not, at first sight, seem to predestine him to be a defender of peace. If he became one of its most influential supporters, it was because the victory of that cause was by no means certain, and he was essentially the defender of unpopular causes."

WORKS IN ENGLISH TRANSLATION: "The International Parliament," The Independent May 14, 1903.

ABOUT: The Independent March 5, 1903; Interparliamentary Union. The Interparliamentary Union From 1889–1939, 1939; Lyons, F. S. L. Internationalism in Europe 1815–1914, 1963.

GOEPPERT MAYER, MARIA
See MAYER, MARIA GOEPPERT

GOLDING, WILLIAM
(September 19, 1911–   )
Nobel Prize for Literature, 1983

The English novelist William Gerald Golding was born in the village of St. Columb Minor in Cornwall. His schoolmaster father, Alec Golding, later described by his son as a polymath, was a rationalist; his mother was a suffragette. The young man attended the Marlborough Grammar School and Oxford University, where for two years, following the wishes of his parents, he studied the natural sciences. Golding, who had been writing since the age of seven, subsequently switched to the study of English and published a collection of poems in 1934, a year before receiving his B.A.

After graduation, Golding became a settlement house social worker; during this time he wrote, produced, and acted in plays for a small London theater. In 1939 he married Ann

WILLIAM GOLDING

Brookfield, an analytical chemist, and began teaching English and philosophy at Bishop Wordsworth's School in Salisbury, where he remained, with the exception of the years during World War II, until 1961.

Between 1940 and 1945 Golding served in the Royal Navy; near the end of World War II he commanded a rocket-launching ship and took part in the Normandy invasion. On his discharge from the navy, he returned to his teaching position in Salisbury. There he also learned ancient Greek and wrote four novels, none of them published. Yet he persisted in his literary efforts, and in 1954, after the manuscript had been turned down by twenty-one publishers, *Lord of the Flies* was brought out by Faber and Faber. It immediately became a best-seller in Britain. Although it was published the next year in the United States, *Lord of the Flies* became popular among American readers only after it was reprinted in 1959. The novel achieved even greater recognition in 1963 when it was released as a film by the British director Peter Brooks.

World War II had greatly affected Golding's view of the human condition. As a result of his wartime experiences, he said, "I began to see what people are capable of doing . . . . Anyone who moved through those years without understanding that man produces evil as a bee produces honey must have been blind or wrong in the head." The flawed nature of mankind provided Golding with the underlying theme of *Lord of the Flies*. This novel, which has rivaled the popularity of J. D. Salinger's *Catcher in the Rye* as a classic on school campuses, has sold more than 20 million copies. The book originated as an ironic comment on R. M. Ballantyne's *Coral Island,* a boys' adventure story in which the protagonists represent the optimistic and colonialistic view of mid-nineteenth-century England.

On a narrative level, *Lord of the Flies* describes the inevitable process whereby a group of middle-class adolescent boys, marooned on an island, revert to savagery. Their behavior degenerates from democratic, rational, and moral to tyrannical, bloodthirsty, and evil—complete with primitive rites and human scapegoats. On a symbolic level, the novel suggests a religious, political, or psychological fable rather than a work of realistic fiction. The mythical character of Golding's fiction has provoked much critical debate, with some critics arguing that the symbolic level not only overwhelms the narrative level but is also forced, confused, or pretentious.

In 1961, after a year as writer-in-residence at Hollins College in Virginia, Golding resigned from teaching and devoted his full time to writing. By this time, he had published three more novels—*The Inheritors* (1955), *Pincher Martin* (1956), and *Free Fall* (1959)—as well as several short stories and a play, *The Brass Butterfly* (1958).

Like *Lord of the Flies, The Inheritors* also refutes an earlier work, H. G. Wells's *Outline of History,* which expresses an optimistic belief in rationalism and progress. Golding has noted that Wells's book played "a great part" in his life because his father "was a rationalist, and the *Outline* . . . was something he took neat." *The Inheritors* describes the extermination of Neanderthal man by Homo sapiens; Golding conceives of the former as our gentle, guileless, unfallen ancestors, and of the latter as brutal, bloodthirsty killers.

The writer's third survival story, *Pincher Martin,* tells the tale of the title character, a shipwrecked naval officer and one-time actor, clinging to a crag on what he believes is an island. At first the reader is led to applaud Martin's courageous efforts to survive. Finally, however, learning more about his selfish and loveless life, the reader begins to condemn him for his tenacity, which Golding links ironically with that of Prometheus. The novel ultimately reveals that Martin is already dead and that his apparent existence is a self-imposed purgatory, a refusal to accept God's mercy and die.

Unlike Golding's first three novels, *Free Fall* is set in contemporary society and has no mythical substructure. Yet its themes resemble those of Golding's other works: the fall from childlike innocence into adult guilt and the conflict between religion and rationalism, myth and history.

The Spire (1964), set in a fourteenth-century English cathedral town, is regarded by some critics as a culmination of the themes and techniques of Golding's first four novels—a richer amalgam of narrative and myth than *Lord of the Flies*. In it, Golding again questions humanity's essential nature and the problem of evil, issues reflected in the determination of Dean Jocelin, the protagonist, to add a spire to his cathedral in order to raise his "prayer in stone," regardless of its cost in money, happiness, life, or even faith itself. At another level, Jocelin's attempt to impose shape upon recalcitrant rock parallels Golding's attempt to shape his novel.

English critics Mark Kinkead-Weekes and Ian Gregor believed that *The Spire* marked a turning point in Golding's career, for the novels that followed developed in two separate directions: the metaphysical and the social. The two critics pointed out that Americans prefer the metaphysical mode of *Darkness Visible* (1979), whereas English readers prefer the social analysis of *Rites of Passage* (1980), which won England's Booker Prize the year it was published.

In 1982 Golding published a collection of essays entitled *A Moving Target*. An earlier collection, *The Hot Gates* (1965), had brought together various nonfiction pieces written between 1960 and 1962, when Golding was a book reviewer for *The Spectator.*

Golding was awarded the 1983 Nobel Prize for Literature "for his novels which, with the perspicuity of realistic narrative art, and the diversity and universality of myth, illuminate the human condition in the world of today." To many, the choice of Golding was unexpected; the English candidate who had received the most public speculation was the novelist Graham Greene. In the controversy, one member of the Swedish Academy, the scholar Artur Lundkvist, broke tradition by voicing disapproval of Golding's selection and calling his works "a little English phenomenon of no special interest."

"William Golding's novels and stories are not only somber moralities and dark myths about evil and treacherous, destructive forces," said Lars Gyllensten of the Swedish Academy in his presentation speech. "They are also colorful tales of adventure which can be read as such, full of narrative joy, inventiveness, and excitement."

In his Nobel lecture, Golding humorously refuted his reputation as an unrelieved pessimist, describing himself as "a universal pessimist but a cosmic optimist." When considering a universe inexorably governed by scientific rules, he said, "then I am a pessimist. . . . I am optimistic when I consider the spiritual dimension which the scientist's discipline forces him to ignore." It is possible that through literature, Golding continued, man can become more "aware of what he is doing. . . . We need more humanity, more care, more love."

At the time he received the Nobel Prize, Golding was at work on *The Paper Men,* which was published in Great Britain and in the United States in 1984. This novel recounts a psychological and spiritual struggle between an aging British novelist (Wilfred Barclay) and an ambitious American academic (Rick Tucker), who hounds Barclay in pursuit of the writer's authorized biography. At one level, wrote the English critic Blake Morrison, it is "a defense of the individual imagination against the threat posed to the living . . . writer by the dead hand of . . . scholarship." At another level, Morrison pointed out, Tucker can be seen either as a "Christ-figure who offers [Barclay] redemption," or as "Satan . . . whose temptations Barclay must refuse." *The Paper Men* received mixed reviews on both sides of the Atlantic.

Throughout his career, Golding's critical reputation has been subject to widely differing opinions. According to the Amercian critic Stanley Edgar Hyman, Golding "is the most interesting British writer today," a view shared by the English critic and short story writer V. S. Pritchett. Frederick Karl, however, has criticized Golding for "his inability . . . to give intellectual substance to his themes, and his didactic intrusion in nearly all of the narratives. . . . His eccentric themes . . . rarely convey the sense of balance and ripeness that indicate literary maturity."

Golding was elected to the Royal Society of Literature in 1955 and knighted in 1966. He and his wife live in Wiltshire, near Salisbury; they have a son, David, and a daughter, Judith. Once an avid sailor, Golding still enjoys playing the piano, studying Greek, and reading about archaeology.

ADDITIONAL WORKS: Poems, 1934; The Pyramid, 1967; The Scorpion God, 1971; An Egyptian Journal, 1985; Close Quarters, 1987.

ABOUT: Anderson, D., et al. William Golding: Some Critical Considerations, 1978; Babb, H. S. The Novels of William Golding, 1973; Baker, J. R. William Golding, 1965; Biles, J. I., and Golding, W. Talk: Conversations With William Golding, 1970; Briggs, J., and Crompton, D. A View From the Spire, 1985; Carey, J. (ed.) William Golding: The Man and His Books, 1986; Dick, B. F. William Golding, 1967; Elmen, P. William Golding, 1967; Gregor, I., and Kinkead-Weekes, M. William Golding: A Critical Study, 1967; Hodson, L. William Golding, 1969; Hynes, S. William Golding, 1964; Johnston, A. Of Earth and Darkness, 1980; Medcalf, S. William Golding, 1975; Oldsey, B. S., and Weintraub, S. The Art of William Golding, 1965; Redpath, P. William Golding, 1986; Whitley, J. S. Golding: Lord of the Flies, 1970.

GOLDSTEIN, JOSEPH L.
(April 18, 1940–)
Nobel Prize for Physiology or Medicine, 1985
(shared with Michael S. Brown)

The American geneticist Joseph Leonard Goldstein was born in Sumter, South Carolina, to Isadore E. and Fannie A. Goldstein. He received a B.S. from Washington and Lee University in Lexington, Virginia, in 1962 and an M.D. from the University of Texas Southwestern Medical School in Dallas four years later. Goldstein was such an outstanding medical student that before graduation he was offered a future faculty position by Dr. Donald Seldin, chairman of the university's Department of Medicine. While serving as an intern and resident in medicine at the Massachusetts General Hospital in Boston from 1966 to 1968, Goldstein became acquainted with MICHAEL S. BROWN, a fellow medical house officer.

Following his residency, he spent two years at the National Institutes of Health as a clinical associate under MARSHALL W. NIRENBERG in the Laboratory of Biochemical Genetics. From 1970 to 1972 Goldstein was a postdoctoral fellow in medical genetics at the University of Washington in Seattle. There, working under Arno G. Motulsky, he discovered a new disease—familial combined hyperlipidemia. In 1972 Goldstein returned to Southwestern Medical School to become head of the Division of Medical Genetics and assistant professor in the Department of Internal Medicine. He was named associate professor two years later, then senior attending physician at Parkland Memorial Hospital (1974), professor of internal medicine (1976), professor and chairman of the Department of Molecular Genetics, professor of medicine and genetics (1977), and nonresident fellow at the Salk Institute in San Diego, California (1983). Michael Brown had already joined the Southwestern Medical School, and the two sci-

JOSEPH L. GOLDSTEIN

entists soon began to collaborate on a study of cholesterol metabolism.

Cholesterol, essential for human life, forms a major part of cell membranes and is required for the manufacture of bile acids and steroid hormones. However, too much cholesterol may accumulate in the walls of blood vessels and block the flow of blood, causing heart attacks and strokes. Some cholesterol is absorbed from dietary fat, and some is synthesized within the body. Most cholesterol in the bloodstream is carried by particles of low-density lipoprotein (LDL).

Familial hypercholesterolemia is a hereditary disease characterized by extremely high blood levels of cholesterol and LDL. Approximately 1 in 500 Americans and Europeans have the less severe heterozygous (one abnormal gene) form of this disease and commonly suffer heart attacks when they reach thirty to fifty years of age; of this group, 85 percent, particularly the males, suffer heart attacks by the age of sixty. Those with the more severe homozygous form, which results from inheritance of two mutant genes and occurs in approximately 1 in 1 million people, have coronary disorders beginning in childhood.

In their study of cholesterol generation and regulation, Goldstein and Brown used tissue culture techniques to grow skin cells taken from individuals with familial hypercholesterolemia. These cells were found to have extremely high levels of 3-hydroxy-3-methyl glutaryl coenzyme A reductase (HMG-CoA reductase), the enzyme that controls the rate of cho-

lesterol synthesis. Because the enzyme was so active, the cells were producing far more cholesterol than was used.

Goldstein and Brown then discovered that cell surfaces, especially in the liver, have specific receptors for the LDL-cholesterol complex. Together with Richard G. Anderson, a colleague at Southwestern, they found that the LDL receptors cluster in cell-surface pits coated with the protein clathrin. In a process called receptor-mediated endocytosis, protective coverings in the cell membrane engulf the LDL and pinch off to form vesicles that carry the particles into the interior of the cell. The receptor then separates from the LDL and returns to the cell surface. In the cell, LDL is broken down and cholesterol is released. Excess cholesterol inhibits HMG-CoA reductase (and therefore synthesis of more cholesterol); at the same time, it activates acyl-CoA: cholesterol acyltransferase (ACAT), the enzyme responsible for storing cholesterol within the cell. Increased cellular cholesterol also shuts off production of more LDL receptors. In this manner, a normal cell can balance cholesterol uptake from the diet with synthesis by the cells. When cells become overloaded with cholesterol, however, arteriosclerotic deposits form in blood vessels.

Patients with familial hypercholesterolemia have abnormal LDL receptors that fail to remove enough cholesterol from the blood. In 1984 Goldstein and Brown described several mutations of the gene responsible for the LDL receptor. Familial hypercholesterolemia can be caused by defective synthesis of the receptor, defective binding of LDL, inadequate endocytosis or transport of the receptor within the cell, or failure of the surface receptor to migrate to the coated pits.

In certain patients with heterozygous familial hypercholesterolemia, who have only one functional gene for the LDL receptor, resin treatment with drugs such as compactin or mevinolin increases the number of LDL receptors produced by the single functioning gene, thus reducing the levels of LDL and cholesterol in the blood. This form of therapy does not work, however, in homozygous patients, who have no functioning gene for the LDL receptor. In 1984 a liver transplant was performed in a six-year-old girl with homozygous familial hypercholesterolemia, and—as Goldstein and Brown's theories had predicted—the presence of normal LDL receptors on the transplanted liver produced a marked lowering of the blood cholesterol level.

Goldstein and Brown received the 1985 Nobel Prize for Physiology or Medicine for their research, which, according to the Karolinska Institute in Stockholm, has "drastically widened our understanding of the cholesterol metabolism and increased our possibilities to prevent and treat atherosclerosis."

Goldstein, who is unmarried, enjoys listening to classical music during his leisure time.

With Brown, Goldstein has also received the Pfizer Award for Enzyme Chemistry of the American Chemical Society (1976), the Lounsbery Award of the National Academy of Sciences (1979), the Gairdner Foundation International Award (1981), the V. D. Mattia Award of the Roche Institute of Molecular Biology (1984), and the Louisa Gross Horwitz Prize of Columbia University (1984). A member of numerous medical and scientific societies, Goldstein is also active in the American Federation for Clinical Research, the Mammalian Cell Lines National Advisory Committee, the Physiological Chemistry Research Study Section of the American Heart Association, the American Society for Clinical Investigation (president, 1985–1986), and the Medical Advisory Board of the Howard Hughes Medical Institute. He currently serves on the editorial boards of *Atherosclerosis Reviews, Arteriosclerosis, Cell, Molecular Biology and Medicine,* and *Science.* He was a co-editor of *The Metabolic Basis of Inherited Disease.*

ABOUT: New York Times October 15, 1985; Science January 10, 1986.

GOLGI, CAMILLO
(July 7, 1843–January 21, 1926)
Nobel Prize for Physiology or Medicine, 1906
(shared with Santiago Ramón y Cajal)

The Italian histologist and pathologist Camillo Golgi (gôl′ jē) was born in Corteno. His father, Alessandro, a native of Pavia, was a doctor. Golgi studied medicine at the University of Pavia under Eusebio Oehl, the first scientist at Pavia to use the microscope for systematic study of cell structures. After receiving his medical degree in 1865, Golgi remained in Pavia to work in a psychiatric clinic at the Hospital of St. Matteo. He also conducted research on the structure of the brain and nervous system in a microscope laboratory run by Giulio Bizzozero, one of his former teachers at the university.

CAMILLO GOLGI

As improved microscopes were developed during the early nineteenth century, scientific knowledge of the structure of cells in different tissues expanded rapidly, and after the publication of Rudolf Virchow's *Cellular Pathology* in 1850, microscopic studies became increasingly popular. When the early histologists turned their instruments to the nervous system, however, they could gain no clear idea of cell structure. While nonnerve cells are restricted in size and appear in a few consistent shapes, nerve cells (called neurons) can be extremely long and thin—certain cells, for example, extend from the toe to the spinal cord—and are much thinner than hairs. Nerve cells are also elaborately branched, and these radiating fibers intertwine with the branches from other nerve cells. Early microscopists who examined the nervous system found only a tangled mass of semitransparent cells and fibers.

Golgi's first studies of microscopic neuroanatomy were published in the late 1860s, while he was in Pavia. In 1872 he became chief medical officer at the Hospital for the Chronically Sick in the town of Abbiategrasso. Since the position involved no research, Golgi pursued his microscopic studies in a converted kitchen, where he managed to devise a method for staining individual nerve cells within the next year.

Tissues must be thinly sliced for microscopic observation. The tissues are usually hardened first with bichromate in order to produce fine, uniform slices. Golgi found that by immersing the hardened slices of nerve tissues in a silver nitrate solution, the neurons were stained black, which made them stand out boldly against the background. By carefully controlling the time of hardening in the bichromate, Golgi could stain just a few neurons, only their fibers, or many cells at once.

After returning to Pavia as a lecturer in histology in 1875, Golgi taught anatomy at the University of Siena in 1879. The next year he moved back to Pavia to become professor of histology. He then succeeded Bizzozero, his former teacher, in the chair of general pathology and made a number of contributions to that field. He married Bizzozero's niece, Donna Lina Aletti; they had no children but adopted Golgi's niece.

Because Golgi's technique required skill and experience, his silver nitrate method did not create a scientific sensation overnight. Eventually, as the method was adopted by other neuroanatomists in the early 1880s, knowledge of nerve-cell structures grew rapidly. Golgi himself classified different types of neurons and made many important discoveries about the structure of individual neurons and the whole central nervous system.

The silver nitrate staining method demonstrated the extreme complexity of nerve connections. A single neuron in the human brain, for example, may make connections with over 10,000 other cells. Theoretically, all the fibers of a single neuron could be traced by Golgi's method, but in practice it may be impossible to distinguish the interconnected cells. Golgi believed that his preparations showed a "diffuse nerve network," in which the fibers "gradually lose their individuality while dividing to become extremely fine filaments."

Of the many neuroanatomists who adopted Golgi's staining technique, SANTIAGO RAMÓN Y CAJAL was the most talented. In contrast to Golgi, however, Ramón y Cajal favored the "neuron theory," which postulated that each nerve cell is an independent unit, both in structure and function.

Although Ramón y Cajal could not prove that nerve fibers from different cells remain separate and individual, because the synapse (the gap between nerve cells) is too small to be distinguished by an optical microscope, the illustrations he drew of nerve networks made them appear as individual cells with complicated interconnections, whereas Golgi saw them as resembling a fine web of undifferentiated fibers. Ramón y Cajal studied his preparations under higher magnification and paid closer attention to details than Golgi, who, nevertheless, was an acute observer and knew that it is difficult to tell whether a particular structure exists in the living cell or is merely an artifact of the fixation and staining process.

These problems are illustrated by the fate of Golgi's most familiar discovery. In 1898 he observed that the interior of the nerve cell contains a fine network of interlaced threads. This "Golgi apparatus" was studied for many years in a variety of cells. Then, during the 1930s and 1940s, and after the advent of the electron microscope—a thousand times more powerful than the best optical microscope—the Golgi apparatus was thought to be only an artificial structure produced by staining techniques. Finally, however, as electron microscopy improved, the reality of the Golgi apparatus was once more accepted; it is now considered to function in the modification and secretion of proteins.

At the turn of the century, Golgi and Ramón y Cajal disagreed over the nature of nerve-cell structure, even though they shared the 1906 Nobel Prize for Physiology or Medicine "in recognition of their work on the structure of the nervous system." Golgi, the pioneer of modern research in the nervous system, chose the occasion to attack Ramón y Cajal's neuron doctrine, saying that the idea of independent nerve cells was only "one interpretation of nerve function." In his Nobel lecture he showed many illustrations of a closed latticework structure that, he believed, established the functional and anatomical continuity among nerve cells. Support for such a network theory diminished, however, as the concept of structurally independent neurons complemented CHARLES S. SHERRINGTON's studies of nerve physiology.

In addition to his work on the nervous system, Golgi turned his attention toward malaria during the period of 1885–1893. His work in that area brought him into conflict with another malaria investigator, RONALD ROSS. Despite their bitter dispute, Golgi enjoyed considerable prestige in Italy as a result of his work on the nervous system and his malaria research. Golgi's investigation of malaria led to a remarkable discovery: all of the malarial parasites in the blood divide almost simultaneously and at regular intervals. Moreover, the moment of division coincides with the onset of fever. Golgi worked first with quartan fever, so named because the victim's temperature peaks every fourth day, counting the first attack as the first day. (The interval between attacks is seventy-two hours.) Using a series of blood slides, he showed that a new generation of quartan parasites (now known as *Plasmodium malariae*) appeared every seventy-two hours.

GRANIT

Golgi was elected a senator in 1900, and he was also named dean of the faculty of medicine and president of the University of Pavia. Considered the leading figure in Italian neuroscience after his retirement in 1918, he died in Pavia on January 21, 1926.

ABOUT: Cook, G. M. The Golgi Apparatus, 1975; Dictionary of Scientific Biography, volume 5, 1972; Haymaker, W. (ed.) The Founders of Neurology, 1953.

GRANIT, RAGNAR
(October 30, 1900–   )
Nobel Prize for Physiology or Medicine, 1967
(shared with H. Keffer Hartline and George Wald)

RAGNAR GRANIT

The Swedish neurophysicist Ragnar Arthur Granit was born in Helsinki, Finland, the eldest son of Albertina Helena (Malmberg) Granit and Arthur Granit, a forester for the government. Shortly after his birth, the family started a forest-products business in Helsinki, where the boy, whose parents were of Swedish origin, attended the Swedish Normal School. While still in school, Granit fought in Finland's war of liberation from the Soviet Union in 1918 and was awarded the Finnish Cross of Freedom. Entering the University of Helsinki the next year to study experimental psychology, he decided to give his interest a firm base by studying medicine as well. He received a master's degree in 1923 and a medical degree in 1927.

During his studies Granit became particularly interested in vision. Until the mid-1920s, vision studies were conducted indirectly and concentrated chiefly on the relationship between physical properties, such as the wavelength or the intensity of a light source, and conscious perceptions in human beings. In 1926 EDGAR D. ADRIAN made the first recordings of electrical impulses in single nerve fibers and soon extended his studies to record impulses from the conger eel's optic nerve, which is actually a bundle of many thousands of individual fibers. SANTIAGO RAMÓN Y CAJAL, one of the founders of microscopic neuroanatomy, had pointed out in 1894 that the retina of the eye is a true nervous center and that it differs from other sense organs in that it is a direct extension of the brain. The Italian histologist CAMILLO GOLGI perfected a system for staining nerve cells with silver nitrate and discovered a fine network within cells that is now known as the Golgi apparatus.

Granit realized that much important information about the nervous system in general, and about vision in particular, could be gained by studying the retina using Adrian's recording techniques. With this purpose in mind, Granit went to Oxford University in 1928 to work not only with Adrian but also with Adrian's mentor, CHARLES S. SHERRINGTON. Sherrington had discovered that the nerves that control the two sets of muscles in the leg are connected in such a way that stimulation of one inhibits the other. The idea that inhibitory processes play a role in governing the behavior of nerve cells led Granit to investigate their possible function in vision, specifically in the retina.

After mastering the techniques of electroneurophysiology, Granit spent the academy year 1929–1932 at the Johnson Foundation for Medical Physics at the University of Pennsylvania. While continuing his research on vision, he became acquainted with H. KEFFER HARTLINE and GEORGE WALD, who were engaged in similar investigations. In his early experiments Granit used traditional indirect methods (for example, the sensitivity a human subject reports to flickering lights) to discover that strong illumination of parts of the retina inhibits the response of adjacent regions. The net effect of this phenomenon is to enhance the perception of contrasts by the eye. (The importance of such lateral inhibition in the processing of visual information was clarified by Hartline's studies of individual retinal cells and, much later, by the research of DAVID H. HUBEL and TORSTEN WIESEL on the visual centers of the brain.) Granit used the electroretinogram (ERG), a record of the activity of the retina as a whole, to confirm that "the details of the visual image" are "elaborated by the interplay of excitation and inhibition in the nervous center of the retina itself."

Many of Granit's ERG experiments were performed after he returned to the University of Helsinki in 1935 to assume the position of professor of physiology. Other topics in vision studies were beginning to attract his interest, however, and the one that appealed most to him was color vision.

In the nineteenth century, the German physician Ferdinand von Helmholtz and the English scientist Thomas Young had proposed that the human ability to discriminate a spectrum of colors could be explained if it could be proven that the eye contains receptors (cone cells) with pigments sensitive to different wavelengths of light. The Young-Helmholtz theory of color vision postulated that there are three sets of color-perceiving elements in the retina—red, green, and violet—with the perception of other colors arising from the combined stimulation of these elements. Granit's first experiments in color vision, performed in 1937, employed the ERG to confirm the extent of spectral differentiation.

Granit's research was interrupted when the Soviet Union invaded Finland in 1939. During the conflict he served as a physician on the island of Korpo in the Baltic Sea, the home of his ancestors, as well as for two other nearby Swedish-speaking island parishes, including the military personnel within these regions. After the war, he was offered a position at both Harvard University and the Karolinska Institute; choosing the latter, he moved to Stockholm in 1940.

In Sweden, Granit and his colleagues developed a method of using microscopic electrodes to record the electrical responses of nerves and individual cells without the necessity for dissection—a noninvasive technique that has since been widely adopted for use in neurophysiological research of all types. Granit himself used it to study the response of the optic nerve—and later of individual cells in the retina—to specific colors. His work established the spectral sensitivities of the three types of cone cells: blue, green, and red. The biochemical proof of Granit's theory was provided in the 1950s when George Wald isolated the three cone pigments.

Finding that "the somewhat monotonous work of recording spectral sensitivities and the absence of photochemical data" gave him a "distaste for the whole field," Granit shifted

his attention in 1945 to muscle spindles, which are specialized sense organs that respond to muscular tension and provide the feedback the body uses to control muscle response. Sherrington and JOHN C. ECCLES had already delineated the role of the spindles in reflex action and the control of posture. Building on their work, Granit further defined spindle function and the relationships among various groups of spindles. He then extended his research to include examination of the interactions among muscles, motor neurons, and spindle nerves in the spinal cord and in the brain itself.

From 1945, when the Karolinska Institute made Granit's laboratory a department of the Medical Nobel Institute, he served as director of the Nobel Institute for Neurophysiology and professor at the Karolinska Institute until his retirement in 1967. Granit shared the 1967 Nobel Prize for Physiology or Medicine with Hartline and Wald "for their discoveries concerning the primary physiological and chemical visual processes in the eye." In his presentation address, Carl Gustaf Bernhard of the Karolinska Institute described Granit's work and noted that it had "led to the conclusion that there are different types of cones representing three characteristic spectral sensitivities," a conclusion that was confirmed by Wald and his colleagues. "The discovery implies that patterns which the optic nerve transmits to the brain and which result in perception of colors are dependent on the contributions from the three types of cone cells," Bernhard said.

Although he has not been actively engaged in vision research for some time, Granit's pioneering studies—of the role of inhibition in visual processing, of the ERG, and of color vision—exerted a profound influence on the development of the field. Before leaving to conduct research at the Johnson Foundation at the University of Pennsylvania in 1929, Granit married Baroness Marguerite Emma (Daisy) Bruun, who accompanied him to the United States; they have one son. Still active in retirement, he currently serves as visiting professor of neurophysiology at St. Catherine's College, Oxford, and spends much of his leisure time sailing on the Baltic Sea.

Among his many honors are the Jubilee Award of the Swedish Society of Physicians (1947), the Anders Retzius Gold Medal of the University of Stockholm (1957), and the F. C. Donders Medal of the University of Utrecht (1957). He is a member of the Royal Swedish Academy of Sciences and served as its president from 1963 to 1965. An honorary member of the American Academy of Arts and Sciences, he holds foreign membership in the Royal Society of London, the American National Academy of Sciences, and other professional societies.

SELECTED WORKS: Sensory Mechanisms of the Retina, 1947; Receptors and Sensory Perceptions, 1955; Charles Scott Sherrington: An Appraisal, 1966; The Basis of Motor Control, 1970; The Purposive Brain, 1977.

ABOUT: The Excitement and Fascination of Science, volume 2, 1978; New York Times October 19, 1967; Science October 27, 1967.

GRIGNARD, VICTOR
(May 6, 1871–December 13, 1935)
Nobel Prize for Chemistry, 1912
(shared with Paul Sabatier)

VICTOR GRIGNARD

The French chemist François Auguste Victor Grignard (grēn yär') was born in Cherbourg to Théophile Henri Grignard and the former Marie Hébert. His father was a sailmaker and later a foreman at the local marine arsenal. The boy attended the local lycée in Cherbourg and displayed his intellectual gifts early. A scholarship enabled him to study mathematics at the École Normale Spéciale at Cluny. When that school was closed two years later, he transferred to the University of Lyons, completing his studies in 1892. After failing his licentiate examinations, which would have qualified him to teach in the secondary schools, Grignard joined the army to fulfill his compulsory military service.

Upon his discharge the following year, Grignard returned to Lyons and passed his examinations. It was around this time that a friend and fellow student at Cluny aroused Grignard's interest in chemistry, and in 1894 he took a position as an assistant in the chemistry department at the university. Quickly showing an aptitude for this field, Grignard received his *licence* (M.A.) in the physical sciences in 1898, the same year that he was appointed senior demonstrator under Philippe Antoine Barbier, head of the chemistry department at Lyons.

Barbier had just begun investigating a technique in which a metal is used to transfer organic material from one molecule to another. Compounds that result from the union of the metal with one or more organic radicals (groups of atoms that remain unchanged during a series of reactions) are called organometallic compounds. The only organometallic compounds then known to be effective transfer agents were the organic zinc compounds. The process was time-consuming, however, and the results tended to be unstable.

Only a few years earlier, several German chemists had substituted magnesium for zinc but obtained only low yields of erratic, unstable compounds that were largely insoluble in inert solvents. Even though magnesium appeared to be an impractical transfer agent, Barbier decided to use it, but he approached the problem in a different way. Rather than preparing organic magnesium compounds in advance, as the German experimenters had done, he simply brought the two organic reactants together in the presence of magnesium and in this way obtained a reaction. Once again, however, the results were inconsistent, and Barbier, abandoning the problem, suggested it to Grignard as the topic for his doctoral thesis.

Grignard knew that earlier in the century the British chemists Edward Frankland and James Wanklyn had prepared organic zinc compounds by heating organic substances together with the metal in the presence of anhydrous ether. Because magnesium is more reactive than zinc, Grignard reasoned, it should react more easily and more thoroughly in a similar process. When this proved to be true, he used the method to produce a variety of organometallic compounds, some of which were entirely new.

In 1900 Grignard published the results of his research, for which he was awarded his doctorate the following year. The Grignard reaction, as it is known, became the focus of

Grignard's career as well as the subject of many experiments in organic chemistry. Using Grignard's method, other researchers were able to synthesize a wide range of organic compounds efficiently and inexpensively.

In 1905 Grignard was appointed a lecturer in chemistry at the University of Besançon, near Dijon, but he returned to Lyons the following year to accept a position as Barbier's research associate. He became an associate professor in 1908. A year later he joined the faculty at the University of Nancy, where he was named professor of organic chemistry in 1910.

Grignard was awarded the 1912 Nobel Prize for Chemistry "for the discovery of the so-called Grignard reagent, which in recent years has greatly advanced the progress of organic chemistry." He shared the prize with PAUL SABATIER. In his presentation address, H. G. Söderbaum of the Royal Swedish Academy of Sciences hailed Grignard for "push[ing] back appreciably the frontiers of our knowledge, of our ability to observe" and for "opening up prospects of new conquests for our science."

When France declared war in 1914, Grignard was called for service as a corporal and posted to Normandy. After serving sentry duty for a short time, he was assigned to conduct research into methods of producing toluene, an explosive. In 1917, while working on the development of chemical weapons, he visited the United States to coordinate joint French and American efforts. During this trip he lectured at the Mellon Institute (now Carnegie Mellon University) on the collaboration of science and industry.

Grignard was discharged from military service in 1919. After spending several months at the University of Nancy, he succeeded Barbier as professor of chemistry at the University of Lyons, where he remained for the duration of his career. In 1921 he assumed a concurrent position as director of the School of Industrial Chemistry in Lyons, and in 1929 he was named dean of its Faculty of Science.

At Lyons, Grignard investigated a wide range of problems in addition to his work with organic compounds of magnesium. These included the condensation of aldehydes and ketones, hydrocarbon cracking, the constitution of unsaturated compounds, catalytic hydrogenation, and dehydrogenation under reduced pressures. During the later stages of his career, administrative responsibilities forced him reluctantly to restrict his research.

In 1910 Grignard married Augustine Marie Boulant, with whom he had a daughter and a son, who also became a chemist. A dedicated and versatile researcher, Grignard was also highly esteemed as a teacher. After a brief illness, he died in Lyons on December 13, 1935.

Among Grignard's many honors were the Berthelot Medal (1902) and Jecker Prize (1905) of the French Academy of Sciences, and the Lavoisier Medal of the French Chemical Society (1912). He was named a commander of the Legion of Honor and held honorary degrees from the universities of Brussels and Louvain. He was a member of many chemical societies, including those of England, the United States, Belgium, France, Romania, Poland, the Netherlands, and Sweden.

SELECTED WORKS: The Collaboration of Science and Industry, 1918.

ABOUT: Dictionary of Scientific Biography, volume 5, 1972; Journal of Chemical Education, September 1950; Scott, A. F. (ed.) Survey of Progress in Chemistry, 1963.

GUILLAUME, CHARLES
(February 15, 1861–June 13, 1938)
Nobel Prize for Physics, 1920

The Swiss physicist Charles Édouard Guillaume (gē yōm′) was born in Fleurier, the son of Édouard Guillaume, a watchmaker. His father had returned to the family's original home in Switzerland after managing a watchmaking business established in London by his own father, who had fled France during the French Revolution. Young Charles was tutored by his father before beginning school in Neuchâtel. At the age of seventeen, Guillaume entered the Federal Institute of Technology in Zurich, where he studied science as well as German and French literature. He later said his interest in science had been stimulated by reading François Arago's Éloges académiques (Academic Praises), with its essays on astronomy, magnetism, and optics. In 1882 Guillaume earned a Ph.D. with a dissertation on electrolytic capacitors.

After serving for a year as an artillery officer in the Swiss army, Guillaume in 1883 joined the newly formed International Bureau of Weights and Measures at Sèvres, near Paris, as an assistant. Rising to associate director in 1902, he became director in 1905, a position he held until his retirement in 1936, when he was named an honorary director.

Guillaume's first project at the bureau dealt with the accuracy of the mercury thermome-

CHARLES GUILLAUME

ter. In this device, a relatively large amount of mercury is contained in a glass bulb, to which is connected a long, cylindrical glass tube of small diameter. An increase in temperature increases the volume of the mercury, causing a great change in position of the cylindrical column of mercury. To achieve accurate measurements with the mercury thermometer, it is necessary to correct for temperature-induced changes in bulb volume (brought on by expansion or contraction of the glass) and for changes in the area and length of the mercury column, so that the thermometer may be properly calibrated. The rate of change of length and volume with change in temperature itself depends on the temperature. Guillaume summarized his careful evaluation of all the relevant factors in *Traité de thermométrie* (Treatise on Thermometry) in 1889.

Turning next to the measurement of length, Guillaume searched for some alloy that could be used to fashion, for use in local metrology laboratories, affordable and reliable substitutes for the very expensive platinum-iridium standard meter bar owned by each of the nations that had participated in the first Conference on Weights and Measures in 1889. The measuring rules used in the field at varying temperatures were calibrated in local metrology laboratories at a fixed temperature against local standard meters that experienced thermal expansion and contraction. Both the poor quality of the local standards and the difference in temperature between field and laboratory resulted in systematic errors in measurements.

In his careful investigations of alloys, Guillaume noted that steel alloys with high nickel content had an anomalously low thermal expansivity. This observation led him to invent a nickel steel alloy containing 36 percent nickel, 0.4 percent manganese, 0.1 percent carbon, and 63.5 percent iron and having a coefficient of expansion less than one-tenth that of iron. He named it invar because it is almost invariable under the action of heat and other influences. Guillaume developed a number of methods, such as tempering, drawing, and rolling, to process invar in a way that would control its thermal expansivity. Standard invar meters were rapidly adopted for use in local metrology laboratories. In the field, surveyors and cartographers used tapes or long wires made of invar to establish surveying baselines. Invar was adopted for use in pendulum clocks, the timekeeping standard of that period.

Continuing his metallurgical research, Guillaume developed an alloy containing 36 percent nickel, 12 percent chromium, and 52 percent iron. His name for this alloy, which has a much lower thermoelastic coefficient than does steel, was elinvar, denoting an invariable elasticity modulus. Errors in the frequencies of steel tuning forks (used as precise oscillators) and in steel balance wheels of watches, brought about by changes in their stiffness (elasticity) resulting from fluctuations in temperature, were eliminated when these objects were fabricated of elinvar.

Guillaume received the 1920 Nobel Prize for Physics "in recognition of the service he has rendered to precision measurements in physics by his discovery of anomalies in nickel steel alloys." Guillaume, said A. G. Ekstrand of the Royal Swedish Academy of Sciences in his presentation speech, "is undeniably the foremost metrologist of today. . . . [His discovery] is of great significance for the precision of scientific measurements and thereby even for the development of science in general." Moreover, Ekstrand added, Guillaume's work on the properties of nickel steel have contributed to the theoretical understanding "of the composition of solid matter."

An early champion of international use of the metric system, Guillaume employed his notable courtesy and tact to further adoption of the system.

Despite his long residence in France, Guillaume retained his Swiss citizenship. In 1888 he married A. M. Taufflieb, with whom he had three children. He died in Sèvres, France, on June 13, 1938.

Guillaume's awards included honorary degrees from the universities of Geneva, Neuchâtel, and Paris. He served as president of the French Physical Society, was a member of more than a dozen scientific academies and societies, and was made a grand officer of the Legion of Honor.

SELECTED WORKS: Mechanics, 1914.

ABOUT: Dictionary of Scientific Biography, volume 5, 1972.

GUILLEMIN, ROGER
(January 11, 1924–   )
Nobel Prize for Physiology or Medicine, 1977
(shared with Andrew V. Schalley and Rosalyn S. Yalow)

ROGER GUILLEMIN

The French-American physiologist Roger Charles Louis Guillemin (gē maN') was born in Dijon, France, to Raymond and Blanche Guillemin. He received his early education in the public schools of Dijon and in 1942 received a bachelor of arts and sciences degree from the University of Dijon. He entered medical school in 1943 under a program that was jointly administered by the faculties of the universities of Dijon and Lyons; however, he had no opportunities for research. After completing three years of clinical training in what was the equivalent of a rotating internship, he practiced medicine briefly and then served in the Resistance during the Nazi occupation of France (1940–1944).

After hearing a lecture in 1948 by Hans Selye, the stress physiologist from Montreal, Canada, Guillemin persuaded Selye to employ him as a research assistant at the Institute of Experimental Medicine and Surgery at the University of Montreal. There Guillemin conducted experimental research on hypertension. This work became the subject of his dissertation, which he defended before the Faculty of Medicine of Lyons and for which he received his medical degree in 1949.

The following year, Guillemin returned to the institute in Montreal to conduct research in experimental endocrinology, the branch of biology and medicine that deals with the endocrine glands and their secretions. These glands secrete hormones that circulate in the blood and regulate the secretions of other endocrine glands and the functioning of certain tissues. Guillemin was interested in the role of the hypothalamus in regulating the hor-

monal secretions of the pituitary gland. The hypothalamus is located at the base of the brain above the pituitary gland and is connected to the anterior lobe of that gland by the portal blood vessels. In the 1930s the British physiologist G. W. Harris had observed that when the portal vessels were severed, the secretory activity of the anterior lobe of the pituitary gland was decreased. He therefore proposed that the pituitary gland was regulated by bloodborne chemical substances, or hormones, originating in the hypothalamus. No one had yet identified these hypothalamic hormones, and Guillemin made that task his goal.

An appointment as assistant professor of physiology at the Baylor University School of Medicine in Houston, Texas, was offered to Guillemin in 1953, and he accepted. Two years later he was joined there by ANDREW V. SCHALLEY, who had recently discovered the first of the hypothalamic hormones. Schalley called this hormone corticotropin-releasing factor, or CRF; it is now known as corticotropin-releasing hormone, or CRH. The hormone is secreted by cells in the hypothalamus and transported via the portal vessels to the pituitary gland, where it causes the release of adrenocorticotropic hormone, or ACTH. ACTH in turn causes the release of the adrenal hormones cortisol and cortisone, which are involved in the body's response to stress.

At Baylor, in the late 1950s, Guillemin and Schalley attempted to isolate and determine the chemical structure of CRF. However, the structure eluded them, and it was not until 1981 that it was determined that CRF is a peptide (a compound made up of amino acids, the building blocks of proteins) containing forty-one amino acids. The failure of Guillemin and Schalley to identify CRF aroused some skepticism among their professional colleagues. Nevertheless, they continued their research on the hypothalamic hormones, convinced of the validity of Harris's original hypothesis.

In 1962 Schalley moved to the Veterans Administration Hospital in New Orleans and Tulane University. Guillemin remained at Baylor and held a concurrent appointment at the Collège de France in Paris, where he was director of the Department of Experimental Endocrinology from 1960 to 1963, when he was appointed professor of physiology and director of the Laboratory for Neuroendocrinology at Baylor. He also became an American citizen that same year. In Houston he became a consultant at the Veterans Administration Hospital and at the M. D. Anderson Hospital and Tumor Institute.

By this time Guillemin and Schalley were working independently and competitively, both getting close to identifying three more hypothalamic hormones. One difficulty Guillemin encountered in his work was obtaining enough hypothalamic tissue from which to extract the hormones he studied. Since only small quantities of these hormones are produced by the body, hundreds of thousands of hypothalami were needed. Guillemin used sheep hypothalami obtained from slaughterhouses. The organs had to be removed from the animals immediately after they were killed to prevent the hormones from breaking down.

The hypothalamic hormone that causes the release of thyrotropin from the pituitary gland was isolated by Guillemin and his colleagues in 1968. Because thyrotropin causes the release of thyroid hormones by the thyroid gland, it is also called thyroid-stimulating hormone, or TSH. Schalley had named the hypothalamic hormone thyrotropin-releasing factor, or TRF. It is now known as thyrotropin-releasing hormone, or TRH. In 1969 Guillemin and Schalley, working independently, determined that TRF is a peptide (amino acid compound) containing three amino acids. According to Guillemin, the determination of the chemical structure of TRF marked the beginning of neuroendocrinology as an established scientific discipline. TRF is now used clinically in the diagnosis and treatment of certain hormone-deficiency diseases.

Another hypothalamic hormone, one that causes the release of gonadotropins from the pituitary gland, was isolated in the late 1960s by Guillemin and his colleagues. Gonadotropins cause the release of male and female sex hormones from the testicles and ovaries. The hypothalamic hormone is now called growth-hormone-releasing hormone (GRH). Guillemin and his colleagues also found that GRH is a peptide containing ten amino acids. Subsequent researchers synthesized several GRH analogues, compounds similar in structure but differing in one component, some of which proved to be effective in treating infertility caused by an inability to ovulate; others may be useful as birth-control agents.

In 1970 Guillemin moved to the Salk Institute in San Diego, California, where during the next four years, he and his colleagues isolated a third hypothalamic hormone, one that inhibits the release of growth hormone from the pituitary gland. Guillemin called this new hypothalamic hormone somatostatin. His research group discovered that somatostatin is a peptide containing fourteen amino acids. Since somatostatin has a variety of biological effects and a very short lifetime in the body, it is of no use in clinical medicine. However, if longer-acting analogues of somatostatin with specific biological functions can be synthesized, they may prove useful in the treatment of diabetes, peptic ulcer disease, and acromegaly (a condition caused by an excess of growth hormone). By the mid-1970s Guillemin had turned his attention to a recently discovered class of neuropeptides (peptides that act at nerve synapses in the hypothalamus and elsewhere in the brain), the endorphins and enkephalins. The endorphins appear to play a role in an organism's perception of pain.

Guillemin and Schalley shared half of the 1977 Nobel Prize for Physiology or Medicine "for their discoveries concerning the peptide hormone production of the brain." The other portion of the prize was awarded to ROSALYN S. YALOW. In concluding his Nobel lecture, Guillemin stated that the observations made by him and other workers on the peptide hormone production of the brain "will lead to profound reappraisals of the mechanisms involved in the function of the normal brain, but also of mental illness."

Since 1970 Guillemin has been a resident fellow and chairman of the neuroendocrinology laboratory at the Salk Institute in San Diego, California. His other research interests include the neurochemistry of the brain and methods for improving population control with antagonists to hypothalamic hormones.

In 1951 Guillemin married Lucienne Jeanne Billard. They have one son and five daughters.

Guillemin has received honorary doctorates from the universities of Rochester, Chicago, Ulm, Dijon, and Montreal and from Baylor College of Medicine and the Free University of Brussels. His awards include the Gairdner Foundation International Award (1974), the Dickson Prize in Medicine of the University of Pittsburgh (1976), the Passano Award in Medical Science of the Passano Foundation (1976), the National Medal of Science of the National Science Foundation (1977), and the Dale Medal of the Society for Endocrinology in London (1980). He is a member of the National Academy of Sciences, the American Academy of Arts and Sciences, the American Physiological Society, the Society for Experimental Biology and Medicine, the International Brain Research Organization, the International Society for Research in Biology and Reproduction, the Swedish Society of Medical Sciences, and the French National Academy of Medicine.

SELECTED WORKS: "The Hormones of the Hypothalamus," Scientific American November 1972.

ABOUT: New Scientist October 20, 1977; New York Times October 14, 1977; Science November 11, 1977; Wade, N. The Nobel Duel, 1981.

GULLSTRAND, ALLVAR
(June 5, 1862–July 21, 1930)
Nobel Prize for Physiology or Medicine, 1911

The Swedish ophthalmologist Allvar Gullstrand was born in Landskrona to Sophia Mathilda (Korsell) Gullstrand and Pehr Alfred Gullstrand, the city's chief medical officer. Although the boy demonstrated an aptitude for mechanics and considered a career in engineering, he decided to follow his father into the medical profession. After attending public schools in his hometown and at Jönköping, he entered the University of Uppsala in 1880.

He completed his medical course in 1885 and then continued his studies in Vienna, returning to Sweden the following year. After two years at the Karolinska Institute in Stockholm, Gullstrand passed the examinations that qualified him to practice medicine and, deciding to specialize in ophthalmology, did graduate work at the Seraphim Hospital in Stockholm. For a dissertation on astigmatism, a condition caused by imperfections in the shape

ALLVAR GULLSTRAND

of the lens of the eye, he received his Ph.D. from the Karolinska Institute in 1890.

The following year Gullstrand became a lecturer in ophthalmology at the Karolinska Institute, as well as chief physician at the Stockholm Eye Clinic, where he became director in 1892. It was not until his appointment as professor of ophthalmology at the University of Uppsala in 1894, however, that he was able to pursue research on geometric and physiological optics, and problems associated with optical image formation in biological systems.

At the time Gullstrand began his investigations, the optics of glass lenses had been worked out in considerable detail, especially by Ernst Abbe, a German physicist whose calculations enabled lens makers to produce optical systems of great accuracy by avoiding refractive errors. The eye, however, differs from glass lenses in several significant ways. Whereas a glass lens is composed of a homogeneous medium that refracts, or bends, light in a predictable fashion, the lens of the eye is composed of many layers of transparent fibers that refract light in ways that were not fully understood in the 1890s. Moreover, the lens of the eye is attached to ligaments and muscles that enable it to change shape and thereby focus an image, a capacity known as accommodation. It was Gullstrand's goal not only to elucidate the refractive index of the eye and the mechanism of accommodation but also to combine them into a general mathematical model of visual reproduction.

Through a series of highly complex mathematical operations, Gullstrand determined that the lens of the eye continually changes its refractive index in order to produce an accurate image on the retina. His work facilitated more reliable and accurate correction of such problems as aberration, astigmatism, and coma than had previously been possible. He summarized the results of his work in commentaries on Hermann von Helmholtz's *Treatise on Physiological Optics* (1924–1925), which Gullstrand had re-edited in 1909.

Two years later Gullstrand introduced two new instruments for use in the clinical examination of the eye—the slit lamp and the Gullstrand ophthalmoscope, both of which he developed in collaboration with the Zeiss Optical Works in Jena, Germany. The slit lamp, which is typically used in combination with a microscope, permits ophthalmologists to examine the cornea and the lens, and to determine whether the aqueous humor (the fluid that fills the eyeball) contains foreign objects. The ophthalmoscope is used by physicians to examine the eye for such clinical conditions as arteriosclerosis and diabetes mellitus.

Gullstrand was awarded the 1911 Nobel Prize for Physiology or Medicine "for his work on the dioptrics of the eye." In the presentation address, K. A. H. Mörner of the Karolinska Institute stated, "The pioneer work of von Helmholtz threw so much light on the subjects of refraction and image formation in the eye that it seemed most unlikely that after him work could be produced of such revolutionary impact on the science as that of Gullstrand."

In his Nobel lecture Gullstrand described the lens of the eye as consisting "throughout of an infinite number of skillfully arranged, microscopically fine fibers, which terminate at various depths below both surfaces of the lens, and which run from one end to the other in coils." At the time he initiated his research, Gullstrand added, "the laws governing optical image formation in such a media were completely unknown, and much of what was thought to be known, proved to be wrong." He then reviewed the work for which he had been awarded the prize and summarized his findings.

In 1914 a chair in physical and physiological optics was created for Gullstrand at the University of Uppsala. There he concentrated his research on calculations intended to improve the refracting surfaces of optical instruments, and to the field of geometric optics. From 1911 to 1929 he served as a member of the Nobel Physics Committee of the Royal Swedish Academy of Sciences. After his retirement from

Uppsala in 1927, his health declined and his mental powers weakened.

The rigor and intellectual discipline that Gullstrand brought to his work made him a highly respected figure in his field. A tall, slender man who often appeared distant and aloof at first impression, he was known among his colleagues to be cordial and generous with his advice.

In 1895 Gullstrand married Signe Christina Breitholtz. They had one daughter, who died at an early age. Gullstrand died in Stockholm on July 21, 1930, following a stroke.

Gullstrand received honorary degrees from the universities of Uppsala, Jena, and Dublin and was awarded the Björken Prize of the Uppsala Faculty of Medicine (1905), the Centenary Gold Medal of the Swedish Medical Association (1908), and the Graefe Medal of the German Ophthalmological Society (1927), in addition to numerous other honors.

SELECTED WORKS: An Illustrated Guide to the Slit-Lamp, 1927, with T. H. Butler.

ABOUT: Dictionary of Scientific Biography, volume 5, 1972; Lindroth, S. (ed.) Swedish Men of Science, 1952.

HABER, FRITZ
(December 9, 1868–January 29, 1934)
Nobel Prize for Chemistry, 1918

The German chemist Fritz Haber (häb' ər) was born in Breslau, (now Wrocław, Poland), the only son of Siegfried Haber and his first cousin Paula Haber, who died in childbirth. When the boy was nine, his father, a prosperous merchant of pigments and dyes, married Hedwig Hamburger, with whom he had three daughters. Although Haber's father was cold and severe toward him, Haber enjoyed a warm relationship with his stepmother. After attending a local elementary school, he entered the St. Elizabeth Gymnasium in Breslau, where he cultivated a love of literature, especially the works of Goethe. As a boy he enjoyed writing verses and entertained the idea of becoming an actor, but chemistry eventually proved to be his dominant interest.

In 1886 Haber entered the University of Berlin to study chemistry, but after one semester he transferred to the University of Heidelberg, where he studied with Robert Bunsen, inventor of the laboratory burner that bears his name. Bunsen's interest in physical chemistry turned Haber to the study of mathematics

FRITZ HABER

namics of Technical Gas Reactions, published in 1905, established Haber as a worldwide authority on science and technology. In it, he showed how theoretical thermodynamic calculations for free energy changes of gas equilibria could have practical uses in important industrial reactions.

Haber's most significant laboratory efforts began in 1905, when he turned his attention to the production of ammonia, which could in turn be further processed into nitrates. The need for nitrogen-rich fertilizers was becoming acute as the world's population expanded and natural sources of fertilizer diminished. Hence the importance of nitrates. Haber began by attempting to combine atmospheric nitrogen with hydrogen to produce ammonia. Other chemists had considered the synthesis of ammonia through a direct chemical union of its constituents, hydrogen and nitrogen, but this method required temperatures approaching 1,000°C, too high for economical results. Through his own experiments, Haber realized that ammonia could be synthesized at temperatures as low as 300°C.

The German chemist WALTHER NERNST had recently demonstrated that ammonia could also be produced by subjecting hydrogen and nitrogen to extremely high pressures. Haber combined the techniques of lower temperature and high pressure. He also discovered that substituting osmium and uranium for the standard iron catalyst increased the yield of ammonia substantially. He increased the efficiency of his method still further by using the heat produced by the union of the gases to sustain the reaction.

Haber's research on ammonia synthesis was supported by the German industrial corporation Badische Anilin- und Sodafabrik (BASF). A BASF engineer, CARL BOSCH, perfected Haber's method and put it into commercial use at the company's Oppau and Leuna ammonia works in 1910. Called the Haber-Bosch process, it is still the basis of large-scale ammonia production worldwide.

The following year, Haber and RICHARD WILLSTÄTTER were appointed codirectors of the Kaiser Wilhelm Institute for Physical Chemistry and Electrochemistry in Berlin. With the outbreak of World War I in 1914, Haber offered his services to the German government. As a consultant to the German War Office, he was assigned to find a chemical irritant that would force enemy troops out of the trenches. Within a few months, Haber's team had devised a chlorine gas weapon that went into production in January 1915. It was

and physics, subjects he further pursued at the technical university in Berlin. After receiving his Ph.D. in 1891, he worked briefly in several industrial chemistry laboratories but found the lack of intellectual stimulation stifling. He then entered the Federal Institute of Technology in Zurich, where he familiarized himself with the new chemical and engineering processes that were making Germany a world leader in the chemical industry.

After working two years for his father, Haber resumed his studies, first at the University of Jena and then at the University of Karlsruhe, where in 1894 he accepted a position as assistant to Hans Bunte, a professor of chemical technology. Haber's work, summarized in 1896 in his book *Experimentelle Untersuchungen über Zersetzung und Verbrennung von Kohlenwasserstoffen* (Experimental Studies on the Decomposition and Combustion of Hydrocarbons), qualified him to become a lecturer at Karlsruhe that year. In 1906 he was named professor of physical chemistry and electrochemistry, with a concurrent appointment as director of a university institute devoted to research in those fields.

At Karlsruhe, Haber's initial research ranged across many fields, including the electrochemistry of fuel cells, the loss of energy through heat in steam engines, and the development of several kinds of electrodes to record oxidation-reduction processes. He discussed this work in *Grundriss der technischen Elektrochemie auf theoretischer Grundlage* (Outline of Technical Electrochemistry on a Theoretical Basis, 1898). His third book, *Thermody-*

used that spring against the Allies at Ypres, Belgium, producing 150,000 casualties.

Although he abhorred war, Haber believed that by breaking the stalemate that trench warfare had brought about along the western front, chemical weapons might save lives. His wife, the former Clara Immerwahr, also a chemist, vehemently opposed his wartime work. In 1915, after a bitter argument with Haber, she took her own life. They had been married in 1901 and had one son. Haber married Charlotte Nathan in 1917; they had a son and a daughter and were divorced in 1927.

In 1916 Haber was named chief of the German Chemical Warfare Service, responsible for all research and production of chemical weapons. After the United States entered the war, Haber's nitrogen-fixation process became even more critical to the German war effort, not only as a source of artificial fertilizers but also for producing explosives.

The Nobel Prize for Chemistry was reserved in 1918, but the following year it was awarded to Haber "for the synthesis of ammonia from its elements." Haber's discoveries, said A. G. Ekstrand of the Royal Swedish Academy of Sciences in his presentation speech, represented "an exceedingly important means of improving the standards of agriculture and the well-being of mankind." The award was sharply criticized by many in the Allied nations who considered Haber a war criminal for his participation in the development of chemical weapons.

Germany's defeat, his first wife's suicide, and his condemnation by British, American, and French scientists plunged Haber into profound depression. He also developed diabetes insipidus. Nevertheless, he set about reorganizing the Kaiser Wilhelm Institute, despite Germany's postwar deprivations. In 1920 he began a project designed to recover gold from seawater, hoping that the success of this method would enable Germany to pay its reparations to the Allies. Nineteenth-century estimations of the amount of gold in seawater proved overoptimistic, however, and the project ended in failure six years later.

At the same time, Haber's work at the institute produced significant advances in atomic physics, biology, and chemistry. The scientific colloquia that Haber organized attracted some of the most outstanding scientists of the age, including NIELS BOHR, OTTO WARBURG, OTTO MEYERHOF, PETER DEBYE, and many others. By the early 1930s, the institute had become one of the world's foremost research centers and training institutions.

After Hitler came to power in 1933, Haber's position became precarious, for although his parents were not religious, they were Jewish in origin. One of the Nazi government's earliest acts was the imposition of civil service laws that expelled Jews from academic and government positions. Because he had served Germany during World War I, Haber was exempted, but in April of that year he refused to dismiss his Jewish staff members and submitted a letter of resignation to the Ministry of Art, Science, and Popular Education. "For more than forty years I have selected my collaborators on the basis of their intelligence and their character and not on the basis of their grandmothers," he wrote, "and I am not willing for the rest of my life to change this method."

Fleeing to England, Haber worked for four months with his former associate William Pope at Cambridge University. Then the chemist and first president of Israel, Chaim Weizmann, offered Haber a position at the Daniel Sieff Research Institute in Rehovot, Israel. Haber's health was failing. He suffered a heart attack but recovered and set out for Israel in January 1934. While stopping to rest in Basel, Switzerland, he died. His friend Willstätter delivered his funeral oration. One year later, on the first anniversary of his death, more than 500 former students and colleagues defied Nazi threats and met at the Kaiser Wilhelm Institute to pay tribute to his life and work.

SELECTED WORKS: Practical Results of the Theoretical Development of Chemistry, 1924.

ABOUT: Dictionary of Scientific Biography, volume 5, 1972; Farber, E. (ed.) Great Chemists, 1961; Goran, M. The Story of Fritz Haber, 1967; Nachmanson, D. German-Jewish Pioneers in Science 1900–1933, 1979.

HAHN, OTTO

(March 8, 1879–July 28, 1968)
Nobel Prize for Chemistry, 1944

The German chemist Otto Hahn was born in Frankfurt am Main, one of three sons of Heinrich Hahn, a glazier, and the former Charlotte Giese Stutzmann, who had a son by a previous marriage. After receiving his early education at the Klinger Realschule, Hahn entered a technical university on his parents' hopes that he would become an architect. Finding chemistry more to his liking, he transferred to the University of Marburg. After one year there, he transferred to the University of Munich to study physical chemistry, inorganic chemistry, zoology, and art. He returned to Marburg for graduate work, receiving his Ph.D. in 1901. After a year of military service with the Eighty-first Infantry Regiment in Frankfurt, he resumed academic life as a lecture assistant at Marburg.

To improve his command of English, which he would need in order to take an industrial position, Hahn spent part of 1904 in the laboratory of WILLIAM RAMSAY at University College in London. Given the assignment of separating pure radium from barium carbonate ore, Hahn discovered a new radioactive species of the element thorium, which he called radiothorium. Ramsay was impressed by the young chemist and recommended him to EMIL FISCHER, director of the Chemical Institute at the University of Berlin. Fischer agreed to accept Hahn as soon as Hahn returned from six months of additional work on radioactivity under ERNEST RUTHERFORD at McGill University in Montreal, Canada.

W. H. BRAGG had found that the range of alpha particles emitted by radioactive atoms is characteristic of each atomic species. At McGill, Hahn measured the alpha-particle range of radiothorium samples and thereby discovered a new radioactive species with very energetic alpha particles. This element, which he called thorium C, had a very short lifetime and could not be chemically separated from radiothorium. Now known to be polonium 214, it has a half-life (the time for half of the material to decay) of about one-third of a millionth of a second. In addition to his investigation of polonium 214, Hahn described properties of radioactinium.

Returning to Germany, Hahn continued his research on radioactive elements at the Chemical Institute. There he confirmed the existence of the intermediate radioactive substance mesothorium. In 1907 Lise Meitner, a physicist from Vienna, came to Berlin to study under MAX PLANCK and to do experimental research. Because women were not permitted to work with male students, she was allowed to join Hahn in his laboratory. Their collaboration lasted more than thirty years. Hahn and Meitner investigated the emission of electrons from radioactive nuclei (beta decay) and identified several previously unknown radioactive transformation products. When the Kaiser Wilhelm Institute for Chemistry was founded in 1912, Hahn was named director of its radiochemistry group. The institute's facilities enabled Meitner and Hahn to study rubidium

OTTO HAHN

and potassium, naturally occurring elements that are weakly radioactive. Finding the half-life of rubidium to be 230 billion years, Hahn determined that the ages of rubidium-containing minerals could be calculated by analysis of the decay of rubidium into strontium.

At the outbreak of World War I, Hahn was called up for active duty in an infantry regiment and saw combat on the western front, for which he was decorated. Because of his training in chemistry, however, he was transferred to service in the development of chemical weapons, working under FRITZ HABER, who overcame Hahn's initial objections to the project by pointing out that such weapons might save lives by shortening the war. Hahn participated in preparations for gas attacks in several locations and was distressed by the effects he observed. Posted in Berlin in 1917, Hahn was able to resume his work on radioactive decay products with Meitner; during this time he discovered the unstable element protoactinium.

Returning to his radioactive researches after the end of the war, Hahn noted that many different radioactive species appeared to have identical chemical properties. This phenomenon was explained by the work of English scientists FREDERICK SODDY, J. J. THOMSON, and FRANCIS W. ASTON, who demonstrated that isotopes of an element are forms that have different numbers of neutrons in the nucleus, causing changes of the nuclear properties and behavior. Hahn discovered uranium Z, the first example of an isomer of radioactive atoms. He then became interested in chemical applications of radioisotopes, including crystal formation and tracers of chemical reactions.

Hahn was appointed director of the Kaiser Wilhelm Institute for Chemistry in 1928. In 1933 he visited the United States to deliver the George Fisher Baker lectures at Cornell University. Learning that under the Nazi civil service laws Jewish scientists were being dismissed from the Kaiser Wilhelm Institute and that Haber had resigned in protest, Hahn hurried back to Germany. The following year he participated in a meeting to memorialize Haber after his death in Switzerland. Despite Hahn's refusal to join the Nazi party, he was permitted to retain his position at the institute.

In 1934 Hahn and Meitner, joined a year later by Fritz Strassmann, began to study the effects of neutron irradiation on uranium and thorium. It was believed that new elements, heavier than uranium, would be created. Before the team of researchers could verify this hypothesis, Austria fell to Germany, and Meitner, who was an Austrian Jew, fled to Sweden. After she settled in Stockholm, Meitner, joined by her nephew Otto Frisch, also a physicist, continued her collaboration with Hahn by mail. To their surprise, they found that neutron bombardment of uranium resulted in the formation of radioactive substances that were chemically identical to barium, lanthanum, and cerium. Since these elements have about half the weight of the original uranium atom, it became evident that the uranium nucleus had been split by the bombarding neutrons. It was soon recognized that the process, which they called nuclear fission, also releases large amounts of energy in a chain reaction.

Like the Allies, the German government was highly interested in exploiting nuclear fission for its military potential, and soon after the outbreak of World War II the German War Department created a nuclear research office. Hahn became involved in its efforts, although he managed to limit his research to basic studies of the radioactive fission products. Near the end of the war the Kaiser Wilhelm Institute was hit by Allied bombs and was moved to the town of Tailfingen in southern Germany. There, after French troops occupied the area, Hahn and his colleagues were detained by a special British-American intelligence unit, taken to England, and interrogated about their wartime research. Hahn was distressed a few months later when he learned that the United States had used nuclear weapons on the Japanese cities Hiroshima and Nagasaki in 1945.

While interned in England, Hahn was awarded the 1944 Nobel Prize for Chemistry "for his discovery of the fission of heavy nuclei." He was permitted to return to Germany in 1946 and received the Nobel Prize in Stockholm at the end of the year. In his presentation speech, ARNE TISELIUS of the Royal Swedish Academy of Sciences said, "The discovery of the fission of heavy nuclei has led to consequences of such a nature that all of us, indeed the whole of humanity, look forward with great expectations, but at the same time with great dread, to further developments."

Hahn's Nobel lecture traced the course of scientific research that led from the natural transmutations of uranium discovered by HENRI BECQUEREL to nuclear fission. In conclusion, he read part of FRÉDÉRIC JOLIOT's 1935 Nobel lecture, in which the French physicist had warned against the potential hazards of atomic energy. "What was ten years ago only a figment of what [Joliot] called our 'wandering imagination' has already become to some extent a threatening reality." Asking his audience whether nuclear energy would be used for peaceful or destructive purposes, Hahn stated, "The answer must be given without hesitation, and undoubtedly the scientists of the world will strive toward the first alternative."

In 1946 Hahn became president of the Kaiser Wilhelm Society, which was renamed the Max Planck Society, and he devoted himself to the rebuilding of the German scientific community. Vocal in his public warnings of the dangers posed by the atomic bomb, he was joined by many other physicists who feared the consequences of developing this weapon. In 1959, on his eightieth birthday, it was announced that the Institute of Nuclear Research in Berlin would be renamed the Hahn-Meitner Institute and that the Max Planck Institute for Chemisty in Mainz would become the Otto Hahn Institute. The following year Hahn retired as president of the Max Planck Society.

In 1913 Hahn married Edith Junghans, daughter of the chairman of the Stettin City Council. They had one son. Shortly after Hahn's retirement at the age of eighty-one, his son and daughter-in-law were killed in an automobile accident in France, leaving Hahn to care for a grandson as well as his own wife, who by this time was an invalid. Hahn died on July 28, 1968, from the aftereffects of a fall in which he fractured a neck vertebra.

Among Hahn's many honors were the Emil Fischer Medal (1922) of the German Chemical Society, the Stanislao Cannizzaro Prize of the

Royal Academy of Sciences in Rome (1938), the Max Planck Medal of the German Physical Society (1949), the Golden Paracelsus Medal of the Swiss Chemical Society (1953), and the Faraday Medal of the British Chemical Society (1956). He was a member of scientific academies worldwide, received numerous honorary degrees, and was an officer of the Legion of Honor of France.

SELECTED WORKS: Applied Radiochemistry, 1936; New Atoms, Progress, and Some Memories, 1950; Otto Hahn, A Scientific Autobiography, 1966; My Life, 1970.

ABOUT: Biographical Memoirs of Fellows of the Royal Society, volume 16, 1970; Frisch, O. R. (ed.) Trends in Atomic Physics, 1959; Hermann, A. The New Physics, 1979; Irving, D. The Virus House, 1967; Shea, W. R. (ed.) Otto Hahn and the Rise of Nuclear Physics, 1983.

DAG HAMMARSKJÖLD

HAMMARSKJÖLD, DAG
(July 29, 1905–September 18, 1961)
Nobel Prize for Peace, 1961

Dag Hjalmar Agne Carl Hammarskjöld (häm' är shûld), Swedish statesman, economist, and secretary-general of the United Nations, was born in the town of Jönköping, the son of Knut Hjalmar Leonard Hammarskjöld and the former Agnes Almquist. One of Sweden's most prominent families, the Hammarskjölds had served as statesmen and soldiers since 1610, when Peder Hammarskjöld was knighted by King Charles IX for bravery in battles against the Danes. Dag Hammarskjöld's father, a noted jurist and university professor, served as prime minister of Sweden from 1914 to 1917.

This heritage influenced Hammarskjöld's career, as he recalled in 1953: "From generations of soldiers and government officials on my father's side I inherited a belief that no life was more satisfactory than one of selfless service to your country—or humanity. This service required a sacrifice of all personal interests, but likewise the courage to stand up unflinchingly for your convictions."

Hammarskjöld graduated from the University of Uppsala in 1925 with a humanities degree; his studies emphasized linguistics, literature, and history. Uppsala also awarded him a degree in economics in 1928, a law degree in 1930, and in 1935 a doctoral degree in political economy, a subject that became for some time his major interest. The topic of his doctoral thesis was a theoretical and historical survey of market trends.

Upon leaving the university in 1930, Hammarskjöld became secretary to the Royal Commission on Unemployment, continuing in this post until 1934. He also served as associate professor of political economics at the University of Stockholm during 1934–1935. He was named secretary of the Bank of Sweden in 1935 and the following year was appointed under secretary of the Department of Finance. In this position and in subsequent appointments, Hammarskjöld, with his brother Bo, an under secretary in the Ministry of Social Welfare, drafted much of the legislation that laid the foundation for the Swedish welfare state. In 1937 he joined the Department of Finance Advisory Board. Three years later, he became a member of the Board of Foreign Exchange, a position he held until 1948. In addition, for seven years beginning in 1941 he headed the Bank of Sweden.

Neutral throughout World War II, Sweden nevertheless aided Norway, which fell to the Nazis in 1940. As a member of the Department of Finance, Hammarskjöld traveled to London to arrange wartime credits for Norway's government-in-exile, a task that required the utmost tact and discretion to avoid provoking Germany. In 1945 Hammarskjöld negotiated the first trade agreement between Sweden and Great Britain.

Hammarskjöld approached these negotiations as exercises in problem solving, a technique he developed as a policymaker in the Finance Ministry. There he led discussions with teams of experts, exploring a problem from every angle. Then he digested the recommendations of his advisers. Finally, he analyzed the problem again and proposed a solution. In a similar fashion, he encouraged the parties to a negotiation to explore all possible solutions and then, through compromise, to forge an agreement. This approach served him well in his later career in international diplomacy.

In 1946 he was appointed a finance specialist in the Foreign Office, where he promoted European economic cooperation. He was Sweden's delegate to the 1947 organizational meeting for the Marshall Plan, a program developed by United States Secretary of State GEORGE C. MARSHALL to make substantial loans to European countries whose economies were devastated during World War II. As vice-chairman of the executive committee of the Organization for European Economic Cooperation (OEEC), in 1948 Hammarskjöld helped develop joint economic projects "to change the entire structure of European trade." This called for discarding the rigid production targets favored by some nations in favor of policies that would increase production and aid the European economy as a whole.

Hammarskjöld was appointed Sweden's assistant foreign minister in 1948. In 1951 he became minister of state in charge of foreign economic relations. In this nonpartisan cabinet post, he devised a system of low-interest loans to European nations aimed at benefiting Sweden by rebuilding the stability of international currency. Generous government loans to Norway drew sharp criticism from opposition leaders and several cabinet members. He eventually convinced the cabinet to back the loans, however, and the program was widely credited with helping Sweden obtain a favorable balance of payments earlier than other European nations after World War II.

Although he promoted economic and political cooperation, Hammarskjöld resisted military commitments. He preferred Sweden to remain neutral between East and West as it had been in European conflicts for 150 years. This conviction led him to steer Sweden away from membership in the North Atlantic Treaty Organization (NATO) while advocating participation in the Council of Europe and the OEEC. In 1950 he was made chairman of United Kingdom–Scandinavia (UNISCAN), an organization made up of the Scandinavian countries and England to promote cooperation in economic affairs.

In 1952 Hammarskjöld first went to the United Nations (UN) as vice-chairman of the Swedish delegation to the General Assembly. The following year, he led the Swedish dele-

gation, and that April he was elected secretary-general of the organization. He said at the time that his election showed a "more cooperative spirit on the part of the Big Five" (the United States, the Soviet Union, Great Britain, France, and the Republic of China), and he promised to make the office "active as an instrument, a catalyst, an inspirer."

At the time Hammarskjöld took office, international confidence in the United Nations had reached a low point. The United States had dismissed some of its United Nations staff members because of suspected Communist leanings. Despite its initial endorsement of Trygve Lie, the first secretary-general, the Soviet Union had later broken with him, claiming that he favored the United States in the Korean War. As a result of these actions, several member nations agreed that the Secretariat was no longer the independent, impartial body described in the United Nations Charter.

To reverse this trend, Hammarskjöld reorganized the Secretariat to restore its independence from member nations. He demoted the deputy secretaries–general from policymakers to administrators, ending the influence they wielded over the secretary-general and the General Assembly. He signaled his independence from the American delegation by revoking the authority of the Federal Bureau of Investigation to conduct security checks on American employees of the United Nations.

Hammarskjöld next sought to broaden the role of the United Nations in international diplomacy. In his view, the charter allowed him to discuss with heads of state any matter he believed might lead to an international dispute. As he assumed the role of chief negotiator of the United Nations, the Security Council and the General Assembly gave him increased latitude to work out settlements to international crises. In 1954, for example, he flew to Peking to negotiate the release of eleven American prisoners who had been held by the Chinese since the end of the Korean War. They were freed by the Chinese government six months later.

In September 1956 Egypt nationalized the Suez Canal, precipitating a confrontation with France, England, and Israel. On November 3, as the British fleet steamed toward Egypt to open the canal by force, Hammarskjöld announced the creation of a United Nations peacekeeping force headed by RALPH BUNCHE. Organized by Hammarskjöld in only forty-eight hours, this was the first United Nations military force assembled to guarantee a peace settlement. When he persuaded all four nations to accept the force, the crisis came to an end.

Another Middle East crisis occurred in 1958 when Lebanon and Jordan appealed for military aid from Britain and the United States, convinced that their security was threatened by neighboring Arab states. Hammarskjöld persuaded the parties to settle the dispute among themselves. He set up a United Nations observation group in Lebanon and a United Nations office in Jordan, thus allowing for the withdrawal of British and American troops that had been sent there.

During his second term as secretary-general, Hammarskjöld broadened the United Nations mandate still further by inviting member nations to consult him about disputes in a spirit of what he termed "preventive diplomacy." Contending that "it is diplomacy and not speeches and votes that has the last word in peacemaking," he tried to transform the United Nations from a forum for international grievances to an active negotiator of international peace.

With the move for independence among African nations, a new crisis arose when the Congo (now Zaire) was liberated from Belgium in 1960. As the Congo's internal administration broke down, the army mutinied, the province of Katanga (now Shaba) seceded, and Belgian troops intervened. In July the new Congolese government requested United Nations military aid to restore peace and stability. In a unanimous resolution, the Security Council called on Belgium to withdraw its troops, but the order was ignored. Congolese Prime Minister Patrice Lumumba further complicated the situation by cabling Soviet Premier Nikita Khrushchev, stating that he would seek Soviet aid if Western powers did not cease their "aggression in the Congo." In response, the Soviet Union denounced Hammarskjöld as a protector of Western colonial interests.

As the situation deteriorated further in 1961, the Congolese government asked Hammarskjöld to come to Léopoldville (now Kinshasa) for discussions on United Nations aid. Unable to negotiate a truce there and hoping to unite the rebel province with the central government, he decided to fly to Katanga to meet with Moise Tshombe, the rebel president. On the flight, the plane crashed, killing Hammarskjöld and everyone else on board.

Dag Hammarskjöld was awarded the 1961 Nobel Peace Prize—the only time the prize had been awarded posthumously. In his presentation speech, delivered on December 10 in Oslo, Gunnar Jahn of the Norwegian Nobel Committee stated, "Dag Hammarskjöld was exposed to criticism and violent, unrestrained attacks, but he never departed from the path he had chosen from the very first: the path that was to result in the UN's developing into an effective and constructive international organization, capable of giving life to the principles and aims expressed in the UN Charter, administered by a strong Secretariat served by men who both felt and acted internationally. The goal he always strove to attain was to make the UN Charter the one by which all countries regulated themselves."

The prize was accepted in the name of the Hammarskjöld family by Rolf Edberg, Swedish ambassador to Norway; and the prize money was placed in a fund bearing Hammarskjöld's name.

A very well-read man, Hammarskjöld was especially interested in philosophy, classical and modern literature, and Christian theology. He had a deep understanding and appreciation of poetry. As a hobby, he translated many classics into Swedish. At his death, he was preparing a translation of a little-known book written by Martin Buber.

After his father's death in 1953, Hammarskjöld replaced him on the eighteen-member Swedish Academy, which awards the Nobel Prize for Literature. Many observers think he was the primary advocate of the controversial 1958 award to BORIS PASTERNAK, author of *Doktor Zhivago,* a novel describing the hardships of life in revolutionary Russia. Hammarskjöld was also partly responsible for the 1960 prize given to SAINT-JOHN PERSE, whose poem *Chronique* Hammarskjöld had translated into Swedish. This was Hammarskjöld's only published work, except for articles on finance, during his lifetime. In 1964, however, his personal diary was published in English under the title of *Markings.* He once described the entries in his diary as constituting "a sort of 'white book' concerning my negotiations with myself—and with God."

Fluent in English, French, and German, Hammarskjöld was a brilliant orator who was known for his wit and the ease with which he established personal relationships. An avid sportsman, he excelled in gymnastics. He had a great love for the Swedish countryside and returned there over the years for skiing and mountaineering. For some time, he was president of the Swedish Alpinist Club.

Shortly after Hammarskjöld's death, a spontaneous collection of funds was begun by his Swedish compatriots—later joined by colleagues and donors in other countries—to establish a living memorial to the man and his ideals. In 1962 an international board was established to form the Dag Hammarskjöld Foundation. Its objective, as described in its statutes, is "the promotion of social, political, economic, and cultural progress within the nations whose development Dag Hammarskjöld had so closely at heart, by providing training for citizens of those countries to hold responsible positions." The foundation, with headquarters in Uppsala, organizes seminars, conferences, and courses on issues facing the Third World countries. It also publishes relevant books and monographs and a semiannual journal called *Development Dialogue—Journal of International Development Cooperation*. In 1965 ALVA MYRDAL, president of the organization at that time, wrote, "The foundation . . . is attempting at one and the same time to fill pressing practical needs in the new countries and to maintain the concepts and efforts of the late Dag Hammarskjöld."

KNUT HAMSUN

The Bettmann Archive

ADDITIONAL WORKS IN ENGLISH TRANSLATION: Servant of Peace: A Selection of the Speeches and Statements of Dag Hammarskjöld, 1962; Castle Hill, 1971; Public Papers of the Secretaries-General of the United Nations, volumes II–V, 1972–1975.

ABOUT: Aulen, G. Dag Hammarskjöld's White Book, 1969; Beskow, B. Dag Hammarskjöld: Strictly Personal, 1969; Cordier, A. W., and Foote, W. (eds.) The Quest for Peace, 1964; Cordier, A. W., and Maxwell, K. L. (eds.) Paths to World Order, 1967; Gavshon, A. L. The Last Days of Dag Hammarskjöld, 1963; Henderson, J. L. Hammarskjöld, 1969; Jordan, R. S. (ed.) Dag Hammarskjöld Revisited, 1982; Kelen, E. Hammarskjöld: The Political Man, 1968; Lash, J. P. Dag Hammarskjöld: Custodian of the Brushfire Peace, 1961; Lichello, R. Dag Hammarskjöld: A Giant in Diplomacy, 1971; Miller, R. I. Dag Hammarskjöld and Crisis Diplomacy, 1962; Settel, T. S. (ed.) The Light and the Rock, 1966; Simon, C. M. Dag Hammarskjöld, 1967; Stolpe, S. Dag Hammarskjöld: A Spiritual Portrait, 1966; Thorpe, D. Hammarskjöld: Man of Peace, 1969; Urquhart, B. E. Dag Hammarskjöld, 1972; Van Dusen, H. P. Dag Hammarskjöld: The Statesman and His Faith, 1967; Zacher, M. W. Dag Hammarskjöld's United Nations, 1969.

HAMSUN, KNUT

(August 4, 1859–February 19, 1952)
Nobel Prize for Literature, 1920

The Norwegian novelist Knut Pedersen Hamsun was born Knut Pedersen in Lom in the Gudbrandsdalen Valley, a farming region in central Norway. His parents, Tora (Oldsdatter) and Peder Pedersen, had settled on Garmotreet, a small holding where Hamsun, his three older brothers, and two younger sisters spent their early years. When the boy was three years old the family moved to the town of Hamarøy in the Nordland region, some 100 miles north of the Arctic Circle, where they rented Hamsund, a farm owned by Hamsun's maternal uncle, Hans Olsen. For the next six years the boy led an idyllic life herding cows, gazing at the clouds, and absorbing the rugged beauty of Nordland's fjords and snowcapped mountains.

The family, however, soon fell in debt to Olsen, and at the age of nine Hamsun was obliged to work for his uncle, a stern, pious man who beat the boy and gave him little to eat. Unable to endure this abuse, Hamsun ran away to Lom in 1873, but returned to Hamarøy the following year and worked for a merchant. He spent 1875 as an itinerant peddler, after which he apprenticed himself to a shoemaker in the northern town of Bodø. It was there that he wrote his first work of fiction, *Den Gaadefulde* (The Enigmatic Man), a short novel that was published in 1877, when Hamsun was eighteen years old.

For the next year Hamsun taught school in Vesterålen and then became an assistant to the district bailiff, in whose library he discovered the works of BJØRNSTJERNE BJØRNSON, Henrik Ibsen, and other leading Scandinavian writers. During this time, Hamsun published a poem and the novel *Bjørger* (1878), whose eponymous hero is inspired to write great poetry by the hardships he suffers.

With support from a Nordland merchant, Hamsun moved to Christiania (now Oslo) in 1878. Unable to support himself as a writer, he depleted his funds, lived in considerable poverty, and eventually became a highway construction worker in eastern Norway. In 1882, armed with letters of introduction to prominent Norwegian émigrés, he embarked for the United States. His connections proved to be of little value, however, and he was forced to work as a farmhand in Wisconsin and later as secretary to a Norwegian minister in Minneapolis. There he contracted a serious illness that was mistakenly diagnosed as terminal tuberculosis, and he returned to Norway.

By the time Hamsun reached Oslo in 1884, all symptoms of the disease, which had probably been bronchitis, had vanished. For a time Hamsun lived in Valders, where he published a piece on Mark Twain, written under the name Knut Pedersen Hamsund, after the family farm. A typographical error altered the name to Hamsun, which he whimsically adopted as his pseudonym. Hamsun pursued a literary career in Oslo without success and suffered great hardships before traveling again to the United States in 1886. Arriving in Chicago, he first worked as a streetcar conductor and then spent a summer as a farmhand in the wheat fields of North Dakota. Discouraged over his literary prospects, he again returned to Europe, bringing with him the beginning of a novel, which he took to Edvard Brandes in Copenhagen, then the center of Scandinavian publishing. Brandes, the brother of the influential Danish literary critic Georg Brandes and the editor of a daily newspaper, was struck by Hamsun's emaciated appearance as well as by the originality and power of the novel fragment. It appeared later that year in a Danish literary journal; when completed, it was published in Copenhagen in 1890 as *Sult* (*Hunger*).

Hunger produced an immediate sensation and established Hamsun as a writer of note. In the novel, Hamsun broke with the tradition of social realism that then dominated Scandinavian fiction and rejected the prevailing tenet that the duty of literature was to better the human condition. A virtually plotless novel, *Hunger* is a first-person account of a young man from the provinces who seeks to establish himself as a writer in Oslo. Utterly confident of his genius, he willingly suffers starvation rather than compromise his ambitions. "He is a Dostoevskyan hero," writes the American critic Alrik Gustafson, "sick in body and soul, the pangs of lacerating hunger having forced upon his inner life a series of violently nervous, grotesquely hectic, otherworldly hallucinations." Deprived not only of food, the protagonist of *Hunger* also suffers from a want of social contact and sexual fulfillment as well as from the lack of artistic expression. In his alienation, this character foreshadows the antihero that dominates much of twentieth-century fiction.

According to one of Hamsun's translators, the contemporary American poet Robert Bly, "The swiftness and pungency of [Hamsun's] prose astounded everyone." Written in short, vigorous sentences, *Hunger* alternates descriptions of startling clarity with intensely subjective, hallucinatory passages. Hamsun composed the novel at a time when such writers and thinkers as Arthur Schopenhauer, Eduard von Hartmann, Friedrich Nietzsche, and August Strindberg were calling attention to the complex unconscious forces underlying the human personality. Hamsun articulated his own concept of subjective fiction in an essay titled "Fra det ubevidste Sjaeleliv" (From the Unconscious Life of the Soul), which was published the same year that *Hunger* appeared. Rejecting the conventions of objective fiction, he proposed to explore "the secret stirrings that go on unnoticed in the remote parts of the mind, the incalculable chaos of impressions, the delicate life of the imagination seen under the magnifying glass; the random wanderings of those thoughts and feelings."

Hamsun again employed this subjective mode in *Mysterier* (*Mysteries,* 1892), a novel about a charlatan who appears in a coastal village and baffles the residents with his singular conduct. The novel *Pan,* published in 1894, takes the form of the memoirs of Thomas Glahn, who has withdrawn from urban civilization to live by fishing and hunting near a provincial Nordland town. "I am trying to present something of the nature worship, the sensibility, the supersensitiveness of a Rousseau-like soul," Hamsun confided to a friend while writing the novel. In its exalted descriptions of nature, *Pan,* published in English under the same title in 1920, expresses the euphoria that Hamsun sought in his own inner life as well as his protagonist's mystical and pantheistic identification with the Nordland countryside. Glahn's obsessive attraction to Edvarda, the spoiled daughter of a local merchant, pitches him into emotional chaos, which eventually leads him to commit suicide.

In addition to novels and essays, Hamsun also wrote poetry and drama. Between 1895 and 1898, he composed a trilogy of plays about the life of a philosopher: *Ved rikets port* (*At the Gate of the Kingdom,* 1895), *Livets spill* (*The Game of Life,* 1896), and *Aftenrøde* (Sunset, 1898). Critics generally agree that in his plays Hamsun was unable to provide his protagonists with the psychological depth exhibited by the characters in his novels. Hamsun burned much of his poetry before it could be published, but his 1904 collection *Det vilde kor* (The Wild Choir) contains work that can be compared with his best prose.

After the beginning of the twentieth century, Hamsun's novels shifted to a third-person narrative style, through which a multitude of characters and entire communities are depicted. *Børn av tiden* (*Children of the Age*, 1913) and its sequel, *Segelfossby* (1915, translated as *Segelfoss Town*), chronicle the decadence that industrialization brings to a Nordland town. According to James W. McFarlane, another of Hamsun's translators, these and subsequent novels "become imaginative demonstrations through fiction of a settled and, on the whole, pastoral (even feudal) scheme of values: anti-intellectual, antipolitical, with a strong animus against commercialism."

Hamsun's move to a farm in 1911 reflected his own increasing withdrawal from society and his rejection—deepened by the events of World War I—of the industrial age. These attitudes permeate *Markens grøde* (*Growth of the Soil*), a novel published in 1917. In unadorned language, *Growth of the Soil* tells the story of Isak and Inger, Norwegian peasants who clear a plot of land and thrive by their unremitting labor, attachment to the soil, and stubborn adherence to patriarchal values. "The novel . . . does not give an actual picture of a Norwegian settler," wrote the Norwegian-American scholar Harald Næss, "but rather Hamsun's dream of one."

It was "for his monumental work, *Growth of the Soil*," that Hamsun was awarded the 1920 Nobel Prize for Literature. According to Harald Hjärne of the Swedish Academy in his presentation speech, "Those who want to find in literature . . . a faithful reproduction of reality will recognize in *Markens grøde* the representation of a life that forms the basis of existence and of the development of societies wherever men live and build." Hjärne went on to compare the novel to the agrarian idylls of the Roman poet Hesiod. Hamsun did not deliver a Nobel lecture.

A year after publishing *Growth of the Soil*, Hamsun purchased an estate, Nörholmen, in southern Norway, where he divided his time between writing and farming. The novel *Konerne ved vandposten* (*Women at the Pump*) appeared in 1920. Cynical and disillusioned in tone, it portrays the pettiness and decline of a small harbor village infected with what Hamsun considered to be the false values of the modern age. It was followed in 1923 by *Siste kapitel* (*Chapter the Last*), a brooding novel set in a rural sanatorium.

Depressed by increasingly unfavorable reviews of his work, Hamsun underwent a brief period of psychoanalysis in 1926, after which he completed *Landstrykere* (*Vagabonds*, 1927). *August* (*August,* 1930) and *Men livet lever* (*The Road Leads On,* 1933) completed this trilogy, which is named after its central character, the vagabond August. Although Hamsun again takes up the social outcast in these novels, August's restlessness assumes a futile, destructive aspect. Hamsun's final novel, *Ringen sluttet* (*The Ring Is Closed*), published in 1936, follows the aimless life of a man whose hopes are foreclosed but who survives nevertheless, as Hamsun wrote, "a sovereign in his own way."

As he grew older, Hamsun became increasingly reactionary, and in 1934 he publicly declared his support of the Nazis. Although he never joined the Norwegian Nazi party, Hamsun wrote a series of pro-Fascist articles during the German occupation of Norway, and in 1943 he met both Joseph Goebbels and Adolf Hitler in Germany. Thousands of readers returned their copies of Hamsun's novels in protest. At the end of the war, Hamsun and his wife Marie were arrested. In the fall of 1945 he was transferred to a psychiatric clinic in Oslo and held there for four months before he was returned to an old-age home in Landvik. He was placed on trial in 1947, found guilty of supporting the enemy, and fined 425,000 Norwegian crowns (about $80,000 at the time). Having been declared "a person with permanently impaired mental faculties," he escaped a prison sentence. *På gjengrodde stier* (*On Overgrown Paths*), an unrepentant account of his trial, appeared in 1949, when Hamsun was ninety years old. A book of remarkable vigor—Robert Bly called its prose "still swift, intense, and collected"—*On Overgrown Paths* made no effort to justify Hamsun's wartime activities, but it did help to revive interest in his fiction.

In 1898 Hamsun had married Bergljot Bech, with whom he had a daughter. They were divorced in 1906, and two years later he fell in love with Marie Andersen, an actress twenty-three years his junior. They married in 1909 and had two daughters and two sons. During the Hamsuns' interrogation in 1946, Marie disclosed intimate details about the marriage, and in anger Hamsun refused to see her for the next four years. Subsequently, the two remained together from 1950 until Hamsun's death at Nörholmen on February 19, 1952.

"Hamsun belonged to that select group of writers who not only interested a reader but virtually hypnotized him," wrote ISAAC BASHEVIS SINGER in his introduction to Robert Bly's 1967 translation of *Hunger*. Throughout pre–World War I Europe, Singer continued, "hosts of readers awaited Hamsun's each new book with impatience. . . . Few writers were as imitated as Hamsun." Critics generally agree with Singer's view that Hamsun "is the father of the modern school of literature in his every respect—his subjectiveness, his fragmentariness, his use of flashbacks, his lyricism."

Like many critics, however, Singer detected a decline in Hamsun's work after *Growth of the Soil*. Calling this view of the novelist's oeuvre "narrow and unjust," Harald Næss has praised Hamsun's lifelong mastery of style. Writing in 1940, Alrik Gustafson declared that Hamsun's greatness as a writer is not to be found in his social criticism but "in his more purely literary qualities, . . . in a succession of magnificently living individual characters, in a narrative fertility such as the world of literature has seldom seen, and perhaps above all in a prose style which in its sensitivity of utterance often comes as close to sheer, pulsing poetry as any prose well can." According to Næss, "[Hamsun] is today the only Norwegian writer besides Ibsen and [SIGRID] UNDSET who belongs to world literature." Næss echoed widespread critical opinion when he stated that Hamsun "is also the best-known Scandinavian novelist, with an international reputation surpassed only by such towering names as Hans Christian Andersen, Henrik Ibsen, and August Strindberg."

ADDITIONAL WORKS IN ENGLISH TRANSLATION: Shallow Soil, 1914; Victoria, 1923; In the Grip of Life, 1924; Children of the Age, 1924; Benoni, 1925; Rosa, 1925; Look Back on Happiness, 1940; The Cultural Life of Modern America, 1969.

ABOUT: Beyer, H. A History of Norwegian Literature, 1956; Ferguson, R. Enigma: The Life of Knut Hamsun, 1987; Gustafson, A. Six Scandinavian Novelists, 1940; Larsen, H. A. Knut Hamsun, 1922; Lavrin, J. Aspects of Modernism, 1935; Lowenthal, L. Literature and the Image of Man, 1957; Næss, H. Knut Hamsun, 1984; Rovinsky, R. T., and Weinstock, J. M. (eds.) The Hero in Scandinavian Literature, 1975; Updike, J. New Yorker May 31, 1976.

HARDEN, ARTHUR

(October 12, 1865–June 17, 1940)
Nobel Prize for Chemistry, 1929
(shared with Hans von Euler-Chelpin)

The English chemist Arthur Harden was born in Manchester, the third of nine children and the only son of Albert Tyas Harden, a businessman, and Eliza (MacAlister) Harden. Both his parents were devout nonconformists who raised their children in a pious, puritanical atmosphere in which even Christmas festivities were disapproved. After receiving his early education at the Victoria Park School in Manchester, he entered Tuttenhall College in Staffordshire in 1877, from which he graduated four years later. He then enrolled at Owens College at the University of Manchester and received a bachelor's degree in chemistry with first-class honors in 1885.

The following year Harden was awarded a Dalton Scholarship, which he used for graduate studies in Germany under Otto Fischer at the University of Erlangen in 1887 and 1888. There he investigated the properties of the chemical compound nitrosonaphthylamine, for which he received his doctoral degree. That year Harden became a lecturer and demonstrator in chemistry at the University of Manchester. Harden remained there until 1897, when he accepted an appointment as a chemist at the Jenner (later the Lister) Institute of Preventive Medicine in London. Initially, he taught chemistry and bacteriology and pursued his interest in the history of science. After a few years, however, he was able to devote most of his attention to research, particularly into the fermentation of sugar.

During fermentation an energy-rich compound like sugar breaks down, in the absence of available oxygen, into either carbon dioxide and alcohol or a carbon-based acid. Harden was particularly interested in fermentation caused by the action of certain bacteria, and starting in 1899 he published several papers on this topic. Fermentation also occurs as sugar is digested—broken down—by yeast, a one-celled fungus. It was generally believed that only intact and living yeast cells could induce fermentation. However, Harden learned that EDUARD BUCHNER, a German chemist, had shown in 1896 that fluid extracted from yeast caused fermentation even though the fluid contained no living yeast cells. Furthermore, Buchner had demonstrated that one component of the extract, an enzyme he called zymase, causes sugar molecules to fragment. An enzyme is a product of living cells that functions as a catalyst; that is, it speeds up specific chemical reactions within the cell without being used up in the reaction.

Some scientists still believed that fermentation resulted from a mysterious "vital force" within the living cell, but by 1904 it was clear to Harden that it was produced by chemical

ARTHUR HARDEN

processes. To confirm his hypothesis he obtained a sample of zymase and filtered it under high pressure through porous porcelain impregnated with gelatin. He discovered that the enzyme zymase itself consisted of two components, one of which passed through the filter and one of which did not. Harden also observed that fermentation ceased when he removed either component from the yeast extract. This was the first indication that one enzyme needed another in order to function effectively. Harden retained the name *zymase* for one component; the other component, or coenzyme, became known as cozymase. Furthermore, he found that zymase is made of protein, whereas the cozymase is not a protein.

In 1905 Harden made his second major discovery: that fermentation requires the presence of phosphate, which is a combination of one molecule of phosphorus and four of oxygen. He noticed that the breakdown of sugar and the formation of carbon dioxide and alcohol slowed down after fermentation had proceeded for a while. When he added phosphate to the solution, however, fermentation activity proceeded with increased vigor. From this observation, Harden concluded that the phosphate molecules joined with the sugar molecules to produce a condition that permitted the enzymes to induce fermentation. Furthermore, he found that the phosphate broke free from the products of fermentation at the conclusion of a complex series of reactions.

Harden's work on the role of phosphate in fermentation contributed to the development of what would later be called intermediary metabolism—the study of compounds formed during chemical reactions in living tissue. During fermentation, many of these intermediary compounds act like phosphorus, briefly entering into reactions and then dropping out of them before the completion of a chemical process. Harden's study of the fermentation of sugar (a carbohydrate) provided a model for later experimenters who studied the decomposition of carbohydrates in plants and in human muscle tissue.

In recognition of the importance and quality of his work, Harden was asked in 1907 to direct the biochemical department of the Lister Institute. Five years later the University of London appointed him emeritus professor of biochemistry, a position that he held concurrently with his directorship of the Lister Institute. In 1913 Harden became coeditor (with M. W. Bayliss) of the *Biochemical Journal,* with which he was associated for twenty-six years. Except for the period 1914–1918, when he conducted war-related research on the chemistry of the two water-soluble vitamins then known, Harden devoted the remainder of his professional life to the study of fermentation.

Harden shared the 1929 Nobel Prize for Chemistry with HANS VON EULER-CHELPIN "for their investigations of the fermentation of sugar and fermentative enzymes." In his presentation speech, H. G. Söderbaum of the Royal Swedish Academy of Sciences pointed out that both Harden and Euler-Chelpin had extended and refined the earlier work of Eduard Buchner. "What gives special interest to the study of the complicated reaction mechanism of the fermentation of sugar," Söderbaum concluded, "is that it has been possible to draw from it important conclusions concerning carbohydrate metabolism in general in both the vegetable and the animal organism."

The year after he received the Nobel Prize, Harden retired from the Lister Institute and during the next decade devoted himself entirely to research.

In 1900 Harden married Georgina Sydney Bridge of Christchurch, New Zealand. They had no children. After suffering the progressive deterioration of a nervous disorder for several years, Harden died at his home at Bourne End, Buckinghamshire, on June 17, 1940.

Known as an extremely reserved person, Harden had a dry sense of humor. According to FREDERICK GOWLAND HOPKINS, "Harden's outstanding qualities as an investigator were clarity of mind, precision of observation, and a capacity to analyze dispassionately the results of an experiment and define their significance."

Harden was knighted in 1926 and received, in addition to the Nobel Prize, the Davy Medal of the Royal Society (1935) as well as honorary degrees from the universities of Manchester, Liverpool, and Athens.

SELECTED WORKS: A New View of the Origin of Dalton's Atomic Theory, 1896, with H. E. Roscoe; An Elementary Course of Practical Organic Chemistry, 1897, with F. C. Garrett; Alcoholic Fermentation, 1911.

ABOUT: Dictionary of National Biography, 1931–1940, 1949; Dictionary of Scientific Biography, volume 6, 1972; Findlay, A. (ed.) British Chemists, 1947; Obituary Notices of Fellows of the Royal Society, volume 4, 1942.

H. KEFFER HARTLINE

HARTLINE, H. KEFFER

(December 22, 1903–March 17, 1983)
Nobel Prize for Physiology or Medicine, 1967
(shared with Ragnar Granit and George Wald)

The American biophysicist Haldan Keffer Hartline was born in Bloomsburg, Pennsylvania, to Daniel and Harriet (Keffer) Hartline. His father, a professor of biology at the State Normal School, encouraged him to take an interest in the natural sciences. While attending Lafayette College in Easton, Pennsylvania, he began studying the visual responses of the isopod, a type of terrestrial crustacean. During the summers, this work took him to the Marine Biological Laboratory in Woods Hole, Massachusetts, where he became acquainted with several prominent neurophysiologists. After receiving his B.S. from Lafayette in 1923, Hartline entered the Johns Hopkins School of Medicine. There he continued to conduct research on vision, mastered methods of studying the electrical properties of the nervous system, and received his medical degree in 1927.

Only a year earlier EDGAR D. ADRIAN had made the first recordings of the electrical impulses in individual nerve cells. In 1927 Adrian measured the discharge in the conger eel's optic nerve, which in fact is not a single nerve but a bundle of many thousands of individual nerve fibers. Upon learning of Adrian's research, Hartline, as he later wrote, "aspired to the obvious extension of this study: appli-

cation of unitary analysis to the receptors and neurons of the visual system." To give his future research in biophysics a solid grounding, Hartline studied physics at Johns Hopkins for two years, with the assistance of a National Research Council Fellowship. An Eldridge Reeves Johnson Traveling Fellowship enabled him to spend a semester studying with WERNER HEISENBERG at the University of Leipzig, followed by an additional two semesters at the University of Munich.

Returning to the United States in the spring of 1931, Hartline took a position at the University of Pennsylvania in Philadelphia, in the Johnson Foundation for Medical Physics, where he began to study electrical impulses in single visual elements. His research was greatly aided, he later said, by "a fortunate choice of experimental animal," the horseshoe crab. The visual system of the horseshoe crab consists of bundles of receptor cells arranged in coarsely faceted compound eyes, which are connected to the brain by long optic nerves. The optic nerve can be frayed into thin bundles that are easily split until only one active fiber remains. In this way Hartline and a colleague, C. H. Graham, were able to produce in 1932 the first recordings of the activity of single optic-nerve fibers.

As Adrian had found with other sensory and motor nerves, Hartline discovered that information recorded by the visual receptors constitutes a kind of code—a collection of uniform signals that reflect the intensity of the light shining on a particular visual receptor. Like other sense organs, these receptors respond

415

most strongly when a light goes on or off. As Hartline later said, "The basic mechanism of the receptor is one that emphasizes change."

By 1938 Hartline had shifted his research from the visual system of the horseshoe crab to the far more complex eyes of vertebrates. Painstakingly, he dissected individual fibers from the optic nerves of frogs and recorded their electrical activity. "The findings were unexpected," he reported; "different optic nerve fibers responded to light in different ways." Unlike horseshoe crab fibers, which act in a fairly uniform manner, certain frog fibers responded only to dimming, some to increased light, and others to movement of a small spot or shadow.

At the Johnson Foundation, Hartline had become acquainted with RAGNAR GRANIT, who had developed a technique for recording the activity of individual cells in the retina. Granit was particularly interested in the role of inhibition, that is, the prevention of the action of an effector substance or agent by another substance or agent. Hartline's studies demonstrated that individual retina ganglion cells, which are located several layers above the visual receptors and send fibers to the optic nerves, respond best to particular combinations of excitation and inhibition in the receptors from which they receive input. "It is evident," Hartline concluded, "that a great deal of elaborate and sophisticated 'data processing' takes place in the thin layer of nervous tissue that is the retina."

Hartline spent 1940–1941 as associate professor of physiology at Cornell Medical College in New York City and then returned to the Johnson Foundation, where he continued his research for the next eight years. When the United States entered World War II, Hartline became involved in military research on human night vision. In 1949 he became chairman of the department of biophysics at Johns Hopkins University.

Although Hartline had demonstrated that visual information is heavily processed in the retina before being sent to the brain, his research had offered few clues to the mechanisms involved. In the early 1950s he took advantage of improved electronic technology to record responses to light from within individual visual receptors. For these studies he abandoned the frog and returned to the horseshoe crab, because, as he later explained, "interaction in [its] retina is complex enough to be interesting, yet simple enough to be analyzed with relative ease."

Hartline found that the response of an individual receptor unit to light is heavily dependent upon the degree to which the neighboring receptors are illuminated. If these neighboring receptors are brightly lit, the firing of the receptor being studied is inhibited. Therefore, diffuse light usually produces weak visual responses, while responses to lines and edges are strong. All of the neuronal interactions Hartline observed in the retina are inhibitory; his studies emphasized that the "molding influence" of inhibition, which CHARLES S. SHERRINGTON had found to be crucial in controlling the motor nerves, is central to visual processing as well. The net effect of visual inhibition, Hartline noted, is enhancement of contrast in which "steep intensity gradients in the retinal image—edges and contours—will be accentuated." DAVID H. HUBEL and TORSTEN WIESEL later showed that visual information that is passed to higher levels of the vertebrate nervous system, including the brain itself, is manipulated by essentially the same processes of image enhancement Hartline found in the eye of the horseshoe crab. Much of his research on "wiring" in the horseshoe crab retina was performed in collaboration with Floyd Ratliff at the Rockefeller University, where Hartline was a professor from 1963 until his retirement in 1974.

Hartline shared the 1967 Nobel Prize for Physiology or Medicine with Granit and GEORGE WALD for "discoveries concerning the primary physiological and chemical visual processes in the eye." In presenting the award, Carl Gustaf Bernhard of the Karolinska Institute declared that Hartline's publications "have given us the basic knowledge about the impulse coding in the visual receptors and presented discoveries of the most fundamental principles for data processing in neuronal networks which serve sensory functions." Bernhard concluded that "in the case of vision they are vital for the understanding of the mechanisms underlying perceptions of brightness, form, and movement."

In 1936 Hartline married Elizabeth Kraus, an instructor in comparative psychology at Bryn Mawr College; they had three sons, all of whom became biological scientists. His work was notable for the elegance of its design and for its clarity. A lover of the out-of-doors, Hartline enjoyed mountain climbing in the Rocky Mountains and flying an open-cockpit plane. In later years, he relaxed by sailing near his summer home in Maine and, occasionally, with Ragnar Granit on the Baltic Sea. He died of a heart attack on March 17, 1983.

Hartline's many awards and honors included the Howard Crosby Warren Medal of the American Society of Experimental Psychologists (1948) and the Albert A. Michelson Award of the Case Institute of Technology (1964). He held honorary degrees from Lafayette College, the University of Pennsylvania, Rockefeller University, the University of Freiburg, and Johns Hopkins University, and he was a member of the National Academy of Sciences, the American Association for the Advancement of Science, the American Physiological Society, the American Philosophical Society, and the American Academy of Arts and Sciences.

SELECTED WORKS: Studies on Excitation and Inhibition in the Retina, 1974.

ABOUT: New York Times October 19, 1967; March 19, 1983; Science October 27, 1967.

ODD HASSEL

HASSEL, ODD

(May 17, 1897–May 15, 1981)
Nobel Prize for Chemistry, 1969
(shared with Derek Barton)

The Norwegian chemist Odd Hassel was born in Oslo to Ernst Hassel, a gynecologist, and Mathilde (Klaveness) Hassel. After attending elementary and secondary schools in Oslo, he studied chemistry, mathematics, and physics at the University of Oslo, graduating in 1920.

After a year of travel through France and Italy, then a common practice among students, Hassel resumed his studies at the University of Munich and then transferred to the University of Berlin, a leading center for the study of physics and chemistry. While there, he also worked at the Kaiser Wilhelm Institute for Physical Chemistry and Electrochemistry in Berlin.

At the institute, Hassel became familiar with the new technique of X-ray crystallography. This method, first employed by the English physicists W. H. BRAGG and W. L. BRAGG, enables researchers to deduce the three-dimensional structure of molecules by directing an X-ray beam at a pure crystal of a substance. Some of the X rays are deflected, or diffracted, by electrons within the substance, and the pattern they form on photographic film can be used to determine the atomic structure of the substance. On the recommendation of the institute's director, FRITZ HABER, Hassel received a Rockefeller Fellowship while still a student at Berlin.

After obtaining his Ph.D. from the University of Berlin in 1924, Hassel accepted a position as instructor at the University of Oslo in 1925 and the following year became assistant professor of physical chemistry and electrochemistry. In 1934 Hassel was appointed to a newly created chair of physical chemistry at Oslo and named chairman of the university's new Department of Physical Chemistry.

In 1930 Hassel began investigating ways to determine the three-dimensional structure of molecules. At the time, molecules were classified according to their constitution (the identity of their constituent atoms) or by their configuration (the arrangement of molecules into left- and right-handed patterns, analogous to left- and right-handed gloves or shoes). A knowledge of molecular structure would cast much light on the chemical behavior of substances and on the nature of chemical reactions.

Hassel was interested in organic molecules, especially the structure of cyclohexane. This substance is composed of an unbroken chain, or ring, of six carbon atoms to which twelve atoms of hydrogen are attached. Its ringlike structure resembles that of many other important organic molecules, including the steroids and most carbohydrates. Through X-ray crystallographic studies, Hassel confirmed earlier research indicating that a six-member carbon ring, such as that of cyclohexane, could

417

assume one of two possible structures, commonly called the boat and chair forms.

In 1938, recognizing the limitations of X-ray crystallography, Hassel began using new techniques, such as electron diffraction. He found that even when cyclohexane was not chemically active, its molecules oscillated between the boat and chair forms about a million times a second, assuming the chair form most often. Hassel proposed that this predominance occurred because the chair form was more energy-efficient. By determining that the form of a cyclohexane molecule affected the arrangement of its atoms, he made it possible to predict the chemical properties of the substance. His work was particularly important because cyclohexane is the base of many organic substances.

Continuing his cyclohexane research into the early 1940s, Hassel succeeded in generalizing a number of his conclusions. With the outbreak of World War II, however, he refused to publish in German scientific journals, and his work went largely unnoticed by chemists elsewhere in Europe and the United States. During the German occupation of Norway, the University of Oslo was closed, and Hassel, with other Norwegian patriots, was arrested by the Nazis and imprisoned for the remainder of the conflict.

After the war, Hassel resumed his work on molecular shapes. In the 1950s, he began investigating the physical structure of charge-transfer compounds. These compounds are formed by the interaction of electron-donating molecules, such as ethers, with electron-accepting molecules, such as those of chlorine and fluorine. He eventually developed rules to explain the geometry of certain types of charge-transfer compounds. Subsequently, the British chemist DEREK BARTON used Hassel's cyclohexane results to expand and generalize the laws governing the structure and consequent behavior of a wide range of organic molecules. Although Hassel officially retired from the University of Oslo in 1964, he continued active research for several years.

Hassel and Barton shared the 1969 Nobel Prize for Chemistry "for their contributions to the development of the concept of conformation and its application in chemistry." Arne Fredga of the Royal Swedish Academy of Sciences said in his presentation speech, "Hassel's elegant work on six-membered rings has laid a solid foundation for a dynamic chemistry in three dimensions."

A quiet, extremely reserved man, Hassel was personally known to only a few colleagues in his field and rarely attended international scientific conferences. He never married. He died in Oslo on May 15, 1981, two days before his eighty-fourth birthday.

In addition to the Nobel Prize, Hassel received the Guldberg and Waage's Law of Mass Action Memorial from the Norwegian Chemical Society (1964) and the Gunnerus Medal from the Royal Norwegian Academy of Sciences (1964). He was an honorary fellow of the Norwegian Chemical Society and of the British Chemical Society as well as a fellow of the Royal Norwegian Academy of Sciences, the Royal Danish Academy of Science, and the Royal Swedish Academy of Sciences. In 1967 an annual Hassel lecture series, to be delivered by distinguished scientists from abroad, was established at the University of Oslo in his honor. He was made a knight of the Order of Saint Olav by the Norwegian government.

SELECTED WORKS: Crystal Chemistry, 1935.

ABOUT: Anderson, P., et al. (eds.) Selected Topics in Structural Chemistry, 1967; New York Times October 31, 1969; Science November 7, 1969.

HAUPTMAN, HERBERT A.
(February 14, 1917–)
Nobel Prize for Chemistry, 1985
(shared with Jerome Karle)

The American biophysicist Herbert Aaron Hauptman was born in New York City to Israel and Leah (Rosenfeld) Hauptman. He was raised in the Bronx and received his secondary education at Townsend Harris High School, from which he graduated in 1933. He went on to study mathematics at the City College of New York, where he met JEROME KARLE, a student from Brooklyn. Hauptman received a B.S. in mathematics from City College in 1937 and an M.A. from Columbia University in 1939.

After working briefly as a statistician for the Census Bureau, Hauptman served in the United States Army Air Force, first as an electronics instructor and then as a weather officer. In 1947 he joined the staff of the Naval Research Laboratory in Washington, D.C., as a physicist-mathematician, at which time he renewed his friendship with Karle. The two men began collaborating on research involving direct methods of interpreting X-ray crystallography. In 1955 Hauptman obtained a Ph.D. in mathematics from the University of Maryland for a dissertation on X-ray crystallography.

X-ray crystallography is used to determine

418

HERBERT A. HAUPTMAN

the time needed to construct a three-dimensional structure from months (or even years) to only a day or two. Nevertheless, when the two scientists reported their method in 1950, few chemists were able to grasp the mathematics underlying it. Their work was greeted with considerable skepticism and remained unused for the next fifteen years. Acceptance came in the late 1960s, after Isabella Karle, Jerome Karle's wife and a physical chemist at the Naval Research Station, demonstrated the practicality of the direct method in the analysis of large molecules.

During his years at the Naval Research Laboratory, Hauptman served as head of the Mathematical Physics Branch (1965–1967), acting superintendent of the Mathematics and Information Sciences Division (1967–1968), head of the Applied Mathematics Branch (1968–1969), and head of the mathematics staff of the Optical Sciences Division (1969–1970). From 1970 to 1972 he was deputy research director of the Medical Foundation of Buffalo in Buffalo, New York, a small, privately funded institution that sponsors basic research on endocrine function and disorders caused by hormonal dysfunction. Since 1972 he has been vice president and research director of the foundation, and from 1970 he has served concurrently as research professor of biophysical sciences at the State University of New York at Buffalo.

Hauptman and Karle shared the 1985 Nobel Prize for Chemistry "for their outstanding achievements in the development of direct methods for the determination of crystal structures." The direct methods they developed have been responsible for major advances in crystallography and are now the principal system used in the analysis of most new compounds. They have proven particularly useful in the study of large, complex organic molecules involved in life processes. By enabling chemists to identify the biologically active components of molecules, these methods have given rise to countless new drugs, such as artificial counterparts of steroid hormones for treatment of breast cancer. Researchers have used these methods to study enkephalins (natural painkillers produced by the brain) and to design drugs based on them.

Hauptman is married to the former Edith Citrynell, a first-grade teacher; they have two daughters and live in Buffalo. Hauptman enjoys hiking, swimming, listening to classical music, and constructing polyhedrons from stained glass, a hobby that requires skills similar to those used in his work on molecular

the three-dimensional configuration of molecules by directing an X-ray beam at a pure crystal of a substance. Some of the X rays pass through the substance, while others are deflected, or diffracted, when they pass close to the electrons surrounding the nucleus of an atom, a phenomenon that the German physicist MAX VON LAUE discovered in 1912. Patterns formed when X rays are recorded on photographic film can be used to deduce the atomic structure of the substance. Using this method W. L. BRAGG and his father, W. H. BRAGG, determined the atomic structure of many kinds of crystals. The work done by Laue and the Braggs provided a fundamental basis for Hauptman and Karle's research.

Hauptman and Karle developed a mathematical method for determining three-dimensional crystal structures of important molecules, such as hormones, antibiotics, and vitamins. By analyzing the intensity of the dots shown on film, they were able to calculate the angles at which the X-ray beams were deflected and from these calculations to construct an accurate picture of the molecular structure of the substance under observation.

X-ray crystallography had enabled DOROTHY C. HODGKIN, JAMES D. WATSON, FRANCIS CRICK, MAX PERUTZ, and other researchers to elucidate the structure of important protein molecules. The methods available to them, however, required a laborious and time-consuming analysis of the pattern of dots on photographic emulsion. Karle and Hauptman's method directly relates the dots to the position of atoms within the molecule, thus reducing

structure—the abilities to think in three dimensions and to calculate with great accuracy.

In addition to the Nobel Prize, Hauptman has received the Award in Pure Sciences of the Research Society of America (1959) and, with Jerome Karle, the A. L. Patterson Memorial Award of the American Crystallography Association (1984). He is a member of the United States National Committee for Crystallography and the American Association of Independent Research Institutes. In 1986 the City College of the City University of New York presented him with an honorary degree.

SELECTED WORKS: Solution of the Phase Problem I: The Centrosymmetric Crystal, 1953, with Jerome Karle; Crystal Structure Determination: The Role of the Cosine Semivariants, 1972.

ABOUT: New York Times October 17, 1985; Physics Today December 1985; Science January 24, 1986.

GERHART HAUPTMANN

HAUPTMANN, GERHART
(November 15, 1862–June 6, 1946)
Nobel Prize for Literature, 1912

The German dramatist and novelist Gerhart Johann Robert Hauptmann was born in Obersalzbrunn (now Szczawno Zdrój, Poland), a popular spa in Silesia. He was the youngest of four children of Robert Hauptmann, the owner of a fashionable hotel, and the former Marie Straehler. He attended the village school, where he was tutored in Latin, and the gymnasium in Breslau (now Wrocław, Poland). However, he displayed little interest in his studies, finding school "torture," and at the age of fifteen was sent to learn farming on his uncle's estate, where he remained for a year. Although his stay was brief, his experiences there had a profound effect on his life. "I grew conscious of myself, my value, and my rights," he wrote over thirty years later; "I gained independence, firmness, and a freedom of intellect that I still enjoy."

In 1880, at the suggestion of his brother Carl, Hauptmann entered the art academy in Breslau to study sculpture. The next year he became engaged to Marie Thienemann, a wealthy woman who supported him while he searched for a career. During a year at the University of Jena, where he studied history, Hauptmann came into contact with the noted German biologist and philosopher Ernst Haeckel, who introduced him to the ideas of Charles Darwin—ideas that were already beginning to turn literature toward greater realism.

While studying sculpture in Rome in 1883–1884, Hauptmann found his imagination stirred by classical culture, and he wrote a romantic epic poem based on the myth of Prometheus. In 1885 he married Marie Thienemann and settled in the town of Erkner, a suburb of Berlin, where he fell in with a group of progressive Berlin intellectuals and avidly read the works of Karl Marx, Friedrich Engels, Leo Tolstoy, Émile Zola, and Henrik Ibsen.

Although the tenets of naturalism were by this time well established in the literature of Russia, France, and the Scandinavian countries, they were slow to take root in Germany, where romanticism remained the dominant literary genre. In 1889 a group of writers and critics established Die Freie Bühne (The Free Stage), a Berlin theater club, for the presentation of new plays. The club's initial production, Ibsen's *Ghosts,* was followed by Hauptmann's first play, *Vor Sonnenaufgang* (*Before Dawn,* 1889), a grim depiction of the sudden rise to wealth and subsequent corruption of a peasant family written in the Silesian dialect. Regarded as the first naturalist German drama, *Before Dawn* jolted the German public with its sordidly realistic plot and colloquial dialogue; it was a succès de scandale that immediately established Hauptmann as an important playwright.

Hauptmann's next two plays, *Das Friedensfest* (*The Coming of Peace,* 1890) and *Einsame Menschen* (*Lonely Lives,* 1891), reflect the influence of Ibsen. But it was the production of

Die Weber (*The Weavers*) in 1893 that brought Hauptmann recognition as the leading dramatist of his generation. An account of a strike by Silesian weavers in 1844, it contains neither conventional hero nor villain. The action proceeds as it might in real life, with the writer making no moral judgments about his characters.

Der Biberpelz (*The Beaver Coat,* 1893), a satirical comedy about a conniving washerwoman, is also written in the naturalist mode. However, in his next work, *Hanneles Himmelfahrt* (*Hannele,* 1894), Hauptmann surprised both audiences and critics by turning from naturalism to symbolism and fantasy. In this play, naturalist scenes in prose, depicting the life of a brutalized fourteen-year-old girl, alternate with mystical passages in verse, portraying her visionary dreams. Returning to naturalism in *Florian Geyer* (*Florian Geyer,* 1896), Hauptmann wrote a vast, panoramic historical drama about the Peasants' War of 1524–1525. *Die versunkene Glocke* (*The Sunken Bell*), published in 1897, is filled with fairy-tale and surreal elements in its depiction of an artist's struggles.

A period of domestic turmoil followed these early successes. In 1900 Margarete Marschalk, a young violinist and actress, bore Hauptmann a son. The following year Hauptmann built a mansion in Agnetendorf (now Jagniakow, Poland) and moved there with Marschalk. In 1904, after being divorced by his wife, with whom he had had three children, Hauptmann married Marschalk.

Discouraged by the diminishing popularity of his work and by his flagging creativity, Hauptmann traveled to Greece in 1907, a trip that inspired *Griechischer Frühling* (Greek Spring, 1908). Ostensibly a travel diary, this work actually represents Hauptmann's attempt to reconcile the conflict he experienced between his commitment to his Christian heritage and his attraction to the paganism of classical culture. These themes are also explored in two novels: *Der Narr in Christo Emmanuel Quint* (*The Fool in Christ, Emmanuel Quint,* 1910), the story of a Silesian carpenter, a modern mystic whose life parallels that of Jesus; and *Die Insel der grossen Mutter* (*The Island of the Great Mother,* 1912).

Hauptmann was awarded the 1912 Nobel Prize for Literature "primarily in recognition of his fruitful, varied, and outstanding production in the realm of dramatic art." The presentation speech, given by Hans Hildebrand of the Swedish Academy, praised Hauptmann for "his penetrating and critical insight into the human soul. . . . The realism in Hauptmann's plays leads necessarily to brighter dreams of new and better conditions and to the wish for their fulfillment."

Thanking the Nobel committee in a brief acceptance speech, Hauptmann paid tribute to "the ideal that underlies this foundation, I mean the ideal of world peace, which comprehends the final ideals of art and science."

A lifelong pacifist, Hauptmann retained his beliefs throughout World War I and supported the Weimar Republic after Germany's surrender in 1918. Many of the plays he wrote during the 1920s incorporate fantasy and folklore. Although repelled by Hitler and Nazism, Hauptmann chose to remain in Germany throughout the Nazi regime and World War II rather than go into exile—a decision that was bitterly denounced by many of his admirers.

Largely ignored by the Third Reich, Hauptmann's plays were infrequently performed during this period, although the Nazi government sponsored a complete seventeen-volume edition of his works in 1942. His literary output in these years includes a visionary poem, *Der grosse Traum* (The Great Dream, 1942), and *Die Atriden-Tetralogie* (The House of Atreus Tetralogy, 1949), a series of four verse plays in which the harshness and violence of the tales from Greek mythology reflect the horrors of World War II.

When Dresden, a city Hauptmann loved dearly, was destroyed by Allied bombing in 1945, he was profoundly shocked and fell into a period of deep pessimism. In 1946 he died of pneumonia at his home in Agnetendorf.

Since his death, Hauptmann's critical reputation has greatly diminished. Although his plays are staged periodically in Germany, they are rarely seen elsewhere. "No particular importance can be attached to the plays written during the last twenty-five years of his life," the critic John Gassner has said, "and today even the bulk of his work rings hollow outside, and apparently inside, Germany."

Even Hauptmann's advocates concede that the early dramas constitute his best work. Nonetheless, in a summation of his achievements, biographer Hugh F. Garten calls Hauptmann "one of the last humanists, in the fullest sense of the term, who embraced, and recreated in a multitude of living characters, the great European heritage."

ADDITIONAL WORKS IN ENGLISH TRANSLATION: Three Plays, 1901; Führman Henschel, 1909; Atlantis, 1912; The Dramatic Works (9 vols.) 1912–1929; The Rats, 1913; The Maidens of the Mount, 1915; Parsival,

HAWORTH

1915; Gabriel Schilling's Flight, 1915; Pastoral, 1917; Phantom, 1922; The Heretic of Soana, 1923; Flagman Thiel, 1933.

ABOUT: Clark, B. H. A Study of the Modern Drama, 1925; Garten, H. F. Gerhart Hauptmann, 1954; Heller, O. Studies in Modern German Literature, 1905; Holl, K. Gerhart Hauptmann: His Life and Work, 1862–1912, 1973; Kipa, A. A. Gerhart Hauptmann in Russia, 1889–1917, 1974; Knight, K. G. (ed.) Hauptmann Centenary Lectures, 1964; Maurer, W. R. Gerhart Hauptmann, 1982; Mellen, P. A. Gerhart Hauptmann and Utopia, 1976; Mellen, P. A. Gerhart Hauptmann, 1984; Shaw, L. R. Witness of Deceit, 1958; Sinden, M. Gerhart Hauptmann: The Prose Plays, 1957.

WALTER N. HAWORTH

HAWORTH, WALTER N.
(March 19, 1883–March 19, 1950)
Nobel Prize for Chemistry, 1937
(shared with Paul Karrer)

The English chemist Walter Norman Haworth was born at Chorley, a small town in the county of Lancashire, the second son and fourth child of Thomas and Hannah Haworth. Haworth attended the local schools until he was fourteen, when he began working at the linoleum factory his father managed. Even though Haworth found the job stultifying, his work with the dyes used in the factory stimulated his interest in chemistry. He began studying with a private tutor from the nearby town of Preston. After passing the entrance examinations at the University of Manchester in 1903, he became a student of W. H. Perkin Jr., head of the university's chemistry department. He graduated with first-class honors in 1906 and for the next three years assisted Perkin in research on terpenes, hydrocarbons that are found in certain plant oils and are used as solvents.

A scholarship enabled Haworth to spend the year 1909 working with OTTO WALLACH at the University of Göttingen, where he received his Ph.D. Returning to Manchester, he completed a second Ph.D. in 1911 and was appointed senior demonstrator in chemistry at the Imperial College of Science and Technology in London. The next year he was appointed lecturer in chemistry at United College of the University of St. Andrews in Scotland. At St. Andrews he became acquainted with the work of Thomas Purdie and James C. Irvine, pioneers in the field of carbohydrate structure. Carbohydrates constitute a large family of substances, from starch to cellulose, that are essential to living organisms. They consist of one or more molecules of simple sugars, which in turn are composed of carbon,

hydrogen, and oxygen, arranged in a variety of ways. At the time, the components of carbohydrates had been identified, but the three-dimensional structure of many sugars had not been elucidated. Soon after arriving at St. Andrews, Haworth began to shift his efforts from the study of terpenes to that of carbohydrates, especially the saccharides, or sugars.

Haworth's research was interrupted by the outbreak of World War I in 1914. For the next four years, the chemistry laboratories at St. Andrews produced drugs and chemicals required by the British war effort. After the armistice, Haworth and his colleagues resumed academic research, and Haworth plunged into an ambitious study of saccharides.

In 1920 he accepted a position as professor of organic chemistry at Armstrong College (now King's College) at the University of Durham, Newcastle upon Tyne, and became head of the chemistry department the following year. He moved to the University of Birmingham in 1925 to be Mason Professor of Chemistry.

During the 1920s Haworth directed research into the structure of monosaccharides (simple sugars) and oligosaccharides, the somewhat more complex sugars built from a small number of simple sugars. In 1925 he proposed that the structure of glucose, a common form of sugar that supplies carbohydrates (and hence energy) in mammals, was composed of six atoms attached to one another in a ring. His model differed from EMIL FISCHER's earlier proposal that sugars were linear, open-chain structures. As a result of this and further work,

Birmingham became an important center for hydrocarbon research during the late 1920s.

While continuing their investigations of sugars and related hydrocarbons during the 1930s, Haworth and his associates also began to examine the study of hexuronic acid, a substance that had been isolated by ALBERT SZENT-GYÖRGYI from the adrenal glands of animals and from paprika. By 1932 Haworth had established that this carbohydrate consists of six carbon, eight hydrogen, and six oxygen atoms, arranged in a five-sided ring with three short branches. Because of its antiscorbutic properties, Haworth renamed hexuronic acid, calling it ascorbic acid, or vitamin C. With this achievement, Haworth became the first person to synthesize a vitamin. Not long after his synthesis of vitamin C, Haworth supervised the construction of new facilities for the chemistry department at Manchester. Upon their completion the buildings were opened by FREDERICK GOWLAND HOPKINS in 1937.

Haworth received the 1936 Nobel Prize for Chemistry "for his investigations on carbohydrates and vitamin C." He shared the prize with PAUL KARRER. In his presentation address, K. W. Palmær of the Royal Swedish Academy of Sciences reminded his audience of the importance of vitamin research. Haworth's synthesis of vitamin C, he said, "opens the way to the artificial production of the compound, a thing of very great importance in the case of vitamins which do occur in nature only in a state of very great dilution." As a result, Palmær added, "vitamin C is already produced on a technical scale and at a price very much lower than that of the natural product."

Overexertion brought about a breakdown in Haworth's health in 1938, and he was forced to curtail his activities. By 1941, however, he had regained his strength and was appointed chairman of the British Chemical Panel for Atomic Energy. In this capacity, he directed the preparation of highly refined metallic uranium and of organic fluorine compounds. At the same time, he became chairman of the Chemical Research Board of the Department of Scientific and Industrial Research as well as an influential organizer of both the Rubber Producers Research Association and the Colonial Products Research Association. From 1943 to 1946 he served as dean of the faculty at Birmingham, and from 1944 to 1946 he was president of the British Chemical Society.

After retiring from Birmingham in 1948, Haworth remained active on several corporate and governmental boards and committees. He represented the Royal Society at the seventh

Pacific Science Congress in New Zealand in 1949 and then delivered a series of lectures in Adelaide, Sydney, and Melbourne. The following year, only a few days after attending a Chemical Society meeting on carbohydrate nomenclature, Haworth died of a heart attack at his home. He was survived by his wife, the former Violet Chilton Dobbie, whom he had married in 1922, and by their two sons.

Extremely reserved in manner, Haworth was known to his colleagues and friends as generous, understanding, and kind. In addition to his love of travel, he cultivated an extensive knowledge of antiques, painting, and classical literature. He received the Longstaff Medal of the British Chemical Society (1933) and the Davy Medal (1934) and Royal Medal (1942) of the Royal Society. He held membership in the British Chemical Society as well as honorary membership in the Swiss Chemical Society, the Bavarian Academy of Sciences, and the Academy of Science of Vienna, among others. He was awarded honorary degrees from Manchester University; Cambridge University; Queen's University, Belfast; and the University of Zurich.

SELECTED WORKS: The Constitution of Sugars, 1929.

ABOUT: Dictionary of National Biography 1940–1951, 1959; Dictionary of Scientific Biography, volume 6, 1972; Obituary Notices of Fellows of the Royal Society, volume 7, 1951.

HAYEK, FRIEDRICH A. VON
(May 8, 1899–)
Nobel Memorial Prize in Economic
  Sciences, 1974
(shared with Gunnar Myrdal)

The English economist Friedrich August von Hayek (hī′ yek) was born in Vienna, the son of August von Hayek, a local health official and part-time biology professor at the University of Vienna, and the former Felicitas Juraschek. His maternal grandfather was professor of public law at the University of Vienna and chief of Austria's Central Statistical Authority. In 1917, after completing high school, Hayek was drafted into the Austrian army and served as an artillery officer on the Italian front.

Returning to Vienna after the armistice in 1918, Hayek entered the University of Vienna, where he studied law, economics, philosophy, and psychology. Although initially attracted to socialism and nationalism, which were popular

FRIEDRICH A. VON HAYEK

political movements in postwar Vienna, he later became an ardent opponent of both. Hayek's first step in what was to become a lifelong struggle against those ideologies was to found the Association of Democratic Students at the university.

After receiving a doctorate in law from the University of Vienna in 1921, Hayek began working for the Austrian War Claims Settlement Office, then directed by the economist Ludwig von Mises. At the same time, he resumed his studies at the University of Vienna and received a doctorate in economics in 1923. Upon completion of his thesis, Hayek spent a year in the United States as a research assistant to Jeremiah Jenks at New York University. He also attended lectures on business cycles by the American economists Wesley C. Mitchell and John M. Clark at Columbia University and helped compile statistical data for the American journal *Business Annals.*

Returning to his civil service post in Austria in 1924, Hayek became a member of Mises' private seminar, a select group of influential economists and philosophers who met several times a month to discuss current economic research. Impressed by the empirical research on business cycles then taking place in the United States, in 1927 Hayek persuaded the Austrian government to set up an institute to conduct similar research in Austria.

Throughout the 1920s, Hayek published numerous articles on the trade cycle and on monetary theory and policy. He began lecturing at the University of Vienna in 1929 and was invited the following year to give four lectures

at the London School of Economics (LSE). The lectures, published in 1931 as *Prices and Production,* won Hayek a visiting appointment at the LSE, where he was then appointed to the Tooke Professorship of Economic Science and Statistics.

In London, Hayek initiated one of the most enduring economic controversies of the 1930s. In 1930 John Maynard Keynes published his *Treatise on Money,* which Hayek reviewed for the British journal *Economica.* Keynes, in turn, asked the Italian Marxist Piero Sraffa to review Hayek's *Prices and Production* for the *Economic Journal,* which Keynes edited. A protracted and contentious series of comments, replies, and rejoinders ensued. Virtually every important figure in British economics contributed to the debate. In essence, Hayek's trade cycle theory was based on Austrian capital theory. According to Hayek, there is an equilibrium pattern of capital formation. During boom times (as in the late 1920s) there is much forced saving due to credit expansion (even when price levels are kept constant), implying a larger capital stock than is desirable. Sooner or later this overinvestment in relation to voluntary savings leads to a crisis. Hayek's concept anticipated MILTON FRIEDMAN's monetarist interpretation of the Great Depression. At the same time, Hayek argued that the Depression was characterized by overconsumption combined with misguided policy. High unemployment was not caused, as Keynes argued, by inadequate aggregate demand but rather, Hayek insisted, by distortions in relative prices. These distortions had, in turn, been brought about by unanticipated changes in the money supply, causing imbalances in labor supply and demand throughout the economy. Only the market mechanism, he concluded, could correct such imbalances and bring the system into equilibrium; expansionist and interventionist government policies were unnecessary or counterproductive.

Although most observers believed that this dispute had concluded in favor of the Keynesians, Hayek's theories foreshadowed developments in macroeconomics that occurred nearly forty years later. For example, he contended that expansionist fiscal and monetary policies might raise aggregate output in the short run but, owing to their effects on relative prices, would eventually cause both unemployment and inflation to rise. This view prefigured Friedman's theory of the "natural rate" of unemployment and provided an accurate description of the "stagflation" of the 1970s. Hayek's insistence that a sound theory of macroeconomic events requires microeconomic foundations and his focus on the difficulty of distinguishing between changes in relative prices and changes in the absolute price level (caused by changes in the money supply) are at the heart of the "rational expectations" revolution in macroeconomics.

The Pure Theory of Capital, published in 1941, was Hayek's other chief contribution to economic theory. Here, rather than identifying capital as a measurable, tangible factor, Hayek looked instead at the length of time (or the number of intermediate stages or products) between raw materials and finished goods, a view in accordance with the earlier Austrian theory of capital. According to Hayek, a decrease in interest rates (or a rise in the productivity of new investment) will lengthen the period of production: firms will adopt more roundabout technologies and a greater division of labor. An increase in interest rates will result in fewer intermediate stages of development and less complex products. Unorthodox for its time and often difficult to understand, Hayek's reintroduction of his classical version of capital theory was not easily assimilated into modern economic analysis.

While his monetary economics were being all but supplanted by Keynesianism, Hayek turned his attention to the economics of socialism. His critique of socialism rests not on the efficiency of capitalism (which is stressed in neoclassical welfare economics) but on the idea that socialist central planning can never respond as quickly as the marketplace to continuously fluctuating levels of supply and demand. Moreover, according to Hayek, the information on consumer preferences and commercial production technologies needed to calculate equilibrium prices and quantities is not available. The principal advantage of free markets is that prices convey all the information necessary for consumers and firms to make rational economic decisions—and at a much lower cost than in any other system. Furthermore, government cannot improve on market outcomes. In Hayek's view, the notion of "market failure" or "imperfect competition" (except that arising by government fiat, as when governments give legal rights and powers to trade unions) is utterly meaningless.

Hayek's 1944 book *The Road to Serfdom* presented his attack on socialism for the lay reader and extended his arguments to the political arena. He argued that democratic governments that adopted socialist goals, such as an equal distribution of income, and socialist tactics of intervening in the marketplace, such

as price controls, were destined to become totalitarian states. Likewise, any attempt to introduce competitive markets into a totalitarian state would end violently, since the freedom of choice underlying the market was antithetical to totalitarian aims. With the Soviet invasions of Hungary in 1956 and Czechoslovakia in 1968—both countries that had attempted to liberalize along free-market lines—Hayek's grim vision seemed to have been vindicated. Much of his later work in political philosophy and legal theory, published in such books as *Constitution of Liberty* (1960) and the three-volume *Law, Legislation, and Liberty* (1972), refined his argument that totalitarianism could be avoided by reliance on free markets and by judicious legal restrictions on government interference.

The popular success of *The Road to Serfdom* brought several invitations to visit the United States after World War II. In 1950 Hayek resigned his post at the LSE to become professor of social and moral sciences at the University of Chicago, where he remained until 1962.

Hayek's years at Chicago were extremely productive. He conducted an interdisciplinary seminar whose participants included GEORGE STIGLER and Milton Friedman. He also published numerous books, articles, and pamphlets on intellectual history, legal theory, scientific methodology, and even psychology. He returned to Europe in 1963 to accept an appointment as professor of economic policy at the University of Freiburg in West Germany. After retiring in 1968, he moved to the University of Salzburg, where he spent nine disappointing years. Not only did the university lack a degree program in economics, but few of its faculty or students seemed interested in Hayek's views on economics or political philosophy. He returned to Freiburg in 1977 and has remained there since.

Hayek shared the 1974 Nobel Memorial Prize in Economic Sciences with GUNNAR MYRDAL "for their pioneering work in the theory of money and economic fluctuations and for their penetrating analysis of the interdependence of economic, social, and institutional phenomena." In his Nobel lecture Hayek took economists to task for their uncritical acceptance of "scientism" (by which he meant crude but quantifiable economic models, no matter how irrelevant or incorrect their assumptions) and for their willingness to predict the effects of expansionist monetary and fiscal policy based on what he called a mere "pretense of knowledge."

Hayek and Helen von Fritsch married in

425

1926; they had a son and a daughter. Following a divorce from his first wife in 1950, he married Helene Bitterlich. He became a British citizen in 1938.

In addition to the Nobel Prize, Hayek has received many honors and awards, including the Austrian government's Medal of Honor for Science and Art (1976). He is a member of the British Academy, the Austrian Academy of Sciences, and the Argentine Academy of Economic Science. He has been awarded numerous honorary degrees.

ADDITIONAL WORKS: Monetary Theory and the Trade Cycle, 1933; Collectivist Economic Planning, 1935; Monetary Nationalism and International Stability, 1937; Profits, Interest, and Investment, 1939; Freedom and the Economic System, 1939; Individualism and Economic Order, 1948; The Counterrevolution of Science, 1952; The Sensory Order, 1952; The Political Ideal of the Rule of Law, 1955; Studies in Philosophy, Politics, and Economics, 1967; Economic Freedom and Representative Government, 1973; Denationalization of Money, 1976; New Studies in Philosophy, Politics, Economics, and the History of Ideas, 1978; The Three Sources of Human Values, 1978; The Political Order of a Free People, 1979; Money, Capital, and Fluctuations: Early Essays, 1984.

ABOUT: Barry, N. P. Hayek's Social and Economic Philosophy, 1979; Butler, E. Hayek: His Contribution to the Political and Economic Thought of Our Time, 1983; Current Biography June 1945; Gary, J. Hayek on Liberty, 1984; Hoy, C. M. A Philosophy of Individual Freedom, 1984; Leube, K. R., and Zlabinger, A. H. (eds.) The Political Economy of Freedom, 1985; Machlup, F. (ed.) Essays on Hayek, 1976; Streissler, E. (ed.) Roads to Freedom, 1969; Walker, G. The Ethics of F. A. Hayek, 1986.

HEIDENSTAM, VERNER VON
(July 6, 1859–May 20, 1940)
Nobel Prize for Literature, 1916

The Swedish poet and novelist Carl Gustaf Verner von Heidenstam was born at Ölshammar, his grandmother's estate on the shores of Lake Vättern in southern Sweden, into an ancient, aristocratic, and wealthy family. His father, Nils Gustaf von Heidenstam, was an engineer, a lighthouse builder, and (like many of his forebears) an army officer. His mother, the former Magdalena Charlotta Rütterskiöld, came from a local family of mill-owning aristocrats. A shy and physically frail only child, Heidenstam lived with his parents in Stockholm most of the year and spent the summers with his extended family at Ölshammar, where he passed much of his time reading poetry and heroic sagas.

Hoping that the Mediterranean climate might improve their son's health, Heidenstam's par-

VERNER VON HEIDENSTAM

ents sent him abroad when he was sixteen years of age. Traveling in the Middle East, Greece, and Italy, he was, as he later put it, "exposed at the age of greatest receptivity to the cosmopolitan atmosphere of the southern countries. Instead of studying antiquity in the lecture halls of the provincial university, I was treading the soil of the Athenian acropolis. Instead of taking root definitively in modern Christian culture, I got to know the Orient."

After returning to Sweden in 1880, Heidenstam married Emilia Uggla, a Swiss woman. He had no particular plans for the future, but travel had stimulated his interest in art, and his father agreed to send the young man to Paris for art studies. Traveling first to Rome, Heidenstam and his bride went on to Paris, where he studied painting under Jean Léon Gérôme at the École des Beaux Arts.

In the summer of 1886 the couple leased Schloss Brunegg, a medieval castle in the canton of Aargau in northern Switzerland, where the Swedish playwright August Strindberg became a frequent visitor. Although Strindberg was several years older than Heidenstam and already famous, the two soon became close friends. In a series of intense discussions, the two writers analyzed their own ambitions and attempted to assess the future of Swedish literature and culture. Around this time Heidenstam realized that poetry, rather than painting, was his true vocation.

In 1887 the Heidenstams returned to Sweden, settling on the family estate at Ölshammar. The following year Heidenstam published his first collection of poems, *Vallfart och van-*

dringsår (Pilgrimage: The Wander Years), which became an immediate success and established his reputation. Inspired by Heidenstam's Mediterranean experiences, the poems offer a summary of his childhood education. As the Swedish critic Steffan Björck wrote, "His criticism of contemporary authority . . . [and] of establishment morals . . . was presented in the guise of stories, fables, and oriental scenes whose sensuous, seductive colors were the feature most appealing to his public." In addition to their exotic subject matter and their celebration of beauty, these poems are also marked by lush, pictorial imagery, standing in dramatic contrast to the somber, naturalistic literature of the time.

During the next decade Heidenstam's output was prolific. The classical Mediterranean world figures prominently in his first novel, *Endymion,* published in 1889. This work was followed by the pamphlet *Renässans* (Renaissance, 1890), a manifesto that addresses the limitations of naturalism as a literary method and calls for a new aesthetic based on a rich imagination, a lively sense of the beautiful, and a bold (but not overly gloomy) realism. These views are embodied in Heidenstam's prose-and-verse novel *Hans Alienus* (1892), in which the Faust-like hero searches the world for the meaning of life. In this novel Charles W. Stork, a translator of Heidenstam's work, found "an earnestness, a depth of vision that holds the reader even though he be out of sympathy with the immediate subject in hand."

Three years after the death of his first wife in 1893, Heidenstam married Olga Wiberg. However, this second marriage, unstable from the beginning, soon ended in divorce.

The publication in 1895 of Heidenstam's second volume of verse, *Dikter* (Poems), confirmed him as a leading figure in contemporary Swedish literature and displayed his poetic gifts at their most fully developed. In the view of the American critic Alrik Gustafson, these poems "give way to a new spirit of optimism, restrained, dignified, characterized by a deep, flowing, quietly vigorous zest for life. . . . [They are] filled with a . . . humanity that finds its deepest roots in a feeling for Sweden's national past."

Heidenstam's growing preoccupation with Sweden's history and his attempt to create a new national myth culminated in his best-known work, *Karolinerna* (The Charles Men, 1897–1898), a series of thematically linked stories. Karolinerna were the soldiers of Charles XII, the eighteenth-century Swedish king who won mastery of the Baltic Sea and transformed his nation into a major European power before he was defeated in the disastrous campaign in which he lost his own life. In presenting King Charles as an uncompromising, self-sacrificing hero who represents a moral ideal, Heidenstam indirectly provided, as Gustafson noted, "a severe critical analysis of the cultural materialism of Sweden at the turn of the century."

Sweden's past provided the background for Heidenstam's succeeding works. The novel *Heliga Birgittas pilgrimsfärd* (The Pilgrimage of St. Bridget, 1901), the two-volume novel *Folkunga Trädet* (The Tree of the Folkungs, 1905–1907), and the two-volume prose poem *Svenskarna och deras hövdingar* (The Swedes and Their Chieftains, 1908–1910) employ historical figures and events and are distinguished by a profound idealism and nationalistic spirit.

While working on these books, Heidenstam (who, in 1900, had married Greta Sjöberg, a woman nearly twenty years his junior) gradually abandoned the radical ideals he had espoused while influenced by the intellectual currents of the Continent and by the friendships he had made there, and he returned to the aristocratic world in which he had been raised. When Strindberg, presenting himself as a progressive and a champion of the working class, attacked Heidenstam in the press in 1910, a public controversy ensued. Heidenstam was subsequently labeled by his enemies as "the Junkers' poet" (the Junkers were the conservative, militaristic landowners of Prussia), and indeed he did speak out strongly in defense of the aristocracy.

Nevertheless, the publication in 1915 of Heidenstam's *Nya Dikter* (New Poems) crowned his reputation as Sweden's foremost lyric poet. In these spare, classical poems, written mostly between 1895 and the break with Strindberg, critics noted a purity of tone and a serenity that gave little hint of acrimony or of diminished creative powers.

Heidenstam was awarded the 1916 Nobel Prize for Literature "in recognition of his significance as the leading representative of a new era in our literature." During World War I, writers who lived in the warring countries were nominated by citizens of neutral nations; among the year's nominees was Henry James, whose name was proposed by a Finnish committee but who died before the voting took place. Because of the war, no award ceremonies were held. In an official critical and biographical essay prepared on this occasion for the Swedish Academy, the Swedish critic Sven Söderman hailed Heidenstam as "the most brilliant star . . . in the constellation of original artists who regenerated Swedish poetry at the end of the last century."

From the time he received the Nobel Prize until his death, Heidenstam published no further works. He did, however, complete *När kastanjerna blommade* (When Chestnuts Blossomed), an idealized memoir of his childhood that was published posthumously in 1941. In the 1920s he designed and had constructed a home at Övralid, near Lake Vättern, where he lived comfortably and quietly until his death on May 20, 1940, at the age of eighty.

During his active career, Verner von Heidenstam was considered one of Sweden's two most important writers, along with his one-time friend and later adversary, Strindberg. However, since his death, Heidenstam has largely passed from the public's attention, and his reputation has declined virtually to the point of eclipse. Today he is recalled much more for his contributions to the development of modern Swedish literature than for the quality of the works themselves.

ADDITIONAL WORKS IN ENGLISH TRANSLATION: A King and His Campaigners, 1902; The Soothsayer, 1919; The Birth of God, 1920.

ABOUT: American-Scandinavian Review March 1961; Gustafson, A. Six Scandinavian Novelists, 1940; Gustafson, A. A History of Swedish Literature, 1961; Stork, C. W. (ed.) Sweden's Laureate, 1919.

HEISENBERG, WERNER

(December 5, 1901–February 1, 1976)
Nobel Prize for Physics, 1932

The German physicist Werner Karl Heisenberg (hīz' ən berg) was born in Duisburg to August Heisenberg, who became a professor of Greek languages at the University of Munich, and the former Annie Wecklein. Raised in Munich, he attended the Maximilian School until 1920, when he entered the University of Munich. An outstanding student, Heisenberg studied physics under the renowned physicist Arnold Sommerfeld and received a Ph.D. in 1923. His thesis dealt with aspects of quantum theory. That year he went to the University of Göttingen as an assistant to MAX BORN, and the following year received a Rockefeller Foundation grant to study with NIELS BOHR in Copenhagen, where he remained until 1927 except for lengthy visits to Göttingen to work with Born. One of his primary interests was unsolved problems in atomic structure and the

WERNER HEISENBERG

increasing inadequacy of the Bohr model of the atom. In 1925, while at the seashore recovering from an attack of hay fever, he had "a moment of inspiration" that clarified his thoughts on a new way to apply quantum theory toward a solution of the difficulties. Within a few weeks he expressed his ideas in an important paper.

MAX PLANCK had planted the seed of quantum theory in 1900 when he explained the relationship between a body's temperature and its emitted radiation by assuming that the radiation was emitted in small discrete units of energy. The energy in each quantum, as ALBERT EINSTEIN referred to these units, was proportional to the frequency of the radiation. This was a radical notion, since centuries of evidence had demonstrated that radiation such as light traveled as a continuous wave. In 1905 Einstein used the quantum to account for puzzling features of the photoelectric effect, the emission of electrons by a metal surface irradiated with ultraviolet rays. More intense radiation produced more numerous, but not more energetic, electrons. Einstein proposed that each quantum (later called a photon, for light or other radiant energy) conveyed its energy to one electron. Some of the energy enabled the electron to break free; any surplus appeared as electron velocity (kinetic energy). More intense radiation supplied more photons, which liberated more electrons, but each photon's energy remained fixed and set a limit on electron velocity.

Then, about 1913, Bohr proposed his atomic model of a dense, central nucleus orbited by electrons at various distances. Using quantum theory, he showed how the atom, excited by burning or by an electric discharge, radiated at certain specific frequencies. According to Bohr, only certain electron orbits were allowed. When an electron jumped from one orbit to another of less energy, the drop in energy was transformed into a quantum of emitted radiation whose frequency, in accordance with Planck's theory, was uniquely determined by the quantum. Bohr's model met with initial success, but it soon began to be modified to eliminate discrepancies between theory and experimental results and to meet objections by physicists that its appealing simplicity failed to provide a systematic basis for attacking many problems in quantum physics.

Heisenberg's insight was to regard quantum events as a different level of phenomena from those of classical physics, that is, as ones not accurately pictured by easily visualized models such as orbiting electrons. Instead, in 1925 he offered purely mathematical representations based only on "fundamentally observable" quantities such as the frequencies of the line spectra. The terms in his equations were tabulated lists of such variables as frequency, position, and momentum, and he prescribed ways of mathematically manipulating them. Born recognized that they could be expressed as arrays called matrices and operated on by the rules of matrix mathematics, an established field but little known to physicists at that time. Born, his student Pascual Jordan, and Heisenberg then developed Heisenberg's conception into matrix mechanics, a method for applying quantum theory to such problems as atomic structure.

A few months later, ERWIN SCHRÖDINGER presented an alternative formulation of quantum mechanics, which described quantum phenomena in terms of waves. Schrödinger's approach was an outgrowth of work by LOUIS DE BROGLIE, who had proposed that just as radiation, traditionally regarded as waves, could exhibit particle properties (quanta), so particles could have wave properties. Matrix mechanics and wave mechanics were later shown to be fundamentally equivalent; matrix and wave mechanics together became known as quantum mechanics. Quantum mechanics was soon extended and made more general by P. A. M. DIRAC, who incorporated elements of Einstein's relativity theory into the wave equation with highly consequential results.

In 1927 Heisenberg became professor of theoretical physics at the University of Leipzig. That year he published a paper expressing the uncertainty principle, with which his name is most closely associated. The principle revealed itself as a consequence of matrix multiplications. In multiplying ordinary mathematical quantities, order is irrelevant; with matrices, however, the order does matter. In dealing with certain pairs of quantities, such as particle momentum and position, the answer in matrix mechanics is different depending on whether momentum or position is placed first. This concept proved to have profound significance: it meant that the specification of one of the quantities affects the value of the other, so that it is impossible to know both with extreme precision at the same time. The quantities are usually the result of measurements. Every measurement has some degree of error, but the experimenter always hopes that better equipment or a more clever procedure will reduce the uncertainty. Heisenberg's principle sets an insurmountable limit on precision. It states that the mathematical product of the two errors cannot be less than a fixed number, Planck's constant. The number is rooted in quantum theory because the energy in a quantum of radiation equals Planck's constant times the frequency.

When both errors are relatively large, as they are in the everyday world, the uncertainty principle has little effect. At the atomic level, however, it can have significant consequences. For example, the more an electron can be pinned down to a known position, the more vague its velocity becomes. Even in theory, the electron cannot be imagined in a narrow confinement and assigned a particular velocity at the same time. Heisenberg suggested an illustration. To "see" an electron under a hypothetical supermicroscope, it must be illuminated by "light" of a wavelength comparable with the electron's size. However, quantum theory dictates that a quantum of such radiation would have so much energy that its impact would drive the electron away. The observation disturbs and alters what is being observed. According to the Copenhagen interpretation (so named because Bohr, who did extensive work on the concept, was in Copenhagen), which prevails in modern physics, the uncertainty principle limits quantum-mechanical descriptions to a statement of relative probabilities of possible experimental outcomes rather than exact numerical predictions.

Another success of the new quantum mechanics was the prediction of two forms of the hydrogen molecule. In ordinary hydrogen gas, each molecule consists of two linked atoms, each with a nucleus consisting of one proton.

The proton is assumed to be spinning like a top (quantum mechanics dispenses with such a simple picture but retains the property of spin). Since the proton carries a positive electric charge, its spin has the character of an electric current and generates a magnetic field that interacts with other charged particles and magnetic fields. In one form of the hydrogen molecule, the spins of the two nuclei are in the same direction (clockwise or counterclockwise). In the other form, the spins are opposite. The two forms were discovered shortly after by observation of line spectra. Since the spin alignment affects the energy levels, transitions between slightly different levels emit radiation of slightly different frequencies. This confirmation of Heisenberg's prediction gave strong support to his theoretical approach.

In 1933 Heisenberg was awarded the 1932 Nobel Prize for Physics "for the creation of quantum mechanics, the application of which has, among other things, led to the discovery of the allotropic forms of hydrogen."

Heisenberg remained at the University of Leipzig until 1941. While there he contributed to the understanding of ferromagnetism (the form of magnetism exhibited by strongly magnetic materials such as iron) and collaborated with WOLFGANG PAULI on quantum electrodynamics. When JAMES CHADWICK discovered the neutron in 1932, Heisenberg immediately recognized that atomic nuclei must be composed of protons and neutrons held together by nuclear exchange forces, then poorly understood.

In 1941 Heisenberg was appointed professor at the University of Berlin and director of the Kaiser Wilhelm Institute for Physics. Although not a supporter of the Nazi regime, he headed the German atomic research project. American physicists, who knew Heisenberg's capabilities, feared that he would develop for Germany the bomb they were working on for the United States. He did hope to develop nuclear power, but the government's incompetence, lack of vision, banishment of Jewish scientists, and alienation of others so hindered research that the German atomic project was unable even to build a nuclear reactor. After the war, Heisenberg was taken prisoner along with other leading German physicists and interned in England. He returned to Germany in 1946 as professor of physics at the University of Göttingen and director of the Max Planck Institute (the former Kaiser Wilhelm Institute) for Physics. In this capacity, he participated in the development of nuclear power, publicly criticizing German Chancellor Konrad Adenauer for inadequate financial support of nuclear technology. He was among the nuclear scientists who expounded upon the dangers of nuclear warfare, and he opposed arming German troops with nuclear weapons. His other research included work on fluid turbulence, superconductivity, and the theory of elementary particles.

In 1937 Heisenberg married Elisabeth Schumacher, with whom he had four daughters and three sons. An avid pianist, Heisenberg frequently played chamber music with his family, all of whom played instruments. He died in Munich on February 1, 1976.

Heisenberg's honors included the Barnard Gold Medal for Meritorious Service to Science of Columbia University (1929), the Matteucci Gold Medal of the National Academy of Sciences of Italy (1929), the Max Planck Medal of the German Physical Society (1933), the Bronze Medal of the American National Academy of Sciences (1964), and the Niels Bohr International Gold Medal of the Danish Society of Civil, Electrical, and Mechanical Engineers (1970). He was awarded honorary degrees by the universities of Brussels, Budapest, Copenhagen, and Zagreb and by the Technical University of Karlsruhe. He held membership in the academies of science of Norway, Göttingen, Spain, Germany, and Romania as well as in the Royal Society of London, the American Philosophical Society, the New York Academy of Sciences, the Royal Irish Academy, and the Japanese Academy.

SELECTED WORKS: The Physical Principles of the Quantum Theory, 1930; Cosmic Radiation, 1946; Philosophic Problems of Nuclear Science, 1952; Nuclear Physics, 1953; The Physicist's Conception of Nature, 1958; Physics and Philosophy: The Revolution in Modern Science, 1958; On Modern Physics, 1961, with others; Introduction to the Unified Field Theory of Elementary Particles, 1966; Natural Law and the Structure of Matter, 1970; Physics and Beyond: Encounters and Conversations, 1971; Across the Frontiers, 1974; Tradition in Science, 1978; Collected Works, 1984.

ABOUT: Biographical Memoirs of Fellows of the Royal Society, volume 23, 1977; Buckley, P., and Peat, F. D. (eds.) A Question of Physics, 1979; Current Biography April 1957; Heisenberg, E. Inner Exile: Recollections of Life With Werner Heisenberg, 1984; Hermann, A. Werner Heisenberg, 1976; MacPherson, M. C. Time Bomb: Fermi, Heisenberg and the Race for the Atomic Bomb, 1986.

HEMINGWAY, ERNEST
(July 21, 1899–July 2, 1961)
Nobel Prize for Literature, 1954

Ernest Miller Hemingway, American novelist and short story writer, was born in Oak

Park, Illinois, an upper-class Chicago suburb. His mother, the former Grace Hall, had given up an operatic career to marry Dr. Clarence Edmonds Hemingway, a general practitioner and sportsman who took his own life in 1928. The eldest son and second of six children, the young Hemingway attended public schools in Oak Park, where his earliest stories and verse appeared in his high school newspaper.

Upon his graduation in 1917, Hemingway planned to enlist in the army and fight in World War I, but after being rejected because of an injured eye, he became a reporter for the *Kansas City Star* instead. Quitting that job after six months, he joined the Red Cross in Italy as an ambulance driver. In July 1918 he suffered a severe leg wound, but nevertheless managed to carry an injured Italian soldier to safety. For his valor, Hemingway was twice decorated by the Italian government. While recuperating in Italy, he fell in love with an American nurse; a decade later this affair and his war experiences would furnish the background for his novel *A Farewell to Arms* (1929).

Returning to Oak Park as a war hero, Hemingway found suburban life unbearably dull and soon took a steady job on a monthly magazine in Chicago, where he met the novelist Sherwood Anderson. Anderson urged him to go to Paris to escape what he regarded as the intellectually stifling atmosphere of the American Midwest. Shortly after marrying Hadley Richardson (with whom he later had one son) in September 1921, Hemingway followed Anderson's advice and left for Europe.

During his first year abroad, Hemingway traveled extensively while writing articles on a wide range of topics for the *Toronto Star*. Between assignments he became part of a social milieu that included Gertrude Stein, Ezra Pound, F. Scott Fitzgerald, and other American literary expatriates then living in Paris. At the same time, he began to write fiction, applying the dictum that "all you have to do is write one true sentence . . . and then go on from there." His first book, *Three Stories and Ten Poems* (1923), influenced by Anderson's work, was published in Paris, as was his next, *In Our Time* (1924), a collection of short stories that appeared in an expanded version in the United States the next year. In this work, Hemingway's deceptively simple prose style, spare and understated, was already evident. These stories also introduced the prototypical Hemingway hero, the man who exhibited, in the author's famous phrase, "grace under pressure."

The Torrents of Spring (1926), a hastily writ-

ERNEST HEMINGWAY

ten parody of a Sherwood Anderson novel, was turned down by Anderson's publishers but accepted soon after by the noted editor Maxwell Perkins of Charles Scribner's Sons. In October 1926 Hemingway published his first serious novel, *The Sun Also Rises,* which was extraordinarily well received by critics and which established Hemingway as one of the most promising new literary talents. A portrait of a group of British and American expatriates in Paris and Spain, it was viewed by Hemingway's friends as a roman à clef. According to Carlos Baker, one of his most authoritative biographers, its depiction of the postwar generation formed "an aspect of the social history of the 1920s." The central characters, members of what Gertrude Stein called the lost generation, are all wounded spiritually (and physically, in the case of the impotent narrator, Jake Barnes). They seek to recover some meaning in their lives through ceaseless involvement in activities Hemingway considered elemental, such as fishing, boxing, bullfighting, drinking, and making love.

By 1927 Hemingway was deeply involved in an affair with Pauline Pfeiffer, whom he married that year, soon after divorcing his first wife; they had two sons. After the publication of another book of short stories, *Men Without Women* (1927), Hemingway returned to the United States. Settling in Key West, Florida, he completed his next novel, *A Farewell to Arms,* which quickly became an enormous critical and commercial success. Many critics rate this novel (along with the later book *For*

Whom the Bell Tolls, published in 1940) as his finest work. Here his prose style—matter-of-fact, hard, and concise, with immense power—reaches its perfection.

During the 1930s, however, critics began to note a decline in the quality of Hemingway's writing. It was during this period that he began to play the role of public celebrity. His preoccupation with an exaggerated masculinity, as exemplified by his interest in bullfighting in Spain, big-game hunting in Africa, and brawling everywhere, was regarded by many as a pose that affected and severely undermined the quality of his art. The major works from this time include *Death in the Afternoon* (1932), a nonfiction account of Spanish bullfighting; *The Green Hills of Africa* (1935), a description of an actual hunting safari in Tanganyika; and *To Have and Have Not* (1937), a novel set in Florida, whose main character is forced to become a smuggler by the hardships of the Depression. His only works to escape the reservations of critics during this period were two masterful short stories, both set in Africa and both published in 1936: "The Short and Happy Life of Francis Macomber" and "The Snows of Kilimanjaro."

The Spanish Civil War signaled a new peak in Hemingway's life and in his writing. In 1937, after raising money for the Loyalist (anti-Franco) cause, he went to Spain to report on the war for the North American Newspaper Alliance and to write a script for a documentary film, *The Spanish Earth,* by the Dutch director Joris Ivens. A second visit to Spain later that year resulted in the play *The Fifth Column,* a realistic picture of Madrid under siege in the autumn of 1937, and led to a romance with Martha Gellhorn, who was in Madrid as a war correspondent. Hemingway's novel of the Spanish Civil War, *For Whom the Bell Tolls,* spans the final three days in the life of an American volunteer fighting with the Loyalists. It is, as the title suggests, a plea for and a celebration of human brotherhood, and proved to be his most commercially successful work to date. According to Carlos Baker, "It is still the one indubitable classic among the accounts, both fictional and nonfictional, which took Spain's civil tragedy as subject matter."

Following his divorce from Pauline Pfeiffer, Hemingway married Martha Gellhorn in November 1940 and bought Finca Vigia, a house outside Havana, Cuba. With his new wife he went to China briefly to cover the Sino-Japanese War. After returning to Havana, he set up an intelligence network to monitor Nazi activities in the area, and he armed his forty-foot fishing boat, the *Pilar,* to patrol Cuban waters for German submarines. His third marriage ended in divorce in 1944, the same year he went to London as a war correspondent. He subsequently flew on several Royal Air Force missions, covered the Allied invasion of Normandy, and entered Paris with the American forces on August 25, 1944. So extensive was his involvement in Allied military activities that he was nearly court-martialed for violating the rules of the Geneva Convention on the conduct of war correspondents. Instead, however, he received a Bronze Star for bravery. Returning to Havana on March 14, 1946, he married Mary Welsh, a correspondent for *Time* magazine, whom he had met in London in 1944, and who was to remain his wife until he died.

After several restless years, Hemingway settled down to finish *Across the River and Into the Trees* (1950), a novel set in Italy during World War II. Attacked as sentimental, self-serving, and overly mannered, the book received overwhelmingly negative reviews. A *New Yorker* profile by Lillian Ross, in which Hemingway made an extremely unfavorable impression, and E. B. White's devastating parody, "Across the Street and Into the Grill," added to the critical debacle.

In 1952 *Life* magazine published *The Old Man and the Sea,* one of several sea narratives Hemingway had been working on for some time. A lyrical account of an old fisherman who catches—and then loses—the biggest fish of his life, the tale was an immediate success with both the public and the critics. It restored his reputation and earned him the 1953 Pulitzer Prize for fiction.

Hemingway was awarded the 1954 Nobel Prize for Literature "for his mastery of the art of narrative, most recently demonstrated in *The Old Man and the Sea,* and for the influence that he has exerted on contemporary style." In his presentation speech, Anders Österling of the Swedish Academy called Hemingway "one of the great authors of our time." Praising the author's celebrated novella, Österling remarked, "Within the frame of a sporting tale, a moving perspective of man's destiny is opened up; the story is a tribute to the fighting spirit, which does not give in even if the material gain is nil, a tribute to the moral victory in the midst of defeat." Ill health prevented Hemingway from attending the award ceremonies in Stockholm. In his acceptance speech, read by John C. Cabot, the American ambassador to Sweden, Hemingway confessed that "writing, at best, is a lonely life. . . . [The writer] grows in public stature as he sheds his loneliness, and often his work deteriorates. For he does his work alone and if he is a good enough writer, he must face eternity, or the lack of it, each day.''

In 1960 Hemingway was hospitalized at the Mayo Clinic in Rochester, Minnesota, for treatment of depression and serious mental disturbance. Released in 1961, but convinced that he could no longer write, Hemingway went to his home in Ketchum, Idaho, and there, on July 2, he placed a shotgun to his forehead, emptied both chambers, and ended his life. Remarking on Hemingway's death, the distinguished American literary critic Edmund Wilson wrote, "It is as if a whole corner of my generation had suddenly and horribly collapsed.''

Several of his works, including a novel, *Islands in the Stream* (1970), were published posthumously. However, with the exception of *A Moveable Feast* (1964), Hemingway's memoir of his life among writers in Paris in the 1920s, most of his posthumously released work adds little to his reputation, which declined in the decades following his death. Objecting specifically to *The Old Man and the Sea,* the critic Ken Moritz protested that "we desperately need the courage of intelligence, not romantic myths of individual self-reliance on the frontier.'' Hemingway's detractors, explained the critic Robert P. Weeks in his introduction to *Hemingway: A Collection of Critical Essays* (1962), feel that "Hemingway is too limited. . . . His characters are mute, insensitive, uncomplicated men; his 'action' circles narrowly about the ordeals, triumphs, and defeats of the bullring, the battlefield, the trout stream, and similar male proving grounds; his style . . . has stripped so much away that little is left.''

Despite such criticisms, Hemingway has retained his standing as one of America's greatest writers and the one most widely translated into other languages. Even while noting his limitations, Weeks declared that "within and because of these limits, he has in his best work uttered a lyric cry that—although it may not resemble the full orchestra of Tolstoy or the organ tones of Melville—is nonetheless a moving and finely wrought response to our times.'' Reviewing two new biographies of Hemingway in 1985, the American short story writer Raymond Carver remarked on "how clear, serene, and solid the best work still seems; it's as if there were a physical communion taking place among the fingers turning on the page, the eyes taking in the words, the brain imaginatively recreating what the words stand for. . . . Hemingway did his work, and he'll last.''

ADDITIONAL WORKS: Present-Day American Stories, 1929, with others; Complete Stories, 1954; By-Line: Ernest Hemingway, 1967; The Nick Adams Stories, 1972; 88 Poems, 1979; Selected Letters, 1917–1961, 1981; The Dangerous Summer, 1985; Dateline: Toronto, 1985; Garden of Eden, 1986.

ABOUT: Astro, R., and Benson, J. J. (eds.) Hemingway in Our Time, 1974; Atkins, J. A. The Art of Ernest Hemingway, 1952; Baker, C. Ernest Hemingway: A Life Story, 1969; Bruccoli, M. J. (ed.) Conversations With Ernest Hemingway, 1986; Burgess, A. Ernest Hemingway and His World, 1985; Donaldson, S. By Force of Will, 1977; Fenton, C. A. The Apprenticeship of Ernest Hemingway, 1954; Ferrell, K. Ernest Hemingway, 1984; Grebstein, S. N. Hemingway's Craft, 1973; Griffin, P. Along With Youth, 1985; Hemingway, L. My Brother, Ernest Hemingway, 1962; Hemingway, M. How It Was, 1976; Hotchner, A. E. Papa Hemingway, 1955; Hovey, R. B. Hemingway: The Inward Terrain, 1968; Kert, B. The Hemingway Women, 1983; Lynn, Kenneth. Hemingway, 1987; Meyers, J. Hemingway: A Biography, 1985; Nelson, G. B., and Jones, G. Hemingway, Life and Works, 1984; Plimpton, G. (ed.) Writers at Work, volume 2, 1963; Ross, L. Portrait of Hemingway, 1961; Rovit, E. Ernest Hemingway, 1963; Stephens, R. O. Hemingway's Nonfiction, 1968; Wagner, L. W. (ed.) Ernest Hemingway: Five Decades of Criticism, 1974; Williams, W. The Tragic Art of Ernest Hemingway, 1981; Wylder, D. E. Hemingway's Heroes, 1969; Young, P. Ernest Hemingway: A Reconsideration, 1966.

HENCH, PHILIP S.
(February 28, 1896–March 30, 1965)
Nobel Prize for Physiology or Medicine, 1950
(shared with Edward C. Kendall and Tadeus Reichstein)

The American pathologist Philip Showalter Hench was born in Pittsburgh, Pennsylvania, the son of Clara John (Showalter) Hench and Dr. Jacob Bixler Hench, a classical scholar and educator. After obtaining his early education at the Shadyside Academy and the University School in Pittsburgh, Hench enrolled in Lafayette College in Easton, Pennsylvania, in 1912. He received a B.A. four years later and then enrolled in the University of Pittsburgh medical school. Receiving a medical degree in 1920, he served for a year as a medical intern at St. Francis Hospital in Pittsburgh. In 1921 he was appointed a fellow in medicine at the Mayo Foundation of the University of Minnesota School of Medicine in Rochester. He became an assistant there in 1923, an associate in 1925, and chief physician in the Department of Rheumatic Diseases in 1926.

During the academic year 1928–1929 Hench

PHILIP S. HENCH

studied with Ludwig Aschoff, an authority on rheumatic fever, at Freiburg University and with Friedrich von Müller at the Ludwig-Maximilians University in Munich. Returning to Rochester, he began research in the diagnosis and treatment of rheumatic diseases, specifically rheumatoid arthritis. Rheumatoid arthritis, first described in the medical literature of the mid-nineteenth century, is a chronic disease that causes inflammation and swelling of the connective tissue of the joints. The joints of the fingers, hands, wrists, feet, and spine are most commonly affected. The inflammatory process not only is painful but also may lead to permanent deformity of the joints. Patients with severe forms of the disease may be bedridden. Spontaneous remission has been known to occur but is uncommon, and at the time Hench began his medical practice, no satisfactory treatment had been found.

In April 1929 a sixty-five-year-old patient with severe rheumatoid arthritis told Hench that during a recent bout of jaundice, the pain in his joints had diminished and the range of motion of his joints had improved. Jaundice is a yellowish appearance of the skin and whites of the eyes caused by excessive levels of bilirubin in the blood and tissue. Bilirubin, a metabolic product of hemoglobin, the oxygen-carrying molecule in red blood cells, is metabolized and excreted by the liver. Cirrhosis, hepatitis, and other liver diseases are the most common causes of jaundice. Over the next five years Hench and a colleague, Charles Slocum, observed similar remissions of rheumatoid arthritis during episodes of jaundice

in a total of sixteen patients. Moreover, Hench noted that the degree of improvement in symptoms and function correlated roughly with the severity of the jaundice. From these findings he postulated that an unknown substance ·(which he called substance X) in patients with both jaundice and rheumatoid arthritis caused a remission of the arthritic symptoms. In 1934 he and Slocum published their observations, citing the correlation between jaundice and symptomatic relief of rheumatoid arthritis and suggesting the possible existence of a substance X.

In an effort to produce remission of symptoms, Hench carried out several therapeutic trials in patients with rheumatoid arthritis. With his colleagues he tried oral administration of bile, blood transfusions from donors with jaundice, intravenous infusions of bilirubin, and other means, none of which produced the desired results. The researchers observed that women with rheumatoid arthritis often experienced remission during pregnancy, followed by flare-ups in the postpartum period. In 1938, after observing this phenomenon in thirty-four pregnancies in twenty women with rheumatoid arthritis, Hench and Slocum reported their observations, concluding that the association of remissions with both jaundice and pregnancy suggested that the still-mysterious substance X was "neither bilirubin nor a strictly female sex hormone."

Another researcher at the Mayo Clinic, the biochemist EDWARD C. KENDALL, had isolated thyroid hormone from thyroid tissue in 1914. In the 1930s Kendall turned his attention to the isolation and identification of the hormones of the adrenal glands, which are located at the upper poles of each kidney and consist of an outer cortex and a central medulla. The cells of the medulla are continuous with the sympathetic division of the autonomic (involuntary) nervous system and synthesize and secrete epinephrine (adrenaline) into the bloodstream. Epinephrine, a potent stimulator of the sympathetic nervous system, increases blood pressure and stimulates the heart muscle, leading to an accelerated heart rate and increased oxidation.

The cells of the adrenal cortex, which synthesize and secrete adrenal corticosteroids into the bloodstream, are controlled by adrenocorticotropic hormone (ACTH), a hormonal secretion of the pituitary gland. When blood levels of cortisol are low, the pituitary produces ACTH; this in turn stimulates the adrenal cortex to synthesize and release cortisol. When the blood levels of cortisol are high, the production of ACTH by the pituitary is reduced, and the adrenal production of cortisol falls off. There are two categories of adrenal corticosteroids: the glucocorticoids (cortisone and cortisol), which are involved in the metabolism of carbohydrate, fat, and protein; and the mineralocorticoids, which are involved in the regulation of electrolyte-and-water balance. Cortisone and cortisol also block the biochemical reactions that are involved in the inflammatory response of tissue to injury or infection.

As early as the 1930s, Hench and Kendall began to consider the possibility of treating rheumatoid arthritis patients with adrenal corticosteroids, but it was more than a decade before the substance became available for clinical use. In 1941, while Kendall was organizing a high-priority program aimed at the mass production of adrenal corticosteroids for use during World War II, Hench made the following entry in his notebook after one of their conferences: "Try compound E [cortisone] in rheumatoid arthritis."

In 1942 Hench became a lieutenant colonel in the United States Army Medical Corps, serving as chief of the medical service and director of the army's rheumatism center at the Army-Navy Hospital. After the war, he became a civilian consultant to the surgeon general of the army. He and Slocum published an extensive review of the relation of jaundice and pregnancy to symptomatic relief in patients with rheumatoid arthritis. In the paper they noted that symptomatic relief sometimes occurred after general anesthesia for surgery. They had treated a few patients with general anesthesia with some benefit and had also induced jaundice in several patients by administering lactophenin, a drug that also produced some improvement in symptoms.

In August 1948 Hench and Slocum treated a woman who was suffering from severe rheumatoid arthritis with lactophenin in an attempt to induce jaundice and symptomatic relief. The treatment was unsuccessful, however, and in September, they administered cortisone (in the form of crystalline suspension in saline solution) by intramuscular injection and continued to inject 100 milligrams of cortisone intramuscularly each day. Hench later recalled that "within three days the patient was markedly improved and continued to improve until the daily dose was reduced to 25 milligrams." This was the first clinical evidence of the therapeutic benefits of adrenal corticosteroids in rheumatoid arthritis. The following year, Hench and Slocum administered the pituitary hormone ACTH, which had recently become available, to a patient with rheumatoid arthritis and found it to be therapeutically beneficial. It was soon discovered, however, that the arthritic symptoms recurred after discontinuance of either drug and that the use of cortisone and ACTH was associated with unpleasant and disturbing side effects, including high blood pressure, high blood glucose, and a form of obesity similar to that caused by tumors of the adrenal or pituitary gland.

Hench and Kendall received the 1950 Nobel Prize for Physiology or Medicine "for their discoveries relating to the hormones of the adrenal cortex, their structure and biological effects." They shared the award with TADEUS REICHSTEIN (a Polish-Swiss chemist who had independently isolated and identified the hormones of the adrenal cortex). In his presentation speech, Göran Liljestrand of the Karolinska Institute predicted "a new epoch in the treatment of [rheumatoid arthritis], one of the groups of diseases which . . . are among the most important and the most difficult to cure."

In 1927 Hench married Mary Genevieve Kahler, with whom he had two sons and two daughters. Regarded as an authority on the conquest of yellow fever, he was interested in the history of medicine and published many articles on this subject. He enjoyed photography, tennis, opera, and the stories of Sir Arthur Conan Doyle. Hench died in 1965 at St. Ann's Bay, Jamaica, while on holiday in the Caribbean.

Hench's other awards included the Albert Lasker Award of the American Public Health Association (1949) and the Passano Award in Medical Science of the Passano Foundation (1951). He was a fellow of the American Medical Association and the American College of Physicians, a founding member of the American Rheumatism Association, and an honorary member of the Royal Society of Medicine in London. He received honorary degrees from Lafayette College, Washington and Jefferson College, Western Reserve (now Case Western Reserve) University, and the University of Pittsburgh.

SELECTED WORKS: Acute and Chronic Arthritis, 1935; Effects of Cortisone Acetate, 1950, with others.

ABOUT: Current Biography December 1950; Nature June 19, 1965; Rowntree, L. G. Amid Masters of Twentieth Century Medicine, 1958.

HENDERSON, ARTHUR
(September 13, 1863–October 20, 1935)
Nobel Prize for Peace, 1934

Arthur Henderson, English labor leader and statesman, was born in Glasgow, Scotland, the younger son of David Henderson, a cotton spinner. He grew up in extreme poverty and, after his father's death in 1872, had to leave school to help support the family. When his mother remarried, the family moved to the industrial port city of Newcastle in northeastern England. There Henderson briefly resumed his formal education until, at the age of twelve, he became an apprentice iron molder.

Henderson was sixteen years old when he joined the Methodist church, whose creed of discipline, cooperation, and duty became a major influence on his character and would later guide his career in public service. As a lay preacher, he developed great powers of speech and persuasion, which he exercised by reading political news items to his colleagues at the ironworks. He also developed his speaking skills as a member of the Tyneside Debating Society. By his eighteenth year, when he attained journeyman status and joined the Ironfounders' Union, Henderson's commitment to the working class and to the labor movement had been sealed. Indeed, his reputation as a union agitator was such that he was frequently laid off by factory managers who resented his efforts.

In 1888 Henderson married Eleanor Watson, a member of his church. The couple had one daughter and three sons; their eldest son was killed in World War I.

After serving as an unpaid secretary of his union's Newcastle lodge, in 1892 Henderson was selected to be a full-time salaried delegate for a district covering three northern counties. That year he was also elected a city councillor. Four years later, he moved to the manufacturing town of Darlington, some thirty miles south of Newcastle, and successfully stood for a seat on the Durham County Council. By 1899, when he attended the historic conference of socialists and trade unionists in London, he had reached national prominence. The following year he helped establish the Labour Representation Committee (LRC)—the foundation of the Labour party. He became secretary of the LRC in 1903. In the same year, he was elected as Darlington's first Labour party mayor and, in a three-party contest, won election to Parliament as member for the district of Barnard Castle.

Until the beginning of the twentieth cen-

ARTHUR HENDERSON

tury, the fledgling British labor movement made its political influence felt through the Liberal party. Indeed, in his youth, Henderson was a fervent admirer of the Liberal party leader William Ewart Gladstone. This alliance gradually dissolved, however, as labor leaders moved beyond such traditional demands as the eight-hour workday to embrace socialist calls for the nationalization of industry and land.

Henderson's early career closely paralleled these developments. In 1906 he chaired the first Labour party conference. That year he was returned to Parliament in a general election that saw a total of twenty-nine Labour members elected to the House of Commons—twenty-three of them trade unionists. During the years before World War I, Henderson molded the Labour members of Parliament into a disciplined and effective group. He was the party's parliamentary leader from 1908 through 1911, when he became party secretary, a post he held until the year before his death.

Although many socialists held pacifist views, Henderson openly supported Britain's entry into World War I in 1914. When Labour party leader Ramsay MacDonald resigned from the House of Commons rather than endorse the government's war policy, Henderson succeeded him as party leader. The following year Henderson joined Herbert Asquith's coalition government as president of the Board of Education. In 1916 he became the first Labour party member to hold a cabinet position when he was named paymaster general. He later served as minister-without-portfolio in David Lloyd George's five-member war cabinet.

At Prime Minister Lloyd George's request, Henderson went to Russia in 1917 to urge the new revolutionary government of Alexander Kerensky to remain in the war. Later that year, with a view to further influencing Russia in this direction, Henderson proposed that Britain send delegates to the International Socialist Congress in Stockholm. However, he was not admitted to the cabinet session at which his proposal was discussed, and when Lloyd George formally rebuked him for the plan, Henderson resigned.

Following this so-called doormat incident, Henderson directed his energies toward building the Labour party into a cohesive political force with nationwide appeal. With the assistance of party intellectuals, including Fabian socialist Sidney Webb, Henderson devised a postwar foreign policy for the party. In a "Memorandum on War Aims," Labour demanded the establishment of an international organization that would oversee the peaceful mediation of disputes. Eager to broaden the party's base, Henderson and Webb also wrote a new Labour party constitution, which was adopted in February 1918. Espousing "common ownership of the means of production," this document not only welded together the socialist and trade union elements of the party but also opened the ranks to women and the middle class by stipulating that members could be "workers by hand and by brain." Under Henderson's leadership, Labour emerged from the war with a peace program, a platform, and an organization that had transformed it into a viable opposition party.

To implement Labour's peace policy, Henderson gradually persuaded rank-and-file party members to support the League of Nations, the formation of which was officially proposed at the Paris Peace Conference. In 1919 Henderson acted as party chairman at the National Industrial Conference, and in 1923 he chaired the Labour-Socialist International Conference held at Hamburg. He served various terms in Parliament from 1919 to 1923. Then in February 1924, when the Labour party won a majority of seats in the parliamentary election, he was named home secretary in the first Labour government in Britain's history.

Although his portfolio gave him responsibility for domestic matters, Henderson was chiefly concerned with international affairs. Because of the recent war, one biographer wrote, Henderson "saw war as the greatest danger to mankind and enlisted against it."

Thus, in 1924 he strongly supported the negotiations chaired by CHARLES DAWES to reduce German reparations. He also became a delegate to the Assembly of the League of Nations and negotiated the drafting of the Geneva Protocol, concerning settlement of international disputes by arbitration. However, Henderson's personal political fortunes suffered a setback when Labour was driven from office in the general election of December 1924. Undaunted, he returned to his former task of making the party an effective opposition force.

When the Labourites returned to power in 1929, Prime Minister Ramsay MacDonald chose Henderson as foreign secretary. Although the prime minister reserved Anglo-American and certain other issues for himself, he left the conduct of most matters to Henderson. Henderson's objective in office was to ensure collective security among the European nations.

At a conference on reparations held at The Hague in 1929, Henderson advocated reconciliation with Germany. His persistence and tact in dealing with statesmen ARISTIDE BRIAND and GUSTAV STRESEMANN resulted in agreements to evacuate Allied troops from the Rhineland and to reduce Germany's war reparations. "Mr. Arthur Henderson, insisting on the speedy evacuation of foreign garrisons," wrote J. L. Gavin, editor of the *Observer*, "accomplished the best single stroke for peace that any foreign minister has achieved since the armistice."

At the Tenth Assembly of the League of Nations, which met in Geneva in 1929, Henderson played a leading role in the public deliberations. Henderson also signed the Optional Clause to the League of Nations Covenant, which accepted compulsory arbitration of all justiciable disputes; eventually over forty nations joined Great Britain. The following year, Great Britain and its dominions signed the General Act of Arbitration. Also in 1930, Henderson strongly supported disarmament, telling the Assembly: "We can never fulfill the purpose for which the league has been created unless we are prepared to carry through a scheme of general disarmament by international agreement."

Disarmament consumed Henderson's remaining years as an international statesman. At the invitation of the league Council, in May 1931 Henderson became chairman of the World Disarmament Conference, which convened early the following year. The conference, representing over sixty nations, took place in disheartening circumstances. The Labour government had fallen in the midst of a severe financial crisis; there was a worldwide economic depression; Japan had invaded Manchuria; and Franco-German mistrust had revived over the proposed customs union between Germany and Austria. Despite failing health and a complete lack of cooperation from the British delegation, now representing a new coalition government in which he played no part, Henderson pursued his goal with single-minded persistence. His faith was not shared by leaders of the other great powers, however, who fundamentally mistrusted the idea of international disarmament. When Adolf Hitler was named German chancellor in January 1933, the German delegation withdrew from the conference. By 1934 it was clear, even to Henderson, that too many unsolved problems remained to make any consensus on disarmament possible.

For his persistence in pursuing disarmament, Henderson received the 1934 Nobel Prize for Peace. In his presentation address, Johan Ludwig Mowinckel of the Norwegian Nobel Committee praised Henderson's tact and unfailing courtesy, his prudent reserve, and his ability to act decisively. While recognizing the paradox that "the very nations that are chiefly responsible for starting and for maintaining the Disarmament Conference are also the nations that have begun a new arms race," Henderson in his Nobel lecture remained optimistic about the future. "Our ultimate ideal," he declared, "is the creation of nothing less than a world commonwealth."

Within the year, however, Italy had invaded Ethiopia, and Germany had begun rearming. Henderson's health, which had been deteriorating for several years, declined rapidly, and he died on October 20, 1935, following an operation.

Summing up his contribution to the search for world peace, Henderson's biographer Mary Agnes Hamilton wrote, "To him, words of failure did not apply. His long service, never motivated by personal ambition, had, throughout, been done in the light of a faith to which temporary setback was no more than an incident, irrelevant to the duty of faithfulness. That duty had never been neglected."

WORKS BY: The Aims of Labour, 1917; The League of Nations and Labour, 1918; Consolidating World Peace, 1931; Labour's Foreign Policy, 1933; Labour's Peace Policy, 1934; Labour's Way to Peace, 1935; Conference for the Reduction and Limitation of Armaments, 1936.

ABOUT: Carlton, D. MacDonald Versus Henderson, 1970;

Dictionary of National Biography 1931–40, 1949; Graubard, S. British Labour and the Russian Revolution, 1956; Hamilton, M. A. Arthur Henderson, 1938; Jenkins, E. A. From Foundry to Foreign Office, 1933; Times (London) October 21, 1935; Walters, F. P. A History of the League of Nations, 1952; Wood, T. M. British Finance and Prussian Militarism, 1917.

HERSCHBACH, DUDLEY R.
(June 18, 1932–)
Nobel Prize for Chemistry, 1986
(shared with Yuan T. Lee and John C. Polanyi)

The American chemist Dudley Robert Herschbach was born in San Jose, California, the eldest of six children of Robert Dudley Herschbach, a building contractor, and Dorothy Edith (Beer) Herschbach. Growing up in what was then rural California, Herschbach took part in outdoor activities, scouting, and athletics. His success as a football player for the Campbell Union High School team led to an offer of both academic and football scholarships by Stanford University, where he played on the freshman team and was invited to try out for the Los Angeles Rams professional club. Absorption in his studies soon took precedence over athletic activities.

Following his second year at Stanford, Herschbach began research in experimental chemical kinetics under the American chemist Harold S. Johnston. At that time, most experimental tests of the transition-state theory of chemical reactions relied on data from complex chemical reactions; Johnston assigned Herschbach to measure the rates of simple chemical reactions to test the theory more directly. Herschbach received his B.S. in mathematics in 1954, even though he could also have qualified for a degree in chemistry or physics. He obtained an M.S. in chemistry in 1955, devising for his master's thesis approximation methods for making more accurate calculations of preexponential factors for a series of simple reactions to test transition-state theory. He continued his graduate study at Harvard University, where he received an M.A. in physics in 1956 and a Ph.D. in chemical physics in 1958. He did his doctoral research with the American chemist E. Bright Wilson's group, which was then developing elegant new ways, using microwave spectroscopy, to study molecular structure and barriers to internal molecular rotation. Herschbach made significant theoretical and experimental contributions, among them an important paper on the calculation of energy levels for internal torsion and overall rotation of molecules.

Harvard University

DUDLEY R. HERSCHBACH

After a term as a junior fellow in the Society of Fellows at Harvard (1957–1959), Herschbach became an assistant professor (1959–1961) and then an associate professor (1961–1963) of chemistry at the University of California at Berkeley. He became a professor of chemistry at Harvard in 1963 and since 1976 has been Frank B. Baird Jr. Professor of Science. At Harvard he served as chairman of the chemical physics program (1964–1977) and of the chemistry department (1977–1980) and was a member of the Faculty Council (1980–1983).

When Herschbach came to Berkeley in late 1959, the understanding of chemical reactions had progressed only moderately beyond pre-World War II ideas. Quantum theory, born in 1900, provided a better picture of the structure of atoms and molecules and explained many aspects of observed chemical behavior. However, chemists essentially were still limited to mixing substances, controlling conditions such as temperature and pressure, and identifying the reaction products. Theoretical models remained basically static, viewing reacting molecules as coexisting side by side and occasionally bouncing against each other, sometimes creating new arrangements. As a student, Herschbach had been intrigued by a remark made by one of his professors about molecular beams, directed streams of molecules projected across a vacuum chamber with controlled energies. The technique appealed to him as a possible way to look more closely at individual molecules in the process of reacting.

Herschbach began research in molecular beam dynamics at Berkeley at about the same

time that JOHN C. POLANYI was beginning his study of chemical dynamics at the University of Toronto using a different method, called chemiluminescence, which was to prove complementary to Herschbach's work. Herschbach and a small group of students and postdoctoral fellows built an apparatus in which two molecular beams crossed each other, one beam consisting of potassium atoms and the other composed of molecules of carbon, hydrogen, and iodine. Details of the reaction taking place at the intersection of the beams were studied with a device called a surface ionization detector. The beam constituents were specially chosen because Michael Polanyi, John C. Polanyi's father, had long ago shown that they reacted efficiently and because other researchers had recently found that the detector was suitable for observing the reaction products under the conditions of the experiment. Herschbach's initial experiments gave the first glimpse into the detailed dynamics of a reactive molecular collision in the form of the directions and recoil energies at which the reaction products emerged. This information enabled the group to characterize the mechanism of reaction (called rebound) and revealed that much of the released chemical energy appeared as vibrations in the reaction products.

With considerable difficulty, the experiments were extended to more complicated versions of the same class of substances. The results were somewhat different, having a mechanism of reaction called stripping. However, again the released energy appeared more in the form of internal excitation of the product molecules than in the velocities at which the molecules traveled. Many more reactions were studied, and Herschbach continued the work when he moved to Harvard in 1963. The experiments disclosed a wide variety in the reactions, including those that were intermediate between rebound and stripping and those that proceeded by way of the formation and subsequent decomposition of a long-lived complex before creation of the final products. This information presented a good opportunity to test statistical theories of chemical reactions and to illuminate the important role of angular momentum.

Despite the success of the experiments with the class of compounds called alkalis (compounds that combine with acids to form salts), the limitations of the equipment became increasingly restrictive, calling for more versatile capabilities. In 1967 YUAN T. LEE joined Herschbach at Harvard as a postdoctoral fellow. With several students, Lee began to design and construct a new "supermachine" that used supersonic nozzles to create beams, a movable mass spectrometer detector (which applied oscillating electric and magnetic fields to deflect different products along different paths so they could be collected and identified), improved differential pumping to provide better vacuums, time-of-flight product velocity analysis, and computers for data acquisition. Completing the apparatus within ten months, Lee, Herschbach, and their coworkers revolutionized the field. Many other reactions of more complex molecules could then be studied, and with far greater precision. In one reaction, involving hydrogen and chlorine, Herschbach's group obtained angular and recoil velocity distributions for compounds whose internal vibrations John Polanyi had determined by chemiluminescence. The results of the two groups gave a uniquely comprehensive view of the detailed dynamics of the reaction. Throughout the work, Herschbach was considered by his colleagues as an innovator in the field, a source of scientific insights, and an enthusiastic and inspirational leader.

Herschbach shared the 1986 Nobel Prize for Chemistry with Lee and Polanyi for fundamental contributions to the development of a new field, the dynamics of chemical reactions, which has provided a more detailed understanding of how chemical reactions take place. Before this pioneering work, the study of chemical reactions mostly involved bulk systems and averages of many random molecular collisions; the details of a single reactive collision were lost. Herschbach has likened this situation to observing a baseball game where "zillions of pitchers throw zillions of balls at zillions of batters at the same time; it would be very hard to tell what is going on." The field of reaction dynamics has simplified the game so that an observer can watch how "one pitcher throws one ball to one batter."

In 1964 Herschbach married Georgene Lee Botyos, also a chemist and now an assistant dean at Harvard College. The Herschbachs, who have two daughters, enjoy outdoor activities and share a love of chamber music, forming a family string quartet. Highly regarded as a teacher as well as a scientist, Herschbach has influenced many students and colleagues with his sharp insights and broad view of science. For five years he and his wife were comasters of Currier House, a Harvard undergraduate residence, living with students and tutors and directing many of the academic and extracurricular activities.

In addition to the Nobel Prize, Herschbach

has received the Pure Chemistry Prize of the American Chemical Society (1965), the Spiers Medal of the Faraday Society (1976), the Centenary Medal of the British Chemical Society (1977), the Linus Pauling Medal of the American Chemical Society (1978), and the Irving Langmuir Prize in Chemical Physics of the American Physical Society (1983). He is a member of the National Academy of Sciences, the American Academy of Arts and Sciences, the American Chemical Society, the American Physical Society, and the American Association for the Advancement of Science. He holds an honorary degree from the University of Toronto.

ABOUT: Harvard Gazette January 18, 1985; New York Times October 16, 1986; Research and Development December 1986; Science November 7, 1986; Scientific American December 1986; Time October 27, 1986.

HERSHEY, ALFRED
(December 4, 1908–)
Nobel Prize for Physiology or Medicine, 1969
(shared with Max Delbrück and Salvador Luria)

The American biologist Alfred Day Hershey was born in Owosso, Michigan, to Alma (Wilbur) and Robert D. Hershey. He attended public schools in Owosso and Lansing before entering Michigan State College (now Michigan State University), where he obtained a B.S. in chemistry in 1930. Remaining at Michigan State for graduate studies, he received a Ph.D. in bacteriology in 1934 and was then appointed to the staff of the Department of Bacteriology at Washington University in St. Louis, Missouri. After serving as an assistant bacteriologist for two years, he became an instructor; he was appointed assistant professor in 1938 and associate professor in 1950.

During his early years at Washington University, Hershey worked under J. J. Bronfenbrenner, who had been investigating bacteriophages since their discovery in 1915. The bacteriophage, a type of virus that infects bacterial cells, is the simplest form of life and, like other viruses, consists of protein and nucleic acid.

Early in the twentieth century, scientists demonstrated that the inheritance of physical characteristics is governed by genes, which reside on chromosomes in the nucleus of each cell. Chromosomes contain proteins associated with nucleic acids, large molecules com-

ALFRED HERSHEY

posed of units of sugar, phosphate, and nitrogenous bases known as purines or pyrimidines. Biochemical studies revealed two kinds of nucleic acids: ribonucleic acid (RNA) and deoxyribonucleic acid (DNA). It had been believed that only proteins, consisting of amino acids linked together in chains, were sufficiently complex to carry the genetic information; DNA molecules were considered too uniform and repetitive. In the 1940s, however, it was discovered that genes are made of DNA and that DNA directs the biosynthesis of cellular proteins, enzymes, and coenzymes (the heat-stable, water-soluble portion of an enzyme), thus establishing the role DNA plays in controlling the biochemical processes of the cells.

Between 1940 and 1947 MAX DELBRÜCK at Vanderbilt University in Nashville, Tennessee, was analyzing the life cycle of the bacteriophage. In collaboration with SALVADOR LURIA at Columbia University, he demonstrated that bacterial cells undergo spontaneous mutation to resist destruction by bacteriophages. Their findings, published in 1943, became a standard for the analysis and presentation of experimental results in bacteriological research. Delbrück, Luria, and Hershey formed the cadre of the Phage Group, an informal group dedicated to bacteriophage research—specifically, the mechanisms of phage replication. Encouraging free exchange of ideas among independent investigators, the Phage Group urged other scientists to concentrate on seven strains of bacteriophage that infect the colon bacillus *Escherichia coli* strain B,

so that experimental results could be easily compared.

In 1946 Hershey and Delbrück, working independently, discovered that different strains of bacteriophage may exchange genetic material if more than one strain infects the same bacterial cell. Delbrück was a brilliant theoretician, whereas Hershey was a better experimentalist, and it was Hershey who obtained unequivocal evidence of genetic exchange, which he called genetic recombination. It was the first laboratory demonstration of recombination of genetic material in viruses.

Hershey left Washington University in 1950 to join the staff of the Genetics Research Unit of the Carnegie Institute at Cold Spring Harbor on Long Island, New York. Electron microscopic analysis had revealed the bacteriophage structure to be a protein head, encapsulating a DNA core, and a slender protein tail. In 1952, together with Martha Chase, a geneticist, Hershey discovered how bacteriophages infect bacterial cells. The method employed by Hershey and Chase was based on the fact that phage protein contains no phosphorus and DNA has no sulfur. After cultivating two batches of bacteriophage—one with radioactive phosphorus, the other with radioactive sulfur—the two researchers traced the isotopes during the process of infection and determined that the bacteriophage first attached itself to the bacterial-cell membrane by its protein tail; the nucleic acid core was then injected into the bacterial cell. To separate the empty bacteriophage coats (containing the sulfur isotope) from the bacterial cells (labeled with phosphorus), the suspension was spun in a blender to break the attachment of the viral tails to the bacterial membranes. The suspension was finally centrifuged to separate cellular and fluid fractions. These blender experiments confirmed that DNA is the genetic material of the bacteriophage and, by inference, of all other organisms as well.

During the 1950s and 1960s Hershey continued to investigate the biochemical structure and function of bacteriophage DNA. His work established that bacteriophage DNA is single-stranded—unlike the DNA of higher organisms—and that some bacteriophagic DNA is circular. Moreover, he demonstrated that DNA differs from one species to another.

The 1969 Nobel Prize for Physiology or Medicine was awarded to Hershey, Luria, and Delbrück "for their discoveries concerning the replication mechanism and the genetic structure of viruses." On presenting the award, Sven Gard of the Karolinska Institute noted the significance of these discoveries for biochemistry, genetics, and other fields of research, adding that the three laureates "must . . . be regarded as the original founders of the modern science of molecular biology."

From 1962 until his retirement in 1974, Hershey served as director of the Genetics Research Unit at Cold Spring Harbor. "Although it would be difficult to imagine three personalities more unlike than those of Delbrück, Luria, and Hershey," wrote Gunther Stent of the Harvard Medical School, "they have one trait in common—total incorruptibility—and it is just this trait . . . that these three men managed to impose on an entire scientific discipline."

After their first meeting in 1943, Max Delbrück described Hershey in a note to Luria: "Drinks whiskey but not tea, simple, to the point, likes living in a sailboat for three months, likes independence." In 1946 Hershey married Harriet Davidson, with whom he had a son.

Hershey has received an honorary degree from the University of Chicago as well as the Lasker Award of the American Public Health Association (1958) and the Kimber Genetics Award of the National Academy of Sciences (1965). He is a fellow of the American Academy of Arts and Sciences and a member of the National Academy of Sciences.

ABOUT: Current Biography July 1970; New York Times October 17, 1969; Science October 24, 1969.

HERTZ, GUSTAV

(July 22, 1887–October 30, 1975)
Nobel Prize for Physics, 1925
(shared with James Franck)

The German physicist Gustav Ludwig Hertz was born in Hamburg to Gustav Hertz, a lawyer, and Auguste (Arning) Hertz. His uncle, Rudolph Heinrich Hertz, was one of the most influential physicists of the late nineteenth century. After receiving his secondary education at the *Johanneum* in Hamburg, Hertz entered the University of Göttingen in 1906, studying mathematics and mathematical physics with David Hilbert and Carl Runge. He then studied with Arnold Sommerfeld at the University of Munich, where he was introduced to the new quantum theory, and with JAMES FRANCK and Robert Pohl at the University of Berlin, where he became interested in experimental physics. In 1911 he received his Ph.D. from Berlin with a dissertation on infrared absorption of carbon dioxide.

In 1913 Hertz was appointed research assistant at the Physics Institute of the University of Berlin, where he and Franck began research on the energy changes that occur when an atom is struck by an electron. Although they did not realize it at the time, their work had direct bearing on the validity of NIELS BOHR's model of the atom, which Bohr had presented earlier in 1913.

Bohr theorized that electrons could revolve about the nucleus only in certain prescribed orbits, each of which corresponds to a specific energy state of the electron. According to Bohr, when an electron absorbs a discrete amount of energy, or quantum, it "jumps" to a higher-energy orbit farther from the nucleus. Conversely, an electron in a higher-energy orbit emits a quantum when it falls to an orbit nearer the nucleus. The energy in the quantum equals the energy difference between the orbits. Bohr's model partially explained the hitherto mysterious line spectra of the elements. When a gas is energized, for example, by an electric discharge, its atoms release the absorbed energy in the form of light. The atoms of each element give off light of specific colors, corresponding to specific frequencies and wavelengths, which can be separated by a spectroscope to produce a series of colored lines, or line spectrum, characteristic of the element. MAX PLANCK, the founder of quantum theory, had shown in 1900 that the frequency is proportional to the energy in a quantum of the light. Thus, according to the Bohr theory, each spectral line corresponds to the energy difference between a specific pair of orbits. Line spectra therefore offer clues to atomic structure.

Hertz and Franck accelerated electrons (which are negatively charged) in a closed tube by applying a positive voltage to an electrode opposite the electron source. The electrons, whose maximum acquired kinetic energy was known (voltage multiplied by electron charge) and could be varied at will, passed through low-pressure mercury vapor. Another electrode could detect the loss of energy by electrons in collisions with mercury atoms. It was found that the energy loss was negligible until the voltage reached 4.9 volts. This finding confirmed at least one aspect of the Bohr theory by demonstrating that energy was absorbed by an atom only in specific amounts. Similar results were obtained with other gases such as helium and neon. Hertz and Franck calculated the frequency associated with a quantum equal to the electron energy at 4.9 volts and found that it coincided with one of the lines (ultra-

GUSTAV HERTZ

violet) in the mercury line spectrum. However, since the Bohr theory was only a few months old at the time and not well understood, they misinterpreted the 4.9 volts as the ionization potential, that is, the energy required to knock an electron out of the atom, disrupting the neutral balance between negative electrons outside the nucleus and positive protons inside, and leaving behind a positively charged ion. They erroneously believed that the ultraviolet mercury line was emitted when the ion captured a free electron and filled the vacancy. A major problem was that the Bohr model predicted an ionization potential of 10.36 volts.

After some confusion, the model was better understood, and it was realized that the line was due to an atomic electron transition between the two lowest orbits in the spectral series, not to the loss and restoration of an outer electron. The 4.9 volts represented, not an ionization potential, but an excitation potential, that is, the energy, or quantum, required to boost (excite) an electron from one energy state to another without severing its attachment to the atom. With refinements of experimental technique and more accurate interpretation by Hertz, Franck, and others, more excitation potentials were measured, at higher voltages, and were found to correspond to other observed lines in the mercury spectrum. The true ionization potential was also confirmed, and the Bohr theory was convincingly verified. Hertz and Franck were the first to measure directly the energy in a quantum.

Franck later admitted that they had "failed to recognize the fundamental significance of Bohr's theory, so much so, that we never even mentioned it once in the relevant paper." However, Bohr and others did realize the significance of Hertz and Franck's experiments and cited them to corroborate Bohr's ideas.

In 1926 Hertz and Franck were awarded the 1925 Nobel Prize for Physics "for their discovery of the laws governing the impact of an electron upon an atom." Until very recently, said C. W. Oseen of the Royal Swedish Academy of Sciences in his presentation speech, "there is nobody who would have thought it advisable to proceed from the assumption that the atom can exist in different states, each of which is characterized by a given energy level, and that these energy levels govern the spectral lines." Bohr's theory has established these hypotheses, Oseen went on, adding that "the methods of verifying these hypotheses are the work of James Franck and Gustav Hertz."

Both Hertz and Franck served in the German army during World War I, and Hertz was wounded severely in 1915. After an extended convalescence, he returned to the University of Berlin in 1917 as a privatdocent (unsalaried lecturer). From 1920 to 1925, Hertz worked in the physics laboratory of the Philips' Incandescent Lamp Works at Eindhoven, in the Netherlands. (Philips' was one of the first private companies to sponsor basic research.) In 1925 he was appointed resident professor of physics at the University of Halle and director of its Physics Institute. Three years later Hertz returned to Berlin as director of the Physics Institute at the Charlottenburg Technical University, where his most noteworthy achievement was the development of a gas diffusion process for separating the isotopes of neon.

When the Nazis came to power in Germany in 1933, Hertz was unwilling to take a loyalty oath, and he resigned from Charlottenburg in 1934 and served as director of the research laboratory of the Siemens and Halske Company in Berlin until the end of World War II. It is not clear why Hertz, whose father was Jewish and whose first wife was a known anti-Nazi, was allowed to remain in such an important position under Nazi rule.

At the end of the war, when Germany was divided, Hertz was one of a group of East German scientists who were sent to the Soviet Union on a ten-year contract. He had once told friends in the United States on a 1939 visit that he found physics in America so advanced that he felt he could make a greater contribution in the Soviet Union. He also hoped his family might become integrated into Russian society. However, he and the other German scientists were segregated from society in a laboratory compound. In the Soviet Union he directed research on atomic energy and radar at a laboratory in Sukhumi on the Black Sea, and he also improved his method of isotope separation so that it could be carried out on a commercial scale. In 1955 Hertz left Sukhumi for Leipzig, in East Germany, where he was appointed professor at the Karl Marx University of Leipzig. As director of the university's Physics Institute, he supervised the building of a modern institution to replace the one destroyed during the war. In 1961 he retired to East Berlin, where he died fourteen years later.

Hertz married Ellen Dihlmann in 1919; they had two sons, both of whom became physicists. In 1943, two years after the death of his first wife, Hertz married Charlotte Jollasse. Hertz was a quiet man, and little is known of his attitudes and views. He was an accomplished photographer.

In addition to the Nobel Prize, Hertz received many honors including the Max Planck Medal of the German Physical Society and the Lenin Prize of the Soviet government. He belonged to the German Academy of Sciences in Berlin and the Göttingen Academy of Sciences, as well as the scientific academies of Hungary, Czechoslovakia, and the Soviet Union.

SELECTED WORKS: New Results in the Isotope Separation of Heavy Gases in the Gas Ultracentrifuge, 1961, with E. Nann; On the Dependence of the Separation Effect on the Countercurrent Circulation in the Gas Centrifuge, 1961, with E. Nann.

ABOUT: Nachmanson, D. German-Jewish Pioneers in Science, 1900–1933, 1979; New York Times October 31, 1975; Physics Today January 1976; Trigg, G. L. Crucial Experiments in Modern Physics, 1971.

HERZBERG, GERHARD
(December 25, 1904–)
Nobel Prize for Chemistry, 1971

The German-Canadian physicist Gerhard Herzberg was born in Hamburg, to Ella (Biber) and Albin Herzberg. His early schooling took place in Hamburg, and he received his bachelor's degree (1927) and his Ph.D. (1928), both in engineering, from the Darmstadt Institute of Technology. His thesis, completed while he was a student of Hans Rau, concerned the interaction of matter with electromagnetic radiation. The following year he

GERHARD HERZBERG

studied under MAX BORN and JAMES FRANCK at the University of Göttingen, followed by a year with A. M. Tyndall at the University of Bristol in England. By 1929, at the age of twenty-four, he had already published twenty scientific papers. In 1930 he was appointed privatdocent (unsalaried lecturer) and senior assistant in physics at the Darmstadt Institute of Technology.

Electromagnetic radiation is energy in the form of a wave produced by electrical charges. The electromagnetic spectrum includes infrared, visible, and ultraviolet light; long radio waves; microwaves; X rays; and gamma rays. When isolated atoms are subjected to electromagnetic radiation, light is either absorbed or emitted by the atoms, depending on whether their electrons move to a higher or lower energy level. This light forms line spectra of characteristic wavelengths. Molecules exhibit more complex spectra than do atoms. Excitation of molecules involves interatomic vibration, bending of molecular bonds, and rotational changes. Molecules also emit and absorb light over a wider range of wavelengths. Spectroscopy, or analysis of line spectra with spectroscopic instruments, may reveal information about the structure and energy levels of atoms and molecules.

In 1929, by analyzing the spectra of molecular nitrogen, Herzberg and Werner Heitler, a colleague at Darmstadt, demonstrated that the nitrogen nucleus could not be composed only of protons and electrons, as had been generally thought. Shortly thereafter, the British physicist JAMES CHADWICK found that an uncharged particle, the neutron, was a major component of atomic nuclei. Herzberg also discovered line spectra of diatomic oxygen, now designated Herzberg bands, which have become important in the study of the upper atmosphere.

The Nazi persecution of Jews forced Herzberg to emigrate to Canada in 1935, where he became a research professor at the University of Saskatchewan. Although no experimental facilities existed when he arrived, he was able to establish a spectroscopy laboratory. Since he was classified as an enemy alien, he played no role in military research projects during World War II.

In 1945 Herzberg became a Canadian citizen and accepted a position as professor at the Yerkes Observatory of the University of Chicago. Working with advanced graduate students, he quickly built up an outstanding laboratory for the investigation of molecular spectra from stars, comets, and planets. Using infrared techniques, he showed that some planetary atmospheres contain hydrogen and also confirmed the presence of water in comets. Three years later he returned to Canada as principal research officer in the Division of Physics at the National Research Council in Ottawa. The following year he was named director of the division, and in 1955 he became director of the Division of Pure Physics. In 1969 he was appointed distinguished research scientist at the research council's Herzberg Institute of Astrophysics.

Until the 1950s, Herzberg primarily studied the structure and properties of stable molecules. In the early 1950s, however, he turned to the more difficult spectroscopic analysis of free radicals (atoms or molecules with at least one unpaired electron). Although their existence as intermediates in chemical reactions had been postulated, free radicals are so extremely reactive and have such fleeting lifetimes that they had not yet been observed. In an attempt to do so, Herzberg and his colleagues used the flash-photolysis techniques developed by RONALD NORRISH and GEORGE PORTER, in which light or other radiant energy causes chemical decomposition. The researchers made their first successful spectroscopic studies of free methyl in 1956 and of methylene three years later.

Herzberg was awarded the 1971 Nobel Prize for Chemistry for "his contributions to the knowledge of electronic structure and geometry of molecules, particularly free radicals." In his presentation speech, Stig Clæsson of the Royal Swedish Academy of Sciences stated,

"Herzberg's elegant experimental investigations combined with his theoretical insight into their interpretation contributed to the progress of quantum mechanics while being decisive for the rapid development of molecular spectroscopy." Around 1950, Clæsson noted, "molecular spectroscopy had progressed so far that one could begin to study even complicated systems of great chemical importance. This is brilliantly demonstrated by Herzberg's pioneering investigations of free radicals. Knowledge of their properties is of fundamental importance to our understanding of how chemical reactions proceed."

In 1929 Herzberg married Luise Oettinger, also a physicist; they had one son and one daughter. A year after his first wife's death in 1971, he married Monika Tenthoff. Herzberg has been described by A. E. Douglas, one of his colleagues at the National Research Council, as "a dynamic scientist" and "an unassuming and generous man."

Herzberg has received the Tory Medal of the Royal Society of Canada (1953), the Gold Medal of the Canadian Association of Physicists (1957), the Companion of the Order of Canada (1968), the Willard Gibbs (1969) and Linus Pauling (1971) medals of the American Chemical Society, the Frederick Ives Medal of the Optical Society of America, and the Faraday Medal of the British Chemical Society (1971). In addition to memberships in professional physical and chemical associations, Herzberg has served as an officer of international commissions on spectroscopy, and was president of the Canadian Association of Physicists (1956–1957), the International Union of Pure and Applied Physics (1957–1963), and the Royal Society of Canada (1966–1967).

SELECTED WORKS: Atomic Spectra and Atomic Structure, 1937; Molecular Spectra and Molecular Structure (4 vols.) 1939–1979, with Klaus-Peter Huber; The Spectra and Structures of Simple Free Radicals: An Introduction to Molecular Spectroscopy, 1971.

ABOUT: Current Biography February 1973; New York Times November 3, 1971; Science November 12, 1971.

HESS, VICTOR F.
(June 24, 1883–December 17, 1964)
Nobel Prize for Physics, 1936
(shared with Carl D. Anderson)

The Austrian-American physicist Victor Franz Hess was born at Waldstein Castle in Styria, Austria, to Vinzens Hess, chief forester on the estate of Prince Öttingen-Wallerstein, and the former Serafine Edle von Grossbauer-Waldstätt. After attending the gymnasium in Graz between 1893 and 1901, he entered the University of Graz and received his Ph.D. in physics summa cum laude in 1906.

Hess had planned to do postgraduate work in optics under Paul Drude at the University of Berlin, but after Drude committed suicide, Hess went to the University of Vienna instead. At Vienna, while serving as demonstrator and lecturer, Hess became interested in research that Franz Exner and Egon von Schweidler were conducting on radioactive radiation and atmospheric ionization. Radioactive radiation occurs when atoms of unstable elements, such as uranium and thorium, emit intense bursts of energy together with positively and negatively charged particles. After such emissions, the surrounding atmosphere becomes electrically conductive, that is, ionized. This form of radioactivity can be detected by an electroscope, an electrically charged instrument that loses its charge in air that has been exposed to radiation.

Working at the university's Institute for Radium Research, where he had been appointed a research assistant in 1910, Hess learned of studies by the staff to determine the source of ionizing radiation in the atmosphere. He also learned that Theodor Wulf had measured atmospheric ionization several months earlier in Paris. Wulf's measurements, taken from the Eiffel Tower, indicated the presence of far greater levels of radiation at the top of the tower, 320 meters up, than on the ground. His finding was at odds with the then current theory that radioactivity emanated only from within the earth. To explain the disparity in levels of radioactivity, Wulf suggested that radiation from above the earth's atmosphere had caused the difference in measurements. He also urged other scientists to test his hypothesis by sending instruments into the atmosphere by balloons.

The following year Hess designed instruments capable of withstanding great changes in both temperature and pressure at high elevations. Calculating the maximum height at which terrestrial radiation might ionize the atmosphere, he reached the figure of 500 meters. During the next two years, with assistance from the Austrian Air Club, he made ten balloon ascents. By this means, he later recalled, "I was able to demonstrate . . . that the ionization [in an electroscope] was reduced with increasing height from the earth (reduction in the effect of radioactive substances in the earth),

VICTOR F. HESS

but that it noticeably increased from 1,000 meters onwards, and at 5 kilometers height reached several times the observed value at earth level." These findings led him to conclude that the ionization "might be attributed to the penetration of the earth's atmosphere from outer space by hitherto unknown radiation."

That this radiation came from outer space rather than from the sun seemed likely to Hess because he observed no decrease in atmospheric ionization during nighttime ascents. In 1925 the radiation was given the name *cosmic rays* by the American physicist ROBERT A. MILLIKAN. The experiments Hess conducted stimulated others to examine cosmic radiation, including CARL D. ANDERSON, who discovered the positron (a positively charged particle with a mass equal to that of the electron) and, with S. H. Neddermeyer, the mu-meson. The latter, now called a muon, is an exceptionally short-lived particle with a mass approximately 200 times that of the electron.

In 1919 Hess was appointed an assistant professor of physics at the University of Vienna but accepted a position as associate professor of experimental physics at the University of Graz in 1920, the same year he married Marie Bertha Warner Breisky. Taking a leave of absence in 1921, Hess traveled to the United States, where he directed the research laboratory of the United States Radium Corporation in Orange, New Jersey, and served as a consultant to the Bureau of Mines of the United States Department of the Interior.

Hess returned to Graz in 1923, was named full professor two years later, and became dean of the faculty in 1929. In 1931 he became professor of experimental physics and director of the Institute for Radiation Research at the University of Innsbruck and also established a station for the study of cosmic rays at nearby Hafelekar.

In recognition "of his discovery of cosmic radiation," Hess shared the 1936 Nobel Prize for Physics with Carl Anderson. His discovery, said Hans Pleijel of the Royal Swedish Academy of Sciences in his presentation address, "has offered us new, important problems on the formation and destruction of matter, problems which open up new fields for research."

In 1938, two months after Nazi Germany's annexation of Austria, Hess was dismissed from his post at Graz because his wife was Jewish and because he had been a scientific adviser to the government of the recently deposed Austrian chancellor, Kurt von Schuschnigg. Warned that he and his wife would soon be arrested, Hess fled to Switzerland only weeks before the order was issued.

An invitation from Fordham University brought Hess and his wife to New York City in 1938, where he taught physics at Fordham and, six years later, became an American citizen. In 1946 he was asked to conduct the world's first test to measure radioactive fallout in the United States from the atomic bombing of Hiroshima. The following year, he and the physicist William T. McNiff devised a gamma-ray method to detect minute amounts of radium in the human body.

After his first wife died in 1955, Hess married Elizabeth M. Hoencke the same year. Although he retired from Fordham in 1956, Hess continued to conduct research on cosmic radiation and radioactivity until his death in Mount Vernon, New York, in 1964.

During his long career, Hess received many awards and honors, including the Lieben Prize of the Austrian Academy of Sciences (1919), the Ernst Abbé Memorial Prize of the Carl Zeiss Foundation (1932), the Austrian government's Honorary Insignia for Art and Science (1959), and honorary degrees from the University of Vienna, Loyola University in Chicago, Loyola University in New Orleans, and Fordham University.

SELECTED WORKS: The Electrical Conductivity of the Atmosphere and Its Causes, 1928; Cosmic Radiation and Its Biological Effects, 1949, with Jakob Eugster.

ABOUT: Current Biography October 1963; Dictionary of Scientific Biography, volume 6, 1972.

HESS, WALTER R.

(March 17, 1881–August 12, 1973)
Nobel Prize for Physiology or Medicine, 1949
(shared with Egas Moniz)

The Swiss physiologist Walter Rudolf Hess was born at Frauenfeld, a small town in German-speaking eastern Switzerland, to Clemens and Gertrud (Fischer Saxon) Hess. Hess was very young when his father, a university physics teacher, first introduced him to scientific experimentation. Hess, who combined a strong interest in biological processes with a pronounced practical bent, entered the University of Lausanne in 1900 to study medicine. He continued his studies at the universities of Bern, Zurich, Berlin, and Kiel, and he received his medical degree from the University of Zurich in 1906. His dissertation concerned the relationship between the viscosity of the blood and the work of the heart. Hemodynamics (the physical forces governing the circulatory system) remained his major research interest for many years.

Lacking the financial means to undertake full-time medical research, Hess served his residency in surgery and ophthalmology at the state hospital in his home canton. The experience gave him the opportunity to see parts of the vascular system in vivo. In 1908 he established his own ophthalmology practice, which quickly became lucrative and made heavy demands on his time. Giving up his practice in 1917, he accepted a poorly paid assistantship in the University of Zurich's Physiology Institute in order to continue research in hemodynamics.

For more than a decade, Hess investigated the regulation of the heart rate and blood pressure, and their relationship to other physiological processes, such as respiration. His research was interrupted by a tour of duty in the Swiss army during World War I, but in 1917 he was named both professor and director of the Department of Physiology, positions he held concurrently for the rest of his career.

By 1925 Hess wished to broaden his examination of isolated activities of the circulatory and respiratory systems for a better understanding of what he called "the neural mechanisms by which the activity of the internal organs is adapted to constantly changing conditions, and by which they are adjusted to one another." The internal organs are not normally under conscious control; their functions are coordinated by the so-called autonomic, or vegetative, nervous system. Previous clin-

WALTER R. HESS

ical observations of patients with brain damage and experiments performed on animals indicated that the diencephalon—a group of brain structures lying directly underneath the cerebral cortex—was the central clearinghouse for the autonomic nervous system. "Something which still, however, lay in obscurity, when my own investigations were started," Hess later said, "was the allocation of definite functions to particular morphological substrata . . . , in other words, the organic structure of the diencephalic vegetative control system. To throw as much light as possible on this was the task which I set myself."

A standard method for studying the function of a particular region of the brain is to observe the response of an experimental animal to electrical stimulation in that area. It had been difficult, however, to use this technique to study the diencephalon, which lies deep within the brain, except by removing a crippling amount of the surrounding cerebral cortex.

Using a stereotaxic instrument (one that can be directed on three planes toward a specific locus in the brain), Hess guided electrodes through small openings in the skull to precise locations, without having to see the internal structures directly. By employing very fine electrodes and careful surgical techniques, the procedure did so little damage that his experimental animals, restrained only by the wires leading to their skulls, could be observed without their being anesthetized. Initially, Hess hoped that a relatively brief series of experiments would enable him to discover the basic functions of the diencephalon (particularly the

hypothalamus, which is located at the very base of the brain). The hypothalamus, however, has a diverse array of functions in a restricted space, and at first it was impossible to predict what effect stimulation at a certain point would produce. Hess thus embarked on a long, extremely meticulous course of work. He supplemented his original experiments with dissections and histological studies, films of the behavior of the stimulated animals, and comparisons of that behavior with the effects of small lesions at the same brain locations.

By this work, Hess showed that electrical stimulation of different regions of the hypothalamus can cause changes in blood pressure, respiration, body temperature, and other internal functions. He also found that the hypothalamus appears to control emotional responses, and that stimulation of some areas provokes anger, fear, sexual arousal, relaxation, or sleep.

Hess continued his experiments from 1925 through the 1940s. Since Switzerland is a neutral nation, his research suffered no interruption during World War II, although his results did not reach the scientific community abroad until after the war. In 1948 Hess was at last able to present in his book, *The Functional Organization of the Diencephalon,* the vast array of data he had assembled over almost twenty-five years. This work summarized Hess's research, and explained how the diencephalon acts as a bridge between the internal and external environments.

According to Hess, for example, if an animal is exposed to a frightening situation, it is the cortex—the conscious part of the brain—that identifies the situation as frightening, but it is the diencephalon that stimulates the fear responses such as snarling, raised hair, and accelerated heart rate. Conversely, it is the diencephalon that, by controlling blood sugar concentration and stomach distension, determines whether the animal feels hungry and, by stimulating the cortex, leads the animal to look for food. The upper part of the diencephalon controls such motor functions, while the lower part, especially the hypothalamus, regulates internal responses. Hess's book became a scientific classic, not only because of his description of the diencephalon but also because his research was a model of precision, care, and thoroughness.

Hess was awarded the 1949 Nobel Prize for Physiology or Medicine "for his discovery of the functional organization of the interbrain as a coordinator of the activities of the internal organs." He shared the prize with the neurosurgeon EGAS MONIZ. In his presentation speech, Herbert Olivecrona of the Karolinska Institute remarked that Hess's investigations had revealed "that in the midbrain we have higher centers of autonomic functions which coordinate these with reactions of the skeletal musculature adapted to the individual functions." Olivecrona went on to declare that "through his research, Hess has brilliantly answered a number of difficult questions regarding the localization of body functions in the brain."

After retiring from the Physiology Institute in 1951, Hess continued to investigate the function of the diencephalon and the integration of the nervous system with the rest of the body.

In 1908 Hess married Louise Sandmeir, with whom he had a son and a daughter. At his summer home in the southern Alps, he enjoyed gardening, cultivating grapes, and learning the traditional skills practiced by local farmers. He died in 1973 at Ascona, near Locarno, Switzerland, at the age of ninety-two.

In addition to his many awards, Hess received honorary degrees from McGill University and the universities of Bern, Geneva, and Freiburg. He was a member of numerous professional societies and was appointed to the Pontifical Academy of Science.

SELECTED WORKS: The Biology of Mind, 1964; Hypothalamus and Thalamus, 1969; Biological Order and Brain Organization, 1981.

ABOUT: Ingle, D. J. A Dozen Doctors, 1963; New York Times August 18, 1973.

HESSE, HERMANN
(July 2, 1877–August 9, 1962)
Nobel Prize for Literature, 1946

The German novelist Hermann Hesse was born into a family of Pietist missionaries and religious publishers in the Black Forest town of Calw in the German state of Württemberg. His mother, Marie (Gundert) Hesse, was a philologist and missionary who had spent decades in India. She was a widow with two sons when she married Hesse's father, Johannes Hesse, who in his youth had also served as a missionary in India. Hermann was the second of their six children.

When Hesse was three years old, his family moved to Basel, Switzerland, where his father taught in a mission institute until 1886, when

HERMANN HESSE

the family returned to Calw. Even though Hesse had aspired from the age of twelve to be a poet, his parents expected him to follow the family tradition by preparing for a career in theology. In accordance with their wishes, he entered the Latin grammar school (preparatory school) in Göppingen in 1890, and the following year he attended the Protestant seminary at Maulbronn. "I was a good learner," he recalled later, "but I was not a very manageable boy, and it was only with difficulty that I fitted into the framework of a Pietist education." In fact, he did not fit in at all, and after an unsuccessful attempt to run away he was expelled from the seminary. His subsequent experiences at secular schools proved equally unhappy.

After working for his father for a time, he served a series of apprenticeships: as a bookshop clerk, as a mechanic in the clockworks at Calw, and finally, in 1895, as a book dealer in the university town of Tübingen. There he had a chance to read widely, particularly the works of Goethe and the German romantics, and to continue his self-education. Joining a literary circle called Le Petit Cénacle (The Little Coterie), in 1899 he published his first two works, *Romantische Lieder* (Romantic Songs), a volume of poems, and *Eine Stunde hinter Mitternacht* (An Hour Beyond Midnight), a collection of vignettes and prose poems. The same year, he became a book dealer in Basel.

Hesse's first novel, *Hinterlassene Schriften und Gedichte von Hermann Lauscher* (The Posthumous Writings and Poems of Hermann Lauscher), appeared in 1901, but it was not until the publication of the novel *Peter Camenzind* in 1904 that he achieved literary success. He then left his job, moved to the country, and began to support himself entirely by his writing. In 1904 he also married Maria Bernoulli, with whom he had three children.

Like all of Hesse's subsequent novels, *Peter Camenzind,* published in English under the same title in 1961, is markedly autobiographical and deals with one of Hesse's recurrent themes, the quest for personal fulfillment and wholeness. In 1906 he brought out *Unterm Rad* (translated as *The Prodigy*), a novel that draws on his seminary experiences and explores the conflicts of the artistic personality under the constraints of a bourgeois society. In these early years Hesse wrote prolifically, contributing reviews and essays to many periodicals and serving as coeditor of the journal *März* until 1912. His novel *Gertrud* (translated as *Gertrude and I*) appeared in 1910. The next year he visited India, a journey that resulted in *Aus Indien* (Out of India, 1913), a collection of stories, essays, and poems. This book was followed in 1914 by the novel *Rosshalde* (*Rosshalde*).

Hesse and his family took up permanent residence in Switzerland in 1912, a move that eventually led him to acquire Swiss citizenship in 1923. As a pacifist, Hesse was opposed to the aggressive nationalism of his native land; this stance brought about a severe decline in his popularity and an outpouring of personal and critical abuse. Nevertheless, during World War I he volunteered his services to the Prisoners of War Welfare Organization in Bern and edited a newspaper and a series of books for German POWs. Hesse took the view that the war was the inevitable outcome of a spiritual collapse of European civilization and that it was the duty of the writer to work toward a new order.

In 1916, trying to cope with the crisis of the war, his son Martin's poor health, his wife's mental illness, and his father's death, Hesse suffered a nervous collapse. He subsequently underwent psychoanalysis by a disciple of C. G. Jung, an experience that inspired his novel *Demian* (1919), published under the pseudonym Emil Sinclair. The novel gained great popularity among young veterans trying to rebuild their lives in postwar Germany. According to THOMAS MANN, it was "no less daring than [James Joyce's] *Ulysses* and [ANDRÉ GIDE's] *The Counterfeiters,*" while it "struck the nerve of the times and called forth grateful rapture from a whole youthful generation who believed that an interpreter of their innermost life had risen from their own midst." Torn

between the order of home and the dangerous world of sensual experience, the novel's narrator confronts the dualism of his own nature. This theme was to be further developed in Hesse's later work, as he explored the dilemma of nature versus spirit, body versus mind. *Demian* was published in English under the same title in 1923.

Leaving his family in 1919, Hesse moved to Montagnola, in southern Switzerland; the separation from his wife was formalized by divorce in 1923, a year after the publication of *Siddhartha*. This novel, set in India in the time of Gautama Buddha, reflects both Hesse's Indian journey and his study of Eastern religions. The novel appeared in English under the same title in 1951. In 1924 Hesse married Ruth Wenger, but the union lasted only three years.

In *Der Steppenwolf* (*Steppenwolf*, 1927), his next important novel, Hesse continued his exploration of Faustian duality in the person of the protagonist, Harry Haller, and in the story of his symbolic voyage of discovery. According to the contemporary scholar Ernst Rose, this influential work "was the first German novel to include a descent into the cellars of the subconscious in its search for spiritual integration." *Narziss und Goldmund* (*Narcissus and Goldmund*, 1930; first translated as *Death and the Lover*) deals with the antitheses of spirit and life, of asceticism and vitality, in a medieval German setting.

Hesse married his third wife, Ninon Dolbin, in 1931. That same year he began work on his masterpiece *Das Glasperlenspiel* (*The Glass Bead Game;* first translated as *Magister Ludi*), which was ultimately published in 1943. A futuristic, utopian novel, it is the fictional biography of Joseph Knecht, the *magister ludi,* or master of the glass bead game, a spiritual discipline practiced by an intellectual elite in the symbolic realm of Castalia at the beginning of the twenty-fifth century. Considered central to an understanding of Hesse's thought, the book reiterates the major themes and problems of the earlier novels. According to the American scholar Theodore Ziolkowski, *The Glass Bead Game* "makes it clear that Hesse advocates . . . responsible action over mindless revolt; . . . it is not a telescope focused on an imaginary future, but a mirror reflecting with disturbing sharpness a paradigm of present reality."

Hesse was awarded the 1946 Nobel Prize for Literature "for his inspired writings, which, while growing in boldness and penetration, exemplify the classical humanitarian ideals and

high qualities of style." In his presentation address, Anders Österling of the Swedish Academy noted that Hesse's award "honors a poetic achievement that presents, throughout, the image of a good man in his struggle, . . . who in a tragic epoch succeeds in bearing the arms of true humanism." Prevented by poor health from attending the award ceremonies, Hesse was represented by the Swiss minister, Henri Vallotton, who in the acceptance speech quoted Sigurd Clurman, president of the Swedish Royal Academy of Sciences: "Hermann Hesse-
. . . shouts to all of us. . . . Advance, mount higher, conquer yourself! For to be human is to suffer an incurable duality, to be drawn toward both good and evil."

Hesse wrote no major works after receiving the Nobel Prize, although editions of his essays and letters, along with new translations of his novels, continued to appear. He remained quietly at his country home in Switzerland, where in 1962, at the age of eighty-five, he died in his sleep of a cerebral hemorrhage.

In addition to the Nobel Prize, Hesse was awarded the Gottfried-Keller Prize for Literature of the city of Zurich, the Goethe Prize of the city of Frankfurt, the Peace Award of the West German Association of Book Publishers and Sellers, and an honorary doctorate from the Univerity of Bern. Elected to the Prussian Academy of Writers in 1926, he resigned his membership in 1930 as a gesture of his disillusionment with the German political scene.

Although Hesse's work was highly esteemed during his lifetime by such distinguished writers as Mann, Gide, and T. S. ELIOT, his reputation at the time of the Nobel Prize was largely confined to German-speaking readers in Western Europe. During the following twenty-five years, as his works were translated throughout the world, a substantial body of new critical material emerged, establishing Hesse's reputation as one of the major writers of the century. According to Ziolkowski, Hesse, like "every major artist of his generation, . . . faced the central problem of the early twentieth century: the breakdown of traditional reality in every area of life. . . . It is his achievement to have shown to what extent modernity is traditional, in its thought and in its form; his works bridge the gap, so to speak, between romanticism and existentialism."

In the 1960s and 1970s Hesse's fame moved beyond the sphere of the literary elite to encompass the popular youth culture, an ironic distinction in the view of those critics who found the adoption of Hesse as the prophet of the young to be based on an incomplete or inaccurate understanding of his work. His popularity among the youthful masses grew, especially in the United States, where he became a culture hero to a worshipful cult of young readers. Meanwhile, Hesse was taken to task by a number of scholars and critics, notably George Steiner and Jeffrey Sammons. "It is one thing to seek after unity," Sammons wrote; "it is another to postulate ultimate unity and to regard all disharmonies as . . . ignorable and trivial aspects of an unimportant 'reality.' It is not wholly clear just where Hesse stands in this matter." By the 1980s the Hesse cult had all but subsided, and critical interest in the novelist declined. Nonetheless, Hesse's place in twentieth-century literature seems assured.

ADDITIONAL WORKS IN ENGLISH TRANSLATION: In the Old Sun, 1914; Youth, Beautiful Youth, 1955; Poems, 1969; Klingsor's Last Summer, 1970; Knulp, 1971; If the War Goes On, 1971; Autobiographical Writings, 1972; Strange News From Another Star, 1972; Wandering, 1972; Reflections, 1974; Stories of Five Decades, 1974; My Belief, 1974; Treatise on the Steppenwolf, 1975; Crisis, 1975; The Hesse-Mann Letters, 1975, with Thomas Mann; Tales of Student Life, 1976; Hours in the Garden, 1979; Pictor's Metamorphosis and Other Fantasies, 1982.

ABOUT: Baumer, F. Hermann Hesse, 1969; Boulby, M. Hermann Hesse: His Mind and Art, 1967; Brunner, J. W. Hermann Hesse, 1957; Casebeer, E. F. Hermann Hesse, 1972; Fickert, K. J. Hermann Hesse's Quest, 1978; Field, G. W. Hermann Hesse, 1970; Freedman, R. Hermann Hesse: Pilgrim of Crisis, 1978; Glenn, J. Hermann Hesse's Short Fiction, 1974; Liebmann, J. (ed.) Hermann Hesse: A Collection of Criticism, 1978; Mileck, J. Hermann Hesse, 1978; Mileck, J. Hermann Hesse and His Critics, 1958; Rose, E. Faith From the Abyss, 1965; Serrano, M. C. J. Jung and Hermann Hesse, 1966; Sorell, W. Hermann Hesse, 1974; Weaver, R. Spinning on a Dream Thread, 1977; Zeller, B. Portrait of Hesse, 1971; Ziolkowski, T. Hermann Hesse, 1966; Ziolkowski, T. (ed.) Hesse: A Collection of Critical Essays, 1973.

HEVESY, GEORGE DE
(August 1, 1885–July 5, 1966)
Nobel Prize for Chemistry, 1943

The Hungarian-Swedish chemist George Charles de Hevesy was born in Budapest, Austria-Hungary, one of eight children of Louis de Hevesy, a councillor at the Austro-Hungarian court who also managed a mining company and several family farms, and the former Eugénie Schlosberger. Hevesy graduated in 1903 from the school of the Piarist Order in Budapest, where he had concentrated on mathematics and physics. He attended the

GEORGE DE HEVESY

University of Budapest for a year. Then, deciding to become a chemical engineer, he enrolled in the technical university in Berlin (equivalent to an engineering college). Forced to seek a warmer climate when he contracted pneumonia after a few months, he transferred to the University of Freiburg in southern Germany, where his main interest became physical chemistry. He received his doctorate in 1908 with a thesis on the interaction between the metal sodium and molten sodium hydroxide.

Hevesy then studied for two years at the Federal Institute of Technology in Zurich with Richard Lorenz, a leading authority on the chemistry of molten salts. In Zurich, Hevesy attended a lecture by ALBERT EINSTEIN, who was appointed to the nearby university in 1909, and had the opportunity to show Einstein around his laboratory. In 1910 Hevesy spent three months studying with FRITZ HABER at Karlsruhe, Germany, and then received an honorary research fellowship to study at ERNEST RUTHERFORD's laboratory at the University of Manchester in England. There he began what became a lifelong friendship with NIELS BOHR. At Rutherford's suggestion Hevesy investigated the chemical properties of actinium, a recently discovered radioactive element.

Rutherford was then developing his concept of the atom as a dense nucleus, which contained nearly all the mass of the atom, surrounded by much lighter electrons. Knowledge of the radioactive elements was still rudimentary, but it was known that their atoms had unstable nuclei that decayed with the emission of radiation. It was also known that they had characteristically different average decay rates. The rates were expressed in terms of a half-life, the time in which half the initial number of nuclei underwent radioactive decay. The problem Rutherford presented to Hevesy was made difficult by actinium's half-life of only three seconds. However, it gave Hevesy the opportunity to learn techniques for investigating short-lived substances and later led to his interest in the electrochemistry of radioactive elements.

After Hevesy completed his actinium study, Rutherford asked him to separate radioactive radium D, one of the so-called daughter products of the decay of radium, from a large quantity of lead given to the laboratory by the Austrian government. Rutherford was eager to study the radiation from daughter products but frustrated that the radium D was embedded in so much lead. Although he failed to separate the radium D, Hevesy conceived an idea that was to prove productive. If radium D could not be separated from lead because they were so chemically similar, he suggested, then radium D could be added to lead as a detectable marker, or label. The behavior of lead in chemical reactions could then be followed by measuring radioactive emissions from its label.

On a visit to the Vienna Institute for Radium Research, Hevesy learned that Adolph Paneth, an assistant at the institute, had also attempted unsuccessfully to separate radium D from lead. After an exchange of letters, they agreed to work together, and Hevesy went to Vienna in 1913. He and Paneth soon showed the value of radium D labeling, which enabled them to measure the activity of exceedingly minute amounts of lead, below the detection threshold of other tests. Labeling made it possible to determine the slight solubility of lead and lead compounds in water and other solvents and the diffusion of lead atoms through a parent body.

By 1913 the work of FREDERICK SODDY, FRANCIS W. ASTON, and J. J. THOMSON had revealed the existence of isotopes, atoms of the same element having different atomic weights. An element is defined by the number of protons (positive charges) in the nuclei of its atoms, which equals the number of electrons (negative charges) circling the nucleus in an electrically neutral atom. Since chemical reactions involve only the electrons, and atoms of the same element (regardless of differences in weight) have the same number of electrons, isotopes of an element have the same chemical properties. It became clear that radioactive radium D and inert lead were chemically inseparable because they were isotopes of the same element and therefore chemically identical. Hevesy's and Paneth's last joint effort involved measurement of an electrical property of radium D that showed it to be identical to that of lead.

The differences in weight between different isotopes of the same element were also explained in 1932 when JAMES CHADWICK discovered neutrons. Neutrons are almost identical to protons in mass but carry no charge. Thus, they add weight but do not affect chemical properties.

Shortly after returning to Manchester in 1913 to pursue research on radioactive ions (charged atoms with too few or too many electrons to neutralize the nuclear protons), Hevesy was invited to join the staff at Oxford University, but the outbreak of World War I in 1914 forced him to go back to Vienna. Two years later he was conscripted for military service. He spent the next year as technical supervisor of an electrochemical plant near Budapest and another year at the Hungarian state copper works in the Carpathian Mountains. At the end of the war he was appointed professor of physical chemistry and then temporary director of the Second Physical Institute at the University of Budapest. But in 1919, with the outbreak of Austria's second revolution, he fled to Bohr's Institute for Theoretical Physics in Copenhagen. After arranging for a permanent position with Bohr, he returned to Hungary to complete his experimental work. These studies demonstrated that, in mixed solutions, lead chloride, lead nitrate, and other ionic lead salts can exchange atoms with one another, whereas organic lead compounds such as tetraethyl lead cannot.

In 1920 Hevesy finally assumed his position at Bohr's institute. There he devoted much of his effort to separating isotopes of mercury and chlorine using differences in their boiling points and diffusion rates, physical properties that vary with atomic weight. He also sought the elusive element 72. Although this 72-electron element had not yet been found, its chemical properties had been predicted theoretically. Hevesy expected to find small quantities of the element in minerals containing large amounts of zirconium, which was thought to be chemically similar to element 72 and so possibly to be found in association with it. Working with Dirk Coster, a Dutch expert on X-ray research, Hevesy identified the new element and named it hafnium, from the Latin name for

Copenhagen. After investigating the chemical behavior of hafnium, Hevesy returned to the problem of separating isotopes.

Although Hevesy enjoyed his work in Copenhagen, especially his association with Bohr, in 1926 he accepted a position as professor of physical chemistry at the University of Freiburg, where he still had many friends and professional colleagues. At Freiburg he worked on the analysis of minerals by the characteristic X rays they emit when bombarded by a powerful X-ray beam. He and his associates also used radioactive isotopes as a tool to investigate chemical and biological systems.

When Adolf Hitler became chancellor of Germany in 1933, Hevesy submitted his resignation at Freiburg but was persuaded to remain for another year so that some of his students could complete their doctoral theses. In 1934 he returned to the Institute for Theoretical Physics in Copenhagen, where laboratories in which some of his students could also work were put at his disposal.

While in Freiburg, Hevesy had begun biological research using heavy water as a tracer. Heavy water is hydrogen oxide, or H_2O, in which common hydrogen has been artificially enriched with a heavier hydrogen isotope, deuterium, discovered by HAROLD C. UREY in 1932. The nucleus of deuterium, or heavy hydrogen, contains a neutron in addition to the proton. The presence of deuterium, a stable isotope, is detected by an increase in the density of the water rather than by a measurement of radioactivity, although heavy water may also contain a minuscule fraction of a third hydrogen isotope, tritium (two neutrons in the nucleus), which is radioactive. Urey had met Hevesy at Bohr's institute in 1923 and now generously supplied a few liters of water that was 0.6 percent heavy water. Hevesy measured the interchange of water molecules between goldfish and the surrounding water, the water content of the human body, and the length of time that water molecules survive in the body. This research was interrupted by his move to Copenhagen. Although he did further work with heavy water some years later, his plans for research in Copenhagen were dramatically affected by the discovery of artificial radioactivity by FRÉDÉRIC JOLIOT and IRÈNE JOLIOT-CURIE in 1934.

Hevesy's previous use of radioactive tracers had been limited by the scarcity of suitable naturally occurring isotopes. Now that radioactive isotopes could be created, his choice broadened. Turning first to a radioactive isotope of phosphorus, he measured the deposition rate and distribution pattern of phosphorus incorporated in bone. His later work included a demonstration that potassium enters red blood cells, a study of the incorporation of phosphorus in tooth enamel, and an investigation, using radioactive phosphorus, of the rate of formation of deoxyribonucleic acid (DNA) in rat cancers and the blocking effect of therapeutic X rays. His pioneering application of radioactive isotopes to biochemistry and physiology provided the first insights into the dynamic nature of chemical and physical reactions in living systems.

When the German army occupied Denmark in 1940, many Danish scientists were fired from their jobs or placed under arrest. Hevesy, however, was permitted to work without interruption until 1943. That summer German troops occupied the institute, hoping to find research papers on atomic weapons, but in fact no such work had been conducted there. Bohr had already fled to neutral Sweden, and Hevesy quickly followed. Given a position at the Institute for Research in Organic Chemistry and Biochemistry in Stockholm, he undertook research into iron metabolism, among other topics.

The 1943 Nobel Prize for Chemistry was not awarded that year, but the following year it was presented to Hevesy "for his work on the use of isotopes as tracers in the study of chemical processes." Because award ceremonies were suspended during the war, he received the prize at a meeting of the Royal Swedish Academy of Sciences. In his Nobel lecture, he reviewed his extensive research into living systems. "The most remarkable result obtained in the study of the application of isotopic indicators," Hevesy said, "is perhaps the discovery of the dynamic state of the body constituents. The molecules building up the plant or animal organism are incessantly renewed."

At the end of the war Hevesy chose to remain in Sweden and became a Swedish citizen in 1945. He continued to use isotopic tracers to elucidate various aspects of physiology and biochemistry until his retirement in 1961 at the age of seventy-six.

Hevesy married Pia Riis in 1924; they had one son and three daughters. A man of medium height and build, Hevesy enjoyed hiking and skiing during his active years. He was a prolific writer of articles for scientific journals, to which he contributed for over thirty years. His health failing, he spent the final months of his life at a medical clinic in Freiburg, where he died of a heart attack on July 5, 1966.

In addition to the Nobel Prize, Hevesy received the Stanislao Cannizzaro Prize of the National Academy of Sciences of Italy (1929), the Copley Medal of the Royal Society of London (1949), the Faraday Medal of the British Chemical Society (1950), and the Niels Bohr Medal of the Danish Engineering Society (1961), among others. He held honorary degrees from Cambridge University and the universities of Uppsala, Freiburg, Gent, Budapest, and nine other institutions of higher learning. He was a member of numerous scientific societies and a foreign member of the Royal Society of London.

SELECTED WORKS: A Manual of Radioactivity, 1926; Radioactive Indicators: Their Application in Biochemistry, Animal Physiology, and Pathology, 1948; Adventures in Radioisotope Research: The Collected Papers of George Hevesy (2 vols.) 1962; Selected Papers, 1967.

ABOUT: Biographical Memoirs of Fellows of the Royal Society, volume 13, 1967; Current Biography April 1959; Dictionary of Scientific Biography, volume 6, 1972; Ingle, D. J. (ed.) A Dozen Doctors, 1963; Levi, H. George de Hevesy: Life and Work, 1985.

HEWISH, ANTONY

(May 11, 1924–   )
Nobel Prize for Physics, 1974
(shared with Martin Ryle)

The English radio astronomer Antony Hewish was born in Fowey, Cornwall, the youngest of three sons of Ernest William Hewish, a banker, and the former Frances Grace Lanyon Pinch. After spending his childhood in Newquay on the northern coast of Cornwall, he attended King's College in Taunton from 1935 until 1942, when he entered Cambridge University. The following year, however, Hewish left college for wartime work on airborne radar–countermeasure devices at the Telecommunications Research Establishment in Malvern, where he first worked with MARTIN RYLE. In 1946 Hewish returned to Gonville and Caius College, Cambridge, from which he graduated in 1948. He then joined Ryle's radio astronomy research group at the Cavendish Laboratory at Cambridge.

Continuing his studies, he earned a Ph.D. from Cambridge in 1952 for his radio studies of the upper atmosphere. Hewish spent his entire career at Cambridge, at the Cavendish Laboratory and at the Mullard Radio Astronomy Observatory, holding successive posts as research fellow (1952–1954), supernumerary fellow (1955–1961), fellow and director of

ANTONY HEWISH

studies at Churchill College and university lecturer (1961–1969), reader (1969–1971), and professor of radio astronomy (1971). In 1972 he was visiting professor in astronomy at Yale University.

After receiving his doctorate, Hewish continued with research that utilized radio waves to study the earth's upper atmosphere and the solar wind, the stream of gas emitted by the surface of the sun. In his early work with Ryle, Hewish assisted in developing antenna arrays and made some observations of radio emission from the solar corona. As early as 1954, he predicted that radio sources with small angular diameters would scintillate, because the waves emanating from them would bend slightly as they traveled through interplanetary space occupied by gas of variable density (the slightly blotchy solar wind). The result would be rapid (about 1-second) variations in strength of the received signal. This effect, which came to be known as interplanetary scintillation (IPS), is analogous to the twinkling of stars as their light passes through the variable density of the earth's atmosphere. Sources of waves (whether radio or light) with large enough angular diameters do not scintillate, because signals from different parts of the source arrive as a composite image in which the separate scintillations are averaged out.

Because there were no known compact radio sources at the time, Hewish did not seek evidence of IPS. Later, however, in 1964, Hewish and his colleagues P. F. Scott and Derek Wills did observe IPS. Realizing that IPS offered a valuable tool for probing the inter-planetary gas, as well as for determining the angular diameter of compact radio sources, Hewish succeeded within two years in measuring the velocity of the solar wind, both within and perpendicular to the planetary plane.

A Hewish-designed radio telescope, intended for using IPS to study the influence of the solar corona on radiation from remote point sources, was completed in 1967. Jocelyn Bell Burnell, a graduate student, helped build the telescope and used it to survey radio sources that showed marked and rapid variability in signal strength. Such variability would indicate that the source was subject to a large amount of IPS. Within two months Bell found such a radio source; more detailed examination revealed that it was emitting pulses of radio waves of a very stable frequency. Bell soon found other pulsars (pulsing stars), all of which were smaller in diameter than a planet and more than 300 parsecs distant (1 parsec = 19.2 × 10^6 miles). Before the nature of pulsars was known, Hewish speculated that these signals might possibly be from a distant civilization. A wry reference to that remote possibility appears on the original data sheets, in Hewish's designation of the first four pulsars as "LGM 1," "LGM 2," and so on, LGM being an abbreviation for "Little Green Men."

Of the very few astronomical objects as small as these pulsars, the most familiar are white dwarf stars, with masses approximately that of the sun and diameters like that of the earth. Although astronomers had predicted the existence of neutron stars, with masses up to twice that of the sun and diameters of about 10 kilometers, none had ever been found. Some astronomers had also predicted the existence of black holes even smaller in size, but Hewish did not believe a black hole could emit radio waves. In 1968 he speculated, therefore, that radio waves from pulsars result from either high-frequency oscillation of an excited white dwarf (the natural frequency of oscillation of white dwarfs was known to be much lower) or the oscillation of a neutron star at its natural frequency. That year, the British astronomer Thomas Gold proposed the theory, subsequently confirmed, that a pulsar is a spinning neutron star (with nuclei converted to a sea of neutrons), accompanied by an enormously powerful magnetic field (10^{15} times that of the earth) and surrounded by an electrically conducting gas cloud of low density (a plasma), emitting a rotating beam. As many as 130 pulsars have since been discovered.

Hewish and Ryle shared the 1974 Nobel Prize for Physics "for their pioneering research in

455

radio astrophysics." In particular, Hewish was cited "for his decisive role in the discovery of pulsars." "Radio astronomy offers unique possibilities for studying what is taking place, or in reality what occurred very long ago, at enormous distances from Earth," said Hans Wilhelmsson of the Royal Swedish Academy of Sciences in his presentation address. "Antony Hewish played a decisive role in the discovery of pulsars," Wilhelmsson continued. "This discovery, which is of extraordinary scientific interest, opens the way to new methods for studying matter under extreme physical conditions."

Since receiving the Nobel Prize, Hewish has continued to study IPS of distant radio sources and has shown that the most powerful are also very compact. He has tested cosmological theories by observing compact radio sources at ever-greater distance from the galaxy.

In 1950 Hewish married Marjorie Richards; they have a son and a daughter. Hewish likes to sail, swim, garden, work with his hands, and listen to music.

Hewish holds honorary doctorates from the universities of Leicester and Exeter. He is a member of the Royal Society, the Royal Astronomical Society, and the American Academy of Arts and Sciences. His numerous awards include the Eddington Medal of the Royal Astronomical Society (1969), the Michelson Medal of the Franklin Institute (1973), the Holweck Medal and Prize of the French Physical Society (1974), and the Hughes Medal of the Royal Society (1977).

ABOUT: New York Times October 16, 1974; Nova: Adventures in Science, 1983; Physics Today December 1974; Science November 15, 1974.

HEYMANS, CORNEILLE

(March 28, 1892–July 18, 1968)
Nobel Prize for Physiology or Medicine, 1938

The Belgian pharmacologist Corneille Jean François Heymans was born in Ghent to Jan and Marie-Henriette (Henning) Heymans. His father was a professor of pharmacology and rector of the University of Ghent. Heymans received his secondary education in Turnhout and in Ghent. His medical studies at the University of Ghent were interrupted by World War I, during which he served as a field artillery officer in the Belgian army and was awarded the Belgian War Cross, the Civil Cross,

CORNEILLE HEYMANS

and the Fire Cross with Eight Bars, as well as the French War Cross.

After the armistice in 1919 he resumed his medical studies, and two years later received his medical degree from the University of Ghent. In 1922 Heymans was appointed lecturer in pharmacology at the University of Ghent, and during the rest of that decade he did postgraduate work in Paris, Lausanne (Switzerland), Vienna, and London, as well as at Western Reserve University (now Case Western Reserve) in Cleveland, Ohio.

In the laboratory at the J. F. Heymans Institute of Pharmacology and Therapeutics (named for his father), Heymans and his colleagues performed an extensive series of experiments on the pathophysiology of the cardiovascular and respiratory systems—specifically, the function of nervous system reflexes on the rate and rhythm of the heart, the level of pressure in the circulation, and the rate of respiration. Many of these experiments were conducted in collaboration with his father, who had developed experimental methods for isolating nerve fibers and detecting nerve reflexes involved in the regulation of the respiratory and cardiovascular systems.

The standard preparation for these experiments utilized two anesthetized dogs, one acting as donor, the other as recipient. Circulation to and from the head of the recipient dog was shut off from the circulation in its chest, abdomen, and extremities. A flow of blood to the head of the recipient dog was then supplied by means of plastic tubes connecting the carotid arteries of the donor dog to those of the recipient dog, and the blood that flowed from the head of the recipient dog was drained from its jugular veins back to those of the donor dog. (The carotid arteries and jugular veins are located in the neck.) The nerve fibers between the head and trunk of the recipient dog were either left intact or selectively obliterated, depending on the research problem under investigation.

Before Heymans began these studies, scientists believed that the cardiovascular and respiratory centers in the medulla (lowest part of the brain stem) regulated the rate of blood flow, the level of blood pressure, and the concentration of respiratory gases in the blood. These processes take place according to the immediate physiological needs of the body and without the intervention of nervous system reflexes. Between 1924 and 1927, Heymans and his colleagues demonstrated that the respiratory rate is regulated by nervous system reflexes carried in the vagus and aortic nerves. The vagus nerve (the tenth nerve that emanates from the medulla) passes through the neck and thorax to the upper part of the abdomen and is associated with the autonomic (involuntary) nervous system. The aortic nerve is located in the abdomen.

In one series of experiments, in which they lowered the blood pressure in the trunk of the recipient dog, the respiratory center in the medulla was stimulated, with a resultant increase in the respiratory rate. When they raised the blood pressure in the trunk of the recipient dog by infusing adrenaline, the respiratory center in the medulla was inhibited and the respiratory rate decreased. Finally, if blood pressure was sufficiently elevated, respiration ceased entirely, a condition known as apnea. In another series of experiments, Heymans severed all the nerves in the trunk of the recipient dog except those from the cardioaortic body—a specialized network of cells, nerve fibers, and blood vessels located in the wall of the aorta, near the origin of the carotid arteries. The results were similar, thus showing that nervous reflexes originating in the cardioaortic body intervene in the response of the respiratory system to changes in blood pressure.

Another series of experiments conducted by Heymans involved the nervous system reflexes between the carotid sinuses and the cardiovascular and respiratory centers in the brain stem, which includes all of the brain except the cerebellum, cerebrum, and white matter. The carotid sinus consists of a specialized network of cells, nerves, and vessels in the wall of the carotid artery, near the point where the

carotid artery divides into its internal and external branches. Heymans and his father discovered that the carotid sinuses contain pressure receptors (or baroreceptors), which are sensitive to changes in blood pressure. Moreover, when blood pressure rises, the frequency of nerve impulses from the carotid sinus receptors to the cardiovascular and respiratory centers in the brain stem increases, and the respiratory rate, heart rate, and blood pressure decrease. Conversely, when blood pressure falls, the frequency of nerve impulses from the receptors to the brain stem decreases and respiratory rate, heart rate, and blood pressure increase.

According to earlier concepts, it was believed that the chemical composition of the blood—specifically, its oxygen and carbon dioxide content and the concentration of hydrogen ion, or the acid-base balance—directly altered the neural activity of the respiratory center in the brain stem. In 1926 Heymans and his colleagues showed that the carotid sinuses and the cardioaortic body contain chemical receptors (chemoreceptors) that are similar in structure to baroreceptors and are sensitive to certain stimuli. They next demonstrated that both the respiratory gases and the hydrogen ion concentration of blood are maintained in equilibrium by nervous system reflexes, interconnecting vascular chemoreceptors, the medullary respiratory center, and the lungs. They also noticed that when the partial pressure of oxygen falls, the partial pressure of carbon dioxide rises, or the hydrogen ion concentration falls, nerve impulses from vascular chemoreceptors to the medulla reflexly stimulate the rate of breathing; during this process the respiratory gas and acid-base abnormalities are corrected. When the opposite occurs, nerve impulses from chemoreceptors to the medulla reflexly inhibit the rate of breathing, and the respiratory gas and acid-base abnormalities are also corrected.

Further study by Heymans revealed that the partial pressure of oxygen—not the oxygen content of hemoglobin—is the effective stimulus of vascular chemoreceptors. This observation explained why the rate of breathing is unaltered by anemia and carbon monoxide poisoning. In anemia, the hemoglobin concentration is abnormally low; in carbon monoxide poisoning, carbon monoxide displaces oxygen from the hemoglobin, resulting in low levels of oxygen.

Heymans succeeded his father at the University of Ghent and as director of the Heymans Institute in 1925. The author of numerous books and monographs, he delivered the Herter lecture at New York University in 1934 and three years later was the Dunham lecturer at Harvard University.

The 1938 Nobel Prize for Physiology or Medicine was awarded to Heymans in 1939 "for the discovery of the role played by the sinus and the aortic mechanisms in the regulation of respiration." In his presentation address, Göran Liljestrand of the Karolinska Institute stated that "Heymans not only discovered the role . . . of certain organs . . . , he also greatly enlarged our field of knowledge concerning the regulation of respiration. He showed that the various methods used for stimulating respiration had quite different mechanisms." In his Nobel lecture, Heymans pointed out that "it has been known for some time that variations in blood pressure affect respiration." He went on to say that "it was generally believed that this interaction . . . involved a direct action on the respiratory center exerted by either the blood pressure or the rate of flow in the cerebral circulation." He stated that "this classical theory should be reconsidered and rejected." He then summarized his research on respiratory control.

In 1921 Heymans married Berthe May, a physician; they had two sons and two daughters. For many years, Heymans published and edited *Archives Internationales de Pharmacodynamie et de Thérapie* (International Archives of Pharmacodynamics and Therapy), a journal his father had founded in 1895. He was an avid student of literature, art history, and the history of medicine. Heymans died in Knokke, Belgium, on July 18, 1968.

Among Heymans's awards and honors were the Alvarenga de Piauhy Prize of the Royal Belgian Academy of Medicine (1931), the Théophile Gluge Prize of the Royal Belgian Academy of Sciences (1931), the Quinquennial Prize for Medicine of the Belgian government (1931), the Montyon Prize for Physiology of the French Academy of Sciences (1934), the Pope Pius XI Prize of the Pontifical Academy of Science (1938), and the Burgi Prize of the University of Bern. Heymans was an honorary member of the Royal Society of London, the French Academy of Sciences, the Academy of Medicine of Paris, and the New York Academy of Sciences.

SELECTED WORKS: Introduction to the Regulation of Blood Pressure and Heart Rate, 1950; Reflexogenic Areas of the Cardiovascular System, 1958.

ABOUT: The Excitement and Fascination of Science, 1965; Fishman, A. P., and Richards, D. W. (eds.) Circulation of the Blood—Men and Ideas, 1964; New York Times July 19, 1968.

HEYROVSKÝ, JAROSLAV
(December 20, 1890–March 27, 1967)
Nobel Prize for Chemistry, 1959

The Czech chemist Jaroslav Heyrovský (hā′ rôf skē) was born in Prague, the fifth of six children of Leopold Heyrovský, a professor of Roman law at Charles University in Prague, and the former Klára Hanlová. His father was an ardent Czech nationalist and a friend of Tomáš Masaryk, the first president of Czechoslovakia. After receiving his early education at a primary school, Heyrovský attended the gymnasium in Prague, where he developed a strong interest in physics and mathematics.

After a year at Charles University, where his father had become rector, Heyrovský transferred to University College, London, to attend the lectures given there by WILLIAM RAMSAY. He received his B.S. in 1913 and remained at University College as research assistant to Ramsay's successor, F. G. Donnan. Under Donnan's direction, he began doctoral research on the electrochemistry of aluminum. While he was visiting his parents in Prague in 1914, World War I broke out, and Heyrovský was forced to remain in Czechoslovakia. Inducted into the Austro-Hungarian army, he was exempted from combat because of poor health and assigned to a military hospital as a chemist and radiologist. Despite his wartime duties, he completed a thesis on the electroaffinity of aluminum and received a Ph.D. from Charles University in 1918, shortly before the end of the war.

Heyrovský became an assistant professor of chemistry at the university in 1919 and a lecturer in 1920. The papers he published on his thesis topic during these years earned him a doctor of science degree from University College in 1921. The following year, he became an associate professor and head of the chemistry department at Charles University.

It was during the early 1920s that Heyrovský developed a new method of analyzing chemical solutions. It had long been known that any substance present in a solution alters in a characteristic (and hence identifiable) way an electric current that is passed through the solution. However, conventional electrodes were unsuitable for precise measurements because solutions tended to adhere to the surface of such electrodes, and the accretions distorted the

JAROSLAV HEYROVSKÝ

readings obtained. In Heyrovský's apparatus the electrodes consisted of drops of mercury falling from a tube into a mercury reservoir. Each successive drop presented an uncontaminated surface, so that by measuring both voltage and current, Heyrovský was able to determine very accurately not only the quantity but also the percentage of extremely small samples.

Heyrovský devoted the rest of his scientific career to this analytic technique, which he called polarography. Working with a colleague, Masuzo Shikata, in 1924, he devised the polarograph, an automatic recording instrument that quickly and efficiently determines the composition of a solution, leaving it unchanged and thus available for further use. Two years later, Heyrovský was appointed the first professor of physical chemistry at the university, which subsequently became a leading center for polarographic research. A Rockefeller Fellowship enabled him to work at the University of Paris in 1926. In 1933 he lectured on polarography at several universities in the United States and published his first definitive work on the application of his method.

With the German occupation of Czechoslovakia in 1939, all institutions of higher learning were closed and their faculties replaced with Germans. Fortunately, Heyrovský's position was taken by an opponent of the Nazi regime who supported his work throughout the years of occupation. By the end of the war, Heyrovský had completed a textbook and begun investigations into oscillopolarography. In 1950 he became director of the newly founded Central Polarographic Institute at Charles University. Two years later, as its staff grew, the center became the Polarographic Institute of the Czechoslovak Academy of Sciences. In 1964 it was renamed the J. Heyrovský Institute of Polarography.

"For his discovery and development of the polarographic methods of analysis," Heyrovský received the 1959 Nobel Prize for Chemistry. The award was presented by G. A. Ölander of the Royal Swedish Academy of Sciences. "Almost all chemical elements can be analyzed with the aid of the polarographic method," Ölander said, "and in organic chemistry it is equally useful for the most diverse groups of substances." In his Nobel lecture Heyrovský explained why he had devoted his life to the dropping mercury electrode. "Its physical conditions of dropping as well as the chemical changes during the passage of the electric current are well defined," he said, "and the phenomena displayed at the dropping mercury electrode proceed with strict reproducibility. The processes at the electrode can be exactly expressed mathematically."

In 1926 Heyrovský married Marie Kořánova, the daughter of a brewer. Their daughter, Jitka, became a biochemist; their son, Michael, works at the institute named in honor of his father. A talented pianist, a lover of opera, and a sports enthusiast, Heyrovský had given up most of his leisure activities to pursue polarographic research, customarily working in the laboratory from eight o'clock in the morning until seven o'clock in the evening and on every weekend. After a serious illness, he retired in 1963 but remained active at the institute. Known for his generous hospitality, lively sense of humor, and love of good food and wine, he was widely honored for his scientific contributions. Heyrovský died in Prague on March 27, 1967.

Heyrovský held honorary degrees from the universities of Warsaw, Aix-Marseilles, and Paris. A fellow of University College, he held honorary membership in the American Academy of Arts and Sciences and the Leopoldina German Academy of Researchers in Natural Sciences, among others. He was awarded the Czechoslovak government's State Prize in 1951 and the Order of the Czechoslovak Republic in 1955.

SELECTED WORKS: Principles in Polarography, 1965, with Jaroslav Kuta; Practical Polarography, 1968, with Petr Zuman.

ABOUT: Biographical Memoirs of Fellows of the Royal

HEYSE

Society, volume 13, 1967; Current Biography July 1961; Dictionary of Scientific Biography, volume 6, 1972; Zuman, P., and Kolthoff, I. M. (eds.) Festschrift: Progress in Polarography (2 vols.) 1962.

HEYSE, PAUL
(March 15, 1830–April 2, 1914)
Nobel Prize for Literature, 1910

PAUL HEYSE

The German poet, novelist, and short story writer Paul Johann Ludwig von Heyse (hī′ zə) was born in Berlin to Karl Ludwig Heyse, a philologist who taught at the University of Berlin, and Julie (Saaling) Heyse, the daughter of a prominent Jewish family. From his mother, whom he later described as "passionate and imaginative," Heyse is thought to have acquired his lively imagination and delight in storytelling. The Heyse household was a salon for scholars, writers, and artists, among them the art historian Franz Kugler, who became a mentor to the young Heyse.

At the University of Berlin, Heyse studied classical literature and philology; two years later, he attended lectures in the philology of Romance languages at the University of Bonn. After receiving his doctorate from Berlin in 1852, he traveled to Italy on scholarship. The trip instilled in him a lifelong love of the Italian countryside and introduced him to the work of such Italian writers as Dante, Boccaccio, and Giacomo Leopardi. At the same time, Heyse began to write lyric poems, dramas, and prose tales.

Heyse's future was assured in 1854, when King Maximilian II offered him a large stipend to live in Munich and become a member of the Bavarian court, with no duties other than to attend intellectual symposia in which the king participated. Freed from financial responsibilities, Heyse was able to marry Margaret Kugler, his mentor's daughter. The couple, who eventually had four children, settled in a villa in Munich, where Heyse remained for the rest of his life.

The prosperous, unhurried atmosphere of preindustrial Munich suited Heyse's temperament, and he diligently pursued his literary interests, publishing the novella L'arrabbiata in 1855. Written during his travels in Italy and set in Sorrento, this work, whose title means "the angry girl," tells the idyllic story of a fisher maiden who first repulses the advances of a young ferry operator only to fall in love with him. An English translation of this novella under the title of La rabbiata was published in 1857. Its romantic mood and setting, characterization of the dark-eyed maiden, and

simple story set the pattern for much of Heyse's subsequent work. The novella Marion appeared in 1855, followed by such others as Das Mädchen von Treppi (The Maiden of Treppi) in 1858 and Andrea Delfin (Andrea Delfin) and Bild der Mutter (The Mother's Portrait) in 1859.

When his friend, the poet Emanuel Geibel, was dismissed from the court in 1864 by Maximilian's successor, Ludwig II, Heyse resigned in protest but continued to live in Munich. In 1866, four years after the death of his first wife, Heyse married Anna Schubart.

In addition to novellas, Heyse wrote many works for the stage. The historical play Hans Lange (Hans Lange, 1866) and the tragedy Maria von Magdala (Mary of Magdala, 1899) enjoyed a brief popularity, but he remains best known as a novelist. His full-length novels, which include Kinder der Welt (Children of the World, 1873), Im Paradiese (In Paradise, 1875), and Merlin (1892), deal chiefly with ethical dilemmas. Though his own verse fell into obscurity, Heyse was celebrated for his translations of the works of a number of Italian poets, including Alessandro Manzoni and Leopardi.

With the rise of naturalism, as exemplified in the works of such late-nineteenth-century writers as Henrik Ibsen and Émile Zola, younger critics began to dismiss Heyse's romanticism and artificiality. Although he attempted to incorporate some realistic elements in his later fiction, Heyse never lost his devotion to beauty and the world of the senses and continued to reject the naturalists' portrayals of a grim reality.

Heyse was awarded the 1910 Nobel Prize for Literature "as a tribute to the consummate artistry, permeated with idealism, which he has demonstrated during his long, productive career as a lyric poet, dramatist, novelist, and writer of world-renowned short stories." He was the first German writer to receive the prize. "It has rightly been said that Heyse is the creator of the modern psychological novella," said C. D. af Wirsén of the Swedish Academy in his presentation speech. Wirsén also praised Heyse as "the most important lyrical poet of contemporary Germany." Because of an illness, Heyse was unable to travel to Stockholm to receive the award, which was accepted by Count von Puckler, the German minister, in Heyse's absence.

The same year that he was honored with the Nobel Prize, Heyse was made an honorary citizen of Munich, where he died of pneumonia four years later.

An exceptionally prolific writer, Heyse produced twenty-four volumes of novellas, six novels, some sixty plays, and nine volumes of poetry during his lifetime. His literary reputation, however, already in eclipse at the time of the Nobel Prize, declined rapidly after his death. While conceding that Heyse's novellas "make on the whole pleasant reading," the British critic E. K. Bennett, in a 1934 study, suggested that Heyse "contributes hardly anything which is really original and fruitful" in this genre. Writing two years later, the American critic Henry Stafford King disagreed; pointing to Heyse's concern for his women characters and terming him "a feminist," King claimed that "Heyse's problems, instead of being outdated, are up-to-the-minute in modernity." Reappraising Heyse in 1976, the German scholar Christiane Ullmann found that "there is indeed much in Heyse's literary work . . . that ought to be read again, not just for its technical brilliance but as the work of a notable writer of the later nineteenth century, whose delineation of the *condition humaine* belongs to the great realist tradition of [Honoré de] Balzac and [Gottfried] Keller."

ADDITIONAL WORKS IN ENGLISH TRANSLATION: Four Phases of Love, 1857; L'Arrabbiata and Other Tales, 1867; Barbarossa and Other Tales, 1874; The Witch of Corso, 1882; Selected Stories, 1886; La Marchesa and Other Tales, 1887; Two Prisoners, 1893; Tales From Paul Heyse, 1903.

ABOUT: Adrian, J. Paul Heyse and Three of His Critics, 1972; Bennett, E. K. A History of the German Novelle, 1934; Brandes, G. Creative Spirits of the Nineteenth Century, 1923; Phelps, W. L. Essays on Books, 1914; Silz, W. Realism and Reality, 1954.

HICKS, JOHN
(April 8, 1904–   )
Nobel Memorial Prize in Economic
   Sciences, 1972
(shared with Kenneth Arrow)

The English economist John Richard Hicks was born in Warwick, near Birmingham. His father, Edward Hicks, was a journalist with the local newspaper. Supported by mathematical scholarships, Hicks attended Clifton College from 1917 to 1922 and Balliol College, Oxford, from 1922 to 1926. After a year's study of mathematics at Oxford, his interests shifted toward politics, philosophy, and especially economics, although his college record reveals few signs of his future achievements. As Hicks put it later, he "finished with a second-class degree and no adequate qualifications . . . in any of the subjects . . . studied."

Fortunately, the demand for economists outstripped the supply, and Hicks quickly landed a temporary lectureship at the London School of Economics (LSE) in 1926. Originally calling himself a labor economist, he soon switched to economic theory, where his mathematical ability proved to be a powerful tool. His influences then included the nineteenth-century French economist Léon Walras, the father of general equilibrium theory, and the nineteenth-century Italian economist Vilfredo Pareto, the originator of welfare economics. Through the writings of FRIEDRICH A. VON HAYEK, who arrived at the LSE in 1931, and Lionel Robbins, Hicks was introduced to macroeconomic issues. He remained at the school until 1935, when he was appointed a fellow at Gonville and Caius College, Cambridge. That year he married the economist Ursula Webb; through the years the two have worked together extensively, mainly on policy issues.

Hicks's first book, *The Theory of Wages* (1932), made two fundamental contributions to economic analysis. First, it defined the "elasticity of substitution," a measure of the relative ease of substituting one productive factor for another. If elasticity was zero, no substitution was possible; if it was infinite, the two factors were perfect substitutes. Second, it showed the relevance of this notion of elasticity to questions of income distribution and economic growth. Marxists, for instance, commonly assumed that laborsaving technical progress—a characteristic of modern indus-

461

JOHN HICKS

trialized economies—would reduce labor's share of national income. But this proposition would hold only if the elasticity of substitution between labor and capital were less than one. In fact, labor's share had been more or less constant over the past century (the so-called Bowley's law), consistent with a long-run elasticity of substitution equal to one.

Between 1935 and 1938 Hicks wrote his most influential book, *Value and Capital,* which helped resolve basic conflicts between business cycle theory and equilibrium theory. Published in 1939, it is often considered an earlier, British version of PAUL SAMUELSON's *Foundations of Economic Analysis.* The beginning chapters set forth what is now orthodox theory about consumers' and producers' behavior and its consequences. Hicks argued that change in the price of a good has a "substitution" effect that is always negative and an "income" effect that can be positive or negative. The book also laid the groundwork for later investigations of the "compensation" principle in cost-benefit analysis. A policy of free trade, for example, might benefit American consumers of Japanese automobiles but hurt members of the United Auto Workers. If the benefit to consumers exceeded the cost to workers, however, consumers could "compensate" (that is, transfer income to) the workers, leaving everyone better off. Dollar benefits were measured by "consumers' surplus" (the difference between what consumers would be willing to pay for a commodity and what they must pay)—a notion, Hicks admitted, that could not be unambiguously defined. Although

Hicks's version of the compensation principle was later criticized by Samuelson and other economists for ignoring distributional issues, its usefulness as a tool in cost-benefit analysis remains undiminished.

Another contribution of *Value and Capital* was its treatment of dynamic stability in general equilibrium models. In this work Hicks attempted to derive the conditions under which an economic system in disequilibrium would return to equilibrium. Although his conditions for dynamic stability were later shown by Samuelson to be neither necessary nor sufficient, their value was subsequently proved in research by GERARD DEBREU and KENNETH ARROW. (One of Hicks's key dynamic concepts, "temporary equilibrium," is now widely employed in theoretical macroeconomics.) In general, Hicks's influence owes more to his methods of analysis—for example, his use of comparative statistics and his application of dynamic analysis to the study of economic growth and the trade cycle—than to his results.

The late 1930s saw the beginnings of the Keynesian revolution, and, swept up by it like many other economists, Hicks wrote two reviews of Keynes's *General Theory of Employment, Interest, and Money.* The first is little remembered today, but the second, "Mr. Keynes and the Classics," published in the journal *Econometrica* in 1937, was deeply influential. Here Hicks introduced his famous investment savings–money market (IS-LM) diagram, reproduced in nearly every macroeconomics textbook since then. The LM (monetary equilibrium) curve shows all combinations of national income and interest rate that are consistent with a situation in which money demand equals money supply. The IS (investment savings) curve shows all combinations of national income and interest rate that are consistent with a situation in which savings equals investment. The intersection of the two curves indicates the point at which interest rate and national income are in equilibrium.

Hicks's theory of money and derivation of the LM curve prefigured modern portfolio and transactions theories of money demand, later elaborated by JAMES TOBIN. Hicks also showed that an autonomous increase in government spending would shift the IS curve to the right, thereby increasing national income. The interest rate would also rise, except where the LM curve was flat (the region known as the Keynesian "liquidity trap"). Believing that the liquidity trap characterized money markets during the Great Depression of the 1930s, many Keynesians urged that fiscal policy be used to stimulate aggregate demand.

It is no exaggeration to say that much of Keynesian macroeconomics in the 1950s and 1960s consisted of little more than variations on Hicks's theme. During this time, policy debates on the effectiveness of monetary versus fiscal policy were frequently conducted within the IS-LM framework. In the early 1970s, however, Hicks's diagram came under attack from a number of Keynesians, including Robert Clower, one of Hicks's former students. These opponents argued that the static, equilibrium character of the IS-LM curves misrepresented the essentially dynamic, disequilibrium nature of Keynes's theory. In fact, however, Hicks had already demonstrated—in his 1950 theory of the trade cycle—the dynamic nature of short-term development, especially with respect to the determination of investment. The IS-LM diagram, properly applied, remains a potent tool. The economic historian Peter Temin, for example, used it to show that the monetarist explanation of the onset of the Great Depression in the United States—a sharp drop in the money supply—was contradicted by empirical evidence on interest rates and national income.

From 1939 to 1946 Hicks was a professor of economics at Manchester University. In 1946 he was appointed a fellow at Nuffield College, Oxford, and in 1952 he became the Drummond Professor of Political Economy at Oxford, a post he held until his retirement in 1965.

During the 1950s and 1960s, Hicks participated little in the debates over his contributions to general equilibrium and welfare theory. Instead, he and his wife "became the servant[s] of applied economics." Continuing work begun during World War II, they advised the British government on tax policy. They also helped officials from a number of former British Commonwealth nations, such as India and Jamaica, to manage the economic problems associated with independence. Hicks's contributions to economic theory continued at a rapid pace, although much of his work since *Value and Capital* has yet to be fully absorbed into the mainstream of economic thought. His 1965 book *Capital and Growth* used the notion of comparative dynamics to study stable and optimal growth paths. In it he introduced the concept of "fix-price" and "flex-price" markets, a distinction that has proved fruitful in macroeconomics.

Hicks shared the 1972 Nobel Memorial Prize

in Economic Sciences with Kenneth Arrow "for their pioneering contributions to general equilibrium theory and welfare theory." In his presentation speech Ragnar Bentzel of the Royal Swedish Academy of Sciences stated that Hicks's *Value and Capital* "breathed fresh life into general equilibrium theory." Moreover, Bentzel said, Hicks's equilibrium model "gave greater concreteness to the equations included in the system and made it possible to study the effects produced within the system by impulses coming from outside it."

In *A Theory of Economic History* (1969), Hicks applied his theories to the analysis of economic history, thereby offering new ways of viewing economic facts. For example, he considered the sequence of events through which the diffusion of new technology led to economic growth. He elaborated this idea in *Capital and Time* (1973). In *Causality in Economics* (1979) he analyzed the dynamics of sequential economic processes, the distinction between economic stocks and flows, and the problem of inferring causal relationships between economic variables.

Since his retirement in 1965, Hicks has been professor emeritus at All Souls College, Oxford. The recipient of many honors and awards in addition to the Nobel Prize, he is a member of the British Academy, the Royal Swedish Academy, and the National Academy of Sciences of Italy and a fellow of the American Academy of Arts and Sciences. He has received numerous honorary degrees, has served as president of the Royal Economic Society from 1960 to 1962, and was knighted in 1964.

ADDITIONAL WORKS: The Social Framework: An Introduction to Economics, 1942; A Contribution to the Theory of the Trade Cycle, 1950; A Revision of Demand Theory, 1956; Essays in World Economics, 1959; Monetary Theory and Policy: A Historical Perspective, 1967; The Crisis in Keynesian Economics, 1974; Economic Perspectives: Further Essays on Money and Growth, 1977; Collected Essays in Economic Theory, 1981; Money, Interest, and Wages, 1982; Classics and Moderns, 1983; Methods of Dynamic Economics, 1985.

ABOUT: Collard, D. (ed.) Economic Theory and Hicksian Themes, 1984; Shackleton, J. R., and Locksley, G. Twelve Contemporary Economists, 1981; Swedish Journal of Economics December 1972; Wolfe, J. N. (ed.) Value, Capital and Growth: Papers in Honour of Sir John Hicks, 1968.

HILL, ARCHIBALD V.
(September 26, 1886–June 3, 1977)
Nobel Prize for Physiology or Medicine,
1922
(shared with Otto Meyerhof)

ARCHIBALD V. HILL

The English physiologist Archibald Vivian
Hill was born in Bristol to Ada Priscilla (Rum-
ney) Hill and Jonathan Hill, a fifth-generation
timber merchant who abandoned the family
when his son was three. Hill and his younger
sister Muriel (who later became a biochemist)
were raised by their mother, a resourceful
woman of great determination and good humor. He was taught at home by his mother
until he reached the age of seven, at which
time the family moved to nearby Weston-super-
Mare, where he attended a small preparatory
school. Another move followed in 1899, this
time to Tiverton, in Devonshire, so that Hill
could prepare for college at Blundell's School,
where he excelled in mathematics, joined the
debating society, and ran cross-country.

A scholarship enabled Hill to enter Trinity
College, Cambridge, in 1905 to study mathematics. He was an excellent student and completed the course in two, rather than the
customary three, years, but his interest in the
subject waned and he sought advice from his
tutor, Walter Morley Fletcher. Fletcher, a
physiologist who had recently conducted research on the chemistry of frog muscle with
FREDERICK GOWLAND HOPKINS, suggested
that physiology might better suit Hill's intellectual temperament. Taking Fletcher's advice, Hill plunged into the study of physiology,
augmenting it with courses in chemistry and
physics, and completed his natural science examinations with honors in 1909.

Following graduation, and with support from
a George Henry Lewes Studentship, Hill began work at the Cambridge Physiological Laboratory. J. N. Langley, the laboratory's director,
suggested that Hill pursue the work on frog
muscle initiated by Fletcher and Hopkins by
investigating the role of heat in muscular contraction. Using a thermocouple recorder (a device that measures temperature by means of
electrical current), Hill determined that "the
muscular machine is concerned with the transformation of chemical energy into the potential energy of increased tension."

In 1911, a year after he was elected a fellow
of Trinity, Hill went to Germany to acquaint
himself with the recent physiological advances
that had been made there. From Karl Burker
at the University of Tübingen he learned how
to construct thermopiles (arrays of thermo-
couples), and from Friedrich Paschen he learned
how to improve the design of galvanometers
(instruments for measuring small electric currents). Returning to Cambridge after four
months, Hill continued his efforts to elucidate
the energy exchanges that occur in muscle. For
the next three years his research focused on
measuring the heat and mechanical work produced by muscular contractions and relating
this information to the chemistry of muscle
activity.

Shortly after Hill accepted an appointment
as lecturer in physical chemistry at Cambridge,
World War I broke out, and he joined the
Cambridgeshire Regiment, serving as captain
and then brevet major. When his fellowship
at Trinity ended in 1916, he received a grant
from King's College, Cambridge. At the same
time he was put in charge of a government
program to improve antiaircraft artillery. For
this work he was knighted in 1918, the same
year that he was elected to membership in the
Royal Society.

After the armistice, Hill resumed his research on muscle physiology at Cambridge but
left in 1920 to accept the Brackenbury Chair
of Physiology at Manchester University. There
he confirmed his earlier finding that the thigh
muscle of a frog produces heat in two separate
phases of activity. The heat associated with
muscular contraction had previously been regarded as a single event that took place only
during contraction. Hill showed, however, that
in the initial phase, heat is produced during
contraction; in the second, or recovery phase,
it is produced after contraction is completed.

He also demonstrated that oxygen is not

necessary for the production of heat during the initial phase; in the recovery phase, however, oxygen is needed for the production of heat. Prior to Hill's investigations, Fletcher and Hopkins had shown that contracting frog muscle not only forms lactic acid but also removes it, in the presence of oxygen. Drawing on their observations, Hill associated the production of initial heat with the formation of lactic acid from a precursor, and the production of recovery heat with the oxidative removal of lactic acid.

His finding that the heat produced during both phases of contraction was enough to burn only a small amount of lactic acid suggested that the unconsumed portion was restored to its precursor. In this research, Hill worked closely with the German-American biochemist OTTO MEYERHOF, who, approaching muscle dynamics from a chemical perspective, demonstrated that lactic acid is formed from glycogen, the principal storage form of carbohydrates in tissue. Meyerhof found that only a small amount of lactic acid is oxidized after contraction, and thus the energy developed from combustion reconverts the surplus lactic acid to glycogen.

In 1923 Hill received the 1922 Nobel Prize for Physiology or Medicine "for his discovery relating to the production of heat in the muscle." He shared the prize with Meyerhof. After reviewing the course of his work in his Nobel lecture, Hill reminded his audience of the intricate complexity of muscle physiology and pointed to the many experiments that remained to be done in the fields of "statics, dynamics, thermodynamics, [and] the design and employment of instruments."

The same year that he received the Nobel Prize, Hill was appointed Jodrell Professor of Physiology at University College, London. Three years later he became Foulteron Research Professor of the Royal Society. Turning to the study of muscular activity in humans, he found that most of the lactic acid formed during moderate exercise is oxidized in the muscle shortly after the exertion stops and that recovery is therefore rapid. During strenuous exercise, however, large amounts of lactic acid accumulate in the muscle and are diffused into the blood and other body tissues. Since lactic acid must diffuse back to the muscle tissue before being removed by resynthesis or oxidation, recovery may require several hours.

To describe the shortage of oxygen and the excess buildup of lactic acid during periods of heavy exercise, Hill devised the term *oxygen debt*. This deficit must be repaid when exercise ceases, as is accomplished by deep breathing. Hill's concept explains how an athlete can exercise strenuously and later repay the oxygen debt during the recovery period. Some of Hill's investigations were conducted at Cornell University at Ithaca, New York, while he was a visiting lecturer in chemistry in 1927. In subsequent research, Hill turned his attention to the mechanism of the passage of nerve impulses and found that they produce heat.

As the political situation in Germany deteriorated, he became an outspoken opponent of Nazi policies. In 1933, when his colleague and friend Paschen was dismissed from the University of Tübingen and was replaced by JOHANNES STARK, a Nazi apologist, Hill denounced Hitler's government and the persecution of Jewish and dissident scientists. That year he helped found the Academic Assistance Council (later the Society for the Protection of Science and Learning), a group that helped refugee scientists escape Nazi persecution.

As the prospects of war deepened, the demands on Hill's time increased. He served briefly on the Committee for the Scientific Survey of Air Defense (the Tizard Committee) and was a leading participant in the Central Register of Scientific and Technical Personnel, which was charged with making the most effective use of Britain's scientists and technicians in the event of war. With the declaration of war in 1939, Hill's laboratory was closed, and the following year he joined the War Cabinet Scientific Advisory Committee. The same year he was elected a member of Parliament from Cambridge University, and a few days later he went to Washington, D.C., as part of an effort to establish wartime cooperation among Great Britain, the United States, and Canada. In addition, Hill served as a member of the University Grants Commission, the Research Defense Society, and the Advisory Council of the Department of Scientific and Industrial Research. In 1943–1944 Hill visited India, where he gathered information for an influential report that recommended measures for organizing the nation's scientific and industrial research. At the end of the war, Hill set about reorganizing his laboratory and gathering a staff at University College. After his retirement at the end of 1952, he continued his research into muscle physiology.

In 1913 Hill married Margaret Neville Keynes, a social worker and the sister of the English economist John Maynard Keynes. The couple had two sons and two daughters. Hill died on June 3, 1977, from complications following a viral infection.

HINSHELWOOD

"A. V. was a person of old-fashioned tastes and virtues," wrote BERNARD KATZ in a memoir of Hill, "dedicated to simple common sense and straight dealings, and very allergic to pomposity. His literary preferences were for the Scriptures, the classics, and for [RUDYARD] KIPLING (in moderation), and Mark Twain." Hill held membership in more than forty scientific associations and received honorary degrees from seventeen universities, including Edinburgh, Oxford, Johns Hopkins, and Columbia. He was awarded the Companion of Honor (1946) and the Copley Medal of the Royal Society (1948), in addition to many other medals and prizes.

SELECTED WORKS: Lectures on Nutrition, 1925; Living Machinery, 1927; Adventures in Biophysics, 1931; The Ethical Dilemma of Science, 1960; Trails and Trials in Physiology, 1965; First and Last Experiments in Muscle Mechanics, 1970.

ABOUT: Biographical Memoirs of Fellows of the Royal Society, volume 24, 1978; The Excitement and Fascination of Science, 1965; Oxbury, H. (ed.) Great Britons, 1985.

HINSHELWOOD, CYRIL N.
(June 19, 1897–October 9, 1967)
Nobel Prize for Chemistry, 1956
(shared with Nikolay N. Semenov)

The English biochemist Cyril Norman Hinshelwood was born in London, the only child of Ethel (Smith) and Norman Hinshelwood. His father, an accountant, moved the family to Canada for business reasons, but because of the boy's poor health, Cyril and his mother returned to England shortly before the elder Hinshelwood's death in 1904. As a young student in London, Hinshelwood attended Westminster City School. In 1916 he was awarded a Brackenbury Scholarship to Balliol College, Oxford University, but was unable to accept it immediately because of World War I. Instead, he became the "boy wonder" of the Queensferry Explosive Supply Factory, where he was made assistant chief chemist in 1918. His work there on the decomposition of solid explosives marked the beginning of a lifelong interest in chemical kinetics.

Hinshelwood finally entered Oxford in 1919, and while he was a student there three papers on his research at Queensferry were accepted for publication by the Chemical Society. He became a fellow of Balliol upon graduation in

CYRIL N. HINSHELWOOD

1920 and a fellow and tutor of Trinity College in 1921. What he called his "joint laboratory" consisted of some cellars at Balliol and several outbuildings at Trinity, which served not only for doing research but also for teaching physical chemistry.

In the early 1920s Hinshelwood, like J. W. STRUTT (Lord Rayleigh) and IRVING LANGMUIR before the war, became interested in applying kinetic theory to explain the dynamics of chemical reactions occurring in gases. The thermal decomposition of various organic vapors was known to occur in the gas phase as either a unimolecular or a bimolecular reaction. In the latter case kinetic theory often provided a relatively good explanation of the initiation of the reaction through the collision of two molecules, but it was more difficult to imagine how a single molecule obtained the necessary activation energy for a unimolecular reaction. It had been shown that radiation does not initiate such reactions; even though the reaction rate is independent of the number of molecules present, Hinshelwood was determined to find an explanation in collisional activation. While many of his contemporaries focused their attention on specific reactions, he abstracted the generalities from a wide range of reactions. After conceiving the idea of a quasi-unimolecular reaction, he was able to predict, on the basis of the particular relationship between collisional activation and deactivation processes, whether a reaction would be unimolecular or bimolecular.

Hinshelwood incorporated much of this research in his first book, The Kinetics of Chem-

ical Change in Gaseous Systems (1926). He felt that the book represented the first of what he described as three stages of a scientific theory, "that of gross oversimplification, reflecting partly the need for practical working rules, and even more a too enthusiastic aspiration after elegance of form." Subsequent editions would proceed to the second stage, in which "the symmetry of the hypothetical systems is distorted and the neatness marred as recalcitrant facts increasingly rebel against conformity." Hinshelwood added that in "the third stage, if and when this is attained, a new order emerges, more intricately contrived, less obvious, and with its parts more subtly interwoven, since it is of nature's and not of man's conception."

In 1927 Hinshelwood began a detailed study of the reaction between hydrogen and oxygen gases. He showed that the reaction proceeds very slowly over a certain pressure range and quickly becomes explosive beyond this range. Using the concept of chain or branched-chain reactions, which his friend and colleague NIKOLAY N. SEMENOV had just applied to the oxidation of phosphorus, Hinshelwood was able to explain the behavior of the hydrogen-oxygen reaction.

Upon the retirement of FREDERICK SODDY from Oxford in 1937, Hinshelwood succeeded him as Dr Lee's Professor of Inorganic and Physical Chemistry. In addition to his responsibilities as professorial tutor of Exeter College, Hinshelwood continued his research in the Balliol-Trinity laboratory until 1941, when a new facility was finally provided for him. Although he intensely disliked the administrative duties associated with this position, he did not shirk them. In fact, Hinshelwood contributed significantly to Oxford's reputation as an important teaching and research center in the sciences, and he helped strike a better balance between the liberal arts and the sciences within the university. He trained and influenced scores of physical and organic chemists who later became pioneers in theoretical chemistry and biology. As a delegate to the Oxford University Press, he advocated and assisted a program of scientific publication, which began before World War II.

In the late 1930s Hinshelwood began to study bacterial growth with the methods of chemical kinetics, a project that remained his chief scientific pursuit. Hinshelwood regarded the living cell as a complicated set of interrelated chemical reactions, which he likened "to so many simple musical themes, each played on a different instrument, ...The operation of a living cell depends upon the combination of all these elements into a symphony. Knowing something of the theory of the simple elements, can we find something about the rules of composition of the symphony?" Hinshelwood believed that adaptations made by a bacterium to environmental change occurred at the molecular level and were thus inheritable. Although his model of cellular response initially encountered opposition from some biologists, many of his seemingly heretical ideas, now integrated into cell regulation theories, have played an important role in the study of immunology.

"For their research into the mechanics of chemical reactions," particularly their work on chain reactions, Hinshelwood and Semenov were awarded the 1956 Nobel Prize for Chemistry. In his Nobel lecture Hinshelwood paid homage to Semenov: "The study of the hydrogen-oxygen reaction was the first point at which the work in Oxford came into close contact with that of Semenov. Our indebtedness to his ideas was at once recognized, and the early exchanges opened friendly relations between Semenov and myself which have lasted ever since." Hinshelwood was deeply respected for his teaching abilities and, characteristically, much of his acceptance speech was devoted to an exposition of some of the intriguing questions that still awaited young theoretical chemists.

After retiring from his chair at Oxford in 1964, Hinshelwood moved to the London apartment where his mother had resided from her return from Canada until her death in 1959. His lifelong devotion to her may explain why he never married. As a senior research fellow at London's Imperial College, he continued his study of bacterial growth; he served as a trustee of the British Museum and council chairman of Queen Elizabeth College in London. Hinshelwood was well versed in literature and the classics and knew at least eight foreign languages, including Greek and Latin. His students joked that he learned a new language during each long vacation. He was a member of Oxford's Dante Society and president of the Oxford branches of both the Modern Language Association and the Classical Association. In 1921, while a tutor at Trinity, he had taken up oil painting, using the little palette that he had bought as a nine-year-old boy. A 1968 posthumous exhibition of over 100 of his paintings included interiors at Oxford, outdoor scenes from London and Oxford, and portraits. His other interests included music, especially Beethoven and Mozart; Chinese

467

porcelain; and Persian rugs. Hinshelwood died in London on October 9, 1967.

In addition to the Nobel Prize, Hinshelwood received the Davy Medal (1942), the Royal Medal (1947), and the Copley Medal (1962) of the Royal Society. He was knighted in 1948 and awarded honorary degrees from numerous universities. He was a member of the Royal Academy and nearly a dozen other professional societies.

SELECTED WORKS: The Reaction Between Hydrogen and Oxygen, 1934; The Chemical Kinetics of the Bacterial Cell, 1946; Some Relations Between Chemistry and Biology, 1949; The Structure of Physical Chemistry, 1951; The Vision of Nature, 1961; Growth, Function, and Regulation in the Bacterial Cell, 1966, with A. C. R. Dean.

ABOUT: Biographical Memoirs of Fellows of the Royal Society, volume 19, 1973; Current Biography April 1957; Dictionary of National Biography, 1961–1970, 1981; Dictionary of Scientific Biography, volume 6, 1972; Oxbury, H. (ed.) Great Britons, 1985; Times (London) October 12, 1967.

HODGKIN, ALAN

(February 5, 1914–   )
Nobel Prize for Physiology or Medicine, 1963
(Shared with John C. Eccles and Andrew Huxley)

The English biophysicist Alan Lloyd Hodgkin was born in Banbury, Oxfordshire. After his father, George L. Hodgkin, died in Baghdad during World War I, he and his two younger siblings were raised by their mother, Mary (Wilson) Hodgkin. Hodgkin attended the Downs School in Malvern and Greshams School in Holt before entering Trinity College, Cambridge, in 1932. From an early age he had been interested in history and natural history, especially ornithology, but at Cambridge he gravitated toward physiology, particularly the function of nerve cells.

The electrical nature of nerve impulses had been recognized since Luigi Galvani's experiments at the end of the eighteenth century. Early in the twentieth century the German physiologist Julius Bernstein proposed that unstimulated nerve cells are batteries with a resting potential (the difference in electrical tension or pressure between the outside and inside of a cell at rest) that is determined by the unequal distribution of ions (charged particles) across the cell membrane. Bernstein suggested that the nerve impulse is an action potential—that the membrane temporarily

ALAN HODGKIN

breaks down, and ions from both sides come into contact with and neutralize the resting potential; when the membrane re-forms, the original resting potential is restored. "A central point in the theory," Hodgkin later said, "is that propagation of the impulse from one point to the next is brought about by the electric currents which flow between resting and active regions. The action potential is not just an electrical sign of the impulse but is the causal agent in propagation."

While at Trinity, Hodgkin conducted some preliminary research on the electrical properties of nerves. One of his teachers, the physiologist EDGAR D. ADRIAN, suggested that he use the comparatively large and tough axons (nerve fibers) from the shore crab *Carcinus maenas*. Hodgkin took his advice and found that single fibers could easily be isolated for study. In 1936 he became a fellow of Trinity College, working under ARCHIBALD V. HILL, who sent a copy of Hodgkin's fellowship thesis to HERBERT S. GASSER. Gasser invited him to spend 1937–1938 at the Rockefeller Institute (now Rockefeller University) in New York City. During this time Hodgkin visited the Woods Hole Oceanographic Institute in Massachusetts, where he met Kenneth S. Cole and H. J. Curtis, who were working with single nerve fibers isolated from squid. Squid axons are among the largest known, measuring up to 1.0 millimeter in diameter, whereas shore crab axons are no larger than .03 millimeter in diameter, and mammalian axons are even smaller. "Cole and Curtis had developed a technique which allowed them to measure

468

changes in the electrical conductivity of the membrane during the impulse," Hodgkin wrote later; "when analyzed, their experiment proved that the membrane undergoes a large increase in conductance which has roughly the same time course as the electrical change." These results were of particular interest to Hodgkin because they suggested that the membranes were permeable to ions. If this proved to be true, it offered a clue to the cause of the resting potential.

Hodgkin returned to Cambridge in 1938 and began working with ANDREW HUXLEY, a talented undergraduate. They employed techniques Hodgkin had learned in the United States in experiments on *Carcinus* axons. "To our surprise, we found that the action potential was often much larger than the resting potential," Hodgkin reported later. They ascertained that, contrary to Bernstein's prediction, the action potential not only neutralized (or depolarized) the resting potential but significantly exceeded it.

Hodgkin and Huxley then began to use squid axons, which are large enough to allow the insertion of a microelectrode entirely within their membranes. These studies confirmed the results of the crab axon experiments by showing that the inner surface of a nerve-cell membrane is more negative than the outer surface. Instead of finding a difference in the action potential of 60 millivolts, as they had expected, however, Hodgkin and Huxley recorded differences of 90 millivolts or greater, which indicated that the inner surface of the axonal membrane temporarily becomes more positive than the outer surface.

Efforts to explain these data were interrupted by World War II. Hodgkin spent most of the war years working on scanning and display systems for airborne radar.

Back at Cambridge after the war, Hodgkin taught at the Physiology Laboratory, and in 1945 he and Huxley published the results of their prewar research. Their work on the ionic mechanisms in living organisms attracted the interest of others at Cambridge, and soon a small research group had formed to pursue the topic. Their efforts were supported by Adrian, who reduced the teaching duties of the researchers and obtained a grant from the Rockefeller Foundation.

The resting potential arises because the axonal membrane is permeable only to certain ions, a condition that results in different concentrations of various ions on either side of the membrane. The concentration of positively charged sodium ions is lower inside the

membrane than outside; the reverse is true for positively charged potassium ions. Many of the large organic molecules inside the cell are negatively charged, and although the pores in the membrane permit potassium ions to move back and forth, sodium and organic ions, which are larger, cannot pass through the membrane. The net result is a resting potential, which arises from the tendency of positively charged potassium ions to move from an area within the cell (where they are highly concentrated) to one outside the cell (where they are less highly concentrated). Hodgkin and Huxley's prewar data indicated that the action potential cannot be caused by the movement of potassium ions alone; another ion must be involved to make the action potential exceed the potassium-based resting potential, and the most likely ion, they believed, was sodium.

According to the sodium hypothesis, first the cell membrane becomes much more permeable to sodium than to potassium through the opening of a sodium channel, or gate. Sodium rushes into the cell, making the inside of the axonal membrane temporarily positive, as Hodgkin and Huxley had found. "A simple consequence of the sodium hypothesis is that the magnitude of the action potential should be greatly influenced by the concentration of sodium ions in the external fluid," Hodgkin said. He and BERNARD KATZ performed the first experiments to test this supposition in 1947 and proved that the action potential—but not the resting potential—fluctuates in tandem with the external sodium concentration.

Hodgkin, Huxley, and Katz began a series of experiments to test the permeability of the axonal membrane to different ions at various electrical voltage levels. In 1952 they presented a mathematical theory, the details of which were worked out by Huxley, to explain the action potential as the movement of sodium ions into the cell, followed by the movement of potassium ions out of the cell to restore the resting potential. That year Hodgkin became Foulerton Research Professor of the Royal Society. The theory proposed by Hodgkin and Huxley offers an essentially complete biophysical description of the action potential, although techniques for examining the molecular mechanisms underlying the nerve impulse (the membrane structures that control the movement of ions) did not become available until the 1980s.

Hodgkin and Huxley received the 1963 Nobel Prize for Physiology or Medicine "for their discoveries concerning the ionic mechanisms involved in excitation and inhibition in the peripheral and central portions of the nerve cell membrane." They shared the prize with JOHN C. ECCLES. In his presentation speech, RAGNAR GRANIT of the Karolinska Institute pointed out that "Hodgkin and Huxley's ionic theory of the nerve impulse embodies principles applicable also to the impulses in muscles, including the electrocardiograph of the heart muscle, a fact of clinical significance." Their discovery, Granit declared, "is a milestone on the road towards the understanding of the nature of excitability."

From 1970 to 1981 Hodgkin was John Humphrey Plummer Professor of Biophysics. He also served as master of Trinity College between 1978 and 1984, was president of the Marine Biological Association from 1966 to 1976, and was a member of the Medical Research Council from 1959 to 1963.

During his first visit to the United States, Hodgkin met Marion de Kay Rous, daughter of PEYTON ROUS, at the Rockefeller Institute. They were married in 1944 while Hodgkin was in the United States on wartime business. The Hodgkins have one son and three daughters.

In addition to the Nobel Prize, Hodgkin has received the Royal Medal (1958) and the Copley Medal (1965) of the Royal Society. The recipient of numerous honorary degrees, he is a member of the Royal Society and the Royal Danish Academy of Sciences and Letters and a foreign member of the American Academy of Arts and Sciences, the Indian National Science Academy, the Soviet Academy of Sciences, and the Royal Irish Academy.

SELECTED WORKS: The Conduction of the Nerve Impulse, 1963; The Pursuit of Nature, 1977, with others.

ABOUT: New York Times October 18, 1963; Science October 25, 1963.

HODGKIN, DOROTHY C.
(May 12, 1910–)
Nobel Prize for Chemistry, 1964

The English chemist Dorothy Mary Crowfoot Hodgkin was born in Cairo, Egypt, which was then under British rule. Her father, John Winter Crowfoot, was a distinguished British classical scholar and archaeologist in the Egyptian Education Service. He was often assisted by his wife, the former Grace Mary Hood, a talented amateur botanist who later described the flora of the Sudan and also became an international authority on Coptic textiles.

DOROTHY C. HODGKIN

Dorothy, the eldest of four daughters, was four years old when World War I broke out. Fearing a possible attack by Turkish troops, her parents sent the children to England to live with their paternal grandmother in Worthing, a few miles from Brighton on the English Channel. After the armistice in 1918, Hodgkin's mother returned to England and settled the family in Lincoln, where she taught the children history, natural science, and literature at home. For the next three years her mother divided her time between England and the Middle East before moving to Geldeston, East Suffolk, where Crowfoots had lived for several centuries.

Hodgkin attended the Sir John Leman School in nearby Beccles until 1928. At Leman her fascination with crystals led her to study the history of crystallography as well as chemistry, a subject normally taught only to boys at that time. At the age of thirteen, while visiting her father in Khartoum, where he had just been appointed director of education and antiquities for the Sudan, she met A. F. Joseph, a soil chemist, who helped her perform the quantitative analysis of some local minerals.

In 1926 her father became director of the British School of Archaeology in Jerusalem, and after graduation from Leman, Hodgkin joined her parents in Palestine. Excavating Byzantine churches at Jerash in Transjordan (now Jordan), she felt drawn to archaeology but went back to England that fall to study chemistry at Somerville College, Oxford.

Hodgkin had read about X-ray diffraction of crystals in Concerning the Nature of Things, a book written by W. H. BRAGG for school-children. Bragg and his son, W. L. BRAGG, with MAX VON LAUE, were pioneers of the new science of X-ray crystallography. Laue had discovered that X rays passing through crystals could be diffracted to form characteristic patterns of spots on photographic plates. The Braggs then demonstrated that such reflect the internal structure of each crystal. With the aid of complex mathematical calculations, X-ray crystallography became an important technique for determining the sizes, shapes, and positions of the atoms and molecules in a crystal.

Intrigued by the relatively new process, Hodgkin studied crystallography under H. M. Powell at Somerville. She then spent a summer in Heidelberg in the laboratory of Victor Goldschmidt, another pioneer in crystallography.

After graduation from Somerville in 1932, Hodgkin received a small research grant that, with additional support from her aunt, enabled her to work at Cambridge University with the noted physicist J. D. Bernal. Bernal was conducting X-ray analyses of crystals of sterols (solid cyclic alcohols, such as cholesterol, found in biological tissues), a topic of particular interest to her. After two years, she returned to Somerville to the Department of Mineralogy and Crystallography and remained there for most of her professional life.

Obtaining funds for X-ray apparatus with the aid of the organic chemist ROBERT ROBINSON, Hodgkin continued analyzing sterols, particularly cholesteryl iodide. For a dissertation on this topic she received her doctorate in 1937. This work was cited by W. H. Bragg as an example of a physical method that passed beyond the limits of organic chemistry in the determination of complicated three-dimensional structures.

Three years after the outbreak of World War II, Hodgkin turned to the study of penicillin, an antibiotic that had been discovered in 1928 by ALEXANDER FLEMING and purified later by ERNST B. CHAIN (whom she had met at Cambridge) and HOWARD W. FLOREY. The wartime need for this drug in the treatment of infections caused by bacteria was acute. Since its chemical structure was essentially unknown, however, penicillin could not be synthesized and mass-produced.

With a small team at Oxford, Hodgkin set about analyzing penicillin by means of X-ray crystallography. Passing X rays through penicillin crystals from all possible angles, they examined the resulting diffraction patterns recorded on photographic plates and calculated the positions of key atoms in the crystal lattice. Later, use of an IBM card-punch machine facilitated the laborious task of plotting the electron-density maps by which Hodgkin and her colleagues determined the molecular structure of penicillin in 1949.

In 1948, even before completing her work on penicillin, Hodgkin had applied X-ray crystallography to the analysis of vitamin B_{12}, which prevents pernicious anemia, a potentially fatal blood condition. By this time electronic computers had become available to aid in performing the calculations. Hodgkin finally elucidated the molecular structure of vitamin B_{12} in 1957, one year after she was appointed a university reader in X-ray crystallography at Oxford. In 1958 her laboratory was moved from scattered rooms in the university's natural history museum to a modern wing of the chemistry building.

"For her determination by X-ray techniques of the structures of important biochemical substances," Hodgkin received the 1964 Nobel Prize for Chemistry. In his presentation speech, Gunnar Hägg of the Royal Swedish Academy of Sciences said, "Knowledge of a compound's structure is absolutely essential in order to interpret its properties and reactions and to decide how it might be synthesized from simpler compounds. . . . The determination of the structure of penicillin . . . has been described as a magnificent start to a new era of crystallography." Hägg continued, "The determination of the structure of vitamin B_{12} has been considered the crowning triumph of X-ray crystallographic analyses, both in respect of the chemical and biological importance of the results and the vast complexity of the structure."

Due largely to Hodgkin's pioneering efforts, X-ray crystallographic techniques were utilized by MAX PERUTZ and JOHN C. KENDREW in their studies of protein structure, and by Rosalind Franklin, MAURICE H. F. WILKINS, JAMES D. WATSON, and FRANCIS CRICK in their analysis of the spiral structure of deoxyribonucleic acid (DNA).

Despite advancing arthritis, Hodgkin continued investigations of the hormone insulin and in 1972, after forty years of work, completed an analysis of zinc insulin. The work on this complex molecule, which contains almost 800 atoms (vitamin B_{12} is composed of 90 atoms), was further complicated because insulin crystallizes in several different forms.

Between 1960 and 1977, Hodgkin was Wolfson Research Professor of the Royal Society. She was named a fellow of Wolfson College,

Oxford, in 1977. She has also been chancellor of Bristol University since 1970 and president of the Pugwash Conference on Science and World Affairs since 1975.

In 1937 she married Thomas Hodgkin, son of a historian at Oxford, grandson of two other historians, descendant of Thomas Hodgkin (for whom Hodgkin's disease—cancer of the lymphatic system—is named), and cousin of the physiologist ALAN HODGKIN. A schoolteacher in their early married life, Thomas Hodgkin served for many years as director of the Institute of African Studies at the University of Ghana. The Hodgkins have two sons and a daughter. They live in Ilmington, Warwickshire, England. Hodgkin remains active in the laboratory, saying, "There are still crystals with complexities which challenge us."

The recipient of numerous awards, Hodgkin holds honorary degrees from Cambridge, Harvard, and Brown universities and from the universities of Leeds, Manchester, Sussex, Ghana, and Chicago, among others. She was the second Englishwoman to be awarded the Order of Merit (1965) and has received the Royal Medal (1957) and the Copley Medal (1976) of the Royal Society and the Lomonosov Gold Medal of the Soviet Academy of Sciences (1982). She holds foreign membership in the American, Soviet, Netherlands, Yugoslav, Ghanaian, Puerto Rican, and Australian academies of sciences. She was instrumental in the founding of the International Union of Crystallography and served as its president from 1972 to 1975.

SELECTED WORKS: Birkbeck: Science and History, 1970.

ABOUT: Campbell, W. A., and Greenwood, N. N. Contemporary British Chemists, 1971; Haber, L. Women Pioneers of Science, 1979; Journal of Chemical Education April 1977; Science November 6, 1964.

HOFFMANN, ROALD
(July 18, 1937–   )
Nobel Prize for Chemistry, 1981
(shared with Kenichi Fukui)

The American chemist Roald Hoffmann was born Roald (after the Norwegian explorer Roald Amundsen) Safran in Zloczow, Poland (now Zolochëv in the Soviet Ukraine) to the former Clara Rosen, a schoolteacher, and Hillel Safran, a civil engineer. From the outbreak of World War II to June 1941, the region was occupied by Soviet troops. When the German

ROALD HOFFMANN

army occupied the area, the Safrans, who were Jewish, were forced into a ghetto and then into a labor camp. In 1943 the elder Safran managed to smuggle the boy and his mother out of the camp, and the two spent the rest of the war hidden in a schoolhouse attic in a nearby Ukrainian village. The father remained in the camp and, like most of the family, was executed by the Nazis. Hoffmann and his mother managed to survive and were liberated by the Red Army in June 1944. Later that year, they moved to Kraków, where the boy was finally able to attend school and where his mother married Paul Hoffmann.

For the next three years the Hoffmanns lived in displaced-persons' camps in Austria and Germany. They were able to emigrate to the United States in 1949, where they settled in New York City. Hoffmann learned English, his sixth language, while attending public schools in Brooklyn, and subsequently entered Stuyvesant High School, a selective public high school with a science-oriented curriculum. He began premedical studies at Columbia University in 1955 and received his B.A. three years later, after which he began graduate studies in chemistry at Harvard University. In 1959 Hoffmann attended a summer program in quantum chemistry sponsored by the University of Uppsala in Sweden. During this time he met Eva Börjesson, and they were married in 1960, after Hoffmann had returned to Harvard. Soon afterward the couple spent a year in the Soviet Union, where Hoffmann was an exchange student at Moscow University.

Back at Harvard, Hoffmann began studying

472

with WILLIAM N. LIPSCOMB, using computers to help solve problems of energy barriers in organic molecules. He extended the Hückel rule (which identifies the number of electrons in orbiting clouds around a given molecule) into calculations of the electronic structure of boron hydrides and polyhedral molecules. After receiving his Ph.D. in 1962, Hoffmann spent three years as a junior fellow at Harvard. Influenced by the organic chemists E. J. Corey and R. B. WOODWARD, he switched his field of study from theoretical chemistry to applied theoretical organic chemistry.

Quantum theory, developed in the 1920s principally by LOUIS DE BROGLIE, ERWIN SCHRÖDINGER, and WERNER HEISENBERG, is a mathematical concept of atomic and subatomic behavior. Quantum mechanics is the application of this theory to the motion of particles. In 1965, seeking to explain an unexpected reaction observed by Woodward in his synthesis of vitamin B_{12}, Woodward and Hoffmann developed rules, based on quantum mechanics, to predict whether a particular combination of chemicals will result in a reaction.

Basic to the Woodward-Hoffmann rules is the idea, known since the 1870s, that systems tend toward a configuration having the least energy. If a set of reactants will have less energy as a new compound than as discrete chemicals, the reaction will take place, given the requisite atmospheric conditions (such as pressure and temperature). Should the product of a reaction have a higher energy level than the aggregate of the individual substances, no reaction will occur.

Bonding between atoms occurs when their orbiting electrons overlap, that is, when the orbitals (the regions in space where electrons are likely to be found) of the reactants are symmetrical. In other words, they must be occupying the same space and must be in the same phase. The Woodward-Hoffmann rules provide a mathematical prediction of whether a particular chemical reaction will maintain the symmetry involved and consequently result in a product of greater bonding and stability than the starting reagents.

Woodward and Hoffmann analyzed these effects of orbital symmetry in concerted reactions, in which several bonds are broken or formed simultaneously, rather than sequentially with involvement of intermediate compounds. The Woodward-Hoffmann rules are widely considered to be the most important theoretical advance in organic chemistry since World War II. Because they were formulated simply and do not require complex computa-

tions by laboratory chemists, they have had numerous practical applications in medicine and industry. Their relative simplicity accords with Hoffmann's belief that the ability to make qualitative predictions without laborious calculations is the essence of understanding. "If you have to go back to the computer, you don't understand it," he has said. Woodward and Hoffmann described their findings in their 1970 book *The Conservation of Orbital Symmetry*.

At the end of his fellowship in 1965, Hoffmann went to Cornell University as associate professor of chemistry (1965–1968) and then full professor. Since 1974 he has been John A. Newman Professor of Physical Science.

Hoffmann shared the 1981 Nobel Prize for Chemistry with KENICHI FUKUI "for their theories, developed independently, concerning the course of chemical reactions." Although Fukui had developed his ideas before Hoffmann, his highly mathematical publications appeared in Japanese journals read by few Western chemists. "The concepts of frontier orbitals and conservation of orbital symmetry have revealed completely new aspects of the interaction between molecules in collision," noted Inga Fischer-Hjalmars of the Royal Swedish Academy of Sciences in her presentation speech. "From your theoretical work new tools have emerged of the greatest importance for the design of chemical experiments."

Since receiving the Nobel Prize, Hoffmann has investigated the structure and reactivity of inorganic and organometallic molecules, from small diatomic complexes to clusters containing several transition metal atoms. Using molecules built from metal-ligand fragments, Hoffmann also studied cluster bonding and the geometry of olefin and polyene metal carbonyl complexes. His predicted new structural types of triple-decker and porphyrin sandwiches have been synthesized by others. He and his colleagues are also studying extended solid-state structures.

Hoffmann's other interests include the relationship between the arts and sciences and the similarities in the creative processes of the two disciplines. The Hoffmanns, who have a son and a daughter, live in Ithaca, New York. Hoffmann is a naturalized American citizen.

In addition to the Nobel Prize, Hoffmann has received the Pure Chemistry Award (1969), the Harrison E. Howe Lectureship (1970), the Arthur C. Cope Award (shared with Woodward in 1973), the Pauling Award (1974), the Nichols Medal (1981), and the Award for Distinguished Service in the Advancement of Inorganic Chemistry (1982), all given by the

HOFSTADTER

American Chemical Society, as well as the International Academy of Quantum Molecular Science Award (1971). He is a member of the National Academy of Sciences, the American Association for the Advancement of Science, the International Academy of Quantum Molecular Science, and the American Physical Society. He holds honorary degrees from the Royal Institute of Technology in Sweden and from Yale University.

ABOUT: New York Times October 20, 1981; Physics Today December 1981; Science November 6, 1981.

ROBERT HOFSTADTER

HOFSTADTER, ROBERT
(February 5, 1915–   )
Nobel Prize for Physics, 1961
(shared with Rudolf L. Mössbauer)

The American physicist Robert Hofstadter was born in New York City, the third son and one of four children of Louis Hofstadter, a salesman, and the former Henrietta Koenigsberg. Growing up in New York, the boy received his early education in the public school system before entering the City College of New York (CCNY), where he majored in physics and mathematics. He received a B.S. with high honors in 1935, winning the school's Kenyon Prize in physics and mathematics. He has credited an inspiring professor at CCNY for shifting his primary interest from philosophy to physics. A Coffin Fellowship from the General Electric Company enabled Hofstadter to attend Princeton University, where he received both his M.A. and Ph.D. in 1938. During the following year, as a Procter Fellow at Princeton, he studied photoconductivity in crystals. Hofstadter was an instructor in physics at the University of Pennsylvania in 1940 and at CCNY in 1941. As a Harrison Fellow at the University of Pennsylvania, 1940–1941, he helped construct a large Van de Graaff generator.

In 1942 and 1943 Hofstadter served as a physicist at the National Bureau of Standards, helping develop photoelectric proximity fuses for antiaircraft shells. Between 1943 and 1946 he was assistant chief physicist at Norden Laboratories Company, maker of the famous Norden bombsight. Returning to academic life after the war, Hofstadter became assistant professor of physics at Princeton in 1946. There his research centered on crystals used as detectors of high-energy particles and radiation. In 1948 he developed a scintillation detector based on a crystal of the salt sodium iodide "doped" with a small quantity of the element thallium. When the crystal is struck by an energetic atomic particle or by a photon (a particle of light energy), it emits a burst of light whose intensity is proportional to the energy of the particle or photon. Measurement of the light intensity provides a measure of particle energy. This is the basis of the scintillation spectrometer, one of the basic measuring tools for nuclear radiation studies.

In 1950 Hofstadter was appointed associate professor of physics at Stanford University. There he turned to studies of nuclear structure, utilizing a newly constructed electron accelerator at Stanford's High-Energy Physics Laboratory. It had already been shown by G. P. THOMSON, CLINTON J. DAVISSON, and others that electrons possess a wavelike nature. It was also known that the wavelength of an electron decreases as its energy increases. The Stanford accelerator could accelerate electrons to energies of 100 to 500 million electron volts, resulting in electron wavelengths smaller than most atomic nuclei. Thus the accelerator could be employed as a giant electron microscope, capable of exploring the structure of the atomic nucleus. When an energetic electron struck a nucleus, the electron would be deflected like a billiard ball; in some cases, the nucleus itself would be broken up, and additional electrons and other particles would be emitted. By studying the debris of such collisions, Hofstadter hoped to gradually develop an image of the nucleus.

In his investigation of nuclear structure,

Hofstadter wished to measure the deflection of electrons that had not generated additional particles in their encounter with a nucleus. To accomplish this, he employed a pair of massive (250-ton) magnetic spectrometers, which are instruments that sort out electrons according to their energy and their angle of deflection from their original path. By this means, Hofstadter measured the size and shape of many atomic nuclei and found that all of them have approximately the same average density. The volume of the nucleus is proportional to the total number of protons and neutrons, which means these particles are not packed any more tightly in the large and heavy nuclei than they are in the small and light ones. The relatively uniform nuclear density was found to be 150 million kilograms per cubic meter; if a drop of water had that density, it would weigh 2 million tons.

Although Hofstadter found that the average density of all nuclei is approximately the same, his experiments showed that the nucleus is not simply a hard-edged sphere. It has a soft "skin" whose thickness is the same for all nuclei regardless of size. The skin thickness is about 2.4×10^{-13} centimeter.

When the Stanford accelerator was upgraded to accelerate electrons to energies of 1 billion electron volts, Hofstadter decided to probe the internal structure of protons and neutrons, the constituent particles of the nucleus. In 1956 and 1957 he and his group determined the size and shape of the proton and the neutron and concluded that the two particles are different aspects of a single entity, called the nucleon. Although the proton and the neutron differ in electric charge, they are identical in all interactions mediated by the strong nuclear force (which holds the nucleus together). Hofstadter's discovery revealed some inadequacies of contemporary nuclear theory and led Yoichiro Nambu of the University of Chicago to propose important revisions. Up to then, the force between nucleons was known to be transmitted by pi-mesons, particles which have about half the mass of a proton. Nambu argued that there must also be heavier and shorter-lived carriers of the nuclear force; such particles were discovered in 1961.

Hofstadter received half the 1961 Nobel Prize for Physics "for his pioneering studies of electron scattering in atomic nuclei and for his thereby-achieved discoveries concerning the structure of the nucleons." He shared the prize with RUDOLF L. MÖSSBAUER. In his presentation speech, Ivar Waller of the Royal Swedish Academy of Sciences hailed Hofstadter for work "characterized by a precision that has scarcely been attained before in high-energy physics." Hofstadter's results, he said, have "stimulated the discovery of new particles that seem to be essential for the understanding of the forces acting in the atomic nuclei."

Since 1971 Hofstadter has been Max H. Stein Professor of Physics at Stanford University, where he has continued his investigations in high-energy physics. He married Nancy Givon in 1942; the couple has three children, one of whom, Douglas, has become prominent in the field of artificial intelligence. Regarded by his colleagues as a relaxed, modest man, Hofstadter enjoys listening to classical music and jazz, taking photographs, reading, and skiing.

A member of the National Academy of Sciences, the Italian and American physical societies, and the Physical Society of London, Hofstadter was named California Scientist of the Year in 1959. In 1962 CCNY struck a medal in his honor. He has received honorary degrees from CCNY, the University of Padua, and Carleton University.

SELECTED WORKS: High-Energy Electron Scattering Tables, 1960, with Robert Herman; Nucleon Structure, 1964, with L. I. Schiff.

ABOUT: Current Biography October 1962; Osiatynski, W. Contrasts, 1984; Science November 10, 1961.

HOLLEY, ROBERT W.

(January 28, 1922–   )
Nobel Prize for Physiology or Medicine, 1968
(shared with Har Gobind Khorana and Marshall W. Nirenberg)

The American biochemist Robert William Holley was born in Urbana, Illinois, one of four sons of Viola Esther (Wolfe) and Charles Elmer Holley, both of whom were teachers. He received his early education in the public school systems of Illinois, California, and Idaho. In his youth he developed a love of the outdoors and a lasting interest in biology. After graduating from Urbana High School in 1938, he enrolled in the University of Illinois, Urbana, to study chemistry. He received a B.A. four years later and entered Cornell University for graduate work in organic chemistry. During his graduate program, he served as an assistant chemist for two years and as a research chemist in the medical college.

During World War II Holley postponed his

ROBERT W. HOLLEY

studies and joined the United States Office of Research and Development research team that first synthesized penicillin. This antibiotic, discovered by ALEXANDER FLEMING in 1928, was vitally needed during the war. After the war, Holley was appointed a National Research Council Fellow at Cornell, where he obtained his Ph.D in 1947.

A postdoctoral fellowship from the American Chemical Society enabled Holley to continue his research at Washington State College (now University) in Pullman, Washington, for two years. He returned to Cornell in 1948 as assistant professor of organic chemistry at the New York State Experimental Station. During these years his research led him to study the biochemistry of the nucleic acids, substances that control the body's production of proteins. On sabbatical leave from Cornell in 1955, he pursued his investigation of nucleic acids as a Guggenheim Fellow at the California Institute of Technology in Pasadena (Caltech). There he initiated a series of experiments that were an outgrowth of his earlier work and which, after ten years, led to a determination of the chemical structure of ribonucleic acid (RNA).

In addition to playing a crucial role in the synthesis of proteins, RNA transmits genetic information from the nucleus of the cell. The science of genetics originated in 1866 when Gregor Mendel published his observations on the inheritance of flower color in the garden pea. Mendel believed that "elements," now called genes, govern the inheritance of an organism's physical traits. The discovery of nu-

cleic acids in 1869 gradually led to the discovery of RNA and deoxyribonucleic acid (DNA) in the twentieth century.

Genes consist of DNA, which directs the synthesis of proteins within the cell and thus controls its biochemical processes. In 1953 FRANCIS CRICK and JAMES D. WATSON determined the double helix structure and developed a three-dimensional model of the DNA molecule, which resembles a ladder twisted into a spiral. The DNA helix consists of two strands of nucleotides joined by pairs of bases within the "rungs" of the "ladder": adenine, thymine, guanine, and cytosine. Each base is always paired with a matching base on the opposite strand; this sequence of bases forms the genetic code of DNA. A triplet of bases contains genetic instructions for the incorporation of a single amino acid into a molecule of protein, which is a chain of amino acids. A gene contains many base triplets and genetic instructions for the synthesis of an entire protein molecule.

Like DNA, RNA is composed of nucleotide chains. There are three types of RNA: messenger, ribosomal, and transfer. Messenger RNA copies the genetic code of DNA in the cell nucleus and carries genetic instructions for protein synthesis to ribosomes, where proteins are formed in the cytoplasm of the cell. Transfer RNA (tRNA), which contains specific nucleotide sequences for each amino acid, picks up the amino acid designated by its nucleotide code and transports it to ribosomes. The three types of RNA then cooperate in the synthesis of protein molecules.

In 1964 Holley was named professor of biochemistry and molecular biology and chairman of the Department of Biochemistry and Molecular Biology at Cornell University. Only three years earlier, MARSHALL W. NIRENBERG had discovered the base triplet code of the amino acid phenylalanine. At Cornell, Holley and his colleagues extended Nirenberg's work by synthesizing molecules of transfer RNA with a nucleotide sequence specific for phenylalanine. They then determined the nucleotide sequence of the phenylalanine transfer RNA, a task comparable to establishing the meaningful sequence of a run-on sentence written in a foreign language by dividing the sentence into words and the words into letters. They published their findings in *Science* in 1965. "The complete nucleotide sequence of an alanine transfer RNA, isolated from yeast, has been determined," the article began. "This is the first nucleic acid for which the structure is known."

Holley and his colleagues also found that transfer RNA has a biologically active secondary structure in addition to its primary structure. The primary structure is the sequence of bases in the nucleotide strand. The secondary structure of transfer RNA shows where twisting of the strand brings it in contact with itself. The secondary structure resembles a three-leaf clover, with the base sequence of the middle leaf complementing that of messenger RNA. This complementarity between transfer and messenger RNA assures that amino acids are inserted into protein molecules in the correct order.

Holley shared the 1968 Nobel Prize for Physiology or Medicine with HAR GOBIND KHORANA and Marshall Nirenberg "for their interpretation of the genetic code and its function in protein synthesis." In his presentation speech, Peter Reichard of the Karolinska Institute pointed out that "[Holley] is one of the discoverers of a special type of nucleic acid which . . . has the capacity to read off the genetic code and to transform it to the protein alphabet." He added that "Holley's work represents the first determination of the complete chemical structure of a biologically active nucleic acid. The interpretation of the genetic code and the elucidation of its function are the highlights of the last twenty years' explosive evolution of molecular biology."

Under a National Science Foundation Fellowship, Holley spent 1966 at the Salk Institute for Biological Studies in San Diego, California. Since 1968 he has been the American Cancer Society Professor of Molecular Biology and a resident fellow of the Salk Institute. In this capacity he has sought to elucidate the biological control mechanisms that govern the growth of mammalian cells. In 1969 he also became an adjunct professor at the University of California at San Diego.

In 1945 Holley married Ann Dworkin, a mathematics teacher, with whom he had one son. Still an outdoor enthusiast, he enjoys hiking with members of his family.

Holley's many honors include the Albert Lasker Basic Medical Research Award (1965), the Distinguished Service Award of the United States Department of Agriculture (1965), and the United States Steel Foundation Award in Molecular Biology of the National Academy of Sciences (1967). He is a member of the National Academy of Sciences, the American Association for the Advancement of Science, the American Chemical Society, the American Society of Biological Chemists, and the American Academy of Arts and Sciences. Keuka College and the University of Illinois have conferred honorary degrees on him.

ABOUT: Current Biography January 1967; National Observer March 22, 1965; New York Times October 17, 1968; New York World-Telegram November 11, 1965; Science October 26, 1968.

HOPKINS, FREDERICK GOWLAND
(June 20, 1861–May 16, 1947)
Nobel Prize for Physiology or Medicine, 1929
(shared with Christiaan Eijkman)

The English biochemist Frederick Gowland Hopkins was born in Eastbourne, East Sussex, to Elizabeth (Gowland) and Frederick Hopkins. His second cousin was the poet Gerard Manley Hopkins. His father, a bookseller and amateur scientist, died shortly after the boy's birth. A lonely, scholarly child, Hopkins spent much of his time reading Dickens and writing poetry. At the age of eight, he was first permitted to use his father's microscope to examine life from the nearby sea. What he saw stimulated him more than his indifferent schooling, although there was nobody to explain it to him.

In 1871 his mother moved to Enfield in the countryside near London to live with her mother and brother. That year Hopkins was sent to the City of London School, where he won awards in chemistry and English. Bored and lonely, he preferred visiting museums and libraries to going to school, and although not formally expelled, he was advised to leave. He was enrolled in a private school for the next three years. Considering his education complete when the boy was seventeen, the family found him a job as an insurance clerk. Shortly after leaving school, however, he wrote a paper on the purple vapor ejected by bombardier beetles that was accepted for publication by *The Entomologist*. "I became there and then a biochemist at heart," he wrote later. There followed three years of apprenticeship to an analytical chemist at a pharmaceutical firm. Using a small inheritance from his grandfather, Hopkins was able to study chemistry first at the Royal School of Mines in South Kensington, and later at University College, London. His high score in a final chemistry examination led to an assistantship with Sir Thomas Stevenson, an expert on poisoning and forensic medicine at Guy's Hospital. While working for Stevenson, whom he found to be a "congenial and considerate chief," Hopkins

NATURE, AIP Niels Bohr Library

FREDERICK GOWLAND HOPKINS

received a B.S. from the University of London. On Stevenson's advice, he enrolled in Guy's Medical School in 1888, having received the Gull Studentship for research.

At Guy's, Hopkins was encouraged to pursue laboratory investigations related to patient cases. In 1891 he published a description of the ammonium chloride precipitation of uric acid from urine, an analytical method that remained in use for many years. He also showed that uric acid was a component of the white pigment of some butterflies, for he retained his childhood curiosity about insects throughout his life; in fact, his last publication was about insect pigmentation.

After receiving his medical degree from Guy's in 1894, Hopkins remained at the school another four years to teach physiology, chemistry, toxicology, and physics. During his last two years there he headed the Clinical Research Association, which performed laboratory tests to aid in diagnosis and treatment. Through his own research in protein chemistry, he helped to develop methods for isolating protein from blood and egg white and for crystallizing proteins in large quantities for further study.

In 1898 Hopkins was invited by Michael Foster to join the staff of Cambridge University as a researcher and teacher of chemical physiology, which is known today as biochemistry. Foster, a highly influential researcher and teacher, encouraged Hopkins to develop the field. The position paid poorly, and Hop-

kins supplemented his income by supervising medical students at Emmanuel College, where he was named a fellow and tutor in 1906.

At Cambridge, a routine teaching experiment about proteins led to the discovery of tryptophan, an amino acid. When a student's protein sample failed to turn blue in the standard Adamkiewicz color test, Hopkins surmised that analysis of such a color reaction could lead to new knowledge of protein structure. He therefore isolated and identified tryptophan, which was added to the growing list of other amino acids (the building blocks of protein) that had already been discovered by EMIL FISCHER, ALBRECHT KOSSEL, and other researchers. In 1906 Hopkins showed that different proteins fed to mice had varying effects on body growth. In particular, he found that proteins lacking tryptophan were insufficient for the needs of the body. He concluded that protein quality depended on the types of amino acids present. Believing that more than protein quality determined an adequate diet, he fed mice a basic diet of lard, starch, and casein (milk protein). When the animals stopped growing, he added small amounts of milk, which supplied some missing factors for growth. These "accessory food factors," as he called them, were later given the name *vitamines* by the Polish chemist Casimir Funk. Hopkins's work was interrupted briefly in 1910, when he suffered a breakdown brought on by overwork. In 1912 he reported the results of his feeding studies in a paper titled "Feeding Experiments Illustrating the Importance of Accessory Factors in Normal Dietaries."

Hopkins considered his work with vitamins secondary to his studies of intermediary metabolism, the complex series of oxidation and reduction reactions by which cells obtain energy. The prevailing theory held that a giant molecule, the biogen, hosted such reactions, but available chemical methods were inadequate to study them. Hopkins showed that intermediary metabolism is a series of ordinary chemical steps. By demonstrating that lactic acid accumulates in muscles when oxygen is depleted, he and his colleague Walter Fletcher laid the foundation for the discovery that energy from a carbohydrate metabolic cycle is used in muscle contraction, a finding made by ARCHIBALD V. HILL and OTTO MEYERHOF.

In 1921 Hopkins isolated and named glutathione, a tripeptide—a product formed by the union of three amino acids—important as an oxygen carrier in both plant and animal cells. He also discovered the enzyme xanthine oxidase, which catalyzes the oxidation of the purines xanthine and hypoxanthine (colorless crystalline substances) to uric acid.

His ability to pioneer in a field, identify its chief issues, and then arouse interest among others was considered one of Hopkins's greatest assets. Even after his appointment as chairperson of the Cambridge biochemistry department in 1914, Hopkins worked in an inferior one-room laboratory at Cambridge. In 1925, however, he moved to the newly built Dunn Institute of Biochemistry.

Hopkins shared the 1929 Nobel Prize for Physiology or Medicine with CHRISTIAAN EIJKMAN "for their discovery of the growth-stimulating vitamins." In his Nobel lecture, "Earlier History of Vitamin Research," Hopkins reminded his listeners that his 1912 paper had emphasized "the indispensable nature of food constituents, which were then receiving no serious consideration as physiological necessities." While giving full credit to Casimir Funk for his contributions to vitamin research, Hopkins pointed out that it was he himself who had been "the first to realize the full significance of the facts."

From 1930 until 1935 Hopkins served as president of the Royal Society, a post that left him little time for research. After 1935 he resumed his study of insect pigments and intermediary metabolism, though his sight was failing and his health declining.

In 1898 Hopkins married Jessie Ann Stevens; they had one son, who became a physician, and two daughters, one of whom became a biochemist. His colleague HENRY H. DALE described Hopkins as "a man of small physique, with slender bones. . . . His face . . . had habitually a pondering expression, but the mobile features were easily lit by eager attention, relishing humor, or by the sympathy which made him so ready to share the troubles of others." He died in Cambridge on May 16, 1947.

Hopkins was knighted in 1925 and awarded the Order of Merit in 1935. His many awards included the Royal Medal (1918) and the Copley Medal (1926) of the Royal Society.

SELECTED WORKS: Food Economy in Wartime, 1915, with Thomas Woods.

ABOUT: Baldwin, E., and Needham, J. (eds.) Hopkins and Biochemistry, 1949; Crowther, J. G. British Scientists of the Twentieth Century, 1952; Dictionary of National Biography 1941–50, 1959; Dictionary of Scientific Biography, volume 6, 1972; Obituary Notices of Fellows of the Royal Society, volume 6, 1948; Oxbury, H. (ed.) Great Britons, 1985.

HOUNSFIELD, GODFREY

(August 28, 1919–   )
Nobel Prize for Physiology or Medicine, 1979
(shared with Allan Cormack)

The English research scientist Godfrey Newbold Hounsfield was born in Newark, Nottinghamshire. His father, Thomas Hounsfield, had been an engineer in the steel industry, but after World War I he bought a small farm in Nottinghamshire and changed his occupation to farming. As the youngest of five children, Hounsfield was often left out of the activities of his siblings and therefore had ample time to convert the farm into a personal playground where, as he said later, he could "go off and follow my own inclinations." Playing around farm machinery as a child, he enjoyed figuring out how it worked; from such early experience was born his penchant for engineering. During his adolescent years, he managed to build a glider on which he sailed off the roof of the barn, a water fountain powered by acetylene, and a phonograph and radio set.

At the Magnus Grammar School in Newark, young Hounsfield was interested chiefly in physics and mathematics. After attending City and Guilds College in London in 1939, at the outbreak of World War II, he enlisted as a reservist in the Royal Air Force and served as instructor in radar mechanics at the Royal College of Science in South Kensington. He also lectured at the air force's Cranwell Radar School, where he developed a large-screen oscilloscope and other educational equipment. In 1945 he was awarded the Certificate of Merit for his work during the war and the following year was discharged from the air force.

A year after his discharge, Hounsfield obtained a grant that enabled him to enroll in the Faraday House Electrical Engineering College in London. After graduating in 1951, he went to work for Electrical and Musical Instruments Limited (EMI), a company involved in research and development of electronic products for commercial use. For a time he worked on radar and weapons guidance systems, and in the early 1950s he became interested in computer design. After designing various computer data storage systems, he spent 1958 and 1959 as a project engineer for a team that designed and constructed the first solid state (transistor) computer in England. The first transistors offered no great advantage over earlier electron tubes, however, until Hounsfield designed a system capable of "driving the

479

GODFREY HOUNSFIELD

transistor with a magnetic core," as he described it.

After completing this work in the early 1960s, Hounsfield worked in EMI's central research laboratories on a design for a thin-film, large-scale memory system to increase the memory capacity of EMI computers, a project that was abandoned as commercially unfeasible. He was also involved in research on computers capable of pattern or print recognition. Contemplating future topics of research, Hounsfield conceived of a computer that could compute the X-ray absorption patterns of biological tissue and overcome some of the limitations of conventional X rays.

The science of medical radiology originated at the end of the nineteenth century, when WILHELM RÖNTGEN discovered and named X rays and produced the first X-ray images. In conventional X-ray imaging, the X rays pass through the part of the body being examined and strike photographic film. Since bones absorb more X-ray energy than do soft, less dense tissues, bones appear as prominent white shadows on the developed film. The margins of soft tissues superimposed on each other, however, are poorly delineated. The distinction between normal and abnormal soft tissue (for example, a tumor) may therefore be impossible by usual X-ray procedures.

Unknown to Hounsfield, in the late 1950s and early 1960s ALLAN CORMACK, a medical physicist at Tufts University in Massachusetts, had developed a mathematical method for determining X-ray absorption patterns in bio-

logical tissues. Cormack's method relied on the analysis of many measurements of absorption of a thin, pencillike X-ray beam passed through a body at different angles, thus defining a thin slice, or cross section. Since the beam probed the slice from many points of view, the accumulated information contained the absorption properties of each individual part. In conventional X-ray images, only total absorption along a ray path determines what appears on the film. Internal tissues in line with the path are hidden behind each other.

Cormack's method permitted reconstruction of the interior details of a body on the basis of different X-ray absorption by different regions. Although published, Cormack's work had attracted almost no attention, and his method remained a primitive laboratory demonstration using simulated models rather than biological tissues. Moreover, computers that could perform the large number of mathematical steps needed to analyze the data were not yet available, so the method was slow and cumbersome. The making of such X-ray images of a slice of the body is called tomography, from the Greek *tomos,* meaning "section." Eventually, with the development and availability of fast computers, the method came to be known as computer-assisted (or computerized axial) tomography (CAT), or CAT scanning. It is also called simply computerized tomography (CT), or CT scanning.

In 1967 Hounsfield independently began work on his CAT system, arriving at a scheme very similar to Cormack's, beginning with a gamma-ray source just as Cormack did. (The same principle holds for gamma and X rays.) Hounsfield developed somewhat different mathematics, used a large computer to process the data, and, with his engineer's frame of mind, brought the tomographic method to a practical stage.

Early models took nine days to scan an object because the low-intensity gamma-ray source required long exposures. A powerful X-ray tube reduced the time to nine hours. Successful pictures were made of a preserved human brain, the fresh brain of a young bull, and a pig's body in the area of the kidneys. The resolution was good enough to show brain and body tissues, but it was not certain that the technique could distinguish diseased from normal tissue, thus revealing tumors. In order to achieve this goal, a faster and more sophisticated machine, the first clinical CAT scanner, was built and installed at Atkinson Morley's Hospital in Wimbledon in 1971. In 1972 the first patient, a woman with a suspected brain lesion, was scanned, and the resulting image clearly showed a dark, circular cyst. Larger and faster scanners were subsequently designed that reduced scanning time first to 18 seconds and then to 3 seconds or less, and were capable of producing high-resolution pictures of the body.

Hounsfield described the operation of the CAT scanner at the annual conference of the British Institute in London and in December 1973 published a paper, "Computerized Transverse Axial Scanning (Tomography)," which reported results of clinical tests with the first commercial scanner, the EMI CT 1000. It was evident at once that the CAT scanner represented a significant advance over other techniques then available for making images of biological tissue. It revealed internal details of soft tissue previously unattainable; it facilitated treatment by locating abnormalities such as tumors with greater precision; and it permitted accurate measurement of the X-ray absorption properties of body tissues, which is valuable information for diagnosis and therapy. Hounsfield estimated that the CAT scanner is a hundred times as efficient as a conventional X ray because it uses all the information gathered, whereas the ordinary X ray records only about 1 percent. The scanner is also more sensitive and requires less X-ray energy per view than a standard X ray, although the total radiation exposure is about the same for both because scanning requires so many views.

A commercial CAT scanner consists of an X-ray generator, a scanning unit containing the X-ray tube and detector, a computer for processing the measurements, and an oscilloscope and printout system for displaying the computed patterns. The scanning unit rotates around the head or body, taking up to a million separate measurements of beam attenuation at many different angles. (In some machines a large number of detectors are fixed in a circle, and only the X-ray source rotates.) From this enormous mass of information, the appropriately programmed computer reconstructs a cross section of the head or body part being examined. The patient can then be moved in small increments of displacement through the ring of the scanner, while scanning is repeated at each step. The result is a series of closely spaced cross sections that provide a three-dimensional representation.

In 1972 Hounsfield was appointed head of the Medical Systems Section at EMI, advanced to chief staff scientist in 1976, and soon thereafter to senior staff scientist. In 1978 he was appointed professional fellow in imaging sciences at the University of Manchester.

Hounsfield and Cormack were awarded the 1979 Nobel Prize for Physiology or Medicine "for the development of computer assisted tomography." Speaking of the development of computer axial tomography in his Nobel lecture, Hounsfield explained that "the method of picture reconstruction, I like to think, was obtained by commonsense practical steps. Most of the available mathematical methods at the time were of an idealized nature and rather impractical."

Hounsfield's subsequent research has included further advances in CAT technology and related fields of diagnostic imaging such as nuclear magnetic resonance, a more recent development in medical imaging that does not use X rays. He has remained a bachelor. He enjoys long walks, which he calls "rambles," in the Lake District of England, plays the piano in a "self-taught way," and is fond of "lively, way-out discussions." He has not only become interested in biology but also renewed an early interest in physics.

Among Hownsfield's other awards are the MacRobert Award of the Fellowship of Engineering (1972), the Barclay Prize of the British Institute of Radiology (1974), the Albert Lasker Basic Medical Research Award (1975), the Duddell Medal and Prize of the Institute of Physics (1976), and the Gairdner Foundation International Award (1976). He has received honorary degrees from the University of Basel and the City University of London. He is an honorary fellow of the Royal College of Physicians and a fellow of the Royal College of Radiologists.

ABOUT: Current Biography March 1980; New Scientist October 18, 1979; New York Times October 12, 1979; Physics Today December 1979; Science November 30, 1979.

HOUSSAY, BERNARDO

(April 10, 1887–September 21, 1971)
Nobel Prize for Physiology or Medicine, 1947
(shared with Carl F. Cori and Gerty T. Cori)

The Argentine physiologist Bernardo Alberto Houssay (o͞o sī′) was born in Buenos Aires, the fourth of eight children of Clara (Laffont) Houssay and Alberto Houssay, a barrister. His parents, both of whom were French, had immigrated to Argentina the year before his birth. As a result, Houssay, a pre-

481

BERNARDO HOUSSAY

cocious child, spoke both French and Spanish at an early age. Attending private schools in Buenos Aires, he impressed his teachers with his intelligence, his commitment to hard work, and his remarkable memory.

After completing his secondary education at the Colegio Británicó in 1901 at the age of fourteen, Houssay enrolled in the School of Pharmacy at the University of Buenos Aires. Three years later he received a bachelor's degree in pharmacy, graduating first in his class, and entered the university's medical school. To support himself he worked as a pharmacist at a local hospital, but he also found time to participate in track and field, winning a championship in the 800-meter run. As part of his medical training Houssay helped care for a patient with acromegaly, a disease caused by excessive secretion of growth hormone by the anterior lobe of the pituitary gland. The work stimulated his interest in endocrinology, the study of the endocrine glands and their secretions (hormones), which circulate in the bloodstream. The principal endocrine glands of the mammalian body are the thyroid, the parathyroid, the pituitary and adrenal glands, and the pancreas, ovaries, and testicles. The pituitary serves as a master gland that regulates not only the hormonal secretions of the other endocrine glands but also the metabolism of other tissues.

While still a medical student, Houssay developed an experimental method for studying the pituitary gland hormones; he later wrote his doctoral dissertation, "Studies of the Physiological Action of Pituitary Extracts," which was published in 1910. In the same year he won the Science Prize of the Faculty of Medical Science for his research on the pituitary gland.

In 1909, a year before he received his medical degree from the University of Buenos Aires, he was appointed acting professor of physiology on the faculty of veterinary science at the same university. The appointment aroused opposition because at the time Houssay had neither an M.D. nor a degree in veterinary medicine. Nevertheless, his enthusiasm, intelligence, and ability as a teacher and investigator soon made him a popular figure in the school of veterinary science, and in 1912 he became a full professor of physiology at the age of twenty-five.

Meanwhile, he had established a private practice in medicine and endocrinology; in 1913 he was appointed chief of the Unit of Clinical Medicine at the Alvear Hospital in Buenos Aires. He also continued to teach and conduct research at the University of Buenos Aires. Between 1915 and 1919 Houssay was chief of the Section of Experimental Pathology at the Institute of Bacteriology, a government laboratory, where he studied the physiologic effects of the venom of snakes, spiders, and scorpions and developed specific antidotes to them. For his investigation of the physiological effects of curare, a muscle relaxant used in anesthesia, he eventually acquired an international reputation.

On his appointment as professor of physiology at the University of Buenos Aires in 1919, Houssay gave up his private practice and his research at the Institute of Bacteriology to devote full time to his faculty responsibilities and medical research. In this position, he made many administrative reforms, converting the physiology department into an Institute of Physiology capable of engaging in experimental investigations. As part of his effort to improve the quality of teaching at the medical school, he replaced the traditional part-time faculty with a full-time staff, a policy that was eventually adopted by universities throughout Latin America. Under the training program he developed, as many as 250 doctoral students worked in his laboratories during a given term.

During the 1920s and the 1930s Houssay made a thorough investigation of the endocrine system, the heart and circulation, the lungs and respiratory system, and the liver and gastrointestinal tract. This work established his reputation as a brilliant physiologist who was always at the forefront of medical research.

"Never worry about priorities," one of his colleagues once remarked; "Houssay has always done it first."

Perhaps his most significant research was on the endocrine system. The first researcher to show that the pituitary is the master gland, Houssay determined its hormonal and regulatory relationships to the other glands in the endocrine system. His early work in this field involved the surgical removal of the pituitary gland (or hypophysis) of experimental animals, followed by the preparation of extracts of pituitary tissue, which in turn were injected into other experimental animals to ascertain the resulting physiological effects.

Houssay was particularly interested in the effects of pituitary hormones on carbohydrate metabolism and their relation to diabetes mellitus, a disorder caused by a deficiency in insulin secretion by the islet cells of the pancreas. This deficiency in turn causes high blood glucose levels, diminished utilization of glucose by cells, and excessive urine formation, accompanied by thirst and weight loss. In 1921 insulin was isolated and first prepared for clinical use by FREDERICK G. BANTING and JOHN J. R. MACLEOD of the University of Toronto. In the early 1920s Houssay prepared and standardized the dose of insulin in extracts of pancreatic islet cell tissue.

In 1924 he and his colleagues discovered that removal of the pituitary gland from experimental animals (mostly dogs and a species of indigenous toads) resulted in hypersensitivity to insulin; that is, in the absence of circulating pituitary hormones, a given dose of insulin was effective in lowering blood glucose levels. From this finding, Houssay concluded that insulin and the hormones of the pituitary gland have antagonistic and opposing effects on blood levels of glucose and its cellular utilization; moreover, the maintenance of normal levels and metabolism results from an interplay of pituitary hormones and insulin. In further research, Houssay determined that surgical removal of the pituitary gland in experimental animals lessened the severity of diabetes and that storage of glucose in the liver in the form of glycogen is a prerequisite for the development of that disorder. Furthermore, he established that diabetes cannot be produced after the liver has been removed from laboratory animals. These findings laid the foundation for major discoveries about hormonal regulation systems.

Houssay was awarded the 1947 Nobel Prize for Physiology or Medicine "for his discovery of the part played by the hormone of the ante-rior pituitary lobe in the metabolism of sugar." He shared the prize with CARL F. and GERTY T. CORI. At the conclusion of his Nobel lecture, Houssay summarized his findings on the role of the pituitary gland. "Carbohydrate metabolism and other metabolic processes are regulated by the balance maintained between the secretion of several endocrine glands," he said. "Diabetes and other metabolic diseases are a disturbance in this endocrine equilibrium. There are still many problems to be solved, but undoubtedly the hypophysis [pituitary gland] is one of the most important organs in the regulation of metabolism and the center of the endocrine constellation."

When the Argentine government of President Ramon Castillo fell in a military coup in 1943, Houssay joined many other academics in signing a petition of protest that called for a return to constitutional government and democratic elections. Like all of those who signed, Houssay was promptly dismissed from the university. He and several colleagues then founded the Institute of Biology and Experimental Medicine, a private research laboratory, which he directed. Two years later, a general amnesty was granted, and Houssay was reappointed professor of physiology at the University of Buenos Aires. Under new laws enacted shortly after his reinstatement, Houssay was asked to retire in 1946. He continued to conduct research at the institute, and in 1955 he was again given an academic appointment at the University of Buenos Aires. After retiring the following year, Houssay remained as director of the institute and was also named president of the National Council of Technical Research of Argentina. In that capacity he actively promoted the development of science and technology in Argentina.

An indefatigable worker, Houssay published over 2,000 scientific papers within his lifetime, either alone or in collaboration. In 1970 he was named honorary president of the Eighth Congress of the International Diabetes Foundation, which was convened in Buenos Aires, with admiring colleagues from around the world in attendance to pay him tribute.

While he was employed by the Institute of Bacteriology in Buenos Aires, Houssay worked with María Angélica Catán, a chemist, whom he married in 1920; they had three sons, all of whom became physicians. Houssay died in 1971 at the age of eighty-four.

Widely honored for his achievements, Houssay received the Baly Medal of the Royal College of Physicians in London (1947) and the Dale Medal of the Society for Endocrinology in London (1960). He was awarded honorary degrees from twenty-eight universities, including Oxford, Cambridge, Harvard, and the University of Paris. He was a member of the Argentine National Academy of Medicine, the Academy of Moral and Political Sciences of Buenos Aires, and the Pontifical Academy of Science and held foreign or honorary memberships in numerous professional societies in the United States and Europe.

SELECTED WORKS: Collected Papers on Medical Subjects (2 vols.) 1924–1934; Functions of the Pituitary Gland, 1936; Human Physiology, 1951, with others.

ABOUT: Biographical Memoirs of Fellows of the Royal Society, volume 20, 1974; Cori, C. F. (ed.) Perspectives in Biology, 1963; Current Biography January 1948; Dictionary of Scientific Biography, volume 15, 1978; The Excitement and Fascination of Science, 1965; Journal of the History of Medicine October 1980.

DAVID H. HUBEL

HUBEL, DAVID H.
(February 27, 1926–   )
Nobel Prize for Physiology or Medicine, 1981
(shared with Roger W. Sperry and Torsten Wiesel)

The American neurobiologist David Hunter Hubel was born in Windsor, in the Canadian province of Ontario. His parents, both Americans, were Elsie M. (Hunter) and Jesse H. Hubel, a chemical engineer. In 1929 the family moved to Montreal. David acquired an interest in science from his father and enjoyed chemistry and electronics as a youth. He also showed musical talent and later remarked, "Since the age of five I have spent a disproportionate amount of time on music." From 1932 until 1944 he attended the Strathcona Academy in Outremont, Ontario.

In 1944 Hubel entered McGill University, where he took honors in mathematics and physics. After receiving a B.S. in 1947, he entered McGill University Medical School, "almost on the toss of a coin, despite never having taken a course in biology." He spent his summers at the Montreal Neurological Institute studying the nervous system. After receiving his medical degree in 1951, he took four years of clinical training in neurology, spending two years in the Montreal Neurological Institute and the year 1954 at the Johns Hopkins University in Baltimore, Maryland.

The following year, Hubel was drafted into the United States Army and assigned to the

Neurophysiology Division of the Walter Reed Army Institute of Research in Washington, D.C. There he developed a tungsten microelectrode (a device used to record the electrical impulses of nerve cells). By implanting it in the brains of cats for extended periods, he was able to record the spontaneous level of nerve-cell activity in the brains of sleeping and waking animals.

After his discharge from the army in 1958, Hubel continued his research in the laboratory of Vernon Mountcastle at Johns Hopkins University. Mountcastle was an authority on the neurophysiology of the sensory area of the cerebral cortex, the gray matter on the surface of the brain. While Mountcastle's research facilities were being renovated, Hubel joined the research team of Stephen Kuffler at the Wilmer Institute, also at Johns Hopkins.

Kuffler, an authority on the neurophysiology of vision, had studied the nervous activity (or microelectrical discharges) of nerve cells in the retina (the innermost layer of the eye) of the cat. He had discovered that retinal nerve, or ganglion cells respond to contrasts of light and not to evenly distributed illumination. Kuffler also described the receptive fields of these cells, the area of the retina which, when stimulated, produces a change in the spontaneous nervous activity of the cell. Kuffler discovered that retinal ganglion cells are stimulated or inhibited when a circular spot of light is shone on the corresponding receptive field of the retina. If the light stimulates the retinal cell, light falling on the doughnut-shaped area surrounding this central spot inhibits the cell, and vice versa.

Hubel and his colleague TORSTEN WIESEL set out to investigate the receptive fields of other nerve cells in the visual nervous system, specifically those in the visual cortex of the brain. The visual cortex is one of the many functional areas of the cerebral cortex where the higher cognitive activities of the brain, such as memory and perception, are performed. The visual nervous system begins in the photoreceptor (light-sensitive) cells of the retina, the rods and the cones. The nerve terminals of the rods and the cones project to other cells in the retina, and from there, nerve impulses travel along the optic nerves to the lateral geniculate nuclei, structures in the brain that relay the impulses to the visual cortex. Consisting of millions of nerve cells arranged in several layers, the visual cortex decodes the neural messages that originate in the retina.

One of the first observations that Wiesel and Hubel made led to significant advances in our understanding of how the visual nervous system functions. They placed a microelectrode in the visual cortex of a cat and began recording the spontaneous nervous activity (or microelectrical discharges) of a nerve cell. Attempting to evoke nervous activity in the cortical cells, they tried a variety of visual stimuli. Unintentionally, Hubel moved a microscope slide past the receptive field of the nerve cell in which the microelectrode was implanted and noticed that the cell began to discharge. At first the two researchers were puzzled by this behavior, but they soon realized that the cell was responding to the linear edge of the slide. Whereas Kuffler's retinal cells responded to circular images, the nerve cells in the visual cortex responded to linear patterns.

In 1959 Kuffler became professor of pharmacology at the Harvard Medical School in Boston, Massachusetts. His research team, including Hubel and Wiesel, followed. A Department of Neurobiology, with Kuffler as its chairman, was created at Harvard in 1964. In 1967 Hubel became department chairman, and the next year he was named George Packer Berry Professor of Physiology at Harvard. During their years at Harvard, Hubel and Wiesel devised an experiment in which they placed a microelectrode in the visual cortex of live cats and monkeys and recorded the spontaneous nervous activity of the cell in which the microelectrode was implanted. In this way they hoped to stimulate the retinal fields with linear images of light at various angles of orientation until they found the most effective

stimuli for a series of cells along the path of the electrode. Sometimes they made vertical penetrations, with the electrode perpendicular to the surface of the brain; at other times they made oblique penetrations. After autopsy of the experimental animals, they compared their findings about the nervous activity of the tissue with its anatomy. They also developed techniques for injecting the eyes with radioactive substances. Traveling along the optic-nerve fibers from the retina to the visual cortex, these tracers further delineated the anatomy of nervous tissue in the visual cortex.

As a result of this and other work, Hubel and Wiesel discovered that the visual cortex of the brain is organized into periodic vertical subdivisions, which they called ocular dominance columns and orientation columns. These columns of nerve cells perform two essential transformations on information transmitted from the retina to the visual cortex. The ocular dominance columns combine the neural input from the two eyes, and the orientation columns transform the circular receptive fields of retinal and geniculate nerve cells into linear receptive fields. Hubel and Wiesel classified cortical nerve cells into simple, complex, and hypercomplex groups and established that the cells perform their transformations through a process of increasing or progressive convergence. The principle of progressive convergence explains how the visual cortex is able to generate large images from the many fragments of neural information transmitted from the retina. Other functional areas of the cerebral cortex may be organized in a similar manner.

Hubel and Wiesel's research on the neurophysiology of vision has had significant effects on clinical ophthalmology (the branch of medicine dealing with the eyes), especially in the treatment of congenital cataracts. For example, they discovered that such cataracts must be removed early in the patient's life in order to preserve vision.

Hubel and Wiesel shared half of the 1981 Nobel Prize for Physiology or Medicine "for their discoveries concerning information processing in the visual system." The other half of the prize was awarded to ROGER W. SPERRY. In his presentation speech, David Ottoson of the Karolinska Institute reminded his listeners that Hubel and Wiesel had shown "how the various components of the retinal image are read out and interpreted by the cortical cells. . . . The cells are arranged in columns, and the analysis takes place in a strictly ordered sequence from one nerve cell to another and every nerve cell is responsible for one particular detail in the picture pattern." Ottoson pointed out that the two investigators had also learned that the ability to decode messages from the retina is developed immediately after birth, a discovery of some importance, since suturing one eye during this period "even for a few days . . . can result in permanently impaired vision."

Hubel was married in 1953 to Shirley R. Izzard. They have three sons.

The recipient of an honorary degree from McGill University, Hubel has also been awarded the Lewis S. Rosenstiel Award for Basic Medical Research given by Brandeis University (1972), the Jonas S. Friedenwald Memorial Award of the Association for Research in Vision and Ophthalmology (1975), the Karl Spencer Lashley Prize of the American Philosophical Society (1977), the Louisa Gross Horwitz Prize of Columbia University (1978), the Dickson Prize in Medicine of the University of Pittsburgh (1979), and the George Ledlie Prize of Harvard University (1980). He is a member of the National Academy of Sciences and is a fellow of the American Academy of Arts and Sciences.

SELECTED WORKS: "Brain Mechanism of Vision," Scientific American September 1979, with Torsten Wiesel.

ABOUT: Harvard Magazine November–December 1984; New York Times October 10, 1981; Science October 30, 1981.

HUGGINS, CHARLES B.

(September 22, 1901–)
Nobel Prize for Physiology or Medicine, 1966
(shared with Peyton Rous)

The American surgeon and cancer researcher Charles Brenton Huggins was born in Halifax, Nova Scotia, the elder son of Bessie (Spencer) Huggins and Charles Edward Huggins, a pharmacist. After receiving his early education in the local public schools, he entered Acadia University in Wolfville, Nova Scotia, from which he graduated with a B.A. in 1920. He then enrolled in the Harvard Medical School in Boston, Massachusetts, and he received his medical degree four years later.

For the next two years Huggins was a surgical intern at the University of Michigan Hospital in Ann Arbor. In 1926 he was appointed an instructor in surgery at the University of

CHARLES B. HUGGINS

Michigan Medical School, and in 1927 he joined the original faculty of the University of Chicago School of Medicine, also as an instructor in surgery. He became an assistant professor in 1929, an associate professor in 1933, and a full professor in 1936.

At Chicago, Huggins specialized in clinical urology, and to obtain further training in this field, he visited the Lister Institute in London in 1930 and then worked under OTTO WARBURG in Germany. Only a few years earlier, Warburg had discovered that tumor cells, unlike normal cells, obtain energy from the combustion of carbohydrates in the absence of oxygen. As Huggins became more deeply involved in cancer research, his association with Warburg developed into a lasting friendship.

Returning to the University of Chicago after his year abroad, Huggins worked with his colleagues for several years on the development of an experimental method for transforming normal connective tissue cells into tumor cells. Soon, however, his interest in the male genitourinary system led him to the study of the male accessory gland of reproduction, the prostate gland. The normal function of this gland, which is situated at the base of the urethra, is to secrete an alkaline fluid that forms a major component of the ejaculatory fluid. His initial experiments were conducted with dogs, the only species besides humans known to develop cancer of the prostate.

By 1939 Huggins and his co-workers had succeeded in surgically isolating the prostate gland in dogs. By measuring the quantity and chemical content of canine prostatic secretions under varying hormonal conditions, they found that testosterone, the male sex hormone and steroid, stimulates growth and secretory activity of the prostate. Moreover, they learned that estrogen, the female sex hormone, inhibits prostate growth.

These discoveries offered promising possibilities for treatment of cancer of the prostate, which is the most common form of cancer afflicting males over the age of fifty. Typically, prostate cancer produces pain and obstruction of the lower urinary tract, and it often metastasizes to bone, the liver, and the lungs. In 1941 Huggins and two of his students, C. V. Hodges and W. W. Scott, published three papers on the effects of testosterone therapy, estrogen therapy, and castration in a group of patients with prostate cancer. Testosterone, Huggins found, tends to promote the growth and metastasis of the cancer, whereas estrogens and castration often inhibit these processes. Among the first twenty patients in the group who were treated with estrogens or castration, four survived for more than twelve years.

Huggins also measured blood levels of acid phosphatase (an enzyme normally secreted by the prostate) and alkaline phosphatase (another enzyme secreted by the bone-forming cells in bone tissue), both of which are highly concentrated in the blood of patients with metastatic cancer of the prostate. Huggins therefore proposed that the level of the enzymes in the blood provides a useful clinical index of the cancer's activity and the efficacy of treatment. The discovery that estrogen therapy can control the growth and spread of prostate cancers provided the first clinical evidence that some human tumors respond to their hormonal environment. The form of treatment that Huggins devised rapidly became—and continues to be—a common therapy for metastatic cancer of the prostate. The first pharmacological estrogen preparation to be used in the clinical treatment of cancer of the prostate was diethylstilbestrol, a synthetic estrogen originally produced in Great Britain. The results of his clinical experience led Huggins to formulate two hypotheses concerning the biological behavior of cancer: first, cancers are not always autonomous and self-perpetuating; second, the growth of some forms of cancer depends upon a hormonal environment that is normal in quality and quantity.

In 1951 Huggins was appointed director of the Ben May Laboratory for Cancer Research at the University of Chicago, where he turned his attention to the study of hormonal regulation of cancer of the breast. During the 1950s he and his colleagues were able to show that in 30 to 40 percent of patients with advanced metastatic cancer of the breast, bilateral adrenalectomy (removal of the adrenal gland) when combined with bilateral ovariectomy (surgical removal of both ovaries) was associated with objective clinical improvement.

Huggins was awarded the 1966 Nobel Prize for Physiology or Medicine "for his discoveries concerning hormonal treatment of prostatic cancers." He shared the award with PEYTON ROUS, another pioneer in cancer research. In his presentation address, Georg Klein of the Karolinska Institute declared that Huggins's discoveries constituted "a completely new type of cancer therapy, [one] capable of helping a previously unaccessible category of patients, by the administration of nontoxic, naturally occurring hormones rather than by toxic or radioactive agents, and with few side effects."

Huggins summarized his work in his Nobel lecture, "Endocrine-Induced Regression of Cancers." "The control of cancer by endocrine methods can be described in three propositions," he said. "(1) Some types of cancer cells differ in a cardinal way from the cells from which they arose in their response to change in their hormonal environment. (2) Certain cancers are hormone-dependent, and these cells die when supporting hormones are eliminated. (3) Certain cancers succumb when large amounts of hormones are administered."

Huggins was named William B. Ogden Distinguished Service Professor in 1962, and in 1969 he retired as director of the Ben May Laboratory for Cancer Research. In his later years at the University of Chicago, Huggins returned to the research laboratory, where he studied experimental tumor models, including mammary tumors in mice, with emphasis on hormonal and chemical dependency and responsiveness. The Charles Huggins Cancer Research Laboratory was founded in his honor in Genzano di Roma, Italy, in 1971, and the following year Huggins was appointed chancellor of Acadia University in Nova Scotia, a post he held until he retired permanently in 1979.

Huggins became an American citizen in 1933. He was married in 1927 to Margaret Wellman, with whom he had a son and a daughter. The Hugginses, who live in Chicago, enjoy music, especially the works of Bach and Mozart. Huggins was once described by a colleague as "a man of wide culture and simple habits."

Huggins is a member of the American College of Surgeons, the Royal College of Surgeons in London, the National Academy of Sciences, and the American Philosophical Society. He holds honorary degrees from Acadia, Washington, Turin, Trinity, and Aberdeen universities as well as from Yale University and the University of Leeds. His work has also earned him the Charles L. Mayer Award of the National Academy of Sciences (1944), the Gold Medal of the American Cancer Society (1953), the Walker Prize of the Royal College of Surgeons in London (1961), the Albert Lasker Award for Clinical Research (1963), and the Gairdner Foundation International Award (1966), among others.

SELECTED WORKS: The Scientific Contributions of the Ben May Laboratory for Cancer Research, 1961; Experimental Leukemia and Mammary Cancer, 1979.

ABOUT: Current Biography February 1965; New York Times October 14, 1966; October 16, 1966; Science October 21, 1966.

CORDELL HULL

HULL, CORDELL
(October 2, 1871–July 23, 1955)
Nobel Prize for Peace, 1945

Cordell Hull, the American statesman known as the "father of the United Nations," was born in a log cabin near Byrdstown, Tennessee, the third of five sons. His parents were William Hull, a successful farmer and lumber merchant, and the former Elizabeth Riley. As a child, Hull assisted his father in the lumber business. After persuading his parents to send him for higher education, he attended various academies and colleges until the age of eighteen. In 1889 Hull worked briefly in law offices in Celina and Nashville before enrolling in Cumberland University, where he obtained his law degree in 1891. A year later he was admitted to the bar.

Even as a student, Hull had taken part in Democratic politics. In 1892 he was elected to the Tennessee House of Representatives, where he served two terms. During the Spanish-American War, he was the captain of a volunteer company stationed in Cuba in 1898–1899. Afterward, he resumed his law practice in Tennessee, and from 1903 to 1907 he held a judgeship in the Fifth Judicial District.

An able and respected public servant, Hull was soon propelled into national politics. In 1906 he was elected to the United States House of Representatives, where he served (with the exception of one term) until 1931. From 1921 to 1924 he was also chairman of the Democratic National Committee. Instrumental in enacting fiscal reform during the Progressive Era, Hull allied himself with WOODROW WILSON's bloc of Southern supporters. During Wilson's first term as president, Hull played a major role in drafting the income tax sections of the 1913 Underwood-Simmons Tariff and the 1916 inheritance law. After the United States entered World War I, he contributed to financial legislation dealing with the war, and in 1919 he took part in drafting the victory loan law that helped liquidate the national debt.

In foreign policy, Hull strongly shared Wilson's idealistic international outlook, vigorously supporting the League of Nations. With his economic ideas rooted in nineteenth-century liberalism, Hull believed that economic nationalism was a major cause of war. He therefore opposed Herbert Hoover's high tariff policy. Elected to the Senate in 1930, Hull was an important figure at the 1932 Democratic Convention, writing portions of the Democratic platform, including a low-tariff plank.

Hull relinquished his Senate seat on March 4, 1933, to become President Franklin D. Roosevelt's secretary of state. Although inexperienced in diplomatic affairs, Hull, with his white hair, dignified bearing, and habit of speaking in absolutes, inspired trust. "Today nearly all the nations of the world, including our own, have no fundamentals, either political, moral, or economic," he asserted in his first speech as secretary of state. Adhering to

Wilsonian principles, Hull assumed that right ideals held the key to world peace and mutual cooperation.

Hull's accomplishments as a member of Roosevelt's cabinet revived several themes of Wilson's administration: lower trade barriers, friendly relations with Latin America, and the establishment of an international organization under world law. One of his most successful efforts was the reciprocal trade program, passed in June 1934 as the Trade Agreements Act. Under its authority, Hull, who believed that trade would reduce international tensions, negotiated reciprocal trade agreements with twenty-two nations. He also used tariff policy as an instrument of coercion, placing an extra duty on German goods after Adolf Hitler's occupation of Czechoslovakia and, in 1939, repudiating the United States–Japanese trade agreement of 1911 in retaliation for Japan's incursions into China.

Hull enjoyed diplomatic success in implementing Roosevelt's Good Neighbor policy, which sought to improve ties with Latin America. He convened the seventh Pan-American Conference in Montevideo, Uruguay, in December 1933. Like ELIHU ROOT, his predecessor under President THEODORE ROOSEVELT, Hull led the delegation and paid goodwill visits to several Latin American countries. Agreeing to Article Eight of the Convention on the Rights and Duties of States, he committed the United States to a policy of nonintervention in the domestic affairs of Latin America. To implement this pledge, United States marines were removed from Haiti in 1934, and Congress signed a new treaty with Cuba nullifying the 1903 Platt Amendment, which had authorized United States intervention there. At the Conference for the Maintenance of Peace, held in Buenos Aires in 1936, the American nations agreed that any threat to the security of the hemisphere would be cause for mutual consultation. Two years later, at the eighth Pan-American Conference in Lima, Peru, Hull, concerned by Germany's annexation of Austria, obtained a resolution reasserting that a threat to any American republic would be regarded as a threat to all.

After the advent of World War II, Roosevelt dominated United States policy-making for Europe but left Hull with a good deal of authority for the Pacific. From 1939 to 1941 Hull patiently but unsuccessfully carried on negotiations to effect peace between Japan and China and to prevent further Japanese incursions into Indochina. Throughout this time, he tried to strengthen the position of moder-

ates and weaken that of militarists within the Japanese government.

Shortly after the outbreak of the war, Hull proposed the formation of a new world organization in which the United States would participate after the war. To accomplish this aim, he formed in 1941 an Advisory Committee on Postwar Foreign Policy composed of both Republicans and Democrats. Mindful of Wilson's failure with the League of Nations, Hull took pains to keep discussion of the organization nonpartisan. As different plans were considered, Hull argued for an international structure rather than a system of regional groups, a plan that eventually prevailed. By August 1943 the State Department had drafted a document entitled "Charter of the United Nations," which became the basis for proposals submitted by the United States at the 1944 Dumbarton Oaks Conference. Ill health forced Hull to resign from office on November 27, before final ratification of the United Nations Charter in San Francisco the following year. Nevertheless, Roosevelt praised the secretary as "the one person in all the world who has done the most to make this great plan for peace an effective fact."

The Norwegian Nobel Committee presented the 1945 Nobel Prize for Peace to Hull in recognition of his work in the Western Hemisphere, for his international trade agreements, and for his efforts in establishing the United Nations. Too ill to receive the award in person, Hull sent a brief acceptance speech that was delivered by the United States ambassador to Norway, Lithgow Osborne. "Under the ominous shadow which the Second World War and its attendant circumstances have cast on the world," Hull wrote, "peace has become as essential to civilized existence as the air we breathe is to life itself. There is no greater responsibility resting upon peoples and governments everywhere," he continued, "than to make sure that enduring peace will this time—at long last—be established *and maintained.*" He expressed his hope that "the searing lessons of this latest war and the promise of the United Nations organization will be the cornerstones of a new edifice of enduring peace and the guideposts of a new era of human progress."

Remaining single into his forties, Hull married Rose Frances Witz Whitney in 1917; they had no children. Leading a quiet personal life, Hull eschewed the Washington social scene, devoting himself primarily to his work. Until his physician ordered him to stop, he even met with key personnel on Sunday mornings. His nearly twelve-year tenure as secretary of state was the longest in that office until that time.

Critics have accused Hull of being an ineffectual Wilsonian, out of step with the times in his disregard for the importance of spheres of influence and in his failure to understand the nature of power. Others have faulted his lack of imagination and failure to act decisively. During the critical war period, Roosevelt often limited Hull's influence by preempting or bypassing him. Nonetheless, Hull is given high marks for his contributions to the Good Neighbor policy and for his single-mindedness in working to establish the United Nations. His contemporary, the British diplomat Lord Halifax, praised Hull as "a great public servant to his country and a great example to statesmen of any country—universally respected, known, and trusted."

WORKS BY: Addresses and Statements by the Hon. Cordell Hull, 1937; Economic Barriers to Peace, 1937; The War and Human Freedom, 1942; The Moscow Conference, 1943; The Memoirs of Cordell Hull (2 vols.) 1948.

ABOUT: Buell, R. L. The Hull Trade Program and the American System, 1938; Feis, H. The Road to Pearl Harbor, 1965; Graebner, N. A. (ed.) An Uncertain Tradition: American Secretaries of State in the Twentieth Century, 1961; Hinton, H. B. Cordell Hull: A Biography, 1942; Pratt, J. W. Cordell Hull (2 vols.) 1964; Times (London) July 25, 1955; Utley, J. G. Going to War With Japan, 1985.

HUXLEY, ANDREW
(November 22, 1917–)
Nobel Prize for Physiology or Medicine, 1963
(shared with John C. Eccles and Alan Hodgkin)

The English physiologist Andrew Fielding Huxley was born in the Hampstead district of London, the son of Leonard Huxley, a classics teacher and writer. His grandfather was Thomas Henry Huxley, the nineteenth-century scientist and writer whose work was instrumental in establishing Darwin's theory of natural selection. Huxley, the younger of two sons from his father's second marriage, to the former Rosalind Bruce, is the half brother of the novelist Aldous Huxley and the biologist Julian S. Huxley. He was educated at University College School and at Westminster School, where he developed a strong interest in physics and engineering, fields he intended to pursue when he entered Trinity College, Cambridge, in 1935. After taking a course in physiology, however,

ANDREW HUXLEY

he transferred to the medical program in 1937, and two years later he became a research assistant to ALAN HODGKIN at the Marine Biology Laboratory in Plymouth.

At the time, Hodgkin was studying the movement of electrical impulses along axons (nerve fibers). Early in the twentieth century, Julius Bernstein, building on the work of Luigi Galvani and WALTHER NERNST, had proposed that unstimulated nerve cells are batteries with a resting potential (the difference in electrical tension or pressure between the outside and inside of a cell at rest) that is determined by the unequal distribution of ions (charged particles) across the cell membrane. The concentration of positively charged sodium ions is lower inside the membrane than outside; the reverse is true for positively charged potassium ions. Many of the large organic molecules inside the cell are negatively charged. The pores in the membrane permit potassium ions to move back and forth, but sodium and organic ions, which are larger, cannot pass through the membrane. The resting potential arises from the tendency of positively charged potassium ions to move from an area in which they are highly concentrated (inside the cell) to one in which they are less highly concentrated (outside the cell).

Bernstein suggested that a nerve impulse is an action potential. When the membrane temporarily breaks down, ions from both sides come into contact with and neutralize the resting potential; the membrane then re-forms, and the original resting potential is restored. To test Bernstein's theory Hodgkin and Huxley inserted microscopic electrodes into single, isolated axons from crabs and measured the relative sizes of the resting and action potentials. To their surprise, they found that the change in membrane voltage during the action potential was, in fact, much greater than the resting potential. The action potential did not merely bring the cell membrane to electrical neutrality; it actually exceeded the resting potential and changed the direction of the voltage difference between the inner and outer surfaces of the membrane.

At the outbreak of World War II, Huxley and Hodgkin set aside their investigations, and from 1940 to 1942 Huxley conducted operational research for the Anti-Aircraft Command, followed by similar work for the Admiralty between 1942 and 1945. After the war he became a demonstrator in the physiology department at Trinity College and, with support from a Trinity research fellowship he had received in 1941, resumed his work with Hodgkin on the transmission of nerve impulses.

The results of Hodgkin and Huxley's studies, published in 1945, disproved Bernstein's theory by showing that the action potential cannot be caused by the movement of potassium ions alone. Another ion must be involved to make the action potential exceed the potassium-based resting potential. Of the various ions that Huxley and Hodgkin considered for this role, sodium seemed the most likely. They postulated that the cell membrane contains voltage-sensitive sodium channels, or gates, which remain closed at the resting-potential stage and open when the axon is depolarized. When the gates open, sodium ions rush from an area of relatively high concentration (outside the axon) to one of relatively low concentration (inside the axon), making the inside of the axonal membrane temporarily positive.

If their sodium hypothesis was correct, the size of the action potential, but not that of the resting potential, would depend strongly on the sodium concentration outside the cell. Testing this consequence in 1947, Hodgkin and BERNARD KATZ showed that they could in fact change or eliminate the action potential by manipulating external sodium concentration.

Huxley, Hodgkin, and Katz then turned their attention to ionic movements across the axonal membrane under different electrical conditions. Using a voltage-clamp apparatus, a system for maintaining the membrane potential at desired levels while observing the current flow, they traced the movement of different ions via radioactive isotopes and manipulation

of the ionic concentration. The studies were performed on squid axons, which are large enough (up to a millimeter in diameter) to allow the insertion of an electrode inside the membrane, and tough enough to withstand replacement of the internal fluid with different combinations of ions without damage to the membrane.

Data from the voltage-clamp experiments enabled the researchers to construct a mathematical model of the action potential. Huxley performed many of the calculations on a hand-cranked adding machine; later, more complex and realistic simulations were calculated with one of the first digital computers. According to their model, which they reported in a series of articles in 1952, the action potential in the squid axon begins when the membrane depolarizes to a certain threshold value. Depolarization opens the sodium gates, sodium ions rush in, and the interior of the membrane briefly becomes positive. Meanwhile, voltage-sensitive potassium gates open, though more slowly than the sodium gates, and the sodium gates eventually close. Potassium rushes out of the axon's interior, which thus becomes more negative. During a brief refractory period, the membrane is hyperpolarized (more negative than usual) as the outrush of potassium exceeds the resting potential. The resting potential is then restored by a sodium-potassium pump, which uses cellular energy to move potassium into the cell and sodium outside it, and thus maintains the resting potential at equilibrium. Huxley and Hodgkin's model was remarkable because biochemical methods for studying the membrane components (channels, gates, and pump) were not devised until the 1980s.

After developing a mathematical model of the action potential, Huxley became interested in the mechanism of muscle contraction through his friendship with ARCHIBALD V. HILL. In the course of this work, he designed a new type of interference light microscope to study living, unstained muscle preparations.

"For their discoveries concerning the ionic mechanisms involved in excitation and inhibition in the peripheral and central portions of the nerve cell membrane," Huxley and Hodgkin were awarded the 1963 Nobel Prize for Physiology or Medicine; they shared the award with JOHN C. ECCLES, who had performed related research on nerve impulses. "By elucidating the nature of the unitary electrical events in the peripheral and central nervous system," said RAGNAR GRANIT of the Karolinska Institute on presenting the prize, "you have brought understanding of nervous action to a level of clarity which your contemporaries did not expect to witness in their lifetime."

From 1952 to 1960 Huxley was director of studies at Trinity College; he served as assistant director of research from 1951 to 1959 and was reader in experimental biophysics between 1959 and 1960. He became Jodrell Professor of Physiology at University College, London, in 1960, and in 1969 he was appointed Royal Society Research Professor at the University of London, where he has been professor emeritus since 1983. From 1974 to 1980 he was chairman of the Medical Research Committee of the Muscular Dystrophy Group; he has been a member of the Agricultural Research Council (1977–1981), the Council of the International Union of Physiological Sciences (1983–), and the British National Committee for Physiological Sciences (1979–1980). He is a trustee of the British Museum and the Science Museum.

Huxley's marriage in 1947 to Jocelyn Richenda Gammell Pease produced one son and five daughters. For relaxation he enjoys walking and designing scientific instruments.

The recipient of the Copley Medal of the Royal Society (1973), Huxley is a member of the Royal Society and holds honorary or foreign memberships in the Royal Society of Edinburgh, the American Academy of Arts and Sciences, and the Royal Academy of Medicine of Belgium. He has received honorary degrees from Oxford University and the universities of Sheffield, Leicester, London, St. Andrews, Aston, Cambridge, Birmingham, Marseilles, York, and West Australia.

SELECTED WORKS: Reflections on Muscle, 1980.

ABOUT: New York Times October 18, 1963; Science October 25, 1963.

INSTITUTE OF INTERNATIONAL LAW
(founded September 11, 1873)
Nobel Prize for Peace, 1904

The Institute of International Law was one of the earliest world organizations to identify principles of international law, to undertake their codification, and to propose ways of solving international problems. Its origins lay in various mid-nineteenth-century European peace movements and in the belief that the codification of international law was a prerequisite for peaceful relations among nations. The immediate impetus for codification came from the Franco-Prussian War of 1870–1871 and the successful arbitration of the *Alabama* claims between the United States and England, in which the principles of international law applied by the arbitrators were elaborated in the final treaty. At this time, most universities did not offer international law as an independent subject of study.

Although various individuals made proposals for judicial conferences to draw up a code of international law, perhaps first with the idea was Francis Lieber, a professor of law at Columbia University. Lieber began urging the establishment of a congress to settle international questions as early as the 1861 *Trent* controversy between England and the United States. He repeated his proposal in an 1871 letter to Gustave Rolin-Jaequemyns, editor of the *Revue de Droit International et de Législation Comparée* (Journal of International Law and Comparative Legislation), the first scholarly review of international law.

In the spring of 1873, Rolin-Jaequemyns issued invitations to a conference whose purpose was to found an international institute of the law of nations. Through the *Revue*, Rolin-Jaequemyns publicized his plans, explaining that the time was opportune "to found a permanent institution, purely scientific, which . . . can . . . aspire to serve as the organ, in the realm of the law of nations, of the legal conscience of the civilized world."

The conference, which convened on September 8, 1873, in Ghent, Belgium, was attended by eleven scholars in international law representing Argentina, Belgium, Germany, Italy, the Netherlands, Russia, Scotland, and the United States. After three days' deliberation, the founders agreed that the Institute of International Law was to be a private organization composed solely of experts who would meet once a year. Its primary objective was to promote the recognition and codification of the principles of international law, the maintenance of peace, the study of international legal problems, and the support of justice and humanity in international relations. Taking a practical attitude toward these idealistic aims, its first president, Pasquale Stanislao Mancini, explained: "We are placed at an equal distance from the virtuous utopians who hope for the immediate and permanent abolition of war, eternal peace, and the timid souls, without faith in the moral progress of humanity, who are struck by a state of things which they believe to be practically inherent in the nature of human societies."

Among its early efforts, the institute endeavored to minimize the difficulties arising from the different judicial systems of various nations. The subjects of its deliberations included the extradition of criminals, marriage and divorce, trusteeship, the coming of age of foreign nationals, and the rights of citizenship. To its 1880 annual meeting the institute invited national governments to incorporate in their own legislation the rules formulated by the institute. In the sphere of criminal law, for instance, the institute's efforts led to treaties of extradition among many Western powers.

At its first annual meeting in 1874, the institute began the arduous task of formulating rules for the competency of tribunals, the forms of procedure, and the rendering of judgments in international judicial proceedings. These principles laid the groundwork for an agreement about international proceedings that was adopted at the International Hague Conference in 1894. At the instigation of one of the institute's founders, TOBIAS ASSER, the Dutch government sponsored conferences on international private law in 1893, 1894, 1900, and 1904. Asser expressed his hope that these and other conferences would pave the way for an international organization that, "without interfering with the complete autonomy of the nations in the domain of legislation, would contribute greatly to the codification of international civil law."

While striving to reduce the conflicts that lead to war, in its early years the institute tacitly accepted the inevitability of armed conflict. In 1879 it published *A Handbook of Rules and Observances of War* in the belief that warfare should be regulated to reduce its destructive effects. The institute also formulated international arbitration procedures and went on record as favoring neutrality for all areas vital to international communication, such as international waterways. After the Russo-Turkish War began in 1877, the institute studied the problem of the Suez Canal and recommended open access to it by all nations, even during wartime. As a result, in 1888 nine nations meeting in Constantinople signed the Suez Canal Convention, an agreement stating that the waterway would "always be free and open." Four years earlier, twenty-seven nations had signed a similar treaty in Paris placing underwater cables under international protection.

The Institute of International Law was awarded the 1904 Nobel Prize for Peace. No presentation speech was given at the ceremonies. However, when the institute held its twenty-seventh annual meeting in Oslo in 1912, the Norwegian statesman Georg Francis Hagerup, then president of the institute, gave an opening address that constituted the usual Nobel lecture. In it, he stated that the institute's efforts were important because they provided "the basis necessary for all pacifist work . . . . We cannot hope to achieve peace until law and justice regulate international as well as national relations." Noting the direct link between the institute's accomplishments and the results of the conferences in The Hague, he reminded his audience that independence from political pressures had given the institute an advantage over large, official diplomatic conferences. Its unofficial character, Hagerup argued, allowed members to serve law and justice first.

In later years, the League of Nations, the United Nations, the International Court of Justice, and the International Law Commission became the principal forums for considering international problems and applying international law. Nevertheless, the Institute of International Law continued to study international issues in an effort to resolve differences among legal systems throughout the world. At its New York plenary session in 1929, the institute adopted a Declaration of the International Rights of Man. In the context of that statement, the organization elucidated the rights of emigration and of admission and reception in order to deal with the persistent problem of refugees, stateless persons, and exiles. These and other institute studies made valuable contributions to the League of Nations Codification Conferences held at The Hague in 1930 and 1931.

At its 1971 annual session in Zagreb, the members passed a series of resolutions dealing with armed conflicts in which United Nations forces might participate. In these articles, the institute recommended application of the humanitarian rules of the 1949 Geneva Convention to hostilities in which United Nations forces might be engaged. Other issues the institute has studied include airline hijackings, the protection of civilian populations from weapons of mass destruction, protection of the seas, measures to be followed in the event of accidental pollution, and situations in which a party has legal grounds not to honor a treaty. From their language and introductory explanations, it is clear that many resolutions resulting from these studies were passed with awareness of the United Nations positions on the case in point and with an eye toward refining, clarifying, or updating that position. More recently, the institute has turned its attention to the problem of bringing multinational entities under the rule of international law and other issues arising from contemporary developments.

International law has been a slowly evolving accretion of treaties, conventions, practices, and customs that govern conduct among nations, and it remains a fragile legal instrument. Within this framework, however, most historians agree that the Institute of International Law played a seminal role in developing the body of law available to the international community. Some would argue that its importance has diminished as more democratic, politically oriented bodies have come to dominate the international lawmaking stage. Some have criticized the institute for its elitism, for the preponderant influence of Western nations and corresponding lack of representation of Third World nations in its deliberations, and for its minor impact on the acceptance and application of international law. Disagreeing with such criticisms, in 1981 the vice president of the International Court of Justice, T. O. Elias, praised the "immense contributions" of the institute and similar societies. The reports of these bodies, he pointed out, "often create landmarks in the development of the law; at least, some of the formulations often constituted the basis of future codification and progressive development of international law by such institutions as the United Nations International Law Commission."

The Institute of International Law, headquartered in Geneva, Switzerland, continues to operate as an unofficial learned society dedicated to the study and improvement of international law. It is funded by annual membership fees and by private grants and donations. Membership, which is attained by recommendation and election, is limited to 132 members and associates. The process is highly selective, and only the most qualified scholars of international law gain admission. As recommended by Oscar Schachter at the 1973 centenary meeting, however, the institute has attempted to make its membership more heterogeneous by recruiting representatives from a wider range of nations.

On the whole, the institute continues to view itself as an academic organization whose role is one "of persuasion and influence." "If our work has had some success," Georg Hagerup told his 1912 Oslo audience, "it is undoubtedly because of our efforts to 'calculate the limits of the possible,' . . . because of our patience in refusing to advocate premature solutions, and because of our belief in the necessity of developing *gradually* and *progressively* as our statutes bid us." However, he said, "The goal, the undisputed and inviolable reign of law in international relations, is most certainly still a long way off."

SELECTED PUBLICATIONS: The Court of Arbitral Justice, 1912; Manual of the Laws of Naval War, 1913; International Law Topics and Discussions, 1914; Resolutions of the Institute of International Law, 1916; Hijacking of Aircraft, 1971; Livre du Centenaire, 1973.

PERIODICALS: (annual) Yearbook/Annuaire.

ABOUT: American Journal of International Law April 1972, October 1978, January 1982; Nussbaum, A. Concise History of the Law of Nations, 1954; Review of Politics July 1957.

INTERNATIONAL COMMITTEE OF THE RED CROSS
(founded 1863)
Nobel Prize for Peace, 1917, 1944
Nobel Prize for Peace, 1963
(shared with League of Red Cross Societies)

The idea of an international movement to aid victims of war and natural disasters is attributed to HENRI DUNANT, a Swiss businessman and humanitarian. In 1859 Dunant hastily assembled a corps of volunteers to treat the wounded in the bloody Battle of Solferino, in northern Italy, when 160,000 French and Italian troops fought an equal number of Austrian soldiers in the long struggle for Italian unification and independence. Dunant's improvised relief work was responsible for saving many of the wounded, for whom he helped find food, water, and medical attention.

In *Un Souvenir de Solferino* (*A Memory of Solferino*), published in 1862, Dunant proposed ways to assist the sick and the wounded during wartime. His book stirred widespread concern over war victims, and in February 1863 the Geneva Public Welfare Society, a small charitable organization providing welfare to the needy and the sick, appointed a five-person committee to study how Dunant's suggestions might be implemented. The committee, which included Dunant, sponsored an international conference in Geneva in October 1863. There, representatives of sixteen nations laid the foundation for the formation of national war relief organizations and unofficially chose a red cross on a white background (the reverse of the Swiss flag) as their emblem. The five-member study committee evolved into the International Committee of the Red Cross (ICRC), the administrative body responsible for coordinating the activities of individual relief groups.

The conference inspired the Swiss government to convene a subsequent conference in Geneva in 1864 to formulate international standards for dealing with war casualties. On August 24 the twelve nations represented signed the Convention for the Amelioration of the Condition of the Wounded and Sick in Armed Forces in the Field. This agreement, also called the 1864 Geneva Convention, guaranteed neutrality for medical personnel and equipment and officially adopted the red cross as the identifying emblem. Eventually, most other nations also agreed to the convention's standards and those of later conventions.

The nascent Red Cross met its first challenge later in 1864, when it cared for the wounded during the conflict between Denmark and Prussia over the duchies of Schleswig and Holstein. It expanded its efforts in the Franco-Prussian War of 1870–1871, even though French officials were not impressed by Dunant's humanitarianism, and France, unlike Prussia, was not motivated by the Geneva Convention.

ICRC activities, although limited, continued through the Russo-Turkish War in 1877, the Serbo-Bulgarian War in 1885, and the Balkan Wars of 1912–1913. During this period, many national Red Cross societies were established. The American Red Cross, for example, was founded in 1881 by Clara Barton, who also served as its first president until 1904. But it was the work of the Red Cross during World War I that was responsible for its development into an international relief agency of major significance.

At the outbreak of the war in August 1914, the ICRC notified national Red Cross societies that it would act as a clearinghouse for messages and gifts sent to prisoners of war. With a volunteer staff of eight, the committee set up the International Prisoners' Relief and Information Agency in Geneva. By September the first major battles of the war had produced thousands of prisoners, and inquiries about missing soldiers poured into the understaffed office. Within several months, the agency had enlisted and trained more than 1,000 new volunteers, who worked in a building lent by the city of Geneva.

During the war, the International Prisoners' Relief and Information Agency listed and traced the names of more than seven million prisoners while tracking hundreds of thousands of others who had been reported missing in action. In addition, it forwarded more than two million parcels to prisons and monitored adherence to the regulations of The Hague Peace Conference of 1907, which governed treatment of prisoners of war. Although ICRC workers lacked authority to enter prison camps, they often obtained permission to do so. As a result of ICRC monitoring, conditions for many prisoners improved significantly. The ICRC also negotiated repatriation agreements under which many prisoners returned home. Others were sent under ICRC care to Switzerland to wait out the war.

For this work, the ICRC received the 1917 Nobel Prize for Peace, the only Nobel Peace Prize awarded during World War I. Although presentation ceremonies were suspended during the war years, the awarding of the prize was announced at a special meeting in Oslo, attended by the king of Norway, members of the Norwegian Nobel Committee, and representatives from the Norwegian Parliament. The secretary of the Norwegian Nobel Committee, Ragnvald Moe, delivered a few words on the origins of the ICRC and on its wartime efforts.

After the armistice, the ICRC repatriated millions of refugees who had been displaced by the fighting. In 1919 the national Red Cross societies, which had worked separately during the war, met to form the LEAGUE OF RED CROSS SOCIETIES (now called the League of Red Cross and Red Crescent Societies), an umbrella organization created to coordinate the activities of the national societies and to extend Red Cross relief to victims of natural disasters. The ICRC, the League of Red Cross Societies, and the national Red Cross societies were known collectively as the International Red Cross. The name was changed in 1986 to the International Movement of the Red Cross and Red Crescent.

Between the two world wars, the ICRC refined the codes protecting prisoners of war. It was instrumental in obtaining ratification of the Prisoner of War Convention in 1929 by all major nations except Japan and the Soviet Union. During this time, the ICRC also worked to alleviate suffering during such conflicts as the Italian-Ethiopian War, which began in 1935, and the Spanish Civil War, which began in 1936.

When World War II broke out in 1939, the

ICRC established the Central Prisoners of War Agency. More than 3,000 agency volunteers handled as many as 200,000 pieces of mail daily. The ICRC delivered more than 34 million parcels and more than 1.3 million books to prisoners. The agency also monitored conditions in prisoner-of-war camps, including some Japanese camps, even though Japan had not ratified the 1929 Prisoner of War Convention.

A joint commission of the ICRC and the League of Red Cross Societies delivered relief shipments to civilians in many war-ravaged nations. Although efforts to aid Jewish victims of the Nazi Holocaust were thwarted by the German government, the ICRC managed to furnish food, clothing, and medical supplies to a few concentration camps. In addition, more than 30,000 Jews received letters of protection from the Red Cross, permitting most bearers to escape.

The ICRC's second Nobel Peace Prize was awarded in 1945 for the year 1944. In his presentation speech, Gunnar Jahn of the Norwegian Nobel Committee quoted the words of PHILIP NOEL-BAKER in which Noel-Baker proposed that the International Committee of the Red Cross be awarded the prize because " 'by its action throughout [World War II the ICRC] has held aloft the fundamental conceptions of the solidarity of the human race, and the identity of the vital interests of different nations and of the need for true understanding and reconciliation, if peace is ever to be brought about.' " Jahn added, "In doing so, [the ICRC] has contributed to the promotion of the concept of that 'fraternity among nations' referred to in Nobel's testament."

Max Huber, a former president of the ICRC, accepted the prize for the organization, and in his acceptance speech he stated, "Although there seems to be a big difference between constructive peace and aid to war victims— indeed, in the eyes of some, an antagonism— there is this implicit and fundamental bond. Helping the victims of war is not the only objective set by the Red Cross; in giving aid, it serves another purpose no less important, that of rescuing in the dark storm of war the idea of human solidarity and respect for the dignity of every human being—precisely at a time when the real or alleged necessities of war push moral values into the background." The Nobel lecture was delivered by Édouard Chapuisat, a Swiss jurist and ICRC member, who offered an account of the activities of the ICRC during World War II.

After World War II, the ICRC helped relocate millions of former prisoners of war and civilian internees. These efforts, which continued until 1948, were facilitated by a Red Cross "travel document" that replaced passports for those whose papers had been lost or invalidated. The ICRC also supervised the allocation of compensation payments for wartime prisoners of Japan and supervised the repatriation of about 75,000 Koreans who had been prisoners of the Japanese.

The ICRC continued to seek more effective protection of noncombatants, especially civilian internees, whose plight was underscored by the full disclosure of the Holocaust. These efforts helped broaden the 1949 Geneva Convention to protect civilian war prisoners, the shipwrecked, and victims of naval warfare.

The limited conflicts that erupted after World War II placed many demands on the Red Cross. During the Korean War, the ICRC assisted prisoners of war and civilians in South Korea but was prohibited from entering North Korea. ICRC officials were involved in repatriation efforts following the July 1953 armistice, accompanying prisoners of war arriving in the south and helping arrange repatriation of 85 Chinese and 600 North Korean soldiers from South Korea, although, again, the officials were not admitted into North Korea.

When Israel, Great Britain, and France invaded Egypt during the Suez crisis of 1956, the ICRC delivered food and other supplies to Port Said, Egypt, and rescued the wounded. During the 1956 Hungarian uprising, it airlifted more than ninety tons of food and medical supplies into Budapest, while the League of Red Cross Societies aided thousands of Hungarian refugees who streamed into Austria. Between 1955 and 1961, during the Algerian revolt against French rule, the ICRC monitored conditions in prisoner-of-war camps, and the league delivered medical supplies, food, and clothing to 285,000 refugees.

When Belgium created the Democratic Republic of the Congo (now Zaire) in 1960 and the secessionist province of Katanga (now Shaba) began a civil war, the ICRC sought to establish neutral medical zones and interceded on behalf of prisoners of war and displaced persons. The league's appeal to various national Red Cross societies summoned more than 100 volunteer doctors and nurses to tend the wounded in the Congo.

The ICRC was awarded a third Nobel Peace Prize in 1963, its centennial year, this time sharing the prize with the League of Red Cross Societies. Léopold Boissier, Swiss jurist and president of the ICRC, represented the organization at the award ceremony and delivered a Nobel lecture in which he discussed aspects of the ICRC's mission. Noting that governments had long considered the existence of the ICRC as useful, he explained, "They know that, in a world where selfish or ideological interests are in conflict, one institution alone stands apart from struggles of this nature, even in the climax of war, and that it will always act, without any thought of self-interest, in complete independence and in obedience to its belief that suffering, being a cruel reality, must be alleviated without prejudice of any kind." Considering the activities of the organization on a moral plane, Boissier commented that the "Red Cross promotes understanding amongst peoples by developing an active sense of brotherhood and by promoting a feeling of mutual responsibility for the good of mankind. . . . The achievements of the Red Cross have a symbolic value and stand out as an example. Its accomplishments at the height of battle are acts of peace."

Since receiving its third Nobel Peace Prize, the ICRC has continued its role as an independent, nonpartisan humanitarian agency. Its activities are governed by twenty-five prominent professional, academic, and business leaders, all of whom must be Swiss citizens, in accordance with the committee's regulations. Committee decisions are carried out by its 500-member headquarters staff and by an additional 500 delegates in the field. Approximately 75 percent of the committee's budget is provided by a contribution from the Swiss government, and the balance is supplied by donations from other governments, the national Red Cross societies, and individual contributors.

The Red Cross as a whole is overseen by the nine-member International Red Cross Commission, which consists of two members from the league, two from the ICRC, and five from the national societies. Every four years, the International Red Cross Conference meets to discuss policy; it is attended by representatives of the league, the ICRC, each national society, and the signatories of the Geneva Conventions.

SELECTED PUBLICATIONS: The Red Cross: Its International Organization, 1930; The International Red Cross Committee in Geneva 1863–1943, 1943; The Work of the International Committee of the Red Cross, 1945; Inter arma Caritas: The Work of the International Committee of the Red Cross During the Second World War, 1947; The International Committee of the Red Cross in Palestine, 1948; The Geneva Conventions (2 vols.) 1950; The ICRC and the Yemen Conflict, 1964.

PERIODICALS: (annual) Annual Report. (monthly) International Review of the Red Cross.

ABOUT: Barton, C. The Red Cross in War and Peace, 1898; Best, S. H. The Story of the British Red Cross, 1938; Bicknell, E. P. Pioneering With the Red Cross, 1935; Bicknell, E. P. With the Red Cross in Europe 1917–22, 1938; Boardman, M. T. Under the Red Cross Flag at Home and Abroad, 1915; Bory, F. Origin and Development of International Humanitarian Law, 1982; Buckingham, C. E. For Humanity's Sake, 1964; Cousier, H. The International Red Cross, 1961; Draper, G. The Red Cross Conventions, 1958; Dunant, H. A Memory of Solferino, 1939; Forsythe, D. Humanitarian Politics, 1977; Gigon, F. The Epic of the Red Cross, 1946; Gumpert, M. Dunant: The Story of the Red Cross, 1938; International Review of the Red Cross August 1963; Joyce, J. A. Red Cross International and the Strategy of Peace, 1959; Junod, M. Warrior Without Weapons, 1951; Magill, J. The Red Cross, the Idea and Development, 1926; Pictet, J. S. Red Cross Principles, 1956.

INTERNATIONAL LABOUR ORGANISATION
(founded April 11, 1919)
Nobel Prize for Peace, 1969

The International Labour Organisation (ILO) was created in 1919 by Part 13 of the Treaty of Versailles at the end of World War I. An autonomous organization of the League of Nations, the ILO had as its original purpose the establishment of international guidelines aimed at improving working conditions, raising labor standards, and promoting economic and social stability throughout the world.

The ILO originated as an outgrowth of nineteenth-century European social reform and the rise of the labor movement. As early as 1864, with the founding of the First International in London, labor leaders demanded international measures to improve working conditions. A series of international labor conferences in Europe during the 1890s led to the founding in 1900 of the International Association for Labour Legislation, a forerunner of the ILO, which gathered and published noteworthy labor legislation from various nations. At the end of World War I, European and United States trade unions, which had grown increasingly influential in the prewar years, demanded a voice in the peace treaty. They succeeded in compelling the Paris Peace Conference to establish the unprecedented International Labour Legislation Commission, through which they participated in the negotiations.

The fifteen-member commission included Samuel Gompers, president of the American Federation of Labor, as chairman; LÉON JOUHAUX, a French labor leader; Harold B. But-

497

ler of Great Britain, later director-general of the ILO; and Eduard Beneš, the foreign minister of Czechoslovakia. The aim of the commission was to secure peace not only among nations but also among classes within nations. This goal is reflected in the ILO constitution, which states that "a universal and lasting peace can be established only if it is based on social justice."

An innovative feature of the ILO—still unique among world organizations—is its tripartite structure, giving representatives of workers and employers an equal voice with those of government in the formulation of policies. Representatives of each member country—two government delegates, one worker delegate, and one employer delegate—convene in the annual International Labour Conference, held usually in Geneva, Switzerland, where the ILO has its headquarters. The first meeting of the conference was held in Washington, D.C., in 1919. There Albert Thomas of France was elected the first ILO director-general. Originally, 45 nations were represented; by 1985 membership had grown to 151.

The principal function of the conference is to formulate and adopt labor standards, called conventions or recommendations, that form the International Labour Code. Conventions require ratification and bind members to put their provisions into practice. Recommendations do not, although they do provide guidance on such matters as policy and legislation. An unusual system of enforcement, pioneered by the ILO, includes a committee of experts that reviews complaints about the degree of compliance to the code practiced by member nations. Their findings are then submitted to the International Labour Conference.

Since 1919, 159 conventions and 169 recommendations have been adopted. The earliest conventions, considered the Magna Charta of the working class, focused on nine points, including the right to a reasonable wage, the establishment of an eight-hour day or forty-eight-hour week, equal pay for men and women for equal work, and a ban on child labor. In subsequent conventions, the ILO has called for abolition of forced labor; elimination of discrimination in employment; and establishment of social security protection, minimum-wage scales, standards of occupational health and safety, and measures to protect migrant and seafaring workers.

In addition to expanding the International Labour Code to meet new needs as they arise, the conference also elects the Governing Body, or executive council, of the ILO. Composed of fifty-six members who serve three-year terms—twenty-eight government representatives and another twenty-eight divided equally between workers and employers—the Governing Body normally holds three sessions a year in Geneva. Its responsibilities include drawing up the agenda for the annual conference and other meetings; electing a director-general, who serves a five-year term; and approving the budget, which is underwritten by contributions from member nations.

The Governing Body also directs the activities of the International Labour Office, the ILO's permanent secretariat in Geneva, which acts as a clearinghouse for a vast array of information on social and economic policy and as a publishing house as well. Among its publications are the bimonthly *Legislative Series,* a selection of labor legislation and regulations formerly published by the International Association for Labour Legislation, and the *Year Book of Labour Statistics.* The ILO employs nearly 2,000 officials representing 110 nationalities and has about 800 technical experts serving around the world.

At an International Labour Conference meeting in the United States in 1944, the year of its twenty-fifth anniversary, the ILO annexed to its constitution the Declaration of Philadelphia, a ringing redefinition of its goals that United States President Franklin D. Roosevelt likened to America's Declaration of Independence. Proclaiming that "poverty anywhere constitutes a danger to prosperity everywhere," the declaration upheld the right of all human beings "to pursue their material well-being and their spiritual development in conditions of freedom and dignity, of economic security and equal opportunity."

After World War II and the dissolution of the League of Nations, the ILO in 1946 became the first specialized agency of the United Nations. Working closely with that organization, the ILO set as a top priority building bridges between the rich nations and the poor nations that attained independence in the wake of the war. A number of subsequent ILO projects have contributed to this goal. The International Institute for Labour Studies, opened in Geneva in 1960, brings together government administrators, trade union officials, and management and industrial experts from all over the world for advanced education and research in social and labor policy. Since opening in 1965, the International Centre for Advanced Technical and Vocational Training in Turin, Italy, has trained personnel from more than 120 countries.

On the fiftieth anniversary of its founding, the ILO was awarded the 1969 Nobel Prize for Peace. In her presentation remarks, Aase Lionæs of the Norwegian Nobel Committee reminded the audience of Alfred Nobel's specification that "the Peace Prize is to be awarded to the person who has done the most to promote fraternity among the nations." She continued, "Beneath the foundation stone of the ILO's main office in Geneva lies a document on which is written: *'Si vis pacem, cole justitiam.'* If you desire peace, cultivate justice. There are few organizations that have succeeded to the extent that the ILO has in translating into action the fundamental moral idea on which it is based."

David A. Morse, then director-general of the ILO, delivered the Nobel lecture. He emphasized the role of social justice in the attainment of world peace and briefly described the ILO's half century of work to build among the nations "an infrastructure of peace." "The ILO has provided the nations of the world with a meeting ground," he stated, "an instrument for cooperation and for dialogue among very different interests, at times when men were more disposed to settle their differences by force than by talk." He also reiterated the two essential features of the ILO's structure: tripartism and universality. Morse concluded by pointing out that "the challenge before us now is to make industrialized societies more human, to make man the master rather than the slave of modern technology, to offer more possibilities for the constructive use of leisure, for greater freedom, for greater participation, for more effective dialogue."

Since 1969, the ILO has continued to introduce and strengthen programs to meet the needs of a rapidly growing world population. In 1976 the World Employment Programme was inaugurated to help developing countries select policies and programs conducive to greater utilization of human resources. For this purpose, specialists have been provided to assist governments on human resource questions, especially in Asia, Africa, and Latin America.

To promote occupational safety and health, the ILO has operated since 1976 the International Programme for the Improvement of Working Conditions and Environment. This program offers assistance to governments, employers' and workers' organizations, and research and training institutes throughout the world in creating safe, healthful workplaces. In this effort, some 700 ILO experts are involved in nearly 500 technical cooperation programs in more than 100 countries.

In the ILO's Medium-Term Plan for 1982–1987, emphasis was placed on improvement of working conditions, development of social security, further development of labor-management relations, and development of vocational and managerial training. Global issues such as rural development, underemployed urban workers, women workers, international migration, and new technologies have increasingly become concerns of the ILO.

SELECTED PUBLICATIONS: ILO: The First Decade, 1931; Partnership for Peace: Workers, Employers, Governments, 1952; Equal Pay for Equal Work, 1960; Discrimination in Employment and Occupation, 1967; The Story of Fifty Years, 1969; The ILO in the Service of Social Progress, 1969; ILO: The Impact of International Labour Conventions, 1976; International Labour Standards: A Worker's Education Manual, 1978; Employment, Trade, and North-South Cooperation, 1981; International Labour Conventions and Recommendations, 1919–1981, 1982.

PERIODICALS: (annual) Year Book of Labour Statistics; CIRF Abstracts. (semiannual) Women at Work. (quarterly) Bulletin of Labour Statistics; Official Bulletin; Labour Education; Social and Labour Bulletin. (bimonthly) ILO-Information; Legislative Series.

ABOUT: Alcock, A. History of the International Labour Organisation, 1971; Galenson, W. The International Labour Organisation—An American View, 1981; Gibberd, K. ILO: The Unregarded Revolution, 1937; Jenks, C. W. Social Justice in the Law of Nations, 1970; Johnston, G. A. The International Labour Organisation, 1970; Landy, E. A. The Effectiveness of International Supervision: Thirty Years of ILO Experience, 1966; Morse, D. A. The Origin and Evolution of the ILO, 1969; Phelan, E. J. Yes and Albert Thomas, 1936; Valticos, N. International Labor Law, 1979.

INTERNATIONAL PEACE BUREAU
(founded 1891)
Nobel Prize for Peace, 1910

The International Peace Bureau (IPB) was founded at a time when pacifism was attracting international attention as an alternative to the burgeoning armaments race among European nations. During the various international peace conferences held late in the nineteenth century, the need for a center of information and a bond of union among the participating nations of the world was recognized. At the International Peace Congress in London in 1890, this idea was put forth by FREDRIK BAJER, a former Danish army officer who had turned to pacifism. At the next International Peace Congress held in Rome in 1891, an organizing committee was named. It charged ÉLIE DU-

COMMUN, a Swiss railway administrator and prominent pacifist, with creating a permanent peace bureau at Bern. The International Peace Bureau began work in December 1891, and its statutes were approved the following year at the fourth International Peace Congress in Chicago.

The bureau was organized as the central office of the International Union of Peace Societies (IUPS) "to coordinate the activities of the peace societies and promote the concept of peaceful settlement of international disputes." Its function was to arrange annual peace conferences, prepare material for discussion, and see that resolutions passed by the congresses were implemented. In the early years, financing of the bureau's activities depended on subsidies from peace societies and on voluntary contributions from individuals. The award of the 1910 Nobel Peace Prize to the bureau helped improve its financial position.

At the presentation of the Peace Prize, Jørgen Løvland of the Norwegian Nobel Committee said, "We are convinced that this award is in the spirit of Alfred Nobel's plan; he wanted his money to be used to support, accelerate, and promote the peace movement. We firmly hope and expect that this year's prize will further this aim and that the fruits of the award will be harvested in the years to come." No Nobel lecture was delivered.

With the outbreak of World War I, the work of the IUPS ended. After the war, the IPB concentrated its efforts on the task of coordinating the peace and humanitarian efforts of nongovernmental organizations and communicating their ideas and proposals to those responsible for governmental decisions and to officials of the League of Nations, whose founding was credited in part to the IPB. In 1924 the bureau moved its headquarters to Geneva in order to be near the league. The bureau continued to organize congresses of pacifists, to add materials to its already extensive library, and to issue publications.

Because the bureau did not operate during World War II, IPB assets were temporarily placed under the supervision of Swiss authorities, as Switzerland was a neutral country. Former member organizations met after the war to reestablish the bureau, and they formed the International Liaison Committee of Organizations for Peace (ILCOP), which in 1961 was recognized by the Swiss Federal Council as the legal successor to the IPB. ILCOP received IPB's assets, while books and archival materials were deposited in the United Nations library in Geneva. The following year,

ILCOP reassumed its original name of International Peace Bureau.

Since World War II, while adhering to its original purpose as stated in its constitution, "to serve the cause of peace by the promotion of international cooperation and the nonviolent solution of international conflicts," the IPB has become somewhat differently oriented. However, it is still involved in promoting communication between member organizations, organizing international peace events, supplying information and other support to member organizations, establishing links to governments, and representing its member organizations at the United Nations level. The IPB has a consultative status with the United Nations Economic and Social Council.

The comprehensive congresses formerly organized by the bureau have been replaced by conferences designed to familiarize participants with specific issues. In connection with these conferences, the bureau prepares documentation and arranges the meeting, which is usually attended by representatives of governments, peace research workers, experts in specific fields, and representatives of peace and other national and international organizations. The bureau then edits, publishes, and distributes a conference report and follows up on conference findings and decisions, often transmitting proposals to governments and intergovernmental bodies. Among subjects studied in this way have been aspects of nonviolence, requirements of a world at peace, United Nations peacekeeping, alternatives to military defense, the right to refuse military service and orders, the call for a world disarmament conference, and the aftereffects of the atomic bombs on Hiroshima and Nagasaki.

A major undertaking of the bureau was a nongovernmental organization conference on disarmament held at Bradford University, England, in 1974. The conference produced the so-called Bradford Proposals, which were published as "A Call for a World Disarmament Conference." This widely distributed manifesto became one of the initiatives that led to the United Nations First Special Session on Disarmament in 1978. Among its proposals were general and complete disarmament as the prime objective of the United Nations; identification of the vested interests opposing disarmament and ways of overcoming their influence; the outlawing of nuclear weapons; the control and licensing of sales and transfers of arms and ammunition; effective machinery for settlement of disputes by the International Court of Justice; and the introduction of steps into the educational process that would mobilize world opinion against war.

Another conference produced a draft convention entitled "The Right to Refuse Military Service and Orders," which, with a draft resolution, was sent to the secretary-general of the United Nations and taken up by some members of the Human Rights Commission. Subsequently, a booklet, "The Right to Refuse to Kill," was published in 1971 and widely distributed.

The question of human rights as a condition of peace has been frequently discussed at IPB-sponsored conferences, especially at the World Congress of Peace Forces in Moscow in 1973. With respect to disarmament, the bureau believes that the mobilization of public opinion is now necessary to persuade governments to take this step. Since 1969 the IPB has served as the secretariat of the Special Nongovernmental Organization Committee on Disarmament and has sponsored several forums on the subject, notably in Helsinki in 1976.

Disarmament negotiations have also been an IPB concern. It promoted the joint statement of Agreed Principles for Disarmament declared by the United States and the Soviet Union in 1961 in which it was stated that all negotiations should be for general and complete disarmament and not merely for arms control or arms limitation. Since then, the bureau has supported meetings between the leaders of the two countries. In addition, the bureau favors ratification of a treaty outlawing the use of nuclear weapons and declaring that their use is a crime against humanity punishable under international law.

Not only the IPB has been honored with a Nobel Peace Prize; numerous individuals closely associated with its work have also been similarly honored. In addition to Bajer and Ducommun, FRÉDÉRIC PASSY, HENRI DUNANT, and ALBERT GOBAT were organizers and leaders of the bureau in its first years. Others involved in its early work were WILLIAM CREMER, BERTHA VON SUTTNER, ERNESTO MONETA, KLAS ARNOLDSON, ALFRED FRIED, TOBIAS ASSER, and HENRI LA FONTAINE, a former IPB president. Later Nobel Peace Prizes went to PHILIP NOEL-BAKER, a bureau vice president; SEAN MACBRIDE, a president; LINUS C. PAULING, a vice president; and ALVA MYRDAL, a vice president.

The bureau publishes conference reports; books and pamphlets on its special interests; and *Geneva Monitor—Disarmament,* which is distributed six times a year to members, other peace organizations, diplomatic missions, research institutes, and a wider public. Membership in the bureau is open to international, national, and local organizations working for peace and international cooperation and to national peace councils or other federations coordinating the peace movements of their countries. Associate membership without voting rights is open to organizations and individuals who support the aims of IPB.

SELECTED PUBLICATIONS: Report on Questions Relating to Nationalities, 1893; Proceedings of the Tenth Universal Peace Congress, 1902; "We the People" and United Nations Peacekeeping, 1966; The International Peace Bureau: History, Aims, Activities, 1969; The Right to Refuse to Kill, 1971; The International Peace Bureau, 1977; Children and War, 1983; Campaigns Against European Peace Movements, 1984.

PERIODICALS: (bimonthly) Geneva Monitor. (irregular) Conference Reports.

ABOUT: American Law Review January 1873; Independent March 19, 1903; Lorimer, J. Studies National and International, 1890.

INTERNATIONAL PHYSICIANS FOR THE PREVENTION OF NUCLEAR WAR
(founded December 1980)
Nobel Prize for Peace, 1985

International Physicians for the Prevention of Nuclear War (IPPNW), a worldwide federation of medical doctors and health professionals, was founded in 1980 to mobilize professional medical opinion against the threat of nuclear warfare. Its founders, Bernard Lown, a professor of cardiology at the Harvard School of Public Health, and Yevgeny Chazov, director-general of the Cardiology Research Center in Moscow, are internationally renowned physicians. The two men shared common interests in cardiology and Soviet-American relations from the time they met in 1960, and they collaborated in Moscow on research into the mechanism of sudden death.

Bernard Lown became interested in the medical aspects of nuclear war after hearing PHILIP NOEL-BAKER give a speech about the nuclear arms race in 1961. Shortly afterward, Lown and several other physicians founded Physicians for Social Responsibility, which Lown served as first president. It later became one of the major affiliates of IPPNW. In 1979 Lown proposed to Chazov that they organize an international movement of physicians against the nuclear arms race as part of their professional duty to "address the greatest threat to human life." Meeting the next year in Geneva, they founded IPPNW in collaboration with four other physicians, two Soviet and two American. Among the guiding principles the group adopted were agreements to restrict its focus to nuclear war, to include physicians from all over the world, and to refrain from either supporting or attacking the position of any government.

The federation, sometimes popularly called Doctors Against Nuclear War, maintains headquarters in Boston and London. By 1985 it had more than 135,000 members in forty-one countries, including 28,000 in the United States and 60,000 in the Soviet Union. Since its founding, IPPNW has held annual international congresses to publicize the medical aspects of nuclear war. At its third meeting, held in Amsterdam in 1983, the federation wrote and ratified a constitution and created a new structure that placed governance of the organization in an international council. The council consists of one representative from each national affiliate. It elects copresidents from the United States and the Soviet Union and an executive committee.

In addition to the international congresses, IPPNW has undertaken a variety of programs aimed at alerting the public to the dangers of the nuclear arms race. It has issued what it calls a "medical prescription" for a moratorium on all nuclear testing. It has advocated a verifiable freeze on the development and deployment of all atomic weapons, a declaration of no-first-use by the world's nuclear powers, and a diversion of funds from developing nuclear weaponry to solving such critical problems as poverty, illiteracy, and disease.

In June 1982 six American and Soviet physicians participated in an unprecedented hour-long discussion on Soviet National Television of the medical aspects of nuclear war. The program, sponsored by IPPNW, was broadcast to 100 million viewers throughout the Soviet Union and was later aired in the United States and Europe. The same year, the group published *Last Aid: The Medical Dimensions of Nuclear War*, a collection of essays by American, Soviet, British, and Japanese medical experts that was widely circulated and used as a text in many universities and medical schools.

Since then, in collaboration with the Center for Nuclear Psychology, IPPNW has cosponsored a study of the reactions of American and Soviet children to the threat of nuclear war. At the center of its educational activities is the

Soviet-American Physicians Campaign, in which teams of doctors tour each other's countries to speak at medical meetings and public forums. The IPPNW encourages its affiliates to carry out programs on a national basis, and it supports this work by supplying them with medical and scientific papers, pamphlets, posters, audiovisual materials, and two regularly published periodicals. In 1984, in recognition of its efforts "to inform public opinion and mobilize the conscience of mankind for peace," IPPNW was awarded the Peace Education Prize of the United Nations Educational, Scientific, and Cultural Organization (UNESCO).

In October of the following year, the Norwegian Nobel Committee announced that the IPPNW had been awarded the 1985 Nobel Prize for Peace. "This organization has performed considerable service to mankind by spreading authoritative information and by creating an awareness of the catastrophic consequences of atomic warfare," the Nobel committee stated. The official statement continued, "The committee believes that this, in turn, contributes to an increase in the pressure of public opposition to the proliferation of atomic weapons and to a redefining of priorities, with greater attention being paid to health and other humanitarian issues. Such an awakening of public opinion as is now apparent both in the East and the West, in the North and in the South, can give the present arms limitation negotiations new perspectives and a new seriousness. In this connection, the committee attaches particular importance to the fact that the organization was formed as a result of a joint initiative by Soviet and American physicians and that it now draws support from physicians in over forty countries all over the world." The committee invited Bernard Lown and Yevgeny Chazov, copresidents of IPPNW, to receive the prize on behalf of their organization.

Lown is a pioneer in research on sudden cardiac death and the inventor of the cardioverter and the defibrillator, a machine that stimulates a damaged heart into resuming a regular beat. He was one of the first doctors to prescribe the drug lidocaine, later used worldwide, to control disturbances of the heartbeat. He has also investigated the role of psychological and behavioral factors in the regulation of the heart. He is a native of Lithuania, a graduate of the University of Maine and the Johns Hopkins University School of Medicine, and the author of two books and more than 300 scientific articles.

In his acceptance speech in Oslo on December 10, Lown stated, "If we are to succeed in our goal of ridding military arsenals of instruments of genocide, we need the extraordinary energizing strength that comes when mind and heart are joined to serve humankind. We physicians who shepherd human life from birth to death have a moral imperative to resist with all our being the drift toward the brink."

Chazov, besides directing one of the world's largest heart centers, is Soviet deputy public health minister and chief of the Fourth Administration of the Ministry of Health, the agency responsible for the health care of top Soviet leaders. In this post, which he has held since 1967, he is known popularly as the Kremlin Doctor. He has written more than 300 articles as well as several books on cardiology, including a description of his efforts to develop compounds that may help dissolve potentially fatal blood clots. A member of the Communist party's Central Committee since 1982, he has received many Soviet awards for his achievements in the field of medicine. He is also chairman of the Soviet Committee of Physicians for the Prevention of Nuclear War, the Soviet counterpart of the American Physicians for Social Responsibility.

"True to the Hippocratic oath," he stated in his Nobel acceptance speech, "we cannot keep silent knowing what the final epidemic—nuclear war—can bring to humankind. The bell of Hiroshima rings in our hearts not as a funeral knell but as an alarm bell calling out to actions to protect life on our planet." The award of the Peace Prize to IPPNW, he said, "invigorates all the forces calling for the eradication of nuclear weapons from the earth."

Almost on the eve of the presentation ceremony in Oslo, the award provoked a heated controversy over Chazov, even though the IPPNW, not Chazov, was the prizewinner. Joined by Chancellor Helmut Kohl of West Germany, ten European leaders from Christian Democratic or affiliated parties asked that the medal not be given to the Soviet doctor because in 1973 he had, along with twenty-four other members of the Soviet Academy, signed a letter denouncing Soviet physicist and dissident ANDREI SAKHAROV for anti-Soviet activities. In reply, Chazov noted that the Nobel Prize was not a personal tribute to him. He also pointed out that the letter was merely an expression of a difference of opinion with Sakharov.

Undaunted by the protests and gestures of disapproval, Egil Aarvik of the Norwegian Nobel Committee announced, "We have not forgotten Sakharov. The prize was not a reward to Dr. Chazov for signing that letter. The prize was for the organization, because it bridged the ideology gap and because it brought people together."

PERIODICALS: (quarterly) IPPNW Report. (three a year) IPPNW Update.

ABOUT: Adams, R., and Cullen, S. (eds.) The Final Epidemic, 1981; Chazov, E. I., et al. The Danger of Nuclear War: Soviet Physicians' Viewpoint, 1982; New England Journal of Medicine May 31, 1962; New York Times December 6, 1981; October 12, 1985; December 12, 1985; December 15, 1985; December 31, 1985; Warner, G., and Shuman, M. Citizen Diplomat, 1987.

JACOB, FRANÇOIS

(June 17, 1920–   )
Nobel Prize for Physiology or Medicine, 1965
(shared with André Lwoff and Jacques Monod)

The French biologist François Jacob (zhə kôb') was born in Nancy, to Simon Jacob, a merchant, and Thérèse (Franck) Jacob. After receiving his elementary school education near home, he attended the Lycée Carnot in Paris. An excellent student who wanted to become a surgeon, Jacob enrolled in the University of Paris (the Sorbonne), but his medical studies were interrupted in 1940 when the German army invaded France. He escaped, joined the Free French forces in London, and served during World War II as a medical officer with General Paul Leclerc in North Africa and later with the United States Second Armored Division in Normandy. Both in Africa and in Normandy he was wounded, sustaining severe injuries to his hands that prevented his becoming a surgeon. Jacob was awarded the highest French military honors, including the War Cross and the Companion of the Liberation.

Returning to the Sorbonne after the war, Jacob received his medical degree in 1947. Continuing his studies, Jacob became an assistant at the Pasteur Institute in 1950, working under ANDRÉ LWOFF. At the time, Lwoff was studying lysogenic bacteria, which are destroyed when infected with bacteriophages, virus particles that infect bacterial cells. The multiplication of bacteriophages within the cell causes lysis (destruction) of the cell and the release of phage particles. Lwoff had shown that the bacteriophage first exists in the bacterial cell in a noninfectious, or temperate, phase, which he called the prophage. Lyso-

503

FRANÇOIS JACOB

genic bacteria and the concept of the prophage were the subjects of Jacob's doctoral dissertation, for which he received a Ph.D. from the University of Paris in 1954. His research efforts for the next ten years were devoted to investigating the cellular genetics of bacteria.

The science of genetics originated with Gregor Mendel's studies of the laws of inheritance in the nineteenth century. Mendel suggested that an organism inherits its physical traits through "elements," now called genes. By the beginning of the twentieth century, it was known that genes reside on chromosomes in the nucleus of the cell; during the next several decades, biochemists gradually determined the chemical structure of the nucleic acids—ribonucleic acid (RNA) and deoxyribonucleic acid (DNA). In the 1940s it was found that genes are made of DNA, which directs the biochemistry of the cell. After FRANCIS CRICK and JAMES D. WATSON deduced the chemical structure of DNA in 1953, it was possible to learn not only how the DNA molecule duplicates itself but also how traits are inherited by means of the genetic code contained in DNA.

During the early 1950s at the Pasteur Institute, Jacob and his colleague Élie Wollman determined that the bacterial cell chromosome is a circular structure attached to the membrane of the cell and that smaller genetic fragments may be added to or subtracted from it. Near the end of the decade Jacob, working with JACQUES MONOD, discovered one of the three types of RNA, messenger RNA (the other two types are ribosomal RNA and transfer RNA). Each of the three performs a specific

function in the normal gene control sequence—from DNA to RNA to the manufacture of protein. Messenger RNA receives genetic information from DNA lodged in the nucleus of the cell and conveys it to ribosomes—the sites of protein synthesis—in the cytoplasm, the protoplasm of the cell outside the nucleus. Transfer RNA carries amino acids, the building blocks of protein, to the ribosomes. The blueprint carried by messenger RNA orders the amino acids in the correct sequence to form protein molecules.

Furthermore, Jacob and Monod discovered that DNA contains two different types of genes, structural and regulatory. Structural genes transmit the genetic code from one generation of cells to the next and direct protein synthesis. Regulatory genes communicate with the structural genes and regulate all biochemical processes of the cell, enabling it to adapt to environmental changes, for example, to a change in the supply or type of nutrients available to it. In a stable environment, the regulatory genes inhibit or suppress the structural genes. When the environment changes, the structural genes are activated to adapt the cell to the new conditions. Jacob and Monod called the sets of structural and regulatory genes operons, and the gene responsible for suppression and activation the operator gene.

In the course of their work, Jacob and his colleagues established that bacteriophage particles contain structural and regulatory genes. During the noninfectious prophage phase of the bacteriophage, the structural gene responsible for phage replication is inhibited or suppressed. Lwoff had shown that ultraviolet light can induce phage multiplication, leading to bacterial cell disintegration, or lysis, by activating the structural gene that causes the phage to multiply.

Jacob and his associates at the Pasteur Institute adhere to the viral theory of carcinogenesis, or cancer production. They believe that viral particles may lie dormant in human cells as the prophage does in bacterial cells and that the cancer-causing potential of the virus may later be induced by a variety of factors. Once activated, the virus can insert itself into the biochemical machinery of the cell, causing cancerous growth.

The Pasteur Institute appointed Jacob chief of its department of cellular genetics in 1960, and four years later the Collège de France established a chair for him in cellular genetics.

Jacob shared the 1965 Nobel Prize for Physiology or Medicine with Lwoff and Monod "for their discoveries concerning genetic control of enzyme and virus synthesis.'' Before these discoveries, ''it was not known how the genetic information was put into effect or transformed into chemical activity,'' said Sven Gard of the Karolinska Institute in his presentation speech. ''The French workers were able to demonstrate how the structural information of the genes was used chemically.'' Their efforts, Gard said, have ''opened up a field of research which in the truest sense of the word can be described as molecular biology.''

In 1947 Jacob married Lise Bloch, a pianist; they have four children.

Jacob's many honors included the Charles Leopold Mayer Prize of the French Academy of Sciences (1962). He is a member of the French Academy of Sciences and a foreign member of the Royal Society of London, the Danish Academy of Sciences and Letters, and the American Academy of Arts and Sciences.

SELECTED WORKS: Sexuality and the Genetics of Bacteria, 1961; Viruses and Genes, 1961, with Élie Wolman; The Logic of Life, 1974; The Possible and the Actual, 1982.

ABOUT: Borek, E., and Monod, J. (eds.) Of Microbes and Life, 1971; Current Biography December 1966; Lwoff, A., and Ullman, A. (eds.) Origins of Molecular Biology, 1979; New York Times October 15, 1965; New Yorker January 13, 1975; Science October 22, 1965; Scientific American July 1956.

JENSEN, J. HANS D.

(June 25, 1907–February 11, 1973)
Nobel Prize for Physics, 1963
(shared with Maria Goeppert Mayer and
    Eugene P. Wigner)

The German physicist Johannes Hans Daniel Jensen was born in Hamburg to Karl Jensen, a gardener, and the former Helene Ohm. The boy's early brilliance in school led to a scholarship to the *Oberrealschule* in Hamburg. He graduated in 1926 and went on to study physics, mathematics, physical chemistry, and philosophy at the universities of Freiburg and Hamburg. After earning his Ph.D. in physics at the University of Hamburg in 1932, he remained as a scientific assistant, was awarded a doctor of science degree in 1936, and became a privatdocent (unsalaried lecturer) in 1937. Jensen became professor of theoretical physics at the Technical University of Hannover in 1941, then professor of physics at the University of Heidelberg in 1949 where he was appointed dean of the science faculty in 1955. He became professor emeritus in 1969.

J. HANS D. JENSEN

Jensen's early research concerned the theory of materials (quantum-mechanical studies of ionic lattices, the systematic arrangements of atoms in crystals) and their properties under extremely high pressures. The work on ionic lattices led in 1947 to an investigation of the recoil distribution of nuclear radiation in molecules and crystals (the backward movement of radioactive atoms locked in a lattice when their nuclei emit a particle or ray, akin to the recoil of a rifle upon discharging a bullet). The significance of these studies was underscored in 1958 by RUDOLF L. MÖSSBAUER's discovery of recoilless emission of gamma rays in which the gamma ray carries all the energy of the nuclear transition and so is very sharply defined (the Mössbauer effect).

From the outset of his career, Jensen was aware of the emerging views of the nucleus. After the discovery of the neutron by the English physicist JAMES CHADWICK in 1932, the nucleus was shown to consist of protons (heavy particles with a unit positive charge of electricity) and neutrons (particles almost identical in mass to the protons but without electric charge). Many models were proposed for a nuclear structure of protons and neutrons that would explain nuclear behavior. In particular, early observations showed that nuclei with certain numbers (dubbed ''magic'' by EUGENE P. WIGNER) were unusually stable (unlikely to change to other nuclei by radioactive emissions or to engage in nuclear reactions) and relatively abundant (stability and abundance are related since stable nuclei tend to persist and accumulate). In 1933 the German physicist Walter Elsasser suggested a model of protons and neutrons somehow in orbital motion, with the orbits corresponding to discrete energies in accordance with quantum theory. As protons or neutrons are added to the nucleus, the number of orbits multiplies. The orbital energies are not equally spaced, but cluster in groups, or shells, with relatively large energy gaps between shells. When an added proton or neutron occupies the last allowed energy level in a shell, the shell is said to be closed, and the nucleus is especially stable. Removal of a nucleon (the collective name for protons and neutrons) is difficult from a closed shell, and the addition of a nucleon requires the relatively large energy necessary to step up to the beginning of the next shell. Elsasser's model had some success in describing a few light nuclei but failed for heavier nuclei or nuclei in highly excited states.

Physicists were encouraged to think in terms of shells because of an analogous situation in the atom as a whole concerning the electrons moving about the nucleus. (Refined quantum theory rejects the appealingly simple picture, first proposed by NIELS BOHR, of electrons orbiting at various discrete distances from the nucleus, but the model can still be useful.) The energies of the electrons, associated with their positions and motions, are quantized—that is, they have only certain discrete values, or energy levels. The energies are associated particularly with the angular momenta of the electrons related to their orbital motion. Quantum theory (whose predictions are confirmed by observations) prescribes a specific number of energy levels to each allowed angular momentum. In addition, electrons spin around their own axes like tops. Since moving electrons constitute an electric current, they generate a magnetic field. Just as two magnets attract or repel each other, the angular momenta and the spins of the electrons interact (spin-orbit coupling), tending to line up in the same direction. The result is additional possible energy levels.

The atomic energy levels cluster naturally in shells separated by relatively large steps of energy between the electron that fills one shell and the electron that begins the next higher shell. A closed shell signifies stability, in this case, chemical stability, since chemical reactions are associated with the loss, gain, or sharing of electrons. The shell model explains the periodic table, which arranges elements according to atomic number and groups them according to similarity of chemical behavior. The table shows that properties recur in cycles, or periods, as the atomic number rises. For certain numbers, the atoms are particularly stable, for example, those of the elements called noble gases, such as helium, neon, argon, xenon, and radon, which are chemically almost inert. The periodic recurrence of chemical properties, related to the filling of shells and the beginning of new ones, follows naturally from the principles of quantum physics applied to electronic energy levels.

Jensen's consideration of the possibility of shells in nuclear structure increased when the geochemist Hans E. Suess and the experimental nuclear physicist Otto Haxel asked him to try to account for the peculiar regularities they had observed in their different fields. Suess had noted an unusual abundance of certain elements and their isotopes (nuclei of atoms that have the same number of protons but different numbers of neutrons). He had discussed this with Haxel, who had observed unusual nuclear behavior in the same isotopes. Abundance and nuclear stability coincided in nuclei that had magic numbers of protons or neutrons. At the time, however, Jensen did not know what to make of the idea of magic numbers and was not thoroughly convinced of their importance.

The outbreak of World War II hampered Jensen's investigations and, as he put it, "brought the physicists in Germany into a stifling isolation." A few years after the war, he was able to resume visits to Copenhagen and discussions with Niels Bohr, whom he held in high regard.

In Copenhagen, Jensen read a paper by MARIA GOEPPERT MAYER, titled "On Closed Shells in Nuclei," which presented empirical evidence she had gathered suggesting the significance of the magic numbers. Her paper rekindled his interest in the topic. Among the models he considered was a nucleus of orbiting protons and neutrons with strong spin-orbit coupling. This notion was contrary to the prevailing opinions of leading physicists, some of whom had argued persuasively that such strong coupling was unlikely to exist in the nucleus. As Jensen said, "Fortunately, I was not too well versed" in this view and "did not remember the old arguments against a strong spin-orbit coupling too well." Despite some early success in predicting a higher magic number, he felt uncomfortable being in conflict with the mainstream and was not surprised when a serious journal rejected a letter on his findings as "not really physics but rather playing with numbers."

Gaining confidence from discussions with

Bohr and others, Jensen developed his theory of nuclear energy levels related to orbital angular moments and the effect of nucleon spin and was able to explain the existence of all seven known magic numbers: 2, 8, 20, 28, 50, 82, 126. The scheme somewhat resembled that for atomic electrons, but required necessary modifications because of the differences between the nucleus and the atom as a whole. For example, the electrons are relatively distant from the nucleus and each other (the atom is largely empty space), whereas the nucleons are closely packed. The forces on the electrons are the well-known electric forces, which can act at long distances. The forces between nucleons were more mysterious in the 1950s, acted only at very close range, and then were about a million times stronger than the electric forces. The electrons moved within a field of forces that included a center of attraction in the positively charged nucleus. Within the nucleus, there was no such obvious center.

When Jensen submitted his paper on nuclear shell theory for publication in the *Physical Review* in 1949, he learned that Mayer had independently reached the same conclusions and had also submitted a paper to the same journal. The papers were published in consecutive issues. Jensen and Mayer eventually met in Germany, became friends, and collaborated on a book, *Elementary Theory of Nuclear Shell Structure* (1955). Their theory explained the excitation of nuclei by incident particles and gamma rays, predicted that so-called magic nuclei would not readily capture slow neutrons, and indicated that numerous nuclear isomers should exist for nuclei with large values of angular momentum. (Isomers are nuclei that have the same numbers of protons and neutrons but differ in state of excitation and rate of radioactive decay.) The predictions were later experimentally confirmed.

Jensen and Mayer shared half of the 1963 Nobel Prize for Physics "for their discoveries concerning nuclear shell structure." The other half was awarded to Eugene P. Wigner. In his presentation speech, Ivar Waller of the Royal Swedish Academy of Sciences declared that Mayer's and Jensen's discoveries had "cast new light on the structure of atomic nuclei" and constituted "a most striking advance in the correlation of nuclear properties."

In his Nobel lecture, Jensen referred to the wartime isolation of physicists in Germany, his discussions with Haxel and Suess over the significance of the magic numbers, and his encounter with Mayer's paper after the war.

Encouraged by her findings, Jensen said, he met with Bohr, and "from that hour I began to consider seriously the possibility of a 'demagification' of the 'magic numbers.'"

In addition to the work for which he received the Nobel Prize, Jensen investigated the so-called giant resonance in the nuclear photoeffect and, in 1955, suggested the so-called gamma invariance of the weak interaction (the "weak" force is related to radioactivity, in contrast to the "strong" force that holds nucleons together). The latter involved questions of violations of the law of parity, a rule governing the conservation of certain symmetries when a nucleus undergoes a transition. (CHEN NING YANG and TSUNG-DAO LEE were awarded the Nobel Prize for Physics in 1957 when they showed theoretically the possible significance of violations of the law of parity, argued that no experiments had yet checked weak interactions for parity conservation, and suggested new experiments.)

Jensen was a visiting professor of physics at the University of Wisconsin in 1951; at the Institute for Advanced Study in Princeton, New Jersey, in 1952; at the University of California at Berkeley in 1952; at Indiana University in 1953; at the University of Minnesota in 1956; and at the University of California at La Jolla in 1961.

Known as a modest, reticent man, Jensen, who remained a bachelor, lived in an apartment above the Institute for Theoretical Physics in Heidelberg. He enjoyed tending the institute's garden and raising pet turtles. He served as coeditor of the journal *Zeitschrift für Physik* (Journal of Physics) from 1955 until his death on February 11, 1973.

Jensen was a member of the Heidelberg Academy of Sciences and the Max Planck Society and held an honorary degree from the Technical University of Hannover.

ABOUT: New York Times November 6, 1963; Science November 15, 1963.

JENSEN, JOHANNES
(January 20, 1873–November 25, 1950)
Nobel Prize for Literature, 1944

The Danish novelist Johannes Vilhelm Jensen was born in the town of Farso, in the Himmerland region of northern Jutland. He was the second son of Hans Jensen, the district veterinarian, and Marie (Kirstine) Jensen. His father's wide-ranging interests in science, history, anthropology, and other subjects stimulated young Jensen's intellectual curiosity and encouraged him to read avidly during childhood. Growing up in the desolate, windswept Himmerland region, Jensen acquired a deep love for the natural world and a lasting interest in Danish peasant life. Until the age of eleven, he was taught by his mother. For two years, he attended the local school, followed by private tutoring and preparatory study for the Viborg Cathedral School, which he entered in 1890.

Three years later, Jensen was admitted to the University of Copenhagen, where he studied medicine and the natural sciences. Throughout his years in school, Jensen took a greater interest in literature than in his formal studies. In addition to Danish writers, he read Heinrich Heine, Émile Zola, and William Shakespeare. It was during these years that KNUT HAMSUN's novels began to appear. "He made a huge impression . . . through his style and the entirely new attitude he assumed toward life," Jensen wrote later. Perhaps even more influential was RUDYARD KIPLING, whose writings, Jensen said, "threw open the gates to the big wide world" and inspired in him a lifelong love of travel and faraway places.

To support himself as a student, Jensen wrote a series of ten detective novels, serialized in a weekly periodical under the pen name Ivar Lykke. During this time he also began a serious novel, *Danskere* (Danes), which was published in 1896. With his earnings from the book, Jensen made a brief visit to the United States that year. He was fascinated by American life and saw in the nation's reliance on technology a fulfillment of what he considered to be the evolutionary impulse of the human race in the direction of progress. He was particularly interested in observing how Danish immigrants had adapted to the New World. After returning to Copenhagen, he wrote *Einar Elkær,* an intensely introspective novel about a young man's futile quest for love and a new life. The book was well received when it appeared in 1897, but Jensen later dissociated himself from the preoccupation with self-expression that is found in these early novels.

Encouraged by his success, Jensen abandoned the study of medicine in 1898 and became a correspondent for the Danish newspaper *Politiken* (Politics), which dispatched him to Spain to cover the Spanish-American War. He then served a brief period of compulsory military service, followed by a trip to Paris and, in 1902–1903, a trip around the world, all the time continuing to produce fiction and con-

JOHANNES JENSEN

tribute articles to *Politiken.* After his marriage to Else Marie Ulrik in 1904, he settled in Copenhagen and eventually became the father of three sons.

The first of Jensen's works to attract substantial critical attention was *Himmerlandsfolk* (Himmerland People, 1898), a collection of realistic stories about the people of his native Jutland. Subsequent volumes—*Nye Himmerlandshistorier* (New Himmerland Stories, 1904) and *Himmerlandshistorier, Tredie Samling* (Himmerland Stories, Third Collection, 1910)—continued in the same vein. In his three-volume novel *Kongens Fald* (*The Fall of the King,* 1901), Jensen blended mythical and realistic elements in a fictional account of the life of Danish King Christian II. It is generally considered Denmark's greatest historical novel. During this time, Jensen's first collection of poems, *Digte* (Poems, 1906), also appeared.

Setting out on another trip around the world in 1912, Jensen traveled to Ceylon (now Sri Lanka), Singapore, Peking, Mongolia, and finally New York City, from which he embarked for Copenhagen, arriving home April 1914. His vivid impressions and thoughts about travel were the subject of *Introduktion til vor Tidsalder* (Introduction to Our Epoch), which was published in 1915.

Between 1908 and 1922 Jensen published the six-volume cycle *Den lange rejse* (*The Long Journey,* 1922–1924), a large-scale fictional rendering of his evolutionary theories. In these novels, Jensen depicted the rigors of nature as the force that drives humanity to seek an ideal lost land. The cycle begins with the early inhabitants of primeval Jutland and culminates with the discovery of the New World by Christopher Columbus. Antecedents for certain aspects of *The Long Journey* can be found in the early volumes of *Myter* (Myths), a series of eleven books published between 1907 and 1944. Not strictly myths, but rather a wide variety of prose sketches, they present Jensen's impressions of the world as well as his scientific and philosophical notions.

A third period of extended travel began in 1925, when Jensen set out for Egypt, Palestine, and North Africa. He returned in 1928 and completed *Åndens Stadier* (The Stages of the Mind), a philosophical treatment of his ideas about evolution and human development, which was published later that year. Although he continued to write fiction and poetry, Jensen now devoted more effort to essays based on his own extrapolations from Darwinian theory. Because his scientific training was often unequal to his ambitious theorizing, the essays are more highly regarded for their prose style than for their scientific content. Jensen also issued expanded editions of his poems in 1917, 1921, 1923, and 1948.

Jensen visited the United States again in 1939, but illness forced him to return to Denmark after only a few months. He considered himself essentially apolitical but was strongly critical of Fascism and anti-Semitism. After the German army invaded Denmark in 1940, he destroyed his diaries and much of his personal correspondence.

Jensen was awarded the 1944 Nobel Prize for Literature "for the rare strength and fertility of his poetic imagination, with which is combined an intellectual curiosity of wide scope and a bold, freshly creative style." Because of World War II, no presentation ceremonies were held in Stockholm that year. A luncheon was given in New York under the auspices of the American-Scandinavian Foundation.

At the official ceremonies in 1945, Anders Österling of the Swedish Academy gave the presentation address. He said of Jensen, "He has constructed a vast and imposing literary oeuvre, comprising the most diverse genres: epic and lyric, imaginative and realistic works, as well as historical and philosophical essays. . . . His example reveals to us both the attraction of the primitive for a sensitive man and the necessity of transforming brute force into tenderness."

In his acceptance speech, Jensen paid tribute not only to Alfred Nobel but also to Carl Linnaeus, the Swedish botanist whose "designation of species," he said, "was the foun-

dation which subsequently enabled Darwin to form his conclusions on their origin." Jensen continued writing "myths" and essays until his death in Copenhagen in 1950.

Widely admired as a leading exponent of naturalistic literature in Denmark, Jensen was referred to by Knut Hamsun as "a visionary by means of all his five senses." Also highly regarded by other contemporaries, Jensen was described by the American writer Hamilton Basso in 1945 as "a Danish writer whose position in his country is comparable to that of SIGRID UNDSET in hers and of THOMAS MANN in pre-Nazi Germany." Nonetheless, Basso compared Jensen to a pitcher who is brought from the minor leagues to star in the majors, commenting, "Jensen isn't as good as that, prize or no prize, but . . . he doesn't belong in the Buckeye League, either." In a more enthusiastic appraisal written a decade later, one of Jensen's biographers, Marion Nielsen, notes that "few writers have done so much to interpret in imaginative terms the past of their own race and to point up the interdependence of past, present, and future. And perhaps no writer has caught the intimate charm of the Danish nature quite as he has." Many of today's specialists in Scandinavian literature continue to regard Jensen's work highly. For instance, in an essay published in 1980, the Danish-American scholar Sven H. Rossel wrote that "Jensen's production, one of the most important in European literature, combines the present with eternity in a mythical vision."

ADDITIONAL WORKS IN ENGLISH TRANSLATION: Friis, O. (ed.) A Book of Danish Verse, 1922; Fire and Ice, 1923; The Cimbrians, 1923; Christopher Columbus, 1924; The Waving Rye, 1958.

ABOUT: Claudi, J. Contemporary Danish Authors, 1952; Heepe, E., and Heltburg, N. (eds.) Modern Danish Authors, 1946; Nielsen, M. L. Denmark's J. V. Jensen, 1955; Rossel, S. H. Johannes V. Jensen, 1984.

JERNE, NIELS K.

(December 23, 1911–)
Nobel Prize for Physiology or Medicine, 1984
(shared with Georges Köhler and César Milstein)

The English immunologist Niels Kai Jerne (yûrn′ ə) was born in London to Else Marie (Lindberg) and Hans Jessen Jerne; he is both a British subject and a Danish citizen by reason of his birthplace and parentage. At the beginning of World War I the family moved to the Netherlands, where Jerne eventually received his baccalaureate in Rotterdam in 1928, at the age of seventeen.

In 1943 Jerne was employed as a research worker at the Danish State Serum Institute. After studying physics at the University of Leiden for two years, he transferred to the University of Copenhagen, where he presented his thesis on the strength and affinity of antibodies and received his medical degree in 1951.

Jerne continued as a research worker at the Danish State Serum Institute until 1956. The study of antibodies (and other features of the immune system) was a major field of research at the institute. In the late nineteenth century EMIL VON BEHRING had shown that blood serum contains antibodies, substances that chemically attack foreign bodies or antigens. In general, an antibody will bind onto a specific antigen; thus antibody-antigen interactions are specific. It was learned that the animal body produces large numbers of antibodies the first time it is exposed to an unfamiliar antigen. Jerne discovered that if the animal body continues to be exposed to the antigen, there is a change in the form of antibodies, with the newer antibodies binding more tightly to the antigen than the earlier forms had.

Through this early research, Jerne showed that antibodies are not just molecular bodies that happen to interact with antigens but components of a dynamic immune system. He pointed out that the main issue was not how the body produces specific antibodies against a previously unknown antigen but how the body controls the production of a series of specific antibodies.

The question of antibody specificity arose from the research of KARL LANDSTEINER in the 1930s. Landsteiner found that he could stimulate mice to produce antibodies that were specific for tens of thousands of different chemicals. Most researchers did not accept the idea that the animals contained millions of different preformed antibodies from which the specific antibody for a given antigen could be selected. It seemed more logical to conclude that the immune system used the antigen as a template to design an antibody as it was needed for an invader.

Jerne, however, did not agree with these "instructional" theories. He suggested that as the immune response developed, the antibodies were being selected, or progressively modified. Indeed, "the phenomenon had Darwinian overtones," he wrote later. It seemed as though the antibodies were being evolved

NIELS K. JERNE

by natural selection. Jerne continued his work on avidity, or antigen binding, at the Danish State Serum Institute until 1954; he then spent a year as a research fellow at the California Institute of Technology at Pasadena, where he worked with MAX DELBRÜCK.

During his stay in the United States, Jerne formulated a theory of selective antibody production. He suggested that the blood always contains a wide variety of antibodies and, further, that when an antibody happens to bind to an antigen, the resultant combination is recognized by white blood cells, which then make additional copies of the bound antibody. In 1957 MACFARLANE BURNET elaborated on Jerne's theory; he hypothesized that every antibody-producing cell can produce only one type of antibody that is specific for a single antigen. Clones of these cells are stimulated to produce large numbers of antibodies when they encounter their specific antigens.

Burnet's clonal selection theory (which was also investigated by JOSHUA LEDERBERG and David Talmadge of the University of California) dominated immunological thinking in the late 1950s. Jerne's major role in this transformation was as a theoretician, clarifying the consequences of various suggestions and proposing a clear, uniform terminology that enabled immunologists to communicate their ideas more effectively.

Jerne performed little research between 1956 and 1962, during which time he headed the sections of biological standards and of immunology at the headquarters of the World Health Organization in Geneva. He also served as a member of the biophysics department of the University of Geneva from 1960 to 1962, after which he joined the faculty of the University of Pittsburgh as head of the microbiology department.

In 1966 Jerne moved to Goethe University in Frankfurt, where he directed the Paul Ehrlich Institute. While in Frankfurt, Jerne was approached by the Hoffmann–La Roche pharmaceutical company and invited to organize a new immunology research center in Basel, Switzerland. Jerne served as director of the Basel Institute for Immunology from its foundation in 1969 until his retirement in 1980.

Despite his administrative responsibilities, Jerne continued to make important contributions to immunology. In the early 1960s JEAN DAUSSET, BARUJ BENACERRAF, and their colleagues had discovered that the same cellular proteins that stimulate the immune system to reject transplanted organs seemed to determine the level of immune response to other antigens as well. In 1971 Jerne proposed that antibodies develop to recognize altered histocompatibility antigens—antigens that are not antagonistic or toxic—and that the process of selecting appropriate antibodies takes place in the thymus, a ductless gland situated in the front part of the upper body cavity, above the diaphragm. His proposal was not confirmed in the case of antibody-producing cells; however, it turned out to be an accurate description of the behavior of T cells, the component of the immune system that eliminates infected or cancerous cells.

Jerne's most significant contribution to immunology was his "network" theory, introduced in 1974. It is the most elaborate and logical explanation yet offered of the interactive processes by which the body's immune system musters its forces to combat disease and then recedes into inactivity when no longer needed. Jerne emphasized that there are many more types of antibodies than there are kinds of proteins and that "in its dynamic state, our immune system is mainly self-centered, generating anti-ideotype antibodies [opposed to their antigenic profiles] to its own antibodies." Thus, the response to an invader is not a matter of simply increasing the production of a specific antibody but rather one of creating a disturbance in a highly complex, self-regulating system.

In recognition of the impact that his pioneering theories have had in stimulating research in immunology, Jerne shared the 1984 Nobel Prize for Physiology or Medicine with GEORGES KÖHLER and CÉSAR MILSTEIN. Although Jerne's network theory has not led to any spectacular advances, it and his other theories form the immunological structure into which Köhler and Milstein were able to fit their discoveries.

Colleagues of Jerne have praised him for his preoccupation with the "philosophical problems of immunology," his unusual ability to select the observations that are the most closely allied to the problems, his capacity to propose bold but clear hypotheses, and "his tendency to be proved right."

Now retired from the Basel Institute for Immunology, Jerne lives in southern France with his wife, the former Ursula Alexandra Kohl, whom he married in 1964 and with whom he has two sons.

Among the other awards and honors bestowed on Jerne are the Gairdner Foundation International Award (1970) and the Paul Ehrlich Gold Medal of the University of Frankfurt (1982). He was a member of the World Health Organization (WHO) Advisory Committee on Medical Research from 1949 to 1968 and of the Advisory Committee on Medical Research of the Panamerican Health Organization from 1963 to 1966; he has been a member of the Expert Advisory Panel of Immunology of the WHO since 1962. He is also an honorary member of the Robert Koch Institute in Berlin, a foreign honorary member of the American Academy of Arts and Sciences, and a member of the Royal Danish Academy of Sciences. He has received honorary degrees from the University of Chicago, Columbia University, the universities of Copenhagen and Basel, and Erasmus University, Rotterdam.

SELECTED WORKS: A Study of Avidity, 1951.

ABOUT: Cairns, J. (ed.) Phage and the Origins of Molecular Biology, 1966; New York Times October 16, 1984; Science November 30, 1984.

JIMÉNEZ, JUAN

(December 23, 1881–May 29, 1958)
Nobel Prize for Literature, 1956

The Spanish poet Juan Ramón Jiménez (hē me′ neth) Mantecón was born in Moguer, a small town in that part of Andalusia which is now the province of Huelva. One of three children of Victor Jiménez, a banker with interests in the wine trade, and Purificación Mantecón y Lopez Parejo, the young Jiménez also had a stepsister from his father's first mar-

JUAN JIMÉNEZ

riage. Despite his frail health, he was sent to a Jesuit academy in Cádiz from 1891 to 1896. Upon leaving the academy, Jiménez began law studies at the University of Seville but gave little attention to his classes, preferring to paint, write poetry, and read—particularly French and German romantic poetry and the Spanish poetry of Rosalía de Castro and Gustavo Bécquer. His earliest poems, published in the Madrid review *Vida nueva* (New Life) when he was seventeen years old, attracted the notice of some of the most important Spanish-language poets of the day, including the Nicaraguan Rubén Darío, then living in Spain, and Jiménez's countryman Francisco Villaespesa, who both invited him to move to Madrid.

Accepting their invitation, Jiménez abandoned his desultory legal studies and went on to help found two influential modernist literary reviews, *Helios* (Helium) in 1902 and *Renacimiento* (Renaissance) in 1906. His earliest books of poetry, *Almas de violeta* (Violet Souls) and *Ninfeas* (Water Lilies), appeared in 1900. Although derivative, sentimental, and tinged with adolescent melancholy, the poems in these collections demonstrated Jiménez's mastery of various metrical forms and were, at the same time, exuberantly sensual and subtly lyrical. The images of nature that pervade the early poems were to color his entire life's work.

The sudden death of Jiménez's father in the summer of 1900, shortly after the poet had returned to Moguer, plunged him into depression. Sent to a sanatorium in Bordeaux, France, for the treatment of neurasthenia, he soon recovered, although he became semireclusive and

acquired a morbid preoccupation with death that lasted the rest of his life. He wrote little poetry during his recuperation but closely studied the works of the French symbolists Paul Verlaine, Arthur Rimbaud, and Stéphane Mallarmé.

Returning to Madrid in 1902, Jiménez wrote his first mature poems. Imbued with a then-fashionable modernist tone of fin-de-siècle malaise, the poems contained in the volumes titled *Rimas* (Rhymes, 1902), *Arias tristes* (Sad Arias, 1903), *Jardines lejanos* (Distant Gardens, 1904), and *Pastorales* (Pastorals, 1905) nevertheless exhibit an original voice that is elegant, musical, and infused with a sense of mystery.

From 1905 to 1911 Jiménez again lived in Moguer and wrote, among other volumes of poetry, *Elejías puras* (Pure Elegies, 1908), *Baladas de primavera* (Ballads of Spring, 1910), and *La soledad sonora* (The Sonorous Solitude, 1911). With their ornate imagery and intricate meters (especially the alexandrine), these poems are almost baroque in style.

In 1912 Jiménez moved to Madrid's Students' Residence, a center of liberal culture, where he met the vibrant, American-born Zenobia Camprubí. Together they translated the work of the Indian poet RABINDRANATH TAGORE. During this time, Jiménez also published *Laberinto* (Labyrinth, 1913), poems dedicated to seven women he knew, and the extremely popular *Platero y yo* (*Platero and I*, 1914), a series of prose poems ostensibly about the poet and his donkey. The book's underlying theme, as the American literary critic Michael P. Predmore wrote in 1970, is "death and rebirth as a process of metamorphosis."

In 1915 he published *Estío* (Summer), a book of idealized love poems inspired by Zenobia Camprubí, with whom he had fallen in love; the following year he sailed for New York, where she was then living, and married her. The ocean voyage became a significant metaphor for a change of poetic direction. His next collection, *Diario de un poeta recién casado* (Diary of a Newlywed Poet, 1917), not only recounts this odyssey but also marks the first major use of free verse in Spanish poetry. Although love plays a vital role in *Diario,* it is the presence of the sea that pervades this mixture of poetry and prose. The rhythms of the sea—its continual flux and movement—reflected Jiménez's impatience with restrictive poetic structures. At the same time, the sea, in its solitude and timelessness, represented his yearning for permanence.

During the next twenty years, while working as a critic and editor for various literary journals in Spain, Jiménez earnestly tried to communicate what he called an "avidity for eternity" in his poetry. In *Eternidades* (Eternities, 1918) he renounced all his past verse and strove for *la poesía desnuda*—"naked," or "pure," poetry. Thus, the poems of *Eternidades* are slender and epigrammatic, stripped of the ornate detail that had marked his earlier work. In the poetry that followed, including *Piedra y cielo* (Stone and Sky, 1919) and *Belleza* (Beauty, 1923), Jiménez explored the relationships between beauty and death, creativity and salvation. In an essay on aesthetics and ethics that dates from this time, he declared that there is indeed a connection between the moral and the beautiful. His eloquent anthology *La estación total con las canciones de la nueva luz* (The Total Season With Songs of New Light) occupied him from 1923 to 1936. In this work, not published until 1946, Jiménez displayed a keen awareness of the splendid harmony in nature. "The title is meaningful," explains the American scholar C. W. Cobb in his 1976 book, *Contemporary Spanish Poetry (1898–1963)*, because "a 'season' is a temporal period of growth and decay, but 'total' suggests the poet's attempt to fuse all seasons into one, into a difficult eternity."

The outbreak of the Spanish Civil War in 1936 disrupted Jiménez's long period of poetic development. The Republican government dispatched him to the United States as honorary cultural attaché; although he went willingly, Jiménez, a strictly apolitical poet, regarded his absence from Spain as a form of exile. At this time, he also began a late career as a lecturer, speaking at several universities in Cuba, Puerto Rico, and the United States. After Francisco Franco's forces won absolute control of Spain in 1939, Jiménez and his wife decided to remain abroad.

Although from this time the quantity of Jiménez's literary output diminished markedly, his poetic search for truth continued, reaching an almost religious intensity in his powerful spiritual testament *Animal de fondo* (Animal of Depth, 1949). The product of another sea voyage, this time to Argentina, this volume is a poetic consummation of Jiménez's lifelong quest to express the metaphysical. Writing in 1964, the American scholar Howard T. Young called it "a spiritual autobiography . . . , a fusion of his poetic ideals in a new sense of creative unity with the world."

In 1951 Jiménez and his wife settled in San Juan, Puerto Rico, where he continued teaching. He also worked on another poetic sequence, *Dios deseado y deseante* (God Desired and Desiring), a projected sequel to *Animal de fondo* that was never completed. Fragments of this work appeared in his *Tercera antolojía poética* (Third Poetic Anthology, 1957).

In 1956, as his wife was dying, Jiménez received the Nobel Prize for Literature "for his lyrical poetry, which in the Spanish language constitutes an example of high spirit and artistic purity." In his presentation speech, Hjalmar Gullberg of the Swedish Academy declared, "When the Swedish Academy renders homage to Juan Ramón Jiménez, it renders homage also to an entire epoch in the glorious Spanish literature." In a brief acceptance note read to the Stockholm audience by the rector of the University of Puerto Rico, Jiménez said, "My wife Zenobia is the true winner of this prize. Her companionship, her help, her inspiration made, for forty years, my work possible. Today, without her, I am desolate and helpless." Profoundly saddened by his wife's death, Jiménez steadily declined in health; he died in Puerto Rico less than two years later, at the age of seventy-six.

Jiménez's reputation as a poet absolutely devoted to his vision and his craft has remained high. C. W. Cobb stated that "Jiménez's position as a lyric poet in Spanish literature has been complicated by his insistence upon seeking purity, universality, and timelessness in his poetry," and he believed that in this respect Jiménez can be justly compared to WILLIAM BUTLER YEATS and Rainer Maria Rilke. Like them, added Howard T. Young, Jiménez "espoused a secular religion in which poetry was the only rite, and its creation the only form of worship."

ADDITIONAL WORKS IN ENGLISH TRANSLATION: Fifty Spanish Poems, 1950; Selected Writings, 1957; Three Hundred Poems, 1903–1953, 1962; Forty Poems, 1967; Stories of Life and Death, 1986; Space and Time: A Poetic Autobiography, 1987.

ABOUT: Cobb, C. W. Contemporary Spanish Poetry (1898–1963), 1976; Coke-Enguidanos, M. Word and Work in the Poetry of Juan Ramón Jiménez, 1982; Cole, L. R. The Religious Instinct in the Poetry of Juan Ramón Jiménez, 1967; Current Biography February 1957; Olson, P. R. Circle of Paradox, 1967; Wilcox, J. C. Self and Image in Juan Ramón Jiménez, 1986; Young, H. T. Juan Ramón Jiménez, 1967; Young, H. T. The Line in the Margin, 1980.

JOHNSON, EYVIND
(July 29, 1900–August 25, 1976)
Nobel Prize for Literature, 1974
(shared with Harry Martinson)

EYVIND JOHNSON

Eyvind Olof Verner Johnson (yōn' son), Swedish novelist and short story writer, was born at Saltsjobaden in Norrbotten, Sweden's northernmost province. His father, Olof, who had settled at the edge of the Arctic Circle to work as a laborer on the Lapland iron ore railroad, suffered a mental breakdown shortly after his son's birth. Unable to care for both her son and a sick husband, Johnson's mother, the former Cevia Gustafsdatter, entrusted the boy's upbringing to relatives.

Leaving school at the age of thirteen, Johnson began working as a laborer at a macadam factory. During his adolescence, he educated himself by reading the classics, especially those of ancient Greece. Before he was nineteen, Johnson had worked as ditchdigger, handyman to an electric fitter, engine roughcaster, timber floater, sawmill laborer, candy salesman, film projectionist, and secretary to a trade union. While employed in the woodworking industry, he organized a workers' strike, which eventually led to his dismissal.

In 1919 Johnson made his way south to Stockholm, where he became actively involved in trade unionism and socialist politics. There he also began to write. Two years later, financially destitute and disillusioned, he went to Berlin to embark on a career as a newspaper correspondent. After two years, he moved on to Paris, where he managed to support himself for the next seven years by writing newspaper articles for publication in Sweden, as well as by publishing short stories and novels. In 1927 he married Aase Christoffersen; they had no children.

As a young man, Johnson was filled with revolutionary fervor, seeking to improve the world through both political action and writing. A graduate of what the Swedish-American scholar and critic Leif Sjöberg termed "life's own university," Johnson continued to compensate for his lack of formal education by reading extensively. Not surprisingly, the work of other writers strongly influenced his early work. His first three novels, *Timans och rättfärdigheten* (Timans and Justice, 1925), *Stad i mörker* (Town in Darkness, 1927), and *Stad i ljus* (Town in Light, 1928), are quite derivative in style and substance, owing much to the literary and intellectual innovations of ANDRÉ GIDE, Marcel Proust, James Joyce, Sigmund Freud, and HENRI BERGSON. *Stad i mörker* is

a series of predominantly satirical vignettes of life in an Arctic town. *Stad i ljus* is the story of a downtrodden young writer in the bohemian quarter of a festive Paris. In these early novels, the characters' Hamlet-like musings, diffidence, and frustration reflect Johnson's profound sense of personal disappointment.

In the novel *Minnas* (Remembering, 1928), Johnson drew on the work of Proust and Freud to illustrate the ways individuals are haunted by repressed sexual desires and unpleasant memories. In *Kommentar till ett stjärnfall* (Commentary on a Falling Star, 1929), a bleak novel of corruption in a decadent capitalist society, Johnson, for the first time in Swedish literature, employed the stream-of-consciousness technique developed by James Joyce. The English critic Gavin Orton characterized this book as "a work of imagination, not a psychological document, for the author . . . comments on the course of events, plays with his characters, indulges in strange flights of fancy."

Returning to Sweden in 1930 as an established writer, Johnson became associated with the reform politics of the Social Democrats. A positive tone of social commitment pervades his next novel, *Avsked till Hamlet* (Farewell to Hamlet, 1930). However in *Bobinack* (1932), a satire of the Swedish middle classes, and in *Regn in gryningen* (Rain at Dawn, 1933), a lyrical lampoon of primitivist society, Johnson returned to caustic social criticism. Rich imagination is the hallmark of two short story collections from this period, *Natten är här* (The Night Is Here, 1932), which includes some unconventional tales of ancient Greece, and *Än en gång, kapten* (Once More, Captain, 1934), which contains tales derived from the author's youth in northern Sweden.

Between 1934 and 1937 Johnson wrote *Romanen om Olof* (The Novel About Olof, 1934–1937), a four-volume epic of adolescence that has become a classic of Swedish literature. Autobiographical in nature, the Olof quartet traces the development of its protagonist, Olof Persson, from a raw, sensitive youth of fourteen into a bloodied but unbowed strike leader of nineteen. A penetrating profile of a young man's development, it is also a detailed chronicle of the rise of the Swedish proletariat. Its first volume, *Nu var det, 1914,* was translated into English in 1970 by Mary Sandbach and published under the title *1914.*

Two years after the death of his first wife in 1938, Johnson married Cilla Frankenhäuser, a writer and translator; they had three children. Their professional collaboration produced Swedish translations of works by AL-BERT CAMUS, ANATOLE FRANCE, JEAN-PAUL SARTRE, and Eugène Ionesco, as well as works by Danish, German, and British writers.

Horrified at the spread of Nazism in the late 1930s, Johnson attacked the Nazis and their Swedish sympathizers in *Nattövning* (Night Maneuvers, 1938). During World War II, he and WILLY BRANDT coedited the newspaper *Et Handslåg* (A Handshake) for the Norwegian Resistance.

From 1941 to 1943 Johnson was immersed in writing the lengthy and textually complex *Krilon* trilogy, published in 1941, 1943, and 1945. On a purely narrative level, it is the story of the Stockholm estate agent Johannes Krilon and his associates as they strive to maintain their integrity in neutral Sweden during the war. On an allegorical level, it is a symbolic description of the war and of humanity's ceaseless struggle with evil. *Krilon* is in essence a multilayered fairy tale, or myth. Johnson came to favor this form over a strictly realistic presentation for communicating his notion of the truth.

Johnson used the same form in his next novel, *Strändernas svall,* published in 1946. Probably his best-known work in the English-speaking world, it was translated in 1952 by M. A. Michael as *Return to Ithaca: The Odyssey Retold as a Modern Novel.* Johnson used the Homeric legend as the basis for a treatment of twentieth-century values and problems, demonstrating the truth of the adage that "the more things change, the more they remain the same." Leif Sjöberg noted that this preoccupation with the mysterious repetition of events from one epoch to another was to become the dominant theme of Johnson's postwar historical novels, a stark and startling series published over the next thirty years, beginning with *Return to Ithaca.*

In the late 1940s, Johnson moved about Europe as a member of the Swedish delegation to the United Nations Educational, Scientific, and Cultural Organization (UNESCO). He also found time to write *Drömmar om rosor och eld* (1949), translated into English in 1984 as *Dreams of Roses and Fire.* The novel is an account of the witchcraft trial at Loudun in seventeenth-century France, a subject that was also to attract the writers Aldous Huxley and John Whiting, as well as the filmmaker Ken Russell.

Johnson received an honorary doctorate from the University of Göteborg in 1953. The publication in 1957 of his novel *Molnen över Metapontion* (The Clouds Over Metapontion), which combines an account of an Italian journey set in the 1950s with a retelling of Xenophon's *Anabasis,* helped ensure Johnson's election to the Swedish Academy the same year. In 1960 *Hans Nådes tid* was published. Translated into English as *The Days of His Grace* in 1968, this analysis of the totalitarian ethos—as perceived by the inhabitants of a nation conquered by Charlemagne—earned Johnson the Nordic Council Prize for Literature in 1962. It was followed by the harrowing novel *Några steg mot tystnaden* (A Novel About Imprisoned Ones, 1973), which also juxtaposes barbaric historical events with those of the seemingly civilized twentieth century.

Johnson received the 1974 Nobel Prize for Literature "for a narrative art, farseeing in lands and ages, in the service of freedom." He shared the award with his countryman HARRY MARTINSON. Some dissenting voices were raised to condemn the choice of the co-winners as shortsighted and parochial. Nevertheless, Karl Ragnar Gierow, speaking for the Swedish Academy in his presentation address, hailed the "influx of experience and creative energy" that the two brought with them when they "broke into our literature, not to ravage and plunder, but to enrich it with their fortunes." In his acceptance speech, Johnson reaffirmed his belief that "at the center of all the good writing that has been and is being created stands man."

Born with the century whose issues preoccupied him as a writer, Johnson died in Stockholm at the age of seventy-six. Of his forty-six books, thirty are novels; only four have been translated into English.

515

While Johnson's work remains little known to readers outside of Scandinavia, it is generally well regarded by the scholarly community. Lars G. Warme, a Swedish literary critic, has characterized Johnson as a "rationalist and a humanist" who in "novel after novel pleads for a liberal democracy and for common sense and common decency. With passionate anger, disguised as irony, he opposes violence, oppression, and power-hungry tyranny." Sjöberg has noted Johnson's interest in "the problems of time, . . . [especially] parallelisms and simultaneity" and has praised the ingenious way he "varies his techniques and devices, . . . mixing the styles of classical writers with those of such moderns as THOMAS MANN and WILLIAM FAULKNER, yet maintaining his integrity and his own personal style."

ABOUT: Books Abroad Summer 1975; Gustafson, A. A History of Swedish Literature, 1961; Orton, G. K. Eyvind Johnson, 1972; Stanford, W. B. The Ulysses Theme, 1963.

FRÉDÉRIC JOLIOT

JOLIOT, FRÉDÉRIC
(March 19, 1900–August 14, 1958)
Nobel Prize for Chemistry, 1935
(shared with Irène Joliot-Curie)

The French physicist Jean Frédéric Joliot (zhô lyō') was born in Paris, the youngest of six children of Henri Joliot, a prosperous merchant, and Émilie (Roederer) Joliot, the daughter of a middle-class Protestant family from Alsace. The boy entered the Lycée Lakanal, a suburban boarding school, in 1910 but after his father's death seven years later he returned to Paris to attend the École Primaire Supérieure Lavoisier. Having decided upon a scientific career, he entered the École Supérieure de Physique et de Chimie Industrielle in Paris in 1920 and graduated first in his class three years later with a degree in engineering.

Although his education had emphasized applied chemistry and physics, Joliot's interests had gravitated increasingly to basic scientific research, in large part due to the influence of one of his teachers at the École Supérieure de Physique et de Chimie Industrielle, the French physicist Paul Langevin. After completing his compulsory military service, Joliot discussed his future plans with Langevin, who advised him to apply for a position as an assistant to MARIE CURIE at the Radium Institute of the University of Paris.

Joliot was accepted, and early in 1925 he assumed his new responsibilities at the insti-tute, where he not only served as a preparator but also continued his study of chemistry and physics. The following year he married Irène Curie, the daughter of Marie and PIERRE CURIE, who was also employed at the institute. She then used the name IRÈNE JOLIOT-CURIE. The couple had a son and a daughter, both of whom became scientists. After completing his requirements for a *licence* (equivalent to a master's degree), Joliot went on to obtain his Ph.D. in 1930 for research on the electrochemical properties of the radioactive element polonium.

Unable to find an academic position, Joliot was on the verge of returning to industrial work when JEAN PERRIN helped him win a government scholarship that enabled Joliot to remain at the institute and pursue his research on the effects of radiation. In 1930 the German physicist WALTHER BOTHE had discovered that certain light elements, notably beryllium and boron, emitted a strong penetrating radiation when bombarded by swift-moving helium nuclei (or alpha radiation, as it was called at the time) spun off from radioactive polonium. Drawing on his engineering experience, Joliot constructed a sensitive cloud-chamber detector to record these penetrating radiations and prepared an unusually strong concentration of polonium. Using this apparatus, the Joliot-Curies (as they called themselves), who began to collaborate in 1931, discovered that a thin sheet of hydrogen-containing material placed between the irradiated beryllium or boron and the detector nearly doubled the measurable radiations. Additional experiments showed them that this increase consisted of hydrogen atoms being ejected at extremely high velocities after colliding with particles of penetrating radiation. Although neither of the two researchers understood the process, their precise measurements led in 1932 to JAMES CHADWICK's discovery of the neutron, an uncharged constituent of typical atomic nuclei.

Among the atomic by-products created when alpha particles bombard boron or aluminum are positrons (positively charged electrons), which were detected by the American physicist CARL D. ANDERSON, also in 1932. The Joliot-Curies studied these particles from late 1932 to 1933 and in early 1934 began a new experiment. Covering the opening of the cloud chamber with a thin sheet of aluminum foil, they irradiated samples of boron and aluminum with alpha radiation and observed the results. As they expected, positrons were emitted, but to their surprise positron emissions continued for several minutes after the polonium source was removed.

The Joliot-Curies subsequently discovered that some of the aluminum and boron in their exposed samples had been transmuted into new chemical elements. Moreover, these new elements were radioactive: aluminum, absorbing the two protons and two neutrons of the alpha particle, had been transformed into radioactive phosphorus, while the boron had become a radioactive isotope of nitrogen. Because these short-lived radioactive elements were unlike any that occurred naturally, it was clear that they had been created artificially. Subsequently, the Joliot-Curies produced a large number of new radioactive elements.

Frédéric Joliot and Irène Joliot-Curie shared the 1935 Nobel Prize for Chemistry "for their synthesis of new radioactive elements." K. W. Palmær of the Royal Swedish Academy of Sciences said in his presentation speech, "Thanks to your discoveries it has become possible, for the first time, to transform artificially one element into another hitherto unknown. The results of your researches are of capital importance for pure science." Palmær continued, "But in addition, physiologists, doctors, and the whole of suffering humanity hope to gain from your discoveries, remedies of inestimable value."

In his Nobel lecture Joliot noted that the use of synthetic radioactive elements as tracers "will simplify the problems of the location and elimination of the various elements introduced into living organisms." From the evidence that has been accumulated, he said, "we can realize that the few hundreds of atoms . . . which form our planet must not be considered as having been created all at one time and to last forever." Moreover, he added, "we are entitled to think that scientists . . . will be able to bring about transmutations of an explosive type, true chemical chain reactions" that liberate vast amounts of usable energy. "But . . . if the contagion spreads to all the elements of our planet," he warned, "the consequences of unloosing such a cataclysm can only be viewed with apprehension."

In 1937 Joliot accepted a concurrent position as a professor at the Collège de France in Paris. There he built a center of research in nuclear physics and chemistry and established a new laboratory where the departments of physics, chemistry, and biology could work in close collaboration. In addition he supervised construction of one of France's first cyclotrons to replace radioactive elements as a source of alpha particles for research.

In 1939, following the discovery by the German chemist OTTO HAHN that the uranium atom could be split, or fissioned, Joliot provided direct physical proof that this division was explosive. Recognizing that the immense amount of energy liberated by atomic fission could be harnessed as a source of power, he obtained from Norway the only sizable stock of heavy water then in existence, but the outbreak of World War II and the German occupation of France interrupted his research. At considerable personal risk, Joliot managed to smuggle his supply of heavy water to England, where it was used in the British effort to develop an atomic weapon.

Remaining in Paris throughout the occupation, Joliot retained his posts at the Radium Institute and the Collège de France. As an active member of the Resistance, he used his laboratory's facilities to manufacture explosives and radio equipment for Resistance fighters before he was forced into hiding in 1944.

After the liberation of Paris, Joliot was appointed director of the National Center for Scientific Research and given responsibility for rebuilding the nation's scientific capacity. In October 1945 Joliot persuaded President Charles de Gaulle to create a French Atomic Energy Commission. Three years later he started France's first atomic pile. Although Joliot was an influential scientist and administrator, his association with the Communist party, which he had joined in 1942, became controversial, and in 1950 he was removed from his post on the Atomic Energy Commission.

JOLIOT-CURIE

Thereafter, Joliot devoted most of his time to laboratory research and to teaching. Remaining active in politics, he also served as president of the World Organization of the Partisans of Peace. Irène Joliot-Curie's death in 1956 dealt a severe emotional blow to Joliot. Succeeding her as director of the Radium Institute and assuming her teaching responsibilities at the Sorbonne, he also began supervising the construction of new facilities for the institute at Orsay, south of Paris. His health failing, and weakened by an attack of viral hepatitis two years earlier, Joliot died in Paris on August 14, 1958, after an operation for internal hemorrhaging.

Described as sensitive, kind, and patient, Joliot enjoyed playing the piano, painting landscapes, and reading. During his later years he devoted much of his time to political causes. A recipient of the Barnard Gold Medal for Meritorious Service to Science of Columbia University (1940), he held membership in the French Academy of Sciences and the Academy of Medicine as well as foreign membership in many scientific societies.

SELECTED WORKS: A New Type of Radioactivity, 1962, with Irène Joliot-Curie.

ABOUT: Biographical Memoirs of Fellows of the Royal Society, volume 6, 1960; Biquard, P. Frédéric Joliot-Curie: The Man and His Theories, 1965; Dictionary of Scientific Biography, volume 7, 1973; Goldsmith, M. Frédéric Joliot-Curie: A Biography, 1976; Goldsmith, M. Three Scientists Face Social Responsibility, 1976.

JOLIOT-CURIE, IRÈNE
(September 12, 1897–March 17, 1956)
Nobel Prize for Chemistry, 1935
(shared with Frédéric Joliot)

The French physicist Irène Joliot-Curie (zhô lyō′ kü rē′) was born in Paris, the first of two daughters of PIERRE CURIE and MARIE (Sklodowska) CURIE. Her mother first isolated radium when the girl was one year old. It was around this time that Irène's paternal grandfather, Eugène Curie, came to live with the family. A physician who had volunteered his services during the revolution of 1848 and in the Paris Commune in 1871, Eugène Curie provided companionship for Irène while her mother was occupied in the laboratory. Both his liberal socialist convictions and his anticlericalism deeply influenced Irène's subsequent political views.

At the age of ten—just a year after her

IRÈNE JOLIOT-CURIE

father died—Irène began studying at a cooperative school organized by her mother and several colleagues, including the physicists Paul Langevin and JEAN PERRIN, who also taught there. Two years later she entered the Collège Sévigné, graduating on the eve of World War I. She continued her education at the University of Paris (the Sorbonne) but interrupted her studies for several months to serve as an army nurse, helping her mother with radiographic equipment.

At the end of the war, Irène Curie became a research assistant at the Radium Institute, which her mother directed, and in 1921 she began her own research. Her initial efforts involved a study of radioactive polonium, the element her parents had discovered more than twenty years earlier. Because the phenomenon of radiation involved the disintegration of atoms, its study promised to elucidate the structure of atoms. Curie investigated observed fluctuations in the numbers of alpha particles ejected, typically at very high velocities, during the breakdown of polonium atoms. Alpha particles, which consist of two protons and two neutrons and are thus identical to helium nuclei, had first been pointed out for use as a tool for probing atomic structures by the English physicist ERNEST RUTHERFORD. For her studies of these particles, Curie received her Ph.D. in 1925.

Her most significant research began several years later, after her marriage in 1926 to a fellow assistant at the Radium Institute, FRÉDÉRIC JOLIOT. In 1930 the German physicist WALTHER BOTHE found that certain light elements (beryllium and boron among them) produced a powerful form of radiation when exposed to a bombardment of alpha particles. Attracted to the questions this discovery posed, the Joliot-Curies (as they called themselves) prepared an especially strong source of polonium for the generation of alpha particles and used a sensitive cloud chamber built by Joliot to record the penetrating radiation thus produced. The Joliot-Curies found that when a sheet of material containing hydrogen was placed between the target beryllium or boron and the detector, the observed output of radiation nearly doubled. This effect, they conjectured, was caused by penetrating radiation striking individual atoms of hydrogen and setting them free with an enormous velocity. Although neither one of them understood the process, their careful measurements paved the way for JAMES CHADWICK's discovery in 1932 of the neutron, an electrically neutral constituent of most atomic nuclei.

Continuing their research, the Joliot-Curies reached their most important discovery. Using boron and aluminum as their targets for alpha-particle bombardment, they investigated the production of positrons (positively charged particles otherwise resembling the negatively charged electron), first discovered in 1932 by the American physicist CARL D. ANDERSON. Covering the opening of the detector with a fine layer of aluminum foil, they irradiated samples of aluminum and boron with alpha particles. To their surprise, the production of positrons continued for several minutes after the polonium alpha-particle source was removed. The Joliot-Curies later determined that some of the aluminum and boron in their exposed samples had been changed into new chemical elements. Moreover, these new elements were radioactive; by absorbing the two protons and two neutrons of the alpha particle, the aluminum had been transmuted into radioactive phosphorus, while the boron had become a radioactive isotope of nitrogen. Within a short time, the Joliot-Curies had produced many new radioactive elements.

"For their synthesis of new radioactive elements," Irène Joliot-Curie and Frédéric Joliot shared the 1935 Nobel Prize for Chemistry. In his presentation address, K. W. Palmær of the Royal Swedish Academy of Sciences reminded Joliot-Curie that twenty-four years ago she had been present on a similar occasion, when her mother received the Nobel chemistry prize. "In collaboration with your husband," Palmær said, "you have worthily maintained those brilliant traditions."

A year after receiving the Nobel Prize, Joliot-Curie became a full professor at the Sorbonne, where she had been lecturing since 1932. She also retained her position at the Radium Institute and continued her research on radioactivity. During the late 1930s she made several important findings while working with uranium and came close to the discovery that bombardment by neutrons could cause the splitting, or fission, of the uranium atom. Repeating these same experiments, the German physicist OTTO HAHN and his colleagues Fritz Strassman and Lise Meitner achieved fission in 1938.

Meanwhile, Joliot-Curie had also become increasingly involved in political activities and in 1936 had served four months as under secretary of state for scientific research in the government of Léon Blum. Despite the German occupation of France in 1940, Joliot-Curie and her husband remained in Paris, where Joliot worked in the Resistance movement. By 1944 the Gestapo had become suspicious of his activities, and when he went underground that year, Joliot-Curie and their two children fled to Switzerland, where they remained until the liberation of France.

In 1946 she was appointed director of the Radium Institute, and from 1946 until 1950 she served as a director of the French Atomic Energy Commission. Always deeply committed to the social and intellectual advancement of women, she participated in the National Committee of the Union of French Women and served on the World Peace Council. By the early 1950s her health had begun to deteriorate, probably as a result of exposure to radioactivity. She died in Paris on March 17, 1956, of acute leukemia.

A tall, slender woman known for her patience and even temper, Joliot-Curie enjoyed swimming, skiing, and mountain climbing. In addition to the Nobel Prize, she received honorary degrees from many universities and held membership in numerous scientific societies. In 1940 she received the Barnard Gold Medal for Meritorious Service to Science of Columbia University; she was also an officer of the Legion of Honor of France.

SELECTED WORKS: Nuclear Physics, 1938, with others; A New Type of Radioactivity, 1962, with Frédéric Joliot.

ABOUT: Biquard, P. Frédéric Joliot-Curie: The Man and His Theories, 1965; Dictionary of Scientific Biography, volume 7, 1973; McKown, R. She Lived for Science: Irène Joliot-Curie, 1961.

JOSEPHSON, BRIAN D.
(January 4, 1940–   )
Nobel Prize for Physics, 1973
(shared with Leo Esaki and Ivar Giaever)

The Welsh physicist Brian David Josephson was born in Cardiff to Abraham and Mimi Josephson. After completing his secondary education at the local high school, he entered Trinity College, Cambridge, where he received his B.A. in physics in 1960 and both an M.A. and a Ph.D. in 1964. From 1962 until 1969 he held a junior research fellowship at Trinity College.

Josephson first came to prominence as an undergraduate when, in 1960, he realized that researchers using the Mössbauer effect (named for RUDOLF L. MÖSSBAUER) to measure the gravitational red shift of gamma rays (which may be viewed as energetic particles of light) had ignored a major source of error in their experiments. ALBERT EINSTEIN's general theory of relativity predicted that photons, such as gamma rays, would change their energy as they traveled in gravitational fields. Experimentalists were attempting to measure any change in the wavelength of gamma rays as they traveled up or down a tower. Josephson realized that differences as small as 1°C in the temperature of the gamma-ray source and of the detector could result in wavelength shifts as large as those they were trying to measure. Josephson's discovery caused experimentalists to repeat their measurements while controlling precisely the temperatures of their pieces of apparatus.

By 1962 Josephson had begun conducting research in superconductivity, a phenomenon in which materials, when they are cooled below a critical temperature, lose all resistance to the flow of electricity. Superconductivity arises from the ability of pairs of electrons in the superconductor to interact with each other by means of atomic vibrations (phonons) that they excite in the material. Working at the General Electric Company, IVAR GIAEVER had recently found that when an electrical contact was made between a superconducting material and a normal metal with a very thin insulating layer separating the two conductors, the electrical behavior of the contact provided a great deal of information about the properties of the superconductor. In 1962 Josephson calculated the behavior of such a junction between two superconductors. He found that current could flow through the insulator without any voltage difference between the two conductors (the DC Josephson effect), a totally unexpected

BRIAN D. JOSEPHSON

result that was not in accordance with classical physical models. He also predicted that when a voltage was applied across the junction, an oscillating current would flow across the junction with a frequency dependent only on the applied voltage (the AC Josephson effect). Both effects were extremely sensitive to the magnetic field at the junction. These effects were soon observed and were found to behave as predicted by Josephson's theory. In fact, some experimentalists using Giaever's technique had already seen the effects but had discarded them as "noise."

Discovery of the Josephson effects had a substantial impact on modern physics. The frequency of the alternating current is dependent on the voltage across the junction and the ratio of the electronic charge to MAX PLANCK's constant (a basic physical constant that determines the behavior of systems of atomic scale or smaller). The Josephson effects allowed a great increase in the precision with which this ratio (e/h) is known. They also permitted the creation of a new primary quantum standard for voltage, now used in many national standards laboratories, that is dependent on the Josephson effects. By putting two Josephson junctions in a loop, it became possible to develop sensors for magnetic fields that are extraordinarily sensitive. Such a device, called a *su*perconducting *qu*antum *i*nterference *de*vice (SQUID), is the most sensitive detector of magnetic fields known and has been used for magnetic investigations of living organisms, as well as for magnetic mapping and detection of subsurface objects. Similar sensitive detectors of extremely small voltage changes have been made by using Josephson-effects devices. Other Josephson-effects devices show promise for use as computer circuitry elements with extremely high speed and very low power consumption.

In 1969 Josephson was appointed senior research fellow at Cambridge. During 1965–1966, he was a visiting research professor at the University of Illinois. From 1967 until 1972 he served as assistant director of research at Cambridge. He held the post of reader in physics from 1972 until 1974, when he was made professor of physics.

Josephson was awarded half of the 1973 Nobel Prize for Physics "for his theoretical predictions of the properties of a supercurrent through a tunnel barrier, in particular those phenomena which are generally known as the Josephson effects." The other half of the prize was shared by LEO ESAKI and Ivar Giaever. On presenting the award, Stig Lundqvist of the Royal Swedish Academy of Sciences noted that Esaki's pioneering work laid the foundation for Giaever's discovery, which in turn provided the impetus that led to Josephson's theoretical predictions.

In the years following his discovery, Josephson investigated superconductivity and the critical phenomena that occur when systems are near to transition points, such as the critical point of water (where the distinction between fluid and gaseous phases disappears) and similar transitions between superconductivity and normal conductivity in systems that exhibit such transitions. In the late 1960s, he developed an interest in problems of mind and intelligence. He became a practitioner of transcendental meditation in the early 1970s, hoping to synthesize modern physics and mathematics with the mental theory of the spiritual leader Maharishi Mahesh Yogi, who was largely responsible for spreading transcendental meditation in the Western world. Josephson stopped his research in mainstream physics to devote himself to transcendental meditation and mental theory. Of this undertaking, he has said, "I am taking a rather unconventional theoretical approach to the phenomenon of intelligence, in that I believe that the most basic concepts underlying intelligence were discovered in ancient times. In particular," he continued, "I am basing my research to a considerable extent on the formulations which have been given in numerous lectures by the Maharishi Mahesh Yogi. It is hoped that the usefulness and validity of these concepts can be confirmed by computer simulation."

Josephson married Carol Anne Oliver in 1976; they have one daughter. During his leisure time, Josephson enjoys walking in the mountains, astronomy, ice skating, and taking photographs.

Josephson's awards include the Science Award of the Research Corporation of America (1969) and the Hughes Medal of the Royal Society of London (1972). He is a fellow of the Royal Society of London and a foreign member of the American Institute of Electrical and Electronics Engineers and the American Academy of Arts and Sciences.

ABOUT: Cousins, N. Nobel Prize Conversations, 1985; Physics Today December 1973; Science November 16, 1973; Weintraub, P. (ed.) The Omni Interviews, 1984.

JOUHAUX, LÉON
(July 1, 1879–April 28, 1954)
Nobel Prize for Peace, 1951

The French labor leader Léon Jouhaux (zhoō' ō) was born into a working-class family in Paris, where his father worked in a slaughterhouse. He grew up in a household imbued with the radical ideals that had led his grandfather to fight in the revolution of 1848 and his father to participate in the Commune of Paris in 1871. Shortly before Léon was two years old, his father took a job at a match factory in Aubervilliers, outside Paris. When he was not quite twelve years of age, the boy was withdrawn from the local primary school and put to work at the Central Melting House because his father was out on strike. This experience, he recalled later, "had a considerable influence on my future."

A scholarship enabled young Jouhaux to enter the Lycée Colbert in preparation for training as an engineer, but within nine months, further family troubles drove him back to work, this time at the Michaux Soap Works. Though he managed to attend the Diderot Vocational School for one year, he soon joined his father at the match factory—"a wage earner of the humblest order"—and completed his apprenticeship at the age of sixteen. Hungry for learning and outraged at "having been unjustly treated," Jouhaux devoted his free hours to reading.

Called up for military service in 1900, he was posted to Algeria with the First Regiment of Zouaves and was released three years later when his father became blind after years of exposure to white phosphorus in the match factory. Already active in the trade union

LÉON JOUHAUX

movement as administrative secretary in the local chapter of the National Federation of Match Factory Workers, Jouhaux eagerly joined a strike aimed at prohibiting the use of the substance that had disabled his father. The monthlong walkout achieved its goal but cost Jouhaux his job. Blacklisted throughout France, he eked out an income for the next six years until the union succeeded in getting him reinstated at the match factory.

In 1906 Jouhaux was elected by his local union as its delegate to the General Confederation of Labor. (This organization was commonly referred to as the CGT, for its French name, Confédération Générale du Travail.) Established in 1895, the CGT represented the majority of French workers, most of whom were socialists and felt strong bonds with their fellow workers throughout Europe. Rising rapidly in the organization, Jouhaux became interim treasurer in 1909 and, in the same year, secretary-general. As a speaker and as editor of *La Bataille syndicaliste* (The Syndicalist Struggle), the CGT's journal, Jouhaux advocated not only improved working conditions but also better international relations.

During the tense months preceding World War I, Jouhaux urged European trade unions to join forces to avert war. When war came in August 1914, however, he set aside his pacifism and threw his support behind the French war effort. Speaking at an Allied trade union conference in Leeds, England, in 1916, he expressed his hope that the end of the war might bring "liberty, political and economic independence, disarmament, compulsory international arbitration, and the abolition of secret diplomacy" to all the nations of Europe. Moreover, he said, "if the peace treaty establishes these things on a permanent basis, it may be the first step toward a United States of Europe," one in which "the working class will be entitled to claim a higher standard of well-being and freedom."

An opportunity to advance these views came after the war, when Jouhaux was named a technical expert to the International Labor Legislation Commission at the Paris Peace Conference. With Samuel Gompers and other labor leaders, he helped draft Part 13 of the Treaty of Versailles, which established the INTERNATIONAL LABOUR ORGANISATION (ILO) in 1919. Appointed to the ILO's governing body, Jouhaux was elected the first vice president of the newly formed International Federation of Trade Unions, an office he held until 1945. As one of its first official acts, the federation appealed to its 20 million members to aid the victims of war, especially in Austria, where famine threatened thousands of people.

During the postwar years, French Communists, encouraged by the Russian Revolution, sought control of the CGT. In 1921, when all other tactics had failed, Jouhaux—once described by a colleague as a man who "loved a fight and was probably most in his element when taking action"—expelled the Communists from the organization. So great was his prestige that protest quickly died, and Jouhaux remained in full control.

The period between the two world wars was a time of strenuous activity for Jouhaux. A burly man with a forceful speaking voice, he served on the French delegation to the League of Nations, drafted proposals for arms control measures, attended economic conferences, took an active part in the 1931 Unemployment Committee of the Commission of Inquiry for European Union, and represented labor at the 1932 Conference for the Limitation and Reduction of Armaments. In *Le Désarmement* (The Disarmament), published in 1927, he argued that the arms industry should be brought under state control.

Alarmed by the possibility of another world war and increasingly convinced that the League of Nations was impotent to avert it, Jouhaux tried to rally opposition to the Italian invasion of Ethiopia, civil war in Spain, and Nazi aggression in Czechoslovakia and Austria. In a 1938 meeting with Franklin D. Roosevelt, he urged the president to take action against Germany. War broke out the following year, and when France fell to Germany in 1940, the

CGT was dissolved. Refusing an invitation to join the Free French in England, Jouhaux fled to the south of France, worked in the Resistance, and was arrested in Marseilles in December 1941. After two years under house arrest in Cahors, he and his wife were deported to the Buchenwald concentration camp but managed to survive until Allied troops liberated them in May 1945.

After returning to Paris, Jouhaux resumed his position with the ILO and was named president of the French Economic Council, one of the preeminent offices in the Fourth Republic. Once again he vied with the Communists for control of the CGT, and in 1947 he reluctantly broke with the organization when his opponents refused to support the European Recovery Program (better known as the Marshall Plan, after GEORGE C. MARSHALL, who proposed it). With other labor leaders, he helped establish the CGT–Force Ouvrière (CGT–Work Force), and as its president, he advocated a United States of Europe, a unified labor movement throughout Europe, and improved standards for workers.

In recognition of his lifelong efforts for peace, Jouhaux was awarded the 1951 Nobel Prize for Peace. According to Gunnar Jahn of the Norwegian Nobel Committee, Jouhaux "has never faltered in the fight to attain the goal which he set himself in his youth: to lay the foundations of a world which could belong to all men alike, a world where peace would prevail." Although he was surprised and deeply moved by the committee's choice, Jouhaux said in his Nobel lecture, "Not for the briefest instant did I believe that it was I alone who was the recipient of this great reward, for it belongs to all those in the trade union movement." After giving a long and often personal account of the European labor movement, Jouhaux asserted his belief that "the free trade union movement is called on to play an essential part in the fight against international crisis and for the advent of true peace. The scope of the task is enormous, matched only by its urgency. Our movement intends to devote its efforts to this task regardless of the cost." The awarding of the prize to Jouhaux was hailed by political and labor leaders around the world, among them George Meany, who called it "a source of encouragement and a joy to all who believe in the liberty of man."

After suffering a heart attack, Jouhaux died suddenly in Paris on April 28, 1954, having remained active in the CGT–Force Ouvrière and the Economic Council until his death. Robert Bothereau, his successor in the CGT–

Force Ouvrière, recalled the days when Jouhaux was "a taciturn young man who used to sit on the back benches of the national committees of the old CGT. . . . He hardly ever spoke, but when he did, the clarity of his intelligence and the power of his mind became obvious with his first few words. The life of Jouhaux," said Bothereau, "was inseparable from the life of the trade union movement."

WORKS IN ENGLISH TRANSLATION: "The Economic Labour Council in France," International Labour Review February 1921; The International Federation of Trade Unions and Economic Reconstruction, 1922; "The Work of the General Conference," International Labour Review March 1922.

ABOUT: Current Biography January 1948; Dale, L. A. Marxism and French Labor, 1956; Earle, E. M. (ed.) Modern France: Problems of the Third and Fourth Republics, 1951; Galenson, W. Comparative Labor Movements, 1952; Godfrey, E. D. The Fate of the French Non-Communist Left, 1955; International Labour Review September–October 1954; Lorwin, L. L. The International Labor Movement, 1953; Lorwin, V. R. The French Labor Movement, 1954; New York Times April 29, 1954; Times (London) April 28, 1954.

KAMERLINGH ONNES, HEIKE
(September 21, 1853–February 21, 1926)
Nobel Prize for Physics, 1913

The Dutch physicist Heike Kamerlingh Onnes (käm′ ər ling ôn′ əs) was born in Groningen in the northern Netherlands. His father, Harm Kamerlingh Onnes, was a prosperous brick manufacturer; his mother, the former Anna Gerdina Coers, was the daughter of an architect.

After attending secondary school in Groningen, Kamerlingh Onnes entered the University of Groningen in 1870 to study mathematics and physics. He received his candidate's degree (roughly equivalent to a bachelor's degree) in 1871. After three semesters at the University of Heidelberg, in Germany, where he studied under the chemist Robert Bunsen and the physicist Gustav Kirchhoff, he returned to Groningen in 1873. Six years later, he completed his doctoral work magna cum laude with a thesis offering new proof of the earth's rotation.

Between 1878 and 1882, Kamerlingh Onnes lectured at the Polytechnic School (later the Technical University) in Delft. There he became interested in JOHANNES VAN DER WAALS's theory of gases, which involves pressure, temperature, and volume and which ac-

HEIKE KAMERLINGH ONNES

assistants, in 1901 he founded a school of instrument makers and glassblowers, and soon Leiden-trained technicians were at work in physics laboratories all over the world. Kamerlingh Onnes's laboratory served as a model for twentieth-century research institutions.

Although the Scottish scientist James Dewar had liquefied hydrogen in 1898, it was not until 1906 that Kamerlingh Onnes produced liquid hydrogen in significant quantities, using a factory-scale device that could produce 4 liters of liquid hydrogen per hour. The device required the expertise of his machinists' workshop to build pumps and his glassblowers' workshop to make transparent vessels allowing substances to be observed at low temperatures.

Two years later, Kamerlingh Onnes liquefied helium for the first time, at only 4 degrees above absolute zero. Some physicists had doubted that this widely sought goal could ever be attained. "I was overjoyed when I could show liquefied helium to my friend van der Waals, whose theory had been my guide in the liquefaction up to the end," he later recalled. As a result of this accomplishment, a vast new temperature region was opened for research.

Using liquid helium, Kamerlingh Onnes achieved still lower temperatures—1.38°K in 1909 and 1.04°K in 1910. His main concern, however, became the properties of substances at these low temperatures. He investigated absorption spectra of elements, phosphorescence of various compounds, viscosity of liquefied gases, and magnetic properties of substances. Because temperature is a measure of the random motion of the molecules of a substance and because large random motion obscures some phenomena, lowering the temperature can, as he put it, "lift the veil which thermal motions at normal temperatures spread over the inner world of atoms and electrons."

His most striking discovery came in 1911, when he observed that the electrical resistance of some metals completely vanishes at low temperatures. He called this phenomenon, which no one had predicted, superconductivity. Kamerlingh Onnes correctly predicted that superconductivity would eventually be explained by quantum theory, as it was in 1957, when JOHN BARDEEN, LEON N COOPER, and J. ROBERT SCHRIEFFER offered a theoretical explanation of this phenomenon.

Kamerlingh Onnes was awarded the 1913 Nobel Prize for Physics "for his investigations on the properties of matter at low temperatures which led, inter alia, to the production of liquid helium." "The attainment of these

counts for the differences in behavior of real gases and ideal gases. At the time, van der Waals was teaching in Amsterdam, and Kamerlingh Onnes corresponded with him about molecular theory.

In 1882, at the age of twenty-nine, Kamerlingh Onnes was appointed professor of experimental physics at the University of Leiden and head of its physics laboratory. His inaugural address expressed the principle that was to guide him during the forty-two years he held this post: "Through measurement to knowledge." Physics laboratories, he believed, must take quantitative measurements as well as do qualitative experiments; purely verbal descriptions should be supplemented by precise measurements, such as those made in astronomy.

According to van der Waals's theory of corresponding states, all gases behave in the same way when the units of pressure, temperature, and volume are adapted to account for weak forces of attraction between the molecules. By studying gases at low temperatures, Kamerlingh Onnes believed important information could be obtained to verify the conformity of substances. To do so, he had to liquefy gases. Kamerlingh Onnes dedicated his laboratory to the specialized area of cryogenics, the study of the effects of low temperature. He built a large-scale liquefaction plant for oxygen, nitrogen, and air that was capable of continuous production of large amounts of low-temperature liquids. These liquids were vital to experiments on properties of materials as well as to the achievement of still lower temperatures. To develop a staff of specially trained

low temperatures is of the greatest importance to physics research," said Theodor Nordström of the Royal Swedish Academy of Sciences in his presentation speech, predicting that Kamerlingh Onnes's achievements would contribute to new theories of the electron.

Affectionately known as the "gentleman of absolute zero," Kamerlingh Onnes did much to promote international cooperation in science, and he always welcomed foreign scientists to his laboratory. *Communications From the Physical Laboratory of the University of Leiden,* which he founded, became the foremost publication for low-temperature research; and Leiden was, during the first three decades of the twentieth century, the world center for low-temperature physics. Kamerlingh Onnes was also active in applying the technology he developed in the laboratory to practical areas such as food preservation, refrigerated transport, and ice production.

In 1887 Kamerlingh Onnes married Elizabeth Bijleveld, with whom he had one son. Although he had few interests outside the laboratory, he was devoted to his family and was known to colleagues as a man of great charm and modesty. During World War I, he was active in aiding starving children of other countries. The magnitude of his accomplishments and the intensity of his scientific work belied the frail health that he suffered throughout most of his life. After a brief illness, Kamerlingh Onnes died in Leiden on February 21, 1926.

His many awards include the Matteucci Gold Medal of the National Academy of Sciences of Italy, the Rumford Medal of the Royal Society of London, and the Franklin Medal of the Franklin Institute, as well as an honorary degree from the University of Berlin. Before the age of thirty, he was elected to membership in the Royal Academy of Sciences of Amsterdam. He was also a member of the academies of science in Copenhagen, Göttingen, Halle, Uppsala, Turin, and Vienna.

SELECTED WORKS: On the Measurement of Very Low Temperatures, 1900, with M. Boudin.

ABOUT: Dictionary of Scientific Biography, volume 7, 1973; Lorentz, H. A., et al. In Memorium: Heike Kamerlingh Onnes, 1926.

KANTOROVICH, LEONID
(January 19, 1912–April 7, 1986)
Nobel Memorial Prize in Economic
  Sciences, 1975
(shared with Tjalling C. Koopmans)

The Russian economist Leonid Vitaliyevich Kantorovich (kän tə rô′ vich) was born in St. Petersburg (now Leningrad), Russia. The Russian Revolution began when he was five, and during the civil war that followed, his family fled to Byelorussia for a year. In 1922 his father, Vitalij Kantorovich, died, leaving the boy to be raised by his mother, the former Paulina Saks.

Kantorovich showed an interest in the sciences long before he entered Leningrad University in 1926, at the age of fourteen. There he studied not only science but political economy, modern history, and abstract mathematics. His aptitude for mathematics was evident in a paper he presented on set theory at the First All-Union Mathematical Congress in 1930. After graduating that year, he remained at Leningrad University to teach and to continue his research in the mathematics department. By 1934 he had been promoted to full professor, and a year later (when the system of academic degrees was restored) he received his doctoral degree.

During the 1930s, a period of intense economic and industrial development in the Soviet Union, Kantorovich was at the forefront of mathematical research and was eager to apply his theoretical work to help meet the needs of the expanding Soviet economy. Such an opportunity came in 1938, when he was engaged as a consultant to the Laboratory of the Plywood Trust. Assigned the task of devising a technique for distributing raw materials in order to maximize equipment productivity, Kantorovich framed the problem in mathematical terms: maximization of a linear function subject to a large number of constraints. Although he had almost no formal training in economics, he knew that maximization subject to multiple constraints was a basic economic problem and that a technique to facilitate planning in the plywood factories could be used in a host of other cases, such as determining the optimal use of sowing area or the most efficient distribution of transport flows.

Kantorovich's technique for solving the Plywood Trust's problem—known today as linear programming—has since found numerous economic applications throughout the world. In *The Mathematical Method of Production Planning and Organization,* published in 1939,

525

KANTOROVICH

LEONID KANTOROVICH

Kantorovich demonstrated that all economic allocation problems could be approached as problems of maximization subject to multiple constraints and hence could be solved using linear programming. In the Plywood Trust case, he represented the variable to be maximized as the sum of the values of the output of all machines. The constraints were represented by equations that related quantities of each input employed (for example, wood, power, and labor time) to the output of each machine, where the total quantity of each input must not exceed the total quantity available. Kantorovich then introduced new variables (called resolving multipliers) as the coefficients of each input in the constraint equations and demonstrated that the values of the input and output variables could be determined easily once the values of the multipliers were known. Next he presented an economic interpretation of these multipliers, showing that they are essentially the marginal values (or "shadow prices") of the limiting factors; consequently, they are analogous to the scarcity price of each input in a regime of perfectly competitive markets. Although superior computational techniques have since been developed to find the value of the multipliers (Kantorovich used a method of step-by-step approximation), his original insight into the economic and mathematical significance of the multipliers laid the foundation for all subsequent work in the field in the Soviet Union. Later a similar methodology was developed independently in the West by TJALLING C. KOOPMANS and other economists.

Even under the adverse conditions of World War II, when Kantorovich served as a professor at the Higher School for Naval Engineers in besieged Leningrad, he was able to prepare a major study, *On the Translocation of Masses* (1942). In this work he used linear programming to plan the optimal location of consumption and production activity.

Returning to his post at the University of Leningrad in 1944, Kantorovich served concurrently as head of the Department of Approximate Methods at the Mathematical Institute of the Soviet Academy of Sciences, Leningrad. From these positions of influence he encouraged the development of new mathematical planning techniques for the Soviet economy. In 1951, with the geometrist V. A. Zalgaller, he published a book describing their work using linear programming to increase efficiency at the Leningrad Carriage-Building Works. Eight years later he published what is perhaps his most widely known work, *The Best Use of Economic Resources*. In it he drew far-reaching conclusions concerning the ideal way to organize a socialist economy in order to achieve high efficiency in the use of resources. Specifically, he recommended the wider use of shadow prices in allocating Soviet resources—even suggesting the use of an interest rate to represent the shadow price of time when planning investments.

Although some Soviet economists approached these new planning techniques guardedly, Kantorovich's methods were gradually adopted in the Soviet economy. He was awarded the Soviet government's Stalin Prize for work in mathematics in 1949, and in 1958 he was elected a corresponding member of the Soviet Academy of Sciences, in which he won full membership six years later. Moving in 1960 to Novosibirsk, site of the Soviet Union's most advanced computation center, he became director of the Department of Mathematical Economic Methods at the Siberian Division of the Soviet Academy of Sciences. With his fellow mathematical economists V. V. Novogilov and V. S. Nemchinov, Kantorovich won the Soviet government's Lenin Prize in 1965, and in 1967 he was awarded the government's Order of Lenin. In 1971 he became laboratory chief of the Institute of National Economic Management in Moscow.

Kantorovich and Tjalling C. Koopmans shared the 1975 Nobel Memorial Prize in Economic Sciences "for their contributions to the theory of optimum allocation of resources." In his presentation address, Ragnar Bentzel of the Royal Swedish Academy of Sciences pointed to the work of the two laureates as evidence that "the basic economic problems" could be addressed "in a scientific manner that is independent of the political organization of the society under consideration." Koopmans's work on linear programming and activity analysis had closely paralleled Kantorovich's, and the American scholar had arranged the first English publication of the Soviet economist's 1939 book. In his Nobel lecture, "Mathematics in Economics: Achievements, Difficulties, Perspectives," Kantorovich discussed "the problems and experience of a planned economy, especially of the Soviet economy."

The following year Kantorovich became director of the Institute for System Studies at the Soviet Academy of Sciences. Besides conducting his own research, he also encouraged and trained a generation of Soviet economists.

In 1938 Kantorovich married Natalia V. Ilyina, a physician. Their son and daughter are both economists. Kantorovich died on April 7, 1986, at the age of seventy-four.

In addition to the Nobel Prize and the awards he received in the Soviet Union, Kantorovich received honorary degrees from the universities of Glasgow, Grenoble, Nice, Helsinki, and Paris and held membership in the American Academy of Arts and Sciences.

ADDITIONAL WORKS IN ENGLISH TRANSLATION: Approximate Methods of Higher Analysis, 1936, with V. I. Kaylor; Management Science, 1960; On the Calculation of Production Inputs, 1960; On the Method of Newton, 1963; Essays in Optimal Planning, 1976; Problems of Application of Optimization Methods in Industry, 1976, with Tjalling C. Koopmans; Functional Analysis, 1981.

ABOUT: New York Times October 15, 1975; April 11, 1986; Scandinavian Journal of Economics, number 1, 1976; Science November 14, 1975.

KAPITZA, PYOTR

(July 9, 1894–April 8, 1984)
Nobel Prize for Physics, 1978
(shared with Arno A. Penzias and Robert W. Wilson)

The Russian physicist Pyotr Leonidovich Kapitza (kä′ pyi tsu) was born at Kronstadt, the island naval fortress near St. Petersburg (now Leningrad), where his father, Leonid Petrovich Kapitza, served as a lieutenant general in the czarist corps of engineers. His mother, Olga Ieronimovna (Stebnitskaya) Kapitza, was a noted teacher and collector of folktales. After attending secondary school at Kronstadt, he started the long, arduous electrical engineer-

PYOTR KAPITZA

ing course at the Polytechnic Institute of Leningrad, graduating in 1918. He remained at the institute for another three years as a lecturer. Under the direction of Abram F. Ioffe, Russia's first atomic researcher, Kapitza and a fellow student, NIKOLAY N. SEMENOV, developed a method for measuring the magnetic moment of an atom in a nonhomogeneous magnetic field, a technique further refined by OTTO STERN in 1921.

The years of Kapitza's schooling and membership on the staff of the institute coincided with the Russian Revolution and the ensuing civil war, also a time of famine and epidemics, during which his young wife, Nadezhda Tschernosvitova, whom he had married in 1916, and his two small children died. Ioffe urged him to study abroad, but the revolutionary government refused permission until prevailed upon by Maxim Gorky, then the most influential Russian writer. In 1921 Kapitza was allowed to leave for England, where he joined ERNEST RUTHERFORD's research group in the Cavendish Laboratory at Cambridge University. He quickly gained the respect and friendship of Rutherford.

Kapitza's early research at Cambridge, on the magnetic deflection of alpha and beta particles emitted by radioactive nuclei, led to his interest in developing powerful electromagnets. By discharging an electric battery into a small copper magnet coil (effecting a short circuit), he was able to produce magnetic fields six or seven times as strong as any previously achieved. The discharges did not overheat or shatter the apparatus because they lasted only about 0.01 second.

In the course of devising unique equipment to measure the temperature-dependent effects of high-strength magnetic fields on the properties of matter, such as the magnetoresistance of metals (magnetically induced changes in resistance to electric current), he was drawn into the field of low-temperature physics. This work involved the use of liquefied gases, which were not readily available in large quantities, to attain very low temperatures. Kapitza applied his considerable physics and engineering skills to the building of novel machines, culminating in 1934 in the design of a remarkably efficient apparatus for liquefying the gas helium, which boils (changes from liquid to a gas or gas to liquid) at about $4.3°K$ (absolute temperature) and which traditionally presented the greatest difficulty. Helium was first liquefied in 1908 by the Dutch physicist HEIKE KAMERLINGH ONNES. Kapitza's apparatus, however, was capable of producing 2 liters per hour, compared with Kamerlingh Onnes's method, which took several days to produce only small amounts of impure liquid helium. In Kapitza's design, the helium was allowed to expand rapidly, thus cooling before heat could flow in from the surroundings; as it expanded, the helium was sent into a machine for further processing. He overcame the problem of conventional lubricants' freezing at such temperatures by using helium itself to lubricate moving parts.

At Cambridge, Kapitza's reputation and career advanced rapidly. In 1923 he received a Ph.D. as well as the prestigious James Clerk Maxwell Fellowship; in 1924 he became assistant director of magnetic research at the Cavendish; and in 1925 he was made a fellow of Trinity College. The Soviet Academy of Sciences awarded him a doctorate in 1928 and elected him a corresponding member in 1929. The following year he became Messel Research Professor of the Royal Society of London. At Rutherford's urging, the Royal Society built a new laboratory specifically for Kapitza. Named the Mond Laboratory after the German-born chemist and industrialist Ludwig Mond, who endowed it, the facility opened in 1933 with Kapitza as director. He was to work there for only one year.

Kapitza's relations with the Soviet government were problematic and never completely revealed. During his thirteen years in England, Kapitza returned to the Soviet Union several times, accompanied by his second wife, the former Anna Krylova, to lecture, visit his mother, and vacation at a Russian resort. Soviet leaders had repeatedly asked him to stay permanently. While showing interest, he set conditions, particularly the freedom to travel to the West, that prevented a resolution. Late in the summer of 1934, he again visited Russia with his wife; but when the couple prepared to return to England, they found that their exit visas had been canceled. After a fruitless confrontation with officials in Moscow, Kapitza remained while his wife returned to their children in England. (She rejoined him later in Moscow, followed after a time by the children.) Rutherford and other friends wrote to the Soviet government to help Kapitza in his negotiations for release, but to no avail.

In 1935 Kapitza was offered complete control over the Soviet Academy of Science's proposed Institute for Physical Problems, a position he refused for nearly a year before accepting. He was also offered the equipment he had left behind in England; for Rutherford, resigned to the loss of his protégé, allowed the Soviet authorities to purchase the Mond Laboratory and ship it to Moscow. The negotiations, transfer, and installation of the laboratory in Moscow took several years.

Kapitza resumed his low-temperature research, including a study of the properties of liquid helium and the design of machines to liquefy other gases. By 1938 he had perfected a small turbine that liquefied air more efficiently than any previous method. He also measured the extraordinary drop in viscosity of liquid helium when it is cooled below $2.17°K$ and becomes a form called helium 2. Loss of viscosity allows helium 2 to pass through the tiniest openings and even to climb the walls of a container in apparent defiance of gravity. It is also accompanied by an increase in heat conductivity. Kapitza coined the name *superfluid* to describe the phenomenon. Two of his former colleagues at the Cavendish Laboratory, J. F. Allen and A. D. Misener, had independently done similar work, and they and Kapitza published their papers in the same issue of the British journal *Nature*. Kapitza's 1938 paper and two others published in 1942 are considered among his most important contributions to low-temperature physics.

Kapitza had attained a reputation for speaking his mind, even during the purges Joseph Stalin conducted during the late 1930s. When a colleague, LEV LANDAU, who was Jewish, was arrested in 1938 on charges of being a Nazi spy, Kapitza obtained his release by going to the Kremlin and threatening to resign as director of the institute. In his reports to government supervisors, Kapitza was outspoken about decisions he considered wrong. Little is known in the West about Kapitza's activities during World War II. In October 1941 he attracted attention by warning that an atomic bomb might be achievable, possibly the first physicist to do so publicly. He later denied having worked on either the atomic bomb or the hydrogen bomb, and the evidence for this denial is convincing. However, it is not clear whether his refusal was due to moral principle or a dispute over the suitability of the work assigned to the institute. It is known, however, that in 1945, after the Americans dropped an atomic bomb on Hiroshima, when the Soviet Union intensified its efforts to develop nuclear weapons, Kapitza was removed as director of the institute, placed under house arrest for eight years, and barred from certain research institutions. He improvised a laboratory in his home in order to continue work. Reinstated as director of the institute in 1955, two years after Stalin's death, he remained there the rest of his life.

Kapitza's postwar scientific papers treated a wide variety of topics, such as the hydrodynamics of thin layers of fluid and the nature of ball lightning; but his research focused primarily on microwave generators and the characteristics of plasmas. Plasmas are gases heated to such high temperatures that they are stripped of their electrons and become electrified ions. Unlike the neutral molecules of an ordinary gas, ions impose relatively strong electric forces on each other and respond to electric and magnetic fields from an outside source; they are, therefore, sometimes regarded as a separate form of matter. They are used in fusion reactors that require very high temperatures. While developing a microwave generator in the 1950s, Kapitza discovered that high-intensity microwaves produced well-defined luminescent discharges in helium. Measuring the temperatures at the center of the discharge, he found changes of approximately 2 million degrees kelvin over a distance of a few millimeters at the boundary of the discharge. His observations were the basis of a reactor design in which the plasma is continuously heated, which may be simpler and less costly than the pulsed heating methods used in other experimental fusion reactors.

In addition to his achievements as a researcher, Kapitza excelled as an administrator and educator. He developed the Institute for Physical Problems into one of the Soviet Academy's most productive and prestigious research facilities, attracting many of the Soviet Union's top physicists. Kapitza also helped establish Akademgorodok, the academy's research city near Novosibirsk in western Siberia, as well as the Moscow Physical Technical Institute, an innovative teaching institution. His gas liquefaction machines proved to have valuable industrial applications. The use of oxygen, extracted from liquid air, in blast furnaces revolutionized the Soviet steel industry.

With the weight of his prestige of later years, Kapitza (who never joined the Communist party) criticized the Soviet tendency to make scientific judgments on nonscientific grounds; argued against the construction of paper factories that would have polluted Lake Baikal; condemned the Communist party's proposal in the mid-1960s to rehabilitate Stalin; and, with ANDREI SAKHAROV and other intellectuals, signed a letter of protest against the psychiatric detention of the biologist Zhores Medvedev. Kapitza was a member of the Soviet committee of the Pugwash Movement for Science and World Affairs, which worked for peace and disarmament. He also suggested ways to bridge the gap between Soviet and American science.

In 1965, for the first time in thirty-one years, Kapitza was allowed to leave the Soviet Union for Denmark to receive the Niels Bohr International Gold Medal of the Danish Society of Civil, Electrical, and Mechanical Engineers; visit Danish laboratories; and lecture on high-energy physics. In 1966 he revisited England, toured his old laboratories, and reminisced about Rutherford in an address to the Royal Society. In 1969 Kapitza and his wife traveled to the United States for the first time.

Kapitza was awarded the Nobel Prize for Physics in 1978 "for his basic inventions and discoveries in the area of low-temperature physics." He shared the prize with ARNO A. PENZIAS and ROBERT W. WILSON. Lamek Hulthén of the Royal Swedish Academy of Sciences added that "Kapitza stands out as one of the greatest experimenters of our time, in his domain the uncontested pioneer, leader, and master."

In 1927, while still in England, Kapitza married Anna Krylova. Her father, the prominent mathematician Alexei Krylov, was on a mission from the Soviet government to oversee the building of ships ordered from English shipyards. The Kapitzas had two sons, both of whom became scientists. As a young man in Cambridge, Kapitza had ridden a motorcycle, smoked a pipe, and worn tweeds; and he never lost his English habits. In Moscow an English-style cottage was built for him near the institute, and he received clothing and tobacco from England. In his leisure time, he liked to play chess and was interested in antique clocks. He died on April 8, 1984.

Kapitza was honored by his own country as well as by nearly every other scientifically advanced nation. He received eleven honorary degrees on four continents; held memberships in many scientific societies and academies of the United States, the Soviet Union, and most European countries; and was given numerous awards and prizes, both scientific and political, including seven Orders of Lenin from the Soviet government.

SELECTED WORKS: Science and War, 1942; High-Power Microwave Electronics, 1964; Collected Papers (3 vols.) 1964–1967; High-Power Electronics, 1966; Experiment, Theory, Practice: Articles and Addresses, 1980.

ABOUT: Badash, L. Kapitza, Rutherford, and the Kremlin, 1985; Blew, A. M. Kapitza, 1956; Current Biography October 1955; Kedrov, F. Kapitza, 1984; New York Review of Books December 5, 1985; New York Times October 18, 1978; Parry, A. (ed.) Peter Kapitza on Life and Science, 1968; Parry, A. The Russian Scientist, 1973; Science December 1, 1978.

KARLE, JEROME

(June 18, 1917–   )
Nobel Prize for Chemistry, 1985
(shared with Herbert A. Hauptman)

The American chemist Jerome Karle was born in New York City to Louis and Sadie (Kun) Karfunkle. He was raised in Brooklyn and attended Abraham Lincoln High School, graduating in 1933. He enrolled in the City College of New York, where he met HERBERT A. HAUPTMAN, a student from the Bronx. Majoring in chemistry and biology, Karle obtained a B.S. in 1937. He continued his education at Harvard University and received an M.A. in biology the following year. For the next eighteen months, Karle worked for the New York State Health Department. He then entered the University of Michigan, where in 1943 he received both an M.S. and a Ph.D. in physical chemistry, the latter for his dissertation on gas electron diffraction.

During World War II, Karle worked on a United States Navy project and later served as a research assistant on the Manhattan Project, the scientific effort that produced the atomic bomb. After the war, in 1946, Karle joined the staff of the Naval Research Laboratory in Washington, D.C., where he renewed his

JEROME KARLE

friendship with Hauptman. During the 1950s Karle and Hauptman collaborated in developing direct methods for interpreting three-dimensional molecular structure by means of X-ray crystallography.

When a beam of X rays is directed at a crystal of a substance, some of the rays pass through the crystal and others are deflected by the electrons surrounding the nuclei of atoms. The deflected rays are recorded on film as thousands of dots that form a characteristic pattern. The pattern bears little resemblance to the exact arrangement of atoms within the crystal, but by analyzing the intensity and position of the dots and applying mathematical formulas, Karle and Hauptman were able to calculate the phase of the X-ray beam, that is, how much each of the rays had been displaced when traveling through the crystal. From these calculations, an electron-density map of the crystal was produced showing the exact position of the atoms and therefore the molecular structure of the substance.

X-ray crystallography had been in use for a number of years as a means of examining the internal structure of large molecules. The German physicist MAX VON LAUE discovered the diffraction of X rays by crystals in 1912; later, W. L. BRAGG and his father, W. H. BRAGG, determined the atomic structure of many kinds of crystals. JAMES D. WATSON and FRANCIS CRICK used X-ray crystallography in their work on the structure of deoxyribonucleic acid (DNA). Whereas earlier researchers deduced the form of the molecule from the pattern of dots shown on photographic film, the methods

Karle and Hauptman developed directly related the dots to the position of atoms within the molecule.

In 1953 Karle and Hauptman published a paper on their work. This extremely difficult mathematical treatise seemed unrelated to chemistry, and its solution to a previously stubborn problem was met with skepticism and even hostility from many crystallographers. A major barrier to its acceptance was that few chemists understood the mathematics involved in the procedure. As a result, Karle and Hauptman received no support from others in the field, and the direct-method system remained unused for fifteen years.

Three-dimensional structure is a vital part of chemistry. To understand a molecule's reactions and interactions with other molecules, it is necessary to know exactly how the atoms within it are arranged. Although other methods of deducing molecular structures are available, Karle's and Hauptman's direct methods not only are more efficient but also provide an accurate, detailed picture of the entire structure of a molecule.

The most significant contributions Karle and Hauptman have made since 1956 involve the practical use of the direct-method system, particularly its application to crystals that are not radially symmetrical. In 1968 the Naval Research Laboratory established a chair of science for Karle and appointed him chief scientist of the Laboratory for the Structure of Matter. Acceptance of his and Hauptman's work came in the late 1960s, after Karle's wife Isabella, a physical chemist employed by the Naval Research Station, demonstrated the practicality of direct methods by analyzing large molecules. The results of these tests convinced many crystallographers of the usefulness and high degree of accuracy of direct methods.

While continuing his research at the Naval Research Laboratory, Karle lectured occasionally on mathematics and physics at University College, University of Maryland. He lectured widely in England, Germany, Italy, Canada, Poland, Brazil, and Japan. In addition he conducted the Washington Crystal Colloquium, a monthly meeting at the Geophysical Laboratory of the Carnegie Institution.

Karle and Hauptman shared the 1985 Nobel Prize for Chemistry "for their outstanding achievements in the development of direct methods for the determination of crystal structures." With increased acceptance of direct methods, chemists can quickly identify the biologically active components of molecules, thus allowing them to develop new compounds with similar properties, a procedure that has led to the development of many drugs. In recent years, artificial counterparts of steroid hormones that are helpful in the treatment of breast cancer have been developed through analysis of molecular structure by way of direct methods. Direct methods have also been used to study enkephalins (natural painkillers produced by the brain) and to develop new drugs based on the structure of enkephalins.

In 1942 Karle married Isabella Lugoski, a chemist; they have three daughters.

Karle's many awards and honors include the Distinguished Public Service Award of the United States Navy (1968), the Hillebrand Award of the American Chemical Society (1970), and the A. L. Paterson Memorial Award of the American Crystallographic Association (1984). He is a member of the American Physical Society, American Chemical Society, American Crystallographic Association, American Association for the Advancement of Science, and the American Mathematical Society. He was given an honorary degree by the City College of the City University of New York in 1986.

SELECTED WORKS: Solution of the Phase Problem I: The Centrosymmetric Crystal, 1953, with Herbert A. Hauptman.

ABOUT: New York Times October 17, 1985; Physics Today December 1985; Science January 24, 1986.

KARLFELDT, ERIK
(July 20, 1864–April 8, 1931)
Nobel Prize for Literature, 1931

The Swedish poet Erik Axel Karlfeldt was born in Folkärna, in the rural Dalecarlia region of central Sweden that forms the setting for much of SELMA LAGERLÖF's work. Although his ancestors were farmers, Karlfeldt's father, Erik Ersson Karlfeldt, was a self-taught lawyer. His mother, the former Anna Jansdotter, had been married once before. Karlfeldt had an idyllic childhood in the Dalecarlia countryside. Shortly after he entered the University of Uppsala, however, his father suffered financial ruin, lost the family home, Tolvmansgården, and died soon after. While supporting himself as a teacher, Karlfeldt slowly completed his university requirements and graduated in 1902. After a year of teaching, he took a position as librarian at the Academy of Agriculture at Stockholm.

Karlfeldt published the first of his six volumes of poetry, *Vildmarks—och kärleksvisor* (Songs of the Wilderness and of Love), in 1895. Like most of his work, these poems describe the Dalecarlia countryside and the lives of its peasants. Many of the poems have mystical undertones, as if in oblique reference to the pagan origins of the Swedish peasantry. Karlfeldt's poetry, regional and deeply traditional in nature, is imbued with nostalgia for a simpler way of life, for the peasant culture that was vanishing in the face of Sweden's increasing industrialization and urbanization.

Karlfeldt's so-called Fridolin collections, *Fridolins visor* (Fridolin's Songs, 1898) and *Fridolins lustgård* (Fridolin's Pleasure Garden, 1901), take their name from their central figure, Fridolin, the author thinly disguised. Through this persona—part poet, part peasant—Karlfeldt was able to write about himself in the third person, a man who "can talk in the peasant style with a churl, / And in Latin with men of degree." *Fridolins lustgård* includes the group of poems "Dalmålningar, utlagda på rim" (Dalecarlia Wall Paintings in Rhyme), the most original of his Dalecarlia poems. It describes the traditional folk paintings that decorated the walls of farmhouses with scenes from the Bible and ancient legends. Although Karlfeldt never ceased writing about Dalecarlia, his poetry matured in style, the blithe serenity of his earlier poems giving way to a more complex, ambivalent tone and to dark, demonic undercurrents.

In 1904 Karlfeldt was elected to the Swedish Academy and in 1907 joined the Nobel Committee for Literature, to which he was appointed permanent secretary in 1912. While serving in this capacity, he was offered the Nobel Prize for Literature several times. He declined on the grounds of his position in the academy, his relative anonymity outside Sweden, and the high proportion of Swedish writers who had already received the award. He was the first person to refuse the prize.

Karlfeldt wrote little prose. His most famous prose works are his funeral address for the Swedish poet Gustaf Fröding, who died in 1911, and his 1930 Nobel Prize presentation address to SINCLAIR LEWIS. Although he maintained an eminent position in Swedish letters, he never became well known outside his native country. His poems are difficult to translate, particularly because of their use of colloquialisms and archaisms, evoking the idiom of the Swedish peasant.

ERIK KARLFELDT

In 1916 Karlfeldt married Gerda Holmberg, a woman twenty years his junior; the couple had two daughters.

Karlfeldt died suddenly in 1931. Six months later, the Swedish Academy voted to award him the Nobel Prize for Literature, a decision urged by NATHAN SÖDERBLOM, archbishop of Uppsala and himself a member of the academy. The award provoked widespread criticism, especially in Sweden. In reply, the academy pointed out that the statutes governing the Nobel Prize permit the prize to be given posthumously if it is proposed before the laureate's death. The prize money was given to Karlfeldt's family.

"In an age in which handmade things have become rare," said Anders Österling of the Swedish Academy in his presentation address, "there is a new and almost moral value in the masterly, chiseled, and resonant language of Karlfeldt's verse. We may rejoice that this poet, whose inspiration is drawn predominantly from a past that is disappearing . . . is thoroughly unconventional in his means of expression and shows daring innovations, whereas busy modernists often content themselves with following the latest trends and fads."

American literary scholar Alrik Gustafson summed up Karlfeldt's contribution with these words: "In his verse and other formal poetic endeavors, Karlfeldt is one of the great Swedish masters. . . . That quality which particularly distinguishes [his] verse is its deliberate, conscious artistry, its solid, honest, and yet richly imaginative craftsmanship. . . . Traditional as Karlfeldt's poetic style is in many ways, it is traditional with a difference." Writing in 1940, his American translator Charles Wharton Stork declared that Karlfeldt "represents, more than any other Swedish poet, the land and the people that produced him. . . . He is tempered with learning, but his themes are directly his earth and his heaven."

Today, however, Karlfeldt is virtually unknown outside Sweden. His works are generally unavailable, and he receives almost no critical attention.

ADDITIONAL WORKS IN ENGLISH TRANSLATION: Arcadia Borealis, 1938.

ABOUT: American-Scandinavian Review January 1925, October 1931; Gustafson, A. A History of Swedish Literature, 1961; Saturday Review of Literature October 24, 1931.

PAUL KARRER

KARRER, PAUL

(April 21, 1889–June 18, 1971)
Nobel Prize for Chemistry, 1937
(shared with Walter N. Haworth)

The Swiss chemist Paul Karrer was born in Moscow, Russia, where his father, after whom he was named, was practicing dentistry. When the boy was three, his family returned to their native Switzerland and lived briefly in Zurich before settling in the parish of Wildegg in Aargau canton. Karrer attended primary school in nearby Möriken and went on to the district school in Lenzburgh and the gymnasium in Aarau. It was during his secondary education that he developed a serious interest in science.

Entering the University of Zurich in 1908, Karrer studied chemistry under ALFRED WERNER. After receiving his Ph.D. in 1911 for a dissertation on cobalt complexes, he became Werner's assistant at the university's Chemical Institute. His first scientific paper, on organic arsenical compounds, so impressed PAUL EHRLICH that in 1912 he invited Karrer to become his assistant at the Research Institute for Chemotherapy in Frankfurt am Main, Germany.

After the outbreak of World War I in 1914, Karrer was called back to Switzerland to serve as an artillery officer in the Swiss army, but when Ehrlich died in 1915, he returned to Frankfurt to direct chemical research at the Research Institute for Chemotherapy. For the next three years, he investigated the chemistry of plant products. He then accepted a position as associate professor of organic chemistry in Zurich. In December 1919 he succeeded Werner as professor of chemistry and director of the Chemical Institute. In this capacity he conducted research into sugars, amino acids, and proteins. He was particularly interested in the stereochemistry (the spatial arrangement of atoms into molecules) of these and other organic substances.

In 1927 Karrer turned his attention to the anthocyanins, a group of pigments that is responsible for most of the red and blue flowers. RICHARD WILLSTÄTTER, working at the Federal Institute of Technology in Zurich, had already isolated these compounds and examined their molecular structures. Karrer further elucidated the composition of the anthocyanins. The following year he investigated crocin, a yellow pigment that occurs in such plants as the crocus and gardenia, and in 1930 he determined the structure of beta-carotene, a constituent of carrots and other plants that RICHARD KUHN had only recently isolated. Karrer found that the beta-carotene molecule consists of two symmetrical parts, each of which mirrors the other across an imaginary vertical axis.

Karrer's research on plant pigments led him to the study of vitamins, a topic of considerable interest since the early part of the twentieth century and one that was only beginning to yield clues to the body's nutritional needs. Learning that the body transforms carotene into vitamin A, he isolated that vitamin from fish-liver oil and by 1931 had determined not only its constituents but its molecular structure as well. He found that vitamin A comprises twenty carbon atoms, thirty hydrogen atoms, and one oxygen atom in a six-sided, closed ring, with three small molecules attached at two points and a long zigzag chain at a third point. This configuration was, in fact, one-half of the beta-carotene molecule attached to a molecule of water. With this discovery, Karrer became the first scientist to describe the molecular structure of a vitamin.

During the early 1930s, Karrer applied his knowledge of organic pigments to additional vitamin research. From more than 100 tons of whey, he isolated a tiny amount of a yellow, water-soluble, nitrogen-containing pigment called lactoflavin, which later became known as riboflavin, or vitamin B_2. Through chemical analysis he then deduced its formula and molecular structure, and in 1935 he synthesized the substance.

Karrer received the 1937 Nobel Prize for Chemistry "for his investigations on carotenoids, flavins, and vitamins A and B_2." He shared the award with the English chemist WALTER N. HAWORTH. In his Nobel lecture Karrer pointed out that in the space of only a few years new analytical methods had disclosed the existence of some forty carotenoids. He reminded his audience that "scarcely ten years have elapsed since the time when many research scientists doubted the material specificity of the vitamins and were of the opinion that a special state of matter . . . was the cause of the peculiar vitamin effects which had been observed." He concluded, "The chemical side of the vitamin problem is solved in its essential points. It is the task of physiology . . . to explain the intervention of these agents in the cell processes."

One year after receiving the Nobel Prize, Karrer synthesized vitamin E, an achievement that he quickly followed by preparing pure vitamin K. He next turned to the study of nicotinamide adenine dinucleotide (NAD), an enzymatic substance that regulates the transfer of hydrogen between molecules within the cell and thereby produces cellular energy. By 1942 he had determined its structure. Later in the decade he returned to the carotenes, and by 1950 had completed the synthesis of all these compounds. At the same time, he directed research into curare, a naturally occurring poison, derivatives of which have since been used in surgery as muscle relaxants.

Between 1950 and 1953 Karrer served as rector of the University of Zurich. After re-

tiring in 1959, he remained active in various scientific pursuits.

In 1914 Karrer married Helene Frölich, whose father directed a psychiatric clinic in Königsfelden. The couple had three sons, one of whom died in infancy. A highly disciplined researcher, Karrer was also highly respected for his personal kindness and his unassuming nature. Although he had become wealthy, he refused to own an automobile and took the bus to work every day. After a brief illness, he died in Zurich on June 18, 1971.

In addition to the Nobel Prize, Karrer received the Marcel Benoist Foundation Prize (1923) and the Stanislao Cannizzaro Prize of the National Academy of Sciences of Italy (1935), among many others. He held membership in scientific societies on three continents, including the Royal Society of London, the Academy of Sciences in Paris, the National Academy of Sciences of Italy, and the American National Academy of Sciences. He received honorary degrees from universities in Paris, London, Zurich, Basel, Strasbourg, Breslau, Brussels, Turin, and Madrid.

SELECTED WORKS: Organic Chemistry, 1938; Carotenoids, 1950, with Ernst Jucker.

ABOUT: Biographical Memoirs of Fellows of the Royal Society, volume 24, 1978; Chemistry April 1974; Dictionary of Scientific Biography, volume 15, 1978.

KASTLER, ALFRED

(May 3, 1902–January 7, 1984)
Nobel Prize for Physics, 1966

The French physicist Alfred Kastler was born in the village of Guebwiller in Alsace, then part of Germany, to Anna (Frey) and Frédéric Kastler. His childhood interest in nature and his excitement upon witnessing a solar eclipse led to an early attraction to science. After attending primary school in Guebwiller, the boy prepared for university studies at the *Oberrealschule* (renamed Lycée Bartholdi when France regained Alsace after World War I) in nearby Colmar. In 1920 Kastler was admitted to the prestigious École Normale Supérieure in Paris.

After graduation, Kastler taught physics at lycées in Mulhouse, Colmar, and Bordeaux before beginning his graduate studies and work as a research assistant at the University of Bordeaux in 1931. He received his doctorate in physical sciences from Bordeaux in 1936, writ-

ALFRED KASTLER

Photo-Clairet-Dimasoni, AIP Niels Bohr Library

ing his thesis on the excitation of mercury atoms. For the next two years he served as a lecturer at Clermont-Ferrand University, and in 1938 he was appointed as full professor of physics at the University of Bordeaux. Returning to Paris in 1941, he taught at the École Normale Supérieure, where he was promoted to professor in 1945, a position he held until his retirement. From 1953 to 1954 he was visiting professor at the University of Louvain in Belgium.

Kastler's initial work concerned the interaction between light and the electrons in atoms. The electrons may be thought of as circling the nucleus in various orbits while also spinning like tops. Quantum theory restricts the electrons to certain orbits, corresponding to discrete energy levels. When they absorb energy from incident light, electrons rise to higher energy levels. They then fall back to lower levels, releasing the previously gained energy in the form of emitted light. Light, like all electromagnetic radiation, consists of units of energy called photons. The energy in an absorbed or emitted photon, which is proportional to the frequency of the absorbed or emitted light, equals the energy difference between the two levels that bracket an electron transition.

A set of allowed energy levels is unique to the atoms of a particular element. Since excited atoms emit light only at frequencies corresponding to the energy differences between levels, the spectrum of emission as displayed by a spectroscope consists of a series of colored lines (color correlates with frequency for visible light). A spectrum not only identifies a particular element but also conveys information about its atoms' characteristic energy levels, that is, atomic structure. Close inspection reveals that the lines are actually bands of closely spaced lines (fine or hyperfine structure); atomic energy levels are in fact clusters of sublevels, or substates. Substates may represent different contributions from electron properties such as spin. A study of the effect of electromagnetic fields on the substates, as evidenced by shifts in the spectral lines, can disclose details of atomic structure. However, optical spectroscopy could not resolve close line spacings with sufficient precision.

By the late 1940s the most advanced techniques used radio-frequency spectroscopy. One method, known as the atomic beam–magnetic resonance technique, was associated with I. I. RABI and his group at Columbia University. Rabi and his colleagues used the method to make precise measurements of atomic energy levels in the ground state (lowest energies). In general, the ground state has several magnetic substates that can be slightly separated by a magnetic field. Atoms can then be induced to undergo transitions from one substate to another with a stimulating field of the appropriate frequency, that is, one that supplies photons whose energy equals the energy difference between the substates. This happens to be in the radio-frequency range. The Columbia group used an arrangement of magnets and slits to produce a narrow beam of atoms in a few magnetic substates of which only atoms in particular substates could reach a detector. When the field was tuned to the correct frequency, the number of atoms reaching the detector changed, indicating that transitions had occurred. Knowing the photon energy that caused the transitions, the group could calculate the substate energy levels. Such correspondence between the radio frequency of the stimulating field and the energy difference between substates is called Hertzian resonance, after Heinrich Hertz who gave the first experimental demonstration of the existence of radio waves and whose name is now the unit of frequency.

The atomic beam–magnetic resonance technique had limitations: the average lifetime of an excited state before it emitted energy and returned to the undisturbed ground state was short (of the order of one ten-millionth of a second), and only a small number of atoms were affected by the resonance-induced transition. Kastler, with a former student, Jean Brossel, developed several powerful methods of using light to overcome some of these limitations. His method subsequently became known as double resonance.

In this method, a beam of light of appropriate frequency excites atoms to a particular energy level. However, not all of the sublevels become occupied. Consequently, light is not emitted equally in all directions when the atoms fall back to the ground state, and the light emitted in any one direction is partially polarized. If an electromagnetic field is applied to the excited atoms of exactly the right frequency (photon energy) to induce transitions between occupied and unoccupied sublevels, then the subsequently emitted light changes in directional distribution and polarization. This change indicates that the radio frequency is tuned to (in resonance with) the energy difference between sublevels. The method is a precise tool for mapping the sublevels of excited atomic states.

In 1950 Kastler reported another method, called optical pumping, that enabled him to shift electrons in atoms from one magnetic sublevel of the ground state to another. In this method, specially polarized light is directed at a group of atoms. If the ground state has two magnetic sublevels, atoms in one sublevel absorb the light and achieve an excited state while atoms in the other sublevel do not. When the excited atoms emit radiation and return to the ground state, they occupy both the absorbing and nonabsorbing levels. The light is said to have "pumped" atoms into the nonabsorbing ground state.

To further refine their techniques, Kastler and Brossel organized a research team at the physics laboratory of the École Normale Supérieure in 1951. Over the next fifteen years, their group and other researchers advanced the knowledge of atomic sublevels and quantum-mechanical phenomena.

In addition to gaining knowledge of the sublevels of the ground states of many atoms, physicists learned how to orient the nuclei of mercury and cadmium vapor atoms in desired directions. In this way they were able to precisely measure certain magnetic properties of the nuclei. Optical pumping has been used to create targets consisting of polarized atoms, which were then bombarded by beams of particles in nuclear physics experiments.

Kastler received the 1966 Nobel Prize for Physics "for the discovery and development of optical methods for studying Hertzian resonances in atoms." In his presentation speech, Ivar Waller of the Royal Swedish Academy of Sciences described the nature of Kastler's work and some of its consequences. "A large number of nuclear moments have been determined with high precision," Waller said, and added, "Kastler's ideas about optical pumping played an important part in the development of the laser. Optical pumping has permitted the construction of easy-to-use and very sensitive magnetometers as well as atomic clocks."

After retiring from the École Normale Supérieure in 1968, Kastler served as director of research at the National Center for Scientific Research until 1972.

In 1924 Kastler married Élise Cosset, a schoolteacher. The couple had two sons and a daughter. Known as an extremely modest, self-effacing man, he nevertheless took an active role in a number of political causes. He was a vocal supporter of the state of Israel, an opponent of nuclear weapons, and a critic of the American role in the Vietnam War. He also lent his support to the Algerian independence movement. He died on January 7, 1984, in Bandol on the French Riviera.

In addition to the Nobel Prize, Kastler received the Holweck Prize of the Physical Society of London (1954), the Scientific Research Prize of the French Academy of Sciences (1956), and the C. E. K. Mees International Medal of the Optical Society of America (1962), among other honors. He was elected to the French Academy of Sciences in 1964 and was an honorary member of scientific societies in Poland, Germany, Hungary, and Belgium. In 1952 he was made a chevalier of the Legion of Honor, and in 1977 he was made a commander. He was given honorary degrees by the universities of Louvain and Pisa and by Oxford University.

ABOUT: Current Biography December 1967; New York Times January 8, 1984; Science November 11, 1966.

KATZ, BERNARD

(March 26, 1911–   )
Nobel Prize for Physiology or Medicine, 1970
(shared with Julius Axelrod and Ulf von Euler)

The English biophysicist Bernard Katz was born in Leipzig, Germany, the only son of Eugenie (Rabinowitz) and Max Katz. After graduating from the Albert Gymnasium (a college preparatory school) in 1929, he entered the University of Leipzig to study medicine. In medical school he became particularly interested in the function and electrical properties of nerves and received the Siegfried Garten Prize for physiological research in 1933, a year before he obtained his medical degree.

BERNARD KATZ

By that time, Hitler had come to power and the Nazi government had begun to dismiss Jews from universities, research laboratories, and other institutions. As a Jew, Katz had no future in Germany, and in 1935 he moved to England. There he continued his neurophysiologic research under ARCHIBALD V. HILL at the University of London and received a Ph.D. in 1938.

The following year, when war was imminent, Katz accepted an offer from JOHN C. ECCLES to move to the isolation—and presumable safety—of Sydney Hospital in Australia, where he became a naturalized subject of the British Commonwealth in 1941. The following year, however, when it became clear that Australia was threatened by a Japanese invasion, he joined the Royal Australian Air Force and served as a radar officer in the Pacific until the war ended.

In the early 1940s Katz, Eccles, and a colleague, Steven Kuffler, investigated the transmission of nerve impulses to muscles. Before World War I most neurophysiologists believed that nerves stimulated muscles or other nerves by a direct electrical process similar to the movement of electrical impulses within individual nerve cells. The research of OTTO LOEWI and HENRY H. DALE in the 1920s and the early 1930s provided substantial evidence that the motion of an impulse across the synapse (the point at which a nervous impulse passes from one neuron to another or from a nerve to a muscle or other tissue) usually occurs through a chemical neurotransmitter.

Among those who adhered to a purely elec-trical theory of synaptic transmission well into the 1940s, Eccles was the most outspoken and insightful. His confidence in electrical transmission was shaken, however, when he, Katz, and Kuffler examined the effects of chemicals on neuromuscular transmission. At the end of World War II Eccles moved to New Zealand, where he conducted experiments that conclusively destroyed his own electrical hypothesis.

Upon returning to London in 1946, Katz rejoined Hill's laboratory at University College. Since Katz was an expert at utilizing electrical techniques in the study of nerve function but was not well versed in biochemistry, he temporarily interrupted his research on chemical synapses to join ALAN HODGKIN and ANDREW HUXLEY in analyzing the properties of the impulse (the action potential) within an individual nerve. This process, they discovered, could be described in purely biophysical terms.

Resuming his investigation of the neuromuscular junction in 1950, Katz and a colleague, Paul Fatt, employed new techniques in recording electrical impulses within individual neurons. They were interested in examining the electrical activity in the end plate of muscles, directly across the synapse from activating neurons. As Dale had shown, this activity occurs when the neurons release the chemical neurotransmitter acetylcholine. Interactions between acetylcholine and the muscle fiber cause electrical excitation and muscle contraction. In the course of these experiments, Katz later said, the researchers "came across something quite unexpected. In the absence of any form of stimulation, the end-plate region of the muscle fiber is not completely at rest but displays electrical activity in the form of discrete, randomly recurring 'miniature' end-plate potentials."

Further investigation—especially in collaboration with Jose del Castillo—showed that "each miniature end-plate potential arises from the synchronous impact of a large, multimolecular quantum of acetylcholine spontaneously discharged by the adjacent nerve terminal." These results were published in 1954, the same year that a number of electron microscopists, including GEORGE PALADE, first described the fine structure of synapses. One striking feature of the synapse is that the presynaptic (or transmitting) region contains many small vesicles. Two years later, Katz and del Castillo proposed that these vesicles contain acetylcholine. When a vesicle merges with the synaptic membrane, one quantum of neurotransmitter is discharged; it moves across the synapse and then stimulates the muscle to a single miniature end-plate potential. It was thus clearly established, as Katz later said, that "the normal end-plate potential is made up of a statistical fusion of quantal components, which are identical with the spontaneously occurring units."

Next, Katz turned to a question of great interest: "*How* does the nerve impulse . . . raise the probability of occurrence of this quantal event?" During the next decade, Katz and his colleague Ricardo Miledi sought the answer using methods similar to those used by Katz, Hodgkin, and Huxley in their investigation of the action potential. Whereas action potentials arise from the movement of sodium and potassium ions across the nerve-cell membrane, Katz and Meledi showed in 1967 that neurotransmitter release depends on the movement of calcium ions.

Utilizing his extremely careful techniques and ability to study small-scale phenomena, Katz and his colleagues measured the electrical activity caused by a single molecule of acetylcholine and showed that each miniature end-plate potential corresponds to the action of a few thousand such molecules—just enough to fit into a synaptic vesicle.

"For their discoveries concerning the humoral transmitters in the nerve terminals and the mechanism for their storage, release, and inactivation" Katz shared the 1970 Nobel Prize for Physiology or Medicine with ULF VON EULER, who discovered that noradrenaline (norepinephrine) is the neurotransmitter in the sympathetic nervous system (the involuntary nerves that control the body's response to stress), and JULIUS AXELROD, who showed how noradrenaline is produced, released from synaptic vesicles, and recycled. Axelrod had also explored the effects of psychoactive drugs on neurotransmitter activity and established that noradrenaline, like acetylcholine, is released from the synapse in discrete units. These and other discoveries demonstrated that Katz's theories about the mechanism of neurotransmitter release do not apply exclusively to acetylcholine synapses but to the nervous system as a whole.

Katz remained at University College, London, from 1946, first as assistant director of research in biophysics and then as reader in physiology during 1950 and 1951. The next year he was appointed professor of biophysics and head of the biophysics department.

In 1945 Katz married Marguerite Penly; they have two sons.

Katz, who was knighted in 1969, is the recipient of the Baly Medal of the Royal College of Physicians (1967) and the Copley Medal of the Royal Society (1967). He holds memberships in the National Academy of Sciences of Italy, the Royal Danish Academy of Sciences and Letters, the American Academy of Arts and Sciences, and the American National Academy of Sciences. He has also received honorary degrees from Cambridge University and the Weizmann Institute of Science (Israel).

SELECTED WORKS: Electric Excitation of Nerve, 1939; Nerve, Muscle, and Synapse, 1966; The Release of Neural Transmitter Substances, 1969.

ABOUT: New York Times October 16, 1970; Science October 23, 1970.

KAWABATA, YASUNARI
(June 11, 1899–April 16, 1972)
Nobel Prize for Literature, 1968

The Japanese novelist and short story writer Yasunari Kawabata was born in Ōsaka into a prosperous and cultured family. When he was only two years old, his father, a physician, died. After his mother's death the following year, Kawabata was raised by his maternal grandparents; but a few years later both his grandmother and his sister died, and he was left with his grandfather, whom he loved deeply. Although he considered a career as a painter, around the age of twelve Kawabata decided to become a writer instead; and in 1914, just before his grandfather's death, he began writing an autobiographical account that was published in 1925 as *Jūrokusai no Nikki* (Diary of a Sixteen-Year-Old).

While living with relatives, Kawabata attended high school in Tokyo and began studying Western culture, reading Scandinavian literature, and acquainting himself with the work of such European artists as Leonardo da Vinci, Michelangelo, Rembrandt, and Paul Cézanne. In 1920 he enrolled at Tokyo University to study English literature but changed to Japanese literature in his second year. One of his articles in the student newspaper *Shinshichō* (New Trend) came to the attention of the writer Kan Kikuchi, who was so impressed that he invited Kawabata to join the staff of the literary journal *Bungei Shunjū* (Literature of the Times) in 1923, a year before Kawabata graduated from the university. With a group of other young writers, Kawabata founded the

YASUNARI KAWABATA

journal *Bungei Jidai* (Contemporary Literature). This group made up the Shinkankaku-ha—the neoperceptionist or neosensualist—movement in Japanese literature, one that was heavily influenced by modernist writers of the West, in particular James Joyce and Gertrude Stein.

Kawabata's first literary success was the novella *Izu no Odoriko* (Dancer at Izu City, 1925), which is about a student who falls in love with a young dancing girl. The two central characters, the autobiographical hero and the virginal heroine, are prototypes for figures that recur throughout Kawabata's body of work. Later, his protégé Yukio Mishima wrote of Kawabata's "worship of virgins": "This is the source of his clean lyricism, but below the surface it has something in common with the themes of death and impossibility. Because a virgin ceases to be a virgin once she is assaulted, impossibility of attainment is a necessary premise for putting virginity beyond agnosticism. And does not impossibility of attainment put eroticism and death forever at that same point?"

Kin jū (*Of Birds and Beasts*, 1933) tells of a bachelor who rejects social interchange with people and finds peace among animals, cherishing the memory of a young virgin he had loved in his youth. During the 1930s Kawabata's work grew increasingly traditional as he eschewed the experimentation of his early efforts. In 1934 he began writing *Yukiguni* (*Snow Country*), the story of a relationship between a middle-aged playboy from Tokyo and an aging country geisha. Written in an understated,

elliptic style (comparable to haiku, the seventeen-syllable Japanese poetic form), *Snow Country* does not rely on a strong plot structure but rather emerges as a series of linked episodes. Kawabata had difficulty finishing the novel; an incomplete form appeared in 1937, but the final version was not published until ten years later.

During World War II and the period afterward, Kawabata remained neutral, offering no comment on the turmoil around him. He spent much of his time traveling in Manchuria and immersed himself in the study of *The Tale of Genji*, a classic eleventh-century Japanese novel. His enigmatic *Sembazuru* (*Thousand Cranes*, 1949), which uses the traditional Japanese tea ceremony as a background, draws on elements of *The Tale of Genji*. It is Kawabata's best-known work in the West, although many critics consider *Yama no Oto* (*The Sound of the Mountain*, 1954), which presents a family crisis in a series of sixteen linked episodes, to be superior. *Mizuumi* (*The Lake*, 1954) is a novel about erotic obsession that uses stream-of-consciousness devices. The American novelist and essayist Edmund White called it "as compact and immense, as natural and contrived, as the ideal tea garden."

Nemureru Bijo (*House of Sleeping Beauties*, 1961) tells of an old man who, in a final burst of desperation, makes a series of visits to a brothel filled with young girls who have been so drugged that they remain unaware of his presence. There he seeks the meaning of his existence and confronts his own loneliness. In this work, wrote the critic Arthur G. Kimball, "Kawabata's artistry manifests itself in the way he combines the suggestions of death with bits of setting, builds up suspense, and uses indirection to achieve a unified tone. The result would satisfy [Edgar Allan] Poe's criterion for the ideal short story, one which has a 'unique or single effect.'"

After their marriage in 1931, Kawabata and his wife Hideko lived in the ancient samurai capital of Kamakura, north of Tokyo; they had one daughter. They spent their summers in a Western-style cottage in Karuizawa, a mountain resort; during the winter they lived in a Japanese-style home in Zushi. Near there, Kawabata kept an apartment where he wrote, usually dressed in the traditional Japanese garb of kimono and wooden sandals.

In 1960, under the aegis of the United States State Department, Kawabata made a tour of several American universities, including Columbia, where he led seminars on Japanese literature. He described the unbroken development of Japanese writing from the eleventh to the nineteenth centuries and the profound changes wrought by the opening of Japan to the West in the late 1800s, when Japanese writers began to be influenced by their Western counterparts.

Possibly as a result of the growing influence of Mishima (who had become a writer, film actor, and right-wing political activist), Kawabata abandoned his political neutrality in the late 1960s and, with Mishima and two other leading writers, signed a petition denouncing Communist China's Cultural Revolution. He also campaigned for conservative political candidates.

Kawabata received the 1968 Nobel Prize for Literature "for his narrative mastery which, with great sensibility, expresses the essence of the Japanese mind." The first Japanese writer to be so honored, Kawabata said in his acceptance speech, "All my life I have been striving for beauty, and this I will continue until I die." With typical Japanese humility, he said he could not understand why he had been chosen but expressed his gratitude nonetheless, while adding that for the writer, "an honor becomes a burden."

In 1970, after his failure to incite an uprising at a Japanese military base, Mishima committed hara-kiri (ritual suicide). Two years later, Kawabata, who had been in poor health and had recently been hospitalized for barbiturate dependence, also committed suicide by gassing himself in his apartment in Zushi, an act that shocked Japan and the literary world. Because he left no note, his reasons are unknown, although it has been speculated that his death was linked to that of his protégé, by which he had been profoundly shaken. Ironically, in his Nobel acceptance speech, Kawabata had said, "However alienated one may be from the world, suicide is not a form of enlightenment. However admirable he may be, the man who commits suicide is far from the realm of the saint."

With their understated reticence, intensity, and blending of traditional Japanese elements and modernist devices, Kawabata's novels constitute an original and individual genre of Japanese literature. Takashi Oka observed in the *New York Times* that Kawabata's writing "assimilated and distilled influences coming from the West into an essence thoroughly Japanese, yet unmistakably within the mainstream of world literature." Arthur Kimball alluded to Kawabata's "tension of opposites," to which he attributed his narrative skill, achieved through the use of "countless examples of paradoxical or contradictory thoughts and appearance/reality opposites." Masao Miyoshi, who found a "traditional sensibility of sadness . . . over the transience of men and things" in Kawabata's work, also praised its "vibrant silence . . . , the delicate strength in the leap of images," and Kawabata's "refusal to connect things into an easy meaning, his embrace of the shambled world."

In addition to the Nobel Prize, Kawabata also received the Literature Promotion Prize (1937) and the Art Academy Literary Prize (1952). Inducted into the Japanese Academy of Arts in 1954, he was awarded the Goethe Medal of the city of Frankfurt in 1959, the Order of Arts and Letters of France in 1960, and both the French Prize for the Best Foreign Book and the Cultural Medal of the Japanese government in 1961. He served as president of the PEN (Poets, Essayists, Novelists) Club of Japan from 1948 to 1965 and, after 1959, as the vice president of the International PEN Club.

ADDITIONAL WORKS IN ENGLISH TRANSLATION: The Existence and Discovery of Beauty, 1969; Japan the Beautiful and Myself, 1969; The Master of Go, 1972; Beauty and Sadness, 1975; The Old Capital, 1987.

ABOUT: Current Biography March 1969; Miyoshi, M. Accomplices of Silence: The Modern Japanese Novel, 1974; Petersen, G. B. The Moon in the Water, 1979; Rimer, J. T. Modern Japanese Fiction and Its Traditions, 1978; Swann, T. E., and Tsuruta, K. (eds.) Approaches to the Modern Japanese Novel, 1976; Tadeka, K. Essays on Japanese Literature, 1977.

KELLOGG, FRANK
(December 22, 1856–December 21, 1937)
Nobel Prize for Peace, 1929

The American lawyer and statesman Frank Billings Kellogg was born in Potsdam, New York, the son of Abigail (Billings) Kellogg and Asa Farnsworth Kellogg. Just after the Civil War, when he was nine years old, the family moved west and settled on a wheat farm near Elgin, Minnesota. After attending a country school for five years, Kellogg worked on the family farm until his younger brother was old enough to take over the property.

Determined to give up farming, Kellogg moved to Rochester, Minnesota, took an unpaid position as a clerk in a law office and, while supporting himself as a handyman, taught himself history, Latin, German, and law. After only two years, in 1877, he passed the Min-

FRANK KELLOGG

nesota bar examination and formed a law practice with another attorney. The two partners had so few clients, however, that they ran for city attorney, each on the opposite ticket so that one of them would be sure to win. Kellogg, who was the victor, went on to win the race for district attorney in 1881 and held this position until 1886, the same year he married Clara M. Cook of Rochester.

As district attorney, Kellogg represented the towns of Elgin, Plainview, and Viola in a suit against a railroad company to recover bonds that had been issued illegally. With his co-counsel (and cousin), Cushman K. Davis, he won the case on an appeal to the United States Supreme Court. Capitalizing on their success, he and Davis established the firm Davis, Kellogg, & Severance in 1887 and soon became counsel for major corporations throughout the Northwest, especially railroad and mining companies that were reaping large profits during the years of rapid industrial expansion.

In 1900 the editor of the *St. Paul Pioneer Press* asked Kellogg to act as general counsel in the paper's antitrust suit against the General Paper Company of Minnesota. Kellogg's successful handling of the case brought him to national prominence, and four years later President THEODORE ROOSEVELT appointed him special counsel to the United States attorney general for antitrust cases. In this capacity, Kellogg played a major role in *Standard Oil Co.* v. *United States* (1911), in which the Supreme Court declared Standard Oil a monopoly and ordered the corporation dissolved. As special counsel to the Interstate Commerce

Commission, Kellogg also investigated the railroad holdings of Edward H. Harriman.

Throughout this time, Kellogg maintained his lucrative private practice and in 1912 was elected president of the American Bar Association. After serving as a delegate to the Republican national conventions of 1904, 1908, and 1912, he was elected to the United States Senate in 1916 but failed in his bid for reelection in 1922. The following year, President Warren G. Harding selected Kellogg as United States delegate to the fifth Pan-American Conference in Santiago, Chile.

As American ambassador to Great Britain in the period 1924–1925, during the administration of President Calvin Coolidge, Kellogg urged British support for the Dawes Plan, named for CHARLES DAWES, head of an international commission established to reevaluate Germany's reparations payments. After Kellogg was named United States secretary of state in 1925, he helped settle a border dispute between Chile and Peru, advocated American military intervention to suppress a revolution in Nicaragua, and was instrumental in convening a naval armaments conference between Great Britain and Japan. During his tenure in the State Department, some eighty treaties and conventions were negotiated with foreign governments, including the Pact of Paris.

Better known as the Kellogg-Briand Pact, the Pact of Paris originated in 1927 when ARISTIDE BRIAND, the French foreign minister, proposed in a speech that his nation and the United States sign a mutual treaty of friendship prohibiting war between the two nations. Although Briand's suggestion received wide popular support in the United States, the Coolidge administration wanted no alliance that might bind the United States to French interests, and Kellogg countered with a proposal designed to render such a treaty meaningless: an international declaration by all major powers "renouncing war as an instrument of national policy."

Outmaneuvered, Briand at last agreed to the expanded treaty, which was signed initially by fifteen nations in Paris in August 1928 and eventually by a total of sixty-five governments. In the United States, the document was ratified with only one opposing vote in the Senate, where one member called it an "international kiss."

For his role in negotiating the Pact of Paris, Kellogg received the 1929 Nobel Prize for Peace, which was awarded to him the following year. In his presentation speech, Johan Mowinckel of the Norwegian Nobel Committee noted that although many nations harbored "significant reservations" about the pact, the document "must be extended to fields other than the purely political," including the German war debt. "I know of no greater work for humanity than in the cause of peace," Kellogg stated in his acceptance speech. "There is no short and easy road, no magic cure for those ills which have afflicted mankind from the dawn of history." At a banquet after the presentation ceremonies, Kellogg, who did not deliver a Nobel lecture, assured his listeners that "there is no country in the world more interested in peace than is the United States."

The same year that he received the Nobel Prize, Kellogg was chosen to complete the term of the deceased Charles Evans Hughes on the Permanent Court of International Justice at The Hague. Elected to his own term shortly thereafter, he was forced by ill health to retire in 1935. After suffering a stroke, he died of pneumonia on December 21, 1937, shortly after having donated $500,000 to Carleton College in Minnesota for the establishment of a foundation for the study of international relations.

Even though it was clear long before his death that the Kellogg-Briand Pact could not abolish war, Kellogg never lost faith in the treaty he had initially drafted as a stratagem. Often criticized during his years in the State Department for being at once vacillating and obstinate, Kellogg was also praised for his diplomacy. No one, wrote his biographer Robert Ferrell, can contemplate his career "without respect for the undoctrinaire nature of Frank B. Kellogg, his willingness to listen to advice, his ability to treat diplomatic problems with reason and rare common sense."

WORKS BY: Lincoln and Roosevelt, 1908; Some Objectives of American Foreign Policy, 1926; The Settlement of International Controversies by Pacific Means, 1928; "The Renunciation of War," Review of Reviews December 1928; "The War Prevention Policy of the United States," American Journal of International Law April 1928.

ABOUT: Bryn-Jones, D. Frank B. Kellogg: A Biography, 1937; Dictionary of American Biography, supplement 2, 1958; Ellis, L. E. Frank B. Kellogg and American Foreign Relations, 1961; Ferrell, R. H. Peace in Their Time: The Origins of the Kellogg-Briand Pact, 1952; Ferrell, R. H., and Bemis, S. F. (eds.) American Secretaries of State and Their Diplomacy, volume XI, 1963; Miller, D. H. The Peace Pact of Paris, 1928; National Cyclopedia of American Biography, volume A, 1930; New York Times December 22, 1937.

KENDALL, EDWARD C.
(March 8, 1886–May 4, 1972)
Nobel Prize for Physiology or Medicine, 1950
(shared with Philip S. Hench and Tadeus Reichstein)

The American biochemist Edward Calvin Kendall was born in South Norwalk, Connecticut, the third of eight children, to the former Eva Frances Abbott and George Stanley Kendall, a dentist. After receiving his early education at the Franklin Elementary School, he attended South Norwalk High School for two years and then transferred to Stamford High School, where he became interested in chemistry. He also was intrigued by electricity, machines, and mathematics.

Enrolling in Columbia University in 1904, Kendall studied chemistry and conducted undergraduate research under the guidance of H. C. Sherman. He received a B.S. in chemistry in 1908 and that summer worked as a laboratory assistant in Columbia's biochemistry department before enrolling in graduate school to study that subject. As the university's first Goldschmidt Fellow, Kendall performed research on amylase, an enzyme which is synthesized and secreted by the pancreas and which converts starch into simple sugar molecules in the intestinal tract. After observing that the quantity of sugar produced from a given amount of starch by the enzymatic action of amylase was related to the concentration of salt in the intestinal tract, he published the results of his research in the Journal of the American Chemical Society. He received a Ph.D. in biochemistry from Columbia in 1910.

Later that year, Kendall was hired as a research chemist by Parke-Davis and Company, a pharmaceutical firm in Detroit, where he was assigned the task of extracting thyroid hormone from the thyroid gland. Upon learning that he was expected to compete with another chemist on the same project, he resigned after only five months and accepted an offer to set up a chemistry laboratory at St. Luke's Hospital in New York City. There he continued his efforts to extract hormones from the thyroid gland.

The thyroid gland is situated in front of and on either side of the trachea, or windpipe. Its function—first described in the last quarter of the nineteenth century by THEODOR KOCHER, a Swiss surgeon—is the synthesis and secretion of thyroid hormones. It was later discovered that there are two thyroid hormones,

EDWARD C. KENDALL

thyroxine and triiodothyronine, whose function is the maintenance of the normal consumption of oxygen and the production of carbon dioxide. The first crude extracts of the thyroid gland for clinical use were produced by Eugen Baumann, a German biochemist, near the end of the nineteenth century.

In 1913 Kendall was able to increase the concentration of thyroid hormone in thyroid gland extracts 100-fold. The clinical efficacy of these extracts was soon demonstrated in patients with such diseases as hypothyroidism (deficiency of thyroid activity), myxedema (swelling of the face and hands), and cretinism (arrested physical and mental development). The importance of his work was not immediately appreciated at St. Luke's Hospital, however. Seeking a more academic and scholarly environment, in 1914 Kendall accepted a position in the research laboratories of the Mayo Clinic in Rochester, Minnesota.

At the Mayo Clinic, Kendall continued his research on the thyroid gland by attempting to isolate and purify its biologically active hormones, a task he eventually accomplished by accident. After preparing an extract of thyroid tissue in ethanol, he inadvertently left it in his laboratory for several hours while the ethanol evaporated, leaving, as it turned out, a pure crystalline form of thyroid hormone. Kendall later proposed a chemical formula for the hormone, which subsequently was found to be incorrect. He and his colleagues at the Mayo Clinic also isolated glutathione, which acts as a respiratory carrier of oxygen. They determined that it is a tripeptide containing the three amino acids glutamine, glycine, and cysteine.

Upon his appointment as professor of biochemistry at the Mayo Clinic in 1921, Kendall turned his attention to the isolation and identification of the hormones of the adrenal glands. Located at the upper poles of each kidney, these glands discharge epinephrine, or adrenaline, into the bloodstream. Epinephrine, a potent stimulator of the sympathetic nervous system, increases blood pressure and stimulates the heart muscle, leading to an accelerated heart rate and increased oxidation.

The cells of the adrenal cortex, which synthesize and discharge adrenocortical hormones into the bloodstream, are controlled by the pituitary gland—specifically, by a secretion called adrenocorticotropic hormone (ACTH). When the blood levels of adrenocortical hormones (specifically, cortisol) are low, ACTH is released by the pituitary gland, an action which, in turn, stimulates the adrenal cortex to release adrenocortical hormones. When the blood levels of adrenocortical hormones are high, the pituitary gland releases less ACTH and the adrenal gland releases less adrenocortical hormone.

There are two categories of hormones of the adrenal cortex: the glucocorticoids (cortisone and cortisol), which are involved in the metabolism of carbohydrate, fat, and protein; and the mineralocorticoids, which are involved in electrolyte and water balance. Cortisone and cortisol also block biochemical reactions that intervene in the inflammatory response of tissue to injury or infection. The adrenocortical hormones are steroids, as are the male and female sex hormones and cholesterol.

A deficiency of adrenocortical hormones can lead to Addison's disease, named after the English physician Thomas Addison, who published the first description of the condition. By the 1920s it had been established that surgical removal of the adrenal glands in experimental animals causes a condition that is identical to Addison's disease in human beings. It had also been shown that extracts of adrenal gland tissue will correct the abnormalities produced by a deficiency of adrenocortical hormones. Since there are so many precursor forms of the hormones of the adrenal gland, their isolation and identification—particularly those of the adrenal cortex—posed a difficult task for Kendall and other investigators.

In 1934 Kendall reported the isolation and preparation in crystalline form of what he thought was a single adrenal corticosteroid, which he called cortin. Kendall and his col-

543

leagues then isolated twenty-eight different steroids from the adrenal cortex, most of which were biochemical precursors and biologically inactive. However, they isolated and identified six biologically active forms of adrenal corticosteroids, which they called compounds A, B, C, D, E, and F, in the order of their discovery. It was later determined that compound E (cortisone) and compound F (cortisol, also called hydrocortisone) are the most important hormones of the adrenal cortex (along with aldosterone, which was isolated in the 1950s).

In the early 1940s Kendall was appointed to the Adrenal Subcommittee of the Committee on Medical Research of the United States Office of Scientific Research and Development with the idea that he might be able to direct the production of large quantities of compound E, or cortisone. Kendall believed that cortisone showed great promise as a therapeutic agent in the treatment of various skin and eye diseases. He had also discussed with PHILIP S. HENCH, a colleague at the Mayo Clinic, the possible use of cortisone in the treatment of rheumatoid arthritis, a chronic disease characterized by inflammation and swelling of the joints. Although cortisone has proved effective in the treatment of rheumatoid arthritis, its use (and that of ACTH) often produces undesirable side effects, such as high blood pressure, high glucose levels, and a peculiar form of obesity.

By the end of World War II, Kendall and his colleagues had clarified thirty of the thirty-eight biochemical steps in the biosynthesis of cortisone. At that point Lewis Sarett of Merck and Company was sent to the Mayo Clinic to help work out the final steps in the biosynthesis of cortisone. In late 1945 the first small quantities of cortisone were synthesized in Kendall's laboratory. Two years later, when a simpler method of synthesizing cortisone was devised, its large-scale production became more feasible. At that time, ACTH (which stimulates the adrenal glands to secrete cortisone and cortisol) was isolated from extracts of pituitary gland tissue by biochemists at Yale University and the University of California.

In 1950 Kendall shared the Nobel Prize for Physiology or Medicine with Hench and TADEUS REICHSTEIN "for their discoveries relating to the hormones of the adrenal cortex, their structure and biological effects." In his Nobel lecture Kendall stated that there "is no doubt that the use of this hormone [cortisone] of the adrenal cortex will continue to increase. Its effect is unique in rheumatoid arthritis,

rheumatic fever, asthma and hay fever, and other allergic conditions." Kendall shared his portion of the prize with several associates who had contributed to his work on cortisone.

After retiring from the Mayo Clinic in 1950, Kendall became visiting professor of chemistry at Princeton University, where he continued to conduct research.

In 1915 Kendall married Rebecca Kennedy; they had three sons and one daughter. His later years were darkened by his wife's mental illness, the death of one of his sons from cancer, and the suicide of another son. During a conference with several associates in 1972, Kendall rose to write a chemical formula on the blackboard and was stricken with a heart attack. He was hospitalized due to coronary insufficiency and died three days later.

Kendall was the recipient of the John Scott Award given by the city of Philadelphia (1921), the Charles Frederick Chandler Medal of Columbia University (1925), the Lasker Award of the American Public Health Association (1949), the Passano Award in Medical Science of the Passano Foundation (1950), and the Kober Medal of the Association of American Physicians (1952). He was awarded honorary degrees by Yale University, the University of Cincinnati, and Columbia University, among others. He held membership in the American Physiological Society, the Association of American Physicians, the American Chemical Society, the American Society of Experimental Pathology, the American Association for the Advancement of Science, the National Academy of Sciences, the American Philosophical Society, the Society of Biological Chemistry, and the Harvey Society.

SELECTED WORKS: Thyroxine, 1929; Vitamins and Hormones, 1943, with others; Cortisone, 1971.

ABOUT: Biographical Memoirs of the National Academy of Sciences, volume 47, 1975; Chittenden, R. H. The Development of Physiological Chemistry in the United States, 1930; Dictionary of Scientific Biography, volume 15, 1978; Robinson, D. The Miracle Finders, 1976; Rowntree, L. G. Amid Masters of Twentieth-Century Medicine, 1958.

KENDREW, JOHN C.
(March 24, 1917–)
Nobel Prize for Chemistry, 1962
(shared with Max Perutz)

The English biochemist John Cowdery Kendrew was born in Oxford, the only son of Wilfrid George Kendrew, a noted climatologist who taught at Oxford University, and the former Evelyn May Graham Sandberg, an art historian who published studies on the Italian primitive painters. He received his early education at the Dragon School in Oxford and his secondary education at Clifton College in Bristol. By the time he graduated from Clifton, he had already decided upon a scientific career and therefore chose to enter Cambridge University, despite his father's connections with Oxford. He received his B.A. with first-class honors in the natural sciences in 1939 and his M.A. in 1943.

A year after Great Britain declared war in 1939, Kendrew joined the Ministry of Aircraft Production as a junior scientific officer. In 1944 he became scientific adviser to the Allied air commander in chief, based in Southeast Asia. During the latter part of World War II, after becoming acquainted with the British chemist J. D. Bernal and the American chemist LINUS C. PAULING, Kendrew developed an interest in solving the molecular structure of proteins. After leaving government service, he returned to Cambridge in 1946 and began working with MAX PERUTZ at the Cavendish Laboratory. He obtained his Ph.D. in 1949 and his doctor of science degree in 1962.

At the time Kendrew joined the Cavendish, Perutz had resumed his earlier investigations into the molecular structure of globular proteins, using the technique of X-ray crystallography. In this method, a beam of X rays is passed through a crystal and recorded on a photographic plate. Because the rays are diffracted by the electrons of the atoms composing the crystal, the pattern they form on the plate offers clues to the atomic structure of the crystal.

While Perutz continued his study of hemoglobin, Kendrew attempted to determine the structure of myoglobin, a substance that retains oxygen in muscles. Although considerably simpler in structure than hemoglobin, myoglobin nevertheless posed a formidable challenge, for it consists of some 150 amino acids that are made up of approximately 2,600 atoms. The task of plotting the position of these atoms was further complicated by the fact that X-ray crystallography techniques depended largely on trial and error for their interpretation.

In 1947 Kendrew followed Perutz to the Unit for Molecular Biology, established that year at the Cavendish Laboratory by the Medical Research Council. Working alone at first in an unused shed, Kendrew and Perutz were joined later by FRANCIS CRICK, JAMES D.

JOHN C. KENDREW

WATSON, FREDERICK SANGER, and other researchers.

Kendrew's work on myoglobin received a decisive impetus in 1953, when Perutz discovered that the introduction of mercury atoms into hemoglobin crystals altered the diffraction patterns produced by X rays. By comparing the original and modified patterns, it was now possible to derive the structure of the molecule. Applying this heavy-atom replacement technique to his own research, Kendrew found that myoglobin would not retain mercury atoms, and he was forced to search for other heavy atoms as a substitute.

In a diffraction pattern, the spots nearest the center of the plate represent X rays that have been deflected from widely spaced atoms, and it was in this area that Kendrew and his colleagues focused their efforts. By 1957 they were able to distinguish objects with a width of 6 angstroms (6 ten-billionths of a meter). Although at this scale the diffraction patterns could not disclose individual atoms, they did reveal "something no one had ever seen," as Kendrew later recalled—"a three-dimensional picture of a protein molecule in all its complexity."

The work of Frederick Sanger had recently shown that proteins are composed of chainlike arrangements of amino acids linked by a form of chemical connection called a peptide bond; hence the protein strings are called polypeptide chains. At 6 angstroms, Kendrew could make out the winding course of the myoglobin polypeptide chain. "The most striking features of the molecule," he reported, "were its irregularity and its total lack of symmetry." These features became further clarified in 1959 when Kendrew obtained an image of myoglobin at a resolution of 2 angstroms, an achievement made possible by the use of powerful computers to perform the mathematical calculations required in studying the 10,000 X-ray plates involved.

Kendrew and Perutz were awarded the 1962 Nobel Prize for Chemistry "for their studies of the structures of globular proteins." "Proteins are unique in combining great diversity of function and complexity of structure with a relative simplicity and uniformity of chemical composition," Kendrew remarked in his Nobel lecture. "In determining the structures of only two proteins, we have reached, not an end, but a beginning," he continued; "we have merely sighted the shore of a vast continent, waiting to be explored."

From 1953 until 1974, Kendrew served as deputy director of the Laboratory of Molecular Biology (formerly the Unit for Molecular Biology) at Cambridge, and in 1975 he became the first director of the European Molecular Biology Laboratory in Heidelberg, Germany, a position he held until 1982. He was named president of St. John's College, Oxford, in 1981. Kendrew, who is unmarried, has been described as sensitive, quiet, and unassuming. During his leisure time he enjoys listening to music and adding to his substantial collection of classic recordings.

In addition to the Nobel Prize, Kendrew has been awarded the Royal Medal of the Royal Society (1965). He was knighted in 1963. A member of the British Association for the Advancement of Science and a trustee of the British Museum (1974–1979), he holds honorary memberships in the American Academy of Arts and Sciences, the Leopoldina German Academy of Researchers in Natural Sciences, the Heidelberg Academy of Sciences, the Bulgarian Academy of Sciences, and the Royal Irish Academy. He has received honorary degrees from the universities of Keele, Reading, Buckingham, and Exeter.

SELECTED WORKS: "The Three-Dimensional Structure of a Protein Molecule," Scientific American December 1961; The Thread of Life: An Introduction to Molecular Biology, 1963.

ABOUT: Current Biography October 1963; New York Times November 2, 1962.

KHORANA, HAR GOBIND
(January 9, 1922–)
Nobel Prize for Physiology or Medicine, 1968
(shared with Robert W. Holley and Marshall W. Nirenberg)

The Indian-American biochemist Har Gobind Khorana (kə rä′ na) was born in Raipur, a small village in Punjab, now a part of Pakistan. He was the youngest son of five children of Ganpat Rai Khorana, a tax clerk for the British colonial government, and Krishna (Devi) Khorana, both of whom were Hindus. Although poor, the Khoranas were one of the few literate families in Raipur. Educated in an outdoor class conducted by the village teacher, Khorana later attended D. A. V. High School in Multan, Punjab. After graduation, he studied chemistry at Punjab University in Lahore, from which he received a B.S. with honors in 1943 and an M.S. with honors two years later.

A Government of India Fellowship enabled him to enter the University of Liverpool in 1945 to study organic chemistry. For a dissertation on the chemical pigment violacein, which colors certain bacterial cells, he was awarded a Ph.D. in organic chemistry in 1948, after which he spent a year studying the chemical structure of certain alkaloids (organic bases) with VLADIMIR PRELOG at the Federal Institute of Technology in Zurich, Switzerland. After visiting India briefly in the fall of 1949, he returned to England and was named a Nuffield Fellow at Cambridge University. Working with ALEXANDER TODD at Cambridge, he became interested in the biochemistry of nucleic acids, large molecules found in the nucleus of the cell.

In 1952 Khorana was appointed director of the Section of Organic Chemistry of the British Columbia Research Council at the University of British Columbia in Vancouver, Canada, where he studied the chemical structure of acetyl coenzyme A. Enzymes are protein molecules that facilitate the biochemical reactions of the cell; coenzymes are molecules necessary for the efficient performance of enzymes. Discovered in 1945 by FRITZ LIPMANN, acetyl coenzyme A is a complex molecule essential to the cellular biochemistry of carbohydrates, fats, and proteins. In 1959 Khorana and a colleague, John Moffatt, synthesized acetyl coenzyme A. Since the method they developed was considerably simpler and less expensive than the previously available techniques for isolating the compound from yeast, it made the coenzyme readily available

HAR GOBIND KHORANA

for research on such cellular processes as the breakdown of sugar molecules to release energy. The work earned Khorana international recognition.

In 1960 Khorana was appointed co-director of the Institute for Enzyme Research at the University of Wisconsin in Madison. The following year he published *Some Recent Developments in the Chemistry of Phosphate Esters of Biological Interest*. In 1963 he was named an editor of the *Journal of the American Chemical Society*. The following year he was appointed Conrad A. Elvelijem Professor of the Life Sciences at Wisconsin. Khorana then directed his research to the central questions of contemporary genetics: the biochemistry of the nucleic acids, the biosynthesis of cellular proteins (enzymes), and the nature of the gene.

The science of genetics began in 1866 when Gregor Mendel published his observations on the inheritance of flower color in the garden pea. Mendel postulated that "elements," now called genes, govern the inheritance of the physical traits of an organism. In 1869 Friedrich Miescher discovered that genes reside on chromosomes in the nucleus of the cell. During the first half of the twentieth century, the work of many researchers clarified the biochemistry of the two nucleic acids, ribonucleic acid (RNA) and deoxyribonucleic acid (DNA). Genes are made of DNA, which directs the biosynthesis of cellular proteins, enzymes, and coenzymes, thus controlling the biochemical processes of the cell.

FRANCIS CRICK and JAMES D. WATSON determined the three-dimensional structure of DNA in 1953, demonstrating that it is shaped like a double helix, a structure that resembles a rope ladder twisted into a spiral. The double helix of DNA consists of two strands of nucleotides, which in turn comprise deoxyribose (a sugar), a nitrogenous base, and a molecule of phosphate. The phosphate molecule links the nucleotides together, and the two nucleotide strands are linked to each other by pairs of bases—or "rungs" of the "ladder"—inside the double helix. The sequence of the four nucleotide bases constitutes the genetic code of DNA. A triplet of bases contains genetic instructions for the incorporation of a single amino acid into a molecule of protein, which consists of amino acids linked together in chains. A gene furnishes instructions for the biosynthesis of an entire protein molecule.

Molecules of RNA, also composed of nucleotide strands, duplicate the genetic code in DNA in the nucleus of the cell and carry it to ribosomes in the cytoplasm, where protein molecules are formed. Another function of RNA is to transfer amino acids to the site of protein synthesis.

In the early 1960s Khorana set out to decipher the genetic code. Because there are four nucleotide bases in DNA that encode for the twenty different amino acids, a code consisting of a triplet of bases has sixty-four possible triplet combinations ($4 \times 4 \times 4 = 64$). To achieve his goal, Khorana therefore had to determine the bases and base sequences in the base-triplet codes for each of the twenty amino acids. MARSHALL W. NIRENBERG of the National Institutes of Health had recently developed a system for the synthesis of protein molecules that consisted of a mixture of DNA, RNA, amino acids, ribosomes, and the essential enzymes.

Using Nirenberg's system, Khorana performed a series of experiments that enabled him to determine the base sequence in the triplet codes for all twenty amino acids. He discovered that some of the amino acids were represented by more than one base triplet; it was therefore said that the genetic code was not perfect from an evolutionary point of view. Khorana and his colleagues synthesized nucleotide strands of DNA and RNA with all 64 base triplets and identified the base-triplet codes that signal the initiation and termination of the biosynthesis of a specific protein. They also studied the secondary chemical structure of transfer RNA, a type of RNA that carries amino acids to the ribosomes. The primary structure is simply the sequence of bases in the nucleotide strand; the secondary structure, which is three-dimensional, shows where twisting of the strand causes it to come in contact with itself. The secondary structure of transfer RNA resembles a three-leaf clover. The base sequence of the middle leaf of transfer RNA is complementary to the base sequence of messenger RNA, which copies the genetic code from DNA and carries it to the ribosomes. This transfer assures that amino acids are inserted into protein molecules in the correct order.

"For their interpretation of the genetic code and its function in protein synthesis, Khorana, ROBERT W. HOLLEY, and Nirenberg were awarded the 1968 Nobel Prize for Physiology or Medicine. In presenting the prize, Peter Reichard of the Karolinska Institute compared nucleic acid and proteins to language and their building blocks to the letters of the alphabet. "It is the chemical structure of the nucleic acid which determines the chemical structure of the protein," Reichard said; "the alphabet of nucleic acids dictates the alphabet of proteins. The genetic code is the dictionary which gives us the translation of one alphabet into the other." Khorana's synthesis of nucleic acids was "a prerequisite for the final solution of the genetic code," Reichard added.

Two years after receiving the Nobel Prize, Khorana and his colleagues were the first researchers to synthesize a DNA gene of yeast, consisting of twenty-seven nucleotide molecules. Later they synthesized a gene of the intestinal bacterium *Escherichia coli*. Since 1971 Khorana has been Alfred P. Sloan Professor of Biology and Chemistry at the Massachusetts Institute of Technology.

He married Esther Elizabeth Sibler of Switzerland in 1952; they have a son and two daughters. Khorana became an American citizen in 1966. Known for his dedication to scientific research, he once worked for twelve consecutive years without a vacation. He enjoys listening to music and going on hikes, during which he jots down ideas that occur to him.

Khorana's many honors include the Merck Award of the Chemical Institute of Canada (1958), the Louisa Gross Horwitz Prize of Columbia University (1968), the Albert Lasker Basic Medical Research Award (1968), and the Willard Gibbs Medal of the American Chemical Society (1974). He is a member of the National Academy of Sciences, the American Association for the Advancement of Science, the American Chemical Society, and the American Society of Biological Chemists.

ABOUT: Current Biography December 1970; New York Times October 17, 1968; Science October 26, 1968; Washington Post June 8, 1970.

KING, MARTIN LUTHER, JR.
(January 15, 1929–April 4, 1968)
Nobel Prize for Peace, 1964

Martin Luther King Jr., American clergyman and civil rights leader, was born Michael Luther King in Atlanta, Georgia, the middle sibling and elder son in a family of three children. His father, who changed his own first name and his son's to Martin when the boy was six years old, was pastor of Atlanta's Ebenezer Baptist Church. His mother, the former Alberta Christine Williams, taught school before her marriage. King grew up in Atlanta during the Depression, in loving, middle-class surroundings.

While attending David T. Howard Elementary School, Atlanta University School, and Booker T. Washington High School, King skipped several grades. In 1944, having passed the entrance examination without graduating from high school, he entered the all-black Morehouse College in Atlanta. At college he became a member of the National Association for the Advancement of Colored People (NAACP). In 1947 he was ordained in his father's church and became his assistant. Graduating from Morehouse with a B.A. in sociology in 1948, King entered Crozer Theological Seminary in Chester, Pennsylvania, and received a B.D. in 1951. A fellowship enabled him to pursue graduate studies at Boston University, where in 1955 he was awarded a Ph.D. in systematic theology with a thesis called "A Comparison of the Conceptions of God in the Thinking of Paul Tillich and Henry Nelson Wieman." During his graduate studies, King was deeply influenced by his reading of the clergyman and social reform leader Walter Rauschenbusch as well as by the works of Georg Hegel, Henry David Thoreau, Edgar S. Brightman, Paul Tillich, and Reinhold Niebuhr. "The projection of a social gospel," he once said, "is the true witness of a Christian life."

King married Coretta Scott, a music student, in 1953. The couple had two sons and two daughters.

In 1954 King accepted a ministry at the Dexter Avenue Baptist Church in Montgomery, Alabama, and remained there until January 1960, when he became co-pastor with his father at the Ebenezer church. In Montgomery, King organized committees for a variety of social-

MARTIN LUTHER KING JR.

action programs, raised money for the NAACP, and served on the Executive Committee of the local NAACP chapter.

After seamstress Rosa Parks was arrested for refusing to yield her seat on a bus to a white passenger, the Montgomery Improvement Association was organized in December 1955, with King as president. Doubtful about the moral rightness of a proposed boycott by blacks of the Montgomery bus system, King hesitated about accepting this position until he remembered a statement of Thoreau: "We can no longer lend our cooperation to an evil system." On the evening of December 5, King made what he later considered to be the most decisive speech of his life. Telling his audience that they had no choice but resistance, King promised that the protest would save them "from that patience that makes us patient with anything less than freedom and justice." Under King's direction, the black community boycotted the Montgomery bus system for 382 days. In November 1956 the United States Supreme Court declared the Alabama segregation law unconstitutional. In December blacks and whites rode Montgomery buses on an integrated basis for the first time. King became a national figure, and his portrait appeared on the cover of *Time* magazine in February 1957.

The mid-twentieth-century civil rights movement into which King was drawn had its roots in the years preceding World War II. Then, such organizations as the NAACP and the Congress of Racial Equality and such labor leaders as A. Philip Randolph took action to win civil rights for blacks. Their early achievements culminated in the 1954 landmark decision *Brown* v. *Board of Education of Topeka*. In that decision, the Supreme Court reversed decades of segregated education by declaring that separate schools for whites and blacks were inherently unequal and therefore in violation of the Fourteenth Amendment.

King's unique contribution to the civil rights movement stemmed from his reliance on Christian philosophical principles. Onto these principles, he grafted the example of Mohandas Gandhi, leader of the passive resistance movement that helped free India from British domination. "I found in the nonviolent resistance philosophy of Gandhi," King once said, "the only morally and practically sound method open to oppressed people in their struggle for freedom."

The Montgomery bus boycott, during which he was jailed and his home was bombed, established King as a hero to the nation's black community. In January 1957 southern black leaders formed an alliance of church-affiliated civil rights organizations, later named the Southern Christian Leadership Conference (SCLC), and elected King its president. It was during this period that King, now the acknowledged spokesman for blacks in the United States, wrote *Stride Toward Freedom: The Montgomery Story*. While signing copies of the book in Harlem in September 1958, he was stabbed by a deranged woman and sustained a severe chest wound.

Using the SCLC as his base of operations, King mounted a series of civil rights campaigns aimed at eliminating racial segregation in transportation, theaters, restaurants, motels, and other public facilities. He traveled and lectured widely and was arrested more than fifteen times. In 1960 he spent a month in India studying Gandhi's techniques, as a guest of Prime Minister Jawaharlal Nehru. During March and April of 1963, he led a mass protest in Birmingham, Alabama, to appeal for fair hiring practices, desegregation of facilities, and the establishment of a biracial citizens' committee. The demonstrators, many of them children, were met by official force in the form of police dogs, water cannons, and clubs.

After defying a court injunction barring public demonstrations, King was jailed for five days. At this time he wrote his "Letter From Birmingham Jail" to the city's white religious leaders who had criticized him for "unwise and untimely" action. "Actually, time itself is neutral," he wrote. "Human progress never rolls in on wheels of inevitability. It comes through the tireless efforts of men, willing to be co-workers with God; and without this hard work, time itself becomes an ally of the forces of social stagnation." Despite sporadic bombings, tensions in Birmingham eased when white and black leaders agreed to a plan for desegregation.

In 1963 King worked with Ralph Abernathy, his second-in-command and later successor at the SCLC; Bayard Rustin, a founder of the Congress of Racial Equality; and other leaders, to mobilize the largest civil rights demonstration in United States history. On August 28 an estimated 250,000 people, black and white, gathered in Washington, D.C., to act as witnesses for civil rights legislation pending in Congress. On that day, black leaders conferred with President John F. Kennedy. Later, on the steps of the Lincoln Memorial, King gave testimony to his faith in brotherhood. The speech, known by its refrain, "I Have a Dream," expressed King's hope that the nation's ideals would become a reality for all.

King's book *Why We Can't Wait* was published in 1964. During May and June of that year, he joined SCLC members in demonstrations for integration of public accommodations in St. Augustine, Florida. In July he was invited to the White House by President Lyndon B. Johnson to witness the signing of the Public Accommodations Bill, part of the Civil Rights Act of 1964. This act outlawed segregation in public facilities and prohibited discrimination in hiring practices, working conditions, and wages. Later that year, King was awarded the 1964 Nobel Prize for Peace.

In his presentation speech, Gunnar Jahn of the Norwegian Nobel Committee stated, "Though Martin Luther King has not personally committed himself to the international conflict, his own struggle is a clarion call to all who work for peace. . . . He is the first person in the Western world to have shown us that a struggle can be waged without violence."

In his Nobel lecture King said: "Nonviolence has also meant that my people, in the agonizing struggles of recent years, have taken suffering upon themselves instead of inflicting it on others. . . . It has meant . . . that we are no longer afraid, and cowed. But in some substantial degree it has meant that we do not want to instill fear in others or into the society of which we are a part. The Movement does not seek to liberate Negroes at the expense of the humiliation and enslavement of whites. It seeks no victory over anyone. It seeks to liberate American society and to share in the self-liberation of all the people."

King organized a march from Selma, Alabama, to Montgomery in March 1965 to dramatize the need for a federal voting rights law, but he did not lead the demonstrators. When the marchers were turned back at the Pettus Bridge in Selma, after being beaten by state highway patrolmen and sheriff's deputies, King called for a second march. Over 3,000 blacks and whites began the march, and 25,000 more joined them along the way. When they reached the capitol in Montgomery, they were addressed by King. On August 6 the Voting Rights Act was signed by President Johnson. King was invited to Washington, D.C., to witness the signing.

A controversial figure, King had many detractors, not only in the South but also in other parts of the country. Perhaps his most powerful critic was the director of the Federal Bureau of Investigation (FBI), J. Edgar Hoover. Hoover called King a Communist, a traitor, and a deeply immoral man. Hoover also called King the "most notorious liar in the country" after King charged that FBI agents took no action on civil rights complaints in Albany, Georgia, because the agents were Southerners. The FBI tapped the phones of King and the SCLC and compiled an extensive file on King's public life and on his personal life as well. The file included details of King's extramarital activities at a time when King traveled widely and was frequently absent from his family.

In 1967 King published *Where Do We Go From Here?* That April he openly declared his opposition to the Vietnam War. He sent a statement to a large Washington rally protesting the war, and he became cochairman of Clergy and Laymen Concerned About Vietnam.

In the last years of his life, King enlarged his area of concern from racism alone to unemployment, hunger, and poverty among all Americans. Among the factors that led him to this broader vision was the need for the support of younger, more radical blacks at a time when urban riots in the ghettos of Watts, Newark, Harlem, and Detroit were challenging his nonviolent precepts. King came to realize that racial discrimination was closely tied to poverty. That he had not formed a comprehensive philosophy or program in this connection may explain the failure of his efforts to improve slum conditions in Chicago in 1966. But in November 1967 he announced the SCLC's formation of a Poor People's Campaign, which would dramatize the problems of poor blacks and whites by a camp-in in Washington, D.C., in April 1968.

On March 28, 1968, King led a march of 6,000 protestors through downtown Memphis, Tennessee, in support of striking sanitation workers. Speaking at the Memphis Masonic Temple a few days later, King said, "We've got some difficult days ahead. But it really doesn't matter with me now. Because I've been to the mountaintop. . . . And I've looked over and I've seen the Promised Land. I may not get there with you, but I want you to know tonight that we as a people will get to the Promised Land." The following day, King was assassinated by a sniper as he stood on the balcony of his second-floor room at the Lorraine Motel in Memphis. He died from the gunshot wound at St. Joseph's Hospital and was buried in Atlanta.

King's work is studied and carried on at the Martin Luther King Jr. Center for Nonviolent Social Change in Atlanta. In 1983 Congress set aside the third Monday in January to commemorate King's birthday. On January 16, 1986, a bust of King was unveiled in the Great Rotunda of the Capitol in Washington, making him the first black to be so honored. On January 20, 1986, the nation celebrated the first Martin Luther King Day.

ADDITIONAL WORKS BY: The Measure of a Measure, 1959; Strength to Love, 1963; The Trumpet of Conscience, 1968.

ABOUT: Ansboro, J. Martin Luther King Jr.: The Making of a Mind, 1982; Beifuss, J. T. At the River I Stand, 1985; Bennett, L. What Manner of Man, 1964; Bishop, J. A. The Days of Martin Luther King Jr., 1971; Bleiweiss, R. M. (ed.) Marching to Freedom, 1971; Clayton, E. Martin Luther King: The Peaceful Warrior, 1985; Collins, D. R. Not Only Dreamers, 1986; Davis, L. G. I Have a Dream, 1969; Faber, D., and Faber, H. Martin Luther King Jr., 1986; Garrow, D. J. Protest at Selma, 1978; Garrow, D. J. Bearing the Cross, 1986; Goodwin, B. E. Martin Luther King Jr., 1976; Hanigan, J. P. Martin Luther King Jr. and the Foundations of Nonviolence, 1984; Harris, J. L. Martin Luther King Jr., 1983; Haskins, J. The Life and Death of Martin Luther King Jr., 1977; King, C. S. My Life With Martin Luther King Jr., 1969; Lewis, D. L. King: A Critical Biography, 1971; Lincoln, C. E. (ed.) Martin Luther King Jr.: A Profile, 1970; Miller, W. R. Martin Luther King Jr., 1968; Oates, S. B. Let the Trumpet Sound, 1982; Schulke, F., and McPhee, P. King Remembered, 1986; Smith, K. L., and Zepp, I. A. The Search for the Beloved Community, 1974; Westin, A., and Mahoney, B. The Trial of Martin Luther King, 1974; Witherspoon, W. R. Martin Luther King Jr., 1985.

KIPLING, RUDYARD
(December 30, 1865–January 18, 1936)
Nobel Prize for Literature, 1907

Joseph Rudyard Kipling, English poet, novelist, and short story writer, was born in Bombay, India, to John Lockwood Kipling, the principal and professor of architectural sculpture at the Bombay School of Art, and Alice (Macdonald) Kipling. His father was a sculptor and designer; his mother wrote occasional magazine pieces.

At the age of six, following the custom among Anglo-Indian families, Kipling and his younger sister were sent to England to attend school. They lived in a foster home and during holidays stayed with their maternal relatives, the family of the Pre-Raphaelite painter Edward Burne-Jones. Kipling's unhappiness at the unkind treatment he received in the foster home was later expressed in the short story "Baa Baa, Black Sheep" (1888), in the novel The Light That Failed (1890), and in his autobiography (1937).

In 1878 Kipling was sent to board at the United Services College in Devon, an inexpensive secondary school that specialized in training sons of officers for entry into exclusive military academies. Its headmaster was a member of the aesthetic circle that included Burne-Jones and William Morris. Despite an initial year of being bullied and beaten, Kipling grew to like the school; he gave a fictionalized account of it in the volume of stories Stalky & Co (1899). Since the school did not offer preparation for scholarships to Oxford or Cambridge universities, and because Kipling's nearsightedness precluded a military career, the college marked the end of his formal education. His father, impressed by what Kipling had written at school, found him a job on the staff of the Civil and Military Gazette, an English-language newspaper published in Lahore, India (now in Pakistan). In October 1882, after eleven years in England, Kipling returned to India.

In Lahore, Kipling used his knowledge of Hindustani—which he had retained during his absence—and of Anglo-Indian society to build up the picture of India he employed later in his fiction. Kipling wrote weekly stories on regional life, as well as poetry, for the Gazette. His first collection of poems, Departmental Ditties, was published in 1886. It sold out quickly in a limited edition and was republished the same year. Plain Tales From the Hills, a collection of stories, appeared two years later, and it, too, sold out quickly in India. Between 1887 and 1889 Kipling brought out six volumes of short stories in the Indian Railway Library series, editions that were marketed to travelers. His work thus became widely known in India and throughout the British Empire.

RUDYARD KIPLING

Determined to make his mark as a writer in England, Kipling returned there via Japan and North America; during his trip, he was under assignment to send back travel articles to the Allahabad *Pioneer.* In October 1889 he arrived in London, where his work had already made him famous, and he was hailed as a literary heir to Charles Dickens. The volumes from his Indian Railway Library series were printed in England and, in 1890, enthusiastically reviewed by the London *Times.*

In London, Kipling became friends with Wolcott Balestier, a young American publisher, with whom he collaborated on a novel, *The Naulahka* (1892). Shortly after Balestier died of typhoid fever in 1892, Kipling married his sister, Caroline Balestier. *Barrack-Room Ballads,* published in the same year, contained two of his best-known poems, "Gunga Din" and "Mandalay."

The young couple moved to Brattleboro, Vermont, where Caroline's family owned property and where the Kiplings' two daughters were born. In Vermont, Kipling produced a book of short stories, *Many Inventions* (1893); two volumes of short stories and verse, *The Jungle Book* (1894) and *The Second Jungle Book* (1895); and a book of verse, *The Seven Seas* (1896). His novel *Captains Courageous,* published in 1897, is a tale about New England fishermen.

In 1896, dissatisfied with life in Vermont and involved in a bitter quarrel with his brother-in-law, Kipling left the United States and took his family back to England, where he soon reestablished his literary prominence. In newspapers, he published a number of poems, in-

cluding the celebrated "Recessional" (1897), a warning about the irresponsible use of national power. *Kim,* the picaresque adventures of an adolescent boy and a Buddhist monk traveling in India, published in 1901, is widely considered Kipling's best novel.

On a visit to New York in January 1898 with his family, which now included a son, Kipling almost died of pneumonia, and his elder daughter succumbed to it, a loss reflected in a number of his subsequent stories. After the outbreak of the Boer War in 1899, Kipling spent several months in South Africa, editing an army newspaper and serving as a consultant to British political and military leaders.

In 1902 Kipling took a country house in Sussex, England, where he remained for the rest of his life. That year he published the *Just So Stories* for children. *Puck of Pook's Hill,* tales of ancient British history for children, appeared in 1906, followed by a sequel in 1910. Kipling also became politically active, speaking for the Conservative party, writing about the danger of war with Germany, and opposing both women's suffrage and home rule for Ireland.

Kipling received the 1907 Nobel Prize for Literature "in consideration of the power of observation, originality of imagination, virility of ideas, and remarkable talent for narration" that the members of the Swedish Academy found in his work. Although he traveled to Stockholm to receive the award, Kipling did not deliver a Nobel lecture. At this point Kipling had written thirteen volumes of short stories, four novels, three books of children's stories, several travel books, political and social essays, newspaper articles, and hundreds of poems. In 1907 Kipling also received honorary degrees from Oxford, Cambridge, Edinburgh, and Durham universities; the universities of Strasbourg, Paris, and Athens honored him as well, as did McGill University in Toronto.

Soon after Kipling received the Nobel Prize, his output of fiction and poetry began to decline. During World War I, in which his son was killed, Kipling and his wife worked briefly with the Red Cross. He published *A Diversity of Creatures,* a collection of verse and short stories, in 1917. After the war he traveled extensively, sometimes on behalf of the War Graves Commission. On one such trip to France in 1922, he met and became a friend of King George V. During this period he became more closely associated with the right wing of the Conservative party, and in 1923 he published *The Irish Guards in the Great War,* a history of his son's regiment.

Kipling produced two more collections of stories, in 1926 and 1932. Since 1915 he had suffered from gastritis, later diagnosed as ulcers. He died in London of an intestinal hemorrhage in 1936, two days before his friend George V; he was buried in Poets' Corner at Westminster Abbey. An autobiographical work, *Something of Myself,* appeared posthumously the following year.

Kipling was hailed by Oscar Wilde in 1890 as "a genius who drops his aspirates," and he was considered by Henry James to contain perhaps "the seeds of an English Balzac." By 1907, however, critical reaction in England and the United States had grown lukewarm. One reason for the eclipse of Kipling's reputation may have been his imperialistic and conservative political views; perhaps another reason was his accessibility to ordinary readers. Members of the modernist literary movement felt that Kipling was out of step with the themes, language, and aesthetic principles that they embraced.

Starting in the 1940s, Kipling's works began to undergo a critical reassessment. His reputation received a powerful boost in 1943 when T. S. ELIOT edited a selection of Kipling's poems for Faber and Faber. In a lengthy essay included in the book, Eliot asserted that "Kipling's craftsmanship is more reliable than that of some greater poets, and . . . there is hardly any poem, even in the collected works, in which he fails to do what he has set out to do." Eliot explained that "the notion of Kipling as a popular entertainer is due to the fact that his works have been popular and that they entertain"; he claimed that Kipling's greatest gift lay in his ability "to make people see." According to the Indian critic Nirad C. Chaudhuri (writing in *Encounter,* 1957), in *Kim* "Kipling wrote not only the finest novel in the English language with an Indian theme, but also one of the greatest of English novels." In his 1977 biography, *The Strange Ride of Rudyard Kipling: His Life and Works,* English novelist and critic Angus Wilson wrote, "Kipling's passionate interest in people and their vocabularies and their crafts is . . . the essence of the magic of all his work."

ADDITIONAL WORKS: Soldiers Three, 1888; The Story of the Gatsbys, 1888; In Black and White, 1888; Wee Willie Winkie, 1888; Under the Deodors, 1888; The Courting of Dinah Shadd, 1890; The City of Dreadful Nights, 1891; Letters of Marque, 1891; American Notes, 1891; Mine Own People, 1891; Life's Handicap, 1891; Out of India, 1895; The Day's Work, 1898; A Fleet in Being, 1898; Kipling's Poems, 1899; From Sea to Sea (2 vols.) 1898; The Five Nations, 1903; Traffics and Discoveries, 1904; Letters to the Family, 1908; Actions and Reactions, 1909; Abaft the Funnel, 1909; Rewards and Fairies, 1910; A History of England, 1911, with C. R. L. Fletcher; France at War, 1915; The Fringes of the Fleet, 1915; The Eyes of Asia, 1918; Twenty Poems, 1918; The Graves of the Fallen, 1919; The Years Between, 1919; Letters of Travel, 1920; Land and Sea Tales, 1923; They and the Brushwood Boy, 1923; Songs for Youth, 1924; A Choice of Songs, 1925; The Art of Fiction, 1926; Debits and Credits, 1926; Sea and Sussex, 1926; Songs of the Sea, 1927; A Tour of Inspection, 1928; Poems 1886–1929 (3 vols.) 1929; Limits and Renewals, 1932; Souvenirs of France, 1933; The Maltese Cat, 1936; Teem, 1938; Kipling's India, 1986; Early Verse, 1986.

ABOUT: Amis, K. Rudyard Kipling and His World, 1975; Beresford, G. C. Schooldays With Kipling, 1936; Birkenhead, Lord. Rudyard Kipling, 1978; Bodelson, A. C. Aspects of Kipling's Art, 1964; Brown, H. Rudyard Kipling, 1945; Carrington, C. E. Rudyard Kipling, 1955; Charles, C. Rudyard Kipling, Life and Work, 1911; Cornell, L. L. Kipling in India, 1966; Croft-Cook, R. Rudyard Kipling, 1948; Dobrée, B. Rudyard Kipling: Realist and Fatalist, 1967; Eliot, T. S. (ed.) A Choice of Kipling's Verse, 1943; Fido, M. Rudyard Kipling, 1974; Gilbert, E. L. (ed.) Kipling and His Critics, 1965; Green, R. L. (ed.) Kipling: The Critical Heritage, 1971; Gross, J. (ed.) The Age of Kipling, 1972; Harrison, J. Rudyard Kipling, 1982; Hart, W. M. Kipling, The Story Writer, 1918; Henn, T. R. Kipling, 1967; Kamen, G. Kipling, Storyteller of East and West, 1985; Laski, M. From Palm to Pine: Rudyard Kipling Abroad and at Home, 1987; LeGallienne, R. Rudyard Kipling, A Criticism, 1900; Mason, P. Kipling, 1975; Rao, K. B. Rudyard Kipling's India, 1967; Rutherford, A. (ed.) Kipling's Mind and Art, 1964; Stewart, J. I. M. Rudyard Kipling, 1946; Tompkins, J. M. S. The Art of Rudyard Kipling, 1959; Wilson, A. The Strange Ride of Rudyard Kipling, 1977.

KISSINGER, HENRY

(May 27, 1923–)
Nobel Prize for Peace, 1973
(shared with Le Duc Tho)

The American political scientist and statesman Henry Alfred Kissinger (kis' inj ur) was born Heinz Alfred Kissinger in the Bavarian city of Fürth, Germany. He was the elder of two sons of Louis Kissinger, a teacher in a girls' secondary school, and Paula (Stern) Kissinger. Of Jewish ancestry, Kissinger grew up in a cultured middle-class family during the years of Germany's turbulent recovery from the bitter defeat of World War I. After Hitler's rise to power in 1933, government persecution of Jews cost Kissinger's father his job. Young Kissinger was expelled from the local gymnasium and forced to attend a segregated Jewish school. In 1938, as Nazi anti-Semitism grew worse, Kissinger and his family escaped from Germany and emigrated to the United States, where they settled in New York City.

In 1943, two years after his graduation from George Washington High School, Kissinger

KISSINGER

Diane Walker, 1983

HENRY KISSINGER

was drafted into the United States Army for service in World War II and thus became a naturalized citizen. He was assigned as an interpreter and interrogator to the 970th Counter-Intelligence Corps. After Germany surrendered to the Allies in 1945, Kissinger was appointed a district administrator with the military government in occupied Germany. For his services in this capacity, the young staff sergeant was awarded the Bronze Star.

After the war, Kissinger entered Harvard University. There he specialized in political science and received a B.A. in 1950. Continuing his graduate studies at Harvard, he was awarded an M.A. in 1952 and a Ph.D. in 1954. His dissertation on the European peace settlement after Napoleon's defeat, was published in 1957 as *A World Restored: Castlereagh, Metternich, and the Problems of Peace.*

Remaining at Harvard, Kissinger served as a member of the faculty with responsibilities in both the Department of Government and the Center for International Affairs. Although Kissinger was regarded by many of his colleagues and students as shy and aloof, his course in foreign policy was well attended. He was appointed associate professor of government in 1959 and full professor in 1962. From 1959 to 1969 he also headed Harvard's Defense Studies Program.

At Harvard, Kissinger quickly established himself as an authority on foreign policy and strategic defense. One of his colleagues, the American historian Arthur M. Schlesinger Jr., recommended him as director of a study sponsored by the Council on Foreign Relations.

The result of this eighteen-month study was *Nuclear Weapons and Foreign Policy* (1957), in which Kissinger examined alternatives to the strategy of massive nuclear retaliation that had been formulated by Secretary of State John Foster Dulles. Kissinger advanced the notion of a "flexible response" to the Soviet Union, which included the possible use of tactical nuclear weapons. The study not only earned Kissinger a WOODROW WILSON Prize but also brought him to the attention of Nelson Rockefeller, who in 1956 appointed him director of the Rockefeller Brothers Fund Special Studies Project. His publications during the late 1950s earned Kissinger a controversial reputation as a hard-line anti-Communist who was cautious over the prospects of détente.

During the administration of President Dwight D. Eisenhower, Kissinger served as a consultant to the Operations Coordinating Board (1955–1956) and the Weapons Systems Evaluation Group of the Joint Chiefs of Staff (1955–1960). Despite his differences with Presidents John F. Kennedy and Lyndon B. Johnson, he continued to act as a consultant during their administrations, to the National Security Council (1961–1963), the Arms Control and Disarmament Agency (1961–1967), and the State Department (1965–1967).

At the invitation of Henry Cabot Lodge, United States ambassador to South Vietnam, Kissinger visited South Vietnam in 1965, shortly after the United States began bombing targets in North Vietnam. Two years later, as the Johnson administration explored the possibility of a negotiated settlement in Vietnam, Kissinger conducted a four-month exchange of messages between the United States and North Vietnam. His efforts led to formal peace talks in Paris in 1968. During that year, Kissinger also served as an adviser to Nelson Rockefeller in his unsuccessful bid for the Republican presidential nomination.

When Richard M. Nixon became president in 1968, Kissinger joined his administration. Consequently, in January of the following year, Kissinger took a leave of absence from Harvard and assumed the position of assistant to the president for national security affairs, with responsibility for advising the president on foreign relations and military policy. In this capacity, he helped Nixon formulate the so-called Vietnamization policy whereby United States troops were progressively disengaged and replaced by South Vietnamese. At the same time, Kissinger advocated increased bombing of North Vietnam and secret air raids against North Vietnamese supply lines in Cambodia.

This much-disputed strategy was allegedly intended to strengthen the United States bargaining position with Hanoi.

During 1970 and 1971, Kissinger made a dozen trips to Paris to meet secretly with North Vietnamese representatives. On January 27, 1973, he reached a cease-fire agreement with the chief North Vietnamese negotiator, LE DUC THO. It was agreed that the United States would withdraw its troops while continuing to send aid to South Vietnam. North Vietnam, in turn, would release American prisoners of war. The two men were awarded the 1973 Nobel Peace Prize for their efforts to end the fighting. The choice stirred considerable controversy. Two of the five Norwegian Nobel Committee members resigned after the selection, and its announcement met with widespread international criticism. Kissinger did not attend the ceremony, and there were protest demonstrations in Oslo when the American ambassador arrived to accept the prize in Kissinger's name.

Aase Lionæs of the Norwegian Nobel Committee addressed this criticism in her presentation speech. "The Nobel committee . . . was fully aware that a cease-fire and not a peace agreement was involved," she said. "They realized that peace has not yet come to Vietnam and that the sufferings of the population of Vietnam are not at an end. They were also aware that events in Vietnam may yet endanger the détente in the world. The cease-fire agreement was only the first but tremendously important step on the laborious road to full peace in Vietnam." She added, "In awarding the prize in 1973 . . . to two responsible politicians at the center of events, the Nobel committee . . . emphasizes its belief that the approach to a solution of the many controversies that have led to or may lead to war must be via negotiations, not through total war aiming at total victory."

In a letter to the Nobel committee, Kissinger wrote, "The people of the United States, and indeed of the whole world, share the hope expressed by the Nobel Peace Prize committee 'that all parties to this conflict will feel morally responsible for turning the cease-fire in Vietnam into a lasting peace for the suffering peoples of Indochina.' Certainly my government, for its part, intends to continue its policies in such a way as to turn this hope into reality." The last American troops were withdrawn from Vietnam on March 29, 1973.

As chief foreign policy adviser to President Nixon, Kissinger initiated the Strategic Arms Limitation Talks (SALT) in 1969. Two years later he played a prominent role in negotia-tions that led to the Soviet Union's promising access to West Berlin in exchange for recognition of East Germany. During the summer of 1971, Kissinger secretly met with Premier Chou En-lai in Peking to pave the way for Nixon's trip to the People's Republic of China in February 1972.

When Nixon began his second term as president in 1973, he named Kissinger secretary of state. That fall, when the Yom Kippur War broke out between Israel and the Arab states of Egypt and Syria, Kissinger made numerous visits to seven Middle Eastern capitals in an effort to end the fighting. This "shuttle diplomacy," as it came to be known, led to a cease-fire agreement between Egypt and Israel, resumption of full-scale diplomatic relations between the United States and Egypt, reopening of the Suez Canal, and in May 1974 the signing of an agreement between Israel and Syria.

In 1974, when President Nixon resigned from office in the wake of the Watergate scandals, Kissinger remained secretary of state under President Gerald Ford until 1977. Then, leaving government service, he taught at Georgetown University's School of Foreign Service. In addition to writing and lecturing, Kissinger now serves as a senior fellow at the Aspen Institute and is widely employed from his New York office as a private consultant to television and other business interests.

Kissinger married Ann Fleischer in 1949; they had a son and a daughter and were divorced in 1964. He married Nancy Maginnes, a former aide to Nelson Rockefeller, in 1974.

Kissinger, who speaks with a slight German accent and has been described as owlish in appearance, serves as a trustee of the Metropolitan Museum of Art in New York and as a board member of the Houston Ballet. He holds membership in the American Political Science Association, the American Academy of Arts and Sciences, and the United States Army Association. He has received a Guggenheim Fellowship (1965–1966), the American Institute of Public Service Award (1973), and an honorary doctorate from Brown University, among other awards and honors.

ADDITIONAL WORKS: The Necessity for Choice: Prospects for American Foreign Policy, 1961; The Troubled Partnership: A Reappraisal of the Atlantic Alliance, 1965; Agenda for the Nation, 1968; Bureaucracy, Politics, and Strategy, 1968, with Bernard Brodie; American Foreign Policy, 1969; White House Years, 1979; For the Record: Selected Statements, 1981; American Foreign Policy: A Global View, 1982; Years of Upheaval, 1982; Three Addresses on Foreign Policy, 1982, with Arthur F. Burns and Jeane J. Kirkpatrick; Observations: Selected Speeches and Essays, 1985.

KLEIN

ABOUT: Ashman, C. R. Kissinger, 1972; Bell, C. The Diplomacy of Détente, 1977; Blumenfeld, R. Henry Kissinger, 1974; Brandon, H. The Retreat of American Power, 1973; Brown, S. The Crisis of Power, 1979; Caldwell, D. (ed.) Henry Kissinger: His Personality and Politics, 1983; Davis, V. Henry Kissinger and Bureaucratic Politics, 1979; Dickson, P. W. Kissinger and the Meaning of History, 1978; Graubard, S. R. Kissinger: Portrait of a Mind, 1973; Hersh, S. M. The Price of Power, 1983; Israel, F. L. Henry Kissinger, 1986; Joiner, H. M. American Foreign Policy: The Kissinger Era, 1977; Kalb, B., and Kalb, M. Kissinger, 1974; Landau, D. Kissinger, 1972; Mazlish, B. Kissinger: The European Mind in American Policy, 1976; Morris, R. Uncertain Greatness, 1977; Starr, H. Henry Kissinger, 1984; Strong, R. J. Bureaucracy and Statesmanship, 1986; Sullivan, B. R., and Balaan, H. The Kissinger Years, 1981; Szulc, T. The Illusion of Peace, 1978; Valeriani, R. Travels With Henry, 1979.

LAWRENCE KLEIN

KLEIN, LAWRENCE
(September 14, 1920–   )
Nobel Memorial Prize in Economic
   Sciences, 1980

The American economist Lawrence Robert Klein was born in Omaha, Nebraska, the second of three children of Blanche (Monheit) and Leo Byron Klein, clerks at a wholesale grocery. After attending public school in Omaha, Klein studied mathematics at Los Angeles City College. He completed his undergraduate training in advanced mathematics and economics at the University of California at Berkeley, where he received his B.A. with honors in 1942. "Although I was not aware of it at the time," he recalled later, "the experience of growing up during the Great Depression was to have a profound impact on my intellectual and professional career."

Klein's graduate studies at the Massachusetts Institute of Technology (MIT) laid the foundation for his later work. Working under PAUL SAMUELSON, Klein translated the revolutionary theories of the British economist John Maynard Keynes into a system of mathematical equations. In The General Theory of Employment, Interest, and Money, published in 1936, Keynes had argued that the total effective demand of an economy—total consumption expenditures, investment expenditures, and government expenditures—determines the level of national income and employment. According to Keynes, when total demand falls below an economy's capacity to produce, unemployment and depression follow.

Working from Keynes's ideas, Klein devised a set of equations to estimate the future output of an economy based on historical relationships among such economic variables as tax-

ation, wages, investment levels, and disposable income. This numerical systematizing of Keynes's theories marked Klein's entry into the field of econometrics, a branch of economics with which economic theories are transformed into mathematical models with which predictions can be statistically tested. By 1944, when Klein received the first Ph.D. in economics awarded by MIT, he had published in the journal Econometrica a series of equations for analyzing investment functions. His doctoral thesis, published in 1949 as The Keynesian Revolution, became an international success.

After completing his doctorate, Klein became a research associate in econometrics at the Cowles Commission for Research in Economics at the University of Chicago. There he joined such noted economists as Theodore Anderson, Herman Rubin, KENNETH ARROW, TJALLING C. KOOPMANS, Don Patinkin, and HERBERT SIMON. Unlike his more theoretical colleagues, Klein sought practical uses for econometric models. The commission's director, Jacob Marschak, assigned Klein the task of revising the early econometric models of JAN TINBERGEN. In building his model of the American economy, Klein departed radically from Tinbergen's work. Using a different economic theory and different statistical techniques, he sought a means for forecasting business fluctuations and for assessing the effects of economic policy measures.

A model Klein developed in 1946 at Cowles countered the widely held notion that the American economy would sink into a depression after World War II as it had after World War I. Klein correctly predicted that the economy would thrive because of an unsatisfied demand for consumer goods magnified by the purchasing power of returning servicemen. Similar assumptions about a post–Korean War depression were contradicted by one of Klein's later models, which forecast only a modest recession. "Although Klein was not the first to build the models," F. Gerard Adams of the University of Pennsylvania later commented, "he was the first to take them and transform them into useful tools."

In 1947 Klein traveled to Ottawa, where he constructed his first models of the Canadian economy, and then to Norway to spend an academic year working with the economists RAGNAR FRISCH and Trygve Haavelmo.

On returning to the United States in 1948, Klein accepted Arthur F. Burns's invitation to join the National Bureau of Economic Research, where he became interested in the effect of wealth, especially liquid assets, on savings behavior. The following year, seeking relevant data from consumer finance surveys, Klein joined the staff of the Survey Research Center at the University of Michigan as a research associate. At Michigan, he resumed his macroeconomic model building and, with a graduate student, Arthur Goldberger, completed the Klein-Goldberger model of the American economy. The basic structure of this model was typical of Klein's later efforts. It consisted of an interdependent series of simultaneous, layered equations that could be solved to establish the output of an economy. Reviewing Klein's work, R. J. Ball of the London Business School observed, "As an empirical representation of an essentially Keynesian system . . . [the Klein-Goldberger model] became perhaps the best known model of a large economy until other developments in the 1960s."

Despite his pioneering work at the University of Michigan, Klein was denied tenure when Senator Joseph McCarthy revealed that the young economist had been a member of the Communist party from 1946 to 1947. Leaving Michigan in 1954, he spent the next four years at Oxford University's Institute of Statistics in England, where he worked on data from the Oxford Savings Survey, constructed the first substantial scale model of the United Kingdom's economy, and began to study methods of statistical inference.

In 1958 Klein joined the Department of Economics of the University of Pennsylvania, where he began constructing models both of the American economy and of international economic systems. The first of these, based on the extensive Brookings–Social Science Research Council project, was designed to forecast short-term developments in the American economy. It became the basis for Klein's subsequent and considerably improved Wharton annual and quarterly models. These are still regarded as significant instruments for predicting how changes in taxation, public expenditures, or variables such as oil price movements might affect gross national product, investment levels, and consumption.

The Wharton models are enormously complex. Whereas an econometric model of a developing nation might have only 30 equations, Klein's quarterly model of the American economy includes more than 1,000 equations, which must be solved simultaneously. Computer facilities at the University of Pennsylvania made the construction of such complex, large-scale models possible and freed Klein and his staff from the laborious task of working out calculations by hand.

In the early 1960s, with financial and journalistic support from *Business Week* magazine, Klein took the pioneering step of selling his econometric models to corporations and public agencies. The commercial success of this venture created a market for later forecasting models, such as those created by Data Resources, Inc., and Chase Econometrics. When Wharton Econometric Forecasting Associates was sold in 1979, all profits were donated to the University of Pennsylvania.

During the 1960s Klein developed econometric models for several other nations, including Israel, Mexico, and Japan. In the course of this international work, he learned how diverse institutional conditions in various nations affected both the choice and the form of the equations he applied. In 1968, seeking to create a model for international economic interdependence, Klein founded Project Link in collaboration with Bert Hickman of Stanford University, Rudolf Rhomberg of the International Monetary Fund, and Aaron Gordon of the University of California. According to the English economist R. J. Ball, Project Link was designed "to integrate the statistical models of different countries, including the Third World and the socialist nations, in a total system, with the object of improving our understanding of international economic linkages and to make improved forecasts of world trade." With Project Link's central coordinating facility and computer software under his supervision at the

University of Pennsylvania, Klein is still adding countries to the project.

In 1975 Klein served as an economic adviser to Jimmy Carter, who was then seeking nomination as the Democratic presidential candidate. Klein gathered a group of fellow economists that drafted a series of position papers under his direction. In 1976, after Carter's election, however, Klein declined an invitation to join the new administration.

Klein was awarded the 1980 Nobel Memorial Prize in Economic Sciences "for the creation of economic models and their application to the analysis of economic fluctuations and economic policies." In his presentation speech, Herman Wold of the Royal Swedish Academy of Sciences summarized Klein's achievements: "Lawrence Klein has created and established a paradigm for econometric macromodels, a general pattern for their theoretical construction and practical application. Klein's paradigm includes the institutional organization," Wold continued, "with a regular procedure for the generation of economic forecasts, with a service system for policy consultations, and with an approach to model adjustment to account for longer-run changes in the economic world." In his Nobel lecture Klein projected some economic scenarios for the 1980s, drawing upon both the Wharton model and Project Link. Of his own work he observed, "From my student days, the concept of public service and the relationship of theoretical economics or econometrics to real-world problems has appealed to me, and I have tried to follow the footsteps of my teachers in practicing economics in this way."

Klein has been Benjamin Franklin Professor of Economics and Finance at the Wharton School of the University of Pennsylvania since 1968. He is regarded by his colleagues as modest, hardworking, and quick to help students and associates. Once described by Paul Samuelson as "rather unworldly," Klein devotes most of his time to work, except for listening to music or playing golf on occasion. He married Sonia Adelson in 1947; they have three daughters and one son.

In addition to the Nobel Prize, Klein has received the John Bates Clark Medal of the American Economic Association (1959) and the William F. Butler Award of the New York Association of Business Economists (1975). He is a member of the American Economic Association, the American Association for the Advancement of Science, and the American Philosophical Society.

ADDITIONAL WORKS: Economic Fluctuations in the United States, 1921–1941, 1950; A Textbook of Econometrics, 1953; An Introduction to Economics, 1962; The Wharton Econometric Forecasting Model, 1967, with Michael K. Evans; An Essay on the Theory of Economic Prediction, 1968; Expanding the Benefits of Manpower Research, 1973; Techniques of Model Building for Developing Economies, 1975, with Stefan Schlecher; Econometric Model Performance, 1976, with Edwin Burmeister; An Introduction to Econometric Forecasting and Forecasting Models, 1980, with Richard Young; Econometric Models as Guides for Decision Making, 1981; Industrial Policies for Growth and Competitiveness, 1983, with Frances Adams; The Economics of Supply and Demand, 1983; Lectures in Econometrics, 1983, with Wladyslaw Welde; Economic Theory and Econometrics, 1985.

ABOUT: Adams, F. G., and Hickman, B. G. (eds.) Global Econometrics: Essays in Honor of Lawrence R. Klein, 1983; Breit, W., and Spencer, R. W. (eds.) Lives of the Laureates, 1986; New York Times October 16, 1980; Scandinavian Journal of Economics, number 1, 1981; Science November 14, 1980.

KLITZING, KLAUS VON
(June 28, 1943–)
Nobel Prize for Physics, 1985

The German physicist Klaus-Olaf von Klitzing was born during World War II in the town of Schroda, which was then in a part of Germany close to the Polish border. He was the third of four children of Bogislav von Klitzing, a forestry official, and the former Anny Ulbrich. Soon after Klaus was born, it became apparent that as the German military position deteriorated, the Soviet army would reach the region of Posen (now Poznań) in which his family lived. Fleeing west, they eventually resettled in Lutten in April of 1945, shortly before the end of the war. The family moved again in 1948 to Oldenburg and then settled in Essen in 1951. Klaus's secondary education at the Artland Gymnasium in Quakenbrück prepared him for specialization in physics at the Technical University of Braunschweig in 1962.

At Braunschweig, Klitzing was first introduced to the problems of the physics of semiconductors. Although he had taken an interest in X-ray spectroscopy (and had traveled to Darmstadt to take a course in computer programming with this topic in mind), it was the technique of luminescence measurement that seized his attention. He used this method to determine the lifetimes of carriers in the semiconductor indium antimonide and reported this work in a thesis written under the guidance of F. R. Kessler in 1969. He then moved to the University of Würzburg, where after briefly

KLAUS VON KLITZING

teaching laboratory physics to premedical students, he spent the next decade honing his skills in semiconductor research. Klitzing spent 1975 at Oxford University, where, at the time, the finest superconducting magnets were manufactured. They were of particular interest to Klitzing because strong, homogeneous magnetic fields are an essential tool for the study of electrons in semiconductors.

Seeking still stronger magnetic fields, Klitzing left Würzburg in 1979 to work at the high-field laboratory in Grenoble. In 1980 he took a new position as professor at the Technical University of Munich, where he remained until becoming director of the Max Planck Institute for Solid-State Physics in Stuttgart in 1985. The combination of low temperatures and strong magnetic fields to which he gained access at Grenoble played an important role in his discoveries concerning the Hall effect. This phenomenon, first observed in 1880 by the American physicist Edwin H. Hall, had previously been considered as only a rough means of measuring the concentration of electrons in semiconductors. In Hall-effect measurements, an electric current is passed through a sample in the presence of a magnetic field applied in a perpendicular direction. A voltage then appears across the sample at right angles to both the current and the magnetic field. This Hall voltage is generally proportional to the magnetic field and inversely proportional to the concentration of electrons. Uncertainties of the order of 10 percent are typical in the interpretation of these results as a consequence of a variety of interactions between the electrons and the atoms forming the crystalline lattice of the semiconductor.

At Grenoble, working in collaboration with Michael Pepper of the Cavendish Laboratory at Cambridge University and with Gerhard Dorda of the Siemens Corporation research laboratories in Munich, Klitzing conducted an experiment that differed from traditional measurements, primarily in the nature of the sample he used. The silicon that he studied formed part of a transistor in which the mobile electrons were confined to a thin layer near one of the surfaces of the device. The electrons were then able to move in only two dimensions rather than the three dimensions available in a uniform sample. Constrained in this way by the voltage applied to the device, the electrons behaved in a markedly different way from their behavior in bulk material.

The most startling aspect of Klitzing's measurement was the departure of the Hall voltage from its normal smooth variation with the applied magnetic field and electron concentration. As the number of electrons in the two-dimensional layer was steadily increased, the Hall voltage at first dropped smoothly, then held constant for a while until dropping to another plateau where it again remained steady before repeating its drop to a new level. The Hall voltages at these plateaus were then divided by the current passing through the sample to give a set of numbers with the dimensions of an electrical resistance. When the numbers were compared, they were found to be simple fractions of a very special resistance; namely 25,813 ohms. This resistance is the ratio of two fundamental constants of nature—Planck's constant, which governs all quantum-mechanical behavior, and the square of the electrical charge on the electron.

The important feature of this result was the great precision with which the relationship was obeyed. In repeated experiments using not only differently shaped samples but also devices made from different materials, the same numbers have been observed with a precision of one part in 10 million. The results immediately led Klitzing to suggest that the phenomenon, now known as the quantum Hall effect, could form the basis for a new absolute standard of electrical resistance. Klitzing and his colleagues reported their findings in August 1980 in the journal *Physical Review Letters*.

The work that Klitzing published in 1980 was remarkable in at least three ways. First, it showed the effects of the quantum theory, which most commonly is relevant only to the behavior of microscopic entities like single electrons, in a measurement of a laboratory-scale electric current. Second, it was totally unexpected by theoretical physicists who had been studying semiconductors for decades. And third, it yielded reproducible measurements of such great precision that they immediately suggested themselves as a new international standard for the unit of electrical resistance, the ohm.

For his discovery of the quantum Hall effect, Klitzing was awarded the 1985 Nobel Prize for Physics. According to the Royal Swedish Academy of Sciences, his work "opened up a new research field of great importance and relevance." The academy went on to add that "we are dealing here with a new phenomenon in quantum physics, and one whose characteristics are still only partially understood."

The precision and reproducibility with which the quantum Hall effect can be measured give the phenomenon an importance that extends far beyond the realm of either metrology or the physics of semiconductor devices. Because the measured unit of resistance appears to be determined only by the most fundamental constants of nature, the result has implications for many other areas of physics. The fine structure in the emission spectra of hot gases, for example, is governed by the same combination of fundamental constants found by the quantum Hall effect. As a result, the measured Hall resistance has provided a verification of the long, difficult calculations that predict the fine-structure constant of atomic spectroscopy.

In some ways, Klitzing's discovery of the quantum Hall effect can be compared with the prediction two decades earlier by BRIAN D. JOSEPHSON of the phenomenon of superconductive tunneling. Both effects demonstrate in a laboratory-scale experiment the quantum-mechanical behavior normally limited to systems of atomic size. Both have led to new absolute standards for electrical quantities—the volt in the case of the Josephson theory and the ohm in the case of the quantum Hall effect. The particular importance of Klitzing's work lies, perhaps, in the stimulus it has given to the study of electrons effectively confined to two dimensions. The wealth of new phenomena that have been found and new questions raised in the physics of electron layers owes much to the remarkable observations made by Klitzing in 1980.

In 1971 Klitzing married Renate Falkenberg, with whom he has two sons and a daughter. Besides the Nobel Prize, he has also received the Walter-Schottky Prize for Solid-State Physics of the German Physical Society (1981) and the Hewlett-Packard Prize of the European Physical Society (1982).

ABOUT: New York Times October 17, 1985; Physics Today December 1985; Science February 21, 1986.

KLUG, AARON

(August 11, 1926–)
Nobel Prize for Chemistry, 1982

The English physicist and molecular biologist Aaron Klug was born in Zelvas, Lithuania, to Lazar Klug, a cattle dealer, and Bella (Silin) Klug. When the boy was two, the family moved to Durban, South Africa, where members of his mother's family had emigrated earlier in the century and where he was educated in the public schools. It was while attending Durban High School between 1937 and 1941 that Klug developed an interest in science, especially after reading *Microbe Hunters,* a popular book by the American science writer Paul de Kruif.

Entering the University of Witwatersrand in Johannesburg in 1942, Klug took the premedical course as well as classes in biochemistry, physics, and mathematics. By the time he graduated with a B.S. in 1945, his interest had shifted to physics. While doing graduate work in this field at the University of Cape Town, which he attended on scholarship, he learned the techniques of X-ray crystallography from one of his teachers, R. W. James. This method, devised by W. L. BRAGG and W. H. BRAGG, records on a photographic plate the patterns produced when a beam of X rays is passed through a crystal. Because the X rays are diffracted, or bent, in a characteristic way, the pattern they form can be used to deduce the arrangement of atoms within the crystal. After receiving his M.S. in 1946, Klug remained at the University of Cape Town to continue his work with James on X-ray diffraction studies of organic compounds. "During this time," he later recalled, "I developed a strong interest . . . in the structure of matter, and how it was organized."

A British 1851 Exhibition Scholarship and a research grant from Trinity College, Cambridge, enabled Klug to move to England in 1949. At Cambridge University's Cavendish Laboratories, Klug applied for a research position with MAX PERUTZ and JOHN C. KENDREW, both of whom were using X-ray crystallography in an effort to determine the structure of large protein molecules. No open-

had determined that the tobacco mosaic virus consists of a thick coil of the repeating structural protein, with the genetic material spiraling along the inner surface.

At the same time, Klug and his colleagues were investigating another group of viruses, such as those that cause polio, which appeared to be spherical but could not be seen clearly enough to determine their structure accurately. Drawing on his knowledge of physics and X-ray analysis, Klug devised a technique called crystallographic electron microscopy, in which images obtained with an electron microscope are subjected to diffraction by laser light. The resulting pattern can then be interpreted to reveal the structure of the object.

With this method Klug acquired not only the technical means but also a procedure for conducting studies that would connect cellular and molecular organization. He could examine a complex biological system by first dissecting it out of the cell, then obtaining a detailed picture by X-ray and chemical analysis, and finally producing a complete image of the intact assembly by means of electron microscopy. In 1972 he began applying this procedure to the study of chromatin, the compound of histones (special proteins) and DNA that makes up the chromosomes of higher organisms. By 1981 he and his colleagues were able to show that each of the many histones is a stubby cylindrical molecule around which a section of continuous DNA is coiled. The histones themselves are gathered into coils so tight that a single strand of human DNA, which is about two meters in length, fits within the nucleus of the cell, which is less than a hundredth of a millimeter in diameter.

Klug was awarded the 1982 Nobel Prize for Chemistry "for his development of crystallographic electron microscopy and his structural elucidation of biologically important nucleic acid–protein complexes." In his presentation address, Bo G. Malmström of the Royal Swedish Academy of Sciences declared that Klug's "virus studies have illuminated an important biochemical principle, according to which the complicated molecular aggregates in the cell are formed spontaneously from their components. The chromatin investigations have provided clues to the structural control of the reading of the genetic message in DNA. In a long-term perspective, they will undoubtedly be of crucial importance for our understanding of the nature of cancer."

Since 1978 Klug has been joint head of the Medical Research Council Laboratory of Molecular Biology at Cambridge. His research

AARON KLUG

ings were available at the Cavendish, however, and he worked instead under D. R. Hartree on the molecular structure of steel, for which he received his doctorate in 1952.

Transferring to the colloid science department at Cambridge, Klug then spent 1953 investigating the biophysical processes by which oxygen and carbon dioxide are exchanged in hemoglobin. These studies further whetted his enthusiasm for X-ray analysis of biological molecules, and near the end of the year he obtained a Nuffield Fellowship to work at Birkbeck College in London under J. D. Bernal, Perutz's former teacher at Cambridge. After participating briefly in a study of the protein ribonuclease, Klug met Rosalind Franklin, whose X-ray analysis of deoxyribonucleic acid (DNA) had helped FRANCIS CRICK and JAMES D. WATSON to determine the double-helical structure of this complex molecule.

Franklin had recently begun to investigate the tobacco mosaic virus, which blights the leaves of the tobacco plant. Although a great deal was known about the virus—especially through the earlier work of JOHN H. NORTHROP and WENDELL M. STANLEY—molecular structure had not yet been elucidated. Fascinated by Franklin's X-ray images, in which he could vaguely discern traces of curved layer lines, Klug joined the project. After Franklin died in 1958, he became director of the Birkbeck Virus Structure Research Group. Four years later he accepted Crick's invitation to return to Cambridge, this time as a member of the Medical Research Council Laboratory of Molecular Biology. Within a short time Klug

there and the information that other researchers have obtained by using his methods have cast much light on the processes that take place within the living cell. Despite his research and administration duties, he has chosen to teach as much as possible.

In 1949 Klug married Liebe Brobow, with whom he has two sons. Klug, who has been described as short, slender, and intellectually aggressive, is popular among his students and colleagues.

In addition to the Nobel Prize, Klug has received honorary degrees from Columbia University, the University of Chicago, Strasbourg University, and the University of Stockholm. He has also been awarded the Dr. H. P. Heineken Prize of the Royal Netherlands Academy of Arts and Sciences (1979) and the Louisa Gross Horwitz Prize of Columbia University (1981). He is a fellow of the Royal Society and an honorary foreign fellow of the American Academy of Arts and Sciences.

SELECTED WORKS: "The Nucleosome," Scientific American February 1981.

ABOUT: New Scientist October 21, 1982; New York Times October 19, 1982; April 24, 1983; Science November 12, 1982.

KOCH, ROBERT

(December 11, 1843–May 27, 1910)
Nobel Prize for Physiology or Medicine, 1905

The German physician and bacteriologist Heinrich Hermann Robert Koch (kôk) was born in Clausthal, the third oldest of thirteen children of Hermann Koch, a mining official, and Mathilde Julie Henriette (Biewend) Koch, the daughter of an iron-mine inspector. A precocious child, Robert showed an early interest in nature and acquired a collection of mosses, lichens, insects, and minerals. His maternal grandfather and uncle, both amateur naturalists, encouraged the boy's interest in natural history. By the time he entered the local elementary school in 1848, Robert had taught himself to read and write. A quick learner, he was transferred to the Clausthal Gymnasium in 1851, where he headed his class four years later and from which he graduated in 1862.

That same year, Koch entered the University of Göttingen, where he studied the natural sciences, physics, and botany for two semes-

ROBERT KOCH

ters before he transferred to the medical program. Several of his teachers at the university— including the anatomist Jacob Henle, the physiologist Georg Meissner, and the clinician Karl Hasse—were instrumental in fostering his interest in scientific investigation. These teachers were engaged in debates about microbes and the nature of disease, and young Koch developed an interest in these subjects.

While Koch was at Göttingen, Louis Pasteur was publishing his famous papers that disproved the theory of spontaneous generation, the creation of living organisms from nonliving matter, which he supplanted with a microbial theory of fermentation. Although Pasteur had not yet investigated the role of microbes in human diseases, the possibility of such a role was the subject of considerable debate. Twenty years before Pasteur's papers on spontaneous generation, Jacob Henle, in an essay titled "Von den Miasmen und Contagion" (On Miasmas and Contagion), had set down guidelines for proving that specific microbes cause particular diseases. Although the essay was a conceptually straightforward argument, his protocols seemed beyond the abilities of the then current technology.

After obtaining his medical degree in 1866, Koch underwent an unsettled period, during which he held positions at various hospitals and tried to establish private practices in five different cities in Germany. Although he wished to become a military physician or to travel around the world as a ship's doctor, he found no opportunity to do so. Eventually, Koch settled in Rakwitz, Germany, where his practice soon flourished and he became a popular and respected physician. This interlude was interrupted by the outbreak of the Franco-Prussian War in 1870.

Even though Koch was severely myopic, he volunteered for service as a field hospital physician and in that capacity gained valuable experience with epidemic diseases, especially cholera and typhoid fever. At the same time, he was involved in microscopic studies of algae and large microbes and polished his microphotography skills. He was discharged from the army in 1871 and the following year was appointed district medical officer in Wollstein (now Wolsztyn, Poland). He found that anthrax (a disease caused by the bacterium *Bacillus anthracis,* which affects cattle and sheep and is characterized by emphysema, subcutaneous swellings, and nodules) was endemic in the Wollstein region. He soon turned his microscopic studies to the bacillus that was believed to be associated with the disease.

In a series of meticulous and methodical experiments, Koch proved that the anthrax bacillus was the sole cause of the disease. He also demonstrated that its epidemiology (the relationship of the various factors that determine the frequency and distribution of an infectious disease) was a result of the natural history of the bacterium. Koch's investigation of the anthrax bacillus was the first unequivocal demonstration of a bacterial cause of any disease. His first papers on anthrax were published in 1876 and 1877, under the auspices of the botanist Ferdinand Cohn and the pathologist Julius Cohnheim at the University of Breslau (now Wrocław, Poland). Koch also published a description of his laboratory methods, including the staining of bacterial cultures and the use of microphotography to record bacterial structures. Many of his results were presented to scientists in Cohnheim's laboratory, including PAUL EHRLICH.

Koch's discoveries brought him instant acclaim, and in 1880 Cohnheim was instrumental in having him appointed government adviser to the Imperial Department of Health in Berlin. In 1881 Koch published his *Methods for the Study of Pathogenic Organisms,* in which he introduced the techniques of culturing microbes on solid media, an advance that was critical to the isolation and study of pure bacterial cultures. It was during this time that he became involved in an acrimonious dispute with Pasteur, whose superiority in microbiology Koch's work had challenged. When Koch published some harsh criticisms of Pasteur's research on anthrax, the two distinguished scientists quarreled in print and public appearances for several years.

Koch achieved his greatest triumph on March 24, 1882, when he announced that he had isolated the bacterium that causes tuberculosis, one of the major causes of death at the time. His publications on tuberculosis included the first formal presentation of what became known as Koch's postulates. These principles for "obtaining a perfect proof . . . that the parasite is the actual direct cause of the disease," derived from Henle's guidelines, are still the theoretical foundations of medical microbiology.

His research on tuberculosis was interrupted by a scientific expedition to Egypt and India sponsored by the German government in the hope of finding the cause of cholera. While in India, Koch announced that he had isolated the microbe responsible for cholera. As a result of his discoveries, Koch became involved in formulating public health policies and eventually was responsible for coordinating research and public health measures for most of the important infectious diseases, including typhoid fever, typhus, malaria, rinderpest (a plaguelike disease of cattle), sleeping sickness, and plague.

In 1885 Koch was appointed professor at the University of Berlin and director of the newly established Institute of Hygiene. Despite his many responsibilities, he continued his research on tuberculosis, concentrating on finding a cure for the disease, which he announced in 1890. The compound he isolated, tuberculin (a sterile liquid containing the growth products of the tubercule bacillus), produced an allergic reaction in those persons exposed to tuberculosis. In fact, however, it was not a cure for tuberculosis; the compound lacked therapeutic value, and the toxic reactions it produced resulted in a storm of controversy. Protests over the use of tuberculin abated only when it became apparent that reactions to the compound were useful in diagnosing tuberculosis. This discovery—an important step in the effort to eliminate bovine tuberculosis—was a major consideration in Koch's nomination for a Nobel Prize.

The 1905 Nobel Prize for Physiology or Medicine was awarded to Koch for "his investigations and discoveries in relation to tuberculosis." In his Nobel lecture Koch stated, "if we look back on what has happened in recent years in the fight against tuberculosis as widespread infectious disease, then we cannot help but gain the impression that quite an important beginning has been made."

Although Koch seemed to be suspicious and

aloof when among strangers, he was regarded by his friends and colleagues as a kind and considerate man. He was an admirer of Goethe and an ardent chess player.

In 1867 Koch married Emmy Adolfine Josefine Fraatz, the daughter of a general superintendent at Clausthal; they had one daughter. After divorcing his first wife in 1893, he married Hedwig Freiburg, a young actress. Koch died in Baden-Baden of heart failure on May 27, 1910.

Among Koch's many awards were the Prussian Order of Merit given by the German government (1906) and honorary doctorates from the University of Heidelberg and the University of Bologna. He was a foreign member of the French Academy of Sciences, the Royal Society of London, the British Medical Association, and numerous other learned societies.

THEODOR KOCHER

SELECTED WORKS: The Aetiology of Tuberculosis, 1932.

ABOUT: Brock, T. D. Milestones in Microbiology, 1961; De Kruif, P. Microbe Hunters, 1926; Dictionary of Scientific Biography, volume 7, 1973; Dolan, E. F. Adventure With a Microscope, 1964; Dubos, R. The Unseen World, 1962; Knight, D. C. Robert Koch, Father of Bacteriology, 1961; Metchnikoff, E. The Founders of Modern Medicine, 1939; Paget, S. Pasteur and After Pasteur, 1914; Walker, M. Pioneers of Public Health, 1930.

KOCHER, THEODOR

(August 25, 1841–July 27, 1917)
Nobel Prize for Physiology or Medicine, 1909

The Swiss surgeon Emil Theodor Kocher (kôk′ ər) was born in Bern into an upper-middle-class family. His father, Jacob Alexander Kocher, an engineer, demanded that his son work hard, while his devout mother Maria (Wermuth) Kocher encouraged in him a lasting concern for religious philosophy. After attending primary and secondary school in Bern, Kocher entered the University of Bern medical school, from which he was graduated in 1865 with honors.

Since his family was well off financially, Kocher was able to travel and obtain postdoctoral surgical training with several well-known European surgeons. During the next five years he served surgical internships and residencies in Vienna, Paris, Berlin, and finally London, where he studied with the English surgeon Sir Joseph Lister. Lister, who in the early years of his surgical practice had been

astonished by the frequency of postoperative infections and deaths, was instrumental in the development of antiseptic surgical techniques. Before Lister's time it had been the practice for surgeons to enter the operating room directly from the wards and autopsy rooms, where they might have been handling contaminated materials or cadavers. Moreover, it was their habit to operate in street clothes, without washing their hands or wearing sterile gloves.

Aware of the experiments of Louis Pasteur, who had formulated the bacterial theory of disease, Lister postulated that postoperative wound infections were caused by bacteria that had been introduced into surgical wounds by contaminated surgical instruments and careless operating techniques. Even though his theory was initially unpopular among his colleagues, Lister introduced antiseptic techniques into his operating room, where he insisted upon preoperative washing of hands and forearms, the rinsing of surgical instruments in a carbolic acid solution, and the wearing of surgical gowns and gloves. The reduced rate of postoperative infection among Lister's surgical patients convinced his colleagues of the value of antisepsis. As a surgical intern under Lister's supervision, Kocher became an advocate of antiseptic surgical procedures.

In Vienna, Kocher served as a surgical resident under Theodor Billroth, who pioneered techniques for operating on the gastrointestinal tract that are used today for the surgical treatment of peptic ulcers. As a resident Kocher assisted Billroth in surgery, conducted research on the causes of postoperative wound infections, and performed autopsies in an effort to correlate the clinical presentation of certain diseases and their postmortem pathology. Kocher also designed surgical instruments, in particular a surgical clamp now known as the Kocher clamp, which is still used in vascular surgery. At the same time, he acquired a reputation for modesty and inventiveness. Impressed by Kocher's knowledge and surgical skills, Billroth invited the young man to join the Vienna Clinic when he finished his residency. Although tempted by Billroth's offer, Kocher wrote to a friend in Switzerland: "My heart urges me to return home and share what I have learned with others while I administer to the ill." Acting on his own advice, he returned to Bern in 1870.

Two years later, Kocher was appointed professor of surgery and director of the surgical clinic at the University of Bern, where he introduced Lister's antiseptic surgical techniques and Billroth's impeccable operating skills. Often spending many hours in the operating room, he performed chest and abdominal surgery; corrected inguinal hernias; operated for trauma, fractures, and dislocations; and performed neurosurgical operations. He also conducted research in biochemistry and continued his research in bacteriology as well as the clinical pathological correlations in the autopsy room.

Among his original contributions was the introduction of a method of treating wounds with chlorine solutions. For the treatment of certain injuries and diseases of the brain, he developed the technique of trephination, which involves the surgical removal of a small section of the skull to relieve intracranial pressure. He described the conditions required for adequate wound healing, including antiseptic conditions, and became an authority on gunshot wounds. He presented a review of his clinical and experimental observations to the International Medical Congress in Rome and later published two books on the subject: *On Gunshot Wounds* (1880) and *The Theory of Gunshot Wounds Due to Projectiles of Small Caliber* (1895). His *Theory of Surgical Operations,* which went through six editions and was translated into many languages, became a standard textbook of surgery in the United States and Europe. His other scientific papers and books covered a wide range of subjects, including acute osteomyelitis (infections of bone and bone marrow) and the surgical treatment of gastric disease, peptic ulcers, gallbladder disease, cancer of the rectum, epilepsy, and inguinal hernias.

Kocher's major contribution, however, was his explanation of the function of the thyroid gland and the development of surgical procedures to correct malfunctions of the gland, including the formation of goiters. It was previously thought that the thyroid gland had no significant biological function; thus, in the early years of Kocher's practice, when a goiter developed, often the entire thyroid gland was removed, with scant attention paid to the four parathyroid glands or the surrounding tissue. (The four parathyroid glands, located at the four corners of the thyroid gland, are essential to the normal metabolism of calcium in bones and other bodily tissues.)

It is now known that the thyroid gland synthesizes and secretes thyroid hormones into the bloodstream. These hormones—thyroxine and triiodothyronine—are essential to normal cellular metabolism (specifically, oxygen consumption, energy levels, and carbon dioxide production). If the thyroid gland secretes too much thyroid hormone, cellular metabolism and respiration are abnormally high, causing a condition known as hyperthyroidism. If it secretes too little, cellular metabolism and respiration are abnormally low, producing a condition called hypothyroidism in adults and cretinism in children. When the supply of iodine in the human diet is too low, the thyroid gland may enlarge and remain in a chronically enlarged state—a goiter—which, if sufficiently large, may interfere with vocal cord nerves, lung airway, and other surrounding structures. A goiter may also be disfiguring.

In the early years of his practice, Kocher followed traditional procedure and removed the entire thyroid gland, but he soon observed that patients whose thyroid gland had been completely excised developed a clinical disease resembling cretinism. Cretinism is a chronic condition caused by a congenital lack of thyroid secretion. It is marked by arrested physical and mental development, with dystrophy of the bones and soft parts of the body, and lowered metabolism; the adult form is known as myxedema. "As a rule," he wrote, "patients begin to complain of fatigue . . . weakness and heaviness . . . a sensation of coldness in the extremities . . . slowness of thinking . . . increasing slowness of speech and of all other movements . . . swellings . . . involving the face, hands, and feet . . . a puffiness of the face. . . . If we are to give a name to this picture, we cannot fail to recognize its relation to . . . cretinism."

These were extremely important observations, for Kocher had established not only the function of the thyroid gland but the cause of cretinism and myxedema. He further observed that patients who underwent goiter surgery did not develop hypothyroidism if part of the thyroid gland was left in place at the time of surgery. Moreover, he pointed out the need to preserve the parathyroid glands and to avoid damaging the nerves to the vocal cords in thyroid surgery. During his long career Kocher performed more than 5,000 thyroidectomies (removal of the thyroid gland) and became the foremost thyroid surgeon in Europe. He also studied the clinical and biochemical abnormalities caused by hyperthyroidism and hypothyroidism unrelated to thyroid surgery. By the beginning of the twentieth century Eugen Baumann, a German biochemist, had prepared a crude extract of thyroid tissue that was used to treat patients with mxyedema and cretinism, conditions that today are treated with thyroid hormone.

Kocher was awarded the 1909 Nobel Prize for Physiology or Medicine "for his work on the physiology, pathology, and surgery of the thyroid gland." "Through his research," said K. A. H. Mörner of the Karolinska Institute in his presentation speech, "Kocher has carried out pioneering work of an enduring nature which is of the greatest importance to medical science and of the greatest value in the service of suffering humanity."

Kocher was married to Marie Witchi; they had three sons, one of whom became a surgeon and an associate of his father. Theodor Kocher died in 1917, in Bern.

An honorary fellow of the Royal College of Surgeons in London and an honorary member of numerous medical societies throughout the world, Kocher was elected president of the German Society of Surgeons in 1902, and three years later he was made president of the First International Surgical Congress in Brussels.

SELECTED WORKS: Textbook of Operative Surgery, 1895.

ABOUT: Surgery June 1969; Zimmerman, L. M. and Veith, I. Great Ideas in the History of Surgery, 1961.

KÖHLER, GEORGES

(April 17, 1946–   )
Nobel Prize for Physiology or Medicine, 1984
(shared with Niels K. Jerne and César Milstein)

The German immunologist Georges Jean Franz Köhler (kû′ lər) was born in Munich to a French mother and a German father. He was raised in the town of Kehl on the French-German border, where he received his early education. He entered the University of Freiburg in 1965 to study biology and obtained his diploma in biology in 1971 for research on deoxyribonucleic acid (DNA) repair in the bacterium *Escherichia coli,* one of the bacteria normally present in the bowel. By the time he received his diploma, however, his interest had shifted from bacteriology to immunology. Consequently, he asked Fritz Melchers of the Institute for Immunology in Basel to supervise his doctoral work. Melchers agreed, and in 1971 Köhler began his immunological studies of the enzyme beta-galactosidase. The Institute for Immunology, founded in 1969, was under the direction of NIELS K. JERNE.

In the 1930s KARL LANDSTEINER had demonstrated that animals can produce thousands of antibodies that are specific for different foreign bodies or antigens. Antibodies are proteins produced by the immune system; they bind to and inactivate antigens. A major problem in immunology in the 1960s and 1970s was to determine how the body produces so many different and specific antibodies. In his doctoral work, Köhler attempted to define the problem by studying the variety of antibodies produced to fight a single antigen; he used the bacterial enzyme beta-galactosidase as the antigen. Even though Köhler found it difficult to keep the cells alive, even for short periods of time, he learned that mice can manufacture at least 1,000 different antibodies that act on a single part of the beta-galactosidase molecule, which meant that these different antibodies recognize a single antigenic determinant.

A prevalent theory of antibody diversity stated that all of the different antibodies derived from mutations in antibody genes in a particular group of cells. To test this theory, Köhler wanted to examine a population of identical antibody-producing cells (clones) to determine how often mutations appeared; he also wanted to learn the effect of mutations on the types of antibodies produced by the cells. He obtained a long-term fellowship from the European Organization of Molecular Biology (EMBO) to work under CÉSAR MILSTEIN at the Medical Research Council (MRC) Laboratory of Molecular Biology at Cambridge University; he began his research in the spring of 1974.

At the time, Milstein was searching for mutations in myeloma cells grown in laboratory cultures (myelomas are cancers of the antibody-producing cells). Generally, all myeloma

GEORGES KÖHLER

cells from one individual are genetically identical descendants of a single, cancerous ancestor; therefore, they produce identical antibodies. The difficulty in using myeloma cells for Köhler's research was that the cancers appear randomly; thus there is no way of predicting the antigen to which a given myeloma's antibodies will bind.

Milstein suggested that Köhler take one of the established myeloma cell lines at the MRC and find its corresponding antigen by trial and error. Köhler, however, still hoped to find a line that was specific for a given antibody. He decided instead to work with a technique developed by a former member of Milstein's laboratory, R. G. H. Cotton, who had discovered that he could fuse two different myeloma cells to produce a hybrid that possessed proteins from both parent myelomas.

Köhler immunized a mouse against a known antigen, extracted the antibody-producing cells from the mouse's spleen, and fused them with myeloma cells. The resulting hybrid myeloma (or hybridoma) combined the useful properties of both its parents; it continuously produced antibodies against a known antigen, as in the case of normal antibody-producing cells. Köhler also developed a way to isolate hybridomas as clones descended from a single fusion. The products were identical monoclonal antibodies.

When Köhler and Milstein published their hybridoma-producing technique in 1975, its practical potential was immediately apparent. As Köhler's doctoral thesis had illustrated, animals naturally produce many different varieties of antibodies to a single antigen. The antiserums isolated from immunized human beings or animals are always mixtures of different antibodies that vary among different individuals or even within the same individual at different times.

Reactions to antiserums can be used to test for the presence of any compound to which an animal can be immunized, but only after each sample of serum has been separately tested to determine its particular pattern of antibody reactivity. Therefore, the production of standardized immunological tests is difficult and time-consuming. A batch of monoclonal antibodies, however, is automatically standardized, and all the antibodies in the sample are identical.

Another problem posed by use of conventional antiserums is that they are useful only if the antibodies to a given antigen predominate in the serum. Monoclonal antibodies, however, can be produced even if the antigen does not stimulate a strong immune response. The only requirement is to screen hybridomas until a useful one is isolated.

By the early 1980s a substantial commercial trade in monoclonal antibodies for diagnostic testing had begun. Since specific monoclonal antibodies can be produced to act with any substance, they are now used by molecular biologists to study problems ranging from enzyme structures to the function of the nervous system. An especially important group of monoclonal antibodies react only to cancer cells. These antibodies can be used to transport toxic materials directly to tumors, destroying the cancers without disturbing other cells.

Köhler and Milstein received half of the 1984 Nobel Prize for Physiology or Medicine for their "discovery and development of principles for production of monoclonal antibodies by hybridoma technique." The other half was awarded to Niels K. Jerne. In his presentation speech, Hans Wigzell of the Karolinska Institute declared that Köhler and Milstein's development of the hybridoma technique had "revolutionized the use of antibodies in health care and research. Rare antibodies with a tailor-made . . . fit for a given structure can now be made in large quantity," Wigzell went on. "The hybridoma cells can be stored in tissue banks and the very same monoclonal antibody can be used all over the world with a guarantee for eternal supply."

Monoclonal antibodies have been used to treat leukemia and a wide range of infectious diseases such as hepatitis B and streptococcal infections. They also played an important role in helping researchers identify cases of acquired immune deficiency syndrome (AIDS) in 1981. Other potential applications include improved techniques for tissue typing, advances in allergy treatment, and the treatment of such autoimmune disorders as rheumatoid arthritis and lupus.

Not wanting to become what he called "a monoclonal antibody maker," Köhler preferred to use hybridomas to conduct research on antibody production. He remained at the Basel Institute for Immunology until 1985, when he became director of the Max Planck Institute for Immunobiology in Freiburg.

Köhler and his wife Claudia have three children. Bearded and given to casual dress, Köhler entertains a keen interest in architecture and enjoys restoring old houses. He has been described by colleagues as quiet, modest, and imperturbable.

Köhler is a member of the European Organization of Molecular Biology and has received the Gairdner Foundation International Award (1981), among other honors and awards.

ABOUT: New Scientist October 18, 1984; New York Times October 16, 1984; Science February 26, 1982; November 30, 1984.

KOOPMANS, TJALLING C.

(August 28, 1910–February 26, 1985)
Nobel Memorial Prize in Economic
 Sciences, 1975
(shared with Leonid Kantorovich)

The American economist Tjalling Charles Koopmans (küp' mənz) was born in 's Graveland, the Netherlands, the third son of Sjoerd Koopmans and the former Wijtske van der Zee. Both of his parents, who were trained as schoolteachers, placed great importance on their children's education. At the age of fourteen Koopmans was awarded a fellowship that enabled him to attend the University of Utrecht from 1927 to 1933. At first he concentrated on mathematics and theoretical physics—he published a paper on quantum mechanics in 1934—but, increasingly dissatisfied with the abstract nature of his studies, he sought a field in which the subject matter was, as he put it later, "closer to real life." His interests shifted to economics after the Great Depression that began in 1929 convinced him "that the economic world order was unreliable, unstable, and, most of all, iniquitous." Around this time, he became friendly with a number of socialist students and studied his first economics book, Karl Marx's *Capital*.

In 1933, when Koopmans was introduced to

TJALLING C. KOOPMANS

the field of mathematical economics, he found a way to apply his mathematical training, and his interest in economics deepened. The following year he went to the University of Amsterdam to study under the leading Dutch mathematical economist, JAN TINBERGEN. Under Tinbergen's guidance he read the works of leading general equilibrium theorists such as Gustav Cassel and Knut Wicksell. In 1935 he spent four months in Oslo working with the noted mathematical economist and econometrician RAGNAR FRISCH. For the dissertation "Linear Regression Analysis of Economic Time-Series," he received his doctorate from the University of Leiden in 1936.

From 1936 to 1938, Koopmans was employed first by the School of Economics in Rotterdam as a substitute lecturer for Tinbergen and then by the Financial Section of the League of Nations. In 1938 he succeeded Tinbergen at the league, where he worked on a business cycle model for the United Kingdom. He remained in Geneva until Germany invaded the lowlands and France in 1940, when he moved to the United States. For the next two years he conducted research at Princeton University before assuming what he called the "humble role" of statistician for the British Merchant Shipping Mission in Washington, D.C. It was this work—fitting information on losses, new construction, and the employment of Allied ships into a comprehensive scheme—that led to his most important contributions in economic analysis.

At the Merchant Shipping Mission, Koopmans sought to improve the routing of Allied shipping in order to minimize cargo delivery costs. The problem was extremely complex, involving thousands of merchant ships carrying millions of tons of cargo on sea lanes connecting hundreds of ports around the world. It afforded Koopmans an opportunity to apply his mathematical training to a fundamental economic problem: the optimal allocation of scarce resources among competing uses.

The analytical technique Koopmans developed, called activity analysis, has transformed the way economists and production managers approach allocation. He first described the technique in a 1942 memorandum, "Exchange Ratios Between Cargoes on Various Routes," which showed how allocation problems can be approached as mathematical problems of maximization subject to constraint. The variable to be maximized is the value of delivered cargo, represented by the sum of the values of cargoes delivered to each port. The constraints are represented by equations that relate the quantities of different inputs (for example, ships, time, labor) to the quantity of cargo delivered to different locations, where the quantity of each input employed must be no more than the total amount available.

To solve this maximization problem, Koopmans developed mathematical solutions that have had broad application in both economic theory and managerial practice. These solutions yield coefficients for each input that are equivalent to the price of the input in a regime of perfectly competitive markets. Thus, a vital link was established between theories of efficient production and theories of allocation through competitive markets. Koopmans's equations, moreover, are of great value to central planners, who can use them to determine the appropriate prices for various inputs, leaving the selection of optimal routes to the charge of local managers instructed to maximize profits. Activity analysis is also widely used by managers in planning production procedures. Automobile manufacturers use it, for example, to plan assembly lines and truck routing.

In 1944 Koopmans left the Merchant Shipping Mission to join the staff of the Cowles Commission for Research in Economics, then affiliated with the University of Chicago. Becoming a United States citizen in 1946, he remained at Chicago for more than a decade. When the Cowles Commission moved to Yale University, he followed and in 1955 accepted a position as Alfred Cowles Professor of Economics there.

In his postwar research, Koopmans developed activity analysis as a tool for economic planning, publishing the results in two collections of seminal papers—*Statistical Inference in Dynamic Economic Models* (1950) and *Activity Analysis of Production and Allocation* (1951)—in numerous articles, and in *Three Essays on the State of Economic Science* (1957). During the 1960s and 1970s he made important contributions to the study of economic growth. In this field he considered the allocation of economic resources over time, from current consumption to the creation of capital as machinery and facilities for the production of future consumer goods. A pioneer in development programming, he has demonstrated the importance of the discount rate (the rate at which a society evaluates the present value of future consumption) for planning a society's economic growth.

The 1975 Nobel Memorial Prize in Economic Sciences was awarded jointly to Koopmans and LEONID KANTOROVICH "for their contributions to the theory of optimum allocation of resources." With respect to politics, Koopmans's work has been essentially neutral in that his theory applies regardless of a society's political and social institutions. Thus, Ragnar Bentzel of the Royal Swedish Academy of Sciences noted in his presentation speech that "the basic economic problems are the same in all societies." The nearly simultaneous development of activity analysis by Kantorovich and Koopmans, one working in the Soviet Union and the other in the United States, was cited as evidence that those problems "can be treated in a scientific manner that is independent of the political organization of the society under consideration."

Koopmans continued his research and teaching after receiving the Nobel Prize. Never one to seek the limelight, throughout his life he remained a modest and careful scholar. In 1978 he served as president of the American Economic Association, but only in deference to membership pressure and as a gesture in memory of his close friend Jacob Marschak, who had died shortly before he was to assume the office. Koopmans became professor emeritus at Yale University in 1981.

In 1936 Koopmans married Truus Wanningen, a fellow student in Amsterdam, whom he had tutored in mathematics. They had two daughters and a son. A great lover of music, he occasionally wrote musical compositions, particularly for voice. He died on February 26, 1985, in New Haven.

Koopmans was a member of the Royal Netherlands Academy of Sciences, the American Mathematical Society, the Institute of

KORNBERG

Management Sciences, the Mathematical Programming Society, the American Association for the Advancement of Science, the International Association of Energy Economists, and the American Economic Association. He held honorary degrees from the Netherlands School of Economics, the Catholic University of Louvain, Northwestern University, and the University of Pennsylvania.

ADDITIONAL WORKS: Optimum Utilization of the Transportation System, 1947; Systems of Linear Production Function, 1948; Assignment Problems and the Location of Economic Activities, 1957, with Martin Beckman; On the Concept of Optimal Economic Growth, 1963; Proportional Growth and Turnpike Theorems, 1963; Objectives, Constraints, and Outcomes in Optimal Growth Models, 1966; Scientific Papers of Tjalling C. Koopmans (2 vols.) 1970–1985; Examples of Production Relations Based on Microdata, 1978.

ABOUT: New York Times October 15, 1975; March 2, 1985; Scandinavian Journal of Economics, number 1, 1976; Science November 14, 1975.

ARTHUR KORNBERG

KORNBERG, ARTHUR
(March 3, 1918–   )
Nobel Prize for Physiology or Medicine, 1959
(shared with Severo Ochoa)

The American biochemist Arthur Kornberg was born in Brooklyn, New York, to Lena (Katz) and Joseph Kornberg. He received his early education in the New York City public school system, proving himself a brilliant student and graduating from Abraham Lincoln High School at the age of fifteen. A scholarship enabled him to enter the City College of New York, where he enrolled in the premedicine course and concentrated on biology and chemistry. After receiving a B.A. with honors in 1937, he entered the University of Rochester School of Medicine, where he became interested in medical research and the biochemistry of enzymes (protein compounds that act as catalysts, or accelerators for biochemical reactions of cells). During one of his terms at Rochester, Kornberg contracted hepatitis and, while convalescing, wrote his first scientific paper: "The Occurrence of Jaundice in an Otherwise Normal Medical Student."

Upon receiving his medical degree in 1941, he began a year's internship at Rochester's Strong Memorial Hospital, a facility attached to the university. At the outbreak of World War II he was commissioned a lieutenant in the United States Coast Guard; by the end of 1942, because of his medical expertise, he had been appointed an officer in the United States Public Health Service and assigned to the nutrition section of the Division of Physiology at the National Institutes of Health (NIH) in Bethesda, Maryland.

When the war was over Kornberg joined the laboratory of Professor SEVERO OCHOA at the New York University School of Medicine as a research assistant. In 1947 he spent time as a visiting investigator in the laboratory of CARL F. and GERTY T. CORI at the Washington University School of Medicine in St. Louis, Missouri. That year he also was appointed chief of the enzymes and metabolism section at the NIH, and three years later he was given a position as visiting researcher at the University of California in Berkeley.

During these years Kornberg became an authority on the biochemistry of enzymes. He also studied the cellular production of coenzymes, the heat-stable, water-soluble portion of enzymes. Coenzymes participate in enzymatic reactions by transferring small chemical groups from one molecule to another. Kornberg discovered that two coenzymes, diphosphopyridine nucleotide (DPN) and flavin-adenine dinucleotide (FAD), are produced in a condensation reaction, during which inorganic phosphate is eliminated from the molecule from which the coenzyme is formed. Kornberg subsequently postulated that the biosynthesis of deoxyribonucleic acid (DNA) might also involve a similar condensing step.

The means by which DNA is formed within the cell was at that time one of the central problems in biology and genetics. In the 1940s researchers learned that genes are made of the nucleic acid DNA. Because genes direct the biosynthesis of cellular proteins, or enzymes, they also control the biochemical processes of the cell. A major breakthrough occurred in 1953 when FRANCIS CRICK and JAMES D. WATSON, working at Cambridge University, discovered the chemical structure of DNA. They found that the DNA molecule is shaped like a double helix, a structure resembling a ladder twisted into a spiral. On the outside of the double helix, two strands of deoxyribose, a five-carbon sugar, are joined by phosphate bridges. The two strands of deoxyribose-phosphate are joined by pairs of nitrogenous bases inside the helix (the "rungs" of the "ladder"), and the bases are attached to one another by hydrogen bonds. With the aid of a three-dimensional model constructed by Crick and Watson, the biosynthesis of DNA could at last be visualized. First, the two halves of the DNA molecule separate from each other, like an opened zipper. A new, mirror-image half molecule of DNA is then synthesized opposite each old one. This sequence of nitrogenous bases, or nucleotides (one of the compounds into which nucleic acid is split by the action of nuclease) acts as a template for the new molecules.

In 1953 Kornberg was appointed professor of microbiology and chief of the Department of Microbiology at Washington University School of Medicine in St. Louis. There he isolated and purified the enzyme responsible for synthesis of DNA in the bacterium *Escherichia coli.* He called the enzyme DNA polymerase. Using DNA polymerase, Kornberg and his colleagues synthesized DNA molecules in 1957, but impurities in the test tube mixture interfered with exact replication. Because the sequence of nucleotides in the synthesized molecule was incorrect, the DNA molecule was biologically inactive; that is, it could not be used as a template to synthesize more DNA. Meanwhile, Severo Ochoa had synthesized molecules of ribonucleic acid (RNA), a nucleic acid similar to DNA. One of the functions of RNA is to carry genetic information from DNA to the sites of protein synthesis.

Kornberg and Ochoa shared the 1959 Nobel Prize for Physiology or Medicine "for their discovery of the mechanisms in the biological synthesis of ribonucleic acid and deoxyribonucleic acid." At the award ceremony in Stockholm, Ochoa described Kornberg as his "best student." In Kornberg's Nobel lecture, "The Biologic Synthesis of Deoxyribonucleic Acid," he compared DNA in lay terms to "a

tape recording that carries a message in which there are specific instructions for a job to be done" and from which "exact copies can be made . . . so that this information can be used again and elsewhere in time and space."

The awarding of the Nobel Prize coincided with Kornberg's appointment as professor of biochemistry and chairman of the Department of Biochemistry at Stanford University in Palo Alto, California, where he continued his research on the biosynthesis of DNA. He and a colleague, Mehran Goulian, were assisted in their work by Robert Sinsheimer, then at the California Institute of Technology in Pasadena, who had been studying a virus that infects the *E. coli* bacillus. In 1967, using the DNA of Sinsheimer's virus as a template, Kornberg and Goulian were the first experimenters to synthesize biologically active DNA in a test tube. At a news conference called to announce their achievement, Kornberg said that the goals of future DNA research in his laboratory would be twofold: "to understand in finer chemical detail . . . DNA polymerase" and "to understand what regulates DNA synthesis in the cell."

The isolation and purification of the enzyme polymerase and the replication of DNA were outstanding achievements in the field of biochemistry; they provided the means and guidelines for the replication of the genetic material of the cell. The key step in Kornberg's synthesis of DNA required a catalytic agent, which he found in the enzyme polymerase, a protein compound that catalyzed the synthesis of a DNA chain in response to directions from a DNA template. These directions were dictated by the hydrogen-bonding relationship of adenine to thymine and guanine to cytosine— nucleotides or bases of DNA. Kornberg's discoveries opened up new avenues for research not only in biochemistry and genetics but also for the treatment of hereditary diseases and the control of cancer.

In 1943 Kornberg married Sylvy Ruth Levy, a biochemist; they have three sons.

Kornberg is the author of *Enzymatic Synthesis of DNA* (1961), *Biosynthesis of DNA* (1964), and *DNA Synthesis* (1974). He is the recipient of the Paul-Lewis Laboratories Award in Enzyme Chemistry of the American Chemical Society (1951), the Scientific Achievement Award of the American Medical Association (1968), the Lucy Wortham James Award of the Society of Medical Oncology (1968), the Borden Award in the Medical Sciences of the Association of American Medical Colleges (1968), and the National Medal of Science of

the Royal Society of London (1979). He is a member of the National Academy of Sciences, the American Academy of Arts and Sciences, and the American Society of Biological Scientists, as well as a foreign member of the Royal Society of London.

SELECTED WORKS: DNA Replication (2 vols.) 1980–1982.

ABOUT: Current Biography September 1963; New York Times October 16, 1959; Science May 20, 1960.

KOSSEL, ALBRECHT
(September 16, 1853–July 5, 1927)
Nobel Prize for Physiology or Medicine, 1910

ALBRECHT KOSSEL

The German physiologist Ludwig Karl Martin Leonhard Albrecht Kossel (kō′ sel) was born in Rostock, the only son of Albrecht Kossel, a merchant, and Clara (Jeppe) Kossel. The boy's scientific interest was in the study of botany, and he often led excursions to view the plants in the Rostock area. Although Kossel hoped to pursue his interest in botany, his father considered it an unpromising career and urged his son to study medicine. Kossel complied with his father's wishes and enrolled in 1872 in the newly formed Imperial University at Strasbourg, where he could attend the lectures of the mycologist Anton de Bary.

At Strasbourg, Kossel studied under the physiological chemist Felix Hoppe-Seyler. After passing the state medical examination in Rostock in 1877, Kossel received his Ph.D. in medicine and returned to Strasbourg as Hoppe-Seyler's assistant at the Institute of Physical Chemistry. Their research dealt with salt diffusion and the digestion of proteins by the enzyme pepsin.

Kossel then began to study the chemical constituents of nuclein, a phosphorus-rich material discovered in the nuclei of pus cells by Friedrich Miescher in 1869. Ten years later Kossel isolated nuclein from yeast. He and his students then determined the constituents of nucleic acids to be nitrogen-containing bases known as pyrimidines, which included thymine, cytosine, and uracil. Adenine and guanine, called purines, which are also fundamental components of nucleic acids, were first isolated by EMIL FISCHER in 1897. As a result of this work, most of the key elements of the nucleic acids had been identified by the end of the nineteenth century. Only the carbohy-

drate component was undefined, although Kossel speculated that it was a mixture of a hexose and a pentose, both simple sugars or monosaccharides.

One of Kossel's goals was to link the chemistry of a cellular substance with its biological function. From physiological studies of nuclein, he deduced that it plays a role in the growth of tissues rather than acting as a storage substance or energy source for muscle cells. His finding that embryonic tissue contains especially high amounts of nuclein supported this conclusion.

In 1883 Kossel was appointed director of the chemical division, and four years later he was made an assistant professor at the Physiological Institute in Berlin, where he remained until 1895, even though his teaching responsibilities left little time for research. When he moved to Marburg in Hesse as a professor of physiology and director of the Institute for Physiology, he was able to devote more time to his research interests, and collaborators from many other countries joined him there.

While analyzing another component of nuclein, Kossel isolated a proteinaceous substance, histone, from the nuclei of goose red blood cells and found that it resembled the protamine in fish spermatozoa discovered by Miescher. Both histone and protamines from various fish species were found to be basic, simple proteins.

In 1901 Kossel succeeded Wilhelm Kühne as head of the Physiological Institute at Heidelberg, where he remained until his retirement. He presided as chairman of the Seventh

International Congress of Physiology in 1907, held in his honor.

Kossel was awarded the 1910 Nobel Prize for Physiology or Medicine for "contributions to our knowledge of cell chemistry made through his work on proteins, including the nucleic substances." At the time of the award, the role of the nucleic acids in encoding and transmitting genetic information was unknown, and Kossel did not anticipate how his research findings would affect the concepts of genetics. Although he had reported in 1893 that chromosomes consist of nucleic acid with varying proportions of a protein (histone), he was not concerned with the identity of the hereditary substance. Later, in a 1912 lecture, he pointed out the diversity of polypeptides and suggested a chemical basis for the transmission of hereditary information in the structure of proteins.

Kossel also is credited with originating the concept of building blocks of the cell. He noted that certain substances—amino acids, sterols, purines, and pyrimidines—that are always found in the tissue of plants and animals are fundamental building blocks for various biological processes. Kossel and his students discovered several of the amino acids between 1885 and 1901.

In 1886 Kossel married Luise Holzmann; they had a daughter and a son.

After his retirement from the Physiological Institute at Heidelberg in 1924, Kossel worked at the Institute for Protein Chemistry and under Ludwig Krehl at the new Heidelberg medical clinic. He died of cardiac arrest on July 5, 1927, at the age of seventy-three.

Among Kossel's many awards were honorary degrees from the universities of Cambridge, Dublin, Edinburgh, Ghent, Greifswald, and St. Andrews. He was a member of numerous scientific academies, including the Royal Swedish Academy of Sciences and the Royal Society of Sciences of Uppsala. For more than thirty years, he was the editor of the *Zeitschrift für Physiologische Chemie* (Journal of Physiological Chemistry).

SELECTED WORKS: The Protamines and Histones, 1928.

ABOUT: Dictionary of Scientific Biography, volume 7, 1973; Farber, E. (ed.) Great Chemists, 1961; Levene, P. A., and Bass, L. W. Nucleic Acids, 1931; Neurath, H., and Bailey, K. (eds.) The Proteins, 1954.

KREBS, HANS

(August 25, 1900–November 22, 1981)
Nobel Prize for Physiology or Medicine, 1953
(shared with Fritz Lipmann)

The German-English biochemist Hans Adolf Krebs was born in Hildesheim, Germany, to Georg Krebs, an ear, nose, and throat specialist, and the former Alma Davidson. He received his early education in the Gymnasium Andreanum in Hildesheim. After graduating in 1918 he served in the Signals Regiment of the Prussian army during the last months of World War I. He then studied medicine at the universities of Göttingen, Freiburg, Munich, and Berlin, and he received his medical degree in 1925 from the University of Hamburg. After studying chemistry for a year at the Institute of Pathology of the University of Berlin, he was appointed laboratory assistant to OTTO WARBURG at the Kaiser Wilhelm Institute of Biology in Berlin.

Warburg had developed a useful experimental method for investigating cellular respiration—the uptake of oxygen and the production of carbon dioxide in the metabolism of carbohydrates, fats, and proteins. Instead of studying the respiration of intact animals or organs, Warburg used thin slices of fresh tissue placed in an airtight flask equipped with a pressure gauge. If the tissue utilized oxygen in its biochemical reactions, the gas pressure in the flask decreased and provided an objective measurement of respiratory activity.

Upon returning to clinical medicine in 1930, Krebs served as assistant in the municipal hospital at Altona (Hamburg) and as privatdocent (unsalaried lecturer) in the medical clinic at the University of Freiburg. During this time he continued his biochemical research. Using an experimental system similar to that employed by Warburg, he discovered the urea cycle, the process by which nitrogen and ammonia are eliminated from the body. He learned that the amino acid ornithine, when added to liver slices, acted as a catalyst; that is, it promoted the synthesis of urea without being consumed. Ornithine was transformed into the related amino acid citrulline, which in turn became the amino acid arginine, which released the end products urea and ornithine; then the cycle could begin again. His introduction of the concept of cyclical processes in biochemistry established Krebs's international reputation.

When Adolf Hitler came to power in Ger-

HANS KREBS

many in 1933, Krebs's appointment at the University of Freiburg was terminated because he was Jewish. However, a Rockefeller Research Fellowship enabled him to study biochemistry under FREDERICK GOWLAND HOPKINS at the Institute of Biochemistry at Cambridge University in England. After arriving in Cambridge in 1933—with "virtually nothing but a sigh of relief, a few books, and sixteen crates of Warburg flasks"—Krebs served as a demonstrator in biochemistry and received an M.S. from Cambridge University. In 1935 he was appointed lecturer in pharmacology at the University of Sheffield. In the following year, the scientist and Zionist leader Chaim Weizmann invited Krebs to join a biochemistry institute of the Hebrew University to be built at Rehovot, Palestine. Although Krebs was fascinated by the idea of pioneer life, especially in the kibbutzim (collective farms), the research facilities at the Hebrew University were meager, and Arab-Jewish hostilities had resumed; so Krebs decided to remain in England, where he was appointed lecturer in charge of the biochemistry department at Sheffield.

While studying the intermediate stages of carbohydrate metabolism in 1937, Krebs made his second important biochemical discovery: the citric acid or tricarboxylic acid cycle, now called the Krebs cycle. This final common pathway in the breakdown of carbohydrates, proteins, and fats into carbon dioxide and water furnishes the main source of energy for most organisms. Earlier work by ALBERT SZENT-GYÖRGYI, Franz Knoop, Carl Martius, and others indicated that in the presence of oxygen, citric acid (a six-carbon tricarboxylic acid) is converted in a series of reactions to oxaloacetic acid (a four-carbon dicarboxylic acid) and carbon dioxide.

Simply stated, the Krebs cycle explains how the body converts food into energy. Krebs investigated the method of food energy conversion by the body in order to determine the process by which sugar is converted into other compounds. Manipulating the formulas of more than twenty organic acids related to sugar, he ascertained that lactic and pyruvic acids were capable of making a specific series of transformations by themselves. Eventually, he utilized pyruvic acid in his experiments on the metabolic process.

In his experiments Krebs found out that when pyruvic acid is oxidized, it forms an intermediate chemical called acetyl coenzyme A (a coenzyme is that portion of an enzyme necessary to produce digestion or fermentation); he also observed that carbon dioxide is released during oxidation. Other acids are formed during oxidation and the whole process continues until another molecule of coenzyme A is reinvigorated. In this manner energy is released. Krebs stated that the basic principle of his cycle could also be applied to other foods, particularly fatty acids.

The discovery of the cyclic nature of intermediary metabolic reactions was an important milestone in biochemistry, for it provided a clue to the understanding of metabolic pathways; furthermore, this finding stimulated additional experimental work and reinforced the concepts of cellular reaction sequences.

Krebs became a British subject in 1939. During World War II he supervised research for the British Medical Research Council on nutrition, including work on the dietary requirements for vitamins A and C. In 1945 he was appointed professor and chairman of the Department of Biochemistry and director of the Medical Research Council Unit for Research in Cell Metabolism at the University of Sheffield.

Krebs was awarded the 1953 Nobel Prize for Physiology or Medicine "for his discovery of the citric acid cycle"; he shared the award with FRITZ LIPMANN. "The Krebs cycle explains two simultaneous processes," said Erik Hammarsten of the Karolinska Institute in his presentation address: "the degradation reactions which yield energy and the building up processes which use up energy." In his Nobel lecture Krebs summarized his findings on the citric acid cycle. Concluding his talk with "an excursion into general biology," he discussed the broader implications of his findings. "The presence of the same mechanism of energy production in all forms of life suggests two other inferences," he said, "firstly, that the mechanism of energy production has arisen very early in the evolutionary process, and secondly, that life, in its present form, has arisen only once."

A year after receiving the Nobel Prize, Krebs was appointed Whitley Professor of Biochemistry at the Nuffield Department of Clinical Medicine, Oxford University, whereupon the Medical Research Council Unit in Cell Metabolism was transferred there. Three years later, he and a former pupil, Hans L. Kornberg, discovered a modification of the citric acid cycle, the glyoxylate cycle, in which two molecules of acetyl coenzyme A are converted to succinic acid. The glyoxylate cycle is of greater metabolic importance in plant and microbial cells than in animal cells. Krebs and Kornberg collaborated on *Energy Transformation in Living Matter: A Survey* (1957), a discussion of the citric acid system and its function in biological organisms.

Upon his retirement from Oxford University in 1967, Krebs was appointed visiting professor of biochemistry at the Royal Free Hospital School of Medicine in London. He continued research at the Nuffield Department of Clinical Medicine at Oxford on the control of rates of metabolic reactions, "inborn errors of metabolism," and preservation of livers for transplantation. He was increasingly critical of "wasteful and unproductive" university research and government policies. Krebs once described his involvement in biochemical research as that of a biologist trying to clarify chemical events taking place in living cells—of striving to discover the missing pieces in a jigsaw puzzle.

In 1938 Krebs married Margaret Cicely Fieldhouse; they had two sons and a daughter. He died in Oxford on November 22, 1981, at the age of eighty-one.

His many honors included the Lasker Award of the American Public Health Association (1953), the Royal Medal (1954) and Copley Medal of the Royal Society (1961), and the Gold Medal of the Royal Society of Medicine (1965). In 1958 Krebs was knighted by Queen Elizabeth II. He was elected to foreign membership in the American Academy of Arts and Sciences and the American National Academy of Sciences. He was also a fellow of the American College of Physicians and a member of the Weizmann Institute in Israel.

SELECTED WORKS: The Advent of Biochemistry, 1946; Reminiscences and Reflections, 1981.

ABOUT: Bartley, W., et al. (eds.) Essays in Cell Metabolism, 1970; Biographical Memoirs of Fellows of the Royal Society, volume 30, 1984; Current Biography March 1954; Nachmanson, D. German-Jewish Pioneers in Science 1900–1933, 1979; Podell, J. (ed.) Annual Obituary 1981, 1982; Richter, D. (ed.) Dahlem in the Late Nineteen Twenties, 1974.

KROGH, AUGUST

(November 15, 1874–September 13, 1949)
Nobel Prize for Physiology or Medicine, 1920

The Danish physiologist Schack August Steenberg Krogh (krôg) was born in Grenaa, Jutland, to Viggo Krogh, who was a shipbuilder, brewer, and newspaper editor, and Marie (Drechmann) Krogh, a descendant of gypsies. Displaying an early interest in the natural sciences, young Krogh spent much time examining insects in the fields surrounding his home. Around the age of fourteen he left school and, hoping for a career as a naval officer, served on a Danish naval ship that patrolled the fisheries of Iceland. The experience gave him a lifelong love of the sea and ships. After a year he resumed his education at the Cathedral School in Århus, and in 1893 he entered the University of Copenhagen to study physics and medicine.

Encouraged by the zoologist William Sørensen, Krogh began research on the larvae of an aquatic organism, *Corethra*. He determined that their air bladders functioned "like the diving tanks of a submarine." He was also influenced by the lectures of Christian Bohr (father of the physicist NIELS BOHR), an authority on the physiology of blood and respiration, under whom Krogh began to work in 1897 in the medical physiology laboratory. After receiving a master of science degree in zoology from the University of Copenhagen two years later, Krogh was appointed Bohr's assistant.

To aid his studies on *Corethra,* Krogh invented a microtonometer, an instrument that measures the partial pressure or tension of a gas dissolved in a fluid (for example, oxygen in blood). On a sailing expedition to Greenland in 1902, he analyzed the amounts of oxygen and carbon dioxide contained in sea and fresh water and further developed the technique for tonometric measurement of dissolved gases. This work threw new light on the role of the oceans in the regulation of atmospheric carbon dioxide.

AUGUST KROGH

The following year, Krogh received a Ph.D. in zoology from the University of Copenhagen for a dissertation on pulmonary (lung) and cutaneous (skin) respiration in the frog. Respiration is the exchange of oxygen and carbon dioxide between cells and the external environment. Krogh demonstrated that, although respiration in the skin of the frog is relatively constant, respiration in the lungs is variable and is regulated by the vagus nerve of the autonomic (involuntary) nervous system. In the respiratory cycle, oxygen passes from the air sacs, or alveoli, of the lungs across a membrane into the capillaries. The oxygen is then carried to tissues throughout the body, where it is burned to form carbon dioxide. In reverse order, carbon dioxide passes from the blood into the alveoli and is eliminated from the body through the lungs.

When Krogh began his work, the mechanisms of respiration were still unclear, and physiologists were divided between two hypotheses. Did the cells in the alveolar-capillary membrane actively secrete pulmonary gases in one direction or the other? Or were pulmonary gases passively diffused across the alveolar-capillary membrane? Bohr, believing that the lung functioned as a gland, favored the former theory. However, using the microtonometer to measure the partial gas pressures of oxygen and carbon dioxide in the blood and lungs, Krogh and his colleagues demonstrated that the exchange of gases in the lungs takes place by diffusion alone. Krogh and Bohr also described the effects of varying carbon dioxide concentrations on the dissociation of oxygen

from its carrier molecule, hemoglobin, in the blood (a phenomenon called the Bohr effect).

In 1905 Krogh married Marie Jørgensen, a physiologist who also worked in Bohr's laboratory. Their son later became prosector of anatomy at the University of Århus; their two eldest daughters were trained as dentists, and the youngest became a physiologist in the United States.

The year after his marriage, Krogh was awarded the Seegen Prize by the Academy of Sciences of Vienna for demonstrating that gaseous nitrogen is not involved in the normal metabolism of animals. His international reputation was further enhanced when in 1907 he discussed his research on the diffusion of pulmonary gases at the International Congress of Physiology at Heidelberg, Germany.

An associate professorship of zoophysiology was established especially for Krogh at the University of Copenhagen in 1908, the same year in which he and his wife made a second expedition to Greenland to study the metabolic and respiratory effects of the nearly all-meat diet of the Eskimo population. Two years later the University of Copenhagen provided Krogh with a physiological laboratory at Ny Vestergade, where the couple continued to collaborate.

With Johannes Lindhard, later a professor of gymnastic theory, Krogh determined the output of the heart at rest and during muscular exercise by using a nitrous oxide method to measure blood flow. The two researchers also showed that arterial blood flow from the left side of the heart is dependent on the quantity of venous blood flow into the right side of the heart.

In 1916 Krogh was named professor of zoology at the University of Copenhagen. In other research, he investigated the physiological regulation of capillary blood flow (and therefore of oxygen delivery) to tissues and cells. Capillaries are small blood vessels, a few micrometers in diameter, that connect arteries with veins in all tissues of the body. Unlike arterial and venous walls, which are multilayered, capillary walls are a single cell in thickness. Oxygen, carbon dioxide, nutrients, and other substances are exchanged between the blood and body tissues across the capillary walls. Previous examinations of muscle capillaries under a binocular microscope had shown that the capillaries open and close asynchronously, that is, out of rhythm rather than in rhythm with arterial pressure changes. Moreover, researchers knew that any increase in blood flow caused by higher arterial blood pressure was offset by increased blood flow through the capillary circulation.

Concluding that the surface area of open or functioning capillaries (the capillary diffusion surface) was directly related to oxygen consumption, Krogh demonstrated that the number of functioning capillaries, or the diffusion surface area, was in turn controlled by local mechanical, chemical, and temperature stimuli. In experiments on the tongue of a frog, he found that capillaries that were visible and filled with blood when the muscle was working seemed to empty and disappeared from sight at rest. Bjovolf Vimtrup, one of Krogh's students, later reported that specialized Rouget cells in capillary walls contained contractile elements that caused capillaries to open and close. Krogh's analysis of pulmonary gas exchange and the regulation of capillary blood flow led to medical applications of tracheal breathing and the use of hypothermia during open heart surgery.

Krogh was awarded the 1920 Nobel Prize for Physiology or Medicine "for his discovery of the capillary motor regulating mechanism," proving that at rest only some of the capillaries are open, while in active work their number increases according to oxygen consumption. His discovery that this phenomenon applies to all organs and tissues of the body had a great impact on modern science. In his Nobel lecture Krogh discussed the physiology of the capillaries based on his observations during experiments with frogs.

While visiting the United States in 1922 to deliver the Silliman lectures at Yale University, Krogh studied insulin, which had been discovered the previous year by FREDERICK G. BANTING and JOHN J. R. MACLEOD. Because his wife had diabetes, the new substance was of particular interest to Krogh, and he played a prominent role in establishing laboratories and manufacturing facilities in Denmark. His later research interests included the permeability of cell membranes to water and salt, respiratory differences during flight among various species of insects, and the history of science. He took a keen interest in the sociobiology of bees and wrote on KARL VON FRISCH's discoveries concerning communication among honeybees.

After the German occupation of Denmark during World War II, Krogh, an outspoken opponent of Nazism, fled to Sweden, where he remained until 1945. Returning to Denmark that year, he resigned his chair at the University of Copenhagen and continued his research at a laboratory provided by the Carlsberg and Scandinavian Insulin Foundations. The author of many popular works on science, Krogh read widely and was particularly fond of the novels of RUDYARD KIPLING. He died on September 13, 1949, in Copenhagen.

"Krogh was an extremely accomplished experimenter, an ingenious designer of instruments," wrote ARCHIBALD V. HILL; "but his personal skill and his delight in beautiful techniques never led him far away from his interest in fundamental scientific problems."

Krogh's numerous awards included the Baly Medal of the Royal College of Physicians in London (1945), as well as honorary degrees from the universities of Edinburgh, Budapest, Lund, Göttingen, and Oslo and from Harvard, Rutgers, and Oxford. He was a foreign member of the Royal Society of London as well as numerous other scientific societies.

SELECTED WORKS: Physiological Papers, 1924; The Anatomy and Physiology of Capillaries, 1924; Osmotic Regulation in Aquatic Animals, 1939; The Comparative Physiology of Respiratory Mechanisms, 1941.

ABOUT: Dictionary of Scientific Biography, volume 7, 1973; Obituary Notices of Fellows of the Royal Society, volume 7, 1950; Rowntree, L. G. Amid Masters of Twentieth Century Medicine, 1958.

KUHN, RICHARD
(December 3, 1900–July 31, 1967)
Nobel Prize for Chemistry, 1938

The Austrian chemist Richard Kuhn (kün) was born in Vienna to Richard Clements Kuhn, an engineer, and Angelika (Rodler) Kuhn, an elementary school teacher. First educated at home by his mother, Kuhn was nine years old when he entered the Döbling Gymnasium, where one of his classmates was WOLFGANG PAULI. After graduating from the gymnasium in 1917, he was drafted into the German army and served until the armistice in November 1918.

After being discharged from military service, Kuhn entered the University of Vienna but moved to the University of Munich three semesters later. At Munich he studied chemistry under RICHARD WILLSTÄTTER and received his Ph.D. in 1922 for the thesis "On the Specificity of Enzymes in Carbohydrate Metabolism." He continued his studies at Munich before accepting an invitation to join the Federal Institute of Technology in Zurich in 1926.

In 1929 Kuhn left Zurich to become director

RICHARD KUHN

of the chemistry department at the University of Heidelberg's newly established Kaiser Wilhelm Institute for Medical Research (since 1950 the Max Planck Institute), with a concurrent appointment as professor of chemistry at the university. In 1937 he became director of the institute, where he remained for the rest of his career.

Greatly influenced by Willstätter's work, Kuhn was particularly interested in how the chemistry of organic compounds was related to their function in biological systems. Enzymes, the subject of his earliest research, are catalysts—proteins that accelerate the rates at which chemical reactions occur in cells. The characteristic shape of an individual enzyme allows it to react in a specific way with a specific chemical (the substrate). Kuhn wanted to determine the configuration of atoms in certain organic molecules and how these molecules are able to bend light passing through them (their optical isomerism). He was also interested in conjugated double bonds, a molecular structure in which doubly bonded and singly bonded carbon atoms alternate with one another.

Kuhn united both of these interests in his investigation of the carotenoids, biological pigments that are important components of living cells. One such substance is carotene, the pigment found in carrots, whose chemical formula had been determined earlier by Willstätter. In 1931, working independently, Kuhn and PAUL KARRER found two distinct compounds in carotene: beta-carotene, which bends light, and alpha-carotene, which does not. Two

years later Kuhn discovered yet a third form, gamma-carotene. These three forms, or isomers, have identical chemical formulas but different molecular configurations, from which their properties arise.

In further investigations, Kuhn learned that carotene is a precursor of vitamin A; that is, it is a necessary starting material in the production of the vitamin by biological systems. Vitamin A is essential for growth in higher animals and for maintenance of the body's mucous membranes. In addition, Kuhn found that the liver can produce two molecules of vitamin A from either one molecule of beta-carotene or two molecules of alpha-carotene. As he and his associates discovered the presence of carotenoids in many plants and animals, they greatly improved the use of chromatography, a major analytical tool.

Next, Kuhn turned his attention to members of the water-soluble vitamin B group. Working with ALBERT SZENT-GYÖRGYI and JULIUS WAGNER VON JAUREGG, he isolated about one gram of lactoflavin from thousands of liters of milk. By determining the structure of lumiflavin, a breakdown product of lactoflavin, Kuhn was able to elucidate the chemical composition of lactoflavin itself and eventually to synthesize both compounds. By showing that lactoflavin (now known as riboflavin, or vitamin B_2) plays a primary role in respiratory enzyme action, Kuhn provided crucial insights into the function of vitamins in living systems. By 1939, he had isolated adermin, now called vitamin B_6, and determined both the chemical composition and molecular structure of this substance, which helps to regulate the metabolism of the nervous system.

Kuhn received the 1938 Nobel Prize for Chemistry in 1939 "for his work on carotenoids and vitamins." As a German citizen, he was forbidden by the Nazi government from accepting the award, a policy that stemmed from Adolf Hitler's anger that the German political dissident CARL VON OSSIETZKY had received the Nobel Peace Prize four years earlier. It was not until 1949 that Kuhn was able to accept the Nobel medal and certificate at ceremonies in Stockholm.

During the remainder of his career, Kuhn went on to identify para-aminobenzoic acid (PABA), a compound that proved useful in the synthesis of anesthetics, and pantothenic acid, important in hemoglobin formation and the release of energy from carbohydrates. After becoming professor of biochemistry in the medical faculty of the Max Planck Institute in 1950, Kuhn focused much of his effort on the study of organic substances that are instrumental in the body's resistance to infection. His investigations of influenza, cholera, and the potato beetle larva led to valuable insights into the molecular interaction between an organism and its assailants.

Throughout his career, Kuhn demonstrated an ability to combine precision and persistence with great intuition and creativity. He was intensely interested in the practical applications of his work to agriculture and medicine. Known as a cheerful man, Kuhn was an accomplished tennis, chess, and billiards player. He was also a talented violinist who gave occasional public concerts with a chamber ensemble. His marriage in 1928 to Daisy Hartmann produced four daughters and two sons. Kuhn died in Heidelberg on July 31, 1967, at the age of sixty-six.

Kuhn, who held membership in scientific societies around the world, received honorary degrees from the Munich Technical University, the University of Vienna, and the University of St. Maria, Brazil, among others. Two years before his death, he was awarded the first commemorative medal struck by the University of Heidelberg to honor a scientist. He served as president of the German Chemical Society and vice president of the Max Planck Society.

SELECTED WORKS: Biochemistry (2 vols.) 1947–1948, with others.

ABOUT: Dictionary of Scientific Biography, volume 7, 1973.

POLYKARP KUSCH

KUSCH, POLYKARP
(January 26, 1911–)
Nobel Prize for Physics, 1955
(shared with Willis E. Lamb Jr.)

The American physicist Polykarp Kusch was born in Blankenburg, Germany, to John Matthias Kusch, a Lutheran missionary, and the former Henrietta van der Haas. A year after his birth, the family immigrated to the United States and eventually settled in Cleveland, Ohio. Kusch attended public school in Cleveland, became a naturalized American citizen in 1922, and got his first job—as a page at the Cleveland Public Library—in 1926. He earned a B.S. in physics in 1931 at the Case Institute of Technology (now Case Western Reserve University) in Cleveland. Moving to the University of Illinois, Kusch received an M.S. in

physics in 1933 and a Ph.D. in 1936, with a thesis on optical molecular spectroscopy.

Kusch began his long teaching career during his graduate study at the University of Illinois, as an assistant instructor in physics from 1931 to 1936. In 1936 he became a research assistant at the University of Minnesota, and in 1937 he was appointed an instructor in physics at Columbia University. During World War II, Kusch conducted military research as development engineer at Westinghouse Electric Corporation (1941–1942), on microwave vacuum tubes for radar; as a staff member at Columbia University's Division of War Research (1942–1944), on high-frequency oscillators; and as a staff member at Bell Telephone Laboratories (1944–1946), on vacuum tubes and microwave generators. After the war, he was named associate professor at Columbia, and in 1949 he became full professor. He was vice president and dean of faculties in 1969–1970 and executive vice president and provost in 1970–1971.

During his early years at Columbia, Kusch worked closely with I. I. RABI on applications of the resonance method of studying atomic and molecular properties, using molecular beams. Rabi had invented the magnetic resonance method in 1937. The method entails simultaneously passing a beam of particles through a magnetic field and bombarding it with pulses of radiation. The high resolution and great precision afforded by this method permit its use in the study of such subtle particle properties as atomic energy levels and nuclear magnetic moments. The magnetic moment of the electron is a property that appears frequently in atomic physics calculations. The electron has an intrinsic magnetic moment due to rotation about its own axis and, if it is bound to an atom, it also has an orbital magnetic moment caused by its revolution around the nucleus. In 1925 the Dutch physicists Samuel A. Goudsmit and George E. Uhlenbeck had postulated that the intrinsic magnetic moment of the electron is equal to the quantity known as the Bohr magneton, after NIELS BOHR. All measurements of atomic properties made before 1947 supported their postulate. Furthermore, the postulate followed as a direct consequence of the relativistic quantum-mechanical equation (formulated in 1928 by P. A. M. DIRAC), which described all the known properties of an electron. In 1947, however, Rabi and his colleagues measured the difference between certain of the energy levels of hydrogen and compared the result with a calculated prediction. The calculation used both the Goudsmit-Uhlenbeck value for the electron's intrinsic magnetic moment and a quantity for the proton's magnetic moment that depended on the value for the electron. When the experimental result differed from the prediction, the American physicist Gregory Breit suggested that the Goudsmit-Uhlenbeck value might be wrong.

Using magnetic resonance, Kusch and the American physicist Henry Foley studied the magnetic moment of the electron and were able to measure the ratio of the total intrinsic and orbital magnetic moments of beams of atoms in different energy states. (These total moments depend upon the intrinsic and orbital moments of the individual electrons and are uniquely determined by the atom's energy state.) Any variation of the observed ratio from the predicted one must indicate that the intrinsic and orbital magnetic moments of the electron are not equal. Because it is difficult to prepare pure atomic states, Kusch and Foley performed the experiment with several different combinations of states and with different atoms in the same energy state. The result was always the same—the intrinsic magnetic moment of the electron is larger than its orbital magnetic moment by a little more than one-tenth of a percent. The findings agreed closely with theoretical calculations made about that time by SIN-ITIRO TOMONAGA, JULIAN S. SCHWINGER, and RICHARD P. FEYNMAN and were quickly incorporated into the fundamental theory of quantum electrodynamics.

Kusch was awarded the 1955 Nobel Prize for Physics "for his precision determination of

the magnetic moment of the electron." He shared the prize with WILLIS E. LAMB JR. Their independent studies, said Ivar Waller of the Royal Swedish Academy of Sciences in his presentation speech, led to "a reshaping of the theory of the interaction of the electrons and the electromagnetic radiation, the so-called quantum electrodynamics."

Later determinations by Kusch and others of the orbital and intrinsic magnetic moments of the electron have been of even greater precision and show excellent agreement with current theory. In 1972 Kusch became Eugene McDermott Professor of Physics at the University of Texas in Dallas, followed by an appointment as regental professor in 1980. He was made professor emeritus in 1982.

Kusch and his first wife, the former Edith Starr McRoberts, who were married in 1935, had three daughters. A year after her death in 1959, he married Betty Pezzoni, with whom he has two children. A voracious reader with wide-ranging tastes, Kusch also enjoys listening to music.

Kusch is a member of the National Academy of Sciences, the American Philosophical Society, and the Association of Physics Teachers. He holds honorary degrees from Case Western Reserve University, Ohio State University, the University of Illinois, Yeshiva University, Colby College, Gustavus Adolphus College, and Incarnate World College.

SELECTED WORKS: The Magnetic Moment of the Proton, 1949, with Herbert Taub; Style and Styles in Research, 1966.

ABOUT: Current Biography March 1958; National Cyclopedia of American Biography, volume I, 1960.

KUZNETS, SIMON
(April 30, 1901–July 10, 1985)
Nobel Memorial Prize in Economic
    Sciences, 1971

The American economist Simon Smith Kuznets was born in the Ukrainian city of Kharkov, the second of three sons of Abraham and Pauline (Friedman) Kuznets. When the boy was six, his father, a fur dealer, left for the United States, intending to send for his family as soon as he had established himself. However, the outbreak of World War I in 1914, followed by the Russian Revolution, interrupted these plans. Meanwhile, Kuznets attended the local gymnasium, where he began his study of economics.

It was not until 1922 that Kuznets and his younger brother Solomon joined their father in New York City. During the summer, the two brothers taught themselves English, and that fall Kuznets entered Columbia University. The following year he received a B.A. in economics followed by an M.A. in 1924. He continued his graduate studies under the Columbia economist Wesley C. Mitchell, and their association lasted long after he completed his graduate studies. Mitchell's skepticism about the reliance of economics on deductive theory and his interest in advancing economics as an empirical science reinforced Kuznets's own convictions. Kuznets received his Ph.D. in 1926 with a dissertation titled "Cyclical Fluctuations: Retail and Wholesale Trade, United States, 1919–1925." Prepared under Mitchell, it reflects their shared desire to understand economic behavior by gathering statistical information and empirically discovering the regularities in economic development.

After completing his graduate studies, Kuznets spent a year and a half as a research fellow of the Social Science Research Council (SSRC), work that led to his 1930 book *Secular Movements in Production and Prices*. In 1927 Mitchell persuaded Kuznets to join the staff of the National Bureau of Economic Research (NBER), where he soon headed the program of national income studies. Kuznets's work at the NBER on national income accounting became one of his principal contributions to economic science. He was a pioneer in the study of the interrelationships between economic fluctuations and long-term growth.

At the NBER, Kuznets developed techniques for measuring the national income (the volume of goods and services produced) of the United States, although he was not the first scholar to attempt such measurements. As early as 1696, Gregory King had tried to measure England's level of prosperity by computing estimates of that country's "national revenue." In 1921 and 1922 the NBER had published estimates by W. I. King and Oswald Knauth of the national income of the United States for 1909–1918. Kuznets's first national income accounting report, *National Income, 1929–1932*, was published in 1934 by the United States Department of Commerce. This was followed by a series of NBER publications, including *National Income and Capital Formation, 1919–1935* in 1937, *Commodity Flow and Capital Formation* in 1938, the two-volume *National Income and Its Composition, 1919–1938* in 1941,

SIMON KUZNETS

and the more accessible *National Income: A Summary of Findings* in 1946.

Kuznets's contribution to the study of national income accounting rested upon a solid theoretical conception of the relationship between the measured value of a nation's output in any given year and the defined level of economic welfare that accompanies it. He paid scrupulous attention to the connection between welfare and income, resolving such tangled empirical problems as the contribution to income of activities outside the scope of markets and the changing value of the output of varied products with changes in relative prices, including new products not previously available. He dealt thoroughly with the public sector and strove for a consistent treatment of intermediate goods. He also clarified the crucial concepts of gross and net national product and investment and their measurement.

In his national income research Kuznets aimed at what he called analytic description of economic development, through a research process he saw as moving "from measurement to estimation to classification to explanation to speculation." With remorseless logic, indefatigable cross-checking, and bold judgment, he extracted from a wide range of data evidence for a coherent and consistent picture of production and income. In the field of national income, he was the leading researcher for many countries.

Kuznets also provided the statistical background for a Keynesian approach to macroeconomics. With his "double-entry" accounting of national income, he measured national income from two perspectives. First he computed a measure such as the Keynesian aggregate demand (the sum of expenditures on consumer goods and services, investment products, and government). Then he computed a measure of total income from the supply side: the sum of wages, profits, and rents. His national income accounting thus provided empirical content for the Keynesian definition of policy problems. Although he described and discussed trends of development, Kuznets did not make forecasts, a decision many considered wise.

Kuznets remained affiliated with the NBER even after becoming a professor of economics and statistics at the University of Pennsylvania in 1931 and while serving as an associate director of the Bureau of Planning and Statistics of the War Production Board between 1944 and 1946. In the 1940s he extended his estimates of national income retrospectively. He published historical estimates of the growth in income over a seventy-year period in *National Product Since 1869* (1946). In 1949 he became chairman of the Committee on Economic Growth of the SSRC, where he directed a large comparative study of national income growth over time for different countries. In conducting the study he was aided by a team of graduate students and other researchers at the SSRC, at Johns Hopkins University, where he was a professor of political economy from 1954 to 1960, and at Harvard University, where he became professor of economics in 1960.

The results of Kuznets's comparative project were published as a series of ten landmark studies under the title "Quantitative Aspects of the Economic Growth of Nations" in the journal *Economic Development and Cultural Change* between October 1956 and January 1967. Kuznets also published many of his findings in *Modern Economic Growth* (1966) and *Economic Growth of Nations* (1971). Providing a long historical perspective on the economic growth process, these studies identified, first for the United States and later for other countries, a variety of empirical regularities. For example, they identified long waves in the economic growth rates of several nations (the so-called Kuznets cycles)—twenty-year periods of alternating rapid and slow growth in technological progress, population, and national income. In his last major work, *Growth and Structural Shifts,* published in 1979, Kuznets dealt with the development of Taiwan since 1895. He pointed out that rapid growth (10 percent per year) means a continuous disruptive process, with large structural shifts in the economy and concomitant changes in institutions as well as in working and living conditions. As in his earlier works, Kuznets emphasized the importance of related demographic changes; in the case of Taiwan, a rapid decline in fertility is a striking example of such a change.

In most of his studies Kuznets discussed the role of savings and investment and the contribution of capital and of technological changes to the growth process. He took up these issues in *Capital and the American Economy* (1961), showing that, in the long term, the stability of the savings process determines the investment ratio of the economy. He also provided new measurements of marginal capital-output ratios. Demonstrating that the relative size of capital stock usually increased in the course of economic development but that the capital share of income declined over time, Kuznets noted that the contribution of capital to the growth of national productivity was relatively low. A pioneer in stressing the crucial role of "human" capital, Kuznets showed that technological change, the reallocation of labor between productive and less productive sectors, and improvements in the quality of labor input account for most of the historical rise in labor productivity.

Kuznets studied with great attention the relationship between economic growth and income distribution. In both *Shares of Upper Income Groups in Income Saving* (1953) and *Modern Economic Growth* (1966), Kuznets showed that increases in the ratio of size of capital stock to total output and declines in the return on capital raise labor's share of national income. Drawing on income data from ten countries, he demonstrated that the distribution of personal income often tends to equalize over time. Similarly, he proposed "Kuznets's law" for the economies of developing countries: during the first decades of development there will be sharply rising inequalities of income distribution, followed by tendencies toward equalization. Taiwan provided a good example of these tendencies.

Kuznets was awarded the 1971 Nobel Memorial Prize in Economic Sciences for "his empirically found interpretation of economic growth, which has led to new and deepened insight into the economic and social structure and process of development." In his presentation speech, BERTIL OHLIN of the Royal Swedish Academy of Sciences stated: "Kuznets has consistently addressed himself to giving quantitative precision to economic magnitudes which seem to be relevant to an understanding of processes of social change. He has collected an extraordinarily large body of statistical material, which he has analyzed carefully and with a keen and shrewd intelligence," Ohlin went on, "and he has used this to shed new light on economic growth."

In 1971 Kuznets was named professor emeritus at Harvard.

In 1929 Kuznets married Edith Handler, a fellow economist at the National Bureau of Economic Research. They had a son and a daughter. Kuznets, who enjoyed listening to classical music, was known to his colleagues as extremely modest. He died in Cambridge on July 10, 1985. Among his numerous honors were degrees from Harvard, Princeton, and Columbia universities; the Hebrew University; and the University of Pennsylvania.

ADDITIONAL WORKS: Seasonal Variations in Industry and Trade, 1933; National Product in Wartime, 1945; Economic Change, 1953; Six Lectures on Economic Growth, 1959; Quantitative Economic Research: Trends and Problems, 1972; Population, Capital, and Growth, 1973; Essays in Growth, Population, and Income Distribution, 1979.

ABOUT: Current Biography May 1972; New York Times July 11, 1985; Science October 27, 1971; Sills, D. L. (ed.) International Encyclopedia of the Social Sciences: Biographical Supplement, 1979; Swedish Journal of Economics December 1971.

LA FONTAINE, HENRI

(April 22, 1854–May 14, 1943)
Nobel Prize for Peace, 1913

The Belgian politician and peace advocate Henri La Fontaine was born in Brussels, the elder child of Alfred La Fontaine and Marie (Philips) La Fontaine. His father was a finance official in the Belgian government. After receiving his early education in Brussels, La Fontaine entered the Free University there, earning a doctorate in law. In 1877, after graduation, he became an advocate in the Brussels Court of Appeal.

The following year, La Fontaine began to combine the practice of law with a career in education when he was appointed secretary of the Technical School for Young Women, then an experimental institution. So successful were his methods that they later furnished a model for similar schools in Belgium and elsewhere. Drawing on his experience as a school administrator, La Fontaine helped found the New University, a branch of the Free University. From 1893 until 1940 he occupied the chair of

HENRI LA FONTAINE

international law at the New University, specializing in the origins and development of world judicial structures. He also lectured to the public on such topics as international relations and disarmament.

It was in the 1880s that La Fontaine encountered the ideas of Hodgson Pratt, an English pacifist. Pratt visited Belgium in 1883 to promote the cause of peace and to establish a Belgian branch of the International Arbitration and Peace Association. Stirred by Pratt's ideas, La Fontaine accepted a position as secretary-general of the Belgian branch when it was organized in 1889. Two years later, he joined the Socialists and became active in party affairs, speaking at meetings, writing articles, and helping to found the journal La Justice.

In 1895 La Fontaine ran for election to the Belgian Senate and won a seat as a representative from Hainaut. During the next four decades, he served the Senate as secretary (1907–1919) and vice president (1919–1932). He supported educational reform, the eight-hour workday, and reforms to promote safety in the workplace. As an internationalist, he used his legislative position to support the League of Nations, form an economic union with Luxembourg, promote disarmament, and encourage arbitration of international disputes.

Throughout these years, La Fontaine participated actively in the peace movement. He succeeded FREDRIK BAJER as president of the INTERNATIONAL PEACE BUREAU in 1907 and joined the Interparliamentary Union (founded in 1888 by WILLIAM CREMER and FRÉDÉRIC PASSY). In the Interparliamentary Union, La Fontaine saw the beginnings of a world parliament that could govern all nations peacefully. He was chairman of the organization's juridical committee and sat on commissions set up to prepare a model world parliament and to draft a model treaty of international arbitration.

In the belief that a ready source of information about international affairs would promote the cause of peace, La Fontaine joined with Paul Otlet in 1895 to found the House of Documentation. Located in Brussels, it undertook the ambitious task of collecting, indexing, and filing all notable publications on international issues from all over the world. With funds from the Belgian government, it began by developing a system of universal classification (based on methods recently devised by Melvil Dewey, the American library reformer). It went on to compile bibliographies of international issues in the social sciences, especially literature pertaining to the peace movement.

An outgrowth of the House of Documentation was the Union of International Associations, founded in 1907 by La Fontaine and Otlet. Directed by La Fontaine until his death, the union published numerous directories, bibliographies, documents, and other reference works, including a periodical, *La Vie Internationale* (International Life), and the *Yearbook of International Organizations*. In 1951 the union became affiliated with the United Nations.

La Fontaine also contributed to the peace movement as a scholar and writer. His *Pasicrisie internationale: Histoire documentaire des arbitrages internationaux, 1794–1900,* published in 1902, is a documentary history of every international arbitration treaty in the Western world during a period of 106 years. It remains a standard reference work. In *Bibliographie de la paix et de l'arbitrage international* (Bibliography of Peace and International Arbitration), which appeared two years later, La Fontaine listed more than 2,000 references to works in this field.

In *The Great Solution: Magnissima Charta,* published in Boston in 1916, La Fontaine outlined organizing principles for the conduct of international relations. He also proposed plans for a world constitution, a world parliament, a world bank, a universal language, and clearinghouses for statistical data on labor, trade, and other matters. His plan for a world court had been set forth a year earlier in an article,

"International Judicature." These and other writings are widely regarded as an important influence on the development of some of the auxiliary bodies of the League of Nations.

When he was awarded the 1913 Nobel Peace Prize, La Fontaine was hailed as "the true leader of the popular peace movement in Europe" by Ragnvald Moe of the Norwegian Nobel Committee. "He is one of the best-informed men working for peace," said Moe in his presentation speech, "and his initiative and energy have done much to promote the international peace movement, particularly in the interparliamentary and peace conferences of recent years." La Fontaine did not attend the award ceremony and did not deliver a Nobel lecture.

When the German army invaded Belgium the following year, La Fontaine fled to England and then to the United States, where he took up residence in Washington, D.C. He entertained little optimism for the prospects of internationalism, even beyond the end of the war. "I foresee the renewal of . . . the secret bargaining behind closed doors," he wrote to David S. Jordan, president of Stanford University, in 1916. "People will be as before, the sheep sent to the slaughterhouses or to the meadows, as it pleases the shepherds."

Despite his pessimism, La Fontaine returned to Europe after the war and continued his peace efforts. He was a member of the Belgian delegation to the Paris Peace Conference in 1919 and to the first Assembly of the League of Nations from 1920 to 1921. During the debate over whether member nations should be required to take part in league sanctions, even when such action might endanger national security, he insisted that all must perform "the sacred task of defending justice, even at the peril of their own existence." Meanwhile, he continued his work at the House of Documentation and at the Interparliamentary Union, serving as president of the union's council and remaining a member of its committee on juridical questions.

A man of wide-ranging interests, La Fontaine advocated women's rights, urged an increased role for women in the legal profession, and served as president of the Association for the Professional Education of Women. In his youth he published a volume of poetry, and in 1885 he translated portions of the libretto for Richard Wagner's opera *Die Walküre;* he also lectured on art. An avid mountaineer, he wrote about climbing and served as president of the Belgian Alpine Club. He married Mathilde Augustine Isabelle Lhoest in 1903.

La Fontaine retired from the Belgian Senate

in 1936, four years before Germany again overran his nation. He died on May 14, 1943.

According to *Nobel, The Man and His Works*, edited by the Nobel Foundation, La Fontaine "tried to bridge the gap between the bourgeois and socialist conceptions of the peace problem" and strove "to arouse the interest of the workers' organizations in the peace movement, of which they had up to then been rather skeptical, while as an assiduous delegate to the Interparliamentary conferences, he also managed to win over many of his colleagues."

ADDITIONAL WORKS IN ENGLISH TRANSLATION: "The Existing Elements of a Constitution of the United States of the World," International Conciliation October 1911; "The Neutralization of States in the Scheme of International Organization," American Society of International Law 1917.

ABOUT: American Journal of International Law January 1914; Hayne, D. Among the World's Peace-Makers, 1907; Rappard, W. E. The Quest for Peace Since the World War, 1940.

LAGERKVIST, PÄR
(May 23, 1891–July 11, 1974)
Nobel Prize for Literature, 1951

The Swedish novelist, poet, and dramatist Pär Fabian Lagerkvist (lä' gər kvist) was born in the small town of Växjö, in southern Sweden, the youngest of seven children born to Johanna (Blad) Lagerkvist and Anders Johan Lagerkvist. His father had given up farming to work as a lineman at the Växjö railway station. While attending secondary school, Lagerkvist read Charles Darwin's *Origin of Species* and other works that offered him perspectives far removed from his family's Lutheran conservatism. After graduating from secondary school in 1910, he studied art and literature for two years at the University of Uppsala.

Lagerkvist made his literary debut in 1912 with the publication of several fiery poems and the novella *Människor* (People). In 1913 he visited Paris, where he was strongly affected by modern painting; he particularly admired the daring vitality of the fauves and the intellectual discipline of the cubists. During the same year, he published *Ordkonst och bildkonst* (The Art of Words and the Pictorial Arts), in which he rejected literary naturalism in favor of the sparse vigor that he found in folktales and Greek tragedies. This critical essay was the first of Lagerkvist's works to attract

PÄR LAGERKVIST

attention, and he was quick to apply its theories to the series of poems and prose pieces collected in *Motiv* (Motifs, 1914) and to the short story collection *Järn och människor* (Iron and People, 1915).

In 1916 Lagerkvist established himself as an author of merit with the poetry collection *Ångest* (*Anguish*), which has been called Sweden's first expressionist work of literature. The book's brilliant imagery and disjointed style relate to Lagerkvist's interest in fauvism and cubism and communicate the despair and pain brought about by the slaughter of World War I. The American poet and critic Kenneth Rexroth, writing in *American Poetry Review* (1978), said that *Anguish* spoke not just of the political disillusionment of the time, but of "an awakening to the duplicity in the heart of man."

Living and writing in neutral Denmark throughout most of World War I, Lagerkvist produced many works for the theater. His first published play, *Den sista människan* (The Last Man, 1917), depicts the pain in the heart of the last man on earth and continues Lagerkvist's theme of despair over the war. However, in an essay included in his collective work *Teater* (Theater, 1918), Lagerkvist struck out against naturalistic drama and revealed an admiration for the late symbolic plays of August Strindberg. It is Strindberg's influence that forms a link between Lagerkvist's dramatic writings and the German expressionists.

In 1919, while serving as theater critic for the Stockholm daily newspaper *Svenska Dagbladet*, Lagerkvist published *Kaos* (Chaos), a collection of poetry, and *Himlens hemlighet*

(Secret of Heaven), the most successful of his early plays. This drama expresses Lagerkvist's desperate pessimism and his conviction that while life may seem supremely important to mankind, it is a matter of total indifference to God. He explored this theme further in the novella *Det eviga leendet* (*The Eternal Smile,* 1920), in which the characters, in a dialogue with God, inquire about his purpose in creating them. God replies that he had no particular objective in mind, but had done his best. This response leaves the characters bereft of the spiritual affirmation they crave, forcing them to seek spirituality from within rather than from an external deity.

Lagerkvist traveled extensively in France and Italy in the 1920s, a time during which his pessimism began to soften and his style became more concrete and far less mannered. The poetry of this period, *Den lyckliges väg* (The Happy Man's Way, 1921) and *Hjärtats sånger* (Songs of the Heart, 1926), reflects a simplicity and optimism not present in his earlier writing.

In addition to the collection of short stories *Onda sagor* (Evil Tales, 1924), Lagerkvist produced what many critics consider to be his two most self-revealing prose works in this same era of creative activity. They are *Gäst hos verkligheten* (*Guest of Reality,* 1925) and *Det besegrade livet* (The Conquered Life, 1927). *Guest of Reality* deals with Lagerkvist's boyhood and his early obsession with death. *Det besegrade livet,* a volume of philosophical meditations, offers Lagerkvist's personal view of his own work and of the world. According to the American critic Alrik Gustafson, these two works affirm Lagerkvist's faith in "the indestructible spirit of man" and in "the ultimate triumph of good over evil." They also illustrate Lagerkvist's distinctive narrative technique, in which a simple, concrete style is combined with a concentration on a single theme in order to achieve unity and wholeness. Lagerkvist continued his dramatic writing with *Han som fick leva om sitt liv* (*The Man Who Lived His Life Over,* 1928). In this play and in others written during the 1930s, he adopted a more realistic stage technique and began to employ everyday language in his dialogue.

As the threat of fascism and war grew during the 1930s, Lagerkvist's work became increasingly humanistic in tone, thematically stressing the need to confront evil. Although he declared his humanism in the poetry of *Vid lägerelden* (At the Campfire, 1932) and in the play *Konungen* (*The King,* 1932), his most no-table condemnation of tyranny occurs in the novella *Bödeln* (*The Hangman,* 1933). Recast as a play with the same title in 1934 (and translated into English in 1966), *The Hangman* contrasts medieval with modern times, providing a haunting allusion to the timelessness of evil. The political and social issues raised by the terrible events taking place in contemporary Europe continued to dominate Lagerkvist's work throughout the 1930s. *Mannen utan själ* (*Man Without a Soul,* 1936) examines how love turns a political terrorist from evil to an acceptance of humanism. *Seger i mörker* (Victory in Darkness, 1939) contrasts twin brothers—one a statesman devoted to democracy, the other a corrupt demagogue.

Germany's invasion of Denmark and Norway inspired many of the poems in *Sång och strid* (Song and Struggle, 1940), published in the same year that Lagerkvist was elected to the Swedish Academy. Although he continued to write poems and plays, one of his seminal works, the allegorical novel *Dvärgen* (*The Dwarf,* 1944), the fictional autobiography of a malevolent dwarf at an Italian Renaissance court, constitutes one of Lagerkvist's most stinging attacks on fascism and humanity's will to greed, hypocrisy, and evil. In the drama *Låt människan leva* (*Let Man Live,* 1949) fictional characters and historical figures, including Socrates, Christ, and Joan of Arc, enact the fate of those who are victimized by intolerance.

The novel *Barabbas* was published in 1950 and was immediately hailed by many writers and critics, including ANDRÉ GIDE, who called it "a remarkable book." The story of the brutish condemned thief released when Jesus was crucified, the novel explores humanity's search for God and seems to affirm the need for faith. Reviewing *Barabbas* in the *Atlantic Monthly,* Charles Rolo called it "nothing short of a masterpiece." Others agreed that seldom has a biblical story been told with such vivid realism or spiritual intensity. Translated into nine languages (including English in 1952) and made into a film in 1952, *Barabbas* is Lagerkvist's most critically acclaimed, and by far most popular, work.

Lagerkvist was awarded the 1951 Nobel Prize for Literature "for the artistic vigor and true independence of mind with which he endeavors in his poetry to find answers to the eternal questions confronting mankind." He belongs, said Anders Österling of the Swedish Academy, "to the group of writers who, boldly and directly, have dedicated themselves to the vital questions of humanity and to the fundamental problems of our existence." Known as a shy, reserved man, Lagerkvist refrained from making an acceptance speech. Instead, after a brief statement of his gratitude for the award, he read from *Myten om människorna* (The Myth of Mankind), an unpublished work he had written thirty years earlier.

In the years following his reception of the Nobel Prize, Lagerkvist continued to write prolifically, completing his ninth (and final) volume of poetry, *Aftonland* (1953, translated by W. H. Auden and Leif Sjöberg as *Evening Land* in 1975), as well as five novels. The novels—*Sibyllan* (*The Sibyl*, 1956), *Ahasverus död* (*The Death of Ahasuerus*, 1960), *Pilgrim på havet* (*Pilgrim at Sea*, 1962), *Det heliga landet* (*The Holy Land*, 1964), and *Mariamne* (*Herod and Mariamne*, 1967)—form a closely linked sequence. In them, Lagerkvist examines ambivalent attitudes toward love through the use of contrasting symbols such as light and dark.

An extremely private man, Lagerkvist kept his personal life strictly separate from his professional life. In 1918 he married Karen Dagmar Johanne Sörenson. They were divorced in 1925, and in the same year he married Elaine Luella Hallberg, widow of the Swedish painter Gösta Sandels. On July 11, 1974, after suffering a stroke, Lagerkvist died in a hospital in Stockholm at the age of eighty-three.

"The sense of alienation from existence is a major theme in twentieth-century literature, and as one of its interpreters Lagerkvist is akin to writers like [Franz] Kafka and [ALBERT] CAMUS," wrote the Swedish critic Gunnel Malmström in 1971. "He belongs among those whose struggle against the dehumanization of mankind has led them to seek for *the hidden God,* a solution to the metaphysical riddles of life."

ADDITIONAL WORKS IN ENGLISH TRANSLATION: The Masquerade of Souls, 1930; Midsummer Dream in the Workhouse, 1953; Marriage Feast and Other Stories, 1955; The Philosopher's Stone, 1966; The Difficult Hour I–III, 1966; Modern Theater: Seven Plays and an Essay, 1966.

ABOUT: Buckman, T. R. Modern Theater, 1965; Gustafson, A. A History of Swedish Literature, 1961; Scandinavica May 1971; Scobbie, I. Pär Lagerkvist: An Introduction, 1963; Sjöberg, L. Pär Lagerkvist, 1976; Spector, R. D. Pär Lagerkvist, 1973; Weathers, W. Pär Lagerkvist: A Critical Essay, 1968.

LAGERLÖF, SELMA

(November 20, 1858–March 16, 1940)
Nobel Prize for Literature, 1909

The Swedish novelist Selma Ottiliana Lovisa Lagerlöf (lä′ gər lûv) was born in the province of Värmland in southern Sweden, the fourth of five children of Lieutenant Erik Gustav Lagerlöf, a retired army officer, and the former Lovisa Walroth. At the age of three, Lagerlöf contracted what may have been infantile paralysis; unable to walk for nearly a year, she was left with a limp. Tutored at home, she grew up largely under the care of her paternal grandmother, who filled the child's imagination with fairy tales and folklore. Lagerlöf spent much of her childhood reading voraciously and writing poetry.

To prepare for a teaching career, Lagerlöf entered the Royal Women's Superior Training Academy in Stockholm, graduating in 1882. In the same year, her father died, and the family estate, Mårbacka, was sold to settle his debts. The double loss of her father and the family home was a severe blow to the young woman, who subsequently accepted a teaching position at a girls' school at Landskrona in southern Sweden, where she was popular with the students. Inspired by the folktales and picturesque scenery of the Värmland region, she began writing a novel and entered the first several chapters in a literary contest sponsored by the Swedish magazine *Idun*. The magazine's editor not only awarded Lagerlöf the prize but also offered to publish the novel in its entirety.

Supported by her friend Baroness Sophie Aldesparre, Lagerlöf took a leave of absence and completed the novel, *Gösta Berlings saga* (*The Story of Gösta Berling*), in 1891. In a romantic style at odds with the realism that prevailed in the works of August Strindberg, Henrik Ibsen, and other naturalist Scandinavian writers of the time, the novel recounts the adventures of its Byronic hero, a renegade priest. Poorly received in Sweden upon its publication, *The Story of Gösta Berling* became immensely popular after the well-known Danish critic Georg Brandes hailed it as a notable revival of the romantic movement.

After the publication of her first novel, Lagerlöf returned to her teaching position but quit after her second book, *Osnliga länkar* (*Invisible Links*), appeared in 1894. That year she met Sophie Elkan, a widow and writer, who became a lifelong companion. With a fellowship granted by King Oscar and financial assistance from the Swedish Academy, Lagerlöf

SELMA LAGERLÖF

was now able to write full-time. Traveling to Italy and Sicily with Elkan, she gathered material for her next novel, *Antikrists mirakler* (*The Miracles of Antichrist,* 1898), a fictional examination of socialism in a Sicilian setting.

A trip to Palestine and Egypt in 1899–1900 occasioned Lagerlöf's third novel, published in two volumes as *Jerusalem: I Dalarne* (1901) and *Jerusalem: In det heliga landet* (1902). The novel was published in English in 1903 as *Jerusalem.* This story of Swedish farm families who emigrate to Palestine was widely praised for its psychological insight into the lives of stolid peasants in quest of a spiritual ideal.

So popular were Lagerlöf's books that she was able to buy back Mårbacka in 1904, the same year she received the Gold Medal of the Swedish Academy. Two years later, her popular children's novel, *Nils Holgerssons underbara resa genom Sverige* (*The Wonderful Adventures of Nils*), was published, followed in 1907 by *Tösen från Stormyrtorpet* (*The Girl From the Marsh Croft*). Both works, which feature stories of folk heroes, combine the dreaminess of fairy stories with the peasant realism of folktales.

Lagerlöf was awarded the 1909 Nobel Prize for Literature "in appreciation of the lofty idealism, vivid imagination, and spiritual perception that characterize her writings." The presentation address was delivered by Claes Annerstedt of the Swedish Academy, who called *The Story of Gösta Berling* "significant not only because it broke decisively with the unhealthy and false realism of the times, but also because of its own original character."

Lagerlöf's work, said Annerstedt, combines "purity and simplicity of diction, beauty of style, and power of imagination" with "ethical strength and deep religious feeling."

In her acceptance speech, Lagerlöf told the audience a story—a whimsical daydream in which she imagines her father appearing to her "on a veranda, with a garden full of sunshine and flowers and birds in front of him." In the conversation that ensues, Lagerlöf expresses the fear that she will be unable to repay the great honor bestowed upon her by the Nobel committee. At length, banging his fist on the arm of his rocking chair, her father declares, " 'I will not rack my brains about problems that no one in heaven or on earth can solve. I am too happy that you have been given the Nobel Prize to worry about anything!' "

After receiving the Nobel Prize, Lagerlöf continued to write about her native land, its myths, and the values represented by the home. She also devoted much of her time to women's causes, addressing an international women's suffrage conference in Stockholm in 1911 and traveling to the United States in 1924 as a delegate to the Women's Congress. In 1914 she was elected to membership in the Swedish Academy. By the 1920s Lagerlöf was firmly established as one of Sweden's leading writers. During this time she published several popular volumes of autobiography and childhood recollections, including *Mårbacka* (1922), and saw some of her novels adapted to film.

As World War II approached, some publications in Nazi Germany praised Lagerlöf as a "Nordic poetess," but when she began helping German artists and intellectuals escape Nazi persecution, the German government denounced her. In the last year of her life, Lagerlöf helped arrange a Swedish visa that saved the German poet NELLY SACHS from Nazi death camps. Deeply distressed by the outbreak of the war—especially by the Soviet invasion of Finland—Lagerlöf donated her gold Nobel Prize medal to a Swedish national fund to benefit Finland. After a long illness, Lagerlöf died of peritonitis at her home at the age of eighty-one.

Immensely popular in Sweden, where she was cherished for her vivid evocations of the Swedish landscape and traditional Swedish culture, Lagerlöf was also admired abroad, although not without reservations. In her preface to a critical study of Lagerlöf, the English writer Victoria Sackville-West wrote that "she is at her happiest and most secure so long as she keeps to myth, saga, and story. . . . Human events, human psychology, in the ordinary sense, are not her strong line." Contrasting Lagerlöf with the Danish writer Isak Dinesen, literary scholar Eric O. Johannesson remarked in *Scandinavian Studies* (1960) that "Lagerlöf's universe is essentially a moral one, in which the conflict is between good and evil, and in which God guides all for the best. For this reason, her stories tend to be didactic in tone." For the Swedish composer Hugo Alfen, "Reading her books is like sitting in the dusk of a Spanish cathedral. You do not know whether what you saw or felt was a dream or reality. You certainly were on holy ground."

ADDITIONAL WORKS IN ENGLISH TRANSLATION: From a Swedish Homestead, 1901; Christ Legends, 1908; Further Adventures of Nils, 1911; Lilliecrona's Home, 1914; Short Stories, 1915; The Emperor of Portugallia, 1916; The Outcast, 1920; Herr Arne's Hoard, 1923; The Treasure, 1925; Charlotte Lowenskold, 1927; The General's Ring, 1928; The Queens of Kungahalla, 1930; The Ring of the Lowenskolds, 1931; Memories of My Childhood, 1934; Harvest, 1935; The Diary of Selma Lagerlöf, 1936.

ABOUT: Berendsohn, W. A. Selma Lagerlöf: Her Life and Work, 1932; Edström, V. B. Selma Lagerlöf, 1984; Gustafson, A. Six Scandinavian Novelists, 1940; Larsen, H. A. Selma Lagerlöf, 1975.

LAMAS, CARLOS SAAVEDRA
See SAAVEDRA LAMAS, CARLOS

LAMB, WILLIS E., JR.
(July 12, 1913–)
Nobel Prize for Physics, 1955
(shared with Polykarp Kusch)

The American physicist Willis Eugene Lamb Jr. was born in Los Angeles, California. His father and namesake was a telephone engineer, and his mother, Marie Helen (Metcalf) Lamb, was a teacher. He attended elementary schools in Oakland and Los Angeles and graduated from Los Angeles High School, where he showed a marked aptitude for chemistry. He received a B.S. in chemistry in 1934 from the University of California at Berkeley, remaining there to earn a Ph.D. in physics under J. Robert Oppenheimer in 1938. His doctoral thesis on the electromagnetic properties of nuclear particles predicted that because the proton has a definite size, its electric field should differ slightly from that of a particle of indefinite size, such as the electron.

Lamb has taught physics throughout his entire career: at Columbia University (1938–1951); Stanford University (1951–1956); Harvard

WILLIS E. LAMB JR.

University (1953–1954); Oxford University (1956–1962); Yale University (1962–1974); and the University of Arizona, where he has been professor of physics and optical sciences since 1974. His attitude toward the responsibilities of a teacher was evident when he was first informed of his Nobel Prize; he went to teach his class in quantum mechanics before going to meet the press.

Concurrently, between 1943 and 1952, Lamb worked at Columbia University's Radiation Laboratory on projects sponsored by the Army Signal Corps, the Office of Naval Research, and the Office of Scientific Research and Development. His research was principally in radar and microwaves.

Working with I. I. RABI and the molecular-beam group at Columbia, Lamb became interested in metastable states of atoms. Ordinarily, an excited, or high-energy, state of an atom quickly decays to a lower-energy state by emitting radiation. Most excited states decay with the emission of a single photon, or quantum of light, in about 10^{-8} second. Metastable states endure much longer. For example, a state of atomic hydrogen called the second excited state has a lifetime about 700 million times longer than those of other excited states. The reason is that the second excited state cannot emit a single photon. In order to conserve angular momentum and the property called parity, it must emit two photons simultaneously. This process is less probable than single-photon emission and hence is slower.

Lamb was originally a theoretical physicist, but his best-known work entailed a series of

589

extremely delicate experiments, most of them carried out in collaboration with Robert C. Retherford at Columbia University. As an outgrowth of his wartime research, Lamb became interested in the absorption and emission of microwave radiation by atoms. When he read of unsuccessful attempts in the 1930s to detect the absorption of microwave radiation in a gas made up of excited hydrogen atoms, he first ascribed the failure to inadequate microwave techniques. He later concluded that the method used to excite the atoms had prevented detection of the absorption. Lamb decided to use the advanced microwave technology that was then newly available to reevaluate the spectroscopic measurements of the various energy levels of the hydrogen atom.

In the hydrogen atom, a single electron moves around the nucleus in one of a series of orbits; in each orbit the electron has a definite energy. For the electron to rise from a lower to a higher orbit, the atom must absorb a photon whose energy exactly corresponds to the energy difference between the orbits. Likewise, when the electron falls from a higher to a lower orbit, the atom emits a photon of the appropriate energy. Such transitions give atomic hydrogen a spectrum of distinct, sharply defined lines.

Many of the lines in the hydrogen spectrum exhibit a "fine structure": when examined at high resolution, they are seen to consist of two or more very closely spaced lines, indicating that the orbital energy levels are similarly split into finely divided sublevels. Transitions between adjacent fine-structure levels require the absorption or emission of radiation at microwave wavelengths.

In an equation published in 1928, the English physicist P. A. M. DIRAC described all the known properties of the electron: its wave properties, electric charge, spin, magnetic moment, and the relativistic variation of mass with velocity. As a foundation of much of quantum mechanics, the Dirac equation predicted with great precision the energy levels of the hydrogen atom. In particular, it predicted that two specific levels, one of them metastable, are equivalent: that they are distinct states which nevertheless have exactly the same energy. Lamb prepared a beam of hydrogen atoms in the metastable state; the atoms remained in this state long enough for convenient experimentation. He then exposed the beam to microwave radiation in the presence of a magnetic field. Some of the atoms absorbed the radiation, making a transition to the shorter-lived state. This result showed that the two energy levels are not identical but are separated by a small amount of energy now called the Lamb shift. The discovery of the Lamb shift inspired JULIAN S. SCHWINGER, SIN-ITIRO TOMONAGA, and RICHARD P. FEYNMAN to reexamine Dirac's theory of the electron and formulate a new theory called quantum electrodynamics, which predicts the Lamb shift with remarkable precision. Lamb himself, in collaboration with Norman M. Kroll, made a theoretical calculation of the effect he had discovered experimentally.

Lamb received the 1955 Nobel Prize for Physics "for his discoveries concerning the fine structure of the hydrogen spectrum." He shared the prize with POLYKARP KUSCH who carried out related, but independent, experiments, also at Columbia. Addressing the two scientists in his presentation speech, Ivar Waller of the Royal Swedish Academy of Sciences said, "Your discoveries led to a reevaluation and a reshaping of the theory of the interaction of electrons and electromagnetic radiation [quantum electrodynamics], thus initiating a development of utmost importance to many of the basic concepts of physics."

Lamb's many years of research have involved such diverse topics as theories of beta decay, range of fission fragments, fluctuations in cosmic-ray showers, ejection of electrons by metastable atoms, field theories of nuclear structure, theories of the interactions of neutrons and matter, theory and design of magnetron oscillators, and diamagnetic corrections for nuclear resonance experiments. He has also contributed to the theory of lasers.

Since 1939 Lamb has been married to Ursula Schaefe, an historian. His leisure interests include swimming, sailing, playing chess, and photography.

Lamb is a member of the National Academy of Sciences and the American Physical Society and an honorary fellow of the Institute of Physics in London and the Royal Society of Edinburgh. His awards include the Rumford Medal of the American Academy of Arts and Sciences (1953) and the Science Award of the Research Corporation of America (1955). He holds honorary degrees from the University of Pennsylvania, Yeshiva University, and Gustavus Adolphus College.

SELECTED WORKS: Lectures on Masers, 1960; Laser Physics, 1974, with others.

ABOUT: Current Biography March 1956; National Cyclopedia of American Biography, supplement J, 1964.

LANDAU, LEV
(January 22, 1908–April 1, 1968)
Nobel Prize for Physics, 1962

LEV LANDAU

The Russian physicist Lev Davidovich Landau was born of Jewish parents, David and Lubov Landau, in the city of Baku, now the capital of the Azerbaijan Soviet Socialist Republic. His father was a well-known petroleum engineer in the local oil fields, and his mother was a physician and research worker in physiology. Landau's older sister became a chemical engineer. Although he did exceptionally well in high school, graduating by the age of thirteen, his parents thought he was too young for college and sent him to the Baku Economic-Technical School for a year. In 1922 he entered Baku University, where he studied physics and chemistry; two years later he transferred to the physics department at the University of Leningrad. By the age of nineteen Landau had published four scientific papers, which included the first use of the density matrix for a mathematical expression of quantum energy states, now widely applied in quantum mechanics. After completing college in 1927, he began graduate study at the Leningrad Physical-Technical Institute, working on the magnetic theory of the electron and on quantum electrodynamics.

From 1929 until 1931 Landau studied in Germany, Switzerland, England, the Netherlands, and Denmark, meeting some of the pioneers of the new science of quantum mechanics, including WERNER HEISENBERG, WOLFGANG PAULI, and NIELS BOHR. He formed a lifelong friendship with Bohr, acknowledging him as one of the foremost influences on his life. While abroad, Landau did important investigations on the magnetic properties of free electrons and, with Ronald F. Peierls, on relativistic quantum mechanics, which established him as a leading theoretical physicist. He also learned how to manipulate complex theoretical systems that were useful in his later work in low-temperature physics.

Landau returned to Leningrad in 1931 but was soon called to Kharkov, then the capital of the Ukrainian Soviet Socialist Republic, as director of theoretical physics at the Ukrainian Physical-Technical Institute. He also occupied the chair of theoretical physics at both the Kharkov Mechanical Engineering Institute and Kharkov University. The Soviet Academy of Sciences awarded him a doctorate in physical and mathematical sciences in 1934, without a dissertation, and the following year he received the title of professor. At Kharkov, Landau earned a reputation as an extremely versatile theorist with publications on such diverse topics as the origin of the energy of the stars, sound dispersion, energy transfers in collisions, light scattering, magnetic properties of materials, superconductivity, structural transitions of substances from one form to another, and the motions of streams of electrically charged particles. His work on electrically interacting particles was useful in later investigations involving plasmas, hot electrically charged gases (ions). With concepts borrowed from thermodynamics, he developed many novel ideas about low-temperature systems. A unifying characteristic of Landau's work was his ingenious application of mathematical techniques to solve complex problems. He made important contributions to quantum field theory and to studies of the nature and interactions of elementary particles.

The breadth of his research, touching on almost every area of theoretical physics, attracted many outstanding students to Kharkov, including Evgeny M. Lifshitz, who became not only a professional colleague but also a personal friend. The school that grew up around Landau established Kharkov as the leading Soviet center of theoretical physics. Convinced that a firm grounding in all areas of physics was a necessary basis for theoretical research, Landau developed a rigorous program of study he called the "theoretical minimum." The examinations for acceptance into his group were so difficult that in thirty years, despite a steady stream of applicants, only about forty students passed them. To these students, however, Landau gave generously of his time, allowing them much freedom in their choice of subjects. He maintained friendly, informal relations with them and with his close associates, all of whom affectionately called him Dau. To help his students, Landau created a comprehensive course in theoretical physics in 1935, which he and Lifshitz published in a series of textbooks that they revised and updated over the next twenty years. The books, which have been translated into nearly a dozen languages, are considered classics throughout the world and earned the authors the Soviet government's Lenin Prize in 1962.

In 1937 Landau was invited by PYOTR KAPITZA to direct the theoretical physics section of the newly created Institute for Physical Problems in Moscow. The next year, during Joseph Stalin's Great Purge, Landau was arrested on false charges of being a German spy. He was released only through Kapitza's direct intervention with the Kremlin.

When Landau arrived in Moscow, Kapitza's experiments on liquid helium were already underway. Helium gas becomes liquid when cooled below 4.2°K (degrees kelvin above absolute zero, or −273.18°C). It is then called helium 1. If cooled below 2.17°K, it becomes a liquid called helium 2 and exhibits strange properties. Helium 2 flows through the narrowest openings as if it had no viscosity, climbs the walls of its container in apparent defiance of gravity, and conducts heat hundreds of times better than copper. Kapitza gave it the name *superfluid*. Yet, when tested by standard methods, such as to make a determination of its drag on the motion of a disk rotating back and forth at a measured frequency, it displays a finite viscosity. Scientists suspected that the odd behavior was due to effects in the realm of quantum theory rather than classical physics, which became evident only at very low temperatures and usually in solids, since almost all substances are frozen under such conditions. Helium is special because it remains liquid down to absolute zero unless subjected to very high pressure. Laszlo Tisza proposed, in 1938, that liquid helium was, in fact, a mixture of the two forms, helium 1 (which accounted for normal behavior) and helium 2 (which was superfluid). As the temperature fell near absolute zero, helium 2 became more dominant. This helped account for the different viscosities observed under different conditions of measurement.

Landau explained superfluidity with a novel mathematical treatment. Whereas others usually applied quantum mechanics to the behav-

ior of individual atoms, he treated the quantum states of the bulk liquid almost as if it were a solid. He proposed the existence of two components of motion, or excitation: "phonons," representing the relatively normal straight-line propagation of sound waves at low values of momentum or energy, and "rotons," representing rotational motion, a more complex manifestation of higher momenta and energy values. Observed phenomena were caused by phonon and roton contributions and their interaction. The result was regarded as a "normal" component embedded in a superfluid background. In a narrow-slit experiment, the superfluid flowed through while phonons and rotons collided with the walls and were held back. In a rotating disk experiment, the superfluid had negligible effect while the phonons and rotons collided with the disk and retarded its movement. The ratio of the two components varied with temperature, rotons predominating above 1°K and phonons below 0.6°K.

Landau's theory, with later refinements, not only accounted for observed behavior but also predicted other unforeseen phenomena such as the propagation of two different waves, called first and second sound, with different properties. The first turned out to be conventional sound waves. The second proved to be a temperature wave. In addition, Landau's theory provided valuable insights into the nature of superconductivity.

During World War II, Landau studied combustion and explosions, particularly shock waves at a large distance from their origin. From the end of the war until 1962, he investigated many subjects, notably a rare isotope of helium having an atomic weight of 3 instead of the common value of 4, for which he predicted a new type of wave propagation called "zero sound," in which the velocity of the second sound in a mixture of the two isotopes tends toward zero at absolute zero temperature. He also contributed to the development of the Soviet atomic bomb.

Shortly before his fifty-fourth birthday, Landau was critically injured in an automobile accident. Physicians from Canada, France, Czechoslovakia, and the Soviet Union managed to save his life, although he was unconscious for six weeks and unable to recognize his family for nearly three months. His condition prevented him from traveling to Oslo to accept the 1962 Nobel Prize for Physics, which had been awarded to him "for his pioneering theories for condensed matter, especially liquid helium." The prize was presented to him in Moscow by the Swedish ambassador to the Soviet Union. Landau lived another six years, unable to resume his work; he died in Moscow from complications arising from his injuries.

In 1937 Landau married Konkordia Drobanzeva, a food technologist from Kharkov. They had one son, who is an experimental physicist at the Institute for Physical Problems where his father did so much of his life's work. Landau's dislike of pretense and his sharp, often witty, criticisms sometimes gave the impression of a cold and even hostile individual, but Kapitza, who knew him well, described him as "a very kind and responsive man, always ready to help people who had been unjustly wronged." After Landau's death, Evgeny Lifshitz remarked that Landau "always aimed to simplify complicated matters and to show as clearly as possible the fundamental simplicity inherent in the basic phenomena of natural laws. He took a certain pride in what he termed 'trivializing' matters."

In addition to the Nobel and Lenin prizes, Landau received three State Prizes and was named a Hero of Socialist Labor by the Soviet government. He was elected to the Soviet Academy of Sciences in 1946 and held membership in the Danish, Dutch, and American academies of science, as well as in the American Academy of Arts and Sciences, the French Physical Society, the Physical Society of London, and the Royal Society of London.

SELECTED WORKS: Statistical Physics, 1938, with others; The Classical Theory of Fields, 1951, with others; Course on Theoretical Physics (9 vols.) 1958–1960, with E. M. Lifshitz; What Is Relativity? 1961, with G. B. Rumer; Collected Papers, 1965; General Physics, 1967, with others; A Shorter Course on Theoretical Physics (2 vols.) 1972–1975; Physics for Everyone: Molecules, 1978, with A. I. Kitaigorodsky.

ABOUT: Biographical Memoirs of Fellows of the Royal Society, volume 15, 1969; Current Biography July 1963; Dictionary of Scientific Biography, volume 7, 1973; Dorozynski, A. The Man They Wouldn't Let Die, 1965; Haar, D. T. (ed.) Men of Physics: L. D. Landau (2 vols.) 1965–1969; Livanova, A. L. Landau: A Great Physicist and Teacher, 1978.

LANDSTEINER, KARL

(June 14, 1868–June 26, 1943)
Nobel Prize for Physiology or Medicine, 1930

The Austrian-American bacteriologist and immunologist Karl Landsteiner was born in Vienna to Leopold Landsteiner, a newspaper publisher and journalist, and the former Fanny Hess. Landsteiner's father died when the boy was six years old, leaving him to be raised by his mother.

After attending a gymnasium, Landsteiner entered the University of Vienna medical school in 1885 and received his medical degree in 1891. By that time he had developed an interest in chemistry, which he studied for another five years in Würzburg, Munich, and Zurich. He returned to Vienna in 1896 to work in the Department of Hygiene at the University of Vienna, where he became interested in immunology.

Immunology was just beginning to take form as a discipline when Landsteiner entered the field. In 1890 EMIL VON BEHRING had discovered that immunity to disease that is conferred by vaccines or by a previous exposure occurs because the body is stimulated to produce antibodies that bind themselves to invading organisms or the toxins produced by them, thus inactivating the organisms. Six years later JULES BORDET demonstrated that injecting an animal with blood from a different species usually resulted in the clumping and breaking up of the blood. Bordet realized that this change in blood structure was caused by antibodies produced by the receiving animal to attack proteins or antigens in the blood of the donor animal.

In his first studies of antibody action, conducted in 1896, Landsteiner learned that laboratory cultures of bacteria can be clumped by the addition of immune blood serum. Since he wished to concentrate on immunological research, Landsteiner transferred to the Department of Pathological Anatomy at the University of Vienna in 1898. There he worked under Anton Weichselbaum, who had discovered the bacteria that cause meningitis and pneumonia. While serving as Weichselbaum's assistant, Landsteiner conducted 3,639 postmortem examinations, which provided him with a comprehensive view of medicine and pathology, as well as considerable experience as a pathological anatomist. Although the purpose of Weichselbaum's department was the study of the anatomy of disease, he permitted Landsteiner to pursue studies in physiology and immunology.

To an article published in 1900 Landsteiner appended a note containing one of his most important discoveries: the fact that the interagglutination (agglutination occurs when cells in a fluid clump together) that takes place between serum (the waterlike liquid that is sep-

KARL LANDSTEINER

arated from the clot and corpuscles during the clotting of blood) and blood cells of different human beings is a physiological phenomenon.

A year later he described a simple method of dividing human blood into three groups: A, B, and C (later changed to O). A fourth group, AB, was added later. The blood grouping was accomplished by mixing suspensions of red blood cells with the test serums known as anti-A and anti-B. Landsteiner found that group O was not agglutinated by either of the serums; group AB was agglutinated by both serums; group A was agglutinated by anti-A serum but not by anti-B serum; and B group was agglutinated by anti-B serum but not by anti-A serum. The serum of group O contains anti-A and anti-B antibodies. That of group A has only anti-B, group B has only anti-A, while group AB has neither. Thus, according to Landsteiner's formula, blood serum contains only those antibodies (isoagglutinins) that do not act against their own blood group.

Although several years passed before Landsteiner's blood-grouping technique was put to practical use, it made possible the safe transfusion of blood from one human being to another based on blood groups. In 1914, when Richard Lewisohn discovered the anticoagulant properties of sodium citrate and learned that adding it to blood prevented the blood from coagulating, a method of preserving blood was found; human blood could now be stored as long as three weeks under refrigeration. These were significant achievements, for operations on the heart, lungs, and circulatory system—previously impracticable because of the great loss of blood—were now feasible, as was the performance of complete blood changes in cases of intoxication and severe jaundice in newborn babies.

The possibility that there were other differences in human blood attracted Landsteiner's attention, and he postulated that the individual characteristics of blood were reflected in antigen differences. He reasoned that these differences could be used to distinguish one human being from another, in much the same way that fingerprints differentiate one person from another.

When he conceived the idea of serological identification, Landsteiner was not aware that blood types were inheritable, because Gregor Mendel's laws of heredity had been ignored since their publication in 1866. After Mendel's work was rediscovered in 1900, more attention was paid to inheritance, and in 1910 Emil von Dungern and a co-worker postulated the first hypothesis for the inheritance of blood groups. When this theory was amended in 1924 by the mathematician B. A. Bernstein, the concept of the inheritance of blood groups was firmly established. Serological genetics is still used to settle cases of disputed paternity.

During the time he was experimenting with serological identification, Landsteiner also worked on the characterization and evaluation of the physiological meaning of cold agglutinations in human blood serum. He and Julius Donath described a test for the diagnosis of paroxysmal cold hemoglobinuria. In this disease, after the victim has been exposed to cold, hemoglobin appears in the urine because some of the red blood cells have been destroyed. PAUL EHRLICH believed that this phenomenon was caused by a pathological change in the endothelium of the blood vessels. However, Landsteiner postulated that the disease was caused by an antibody that, when exposed to cold, combines with the red cells and, eventually, under warm conditions, causes their breakdown in the body. He demonstrated this process in a test tube in what has become known as the Donath-Landsteiner test.

Between 1908 and 1919, when he was prosector (chief dissector) at the Royal-Imperial Wilhelmina Hospital in Vienna, Landsteiner concentrated on poliomyelitis. After conducting a postmortem examination of a child who had died from the disease, he injected a mixture of the child's brain and spinal cord into the abdominal cavity of rhesus monkeys. On the sixth day following the injections, the monkeys developed symptoms of paralysis similar to those in poliomyelitis patients. The appearance of central nervous system tissue taken from the monkeys was also similar to that of human beings who had died from the disease. Since he was unable to demonstrate the presence of bacteria in the spinal cord of the deceased child, Landsteiner postulated a virus as the cause of poliomyelitis. "The supposition is hence near," he said, "that a so-called invisible virus, or a virus belonging to the class of protozoa, causes the disease."

In 1923 Landsteiner was invited to join the staff of the Rockefeller Institute for Medical Research (now Rockefeller University). Accepting the offer, he moved to the United States, and in 1929 he became an American citizen.

The 1930 Nobel Prize for Physiology or Medicine was awarded to Landsteiner "for his discovery of human blood groups." Referring to his blood groups, in his Nobel lecture Landsteiner said, "the surprising thing was that agglutination, when it occurred at all, was just as pronounced as the already familiar reactions that take place during the interaction between serum and cells of different animal species." Landsteiner's discovery of blood groups opened new routes of research in several branches of science and made possible many important advances in practical medicine.

In 1940 Landsteiner and his associates Alexander Wiener and Philip Levine described a new factor in human blood: the rhesus, or Rh, factor. This factor was linked to jaundice in newborn infants. A mother lacking the Rh factor (who thus is Rh negative) can be stimulated by an Rh-positive fetus to form antibodies against the Rh factor. The red cells of the fetus are then destroyed by the antibodies, and the decomposition of the hemoglobin forms bilirubin, which causes jaundice.

In 1916 Landsteiner married Helene Wlatso; they had a son. After suffering a heart attack while working in his laboratory, Landsteiner died in New York City on June 26, 1943.

Among Landsteiner's awards and honors were the Hans Aronson Foundation Prize of Berlin (1926), the Dutch Red Cross Society Gold Medal (1933), and the Cameron Prize and Lectureship of the University of Edinburgh (1938); he was also made a chevalier of the Legion of Honor of France. He was elected to membership in the National Academy of Sciences, the American Philosophical Society, the American Society of Naturalists, the American Association of Immunologists, the French Academy of Sciences, the New York Academy of Medicine, the Pathological Society of Philadelphia, the Pathological Society

of Great Britain and Ireland, the Royal Society of London, the Royal Society of Medicine in London, the Royal Danish Academy of Sciences, the Royal Swedish Academy of Sciences and Letters, and the Swedish Society of Medicine.

SELECTED WORKS: The Specificity of Serological Reactions, 1936.

ABOUT: Biographical Memoirs of the National Academy of Sciences, volume 40, 1969; Dictionary of Scientific Biography, volume 7, 1973; Mazumdar, P. Karl Landsteiner and the Problem of Species, 1976; Obituary Notices of Fellows of the Royal Society, volume 5, 1947; Simms, G. R. The Scientific Work of Karl Landsteiner, 1963; Speiser, P., and Smekal, F. Karl Landsteiner, 1975.

LANGE, CHRISTIAN
(September 17, 1869–December 11, 1938)
Nobel Prize for Peace, 1921
(shared with Karl Branting)

Christian Lous Lange (läng' ə), Norwegian internationalist, was born in the seaport city of Stavanger in southwestern Norway. His grandfather was a distinguished historian and archivist; his father, Colonel Halvard Lange, was an engineer in the Norwegian army, married to the former Thora Marie Lous. An excellent student, Lange majored in history and languages at the University of Oslo. After completing his thesis, "The History of Internationalism," he received the Norwegian equivalent of an M.A. in 1893. The following year he married Bertha Manthey, the daughter of a judge.

After receiving his degree, Lange taught in the secondary schools of Oslo for seven years, increasing his proficiency in languages by traveling during the summer months. He also wrote a survey of world history that later was widely used as a school text. While teaching, he became involved in the movement to secure Norway's independence from Sweden.

When the Interparliamentary Union held its conference in Oslo in 1899, Lange was invited to serve as secretary to the Committee on Arrangements. Founded in 1888 by WILLIAM CREMER and FRÉDÉRIC PASSY, the union advocated arbitration as a means of resolving international disputes. Displaying considerable tact and organizational skill during the Oslo conference, Lange was appointed secretary to the newly founded Norwegian Nobel Committee the following year, a position that in-

CHRISTIAN LANGE

volved him in administration of the Nobel Peace Prize.

Lange continued to serve as an adviser to the Nobel committee after he resigned in 1909 to become secretary-general of the Interparliamentary Union at the organization's headquarters in Brussels. Responsible for coordinating and administering the union's activities, he served as liaison among its branches, frequently visiting representatives of the fourteen member nations, and he drew up the agenda for annual meetings. During this period he also lectured, raised funds, wrote reports, and edited several of the union's publications.

The outbreak of World War I threw the union into disarray. When German troops invaded Brussels in 1914, the organization's funds were impounded. Lange moved its headquarters to neutral Norway to avoid destruction of its records and administered the union almost single-handedly while supporting himself by teaching at the Nobel Institute. In response to a plea from Lange, the Carnegie Endowment for International Peace (whose officials included NICHOLAS MURRAY BUTLER) lent the union enough money to survive.

During the war Lange also served as a delegate to the Stockholm Conference of Neutrals, which worked to end the war, and he participated in the Central Organization for a Lasting Peace, a Dutch group that sought to promote world peace. As a special correspondent to the Carnegie Endowment, he wrote a report on conditions in the warring nations.

After the war Lange set about rebuilding the union, a task complicated by a shortage of funds and by the desire of some member nations to exclude their recent enemies. Nevertheless, Lange managed to convene the organization's first postwar conference in Geneva in 1921.

That year, he received the 1921 Nobel Prize for Peace, which he shared with KARL BRANTING. The title of Lange's Nobel lecture was "Internationalism," a term he preferred to *pacifism.* "Today," he said, "we stand on a bridge leading from the territorial state to the world community." Because "we live under the auspices of worldwide communications and worldwide markets," he continued, "international war . . . is suicide." An advocate of a world federation, he hailed the recent formation of the League of Nations as "the first serious and conscious attempt to approach that goal."

Lange was active in the League of Nations from its inception, serving as a delegate from Norway on many occasions and sitting on several committees. Convinced that war could not be made more humane, he devoted most of his efforts in the league to disarmament. He headed one committee on political questions and another that kept the league informed about the developing conflict between China and Japan. Meanwhile, he continued his work for the Interparliamentary Union, writing and publishing articles, books, and pamphlets on arms control and arbitration. He made some 500 lecture appearances before and after World War I. In 1925 he toured the United States, where he spoke before thirty university and professional groups. In 1938 he delivered the Merttens Peace lecture at Friends House, London, which was later published as *Imperialism and Peace.*

At the age of sixty-five, Lange resigned as secretary-general of the Interparliamentary Union. The following year, he was elected to membership on the Norwegian Nobel Committee. Lange died at his home in Oslo on December 11, 1938. His son, Halvard Lange, continued his work, serving as Norwegian foreign minister between 1946 and 1965.

"Lange's devotion to the cause of peace remained unwavering and unalloyed," wrote the historian Oscar J. Falnes. "It was sustained through . . . the euphoria of prewar days, the anguish of World War years, and the guarded optimism of the League of Nations days. The service he gave the cause was a full-time one, in the richest sense of the word."

ADDITIONAL WORKS IN ENGLISH TRANSLA-

TION: "The Future of the Norwegian Nobel Institute," The Independent May 9, 1907; The Conditions of a Lasting Peace, 1917; Russia, the Revolution, and the War, 1917.

ABOUT: American-Scandinavian Review September 1969; Derry, T. K. A History of Modern Norway, 1973; Falnes, O. J. Norway and the Nobel Peace Prize, 1938; Jones, S. S. The Scandinavian States and the League of Nations, 1939; New York Times December 12, 1938.

LANGMUIR, IRVING
(January 31, 1881–August 16, 1957)
Nobel Prize for Chemistry, 1932

IRVING LANGMUIR

The American chemist Irving Langmuir was born in Brooklyn, New York, the third of four sons of Charles Langmuir and the former Sadie Comings. His father was an insurance executive of Scottish descent, and his mother traced her ancestry back to the *Mayflower*. After attending schools in Paris, New York, and Philadelphia, he graduated from Pratt Institute in Brooklyn in 1899.

Entering Columbia University, Langmuir enrolled in the School of Mines because, he explained later, "the course was strong in chemistry. It had more physics than the chemical course, and more mathematics than the course in physics—and I wanted all three." In 1903 he received a metallurgical engineering degree and then went to Germany for graduate study at the University of Göttingen under the physical chemist WALTHER NERNST. At Göttingen Langmuir's research focused on the dissociation of various gases in contact with a glowing platinum wire, a topic closely related to his future industrial research in electric lighting. He was awarded a Ph.D. from Göttingen in 1906.

Having been trained in both chemistry and mathematical physics, Langmuir now faced a choice. Should he begin his career in the high-paying field of commercial chemistry, as his elder brother Arthur had done, or should he devote his life to basic research? Choosing the latter, he returned to America and for three years served as an instructor in chemistry at the Stevens Institute of Technology in Hoboken, New Jersey.

Because Langmuir found little time to pursue his own research, he resigned from Stevens in the summer of 1909 and went to work at the research laboratory of the General Electric Company in Schenectady, New York. The General Electric laboratory, then under the direction of Willis R. Whitney, represented a new concept of industrial research. The electrical industry had initially capitalized on knowledge gathered by academic scientists in the nineteenth century. Then, in the first decade of the twentieth century, General Electric executives decided that the company itself should contribute to the advancement of scientific knowledge. Whitney, who had been recruited from the faculty of the Massachusetts Institute of Technology, encouraged Langmuir to develop his own research program. "When I joined the laboratory," Langmuir said later, "I found that there was more academic freedom than I had ever encountered in any university." This freedom and the laboratory's superb research facilities provided Langmuir with challenging and important problems for the rest of his professional life.

His first major contributions to science were based on his doctoral research into the characteristics of filaments burned in various gases. Three years after joining General Electric, Langmuir challenged the notion, common among lamp engineers, that a perfect vacuum would make a perfect lamp. He showed instead that a light bulb filled with nitrogen was stronger and brighter than any yet made. The simplicity and efficiency of the new bulb saved vast amounts of energy (which in turn saved consumers approximately $1 million a day in electric bills) and yielded large profits for General Electric.

Langmuir's interest in vacuum phenomena led to his invention of the mercury pump in 1916. One hundred times more powerful than any previous pump, it enabled him to create the low pressures needed to manufacture the vacuum tubes used in radio. Around this time

Langmuir tested a strip of tungsten coated with thoria (an oxide of thorium) for its electron-emitting powers; he discovered that the filament behaved best if coated with a layer of thoria only one molecule thick. This finding led him to investigate surface phenomena, the molecular activity occurring in a thin film, or surface. In this virtually two-dimensional world he studied absorption and the surface tension and behavior of thin films on liquids and solids. Absorption, the power of certain materials to retain other molecules on their surfaces, had been investigated in the nineteenth century by the Scottish chemist James Dewar and by the American physicist Josiah Willard Gibbs, but a comprehensive and successful theory had not yet been proposed. Using insights gained from atomic theory, Langmuir described the chemical behavior of surfaces in terms of individual atoms and molecules assuming definite positions as if they were pieces on a chessboard. He also recognized that six forces take part in absorption phenomena: Coulomb forces, forces between dipoles, valence forces, attractive van der Waals forces (named for JOHANNES VAN DER WAALS), repulsive forces caused by the impenetrability of completed electron shells, and electron pressures that counterbalance Coulomb attraction. During World War I, when his research on surface chemistry was interrupted, Langmuir worked on submarine-detecting devices for the United States Navy.

After the war Langmuir became interested in atomic structure. His contributions to atomic theory stem from his fascination with the boundary between chemistry and physics. Using the model of the atom proposed by NIELS BOHR and the chemical theories of Gilbert N. Lewis, Langmuir advanced a theory describing chemical valence (the measurement of the differential tendency of atoms to combine) as the effect of electrons filling up electron "shells," or orbits, surrounding the atomic nuclei.

In 1923 Langmuir began a nine-year investigation of the properties of electronic discharges in gases. He coined the term *plasma* for the ionized gas he observed when he used extremely powerful alternating currents during these experiments. He also developed the concept of electron temperature as well as a method of measuring both electron temperature and ion density with a special electrode, now called the Langmuir probe. The field of controlled thermonuclear fusion depends on the basic theories of plasma first reported by Langmuir.

Langmuir received the 1932 Nobel Prize for Chemistry "for his outstanding discoveries and investigations within the field of surface chemistry." His contributions to the chemistry of surface processes were of great importance in many technical fields: in biology, for the study of complex viruses; in chemistry, for the study of giant molecules; and in optics, for the study of the transmission of light. The same year that he received the Nobel Prize, Langmuir was named associate director of the General Electric laboratory.

From 1938 into his retirement years Langmuir devoted himself to studying the natural world, especially the atmosphere. He studied such phenomena as windrows, which are regular patterns of seaweed on the windblown surface of the sea, and cloud nucleation, which is the formation of liquid particles of various sizes in the air. During World War II he helped produce a smoke-making machine that was used to screen troops and ships from enemy observation. He also studied methods for preventing the formation of ice on airplanes. After the war Langmuir continued his interest in meteorology and became an advocate of weather control through seeding clouds with dry ice (solid carbon dioxide) and silver iodide.

In 1912 Langmuir married Marion Mersereau, with whom he shared interests in mountain climbing, sailing, aviation, and classical music. They adopted a son and a daughter. Much in demand as a lecturer and popularizer of science, Langmuir enjoyed sharing his views on the philosophy of science and on the interrelationship of science and society. One of his favorite themes was "the freedom that characterizes democracy is necessary for making discoveries." He died on August 16, 1957, at Woods Hole, Massachusetts.

In addition to the Nobel Prize, Langmuir received many other honors, including the Hughes Medal of the Royal Society of London (1918), the Rumford Medal of the American Academy of Arts and Sciences (1920), the Nichols Medal (1920) and Willard Gibbs Medal (1930) of the American Chemical Society, the Franklin Medal of the Franklin Institute (1934), and the Faraday Medal of the Institution of Electrical Engineers in London (1944). He was elected to the National Academy of Sciences and the Royal Society of London and served as president of the American Chemical Society (1929) and the American Association for the Advancement of Science (1941). He was the recipient of fifteen honorary degrees. Mount Langmuir in Alaska is named for him, as is a residential college at the State University of New York at Stony Brook.

SELECTED WORKS: Molecular Films, the Cyclotron and the New Biology, 1942; Surface Phenomena, 1946; Phenomena, Atoms and Molecules, 1950; The Collected Works of Irving Langmuir (12 vols.) 1960–1962.

ABOUT: Biographical Memoirs of Fellows of the Royal Society, volume 4, 1958; Biographical Memoirs of the National Academy of Sciences, volume 45, 1974; Dictionary of Scientific Biography, volume 8, 1973; Farber, E. (ed.) Great Chemists, 1961; Jaffe, B. Crucibles: The Story of Chemistry, 1930; Rosenfeld, A. The Quintessence of Irving Langmuir, 1966; Westervelt, V. The Incredible Man of Science, 1968.

LAUE, MAX VON
(October 9, 1879–April 24, 1960)
Nobel Prize for Physics, 1914

MAX VON LAUE

The German physicist Max Theodor Felix von Laue (lou′ ə) was born in Pfaffendorf to Julius Laue, a civil official of the military court system, and the former Minna Zerrenner. The family name became von Laue in 1913 when Laue's father was raised to hereditary nobility. Because his father moved frequently, Max received his education in many different schools, principally at the Protestant Gymnasium in Strasbourg. At about the age of twelve, he developed an intense interest in physics, and his mother arranged many visits for him to the Urania, a popular science society in Berlin that exhibited working models of scientific apparatus with explanatory demonstrations.

After Laue graduated from the gymnasium in 1898, he was able to attend classes in physics, chemistry, and mathematics at the University of Strasbourg while simultaneously serving a year of compulsory military service. At Strasbourg his interest in physics was stimulated by the lectures of FERDINAND BRAUN. In rapid succession, Laue studied at the universities of Göttingen, Munich, and Berlin. With MAX PLANCK as his mentor, he received a Ph.D. magna cum laude in physics from Berlin in 1903, writing his dissertation on the theory of interference in plane parallel plates. Interference is the interaction between intersecting light waves, which tend to destroy or reinforce each other depending on their relative phases (points in the cycles of fluctuating electric and magnetic fields). This work reflected Laue's early attraction to the field of optics.

After two years as a postdoctoral student at the University of Göttingen, Laue passed the examination that qualified him to teach in secondary school. From 1905 to 1909 he was Planck's assistant at the Institute for Theoretical Physics in Berlin. There his research dealt with the application of the concept of entropy to radiation fields and with the thermodynamic significance of the coherence of light waves. Entropy, in thermodynamics, is a physical property related to energy changes and the degree of equilibrium of a system. Coherence between light waves is the existence of a fixed and persisting relationship between their phases; that is, the degree to which their fluctuating electromagnetic fields are in or out of step does not change. In the course of their collaboration, Laue and Planck developed a lifelong friendship. After serving as a privatdocent (unsalaried lecturer) at the University of Berlin from 1906 to 1909, Laue joined the physics faculty at the University of Munich under Arnold Sommerfeld. At Munich he lectured on optics and thermodynamics and, in 1911, published the first comprehensive monograph on ALBERT EINSTEIN's still controversial theory of relativity.

The following year Laue was named to the chair of theoretical physics at the University of Zurich, where he remained for two years before moving to the University of Frankfurt. During World War I, he spent much of his time at the University of Würzburg under WILHELM WIEN, doing research on vacuum tubes used in telephone and wireless communications. In 1917 he accepted the position of deputy director of the new Kaiser Wilhelm Institute for Physics in Berlin, of which Einstein was director. Continuing his largely administrative duties at the institute, Laue accepted an appointment as a professor of physics at the University of Berlin in 1919, where he remained until 1943.

Shortly before moving to Zurich, Laue took up a problem that had remained unresolved ever since WILHELM RÖNTGEN's discovery of X rays in 1895: whether or not X rays were a form of electromagnetic radiation with a very short wavelength. At the time, Laue was writing the chapter on wave optics for the multivolume *Enzyklopädie der mathematischen Wissenschaften* (Encyclopedia of Mathematical Sciences). This project required him to express mathematically the action of a diffraction grating on light waves. A diffraction grating is a set of closely spaced, equidistant grooves on a glass plate or mirror, which breaks up incident light into a large number of individual new sources. The secondary light waves start out from the grating in phase; when rays from different parts of the many sources arrive at a point on a screen, they have traveled different distances. Since a given phase recurs with each wavelength of progress along the light path (like the distance from crest to crest of an ocean wave), various rays converge at a point in various phases, depending on the number and fractions of wavelengths in the paths they have traveled. The result is a pattern of light and dark bands representing points where the waves arrive in phase and reinforce each other or arrive in opposite phases and cancel each other. Laue was extending the mathematics to cover two-dimensional gratings containing two sets of grooves.

At that time, a colleague requested Laue's help on a mathematical investigation of the behavior of light waves in a crystal presumed to consist of a three-dimensional array (lattice) of atoms in a regular, repetitive pattern. Laue was not then able to help him, but during their conversation he was struck by the question of how such waves would behave if their wavelengths were very short (much shorter than those of visible light) compared with the spacings between atoms in the crystal lattice. Existing knowledge suggested that the lattice spacings in crystals were about ten times as large as the suspected wavelengths of X rays. Laue immediately expressed his intuitive feeling that, if X rays were indeed electromagnetic waves like light, the crystal would act like a three-dimensional grating. X rays scattered by individual atoms would emerge from the crystal in many directions and create a diffraction pattern consisting of points of reinforcement, where rays converged in phase, and areas of destructive interference, where rays converged more or less out of phase.

Laue suggested an experiment to explore his idea and had to overcome theoretical objections before personnel and equipment were made available. At Munich in April 1912, Walter Friedrich, an assistant to Sommerfeld, and Paul Knipping, a graduate student, irradiated a copper sulfate crystal with a pencillike beam of X rays and recorded the results on a photographic plate. Their first success showed a pattern of dark points on the developed plate (dark on the negative image indicating intense exposure), now known as a Laue diagram. Among other confirmations that true electromagnetic wave interference had taken place was the fact that even when the incident X rays contained a mixture of different wavelengths, the rays passing through the dark points all had the same wavelength. Phase relationships between rays of different wavelengths are too complex to produce clear diffraction patterns, whereas rays of a given wavelength in a mixture can selectively produce such a pattern discernible from the background. Buoyed by verification of his intuitive expectation, Laue worked out the mathematics, finding that he merely had to repeat one more time what he had done to go from a one-dimensional to a two-dimensional grating.

The equations related the observed Laue diagram to the actual positions of atoms in crystals and to the X-ray wavelength. This accomplishment opened a particularly fruitful field of research using X rays to determine the structure of crystals and crystals of known structure to determine the wavelengths of X rays. Analysis of X rays emitted by atoms (X-ray spectroscopy) was of great value in the pursuit of an understanding of atomic structure. Einstein called Laue's discovery "one of the most beautiful in physics."

"For his discovery of the diffraction of Röntgen [X] rays by crystals," Laue was awarded the 1914 Nobel Prize for Physics. "As a result of von Laue's discovery . . . ," said G. D. Granqvist of the Royal Swedish Academy of Sciences in his presentation speech, "proof was thus established that these light waves are of very small wavelengths. However, this discovery also resulted in the most important discoveries in the field of crystallography." Granqvist went on, "It is now possible to determine the position of atoms in crystals, and much important knowledge has been gained in this connection."

Laue's work laid the foundation for the methods of X-ray crystallography worked out by W. L. BRAGG and for the eventual elucidation of the molecular structure of penicillin by DOROTHY C. HODGKIN and of amino acids by JOHN C. KENDREW and MAX PERUTZ. Moreover, it led to the further development of spectroscopy and solid-state physics. Extending his theory of X-ray interference, Laue investigated the interaction between atoms within a crystal and the incident electromagnetic field. Late in life, he approached the theory of diffraction in an entirely novel way by considering energy flow instead of wave amplitudes. During the 1930s he also contributed to Walter Meissner's discovery that a superconductor eliminates the entire magnetic field in its interior.

At a physics congress held at the University of Würzburg in 1933, Laue attacked the new National Socialist government of Adolf Hitler for its dismissal of Einstein as director of the Kaiser Wilhelm Institute for Physics in Berlin, comparing it to the seventeenth-century censure of Galileo. He not only defended Einstein's theory of relativity against Nazi apologists such as PHILIPP VON LENARD and JOHANNES STARK, but also worked actively to block Stark's appointment to the Prussian Academy and the German Research Association. Despite these actions, Laue was permitted to teach and conduct research throughout World War II.

When Berlin was bombed in 1944, Laue moved with the Kaiser Wilhelm Institute to the town of Hechingen in Württemberg. The following year he was taken prisoner by the Allies and sent with other German scientists to England, where they were questioned about Germany's wartime scientific programs. Laue was permitted to return to Germany in 1946, when he became acting director of the Max Planck (formerly Kaiser Wilhelm) Institute and professor of physics at the University of Göttingen. In these capacities and as consultant to the State Physical-Technical Institute in Berlin, he played a major role in rebuilding German science after the war. From 1951 until his retirement seven years later, Laue was director of the Fritz Haber Institute for Physical Chemistry in Berlin.

Laue was married in 1910 to Magdalena Degan; they had a son and a daughter. He enjoyed sailing, mountain climbing, and listening to classical music. He was particularly fond of driving his car or motorcycle at high speeds. While traveling to a meeting at Wannsee on April 8, 1960, he collided with a motorcyclist and was trapped in his overturned car. After seeming to recover, he died in the hospital and was buried in Göttingen with Max Planck, WALTHER NERNST, and several other notable German scientists.

Laue was the recipient of many awards in addition to the Nobel Prize, including the Max Planck Medal of the German Physical Society (1932) and the Grand Cross for Federal Service of the West German government (1953). He held honorary degrees from the universities of Bonn, Stuttgart, Munich, Berlin, Manchester, and Chicago and was a member of numerous scientific societies, including the American Physical Society, the German Physical Society, the Academy of Sciences of Vienna, and the French Physical Society. He was made honorary president of the International Union of Crystallographers in 1948 and an officer of the Legion of Honor of France in 1953.

SELECTED WORKS: History of Physics, 1950; Theory of Superconductivity, 1952.

ABOUT: Biographical Memoirs of Fellows of the Royal Society, volume 6, 1960; Dictionary of Scientific Biography, volume 8, 1973; Frisch, O. R. (ed.) Trends in Atomic Physics, 1959; Segrè, E. From X Rays to Quarks: Modern Physicists and Their Discoveries, 1980.

LAVERAN, CHARLES
(June 18, 1845–May 18, 1922)
Nobel Prize for Physiology or Medicine, 1907

The French biologist and parasitologist Charles Louis Alphonse Laveran (läv rän′) was born in Paris, the descendant of doctors on his father's side of the family and army commanders on his mother's. His father, Louis Laveran, an army medical inspector, was director of the École du Val-de-Grâce. Following his father's example, Laveran entered the École Impériale du Service de Santé Militaire in Strasbourg, from which he graduated in 1867 with a degree in public health. He served as a military doctor during the Franco-Prussian War and in 1874 won a competitive examination to succeed his father, who held the chair in military disease and epidemics at the École du Val-de-Grâce. A year later, the younger Laveran wrote a treatise on military diseases, including malaria. Although it rarely occurred in France, malaria posed a serious threat to French soldiers who were on duty in Algeria. When his period of office ended in 1878, the army posted Laveran to Algeria to study the disease.

Acceptance of Louis Pasteur's germ theory of fermentation laid the foundation for a germ theory of disease. To devise such a theory, not only would researchers have to find the bac-

CHARLES LAVERAN

terium or other organism responsible for a particular disease; they would also have to establish the relationship between the disease and the germ. It was through his investigations of anthrax in 1876 that ROBERT KOCH accomplished this task and launched the search for disease-causing bacteria.

Laveran spent his first two years in Algeria familiarizing himself with the research of Achille Kelsch, a German pathologist, who had investigated the phenomenon of innumerable tiny black particles found in the blood vessels, spleen, and liver of people who had died from malaria. Kelsch, accustomed to examining dead tissue, was more concerned with the physiological changes caused by a disease than with its processes. However, he did recognize that the presence of the black particles was a valuable diagnostic clue. Laveran confirmed that the black particles characterized only malaria and then set about determining what role they played in the disease.

Whereas Kelsch and other researchers had studied the black particles on slides of dried, stained blood, Laveran examined fresh blood drawn from malarial patients. He noted leukocytes, or white blood cells, with black pigment but saw that next to them were clear bodies that showed some black fragments. These bodies, which did not resemble the familiar white blood cells, were visible in two basic shapes: crescents and spheres.

On November 5, 1880, Laveran took blood from a young soldier suffering from a relapse of a fever. In previous blood samples from the same patient, Laveran had found crescent-shaped bodies; this time, however, he observed spherical bodies. He later wrote that "at the periphery of this body was a series of fine, transparent filaments that moved very accurately and beyond question were alive." Laveran had discovered the malarial parasite, now known as *Plasmodium,* a genus of protozoans, or one-celled animals, that lives inside red blood cells.

However, Laveran's discovery was ignored or rejected for four years, with most researchers refusing to believe that flagellate organisms, such as reported by Laveran, could exist in the blood. Furthermore, researchers not only excluded the possibility of flagellate organisms in the blood but maintained that the cause of malaria was a bacterium. As more researchers became interested in the cause of malaria, the skepticism of both military and civilian physicians regarding the existence of protozoan parasites in the blood of malaria victims began to abate. By 1885 acceptance of Laveran's discovery had spread throughout the world. Among the converts to the *Plasmodium* theory was the noted Canadian clinician and teacher William Osler, professor at the Johns Hopkins School of Medicine.

The difficult and time-consuming task of tracing the development and mode of transmission of the malaria *Plasmodium* was accomplished in 1897 by RONALD ROSS, who credited Laveran and Patrick Manson (England's leading authority on tropical diseases) with guiding his research in the right direction.

In 1884 Laveran was appointed professor of military medicine at Val-de-Grâce, a position he held for ten years. By that time, his *Plasmodium* theory was so widely accepted and his published works on protozoans and malaria so widely read that the French Academy of Sciences awarded him its prestigious Breant Prize. Even though Laveran had won over the scientific community, French army physicians were not completely convinced, and he was given little opportunity for research. When his tenure at Val-de-Grâce ended, he was not assigned to a military medical laboratory. Disappointed, Laveran resigned from the army in 1896 and accepted a position at the Pasteur Institute.

There Laveran had the time and facilities to conduct research on other protozoan diseases. His most important work at that time was on the trypanosomes, protozoans that are transmitted to human beings through the bite of flies. Trypanosomiasis, or African sleeping sickness, was one of the diseases caused by the presence of trypanosomes in the body. The trypanosomic diseases, like malaria, are normally confined to the tropics. Laveran's geographic distance from the source of the disease, however, did not hinder his research, because he could now draw upon the resources of the Pasteur Institute in order to conduct artificial infection experiments on animals. Although he did not discover the trypanosome of sleeping sickness, he was responsible for improving the understanding of the morphology, biology, and pathological activity of protozoan parasites.

The 1907 Nobel Prize for Physiology or Medicine was awarded to Laveran for "his work on the role played by protozoa in causing diseases." Awards ceremonies were canceled that year in observance of the death of Sweden's King Oscar II. In a lecture written for the occasion, Laveran recounted his research activities and the obstacles that his theory had encountered and summarized his work on the trypanosomes. "For twenty-seven years," he stated, "I have not ceased to busy myself with the study of the parasitic protozoa of man and animals and I can say, I believe without exaggeration, that I have taken an important part in the progress which has been made in this field."

Malaria was the most important of the diseases caused by protozoans, but Laveran's work on the trypanosomes was also significant. He used his Nobel Prize money to organize a laboratory for the study of tropical medicine at the Pasteur Institute. He continued his research on protozoa, which included a study of leishmaniasis, a tropical disease caused by *Leishmania,* a genus of flagellate protozoans. A dedicated scientist and an egotistical man, Laveran was endowed with seemingly unlimited energy, patience, and optimism. He continued his research on protozoans in animals and human beings until a few months before his death in Paris in 1922.

Laveran's family consisted of his wife, whom he had married in 1885, and his sister; the Laverans had no children.

In addition to the Nobel Prize, Laveran received the Jenner Medal of the Epidemiological Society of London (1902) and the Moscow Prize of the International Congress of Medicine (1906). He was a member of the Academy of Sciences and the Academy of Medicine and held foreign membership in the Royal Society of London, the Pathological Society of Great Britain and Ireland, the Royal College of Physicians of Edinburgh, and the Medical and Surgical Society of London.

SELECTED WORKS: Paludism, 1893.

ABOUT: Charles, T. E. Letters From Rome, 1929; Dictionary of Scientific Biography, volume 8, 1973; Hackett, L. W. Malaria in Europe, 1937; Walker, M. Pioneers of Public Health, 1930.

LAWRENCE, ERNEST O.
(August 8, 1901–August 27, 1958)
Nobel Prize for Physics, 1939

The American physicist Ernest Orlando Lawrence was born in Canton, South Dakota, the elder son of Carl Gustav and Gunda (Jacobson) Lawrence, both of whose parents had emigrated to the United States from Norway. The boy's father was the local superintendent of schools and later became state superintendent of education and the president of several teachers' colleges; his mother was also an educator. Lawrence attended public schools in Canton and Pierre. In his spare time he and his best friend and neighbor, Merle Tuve, who also became a noted physicist, built gliders and devised their own wireless telegraph systems.

When one of his cousins died of leukemia, Lawrence decided to pursue a medical career. With the aid of a scholarship, he entered St. Olaf College in Northfield, Minnesota, in 1918, but after a year he switched to the University of South Dakota. There Lewis E. Akely, a professor of electrical engineering, encouraged Lawrence to study physics. After receiving a B.S. with high honors in 1922, Lawrence began graduate studies at the University of Minnesota under W. F. G. Swann. There he did experimental work on electrical induction and received an M.S. in 1923.

Later that year, he followed Swann to the University of Chicago, where his interest in physics was further stimulated by encounters with NIELS BOHR, ARTHUR H. COMPTON, ALBERT A. MICHELSON, H. A. Wilson, and other leading scientific figures. Transferring to Yale University in the fall of 1924, Lawrence was awarded a Ph.D. the following year. His dissertation on the photoelectric effect in potassium vapor was the first of several major contributions he made in the field of photoelectricity. For the next two years he conducted research at Yale as a National Research Council fellow and in 1927 was appointed assistant professor of physics. In 1928, however, Lawrence left Yale to accept an appointment as associate professor at the University of California at Berkeley.

In California, Lawrence at first continued

ERNEST O. LAWRENCE

the work he had begun at Yale on such subjects as photoelectricity and the measurement of extremely short time intervals. Among other achievements, he gave a practical demonstration of WERNER HEISENBERG's uncertainty principle. The principle predicts that a measurement of energy, such as that in a photon of light (a photon is a unit, or particle, of electromagnetic energy), becomes more uncertain as the time available for the measurement becomes shorter. Since the photon energy is proportional to the frequency of the light, an uncertainty in energy amounts to an uncertainty in frequency. A line in an optical spectrum represents a narrow (that is, well-defined) band of light frequencies. By turning the light on and off again in an extremely short time while observing a spectral line, Lawrence and a colleague showed that the line became broader. Although the light source had not changed, the indication of its frequency had become less definite, just as the uncertainty principle predicted.

Lawrence then turned to nuclear physics, a field that was developing rapidly. In 1919 ERNEST RUTHERFORD had split the atomic nucleus by bombarding it with alpha particles from radium. Rutherford found that the debris left by the collisions contained atoms of lower atomic weight than the original, some of them isotopes of well-known elements, that is, having the same chemical properties, or nuclear charge, but different weight.

Rutherford's methods had serious drawbacks; radium was scarce, alpha particles emerged in all directions at random, the number of collisions to be observed was extremely small, and the procedure was tedious. What was needed was an abundance of controllable, high-energy particles. Since both the bombarding particles and the target nuclei were positively charged (electrons played a very small role), the incoming particles needed enough energy to overcome not only the electric repulsion but also the binding energy holding the nucleus together. JOHN COCKCROFT and ERNEST WALTON had recently developed linear particle accelerators that used extremely high voltages. In these devices, positively charged particles raced in straight lines toward the negative electrode that attracted them, accelerated to an energy equal to the voltage.

Linear accelerators did not appeal to Lawrence because their insulating materials tended to break down and their voltage sometimes discharged through the surrounding air in a lightninglike arc. In 1929 he happened upon a paper in German by Rolf Wideröe, a Norwegian-born engineer, based on a particle-accelerator scheme proposed earlier by the Swedish physicist Gustaf A. Ising. Although Lawrence could not read German well, the illustrations clearly showed that the particle was accelerated in a series of steps rather than in one large, high-voltage surge. He quickly realized that the linear path could be bent into a circle, and after a few calculations, Lawrence and several colleagues proceeded to design and build the first cyclotron, the invention for which Lawrence is best known.

The design depends on the fact that charged particles in a uniform magnetic field travel in circles. They do so because the moving charge constitutes an electric current which, like the current in the windings of an electromagnet, generates a magnetic field. Like two magnets brought close together, the particle and the external magnet exert a force on each other, but only the particle is free to move (equivalent to holding one magnet fixed so that only the other one moves). The direction of the force is always at right angles to both the magnetic field and the direction of motion of the particle. Because the direction of the particle is constantly deflected, the particle travels in a circle. An important feature of the particle's motion is that it always completes a circle in the same time, regardless of its speed (or kinetic energy). However, the diameter of the circle is larger for faster speeds. Lawrence exploited these features in his design.

The heart of the cyclotron is a large, hollow, circular disk, divided along a diameter into two D-shaped semicircles (now called dees).

The two-part disk is placed between the flat pole faces of a large magnet. An electric oscillator is connected between the dees so that an alternating voltage is impressed across the gap. When a charged particle such as a proton is injected into the gap, it is attracted to the dee that happens to have negative voltage at the time and thus picks up speed. Entering the dee, it travels in a circle and emerges at a point diametrically opposite its entrance point. The oscillator frequency is tuned so that the voltage has reversed, and the proton emerges toward a now negative opposite dee, attracted and accelerated by the voltage across the gap. It enters the opposite dee at an increased speed and therefore travels inside the dee in a wider circle than before. When it emerges, the voltage has again reversed, so the proton is accelerated once more and reenters the first dee at higher speed in a wider circle. The proton therefore receives an energy "kick" each time it crosses the gap between the dees and moves in ever-widening circles and with increasing speeds until it reaches the perimeter of the disk. It then emerges and is directed at the desired target. Larger-diameter disks can produce higher speeds but also require larger, more costly magnets. The dees must be made of nonmagnetic material that does not shield out the magnetic field, and the chamber must contain a vacuum so that the particle does not lose its energy in collisions with gas molecules.

After the first crude cyclotron was built in 1930, Berkeley scientists quickly built successively larger models. Using an 80-ton magnet contributed by the Federal Telegraph Company, Lawrence accelerated particles to energies of many million electron volts, more than had ever been achieved. Cyclotrons proved to be ideal experimental instruments. Unlike radiation from radioactive nuclei, the particle beam from a cyclotron was unidirectional, had adjustable energy, and was far more intense than from any radioactive source. The high energies achieved by Lawrence and his colleagues opened a vast new field of research. Bombardment of the atoms of many different elements disintegrated their nuclei into fragments that proved to be isotopes, often radioactive, of known elements. Sometimes the particles stuck to the target nuclei or caused nuclear reactions that produced new elements not found naturally on earth. The results indicated that almost any nuclear reaction could occur if sufficient energy were available. The cyclotron was also used to measure the binding energies of many nuclei and, by a comparison of the difference in masses before and after a

reaction with the energies involved, to verify ALBERT EINSTEIN's equation relating mass to energy.

With the cyclotron, it was possible to create radioactive isotopes for medical use. Lawrence worked closely with his younger brother, John, a physician and director of the Berkeley Biophysics Laboratory, on the biomedical applications of nuclear physics. John Lawrence successfully used isotopes to treat cancer, including the inoperable cancer of their mother, who lived another twenty years.

Lawrence was awarded the 1939 Nobel Prize for Physics "for the invention and development of the cyclotron and for results obtained with it, especially with regard to artificial radioactive elements." Because of the outbreak of World War II, however, presentation ceremonies were canceled. In an account of Lawrence's work, MANNE SIEGBAHN of the Royal Swedish Academy of Sciences declared that the invention of the cyclotron had brought about an "explosive development of nuclear research. . . . Within the history of . . . experimental physics, the cyclotron takes an exceptional position. It is, without comparison, the most extensive and complicated apparatus construction carried out so far." The prize was presented to Lawrence in ceremonies held at Berkeley in 1940, and he delivered a Nobel lecture in Stockholm in 1951.

In 1940 Lawrence helped establish the Radiation Laboratory at the Massachusetts Institute of Technology and induced many former students to join the staff. The purpose of the laboratory was improvement of radar technology, first developed in England, for the electronic detection of military aircraft during World War II. In 1941 Lawrence also recruited staff for an underwater sound laboratory in San Diego to develop antisubmarine warfare systems against German submarines then destroying convoys of material being sent from the United States to aid Great Britain. Lawrence, who remained only informally associated with these laboratories, turned his efforts at Berkeley to converting the 37-inch cyclotron into a mass spectrometer for separating fissionable uranium 235 from ordinary uranium. The mass spectrometer also employs a combination of electric and magnetic fields, but they are used to send particles into different trajectories according to their masses and the electric charges they carry. Since isotopes have slightly different masses, they follow slightly different paths and can be collected separately, although not with great efficiency.

Lawrence attained enough success in isotope separation to commit his laboratory to the work. As a result, hundreds of mass spectrometers, modeled on the 184-inch cyclotron magnet at Berkeley, were built at Oak Ridge, Tennessee, as part of the Manhattan Project, the secret effort to develop an atomic bomb. From 1941 to 1945 Lawrence and his Berkeley associates produced almost all the uranium in the bomb that was dropped on the Japanese city of Hiroshima in August 1945. The Oak Ridge mass spectrometer plant was later closed, superseded by a more efficient gaseous diffusion system.

At the end of the war, Lawrence and his colleagues returned to basic research. Lawrence also remained involved in the development of nuclear weapons. He obtained funds for a second weapons research facility at Livermore, near Berkeley, separate from the Los Alamos laboratory established for the Manhattan Project. Later called the Lawrence Livermore Laboratories, it became a major center for advances that led to the development of the hydrogen bomb.

At Berkeley, Lawrence supervised the construction of accelerators capable of propelling particles to energies reaching billions of electron volts. Such a device, called a bevatron, enabled EMILIO SEGRÈ and others to investigate the properties of mesons (fundamental particles with a mass between those of the electron and the proton) and to discover the antiproton (a twin of the proton but with a negative charge).

In his capacity as a government consultant, Lawrence was invited by President Dwight D. Eisenhower to take part in the Conference of Experts to Study the Possibility of Detecting Violation of a Possible Agreement on Suspension of Nuclear Tests that was convened in Geneva in 1958. Returning home, Lawrence underwent surgery for ulcerative colitis and died in a hospital at Palo Alto, California, on August 27, 1958.

In 1932 Lawrence married Mary Kimberly Blumer, daughter of the dean of the Yale University School of Medicine. The couple had six children. In addition to his many contributions to nuclear physics, Lawrence devised a novel television tube, the Lawrence Chromatron, which was eventually manufactured in Japan and the United States. Although he devoted long hours and many weekends to his work, Lawrence enjoyed boating, tennis, ice skating, and listening to music. "The important ingredients of his success," LUIS W. ALVAREZ wrote, "were native ingenuity and basic good judgment in science, great stamina, an enthusiastic and outgoing personality, and a sense of integrity that was overwhelming."

Lawrence's many honors included the Elliott Cresson Medal of the Franklin Institute (1937), the Hughes Medal of the Royal Society of London (1940), and the Holley Medal of the American Society of Mechanical Engineers (1942). He received honorary degrees from the universities of South Dakota, Chicago, Pennsylvania, British Columbia, Southern California, and Glasgow, as well as from Yale, Harvard, Rutgers, and McGill, among others. He held membership in the National Academy of Sciences, the American Philosophical Society, and the Physical Society of Japan, in addition to numerous honorary and foreign memberships.

SELECTED WORKS: Molecular Films, the Cyclotron and the New Biology, 1942, with others.

ABOUT: Biographical Memoirs of the National Academy of Sciences, volume 41, 1970; Childs, H. An American Genius, 1968; Davis, N. P. Lawrence and Oppenheimer, 1968; Dictionary of Scientific Biography, volume 8, 1973; Heilbron, J. L., et al. Lawrence and His Laboratory, 1981; Jaffe, B. Men of Science in America, 1958; Jungk, R. Brighter Than a Thousand Suns, 1960.

LAXNESS, HALLDÓR
(April 23, 1902–)
Nobel Prize for Literature, 1955

The Icelandic novelist and essayist Halldór Kiljan Laxness (läks' nes) was born Halldór Guðjónsson in Reykjavík, the son of Guðjón Helgi Helgason, a road construction supervisor, and the former Sigríður Halldórsdóttir. When the boy was three years old, his family moved to Mosfellssveit, just northeast of Reykjavík, to raise sheep on a farm called Laxness (salmon peninsula), a name he later adopted. As a boy, Laxness listened to his father recite the great Icelandic sagas and read volumes of epic poetry in the family library. During this time his father also taught him to play the violin, and the boy went to Reykjavík for school and piano lessons. While still in high school, he secretly wrote romantic stories, one of which, the short novel Barn náttúrunnar (The Child of Nature), was published in 1919, under the pen name Halldór frá Laxnesi.

After his father died in 1919, Laxness went abroad for the first of many trips, spending most of his time in Copenhagen. He traveled through Austria and Germany in 1921–1922, and later in 1922 went to France, where he

HALLDÓR LAXNESS

this same period, Laxness was leaning toward a leftist political philosophy, having largely relinquished his involvement with Catholicism. While in the United States, influenced by the writer Upton Sinclair, Laxness became a Socialist, a political change reflected in the essay collection *Alþýðubókin* (The Book of the People, 1929).

In 1930, on the occasion of the thousandth anniversary of Iceland's Parliament, Laxness returned to Iceland and while there married Ingibjörg (Inga) Einarsdóttir. In 1931–1932 he published the two-volume novel *Salka Valka*. The first of his works to be translated into English (it appeared under the same title in 1936), it made a strong impression on some American critics. This was to be the first in a two-decade series of epic novels in which Laxness depicted the Icelandic lower classes, addressing a myriad of social problems in a bleakly realistic style. In 1934–1935 he published the two-volume *Sjálfstætt fólk* (*Independent People*), the story of a poor farmer's struggles to retain his land against the harsh onslaughts of nature and social oppression. When *Independent People* was published in the United States, it established Laxness's American reputation as Iceland's foremost writer. *Heimsljós* (*World Light*, 1937–1940) is the four-volume saga of an impoverished poet. It portrays the conflict between the poet's love of beauty and his abhorrence of social injustice; Laxness considers *World Light* the most significant of his novels. He followed it with the historical trilogy *Íslandsklukkan* (Iceland's Bell, 1943–1946), set in the eighteenth century, in which he criticized Danish rule in Iceland. Although these major novels of the 1930s and 1940s describe harrowing social conditions, they leaven their trenchant observations with irony and compassion.

Other works by Laxness during this period include *Í Austurvegi* (Going East, 1933), describing his impressions of a journey to the Soviet Union, and another Russian travel book, *Gerska æfintýrið* (The Russian Adventure, 1938). He also published several volumes of short stories, the play *Straumrof* (Short Circuit, 1934), the poetry collection *Kvæðakver* (Poems, 1930), and a translation of ERNEST HEMINGWAY's *A Farewell to Arms* (*Vopnin kvödd*, 1941).

In 1940 Laxness divorced Inga Einarsdóttir; five years later he married Auður Sveinsdóttir, a hospital technician. They moved into Gljúfrasteinn, a house Laxness built on his family's farm, spending their winters in Reykjavík. Recognizing that the population of Iceland was

became acquainted with the surrealist movement. A period of spiritual questioning during this trip led Laxness to seek refuge in the Benedictine monastery of Clairvaux in Luxembourg. There, in January 1923, he converted from Lutheranism to Catholicism and formally adopted the name Laxness.

While abroad, Laxness continued to write. In 1923 he published the collection *Nokkrar sögur* (Some Stories), and in 1924 he published the novel *Undir Helgahnúk* (Under the Holy Mountain), which follows an Icelandic boy through his childhood. Laxness also began work on an autobiography, *Heiman ég fór* (From Home I Went), which was eventually published in 1952. In 1925 he published a defense of Catholicism, *Kapólsk viðhorf* (From a Catholic Point of View). In the same year, after a brief return to his homeland, Laxness went to Sicily, where he wrote his first long novel, *Vefarinn mikli frá Kasmír* (The Great Weaver From Kashmir, 1927), in which he described the spiritual development of a young writer from Reykjavík. Strongly autobiographical and surrealistic in tone, this work is now seen as an important literary breakthrough for Laxness. At the time, however, it was criticized in Iceland for its stylistic experimentation, for the decadence it portrayed, and for its use of foreign phrases, which was considered to be an undesirable admission of outside influences into Icelandic culture.

In 1927–1929 Laxness visited North America. A story he wrote while visiting Canada about the poverty of Icelandic immigrants in Manitoba led to threats of deportation. During

too small to enable even the most distinguished native writer to support himself solely from the royalties generated by his books, the government supplemented Laxness's income with a yearly stipend. Occasional reductions in the amount of the stipend eventually caused Laxness to refuse the money as an insult to his honor as a writer.

In 1948 Laxness published *Atómstöðin* (*The Atom Station*), a satirical novel about the atomic age, which did not attain the popular success of his earlier works. *The Atom Station* was not published in the United States until 1982, possibly because of what were regarded as Laxness's pro-Communist leanings. Strongly pro-Soviet at the time the book was written, Laxness served as chairman of the Iceland-USSR Society in 1950.

Laxness was awarded the 1955 Nobel Prize for Literature "for his vivid epic power which has renewed the great narrative art of Iceland." Citing *World Light* as Laxness's masterpiece in his presentation address, E. Wessén of the Swedish Academy paid tribute to the rich heritage of Icelandic literature. He noted that "Halldór Laxness has guided literary development back to common and traditional ground . . . [and] renewed the Icelandic language as an artistic means of expression for a modern content." In his acceptance speech, Laxness acknowledged his indebtedness to "the old Icelandic storytellers" whose epics created "not only a literary language, which is among the most beautiful and subtlest there is, but a separate literary genre."

The novel *Brekkukotsannáll* (*The Fish Can Sing,* 1957) marked a change in Laxness's style. A lyrical, introspective novel, it embodies his faith in the human capacity for dignity and goodness. In this book and in the novels that followed, Laxness moved away from the social and political concerns that had dominated his writing during the three previous decades. In addition, his denunciation of Soviet Communism in the autobiographical *Skáldatími* (Poetic Age, 1963) became something of an international cause célèbre. Laxness has continued to produce novels, memoirs, essays, plays, and translations.

Laxness remains a prominent and respected figure in Scandinavian literature. In his 1971 biography, Peter Hallberg pointed out that "the Icelandic heritage has constantly been a living force in his work, contrasting or combining in various ways with his modernism and preoccupation with the problems of his time. The tension between the native and the foreign, the national and the cosmopolitan, has formed one of the fruitful contrasts which run through all his writing."

In a 1980 essay, the Icelandic scholar Sveinn Skorri Höskuldsson hailed Laxness as "by far the most famous Icelandic writer of the twentieth century" and noted that "his creative powers are unequaled: no other author has dealt so imaginatively with practically all aspects of human life in Iceland." "With his narrative skill and vivid style, [Laxness] has done more than any modern novelist to renew Icelandic prose," wrote the Icelandic critic Sigurður A. Magnússon in 1982. "He has a surprisingly large range of styles and subjects," Magnússon added, "so that no two of his novels resemble one another in anything but their felicity of expression and power of character portrayal." In spite of such critical acclaim, great popularity with Icelandic readers, and the acknowledgment of his achievements by scholars, Laxness remains little known to contemporary audiences outside Scandinavia.

ADDITIONAL WORKS IN ENGLISH TRANSLATION: The Happy Warrior, 1958; The Honour of the House, 1959; Paradise Reclaimed, 1962; Christianity at Glacier, 1972; A Quire of Seven, 1974.

ABOUT: Books Abroad Spring 1970, Winter 1971; Einarsson, S. History of Icelandic Prose Writers, 1948; Hallberg, P. Halldór Laxness, 1971; Höskuldsson, S. (ed.) Ideals and Ideologies in Scandinavian Literature, 1975.

LEAGUE OF RED CROSS SOCIETIES
(founded May 5, 1919)
Nobel Prize for Peace, 1963
(shared with the International Committee of the Red Cross)

The League of Red Cross Societies, a voluntary humanitarian organization headquartered in Geneva, Switzerland, is a federation of national Red Cross societies that administers relief around the world. It has been known since 1983 as the League of Red Cross and Red Crescent Societies. It is one of three components of the International Movement of the Red Cross and Red Crescent (until 1986 the International Red Cross); the other two entities are the INTERNATIONAL COMMITTEE OF THE RED CROSS (ICRC) and the various national Red Cross societies themselves.

The league was founded in Paris in the aftermath of World War I by, among others, the five large Red Cross societies of the victorious Allies (the United States, Great Britain, France, Italy, and Japan). Although the group had no formal affiliation with the League of Nations, and indeed stressed its nonpolitical, nongovernmental, and nonsectarian nature, it did envision cooperating with that body as well as with the governments of the world. Similarly, it was intended to complement the work of the all-Swiss ICRC, which had focused on assisting victims of war since its founding in 1863.

The League of Red Cross Societies was the brainchild of American financier Henry P. Davison. At the request of President WOODROW WILSON, Davison had served during World War I as president of the War Council of the American Red Cross, established to provide expanded voluntary services to the armed forces. Davison proved to be an able organizer. By the end of the war, the American Red Cross had raised over $400 million, and its 3,724 chapters had helped to feed European orphans, relocate refugees, clothe the needy, combat epidemic diseases, reconstruct destroyed villages, build hospitals, rehabilitate the wounded, and reunite families. By the time of the armistice, Davison was reluctant to reduce his mighty organization to its prewar status. "The war program of the American Red Cross," he said, "will thus steadily and rapidly merge itself into a peace program." Moreover, Davison began to formulate plans to unite the American Red Cross with the Red Cross societies of the victorious Allies.

With the enthusiastic support of President Wilson, Davison left for Europe in December 1918 hoping to unite the national Red Cross societies into a permanent international organization. He encountered many obstacles. His own national society seemed intent on shrinking back to its prewar status. The British Red Cross could not conceive of joining an organization that required cooperation with the German Red Cross. Conversely, the ICRC had reservations about Davison's lack of neutrality in restricting the formative planning to the five Allies. Eventually, Davison's idea was accepted and incorporated into Article 25 of the League of Red Cross Societies Covenant. It urged national Red Cross societies "to combine with each other in an international Red Cross league" for the purposes of improving health, preventing disease, and mitigating suffering throughout the world.

At a dinner given for him in Paris in February 1919, Davison announced that his committee of representatives from the five Allied Red Cross societies would prepare a peacetime program for submission to an international conference of national Red Cross societies. The conference convened in Cannes, France, on April 1, 1919. In the judgment of Lillian Wald, founder of the Henry Street Settlement and a member of the American delegation, the gathering of eminent specialists in public health and public welfare far outshone the gathering of political leaders that was drafting the peace treaty in Paris. After preliminary discussions, the conference recommended that an international Bureau of Public Health and Hygiene be established in conjunction with the League of Red Cross Societies. Subsequently, disease prevention became a major concern of the league.

When the League of Red Cross Societies was founded, Davison was elected chairman of the board of governors. Lieutenant General David Henderson, who had been director of Britain's wartime aircraft production, was appointed vice-chairman of the board and director-general, which put him in charge of the league's day-to-day administrative duties. Stockton Axson, brother-in-law of President Wilson and former secretary of the War Council of the American Red Cross, was appointed acting secretary-general. Other board members represented Red Cross organizations from Great Britain, France, Italy, and Japan.

As set forth in its Articles of Association, the league's purposes included encouraging new Red Cross national organizations for the improvement of health and mitigation of suffering, promulgating information about science and medicine, and coordinating relief work in times of national and international disasters. A press release stated that, while cooperating with the League of Nations, the new organization had no formal affiliation with that body.

By July 1919 headquarters had been opened in Geneva, and staff members were beginning to tackle the enormous problems of relief and reconstruction in postwar Europe. A massive relief effort was begun in Central Europe in cooperation with the League of Nations. Particularly concerned about the threat of epidemics, the leagues distributed vast quantities of medical supplies in addition to food and clothing. Moreover, the number of war orphans, which was estimated at 10 million, prompted special plans for the care of children. During this reconstruction period, more than 100 child-health centers operated in Austria alone. As a result of this emphasis, the Red Cross Youth movement started in the United States in 1923.

The League of the Red Cross Societies has since participated in hundreds of relief, rescue, and disease-prevention programs throughout the world. For example, in 1956 it coordinated relief and administered temporary camps to house the thousands of refugees who fled their country after the failed Hungarian uprising. For this work, the league received the Nansen Medal (established in honor of FRIDTJOF NANSEN). In the year 1960 alone, the league sent medical teams to assist hospitals in the Congo, provided relief to Angolan refugees, and helped resettle and equip Watusi tribes from Ruanda-Urundi. The organization has also aided victims of natural disasters. Following the earthquake that virtually leveled Skopje, Yugoslavia, in July 1963, the league assisted the Yugoslav Red Cross in providing food and clothing to families whose homes were being rebuilt.

The league's motto—*Per Humanitatem Ad Pacem* (Peace Through Humanity)—reflects its emphasis on activities that promote peace. The league helps foster understanding among national Red Cross societies by encouraging the exchange of technical experts, conducting international study seminars, and introducing peace resolutions to be debated at various conferences. On occasion, the league intervenes directly to remedy the consequences of conflict. In 1952 the league arranged discussions between the Red Cross societies of the People's Republic of China and Japan, talks that led to the return of some 30,000 Japanese detained in China. Junior Red Cross societies have played a particularly prominent role in Red Cross peace work.

On the centennial of the founding of the ICRC, the Norwegian Nobel Committee divided the 1963 Nobel Peace Prize between the League of Red Cross Societies and the International Committee of the Red Cross. In his presentation speech, Carl Joachim Hambro of the Nobel committee observed that "the great worldwide humanitarian work of the league falls outside the sphere of the Peace Prize, but the cooperation between the Red Cross societies of ninety different countries of different races, creeds, and color is of very real importance for international understanding and peace." The award was accepted by John A. MacAulay, a Canadian jurist, member of the Central Council of the Canadian Red Cross, and chairman from 1959 to 1965 of the league's board of governors.

At that time, the league was composed of 102 national societies with a combined membership of 170 million. In his acceptance speech, MacAulay paid tribute to these volunteers and expanded on Hambro's theme. "Throughout the world, volunteers of different nationalities, races, and ideologies unite in one and the same impulse to serve the same cause," he said, "and thereby create a vast network of international agreement, a climate of understanding conducive to the establishment of lasting peace." In his Nobel lecture, MacAuley noted that through the expansion of knowledge, the rise of ecumenism, and improvements in communication, the habit of cooperation was growing among nations. "Idealism is no longer 'far out': it is approaching a norm," he told the audience.

The awarding of the Nobel Peace Prize to both organizations tended to mask the problems that can arise from competition among various Red Cross groups. In his 1977 book *Humanitarian Politics,* David Forsythe pointed out that while the ICRC and the league were discussing which group would deliver humanitarian aid to Bangladesh, the Soviet Union's national Red Cross society dispatched a medical team to the area without waiting for the agencies to resolve their differences. Although technically the ICRC concerns itself with problems of war whereas the league deals with peacetime issues, the blurred boundary between war and peace has made it difficult to determine jurisdiction in cases of internal strife, civil war, and undeclared war. Moreover, the ICRC tends to guard its institutional independence, refusing to merge its administrative operations with those of the league in a single headquarters. Despite these problems, delegates from the ICRC, the league, and the national Red Cross societies, as well as from all states signatory to the Geneva Conventions, meet every four years, issue joint resolutions, and iron out problems requiring coordinated effort among agency bodies.

Today the league includes approximately 144 national groups with a combined membership of 250 million people. Its humanitarian efforts have included disaster relief in Ethiopia, Chad, the Sudan, Bangladesh, Madagascar, and Mauritania. Much of the league's assistance has centered in South America, Africa, and the Middle East. It has founded a youth-care center in Chile, a day-care center in Costa Rica, and centers for the handicapped in Uruguay and Lebanon. It has sponsored blood transfusion programs in Burma, China, Indonesia, Sri Lanka, Angola, Ethiopia, Mozambique, Somalia, and Uganda.

Most of the league's annual operating budget, which exceeds $125 million, consists of contributions from national Red Cross societies, governments, and various relief agencies. The rest comes from investments and donations from private individuals and groups. Some three-quarters of these contributions are provided by countries in Europe and North America. In recent years, the largest share of the league's expenditures for aid, some 75 percent, has gone to African nations.

Responding to an appeal by the UNITED NATIONS CHILDREN'S FUND (UNICEF) in 1984, the league established the Child Alive program, through which it has promoted breast-feeding, appropriate weaning and sanitary practices, and massive child immunization efforts. In recognition of the league's work on behalf of child survival and welfare, UNICEF bestowed its Maurice Pate Memorial Award on the league in 1986.

Whether through relief activities, humanitarian programs, or the care of refugees, the league continues its efforts to promote world peace. In a glowing tribute, the late secretary-general of the United Nations DAG HAMMAR-SKJÖLD said, "The Red Cross, with its affiliated Red Crescent and Red Lion and Sun societies, has become the symbol of complete impartiality in rendering help wherever help is needed. The technical achievements of the league have been outstanding, but even greater has been its work in strengthening the ideal of the human race as one family by translating into practical terms the humanitarian concern for the welfare of our fellow man."

SELECTED PUBLICATIONS: The League of Red Cross Societies, 1920; Disaster Relief and the Red Cross, 1924; The Red Cross: Its International Organization, 1930; Universality in Action, 1957.

PERIODICALS: (annual) Report. (semiannual) Nursing. (quarterly) Transfusion International. (monthly) LORCS Secretariat. (irregular) The League.

ABOUT: Barton, C. The Red Cross in War and Peace, 1898; Best, S. H. The Story of the British Red Cross, 1938; Bicknell, E. P. Pioneering With the Red Cross, 1935; Bicknell, E. P. With the Red Cross in Europe 1917–22, 1938; Boardman, M. T. Under the Red Cross Flag at Home and Abroad, 1915; Bory, F. Origin and Development of International Humanitarian Law, 1982; Buckingham, C. E. For Humanity's Sake, 1964; Cousier, H. The International Red Cross, 1961; Draper, G. The Red Cross Conventions, 1958; Dunant, H. A Memory of Solferino, 1939; Forsythe, D. Humanitarian Politics, 1977; Gigon, F. The Epic of the Red Cross, 1946; Gumpert, M. Dunant: The Story of the Red Cross, 1938; International Review of the Red Cross August 1963; Joyce, J. A. Red Cross International and the Strategy of Peace, 1959; Junod, M. Warrior Without Weapons, 1951; Magill, J. The Red Cross, the Idea and Development, 1926; Pictet, J. S. Red Cross Principles, 1956.

LEDERBERG, JOSHUA
(May 23, 1925–   )
Nobel Prize for Physiology or Medicine, 1958
(shared with George W. Beadle and Edward L. Tatum)

The American geneticist Joshua Lederberg was born in Montclair, New Jersey, to Zwi Hirsch Lederberg, a rabbi, and Esther (Goldenbaum) Lederberg, who had emigrated from Palestine two years earlier. Lederberg received his early education in the New York City public school system, graduating from Stuyvesant High School in 1941. He studied zoology as a premedical student at Columbia University and received his B.A. with honors at the age of nineteen. He went on to medical school at the College of Physicians and Surgeons, Columbia University, but continued to do research with F. J. Ryan of the department of zoology at Columbia.

After two years in medical school, Lederberg went to Yale University during the summer of 1944 as a research assistant in the department of microbiology. Although he had planned to return to medical school that fall, he stayed on at Yale to continue his research and study for a Ph.D. in microbiology under EDWARD L. TATUM, a microbiologist and biochemist.

At Stanford, Tatum and his colleague GEORGE W. BEADLE had done pioneering work in the field of biochemical genetics, a subdiscipline of genetics that seeks to determine the biochemical processes involved in the translation of the genotype (a specific set of genetic instructions) of an organism into its phenotype (a specific set of physical traits). The science of genetics began in 1865, when Gregor Mendel, a Dominican monk, published his studies of the laws of inheritance. Mendel postulated that "elements," now called genes, govern the inheritance of physical traits.

At the turn of the century Mendel's work, which had been rejected in his lifetime, became the basis for new research. Scientists found that genes reside on chromosomes, strands of material in the nucleus of the cell. Yet it was not until 1940 that researchers discovered that genes are made of the nucleic acid deoxyribonucleic acid (DNA). From HERMANN J. MULLER's work in the 1920s, it was known that X rays produce genetic mutations, and thus Tatum and Beadle were able to produce mutations in a fungus in the early 1940s. They proved that genes, or DNA, direct the production of cellular enzymes (proteins neces-

JOSHUA LEDERBERG

sary for a variety of chemical reactions in the body), and thus control the biochemical processes of the cell.

At the time Lederberg began studying the genetics of bacteria with Tatum, scientists believed that bacteria reproduced asexually, one bacterial cell dividing into two cells. From the work of Tatum and Beadle and from his own research at Columbia, however, Lederberg knew that fungal organisms reproduce sexually by the temporary combination, or conjugation, of two separate fungal organisms to form a third, or daughter, cell. Lederberg suspected that bacteria also reproduced sexually, and to find out whether this was true, he and Tatum investigated the colon bacillus, the rod-shaped bacterium *Escherichia coli,* which resides in the gastrointestinal tract of humans and other animals. They discovered that this bacterium may reproduce sexually by the conjugation of two separate bacterial cells. The bacterial daughter cell that is produced in this way divides, and new generations of cells are produced by successive divisions of its offspring. When Lederberg and Tatum mated two different strains of colon bacillus, they discovered that the offspring cells inherited certain traits from each parent strain, a process they called sexual genetic recombination. Genetic recombination of bacterial cells involves the transfer of a full complement of chromosomes, and their genes, from one cell to the other.

Lederberg left Yale in 1947 to become professor of genetics at the University of Wisconsin, where he continued to investigate genetic recombination of bacteria. The following year he received his Ph.D. in microbiology from Yale. At Wisconsin Lederberg developed the technique of replica plating, a laboratory method that isolates mutations of a bacteria species by using ultraviolet light or other mutant-inducing agents. He proved that genetic mutations occur spontaneously, thus confirming a long-held hypothesis in the field of evolutionary genetics. By using the replica plating technique to mate bacteria that were resistant to penicillin with others that were resistant to streptomycin, he produced bacteria that were resistant to both antibiotics. He also demonstrated that by similar methods clinically weak bacteria could be made virulent, and clinically virulent bacteria could be made weak.

In collaboration with Norton Zinder, a graduate student at the University of Wisconsin, Lederberg discovered the phenomenon of transduction in bacteria. Transduction, the transfer of fragments of chromosomal material from one cell to another, alters the genetic code of the recipient cell. Some scientists believe that viruses may also alter the genetic code of bacteria by a process resembling transduction. Because determination of the order of genes on chromosomes depends on methods related to transduction, Lederberg's work contributed to subsequent research and discoveries in the genetics of bacteria. It also prepared the way for the development of modern recombinant genetics, the study of processes whereby the genetic code of bacterial cells can be manipulated to produce certain biochemical substances.

In 1957 Lederberg was asked to organize the department of genetics at Wisconsin and serve as its chairman. A Fulbright Fellowship enabled him to conduct research at Melbourne University in Australia before assuming his new responsibilities.

Lederberg was awarded the 1958 Nobel Prize for Physiology or Medicine "for his discoveries concerning the genetic recombination and the organization of the genetic material of bacteria." The other half of the prize was divided between Beadle and Tatum for their work on the role of genes in specific chemical events.

The same year he received the Nobel Prize, Lederberg was named the Joseph Grand Professor of Genetics and chairman of the newly created department of genetics at Stanford University, where, in 1962, he was also appointed director of the Joseph P. Kennedy Jr. Laboratories for Molecular Medicine.

During the early years of the American space program, Lederberg speculated on the scientific and medical consequences of space exploration and served as a consultant to the

Viking program that sent a spacecraft to Mars. He was also a scientific adviser to the World Health Organization on biological warfare and biological weapons.

In 1978 Lederberg left Stanford to become president of Rockefeller University. In addition to his work on genetics, he has written extensively on the biological sciences and the future of the human species.

In 1946 Lederberg married Esther Zimmer, a former graduate student of Tatum's. After their divorce, he married Marguerite Stein Kirsch in 1968; they have one son and one daughter.

In addition to the Nobel Prize, Lederberg has received the Eli Lilly Award of the Society of American Bacteriologists (1953) and the Alexander Hamilton Medal of Columbia University (1961). He has received honorary degrees from Yale, Columbia, and New York universities and from the University of Turin. He is a member of the National Academy of Sciences, the American Chemical Society, and the Genetics Society of America. He was elected a foreign member of the Royal Society of London in 1979.

SELECTED WORKS: Papers in Microbial Genetics, 1951; Man and His Future, 1962, with others; Health in the World of Tomorrow, 1969.

ABOUT: Current Biography March 1959; Dunn, L. C. (ed.) Genetics in the Twentieth Century, 1951; National Cyclopedia of American Biography, volume J, 1964.

LE DUC THO
(October 14, 1911–)
Nobel Prize for Peace, 1973
(shared with Henry Kissinger)

Le Duc Tho (lā duk tō), Vietnamese political leader, was born and reportedly given the name Phan Dinh Khai in the village of Dich Le in Nam Ha Province of northern Vietnam. At the time of his birth, all of Vietnam, as well as other areas of Indochina, was under French control. Because his father worked as a middle-echelon civil servant in the French colonial administration, Tho, along with the other children in the family, had the opportunity to obtain an education. Tho himself was trained as a radiotelegrapher.

Still a teenager during Vietnam's struggle to break free of French colonial rule, Tho joined a revolutionary youth movement dedicated to Vietnamese independence in 1928. During these early years of political activity, he is thought to have taken the name Le Duc Tho as a nom

LE DUC THO

UPI/Bettmann Newsphotos

de guerre, a common practice among young revolutionaries. Tho organized often-violent demonstrations against the French, and in 1930 he and other young radicals led by Ho Chi Minh founded the Indochinese Communist party. The same year these activities led the French authorities to sentence Tho to forced labor on the prison island of Poulo Condore (now Con Son). After his release in 1936, he headed the Communist information organization in the northern city of Nam Dinh. At this time, the Vietnamese Communists, with material aid from the Soviet Union and China, were conducting a guerrilla war against the French. After the outbreak of World War II in 1939, the French again imprisoned Tho, this time in Nam Dinh. "Rage grips me against those barbaric imperialists," Tho wrote from his cell, "so many years their heels have crushed our country."

Accounts of Tho after his second confinement differ. Some report that during most of the Japanese occupation of Vietnam (1940–1945) he was in prison at Sonla near the Chinese border. Others claim that he escaped to China in 1940 and a year later helped Ho Chi Minh found the Viet Minh, a large, diverse coalition of Communist and non-Communist groups dedicated to the removal of Japanese occupational forces and independence for Vietnam.

By the end of the war, Tho was on several prominent committees in the Indochinese Communist party. After the Japanese surrender in 1945, Ho Chi Minh declared Vietnam independent and became president of the new nation. Le Duc Tho became a member of the government's Central Committee and of the Communist party's Standing Committee. When the French attempted to reestablish control of Vietnam in 1946, the war for liberation was resumed. Tho became deputy secretary of the Central Office of the Communist party in the southern part of Vietnam, where he directed revolutionary activities. At Dien Bien Phu in 1954, after eight years of guerrilla warfare, the Viet Minh defeated the French, who withdrew from Vietnam.

An international conference held in Geneva, Switzerland, in 1954 promulgated the Geneva Accords, which ruled that until the holding of national elections in 1956, Vietnam would be temporarily divided at the seventeenth parallel. The Democratic Republic of Vietnam in the north (North Vietnam) would be headed by Ho Chi Minh, and the Republic of Vietnam in the south (South Vietnam) by the former emperor, Bao Dai. Returning to North Vietnam in 1955, Tho was named to the politburo of the newly reorganized Communist organization, the Workers' party. By 1960 he had been elected to the secretariat of the Central Committee, which placed him among the most powerful of North Vietnam's leaders.

Tho reportedly took a hard line on the issue of reunification and on the renewed war that soon erupted between North and South Vietnam. In 1956, when South Vietnam's new leader, Ngo Dinh Diem, refused to participate in the national elections mandated by the Geneva Accords, the National Liberation Front of South Vietnam (Viet Cong) launched a guerrilla war against the South Vietnamese army. Although it represented a broad constituency, the Viet Cong was dominated by the Communists. During the late 1950s and early 1960s, fearing a Communist takeover, the United States, under presidents Dwight D. Eisenhower and John F. Kennedy, sent increasing amounts of military and economic aid to the Diem regime. By the mid-1960s, President Lyndon B. Johnson's administration had committed hundreds of thousands of American troops to South Vietnam. Tho is thought to have favored heavy North Vietnamese participation in the conflict, but his precise role in the prosecution of the war is unclear. According to the *New York Times,* in 1967 Tho was reported to be chairman for the supervision of the South. Evidently, Tho's strategy of total commitment to unification met with severe criticism from other party members, for in 1972 he is alleged to have engineered a "purification campaign" during which thousands of his opponents were executed.

Meanwhile, faced with increasing domestic opposition to the war, in 1968 President Johnson authorized negotiations aimed at achieving a cease-fire. The talks began in Paris on May 13, and on June 3 Le Duc Tho arrived as a special adviser to his delegation. After President Richard M. Nixon took office in January 1969, the talks were expanded to include representatives of South Vietnam and of the Viet Cong. The addition of these two delegations effectively ended any hope of real progress. As preconditions of a cease-fire, the North Vietnamese demanded the withdrawal of United States troops and the replacement of the government of Nguyen Van Thieu (successor to Diem) with a provisional regime that included Communists. At the same time, however, Tho and HENRY KISSINGER began a series of secret talks in Paris on August 4, 1969. Of Tho, Kissinger wrote in his memoirs, "He was there to wear me down. As the representative of the truth, he had no category for compromise." Indeed, the secret talks dragged on for three years, with neither side willing to make substantial concessions.

Tho and Kissinger finally reached an agreement, which they signed on January 27, 1973. The North Vietnamese agreed to recognize the legitimacy of Thieu's government in sectors held by the South Vietnamese army and to accept a National Council of Reconciliation that would arrange elections. For its part, the United States agreed to the total withdrawal of American troops and an in-place cease-fire for units of the North Vietnamese army. Other provisions dealt with the exchange of prisoners of war and the supervision of the cease-fire by a four-nation team. At a press conference, Tho stated, "For centuries, Vietnam has been one: the Vietnamese nation has been one and indivisible. The Vietnamese people from north to south aspire with all their heart not only to a peaceful settlement of the Vietnam problem but also to the reunification of their country."

Le Duc Tho shared the 1973 Nobel Prize for Peace with Henry Kissinger in recognition of their work in negotiating the armistice. In her presentation speech, Aase Lionæs of the Norwegian Nobel Committee acknowledged that the cease-fire agreement was "only the first but a tremendously important step on the laborious road to full peace." She added, however, that "the two negotiators who were awarded the prize represent widely differing systems—one an essentially Western system . . . the other a Communist system. We are under no illusion that the differences between systems and ideologies can be ignored;

but the Nobel committee has been anxious to emphasize that in a world yearning for peace, no one can assume the right to force his particular system on others by armed might. Nations with different systems of government must be able to live together in peace and solve their controversies by negotiation."

The awards were among the most controversial in the history of the Nobel Prize. Two members of the Nobel committee resigned in protest, and worldwide press reaction was critical. In a letter to the Nobel committee, Tho himself refused the prize, charging the United States and South Vietnam with violating the Paris Accords.

In part, the controversy arose because the cease-fire never actually went into effect. Although the American troop withdrawal was completed on March 29, 1973, the civil war in Vietnam continued to claim high casualties. In January 1975 the expected Communist offensive against South Vietnam began. In April the Saigon government collapsed, and a year later, on July 2, 1976, North Vietnam and South Vietnam were reunited as the Socialist Republic of Vietnam. Le Duc Tho continued to serve on the politburo of the new nation.

During the late 1970s, Tho's three younger brothers rose rapidly to top positions within the party. His cousin Nguyen Duc Tam later replaced Tho as head of the party's influential Central Organization Department. These signs of nepotism reportedly produced serious tensions in party leadership. Tho's resignation from the politburo was announced in December 1986.

Little is known about Tho's private life. Newspaper accounts report that he has been married twice. According to the *New York Times,* he "apparently lives with the austerity and strict morality demanded by the Vietnamese revolutionary ethos." A handsome man, five feet eight inches tall with gray hair, at the negotiations he wore plain black Mao suits and impressed observers as quiet, serious, and purposeful. Kissinger once characterized him as a man "always composed," with impeccable manners, whose "large luminous eyes only rarely revealed the fanaticism that had induced him as a boy of sixteen to join the anti-French Communist guerrillas."

ABOUT: Bouscaren, A. T. (ed.) All Quiet on the Eastern Front, 1979; Current Biography March 1975; New Statesman March 21, 1980; Newsweek October 29, 1973; New York Times February 11, 1969; January 24, 1973; December 18, 1984; Nguyen, V. C. Vietnam Under Communism, 1983; Thai, Q. T. Collective Leadership and Factionalism, 1985; Time November 13, 1972.

LEE, TSUNG-DAO

(November 25, 1926–)
Nobel Prize for Physics, 1957
(shared with Chen Ning Yang)

The Chinese-American physicist Tsung-Dao Lee was born in Shanghai, the third of six children of Tsing-Kong Lee, a businessman, and the former Ming-Chang Chang. After graduating in 1943 from Kiangsi Middle School in Kan-chou, he entered National Chekiang University in Kweichow. When the Japanese invasion forced the university to move to K'unming to become part of a consolidation of relocated institutions called the National Southwest Associated University, Lee moved with it in 1945. Also at the university in K'un-ming, for similar reasons, was CHEN NING YANG, who later became a colleague of Lee's. Lee earned a B.S. in physics in 1946. That year, on a Chinese government fellowship, he entered the University of Chicago where he studied under ENRICO FERMI and became friendly with Yang, who was also there on a fellowship. Lee's 1950 Ph.D. thesis was entitled "Hydrogen Content of White Dwarf Stars."

In 1950 Lee spent several months as a research associate in astrophysics at the Yerkes Astronomical Observatory in Lake Geneva, Wisconsin. The following year he served as a research associate in physics at the University of California at Berkeley. Lee was reunited with Yang in 1951 when he joined the Institute for Advanced Study in Princeton, New Jersey. In 1953 he joined the faculty of Columbia University as an assistant professor, becoming a full professor in 1956 at the age of twenty-nine, the youngest person ever to attain that rank at the university. From 1960 to 1963, Lee was a professor at the Institute for Advanced Study, but returned to Columbia in 1963 as Enrico Fermi Professor of Physics.

The friendship between Lee and Yang grew during their two years together in Princeton and continued after Lee went to Columbia and Yang remained at the Institute for Advanced Study. During weekly meals together, they discussed current problems in physics. One in particular involved two apparently different kinds of K-mesons, unstable particles found in the debris created by high-energy bombardment of atomic nuclei. The two particles seemed different in the characteristics of their decay into other particles; for example, one K-meson (named theta) decayed into two pi-mesons, whereas the other (named tau) decayed into three pi-mesons. Some experimental evidence, however, implied that the two

TSUNG-DAO LEE

particles were the same; for example, they seemed to have the same mass and lifetime. The strongest basis for considering them different was the law of conservation of parity, which arose from one of the fundamental symmetries of nature recognized by physicists.

Conservation of parity means, among other things, that particle interactions and the mirror image of such interactions obey the same physical laws and are indistinguishable from each other. In effect, nature is regarded as neither right-handed nor left-handed and is expected to exhibit no right or left bias in the outcome of an experiment. Particles or energy states each have a distinct parity, called even ($+1$) or odd (-1). The parity conservation law stated that the parity of a decaying particle will be the same as the product of the parities of the particles it decays into, so that overall parity remains unchanged. Since a pi-meson has odd parity (-1), the combined parity of two pi-mesons is even ($-1 \times -1 = +1$). Therefore, a theta particle, the parent of two pi-mesons, must also have even parity. Since a tau particle decays into three pi-mesons, it must have odd parity ($-1 \times -1 \times -1 = -1$). Conservation of parity therefore demands that theta and tau mesons be different particles. However, respected experimental evidence of their similarity conflicted with this conclusion and presented an unresolved puzzle when Lee and Yang began their deliberations.

The law of conservation of parity was first expressed explicitly in 1925. It had since gained universal acceptance because its application in theoretical and experimental investigations of physical interactions had proved fruitful, and probably also because it seemed intuitively reasonable. Why should nature play favorites? Known physical interactions involve four forces: the strong force (which holds the nucleus together), the electromagnetic force (which acts on charged particles), the weak force (which acts in the emission of particles during radioactive decay), and gravitation (the force that affects all masses). In seeking a way out of the theta-tau impasse, Lee and Yang explored the experimental evidence for conservation of parity. To their surprise, they discovered that evidence was abundant for conservation of parity in strong or electromagnetic interactions but nonexistent for weak interactions. Gravitation, the weakest of the four forces, is generally negligible in subatomic particle interactions. Experimental observers had never performed tests that explicitly challenged the law in weak interactions, an oversight possibly influenced by their conviction of its intrinsic validity. Theta and tau disintegrations into pi-mesons were weak interactions.

Lee and Yang were primarily theorists, but they proposed several experiments designed to test conclusively right-left symmetry in weak interactions. One was performed in 1956–1957, after six months of difficult preparation to meet the novel requirements, by Chien-Shiung Wu of Columbia University, who worked with physicists at the United States National Bureau of Standards. Radioactive cobalt, which decays into nickel and emits the energy difference in the form of a beta ray (electron) and a neutrino (a massless, uncharged particle), was placed within an electromagnetic coil and cooled to a temperature near absolute zero to minimize the influence of thermal effects. Since atoms and their nuclei behave in some respects like minuscule magnets, the cobalt atoms were preferentially aligned parallel to the strong magnetic field in the coil, establishing a reference direction. Beta emission is the result of a weak interaction; if parity were conserved in cobalt decay, equal numbers of electrons would be emitted in the directions of the north and south magnet poles. Wu found beyond doubt that more electrons emerged from the south end. Parity was not conserved, an outcome that Lee and Yang had not expected, despite their daring proposal.

Confirmation followed almost immediately in other experiments performed at Columbia by Richard L. Garwin, Leon Lederman, and Marcel Weinrich, using the decay of pi-mesons into mu-mesons and the subsequent decay of the mu-mesons into electrons and neutrinos (or antineutrinos). They found that the mu-mesons and electrons failed to exhibit the forward-backward symmetry expected if parity were conserved. Still other experiments established that parity was not conserved in the decay of other particles.

The fall of the time-honored law of conservation of parity made it easier to explain the theta-tau puzzle as the decay of the same particle by two different routes. Abolition of the law also opened new fields of research and held out hope of progress toward ALBERT EINSTEIN's goal of combining the four known forces into a single unified theory.

Lee and Yang shared the 1957 Nobel Prize for Physics "for their penetrating investigation of the so-called parity laws, which has led to important discoveries regarding the elementary particles." On presenting the award, O. B. Klein of the Royal Swedish Academy of Sciences declared, "Through your consistent and unprejudiced thinking, you have been able to break a most puzzling deadlock in the field of elementary particle physics where now experimental and theoretical work is pouring forth as a result of your brilliant achievement."

Lee's other research interests include such diverse topics as field theory, statistical mechanics (the science of the atomic origin of thermal phenomena), hydrodynamics, turbulence, and astrophysics.

Lee married Hui-Chung Chin (known as Jeannette) in 1950; they have two sons. Lee is described by his colleagues as shy and reserved. Although he considers thinking his main activity, he likes to relax by reading mystery novels and listening to music. He became a United States citizen in 1963.

In 1957 Lee received the Albert Einstein Commemorative Award of Yeshiva University. Princeton University awarded him an honorary degree in 1958. He is a member of the National Academy of Sciences and a fellow of the American Physical Society.

SELECTED WORKS: Conservation Laws in Weak Interactions, 1957, with Chen Ning Yang; Elementary Particles and Weak Interactions, 1957, with Chen Ning Yang; Remarks on Nonvariance Under Time Reversal and Charge Conjugation, 1957, with Chen Ning Yang; Theory of Charged Vector Mesons Interacting With the Electromagnetic Field, 1963, with Chen Ning Yang; Particle Physics and Introduction to Field Theory, 1979.

ABOUT: Crease, R. P., and Mann, C. C. The Second Creation, 1986; Current Biography November 1958; New Yorker May 12, 1962.

LEE, YUAN T.
(November 29, 1936–)
Nobel Prize for Chemistry, 1986
(shared with Dudley R. Herschbach and John C. Polanyi)

The Chinese-American chemist Yuan Tseh Lee was born in the city of Hsinchu, Taiwan, to Tse Fan Lee, an artist and art teacher, and the former Pei Tsai, an elementary schoolteacher. His parents' ancestors had moved from mainland China in the sixteenth century. Lee's childhood education was interrupted during World War II when the Japanese occupied Taiwan, and Hsinchu's population was relocated to the mountains to avoid daily bombings by Allied aircraft. After the war, Lee was able to finish elementary school and enter Hsinchu High School, where he was an excellent student and played in the brass band. He graduated in 1955 with an outstanding academic record that gained him acceptance to the National Taiwan University without the normally required entrance examination.

As Lee later recalled, he was strongly impressed by a biography of MARIE CURIE, and it was her "beautiful life as a wonderful human being, her dedication toward science, her selflessness, and her idealism that made me decide to become a scientist." By the end of his freshman year, he had chosen a career in chemistry. Shortcomings in university facilities were offset by a free and exciting atmosphere, some dedicated professors, and student camaraderie. Lee obtained a B.S. in 1959, doing a research thesis on separation of the elements strontium and barium by paper electrophoresis (differential migration under the influence of an electric field).

Lee began graduate studies at the National Tsinghua University, where he received an M.S. in 1961 for research on natural radioisotopes (radioactive forms of elements) in Hokutolite, a mineral found in hot spring sediments. As a research assistant to C. H. Wong, he then used X-ray crystallography to determine the molecular structure of the organolanthanide compound tricyclopentadienyl samarium.

In 1962 Lee entered the University of California at Berkeley to continue his graduate studies. He considered working for DUDLEY R. HERSCHBACH but chose research under Bruce H. Mahan; he worked on chemi-ionization processes involving electronically excited alkali atoms and developed a special interest in ion-molecule reactions and the dynamics of molecular scattering. He received his Ph.D. in 1965 and remained in Mahan's

YUAN T. LEE

laboratory as a postdoctoral fellow for a year and a half, mastering the art of designing and constructing a powerful and sophisticated apparatus for measuring the scattering of atoms and molecules. He was able to achieve a remarkable and complete map of the distribution of the products of the reaction between positive nitrogen ions and neutral hydrogen molecules.

Meanwhile, Herschbach had moved to Harvard University in 1963 and performed successful experiments to explore the dynamics of reactions between neutral atoms and molecules using crossed molecular beams. Because the method at that time relied on a device called a surface ionization detector, it was limited to the study of systems containing alkali atoms. Lee joined Herschbach's group at Harvard in 1967 and began the design of a new, highly complicated apparatus to allow a wider range of scattering studies. His previous experience in building an ion-molecule scattering instrument proved invaluable. Aided by Herschbach's encouragement and enthusiasm, Lee succeeded in overcoming many technical difficulties by ingenious and imaginative innovations, particularly in advancing the art of differential pumping and the use of three pumping stages to achieve a rotatable ultrahigh-vacuum detector. The detector was a mass spectrometer, which applies magnetic and electric fields to deflect different ions along different paths, thus separating and identifying them. Within ten months, the apparatus was completed and the first study made of a hal-

ogen atom exchange reaction between chlorine and bromine. The alkali limit had been lifted. The new instrument was the first truly successful universal crossed-molecular-beam apparatus. Several orders of magnitude more sensitive than its competitors, it revolutionized the crossed-beam study of reaction dynamics and provided a powerful tool for modern chemical research.

Before Herschbach and Lee achieved their success with crossed molecular beams, only moderate progress had been made toward the understanding of chemical reactions since the nineteenth century. Quantum theory, which was introduced at the beginning of the twentieth century, enabled scientists to elucidate atomic and molecular structure and to explain many of the observations of chemical behavior. Many details were lacking, however, and chemists were still limited primarily to mixing substances under various conditions and tallying the products of reactions. Theoretical models were essentially static, viewing collections of interacting molecules as small balls occupying the same volume, bouncing against each other, and occasionally merging to form new arrangements. Data were generally statistical, dealing with averages rather than individual events. The crossed-beam technique directed streams of relatively free molecules of different kinds to a region of intersection where reaction took place. Using ingenious detectors, experimenters then analyzed the velocities, directions, and energies of reaction products from which they could deduce the mechanisms of reaction and the dynamics of collisons between individual molecules. This method provided unique and detailed insights previously unattainable, such as the role played by angular momentum in the reactions and the distribution of chemically released energy between the velocity of flight and internal vibrations of the reaction products.

Lee became an assistant professor of chemistry at the University of Chicago in 1968, associate professor in 1971, and full professor in 1973. In 1974 he returned to California as professor of chemistry and principal investigator at the University of California's Lawrence Berkeley Laboratory. Lee's laboratory quickly became noted for its outstanding work in physical chemistry and chemical physics. His studies of reactions between oxygen and hydrocarbon molecules as large as benzene and toluene laid a fundamental basis for advances in combustion chemistry. Lee imaginatively combined molecular beam chemistry with laser technology to solve many chemical problems, such as the mechanism of the glyoxal triple dissociation.

Lee shared the 1986 Nobel Prize for Chemistry with Herschbach and JOHN C. POLANYI "for their contributions concerning the dynamics of elementary chemical processes." The presentation cited Lee specifically for his contributions to making the crossed molecular beam applicable to relatively large molecules.

In 1963 Lee married Bernice Chinli Wu, whom he had known since elementary school. They have two sons and a daughter. He is known as a modest man, intensely devoted to his research. The spirit and sense of excitement in his laboratory have attracted bright young scientists from all over the world. Lee became a United States citizen in 1974.

In addition to the Nobel Prize, Lee has received many awards and prizes, including the Ernest Orlando Lawrence Memorial Award for Physics of the United States Energy Research and Development Agency (1981), the Harrison E. Howe Lectureship (1983) and the Peter Debye Award in Physical Chemistry (1986) of the American Chemical Society, and the National Medal of Science of the National Science Foundation (1986). He has also received an honorary doctorate from the University of Waterloo, Canada.

ABOUT: New York Times October 16, 1986; Research and Development December 1986; Science November 7, 1986; Scientific American December 1986; Time October 27, 1986.

LEGER, ALEXIS SAINT-LEGER
See PERSE, SAINT-JOHN

LELOIR, LUIS F.
(September 6, 1906–   )
Nobel Prize for Chemistry, 1970

The Argentine biochemist Luis Federico Leloir (lā lwär') was born in Paris while his parents, Federico Leloir and Hortensia (Aguirre) Leloir, were visiting France. When the boy was two the family returned home to Buenos Aires, where Leloir attended elementary and secondary schools. Entering the University of Buenos Aires to study medicine, he received his medical degree in 1932. Subsequently he worked in the hospital of the university for two years, but, feeling dissatisfied with the limited medical treatment then available, he began working at the university's Institute of Physiology under BERNARDO

HOUSSAY on the role of adrenal glands in carbohydrate metabolism.

His interest in biochemistry increasing, Leloir went in 1936 to the Biochemical Laboratory of Cambridge University, England, an important research center directed by FREDERICK GOWLAND HOPKINS. After a year of research on the biochemistry of enzymes, Lelior returned to the Institute of Physiology in Buenos Aires, where he studied ethanol metabolism and the oxidation of fatty acids in cell-free liver extracts. Such study was unusual because intact cell structures were then thought to be necessary for this process. Leloir then joined a group of scientists studying the role of the kidney in the regulation of blood pressure. This work led to the discovery of the peptide angiotensin, which is split by renin, an enzyme secreted by the kidney, from angiotensinogen, a protein formed by the liver.

Following the rise of Juan Perón in Argentina in 1943, Houssay was dismissed and his research team disbanded. Leaving for the United States, Leloir worked as a research assistant in the biochemical laboratories of CARL F. CORI at Washington University in St. Louis, Missouri, and then under David E. Green at the College of Physicians and Surgeons of Columbia University in New York. Returning to Argentina two years later, Leloir conducted research at the Institute of Biology and Experimental Medicine, a private institution in Buenos Aires headed by Houssay. With financial support from Jaime Campomar, owner of a textile company, the Institute for Biochemical Investigations was established in 1947, with Leloir as its director.

The initial goal of research at the new institute was the synthesis of milk sugar, or lactose. At the time, biochemists knew that the body's process of breaking down carbohydrates (polysaccharides and starches) into simpler sugars provides energy and is vital for life. However, far less was known about how these complex organic molecules are synthesized by living systems.

In the search for an enzyme to catalyze the reversible synthesis of lactose, a form of sugar present in milk, Leloir and his colleagues found that the process required the presence of heat-labile enzymes and two heat-stable cofactors, which he identified as glucose-1,6-diphosphate and a nucleoside, uridine diphosphoglucose (UDPG). As Leloir later said, "The presence of uridine in a cofactor was rather novel because in other compounds . . . the nucleoside present was adenine. The occurrence of a sugar

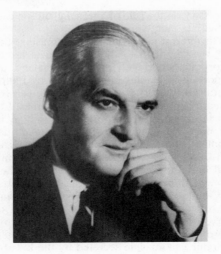

LUIS F. LELOIR

derivative combined with a nucleoside was also novel."

Believing that UDPG must have other functions besides acting as a cofactor in galactose metabolism, Leloir and his associates found that it serves as a glucose donor in the formation of the disaccharides trehalose phosphate and sucrose phosphate. Workers in different laboratories soon discovered numerous other sugar nucleotides and demonstrated their two principal functions: first, to serve in the interconversion of simple sugars, and second, to act as donors in glucose-transfer reactions, leading to the synthesis of di- and polysaccharides. In 1959, after finding that glycogen (the storage form of glucose in animals) is formed from UDPG, Leloir and his colleagues analyzed the synthesis of starch in plants and demonstrated that the sugar nucleotide involved is adenosine diphosphate (ADP) glucose.

When Perón's dictatorship was overthrown in 1955, the new government provided a larger building for the Institute of Biochemical Research. In 1962 the institute became affiliated with the University of Buenos Aires, with Leloir as chairman of the Department of Biochemistry, an administrative position he later gave up to spend more time in the laboratory.

"For his discovery of sugar nucleotides and their role in the biosynthesis of carbohydrates," Leloir was awarded the 1970 Nobel Prize for Chemistry. "Leloir established that the transformation reaction does not occur in the sugars as such," said Karl Myrbäck of the Royal Swedish Academy of Sciences in his presentation address, "but in the corresponding sugar nucleotides. . . . Other scientists were quick to grasp the fundamental importance of Leloir's discovery," Myrbäck continued. "Today more than one hundred sugar nucleotides, which are essential participants in various reactions, are known and well characterized." After receiving the prize, Leloir became a national hero in Argentina, and a postage stamp with his portrait was issued.

In his recent biochemical research, Leloir has investigated the role of lipid intermediates in the synthesis of polysaccharides from nucleotide sugars, as well as the participation of dolichol, a polyisoprene substance, in the synthesis of glycoproteins, which are components of biological membranes and immunological blood group substances.

Described as a courteous, accessible man by his students and colleagues, Leloir has been praised for his ability to conduct significant scientific research with limited financial resources. Leloir married Amelie Zuherbuhler in 1943. The couple have one daughter. He and his wife continue to live in Buenos Aires.

In addition to playing a substantial role in the development of the Argentine Society for Biochemical Research and the Panamerican Association of Biochemical Societies, Leloir has received prizes and honorary degrees from universities worldwide and is a member in the American National Academy of Sciences, the American Academy of Arts and Sciences, the American Philosophical Society, and the Pontifical Academy of Sciences, and the Royal Academy of London.

SELECTED WORKS: Renal Hypertension, 1946, with others; The Biosynthesis of Glycoproteins, 1976.

ABOUT: The Excitement and Fascination of Science, volume 2, 1978; New York Times November 6, 1970; Science November 6, 1970.

LENARD, PHILIPP VON
(June 7, 1862–May 20, 1947)
Nobel Prize for Physics, 1905

The German physicist Philipp Eduard Anton von Lenard was born in Pressburg, Austria-Hungary (now Bratislava, Czechoslovakia), the only child of Philipp von Lenard, a prosperous wine merchant, and the former Antonie Baumann. When he was young, his mother died, and Lenard was brought up by an aunt who later married his father. Lenard was taught at home until he was nine years old, then attended the cathedral school and later the Pressburg secondary school. His favorite subjects were mathematics and physics, and he supplemented school studies by reading college textbooks and doing chemistry and physics experiments on his own.

Despite Lenard's interest in science, his father wanted him to join the family business and permitted him to continue his studies only at technical universities in Budapest and Vienna, primarily to learn the chemistry of winemaking. In 1882 Lenard reluctantly began to work for his father. After a year, he used his savings for a trip to Germany where he attended lectures by the famous chemist Robert Wilhelm Bunsen (originator of the Bunsen burner), which reinforced his ambition to become a scientist. In the winter of 1883 he entered the University of Heidelberg to study physics. After four semesters at Heidelberg and two at the University of Berlin, studying under such noted scientists as Bunsen and the physicist and physiologist Hermann von Helmholtz, Lenard received his doctoral degree with highest honors from Heidelberg in 1886. His dissertation was on the vibration of water drops. He remained at Heidelberg for three more years as an assistant to the German physicist Georg Quincke.

Lenard had begun doing research on phosphorescence several years before with his secondary school physics teacher Virgil Klatt, working with him during university vacations. They found that some materials phosphoresced only if they contained trace amounts of certain metals. Lenard was to study the subject for more than forty years while working on other projects.

After leaving Heidelberg, he worked briefly in London and Breslau (now Wrocław, Poland) and, in April 1891, became Heinrich Hertz's assistant at the University of Bonn. Hertz, who was already famous for having discovered the electromagnetic radiation predicted by James Clerk Maxwell, had accidentally discovered the photoelectric effect (emission of electricity by surfaces struck by radiation, in this case ultraviolet rays). One of Hertz's main interests had become the mysterious cathode rays that traveled from the negative electrode (cathode) of a glass vacuum discharge tube to the opposite end. Many scientists were pursuing similar investigations, notably the English physicist William Crookes. The topic had attracted Lenard's attention in 1880 when he had read Crookes's paper "Radiant Matter, or the Fourth Physical State."

PHILIPP VON LENARD

Hertz and Lenard sought to study the cathode rays more conveniently outside the discharge tube. Since Hertz had found that the rays penetrated thin aluminum foil, Lenard constructed a glass vacuum tube sealed at the anode (positive electrode) end by a thin piece of aluminum, which came to be known as a Lenard window. Using a phosphorescent screen as a detector (it glowed when struck by the rays), Lenard found that the rays emerged for a short distance into the air outside the aluminum window. By replacing the air with a second vacuum tube, he produced a longer beam of cathode rays, separated from their origin and more accessible to experiment. He deflected the beam with magnetic and electric fields, showing that they carried a negative electric charge, and was able to measure the ratio of charge to mass of particles he had previously believed to be nonmaterial radiation. He also found that the particles penetrated air and other substances to different depths, that absorption was approximately proportional to thickness and density, and that the rays were more penetrating at higher tube voltages, which corresponded to greater velocities and energies.

Lenard's research on cathode rays continued for twelve years while he moved from one academic position to another. Upon Hertz's death in 1894 at the age of thirty-six, Lenard briefly became acting director of the Physical Institute of the University of Bonn. He then spent periods of one or two years teaching at the universities of Breslau, Aachen, and Heidelberg before becoming a full professor and director of the physics laboratory at the University of Kiel in 1898. Despite the recognition given his work, Lenard was sensitive to perceived slights and jealous of the success of others. Although he had greatly respected Hertz, he had sometimes felt neglected at Bonn. When WILHELM RÖNTGEN discovered X rays (created by the impact of cathode rays with parts of the discharge tube) in 1895, Lenard was depressed that he had not found them first. He referred to them only as "high-frequency radiation" and never called them by their common name, Röntgen rays. He even felt that his loan of a tube to Röntgen should have been acknowledged as a contribution to the discovery. When J. J. THOMSON was credited in 1897 with discovering the electron in cathode rays, Lenard claimed priority, even though Thomson had given the modern description of the particle while Lenard, as late as 1906, was still calling the electron "electricity without material, electrical charges without charged bodies" and said it was "*electricity itself.*"

One of Lenard's major scientific contributions was his observation, in 1902, that a free electron (which he called a cathode ray) must have at least a certain energy to ionize a gas (cause it to be electrically charged) by knocking a bound electron out of an atom (he called the displaced atomic electrons secondary cathode rays). His estimate of the ionization potential (required energy) for hydrogen was remarkably accurate. Also in 1902, he showed that the photoelectric effect produces the same electrons found in cathode rays, that the photoelectrons are not merely dislodged from the metal surface but ejected with a certain amount of energy (velocity), and that the number of emitted electrons rises with the intensity of radiation but that their velocities never exceed a certain limit. These experimental data were explained by ALBERT EINSTEIN in 1905 in his remarkable application of MAX PLANCK's quantum theory. (According to Einstein, light consists of small discrete packets of energy that later became known as photons. The energy in a photon is proportional to the frequency of the light. In the photoelectric effect, each photon conveys its energy to an electron in the irradiated metal surface, enabling it to break free. A more intense light has more photons, which liberate more electrons, but the fixed energy in each photon sets a limit on each electron's escaping velocity.)

In 1903 Lenard presented his hypothesis that the atom is largely empty space, based on his observation of how electrons passed through a Lenard window and penetrated air and other substances. He proposed that negative and positive electric charges in the atom (the amounts must be equal to maintain electric neutrality) were arranged tightly in pairs he called dynamids. This concept was interesting and an advance over previous views. However, it was incorrect, as ERNEST RUTHERFORD demonstrated some eight years later with his atomic model consisting of a very dense positive nucleus orbited by relatively distant negative electrons.

Although Lenard narrowly missed making several discoveries that brought acclaim to others, he was awarded the 1905 Nobel Prize for Physics "for his work on cathode rays." On presenting the award, Arne Lindstedt of the Royal Swedish Academy of Sciences said, "It is clear that Lenard's work on cathode rays has not only enriched our knowledge of these phenomena, but has also served in many respects as a basis for the development of the electron theory."

In 1907 Lenard became Quincke's successor as professor of experimental physics at the University of Heidelberg. In 1909 he assumed the added duties of director of Heidelberg's newly formed Radiological Institute. His most productive work at the institute involved spectral analysis of the light emitted by excited atoms and molecules.

Although Lenard's reputation remained high in some German circles, it began to suffer among the modern physicists. Einstein described as "infantile" a 1910 speech by Lenard on the largely discredited ether that was supposed to permeate space. Moreover, at the outbreak of World War I, Lenard became an ardent nationalist who accused the English of usurping the achievements of German scientists. After Germany's defeat, he despised the democratic Weimar Republic as peacefully accepting dishonor and tried to incite students against it. He was an early supporter of Adolf Hitler and became a bitter anti-Semite. His anti-Semitism was reinforced by his penchant for experimental investigations, which he called "pragmatic German physics," and by his distaste for the tendency toward difficult mathematical theories, which he called "dogmatic Jewish physics." He seemed to have a particular animosity toward Einstein, whom he sharply attacked at a 1920 science conference, according to MAX BORN, "with an unconcealed anti-Semitic bias." He even retroactively divided his estimation of Hertz's work into good experiment and bad theory, attributing the bad to Hertz's Jewish ancestry. After the Nazis came to power in 1933, Lenard received the title of Chief of Aryan or German Physics and was a personal adviser to Hitler, giving the Führer a racially oriented version of physics.

Lenard married the former Katharina Schlehner in 1897. He left Heidelberg in 1945 to settle in the village of Messelhausen, where he died two years later. Scientists generally have condemned his ideological biases, which clouded his scientific judgment in his later years. Carl Ramsauer, Lenard's pupil and colleague for over thirteen years, called him "a tragic figure," stating that "his achievements were of fundamental importance, and yet his name is not closely or permanently linked with any landmark in the evolution of physics."

In addition to the Nobel Prize, Lenard's many awards included the Franklin Medal of the Franklin Institute and honorary doctorates from the universities of Christiania (now Oslo), Dresden, and Pressburg. He also received the Eagle Shield of the German Reich in 1933.

SELECTED WORKS: Great Men of Science: A History of Scientific Progress, 1933.

ABOUT: Dictionary of Scientific Biography, volume 8, 1973; Nature December 27, 1947.

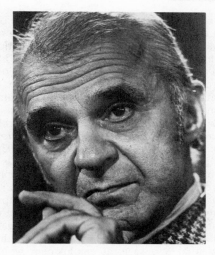

WASSILY LEONTIEF

LEONTIEF, WASSILY
(August 5, 1906–)
Nobel Memorial Prize in Economic
    Sciences, 1973

The American economist Wassily Leontief (lē ōn′ tēf) was born in St. Petersburg (now Leningrad), Russia, to Wassily Leontief, a professor of economics, and the former Eugenia Bekker. The years of Leontief's childhood were a time of great social and political upheaval. He was eight years old when World War I began. He experienced firsthand the turmoil of the Russian Revolution and remembers seeing Lenin address a mass rally at the Winter Palace in Leningrad.

Entering the University of Leningrad in 1921, Leontief first studied philosophy and sociology and then economics. After graduating in 1925, he continued his education at the University of Berlin. While still a graduate student, he began his professional career as a research associate in economics at the University of Kiel in 1927–1928. At the age of twenty-two, he received a Ph.D. in economics.

Leontief spent the following year in Nan-

king as economic adviser to the Chinese Ministry of Railroads. Emigrating to the United States in 1931, he joined the National Bureau of Economic Research. In 1932 he married the poet Estelle Helena Marks. Their only daughter, Svetlana Alpers, later became a professor of art history at the University of California at Berkeley.

Leontief began his long tenure at Harvard University in 1931 as an instructor in economics. In 1946 he was promoted to full professor. Two years later he founded the Harvard Economic Research Project, a center for research in input-output analysis. He directed the project until its closing in 1973. Also at Harvard, Leontief held the Henry Lee Chair of Political Economics from 1953 until he resigned in 1975 to become a professor of economics and director of the Institute for Economic Analysis at New York University.

Since the publication of his first paper on input-output analysis in 1936, Leontief's scientific writing has been characterized by a high degree of analytical rigor and a broad interest in general economic issues. Although he himself is a skilled mathematician, Leontief has consistently criticized attempts to apply advanced mathematical theories to explain world economic problems. In his view, economics is an applied science, and its theories are useful only if they can be empirically implemented.

This view was clearly demonstrated in his first book, published in 1941, *The Structure of the American Economy, 1919–1929: An Empirical Application of Equilibrium Analysis*. This seminal work describing his method of analyzing economic input and output is the basis of Leontief's reputation as an outstanding innovator in the field of economics. Recognition for his system, however, came slowly in a world that was gripped in the Great Depression. Chronic unemployment and the instability of capitalist economies were then the leading economic issues, and the English economist John Maynard Keynes had captured the world's attention with his *General Theory of Employment, Interest, and Money,* published in 1936.

During World War II unemployment as a problem vanished, but afterward it rose sharply. In response to these changes, the first major policy applications of Leontief's input-output analysis were made by the United States Bureau of Labor Statistics. First in 1939 and again in 1947, Leontief's model was used to predict how total and sectoral employment would change as the economy shifted from peace to war and back again. The economics of disarmament subsequently became one of Leontief's lifelong research interests. In less than a decade after the bureau's analyses, Leontief's method had become a basic ingredient in the national accounting systems of most countries, both capitalist and socialist. It is still being applied and refined today in government and international agencies and research institutions around the world.

Input-output analysis belongs to the branch of economics pioneered by the nineteenth-century French economist Léon Walras and known as general equilibrium theory. It focuses on the interdependence of economic relationships through a system of equations representing an economy as a whole. From the beginning of his work, Leontief acknowledged Walras's system of interrelationships. But until Leontief systematically applied these interrelationships, general equilibrium analysis was not a practical tool for policymaking purposes. Before Leontief's innovations, the principal methodology in mainstream economics was *partial* equilibrium analysis, focusing on the effects of a few changing variables. Thus, an economist might examine how a tax on imported oil would affect the demand for automotive gasoline, while ignoring any repercussions such a tax might have on the steel industry. Economists had long been aware that partial equilibrium analysis could be seriously misleading if the industry or the changes being studied were large.

Leontief's adaptation of Walras's system to solve this problem, and the heart of his input-output method of analysis, is a transactions table. This table divides the economy into many sectors (originally forty-four). Sales of intermediate products and finished goods from sectors listed down the left-hand side appear in vertical columns under the same sectors ranged in a row across the top. A second table, or grid, of "technical coefficients" is derived from the closed model transactions table. When these coefficients are placed in a set of equations that are solved simultaneously, a third table, the "Leontief inverse," is produced, revealing what each sector requires to produce one additional dollar's worth of output.

The significance of the Leontief inverse is threefold. First, improvements in international data collection in recent decades are largely attributable to its increasing use, because it requires systematic assembly of an enormous amount of economic data. Second, the inverse reveals the inner workings of an economy in great detail, limited only by the burdens of the calculation. Third, once demands for finished goods are specified or projected into the future, the inverse can be used for policy analysis, because it shows both directly and indirectly what each sector requires in input to increase output.

Leontief improved his system in the 1950s and 1960s. With the advent of more sophisticated computers, he increased the number of economic sectors and relaxed several simplifying assumptions, notably that the technical coefficients held constant despite changing prices or developing technologies. To examine the problems of economic growth and development, Leontief devised a dynamic version of the previously static input-output analysis model by adding capital requirements to the list of so-called final demands or final sales. Because input-output proved to be a useful analytic tool in the emerging field of regional economics, transactions tables were developed for several American cities. Gradually, the construction of such tables became standard. In the United States Department of Commerce, for example, the Interindustry Economics Division began to publish tables at five-year intervals. The United Nations, the World Bank, and most governments, including that of the Soviet Union, also embraced input-output analysis as an essential technique in economic planning and government budgeting.

Input-output analysis also remained a fruitful technique in basic economic research, where Leontief continued to make important contributions. For example, although he started with fixed technical coefficients, as had Walras, Leontief later applied flexible coefficients to price relations and technical development. In the mid-1950s he showed that America's exports were more labor-intensive than its imports, thereby challenging a basic tenet of international trade theory. Known as the "Leontief paradox," this basic concept has led to a deeper understanding of trading patterns among nations.

Leontief's success in applying the input-output model of economic analysis has resulted in part from his outstanding ability as a general economist with interests in several fields, such as the theories of international trade and of monopoly, and in econometrics. Leontief's attitude to methodology has been clear throughout his decades of scientific work. He opposed what he calls "implicit" economic theorizing along the line of the Cambridge School (JOHN HICKS and Keynes). In *Essays in Economics: Theories and Theorizing* (1966), Leontief wrote: "What counts is the relevance of the basic material premises, the capability to exploit effectively all factual data at hand and to identify the promising directions of further theoretical inquiry and empirical research."

Leontief was awarded the 1973 Nobel Memorial Prize in Economic Sciences "for the development of the input-output method and for its application to important economic problems." One of the first economists to consider the impact of economic activity on the quality of the environment, Leontief outlined in his Nobel lecture a simple input-output model of the world economy in which pollution was explicitly treated as a separate sector. "In less developed countries," he concluded, "the inauguration of abatement activities [strict antipollution standards] . . . would bring about expanded employment while requiring some sacrifices in consumption."

Leontief's research into the impact of differing economic strategies on the environment and on world economic development has continued. An interim summary of research in this area, *The Future of the World Economy* by Leontief and others, was published in 1977. His work on world economic problems, especially interindustrial relations, is continuing under the auspices of the United Nations and the Institute for Economic Analysis at New York University. Leontief's input-output analysis has become a classic technique of economics, and he is considered equal to Keynes as a major contributor to twentieth-century economic science.

Leontief is a naturalized American citizen. In addition to being awarded the Nobel Prize, he was made an officer in the Legion of Honor of France. He is a member of the National Academy of Sciences, the American Academy of Arts and Sciences, the British Academy, and the Royal Statistical Society in London. He served as president of the Econometric Society in 1954 and of the American Economic Association in 1970. He holds honorary doctoral degrees from the universities of Brussels, York, Louvain, and Paris, among others.

ADDITIONAL WORKS: Studies in the Structure of the American Economy, 1953, with others; Input-Output Economics, 1966; The New Outlook in Economics, 1967; The Economic System in an Age of Discontinuity, 1976; Essays in Economics, volume 2: Theories, Facts, and Policies, 1977; Military Spending, 1983, with Faye Duchin; The Future Impact of Automation on Workers, 1986, with Faye Duchin.

ABOUT: Agarwal, J. P., et al. The Future of the World Economy: An Appraisal of Leontief's Study, 1978; Current Biography January 1967; Leontief, E. Genia and Wassily: A Memoir, 1983; Science November 9, 1973; Sill, D. L. (ed.) International Encyclopedia of the Social Sciences: Biographical Supplement, 1979; Swedish Journal of Economics, number 4, 1973.

LEVI-MONTALCINI, RITA

(April 22, 1909–   )
Nobel Prize for Physiology or Medicine, 1986
(shared with Stanley Cohen)

The Italian-American biologist Rita Levi-Montalcini (lä′ vē môn täl chē′ nē) was born Rita Levi, one of twin sisters, in Turin. She added her mother's maiden name to her surname when she began her professional career. Although she came from what she characterized as an intellectual Jewish family, her father had the old-fashioned attitude that women should not pursue careers. Nevertheless, after completing her early education, she entered the University of Turin Medical School, much against her father's wishes, and received a medical degree in 1936 and a degree for specialization in neurology and psychiatry in 1940. Among her Turin classmates were RENATO DULBECCO and SALVADOR LURIA. Training in her specialty included service as an assistant to the histologist and embryologist Giuseppe Levi in the University of Turin Clinic of Neurology and Psychiatry and study at the Neurologic Institute of Brussels, Belgium. It was Giuseppe Levi who stimulated her interest in neuroembryological research.

During the war years 1940–1943, when the Fascist government's anti-Semitic laws pre-

RITA LEVI-MONTALCINI

vented her from working at the university, Levi-Montalcini conducted research in her bedroom in a house in the Turin countryside. When the Nazis occupied northern Italy, she moved to Florence, where she managed to work in her small apartment. In 1944, after the Allied liberation of Italy was under way, she provided medical services for the American army in a camp for Italian refugees. She was able to return to her research work in 1945 as an assistant at the University of Turin Institute of Anatomy.

Levi-Montalcini was impressed by research done in the United States by Viktor Hamburger, a developmental neurobiologist at Washington University in St. Louis, even though Hamburger disagreed with her novel idea that the programmed death of nerve cells played a role in the normal development of the nervous system. At Hamburger's invitation, she went to St. Louis in 1947 to collaborate with him as a research associate in the Washington University zoology department. Modifying experiments performed earlier by the American anatomist Elmer Bueker, they grafted mouse tumors onto chick embryos and found that the embryos' nerve cells grew rapidly into the tumors. The same thing happened even when the tumors were not in direct contact with the embryos. Levi-Montalcini's observations suggested to her that the nerve growth was being guided by some unknown stimulating substance in the tumors. Since embryological procedures were slow and difficult, she turned to the then-developing field of tissue culture as a more effective way to demonstrate conclusively the existence of the substance. In 1952 she flew to Rio de Janeiro to learn the required technique from a friend, Herta Meyer. In the Brazilian laboratory, she sliced mouse tumors into small pieces, cultured the pieces in chick blood and embryonic extract, then added chick embryo sensory nerve cells and incubated the mixture. Within twelve hours nerve fibers grew toward and then around the tumor pieces, creating a characteristic halo. Further experiments showed that extracts from the tumors were as effective as the tumors themselves. Existence of the stimulating substance seemed assured, and Levi-Montalcini named it nerve growth factor (NGF).

In 1953 the American biochemist and zoologist STANLEY COHEN joined Levi-Montalcini at Washington University. Their collaboration established that NGF was a protein and that snake venom and the salivary gland of adult male mice were even richer sources than the tumors. Cohen purified NGF, determined its chemical structure, and produced NGF antibodies. The two researchers found that the antibodies not only inhibited the action of NGF but could selectively and permanently destroy sympathetic nerve tissues (related to the contraction of blood vessels and secretions of glands). Cohen also discovered a second substance, first noted as a contaminant in NGF preparations, which he called epidermal growth factor (EGF) because it stimulated the growth of cells in the skin and cornea. Levi-Montalcini continued to study the biological effects and mechanism of action of NGF.

Levi-Montalcini became an associate professor at Washington University in 1951 and a full professor in 1958. In the 1960s she began to spend more time with her family in Italy and set up a laboratory with Pietro Angeletti at the Higher Institute of Health in Rome. The laboratory participated in a joint research program with Washington University from 1961 to 1969. Levi-Montalcini was known as an inspirational leader for whom researchers worked diligently on NGF studies, often at personal sacrifice when funding lapsed. In 1969 she established the Laboratory of Cell Biology of the Italian National Research Council in Rome, served as its director until 1979, and then continued as a full-time researcher. From 1969 to 1977 she was also a professor in the Washington University biology department. At first, her laboratory was alone in its NGF research, but its work opened a broad new field of neurobiological study in which scientists in many countries now participate.

At first, the idea of a growth factor such as NGF was not readily accepted. It is not a conventional hormone, which evokes a transient metabolic response, but a previously unknown type of molecule necessary for the development and survival of a specific cell type. Many other growth factors have been discovered subsequently, including Cohen's EGF, colony stimulating factors (CSFs), platelet-derived growth factor (PDGF), fibroblast growth factor (FGF), and the interleukins (IL-1, IL-2). In the 1980s it was found that oncogenes, cancer-causing genetic elements, carry a code for the manufacture of proteins similar in structure to growth factors and their receptors (chemical groupings on cell surfaces that bind to specific substances). This finding suggested that cancers may involve a failure in the regulation of growth factors. Growth factors for different types of nerve cells have been discovered. Therapeutic applications are being explored, such as the use of NGF to repair damaged nerves and the use of EGF to improve the effectiveness of skin transplants.

The 1986 Nobel Prize for Physiology or Medicine was awarded to Levi-Montalcini and Cohen "in recognition of their discoveries which are of fundamental importance for our understanding of the mechanisms which regulate cell and organ growth." Levi-Montalcini's discovery of NGF was called "a fascinating example of how a skilled observer can create a concept out of apparent chaos."

Levi-Montalcini, who has never married, remains close to her family and lives in Rome with her twin sister, Paola Levi, an artist. She has been described as a vivacious, elegant woman who is warm and considerate in her associations with co-workers and friends. In St. Louis, her intimate dinner parties were distinguished by fine cooking and stimulating conversation. In addition to her work in the Rome laboratory, she helps young scientists and is active in promoting the development of science in Italy. She is a dual citizen of Italy and the United States.

In addition to the Nobel Prize, Levi-Montalcini has received numerous awards and honors in Italy as well as the William Thomson Wakeman Award of the National Paraplegic Foundation (1974), the Lewis S. Rosenstiel Award for Distinguished Work in Basic Medical Research of Brandeis University (1982), the Louisa Gross Horwitz Prize of Columbia University (1983), and the Albert Lasker Basic Medical Research Award (1986). She is a member of the Harvey Society; the American Academy of Arts and Sciences; the American National Academy of Sciences; the Pontifical Academy of Sciences; the Belgian Royal Academy of Medicine; the National Academy of Sciences of Italy; the European Academy of Sciences, Arts, and Letters; and the Academy of Arts and Sciences of Florence. She has also received honorary doctorates from the University of Uppsala, the Weizmann Institute of Science, St. Mary College, and the Washington University School of Medicine.

SELECTED WORKS: Symposium on the Nerve Growth Factor, 1964, with others; "The Nerve Growth Factor," Scientific American June 1979, with Pietro Calissano; Molecular Aspects of Neurobiology, 1986.

ABOUT: Alberts, B., et al. (eds.) Molecular Biology of the Cell, 1983; New York Times October 14, 1986; Science October 31, 1986; Science News May 21, 1977.

LEWIS, SINCLAIR
(February 7, 1885–January 10, 1951)
Nobel Prize for Literature, 1930

The American novelist Harry Sinclair Lewis was born in Sauk Centre, a newly settled village of less than 3,000 inhabitants in the heart of Minnesota's corn-growing region. Lewis scathingly recreated his hometown, calling it Gopher Prairie, in the novel *Main Street* (1920). His father, Edwin J. Lewis, was a country doctor not unlike *Main Street*'s Dr. Kennicott. His mother, Emma (Kermott) Lewis, the daughter of a Canadian physician who fought in the Union army during the Civil War, suffered from tuberculosis and spent winters convalescing in the Southwest. She died when Lewis was five years old, and a year later his father married Isabel Warner. According to Mark Schorer, one of his biographers, Lewis's upbringing was adamantly middle-class and "curiously loveless."

Lewis, the youngest of three sons, was an ungainly, acne-scarred, redheaded boy whose unconventional views and behavior sometimes provoked ridicule from his peers and elders in Sauk Centre. He disliked sports and preferred reading poetry and taking solitary walks to more active pursuits. In 1902, at the age of seventeen, he entered Oberlin Academy. He aspired, however, to Yale University and, after a year, was accepted and moved to New Haven, Connecticut. At Yale, Lewis wrote verse in the pseudomedieval style of such then-popular Victorian poets as Algernon Swinburne and Alfred Lord Tennyson. In a rare distinction for a freshman, one of his gothic ballads

SINCLAIR LEWIS

was accepted by the *Yale Literary Magazine.* Lewis later served on the magazine's editorial staff and was considered a promising young writer. Although he won the respect of several professors who appreciated his intelligence and wit, Lewis later claimed that he felt no more comfortable in the Yale social scene than he did in Sauk Centre. The summer after his sophomore year, finding himself miserable in Sauk Centre, Lewis conceived the idea for a novel about provincial life to be called "The Village Virus," which a decade and a half later evolved into *Main Street.*

During his 1904 and 1906 college summer vacations, he traveled to England by cattle boat and gathered notes for his fiction. After his trip in 1906, he returned to Yale for his senior year. Soon, however, feeling bored and restless, he fled from New Haven to work as a janitor at Upton Sinclair's socialist commune, Helicon Hall, near Englewood, New Jersey. The experience began to pall, however, and by December Lewis had moved to New York City, where he tried his hand at free-lance work. Some of his poems and short stories were published in a number of magazines, and he became assistant editor of *Transatlantic Tales.*

Near the end of the following year, Lewis sailed to Panama, tried unsuccessfully to find a job working on the canal, and returned to New York in December. In January 1908 he resumed his classes at Yale and received his B.A. in June. Meanwhile, a magazine in San Francisco had accepted several of his poems, one of which drew favorable comments from

William Rose Benét, who sent the young writer an encouraging letter. A period of restless wandering ensued. After returning home briefly, Lewis found newspaper jobs in Waterloo, Iowa; San Francisco; and Washington, D.C.; but he either quit them or was fired.

During a brief stay at an artists' colony in Carmel, California, Lewis became acquainted with such writers as George Sterling and Jack London. Unable to sell his own stories, Lewis was reduced to selling plot ideas to London; a few of these ultimately became published stories. In 1910 Lewis moved back to New York City, where for the next five years he worked in book publishing houses and for various magazines. Lewis's first published work was a boys' book, *Hike and the Aeroplane* (1912), which appeared under the pseudonym Tom Graham. A little more than a year later, Lewis published his first serious novel, *Our Mr. Wrenn* (1914). This realistically told tale is the semiautobiographical story of a young dreamer who adventurously journeys to London, where he finds both romance and disillusionment, and from which he returns, somewhat chastened and undoubtedly more worldly. It was followed by *The Trail of the Hawk* (1915), a work that, according to the contemporary American scholar Martin Light, "is a tribute to quixotic romance, a youthful, optimistic novel." Although both books were moderately well received, they failed to provide Lewis with an adequate income.

In 1914 Lewis married Grace Livingstone Hegger. The couple had a son, Wells, named for the British writer H. G. Wells. In 1928 they were divorced, and a few weeks later Lewis married Dorothy Thompson, a well-known journalist with whom he had a son, Michael. The marriage ended in divorce in 1942.

Lewis's career as a professional writer began in earnest in 1915 when the *Saturday Evening Post* paid him $1,000 for his story "Nature, Inc." With other such financial prospects on the horizon, Lewis quit his job at the publishing house of George H. Doran and Company and devoted himself to writing fiction full-time. During the next four years, he wrote scores of stories for popular periodicals as well as three more novels of uneven quality. If *The Job* (1917) is regarded as one of the best of his early books, *The Innocents* (1917) is often considered his worst. By 1919 Lewis had also published *Free Air,* a fictionalized account of a cross-country automobile trip.

It was the appearance of the controversial novel *Main Street* in 1920 that suddenly established Lewis's reputation as a significant novelist and social critic. Until then, most American writers had treated small-town life with humor and sympathy, contrasting its innocence with the decadence and corruption of urban life. *Main Street,* however, brilliantly satirizes the bigotry, narrow-mindedness, and complacency that Lewis observed beneath the surface of small-town, middle-class American life. The novel's heroine, Carol Kennicott, marries a stolid small-town doctor and moves to Gopher Prairie, hoping to infuse the town with her ideals and enthusiasm for culture. Instead, she finds herself infected with the "village virus" of smugness and provincialism.

Alternately praised and damned for its social thesis, *Main Street* was widely acclaimed as a literary work. For instance, the American critic Stanton A. Coblentz, writing a few months after the novel's publication, noted "that neither Jane Austen nor George Eliot depicted the provincial England of the past with more vividness than that with which Mr. Lewis portrays the present-day American small town, its humor and its pathos, its meanness and its potential greatness, its innumerable petty comedies and its hidden, sordid tragedies." According to the American scholar Perry Miller, many of Lewis's creative instincts derived from his familiarity with Charles Dickens. "He knew Dickens by heart," Miller wrote, and in works like *Main Street* sought to apply "Dickensian exaggeration in a modern situation."

Main Street was followed by even more controversial works, each focusing on a separate aspect of American society. *Babbitt* (1922) exposed the hypocrisy and shallowness of middle-class businessmen. *Arrowsmith* (1925) examined the life of a doctor caught between his ideals and a society ridden by Babbittry and commercialism. *Elmer Gantry* (1927) revealed the seamier side of organized religion, especially Evangelicalism. *Dodsworth* (1929) examined the conflict between European and American culture as it is experienced by an ambitious, but artistically inclined, businessman. *Ann Vickers* (1933) assailed the corruption of social services. Throughout these novels, Lewis used wit, satire, and an uncanny gift for mimicry to attack what he saw as the vices of the middle class—smugness, complacency, and crassness.

Lewis researched his best work with almost anthropological thoroughness. To ensure accuracy, he often collaborated with experts in the field; these included the popular science writer Paul De Kruif for *Arrowsmith* and the Kansas City evangelist L. M. Birkhead for *Elmer Gantry.*

Lewis's reputation as a social thinker and as a writer has fluctuated over the years. During the early 1920s many critics agreed with H. L. Mencken that a novel such as *Babbitt* was a "social document of a high order." At the time, Lewis was ranked very high among America's finest writers. When he was awarded the Pulitzer Prize for *Arrowsmith* in 1926, he became even more famous—and controversial as well— by refusing to accept the award, claiming that he did not believe in prizes and that other writers were more deserving. By the end of the decade, he had acquired an international reputation as one of the most daring, witty, and trenchant writers in the United States.

The 1930 Nobel Prize for Literature was awarded to Lewis "for his vigorous and graphic art of description and his ability to create, with wit and humor, new types of characters." "Yes, Sinclair Lewis is an American," remarked ERIK KARLFELDT of the Swedish Academy in his presentation address. "He writes the new language—American—as one of the representatives of 120,000,000 souls." Karlfeldt added, "The new great American literature has started with national self-criticism. It is a sign of health. Sinclair Lewis has . . . the manners of a new settler. . . . He is a pioneer." In his Nobel lecture, "The American Fear of Literature," Lewis railed against those in the United States who "are still afraid of any literature which is not a glorification of everything American, a glorification of our faults as well as our virtues." Dismissing "Emerson, Longfellow, Lowell, Holmes, the Alcotts" as "sentimental reflections of Europe," he praised writers like Hamlin Garland who, in his view, had written honestly about the American experience. "In Mr. Garland's *Main-Travelled Roads* I discovered that there was one man who believed that Midwestern peasants were sometimes bewildered and hungry and vile—and heroic. And, given this vision, I was released; I could write of life as living life."

In the years after Lewis won the Nobel Prize, the quality of his work declined and his critical reputation waned. Although he produced another ten novels, few of them received favorable notice. *It Can't Happen Here,* published in 1935 in the depth of the Great Depression, depicts a United States fallen under a fascist government. Marriage is the subject of *Cass Timberlane* (1945), the story of a middle-aged judge who falls in love with the unfaithful twenty-four-year-old Jinny Marshland. In

629

Kingsblood Royal, which appeared in 1947, Lewis turned to the issue of racial prejudice.

In failing health after a life of heavy drinking, Lewis spent his final years in Europe, mostly in Italy. His last novel, *World So Wide,* was published shortly after he died of a heart attack in Rome on January 10, 1951.

Critics have remained divided in their assessment of Lewis's work. Writing in the 1940s, the American literary critic Alfred Kazin called Lewis "fundamentally uncritical," a writer who enjoys—and identifies with—the targets of his satire. In 1951 the American author Joseph Wood Krutch praised Lewis's gift for mimicry but suggested that "he rarely if ever escaped the limitations of mimicry as an artistic device."

James Lundquist, a more recent critic, saw in Lewis a peculiarly American virtue, a quality he also found in such popular American novelists as John Dos Passos, Gore Vidal, and Terry Southern. "Lewis came on the scene at just the moment when twentieth-century American garishness was becoming apparent—even to Americans," Lundquist wrote. "His fictionalizing of what was happening in the small town and in the city to the housewife, the businessman, the scientist, the preacher, the industrialist was a purgation of fears that were widely and deeply felt, fears that are . . . still with us." "It was the élan that went into the writing of the great novels of the twenties," Perry Miller wrote, "which makes them, in the guise of ferocious attacks upon America, celebrations of it." " 'I wrote Babbitt,' " he quoted Lewis as having told him, " 'not out of hatred for him but out of love.' "

ADDITIONAL WORKS: Mantrap, 1925; The Man Who Knew Coolidge, 1928; Work of Art, 1934; Jayhawker, 1935; Selected Short Stories, 1935; The Prodigal Parents, 1938; Bethel Merriday, 1940; Gideon Planish, 1943; The God-Seeker, 1949; From Main Street to Stockholm, 1952; The Man From Main Street, 1953; I'm a Stranger to Myself and Other Stories, 1962; Storm in the West, 1963.

ABOUT: Bucco, M. Critical Essays on Sinclair Lewis, 1986; Dooley, D. J. The Art of Sinclair Lewis, 1962; Griffin, R. J. (ed.) Interpretations of Arrowsmith, 1968; Kazin, A. On Native Grounds, 1942; Lewis, G. H. With Love From Gracie, 1955; Light, M. The Quixotic Vision of Sinclair Lewis, 1975; Lundquist, J. Sinclair Lewis, 1973; Miller, P. The Responsibility of Mind in a Civilization of Machines, 1979; O'Connor, R. Sinclair Lewis, 1971; Parrington, V. L. Sinclair Lewis, Our Own Diogenes, 1930; Schorer, M. Sinclair Lewis: An American Life, 1961; Schorer, M. (ed.) Sinclair Lewis: A Collection of Critical Essays, 1962; Sheean, V. Dorothy and Red, 1963; Sherman, S. P. The Significance of Sinclair Lewis, 1922; Smith, H. Sinclair Lewis, 1977.

LEWIS, W. ARTHUR

(January 23, 1915–   )
Nobel Memorial Prize in Economic
   Sciences, 1979
(shared with Theodore Schultz)

The West Indian economist William Arthur Lewis was born on the island of St. Lucia, in the British West Indies, to Ida Louise (Barton) Lewis and George Ferdinand Lewis, schoolteachers who had emigrated from Antigua. His father died when Lewis was seven, leaving his mother to bring up five sons. Lewis has described her as "the most highly disciplined and hardest-working person I have ever known, and she passed that on to her children."

When Lewis graduated from St. Mary's College in St. Lucia in 1929, he was only fourteen years of age. Too young for admission to a university, he worked as a government clerk until he was old enough for a government scholarship to the London School of Economics (LSE), to which he was admitted in 1933. His ambition was to become an engineer, but as he later recalled, "This seemed pointless since neither the government nor the white firms would hire a black engineer." He therefore chose a more practical course of study that included accounting, commercial law, and business management. In 1937 he received a bachelor of commerce degree with first-class honors. Despite his lack of appropriate course work in economics and mathematics, he was also awarded a full scholarship for doctoral studies in industrial economics. The following year he received a one-year contract to teach at the University of London, after which he was appointed an assistant lecturer. He received his doctorate from the LSE in 1940 and remained on the faculty of the University of London until 1948, when he became Stanley Jevons Professor of Political Economy at the University of Manchester.

Lewis has described his intellectual career as consisting of three phases: the history of world economics and development, industrial economics, and the economic problems of underdeveloped nations. His work on the first phase began while he was still at the LSE. There, at the suggestion of FRIEDRICH A. VON HAYEK, then chairman of the LSE's economics department, he began to lecture on the period of alternating economic prosperity and depression between the two world wars. The result was an early study of these cycles, *Economic Survey 1919–1939,* published in 1949. He summarized his pioneering work on industrial economics in *Overhead Costs: Some*

W. ARTHUR LEWIS

Essays in Economic Analysis (1950). After its publication, however, he concentrated increasingly on economic issues of the so-called Third World.

The end of World War II and the independence of many former European colonies focused increasing attention on the issue of economic development in the Third World nations, which economists had dubbed "the South" in contrast to the developed capitalist nations they called "the North." At the time, most economic planners believed that developing nations must invest profits from the export of traditional products in the industrial sector to achieve rapid economic growth. Their views were reinforced by the success of the Marshall Plan (named for GEORGE C. MARSHALL), whose massive infusion of investment money and capital equipment, contributed to postwar recovery in Western Europe.

In the course of his studies, Lewis arrived at a different position. He conceived of a developing nation's economy as dual rather than single, with both an agricultural, traditional sector and an industrial, capitalist sector. The Third World generally had a vast supply of uneducated agricultural labor. Once trained, this labor force could be put to work in a rising commercial and manufacturing sector of the economy at relatively little expense. Profits made in that sector could then provide the savings and capital the Third World so badly needed to develop economically and industrially. In Lewis's view, the Third World required something very different from a Marshall Plan. Foreign trade was not, in his opinion,

an engine of growth for typical poor nations. He had little confidence in outside investment of capital but believed in rising profits, in financing industrial investment, and in making a large investment in the education of people—that is, in human capital. Lewis's first approach to his model was published in 1951 as part of a United Nations report, *Economic Development in Low-Income Countries,* to which THEODORE SCHULTZ also contributed.

By 1955, when Lewis published his *Theory of Economic Growth,* he had refined and enlarged his original model. He viewed the economic production of the world as consisting of "steel" (the manufactured products of the developed world), "coffee" (a single-export article based on natural resources of the Third World), and "food" (produced by both). He could not use the Heckscher-Ohlin model (formulated by Eli Heckscher and BERTIL OHLIN) for the terms of world trade, because "coffee" was not found in the developed North. "Food," produced efficiently in the North but with low productivity in the South, was the key and determined the unfavorable terms of trade. The principal way to improve the balance of trade and achieve the development of the Third World was therefore to raise agricultural productivity in the South and invest savings in an expanding industrial sector.

Central to Lewis's theory of economic development is the process whereby a poor, underdeveloped nation could raise its ratio of total savings from about 4 or 5 percent of its national income to about 15 percent over a short time. Lewis showed that this process was chiefly the result of a rising industrial sector with fairly high profits. A large investment in education would also be necessary. Regional as well as world trade would grow under such favorable conditions (as in the 1950s and 1960s), and the North and South would be able to advance together rather than at each other's expense. Lewis viewed economic growth from a broad perspective that considered both social and economic development. Equally important, he stressed the difficulties of central economic planning under dictatorships as well as under democratic governments. He was one of the first economists to question whether econonic growth is always desirable and to argue for the evolution of the world economy as a whole.

Lewis's theories matured in the course of his practical work with Third World countries. From 1957 until 1963 he served as United Nations economic adviser to the prime minister of Ghana; as deputy managing director of the

United Nations Special Fund; and as vice-chancellor of the University of the West Indies, for which he was knighted in 1963. In 1963 he joined Princeton University's Woodrow Wilson School of Public and International Affairs as professor of economics and international affairs. In 1968 he received an additional appointment as James Madison Professor of Political Economy at Princeton, and in 1970 he took a four-year leave to serve as founder and president of the Caribbean Development Bank of Barbados.

Lewis is also interested in the problems of blacks in the United States, which he regards as similar to those of Third World peoples. He has taken issue with the introduction of black studies courses into American universities because of his staunch belief in rigorous traditional education as the road to progress.

Lewis shared the 1979 Nobel Memorial Prize in Economic Sciences with Theodore Schultz "for their pioneering research into economic development . . . with particular consideration of the problems of developing countries." In his Nobel lecture, "The Slowing Down of the Engine of Growth," Lewis wove together his theories on the nature of world trade and its history by suggesting that the least developed countries need no longer remain so dependent for their growth on the continuing growth of the most developed. By increasing their regional trade, he said, they could eventually accelerate their own development even as growth in the developed nations slackens. He also accused the developed countries of "lack of sensitivity" to the "mutual dependence" of both types of economies.

In 1938 Lewis married Gladys Isabel Jacobs, a Grenadian who was then a schoolteacher in London and is now a sculptor; they have two daughters. He has retained his British citizenship. During his leisure time he enjoys listening to classical music and taking long walks.

Lewis has received honorary degrees from many universities in the United States, including Columbia, Howard, and Yale, and from the universities of Manchester, Wales, Bristol, the West Indies, Lagos, and Toronto, among others. He is an honorary fellow of the London School of Economics and a corresponding fellow of the British Academy. He has served on the council of the Royal Economic Society, as president of the Economics Society of Ghana, and as a member of the Economic Advisory Committee of the National Association for the Advancement of Colored People.

ADDITIONAL WORKS: Labour in the West Indies, 1939;

Monopoly in British Industry, 1945; Economic Problems of Today, 1948; Principles of Economic Planning, 1949; Aspects of Industrialization, 1953; Politics in West Africa, 1965; Education and Economic Development, 1965; Development Planning: The Essentials of Economic Policy, 1966; Some Aspects of Economic Development, 1969; The Development Process, 1970; Dynamic Factors in Economic Growth, 1974; The Evolution of the International Economic Order, 1977; Growth and Fluctuations, 1870–1913, 1978.

ABOUT: Breit, W., and Spencer, R. W. (eds.) Lives of the Laureates, 1986; Scandinavian Journal of Economics, number 1, 1980; Science December 21, 1979.

LIBBY, WILLARD F.
(December 17, 1908–September 8, 1980)
Nobel Prize for Chemistry, 1960

The American chemist Willard Frank Libby was born in Grand Valley, Colorado, to Ora Edward Libby, a farmer whose education had ended at the third grade, and Eva May (Rivers) Libby. When the boy was five years old, his family, which included two brothers and two sisters, moved to an apple ranch near Sebastopol in northern California. He attended a two-room grammar school and graduated from high school in 1926. With his parents' encouragement, Libby entered the University of California at Berkeley, intending to become a mining engineer; but he found chemistry more interesting. After studying chemistry, physics, and mathematics, he received a B.S. in chemistry in 1931. A Ph.D. and an appointment as instructor in chemistry followed two years later, after graduate study in the field of low-energy radioactive nuclei under the physical chemists Gilbert N. Lewis and Wendell M. Latimer.

Isotopes are forms of a chemical element with the same atomic number (because there are identical numbers of protons in the nuclei), but with different atomic weights or number of neutrons. They have identical chemical properties but slightly different physical properties. Radioactive isotopes have unstable nuclei, which decay by emitting alpha, beta, or gamma rays. The chemist GEORGE DE HEVESY pioneered the use of radioactive nuclei as tracers of chemical reactions. For sensitive measurements of small numbers of radioactive nuclei, it is necessary to isolate the radiation emitted by the nuclei under investigation from both the background cosmic radiation originating in outer space and radioactive nuclei in the general environment. WALTHER BOTHE, a German physicist, developed a coincidence counter in which numerous electrical detectors measured simultaneous discharges of radia-

WILLARD F. LIBBY

carbon, which is rapidly oxidized to carbon dioxide in the air and is absorbed by plants through photosynthesis. Any organism eating these plants would also incorporate the radioactive carbon atoms. Libby assumed that radioactive carbon is generated at a constant rate and that, once included, it would remain in a molecule. Therefore, he reasoned, all living things have a constant level of radioactivity that decreases after death. The lifetime of a radioactive isotope is designated by its half-life, the length of time required for half of a given quantity of the substance to decay. As determined by Martin Kamen in 1940, the half-life of carbon 14 is 5,730 years, a short time in relation to the age of the earth, but long enough for an equilibrium in the production and decay of carbon 14. "It should be possible," Libby decided, "by measuring the remaining activity, to determine the time elapsed since death, if this occurred during the period between approximately 500 and 30,000 years ago."

To test his hypothesis, Libby built a Geiger counter that was shielded by 8-inch-thick iron walls to absorb terrestrial radiation. An inner barrier of Geiger tubes detected cosmic rays that penetrated the outer shielding. As in his doctoral research, when the shielding Geiger counters registered penetrating particles, the central counter for measuring the radioactivity of the sample was turned off for one-thousandth of a second. Maximum sensitivity to the radiation emitted by the dating sample was achieved by depositing pure carbon (in the form of lampblack) on the inner wall of the sensing detector. Later Libby found that the sensitivity of the method was further increased if the carbon was present as a gas, either carbon dioxide or acetylene. About 1 in 1 trillion carbon atoms was found to be radioactive. Libby checked the accuracy of the method by measuring the radioactivity of samples from redwood and fir trees whose exact ages had been determined by counting annual rings. He also tested historical artifacts for which the ages were known, such as a piece of timber from the funerary boat of King Sesostris of Egypt, donated by the Chicago Museum of Natural History. The excellent agreement that he found rapidly led to use of the dating method in archaeology and geology.

Testing the radioactivity of animal and plant material obtained worldwide from the North Pole to the South Pole, Libby found little variation related to latitude. Archaeological objects that were then accurately dated by Libby's carbon 14 method included linen wrappings of

tion. In the anticoincidence variation of Bothe's arrangement devised by Libby, the measurement chamber contained both inner and outer radiation detectors. This method greatly reduced the effects of background radioactivity on measurements of very low levels of radiation. As a graduate student, Libby discovered that the element samarium is slightly radioactive, a finding also made about the same time by Hevesy.

In 1941 Libby, who was now an associate professor, took a sabbatical and spent the year at Princeton University as a Guggenheim Fellow. In December the United States entered World War II, and Libby joined HAROLD C. UREY at Columbia University as a member of the Manhattan Project, the American effort to develop nuclear weapons. In this effort Libby worked on gaseous diffusion techniques for the separation of uranium isotopes, which were necessary for the production of an atomic bomb. At the end of World War II he accepted a position as full professor in the Department of Chemistry at the University of Chicago, where he also conducted research at the university's Institute of Nuclear Studies.

Serge Korff at New York University had discovered in 1939 that when cosmic rays strike atoms in the upper atmosphere, they create showers of neutrons. Other evidence indicated that nitrogen, which constitutes about 80 percent of the atmosphere, easily absorbs neutrons and then decays into radioactive carbon, also called radiocarbon or carbon 14. Libby theorized that the cosmic-ray bombardment converts atmospheric nitrogen into radioactive

the Dead Sea Scrolls; bread from a house in Pompeii buried by volcanic ashes in 79 A.D.; charcoal from a campsite at Stonehenge, England; and corncobs from a cave in New Mexico. Libby also established that the last Ice Age in North America ended 10,000 years ago, in contrast with the 25,000 years previously estimated by geologists. Radiocarbon dating was quickly recognized as a basic technique for determining dates of events within the last 70,000 years.

Cosmic-ray interactions in the upper atmosphere also produce small amounts of tritium, a radioactive isotope of hydrogen with one proton and two neutrons and a half-life of twelve years. Thus, tritium concentrations could be used as a tracer of atmospheric moisture and the earth's hydrologic system. With this technique Libby analyzed water-circulation patterns, the mixing of oceanic waters, and the ages of wines.

As an appointee of President Dwight D. Eisenhower, Libby served on the United States Atomic Energy Commission (AEC) from 1954 to 1959. At the AEC he worked on problems of radioactive fallout from atomic bombs and was involved in international programs, such as Atoms for Peace, for the peaceful application of nuclear technologies. After resigning from the AEC in 1959, he joined the chemistry department at the University of California at Los Angeles (UCLA). Three years later he was appointed director of the Institute of Geophysics and Planetary Physics, a position he held concurrently with his UCLA post until his retirement in 1976. His scientific interests extended into geochemistry, planetary atmospheres, lunar and space research, environmental and pollution control, earthquake protection, and civil defense.

Libby was awarded the 1960 Nobel Prize for Chemistry "for his method to use carbon 14 for age determination in archaeology, geology, geophysics, and other branches of science." Libby said in his Nobel lecture, "The dating technique itself is one which requires care, but which can be carried out by adequately trained personnel" exercising "cleanliness, care, seriousness, and practice. With these things it is possible to obtain radiocarbon dates, which . . . may indeed help roll back the pages of history and reveal to mankind something more about his ancestors, and in this way," he concluded, "perhaps about his future."

Libby was married in 1940 to Leonor Lucinda Hickey, a teacher; they had twin daughters. After their divorce in 1966, he married Leona Woods Marshall, a professor of environmental engineering at the University of California at Los Angeles. Tall and powerful in build, Libby was once described by GLENN T. SEABORG as "a painstaking, patient, and effective teacher" whose "career was characterized by an extraordinary versatility and breadth of interest, a consequence of his wide-ranging curiosity." Libby died in Los Angeles on September 8, 1980, after contracting pneumonia and suffering a blood clot in his lung.

In addition to the Nobel Prize, his awards included the Charles Frederick Chandler Medal of Columbia University (1954), the Elliott Cresson Medal of the Franklin Institute (1957), the Willard Gibbs Medal of the American Chemical Society (1958), and the Day Medal of the Geological Society of America (1961). He was a member of the National Academy of Sciences, the American Academy of Arts and Sciences, the American Philosophical Society, the Heidelberg Academy of Sciences, the Bolivian Society of Anthropology, and the Royal Swedish Academy of Sciences.

SELECTED WORKS: Radioactivity of Ordinary Elements, 1933; Radiocarbon Dating, 1952; Isotopes in Industry and Medicine, 1957; Science and Administration, 1961; Solar System Physics and Chemistry: Papers for the Public, 1981, with Leona Marshall Libby; Tritium and Radiocarbon, 1981; Collected Papers, 1981, with others.

ABOUT: Berland, T. The Scientific Life, 1962; Current Biography November 1954; National Cyclopedia of American Biography, volume 1, 1960; New York Times September 10, 1980; Physics Today February 1981.

LIPMANN, FRITZ
(June 12, 1899–July 24, 1986)
Nobel Prize for Physiology or Medicine, 1953
(shared with Hans Krebs)

The German-American biochemist Fritz Albert Lipmann was born in Königsberg (now Kaliningrad, Soviet Union) to Gertrud (Lachmanski) Lipmann and Leopold Lipmann, a lawyer. Influenced by an uncle who was a pediatrician, Lipmann began the study of medicine in 1917 at the University of Königsberg. After serving in the army Medical Corps during the last months of World War I, he continued his education at the University of Munich and later at the University of Berlin, which awarded him a medical degree in 1922 for a dissertation on colloid chemistry. Lipmann remained at Berlin for a three-month intensive

FRITZ LIPMANN

biochemistry course, after which he received a research fellowship in pharmacology at the University of Amsterdam, in the Netherlands. Having resolved to become a biochemist, he began graduate studies in biochemistry at the University of Königsberg. For a thesis on biochemical reactions in muscle cells, Lipmann received a Ph.D. in chemistry from the University of Berlin in 1927.

For the next two years, he was a research assistant to OTTO MEYERHOF at the Kaiser Wilhelm Institute for Biology in Berlin. When Meyerhof moved to the Kaiser Wilhelm Institute for Medical Research in Heidelberg in 1929, Lipmann accompanied him. At Heidelberg, Lipmann became acquainted with the nuclear chemist OTTO HAHN as well as the biochemists OTTO WARBURG and HANS KREBS.

By the mid-1920s, scientists had formulated a general scheme of cellular carbohydrate metabolism. The carbohydrates glycogen and glucose were known to be chemically degraded by both an oxidative pathway (aerobic glycolysis, or respiration) and a fermentation pathway (anaerobic glycolysis). In the former, glucose (a six-carbon molecule) is converted to the three-carbon molecule pyruvic acid, which is then oxidized to carbon dioxide and water. In anaerobic glycolysis, the pyruvate is transformed into lactate (also a three-carbon molecule). Meyerhof had shown that a small but significant fraction of lactate produced in active muscle cells is further oxidized to carbon dioxide and water.

Like Meyerhof, Lipmann was interested in elucidating the molecular mechanisms by which living cells generate and utilize energy. He discovered that sodium fluoride inhibits the oxidation of lactic acid. Lipmann also studied the biochemistry of creatine phosphate, the breakdown of which is more closely related to the contraction of muscle cells than is lactic acid. In 1931 Lipmann returned to the Kaiser Wilhelm Institute for Biology in Berlin as an assistant to Albert Fischer, who taught him how to grow fibroblasts (cells of embryonic tissue) in an in vitro culture, a technique useful for studies of cellular metabolism.

Through his older brother, an artist, Lipmann became acquainted with the literary and theatrical life of Berlin. In these circles, while attending a masked ball, that he met Elfreda M. Hall, an American, whom he married in 1931. Later that year the couple went to New York City, where, on a Rockefeller Foundation fellowship, Lipmann studied phosphorylated proteins with the chemist P. A. Levene at the Rockefeller Institute for Medical Research (now Rockefeller University).

In 1932 Lipmann rejoined Fischer in a new laboratory at the Biological Institute of the Carlsberg Foundation in Copenhagen, Denmark. For the next seven years he studied how cells generate energy to power the biochemical reactions required to sustain life. He found that in the presence of oxygen, anaerobic glycolysis is suppressed. To analyze this phenomenon, which is called the Pasteur effect, Lipmann studied the oxidation of pyruvate (an ester, or salt, of pyruvic acid, an intermediary in the metabolic process). Using an enzyme system extracted from the bacteria *Lactobacillus delbrueckii,* he discovered that the conversion of pyruvate to acetate was completely dependent on inorganic phosphate and yielded a phosphorylated form of acetate, acetyl phosphate. He mistakenly concluded that acetyl phosphate was the chemically active form of acetate, which combined with oxaloacetate to form citric acid in the first step of the Krebs cycle, the major series of reactions in the metabolism of carbohydrates and fatty acids.

In the late 1930s Nazi Germany was extending its influence to Denmark. Realizing that, as a Jew, he could neither return to Germany nor remain in Denmark, Lipmann and his wife emigrated to the United States in 1939. There he found a position as a research associate in the Department of Biochemistry under VINCENT DU VIGNEAUD at the Cornell University Medical College in New York City. He remained at Cornell until 1941, when he became a research fellow in surgery at Harvard Medical School and at Massachusetts

635

General Hospital in Boston. Two years later he became an associate in biochemistry and then a professor of biological chemistry at Harvard in 1949. In 1944 he became a naturalized American citizen; the Lipmanns' son was born in the next year.

As a result of his studies of cellular energetics, Lipmann proposed in 1941 that the principal source of energy powering metabolic reactions in the living cell was adenosine triphosphate (ATP), a central compound of the phosphate group that makes up the nucleotide molecular structure. The chemical bond formed by this phosphate group furnishes the energy used by the human cell. How ATP releases cellular energy was not clear, however, until Lipmann and his colleagues discovered coenzyme A in 1945. After isolating and synthesizing this catalytic agent, Lipmann showed how it helps convert phosphate bond energy into other useful forms of chemical energy in the body. His finding further clarified the Krebs cycle, whereby food is transformed into physical energy in the cell. Coenzyme A is found in all living cells, including those of plants, animals, and microorganisms.

Lipmann was awarded the 1953 Nobel Prize for Physiology or Medicine for his "discovery of coenzyme A and its importance for intermediary metabolism." He shared the prize with Hans Krebs. In his presentation speech, Erik Hammarsten of the Karolinska Institute, said: "This is an acknowledgment of vast and significant contributions to the research into the functions of the living cell." Addressing Lipmann, Hammarsten said: "You have removed an obstructive confusion by the clear demonstration of a widespread reaction and have discovered simultaneously a new way for the transmission of energy in the cell."

In 1957 Lipmann became a professor of biochemistry at Rockefeller University. In his research there he investigated the unusual phosphate compounds such as carbamyl phosphate, the structure of cancer cells, the thyroid hormone and how it regulates bodily energy, and the processes involved in intermediate metabolism. Named professor emeritus at Rockefeller in 1970, he remained active as a researcher until his death in Poughkeepsie, New York, on July 24, 1986.

Lipmann, who enjoyed listening to music, was a member of the National Academy of Sciences, the American Society of Biological Chemists, the Harvey Society, and the American Philosophical Society, as well as a foreign member of the Royal Society of London. He was awarded the Carl Neuberg Medal of the American Society of European Chemists (1948), the Mead Johnson Award of the American Academy of Pediatrics (1948), and the National Medal of Science of the National Science Foundation (1966); and he held honorary degrees from the universities of Paris, Aix-Marseilles, Chicago, and Copenhagen, as well as Harvard University, Rockefeller University, and the Albert Einstein College of Medicine.

SELECTED WORKS: Wanderings of a Biochemist, 1971.

ABOUT: Chapeville, F., and Haenni, A. L. (eds.) Chemical Recognition in Biology, 1980; Current Biography March 1954; Kaplan, N. O., and Kennedy, E. P. (eds.) Current Aspects of Biochemical Energetics, 1966; New York Times July 25, 1986; Richter, D. (ed.) Dahlem in the Late Nineteen Twenties 1974.

LIPPMANN, GABRIEL
(August 16, 1845–July 12, 1921)
Nobel Prize for Physics, 1908

The French physicist Gabriel Jonas Lippmann was born in Hollerich, Luxembourg. He was educated at home until the age of thirteen, when his parents, who were French, moved to Paris and enrolled him in the Lycée Napoléon. In 1868 he entered the École Normale Supérieure, where he developed an interest in contemporary research in electricity while preparing abstracts of German papers for the journal *Annales de Chimie et de Physique* (Journal of Chemistry and Physics).

During a government-sponsored mission to Germany in 1873 to study methods of teaching science, Lippmann worked at the University of Heidelberg with the physiologist Wilhelm Kühne and the physicist Gustav Kirchhoff, and then with the physiologist and physicist Hermann von Helmholtz in Berlin. Kühne showed him an experiment in which a drop of mercury covered with sulfuric acid deformed when touched lightly with an iron wire. Lippmann deduced that the metals and the acid formed an electric battery whose voltage changed the shape of the mercury surface. From this insight he developed the capillary electrometer, or voltmeter, a tilted capillary (small-diameter) glass tube of mercury topped with acid. Electrically induced changes in the curved mercury surface caused the column of metal to move in the tube and were capable of indicating differences in electric potential as small as 0.001 volt.

GABRIEL LIPPMANN

Returning to Paris to complete his studies, Lippmann did research on electrocapillarity, the effect of electric fields on the surface tension of liquids, and received a doctor of science degree in 1875 from the Sorbonne, the arts and letters branch of the University of Paris. In 1878 he joined the Faculty of Science in Paris, was appointed professor of mathematical physics in 1883, and became director of the research laboratory in 1886. The laboratory was later transferred to the Sorbonne where Lippmann remained for the rest of his life.

In other research, Lippmann investigated the converse of his capillary electrometer, the production of electricity by mechanically deforming the mercury surface. This work led him to a general theorem, published in 1881, that knowledge of a particular physical phenomenon enables the prediction of the existence and magnitude of its converse. He applied this insight to the phenomenon of piezoelectricity, the generation of electricity by the compression or expansion of certain crystals such as quartz. Since mechanical forces change the crystal dimensions as they produce electric charge (that is, a change in dimensions generates a voltage), Lippmann predicted that applying a voltage to the crystal would change its dimensions. PIERRE CURIE and his brother, Jacques Curie, confirmed this prediction experimentally. The reverse piezoelectric effect is now widely used in science and industry. Applying an alternating voltage to a piezoelectric crystal causes it to vibrate and radiate sound waves, which are applied to sonar (detection of submarines) and ultrasonic devices

such as cleaners, remote controls, and dental drills.

As early as 1879, Lippmann contended that an electric charge increases the inertia of a body, its resistance to a change in velocity. This contention may have been related to observations by Michael Faraday in 1838 and experiments by H. A. Rowland in 1876, which showed that a moving charge is equivalent to an electric current and creates a magnetic field. However, Lippmann neither cited experimental confirmation nor developed the idea further.

In 1891 Lippmann demonstrated a method for producing permanent color photographs. Color photographs had been made in 1848 by the French physicist Edmond Becquerel, using a silver plate covered with a film of silver chloride; but his pictures faded quickly and he could not explain how they worked. Twenty years later, the German physicist Wilhelm Zenker explained that the appearance of color in Becquerel's photographs was an interference phenomenon. Zenker's theory was developed further by the English physicist J. W. STRUTT and proved conclusively by the German experimentalist Otto Wiener in 1890.

Interference is the combining of different light waves arriving simultaneously at the same point. Since light consists of electric and magnetic fields going through repeated cycles of rise, fall, and reversal along a given axis perpendicular to the direction of travel, the light rays reinforce or weaken each other depending on whether their fields are in the same or opposing directions. If the light waves have the same wavelength (and associated frequency), the result is an interference pattern, called fringes, which are bright regions where the waves arrive in step (the same point in a cycle) alternating with dark regions where the waves arrive at opposing points of a cycle. The spacings in the pattern are related to the wavelength. Waves of different lengths interfere in a continuously shifting way that produces a blurred mixture rather than a simple pattern.

In Becquerel's silver chloride film, it was explained, interference between incoming light rays and rays of the same wavelength reflected back from the silver base plate, producing a pattern of bright layers at half-wavelength intervals, separated by dark layers. Since wavelength corresponds to color as perceived by the eye, different colors created interference patterns at different depths, and also at different locations across the plate where they occurred in the incident light. The light energy accumulated at each point in the film during an exposure determined the number of grains of silver metal formed from the chloride during later development of the plate. The metallic grains then became a copy of the interference patterns for the various colors in the form of darkened layers at various depths and lateral positions.

When the photograph was then viewed in ordinary light, which is a mixture of all colors, light was reflected back to the viewer from both the layers of grains and the silver base plate. Light rays reflected from different depths interfered constructively only for specific wavelengths (colors), corresponding to the spacings between layers, and thus reproduced the colors of the photographed object.

When Lippmann devised his way of making color photographs that did not fade quickly after development, he denied that interference was involved in Becquerel's color plates but maintained that it was the underlying principle of his own method. Lippmann's plates were of clear glass coated on one side with a relatively thick photosensitive emulsion consisting of gelatin, silver nitrate, and potassium bromide. The plate holder, during an exposure, backed the uncoated glass face with mercury, which formed a shiny, reflecting surface. Color-linked interference patterns between incoming light from the object and reflected light from the mercury became fixed in the distribution of silver grains produced chemically during development. Lippmann later described the process as making a sort of mold of the luminous rays within the thickness of the photographic film.

"For his method of reproducing colors photographically based on the phenomenon of interference," Lippmann was awarded the 1908 Nobel Prize for Physics. Pointing to what he called "the key position of photographic reproduction in present-day life," K. B. Hasselberg of the Royal Swedish Academy of Sciences declared in his presentation speech that "Lippmann's color photography marks a further step forward . . . in the art of photography." In his Nobel lecture, Lippmann demonstrated that colors were indeed produced by interference in an unpigmented photograph. He moistened the emulsion, causing the gelatin to swell and alter the spacings in the interference patterns. The colors vanished. As the gelatin was allowed to dry, the patterns were restored, and the colors gradually returned. He also pointed out the need for further improvement. "The length of exposure (1 minute in sunlight) is still too long for the portrait. It was 15 minutes when I first began

my work. Progress may continue. Life is short and progress is slow." Modern color photography, with films that require exposures of fractions of a second, is based on a three-color process using absorbent dyes first suggested by the Scottish physicist James Clerk Maxwell in the 1850s.

In subsequent years, as director of the Sorbonne's research laboratory, Lippmann made contributions to the fields of seismology and astronomy. He suggested the use of telegraph signals to give early warning of earth tremors and to enable their velocity of propagation to be measured. He also proposed a new form of seismograph for directly detecting the acceleration of the earth's movement. He designed two astronomical instruments: the coelostat, in which a reflecting mirror rotated slowly to produce a stationary image of a portion of the sky, not merely of one particular star; and the uranograph, which provided a photographic chart of the sky with meridians already marked to indicate equal intervals of time. His textbook on thermodynamics (the study of heat in relation to mechanical energy) became a standard reference work in France.

Lippmann was married in 1888. He died aboard the steamship *La France* while returning home from a trip to Canada. He was a member of the French Academy of Sciences (serving as president in 1912), a fellow of the Royal Society of London, and a commander of the Legion of Honor.

ABOUT: Dictionary of Scientific Biography, volume 8, 1973; New York Times July 14, 1921.

LIPSCOMB, WILLIAM N.
(December 9, 1919–   )
Nobel Prize for Chemistry, 1976

The American physical chemist William Nunn Lipscomb was born in Cleveland, Ohio, to Edna (Porter) and William N. Lipscomb. A year after his birth the family moved to Lexington, Kentucky. After graduation from Picadome High School, Lipscomb entered the University of Kentucky and received his B.S. in chemistry in 1941. That fall he began graduate work in physics at the California Institute of Technology (Caltech), but after a year he returned to the study of physical chemistry at the encouragement of LINUS C. PAULING, one of his professors and later his doctoral adviser. Between 1942 and 1945 Lipscomb interrupted his studies to conduct wartime research for the

WILLIAM N. LIPSCOMB

Harvard University

United States Office of Scientific Research and Development.

Returning to Caltech in 1945, Lipscomb completed his Ph.D. the following year with a dissertation on X-ray crystallography and electron-diffraction studies of organic compounds. He then received an appointment as assistant professor of physical chemistry at the University of Minnesota, where he became associate professor in 1950 and full professor in 1954. In 1959 he moved to Harvard University as a professor, serving as chairman of the chemistry department from 1962 to 1965. Since 1971 he has been the Abbott and James Lawrence Professor of Chemistry at Harvard.

At Caltech, Lipscomb became intrigued by the puzzle of chemical bonding in the boron hydrides, also known as boranes. A number of these compounds, which are rarely found in nature, had been synthesized a generation earlier by the German chemist Alfred Stock. Their molecular structures were unknown, but their empirical formulas suggested some curious bonding patterns. An interpretation of these bonding patterns proposed by Pauling, then the leading authority on chemical bonding, struck Lipscomb as somehow flawed.

When Lipscomb moved to the University of Minnesota in 1946, he set out to prove his mentor wrong. At that time borane chemistry was regarded as not only esoteric but also extraordinarily difficult, since boranes are highly volatile, unstable, and even explosive. After developing new techniques to conduct X-ray diffraction studies of these compounds under high vacuum and low temperature, Lipscomb was able to delineate their structures in detail, describing them as cagelike polyhedrons.

Lipscomb wanted to understand the boranes theoretically as well as empirically, however. The prevailing theory stated that the atoms in borane molecules were held together by covalent (two-center) bonds; that is, the two atoms forming the bond were held together by a shared pair of electrons. The problem was that the borane structures Lipscomb had found could not be explained according to the theory. Boron atoms have too few bonding electrons to share with the number of hydrogen atoms with which they were known to combine. In work performed in 1953 and reported the following year in *Journal of Chemical Physics*, Lipscomb, with the chemists Bryce Crawford and W. H. Eberhardt, proposed that the electron deficiency was only apparent. They suggested that some of the atoms in borane molecules were participating in three-center bonds, in which an electron pair unites either three boron atoms or two boron atoms and one hydrogen atom to form a hydrogen bridge. "We have even ventured a few predictions," the scientists wrote, "knowing that if we must join the ranks of boron hydride predictors later proved wrong, we shall be in the best of company."

Their theory of three-centered bonds, however, not only was correct but proved to be the key to a new topological theory of bonding in the boranes. The theory explained their structures and also predicted the possibility of novel compounds, which have since guided chemists to the creation of large numbers of stable, cagelike molecules. Moreover, Lipscomb applied this new modification of bonding theory to the understanding of reactivity in mixed carbon-boron hydrides (known as carboranes), which were used in the synthesis of polymers that exhibited remarkable resistance to thermal and chemical degradation. Lipscomb's boranes have also shown some promise in radiation cancer therapy. Russell Grimes, writing in *Science* magazine, predicted that carboranes would have profound implications for the future of organic synthesis, following the "revolution" in ideas about the covalent bond that Lipscomb's work with boron chemistry had caused.

Lipscomb received the 1976 Nobel Prize for Chemistry "for his studies on the structure of boranes illuminating problems of chemical bonding." In his Nobel lecture Lipscomb said, "My original intention in the late 1940s was to spend a few years understanding the boranes and then to discover a systematic valence description of the vast numbers of 'electron deficient' . . . compounds. I have made little progress toward this latter objective," Lipscomb added. Instead, the field of boron chemistry has grown enormously, and a systematic understanding of some of its complexities has now begun." Upon notification of the award he remarked, "I knew I had written a lot of nice papers about boranes, but I never actually knew that anyone read them."

When Lipscomb became affiliated with Harvard University, his research program shifted toward biochemistry. His particular focus has been the elucidation of the structures of complex proteins as a means of investigating the mechanisms of their functions in the human body, since function is determined by a protein's shape. This research poses extraordinarily complex problems because protein molecules are so large. Lipscomb's principal approach has been to use innovative computer-assisted X-ray diffraction techniques. His greatest success in this work has been his structural analysis of the digestive enzyme carboxypeptidase A, which has led to a proposed mechanism for the activity of the enzyme. A current challenge is the regulatory enzyme aspartate *trans*-carbamylase (ATCase), which controls a step in the body's synthesis of a basic constituent of the nucleic acids. ATCase, therefore, is an important trigger of cell growth in all living things. Lipscomb has rated his research on the digestive enzyme as his best work, although it will be bested if his attack on ATCase proves successful.

Lipscomb's strength lies not only in his vigorous scientific imagination but also in the versatility and flexibility of his approach. As he has said, "I was raised as a physical chemist; I got my degree in physical chemistry. I worked in inorganic chemistry . . . and I work in biochemistry. But it's not all that different. It's all structure and function."

In 1944 Lipscomb married Mary Adele, with whom he had a son and a daughter. They were divorced in 1983, and in the same year he married Jean Evans, a lettering artist. Described by science writer Rebecca Rawls as a "country farmer who has come to town," Lipscomb is said to direct his laboratory with lively good humor. He is held in great affection by his colleagues and students, who address him as "Colonel" in recognition of his Kentucky upbringing. He plays the clarinet with near-professional skill (he says he is "abnormally interested in chamber music"), has quoted Lewis Carroll in his scientific papers, and belongs to the society of Sherlock Holmes fans known as the Baker Street Irregulars.

Lipscomb's many awards include the Distinguished Service Award of the American Chemical Society (1968), the George Ledlie Prize of Harvard University (1971), and the Peter Debye Award in Physical Chemistry (1973) and Remsen Award (1976) of the American Chemical Society. He is a member of the American Academy of Arts and Sciences and the National Academy of Sciences and a foreign member of the Royal Netherlands Academy of Sciences and Letters. He holds honorary degrees from the University of Kentucky, Harvard University, the University of Munich, Rutgers University, Long Island University, and Marietta College.

SELECTED WORKS: Comprehensive Inorganic Chemistry, 1953, with others; Boron Hydries, 1963; NMR Studies of Boron Hydrides and Related Compounds, 1969, with G. R. Eaton.

ABOUT: Chemistry and Engineering News November 15, 1976; New York Times October 19, 1976; Science November 12, 1976.

LOEWI, OTTO
(June 3, 1873–December 25, 1961)
Nobel Prize for Physiology or Medicine, 1936
(shared with Henry H. Dale)

The German-American pharmacologist and physiologist, Otto Loewi (lō′ ē), was born in Frankfurt am Main, the first child and only son of Jakob Loewi, a wealthy wine merchant, and his second wife, Anna (Willstadter) Loewi. Loewi, who spent much of his youth in the Hardt Mountains, entered the Frankfurt Gymnasium when he was nine years old. The curriculum emphasized Latin, Greek, and classical civilization, and although he did poorly in mathematics and physics, he excelled in the humanities. Loewi planned to become an art historian but, at the urging of his parents, enrolled at the University of Strasbourg in 1891 to study medicine.

In medical school he was influenced by outstanding professors: Gustav Schwalbe in anatomy, Bernhard Naunyn in medicine and experimental pathology, and the pharmacologist Oswald Schmiedeberg in research. Loewi's first experimental work—for his dissertation on the effects of hydrocyanic acid, arsenic, and phosphorus on the isolated heart of the frog— was directed by Schmiedeberg. Loewi attrib-

OTTO LOEWI

uted his interest in biology and physiology in part to Oscar Minkowski, who was conducting research on the role of the pancreas (the gland that secretes insulin) in diabetes. He was influenced too by Friedrich Miescher, the Swiss pioneer in biology.

After graduating from medical school in 1896, Loewi visited Italy, a country he loved all his life. He then returned to Strasbourg in 1897 for a brief period of training in Franz Hofmeister's biochemical institute, to increase his knowledge of chemistry and experimental methods. He became an assistant in the medical department of the City Hospital of Frankfurt, working with tuberculosis and pneumonia patients. The high mortality rate from pneumonia, especially among vigorous young men, discouraged him from clinical medicine. In 1898 he received an assistantship in the department of pharmacology at the University of Marburg under Hans Meyer, who became his friend, collaborator, and academic patron, and with whom he stayed until 1905. In 1900 Loewi was named privatdocent (unsalaried lecturer), signifying the first step in an academic career. Within two years he had published the results of his first important research, including the first in a series of papers on kidney function and the action of diuretics (drugs that increase the secretion of urine).

Loewi spent several months at University College, London, in 1903, in the laboratory of Ernest Starling, where he studied experimental methods in physiology. There he met HENRY H. DALE. In the academic circles in England, he also met the Cambridge physiologists J. N.

Langley and H. K. Anderson, who had described the structure, functions, and relations of the two divisions of the involuntary nervous system, the sympathetic and the parasympathetic. (The involuntary, or autonomic, nervous system controls the activity of the heart, glands, and smooth muscle.) At the time, a number of scientists were exploring the possibility that nerve impulses were transmitted chemically. In 1901 Langley had reported that material from the adrenal glands, which are situated on top of the kidneys, produced effects similar to those of impulses carried by certain nerves in the sympathetic nervous system. T. R. Elliott, also at Cambridge, was a year or two from publishing his work suggesting that nerve impulses in the sympathetic nervous system were transmitted by the hormone adrenaline; and W. E. Dixon, another Cambridge physiologist, was formulating the hypothesis that the chemical muscarine was the transmitter of the parasympathetic nervous system.

After Meyer moved to the University of Vienna in 1904, Loewi became acting chairman of pharmacology in Marburg. A year later, however, he followed Meyer to Vienna and was Meyer's assistant again until 1907, when Loewi was named assistant professor. That year, while on vacation in Switzerland, he met Guida Goldschmidt, who was vacationing with her mother and her father, Guido Goldschmidt, a professor of chemistry in Prague and later Vienna. The couple were married the following year and eventually had four children.

At the University of Vienna, Loewi published on a variety of subjects, mostly in collaboration with others. His work included studies on the effects of adrenaline and noradrenaline on blood pressure, on diabetes, and on the effects on the heart of stimulation of the vagus nerve (the largest nerve in the body). In 1909 Loewi was appointed professor of pharmacology at the University of Graz, where he remained until the Nazi occupation of Austria in 1938.

Although more than fifteen years had passed since Elliott first suggested that nerve impulses were carried by chemical transmitters, by 1921 no decisive evidence for the existence of a transmitter had emerged. During the night before Easter Sunday that year, Loewi awoke from a dream and by his own account "jotted down a few notes on a tiny slip of thin paper." By morning, he said, "I was unable to decipher the scrawl. The next night, at three o'clock, the idea returned. It was of the design of an experiment to determine whether or not the hypothesis of chemical transmission that I had uttered seventeen years ago was correct. I got up immediately, went to the laboratory, and performed a simple experiment on a frog heart according to nocturnal design."

In this experiment, Loewi isolated two frog hearts. After stimulating the vagus nerve of the first heart, he removed some fluid from it and injected the fluid into the second heart, from which he had removed the vagus nerve. The rate of the second heart slowed, as if its vagus nerve had been stimulated. Next, Loewi stimulated in the first heart a nerve that accelerates the heart rate. Transferring fluid to the second heart, he observed that its rate increased. In this way, he proved that not nerves but the chemicals they release directly affect the heart. Having proved the chemical-transmission hypothesis, Loewi named the transmitters *Vagusstoff* (vagus substance) and *Acceleransstoff* (accelerator substance). In the next fifteen years Loewi and his colleagues published fourteen papers on the chemical transmission of nerve impulses.

By 1926, with Ernst Navratil, Loewi had identified *Vagusstoff* as acetylcholine. The same year, because other investigators found it difficult to reproduce the results of Loewi's work, he was asked to perform the experiment at the Twelfth International Congress of Physiology in Stockholm. With some trepidation, he successfully demonstrated it eighteen times on the same heart. Loewi correctly attributed the difficulties in reproducing his results to chemical differences in different species of frogs that were used.

In delivering the 1933 Harvey lecture in New York City, Loewi expressed doubts about the existence of chemical transmitters in the voluntary nervous system. It was left for Henry H. Dale to demonstrate the chemical transmission of nerve impulses at voluntary motor nerve endings. In 1936 Loewi published a report identifying adrenaline (epinephrine) as the transmitter in the sympathetic nervous system. Later, noradrenaline (norepinephrine) was shown to be the principal transmitter of the sympathetic nervous system. However, it was Loewi's simple, convincing demonstration that first brought the chemical-transmission theory within the range of directly experimental proof and investigation, thus opening the way to subsequent research.

Loewi and Dale were awarded the 1936 Nobel Prize for Physiology or Medicine "for their discoveries relating to chemical transmission of nerve impulses." In his presentation speech, Göran Liljestrand of the Karolinska Institute described the "very simple but ingenious experiment" through which Loewi "proved that the nerve stimulus can release substances having the action characteristic for the nerve stimulation." Liljestrand went on to say that "further observations left no doubt whatever that the nerve stimulus itself was passed on to the organ by chemical means."

With the Nazi occupation of Austria in 1938, Loewi and two of his young sons were arrested and imprisoned with many other Jewish citizens. He was released two months later, and his sons were released the following month. After transferring his Nobel Prize monies to a Nazi-controlled bank, Loewi was allowed to leave for Brussels, where he served as a visiting professor at the Free University. While he was visiting England in 1939, World War II broke out, and after several months at Oxford University, he became a research professor of pharmacology at New York University School of Medicine. Loewi arrived in New York City in June 1940; he was joined the following year by his wife and children. In 1946 he became an American citizen.

Continuing his research until 1955, Loewi spent most of his remaining years writing articles and his memoirs and delivering lectures. In 1958 his wife died suddenly, and in 1961 Loewi died in New York City at the age of eighty-eight.

Loewi was the recipient of numerous honors and prizes and was particularly pleased by his election to a foreign membership in the Royal Society of London in 1954. Among his awards were the Cameron Prize and Lectureship of the University of Edinburgh (1944) and honorary degrees from New York University, Yale University, and the universities of Graz and Frankfurt. He was an honorary member of the Physiological Society of London, the Harvey Society, and the Italian Society of Experimental Biology.

SELECTED WORKS: The Secretion of the Urine, 1917; From the Workshop of Discovery, 1953.

ABOUT: Biographical Memoirs of Fellows of the Royal Society, volume 8, 1962; Dictionary of Scientific Biography, volume 8, 1973; The Excitement and Fascination of Science, 1965; Haymaker, W., and Schiller, W. The Founders of Neurology, 1970; Ingle, D. J. (ed.) A Dozen Doctors, 1963; Perspectives in Biology and Medicine Autumn 1960.

LORENTZ, HENDRIK
(July 18, 1853–February 4, 1928)
Nobel Prize for Physics, 1902
(shared with Pieter Zeeman)

The Dutch physicist Hendrik Antoon Lorentz was born in Arnhem to Gerrit Frederik

Lorentz, who owned a nursery, and Geertruida (van Ginkel) Lorentz. The boy's mother died when he was four years old, and five years later his father married Luberta Hupkes. Lorentz attended high school in Arnhem, excelling in all subjects.

In 1870 he entered the University of Leiden and became acquainted with Frederick Kaiser, a professor of astronomy, whose lectures on theoretical astronomy intrigued him. In less than two years, Lorentz earned a B.S. in physics and mathematics. Returning to Arnhem, he taught in the local high school while preparing for his doctoral examination, which he passed summa cum laude in 1873. Two years later he received a Ph.D. from Leiden with a dissertation on the theory of the reflection and refraction of light, in which he investigated some of the implications of James Clerk Maxwell's electromagnetic theory with regard to light waves. His dissertation was soon recognized as a work of considerable importance.

Lorentz continued living at home and teaching high school until 1877, when he was appointed to the chair in theoretical physics at the University of Leiden. Theoretical physics was just emerging as a separate discipline, and the chair at Leiden was one of the first of its kind in Europe. The appointment suited Lorentz, because he was particularly gifted in formulating theory and applying advanced mathematics to the solution of physical problems.

Continuing his investigation of optical phenomena, Lorentz published a paper in 1878 predicting the relation between a body's density and its index of refraction (the ratio of the velocity of light in a vacuum to its velocity in the body, which determines how much the body bends light). It happened that the Danish physicist Ludwig Lorenz had published the same formula earlier, and therefore it became known as the Lorentz-Lorenz formula. Lorentz's paper is particularly interesting, however, because it is based on the assumption that a material object contains oscillating electrically charged particles that interact with the incident light waves. Lorentz's work supported the view that matter is composed of atoms and molecules, a view not completely accepted at the time. During the 1880s his primary research interest was in the kinetic theory of gases, which describes the motion of molecules and relates their temperature to their average kinetic energy.

In 1892 Lorentz began to formulate a theory of what he and others would later call electrons. Electricity, he said, resulted from the

HENDRIK LORENTZ

motion of tiny charged particles, positive and negative electrons. (It was later established that all electrons are negatively charged.) Lorentz deduced that oscillations of these minute charged particles produced electromagnetic waves, including light and the radio waves predicted by Maxwell and discovered by Heinrich Hertz in 1888. During the 1890s, as Lorentz further developed the electron theory and used it to unify and simplify Maxwell's electromagnetic theory, he published important papers on many physics topics, among them one on the splitting of spectral lines in a magnetic field.

When light from a glowing gas is passed through a slit and separated by a spectroscope into its component frequencies, or colors, the different colors appear as a line spectrum, a series of bright lines on a black background whose positions indicate their frequencies. Each spectrum is characteristic of a particular gas. Lorentz assumed that the frequencies of oscillations of electrons determined the frequencies in the emitted light. Furthermore, he suggested that a magnetic field should alter the motion of the electrons and slightly vary the oscillation frequencies, splitting the single spectral lines into multiples. In 1896 Lorentz's colleague at Leiden, PIETER ZEEMAN, placed a sodium flame between the poles of an electromagnet and found that sodium's two most prominent spectral lines broadened. After further painstaking observations with various flames, Zeeman confirmed the implications of Lorentz's theory by establishing that broadened spectral lines were actually groups of separate components. The splitting of spectral lines in a magnetic field became known as the Zeeman effect. Zeeman also confirmed Lorentz's prediction that the emitted light would be polarized in certain ways.

Although the Zeeman effect was not fully explained until the advent of quantum theory in the twentieth century, Lorentz's explanation based on electron oscillations accounted for its simpler manifestations. At the end of the nineteenth century, many physicists believed—correctly, as it happened—that the spectra would prove to be keys to the mystery of atomic structure. Lorentz's use of electron theory to explain a spectral phenomenon was therefore considered an extremely important step toward elucidating the structure of matter. In 1897 J. J. THOMSON discovered the electron in the form of a free-moving particle in electric discharges in vacuum tubes. Its properties proved to be the same as Lorentz's postulated electrons oscillating in atoms.

Lorentz and Zeeman were awarded the 1902 Nobel Prize for Physics "in recognition of the extraordinary services they rendered by their researches into the influence of magnetism upon radiation phenomena." "The greatest credit for the further development of the [Maxwell] electromagnetic theory of light is due to Professor Lorentz," said Hjalmar Théel of the Royal Swedish Academy of Sciences in his presentation speech. "While Maxwell's theory is free from any assumptions of an atomistic nature, Lorentz starts from the hypothesis that in matter extremely small particles, called electrons, are the carriers of certain specific charges," Théel went on.

At the end of the nineteenth century and the beginning of the twentieth, Lorentz was recognized as the world's leading theoretical physicist. His work, which extended beyond electricity, magnetism, and optics to embrace kinetics, thermodynamics, mechanics, statistical analysis, and hydrodynamics, developed physical theory as far as it could be taken within the limits of classical physics and profoundly affected the development of modern relativity and quantum theory.

In 1904 he published his best-known equations, called the Lorentz transformations, which described a shortening in the dimensions of a moving body along the direction of motion and a change in the perception of time. The effect was very small but increased as the velocity approached the velocity of light. This work was an attempt to explain the failure to detect the influence of the ether, a mysterious, hypothetical substance then thought to fill all space. The ether was considered necessary as a medium for propagating electromagnetic waves such as light, just as the molecules of air are necessary to propagate sound waves. Despite the many difficulties encountered in defining the properties of a medium that was everywhere yet eluded observation, scientists were convinced it existed. One consequence of the ether seemed unavoidable. If the speed of light is measured with a moving instrument, then the measured speed should be faster when the motion is toward the light source and slower when the motion is away from the source. The ether could be conceived as a wind carrying the light, making the light travel faster past an observer heading into the wind and more slowly past an observer for whom the ether is a tail wind.

In a famous experiment performed in 1887 by ALBERT A. MICHELSON and Edward W. Morley, using an extremely precise instrument called an interferometer, light rays were made to travel a fixed distance in the direction of the earth's motion and returned traveling in the opposite direction. They were then compared with rays that traveled the same distance at right angles to the earth's motion. If the ether exerted any effect, the times of travel of the two beams would be sufficiently different, due to differences in effective velocity, for the instrument to detect. Astonishingly, for ether proponents, no difference was found.

Various explanations, such as the earth's dragging the ether along with it so that no relative motion existed, were ultimately unsatisfactory. To resolve the problem, Lorentz (and, independently, the Irish physicist G. F. FitzGerald) proposed that motion through the ether caused the structure of the interferometer (and, by inference, any moving body) to shorten by an amount that accounted for the apparent absence of a measurable difference in velocity between the light rays in the experiment. The Lorentz transformations had far-reaching consequences for physical theory and strongly influenced the development of the special theory of relativity the following year by ALBERT EINSTEIN, who had great respect for Lorentz. However, whereas Lorentz believed the deformation of moving bodies to be caused by molecular forces of some kind, the change in time to be a mathematical device, and the constancy of the speed of light for all observers to be a consequence of his theory, Einstein presented relativity and the constancy of the speed of light as basic principles rather than as problems. From a radically altered view of space and time and with the assumption of a few fundamental postulates, Einstein was able to derive the Lorentz transformations and eliminated the need for an ether.

Sympathetic to innovative ideas, Lorentz was among the first scientists to support Einstein's theory of special relativity and MAX PLANCK's quantum theory. During the first three decades of the twentieth century, Lorentz took great interest in the development of modern physics, recognizing that the new ideas about time, space, matter, and energy resolved many of the problems he had encountered in his own research. So highly esteemed was Lorentz by his colleagues that he was asked in 1911 to serve as chairman of the first Solvay Physics Conference, an international gathering of eminent physicists; he performed this function annually until his death.

In 1912 Lorentz resigned from the University of Leiden to devote most of his time to research, but he continued to lecture there once a week. Moving to Haarlem, he served as curator of the physics collection of the Teyler's Stichting Museum, which provided him with a laboratory. In 1919 he became involved in one of the world's largest land reclamation and flood control projects, heading a committee to study the movement of sea water during and after the draining of the Zuider Zee (an inlet of the North Sea). Following World War I, he became active in the cause of restoring scientific cooperation, trying to persuade international scientific organizations to readmit citizens of the Central Powers. He was elected in 1923 to the League of Nation's International Commission on Intellectual Cooperation, consisting of seven of the world's most eminent scholars; two years later he became the commission's president. Lorentz remained intellectually active until his death in Haarlem on February 4, 1928.

Lorentz married Aletta Catherina Kaiser, the niece of his former astronomy professor, in 1881. They had four children, one of whom died in infancy. Lorentz was known as a man of great personal charm and modesty; these traits, along with his gift for languages, suited him to his positions of leadership in international organizations and conferences.

In addition to the Nobel Prize, Lorentz received the Copley Medal and the Rumford Medal of the Royal Society of London. He was awarded doctorates from the University of Paris and from Cambridge University and was elected to membership in the Royal Society of London and the German Physical Society. He became secretary of the Dutch Society of Sciences in 1912.

SELECTED WORKS: The Theory of Electrons, 1909; The Einstein Theory of Relativity, 1920; The Principle of Relativity, 1923, with others; Problems of Modern Physics, 1927; Lectures on Theoretical Physics (8 vols.) 1931; Collected Papers (9 vols.) 1934–1939.

ABOUT: Dictionary of Scientific Biography, volume 8, 1973; Einstein, A. H. A. Lorentz: His Creative Genius and His Personality, 1953; de Haas-Lorentz, G. L. (ed.) Hendrik Lorentz: Impressions of His Life and Work, 1957; Thomson, G. The Inspiration of Science, 1961.

LORENZ, KONRAD

(November 7, 1903–   )
Nobel Prize for Physiology or Medicine, 1973
(shared with Karl von Frisch and Niko Tinbergen)

The Austrian zoologist and ethologist Konrad Zacharias Lorenz was born in Vienna, the younger of two sons, to Emma (Lecher) Lorenz and Adolf Lorenz. His father, the son of a harness maker, had risen from an impoverished childhood to become a wealthy orthopedic surgeon who built an ornate mansion in Altenberg, near Vienna, which he had decorated with huge paintings and Roman statues. Roaming the grounds and marshes around Lorenz Hall, Lorenz developed what he later called an "inordinate love for animals."

It was while raising domestic ducks that the young Lorenz discovered imprinting, a rapid form of learning which occurs in early life and by which social attachment and identification are established in animals. "From a neighbor," he recalled later, "I got a one-day-old duckling and found, to my intense joy, that it transferred its following response to my person. At the same time, my interest became irreversibly fixated on waterfowl, and I became an expert on their behavior even as a child."

Soon the boy had collected a remarkable variety of animals, both domestic and wild, that lived in the house and on the extensive grounds of Lorenz Hall as though it were a private zoo. Under these circumstances Lorenz familiarized himself with many kinds of animals and became disinclined to think of them as mere living machines. His objectivity, however, prevented him from interpreting animal behavior according to human thoughts and feelings; rather, he became absorbed with problems of instinct—how and why animals behave in appropriate and complex ways without having human intelligence.

After receiving his early education at a pri-

KONRAD LORENZ

vate school conducted by his aunt, Lorenz entered the Schottengymnasium, where the level of scientific instruction was exceptionally high. In addition, Lorenz's habits of observation were supplemented by training in zoological methods and the principles of evolution. "On finishing high school," Lorenz wrote later, "I was still obsessed with evolution and wanted to study zoology and paleontology. However, I obeyed my father, who wanted me to study medicine."

In 1922 Lorenz enrolled at Columbia University in New York City, but he returned to Austria six months later and entered the University of Vienna's medical program. Although he had little interest in becoming a physician, he found the medical instruction pertinent to his preferred vocation: ethology, the study of animal behavior under natural conditions. According to Lorenz, the university's anatomy teacher, Ferdinand Hochstetter, provided "a very thorough instruction in the methodological procedure of distinguishing similarities caused by common descent from those due to parallel adaptation," and Lorenz was "quick to realize . . . that the comparative method was as applicable to behavior patterns as it was to anatomical structure."

While working toward his medical degree, Lorenz began systematically to compare instinctive animal behavior patterns; he also served as a demonstrator in the University of Vienna's anatomy department. Upon receiving his medical degree in 1928, Lorenz was promoted to assistant in the anatomy department, although his interest still lay with eth-

ology rather than medicine. He began graduate work in zoology while teaching comparative animal behavior.

Before 1930 two established but opposing viewpoints dominated the study of instinct: vitalism and behaviorism. Vitalists (or instinctivists) watched the complex actions of animals in their natural habitats and were struck by the way in which an animal's instincts suited the performance of its natural tasks. They either attributed instincts to a vague concept of "nature's wisdom" or assumed that animal behavior is motivated by the same factors that shape human actions. Behaviorists, on the other hand, studied animal behavior in the laboratory, testing the capacity of animals to solve artificial problems, such as mazes. The behaviorists attributed animal behavior to chains of reflex responses (similar to those defined by CHARLES S. SHERRINGTON), held together by the classical conditioning studied by IVAN PAVLOV. Behaviorists, whose studies focused on learned actions, were uncomfortable with the concept of instinct, a complex set of completely unlearned, innate responses.

Initially favoring the behaviorists, Lorenz assumed that instincts were based on chain reflexes. In his research, however, he gathered increasing evidence that instinctive behavior is internally generated. For instance, animals do not normally exhibit mating behavior unless they are exposed to a member of the opposite sex, and not always even then—stimulation must pass a certain threshold for the instinct to be activated. If an animal is kept in isolation long enough, however, the threshold declines—that is, less stimulation will be needed to activate the instinct—until eventually the animal will exhibit mating behavior even when no stimulation is available. Lorenz reported his findings in a series of papers between 1927 and 1938.

It was not until 1936, however, that Lorenz accepted the import of his own evidence and took the position that instincts are caused not by reflexes but by internally generated drives. At a symposium in Leiden later that year, Lorenz met NIKO TINBERGEN; their "views coincided to an amazing degree," Lorenz said later. "In [our] discussions some conceptualizations took form which later proved fruitful to ethological research." In fact, the concept of instinct that Lorenz and Tinbergen worked out over the course of the next few years laid the foundation of modern ethology.

Later, Lorenz and Tinbergen hypothesized that instinctive behavior begins with internal drives, which motivate an animal to seek a particular set of environmental or social stimuli. This so-called orientation behavior is often highly variable; once the animal encounters certain cues (the sign stimuli or releasers), it automatically performs a stereotypical set of movements called the fixed action pattern (FAP). Every animal has a distinctive system of FAPs and associated releasers which are integral to its species and which evolve in response to natural selection.

In 1937 Lorenz began lecturing on animal psychology at Vienna. At that time, he was studying the domestication process in geese, which involves the loss of social skills and an increase in the power of the hunger and sex drives. He found the possibility that such a process might be occurring in the human race profoundly disturbing. Shortly after the annexation and invasion of Austria by Germany in 1938, Lorenz did what he later called "a very ill-advised thing. . . . I wrote about the dangers of domestication and . . . couched my writing in the worst of Nazi terminology." Some of Lorenz's critics have termed this aspect of his work racist; others consider it the result of political naiveté.

Two years after receiving an appointment to the chair of psychology at the University of Königsberg (now Kaliningrad, USSR), Lorenz was inducted into the German army as a physician, even though he had never practiced medicine. After being sent to the eastern front in 1942, he was captured by the Soviets and put to work in a hospital for prisoners of war. He was not repatriated until 1948, long after many of his friends and relatives had given him up for dead.

During the first few years after his return to Austria, Lorenz was unable to obtain an official position but managed to continue his research in Altenberg with financial aid from friends. In 1950 he and Erich von Holst established the Max Planck Institute for Behavioral Physiology.

For the next two decades Lorenz continued basic ethological research, concentrating on the study of waterfowl. His status as the founder of modern ethology was unchallenged, and as such he took a leading role in disputes between ethologists and those of other disciplines, particularly behavioral psychologists.

Some of Lorenz's most controversial views are expressed in *Das sogenannte Böse: zur Naturgeschichte der Aggression* (1963, translated as *On Aggression*). As the German title suggests, Lorenz regards aggression as no more than a "so-called evil" because, despite its often destructive consequences, this instinct serves

such essential functions as the selection of mates, the establishment of social hierarchies, and the maintenance of territories. Critics of the book have objected that its conclusions encourage the acceptance of violence in human behavior, even though Lorenz himself agrees that innate human aggression is all the more dangerous because "the invention of artificial weapons upset the equilibrium of killing potential and social inhibitions."

The 1973 Nobel Prize for Physiology or Medicine was shared by Lorenz, Tinbergen, and KARL VON FRISCH "for their discoveries concerning organization and elicitation of individual and social behavior patterns." Lorenz, in particular, was cited for having "observed behavior patterns that could not reasonably have been learned but were to be interpreted as being genetically programmed." More than any other researcher, Lorenz is responsible for the recognition that behavior arises from the same genetic foundation as other animal characteristics and is thus subject to natural selection.

Since his retirement from the Max Planck Institute in 1973, Lorenz has continued his research at the Department for Animal Sociology, Institute for Comparative Ethology, of the Austrian Academy of Science in Altenberg, where he also lives.

In 1927 Lorenz married Margarethe (Gretl) Gebhardt, a childhood friend; they have two daughters and a son.

Among the awards and honors bestowed on Lorenz are the Gold Medal of the New York Zoological Society (1955), the Vienna Prize for Science given by the Vienna City Council (1959), and the Kalinga Prize given by UNESCO (1970). Lorenz is a foreign member of the Royal Society of London and the American National Academy of Sciences.

SELECTED WORKS: My Life and Work, 1936; King Solomon's Ring, 1952; Man Meets Dog, 1954; The Evolution and Modification of Behavior, 1965; Studies in Animal and Human Behavior (2 vols.) 1970–1971; Motivation of Human and Animal Behavior, 1973, with Paul Leyhausen; Civilized Man's Eight Deadly Sins, 1974; This Land of Europe, 1976, with Dennis Stock; Behind the Mirror, 1977; The Year of the Greylag Goose, 1979; The Foundations of Ethology, 1981; The Waning of Humaneness, 1987.

ABOUT: Evans, R. I. (ed.) Konrad Lorenz: The Man and His Ideas, 1975; Fromm, E. The Anatomy of Human Destructiveness, 1974; Montagu, A. (ed.) Man and Aggression, 1973; Nisbett, A. Konrad Lorenz, 1976; Sills, D. (ed.) International Encyclopedia of the Social Sciences: Biographical Supplement, 1979; Thorpe, W. H. The Origin and Rise of Ethology, 1979.

LURIA, SALVADOR

(August 13, 1912–   )
Nobel Prize for Physiology or Medicine,
 1969
(shared with Max Delbrück and Alfred
 Hershey)

SALVADOR LURIA

The Italian-American biologist Salvador
Edward Luria was born in Turin, Italy, to Ester (Sacerdote) and David Luria. In 1929, after
receiving his early education in the local public
schools, he enrolled in the medical school of
the University of Turin. While studying under
Giuseppe Levi, a professor of anatomy and
histology, Luria developed a technical facility
for the culturing of living cells. After he received his medical degree summa cum laude
in 1935, he served as a medical officer in the
Italian army for three years. At that time he
began reading in physics and mathematics, and
after being discharged from the army, he studied medical physics and radiology at the Curie
Laboratory of the Institute of Radium in Paris.

In 1938 Luria developed an interest in bacteriophages (viruses that attack bacteria) and
soon became involved with experiments on the
X-ray radiation of bacteriophage particles, in
an attempt to produce genetic mutations. When
it became apparent in 1940 that Italy was about
to join Germany in World War II, Luria departed for France. After a brief stay, he traveled to the United States to accept an
appointment as a research assistant at the College of Physicians and Surgeons of Columbia
University in New York City. At a meeting of
the American Physical Society in Philadelphia
the following year, he met MAX DELBRÜCK,
who later spent a few days in Luria's laboratory in New York, where the two scientists
planned a series of collaborative experiments.
During the period of 1942–1943 a Guggenheim Fellowship enabled Luria to spend part
of his time working at Princeton University
and the rest at Vanderbilt University in Nashville, Tennessee, working with Delbrück. In
1943 he was appointed instructor in the Department of Bacteriology at Indiana University in Bloomington. He became assistant
professor two years later and an associate professor in 1947.

For some time bacteriologists had recognized the phenomenon of resistance, the appearance of bacterial variants resistant to both
viruses and bactericidal drugs. There was speculation that resistance appeared to be either
an adaptation of the bacteria in response to
something in the environment or a spontaneous genetic change, a mutation that allowed
a new hereditary strain to survive. In his work
with Delbrück, Luria's first problem "was to
decide whether the resistant bacteria were
spontaneously arising mutants or were cells
that became resistant as a result of an action
of the phage on otherwise normal bacteria,"
as he wrote later.

While attending a faculty dance at the
Bloomington Country Club, Luria happened
to watch a colleague playing a slot machine.
It suddenly occurred to him that there was an
analogy between the payoff of a slot machine
and the clustering of mutant bacteria. A slot
machine returns most of the money put into
it, but at random—sometimes a few coins at
a time, and on rare occasions a great many.
Similarly, in a bacteria culture colonies are
clustered in groups of one, two, four, eight,
and so on, "plus some larger clusters—the
jackpots," as Luria said, "each due to a mutation that happened some generation earlier
than might be expected by pure chance." Based
on his observations of the fluctuating returns
from slot machines, Luria devised an experiment to distinguish between induced resistance and resistance from a previous spontaneous mutation. This so-called fluctuation
test, published jointly in 1943 with Delbrück
(who supplied the mathematical analysis),
provided the first evidence for bacterial mutation. "This was a major step forward in genetics," Luria said later. "With no other
organism had it been possible to calculate the
spontaneous mutation rate for one specific gene,
or in fact, for all genes. If genes of bacteria
were the same kinds of structures as genes of

other organisms, bacteria became overnight a choice organism for genetic research," superior even to fruit flies or molds in their vast numbers and the speed with which new generations can be bred.

Around the same time, Luria and Delbrück began to collaborate with ALFRED HERSHEY, a biologist who was conducting bacteriophage research at Washington University in St. Louis, Missouri. The three scientists formed the core of the Phage Group. This informal circle of investigators drafted an agreement to work only with seven strains of bacteriophage that infect the colon bacillus *Escherichia coli* strain B, so that experimental results from different laboratories could be compared. Working independently, Delbrück and Hershey showed in 1946 that different strains of bacteriophage may exchange genetic material if more than one strain infects the same bacterial cell.

In 1950 Luria was appointed professor of bacteriology at the University of Illinois at Champaign-Urbana. The next year he published unequivocal proof that bacteriophage (and viral) genes undergo spontaneous mutations in a process similar to that of bacteria. He planned to present a paper at the 1953 meeting of the Society for General Microbiology in Oxford, England. However, American politics were dominated by Joseph McCarthy at that time, and although Luria had been a naturalized citizen since 1947, he was denied a visa for travel. His paper, which was read by his former student JAMES D. WATSON, discussed Luria's belief that the phage protein, rather than deoxyribonucleic acid (DNA), carried the genetic information. From the model of DNA proposed by Watson and FRANCIS CRICK it was clear that mutations involved deletions or substitutions in the purine-pyrimidine bases of the DNA molecule.

Luria was appointed professor and chairman of the Department of Microbiology at the Massachusetts Institute of Technology (MIT) in Cambridge in 1959. There he developed a training program for young scientists interested in bacterial and viral genetics. He also studied the biochemistry of bacterial cell membranes. In 1964 he was named Sedgwick Professor of Biology at MIT and, in 1965, he became a nonresident fellow of the Salk Institute for Biological Studies in San Diego.

Luria, Delbrück, and Hershey shared the 1969 Nobel Prize for Physiology or Medicine "for their discoveries concerning the replication mechanism and the genetic structure of viruses." "These discoveries have decisively influenced the development within many fields

of biological research," said Sven Gard of the Karolinska Institute in his presentation speech. "The charting of the fundamental processes in the life cycle of the bacteriophages was a necessary condition for attempts to define them in chemical terms, on the molecular level," Gard went on. Noting the significance of the laureates' work for the field of genetics, Gard pointed out that it had revealed "the mechanisms of the genetic regulation of the vital processes. . . . Last but not least, bacteriophage research has given us the better insight into the nature of viruses, which is necessary for the understanding and combatting of virus diseases of higher beings."

In 1970 Luria was named institute professor in the Department of Biology at MIT. Since 1974 he has also been director of the Center for Cancer Research. In discussing genetic manipulation, Luria has warned that "we need to create a society in which technology is purposefully directed toward socially chosen goals." Critical of the high cost of national defense and the American lunar programs, he donated part of his Nobel Prize money to various antiwar groups.

Luria married Zella Hurwitz, a psychologist, in 1945; they have a son. An amateur painter and sculptor, Luria also teaches a course in world literature.

Luria's awards and honors include the Lenghi Prize of the National Academy of Sciences of Italy (1965), and the Louisa Gross Horwitz Prize of Columbia University (1965). He holds memberships in the American Society of Microbiology, the National Academy of Sciences, the American Association for the Advancement of Science, and the American Philosophical Society.

SELECTED WORKS: General Virology, 1953; Life: The Unfinished Experiment, 1973; Thirty-six Lectures in Biology, 1975; A View of Life, 1981, with others; A Slot Machine, a Broken Test Tube: An Autobiography, 1985.

ABOUT: New York Times October 17, 1969; Science October 24, 1969; Washington Post October 17, 1969.

LUTHULI, ALBERT
(1898–July 21, 1967)
Nobel Prize for Peace, 1960

Albert John Mvumbi Luthuli (also spelled Lutuli), a South African political leader, was born at a Seventh Day Adventist mission near Bulawayo, Rhodesia (now Zimbabwe). Although the exact date of his birth was not recorded, it is estimated to have been 1898. Luthuli, whose Zulu name was Mvumbi (Constant Rain), belonged to a high-ranking family in the Zulu community. His parents, John Bunyan Luthuli and Mtonya (Gumede) Luthuli, were born in South Africa but later moved to Rhodesia, where the elder Luthuli became an evangelist and interpreter. He died shortly after his son's birth.

Around 1908 Luthuli's mother returned to Natal Province, a former British colony in South Africa, and the family settled on a farm run by Christian missionaries. Intending her son to have a good education, Mtonya Luthuli sent him to live with his uncle, Martin Luthuli, the chief of Groutville. There Luthuli attended school for the first time. After a year at the Ohlange Institute, a preparatory school, Luthuli entered Edendale, a Methodist teacher-training institute, in 1915. Graduating two years later, he became the principal and sole faculty member of a small intermediate school in Blaauwbosch, Natal. During this time, he was also confirmed and became a lay preacher in the Methodist church.

Winning a Natal Department of Education award in 1920, Luthuli studied for two additional years at Adams Mission Station College. He subsequently accepted a faculty appointment and taught there for the next thirteen years, also founding the Zulu Language and Cultural Society, serving as choirmaster, and acting as secretary of the South African Football Association. In 1927 he married Nokukhanya (The Bright One) Behengu, a teacher and granddaughter of a Zulu chief; they had seven children.

In 1933 a group of tribal elders from Groutville approached Luthuli to ask him to stand for election as chief of the Umvoti Mission Reserve. After resisting their persistent entreaties for two years, he finally resigned from Adams at the end of 1935 and became chief the following year. In Groutville, the administrative center of the reserve, Luthuli administered the affairs of about 5,000 people. Their economic hardships and exploitation at the hands of the white minority stirred his political conscience.

The same year that Luthuli became chief, the South African government passed two laws that severely curbed the rights of blacks. Although making up 80 percent of the population, blacks were stricken from the common voting rolls in Cape Province. Also, in the House of Assembly, blacks were allowed only 3 representatives (who were whites), whereas

ALBERT LUTHULI

the white population had 150 representatives. In addition, black families were allotted only 4 or 5 acres of land in contrast to the 375 acres granted to each white citizen.

Although Luthuli was able to organize sugarcane farmers and win a few economic concessions from the government, he began to realize that under white rule blacks could never achieve significant progress. He also came to feel that the tribal system was "a velvet-glove act," as he later described it, "designed to give Africans in the reserves some feeling of autonomy" while whites held the actual reins of power. As yet, he had formulated no plan of action to oppose the government, but his confidence in the church as an agent of political and social change had begun to ebb. In 1945 he joined the Natal chapter of the African National Congress (ANC), an organization formed in 1912 to unite the tribes and obtain black suffrage.

During World War II, nonwhites in South Africa strongly supported the government, which encouraged them to believe that their loyalty would be rewarded after the war with an expanded program of civil rights. In 1946, however, Prime Minister Jan Smuts initiated the policy of apartheid, or separate development of the races. A series of laws stripped blacks of their voting rights, set up a pass system requiring blacks to carry travel permits, and banned interracial sex. These laws also sharply restricted the rights of coloreds (people of mixed race) and Asians, thousands of whom voluntarily went to jail in protest.

Luthuli became increasingly involved in political causes. He spoke to South African groups and in 1948 traveled to the United States to warn that South Africa was on "the crest of a crisis" and to ask for support of the black cause. Returning home, he was elected president of the Natal chapter of the ANC, which launched a Defiance Campaign the following year "to bring the white man to his senses," as Luthuli later said. Using the techniques of civil disobedience, blacks violated segregation and curfew laws and willingly went to jail. Luthuli himself was jailed in Natal, although the case against him was postponed indefinitely. When government representatives asked Luthuli to resign either as president of the Natal ANC or as chief of the reserve, he refused. Consequently, he was dismissed from his tribal duties in Groutville. Nevertheless, supporting himself and his family on a few acres of farmland, he continued his political activities.

One month after his dismissal, Luthuli was elected president-general of the ANC. He began touring South Africa, denouncing the pass laws and the Bantu Education Act, which abolished mission schools, and urging nonviolent protest. In retaliation, the government banned his appearance in major cities or at gatherings for two years. At the end of this time, he resumed his speaking engagements. He was about to lead a protest against the forced removal of 75,000 blacks from Sophiatown when the government ordered him confined to the Groutville area for another two years. He was reelected president of the ANC in 1955.

Five months after the second ban expired, Luthuli and 155 others were arrested for treason, a capital crime, and imprisoned in Johannesburg. Their trial, which dragged on for months, solidified Luthuli's status as de facto leader of South Africa's black population and brought him to international prominence. During the proceedings, he managed to organize peaceful protests. These included "stay-at-homes," in which blacks boycotted their jobs. Eventually, the charges against Luthuli and sixty-four others were dropped.

Luthuli set out again on a speaking tour, addressing both blacks and whites throughout Natal and Cape provinces. Again, the government issued a ban, this time for five years, "for promoting feelings of hostility between the European . . . and non-European inhabitants." After the Sharpeville Massacre in 1960, in which sixty-nine unarmed blacks were killed by the police during a demonstration against the pass laws, Luthuli burned his passbook and urged other Africans to follow his example. The government declared a state of emergency, outlawed the ANC, and arrested more than 18,000 Africans, including Luthuli. Luthuli received a six-month prison sentence that was suspended in view of his ill health and high blood pressure.

The following year, the prime ministers of the British Commonwealth nations were meeting in London. Luthuli, again confined to Groutville, cabled the *Times* of London, urging the prime ministers to deny South Africa's application for continued membership in the Commonwealth. Opposition to its membership grew so intense that the South African government withdrew before a vote could be taken. In the spring of 1961, South Africa's white leaders promulgated a new constitution and declared the nation (formerly the Union of South Africa) to be fully independent as the Republic of South Africa.

Luthuli received the 1960 Nobel Peace Prize in 1961 for his efforts "to promote the idea of justice in the individual, in the nation, and among the nations." Gunnar Jahn of the Norwegian Nobel Committee said of Luthuli that his "activity has been characterized by a firm and unswerving approach: never has he succumbed to the temptation to use violent means in his struggle for his people." The first black African to receive a Nobel Prize, Luthuli accepted the award as a "welcome recognition of the role played by the African people during the last fifty years to establish, peacefully, a society in which merit, and not race, would fix the position of the individual in the life of the nation." He also described the prize as "a democratic declaration of solidarity with those who fight to widen the area of liberty in my part of the world." But the fight was not over, he reminded the audience. "To us all, free or not free, the call of the hour is to redeem the name and honor of Mother Africa."

Upon his return to South Africa, Luthuli was greeted by cheering crowds but was prohibited from addressing them and was forced to resume his confinement in Groutville. He published his autobiography, *Let My People Go,* the following year. Under the terms of the Sabotage Act, the book was banned in South Africa, and Luthuli was barred from giving speeches of any kind. Even to quote or publish his remarks was a serious crime. His hearing and eyesight began to fail, and on July 21, 1967, while attempting to cross a railroad bridge, he was struck by a train and fatally injured. He was buried nine days later in Groutville.

651

ADDITIONAL WORKS: "What I Would Do If I Were Prime Minister," Ebony February 1962; Africa's Freedom, 1964, with others.

ABOUT: Atlantic Monthly April 1959; Benson, M. Chief Albert Lutuli of South Africa, 1963; Callan, E. Albert John Luthuli and the South African Race Conflict, 1965; Legum, C., and Legum, M. The Bitter Choice: Eight South Africans' Resistance to Tyranny, 1968; New York Times July 22, 1967; Sampson, A. The Treason Cage, 1958; Times (London) July 22, 1967.

LWOFF, ANDRÉ
(May 8, 1902–)
Nobel Prize for Physiology or Medicine, 1965
(shared with François Jacob and Jacques Monod)

ANDRÉ LWOFF

The French microbiologist André Michel Lwoff (lə wôf′) was born in Ainay-le-Château, a small village in central France, to parents who had emigrated from Russia in the late nineteenth century. His father, Salomon Lwoff, who was a psychiatrist, was chief physician at a psychiatric hospital, and his mother, Marie (Siminovitch) Lwoff, was a sculptor. His father was appointed to another hospital in Neuilly-sur-Marne, near Paris, when Lwoff was a child. Growing up in this rural environment, the boy swam, played tennis, and became a decent marksman. As part of Lwoff's education, his father had the boy accompany him on hospital rounds and visits to other institutions. On one such occasion he met his father's friend ILYA METCHNIKOFF, who showed him a typhoid bacillus under a microscope. He also recalled the outbreak of World War I when he was twelve years old. Fighting advanced to within twenty miles of his home. "The antiaircraft guns were close and the splinters [shrapnel] were whistling and drumming on the roof," he remembered. "I listened to the strange music with curiosity, perfectly unaware of the danger. . . . I was not mature enough to realize the depth of the war tragedy."

Although Lwoff wanted to study biology in order to do research, his father advised him to study medicine so that he could earn a living. At the age of seventeen, Lwoff enrolled in the University of Paris (the Sorbonne) under the Faculté des Sciences to study medicine and biology and spent the next three summers at the Marine Biology Laboratory at Roscoff in Brittany. In 1921 he became an assistant at the Pasteur Institute in Paris, where he worked under the famous microbiologists Édouard Chatton and Félix Mesnil. The same year he received a fellowship that enabled him to work part-time at the institute while he completed his medical studies. His doctoral dissertation, based on his research at the Marine Biology Laboratory, was a study of the eye pigment of copepods, small parasitic animals that live in fresh or salt water.

During the 1920s Lwoff studied ciliates, one-celled animals covered with hairlike structures called cilia, to determine their nutritional requirements and morphology (the formation of their tissues and organs). In the course of his research, he discovered new species of ciliated protozoa. While working at the Pasteur Institute he met a fellow microbiologist, Marguérite Bourdaleix, whom he married in 1925 and with whom he was to collaborate for many years. Two years later Lwoff received his medical degree from the University of Paris, was appointed chief of a laboratory at the Pasteur Institute in 1929, and in 1932, received his Ph.D. from the University of Paris. With a Rockefeller Foundation fellowship the following year, he studied with OTTO MEYERHOF at the Kaiser Wilhelm Institute for Medical Research in Heidelberg.

Some twenty years earlier, in 1911, Casimir Funk, a Polish chemist, had proposed the term *vitamine* to describe unidentified substances necessary for human and animal growth. However, very few of these elements had been isolated or identified by the early 1930s. At Heidelberg, Lwoff investigated hematin, a growth factor in flagellates, another type of protozoa. As a result of his research, growth factors were defined for the first time as "specific substances which the organism is unable to synthesize and which are necessary for its growth and multiplication." Lwoff went on to study the biochemistry of thiamine (vitamin B_1) in certain protozoa and the physiology of nicotinamide (vitamin P, a member of the B complex). He proved that nicotinamide is present in colostrum, a watery fluid that is secreted in small amounts by female mammary glands immediately before the production of human milk.

With another Rockefeller grant in 1936, Lwoff continued his work on growth factors at the Molteno Institute in Cambridge, England. At the time, hematin, called growth factor X, was known to be essential for the growth of the bacterium *Haemophilus influenzae*. The Lwoffs identified growth factor X and demonstrated that it is a limiting factor in the growth of this bacterium.

Returning to Paris in 1938, Lwoff was appointed chief of the Department of Microbial Physiology at the Pasteur Institute, where he continued his research throughout World War II. After the war, in 1946, he attended a nomenclature conference in Cold Spring Harbor, New York, and helped establish a system of classification of microorganisms based on energy sources and synthetic processes. In the 1940s he also wrote two books, *Problems of Morphogenesis in Ciliates,* published in 1950, and *Biochemistry and Physiology of Protozoa,* published in 1951.

In his early research in the 1930s, Lwoff had described the characteristics of a previously misclassified genus of bacterium, which he renamed *Moraxella,* a species of which was later named *Moraxella lwoffii* in his honor. In the late 1940s Lwoff turned to research in the genetics of bacteria and viruses. The science of genetics began in 1866, when Gregor Mendel published his studies of the law of inheritance and postulated that physical traits of an organism are determined by "elements," later called genes. At the beginning of the twentieth century, it was discovered that genes reside on chromosomes, strands of genetic material in the nucleus of the cell. However, it was not until the 1940s that it was established that genes consist of deoxyribonucleic acid (DNA).

By that time, too, the first generation of virologists were able to describe the life cycle of bacteriophages. These virus particles infect bacterial cells, and after a noninfectious, or temperate, phase in the cell may multiply and cause lysis, or cell destruction. As the cell is destroyed, bacteriophage particles are released. Bacteria infected by phage particles are called lysogenic bacteria; the process of cell destruction (lysis) is called lysogeny.

Encouraged by two of his colleagues at the Pasteur Institute, FRANÇOIS JACOB and JACQUES MONOD, Lwoff began to study lysogenic bacteria and the process of lysogeny and, in 1950, made a remarkable discovery. He placed a lysogenic bacterium in a culture medium, watched it divide through nineteen generations of daughter cells, and then demonstrated that the daughter cells were also lysogenic, thus proving that lysogeny is a genetic trait. He also discovered that the lysogenic bacteriophage and the noninfectious, or temperate, phage particles differ; to describe the noninfectious phage, he coined the term *prophage.* After further research, Lwoff and his colleagues found that when subjected to ultraviolet light, the noninfectious prophage can be made to multiply and cause cell destruction.

Phage particles and most other virus particles consist of an inner core of DNA and an outer coat of protein. In 1952 ALFRED HERSHEY proved that bacteriophage particles reproduce themselves by replication of their inner core of DNA. Searching for the way bacteriophage genes are organized and regulated, Lwoff, Monod, and Jacob discovered that when a bacterial cell is infected, the prophage particle attaches itself to the chromosome of the cell, where the genes normally are, and, as Lwoff put it, "behaves as if it were a bacterial gene." The phage DNA has two kinds of genes, structural and regulatory. Structural genes transmit the genetic code from one generation to the next. During the prophage stage, the structural gene is suppressed by the regulatory gene, and as a result, the phage particle cannot reproduce. Lwoff found that ultraviolet light and other inducers counteract this effect, allowing phage multiplication and lysis, or destruction, of the bacterial cell.

This basic research led Lwoff to propose hypotheses about cancer and poliomyelitis. Lwoff and his colleagues at the Pasteur Institute believed that viruses cause cancer. According to their hypotheses, viruses may reside in human cells like the phage particles in bacterial cells. Lwoff correctly postulated that the carcinogenic properties of viruses reside in their protein coats and that the cancer-causing potential of viruses may be induced by a variety of factors, as the prophage stage could become lysogenic when subjected to ultraviolet light. Studying poliomyelitis in the 1950s, Lwoff demonstrated that, unlike the sensitive vaccine strains, some poliovirus strains are relatively insensitive to fluctuations in temperature.

Invited to deliver the prestigious Harvey lecture in New York in 1954, he discussed "control and interrelations of metabolic and viral diseases of bacteria." Three years later he published a paper, "The Concept of Viruses," and took part in a meeting of the Society of General Microbiology in London that sought to define the differences between viruses and small bacteria. He was appointed professor of microbiology at the University of Paris in 1959.

Lwoff shared the 1965 Nobel Prize for Physiology or Medicine with Jacob and Monod "for their discoveries concerning genetic control of enzyme and virus synthesis." "Action, coordination, variation—these are the most striking manifestations of living matter," said Sven Gard of the Karolinska Institute in his presentation speech. "By placing more emphasis on dynamic activity and mechanisms than on structure, you have laid the foundations for the science of molecular biology in the truest sense of the term."

Three years after receiving the Nobel Prize, Lwoff retired from the Pasteur Institute to become director of the Cancer Research Institute at Villejuif, near Paris. A member of the French Academy of Sciences, he served as president of the French Family Planning Movement in 1970. He is a foreign member of the American National Academy of Sciences, the Royal Society of London, and the Soviet Academy of Medicine. Honors from his native France include the Grand Cross and membership in the Legion of Honor. He received the Leeuwenhoek Medal of the Royal Netherlands Academy of Arts and Sciences (1960) and the Keilin Medal of the Biochemical Society in London (1964), and he was granted honorary degrees by several universities, including Harvard and Oxford.

SELECTED WORKS: Biological Order, 1962; Reflections on Patterns and Problems, 1967, with others.

ABOUT: Borek, E., and Monod, J. (eds.) Of Microbes and Life, 1971; The Excitement and Fascination of Science, volume 2, 1978; New York Times October 15, 1965; Science October 22, 1965.

LYNEN, FEODOR

(April 6, 1911–August 6, 1979)
Nobel Prize for Physiology or Medicine, 1964
(shared with Konrad Bloch)

The German biochemist Feodor Lynen (lü' nen) was born in Munich to Frieda (Prym)

FEODOR LYNEN

Lynen and Wilhelm Lynen, a professor of engineering at the Munich Technical University. Lynen, who received his early education in Munich, became interested in chemistry when his older brother installed a small chemistry laboratory in their home.

At the University of Munich, which he entered in 1930, Lynen studied chemistry under HEINRICH WIELAND. For a doctoral dissertation on the poisonous substance in the mushroom *Amanita phalloides,* Lynen received a Ph.D. in chemistry in 1937. A scholarship enabled him to remain at Munich to conduct research on the biochemistry of tumor tissue. He did not serve in the military during World War II, having been exempted because of permanent knee damage he suffered as a result of a skiing accident in 1932. He was appointed privatdocent (unsalaried lecturer) at the University of Munich in 1942. Wartime shortages and bombing raids made conditions increasingly difficult, and in 1942 his laboratory was moved to Schöndorf, a small village outside Munich. The following year the chemistry department at the University of Munich was destroyed. After Germany surrendered, Lynen's political integrity was proved, and he was allowed to resume his university teaching. In 1947 he became assistant professor of chemistry at the University of Munich, and in 1953 he was appointed full professor. The next year he accepted a concurrent appointment as director of the Max Planck Institute for Cell Chemistry.

Lynen expressed his attitude toward scientific research in his autobiographical notes: "I have the philosophy that persistence is an essential element in science which, however, should not exclude tackling more than one problem at a time. Also, a scientist wants to be happy, and if he does not progress with one problem, he might be more successful with others." Over the years Lynen's research at the University of Munich focused on intermediary metabolism, fatty acid oxidation, fatty acid biosynthesis, cholesterol synthesis, and the synthesis of rubber.

Intermediary metabolism involves the biochemical degradation of glucose (sugar) and fat molecules, with the generation of cellular energy in high-energy phosphate molecules that drive other biochemical reactions in the cell. Fatty acids are long chains of carbon atoms with an acid group at one end. Saturated fatty acids have single chemical bonds between all carbon atoms, whereas unsaturated fatty acids have one or more double bonds between adjacent carbon atoms. Cholesterol is a complicated lipid (fat) molecule containing twenty-seven carbon atoms, arranged in four rings, with an eight-carbon side chain. Fatty acids and cholesterol contribute to the stability of cell membranes and may be involved in the development of heart attacks and strokes. Cholesterol is the biochemical precursor of steroid hormones and bile acids.

The biosynthesis of both fatty acids and cholesterol begins with a chemically active form of acetate, a two-carbon molecule. Lynen had begun to study the nature of active acetate before his work was disrupted by World War II; later, in 1951, he discovered that the active form of acetate is acetyl coenzyme A (a coenzyme is a heat-stabilized, water-soluble portion of an enzyme). The chemical structure of acetyl coenzyme A was determined to be a thiol (sulfur-containing) ester of acetate.

Lynen and his colleagues also elucidated the mechanism of fatty acid biosynthesis. The process begins with acetyl coenzyme A, which combines with carbon dioxide in an irreversible step to form malonyl coenzyme A, a three-carbon molecule and the chemically active form of malonyl. (Malonyl is a radical, or group of atoms that takes part in chemical changes without being altered.) The formation of long-chained fatty acids proceeds by the repetitive addition of malonyl coenzyme A to the acetyl coenzyme A end of the growing fatty acid molecule. A multiple enzyme complex (fatty acid synthetase) contains all the enzymes required for fatty acid synthesis, which proceeds as though on an assembly line. The regulation of fatty acid biosynthesis occurs through negative

feedback; for example, as fatty acid molecules accumulate in the cell, the carboxylase system is suppressed and less fatty acid is synthesized. (Carboxylase is an enzyme that catalyzes the removal of carbon dioxide from the carboxyl group of certain acids.) Lynen clarified the function of coenzymatic biotin, a growth vitamin of the B complex, which is involved in the transfer of carbon dioxide to acetyl coenzyme A to form malonyl coenzyme A. The role of acetyl coenzyme A in the breakdown of the fatty acid chain was also determined by Lynen.

In the course of investigating cholesterol biosynthesis, Lynen and his colleagues demonstrated that the formation of cholesterol begins with the condensation of two molecules of acetyl coenzyme A to form acetoacetyl coenzyme A, a four-carbon molecule. The two coenzymes then combine to form coenzyme A (beta-hydroxy-beta-methylglutarate, or HMG), which is converted to mevalonic acid in a catalytic reaction caused by HMG coenzyme A reductase (an enzyme that has a reducing action on chemical compounds). Lynen showed that mevalonic acid is converted into chemically active isoprene, a hydrocarbon that is the basic building block of cholesterol and other terpene (hydrocarbon) molecules, such as carotenes and rubber. Cholesterol biosynthesis is also regulated by negative feedback. As cholesterol accumulates in the cell, the HMG coenzyme A reductase system is suppressed and less cholesterol is synthesized.

Over the years Lynen corresponded about his work with the German-born biochemist KONRAD BLOCH, who had immigrated to the United States in 1936 and pursued related research. Lynen and Bloch shared the 1964 Nobel Prize for Physiology or Medicine "for their discoveries concerning the mechanism and regulation of cholesterol and fatty acid metabolism." "Mainly through the basic biochemical work of this year's prizewinners, we know today in detail how cholesterol and fatty acids are synthesized and metabolized in the body," said SUNE BERGSTRÖM of the Karolinska Institute in his presentation speech. "These processes comprise a series of reactions with a great number of individual steps. For instance, the formation of cholesterol from acetic acid is a process involving some thirty different steps," Bergström went on. "Derangements of this complicated mechanism . . . are in many cases responsible for the genesis of some of our most important diseases, especially in the cardiovascular field."

In 1937 Lynen married Eva Wieland, the

daughter of his professor at the University of Munich; the couple eventually had five children. Lynen was known for his personal warmth, gregarious nature, and love of life. "On social occasions," wrote HANS KREBS, "his conversation was vivacious, direct, and sometimes mingled with sarcasm. In personal dialogue he was open to any topic of discussion; he was stimulating, entertaining, and profound." According to Krebs, "an important factor contributing to Lynen's monumental achievements was his quality of leadership. He had the ability to inspire and guide a large number of junior and senior collaborators." "Lynen," Krebs went on, "was probably the last representative of a long tradition . . . of the professor organizing a large team of researchers towards his specific personal interests. It was his example, his authoritative competence, his openness, and his personal warmth that made his associates willingly accept his undisputed leadership."

Between 1974 and 1976, Lynen served as acting director of the Max Planck Institute. He died in 1979 after an operation for an aneurysm of the abdominal aorta.

Among his many awards, Lynen received the Carl Neuberg Medal of the American Society of European Chemists (1954) and the first Otto Warburg Medal of the German Society for Biological Chemistry (1963). He was a member of numerous scientific societies and held honorary degrees from seven universities.

ABOUT: Biographical Memoirs of Fellows of the Royal Society, volume 28, 1982; Current Biography June 1967; Kornberg, A., et al. (eds.) Reflections on Biochemistry, 1975; New York Times October 16, 1964; Science October 23, 1963.

MACBRIDE, SEAN
(January 26, 1904–   )
Nobel Prize for Peace, 1974
(shared with Eisaku Sato)

Sean MacBride, Irish lawyer, politician, and United Nations official, was born in Paris. His father was Irish nationalist John MacBride, who vehemently opposed British rule over Ireland and founded the Irish Brigade, which fought in South Africa against Great Britain in the Boer War during the 1890s. MacBride's mother, the former Maud Gonne, was a noted beauty who inspired much of the poetry of WILLIAM BUTLER YEATS. She was also a leading figure in Irish nationalist politics.

In 1905 the elder MacBride returned to

SEAN MACBRIDE

Dublin, leaving the boy and his mother in Paris. In Paris, young MacBride attended the Jesuit school of St. Louis de Gonzague, where he became fluent in French but learned little English. While vacationing in southern France in 1914, ten-year-old MacBride and his mother nursed soldiers wounded in the First Battle of the Marne. MacBride's father took part in the 1916 Easter uprising against the British and was captured and executed. MacBride and his mother then moved to Dublin, where she was arrested several times for her political activities. On two occasions, MacBride helped her escape from British prisons and was twice arrested for his own revolutionary activities.

In 1917 MacBride joined the Irish Republican Army (IRA). Despite his youth, he served as an officer during the war that was waged against the British from 1919 to 1921. He was also briefly secretary to the Republican leader Eamon De Valera. The peace settlement that followed the war partitioned Ireland into the Irish Free State and the six predominantly Protestant counties of Northern Ireland, which remained part of Britain. The IRA leadership, opposed to the treaty, launched a civil war against the government of the Irish Free State. During this period MacBride was arrested several times but always managed to escape. Although distinguished by his unusual height, a characteristic slouch, and a pronounced French accent, he nevertheless disguised himself while living underground for the next fourteen years.

MacBride married Catalina Bulford, an Irishwoman from Argentina, in 1926; they have one daughter and one son. After living in Paris for a year, the couple returned to Ireland. In 1929 MacBride traveled briefly to the United States seeking support for the IRA. He became commander in chief of the organization in 1936 but resigned the following year after objecting to a proposed terror campaign in England and Northern Ireland.

During his years underground, MacBride completed law studies at Mount St. Benedict in Dublin, and he was admitted to the bar in 1937. He soon earned a reputation as the best trial lawyer in Dublin and gained the title of senior counselor in a record seven years instead of the usual fifteen. With the outbreak of World War II in 1939, the Irish government, now headed by De Valera, proclaimed its neutrality. When IRA members refused to observe the neutrality decree by showing support for Hitler in his fight against Britain, the Irish government imprisoned numerous IRA members without writ of habeas corpus. Although he had broken with the IRA, MacBride defended several men who had been condemned to death and, working without fee, saw the government's decrees ruled unconstitutional in the Irish Supreme Court.

After World War II, MacBride formed the Republican party, whose platform called for economic reforms similar to those of the New Deal in the United States. It also asked the Irish government to sever its political ties to the British crown and declare Ireland a republic. In the 1948 election, MacBride's party, showing surprising strength, helped unseat De Valera's ruling Fianna Fail party. A coalition government was then installed under the former opposition leader John Costello, with MacBride as minister of external affairs. In this capacity, MacBride signed an agreement with the United States that made Ireland a participant in the European Recovery Program. The following year, he represented Ireland at a meeting in Paris where the nineteen Marshall Plan nations set up the Office for European Economic Cooperation (OEEC), the steering committee for administering the massive plan for rebuilding postwar Europe.

At home, MacBride threw his weight behind the Republic of Ireland Act. With its passage on April 18, 1949, Ireland became a republic, withdrew from the British Commonwealth, and asserted its jurisdictional claims over Northern Ireland.

MacBride served as minister of external affairs until 1951 and was reelected to the Irish Parliament in 1951, 1954, and 1955. At the Council of Europe in 1950, he played an important role in the adoption of the European Convention on Human Rights, the first international recognition of individual rights, which was signed in November 1950.

From this point forward, MacBride turned his energies toward promoting the cause of human rights. In 1961 he was elected chairman of the International Board of AMNESTY INTERNATIONAL, a post he held until 1974. Traveling around the world to apply pressure to nations accused of political persecution, he won wide respect for Amnesty International as a neutral voice of the politically oppressed. From 1968 to 1970 he served as secretary-general of the International Commission of Jurists, originally established in West Berlin in 1952 to monitor human rights violations in East Germany and other Eastern European nations. He was also a member of the INTERNATIONAL PEACE BUREAU and chairman of the bureau's executive board from 1968 to 1974.

In 1973 MacBride became United Nations commissioner for Namibia (also known as South-West Africa), a territory claimed by the Republic of South Africa in defiance of a United Nations mandate. During his tenure as commissioner, MacBride pressed South Africa to grant Namibia independence despite criticism from some of his United Nations colleagues who objected to his proposal to impose sanctions against South Africa.

MacBride shared the 1974 Nobel Prize for Peace with EISAKU SATO, largely in recognition of his efforts to create international mechanisms for guaranteeing political rights to all persons. "Sean MacBride is of the opinion that no state can claim absolute national sovereignty where human rights that are universally recognized are concerned," said Aase Lionæs of the Norwegian Nobel Committee in her presentation speech. Lionæs noted that MacBride advocated the establishment of an international human rights court empowered to supersede governments in ensuring individual rights. She also cited his work with the European Convention of Human Rights, Amnesty International, the International Commission of Jurists, and the International Peace Bureau.

In his acceptance speech, MacBride voiced his despair over the advent of nuclear weapons and government callousness toward human life. "From a survey of the contemporary scene," he said, "it is only too obvious that it is often those in authority who set the bad example. If those vested with authority and power practice injustice, resort to torture and killing, is it not inevitable that those who are the victims will react with similar methods?" Calling for a new world order based on disarmament and world government, as well as for a new Geneva Convention to discuss a ban on nuclear weapons, MacBride asked: "Why outlaw a dumdum bullet and not an atomic bomb?"

The selection of MacBride for a Nobel Peace Prize was not without controversy. Some critics found the choice highly ironic in view of his former long association with the IRA. Others were puzzled that he should personally receive the award the year after it was given to Amnesty International, an organization with which he was closely connected.

During the years following his receipt of the prize, MacBride has remained active in international affairs. Although he served in his United Nations commissioner's post until 1976, he failed to break the stalemate with South Africa. In 1977 he chaired a commission on international communications for the United Nations Educational, Scientific, and Cultural Organization (UNESCO). Shortly after the 1982 Israeli invasion of Lebanon, he was appointed chairman of an international commission inquiring into possible violations of international law by Israel.

In addition to the Nobel Prize, MacBride has received the Lenin Peace Prize (1977), the American Medal of Justice (1978), and the UNESCO Silver Medal (1980). His publications include *Civil Liberty* (1948) and *Our People—Our Money* (1951).

ADDITIONAL WORKS: The Right to Refuse to Kill, 1971; Is Nuclear Survival Possible? 1977.

ABOUT: Advertising Age December 13, 1982; Current Biography June 1949; New York Times October 9, 1974; New York Times Magazine March 11, 1951; Saturday Evening Post April 23, 1949; UN Monthly Chronicle March 1974, March 1975, June 1980, August 1981.

MACLEOD, JOHN J. R.

(September 6, 1876–March 16, 1935)
Nobel Prize for Physiology or Medicine, 1923
(shared with Frederick G. Banting)

The Scottish physiologist John James Rickard MacLeod was born at Cluny near Dunkeld, Perthshire, to Jane Guthrie (McWalter) MacLeod and Robert MacLeod, a minister. MacLeod received his early education at the Aberdeen Grammar School and in 1893 enrolled in the Marischal College of the University of Aberdeen to study medicine. An outstanding student, he graduated in 1898 with honors, receiving a bachelor's degree in medicine and a degree in surgery.

An Anderson Traveling Fellowship enabled him to spend the next year at the Institute of Physiology of the University of Leipzig in Germany. He then served as demonstrator in physiology at the London Hospital Medical School, where after two years he was appointed lecturer in biochemistry. While there, he won the McKinnon Research Studentship of the Royal Society of London. In 1903 MacLeod and others published a textbook, *Practical Physiology,* after which he moved to the United States, where, although only twenty-seven years old, he was appointed professor of physiology at Western Reserve (now Case Western Reserve) University in Cleveland, Ohio. Two years later he collaborated with Sir Leonard Hill in writing *Recent Advances in Physiology;* he also began research on carbohydrate metabolism and the disease now known as diabetes mellitus.

The first clinical descriptions of diabetes date to the first century A.D., when the Roman physicians Celsus and Araeteus described a disease with symptoms of copious urine, excessive thirst, and weight loss. In the seventeenth century the English physician Thomas Willis observed that the urine of patients with those same symptoms tasted sweet. Later, in the nineteenth century, it was learned that starchy foods are converted into glucose (sugar) in the intestinal tract, and that glucose is absorbed from the bloodstream by the liver, where it is then stored as glycogen (a starchlike substance consisting of glucose molecules linked together in chains). In 1889 the German physiologists Joseph von Mering and Oscar Minkowski surgically removed the pancreas from dogs and observed that the animals developed abnormally high levels of glucose in the blood and urine, in addition to signs and symptoms resembling those of clinical diabetes mellitus.

The pancreas is a gland with two basic types of cells: acinar and islet cells. Acinar cells synthesize and discharge peptide enzymes into the pancreatic ducts, which carry the enzymes to the small intestine, where they participate in the digestion of foods. Islet cells (located in the islets of Langerhans, irregular structures in the pancreas) synthesize and discharge insulin into the bloodstream, an action that promotes the transfer of glucose into cells of the body, where it is utilized as a source of energy. When glucose is unavailable to cells, fat (in the form of fatty acids) is utilized instead, and its biochemical degradation results in the formation of abnormally high acid levels, or di-

JOHN J. R. MACLEOD

abetic acidosis; before the availability of insulin for clinical use the condition was usually fatal.

At Western Reserve University, MacLeod developed an experimental model of glycosuria (glucose in the urine, which is normally glucose free) and performed experiments to determine the role of the central nervous system in the development of diabetes mellitus. He also wrote numerous papers on carbohydrate metabolism and a series of twelve papers on experimental glycosuria. In 1916 the British physiologist Edward A. Sharpey-Schäfer suggested that a hypothetical pancreatic substance with blood-glucose-lowering effects be called insuline (a term that MacLeod later changed to insulin). Although MacLeod believed that the pancreas was involved in diabetes, he had not been able to ascertain its exact role in the disease.

In 1918 MacLeod was appointed professor of physiology at the University of Toronto in Canada. The following year he was approached by FREDERICK G. BANTING, a young Canadian surgeon, who asked him to provide research facilities for an experimental project on diabetes mellitus. Banting was particularly interested in isolating insulin from the islet cells of the pancreas. The previous October, Banting had read an article by Moses Barron describing how blockage of the pancreatic duct by gallstones resulted in atrophy of the acinar cells. It was Banting's hope that "by ligating [tying off] the duct and allowing time for the degeneration of the acinus cells, a means might be provided for obtaining an extract of the islet cells free from the destroying influence of tryp-

sin and other pancreatic enzymes." At the suggestion of F. R. Miller, one of his professors at the University of Western Ontario, Banting took his idea to MacLeod, who was in a position to provide facilities for conducting the project at the University of Toronto.

According to Banting, MacLeod scoffed at the idea, and it was only after several visits to MacLeod's office that Banting was provided with the support necessary for his research. Eventually, laboratory facilities, ten dogs, and the assistance of Charles Best, an undergraduate medical student who was skilled at determining the glucose content of blood and urine, were made available. In May 1921, Banting, assisted by Best, began a series of experiments at the University of Toronto, while MacLeod left for a holiday in Scotland. By the time MacLeod returned in August, Banting and Best had succeeded in extracting insulin from the islet cells of the pancreas of dogs. They had also removed the pancreas of a dog and, as the dog lay dying of diabetic acidosis, injected it with their extract of pancreas. The dog recovered—its blood glucose returned to normal and its urine became free of glucose.

Later that year, Banting and Best reported their research to the Physiological Journal Club at the University of Toronto. The next month they again presented their findings, this time at a meeting of the American Physiological Society in New Haven, Connecticut, with MacLeod participating in the presentation. MacLeod then made available all of the resources of his department for the task of isolating more insulin and purifying it; he enlisted the aid of J. B. Collip, a biochemist, in this effort. In January 1922, a fourteen-year-old boy with severe diabetes mellitus of two years' duration was successfully treated with insulin at the Hospital for Sick Children. The insulin had been extracted from the pancreas of slaughtered beef cattle.

By late 1922 insulin was commercially available from the Connaught Laboratories of the University of Toronto and from Eli Lilly and Company, an American pharmaceutical firm. The patent rights for the production of insulin were assigned to the Medical Research Council of Canada, with none of the research team profiting from its manufacture.

MacLeod and Banting shared the 1923 Nobel Prize for Physiology or Medicine "for the discovery of insulin." When he learned that Best had not been included in the honor, Banting threatened to refuse the award but was dissuaded from doing so; instead, he accepted the award and gave half of his prize money to

659

Best, publicly acknowledging Best's contribution to the discovery of insulin. Later, MacLeod gave an unknown sum to Collip. (Members of the Nobel committee privately admitted in later years that Best should have been awarded a share of the Nobel Prize.)

Two years after receiving the Nobel Prize, MacLeod published *Insulin and Its Uses in Diabetes* and served as president of the Royal Canadian Institute for one year. In 1926 he published *Carbohydrate Metabolism and Insulin,* and two years later his Vanuxem lectures, which had been delivered at Princeton University, were published under the title of *Fuel for Life.* That year he was appointed Regius Professor of Physiology at the University of Aberdeen, where he eventually became dean of the Faculty of Medicine. MacLeod was respected for his organizational abilities, high standards of research, and skill in conveying ideas and information in a way that stimulated his students. A victim of crippling arthritis, MacLeod died on March 16, 1935.

In 1903 MacLeod married Mary Watson McWalter; they had no children.

MacLeod held memberships in the American Physiological Society and the Royal Canadian Institute. He was also a foreign associate fellow of the College of Physicians of Philadelphia, an honorary academician of the Royal Academy of Medicine of Rome, and a fellow of the Royal Society of Canada, the Royal Society of London, and the Royal College of Physicians.

MAURICE MAETERLINCK

SELECTED WORKS: Organic Chemistry, 1907, with Howard Haskins; Diabetes: Its Pathological Physiology, 1913; Physiology and Biochemistry in Modern Medicine, 1918, with others; Fundamentals of Human Physiology, 1936, with others.

ABOUT: Bliss, M. The Discovery of Insulin, 1982; Chittenden, R. H. The Development of Physiological Chemistry in the United States, 1930; Dictionary of Scientific Biography, volume 8, 1973; Obituary Notices of Fellows of the Royal Society, volume 1, 1935; Science September 17, 1982.

MAETERLINCK, MAURICE

(August 29, 1862–May 6, 1949)
Nobel Prize for Literature, 1911

The Belgian dramatist and essayist Maurice Polydore Marie Bernhard Maeterlinck was born into a prosperous family of ancient Flemish stock in Ghent in 1862. His father was a retired notary, and his mother was the daughter of an affluent lawyer. From 1874 to 1881, Maeter-

linck attended the Jesuit Collège de Ste.-Barbe. Although he became interested in poetry and literature during this period, his family wanted him to study law at the University of Ghent. After receiving his degree in 1885, he went to Paris to continue his legal studies, but instead he devoted most of the six-month visit to literary pursuits. In Paris he met the symbolist poets Stéphane Mallarmé and Villiers de l'Isle-Adam. Encouraged by Joris Karl Huysmans, a novelist of the Decadent literary movement, he read the works of the fourteenth-century Flemish mystic Jan van Ruysbroeck. *L'Ornement des noces spirituelles* (The Adornment of Spiritual Nuptials), Maeterlinck's French translation of a work by Ruysbroeck, was published in 1891.

Maeterlinck returned to Ghent and began to practice law while continuing to pursue his literary interests. The Paris monthly *La Pléïade* (The Pleiad) published his short story "Le Massacre des innocents" ("The Massacre of the Innocents") in 1886. In 1889 Maeterlinck published a volume of poetry, *Serres chaudes* (Hothouses), and that year he wrote his first play, *La Princesse Maleine* (*Princess Maleine*). The influential French realist critic Octave Mirbeau read the play and reviewed it in the newspaper *Le Figaro,* calling it a "masterpiece" and comparing its author to Shakespeare. The praise encouraged Maeterlinck to drop his law practice and devote his full attention to literature.

Over the next few years, Maeterlinck wrote a series of symbolist plays. *L'Intruse* (*The Intruder,* 1890), a virtually actionless drama in which a family waits while a woman dies after childbirth, is the first of several Maeterlinck dramas to center around death (the "intruder" of the title). *Les Aveugles* (*The Blind,* 1890) is another examination of death, using the metaphor of a group of blind people trapped in a dark forest without a guide. *Les Sept Princesses* (*The Seven Princesses,* 1891) is a fairy tale about a prince who must awaken seven princesses from a sleep that will bring death; he arrives in time to save all but his beloved. *Pelléas et Mélisande* (*Pelleas and Melisande,* 1892), the story of a doomed, adulterous passion ending in death, later served as the libretto for Claude Debussy's 1902 opera of the same name. Aside from their preoccupation with death, these plays are all characterized by a hushed, brooding, fairy-tale atmosphere. The language is understated and restrained; as much is conveyed by what is left unsaid as by what is said.

In 1894 Maeterlinck wrote three plays for marionettes: *Alladine et Palomides* (*Alladine and Palomides*), *Intérieur* (*Interior*), and *La Mort de Tintagiles* (*The Death of Tintagiles*). He was drawn to puppet theater because, unlike actors, who are limited by their specifically human characteristics, puppets could illustrate the archetypal aspects of his characters.

In 1895 Maeterlinck met Georgette Leblanc, an actress and singer who became his mistress and companion during a liaison that lasted twenty-three years. Leblanc, a strong-willed, well-read woman, served as Maeterlinck's secretary and impresario and kept outsiders from disturbing his privacy. She was also his leading actress. The plays Maeterlinck wrote for her revolve around powerful women: *Aglavaine et Sélysette* (*Aglavaine and Selysette,* 1896), *Ariane et Barbebleue* (*Ariadne and Bluebeard,* 1901), *Monna Vanna* (1902), and *Joyzelle* (1903). These plays are more realistic and conventional than the works that preceded them and, in the opinion of Maeterlinck's biographer Bettina L. Knapp, are inferior to them.

Maeterlinck and Leblanc moved in 1896 from Ghent, where his works were ridiculed, to Paris. During this period, Maeterlinck wrote metaphysical essays that were collected in the volumes *Le Trésor des humbles* (*The Treasury of the Humble,* 1896); *La Sagesse et la destinée* (*Wisdom and Destiny,* 1898); and *La Vie des abeilles* (*The Life of the Bee,* 1901), which draws analogies between the activity of the bee and human behavior.

L'Oiseau bleu (*The Blue Bird*), perhaps Maeterlinck's most popular play, was first produced in 1909 by Konstantin Stanislavski at the Moscow Art Theater; there were subsequent productions in London, New York, and Paris. Recounting the spiritual odyssey of two children, *The Blue Bird* marks a return to Maeterlinck's symbolic fairy-tale manner, and it remains popular as much for its charming fantasy as for its metaphysical content. A sequel, *Les Fiançailles* (*The Betrothed*), appeared in 1918.

Maeterlinck was awarded the Nobel Prize for Literature in 1911 "in appreciation of his many-sided literary activities, and especially of his dramatic works, which are distinguished by a wealth of imagination and by a poetic fancy, which reveals, sometimes in the guise of a fairy tale, a deep inspiration, while . . . they appeal to the readers' own feelings and stimulate their imaginations." In his presentation speech, C. D. af Wirsén of the Swedish Academy singled out *Aglavaine and Selysette* as Maeterlinck's "masterpiece"—an interesting appraisal, considering the play's uncertain latter-day reputation. Illness prevented Maeterlinck from traveling to Stockholm to attend the award ceremonies; the prize was accepted on his behalf by Belgium's minister to Sweden, Charles C. M. A. Wauters. The French Academy subsequently offered Maeterlinck a membership, which he declined because acceptance would have required him to renounce his Belgian citizenship.

During World War I, Maeterlinck tried to enlist in the Belgian civil guard but was rejected because of his age. He channeled his patriotic energy into lecturing for the Allied cause throughout Europe and in the United States. His relationship with Leblanc deteriorated during this period, and the two separated after the war. In 1919 Maeterlinck married Reneé Dahon, an actress who had appeared in *The Blue Bird*.

In his later years, Maeterlinck wrote more essays than plays, publishing twelve volumes between the years 1927 and 1942. The most interesting is *La Vie des termites* (*The Life of the White Ant,* 1926), an oblique denunciation of communism and totalitarianism that likens the future of humanity to the life of the termite—rigidly organized and unknowing. Other volumes of essays from this period include *La Vie de l'espace* (*The Life of Space,* 1928), *La Grande féerie* (*The Great Fairyland,* 1929), and *La Grande Loi* (*The Great Law,* 1933).

In 1939, as Nazi Germany was on the point of conquering Europe, Maeterlinck went to Portugal under the protection of Antonio Salazar, dictator of Portugal. When it began to appear that Portugal might also fall to the Nazis, Maeterlinck fled with his wife to the United States. He stayed there throughout the war and returned to Les Abeilles, his home in Nice, in 1947. He died of a heart attack on May 6, 1949. A lifelong agnostic, he was buried in a civil ceremony devoid of religious ritual.

In addition to the Nobel Prize, Maeterlinck received an honorary doctorate of law from Glasgow University, Belgium's Grand Cross in the Order of Leopold (1920), and Portugal's medal of the Order of St. James of the Sword (1939). The king of Belgium named him a count in 1932.

Maeterlinck's contemporary reputation rests on his plays, which continue to be performed. He is looked upon as one of the ancestors of the theater of the absurd, and his works have exerted special influence over the plays of SAMUEL BECKETT. Moreover, *Pelléas et Mélisande* in Debussy's setting has maintained a firm position in the repertories of the world's opera houses.

"The internal argument of Maeterlinck's work pleads no cause and makes no judgments," wrote critic Joan Pataky Kosove in 1967. "His art never becomes propaganda because he is concerned with fundamentals outside the reach of politics and psychiatry." In *Maurice Maeterlinck* (1975), the critic Bettina Knapp suggested that Maeterlinck often chose the fairy-tale structure because it "is the profoundest and simplest expression of the collective unconscious. It brings forth a world of feeling."

ADDITIONAL WORKS IN ENGLISH TRANSLATION: The Buried Temple, 1902; The Double Garden, 1904; Old-Fashioned Flowers, 1905; Life and Flowers, 1907; Chrysanthemums, 1907; The Measures of the Hours, 1907; Mary Magdalene, 1910; Death, 1911; On Emerson, 1912; Hours of Gladness, 1912; News of Spring, 1913; Our Eternity, 1913; The Unknown Guest, 1914; Poems, 1915; The Wrack of the Storm, 1916; A Miracle of St. Anthony, 1917; The Light Beyond, 1917; The Burgomaster of Stilemonde, 1918; Mountain Paths, 1919; The Great Secret, 1922; The Cloud That Lifted, and The Power of the Dead, 1923; Ancient Egypt, 1925; The Magic of the Stars, 1930; The Supreme Law, 1934; Pigeons and Spiders, 1935; Before the Great Silence, 1935; The Hour Glass, 1936; The Great Beyond, 1947.

ABOUT: Bailley, A. Maeterlinck, 1931; Bithel, J. Life and Writings of Maurice Maeterlinck, 1913; Clark, M. Maurice Maeterlinck, Poet and Philosopher, 1915; Halls, W. D. Maurice Maeterlinck, 1960; Harry, G. Maurice Maeterlinck, 1910; Heller, O. Prophets of Dissent, 1968; Huneker, J. Iconoclasts, 1905; Knapp, B. L. Maurice Maeterlinck, 1975; Konrad, L. B. Modern Drama as Crisis, 1986; Leblanc, G. Souvenirs: My Life With Maeterlinck, 1932; Mahony, P. Magic of Maeterlinck, 1951; Moses, M. J. Maurice

Maeterlinck, A Study, 1911; Rose, H. Maeterlinck's Symbolism, 1977; Taylor, U. Maurice Maeterlinck: A Critical Study, 1914; Thomas, E. Maurice Maeterlinck, 1911.

MANN, THOMAS
(June 6, 1875–August 12, 1955)
Nobel Prize for Literature, 1929

The German essayist and novelist Thomas Mann was born in the historic port and commercial city of Lübeck, on the Baltic Sea, in what is now West Germany. His father, Johann Heinrich Mann, was a prosperous grain merchant and senator of Lübeck; his mother, the former Julia da Silva Bruhns, was an accomplished musician who had been born in Brazil to a German plantation owner and his Creole (Portuguese-Indian) wife. Perhaps partly as a result of this mixed background, Mann grew up associating northern Europe with "the bourgeois home, . . . deeply rooted emotion, and intimate humanity," whereas southern Europe stood for "sensual, intellectual adventure, . . . the cold passion of art." This dichotomy between the northern and southern parts of Europe, between bourgeois values and aestheticism, played an important part in Mann's life and work.

Mann was designated to take over the family grain firm, but upon his father's untimely death in 1891, the business was liquidated, and Mann completed school, as he later put it, "rather ingloriously."

When Mann was sixteen years old, the family moved to Munich, then as now a leading intellectual and artistic center. There he worked briefly for an insurance company and studied journalism with the intention of becoming a writer like his older brother, Heinrich. Mann soon obtained a position as writer and editor for *Simplizissimus,* a satirical weekly. He also wrote short stories, which were first collected as *Der kleine Herr Friedemann (The Little Mr. Friedemann,* 1898). Like many of Mann's later works, these tales present, in an ironic and somewhat disillusioned fashion, the problems of the self-consciously "modern" artist who struggles to find meaning and purpose in life. They also reflect Mann's characteristic nostalgia for the bourgeois existence that his artist heroes find wanting.

These themes appear with compelling force in Mann's first and most popular novel, *Buddenbrooks* (1901), which was translated into English under the same title in 1924. Partly autobiographical, *Buddenbrooks* examines the decline and fall of a great Lübeck trading firm

THOMAS MANN

nor did it quell the homosexual urges that persisted throughout his life.

The theme of homosexuality figures significantly in *Der Tod in Venedig* (*Death in Venice,* 1913), generally considered one of the finest novellas ever written. Its protagonist, the middle-aged artist Gustav von Aschenbach, has devoted himself to the classical ideal of art and living—detachment and self-renunciation—only to find himself embroiled in a self-destructive and unrequited love for a handsome young boy. This exquisitely written tale embodies many of the themes found in Mann's mature works: the isolation of the artist, the equation of physical and spiritual disease, and the debilitating effects of art on the individual psyche.

Mann's literary endeavors were interrupted by World War I, an event that plunged him into a profound moral and spiritual crisis. During these years, he labored on a 600-page critique of liberal optimism, *Betrachtungen eines Unpolitischen* (*Reflections of a Nonpolitical Man,* 1918), in which he argued against the influence of rationalist, Enlightenment philosophy in favor of the German national spirit, which Mann regarded as essentially musical and irrational. Yet, with typical irony, Mann concluded by admitting that his own literary efforts would probably contribute to the rational, humanist trends he deplored.

After the war, Mann resumed writing fiction and produced *Der Zauberberg* (*The Magic Mountain,* 1924), one of the most brilliant and ironic novels in the tradition of the bildungsroman, or story of a person's intellectual and spiritual education. Its protagonist is Hans Castorp, a mediocre but good-natured engineer from northern Germany who visits his cousin in a Swiss tuberculosis sanatorium only to find that he, too, has a lung problem. The longer Castorp remains with the well-to-do invalids and is exposed to the intellectuals among them, the more fascinated he becomes by a mode of life very different from his own "flatland," middle-class milieu. On the surface an account of Castorp's enlightenment, the novel is also a profound and subtle analysis of pre–World War I European culture. Many of the themes Mann had belabored in *Reflections of a Nonpolitical Man* are dramatized in *The Magic Mountain* with wit, irony, and deep sympathy for human fallibility.

Mann's work exerted a strong influence on educated readers, who saw in its carefully orchestrated complexities a reflection of their own intellectual and moral struggles. He was awarded the 1929 Nobel Prize for Literature "principally for his great novel, *Budden-*

over the course of three generations. Using a traditional literary form, the Scandinavian family saga, Mann imparts to his narrative an almost epic scope, so that the fate of his characters seems to represent that of bourgeois culture. Realistic and at the same time mythical, *Buddenbrooks* reveals the author's ambivalence toward both the artistry the novel brilliantly displays and the bourgeois culture it painstakingly chronicles. As each generation of the Buddenbrooks family becomes more self-conscious and "artistic," its ability to act effectively diminishes. Significantly, the family line ends when Hanno, a precocious musician, dies of a fever that seems somehow related to his thwarted will to live.

The ambiguous relation of knowledge to life also appears in *Tonio Kröger* (1903), Mann's first successful novella. (The English version appeared in 1925 under the same title.) Like Hamlet, Tonio finds that his overrefined sensibility makes him unable to act. Nothing but love, Tonio comes to see, can rescue him from the moral paralysis caused by his hyperactive intellect.

Perhaps with this hopeful resolution in mind, in 1905 Mann married Katja Pringsheim, the daughter of a distinguished mathematics professor who came from a long line of Jewish bankers and merchants. They had six children: three girls, of whom the eldest became an actress, and three boys, of whom the eldest became a writer. However, the marriage did not provide the intellectual resolution Mann sought,

brooks, which has won steadily increased recognition as one of the classic works of contemporary literature." In his presentation speech, Fredrik Böök of the Swedish Academy noted that Mann was the first German novelist to achieve the stature of Charles Dickens, Gustave Flaubert, or Leo Tolstoy. Böök also observed that Mann "wrestled with ideas and created painful beauty though . . . convinced that art is questionable." According to Böök, Mann's greatness lay in his ability to reconcile "the loftiness of poetry and the intellect with a yearning love for the human and for the simple life."

After Mann won the Nobel Prize, his career took a political turn. In 1930 he delivered a speech in Berlin entitled "Ein Appell an die Vernunft" (An Appeal to Reason), calling for a common front of socialist workers and middle-class liberals to oppose the Nazi threat. He also wrote *Mario und der Zauberer* (*Mario and the Magician,* 1930), a political allegory in which a corrupt hypnotist symbolizes leaders such as Adolf Hitler and Benito Mussolini. In essays and speeches he delivered throughout Europe, Mann valiantly attacked Nazi policies and expressed sympathy for socialism and communism insofar as they supported human freedom and dignity. When Hitler became chancellor in 1933, Mann and his wife, who were in Switzerland at the time, decided not to return to Germany. They made their home near Zurich but traveled widely and, in 1938, settled in the United States. After spending three years at Princeton University as a lecturer in the humanities, Mann lived in southern California from 1941 to 1952. He also served as consultant in Germanic literature at the Library of Congress.

In 1936 Mann was stripped of his German citizenship as well as of the honorary doctorate he had received from the University of Bonn in 1919 (the latter was restored in 1949). Mann became a United States citizen in 1944. During World War II, he made frequent broadcasts to Germany, denouncing Nazism and calling for Germans to reclaim their native sanity. After the war, Mann visited both East Germany and West Germany and received honors from both, but he refused to return to either Germany to live, choosing instead to settle near Zurich, where he spent his last years.

During the final stage of his career, Mann worked more than thirteen years composing a tetralogy of novels based on the biblical story of Joseph. Told from a modern viewpoint, and bristling with irony and humor, *Joseph und seine Brüder* (*Joseph and his Brothers,* 1933–

1943) examines the development of individuated consciousness from its collective roots. "The triumph of Mann is that we love on every page the hero he himself loves this side idolatry," wrote Mark Van Doren of the vain, yet engaging, Joseph.

Searching for a different kind of hero for his time, Mann celebrated Goethe in essays and in *Lotte in Weimar* (1939, translated as *The Beloved Returns*), a novel that explores Goethe and his career from the viewpoint of his ex-lover. In contrast to these somewhat idyllic works, *Doktor Faustus* (*Doctor Faustus,* 1947) presents a caustic treatment of its artist-hero, a brilliant but deranged composer, whose career epitomizes the spiritual malaise of his era. A bitter critique of European high culture, *Doctor Faustus* contains some of Mann's most ambitious experiments in style.

Mann's final work, *Bekenntnisse des Hochstaplers Felix Krull* (*Confessions of Felix Krull, Confidence Man,* 1954), was a reworking of a manuscript he had abandoned in 1911. It stands as an ironic coda to a career dedicated to ironic self-reflection. An extravagant parody, *Felix Krull,* in Mann's words, takes the "Goethean, self-stylizing, autobiographic, and aristocratic confession" and translates it "into the sphere of the humorous and criminal." The artist is presented as comically doomed; he can dazzle and deceive, but he cannot change the world. Mann considered *Felix Krull* to be his "best and most felicitous achievement," as well as the most personal work he had ever written, since it "is simultaneously loving and destructive" toward tradition.

Critical opinion of Mann's literary achievement has remained consistently high, even if his Germanic sensibility has not always appealed to English and American tastes. The German poet Rainer Maria Rilke gave *Buddenbrooks* his highest praise, noting that in this work Mann combined the realistic novelist's "colossal labor" with the "poet's gift of seeing," a view of Mann's work shared by many later critics. On the other hand, the Marxist critic György Lukács viewed Mann's work as a complex and brilliantly orchestrated "critique of capitalist society." Critics agree that Mann displayed courage in facing and depicting the moral crisis of his age and the transformation of values brought about by the insights of Nietzsche and Freud.

In addition to the Nobel Prize, Mann received the Goethe Prize (awarded jointly in 1949 by East Germany and West Germany) as well as honorary degrees from Oxford and Cambridge universities.

ADDITIONAL WORKS IN ENGLISH TRANSLATION: The Royal Highness, 1916; Bashan and I, 1923; Tristan, 1925; Children and Fools, 1928; Disorder and Early Sorrow, 1929; Three Essays, 1929; A Man and His Dog, 1930; A Sketch of My Life, 1930; A Christmas Poem, 1932; Past Masters and Other Essays, 1933; Nocturnes, 1934; Sleep, Sweet, Sleep, 1934; Stories of Three Decades, 1936; Freud, Goethe, and Wagner, 1937; Measure and Value, 1937; The Problem of Freedom, 1939; War and Democracy, 1940; Stories and Episodes, 1941; The Transposed Heads, 1941; Order of the Day, 1942; Germany and the Germans, 1945; Essays of Three Decades, 1947; Nietzsche's Philosophy, 1947; Goethe and Democracy, 1950; The Holy Sinner, 1951; The Black Swan, 1954; On Schiller, 1958; Last Essays, 1959; Stories of a Lifetime, 1961; The Story of a Novel: The Genius of Dr. Faustus, 1961; Letters of Thomas Mann, 1970; The Hesse-Mann Letters, 1975, with Hermann Hesse; Diaries, 1982.

ABOUT: Apter, T. E. Thomas Mann, The Devil's Advocate, 1979; Bauer, A. Thomas Mann, 1971; Berendsohn, W. A. Thomas Mann: Artist and Partisan, 1973; Bloom, H. Thomas Mann, 1986; Brennan, J. G. Thomas Mann's World, 1942; Cleugh, J. Thomas Mann, A Study, 1933; Feuerlicht, I. Thomas Mann, 1969; Hamilton, N. The Brothers Mann, 1975; Hatfield, H. C. Thomas Mann, 1951; Hatfield, H. C. (ed.) Thomas Mann: A Collection of Critical Essays, 1964; Heller, E. The Ironic German, 1958; Hollingdale, R. J. Thomas Mann: A Critical Study, 1971; Kahler, E. Orbit of Thomas Mann, 1969; Kaufmann, F. Thomas Mann, 1957; Lindsay, J. M. Thomas Mann, 1954; Mann, E. The Last Years of Thomas Mann, 1958; Mann, K. Unwritten Memories, 1975; Neider, C. (ed.) The Stature of Thomas Mann, 1947; Reed, T. J. Thomas Mann: The Uses of Tradition, 1974; Stern, J. P. Thomas Mann, 1967; Swales, M. Thomas Mann: A Study, 1980; Thomas, R. H. Thomas Mann: The Meditation of Art, 1956; Von Gronicka, A. Thomas Mann: Profile and Perspective, 1970; Winston, R. Thomas Mann: The Making of an Artist, 1981.

MARCONI, GUGLIELMO

(April 25, 1874–July 20, 1937)
Nobel Prize for Physics, 1909
(shared with Ferdinand Braun)

The Italian electrical engineer and inventor Guglielmo Marconi (mär kō′ nē) was born in Bologna, the second son of Giuseppe Marconi, a landowner, and his second wife, the former Annie Jameson of Ireland. He was tutored privately in Bologna and Florence before entering a technical school in Livorno. By the age of twenty, he had developed a strong interest in the physical sciences, especially the electrical researches of James Clerk Maxwell, Heinrich Hertz, Édouard Branly, Oliver Lodge, and Augusto Righi.

Marconi's involvement with wireless telegraphy began in 1894, when he read a description of Hertz's 1888 demonstration that an electric spark made to cross a gap between two metal spheres generates periodic oscillations or impulses (Hertzian waves). Marconi immediately conceived of using these waves to transmit signals through the air without the use of wires. For the next forty years, he devoted himself to wireless telegraphy, achieving ever greater goals of efficiency and distance of transmission.

GUGLIELMO MARCONI

After an initial consultation with Righi, Marconi used a Hertz oscillator and a Branly coherer (a detector of Hertzian waves that converts the oscillations into electric current) to ring an electric bell across the distance of the lawn of his father's estate. By mid-1895, he had devised a more sensitive and reliable coherer, incorporated a telegraphy key into the transmission circuit, grounded the oscillator, and connected one of its terminals to a metal plate far above the ground. In this way, he was able to send a message 1.5 miles. After failing to interest the Italian government in his invention, Marconi traveled to England, where he hoped to find funding for research and eventual commercialization. A cousin, Henry James Davis, helped him prepare the first patent ever granted for radiotelegraphy, in 1896.

Marconi's stay in England began inauspiciously when suspicious customs officials smashed his wireless apparatus. After rebuilding it, he was able to attract the attention of British entrepreneurs and government officials. With improvements to his system, he sent a message almost 2 miles in September 1896. When the Italian government called him for three years of military service, he was able to secure a nominal assignment as a naval student at the Italian embassy in London. In May 1897 Marconi sent messages across the Bristol Channel, a distance of 9 miles. That July, he and a small group of investors formed the Wireless Telegraph and Signal Company to install wireless telegraphy on lightships and lighthouses along the English coast.

In the course of his work, Marconi found that the range of transmission was proportional to the number and length of antennas used. To send a message 28 miles across the English Channel, he used a battery of antennas each 150 feet high. In 1900, applying the discoveries of FERDINAND BRAUN, Marconi added a condenser and tuning coils to his transmitter, giving the signal more energy. The condenser magnified the effect of the oscillations produced by the sparking apparatus and the coils induced the antenna to oscillate precisely to the period of the enhanced oscillations. These two circuits were now tuned to one another, preventing destructive interference and minimizing signal diminution. At the same time, he improved signal reception by adding tuning coils to the receiver, so that the receiving aerial passed on to the coherer only tuned oscillations identical to those transmitted, thus eliminating indiscriminate reception by every aerial of the transmission of every antenna. With Patent No. 7777, filed in April 1900, Marconi secured a virtual monopoly on the use of transmitters and receivers tuned within themselves and to one another. His company was renamed Marconi's Wireless Telegraph Company, Ltd.

By the end of 1900 Marconi had transmitted messages as far as 150 miles. In January 1901 he established wireless contact between points 186 miles apart along the English coast. At the end of the year, while in St. John's, Newfoundland, he received a signal sent 2,100 miles across the Atlantic Ocean from Cornwall, England; and in 1902 he sent the first wireless message across the Atlantic from west to east. In 1905 Marconi patented a directional aerial. In 1907 he opened the first transatlantic commercial wireless service, and in 1912 he patented an improved "timed spark" system for generating transmission waves.

Marconi and Braun shared the 1909 Nobel Prize for Physics "in recognition of their contributions to the development of wireless telegraphy." Noting the theoretical work of Michael Faraday, Hertz, and others who preceded Marconi, Hans Hildebrand of the Royal Swedish Academy of Sciences pointed out that "Marconi's first success was gained as a result of his ability to shape the whole thing into a practical, usable system, added to his inflexible energy with which he pursued his self-appointed aim."

During World War I, Marconi received a series of military commissions, eventually becoming a commander of the Italian navy. He also directed the program of telegraphy of the Italian armed forces. In 1919 he was named Italian plenipotentiary delegate to the Paris Peace Conference, signing for Italy the peace treaties with Austria and Bulgaria.

After converting his steam yacht *Elettra* into a home, laboratory, and office in 1921, Marconi began an intensive study of shortwave telegraphy. By 1927 Marconi's company had established an international network of commercial shortwave telegraph links. In 1931 Marconi began to study the transmission of microwaves, and by the following year he established the first microwave radio telephonic linkup. In 1934 he demonstrated the utility of microwave telegraphy for navigation at sea.

Marconi married the Irish-born Beatrice O'Brien in 1905; they had three children. Three years after the marriage was annulled in 1924, he married Countess Maria Bezzi-Scali, with whom he had one daughter. Marconi died in Rome on July 20, 1937.

Marconi's awards included the Franklin Medal of the Franklin Institute and the Albert Medal of the Royal Society of Arts in London. In Italy he received the hereditary title of Marchese, an appointment to the Senate, and the Grand Cross of the Order of the Crown of Italy.

SELECTED WORKS: Improvements in Apparatus Employed in Wireless Telegraphy, 1899; Transatlantic Wireless Telegraphy, 1908; The Progress of Wireless Telegraphy, 1912; Radio Communications, 1925.

ABOUT: de Boinod, B. L., and Collier, D. M. Marconi, Master of Space, 1935; Clayton, H. Atlantic Bridgehead, 1968; Coe, D. Marconi, Pioneer of Radio, 1943; Dictionary of Scientific Biography, volume 9, 1974; Dunlap, O. E. Marconi: The Man and His Wireless, 1937; Gunston, D. Marconi, Father of Radio, 1965; Jolly, W. P. Marconi, 1972; Marconi, D. My Father Marconi, 1962.

MÁRQUEZ, GABRIEL GARCÍA
See GARCÍA MÁRQUEZ, GABRIEL

MARSHALL, GEORGE C.
(December 31, 1880–October 16, 1959)
Nobel Prize for Peace, 1953

George Catlett Marshall, American statesman and general, was born in Uniontown, Pennsylvania. Descended from Chief Justice John Marshall, he was the third child and second son of George Catlett Marshall, a prosperous coal merchant, and the former Laura Bradford. He was a reserved, serious child, with a strong desire to excel. Despite parental opposition, he decided on a military career and enrolled in the Virginia Military Institute in 1897. Although poorly prepared for college, he graduated in 1901 as senior first captain of the Cadet Corps and was commissioned a second lieutenant of infantry in the United States Army.

After serving eighteen months in the Philippines, Marshall returned to the United States and was posted to Fort Reno, Oklahoma. He then spent one year at the Infantry-Cavalry School in Fort Leavenworth, Kansas, graduating with honors in 1907. He completed Army Staff College the following year and taught military engineering and planned maneuvers at various militia and training camp posts. He was recalled from a second tour of duty in the Philippines in 1916 for service in San Francisco and in Fort Douglas, Utah. At that time, his commanding officer wrote, "In my judgment there are not five officers in the army so well qualified as he to command a division in the field."

Serving with the First Infantry Division during World War I, Marshall saw action near Lunéville and the Picardy and Cantigny fronts in 1917. Called to General Headquarters the next year, he helped plan strategy for the battles of St.-Mihiel and Meuse-Argonne. That year, with the rank of colonel, he was also appointed chief of operations of the First Army. He held that post until recalled to headquarters in 1919 to help plan the anticipated advance into Germany. There he caught the eye of General John J. Pershing. Dubbed "Wizard" by his colleagues, Marshall was decorated with the United States government's Distinguished Service Medal and the French government's War Cross with Palms, for his service during the war.

Under peacetime regulations, Marshall's rank reverted to captain, and he continued to distinguish himself in important assignments. After serving as Pershing's aide-de-camp from 1919 to 1924, he was stationed for three years in Tientsin, China, where he learned to speak and write Chinese. These skills served him later in his career. Upon returning to the United States in 1927, he was named assistant commandant of the Army Infantry School at Fort Benning, Georgia, where he remained almost five years. In this and other training positions, Marshall gained a reputation for revolutionizing infantry tactics and increasing combat ef-

GEORGE C. MARSHALL

ficiency. During the Great Depression, he also commanded a number of Civilian Conservation Corps camps. In this role, he was as highly regarded for his fairness and compassion as for his efficiency.

Marshall moved to Washington, D.C., in 1938 when he became assistant chief of staff in the War Plans Division of the General Staff. Within a few months, he was promoted to deputy chief of staff. The following year, he was named acting chief of staff with the rank of general. And when World War II broke out in Europe in September 1939, he was appointed army chief of staff. Convinced that the army had fallen "to the status of a third-rate power," he set about modernizing equipment and increasing troop strength. Urging military preparedness, in 1940 he convinced Congress to pass the Selective Service Act and to nationalize units of the National Guard. On inspection tours, he insisted that officers demonstrate the stamina, imagination, and leadership qualities that inspire men to action. In Washington, he reorganized the War Department to increase control and efficiency of command. Like Secretary of State CORDELL HULL, Marshall warned army commanders in the Pacific to be on the alert against a surprise attack from Japan.

In addition to molding an effective fighting force, Marshall, more than anyone else, devised the operations and defined the objectives for global war. After the Japanese attack on Pearl Harbor, President Franklin D. Roosevelt made Marshall directly responsible to him in matters of strategy and tactics. As the president's chief military adviser, Marshall accompanied Roosevelt to Allied conferences in Argentina, Casablanca, Quebec, Cairo, Tehran, and Yalta. In keeping with the Europe First policy of the Allies to defeat Germany first, then Japan, Marshall, in cooperation with the British, coordinated campaigns in North Africa and Sicily, supplied the besieged Soviets with arms and food, and engineered Italy's defeat, in addition to planning history's largest amphibious expedition, which culminated in the cross-channel assault on Normandy and Germany's surrender.

Throughout the war, Marshall served on the policy committee that supervised the British and American development of the atomic bomb. In 1945 he recommended to President Harry S Truman that the United States use this weapon on the Japanese cities of Hiroshima and Nagasaki. "The bomb stopped the war," he later said. "Therefore it was justifiable." After Japan's surrender, Marshall resigned as chief of staff. Six days later, Marshall's career as a diplomat began when, at Truman's request, he went to China in an attempt to prevent civil war and forge a coalition government between Nationalist and Communist leaders. At first it appeared that Marshall had achieved a truce, but the cease-fire proved impossible to implement. In January 1947 Marshall reported to Truman that his mission had failed and recommended that United States troops be withdrawn.

The following month, Truman appointed Marshall secretary of state and charged him with the enormous tasks involved in the postwar reconstruction of Europe. By the spring of 1947, the United States and the Soviet Union had failed to reach agreement on the future of Europe, and Truman's determination to counter Soviet expansion was being translated into military assistance for Turkey and Greece. Concerned about Europe's economic instability and the gains Communist parties were making as a result, Marshall announced, in a 1947 commencement speech at Harvard, a plan of massive economic aid for Europe. "Our policy is directed not against any country or doctrine," said the new secretary of state, "but against hunger, poverty, desperation, and chaos." In September 1947 sixteen European nations formed a Committee of European Economic Cooperation, which drafted a joint program to make Europe economically viable. Over a three-year period, Congress authorized the expenditure of more than $12 billion to stimulate recovery in Europe. The Marshall Plan was the most massive international economic assistance program undertaken up to that time, and is credited with alleviating much of the immediate suffering in postwar Western Europe and with making possible the so-called economic miracle in Germany in the 1950s.

Assistance to Europe was only one of the many problems Marshall faced in this cold war period. As relations with the Soviet Union deteriorated, four-power rule in Germany broke down, and the nation was divided into two states. In 1948 Marshall countered a Soviet blockade of Berlin with a successful airlift. In Korea, similar disagreements between the United States and the Soviet Union over the provisional government prompted the State Department to take the issue to the United Nations in 1947. The United Nations supervised elections in the southern part of Korea and helped establish the Republic of Korea the following year. In an effort to win new allies, Marshall cemented relations with Italy and established diplomatic missions in Ceylon (now Sri Lanka), Israel, and Korea. He also participated in the formation of the Organization of American States and supported initial negotiations for a European security alliance, which later resulted in the North Atlantic Treaty Organization (NATO). On January 20, 1949, he resigned from office because of poor health.

When hostilities erupted in Korea in 1950, Truman asked Marshall to return to government service as secretary of defense. Marshall began that September by reorganizing the defense bureaucracy. He persuaded Congress to extend the selective service system. He also directed that basic training be racially integrated in all military branches, that racial quotas be removed in military schools, and that segregated units in Korea be abolished. When the president relieved General Douglas MacArthur of his command in 1951, Marshall supported Truman in testimony before Congress. During his last months in office, when attacked by Senator Joseph McCarthy for being "soft on Communism," Marshall considered it beneath his dignity to reply.

Marshall retired as secretary of defense in September 1951, at the age of seventy. Two years later, he was awarded the 1953 Nobel Prize for Peace, the first professional soldier to receive the award. As Norwegian Nobel Committee member Carl Joachim Hambro said in his presentation speech, the prize was not given for what Marshall accomplished during the war, but for his accomplishments after the war through the Marshall Plan. Responding to those who criticized the selection of a military leader, Marshall said, "The cost of war in human lives is constantly spread before me, written neatly in many ledgers whose columns are gravestones. I am deeply moved to find some means or method of avoiding another calamity of war."

Marshall married Elizabeth Carter of Lexington, Virginia, in 1902; a heart defect prevented her from having children, and she died after surgery in 1927. Three years later, Marshall married Katherine Tupper Brown, a widow, and became stepfather to her three children. Allen, Marshall's favorite, was killed by a German sniper in Italy in May 1944. Reserved and dignified, Marshall lived quietly in retirement in Leesburg, Virginia, until his death in Washington, D.C., on October 16, 1959. He was buried at Arlington Cemetery.

Marshall's life exemplified the best in the American military tradition. Secretary of Defense Henry Stimson considered him "the finest soldier I have ever known." Truman called him "the greatest living American" and the one to whom "the United States owes its future." British Prime Minister WINSTON CHURCHILL described him as "the true organizer of victory." Most of his contemporaries, however, focused less on Marshall's military achievements than on his character. Colleagues agreed that he was without political ambition, a man dedicated to duty, discipline, self-sacrifice, and excellence. His integrity was unimpeachable. "It is morale that wins the war," he said in a rare statement of his principles. "It is not enough to fight. It is the spirit which we bring to the fight that decides the issue. The soldier's heart, the soldier's spirit, the soldier's soul are everything . . . . It is what men believe that makes them invincible."

WORKS BY: Report on the Army, 1941; The Winning of the War in Europe and the Pacific, 1945; Selected Speeches and Statements, 1945; Memoirs of My Services in the World War 1917–1918, 1976; The Papers of George Catlett Marshall (2 vols.) 1981–1986.

ABOUT: Beal, J. R. Marshall in China, 1970; Ferrell, R. H. George C. Marshall, 1966; Frye, W. Marshall, Citizen Soldier, 1947; Hobbs, J. P. Dear General, 1971; Marshall, K. T. Together: Annals of an Army Wife, 1946; Mosley, L. Marshall, Hero for Our Time, 1982; Payne, R. The Marshall Story, 1951; Pogue, F. C. George C. Marshall: Education of a General, 1963; Pogue, F. C. George C. Marshall: Ordeal and Hope, 1966; Pogue, F. C. George C. Marshall: Global Commander, 1968; Pogue, F. C. George C. Marshall: Organizer of Victory, 1973; Watson, M. Chief of Staff, 1950; Wilson, R. P. George Marshall Remembered, 1968.

MARTIN, ARCHER
(March 1, 1910–)
Nobel Prize for Chemistry, 1952
(shared with Richard Synge)

The English biochemist Archer John Porter Martin was born in London, the only son and youngest of four children of Lilian Kate (Brown) Martin, a nurse, and William Archer Porter Martin, a physician. At the age of nineteen, he entered Cambridge University with a scholarship to study chemical engineering. After meeting the biologist J. B. S. Haldane, however, Martin became interested in the biological sciences and, changing his field of study, received a B.A. in biochemistry in 1932, an M.A. three years later, and a Ph.D. in 1936.

As a student at Cambridge, Martin worked at the Dunn Nutritional Laboratory on the separation and isolation of vitamins. Through this work he developed considerable expertise in separating closely related chemical compounds by such methods as fractional distillation, solvent extraction, and similar techniques that involve the distribution of material between two phases. In countercurrent distribution, the mixture to be separated is repeatedly dissolved in two immiscible solvents that flow past each other in opposite directions. Because the components of the mixture have slightly different affinities for the solvents, they are eventually separated by the two fluids. In the chromatographic method, one phase flows past another stationary one of solids that have special affinities for the substances to be analyzed. Mixtures are separated into their components, depending on the differing attraction for the two phases. Because separate bands may be seen when colored substances are tested, the technique is known as chromatography. Colorless substances may be detected by ultraviolet light or chemical indicators that produce a color reaction.

In 1906 the Russian botanist Mikhail Tsvet had developed a technique called absorption or column chromatography, in which complex mixtures were poured into a long glass tube filled with finely powdered substances. The mixture's rate of travel from the top of the tube downward depended on the attraction of the molecules for the filling material and on the velocity of the solvent. Although this method was useful for the separation of plant pigments, it was restricted by the choice of filling materials. While still a schoolboy, Martin had built a fractional distillation column out of coffee cans soldered together in his basement laboratory. Later, Sir Charles Mar-

ARCHER MARTIN

tin, Martin's research adviser, suggested that he collaborate with RICHARD SYNGE, then a graduate student at Cambridge, on the separation of amino acids, the building blocks of protein molecules. Attempts to build countercurrent extraction devices for analysis of these compounds had failed because a satisfactory mixture of the suitable solvents could not be achieved as they flowed past each other.

Martin and Synge applied the principle of countercurrent distribution to column chromatography. In this method, columns of silica gel, which retains water strongly, served as the stationary phase, chloroform was used for the mobile phase, and methyl orange was used as an indicator. Examination of the separated amino acids by reaction with ninhydrin (a crystalline oxidizing agent) and comparison of the individual bands with similar measurements made with pure compounds allowed the determination of the composition of mixtures of amino acids. This analytical technique was named partition chromatography because it uses chromatographic techniques but is dependent on the chemical partition of the solute between the two solvents used in the column. The carrier, which is used to pack the column, is inert and serves only to hold one of the solvents. Unlike absorption chromatography, partition chromatography allows a wide choice of solvents and packing materials.

In 1938 Martin accepted a position as biochemist at the Wool Industries Research Association laboratory at Leeds, where Synge later was also employed. Continuing their collaboration, the two scientists found that cel-

lulose was a good water-holding medium for column chromatography. The discovery led them to the invention in 1944 of paper chromatography, in which filter paper is used as the supporting material. In this method, a drop of the mixture to be analyzed is placed at one end of a strip of filter paper, which is then put into a sealed glass cylinder containing an organic solvent saturated with water. The paper binds the water, while the other phase travels along the paper by capillary action. Amino acids that are more soluble in the organic phase move with the organic solvent; those more soluble in the aqueous phase remain closer to the starting point. After the paper is removed and dried, it may be sprayed with a chemical indicator to show the location of each compound, the migration of which is a characteristic constant for every solvent system.

Two-dimensional paper chromatography (chromatograms run in succession in two directions at right angles in different solvent systems) gives even further separation and allows the analysis of complex mixtures at low cost and with little effort. Paper chromatography was rapidly adopted in all branches of chemistry and led to important discoveries about protein structure, antibiotics, vaccines, polysaccharides, and rare earths.

In 1946 Martin became head of the biochemical research division of the Boots' Pure Drug Company in Nottingham. For the next two years he studied partition chromatography of fatty acids at the Medical Research Council of the Lister Institute in London. He then became a biochemist and head of the physical chemistry department at the National Institute for Medical Research, Mill Hill, London.

Martin and Synge were awarded the 1952 Nobel Prize in Chemistry "for their invention of partition chromatography." ARNE TISELIUS of the Royal Swedish Academy of Sciences said in his presentation speech, "Your invention of partition chromatography has given to science a new tool which has already proved its usefulness in an impressive number of important investigations. This tool has enabled research workers in chemistry, biology, and medicine to tackle and solve problems which earlier were considered almost hopelessly complicated."

In 1953 Martin, together with A. T. James, developed gas-liquid chromatography. In this technique, an inert gas, such as argon, helium, or nitrogen, serves as the mobile phase flowing over an inert solid (diatomaceous earth) impregnated with a nonvolatile liquid (silicone oils or high-molecular-weight alcohols). The method has been particularly useful for the characterization of fatty acid and steroid mixtures in microgram amounts.

From 1959 to 1970 Martin was director of Abbotsbury Laboratories, Ltd., then consultant to the Wellcome Foundation, Ltd., for three years, after which he received the Medical Research Council Professional Fellowship of Chemistry at the University of Sussex.

Martin's marriage in 1943 to Judith Bagenal, a teacher, produced three daughters and two sons. As a young man, he enjoyed mountaineering, gliding, and jujitsu.

Martin's many awards include the Berzelius Medal of the Swedish Medical Society (1951), the John Scott Award given by the city of Philadelphia (1958), the John Price Wetherill Medal (1959) and Franklin Medal (1959) of the Franklin Institute, the Order of the Rising Sun given by the Japanese government (1972), and the Randolf Major Medal of the University of Connecticut (1979). Martin is a fellow of the Royal Society, in addition to memberships in many other scientific societies.

ABOUT: Campbell, W. A., and Greenwood, N. N. Contemporary British Chemists, 1971; Journal of Chemical Education February 1977.

MARTIN DU GARD, ROGER
(March 23, 1881–August 23, 1958)
Nobel Prize for Literature, 1937

The French novelist and playwright Roger Martin du Gard (mär taN dü gär′) was born in the Paris suburb of Neuilly-sur-Seine, the elder of two children in a prosperous family that had its roots in Burgundy and Lorraine. His father, Paul-Émile Martin du Gard, and his grandfather were both lawyers; his mother, the former Madeleine-Jeanne Wimy, came from a family of stockbrokers. At about the age of ten, the boy became the friend of a schoolmate who was an aspiring dramatist; he later attributed to this acquaintance the birth of his own ambition to be a writer.

When he was eleven years old, Martin du Gard was sent to the École Fénelon, a Catholic school where he came under the influence of Abbé Marcel Hébert, a leading member of the Catholic modernists, a dissident movement within the Catholic church which sought to reinterpret church dogma in the light of modern science and philosophy and which was officially censured in the early years of the twentieth century. Although he gradually drew away from the tenets of Roman Catholicism,

ROGER MARTIN DU GARD

Martin du Gard established a close friendship with Hébert that was to last until the priest's death in 1916.

An indifferent student, Martin du Gard made slow academic progress. To improve his work, his father sent him to live in the home of Professor Louis Mellerio, who became his private tutor for several months. Stimulated by an invigorating academic atmosphere in which he was encouraged to read and to question rigorously whatever he was taught, Martin du Gard developed work habits that sharpened what he later characterized as his inherited propensity for analysis and investigation.

At the age of seventeen, at Hébert's suggestion, Martin du Gard read Leo Tolstoy's War and Peace, a novel which became an immediate and enduring inspiration and which fired his own literary ambitions. Shortly thereafter, he entered the Sorbonne in Paris, but was forced to withdraw after failing an important examination. He subsequently took and passed the qualifying examination for the École des Chartes in Paris, a specialized institution that trained paleographers and archivists by a rigorous and lengthy course of study. Although Martin du Gard later claimed that he was not sure why he had chosen this particular discipline, it was to have enormous significance in the development of his literary technique, building on the foundations laid down by Professor Mellerio in its meticulous scientific methodology. Martin du Gard received his diploma as a paleographer-archivist in 1905 after completing a thesis on the Abbey of Jumièges, near Rouen. The following year he married Hélène Foucault, the daughter of a Paris lawyer.

Settling in Paris, Martin du Gard attempted to begin a career as a professional novelist. He planned a long Tolstoyan novel about a country priest, a character very likely inspired by his mentor, Hébert. After a year and a half of hard work, he realized that a novel of such scope was beyond his ability, and he abandoned his effort. Profoundly discouraged, he entertained grave doubts about his intended vocation. He also had to consider the responsibility of providing for a daughter, Christiane, born in 1907. In an attempt to prove himself, he managed, in the space of a few weeks in the spring of 1908, to complete *Devenir!* (To Become), the story of a would-be man of letters who fails both in his effort to write and in his quest for personal happiness. Published later in the year at his own expense, *Devenir!* marked the beginning of Martin du Gard's literary career.

With his next intended work, which he planned to call *Marise,* Martin du Gard once again felt his ability unequal to his ambition. After a sustained effort, he abandoned the novel to seek a subject more appropriate to his experience. Such exacting perfectionism was to characterize Martin du Gard's entire career; on a number of occasions he burned manuscripts that he found unsatisfactory. In this case, his perfectionism led him to begin a new novel, *Jean Barois* (1913), his first major work and literary success. Using the then largely experimental technique of juxtaposing dialogue and historical documentation, Martin du Gard described the conflict of reason and faith in the person of his young hero, Barois. In considering problems of conscience during the course of the novel, he drew a perceptive portrait of the political scandal involving French army officer Alfred Dreyfus, which had a devastating effect on the entire structure of French society during the end of the nineteenth century and the beginning of the twentieth. *Jean Barois* was published on the recommendation of ANDRÉ GIDE, who became Martin du Gard's close friend and literary correspondent. The English version was published in 1949 under the same title.

During World War I, Martin du Gard served in the French army on the western front. Demobilized in 1919, he worked briefly in the theater in Paris and in 1920 moved to his parents' country estate in central France. There he began work on what is considered his masterpiece, the eight-volume novel *Les Thibault,* published between 1922 and 1940 (volumes 1–

6 translated as *The Thibaults;* volumes 7–8 translated as *Summer 1914*). Set during the first two decades of the twentieth century, *Les Thibault* is a powerful account of two bourgeois families, one Roman Catholic and one Protestant. It depicts the decline of pre–World War I society by tracing the lives of its two principal characters, the brothers Thibault— Jacques, a socialist revolutionary, and Antoine, a doctor who follows a more conservative path. As was his custom, Martin du Gard planned this roman-fleuve according to a detailed and historically documented outline. In 1931, however, following a severe automobile accident that required a two-month period of hospitalization, he revised the scheme for the remaining volumes, changing the planned ending and altering its emphasis by adopting a documentary technique similar to that used in *Jean Barois*. In the view of the English critic Martin Seymour-Smith, *Les Thibault* is "massive in its detail, its grasp of its main characters, its honesty," and "one of the most tragic major novels of the century."

Martin du Gard received the 1937 Nobel Prize for Literature "for the artistic power and truth with which he has pictured human conflict as well as some fundamental aspects of contemporary life." Describing *Les Thibault* in detail in his presentation address, Per Hallström of the Swedish Academy declared that "after his pointed and skeptical analysis of the human soul . . . through the most minute realism possible, Martin du Gard finally pays homage to the idealism of the human spirit." In his acceptance speech, Martin du Gard spoke out against the dogmatism that, in his view, pervaded twentieth-century life and thought, praising instead the "independent minds that escape the fascination of partisan ideologies and whose constant care is to develop their individual consciences." At a time when Adolf Hitler's demands threatened to plunge the world into another war, Martin du Gard expressed his hope that his work "might serve not only the cause of letters, but even the cause of peace."

During the years in which he produced *Les Thibault,* Martin du Gard also wrote *Confidence africaine (African Secret,* 1931), a daring story of incest; *Un Taciturne (A Silent Man,* 1932), a play dealing with the theme of homosexuality; and *Vieille France (The Postman,* 1933), a cynical and biting look at the French peasantry that is unique in Martin du Gard's body of work for both its tone and its subject. After 1940 he worked for seventeen years on *Les Souvenirs du colonel Maumort (The Mem-*

oirs of Colonel Maumort), another work conceived on the grand scale. It remained unfinished when he died of a heart ailment at his home in Bellême, in Normandy, at the age of seventy-seven.

Throughout his life, Martin du Gard remained an intensely private, reticent man, believing that the writer reveals what is best in himself through his work. In the months before his death, he organized his papers, including his voluminous correspondence and a journal he had kept from 1919 to 1949, which at his direction were subsequently deposited in the Bibliothèque Nationale in Paris, where they remained sealed for twenty-five years. But despite his reluctance to stand in the spotlight, Martin du Gard was, as his biographer Catherine Savage wrote, "one of the rare artists of his generation—or any—to receive the unanimous respect of his contemporaries." Moreover, Savage stated, by "applying realism to contemporary social problems, Martin du Gard . . . maintained a nineteenth-century tradition and also pointed toward subsequent contemporary development of the novel as a tool and an act."

ADDITIONAL WORKS IN ENGLISH TRANSLATION: Papa Leleu's Will, 1921; Recollections of André Gide, 1953.

ABOUT: Boak, D. Roger Martin du Gard, 1963; Brombert, V. The Intellectual Hero, 1961; Gibson, R. Roger Martin du Gard, 1962; Howe, I. The Decline of the New, 1970; Jouejati, B. R. The Quest for Total Peace, 1977; O'Nan, M. Roger Martin du Gard Centennial, 1981; Rice, H. C. Roger Martin du Gard and the World of the Thibaults, 1941; Savage, C. Roger Martin du Gard, 1968; Shalk, D. Roger Martin du Gard: The Novelist and History, 1967; Taylor, M. J. Roger Martin du Gard-Jean Barois, 1974.

MARTINSON, HARRY
(May 6, 1904–February 11, 1978)
Nobel Prize for Literature, 1974
(shared with Eyvind Johnson)

Harry Edmund Martinson (mär' tin sôn), Swedish poet, novelist, essayist, and journalist, was born in Jämshög, in the southern Swedish province of Blekinge. His father, Martin Olofsson, a retired sea captain, died when the boy was only six years old; shortly thereafter, his mother abandoned Martinson and his six sisters and emigrated to America. As wards of the state in prewelfare Sweden, the children were assigned to the care of the lowest bidders. Martinson spent most of his

HARRY MARTINSON

childhood in a succession of foster homes, from which he frequently fled.

At the end of World War I, while still in his teens, Martinson wandered to Göteborg, where he signed on as a ship's cabin boy. From 1920 to 1927 he worked intermittently on board a total of fourteen ships as a stoker and seaman. He often jumped ship, however, at ports in India, China, and South America, subsequently spending long periods as a laborer or vagrant. A bout of tuberculosis, which was later arrested, finally forced him to give up the seafaring life. It was about this time that he began to write poetry.

In 1929 Martinson married Moa Swartz, a writer who was fourteen years his senior. That year he published *Spökskepp* (Ghost Ship), a collection of poems inspired by RUDYARD KIPLING's *The Seven Seas* but also influenced by the Swedish modernist poet and critic Artur Lundkvist. Although Martinson's poetic contributions to the anthology *Fem Unga* (Five Young Men, 1929) also showed the imprint of Kipling—as well as of Walt Whitman, Carl Sandburg, and Edgar Lee Masters—they were considered less derivative than his first efforts.

His first mature work, *Nomad* (1931), a volume of brief lyrics in free verse, confirmed his reputation as a poet of promise. Although purists objected to its unorthodox diction and syntax, many critics were impressed with its freshness and the startling contrasts in its imagery. The American poet and critic Alrik Gustafson has attributed the innovative and occasionally obscure aspects of Martinson's work to "the inability of language to express the overwhelming intensity and complexity of his impressions." Thematically, *Nomad, Modern lyrik* (Modern Poems, 1931), and *Natur* (Nature, 1934) are imbued with primitivism. Throughout the poems, Martinson's belief in nature's goodness and the nobility of the common laborer is juxtaposed with what he perceives to be the contrivances and evils of modern society.

The image of the carefree wanderer pervades his travelogues *Resor utan mål* (Journeys Without a Goal, 1932) and *Kap Farväl!* (*Cape Farewell*, 1933). These prose sketches, based on Martinson's observations during his travels, were generally well received. The critic for the *Daily Mail* of London compared *Cape Farewell* with Joseph Conrad's *Nigger of the Narcissus*.

After the loosely autobiographical sketches, Martinson wrote his first novel, *Nässlorna blomma* (*Flowering Nettle*, 1935), inspired by his wretched childhood as a runaway orphan. Another novel, *Vägen ut* (The Way Out, 1936), based on his adolescence, followed shortly. Despite the hardships of his early years, these two personal, yet imaginative, works are surprisingly devoid of bitterness. During the late 1930s, he published three volumes of nature studies and essays, idiosyncratic in style and often in content, in which he again defended the simple, natural world against the relentless momentum of the industrial age.

Visiting the Soviet Union in 1934 with his wife to attend a writers' conference, Martinson was not favorably impressed by what he observed of Soviet life. The Soviet invasion of Finland in 1939 impelled him to enlist in the Swedish Volunteer Corps to fight for the liberation of Finland, but poor health soon forced him to resign. While recuperating, he wrote about the struggle against totalitarian forces in Europe in *Verklighet till döds* (Realism Unto Death), which was published in 1940, the same year he and his wife were divorced.

Although World War II and the years preceding it constituted a depressed period in Martinson's life, the mood of the poems in his collection *Passad* (Trade Wind, 1945) is predominantly one of meditative calm. Like his earlier writings, *Passad* is full of journeys and wanderings, but this time of the spirit. The trade wind is, as Martinson expressed it, "the best symbol of human reasonableness and human desire for airing things."

Among Martinson's most significant postwar works are a novel, *Vägen till Klockrike* (1948, translated as *The Road*), and an epic poem, *Aniara: En revy om människan i tid och rum,* published in 1956 and adapted in English by Hugh MacDiarmid and Elspeth Schubert in 1963 as *Aniara: A Review of Man in Time and Space.* The novel is a rather formless account of the adventures of Bolle, a middleaged vagabond, as he wanders through Sweden. Folktale-like in tone, it was well received in its English translation, despite its apparent structural weaknesses, and ensured Martinson's election to the Swedish Academy in 1949—an extraordinary honor for a writer without formal education.

Aniara is a brooding philosophical poem of 103 cantos about a spaceship that becomes eternally lost in space when it goes off course while taking 8,000 refugees from a dying Earth to Mars. At the same time, it is a symbolic review of human cultural history and alienation from spiritual values. If Martinson did not fear technological progress, he envisioned progress for its own sake as an endless voyage into darkness. Although some critics, including Michael Meyer, consider the poem confusing and pretentious, others, such as the Swedish-American critic Leif Sjöberg and the American poet Robert Bly, have hailed *Aniara* as Martinson's masterpiece while taking its English translation to task for failing to do it justice. Martinson himself termed the English translation "a scandal." An operatic adaptation of the poem by Karl Birger Blomdahl has been performed frequently.

In his poems, according to the critic Christopher Howell, "using precision, stillness, and the solitude of travelers, Martinson strings a tense, thin field between the mechanized, human-dominated world and the dance of nature." Indeed, this theme of estrangement permeates many of his later poetry cycles, including *Cikada* (Cicada, 1953), *Gräsen i Thule* (The Grasses in Thule, 1958), and *Vagnen* (The Wagon, 1960). When the reception of *Vagnen* was mixed, Martinson vowed not to publish any more poetry, but *Dikter om ljus och mörker* (Poems About Light and Darkness) appeared in 1971 and *Tuvor* (Tussocks) in 1973. Of the several plays he wrote, the most notable is *Tre Knivar från Wei* (Three Knives From Wei, 1964).

When Martinson was awarded the 1974 Nobel Prize for Literature (which he shared with his fellow countryman EYVIND JOHNSON) "for writings that catch the dewdrop and reflect the cosmos," the announcement was met with some skepticism, particularly in Sweden. Dissenting voices complained that the academy's decision displayed favoritism, though in fact Martinson and Johnson were the first Swedish recipients since PÄR LAGERKVIST in 1951. In his presentation speech, Karl Ragnar Gierow of the Swedish Academy praised Martinson and Johnson as "representatives of the many proletarian writers or working-class poets who, on a wide front, broke into our literature . . . to enrich it with their fortunes." He further lauded their "creative energy," which transcends parochial considerations and the limited distribution of their works.

Summing up the literary contributions of Martinson—whom he called "the first poet of the space age"—Leif Sjöberg considered *Aniara* one of "the great poems of our time." Writing about Martinson's use of poetic language, Christopher Howell noted its "precision and overall exactitude." For a man who was self-taught, Martinson's erudition was impressive. Sjöberg adds that he was a "stylistic innovator comparable to Strindberg and an imaginative coiner of words." Martinson died in Stockholm in 1978 at the age of seventy-three.

In addition to the Nobel Prize, Martinson was awarded an honorary doctorate by the University of Göteborg in 1954. In 1972 *Dikter om ljus och mörker* received the International Henrik Steffens Prize.

ADDITIONAL WORKS IN ENGLISH TRANSLATION: Fleischer, F. (ed.) Seven Swedish Poets, 1963; Wild Bouquet: Nature Poems, 1985.

ABOUT: American-Scandinavian Review December 1972; Bly, R. (ed.) Friends, You Drank Some Darkness, 1975; Books Abroad Summer 1974, Summer 1975; Gustafson, A. A History of Swedish Literature, 1961; Holm, I. Harry Martinson, 1960; Swenson, M. Half Sun Half Sleep, 1967.

MAURIAC, FRANÇOIS

(October 11, 1885–September 1, 1970)
Nobel Prize for Literature, 1952

François Charles Mauriac (mô ryäk´), French novelist, dramatist, and poet, was born in the city of Bordeaux, the youngest of five children of Jean-Paul Mauriac, a wealthy businessman, and the former Marguerite Coiffard. After his father died from a brain abscess when Mauriac was not quite two years old, the family lived with young Mauriac's maternal grandparents. According to his memoirs, the bashful Mauriac was deeply unhappy at Ste. Marie, a school run by the Marianite Order, where he was sent at the age of seven. Three years later he entered the College of the Marianites, where he discovered the work of Racine and Pascal, who

The Bettmann Archive

FRANÇOIS MAURIAC

became his favorite writers. Summers were spent on the family's property in the countryside around Bordeaux, a landscape that appears in many of his novels. After passing his baccalaureate examination, Mauriac went to the University of Bordeaux, where he took his *licence* (the equivalent of an M.A.) in letters in 1905.

The next year Mauriac went to Paris to prepare for entrance in the École des Chartes, a school for medievalists and curators of French archives. He was accepted in November 1908, but he resigned after six months to devote himself to literature. This decision was precipitated when the review *Le Temps Présent* (The Present Time) offered to publish Mauriac's first volume of poems, *Les Mains jointes* (*The Clasped Hands*), which appeared in November 1909. In March 1910 a eulogistic review of the book was written by the celebrated novelist Maurice Barrès.

The following year Mauriac worked on a second volume of poetry. His first novel, *L'Enfant chargé de chaînes* (*Young Man in Chains*), appeared in the magazine *Mercure de France* (Mercury of France) and was published by Grasset in 1913. That year he married Jeanne Lafont, the daughter of a banker; they had two daughters and two sons, one of whom, Claude, became a well-known novelist and critic. When France declared war on Germany in 1914, Mauriac was rejected by the army because of a physical disability, but he joined the Red Cross and served in the Balkans for two years as a hospital orderly.

After he was demobilized in 1918, Mauriac

wrote two more novels, but it was not until 1922 that he produced his first great success, *Le Baiser au lépreux* (*A Kiss to the Leper*). *A Kiss to the Leper* concerns the failure of an arranged marriage between a hideously ugly, but wealthy, man and a beautiful peasant girl. "What is brought out with great force," wrote the English critic Cecil Jenkins in 1965, "is the sacrifice of love and of youth in this society by the alliance of the family and an organized church colored by its values."

Mauriac's next two novels, *Le Fleuve de feu* (*The River of Fire*) and *Genitrix* (*The Family*), both published in 1923, were denounced as morbid, even pornographic, by spokesmen of the Catholic right wing. Set in a gloomy country house near Bordeaux similar to the one in *A Kiss to the Leper* (actually, the house of Mauriac's grandfather), *The Family* is a nightmarish study of the tyrannical love of a mother for her son, her destruction of his marriage, his revenge, and his final unhappiness.

Mauriac's next major novel, *Le Désert de l'amour* (*The Desert of Love*, 1925), won the First Prize for Novels of the French Academy. Longer and more complex than its predecessors, *The Desert of Love* describes the frustrated loves of father and son for the same sexually frigid woman, Maria Cross, a character the Irish critic Conor Cruise O'Brien described as an example of the dominant mother figure employed by many other Catholic writers.

Thérèse Desqueyroux (*Thérèse*, 1927), selected by a jury of eminent French literary critics as one of the best novels written since 1900, is based on an actual murder trial of 1906. The protagonist, who is mistakenly acquitted of attempting to murder her husband by arsenic poisoning, does not understand what motivated her crime. However, as Maxwell A. Smith stated, most readers conclude "that in attempting to destroy Bernard [her husband] it was not so much hatred for Bernard himself . . . as a despairing effort to escape from the bonds of family, of deadening routine, of bourgeois cant and futility."

In his 1928 essay "Souffrances du chrétien," Mauriac despaired that Christianity, because it suppressed the flesh for the spirit, was not a practicable religion. He subsequently underwent a religious crisis precipitated by widespread condemnation of his writing among Catholics, his pious mother's disapproval, and an extramarital affair that threatened his marriage. After discussions with a priest, Mauriac reaffirmed his faith. He declared his spiritual serenity in *Souffrances et bonheur du chrétien* (*Anguish and Joy of the Christian Life*, 1931).

Ce qui était perdu (*Suspicion*, 1929) shows the effects of his new religious orientation; *Le Nœud de vipères* (*Viper's Tangle*, 1932), one of his greatest novels, was hailed by the critic Charles Du Bos as "the accomplished success of a great Catholic novel." This family drama, whose greatness lies in Mauriac's psychological portrayal of his tragic protagonist, a miser, depicts the hypocrisy prevalent among respectable, conventional Catholics of the bourgeoisie, while it traces the spiritual regeneration of its central character. After publication of *Viper's Tangle*, Mauriac underwent surgery for cancer of the throat. The removal of a vocal chord left his voice permanently impaired. The next year he was elected to the French Academy.

Although Mauriac continued to write novels and attempted a great Catholic novel of salvation, many critics perceive a gradual decline in his work. *La Pharisienne* (*A Woman of the Pharisees*, 1941) recounts the story of Brigitte Pien, a deeply religious and domineering woman who destroys other people's lives by her interference and, as the literary scholar Henri Peyre observed, "turns her own religion into a caricature of Christian mercy." At last, however, she recognizes her sin and achieves salvation.

After his 1929 *Dieu et Mammon* (*God and Mammon*), Mauriac wrote a series of religious essays that culminated in 1936 with *Vie de Jésus* (*Life of Jesus*). During this period he turned to the theater. The first of his four plays, *Asmodée*, staged by Jacques Copeau, was performed 100 times during the 1937–1938 season at the Comédie Française. It was translated into English in 1939 under the title *Asmodée; or, The Intruder*. Two collections of his short stories, *Trois Récits* (*Three Tales*) and *Plongées* (*Dives*), appeared in 1929 and 1938, respectively.

During the German occupation of France in World War II, Mauriac contributed occasional articles to the clandestine journal *Les Lettres Françaises* (French Literature). When one of the journal's organizers was arrested by the Gestapo and shot in 1942, Mauriac wrote *Le Cahier noir* (*The Black Notebook*, 1943), an eloquent protest against German tyranny and French collaboration. Its publication, even though under a pseudonym, forced Mauriac into hiding for a time. Despite these experiences, after the war he urged his fellow citizens to show mercy toward collaborators.

Mauriac was first nominated for the Nobel Prize for Literature in 1946, and his name was mentioned in subsequent years. He finally received the prize in 1952 "for the deep spiritual insight and the artistic intensity with which he has in his novels penetrated the drama of human life." In his presentation address, Anders Österling of the Swedish Academy explained that Mauriac "uses the novel to expound a particular aspect of human life in which Catholic thought and sensitivity are at the same time background and keystone." In addition, he noted that Mauriac "remains unequaled in conciseness and expressive force of language; his prose can in a few suggestive lines shed light on the most complex and difficult things. His most remarkable works are characterized by a purity of logic and classic economy of expression that recall the tragedies of Racine."

In his acceptance speech, Mauriac emphasized the need for hope in a world permeated by horror and "the mystery of evil." He stated, "A humanity which does not doubt that life has a direction and a goal cannot be a humanity in despair. The despair of modern man is born out of the absurdity of the world; out of his despair as well as his submission to surrogate myths: the absurd delivers man to the inhuman."

After receiving the prize, Mauriac published his penultimate novel, *L'Agneau* (*The Lamb*), in 1954. Turning to journalism, he expressed his support for Charles de Gaulle's anticolonial policies in Morocco and for Algerian independence, allying himself with Catholics on the left. When de Gaulle returned to power in 1958, Mauriac was awarded the Grand Cross of the Legion of Honor upon the general's personal recommendation. From the late 1950s to the late 1960s, Mauriac published a series of personal memoirs and a biography of de Gaulle. His celebrated weekly newspaper column, *Bloc-Notes,* contained witty and malicious comments on politics, literature, and people; it ran from the mid-1950s until July 27, 1970, and reached a far larger audience than his novels. Mauriac's eightieth birthday was celebrated in 1965 in the paper *Le Figaro littéraire* (The Literary Figaro) by a complete issue of eulogies from French critics. He published a final novel, *Un Adolescent d'autrefois* (translated as *Maltaverne*), in 1969. He died on September 1, 1970, in Paris.

Henri Peyre wrote that between 1930 and 1945 French critics would have ranked Mauriac as the twentieth-century novelist second in line to Marcel Proust, but that after 1945 he lost ground to experimental writers. Critics generally agree that Mauriac's fiction is limited by an "obsession with his own childhood memories," the narrow social range of his characters, the continual reappearance of the same character "whose consuming passion is dominance over all who surround him or her," the frequency of miraculous conversions of sinners, and the "pessimistic and sulfurous atmosphere" of the world Mauriac portrays. Yet in Peyre's estimation, "Out of the score of novels he has published, four or five seem clearly destined for survival. Few are the novelists in any language of whom such a prophecy could be ventured."

ADDITIONAL WORKS IN ENGLISH TRANSLATION: Destinies, 1929; Maundy Thursday, 1932; Communism and Christians, 1938; The Eucharist, 1944; The Unknown Sea, 1948; Saint Margaret of Cortona, 1948; Proust's Way, 1950; Men I Hold Great, 1951; The Little Misery, 1952; The Stumbling Block, 1952; The Weakling and the Enemy, 1952; The Frontenac Mystery, 1952; The Loved and the Unloved, 1952; Mask of Innocence, 1953; Letters on Art and Literature, 1953; Flesh and Blood, 1955; Words of Faith, 1955; Lines of Life, 1957; Questions and Precedence, 1958; Mémoires intérieur, 1960; Second Thoughts, 1961; Cain, Where Is Your Brother? 1962; What I Believe, 1963; Young Man in Crisis, 1963; De Gaulle, 1966; The Holy Terror, 1967; The Inner Presence, 1968.

ABOUT: Brée, G., and Guiton, M. O. An Age of Fiction, 1957; Caspary, A. M., and Peyre, H. François Mauriac, 1968; Cowley, M. (ed.) Writers at Work, volume 1, 1958; Flower, J. E. Intention and Achievement, 1969; Greene, G. The Lost Childhood and Other Essays, 1951; Heppenstall, R. The Double Image, 1947; Jarret-Kerr, M. François Mauriac, 1954; Jenkins, C. Mauriac, 1965; Kellogg, G. The Vital Tradition, 1970; Moloney, M. F. François Mauriac: A Critical Study, 1958; Pell, E. François Mauriac: In Search of the Infinite, 1947; Peyre, H. French Novelists of Today, 1955; Scott, M. Mauriac: The Politics of a Novelist, 1980; Smith, M. A. François Mauriac, 1970; Stratford, P. Faith and Fiction, 1964; Turnell, M. The Art of French Fiction, 1959.

MAYER, MARIA GOEPPERT
(June 28, 1906–February 20, 1972)
Nobel Prize for Physics, 1963
(shared with J. Hans D. Jensen and Eugene P. Wigner)

The German-American physicist Maria Goeppert Mayer (mī' ər) was born Maria Göppert in Kattowitz (now Katowice, Poland), the only child of Friedrich Göppert, a professor of medicine, and the former Maria Wolff, a schoolteacher. (Mayer anglicized the spelling of her maiden name when she came to the United States.) When Maria was four years old, her family moved to Göttingen, where her father had been appointed professor of pediatrics at the university there. Her family

MARIA GOEPPERT MAYER

became close friends of MAX BORN and JAMES FRANCK and social acquaintances of other scientists at the university who were to revolutionize physics with the development of quantum mechanics. Her father encouraged Maria's early love of science, taking her on nature walks, showing her eclipses of the sun and the moon, and collecting fossils with her.

Young Maria was an excellent student in public school, but the course did not prepare girls for her goal of studying mathematics at the university. Therefore, in 1921 she enrolled in the Frauenstudium, a private preparatory girls' school run by suffragettes. Although the school closed for lack of funds before she could complete the three-year program, she studied on her own, passed the university entrance examination, and was admitted in 1924.

The University of Göttingen was then a leading center for developments in the new field of quantum physics. When Max Born invited her to join his physics seminar, she switched from mathematics to physics, concentrating on quantum mechanics, which deals with the behavior of atoms, nuclei, and their components. Soon after starting her physics studies, she spent one term at Cambridge University in England, where she met the noted English physicist ERNEST RUTHERFORD and learned the English language. She received her Ph.D. at Göttingen in 1930 with the doctoral thesis "On Elemental Processes With Two Quantum Jumps." Her examining committee included Max Born, James Franck, and ADOLF WINDAUS.

After the death of Maria's father in 1927,

her mother had taken in boarders, a common practice in Göttingen. One was Joseph E. Mayer, an American chemist from the California Institute of Technology. Maria and Joseph fell in love and were married in January 1930, shortly before she received her Ph.D. They eventually had a son and a daughter. After her marriage, she signed her name Maria Goeppert Mayer because of her pride that she was, as she put it, "the seventh straight generation of university professors" on her father's side. One month after their marriage, the couple sailed to the United States, where Joseph Mayer had been offered a position as assistant professor of chemistry at Johns Hopkins University in Baltimore, Maryland.

Despite the academic credentials of Maria Mayer, university policy and the prevailing attitude toward faculty wives denied her a paid teaching position at Johns Hopkins. However, she was assigned to help a member of the physics department with German correspondence, given a small salary and an attic office, and permitted to participate in the university's scientific activities.

Although Mayer chose to study chemical physics to learn the physics of molecules and their interactions, she also took advantage of other opportunities in both the physics and mathematics departments. With the physicist Karl F. Herzfeld, who became a lifelong friend, she worked on energy transfer on solid surfaces and the behavior of hydrogen dissolved in the metallic element palladium. After Herzfeld left Johns Hopkins, Mayer worked with one of his former students, Alfred Sklar, on the quantum-mechanical electronic levels of benzene and the structures of several organic dyes, applying group theory and matrix methods from her special mathematical background. During the summers of 1931, 1932, and 1933, partly out of homesickness, she returned to Göttingen to study with Born.

Mayer became a naturalized American citizen in 1933, the year the Nazis came to power in Germany. Anti-Semitism and the racially oppressive Nazi civil service laws had a disastrous effect on German scientists, especially academic Jews like Born and Franck, who fled Germany. The Mayers opened their Baltimore home to a stream of German exiles, most of them Jewish refugees.

At Johns Hopkins, the Mayers did important work together, notably on the theory of condensation. In 1938 they collaborated on a book, *Statistical Mechanics,* describing the behavior of enormous numbers of interacting particles, for example, in gases and liquids.

When the book was published in 1940, Joseph Mayer was associate professor of chemistry at Columbia University in New York City. Columbia offered Maria Mayer even less official recognition than she had received at Johns Hopkins. Although the chairman of the physics department provided an office, she received neither an appointment nor a salary. Nevertheless, she worked at Columbia with ENRICO FERMI and HAROLD C. UREY (the Mayers became close friends of the Ureys) on chemical and atomic structure, and Urey gave her the title of lecturer in chemistry.

In 1941 Mayer received her first paid teaching appointment, a part-time position at Sarah Lawrence College. The following year, when Urey brought her into the Manhattan Project (the massive effort to develop the atomic bomb), she headed a team that investigated the possibility of separating fissionable uranium isotopes from natural uranium by photochemical reactions. In 1945 she spent several months at the Manhattan Project's laboratory in Los Alamos, New Mexico, working with the Hungarian-American physicist Edward Teller.

After the war, Joseph Mayer became professor of chemistry at the University of Chicago. Although Maria Mayer was named associate professor of physics there in 1946, she received no salary because university antinepotism regulations forbade it. In 1946 she also became a part-time senior physicist at the Argonne National Laboratory near Chicago, where a nuclear reactor was being built. There she worked with Fermi, Urey, Franck, and Teller and worked on the calculations needed to solve the criticality problem for a liquid-metal breeder reactor. The calculations were performed on the first electronic computer, the electronic numerical integrator and computer (ENIAC), which had recently been installed at the United States Army's Ordnance Department at Aberdeen, Maryland.

It was during this time, while collaborating with Teller on a theory of the origin of the elements, that Mayer encountered the subject of "magic" numbers, first referred to in 1933 by the German physicist Walter Elsasser. Atomic nuclei contain protons (positively charged particles over 1,800 times as heavy as negative electrons) and neutrons (electrically neutral particles whose mass is almost identical to that of protons). Mayer found that certain nuclei were unaccountably abundant and therefore must be unusually stable. Abundance and stability tend to coincide because an unstable nucleus is likely to change by radioactive decay into another one. If the decay product is also unstable, it, too, will change over time, until a stable product is formed. Stable nuclei persist and accumulate. In the especially abundant nuclei, either the number of protons or the number of neutrons equals one of the magic numbers, which proved to be 2, 8, 20, 28, 50, 82, 126, and some others to a lesser degree.

Mayer knew that an analogous situation existed for atomic electrons surrounding the nucleus. Stability for atoms is chemical, since it is the loss, gain, or sharing of electrons that governs chemical reactions; the nuclei remain unaffected. The periodic table shows that chemical properties recur in cycles, or periods, as the atomic number increases. The atomic number is the number of protons (positive) in the nucleus, which equals the number of electrons (negative) around the nucleus in an undisturbed atom, so that the atom as a whole is electrically neutral.

The recurring stability at certain atomic numbers was explained on the basis of atomic energy levels related to the angular momentum of the electrons moving around the nucleus. In accordance with quantum theory, the energy levels are restricted to certain discrete values. The angular momenta arise from electron motion around the nucleus (orbital) and electron spin about its own axis, like a top. (Such simple images are rejected by quantum physics but can still be useful.) Since moving electrons constitute an electric current, they generate a magnetic field. Just as two magnets repel or attract each other, the angular momenta and spins of the electrons interact (spin-orbit coupling). Quantum theory describes a specific number of discrete energy states for each allowed level of angular momentum. When these states are coupled with the effects of electron spin, the result is a system of energy levels, each identified by a set of four quantum numbers. To this is added the restriction of the principle discovered by WOLFGANG PAULI that only one electron can occupy a quantum state of a given set of quantum numbers. The outcome is that, as the atomic number rises, and electrons are added one by one, each additional electron occupies the next available level. The total energy rises step by step.

The energy steps are not equal, but occur in clusters of smaller steps separated by unusually large steps. On the basis of an early picture of the electrons circling the nucleus at various distances, the clusters were called shells. The chemical element in whose atom the outermost electron occupies the last level before a large step is said to close the shell. The element of next higher atomic number (one more electron) starts the next shell. A closed shell represents a stable element. Because the addition or removal of an electron requires an unusually large amount of energy, chemical reaction is inhibited.

This scheme was applied to the nucleus, under the assumption that the protons and neutrons could be regarded as orbiting around each other, but with limited success. The nucleus is very different from the atom as a whole. In the atom, the dominant central attraction occurs between the protons in the nucleus and the electrons, the well-known electric force. The electrons are relatively distant from each other and their mutual repulsion is weak; as a result, the energy of one electron does not depend very much on the positions of the others. The nuclear forces between protons and between protons and neutrons act at short range, and the energy of one particle might be expected to depend strongly on the positions of the others. No single dominant center of attraction exists. Such differences led earlier theorists to expect that spin-orbit coupling would be almost negligible for protons and neutrons in the nucleus.

Mayer struggled with the nucleus problem. At the beginning of her research, she had found two magic numbers, 50 and 82. In studying the data she found five more, but no explanation for them. The crucial moment came in 1948 when Fermi asked her, "Is there any indication of spin-orbit coupling?" Recognizing at once that this was the clue, she was able to explain nuclear magic numbers by that evening. She showed that the nucleus, too, could be depicted as having shells and described it as "built up like an onion in layers, with the protons and neutrons revolving around each other and spinning in orbit, like couples in a waltz around a ballroom." Nuclei were stable when the shells of protons or neutrons were full. The magic numbers were different from those for atomic electrons, but the parallel, with necessary modifications, held.

Mayer reported her work on nuclear shell theory in two papers in the journal *Physical Review* in 1948 and 1949. They coincided with the publication of an almost identical theory by J. HANS D. JENSEN at the University of Heidelberg, working independently with Otto Haxel and Hans E. Suess. Mayer and Jensen met in 1950 in Germany, became friends, and began collaborating on a book, *Elementary Theory of Nuclear Shell Structure,* which was published in 1955.

Mayer and Jensen shared half of the 1963

Nobel Prize for Physics "for their discoveries concerning nuclear shell structure." The other half was awarded to EUGENE P. WIGNER. In his presentation speech, Ivar Waller of the Royal Swedish Academy of Sciences reminded his listeners that until Mayer's discoveries, "it was . . . not possible to explain more than the first three magic numbers." Both she and Jensen, he said, "gave convincing evidence for the great importance of the shell model in systematizing this material and predicting new phenomena concerning the ground state and the low excited states of the nuclei."

The Mayers were offered positions at the University of California at San Diego in 1960, she as a full professor of physics and he as professor of chemistry. Shortly after the move to California, Maria Mayer suffered a stroke, apparently due to a viral infection, which impaired her speech and left her partly paralyzed. After her stroke, she was increasingly hampered by ill health, but she continued to teach and to contribute to the development of nuclear theory. She also continued her association with Jensen, publishing her last paper in collaboration with him in 1966, six years before she died in San Diego of a heart attack.

Mayer was elected to the National Academy of Sciences and the American Academy of Arts and Sciences, and she was chosen a corresponding member of the Academy of Sciences in Heidelberg. She received honorary degrees from Smith College, Russell Sage College, and Mount Holyoke College.

ABOUT: Biographical Memoirs of the National Academy of Sciences, volume 50, 1979; Current Biography June 1964; Dash, J. A. Life of One's Own, 1973; Haber, L. Women Pioneers of Science, 1979.

MCCLINTOCK, BARBARA
(June 16, 1902–)
Nobel Prize for Physiology or Medicine, 1983

The American geneticist Barbara McClintock was born in Hartford, Connecticut, the youngest of three daughters of Thomas Henry McClintock, a physician, and the former Sara Handy. In her early years she spent a great deal of time with her paternal aunt and uncle in rural Massachusetts, where she developed a love of the outdoors and nature. When she was eight years old, her family moved to the then semirural neighborhood of Flatbush in Brooklyn, New York, where her father worked for the Standard Oil Company as phy-

BARBARA MCCLINTOCK

sician to the crews on oil tankers. As a girl McClintock enjoyed ice skating and playing other sports with the neighborhood boys. She also developed a lifelong habit of solitary reading and thinking.

McClintock received her early education in the public schools of Brooklyn and graduated from high school in 1918. Although her parents opposed her wish to attend college, they eventually relented, and in 1919 she enrolled in Cornell University in Ithaca, New York, to study biology in the College of Agriculture.

At Cornell she was elected president of the freshman women's class; during her first years there she led an active social life, including playing banjo in a jazz band. She decided not to join a sorority when she learned that her Jewish friends had not also been invited to join. She took the only course in genetics open to undergraduates and so impressed her teachers that she was invited to take a graduate-level course in genetics while still in her junior year. McClintock received a B.S. in 1923 and shortly thereafter continued her studies as a graduate student in the Department of Botany, majoring in cytology (the study of cells) and minoring in genetics and zoology.

The favored organisms for genetic studies were the fruit fly (*Drosophila melanogaster*) and Indian corn, or maize (*Zea mays*). *Drosophila* was popular because it has a short life span, many progeny, and certain prominent physical traits. Maize has a longer life span, but its kernels and leaves are colorful and variegated, rendering it suitable for genetic study.

While McClintock was an undergraduate at Cornell, the geneticists in the university's College of Agriculture were pioneering the development of genetics. Professor R.A. Emerson was studying the genetics of maize and hybrid strains of corn. McClintock worked with him and also developed a stimulating professional association with two other graduate students, GEORGE W. BEADLE and Marcus Rhoades, both of whom became well known as geneticists in later years.

In 1924, in the course of her graduate work, McClintock developed a method of studying individual maize chromosomes under a microscope, which made it possible to study the chromosomes and the phenotypical, or physical, traits of maize concurrently. That year she was appointed assistant in the department of botany, and in 1925 she received her M.A. She wrote her doctoral dissertation on the method that she had developed, for which she received a Ph.D. two years later. She then served as an instructor in the botany department from 1927 until 1931.

During these years McClintock continued to study the morphology of maize chromosomes, as well as their correlation with the phenotypical traits of the fully grown plant. In collaboration with Harriet Creighton, McClintock discovered that maize chromosomes exchange genetic material and information during chromosomal crossing over in the early stages of meiosis. Meiosis is the process of cell division that leads to the formation of germ, or sex, cells, which have half the number of chromosomes of somatic, or tissue, cells; during fertilization the number of chromosomes is doubled.

Between 1929 and 1931 McClintock published nine papers in the biology and genetics literature. In 1931 THOMAS HUNT MORGAN visited Cornell and, impressed with McClintock's research, arranged for her work to be published in the prestigious journal *Proceedings of the National Academy of Science*. Her paper on the exchange of genetic information during meiosis, "A Correlation of Cytological and Genetical Crossing Over in *Zea mays*," appeared in the August 1931 issue. That year she won a National Research Council Fellowship for two years of further research on the genetics of maize. She was also appointed a research fellow in Morgan's department at the California Institute of Technology and spent time at Cornell and at the University of Missouri in Columbia, where she studied the correlation between X-ray-induced genetic mutations in the chromosomes of maize and the phenotypical appearance of the plant. She determined that circular chromosomes correlated with variegated color in maize kernels. She also discovered nucleolar chromosomes, which are involved in the biosynthesis of cellular ribosomes, the sites of cellular protein biosynthesis.

A Guggenheim Fellowship enabled her to study at the Kaiser Wilhelm Institute in Berlin in 1933. The following year, troubled by the rise of Nazism, she returned to Cornell, where she was a research associate in Emerson's department until 1936, when she was appointed assistant professor of botany at the University of Missouri. Realizing that her chances of promotion were limited, she left the university in 1941 and spent the summer working in the biology laboratory of her old friend Marcus Rhoades, in Cold Spring Harbor, New York. That fall she accepted a job as staff member of the Carnegie Institute of Washington in Cold Spring Harbor, where she has been doing research on the genetics of maize ever since.

The 1940s were particularly productive years for McClintock. In the winter months she analyzed her experimental results from the previous summer and planned the next year's research. During the summers she grew maize in her garden outside the laboratory. Earlier experiments had led her to suspect the presence of mobile genetic elements on maize chromosomes. In the winter of 1943–1944 she planned an experiment that she hoped would prove this theory. In the summer of 1944 she noticed that twin plants had opposite leaf patterns: one had deeply colored stripes, and the other had faint stripes. Noticing a similar phenomenon in the kernels of maize, she concluded that one of the daughter plants possessed a genetic system that the other did not. This phenomenon is now called genetic transposition, and the genes involved are called transposable or "jumping" genes.

McClintock correctly formulated a model of the genetic system responsible for producing the experimental results. Two transposable genes were involved: a dissociator gene, which she called the *Ds* gene, and an activator gene, which she called the *Ac* gene. She observed that the genetic system worked in the following way. If the *Ds* gene moved to a chromosomal site next to a structural gene (for example, the structural gene that governs the stripe patterns of maize leaves), the *Ds* gene suppressed the phenotypical expression of the structural gene and the leaf stripes were faint. The suppression of the structural gene was effective, however, only if the *Ac* gene occupied a site near the other two genes. If the *Ac* gene

moved (or was transposed) to a distant site, the *Ds* gene no longer suppressed the structural gene and the leaf stripes were a deep color. One of the two transposable genes was a suppressor gene and the other was a desuppressor of the suppressor.

The discovery by McClintock of transposable genetic systems and genetic regulation anticipated the findings of bacterial geneticists fifteen years later. The influence of her discovery has been far-reaching; for instance, the determination of how resistance to antibiotic drugs can be passed from one kind of bacteria to another through jumping genes owes much to McClintock's work. Her model also explained certain phenomena that were incompatible with strict Mendelian laws of inheritance, which predicted that the phenotypical traits of the progeny of any set of parents would be distributed according to genetic dominance or recessiveness in simple ratios. McClintock's system provided an explanation of how the color pattern of a maize kernel could change from the early to the late stages of development. She also speculated that transposable genetic elements or genes might explain the occasional rapid emergence of new species of plants and animals.

In 1950 McClintock presented a review of her research on maize genetics and transposable genetic systems to a symposium at the Cold Spring Harbor facility. Because her hypothesis of mobile, transposable genes violated a then current dogma of genetics—that genes were stable components of chromosomes—her talk was poorly received. In a certain sense, her research was not taken seriously—possibly because she was a woman, but more likely, simply because it was not understood. McClintock was justifiably disappointed and for a time cut back on publication of her experimental results. From 1958 until 1960 she suspended her research to train cytologists from Latin America under a program administered by the National Academy of Sciences. By the time she resumed her work on the genetics of maize and transposable genes, bacterial geneticists had discovered regulatory genes in bacteria not unlike those discovered by McClintock in corn.

McClintock was awarded the 1983 Nobel Prize for Physiology or Medicine for her discovery of transposable genetic systems—more than three decades after the work for which she was cited.

In an interview with Evelyn Fox Keller, her biographer, McClintock summed up her attitude toward her work: "As you look at these things, they become part of you. And you forget yourself. The main thing about it is you forget yourself." Described by members of the Nobel committee as "a loner," she continues to conduct solitary research on the genetics of maize in her laboratory and garden in Cold Spring Harbor, New York. She has remained unmarried.

In addition to the Nobel Prize, McClintock has received the Kimber Genetics Award of the National Academy of Sciences (1967), the National Medal of Science of the National Science Foundation (1970), the Albert Lasker Basic Medical Research Award (1970), the Wolf Prize in Medicine of the Wolf Foundation in Israel (1981), and the Louisa Gross Horwitz Prize of Columbia University (1982). In 1981 she was awarded a MacArthur Foundation Fellowship. She is a member of the National Academy of Sciences, the American Society of Naturalists, the American Philosophical Society, the Botanical Society of America, and the Genetics Society of America. She holds honorary degrees from the University of Rochester, Smith College, the University of Missouri, Yale University, Williams College, and New York University.

SELECTED WORKS: "The Control of Gene Action in Maize," Brookhaven Symposia in Biology, 1965.

ABOUT: Current Biography March 1984; Hammond, A. (ed.) A Passion to Know, 1984; Keller, E. F. A Feeling for the Organism: The Life and Work of Barbara McClintock, 1983; New York Times October 11, 1983; Science October 28, 1983.

MCMILLAN, EDWIN M.

(September 18, 1907–   )
Nobel Prize for Chemistry, 1951
(shared with Glenn T. Seaborg)

The American physicist Edwin Mattison McMillan was born in Redondo Beach, California, to Edwin Harbaugh McMillan, a physician, and the former Anne Marie Mattison. The family soon moved to Pasadena, and McMillan received his early education there. While at Pasadena High School, he attended public lectures at the California Institute of Technology, where he later majored in physics, receiving a B.S. in 1928 and an M.S. the following year. He was awarded a Ph.D. in 1932 from Princeton University for a thesis on molecular beams. He then worked at the University of California at Berkeley as a National Research fellow. When ERNEST O. LAW-

RENCE founded the Lawrence Radiation Laboratory at Berkeley in 1934, McMillan joined the staff. In his years there, he contributed to the development of cyclotron technology as well as to nuclear physics and chemistry.

The cyclotron, invented by Lawrence, is a particle accelerator that produces protons and atomic nuclei with very high energies. More compact than linear accelerators, the cyclotron uses a magnetic field to bend the particles in a curved path. Charged particles introduced into the center of the chamber are accelerated by an alternating electric field having the same frequency as their orbit. As the velocity of a particle increases, so does the diameter of its orbit, the period of its revolution remaining constant. The oscillating electric field gradually accelerates the spiraling particles to very high energies.

In 1938, while attempting to create new chemical elements by adding neutrons to the uranium nucleus, the German chemists OTTO HAHN, Fritz Strassmann, and Lise Meitner instead produced the fission, or splitting, of uranium nuclei. McMillan used a cyclotron at the Lawrence Radiation Laboratory to conduct similar studies of the effect of neutrons on uranium. In 1940 he and a co-worker, Philip Abelson, found that some of the uranium nuclei bombarded with neutrons did not undergo fission. Instead, as ENRICO FERMI had predicted six years earlier, they decayed, forming a new element with ninety-three protons and electrons. This element, which they named neptunium for the planet Neptune, was the first transuranium (heavier than uranium) element to be synthesized. McMillan's research was continued by GLENN T. SEABORG and his colleagues, who in 1941 discovered plutonium.

During World War II, McMillan conducted wartime research on sonar, microwave radar, and nuclear weapons at Berkeley, the Massachusetts Institute of Technology (1940–1941), the United States Navy Radio and Sound Laboratory in San Diego (1941–1942), and the Manhattan Project in Los Alamos (1942–1945). After the war he was appointed a full professor of physics at the University of California at Berkeley, and in 1954 he became associate director of the Lawrence Radiation Laboratory. From 1958 until his retirement in 1973, he was director of the laboratory, which had been renamed the Lawrence Berkeley Laboratory in 1971.

In 1945 McMillan addressed a problem affecting the cyclotron: the orbital period of a particle in a cyclotron is steady only if the mass of the particle remains constant. According to

EDWIN M. MCMILLAN

ALBERT EINSTEIN's theory of relativity, as the velocity of a moving object approaches the speed of light, its mass increases. It is therefore possible for the kinetic energy of an object to reach very high levels without major increases in its speed, since most of the energy goes to increasing the mass of the object. As the mass of the orbiting particle increases, however, it takes longer to complete each circular revolution and thus falls out of rhythm with the oscillating electric impulses used in the cyclotron. McMillan's solution to this problem was to vary the strength of the magnetic field or the frequency of the electrical impulses to match the decreasing velocity of the orbiting particles, which are kept moving in a circle of constant radius rather than in a spiral, as in the cyclotron. (Unknown to him, since Soviet scientific journals were not distributed in the United States during World War II, the Russian physicist Vladimir I. Veksler had proposed the same concept the previous year.) The energies that can be obtained in such accelerators, which are called synchrotrons, is limited only by the diameter of the accelerator and the strength of the magnetic field that is used to confine the energetic particles within it.

McMillan and Seaborg shared the 1951 Nobel Prize for Chemistry "for their discoveries in the chemistry of the transuranium elements." In his presentation address, A. F. Westgren of the Royal Swedish Academy of Sciences saluted McMillan for establishing the existence of the transuranium elements. "You were the first to succeed in this enterprise,"

Westgren said. "By your discoveries you have opened a field of research in which vast and fundamentally important scientific and technical gains have been made. Later, by your work on the accelerator problem you have also actively furthered the progress in this domain of chemistry."

After receiving the Nobel Prize, McMillan remained active in research until his retirement from Berkeley in 1973..

In 1941 McMillan married Elsie Blumer, the daughter of the dean of the Yale Medical School; they have one daughter and two sons.

In addition to the Nobel Prize, McMillan has received the Science Award of the Research Corporation of America (1951) and the Atoms for Peace Award of the Ford Motor Company Fund (1963). He is a member of the National Academy of Sciences, the American Physical Society, the American Academy of Arts and Sciences, and the American Philosophical Society. He has been a member of numerous organizations involved with science policy and high-energy physics, including the United States Atomic Energy Commission, the Rand Corporation, the International Union for Pure and Applied Physics, and the Stanford Linear Accelerator Center.

SELECTED WORKS: Lecture Series on Nuclear Physics, 1947, with others.

ABOUT: Current Biography February 1952; National Cyclopedia of American Biography, volume H, 1952; Seaborg, G. T. Man-Made Transuranium Elements, 1963.

MEADE, JAMES
(June 23, 1907–   )
Nobel Memorial Prize in Economic
    Sciences, 1977
(shared with Bertil Ohlin)

The English economist James Edward Meade was born in Swanage, Dorset, to Charles Hippsley and Kathleen (Cotton-Stapleton) Meade. His early education at the Lambrook School (1917—1921) and then at Malvern College (1921–1926) concentrated on Latin and Greek, a focus he maintained during his first two years at Oriel College, Oxford. It was in 1928, when he transferred to Oriel's newly established School of Philosophy, Politics, and Economics, that Meade began to study economics. His interest in this field reflected a concern for what he has called the "stupid and wicked" levels of unemployment in Britain be-

JAMES MEADE

tween the wars, as well as the influence of his "much-loved but somewhat eccentric maiden aunt." She was a follower of Major C. H. Douglas, a English economist who expounded the theory that modern economies are plagued by insufficient purchasing power. His proposed solution was to increase purchasing power by controlling prices and distributing "social credit" to consumers. Although Meade's economic studies soon weakened his confidence in Douglas's ideas, they did not dampen his interest in devising policies to improve economic well-being.

After receiving an M.A. in 1930, Meade was elected a fellow of Hertford College, Oxford, which enabled him to continue his studies for an additional year. Accepting an invitation by Dennis Robertson to study at Trinity College, Cambridge, Meade had the opportunity to join a group of economists known as the Circus. It included Robertson, Richard Kahn, Piero Sraffa, and Joan and Austin Robinson and met regularly with John Maynard Keynes, discussing ideas that would ultimately lead to Keynes's *The General Theory of Employment, Interest, and Money* (1936). This "intellectual treat," Meade recalled later, was the "most exciting year of my life."

Returning to Hertford College in 1931 as a fellow and lecturer in economics, Meade maintained his ties with the Keynesian revolution in macroeconomic theory. In 1936 he published *An Introduction to Economic Analysis and Policy,* one of the first textbooks to attempt a systematic explanation of Keynesian theory. His continuing interest in the problem of unemployment, added to an interest in international affairs, led him to accept a position in Geneva with the League of Nations Secretariat in 1937. There, as editor of the *World Economic Survey,* he continued a research program begun by BERTIL OHLIN and involving an impressive group of economists, among them JAN TINBERGEN and TJALLING C. KOOPMANS.

After World War II began, Meade returned to England in 1940 to serve in the Economic Section of the British government's Cabinet Office. With RICHARD STONE he prepared the first official estimates of the United Kingdom's national income accounts. Also at the Cabinet Office, Meade took part in the development of postwar British economic and foreign policy. He helped prepare the government's 1944 white paper on employment policy, which pledged action to maintain low levels of unemployment after the war. He worked, too, as a member of Keynes's team, for the reconstruction of the international financial and trading system through establishment of the International Monetary Fund, the International Bank for Reconstruction and Development, and especially the General Agreement on Tariffs and Trade.

In 1946, the year after the Labour party came to power, Meade was named director of the Economic Section, a position he held until 1947. The same year he returned to academic life as professor of commerce at the London School of Economics (LSE) for the next ten years. During this time he wrote *The Theory of International Economic Policy.* Even the two formidable volumes in the work, *The Balance of Payments* (1951) and *Trade and Welfare* (1955), "did not cover the whole of the international problem," he later said, concluding that his "original project was overambitious."

Meade's pioneering work in international trade theory integrated his theoretical interests with his desire to develop effective instruments of economic policy. The central contribution of *The Balance of Payments* is a policy model for achieving two main objectives: internal balance (full employment) and external balance (balance-of-payments equilibrium). Applying a principle developed by Tinbergen, the book shows that to meet both of these objectives, two policy tools are required. For example, internal and external balance can be attained only by applying both fiscal policy (to promote full employment) and monetary policy (to attract or repel the international flow of capital).

In *Trade and Welfare* Meade developed the welfare implications of multinational trade for countries that lack perfectly competitive domestic markets. He showed, by means of the "theory of second best," that if the conditions necessary for an optimum are not realized, a movement in the direction of free trade may be dysfunctional and even reduce welfare. Moreover, in the event of entrenched trade barriers, the best can be the enemy of the good; restraints on trade may in that case promote a higher level of economic welfare. This work also reflects Meade's view that economics should develop as a policy-oriented science. He drafted much of *Trade and Welfare* using "new welfare economics," a method that rejects the use of comparisons explicitly weighing one person's utility gains against another's losses. Nevertheless, he later concluded that this is an overly restrictive approach for policymaking, since policy inevitably rests on interpersonal comparisons. He therefore returned to the older economic tradition, where interpersonal utility comparisons based on explicit distributional weights reflect the policymaker's evaluation of the importance of increasing the welfare of some individuals. Accordingly, economic policies are judged as to how well they serve total utility, computed as the weighted sum of individual utilities.

From the outset Meade was concerned about the balance between efficiency and equality. Shortly after World War II he wrote an influential book on the efficiency of the free-market system, criticizing the regulations imposed on Britain's postwar economy. At the same time, he was aware of the negative effects on income distribution of a capitalist system. "I have my heart to the left and my brain to the right," he used to say.

Moving to Cambridge University from the LSE in 1957, Meade continued to write prolifically, concentrating on issues of domestic economic policy and income distribution. In *Efficiency, Equality, and the Ownership of Property* (1964), he provided a suggestive account of the forces underlying the accumulation of capital—a subject he discussed further in *The Inheritance of Inequalities* (1974) and *The Just Economy* (1976). Since retiring from Cambridge in 1974, he has remained active in economic research and in policymaking. In 1975 he published *The Intelligent Radical's Guide to Economic Policy,* a book that promotes his vision of "price system socialism." Between 1975 and 1977, he directed the government committee that published *The Structure and Reform of Direct Taxation* in 1978.

Meade and Bertil Ohlin shared the 1977 Nobel Memorial Prize in Economic Sciences "for their pathbreaking contribution to the theory of international trade and international capital movements." In his presentation speech, Assar Lindbeck of the Royal Swedish Academy of Sciences commended Meade for his analysis of "the consequences for international trade and the international division of labor of different types of economic policy" and for having "laid the foundation for the modern theory of employment in open economies." In his Nobel lecture Meade discussed the complex interrelationships of such important economic factors as employment, wages, prices, and foreign exchange.

In 1933 Meade married Margaret Wilson, who at the time was secretary of the Oxford branch of the League of Nations Union. He is known as a highly private person who avoids traveling and attending seminars.

Meade is an honorary fellow of the London School of Economics, of Oriel and Hertford colleges, Oxford, and of Christ's College, Cambridge University. He holds honorary membership in the Belgian Royal Society of Political Economics, the American Economic Association, and the American Association for the Advancement of Science.

ADDITIONAL WORKS: National Income and Expenditure, 1944, with Richard Stone; Planning and the Price Mechanism: The Liberal-Socialist Solution, 1948; A Geometry of International Trade, 1952; The Theory of Customs Unions, 1955; A Neoclassical Theory of Economic Growth, 1961; Principles of Political Economy (4 vols.) 1965–1976; The Theory of Indicative Planning, 1970; The Theory of Economic Externalities, 1973.

ABOUT: New York Times October 15, 1977; Scandinavian Journal of Economics, number 1, 1978; Science November 25, 1977; Sills, D. L. (ed.) International Encyclopedia of the Social Sciences: Biographical Supplement, 1979.

MEDAWAR, P. B.

(February 28, 1915–   )
Nobel Prize for Physiology or Medicine, 1960
(shared with Macfarlane Burnet)

The English biologist Peter Brian Medawar was born in Rio de Janeiro, Brazil, to Nicholas Medawar, an international businessman and naturalized British citizen from Lebanon, and Edith Muriel (Dowling) Medawar. When the boy was four, his family moved to England, where Medawar has continued to live. He received his secondary education at Marlbor-

P. B. MEDAWAR

ough College and entered Magdalen College, Oxford, in 1932.

As an undergraduate Medawar studied zoology and began some original research on the growth of tissues. After obtaining his bachelor's degree in 1935, he was awarded two scholarships from Magdalen to continue his investigations at Oxford's Department of Pathology under HOWARD W. FLOREY. He maintained a full teaching schedule while working on tissue culture, mathematical theories of animal growth and form, and the regeneration of nerves. In 1938 he became a fellow by examination of Magdalen College, where he remained until 1944. At that time, he went to St. John's College, Oxford, for two years as a senior research fellow.

Shortly after the outbreak of World War II, Medawar began studying the problems involved in tissue transplants at the Burns Unit of the Glasgow Royal Infirmary in Scotland. Blood transfusions and antibiotics had made it possible for military casualties with very severe burns to survive. Unfortunately, no way had been found to prevent disfigurement. "The most obvious treatment was to graft the burn areas with skin from voluntary donors," Medawar later said. "But this ambition was absolutely hopeless, because skin grafted from one human being to another simply sloughed off as a result of the 'graft rejection' reaction."

Instead, Medawar developed methods for using the patient's own undamaged skin to cover burn wounds. Skin was made into a kind of "soup" of living cells and applied as a dressing or was frozen and sliced into very thin layers

and placed on the burned areas. However, none of the methods could prevent the disfiguring puckering of the skin.

Continuing transplantation research, Medawar and his colleagues worked with mice and rabbits, as well as with humans, and came to the conclusion that the body rejected "foreign" tissue because of differences in each individual's immunological pattern. Tissue rejection was indeed an immunological process, but it did not depend on the formation of antibodies, as when the body musters its defenses against infection or disease. The agents in tissue rejection were found to be lymphocytes, or small white blood cells.

Medawar's research in immunology showed that all mammalian cells with nuclei contain proteins that can act as antigens (substances that provoke immunological reactions). Blood transfusions, which are, in effect, "transplants," are possible because red blood cells do not have nuclei and thus do not contain the antigenic proteins. The structure and function of these proteins, which are called the major histocompatibility antigens, were established by BARUJ BENACERRAF, JEAN DAUSSET, and GEORGE D. SNELL. It is differences in histocompatibility antigens that cause most grafts to be rejected eventually. The only exception occurs in identical twins, which have identical histocompatibility antigens and can therefore exchange organs without suffering adverse immunological reactions.

Through his attempts to graft peripheral nerves, Medawar developed a biological "glue," a concentrated form of the blood component fibrinogen, that could be used to join the severed nerve endings in skin grafts and other kinds of surgery. This research led to Medawar's election in 1949 as a fellow of the Royal Society, one of the highest distinctions available to a British scientist.

In 1947, after returning to Magdalen College, Oxford, for a year, Medawar became professor of zoology at the University of Birmingham. His studies of the immunological basis of transplant rejection were so successful that, as he later recalled, he and a graduate student, Rupert Billingham, were "goaded by Dr. H. P. Donald into trying to devise a foolproof method of distinguishing monozygotic [identical] from dizygotic [fraternal] twins." Transplanting skin between twin calves, they expected to be able to tell whether the animals were identical or fraternal. If the grafts were accepted, they must be identical; if they were rejected, the twins must be fraternal.

To their surprise, Medawar and Billingham

found that all skin transplants between twin calves were accepted, even when the two animals were not of the same sex and thus not identical. These results were explained by MACFARLANE BURNET in 1949, building on the work of Ray D. Owen of the California Institute of Technology. Four years earlier, Owen had discovered that twin calf embryos have blood systems that join with each other, causing a prolonged exchange of blood before birth. At birth, each animal usually has some of its twin's red blood cells mixed in with its own; the twins may maintain a stable mixture of each other's red cells for the rest of their lives. According to Burnet, Owen's work showed that the ability to distinguish "self" from "not-self" was determined not intrinsically but by experience. That is, the immune system does not automatically "know" that certain tissues are its own and others are foreign; it acts as if any antigen to which the body is exposed at an early age is native and reacts only against other antigens. Burnet predicted that immunological tolerance could be produced in the laboratory by exposing animals to foreign tissue early in life.

Burnet was not able to confirm his own prediction, but Medawar and his colleagues had enough experience in transplantation to test the theory. In 1951 Medawar moved to University College, London, where he and Billingham were joined by a graduate student, Leslie Brent. Two years later, the three scientists reported that they had injected fetal or newborn mice with tissue from an adult mouse of a different strain. When the recipient mice matured, they accepted skin grafts from the original donor as though they had come from an identical twin.

Medawar and Burnet were awarded the 1960 Nobel Prize for Physiology or Medicine "for discovery of acquired immunological tolerance," even though, as the Nobel committee admitted, "application in practical medicine is still in its very early stages." In his presentation speech, however, Sven Gard of the Karolinska Institute said of Medawar's work, "It has opened a new chapter in the history of experimental biology. In a decisive way it has made a direct study of immunologically active tissue feasible, which in turn has created conditions for a further penetration of the problem of the nature of immunity and of such disturbances of immunization processes as might result in serious disease." In his Nobel lecture, Medawar discussed "immunological tolerance," a term he described as "a state of indifference or nonreactivity towards a substance that would normally be expected to excite an immunological response."

In 1962 Medawar was appointed director of the National Institute for Medical Research at Mill Hill, London, where he supervised biomedical research projects and continued his studies of transplantation immunology. From 1968 to 1969 he served as president of the British Association for the Advancement of Science. Forced by a stroke to retire from the institute in 1971, he nevertheless maintained an active laboratory at the clinical research center of the Medical Research Council near London, and he was named the institute's director emeritus in 1975.

Medawar is as well known for his philosophical writings as for his research activities. His first book, *The Uniqueness of the Individual* (1957), dealt with "various aspects of laboratory studies of physiology that bear on evolutionary problems." In it he discussed aging, "natural death," and the work of the French naturalist Lamarck, whose theory of organic evolution asserts that environmental changes cause structural changes in animals and plants that are transmitted to offspring.

Two years later, he reached a wider audience with his series of radio broadcasts *The Future of Man,* published in 1960. These lectures drew on contemporary research to suggest ways in which human beings might increase their ability to control their own evolution. Medawar was the first to predict the "population explosion," and he did so at a time when it was believed that the population of the Western world was in decline. His other widely read books include *The Art of the Soluble* (1967), *Induction and Intuition in Scientific Thought* (1969), and *The Life Science: Current Ideas of Biology,* written with his wife, Jean S. Medawar, and published in 1977.

Not only has Medawar's writing on the philosophy of science greatly influenced the scientific community, but his ideas, presented in lucid prose, have a popular appeal. While some scientists and social critics have found Medawar's ideas (particularly those concerning progress and evolution) controversial, few have disputed his wide knowledge or his powers of analysis. Medawar believes that science is not only inductive—that is, proceeding by generalizing the results of many individual observations—but also "hypothetico-deductive." According to this view, the scientist begins with "an imaginative preconception of what might be true," writes Medawar, and uses observation to test his hypothesis.

In 1937 Medawar married Jean Shinglewood Taylor, a zoologist. They have two sons and two daughters.

Medawar's many honors include the Royal Medal (1959) and Copley Medal (1969) of the Royal Society. He was knighted in 1952 and named a Companion of Honor in 1972. He is a member of the Royal Society, the American Academy of Arts and Sciences, and the Royal College of Physicians.

SELECTED WORKS: The Hope of Progress, 1972; Advice to a Young Scientist, 1979; Pluto's Republic, 1982; Aristotle to Zoos, 1983, with Jean Medawar; The Limits of Science, 1985; Memoir of a Thinking Radish: An Autobiography, 1986.

ABOUT: Current Biography April 1961; Omni January 1984; Robinson, D. The Miracle Finders, 1976; World Authors 1970–75, 1980.

SIMON VAN DER MEER

MEER, SIMON VAN DER
(November 24, 1925–   )
Nobel Prize for Physics, 1984
(shared with Carlo Rubbia)

The Dutch physicist and engineer Simon van der Meer (von dər mãr) was born in The Hague, the third child and only son among the four children of Pieter van der Meer, a schoolteacher, and the former Jetske Groeneveld. His parents greatly valued learning and made sacrifices to ensure a good education for their children. Van der Meer studied science at the local gymnasium and passed his final examination in 1943 during the German occupation of Holland in World War II. Since the Germans had just closed the Dutch universities, he studied humanities at the gymnasium for two more years. However, his interest in physics and technology was growing, and he dabbled in electronics as a hobby, equipping the family home with many gadgets. After the war he was able to enter the technical college in Delft, where he specialized in measurement and control technology and received an engineering degree in 1952. The same year he joined the Phillips Research Laboratory in Eindhoven and was assigned to work on the electronics of electron microscopes and on high-voltage equipment. In 1956 he joined CERN (the European Organization for Nuclear Research) in Geneva, formed two years earlier as a consortium of thirteen European nations.

At CERN, van der Meer's initial work was the technical design of a particle accelerator, the proton synchrotron (PS). He developed a special interest in manipulating particle beams

and spent several years on his invention of a pulsed focusing device called a neutrino horn, which was designed to increase the intensity of beams of neutrinos, which are electrically uncharged, almost massless subatomic particles. Neutrinos are emitted along with other particles in such reactions as the beta decay (electron emission) of radioactive nuclei. In 1965 van der Meer designed a small storage ring (a device using electromagnetic fields to keep charged particles circling in confinement) for use in experiments to measure the magnetic properties of the muon, a particle similar to an electron but much heavier, found originally in cosmic rays. This experience taught him the principles of accelerator design and familiarized him with the working and thinking habits of high-energy physicists. From 1967 to 1976 he was responsible for the magnet power supplies of the CERN intersecting storage rings and the 400-billion-electron-volt super proton synchrotron (SPS). Intersecting storage rings allow particles such as protons to circulate in opposite directions in two separate rings and then collide head-on at the intersection.

In 1976 van der Meer was assigned to a project proposed by CARLO RUBBIA, David Cline, and Peter McIntyre to convert the SPS into a tool for discovering the hypothetical W and Z particles related to nuclear forces. The search had been on for many years and was crucial for the confirmation of theories in quantum mechanics.

Physicists recognized four forces in nature: gravitation, the attraction between masses that holds the universe together; electromagnetism, which binds atomic electrons to the nucleus and atoms to atoms in molecules, and underlies all chemical processes; the weak force, responsible for certain kinds of radioactivity, such as the emission of beta rays (electrons); and the strong force, which holds protons, neutrons, and other subatomic particles together in the nucleus against such opposing forces as the mutual repulsion between closely packed protons. According to quantum field theory, forces act through the exchange of fundamental particles, or quanta of the field. MAX PLANCK, the father of quantum theory, found in 1900 that radiant energy was emitted in discrete units, or quanta, rather than continuously. ALBERT EINSTEIN confirmed the theory in 1905 by showing that light, known from the evidence of centuries to be made of continuous waves, could also act like a stream of individual particles. A quantum of light, and all electromagnetic radiation, is called the photon, and the electromagnetic force acts through the exchange of photons. The photon energy is proportional to the radiation frequency.

The photon has no rest mass; light either moves or does not exist. In 1935 the Japanese physicist HIDEKI YUKAWA suggested that forces within the nucleus might have quanta that did possess mass and calculated its expected value, some 200 times the mass of the electron. The English physicist CECIL F. POWELL found the Yukawa particle in 1947 in high-altitude collisions between cosmic rays and nuclei. Since a similar, but lighter, particle had been found previously at low altitudes, the Yukawa particle was named the pi-meson, or pion, and the lighter particle was named the mu-meson, or muon. The pion plays a role in the strong force binding protons and neutrons together and to each other.

Physicists dislike dealing with four independent forces and have long sought theories that could encompass all four in a unified formulation. In 1960 the American physicist SHELDON L. GLASHOW proposed the electroweak theory, unifying electromagnetism and the weak force, which required the existence of three particles of the class of bosons (named for the Indian physicist Satyendranath Bose): W^+, carrying a positive electric charge; W^-, negatively charged; and Z^0, uncharged. The W particles would be the mediators of the weak force, and all the new particles and the photon would be exchanged in an electroweak interaction. Seven years later, the American physicist STEVEN WEINBERG and the Pakistani physicist ABDUS SALAM, working independently, predicted that the W and Z particles would be ten times as heavy as any previously known subatomic particle and have extremely short lifetimes (less than 10^{-18} second).

Rubbia, an Italian physicist who had joined CERN in 1960 and who had been searching for the W and Z particles at the Fermi National Accelerator Laboratory, located near Chicago, in 1979 convinced CERN to modify the SPS for the search, at an estimated cost of $100 million.

To make the particles observable required the release of enormous energy because of their expectedly large masses. The equivalence of mass and energy derived from Einstein's theory of relativity permitted an estimate of how much energy was needed, an amount beyond the capability of existing particle accelerators, especially since all the energy in a collision of fast-moving particles is not available for new-particle formation. Rubbia and his colleagues proposed to use the SPS as a proton-antiproton collider. Antiprotons are the antimatter counterparts of the proton, twins except for a reversal of charge. P. A. M. DIRAC had predicted the existence of the first antiparticle, the antielectron, in 1928. It was found by CARL D. ANDERSON in 1932 and named the positron. When particle and antiparticle meet, they annihilate each other in a flash of energy such as gamma rays. In the proposed use of the SPS, protons and antiprotons would circle in opposite directions in the same magnetic field in the same ring because of their opposite electric charges. When the particles are caused to collide, the conversion of their masses into energy by annihilation would contribute to the amount needed to produce W and Z particles.

The project faced many difficult problems, in particular the accumulation of sufficient numbers of antiprotons in a sufficiently intense beam (antimatter is extremely rare) and the design of a detector to identify the particles and determine their characteristics. The particles themselves were too short-lived to be observed directly, but their decay products would give telltale evidence. One of the decay products would be the elusive neutrino, whose properties, including a lack of charge and mass, almost totally preclude the interactions with matter necessary to make any detector work. The presence of neutrinos would be detected by summing up the energy and directions of travel of the other decay products and deducing the neutrinos from the missing energy and momentum. Rubbia and over 100 scientists built an intricate, 1,200-ton detection chamber, and a second group built a smaller, 200-ton detector to help confirm the findings. Van der Meer solved the problem of supplying the antiprotons with the use of a special accumulator storage ring.

The antiprotons were produced by bombarding a fixed copper target with bursts of high-energy protons from the older PS and were then accepted in a rapid sequence of batches into the accumulator storage ring. After about a day of accumulation, a large number were reinjected into the PS, given a preliminary acceleration, and then transferred to the SPS, shortly following a similar group of protons also withdrawn from the PS. Protons and antiprotons were then given a final acceleration to energies of the order of 300 billion electron volts. The SPS became a huge, 4-mile-diameter storage ring in which particles and antiparticles, three groups of each, circled in opposing directions and collided head-on at six well-defined points. Two of the points were instrumented with the detectors.

A key to the success of the antiproton accumulator was van der Meer's achievement of what is known as stochastic cooling. The goal was to accept each varied batch of injected antiprotons, compress it into a tight, narrow bunch, and add it to a growing stack flying down the center line of the evacuated accumulator tube. The stack had to be stored out of the way of the stream of new batches. The intricate system included a series of pickup electrodes that sensed the spread in particle orbits and sent appropriately amplified signals ahead to electrodes that applied corrective "kicks" to the batch as it arrived at the correction points. Other kicks changed the velocities in a compacted batch so that it joined the stack. *Cooling* referred to the reduction in particle velocities relative to each other. *Stochastic* referred to statistics inherent in the processing of large numbers of particles. As van der Meer said later, "The process is of a complexity that could only be mastered by the effort and devotion of several hundreds of people."

The collisions of protons and antiprotons racing 50,000 laps per second around a circle over 1,250 miles in circumference were the most violent produced on earth up to that time. The collider began operating in 1982, and the discovery of the W^+ and W^- particles was announced in January 1983, followed within a few months by the discovery of the more elusive Z^0 particle.

Van der Meer and Rubbia shared the 1984 Nobel Prize for Physics "for their decisive contributions to the large project, which led to the discovery of the field particles of W and Z, communicators of the weak interaction." Verification of the weak-force quanta was hailed worldwide as one of the most important physics achievements of the twentieth century. Discovery of the W and Z particles has already proved why the sun does not overheat and wipe out life on earth; has given more proof for the so-called big-bang theory of cosmology; and has brought science closer to the possible realization of Einstein's goal, although considerably modified: a unified field theory that relates all four basic forces of nature. Van der Meer continues to design and build improved storage rings at CERN.

Van der Meer and Catharina M. Koopman were married in 1966; they have a son and a daughter. He is an avid skier and hiker who also enjoys reading for pleasure.

Van der Meer holds honorary doctorates from the University of Geneva, Amsterdam University, and the University of Genoa. He was awarded the Duddell Medal and Prize of the Institute of Physics in London in 1982 and is a member of the Royal Netherlands Academy of Sciences and the American Academy of Arts and Sciences.

ABOUT: New York Times October 18, 1984; Physics Today January 1985; Science January 11, 1985; Sutton, C. The Particle Connection, 1985; Taubes, G. Nobel Dreams, 1987.

MERRIFIELD, R. BRUCE
(July 15, 1921–   )
Nobel Prize for Chemistry, 1984

The American biochemist Robert Bruce Merrifield was born in Fort Worth, Texas, the only son of Lorene (Lucas) and George E. Merrifield. Two years after his birth, the family moved to California, and during the Great Depression of the 1930s, they continued to move frequently while his father sought work as a furniture salesman. Merrifield once estimated that he attended some forty schools before the family settled in Montebello, California. There, while attending the local high school, he became interested in chemistry, joined the school's astronomy club, and built a small telescope.

Graduating from high school in 1938, Merrifield entered Pasadena Junior College but transferred the following year to the University of California at Los Angeles (UCLA) to study chemistry. To help support himself, he worked in the laboratory of Max Dunn, synthesizing dihydroxyphenylalanine (dopa), an amino acid involved in the transmission of nerve

R. BRUCE MERRIFIELD

impulses and used in the treatment of Parkinson's disease.

After receiving his B.A. from UCLA in 1943, Merrifield worked for a year as a chemist at the Philip R. Park Research Foundation. He then returned to UCLA, where a fellowship from Anheuser-Busch Inc. enabled him to continue his graduate studies while he also served as a chemistry instructor. Later, as a research assistant at the UCLA Medical School in 1948–1949, he studied yeast purines and pyrimidines and developed a bioassay system to test their promotion of bacterial growth. (Purines and pyrimidines are cyclic nitrogenous organic bases found in biologically important compounds such as nucleotides and nucleic acids.) Upon receiving a Ph.D. in chemistry in 1949, Merrifield was appointed an assistant biochemist at the Rockefeller Institute for Medical Research (now Rockefeller University) in New York City. Remaining at this institution for the rest of his career, he was named research associate in 1953, associate professor in 1958, full professor in 1966, and John D. Rockefeller Jr. Professor in 1983.

In 1953 Merrifield turned to the study of protein chemistry. "The proteins are key components of all living organisms," he later explained. "All of the enzymes that catalyze biological reactions and many of the hormones that regulate them are proteins. If we are to understand, and eventually control, the events that occur in the body, we must first understand the composition, structure, and function of the individual proteins."

Proteins are chains of amino acids linked by peptide bonds. In an effort to understand the structure of these large and highly complex organic molecules, researchers have attempted to synthesize them from their chemical components. The two classical techniques for linking amino acids were the stepwise and the fragmentation model. In the stepwise method (devised by EMIL FISCHER in the early 1900s), amino acids were added one at a time to a growing peptide chain. In the fragmentation method, amino acids were first linked in short peptide fragments, which were then joined to form larger peptides. In both methods, at each step in the synthetic sequence, it was necessary to protect (or cover) all chemically reactive groups in the growing peptide molecule so that only the desired sites would interact. Moreover, the exposed or unprotected group also had to be activated before the peptide linkage could take place.

The sequence of protection, activation, synthesis, and removal of the protecting group had to be performed repeatedly until a finished peptide molecule of the desired composition was formed. The by-products of the previous reaction and the reagents (protectors, deprotectors, and activators) used in each step had to be washed away and the resulting peptide purified before the next amino acid could be added. Since a small part of the desired product was inevitably lost in each step, the final peptide represented only a small fraction of the potential yield. Although these classical methods permitted VINCENT DU VIGNEAUD to synthesize oxytocin and vasopressin and Merrifield to prepare peptides of twenty to forty amino acids in random sequence, the methods were inefficient, time-consuming, and laborious.

In 1959 Merrifield wrote in his research notebook: "There is a need for a rapid, quantitative, automatic method for synthesis of long chain peptides." He theorized that if the first amino acid were anchored to an insoluble supporting structure, the unwanted by-products and reagents could be washed out of the reaction vessel after each step while the growing peptide remained securely attached. If so, the final yield would be significantly increased. When the synthetic process was complete, the finished peptide could be removed from its anchor and purified by conventional techniques. With encouragement from Dilworth W. Woolley at Rockefeller, Merrifield devoted the next three years to the development of an improved method of peptide synthesis.

The most effective anchoring material for the first amino acid proved to be a polymer of styrene and divinylbenzene. In 1962 Merrifield reported that in a relatively short time the new method, called solid-phase peptide synthesis, produced large yields of synthetic peptides, almost 100 percent of predicted amounts. Using this technique, Merrifield and his colleagues synthesized the nonapeptide (nine-amino-acid) hormone bradykinin, a powerful vasodilator.

Their next task was to design and construct a machine capable of automated peptide synthesis. Working in the basement of his house with an associate, John Stewart, and with the aid of Nils Jernberg of the Rockefeller Institute's instrument shop, Merrifield completed the first working model of an automated solid-phase peptide synthesizer in 1965. It consisted of containers for amino acids and reagents, a reaction vessel with automatic inflow and outflow valves, and a programmer that timed the sequences of the process.

Using this device, Merrifield and his co-workers synthesized several peptide hormones, including bradykinin, oxytocin, and angiotensin (an octapeptide and potent constrictor of arterial smooth muscle). They also produced the small protein insulin (consisting of fifty-one amino acids in two chains) in only twenty days, a process that previously had taken several months. Critics of the new methodology complained that its peptide products were impure. Admitting that there were a few early problems with purity, Merrifield expressed his preference for a pragmatic approach, "using the best methods currently available during synthesis, isolation, and characterization of the products. Improvements in separation methods are appearing regularly," he said; "what cannot be achieved today may seem simple tomorrow." Product purification was soon aided by the development of high-performance liquid chromatography.

In 1969, with Bernd Gutte, Merrifield accomplished the first successful synthesis of a naturally occurring enzyme, ribonuclease. Ribonuclease, whose amino acid sequence was determined by STANFORD MOORE and WILLIAM H. STEIN in 1960, had been the object of research at the Rockefeller Institute for more than thirty years. Merrifield's method involved 369 chemical reactions and 11,931 separate steps, requiring several weeks of continuous operation of the solid-phase synthesizer.

Merrifield's solid-phase synthesis technique, which neither he nor Rockefeller University ever patented, has been widely used by other institutions and commercial laboratories for the preparation of peptide hormones, neuropeptides, toxins, protein growth factors, antibiotics, nucleotides, and nucleic acids. It is used most commonly to synthesize peptides containing up to fifty amino acids. Merrifield's wife, the former Elizabeth Furlong, who works in his laboratory at Rockefeller University, has been using automated solid-phase techniques in an attempt to synthesize the protein interferon. Interferon, which contains 166 amino acids, has potential therapeutic value in the treatment of viral diseases and tumors.

Merrifield was awarded the 1985 Nobel Prize for Chemistry in recognition of his methodology for chemical synthesis on a solid matrix. "[Merrifield's] completely new approach to organic synthesis . . . has created new possibilities in the fields of peptide-protein and nucleic acid chemistry," said Bengt Lindberg of the Royal Swedish Academy of Sciences in his presentation speech. "It has greatly stimulated progress in biochemistry, molecular biology, medicine, and pharmacology. It is also of great practical importance, both for the development of new drugs and for gene technology."

The Merrifields, who were married in 1948, have six children and live in Cresskill, New Jersey. Merrifield spends some of his free time as a Boy Scout leader.

In 1968 Merrifield was the Nobel guest professor at Uppsala University in Sweden. Since 1969 he has been associate editor of the *International Journal of Peptide and Protein Research*. His many awards include the Albert Lasker Basic Medical Research Award (1969); the Gairdner Foundation International Award (1970); and the Award for Creative Work in Synthetic Organic Chemistry (1972) and Nichols Medal (1973), both from the American Chemical Society. He is a member of the National Academy of Sciences and has received honorary degrees from the University of Colorado, Yale University, and Uppsala University.

ABOUT: Current Biography March 1985; New Scientist October 25, 1984; New York Times October 18, 1984; Science December 7, 1984.

METCHNIKOFF, ILYA
(May 16, 1845–July 15, 1916)
Nobel Prize for Physiology or Medicine, 1908
(shared with Paul Ehrlich)

The Russian embryologist and immunologist Ilya Ilyich Metchnikoff (mech′ nē kôf) was born in Ivanovka, a village in the Ukraine near Kharkov. His father, Ilya Ivanovich, an officer of the Imperial Guard in St. Petersburg, gambled away most of his wife's dowry and inheritance before moving to a Ukrainian estate. Metchnikoff's mother, the former Emilia Nevahovna, was the daughter of Lev Nevakhovich, a wealthy Jewish writer. She encouraged Ilya, the last of her five children and the fourth son, to enter a scientific career.

An inquisitive child with a particular interest in natural history, Metchnikoff was a brilliant student at the Kharkov lycée. A paper he wrote at the age of sixteen criticizing a geology text was published in a Moscow journal. Upon graduation from secondary school with a gold medal in 1862, he decided to study protoplasm at the University of Würzburg. Impulsively, he rushed off to Germany without ascertaining that the school's classes did not begin for another six weeks. Lonely and unable to speak German, Metchnikoff returned to the University of Kharkov, bringing with him a Russian translation of Charles Darwin's book *On the Origin of Species by Means of Natural Selection,* which had been published only three years earlier. Upon reading it, Metchnikoff was converted to a believer in the theory of evolution by natural selection.

In Kharkov, Metchnikoff completed the university course in two years instead of the usual four. Already familiar with the anatomical structure of the lower orders of the animal kingdom (worms, sponges, and other simple invertebrates), Metchnikoff realized that, according to Darwin's theory, higher animals should show a structural similarity to the lower ones from which they derived. At that time, vertebrate embryology was much better understood than that of invertebrates. Over the next three years, Metchnikoff pursued his studies of invertebrate embryos throughout various parts of Europe—first on the North Sea island of Heligoland, then in Rudolf Leuckart's laboratory in Giessen, near Frankfurt, and finally in Naples, where he collaborated with a young Russian zoologist, Alexander Kovalevsky. Their demonstration that germ layers in multicellular animals are in fact homologous (exhibiting structural correspondence), as expected for forms united by common descent, won them the Karl Ernst von Baer Prize. Metchnikoff was only twenty-two years old at the time. During this period of intense study, he developed severe eyestrain that hampered his work for the next fifteen years and prevented him from using a microscope.

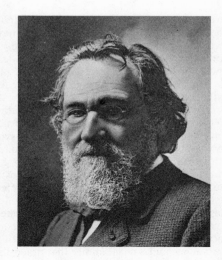

ILYA METCHNIKOFF

In 1867, with a thesis on the embryonic development of fish and crustaceans, Metchnikoff received his doctorate from the University of St. Petersburg (now Leningrad), where he remained to teach zoology and comparative anatomy for the next six years. After accompanying an anthropological expedition to the Kalmyk region near the Caspian Sea, where he carried out comparative physical measurements of the Mongol residents, he accepted a teaching position at the University of Odessa. Odessa's location on the Black Sea was ideal for Metchnikoff's studies of marine animals, and he was a popular teacher. However, the growing political and social unrest in Russia depressed him, and following the assassination of Czar Alexander II in 1881, which resulted in further governmental repression, Metchnikoff resigned his position and moved to Messina, Italy.

"It was in Messina," he later recalled, "that the great event of my scientific life took place. A zoologist until then, I suddenly became a pathologist." The discovery that occasioned this change came from his observations of starfish larvae. In these transparent animals, Metchnikoff could watch mobile cells surround and engulf foreign bodies in a manner similar to the inflammation reaction in humans. If the foreign body was small enough, the wandering cells—which he named phagocytes from the Greek *phagein,* "to eat"— could completely absorb the invader.

Metchnikoff was not the first to observe that white blood cells in animals engulf invading bodies, including bacteria. At the time, however, it was commonly believed that this absorption served mainly for the blood system to spread the foreign material throughout the body. Metchnikoff had a different view because he looked at the cells with the eyes of an embryologist. In starfish larvae, the mobile phagocytes not only surround and absorb an invading object but also resorb or erase other tissues that are no longer needed. Because human white blood cells and the mobile cells in starfish are embryologically homologous—both are of mesodermal origin—Metchnikoff deduced that the blood cells, like the phagocytes, actually function as policing or sanitizing agents. He further demonstrated the activity of phagocytes in transparent water fleas. "On this hypothesis," Metchnikoff said later, "disease would be a fight between the morbid agents, the microbe from outside, and the mobile cells of the organism itself. Cure would come from the victory of the cells, and immunity would be the sign of their action sufficiently to prevent the microbial onslaught." His ideas, however, were not accepted by the scientific community for many years.

In 1886 Metchnikoff returned to Odessa to direct the newly established Bacteriological Institute, where he studied the action of dog, rabbit, and monkey phagocytes on the microbes causing erysipelas and relapsing fever. His staff also investigated vaccines for chicken cholera and sheep anthrax. Harassed by sensationalistic journalists and local physicians who opposed Metchnikoff because of his lack of medical training, he once again left Russia in 1887. A meeting with Louis Pasteur resulted in the great French scientist's offering Metchnikoff the directorship of a new laboratory at the Pasteur Institute in Paris. Continuing his research on phagocytosis, Metchnikoff remained there for the next twenty-eight years.

The dramatic accounts of phagocytic battles reported by Metchnikoff met much resistance from supporters of a humoral theory of immunity, who argued that factors in the blood other than white blood cells played a central role in destroying invaders. Metchnikoff acknowledged the existence of antibodies and antitoxins as described by EMIL VON BEHRING, but he vigorously defended his phagocyte theories. He and his colleagues also investigated syphilis, cholera, and other infectious diseases.

The work Metchnikoff performed in Paris contributed to many fundamental discoveries concerning the nature of the immune response. One of his students, JULES BORDET, clarified the role of complement (a substance found in normal blood serum) in killing microbes targeted by antibodies and in making microbes more susceptible to phagocytosis. Metchnikoff's most important contribution was methodological: his aim was to study "the immunity in infectious diseases . . . as a section of cellular physiology."

As the role of phagocytosis and of white blood cells in general became more widely accepted among immunologists, Metchnikoff turned to other projects, particularly the problems of aging and death. In 1903 he published a book on orthobiosis, or "right living," *The Nature of Man,* in which he discussed diet and advocated the consumption of large quantities of fermented milk or yogurt made with a Bulgarian bacillus. His name was associated with a popular commercial preparation of yogurt, but he received no payment for it.

Metchnikoff was awarded the 1908 Nobel Prize for Physiology or Medicine jointly with PAUL EHRLICH "for their work on immunization." In his presentation speech, K. A. H. Mörner of the Karolinska Institute pointed out that after the discoveries of Edward Jenner, Louis Pasteur, and ROBERT KOCH, a fundamental question in immunology remained: "By what means does the organism vanquish the disease-bearing microbes attacking the organism in which they have succeeded in establishing themselves and developing?" Through his efforts to answer this question, Mörner said, Metchnikoff had initiated "modern research into . . . immunology" and profoundly influenced the course of its development.

In 1869 Metchnikoff married Ludmilla Federovna, who was ill with tuberculosis; they had no children. When she died four years later, Metchnikoff attempted suicide unsuccessfully by taking morphine. While teaching at the University of Odessa in 1875, he met and married Olga Belokopitova, a fifteen-year-old student. When she contracted typhoid fever, Metchnikoff again attempted suicide, this time by injecting himself with relapsing-fever microorganisms. After a serious illness, however, he recovered—his lifelong pessimism abated, and his eyesight improved. It was during this period of personal crisis that he developed an interest in infectious diseases. Although he and his second wife had no children of their own, her parents died within a year of each other, and the Metchnikoffs became the guardians of her two brothers and three sisters. After suffering a series of heart attacks, Metchnikoff died in Paris on July 15, 1916, at the age of seventy-one.

Among Metchnikoff's many awards and

honors were the Copley Medal of the Royal Society of London, memberships in the French Academy of Medicine and the Swedish Medical Society, and an honorary doctorate from Cambridge University.

SELECTED WORKS: Lectures on the Comparative Pathology of Inflammation, 1893; Immunity in Infective Diseases, 1905; The New Hygiene, 1906; The Prolongation of Life: Optimistic Studies, 1908; The Founders of Modern Medicine: Pasteur, Koch, Lister, 1939.

ABOUT: De Kruif, P. Microbe Hunters, 1926; Dictionary of Scientific Biography, volume 9, 1974; Karnovsky, M., and Bolis, L. (eds.) Phagocytosis: Past and Future, 1982; Mardus, E. Man With a Microscope: Elie Metchnikoff, 1968; Metchnikoff, O. Life of Elie Metchnikoff, 1845–1916, 1921; Parry, A. The Russian Scientist, 1973.

OTTO MEYERHOF

MEYERHOF, OTTO
(April 12, 1884–October 6, 1951)
Nobel Prize for Physiology or Medicine, 1922
(shared with Archibald V. Hill)

The German-American biochemist Otto Fritz Meyerhof (mī′ ər hōf) was born in Hannover to Felix Meyerhof, a Jewish merchant, and Bettina (May) Meyerhof. The family, which included an older sister and two younger brothers, moved to Berlin, where Otto received his secondary education at the Wilhelms Gymnasium. When he was sixteen years of age, a kidney disease kept him bedridden for many months, during which time he read extensively, particularly the works of Goethe. While Otto was recuperating, he and his cousin Max, a physician, traveled for four months in Egypt, where Meyerhof acquired a lasting interest in archaeology.

His health restored, Meyerhof studied medicine at the universities of Freiburg, Berlin, Strasbourg, and Heidelberg, in keeping with the German tradition of studying at more than one university. In 1909 Meyerhof received his medical degree from the University of Heidelberg, with a dissertation on the psychological theory of mental disturbances, and began writing *Beiträge zur psychologischen Theorie der Geistesstörungen* (Contributions to a Psychological Theory of Mental Disturbances), which was published in 1912. He also published an essay on Goethe's methods of scientific research, which he found insufficiently inductive. For the next three years Meyerhof was an assistant in internal medicine at the Heidelberg Clinic under Ludwig Krehl. It was

there that he met OTTO WARBURG, who was influential in shifting Meyerhof's interest from psychology and psychiatry to experimental biochemical research. Later he worked at the zoological station in Naples, Italy, an international center for biological research. In 1912 he joined the staff of the physiology department at the University of Kiel, and he received an appointment as university lecturer in physiology the following year.

Meyerhof was the first person to apply thermodynamic concepts to the analysis of cell reactions, a theory he introduced in a lecture on the bioenergetics of cell processes, given in July 1913. (An expanded version of the lecture was published by the Rockefeller Institute in New York in 1924 as *Dynamics of Life Phenomena.*) At the time, the details of carbohydrate metabolism had not yet been elucidated. It was known that carbohydrates are stored in liver and muscle cells as glycogen, a starchlike compound made up of chains of glucose molecules, and that the biochemical degradation of glycogen and glucose (glycolysis) proceeds in two ways: along an aerobic pathway requiring oxygen and via an anaerobic process in the absence of oxygen. The aerobic degradation of carbohydrates results in the formation of carbon dioxide and water; anaerobic degradation produces lactic acid or lactate. Meyerhof's experimental approach involved comparisons and determinations of correlations among cellular oxygen consumption (respiration), cellular heat production (thermodynamics), the biochemical events in cells, and the mechanical work performed by

696

specialized muscle cells. In 1917 he demonstrated that the carbohydrate enzyme systems in yeast and animal cells are similar, thus supporting the concept of the biochemical unity of life.

In 1918, near the end of World War I, Meyerhof served briefly on the French front as a medical officer in the German army. After the war he was appointed assistant professor at the University of Kiel. Resuming his research, he sought to explain cellular function in physicochemical terms. While studying the contraction of frog muscle, he measured oxygen consumption and lactic acid production in both the presence and absence of oxygen. He demonstrated that anaerobic glycolysis yields lactic acid and that in the presence of oxygen, only one-fifth of the cellular lactic acid (lactate) is fully oxidized to carbon dioxide and water. From this he concluded that the cellular energy generated by the oxidative process is used by the cell in a cyclic reaction to resynthesize glucose molecules from the residual lactate in the cells.

In 1923 Meyerhof was awarded the 1922 Nobel Prize for Physiology or Medicine "for his discovery of the fixed relationship between the consumption of oxygen and the metabolism of lactic acid in the muscle." He shared the prize with ARCHIBALD V. HILL, who studied the production of heat during muscle contraction. "The true life of science does not consist of applications and exploitations," Meyerhof said in his Nobel lecture; "they are only an end product or even a by-product. It consists in revolutionary thought, in the concept of new theories, and in the basic discoveries which are made by single prepared minds in a creative act, like a piece of art." Meyerhof also paid tribute to Hill's work, "which, shining out like a beacon light through a sea mist, made it possible for me to steer a safe course through the shallows."

Shortly before receiving the Nobel Prize, Meyerhof had been rejected for the chairmanship of his department at the University of Kiel, probably because of anti-Semitism. However, laboratory space was created for him by members of the Kaiser Wilhelm Society, and in 1924 he was appointed professor at the Kaiser Wilhelm Institute for Biology in Berlin. There he trained numerous biochemists, including HANS KREBS, FRITZ LIPMANN, and SEVERO OCHOA. After one of his colleagues, Karl Lohmann, discovered that the most important molecule that powers the biochemical reactions of the cell is adenosine triphosphate (ATP), Meyerhof and Lohmann described the role of ATP in muscle contraction. In 1929 Meyerhof was named director of the newly established Kaiser Wilhelm Institute for Medical Research in Heidelberg. In *Biochemical Investigations in Muscle Cells* (1930), he suggested that all biological phenomena, excepting certain mental processes, could theoretically be explained in physicochemical terms.

By 1932 Meyerhof and his colleagues had extracted the enzymes for principal biochemical reactions in the conversion of glucose to lactic acid. This basic cellular pathway is known as the Embden-Meyerhof pathway of carbohydrate metabolism. (Gustav Embden, who died suddenly in 1933, made significant contributions to the theoretical formulation of the scheme.)

Alarmed by the rise of Nazism, Meyerhof and his wife left Germany in 1938, moving first to Switzerland and then to Paris, where Meyerhof continued his research at the Institute of Physicochemical Biology. With the German invasion of Paris in June 1940, the couple fled to southern France, then across the Pyrenees into Spain, and finally to the United States to join his colleague Hill, who had obtained funds from the Rockefeller Foundation to create a professorship for Meyerhof at the University of Pennsylvania. During the summer months Meyerhof continued to study the bioenergetics of cellular processes at the Marine Biology Laboratory in Woods Hole, Massachusetts. A severe heart attack hospitalized him for ten months in 1944. Two years later he became an American citizen. His colleagues and pupils contributed to a festschrift, *Metabolism and Function,* presented to him on his sixty-fifth birthday in 1949, when he was also elected to membership in the National Academy of Sciences.

In 1914 Meyerhof married Hedwig Schallenberg, a painter; they had two sons and a daughter. An amateur poet, Meyerhof had an avid interest in philosophy, art, and archaeology. He was also concerned with the impact of science on society. After a second heart attack, he died on October 6, 1951, in Philadelphia, at the age of sixty-seven.

Meyerhof, who held memberships in the Royal Society of London and the Harvey Society, received an honorary degree from the University of Edinburgh, in addition to many other awards and honors.

ABOUT: Biographical Memoirs of the National Academy of Sciences, volume 34, 1960; Dictionary of American Biography, supplement 5, 1977; Dictionary of Scientific Biography, volume 9, 1974; Nachmanson, D. German-Jewish

MICHELSON

Pioneers in Science 1900–1933, 1979; Obituary Notices of Fellows of the Royal Society, volume 9, 1954.

MICHELSON, ALBERT A.
(December 19, 1852–May 9, 1931)
Nobel Prize for Physics, 1907

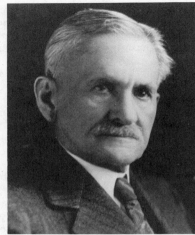

ALBERT A. MICHELSON

The American physicist Albert Abraham Michelson was born in Strelno, Germany, near the Polish border, to Samuel Michelson, a merchant, and Rosalie (Przlubska) Michelson, the daughter of a physician. He was the oldest of three children. When he was two years old, the family moved to the United States, where Michelson's father became a dry goods merchant to gold rush miners in California and Nevada. Sent to relatives in San Francisco to attend Boys' High School, Michelson later boarded with the school's principal, who sparked his interest in science and suggested that he apply to the United States Naval Academy in Annapolis, Maryland. Armed with a letter from his congressman, Michelson appealed personally to President Ulysses S. Grant for a position at the academy, even though they had all been filled. His perseverance so impressed officials that an additional position was created especially for him in 1869. Michelson graduated in 1873, served as a midshipman for two years, and in 1875 was appointed as an instructor in physics and chemistry at the academy, a post he held for four years.

In 1878, while teaching physics, Michelson became interested in measuring the speed of light. Light and the field of optics were to remain his life's work. Although the speed of light had been measured earlier by the French physicists Hippolyte Fizeau, Léon Foucault, and Marie Alfred Cornu, their results were not regarded as accurate. Using a $2,000 gift from his father-in-law, he significantly improved on Foucault's measurement technique and measured the speed of light with an accuracy never before achieved. His work attracted international attention, and Michelson left Annapolis in 1880 to study optics in Europe for two years. There he designed the interferometer, an apparatus that uses the interference of light waves to measure various phenomena involving light.

A master of instrumentation, Michelson invented the interferometer to detect the earth's motion through the stationary ether that was believed to fill the universe. The Scottish physicist James Clerk Maxwell, who had shown that light is an electromagnetic wave, had assumed that a wave must be propagated by a medium of some sort; the success of his electromagnetic theory seemed to confirm the existence of the ether. Maxwell had suggested that the ether might be detected by measuring the speed of light with respect to the earth's motion. If the ether is the light-carrying medium and if the earth moves with respect to the ether, the speed of light should vary according to whether light is moving toward, away from, or at an angle to the earth. No one had succeeded in detecting the earth's motion through the ether, but this was assumed to be due to the lack of adequate measuring devices. It was this lack that Michelson proposed to remedy with his interferometer.

Michelson's precision interferometer used a half-silvered mirror to split a beam of light in two and then to recombine the two beams. He reasoned that if the two beams followed different paths, they would travel at different speeds relative to the earth's motion. Hence, the waves of the two beams would be out of phase when they rejoined, and they would interfere with one another like intersecting waves in a pond. Such interference produces alternating dark and light bands called interference patterns. In 1881, working under Hermann von Helmholtz in Berlin, Michelson first used the interferometer in an effort to detect the earth's motion through the ether. To his surprise, he found no interference patterns: the two beams appeared to travel at the same speed. So confident was Michelson of the accuracy of his measurements that in his report of the experiment in the *American Journal of Science* he asserted that "the hypothesis of a stationary ether is thus shown to be incorrect." Although the importance of the experiment was widely recognized, some physicists pointed out possible sources of error in its design, casting doubt on Michelson's conclusion.

Before returning to the United States in 1882, Michelson resigned from the Naval Academy to accept a physics professorship at the Case School of Applied Science (now Case Western Reserve University) in Cleveland, Ohio. There he began a collaboration with Edward W. Morley of Western Reserve. Their famous Michelson-Morley experiment of 1887 was a repetition of Michelson's 1881 experiment, using an improved interferometer designed to overcome the earlier sources of error. Once more the results were negative—no interference patterns were produced. The speed of light seemed to be unaffected by the motion of the earth.

Although the Michelson-Morley experiment cast doubt on the existence of a totally stationary ether, it did not lead physicists to reject the concept of the ether altogether. As Michelson himself pointed out, the results could be explained if the ether were dragged along at almost the speed of the earth. There were problems with this theory, however, and the matter aroused the interest of such eminent physicists as HENDRIK LORENTZ. Classical ideas of motion depended on the existence of a stationary reference frame (in this case, the ether) against which absolute motion could be measured, and the continuing failure to demonstrate the existence of such a reference frame was one of the thorny problems confronting classical physicists at the end of the nineteenth century. Lorentz's work on the subject influenced ALBERT EINSTEIN, who published his special theory of relativity in 1905. This theory rejected stationary reference frames and absolute motion, thus abolishing the need for the ether. Motion, according to Einstein's theory, is describable only in terms of the motion of the observer. Light, on the other hand, travels at a constant speed, regardless of the motion of the observer or the light source. Although the Michelson-Morley experiment contributed only indirectly to the development of special relativity (in 1905 Einstein was unaware of their experiment) it served in retrospect as an important confirmation of the theory's predictions.

Although puzzled by the results of his experiment, Michelson was pleased with the precision he had achieved with the interferometer, and he thought of many other uses for the instrument. From 1889 to 1893 he was professor of physics at Clark University in Worcester, Massachusetts. There he used the interferometer to define the length of a meter in terms of the wavelength of one of the spectral lines of cadmium. This international standard permitted laboratories to dispense with physical standards such as metal bars, which are affected by handling and temperature. This metrological project, completed in 1892, gained Michelson further international recognition. In 1893 Michelson became head of the new physics department at the University of Chicago.

Michelson's work on the metric standard was an offshoot of the research he conducted between 1887 and 1897 on the light emitted by excited atoms (atoms that have absorbed energy—by being heated, for example). It was known that when the emitted light is broken into its component wavelengths, or colors, by means of a spectrograph, the resulting line spectrum (series of colored lines) is unique for each element. The spectra of atoms were widely—and correctly—regarded by physicists as keys to the mystery of atomic structure. When Michelson studied spectral lines by means of his interferometer, he discovered that almost all were composed of a number of closely spaced sublines. This fine structure could not be explained until quantum mechanics was developed in the 1920s. Today, Michelson's interferometer is routinely used to analyze light and remains a powerful tool in modern analytic techniques.

Michelson received the 1907 Nobel Prize for Physics "for his optical precision instruments, and the spectroscopic and metrological investigations carried out with their aid." In his presentation speech, K. B. Hasselberg of the Royal Swedish Academy of Sciences declared that Michelson's interferometer had made possible measurements with an "extraordinarily high degree of accuracy."

In his zeal to develop instruments capable of ever greater precision, Michelson set out to improve the resolution capabilities of spectrographs by making bigger and better diffraction gratings. These gratings, essential components of spectrographs, break up an incident light beam into its component wavelengths; the type of diffraction grating Michelson was concerned with is a mirror on which many finely spaced lines are drawn. Michelson's work resulted in some of the largest and finest diffraction gratings ever made. Although he initially thought this effort might take a few years, Michelson worked on the problem of ruling diffraction gratings for the rest of his life.

Interrupted by work for the United States Navy in Washington, D.C., during World War I, Michelson returned to his research with a greater interest in astronomy. He devised ways to use the interferometer to measure the diameter of small objects such as asteroids, of minor moons within the solar system, and of large, bright stars. Michelson, who was the first scientist to measure the diameter of a distant star, reported in 1920 that the giant star Betelgeuse was 240 million miles in diameter. This work, done at the Mount Wilson telescope near Pasadena, California, increasingly brought Michelson to California, where he worked at the California Institute of Technology. Michelson also provided the first measurement of the rigidity of the earth, using the interferometer to measure the tidal displacement of water in buried pipes.

Michelson was appointed to the University of Chicago's first Distinguished Service Professorship in 1925, but in 1929 he left Chicago to devote himself to his research in California.

Michelson's marriage in 1877 to Margaret Heminway, which produced a daughter and two sons, ended in divorce in 1897. Two years later he married Edna Stanton, with whom he had three daughters. A noted amateur watercolor artist, Michelson was also a talented violinist who taught his children music. Skilled at tennis, billiards, chess, and bridge, he also enjoyed sailing.

During the last year of his life, after suffering several strokes, he continued to direct his research from his sickbed. His final project, which he did not live to see completed, was another attempt to refine the measurement of the speed of light. Michelson died of a cerebral hemorrhage on May 9, 1931, in Pasadena.

Known for his singleness of purpose, Michelson always preferred research to his administrative and teaching responsibilities. He disliked interacting with graduate students and lectured only occasionally.

Although Michelson never earned a doctoral degree, he received eleven honorary doctorates from major European and American universities for his accomplishments. His many awards in addition to the Nobel Prize included the Copley Medal of the Royal Society of London (1907), the Henry Draper Medal of the National Academy of Sciences (1916), the Franklin Medal of the Franklin Institute (1923), the Gold Medal of the Royal Astronomical Society of London (1923), and the Duddell Medal of the Physical Society of London.

Michelson was a member of many scientific societies and learned academies, including the National Academy of Sciences, the Royal Society of London, the French Academy of Sciences, and the Soviet Academy of Sciences. He was president of the American Physical Society (1901–1903) and of the National Academy of Sciences (1916).

SELECTED WORKS: Experimental Determination of the Velocity of Light, 1879; The Echelon Spectroscope: Investigations on Light and Heat, 1899; Light Waves and Their Uses, 1902; Studies in Optics, 1927.

ABOUT: Biographical Memoirs of the National Academy of Sciences, volume 19, 1938; Dictionary of Scientific Biography, volume 9, 1974; Jaffe, B. Michelson and the Speed of Light, 1960; Livingston, D. M. The Master of Light, 1973; McCallister, D. T. Albert Abraham Michelson, 1970; Swenson, L. S. The Ethereal Aether, 1972; Wilson, J. H. Albert A. Michelson: America's First Nobel Prize Physicist, 1958.

MILLIKAN, ROBERT A.
(March 22, 1868–December 19, 1953)
Nobel Prize for Physics, 1923

The American physicist Robert Andrews Millikan was born in Morrison, Illinois, the second son of Silas Franklin Millikan, a Congregationalist preacher, and Mary Jane (Andrews) Millikan, a former dean of women at Olivet College in Michigan. In 1875 the family moved to Maquoketa, Iowa, a small town near the Mississippi River, where Millikan grew up with his two brothers and three younger sisters.

After graduation from Maquoketa High School, Millikan enrolled in his mother's alma mater, Oberlin College, in Ohio; his chief interests there were mathematics and Greek. Although he had taken only a twelve-week physics course, which he described as a complete loss, his Greek teacher asked him to teach physics in the preparatory school run by the college. Millikan accepted for the sake of the salary, and after receiving his B.A. in 1891, he continued to teach physics for two years, keeping ahead of his students by studying available textbooks. The Oberlin faculty awarded him an M.A. in physics in 1893 and, without his knowledge, sent his transcript to Columbia University, which awarded him a graduate fellowship.

At Columbia, Millikan studied with the noted physicist and inventor Michael I. Pupin, and he spent a summer at the University of Chicago, studying with the prominent experimen-

ROBERT A. MILLIKAN

tal physicist ALBERT A. MICHELSON. In time, he became convinced that physics was his true calling, and in 1895 he received a Ph.D. from Columbia with a thesis on the polarization of light. He then spent a year in Europe at the universities of Jena, Berlin, Göttingen, and Paris, where he met HENRI BECQUEREL, MAX PLANCK, WALTHER NERNST, and Henri Poincaré. On his return in 1896 he became an assistant in physics at the University of Chicago under Michelson. During the next twelve years he wrote several physics textbooks, the first for American students that were not translations of French or German texts. Millikan's works became standard texts in colleges and high schools and (with revisions) remained in use for more than half a century. In 1907 Millikan was appointed associate professor of physics, and he became full professor in 1910.

In 1908 Millikan stopped writing textbooks in order to devote more time to original research. Like many physicists of that time, he was interested in the newly discovered electron, particularly in the magnitude of its charge, which had not yet been measured. The English physicist H. A. Wilson had tried to measure the charge of the electron by studying the effect of an electric field on a charged cloud of ether vapor, but his calculations were based on the average behavior of microscopic ether droplets, because he was unable to devise a method for making all the measurements on a single droplet. The results of Wilson's measurements varied so widely that some physicists suspected that different electrons had different charges, which would mean that the electron was not an indivisible charged particle. Millikan set out to determine whether all electrons have the same charge and to measure their charge precisely. Eventually, he developed the oil-droplet method of observation, a classic example of elegant experimentation and one of the accomplishments for which he won the Nobel Prize.

Millikan first improved on Wilson's experimental apparatus by building a powerful battery that could generate a far stronger electric field. He was then able to isolate a few charged water droplets between two metal plates. When the field between the plates was turned on, the droplet moved slowly upward by magnetic attraction; and when it was turned off, the droplet moved downward by the force of gravity. By turning the field on and off, Millikan could study suspended droplets individually for as long as 45 seconds before they evaporated. By 1909 he had determined that any charge on a droplet was always a whole-number multiple of an irreducible value, e—the charge of an electron. This observation provided persuasive evidence that electrons were fundamental particles of identical charge and mass.

Millikan's efforts to determine the exact value of e were beset by experimental problems that he worked patiently to resolve. Eventually, he substituted droplets of a virtually nonvolatile oil for the water droplets, and he was then able to make observations for up to 4.5 hours. In 1913, after eliminating the sources of error one by one, he published his final calculation of the electron's charge: $e = (4.774 \pm 0.009) \times 10^{-10}$ esu (electrostatic units). This value stood for over seventy years; with more sensitively calibrated equipment it has recently been corrected to $e = 4.80298 \times 10^{-10}$ esu.

While still engaged in writing textbooks, Millikan had begun to investigate the photoelectric effect, in which light striking the surface of a metal causes electrons to be ejected. In 1905 ALBERT EINSTEIN tried to explain some peculiarities of this effect by proposing that light consists of particles he called quanta. This was an extension of a suggestion by MAX PLANCK that the energy of vibrating atoms is quantized (composed of indivisible units). Because Einstein's theory contradicted the accepted description of light as a wave (which was based on strong experimental evidence), most physicists did not believe it. In 1912 Millikan set out to test Einstein's photoelectric equation, which related the energy of the ejected electrons to the frequency of the incident light quanta. Again he devised elaborate apparatus to overcome the many sources of experimental error, and he showed, to his own surprise, that the equation was entirely correct. Furthermore, as a result of this experiment, he was able to determine the value of Planck's constant (a fundamental constant of the quantum theory) much more precisely than had been done before. Millikan's results, published in 1914, helped convince physicists of the validity of the quantum theory.

Millikan was awarded the 1923 Nobel Prize for Physics "for his work on the elementary charge of electricity and on the photoelectric effect." In his Nobel lecture Millikan used his work in both areas to illustrate the fact that "science walks forward on two feet, namely theory and experiment. . . . Sometimes, it is one foot that is put forward first, sometimes the other, but continuous progress is only made by the use of both."

Among Millikan's other important achievements during his years at Chicago were his investigations of portions of the electromagnetic spectrum by means of hot-spark spectrography and his work on Brownian movements in gases, which helped confirm the molecular theory. His work won him an international reputation, and industry began seeking his services. In 1913 he became a consultant on vacuum-tube theory to Western Electric; from 1916 to 1926 he served as an expert witness in patent litigation. In 1917, at the invitation of astronomer George Ellery Hale, Millikan went to Washington, D.C., to serve as vice-chairman and director of research of the National Research Council, a branch of the National Academy of Sciences set up by the government for the mobilization of scientists during World War I. He also served in the Army Signal Corps, where he coordinated the work of scientists and engineers, especially in the vital field of antisubmarine warfare.

After the war, Millikan returned to the University of Chicago, but only briefly. Hale, a trustee of the California Institute of Technology (Caltech) in Pasadena, lured him to Caltech in 1921 with the offer of a new laboratory and $90,000 a year in research funds. Millikan was appointed director of the new Norman Bridges Laboratory of Physics and also chairman of the executive council of Caltech—in effect, president of the school. He devoted the rest of his career to building Caltech into one of the world's finest scientific and technological institutions. Millikan's contacts with business leaders made him a highly successful fundraiser, but his greatest contribution lay in his ability to attract an outstanding faculty and student body. Even after he retired as chief

executive of Caltech in 1946, he remained active there until his death.

Millikan's chief research project at Caltech was the study of the radiation from outer space that had first been detected by the Austrian physicist VICTOR F. HESS. It was Millikan who gave this radiation the name *cosmic rays,* a term that was quickly adopted by both scientists and the public. He and his associates hauled scientific instruments to the tops of mountains, sent them up in balloons, and sank them deep in lakes to detect the mysterious rays. Millikan's student CARL D. ANDERSON discovered the positron and the muon in the course of investigating cosmic radiation.

In 1902 Millikan married Greta Irvin Blanchard, who had graduated from the University of Chicago with a degree in Greek. They had three sons, all of whom became prominent scholars. He died in San Marino, California, on December 19, 1953.

A political conservative, Millikan opposed President Franklin D. Roosevelt's New Deal policies, believing that the cooperation of science and industry was the surest formula for recovery from the Depression. However, unlike many conservatives of his time, he opposed isolationism, and he was instrumental in converting Caltech's research program to military endeavors during World War II. Millikan was a religious modernist who wrote several books on the relationship of science and religion. For recreation he played tennis and golf.

Millikan's many awards included the Hughes Medal of the Royal Society of London (1923) and the Faraday Medal of the British Chemical Society (1924); he was a commander of the Legion of Honor of France and a recipient of the Chinese government's Order of Jade. He held honorary doctorates from twenty-five universities. Millikan served as president of the American Association for the Advancement of Science and the American Physical Society and was a member of the American Philosophical Society. From 1903 to 1916 he was assistant editor of the *American Physical Review.* At the time of his death Millikan was a member of twenty-one foreign scientific academies.

SELECTED WORKS: The Electron, 1917; Elements of Electricity, 1917; Science and Life, 1924; Elements of Physics, 1927, with Henry Gale; Evolution in Science and Religion, 1927; Science and the New Civilization, 1930; Time, Matter and Values, 1932; Electrons, Protons, Photons, Neutrons and Cosmic Rays, 1935; Cosmic Rays, 1939; Science, War and Human Progress, 1943; The Autobiography of Robert A. Millikan, 1950.

ABOUT: Biographical Memoirs of the National Academy of Sciences, volume 33, 1959; Current Biography June 1952; Dictionary of Scientific Biography, volume 9, 1974; Kargon, R. H. The Rise of Robert Millikan, 1982.

MIŁOSZ, CZESŁAW
(June 30, 1911–   )
Nobel Prize for Literature, 1980

CZESŁAW MIŁOSZ

The Polish-American poet and essayist Czesław Miłosz (mē′ lôsh) was born in Šeteiniai, a rural town in Lithuania then under the domination of the Russian czarist government. His father, Aleksander, and his mother, the former Weronika Kunat, were ethnic Poles in a land rich in contrasting traditions, where the boy grew up speaking not only his native Polish but also Lithuanian, Yiddish, and Russian.

When the German army invaded Lithuania in 1914, Miłosz's father, a civil engineer, was mobilized by the Russians. The family began an eastward trek with the czarist army, living in constant danger for six disruptive years, until the armed conflict between Soviet Russia and Poland, which followed in the wake of World War I, ended in 1920.

After the war the family settled in Vilna (now Vilnius, Lithuanian Soviet Socialist Republic), a city of many nationalities and traditions known to its Jewish population as the Jerusalem of Lithuania. By 1921, when Miłosz began school there, Vilna had been incorporated into Poland. Miłosz received a strict Roman Catholic education, studying and translating Latin for seven years. In 1929 he entered the University of Vilna. Though sure of his vocation as a poet, he chose to study law. His first collection of verse, *Poemat o czasie zastygłym* (Poem of the Frozen Times), was published in 1933. Subsequently, he helped found Zagary, a literary group that later became known as the Catastrophists because of its members' abiding belief in an imminent cosmic disaster.

After receiving his master of laws degree in 1934, Miłosz won a fellowship to study literature in Paris, where he formed a close relationship with his uncle, Oscar Miłosz, a diplomat and poet who wrote in French and who had a reputation for living the life of a reclusive visionary. The year in Paris was significant in Miłosz's development as a poet; as he said later, Oscar Miłosz "inculcated a need for a strict, ascetic hierarchy in all matters of mind, including everything that pertains to art." Perhaps even more significantly, Miłosz said, "he taught me not to despair" in the face of an intuition that catastrophe was indeed close at hand.

Returning to Vilna, Miłosz published his second volume of poetry, *Trzy zimy* (Three Winters), in 1936 and accepted a post as director of programming at a radio station in Vilna. Dismissed the following year because of his leftist sympathies, he moved to Warsaw, the capital. It was a politically ominous time in Poland, with ample justification for the dire prophecies of the Catastrophists. For centuries Poland's borders had shifted as rival foreign powers sought domination of the country. Although an independent Poland was established after World War I, by the late 1930s Adolf Hitler and Joseph Stalin were moving toward a secret agreement that would divide the country between them. Because of Poland's turbulent, divisive history, its national identity has been enshrined more in its literature than in its political institutions. In Poland the poet, therefore, occupies a special place, and it was as a poet that Miłosz thought of himself, rather than as a leftist (or as a Marxist, as some believed).

When the German army invaded Poland in September 1939, precipitating the long-anticipated disaster, Miłosz met the special obligation of his chosen vocation "to look at the world from his own independent viewpoint." Throughout World War II he was active as a writer in the Resistance movement, an underground more highly developed in Poland than elsewhere in Europe. The experience of the Holocaust, which Miłosz witnessed first-

703

hand in the streets of Warsaw, altered both his personal life and his artistic development. During the war, in 1944, Miłosz married Janina Dluska; they have two sons.

After the war Miłosz served in the Polish diplomatic service in Washington, D.C., and in Paris between 1946 and 1951, but he finally broke with the regime after the suppression of the coalition government by the Communists. Reluctantly, in 1951 he chose exile, finding himself unable to accept "the erosion of truth" and the moral relativism of the totalitarian state, which encroached on his obligation as a writer. Settling in Paris, he wrote *Zniewolony umysł* (*The Captive Mind*, 1953), an examination of the effects of totalitarianism on the artistic personality. It was this work that brought him his first prominence in the West.

The experience of exile was wrenching; as Miłosz has said, he seemed to have chosen "sterility and inaction" in separating himself from his native land and language, the poetic source and impetus. Temporarily unable to write poetry, he produced a novel, *Dolina Issy* (*The Issa Valley*, 1955), an invocation of his childhood in Lithuania and an elegiac account of a boy's coming of age. During this period he also published *Zdobycie Władzy* (*The Seizure of Power*, 1953), a novelistic counterpart to *The Captive Mind*, for which he won the European Literary Prize. Following the award, Miłosz might have chosen, as he put it, to "push the gas and publish constantly." But he was unable to accept the position of French intellectuals of the Left, who still looked to Soviet Communism for worldly salvation and failed to see its reality. In 1960 he moved to the United States, and the following year he was appointed professor of Slavic languages and literature at the University of California at Berkeley. He became a naturalized citizen in 1970.

Though Miłosz feared the sterility of exile, his output has been prolific. His writing since moving to the United States includes translations from Polish; Polish translations of the Bible (Psalms), Walt Whitman, William Shakespeare, John Milton, T. S. ELIOT, and Charles Baudelaire; and acclaimed works of autobiography and literary history, as well as essays and poetry.

Miłosz has received the Marian Kister Literary Award (1967), the Jurzykowski Foundation Award for creative work (1968), an award for poetry translation from the Polish PEN (Poets, Essayists, Novelists) Club in Warsaw, the Neustadt International Literary Prize (1978), a Guggenheim Fellowship (1974),

and an honorary doctorate from the University of Michigan.

The 1980 Nobel Prize for Literature was awarded to Miłosz, "who with uncompromising clear-sightedness voices man's exposed condition in a world of severe conflicts." "The world that Miłosz depicts," said Lars Gyllensten of the Swedish Academy in his presentation address, "is the world in which man lives after having been driven out of paradise." Gyllensten told Miłosz, "To read your writings and be confronted with their challenges means to become enriched with important, new experiences—in spite of all alienation."

After speaking of his childhood in his Nobel lecture, Miłosz turned to the issues of politics and exile. "The exile of a poet," he said, "is today a simple function of a relatively recent discovery: that whoever wields power is also able to control language, and not only with the prohibitions of censorship, but also by changing the meaning of words." It is the writer's obligation, then, to remember. "Memory is our force," he said. "Those who are alive receive a mandate from those who are silent forever. They can fulfill their duties only by trying to reconstruct precisely things as they were and by wrestling the past from fictions and legends."

Miłosz is considered one of the greatest of Polish poets, and—without reference to his national origin or language, in which he has always chosen to write—he is, in the view of the Soviet émigré and poet Joseph Brodsky, perhaps the greatest poet of our time. In the West, Miłosz's reputation has grown steadily as his work has become available in translation. In Poland his work circulated in the underground press during the years it was banned; when Miłosz returned to his native land shortly before he was honored with the Nobel Prize, he was given a hero's welcome.

His poetry is particularly esteemed for its thematic range and intellectual content; for its cerebral, wry, or lyrical tone; for its concrete, sensual imagery and its dialectical power; for its moral weight and conviction. Shaped by the particular traditions of Eastern Europe—of his native soil and of Christianity, Judaism, and Marxism—and informed by the terrible history of his time, Miłosz's poetic sensibility was honed in the painful experience of exile. As the American poet and editor Jonathan Galassi has remarked, "[Miłosz's] entire effort is directed toward a confrontation with experience—and not with personal experience alone, but with history in all its paradoxical horror and wonder." Terrence Des Pres, writing in *The Nation* (1978), concurred, declaring that "people, places, objects, everything for Miłosz is densely historical. Destiny for him is *human destiny.* . . . I know of no poet more driven to celebration . . . and therefore no poet more tormented. . . . Clearly, through his art, Miłosz has earned a solution to the most pressing spiritual dilemma today: how to bear the burden of historical consciousness without despair." Similarly, Paul Zweig has underlined "Miłosz's conviction that poetry must be a moral as well as an esthetic discipline, that poetry must translate the anguish of personal experience into a framework of values which defend against 'skepticism' and 'sterile anger' and therefore defend against the lure of ideology."

ADDITIONAL WORKS IN ENGLISH TRANSLATION: Polish Postwar Poetry, 1965; Native Realm, 1968; The History of Polish Literature, 1969; Selected Poems, 1973; Emperor of the Earth, 1977; Bells in Winter, 1978; Visions From San Francisco Bay, 1982; The Witness of Poetry, 1983; The Separate Notebooks, 1984; The Land of Ulro, 1984; Unattainable Earth, 1986.

ABOUT: Commentary April 1983; Current Biography October 1981; Davie, D. Czesław Miłosz and the Insufficiency of Lyric, 1986; Gillon, A., and Krzyzanowski, L. (eds.) Introduction to Modern Polish Literature, 1964; Gömöri, G. Polish and Hungarian Poetry, 1966; New York Times June 28, 1981; January 17, 1982; World Literature Today Summer 1978.

MILSTEIN, CÉSAR
(October 8, 1927–   )
Nobel Prize for Physiology or Medicine, 1984
(shared with Niels K. Jerne and Georges Köhler)

The Argentine biochemist César Milstein was born in Bahía Blanca, the second of three sons of Lázaro and Máxima Milstein, a schoolteacher. Milstein attended the Colegio Nacional in Bahía Blanca from 1939 to 1944, then entered the University of Buenos Aires in 1945 to study science. While attending the university, he became heavily involved in student political activities and was also employed at the Liebeschutz Laboratories as a clinical analyst, a position that he held until 1956. After obtaining a degree in chemistry from the University of Buenos Aires in 1952, despite a mediocre undergraduate scholastic record, Milstein decided to work for a doctorate in biochemistry and enrolled as a research student in the Institute of Biological Chemistry at the University of Buenos Aires.

CÉSAR MILSTEIN

Milstein's doctoral research, completed in 1957, concentrated on the chemistry of the enzyme aldehyde dehydrogenase, one of the alcohol enzymes that catalyze the oxidation of ethyl alcohol to acetaldehyde and water. The work of FREDERICK SANGER at Cambridge University during the 1950s had made it clear that the function of an enzyme depends on the arrangement of amino acids within it, especially in a certain antigen-combining region of the enzyme molecule known as the active site.

Milstein obtained a British Council fellowship that enabled him to work in Sanger's laboratory from 1958 to 1961. Under Sanger's guidance, Milstein conducted a number of studies involving the enzyme active sites. After receiving a Ph.D. from Cambridge University in 1960, he joined the staff of the Medical Research Council (MRC) at the Department of Biochemistry (now the MRC Laboratory of Molecular Biology), Cambridge University. He returned to Argentina in 1961 to head the new Division of Molecular Biology at the National Institute of Microbiology in Buenos Aires, where he planned to continue the same line of research. However, a military coup soon led to the dismissal of many members of the institute, including its director, Ignacio Pirosky. Milstein and several other young members of the institute resigned in protest over the dismissal of Pirosky, and in 1963 Milstein returned to Sanger's laboratory at Cambridge University.

At the suggestion of Sanger, Milstein switched from the study of enzymes to research on antibodies, protein bodies produced by the immune system to bind to and inactivate foreign bodies, or antigens. KARL LANDSTEINER's research of the 1930s had revealed that animals can produce thousands of different kinds of antibodies, each able to combat specific antigens; all of the antibodies are similar in their chemistry. Sanger thought that Milstein could use his enzymological methods to study the amino acids in the active sites of different antibodies. "The idea was to find out whether two different antibodies differed in [amino acid sequence], and, if they did, what the difference was," Milstein said. The experiment failed, however.

The main difficulty Milstein encountered was the virtual impossibility of isolating only two different antibodies. RODNEY R. PORTER had shown that even an antiserum that reacted with only one antigen was a mixture of antibodies with different active sites. Porter, GERALD M. EDELMAN, and other scientists investigating the chemical structure of antibodies bypassed this difficulty by studying myeloma proteins. A myeloma is a tumor of the antibody-producing cells. The cells in a given myeloma form a clone and are genetically identical descendants of a single, cancerous ancestor. As MACFARLANE BURNET had predicted some years earlier, all of these cloned cells produce the same antibody.

Milstein and his colleagues in the MRC Laboratory spent the greater part of the 1960s analyzing the amino acids of different myeloma proteins. They moved on to the study of antibody deoxyribonucleic acid (DNA) and ribonucleic acid (RNA) in the early 1970s, with Milstein making many important contributions to the understanding of how antibodies and their genes are constructed.

The major question of antibody research during the 1960s and early 1970s was how the immune system is able to produce an apparently infinite variety of antibodies from a finite amount of antibody DNA. Many researchers believed that antibody genes were subject to high rates of mutation. In the early 1970s Milstein and his colleagues searched for mutations in myeloma cells grown in laboratory cultures. Their results were only moderately successful, mainly because determining that a cell has mutated is a difficult process. "It became increasingly clear that . . . the only way ahead was to use a culture of a myeloma cell capable of expressing an antibody," Milstein wrote later. The myeloma cells they used did produce antibodies, but Milstein and his co-workers failed to find any antigens with which those antibodies would combine. What they needed was

some way to start with an antigen and then find a myeloma that would produce the corresponding antibody. It would be easy to isolate mutants from among this myeloma's descendants, because the mutants would have lost the ability to bind the antigen.

Milstein began research into this problem in 1974 in collaboration with GEORGES KÖHLER, a postdoctoral student who had recently come to Cambridge from Switzerland. The two researchers employed a technique devised by another of Milstein's colleagues, R. G. H. Cotton, who had discovered that he could fuse two different myeloma cells and that the process resulted in a hybrid that produced both proteins from the parent myelomas. Köhler immunized a mouse against a certain antigen, removed its antibody-producing white blood cells, and fused these cells with myeloma cells. The result was a hybrid myeloma, or hybridoma, that possessed the antibody-producing ability of its normal parent but grew forever like its cancerous myeloma parent. When the procedure is done properly, hybridomas can be isolated as clones that are descended from a single fusion. Their products are identical monoclonal antibodies.

Milstein and Köhler published their procedure for the production of monoclonal antibodies in 1975. It soon became apparent that the implications of their technique went far beyond the problem of mutation in antibody-producing cells. It is possible to produce monoclonal antibodies that give extremely clear, specific, standardizable tests for any antigen. By the early 1980s a substantial commercial trade had begun in monoclonal antibodies for diagnostic tests, and hybridoma-based controlled vaccines and cancer therapies were under development.

During the late 1970s Milstein refined his methods for producing monoclonal antibodies and promoted their use. He then returned to his original goal: the study of the genetic basis of antibody diversity and the way the immune response changes with exposure to an antigen. Milstein was appointed head of the Protein and Nucleic Acid Chemistry Division at the MRC Laboratory in 1983.

Milstein shared the 1984 Nobel Prize for Physiology or Medicine with Köhler and NIELS K. JERNE. "We are at the beginning of a new era of immunochemistry, namely the production of 'antibody-based' molecules," Milstein declared in his Nobel lecture. He added that the hybridoma technology he and his colleagues devised "was a by-product of basic research. Its success in practical applications is to a large extent the result of unexpected and unpredictable properties of the method. It thus represents another clear-cut example of the enormous practical impact of an investment in research which might not have been considered commercially worthwhile, or of immediate medical relevance."

In 1953 Milstein married Celia Prilleltensky, a biochemist. They have no children.

Among Milstein's honors are the Wolf Prize in Medicine of the Wolf Foundation in Israel (1980), the Louisa Gross Horwitz Prize of Columbia University (1980), the Gairdner Foundation International Award (1981), the Royal Medal of the Royal Society of London (1982), the Albert Lasker Basic Medical Research Award (1984), and the Dale Medal of the Society for Endocrinology in London (1984). He is a member of the European Molecular Biology Organization, the Royal Society of London, the American National Academy of Sciences, the American Academy of Arts and Sciences, and the Royal College of Physicians in London.

ABOUT: Ahmad, F. (ed.) From Gene to Protein, 1982; New Scientist October 18, 1984; New York Times October 16, 1984; Science February 26, 1982; November 30, 1984.

MINOT, GEORGE R.

(December 2, 1885–February 25, 1950)
Nobel Prize for Physiology or Medicine, 1934
(shared with William P. Murphy and
George H. Whipple)

George Richards Minot, American physician and pathologist, was born in Boston to a prominent New England family of intellectuals and physicians whose ancestors had emigrated from England in the 1630s. Minot was the eldest of three sons of Elizabeth (Whitney) Minot and Jämes Jackson Minot, a physician. Believed by his parents to be a delicate child, he was taken in winters to Florida and California, where he developed a lifelong interest in natural history. While still a youth, he published two articles on butterflies: "The Chrysalis of *Melitaea gabbe*" (1902) and "The Tussack Moth Peril" (1903).

After attending private schools in Boston's Back Bay section, Minot entered Harvard University and received a B.A. in 1908, followed by a medical degree four years later. As a medical student working in an outpatient clinic, he became interested in hematology, the study of blood. One of his teachers at Har-

vard was Homer Wright, a physician who developed staining techniques for microscopic study of blood. While interning at Massachusetts General Hospital, Minot studied blood diseases and acquired a lifelong interest in the diets of anemic patients. He spent the period 1913–1915 at the Johns Hopkins Hospital in Baltimore, Maryland, as a resident physician working in the laboratory of William Howell, a physiologist who was investigating blood clotting. Minot's work on the antithrombin content of blood later enabled Howell to isolate heparin, an anticoagulation drug.

In 1915 Minot joined the Harvard Medical School staff; at the same time, he joined Massachusetts General Hospital as an assistant in medicine. The atmosphere at Massachusetts General encouraged the use of scientific methods in clinical medicine. In the course of their work, Minot and Roger Lee, a professor of clinical medicine, discovered that platelets, small bodies in the blood, were involved in clotting. Minot also classified blood characteristics of various types of anemia; pernicious anemia in particular interested him. As their red blood cell levels became dangerously low, patients with pernicious anemia exhibited what at that time was called blood thinning. It was assumed that an unknown destroyer of blood cells was responsible for the condition. Unexplained relapses were common and arsenic treatment or splenectomy (removal of the spleen) brought only temporary relief; no cure was available, and death was almost always inevitable. At Johns Hopkins in 1914, Minot had noted that during remissions, reticulocytes (new red blood cells) inundated the blood. He concluded that an increased number of reticulocytes was a sign of clinical improvement, an observation that proved to be important several years later.

During World War I, Minot investigated anemia in industrial workers whose blood cells were being poisoned by exposure to chemicals. In 1917 he was appointed physician in chief at the Collis P. Huntington Memorial Hospital, a clinical cancer research center at Harvard, where he studied leukemia (blood cancer) and continued his investigation into the diets of patients suffering from pernicious anemia.

A setback in Minot's own health occurred when he developed diabetes in 1921, a year before the discovery of insulin by FREDERICK G. BANTING and Charles Best. The prevailing treatment for the disease was a regimen of semistarvation, but the Boston diabetes specialist Elliott Joslin arranged for Minot to receive some of the first insulin, produced in

GEORGE R. MINOT

1922. Strict dietary control and insulin injections prolonged Minot's life for many years.

In 1921 he also became affiliated with a group of physicians in private practice, one of whom, WILLIAM P. MURPHY, later became his collaborator. Two years later, Minot became chief of medical services at Huntington Memorial Hospital and was appointed to the staff of Peter Bent Brigham Hospital in Boston. At this time, his interest in pernicious anemia became more concentrated. His early inquiries about diet led him to suspect "that something in food might be of advantage to patients with pernicious anemia." In his previous investigations Minot had noted that many pernicious anemia patients had particularly unbalanced diets. Moreover, he observed that symptoms of pernicious anemia were similar to those of sprue, pellagra, and other forms of anemia—all of which had dietary cures.

Meanwhile, GEORGE H. WHIPPLE, an acquaintance at Johns Hopkins Hospital, had completed experiments in which he bled dogs to make them anemic and then determined which foods restored red blood cells. He had found that although red meat and certain vegetables proved effective, liver was best. After Minot fed liver to some private patients and observed improvements in their health, he and Murphy began giving it to hospitalized patients. At a meeting of the Association of American Physicians in 1926, Minot and Murphy reported that in forty-five patients "clinical improvement has been obvious, usually within two weeks." An increase in the numbers of reticulocytes also was a gauge of im-

provement, but to achieve the best results, patients had to consume as much as half a pound of liver daily.

While working at the Harvard Medical School, the physical chemist Edwin Cohn condensed and purified a liver extract suitable for oral and intravenous use. Between 50 and 100 times as potent as liver, the extract was not only easier to use but less expensive. The rise in the numbers of reticulocytes of patients was monitored to determine the potency of the extract that should be administered. When pharmaceutical manufacturers began producing the extract, variations among batches were supervised by the newly formed Committee on Pernicious Anemia at Harvard, of which Minot was a member. In 1936 Minot joined the Anti-Anemia Preparations Advisory Board established by the United States Pharmacopeia to standardize the unit of dosage by using a specific reticulocyte response as an index of potency for each manufactured product.

In 1928 Minot was appointed professor of medicine at Harvard University, with a concurrent appointment as director of the Thorndike Memorial Laboratory at Boston City Hospital. In these capacities he continued to study other forms of anemia and nutritional diseases; supervised medical students, urging them to be especially concerned with the social and economic problems of their patients; and consulted extensively and on a worldwide basis with other physicians about blood diseases.

For "their discoveries concerning liver therapy in cases of anemia," Minot, Murphy, and Whipple were awarded the 1934 Nobel Prize for Physiology or Medicine. On presenting the award, Israel Holmgren of the Karolinska Institute summarized the discoveries of the three laureates. "You have spread a new light over the process of regeneration of the blood," he declared, "you have discovered a function of the liver, before you unknown to science, you have invented and elaborated a new method for the treatment of anemia. . . . This new method . . . has already saved thousands of lives, and will in the future save innumerable human beings from death."

At the time the award was presented, three-quarters of the forty-five patients treated eight years earlier were still alive. It was not until 1948 that the cause of pernicious anemia was shown to be a deficiency of vitamin B_{12}, the compound in liver that stimulates reticulocyte formation.

During the early 1940s, Minot developed vascular and neurological complications brought about by diabetes, followed in 1947 by a stroke that left him partially paralyzed. After resigning as director of the Thorndike Laboratory in 1948, he maintained an active interest in medical research. In addition to his appointments at Harvard and the Thorndike Laboratory, Minot served as visiting physician at Boston City Hospital (1928–1948), as consulting physician at Peter Bent Brigham Hospital in Boston (1928–1950), and as consulting physician at Beth Israel Hospital in Boston (1928–1950).

In 1915 Minot married Marian Linzee Weld, with whom he had two daughters and a son. An avid sailor and gardener, Minot was also a serious stamp collector and a keen observer of the natural world. According to W. B. Castle, one of Minot's colleagues at Harvard, Minot "was in essence a naturalist whose interests included flowers, insects, and every organic aspect of his patients as well as their emotional and social problems." Minot died in Brookline, Massachusetts, on February 25, 1950.

Among his many awards and prizes were the Kober Medal of the Association of American Physicians (1929), the Cameron Prize and Lectureship of the University of Edinburgh (1930), the Moxon Medal of the Royal College of Physicians in London (1933), and the Distinguished Service Medal of the American Medical Association (1945). He was a member of the American Society for Clinical Investigation, the Association of American Physicians, the American Clinical and Climatological Association, the American Academy of Arts and Sciences, and the National Academy of Sciences. He also was a fellow of the American Medical Association, of the American College of Physicians, and of the American Philosophical Society. Harvard University awarded him an honorary doctorate in 1928.

SELECTED WORKS: Early Papers on Pernicious Anemia, 1933, with William Murphy; Pathological Physiology and Clinical Description of the Anemias, 1936, with W. B. Castle.

ABOUT: Biographical Memoirs of the National Academy of Sciences, volume 45, 1974; De Kruif, P. Men Against Death, 1932; Dictionary of Scientific Biography, volume 9, 1974; Rackemann, F. M. The Inquisitive Physician, 1956.

MISTRAL, FRÉDÉRIC
(September 8, 1830–March 25, 1914)
Nobel Prize for Literature, 1904
(shared with José Echegaray)

The Provençal poet Frédéric Mistral (mēs-träl′) was born in Maillane, a village in the Rhone Valley of southern France. The only child of François Mistral, a prosperous farmer, and his second wife, the former Delaide Poulinet, the young Mistral grew up speaking Provençal, an ancient form of French that differs considerably from the standard language. He attended the local schools but was truant so often that his parents sent him to a boarding school in Avignon. Ridiculed by the other students for his Provençal dialect, Mistral developed a passionate attachment to the language of his region and translated Virgil's first eclogue into his native tongue. He shared this interest with one of his teachers, Joseph Roumanille, himself a poet who wrote in Provençal and who aspired to reestablish the language as a literary medium.

Returning to Maillane in 1847, Mistral began to compose a Provençal poem in four cantos. Recognizing the boy's intellectual gifts, his father sent him to Aix-en-Provence to study law. After receiving his law degree in 1851, Mistral embarked on a literary career, publishing his first poem the following year. In 1854 Mistral, Roumanille, and several other writers formed a group dedicated to reviving the great tradition of Provençal literature that had flourished during the twelfth and thirteenth centuries. Calling themselves the Félibres, these writers published an annual journal, *Armana Prouvençau* (Almanac of Provence), which offered a platform for the group's ideas and which in time reached a circulation of 10,000.

The pastoral epic *Miréio* (1859) was Mistral's first major contribution to the Provençal literary movement, which was called Felibrige. In 748 seven-line stanzas, the poem recounts the story of a young woman who, unable to obtain parental consent to marry the man she loves, flees home to seek solace at the Church of the Three St. Marys on the island of La Camargue in the Rhone Delta. Stricken by sunstroke, she sees a vision of the three Marys before dying. Into this poem, which was published in English in 1872 under the same title, Mistral wove many colorful scenes from his youth on the family farm and from the daily peasant life that surrounded him.

Encouraged by Adolphe Dumas, a Provençal writer living in Paris, Mistral presented a copy of *Miréio* to the French poet Alphonse de Lamartine, who praised it enthusiastically, exclaiming, "A great poet is born!" Other writers and critics shared Lamartine's enthusiasm, including Stéphane Mallarmé, who called Mistral "one of the diamonds of the Milky Way." The poem was subsequently adapted

FRÉDÉRIC MISTRAL

by the composer Charles Gounod for his opera *Mireille*, which had its debut in Paris in 1864.

After two months in Paris, Mistral returned to Provence and began polishing and revising *Calendau,* a work he had begun before *Miréio* but which did not appear until 1867. It was followed in 1875 by *Lis Isclo d'Or* (The Golden Isles), a collection of short lyric poems. The next year, Mistral married Marie Riviere, a young woman from Dijon.

The activities of the Félibres consumed much of Mistral's time. He presided at meetings of the group, handled correspondence, furnished introductions to books published in Provençal, and worked to standardize Provençal orthography and grammar. *Lou Tresor dóu Felibrige* (The Treasury of the Félibres), his comprehensive Provençal-French cultural lexicon, was issued between 1880 and 1886. More than a dictionary, this scholarly work contains all the dialects of the language and a wealth of Provençal folklore, traditions, and beliefs.

Mistral's narrative poem about the last days of the popes in Avignon, *Nerto,* was published in 1884. Six years later he completed his only drama, *La Réino Jano* (Queen Jano). His last great epic, *Lou Pouèmo dou Rose* (translated as *Anglore: The Song of the Rhone*), which appeared in 1897, celebrates the Rhone River and the towns through which it flows.

On the fiftieth anniversary of the Felibrige movement, Mistral received the 1904 Nobel Prize for Literature (which he shared with JOSÉ ECHEGARAY) in recognition of the "fresh originality and true inspiration of his poetic production, which faithfully reflects the natural spirit of his people." In the presentation speech, C. D. af Wirsén of the Swedish Academy reminded his listeners that idealism was Alfred Nobel's criterion for the award, a quality "amply found," he said, "in a man who has devoted his entire life to an ideal, the restoration and development of the spiritual interests of his native country, its language, and its literature." Mistral was unable to travel to Stockholm because of his physical frailty, and he sent no formal acceptance speech.

Two of Mistral's final works were *Moun espelido (Memoirs of Mistral,* 1906), reminiscences of his youth, and *Les Olivadou* (The Olives, 1912), a collection of short lyric poems. Using his own funds, Mistral founded the Muséon Arlaten, a museum of Provençal popular culture, for which he collected specimens of flowers, rocks, and archaeological artifacts.

While inspecting a new inscription on the church bell in Maillane, Mistral contracted bronchitis and died on March 25, 1914, at the age of eighty-three.

Comparing Mistral with such regional writers as Robert Burns and Sir Walter Scott, the English novelist and poet Richard Aldington wrote that "Mistral 'represents' modern Provence with a power and thoroughness and felicity hardly to be equaled" by other comparable figures. His most severe critics, according to the French historian and novelist André Chamson, have been those in France who regard Mistral's work as only "the last offshoot of an outmoded art."

If, as Chamson points out, "Mistral has not sought to express what is of universal interest" in his depiction of Provence, his poetry nevertheless offers a universal lesson. As we read it, Chamson says, "we can learn that civilizations are mortal—but we learn, too, that they cannot disappear."

ABOUT: Aldington, R. Introduction to Mistral, 1956; Downer, C. Frédéric Mistral, 1901; Edwards, T. The Lion of Arles, 1964; Lyle, R. Mistral, 1953.

MISTRAL, GABRIELA
(April 7, 1889–January 10, 1957)
Nobel Prize for Literature, 1945

Gabriela Mistral (mēs träl ') is the pen name of the Chilean poet and educator Lucila Godoy Alcayaga, who was born in the high Andean village of Vicuña, the only child of Jerónimo Godoy Villanueva, a part-Indian elementary school teacher in the village of La Unión, and Petronila Alcayaga de Molina, a widow of Basque descent who had a fifteen-year-old daughter by a previous marriage. Mistral's father was also a *pallador* (minstrel) who composed verses for local festivals; something of a vagabond, he permanently abandoned his family when his daughter was three years old.

In 1892 Mistral and her mother settled in the town of Monte Grande. Nine years later, when Mistral was twelve years old, the two moved to the village of La Serena, where her older half-sister, Emelina, had taken a teaching position. Tutored by her half-sister, Mistral soon became aware of her own strong desire to become a teacher. In the ensuing years, she developed a keen political awareness and openly expressed her views in poems and newspaper articles published in the provincial press. In 1907, while serving as an assistant teacher in the village of La Cantera, she met a young railroad worker, Romelio Ureta, to whom she became briefly engaged. They canceled their wedding plans, however, because they frequently disagreed and quarreled. Two years later, Ureta committed suicide, an event that left deep psychological scars on Mistral and inspired her first significant poetic work, *Sonetos de la muerte* (Sonnets of Death), published in 1914. This volume won the first prize in the Floral Games, a Chilean literary contest. Fearful that her passionate lyrics might be detrimental to her teaching career, the young poet published her work under the pen name of Gabriela Mistral. This pseudonym, soon to become famous throughout the Spanish-speaking world and used by the poet thereafter, was created to honor two of her favorite writers, the Italian Gabriele d'Annunzio and the Provençal poet FRÉDÉRIC MISTRAL.

In the year following Ureta's suicide, Mistral passed an examination at the Santiago Normal School and began her rapid rise through the Chilean education system. Her first important job was as chief inspector and instructor in history, geography, and Spanish in the northern Chilean city of Antofagasta.

Another youthful love affair also ended badly, although little is known of the details—not even the name of the young Santiagan poet with whom she was in love. It is known, however, that he married a wealthy woman, leaving Mistral once again immersed in grief. She requested a transfer to Punta Arenas on the Strait of Magellan. There, during a two-year period of intense creativity, she wrote a series of poems that gave vent to her extreme emotional turmoil.

Her next appointment was as principal of a

GABRIELA MISTRAL

girl's high school in Temuco, a city in the Indian region of south-central Chile. It was there that she met PABLO NERUDA who, at only sixteen years of age, was president of the local literary society. Recognizing his precocious talents, Mistral made the facilities of her school library available to the young poet and actively encouraged his development as a writer.

In 1921 she became principal of Santiago High School. Those who knew her at the time have commented on her dual nature, in which a solitary, majestic, and sorrowful personality was combined with a joyful and often capricious one. Mistral's move to the capital coincided with the discovery of her poetry by Federico de Onís, a professor at Columbia University, who was instrumental in having her collected poems published in 1922 by the Hispanic Institute of Columbia University under the title *Desolación* (Desolation). The title is derived from one of the poems in the volume, a verse that describes a desolate landscape of heavy winds and dense fog, symbols of the poet's own mental and spiritual anguish. More than two decades later, the American critic Mildred Adams wrote in the *Nation:* "[*Desolación*] is full of passion and tragedy—the suicide of a lover; the anguish of the woman who quarreled with him and lost him; the deep longing for his child, which she would never bear. With these themes go her love for and keen observation of country places and country children and her sense of the teacher as a consecrated being. The tone is simple, direct, almost primitive."

Because of the prestige of the Hispanic Institute and of Columbia University, coupled with the power of her poetry, this first publication of her verse outside Chile brought Mistral almost immediate international acclaim. The American literary scholar Alfred Ortiz-Vargas wrote in *Poet Lore* that the appearance of Mistral as a poet was "an epoch-making event, for it initiated a poetry that from the beginning bore the unmistakable stamp of things that endure. . . . [Her poetry] elevates the mind by the nobility of its thought, by its high ideals, by its deep feeling for all that is frail and that suffers and dies."

Soon after she had assumed her post at the school in Santiago, a law was passed in Chile prohibiting persons without a university degree from serving as teachers. Mistral resigned and was invited by José Vasconselos, the Mexican minister of education, to work on a plan for the reform of Mexico's schools and libraries. The project later proved to be successful. In Mexico she also found time to study Indian history and to travel widely throughout the country.

Mistral then journeyed to the United States and after addressing the Pan-American Union in Washington, D.C., she went on to visit Spain, Switzerland, and Italy. When she returned to Chile, she was hailed as a cultural and an educational heroine, granted a pension for her work as a teacher, and appointed by the Chilean government as a kind of ambassador-at-large for Latin American culture.

Her second volume of poems, *Ternura* (Tenderness, 1924), was also widely acclaimed. Loving in tone, many of its poems reflect Mistral's own longing for the children she never had. Two years later she traveled to Paris as the Chilean delegate to the Committee for Intellectual Cooperation of the League of Nations. In connection with this work, she was responsible for the selection of works by Latin American authors for a series of volumes to be published in Europe; among those she selected were works by Neruda, who was then serving as the Chilean consul in Saigon. In 1930–1931 she taught Hispanic-American literature at Barnard College of Columbia University in New York. Around this same time she lectured at Vassar College and Middlebury College and spent a term teaching at the University of Puerto Rico. Her dual career as a writer and diplomat also prospered, and she served as Chilean consul in Italy (1932) and Spain (1934).

In 1938 she published *Tala* (Devastation), a volume of poems strongly antifascist in character, inspired by her deep distress over the suffering brought about by the Spanish Civil War. That year she received a consular assignment to France but, because of the threat of World War II, she soon requested a transfer to Brazil. There Mistral became an intimate friend of Stefan Zweig, the exiled Austrian-born writer, and his wife. Despondent over the Nazi persecution of the Jews, the Zweigs committed suicide in 1942. A year and a half later, Mistral's eighteen-year-old nephew, Juan Miguel, who had lived with her since the age of four, killed himself in despair—presumably caused by his grief for the Zweigs and by the xenophobic reaction of his fellow students to his foreign education. The tragedy was comparable to the loss of her own son.

Mistral was awarded the 1945 Nobel Prize for Literature "for her lyric poetry which, inspired by powerful emotions, has made her name a symbol of the idealistic aspirations of the entire Latin American world." In his presentation address, Hjalmar Gullberg of the Swedish Academy commented, "In rendering homage to the rich Latin American literature, we address ourselves . . . to its queen, the poet of *Desolación*, who has become the great singer of sorrow and of motherhood." Mistral was the first writer from Latin America to win the Nobel Prize for Literature. In her acceptance speech, she declared herself a representative of Latin American culture and saluted "the spiritual pioneers of Sweden." Mistral later remarked that perhaps she had won the prize because she was "the candidate of the women and the children."

In 1946 Mistral became the Chilean consul in Los Angeles. She also served a term as Chilean delegate to the United Nations Subcommittee on the Status of Women of its Commission of Human Rights. She was awarded the Chilean National Prize for Literature in 1951 and that same year resumed her consular duties in Italy. Poor health soon forced her to retire to her home in New York, although in 1954 she was able to travel to her native land to receive an honorary doctorate from the University of Chile and to speak at the presidential palace before 200,000 Chileans. Upon her return to New York, she was awarded an honorary degree from Columbia University.

In 1954 Mistral published her final book of poems, *Lagar* (Wine Press), which was largely devoted to the tragedy of the suicides of the Zweigs and her nephew. "Exile and return, mourning and rebirth," wrote the Chilean critic Fernando Alegría in a discussion of *Lagar*, "these are the common forms used by the poet to describe her life and to suggest, at the same time, the faith that will save her."

Mistral died of cancer in Hempstead, Long Island, New York, at the age of sixty-seven. Funeral services were held at St. Patrick's Cathedral in New York City, after which the body was taken to Chile and, following three days of national mourning, was interred at Monte Grande, where the poet had spent her early childhood. Her tomb is inscribed with one of her axioms: "What the soul is to the body, so is the artist to his people."

"Almost all of Gabriela Mistral's poems have the accent of a prayer," wrote Francisco Donoso, a Chilean author and priest, in the 1930s, "a loving or confident prayer at times, a desperate petition on other occasions when her feelings are overwhelmed by some tragic vision." "In Spanish-speaking countries Gabriela's name . . . had long been a household word," remarked the American poet Langston Hughes in an introduction to *Selected Poems of Gabriela Mistral* (1957), his translation of some of her works. He continued, "Much of her poetry is simple and direct in language, never high-flown or flowery." In *Gabriela Mistral* (1962), the biographer and critic Arturo Torres-Ríoseco described the poet as "a distinguished teacher and a writer who crystallized an era. The strength of her renovation of literature is a model for young writers."

"By comparison with Hispanic-American literature generally," said the literary critic and biographer Margot Arce de Vázquez in her study of Mistral's work, "Gabriela's poetry possesses the merit of consummate originality, of a voice of its own, authentic and consciously realized." According to the American literary scholar Margaret Bates in her introduction to *Selected Poems of Gabriela Mistral* (1971), "Gabriela, in true Hispanic fashion, turned her back on easy elegance, deliberately eschewed the smooth-flowing, and reveled in the rough-hewn and rugged." Bates continued, "She differs from other women poets of her time, often painfully self-centered and extremely conscious of their 'femininity,' in that she seldom mentions herself unless it is to tell us of her plainness. In her poems, as in her life, she is the arch enemy of *vanitas*."

ADDITIONAL WORKS IN ENGLISH TRANSLATION: Blackwell, A. S. (ed.) Some Spanish-American Poets, 1938; Crickets and Frogs: A Fable, 1972; The Elephant and His Secret, 1974.

ABOUT: Arce de Vázquez, M. Gabriela Mistral: The Poet and Her Poetry, 1964; Caimano, R. A. Mysticism in Gabriela Mistral, 1969; Castleman, W. J. Beauty and the Mission of the Teacher, 1982; Gazarian-Gautier, M. Gabriela Mistral, 1975; Ladrón de Guevera, M. Gabriela Mistral: Magnificent Rebel, 1962; Peers, E. A. Gabriela Mistral, 1946; Rosenbaum, S. C. Modern Women Poets of Spanish America, 1945; Taylor, M. C. Gabriela Mistral's Religious Sensibility, 1968.

MITCHELL, PETER D.
(September 29, 1920–)
Nobel Prize for Chemistry, 1978

The English biochemist Peter Dennis Mitchell was born in Mitcham, Surrey, to Christopher Gibbs Mitchell, a civil servant, and Beatrice Dorothy (Taplan) Mitchell. He received his early education at Queen's College in Taunton, where he studied under C. L. Wiseman, a mathematician and musician. However, he did so poorly on his scholarship examinations that only a personal letter from Wiseman secured his admission to Jesus College, Cambridge, which he entered in 1939.

At Cambridge, Mitchell studied chemistry, physiology, mathematics, and biochemistry, obtaining a B.A. with honors in 1943. That year he enrolled as a doctoral candidate in biochemistry under the direction of J. F. Danielli, in whose laboratory he investigated the transport of biochemical substances across cell membranes. He also taught biochemistry. In 1950 he received his Ph.D. for a dissertation on the mechanism of the action of penicillin, an antibiotic discovered in 1928 by ALEXANDER FLEMING that attacks the cell membranes of susceptible bacteria.

Mitchell was then appointed demonstrator in the biochemistry department at Cambridge, where he concentrated his research on the mechanism of oxidative phosphorylation (by which 95 percent of the energy of aerobic organisms is obtained) and the similar mechanism of photosynthetic phosphorylation (by which a large amount of the energy available from plants is initially harvested from the sun). At the time, these two mechanisms were regarded as among the great unsolved problems of biochemistry.

How organisms generate energy and harness it to such functions as movement, transport, and biosynthesis was a question that intrigued Mitchell and many other biochemists. By 1955 FRITZ LIPMANN's theory that adenosine triphosphate (ATP) serves as a universal energy currency had been accepted by biochemists. The functions of the major pathways of metabolism (respiration, fermenta-

713

PETER D. MITCHELL

tion, and photosynthesis) were considered to arise from ATP, which supported various activities by means of its energy-rich phosphoryl bonds. Thus, at least the main outline of bioenergetics (the study of energy transformation in living organisms) seemed to be comprehensible, and all that remained was to work out the molecular details.

This task was extremely difficult, however, largely because the enzymes of oxidative and photosynthetic phosphorylation are tightly linked with the lipoprotein membranes of mitochondria (small granules or rod-shaped structures in the cytoplasm of cells) and chloroplasts (chlorophyll-bearing bodies of plant and animal cells). This close linkage prevented any studies of the molecular details in solutions.

A number of researchers devoted themselves to describing the basic features of oxidative phosphorylation. They learned that respiration is brought about by a kind of cascade of enzymes and coenzymes that carry electrons from various substrates (substances acted upon by enzymes) to oxygen. The synthesis of ATP follows catalytic action by a distinct enzyme complex known as ATPase (adenosine triphosphatase). In the case of chloroplasts, electrons thrown out when light is absorbed by chlorophyll move along a series of carriers to the ultimate target, water. The synthesis of ATP is brought about by an ATPase complex with a molecular structure that closely resembles that of mitochondrial membranes. In the course of this research, an important question arose: How does the free

energy that is released during electron transportation force the ATPase in the direction of ATP synthesis?

The search for molecular mechanisms was based on the theory that the respiratory chain and ATPase are connected by high-energy intermediates corresponding to those in reactions catalyzed by soluble enzymes. Mitchell was not a mitochondriologist; his expertise lay in the study of metabolite transport over the cytoplasmic membrane of bacteria, the topic he had pursued while a student at Cambridge. In 1958 Mitchell and a co-worker, Jennifer Moyle, pointed out that enzymic reactions are essentially vectorial; that is, they transport or carry something. The two researchers further suggested that the direction of these reactions, though obscured in solution, might become apparent when enzymes were taken into membranes. In fact, an enzyme complex might be set so firmly in a membrane that the reaction route would traverse the barrier, immediately catalyzing the dislocation of a chemical group. They called this process vectorial metabolism.

Between 1961 and 1966, Mitchell formulated what he called the chemiosmotic hypothesis, an extreme solution to the problem of energy coupling in the mechanisms of oxidative and photosynthetic phosphorylation. He proposed that the respiratory chain is an alternating sequence of carriers for hydrogen and electrons. These carriers are so arranged in the inner mitochondrial membrane that they transport protons (tripeptides) across the membrane. Since the mitochondrial membrane does not permit a passive flow of protons, respiration generates an electrochemical potential ramp or slope for hydrogen ions, with the inner matrix being electrically negative and alkaline relative to the exterior. Protons on the outer surface gravitate back into the matrix, traveling down the potential ramp. It is this proton current—comparable to the electron current produced by a battery—that can be called upon to perform work.

According to the chemiosmotic hypothesis, the existence of chemical links between the respiratory chain and ATPase is impossible, a conclusion that made the theory unpopular among many biochemists, some of whom questioned the validity of Mitchell's propositions. Continuing skepticism and controversy over the radical hypothesis convinced Mitchell that he would have to defend it with concrete data. Such data were not easily accessible and required new investigative methods. Nevertheless, Mitchell and Moyle eventually produced a network of quantitative methods and observations designed to expose the predictions of the chemiosmotic hypothesis to rigorous testing.

A period of great productivity, both experimental and theoretical, ensued, accompanied by often-heated debates within the small circle of bioenergeticists. The chief issue was whether Mitchell's chemiosmotic principles and practices conformed to accepted standards. By 1970 the weight of evidence had shifted in favor of the chemiosmotic hypothesis, and a number of believers came forward in Great Britain, the United States, and the Soviet Union in its support.

The 1978 Nobel Prize for Chemistry was awarded to Mitchell "for his contribution to the understanding of biological energy transfer through the formulation of the chemiosmotic theory." In his presentation speech, Lars Ernster of the Royal Swedish Academy of Sciences noted the controversy that Mitchell's theories had provoked but pointed to the wealth of experimental data that had been produced in response. In conclusion he pointed to some of the practical benefits of Mitchell's work. "Chloroplasts, mitochondria, and bacteria may be regarded as naturally occurring solar cells and fuel cells," he said, "and may as such serve as models and in the future perhaps also as tools in energy technology."

Since 1964 Mitchell has been director of research at the Glynn Research Laboratories in Cornwall. In 1958 he married Helen French, with whom he has three sons and a daughter. Despite his professional duties, he finds time to participate in local community affairs, work for conservation of natural resources, and restore medieval farmhouses.

In addition to the Nobel Prize, Mitchell has received the Louis and Bert Freedman Award of the New York Academy of Sciences (1976), the Lewis S. Rosenstiel Award for Distinguished Work in Basic Medical Research of Brandeis University (1977), the Copley Medal of the Royal Society (1981), and the Medal of Honor of the Athens Municipal Council (1982). He is a fellow of the Royal Society and holds foreign membership in the National Academy of Sciences and the Royal Society of Edinburgh. He has been awarded honorary degrees by the Technical University of Berlin, the universities of Chicago and East Anglia, and Liverpool, Bristol, and Edinburgh universities, among other institutions.

SELECTED WORKS: Chemiosmotic Coupling and Energy Transduction, 1968.

ABOUT: Chemistry January 1979; New York Times October 18, 1978; Science December 15, 1978.

MODIGLIANI, FRANCO

(June 18, 1918–   )
Nobel Memorial Prize in Economic
   Sciences, 1985

The American economist Franco Modigliani (mō dēl yä′ nē) was born in Rome, Italy, the son of Enrico Modigliani, a Jewish pediatrician, and the former Olga Flaschel, a child development specialist. After attending the Liceo Visconti, Modigliani entered the University of Rome to study medicine. Finding that he was unable to tolerate the sight of blood, however, he took up the study of law and received a doctor of jurisprudence degree from the University of Rome in 1939. He also studied economics, motivated in part by curiosity about the causes of the Great Depression. His interest deepened when in 1939 he took first prize in a national essay competition among university students on the effect of price controls.

Because Modigliani's antifascist politics and Jewish heritage made it impossible for him to remain in Italy, he fled in 1939, first to France and then to the United States. The next year he renewed his work in economics in New York City at the New School for Social Research, then a leading center of émigré scientific research. Working under Jacob Marschak, he developed a lasting interest in Keynesian macroeconomics and in the use of formal models in economic analysis.

While completing his graduate work at the New School, Modigliani taught at the New Jersey College for Women (1942) and was an associate in economics and statistics at Bard College, Columbia University (1942–1944). He was also a lecturer at the New School in 1943–1944. He received his Ph.D. in social science in 1944 and became assistant professor of mathematical economics and econometrics at the New School in 1946, a position he held for two years. Between 1945 and 1948 he also served as research associate and chief statistician at the Institute of World Affairs in New York City.

Moving to the University of Chicago in 1949, Modigliani joined the staff of the Cowles Commission for Research in Economics as a research consultant, remaining there until 1954. Concurrently, he was first an associate economics professor (1949) and then full professor of economics (1950–1952) at the University of Illinois.

MODIGLIANI

FRANCO MODIGLIANI

Between 1952 and 1960, Modigliani was professor of economics and industrial administration at the Carnegie Institute of Technology and visiting professor at Harvard University (1957–1958). In 1960 he became a professor at Northwestern University, but he left two years later to join the faculty at the Massachusetts Institute of Technology (MIT) as professor of economics and finance. In 1970 he was appointed institute professor at MIT.

Throughout his career, Modigliani has been a leader in the effort to integrate Keynesian economics into orthodox neoclassical economic theory and monetary analysis by reconciling Keynesian macroeconomic theory with theories that assume that individuals act efficiently to maximize their welfare. In his early work Modigliani explained the onset and persistence of periods of economic depression and high unemployment by using the Keynesian concept of "wage rigidity" (the hypothesis that wages do not instantaneously adjust to changes in demand conditions). In his 1944 article "Liquidity Preference and the Theory of Interest and Money," he showed that if wages do not instantaneously adjust to changing market conditions, workers can overprice themselves in a weakening economy, thus producing unemployment. In this way he related a monetary problem in financial markets to unemployment and a decline in real economic activity.

In the long debate between monetarists and Keynesians, Modigliani did not take a dogmatic position. He clearly recognized the role

of money, but in contrast to MILTON FRIEDMAN, he was at the time seeking the effects that money exerts on economic activity through the various channels of financial markets. He worked on these problems while constructing the financial sector of the MIT econometric model and therefore could not accept the reduced forms of Friedman's simplified method. In general, however, Modigliani is close to modern versions of Keynesian theory and to its policy conclusions. He expressed his credo in the 1960s in these words: "The private market economy needs to be stabilized, should be stabilized, and can be stabilized."

Interested in improving on Keynes's "consumption function" and finding a rational individual basis for macroeconomic behavior, Modigliani undertook pioneering work on "life cycle" models designed to explain personal savings. In this work he argued that "the main motive [of savings] is to maintain a fairly fixed standard of living." Savings, he said, reflects the difference between this stable desired consumption level and a variable income level that systematically rises from an initially low level to a peak during one's later working years before declining to a very low level in retirement. Reflecting on this attempt to maintain a constant consumption level despite fluctuations in income, Modigliani claimed that "young people save, old people dissave."

Modigliani first presented a form of the life cycle savings model in a 1949 article, "Fluctuations in the Saving-Income Ratio," and a 1954 article, "Utility Analysis and the Consumption Function," which he wrote with his student Richard Brumberg. He developed the model further in a series of papers written with Albert Aldo, notably "Tests of the Life Cycle Hypothesis of Savings" (1957), "The 'Permanent Income' and the 'Life Cycle' Hypothesis of Savings Behavior" (1960), and "The 'Life Cycle' Hypothesis of Saving: Aggregate Implications and Tests" (1963). In these papers Modigliani shows that savings rates are closely tied to rates of population growth, since such growth affects the ratio of young people and retirees to those of prime working age. He also shows that high rates of economic growth raise the savings rate by increasing the income of working people (out of which they save) without raising the consumption of retirees, whose spending reflects the past's lower levels of income. Modigliani uses these insights to account for variations in international savings rates in a 1970 article, "The Life Cycle Hypothesis of Saving and Intercountry Differences in the Saving Ratio." His theory of long-term savings has also been used for testing alternative pension schemes.

Modigliani's interest in monetary theory and financial markets also led to his pioneering work associated with the Modigliani-Miller theorem. Developed with Merton H. Miller, who was then at Carnegie-Mellon University, and presented in their 1958 paper "The Cost of Capital, Corporation Finance, and the Theory of Investment," it asserts that rational investors will focus only on the future profitability of a company and not on the size and structure of its debt. The theory puts forth new ideas concerning the total cost of capital and revises models for individual firms' investment decisions in such a way that they can be distinguished from their financial decisions. Originally rejected by many, this theorem is now taken as self-evident and is one of the cornerstones in modern theories of corporate finance. Modigliani and Miller showed that individual investors can always mix their own portfolios to balance the expected risks and returns from any degree of company leverage. A technique they used to compute the value of anticipated future earnings is now standard. However, the simplest version of the Modigliani-Miller theorem is based on a number of simplifying assumptions, such as perfect financial markets, that must be kept in mind.

Since the 1940s Modigliani has been one of the leading figures in the development of macroeconomic theory and policy. His theoretical work has invoked a high level of abstraction to derive the implications of welfare-maximizing economic theory for macroeconomic behavior. His work thus contributed to the introduction in the late 1960s and 1970s of the "rational expectations" school of macroeconomics. Some date this approach to Modigliani's 1954 article with Emile Grunberg, "The Predictability of Social Events." Later rational expectation theorists have taken Modigliani and Grunberg's arguments much further than the authors intended, arguing that government policy can never improve the operation of the economy because rational people will always anticipate the government's actions and act to negate its effects. However, Modigliani has been highly critical of these views and has resisted drawing this conclusion. In his applied work, as a designer, with Lawrence Klein and others, of the Keynesian-inspired MIT-Pennsylvania model of the economy and in his regular economics column in the Italian newspaper *Corriere della sera* (The Evening Courier), Modigliani argues that persisting rigidities in the adjustment of prices and expectations limit the value of rational expectation models when applied to the interpretation of macroeconomic events.

Modigliani received the 1985 Nobel Memorial Prize in Economic Sciences "for his analysis of the behavior of household savers," work that has had "extremely important" implications for national pension programs, "and for his work on the relationship of a company's financial structure to the value placed on its stock by investors."

In 1939 Modigliani married Serena Calabi, with whom he has two sons. Once described as "a small, bouncy man with silver hair," Modigliani makes his home in Belmont, Massachusetts. His recreational activities include tennis, skiing, sailing, and swimming. He is a naturalized American citizen.

In addition to the Nobel Prize, Modigliani has received the Graham and Dodd Plaque of the Financial Analysts Federation (1974, 1979) and the James R. Killian Jr. Faculty Achievement Award of MIT (1985). He is a member of the American Economic Association, the American Finance Association, the Econometric Society, and the Italian Economics Society. He holds honorary degrees from the University of Chicago, the Catholic University of Louvain, the University Institute of Bergamo, and Bard College. Since 1966 he has been an academic consultant to the Board of Governors of the Federal Reserve System and since 1971 has been a senior adviser to the Brookings Panel on Economic Activity, in addition to many other professional positions.

ADDITIONAL WORKS: National Incomes and International Trade, 1953, with Hans Neisser; Planning Production Inventories and Work Forces, 1960, with others; Role of Anticipations and Plans in Economic Behavior and Their Use in Economic Analysis and Forecasting, 1961; The Reform of the International Payments System, 1971, with Hossein Askari; The Collected Papers of Franco Modigliani (3 vols.) 1980.

ABOUT: Economist October 19, 1985; Klamer, A. Conversations With Economists, 1981; New York Times October 16, 1985; November 3, 1985; Science March 21, 1986.

MOISSAN, HENRI

(September 28, 1852–February 20, 1907)
Nobel Prize for Chemistry, 1906

The French chemist Ferdinand-Frédéric-Henri Moissan (mwä säN′) was born in Paris. His father was an official of the Eastern Railways Company, and his mother was a seam-

HENRI MOISSAN

stress. When the family moved to Meaux in 1864, Moissan entered the municipal academic school, where an outstanding teacher of mathematics and sciences gave him additional free private instruction. So single-minded was Moissan's interest in chemistry that he neglected his other subjects and was not accepted at a university when he graduated in 1870. After two years as an apprentice pharmacist in Paris, he went to work for the chemist Edmond Frémy at the Museum of Natural History. In 1874 he transferred to the laboratory of Pierre-Paul Dehérain at the École Pratique des Hautes Études, a prestigious institute of technology, where he worked on plant physiology. Persuaded by Dehérain to complete his education, he entered the University of Paris, where he received a *baccalaureate* in 1874 and a *licence* (M.A.) three years later. In 1880 he was awarded a doctoral degree in inorganic chemistry for a thesis on chromium oxides.

To support himself, Moissan served for a time as director of a commercial laboratory, and between 1879 and 1883 he was lecture assistant and senior demonstrator at the École Supérieure de Pharmacie in Paris. In 1882 he married Léonie Lugan, the daughter of a pharmacist friend from Meaux. The couple had one son. Moissan's wife's family provided the financial support that enabled him to continue his research without financial pressure. He was appointed professor of toxicology at the École Supérieure de Pharmacie in 1886 and became professor of inorganic chemistry there three years later.

Freed from financial restraints, Moissan devoted himself to a problem that had resisted chemical analysis for eighty years. The similarity between hydrochloric acid and hydrofluoric acid implied the existence of fluorine, an extremely reactive element belonging to the halogen group (which also includes chlorine, bromine, and iodine). All attempts to isolate free fluorine from molten fluoride salts by electrolysis had failed, however, because at the high temperatures that were required, the released fluorine reacted with water, the container, and the electrodes.

Anhydrous hydrogen fluoride alone does not conduct an electrical current. Thus, in 1886 Moissan was able to prepare free fluorine by using an electrolyte of dry potassium acid fluoride dissolved in anhydrous hydrofluoric acid, with platinum-iridium electrodes. Because of the technical difficulties associated with the preparation of fluorine at high temperatures, Moissan investigated the chemical properties of fluorine compounds at very low temperatures. Together with the Scottish chemist James Dewar, Moissan liquefied fluorine at $-185°C$, at which temperature it still attacked hydrogen and hydrocarbons. The study of this most reactive known element eventually led to the discovery of carbon tetrafluoride; methyl, ethyl, and isobutyl fluorides; and sulfuryl fluoride. Modern uses of fluorine include the separation of uranium 235 from uranium 238 in the form of uranium hexafluoride.

In other work, Moissan studied the metal fluorides of platinum, alkaline earths, silver, and manganese and the nonmetallic iodine pentafluoride and nitryl fluoride. Since fluorine and its compounds are highly toxic, the health of previous investigators had been seriously affected, and in his later years Moissan said, "Fluorine has taken ten years of my life."

In addition to his work on fluorine compounds, Moissan improved the techniques used to extract the element boron, yielding a product that was 99 percent pure rather than the previous 70 percent. He also hoped to separate crystalline diamonds from the decomposition of fluorhydrocarbons, since diamond, charcoal, graphite, lampblack, coal, and coke were all known to be different forms of carbon. Although these attempts failed, his subsequent analytical work on diamonds indicated that they were frequently contaminated with iron. Because it was known that iron dissolves carbon and that diamonds are formed under the combined conditions of high temperature and high pressure, Moissan tried to make diamonds by subjecting molten iron saturated with carbon to high pressure. He achieved high pressure by plunging containers of molten carboniferous iron into cold water, relying on the expansion of the carbon-loaded iron upon solidifying to generate high internal pressure against the solid outer shell of the iron that cooled first. Moissan claimed to have made small diamonds by this technique, but the claim has never been verified.

Even though Moissan's work on diamond production was not fruitful, the techniques that he developed had great practical value. To attain extremely high temperatures, he designed an electric arc furnace capable of heating substances to 3,500°C. With this device Moissan became the founder of high-temperature chemistry. He went on to study the melting and vaporizing of materials that had been considered inherently nonvolatile, including zirconium, molybdenum, manganese, chromium, thorium, tungsten, platinum, uranium, titanium, and vanadium. Moissan discovered that at very high temperatures carbon, boron, and silicon, which are inactive at ordinary temperatures, react with many elements to form carbides, borides, and silicides, respectively. He also prepared silicon carbide, or carborundum. Moissan's findings had immediate industrial applications, as in the production of acetylene from calcium carbide.

Moissan was awarded the 1906 Nobel Prize for Chemistry "in recognition of the great services rendered by him in his investigation and isolation of the element fluorine, and for the adoption in the service of science of the electric furnace called after him." On presenting the award, J. P. Klason of the Royal Swedish Academy of Sciences declared, "The whole world has admired the great experimental skills with which you have isolated and studied fluorine. . . . With the aid of your electric furnace, you have solved the riddle of how diamonds are formed in nature. You have unleashed a mighty wave into the world of technology, a wave which has not yet attained its full height." Moissan did not deliver a Nobel lecture.

A man of wide-ranging interests, Moissan loved art, music, and literature. As a student, he even wrote a play. He was a collector of paintings, engravings, and autographs—particularly from the era of the French Revolution—and enjoyed traveling.

After suffering an attack of acute appendicitis, Moissan underwent surgery on February 16, 1907. Weakened by a chronic heart condition and by his years of exposure to toxic chemicals, he died four days later at the age of fifty-four.

In addition to the Nobel Prize, Moissan received the Davy Medal of the Royal Society of London (1896) and the August Wilhelm von Hofmann Medal of the German Chemical Society (1903). He was a member of the French Academy of Medicine and the French Academy of Sciences and was a foreign member of the Royal Society of London and the British Chemical Society, among others. He was made a commander of the Legion of Honor in 1900.

SELECTED WORKS: The Liquefication of Fluorine, 1897; The Electric Furnace, 1904; Collection of Works on Chemistry, 1904–1906.

ABOUT: Dictionary of Scientific Biography, volume 9, 1974; Farber, E. (ed.) Great Chemists, 1961; Harrow, B. Eminent Chemists, 1927; Weeks, M. E. Discovery of the Elements, 1956.

MOMMSEN, THEODOR
(November 30, 1817–November 1, 1903)
Nobel Prize for Literature, 1902

The German historian Christian Matthias Theodor Mommsen was born in the village of Garding in the duchy of Schleswig (then part of Denmark, now in West Germany). When he was four, the family moved to the small town of Oldesloe (now Bad Oldesloe), in Holstein, another duchy then under Danish rule. His father, Jens Mommsen, a Protestant minister of modest means, encouraged the boy's love of literature, introducing him to German poetry and supervising his translations of Victor Hugo, Lord Byron, and William Shakespeare into German, the family's native tongue. Both at home and later at the Gymnasium Christianeum in Altona, he received an intensive education in the classics, philosophy, rhetoric, and German literature.

Entering the University of Kiel in 1838, Mommsen elected to study jurisprudence, a course that consisted largely of Roman law. At Kiel the young lecturer Otto Jahn trained Mommsen in the study and interpretation of classical inscriptions. During his years at the university Mommsen maintained an interest in literature, publishing the *Liederbuch dreier Freunde* (Songbook of Three Friends), a collection of poems written by him, his brother Tycho, and their friend Theodor Storm.

Before his graduation from Kiel in 1843, Mommsen wrote a treatise, "De collegiis et sodaliciis Romanorum" (On the Colleges and Corporations of the Romans). On the strength of this paper and the general distinction of his

THEODOR MOMMSEN

work as a student, Mommsen's professors recommended him for a Danish government scholarship that enabled him to spend the next three years in Italy. There he wrote numerous articles and began gathering material for his *Corpus Inscriptionum Latinarum,* a comprehensive collection of Latin inscriptions that was published in sixteen volumes between 1863 and 1936. The first volume was dedicated to Count Bartolomeo Borghesi, an Italian statesman and scholar who had supported Mommsen's early work.

After returning to Schleswig in 1847, Mommsen became involved in the movement to free from Danish rule the German-speaking duchies north of the Elbe. During the revolution of 1848 he edited a liberal newspaper, the *Schleswig-Holsteinische Zeitung,* but he resigned at the end of the year to become a professor of civil law at the University of Leipzig in Germany. His participation in an uprising in Saxony that year cost him his appointment, and in 1852 he went to Zurich. There he began to write a history of Rome which, although scholarly, was intended for the general reader.

The first volume of Mommsen's *Römische Geschichte* (*The History of Rome*) appeared in 1854, the same year that he returned to Germany to accept a professorship at the University of Breslau, in Prussia. That year he also married Marie Reimer, the daughter of a bookseller; they eventually had sixteen children. The first three volumes of *The History of Rome* (two more having been published in 1855 and 1856) spanned the Roman republic

from its origins to 46 B.C., the year Julius Caesar defeated the Senate's armies in North Africa. This work, distinguished by its masterful prose and Mommsen's encyclopedic knowledge of ancient Rome, brought him acclaim throughout Europe. To paint a vivid portrait of Rome, Mommsen often compared historical figures to their nineteenth-century counterparts. An English-language edition of the work, translated by W. P. Dickson, appeared in four volumes from 1862 to 1875. Advances in historical research have dated some of Mommsen's scholarship, but *The History of Rome* is still considered an impressive work of history and literature.

Although Mommsen planned a fourth volume, on the history of the Roman emperors, he never fulfilled his intention, because he felt his work on this subject would not measure up to his previous writing on the Roman republic. His account of the Roman provinces during the first three centuries of the empire, *Die Provinzen, von Caesar bis Diocletian* (*The Provinces of the Roman Empire*), was published in 1885 as volume 5 of *The History of Rome.*

In 1858 Mommsen joined the faculty of the University of Berlin as professor of Roman history, and he remained in Berlin for the rest of his life. He was also elected to membership in the Prussian Academy of Sciences, whose support enabled him to continue his work on the *Corpus Inscriptionum.* During these years he remained active in political affairs, serving as a member of the Progressive party in the state parliament of Prussia from 1863 to 1866 and again from 1873 to 1879. After Otto von Bismarck unified the independent German states as the German Empire, Mommsen sat in the Reichstag (German imperial parliament), where he opposed Bismarck's domestic policies as well as the anti-Semitism that he found among many of his colleagues.

Between 1871 and 1888 Mommsen published *Römisches Staatsrecht* (Roman Constitutional Law), a three-volume study that codified the legal system on which the Roman constitution was based and placed it in the context of the republic's history. It was followed in 1899 by *Römisches Strafrecht* (Roman Criminal Law).

Although in 1902 Leo Tolstoy was a prominent candidate for the Nobel Prize for Literature, many of his views were unpalatable to the Nobel committee of the Swedish Academy, which extended its definition of literature to encompass historical writings and awarded the prize to Mommsen, calling him "the greatest living master of the art of historical writing, with special reference to his monumental work, *The History of Rome.*" In his presentation speech, C. D. af Wirsén of the Swedish Academy praised Mommsen's "thorough and comprehensive scholarship" as well as his "vigorous and lively style." Mommsen, who was then eighty-five, made no formal acceptance speech.

The next year Mommsen died at Charlottenburg, outside Berlin, on November 1.

A slender man with a thin face and piercing eyes, Mommsen was said to be a riveting lecturer. He conducted his work with the help of many of his students, whose careers he assisted generously. The historians James Thompson and Bernard Holm, coauthors of *A History of Historical Writing,* called him "one of the marvels of German scholarship." In the opinion of the English historian Francis J. Haverfield, Mommsen was "a poet who was also a lawyer, a critic who was also a creator, emotional, excitable, and imaginative."

ERNESTO MONETA

ADDITIONAL WORKS IN ENGLISH TRANSLATION: The Roman Catacombs, 1871; Letters on the War Between Germany and France, 1871, with others; Rome From Earliest Times to 44 B.C., 1907.

ABOUT: Buchan, J. Some Eighteenth-Century Byways, 1908; Gossman, L. Orpheus Philologus, 1983; Thompson, J. W., and Holm, B. J. A History of Historical Writing (2 vols.) 1942; Warde Fowler, W. Theodor Mommsen: His Life and Work, 1909; Wilamowitz-Möllendorff, V. My Recollections, 1930.

MONETA, ERNESTO

(September 20, 1833–February 10, 1918)
Nobel Prize for Peace, 1907
(shared with Louis Renault)

The Italian journalist and peace advocate Ernesto Teodoro Moneta (mô nā' tä) was born in Milan, the third of eleven children in the aristocratic family of Carlo Aurelio Moneta and the former Giuseppina Muzio. By the time of Moneta's birth, the family's fortunes were in decline. He received his early education at the Liceo di Brera and the Liceo Parini in Milan, a city that had been under Austrian rule since 1713. In 1848 Moneta fought alongside his father and brothers in the unsuccessful Italian revolt against Austria. When the Austrians crushed the Milan uprising and others like it throughout northern Italy, Moneta, fearing for his life, fled to the independent kingdom of Piedmont. There he attended the military academy at Ivrea and participated in a secret society that maintained contacts with Italian nationalists in Milan.

When Piedmont went to war with Austria in 1859, Moneta and four of his brothers joined the forces of the nationalist leader Giuseppe Garibaldi and saw action during the Battle of Volturno in Calabria. During his service in the Italian army, Moneta became a member of Garibaldi's general staff. He stopped fighting for Italian unification after Italy's defeat at Custoza in 1866. Discouraged by rivalry and disorganization within the army, he resigned his commission and turned to journalism.

Settling in Milan, Moneta began contributing drama reviews to the daily newspaper *Il secolo* (The Century). The following year, two of Moneta's friends took control of the paper and invited him to serve as editor in chief, a position he held for twenty-eight years. Under his direction, *Il secolo* became Italy's leading newspaper and a powerful voice in the nation's intellectual and political affairs.

In the pages of *Il secolo,* Moneta took strong and often controversial stands on a number of issues of national and international importance. Although a Catholic, he regularly printed anticlerical articles in the belief that criticism of the church was essential for the reform and unification of Italy. Sympathetic to the army, he nevertheless argued vigorously for reducing its size and developing a home guard that would be less costly to maintain and less militaristic in attitude. An ardent supporter of Italian nationalism, he nevertheless urged his readers to moderate their hatred of Austria and advocated closer cooperation between Italy and France.

In 1874 Moneta married Ersilia Caglio, who died in 1899. The couple had two sons.

During the 1870s Moneta's articles in *Il secolo* reflected his increasing commitment to international peace. Extending this commitment beyond journalism, he convened a peace conference in Milan in 1878. Nine years later, he helped found the Lombard Union for International Peace and Arbitration, to which he contributed the money he received from the publisher of *Il secolo* on the occasion of his twentieth anniversary with the paper. To disseminate information about the peace movement, he began issuing *L'amico della pace* (Friend of Peace), an almanac of the movement's activities, in 1890. Five years later, he became the Italian representative to the INTERNATIONAL PEACE BUREAU.

In 1896, after one of the most illustrious careers in Italian journalism, Moneta retired from *Il secolo,* though he continued writing for the paper. Two years later, he founded *La vita internazionale* (International Life), a highly respected forum for articles on peace and international arbitration. Its discussion of Franco-Italian relations was widely credited with encouraging a climate of opinion that made possible an arbitration treaty between France and Italy in 1903.

For his long and tireless advocacy of peace, Moneta shared the 1907 Nobel Prize for Peace with LOUIS RENAULT. "Special emphasis must be placed on his work in the press and in peace meetings . . . for an understanding between France and Italy," said Jørgen Løvland of the Norwegian Nobel Committee in his presentation address.

Illness prevented Moneta from attending the award ceremonies; he delivered his Nobel lecture in Oslo two years later. Speaking in French, he addressed the theme "Peace and Law in the Italian Tradition," in which he drew parallels between Italian nationalism and the quest for universal liberty. "Pacifism," he said, "does not seek to obliterate countries by throwing them into the melting pot of cosmopolitanism, but to organize them . . . according to the dictates of justice." Confessing to moments of discouragement, he reaffirmed his conviction that peace and justice were not illusions. "Reasonable ideas which find their sanction in the conscience of the righteous do not die," he declared. "They are consequently realities and active forces, but they are so only to the extent that those who profess them know how to turn them to account." Because Moneta

found no contradiction between defending a nation's right to fight for self-government and working to improve international relations, his selection as the 1907 Peace laureate drew negative comment in some quarters.

After 1900 Moneta was forced to spend long periods in the country recuperating from eye operations that failed to halt the advance of glaucoma. Although virtually blind near the end of his life, he remained active in journalism and politics. He supported Italy's annexation of Libya in 1911 and endorsed Italy's entry into World War I because he opposed the aggressive policies of Germany and Austria. "I, as an Italian, cannot put myself *au-dessus de la mêlée* [above the battle]," he said in 1918. "I must participate in the life of my country, rejoice in her joys, and weep in her sorrows."

In addition to countless newspaper articles, pamphlets, and editorials, Moneta wrote *Le guerre, le insurrezioni, e la pace nel secolo XIX* (Wars, Insurrections, and Peace in the Nineteenth Century), a historical survey in four volumes published between 1903 and 1910.

After contracting pneumonia, Moneta died in Milan on February 10, 1918, at the age of eighty-eight.

ABOUT: Cooper, S. E. (ed.) Internationalism in Nineteenth-Century Europe: The Crisis of Ideas and Purpose, 1976; Times (London) February 11, 1918.

MONIZ, EGAS

(November 29, 1874–December 13, 1955)
Nobel Prize for Physiology or Medicine, 1949
(shared with Walter R. Hess)

The Portuguese neurologist Egas Moniz was born Antonio Caetano de Abreu Freire to Fernando de Pina Rezende Abreu and his wife Maria do Rosario de Almeida e Sousa at their ancestral home at Avanca, an estate that had been in the Abreu family for five centuries. After receiving his early education from his uncle, an abbot, he entered the University of Coimbra in 1891 and became part of an academic community that enjoyed the highly regimented, protective pace of medieval-style learning. There, under the pen name Egas Moniz, after a twelfth-century Portuguese patriot, he wrote political pamphlets for the liberal republicans who were struggling to overthrow the Portuguese monarchy. Although he soon abandoned his attempt at anonymity, he was known as Moniz throughout his career.

Undecided at first between mathematics and medicine as a career, he chose the latter and received his medical degree in 1899 for a thesis on diphtheria. In the same year he suffered his first attacks of gout, an arthritislike disease that eventually crippled his hands. He studied neurology for two years in Bordeaux and Paris, and in 1902 he wrote a monograph on the physiological pathology of sexual activity. The same year, he accepted an appointment to the medical faculty at the University of Coimbra and married Elvira de Macedo Dias. The couple had no children.

Concurrently with his academic career, Moniz was active politically. The first decade of the twentieth century was one of great political turmoil in Portugal. The monarch was overthrown in 1910, and a republic was founded in 1911. That year Moniz was appointed professor in the newly formed Department of Neurology at the University of Lisbon, a position he held until his retirement in 1945. As a leading liberal activist, Moniz was deeply involved in the nation's political reconstruction. He served as a deputy in the Portuguese Parliament from 1903 until 1917, when he was named ambassador to Spain and, later that year, minister for foreign affairs. As Portugal's representative at the peace conference following the end of World War I, he signed the Treaty of Versailles. In 1917 he also published *A neurologia na guerra* (Neurology in War), which summarized his studies of head injuries during the war. When a conservative government came to power in 1922, Moniz abandoned politics.

Like many neurologists, Moniz was frustrated by the lack of techniques available for studying the living human brain. WILHELM RÖNTGEN's discovery of X rays for photographing bones and organs of the body and noting their various densities had made certain diagnoses possible, but X rays had not advanced neurology. Since the brain has a uniform density, normally no individual structures can be distinguished by X ray. In 1927 Moniz developed cerebral angiography, a procedure that uses X rays and radioactive iodine to make the blood vessels of the brain contrast with the surrounding tissues. The angiogram, which established Moniz as a leading neurologist, remains the most useful method for diagnosing such brain disorders as tumors, strokes, and injuries.

Since the early part of the twentieth century, psychiatrists, following the theories of Sig-

EGAS MONIZ

mund Freud and others, have regarded mental and emotional disturbances as diseases of the mind, and most have attempted to treat them by investigating the patient's mind through various forms of psychoanalysis. Some neurologists in the 1920s and 1930s, however, considered psychological problems as diseases of the brain and searched for physical cures for mental illnesses. In 1935 Moniz attended the International Neurological Conference in London, where the American neurophysiologists John Fulton and Carlyle Jacobsen presented their study of two monkeys from which they had removed most of the prefrontal lobe of the brain (the part directly behind the forehead). After the experimental procedure, the monkeys no longer became upset if they made mistakes carrying out one of the complex tasks they had learned. Although their problem-solving ability was almost nonexistent after the devastating surgery, they seemed not to care; they were immune to anxiety and frustration. These results suggested to Moniz that certain psychiatric patients might also be helped if their prefrontal lobes were severed from the rest of the brain, particularly those patients hospitalized with severe anxiety, or those whose aggression made them dangerous.

Earlier—and unsuccessful—somatic (physical) treatments for mental disorders were diverse and often extreme. Hydrotherapy, sleep therapy, fever therapy, oxygen therapy, hypothermia, the use of arsenic, and the removal of endocrine glands, teeth, tonsils, or other organs are a few examples. Desperation goaded research. Psychotherapy, still in its infancy, was slow and costly, and most families, their savings depleted or their physical resources exhausted, were forced to commit their loved ones to state mental hospitals. Hospital stays were reckoned in decades, and many young patients spent the rest of their lives incarcerated. Large state institutions, operating on limited budgets, were often overcrowded and understaffed. Courses of shock therapy, produced either by an electric current to the brain or by a high dose of insulin injected intravenously, rarely cured hospitalized patients, but it made them docile and easier to handle. In this climate, the drastic surgery offered by Moniz appeared to hold out hope.

Moniz was too handicapped by gout to perform the surgery himself, so the first procedures were carried out in 1936 under his direction by his colleague Almeida Lima, a professor of neurosurgery. Moniz called the operation a leucotomy (from the Greek word for white), because the prefrontal lobes themselves were not severed; only the white-matter, neuronal-association fibers connecting the lobes to other parts of the brain were cut. (The operation is now known as a lobotomy.) Postoperatively, seven of the first twenty lobotomized patients were pronounced cured, eight seemed improved, and five were unchanged. The operation also appeared to relieve patients suffering from intractable pain. Curiously, the pain itself did not diminish; the individual simply became indifferent to it. Moniz published his results in 1936 and presented them before the Medical Psychology Society in Paris the following year.

Lobotomies never became common in Portugal; Moniz and his associates performed a total of no more than 100 operations before the surgery was banned by the government. The procedure had its proponents, but it had its critics as well, including many psychiatrists who favored less drastic treatments for mental illness.

After World War II lobotomies came into wide use, largely through the efforts of Walter Freeman, an American neurologist, who developed variations of the original operation. Although most lobotomized patients were not completely cured, many were able to live semi-independent lives without institutional care.

Near the end of his life, Moniz was awarded the 1949 Nobel Prize for Physiology or Medicine "for his discovery of the therapeutic value of leucotomy in certain psychoses"; he shared the prize with WALTER R. HESS, who used precise surgical and electrical techniques to investigate functions of the hypothalamus.

Moniz was unable to attend the awards ceremony. In his presentation speech, Herbert Olivecrona of the Karolinska Institute made note of "the great subjective suffering and invalidism" characteristic of severe mental illness. "When it is remembered that other methods of treatment have failed or have been followed by recurrence of the disease," he continued, "it is easy to understand the importance of Moniz' discovery for the problems of psychiatric treatment."

Despite growing protest from psychologists, psychiatrists, and neurologists, the number of lobotomies being performed increased. Exaggerated reports in the press, often supported by Freeman and his colleagues, furthered the cause of the procedure that had been legitimized by the awarding of the Nobel Prize. Between 1949 and 1952 some 5,000 lobotomies were performed annually in the United States. By 1960, however, the use of the procedure was greatly curtailed when it was realized that these operations were leaving in their wake many brain-damaged people. The use of new psychoactive drugs has provided a simple and inexpensive alternative to lobotomies, and the procedure born of desperation has fallen into disrepute.

Moniz was an ambitious man, the last survivor of a long and distinguished line of Portuguese aristocrats. He has been described by some as vain and hungry for the immortality that the development of his drastic surgery, devised when he was in his sixties, would assure. Others have described him as a quiet man who suffered intractable pain from gout all his life. One historian suggested that his hands may have been disfigured by the ulcerating effects of handling radioactive dye during the development of cerebral angiography. Moniz retired to his ancestral home in Avanca in 1945 and died ten years later at the age of eighty-one.

A man of wide interests, Moniz wrote several biographies as well as a history of playing cards, while pursuing an active interest in sculpture and painting. He held membership in the Royal Academy of Science of Lisbon and the American Society of Neurology and was an honorary member of the Royal Society of Medicine in London. In addition to the Nobel Prize, he received honorary degrees from the universities of Bordeaux, Toulouse, and Lyons.

SELECTED WORKS: How I Came to Perform Prefrontal Leucotomy, 1948.

ABOUT: American Journal of Psychiatry April 1956; Dictionary of Scientific Biography, volume 4, 1971; Valenstein, E. S. Great and Desperate Cures, 1986.

MONOD, JACQUES
(February 9, 1910–May 31, 1976)
Nobel Prize for Physiology or Medicine, 1965
(shared with François Jacob and André Lwoff)

JACQUES MONOD

The French biologist Jacques Lucien Monod (mo nō′) was born in Paris, the son of Charlotte Todd (MacGregor) Monod, a Scottish-American, and Lucien Monod, a painter and intellectual whose ancestors were Swiss Protestant Huguenots. The family moved to Cannes when Monod was seven years old, and throughout his life Monod thought of himself as a native of the south of France rather than a Parisian.

In his youth, Monod attended the Lycée de Cannes, where he studied under Dor de la Souchère, a humanities scholar who was later founder and curator of the Antibes Museum. After he was graduated in 1928, Monod enrolled in the Faculté des Sciences of the University of Paris (the Sorbonne), to study natural science. He later credited his father with influencing his choice of career: "He fostered a positivist faith in the joint progress of science and society. It is to him, a reader of Darwin, that I owe my early interest in biology." However, Monod discovered that the biology taught at the university was several decades behind the times, so he set about acquiring a more thorough education. He studied microbiology and microbial nutrition under ANDRÉ LWOFF, with whom he established a lifelong association. He learned biochemical genetics from Boris Ephrussi, and from Louis Rapkine he gained an understanding of the need for a molecular biological approach to the mysteries of the living cell. Monod received a B.S. from the Sorbonne in 1931, and he stayed on for graduate studies.

The following year he became an assistant in the Laboratory of the Evolution of Organic Life at the Sorbonne. He moved to the Sorbonne's zoology laboratory as an assistant in 1934 and a year later, was appointed assistant professor of zoology. In the summer he joined a natural history expedition to Greenland that sailed from France aboard the ship *Pourquoi Pas?* Monod was planning a second expedition to Greenland two years later aboard the same ship, but he received a Rockefeller Fellowship

and embarked for the United States with Ephrussi instead. That summer the *Pourquoi Pas?* and all hands aboard her were lost at sea.

In the United States during 1936 and 1937, Monod and Ephrussi studied the genetics of the fruit fly (*Drosophila melanogaster*) under THOMAS HUNT MORGAN at the California Institute of Technology. Monod was impressed with the high quality of research and the free exchange of ideas and experimental results by members of Morgan's department, a situation in sharp contrast to the more rigid academic climate of the Sorbonne. Returning to Paris, Monod worked for a few months in Ephrussi's laboratory at the Institute of Physicochemical Biology on the biochemical genetics of the fruit fly, after which he resumed his responsibilities at the Sorbonne.

While conducting experiments involving the colon bacillus (*Escherichia coli*), Monod discovered that cellular energy is primarily used for biosynthetic processes rather than for maintenance of cellular structures. He observed two distinct growth curves in colonies of *E. coli* when the organism was given two different sugars in its nutrient. Lwoff suggested that Monod was observing enzyme adaptation, in which first one enzyme is activated and synthesized while the second is repressed and then the second enzyme is activated and synthesized. "From this very day of December 1940, all my scientific activity has been drawn to the study of enzymatic adaptation," Monod later wrote.

The following year Monod received a Ph.D. from the Sorbonne, with a dissertation based on this research, but the director of the laboratory was not interested in supporting his work, and Monod continued his investigations at the Pasteur Institute while serving in the French Resistance. He was captured by the Gestapo, managed to escape, and after the liberation of Paris, received several military honors. As a member of the staff of General de Lattre de Tassigny, he met American medical officers who shared their scientific journals with him. He came across two papers that described results of experiments done in the United States during the war. One—by MAX DELBRÜCK and SALVADOR LURIA—revealed that bacteria undergo spontaneous genetic mutations. "I think I have never read a scientific article with such enthusiasm," Monod later recalled; "for me, bacterial genetics was established." The other paper identified deoxyribonucleic acid (DNA) as the transforming principle. These new discoveries would form the basis of his later research in DNA and RNA.

After the liberation of Paris, Monod managed to locate his family and then returned briefly to the Sorbonne, where he worked alone in the zoology laboratory. In 1945 André Lwoff gave him a position as laboratory chief in the department of microbic physiology at the Pasteur Institute, one of the teaching and research units within the National Center for Scientific Research. Over the next two decades, he and his colleagues studied the molecular biology of bacterial genetics and bacterial cell enzymology. He was named director of the Cell Biochemistry Department in 1954.

Monod and the other researchers at the Pasteur Institute developed an experimental system for analyzing the biochemical genetics of the cell. They discovered a mutant strain of *E. coli* that contains beta-galactosidase, an adaptive enzyme that is activated by the presence of lactose in the nutrient solution and causes lactose to break up into its component sugars. Monod's team then sought to determine what triggers the cell to activate a specific enzymatic system such as this one. They postulated two theories: either the enzyme is inhibited in its surroundings, and induction (activation) involves freeing that inhibition; or the gene is inhibited, and induction involves deinhibition of the gene, which directs the synthesis of a specific enzyme. Monod favored the latter explanation.

Appointed director of the Department of Cellular Biology at the Pasteur Institute in 1953, Monod began research with FRANÇOIS JACOB later in the decade in an association that FRAN-

CIS CRICK would call the "great collaboration." Monod and Jacob postulated and proved the existence of messenger RNA, the RNA molecule that carries genetic instructions from DNA in the nucleus of the cell to the cytoplasm. Living cells contain three types of RNA: messenger, transfer (soluble), and ribosomal. Messenger RNA carries the genetic code to ribosomes in the cytoplasm. Transfer RNA picks up amino acids in the cytoplasm and carries them to the ribosomes, after which the three types of RNA cooperate in the synthesis of proteins and enzymes at the ribosomal sites.

The work of Monod and Jacob on DNA demonstrated that it is organized into sets of genes, which they called operons. An operon consists of a structural gene, which directs and controls the synthesis of a specific cellular enzyme, and a regulatory, or operator, gene. Normally, the structural gene is inhibited, or repressed, by the regulatory gene. When enzymes are activated, the regulatory gene is repressed by a cellular protein called the repressor protein, thereby freeing the structural gene to synthesize messenger RNA. This system of biochemical genetics allows the cell to adapt to new conditions in its environment (for example, a different sugar in its supply of nutrients). Monod and his colleagues also demonstrated that similar systems are present in bacteriophages, the viruses that infect bacterial cells.

Monod, Jacob, and Lwoff shared the 1965 Nobel Prize for Physiology or Medicine "for their discoveries concerning genetic control of enzyme and virus synthesis." Their work, said Sven Gard of the Karolinska Institute in his presentation speech, "has opened up a field of research which in the truest sense of the word can be described as molecular biology."

In 1959 Monod had been appointed full professor of the chemistry of metabolism at the Sorbonne, and in 1967 he became a professor at the Collège de France. His book *Chance and Necessity,* which illuminates the nature of cellular biochemical processes and expresses the view that the origin of life and the process of evolution are the result of chance, was published in 1971. That same year Monod became director of the Pasteur Institute and gave up his research work to reorganize and modernize the institute's research facilities.

In 1938 Monod married Odette Bruhl, an archaeologist and orientalist who later became curator of the Guimet Museum in Paris; they had twin sons. A passionate lover of music who once seriously considered pursuing a conducting career, Monod played the cello in a quartet and directed a Bach choir for many years. Athletic as well as musical, he enjoyed mountain climbing in the Alps and sailing.

After the death of his wife in 1972, Monod fell ill. Four years later, knowing that death was imminent, he returned to the south of France. He spent his last days in Cannes and died at the age of sixty-six. His last words were, "Je cherche à comprendre" (I am trying to understand).

"[Monod] commanded attention by his intelligence, his clarity, his incisiveness, and by the obvious breadth and depth of his interest," FRANCIS CRICK said. "Never lacking in courage, he combined a debonair manner and an impish sense of humor with a deep moral commitment to any issue he regarded as fundamental." According to Lwoff, Monod was "an excellent experimentalist. Rigor and precision were served by an implacable deductive logic. Critical sense never hindered imagination nor audacity."

Monod received many honors throughout his lifetime, including the Legion of Honor and the Bronze Star Medal from the French government for his military service; the Montyon Prize for Physiology (1955); and the Charles Leopold Mayer Prize of the French Academy of Sciences (1962). He was awarded honorary doctorates by two universities: Chicago and Rockefeller.

SELECTED WORKS: Adaptation in Microorganisms, 1953, with Melvin Cohn; Enzymes, 1956; From Biology to Ethics, 1969; Selected Papers in Molecular Biology, 1978.

ABOUT: Biographical Memoirs of Fellows of the Royal Society, volume 23, 1977; Chiari, J. The Necessity of Being, 1973; Current Biography July 1971; Lwoff, A., and Ullman, A. (eds.) Origins of Molecular Biology, 1979.

MONTALE, EUGENIO

(October 12, 1896–September 12, 1981)
Nobel Prize for Literature, 1975

The Italian poet and critic Eugenio Montale (mōn tä′ lē) was born in Genoa, the youngest of five children of Domenico Montale and Giuseppina (Ricci) Montale. Until the age of thirty, Montale spent his summers at the family villa on the Ligurian Riviera, whose rugged coastline supplied much of the imagery that pervades his poetry.

When the boy was fourteen years of age, his formal education was cut short by ill health, and he spent his teenage years reading the Italian classics, French fiction, and the works of Arthur Schopenhauer, Benedetto Croce, and HENRI BERGSON. He was expected to succeed his father in the family's import business, but the world of commerce did not appeal to the young man. As he entered adulthood, Montale felt unprepared for any practical career. For a time he thought of becoming an opera singer but gave up the idea, along with his musical studies, in his late teens.

With Italy's entry into World War I in 1917, Montale was drafted and saw action as an infantry officer on the Austrian front. After his discharge two years later, he returned to Genoa and began his literary career in earnest, helping to found a short-lived literary magazine in 1922. During this time his work also began to appear in other magazines and in newspapers. The publication in 1925 of his essay on the prominent Italian novelist Italo Svevo attracted national attention and initiated a correspondence between the two writers that lasted until Svevo's death four years later.

The appearance in 1925 of *Ossi di seppia* (*Bones of the Cuttlefish*), Montale's first collection of poetry, established his reputation as a poet. At that time, Italian poetry was dominated by the grandiose style of Gabriele d'Annunzio. In contrast, Montale's work was devoid of rhetorical excess, displaying a quiet concern for precision and exactness of expression and an imagery that is often startling, unconventional, and concrete. "My desire was to be naked and essential," he wrote in one poem; in another he declared his intention "to know at once variation and unity: / and thus to rid myself of all waste." Critics throughout Italy praised *Bones of the Cuttlefish* as an accomplished, original body of work and as an important departure from prevailing literary conventions.

In Florence, where Montale moved in 1927, he discovered "culture, ideas, tradition, humanism." There he worked briefly in a publishing house before being appointed director of the prestigious Gabinetto Vieusseux research library in 1928, a post he held for ten years. Although the job paid poorly, Montale found the work congenial and enjoyed having the library's large collection of contemporary literature at his disposal. During these years his poems and critical essays appeared regularly in literary journals.

In the early 1930s Montale had an affair with a beautiful foreign woman, who ultimately abandoned him; later in the decade, he met Drusilla Tanzi, with whom he lived for a number of years before they married in the 1950s.

EUGENIO MONTALE

The couple had no children. Drusilla Montale died in 1963.

Montale was dismissed from his library directorship in 1938 for refusing to join the Fascist party. His second volume of poems, *Le occasioni* (The Occasions), which appeared in 1939, expressed attitudes at odds with fascism, although it was not explicitly political in aim or content. For the most part, these poems examine personal emotions, primarily love, seen in contrast with the fateful public events that were happening in Europe on the eve of World War II.

As Mussolini strengthened his grip on Italy, Montale withdrew from public life. He used this time of inner exile to study the great literature of the Western world and to translate such writers as Shakespeare, Herman Melville, EUGENE O'NEILL, T. S. ELIOT, and WILLIAM BUTLER YEATS into Italian. During the early years of World War II, he wrote a brief series of intensely lyrical poems, collected under the title *Finisterre* and published in neutral Switzerland in 1943.

After the war Montale moved to Milan, where he served as literary editor, music critic, and journalist-at-large for one of Italy's leading newspapers, *Corriere della sera* (The Evening Courier). His third major collection, *La bufera e altro* (*The Storm and Other Poems*), appeared in 1956; many critics consider it his finest and most representative work. The main themes, as throughout Montale's poetry, are exile, dislocation, isolation, and identity. Montale's later volumes, including *Satura, 1962–1970* (Satires, 1971), *Diario del '71 e del '72* (Diary of 1971 and of 1972, 1973), and *Quaderno di quattro anni* (1977, literally "a notebook of four years," but translated as *It Depends: A Poet's Notebook*), are more personal, colloquial, and humorous than their predecessors.

Montale was awarded the 1975 Nobel Prize for Literature "for his distinctive poetry which, with great artistic sensitivity, has interpreted human values under the sign of an outlook on life with no illusions." Although acknowledging Montale's fundamental pessimism, Anders Österling of the Swedish Academy noted in his presentation speech that the poet's "resignation does contain a spark of confidence in life's instinct to go on, to overcome the accumulated obstacles." The title of Montale's Nobel lecture—"Is Poetry Still Possible?"—underscored his pessimistic outlook. Yet in questioning the destiny of the arts, Montale affirmed their survival throughout recorded history.

In his poetry, critics have noted, Montale answers despair not by capitulating but by continuing his search. In 1975 Wallace Craft in *Books Abroad* wrote that "Montale's desire to escape a sense of homelessness and alienation . . . will, in truth, never be satisfied, for man is permitted neither to recover his past nor to understand fully the roots of his existence." What Montale sought was not literal truth but imaginative truth.

Montale is often grouped with his contemporaries Giuseppe Ungaretti and SALVATORE QUASIMODO as a cofounder of the hermetic school of poetry in Italy, one of whose characteristics is deliberate obscurity. A number of critics have also pointed out his affinities with T. S. Eliot. Admitting that Montale was not an "easy" poet, the English novelist and critic Rebecca West felt that he belonged to no school. "His difficult poetry," she wrote, "does not offer any sure solutions to the existential and spiritual problems with which it deals, but rather finds its abiding power in . . . its commitment to the importance of the individual, to what Montale has called 'daily decency.' "

Montale believed it is the poet's duty to make the poem "the most solid, unique, and precise correlative of his own inner experience." The critic Vinio Rossi has asserted that "Montale owes his stature in Italian poetry mainly to his success in dusting off old rhythmic and imagistic models and recasting them with modern sensibility. He returns us to an older, pristine tradition when language and its literary forms were fresh and vibrant." Throughout his career Montale resisted the temptation to write "beautiful" poetry. The music of his verse is closer to contemporary colloquial Italian speech than to "literary" Italian. Of his method of composition Montale once remarked, with characteristic terseness and understatement, "I do not go in search of poetry. I wait for poetry to visit me."

In addition to poetry, Montale published collections of essays. In 1967 he became a member-for-life of the Italian Senate, a largely ceremonial body. He won several literary prizes in Italy and received honorary degrees from the universities of Milan and Rome and from Cambridge University.

Montale died quietly in Milan on September 12, 1981.

ADDITIONAL WORKS IN ENGLISH TRANSLATION: Poems From Eugenio Montale, 1959; Poesie/Poems, 1964; Selected Poems by Eugenio Montale, 1965; Selected Poems, 1966; Selected Poems of Eugenio Montale, 1969; Provisional Conclusions, 1970; Xenia, 1970; The Butterfly of Dinard, 1971; Mottetti, 1973; New Poems, 1976; Poet in Our Time, 1976; The Second Life of Art: Selected Essays, 1982; Otherwise: Last and First Poems of Eugenio Montale, 1984.

ABOUT: Almansi, G., and Merry, B. Eugenio Montale: The Private Language of Poetry, 1977; Becker, J. Eugenio Montale, 1986; Books Abroad Winter 1975; Cambon, G. Eugenio Montale, 1972; Cambon, G. Eugenio Montale's Poetry: A Dream in Reason's Presence, 1982; Cary, J. Three Modern Italian Poets: Saba, Ungaretti, Montale, 1969; Current Biography April 1976; Huffman, C. Montale and the Occasions of Poetry, 1983; Pipa, A. Montale and Dante, 1968; Singh, G. Eugenio Montale: A Critical Study, 1973; West, R. Eugenio Montale: Poet on the Edge, 1981.

MOORE, STANFORD
(September 4, 1913–August 23, 1982)
Nobel Prize for Chemistry, 1972
(shared with Christian Anfinsen and
   William H. Stein)

The American biochemist Stanford Moore was born in Chicago, Illinois, to John Howard Moore and the former Ruth Fowler. Shortly after his birth the family moved to Nashville, Tennessee, where his father taught law at Vanderbilt University. Raised in an intellectually stimulating atmosphere, Moore developed an interest in chemistry that was encouraged by a high school science teacher. Upon entering Vanderbilt in 1931, he wavered between chemistry and aeronautical engineering but was drawn to organic chemistry after studying molecular structure under Arthur Ingersoll.

After receiving his B.A. summa cum laude

STANFORD MOORE

in 1935, Moore was awarded a Wisconsin Alumni Research Foundation Fellowship for graduate study at the University of Wisconsin. There he wrote his thesis under the direction of Karl Paul Link, who had recently worked in Europe with FRITZ PREGL on microanalytical techniques for determining the atomic structure of organic compounds. For a dissertation on the characterization of carbohydrates as benzimidazole derivatives, Moore received his Ph.D. in 1938.

So outstanding was Moore's graduate work that Link recommended him to the German chemist Max Bergmann, who had recently arrived in the United States to join the Rockefeller Institute for Medical Research (now Rockefeller University) in New York City. Bergmann, a former research associate of EMIL FISCHER, was regarded as one of the foremost investigators of protein chemistry. At the time, little was known about the structure of these extremely large organic molecules. According to the prevailing view, proposed by Fischer in 1908, proteins consisted of strings of amino acids linked into polypeptide chains. At Bergmann's invitation, Moore joined the Rockefeller Institute in 1939 and began working on methods for determining the amino acid composition of proteins. One of his collaborators on this project was the American biochemist WILLIAM H. STEIN.

When the United States entered World War II in 1941, Moore took a leave of absence from the Rockefeller Institute to serve as a junior administrative officer for the United States Office of Scientific Research and Development. Later in the war he was assigned to the Armed Forces Operational Research Section in Hawaii.

When Moore returned to civilian life at the end of the war in 1945, Bergmann had died, and his own future at the Rockefeller Institute appeared uncertain. However, the director of the institute, HERBERT S. GASSER, invited Moore and Stein to resume their earlier investigations into quantitative amino acid analysis. Equipped with their own laboratory facilities, the two scientists set to work. During the war years, a number of advances had been made in protein separation and purification, notably the first biochemical application of paper chromatography (the separation of complex mixtures by percolation through an absorbing medium) by the English researchers ARCHER MARTIN and RICHARD SYNGE. Martin and Synge had found that, after breaking a polypeptide chain into its component amino acids, they could sort out the amino acids by observing the characteristic rates at which they moved through special filter paper. At the same time, the British chemist FREDERICK SANGER had begun using paper chromatography to clarify the types and proportions of amino acids present in insulin.

Although these new applications of paper chromatography furnished useful data, Moore and Stein sought a separation technique that would yield greater amounts of each amino acid. The method they chose was column chromatography, in which the solution to be analyzed is poured into a tube packed with a substance that absorbs the different molecules at differing rates. In this way, the results can be observed as distinct bands in the absorbent packing. Passing amino acid solutions through columns packed with potato starch, Moore and Stein obtained their first successful results in 1948. The process took almost two weeks, however, and they sought a more efficient technique.

In the early 1950s Moore and Stein turned to ion-exchange chromatography, in which ion-exchange resins sort out molecules according to their electrical charge and size. The method not only speeded up the analytical process but produced sharper separations than the starch-column technique. Combining both methods, Moore and Stein analyzed the amino acids present in a variety of proteins.

In 1950 Moore interrupted this work to spend six months at the Free University of Brussels, where he held the Francqui Chair, followed by another six months in England working with Sanger at Cambridge University. After re-turning to the Rockefeller Institute, Moore, again in collaboration with Stein, turned most of his attention to ribonuclease, an enzyme, or organic catalyst, that breaks down ribonucleic acid (RNA). During the 1930s, the American chemists JAMES B. SUMNER and JOHN H. NORTHROP had established conclusively that enzymes are proteins. Very little was known about their structure, however, and Moore and Stein set out to determine the relationship between the structure and function of ribonuclease.

Using samples supplied by the Chicago meat-packing firm of Armour, Inc., Moore, Stein, and their colleagues further purified bovine ribonuclease through the ion-exchange method. From this highly purified enzyme preparation, they broke the polypeptide chain into pieces, separated the pieces by chromatography, and identified the amino acids present in each one. The process became even more efficient when in 1958 Moore, Stein, and Darrel Spackman developed automatic techniques for amino acid analysis that subsequently became standard tools in protein biochemistry.

By 1960 the team had delineated the complete amino acid sequence of ribonuclease. It was the second protein sequence ever to be determined and the first enzyme sequence. From these results Moore and Stein were able to locate and determine the components of the active center of ribonuclease, where RNA is broken down. After spending 1968 as a visiting professor of health sciences at Vanderbilt University School of Medicine, Moore returned to the Rockefeller Institute, where he and Stein supervised analytical work on deoxyribonuclease, the enzyme that breaks down deoxyribonucleic acid.

Moore and Stein shared half of the 1972 Nobel Prize for Chemistry "for their contribution to the understanding of the connection between chemical structure and catalytic activity of the active center of the ribonuclease molecule." The other half of the prize was awarded to CHRISTIAN ANFINSEN for related work. In his presentation speech, Bo G. Malmström of the Royal Swedish Academy of Sciences pointed out that an understanding of an enzyme's catalytic activity depends on locating its active site. "Through these investigations," he said, "Moore and Stein were able to provide a detailed picture of the active site of ribonuclease long before the three-dimensional structure of the enzyme had been determined." In their Nobel lecture Moore and Stein stated that "very few macromolecules can be discussed in the detail with which ribonuclease or hemoglobin can be defined. Such knowledge of structure-function relationships is basic to the rational approach to the intricate synergisms of living systems."

After receiving the prize Moore continued enzyme research at the Rockefeller Institute. Suffering from amyotrophic lateral sclerosis, a degenerative disease of the muscles and nerves, he took his life at his home in New York City on August 23, 1982, at the age of sixty-eight.

A tall, thin man who never married, Moore was firmly committed to biological research and the benefits it offered. "Man's understanding of man," he remarked at the time the Nobel Prize was bestowed on him, "is an even higher priority of research than man's understanding of the universe."

In addition to the Nobel Prize, Moore and Stein shared the Award in Chromatography and Electrophoresis (1964) and the Theodore William Richards Medal of the American Chemical Society (1972). Moore was awarded honorary degrees from the universities of Brussels and Paris. He held membership in the American Association for the Advancement of Science, the National Academy of Sciences, the American Chemical Society, the American Society of Biological Chemistry, and the American Academy of Arts and Sciences.

ABOUT: New York Times October 21, 1972; August 24, 1982; Science November 3, 1972.

MORGAN, THOMAS HUNT
(September 25, 1866–December 4, 1945)
Nobel Prize for Physiology or Medicine, 1933

The American zoologist and geneticist Thomas Hunt Morgan was born in Lexington, Kentucky, the elder son and first of three children of Charlton Hunt Morgan, a diplomat, and the former Ellen Key Howard, the granddaughter of Francis Scott Key, composer of the American national anthem. As a boy, Morgan's enthusiasm for natural history and science led him to explore the countryside and collect birds and fossils during summer vacations. Later he worked for two summers in the mountains of Kentucky with the United States Geological Survey, doing geological and biological field surveys.

In 1886 he received a B.S. from the State College (now the University) of Kentucky. Morgan was particularly interested in the ev-

olution of species. According to the prevailing theory, Charles Darwin's concept of natural selection, there is a range of variability for every trait within a population. Generation by generation, through inheritance within the population, the demands and opportunities presented by the environment tend to ensure the spread of traits that enable individual members of a species to survive. At the time Morgan completed his undergraduate work, virtually nothing was known about the actual mechanism of inheritance, and the accepted procedure for studying evolution and heredity was to examine the morphology and physiology (the physical shape and functions) of individuals of different species, in an effort to deduce the basis of their similarities and differences. The study of embryonic development was an important part of such study.

Accordingly, Morgan studied morphology and physiology when he entered the Johns Hopkins University in 1887. Three years later he obtained his Ph.D. there for research on the embryology of sea spiders. When he became an associate professor of biology at Bryn Mawr College in 1891, he was familiar with comparative, descriptive methods. Like Darwin's theory, however, such methods furnish no explanation for the transmission of inherited traits. Morgan therefore turned to an experimental approach, in the hope that more testable and rigorous data might eventually produce an answer. In 1897, while studying the capacity of certain animals to regenerate lost body parts—an ability that seemed clearly connected to survival success—he published the first of his lifelong series of articles on this topic. In his first major book, *Regeneration* (1901), he emphasized the relationship between the events of regeneration and early embryonic development. Morgan was appointed professor of experimental zoology at Columbia University in 1904. His early work there continued to focus on experimental embryology.

Morgan's interest in the emerging discipline of genetics was stimulated by the rediscovery in 1900 of the 1866 research by Gregor Mendel on inheritance in pea plants. Mendel's research showed that traits are inherited in strict mathematical ratios, which suggested that each trait was a discrete, independent entity. In 1902 the American biologist William S. Sutton had theorized that Mendel's hypothetical "factors," the units of heredity now called genes, are located in or on the cell-nucleus structures called chromosomes. More direct proof of this chromosomal theory of heredity was needed,

THOMAS HUNT MORGAN

covered four such linkage groups of genes in the fruit fly, which corresponded with its four chromosome pairs.

Early in 1912 two Columbia undergraduates, Alfred H. Sturtevant and Calvin B. Bridges, joined the team of researchers in Morgan's "fly room," followed two years later by a graduate student, HERMANN J. MULLER. To their surprise, Morgan and his colleagues observed that genes located on the same chromosome were inherited together less often than they could predict. Most cells in the body have two of each type of chromosome, and Morgan suspected that chromosomes in a pair could break and recombine, thus allowing them to exchange genes. This idea was consistent with microscopic evidence of intertwining chromosomes that had been presented in 1909 by a Belgian researcher, F. A. Janssens, who believed that a pair of chromosomes may occasionally exchange pieces.

The greater the distance between two genes on a chromosome, Morgan reasoned, the more likely it was that a break could occur. If so, the genes would not be inherited together. Conversely, genes that were close together on a chromosome would be less likely to be separated. By 1911 Sturtevant realized that the degree of linkage of two genes on a chromosome provides a measure of the linear distance between them. Using this principle, Morgan and his colleagues made "maps" showing the relative positions of the genes on the fruit fly's chromosomes. The concept that genes are located in a specific linear arrangement on a chromosome, and further, that the basis of linkage is the proximity of two genes on a chromosome, represented a major advance in genetic theory. In 1915 Morgan, Bridges, Sturtevant, and Muller reported their findings in *The Mechanism of Mendelian Heredity,* in which they demonstrated that heredity follows predictable rules and can be treated in a quantitative, rigorous manner.

In 1928 Morgan left Columbia to help establish a division of biology at the California Institute of Technology (Caltech) in Pasadena. He brought several of his former students and associates with him, and he recruited an outstanding staff. The work conducted by Morgan's group and other researchers at Pasadena earned the institute a reputation for distinguished work in experimental biology, even after Morgan turned to other research topics, chiefly embryology.

Morgan received the 1933 Nobel Prize for Physiology or Medicine "for his discoveries concerning the role played by the chromosome

however. Morgan was skeptical of the theory, believing instead that the chromosomes were not carriers of inheritance but simply products of an early stage of development. He also was skeptical of the "gradual change" described by Darwin, preferring the theory of the Dutch botanist Hugo de Vries, who suggested that new species result from mutations.

In 1908 Morgan began genetic studies on the fruit fly, *Drosophila melanogaster,* a tiny organism whose characteristics are ideally suited to genetics research. The fly has only four chromosomes and starts breeding about two weeks after birth; it can easily be studied during its three-month lifetime. As he and his colleagues at Columbia bred and studied millions of *Drosophila,* Morgan came to believe that chromosomes were in fact directly involved in heredity.

The results of certain breeding experiments conducted by Morgan appeared to violate Mendel's law of independent assortment. According to this law, each organism possesses genes that control a given trait, and the inheritance of one trait, such as the animal's sex, is independent of the inheritance of another trait, such as eye color. Morgan's team found that certain traits seemed to be linked; that is, they appeared together in offspring more frequently than Mendel's statistics predicted. A mutant trait for white eye color, for example, was almost always observed only in male flies, a phenomenon that Morgan called sex linkage. This linking tendency suggested to Morgan that the genes might be located close together on the same chromosome. Morgan's team disin heredity." In his Nobel lecture Morgan declared that the most important contribution of genetics to medicine was an intellectual one. "The whole subject of human heredity in the past has been so vague and tainted by myths and superstition that a scientific understanding of the subject is an achievement of the first order," he said. He went on to predict that the phenomenon of linkage might someday be helpful in the diagnosis of genetic diseases.

After receiving the Nobel Prize, Morgan continued his administrative duties at Caltech while conducting research on such wide-ranging topics as biological regeneration, inheritance in pigeons, secondary sexual characteristics of the salamander, and cross-strains of deer mice.

Although considered to be tightfisted with his institutional funds, Morgan showed great personal generosity and often quietly financed fellowships for deserving students out of his own pocket.

In 1904 Morgan married Lillian Vaughan Sampson, a cytologist who had been one of his students at Bryn Mawr; they had four children. In 1941 Morgan became emeritus professor of biology in residence at Caltech. He died four years later in Pasadena of a ruptured stomach artery.

Morgan's many honors included the Darwin Medal (1924) and Copley Medal of the Royal Society of London (1939). He held membership in the Royal Society of London, the National Academy of Sciences, the American Association for the Advancement of Science, the American Philosophical Society, the Genetics Society of America, and the American Society of Naturalists.

SELECTED WORKS: Early Papers (4 vols.) 1903–1915; Evolution and Adaptation, 1903; Experimental Zoology, 1907; Heredity and Sex, 1913; A Critique of the Theory of Evolution, 1916; The Physical Basis of Heredity, 1919; Some Possible Bearings of Genetics on Pathology, 1922; Human Inheritance, 1924; Experimental Embryology, 1927; What Is Darwinism? 1929; The Scientific Basis of Evolution, 1932; Embryology and Genetics, 1934.

ABOUT: Allen, G. E. Thomas Hunt Morgan, 1978; Biographical Memoirs of the National Academy of Sciences, volume 33, 1959; Dictionary of Scientific Biography, volume 9, 1974; Oleson, A., and Voss, J. (eds.) The Organization of Knowledge, 1979; Shine, I., and Wrobel, S. Thomas Hunt Morgan: Pioneer of Genetics, 1976; Sturtevant, A. H. A History of Genetics, 1965; Teas, H. J. (ed.) Genetics and Developmental Biology, 1969.

MÖSSBAUER, RUDOLF L.

(January 31, 1929–   )
Nobel Prize for Physics, 1961
(shared with Robert Hofstadter)

The German physicist Rudolf Ludwig Mössbauer (mûs′ bou ər) was born in Munich, one of two children and the only son of Ludwig Mössbauer, a phototechnician, and the former Erna Ernst. After receiving his early education in the local schools, he attended the Munich-Pasing Oberschule (nonclassical high school) and graduated in 1948. For the next few months he worked at an optical firm before entering the Munich Technical University, earning a B.S. in 1952, an M.S. in 1955, and a Ph.D. in 1958. During the academic year 1953–1954 he served as an instructor in mathematics at the same institution. From 1955 to 1957 he was a research assistant at the Physics Institute of the Max Planck Institute for Medical Research in Heidelberg, and in 1958 Mössbauer became a research fellow at the Munich Technical University.

Mössbauer's doctoral studies, although carried out principally at the Max Planck Institute, were guided by his mentor in Munich, Heinz Maier-Leibnitz. They concerned the emission and absorption of gamma rays by atomic nuclei. Gamma rays are the most energetic form of electromagnetic radiation, more powerful even than X rays; they are emitted by unstable (radioactive) atomic nuclei.

Since the 1850s it had been known that some gases, liquids, and solids (such as the mineral fluorite) absorb electromagnetic radiation (typically visible light) and immediately reradiate it, a phenomenon called fluorescence. In the special case known as resonance fluorescence, both the absorbed and the reemitted radiation have the same energy, wavelength, and frequency. Important information about atomic structure has been obtained from studies that utilize the analogous phenomenon of X-ray fluorescence, in which a material excited by the absorption of X rays emits X rays of identical wavelength and frequency. X-ray fluorescence was demonstrated and quantified between 1915 and 1925 by CHARLES G. BARKLA and KAI SIEGBAHN.

Fluorescent absorption occurs only if the energy of the exciting photon (the particle of electromagnetic radiation) equals that needed to excite an atom or its nucleus. The apparent energy of a photon, however, depends on the motion of the atom that absorbs or emits it: if the atom and the photon are approaching head-on, the energy is increased; and if the

RUDOLF L. MÖSSBAUER

atom is moving away from the photon, the energy is decreased. This effect introduces a complication, because the emission or absorption itself imparts motion to the atom.

The process of photon emission or absorption must conserve both energy and momentum; that is, the total energy and momentum of the photon and the atom taken together must be the same after the event as they were before. It follows that the atom must recoil when it emits a photon. The energy that goes into the atomic recoil is subtracted from that available to the photon, which therefore has a slightly lower energy than it otherwise would have.

For photons of visible light, which have comparatively little energy and momentum, the effect of atomic recoil is negligible. Gamma-ray photons, on the other hand, have energies from 10,000 to a million times greater than those of visible light, and the recoil is important. When an atomic nucleus emits a photon, the resulting backward movement of the nucleus causes a measurable decrease in the energy of the photon. As a result, the emitted photon does not have the same energy (or wavelength or frequency) as a photon that can be absorbed by the same species of nucleus. For this reason, resonance fluorescence—in which the absorbed and emitted photons must be equal in energy—is not ordinarily observed with gamma rays.

Mössbauer found a way to demonstrate gamma-ray resonance fluorescence. He used

as his source of gamma rays atoms of a radioactive isotope of the metal iridium. The iridium was in the form of a crystalline solid, so that both the emitting and the absorbing atoms were held fast in crystals. When he cooled the crystals with liquid nitrogen, Mössbauer was surprised to find that fluorescence increased markedly. His investigation of this phenomenon revealed that the individual nuclei emitting or absorbing the gamma rays transferred the interaction momentum directly to the surrounding crystal. Because the crystal is far more massive than an individual nucleus, the emitted and absorbed gamma-ray photons showed no frequency shift. This phenomenon, which Mössbauer described as a "recoilless nuclear resonance absorption of gamma-ray radiation," is now called the Mössbauer effect. As a solid-body effect, it is dependent on the crystalline structure of the substance, on the temperature, and even on the presence of minute amounts of impurity. Mössbauer showed that the suppression of nuclear recoil by the Mössbauer effect allowed the generation of gamma rays with wavelengths invariable to one part in 1 billion (10^9); other workers have improved that to an invariability of one part in 100 trillion (10^{14}).

Initially, Mössbauer's results, published in 1958, were ignored, and then doubted. Within a year, however, recognizing the potential importance of the Mössbauer effect, other scientists repeated his experiments and confirmed the results. The fact that recoilless nuclear resonance absorption makes it possible to measure extraordinarily small energy differences between two systems (just large enough to hinder resonance fluorescence) gives the method a broad range of important applications. With their remarkably constant wavelengths and frequencies, fluorescence gamma rays are used as extremely precise measuring tools for gauging the effect of such natural forces as gravity, electricity, and magnetism on infinitesimal particles.

One of the first applications of the Mössbauer effect took place in 1959, when R. V. Pound and G. A. Rebka Jr. of Harvard University used it to confirm ALBERT EINSTEIN's prediction that a gravitational field would change the frequency of electromagnetic radiation. This support for Einstein's general theory of relativity took the form of a measurable change in the frequency of gamma-ray photons produced by the difference in gravity between the top and the bottom of a 70-foot tower. Use of the Mössbauer effect also provides information about the magnetic and electrical properties of nuclei and about the electrons that surround them. Applications of the effect abound in fields as diverse as archaeology, chemical catalysis, molecular structure, valency, solid-state science, atomic physics, and biological polymers.

Mössbauer received half of the 1961 Nobel Prize for Physics "for his researches concerning the resonance absorption of gamma radiation and his discovery in this connection of the effect which bears his name." By Mössbauer's discovery, said Ivar Waller of the Royal Swedish Academy of Sciences in his presentation speech, "it has become possible to examine precisely, numerous important phenomena formerly beyond or at the limit of attainable accuracy of measurement."

Mössbauer was to have been appointed a full professor at the Munich Technical University but, frustrated by what he regarded as the bureaucratic and authoritarian organization of German universities, he refused the promotion and took a leave of absence from Heidelberg in 1960 to become a research fellow at the California Institute of Technology, where he was appointed a professor the following year. In 1964, however, Mössbauer returned to Germany as professor of physics at the Munich Technical University in a department modeled on those found in American universities. Some scientists facetiously referred to this change in German academic organization as "the second Mössbauer effect." From 1972 to 1977 Mössbauer directed the Laue-Langevin Institute in Grenoble, France.

Since 1957, Mössbauer has been married to the former Elisabeth Pritz, a fashion designer, with whom he has a son and two daughters. His leisure time pursuits include playing the piano, bicycling, and photography.

Mössbauer is a member of the American, European, and West German physical societies; the Indian Academy of Sciences; and the American Academy of Arts and Sciences. He holds honorary doctorates from Oxford University and from the universities of Leicester and Grenoble. In addition to the Nobel Prize, he has received the Science Award of the Research Corporation of America (1960), the Röntgen Prize of the University of Giessen (1961), and the Elliott Cresson Medal of the Franklin Institute (1961).

ABOUT: Current Biography May 1962; Frauenfelder, H. (ed.) The Mössbauer Effect, 1962; Science November 10, 1961.

MOTHER TERESA
See TERESA, MOTHER

MOTT, JOHN
(May 25, 1865–January 31, 1955)
Nobel Prize for Peace, 1946
(shared with Emily Greene Balch)

John Raleigh Mott, American leader of the Young Men's Christian Association (YMCA), was born in Livingston Manor, New York. He was the third child and only son of John Stitt Mott and the former Elmira Dodge. When Mott was two years old, the family moved to Postville in northeast Iowa, where his father became a prosperous lumber and hardware merchant and was elected the town's first mayor. Surrounded by books, Mott grew up in an atmosphere of devout Methodism and declared his conversion when he was thirteen.

At the age of sixteen, Mott entered Upper Iowa University, a small Methodist preparatory college in Fayette. He was a keen student of history and literature and won awards as an orator and debater. Planning to make his career in law and politics, he transferred to Cornell University as a sophomore in 1885. There he participated actively in the YMCA. In 1886 he heard a lecture by the English cricketer and evangelist J. Kynaston Studd. "Seekest thou great things for thyself?" Studd asked the audience. "Seek them not. Seek ye first the kingdom of God."

Mott later credited these words with changing his life. After meeting Studd the next day, he wrote to his parents and announced his intention to work on behalf of the Christian student cause. Elected president of the Cornell YMCA that year, he used his speaking and organizing abilities to triple the chapter's membership and raise funds to construct a YMCA building on campus. He graduated in 1888 with a B.A. in history, political science, and philosophy.

That fall Mott became national secretary of the Intercollegiate Committee of the YMCA, a post he held for the next twenty-seven years. Traveling throughout the United States and Canada, he recruited students and promoted YMCA activities among colleges. He also assumed responsibility for the foundering Student Volunteer Movement for Foreign Missions. Merging its activities with YMCA programs, Mott reorganized the group's leadership and became its chairman. Working through college campuses, the organization was soon sending thousands of American and Ca-

JOHN MOTT

nadian volunteers to spread the Christian message to students around the world.

Mott married Leila Ada White, an English teacher, in 1891; they had four children. The year of his marriage, Mott made his first trip overseas, visiting England to study the Christian youth movement. In the next four years, he made great strides for the YMCA both in the United States and in Europe. Membership in YMCA college chapters doubled, and under Mott's leadership, British and Swedish Christians joined to form the World's Student Christian Federation; representatives from ten nations attended its first meeting, held in 1895 in Vadstena, Sweden.

Embarking on a two-year tour in 1895, Mott organized national student movements in India, China, Japan, Australia, New Zealand, the Middle East, and Europe. By this time, he was in great demand as a speaker at college campuses. According to one of his associates, Mott "had an unsurpassed gift of sensing the common mind of a group of people with the most diverse backgrounds. When he gave a lead, almost everyone was ready to follow it." He also wrote books, articles, and pamphlets to promote dedication to Christian ideals and missionary work.

Now recognized as a major evangelical leader, Mott was chosen to preside over the World Missionary Conference in Edinburgh, Scotland, in 1910. As chairman of the Continuation Committee, which directed the organization's activities between conferences, he traveled to Asia in 1912–1913 to attend regional conferences, organize student organi-

zations, and address large audiences. Despite conservative opposition, he insisted that the missionary movement be open to students of all races and nationalities. So great was Mott's commitment to the movement that when President WOODROW WILSON offered him the post of United States ambassador to China in 1913, he declined.

When World War I broke out, Mott tried to maintain links between YMCA groups in Europe. Defeated in his efforts, he began providing assistance to prisoners of war and refugees through the Continuation Committee. He was chosen national executive of the American YMCA in 1915 and appointed general secretary of the National War Work Council the following year. Under his direction, the council raised almost $200 million to support YMCA relief efforts. Mott also served on President Wilson's Mexican Commission that year and as a member of the United States Special Delegation to Russia in 1917. After the war, Mott attended the Paris Peace Conference to plead for religious freedom.

The World Missionary Conference was reorganized in 1921 as the International Missionary Council, with Mott as chairman. Throughout the 1920s and 1930s, he traveled around the world working for the council and the World Committee of the YMCA. In 1926 he resigned from the American YMCA to become president of the world organization.

Although he was seventy-four years old when World War II broke out, Mott worked tirelessly on fund-raising campaigns to support such YMCA programs as relief efforts for prisoners of war.

Mott shared the 1946 Nobel Prize for Peace with EMILY GREENE BALCH. On his way to Oslo to receive the prize, he was cheered by large crowds of West Germans. At the ceremonies, Herman Smitt Ingebretsen of the Norwegian Nobel Committee said of Mott: "He has never been a politician, he has never taken an active part in organized peace work. But he has always been a living force, a tireless fighter in the service of Christ, opening young minds to the light which he thinks can lead the world to peace and bring men together in understanding and goodwill."

In his Nobel lecture, Mott spoke about the need for "the leadership of the constructive forces of the world" in a period of transition. He outlined what was required "to wage a better-planned, more aggressive, and more triumphant warfare against the agelong enemies of mankind—ignorance, poverty, disease, strife, and sin." He concluded by quoting the words of Christ: "He who would be greatest among you shall be the servant of all."

Mott spent the last ten years of his life in retirement in Orlando, Florida. In 1952 his first wife died, and in 1953 he married Agnes Peter. He died in 1955.

ELIHU ROOT once said of Mott: "His powerful personality and . . . self-sacrificing devotion to the cause of peace have, I believe, never been equaled. He does not owe his influence to the official positions he holds; rather, it is the positions which have acquired importance through the work he has accomplished. Over the years, he has traveled over the whole world . . . to create and strengthen a universal sympathy for the fundamental ideas on which peace necessarily depends."

WORKS BY: Evangelization of the World in This Generation, 1900; The Students of North America United, 1903; The Pastor and Modern Missions, 1904; The Future Leadership of the Church, 1909; The Decisive Hour of Christian Missions, 1910; The Present World Situation, 1914; The World's Student Christian Federation, 1920; Confronting Young Men With the Living Christ, 1923; The Present-Day Summons to the World Mission of Christianity, 1931; Leadership of the Constructive Forces of the World, 1931; Liberating the Lay Forces of Christianity, 1932; Cooperation and the World Mission, 1935; Five Decades and a Forward View, 1939; The Larger Evangelism, 1944; Addresses and Papers (6 vols.) 1946–1947.

ABOUT: Ecumenical Review April 1955; Fisher, G. M. John R. Mott: Architect of Cooperation and Unity, 1953; Hopkins, C. H. John R. Mott, 1979; Mackie, R. C., et al. Layman Extraordinary: John R. Mott, 1965; Mathews, B. J. John R. Mott: World Citizen, 1934; Neill, S. C., and Rouse, R. History of the Ecumenical Movement, 1954; Shedd, C. P. History of the World's Alliance of YMCAs, 1955.

MOTT, NEVILL
(September 30, 1905–   )
Nobel Prize for Physics, 1977
(shared with Philip W. Anderson and
    John H. Van Vleck)

The English physicist Nevill Francis Mott was born in Leeds, the son of Lilian Mary (Reynolds) and Charles Francis Mott, director of public education in Liverpool. His parents had met one another while studying physics with J. J. THOMSON at the Cavendish Laboratory of Cambridge University. After attending Clifton College in Bristol, Mott entered St. John's College, Cambridge, to study mathematics and theoretical physics. He received his B.S. in 1927.

Mott's undergraduate years coincided with

NEVILL MOTT

some of the most notable advances in theoretical physics, such as the establishment of the principles of quantum mechanics by WERNER HEISENBERG and, independently, ERWIN SCHRÖDINGER. Plunging into postgraduate research, Mott worked briefly at Cambridge under R. H. Fowler, one of the founders of modern astrophysics, then in Copenhagen under NIELS BOHR and at the University of Göttingen under MAX BORN. Returning to England in 1929, he lectured for one year at Manchester University, where he worked with W. L. BRAGG, and then at Gonville and Caius College, Cambridge, from 1930 to 1933. He received an M.S. from Gonville and Caius in 1930. In Cambridge, working under ERNEST RUTHERFORD, Mott applied quantum mechanics to an analysis of scattering in particle collisions. He was able to derive theoretically Rutherford's famous empirical formula for the scattering of alpha particles by atomic nuclei, and his calculations yielded a surprising result for the case of helium, whose nuclei are identical to alpha particles. At certain angles, the calculated reaction rate doubled, an effect that was later observed experimentally.

In 1933 Mott was appointed Melville Wills Professor of Theoretical Physics at the University of Bristol at the age of twenty-eight. That year he and the English physicist H. S. W. Massey wrote *The Theory of Atomic Collisions,* a book summarizing Mott's work on particle collisions. Mott then turned to a variety of phenomena in solid-state physics, especially the structural properties of metals. He proposed a theory of transition metals (metallic elements, including most of the common metals) in which he identified two groups of electrons, one primarily responsible for electrical conductivity, the other for magnetic and scattering properties. In other research, he investigated age- and work-hardening of metal alloys, rectification of electrical current (AC-to-DC conversion), the structure of ionic crystals, and the photographic process.

By the 1930s quantum mechanics had enabled researchers to explain the distinction between metallic and nonmetallic substances by means of band theory. According to this theory, the energies of electrons in substances are restricted to bands, or ranges, specific to the substances, which mark the boundaries between metals and nonmetals. In metals, electrons can occupy energy states in which they are only loosely bound to nuclei so that they are able to contribute to conductivity and flow as an electric current when a voltage is impressed. While attending a scientific conference at the University of Bristol in 1937, Mott became interested in an apparent discrepancy in band theory. According to the theory, nickel oxide ought to be a metallic conductor; in fact, it is an insulator. Refining band theory to account for interactions between electrons, Mott in 1949 elucidated the properties of nickel oxide and explained why certain substances change from insulators to conductors when their electron density is altered. These changes, now called Mott transitions, became important in the development of semiconductors.

During World War II, Mott conducted work on operations research, a mathematical theory of decision making applicable to strategic planning, and on efforts to compute the range of the German V-2 rocket. After the war, he returned to Bristol where, in 1948, he became director of the university's H. H. Wills Physics Laboratory and was appointed H. O. Wills Professor of Physics. In 1954 he succeeded W. L. Bragg as Cavendish Professor of Physics at Cambridge.

During the early 1960s Mott initiated research into the electrical properties of amorphous (noncrystalline) materials, substances such as glass whose arrangement of molecules is disordered rather than a regular lattice pattern. His interest in this topic began in 1958, when he read a paper by PHILIP W. ANDERSON on amorphous semiconductors. A semiconductor is a substance that behaves like an insulator at low temperatures and a conductor at high temperatures.

At Mott's invitation, Anderson served as a tenured visiting professor at Cambridge from 1967 to 1975. In their work together, Mott and Anderson investigated electrical conduction in semiconductors. Anderson had previously shown that under certain conditions electrons in a disordered solid are not free to diffuse, an effect known as the Anderson localization of electrons.

Initially Anderson's work was largely ignored, except by Mott, who, by extending it, was able to explain a number of electronic properties in disordered materials. Mott's concept of mobility edge describes the critical energy level that separates mobile electrons from trapped electrons. Mott also explained the electrical conductivity caused by the presence of relatively small numbers of foreign atoms as well as minimum conductivity, in which disordered material carries either no electrical current or a current having a strength above a specified value. This work led to the use of semiconductors in solar cells, photocopying machines, and many other devices.

Freed from administrative responsibilities after his retirement from Cambridge in 1971, Mott, "like a dog released from the slips, went hell-for-leather at work on amorphous materials," according to his successor at the Cavendish Laboratory, Brian Pippard.

Mott shared the 1977 Nobel Prize for Physics with Anderson and JOHN H. VAN VLECK "for their fundamental theoretical investigations of the electronic structure of magnetic and disordered systems." "The theory for Mott transitions and Mott-Anderson transitions is today of fundamental importance for the understanding of certain materials and for the construction of new ones," said Per-Olov Löwdin of the Royal Swedish Academy of Sciences in his presentation speech. "Anderson and Mott have shown that properly controlled disorder may be technically as important as perfect order."

In addition to his scientific work, Mott has written papers on science education and served on numerous committees concerned with educational reform. Between 1969 and 1977 he was chairman of the board of directors of Taylor & Francis, Ltd., publishers of scientific books, and from 1959 to 1966 he was master of Gonville and Caius College, Cambridge.

In 1930 Mott married Ruth Eleanor Horder; they have two daughters. Mott's recreational interests include religious history, photography, stained glass, and Byzantine coins.

The recipient of many awards, Mott holds honorary degrees from Oxford University, London University, and the University of Paris, among other institutions. In 1977 the French government made him a chevalier of the National Order of Merit. He was knighted in 1962.

SELECTED WORKS: An Outline of Wave Mechanics, 1930; The Theory of the Properties of Metals and Alloys, 1936, with H. Jones; Electronic Processes in Ionic Crystals, 1940, with R. W. Gurney; Wave Mechanics and Its Applications, 1948, with I. N. Sneddon; Elements of Wave Mechanics, 1952; Atomic Structure and the Strength of Metals, 1956; Electronic Processes in Non-Crystalline Materials, 1971, with E. A. Davis; Elementary Quantum Mechanics, 1972; Metal-Insulator Transitions, 1974; Localization and Metal-Insulator Transitions, 1985, with others.

ABOUT: New York Times October 12, 1977; Physics Today December 1977; Science November 18, 1977.

MOTTELSON, BEN R.
(July 9, 1926–   )
Nobel Prize for Physics, 1975
(shared with Aage Bohr and James
   Rainwater)

BEN R. MOTTELSON

The American-Danish physicist Ben Roy Mottelson was born in Chicago, Illinois, to Goodman Mottelson, an engineer, and the former Georgia Blum. The second of three children, Mottelson grew up in a lively, intellectual family environment. He attended public schools in La Grange, Illinois, and graduated from high school during World War II. After joining the Navy, he received officer training at Purdue University, to which he returned after the war. Receiving his B.S. in 1947, he entered Harvard University where he did graduate work in physics under JULIAN S. SCHWINGER and received his Ph.D. in 1950 for a thesis on nuclear physics.

That year, Harvard awarded Mottelson a Sheldon Traveling Fellowship, which enabled him to study at the Institute for Theoretical Physics in Copenhagen. He continued his work at the institute in 1951 and 1952 under a fellowship from the United States Atomic Energy Commission. From 1953 to 1957 he conducted research in Copenhagen that was sponsored by CERN (the European Organization for Nuclear Research). In 1957, with the founding of the Nordic Institute for Theoretical Atomic Physics (Nordita) in Copenhagen, he became a professor there and continued his research. He succeeded AAGE BOHR as director of Nordita in 1981.

In his early work at the Institute for Theoretical Physics, Mottelson began a lifelong collaboration with Aage Bohr on problems of nuclear theory. Bohr (one of six sons of NIELS

BOHR) had recently returned to Copenhagen from Columbia University where he had shared an office with JAMES RAINWATER in 1949–1950. During this time Rainwater had gained an important insight into the structure of the atomic nucleus, which he had discussed extensively with Bohr. With this insight, Bohr and Mottelson developed a comprehensive theory of nuclear behavior, which they called the collective model.

At the time, scientists attempted to explain the behavior of the many protons and neutrons (together known as nucleons) in a large nucleus by means of two theoretical models. According to the liquid-drop model, proposed by Niels Bohr in 1936, the nucleus is much like a liquid drop, which vibrates and changes shape. The liquid-drop model accounted for nuclear fission but could not explain other properties of the nucleus. In the shell model, offered in 1949, MARIA GOEPPERT MAYER and J. HANS D. JENSEN proposed that nucleons move in independent concentric orbits, or shells, inside the nucleus, much as electrons move in an atom. According to their theory, the force acting on a single nucleon is the sum of the forces exerted by all nucleons in the nucleus. Mayer and Jensen hypothesized that this collective force field is spherical. Experimental data, however, showed that the distribution of electric charge around some nuclei is not spherical, as the shell model said it ought to be.

It was Rainwater's insight that centrifugal forces might distort the orbital shells into a football-like shape, an idea that he published in early 1950. Rainwater's hypothesis paralleled Aage Bohr's own line of thinking, and after returning to Copenhagen later that year, Bohr set out to develop a comprehensive theory of nuclear behavior. Two years later, he and Mottelson published their collective model of the nucleus, based on Rainwater's idea. The model was a synthesis of the liquidlike behavior of the nucleus described in the liquid-drop model with the orbiting-nucleon properties of the shell model.

According to the Bohr-Mottelson model, the aggregate behavior of nucleons causes the surface of the nucleus to behave like the surface of a liquid drop. At the same time, the shell structure of the nucleus can be deformed, giving rise to surface oscillations and rotations. When the outermost shell of a nucleus has a full complement of nucleons, Bohr and Mottelson said, it remains spherical; but when the outer shell is incomplete, the nucleus becomes distorted into the shape of a football. Distorted nuclei, they found, have various new modes of vibration and rotation, including surface waves and "breathing" modes in which the nucleus oscillates in size. Previous models had failed to predict these phenomena because they did not take into account the interactions among nucleons.

The collective model enabled Mottelson and Bohr to predict the properties of deformed nuclei and to confirm the predictions experimentally. The agreement between their theory and the experiments of others was excellent, and the two scientists reported their findings in 1953. After publication of the collective model, Mottelson and Bohr further developed their nuclear theory.

Mottelson shared the 1975 Nobel Prize for Physics with Bohr and Rainwater "for the discovery of the connection between collective motion and particle motion in atomic nuclei and the development of the theory of the structure of the atomic nucleus based on this connection." By confirming the collective theory, said Sven Johansson of the Royal Swedish Academy of Sciences in his presentation speech, Mottelson and Bohr "gave stimulus to new theoretical studies, but, above all, to many experiments to verify the theoretical predictions." The result, said Johansson, has been "a deepened understanding of the structure of the atomic nucleus" that was itself "influenced in a decisive way by Bohr and Mottelson. For example, they showed . . . that the nucleons have a tendency to form pairs. A consequence of this is that nuclear matter has properties reminiscent of superconductors."

Mottelson married Nancy Jane Reno in 1948;

they had three children. In 1971 Mottelson and his family became Danish citizens. Mottelson's wife died of cancer in 1975, shortly before Mottelson was informed that he had won the Nobel Prize. Known as a man of exceptional intellectual strength and range, Mottelson has a wide variety of interests, including cycling, swimming, and music; but he has devoted most of his working life to understanding the atomic nucleus and its behavior.

In addition to the Nobel Prize, Mottelson has received honorary degrees from Purdue University and the University of Heidelberg.

SELECTED WORKS: Collective and Individual Particle Aspects of Nuclear Structure, 1953, with Aage Bohr; Lectures on Selected Topics in Nuclear Structure, 1964; Nuclear Structure (2 vols.) 1969–1975, with Aage Bohr.

ABOUT: New York Times October 18, 1975; Physics Today December 1975; Science November 28, 1975.

MULLER, HERMANN J.
(December 21, 1890–April 5, 1967)
Nobel Prize for Physiology or Medicine, 1946

The American biologist and geneticist Hermann Joseph Muller was born in New York City, the younger of two children. His father and namesake, who was of German Catholic descent, was trained as a lawyer but had taken over the family art metal foundry. His mother, the former Frances Louise Lyons, was the daughter of English Sephardic Jews. Although Muller's father died when the boy was only nine, he had already communicated his enthusiasm for science to his son. Muller and his older sister attended public schools in Harlem, and in 1907 he graduated from Morris High School in the Bronx. An outstanding student, he won a scholarship to Columbia University, a leading center of genetic research. There, as he had done in high school, Muller founded a student biology club. Graduating cum laude in 1910, he received his M.S. in physiology the following year with a thesis on the transmission of nerve impulses.

After graduation Muller held a teaching fellowship in physiology at Cornell University Medical College in New York City. He maintained contact with two younger friends from the Columbia biology club, Alfred Sturtevant and Calvin Bridges, who were studying chromosome heredity in the fruit fly, Drosophila, in the laboratory of the zoologist and geneticist

HERMANN J. MULLER

THOMAS HUNT MORGAN at Columbia. Muller joined the group in 1912 when he became a teaching assistant in the zoology department.

Analysis of the transmission of altered genetic traits (mutations) in *Drosophila* revealed to Morgan and his colleagues that genes are linked into groups, separated, and recombined according to the genetic theories of Gregor Mendel. Muller's doctoral thesis in 1916 demonstrated unequivocally that the four groups of linked genes discovered by purely genetic studies corresponded to the four chromosomes in the nuclei of *Drosophila* cells. This finding convinced the previously doubtful Morgan that Mendelian genes were not merely handy theoretical tools but physical entities carried on chromosomes. The results of the group's research were published under the title *The Mechanism of Mendelian Heredity* (1915), a discussion of the principles of "classic" (prebiochemical) genetics. Feeling that his many contributions—especially the theoretical ones—were not sufficiently appreciated at Columbia, Muller accepted a position offered to him by Julian Huxley at the Rice Institute in Houston, and he moved to Texas in 1915. He later returned to Columbia for two years (1918–1920) before becoming a professor of zoology at the University of Texas at Austin.

In 1923 Muller married Jessie Marie Jacobs, a mathematics instructor at the university, who collaborated in some of Muller's publications; they had one son.

Muller's interest in genetics had been inspired by Charles Darwin's theory of natural selection, which held that new genetic variations (or mutations) arise constantly and randomly in populations of living organisms. According to this view, because the variations are small, evolution proceeds in gradual steps, not in big leaps.

Expecting that most natural mutations should be disadvantageous for the survival of a species, Muller bred stocks of *Drosophila* in which chromosomes were marked with distinctive, nondeleterious genetic variants for identification. Theoretically, a marked chromosome in which harmful mutation had occurred would disappear from the stock; consequently, the frequency of such disappearances would serve as a measure of the mutation rate. Muller and his colleague Edgar Altenburg at Columbia made the first measurements of mutation rates in 1920.

While at Rice Institute, Muller confirmed that most mutations are deleterious or lethal. He further demonstrated that the mutation rate does not depend on the environment and that mutations are produced at a constant rate whether they are needed evolutionarily or not. Muller speculated that environmental factors such as X rays (discovered by WILHELM RÖNTGEN in 1895) might produce a genetic effect. Genes are normally highly stable, and it would take an extremely energetic force such as X radiation to alter them. Because X rays also act on individual molecules, they might alter individual genes, leaving the rest of the organism's heredity intact. In 1926 Muller discovered that X rays could in fact increase the mutation rate in his marked stock to levels hundreds or thousands of times higher than normal.

The discovery that the material of inheritance and evolution could be deliberately changed in the laboratory created a sensation. After reporting his findings in *Science* in 1927, Muller was suddenly famous and honored, but under the strain of overwork, increasing marital problems, and the financial hardships imposed by the Great Depression, he attempted suicide in early 1932. After recovering from his depression, he went to Germany as a Guggenheim Fellow and spent a year at the Kaiser Wilhelm Institute for Brain Research in Berlin, in the genetics department headed by N. W. Timofeev-Ressovsky. He then accepted an invitation by N. I. Vavilov, director of the Institute of Genetics of the Soviet Academy of Sciences, to come to Leningrad as a senior geneticist to conduct research on the mutation of genes. His divorce from Jessie Jacobs became final in 1935.

Muller left the Soviet Union in 1937 to serve

in the Spanish Civil War. He spent the next three years at the Institute of Animal Genetics of the University of Edinburgh, Scotland, where he met Dorothea Johanna Kantorowicz, a German refugee. They were married in 1939 and had one daughter.

Returning to the United States in 1940, Muller took an interim professorship in biology at Amherst College, Massachusetts. He served as an adviser to the Manhattan District Project in 1943 and, after the war, to the United States Atomic Energy Commission. He became professor of zoology at Indiana University at Bloomington in 1945.

Muller was awarded the 1946 Nobel Prize for Physiology or Medicine "for the discovery of the production of mutations by X-ray irradiation." In his Nobel lecture, "The Production of Mutations," Muller summarized his experimental work, which, with the advent of atomic weapons, had taken on new and dire significance. "With the increasing use of atomic energy, even for peacetime purposes," he said, "the problem will become very important of insuring that the human germ plasm . . . is effectively protected from this additional and potent source of permanent contamination." Among those who drew on Muller's research to argue for a nuclear test ban was LINUS C. PAULING.

In his later years, Muller devoted considerable effort to the reform of biology teaching in high schools and to a eugenic program called "germinal choice," in which semen of outstanding men would be frozen for later use in the propagation of healthy and intelligent future generations. He discussed these views in *Out of the Night: A Biologist's View of the Future* (1935). Although known chiefly for his genetic research, Muller also made the first psychological analysis of identical twins raised in separate homes.

Muller, who enjoyed various outdoor sports, had a keen interest in world politics and travel as well as a deep appreciation for literature. He developed congestive heart failure in the mid-1960s and died from the condition in Bloomington in 1967, at the age of seventy-seven.

Muller's many honors included the Kimber Award in Genetics of the National Academy of Sciences (1955) and the Alexander Hamilton Award of Columbia University (1960). He was a fellow of the American Association for the Advancement of Science, a member of the American Academy of Arts and Sciences, the Society for Experimental Biology and Medicine, the American Society of Natural-

ists, the American Society of Zoologists, the Genetics Society of America, the Genetical Society of Great Britain, and the American Philosophical Society and a foreign member of the Royal Society of London.

SELECTED WORKS: Genetics, Medicine, and Man, 1947, with others; Radiation Biology, 1954; Studies in Genetics: The Selected Papers of H. J. Muller, 1962; The Modern Concept of Nature, 1973; Man's Future Birthright, 1973.

ABOUT: Biographical Memoirs of Fellows of the Royal Society, volume 14, 1968; Carlson, E. A. Genes, Radiation, and Society, 1981; Current Biography February 1947; Dictionary of Scientific Biography, volume 9, 1974; Genetics January 1972; Madden, C. (ed.) Talks With Scientists, 1968.

MÜLLER, PAUL

(January 12, 1899–October 13, 1965)
Nobel Prize for Physiology or Medicine, 1948

The Swiss chemist Paul Hermann Müller (mül' ər) was born in Olten, to Gottlieb Müller, a Swiss Federal Railway official, and the former Fanny Leypoldt. Müller spent his early years in Lenzburg, Aargau canton, his father's hometown. When the boy was five years old, the family moved to Basel, where young Paul received his education in the local schools. Leaving school at the age of seventeen, he took a job at a chemical factory, and the following year he worked as a chemical assistant at the research laboratories of the Lonza Company. This exposure to research encouraged him to enter the University of Basel in 1919 to study chemistry; in 1925 he obtained his Ph.D. with a thesis on the organic chemistry of dyes.

Upon graduation, Müller was employed by the J. R. Geigy Company, one of the world's largest chemical corporations. At Basel, he had minored in botany, and one of his first assignments at Geigy was to investigate the properties of natural plant products. Over the next three years, Müller invented several useful tanning compounds before turning his attention to disinfectants, especially those used to protect such plant products as seeds. In 1935 he began research on insecticides. Although there was a great deal of scientific literature on the subject—and many formulas—virtually no insecticides were commercially available. Of the few that were, Müller found they could not compare with known insecticides such as the arsenates, pyrethrum, or rotenone.

Arsenates are synthetic chemicals, whereas

PAUL MÜLLER

pyrethrum and rotenone are natural plant extracts. As insecticides, each of the three compounds has a drawback. Arsenates, for example, are toxic to human beings; and the plant compounds, although nontoxic, are costly. Moreover, the effects of all three compounds are relatively short-lived. Müller sought to produce a synthetic insecticide that would kill insects on contact that would be nontoxic to human beings and plants, inexpensive, and chemically stable.

The research team led by Müller conducted biological studies to test the insecticidal properties of hundreds of chemical compounds. Müller was involved in both the chemical and biological aspects of the work. The Geigy researchers synthesized one compound after another, trying unsuccessfully to predict the insecticidal activity of a chemical from its structure. By September 1939 they had produced diphenyltrichloroethane, a compound in which two benzene rings are joined by a carbon atom to which three chlorine atoms are attached. The substance proved to be an effective contact insecticide, and its chemical structure appeared to be stable. Müller knew that similar diphenyl compounds with sulfur groups in place of the central carbon atom were effective oral poisons if they carried chlorine atoms in the para positions, and accordingly he synthesized p, p-dichloro-diphenyltrichloroethane (DDT) in 1939. Geigy patented DDT in 1940, conducted field tests, and put the compound on the market in 1942.

During World War II, Allied access to supplies of natural insecticides, most of which were produced in the tropics, was reduced or cut off completely while the need for insecticides was acute. Typhus fever and malaria, two of the greatest medical problems the Allies faced, are insect-borne diseases for which no vaccines exist. The work of RONALD ROSS and CHARLES NICOLLE had shown that both malaria and typhus could be contained, but only if the mosquitos and lice that spread the diseases were controlled.

The new insecticide DDT seemed ideal for this purpose. Its toxicity to human beings was so low that it could be sprayed directly on the body to control typhus. It was also sufficiently inexpensive that it could be used to spray entire islands in the Pacific before United States forces landed, thus preventing malaria throughout the invasion. It was so stable that a single spraying was effective for months.

The wartime success of DDT in controlling typhus fever and malaria made Müller a popular choice for the Nobel Prize for Physiology or Medicine, which he received in 1948 "for his discovery of the high efficiency of DDT as a contact poison."

During the next two decades, the unparalleled value of DDT as an insecticide was proven again and again, particularly in tropical regions. The compound not only controlled malaria, the most devastating tropical disease, but in combination with new crop strains (such as those developed by NORMAN BORLAUG), it also led to dramatic increases in agricultural productivity.

It was only later that the adverse effects of DDT became evident. One of the properties that originally made the compound so attractive was its stability when compared with that of natural, plant-produced insecticides. From the outset Müller had recognized that this stability posed potential hazards. Although DDT is not highly toxic to vertebrates, it does not break down gradually into harmless components. As a result it accumulates in soil, water, and the bodies of higher animals. Moreover, it is a broad-spectrum insecticide that kills useful insects, such as bees, in addition to pests. Concern over the environmental effects of DDT grew during the 1960s, and in 1972 its general use was banned in the United States. The deleterious effects of DDT—and the damage done to the environment by this powerful insecticide—led to the work of Rachel Carson and the publication of her book, *Silent Spring*.

In 1927 Müller married Friedel Rügsegger; they had two sons and a daughter. Müller retired from Geigy in 1961 and spent the next four years working in a private laboratory that

MULLIKEN

he set up in his home in Oberswil, near Basel. After a brief illness, he died on October 13, 1965.

Müller received an honorary doctorate from the University of Thessalonica (Greece). He was a member of the Society of Industrial Chemistry in Paris and an honorary member of the Swiss Nature Research Society.

SELECTED WORKS: The Constitution and Toxic Effects of Botanicals and New Synthetic Insecticides, 1945, with others.

ABOUT: Current Biography October 1945; Dictionary of Scientific Biography, volume 9, 1974; Nature December 11, 1965.

ROBERT S. MULLIKEN

MULLIKEN, ROBERT S.
(June 7, 1896–October 31, 1986)
Nobel Prize for Chemistry, 1966

The American chemist Robert Sanderson Mulliken was born in Newburyport, Massachusetts, the son of Samuel Parsons Mulliken, a professor of organic chemistry at the Massachusetts Institute of Technology (MIT), and Katherine (Wilmarth) Mulliken. Mulliken's interest in molecular structure began while he was still in high school, where he gave a graduation oration, "The Electron: What It Is and What It Does." After receiving a B.S in chemistry from MIT in 1917, he worked for two years at the United States Bureau of Mines, the Chemical Warfare Service, and the New Jersey Zinc Company. In 1919 he began the graduate study of chemistry at the University of Chicago. He received a Ph.D. in physical chemistry in 1921 with a thesis on the separation of mercury isotopes by fractional distillation (isotopes are atoms whose nuclei contain identical numbers of protons but different numbers of neutrons). A National Research Council fellowship allowed him to continue his investigations on the behavior of isotopes at Harvard. During his research he became interested in the effect of isotopes on the line spectra of diatomic (two-atom) molecules.

When atoms, the basic units of chemical elements, become excited (by being heated, for example), they emit light in a characteristic spectrum, with lines of specific colors at specific distances from one another. Using the quantum theory developed by MAX PLANCK and ALBERT EINSTEIN in the first decade of the twentieth century, NIELS BOHR proposed

a model of the atom in which electrons have only "allowed" energy levels, or orbitals. Spectral lines represent wavelengths of light energy emitted as electrons "jump" from one allowed state to another.

Molecules, the basic units of a chemical compound, also have characteristic spectra, which are more complex than those of single atoms. The additional modes of excitation in a molecule—interatomic vibration, molecular rotation, and bending of molecular shape—result in the emission of energy over broader wavelength ranges. Therefore, a molecular spectrum consists of broad bands rather than lines.

Realizing that quantum theory was essential to his work on the spectra of molecules, Mulliken went to Europe in 1925 to study with the leading physicists and spectroscopists. In 1926 he returned to the United States as assistant professor of physics at Washington Square College, part of New York University. ERWIN SCHRÖDINGER, MAX BORN, and WERNER HEISENBERG had just published their detailed mathematical treatment of quantum theory, which contained formulations that can be used to describe the behavior of electrons in atoms. However, the electron structure of molecules was much more resistant to analysis. In 1927 Mulliken, working with Friedrich Hund at the University of Göttingen, Germany, proposed that when atoms join to form a molecule, in a process called chemical bonding, their outer electrons become associated with the molecule as a whole. Thus, the outer electrons of a molecule, which determine many of its important properties, are associated with molecular orbitals rather than orbitals of specific atoms. Mulliken showed that molecular orbitals can be described in a rigorous mathematical form that can be used to predict physical and chemical properties in great detail.

In 1928 Mulliken, by then internationally known for his work, became associate professor of physics at the University of Chicago, rising to full professor in 1931. From 1957 until 1961 he was Ernest DeWitt Burton Distinguished Professor at Chicago.

In 1916 Gilbert N. Lewis had postulated that chemical bonding was due to the presence of pairs of electrons located between atoms in a molecule. LINUS C. PAULING and his colleagues adapted this concept to quantum mechanics, creating a theory of chemical bonding that quite accurately describes molecules possessing only single bonds (bonds formed by one pair of electrons). However, this so-called resonance theory was unsatisfactory for describing the behavior of molecules with more complex bonding structures. Resonance theory treats the sharing of electrons by atoms as a local phenomenon, with each atom keeping its essential electron configuration. In molecules with multiple bonds, the electrons are shared over large regions of the molecule, and complex effects occur that cannot be described by a local treatment of bonding. Mulliken was able to demonstrate the superiority of his molecular bonding model for treating complex molecules, and he determined the shapes and relative energies of the orbitals for many compounds.

Mulliken continued his investigations of the basic mechanisms of molecular structure using a combination of spectroscopic observations and sophisticated theoretical calculations. This work greatly extended knowledge about chemical bonding, particularly the behavior of molecules when many electrons and molecular groups interact strongly with one another. The invention of the general-purpose computer provided a powerful tool, and Mulliken and his colleagues pioneered in the development of computer methods for understanding molecular structure. During the 1950s they applied these techniques to delineate the behavior of charge-transfer complexes (relatively weak associations of different molecules that share electrons and that interact strongly with light). Charge-transfer complexes are responsible for most of the known organic semiconductors, photoconductors, conductors, and superconductors of electricity.

During World War II, Mulliken served as director of educational work and information on the Plutonium Project at the University of Chicago. He was a scientific attaché to the United States embassy in London in 1955.

Mulliken was awarded the 1966 Nobel Prize for Chemistry "for his fundamental work concerning chemical bonds and the electronic structure of molecules by the molecular orbital method." "The molecular orbital method means a principally new understanding of the nature of the chemical bond," said Inga Fischer-Hjalmars of the Royal Swedish Academy of Sciences on presenting the award. "Previous ideas started from the assumption . . . that the bonding depends on interaction between complete atoms. The molecular orbital method, on the other hand, starts from quantum mechanical interactions between all the atomic nuclei and all the electrons of the molecule. This method has given exceedingly important contributions to our qualitative understanding of the chemical bond and the electronic structure of molecules."

In addition to his position at the University of Chicago, Mulliken lectured widely. He was the Baker Lecturer at Cornell University in 1960, the Silliman Lecturer at Yale University in 1965, and the Jan Van Geuns Visiting Professor at the University of Amsterdam, also in 1965. After his formal retirement in 1961, he continued as distinguished service professor of physics and chemistry at the University of Chicago. From 1965 to 1971 he was also distinguished resident professor of chemical physics at Florida State University during the winter months.

Mulliken was married in 1929 to Mary Helen von Noé, the daughter of an Austrian geologist who had emigrated to the United States to teach at the University of Chicago. They had two daughters. Mulliken has been described as unassuming and good-natured. He had a wide knowledge of botany and enjoyed driving, oriental rugs, and art. He died on October 31, 1986, in Arlington, Virginia.

In addition to the Nobel Prize, Mulliken received the American Chemical Society's Gilbert Newton Lewis Medal (1960), the Theodore William Richards Medal (1960), the Peter Debye Award in Physical Chemistry (1963), and the Willard Gibbs Medal (1965). He was a member of the National Academy of Sciences, the American Association for the Advancement of Science, and the American Academy of Arts and Sciences and a foreign member of the Royal Society of London. He was presented with honorary degrees by Columbia, Marquette, and Cambridge universities and the University of Stockholm.

SELECTED WORKS: The Separation of Isotopes, 1922; The Interpretation of Band Spectra, 1932; Molecular Electronic Spectra, 1941; Selected Papers of Robert S. Mulliken, 1975; Diatomic Molecules, 1977, with Walter Ermler; Polyatomic Molecules, 1981, with Walter Ermler.

ABOUT: Current Biography September 1967; Libby, L. M. The Uranium People, 1979; New York Times November 4, 1966; November 3, 1986; Science November 12, 1966.

WILLIAM P. MURPHY

MURPHY, WILLIAM P.
(February 6, 1892–   )
Nobel Prize for Physiology or Medicine, 1934
(shared with George R. Minot and George H. Whipple)

The American physician and pathologist William Parry Murphy was born in Stoughton, Wisconsin, to Rose Anna (Parry) Murphy and Thomas Francis Murphy, a Congregational minister. After attending public schools in Wisconsin and Oregon, he received his B.A. from the University of Oregon in 1914. For the next two years he taught high school mathematics and physics in Oregon. He then entered the University of Oregon Medical School, where, in addition to his medical studies, he also served as a laboratory assistant in the anatomy department. He spent the following summer at the Rush Medical School in Chicago. The award of a William Stanislaus Murphy Fellowship enabled him to attend Harvard Medical School in Boston in 1919.

After receiving his medical degree in 1922, Murphy interned at Rhode Island Hospital, Providence, and later served as a resident at Peter Bent Brigham Hospital in Boston. While in private practice in Boston in 1923, he met GEORGE R. MINOT, a Boston physician who was investigating pernicious anemia, a disease that at the time was almost invariably fatal.

The following year Murphy was appointed an assistant instructor in medicine at Harvard Medical School; at the same time he began research on diabetes mellitus and blood diseases, including anemia. Pernicious anemia attacks bone marrow (the site of red blood cell synthesis), with the result that red blood cells fail to mature to their proper size and shape, a condition then described as blood thinning. The disease was thought to be caused by a poison and was therefore treated by doses of arsenic, transfusions, or removal of the spleen, an organ that breaks down red blood cells.

Minot, however, took a different approach, one based on GEORGE H. WHIPPLE's recent discovery that liver stimulated red blood cell production in anemic dogs. After feeding a liver-rich diet to his private patients, Minot observed an increase in their red blood cells. Working together, Murphy and Minot promoted a daily liver diet for patients hospitalized with pernicious anemia. Their experiment aroused skepticism among other physicians, who refused to believe that the disease was caused by a simple dietary deficiency. The treatment was also hindered by the patients' reluctance to eat large quantities of liver.

The two researchers presented the results of their successful program at a medical meeting in Atlantic City in 1926. By that time they had successfully treated forty-five patients and had shared the "thrill of watching the patient through a few days of depression following the institution of liver therapy until remission occurs, with its often sudden and almost unbelievable sense of well-being, simultaneously with the maximum increase of the reticulocytes or new red blood cells," as Murphy recalled later. "Even more dramatic has been the improvement in the disturbances of locomotion resulting from nerve damage."

Until 1926, 6,000 persons died from pernicious anemia yearly. Worldwide usage of the liver diet substantiated its effectiveness, although the treatment had drawbacks. A major problem was that patients had to eat half a pound of liver each day; in the case of very ill patients it was forced through stomach tubes. Methods were therefore sought to make liver more acceptable and palatable, as well as to reduce the cost of the treatment. In 1928 a Harvard physical chemist, Edwin Cohn, prepared a liver extract 50 to 100 times as potent as the natural food. Not only could this concentrated extract be eaten in small amounts or injected into muscle; it was also less costly than a liver diet.

The active ingredient in liver, however, remained a mystery. Another Harvard physician, William Castle, noted that removal of the stomach for cancer often led to death by pernicious anemia. He also observed that red meat other than liver was ineffective when fed to patients, whether alone or digested in a test tube with enzymes. Something in the stomach, he reasoned, was related to the disease. In a novel experiment, Castle ate red meat, vomited, and then mixed the regurgitated stomach contents in a preparation for patients to eat. When the mixture proved as effective as liver, he concluded that the stomach normally contains an "intrinsic factor" that acts with an "extrinsic factor" in meat and is necessary for red blood cell formation in the bone marrow; pernicious anemia patients lack this intrinsic factor.

Soon after Castle's experiment, a commercial extract from hog stomach, called ventriculin, became available to provide the missing factor. The liver factor was isolated in 1948 and named vitamin B_{12}, or cyanocobalamin for its high content of cobalt. The vitamin is now given as a direct muscle injection to treat pernicious anemia. Certain stomach glands produce the intrinsic factor needed for gut absorption of vitamin B_{12}, which, in turn, promotes red blood cell formation in the bone marrow. The liver fed to patients in Minot and Murphy's early experiments was effective because it contains enough vitamin B_{12} to be absorbed without the intrinsic factor.

For "their discoveries concerning liver therapy in cases of anemia," Murphy, Minot, and Whipple were awarded the 1934 Nobel Prize for Physiology or Medicine. In his presentation speech, Israel Holmgren of the Karolinska Institute summarized the significance of the three laureates' research. "We have acquired new knowledge as to the very divergent effects exercised by different food substances in promoting and stimulating the bone marrow's activity in the regeneration of the blood," Holmgren said; "we have been made acquainted with a new internal secretory function possessed by the liver that is of the utmost importance; we have been furnished with a method of treatment of pernicious anemia, and also for other diseased conditions, that will save the lives of many thousands of persons every year."

Between 1935 and 1948, Murphy was an associate in medicine at the Harvard University Medical School, followed by an appointment as lecturer on medicine. Concurrently, he was an associate in medicine at Peter Bent Brigham Hospital from 1928 until 1935 and then senior associate in medicine and consultant in hematology from 1935 to 1958. In 1958 both institutions granted him emeritus status.

In 1919 Murphy married Pearl Harriet Addams; they had a son, who became a physician, and a daughter who died in 1936.

Murphy's many honors include the Cameron Prize and Lectureship of the University of Edinburgh (1930), the Bronze Medal of the American Medical Association (1934), and the Gold Medal of the Massachusetts Humane Society (1937). He is a member of the American Society for Clinical Investigation, the Association of American Physicians, the American Association for the Advancement of Science, the American Medical Association, and the National Institute of Social Sciences.

SELECTED WORKS: Early Papers on Pernicious Anemia, 1933, with George Minot; Anemia in Practice: Pernicious Anemia, 1939.

ABOUT: Current Biography November 1955; De Kruif, P. Men Against Death, 1932; National Cyclopedia of American Biography, volume 6, 1946.

MYRDAL, ALVA
(January 31, 1902–February 1, 1986)
Nobel Prize for Peace, 1982
(shared with Alfonso García Robles)

The Swedish sociologist and United Nations official Alva Reimer Myrdal (mür' däl) was born in Uppsala, the daughter of Albert Reimer, a building contractor, and the former Lowa Larsson. Raised in a socially conscious middle-class family, Myrdal admired the example of her father, a member of the Swedish Social Democratic party (also known as the Labor party) who was active in the movement to establish worker cooperatives.

After studying sociology, philosophy, psychology, and childhood education at Stockholm University, Myrdal graduated with a B.A. in 1924. The same year, she married the econ-

omist GUNNAR MYRDAL, at the time a lawyer
in Stockholm. They had one son and two
daughters: Sissela Bok, an internationally recognized philosopher and author who resides
in the U.S.; Kaj Fölster, a sociologist; and Jan
Myrdal, an author who is active in Swedish
politics.

For the next three years Myrdal pursued her
studies in London, Leipzig, and Stockholm.
She traveled with her husband in the United
States on Rockefeller Foundation scholarships
in 1929–1930, studied in Geneva in 1930–1931,
and earned an M.A. from Uppsala University
in 1934. Also in 1934, she and her husband
published their important study *Kris i befolkningsfrågan* (Crisis in the Population Problem), which contributed to Myrdal's growing
international reputation in the field of population problems.

During the 1930s the Social Democrats gained
enough political power in Sweden to undertake major social reforms that required dynamic state planning. *Kris i befolkningsfrågan*
directly influenced the government's decision
to assume responsibility for the well-being of
all children, regardless of the financial circumstances of their parents. As the study's coauthor and a recognized authority in the field,
Alva Myrdal was appointed to the Government Committee on Social Housing. She was
also made an adviser to the Royal Population
Commission in 1935. In 1936, under the auspices of the Swedish Cooperative Housing Authority, she founded the Training College for
Nursery and Kindergarten Teachers, serving
as its director until 1948. An advocate of progressive educational methods, she was appointed to the Royal Commission on
Educational Reform in 1946 and named chairwoman of the Interim Commission of the World
Council for Early Childhood Education.

During this period Myrdal also played a
leading part in the movement for the political
and economic equality of Swedish women. As
chief secretary of the State Commission on
Women's Work from 1935 to 1938, she edited
a monthly magazine for women members of
the Labor party. As vice-chairwoman of the
Stockholm Organization of Business and
Professional Women in 1935–1936, she sought
to achieve feminist goals through the marketplace rather than through political power or
psychological change. Gradually, her interests
became international in scope. From 1938 to
1947 she served as vice president of the International Federation of Business and Professional Women. She also participated in the
International Federation of University Women

ALVA MYRDAL

between 1945 and 1947, preparing its report
on the implications of married women's work.

During World War II, when Sweden's neutrality attracted an influx of refugees, Myrdal
was vice-chairwoman of the Joint Committee
of Swedish Civic Organizations for Cultural
Relief in Europe. After the war she edited *Via
Suecia* (The Swedish Way), a multilingual
weekly designed to help refugees become assimilated into Swedish society.

Turning increasingly to international affairs,
Myrdal represented Sweden at the United Nations Educational, Scientific, and Cultural Organization (UNESCO) conference in Paris in
1946. The following year she was a consultant
to International Understanding Through
Schools, a project sponsored by the Social Science Department of UNESCO. Three years
later, she was named principal director of the
Department of Social Affairs of the United
Nations. In this position she coordinated projects involving such issues as human rights,
freedom of information, the status of women,
drug abuse, and population growth. "To the
internationally minded men and women of the
world," she told an interviewer, "social ills are
as real and urgent as political and economic
problems."

Although a member of the Social Democratic party, Myrdal had up to this time played
only a limited role in its affairs, serving on a
wartime committee that formulated the party's
postwar goals and representing the party at
the INTERNATIONAL LABOUR ORGANISATION
conference in Paris in 1945. Her first highly
visible international role began in 1955 when

she was appointed Sweden's ambassador to India, despite criticism from the Swedish business community, which objected to her socialist views. An efficient administrator, she soon won the respect of Prime Minister Jawaharlal Nehru and the Indian people.

Returning to Sweden in 1961, Myrdal became a special assistant to the Swedish foreign minister on disarmament. Since disarmament was at the time an unfamiliar field to her, she undertook an intense study of the subject. It soon became her main preoccupation. Elected to the Swedish Parliament in 1962, she headed the Swedish delegation to the United Nations Disarmament Conference in Geneva. As a minister-without-portfolio, she continued her work on behalf of disarmament from 1966 until 1973, when she resigned from government service.

Continuing her active opposition to the arms race, in 1977 Myrdal published *The Game of Disarmament: How the United States and Russia Run the Arms Race*. In it, she made a scathing attack on both superpowers for wasting resources that could otherwise be used for health care, housing, and education. When she was awarded the Albert Einstein Peace Prize from the Albert Einstein Peace Foundation in 1980, she expressed her concern over the climate of despair that was "being forced on the youth of today by the ever-present threat of nuclear war." But, she added, "I have never, never allowed myself to give up."

Myrdal received the 1982 Nobel Prize for Peace in recognition of her "commitment to the service of disarmament," sharing the prize with ALFONSO GARCÍA ROBLES. "More must be done in *concrete* terms in order to promote the cause of disarmament," Myrdal said in her Nobel lecture. After outlining the rapid growth of nuclear arsenals in the United States and the Soviet Union, she declared, "War is murder. And the military preparations now being made for a potential major confrontation are aimed at collective murder. In a nuclear age the victims would be numbered by the millions." She concluded her speech by reminding the audience that "no peace congresses have been held in the nearly 100 years" since Alfred Nobel's will endowed the Peace Prize. She called for such conferences in the future.

A reformer in the tradition of European democratic socialists, Myrdal began her commitment to peace as a social planner at the national level. After she joined the United Nations, her concerns for equality, social justice, and public welfare became international in scope. For her, the most important global concern became the arms race. Although she was proud of the fact that Sweden formally renounced nuclear weapons in 1968, she sometimes expressed her dismay that despite years of disarmament negotiations, the arms race has continued to escalate and the "militarization of the economy and national life of almost all countries has intensified."

Myrdal's leisure activities included reading, cooking, and taking walks. A victim of heart disease, she spent the last two years of her life in a hospital in Stockholm, where she died on February 1, 1986.

ADDITIONAL WORKS IN ENGLISH TRANSLATION: America's Role in International Social Welfare, 1955, with others; Women's Two Roles: Home and Work, 1956, with Viola Klein; Disarmament and the United Nations, 1965; The Right to Conduct Nuclear Explosions, 1975; Strengthening the Readiness to Create a Better Future, 1980.

ABOUT: Current Biography December 1950; Hayes, H. Our Best Years, 1984; Independent Woman June 1949; New York Times October 14, 1982; February 3, 1986; New York Times Book Review March 6, 1977; People August 11, 1980; Sociological Review July 1968.

MYRDAL, GUNNAR

(December 6, 1898–May 17, 1987)
Nobel Memorial Prize in Economic
    Sciences, 1974
(shared with Friedrich A. von Hayek)

The Swedish economist Karl Gunnar Myrdal (mür' däl) was born in Solvarbo, a small village in central Sweden, to Karl Adolf Myrdal, a railroad employee, and the former Sophia Carlson. His childhood experiences on the family farm strongly influenced his adult economic and political philosophy, which he once called a combination of "Jeffersonian liberalism and Swedish peasant democracy." He described himself, at age twenty, as "an ordinary Swedish country boy . . . [who] had inherited [a] puritanical and positive attitude to the value of work."

Entering Stockholm University in 1919, Myrdal received a law degree in 1923 and began practicing law. The following year he married Alva Reimer, also a student at Stockholm, who as ALVA MYRDAL became a world-renowned sociologist and UNESCO official and a frequent collaborator with her husband on social and political projects. She died in 1986. The Myrdals had one son and two daughters: Jan Myrdal, an author prominent in Swedish literature and political debate; Sissela Bok, an

GUNNAR MYRDAL .

internationally recognized philosopher; and Kaj Fölster, a sociologist.

Not fully satisfied with practicing law, Myrdal returned to Stockholm University to study economics under Knut Wicksell and Gustav Cassel. After receiving his doctorate in 1927, he was appointed to a lectureship in political economy. On a Rockefeller Foundation Fellowship, he arrived in the United States the day before the stock market crash of 1929. Witnessing the economic and social crisis of the Depression years kindled his desire to influence economic policies. In 1933, after a sabbatical year in Switzerland, Myrdal returned to Stockholm University, where he spent the major portion of his academic career. He succeeded Cassel in the university's Lars Hierta Chair of Political Economy and Financial Science. Many years later, in 1961, he was appointed professor of international economics at the university and became the founder and director of its Institute for International Economic Studies.

Myrdal's interest in "pure" economic theory occupied him only from about 1925 to 1933. In this period his doctoral dissertation, "Prisbildningsproblemet och föränderligheten" (The Problem of Price Formation Under Economic Change, 1927), examined how the expectation of uncertain future market conditions might influence the behavior of companies at the microeconomic level. Myrdal's formulation of this problem prefigured much research on the economics of risk and uncertainty.

In 1931 Myrdal expanded Wicksell's theories of interest rate and cumulative processes

in an article appearing in the journal *Ekonomisk tidskrift* (Economics Magazine). In this work, which appeared in English as *Monetary Equilibrium* in 1939, he introduced the notions of ex ante and ex post into economic analysis. *Ex ante* refers to the anticipated value of a given economic variable; *ex post* refers to the realized (or actual) value of that variable. These two terms are crucial to the theories of dynamic economics developed in Stockholm during the 1930s. Consumers or companies (so-called economic actors) base their decisions on the ex ante values of economic variables (for example, anticipated prices), thereby, in an equilibrating process, helping to determine the value of ex post variables (for example, actual prices). Myrdal's ideas formed one basis for what became known as the Stockholm School of macroeconomics. In this connection he wrote *Finanspolitikens ekonomiska verkningar* (The Economic Effects of Fiscal Policy, 1934), proposing an active fiscal policy to combat the Depression. In it he argued that, to preserve public confidence, government deficits during the Depression should be matched by corresponding surpluses during the following boom. In fact, the Stockholm School, activated by Myrdal, developed Keynesian policy models before the appearance of John Maynard Keynes's *General Theory of Employment, Interest, and Money*.

After serving on several government committees, Myrdal was elected to the Swedish Parliament in 1935. Together the Myrdals helped design a population policy for Sweden. Their *Kris i befolkningsfrågan* (Crisis in the Population Problem, 1934) analyzed the reasons for Sweden's declining birth rate and proposed a "New Deal," recommending advanced housing policies, with subsidies for large families. Many of these proposals were realized during the following decades. Besides encouraging couples to have larger families, the book advocated universal sex education for high school students in the hope of reducing unwanted pregnancies. As a result, the Myrdals were surrounded by controversy and became the target of abundant satire.

While visiting the United States in 1938 to deliver a lecture series at Harvard University, Myrdal was asked by the Carnegie Corporation to head a large group of scholars studying the "Negro question." The corporation's trustees had requested "a comprehensive study of the Negro in the United States to be undertaken in a wholly objective way as a social phenomenon." Accepting the assignment, Myrdal and his team, which included RALPH

BUNCHE, produced *An American Dilemma: The Negro Problem and Modern Democracy* (1944), a two-volume work considered by many to be one of the most significant analyses of American race relations. In this work Myrdal did not take an exclusively economic approach; he also investigated the sociological, political, historical, legal, and institutional bases of white behavior toward black Americans, as well as the black response to racism. *An American Dilemma* not only shaped subsequent scholarly thought; it also exerted a deep and lasting effect on public policy. Its meticulous discussion of educational discrimination, for example, strongly influenced the United States Supreme Court's 1954 decision in *Brown* v. *Board of Education of Topeka,* which struck down the doctrine of "separate but equal" and outlawed racial segregation in public schools.

Myrdal returned to Sweden in 1940, after the Nazi invasion of Norway, but was posted to the United States in 1943 as an economic adviser to the Swedish embassy. In 1944 he published his famous book *Varning för fredsoptimism* (Warning Against Postwar Optimism), in which he predicted a major postwar depression originating in the United States. As chairman of a government economic commission, he stressed the dangers of continued stagnancy and lack of balance in world markets. Because of these conditions and the unbalanced industrial structure in Sweden, he recommended considerable government planning. He also looked for greater stability in the Eastern bloc's planned economies and suggested increased trade with them.

As a free and outspoken economist, Myrdal could never be a reliable social democrat or obey politicians' rules. In 1947 he left the government and accepted an appointment as secretary-general of the Economic Commission for Europe (ECE), a United Nations agency. There he created an independent economic secretariat whose reports were highly regarded. After completing his work at the ECE in 1957, he joined his wife in India, where she was serving as the Swedish ambassador, and began a ten-year study of the problems of underdeveloped Asian countries (he shunned the term *developing*). The results were published in 1968 as *Asian Drama: An Inquiry Into the Poverty of Nations.* The central thesis of this three-volume work was that only extensive reforms in population control, agricultural land distribution, health care, and education could bring about rapid economic development in Southeast Asia. Moreover, Myrdal concluded, the region's "soft governments" were too weak to combat what he called the cumulative forces of poverty. Although Western foreign aid could be important in special cases, if properly directed, it was generally a marginal factor, according to Myrdal. The book was widely praised for its encyclopedic compilation of facts and for its evenhanded approach, although its conclusions seemed profoundly pessimistic when compared to those of *An American Dilemma.*

This same pessimism about the conditions in Asian countries was reflected in a speech Myrdal made at the Stockholm Conference on Vietnam in the late 1960s. Critical of American policy, he stated that the chief obstacle to Vietnamese self-determination was "American aggression, which provoked a general uprising of the Vietnamese people." Even if a Communist takeover of Southeast Asia were imminent, he argued, communism could hardly worsen the ghastly economic and social conditions in the region.

Compared to PAUL SAMUELSON, GERARD DEBREU, or KENNETH ARROW, Myrdal, who called himself "an institutional economist," has not had a major influence on mainstream economic theory. His international influence, however, was immense, for he was one of the few Nobel economists who tackled the politics of economic and social policy and mastered a wide range of social science disciplines. In his view, an economist who ignores the effects of political and social forces on economic events is dangerous. In *Against the Stream: Critical Essays in Economics* (1973), Myrdal criticized mainstream economists for slighting the moral bases of economic theory. For example, he asserted that belief in the "optimality" of competitive markets (Adam Smith's "invisible hand") is justified only if distributional issues are ignored.

The 1974 Nobel Memorial Prize in Economic Sciences was awarded jointly to Myrdal and FRIEDRICH A. VON HAYEK "for their pioneering work in the theory of money and economic fluctuations and for their penetrating analysis of the interdependence of economic, social, and institutional phenomena." By the following year, when Myrdal delivered his Nobel lecture, the sense of gloom already evident in *Asian Drama* had, if anything, intensified. In his speech the laureate criticized the United States for allowing its foreign aid program to be tied to narrow national interests. He also condemned the "conspicuous consumption" of the West, which, he charged, contributed to the misery of the Third World.

As an academic, Myrdal was celebrated both at home and abroad. During his tenure at

NANSEN

Stockholm University, he was a visiting research fellow at the University of California in Santa Barbara (1973–1974) and the following year was distinguished visiting professor at New York University.

After a brief period of hospitalization, Myrdal died in Stockholm on May 17, 1987.

In addition to the Nobel Prize, Myrdal shared the Peace Prize given by the West German government (1970) with his wife Alva. He was a member of the British Academy, the American Academy of Arts and Sciences, and the Royal Swedish Academy of Sciences. He received more than thirty honorary degrees from European and American universities.

ADDITIONAL WORKS: Population: A Problem for Democracy, 1940; Economic Developments and Prospects in America, 1944; Psychological Impediments to Effective International Cooperation, 1952; The Political Element in the Development of Economic Theory, 1953; An International Economy: Problems and Prospects, 1956; Economic Theory and Underdeveloped Regions, 1957; Economic Nationalism and Internationalism, 1957; Beyond the Welfare State, 1960; Challenge to Affluence, 1963; Objectivity in Social Research, 1969; The Challenge of World Poverty, 1970; Essays and Lectures, 1973; Political and Institutional Economics, 1978.

ABOUT: Contemporary Review March 1974; Current Biography March 1975; New York Times May 18, 1987; Sills, D. L. (ed.) International Encyclopedia of the Social Sciences: Biographical Supplement, 1979; Southern, D. W. Gunnar Myrdal and Black-White Relations, 1987; Swedish Journal of Economics, number 4, 1974; Ulianovskii, R. A., and Pavlov, V. I. Asian Dilemma, 1975.

NANSEN, FRIDTJOF
(October 10, 1861–May 13, 1930)
Nobel Prize for Peace, 1922

The Norwegian explorer and humanitarian Fridtjof Nansen was born in Store-Frøen, on the outskirts of Christiania (now Oslo). His father, a lawyer, was strict with his children but encouraged them to enjoy the freedom of the outdoors. Nansen's mother, who participated in such outdoor sports as skiing, also helped Nansen develop a love of nature. As a youth, he spent many hours roaming the wooded hills of the Norwegian countryside, and he and his brothers lived in the forest for days at a time. In winter they fished through holes in the river ice and hunted on snowshoes. Through these experiences, Nansen developed the endurance and skills he later employed in his Arctic explorations.

Nansen enrolled at the University of Oslo in 1880, choosing to study zoology because it

FRIDTJOF NANSEN

Brown Brothers

would enable him to conduct fieldwork. Two years later he joined the crew of the *Viking,* a sealing ship that plied the Arctic waters, and soon observed the ice-covered mountains of Greenland. This view inspired his first exploratory expedition: the first crossing of Greenland by foot.

To accomplish this feat, Nansen proposed sailing as close as possible to Greenland's uninhabited eastern shore, abandoning the ship at the edge of the ice floes, and trekking across the ice and mountains to the western shore. Rebuffed in his initial attempts to find a sponsor for the expedition, he at last persuaded a Copenhagen philanthropist to underwrite the effort. In May 1888 Nansen and five crew members set sail. Upon reaching an ice floe, they abandoned ship as planned, but the floe broke loose and drifted several hundred miles south before striking land. Forced to march north before turning inland, the party lost valuable time as the Arctic winter set in.

Mountains, glaciers, and subzero temperatures imperiled the crossing, but after thirty-seven days the party reached an Eskimo settlement on the western shore. By then, however, it was late September, and the last ship of the season had just left port. While wintering in the village, Nansen made the most of his time by studying the inhabitants. Learning from the Eskimos and from his own experience, he perfected the classic method of polar travel using skis and dog-drawn sledges. In May 1889 the party returned to Norway, where Nansen received a hero's welcome and international acclaim.

Settling again in Norway, Nansen became curator of the University of Oslo's zoological collection in 1889 and wrote two books based on his adventures: *På ski over Gronland (The First Crossing of Greenland,* 1890) and *Eskimoliv (Eskimo Life,* 1891). Meanwhile, he began planning another expedition, which he hoped would make him the first to reach the North Pole and determine whether a landmass existed there. Reading accounts of an American exploration vessel that had become trapped in Arctic ice and had drifted for more than a year, he theorized that a properly designed ship could use the drifting ice to float over the pole. A grant from the Norwegian government enabled him to build the *Fram* (Forward), a round-bottomed boat designed to ride above the pressures of the ice.

Nansen set out in the summer of 1893 with a crew of twelve. The *Fram* came within 450 miles of the pole but made no further headway. In March Nansen and a crew member went on with a dogsled. Beset by difficulties, they were driven back after reaching 86° 13.6′ north, the farthest north anyone had gone at that time. Not knowing where the *Fram* had drifted, the two men were forced to winter on the archipelago of Franz Josef Land. They hunted walrus and polar bear for food and lived in a hut made of walrus hide. In May 1896 they encountered an English expedition and by August were reunited with the *Fram* and her crew. Nansen chronicled the expedition in his two-volume work *Fram over Polhavet: Den norske polarfærd* (1897, translated as *Farthest North*).

These experiences interested Nansen in the study of the ocean, and in 1908 the University of Oslo created a chair in oceanography for him. In this capacity Nansen helped found the International Council for the Exploration of the Sea, directed its laboratories in Oslo, and participated in several scientific voyages in the Arctic.

By this time an internationally respected public figure, Nansen participated in negotiations over the separation of Norway from Sweden in 1905. Many Swedes adamantly opposed dissolution of the bond between the nations. Nansen was sent to London to argue for recognition of Norway's right to independence. After the separation was accomplished peacefully, he served as his country's first ambassador to Great Britain, a post he held for two years, from 1906 to 1908. During this time he also worked on his book *Nord i taakeheimen (In Northern Mists,* 1910–1911). As the world's foremost authority on polar explora-

tion, Nansen advised the British explorer Robert Falcon Scott (advice Scott largely ignored) on preparations for the latter's fatal expedition to the South Pole. Borrowing Nansen's ship, the *Fram,* and adopting Nansen's methods, his fellow countryman Roald Amundsen reached the South Pole at the end of 1911.

After World War I broke out in 1914, Nansen again took up government service. In 1917 he was sent to the United States to negotiate an agreement providing Norway with essentials for the remainder of the war. Norway strongly supported the League of Nations, and Nansen, who headed the Norwegian League of Nations Society, was chosen to lead his country's first delegation to the league in 1920.

In the same year, Nansen was persuaded by PHILIP NOEL-BAKER, then an assistant to the league's British delegation, to oversee the repatriation of 500,000 German and Austro-Hungarian prisoners of war from Russia. The task was complicated by the chaos that followed the Russian Revolution and by the Soviet government's decision not to recognize the League of Nations. However, Nansen's international stature persuaded the Soviets to grant him authority to deal with the prisoners. Lacking funds to transport and provision the prisoners during repatriation, Nansen appealed to the league to secure loans for this purpose. He persuaded the Soviets to allocate trains to move the former prisoners to the frontier, and he obtained captured German ships from Britain to transport them from Soviet ports. By September some 437,000 prisoners had been returned to their homes.

During this time, Nansen took on the additional task of finding homes for 1.5 million refugees from the Russian Revolution. Many lacked identification papers and were being shuttled from country to country, living in squalid refugee camps where thousands perished from typhus and starvation. Nansen worked out an international agreement to provide papers for these refugees. Fifty-two nations eventually recognized the documents, which were called Nansen passports. Largely through his efforts, which continued until his death in 1930, most of the refugees were eventually resettled.

During the famine that struck the Soviet Union in the summer of 1921, Nansen, who had been appointed the league's high commissioner for refugees in June, appealed to foreign governments to provide humanitarian aid on a nonpolitical basis. When the League of Nations turned down his request for a relief loan, he appealed to the world. The United

States government contributed $20 million. This money, along with donations from other governments and relief organizations, financed a relief effort estimated to have saved as many as 10 million lives. Nansen also took an interest in the refugees from the 1922 war between Greece and Turkey and arranged an exchange of 1,000,000 Greeks living in Turkey for 500,000 Turks living in Greece.

For his efforts on behalf of the helpless, Nansen was awarded the 1922 Nobel Peace Prize. "The Nobel Peace Prize has in the course of the years been given to all sorts of men," a Danish journalist wrote. "It has surely never been awarded to anyone who in such a short time has carried out such far-reaching practical peace work as Nansen." Fredrik Stang of the Norwegian Nobel Committee echoed this sentiment in his presentation speech: "Perhaps what has most impressed all of us is his ability to stake his life time and time again on a single idea, on one thought, and to inspire others to follow him."

In his Nobel lecture, Nansen described the desperate conditions brought about by World War I and pleaded for the League of Nations as the only means of averting future tragedies. "It is because of blind fanaticism for and against—especially against—that conflicts come to a head and lead to heartrending struggles and destruction; whereas discussion, understanding, and tolerance might have turned this energy into valuable progress," he said. Nansen dedicated his prize money to refugee relief.

Nansen never married. He died in Oslo in 1930 after overexerting himself on a skiing trip. He was buried on May 17, the anniversary of Norway's independence.

ADDITIONAL WORKS IN ENGLISH TRANSLATION: The Norwegian North Pole Expedition (6 vols.) 1900–1906, with others; Through Siberia, the Land of the Future, 1914; Russia and Peace, 1923; Adventure and Other Papers, 1927; Armenia and the Near East, 1928.

ABOUT: Christensen, C. A. R. Fridtjof Nansen: A Life in the Service of Science and Humanity, 1961; Hoyer, L. N. Nansen: A Family Portrait, 1957; Innes, K. E. The Story of Nansen and the League of Nations, 1931; Joyce, J. A. Broken Star: The Story of the League of Nations, 1978; Shackleton, E. Nansen: The Explorer, 1959; Sorenson, J. The Saga of Fridtjof Nansen, 1932; Vogt, P. Fridtjof Nansen: Explorer, Scientist, Humanitarian, 1961.

NANSEN INTERNATIONAL OFFICE FOR REFUGEES

(founded 1930)
Nobel Prize for Peace, 1938

The Nansen International Office for Refugees was created to carry on the work of the League of Nations High Commission for Refugees. The high commission was established in 1921 under the direction of the Norwegian explorer FRIDTJOF NANSEN, its high commissioner from then until his death in 1930. The feats of exploration for which Nansen gained worldwide respect, his organizational abilities, his scientific bent, and his growing humanitarianism after observing the squalor resulting from World War I—all these combined to make him a forceful figure in dealing with the problems of international refugees.

Nansen was a leading advocate of the League of Nations and Norway's first league representative. As high commissioner, he was given the responsibility for repatriating some 500,000 prisoners of war held in Russia. This was seen as the league's first noteworthy achievement. Nansen also worked to resettle millions of refugees from the 1917 Russian Revolution, campaigned to ease the effects of the 1921 famine in the Soviet Union, and effected a refugee exchange between Greece and Turkey after their war in 1922. Another compelling refugee problem facing the commission was created by the strife between Turkey and its Armenian minority.

Because many refugees came from countries that no longer existed after World War I, they lacked valid passports and were shuttled from country to country and from camp to camp without hope of repatriation or permanent settlement. This problem was solved by Nansen in 1922 when he won international recognition of a form of identity paper that became known as the Nansen passport. The document was issued to many refugees and eventually gained acceptance by fifty-two nations.

Nansen, who was awarded the 1922 Nobel Peace Prize, dedicated his prize money to refugee assistance. He continued to work on behalf of refugees until his death in May 1930. In the fall of 1930, the League of Nations began setting up the Nansen International Office for Refugees, and on April 1, 1931, the office began operating in Geneva.

Although Nansen had accomplished much of the task of relocating refugees, the office made great strides to complete the work. By the end of 1935, it had resettled more than 40,000 Armenians in Syria and Lebanon and another 10,000 in Yerevan. During the same year, it found refuge in Paraguay for 4,000 people who fled the Saar after a plebescite returned the region to Germany.

Relocation, however, did not solve all refugee problems. Authorities often harassed refugees, and many found themselves excluded from the economic life of their host nations. The bulk of the work of the Nansen Office consisted of aiding refugees with the day-to-day problems they faced after resettlement. Through representatives in several major nations, the office functioned as a kind of consulate for Nansen passport holders in their dealings with authorities. The office also used its scant resources to award loans and grants to needy refugees. Its main source of funding was the 250,000 Norwegian kroner from Nansen's estate. It also collected a small levy each year from holders of the Nansen passport. By 1938 the office had assisted more than 800,000 refugees. It had also campaigned successfully for adoption by fourteen nations of the Refugee Convention of 1933, a document guaranteeing basic human rights to refugees.

The Nansen International Office for Refugees was awarded the 1938 Nobel Prize for Peace. In presenting the prize, Fredrik Stang of the Norwegian Nobel Committee stated, "The work accomplished by the Nansen Office throughout its years of operation is great. And it is easy to see that it has been influenced by the traditions of Fridtjof Nansen's time. It is marked by two characteristics that rarely go together, but which in Nansen were combined: the highest idealism and an exceptional faculty for the practical." Stang spoke of the message carried to refugees by the work of the office. He added that the message was directed not only to refugees but to "those in politics, that political action has a higher goal than that of sowing discord and harvesting hate."

The office was represented at the award ceremonies by Michael Hansson, a Norwegian international jurist who had been its president since 1936. In his Nobel lecture, he described the history of the office and its work. He noted that when Nansen began his work in 1920, he believed the refugee problem could be solved in a decade. Hansson explained why this was impossible. The worldwide economic depression of the 1930s hit refugees hardest, just when they were establishing themselves in their new countries. Moreover, the anti-Semitic policies of Nazi Germany were creating an exodus of German Jews. In 1933 the League of Nations set up the High Commission on Refugees From Germany to deal specifically with this prob-

lem. By 1935 the first steps had been taken to join this body with the Nansen Office, which was originally intended to have a term of ten years. A new High Commission for All Refugees Under League of Nations Protection was eventually created to fulfill the duties of both offices. When this high commission began operating in London on January 1, 1939, the role of the Nansen Office came to an end.

SELECTED PUBLICATIONS: Report by the Governing Body, 1931; Convention Relating to the Status of Refugees, 1938.

ABOUT: Christensen, C. A. R. Fridtjof Nansen: A Life in the Service of Science and Humanity, 1961; Hansson, M. The Refugee Problem and the League of Nations, 1938; Innes, K. E. The Story of Nansen and the League of Nations, 1931; Macartney, C. A. Refugees: The Work of the League, 1930; Proudfoot, M. J. European Refugees, 1939–1952, 1957; Vernant, J. The Refugee in the Post-War World, 1953.

NATHANS, DANIEL
(October 30, 1928–   )
Nobel Prize for Physiology or Medicine, 1978
(shared with Werner Arber and Hamilton O. Smith)

The American molecular biologist Daniel Nathans, the last of nine children of Sarah (Levitan) and Samuel Nathans, both of whom were Russian Jewish immigrants, was born in Wilmington, Delaware. After the Great Depression began, his father's business failed. Among Nathans's earliest memories are the hardships caused by the Depression and his parents' good humor in the face of adversity.

He received his early education in the Wilmington public schools, usually working part-time after school or on weekends. In 1946 he enrolled in the University of Delaware, where he studied mathematics, chemistry, philosophy, and literature, and from which he received a bachelor's degree in 1950. Entering the Washington University School of Medicine in St. Louis on a scholarship that year, he found the faculty to be "scholarly and dedicated." He discovered medical research during "one wonderful summer" under Oliver Lowry, a professor of pharmacology, and, instead of entering medical practice, he decided to pursue a career in research and teaching. After receiving his medical degree in 1954, he interned at the Columbia-Presbyterian Medical Center in New York City, where he at-

The Johns Hopkins Medical Institutions

DANIEL NATHANS

tended to the patients of the "masterful clinician and medical scientist" Professor Robert Loeb.

From 1955 until 1957 Nathans was a clinical associate at the National Cancer Institute (NCI) of the National Institutes of Health in Bethesda, Maryland. There he investigated protein biosynthesis, specifically the myeloma protein that is synthesized by malignant plasma cells in multiple myeloma (bone cancer). Returning to the Columbia-Presbyterian Medical Center, for two years he again assisted Loeb as a medical resident. From 1959 until 1962 he was a guest investigator in FRITZ LIPMANN's laboratory at the Rockefeller Institute for Medical Research (now Rockefeller University) in New York City. At Rockefeller, Nathans continued to study protein biosynthesis and identified certain bacterial factors that promote the incorporation of amino acids—the building blocks of protein—into peptide molecules. While working with the molecular geneticist Norton Zinder, he investigated the role of bacteriophage ribonucleic acid (RNA) in the synthesis of bacteriophage protein in a test tube containing cellular extract.

The genetics and life cycle of the bacteriophage had been elucidated during the 1940s and 1950s. Bacteriophage (viruses that infect bacterial cells) are among the simplest forms of life, consisting of an inner core of nucleic acid and an outer coat of protein. After it enters a bacterial cell, an infective bacteriophage has three possible fates. First, it may appropriate the biochemical apparatus of the bacterial cell and release new phage particles, causing destruction of the cell. Second, it may

be incorporated into the genetic structure, or deoxyribonucleic acid (DNA), of the bacterial cell (in which case it is called a prophage) and then be transmitted to daughter cells during bacterial-cell division. Third, the bacteriophage enzyme system may be broken into its constituent parts by the action of bacterial enzymes, a phenomenon called host-cell-induced variation, or restriction-modification.

Restriction-modification is brought about by the intervention of a pair of bacterial-cell enzymes, a restriction endonuclease and a methylase. The restriction endonuclease recognizes a specific nucleotide sequence on the bacteriophage DNA and cleaves, or cuts, the phage DNA into several parts. Meanwhile, the methylase recognizes the identical nucleotide sequence on the host-cell DNA, methylates the host-cell DNA, and thus protects it from enzymatic cleavage by its own endonuclease enzyme. (Methylation involves the addition of a methyl group—a carbon atom and three hydrogen atoms—to the DNA molecule.)

In the 1960s WERNER ARBER of the University of Geneva in Switzerland postulated that restriction-modification systems are general properties of bacteria. Arber also discovered a restriction endonuclease enzyme in the colon bacillus Escherichia coli. Arber's endonuclease, however, cleaved phage DNA at nonspecific sites. He called it a type I endonuclease and predicted that site-specific restriction endonucleases would be found in other bacterial systems and that they would prove to be useful in analyzing the precise genetic structure of DNA molecules.

In 1962 Nathans became an assistant professor of microbiology at the Johns Hopkins School of Medicine, with a concurrent appointment as head of the genetics division. He rose to associate professor in 1965 and two years later was named full professor. During these years Nathans continued to study the replication of bacteriophages in experimental systems, especially the regulation of the replication process and the location of genes on the DNA and RNA molecules.

During the mid-1960s Nathans lectured medical students on the subject of animal viruses, which resemble bacteriophage viruses except that they infect the cells of animal species. Animal viruses may be infectious or tumorigenic, that is, causing or producing tumors. As Nathans began to investigate animal viruses in more detail, he became particularly interested in simian virus 40, which causes tumors in monkeys, and concentrated on analyzing the location and function of genes of the simian virus DNA, while continuing to read widely on the genetics of animal viruses.

In a letter to Nathans written in 1969, while Nathans was an American Cancer Society Fellow at the Weizmann Institute of Science in Rehovot, Israel, HAMILTON O. SMITH, a colleague at Johns Hopkins, reported that he had isolated and purified a site-specific restriction endonuclease in *Haemophilus influenzae*. This finding caused Nathans to consider the possibility of using restriction enzymes to dissect the genomes (complete set of hereditary factors) of DNA tumor viruses. Upon returning to Johns Hopkins that summer, he spent several months investigating the genetic structure of the DNA of simian virus 40, using Smith's endonuclease and another endonuclease discovered by a different investigator.

The simian virus DNA was suitable because it is small, consisting of only 5,000 nucleotides (one of the compounds into which nucleic acid is split by the action of nuclease) and a few genes. Nathans and his colleagues first cleaved the DNA molecule with the two endonucleases, identified the various parts, and made a map of the cleavage sites. Next they identified the location and function of specific genes and made a detailed genetic map of the DNA molecule, including the sites of origin and termination of the replication process. (Because the DNA molecule of the simian virus is circular, replication proceeds in two directions around the circular DNA and terminates 180 degrees opposite the site of origin.) They also identified the template (or nucleotide mold) for messenger RNA and the location of the genes that direct the synthesis of the protein coat of the virus, using selected mutant strains of the simian DNA to analyze certain gene locations and functions. Nathans's efforts yielded the first genetic map of a DNA molecule. The methods that he developed for analyzing genetic structure were later used in genetic mapping of more complex DNA molecules, as well as in recombinant DNA techniques for the production of bacterial "factories" that synthesize medically useful compounds such as insulin and growth hormones.

Nathans shared the 1978 Nobel Prize for Physiology or Medicine with Arber and Smith for "the discovery of restriction enzymes and their application to problems of molecular genetics." In his Nobel lecture Nathans described his research on simian virus 40. "In time," he concluded, "it should be possible to make out the basic regulatory mechanisms used by plant and animal cells, and eventually to understand some of the complex genetic programs that govern the growth, development, and specialized functions of higher organisms, including man."

Since 1980 Nathans has been Boury Professor of Molecular Biology and Genetics at Johns Hopkins, as well as senior investigator at the Howard Hughes Medical Institute.

Nathans married Joanne Gomberg in 1956; they have three sons. "My field of research is as exciting to me as ever," Nathans has said. "I have talented students who are a source of much enjoyment and I anticipate more to come as their careers develop."

Nathans's awards include the United States Steel Foundation Award in Molecular Biology of the National Academy of Sciences (1976). He is a member of the American Academy of Arts and Sciences.

ABOUT: New York Times October 13, 1978; Science December 8, 1978.

NATTA, GIULIO
(February 26, 1903–May 1, 1979)
Nobel Prize for Chemistry, 1963
(shared with Karl Ziegler)

The Italian chemist Giulio Natta (nät′ tä) was born in Imperia, a resort town on the Mediterranean coast, the son of Francesco Natta, a well-known attorney and judge, and Elena (Crespi) Natta. Raised in the nearby city of Genoa, the boy was twelve when he first came across a chemistry book. He developed an immediate interest in the subject. After graduating from Genoa's high school of science in 1919, Natta entered the University of Genoa to study pure mathematics but soon transferred to the Milan Polytechnic Institute, seeking a field with more practical applications. In chemical engineering he found a suitable combination of theory and practice, and in 1924 he received his doctorate from the Milan Polytechnic Institute.

Remaining at the Polytechnic, Natta rose from instructor to full professor in three years. During this time his research concerned the determination of the structure of inorganic solids by methods of X-ray diffraction. In 1932, Natta visited the University of Freiburg in Germany to study the relatively new technique of electron diffraction. At Freiburg he became acquainted with HERMANN STAUDINGER and his work on the chemistry of polymers—huge molecules linked into chains of repeating small

GIULIO NATTA

molecular units called monomers. Applying his own research results to polymer chemistry, Natta began shifting from inorganic to organic chemistry.

After returning to Italy in 1933, Natta accepted a position as full professor and director of the Institute of General Chemistry at the University of Pavia. Two years later he became chairman of the physical chemistry department at the University of Rome, and in 1937 he was appointed professor of industrial chemistry and director of the Institute of Industrial Chemistry at the Turin Polytechnic Institute. An appointment as professor and director of the Industrial Chemistry Research Center brought him back to Milan in 1938.

Natta's interest in polymer chemistry coincided with the Italian government's pre–World War II program to become self-sufficient in certain essential resources, and in 1938 he received an appointment to direct research into artificial substitutes for commodities, especially rubber. During the war Natta also developed catalytic syntheses for such important chemicals as methanol, butadiene, formaldehyde, and butyraldehyde. After the war, the Montecatini Company, a large chemical company in Milan, began to subsidize Natta's work.

Natta benefited also from the research of the German chemist KARL ZIEGLER, who was likewise interested in polymer catalysis. A lecture delivered by Ziegler in Frankfurt in 1952 inspired Natta to pursue complementary and parallel studies on the reaction mechanisms of polymerizations (the uniting of two or more monomers to form a polymer). Later in the

following year, Ziegler discovered that certain inorganic catalysts such as titanium tetrachloride worked in combination with aluminum alkyls to catalyze the polymerization of ethylene (a type of unsaturated hydrocarbon). The resulting high-density polyethylene plastic had desirable properties that far exceeded those of the crude low-density polyethylene then available. Subsequently Natta turned his attention to the next larger olefin (a class of unsaturated hydrocarbons), propylene, a by-product of petroleum refining that cost ten times less than ethylene. In 1954 he and his colleagues discovered a method of catalytically polymerizing propylene, similar to Ziegler's ethylene process. Natta found that the new plastic was strong, had a high melting point and high crystallinity, and in many respects was superior to Ziegler's high-density polyethylene.

Applying his knowledge of physical chemistry, Natta carried out X-ray and electron-diffraction studies of the new polypropylene to determine its molecular structure. The results showed that Ziegler's catalysts (since known as Ziegler-Natta catalysts) produced macromolecules with extraordinarily regular atomic spatial relationships—the so-called stereoregular polymers. This method of catalysis was the key to the remarkable properties of these polymers. In the case of Natta's polypropylene, all the side chains of each monomer unit were arrayed on the same side of the molecule, rather than being randomly oriented as in the existing but inferior plastics. When Natta asked his wife, the former Rosita Beati, a professor of literature at the University of Milan, for an appropriate term to describe this structure, she suggested *isotactic* (meaning all on the same side), and this neologism promptly entered the chemical literature.

Accompanied by a top official of Montecatini on a trip to New York City in June 1956, Natta held a news conference to announce the discovery of isotactic polypropylene. The items he displayed showed that the material could be cast or extruded into the form of solid objects, spun into fibers as strong as nylon yet light enough to float on water, or spread into films as clear as cellophane. Industrial production of Natta's polypropylene was soon started in Italy and eventually was licensed for production around the world.

While continuing his study of polymerization catalysis, Natta made rapid progress in understanding the reactions and in devising new processes and materials. Among the varieties of new plastics introduced as the result of his research were a new polystyrene and a polybutadiene. Natta's studies provide the polymer chemist with unmatched control of the precise size and shapes of the macromolecules with which they deal.

"For their discoveries in the field of the chemistry and technology of high polymers," Natta and Ziegler shared the 1963 Nobel Prize for Chemistry. In his presentation speech, Arne Fredga of the Royal Swedish Academy of Sciences declared that Natta's discoveries had broken the monopoly of nature in stereoregular polymers. In his Nobel lecture Natta pointed out that "the knowledge acquired in these last ten years in the field of the stereospecificity of the polymerization processes shows that stereoregular and, in particular, isotactic polymers can be obtained in the presence of suitable catalysts acting through an ionic (both anionic and cationic) coordinated mechanism; however," he added, "they cannot generally be obtained by processes characterized by radical mechanism."

Natta proved a perfect complement to Ziegler. Whereas Ziegler was the archetypal organic chemist, interested primarily in pure science, Natta pursued an essentially physical approach to polymer chemistry; he was concerned with both its scientific aspects and the problems of industrial production.

An extremely hard and productive worker, Natta was known as a gentle and pleasant man with a strong love of nature. He married Rosita Beati in 1935. They had a son and a daughter. During the last two decades of his life, Natta's activities were increasingly limited by Parkinson's disease. He died in Bergamo at the age of seventy-six.

In addition to the Nobel Prize, Natta received the Lavoisier Medal of the French Chemical Society (1963) and the Lomonosov Gold Medal of the Soviet Academy of Sciences (1969). He held honorary degrees from the universities of Turin, Mainz, Genoa, Belgium, and Paris, as well as from the Polytechnic Institute of Brooklyn, New York. He was a member of the National Academy of Sciences in Rome and an honorary member of the New York Academy of Sciences.

SELECTED WORKS: Stereochemistry, 1972, with Mario Farina.

ABOUT: Current Biography November 1964; New York Times November 6, 1963.

NÉEL, LOUIS
(November 22, 1904–)
Nobel Prize for Physics, 1970
(shared with Hannes Alfvén)

The French physicist Louis Eugène Félix Néel (nā el′) was born in Lyons, the son of Louis Néel, a director in the civil service, and Marie-Antoinette (Hartmayer) Néel. After receiving his secondary education at the Lycée du Parc in Lyons and at the Lycée St.-Louis in Paris, he attended the prestigious École Normale Supérieure and was appointed a lecturer there upon his graduation in 1928. He then began graduate studies at the University of Strasbourg under Pierre Weiss, earning his doctorate in 1932.

Weiss, like PIERRE CURIE, was a pioneer in the theoretical study of magnetization (the magnetism a substance acquires in an external magnetic field). Although he had given quantitative explanations of many experimental results, he had been unable to explain precisely the interaction of two neighboring elementary magnets (that is, neighboring atoms, which act as tiny magnets). In 1928, as Néel was taking up the study of magnetization, WERNER HEISENBERG successfully explained this interaction, using the recently formulated quantum theory.

At the time, three types of magnetic material were known: diamagnetic, paramagnetic, and ferromagnetic. In diamagnetic substances such as bismuth and antimony (which are slightly repelled by an external magnetic field) and in paramagnetic substances such as aluminum and platinum (which are slightly attracted to an external field), the elementary magnets are essentially independent of one another. Therefore, the magnetic fields of these substances are oriented in different directions, almost canceling each other's effects. In ferromagnetic substances, such as iron and nickel, neighboring atoms interact so that their magnetic fields tend to be oriented in the same direction. Heisenberg was able to show that such interactions produce the large-scale magnetic characteristics exhibited by ferromagnetic substances.

Building on Heisenberg's work, Néel hypothesized that in certain substances the interactions of neighboring atoms cause their magnetic fields to be oriented in opposite directions. He suggested that the crystal lattice of such a substance could be viewed as two identical interpenetrating sublattices, each composed of atoms with magnetic fields oriented in a single direction. This rigid orien-

LOUIS NÉEL

tation of opposed fields, resulting in zero net magnetization, would occur below a certain temperature, now known as the Néel point. Above the Néel point, paramagnetic effects would occur. Probable examples of such antiferromagnetic substances, as they are now called, were first identified in 1937, but it was not until 1949 that Néel's theory was confirmed by neutron diffraction studies.

In 1937 Néel was appointed professor at the Strasbourg Faculty of Science, a position he held until 1945. With the outbreak of World War II, he also began working for the French navy and was assigned to protect warships against magnetic mines. At the end of the war, in 1945, Néel joined the faculty at the University of Grenoble. There he set up the Laboratory of Electrostatics and the Physics of Metals, which he directed until 1976.

Three years after moving to Grenoble, Néel proposed another form of magnetization, which he called ferrimagnetism. It had long been known that ferrites, a class of minerals that includes magnetite (lodestone), exhibit anomalous magnetic behavior in relation to ferromagnetic substances, with which they were classified. Proposing that ferrites constitute a separate class, Néel expanded his earlier theory of antiferromagnetism to explain the behavior of ferrimagnetism. In ferrimagnetic substances, he said, the magnetic fields of the lattices are of different strengths, so that a net magnetic effect occurs. Some of these substances, including magnetite, possess not two but three lattices, two of which cancel each other. Ferrites, which are not electrical con-

ductors, have since proved extremely useful in the coating of magnetic tape, in computer memory cores, in communications technology, and in many other applications. The production of synthetic ferrites for such purposes resulted largely from Néel's research.

In 1956 Néel was asked to establish and direct the Center for Nuclear Studies at Grenoble, where he has worked on neutron diffraction and crystal growth. He was also involved in the establishment of a French-German high-flux reactor in Grenoble. Largely because of Néel's role in Grenoble's scientific institutes, the city has become a major center for physics research.

Néel's other research has included the study of magnetic creep (changes that occur in ferromagnetism over time), the properties of extremely fine-grained ferromagnetic substances, and methods for improving the magnetic properties of substances. His work on paleomagnetism, which helped explain the "magnetic memory" of rocks during changes in the earth's magnetic field, contributed to the first decisive evidence for continental drift and the theory of plate tectonics.

Néel received the 1970 Nobel Prize for Physics "for fundamental work and discoveries concerning antiferromagnetism and ferrimagnetism, which have led to important applications in solid-state physics." He shared the honor with HANNES ALFVÉN, who was cited for his work in magnetohydrodynamics. In presenting the award to Néel, Torsten Gustafsson of the Royal Swedish Academy of Sciences declared that "remarkable observations in the physics of the solid state were explained" by Néel's theories.

Néel married Hélène Hourticq in 1931; they have one son and two daughters. He enjoys taking long walks through the countryside, reading eighteenth-century French literature and mystery stories, and carpentry.

In addition to the Nobel Prize, Néel has been awarded the Holweck Prize of the Physical Society of London (1952) and the Gold Medal of the National Center for Scientific Research in Paris. He holds many honorary degrees, and he is a member of the French Academy of Sciences, the American Academy of Arts and Sciences, the Soviet Academy of Sciences, the Royal Society of London, and scientific academies in other countries. Between 1963 and 1983 Néel was the French representative to the scientific committee of NATO, and from 1963 to 1965 he served as president of the International Union of Pure and Applied Physics. Since 1981 he has been president of the High Council for Nuclear Safety. He was made a grand officer of the Legion of Honor in 1966.

SELECTED WORKS: The Selected Works of Louis Néel, 1983, with Nicholas Kurti.

ABOUT: New York Times October 28, 1970; Science November 6, 1970.

NERNST, WALTHER
(June 25, 1864–November 18, 1941)
Nobel Prize for Chemistry, 1920

WALTHER NERNST

The German chemist Hermann Walther Nernst was born in Briessen, West Prussia (now Wabrzezno, Poland), the third child of Gustav Nernst, a judge in the Prussian civil service, and Ottilie (Nerger) Nernst. At Graudenz Gymnasium he studied natural science, literature, and the classics, graduating first in his class in 1883. Although he aspired to be a poet, his chemistry teacher kindled his interest in science.

Between 1883 and 1887, Nernst studied physics at the universities of Zurich (with Heinrich Weber), Berlin (with Hermann von Helmholtz), Graz (with Ludwig Boltzmann), and Würzburg (with Friedrich W. G. Kohlrausch). Boltzmann, who placed great importance on the atomistic interpretation of natural phenomena, encouraged Nernst to investigate the combined effects of magnetism and heat on electric currents. The work, supervised by Kohlrausch, led to the discovery that a metallic conductor heated at one end generates an electric current when placed perpendicular to a magnetic field. For this research Nernst earned a doctorate in 1887.

It was around this time that Nernst became acquainted with the chemists SVANTE ARRHENIUS, WILHELM OSTWALD, and JACOBUS VAN'T HOFF. Ostwald and van't Hoff had just launched the new *Zeitschrift für physikalische Chemie* (Journal of Physical Chemistry), in which they reported developments in the application of physics to chemical problems. Nernst became Ostwald's assistant at the University of Leipzig in 1887 and soon came to be considered one of the founders of the new discipline of physical chemistry, even though he was much younger than Ostwald, van't Hoff, and Arrhenius.

In Leipzig, Nernst worked on theoretical as well as experimental problems in physical chemistry. In 1888 and 1889 he investigated the behavior of electrolytes (solutions of electrically charged particles, or ions) in the presence of electric currents and developed a fundamental law, known as the Nernst equation, which describes the relationship between electromotive force (voltage) and ionic concentration. The equation makes it possible to predict the maximum work potential that can be generated by an electrochemical interaction (for example, the maximum voltage of a chemical battery) when only simple physical properties of pressure and temperature are known. It thus links thermodynamic and electrochemical theory for problems involving very dilute solutions. For this work Nernst, still in his midtwenties, earned an international reputation.

Between 1890 and 1891 Nernst investigated substances that, when dissolved in liquids, do not mix with each other. He developed the Nernst distribution equation to describe the activity of these substances as a function of concentration. Henry's law, which describes the solubility of a gas in a liquid, was later shown to be a special case of the more general Nernst law. The Nernst distribution equation is important in the fields of medicine and biology because it allows analysis of the distribution of substances in different parts of a living organism.

Nernst was appointed associate professor of physics at the University of Göttingen in 1891. Two years later he published *Theoretical Chemistry From the Standpoint of Avogadro's Rule and Thermodynamics,* an influential textbook on physical chemistry that went through fifteen editions and was used for over three decades. Considering himself a physicist doing chemistry, Nernst defined the new discipline of physical chemistry as "the meeting of two sciences hitherto somewhat independent of each other."

Fundamental to Nernst's physical chemistry was the Italian chemist Amedeo Avogadro's hypothesis that the number of integral molecules in any gas is always the same for equal volumes. Nernst called this a "horn of plenty" for the molecular theory. Equally important was the thermodynamic law of energy conservation that governs all natural processes. By applying these two basic principles to scientific problems, Nernst strengthened the foundations of physical chemistry.

In 1894 Nernst became professor of physical chemistry at Göttingen and established the Kaiser Wilhelm Institute for Physical Chemistry and Electrochemistry. An international group of scholars joined him there to investigate such topics as polarization, dielectric constants, and chemical equilibria.

Nernst left Göttingen in 1905 to become professor of chemistry at the University of Berlin. That year he proposed his "heat theorem," now known as the third law of thermodynamics. This theorem makes it possible to use thermal data to calculate chemical equilibria—that is, to predict how far a given reaction will go before it reaches equilibrium. Over the next decade Nernst defended and tested his theorem, which was subsequently used for such widely differing purposes as verifying the quantum theory and commercially synthesizing ammonia, an important step in the manufacture of explosives.

In 1912 Nernst expressed his heat theorem as the basic unattainability of absolute zero. "It is not possible," he said, "to build a caloric machine that will reduce the temperature of a substance to absolute zero." From this conclusion, Nernst proposed that the physical activities of substances tend to vanish as the temperature approaches absolute zero. The fields of cryogenics (extremely low-temperature physics) and solid-state physics depend on the third law of thermodynamics.

Nernst was an early automobile enthusiast and served during World War I as a driver in the Volunteer Automobile Corps. He also worked on chemical weapons, which he believed to be the most humane insofar as they might break the deadly stalemate on the Western front. After the war, he returned to his laboratory in Berlin.

In 1921 Nernst was awarded the 1920 Nobel Prize for Chemistry "in recognition of his work in thermochemistry." In his Nobel lecture Nernst reported that "in more than 100 experimental studies an abundance of data were collected, which confirmed the new theorem as accurately as allowed by the precision of what were at times very difficult experiments."

From 1922 to 1924 Nernst was president of the Reich Institute for Applied Physics in Jena, but when postwar inflation made impossible the changes he wanted to institute, he returned to the University of Berlin as professor of physics. Toward the end of his career, Nernst examined cosmological questions raised by his third law of thermodynamics (specifically, the so-called heat death of the universe, an idea he opposed), as well as photochemistry and chemical kinetics.

In 1892 Nernst married Emma Lohmeyer, the daughter of a noted Göttingen surgeon. They had two sons, both of whom were killed in World War I, and a daughter. Known for his strong ego, good sense of humor, and interest in life, Nernst had a lasting love of literature and the theater and was especially fond of Shakespeare. An influential organizer of scientific institutions, he helped establish the first Solvay Conference and the German Electrochemical Society as well as the Kaiser Wilhelm Institute.

After Adolf Hitler came to power in 1933, Nernst opposed Nazi efforts to discredit the contributions of ALBERT EINSTEIN and other Jewish scientists, telling his colleagues that the anti-Semitism of PHILIPP VON LENARD, JOHANNES STARK, and others would sabotage progress in physics and chemistry. Increasingly isolated by his anti-Nazi stance, Nernst retired in 1934 to his country home at Lusatia, where he died suddenly of heart failure in 1941. He was a member of the Berlin Academy of Sciences and a fellow of the Royal Society of London.

SELECTED WORKS: Experimental and Theoretical Applications of Thermodynamics to Chemistry, 1907; The Theory of the Solid State, 1914; The New Heat Theorem, 1917.

ABOUT: Dictionary of Scientific Biography, volume 15, 1978; Farber, E. (ed.) Great Chemists, 1961; Mendelssohn, K. The World of Walther Nernst, 1973; Obituary Notices of Fellows of the Royal Society, volume 4, 1942.

NERUDA, PABLO
(July 12, 1904–September 23, 1973)
Nobel Prize for Literature, 1971

The Chilean poet and diplomat Pablo Neruda (nä rōō′ dä) was born Ricardo Eliecer

Neftalí Reyes y Basoalto in the small town of Parral in central Chile. His father, José del Carmen Reyes, worked for the railroad; his mother, Rosa de Basoalto, a schoolteacher, died of tuberculosis when Neruda was an infant. Soon afterward, Neruda's father married Trinidad Candia, and the family moved to Temuco, in the south, where the forests and natural beauty of the region made a lasting impression on the boy.

Attending the Liceo de Temuco, Neruda read widely and at the age of ten began writing verse. Two years later he met the Chilean poet GABRIELA MISTRAL, who befriended him and encouraged his literary efforts. In 1920, the year he completed his secondary education, he began submitting poems to the magazine *Selva Austral* (Southern Jungle), using the pen name Pablo Neruda to avoid conflict with his family, who disapproved of his literary ambitions. Later, he adopted the name legally.

The following year Neruda entered the Instituto Pedagógico in Santiago, the capital, to study French, but he was distracted from his studies by the city's literary life. His own literary aspirations received further encouragement when his poem "La Canción de la fiesta" (The Song of the Feast) won first prize in a contest sponsored by the Federation of Chilean Students. By selling his possessions, Neruda was able to finance the publication of his first volume of poetry, *Crepusculario* (Twilight), in 1923. Conventional in language and form, these poems received favorable notice and helped Neruda find a publisher the following year for another volume, *Veinte poemas de amor y una canción desesperada* (*Twenty Love Poems and a Song of Despair*). Although many reviewers expressed dismay at its explicitly erotic celebration of love, the collection made a celebrity of the twenty-year-old poet, who gave up his studies and devoted himself entirely to poetry. In *Tentativa del hombre infinito* (Venture of the Infinite Man, 1926), he abandoned the conventions of meter and rhyme, expressing his inner turmoil in language and images that verge on the surreal.

In 1927, in accordance with a Latin American tradition of honoring poets with diplomatic assignments, the Chilean government appointed Neruda consul, and he spent the next five years representing his nation in Burma, Ceylon, the Dutch East Indies, India, Japan, and other parts of Asia. During this time he married Maria Antonieta Haagenar Vogelzang, a Dutch woman, in Bali, and wrote the first volume of *Residencia en la tierra* (*Residence on Earth*), which was published in 1933.

PABLO NERUDA

The pessimism and melancholy of this work reflect the loneliness and dissatisfaction Neruda experienced during his years away from Latin America. Expecting the book to be received as a masterpiece, he sought a publisher in Spain; when these plans fell through, Neruda consented to a limited edition in Chile in 1933.

That year Neruda was posted to Buenos Aires where he met and befriended the visiting Spanish poet Federico García Lorca. In 1934 he served as Chilean consul first in Barcelona and then in Madrid, during which time he collaborated with García Lorca and several other Spanish poets in publishing a literary journal, *El Caballo verde para la poesía* (The Green Horse for Poetry), in which Neruda also published essays. While in Madrid he brought out the second part of *Residence on Earth* (1935), in which the dark, introspective mood of the preceding volume gives way to a more outgoing narrative style. Divorcing his first wife in 1936, he married Delia del Carril in Madrid the same year.

With the outbreak of the Spanish Civil War, Neruda's work shifted from the personal to the ideological. *España en el corazón* (*Spain in the Heart*), a tribute to the Loyalists who supported the Republic, was distributed to the Republican front lines. When Neruda declared Chile's support of the Republican cause without official sanction from his own government, he was recalled in 1937; the following year, he served briefly in Paris, where he helped Republican refugees emigrate to Chile.

In Mexico, where he was sent in 1939, Neruda acted as secretary to the Chilean embassy and then as consul (1941–1944). During this time he expressed his increasing attraction to Marxism in several poems; in at least two, he praised those who defended Stalingrad against the Nazis. It was during his tour in Mexico that Neruda joined the Communist party.

Back in Chile in 1944, Neruda entered politics and was elected to the national Senate, where he represented the provinces of Antofagasta and Tarapacá. Two years later, when he published letters denouncing the government and calling Chile's president, Gabriel González Videla, a puppet of the United States, Neruda was charged with treason. After a brief period underground, he fled to Mexico.

In exile Neruda produced *Canto general* (General Song, 1950) a monumental work of 340 poems illustrated by the Mexican artists Diego Rivera and David Alfaro Siqueiros. Widely regarded as his masterpiece, it celebrates the geography and people of his land from a Marxist point of view. Although banned in Chile, the book was circulated secretly by the Communist party.

The moderation of antileftist laws enabled Neruda to return in 1952 to Chile, where he divorced his second wife and married Matilde Urrutia, the inspiration for much of his later poetry, including *Odas elementales* (*Elementary Odes,* 1954), *Tercer libro de las odas* (Odes: Third Book, 1957), and *Estravagario* (*Extravagaria,* 1958). Establishing a permanent home on the Isla Negra, on the Pacific coast, Neruda continued to travel extensively, visiting Cuba in 1960 and the United States in 1966. In 1970 the Chilean Communist party nominated him as its candidate for the presidency of Chile, but when the party withdrew its nomination to back the Socialist candidate, Salvador Allende, Neruda stepped aside. After winning the election, Allende subsequently appointed Neruda as Chile's ambassador to France.

Neruda received the 1971 Nobel Prize for Literature "for a poetry that with the action of an elemental force brings alive a continent's destiny and dreams." The presentation address, delivered by Karl Ragnar Gierow of the Swedish Academy, paid special tribute to Neruda's political and social concerns. In Spain, Gierow said, Neruda "found the fellowship of the oppressed and persecuted," a fellowship which, in turn, fostered an awareness of Chile's "riches, pride over its past, and hope for its future."

In his Nobel lecture, "Toward the Splendid City," Neruda recounted a journey that he once took into the heart of the Andes. On this arduous venture into "a dazzling and secret world of nature" and solitude, said Neruda, "I found the necessary components for the making of the poem," namely, solitude, nature, and solidarity with his companions. "There is no insurmountable solitude," he said. "All paths lead to the same goal: to convey to others what we are" through works of the creative imagination. "I come from a dark region, from a land separated from all others by the steep contours of its geography. I was the most forlorn of poets and my poetry was provincial, oppressed, and rainy. But I always put my trust in man. I never lost hope."

Neruda, who died of leukemia in Santiago in 1973, was also the recipient of the International Peace Prize (1950); the Lenin Peace Prize and the Stalin Peace Prize, both received in 1953; an honorary degree from Oxford University; and other awards.

During his long literary career, Neruda produced more than forty volumes of poetry, translations, and verse drama, constantly experimenting and adopting new styles and attitudes. "There are so many Nerudas," the British critic and translator Alastair Reid has written. "He has always been not so much looking for a new style as discarding his previous one." "Neruda was a poet of many styles and many voices," Rene de Costa wrote in *The Poetry of Pablo Neruda,* "one whose multitudinous work is central to almost every important development in twentieth-century Spanish-American poetry." Writing in 1962, Chilean critic Fernando Alegría asserted that "anyone who approaches his work with the fear of becoming contaminated or with repugnance because of political antagonism commits a grave error, since, attentive only to the fireworks of circumstantial propaganda, he will never grasp the true significance of Neruda's art: his profound attempt to express the soul of the Latin American people in a style that attains even the loftiest heights of Spanish baroque poetry."

Not all critics have sympathized with Neruda's overtly Marxist stance. Writing in *Spanish American Literature: A History,* Anderson Imbert charged that his "conversion to Communist realism . . . causes him to be given to the exaltation of three uglinesses: arrogance, demagoguery, and insincerity." To Reid, however, what distinguishes Neruda's poetry is its commitment to humanity. "If the fact that so absolute and dedicated a lyric poet can still affirm, still communicate his humanity as triumphantly as Neruda does, seems naive and unacceptable to us in the context in which we live, then so much the worse for the context."

ADDITIONAL WORKS IN ENGLISH TRANSLATION: Three Material Songs, 1948; The Man Who Told His Love, 1959; Selected Poems, 1961; Nocturnal Collection, 1966; The Heights of Macchu Picchu, 1967; Twenty Poems, 1967; We Are Many, 1967; Pablo Neruda: The Early Poems, 1969; A New Decade: 1959–1967, 1969; The Captain's Verses, 1972; New Poems: 1968–1970, 1972; The Splendor and Death of Joaquín Murieta, 1972; Bestiary, 1974; Five Decades: 1925–1970, 1974; Fully Empowered, 1975; Song of Protest, 1976; Ode to Typography, 1977; Memoirs, 1978; A Call for the Destruction of Nixon and Praise for the Chilean Revolution, 1980; Isla Negra, A Notebook, 1981; Passions and Impressions, 1983; Still Another Day, 1984; Art of Birds, 1985; One Hundred Love Sonnets, 1986; Winter Garden, 1986.

ABOUT: Agosin, M. Pablo Neruda, 1986; Bellit, B. Adam's Dream, 1978; Bizzaro, S. Pablo Neruda: All Poets the Poet, 1979; Current Biography December 1970; de Costa, R. The Poetry of Pablo Neruda, 1979; Durán, M., and Safir, M. Earth Tones: The Poetry of Pablo Neruda, 1981; Felstiner, J. Translating Neruda: The Way to Macchu Picchu, 1980; Gallagher, D. P. Modern Latin American Literature, 1973; Plimpton, G. (ed.) Writers at Work, volume 5, 1981; Riess, F. The Word and the Stone, 1972; Santi, E. M. Pablo Neruda: The Poetics of Prophecy, 1982.

NICOLLE, CHARLES

(September 21, 1866–February 28, 1936)
Nobel Prize for Physiology or Medicine, 1928

The French physician and bacteriologist Charles Jules Henri Nicolle (nē kôl') was born in Rouen, the younger of two sons of Eugène Nicolle, a physician and professor of natural history. Although he felt a strong literary calling and later wrote a number of novels, Nicolle followed his father and his older brother Maurice, a well-known pathologist, into medicine. After studying in Rouen and Paris, he passed the examination for a medical residency in 1889. His brother persuaded him to enter the Pasteur Institute in Paris, where he studied under Émile Roux, a collaborator of Louis Pasteur. Nicolle wrote his doctoral dissertation in 1893 on the role of Ducrey's bacillus in the development of soft-chancre venereal disease.

After obtaining his medical degree, Nicolle returned to Rouen, where he worked in the municipal hospital, directed the work in a bacteriology laboratory, and lectured at the medical school. Nicolle hoped Rouen would become

CHARLES NICOLLE

a major center for medical research but was frustrated in this ambition by an intransigent city bureaucracy and by increasing deafness that interfered with his relations with his patients and his medical peers. Throughout his life, Nicolle's inability to follow conversation made him socially withdrawn and reinforced a tendency to direct his energies toward research and writing.

When Nicolle was invited to become director of a branch of the Pasteur Institute located in Tunis, North Africa, in 1902, he felt sufficiently discouraged with his life in France to accept. Although that branch of the institute did not have a truly independent status when Nicolle arrived in Africa, he soon converted it from a rabies vaccination unit into a center for medical research and vaccine production. Under Nicolle, the Pasteur Institute of Tunis became a leading laboratory in the study of tropical diseases. Nicolle investigated leishmaniasis and toxoplasmosis (diseases caused by protozoa), examined the role of flies in the transmission of trachoma (an eye disease common in North Africa), and demonstrated that influenza is caused by a virus.

"Of all the problems which were open to me for study," Nicolle later wrote, "typhus was the most urgent and unexplored." Typhus, which had been known in Europe for several hundred years, was notorious for decimating the ranks of armies, jails, and the urban poor. Typhus fever is caused by *Rickettsia* microorganisms; it is a disease that spreads rapidly and often has a very high mortality rate—typically 30 percent, sometimes 70 percent or more. The disease was a major problem in the Napoleonic wars in the early nineteenth century, after which it was limited to eastern Europe. Nicolle had seen few cases before he went to Tunis, but he found that typhus epidemics were a yearly occurrence in North Africa.

Nicolle began his investigations by observing the distribution of typhus within the community. At the native hospital in Tunis, he was struck by the peculiar limits to the spread of the disease within the hospital walls. Until they entered the general wards of the hospital, typhus patients infected their families, their personal physicians, and even the hospital staff in charge of admissions. As soon as they entered the wards, however, patients no longer spread the disease. "I took this observation as my guide," Nicolle said. "I asked myself what happened between the entrance to the hospital and the wards. This is what happened: the typhus patient was stripped of his clothes and linen, shaved, and washed. The contagious agent was therefore something attached to his skin and clothing, something which soap and water could remove. It could only be the louse."

In a series of experiments, Nicolle transmitted typhus to chimpanzees, certain monkeys, and then guinea pigs by the use of infected lice. The discovery that typhus is spread by lice had great practical value. In three years, public health measures to rid the population of Tunis of lice virtually eliminated typhus from the city, which had suffered yearly outbreaks of the disease for centuries. During World War I the armies of both belligerents deloused everyone going to or from the trenches. As a result, the German, French, and British armies suffered few losses from typhus, whereas typhus deaths among the less meticulous Russian and Serbian forces on the eastern front numbered in the millions.

In the course of his work, Nicolle observed that some animals exposed to typhus developed no signs of infection but were still capable of transmitting the disease to others. This phenomenon, called inapparent infection, explained a major problem in the frequency and distribution of typhus and other diseases.

Human beings are the primary hosts for classic epidemic (exanthematous, or European) typhus; the disease is spread directly from person to person by lice, without passing through a stage in other organisms. Diseases that are spread in this manner tend to die out

quickly except in large populations. The reason is that the chain of infection is broken unless the population contains a number of people who have never been exposed to the disease and thus are not immune.

In the case of typhus, however, the disease often persists in areas without a large population, seeming to die out and then return spontaneously. Nicolle's studies showed that this pattern is caused by inapparent infection. A small percentage of the population carry typhus unknowingly until they become infectious and start a new chain of infection, often years later.

The 1928 Nobel Prize for Physiology or Medicine was awarded to Nicolle "for the successful transmission of exanthematous typhus fever to chimpanzees in the acute stages by the injection of a small amount of the body louse." The decision to award Nicolle the Nobel Prize was far from unanimous because his discoveries concerning typhus involved no new principles. In his Nobel lecture Nicolle pointed out that "we have known for a long time that primary infection of typhus confers immunity in man in almost all cases and that this immunity lasts a lifetime. I established that laboratory animals were subject to similar immunity." By 1897 RONALD ROSS's studies of malaria had already demonstrated that insects can transmit human diseases. The factor that tipped the balance in Nicolle's favor, however, was the prevention of typhus during World War I.

Nicolle was appointed to the prestigious chair of experimental medicine at the Collège de France in 1932, where he taught for three years. His lectures on the scientific enterprise, medicine, and human destiny were widely influential among French scientists. He died in Tunis, still at his post as the director of the Pasteur Institute, in 1936. Nicolle, in addition to his outstanding investigations in the fields of bacteriology and immunology, was a poet, philosopher, and scholar.

In 1895 Nicolle married Alice Avice; they had two sons, both of whom entered the medical profession.

Among other awards Nicolle became a commander of the Legion of Honor (1920) and received the Orisis Prize of the Academy of Sciences (1927). He was named an associate in the Academy of Medicine and a correspondent to the Academy of Sciences.

ABOUT: Dictionary of Scientific Biography, volume 15, 1978; Major, T. Classic Description of Disease, 1932.

NIRENBERG, MARSHALL W.
(April 10, 1927–   )
Nobel Prize for Physiology or Medicine,
  1968
(shared with Robert W. Holley and
  Har Gobind Khorana)

MARSHALL W. NIRENBERG

Marshall Warren Nirenberg, American biochemist, was born in New York City, the son of Harry and Minerva Nirenberg. When he was twelve years old his family moved to Orlando, Florida. In 1944 Nirenberg enrolled at the University of Florida, where he studied zoology and biology, subjects that had interested him since his boyhood. He was an assistant in the Department of Biology from 1945 until 1947, when, while still an undergraduate, he became a teaching assistant. He also worked in the Nutrition Laboratory, studying biochemistry and gaining experience in the use of radioisotopes—radioactive forms of certain atoms that can be used to label substances and trace their activity in chemical reactions.

After receiving a B.S. from the University of Florida in 1948, Nirenberg began graduate studies in the Department of Biology. He spent a year as research associate in the Nutrition Laboratory and wrote his master's dissertation on the taxonomy and ecology of the caddis fly, a common insect in Florida. He received an M.S. in biology in 1952. Moving to the University of Michigan in Ann Arbor, he studied biochemistry as a teaching fellow in the Department of Biological Chemistry. With a dissertation on the uptake of hexose (a six-carbon sugar molecule) by tumor cells, he received a Ph.D. in biochemistry in 1957.

That year Nirenberg was awarded a postdoctoral fellowship from the American Cancer Society to study under Dewitt Stetten Jr. at the National Institute of Arthritis and Metabolic Diseases of the National Institutes of Health (NIH) in Bethesda, Maryland. Two years later a fellowship from the United States Public Health Service enabled him to study the biochemistry of compounds that control the biosynthesis of protein. In 1960 he was appointed research biochemist in the Metabolic Enzyme Section of the National Institute of Arthritis and Metabolic Diseases, where he did pioneering work in deciphering the genetic code.

The science of genetics began in 1866 with the publication of Gregor Mendel's studies on the inheritance of flower color in the garden pea. Mendel correctly postulated that "elements," now called genes, govern the inheritance of the physical traits of an organism. In 1869 the Swiss biochemist Friedrich Miescher discovered nucleic acid, but it was not until the first half of the twentieth century that the biochemistry of the nucleic acids was explained. There are two types of nucleic acid: ribonucleic acid (RNA) and deoxyribonucleic acid (DNA). Genes are composed of DNA, which directs the biosynthesis of cellular proteins, enzymes, and coenzymes. Enzymes are protein molecules that facilitate the biochemical reactions of the cell; coenzymes are essential for the efficient function of enzymes.

FRANCIS CRICK and JAMES D. WATSON determined the chemical structure of DNA when in 1953 they showed that the molecule is shaped like a double helix, a structure resembling a rope ladder twisted into a spiral. Each strand of DNA is a chain of nucleotides, compounds made of a deoxyribose molecule (a sugar), a nitrogenous base, and a phosphate molecule. The phosphate molecule links the nucleotides together along the length of the chain. The two strands of DNA are joined by pairs of bases inside the "rungs" of the "ladder." DNA contains four bases: adenine, thymine, guanine, and cytosine. An adenine molecule on one strand of DNA is always paired with a thymine on the other strand; similarly, a guanine is always paired with a cytosine. Thus the two strands of DNA are complementary, and the replication of DNA can be visualized as follows. The two strands separate from each other, and a new nucleotide strand is synthesized opposite each old one. The sequence of bases in DNA constitutes the genetic code;

767

that is, a triplet of bases encodes the genetic instructions for the incorporation of a single amino acid into a protein molecule. (Proteins are made of amino acids linked together in chains.) A gene contains instructions for the biosynthesis of an entire protein molecule.

The RNA molecules, which also are made of nucleotide chains, duplicate the genetic code of DNA in the nucleus of the cell and carry it to ribosomes in the cytoplasm, where protein molecules are formed. RNA is also responsible for the transfer of amino acids to the site of protein synthesis, thus assuring that they are combined in the proper order.

Shortly before Nirenberg began research on the biochemistry of the nucleic acids at the NIH, the enzymes responsible for DNA and RNA biosynthesis were isolated and purified. In the early 1960s Nirenberg and his colleagues performed an important series of experiments that enabled them to decipher the genetic code. First, they synthesized polyuracil, an RNA molecule that contains only uracil bases. (Unlike DNA, RNA has a uracil base instead of a thymine base.) They then placed polyuracil in a cell-free experimental system made by gently grinding bacteria to release a mixture of amino acids, RNA, ribosomes, essential enzymes, and other substances. The polyuracil RNA directed the synthesis of a protein molecule consisting of a chain of molecules of the amino acid phenylalanine. The triplet code for phenylalanine is therefore uracil-uracil-uracil (since uracil is the only base in polyuracil), or UUU. Because DNA contains four bases and the genetic code consists of base triplets, there are sixty-four ($4 \times 4 \times 4 = 64$) possible triplet combinations for DNA. Nirenberg and his colleagues then synthesized RNA with all possible triplet sequences, repeating the cell-free experiment with each one, and in this way they discovered the triplet base codes for all twenty amino acids. Some of the amino acids are encoded by more than one base triplet, and some triplets are known as nonsense triplets because they do not encode any amino acid. Nirenberg found that nonsense triplets, like a period in a sentence, may signal the termination of a biosynthetic process in the cell. He and his colleagues then performed additional experiments to determine the order of the bases in each triplet.

The genetic code controls not only the production of all the proteins the body needs to sustain itself but also the transmission of inherited characteristics. By deciphering the code, Nirenberg provided the basic knowledge that eventually may enable scientists to control heredity and eliminate diseases caused by genetic defects.

Nirenberg shared the 1968 Nobel Prize for Physiology or Medicine with ROBERT W. HOLLEY and HAR GOBIND KHORANA; it was awarded "for their interpretation of the genetic code and its function in protein synthesis." "The translation from nucleic acid to protein proceeds in a sequential fashion according to a systematic code with relatively simple rules," Nirenberg said in his Nobel lecture. "Each unit of nucleic acid defines the species of molecule to be selected, its position relative to the previous molecule selected, and the time of the event relative to the previous event. The nucleic acid therefore functions both as a template for other molecules and as a biological clock."

After the genetic code was broken, Nirenberg turned his attention to cellular control mechanisms, hoping to discover why one set of biosynthetic reactions occurs in a given cell rather than in another. He is also interested in how different types of cells, such as nerve and muscle cells, differentiate their form in embryonic development or during a threat from the environment. His work has led him to speculate that the mammalian genetic code is a few billion years old and is the same in all species.

Since 1966 Nirenberg has been chief biochemist at the Genetics Laboratory of the National Heart, Lung, and Blood Institute. He and his wife, the former Perola Zaltzman, a biochemist whom he married in 1961, live in Bethesda, Maryland. A man who prefers anonymity, Nirenberg has been an outspoken strong advocate of government support for scientific research.

Nirenberg's many honors include the National Medal of Science of the National Science Foundation (1965), the Franklin Medal of the Franklin Institute (1968), the Priestley Medal of the American Chemical Society (1968), and the Louisa Gross Horwitz Prize of Columbia University (1968). He is a member of the National Academy of Sciences, the American Chemical Society, the Biophysical Society, and the Society for Developmental Biology and holds honorary degrees from the universities of Michigan, Chicago, and Windsor, as well as from Yale University, George Washington University, and the Weizmann Institute (Israel).

SELECTED WORKS: "The Genetic Code: II," Scientific American March 1963.

ABOUT: Current Biography April 1965; Newsweek October 28, 1968; New York Times October 17, 1968; Science October 26, 1968; Scientific American March 1963; Washington Post January 3, 1965.

NOEL-BAKER, PHILIP
(November 1, 1889–October 8, 1982)
Nobel Prize for Peace, 1959

The English pacifist and diplomat Philip Noel-Baker was born Philip John Baker in London, one of seven children of Canadian-born parents. (He changed his name to Noel-Baker in 1923, after his marriage to Irene Noel.) His father, Joseph Allen Baker, had been sent to London to open a branch office of the family engineering firm and had settled there permanently. He and his wife, the former Elizabeth Moscrip, were Quakers who participated actively in social and humanitarian causes. Eventually, Joseph Baker became involved in politics as a member of the London County Council (the governing body of metropolitan London). He served on the council for eleven years and was elected to the House of Commons as a Liberal in 1905. Noel-Baker thus grew up in a home where politics and social commitment were mingled with traditional Quaker pacifism.

After receiving his early education at Bootham School in York, Noel-Baker went to the United States to attend Haverford College, a Quaker institution in Pennsylvania. He returned to England to King's College, Cambridge, where he won honors in history (1910) and economics (1912), which opened the way for an academic career. Also an outstanding athlete, Noel-Baker was head of the Cambridge Athletic Club for two years and participated in the 1912, 1920, 1924, and 1928 Olympic Games, winning the Silver Medal in the 1,500-meter run in 1920.

Receiving an M.A. with honors from Cambridge in 1913, Noel-Baker became vice-principal of Ruskin College, Oxford, the following year. Led by his Quaker beliefs to reject combat service during World War I, he organized and commanded the Friends' Ambulance Corps. He served at the front in France and was decorated for valor. Later he was an adjutant in a British ambulance unit in Italy and was decorated with the British Silver Medal for Military Valor and the Italian War Cross.

Noel-Baker married Irene Noel in 1915. They had one son, Francis, born in 1920. Irene Noel-Baker died in 1956.

Following the war, Noel-Baker served as an assistant to ROBERT CECIL at the Paris Peace

PHILIP NOEL-BAKER

Conference, where he helped draft the Covenant of the League of Nations. This work led to a post in the league's Secretariat as chief assistant to the secretary-general, Eric Drummond, until 1922. During this time Noel-Baker was also closely associated with FRIDTJOF NANSEN, the Norwegian explorer and humanitarian who became internationally renowned for his work on behalf of war refugees.

In 1924 Noel-Baker became Cassel Professor of International Relations at London University. That year also marked his first attempt to win elective office. He ran for Parliament as a Labour party candidate in a strongly conservative Birmingham district and lost, but he won as a Labour member for Coventry four years later.

In 1926 Noel-Baker published two books, *The League of Nations at Work* and *Disarmament,* which earned him a reputation as an authority on disarmament. He was invited to the Tenth Assembly of the League of Nations as a member of the British delegation. He was also appointed parliamentary private secretary to ARTHUR HENDERSON, foreign secretary and chairman of the World Disarmament Conference, which convened in Geneva in 1932.

With Ramsay MacDonald's departure from the Labour party, Noel-Baker lost his Coventry seat in Parliament in the election of 1931. However, he was reelected five years later as a member from Derby, a seat he held until his retirement in 1970. Alarmed by the increasing belligerence of Benito Mussolini and Adolf Hitler during the 1930s, Noel-Baker advocated sanctions against Italy for its invasion of

Ethiopia, chastised his own government for accommodating Hitler, and joined WINSTON CHURCHILL in calling for resistance to the threat of fascism and Nazism.

As parliamentary secretary to the Ministry of War Transport in Churchill's coalition government, an appointment he received in 1942, Noel-Baker served as official spokesman for the War Ministry in the House of Commons. When the Labour party was returned to office in 1945, he became minister of state, a noncabinet office below the foreign secretary. In this capacity he headed the British delegation to the fourteen-nation executive committee of the United Nations Preparatory Commission and later served on the subcommittee that drew up a preliminary agenda for the United Nations Assembly. A forceful advocate of arms control, Noel-Baker also held membership on the United Nations Committee for Food and Agriculture and on the Economic and Social Council, where he was instrumental in setting the course not only for these early groups but for others that were to follow.

Despite his United Nations responsibilities, Noel-Baker remained active in British government. He attained cabinet rank as secretary of state for air in 1946 and was elected chairman of the Labour party the same year. As minister of commonwealth relations from 1947 to 1950, he figured prominently in negotiations that led to the independence of India. When the Conservatives regained power in 1951, he once again became a member of the opposition and participated in major foreign policy debates in the House of Commons. Meanwhile, he continued his campaign for disarmament. His book *The Arms Race: A Program for World Disarmament* (1958) was a comprehensive analysis of the history of disarmament negotiations that incorporated practical suggestions based on his long experience in the field.

When Noel-Baker was awarded the 1959 Nobel Prize for Peace, he was cited for his vast knowledge of disarmament, for his lifetime commitment to peace, for his work in the League of Nations and the United Nations, and for his labors on behalf of war refugees. In his Nobel lecture, he outlined the unparalleled threat posed by nuclear weapons and the arms race. He warned about the way "we are continually being 'conditioned' " to the use of weapons of mass destruction. The solution, he declared, lies not in partial measures but in a comprehensive and complete program of disarmament under the United Nations. "Disarmament is . . . for every nation," he

said, "the safest and most practicable system of defense."

After receiving the Nobel Prize, Noel-Baker continued to work actively for peace. On his retirement from the House of Commons at the age of eighty, he declared, "While I have the health and strength, I shall give all my time to the work of breaking the dogmatic sleep of those who allow the nuclear, chemical, biological, and conventional arms race to go on." As president of the British Vietnam Committee he vigorously opposed the war in Vietnam. He was made a life peer as Baron Noel-Baker of Derby in 1977. He died in London in 1982 at the age of ninety-two.

ADDITIONAL WORKS: The Geneva Protocol for the Pacific Settlement of International Disputes, 1925; Disarmament and the Coolidge Conference, 1927; The Present Juridical Status of the British Dominions, 1929; Hawkers of Death, 1934; Jameson, S. (ed.) Challenge to Death, 1934; The Private Manufacture of Armaments, 1936; The Way to World Disarmament—Now! 1963; The First World Disarmament Conference, 1932–1933, and Why It Failed, 1979.

ABOUT: Current Biography February 1946; Guardian (London) October 9, 1982; New Statesman November 14, 1959; Times (London) October 9, 1982; U.S. News and World Report November 19, 1946.

NORRISH, RONALD
(November 9, 1897–June 7, 1978)
Nobel Prize for Chemistry, 1967
(shared with Manfred Eigen and George Porter)

The English chemist Ronald George Wreyford Norrish was born in Cambridge to Herbert Norrish, a pharmacist, and Amy Norrish. He received his early education at a local elementary school and the Perse Grammar School. With a scholarship to Emmanuel College, Cambridge, he began studies of natural sciences in 1915. The following year, he was commissioned in the Royal Field Artillery. He saw combat in France and was captured by German forces in 1918. After being held as a prisoner of war for a year, he returned to Emmanuel College and completed his undergraduate studies, receiving a degree in chemistry in 1921. He received a Ph.D. in chemistry from Cambridge in 1924 and became a fellow of Emmanuel College and a demonstrator in chemistry in 1925. In 1930 he was named Humphrey Owen Jones Lecturer in Physical Chemistry at Cambridge, and in 1937 he was appointed professor of physical chemistry and

RONALD NORRISH

director of the Department of Physical Chemistry, a position he held until his retirement in 1965.

Norrish's doctoral studies concerned the effects of light on the chemistry of potassium permanganate solutions. He was one of the first investigators in the field of photochemistry. He found that when nitrogen peroxide, ketones, aldehydes, ketenes, and diazomethane are exposed to light of short wavelengths, they decompose in one of two ways—into stable molecules or into highly unstable, very reactive free radicals (atoms or molecules with at least one unpaired electron). The production of free radicals is far more common when the reaction occurs in a low-density gas than in a relatively high-density liquid, where the free radicals can react with each other. Norrish investigated the interaction of light with these molecules and also the light emitted by the chemical reactions.

In research on the combustion of methane and ethylene, Norrish determined the role of formaldehyde as an intermediate compound that reacts with ultraviolet light to cause an explosion. He also found that many photochemical processes involve chain reactions in which light creates reactive intermediate compounds. In this process, the catalytic action of small amounts of light produces major chemical effects. Finding that the reactive intermediates created by the interaction of light resulted in polymerization (the joining together of many small molecules to form large molecules), Norrish made extensive studies of

the kinetics of polymerization in numerous chemical systems.

During World War II, as chairman of the government's Incendiary Projectiles Committee, Norrish conducted research on the suppression of gun flash.

After the war, Norrish and a former student, GEORGE PORTER, investigated the chemistry of very fast chemical reactions. Using a powerful burst of short-wavelength light, they dissociated unstable molecules into free radicals. To observe the behavior of these very reactive species, they used a second, weaker spectroscopic flash. This method enabled them to determine the presence of numerous intermediate compounds and also to observe the mechanism of many complex reactions. This measurement technique, called flash photolysis, for the first time allowed the direct investigation of fast transitional reactions that had been theoretically predicted but never observed. Norrish and Porter went on to study the combustion and pyrolysis of hydrogen, hydrocarbons, ammonia, phosphine, and hydrogen sulfide.

Norrish and Porter shared half of the 1967 Nobel Prize for Chemistry "for their studies of extremely fast chemical reactions, effected by disturbing the equilibrium by means of very short pulses of energy." The other half was awarded to MANFRED EIGEN for similar work. In his presentation address, H. A. Ölander of the Royal Swedish Academy of Sciences remarked that the "method developed by Norrish and Porter enabled them to study at first hand many fast reactions" whose existence had been only conjectural. In earlier times, Ölander went on, "the study of these short-lived, high-energy molecules and their chemical characteristics could hardly even have been contemplated as a wild dream."

In 1926 Norrish married Anne Smith, a lecturer on the Faculty of Education at the University of Wales; they had twin daughters. Norrish was known to his associates for his enthusiasm, abundant energy, and insatiable curiosity. He died in 1978 in Cambridge at the age of eighty.

In addition to the Nobel Prize, Norrish was awarded the Meldola Medal of the Institute of Chemistry (1928), the Davy Medal of the Royal Society (1958), the Liversidge (1958) and Faraday (1964) medals of the Chemical Society, the Lewis Gold Medal of the Combustion Institute (1964), and the Longstaff Medal of the Chemical Society (1968). He was a fellow of the Royal Society and a member of eight foreign scientific academies. He served

771

as president of the Faraday Society (1953–1955) and of the British Association for the Advancement of Science in 1961, and he received honorary degrees from the universities of Lancaster, Leeds, Liverpool, Paris, Sheffield, and British Columbia.

ABOUT: Biographical Memoirs of Fellows of the Royal Society, volume 27, 1981; Campbell, W. A., and Greenwood, N. N. Contemporary British Chemists, 1971; Nature September 7, 1978; Science November 10, 1967.

NORTHROP, JOHN H.
(July 5, 1891–May 27, 1987)
Nobel Prize for Chemistry, 1946
(shared with Wendell M. Stanley and
    James B. Sumner)

JOHN H. NORTHROP

The American biochemist John Howard Northrop was born in Yonkers, New York, to Alice Belle (Rich) and John Isaiah Northrop. Shortly before the boy's birth, his father, an instructor in the zoology department at Columbia University, was killed in a laboratory explosion. His mother resumed her position as a botany teacher at Hunter College in New York City, where she was instrumental in introducing nature study into the public school curriculum. Northrop attended elementary and secondary schools in New York and graduated from high school in 1908.

Entering Columbia University, he majored in chemistry and minored in biology. He received his B.S. in 1912 and then began graduate studies in chemistry. During his years as a graduate student, Northrop joined the Columbia fencing team, which won the intercollegiate championship in 1913, the same year he received his M.S. Before completing his Ph.D. in chemistry in 1915, the young biochemist spent a summer as a prospector in Arizona.

A William Bayard Cutting Traveling Fellowship enabled Northrop to work for one year at the Rockefeller Institute for Medical Research (now Rockefeller University) under Jacques Loeb, after which he was appointed first an assistant and then, in 1917, an associate. He became an associate member of the institute in 1920 and a member four years later.

After the United States entered World War I in 1917, Northrop served as a captain in the Army Chemical Warfare Service. In this capacity he discovered a fermentation process for the production of acetone, a solvent with many industrial and scientific applications.

Returning to the Rockefeller Institute after the war, Northrop resumed his studies on proteins and the duration of life, work that led him to the study of enzymes. In 1902 the German chemist EDUARD BUCHNER had discovered a group of proteins that became known as enzymes. Enzymes are catalysts that facilitate chemical reactions such as the digestion of food. When Northrop began his work, little was known about the chemistry of these vital compounds. Although many scientists believed that they were proteins, the influential German chemist RICHARD WILLSTÄTTER had attempted unsuccessfully to obtain pure samples of enzymes and as a result concluded that they were unlike any known organic compound.

Disagreeing with Willstätter's conclusion, Loeb suspected that enzymes were protein and could therefore be elucidated according to the laws of chemistry. At Loeb's suggestion, Northrop tried in 1920 to purify pepsin, an enzyme that regulates gastric digestion. His efforts failed, however, and resuming his initial work with Loeb, he showed that the life span of an organism depends on temperature. The discovery that high temperature leads to a short life span tended to confirm his and Loeb's conviction that life depends on chemical processes.

In 1926, the same year that Northrop joined the Rockefeller Institute's laboratory at Princeton, New Jersey, JAMES B. SUMNER of Cornell University Medical College published his research on urease, an enzyme involved in the breakdown of urea (a waste product formed during protein metabolism). Sumner reported not only that he had crystallized the enzyme, but also that it appeared to be a protein. Although Sumner's findings were assailed by most scientists, they inspired Northrop to resume his research on pepsin, and within four years he had isolated crystals that showed abundant pepsinlike activity.

During the 1930s Northrop and his colleagues—especially Moses Kunitz—isolated trypsin, chymotrypsin, and several other enzymes. Their work furnished experimental confirmation of Sumner's theories and helped initiate intensive research into enzymes. A major advance occurred in 1935 when WENDELL M. STANLEY, another of Northrop's colleagues at Rockefeller, obtained the first crystals of the tobacco mosaic virus, a nucleoprotein. In 1939 Northrop became the first to isolate a bacterial virus, and the following year he crystallized diphtheria antitoxin.

During World War II, Northrop served as consultant to and official investigator for the National Defense Research Committee. His wartime work led to the development of methods for the automatic detection of chemical weapons.

"For their preparation of enzymes and virus proteins in pure form," Northrop and Stanley shared the 1946 Nobel Prize for Chemistry with Sumner. The award was presented by ARNE TISELIUS of the Royal Swedish Academy of Sciences. Addressing Northrup, Tiselius said, "You and your collaborators have developed the crystallization of enzymes and other active proteins into an art, of which you are the masters." In his Nobel lecture Northrop said that the experiments that he and his fellow laureates had conducted "confirm the conclusion that the enzymatic activity is a property of the protein molecule itself, and is not due to a nonprotein impurity."

After receiving the Nobel Prize, Northrop became deeply involved in viral research, especially investigations into the origin and relationship of viruses. He served as visiting professor at the University of California at Berkeley from 1949 to 1958, at which time he became professor and resident biophysicist at the university's Donner Laboratory. He was named professor emeritus at Rockefeller University in 1961 and at Berkeley in 1962.

In 1917 Northrop married Louise Walker, with whom he had a son and a daughter; his son-in-law was FREDERICK C. ROBBINS. Northrop died at his home in Wickenburg, Arizona, on May 27, 1987. An enthusiastic sportsman during his active years, he once enjoyed hunting and salmon fishing.

Northrop's many awards included the Charles Frederick Chandler Medal of Columbia University (1937), the United States government's Certificate of Merit (1948), and the Alexander Hamilton Medal of Columbia University (1961). He was a member of the National Academy of Sciences, the American Philosophical Society, and the American Academy of Arts and Sciences, and he held foreign membership in the British Chemical Society, the Royal Society for the Encouragement of Arts, and the Leopoldina German Academy of Researchers in Natural Sciences.

SELECTED WORKS: Crystalline Enzymes: The Chemistry of Pepsin, Trypsin, and Bacteriophage, 1939; The Chemistry and Physiology of Growth, 1949, with others.

ABOUT: Current Biography June 1947; The Excitement and Fascination of Science, 1965; National Cyclopedia of American Biography, volume G, 1946; New York Times, July 16, 1987.

OCHOA, SEVERO
(September 24, 1905–   )
Nobel Prize for Physiology or Medicine, 1959
(shared with Arthur Kornberg)

The Spanish-American biochemist Severo Ochoa (ō chō′ ä) was born in Luarca, Spain, the youngest son of Severo Ochoa, a lawyer and businessman, and the former Carmen Albornoz. He received his early education in Luarca and Málaga. In his undergraduate years at Málaga College, Ochoa was influenced by the writings of the Spanish neurologist SANTIAGO RAMÓN Y CAJAL. After receiving a B.A. from Málaga in 1921, he enrolled in the medical school of the University of Madrid, from which he graduated with honors in 1929. For the next two years, aided by the Spanish Council of Scientific Research, he studied the biochemistry and physiology of muscle tissue while serving as a research assistant to OTTO MEYERHOF at the Kaiser Wilhelm institutes in Heidelberg and Berlin. He returned to the University of Madrid as lecturer in physiology and biochemistry in 1931 and spent the following year at the National Institute for Medical Research in London, where he concentrated on enzymology, the study of enzymes and their actions.

Upon returning to the medical school of the University of Madrid in 1935, he was appointed chief of the physiology division at the Institute for Medical Research; when the

SEVERO OCHOA

Spanish Civil War began in 1936, Ochoa and his wife left Spain. For the next five years he worked in German and English laboratories: the Kaiser Wilhelm Institute for Medical Research in Heidelberg, the Marine Biology Laboratory in Plymouth, England, and the Oxford University Medical School. During this period Ochoa studied the function of thiamine (vitamin B_1) and intermediary metabolism—the biochemical reactions in which carbohydrates (sugar) and fatty acids generate energy for cellular processes.

After the outbreak of World War II, Ochoa emigrated to the United States in 1941; he was granted citizenship in 1956. He was appointed an instructor and research associate in the Department of Pharmacology at Washington University in St. Louis, where he worked with CARL F. and GERTY T. CORI, authorities on intermediary metabolism of carbohydrates. In 1942, with an appointment as research associate, Ochoa began a long affiliation with the New York University School of Medicine, as an assistant professor of biochemistry (1945), then as professor and chairman of the Department of Pharmacology (1946), and finally as professor of biochemistry (1954). In 1949 he was visiting professor of biochemistry at the University of California at Berkeley.

High-energy phosphate compounds in the form of adenosine triphosphate (ATP) are the principal sources of cellular energy. Amino acids, fats, and carbohydrates are metabolized in the Krebs citric acid cycle, the final common series of reactions leading to the formation of ATP. The citric acid cycle—a chain of chem-

ical reactions in mammalian cells by which food substances are burned with oxygen to yield energy—was discovered by HANS KREBS. Ochoa found that the complete oxidation of one glucose molecule to carbon dioxide yields thirty-six high-energy ATP molecules. He also elucidated the mechanism of the citric acid cycle by isolating the enzymes known as citrate synthetase (originally called condensing enzyme), isocitric dehydrogenase, and malic enzyme. While researching photosynthesis—the biochemical process by which green, chlorophyll-bearing plants convert carbon dioxide and water molecules into carbohydrates by the action of light—Ochoa discovered an additional role for malic enzyme.

Genes residing on the chromosomes of every cell nucleus govern the inheritance of physical traits by directing the synthesis of proteins (enzymes). Genes are composed of deoxyribonucleic acid (DNA), a long macromolecule of the nitrogenous bases (purines or pyrimidines) arranged in a double helical structure with sugars and phosphate groups. When DNA replicates itself, the two halves of the double helix unwind and separate from each other, with a new molecule of DNA then synthesized opposite each old one. The sequence of bases acts as a template or mold for the new molecules. Protein synthesis occurs when the genetic information is passed to ribonucleic acid (RNA), a macromolecule similar to DNA but containing ribose instead of the sugar deoxyribose and uracil rather than thymine.

Three types of RNA are involved in the sequential incorporation of amino acids into protein molecules: messenger RNA, ribosomal RNA, and transfer (or soluble) RNA. The genetic instructions for protein biosynthesis are encoded in the base sequences of DNA and RNA. Groups of three bases, or triplets, encode the incorporation of each amino acid into a molecule of protein.

In 1955 Ochoa isolated the bacterial enzyme polynucleotide phosphorylase, which catalyzes the synthesis of polyribonucleotides from ribonucleoside diphosphates in a reversible reaction. With this enzyme he prepared synthetic RNAs with varying base compositions, work that led him to decipher the triplet code for eleven amino acids. Thus it became possible to synthesize RNA and protein molecules of known base and amino acid composition in a test tube. This achievement—the first in the history of biology—enabled subsequent researchers to decipher the genetic code.

Ochoa shared the 1959 Nobel Prize for Physiology or Medicine with ARTHUR KORN-

BERG "for their discovery of the mechanisms in the biological synthesis of ribonucleic acid and deoxyribonucleic acid." In his presentation speech, HUGO THEORELL described the effort to "find out the procedure whereby Nature forms such complicated substances as nucleic acids" as heroic. "The development turned, for Ochoa's part, in a direction that made him work with systems that produced ribonucleic acids," Theorell explained. "We are sure to witness in the near future several important discoveries in biochemistry, virus research, genetics, and cancer research as a consequence of the works of Ochoa and Kornberg," Theorell concluded. In his Nobel lecture, "Enzymatic Synthesis of Ribonucleic Acid," Ochoa reviewed the work that led to his findings.

In honor of Ochoa's seventieth birthday in 1975, scientific symposia were held in Barcelona and Madrid. Kornberg and others published *Reflections on Biochemistry*, a three-volume book containing all the scientific papers written by Ochoa and his co-workers. Upon his retirement from New York University School of Medicine in 1975, Ochoa became an associate of the Roche Institute for Medical Research in New Jersey.

In 1931 Ochoa married Carmen Garcia Cobian, the daughter of a Spanish lawyer and businessman; they have no children.

Among the awards and honors bestowed on Ochoa are the Carl Neuberg Medal of the American Society of European Chemists (1951), the Charles Leopold Mayer Prize of the French Society of Biochemists (1955), the Borden Award in the Medical Sciences of the Association of American Medical Colleges (1958), the University Medal of New York University (1959), and the Order of the Rising Sun from the Japanese government (1967). He has received honorary degrees from Washington University, Wesleyan University, Oxford University, the University of Pennsylvania, Brandeis University, the University of Michigan, Glasgow University, and Yeshiva University.

Ochoa is a member of the American Association for the Advancement of Science, the American Academy of Arts and Sciences, the New York Academy of Sciences, the New York Academy of Medicine, the American Society of Biological Chemists, the American Chemical Society, the National Academy of Sciences, the Society for Experimental Biology and Medicine, the American Philosophical Society, the Biochemical Society of Great Britain, the royal academies of science of Madrid and Barcelona, and the Leopoldina German Academy of Researchers in Natural Sciences. He is also a foreign member of the Royal Society of London, a member of the Soviet Academy of Sciences, and a member of the Polish Academy of Sciences.

ABOUT: Current Biography June 1962; Kornberg, A., et al. (eds.) Reflections on Biochemistry, 1976; Nachmanson, D. German-Jewish Pioneers in Science 1900–1933, 1979; National Cyclopedia of American Biography, volume L, 1972.

OFFICE OF THE UNITED NATIONS HIGH COMMISSIONER FOR REFUGEES
(founded 1951)
Nobel Prize for Peace, 1954, 1981

The Office of the United Nations High Commissioner for Refugees (UNHCR) was created by the General Assembly to replace the International Refugee Organization, which had been caring for the 30 million Europeans left homeless at the end of World War II. The founding statute of the office charged it with protecting persons who crossed an international border believing they were no longer safe in their native country from persecution for reasons of race, religion, nationality, political opinion, or membership in a particular social group. The office was created to work with governments and voluntary organizations to ensure that the material needs of refugees were met and that their political rights under the 1951 Convention Relating to the Status of Refugees were protected. Furthermore, the office was called upon to find "permanent solutions" for individual refugees by securing their safe and voluntary return home, emigration to another country, or settlement in the country where they first sought asylum.

G. J. van Heuven Goedhart of the Netherlands became the first high commissioner in 1951. By the end of that year, 1.25 million refugees fell under UNHCR protection. The first effort of the office was to provide medical care for Russian and Armenian refugees in Belgium. Then, in 1953, it arranged for the emigration of 33,000 refugees through the Intergovernmental Committee for European Migration, another United Nations agency.

In 1954 the high commissioner submitted a report stating that no aid was being received by many of the 5,000 European refugees stranded in Shanghai after the Chinese Communist victory in 1948 nor by the 1,500 refugees arriving in Austria from Eastern Europe each month. In response, the General Assembly authorized a new United Nations Refugee Emergency Fund to help the office meet these pressing needs. Thus mandated, the office secured a $3.1 million grant from the Ford Foundation to settle refugees locally in Europe. The money was used to build housing, to provide vocational training for young people, and to make loans to help lawyers and doctors reestablish their practices.

Also in 1954 the General Assembly authorized the office to raise $16 million over four years to dissolve the refugee camps of Europe, where only the minimal needs of 70,000 refugees could be met. Hoping to build on the success of the Ford Foundation program, the high commissioner initiated a five-year, $12 million program to resettle 350,000 refugees in the countries where they first sought asylum or elsewhere in Europe.

The Office of the United Nations High Commissioner for Refugees was awarded the 1954 Nobel Prize for Peace. Gunnar Jahn of the Norwegian Nobel Committee commended the office for seeking, "by dint of untiring and sometimes thankless effort, to bring assistance to the refugees and to help the authorities understand their problems. This kind of work cannot be described in terms of figures. But think of what it means to the individual refugee to feel and to know that he has not been forgotten, that in spite of everything there is someone willing to help him."

Accepting the award for the office, High Commissioner van Heuven Goedhart emphasized the dignity of those under his protection. "The refugee problem . . . is not the problem of people to be pitied, far more of people to be admired. It is the problem of people who somewhere, somehow, sometime, had the courage to give up the feeling of belonging . . . rather than abandon the human freedom which they valued more highly." Nobel Prize money received by the UNHCR was used to help resettle several thousand Romanian refugees.

By the end of 1955, three-quarters of all refugees in Europe had been resettled; still, there remained throughout the world 2.2 million refugees under UNHCR protection.

With the outbreak of a revolution in Hungary in October 1956, Soviet troops intervened; by November, Hungarian refugees numbering 160,000, many of them young people and children, had flooded into Austria. In meetings with the Austrian and Hungarian governments, a new high commissioner, Auguste Lindt, stressed the necessity of quickly placing the young in schools and of reuniting them with their families. By January 1957 the UNHCR had coordinated the resettlement of 100,000 of these refugees.

In 1958, as a result of Algeria's war for independence from France, Algerians began to flee their country for Tunisia and Morocco. By 1962 there were 250,000 such refugees. In March of that year, a three-member commission of representatives from the Algerian Provisional Authority, the French government, and the UNHCR agreed that the UNHCR and the LEAGUE OF RED CROSS SOCIETIES would arrange to provide the refugees with food, medical care, clothing, and schools. The refugees—mostly women, children, and elderly men—were returned home by the end of the year.

The United Nations declared 1959 World Refugee Year, and the UNHCR used the occasion to renew its efforts to clear the European refugee camps. For the year 1960 alone, the office raised $16 million. Because new refugee problems had arisen since the end of World War II, the UNHCR in 1961 divided its operations between "a major aid program" to deal with those refugees displaced by the war and a "current program" to aid postwar refugees.

In March 1961 the office received its first request to aid refugees in black Africa. At that time, it was reported that Togo had attempted an invasion of Ghana and that Ghanaians in the border area were fleeing toward Togo. At the same time, rebels in Angola began a rebellion against the Portuguese, who refused to grant Angola independence. After the Portuguese bombed villages controlled by the rebels, there was a mass exodus of Angolans into the Congo (now Zaire) in the spring and summer of 1961. The government of Togo had received an emergency grant for refugees from Ghana by the time the government of the Congo sought UNHCR help for refugees from Angola, who by July numbered 150,000. Despite the magnitude of the problem, land and tools were quickly provided to allow the Angolans to become self-sufficient.

After 1962 the focus of the UNHCR turned from Europe to Africa and Asia. In 1965 the UNHCR provided $250,000 to the United Nations World Program for Makonde refugees from Mozambique, then an overseas province of Portugal. They had sought protection from fighting between Portuguese forces and anti-Portuguese nationalists. The money was spent to clear trees and build an irrigation system so the refugees could continue their lives as self-sufficient tillers. The following year, the UNHCR created a fund for education projects in Senegal and Ethiopia. In 1967 the former Makonde refugees harvested their first crop in Tanzania. Six villages became home to 11,000 former refugees; new arrivals were absorbed into the settlement with no outside aid.

A major crisis for the UNHCR occurred in 1971 when Bengalis in East Pakistan fled into India because of the merciless killing of civilians during the civil war that resulted in East Pakistan's declaring its independence from West Pakistan and becoming Bangladesh. In 1972 the UNHCR sponsored one of the largest airlifts in history to help 10 million refugees return to their newly independent homeland after months in Indian relief camps. Two years later, after several African territories had gained their independence from Portugal, hundreds of thousands of refugees were returned to their homes in Guinea-Bissau, Mozambique, and Angola. The following year, the UNHCR helped return 50,000 Angolans from Zaire, where they had sought protection from a civil war fomented by insurgents backed by the Republic of South Africa.

The achievements of the UNHCR were again honored with the 1981 Nobel Prize for Peace. John Sanness of the Norwegian Nobel Committee emphasized that the prize was awarded both in recognition of the UNHCR's work on behalf of refugees and to call attention to the refugees' enduring plight. "The two Peace prizes which, in the course of a quarter of a century, have been awarded to the Office of the High Commissioner are therefore not merely a recognition of far-reaching work carried out by the office," Sanness said in his presentation speech. "They represent both a symbol and a practical instrument in the long-term work carried out to ensure that the fundamental principles for this refugee work will achieve universal recognition and validity."

The prize was accepted for the office by Poul Hartling, a former prime minister of Denmark who had become high commissioner in 1977. He, like his predecessor of twenty-seven years before, directed his most poignant remarks to the refugees under his protection. "Yes, this Nobel Peace Prize bears witness to the fact that your voices are being heard! If we have allowed ourselves to stop for a moment to rejoice in the memory of the achievements of the past, we realize that the challenges of the present are no cause for joy. . . . But today the world is focusing on your plight and today it renews its commitment to help."

Meanwhile, the UNHCR had become heavily involved in the refugee problem in Southeast Asia. The problem began with the ending of the Vietnam War in 1975 and Communist efforts at social reorganization in South Vietnam. From Vietnam, ethnic Chinese and others set out in makeshift boats to seek refuge in Malaysia, Hong Kong, Indonesia, and Thailand. Many, who drowned or died from attacks by pirates, never reached their destination. In 1979 the exodus of so-called boat people crested, with over 200,000 Vietnamese attempting to make their escape by sea.

In May of that year, the UNHCR and the government of Vietnam agreed to the establishment of an Orderly Departures Program, which provided safe transit by air for any Vietnamese who qualified for both an exit visa from the Vietnamese government and an entry visa to a country abroad. Because many refugees did not meet these requirements, the exodus of boat people continued. In 1984, however, for the first time more people left Vietnam under the Orderly Departures Program than by boat. They resettled mostly in the United States, Canada, France, West Germany, Australia, and the Netherlands. In January 1986 the 100,000th person, who might otherwise have been one of Vietnam's 700,000 boat people, left the country under the program.

The UNHCR program for disabled refugees began in 1973 as the Ten or More plan. Because nations are reluctant to accept refugees who are not self-sufficient, resettling handicapped refugees has been a chronic problem. In 1982, however, Finland, which had been unable to accept large groups of refugees, decided to take in smaller groups to which individual attention, medical care, and counseling could be offered. Following the successful resettling in Finland of thirty-seven handicapped refugees and their immediate families from Vietnam and Cambodia, the Ten or More program was refashioned and renamed the Twenty or More plan. The UNHCR now recommended that the member states of its Executive Committee each accept twenty disabled refugees and their families every year.

A devastating famine in Ethiopia in 1984 forced thousands to flee to neighboring Somalia and Sudan to escape starvation. Later that year, the UNHCR administered a $23 million fund to aid 105,000 Ethiopians returning to their homeland. The fund provided food and shelter for their emergency needs as well as seeds, fertilizer, livestock, and farming tools to enable them to support themselves in the future.

Refugee trouble spots remain in Africa and Asia. In Central America, the office has aided over 104,000 refugees fleeing political violence in El Salvador, Guatemala, and Nicaragua. The largest current problem, however, centers in Pakistan, to which 2.5 million Afghans have fled the Soviet Union's 1979 invasion of their country. In January 1984 the World Bank and the UNHCR signed a three-year agreement to develop economic projects to provide the refugees with jobs and income to reduce the need for further assistance.

In October 1985 the UNHCR faced a $75 million shortfall. High Commissioner Hartling told a group of donors that African drought aid would not be cut but that other programs would be affected. He noted that while the causes of the office's financial straits were many, they had deep roots, particularly in the lack of a political solution to the problems that force people to become refugees in the first place. Until those problems are solved, he maintained, "it is of absolutely primary importance that the UNHCR be given the resources to do the job which is expected, indeed, demanded of us."

Hartling was succeeded as high commissioner in December 1985 by the Swiss Jean-Pierre Hocke of the INTERNATIONAL COMMITTEE OF THE RED CROSS. At that time, the UNHCR, with headquarters in Geneva, employed a staff of about 1,600 in ninety offices around the world.

SELECTED PUBLICATIONS: Memorandum on the International Protection of Refugees, 1953; A United Nations Plan for Refugees, 1955; To Have a Key, 1957; Forty Years of International Assistance to Refugees, 1961; The Opening Door, 1962; The Red Cross and the Refugees, 1963; As They Came in Africa, 1971; A Story of Anguish and Action, 1972; How They Did It, 1973; Nursing a Miracle, 1973; El Refugio: Refugees From Chile, 1975; Refugees in Africa, 1981.

PERIODICALS: (annual) Report of the United Nations High Commissioner for Refugees. (monthly) Refugees.

ABOUT: Elbadrawy, B. M. F. The Refugee: A Problem of International Social Welfare, 1951; Holborn, L. The International Refugee Organization, 1956; Holborn, L. Refugees: A Problem of Our Time, 1975; New York Times January 20, 1986; Proudfoot, M. J. European Refugees, 1939–1952, 1957; Stoessinger, J. G. The Refugee and the World Community, 1956; Vernant, J. The Refugee in the Post-War World, 1953.

OHLIN, BERTIL

(April 23, 1899–August 3, 1979)
Nobel Memorial Prize in Economic
  Sciences, 1977
(shared with James Meade)

The Swedish economist Bertil Gotthard Ohlin was born in Klippan, a village in southern Sweden, one of seven children of Elis Ohlin, a local district attorney, and Ingeborg Ohlin. A child prodigy, Ohlin completed his secondary schooling by the age of fifteen and entered Lund University. There he studied economics, mathematics, and statistics. After receiving his B.A. with highest honors in 1917, he entered the Stockholm School of Economics and Business Administration to study under the international trade theorist Eli Heckscher. Within two years he had received the degree of civil economist. He continued his graduate work in economics at Stockholm University. Meanwhile, in 1918, he had joined the Political Economy Club, an elite group that included such luminaries as Knut Wicksell, David Davidson, and Sven Brisman, as well as Heckscher, Gustav Cassel, and Gösta Bagge. Participating actively in the club's freewheeling seminar debates, Ohlin also presented papers on his own research and took part in public discussion.

Ohlin's economic studies were interrupted by service as assistant secretary to the Swedish Economic Council in 1920 and by military duty in the Swedish navy in 1921. Returning to Stockholm University the following year, he presented his thesis on international trade theory to Cassel and began work on his dissertation. While completing his doctoral dissertation, he spent the summer of 1922 at Cambridge University and the academic year 1922–1923 at Harvard University. After receiving his Ph.D. in 1924, he was appointed professor of economics at the University of Copenhagen. Remaining there five years, he revised his dissertation and translated it into English. Published in 1933 as *Interregional and International Trade,* this work is generally considered one of Ohlin's most significant contributions to economics. The research it generated has revolutionized the field of international trade.

The Heckscher-Ohlin model (as it is now called, in recognition of Heckscher's earlier work on the effects of trade on income distribution) is the centerpiece of Ohlin's trade theory. International trade, Ohlin has shown, will occur between countries with different "factor endowments" (different relative supplies of

BERTIL OHLIN

land, labor, and capital) even if the countries have identical production technologies. This is so because, in the absence of trade, the different factor endowments will produce different relative prices. Ohlin builds on this insight to make assertions about the direction of trade flows, predicting that countries will export goods that would be relatively cheap without trade while importing those that would be relatively expensive without trade. If, for example, land is relatively abundant in Australia while labor is abundant in England, then Australia will export land-intensive goods, such as wool, while England will export labor-intensive goods, such as textiles.

Ohlin thus provides a framework for linking trade theory with the larger field of general equilibrium theory—for investigating the effects of trade on income and its distribution. Indeed, his work led to the development, by Wolfgang Stolper and PAUL SAMUELSON, of the "factor-price equalization theorem," which states that foreign trade tends to equalize the prices of factors of production in different countries. The exchange of Australian goods for English goods, to continue the example, raises the price of Australian land while pulling up English wages. Trade flows then expand, promoting the realignment of prices, until Australian and English land prices and wages are equilibrated. Therefore, trade in commodities can have the same effect on factor prices as would occur if the factors themselves could move freely between countries. A related implication of Ohlin's theory is that tariffs and other trade restrictions will affect

income distribution by restraining the equalization of factor incomes. A British tariff on land-intensive goods, for example, would increase the landowners' share of income in England and labor's share of income in Australia.

Rich in empirical evidence, Ohlin's *Interregional and International Trade* has provided trade theory with a variety of powerful hypotheses susceptible to empirical testing. The first formal test of these predictions came twenty years later in a paper by WASSILY LEONTIEF showing that the United States, with the world's highest relative wage levels, was an exporter of labor-intensive products. Various interpretations of this seeming paradox stimulated additional empirical and theoretical work on international trade, further developing the implications of Ohlin's work.

In 1930, after a year in Geneva at the League of Nations writing a world economic survey, Ohlin succeeded Eli Heckscher at the Stockholm School of Economics and Business Administration. There he contributed to the development of macroeconomic theory and of theories of stabilization policy often associated with John Maynard Keynes. In a 1929 exchange with Keynes over German war reparations, Ohlin first stressed the importance of effective demand changes (instead of relative price shifts), anticipating Keynes's theme in *The General Theory of Employment, Interest, and Money* of 1936. At the time, Keynes failed to appreciate Ohlin's argument, although the independent role of aggregate demand in the determination of national income was to become crucial to Keynes's later work. During the Great Depression, Ohlin continued to argue the importance of demand management and government stabilization policy, urging the Swedish government to adopt expansive fiscal policies to reduce unemployment.

In 1938 Ohlin wrote two influential articles on the so-called Stockholm theory of savings and investment. Describing the Stockholm School's view of the relationship, in ex ante export terms, among national income, savings, investment, and interest rates, he emphasized a dynamic sequential framework. According to the Stockholm School model, national income was the result of a dynamic process whereby one period's investment and consumption plans produced employment levels that led to the next period's plans, and so on ad infinitum. Ohlin's 1949 book *The Problem of Employment Stabilization*, which showed that excess demand pressures stemming from overly expansive government policies could cause chronic inflation, also relied on this dynamic approach.

Elected to the Swedish Parliament in 1938, Ohlin headed the Swedish Liberal party from 1944 to 1967 and served as minister of trade in a coalition government from 1944 to 1945. Throughout this time, his research and political activities helped to shape the Swedish welfare state, in which classic liberalism joined with elements of social democracy. In the 1950s and 1960s the Swedish model represented a balance between capitalism and socialism. In the years following World War II, Swedish Social Democrats (with GUNNAR MYRDAL as their mentor) urged a planned economy. Their main opponent was Ohlin. In the elections of 1948, Ohlin's Liberal party won such a resounding victory that the Social Democrats returned to their usual pragmatism, becoming willing once again to cooperate with private business. The friendly relationship Ohlin maintained with his old friend and rival Gunnar Myrdal, despite their great differences over public policy, was praised by PAUL SAMUELSON as having "set a pattern for economists to emulate all over the world."

Ohlin and JAMES MEADE shared the 1977 Nobel Memorial Prize in Economic Sciences "for their pathbreaking contribution to the theory of international trade and international capital movements." In his presentation speech Assar Lindbeck of the Royal Swedish Academy of Sciences noted that Ohlin's work "has proved to be a firm cornerstone both for further theoretical work and for empirical testing," as well as having "inspired much research in international economics beyond the framework of strict formalized models." In his Nobel lecture Ohlin compared "two cases of serious international depressions in countries with an essential orientation toward a market economy." He also drew attention to the various economic factors at work in the Great Depression and in the worldwide recession of the mid-1970s.

In 1931 Ohlin married Evy Kruse, with whom he had a son and two daughters. He died on August 3, 1979, while vacationing in northern Sweden.

In addition to the Nobel Prize, Ohlin's honors included the Swedish government's Royal North Star (1961) and was made a member of the Danish government's First Order of the Dannebrogen.

ADDITIONAL WORKS: The Reparations Problem, 1928; The Course and Phases of the World Economic Depression, 1931.

ABOUT: History of Political Economy Summer 1981; New York Times August 17, 1979; Scandinavian Journal of Economics, number 1, 1978; Science November 25, 1977; Sills, D. (ed.) International Encyclopedia of the Social Sciences: Biographical Supplement, 1979.

O'NEILL, EUGENE
(October 16, 1888–November 27, 1953)
Nobel Prize for Literature, 1936

The American dramatist Eugene Gladstone O'Neill was born in a New York City hotel, the third son of Ella (Quinlan) O'Neill and James O'Neill, a prominent actor who became famous for his portrayal of the Count of Monte Cristo in a dramatization of the Alexandre Dumas novel. Since Ella O'Neill traveled with her husband on his theatrical tours throughout the United States, the first seven years of young O'Neill's life were spent backstage and "in hotels and railroad trains" as he put it—a way of life both he and his mother came to hate for its constant upheaval and lack of security.

At the age of seven, O'Neill was sent to a Roman Catholic boarding school in New York. Three years later he transferred to a day school and lived at home with his mother in New London, Connecticut. During those years, Ella O'Neill's addiction to morphine left profound emotional scars on her growing son. Steeped in the Catholic tradition of his parents, O'Neill prayed for his mother's recovery; but when his efforts failed, he renounced his ties to the church.

In 1902 O'Neill entered Betts Academy, a nonsectarian boarding school in Stamford, Connecticut. Though only an average student, he was an avid reader with wide-ranging interests and in 1906 won admission to Princeton University. Before completing his first year, however, he was forced to withdraw because he was spending most of his time in dissipation, under the influence of his oldest brother James Jr. (Jamie). It was Jamie, a profligate drinker and womanizer, who introduced the younger O'Neill to the world of New York waterfront bars and brothels.

After leaving Princeton, O'Neill embarked on a lacerating period of self-destructive behavior. In 1909, several weeks before his twenty-first birthday, he married Kathleen Jenkins, against the wishes of his father. Almost immediately after the wedding, he left for Honduras in search of gold, a trip that had been arranged by his father. Shortly after O'Neill returned to New York in 1910, his wife gave birth to a son, Eugene Jr. Abandoning his family, O'Neill left on an eighteen-month sail-

EUGENE O'NEILL

ing journey to England and then to Argentina, where he lived for a time as a derelict and panhandler. His wife divorced him in 1911, and he did not see his son until the boy was twelve years old. Eugene Jr., who subsequently became a drama scholar, committed suicide at the age of forty.

In 1911 O'Neill returned to New York City, where he worked briefly at a series of jobs but frequently drank himself into oblivion. In 1912, while living at Jimmy-the-Priest's (a run-down saloon and rooming house in New York), he attempted suicide but was rescued by some of his fellow derelicts. After his suicide attempt, O'Neill made an effort to recover. He took a job as a reporter on a newspaper in New London, Connecticut, where the O'Neill family maintained a summer residence, the only permanent home he had ever known. Within a few months, however, O'Neill discovered he had contracted tuberculosis. He was sent to recuperate in a private sanatorium, remaining there for six months, time during which he was able to contemplate his life in a state of sobriety and consequently to experience what he was later to term his "rebirth." It was also during this period that O'Neill began to write plays. He had made the decision "to be an artist, or nothing," as he characterized his ambition, and in 1914 he applied for admission to a playwriting course at Harvard that was taught by George Pierce Baker.

Although he did not complete the course, O'Neill wrote seven short plays that year, all eventually published in *Thirst and Other One-*

Act Plays. His first work was not produced for another two years, when *Bound East for Cardiff,* the first of a second series of plays O'Neill wrote, was produced in Provincetown, Massachusetts, in the summer of 1916. The play was staged by a group of young writers and artists who had established an experimental playhouse, the Wharf Theater, in the summer resort town. When the same group opened the Playwrights' Theater in Greenwich Village that fall, *Bound East for Cardiff* became O'Neill's New York debut. Like many of his early one-act plays, it drew on his experience at sea and on his painfully acquired knowledge of human character. In its depiction of the hopeless fate of a dying seaman, the play eschewed the formal elements of action and plot and thereby broke with tradition.

Before he began to write, O'Neill had read the plays of August Strindberg, whom he considered the source of his own inspiration—for giving him "the vision of what modern drama could be," as he acknowledged in his Nobel acceptance speech many years later. Yet his own work evolved, for the most part, out of the wrenching experiences of his own early life. In 1920 his first full-length play, *Beyond the Horizon,* was staged on Broadway. The drama, which centers on the relationship between two brothers, won a Pulitzer Prize, the first of four O'Neill received (the other three were for *Anna Christie, Strange Interlude,* and *A Long Day's Journey Into Night*).

Between 1920 and 1943 O'Neill completed twenty long plays and several shorter ones, including works of realism, expressionism, comedy, tragedy, and adaptation from classical Greek drama. *Anna Christie* (1920) is the story of two men of the sea and a prostitute whose innocence is restored through love. *The Emperor Jones* (1920), an expressionistic drama about Brutus Jones, a black Pullman car porter who commits murder and becomes the ruler of a West Indian island, astonished New York audiences and earned O'Neill an overnight reputation as the leader of a new theatrical movement. *The Hairy Ape* (1922) enhanced this reputation but brought O'Neill another kind of attention when the play was criticized for its use of profanity. *Desire Under the Elms* (1924) explores the themes of incest and adultery coupled with infanticide in a rustic New England setting; the play was immediately acclaimed for its tragic power and is still considered one of the greatest works of the modern theater. *The Great God Brown* (1926) deals with the conflict between materialism and idealism; in its use of symbolism and the theatrical device of masks, it was a precursor of the avant-garde movement in American theater.

By the late 1920s, O'Neill's reputation as a leading American playwright was firmly established, yet his personal life continued to be troubled. In 1918 he had married Agnes Boulton, a short story writer; they had a son, Shane, and a daughter, Oona (who, at the age of eighteen, married Charlie Chaplin despite her father's vehement objections). Between 1920 and 1923 O'Neill lost his father, his mother, and his beloved brother Jamie, and in 1928 his second marriage ended in divorce. The following year, he married Carlotta Monterey, an actress he had first met in the early 1920s.

O'Neill was awarded the 1936 Nobel Prize for Literature "for the power, honesty, and deep-felt emotions of his dramatic works, which embody an original concept of tragedy"; he was the first American playwright to be so honored. Too ill to attend the Nobel award ceremony, O'Neill sent an acceptance speech to be read on his behalf in which he expressed his feeling that "it is not only my work which is being honored, but the work of all my colleagues in America—that this Nobel Prize is a symbol of the recognition by Europe of the coming-of-age of the American theater."

During the preceding decade, he had received an honorary degree from Yale University (1929) and had done some of his most innovative writing. *Marco Millions* (1928), a version of the life and times of Marco Polo, satirizes materialism and religious absurdities. In *Strange Interlude* (1928) the characters reveal their innermost thoughts to the audience through asides that are supposedly inaudible to the others onstage (the play elucidates the title's meaning as "life, the present . . . the strange interlude between the past and what is to come"). The trilogy *Mourning Becomes Electra* (1931), an adaptation of the *Oresteia* trilogy by Aeschylus, is set in New England in the Civil War period; starring Alla Nazimova in its Broadway premiere, it was considered the outstanding drama of its day. O'Neill's only comedy, *Ah, Wilderness!* (1933), presents a nostalgic version of his own youth as it might have been.

While the Nobel award confirmed the Swedish Academy's regard for O'Neill's contribution as "extraordinarily comprehensive in scope, versatile in character, and abundantly fruitful in new departures," three of his major plays were yet to be written—two of which are considered his masterworks: *The Iceman Cometh* (written in 1939 and produced on Broadway in 1946) and the autobiographical *Long Day's*

Journey Into Night (completed in 1941 and produced posthumously in 1956).

The Iceman Cometh draws on O'Neill's experience as a habitué of waterfront bars and on his intimate knowledge of the down-and-out characters who frequent them. It is considered the most complex of his works because of its religious symbolism, metaphysical depth, and emotional range. The themes of the play are the human need for hope and capacity for self-delusion.

Long Day's Journey Into Night, which had its premiere at the Royal Dramatic Theater in Stockholm, is an intensely autobiographical work in which the members of the fictional Tyrone family correspond to O'Neill, his parents, and his brother Jamie. Straightforward in style, the play spans one day in the life of the Tyrones and, with cumulative force, gradually reveals the destructive and shattering relationships between husband and wife, parents and sons. Written, according to its author, "in tears and blood . . . with deep pity and understanding and forgiveness for *all* the four haunted Tyrones," it was later made into a film starring the English actor Sir Ralph Richardson as the father, James, and Katharine Hepburn as the mother, Mary.

A Moon for the Misbegotten (written in 1943 and produced in 1957), which is also autobiographical in nature, can be considered a sequel to *Long Day's Journey*. One of its major characters is the older brother, James Tyrone Jr., and it is set after the death of Mary Tyrone.

The last decade of O'Neill's life was marked by physical decline and creative frustration. He had planned a long cycle of plays depicting the history of the American family, but in 1943 he was incapacitated by a degenerative nervous disorder, similar to Parkinson's disease, that made it impossible for him to hold a pen or pencil, which was the only way he could write. Of the intended cycle, there are only two plays extant: *A Touch of the Poet* (produced in 1957 at the Swedish Royal Dramatic Theater) and *More Stately Mansions* (produced in 1962, also at the Royal).

Although O'Neill's work is uneven and individual plays have been criticized for their melodramatic quality or their lack of verbal distinction, his place as one of America's foremost dramatists is assured. He was, as the English critic Martin Seymour-Smith wrote, "a man who raised his struggle with his own demons to the point at which it could become a metaphor for the struggles of all human beings."

Although the American critic John Gassner

believed that "one possibly serious difference between his effects and those of the greatest tragedians (including Chekhov) is that O'Neill's characters are too often only pseudotragic, since they lack greatness of spirit and stamina," he conceded that "O'Neill . . . practically created American naturalistic drama, . . . and such work as *Tobacco Road* and [JOHN STEINBECK's] *Of Mice and Men* would possibly have remained unaccepted but for his potent example."

The noted American drama critic George Jean Nathan, writing in 1946, called O'Neill "the foremost dramatist in the American theater" and went on to declare that "no other has anywhere near his ability to delve into and appraise character, his depth of knowledge of his fellow men, his sweep and pulse and high resolve, his command of a theater stage. . . . His plays at their best have in them a real universality."

According to his obituary in the *New York Times,* O'Neill, toward the end of his life in a house in Massachusetts overlooking the Atlantic, "brooded over the ghosts of his past, bitterly lamenting his inability to write. . . . Desperately, he joined the Euthanasia Society and willed himself to die, a wish finally granted . . . a month after his sixty-fifth birthday."

ADDITIONAL WORKS: Bread and Butter, 1914; Children of the Sea, 1914; The Long Voyage Home, 1917; In the Zone, 1919; Where the Cross Is Made, 1919; The Rope, 1919; Chris Christophersen, 1919; The Moon of the Caribbees, 1919; Gold, 1920; The Dreamy Kid, 1920; The First Man, 1922; The Fountain, 1923; All God's Chillun Got Wings, 1924; Lazarus Laughed, 1926; Dynamo, 1929; Nine Plays, 1932; Days Without End, 1933; Lost Plays, 1913–15, 1950; Hughie, 1959; Inscriptions, 1960; Ten "Lost" Plays, 1964; Poems, 1912–44, 1979.

ABOUT: Ahuja, C. Tragedy, Modern Temper, and O'Neill, 1984; Alexander, D. The Tempering of Eugene O'Neill, 1962; Berlin, J. E. Final Acts, 1985; Bogard, T. Contour in Time: The Plays of Eugene O'Neill, 1972; Boulton, A. Part of a Long Story, 1958; Cargill, O., et al. O'Neill and His Plays, 1961; Carpenter, F. I. Eugene O'Neill, 1964; Chabrowe, L. Ritual and Pathos, 1976; Clark, B. H. Eugene O'Neill: The Man and His Plays, 1947; Cronin, H. Eugene O'Neill: Irish and American, 1976; Engel, E. A. The Haunted Heroes of Eugene O'Neill, 1953; Floyd, V. The Plays of Eugene O'Neill: A New Assessment, 1985; Frenz, H. Eugene O'Neill, 1971; Gassner, J. (ed.) O'Neill: A Collection of Critical Essays, 1964; Gelb, A., and Gelb, B. O'Neill, 1962; Griffin, E. (ed.) Eugene O'Neill, 1976; Leech, C. O'Neill, 1963; Miller, J. Playwright's Progress: O'Neill and the Critics, 1965; Raleigh, J. H. The Plays of Eugene O'Neill, 1965; Scheaffer, L. O'Neill, Son and Playwright, 1968; Scheaffer, L. O'Neill, Son and Artist, 1973; Scheibler, R. The Late Plays of Eugene O'Neill, 1970; Skinner, R. D. Eugene O'Neill: A Poet's Quest, 1935; Törnqvist, E. Drama of Souls, 1970; Winter, S. K. Eugene O'Neill: A Critical Study, 1934.

ONSAGER, LARS

(November 27, 1903–October 5, 1976)
Nobel Prize for Chemistry, 1968

The Norwegian-American chemist Lars Onsager (ôn' säg ər) was born in Oslo to Erling Onsager, a barrister of the Supreme Court of Norway, and the former Ingrid Kirkeby. In his early schooling in Oslo, he studied literature, philosophy, the fine arts, and the Norwegian epics. He received a degree in chemical engineering in 1925 from the Norwegian Institute of Technology in Trondheim.

Onsager's particular interest was in the chemistry and physics of electrolytes (compounds which, when dissolved, dissociate into charged particles, or ions, that conduct electrical current). At the Federal Institute of Technology in Zurich, PETER DEBYE and an assistant, Erich Hueckel, had developed a general theory to describe the thermodynamic behavior of such solutions. Working independently in Norway, Onsager revised their calculations and in 1925 presented his arguments to Debye. Debye was so favorably impressed that he accepted Onsager as an assistant the next year.

In 1928 Onsager was appointed an associate in chemistry at the Johns Hopkins University in Baltimore, Maryland. Assigned to teach freshman chemistry, he found it impossible to present his lecture in suitably elementary terms and was soon dismissed. He was then offered a position as research instructor at Brown University in Providence, Rhode Island, where he also lectured on statistical mechanics (a course that his students soon dubbed Advanced Norwegian I).

The three laws of classical thermodynamics describe relationships between properties of systems at equilibrium; they do not deal with time or reaction rates. According to the first law (the law of conservation), energy in one form may be converted to another form but cannot be created or destroyed. The second law predicts whether a particular chemical reaction can occur spontaneously and measures the degree of entropy (disorder) of a system. The third law describes the calculation of equilibrium constants.

At Brown, Onsager developed theories to describe irreversible reactions that occur in nonequilibrium conditions. For example, when a cold lump of sugar is dissolved in hot tea,

LARS ONSAGER

heat is conducted from a hot to a cold body while at the same time sugar molecules are diffusing throughout the solution. Using statistical mechanics based on laws of motion, Onsager showed how simultaneous reactions influence each other in relationships now called Onsager's reciprocal relations. Onsager also demonstrated that the reciprocal relations were mathematically equivalent to a more general principle of least dissipation, which states that the rate of increase of entropy in coupled irreversible processes is a minimum. His theoretical description of irreversible processes, published in 1931, was ignored at the time. Indeed, when Onsager submitted this work in Trondheim for his doctoral thesis, it was judged unacceptable. Since the end of World War II, the reciprocal relations (now called the fourth law of thermodynamics) have been recognized for their value in physics, chemistry, biology, and technology.

When the chairman of Brown's chemistry department suggested that Onsager do experimental work in addition to theoretical analysis, Onsager agreed to attempt the separation of isotopes by thermal diffusion (isotopes of an element have the same number of protons but a different number of neutrons). The only equipment needed would have been a platinum tube three stories high. With the economic hardships of the Depression, however, Onsager's position at Brown was eliminated in 1933, and the experiment was not performed until ten years later by researchers on the Manhattan Project.

Onsager next joined the faculty of Yale Uni-

versity as a Sterling and Gibbs Postdoctoral Fellow in the chemistry department. Shortly after his arrival the administration discovered that he had no Ph.D. The chemistry department suggested that Yale would grant him the degree if he submitted a recent publication in lieu of a thesis. Instead he wrote an original paper on the mathematical background for his study of weak electrolytes. The faculties of the chemistry and physics departments declared themselves incompetent to judge the thesis and turned for an opinion to the mathematics department. Onsager received his Ph.D. in chemistry from Yale in 1935, having been appointed assistant professor the previous year.

In 1936 Onsager published a major paper on the behavior of polar liquids (molecules such as water and many acids that are electrically asymmetrical) in applied electrical fields. This work, important for the interpretation of electrical dipoles of amino acids and proteins in solution, involved correcting another theory developed by Debye, who only after many years accepted Onsager's amendments.

Because Onsager did not become a United States citizen until 1945, he played no part in the military work that occupied much of the scientific community during World War II. Instead he spent the war years analyzing a problem of physics widely thought to be insoluble— namely, whether statistical mechanics could account for phase transitions of matter. For example, many systems such as ferromagnetic material exhibit spontaneous ordering when cooled from a high temperature. That is, at high temperatures they are nonmagnetic, but as they are cooled through a critical temperature, they suddenly become magnetic. The Swedish physicist Gustaf Ising had proposed a simple two-dimensional model of a ferromagnetic material: a square grid of atoms oriented either up or down. The total energy of the system is the sum of all the adjacent parallel or antiparallel pairs of particles. As the temperature of the lattice approaches the critical temperature, the effective range of the interaction between atoms increases, and each atom affects every other atom in the system. Using obscure branches of mathematics including quaternion and spinor algebra and the theory of elliptical functions, Onsager showed that the specific heat of the system rises to infinity at the transition point. This conclusion was widely accepted as one of the most important contributions to theoretical physics of the decade.

Onsager continued to make important contributions to the theory of phase transitions for many years. He also studied problems of turbulence, quantum effects of superfluid helium, the electrical and magnetic behavior of metals in strong magnetic fields, the behavior of liquid crystals, and the properties of virus suspensions in water. Two international conferences were inspired by Onsager's discoveries: Irreversible Thermodynamics and the Statistical Mechanics of Phase Transitions, held at Brown University in 1962, and Phenomena in the Neighborhood of Critical Points, held in Washington in 1965.

Onsager was awarded the 1968 Nobel Prize for Chemistry for "the discovery of the reciprocal relations bearing his name, which are fundamental for the thermodynamics of irreversible processes." "You have made a number of contributions to physics and chemistry which can be regarded as milestones in the development of science," noted Stig Clæsson of the Royal Swedish Academy of Sciences on presenting the award. "Your discovery of the reciprocal relations takes a special place. It represents one of the great advances in science during this century."

From 1945 until 1972 Onsager was Josiah Willard Gibbs Professor of Theoretical Chemistry at Yale University. Upon his retirement, he was appointed distinguished university professor at the University of Miami in Coral Gables, Florida, where he joined the Center for Theoretical Studies and the Neurosciences Research Program.

Onsager married Margarethe Arledter in 1933; they had three sons and one daughter. On their farm in New Hampshire, Onsager enjoyed gardening, swimming, and carpentry. He read widely and translated a number of Norse epics into English. He suffered from phlebitis and died at the age of seventy-two in Coral Gables.

Although recognition of his contributions was belated, Onsager reaped many honors. In addition to the Nobel Prize, he received the Rumford Gold Medal of the American Academy of Arts and Sciences (1953), the Lorentz Medal of the Royal Netherlands Academy of Sciences (1958), the Peter Debye Award in Physical Chemistry of the American Chemical Society (1965), the Belfer Award in Pure Science of Yeshiva University (1966), and the National Medal of Science of the National Science Foundation (1968). He held honorary degrees from Harvard, Brown, Ohio State, and Cambridge universities as well as from the Norwegian Institute of Technology and the University of Chicago. He was a member of the American Physical Society, the National

Academy of Sciences, the American Academy of Arts and Sciences, the American Philosophical Society, the American Chemical Society, the Norwegian Academy of Sciences, the Swedish Academy of Sciences, and the Royal Netherlands Academy of Sciences.

SELECTED WORKS: Reciprocal Relations in Irreversible Processes, 1931; Kinetic Energy and Statistical Mechanics, 1952.

ABOUT: Biographical Memoirs of Fellows of the Royal Society, volume 24, 1978; Current Biography April 1958; New York Times October 31, 1968; Science November 8, 1968.

ORR, JOHN BOYD
See BOYD ORR, JOHN

OSSIETZKY, CARL VON
(October 3, 1889–May 4, 1938)
Nobel Prize for Peace, 1935

Carl von Ossietzky (ô sē et' skē), German author and pacifist, was born in Hamburg, the son of a poor merchant who died when the boy was two. Seven years later, his mother married Gustav Walther, a Social Democrat whose liberal views influenced Ossietzky's political outlook. Several of his father's friends offered to pay for Ossietzky's university education, but he refused their assistance, intending instead to become a writer. By the age of twenty he had published poetry in a Munich periodical.

Concerned that the growing spirit of militarism in Germany would lead to war, Ossietzky helped found the Hamburg branch of the German Peace Society in 1912. The following year *Das Freie Volk* (The Free People), a liberal weekly newspaper, published an article by Ossietzky criticizing a court decision that favored the military. The Prussian War Ministry charged him with an "insult to the common good" and fined him.

On August 19, 1913, Ossietzky married Maud Woods, an Englishwoman, a trained nurse, and a worker for women's rights who had left England and was giving English lessons in Hamburg. They had one daughter.

In 1916 Ossietzky was called up for military service in World War I and sent to the trenches of eastern France, an experience that deepened his pacifist convictions. "I know war as it is, not through reading about it," he wrote later. "What I saw thoroughly confirmed my

CARL VON OSSIETZKY

opinion both of war and of the profession of arms. We who are supporters of peace have a duty and a task," he added. "It is to point out, over and over again, that there is nothing heroic in war but that it brings terror and misery to mankind."

After the armistice in 1918, Ossietzky returned to Hamburg, where he resumed his pacifist activities. He became president of the local chapter of the German Peace Society and established a short-lived periodical, *Der Wegweiser* (The Signpost). In 1920 he accepted an invitation from the society's president, LUDWIG QUIDDE, to become secretary of the organization at its headquarters in Berlin.

In Berlin, Ossietzky founded a monthly publication, contributed to other periodicals, and helped establish the Nie Wieder Krieg (No More War) movement. Bored with his administrative duties in the German Peace Society, he resigned in 1924 to become foreign editor of the *Berliner Volkszeitung* (Berlin People's Paper). Two years later, he accepted an editorial position with *Die Weltbühne* (The World Stage), which had been founded and was published by Siegfried Jacobsohn. Upon the latter's death in 1927, Ossietzky was appointed editor in chief. That year he published an article by Berthold Jacob charging the Weimar government with condoning the existence of paramilitary groups. Ossietzky was tried and convicted on charges of libel and sentenced to one month in prison.

Undeterred, Ossietzky continued his attacks on the militaristic spirit that was again spreading among Germans. In May 1929 he published an article by Walter Kreiser, a German aviator, "Queer Happenings in German Aviation." The article detailed the government's secret development of warplanes in violation of the Treaty of Versailles. Ossietzky and Kreiser were arrested and tried for treason for having revealed military secrets, but the trial was deferred.

The following year Adolf Hitler's National Socialist, or Nazi, party won 107 seats in the Reichstag, the German national legislature. When party members celebrated by staging demonstrations against the antiwar film *All Quiet on the Western Front*, Ossietzky lashed out. "Fascism," he wrote, "won its first great victory in the elections. . . . Today it has slain a film; tomorrow it will slay something else."

Ossietzky and Kreiser were brought to trial in 1931, and after secret hearings, each was sentenced to eighteen months in prison. With the announcement of the sentences, protest meetings were held by liberals. Among those who demonstrated for Ossietzky were Ernst Toller, Lion Feuchtwanger, Arnold Zweig, and ALBERT EINSTEIN. While waiting to appeal their case, both Ossietzky and Kreiser were allowed to keep their passports, which would have enabled them to flee Germany. Kreiser went to Paris, but despite pleas from his friends and associates, Ossietzky refused to leave the country. "If you wish to fight effectively against the rottenness in a nation, you must do it on the inside," he said. "I will not flee abroad. A man speaks with but a hollow voice from across a border."

In May of the next year he entered Tegel Prison, walking through a crowd of supporters who detained him for hours trying to dissuade him from remaining. After serving seven months of his sentence, he was freed during a Christmas amnesty.

Hitler became chancellor of Germany in January 1933, and the following month a fire of undetermined origin swept through the Reichstag building. Blaming the fire on his opponents, Hitler effectively dissolved what remained of national democratic institutions and rounded up "enemies of the state," including Ossietzky, who was imprisoned first in Berlin and later at two concentration camps, in Sonnenburg and in Esterwegen. His health, already weakened by a heart condition and tuberculosis, deteriorated rapidly under forced labor and mistreatment. One fellow prisoner stated that Ossietzky was injected with tuberculosis bacilli.

Ossietzky was first suggested for the Nobel

Peace Prize in 1934. Then and later, petitions were submitted to the Norwegian Nobel Committee by, among others, Einstein, THOMAS MANN, NORMAN ANGELL, JANE ADDAMS, and BERTRAND RUSSELL. Mann wrote that the awarding of the prize to Ossietzky would represent a symbolic justice for millions of anxious contemporaries. The prize was reserved in 1935. Awarded to Ossietzky the next year, it "almost paralyzed the German government with anger," as Harold Fey wrote in the *Christian Century*. When the German ambassador to Norway protested to the Norwegian government, the Norwegian foreign minister replied that the Nobel committee was an independent body.

Ossietzky had been transferred from a concentration camp to a prison hospital because of the seriousness of his illness, and there he received notification of the prize. Although he was too ill to travel, the German propaganda ministry announced publicly that he was free to go to Oslo to accept the prize. The German government would not issue him a passport, however. It later denounced him as a traitor, decreed that no German could accept a Nobel Prize, and set up a substitute system of German prizes.

In his presentation speech, Fredrik Stang of the Norwegian Nobel Committee remarked that Ossietzky belonged to no political party and was not motivated in his work by narrow political causes. Rather, Stang found his actions marked by "a burning love for freedom of thought, a firm belief in free competition in all spiritual fields, a broad international outlook, a respect for values created by other nations—and all of these dominated by the theme of peace." Stang also emphasized that Ossietzky was not merely "a symbol of the struggle for peace" but rather a champion of peace.

In the hospital Ossietzky received and read tributes from around the world. Congratulatory messages were sent by Bertrand Russell, Virginia Woolf, J. B. Priestley, Aldous Huxley, Rose Macaulay, and Rebecca West, among others. In the United States, Ossietzky became a celebrated figure. After his imprisonment, outrage at his treatment by the German government and sympathy for his plight had been expressed by journalists and many others. In a message read at a mass meeting honoring Ossietzky at Cooper Union on December 12, 1936, NICHOLAS MURRAY BUTLER said, "Ossietzky has assuredly deserved consideration because of his outspoken support, despite almost every possible type of calumny and per-

secution, of ideals of peace and of the public policies which make for peace."

Ossietzky died in the hospital in Berlin on May 4, 1938. After World War II a street in East Berlin was named for him.

ABOUT: Christian Century May 25, 1938; Deak, B. I. Weimar Germany's Left-Wing Intellectuals, 1968; Living Age July 1938; New York Times May 5, 1938; What Was His Crime? The Case of Carl von Ossietzky, 1937.

OSTWALD, WILHELM
(September 2, 1853–April 4, 1932)
Nobel Prize for Chemistry, 1909

The German chemist Friedrich Wilhelm Ostwald was born in Riga, Latvia (now part of the Soviet Union), the second son of Gottfried Ostwald, a master cooper, and Elisabeth (Leuckel) Ostwald. Receiving his early education at the Riga Realgymnasium, Ostwald was a good student whose unusually wide range of interests included physics, chemistry, literature, and painting. He also played the viola and the piano. Although his father encouraged him to study engineering, Ostwald was drawn to chemistry, and in 1872 he entered the University of Dorpat (now Tartu) as a chemistry student. Four years later he received his bachelor's degree and remained at Dorpat as a doctoral candidate and privatdocent (unsalaried lecturer).

In the 1870s German chemists were actively involved in research into the structure, properties, and synthesis of organic molecules. Ostwald's interest lay in the neglected area of physical chemistry. In this field, chemical activities are analyzed by measuring changes in such physical properties of the reactants as volume, index of refraction, viscosity, color, and electrical conduction. Ostwald's thesis for his master's degree at Dorpat concerned volume changes occurring during neutralization of acids by bases in dilute solutions. In 1878 he received a Ph.D. for a dissertation on the optical coefficient of refraction of acid-base reactions. He continued his research on the application of physical measurements to chemical reactions while serving as an assistant to the physicist Arthur von Oettingen and teaching physics and chemistry in a local school. In 1881 he was appointed professor of chemistry at the Riga Polytechnic Institute. In the years following, he wrote several textbooks and manuals that were instrumental in establishing physical chemistry as a separate discipline. In 1884 Ostwald was sent a controversial

WILHELM OSTWALD

doctoral dissertation by SVANTE ARRHENIUS, a student at the University of Uppsala. In his dissertation Arrhenius proposed a theory to explain the dissociation of acids and bases into electrically charged ions in aqueous solutions. Because prevailing beliefs held that oppositely charged particles could not coexist in solution, Arrhenius's work had been given a low rating by the faculty at Uppsala. Ostwald found his ideas arresting, however, and at once applied them to check his own results on the affinities of acids. Using a "resistance box borrowed from the telegraph office for a few days (they could not do without it for a longer period) . . . I soon made measurements of the whole collection of acids I had on hand from other investigations," Ostwald later recalled. "With ever-growing excitement, I found that one value after another conformed to the predictions and expectations."

Ostwald not only supported Arrhenius's ideas but also disseminated them throughout the chemical community. Moreover, he arranged for Arrhenius to receive a postdoctoral fellowship so that he could continue his research. However, the idea that molecules dissociated into stable, electrically charged particles when dissolved in polar solvents such as water struck many chemists as needlessly complex. Rejecting the ionic view of solutions, they believed that ions with opposite charges must immediately recombine. These doubts were bolstered by the failure of the theory to predict accurately the behavior of very strong acids and bases. In the early twentieth century, PETER DEBYE and LARS ONSAGER extended the

theory of ionization with concepts based on electronic explanations of atomic structure. Much later, the demonstration by X-ray analysis that crystals of strong electrolytes are composed of ionic lattices and are completely ionized at all concentrations convinced the chemical community of the validity of the ionization theory.

In 1887 Ostwald was appointed to the first professorship of physical chemistry in Germany, at the University of Leipzig, where his assistants and co-workers included JACOBUS VAN'T HOFF, Arrhenius, and WALTHER NERNST. In the same year, he founded the *Zeitschrift für physikalische Chemie* (Journal of Physical Chemistry), which he edited for many years. He was also the founder, in 1894, of the German Electrochemical Society, which soon expanded to become the German Bunsen Society for Applied Physical Chemistry.

Ostwald's interest in the theory of ionic dissociation led him to see it as a good explanation for the many chemical reactions that are catalyzed by weak acids or bases. (As with the dissociation of strong electrolytes, the catalytic activity of strong acids and bases was not adequately predicted by the theory.) When chemical equilibrium exists, the forward and backward rates of reaction are equal. Ostwald showed that the presence of a catalyst speeds up the reaction in both directions by an equal amount. He also demonstrated that a system moving from a less stable to a more stable state does so by degrees and does not always move to the most stable state, behavior now called Ostwald's law of stages. Applying his knowledge of catalysis for industrial purposes, he developed the Ostwald process for synthesizing ammonia from hydrogen, using iron wire as a catalyst.

By 1890 Ostwald had become interested in the science of energetics, which viewed energy as the basis of the physical world. Skeptical of all concepts of matter, particularly theories of atoms and molecules, Ostwald believed that natural phenomena could instead be explained by energy transformations. Accordingly, he extended the laws of thermodynamics into a general philosophical outlook.

Following a year as the first exchange professor at Harvard University (during which he studied Esperanto and devised his own artificial language), Ostwald retired in 1906 to devote himself to his interests in energy models, organizational activity, writing, and color research. He developed a quantitative color theory with standards for color measurement that were published in atlases of color, and he developed systems of color harmony.

Ostwald was awarded the 1909 Nobel Prize for Chemistry "in recognition of his work on catalysis and for his investigations into the fundamental principles governing chemical equilibria and rates of reaction." In his presentation speech, Hans Hildebrand of the Royal Swedish Academy of Sciences pointed to the theoretical value of Ostwald's discoveries and also to such commercial applications as the manufacture of sulfuric acid and the synthesis of indigo. He also predicted that catalyst chemistry would shed important light on the function of enzymes.

In his later years Ostwald became involved in a variety of educational, cultural, and reform movements, including internationalism, pacifism, and the conservation of natural resources. He participated actively in numerous international learned societies, including the International Commission on Atomic Weights and the International Association of Chemical Societies. He was also concerned with public education and the training of scientists.

In 1880 Ostwald married Helene von Reyher, the daughter of a Riga surgeon. They had two daughters and three sons, one of whom, Wilhelm Wolfgang Ostwald, became an eminent colloid chemist. Ostwald died at his home near Leipzig on April 4, 1932, at the age of seventy-eight. One of his former students, Wilder Bancroft, wrote: "Ostwald was a great protagonist and an inspiring teacher. He had the gift of saying the right thing in the right way. When we consider the development of chemistry as a whole, Ostwald's name . . . leads all the rest. Ostwald was absolutely the right man in the right place."

SELECTED WORKS: Outlines of General Chemistry, 1890; Scientific Foundations of Analytical Chemistry, 1895; The Principles of Inorganic Chemistry, 1902; Conversations on Chemistry (2 vols.) 1905–1906; Individuality and Immortality, 1906; The Historical Development of General Chemistry, 1906; Letters to a Painter on the Theory and Practice of Painting, 1907; The Fundamental Principles of Chemistry, 1909; Elementary Modern Chemistry, 1909; Natural Philosophy, 1910; Introduction to Chemistry, 1911; Monism as the Goal of Civilization, 1913; Colour Science (2 vols.) 1931–1933; The Color Primer, 1969.

ABOUT: Dictionary of Scientific Biography, volume 15, 1978; Farber, E. (ed.) Great Chemists, 1961; Jacobson, E. Basic Color, 1948.

PALADE, GEORGE E.
(November 19, 1912–   )
Nobel Prize for Physiology or Medicine, 1974
(shared with Albert Claude and Christian de Duve)

The Hungarian-American biologist George Emil Palade (pa lä′ dē) was born in Iaşi, Romania, to Emil Palade, a philosophy professor at the University of Iaşi, and Constanta (Cantemir) Palade, an elementary school teacher. He received his early education at the Al Hasdeu Lyceum in Buzan, and in 1930 he entered the medical school of the University of Bucharest. There he was influenced by André Boivin, a biochemistry professor, and Francisc Rainer, an anatomy professor who gave him a research assistantship. Palade obtained his medical degree in 1940 after six years of clinical training and the completion of a dissertation on the microanatomy of the kidney in a species of sea mammal. After graduation from medical school, he became an assistant in internal medicine at the University of Bucharest. During World War II he served in the Romanian army with an assignment that allowed him to continue his work at the university until the end of the war.

In 1945, with the help of Rainer's successor, Grigore Popa, Palade obtained a research assistantship in a biology laboratory at New York University. After a seminar given by ALBERT CLAUDE, Palade introduced himself, and Claude invited him to join his research group at the Rockefeller Institute (now Rockefeller University). Palade was appointed visiting investigator at the institute in 1946; however, after the Communists assumed political power in Romania, he decided to remain in the United States.

Claude was a pioneer in methods of electron microscopy and cell fractionation. Cell fractionation involves the separation of the constituents of cells from one another by ultracentrifugation, a process by which the cells are first broken into particles of uniform size in a blender apparatus, placed in tubes and spun in a centrifuge. The components of the cells separate according to their size, shape, and density. Each cell fraction can then be removed separately and studied by biochemical methods or under the electron microscope.

It was Claude who introduced the use of the electron microscope in the study of cells. This instrument (devised in 1933 by ERNST RUSKA) delineates objects with beams of electrons.

GEORGE E. PALADE

Images of the cell and its components are greatly magnified by the electron microscope, allowing visualization of very small components of cells, and even large molecules, that cannot be seen with a light microscope. At the Rockefeller Institute, Palade improved the methods then used to prepare tissue for cell fractionation and to preserve tissue for electron microscopy.

After Claude left the institute in 1949, Palade was relatively independent and was well supported by its director, HERBERT S. GASSER. During the next four years Palade made his first important contributions to the new science of cell biology that extended beyond methodology. Since cell fractionation and electron microscopy were new techniques, many discoveries were yet to be made. Using these techniques, Palade and his collaborators reported original descriptions of the ultrastructural (electron microscopic) appearance of the cell and the biochemical functions of the structures (or organelles) within it: the mitochondria, the endoplasmic reticulum (network), the ribosomes, and the Golgi complex (named for CAMILLO GOLGI). Mitochondria are the sites of energy production in the cell; the endoplasmic reticulum is the network of tubular structures that specializes in the formation and transport of fats and proteins; the ribosomes are small particles of ribonucleic acid (RNA); and the Golgi complex is responsible for the modification, sorting, and packaging of larger molecules for transport to other organelles or to the exterior of the cells. These structures are found in the cytoplasm, the living material

in the cell other than the nucleus (the part that contains the chromosomes).

In 1952 Palade became a naturalized American citizen; a year later he was named an associate member of the Rockefeller Institute, and in 1956 he was made full professor of cell biology. By that time he had assembled the laboratory personnel and devised the experimental methods needed to investigate how the living cell synthesizes proteins to sustain itself and the life of the organism. For his experimental model, Palade chose the exocrine cell of the guinea pig pancreas. This cell synthesizes and secretes digestive enzymes (proteins that increase the rate of chemical reactions) into the intestinal tract, where they participate in the breakdown of nutrients.

Over the next several years Palade and his team elucidated the pathways of protein synthesis and enzyme secretion in the pancreatic exocrine cell. The following sequence became apparent. First, the proteins and secretory enzymes of the cell are assembled on the ribosomes, which are attached to the endoplasmic reticulum. Then the proteins are separated from other structures within the tubular spaces of the endoplasmic reticulum; these segregated proteins are transported to vacuoles (small spaces or cavities) in the cytoplasm of the cell by a process that appears to require energy from the mitochondria. Next the proteins are concentrated into particles called mature secretory granules, or zymogen granules; these granules of secretory proteins and enzymes are temporarily stored in the cell in preparation for their release from it. Finally, the protein and enzyme contents of the mature granules are discharged from the cell into the canals of the pancreas and conveyed to the intestine, where they take part in digestion.

Having completed the task of explaining how protein synthesis occurs, Palade left the Rockefeller Institute and became professor of cell biology at Yale University in 1973. By this time Palade had already turned his attention to another process central to biology: the synthesis of cellular and intracellular membranes, the capsules that surround the cell itself and the organelles within it. In the early 1950s the prevailing theory of cellular transport (the movement of substances through cell membranes) was the pore theory, which stated that ions and larger molecules entered the cell through pores in the cell membrane (the plasmalemma). Working with Marilyn Gist Farquhar, a research assistant in his laboratory at the Rockefeller Institute, Palade replaced the pore theory with a vesicular theory. Their electron micrographs showed that ions and larger molecules from outside the cell were probably engulfed by vesicles (sacs) that temporarily fused with the membrane of the cell.

The 1974 Nobel Prize for Physiology or Medicine was shared by Palade, Claude, and CHRISTIAN DE DUVE "for their discoveries concerning the structural and functional organization of the cell." It was largely because of Palade's description of protein synthesis that he shared in the award. In his Nobel lecture, Palade explained that the "functional analysis of the pancreatic exocrine cell gave us a reasonably good representation of the steps generally involved in the secretory process."

In 1940 Palade married Irina Malaxa, with whom he had a son and a daughter. A year after his first wife's death in 1969, Palade married Marilyn Gist Farquhar. When he is not working in the laboratory, Palade enjoys reading history, especially Roman history.

Palade is the recipient of the Passano Award in Medical Research of the Passano Foundation (1964), the Albert Lasker Basic Medical Research Award (1966), the T. Duckett Jones Memorial Award of the Helen Hay Whitney Foundation (1966), and the Gairdner Foundation Special Award (1967). He was awarded an honorary degree by New York University. He is a fellow of the American Academy of Arts and Sciences, a member of the National Academy of Sciences, and a member of the International Society of Cell Biologists; he also serves as an editor of the *Journal of Cell Biology,* which he founded in 1955.

ABOUT: Current Biography July 1967; Hayashi, T. (ed.) Subcellular Particles, 1959; New York Post November 17, 1966; New York Times November 16, 1966; Science November 8, 1974.

PASSY, FRÉDÉRIC
(May 20, 1822–June 12, 1912)
Nobel Prize for Peace, 1901
(shared with Henri Dunant)

Frédéric Passy, French political economist and peace advocate, was born in Paris into a large and prosperous family whose ancestors included many influential civil servants. At the time of his birth, the memory of the Napoleonic wars was still fresh, and the young Passy heard stories about battles in which his relatives had fought. As a boarding student at the Lycée Louis-le-Grand and later as a day student at the Lycée Bourbon in Paris, he studied philosophy, law, and economics. Influenced

FRÉDÉRIC PASSY

by his uncle Hyppolyte, a cabinet minister under King Louis Philippe and Emperor Napoleon III, Passy developed a lifelong interest in political economy. His intellectual outlook was also strongly colored by the free-trade doctrines he encountered in the writings of Richard Cobden, John Bright, Gustave de Molinari, and others who embraced the ideals of rationalism, personal and economic liberty, private property, and internationalism.

In 1844 Passy became an accountant for the State Council, but an inheritance permitted him to resign three years later to pursue the study of political economy. Traveling in Italy in 1843, he met Blanche Sageret; they married in 1846 and eventually had twelve children.

Although familiar with the peace movement then emerging in Europe, Passy's interest in its goals was not awakened until the final year of the Crimean War (1853–1856), in which France fought on the side of Great Britain and Turkey against Russia. The appalling casualties on both sides horrified him. When the Loire River flooded in 1856, he was struck by the ironic contrast between public dismay over the lives it claimed and public indifference to the number that had perished in the war. It occurred to Passy that while natural disasters could not be prevented, warfare could, and he redirected much of his effort from the study of political economy to the furtherance of peace.

In light of Passy's beliefs, this was a logical step. He reasoned that war was not only immoral but unproductive, resulting in "heavy financial charges, setbacks to property and commerce, [and] a violation of the life and

791

liberty of the individual." Passy believed that if individuals and nations properly understood "the material and moral solidarity which ties [them] together," they would renounce war and seek to satisfy their natural self-interest through international agreements and unrestricted trade.

Passy outlined some of his views in *Mélanges économiques* (Problems in Economics), a collection of essays published in 1857, and in a series of lectures over the next several years. He refused any state appointments because they required an oath of allegiance to Emperor Napoleon III, which his conscience forbade him to take. On the same ground, he declined nomination for the Legion of Honor, a chair at the Conservatoire des Arts et Métiers (School and Museum of Arts and Crafts), and a number of other positions.

Increasing friction between France and the German states during the 1860s alarmed Passy and other French liberals. When Napoleon III attempted to seize control of Luxembourg in 1867, war seemed unavoidable. Passy and two influential colleagues wrote a letter to the Paris newspaper *Le Temps* (The Time) urging a peaceful resolution to the conflict and the formation of a French peace society. So enthusiastic was public response to these proposals that Passy and several others established the International League for Permanent Peace later that year. As its director, Passy wrote a bimonthly column for *Le Temps* and supervised publication of the Library of Peace, a series of books that argued the pacifist cause.

Despite Passy's efforts, war broke out between France and Prussia in July 1870. For France, the consequences were swift and disastrous. Its outnumbered army was defeated, Napoleon taken prisoner, and Paris besieged until the government sued for peace early the following year. One of the war's casualties was the league. Nevertheless, from its ruins Passy created the French Society of the Friends of Peace. He also issued *Revanche ou relèvement* (Revenge or Recovery), a manifesto calling for a peace settlement between France and Germany based on voluntary arbitration and proposing neutral status for Alsace-Lorraine.

With the advent of the Third Republic in 1871, Passy felt free to accept public appointment and soon began teaching in the Paris school system. In 1881 he was elected to the Chamber of Deputies where, for two terms, he occupied a center left seat and supported free trade, labor legislation, and resolutions calling for international arbitration. At a time when France was aggressively expanding its colonial empire in North Africa and Southeast Asia, Passy courageously denounced its attempt "to dominate, to enslave, to exploit other peoples . . . who feel their nationality as we do and who are no less attached to their independence and native soil."

In this period Passy became increasingly involved in the movement to encourage arbitration as an alternative to armed conflict among nations. In 1887 WILLIAM CREMER was working to promote an agreement requiring arbitration in any disputes that Great Britain and the United States could not settle by established diplomatic means. Cremer's warm reception in the United States and the support he received in the British Parliament inspired Passy to introduce similar legislation in the French Parliament. He and Cremer organized a meeting of French and British parliamentary representatives in 1888 to discuss a possible arbitration treaty between their governments and the United States. They decided to meet again the following year. Thus, in 1889 representatives from ten European nations and the United States met in Paris during the World Exhibition and founded the Interparliamentary Union, a clearinghouse for arbitration and disarmament proposals. Defeated for reelection that year, Passy devoted much of his time to his duties as the union's president while continuing to write and lecture extensively.

For his tireless crusade for peace, Passy was awarded the first Nobel Peace Prize in 1901, an honor he shared with HENRI DUNANT. Neither presentation nor acceptance speeches were made on the occasion.

Widely regarded as the leader of the European peace movement after the awarding of the prize, Passy worked diligently to promote the goals of the movement. He appealed to Queen Victoria to avoid war with the Boers in the Transvaal region of South Africa. He urged Russia and Japan to settle their territorial dispute through arbitration, which they did in 1906 with the assistance of United States President THEODORE ROOSEVELT. To the end of his life, Passy maintained that "the future, if only we can learn to will it, shall belong to neither war, nor division, nor hatred. It shall belong to peace, to work, and—to arbitration." Passy died at home on June 12, 1912, and was buried at Père-Lachaise Cemetery in Paris.

WORKS IN ENGLISH TRANSLATION: "Peace Movement in Europe," American Journal of Sociology July 1896; "The Advance of the Peace Movement Throughout the

World," American Monthly Review of Reviews February 1898; Pour La Paix: Notes and Documents, 1972.

ABOUT: American Journal of International Law October 1912; Economic Journal September 1919; Interparliamentary Union. The Interparliamentary Union, 1889–1939, 1939; Times (London) June 13, 1912.

PASTERNAK, BORIS
(February 10, 1890–May 30, 1960)
Nobel Prize for Literature, 1958

BORIS PASTERNAK

The Russian poet and novelist Boris Leonidovich Pasternak was born into a prominent Jewish family in Moscow, where his father, Leonid, was a professor at the Moscow School of Painting, Sculpture, and Architecture and a portrait painter whose subjects included such celebrated figures as Leo Tolstoy. Pasternak's mother, the former Roza Kaufmann, an acclaimed concert pianist, largely abandoned her career to raise Boris and his brother and two sisters. Although not wealthy, the Pasternaks moved comfortably in the highest cultural circles of prerevolutionary Russia, and their home was open to a stream of distinguished visitors, including Sergei Rachmaninoff, Aleksandr Scriabin, Rainer Maria Rilke, and Tolstoy. Writing of Tolstoy many years later, Pasternak remarked that "his image stalked me through life."

Inspired by Scriabin, Pasternak entered the Moscow Conservatory to study music theory and composition. Although talented, he lacked perfect pitch and gave up his studies in 1910. Meanwhile, he had become increasingly attracted to philosophy and religion, particularly the teachings of the New Testament as he had heard them interpreted by his Greek Orthodox nanny and by Tolstoy. At the age of twenty-three, Pasternak entered Marburg University, in Germany, where he studied philosophy under Hermann Cohen, an authority on Immanuel Kant and Georg Hegel. But a brief encounter with a young Russian woman stirred Pasternak's blood, reminded him of home, and persuaded him that his talents were more lyrical than logical. After a brief tour of Italy, he returned to Moscow in the winter of 1913–1914.

Once back in Moscow, he associated with prominent representatives of the symbolist school and with Vladimir Mayakovsky, the leading member of the futurist movement, who became both a personal friend and a literary rival. Although music, philosophy, and religion remained important to him, Pasternak discovered his true vocation as a poet during his sojourn in Western Europe. While supporting himself as a tutor, he published his first collection of poems, *Bliznets v tuchakh* (Twin in the Clouds), in 1914, followed three years later by a second collection, *Poverkh baryerov* (Above Barriers). The idyllic atmosphere of his life in Russia on the eve of World War I is evoked in the novella *Povest* (*The Last Summer,* 1934).

A leg injury he had sustained in a childhood riding accident exempted Pasternak from military service during the war, though he volunteered for clerical work at a factory in the Ural Mountains in order to contribute to the war effort. The rich impressions of his journey to the Urals were later to figure vividly in his novel *Doctor Zhivago*.

With the outbreak of the Russian Revolution in 1917, Pasternak rushed back to Moscow, a city in upheaval. His sense of the vibrancy and excitement that was sweeping over Russia at this time found expression in a series of poems published five years later as *Sestra moya zhizn* (*Sister, My Life*), which record the deep personal emotions Pasternak experienced at the time. This volume and its sequel, *Temy i variatsii* (Themes and Variations, 1923), won wide recognition in his homeland and firmly established him as one of Russia's more important poets. The poet Marina Tsvetaeva, an early admirer of Pasternak's work, described his poetry as "a downpour of light," remarking that both his speech and his verse were like "the interruption of a primordial muteness." In one of his poems, Pasternak urged poetry itself to "preserve living exactness—the exactness of mysteries."

Since Pasternak was by nature reticent about his personal affairs and more disposed to write circumspectly about the events he observed, the details of his life after the revolution are sketchy; much of what is known about him comes from his correspondence with friends in the West and from two books, his *Autobiograficheskiy ocherk* (*I Remember: Sketch for an Autobiography*, 1961) and *Okhrannaya gramota* (*Safe Conduct*, 1931). Like many poets and writers during the early days of the revolution, he worked for a time as a librarian at the People's Commissariat for Education.

Although in 1921 his parents and two sisters emigrated to Germany, finally settling in England after Hitler came to power, Pasternak and his brother, Aleksandr, remained in Moscow. Around the time of his parents' departure, Pasternak married Eugenia Muratova, a painter; they had one son. After this marriage ended in divorce in 1931, Pasternak married Zinaida Nikolaevna Neuhaus, with whom he had two more sons. For the remainder of his life, with the exception of several periods during World War II, the couple lived in Peredelkino, the official Soviet writers' colony outside Moscow.

During the 1920s Pasternak wrote two narrative poems praising the revolution, and in 1934 the first All-Union Congress of Writers commended him as one of the nation's leading contemporary poets. This acclaim was short-lived, however, because his reluctance to confine his work to proletarian themes antagonized Soviet authorities. During the purges ordered by Joseph Stalin in the 1930s, Pasternak refused to support the execution of certain Soviet generals for treason even though he was aware of the probable repercussions. Consequently, he published no new books between 1935 and 1943, but his circumspect behavior spared him the internal exile or execution that befell many of his contemporaries.

Having grown up in a cosmopolitan home, Pasternak spoke several languages, and he spent much of the 1930s translating into Russian the works of classic English, German, and French poets. His translations of Shakespeare's tragedies are generally considered the finest versions in Russian. At the same time, Pasternak championed the work of several poets from Soviet Georgia and also translated their poems, work that may have commended him to Stalin, who was himself Georgian.

During World War II, as the Germans pushed deep into the Soviet Union and threatened Moscow, Pasternak was evacuated from Peredelkino. Supporting the Soviet war effort, he wrote patriotic verses and petitioned the government to allow him to go to the front as a war correspondent, a request that was eventually granted. In 1943 his first book in eight years, *Na Rannikh poyezdakh* (*On Early Trains*), a slim collection of twenty-six poems, appeared and quickly sold out. Another book of his poems was published in 1945, followed in 1947 by a selection of earlier poetry.

While continuing to write poetry and do translations through the 1940s, Pasternak contemplated writing a novel "in which, as in an explosion, I would erupt with all the wonderful things I saw and understood in the world." After the war, in the solitude of Peredelkino, he immersed himself in the task of creating this work. *Doktor Zhivago* (*Doctor Zhivago*), the novel that emerged from this effort, follows its protagonist, Yury Andreevich Zhivago, a physician and poet, from his childhood at the turn of the twentieth century through World War I, the Russian Revolution, the civil war, and into the Stalinist era. With his reflective nature, artistic temperament, and philosophical outlook, Zhivago was in direct contrast to the unhesitating and doctrinaire revolutionary hero favored by Soviet authorities. Although the characters of the book adopt diverse approaches to the problems of life, they do not reflect Marxist-Leninist views. To Pasternak, their lives chronicle the generation that grew up just before and during the revolution. Significantly, *zhivago* means "life" in Russian.

In the midst of social upheaval, Zhivago finds deep, idyllic peace in a passionate love affair with Lara, a woman who has suffered as the mistress of a corrupt businessman and as the wife of a fanatical revolutionary. In its lyrical and epic qualities and its emphasis on the spiritual in the face of grave threats to the spirit, *Doctor Zhivago* exhibits parallels to Tolstoy's *War and Peace*.

Initially approved for publication by Soviet authorities, *Doctor Zhivago* was then rejected for expressing "a negative attitude toward the revolution and a lack of faith in social transformation." First published in Milan in 1957 in an Italian translation, by the end of 1958 it had been translated into eighteen languages, including the American edition that year. It was later made into a motion picture by the English director David Lean.

The Swedish Academy awarded Pasternak the 1958 Nobel Prize for Literature "for his important achievement both in contemporary lyrical poetry and in the field of the great Russian epic tradition." *Pravda* (The Truth) and the Soviet *Literaturnaya Gazeta* (Literary Gazette) immediately denounced him as a "traitor," a "malevolent Philistine," a "libeler," a "Judas," and an "extraneous smudge in our socialist country." He was expelled from the Soviet Writers' Union and pressured to reject the prize, which he did. Having first replied to the Swedish Academy that he was "immensely thankful, touched, proud, astonished, abashed," four days later Pasternak sent another telegram: "Considering the meaning this award has been given in the society to which I belong, I must reject this undeserved prize which has been presented to me. Please do not receive my voluntary rejection with displeasure." "This refusal, of course, in no way alters the validity of the award," said Anders Österling of the Swedish Academy in an announcement at the award ceremony. "There remains only for the academy . . . to announce with regret that the presentation of the prize cannot take place."

In a personal letter to Nikita Khrushchev, the Soviet premier, Pasternak expressed his hope that he would be allowed to remain in the Soviet Union. "Leaving the motherland will equal death for me," he said. "I am tied to Russia by birth, by life and work." Profoundly shaken by the continuing attacks against him and his work—a reaction he had not expected when he set out to write *Doctor Zhivago*—he remained at Peredelkino quietly writing, gardening, receiving visitors, and entertaining friends until his death from lung cancer in 1960.

Pasternak's disagreement with Soviet Communism was not political but rather "philosophical and moral," in the words of the critic and literary historian Marc Slonim, who went on to say of Pasternak: "He believes in human virtues formulated by the Christian dream, and he asserts the value of life, of beauty, of love, and of nature. He rejects violence, especially when justified by abstract formulas and sectarian rhetoric." With his early grounding in humanism and in religion, Pasternak was ill-disposed to accept the Soviet credo of materialism, collectivism, and atheism. As Robert Payne, one of his biographers, remarked, "Again and again in his poems and in the novel, Pasternak declares the supremacy of man and of the heart's affections over all the regimentation of dictatorship." In a letter to one of his translators, Pasternak wrote that "art is not simply a description of life but a setting forth of the uniqueness of being. . . . The signifi-

cant writer of his epoch . . . is a revelation, a representation of the unknown, unrepeatable uniqueness of living reality."

Official attitudes toward Pasternak began to relax in the early 1980s, after the poet Andrei Voznesensky published a memoir about him in the literary journal *Novy Mir* (New World). A two-volume selection of Pasternak's poetry, edited by his son Yevgeny, appeared in 1986. The following year Pasternak was reinstated posthumously by the Soviet Writers' Union, shortly after an announcement that *Doctor Zhivago* would be published in full in 1988.

ADDITIONAL WORKS IN ENGLISH TRANSLATION: Bystander, 1936; Childhood, 1941; The Collected Prose Works, 1945; Selected Poems, 1946; Selected Writings, 1949; The Poetry of Boris Pasternak, 1917–1959, 1959; When the Sky Clears, 1960; Poems 1955–59, 1961; The Adolescence of Zhenya Luvers, 1961; In the Interlude: Poems 1945–1960, 1962; Poems 1916–1959, 1964; Letters to Georgian Friends, 1967; The Blind Beauty, 1969; Seven Poems, 1969; Collected Short Prose, 1977; Zhenia's Childhood and Other Stories, 1982; The Correspondence of Boris Pasternak and Olga Freidenberg, 1910–54, 1982; Letters: Summer 1926, with others, 1986; The Voice of Prose, 1986.

ABOUT: Bodin, P. A. Nine Poems From Doktor Zhivago, 1976; Conquest, R. The Pasternak Affair: Courage of Genius, 1962; Davie, D. The Poems of Dr. Zhivago, 1965; Davie, D., and Livingstone, A. (eds.) Pasternak: Modern Judgements, 1969; Dyck, J. W. Boris Pasternak, 1972; Erlich, U. Pasternak: A Collection of Critical Essays, 1978; Gaev, A. G. Boris Pasternak and Dr. Zhivago, 1959; Gifford, H. Pasternak: A Critical Study, 1977; Gladkov, A. K. Meetings With Pasternak: A Memoir, 1977; Hingley, R. Pasternak: A Biography, 1983; Hughes, O. R. The Poetic World of Boris Pasternak, 1974; Ivanskaia, O. V. A Captive of Time, 1978; de Mallac, G. Boris Pasternak: His Life and Art, 1981; Nilsson, N. A. (ed.) Boris Pasternak: Essays, 1976; Payne, R. The Three Worlds of Boris Pasternak, 1961; Plank, D. L. Pasternak's Lyric: A Study of Sound and Imagery, 1966; Plimpton, G. (ed.) Writers at Work, volume 2, 1963; Pomorska, K. Themes and Variations in Pasternak's Poetics, 1975; Rowland, M. F., and Rowland, P. (eds.) Pasternak's "Doctor Zhivago," 1967; Ruge, G. Pasternak: A Pictorial Biography, 1959; Slonim, M. Soviet Russian Literature: Writers and Problems, 1964.

PAULI, WOLFGANG

(April 25, 1900–December 15, 1958)
Nobel Prize for Physics, 1945

The Austrian-Swiss physicist Wolfgang Ernst Pauli (pou′ lē) was born in Vienna. His father, Wolfgang Joseph Pauli, was a noted physician and biochemist who later became a professor of colloid chemistry at the University of Vienna. His mother was Bertha (Schütz) Pauli, a writer associated with theatrical and journalistic circles in Vienna. Pauli's younger sister, Hertha, became an actress and author.

WOLFGANG PAULI

Ernst Mach, an eminent physicist and philosopher, was Pauli's godfather. At secondary school in Vienna, Pauli demonstrated a particular talent for mathematics, but finding many of his classes dull, he gave his attention to independent study of advanced calculus and read ALBERT EINSTEIN's newly published general theory of relativity.

In 1918 Pauli entered the University of Munich, where he studied under the noted physicist Arnold Sommerfeld. At this time, the German mathematician Felix Klein was engaged in publishing an encyclopedia of the mathematical sciences. Klein asked Sommerfeld to write a review of Einstein's special and general theories of relativity, and Sommerfeld in turn asked the twenty-year-old Pauli to write the article. He promptly produced a 250-page article that Sommerfeld described as "simply masterful." Einstein also praised it.

In 1921, after completing his doctoral thesis on the theory of the hydrogen molecule and receiving his Ph.D. in the shortest time allowed by the university, Pauli went to the University of Göttingen for postgraduate studies with MAX BORN and JAMES FRANCK. In late 1922 he went to Copenhagen as an assistant to NIELS BOHR. His studies under Sommerfeld, Born, Franck, and Bohr introduced Pauli to the new field of quantum theory, which was being applied to the study of atoms and subatomic particles, and he became engrossed in the problems facing physicists in this area.

Although the principles of classical physics could satisfactorily explain the behavior of macroscopic physical systems, attempts to ap-ply the same principles to events at the atomic scale had failed. A particularly troubling problem concerned the nuclear model of the atom, in which electrons orbit a central nucleus. According to the principles of classical physics, the orbiting electrons should emit electromagnetic radiation continually, thereby losing energy and spiraling into the nucleus. In 1913 Bohr proposed that the electrons cannot radiate continuously because they are confined to specific allowed orbits; all intermediate orbits are forbidden. An electron can emit or absorb radiation only by making a quantum jump from one allowed orbit to another.

Bohr's model was derived in part from studies of atomic spectra. When an element is heated to create a gas or vapor of individual atoms, it gives off light with a characteristic spectrum. The spectrum is not a continuous range of colors like the spectrum of the sun but rather a sequence of bright lines at specific wavelengths, separated by wider dark regions. Bohr's model of the atom accounted for the basic form of atomic spectra: each line represented light emitted when electrons fell from some specific orbit to a lower-energy orbit. Moreover, the model correctly predicted the major features of the simplest atomic spectrum, that of hydrogen. On the other hand, the model was less successful in describing the spectra of more complex atoms.

Two additional failings of Bohr's atomic theory had an important bearing on Pauli's later contributions to quantum theory. First, the model could not explain certain fine details in the hydrogen spectrum. For example, when an atomic gas is immersed in a magnetic field, some of the spectral lines are split into several closely spaced lines, an effect first observed by PIETER ZEEMAN in 1896. Of more fundamental importance, the stability of the electron orbits had still not been fully explained. Although the electrons could not spiral into the nucleus by continuous radiation, there was no apparent reason why they could not descend by steps through the allowed orbits, all congregating in the lowest energy state.

In 1923 Pauli became assistant professor of theoretical physics at the University of Hamburg. There he conducted theoretical research in atomic structure and the behavior of atoms in magnetic fields, developing a theory of the Zeeman effect and other forms of spectral splitting in early 1925. Pauli suggested that electrons have a property that was later identified by Samuel A. Goudsmit and George E. Uhlenbeck as "spin," or intrinsic angular momentum. In a magnetic field, an electron with spin has two possible orientations—namely, with the spin axis parallel or antiparallel to the direction of the field. The orbital motion of the electron in the atom defines another axis that can be oriented in various ways with respect to an externally imposed magnetic field. Various possible combinations of spin and orbital orientation differ slightly in energy, causing a proliferation in the number of atomic energy states. Transitions between each of the sublevels and some other orbit correspond to slightly different wavelengths of light, thus accounting for the fine splitting of the spectral lines.

Shortly after introducing this "two-valuedness" property of the electron, Pauli extended his analysis to explain why the electrons in an atom do not all occupy the lowest energy level. In Pauli's modification of the Bohr model, the allowed energy states, or orbits, of electrons in atoms are described by the four quantum numbers of each electron. These numbers define the electron's basic energy level, its orbital angular momentum, its magnetic moment, and (Pauli's contribution) its spin orientation. Each of the quantum numbers can assume only certain values; moreover, only certain combinations of values are possible. In a formulation that came to be known as the exclusion principle, Pauli stated that no two electrons in a system can have an identical set of quantum numbers. Thus, each shell in an atom can have only a limited number of electron orbits, determined by the possible values of the quantum numbers.

The Pauli exclusion principle is fundamental to an understanding of the structure and behavior of atoms, the atomic nucleus, the properties of metals, and other aspects of physics. It explains the chemical interaction of the elements and their previously baffling organization in the periodic table. Pauli himself was to use the exclusion principle to understand the magnetic properties of simple metals and certain gases.

Shortly after Pauli's formulation of the exclusion principle, the theory of quantum phenomena was given sound theoretical footing by the work of ERWIN SCHRÖDINGER, WERNER HEISENBERG, and P. A. M. DIRAC. The theoretical techniques they used to treat the behavior of atomic and smaller systems came to be called quantum mechanics. The Bohr model of the atom was replaced by a quantum-mechanical model that was more successful in predicting spectra and other atomic phenomena. Pauli's many contributions helped expand quantum mechanics so that it could describe high-energy particles and the interaction of particles with light and other forms of electromagnetic fields. This field became known as relativistic quantum electrodynamics.

In 1928 Pauli succeeded PETER DEBYE as professor at the Federal Institute of Technology in Zurich, Switzerland, where he remained for the rest of his life except for two periods spent in the United States. Pauli spent the academic year 1935–1936 as a guest lecturer at the Institute for Advanced Study in Princeton, New Jersey. Early in World War II, when he feared that Germany might invade Switzerland, Pauli returned to the institute, where he held the chair of theoretical physics from 1940 to 1946.

During the 1930s he made another major contribution to physics. Observation of the beta decay of atomic nuclei, in which a neutron in the nucleus emits an electron and turns into a proton, had revealed an apparent violation of the principle of conservation of energy. When all detected decay products were taken into account, there was less energy after the decay than there had been before. In 1930 Pauli proposed that an undetected particle (which ENRICO FERMI named the neutrino) was also emitted, accounting for the missing energy and also preserving the conservation law for angular momentum. Neutrinos were eventually detected in 1956.

Pauli was awarded the 1945 Nobel Prize for Physics "for the discovery of the exclusion principle, also called the Pauli principle." Pauli did not attend the ceremonies, and the prize was accepted on his behalf by a member of the American embassy in Stockholm. In his Nobel lecture, delivered in Stockholm the following year, after his return to Zurich, Pauli summarized his work on the exclusion principle and quantum mechanics.

Pauli became a Swiss citizen in 1946. In his later work he sought to elucidate the interactions of energetic particles and the forces by which they interact, a field now known as high-energy physics, or particle physics. He also made profound studies of the role of symmetry in particle physics. Legendary for his critical ability and his insight into physical problems, he was intolerant of obscure arguments and superficial speculation. He subjected his own work to such stringent critical analysis that his publications are remarkably free from error. His colleagues referred to Pauli as "the conscience of physics."

After the dissolution of a brief and unhappy first marriage, Pauli married Franciska Bertram in 1934. Deeply interested in philosophy and psychology, Pauli enjoyed conversations with his friend C. G. Jung. He also had a deep appreciation of art, music, and the theater. For recreation he liked to swim and to hike in the mountains and forests of Switzerland. Pauli's intellectual ability was not matched by manual dexterity; his colleagues used to joke about a mysterious "Pauli effect," whereby the short, stocky scientist's mere presence in a laboratory seemed to cause accidents to happen. In early December 1958 Pauli became ill; he died suddenly on December 15.

In addition to the Nobel Prize, Pauli received the Franklin Medal of the Franklin Institute (1952) and the Max Planck Medal of the German Physical Society (1958). He was a member of the Swiss Physical Society, the American Physical Society, and the American Association for the Advancement of Science, as well as a foreign member of the Royal Society of London.

SELECTED WORKS: Meson Theory of Nuclear Forces, 1946; Continuous Groups in Quantum Mechanics, 1955; Theory of Relativity, 1958; Collected Scientific Papers (2 vols.) 1964; Electrodynamics, 1973; Thermodynamics and the Kinetic Theory of Gases, 1973; Optics and the Theory of Electrons, 1973; Selected Topics in Field Quantization, 1973; Statistical Mechanics, 1973; Wave Mechanics, 1973; General Principles of Quantum Mechanics, 1980.

ABOUT: Biographical Memoirs of Fellows of the Royal Society, volume 5, 1960; Dictionary of Scientific Biography, volume 10, 1974; Fierz, M., and Weisskopf, V. F. (eds.) Theoretical Physics in the Twentieth Century, 1960; Hendry, J. The Creation of Quantum Mechanics and the Bohr-Pauli Dialogue, 1984.

PAULING, LINUS C.

(February 28, 1901–   )
Nobel Prize for Chemistry, 1954
Nobel Prize for Peace, 1962

The American chemist Linus Carl Pauling was born in Portland, Oregon, to Lucy Isabell (Darling) and Herman Henry William Pauling. Pauling's father, a pharmacist, died when the boy was nine years old. Pauling became interested in science as a child, collecting insects and minerals. When he was thirteen years old, a friend introduced him to chemistry, and Pauling began to experiment at home using materials from his mother's kitchen. He attended Washington High School in Portland but did not receive a diploma. Nevertheless, he enrolled in the Oregon Agricultural College (later Oregon State University) in Corvallis, where he majored in chemical engineering,

chemistry, and physics. To help support himself and his mother, he washed dishes and graded papers. It soon became evident that Pauling was a prodigy, and he was appointed an assistant in quantitative analysis in his junior year. In his senior year he became an assistant in chemistry, mechanics, and materials. After receiving a B.S. in chemical engineering in 1922, he began doctoral studies in chemistry at the California Institute of Technology (Caltech) in Pasadena.

Pauling was first a graduate assistant and then a teaching fellow in the Caltech chemistry department. He was awarded a Ph.D. in chemistry summa cum laude in 1925. For the next two years he was a research associate and a fellow of the National Research Council at Caltech. He was appointed assistant professor of chemistry in 1927, associate professor in 1929, and professor in 1931.

During his years as a research assistant, Pauling became adept at the techniques of X-ray crystallography, the passage of X rays through crystallized molecules to produce a characteristic pattern from which the atomic structure of the molecules can be determined. Using these techniques, he studied the nature of chemical bonding in benzene and other aromatic compounds (compounds that contain at least one benzene ring and emit an aroma). A Guggenheim Fellowship enabled him to spend the academic year 1926–1927 studying quantum mechanics with Arnold Sommerfeld in Munich, ERWIN SCHRÖDINGER in Zurich, and NIELS BOHR in Copenhagen. Schrödinger's 1926 formulation of quantum mechanics, called wave mechanics, and WOLFGANG PAULI's exclusion principle, published in 1925, were to have profound effects on the study of chemical bonding.

In 1928 Pauling published his resonance, or hybridization, theory of bonding in aromatic compounds, which was based on the quantum mechanical concept of electron orbitals. In the older model of benzene, still used sometimes for convenience, three of the six chemical bonds (shared electron pairs) between adjacent carbon atoms were single bonds and three were double bonds. Single and double bonds alternated in position in the benzene ring. Thus, benzene could have two possible structures, depending on which bonds were single and which were double. Double bonds, however, were known to be shorter than single bonds, and X-ray diffraction showed that all the bonds in the carbon molecule are equal in length. The resonance theory stated that the bonds between the six carbon atoms in benzene were

LINUS C. PAULING

intermediate in character between single and double bonds. In Pauling's model, benzene rings can be viewed as hybrids of their possible structures, a concept that has proved extremely useful in predicting the properties of aromatic compounds.

Over the next few years Pauling continued to conduct research on the physicochemical properties of molecules, particularly those involving resonance. In 1934 he turned his attention to biochemistry, particularly the biochemistry of proteins. With A. E. Mirsky, Pauling formulated a theory of protein structure and function. With C. D. Coryell he studied the effects of oxygenation on the magnetic properties of hemoglobin, the oxygen-carrying protein in red blood cells.

On the death of Arthur Noyes in 1936, Pauling was appointed chairman of the Department of Chemistry and Chemical Engineering and director of the Gates and Crellin Laboratories of Chemistry at Caltech. In these administrative positions, he initiated studies of the atomic and molecular structure of proteins and amino acids (molecular subunits of proteins) using X-ray crystallography. He spent the academic year 1937–1938 as the George Fisher Baker Lecturer in Chemistry at Cornell University in Ithaca, New York.

In 1942 Pauling and his colleagues succeeded in altering the chemical structure of certain blood proteins known as globulins, producing the first synthetic antibodies. Antibodies are globulin molecules that are made by specialized cells in response to invasion of the body by antigens, or foreign substances such as viruses, bacteria, and toxins. An antibody combines with the specific kind of antigen that stimulated its production. Pauling correctly postulated that the three-dimensional structures of an antigen and its antibody are complementary, thus accounting for the formation of antigen-antibody complexes. In 1947 he and GEORGE W. BEADLE received funding for a five-year investigation of the mechanism by which polioviruses destroy nerve cells. During the following year Pauling was Eastman Professor at Oxford University.

Pauling's work on sickle-cell anemia began in 1949, when he learned that the red blood cells of patients with this hereditary disease became sickle-shaped only in venous blood, where the oxygen content is low. On the basis of his knowledge of hemoglobin chemistry, Pauling immediately postulated that the sickling of a red cell was caused by a genetic defect in the globin portion of the cell's hemoglobin. (The hemoglobin molecule consists of an iron-containing portion called the heme and a protein portion, the globin.) This insight illustrates Pauling's intuitive approach to many scientific problems. Three years later he was able to show that normal hemoglobin and hemoglobin from patients with sickle-cell anemia can be distinguished by electrophoresis, a method for separating different proteins from a mixture. This finding supported his contention that the protein portion of the molecule was responsible for the abnormality.

Pauling and R. B. Corey published the first complete description of the molecular structure of proteins—the product of fourteen years of research—in 1951. Using X-ray crystallographic methods to examine the proteins in hair, wool, muscle, fingernails, and other biological tissues, they found that the chains of amino acids in a protein twisted around one another to form a helix. This description of the three-dimensional structure of proteins marked a major advance in biochemistry.

Not all of Pauling's scientific ventures were successful. During the early 1950s he turned his attention to deoxyribonucleic acid (DNA), the biological molecule that carries the genetic code. In 1953, as scientists in several parts of the world were trying to determine the structure of DNA, Pauling published a paper in which he incorrectly described it as a triple-stranded helix. A few months later FRANCIS CRICK and JAMES D. WATSON published their famous paper describing the DNA molecule as a double helix.

Pauling was awarded the 1954 Nobel Prize for Chemistry "for his research into the nature of the chemical bond and its application to the structure of complex substances." In his Nobel lecture Pauling predicted that future chemists would "come to rely upon a new structural chemistry, involving precise geometrical relationships among the atoms in the molecules and the rigorous application of the new structural principles, and that great progress will be made through this technique in the attack, by chemical methods, on the problems of biology and medicine."

Although Pauling had been a pacifist as a youth in World War I, during World War II he was a staff member of the National Defense Research Commission, working on rocket propellants and on oxygen indicators for submarines and aircraft. As a member of the Office for Scientific Research and Development, he made significant contributions to the development of a substitute human plasma for wartime use. However, soon after the United States dropped atomic bombs on the Japanese cities of Hiroshima and Nagasaki, Pauling began to campaign against the new weapons, and from 1945 to 1946, as a member of the Research Board for National Security, he lectured on the dangers of nuclear war.

In 1946 Pauling became a charter member of the Emergency Committee of Atomic Scientists, organized by ALBERT EINSTEIN and seven other prominent scientists to promote a ban on atmospheric testing of nuclear weapons. Four years later, as the nuclear arms race gathered momentum, Pauling spoke out against his government's decision to develop the hydrogen bomb and advocated an end to all atmospheric testing of nuclear weapons. During the early 1950s, as both the United States and the Soviet Union tested hydrogen bombs, the level of radioactivity in the atmosphere increased, and Pauling used his considerable talent as a public speaker to publicize the possible biological and genetic effects of radioactive fallout. His concern over potential genetic damage stemmed in part from his research on the molecular basis of hereditary disease. Pauling and fifty-two other Nobel Prize winners signed the Mainau Declaration in 1955, appealing for an end to the arms race.

When Pauling drew up an appeal in 1957 that called for an end to nuclear testing, it was signed by more than 11,000 scientists from forty-nine countries, including over 2,000 Americans. In January 1958 he presented this document to DAG HAMMARSKJÖLD, then the secretary-general of the United Nations. Pauling's efforts contributed to the establishment of the Pugwash Movement for Science and World Affairs, which held its first conference in 1957 in Pugwash, Nova Scotia, and which was eventually instrumental in promoting a nuclear test ban treaty. Such great public and private concern was aroused about the dangers of atmospheric radioactivity that in 1958, although no treaty existed, the United States, the Soviet Union, and Great Britain voluntarily stopped testing nuclear weapons in the atmosphere.

Pauling encountered considerable opposition as well as support in his efforts to ban atmospheric testing of nuclear weapons. Such prominent American scientists as Edward Teller and WILLARD F. LIBBY, both members of the United States Atomic Energy Commission, maintained that Pauling exaggerated the biological effects of radioactive fallout. Pauling also encountered political harassment for alleged pro-Soviet sympathies. During the early 1950s he had trouble obtaining a passport and was granted one without restrictions only after he was awarded the Nobel Prize.

Ironically, he came under attack in the Soviet Union during the same period because his resonance theory of chemical bonding was considered not in accord with Marxist principles. (After the death of Joseph Stalin in 1953, it became permissible for Soviet scientists to accept the resonance theory.) Pauling was called before the Internal Security Subcommittee of the United States Senate in 1955 and again in 1960 for questioning about his political views and activities. On both occasions he denied ever having been a Communist or being sympathetic to Marxist views. On the second occasion he risked prosecution for contempt of Congress by refusing to reveal the names of those who had helped him collect signatures for his 1957 appeal. The matter was eventually dropped.

In June 1961 Pauling and his wife convened a conference in Oslo, Norway, against the spread of nuclear weapons. In September of that year, despite Pauling's appeals to Nikita Khrushchev, the Soviet Union resumed atmospheric testing of nuclear weapons, as did the United States the following March. Pauling began to monitor levels of atmospheric radioactivity, and in October 1962 he released information showing that the previous year's tests had increased the level of atmospheric radioactivity by twice as much as the combined tests of the preceding sixteen years. He also drafted a proposed test ban agreement. In July 1963 the United States, the Soviet Union, and Great Britain signed a nuclear test ban treaty based in part on Pauling's draft.

In 1963 Pauling was awarded the 1962 Nobel Prize for Peace. On presenting the award, Gunnar Jahn of the Norwegian Nobel Committee declared that Pauling had "campaigned ceaselessly, not only against nuclear weapons tests, not only against the spread of these armaments, not only against their very use—but against all warfare as a means of solving international conflicts." In his Nobel lecture, "Science and Peace," Pauling expressed his hope that the test ban treaty would be only "the first of a series of treaties that will lead to the new world, from which war has been abolished forever."

The same year that he received his second Nobel Prize, Pauling resigned from Caltech to become a research professor at the Center for the Study of Democratic Institutions in Santa Barbara, California, where he was able to devote more time to problems of international disarmament. In 1967 he took an additional appointment as professor of chemistry at the University of California at San Diego, hoping to spend more time doing research in molecular medicine. He left after two years to become professor of chemistry at Stanford University in Palo Alto, California. At that time he also resigned from the Center for the Study of Democratic Institutions.

During the late 1960s Pauling became interested in the biological effects of vitamin C. He and his wife began taking it regularly, and he began publicly to advocate its use for preventing the common cold. His monograph *Vitamin C and the Common Cold,* which appeared in 1971, summarized current published evidence and theoretical support for vitamin C therapy. In the early 1970s Pauling also formulated a theory of orthomolecular medicine, which emphasized the importance of vitamins and amino acids in the maintenance of an optimal molecular environment for the brain. These theories, which were widely publicized at the time, have not been supported by subsequent research and have been largely rejected by the medical and psychiatric professions. However, Pauling maintains that evidence to the contrary is flawed.

Pauling founded the Linus Pauling Institute of Science and Medicine in Palo Alto in 1973. During its first two years, he served as president and since then has been a professor. He and his colleagues at the institute have continued to conduct research on vitamin therapy, particularly on the effects of vitamin C in the treatment of cancer. In 1979 Pauling published a book, *Cancer and Vitamin C,* in which he claimed that massive doses of vitamin C prolonged the lives and improved the condition of patients with certain types of cancer. However, authorities in the field of cancer research have not found his evidence persuasive.

In 1922 Pauling married Ava Helen Miller, one of his students at the Oregon Agricultural College. They had three sons and a daughter. Since his wife's death in 1981, Pauling has continued to live in their rural cabin in Big Sur, California.

In addition to his two Nobel Prizes, Pauling has received many awards, including the Award in Pure Chemistry of the American Chemical Society (1931), the Davy Medal of the Royal Society of London (1947), the International Lenin Peace Prize given by the Soviet government (1971), the National Medal of Science of the National Science Foundation (1975), the Lomonosov Gold Medal of the Soviet Academy of Sciences (1978), the Award in Chemical Sciences of the National Academy of Sciences (1979), and the Priestley Medal of the American Chemical Society (1984). His honorary degrees include doctorates from the University of Chicago and from Princeton, Yale, Oxford, and Cambridge universities. Pauling is a member of many professional organizations, including the National Academy of Sciences, the American Academy of Arts and Sciences, and scientific societies or academies in Germany, England, Belgium, Switzerland, Japan, India, Norway, Portugal, France, Austria, and the Soviet Union. He has been president of the American Chemical Society (1948) and of the Pacific division of the American Association for the Advancement of Science (1942–1945) and vice president of the American Philosophical Society (1951–1954).

SELECTED WORKS: The Structure of Line Spectra, 1930, with Samuel Goudsmit; Introduction to Quantum Mechanics, 1935, with E. Bright Wilson; The Nature of the Chemical Bond and the Structure of Molecules and Crystals, 1940; General Chemistry, 1947; College Chemistry, 1950; No More War! 1958; The Architecture of Molecules, 1964; The Greatest Experience: The Abolition of War, 1964; The Chemical Bond, 1967; Science and World Peace, 1967; Structural Chemistry and Molecular Biology, 1968; Chemistry, 1975, with Peter Pauling; How to Live Longer and Feel Better, 1986.

ABOUT: Current Biography February 1964; Huemer, R. P. (ed.) The Roots of Molecular Medicine: A Tribute to Linus Pauling, 1986; National Cyclopedia of American Biography, volume 6, 1946; New York Times October 21, 1984; White, F. M. Linus Pauling, Scientist and Crusader, 1980.

PAVLOV, IVAN
(September 27, 1849–February 27, 1936)
Nobel Prize for Physiology or Medicine,
1904

IVAN PAVLOV

The Russian physiologist Ivan Petrovich Pavlov was born in Ryazan, a town located about 125 miles from Moscow. His mother, Varvara Ivanova, came from a family of clergymen; his father, Pyotr Dmitrievich Pavlov, was a priest who originally worked in a very poor parish and by great perseverance eventually became the head of one of the wealthiest parishes in Ryazan. From an early age Pavlov exhibited his father's persistence and constant striving for self-improvement. Following his parents' wishes, Pavlov attended an elementary theological seminary in Ryazan in 1860 before entering a secondary seminary. At school he was allowed to pursue the subjects that interested him most, including debating (in which his passion and tenacity made him a formidable opponent throughout his life) and the natural sciences.

Pavlov was first attracted to the study of physiology through reading a Russian translation of a book on the physiology of common life written by the English critic, George Henry Lewes. His enthusiasm for science, especially biology, was intensified by his reading of the popular writings of Dmitri I. Pisarev, a radical political philosopher and materialist whose works introduced Pavlov to the theories of Charles Darwin.

In the late 1860s the Russian government changed its regulations to permit divinity students to pursue a secular education. Before receiving a degree from the seminary, Pavlov enrolled in St. Petersburg University in 1870 to study natural science. His interest in physiology further increased when he read Ivan M. Sechenov's *Reflexes of the Brain,* but he did not become totally committed to the subject until he studied under E. F. Zion, who had discovered the depressor nerve. Zion specialized in the study of the effects of nerves on the internal organs, and it was at his suggestion that Pavlov undertook his first research project, an investigation of the secretory innervation or distribution of nerves to the pancreatic gland; for this work, Pavlov and a fellow student were awarded the Gold Medal of the university.

After receiving a candidate of natural sciences degree in 1875, Pavlov entered the Military Medical Academy in St. Petersburg (now Leningrad), where he hoped to become an assistant to Zion, who had recently been ap-

pointed to the academy's chair of physiology. Zion, however, left Russia after the government, upon learning that he was of Jewish descent, revoked his professorship. Refusing to serve under Zion's successor, Pavlov resigned and became an assistant at the Veterinary Institute, where for two years he continued his studies of digestion and circulation. During the summer of 1877, he worked in Breslau, Germany (now Wrocław, Poland), with Rudolf Heidenhain, a specialist in digestion. The following year Sergei P. Botkin invited Pavlov to become head of the experimental physiology laboratory at his clinic in Breslau, even before Pavlov received his medical degree in 1879. Working in Botkin's laboratory, Pavlov developed the ability to organize and manage many investigations simultaneously.

After a long struggle with the administration of the Military Medical Academy (his relations remained strained as a result of his reaction to Zion's dismissal), Pavlov obtained his doctoral degree in 1883, with a dissertation describing the nerves that control the action of the heart. He was appointed privatdocent (unsalaried lecturer) at the academy but was granted leave to do additional work in Leipzig with Heidenhain and Carl Ludwig, two of the most distinguished physiologists of the time. Two years later, he returned to Russia.

Much of Pavlov's research during the 1880s involved the circulatory system, especially the control of the heart and blood pressure. His methodology reached its full flower with his studies of digestion, which began in 1879 and

PAVLOV

continued for more than twenty years. By 1890 Pavlov had become so prominent that he was asked to set up the department of physiology at the Institute of Experimental Medicine, where he remained for the rest of his career; concurrently he held the chair of physiology at the Military Medical Academy between 1895 and 1925. Although left-handed like his father, Pavlov practiced the use of his right hand and became so ambidextrous that, according to a colleague, "it was a hard task to assist Pavlov during an operation. One never knew which hand he would use next. He made sutures with the right and the left hand with such rapidity that two men were required to supply him with threaded needles."

In his investigations, Pavlov combined elements of the mechanistic and holistic schools of biology, philosophies that are often considered incompatible. As a mechanist, Pavlov believed that a complex system, such as circulation or digestion, could be understood by examining each of its parts in turn; as a holist, he felt that the parts had to be examined in an intact, living, normal animal. For this reason he was opposed to the traditional techniques of vivisection, in which live laboratory animals were cut open to observe the action of the organs.

Believing that an animal that was dying and in pain was not normal, Pavlov altered the animal surgically in such a way that he could observe the actions of the internal organs without interfering with their function or the animal's well-being. In certain cases, he diverted some of the digestive glands to discharge their contents into containers outside the animal; in others, he inverted part of the lining of the digestive canal to form an exterior pouch. Pavlov's skill at this difficult surgery was unrivaled. Moreover, he insisted on the same level of care, anesthesia, and cleanliness that would be expected in operations on human beings. "After remaking the animal's organism in accordance with our design," he said, "we had to find a modus vivendi for it that would ensure an absolutely normal and long life. Only by observing this condition would the results of our work be regarded as fully conclusive and as having elucidated the normal course of the phenomena."

Using these methods, Pavlov and his colleagues discovered how each part of the digestive system—salivary and duodenal glands, stomach, pancreas, and liver—adds a different combination of chemicals to food, breaking it down into absorbable units of protein, fat, or carbohydrate. After isolating several of the digestive enzymes, Pavlov began to study their regulation and mutual interaction.

Pavlov was awarded the 1904 Nobel Prize for Physiology or Medicine "in recognition of his work on the physiology of digestion, through which knowledge on vital aspects of the subject has been transformed and enlarged." In his presentation speech, K. A. H. Mörner of the Karolinska Institute described Pavlov's contributions to the physiology and chemistry of the digestive organs. "Through Pavlov's work we have obtained a much more extensive and clearer insight than our previous knowledge could give us," Mörner said. "We have now a fairly comprehensive view of the influence which the activity of one portion of the digestive apparatus can exert on another—in other words, how the wheels of the digestive mechanism fit together for the efficient use and advantage of the body."

Throughout his career Pavlov maintained an interest in the influence of the nervous system on the action of the internal organs. During the early years of the twentieth century, his digestive system experiments led to his first observations of conditioned reflexes. Pavlov and his co-workers had found that if a piece of food is placed in a dog's mouth, saliva is produced reflexively. If a dog merely sees a piece of food, salivation occurs automatically, but in this case, the reflex is much less constant and depends on such additional factors as whether the dog is hungry or has been previously teased with the food. Summing up the difference between the reflexes, Pavlov remarked that "the new reflex continually fluctuates and, hence, is *conditioned*." Thus, the mere sight or smell of food acts as a signal for saliva production. "Any phenomenon in the external world can be made a temporary signal of an object stimulating the salivary glands," Pavlov continued, "if the stimulation of the oral mucous membrane by this object has been associated repeatedly . . . with the action of the given external phenomenon on other sensitive body surfaces."

Impressed by the power of conditioned reflexes to illuminate both psychology and physiology, Pavlov made this field the main focus of his research after 1902. Single-minded and highly disciplined in all aspects of his work, whether surgery, lectures, or experiments, Pavlov would have nothing to do with physiology during the summer holidays; instead he devoted himself to other interests, such as gardening and reading works of history. According to one colleague, "he was always on the lookout for joy and he derived it from hundreds of sources." His status as the greatest living Russian scientist protected him from the political upheavals of the Russian Revolution, and after the founding of the Soviet state, his research and freedom were guaranteed by Lenin's personal order, even when all other scientists were subject to censorship and state intervention.

In 1881 Pavlov married Seraphima Vasilievna Karchevskaya, a teacher, with whom he had four sons and a daughter. Known for his tenacity and persistence, Pavlov was regarded by some of his students and colleagues as a martinet. Nevertheless, he was highly respected in the scientific world, and his personal enthusiasm and warmth won him many friends. He died of pneumonia in Leningrad in 1936.

Pavlov was awarded the Order of the Legion of Honor of France in 1915, the same year that he received the Copley Medal of the Royal Society of London. He was elected to membership in the Russian Academy of Sciences and was a foreign member of the Royal Society of London and an honorary member of the Physiological Society of London.

SELECTED WORKS: The Work of the Digestive Glands, 1902; Conditioned Reflexes, 1927; Lectures on Conditioned Reflexes, 1928; Conditioned Reflexes and Psychiatry, 1941; Selected Works, 1955; Essays in Psychology and Psychiatry, 1957; Experimental Psychology and Other Essays, 1957.

ABOUT: Astratyan, E. A. Ivan Petrovich Pavlov: His Life and Work, 1953; Astrup, C. Pavlovian Psychiatry, 1965; Babkin, B. P. Pavlov, 1949; Cuny, H. Ivan Pavlov, 1964; Dictionary of Scientific Biography, volume 10, 1974; Frolov, I. P. Pavlov and His School, 1937; Gantt, W. H., et al. (eds.) Pavlovian Approach to Psychotherapy, 1970; Gray, J. A. Ivan Pavlov, 1971; Nagel, E., and Wolman, B. B. (eds.) Scientific Psychology, 1965.

PEARSON, LESTER
(April 23, 1897–December 27, 1972)
Nobel Prize for Peace, 1957

Lester Bowles Pearson, Canadian statesman and United Nations official, was born of Irish stock in Toronto, Ontario, to E. A. Pearson, a Methodist minister, and the former Anne Sarah Bowles. A bright student, Pearson entered Victoria College at the University of Toronto at the age of sixteen. In 1915 he interrupted his education to enlist in the Canadian army, which was fighting with the Allied forces in World War I. Too young for combat duty, Pearson served in a hospital unit, first in Egypt and then in the Balkans on the

Salonika front. In 1917 he was transferred to the Royal Flying Corps in England and commissioned a lieutenant. During fighter training, he crashed on his first solo flight but was uninjured. A few days later, however, he was hit by a bus during a blackout in London and shipped home in April 1918. It was during the war years that Pearson acquired the nickname Mike.

Back in Canada, Pearson completed his B.A. requirements at the University of Toronto and in 1919 entered Osgood Hall Law School. He decided quickly that he had little aptitude for law and dropped out, taking a job with a meat-packing firm in Hamilton, Ontario, and later in Chicago. When this work proved dissatisfying, he applied for and won a Massey Foundation scholarship that took him to St. John's College, Oxford, in 1920. For the next two years, a period he later described as the happiest in his life, Pearson studied history and distinguished himself as a member of the college lacrosse and ice hockey teams.

Returning to Canada with an M.A. from Oxford, Pearson lectured in modern history at the University of Toronto. In 1925 he married one of his students, Maryon Elspeth Moody; they had a son and a daughter. Pearson became an assistant professor in 1928 but later that year decided to take the entry examination for a position in the Canadian Department of External Affairs. With the highest score in his group, Pearson joined the diplomatic corps as a foreign service officer. He was soon noticed by the prime minister, Richard Bedford Bennett, who asked him to join the Canadian delegation to the Imperial Conference in 1930. Pearson also attended the World Disarmament Conference in Geneva in 1933–1934. In 1935 he was promoted to first secretary and assigned to the office of Canada's high commissioner in London, where he participated in the London Naval Conference.

After six years in London, Pearson returned to Ottawa in May 1941 as assistant under secretary of state for external affairs. The following year, he became minister counselor and was transferred to Washington, D.C. From 1944 to 1946 he served as Canadian ambassador to the United States. During his years in Washington, Pearson also played a role in establishing the United Nations Relief and Rehabilitation Administration. In 1944 he attended the Dumbarton Oaks Conference, where the foundations of the United Nations were laid. At the 1945 San Francisco Conference, which met to draw up the United Nations Charter, Pearson argued unsuccessfully

LESTER PEARSON

against granting veto power to the five permanent members of the Security Council.

Promoted to under secretary for external affairs in 1946, Pearson represented Canada at the 1947 United Nations conference that led to the creation of the state of Israel. The following year, the Liberal party offered him the position of secretary for external affairs, a cabinet post that drew him into electoral politics. In October 1948 he won a seat in the House of Commons, which he held for nine years. As secretary for external affairs, Pearson wrote an influential speech for Prime Minister Louis St. Laurent proposing the formation of the North Atlantic Treaty Organization (NATO). Pearson signed the enabling treaty in 1949 and headed Canada's NATO delegation until 1957. He also served as chairman of the NATO Council in 1951–1952.

Between 1946 and 1956 Pearson led the Canadian delegation to the United Nations, where his genial personality and quick wit made him a favorite choice as mediator in crises between the major powers. In 1950 he was part of a three-member commission that developed a proposal for a cease-fire in the Korean War. The actual truce, signed two years later, closely resembled the commission's recommendations. During the seventh session of the United Nations General Assembly in 1952–1953, Pearson was chosen president.

Pearson again played a role as mediator in 1956 when Egyptian President Gamal Abdel Nasser nationalized the Suez Canal, a move that particularly alarmed the British, French, and Israelis. In retaliation, Israel invaded the

Gaza Strip and Sinai Peninsula. Two days later, France and Great Britain dispatched warships and airborne troops with the intention of retaking the canal. Backed by the Soviet Union, the United States introduced a Security Council resolution calling for a cease-fire and the withdrawal of troops from Egyptian soil. Vetoed by France and Great Britain, the resolution then went to the General Assembly in a somewhat different form and was passed. Believing that this measure alone was insufficient to stop the conflict, Pearson submitted "a plan for the setting up . . . of an emergency international United Nations force to secure and supervise the cessation of hostilities." The plan, which was adopted, replaced French and British troops with soldiers under the command of the United Nations and averted full-scale war.

Pearson received the 1957 Nobel Prize for Peace for his role in resolving the Suez crisis. In his presentation speech, Gunnar Jahn of the Norwegian Nobel Committee described Pearson as the person who had "contributed more than anyone else to save the world" during the tense moments of 1956. "Never, since the end of the last war, has the world situation been darker than during the Suez crisis," said Jahn. He also credited Pearson for his efforts to substitute United Nations actions for military force in resolving international disputes.

In accepting the Nobel Prize, Pearson described "the four faces of peace"—prosperity, power, policy, and people. He called for extended economic cooperation to eliminate the economic incentives for war, and he renounced the use of force, "for there is no effective defense against . . . nuclear missile weapons." Instead, he said, "what is needed is a new and vigorous determination to use every technique of discussion and negotiation that may be available" to achieve cooperation and avoid the risk of war. Finally, he asked, "How can there be peace without people understanding each other?" Only in a climate of political freedom, mutual tolerance, and compromise, he said, can we "solve the problem of peace and war."

Although Pearson's role in the Suez crisis was widely acclaimed, some Canadians charged that his actions prevented Great Britain from recovering the canal. When the Liberal party was defeated in the 1957 elections, Pearson lost his cabinet post. Assuming leadership of the party, Pearson directed parliamentary opposition to the Conservative government of Prime Minister John Diefenbaker. In 1963 the Liberals unseated Diefenbaker's government by a narrow margin, and Pearson was installed as prime minister. During his five years in office, Pearson saw the enactment of social legislation intended to achieve what he called the Good Society, but his administration was marred by minor scandals, including allegations of bribery and corruption. In 1968 he retired from politics to serve as head of the World Bank Commission on International Development. He also encouraged the Liberal party to heed the increasingly vocal demands of French-speaking Canadians. Pearson died of cancer in Ottawa in 1972.

WORKS BY: Democracy in World Politics, 1955; Diplomacy in the Nuclear Age, 1959; The Four Faces of Peace and the International Outlook, 1964; Peace in the Family of Man, 1969; Partners in Development, 1969; The Crisis of Development, 1970; Words and Occasions, 1970; Mike: The Memoirs of the Rt. Hon. Lester B. Pearson (3 vols.) 1972–1975.

ABOUT: Ayre, W. B. Mr. Pearson and Canada's Revolution by Diplomacy, 1962; Beal, J. R. Pearson of Canada, 1964; Bothwell, R. Pearson: His Life and World, 1978; Newman, P. C. Renegade in Power: The Diefenbaker Years, 1963; Nicholson, P. Vision and Indecision, 1968; Stursberg, P. Lester Pearson and the Dream of Unity, 1978; Stursberg, P. Lester Pearson and the American Dilemma, 1980; Thordarson, B. Lester Pearson: Diplomat and Politician, 1974; Times (London) December 29, 1972.

PENZIAS, ARNO A.

(April 26, 1933–)
Nobel Prize for Physics, 1978
(shared with Pyotr Kapitza and Robert W. Wilson)

The American astrophysicist Arno Allan Penzias was born in Munich, Germany, one of two sons of Karl Penzias, a Polish citizen who operated a small leather business, and his German wife, the former Inge Eisenreich.

The family, which was Jewish, managed to leave Germany on the eve of World War II. In the spring of 1939 Arno and his younger brother were sent to England, soon followed by their father; their mother was allowed to leave a few months later, shortly before the war began. Reunited, the family left England in December and arrived in New York City the first week of 1940. Penzias's father worked as a superintendent of various apartment buildings in the Bronx but eventually obtained a job in the carpentry shop of the Metropolitan Museum of Art. To supplement the family income, his mother, who had changed her name to Justine, sewed coats in the garment district.

ARNO A. PENZIAS

In 1947 Arno entered Brooklyn Technical High School where, despite an interest in electronics, he concentrated on chemistry. Four years later he entered the tuition-free City College of New York. During his freshman year he switched his major from chemical engineering to physics because a professor assured him that he could earn a living in this field. He graduated in the top 10 percent of his class in 1954.

Having joined the Reserve Officers' Training Corps in college, Penzias spent the next two years as a radar officer in the Army Signal Corps at Fort Devens, Massachusetts. In the fall of 1956 he began graduate study in physics at Columbia University, whose faculty included I. I. RABI, POLYKARP KUSCH, TSUNG-DAO LEE, and CHARLES H. TOWNES. Two years earlier, Townes had made the first maser, a device for the creation and amplification of high-frequency radio waves. Under Townes's direction, Penzias built the second maser, for use as an amplifier in a microwave receiver, as part of his doctoral work at Columbia. Designed to work at 21 centimeters, the wavelength at which hydrogen emits radio waves, the maser was intended to help Penzias in his attempt to determine the maximum amount of hydrogen in the gas of several clusters of galaxies. He attached the maser to the Naval Research Laboratory's antenna at Maryland Point, Maryland, but the resulting spectral data contained no lines characteristic of hydrogen. He was to comment later that "the equipment-building went better than the observations."

Unsatisfied with his thesis result, Penzias asked Rudolf Kompfner, director of the Bell Telephone Laboratories' Radio Research Laboratory at Crawford Hill, New Jersey, if he could obtain a temporary appointment to do the work over again. He proposed using the 20-foot horn-reflector antenna that the company had built at Holmdel, New Jersey, in 1960 to receive signals from the *Echo* balloon satellite then about to be launched. Instead, Kompfner offered him a permanent job, which Penzias accepted in 1961; the following year he received his Ph.D. from Columbia.

Penzias's first assignment at Bell Labs was to devise a way to point a company antenna in Andover, Maine, with sufficient accuracy to communicate with the AT&T-built *Telstar* communications satellite. For a variety of reasons, among them gravity and weather conditions, the steel antenna could bend. Penzias quickly solved the problem by placing within the antenna a second receiver aimed at a known source of radiation, such as a supernova remnant (an expanding shell of gas resulting from the explosion of a star).

Offered an opportunity to do further satellite communications work with the horn antenna, Penzias chose instead to conduct basic research in radio astronomy, hoping to detect the hydroxyl molecule (containing one hydrogen atom and one oxygen atom) in interstellar space. Although Penzias gained valuable experience from his project, a group at the Massachusetts Institute of Technology was the first to detect this interstellar molecule.

In 1963, working with ROBERT W. WILSON, Penzias began converting the horn antenna into an instrument for radio astronomy. Its precise calibration and the extreme sensitivity of its amplifier enabled the two researchers to measure the intensities of several extraterrestrial radio sources. Moreover, they could distinguish and subtract from their measurements radio noise from local sources such as the ground, the earth's atmosphere, and the structure of the antenna itself. This knowledge allowed them to make absolute measurements of the intensity of background radiation from an area of sky near a source of interest.

In 1964 the two scientists used their system to measure radio signals from Cassiopeia A, a supernova remnant and the brightest radio source in the constellation Cassiopeia. However, the results of background measurements were puzzling, for they indicated more noise than could be accounted for from known sources. During the course of further measurements, the anomalous results persisted.

Reviewing the entire antenna system for possible sources of the extra noise, Penzias and Wilson tried covering a riveted joint with metal tape and cleaned out pigeon droppings, but they could not significantly change the measurements.

Radio waves, like all electromagnetic radiation, are often described in terms of wavelength or frequency. They can also be expressed in the form of a temperature, because all objects radiate at wavelengths characteristic of their temperature, the wavelengths becoming shorter as the temperature rises. Since the radiation from an object depends somewhat on surface color and texture, scientists use a blackbody as a standard reference. A blackbody emits a range, or spectrum, of radiation rather than a single wavelength, but at each temperature one wavelength is dominant. Cold bodies also radiate, but at wavelengths too long for the human eye to see. The eye sees cold bodies by reflected light. In the dark, with no other source of light, cold bodies are invisible. The background radiation, or radio noise, detected by Penzias and Wilson had long wavelengths well below the visible range. They corresponded to the dominant wavelength emitted by a blackbody at 3.5°K (degrees kelvin), just above absolute zero, the temperature at which all thermal motion ceases.

While Penzias and Wilson were encountering the unforeseen radio background noise, a theoretical group at Princeton University, led by Robert Dicke, had been contemplating a cosmological model of the universe that alternately expands and contracts. If the universe originated in the so-called big bang as proposed by George Gamow, Dicke theorized, radiation from this cosmic explosion might still be observable after some 18 billion years of cooling. Dicke's colleague P. J. E. Peebles calculated a present-day background radiation equivalent to 10°K (later refined to approximately 3°K), which he announced in a lecture at the Johns Hopkins University.

Among the scientists who attended Peebles's lecture was Bernard Burke, a radio astronomer at the Massachusetts Institute of Technology. During a telephone conversation with Burke in 1965, Penzias happened to mention the unexplained noise he and Wilson had observed. After learning from Burke about Peebles's efforts, Penzias met not only Peebles but also Dicke and several other colleagues at Princeton who were building an antenna to measure the cosmic background radiation the group had predicted.

As a result of this meeting, the Princeton

807

group collaborated with Penzias and Wilson in the simultaneous publication of two papers—one by the Princeton group on the cosmological theory and the other by Penzias and Wilson on the background radiation measured by their antenna. Over the next few years, additional observations were made, and the radiation was found to exhibit the blackbody wavelength distribution for the temperature predicted by big-bang cosmology. (Gamow and his associates had actually made a similar prediction as early as 1948, but many prominent radio astronomers at the time believed that it could not be detected with available instruments.)

Penzias and Wilson then turned to very different research, including the design of a carbon dioxide laser (a light amplifier that produced an intense monochromatic beam), which they hoped would be able to send communications signals through ground fog. It was unsuccessful. They returned to radio astronomy in the late 1960s, working with a Bell Labs' atomic physicist, Keith Jefferts, to build a receiver capable of detecting radiation with wavelengths of the order of millimeters. In 1970 they connected their receiver to a newly built 36-foot radio telescope at the National Radio Astronomy Observatory's site at Kitt Peak, Arizona. When the telescope was aimed at the Orion nebula, the spectral line (characteristic emission wavelength) of carbon monoxide immediately appeared on the monitor display. Subsequent measurements detected six other interstellar molecules. Penzias has continued to pursue his interests in astrophysics, especially in the origin of the chemical elements.

Penzias and Wilson shared half of the 1978 Nobel Prize for Physics "for their discovery of cosmic microwave background radiation." The other half of the prize was awarded to PYOTR KAPITZA. In his presentation speech, Lamke Hulthén of the Royal Swedish Academy of Sciences noted that "exceptional perseverance and skill in the experiments led [Penzias and Wilson] to a discovery, after which cosmology is a science, open to verification by experiment and observation."

Bell Labs recognized the outstanding organizational abilities Penzias had displayed in the millimeter-wave astronomy project and gave him a series of managerial appointments: head of the Radio Physics Research Department at Crawford Hill in 1972, director of the Radio Research Laboratory in 1976, and vice president for research in 1981. Since 1972 Penzias has also been a visiting member of the Department of Astrophysical Sciences at Princeton University.

Penzias became a naturalized United States citizen in 1946 and adopted the name Allan, by which he had been known since his arrival in America. He retains it now as a middle name. In 1954 he married Anne Pearl Barras, a guidance counselor. They live in Highland Park, New Jersey, and have a son and two daughters.

A member of the National Academy of Sciences, the American Academy of Arts and Sciences, and the American Astronomical Society, among other organizations, Penzias has served as a trustee of Trenton State College and as a member of the astronomical advisory panel of the National Science Foundation. His other honors include the Henry Draper Medal of the National Academy of Sciences (1977), the Herschel Medal of the Royal Astronomical Society in London (1977), and an honorary degree from the Paris Observatory.

ABOUT: Current Biography September 1985; National Cyclopedia of American Biography, volume 63, 1984; New Yorker August 20, 1984; Physics Today December 1978; Science December 1, 1978.

PÉREZ ESQUIVEL, ADOLFO

(November 26, 1931–)
Nobel Prize for Peace, 1980

Adolfo Pérez Esquivel (pā' res es kē vel'), Argentine sculptor and human rights advocate, was born in Buenos Aires. His mother died when he was a young boy. His father, a Spanish fisherman who had emigrated to Argentina and become a sales agent for a coffee firm, was often away on business. Consequently, Pérez Esquivel was raised largely by the nuns and priests in the Roman Catholic schools he attended.

A devout Catholic and a voracious reader, he was shaped by his early reading of the works of Mohandas Gandhi, Saint Augustine, Thomas Merton, and other religious and philosophical writers. During his adolescence, Pérez Esquivel often participated in prayer and discussion groups and became interested in how the teachings of the gospel could be applied to contemporary South American life. At the same time, he began to develop his considerable artistic gifts. He enrolled in the National School of Fine Arts of Buenos Aires and La Plata, graduating in 1956. In October of that year, he married Amanda Pérez, a pi-

ADOLFO PÉREZ ESQUIVEL

anist and composer; the couple have three children.

Over the next fifteen years, Pérez Esquivel pursued a successful career as a sculptor. He also taught art and architecture at the Manuel Belgrano National School of Fine Arts in Buenos Aires and at other local schools. His sculptures were exhibited widely in Argentina, and he won, among other prizes, the prestigious Premio La Nación de Escultura, a sculpture award. He incorporated pre-Columbian motifs into his work, saying "I feel the need to find in our American roots the means of expression in symbols and signs that can fuse with today's concerns." Although he considered himself apolitical, "today's concerns" increasingly came to mean the social and political turmoil that engulfed Argentina through several decades of Pérez Esquivel's life.

During the late 1940s and early 1950s, Argentina was ruled by the popular but demagogic dictator Juan Perón, who had risen to power by recruiting poor urban workers into unions controlled by his party. While instituting a number of social reforms, Perón also used force and intimidation to maintain his rule. His strategy of pitting the working class against the middle and upper classes created deep scars at all levels of Argentine society. Following a military coup in 1955, Perón was exiled to Spain. His political organization remained intact, however, and conditions in Argentina deteriorated as the Peronist unions continually challenged the series of military and civilian leaders who attempted to control the country. Repressive government measures

led many Peronists and leftists to organize urban guerrilla forces, whose often-violent protests brought more reprisals from the military. By the late 1960s, fighting among the various political factions had so escalated that the democratic provisions of constitutional government were effectively dissolved.

In these circumstances, Pérez Esquivel realized that his Christian beliefs would not allow him to remain aloof from social concerns. Shunning party politics, he began meeting informally with other Argentines to discuss ways ordinary Catholics could respond to the deepening social crisis. In 1968 he attended a conference of Argentine church, union, university, and community groups in Montevideo, Uruguay, to consider ways of improving conditions in Argentina through nonviolent means. In 1970 he went on a nearly two-month-long hunger strike to protest violence by members of both the Left and the Right. When a second conference was held in 1971, Pérez Esquivel played a major role in founding the Service for Peace and Justice, an organization that provided a framework for cooperation between socially active Catholic clergy and Catholic lay activists in their work on behalf of the poor.

Later in 1971 Pérez Esquivel joined another local prayer group based on the Gandhian principles of militant nonviolence. Initially, he set about organizing crafts workshops in urban neighborhoods to work toward the Gandhian goal of self-sufficiency for the poor. In 1972 he founded a monthly magazine, *Paz y Justicia* (Peace and Justice), which became the official publication of the Service for Peace and Justice. Two years later, when the headquarters of the organization was moved from Montevideo to Buenos Aires, Pérez Esquivel was named its general coordinator.

Self-effacing, Pérez Esquivel avoided publicity, preferring to work behind the scenes to build support for the Service for Peace and Justice. He gave up teaching and spent less time on his own creative work in order to coordinate the activities of the organization in Argentina and to travel elsewhere in South America promoting nonviolent social change. Believing that poverty was the cause of most of Latin America's problems, he helped Indians and the disadvantaged in Ecuador and Paraguay to obtain their own land. He was briefly jailed in Brazil (1975) and Ecuador (1976) for publicly accusing the governments of those nations of failing to respond to the needs of their people and for attributing crime and violence to poverty.

Meanwhile, unable to restore stability or

improve the national economy, the Argentine military government in 1973 invited Juan Perón to return from his Spanish exile. The former dictator was greeted with popular acclaim and elected president, but he died the following year and was succeeded by his widow, Isabel. Under her presidency, Argentina's economy virtually collapsed. The rate of inflation soared, corruption became even more rampant, and a series of paralyzing strikes brought the country to a standstill. On March 24, 1976, the army deposed Isabel Perón, declared martial law, and once again seized control of the government. When Peronist and left-wing urban guerrillas took to the streets to oppose their military and conservative opponents, the Argentine government encouraged the formation of right-wing vigilante and paramilitary groups to counter them. Thousands of Argentines deemed sympathetic to the left disappeared without any official record of having been arrested. Many of them were assumed to have been killed by death squads. Others were arbitrarily arrested, held indefinitely without formal charges or trials, tortured, and ultimately either consigned to prison or summarily executed.

To protest this government-backed terrorism, Pérez Esquivel, at considerable risk to his own life, led a campaign to publicize the disappearances. In 1975 he was instrumental in organizing the Permanent Assembly for Human Rights, which monitored violations of basic human rights by the government. He also helped form the Ecumenical Movement for Human Rights, whose efforts to provide assistance to prisoners and their families were based on Pérez Esquivel's interpretation of the Gospels as a call to action. Because of his quiet but unyielding opposition to government violations of human rights, Pérez Esquivel himself soon became a target for repression. While he was abroad in 1976, the headquarters of the Service for Peace and Justice were ransacked by the police. In April of the following year, Pérez Esquivel was arrested when he attempted to renew his passport.

Thus began a thirteen-month imprisonment for Pérez Esquivel, a time during which he was neither officially charged nor brought to trial. The government's only response to inquiries about his status was to acknowledge that he was being held for "subversive activities." After his release Pérez Esquivel was reluctant to talk about his treatment in prison, but he confirmed that he had been tortured frequently.

During his imprisonment, Pérez Esquivel was adopted as a prisoner of conscience by Am-

nesty International and nominated for the Nobel Peace Prize by Mairead Corrigan and Betty Williams. These efforts, along with protests to the Argentine government by the administration of United States President Jimmy Carter, eventually helped bring about his release in May 1978. He was restricted to his house for the next nine months but was able to resume his activist role in 1980, when the government (under yet another junta) announced that the "threat from the Left" no longer existed. In addition to his previous activities, he now also called for negotiations to settle a territorial dispute between Argentina and Chile.

Pérez Esquivel was selected from fifty-seven nominees to be awarded the 1980 Nobel Prize for Peace. In the presentation address, John Sanness of the Norwegian Nobel Committee called him "an untiring and consistent champion of the principle of nonviolence in the struggle for social and political liberty. He has lit a light in the dark, which . . . should never be allowed to be extinguished." Among those who hailed Pérez Esquivel's selection was the Soviet physicist Andrei Sakharov who, from his own banishment in Gorky, sent a message to the new laureate: "Your vigorous struggle for justice and the help you have given to people suffering under oppression are cherished by people who live thousands of miles away, in another world." Pérez Esquivel donated most of the prize money to relief agencies and churches to help the needy in South America.

The Nobel Prize brought worldwide attention to the previously little-known Pérez Esquivel and to his work. It was especially effective in focusing public and diplomatic pressure on Argentina to account for its *desaparecidos*—the 10,000 to 20,000 people (according to Pérez Esquivel's own estimate) who had vanished during the late 1970s. Again risking arrest, Pérez Esquivel demonstrated with the Locas de Mayo (Madwomen of May Square), a group of women who gathered weekly in a Buenos Aires plaza to dramatize the disappearance of their relatives and friends. These demonstrations continued until 1984, when a commission appointed by the newly elected civilian government acknowledged that some 9,000 citizens had been illegally imprisoned or executed. A number of military officers were subsequently charged and tried for these crimes.

Although political violence in Argentina has abated significantly since 1984, Pérez Esquivel continues his work to improve conditions for the poor and oppressed throughout Latin America. As he has said, "You cannot talk of human rights solely in terms of torture and imprisonment and killing. . . . We must also look at the case of the peasant who has no land and is dying of hunger."

WORKS IN ENGLISH TRANSLATION: Christ in a Poncho, 1983.

ABOUT: America October 25, 1980; December 27, 1980; Current Biography March 1981; Fellowship October–November 1980; Newsweek October 27, 1980; May 18, 1981; New York Times October 14, 1980.

PERRIN, JEAN
(September 30, 1870–April 17, 1942)
Nobel Prize for Physics, 1926

JEAN PERRIN

The French physicist Jean Baptiste Perrin (pe raN') was born in Lille. He and his two sisters were raised by their mother after their father, an army officer, died of wounds received in the Franco-Prussian War. After attending local schools, Perrin completed his secondary education at the Lycée Janson-de-Sailly in Paris, served a year of compulsory military service, and entered the École Normale Supérieure in 1891. Between 1894 and 1897 he was an assistant in physics at the École Normale, during which time he did research on cathode rays and X rays, the subject on which he wrote his doctoral dissertation.

At the time of Perrin's research there was widespread disagreement over the nature of cathode rays emitted by the negative electrode (cathode) in a vacuum tube during an electric discharge. Some scientists thought the rays were a form of radiation similar to light, but Perrin's investigations indicated in 1895 that they were streams of negatively charged particles. J. J. THOMSON, modifying Perrin's experiment, confirmed Perrin's findings and conclusively characterized the particles in 1897, measuring the ratio of their charge to their mass by means of deflections in electric and magnetic fields. The implied mass was about 2,000 times smaller than that of a hydrogen atom, the lightest of all atoms. It was soon widely supposed that the negative particles, named electrons, were parts of atoms. Perrin's research involved him in the debate over the atomic, or discontinuous, nature of matter. Marcel Brillouin, one of Perrin's teachers, was a vigorous proponent of the atomic theory.

The atomic theory held that elements are made up of discrete particles called atoms and that chemical compounds are made up of molecules, larger particles consisting of two or more atoms. By the end of the nineteenth century, the atomic theory was widely accepted among scientists, especially chemists. However, some physicists contended that atoms and molecules were nothing more than convenient fictions, useful for calculating the results of chemical reactions. The Austrian physicist and philosopher Ernst Mach regarded the ultimate makeup of matter as unknowable and an improper pursuit for scientists. For proponents of atomism, confirmation of the discontinuous nature of matter was one of the great challenges left in physics.

Perrin received his doctorate in 1897 and in the same year began teaching a new course in physical chemistry at the University of Paris (the Sorbonne). The course became a great success; Perrin was given a chair in physical chemistry in 1910 and remained at the Sorbonne until 1940. Continuing his interest in atomic theory, Perrin suggested in 1901 that an atom is like a miniature solar system, but he saw no way to prove it. Ten years later, ERNEST RUTHERFORD presented his model of a dense, positively charged nucleus surrounded by negative electrons, which became the prevailing conception. Thomson had proposed the "plum pudding" atom, a positively charged sphere in which the electrons were embedded like raisins. Although Perrin's work in physical chemistry was a departure from his earlier study of cathode rays, it focused his attention on topics relevant to the molecular nature of compounds, including thermody-

811

namics, osmosis, ion transport, and crystallization. His investigations of colloids (suspensions of fine particles) led him to his celebrated studies of Brownian motion, which would confirm the existence of molecules.

Brownian motion was first described by the English botanist Robert Brown in 1827. When very small particles, such as pollen grains, are suspended in a fluid, they can be observed microscopically to undergo a random, energetic jiggling, as though they were being continually bombarded by invisible objects. Various causes of this motion had been suggested, including electric forces, convection currents, and collisions with constantly moving molecules of the fluid. In 1905 ALBERT EINSTEIN published an important paper on Brownian motion that gave strong theoretical support to the molecular hypothesis. It made quantitative predictions, but the experiments required to verify the hypothesis were so exacting that Einstein doubted they were possible. From 1908 to 1913 Perrin (at first unaware of Einstein's paper) conducted painstaking observations of Brownian movement that confirmed Einstein's predictions.

Perrin realized that if the movements of suspended particles resulted from molecular collisions, he could predict their average displacements during a given observation time from their size and density and from the conditions (such as temperature and density) of the fluid, on the basis of well-known gas laws. If these predictions agreed with measurements, he would have very strong evidence for the existence of molecules. However, obtaining particles of the necessary size and uniformity was not simple. One of Perrin's great experimental achievements was the segregation, after months of tedious centrifuging, of a few tenths of a gram of uniform particles of gamboge (a yellowish material made from vegetable sap). When he observed and measured the Brownian motion of these particles, the results agreed well with the molecular theory.

Perrin also studied the sedimentation, or sinking, of small suspended particles. If the molecular hypothesis is correct, he reasoned, particles below a certain size will not all sink to the bottom of the container: the upward component of momentum gained from molecular collisions will continually oppose the downward force of gravity. So long as the suspension is undisturbed, an equilibrium will eventually be reached, after which the concentrations of particles at various depths will remain unchanged. If the properties of the suspension are known, it should be possible to predict the vertical distribution of the particles at equilibrium.

Perrin made several thousand observations by ingenious and sophisticated microscopic techniques, counting particles at various depths in a single drop of liquid only twelve-hundredths of a millimeter deep. He found that the particle concentration decreased exponentially with height in the liquid in such close quantitative agreement with the predictions of molecular theory that his results were widely accepted as conclusive proof of the existence of molecules. He later devised a means for measuring the rotation as well as the linear displacement of the particles in Brownian motion. Perrin's studies allowed him to calculate molecular sizes and the Avogadro number, that is, the number of molecules in a mole (a quantity whose mass, in grams, equals the molecular weight of the substance). He checked the Avogadro number by five different kinds of observations, all in agreement within experimental error. The accepted value is now approximately 6.02×10^{23}; Perrin's result was about 6 percent too high. By 1913, when Perrin summarized the abundant evidence for the discontinuous nature of matter in his book *Atoms,* the reality of atoms and molecules was almost universally accepted.

Perrin received the 1926 Nobel Prize for Physics "for his work on the discontinuous structure of matter, and especially for his discovery of sedimentation equilibrium." In his presentation speech, C. W. Oseen of the Royal Swedish Academy of Sciences summarized Perrin's work and described the confirming evidence that supported his conclusions.

During World War I, Perrin served as an officer in the Engineering Corps of the French army and worked on such technical innovations as the acoustic detection of submarines. After the war he became interested in nuclear physics and was one of the first to suggest a plausible source of the sun's heat that accounted for its long persistence. He created the National Center for Scientific Research and was influential in the establishment of the Institute of Physicochemical Biology and the Institute of Astrophysics. His interest in popularizing science, especially for young people, led to the founding of the Palace of Discovery at the 1937 International Exposition in Paris.

A socialist and outspoken opponent of fascism, Perrin fled France after the German occupation in 1940 and traveled to the United States, where his son was teaching physics at Columbia University. While in exile, Perrin sought American support for the French war effort and helped establish the French University of New York. He died in New York City in 1942; in 1948 his remains were taken to France and placed in the Panthéon monument in Paris.

Perrin married Henriette Duportal in 1897. They had a son and a daughter. Well liked and considered a lively conversationalist who took a warm interest in young people, Perrin held weekly parties for discussion groups in his laboratory. He had more confidence in experiment than in theory. Once, when pressed by another professor to admit that a new theory had some merit, Perrin responded that "it would be difficult to prepare a theory that was entirely false."

Among Perrin's awards, in addition to the Nobel Prize, were the Joule Prize of the Royal Society of London (1896) and the La Caze Prize of the French Academy of Sciences (1914). Perrin became a member of the French Academy in 1923 and its president in 1938. He held honorary degrees from the universities of Brussels, Liège, Ghent, Calcutta, and Manchester and from New York, Princeton, and Oxford universities. He was a member of the Royal Society of London as well as scientific academies in Italy, Czechoslovakia, Belgium, Sweden, Romania, and China.

SELECTED WORKS: Brownian Movement and Molecular Reality, 1910.

ABOUT: Brush, S. G. The Kind of Motion We Call Heat, 1976; Dictionary of Scientific Biography, volume 10, 1974; Nye, M. J. Molecular Reality: A Perspective on the Scientific Work of Jean Perrin, 1972.

PERSE, SAINT-JOHN
(May 31, 1887–September 20, 1975)
Nobel Prize for Literature, 1960

The French poet and diplomat Saint-John Perse was born Marie-René Alexis Saint-Leger Leger on a small family-owned island off Guadeloupe in the West Indies. His father, Amédée Saint-Leger Leger, a lawyer, was descended from a Burgundian family that had left France at the end of the seventeenth century. His mother, the former Françoise-Renée Dormoy, belonged to a family of planters and naval officers who had resided in the Antilles since the eighteenth century. The only son in a family with four daughters, Leger attended school in Pointe-à-Pitre, Guadeloupe, until the family returned to France in 1899 for economic

SAINT-JOHN PERSE

reasons, settling in Pau. After studying at the University of Bordeaux, he prepared for the foreign service and passed the competitive examination in 1914.

Leger's first slim volume of poems, *Éloges*, appeared in 1910 and drew the attention of ANDRÉ GIDE and Jacques Rivière, among others. (The English translation of this work was published under the same title in 1944.) Throughout his diplomatic career, he used the pseudonym Saint-John Perse to keep his literary activity private. During these years, he allowed the publication of only a few poems, notably *Anabase* (1924), which was published as *Anabasis* in an English translation by T. S. ELIOT in 1930. This epic poem was written during Leger's five-year assignment at the French embassy in Peking. During this time in China, Perse spent his vacations sailing the South Seas and traveling through the Gobi Desert on horseback. *Anabasis* came to life in a remote, unused Taoist temple retreat in the hills near Peking. Placed in the vast deserts of Asia, it is a poem whose theme is the loneliness of the man of action—here the leader of a nomadic people—on his expeditions into unknown spaces and within the human spirit. Arthur J. Knodel, a scholar of Leger's writings, has called it "one of the most austere and baffling of Perse's works." In the preface to his translation of the epic, Eliot wrote, "The reader has to allow the images to fall into his memory successively without questioning the reasonableness of each at the moment; so that, at the end, a total effect is produced."

After returning to Paris in 1921, Leger was

immediately sent to Washington, D.C., for the International Conference on the Limitations of Armaments. There he met ARISTIDE BRIAND, France's prime minister and head of the French delegation, with whom he became a close friend and colleague until Briand's death in 1932. Advancing in the Foreign Office to the highest position, Leger was appointed secretary-general of the Ministry of Foreign Affairs, with the rank of ambassador, in 1933. However, in the troubled period leading to World War II, Leger was outspoken in his opposition to appeasement of Adolf Hitler's increasing demands. This stance won him the enmity of the right wing in French politics and resulted in his removal from office by Premier Paul Reynaud shortly before the fall of France in 1940. In June of that year, barely escaping the German occupation, Leger left France for the United States, by way of Britain and Canada, and remained in voluntary exile until after the end of World War II. The Vichy government stripped him of his citizenship, his rank of ambassador, and all honors. In Washington, Leger accepted a modest, privately funded position as consultant in the Library of Congress.

Amitié du prince (*Friendship of the Prince,* 1924) is the only major poem, besides *Anabasis,* that is available from Leger's diplomatic years. Its English translation was published as *Éloges and Other Poems*. Several unpublished manuscripts were confiscated and presumably destroyed by the Gestapo, which ransacked Leger's Paris apartment in 1940.

Once in the United States, Leger returned to literary activity. *Exil* (translated into English in *Exile and Other Poems*) appeared in 1942, *Vents* (*Winds*) in 1946, *Amers* (*Seamarks*) in 1957, *Chronique* (*Chronique*) in 1959, and *Oiseaux* (*Birds*) in 1962. Even allowing for the silence of his diplomatic years, during which he may have written a good deal that was lost, his final published output was small compared with that of many poets—seven slim volumes in all.

Leger was awarded the 1960 Nobel Prize for Literature "for the soaring flight and the evocative imagery of his poetry, which in a visionary fashion reflects the conditions of our time." In a speech delivered after the ceremony, the poet spoke of the affinities between poetry and science. "Poetry is not only a way of knowledge," he said, "it is even more a way of life—of life in its totality. A poet already dwelt within the cave man: a poet will be dwelling still within the man of the atomic age; for poetry is a fundamental part of man. . . . By his absolute adhesion to what exists, the poet keeps us in touch with the permanence and unity of Being." In the atomic age, Leger concluded, "it is enough for the poet to be the guilty conscience of his time."

Following the war, Leger's citizenship and honors were reinstated, and in 1957 he returned to France for the first time. Although he kept his residence in the United States, in the Georgetown section of Washington, he spent part of each year for the rest of his life in France at his villa in Giens with his American wife, the former Dorothy Milburn Russell, whom he married in 1958. At his death in 1975, he was a grand officer of the Legion of Honor, a commander of the Order of Bath, and a recipient of the Grand Cross of the British Empire.

Saint-John Perse was one of the most original of twentieth-century poets; his language, full of daring and arcane imagery, set him apart. "The pace of his poems is slow and ceremonious, the language is a self-consciously literary one quite apart from the language of everyday intercourse," Arthur Knodel has written. "There is ever present . . . not merely the delight in what is well said, but in what is *better* said."

Because of his identification with the forces of nature, Perse has been compared with Walt Whitman, but his aristocratic diction was of an order entirely different from Whitman's. In reviewing *Winds,* the English poet and critic Stephen Spender called it "a great poem about America," and went on to describe Perse as "a grandiose poet, a kind of Old Testament writer, treating of modern situations. . . . His vision is a generalized one of nature and moral and religious forces moving through history."

During the 1920s Perse was associated with Paul Valéry, Paul Claudel, and the writers connected with the *Nouvelle revue française* (New French Revue). After Claudel died, Perse carried on the tradition of the prose poem with greater success than any of his contemporaries.

"Saint-John Perse is a poet of tremendous power and achievement," wrote Philip Toynbee. The Mexican poet Octavio Paz observed that "images [of the modern poet] have more truth in them than the so-called historical documents. Anyone interested in what took place in the first half of this century had better avoid the dubious accounts of it in our newspapers. Let him get hold instead of a key group of poetical works," Paz continued. "One of them would be Saint-John Perse. . . . His language, a prodigious fountain of images, is one of the freest and richest in all contemporary poetry and one of the most precise and skillful rhythmic constructs we have yet produced."

There are some dissenters from this high praise. The American poet and critic Howard Nemerov wrote, "*Seamarks* is neither a great poem nor even a very good one." In another review of *Seamarks,* John Ciardi wrote, "Perse is a fabulously rich musician, but . . . I must confess to a doubt that English readers will ever kindle into real enthusiasm for him. Whether he is read in the original or in translation, Perse seems incapable of pushing his poem forward; . . . the thing simply goes on too long and too slowly." Ciardi also referred to a review by W. H. Auden of the same work, in which Auden cited Perse as the logical candidate for the Nobel Prize. "Auden notes this slowness but dismisses it. Auden may be right. I certainly do not know what could have been cut, but I wish *something* had been."

The disputed review by Auden, which appeared in the *New York Times Book Review,* July 27, 1958, may, however, provide a useful overview of Perse's work: "If one reads through all of the poems of Saint-John Perse, one is immediately aware that each is, as it were, an instrument of one great oeuvre. He is one of those fortunate poets who discovered both his vision and the proper linguistic means to express it early."

ADDITIONAL WORKS IN ENGLISH TRANSLATION: A Selection of Works for an Understanding of World Affairs, 1943; Rains, 1945; Snows, 1945; Two Addresses, 1966; Chanté par celle qui fut là, 1970; Collected Poems, 1971; Song for an Equinox, 1977; Letters, 1979; Collected Poems, 1983.

ABOUT: Aiken, C. Collected Criticism, 1968; Emmanuel, P. Saint-John Perse: Praise and Presence, 1971; Galand, R. M. Saint-John Perse, 1972; Horry, R. N. Paul Claudel and Saint-John Perse, 1971; Knodel, A. Saint-John Perse: A Study of His Poetry, 1966; Little, R. Saint-John Perse, 1973; Ostrovsky, E. Under the Sign of Ambiguity, 1985.

PERUTZ, MAX

(May 19, 1914–   )
Nobel Prize for Chemistry, 1962
(shared with John C. Kendrew)

The English biochemist Max Ferdinand Perutz (pə rüts′) was born in Vienna, Austria, one of three children of Adele (Goldschmidt) and Hugo Perutz, both of whom came from wealthy textile manufacturing families. Although his parents hoped that the boy would study law and enter the family business, Perutz developed an interest in chemistry while attending secondary school at the Vienna Theresianum. In 1932 he entered the University of Vienna to study inorganic chemistry, but he soon found the subject boring and shifted to organic chemistry. It was through his work in this field that Perutz first learned about the X-ray crystallography studies then being conducted at Cambridge University. After completing his undergraduate requirements at Vienna in 1936, he went to Cambridge to work under J. D. Bernal, the noted physicist, at the Cavendish Laboratory.

The technique of X-ray crystallography originated in 1912 when MAX VON LAUE found that by passing a beam of X rays through a crystal onto a photographic plate he could produce a pattern of spots. This diffraction pattern, as it came to be known, appeared to differ with various types of crystals. Two years later W. H. BRAGG and W. L. BRAGG determined that because the X rays were being diffracted by the atoms composing the crystal, it was possible to interpret the resulting diffraction patterns mathematically and thereby deduce the atomic structure of the diffracting substance.

In their initial work the Braggs examined relatively simple crystals, such as sodium chloride (salt), that are composed of only a few types of atoms. Bernal, however, was interested in the far more complex structure of proteins, and he hoped that diffraction studies would eventually enable him to elucidate the function of a given protein. In 1937, after learning X-ray diffraction techniques from Bernal and from the physicist Isidor Fankuchen, Perutz began investigating hemoglobin, the globular, oxygen-carrying protein of blood.

In 1938, shortly after Perutz began his work on hemoglobin, Bernal left for London University; later that year the Nazi annexation of Austria left Perutz without financial support from his parents. W. L. Bragg, who had recently joined the faculty at Cambridge, helped obtain a Rockefeller Foundation grant that enabled Perutz to remain at the university as Bragg's research assistant and to receive his doctorate in 1940. The following year Perutz was interned in Canada as an enemy alien; however, his side interest in the crystalline properties of glaciers led to his appointment in 1943 to a secret Allied project under the direction of Lord Louis Mountbatten involving the possible use of ice floes as aircraft carriers. The project, however, was never implemented.

After the war Perutz obtained a research

MAX PERUTZ

the assistance of computers until in 1960 he proposed a model of the three-dimensional structure of hemoglobin. His results were published in February of that year in the British journal *Nature,* with Kendrew's findings on the myoglobin molecule.

"For their studies of the structures of globular proteins," Perutz and Kendrew received the 1962 Nobel Prize for Chemistry. "As a result of Kendrew's and Perutz's contributions," said Gunnar Hägg of the Royal Swedish Academy of Sciences on presenting the award, "it is . . . becoming possible to see the principles behind the construction of globular proteins." This achievement, he continued "will mean a big step forward in the understanding of life processes." In his Nobel lecture Perutz emphasized that "the discovery of a marked structural change accompanying the reaction of hemoglobin with oxygen suggests that there may be other enzymes which alter their structure on combination with their substrate, and that this may perhaps be an important factor in certain enzymatic catalysis."

After receiving the Nobel Prize, Perutz continued his investigation of globular proteins. Further refining his model of the hemoglobin molecule, he was able to show how its structure functions to transport oxygen in the blood. Although Perutz retired from his executive position at the Laboratory of Molecular Biology (formerly the Unit for Molecular Biology) in 1979, he has remained active in hemoglobin research.

In 1942 Perutz married Gisela Clara Peiser, a medical photographer. They have a son and a daughter. Once an avid skier and mountaineer, Perutz has described his interest in glaciers as "mainly an excuse for working in the mountains." Perutz, who has been described as shy and diffident, is known to his colleagues as an extremely tenacious researcher.

Perutz has served as an adviser to the British Defense Ministry. From 1963 to 1969 he was chairman of the European Molecular Biology Organization, and from 1974 to 1979 he was Fullerian Professor of Physiology at the Royal Institution in London. He has been awarded the Royal Medal (1971) and the Copley Medal (1979) of the Royal Society. He holds foreign membership in the French Academy of Sciences as well as the American National Academy of Sciences. He has received honorary degrees from the universities of Århus, Edinburgh, Norwich, Salzburg, and Vienna.

fellowship from the Imperial Chemical Industries and resumed his studies of hemoglobin at the Cavendish Laboratory. At the conclusion of the two-year grant, he was named director of the Unit for Molecular Biology at Cambridge, created in 1947 by the Medical Research Council. Initially his only colleague was JOHN C. KENDREW, a former doctoral student who was conducting X-ray studies of the muscle protein myoglobin. As the staff gradually expanded (including FRANCIS CRICK in 1949 and JAMES D. WATSON in 1951), Perutz and his colleagues sought an underlying regularity in the structure of protein molecules. If such regularity did in fact exist, it would enable them to decipher the structure of a protein crystal by a combination of model building and trial and error.

It was not until 1953 that Perutz solved the problem by applying a fundamental X-ray crystallographic technique known as isomorphous heavy-ion replacement. In this method a massive atom, such as mercury, is inserted into the crystal by attaching it to a particular atom. The massive atom produces a greater deflection than those of the substance being examined and therefore presents a different diffraction pattern. By comparing the two patterns, it is possible to determine the location of specific atoms and hence gain important information about the structure of the crystal.

By 1956 Perutz had created half a dozen types of hemoglobin molecules, each with a heavy atom attached at a different location. During the next four years, he made thousands of photographic plates and analyzed them with

SELECTED WORKS: Proteins and Nucleic Acids: Structure and Function, 1962; "The Birth of Protein Engineering," New Scientist June 13, 1985.

ABOUT: Current Biography November 1963; New Scientist October 3, 1974; New York Times November 2, 1962.

PIRANDELLO, LUIGI
(June 28, 1867–December 10, 1936)
Nobel Prize for Literature, 1934

LUIGI PIRANDELLO

Luigi Pirandello (pē rän del' lo), Italian dramatist, short story writer, and novelist, was born in Girgenti (now Agrigento) on the island of Sicily, where his father owned a prosperous sulfur mine. The second of six children, Pirandello revealed his literary talent during his early schooling in Girgenti. While in his teens he wrote poetry as well as a tragedy, *Barbaro* (Barbarian), which no longer survives.

After an unsuccessful stint in his father's business, Pirandello enrolled at the University of Rome in 1887. Dissatisfied with his instructors, he transferred to the University of Bonn the next year. There he studied literature and philosophy, and in 1891 he received a doctoral degree in Romance philology for a thesis on the dialect of his native region. Meanwhile, in 1889, he had published his first volume of poetry, *Mal giocondo* (*Painful Joy*), written largely in the manner of GIOSUÈ CARDUCCI. After his graduation, he remained at Bonn for a year as a lecturer.

Returning to Rome in 1893, Pirandello, with financial help from his father, embarked upon a literary career and wrote his first novel, *L'esclusa* (*The Outcast*). His first collection of short stories, *Amori senz' amore* (*Loves Without Love*), appeared in 1894, the same year that he married Antonietta Portulano, the daughter of his father's business associate. The marriage, arranged by the couple's families, produced two sons and a daughter. In 1898 he became professor of Italian literature at a teachers' college for women in Rome, where he continued to teach until 1922. His first adult play, the one-act *L'epilogo* (*Epilogue*), written in 1898, was not produced until 1910, under the title *La morsa* (*The Vise*).

In 1903 the Pirandellos' fortune was wiped out by a flood that destroyed the family's sulfur mine, and Pirandello was forced to rely solely on his writing and his teaching for income. As a more serious sequel of the catastrophe, his wife suffered a nervous breakdown in 1904. Over the next fifteen years, her mental condition—a persecution mania that manifested itself in hysterical outbursts at Pirandello's supposed infidelities—steadily worsened, and in 1919 Pirandello was forced to place her in a mental institution.

In spite of his marital and financial troubles, Pirandello continued to write and to have his works published. He achieved his first literary success in 1904 with his third novel, *Il fu Mattia Pascal* (*The Late Mattia Pascal*). Two important works of nonfiction followed in 1908: *L'umorismo* (*On Humor*), in which he defined his complex tragicomic vision, and an essay collection, *Arte e scienza* (*Art and Science*).

Until 1915, when his first three-act play, *Se non cosí . . .* (If Not So . . .), was produced, Pirandello wrote mainly short stories and novels. After 1915 he concentrated on the theater, which was financially rewarding and which eventually permitted him to leave his teaching position. In an extremely prolific period between 1915 and 1921, Pirandello wrote sixteen plays, all of which were performed. The 1917 production of *Cosí è (se vi pare)* (*Right You Are—If You Think You Are*), in particular, brought him serious critical attention and popular acclaim.

In 1922 Pirandello attained international fame when *Sei personaggi in cerca d'autore* (*Six Characters in Search of an Author,* 1921) received successful performances in London and New York. Ironically, the opening in Rome of what has since become the most popular of his forty-four plays had occasioned a riot by an audience offended by the dramatist's assertions about the relativity of personality and truth. *Enrico IV* (*Henry IV*), considered by

817

many critics to be Pirandello's masterpiece, was also first performed in 1922.

In his mature work, Pirandello adhered to the basic themes of the illusory nature of experience and the vague and mercurial nature of the personality. In these plays, he sought to go beyond the idea of characters as well-defined creations with stable sets of values. In Pirandello's world, identity was relative; the only truth was that perceived at the moment. Pirandello stripped his characters of masks and illusions. The sources of his preoccupations were both intellectual and personal. He had been deeply influenced by the theory of the subconscious propounded by the French experimental psychologist Alfred Binet, and he was familiar with German idealist philosophy from his university work in Bonn. In addition, his fifteen-year struggle to care for a mentally disturbed wife served to reinforce his belief that the psyche lacked unity.

Pirandello's theatrical successes made him eager to become his own producer, hoping thereby to ensure the integrity of his texts. In 1923 he requested membership in the Fascist party and obtained Mussolini's support in founding the National Art Theater of Rome, which toured Europe in 1925 and 1926 and South America in 1927. Its leading actress, Marta Abba, became a source of inspiration for Pirandello. Despite state subsidies, however, the company ran up a huge deficit and was disbanded in 1928.

Some scholars have regarded Pirandello as an opportunist in his dealings with the Fascists; whether or not these charges are justified, he proclaimed himself an apolitical artist, and on several occasions criticized the Fascist party. As a result, after the closing of the National Art Theater, he found it increasingly difficult to get his plays produced in Italy. After living and traveling abroad, mainly in Paris and Berlin, he ended his self-imposed exile in 1933 at Mussolini's urging.

Pirandello was awarded the 1934 Nobel Prize for Literature "for his bold and ingenious revival of dramatic and scenic art." In his presentation speech, Per Hallström of the Swedish Academy noted that "the most remarkable feature of Pirandello's art is his almost magical power to turn psychological analysis into good theater." In his acceptance speech, Pirandello attributed his creative dramatic powers to "a love and respect for life that were indispensable for the assimilation of bitter disillusions, painful experiences, frightful wounds, and all the mistakes of innocence that give depth and value to our experiences."

Pirandello died in Rome on December 10, 1936; according to his request, the funeral took place without public ceremony, and his ashes were taken to his birthplace.

Although Pirandello's short stories are held in high regard, his most significant contributions to literature lie in his treatment of the personality and his experiments with dramatic structure. The American critic Martin Esslin compared the effect of Pirandello's revolutionary ideas regarding the psyche with that of "[ALBERT] EINSTEIN's discovery of the concept of relativity in physics." The American scholar Robert Brustein explained how Pirandello's experimental trilogy—*Six Characters in Search of an Author*, *Ciascuno a suo modo* (*Each in His Own Way*, 1924), and *Questa sera si recita a soggetto* (*Tonight We Improvise*, 1930)—is "unified by a common purpose. . . . In these plays, the illusions of the realistic theater—where actors pretend to be real people, canvas and lumber pass for actual locations, and forged events are designed to seem real—no longer apply. Now the stage is a stage, actors are actors, and even the audience, formerly silent and half invisible in its willing suspension of disbelief, has been drawn into the action and implicated in the theatrical proceedings." According to the American critic and director Eric Bentley, "The essence of Pirandello is his conversion of the intellect into passion. . . . In Pirandello, passion and intellect torture each other and join in a mutual failure. The quintessence of Pirandellism is this peculiar relation of intellect to feeling."

Pirandello's dramatic body of work is often seen as the culmination of the explorations of personality initiated in the plays of Henrik Ibsen and August Strindberg. In turn, Pirandello's influence on such European playwrights as Jean Anouilh, JEAN-PAUL SARTRE, SAMUEL BECKETT, Eugène Ionesco, and Jean Genet has been compared by Thomas Bishop with the legacy of Shakespeare. Brustein has listed EUGENE O'NEILL, Edward Albee, and Harold Pinter among modern American and English playwrights influenced by Pirandello, concluding that "the extent of even this partial list of influence marks Pirandello as the most seminal dramatist of our time."

ADDITIONAL WORKS IN ENGLISH TRANSLATION: Sicilian Limes, 1922; Shoot, 1926; The Old and the Young, 1928; As You Desire Me, 1931; Horse in the Moon, 1932; Better Think Twice About It, 1933; Naked Truth and Eleven Other Stories, 1934; A Character in Distress, 1938; The Haunted House, 1938; Professor Lamis' Vengeance, 1938; Four Tales, 1939; To Find Oneself, 1943; No One Knows

How, 1949; The Wives' Friend, 1949; Diana and Tudda, 1950; Naked Masks: Five Plays, 1952; Liola, 1952; The Rules of the Game, 1954; Destruction of Man, 1956; The Mountain Giants, 1956; When Somebody Is Somebody, 1956; Cap and Bells, 1957; Man, Beast, and Virtue, 1957; A Dream of Christmas, 1959; Lazarus, 1959; The Life I Gave You, 1959; All for the Best, 1960; The Merry-Go-Round of Love, 1964; The Little Hut, 1965; Signora Frola and Her Son-in-Law, Signor Ponza, 1965; Tales of Madness, 1984.

ABOUT: Bassnett-McGuire, S. Luigi Pirandello, 1983; Bentley, E. In Search of Theatre, 1953; Bishop, T. Pirandello and the French Theatre, 1960; Brustein, R. The Theatre of Revolt, 1964; Budel, O. Pirandello, 1966; Cambon, G. (ed.) Pirandello: A Collection of Critical Essays, 1967; Gilman, R. The Making of Modern Drama, 1974; Giudice, G. Pirandello: A Biography, 1975; Lamm, M. Modern Drama, 1953; MacClintock, L. The Age of Pirandello, 1951; Mathaei, R. Luigi Pirandello, 1973; Oliver, R. Dreams of Passion: The Theater of Luigi Pirandello, 1979; Palmer, J. Studies in the Contemporary Theatre, 1927; Paolucci, A. Pirandello's Theatre, 1974; Poggioli, R. The Spirit of the Letter, 1965; Radcliffe-Umstead, D. The Mirror of Our Anguish, 1978; Ragusa, O. Luigi Pirandello, 1968; Sogiiuzzo, R. A. Luigi Pirandello, Director, 1981; Starkie, W. Pirandello, 1926; Valency, M. The End of the World, 1980; Vittorini, D. The Drama of Luigi Pirandello, 1935.

GEORGES PIRE

PIRE, GEORGES

(February 10, 1910–January 30, 1969)
Nobel Prize for Peace, 1958

Georges Charles Clement Ghislain Pire (pir), Belgian priest and humanitarian, was born in Dinant. He was the eldest of four children of Georges Pire, a schoolteacher, and the former Françoise Laurent. Pire was four years old when World War I began and German forces swept through Belgium. After his grandfather was shot by German troops, the family fled to France until the end of the war. Returning to Dinant in 1918, they found their home burned to the ground.

Pire studied philosophy and classics at the Collège de Bellevue in Dinant before deciding to prepare for a religious life. He entered the Roman Catholic monastery of La Sarte at Huy, Belgium, in 1926, taking the name Henri Dominique. Six years later, he took his final vows as a religious brother. He was then sent to the Collegio Angelico, the Dominican university in Rome, to study for a doctorate in theology, which he received in 1936, two years after being ordained as a priest. Now known as Father Pire, he studied social sciences at the University of Louvain in Belgium and returned to La Sarte the following year to teach sociology and moral theology.

Also serving during this time as curé to poor farm families in the parish of La Sarte, Father Pire founded the Mutual Family Aid Service to assist them, especially the children. Equally concerned about city children, he established a series of open-air camps where youngsters could enjoy country life. After German forces overran Belgium in the spring of 1940, these camps became missions for feeding thousands of children.

During World War II, Father Pire remained in Belgium, serving as chaplain to an underground Resistance group and acting as a Belgian intelligence agent. As part of the underground, he delivered messages to couriers and organized networks to help downed Allied pilots escape German-occupied territory. He also reported to the Allied authorities that the Germans were launching V-1 rockets from the Strait of Dover. After the war he was decorated for these activities with the Belgian Military Cross with Palms, the Resistance Medal with Crossed Swords, the War Medal, and the National Recognition Medal.

In the aftermath of the war, Father Pire began organizing camps for French and Belgian refugee children. He was inspired to these efforts in 1949 after hearing a speech given by Colonel Edward Squadrille, an American army officer who directed a displaced-persons camp in Austria for the United Nations Relief and Rehabilitation Agency. Squadrille's description of the plight of the refugees left stateless and destitute by the war moved Father Pire to make their cause his own.

That year he visited Austrian camps where 60,000 refugees suffered the effects of starvation, disease, and despair. Likening them to "people who have been sitting on their suitcases in a railroad station waiting for a train that will never arrive," he first attempted to break down the wall of isolation surrounding them. He did this through a sponsorship service (*service de parrainage*) whereby volunteers agreed to send letters and parcels to refugee families.

Father Pire's next task was to establish homes in Belgium for elderly refugees who were unable to care for themselves. The first home opened in Huy in 1950, the second in Esneux the following year, a third in Aertselaer in 1953, and a fourth in Braine-le-Comte in 1954.

Father Pire believed that the refugees' greatest obstacle was "a total uprooting, not only from their own countries, but from the world of men." To help them reestablish roots in a community, he conceived of special "European villages" where the displaced persons would form a "neighborhood glued onto a city." Within three years, he had established five of these villages, each with 150 residents, near cities in Belgium, Germany, and Austria. Initially built with private contributions, they gradually became self-supporting as refugee families found jobs and integrated themselves into nearby communities. Two of the villages were named for FRIDTJOF NANSEN and ALBERT SCHWEITZER.

To administer his refugee work, Father Pire created Aid to Displaced Persons and European Villages in 1957, an organization funded chiefly by contributions raised through a series of crusades called Europe of the Heart. However, he still sought funds with which to establish a sixth European village, to be built in Norway and to be named after Anne Frank.

The following year Father Pire was awarded the 1958 Nobel Peace Prize "for his efforts to help refugees leave their camps and return to a life of freedom and dignity," especially the "hard core" of the handicapped, the old, and the infirm "for whom our hard, ruthless world . . . has had no further use," according to Gunnar Jahn of the Norwegian Nobel Committee.

In his Nobel lecture, which he delivered in French, Father Pire stressed the importance of individual concern as the basis for humanitarian relief. "Let us be wary of mass solutions," he said. "We must love our neighbors as ourselves." He went on to declare that "there is perhaps no surer road to peace than the one that starts from little islands and oases of genuine kindness . . . constantly growing in number and being continually joined together until eventually they ring the world."

Father Pire's refugee work increased after he received the Nobel Prize. The next year he established the Heart Open to the World, an organization dedicated to international fraternity. To accomplish its goals, he founded the University of Peace at Huy in 1960. Since then, thousands of people have attended the university to hear lectures on practical measures to promote peace and to participate in workshops. Father Pire also established the World Friendships agency, organized to channel aid to refugee families—especially children—in Africa and Asia.

A visit to Pakistan in 1960 inspired Father Pire to initiate a series of programs he called Islands of Peace. The "islands" were to be rural organizations consisting of several villages joined together to solve specific problems with the assistance of international aid. The first program went into operation in East Pakistan in 1962, and the second began in southern India in 1969.

Father Pire died at Louvain Roman Catholic Hospital on January 30, 1969, following surgery.

WORKS IN ENGLISH TRANSLATION: Europe of the Heart: The Autobiography of Father Dominique Pire, 1960; Building Peace, 1967, with Charles Dricot.

ABOUT: America February 14, 1959; Catholic World April 1959; Christian Century August 9, 1961; Houart, V. The Open Heart: The Inspiring Story of Father Pire and the Europe of the Heart, 1959.

PLANCK, MAX

(April 23, 1858–October 4, 1947)
Nobel Prize for Physics, 1918

The German physicist Max Karl Ernst Ludwig Planck (plängk) was born in Kiel (then in Prussia) to Johann Julius Wilhelm von Planck, a professor of civil law, and Emma (Patzig) Planck. As a child, Planck played the piano and organ, showing considerable musical talent. In 1867 the family moved to Munich, where Planck entered the classical Royal Maximilian Gymnasium and was first attracted to science by an excellent mathematics teacher. Upon graduation in 1874, he contemplated studying classical philology and also tried musical composition, but chose physics instead.

Planck studied mathematics and physics for three years at the University of Munich and

MAX PLANCK

for one year at the University of Berlin. One of his professors at Munich, the experimental physicist Philipp von Jolly, unprophetically advised him that nothing essentially new remained to be discovered in physics. This view, widely held was at the time, fostered by the extraordinary successes of nineteenth-century scientists in acquiring knowledge about physical and chemical processes. Planck received a broader view of science in Berlin from the writings of the eminent physicists Hermann von Helmholtz and Gustav Kirchhoff and from papers by Rudolf Clausius. These readings promoted Planck's lasting concentration on the field of thermodynamics, the science that deals with heat, mechanical energy, and energy transformations on the basis of a few fundamental laws. He received his Ph.D. in 1879 from Munich with a dissertation on the second law of thermodynamics, which states that no continuous self-sustaining process can transfer heat from a colder body to a hotter one.

The following year Planck wrote another paper on thermodynamics, which won him a junior faculty position at the University of Munich. In 1885 he became an extraordinary (associate) professor at the University of Kiel, a position that gave him greater independence, more financial security, and ample time for research. Planck's research in thermodynamics and its applications to physical chemistry and electrochemistry earned him international recognition. In 1888 he became an assistant professor at the University of Berlin and director of the Institute for Theoretical

Physics, a facility created especially for him. He became a full professor in 1892.

From 1896 on, Planck, stimulated by measurements then being made at the State Physical-Technical Institute in Berlin, increasingly devoted his attention to the problem of radiation from hot bodies. Any body radiates electromagnetic energy by virtue of its heat content, and the radiation is visible if the body is hot enough. As its temperature rises, a body first glows red, then orange-yellow, then white. The radiation has a mixture of frequencies (corresponding to colors for visible light). However, a body's radiation depends not only on temperature but, to some extent, on surface characteristics such as color and texture. For an ideal standard for measurement and theoretical investigation, physicists imagine a perfectly black body, defined as one that absorbs all radiation falling on it and reflects none. Radiation from such a body depends only on its temperature. Although the ideal does not exist, a good approximation is a small hole in an enclosure (for example, a suitably constructed furnace) whose walls and contents are at equilibrium at the same temperature. One demonstration of the blackbody characteristics of such an enclosure is that radiation falling on the hole enters the cavity and, bouncing from wall to wall, is partially reflected and partially absorbed. Because the radiation is highly unlikely to find its way back out the hole, it is totally absorbed. Radiation originating in the cavity and emerging from the hole is taken to represent radiation from an area the size of the hole on the surface of a truly black body at the same temperature as the enclosure. Planck read Kirchhoff's work on the properties of such an enclosure in preparation for his own investigation. Accounting quantitatively for the observed energy distribution of the radiation became known as the blackbody problem.

Blackbody experiments had shown that a graph of energy (brightness) versus frequency or wavelength is a characteristic curve, beginning low at low frequencies (long wavelengths), rising to a rounded peak at some intermediate frequency, and then falling off at high frequencies (short wavelengths). As the temperature is raised, the curve retains its shape but shifts toward higher frequencies. Empirical relationships had been found between the temperature and the frequency at the peak of the blackbody curve (Wien displacement law, after WILHELM WIEN) and between the temperature and the total radiated energy (Stefan-Boltzmann law, after the Austrian physicists

821

Josef Stefan and Ludwig Boltzmann), but no one had succeeded in deriving the blackbody curve accurately from the basic principles known at the time. Wien developed a semiempirical formula that could be made to fit the curve at higher frequencies but which failed at lower ones. J. W. STRUTT (Lord Rayleigh) and the English physicist James Jeans applied the principles of the distribution of energies among frequencies of vibration in an enclosed space and arrived at another formula (Rayleigh-Jeans), which matched the blackbody curve at lower frequencies but failed at higher ones.

Planck, convinced by James Clerk Maxwell's theory of the electromagnetic nature of light (published in 1873 and confirmed experimentally by Heinrich Hertz in 1887), approached the blackbody problem from the point of view of the energy distribution among elemental electric oscillators of unspecified physical form. Although his method had a superficial resemblance to the Rayleigh-Jeans derivation, he rejected some of their assumptions. In 1900, after a long, persistent effort to make theory fit facts, he succeeded in deriving a formula that the experimental physicists at the State Physical-Technical Institute found agreed with their measurements to a remarkable degree of accuracy. It also yielded the Wien and Stefan-Boltzmann laws. However, to do so, Planck was obliged to introduce a radical concept that departed completely from established principles. The energy of his oscillators could not vary continuously, as conventional physics allowed, but could have only discrete values that increased in finite steps. Each step of energy equaled a constant number (now called Planck's constant) multiplied by the frequency. The discrete bits of energy later were named quanta. His concept constituted the birth of quantum theory and marked a revolution in physics. The designation *classical*, as opposed to *modern*, physics now generally means "before Planck."

Planck was no revolutionary, and neither he nor other physicists understood the deep significance of the quantum. To Planck it was a necessary device to make the formula work. He tried many ways to fit it into the classical tradition but could not. Nevertheless, he was delighted at the almost immediate success with certain applications. His new theory also involved other fundamental quantities, such as the velocity of light and a number called Boltzmann's constant, in addition to Planck's constant. In 1901, with the help of experimental data on blackbody radiation, Planck found the value of Boltzmann's constant, added other

known information, and calculated the Avogadro number (the number of atoms in a molecular weight of an element). Using the Avogadro number, he was able to calculate the electric charge of the electron with remarkable accuracy.

Quantum theory took on more substantial form in 1905, when ALBERT EINSTEIN used the idea of the photon, the quantum of electromagnetic radiation, to explain the photoelectric effect (ejection of electrons from a metal surface irradiated by ultraviolet rays). Einstein proposed that light had a dual nature; it could behave like a wave, as all previous physics had demonstrated, and it could act like a particle, as in the photoelectric effect. In 1907 Einstein added further support by using the quantum to account for puzzling discrepancies between theory and experiment in the specific heat of solids, the quantity of heat required to raise the temperature of a unit amount of a solid by one degree. Further confirmation of the potential power of Planck's innovation came in 1913 when NIELS BOHR applied quantum theory to atomic structure. In Bohr's model, atomic electrons could have only certain energy levels governed by quantum limitations. A transition between levels released the energy difference in the form of a photon of radiation, whose frequency was the photon energy divided by Planck's constant, thus accounting for the characteristic spectra of radiation emitted by excited atoms.

In 1919 Planck was awarded the 1918 Nobel Prize for Physics "in recognition of the services he rendered to the advancement of physics by his discovery of energy quanta." According to A. G. Ekstrand of the Royal Swedish Academy of Sciences in his presentation speech, "Planck's radiation theory is . . . the most significant lodestar for modern physical research, and it seems that it will be a long time before the treasures will be exhausted which have been unearthed as a result of Planck's genius." In his Nobel lecture, delivered in 1920, Planck summarized his work and acknowledged that "the introduction of the quantum of action has not yet produced a genuine quantum theory."

The 1920s saw the development of quantum mechanics, a complex mathematical treatment of quantum theory, by ERWIN SCHRÖDINGER, WERNER HEISENBERG, P. A. M. DIRAC, and others. Planck was unhappy with the new probabilistic interpretation of quantum mechanics and, like Einstein, sought a way to reconcile predictions based only on probabilities with classical ideas of causality. In this he was unsuccessful: the probabilistic approach has endured. However, Planck's contribution to modern physics did not end with his discovery of the quantum and of the constant named for him. He was greatly impressed with Einstein's theory of special relativity, published in 1905, and his strong support was instrumental in its acceptance by physicists. Among other achievements, Planck derived the Fokker-Planck equation, which describes the behavior of a system of particles subjected to small random impulses. (Adriaan Fokker was a Dutch physicist whose contribution was an improvement on a method first used by Einstein to describe Brownian motion, the zigzag movement of particles suspended in a liquid.) In 1928, at the age of seventy, Planck took mandatory retirement from his professorship but maintained his association with the Kaiser Wilhelm Society for the Advancement of Science, of which he became president in 1930. He continued his research activities well into his eighties.

Planck's personal life was marked by tragedy. His first wife, the former Marie Merck, whom he married in 1885 and with whom he had two sons and twin daughters, died in 1909. Two years later he married her niece, Marga von Hösslin, with whom he had one son. Planck's eldest son was killed in action in World War I, and within the next few years both of his daughters died in childbirth. The surviving son of his first marriage was executed in 1944 for participation in an unsuccessful conspiracy to assassinate Adolf Hitler.

A conservative, religious, and just man, Planck publicly and privately opposed Nazi persecutions. After Hitler came to power in 1933, Planck intervened on behalf of Jewish scientists who were being dismissed from their positions and forced into exile. At a scientific conference he acclaimed Einstein, who had been declared anathema by the Nazis. When Planck, in his capacity as president of the Kaiser Wilhelm Society, was required to visit Hitler, he used the opportunity to try to stop the actions against Jewish scientists. Hitler responded with a tirade against Jews in general. Planck thereafter appeared to become resigned and kept his silence, although the Nazis had no doubt about his views. A strongly patriotic man, Planck could only pray that his nation would eventually return to normal. He continued to serve in German scientific societies, hoping to preserve some German science and education from obliteration. After his house and personal library were destroyed by an Allied air raid on Berlin, he and his wife sought refuge in an estate in Rogätz, near Magdeburg, where they were caught between the retreating German army and advancing Allied forces. They were finally picked up and transported to safety in Göttingen by the American army.

Planck died in Göttingen on October 4, 1947, six months before his ninetieth birthday. His gravestone there bears only his name and the numerical value of Planck's constant.

Like Bohr and Einstein, Planck was deeply interested in philosophical questions concerning causality, ethics, and free will, and he wrote and spoke on these subjects to both professional and nonprofessional audiences. Planck, who served as a lay church officer in Berlin, believed that science complements religion and teaches truthfulness and reverence.

Throughout his life, Planck retained his early love of music. An accomplished pianist, he often played chamber music with his friend Einstein before the latter left Germany. He was also a skilled mountain climber and spent most of his vacations in the Alps.

In addition to the Nobel Prize, Planck was awarded the Copley Medal of the Royal Society of London (1928) and the Goethe Prize of the city of Frankfurt am Main (1946). The German Physical Society named its highest award, the Planck Medal, after him, and he was its first recipient. A planetoid was named Planckiana in honor of Planck's eightieth birthday, and after the end of World War II, the Kaiser Wilhelm Society was renamed the Max Planck Society. Planck was a member of all the German and Austrian scientific academies, as well as the scientific societies and academies in England, Denmark, Ireland, Finland, Greece, the Netherlands, Hungary, Italy, the Soviet Union, Sweden, the Ukraine, and the United States.

SELECTED WORKS: Treatise on Thermodynamics, 1903; The Theory of Heat Radiation, 1914; Eight Lectures on Theoretical Physics, 1915; A Survey of Physics, 1923; The Universe in Light of Modern Physics, 1931; Introduction to Theoretical Physics (5 vols.) 1932–1933; Where Is Science Going? 1932; The Philosophy of Physics, 1936; Scientific Autobiography and Other Papers, 1949; Original Papers in Quantum Physics, 1972.

ABOUT: Dictionary of Scientific Biography, volume 11, 1975; Heilbron, J. L. The Dilemmas of an Upright Man, 1986; Kangro, H. Early History of Planck's Radiation Law, 1976; Obituary Notices of Fellows of the Royal Society, volume 6, 1948.

POLANYI, JOHN C.

(January 23, 1929–   )
Nobel Prize for Chemistry, 1986
(shared with Dudley R. Herschbach and
    Yuan T. Lee)

JOHN C. POLANYI

The Canadian chemist John Charles Polanyi (pō län' ē) was born in Berlin, Germany, to Hungarian parents, Michael and Magda Elizabeth (Kemeny) Polanyi. When Polanyi was four years old, the family moved to Manchester, England, where his father was a professor of chemistry at Manchester University. After receiving his early education at Manchester Grammar School, Polanyi entered Manchester University in 1946, in time to attend the last chemistry lectures given by his father, who shortly thereafter left the chemistry department to become professor of philosophy at Manchester.

Polanyi's father left behind a staff devoted largely to the exploration of the molecular basis of simple chemical reactions. One of his father's former students, Ernest Warhurst, became Polanyi's research supervisor. Warhurst's doctoral thesis had involved experiments with the sodium flame apparatus that had enabled Polanyi's father and co-workers to determine the probability that a collision between a sodium atom and an available molecule would lead to a reaction. Under Warhurst, Polanyi measured the strengths of chemical bonds by means of pyrolysis (thermal dissociation) and received his Ph.D. in chemistry in 1952.

Polanyi's years at Manchester set the course for his subsequent work on the molecular basis of chemical reactions. At Manchester the main focus had been on the mystery of the overall reaction rate, that is, whether a molecular collision of a given force would result in the formation of a new chemical species. Polanyi redirected the question to consider what *types* of forces are most conducive to reaction. He decided that the answer could most easily be found in a study of the motions of newly born reaction products, since the forces operating in the "transition state" (between the coming together of reagents and the emergence of products) should leave an imprint on the products.

During postdoctoral work in 1952–1954 with E. W. R. Steacie at the laboratories of Canada's National Research Council (NRC) in Ottawa, Polanyi became increasingly convinced that he had raised the right question and that he would devote himself to finding the answer. At Manchester, his sense of vocation had been slow in coming. As a student his main interests

had been politics, editing a newspaper, and writing poetry; his interest in science had been only peripheral. In Ottawa, however, he was exhilarated by the sunny climate, and he began to enjoy laboratory work as never before. With Steacie's encouragement, he performed calculations to test whether the reigning transition-state theory of reaction rates had predictive power. He concluded that the theory was unprovable because knowledge of the forces acting in the transition state was lacking. After his two years at NRC, he spent a few months in the laboratory of GERHARD HERZBERG, where he assembled spectroscopic equipment to probe vibrational and rotational excitation in molecular iodine. As he later put it, "Some unseen hand must have been guiding me," since he would later measure in reaction products the types of motion he had been studying in Herzberg's laboratory.

At the invitation of the American chemist Hugh Stott Taylor, Polanyi then spent two years in the United States as a postdoctoral fellow at Princeton University. There he became acquainted with two of Taylor's associates, Michael Boudart and David Garvin, who were studying vibrational excitation in the products of the reaction of atomic hydrogen with ozone. The reaction emitted an orange glow as the reaction product underwent spontaneous transitions from highly excited vibration states directly to very low states of excitation. Although Polanyi did not participate in this experiment, he was greatly influenced by it. The relatively high-frequency radiation (high overtones) from these vibrational transitions suggested to Polanyi that it should be possible to detect the much more probable "fundamental transitions," caused by smaller changes in vibrational state, which would emit lower-frequency infrared radiation. Polanyi took this idea with him when he returned to Canada in 1956 as a lecturer in chemistry at the University of Toronto.

With his first graduate students, he looked for enhanced reaction rates in vibrationally excited hydrogen chloride in the product of the exothermic (heat-releasing) reaction of atomic hydrogen and molecular chlorine. The hydrogen chloride experiment, first reported in 1958, set Polanyi and his group on the path to their main work.

The experiment was simple and inexpensive. Atomic hydrogen formed in an electric discharge (using a neon sign transformer to supply the high voltage) was mixed with a flow of chlorine gas at low pressure in a vessel equipped with sodium chloride windows that transmitted infrared. An infrared spectrometer was borrowed and positioned in front of the window. The reaction vessel, which remained cold to the touch, emitted an infrared spectrum that indicated the presence of hydrogen chloride at a temperature of thousands of degrees. This molecular excitation was chemical in origin and constituted infrared chemiluminescence.

The 1958 report by Polanyi and his student J. K. Cashion ended by stating that "the method promises to provide, for the first time, information concerning the distribution of vibrational and possibly rotational energy among the products of a three-center reaction."

It took ten years and the work of many graduate students to fulfill the promise. One of the problems was vibrational and rotational "relaxation." The problem was overcome by using sprays of reagent gases that crossed in the center of an evacuated chamber, recording the infrared emission from newborn reaction products, and then removing the products by condensation at the liquid-nitrogen–cooled vessel walls before they had time to relax. This arrested relaxation led to the first quantitative determinations of "detailed rate constants," that is, the rates at which the reaction created products with specific states of vibrational, rotational, and (hence) translational excitation.

The measurements related to translational excitation provided a common ground between Polanyi's infrared chemiluminescence and studies of crossed molecular beams, which were the major alternative means of making such measurements. The crossed-beam method, in which the primary measured quantities are product translational and angular distributions, was achieved in 1967 by DUDLEY R. HERSCHBACH and YUAN T. LEE.

A major technological outgrowth of Polanyi's work was first described in his 1960 paper, "An Infrared Maser Dependent on Vibrational Excitation," submitted to *Physical Review Letters* but rejected as lacking scientific interest. This paper extended the 1958 proposal by CHARLES H. TOWNES and ARTHUR L. SCHAWLOW for the device now known as a laser (*l*ight *a*mplification by *s*timulated *e*mission of *r*adiation). Townes and Schawlow had envisioned an electronically excited medium. Polanyi proposed that the medium be composed of vibrationally and rotationally excited molecules. His suggestion had several attractive aspects. First, due to a phenomenon Polanyi called partial population inversion, a lasing medium could be obtained simply by partially cooling a hot gas. Second, a lasing medium could be generated by a chemical reaction; such a device is now known as a chemical laser. Moreover, Polanyi noted that such lasers should exist naturally in the upper atmosphere.

Physical Review Letters also rejected the American physicist Theodore H. Maiman's report of the first operating laser, on the same grounds given for the rejection of Polanyi's paper. When Polanyi learned of this, he submitted his paper, unchanged, to the *Journal of Chemical Physics* in September 1960. It was promptly published. Since then, vibrational lasers (developed by C. K. N. Patel) and chemical lasers in particular (developed by G. C. Pimentel) have become the most powerful sources of infrared radiation. Polanyi enjoys asking sponsors of basic research who insist on evidence of practical applications whether they would have been sufficiently farsighted to support studies of barely detectable luminescence as a means of developing the most powerful lasers in existence.

Despite its simplicity, infrared chemiluminescence has provided the most complete and detailed information available on the energy distributions of chemical reaction products. Such information has been widely used to test theories of the molecular mechanics of simple exchange reactions. Polanyi's group used the tool of computer modeling from the beginning of their experiments. High-speed computers made it possible to solve the complex equations of motion for the reacting particles, and the interplay of theory and experiment yielded significant insights. Infrared chemiluminescence is not restricted to the determination of product excitation, but also can be used to measure how varying reagent vibrational and rotational excitation affect the probability of reactions.

Polanyi shared the 1986 Nobel Prize for Chemistry with Herschbach and Lee for contributions to "the development of a new field of research in chemistry—reaction dynamics." Polanyi was cited for "the method of infrared chemiluminescence, in which the extremely weak infrared emission from a newly formed molecule is measured and analyzed" and for his application of "this method to elucidate the detailed energy disposal during chemical reactions."

More recently, Polanyi's research interests have branched out. He is trying to develop a spectroscopy of the reactive transition state to gain an insight into the "molecular dance" in chemical reactions by observing the participating molecules while they are "on the stage, rather than in the wings before or after the dance is over," as he has put it. Polanyi's group is also developing a photochemistry of the absorbed state, using ultraviolet laser radiation to induce reactions between neighboring molecules clinging to a solid surface. The group hopes to be able to position molecules at will and to induce them to react in a determined way.

In the late 1950s Polanyi became convinced of the need for scientists to involve themselves in public affairs, particularly in relation to the problem of survival in an age of nuclear weapons. He has published some sixty articles and given numerous talks on this subject. In 1960 he became the founding chairman of the Canadian Pugwash Group and remained chairman until 1978. He is an active member of the American National Academy of Sciences' Committee on International Security Studies and of the Canadian Center for Arms Control and Disarmament.

Polanyi was a founding member of the Royal Society of Canada's Committee on Scholarly Freedom and of the Canadian Committee of Scientists and Scholars. He has also found time to participate in the continuing Canadian debate on science policy. He has stressed that high quality science is a necessary investment in the future. To the cry for relevance in basic science, he has responded that "nothing is more irredeemably irrelevant than bad science."

In 1958 Polanyi married Anne Ferrar Davidson of Toronto, a musician and piano teacher. They have a daughter and a son. Polanyi describes himself as "a musical ignoramus," his aesthetic pleasures coming from art,

literature, and poetry. He and his wife have written words and music, respectively, for skits performed professionally. Polanyi has given up his youthful enthusiasms for white water canoeing and aerobatics in favor of skiing and walking.

Polanyi has received many other honors in addition to the Nobel Prize, including the Marlow Medal of the Faraday Society (1962), the Steacie Prize for the Natural Sciences (1965), the Henry Marshall Tory Medal of the Royal Society of Canada (1977), and the Wolf Prize (1982), and he has held a large number of eminent lectureships. He has received twelve honorary degrees from Canadian universities and two from institutions in the United States (Harvard University and Rensselaer Polytechnic Institute). The government of Canada appointed him an officer of the Order of Canada in 1974 and a companion of the Order of Canada in 1979. He is a fellow of the Royal Society of Canada and the Royal Society of London, a foreign member of the American Academy of Arts and Sciences, a foreign associate of the American National Academy of Sciences, and a member of the Pontifical Academy in Rome.

ABOUT: Maclean's October 27, 1986; New Scientist October 23, 1986; New York Times October 16, 1986; Research and Development December 1986; Saturday Night February 1987; Science November 7, 1986; Scientific American December 1986; Time October 27, 1986.

PONTOPPIDAN, HENRIK
(July 24, 1857–August 21, 1943)
Nobel Prize for Literature, 1917
(shared with Karl Gjellerup)

The Danish novelist Henrik Pontoppidan (pon top′ ē dän) was born in the town of Fredericia, on the Jutland Peninsula, the fourth of sixteen children born to Dines Pontoppidan and the former Marie Oxenbøl. Pontoppidan's father, one of a long line of Danish scholars and clergymen, was a follower of N. F. S. Grundtvig, a radical theologian who linked Lutheranism with Danish nationalism. While Pontoppidan maintained a formal relationship with his father, he was much closer to his mother. Well read in history and economics, she believed that Denmark—newly democratic after a long history of autocracy and rigid class structure—was hypocritical in its attitude toward the peasants, who had been given the vote but little help in their battle against poverty. Her outlook and convictions were reflected in Pontoppidan's development

HENRIK PONTOPPIDAN

as a writer and in the sentiments expressed in many of his books.

When Pontoppidan was six years old, the family moved to nearby Randers, in central Jutland. A year later, the city was briefly occupied and sacked by Prussian and Austrian troops. The invasion left a deep impression on Pontoppidan. When southern Jutland, which had been subsumed into the Prussian province of Schleswig-Holstein, was returned to Denmark in 1920, he celebrated the event in a patriotic poem, the first of his many works dealing with the trauma of the invasion.

Although not destitute, Pontoppidan's father endured many financial struggles, and the family lived very modestly. Parochial Lutheran vicarage life grew increasingly distasteful to Pontoppidan. He was exasperated by what he saw as the defeatism of the Danish middle class in the wake of the Prussian invasion and by its apparent aversion to the peasants. He was also critical of the landed gentry and the rising class of capitalists in Copenhagen. Determined to participate in Denmark's emergence as a modern nation, Pontoppidan resolved to become an engineer and, upon high school graduation, entered Copenhagen's Polytechnic Institute.

The move to Copenhagen marked Pontoppidan's first concrete break with his provincial upbringing. He visited museums and galleries and went to hear the city's two most popular orators: the evangelical Pastor Frimodt, whose graphic depictions of hell amused him, and Georg Brandes, the nation's leading critic and historian, who exerted a powerful influence on him. Brandes urged his fellow Danes to

catch up with the more modern, industrialized countries of Western Europe. He championed naturalistic writers, such as Émile Zola, who focused on current social issues. With Hans Christian Andersen, Brandes initiated a nineteenth-century Danish literary renaissance. Pontoppidan, who met Brandes in 1884, partially modeled the main character in one of his major novels (Emmanuel in *The Promised Land*) after this charismatic figure.

During his early years in Copenhagen, Pontoppidan followed parliamentary debates between conservatives, who wished to ensure the primacy of the nobility and upper classes, and the opposition, which sought a more egalitarian, democratic society. Pontoppidan's sympathy with the opposition would later be reflected in his writing.

In 1877, the year he turned twenty, Pontoppidan took a walking tour of Switzerland, where he had his first love affair and wrote some sketches. It was on this holiday that he resolved to become a writer. By 1879 he had completed his preliminary engineering studies, withdrawn from the Polytechnic Institute, and taken a teaching position in a folk high school, a school for peasants run by his brother Morten. This institution, in the rural town of Frerslev, exposed Pontoppidan directly to the lives of landless peasants. "It was, above all, the conditions of the poor that interested me," he wrote. "I was concerned primarily with the inequality in this world's distribution of goods."

During his years as a teacher, Pontoppidan read widely, including philosophical works by Søren Kierkegaard, Harald Høffding, and Friedrich Nietzsche and novels by Fedor Dostoevsky and other Russian, French, and German writers. His teaching career came to an abrupt end in 1882, when his brother was jailed for political activities and the school was closed.

Pontoppidan served in the Danish Army Corps of Engineers during the summer of 1880. The following year, he made his literary debut with the story "Et Endeligt" (The End of a Life), published in the weekly journal *Ude og Hjemme* (Abroad and at Home). His first book, *Stækkede Vinger* (Clipped Wings), a collection of short stories first printed in the journal, was also published that year.

In December 1881 Pontoppidan married Mette Marie Hansen, a young peasant woman he had met while teaching; they had two children. Until 1884 the couple lived in the country, where Pontoppidan wrote steadily, producing stories, novellas, and sketches of rural life. After traveling to Germany and Italy, the couple settled in Copenhagen. There

Pontoppidan began a friendship with Brandes and became active in intellectual and artistic circles.

By 1883 he had conceived the idea of a long novel based on the religious rivalry between followers of Grundtvig and those who favored the evangelical Indre Mission. The project developed into a trilogy, *Det Forjættede Land* (*The Promised Land*), published between 1891 and 1895. With its detailed portraits of peasant life, insightful psychology, and precise descriptions of the landscape, this series exemplifies Pontoppidan's capacity as a writer in the naturalist tradition.

Emmanuel, the trilogy's hero, a well-educated clergyman who marries a peasant woman, labors on the land and lives in isolated surroundings. Like Pontoppidan, Emmanuel advocates constitutional government and an egalitarian society, but his efforts to heal the rift between the upper and lower classes ultimately fail, and he is unable to make a meaningful life for himself. The work is not only a tale of an idealist's disillusionment; it is also a scrupulous rendering of the clashing religious, political, and social forces that prevailed in Denmark from 1849 to 1866. At the same time it reflects Pontoppidan's growing disillusionment with Brandes and his philosophy.

In 1887 Pontoppidan's wife left him in Copenhagen and returned to the country to live with her parents. Pontoppidan was greatly saddened by his failure to unite himself to the Danish peasantry through his marriage. In 1892 he divorced his first wife and married Antoinette C. E. Kofoed. Their marriage lasted until her death in 1928; they had no children.

Pontoppidan's next major work, the eight-volume novel *Lykke-Per* (*Lucky Peter*), was published between 1898 and 1904. Its protagonist, Peter, a young provincial engineer, is a passionate realist, the antithesis of dreamy Emmanuel in *The Promised Land*. Like the author, Peter is raised in a rural parsonage and studies engineering in Copenhagen. He conceives a plan to use the Jutland canals for freight transport, thus creating a free port in Denmark in competition with Hamburg. He becomes engaged to the daughter of a wealthy Jewish financier, writes a book about his canal project, and travels widely to bolster the plan. But he is unable to relinquish his rural, Christian heritage. He eventually abandons his plan for a free port, breaks his engagement, and returns to Jutland to live a life steeped in the Christian romanticism he had tried to escape. *Lucky Peter* has been praised for its portrayal of a man who loses his nerve at a critical juncture in his life. Its penetrating analysis of the differences between Jewish and Christian thought and of various conflicts in contemporary Danish society has also been admired, as well as its criticism of anti-Semitism.

The last of Pontoppidan's three major works, *De Dødes Rige* (*The Kingdom of the Dead*, 1912–1916), is a five-volume narrative cycle. Unlike his earlier works, it has no central protagonist but portrays a social panorama through the struggles of many characters. The complex plot, involving an election campaign and a series of parliamentary scenes, focuses on the efforts of a radical politician to awaken a "people who are sleeping." Written on the eve of World War I and during the conflict, the novel is at once more bitter toward Danish society and more patriotic than his other books. Rushing to complete the massive work, Pontoppidan declared, "I'm not an author, but a loyal soldier."

"For his authentic descriptions of present-day life in Denmark," Pontoppidan received the 1917 Nobel Prize for Literature, which he shared with KARL GJELLERUP. Because of the war, no award ceremony was held, and Pontoppidan delivered no lecture. Swedish critic Sven Söderman wrote an essay to mark the occasion. Declaring that Pontoppidan "assuredly ranks first among contemporary Danish novelists," Söderman further noted that "all his work is a struggle against what seemed to him deceptive and perfidious illusions, false authority, romanticism, superstitious belief in beautiful phrases, and the intoxication of lofty words, exalted sentiments, and moral fear."

Pontoppidan continued to write fiction for the next twenty years. His most significant later work, published between 1933 and 1943, was his five-volume memoir consisting of *Drengeaar* (Boyhood Years, 1933), *Hamskifte* (Sloughing, 1936), *Arv og Gæld* (Inheritance and Debt, 1938), *Familieliv* (Family Life, 1940), and *Undervejs til mig selv* (On the Way to Myself, 1943).

As an older man, Pontoppidan had thick white hair and wore a beard. He was serious in demeanor, with deep-set, gray eyes. After 1910 he lived quietly in Charlottenlund, a suburb of Copenhagen, where he died in 1943.

Although Pontoppidan has never been well known in English, critics generally concur that he is one of Denmark's finest writers. According to Danish literary historian Vilhelm Andersen, "Modern Denmark could be reconstructed entirely from his books." "As an artist, he does not rank among the greatest," said Oscar Geismar, "but in an age of transition, he has lived the fate of his people with a sensitive soul and recorded what he has experienced in clear and intelligible Danish." The American writer and journalist George Strandvold called Pontoppidan "one of the greatest realists and one of the most penetrating novelists of his country; his observation of life is notable for its detail. . . . His style, while originating in anger and criticism, is detached." To THOMAS MANN, writing in 1927, Pontoppidan was "a born epic poet . . . a true conservative, who in a breathless world has preserved the grand style in the novel." Mann continued, "With the winning and delightful severity that is the secret of art, he has judged the times and, like the true poet that he is, pointed toward a purer humanity." More recently in a 1980 essay, the Danish-American scholar Sven H. Rossel remarked, "No other Danish writer has succeeded in portraying his own age, its main currents, and its people so completely and with such artistic precision as Pontoppidan."

ADDITIONAL WORKS IN ENGLISH TRANSLATION: Village Tales, 1883; The Apothecary's Daughter, 1890; From the Huts, 1901; Man's Heaven, 1927; The Royal Guest, 1928.

ABOUT: American-Scandinavian Foundation. Scandinavian Studies: Essays Presented to Dr. Henry Goddard Leach, 1965; Claudi, J. Contemporary Danish Authors, 1952; Mitchell, P. M. Henrik Pontoppidan, 1979; Scandinavian Studies November 1957, February 1965; Töpsoe-Jensen, H. G. Scandinavian Literature, 1929.

PORTER, GEORGE
(December 6, 1920–   )
Nobel Prize for Chemistry, 1967
(shared with Manfred Eigen and Ronald Norrish)

The English chemist George Porter was born in Stainforth, West Yorkshire, to John Smith Porter and the former Alice Ann Roebuck. After receiving his early education in the local primary and grammar schools, he won an Ackroyd Scholarship and entered Leeds University in 1938 to study chemistry. In his final year of college, he studied radio physics and electronics and was commissioned by the Royal Navy as a reserve officer specializing in radar.

After World War II Porter did graduate work at Emmanuel College, Cambridge University, under RONALD NORRISH, a pioneer in photochemical investigations of reactive molecules. In his initial studies of fast chemical

GEORGE PORTER

reactions, Porter mixed two flowing gases in a rapidly moving stream and analyzed their reactions with one another at varying distances. Porter and Norrish found this technique useful for measuring chemical reactions with a duration of several thousandths of a second, but it was not fast enough for the study of reactions involving the production of unstable, highly reactive free radicals (atoms or molecules with at least one unpaired electron).

Drawing on Porter's wartime training in radar electronics, the two scientists developed a technique known as flash photolysis. In this technique, a powerful flash of short-wavelength light first breaks a photosensitive chemical into reactive intermediate components. A second, weaker light flash, triggered at a known interval after the first flash, then illuminates the reaction zone, and the resulting absorption spectra of the short-lived free radicals can be measured. By varying the time between the two flashes, Porter and Norrish were able to determine the course of chemical reactions that occur in millionths of a second. By replacing the second flash with a continuous light source and using a very fast light detector, they could observe the concentration of a chosen chemical continuously as a function of time during a reaction initiated by the primary flash. These methods permitted the first observation and measurement of free radicals and the kinetics of their chemical behavior.

After receiving his Ph.D. in chemistry in 1949, Porter was appointed demonstrator in chemistry at Cambridge. There, in collaboration with Norrish, he continued to study the behavior of free radicals and fast chemical reactions. In 1952 he became assistant director of research in the Department of Physical Chemistry. Using flash photolysis, he recorded the absorption spectra of organic free radicals with a lifetime of 1 millisecond. In 1954, as assistant director of research at the British Rayon Research Association, he worked on problems of dye fading and other light effects on fabrics. The following year, Porter became professor of physical chemistry at Sheffield University, where in 1963 he was made Firth Professor and head of the chemistry department.

At Sheffield, Porter applied high-speed flash techniques to the study of more complex chemical reactions, such as the interaction of oxygen with hemoglobin in animals and the properties of chlorophyll in plants. He improved the flash-photolysis technique by using fast-spark light sources and pulsed lasers, which allow the observation of chemical reactions more than 1,000 times faster than could be observed with flash tubes. In 1966 Porter succeeded W. L. BRAGG as Fullerian Professor and director of the Faraday Research Laboratory of the Royal Institution in London.

Porter and Norrish shared half of the 1967 Nobel Prize for Chemistry for "their studies of extremely fast chemical reactions, effected by disturbing the equilibrium by means of very short pulses of energy." The other half was awarded to MANFRED EIGEN, who had investigated fast chemical reactions by different techniques. "The chief importance to chemists of the methods worked out by Eigen, Norrish, and Porter is their usefulness for the most widely diverse problems," said H. A. Ölander of the Royal Swedish Academy of Sciences on presenting the award. "A great many laboratories around the world are now obtaining hitherto undreamt-of results with these methods."

Porter married Stella Brooke in 1949; they have two sons. In his leisure time he enjoys recreational sailing. Porter has also been concerned with communication between scientists in different fields and between scientists and nonscientists. He has served as an adviser to several film and television productions and is a member of many policy and institutional committees involving science and education.

In addition to the Nobel Prize, Porter's awards include the Corday-Morgan Medal of the British Chemical Society (1955), the Davy Medal of the Royal Society (1971), the Robertson Prize of the American National Academy of Sciences (1978), the Rumford Medal

of the Royal Society (1978), the Faraday Medal of the British Chemical Society (1979), and the Longstaff Medal of the Royal Society of Chemistry (1981). He was knighted in 1972. Porter is a member of numerous academic and scientific academies and societies including the Royal Society, the American National Academy of Sciences, the Pontifical Academy of Sciences, the Göttingen Academy of Sciences, the American Academy of Arts and Sciences, and the Spanish Academy of Sciences.

SELECTED WORKS: Chemistry for the Modern World, 1962.

ABOUT: New York Times October 31, 1967; Science November 10, 1967.

PORTER, RODNEY R.
(October 8, 1917–September 7, 1985)
Nobel Prize for Physiology or Medicine, 1972
(shared with Gerald M. Edelman)

The English biochemist Rodney Robert Porter was born in Newton-le-Willows in the English county of Lancashire, the son of Joseph L. Porter, a railway clerk, and his wife, Isobel. Porter attended Ashton-in-Makerfield Grammar School before entering the University of Liverpool, from which he received a bachelor of science degree in biochemistry with honors in 1939. The following year he joined the army and served with the Royal Engineers and the Royal Army Signal Corps during the invasions of Algeria, Sicily, and Italy in World War II. In January 1946 he was discharged from the Central Mediterranean Forces with the rank of major.

After leaving the military, Porter went to Cambridge University to study biochemistry under FREDERICK SANGER. There he read KARL LANDSTEINER's The Specificity of Serological Reactions, a description of the nature of antibodies, which stimulated Porter's lifelong interest in their structure and function. Antibodies are a class of proteins called immunoglobulins (Ig's) that are found in the blood serum. For many centuries it had been known that there are certain diseases (including measles and smallpox, to name two) that an individual can contract only once. Once a person has had the disease, he or she is immune and will never contract it again. In 1890 EMIL VON BEHRING discovered that immunity is caused by antibodies, which combine with disease organisms

RODNEY R. PORTER

or the toxins they produce, thus rendering them inactive. Any substance that stimulates the production of an antibody is called an antigen.

Antibodies are so specific that immunity to one disease does not grant immunity to others. Landsteiner's work in the 1920s and 1930s showed that an immense variety of compounds can act as antigens and that the body must be able to produce millions of different but highly specific antibodies. When Porter began to study antibodies, little was known about their structure. It appeared that all Ig molecules were of the same size and general composition. "This combination of an apparently infinite range of antibody-combining specificity associated with what appeared to be a nearly homogenous group of proteins astonished me," Porter said later, "and indeed still does."

To determine how antibodies combine diversity of function with uniformity of structure, Porter first attempted to break up purified Ig molecules with various enzymes. The most important Ig variety in the blood, IgG, consists of more than 1,300 amino acids. IgG was much too large to be studied using Sanger's methods for determining the order of amino acids in a protein. (Sanger's work at that time was on insulin, which has only 51 amino acids.) There was evidence, however, that the antibody's active site—the part of the molecule that actually combines with the antigen—was relatively small. Porter hoped that by choosing the proper enzyme he could isolate a piece of antibody that was small enough to examine but that still contained the active site. His initial studies showed that papain, a papaya juice enzyme,

could break IgG into fragments about one-quarter the size of a whole antibody. With this work, he received a Ph.D. from Cambridge University, in 1948.

Porter continued investigating antibodies in Sanger's laboratory for a year before moving to the National Institute of Medical Research at Mill Hill, London, in 1949. Although employed as a biochemist in a microbiology research group, he was determined to continue his studies of antibodies. During the 1950s, he improved methods for purifying protein mixtures and used some of those techniques to show that not all IgG molecules are alike, although the differences are small compared to the variety of their activities.

A breakthrough came in 1957, when Porter obtained pure papain instead of the crude enzyme preparations he had used at Cambridge. Repeating his early experiments, he found that pure papain breaks IgG molecules into three pieces (each about one-third the size of the whole molecule) of two different types. One piece was called the "fragment crystallizable," or Fc. Even the purest IgG available at the time would not crystallize, because it was a mixture of slightly different antibody molecules. Fc crystallizes, however, indicating that this part of the antibody is the same in all IgG molecules. Because Fc does not contain the active site, the ability to bind antigens resides in the other two-thirds of the antibody, the two "fragment antigen-binding," or Fab, pieces.

Porter published the results of his research in 1959. The next year GERALD M. EDELMAN and his associates succeeded in splitting IgG by a method that does not break proteins between amino acids, as papain does, but separates individual amino acid chains. In 1960 Porter moved to St. Mary's Hospital Medical School in London, where, repeating Edelman's experiments under different conditions, he proved that Edelman's techniques split the IgG molecule at right angles to the breaks caused by papain. Porter combined his findings with Edelman's and proposed the first satisfactory model of IgG structure in 1962. Although Porter's model did not show what gives antibodies such a wide range of activities, by predicting that Fab fragments consist of parts of two different amino acid chains, it provided a framework for more detailed biochemical studies.

During the 1960s, many scientists in different institutions attempted to explain antibody function in chemical terms. Porter and Edelman played important roles in this work, not only through their personal research but through

831

their encouragement of other scientists to share ideas and information in a series of informal "antibody workshops." Porter and his colleagues contributed numerous studies of the structures of individual IgG molecules, while Edelman and his associates determined the complete amino acid sequence of a single IgG and published their findings in 1969.

Porter and Edelman were awarded the 1972 Nobel Prize for Physiology or Medicine "for their discoveries on the chemical structure of antibodies." Porter titled his Nobel lecture "Structural Studies of Immunoglobulins." By that time, the chief question about antibody diversity was no longer the structure of the molecules but how they are formed, a problem that was solved only in the late 1970s, when the development of recombinant DNA technology enabled researchers to examine antibody genes directly.

In 1967 Porter was appointed Whitley Professor of Biochemistry and chairman of the department of biochemistry at Oxford University, where he continued to conduct research in immunochemistry. Seeking to confirm MACFARLANE BURNET's prediction that antibodies would be found on the surface of antibody-producing cells, Porter devised ways to label specific cell-surface receptors. He also became an authority on the chemistry and genetics of complement, a group of blood proteins (discovered by JULES BORDET) that bind to the Fc region of Ig and are involved in many important immunological reactions.

A month before he was due to retire from his post at Oxford, Porter was killed in an automobile accident in Winchester. He had been married since 1948 to Julia Frances New; the couple had two sons and three daughters.

In addition to the Nobel Prize, Porter received the Gairdner Foundation Award of Merit (1966) and the Ciba Medal of the Biochemical Society (1967). He was a fellow of the Royal Society and a foreign member of the American National Academy of Sciences.

ABOUT: Head, J. J. (ed.) Chemical Aspects of Immunology, 1976; New Scientist October 19, 1972; New York Times October 13, 1972; September 9, 1985; Science October 27, 1972.

POWELL, CECIL F.
(December 5, 1903–August 9, 1969)
Nobel Prize for Physics, 1950

The English physicist Cecil Frank Powell was born in Tonbridge, Kent, to Elizabeth Caroline (Bisacre) Powell, the daughter of a schoolteacher, and Frank Powell, a gunsmith. A lawsuit over an accidental shooting left the boy's father penniless, and the family suffered financial hardships. Powell attended the local elementary school until, at the age of eleven, he won a scholarship to the Judd School in Tonbridge, where one of his teachers turned Powell's interest toward physics. An excellent student, he won scholarships to Sidney Sussex College, Cambridge, from which he graduated with first-class honors in natural science in 1925.

Although he was offered a teaching position at Uppingham, Powell chose to remain at Cambridge for graduate studies under C. T. R. WILSON and ERNEST RUTHERFORD. In his first research effort, Powell sought to improve the cloud chamber invented by Wilson in 1911, so that he would be able to detect more energetic nuclear particles. His efforts failed, but in the course of his experiments, Powell added significantly to an understanding of how gases condense in the cloud chamber. For this work he was awarded a Ph.D. in 1927.

The following year Powell became a research assistant to A. M. Tyndall at the University of Bristol. In 1931 he became a lecturer in physics, followed by successive appointments as a reader in physics (1946), Melville Wills Professor of Physics (1948), and Henry Overton Wills Professor of Physics and director of the university's physics laboratory (1964). From 1964 to 1967 he also served as the university's vice-chancellor.

At Bristol, Powell's initial research involved measuring the motion of ions in gases. Tyndall believed that the university's future depended on research in nuclear physics, and he asked Powell to supervise the construction of a particle accelerator, a project that occupied him until 1939. Powell interrupted his work for several months in 1936 when he was appointed seismologist on a team of British scientists sent to the island of Montserrat in the West Indies, where the government feared the possibility of a catastrophic volcanic eruption that did not, in fact, occur.

Shortly before completing the particle accelerator, Powell became interested in the use of photographic plates to detect the tracks of electrically charged particles. Although this technique had been employed earlier in the twentieth century, researchers had abandoned it, convinced that photographic emulsions did not provide accurate and reliable results. Most subsequent research relied on the Wilson cloud chamber.

It was Powell's belief that photographic

CECIL F. POWELL

emulsions offered a precision tool for particle physics because they were capable of recording the track of every charged particle that struck them, whereas the cloud chamber was sensitive for only short periods. During the late 1930s, Powell urged photographic technicians to develop new, more sensitive emulsions designed specifically for physics research, and he purchased high-quality German microscopes for examining photographic plates. Despite these efforts, Powell's initial investigations were disappointing.

With the outbreak of World War II in 1939, Powell and his colleagues became involved in measurements of neutron energies for the British Atomic Energy Project. Resuming his work on particle detection after the war, Powell persuaded the photographic firms of Ilford Ltd. and Kodak Ltd. to develop special emulsions and new film-developing techniques for recording the tracks of nuclear particles. In 1946 the Ilford laboratory perfected an emulsion that allowed particle tracks to be seen far more clearly and to be measured with much greater reliability. Using the new emulsion, Powell studied cosmic radiation in the Pyrenees. High altitude (Powell did his work at 9,000 feet) is essential in such studies because the earth's atmosphere prevents many cosmic-ray particles from reaching lower levels.

In 1947 Powell and his colleagues discovered a new charged particle in cosmic radiation: the pi-meson, or pion. Its mass is 273 times that of an electron and about one-seventh that of a proton. It is short-lived, decaying into a muon (a relative of the electron) and a neutrino (a

particle lacking both mass and electric charge). The pion is largely responsible for the forces between protons and neutrons that bind the atomic nucleus together. The discovery of the pion, which had been predicted in 1935 by the Japanese physicist HIDEKI YUKAWA, led to the subsequent detection of many other new subatomic particles. Powell and his colleagues also discovered the K-mesons, which are heavier and even shorter-lived than the pi-meson and which also contribute to the forces holding the atomic nucleus together.

Extending his search for cosmic particles, Powell sent photographic plates still higher into the atmosphere, first in balloons and later in rockets. In 1952 he moved his balloon operation to the Mediterranean, where the weather permitted more extended flights. Scientists throughout Europe collaborated with him to launch, retrieve, and analyze the photographic films for tracks of new particles.

Powell was awarded the 1950 Nobel Prize for Physics "for his development of the photographic method of studying nuclear processes and his discoveries regarding mesons made with this method. Powell's special claim to fame," said A. E. Lindh of the Royal Swedish Academy of Sciences, who presented the prize, "is the fact that he has shown that discoveries of fundamental importance can still be made with the simplest apparatus—in this case special nuclear emulsions developed under his general direction—and microscopes."

After receiving the Nobel Prize, Powell continued to study cosmic rays, expanding the scope of the international projects devoted to this research. He also conducted research that involved the use of particle accelerators. Deeply committed to his social responsibility as a scientist, Powell became increasingly active in scientific organizations concerned with the spread of nuclear weapons. As president of the Association of Scientific Workers (1952–1954), he urged the British government to seek a ban on atomic weapons. In 1955 he joined eight other prominent figures, among them ALBERT EINSTEIN, in signing the Russell Statement, initiated by BERTRAND RUSSELL, which warned of the perils of nuclear arms and calling for disarmament conferences. He was also a founding member of the Pugwash Movement for Science and World Affairs and served at the plenary sessions of the first Pugwash Conference in 1957.

In 1932 Powell married Isobel Therese Artner, of Hamburg, Germany, to whom he was introduced by MAX DELBRÜCK. The Powells had two daughters. Shortly after retiring from

Bristol in 1969, Powell died suddenly while vacationing in Milan, Italy.

Powell was the recipient of many honors and awards, including the Hughes Medal (1949) and the Royal Medal (1961) of the Royal Society and the Lomonosov Gold Medal of the Soviet Academy of Sciences (1967). He was a fellow of the Royal Society and a foreign member of numerous scientific societies around the world. From 1961 to 1963 he served as chairman of the Science Policy Committee of CERN (the European Organization for Nuclear Research). The universities of Dublin, Bordeaux, and Warsaw bestowed honorary degrees on him.

SELECTED WORKS: Nuclear Physics in Photographs, 1947, with G. P. S. Occhialini; The Study of Elementary Particles by the Photographic Method, 1959, with others; Selected Papers, 1979.

ABOUT: Biographical Memoirs of Fellows of the Royal Society, volume 17, 1971; Dictionary of Scientific Biography, volume 11, 1975; Oxbury, H. (ed.) Great Britons, 1985.

PREGL, FRITZ
(September 3, 1869–December 13, 1930)
Nobel Prize for Chemistry, 1923

The Austrian chemist Fritz Pregl (prā′ gəl) was born in Laibach (now Ljubljana, Yugoslavia) to Raimund Pregl, the treasurer of a savings bank, and Friderike (Schlacker) Pregl. While he was still young, his father died, and in 1887, after graduating from the Laibach Gymnasium, the boy moved with his mother to Graz. Entering the University of Graz to study medicine, he proved to be such an outstanding student that his physiology teacher, Alexander Rollet, made Pregl his laboratory assistant.

Receiving his medical degree in 1893, Pregl continued to work in Rollet's laboratory while practicing medicine with a specialty in ophthalmology. Although trained in physiology, Pregl grew increasingly interested in chemistry, particularly the reactions of cholic acid (found in bile) and the reason for the high carbon-nitrogen ratio in human urine. His investigations into these topics led to a position as lecturer in physiology at the university in 1899.

To pursue his study of physiological chemistry, Pregl spent the year 1904 in Germany, working with Carl Hufner at the University of Tübingen, WILHELM OSTWALD at the Uni-

FRITZ PREGL

versity of Leipzig, and EMIL FISCHER at the University of Berlin. Upon his return to Graz in 1905, he was appointed assistant professor in the university's Medical Chemistry Laboratory. Two years later he became forensic chemist for the Graz district.

Continuing his investigation of bile acids and protein chemistry, Pregl grappled with the difficulties presented by extremely small samples. The most advanced analytical methods then available—developed in the 1830s by the chemists Justus von Liebig and Jean-Baptiste-André Dumas—required samples weighing at least 0.15 to 0.20 grams. This meant that, for his research on organic molecules, Pregl would have had to process several tons of source material, a prohibitive task. The alternative was to improve the analytical techniques, and it was this path that Pregl chose.

After Pregl accepted a position as professor of medical chemistry at the University of Innsbruck in 1910, he was able to devote most of his time to microanalysis. One of his first goals was to devise a balance more sensitive than those used in conventional macroanalytical chemistry. By modifying a balance developed by German chemist W. H. Kuhlman so that it was accurate to within a thousandth of a milligram, Pregl increased its accuracy tenfold.

Pregl's studies involved organic molecules, which contain chiefly carbon, hydrogen, and oxygen, often with traces of nitrogen, sulfur, phosphorus, and other elements. Their analysis requires determining the proportions of the constituent elements. The first step is to convert all the carbon to carbon dioxide and all the hydrogen to water. These products are then separated by being absorbed into other materials, which, being weighed before and after, reveal the amount of carbon, oxygen, and hydrogen that were absorbed. Because any contact with air would contaminate the samples, this step of the process proved to be the most difficult. Pregl also found that extraneous byproducts of the process, innocuously small by macroanalytic standards, infiltrated the absorbing materials and contaminated the samples. To circumvent this difficulty, he developed a special filter that retained everything except carbon dioxide and water. In an extension of this work, Pregl devised microanalytic methods for the study of such common organic groups as the halogens, carboxyls, and methyls. In another important contribution, he worked with a glassblower to produce extremely small new pieces of apparatus that would permit the use of boiling points to determine molecular weights.

By 1911 Pregl could apply his methods to analyze 7 to 13 milligrams of sample, an amount he was able to reduce to a mere 3 milligrams within two years. Moreover, he cut the length of time needed for analysis to an hour, about a third of the time previously required. Less complicated and far more exact than earlier methods, his techniques were to prove particularly valuable in the analysis of complex biomedical compounds.

Pregl returned to the University of Graz in 1913 as professor of medical chemistry. He became dean of the medical faculty in 1916 and vice-chancellor in 1920. During these years he continued to refine and simplify his methods of microanalysis. His work on serums, bile acids, and various enzymes produced important results.

Pregl was awarded the 1923 Nobel Prize for Chemistry "for his invention of the method of microanalysis of organic substances." In his Nobel lecture he gave generous praise to his associates for their contributions to his work, adding that he was "very hopeful that in the future quantitative organic microanalysis will find many more fields of application and expansion and that it will make possible much insight and discernment."

After receiving the Nobel Prize, Pregl remained active as a researcher and a teacher. His careful and painstakingly exact experimental attitude was passed along to his students, and his laboratory became a world-famous center for organic microanalysis. Known as an earnest, energetic, and unpretentious man, he helped many of his students complete their education during the lean years after World War I. Pregl, who never married, enjoyed mountain climbing and was an enthusiastic bicyclist and motorist. Before his death he donated a large sum of money to the Vienna Academy of Sciences to establish a prize for achievements in microchemistry. After a short illness, he died in Graz at the age of sixty-one.

In addition to the Nobel Prize, Pregl received the Lieben Prize for Chemistry of the Imperial Academy of Science in Vienna (1914) and an honorary doctorate from the University of Göttingen. He was a corresponding member of the Imperial Academy of Science.

SELECTED WORKS: Quantitative Organic Microanalysis, 1920.

ABOUT: Dictionary of Scientific Biography, volume 11, 1975; Farber, E. (ed.) Great Chemists, 1961; Szabadváry, F. History of Analytical Chemistry, 1966.

PRELOG, VLADIMIR
(July 23, 1906–)
Nobel Prize for Chemistry, 1975
(shared with John W. Cornforth)

The Swiss chemist Vladimir Prelog (prel' ōg) was born to Maria (Cettolo) and Milan Prelog in the Serbian town of Sarajevo, now part of Yugoslavia. It was in Sarajevo that the Austrian Archduke Francis Ferdinand and his wife were assassinated in 1914, an event that precipitated World War I, the dissolution of the Austro-Hungarian Empire, and the creation of Yugoslavia, Czechoslovakia, and other nations. During the war Prelog's family moved to Zagreb, where he attended the local gymnasium. From 1924 until 1929 he studied chemistry at the Institute of Technology in Prague.

Prelog received a diploma in chemical engineering (the equivalent of a bachelor's degree) in 1928 and a doctorate in science and technology the following year, when a worldwide economic depression began. Unable to find an academic position, he worked as a staff chemist for six years at G. J. Dříza, a commercial laboratory that manufactured rare chemicals.

In 1935 he was appointed lecturer and, five years later, associate professor at the University of Zagreb. "I did not know that I had to fulfill there all the duties of a full professor and to live on a salary of an underpaid assis-

VLADIMIR PRELOG

tant, but it would probably not have affected my decision if I had known," he later remarked. Organizing a research laboratory, he synthesized adamantane, a hard crystalline substance resembling a diamond and previously found only in small amounts in Moravian petroleum.

Shortly after the German army invaded Zagreb in 1941, Prelog was invited by RICHARD KUHN to lecture in Germany. On his way, he visited LEOPOLD RUŽIČKA in Zurich, Switzerland. With the help of Ružička, who was then chairman of the organic chemistry department at the Federal Institute of Technology, Prelog remained in Zurich with financial support from the Swiss pharmaceutical company Gesellschaft für Chemische Industrie (Ciba). During World War II, Switzerland remained neutral, and Prelog was able to continue his research on the chemistry of natural products, including alkaloids and the antibiotics rifamycin and boromycin.

In 1942 Prelog was appointed privatdocent (a teacher paid for his lectures directly by his students). He became an associate professor in 1947 and a full professor of organic chemistry five years later. In 1957 he succeeded Ružička as director of the Laboratory of Organic Chemistry.

Stereochemistry is the study of the three-dimensional geometric arrangement of atoms within a molecule. In the nineteenth century, Louis Pasteur separated two optical isomers of tartaric acid crystals by hand. He observed that solutions of each isomer rotated a beam of polarized light either to the left or to the right. Pasteur concluded that tartaric acid exists in two distinct forms, each with identical atomic components, but with different internal geometries. A substance rotating light to the left is called levorotatory; to the right, dextrorotatory. He suggested that these forms were mirror images (or enantiomorphs) of each other. In 1884 W. H. Thomson coined the term *chirality* (from the Greek word *cheir,* for hand) to describe such structural and optical differences. Chiral molecules contain a carbon atom to which four different groups are attached; therefore they are not symmetrical.

Isomers have identical molecular formulas but different structures. For example, the isomers ethanol (CH_3CH_2OH) and dimethyl ether (CH_3OCH_3) both have the molecular formula of C_2H_6O. Because the atoms are joined together in completely different ways, the two isomers have different physical properties. In stereoisomers the same basic configurations of atoms are arranged differently in space. Stereoisomers that are not mirror images are called diastereomers; they contain more than one chiral, or asymmetrical, carbon.

After studying the stereochemistry of the malarial drug quinine and its isomers, Prelog turned his attention to compounds containing medium-sized ring structures (with eight to eleven members) and to the mechanisms of transannular reactions, the stereochemical reactions between segments of medium ring structures. Transannular reactions involve the exchange of atoms or molecular groups between proximate segments that may be separated by four or five carbon atoms. The stereochemical or conformational analyses of medium ring structures were exceedingly difficult and required the use of X-ray crystallography, a technique in which atomic structure is deduced from photographs of diffraction patterns formed by X rays passing through a crystal. While studying the stereochemistry of large cyclic polypeptides, Prelog and a colleague, Hans Gerlach, discovered an entirely new type of stereoisomerism, which they called cyclostereoisomerism.

Because of the inherent difficulties of visualizing and discussing the stereochemical shapes of organic compounds, Prelog, together with two Englishmen, R. S. Cahn and Christopher K. Ingold, developed a system of classification and nomenclature of stereoisomers. The Cahn-Ingold-Prelog system is based on three-dimensional models and, in a set of sequence rules, specifies the stereochemical structure of molecules with more than one asymmetrical center. As a result of determining these rules for describing and cataloging stereochemical compounds, Prelog became interested in other problems of stereochemical descriptions, such as group theory, graph theory, and chemical topography.

Prelog and his colleagues synthesized vespirenes, molecules with a rare type of symmetry, and studied the stereochemistry of nonactin (a fungal metabolite that alters the permeability of cell membranes to potassium) and the enzyme fatty acid synthetase, actually a composite enzyme containing all the individual enzymes required for the biosynthesis of fatty acids.

Prelog was awarded the 1975 Nobel Prize for Chemistry "for his research into the stereochemistry of organic molecules and reactions." He shared the award with JOHN W. CORNFORTH. In his presentation speech Arne Fredga of the Royal Swedish Academy of Sciences noted Prelog's "important contributions to enzyme chemistry," work that made it possible "to construct a 'map' of the active part of the enzyme molecule." In his Nobel lecture Prelog said, "The enantiomorphs involved in life processes are the same in men, animals, plants, and microorganisms, independent on their place and time on Earth. . . . One possible explanation is that the creation of living matter was an extremely improbable event, which occurred only once."

Prelog retired from his chair at the Federal Institute of Technology in 1976 but remains on the board of directors of the pharmaceutical company Ciba-Geigy in Basel.

Prelog and Kamila Vitek of Prague were married in 1933; they have one son. Prelog became a Swiss citizen in 1959. His leisure interests include swimming and skiing.

Prelog is a member of the Royal Society of London, the United States National Academy of Sciences, the American Philosophical Society, the American Academy of Arts and Sciences, the Royal Irish Society, and the Soviet Academy of Sciences. His numerous awards and prizes include the August Wilhelm Hofmann Medal of the German Chemical Society and the Davy Medal of the Royal Society of London. He has received honorary degrees from the universities of Zagreb, Liverpool, Brussels, Paris, and Manchester and from Cambridge University.

ABOUT: New York Times October 18, 1975; Science November 21, 1975.

PRIGOGINE, ILYA
(January 25, 1917–)
Nobel Prize for Chemistry, 1977

The Belgian chemist Ilya Prigogine (prē gō' jeen) was born in Moscow at the start of the Russian Revolution. He was one of two sons of Roman Prigogine, a chemical engineer, and the former Julia Wichman, a musician. His mother taught him to play the piano and later recalled that he could read music before he could read words. In 1921 the family left the Soviet Union as exiles, living in Lithuania and Germany before settling in Belgium in 1929. These years of migration left Prigogine with "a vivid sensitivity to change," as he said later. "I went on to study physics and chemistry. And I was astonished that the time element was missing." Although interested in history and philosophy, he hoped to become a concert pianist.

Prigogine received his early formal education in Berlin and Brussels and then studied chemistry at the Free University of Brussels. He was especially drawn to the study of thermodynamics, the science that deals with heat and other forms of energy. He received his B.S. from the Free University in 1943 and his Ph.D. two years later, with a dissertation on the significance of time and change in thermodynamic systems. He was appointed professor of physical chemistry at the Free University in 1947, and in 1962 he became director of the Solvay International Institute of Physics and Chemistry in Brussels.

The principles of thermodynamics were formulated in the middle of the nineteenth century after the invention of the steam engine, when considerable interest was focused on the interaction of heat, electricity, and mechanical work. One version of the first law of thermodynamics, which is the principle of the conservation of energy, states that in any closed system, energy is neither lost nor gained when it is converted from one form to another. The second law of thermodynamics, the principle of entropy, describes the tendency of systems to move from a state of greater order to one of lesser order. Entropy is a measure of the disorder or randomness of a system; the greater the disorder, the greater the entropy. In the nineteenth century, the American mathematical physicist Josiah Willard Gibbs developed a theory of statistical thermodynamics for reversible systems in equilibrium. Théophile De Donder, Prigogine's professor at the Free University and a founder of the Brussels School

ILYA PRIGOGINE

of Thermodynamics, formulated a theory for nonequilibrium irreversible systems.

An example of reversible equilibrium is the melting of a block of ice at a temperature only slightly above the freezing point of water. The entropy of the block of ice increases as ice crystals on its surface melt to form water; simultaneously, the entropy of the watery surface film of the ice decreases as it is heated by the heat of melting. This process may be reversed by lowering the temperature of the system to the freezing point: the surface water crystallizes, and the entropy of the ice decreases, while the entropy of the water film increases. In each process, melting and freezing at a temperature at or near the freezing point, the total entropy of the system is unchanged. An example of an irreversible nonequilibrium system is the melting of an ice cube in a glass of water at room temperature. The entropy of the ice cube increases until all the crystals have melted. As heat diffuses throughout the water in the glass, to its surface, and into the surrounding air, the entropy of the total system is increased.

Prigogine was most interested in the thermodynamics of nonequilibrium systems, specifically open systems in which matter or energy or both are exchanged with the environment in reactions that increase or decrease with time. To explain the behavior of systems far from equilibrium, he formulated the theory of dissipative structures. Believing that nonequilibrium could be a source of organization and order, he conceived of dissipative structures in terms of a mathematical model with time-dependent nonlinear functions that describes the ability of systems to exchange matter or energy with their environment and to restabilize themselves spontaneously. A now-classic example of dissipative structure in physical chemistry is known as the Benard's instability. This occurs when layers of liquid fluid are heated from below. At sufficiently large temperature gradients, heat is transferred through the fluid by convection, and a large number of molecules in the liquid arrange themselves in specific geometric forms that resemble living cells.

It soon became apparent that human society as well as biology offered examples of dissipative and nondissipative structures. In 1952 the English mathematician Alan M. Turing first suggested that thermodynamic instabilities of the type imagined by Prigogine and his colleagues were characteristic of self-organizing systems. In the 1960s and 1970s Prigogine extended his theory of dissipative structures to descriptions of the formation and development of embryos. Critical bifurcation points in his mathematical model were correlated with the point at which a biological system in chaos becomes coherent and stabilized. Prigogine suggested that his theories and mathematical models of systems that change with time could be applied to evolutionary schemes, social systems, vehicular-traffic patterns, and natural resource management policies, as well as to such fields as population growth, meteorology, and astronomy.

In 1967 Prigogine was appointed director of the Ilya Prigogine Center for Statistical Mechanics and Thermodynamics, which he founded at the University of Texas in Austin. Since then he has divided his time between Brussels and Austin.

For "his contributions to nonequilibrium thermodynamics, particularly the theory of dissipative structures," Prigogine was awarded the 1977 Nobel Prize for Chemistry. "Prigogine's researches into irreversible thermodynamics have fundamentally transformed and revitalized the science," said Stig Clæsson of the Royal Swedish Academy of Sciences in his presentation speech. This work has given thermodynamics "a new relevance and created theories to bridge the gaps between chemical, biological, and social scientific fields of inquiry," Clæsson continued, adding that "his works are also distinguished by an elegance and a lucidity which have earned him the epithet 'the poet of thermodynamics.' "

Prigogine married Marina Prokopowicz in 1961; they have two sons. Known to his colleagues as a gracious, outgoing person with a wide range of interests, including literature and archaeology, he still plays the piano and enjoys listening to music.

In addition to the Nobel Prize, Prigogine has received the Svante Arrhenius Gold Medal of the Royal Swedish Academy of Sciences (1969), the Bourke Medal of the British Chemical Society (1972), the Cothenius Medal of the Leopoldina German Academy of Researchers in Natural Sciences (1975), and the Rumford Medal of the Royal Society of London (1976). He is a member of the Royal Academy of Belgium, the New York Academy of Sciences, the Romanian Academy of Science, the Royal Society of Sciences (Uppsala), and the Leopoldina German Academy of Researchers in Natural Sciences. He is a foreign member of the American Academy of Arts and Sciences, the Chemical Society of Poland, and the American Chemical Society, among other organizations. He has received honorary degrees from the universities of Newcastle upon Tyne, Poitiers, Chicago, Bordeaux, Uppsala, Liège, Aix-en-Provence, Georgetown, Kraków, and Rio de Janeiro.

SELECTED WORKS: The Molecular Theory of Solutions, 1957, with others; Non-Equilibrium Statistical Mechanics, 1962; Introduction to Thermodynamics of Irreversible Processes, 1962; Non-Equilibrium Thermodynamics, 1966, with others; Surface Tension and Absorption, 1966, with others; Kinetic Theory of Vehicular Traffic, 1971, with Robert Herman; Thermodynamic Theory of Structure Stability and Fluctuations, 1971, with P. Glansdorff; The Macroscopic Level of Quantum Mechanics, 1972, with others; Non-Simple Liquids, 1975, with Stuart Alan Rice; Self-Organization in Non-Equilibrium Systems, 1977, with G. Nicolis; From Being to Becoming: Time and Complexity in the Physical Sciences, 1980; Order Out of Chaos, 1984, with Isabelle Stengers.

ABOUT: Cousins, N. Nobel Prize Conversations, 1985; Current Biography February 1987; Griffin, D. R. Physics and the Ultimate Significance of Time, 1986; Hershey, D. Must We Grow Old, 1984; New York Times October 12, 1977; Rice, S. A. (ed.) For Ilya Prigogine, 1978; Science November 18, 1977; Weintraub, P. (ed.) The Omni Interviews, 1984.

PROKHOROV, ALEKSANDR

(July 11, 1916–   )
Nobel Prize for Physics, 1964
(shared with Nikolai Basov and Charles H. Townes)

The Russian physicist Aleksandr Mikhailovich Prokhorov (prô kə rôf′), the son of Mikhail Ivanovich Prokhorov and Mariya Ivanovna Mikhailovna Prokhorova, was born in Atherton, Australia, where the family had fled in 1911 after the elder Prokhorov's escape from exile in Siberia. After the Russian Revolution, the family returned to the Soviet Union in 1923. After graduating with honors from the Department of Physics at Leningrad State University in 1939, Prokhorov began graduate work in the Oscillation Laboratory of the P. N. Lebedev Physical Institute of the Soviet Academy of Sciences in Moscow. There he studied the propagation of radio waves over the earth's surface and, with one of his research directors, the physicist V. V. Migulin, proposed a novel technique for using radio interference to explore the ionosphere, one of the layers of the upper atmosphere.

Inducted into the Soviet army in June 1941, Prokhorov was wounded twice before returning in 1944 to the Lebedev Institute, where he undertook an investigation of frequency stabilization in vacuum-tube oscillators. His candidate's degree (similar to a master's degree) thesis in 1946 was on the theory of nonlinear oscillations. For this work, Prokhorov and two other physicists were awarded the prize named in honor of the academician Leonid I. Mandelshtam, a distinguished Soviet radio physicist. In 1947 Prokhorov began a study of the radiation from electrons in a synchrotron (a device that accelerates charged particles such as protons and electrons in widening circles to very high energies) and demonstrated experimentally that the electrons radiate at wavelengths of the order of centimeters, in the microwave region. This work formed the basis of his 1951 dissertation for the degree of doctor of physical and mathematical sciences and led to many later investigations by others.

After his appointment as assistant director of the Oscillation Laboratory in 1950, Prokhorov became interested in radio spectroscopy. He organized a team of young research scientists who applied radar and radio broadcasting techniques, developed primarily in the United States and England during and after World War II, to study the rotational and vibrational spectra of molecules. Prokhorov focused his research on a class of molecules called asymmetric tops, which have three different moments of inertia and are the most difficult to analyze in terms of their rotational spectra. In addition to purely spectroscopic research, he carried out a theoretical analysis of the application of microwave absorption spectra to improving frequency and time standards. This latter analysis led to his collaboration with NIKOLAI BASOV on research into molecular oscillators, now called masers (an acronym for

PROKHOROV

ALEKSANDR PROKHOROV

microwave amplification by stimulated emission of radiation).

It is a basic principle of quantum physics that atoms and molecules have energies (arising from the locations and motions of their electrons) that are restricted to certain discrete values, or energy levels. A set of allowed energy levels is unique to a particular atom or molecule. Another principle states that electromagnetic radiation, such as light or radio waves, is composed of discrete units of energy (photons) whose energy is proportional to the frequency. If a photon has an energy equal to the difference between two energy levels, the atom or molecule can absorb the radiation and jump from the lower to the higher level. It later spontaneously falls to a lower energy level (not always the one it started from), giving off the energy difference between the two levels in the form of a photon of radiation. The radiation frequency, again, is in accordance with the energy of the emitted photon. In 1917 AL-BERT EINSTEIN, investigating the interaction between radiation and matter in a confined region, developed an equation that described the already known processes of absorption and spontaneous emission. His equation also predicted a third process, called stimulated emission, the transition of an excited atom or molecule in a state of high energy to a lower energy level merely because of the presence of radiation whose photons have an energy equal to the difference between those two levels. The energy lost in the transition is emitted as photons of the same kind that stimulated the emission.

Prokhorov and Basov saw a way to exploit stimulated emission. If they segregated excited molecules from those in the ground state, which can be done with nonhomogeneous electric or magnetic fields, they could then create a population of molecules at some upper energy level. Incoming radiation whose frequency (photon energy) matched the difference between the excited and ground levels would then trigger stimulated emission of radiation of the same frequency, resulting in amplification. By feeding back some of the energy to excite more molecules, the amplifier could be turned into a molecular oscillator capable of generating radiation on a sustained basis.

The two physicists discussed the possibility of such a molecular oscillator at the All-Union Conference on Radio Spectroscopy in May 1952, but they did not publish until October 1954. In 1955 they proposed a new "three-level method" for producing a maser. In this method, atoms or molecules are "pumped" to the highest of three energy levels by absorption of radiation whose photons have an energy corresponding to the difference between the highest and lowest levels. Most of the atoms quickly fall to the intermediate energy level, which becomes relatively densely populated. Maser action then occurs at a frequency corresponding to the energy difference between the intermediate and lowest levels.

Ten months before Prokhorov and Basov published their paper in 1954, CHARLES H. TOWNES, an American physicist at Columbia University who had independently reached similar conclusions, constructed a working maser that confirmed their predictions. Townes used a resonant chamber filled with excited ammonia molecules and achieved enormous amplification of microwaves at 24,000 megahertz. In 1960 the three-level principle was validated when the American physicist Theodore H. Maiman, working at the Hughes Aircraft Company, amplified light waves, using a long crystal of synthetic ruby as a resonant chamber encircled by a spiral tube of xenon gas flashed to provide the stimulating radiation. Because Maiman used light, his device was called a laser, for light amplification by stimulated emission of radiation.

As director of the Oscillation Laboratory at the Lebedev Institute since 1954, Prokhorov continued to develop the laboratory, which eventually gave rise to two new facilities, the Radio Astronomy and the Quantum Radio Physics laboratories. He also consulted for numerous scientific institutions on questions of quantum electronics and established the Radio

Spectroscopy Laboratory at the Nuclear Physics Research Institute of Moscow State University, where he attained the rank of professor in 1957.

Since the mid-1950s, Prokhorov has concentrated on maser and laser development and on the search for crystals with suitable spectral and relaxation properties. His detailed studies of ruby, one of the best crystals for lasers, led to its widespread use at microwave and optical wavelengths. To overcome certain problems in molecular oscillators operating in the sub-millimeter-wavelength region, Prokhorov proposed a new open resonator consisting of two parallel mirrors, a type that was to prove extremely useful in the development of lasers in the 1960s.

The 1964 Nobel Prize for Physics was divided, one half being awarded to Prokhorov and Basov and the other half to Townes "for [their] fundamental work in the field of quantum electronics, which has led to the construction of oscillators and amplifiers based on the maser-laser principle."

As deputy director of the Lebedev Institute since 1972, Prokhorov has continued to expand his research on lasers, including their applicability to the investigation of multiquantum processes and thermonuclear fusion.

Prokhorov married Galina Alekseevna Shelepina, a geographer, in 1941. They have one son.

Elected a corresponding member of the Soviet Academy of Sciences in 1960, Prokhorov became a full academician in 1966 and a member of its Presidium in 1970. He is also an honorary member of the American Academy of Arts and Sciences. In 1969 he was appointed editor in chief of the *Great Soviet Encyclopedia,* and he accepted honorary professorships at Delhi University (1967) and Bucharest University (1971). He was named a Hero of Socialist Labor by the Soviet government in 1969. He has been a member of the Communist party since 1950.

SELECTED WORKS: Problems in Solid-State Physics, 1984, with A. S. Prokhorov.

ABOUT: New York Times October 30, 1964; Science November 7, 1964.

PURCELL, EDWARD M.

(August 30, 1912–)
Nobel Prize for Physics, 1952
(shared with Felix Bloch)

The American physicist Edward Mills Purcell was born in Taylorville, Illinois, to Edward A. Purcell and Mary Elizabeth (Mills) Purcell. Educated in public schools in Taylorville and Mattoon, Purcell entered Purdue University in Lafayette, Indiana, in 1929. By the time he received a B.S. in electrical engineering in 1933, his interest had already turned to physics. After a year as an exchange student at the technical university in Karlsruhe, Germany, Purcell began graduate studies in physics at Harvard University, where he received his M.A. in 1936 and his Ph.D. in 1938. He remained at Harvard as an instructor until 1940.

During World War II, Purcell joined the Massachusetts Institute of Technology Radiation Laboratory, established for the purpose of developing microwave radar. There he supervised the Fundamental Studies Group (1941–1945), which was devising new techniques for the production and detection of microwaves (high-frequency electromagnetic radiation). During this period he was associated with I. I. RABI, who had studied molecular and atomic properties by means of radio waves. Purcell returned to Harvard in 1946 as an associate professor of physics and became a full professor in 1949. At Harvard he applied the knowledge of microwave and radio-frequency radiation he had acquired in the development of radar to the research on nuclear magnetic moments that was to earn him the Nobel Prize.

It had been known since the 1920s that an atomic nucleus spins and that it acts as a tiny magnet. Precise knowledge of the magnetic moments (magnetic strengths) of different nuclei was important to physicists who sought to understand the behavior of the nucleus; in addition, they needed to know the magnetic moment of the proton (a fundamental constituent of the nucleus). In the 1930s Rabi had developed a technique for measuring magnetic moments using radio waves, but his method required vaporizing the sample. Purcell set out to develop a technique that was not only nondestructive but also more precise than Rabi's. At about the same time, FELIX BLOCH of Stanford University (who had also been involved with radar during the war) began working on the same problem. Simultaneously and independently, the two researchers achieved virtually identical methods for measuring nuclear magnetic moments.

The magnetic moment of a nucleus causes it to precess in a magnetic field. Precession is the rotation of the axis of a spinning object when the axis is tilted; a familiar example is the wobbling motion of a spinning top (although this happens under the influence of gravity rather than magnetism). The fre-

EDWARD M. PURCELL

quency, or rate, of nuclear precession depends on the strength of the magnetic field and on the magnetic moment of the particular nucleus. Thus, if the strength of the field is known and the precession frequency can be determined, the magnetic moment can be calculated. The technique Purcell developed in 1946 involved placing the sample to be studied between the poles of a small magnet that could be activated by radio signals. The field of the magnet fluctuated (turned on and off) with a frequency corresponding to that of the controlling radio waves. The small magnet, in turn, was placed in the much stronger field of a large nonfluctuating magnet. The strong fixed field caused the nuclei in the sample to precess at a fixed (though unknown) frequency. When the fluctuation frequency of the weak field exactly matched the precessional frequency of the nuclei, the spin orientation of the nuclei would suddenly reverse—an easily detected effect called nuclear magnetic resonance (NMR). This effect allowed the precession frequency to be determined with great precision: it was the same as the radio frequency being used at the instant NMR occurred. Once the precession frequency of the nuclei in the sample was known, the nuclear magnetic moment could be calculated with equal precision.

Purcell's technique did not alter in any perceptible way the substance being studied, and it allowed calculation of magnetic moments with a precision greater than that of almost any other physical measurement. Furthermore, once an atom's nuclear magnetic moment was determined, it could be used, in turn,

to measure the strength of any magnetic field. Thus, in addition to providing essential information to nuclear physicists, nuclear magnetic resonance provided a convenient and very precise method of measuring magnetism by means of radio waves.

Using NMR, Purcell found that the behavior of the magnetic moments of nuclei in a molecule is altered by the magnetic fields of surrounding electrons. While physicists attempting to determine nuclear properties might view these effects as irritating molecular artifacts, chemists found them to be of great importance and utility, since they reveal a great deal about the structure of the molecule in question. NMR rapidly came to be one of the great analytic tools of chemistry. In addition, NMR measurements can be used to study living organisms without causing damage. Technology developed in the 1970s has allowed the development of NMR scanners that can image specific chemical reactions within human beings or other large mammals. In addition to being extraordinarily useful for research, NMR scanners have become powerful tools for medical diagnosis. Commercially produced NMR diagnostic scanning equipment became available to the medical community in the mid-1980s.

In 1951 Purcell's investigations using NMR revealed that interstellar hydrogen atoms emit electromagnetic radiation at a radio frequency corresponding to a wavelength of 21 centimeters. Purcell quickly realized that this emission presented a new observational window for astronomical studies. Interstellar space was thought to contain vast clouds of hydrogen, but since much of the hydrogen in space does not emit light, it is unobservable by optical methods. Purcell, working with Harold Ewen, was instrumental in building the first radio telescope, designed to detect the 21-centimeter wavelength. Radio telescopes have allowed mapping of the overall structure of the galaxy despite the obscuring galactic dust clouds.

The application of Purcell's research in physics to revolutionary developments in astronomy, chemistry, and medicine is an outstanding example of how basic research can have practical effects that go far beyond the original field of study.

Purcell and Bloch were awarded the 1952 Nobel Prize for Physics "for their development of new methods for nuclear magnetic precision measurements and discoveries in connection therewith." In his Nobel lecture Purcell said of nuclear precession, "I have not yet lost a feeling of wonder, and of delight, that this delicate motion should reside in all the ordinary things around us. . . . I remember, in the winter of our first experiments, . . . looking on the snow with new eyes. There the snow lay around my doorstep—great heaps of protons quietly precessing in the earth's magnetic field. To see the world for a moment as something rich and strange is the private reward of many a discovery."

In 1958 Purcell became Donner Professor of Science at Harvard. He served as a scientific adviser to the United States (1957–1960) and to the President's Scientific Advisory Committee (1957–1960, 1962–1966). In 1960 he became the Gerhard Grade University Professor at Harvard, a position he held until his retirement. During this period Purcell made significant contributions to physics education at the high school and college levels and served on the committee that planned the Physical Science Study Committee revision of the American high school physics curriculum. Purcell was active in the development of the Berkeley university-level introductory physics course, for which he wrote *Electricity and Magnetism* (1965), a book that is widely regarded as a masterpiece of pedagogy. In 1980 he became emeritus professor at Harvard.

Purcell married Beth C. Bussner in 1937, when he was still a doctoral student; they have two sons. For recreation he enjoys hiking, skiing, and visiting modern art museums.

In addition to the Nobel Prize, Purcell has received the Oersted Medal of the American Association of Physics Teachers (1968) and the National Medal of Science of the National Science Foundation (1980). He is a member of the National Academy of Sciences, the American Academy of Arts and Sciences, the American Philosophical Society, and the American Physical Society, of which he was president in 1970. From 1950 to 1971 he was a senior fellow in the Society of Fellows at Harvard University. He holds an honorary degree from Purdue University.

ABOUT: Current Biography September 1954; Science October 16, 1953; Waltz, G. What Makes a Scientist? 1959.

QUASIMODO, SALVATORE
(August 20, 1901–June 14, 1968)
Nobel Prize for Literature, 1959

The Italian poet Salvatore Quasimodo (kwä se mō′ dō) was born in Modica, a small town near Syracuse, Sicily, to Gaetano Quasimodo and Clotilde (Ragusa) Quasimodo. His father was a railroad stationmaster whose job required the family to move frequently from one small Sicilian town to another. In 1916 Quasimodo and his older brother enrolled in technical school in Messina, where the family was living at the time. Although Quasimodo had wanted to study at the *ginnasio,* a high school that offered academic courses, his parents felt that technical training would be more practical. During this period, he became interested in poetry and literature and began reading the classics and contemporary Russian and French literature. He also published his first poems and, with a group of friends, started a short-lived newspaper.

In 1919 Quasimodo left Messina to study engineering at the Polytechnical Institute in Rome. Financial constraints forced him to abandon his engineering studies, however, and he left school with a degree in surveying. In 1920 he married Bice Donetti. He was encouraged to pursue his interest in literature by Monsignor Rampolla, a Sicilian priest in Rome, and Quasimodo began teaching himself to read Greek and Latin. Unsure of his ability as a writer, he held a variety of technical jobs during this period.

Quasimodo was appointed to the government Civil Engineering Department in 1926, a position that required him to travel throughout Italy. His open antipathy to the Fascists made it impossible for him to find work as a journalist, but he began to write poetry in earnest. In 1929 Quasimodo's brother-in-law, Elio Vittorini, later to become a leading novelist, critic, and translator, introduced him into literary circles in Florence. There he met the poets EUGENIO MONTALE and Giuseppe Ungaretti as well as Alessandro Bonsanti, editor of the magazine *Solaria,* which published some of Quasimodo's poems.

In 1930 Bonsanti sponsored the publication of Quasimodo's first collection of poems, *Acque e terre* (Waters and Lands). The poems, which describe scenes from Quasimodo's native Sicily, include at least one acknowledged masterpiece, "Vento a Tindari" ("Wind at Tindari"). Many of the traits of hermetic poetry are already present in this first collection. According to the American critic Thomas G. Bergin, the distinguishing features of hermeticism are "a highly personalized imagery, the cult of the word, and an austere intellectualism, often cryptic and obscure." Quasimodo subscribed to the idea of the "magic of the word," the belief that words have an identity

SALVATORE QUASIMODO

and autonomy apart from their purely descriptive function.

Over the next few years, Quasimodo published several other volumes of poetry: *Oboe sommerso* (The Sunken Oboe, 1932); *Odore di eucalyptus e altri versi* (*The Scent of Eucalyptus and Other Verses,* 1933); *Erato e Apollion* (Aerato and Apollyon, 1936); and *Poesie* (Poems, 1938). His poetry moved further in the direction of hermeticism, abandoning the realism of *Acque e terre* in favor of a more personal, allusive style. Quasimodo won the Florentine Prize of the Antico Fattore in 1932, the year after Montale had won the same prize. Settling in Milan in 1934, he became involved with a group of southern Italian intellectuals known as the "young immigrants." His daughter, Orietta, was born out of wedlock in 1935 to Amelia Specialetti.

Quasimodo resigned from the Civil Engineering Department in 1938 to take a position as assistant to Cesare Zavattini, the editor of several periodicals owned by the publishing house of Mondadori. The next year Quasimodo became literary editor of *Il tempo* (The Time), a weekly magazine. The dancer Maria Cumani bore him a son, Alessandro, that same year. During this period he began translating; his *Lirici greci* (*Greek Lyrics*), a presentation of ancient Greek poetry in a radically modern Italian idiom, was published in 1940. Quasimodo was named professor of Italian literature at Milan's Giuseppe Verdi Conservatory in 1941. In 1942 he published *Ed è subito sera* (And Suddenly It's Evening), a selection and revision of his entire poetic output at that point.

The horrors of World War II and their effects on the land and people of Italy deeply affected Quasimodo and brought a change to his writing style. He became involved in literary groups struggling to bring about liberation, and he was briefly imprisoned in Bergamo for anti-Fascist activity. The resultant change in his work is often described as a shift from hermeticism to engagement. The critic C. A. McCormick described this shift as "a passage from the poetry of the private world, closed in upon itself, to poetry of more open communication."

Although Quasimodo joined the Italian Communist party in 1945, the association was short-lived. When the party insisted that he write political poems, Quasimodo resigned in protest. During the period immediately after the war, he published a spate of essays, translations, and poems, including the poetry collection *Giorno dopo giorno* (Day After Day, 1947), which reflected the change in his style brought about by the war.

After the death of his first wife in 1948, Quasimodo married Maria Cumani. He began writing theater criticism during this time, first for *Omnibus* and then for *Il tempo.* In 1956 his poetry collection *Il falso e vero verde* (The False and True Green), first published in 1954, was issued along with an influential essay, "Discorso sulla poesia" (Discourse on Poetry); in it he argued that the poet has a responsibility to express his ideological convictions in his poetry. In late 1958 Quasimodo visited the Soviet Union where, suffering a heart attack, he remained until May of the following year.

Although a respected figure, Quasimodo was not generally considered at this time the most significant living Italian writer. It therefore came as a surprise in literary circles when Quasimodo was awarded the 1959 Nobel Prize for Literature "for his lyrical poetry, which with classical fire expresses the tragic experience of life in our own times." In his acceptance speech, Quasimodo expressed his belief that "poetry reveals itself in solitude, and . . . from this solitude it moves out in every direction. . . . Poetry, even lyrical poetry, is always 'speech.' The listener may be the physical or metaphysical interior of the poet, or a man, or a thousand men."

Quasimodo and his wife Maria separated permanently in 1960. During the 1960s he published a book of essays, *Il poeta e il politico, e altri saggi* (The Poet and the Politician and Other Essays, 1960), and a final collection of poems, *Dare e avere* (1966, translated into

English as *To Give and to Have, and Other Poems* in 1969 and then as *Debit and Credit* in 1972). In 1968, while presiding over a poetry competition in Amalfi, he suffered a cerebral hemorrhage that resulted in his death.

Although contemporary critics generally regard Quasimodo as an important exponent of hermeticism, he has never entirely escaped comparison with Montale and Ungaretti. Writing in 1959, the American scholar Glauco Cambon remarked that "Quasimodo certainly has an important place [among] contemporary Italian [poets], even if some of his recent work is disappointing." In an article published the following year in *Books Abroad,* the critic Francis Golffing qualified his praise of Quasimodo, calling him a "rather simple poet, compared with such writers as Montale, [T.S.] ELIOT, and [WILLIAM BUTLER] YEATS." Nonetheless, the English scholar C. M. Bowra claimed in 1960 that Quasimodo, "more than any living poet, speaks for the whole of Europe." Quasimodo is also highly regarded for his critical studies and librettos, and especially for his translations of works by Shakespeare; by classical Greek and Latin writers, including Homer, Aeschylus, Sophocles, Virgil, and Catullus; and by European and American contemporaries, including PABLO NERUDA.

In addition to the Nobel Prize, Quasimodo received the Etna-Taormina Prize for Poetry in 1953 (shared with Dylan Thomas), the Viareggio Prize in 1958, and an honorary degree from Oxford University in 1967.

ADDITIONAL WORKS IN ENGLISH TRANSLATION: The Incomparable Earth, 1958; The Selected Writings of Salvatore Quasimodo, 1960; Quasimodo: Selected Poems, 1965; Complete Poems, 1984.

ABOUT: Burnshaw, S. (ed.) The Poem Itself, 1960; Ciardi, J. Dialogue With an Audience, 1963; Cohen, J. M. Poetry of This Age, 1966; Curley, A., and Curley, D. N. Modern Romance Literatures, 1967; Current Biography March 1960; Lind, L. Twentieth-Century Italian Poetry, 1974.

QUIDDE, LUDWIG
(March 23, 1858–March 4, 1941)
Nobel Prize for Peace, 1927
(shared with Ferdinand Buisson)

The German pacifist Ludwig Quidde (kvid′ ə) was born in Bremen, the oldest son of a prosperous merchant. An independent income permitted him to devote his life to the study of history and the cause of peace. As a

LUDWIG QUIDDE

youth Quidde did well in school, and he went on to study medieval German history at the universities of Strasbourg and Göttingen. After receiving a Ph.D., Quidde became a member of the editorial board that was preparing the medieval documents of the Reichstag (German imperial parliament) for publication. In 1889 he founded the *Zeitschrift für Geschichtswissenschaft* (German Review of Historical Sciences), which he edited for six years. From 1890 to 1892 he also served as secretary of the Prussian Historical Institute in Rome.

Quidde was converted to pacifism by his reading of history and by the influence of Margarethe Jacobson, whom he married in 1882. In 1891 he joined the German Peace Society, founded by ALFRED FRIED in 1892 and modeled after a similar society founded in Austria by BERTHA VON SUTTNER. In 1893 he published a pamphlet, *Der Militarismus im heutigen deutschen Reich* (Militarism in Today's Germany), an anonymous attack on the spirit of militarism that was sweeping Germany. Quidde stepped up his criticism in 1894 by publishing under his own name a pamphlet entitled *Caligula: Eine Studie über römischen Cäsarenwahnsinn* (Caligula: A Study in Roman Caesarean Madness). Although the pamphlet purported to be a historical study, it implicitly satirized the German emperor, Wilhelm II. Tried on a charge of libel, Quidde was convicted and sentenced to three months' imprisonment.

In 1984 Quidde solidified his commitment to the ideals of pacifism by forming an antiwar group in Munich and by attending various international peace conferences. He entered the political movement for pacifism the following year by helping to reorganize the German People's party, an antimilitarist and anti-Prussian organization. After giving a political speech in 1896, he was convicted of high treason and served three months in a Munich prison.

Within a few years Quidde became a recognized leader of the international pacifist movement. He was a member of the Council of the INTERNATIONAL PEACE BUREAU in Bern, Switzerland, and head of the World Peace Congress of 1901 in Glasgow, Scotland. The following year he was elected to the Munich City Council. In 1905 he and FRÉDÉRIC PASSY attempted to forge a peace agreement between France and Germany, and in 1907 Quidde organized the World Peace Congress in Munich. In 1907–1908 he held a seat in the Bavarian Parliament as a member of the German People's party.

Quidde was among the pacifists from several nations who sought to curtail the arms race that preceded World War I. When the conflict began in 1914, Quidde's pacifism obliged him to leave Germany. Accounts vary on several incidents in his life. They place him at this time in either Switzerland or The Hague but agree that he maintained his contacts with other international pacifists and attended an antiwar conference in The Hague in 1915. He also continued to publish pamphlets suggesting ways to eliminate war by reordering international relations. For example, he proposed that nations renounce their desire to annex territory and instead seek a peace agreement giving all countries freedom of the seas and the right to unfettered trade.

After the war Quidde returned to Germany and attempted to consolidate the remnants of the peace movement there. He headed the German Peace Cartel, which was composed of twenty-one different peace organizations. In 1919 he was elected a deputy to the Weimar National Assembly. He opposed the Treaty of Versailles because it placed all responsibility for World War I on Germany. He strongly supported the League of Nations as the best hope for world peace. Opposed to rearmament, in 1924 Quidde wrote a series of newspaper articles accusing Germany of secretly building an air force and recruiting youth troops for military training in violation of the Versailles treaty. He argued that such actions gave France an excuse to levy more of the punitive measures that were devastating Germany's economy. He was arrested and imprisoned briefly for "collaborating with the enemy."

Quidde shared the 1927 Nobel Prize for Peace with FERDINAND BUISSON, a French pacifist. The Norwegian Nobel Committee credited the two recipients with fostering "the emergence in France and Germany of a public opinion which favors peaceful international cooperation." As Fredrik Stang of the Nobel committee stated in his presentation speech, "The great organized work for peace must be preceded by the education of the people, by a campaign to turn mass thinking away from war as a recognized means of settling disputes, and to substitute another and much higher ideal: peaceful cooperation between nations, with an international court of justice to resolve any disagreements which might arise between them." Stang went on to say: "It is in the task of reorienting public opinion that Buisson and Quidde have played such prominent roles. They have guided this work in two countries where it has been particularly difficult to accomplish but where the need for it has been commensurately great."

In his Nobel lecture Quidde discussed security and disarmament. "Lightly armed nations," he pointed out, "can move toward war just as easily as those which are armed to the teeth, and they will do so if the usual causes of war are not removed. Even a total and universal disarmament does not guarantee the maintenance of peace. Should the occasion arise, flails and scythes would again come into their own as weapons. Disarmed nations embroiled in war would obtain modern weapons as quickly as possible by converting peacetime industry."

On arms limitation, he said, "The increase in armaments, the endless arms race—this in itself is a potential cause of war. Influential military men want to demonstrate that their profession has some use. Many people who are disturbed by the terrible growth of armaments become accustomed and resigned to the belief that war is inevitable. They say, 'Better a terrible end than an endless terror.' That is the greatest cause of war." Quidde stressed his lifelong conviction that international law could assure peace. "We must learn to recognize that Europe has a choice only between the total devastation that will result from a future war employing gas and other such modern methods of war, and peace secured by rule of law," he said.

When Adolf Hitler came to power in 1933, Quidde was again obliged to flee Germany. He settled in Geneva, where he remained active in the international pacifist movement until his death on March 4, 1941.

WORKS IN ENGLISH TRANSLATION: "The Future of Germany," Living Age April 15, 1924.

RABI, I. I.
(July 29, 1898–   )
Nobel Prize for Physics, 1944

I. I. RABI

The American physicist Isidor Isaac Rabi (rä′ bē) was born in Rymanów, in what was then the Austro-Hungarian Empire (now Poland). He was the first of two children of David Rabi, an unskilled worker, and Jennie (Teig) Rabi. Shortly after Rabi's birth, his father immigrated to the United States, sending for his wife and son a few months later. Rabi grew up on the Lower East Side of New York City and in Brooklyn, where his father eventually owned a small grocery store. His parents were deeply religious Hasidic Jews, and Rabi began attending religious school at the age of three. He received his early education in the New York City public schools. A voracious reader at the public library, he developed an interest in science and technology and set up a neighborhood telegraph system when he was eleven. In his early teens he published an article on making electrical condensers in a popular science magazine. Although his parents had hoped he would take up rabbinic studies, he chose instead to attend Manual Training High School in Brooklyn. Rabi won a New York State Regents scholarship as well as a tuition scholarship to Cornell University in Ithaca, New York.

Although he started in 1916 as an electrical engineering student at Cornell, Rabi graduated three years later with a bachelor of chemistry degree. He worked as a chemist for three years, but he found that anti-Semitism limited his opportunities. In 1922 he returned to Cornell to pursue graduate work in chemistry, but while there he discovered that his true interest lay in physics. Transferring to Columbia University in 1923, he supported himself by teaching at the City College of New York. In 1926 he received his Ph.D. in physics for measurements of the magnetic properties of crystals. In the course of his thesis research, Rabi so improved the method for making these measurements that what had taken several years could now be done in weeks.

Shortly after receiving his Ph.D., Rabi was awarded a fellowship for postgraduate research in Europe. Spending two years in Germany and Denmark, he studied with ERWIN SCHRÖDINGER, Arnold Sommerfeld, NIELS BOHR, WOLFGANG PAULI, and OTTO STERN, who were instrumental in the development of the quantum theory of atomic and subatomic systems. The quantum theory states that the particles in an atom can have only certain discrete energy levels; the energies between these levels are never observed. Around the time Rabi arrived in Europe, Schrödinger, MAX BORN, WERNER HEISENBERG, and P. A. M. DIRAC were developing a general mathematical approach to quantum problems called quantum mechanics; this set of principles explained many phenomena that could not be explained by the principles of classical physics.

Stern and Walter Gerlach had developed a technique for creating beams of atoms or molecules by releasing a heated vapor into a vacuum through a series of slits. When they passed a beam of silver atoms through a magnetic field, they found that the beam, instead of being spread out smoothly as they had expected, was split into two distinct beams. This meant that atoms in the beam could assume only two orientations in a magnetic field, corresponding to two discrete energy levels; the observation could be explained only by quantum mechanics. After discussing this experiment with Stern, Rabi devised an improved method for performing the measurements. He then went to study with Heisenberg, who was greatly impressed with Rabi.

In 1929 Rabi returned to New York to become a lecturer at Columbia, a position he had been offered on Heisenberg's recommendation. He was named assistant professor in 1930 and associate professor in 1932. While directing the theoretical physics program at Columbia, Rabi began his own experimental research

847

with atomic and molecular beams, using funds provided by HAROLD C. UREY, who was then professor of chemistry at Columbia. Stern's experimental observation of atomic orientation in a strong magnetic field had been explained by the discovery that electrons have a property called spin; in a magnetic field the electron's spin axis can be oriented in either of two ways. The energies of these two states depend on the magnetic moment associated with the electron spin, as well as on the magnetic field strength. Later, it was found that the nucleus of an atom also interacts with magnetic fields by means of the nuclear spin and its associated magnetic moment. Calculating the theoretical behavior of atoms in weaker magnetic fields, Rabi predicted that a molecular beam could be split into more than two parts. The number of subbeams would depend upon the interactions of the nuclear and electron spins with each other and with the applied magnetic field; each subbeam would be composed of atoms that shared the same nuclear and electron spins. Rabi proceeded to confirm his prediction experimentally, providing a technique for measuring nuclear spin by counting the splittings of the molecular beam.

In 1937 Rabi found that if he applied a weak radio-frequency signal to a molecular beam in a magnetic field, he could make atoms change their spin orientation. Adjusting the frequency of the radio signal allowed him to make precise measurements of nuclear spin and of the strength of the nucleus's own magnetic field. His first measurements were about 10 times more precise than measurements done by earlier methods, and further development increased the precision of his technique by a factor of 1,000. Since nuclear spin and the associated nuclear magnetic field are basic properties of the nucleus, precise knowledge of their values was needed in order to understand the behavior of the nucleus. Thus, Rabi's measurements were extremely important to the growing field of nuclear physics.

With the outbreak of World War II, Rabi's research group at Columbia was scattered. In 1940 Rabi took a leave of absence to serve as associate director of the Massachusetts Institute of Technology Radiation Laboratory, where he was responsible for the development of microwave sources for use in radar systems. To assist him in these efforts, Rabi recruited many noted physicists, among them JULIAN S. SCHWINGER, EDWARD M. PURCELL, Robert H. Dicke, and George E. Uhlenbeck. Although he had declined an invitation to participate in the Manhattan Project in the

belief that radar offered a more immediate advantage to the Allied war effort than did the atomic bomb, Rabi often visited the project's laboratory at Los Alamos, New Mexico, as an unofficial consultant to J. Robert Oppenheimer. He was among the scientists who observed the first test of the atomic bomb at Alamogordo, New Mexico. After the war, Rabi was active in the successful effort to establish nonmilitary control of nuclear power and its applications.

Rabi was awarded the 1944 Nobel Prize for Physics "for his resonance method for recording the magnetic properties of atomic nuclei." Award ceremonies were suspended during the war years, and Rabi did not deliver a Nobel lecture. In a broadcast lecture, Erik Hulthén of the Royal Swedish Academy of Sciences described Rabi's solution to the problem of how the atom reacts to the magnetic field as both simple and brilliant. "By this method," Hulthén said, "Rabi has literally established radio relations with the most subtle particles of matter, with the world of the electron and of the atomic nucleus."

In 1945 Rabi returned to Columbia University as executive officer of the physics department. Although most of the senior physicists who had been dispersed by wartime assignments did not return to Columbia, Rabi rebuilt the department. Among the notable physicists who worked at Columbia in those years were WILLIS E. LAMB JR. and POLYKARP KUSCH, whose measurements of atomic spectra were inspired in part by Rabi's earlier work. As department head, Rabi helped establish the Brookhaven National Laboratory in Upton, Long Island, an institution for research on peaceful uses of atomic energy operated by several universities under contract to the Atomic Energy Commission. He was named University Professor at Columbia in 1964 and became University Professor Emeritus in 1967.

Rabi married Helen Newhouse in 1926; they have two daughters. The Rabis live near Columbia, where Rabi still lectures occasionally and participates in seminars. For recreation he enjoys travel, walking, and attending the theater.

In addition to the Nobel Prize, Rabi has received the Elliott Cresson Medal of the Franklin Institute (1944), the Niels Bohr International Gold Medal of the Danish Society of Civil, Electrical, and Mechanical Engineers (1967), the Atoms for Peace Award established by the Ford Motor Company Fund (1967), the Pupin Gold Medal of Columbia University (1981), and appointments to the

Brazilian Order of the Southern Cross and the Legion of Honor of France. He holds many honorary doctorates. He is a fellow and former president (1950) of the American Physical Society and a member of the National Academy of Sciences, the American Philosophical Society, the American Academy of Arts and Sciences, and the Brazilian and Japanese scientific academies. He has served on international committees concerned with arms control and the uses of nuclear power. In 1985 Columbia honored his achievements by establishing the Isidor Isaac Rabi Chair in Physics.

SELECTED WORKS: Nuclear Physics, 1941, with others; My Life and Times as a Physicist, 1960; Science and Public Policy, 1963; Man and Science, 1968; Science: The Center of Culture, 1970.

ABOUT: Current Biography April 1948; Libby, L. M. The Uranium People, 1979; Motz, L. (ed.) A Festschrift for I. I. Rabi, 1977; New Yorker October 13, 1975; October 20, 1975; New York Times November 21, 1985; Rigden, J. S. Rabi: American Physicist, 1987.

JAMES RAINWATER

RAINWATER, JAMES

(December 9, 1917–May 31, 1986)
Nobel Prize for Physics, 1975
(shared with Aage Bohr and Ben R.
Mottelson)

The American physicist Leo James Rainwater was born in Council, Idaho, to Leo Jasper Rainwater, a civil engineer and general store manager, and Edna Eliza (Teague) Rainwater. After his father's death in the 1918 influenza epidemic, the family moved to Hanford, California, where his mother remarried. Raised in Hanford, Rainwater was an outstanding student in chemistry, physics, and mathematics. After excelling in a chemistry competition sponsored by the California Institute of Technology (Caltech), he was admitted to the school as a chemistry student; soon, however, he changed his major to physics. At Caltech, he studied physics with CARL D. ANDERSON and took a biology class taught by THOMAS HUNT MORGAN. After receiving his B.S. in physics in 1939, Rainwater entered Columbia University for graduate studies under I. I. RABI, ENRICO FERMI, Edward Teller, and other noted physicists.

When the United States entered World War II, Rainwater interrupted his thesis research to participate in the Manhattan Project as a member of the Office of Scientific Research and Development. Working under J. R. Dunning, he used Columbia's cyclotron (a type of particle accelerator) to investigate the behavior of atomic nuclei under neutron bombardment. After the war, Rainwater's data were declassified, and in 1946 he was awarded a Ph.D. for this work.

Remaining at Columbia as a physics instructor, he pursued research in experimental physics. In 1946 Columbia received funds to build the Nevis Cyclotron Laboratory, containing a synchrocyclotron that produced particles of much higher energy than the earlier cyclotron. From the beginning, Rainwater was involved in the construction of the accelerator, which began operation in 1950. By then, Rainwater and his colleagues William W. Havens Jr. and Chien-Shiung Wu had already measured the strength with which neutrons interact with most nuclei. The new accelerator allowed similar experiments to be carried out with particles other than neutrons, namely with muons (which resemble electrons except that they are approximately 200 times more massive and are unstable, decaying in only 2.2 millionths of a second) and pi-mesons (the short-lived particles that carry the strong nuclear force responsible for holding nuclei together).

In 1949–1950 the Danish physicist AAGE BOHR conducted research at Columbia, where he shared an office with Rainwater. The two scientists had long discussions on the fundamental structure of the nucleus. At the time there were two principal models of the nucleus, the liquid-drop model and the shell

849

model. Both models took as their starting point the fundamental forces known to act between the protons and neutrons (together called nucleons) that make up a nucleus. The problem addressed by the models was to predict the properties of dozens or hundreds of nucleons interacting through these forces.

The liquid-drop model had been advanced by Aage Bohr's father, NIELS BOHR, in 1936. It supposed that the nucleus acts like a liquid drop capable of vibrating and changing shape. Although the liquid-drop model offered a satisfactory explanation of nuclear fission, it failed to account for other important properties of the nucleus. In the shell model, proposed in 1949 by MARIA GOEPPERT MAYER and J. HANS D. JENSEN, the nucleons move in independent concentric orbits, or shells; their motion is much like that of the electrons in an atom, except that there is no central force affecting their movement. According to the shell model, the force acting on one nucleon is the sum of the forces exerted by all the other nucleons in the nucleus. The sum of these forces constitutes a force field, which Mayer and Jensen assumed to be spherical. Although the shell model successfully predicted the energies of certain excited states of the nucleus, it failed elsewhere. In particular, it could not account for the discovery that the distribution of electric charge around some nuclei is not at all spherical.

In late 1949 CHARLES H. TOWNES spoke at Columbia on the disparities between the predictions of the shell theory and experimental data. Listening to Townes's talk, Rainwater thought of a way to explain these discrepancies. It occurred to him that the orbited shells in the nucleus might be distorted by centrifugal forces into a shape more like a football than a sphere. After convincing Aage Bohr that the arguments had merit, Rainwater published his hypothesis in 1950 and then returned to his experimental studies.

Bohr, who had been thinking along similar lines, returned to Copenhagen later that year determined to develop a complete theory of nuclear behavior. He and BEN R. MOTTELSON published their collective model of the nucleus in 1952, using Rainwater's insight to combine the liquidlike behavior of the nucleus described in the liquid-drop model with the orbiting-nucleon properties of the shell model.

According to Bohr and Mottelson, the collective action of the nucleons causes the surface of the nucleus to behave like that of a liquid drop. The nucleus, however, has a shell structure capable of being deformed into a football-like shape; these deformations appear on the surface as oscillations and rotations. When its outermost shell has a full complement of nucleons, the nucleus remains spherical. When the outermost shell is only partly filled, however, the shape of the nucleus is distorted. Bohr and Mottelson found that such distorted nuclei could exhibit oscillations in size, surface waves, and rotation. These new collective modes could not be predicted by the shell model because it ignored interactions among nucleons. Using the collective model to calculate the properties of the deformed nuclei and reviewing a wealth of experimental data, Mottelson and Bohr confirmed Rainwater's hypothesis in 1953.

Meanwhile, Rainwater had returned to his experimental work with the Columbia synchrocyclotron. While collaborating with VAL L. FITCH in 1953 on studies of X rays given off by muons, he discovered that current estimates of the size of the proton were too large.

Rainwater was appointed a full professor at Columbia in 1952 and was named Michael I. Pupin Professor of Physics in 1983. He was associated with the Nevis Cyclotron Laboratory from 1946 until 1978, serving as its director between 1951 and 1953, and again from 1956 until 1961.

Rainwater, Bohr, and Mottelson shared the 1975 Nobel Prize for Physics "for the discovery of the connection between collective motion and particle motion in atomic nuclei and the development of the theory of the structure of the atomic nucleus based on this connection." In his presentation speech, Sven Johansson of the Royal Swedish Academy of Sciences called their work "an inspiration to an intensive research activity in nuclear structure physics." Rainwater's Nobel lecture summarized the background leading to his discoveries and their confirmation.

In 1942 Rainwater married Emma Louise Smith. The couple had a daughter who died in infancy and three sons. Rainwater enjoyed studying geology and astronomy and liked listening to classical music. He died in Yonkers, New York, on May 31, 1986, shortly after retiring from Columbia.

In addition to the Nobel Prize, Rainwater received the Ernest Orlando Lawrence Memorial Award for Physics of the United States Atomic Energy Commission (1963). He was a member of the National Academy of Sciences, the Institute of Electrical and Electronics Engineers, the New York Academy of Sciences, the American Association for the Advancement of Science, and the American Physical Society.

ABOUT: New York Times October 18, 1975; June 3, 1986; Physics Today December 1975; Science November 28, 1975.

RAMAN, VENKATA
(November 7, 1888–November 21, 1970)
Nobel Prize for Physics, 1930

The Indian physicist Chandrasekhara Venkata Raman (rä′ män) was born in the city of Tiruchchirappalli to Chandrasekhara Aiyar, professor of mathematics and physics at the Society for the Propaganda of the Gospel College, and the former Parvati Ammal, whose family included several noted Sanskrit scholars. Raman attended the Mrs. A. V. N. College in Vishakhapatnam from 1901 to 1903 before going on to Presidency College of the University of Madras, from which he graduated in 1904 at the age of sixteen, first in his class, with a gold medal in physics. Remaining there for graduate studies, he received his M.A. in 1907 with highest honors.

Because poor health prevented Raman from continuing his graduate education in Europe, he was denied opportunities to join the Indian academic community. Instead, he entered the Indian civil service in 1907, and during the next ten years he advanced through the ranks of the Finance Department. As a boy, Raman had acquired a love of music, and in addition to his civil service duties, he undertook independent experimental and theoretical research on stringed instruments and Indian drums. By 1917 he had published thirty papers on his work in this field, conducted at the laboratory of the Indian Association for the Cultivation of Science in Calcutta.

Through these publications Raman acquired a reputation in scientific circles, and in 1917 he was offered the newly created Palit Professorship of Physics at the University of Calcutta. He accepted, and soon the university's physics department acquired an international reputation for the quality of its research under the leadership of Raman, Meghnad Saha, and Satyendranath Bose. By this time, Raman's interest had shifted to optics.

In 1921 Raman first visited Europe, where he attended the Congress of British Universities at Oxford. While returning to India by ship, he was struck by the deep blue color of the sea. Back in Calcutta, he set about to find its cause. A year later, he confirmed his theory that the color of the sea is caused by molecular scattering of light by water molecules, just as light scattering by air molecules explains the color of the sky. His observations initiated a

VENKATA RAMAN

seven-year study of how light is scattered by liquids, solids, and gases. While working primarily on this topic, Raman also continued to study the physics of musical sounds. So substantial was his international reputation for his work in this field that in 1924 he was elected to the Royal Society of London.

The previous year Raman and his associates had first observed that scattered light is accompanied by a feebler type of secondary radiation, whose wavelength differs from that of the primary radiation. During the following years, Raman and K. S. Krishnan improved their experimental techniques in order to isolate and observe this type of secondary radiation. The two scientists studied the light scattered when beams of sunlight were focused on purified liquid and dust-free air. In a 1928 paper published in the *Indian Journal of Physics*, they showed that this secondary radiation consists of light at a number of different wavelengths, mostly longer and of lower energy than the original beam of light. They also reported that the wavelengths produced in this way depend on the nature of the molecules doing the scattering and are characteristic of the transmitting substance. When the wavelength of the illuminating light source is changed, they noted, the induced light emissions also change their wavelengths, although the energy shifts between the primary and secondary radiation remain constant. These energy shifts, later known as the Raman effect, provided a sensitive tool for investigating molecular structure. In quantum mechanics, the Raman effect is described as an exchange of energy between molecules of the scattering substance and the incident light.

Later in 1928, the same energy shifts were discovered independently by the Soviet physicists Grigory Landsberg and Leonid Mandelshtam, but because the findings of Raman and Krishnan were more complete, they received credit for the discovery. Although such molecular interactions with light had been predicted by Adolf Smekal in 1923 and by WERNER HEISENBERG, Raman was the first to observe them.

Raman was awarded the 1930 Nobel Prize for Physics "for his work on the scattering of light and for the discovery of the effect named after him." According to Hans Pleijel of the Royal Swedish Academy of Sciences, who made the presentation, "The Raman effect has already yielded important results concerning the chemical constitution of substances. . . . The extremely valuable tool that the Raman effect has placed in our hands will, in the immediate future, bring with it a deepening of our knowledge of the structure of matter."

Because the Raman effect requires monochromatic, highly intense light sources if sensitive investigations are to be performed, it was little used until the invention of lasers in the early 1960s. With these devices and the ideal source of monochromatic light they provide, scientists were able to conduct molecular analysis using the Raman effect, which remains a standard laboratory tool.

In 1933 Raman became director of the Indian Institute of Science in Bangalore. While continuing to study the Raman effect, he also began crystallographic studies of diamonds. He found that the luminescence of a diamond excited by ultraviolet light is not, as was believed earlier, due to impurities or defects, but is rather an intrinsic property of the gem. In addition, he studied the interactions of atoms in crystals with light and sound and the effect of sound waves on light scattering.

After his retirement in 1948, Raman became director of the Raman Research Institute, constructed by the Indian Academy of Sciences on property donated several years earlier by the government of Mysore. There he and his students combined studies of the physiology of vision with their continuing work on optics and crystal structure. In the 1960s they attempted to develop a new theory on human color vision and investigated the colors of flowers. A museum of gemstones at the Raman Research Institute now contains hundreds of diamonds collected by Raman.

In 1907 Raman married Loka Sundari Am-

mal, an accomplished artist who shared his interest in musical instruments; the couple had two sons. A productive and prolific researcher, Raman served as model and leader to the Indian scientific community he helped create, and he encouraged public interest in the sciences. A gifted teacher who played a leading role in the Indian cultural renaissance, Raman was known for his intuitive mind, sense of humor, and love of music. He was active scientifically until his death in Bangalore on November 21, 1970, at the age of eighty-two.

In addition to the Nobel Prize, Raman received the Matteucci Gold Medal of the National Academy of Sciences of Italy (1928), the Hughes Medal of the Royal Society of London (1930), the Franklin Medal of the Franklin Institute (1941), and the Soviet government's International Lenin Prize (1957). In 1954 Raman was given the title Gem of India by the Indian government, one of its highest honors. He received honorary degrees from the universities of Calcutta, Bombay, Madras, Benares, Dacca, Mysore, Delhi, Freiburg, Glasgow, and Paris. As a founding member of the Indian Academy of Sciences, Raman served as its president until his death. He also held foreign membership in the Zurich Physical Society, the Royal Society of London, the Royal Philosophical Society of Glasgow, the Royal Irish Academy, the Optical Society of America, the Mineralogical Society of America, and the Pontifical Academy of Sciences, among others. He was knighted by the British government in 1929.

SELECTED WORKS: Molecular Diffraction of Light, 1922; Aspects of Science, 1948; The New Physics, 1951; Lectures on Physical Optics, 1959; The Physiology of Vision, 1968.

ABOUT: Biographical Memoirs of Fellows of the Royal Society, volume 17, 1971; Current Biography November 1948; Dictionary of Scientific Biography, volume 11, 1975; Indian Academy of Sciences. Sir Chandrasekhara Venkata Raman, 1948; Keswani, G. H. Raman and His Effect, 1980; Pisharoty, P. R. C. V. Raman, 1982.

RAMÓN Y CAJAL, SANTIAGO
(May 1, 1852–October 18, 1934)
Nobel Prize for Physiology or Medicine, 1906
(shared with Camillo Golgi)

The Spanish neuroanatomist and histologist Santiago Ramón y Cajal (rä môn′ ē kä käl′) was born in Petilla de Aragon, a village in the southern Pyrenees, to Antonia and Justo Ra-

SANTIAGO RAMÓN Y CAJAL

món y Casasús. His father was a poor barber-surgeon who, determined to become a physician, took the family to Zaragoza when the boy was five. There Justo Ramón y Casasús completed his medical training while his family lived in considerable poverty. Young Santiago showed early promise as an artist—an aptitude that would later assume great importance in his scientific career—but his father insisted that he join the medical profession.

At the College of the Aesculapian Fathers and at the Institute at Huesca, Ramón y Cajal resisted the strict discipline of his teachers and became truant. His father apprenticed the rebellious young man first to a barber and then to a shoemaker. When he showed ability in the latter trade, his father, pleased with the boy's change in attitude, gave him anatomy lessons, and at the age of sixteen Ramón y Cajal entered the University of Zaragoza, where his father was a professor of applied anatomy.

Upon his graduation in 1873 Ramón y Cajal began military service as an infantry surgeon. Posted to Cuba when rebellion broke out, he fell ill with malaria, was discharged, and returned to the University of Zaragoza's School of Anatomy to study for his doctorate in medicine. He received his degree in 1879 and was appointed director of the University Museum of Anatomy. Weakened by recurrent bouts of malaria, he developed tuberculosis and was forced into many months of convalescence but recovered completely the next year.

So sketchy was Ramón y Cajal's medical training at Zaragoza that his first opportunity to look through a microscope came only when he took his medical examination in histology, held in Madrid. Stunned by what it revealed, he found an unused and antiquated instrument at the University of Zaragoza and began teaching himself microscopic anatomy. These efforts led to his first scientific publication, which focused on inflammation of the mesentery, cornea, and cartilage and which he illustrated with his own lithographs. His many subsequent publications on cell biology and microscopy were outstanding because of the beautiful illustrations he prepared.

Ramón y Cajal was appointed to the chair of anatomy at the University of Valencia in 1883. He continued to write and illustrate books on histology and pathology, which were printed at his own expense because Spain was too isolated from the mainstream of European science for such works to be financially successful. Since non-Spanish periodicals were scarce or unavailable, Ramón y Cajal was constrained to learn histology and microscopy on his own. He examined each tissue in turn, saving the nervous system until last because of its complexity.

In 1886 a neurologist in Madrid showed him a silver nitrate method for staining nerve tissue developed by CAMILLO GOLGI. Seen under the microscope, the results were delineated with startling clarity. "All was sharp as a sketch with Chinese ink on transparent Japan paper," Ramón y Cajal later recalled. "And to think that that was the same tissue which when stained with carmine or logwood left the eye in a tangled thicket. . . . Here, on the contrary, all was clear and plain as a diagram. A look was enough. Dumbfounded, I could not take my eye from the microscope."

The following year Ramón y Cajal accepted the chair of histology at the University of Barcelona, where he began to refine Golgi's method in an effort to eliminate occasional inconsistent results. These improvements, together with his artist's hand and eye, enabled him to publish more detailed and accurate descriptions of the structures of individual neurons than had ever been seen before.

As he developed other innovative staining methods and perceived details of the nervous system that earlier researchers had missed, Ramón y Cajal drew novel conclusions about neuronal organization and function. At the time, most neurobiologists believed that nerve fibers formed a network in which individual cells were interconnected. Golgi remained a leading proponent of this "reticular theory." Ramón y Cajal, however, was able to trace each fiber to a specific nerve cell. He found that although fibers from different cells come into very close contact, they do not fuse together but always end in free terminals. This discovery made him the leading advocate of the "neuron doctrine," the theory that the nervous system consists of many independent cells rather than a single network.

The neuron doctrine was widely accepted because it was useful in neurophysiology. CHARLES S. SHERRINGTON (who had met Ramón y Cajal while they were both investigating a Spanish cholera epidemic in 1886) found that he could describe reflex actions by assuming that there were separate motor and sensory neurons, with distinct functions, that interacted at discrete points, or synapses (the region of contact between processes of two adjacent neurons).

An individual nerve cell consists of anywhere from a few to several thousand protruding fibers known as dendrites. Since the early 1860s, it had been recognized that one of these fibers—the axon—is different from the others, being longer, thicker, and covered with a layer of fatty insulation called myelin. Most neuroanatomists believed that the structural differences between dendrites and axons indicated functional differences as well. When he examined neurons from the nose and the eye, Ramón y Cajal noted that the dendrites were all on one side of the cell, pointing toward the outside, whereas the axons all extended in the direction of the brain. This finding led him in 1891 to introduce what he called the "doctrine of dynamic polarization," which states that nerve impulses are received by the dendrites (or by the cell body directly) but are transmitted only by the axon.

Ramón y Cajal's reputation grew rapidly, both at home and abroad. In 1892, at the age of forty, he was appointed to the chair of histology and pathological anatomy at the University of Madrid, where he remained for the next thirty years. His major works were written in Spanish, a language known to few foreign scientists, but Ramón y Cajal often published in other languages, especially French. Although he wrote over twenty books and 250 scientific papers, he estimated that only a third of them were read by scientists outside Spain. He never ceased to resent the isolation he felt was imposed by foreign ignorance of his native tongue.

Ramón y Cajal and Golgi shared the 1906 Nobel Prize for Physiology or Medicine for "their work on the structure of the nervous system." In his presentation speech, K. A. H. Mörner of the Karolinska Institute hailed the two scientists "as the principal representatives and standard-bearers of the modern science of neurology."

In 1904 Ramón y Cajal summarized his work in a book called *The Nervous System in Man and Vertebrates*. In addition to discussing his theories on the neuron doctrine and the functions of the axon and dendrites, the book described the structure and organization of cells in different parts of the brain. These cytoarchitectonic descriptions (delineations of the cellular structure, or the arrangement of cells in a tissue) are still the foundation for studies of cerebral localization—the determination of the specialized functions of the various regions of the brain.

In subsequent research, Ramón y Cajal investigated nerve degeneration and repair, but, as Spain's greatest living scientist, he was increasingly in demand as an administrator and authority. He was also celebrated as a popular writer. *Conversations at the Café* and *The World as Seen at Eighty: Impressions of an Arteriosclerotic* were collections of his clever, often melancholy aphorisms. "The saddest thing about old age is that its future is behind it," he said. He also wrote that "so long as the brain is a mystery, the universe, the reflection of it, will remain so."

The most significant work of Ramón y Cajal's later years centered on his discovery in 1913 of the gold sublimate method, which he utilized in the staining of neuralgic tissue. This work provided a stepping-stone to current knowledge of the pathology of tumors of the central nervous system.

In 1880 Ramón y Cajal married Silvería Fañanás García, with whom he had four sons and four daughters. Short in stature and dark in complexion, he was considered somewhat shy and reclusive. "He had an intensity of expression to which variety was lent chiefly by the remarkable eyes," Charles S. Sherrington recalled in a biographical memoir. "Full and dark, they lit or gloomed according to each passing mood." A talented amateur photographer, Ramón y Cajal was passionately devoted to chess. He died on October 18, 1934, at the age of eighty-two. After his death the Spanish government reprinted all of his publications, issued postage stamps and bank notes with his likeness, and erected a statue of him in a Madrid public garden.

Ramón y Cajal's many awards included the Fauvelle Prize of the Society of Biology of Paris (1896), the Moscow Prize of the International Congress of Medicine (1900), and the Helmholtz Medal of the Royal Academy of

Sciences of Berlin (1905). He received honorary degrees from Cambridge University, the University of Würzburg, Clark University, and many other institutions. He was a member of numerous professional societies, including the National Science Academy of Lima, the Royal Swedish Academy of Sciences, the Royal Society of London, and the American National Academy of Sciences.

SELECTED WORKS: Collected Pamphlets, 1884–1899; Collected Papers, 1907–1917; Degeneration and Regeneration of the Nervous System (2 vols.) 1928; Histology, 1933; Recollections of My Life (2 vols.) 1937; Precepts and Counsels on Scientific Investigation, 1951; Studies on the Cerebral Cortex, 1955; Studies on Vertebrate Neurogenesis, 1960; Studies on the Diencephalon, 1966; Structure of Ammon's Horn, 1968; Structure of the Retina, 1972; The Neuron and the Glial Cell, 1984.

ABOUT: Cannon, D. F. Explorer of the Human Brain, 1949; Craigie, E. H., and Gibson, W. C. (eds.) The World of Ramón y Cajal, 1968; Dictionary of Scientific Biography, volume 11, 1975; Grisolia, S. (ed.) Ramón y Cajal's Contribution to the Neurosciences, 1983; Obituary Notices of Fellows of the Royal Society, volume 1, 1935; Williams, J. H. Don Quixote of the Microscope, 1954.

WILLIAM RAMSAY

RAMSAY, WILLIAM
(October 2, 1852–July 23, 1916)
Nobel Prize for Chemistry, 1904

The Scottish chemist William Ramsay was born in Glasgow. He was the only child of William Ramsay, a civil engineer and businessman, and the former Catherine Robertson, daughter of an Edinburgh doctor who had written a textbook on chemistry. Raised in a strict Calvinist household, Ramsay attended the Glasgow Academy and in 1866 entered the University of Glasgow to study the classics, general literature, logic, and mathematics.

Although he planned to become a clergyman, Ramsay developed an interest in science during his undergraduate years. He studied anatomy and geology, attended lectures given by the Scottish chemist John Ferguson and by the noted English physicist William Thomson, and worked as an apprentice to a local chemical analyst. Transferring to the University of Tübingen in 1871, Ramsay worked under the German organic chemist Rudolf Fittig. He received his doctorate in 1872 with a thesis titled "Investigations on the Toluic and Nitrotoluic Acids."

Upon returning to Edinburgh that year, Ramsay became an assistant at Anderson College and in 1874 was appointed Ferguson's tu-

torial assistant at the University of Glasgow. During these years Ramsay's interest shifted to physical chemistry. In 1880 he accepted an appointment as professor of chemistry at University College, Bristol, where he began research on vapor pressures and the critical states of liquids.

Following his appointment to the chair of general chemistry at University College in 1887, Ramsay focused his studies on the evaporation and dissociation of vapors and liquids. After confirming a linear relationship between surface tension and temperature in liquids, he took up an anomaly that had been pointed out by the English physicist J. W. STRUTT (Lord Rayleigh): that atmospheric nitrogen has a slightly greater density than artificially produced nitrogen. Like Rayleigh, Ramsay conjectured that this difference might arise from the presence of an unknown atmospheric gas. He produced evidence to confirm Rayleigh's hypothesis by removing oxygen from a sample of air and allowing the remaining gas to pass repeatedly over heated magnesium, thus removing all nitrogen. This experiment, performed in 1894, revealed the presence of the hitherto undiscovered gas. Since it had not entered into chemical reaction with any other elements, Ramsay named the gas argon, from the Greek word meaning "inert."

Learning that William Hillebrand, an American geologist, had obtained a gas believed to be nitrogen by heating certain minerals, Ramsay set out early in 1895 to determine whether this gas also contained argon. Such a finding would mean that argon was a constituent of the earth's crust. Spectral analysis of this gas confirmed the presence of helium with traces of argon. Although the astronomers Pierre Janssen and Joseph Lockyer had identified helium in the spectra of the sun's atmosphere more than thirty years earlier, the gas had never been found elsewhere. Through additional experiments, Ramsay demonstrated that helium, like argon, is inert.

After making a careful study of the periodic table, Ramsay and Rayleigh surmised that argon and helium represented two members of a family of similar elements as yet undiscovered. It seemed clear that these gases would be present in nature in smaller quantities than either argon or helium and therefore would be more difficult to detect. Examining various minerals and meteorites, Ramsay found no evidence of other inert gases. In 1898, however, working with Morris Travers, he applied a different analytic technique. The constituent substances of unknown liquids were commonly revealed by slowly raising the temperature and noting the precise boiling point of each substance. Using a device that could chill and liquefy a large sample of argon gas, Ramsay identified two more inert gases, which he named krypton and neon (from the Greek words meaning "hidden" and "new" respectively). Subsequent refinements revealed yet another inert gas, which he named xenon (from the Greek word meaning "stranger"), bringing the total to five. Over the next two years, he confirmed that these five gases indeed possessed the properties expected of a new class of elements. Thus a new group was added to the periodic table.

Ramsay was awarded the 1904 Nobel Prize for Chemistry "in recognition of his services in the discovery of the inert gaseous elements in air, and his determination of their place in the periodic system." At the same time, Rayleigh received the Nobel Prize for Physics for his work on densities in gases and for his role in the discovery of argon. In his presentation speech, J. E. Cederblom of the Royal Swedish Academy of Sciences hailed the magnitude of Ramsay's achievements. "The discovery of an entirely new group of elements," Cederblom said, "of which no single representative had been known with any certainty, is something utterly unique in the history of chemistry." Not only did Ramsay's work prove crucial to NIELS BOHR's 1913 theory of atomic structure, but his discovery of helium permitted replacement of the highly flammable hydrogen then used in balloons and lighter-than-air ships by an inert, and thus safer, gas.

Shortly after his discovery of the inert gases, Ramsay turned his attention to the gas called "emanation," which had been linked by ERNEST RUTHERFORD and F. E. Dorn to the radioactive elements thorium and radium, respectively. Rutherford's work in 1902 had convinced him that emanation was inert and therefore possibly another member of the argon family. In 1903, working with FREDERICK SODDY, Ramsay observed the spectrum of helium in the emanation from radium bromide. Seven years later Ramsay and Whytlaw-Gray demonstrated that the major component of this emanation was less dense than radium itself by four atomic units—the precise weight of a helium nucleus. These findings added another inert gas, radon, to the periodic table and further confirmed Rutherford's hypothesis that radiation involves the transmutation of one element into another.

In 1881 Ramsay married Margaret Buchanan, with whom he had two children. In addition to his scientific research, Ramsay became deeply involved in educational reform and worked to improve the quality of teaching at University College throughout his twenty-five-year tenure. After his retirement in 1912, Ramsay, who was considered tireless and unfailingly optimistic by his students and colleagues, continued to work from his home in Hazlemere. After Great Britain declared war on Germany in 1914, Ramsay offered his services to the government, but his health was already failing, and he died of cancer at Hazlemere on July 23, 1916.

In addition to the Nobel Prize, Ramsay received the Davy Medal of the Royal Society (1895) and the August Wilhelm von Hofmann Medal of the German Chemical Society (1903) as well as honorary degrees and many other awards. He was knighted in 1902.

SELECTED WORKS: A System of Inorganic Chemistry, 1891; Gases of the Atmosphere: The History of Their Discovery, 1896; Modern Chemistry, 1900; Introduction to the Study of Physical Chemistry, 1904; Essays Biographical and Chemical, 1908; Elements and Electrons, 1912.

ABOUT: Dictionary of National Biography 1912–1921, 1927; Dictionary of Scientific Biography, volume 11, 1975; Tilden, W. A. Sir William Ramsay, 1918; Travers, M. W. A Life of Sir William Ramsay, 1956.

RED CROSS
See INTERNATIONAL COMMITTEE OF
THE RED CROSS and LEAGUE OF RED
CROSS SOCIETIES

REICHSTEIN, TADEUS
(July 20, 1897–)
Nobel Prize for Physiology or Medicine,
1950
(shared with Philip S. Hench and Edward C.
Kendall)

The Polish-Swiss chemist Tadeus Reichstein
(rīk′ shtīn) was born in Włocławek, Poland
(then part of Russia), to the former Gustava
Brockman and Isidor Reichstein, an engineer.
After spending his early years in Kiev, where
his father was employed, Reichstein attended
a boarding school in Jena, Germany. His family moved to Berlin in 1905 and later to Zurich,
where he studied with a private tutor before
attending the *Oberrealschule* (technical junior
college) and the Federal Institute of Technology. Reichstein and his parents became Swiss
citizens in 1914; two years later he passed his
final examinations at the Federal Institute of
Technology and remained there to study
chemistry. After receiving the equivalent of a
bachelor's degree in 1920, he worked as an
industrial chemist for one year and then returned to the Federal Institute of Technology
for graduate work in organic chemistry, receiving a Ph.D. in 1922.

That same year Reichstein began working
with HERMANN STAUDINGER on the chemical
composition of the aromatic substances in coffee, a topic he later investigated for an industrial firm. He also examined the aromatic
substances in chicory, and later in the 1920s
he published the results of his research in a
series of scientific papers.

In 1929 Reichstein received an appointment
as part-time instructor in organic and physiological chemistry at the Federal Institute of
Technology, where he completed his work on
the aroma and flavor of coffee and chicory in
1931 and was appointed assistant to LEOPOLD
RUŽIČKA. In 1933 he synthesized vitamin C
(ascorbic acid), around the same time that
biochemists in England accomplished the same
task. Reichstein's method is still used today in
the commercial synthesis of vitamin C. After
becoming assistant professor and then associate professor, he was appointed professor of
pharmaceutical chemistry and director of the
Pharmaceutical Institute at the University of

TADEUS REICHSTEIN

Basel in Switzerland in 1938. Meanwhile, he
had begun a series of experiments in an effort
to isolate and identify the hormones of the
adrenal glands.

The adrenal glands are paired endocrine organs located at the upper poles of the kidneys.
They are divided into a central portion, known
as the medulla, and an outer portion, called
the cortex. The medulla produces two hormones: epinephrine and norepinephrine (also
known as adrenaline and noradrenaline). Epinephrine acts to stimulate the production of
sugar in the liver and its release into the bloodstream; the hormone also increases the production of body heat and expands the blood
vessels in muscles. Norepinephrine constricts
blood vessels, which in turn causes an elevation of blood pressure.

The cells of the adrenal cortex are controlled by a pituitary gland hormone called
adrenocorticotropic hormone (ACTH). These
cells synthesize and secrete three adrenal corticosteroids—cortisone, cortisol, and aldosterone—into the bloodstream. When the blood
levels of cortisol (also called hydrocortisone)
are low, ACTH is released by the pituitary
gland, an action that in turn stimulates the
release of cortisone and cortisol. When the
blood levels of cortisol are high, the production of ACTH is suppressed, resulting in a
lowering of the blood levels of cortisone and
cortisol.

There are two categories of adrenal corticosteroids: the glucocorticoids (cortisone and
cortisol)—which are involved in the metabolism of carbohydrate, fat, and protein—and

the mineralocorticoids, which are involved in the regulation of electrolyte-and-water balance. Cortisone and cortisol also block certain biochemical reactions involved in the inflammatory response of tissue to injury or infection. A deficiency of the hormones of the adrenal cortex can lead to Addison's disease (named after the English physician Thomas Addison), which is characterized by anemia, weakness and fatigue, digestive disturbances, abnormalities of salt-and-water balance, low blood pressure, and a darkish pigmentation of the skin.

By the 1920s it was clear that the surgical removal of the adrenal glands from experimental animals resulted in a condition similar to Addison's disease in human beings. It had also been shown that extracts of adrenal gland tissue will correct the physiological abnormalities produced by Addison's disease or surgical removal of the glands. Since there are so many precursor forms of the hormones of the adrenal cortex, their isolation and identification proved to be particularly difficult.

When Reichstein began his research on the adrenal cortical hormones in the 1930s, he made two erroneous assumptions—that a single hormone was involved and that this hormone was not a steroid. However, he soon discovered that the adrenal gland cortex contains many different steroids and that most of them are precursor compounds in the biosynthetic pathway of the biologically active adrenal corticosteroids. Reichstein and his colleagues later isolated and identified five of these compounds. In 1935 they isolated aldosterone (although its chemical structure was not determined until 1952), and within the next two years they isolated nine other adrenal corticosteroids in crystalline form, including corticosterone (Kendall's compound B), and deoxycorticosterone (Kendall's compound A). By 1942 Reichstein and his assistants had isolated twenty-seven different adrenal corticosteroids in crystalline form.

During the course of his work Reichstein also studied the relationship of the chemical structure of the adrenal corticosteroids to their biological activity and showed that the latter occurs in the biochemistry of the first ring structure and the side chain. In the late 1930s George Thorn of the Harvard Medical School successfully treated patients with Addison's disease using a combination of corticosterone and deoxycorticosterone. In the latter part of the next decade, Reichstein and his colleagues employed a much simpler method to synthesize cortisone and cortisol from a naturally oc-

curring precursor, deoxycholic acid, which was readily available from the bile ducts of cattle.

In 1943 Reichstein collaborated on writing a chapter of the classic textbook *Vitamins and Hormones* titled "The Hormones of the Adrenal Gland"; that same year he was granted a patent on a method for synthesizing one of the sex hormones. (Androgens and estrogens, the male and female sex hormones, are also naturally synthesized in small amounts in the adrenal cortex.) Three years later he and Ružička went on a lecture tour of the United States, during which they visited several research laboratories, all under the auspices of the American-Swiss Foundation for Scientific Exchange. Later that year Reichstein was appointed director of the organic chemistry division of the University of Basel, where he directed the construction of a new Institute for Organic Chemistry.

Reichstein shared the 1950 Nobel Prize for Physiology or Medicine with PHILIP S. HENCH and EDWARD C. KENDALL "for their discoveries relating to the hormones of the adrenal cortex, their chemical structure and biological effects." In his Nobel lecture he referred to himself as a "devoted gardener of African plants," which he grows for pleasure as well as professional use.

In an effort to find inexpensive methods of producing adrenal corticosteroids, Reichstein's later research involved extraction and evaluation of the biological properties of the compounds of certain African plants. He also investigated plant compounds that affect cardiac activity and are related to the digitalis glycosides. In 1960 Reichstein was appointed director of the Institute of Organic Chemistry at the University of Basel; the university designated him professor emeritus in 1967.

In 1927 Reichstein married Louise Henrietta Quarls van Ufford, the daughter of Dutch nobility; they have one daughter.

Reichstein received honorary degrees from the universities of Geneva, Zurich, Basel, and Leeds, among others; he was elected to membership in the Royal Society of London in 1952 and awarded the society's Copley Medal in 1968.

ABOUT: Current Biography February 1951; Journal of Chemical Education October 1947; New York Times October 27, 1950.

RENAULT, LOUIS
(May 21, 1843–February 8, 1918)
Nobel Prize for Peace, 1907
(shared with Ernesto Moneta)

The French international jurist Louis Renault (rə nō′) was born in the town of Autun, in east-central France. His father, a prosperous bookseller, encouraged the boy's intellectual development. After graduating first in his class at the local lycée, Renault entered the Collège d'Autun, where he earned honors in philosophy, mathematics, and literature. Continuing his studies at the University of Dijon, he received a bachelor's degree in literature in 1861. He then studied law at the University of Paris where, after seven years, he was awarded three degrees with honors, the highest of which was a doctorate in law.

Returning to Dijon, Renault taught Roman and commercial law at the university until 1873, when he accepted an appointment to the faculty of law at the University of Paris. After teaching criminal law for one year, he was named professor of international law. Initially reluctant to change fields, he soon distinguished himself by his brilliant lectures and the publication of a book, *Introduction à l'étude du droit international* (Introduction to the Study of International Law), in 1879. Two years later, he was given the chair in international law at the University of Paris, a position he held concurrently with a professorship in international law at the Free School of Political Sciences.

In 1880 Renault became director of the French diplomatic archives. Through his lectures and papers, he quickly gained a reputation as the nation's foremost authority on international law. He was appointed legal consultant to the French Foreign Office in 1890. In the years that followed, he represented his nation at international conferences on such topics as international transport, military aviation, naval affairs, the circulation of obscene literature, international credit, and the revision of the 1864 Geneva Convention. In recognition of his distinguished service, he was awarded the honorary title of minister plenipotentiary and envoy extraordinary in 1903.

Renault's comprehensive grasp of international law made him a logical choice to accompany LÉON BOURGEOIS as French delegate to The Hague Peace Conference of 1899. There he became involved in discussions on naval warfare. At The Hague Peace Conference of 1907, he served on a committee that defined the rights of neutral nations in maritime combat and on one that considered the application

LOUIS RENAULT

of the Geneva Convention to naval battles. Moreover, his status as an elder statesman enabled him to help smooth relations between various national delegations. At the conclusion of the conference, he helped draft the official summary of the proceedings.

As a member of the Permanent Court of Arbitration at The Hague, Renault was so highly esteemed that he was selected to hear more cases than any other jurist during the tribunal's first fourteen years. Among the international disputes that he helped resolve was the Japanese House Tax case. In its verdict, delivered in 1905, the court ruled that the Japanese government did not have the right to tax improvements made to land that had been set aside for perpetual lease to citizens of foreign nations.

Renault received the 1907 Nobel Prize for Peace, which he shared with ERNESTO MONETA. In his presentation address, Jørgen Løvland of the Norwegian Nobel Committee saluted Renault as "the guiding genius in the teaching of international law in France" and cited "the outstanding part he played" at both conferences at The Hague.

In his Nobel lecture, delivered the following year, Renault described the increasing complexity of international relations, which, he said, called for "the juridical organization of international life." He continued, "Anything that contributes to extending the domain of law in international relations contributes to peace," reminding his listeners that, because war always remains a possibility, measures must be taken "to safeguard . . . the interests of noncombatants and of the sick and the wounded." Although critics may scoff at such efforts, he added, "wars will not become rarer by becoming more barbarous."

After receiving the Nobel Prize, Renault continued to teach, write, and sit on the Permanent Court of Arbitration at The Hague. He participated in the settlement of the Casablanca case (1909), a territorial dispute involving French military authorities, the German consul, and the government of Morocco; the Savarkar case (1911), which involved the custody of an Indian prisoner; and several other notable international conflicts.

Renault married Juliette Thiaffait in 1873; the couple had a son and four daughters. Renault remained active until the very end of his life. After delivering a lecture on February 6, 1918, he went to his villa near Paris for a brief holiday. There he suddenly became ill and died on February 8.

During his long career, Renault received many honors in addition to the Nobel Prize, including being decorated by nineteen foreign nations and awarded honorary degrees by many universities. He was a member of the Legion of Honor and the Academy of Moral and Political Science in France and, in 1914, was chosen president of the Academy of International Law at The Hague.

WORKS IN ENGLISH TRANSLATION: "War and the Law of Nations in the Twentieth Century," American Journal of International Law January 9, 1915; First Violations of International Law by Germany: Luxembourg and Belgium, 1917.

ABOUT: American Journal of International Law July 1918; Hull, W. I. The Two Hague Conferences and Their Contributions to International Law 1908; Scott, J. B. The Hague Peace Conferences (2 vols.) 1909.

REYMONT, WŁADYSLAW
(May 6, 1868–December 5, 1925)
Nobel Prize for Literature, 1924

The Polish novelist Władyslaw Reymont was born Władyslaw Stanislaw Rejment in Kobiele Wielkie, a small town in southern Poland then under Russian rule. His parents, Jozef Rejment and Antonina (Kupezynska) Rejment, were of the lower middle class; his father was the village organist, and his meager income barely supported a family of nine children of whom Władyslaw was the fifth. Leaving school after the third grade, the boy was apprenticed to one of his brothers-in-law, a tailor in War-

WŁADYSLAW REYMONT

saw. He subsequently was admitted to the tailors' guild as a journeyman. Shortly thereafter, however, he was expelled from Warsaw when the Russian authorities suspected him of taking part in a strike in Łódź and placed him in his father's custody. Reymont soon ran afoul of his father's strict discipline and his mother's pious attachment to the Roman Catholic church. He ran away several times, finally joining a theatrical touring troupe as an actor. Although he enjoyed the freedom of theatrical life and later found the experience useful to him as a writer, he decided he had no acting talent and abandoned the troupe after a year.

Over the next few years Reymont unsuccessfully tried his hand at various occupations, to the dismay of his parents. He even became a novice monk for a few months at the monastery at Częstochowa. Eventually, with his father's help, he found a job as a railway supervisor, a position that left him ample time to indulge his passion for reading. According to Reymont, his love of reading was acquired as a young boy when he used to seek relief from the harsh realities of life by escaping to the nearby woods or fields with a novel or a volume of verse. Although largely self-educated, he gained a broad knowledge of literature, not only of the Polish classics, but of nineteenth-century English and French novels as well.

Although Reymont's railroad job paid very little, it provided him with an isolated cottage on a rural railroad line, where he began to fill his spare hours by writing. For two years, as he recalled later, he "wrote feverishly:

dramas, . . . novels without end, stories, . . . poems. Then I tore up everything mercilessly and burned it." Of his writing during this period, he saved only six short stories, which he sent to a critic in Warsaw. The critic reacted favorably, and in 1893, only months after he had sent them out, several of the stories were published in a Warsaw weekly. Around this time Reymont lost his job with the railroad, but heartened by his first luck as an author, he moved to Warsaw. Almost penniless, he lived on the verge of starvation until he received a commission from a local magazine to write a piece about the annual pilgrimage to Częstochowa, an important ritual in Polish communal life. The result, *Pieł grzymka do Jasney Góry* (*Pilgrimage to the Mountain of Life*, 1894), a fictionalized account of the event, was an immediate success, and Reymont's career as a writer was launched.

In 1896 Reymont's first novel, *Komediantka* (*The Comedienne*), was published. It is the story of a young woman's pursuit of fame in a seedy theatrical touring company and is drawn, as many of his novels were, from his own experience. The sequel, *Fermenty* (*Ferments*, 1897), follows the heroine, Janka, from the city to the countryside and uses the woman's railway journey to symbolize her quest for emotional fulfillment.

In his next novel, *Ziemia obiecana* (*The Promised Land*, 1899), Reymont abandoned the naturalist and symbolist techniques of his first two novels, feeling that both styles were overly contrived. In this work he used an objective and realistic narrative to explore the brutal world of industrialization. In *The Promised Land*, according to the Polish-American critic Jerzy Krzyżanowski, Reymont "emerged as a mature novelist, in full control of his technique and able to employ it in a major novel of ambitious scope." This "novel without a hero" focuses on three characters in the city of Łódź. What emerges is a finely detailed account of the predatory nature of capitalism, in which the main character is the city itself.

At the beginning of the twentieth century Reymont was badly injured in a railroad accident that left him incapacitated for over a year. Successfully suing the railway, he received a substantial settlement that brought him financial independence and enabled him to pursue his writing without the need to earn a living from other work.

During his recuperation Reymont began to write *Chlopi* (*The Peasants*), a long novel dealing with peasant life that is considered his major work. The first of its four volumes appeared in 1902, the year he moved to Paris with his wife, the former Aurelia Szacsznajder, whom he had married in 1900. The final volume of *The Peasants* was published in 1909. In this account of the lives of ordinary peasants—basically inhabiting the world of his childhood—Reymont paints an exhaustive portrait that has been compared to the works of Thomas Hardy and Émile Zola. He tells the story of a father and son in love with the same woman, Jagna, in a highly lyrical prose style that imparts a mythical quality to the realism of the narrative. In the view of the American critic Joseph Wood Krutch, Reymont's characters are "at once less and more than individuals: he sees them as natural phenomena, parts of the great whole; . . . there is something pantheistic in his feeling for the oneness of all nature." Although the world of *The Peasants* is indisputably Polish, the novel attains universality. Despite a certain diffuseness, prolixity, and unevenness of structure, the novel brought Reymont an international reputation when it was translated into a number of languages.

After completing his masterwork, Reymont continued to write prolifically, but without the same popular and critical success that greeted *The Peasants*. Among his later books are *Marzyciel* (*The Dreamer*, 1910), a novel that reflects Reymont's years of wandering from job to job, and *Wampir* (*The Vampire*, 1911), a novel of the occult.

Reymont returned to Poland in 1914 and spent the years of World War I in his native country. During this period he wrote *Rok 1794* (*The Year 1794*, 1914–1918), a three-volume historical novel about the uprising led by the Polish patriot and general Tadeusz Kosciuszko against German and Russian rule. The author made visits to the United States in 1919 and 1920. Returning to Poland later that year, he settled on his own estate, Kołaczkowo.

Reymont received the 1924 Nobel Prize for Literature "for his great national epic, *The Peasants*," which, according to Per Hallström of the Swedish Academy, "is characterized by an art so grand, so sure, so powerful, that we may predict a lasting value and rank for it." Reymont was too ill to travel to Stockholm to receive the award in person, and no official ceremony took place. In a short note to the Swedish Academy, Reymont wrote, "In 1922–1923 . . . I began to have heart trouble. I still have many things to say and desire greatly to make them public, but will death let me?" A year later, on December 5, 1925, Reymont died in Warsaw.

RICHARDS

Since his death, Reymont's reputation has waned in the West, and his work is known chiefly to specialists. Nevertheless, he remains a major figure in Polish literature. Many scholars share the view of the British critic Martin Seymour-Smith, who finds *The Peasants* "distinguished by the brilliance of its depiction of a whole community" and feels that Reymont "deserves rediscovery outside Poland."

ABOUT: Boyd, E. Studies From Ten Literatures, 1925; Dyboski, R. Modern Polish Literature, 1924; Krzyżanowski, J. R. Władysław Stanisław Reymont, 1972; Living Age January 19, 1925; Poland December 1925.

RICHARDS, DICKINSON W.
(October 30, 1895–February 23, 1973)
Nobel Prize for Physiology or Medicine, 1956
(shared with André Cournand and Werner Forssmann)

DICKINSON W. RICHARDS

The American physician Dickinson Woodruff Richards was born in Orange, New Jersey, to Sally (Lambert) and Dickinson Woodruff Richards. After attending the Hotchkiss School in Connecticut, he entered Yale University and graduated with a B.A. in 1917. Three months later he enlisted in the United States Army and served in France with the American Expeditionary Force in 1918.

Upon his return to the United States, Richards entered the College of Physicians and Surgeons at Columbia University, from which he received his M.A. in physiology in 1922 and his medical degree the following year. He then became an intern and resident physician at Presbyterian Hospital in New York. After a year in London as a Columbia University research fellow at the National Institute for Medical Research, he returned in 1928 to Presbyterian Hospital and the College of Physicians and Surgeons.

From the work conducted by Lawrence Henderson of Harvard University, on the physical chemistry and respiratory function of the blood, Richards and his associate ANDRÉ COURNAND derived what Richards later described as "the simple but essential concept that lungs, heart, and circulation should be thought of as one single apparatus for the transfer of respiratory gases between outside atmosphere and working tissues." This concept was to have a great influence on his own career.

Richards began his association with Cournand in 1913 while in the medical service of

Dr. James Alexander Miller in Bellevue Hospital, a teaching hospital of the College of Physicians and Surgeons. There he had an opportunity to observe and study many patients with chronic pulmonary insufficiency, a condition in which blood flows backward into the heart because of improper functioning of the tricuspid and pulmonic valves.

In his first three years of clinical investigation, Richards confirmed what others had observed—that it was not possible to achieve an even mixing of air in the lungs of patients with chronic pulmonary disease. Later he, Robert Darling, and Eleanor Baldwin developed methods for measuring the physiological performance of the lungs.

As Richards later recalled, there remained in the study of the heart and circulation "one measurement or set of measurements which were conspicuously in default, viz., the state of blood as it enters the right heart, its respiratory gas contents, its pressure relations, and its rate of flow." During the four decades preceding the work of Richards, researchers had attempted to make these measurements. In 1929 the German physician WERNER FORSSMANN successfully passed a narrow rubber catheter through a vein of his own arm into his right atrium (a chamber of the heart), a distance of some two feet, and observed the progress of the catheter on a fluoroscope.

Knowing that accurate measurements of respiratory gases (oxygen and carbon monoxide) in blood returning from the circulation to the right atrium would permit "a reliable measurement of total blood flow through the lungs," Richards and Cournand attempted to use Forssmann's technique. They began their work on dogs and chimpanzees in 1936 and were able to catheterize the right atrium of the human heart by 1941. In that year they also demonstrated that a catheter could be left in the right atrium for up to seven hours without harm to the patient. This procedure enabled them to measure both blood gases and the cardiac output (the volume of blood pumped out of either ventricle, or lower chamber, of the heart in a given period of time). It also became possible to measure blood pressure in the right atrium, the right ventricle, and the pulmonary artery, as well as total blood volume. These measurements significantly advanced the study of how the heart and circulatory system function. Both the technique of cardiac catheterization and the measurements it allows proved of great value in the diagnosis and treatment of cardiovascular and pulmonary diseases.

During World War II Richards served as chairman of the National Research Council's subcommittee on shock. He and his colleagues had been asked by the government to study the circulatory forces involved in shock, to measure the effects of hemorrhage and trauma on the heart and circulation, and to test the effects of various forms of treatment. Using cardiac catheterization, they significantly increased understanding of shock and determined that whole blood, rather than plasma, should be used in its treatment.

In 1944 Richards was named deputy chief of the Division of Physiology of the Committee on Medical Research of the Office of Scientific Research and Development. He served in this capacity until 1946. In 1945 he was also appointed attending physician at Presbyterian Hospital and director of the Columbia University Medical Division at Bellevue Hospital, a post he held until his retirement in 1961, when he became Emeritus Lambert Professor.

After the war and during the early 1950s, Richards continued his clinical studies at the Columbia Medical Division at Bellevue, investigating the effects of digitalis, a drug that stimulates the heart, and explaining the natural history of pulmonary insufficiency. Throughout these years Richards continued his long-standing collaboration with Eleanor Baldwin, whose work had led to the development of practical clinical methods of measuring pulmonary function. In 1948 and 1949 Richards, Cournand, and Baldwin proposed a system for the physiological classification of pulmonary insufficiency, and in so doing summarized the natural history of the disease from mild through severe forms.

Richards shared the 1956 Nobel Prize for Physiology or Medicine with Cournand and Forssmann "for their discoveries concerning heart catheterization and pathological changes in the circulatory system." In his Nobel lecture Richards paid tribute to the pioneering work of Forssmann and others and remarked of the work he himself had done, "Our findings have been for the most part preliminary, revealing new problems more often than solving old ones." The real value of his work, he concluded, was "the interest which has been aroused and the excellent new work that has been stimulated in many laboratories and clinics in many countries."

Richards spoke out on a number of public health issues. For example, in testimony before the Joint Legislative Committee on Narcotics Study in 1957, he recommended that hospital clinics be established to legally distribute narcotics to addicts. He also accused the New York City administration of neglecting Bellevue Hospital, a charge in which he was supported by 450 interns and resident physicians and five lay committees. After becoming president of the Better Bellevue Association in 1962, he initiated the reconstruction of the hospital. He also urged more generous health care benefits for the aged—a position opposed at that time by the American Medical Association.

Richards married Constance B. Riley in 1931; they had four daughters. He died at his home in Lakeville, Connecticut, on February 23, 1973, after suffering a heart attack.

Among Richards's many awards were the John Phillips Memorial Award of the American College of Physicians (1960), the Trudeau Medal of the National Tuberculosis Association (1968), and the Kober Medal of the Association of American Physicians (1970). He was made a chevalier of the Legion of Honor of France (1963). He was a fellow of the American College of Physicians and a member of the Association of American Physicians, the American Medical Association, and the American Clinical and Climatological Association.

SELECTED WORKS: Medical Priesthoods and Other Essays, 1970.

ABOUT: Current Biography March 1957; National Cyclopedia of American Biography, volume I, 1960; New York

RICHARDS

Times October 19, 1956; February 24, 1973; Robinson, D. The Miracle Finders, 1976.

RICHARDS, THEODORE W.
(January 31, 1868–April 2, 1928)
Nobel Prize for Chemistry, 1914

THEODORE W. RICHARDS

The American chemist Theodore William Richards was born into a Quaker family in Germantown, Pennsylvania, the fourth of six children. His father was William Torst Richards, a successful seascape painter; his mother, the former Anna Matlack, a poet. Dissatisfied with the quality of public education, the boy's mother taught him at home. The family spent the summer months at their home in Newport, Rhode Island, where Josiah Parsons Cooke Jr., a professor of chemistry at Harvard University, was a neighbor. Cooke awakened the boy's interest in science by showing him the planet Saturn through a telescope.

Entering Haverford College as a sophomore at the age of fourteen, Richards excelled in chemistry and astronomy. He graduated at the head of his class in 1885 with a B.S. in chemistry. Moving to Harvard that fall to study with Cooke, he completed his senior year in 1886 and graduated summa cum laude in chemistry. As a graduate student under Cooke, Richards began investigating the relationship between atomic weights. Atomic weight is a measurement that defines the relative masses of the atoms of individual elements. Although at this time the atomic weights of several elements had been calculated, the reliability of these results was doubtful.

Under Cooke's supervision, Richards set out to determine the atomic weights of oxygen and hydrogen. He used an original method, burning a known quantity of hydrogen with copper oxide to form a measurable amount of water. His results—a hydrogen-to-oxygen weight ratio of 1:15.96—contradicted the prevailing belief that the weight of any element should be a whole-number multiple of the atomic weight of hydrogen. Turning to copper, Richards corrected its atomic weight from 63.31 to 63.54.

On receiving his Ph.D. from Harvard in 1888, Richards was awarded a Parker Fellowship that enabled him to continue his studies in Germany at the universities of Göttingen, Munich, and Dresden. When he returned to Harvard the following year, he was appointed an assistant in quantitative analysis. He became an instructor in 1891 and an assistant professor in 1894. With Cooke's death the following year, Richards was sent abroad for one year to work with WILHELM OSTWALD at the University of Leipzig and with WALTHER NERNST at the University of Göttingen. In 1901 he turned down the chair of physical chemistry at the University of Göttingen to become a full professor at Harvard. From 1903 to 1911 he served as chairman of the chemistry department, and from 1912 until his death he was Erving Professor of Chemistry.

By 1905 Richards had become aware that the accepted values for many atomic weights were in error, and he made it his task to correct them. To increase the precision of his measurements, he developed several new instruments, including an apparatus that precluded contamination of his samples by atmospheric moisture, a calorimeter that, unlike other types, was not affected by slight temperature changes caused by the substances under investigation, and the nephelometer, a device that permits visual determination of the concentration or size of particles in solution.

During the next decade, Richards was the impetus for determining the atomic weights of more than thirty elements, twenty-one of which he himself established. Apart from its practical importance, this work was fundamental to chemical theory. For example, by confirming that cobalt has a greater atomic weight than nickel, even though it precedes nickel in the periodic table, he showed that, contrary to accepted theory, atomic weight was not the basis of the chemical order. Perhaps his most notable achievement in the determination of atomic weights was his 1914 proof that lead from radioactive sources has a distinctly lower atomic weight than the normal variety of lead. This was among the earliest confirmations of the existence of isotopes, or atoms of the same element with different atomic weights.

Richards was a leading candidate for the 1914 Nobel Prize for Chemistry. With the outbreak of World War I that year, however, nominations were postponed until the following year, when Richards was awarded the prize "in recognition of his exact determinations of atomic weights of a large number of chemical elements." Richards was unable to accept the award in person. In his remarks at the ceremonies in Stockholm, H. G. Söderbaum of the Royal Swedish Academy of Sciences remarked that "in almost every one of Richards's treatises there are to be found descriptions of methods and manipulations that mark noteworthy improvements as compared with those practiced before his day." Richards delivered a Nobel lecture in Stockholm in 1919. His investigations into atomic weights, he said, "were first inspired by an intense philosophic desire to know more about the fundamental nature of matter and its relations to energy. Later I perceived more and more clearly that a better understanding of the behavior of matter . . . must give mankind more power over the circumstances of living."

In addition to his work on atomic weights, Richards investigated equilibrium, electrochemistry, and chemical thermodynamics. His work on the thermodynamics of elements at low temperatures led in 1902 to observations that anticipated the third law of thermodynamics, developed three years later by Nernst. A topic of particular interest to him was atomic volumes. His theory of compressible atoms, which he articulated in 1907, suggested that atomic volume depends on chemical state. Richards went on to examine variations in atomic volume in many of the elements.

In 1896 Richards married Miriam Stuart Thayer, the daughter of a theology professor at Harvard. They had one daughter and two sons. Described by the science writer Benjamin Harrow as a man "of medium height . . . , eyes that look keenly through his glasses, and a genial manner," Richards enjoyed literature, music, and art during his leisure time. His prodigious commitment to research and teaching helped build Harvard into a leading center for graduate instruction in chemistry. Richards continued to teach until a few days before his death at Cambridge, Massachusetts, in 1928.

In addition to the Nobel Prize, Richards received the Davy Medal of the Royal Society of London (1910), the Willard Gibbs Medal of the American Chemical Society (1912), the Franklin Medal of the Franklin Institute (1916), and the Lavoisier Medal of the French Chemical Society (1922). He served as president of the American Chemical Society, the American Association for the Advancement of Science, and the American Academy of Arts and Sciences and was a member of numerous learned societies. He was awarded honorary degrees by thirteen universities in Europe and the United States.

SELECTED WORKS: The Universally Exact Application of Faraday's Law, 1902, with W. N. Stull; Determinations of Atomic Weights, 1910.

ABOUT: Biographical Memoirs of the National Academy of Sciences, volume 44, 1974; Dictionary of American Biography, volume 15, 1935; Dictionary of Scientific Biography, volume 11, 1975; Harrow, B. (ed.) Eminent Chemists of Our Time, 1927; Journal of the Chemical Society August 1930.

RICHARDSON, OWEN W.
(April 26, 1879–February 15, 1959)
Nobel Prize for Physics, 1928

The English physicist Owen Willans Richardson was born in Dewsbury, Yorkshire, the only son among the three children of Joshua Henry Richardson, an industrial tool salesman, and Charlotte Maria (Willans) Richardson. After early schooling in Askern, near Doncaster, Richardson won a full scholarship at the age of twelve to Batley Grammar School, where he was a prizewinning student. In 1897 he entered Trinity College, Cambridge, on a full scholarship, studying at the Cavendish Laboratory under J. J. THOMSON, with fellow students ERNEST RUTHERFORD, C. T. R. WILSON, H. A. Wilson, and Paul Langevin. Earning first-class honors in physics, chemistry, and botany, he received his B.A. from Cambridge in 1900. Richardson remained at Cambridge for graduate work in physics and chemistry and became a fellow of Trinity College in 1902. Two years later he was awarded a Clerk Maxwell Fellowship and a Ph.D. from University College in London.

Thomson had demonstrated in 1899 that the current from an incandescent carbon filament in a vacuum tube is carried by negatively charged particles (electrons). Richardson sought, both theoretically and experimentally, to describe how heated metal filaments emit streams of charged particles. In 1901 he hy-

OWEN W. RICHARDSON

pothesized, on the basis of his work with heated platinum filaments, that freely moving electrons in the interior of a hot conductor can escape when they reach the surface if their kinetic energy is great enough to overcome the forces that bind them within the material. In other words, an electron gas can evaporate from the hot surface. He formulated an empirical law that relates the rate of electron emission to the composition of the filament and to the temperature of its surface. Experiments over the next twelve years, including those in 1913 with the newly developed ductile form of the element tungsten, confirmed the law fully. Richardson's law states that the rate of electron emission increases very rapidly as the surface temperature is increased.

In 1906 Richardson became professor of physics at Princeton University, where his students included Robert T. Goddard, Karl T. Compton, and ARTHUR H. COMPTON. His mathematician colleague Oswald Veblen and his research assistant CLINTON J. DAVISSON married Richardson's two sisters.

At Princeton, Richardson demonstrated that electrons emitted from a metal surface obey the same statistical relationships as do atomic and molecular gases. His other research concerned the emission of electrons from illuminated matter (the photoelectric effect), the interaction of X rays with matter, the emission of light by matter, the gyromagnetic effect, and thermodynamics, which treats the behavior of systems made up of enormous numbers of particles. In 1909 he coined the term *ther-*

mionics to describe the emission of electric charges from hot bodies.

In 1913, shortly before he was to become a naturalized American citizen, Richardson was elected a fellow of the Royal Society of London and was offered the Wheatstone Professorship of Physics at King's College, University of London. Accepting the post, he returned to London in 1914, where his research was immediately disrupted by the outbreak of World War I. Although much of Richardson's time during the war years was devoted to the development of improved vacuum tubes for use in military telecommunications, he managed to conduct basic research. He performed extensive spectroscopic investigations (measuring with a spectrometer the light emitted at different wavelengths) of the light emitted by excited atoms, in order to test the accuracy of NIELS BOHR's 1913 model of the atom. He also conducted experimental tests of ALBERT EINSTEIN's analysis of electron emission from a metal surface illuminated by ultraviolet radiation. At the end of the war, Richardson returned to full-time teaching and research. He gave up teaching in 1924, however, when he was appointed Yarrow Research Professor of the Royal Society and director of research in physics at King's College.

In 1929 Richardson was awarded the 1928 Nobel Prize for Physics for "his work on the thermionic phenomenon and especially for the discovery of the law named after him." In his Nobel lecture Richardson outlined the course of his discoveries and summarized his findings.

During the 1920s and 1930s Richardson published a series of papers on the connection between physics and chemistry as exemplified by molecular structure. He was active in the application and the experimental verification of the predictions about molecular structure made by quantum mechanics, a newly developed field that describes the behavior of systems at the atomic and subatomic scale.

Richardson was knighted in 1939, and when World War II broke out later that year, he applied his knowledge to research on radar, sonar, electronic test instruments, magnetrons, and klystrons.

In 1906 Richardson married Lillian Maude Wilson, the sister of a fellow student, H. A. Wilson. They had two sons and one daughter. After Richardson retired from King's College in 1944, he moved to Chandos Lodge, his country home near Alton, Hampshire, where he operated a nearby dairy farm. His first wife died in 1945, and three years later Richardson married Henrietta M. G. Rupp, a physicist and an authority on luminescence in solids. Even in retirement, he continued his research on molecular structure. Richardson, who enjoyed the natural world and long walks in the country, was known as an exceptionally pleasant man who assisted colleagues and students generously. He died at home on February 15, 1959.

Richardson was awarded the Hughes Medal of the Royal Society in 1920. He held honorary doctorates from the universities of Leeds, St. Andrew's, and London. He was a member of the American Philosophical Society and the scientific academies of Norway, Sweden, Germany, and India.

SELECTED WORKS: The Electron Theory of Matter, 1914; The Emission of Electricity From Hot Bodies, 1916; Molecular Hydrogen and Its Spectrum, 1934.

ABOUT: Biographical Memoirs of Fellows of the Royal Society, volume 5, 1959; Dictionary of Scientific Biography, volume 11, 1975.

RICHET, CHARLES
(August 26, 1850–December 4, 1935)
Nobel Prize for Physiology or Medicine, 1913

The French physiologist Charles Robert Richet (rē shā′) was born in Paris to Alfred Richet, a professor of clinical surgery in the Faculty of Medicine at the University of Paris, and the former Eugénie Rouard. After receiving the customary elementary and secondary schooling, Richet decided to follow in his father's footsteps and become a doctor. He entered the University of Paris but had not been in medical school long when it became clear that his true interest lay in research rather than in the practice of medicine. Richet had also considered a career in the humanities, in which he maintained an interest throughout his life.

While still a medical student, he studied hypnotism, the fluids involved in digestion, and the effects of pain on muscle and nerve function. He received his medical degree in 1877, followed the next year by a doctor of science degree with a thesis on the first demonstration of the presence of hydrochloric acid in the stomach secretions of mammals, fish, and invertebrates. He also showed that a form of lactic acid is present in the stomach during digestion. That year he was appointed professor on the Faculty of Medicine of the Univer-

CHARLES RICHET

sity of Paris, where he began a study of the different types of muscle contraction.

By 1883 Richet was studying how warm-blooded animals maintain a constant internal temperature, especially by panting and shivering. He demonstrated that specific areas of the brain are involved in the control of body heat and that the heat output of an animal is proportional to its size (for example, the larger the animal, the less heat is produced per unit of weight). He also developed an interest in microbiology, particularly the distribution of bacteria in body fluids, a subject that had been a side issue in his studies of digestion.

In 1880 Louis Pasteur announced that he had found a way to protect chickens against fowl cholera. Watching a demonstration in which Pasteur inoculated chickens with weakened, artificially cultured cholera microbes, Richet was impressed by the idea that microbial diseases may be caused by a toxin that is counteracted by chemical substances in the blood. The next year, he proposed that French sheep, which were susceptible to anthrax, might be protected from the disease by transfusions of blood from resistant Algerian sheep. He was unable to pursue this idea until 1888, when he began to study the properties of blood from infected animals more intensively.

While working with Jules Hericourt, Richet discovered a *Staphylococcus* bacterium that was fatal to rabbits but only produced sores when injected into dogs. Their attempt to transfer resistance to the bacterial substance by direct transfusions of dog blood into rabbit veins proved to be toxic to the rabbits. The transfer succeeded, however, when the dog blood was injected into the rabbits' peritoneal cavity (the space between the layers of membranes lining the abdominal wall), from which the blood could be absorbed slowly. As a result, the rabbits became more immune to further injections of the *Staphylococcus.*

Next, Richet and Hericourt attempted to extend their "hematotherapy" (later called serum therapy) to human diseases. They began their efforts with tuberculosis—an unfortunate choice, Richet later admitted, "for the serum therapy of tuberculosis is doubtful, whilst the serum therapy of diphtheria gives marvelous results; as, two years later, [EMIL VON] BEHRING showed in an admirable piece of work." For ten fruitless years, Richet and his collaborator attempted to develop tuberculosis serum therapy.

During the 1890s Richet was involved in various nonphysiological projects, including an unsuccessful attempt to design an airplane. By the end of the decade, Richet and Hericourt were forced to admit that their original goal—serum therapy for tuberculosis—had eluded them. Meanwhile, however, they had discovered that a diet of raw meat improved the condition of tubercular dogs, and after 1900 Richet argued that "zomotherapy" (feeding with raw meat fluids) was an effective treatment for human tuberculosis.

In 1901, while investigating the phenomenon that muscle plasma is toxic when injected directly into a vein, Richet had another opportunity to expand his knowledge of toxicology. On a scientific expedition in the Mediterranean Sea with Prince Albert of Monaco, he was urged to study the poisonous tentacles of the Portuguese man-of-war. After a few preliminary experiments, he returned to France, where he undertook a comparative study of sea anemone poison. He injected dogs with varying quantities of the poison to determine the toxic dose; the animals that survived the procedure were kept and after a few weeks were injected again. "And then appeared an extraordinary fact," Richet reported, "which at first I had enormous difficulty in believing." When the dogs were reinjected with much smaller doses of the poison, they died very quickly. Richet called this phenomenon anaphylaxis, because its action was opposite to that of the prophylactic (protective) effect produced by normal immunization.

Anaphylaxis had important implications for medical practice. The diphtheria serum therapy developed by Behring, for instance, was not always successful; some patients reacted strongly to the serum injections and died. According to Richet's findings, those patients were victims of anaphylactic shock, an exaggerated allergic reaction to foreign proteins or antigens. For example, horse serum used to immunize people against tetanus toxin causes anaphylaxis in overly sensitive individuals; bee stings and penicillin can cause it in others. Regardless of the kind of antigen, the symptoms of anaphylaxis show certain general characteristics, such as vomiting, itching, lowered blood pressure, paralysis of higher brain function, labored breathing, low temperature, and even death.

In the first decade of the twentieth century, considerable research was conducted on the phenomenon of anaphylaxis by Richet and others. Richet summarized his findings in a 1911 monograph titled *Anaphylaxis.* He explained the phenomenon by postulating that "there exists in anaphylactized blood a substance harmless in itself but which releases a strong poison when mixed with the antigen." Showing that these substances are proteins, Richet developed diagnostic tests specific for those causing hypersensitivity reactions.

Richet received the 1913 Nobel Prize for Physiology or Medicine "in recognition of his work on anaphylaxis." In his Nobel lecture he stated that while anaphylaxis may be a "sorry matter for the individual, it is necessary to the species, often to the detriment of the individual . . . [because] anaphylaxis defends the species against the peril of adulteration." Thus the chemical identity of each species is maintained. As a result of Richet's discovery, physicians not only were made aware of the value of prophylaxis but were given an insight into the opposite of prophylaxis. During World War I, Richet studied problems in blood plasma transfusion.

In 1877 Richet married Amélie Aubry; they had two daughters and five sons (one of whom also became a professor of medicine at the University of Paris and was succeeded in turn by his own son). A man of wide-ranging talents and diverse interests, Richet had a remarkably varied career as a physiologist, bacteriologist, pathologist, psychologist, statistician, engineer, poet, dramatist, and novelist. He also became interested in psychic investigation, and in 1923 an English translation of his experience in this field appeared as *Thirty Years of Psychical Research.* A dedicated pacifist, Richet wrote several books dealing with the evils of war. He died in Paris on December 4, 1935.

Richet was elected to the French Academy of Medicine and the French Academy of Sciences and in 1926 received the Cross of the Legion of Honor. He also served as the coeditor of the *Journal de Physiologie et Pathologie Générale* (Journal of Physiology and General Pathology) for seventeen years and as editor of the *Revue Scientifique* (Scientific Review) for twenty-four years.

SELECTED WORKS: Physiology and History of Cerebral Convulsions, 1879; Peace and War, 1906; The Pros and Cons of Vivisection, 1908; Idiot Man, 1925; The Natural History of a Savant, 1927; The Importance of Man, 1928; Our Sixth Sense, 1929; The Story of Civilization Through the Ages, 1930.

ABOUT: Dictionary of Scientific Biography, volume 11, 1975.

RICHTER, BURTON
(March 22, 1931–)
Nobel Prize for Physics, 1976
(shared with Samuel C. C. Ting)

BURTON RICHTER

The American physicist Burton Richter (rik′ tər) was born in New York City, the only son and elder child of Abraham Richter, a textile worker, and Fannie (Pollack) Richter. Showing an early interest in science, he built a chemistry laboratory in the basement of his home and read widely in physics. Richter attended Far Rockaway High School in Queens, New York, and Mercersburg Academy in Mercersburg, Pennsylvania, before entering the Massachusetts Institute of Technology (MIT) in 1948. Initially, he was undecided about whether to major in physics or chemistry, but one of his professors, Francis Friedman, "opened my eyes to the beauty of physics," as Richter said later.

In his junior year Richter worked with Francis Bitter in MIT's magnetism laboratory, studying the physical system composed of an electron and a positron (the antimatter counterpart of the electron). Twenty-five years later, the work for which he received the Nobel Prize relied on experiments with the same two particles. His senior thesis at MIT, written under Bitter's supervision, examined the effect of strong magnetic fields on the energy level of the hydrogen atom.

After receiving his B.S. in 1952, Richter continued as a graduate student in Bitter's laboratory. His first assignment was to produce a short-lived isotope of mercury by bombarding gold atoms with high-energy nuclei of deuterium (heavy hydrogen). The high-energy nuclei were supplied by a cyclotron, a particle accelerator in which charged particles gain speed as they follow a spiral path. Richter soon became more interested in the cyclotron and in its potential as a tool for nuclear physics and particle physics than he was in the preparation of the mercury isotope.

At this time Richter met the physicist David Frisch, who arranged for him to spend six months at the Brookhaven National Laboratory on Long Island, New York. There he worked with the cosmotron, one of the most powerful particle accelerators then operating. Returning to MIT, he performed experiments with the institute's synchrotron, an accelerator similar in design to the cosmotron, although much smaller. In a synchrotron, the accelerated particles follow a circular path rather than a spiral.

Richter completed his Ph.D. in 1956, using the synchrotron to study the production of certain unstable particles. He then became a research associate in the physics department at Stanford University. At the time, his primary interest was in quantum electrodynamics, the theory of electromagnetic forces acting on charged particles. He proposed to test the theory by observing collisions between moving electrons and stationary ones. His colleagues Wolfgang Panofsky and Sidney Drell suggested a better procedure: examining pairs of electrons and positrons created from gamma rays, the highest-energy form of electromagnetic radiation. Richter's results showed that quantum electrodynamics correctly describes the electromagnetic force at distances as small as one ten-trillionth of a centimeter.

869

A conventional particle accelerator directs a beam of high-energy particles against the atoms of a stationary target. Much higher energies can be attained if two moving particles meet head-on, and in 1957 Gerard K. O'Neill at Princeton University suggested that such head-on collisions might be arranged by storing accelerated particles in circular orbits in a doughnut-shaped vacuum chamber. The following year Richter, O'Neill, and several other colleagues began building a pair of such storage rings at Stanford. An accelerator at the university's High-Energy Physics Laboratory would fill both rings with electrons accelerated to an energy of 700 million electron volts. It took several years to overcome the technical difficulties of making the storage rings work. The team's first results, a confirmation of quantum electrodynamics ten times more accurate than Richter's earlier experiment, were announced in 1965.

In the meantime, in 1960, Richter was promoted to assistant professor at the High-Energy Physics Laboratory. Three years later he moved to the Stanford Linear Accelerator Center (SLAC), a few miles from the university campus, where a two-mile-long electron accelerator was being completed. In 1967 he was appointed a full professor at Stanford while continuing to work at SLAC.

With the higher-energy electrons available from the SLAC accelerator, a new kind of particle storage ring became feasible. Earlier designers had called for two rings in a figure-eight configuration; electrons circulating in the separate rings met head-on in the common segment that joined the rings. The SLAC accelerator, however, could generate positrons as well as electrons, both of which could be stored in a single ring. The same electromagnetic fields that keep the electrons circulating clockwise in the ring would keep the positrons moving counterclockwise. The beams of particles and antiparticles would collide twice during each revolution.

Richter led a group that began construction of an electron-positron storage ring at SLAC in 1970. The device, called the Stanford positron-electron accelerating ring (SPEAR), could reach collision energies of 8 billion electron volts. A year later, a remarkable discovery was announced. The experiments using SPEAR, which began in 1973, were the inverse of those Richter first carried out at Stanford. Whereas he had earlier created electrons and positrons from high-energy electromagnetic radiation, each collision using SPEAR annihilated an electron and a positron to produce an electro-

magnetic "fireball." Out of this fireball new particles were born.

In the summer of 1974 the group was recording the production rate of hadrons (the class of particles, related to the proton and the neutron, that respond to the strong nuclear force) as a function of collision energy. The storage ring was operated for a time at a particular energy, and the number of hadrons produced were counted; the energy was then increased slightly and the count repeated. As the researchers expected, the production rate increased smoothly and gradually. At one particular energy, however, corresponding to about three times the mass of the proton, a tall, sharp peak occurred in hadron production. Such a "resonance" is often the telltale sign of a new particle, one whose mass corresponds to the collision energy where the peak is observed.

Richter and his group spent several months repeating the experiment, checking the equipment and measuring the production rate in smaller energy steps to exclude the possibility of a false alarm. By November all potential sources of error had been ruled out, and the discovery of a particle was announced. A day later Richter learned that SAMUEL C. C. TING's group at MIT had independently and simultaneously identified the same particle, using a different experimental technique. Richter gave the particle the name *psi* because "it was the only Greek letter that hadn't been picked to describe an atomic particle." Ting chose the name *J;* the two names were later combined.

The discovery of a new subatomic particle would not in itself have caused a great deal of excitement in the world of high-energy physics. Since the 1950s, more than 100 hadrons had been identified, and there was every reason to believe that more would be found. All but the least-massive of the hadrons, however, are very short-lived; they are excitations of the lower-mass hadrons, analogous to the excited states of atoms, that quickly decay to yield the lower-mass relatives such as the proton and the neutron. What seemed extraordinary about the J/psi was its lifetime, some 10,000 times longer than would have been expected for such a massive particle. This longevity suggested that the J/psi has some property of matter not shared by any lighter particle. The need somehow to cast off the new property—since no lighter particle could inherit it—would delay the J/psi decay.

Ting's and Richter's discovery of J/psi provided experimental evidence of the existence of a fundamental particle called charm. As early as 1963, the physicists MURRAY GELL-

MANN and George Zweig had speculated that all hadrons might be made up of a few fundamental particles, which Gell-Mann named quarks. Originally, there were three kinds of quarks (up, down, and strange), which could account for all the hadrons known before the discovery of the J/psi. In 1964, however, SHELDON L. GLASHOW and James D. Bjorken had argued that a fourth quark, called the charmed quark, might account for certain peculiarities in the interactions of the known particles. The J/psi confirmed this notion. In fact, it consists of a charmed quark bound to a charmed antiquark. Dozens of other charmed particles have since been found, including many first observed by members of Richter's group.

In 1976 the Nobel Prize for Physics was awarded to Richter and Ting "for their pioneering work in the discovery of a heavy elementary particle of a new kind." In his Nobel lecture Richter described his career as "a long love affair . . . with the electron. Like most love affairs, it has had its ups and downs, but for me the joys have far outweighed the frustrations." It is rare for the Royal Swedish Academy of Sciences to honor an achievement only two years after the work has been completed. Richter pointed out, however, that "my work and Ting's work provided instant confirmation of our individual findings."

Since 1979 Richter has been Paul Pigott Professor of Physics at Stanford, a position he holds concurrently with his responsibilities at SLAC. He is also a consultant to the United States Department of Energy.

In 1960 Richter married Laurose Becker, an administrative assistant at Stanford. They have a son and a daughter. Described by his colleagues as an affable man with a genial sense of humor, Richter enjoys hiking, skiing, playing squash, and tending his garden.

In addition to the Nobel Prize, Richter has received the Ernest Orlando Lawrence Memorial Award for Physics of the United States Energy Research and Development Agency (1975). He is a member of the National Academy of Sciences and a fellow of the American Association for the Advancement of Science and the American Physical Society.

ABOUT: Current Biography September 1977; Nova: Adventures in Science, 1982; Physics Today December 1976; Science November 19, 1976.

ROBBINS, FREDERICK C.

(August 25, 1916–)
Nobel Prize for Physiology or Medicine, 1954
(shared with John F. Enders and Thomas H. Weller)

The American bacteriologist Frederick Chapman Robbins was born in Auburn, Alabama, to William J. Robbins, a plant physiologist who later became director of the New York Botanical Garden, and Christine (Chapman) Robbins, who was a botanical researcher before her marriage. The eldest of three brothers, Robbins grew up in Columbia, Missouri, where his father was professor of botany at the University of Missouri. Majoring in science and medicine, Robbins earned a B.A. in 1936 and a B.S. in 1938 from the University of Missouri, where he distinguished himself as a fine horseman and polo player. He then went to Harvard Medical School, where he roomed with classmate THOMAS H. WELLER. After graduating from medical school in 1940, Robbins was resident bacteriologist at Children's Hospital Medical Center in Boston, serving as an intern in 1941–1942.

In 1942 Robbins and Weller joined the Army Medical Corps, and Robbins was assigned to the Fifteenth Medical General Laboratory. As chief of the Virus and Rickettsial Disease Section, he headed a laboratory for virus diagnosis, studying rickettsial and virus diseases. The diseases are paired in research—even though rickettsias are a form of bacteria and differ from viruses in size and complexity—because both are parasites that grow only within the cells of their host. Robbins's wartime research took him to North Africa and Italy, where he investigated infectious hepatitis and typhus and isolated the rickettsia responsible for Q fever (Queensland or quadrilateral fever), an infectious disease similar to viral pneumonia. In 1945 he was awarded the Bronze Star for Distinguished Service, and a year later he was discharged from the army with the rank of major.

Returning to Boston Children's Hospital in 1946, Robbins completed his pediatric training there two years later. His friend Weller was also at Children's, in the newly organized Research Division of Infectious Diseases headed by JOHN F. ENDERS. Robbins was awarded a Senior National Research Fellowship in virus diseases and, at Weller's suggestion, joined Enders's staff.

Because viruses cannot grow outside living cells, much virus research poses problems of

FREDERICK C. ROBBINS

tissue culture (the cultivation of cells in animal tissue in laboratory dishes). Weller was working with measles and chicken pox viruses; Robbins was trying to isolate the virus responsible for infantile epidemic diarrhea, a potentially dangerous disease common in hospital nurseries. Initially, none of the Enders team was conducting research in poliomyelitis (polio).

Poliomyelitis was the most feared of all virus diseases in the 1940s. While the incidence of other infectious diseases decreased in the twentieth century, poliomyelitis became more common and more virulent. It is now thought that its rise as a serious illness was an ironic result of improved public health. In the past, polio was usually contracted by children when they were very young, and the effects of the disease were mild. With improved sanitation, however, many people were not exposed until their teens or twenties, when the effects of the disease are more devastating.

Research on poliomyelitis proceeded slowly. The poliovirus was first isolated by KARL LANDSTEINER in 1908. Only one of the virus's three types could be grown in mice or other inexpensive laboratory animals; the other two types would grow only in monkeys or in humans. Previous research indicated that the virus was neurotropic—that is, it would grow only in nerve tissue, a difficult medium to cultivate in quantities necessary for research purposes. Enders, however, began to doubt the premise that the virus was exclusively neurotropic. He found that polio patients excreted

far more of the virus in their urine and feces than could be expected if it were produced by the nervous system alone.

Meanwhile, the three men had greatly improved earlier methods for growing cells in tissue cultures. Researching mumps, Enders and Weller proved that viruses could multiply and spread in cultured cells. Robbins prepared tissue cultures of mouse intestine for his first experiments in infantile diarrhea, and human cell cultures were being used by Weller to grow chicken pox virus. "In this way," the three scientists later said, "such cultures were made available while close at hand in the storage cabinet was the Lansing strain of poliomyelitis virus. Thereupon it suddenly occurred to us that everything had been prepared almost without conscious effort on our part for a new attempt to cultivate the agent in extraneural tissue."

Their attempt succeeded. In 1948 Robbins, Enders, and Weller proved that poliovirus could be grown in laboratory cultures of human tissue, even though nerve cells were not present in the preparation. The implications for treating human disease were considerable.

Until then, researchers diagnosed poliomyelitis by injecting a sample of the patient's tissue or body fluid into the brain of a monkey and observing the animal for symptoms. The process was laborious, time-consuming, and costly. With their new technique, Robbins and his colleagues could detect the growth of poliovirus in cultures after eight days. As knowledge of the method spread, other scientists found that tissue cultures could be substituted for experiments in laboratory animals. Not only could viruses be grown in tissue cultures, but changes in the cultures could be used to measure the infectiousness of a given virus strain. It was also discovered that tissues could be protected from virus infection with antiserum from patients with poliomyelitis. Since these protective antibodies are type-specific, the discovery contributed greatly to the study of different types of poliomyelitis in human populations.

The culture method invented by Robbins, Enders, and Weller depended on the use of antibiotics to prevent bacteria from contaminating the cultures. With antibiotics, they could reliably grow poliovirus from samples heavily loaded with other microorganisms. Without antibiotics, the method probably would not have worked. "The discovery of the antibiotics has, as in so many other areas, worked a revolution in the field of tissue culture," the three scientists said. "Here, then, we have another example of how one discovery leads to many others, often of quite a different nature."

As the discovery of antibiotics aided the research of Robbins, Enders, and Weller, their research in turn marked a significant step in the development of a polio vaccine. Their contribution to the production of the vaccine was an important consideration in the awarding of the 1954 Nobel Prize for Physiology or Medicine to the three men "for their discovery of the ability of poliomyelitis viruses to grow in cultures of various types of tissue." In his presentation speech, Sven Gard of the Karolinska Institute called the team's 1949 research report "a paper, modest in size and wording but with sensational content." With the successful cultivation of the poliovirus in a test tube culture of human tissue, he said, "a new epoch in the history of virus research had started."

Appointed professor of pediatrics at Western Reserve (now Case Western Reserve) University School of Medicine in 1952, Robbins served as dean of the medical school from 1966 to 1980. He then moved to Bethesda, Maryland, to become president of the Institute of Medicine, a position he held until 1985.

In 1948 Robbins married Alice Northrop, who, like his mother, was a researcher before her marriage. The couple's two daughters have the distinction of being both the children and the grandchildren of Nobel laureates. Their maternal grandfather, JOHN H. NORTHROP, was co-winner of the 1946 Nobel Prize for Chemistry.

A member of the National Academy of Sciences and the National Philosophical Society, Robbins was elected president of the Society for Pediatric Research in 1961. He shared the Mead Johnson Award of the American Academy of Pediatrics with Weller in 1953. He was awarded honorary doctor of science degrees from John Carroll University, Cleveland, and the University of Missouri and an honorary LL.D. from the University of New Mexico.

ABOUT: Current Biography June 1955; Nature October 30, 1954; New York Times October 22, 1954; Williams, G. Virus Hunters, 1959.

ROBINSON, ROBERT
(September 13, 1886–February 8, 1975)
Nobel Prize for Chemistry, 1947

The English chemist Robert Robinson was born at Rufford Farm, near Chesterfield, Derbyshire. He was the eldest of five children of William Bradbury Robinson and his second wife, the former Jane Davenport. Since 1794 the Robinson family had been successful manufacturers of surgical dressings. Robinson's grandfather, William Robinson, had invented cotton wool, a mechanical linting machine, and a process for the automated cutting of cotton bandages.

When Robinson was three years old, his large family (which included eight children from his father's first marriage) moved to nearby New Brampton. After receiving his early education at Mrs. Wilke's Kindergarten and the Chesterfield Grammar School, Robinson attended Fulneck School, an outstanding academic institution between Leeds and Bradford, run by members of the Moravian church. Robinson, whose family were Congregationalists, remained there until 1902, when he entered Manchester University.

Although Robinson had shown a strong interest in mathematics, his father wanted him to join the family business and insisted that he study chemistry. The chemistry department at Manchester, headed by William H. Perkin Jr., was a leading center of instruction and research. When Robinson enrolled there, the Russian-born chemist Chaim Weizmann, the future first president of Israel and founder of the Rehovot Research Institute, was a faculty member, and Robinson's fellow students included WALTER N. HAWORTH. After graduating in 1905 with first-class honors, Robinson entered Perkin's private research laboratory, where he studied the structure and chemical properties of brazilin, a dye obtained from wood. This natural coloring substance and its derivative hematoxylin were the objects of Robinson's continuing research for the next sixty-nine years. Other lifelong interests stemming from his research with Perkin included pyrylium salts, anthocyanidins, and alkaloid synthesis.

Robinson returned to Manchester University as a university fellow (1906) and an 1851 Exhibition Scholar (1907–1909). He received a doctorate of science in 1910. Two years later, at the age of twenty-six, he became the first professor of pure and applied organic chemistry at the University of Sydney, Australia. That year he also married Gertrude Maud Walsh, a fellow student at Manchester. The couple had a son and a daughter.

Robinson was subsequently appointed chairman of the organic chemistry departments at the universities of Liverpool (1915–1920), St. Andrews (1921), and Manchester (1922–1928), and at University College, London (1928–1930). In 1930 he succeeded Perkin

ROBERT ROBINSON

as Waynflete Professor of Chemistry at Oxford University. In 1920 he served briefly as research director for the British Dyestuff Corporation. He gained a wide knowledge of the chemistry of dyes, which was useful when he became a consultant to the Dyestuffs Division Research Panel of Imperial Chemical Industries Ltd. in 1929.

Robinson's studies of brazilin involved the use of catechol derivatives and led to an attempt to synthesize alkaloids containing isoquinoline, a two-ring carbon and nitrogen structure. Alkaloids, which are complex nitrogenous substances found in plants, include quinine, cocaine, atropine, morphine, and opium. While working in Perkin's laboratory in Manchester, Robinson synthesized papaverine. Because of his relatively easy preparation of the alkaloids hydrastine, narcotine, and tropinone (closely related to atropine and cocaine), Robinson believed that these chemical substances must be synthesized in a similar way by plants. His theory of alkaloid biogenesis, in which three simple molecules combine to form a complicated system, was later confirmed by radioactive tracer studies of reactions in living plants. Robinson synthesized and then determined the structure of many other alkaloids, including morphine, strychnine, brucine, akuammicine, and (in collaboration with R. B. WOODWARD) ajmaline.

Together with his wife, Robinson made a lengthy study of the flower pigments anthocyanin (blue-red) and anthoxanthin (yellow). In the laboratory, they synthesized many pigments that were found to be identical to the naturally occurring substances. The Robinson team devised rapid tests for the identification of pigments using only a few flower petals, and they published catalogs of flower colors. Applying these small-scale tests for plant pigments, the Robinsons also investigated genetic variations in flowers.

Another complex molecular structure of interest to Robinson was the carbon-ring skeleton of steroid hormones. Working with many collaborators, including JOHN W. CORNFORTH, he prepared the female hormone estrone and three synthetic estrogens: stilbestrol, hexestrol, and dienestrol. Robinson also contributed to a qualitative electronic theory of chemical reactions concerning the distribution of electrons and partial valences in aromatic carbon compounds. These ideas, which were further developed by his friend Arthur Lapworth at Manchester, laid the foundation for modern theoretical organic chemistry.

After the outbreak of World War II in 1939, Robinson devoted much of his effort to war-related work, including the development of explosives and defenses against chemical weapons. He also contributed to research on chemotherapy at the Medical Research Council and was particularly interested in efforts to synthesize penicillin, discovered in 1928 by ALEXANDER FLEMING.

Between 1945 and 1950, Robinson was president of the Royal Society. In this capacity, he played a prominent role in the postwar restoration of scientific research and in the reactivation of international scientific unions. For this service he was awarded the Order of Merit in 1949.

"For his investigations on plant products of biological importance, especially the alkaloids," Robinson received the 1947 Nobel Prize for Chemistry. In his presentation speech, Arne Fredga of the Royal Swedish Academy of Sciences noted that elucidating the structure of the alkaloids "is a task as difficult as it is fascinating. It requires great experimental skill, creative power, and sharp logic. In this sphere," Fredga added, "Sir Robert stands out as our foremost contemporary."

When Robinson reached Oxford's official retirement age in 1951, his tenure was extended until 1955. In that year he became president of the British Association for the Advancement of Science. He also served as president of the Society of the Chemical Industry in 1958–1959. World War II had interrupted Robinson's plans to establish a journal that would offer organic chemists a forum for papers of major significance. Finally, with

R. B. Woodward, he founded the journal, called *Tetrahedron,* and the first issue appeared in 1957.

Chaim Weizmann, a friend from the Manchester years, had devised a procedure for petroleum cracking, the basis of the industrial company Petrochemicals Ltd., of which Robinson was a director. In 1955 Petrochemicals was taken over by Shell Chemical Company, which employed Robinson as an active consultant. As a result of his association with the oil industry, Robinson became interested in the composition and origins of petroleum.

Robinson's exceptionally wide interests outside of science included music, photography, and literature. He and his wife were avid gardeners and also shared an enthusiasm for mountain climbing. While working in Australia, they explored the New Zealand Alps, and until the beginning of World War II, they spent their holidays climbing in Britain, the Pyrenees, Norway, and the French and Swiss Alps. When Robinson was eighty years old, he climbed Table Mountain in South Africa. Introduced to chess as a child, he later won several championships and was president of the British Chess Federation from 1950 to 1953. When he became blind in his eighties, he continued to play postal chess, and two years before his death, he collaborated with Raymond Edwards in writing *The Art and Science of Chess.*

Gertrude Robinson died in 1954, shortly before her husband's retirement from Oxford. Three years later he married Stearn Hillstrom. Before his death at the age of eighty-eight in Great Missenden, Buckinghamshire, England, Robinson had begun writing not only a two-volume autobiography but also, in collaboration with E. D. Morgan, *An Introduction to Organic Chemistry,* a textbook that was published posthumously.

Among his many honors, Robinson received the Longstaff (1930) and Faraday (1947) medals of the British Chemical Society; the Davy (1930), Royal (1932), and Copley (1942) medals of the Royal Society; the Lavoisier Medal of the French Chemical Society (1946); the Franklin Medal of the Franklin Institute (1947); and the Medal of Freedom of the United States government (1947). He was a member of the Biochemical Society, the Society of Endocrinology, the Institution of Royal Engineers, the Royal Society of Edinburgh, the Royal College of Surgeons, the Royal College of Physicians of Edinburgh, the Australian Academy of Sciences, the Royal Society of New Zealand, and the Indian Academy of Sciences. He held foreign memberships and fellowships in many other scientific societies. He was awarded honorary degrees by the universities of Belfast, Bristol, London, and Paris, and Cambridge and Oxford universities, among others.

SELECTED WORKS: The Building of Molecules, 1937; The Structural Relations of Natural Products, 1955; Chemistry in Britain, volume 10, 1974.

ABOUT: Biographical Memoirs of Fellows of the Royal Society, volume 22, 1976; Campbell, W. A., and Greenwood, N. N. Contemporary British Chemists, 1971; Discovery January 1946; Times (London) February 10, 1975.

ROBLES, ALFONSO GARCÍA
See GARCÍA ROBLES, ALFONSO

ROHRER, HEINRICH
(June 6, 1933–)
Nobel Prize for Physics, 1986
(shared with Gerd Binnig and Ernst Ruska)

The Swiss physicist Heinrich Rohrer (rôr′ ər) was born in the town of Buchs in eastern Switzerland to Hans Heinrich Rohrer, a distributor of manufactured goods, and the former Katharina Ganpenbein. As a young man he excelled in physics and chemistry and, although he found modern languages difficult, he showed an aptitude for Latin and Greek. After briefly considering advanced studies in classical languages, he enrolled in the Federal Institute of Technology in Zurich to study mathematics and physics. His doctoral research at the institute concerned pressure and volume effects in superconductivity, for which he obtained his Ph.D. in 1960.

Following a year of service in the Swiss army, Rohrer accepted a position as a postdoctoral fellow at Rutgers University, in New Brunswick, New Jersey, where he spent two years investigating superconducting phenomena. In 1963 he returned to Zurich to work at the research laboratory of the International Business Machines Corporation (IBM). Except for the academic year 1974–1975, which he spent as a visiting scientist at the University of California at Santa Barbara, he has remained at the IBM laboratory.

While working at IBM, Rohrer became interested in types of solid-state physics other than superconductivity. He was particularly intrigued by the problems posed by the sur-

International Business Machines Corporation

HEINRICH ROHRER

faces of materials, where chemical and other types of interactions between substances take place. There are methods for exploring the arrangement of atoms in the bulk, but surprisingly little was known about the very different behavior of surface atoms. The complexities involved, which long thwarted advances in understanding, once drove WOLFGANG PAULI to exclaim, "The surface was invented by the devil."

In his efforts to understand surfaces, Rohrer was joined in 1978 by GERD BINNIG, who had just completed graduate studies at the University of Frankfurt. The two scientists soon hit upon a novel approach for probing surfaces by exploiting a quantum-mechanical effect called tunneling. The phenomenon is a direct consequence of the Heisenberg uncertainty principle (named for the German physicist WERNER HEISENBERG), which states that both the position and velocity of a subatomic particle cannot be known simultaneously. As a result, a particle such as an electron behaves not as a particle but as a diffuse "cloud" of matter. The cloudlike nature of a subatomic particle permits it to "tunnel," or diffuse, between two surfaces, even if they are not touching. Tunneling was verified experimentally by IVAR GIAEVER in 1960.

At the time of Rohrer and Binnig's work, tunneling was well known; other physicists had even used the effect to obtain gross data about interfaces between "sandwiches" of materials. The two IBM investigators took a different tack by trying to get electrons to tunnel through a vacuum. Their approach ultimately culminated in the invention of a new instrument called the scanning tunneling microscope. The basic idea underlying such a device is to scan the surface of a solid in a vacuum with a sharp needle tip. If a voltage is applied between the sample and the tip, and if the distance between the two is small enough, electrons will tunnel from one to the other. The flow of electrons can then be measured as a tunneling current. The amount of tunneling current depends on the distance between the sample and tip and is expressed as an exponential function of distance. By sweeping the tip over the sample and monitoring the current, it is possible to map the atomic-sized hills and valleys of the surface.

Despite the formidable technical difficulties they faced, Rohrer and Binnig were optimistic from the outset. As Rohrer said later, "We were quite confident. Even at the beginning, we knew it would be a significant development. The surprising thing is that it went so fast." They conducted their first successful test of the scanning tunneling microscope in the spring of 1981; in collaboration with two other IBM workers, Christoph Gerber and Edmund Weibel, they resolved irregularities only 1 atom high on the surface of calcium-iridium-tin ($CaIrSn_4$) crystals. Ironically, when they first submitted a paper reporting their results, a referee rejected it as "not interesting enough."

The biggest hurdle the IBM team faced was to eliminate all sources of vibrational noise. The sensitive dependence of the tunneling current on the distance between the sample surface and the scanning tip means that the vertical position of the tip must be controlled to within a fraction of the diameter of an atom. Without sufficient preventive measures, street noises and even footsteps can jar the delicate operation of the scanning tunneling microscope. Rohrer and Binnig initially sought to solve the problem by placing the microscope on a heavy stone table, which they insulated from external disturbances in the laboratory building with inflated rubber tires. The microscope itself was suspended over a bowl of superconducting lead with permanent magnets. To move the tip as precisely as possible, piezoelectric materials, which contract or expand upon the application of voltages, were used.

Since its rather primitive beginnings, the instrument has been refined considerably. A scanning tunneling microscope (except for the vacuum chamber) now fits in the palm of the hand and can resolve vertical features as small as 0.1 angstrom (1 hundred-billionth of a meter), or roughly one-tenth the diameter of a hydrogen atom. Scanning tips only a few atoms in width permit lateral features to be resolved within 2 angstroms. Tips only 1 atom wide are now being prepared. By 1986, at least fifty scanning tunneling microscopes were being used in laboratories around the world, and two companies had begun making commercial versions. The instrument works in a variety of environments besides the vacuum, including air, water, and cryogenic fluids. It has been employed to study a variety of materials other than inorganic substances, including virus particles and deoxyribonucleic acid (DNA).

Rohrer and Binnig shared half of the 1986 Nobel Prize for Physics "for their design of the scanning tunneling microscope." The other half was awarded to ERNST RUSKA for his contributions to the electron microscope. In awarding the prize to Rohrer and Binnig, the Royal Swedish Academy of Sciences stated: "The scanning tunneling microscope is completely new, and we have so far seen only the beginning of its development. It is, however, clear that entirely new fields are opening up for the study of the structure of matter. Binnig's and Rohrer's great achievement is that, starting from earlier works and ideas, they have succeeded in mastering the enormous experimental difficulties involved in building an instrument of the precision and stability required."

In 1961 Rohrer married Rose-Marie Eggar, with whom he has two daughters. When asked to comment about himself, Rohrer, who is known as an affable and modest man, once replied: "The ones who know me, understand me; for those who don't, it is hopeless."

In addition to the Nobel Prize, Rohrer and Binnig have shared other honors for their work. In 1984 they received the Hewlett-Packard Prize of the European Physical Society and the King Faisal International Prize in Science of the Saudi Arabian government for their efforts in scanning tunneling microscopy.

SELECTED WORKS: "The Scanning Tunneling Microscope," Scientific American August 1985, with Gerd Binnig.

ABOUT: New York Times October 16, 1986; Science November 14, 1986; Science News October 25, 1986.

ROLLAND, ROMAIN
(January 29, 1866–December 30, 1944)
Nobel Prize for Literature, 1915

Romain Rolland (rô län'), the French novelist and essayist, was born to a comfortable middle-class family in Clamecy, a small town in southern France where he spent his early years. His father, Émile, was a lawyer and local notable. His mother, the former Antoinette-Marie Courot, was a pious and introspective woman at whose urging the family moved to Paris in 1880 in order to obtain better schooling for their son.

From an early age, when his mother taught him to play the piano, Rolland was passionately interested in music, especially the works of Beethoven. Later, while a student at the Lycée Louis-le-Grand, he became equally fond of Richard Wagner. He attended this secondary school in preparation for the highly selective École Normale Supérieure, which he entered in 1886. There he specialized in history, readying himself for the university career that his mother expected of him, and in 1889 he passed his *agrégation* examination, which qualified him to teach.

Rolland studied history as a fellow of the École Française in Rome from 1889 to 1891 on a scholarship. Lacking enthusiasm for the research project that he had been assigned, he instead wrote a cycle of historical dramas based on events and characters from the Italian Renaissance, having been inspired by performances of Shakespearean history plays. While pursuing his studies in Rome, he met Malwilda von Meysenburg, a German woman who was the friend and confidante of such nineteenth-century luminaries as Lajos Kossuth, Giuseppe Mazzini, Friedrich Nietzsche, and Wagner. Her idealist philosophy and interest in German romanticism profoundly influenced Rolland's thinking.

Back in Paris in 1891, Rolland continued writing plays and doing research. In October 1892 he married Clotilde Bréal; the daughter of a distinguished philologist, she shared his love of music. That same year, the couple left for Rome to begin research on Rolland's doctoral thesis, on the origins of opera before Jean-Baptiste Lully and Alessandro Scarlatti. After returning to Paris in 1893, Rolland began to teach while continuing to do research and write plays. Two years later he received his doctoral degree, with highest honors, with the first dissertation on music ever presented at the Sorbonne. Indeed, the chair of musi-

ROMAIN ROLLAND

cology at the Sorbonne was created for Rolland after he received his doctorate.

For the next seventeen years, Rolland wrote during the time available to him after his lectures in music and art at the Sorbonne, the École des Hautes Études Sociales, and the École Normale Supérieure. During this time he made the acquaintance of Charles Péguy, the Catholic poet whose periodical, *Cahiers de la Quinzaine* (Bimonthly Notes), became an important outlet for many of Rolland's early works.

Because Rolland was interested in the cultural history of what he envisioned as heroic or inspired periods, he chose to write cycles of works rather than single works, though he did not always complete his designs. His first cycle of plays, devoted to the Italian Renaissance, remained fragmentary and was never published. *Les Tragédies de la foi* (*The Tragedies of Faith*), his second cycle, comprised three plays—*Saint Louis* (1897), *Aërt* (1898), and *Le Triomphe de la raison* (*The Triumph of Reason,* 1899). His later cycles included plays, biographies, and novels.

The three historical plays in *The Tragedies of Faith* cycle combine art with social criticism, and in them Rolland sought to imbue his fellow citizens with a faith, courage, and hope that he found missing in the France of his time. Even after these plays were published, Rolland's work was largely overlooked by the public, and French theater continued to concentrate on bourgeois sexual intrigues. Accordingly, Rolland began to think about the popular theater; he believed, like Leo Tolstoy, whom he admired and with whom he had corresponded, that the public would respond to heroic problems. Interested in Maurice Pottecher's essay "People's Theatre," Rolland issued a manifesto in 1903 in the *Cahiers de la Quinzaine* aimed at combating the pessimism and materialism of the 1880s. The manifesto, published later as *Le Théâtre du peuple* (*The People's Theater,* 1918), called for inspirational new plays dealing with national historic events that would arouse an aspiration to greatness in popular audiences.

Rolland envisioned a cycle of ten or twelve dramas concerning the French Revolution in the manner of Shakespeare's history plays. Three such plays were collected in *Théâtre de la Révolution* (*Theater of the Revolution*) in 1909. Over the years, Rolland added to the cycle and completed it in 1939 with the publication of *Robespierre*. These didactic and declamatory plays of political and social ideals had very little impact at the time, appearing as they did during a period when naturalism dominated literature; they were more widely appreciated when staged in Germany after World War I and in France during the 1930s.

Rolland also conceived of a cycle of biographies of illustrious men, which would offer heartening examples to readers. His biographer William Thomas Starr believes that Rolland wrote *Vie de Beethoven* (*Beethoven,* 1903), the first in this cycle and the most successful of his works to date, partly in "gratitude for a source of strength in a period of despair." That despair was partially occasioned by his divorce in 1901. After continuing the biographical works with the life of Michelangelo in 1905, Rolland gave up his plan for this cycle, realizing that the historical truth about unhappy heroes was not consonant with his desire to inspire his readers. Even though he abandoned the cycle, biography continued to interest Rolland; he wrote biographies of Handel in 1910, Tolstoy in 1911, Gandhi in 1924, Ramakrishna in 1929, Vivekananda in 1930, and Péguy in 1944, among others.

Jean-Christophe, a ten-volume novel that appeared between 1904 and 1912, is the epic story of a musical genius, modeled partly on Beethoven. It is also the portrait of an entire generation and of the world of Europe in the first decade of the twentieth century. The volumes were published individually in Péguy's *Cahiers de la Quinzaine* and appeared in English translations from 1910 to 1913. Generally regarded as Rolland's masterpiece, *Jean-Christophe* brought him immediate international recognition and enabled him to resign from the Sorbonne in 1912 to write full time.

The Austrian poet, biographer, and novelist Stefan Zweig asserted that *Jean-Christophe* resulted from Rolland's disappointment with biography: "Since history refused to supply him with the image of the consoler, he had recourse to art, fashioning amid contemporary life the hero he desired, creating . . . Jean-Christophe."

It was largely for *Jean-Christophe* that Rolland was awarded the 1915 Nobel Prize for Literature. The decision, however, was delayed until 1916, in part because of the violent controversy Rolland had aroused by settling in Switzerland shortly before the outbreak of World War I. His provocative antiwar essays, collected in 1915 in *Au-dessus de la mêlée* (*Above the Battle*), advocated an international fellowship of the free and impartial spirits of Europe, spoke out against specific injustices committed by both sides, and attacked former pacifists who were now ardent nationalists. Rolland received the Nobel Prize for Literature "as a tribute to the lofty idealism of his literary production and to the sympathy and love of truth with which he has described different types of human beings." Because of the war, no ceremony was held, and Rolland did not deliver a Nobel lecture.

Rolland continued to take controversial political positions, particularly about the Soviet Union, which he championed after the 1917 revolution, while criticizing what he perceived as its mistakes; and he assumed an increasing burden of political obligations in the years following World War I. Nevertheless, he continued to produce a vast body of writing, including musicological treatises, biographies, plays, diaries, memoirs, letters, essays, and novels. In the 1920s he became interested in Indian religious and political thought; Gandhi, the subject of his 1924 biography, visited him in 1931 in Switzerland. The major work of this period, however, was his sixth cycle, *L'Âme enchantée* (*The Enchanted Soul,* 1925–1933), a seven-volume novel that describes a woman's struggle to achieve her spiritual potential as the enchantments of a world of illusion are stripped from her mind.

Rolland married his second wife, Marie Koudachev, in 1934, and they returned to France from Switzerland four years later. In contrast to his position during World War I, he was uncompromisingly pro-French and anti-German in World War II, taking a strong and public stand against Nazism. On December 30, 1944, he succumbed to tuberculosis, an illness that had afflicted him since childhood. His last written message, read aloud at the Sorbonne, was composed on December 9 to commemorate the families of intellectuals who had been victims of the Nazis.

Rolland's personality and the ideals he represented may have influenced his contemporaries more than his works did. His friend Marie Dormoy wrote, "I admired Romain Rolland. I also admired *Jean-Christophe,* but perhaps I liked the man better than the author. . . . He was the guide, the beacon showing the way for those who hesitated, who did not feel strong enough to make their way alone." Some critics have objected to Rolland's prose style, in which individual words are less important than the whole of the work. They have also found that the structure of *Jean-Christophe,* which Rolland thought of as symphonic, lacked form. Speaking of his later works, the English novelist and critic E. M. Forster wrote that Rolland "did not fulfill his earlier promise as a novelist." The most balanced assessments, however, may be those of his biographer Starr, who has remarked that "apart from *Jean-Christophe,* Rolland will be remembered as one of the most active and determined defenders of human dignity and freedom and as an eager advocate of a more just and humane social order." However, Starr also asserted that Rolland "is perhaps still too near to us to be adequately judged; time alone will reveal in him the eternal aspects of what is good and what is ephemeral."

ADDITIONAL WORKS IN ENGLISH TRANSLATION: Michelangelo, 1915; Handel, 1916; Colas Breugnon, 1919; Clerambault, 1921; Pierre and Luce, 1922; Gandhi, 1924; Prophets of a New India, 1930; Goethe and Beethoven, 1931; I Will Not Rest, 1935; The Wolves, 1937; The Living Thoughts of Rousseau, 1939; The Journey Within, 1947; Essays on Music, 1948; A Musical Tour Through the Land of the Past, 1967; Musicians of Today, 1969; Tolstoy, 1972.

ABOUT: Aronson, A. Romain Rolland, 1944; Harris, F. J. André Gide and Romain Rolland, 1973; March, H. Romain Rolland, 1971; Myers, R. H. (ed.) Richard Strauss and Romain Rolland, 1968; Ruitenbeck, H. M. (ed.) Literary Imagination, 1965; Saurat, P. Modern French Literature, 1946; Starr, W. T. Romain Rolland and a World at War, 1956; Starr, W. T. Romain Rolland: One Against All, 1956; Wilson, R. The Pre-War Biographies of Romain Rolland, 1939; Zweig, S. Romain Rolland: The Man and His Work, 1921.

RÖNTGEN, WILHELM

(March 27, 1845–February 10, 1923)
Nobel Prize for Physics, 1901

The German physicist Wilhelm Conrad Röntgen (rûnt′ gən) was born in Lennep, a small town near Remscheid in the Prussian Rhine Province, the only child of Friedrich Conrad Röntgen, a prosperous textile merchant, and Charlotte Constanze (Frowein) Röntgen. In 1848 the family moved to Apeldoorn, the Netherlands, the home of Charlotte's parents. Wilhelm's childhood exploration of the thick forests surrounding the town led to a lifelong enjoyment of the outdoors.

Röntgen entered the Utrecht Technical School in 1862 but was expelled when he refused to identify a fellow student who had drawn an unflattering caricature of an unpopular teacher. Because he lacked a high school graduation certificate, he could not begin formal college studies, but he did audit several courses at the University of Utrecht. After passing the entrance exam, he entered the Federal Institute of Technology at Zurich in 1865 to study mechanical engineering and received his diploma in 1868. August Kundt, a distinguished German physicist and physics professor at the institute, recognized Röntgen's brilliance and encouraged him to enter the field of physics. Röntgen took Kundt's advice, graduated a year later with a Ph.D. in physics from the University of Zurich, and was immediately hired by Kundt as his first laboratory assistant.

When Kundt assumed the chair of physics at the University of Würzburg in Bavaria, he brought his assistant with him. It was the beginning of an intellectual odyssey for Röntgen. He moved again with Kundt to the University of Strasbourg in 1872 and began his own teaching career there in 1874 as a lecturer in physics. Later, after a year as a full professor of physics at the Agricultural Academy in Hohenheim, Germany, Röntgen returned to Strasbourg in 1876 to teach theoretical physics.

His experimental work at Strasbourg on such diverse topics as the heat conductivity of crystals and the electromagnetic rotation of the plane of polarization of light in gases earned him, in the words of his biographer Otto Glaser, a reputation as "a fine classical experimental physicist." In 1879 he was appointed professor of physics at the University of Giessen, where he remained until 1888, turning down offers of the chair of physics at the universities of both Jena and Utrecht. In 1888 he returned to the University of Würzburg as professor of physics and director of the Physical Institute, where he continued extensive experimentation on such problems as the compressibility of water and the electrical properties of quartz.

In 1894, the same year he was elected headmaster of the university, Röntgen started experimenting with electric discharges in glass

WILHELM RÖNTGEN

vacuum tubes. Much work had already been done in this field by others. In 1853 the French physicist Antoine-Philibert Masson had noted that a high-voltage discharge between electrodes in a glass tube containing a gas at low pressure produced a purplish glow. (This was an early ancestor of the modern neon tube.) When other experimenters removed more of the gas from the tube, the glow broke into a pattern of separate strips of light whose color depended on which gas was used. The English physicist William Crookes, applying a vastly improved vacuum pump, achieved much lower pressures and found that the glow vanished, but the glass walls of the tube fluoresced with greenish light. He demonstrated that rays were apparently emanating from the negative electrode (a cross-shaped object placed in the tube cast a shadow on the opposite wall) and that the rays had substance and carried a negative electric charge (their impact turned a small wheel, and the beam was deflected in a particular direction by a magnet). In 1878 Crookes proposed that the rays caused the fluorescence when they struck the glass walls. Since the negative electrode was called a cathode, the emanation was named cathode rays. The German physicist PHILIPP VON LENARD showed that cathode rays could penetrate a thin aluminum window in the tube and electrify the air immediately outside the window. The mystery was clarified later when the English physicist J. J. THOMSON demonstrated the nature of the particles in 1897, and they became known as electrons.

Röntgen repeated some of the earlier experiments, in particular showing that the cathode rays (still undefined at the time) emerging from a Lenard window produced fluorescence in a screen painted with barium platinocyanide. On November 8, 1895, to help his observations, he darkened the room and surrounded a Crookes's tube (without a Lenard window) with a close-fitting opaque black cardboard. To his surprise, a nearby barium platinocyanide screen displayed a band of fluorescence. After taking pains to eliminate possible errors, he found that the fluorescence appeared every time he turned the tube on, that the source was indeed the tube and not some other part of the circuit, and that the screen fluoresced even when moved 6 feet away from the tube, far beyond the short range of cathode rays. Röntgen spent the next seven weeks exploring the phenomenon, which he called X (for unknown) rays. A shadow cast on the fluorescent screen by a wire from the induction coil that produced the high voltage needed for the discharge led him to test the ability of X rays to penetrate a range of different materials. He found that X rays could pass through almost all objects to different extents, depending on their thickness and density. While holding a small lead disk between the tube and the screen, he noted that the lead seemed impenetrable but made the dramatic discovery that the bones in his hand produced a dark shadow surrounded by a lighter shadow of the soft tissues of his hand. He soon learned that X rays not only caused barium platinocyanide to fluoresce but also affected a photographic plate, which darkened after development where it had been struck by the rays. He thus became the first radiologist. In his honor, X rays are often called Röntgen rays. His X-ray photograph (röntgenogram) of his wife's hand became famous. It clearly shows the bones (white because X rays were blocked from reaching the film) within the darker image of soft flesh (X rays were only partly impeded), and the white shadow of the rings on her fingers.

In 1893 the German physiologist and physicist Hermann von Helmholtz had predicted that radiation such as light, but of a sufficiently short wavelength, could penetrate solid materials. No such radiation was then known. After Röntgen's discovery, the German physicist MAX VON LAUE made the brilliant suggestion that the shortwave character of X rays could be demonstrated by using the atomic positions in a crystal as a diffraction grating. (A diffraction grating contains a series of closely spaced grooves that cause electromagnetic radiation such as light to produce patterns related to their wavelength, but optical gratings were inadequate to produce diffraction of radiation with wavelengths as short as those expected for X rays.) In 1913 the experiment suggested by von Laue was conclusively performed by the German physicists Walter Friedrich and Paul Knipping. Röntgen's discovery of X rays thus contributed to the revolution in physics that took place at the turn of the twentieth century.

Röntgen's first publication of his investigations, in a local scientific journal at the end of 1895, aroused great interest among both scientists and the public at large. "We soon discovered that all bodies are transparent to the agent," he wrote, "though in very different degrees." His experiments were immediately confirmed by other scientists. Röntgen published two additional research articles on X rays in 1896 and 1897, but thereafter moved on to other fields. The medical profession immediately realized the diagnostic potential of X rays; at the same time, X rays became a sensation in popular newspapers and magazines around the world, often in hysterical or comic accounts. Röntgen was annoyed by the sudden publicity, which took up his time and hindered further experimental work. It also limited the frequency of, but did not end, his scientific publications. In his lifetime he wrote fifty-eight papers and in 1921, when he was seventy-six years old, published a paper on the electrical conductivity of crystals.

In 1899, shortly after declining the chair of physics at the University of Leipzig, Röntgen accepted the position of professor of physics and director of the Physical Science Institute at the University of Munich. While he was at Munich, he learned that he was the recipient in 1901 of the first Nobel Prize for Physics, "in recognition of the extraordinary services he had rendered by the discovery of the remarkable rays subsequently named for him." On presenting the award, C. T. Odhner of the Royal Swedish Academy of Sciences said, "There is no doubt that much success will be gained in physical science when this strange energy form is sufficiently investigated." Odhner went on to remind his audience that X rays had already found many practical applications in medicine.

In 1872 Röntgen married Anna Bertha Ludwig, the daughter of a scholarly innkeeper, whom he met in Zurich while at the Federal Institute of Technology. Unable to have children of their own, they adopted the six-year-old daughter of Bertha's brother in 1881. A shy, reticent man, Röntgen deeply resented becoming a public personality. He retained a love of outdoor activities, spending many vacations at Weilheim, where he enjoyed climbing in the nearby Bavarian Alps and hunting with friends. He retired from his post at Munich in 1920, shortly after his wife died. He died three years later from cancer of the intestine.

Although Röntgen felt he had received adequate reward in knowing that his discovery proved to have enormous value in medicine (he never sought a patent or any financial return), he was showered with many honors in addition to the Nobel Prize. These included the Rumford Medal of the Royal Society of London, the Barnard Gold Medal for Meritorious Service to Science of Columbia University, and honorary and corresponding memberships in scientific societies throughout the world.

SELECTED WORKS: Röntgen Rays; Memoirs, 1899, with others; X Rays and the Electric Conductivity of Gases, 1958, with others.

ABOUT: Dibner, B. Wilhelm Conrad Röntgen and the Discovery of X Rays, 1968; Dictionary of Scientific Biography, volume 11, 1975; Glasser, O. Dr. Wilhelm Conrad Röntgen, 1958; Grey, V. Röntgen's Revolution: The Discovery of the X Ray, 1973; Hermann, A., et al. Wilhelm Conrad Röntgen, 1973; Nitske, W. R. The Life of Wilhelm Conrad Röntgen, 1971.

ROOSEVELT, THEODORE

(October 27, 1858–January 6, 1919)
Nobel Prize for Peace, 1906

THEODORE ROOSEVELT

Theodore Roosevelt, historian, politician, and twenty-sixth president of the United States, was born in New York City, the second of four children. His parents, Theodore Roosevelt, a glass importer, and the former Martha Bulloch, enjoyed a comfortable income and prominent social position. A sickly, near-sighted, and asthmatic child, Roosevelt undertook such activities as rowing, jogging, boxing, and calisthenics to strengthen his body. He was taught by private tutors and graduated from Harvard Phi Beta Kappa in 1880. In October of that year, he married Alice Hathaway Lee of Massachusetts. He then spent a year studying and traveling in Germany.

Upon his return to the United States, Roosevelt was elected to the New York State Assembly as a reform Republican candidate from New York City. Shortly after the birth of a daughter, Alice Lee (later Longworth), his wife died in 1884 of Bright's disease. In his grief, he withdrew from politics, went west to ranch, and wrote prodigiously.

Returning to politics in 1886, Roosevelt ran for mayor of New York City but lost. That year he married Edith Kermit Carow and settled near Oyster Bay, Long Island. They had five children. During this time, Roosevelt served as a United States civil service commissioner (1889–1895) and as New York City police commissioner (1889–1897). To these offices, he brought a zealous enthusiasm and a flair for dramatizing himself and his causes. As police commissioner, for example, he attacked the alliance between the municipal machine, the police, and the city's underworld. To ensure that his orders were obeyed, he sometimes dressed in a black cape and prowled the slums at night checking on patrolmen, a theatrical gesture that provided grist for cartoonists and publicity for Roosevelt.

Appointed assistant secretary of the navy by President William McKinley in 1897, Roosevelt acted to promote military preparedness for a possible war with Spain. He requested $1.5 million from Congress for ammunition and fuel for the navy. In February 1898 Roosevelt, as acting secretary, secretly telegraphed Commodore George Dewey in Hong Kong and advised him to prepare for an attack against the Spanish fleet in the event of war. With this warning, Dewey's fleet was able to defeat the Spanish at the Battle of Manila Bay two months later. When Congress declared war on Spain in April 1898, Roosevelt obtained a volunteer commission as lieutenant colonel and organized a regiment of cavalry volunteers, chiefly cowboys, who became known as Roosevelt's Rough Riders. Although mainly remembered for leading the charge up Cuba's San Juan Hill (a colorful but militarily insignificant operation), Roosevelt also fought courageously in the Battle of Las Guásimas.

Returning to New York as a national hero, Roosevelt campaigned for governor with an escort of Rough Riders, won by a small majority, and took office in January 1899. As governor, he persuaded the legislature to pass a corporation franchise tax, form a tenement house commission, and establish a civil service system. Republican politicians of the Old Guard, alarmed by his independence and eager to oust him from state politics, helped nominate Roosevelt for the national office of vice president—traditionally a powerless position—and in 1900 he was elected on the Republican ticket with McKinley. When McKinley died from an assassin's bullet on September 14, 1901, Roosevelt became president. At age forty-two, he was the youngest man ever to assume the office. "Now look," Republican party chief Mark Hanna is said to have lamented, "that damned cowboy is president of the United States."

Roosevelt brought a dynamic, decisive style of leadership to the presidency, using the office as a "bully pulpit" from which to air his views. "I did not usurp power," he said later, "but I did greatly broaden the use of executive power." He did so by exerting a moral leadership that mobilized public opinion and impelled political action. In this way, he transformed the federal government into a defender of the public interest and a referee between conflicting economic groups. Nevertheless, he moved cautiously. He advocated supervision and control of trusts "within reasonable limits." In a highly popular move, he sued the Northern Securities Company, a combine of railroads, and won. He also used the government as an arbitrator between capital and labor to settle the anthracite coal strike of 1902.

In foreign affairs, Roosevelt epitomized the confident, imperialistic mood of the times. Believing that sea power held the key to America's position in the world, he strengthened the navy. He supported a Panamanian revolution against Colombia that created the independent nation of Panama and enabled the United States to purchase the Panama Canal Zone for $40 million. As part of his Caribbean defense strategy, Roosevelt revised the Monroe Doctrine, which had been formulated by President James Monroe in 1823 to warn the European powers not to interfere in the Western Hemisphere. Under Roosevelt's corollary to the doctrine, the United States would not only warn European powers to stay away, it would also actively intervene during political or economic crises that might expose unstable nations to European manipulation.

With the support of business leaders and Progressives, Roosevelt was elected president in his own right in 1904, with a popular majority of 2.5 million votes. He interpreted his election victory as a mandate for reform. Progressive measures passed in his second term included the Hepburn Act, to regulate railroads; the Meat Inspection Act; and the Pure Food and Drug Act. Despite opposition from economic developers in the West, Roosevelt added some 148,000 acres to the national forests and reserved additional acres of coal deposits, phosphate beds, and waterpower sites. With the establishment in 1908 of the National Conservation Commission, a systematic inventory and study of the country's natural resources was initiated.

In Asia, Roosevelt sought to maintain a balance of power. When Japan declared war on Russia in 1904, he hoped that Japan's naval successes would halt Russia's encroachment into Manchuria. Yet he did not want either nation to achieve total victory, since this would threaten United States interests in the Pacific. At Japan's request, Roosevelt invited the belligerents to a peace conference in Portsmouth, New Hampshire, in 1905. When a deadlock developed, he appealed to the leader of each nation for a compromise. In September the Treaty of Portsmouth ended the Russo-Japanese War. Although Roosevelt "did not act officially as president of the United States" in supervising the Portsmouth conference, he later acknowledged that "it was nevertheless only because I was president that I was enabled to act at all."

Roosevelt was awarded the 1906 Nobel Prize for Peace for his role in the Treaty of Portsmouth. Peace societies criticized the decision to give the award to an avowed militarist; Roosevelt's supporters pointed out that by helping to end the Russo-Japanese War, he had saved thousands of lives.

Because a heavy work schedule demanded his presence in the United States, Roosevelt was unable to attend the award ceremonies. However, he visited Oslo as a private citizen in 1910, delivering his Nobel lecture on May

5 of that year. "Peace is generally good in itself," he told an audience of more than 2,000, "but it is never the highest good unless it comes as the handmaid of righteousness. . . . Many a tyrant has called it peace when he has scourged honest protest into silence." He suggested that "it would be a masterstroke if those great powers honestly bent on peace would form a League of Peace, not only to keep the peace among themselves, but to prevent, by force if necessary, its being broken by others." The prize money was held in trust until 1917, when Roosevelt asked Congress to donate it to agencies providing relief for victims of World War I.

After leaving the White House in March 1909, Roosevelt went hunting in Africa, lectured at Oxford University and at the Sorbonne, and toured Europe. Drawn back into politics as the breach between conservatives and Progressives widened under his Republican successor, William Howard Taft, Roosevelt made an unsuccessful third-party bid for president in 1912. An outspoken critic of President WOODROW WILSON, he ridiculed Wilson's caution, bristled at the government's refusal to let him volunteer for service during World War I, and opposed the entry of the United States into the League of Nations. At age sixty, Roosevelt died in his sleep.

Roosevelt left an enduring imprint on American government and politics. As a leader, he publicized the need for reform, roused public indignation, and stirred the electorate to action. As president, he interpreted the powers of his office broadly, exercising them decisively and, for the most part, moderately. Addressing problems of corporate concentration, he favored laws that protected consumers and regulated business. He advocated sound management of the nation's natural resources and spoke for the public interest.

In foreign affairs, Roosevelt broke with the isolationist tradition of the United States and entered into diplomatic relationships with nations in Asia, Europe, and the Caribbean. He has been criticized by historians for his imperialism during the Spanish-American War as well as for his strong-arm tactics in building the Panama Canal. Yet he was the first American to be awarded the Nobel Peace Prize, and his legislative achievements initiated the nation's first great period of modern-day reform. The vibrant, competitive, and confident spirit he brought to the presidency reflected the tenor of the times.

WORKS BY: The Naval War of 1812, 1882; Essays on Practical Politics, 1888; The Winning of the West (4 vols.) 1889–1896; New York, 1891; American Big Game Hunting, 1893; American Ideals and Other Essays, 1897; The Rough Riders, 1899; The Strenuous Life, 1900; Addresses and Presidential Messages, 1904; Abraham Lincoln, 1909; The New Nationalism, 1910; Progressive Principles, 1913; Theodore Roosevelt: An Autobiography, 1913; America and the World War, 1915; Fear God and Take Your Own Part, 1916; The Great Adventure, 1918; The Works of Theodore Roosevelt (24 vols.) 1923–1926; The Letters of Theodore Roosevelt (8 vols.) 1951–1954.

ABOUT: Beale, H. K. Theodore Roosevelt and the Rise of America to World Power, 1956; Bishop, J. B. Theodore Roosevelt (2 vols.) 1920; Blum, J. M. The Republican Roosevelt, 1954; Burton, D. H. Theodore Roosevelt: Confident Imperialist, 1968; Chessman, G. W. Theodore Roosevelt and the Politics of Power, 1969; Cooper, J. M. The Warrior and the Priest, 1983; Dennett, T. Roosevelt and the Russo-Japanese War, 1925; Foster, G. Theodore Roosevelt, 1954; Garraty, J. A. Theodore Roosevelt: The Strenuous Life, 1967; Gerson, N. B. TR, 1970; Harbaugh, W. H. Power and Responsibility: The Life and Times of Theodore Roosevelt, 1961; Lorant, S. The Life and Times of Theodore Roosevelt, 1959; Markham, L. Theodore Roosevelt, 1985; Marks, F. W. Velvet on Iron: The Diplomacy of Theodore Roosevelt, 1979; McCullogh, D. G. Mornings on Horseback, 1981; Mowry, G. E. Theodore Roosevelt and the Progressive Movement, 1946; Neu, C. E. An Uncertain Friendship: Theodore Roosevelt and Japan, 1967; Norton, A. A. Theodore Roosevelt, 1980; Pringle, H. F. Theodore Roosevelt, A Biography, 1931; Riis, J. A. Theodore Roosevelt, The Citizen, 1904; Schorr, M. Bully! 1985; Trani, E. P. The Treaty of Portsmouth, 1969; Wagenknecht, E. C. The Seven Worlds of Theodore Roosevelt, 1958.

ROOT, ELIHU
(February 15, 1845–February 7, 1937)
Nobel Prize for Peace, 1912

The American lawyer and statesman Elihu Root was born in Clinton, New York, the third of four sons of Oren ("Cube") Root, a professor of mathematics at Hamilton College, and the former Nancy Whitney Buttrick. Root grew up in a scholarly atmosphere that encouraged intellectual excellence, scientific curiosity, and the love of nature, values he cultivated throughout his life.

At fifteen years of age, Root was admitted to Hamilton College, graduating four years later as valedictorian. With money earned by teaching, he moved to Manhattan in 1864, enrolled in the New York University Law School, and was admitted to the New York bar after graduating in 1867. He spent a year with a prestigious law firm and started his own practice in 1869 at the age of twenty-four. Root's keen analytical mind and ability to extract essential principles from complex legal issues soon established him as one of New York's foremost corporation lawyers. Among his clients

ELIHU ROOT

were banks, railroads, successful businesses, and municipal interests.

Root's thriving and lucrative practice combined with his strong sense of civic responsibility to make him a power in local Republican politics. He allied himself with the reform elements of his party and, in an era characterized by corruption at all levels of government, distinguished himself by his integrity. As United States attorney for the Southern District of New York from 1883 to 1885, he opposed machine politics and spoke out against municipal graft. In 1898 he was a strong supporter of the successful candidacy of THEODORE ROOSEVELT for governor of New York.

Root's legal and political experience made him President William McKinley's choice for secretary of war, a cabinet position he accepted in 1899. Serving in this capacity until 1904, he instituted sweeping reforms in the nation's military system, including the creation of the Army War College in Washington, D.C.; increased federal control over the National Guard; and the establishment of a general staff to supervise, plan, and coordinate departmental actions.

In addition to his domestic duties, Root exercised unprecedented responsibilities abroad. Entering government service after the Spanish-American War had made the United States an imperial power, he became the architect of its colonial policies. Based on British patterns but with less emphasis on representative institutions or future independence, his policies stressed economic benefits and responsible

governance. In the Philippines, for example, Root introduced roads, sanitation, education, and economic enterprise, but he also sent troops to suppress Filipino resistance to occupation by the United States. Moreover, his policy did not envision a future of territorial status, statehood, or eventual autonomy. Likewise, even though the United States withdrew from Cuba in 1902, it withheld unqualified independence from the new republic for almost twenty years under provisions of the Platt Amendment drafted by Root.

After a brief return to private practice in 1904, Root served President Theodore Roosevelt as secretary of state from 1905 to 1909. Like Roosevelt, Root recognized that the power and status of the United States gave it a stake in world peace. Accordingly, he focused on conciliation of national differences, using a restrained, judicial manner in the conduct of diplomacy.

Root's most outstanding contributions as secretary of state were in the fields of arbitration, international cooperation, and world peace. He settled a long-standing dispute with Great Britain over Newfoundland fisheries, and in 1909 he negotiated a treaty creating a permanent American-Canadian joint commission for settling future disputes. In 1908 Root improved strained relations between the United States and Japan by negotiating the Root-Takahira Agreement, in which both governments pledged to maintain the status quo in the Pacific and to honor the Open Door policy with China.

Root made his most innovative and constructive efforts in the promotion of Pan-American cooperation. When he took office as secretary of state, United States expansion into the Caribbean had engendered deep distrust of the United States among Latin American nations. To restore goodwill in the region, in 1906 Root attended the third Pan-American Conference in Rio de Janeiro. There, in a much-praised address, he declared, "We wish for no victories but those of peace; for no territory except our own; for no sovereignty except sovereignty over ourselves. We deem the independence and equal rights of the smallest and weakest member of the family of nations entitled to as much respect as those of the greatest empire."

The following year, the United States and Mexico hosted the Central American Peace Conference in Washington, D.C. The major achievement of the conference, establishment of a Central American Court of Justice, was Root's idea. This court was the first such body for the judicial settlement of disputes among Central American republics.

In 1913 Root was awarded the 1912 Nobel Prize for Peace, which had been reserved, for his contributions to peace in the Western Hemisphere, for his policies in administering new United States colonies, and for his attempts to maintain international peace through treaties, arbitration, and courts of mediation. The outbreak of World War I prevented him from traveling to Norway to deliver his Nobel lecture, which had been scheduled for September 8, 1914. The text was published in 1916 in a collection of Root's *Addresses on International Subjects*.

In his Nobel lecture, Root took a Hobbesian view of human nature and the causes of war. Well-intentioned calls for peace by idealists are insufficient, he declared, because they "appeal to the civilized side of man, while war is the product of forces proceeding from man's original savage nature. To deal with the true causes of war, one must begin by recognizing . . . that civilization is a partial, incomplete, and, to a great extent, superficial modification of barbarism. . . . War is the natural reaction of human nature in the savage state, while peace is the result of acquired characteristics." Root questioned the ability of international bodies to prevent war, believing that independent nations were unlikely to surrender the principles for which they generally go to war. Moreover, he believed that "a great majority of mankind is in favor of war when that is necessary for the preservation of liberty and justice," or when it is perceived to be so.

Nevertheless, with the roots of war so deeply ingrained in the human experience, Root still found "reasons to believe that progress toward the permanent prevalence of peace may be more rapid in the future than in the past." Foremost among such reasons was his perception that "civilized man is becoming less cruel. . . . Human life is held in much higher esteem, and the taking of it . . . is looked upon much more seriously than it was formerly." From his vantage point in progressive, pre–World War I America, Root found "a very widespread sense that men have some sort of responsibility to cause affairs to be so ordered in civilized communities that their fellowmen have a chance to live."

The final phase of Root's career combined public service with continued dedication to the principles and practice of international law. Representing New York in the United States Senate from 1909 to 1915, Root persuaded his colleagues not to exempt United States shipping from standard Panama Canal tolls. During this time, he also became a member of the Permanent Court of Arbitration at The Hague. In 1913, as president of the court, he presided over the resolution of a dispute among Great Britain, France, Spain, and Portugal.

An eloquent advocate of international law, Root was prominent in the founding and development of the American Society of International Law. From 1910 to 1924 he served as president of the Carnegie Endowment for International Peace, an organization that studies the causes of war and their prevention. In the debate over the entry of the United States into the League of Nations, Root supported the Covenant with reservations but failed to persuade his colleagues to his position. In 1920 he served on a committee of jurists that established the framework of a Permanent Court of International Justice, which would rule on disputes between members of the league and interpret the league's Covenant.

In 1878 Root married Clara Frances Wales, the daughter of a well-to-do editor of *Scientific American*. They had three children. Despite financial success and worldwide acclaim, Root lived without ostentation or social pretension. During retirement, he divided his time between New York City and the family home in Clinton, New York.

Root believed that change occurs slowly. Although lacking the zeal of a reformer, he had a clear view of what he was trying to accomplish. "The utmost that any one generation can hope to do is to promote the gradual change of standards of conduct," he wrote to Robert Bacon, his successor at the State Department. "All estimates of such work and its results must be in terms not of individual human life, but in terms of the long life of nations. Inconspicuous as are the immediate results, however, there can be no nobler object of human effort than to exercise an influence upon the tendencies of the race, so that it shall move, however slowly, in the direction of civilization and humanity and away from senseless brutality."

Root died in New York City on February 7, 1937, at the age of ninety-one.

ADDITIONAL WORKS: The Citizen's Part in Government, 1907; Experiment in Government and the Essentials of the Constitution, 1913; Addresses on American Government and Citizenship, 1916; The Military and Colonial Policy of the United States, 1916; Latin America and the United States, 1917; Miscellaneous Addresses, 1917; North Atlantic Coast Fisheries Arbitration at The Hague, 1917;

The United States and War, The Mission to Russia, Political Addresses, 1918; Men and Policies, 1925.

ABOUT: Bemis, S. F. (ed.) American Secretaries of State and Their Diplomacy, volume IX, 1929; Butler, N. M., et al. Addresses Made in Honor of Elihu Root, 1937; Herman, S. R. Eleven Against War, 1969; Jessup, P. C. Elihu Root (2 vols.) 1938; Kuehl, W. F. Seeking World Order, 1969; Leopold, R. W. Elihu Root and the Conservative Tradition, 1954; Scott, J. B. Elihu Root, 1963; Werking, R. H. The Master Architects: Building the United States Foreign Service, 1977.

RONALD ROSS

ROSS, RONALD
(May 13, 1857–September 16, 1932)
Nobel Prize for Physiology or Medicine, 1902

Ronald Ross, an English physician and medical researcher, was born in Almora, Nepal, the eldest of ten children of a British army officer. At the age of eight he was sent to school in England. Although Ross entertained a lifelong desire to be a writer, artist, or musician (eventually he published numerous poems, plays, and novels), in 1874, at his father's insistence, he entered the medical program of St. Bartholomew's Hospital. He graduated five years later and joined the Indian Medical Service in 1881.

During his initial posting abroad, Ross devoted more of his energy to writing poetry and prose and teaching himself mathematics than to practicing medicine. "I was neglecting my duty in the medical profession," he later admitted. "I was doing my current [literary] work, it was true; but what had I attempted towards bettering mankind by trying to discover the causes of those diseases which are perhaps mankind's chief enemies?" In India, the most important of those diseases was malaria.

On his first furlough to England in 1888, Ross prepared himself to investigate the cause of malaria by obtaining a diploma in public health and taking a course in bacteriology. He returned to India in 1889 and began microscopic study of the blood of malaria patients.

In 1880 CHARLES LAVERAN had discovered that malaria is caused by a single-celled parasite, *Plasmodium*. It is now known that in humans *Plasmodium* infects red blood cells, replicates asexually, and then bursts the cells, forms spores, and begins another cycle of asexual replication. Eventually, the parasites assume crescent-shaped adult forms and pass into mosquitoes that bite infected humans. Because sexual reproduction of *Plasmodium* takes place within the insects, humans are said to be secondary hosts.

In the 1880s the stage of asexual *Plasmodium* reproduction in humans was understood (knowledge to which CAMILLO GOLGI made major contributions), yet it was not known how malaria was transmitted. Doubting the widely accepted theory that malaria was acquired from air, especially in swampy regions, Ross wrote several papers arguing that the disease was caused by the accumulation of intestinal poisons in the blood. Ross also rejected Laveran's *Plasmodium* theory because the first accounts he read in India were written by observers who had not actually seen the parasite.

On a second furlough to England in 1894, Ross met Patrick Manson, who showed him Laveran's *Plasmodium* in malarial blood. Manson, a physician at the Seaman's Hospital and a parasitologist, had demonstrated that elephantiasis is caused by a parasitic worm that is transmitted to humans through mosquito bites. Manson proposed to Ross that malaria was also spread by mosquitoes but could not prove his theory. "I was immediately and powerfully struck with this hypothesis," said Ross, "and at once determined to give it close experimental examination on my return to India." Manson took a keen interest in Ross's work and used his influence to urge the government to send Ross back to India the next year.

Ross began histological studies of mosquitoes in Secunderabad, hoping to find *Plasmodium* in them. His research was hampered, however, by his persistent efforts to write novels and poetry, by a lack of cooperation from his superiors, and by his own ignorance of entomology. Moreover, since he could obtain very little scientific literature in India and lacked information on the scientific names of mosquitoes, he found it necessary to develop an improvised taxonomy.

Ross spent two years examining common types of mosquitoes before he came upon a specimen of the genus *Anopheles* and discovered in the wall of its stomach pigmented cysts similar to the parasites Laveran had discovered in malarial blood. The possibility that these cysts were a form of *Plasmodium* was made more credible by Ross's careful experimental methods. He not only captured mosquitoes but bred them to ensure that they were initially free of malaria. He then fed them the blood of malaria patients who were at specified stages of the disease and examined the stomachs of the mosquitoes. His conclusion that *Plasmodium* matures in the bodies of specific mosquito species "solved the malaria problem," Ross said later. "The path led onward full in the light, and it was obvious that science and humanity had found a new dominion."

Shortly after completing these experiments, Ross was posted to Rajputana, a region where human malaria did not occur. There he began studying malaria in birds, a disease known to resemble that in humans. After six months, Manson again used his influence to have Ross transferred to Calcutta, where malaria in humans was common. Ross then tried without success to find the malaria parasite in various kinds of mosquitoes that had bitten malaria patients. Therefore, he resumed his studies in birds, and by 1898 he had elucidated the life cycle of avian malaria, including the crucial stage of infection in mosquito salivary glands. Manson announced these findings at a meeting of the British Medical Association that year.

In 1899 Ross retired from the Indian Medical Service and returned to England. Although his career in experimental medicine ended at that time, his work on avian malaria was being extended to humans by a group of Italian researchers, especially Battista Grassi and Amico Bignami. Grassi and his colleagues reported that both human and avian malaria were spread by *Anopheles* mosquitoes. They described the life cycle of the *Plasmodium* organism in humans, used *Anopheles* to transmit malaria to a previously unexposed person, and proved that in malarious areas, people who used mosquito netting could be protected from the disease. Ross maintained that "the efforts of Bignami and Grassi were . . . obviously hasty and unreliable" and called the demonstration that mosquitoes transmit human malaria "merely a formality of which the success could already be foretold with confidence."

Because his work on avian malaria clearly preceded that of Grassi on human malaria, Ross received the 1902 Nobel Prize for Physiology or Medicine. He was cited "for his work on malaria, by which he has shown how it enters the organism and thereby has laid the foundation for successful research on this disease and methods of combating it." In presenting the award, K. A. H. Mörner of the Karolinska Institute hailed Ross's work for "its importance as a basis for the success of the recent investigations into malaria, [and] its rich contents as regards the art of medical practice and especially hygiene."

Ross devoted the last twenty years of his professional life to the epidemiology and prevention of malaria. Working at the School for Tropical Medicine in Liverpool, the British War Office, and the Ross Institute of Tropical Hygiene in London, which was established in 1926, he campaigned for mosquito destruction as the key to the eradication of malaria. His methods soon proved successful in controlling the disease in Cuba and other parts of the world; they became even more effective several decades later, after the development of DDT by PAUL MÜLLER.

In 1889 Ross married Rosa Bessie Bloxam, with whom he had two sons and two daughters. After a lingering illness, he died at the Ross Institute in London on September 16, 1932.

Ross, who served as president of the Society of Tropical Medicine, was knighted in 1911. He was awarded an honorary medical degree from the Karolinska Institute and held honorary membership in professional societies throughout Europe. In recognition of his services as a consultant to the British War Office during World War I, he was elevated to the rank of knight commander, St. Michael and St. George, in 1918.

SELECTED WORKS: The Story of Malaria, 1906; Fables, 1907; Philosophies, 1910; The Prevention of Malaria, 1910, with others; Psychologies, 1919; Memoirs, 1923; Poems, 1928; Studies on Malaria, 1928.

ABOUT: Crowther, J. G. Six Great Doctors, 1957; De Kruif, P. Microbe Hunters, 1926; Dictionary of Scientific Biography, volume 11, 1975; Mégroz, R. Ronald Ross, Discoverer and Creator, 1931; Obituary Notices of Fellows of the Royal Society, volume 11, 1933; Rowland, J. The Mosquito Man: The Story of Sir Ronald Ross, 1958.

ROUS, PEYTON
(October 5, 1879–February 16, 1970)
Nobel Prize for Physiology or Medicine,
   1966
(shared with Charles B. Huggins)

The American pathologist Francis Peyton Rous was born in Baltimore, Maryland, the only son and eldest of three children of Charles Rous, a grain importer, and Francis Anderson (Wood) Rous, the daughter of a Texas circuit judge. When Rous was eleven his father died, leaving his mother to support the family on a meager income. Rous received his early education in the Baltimore public schools. His prospects for college were dim until he won a scholarship to Johns Hopkins University. After receiving his B.A. in 1900, he entered the Johns Hopkins School of Medicine.

During his second year in medical school, Rous accidentally scraped his finger while performing an autopsy and became infected with tuberculosis. To recuperate he went to Texas, where his maternal uncle got him a job on a ranch near the town of Quanah, north of Abilene on the Oklahoma border. Although frail and slight of build, the young medical student enjoyed his work as a cowboy and returned to Johns Hopkins having discovered, as he recalled later, "that uneducated men can be as greathearted and lovable as those who know much."

After receiving his medical degree in 1905, Rous interned at Johns Hopkins, but finding medical practice dissatisfying, he accepted a position as an assistant in pathology at the University of Michigan. He spent the year 1907 in Dresden, Germany, studying morbid anatomy. Upon returning to the United States, he applied for and received a grant to work under Simon Flexner at the Rockefeller Institute of Medical Research (now Rockefeller University). His first task there was to investigate lymphocytes, cells that specialize in the formation of antibodies to viruses and other foreign substances. At Rockefeller, Rous advanced rapidly from assistant to associate in 1910 and then to associate member in 1912; in 1920 he became a full member of the institute.

In 1909 a farmer brought Rous a Plymouth Rock hen that had a tumor of the breast. Rous performed a biopsy, examined the specimen under a microscope, and discovered a spindle-cell sarcoma (a malignant tumor containing fibrous tissue and abnormal cells shaped like spindles, which are typical sarcoma tumor cells). He minced the tumor tissue, suspended cell-free tissue extracts in a saline solution, in-

PEYTON ROUS

jected the extracts into other Plymouth Rock hens, and observed that one of them developed sarcoma of the breast. He then proceeded to transmit the tumor by similar methods through several generations of hens. Two years later, in an article published in the *Journal of Experimental Medicine,* he stated, "The behavior of the new growth has been throughout that of a true neoplasm, for which reason the fact of its transmission by means of a cell-free filtrate assumes exceptional importance."

The transmissibility of the chicken tumor by cell-free extracts (extracts of tumor tissue that had been filtered to eliminate tumor cells) suggested that the cause of the chicken sarcoma was a living virus. This observation was not altogether original, for a few years earlier two Danish investigators had transmitted a fowl leukemia by cell-free infiltrates. Because leukemia was not then thought to be related to cancer, however, their report was largely ignored. Moreover, prevailing theories about the cause and development of cancer were dominated by the German school of pathological anatomy, led by Rudolf Virchow. Virchow and his followers had argued effectively against an opposing group—led by ROBERT KOCH—that cancer was not caused by infectious agents. Therefore, Rous's hypothesis that his experimental chicken sarcoma was caused by a virus remained unnoticed for two decades. Over the years the tumor became known as the Rous sarcoma, and the hypothetical causative agent as the Rous sarcoma virus. Eventually, in the 1930s, Rous's hypothesis was proved correct, and in the 1940s the Rous sarcoma virus was identified by electron microscopy.

During his early years at the Rockefeller Institute, Rous and his colleagues discovered two more experimental fowl tumors, both of which were caused by a filtrable agent. In 1914 Rous suggested that all three experimental tumors belonged to "a new group of entities which caused in chickens neoplasms of diverse characters." He and his colleagues also attempted to define the biological conditions that promote and impair experimental tumor growth, and they speculated about the similarities and differences between experimental fowl tumors and clinical mammalian tumors.

When World War I began, Rous and a colleague, J. R. Turner, collaborated on methods for preserving blood, which would be needed at the front lines. They soon developed a solution that contained acid, citrate, and dextrose. Known as ACD solution, it preserves red blood cells for three to four weeks, during which time the blood can be safely stored for later use; it is still used for that purpose.

For eight years, beginning in 1918, Rous was a member of the National Research Council, serving as vice-chairman of the medical division and executive committee. Shortly after the end of World War I, he and his colleagues developed a new experimental method for separating cells from tissues by using trypsin, an enzyme synthesized by the pancreas that hydrolyzes protein molecules.

In the early 1920s Rous investigated the physiological function of the liver and gallbladder. He and his associates learned that up to three-quarters of the biliary system can be obstructed before significant amounts of bile pigments accumulate. They also found that bile is reabsorbed by the intestines and recirculated to the liver by means of a special vascular system. They proved that the function of the gallbladder is the absorption of water and the concentration of bile, a finding that established the physiological basis of clinical tests for gallstones. Their research also revealed that hemoglobin breakdown is the source of bilirubin (a red bile pigment), which, when accumulated, causes jaundice.

Returning to experimental cancer research in the early 1930s, Rous and his colleagues studied the malignant evolution of rabbit papillomas (benign tumors) and tumors in rats and mice. They discovered that the growth and malignancy of these tumors were related to an interplay between the causative agent—coal tar was used in their experiments—and certain environmental factors.

In 1942 Rous presented three hypotheses about the biological behavior of cancers: The first suggested that viruses may infect the body in utero (before birth) or at a young age, giving, he said, "no sign of their presence in most instances. . . . But if a provocative carcinogen happened to work on the cells with which such a virus was associated . . . it might undergo variation and give rise to a tumor." According to his second hypothesis, chemical carcinogens (which Rous called provocative carcinogens) may cause tumors that otherwise appear to occur spontaneously. Finally, he suggested that latent viruses and provocative chemical carcinogens may interact and cause tumors that also appear to occur spontaneously.

The 1966 Nobel Prize for Physiology or Medicine was awarded to Rous "for his discovery of tumor-inducing viruses." He shared the award with CHARLES B. HUGGINS. In his Nobel lecture, "The Challenge to Man of the Neoplastic Cell," Rous discussed the unique difficulties that tumors present to the medical researcher. Although progress had been achieved, Rous said, 'the successes thus far obtained have been episodic."

In 1915 Rous married Marion Eckford DeKay; they had three daughters. After World War II Rous and his wife bought a house in West Cornwall, Connecticut, where he spent his summers fishing and gardening. RENATO DULBECCO once described Rous as "a man fully dedicated to his work, a scientist with a vision, a strong although kind person with a good sense of humor." Three years after receiving the Nobel Prize, Rous developed abdominal cancer and died in New York City on February 16, 1970.

Among the many awards and honors received by Rous were the Walker Prize of the Royal College of Surgeons in London (1941), the Jessie Stevenson Kovalenko Medal of the National Academy of Sciences (1954), the Lasker Award of the American Public Health Association (1958), the National Medal of Science of the National Science Foundation (1966), and the Cleveland Medal from the American Cancer Society (1966).

Rous was a member of the Royal Academy of Sciences of Denmark and a fellow of the American Association for the Advancement of Science, the Weizmann Institute of Science in Israel, the National Academy of Sciences, the Association of American Physicians, American Society of Experimental Pathology, the American Philosophical Society, and the American Association for Cancer Research.

ABOUT: Biographical Memoirs of Fellows of the Royal Society, volume 17, 1971; Biographical Memoirs of the National Academy of Sciences, volume 48, 1976; Henderson, J. S., et al. A Notable Career in Finding Out: Peyton Rous, 1971; Science October 21, 1966.

RUBBIA, CARLO
(March 31, 1934–   )
Nobel Prize for Physics, 1984
(shared with Simon van der Meer)

CARLO RUBBIA

The Italian physicist Carlo Rubbia was born in the town of Gorizia, near the Yugoslav border, the oldest son of Silvio Rubbia, an electrical engineer, and Beatrice (Liceni) Rubbia, an elementary schoolteacher. Rubbia developed an early passion for science and engineering and spent much of his childhood learning electronics on communications equipment abandoned during World War II.

Near the end of the war, Yugoslav forces occupied much of the province of Gorizia, and the family fled, first to Venice and then to Udine, finally settling in Pisa. After high school, Rubbia wanted to study physics at the exclusive Scuola Normale Superiore, part of the University of Pisa, but failed the entrance examination because of wartime gaps in his education. Resigned to giving up physics, he became an engineering student at the University of Milan. A few months later he received word that he could return to Pisa to fill a last-minute vacancy. He was to remark in later years that he became a physicist by accident. After receiving an undergraduate degree at Pisa, Rubbia went on to obtain a doctorate there in 1958. His thesis research involved cosmic-ray experiments and participation in the development of instruments to detect elementary particles produced by high-energy collisions in particle accelerators.

To gain more experience, especially in particle accelerators, Rubbia spent the academic year 1958–1959 at Columbia University, where he worked with STEVEN WEINBERG and other leading figures in high-energy particle research. He returned to Italy, furthering his studies at the University of Rome during 1960, and then joined CERN (the European Organization for Nuclear Research), a thirteen-nation consortium headquartered near Geneva, Switzerland. CERN had just built the world's most powerful particle accelerator, the proton synchrotron, with which researchers hoped to produce elementary particles predicted theoretically but not yet confirmed by experiment.

Physicists had come to recognize four forces in nature: gravitational, an attraction between masses; electromagnetic, an interaction between electrically charged or magnetic entities; "strong," the force that holds the nucleus together against the mutual electric repulsion between protons and in the presence of uncharged neutrons; and "weak," the force associated with the radioactive decay of some unstable nuclei, such as the emission of beta particles (electrons). The forces were also regarded as acting through the exchange of particles, or quanta of the force fields, representing the discontinuous units of which energy is composed, as discovered during the early days of quantum theory. The first such particle to be identified was the photon, the quantum of electromagnetic radiation such as light. The unavoidable fact that light, known for centuries to have the character of continuous waves, also acted like discrete particles instigated the development of modern quantum mechanics, which incorporates the wave-particle duality. ALBERT EINSTEIN's theory of relativity introduced the equivalence between mass and energy, which provided both a theoretical and practical tool for analyzing interactions involving particle masses and massless radiation.

The massless photon is exchanged in electromagnetic interactions, for example, between charged particles such as the electron and the proton. In 1935 the Japanese physicist HIDEKI YUKAWA predicted on theoretical grounds that interactions within the nucleus might involve a force whose quantum had mass, and he calculated the mass's probable value. The particle was found in 1947 by the English physicist CECIL F. POWELL in high-altitude collisions between very energetic cosmic rays and nuclei. It became known as the pi-meson, or pion, had a mass more than 200 times that of the electron, and was associated with the strong force. The pion was later produced in the laboratory with powerful particle accelerators. Many different mesons and other subatomic particles have been discovered, and the field is still highly active. Some physicists are proposing theories to organize the bewildering array of particles into a rational order, while others seek to build increasingly powerful accelerators to coax more particles into observability.

Physicists dislike the presence of four independent natural forces and have long tried to find theories to unify them. In 1960 the American physicist SHELDON L. GLASHOW proposed a unification of the electromagnetic and weak forces (electroweak) that required the existence of three previously unobserved particles: W^+, with a positive electric charge; W^-, with a negative charge; and Z^0, with no charge. They are classed as bosons (named for the Indian physicist Satyendranath Bose); the photon, the pion, and nuclei with an even total number of protons and neutrons are also bosons. Steven Weinberg and ABDUS SALAM, working independently, predicted that the Glashow bosons would be short-lived and have masses about ten times as great as any known subatomic particles. Because of their large expected masses, the particles would require collisions of extremely high energy to produce them.

In 1969 Rubbia, in collaboration with Alfred Mann and David Cline, set out to search for the W and Z particles at the Fermi National Accelerator Laboratory (Fermilab) near Chicago. Within two years, they interrupted their efforts to announce that they had found evidence for the existence of neutral currents, the flow of uncharged particles expected as a consequence of the exchange of Z^0 particles, which would strongly support the Glashow-Weinberg-Salam theory. However, after CERN researchers, who had also been hunting for the elusive currents, reported almost conclusive findings in 1973, and shortly after Rubbia had returned to Italy, Rubbia's Fermilab team hastily published a paper stating that they had not, after all, found the currents. Then, the following year, they reversed their position again and published an exhaustive paper on the existence of the currents. Although their conclusions were accepted, the episode temporarily clouded Rubbia's reputation.

With the added confidence of the suggestive experimental findings, Rubbia resumed his search for the W and Z particles. However, no existing accelerator was capable of supplying the energy needed to produce the massive particles. In 1976 Rubbia, Cline, and Peter McIntyre made the radical proposal of modifying an available high-energy accelerator, CERN's super proton synchrotron (SPS), to create a stream of protons and a stream of antiprotons circling in the same ring-shaped tunnel in opposite directions and then to bring them together in a head-on collision. P. A. M. DIRAC had predicted the existence of antimatter in 1928 in the form of an antielectron, a twin of the negatively charged electron but with a positive charge. A meeting of matter and antimatter results in annihilation of the two masses in a flash of energy. The theory was confirmed with the discovery of the antielectron (now called the positron) by CARL D. ANDERSON in 1932.

The Rubbia-Cline-McIntyre scheme required the solution of many difficult problems and aroused considerable skepticism. However, Rubbia, noted for his irresistible enthusiasm and persuasive powers, was able to induce CERN in 1979 to undertake the project for their SPS, at an estimated cost of $100 million.

One major element of the plan was the design of a complicated detector to sense the particles resulting from the collisions and to determine their characteristics, such as energy and direction of travel. Working with a team of over 100 scientists, Rubbia and his colleagues built a 1,200-ton detection chamber capable of conclusively identifying and characterizing the approximately ten sought-after particles expected as the yield of each billion collisions. A smaller, 200-ton detector was built by a second group for other experiments and to confirm the results of the primary detector.

The problem of supplying enough antiprotons (antimatter is extremely scarce) was solved by SIMON VAN DER MEER. With his method, the antiprotons would be produced by bombarding a solid copper target with a rapid series of bursts of very fast-moving protons from the proton synchrotron (PS); the antiprotons would then be harvested and left to accumulate in a special storage ring. There they would be compacted by an intricate system of electrodes and gathered into "stacks."

Antiprotons from the accumulator would then be reinjected into the PS, given a preliminary acceleration, and then transferred to the SPS, along with groups of protons similarly accelerated. There particles and antiparticles would receive final acceleration to the order of 300 billion electron volts. Since they have opposite electric charges, they would travel around the 4-mile-diameter evacuated ring in opposite directions, three separate groups of each, and collide at six well-defined points, two points instrumented with the detectors.

The experiments began in 1982, and within a month five W particles were detected. To avoid another premature announcement, Rubbia waited until 1983, after thorough analysis of experimental results, to report the team's discovery of both the W^+ and W^- particles. A few months later he announced the detection of the Z^0 particle.

Rubbia and van der Meer shared the 1984 Nobel Prize for Physics "for their decisive contributions to the large project, which led to the discovery of the field particles W and Z, communicators of the weak interaction." "An old dream was fulfilled . . . when the discoveries of the W and Z were made at CERN," said Gösta Ekspong of the Royal Swedish Academy of Sciences in his presentation speech, "the dream of better understanding the weak interaction, which turns out to be weak just because the W and Z are so very heavy." Ekspong concluded by predicting that "the discovery of the W and Z particles will go down in the history of physics like the discovery of radio waves and the photons of light, the communicators of electromagnetism."

Shortly before the awarding of the prize was made public, Rubbia and his team announced their discovery of the top quark, an elementary particle believed to be a fundamental constituent of other particles such as protons and neutrons. Rubbia subsequently proposed the addition of a new and vastly more powerful proton accelerator to the large electron-positron collider CERN was planning to put into operation in the late 1980s.

Since 1970 Rubbia has spent half the year teaching at Harvard University, where in 1986 he was named Higgins Professor of Physics, and the other half as senior physicist at CERN. An energetic, restless person who travels frequently, he is noted for his skill not only as a physicist but as a dynamic project leader.

Rubbia married Marisa Romé, a high school physics teacher, in 1957. The Rubbias, who have a son and a daughter, live in Geneva and also have a home in Boston, Massachusetts.

In 1985 Rubbia was made an Italian Knight of the Grand Cross and was awarded the George Ledlie Prize of Harvard University. He is a member of the European Academy of Sci-

ences and the American Academy of Arts and Sciences, as well as a foreign member of the Royal Society of London. He holds honorary degrees from many universities, including Geneva, Genoa, Northwestern, Carnegie Mellon, Udine, and La Plata.

ABOUT: Current Biography June 1985; Discover January 1984; New York Times May 21, 1985; Science January 11, 1985; Sutton, C. The Particle Connection, 1985; Taubes, G. Nobel Dreams, 1987.

RUSKA, ERNST

(December 25, 1906–)
Nobel Prize for Physics, 1986
(shared with Gerd Binnig and Heinrich
  Rohrer)

The German physicist Ernst August Friedrich Ruska (rōōs' kä) was born in Heidelberg, the fifth of seven children of Julius Ferdinand Ruska, a professor of Asian studies, and Elisabeth (Merx) Ruska. In 1925 he began his formal training in the physical sciences at the Technical University of Munich before transferring to the Technical University of Berlin in 1927. He received practical training in Berlin with the Siemens and Halske Company and in Mannheim with Brown, Boveri and Company. After becoming a certified engineer at the Technical University of Berlin in 1931, he went on to earn a doctorate in electrical engineering there two years later under Max Knoll.

While working toward his doctorate, Ruska made a discovery that ultimately led to the invention of the electron microscope. Ruska's breakthrough was based on the fact that the conventional light microscope is limited by the wavelength of visible light. Visible light has a wavelength of about 5,000 angstroms, or one-half millionth of a meter; the diameter of an atom is only about 1 angstrom (1 ten-billionth of a meter). It would be impossible to build a light microscope sufficiently powerful to focus on objects so small.

By the mid-1920s it was well understood that electromagnetic radiation (such as light) exhibits particlelike properties; in 1924 the French physicist LOUIS DE BROGLIE proposed that particles, such as electrons, also exhibit wavelike properties. Broglie calculated that the greater the energy of an electron, the shorter its wavelength should be. An electron with an energy of 100 kiloelectron volts, for instance, has a wavelength of about 0.1 angstrom, or approximately one-tenth the diameter of an

ERNST RUSKA

atom. In 1927 CLINTON J. DAVISSON and Lester H. Germer of the Bell Telephone Laboratories confirmed the wavelike properties of the electron.

Since an electron can have a wavelength ten times smaller than an individual atom, experimentalists conceived of building a microscope that exploited electrons instead of light. Ruska's breakthrough in the late 1920s was the discovery that a magnetic coil could act as a lens for electrons. Moreover, Ruska succeeded in building a magnetic lens with a focal length short enough that it could be used to obtain an image of an object irradiated with electrons.

The earliest electron microscope, developed by Ruska and Knoll in 1931, consisted of two magnetic coils in series. With a magnification of 15, the instrument was considerably less powerful than optical microscopes of the day, but it established the basic principle of electron microscopy. In 1933 Ruska built a version that could reveal features with a size of 500 angstroms, which enabled researchers to explore details ten times smaller than those the most powerful light microscope is capable of revealing.

Upon receiving his doctorate in 1933, Ruska joined the Fernseh Corporation in Berlin, where he worked on perfecting television tube technology. In 1937 he took a position as an electrical engineer at Siemens and participated in the development of the first commercial, mass-produced electron microscope. This instrument, which could resolve features as small as 100 angstroms, was first marketed in 1939. To-

day, electron microscopes with resolutions of 1 angstrom are available.

The electron microscope developed by Ruska is called a transmission microscope. In the operation of such an instrument, the material to be examined—which must be in the form of a thin slice—is bombarded with a narrow beam of electrons. As the electrons travel through the slice, they are deflected according to the composition and structure of the material. By recording where the electrons fall on a piece of photographic emulsion, the user can obtain a magnified image of the material. Ruska's device has been used in a wide range of fields, including the study of metals, viruses, protein molecules, and other biological structures.

The transmission microscope Ruska invented led to the development of other types of electron microscopes, perhaps the most important of which is the scanning electron microscope. In this instrument, a sharply focused beam of electrons is fired at the specimen; instead of looking at the electrons that pass through it, one looks at the electrons that are scattered off it. Magnetic coils are used to sweep the incident beam over the surface in much the same manner that the electron beam in a television tube is swept across its surface. Through recordings of the variations in the emission of the scattered electrons, an image with a large depth of focus—in contrast to the sectional image of the transmission microscope—is obtained. Since the resolution of the scanning electron microscope is lower than that of the transmission microscope, the two types complement each other.

In 1949, while still at Siemens, Ruska became a privatdocent (unsalaried lecturer) at the Technical University of Berlin. In the same year he was named an honorary professor at the Free University of Berlin. In 1954, a year before he left Siemens, Ruska became a member of the Max Planck Society, which appointed him director of its Institute of Electron Microscopy in 1957. Two years later he accepted a concurrent position as professor of electron optics and electron microscopy at the Technical University of Berlin. He continued to contribute actively to his field until his retirement in 1972.

Ruska was awarded half of the 1986 Nobel Prize for Physics for "his fundamental work in electron optics and for the design of the first electron microscope." The other half was shared by GERD BINNIG and HEINRICH ROHRER for their contributions to the scanning tunneling microscope. In awarding the prize to Ruska, the Royal Swedish Academy of Sciences stated:

894

"The significance of the electron microscope in different fields of science such as biology and medicine is now fully established: it is one of the most important inventions of the century. . . . Electron microscopy has developed extremely over the past few decades, with technical improvements and entirely new designs." The statement continued, "Its importance can scarcely be exaggerated, and, against this background, the importance of the earliest, fundamental work becomes increasingly evident. While many researchers were involved, Ruska's contributions clearly predominate. His electron-optical investigations and the building of the first true electron microscope were crucial for future development."

In 1937 Ruska married Irmela Ruth Geigis. The Ruskas, who live in Berlin, have two sons and one daughter.

In addition to the Nobel Prize, Ruska has received the Senckenberg Prize of the University of Frankfurt am Main (1939), the Leibniz Silver Medal of the Prussian Academy of Sciences (1941), the Lasker Award of the American Public Health Association (1960), the Duddell Medal and Prize of the Institute of Physics in London (1975), and the Cothenius Medal of the Leopoldina German Academy of Researchers in Natural Sciences (1975). He has received honorary doctorates from the University of Kiev, the University of Modena, the Free University of Berlin, and the University of Toronto.

SELECTED WORKS: The Early Development of Electron Lenses and Electron Microscopy, 1980.

ABOUT: New York Times October 16, 1986; Science November 14, 1986; Science News October 25, 1986.

RUSSELL, BERTRAND
(May 18, 1872–February 2, 1970)
Nobel Prize for Literature, 1950

The English philosopher, mathematician, and author Bertrand Arthur William Russell was born at Ravenscroft (later Cleiddon Hall), near Trelleck, Monmouthshire (now the county of Gwent, Wales). He was the youngest of three children of John, Viscount Amberley, and Katherine (Stanley) Russell. The Russell family had been in the forefront of British political life since the 1500s. Its most prominent member, Lord John Russell, Bertrand's grandfather, twice served as Liberal prime minister under Queen Victoria, who made him the first

BERTRAND RUSSELL

Earl Russell in 1861. (Bertrand Russell became the third Earl Russell in 1931.) Lord John, who introduced the parliamentary Reform Bill of 1832, held radical views that often clashed with those of Tory conservatives.

When Russell was two years old, his mother and sister died, and his father died only twenty months later. In 1876 Russell and his brother went to live with their grandmother, Countess Russell, at Pembrook Lodge in Richmond Park, overlooking Epsom Downs, where they were taught by German and Swiss governesses and by English tutors. Inspired by Euclid's Geometry, Russell displayed a keen aptitude for pure mathematics and developed an interest in philosophy. Despite his grandmother's pious ministrations, his devotion to the truths of pure mathematics soon led him to reject the existence of God.

At eighteen years of age, Russell entered Trinity College, Cambridge, where he received a B.A. in moral sciences with highest distinction in 1894. He was introduced to the absolute idealism of the German philosopher Georg Hegel by J. M. E. McTaggart, a Trinity friend, but he was far more interested in the analytical philosophy of another classmate, G. E. Moore, whose ideas were in the British empirical tradition of John Locke and David Hume. Russell was elected a fellow of Trinity in 1895 and delivered An Essay on the Foundations of Geometry (1897) as his dissertation.

After graduation in 1894, he went to Paris as honorary attaché to the British embassy. He left the post that December to marry an

American Quaker, Alys Whitall Pearsall Smith, the first of his four wives. The couple went to Berlin in 1895, where Russell studied economics and gathered data for his first book, *German Social Democracy* (1896). After a visit to the United States in 1896, the Russells settled in the county of Sussex, England. Russell's next book, *A Critical Exposition of the Philosophy of Leibniz* (1900), grew out of a series of lectures he gave at Cambridge.

In 1900—his "most important year," as he later called it—Russell attended the International Congress of Philosophy in Paris with a fellow Trinity lecturer, Alfred North Whitehead. Impressed by the work of Italian philosopher Giuseppe Peano and German philosopher Gottlob Frege, two of the founders of symbolic logic, Russell wrote *The Principles of Mathematics* (1903), his first book to receive international acclaim. In it, he argued that mathematics and formal logic are identical and that all of mathematics can be deduced from a handful of principles.

Over the next several years, Russell and Whitehead developed this theory further. Their efforts culminated in *Principia Mathematica,* published in three volumes between 1910 and 1913, a work that influenced Continental philosophers, who had traditionally disagreed with British empirical approaches to metaphysical problems. For Russell and Whitehead, the proper function of philosophy was to construe science, and logic was the essential ingredient of scientific inquiry. In their view, philosophy should have nothing to do with ethics or theology. Instead, it should counter the "corruptive" tendencies of idealistic thought by limiting itself to simple, objective accounts of phenomena. It was the belief of Russell and Whitehead that empirical knowledge was the only path to truth and that all other knowledge was subjective and therefore misleading.

Nevertheless, Russell became skeptical of the empirical method as the sole means for ascertaining truth. In his Lowell lectures, delivered at Harvard in 1914 and published the same year as *Our Knowledge of the External World as a Field for Scientific Method in Philosophy,* as well as in subsequent philosophical explorations, he acknowledged the contradictory nature of logic and admitted that much of philosophy does indeed depend on unprovable a priori assumptions about the universe.

While working on *Principia Mathematica,* Russell also became involved in a number of political activities. For several years, he and his wife belonged to the Fabian Society, founded to promote the growth of socialism in Great Britain. He also participated in the campaign for women's suffrage. In 1910, while still a Trinity lecturer, he tried to stand for Parliament as a Liberal but was turned down by the party because of his views on religion.

Opposed to England's involvement in World War I, Russell became associated with a pacifist group, the No Conscription Fellowship, in 1914. He argued against the war passionately in *Principles of Social Reconstruction* (1916, published in the United States as *Why Men Fight*), *Justice in Wartime* (1916), *Political Ideals* (1917), and *Roads to Freedom* (1918). These books brought Russell some public attention, but he was not thrust into the limelight until he was fined and imprisoned for writing a pamphlet censuring the jailing of a conscientious objector. Consequently, Trinity College dismissed him, he had to sell his library to pay the fine, and, when Harvard offered him a post, the British government refused to grant him a passport. Undeterred, Russell continued to advocate pacifism. He was again imprisoned for four months in 1918 after the Magistrate's Court prosecuted him for criticizing the entry of the United States into the war. While in Brixton Gaol, he worked on *Introduction to Mathematical Philosophy* (1919).

Russell's involvement in politics—particularly with the Labour party—continued during the 1920s. He also produced popular books on various scientific subjects, including *Analysis of Mind* (1921), *The ABC of Atoms* (1923), *The ABC of Relativity* (1925), and *Analysis of Matter* (1927). He spent five weeks in the Soviet Union in 1920, meeting such eminent revolutionary figures as Vladimir Ilyich Lenin, Leon Trotsky, and Maxim Gorky. Although sympathetic to socialism, he expressed strong disapproval of the Soviet regime in *The Practice and Theory of Bolshevism* (1920). He visited Asia in 1920 and 1921, teaching philosophy at the National University of Peking, and expressed his admiration for the Orient in *The Problem of China* (1922). From 1924 to 1931 he made lecture tours of the United States.

After divorcing his first wife, with whom he had no children, Russell married Dora Winifred Black in 1921; they had a son and a daughter. Developing an interest in education, the couple started the experimental Beacon Hill School for young children. Russell expounded his theories on education and human behavior in *On Education* (1926), *Education and the Good Life* (1926), *Marriage and Morals* (1929), and *Education and the Social Order* (1932).

In the 1930s Russell turned his attention to

world affairs in *Freedom and Organization, 1814–1914* (1934), *Which Way to Peace?* (1936), and *Power: A New Social Analysis* (1938). In 1935 he was again divorced. The following year, he married Patricia Helen Spence, his former secretary; they had one son. The couple went to the United States, where he taught philosophy at the University of Chicago (1938) and the University of California at Los Angeles (1939).

After the Nazi invasion of Poland in September 1939, Russell put aside his pacifism to support the British war effort. Although no longer controversial in his own country, he encountered protests in the United States because of his progressive social views. In 1940 his appointment as professor of philosophy at the City College of New York was blocked by the protests of a number of clergymen and members of the city council. Despite demonstrations, he gave the 1940 William James lectures at Harvard, published later that year as *An Inquiry Into Meaning and Truth*. A five-year contract to lecture at the Barnes Foundation in Merion, Pennsylvania, beginning in October 1940, was breached by his dismissal in 1942. Suing for damages, Russell was awarded $20,000. The partly delivered lectures were incorporated into *A History of Western Philosophy* (1945).

Russell returned to Trinity College, Cambridge, on a fellowship in 1944. Further philosophical inquiries formed the basis of *Philosophy and Politics* (1947) and *Human Knowledge, Its Scope and Limits* (1948). In 1948 and 1949 he delivered the Reith lectures, broadcast by the British Broadcasting Corporation (BBC). They were published as *Authority and the Individual* (1949). To add to his many honors—including Fellow of the Royal Society since 1908—the British government awarded him the Order of Merit in 1949.

In 1950, the year his *Unpopular Essays* appeared, Russell received the Nobel Prize for Literature for that year, becoming the third philosopher (after RUDOLF EUCKEN and HENRI BERGSON) to be so honored. Comparing Russell's ideals to those of Alfred Nobel, Anders Österling of the Swedish Academy praised him "as one of our time's brilliant spokesmen of rationality and humanity, as a fearless champion of free speech and free thought in the West." Russell did not deliver a formal lecture.

During the last twenty years of his life, Russell received wide attention as a peace activist, becoming a familiar figure at public demonstrations and committee meetings. Beginning in 1954, after the first hydrogen bomb test, he worked to promote nuclear disarmament. He joined the Campaign for Nuclear Disarmament in 1958 and the Committee of 100 in 1960. In 1961 he served a short prison sentence for breach of the peace during a demonstration outside the houses of Parliament. During the Cuban missile crisis in 1962, he sent messages to United States President John F. Kennedy and Soviet Premier Nikita Khrushchev pleading for a summit conference.

In 1963 he left the Committee of 100 to devote his energies to the Bertrand Russell Peace Foundation and the Atlantic Peace Foundation, which were organized to develop worldwide resistance to the nuclear arms race. In the late 1960s, together with JEAN-PAUL SARTRE and others, he sat on an unofficial tribunal that found the United States guilty of war crimes in Vietnam.

Again divorced, Russell married his fourth wife, Edith Finch, in 1952. They retired to Plas Penrhyn, his residence in North Wales, where he continued to write. He died there of influenza in 1970 at the age of ninety-seven. Important works published after Russell won the Nobel Prize are *The Impact of Science on Society* (1952), *Portraits From Memory* (1956), *Fact and Fiction* (1962), and his three-volume *Autobiography* (1967–1969).

In assessing Russell's long career, critics have been hard-pressed to distinguish between the man and the philosopher. For all his considerable intellectual accomplishments, it is as a controversial public figure that he is likely to be remembered. Reviewing the second volume of Russell's autobiography in 1968, the English critic Michael Holroyd described him as "one of the most extraordinary phenomena of this century . . . [whose] career comprises an astonishing series of paradoxes." While the American philosopher Sidney Hook found in the third volume of the autobiography "a pronounced strain of the aristocrat's contempt for the masses," other critics, including the American philosopher Irwin Edman, have compared Russell to Voltaire in Russell's defense of liberty and iconoclastic declarations. "It was not whimsical of the Nobel Prize committee to give [him] the prize for literature," Edman asserted in a 1951 review of *Unpopular Essays*. "Like some of his most famous predecessors in British philosophy . . . he is a master of English prose."

Russell addressed the complexities of his life in the opening sentence of his autobiography: "Three passions, simple but strong, have governed my life: the longing for love, the search for knowledge, and unbearable pity for the suffering of mankind."

ADDITIONAL WORKS: The Problems of Philosophy, 1912; The Philosophy of Bergson, 1914; Scientific Method in Philosophy, 1914; War, The Offspring of Fear, 1915; Mysticism and Logic, 1917; The Prospects of Industrial Civilization, 1923; Icarus, 1924; What I Believe, 1925; An Outline of Philosophy, 1927; Selected Papers, 1927; Skeptical Essays, 1928; A Liberal View of Divorce, 1929; The Conquest of Happiness, 1930; The Scientific Outlook, 1931; Religion and Science, 1935; In Praise of Idleness, 1935; Determinism and Physics, 1936; Let the People Think, 1941; Is Materialism Bankrupt? 1946; New Hopes for a Changing World, 1951; What Is Democracy? 1953; Satan in the Suburbs, 1953; Human Society in Ethics and Politics, 1954; History as Art, 1954; Logic and Knowledge, 1956; Nightmares of Eminent Persons, 1957; Understanding History, 1957; Why I Am Not a Christian, 1957; The Will to Doubt, 1958; Common Sense and Nuclear Warfare, 1959; My Philosophical Development, 1959; Wisdom of the West, 1959; Bertrand Russell Speaks His Mind, 1960; Has Man a Future? 1961; History of the World in Epitome, 1962; Unarmed Victory, 1963; War Crimes in Vietnam, 1967; The Art of Philosophizing, 1968; My Own Philosophy, 1972; The Collected Stories of Bertrand Russell, 1972; Mortals and Others, 1975.

ABOUT: Aiken, L. W. Bertrand Russell's Philosophy of Morals, 1963; Ayer, A. J. (ed.) Russell, 1972; Clark, R. W. The Life of Bertrand Russell, 1975; Crawshay-Williams, R. Russell Remembered, 1970; Dewey, J., and Kallen, H. M. The Bertrand Russell Case, 1941; Eames, E. R. Bertrand Russell's Theory of Knowledge, 1969; Feinberg, B., and Kasvils, R. Bertrand Russell's America, 1973; Fritz, C. A. Bertrand Russell's Construction of the External World, 1952; Gotlind, E. Bertrand Russell's Theories of Causation, 1952; Hardy, G. H. Bertrand Russell and Trinity, 1942; Jackson, M. L. Style and Rhetoric in Bertrand Russell's Work, 1983; Jager, R. The Development of Bertrand Russell's Philosophy, 1973; Kilmister, C. W. Russell, 1984; Klemke, E. D. (ed.) Essays on Bertrand Russell, 1970; Kuntz, P. G. Bertrand Russell, 1986; Lawrence, D. H. Letters to Bertrand Russell, 1948; Leggett, H. W. Bertrand Russell, 1950; Moran, M., and Spadoni, C. (eds.) Intellect and Social Conscience, 1984; Murray, J. G. (ed.) An Atheist's Bertrand Russell, 1980; Nakhikian, G. (ed.) Bertrand Russell's Philosophy, 1974; Pears, D. Bertrand Russell and the British Tradition in Philosophy, 1967; Russell, D. The Tamarisk Tree, 1975; Sainsbury, M. Russell, 1979; Schlipp, P. A. (ed.) The Philosophy of Bertrand Russell, 1944; Schuenman, R. Bertrand Russell, Philosopher of the Century, 1967; Tait, K. My Father, Bertrand Russell, 1975.

RUTHERFORD, ERNEST

(August 30, 1871–October 19, 1937)
Nobel Prize for Chemistry, 1908

The English physicist Ernest Rutherford was born near Nelson, New Zealand, one of twelve children of James Rutherford, a Scottish-born wheelwright who also worked as a construction hand, and Martha (Thompson) Rutherford, a schoolteacher from England. After attending local schools, Rutherford won a scholarship to Nelson College, a nearby private high school, where he did outstanding work, especially in mathematics. His record won him another scholarship that enabled him to attend Canterbury College in Christchurch, one of New Zealand's largest cities.

At Canterbury, Rutherford was influenced by A. W. Bickerton, who taught physics and chemistry, and G. H. H. Cook, who taught mathematics. After receiving his B.A. in 1892, Rutherford remained at Canterbury for further study on a mathematics scholarship. The following year he received his M.A. with first-class honors in both mathematics and physics. His research was concerned with the detection of high-frequency radio waves, whose existence had been demonstrated less than a decade before. In order to study this phenomenon, he designed and constructed a wireless receiver (several years before GUGLIELMO MARCONI's wireless experiments) and with it received signals transmitted by a colleague from half a mile away.

Rutherford received a B.S. in 1894—it was a tradition at Canterbury that any student with an M.A. who remained at the college should do more research and obtain a B.S.—and then taught briefly at a boy's school in Christchurch. His extraordinary scientific ability then won him a scholarship to Cambridge University in England, where Rutherford entered as a research student at the Cavendish Laboratory, one of the world's leading centers for scientific research.

At Cambridge, Rutherford worked under the English physicist J. J. THOMSON. Impressed by Rutherford's research on radio waves, Thomson asked Rutherford in 1896 to investigate with him the effect of X rays (discovered the previous year by WILHELM RÖNTGEN) on the discharge of electricity in gases. Their collaboration produced several notable results, including Thomson's discovery of the electron, an atomic particle with a negative electrical charge. Based on their investigations, Thomson and Rutherford proposed that as X rays pass through a gas they disrupt its atoms, releasing equal numbers of positively and negatively charged particles, which they called ions. Rutherford now turned to the study of atomic structure.

In 1898 Rutherford accepted a professorship at McGill University in Montreal, Canada, where he began an important series of experiments on the radiation produced by the element uranium. He soon discovered two forms: alpha radiation, which penetrated matter only

ERNEST RUTHERFORD

a short distance before it stopped, and beta radiation, which penetrated much farther. He next found that radioactive thorium emitted a gaseous radioactive product, which he named "emanation." Further studies indicated that at least two other radioactive elements, radium and actinium, also produced emanation. From these and other findings, Rutherford discerned two important clues to the nature of radiation: all known radioactive elements emit alpha and beta radiations; more importantly, every radioactive element decreases in radioactivity over a characteristic period of time. These clues suggested that all radioactive elements belonged to a single atomic family and that they could be ranked by the period of their decreasing radioactivity.

After further research at McGill in 1901 and 1902, Rutherford and his colleague FREDERICK SODDY announced their disintegration theory of radioactivity. According to this theory, radioactivity occurs when an atom expels a small portion of itself at an enormous velocity, the loss transforming the atom from one chemical element to another. The theory conflicted with several prevailing beliefs, including the time-honored concept that atoms were indestructible and unchangeable.

Rutherford went on to marshal additional experimental evidence for his theory. In 1903 he demonstrated that alpha particles are positively charged. Because these particles have a measurable mass, their ejection from the atom is crucial in transforming a radioactive

element into another element. Rutherford's theory also enabled him to predict the rates at which the various radioactive elements would change into what he called the daughter material. Rutherford was convinced that an alpha particle was indistinguishable from the nucleus of a helium atom. Evidence of this came when Soddy, then working with the British chemist WILLIAM RAMSAY, discovered that radium emanation contained helium, the suspected alpha particle.

In 1907, wishing to be closer to the center of scientific research, Rutherford accepted the post of Langworthy Professor of Physics at Manchester University, England. With the assistance of Hans Geiger, later known for his invention of the Geiger counter, Rutherford developed a school at Manchester for research into radioactivity.

Rutherford was awarded the 1908 Nobel Prize for Chemistry "for his investigations into the disintegration of the elements and the chemistry of radioactive substances." In his presentation address, K. B. Hasselberg of the Royal Swedish Academy of Sciences pointed to the connection between Rutherford's work and that of Thomson, HENRI BECQUEREL, and PIERRE and MARIE CURIE. "Rutherford's discoveries led to the highly surprising conclusion that a chemical element . . . is capable of being transformed into other elements," Hasselberg said. In his Nobel lecture Rutherford noted that "there is every reason to believe that the alpha particles, so freely expelled from the majority of radioactive substances, are identical in mass and constitution and must consist of atoms of helium. We are consequently driven to the conclusion that the atoms of the primary radioactive elements like uranium and thorium must be built up in part at least of atoms of helium."

Rutherford now turned his attention to a phenomenon observed when alpha particles expelled from radioactive elements such as uranium bombarded thin sheets of gold foil. The angle at which the alpha particles were deflected proved to be useful for studying the structure of the stable elements in the sheets. According to the then-accepted "plum pudding" model of the atom, positive and negative charges were distributed evenly throughout an atom and therefore could alter the course of alpha particles by only a small amount. Rutherford, however, had observed that certain alpha particles were deflected from their expected paths by a greater amount than the theory allowed. Working with Ernest Marsden, an undergraduate at Manchester, he confirmed that a few alpha particles were indeed deflected farther than expected, some through angles of more than 90 degrees.

After pondering this phenomenon, Rutherford presented a new model of the atom in 1911. According to his theory, which is still generally accepted, positively charged particles are concentrated in a massive center while negatively charged particles (electrons) orbit this nucleus at a relatively great distance from it. This model, similar to that of a minuscule solar system, implies that atoms consist chiefly of empty space. Acceptance of Rutherford's theories grew after 1913, when the Danish physicist NIELS BOHR joined him at Manchester. Bohr demonstrated that the observed physical characteristics of the hydrogen atom, as well as the atoms of several heavier elements, could be understood in terms of Rutherford's proposed structure.

Following the outbreak of World War I, Rutherford served as a civilian committee member of the British Admiralty's Board of Invention and Research, studying the problems of submarine detection by acoustics. After the war, he returned to his Manchester laboratory, and in 1919 he made another fundamental discovery. While probing the interior of hydrogen atoms by firing at them a high-velocity stream of alpha particles, he observed a signal in his particle detector that could be explained as the result of hydrogen nuclei set in motion by collision with an alpha particle. He was puzzled, however, to see the same signal when nitrogen atoms were substituted for hydrogen atoms. Rutherford recognized that this phenomenon was caused by the induced disintegration of a stable atom. That is, in a process paralleling the naturally occurring disintegration caused by radiation, an alpha particle had dislodged a single proton (a hydrogen nucleus) from the normally stable nitrogen nucleus and had given it a tremendous velocity. Further evidence for this interpretation came when FRÉDÉRIC JOLIOT and IRÈNE JOLIOT-CURIE created radioactivity artificially in 1934.

In 1919 Rutherford went to Cambridge University, succeeding Thomson as Cavendish Professor of Experimental Physics and director of the Cavendish Laboratory; and in 1921 he became professor of natural philosophy at the Royal Institution in London. In 1930 he was named chairman of the advisory council to the British government's Department of Science and Industrial Research. Now at the peak of his career, Rutherford attracted many talented young physicists to his laboratory at Cambridge, including P. M. S. BLACKETT, JOHN COCKCROFT, JAMES CHADWICK, and ERNEST WALTON. Even though he found less time for active research, Rutherford's keen interest and guidance helped to sustain a high level of work at the laboratory. He was described by his students and colleagues as warm and outgoing. His theoretical outlook was tempered by a practical streak that enabled him to interpret his observations accurately, no matter how unconventional the implications might appear to be.

Disturbed by the policies of Adolf Hitler's Nazi government, Rutherford in 1933 became president of the Academic Assistance Council, which was established to assist refugees fleeing Germany.

In 1900, on a brief visit to New Zealand, Rutherford married Mary Newton, with whom he had a daughter. Remaining in sound health until nearly the end of his life, he died at Cambridge in 1937 after a short illness. He was buried at Westminster Abbey near the graves of Isaac Newton and Charles Darwin.

Among the awards Rutherford received were the Rumford Medal (1904) and the Copley Medal (1922) of the Royal Society and the British Order of Merit (1925). He was elevated to the peerage in 1931. He received honorary degrees from New Zealand University, Cambridge University, the University of Wisconsin, the University of Pennsylvania, and McGill University. He was a corresponding member of the Royal Society of Göttingen and a member of the New Zealand Philosophical Institute, the American Philosophical Society, the St. Louis Academy of Science, the Royal Society, and the British Association for the Advancement of Science.

SELECTED WORKS: Radioactivity, 1904; Radioactive Transformations, 1906; Radioactive Substances and Their Radiations, 1913; The Natural and Artificial Disintegration of the Elements, 1924; Electricity and Matter, 1928; Radiations From Radioactive Substances, 1930, with others; The Artificial Transmutation of the Elements, 1933; The Newer Alchemy, 1937; Science in Development, 1937; Collected Papers (3 vols.) 1962–1965; Rutherford and Boltwood: Letters on Radioactivity, 1969.

ABOUT: Allibone, T. E. Rutherford: The Father of Nuclear Energy, 1973; Andrade, E. N. C. Rutherford and the Nature of the Atom, 1964; Birks, J. B. (ed.) Rutherford at Manchester, 1962; Dale, H. H. Some Personal Recollections of Lord Rutherford of Nelson, 1950; Evans, I. B. N. Man of Power, 1939; Eve, A. S. Rutherford, 1939; Feather, N. Lord Rutherford, 1940; Howorth, M. Pioneer Research on the Atom, 1958; Kelman, P., and Stone, A. H. Ernest Rutherford: Architect of the Atom, 1969;

McKown R. Giant of the Atom, 1962; Moon, P. B. Ernest Rutherford and the Atom, 1972; Oliphant, M. R. Rutherford: Recollections of the Cambridge Days, 1972; Rowland, J. Ernest Rutherford, Master of the Atom, 1964; Shire, E. S. Rutherford and the Nuclear Atom, 1972; Trenn, T. J. The Self-Splitting Atom: The History of the Rutherford-Soddy Collaboration, 1977; Wilson, D. Rutherford, Simple Genius, 1983.

RUŽIČKA, LEOPOLD
(September 13, 1887–September 26, 1976)
Nobel Prize for Chemistry, 1939
(shared with Adolf Butenandt)

LEOPOLD RUŽIČKA

The Swiss chemist Leopold Stephen Ružička (rü′ zhich kə) was the elder of two sons born to Stjepan Ružička, a cooper, and the former Amalija Sever in the town of Vukovar, then in Austria-Hungary (now part of Yugoslavia). After Ružička's father died in 1891, his family moved to the nearby town of Osijek, where they lived with relatives while Ružička attended primary school and later the local gymnasium.

In 1906, hoping for a career in a new sugar refinery in Osijek, Ružička enrolled in the technical university at Karlsruhe, Germany. He chose the German school to avoid the student unrest then endemic in universities in the Austro-Hungarian Empire as nationalistic fervor swept the Balkan states. In addition, the technical university had no entrance examination, which made it easier to matriculate. After completing his undergraduate studies in only two years, he began his doctoral research under HERMANN STAUDINGER. In 1910 Ružička received both his engineering diploma, for work on the reaction kinetics of ketenes, and his Ph.D., with the dissertation "Phenyl Methyl Ketene." He immediately began work as Staudinger's assistant.

When Staudinger was appointed director of the Federal Institute of Technology in Zurich in 1912, Ružička followed him. For the next four years he assisted Staudinger in research into the chemistry of the natural insecticide produced by the plant *Chrysanthemum cinerariaefolium,* work that ultimately promoted the synthetic pesticide industry. During this time Ružička became intensely interested in the chemistry of natural substances, and in 1916 he announced to Staudinger his intention to conduct research of his own, a decision that cost him Staudinger's support.

In 1917 Ružička became a Swiss citizen. The same year, he received funds from Haarman and Reimer, a German perfume-manufacturing firm, to seek a method for synthesizing irone, a fragrant substance with an odor of violets. At the same time, he became a lecturer at the Federal Institute of Technology, an unsalaried position that nevertheless gave him access to the institute's chemistry laboratories.

From 1918 to 1921, Ružička conducted research for a Swiss chemical firm, the Gesellschaft für Chemische Industrie (Ciba), and in 1920 he became a lecturer in chemistry at the University of Zurich. Even though the Federal Institute promoted him to professor in 1923, Ružička still received no salary. Therefore, he accepted a position in 1926 in the laboratories of Chuit, Naef, and Firmenich, a Geneva perfume manufacturer.

During these years, Ružička became known for his work on terpines, organic compounds found in the oils of plants. He also conducted research on ketones and many other substances. In 1926 he was appointed professor of organic chemistry at the University of Utrecht, a position he held until 1929, when he returned to Zurich as director of the Federal Institute of Technology, succeeding RICHARD KUHN.

Ružička's return to Zurich was motivated in part by the opportunities and resources offered by Switzerland's increasingly prosperous chemical industry. In 1930 he persuaded Ciba to make a sizable financial commitment to the institute, which enabled him to expand the school's staff, graduate enrollment, and research facilities. In an ambitious research program, Ružička and his colleagues further elucidated the structures of complex terpenes and other large-ring hydrocarbons. In 1934 they partially synthesized the male hormones androsterone and testosterone, and the following year, Ružička correctly defined the molecular structure of testosterone.

The 1939 Nobel Prize for Chemistry was awarded to Ružička "for his work on polymethylenes and higher terpines." He shared the award with ADOLF BUTENANDT, one of his chief competitors in the field of sex hormone chemistry. Because the outbreak of World War II made travel difficult, Ružička was given the award by the Swedish ambassador at special ceremonies held at the Federal Institute of Technology in 1940. Ružička delivered his Nobel lecture in Stockholm five years later.

Although he had expressed little previous interest in political matters, Ružička became increasingly concerned over Nazi Germany's policies and the spread of World War II. During the war years he helped several Jewish scientists to escape from Nazi-occupied Europe and provided refuge for others. He actively supported the Yugoslav Resistance movement through charitable organizations in Switzerland and, as the founder of the Swiss-Yugoslav Relief Society, led efforts to aid victims of the conflict both during and after the war.

During the postwar years Ružička devoted time to collecting art, particularly works by seventeenth-century Dutch and Flemish masters. He later donated his sizable collection to the Zurich art museum. Although severely color-blind (especially to the color red), Ružička also enjoyed taking color photographs.

After retiring from the Federal Institute in 1957, Ružička continued to serve as a consultant to a number of Swiss chemical companies and worked to strengthen ties between industry and academia. In retirement he became an avid gardener with a special fondness for roses and alpine flowers. He married Anna Hausmann in 1912; they had no children. They were divorced in 1950, and one year later Ružička married Gertrud Acklin. Ružička "had a strong-willed character and a vigorous—even charismatic—personality," VLADIMIR PRELOG recalled in a biographical sketch. "His candor and direct way of speaking were such that many who came into contact with him were often shocked and sometimes even felt insulted. At the same time, he was able to accept criticism of himself with good grace, provided it was well argued."

In addition to the Nobel Prize, Ružička received the Werner Medal of the Swiss Chemical Society (1923), the Leblanc Medal of the French Chemical Society (1928), the Stanislao

Cannizzaro Prize of the National Academy of Sciences of Italy (1936), the Scheele Medal of the Swedish Chemical Society (1938), and the Faraday Medal of the British Chemical Society (1958). He held honorary degrees from Harvard University and from the universities of Basel, Zagreb, Paris, Bordeaux, Prague, Glasgow, and Geneva. He was a foreign member of, among others, the American Academy of Arts and Sciences; the Yugoslav Academy of Sciences; the Royal Society of London; the American National Academy of Sciences; the Royal Flemish Academy of Sciences, Literature, and Arts; the Serbian Academy of Sciences; the Soviet Academy of Sciences; and the Polish Academy of Sciences.

ABOUT: Annual Review of Biochemistry, volume 42, 1973; Biographical Memoirs of Fellows of the Royal Society, volume 26, 1980.

RYLE, MARTIN

(September 27, 1918–October 16, 1984)
Nobel Prize for Physics, 1974
(shared with Antony Hewish)

The English radio astronomer Martin Ryle (rīl) was born in Oxford, the second of five children of John A. Ryle, a physician and professor of social medicine at Oxford University, and Miriam (Scully) Ryle. Educated at Bradfield College and Oxford, he graduated in 1939 with a first-class degree from the School of Natural Sciences. Between 1939 and 1945 he worked on military airborne radar and radio at the Telecommunications Research Establishment in Malvern, where he first met ANTONY HEWISH. Ryle came to the Cavendish Laboratory at Cambridge University in 1945 on a fellowship to do research under John A. Ratcliffe and W. L. BRAGG. His subject was the emission of radio waves by the sun, a phenomenon discovered accidentally by radar operators during World War II; his equipment consisted of two small antennas.

After the war Ryle remained at Cambridge, including time at the Cavendish Laboratory and the Mullard Radio Astronomy Observatory. In 1948 he became lecturer in physics at Trinity College, in 1949 a fellow of the college, in 1957 reader in physics, and in 1959 Cambridge's first professor of radio astronomy.

Ryle was concerned with improving the resolving power of radio telescopes, because the higher the resolving power, the easier it is to distinguish the wave front coming from a par-

MARTIN RYLE

ticular direction and to ignore those from adjacent directions. The resolving power of any telescope depends on an aperture, or diameter, that is large in relation to the wavelength of the radiation being collected. For light telescopes, ratios of several million to one between aperture and wavelength are easily attainable, because light has a wavelength of less than one-millionth of a meter. Radio wavelengths range from about 1 centimeter upward. To have an aperture of 1 million centimeters, a radio telescope dish (parabolic reflector) would need to be 10 kilometers in diameter.

Spacing his two antennas many wavelengths apart, Ryle connected them to a single receiver. With this simple interferometer, he deduced that radio emission from solar flares occurs in very small regions. By resorting to phase switching (combining the signals from each antenna alternately in phase and in antiphase), Ryle was able to distinguish radio waves emitted by a flare from those emitted by the rest of the sun. Using the same technique to make exploratory studies of stars and galaxies, he reached 6 billion light-years into space, enabling the range of the 200-inch reflecting optical telescope at Mount Palomar Observatory to be tripled. By 1948 Ryle had located several so-called radio stars (celestial objects that emit electromagnetic radiation) accurately enough that they could be observed optically. The use of radio waves in astronomy meant that new and entirely different regions—such as those containing high-energy particles or diffused ionized gas—could be studied for the first time.

In 1952 Ryle and his colleagues set out to design instruments capable not only of extending observations to weaker and weaker sources but also of exploring their internal structure. He found that it was theoretically possible to combine the signals from a pair of antennas (one of them movable) whose separation and orientation are varied systematically between consecutive measurements. The electronic computers available in the mid-1950s were able to carry out some of the necessary calculations. In 1957 Ryle used a large two-antenna telescope he built to conduct a celestial survey that revealed 5,000 radio sources. Because the computational power of the computers was limited, however, the telescope had very high resolution in only one dimension.

Taking advantage of the greatly increased computing power available by 1963, Ryle built a telescope with three steerable, 60-foot parabolic reflector antennas, two fixed 0.5 mile apart and the third mounted on a 2,500-foot track. Combined with the effect of the earth's rotation during the twelve-hour period of observation, this technique allowed the signals of three antennas to be combined to yield a resolution equivalent to that of a radio telescope with a 1-mile aperture. With this 1-mile telescope, Ryle first demonstrated the method of aperture synthesis, which allows both high resolving power in two dimensions and a large effective collecting area to be obtained with a minimum of engineering structure and cost. This instrument was the first to reveal structural details of radio galaxies.

A larger aperture synthesis telescope (equivalent to 3.1 miles in diameter) designed by Ryle was built in 1971. It included eight 42-foot diameter dishes (four on tracks) and was used to study the fine structure of distant radio sources. Its resolution was 0.6-inch arc. Ryle's major surveys of celestial radio sources, most of them too far and too faint to be detected with light telescopes, revealed that some of the most intense were quasars (quasi-stellar objects), remote starlike objects that emit many times more energy than do entire galaxies.

Modern radio telescopes, much larger than those built by Ryle, utilize the accuracy of atomic clocks to permit the recording of signals at antennas thousands of miles apart and their later processing at a separate computer analysis facility; the equivalent aperture is as great as the diameter of the earth.

Ryle and Hewish were awarded the 1974 Nobel Prize for Physics "for their pioneering research in radio astrophysics." Ryle was cited "for his observations and inventions, in particular of the aperture synthesis technique." "The contributions of Ryle and Hewish represent an important step forward in our knowledge of the universe," said Hans Wilhelmsson of the Royal Swedish Academy of Sciences in his presentation address. "Thanks to their work, new fields of research have become part of astrophysics. The gigantic laboratory of the universe offers rich possibilities for future research."

Telescopes designed by Ryle have been built in the Netherlands and New Mexico (the Very Large Array). It is expected that very long base interferometry, using a baseline of several thousand kilometers, will provide a resolution to 0.001-inch arc.

According to Ryle's statistical analysis of radio sources, the universe is not infinite and was once much hotter than it is now. These conclusions lend support to the big-bang theory of cosmology and are not consistent with the steady-state theory.

In 1976 Ryle became actively involved in research on renewable energy sources, especially winds and waves. His work established that wind energy in the United Kingdom could provide a realistic alternative to nuclear power when due account was taken of the large seasonal fluctuation in demand.

In 1947 Ryle married Ella Rowena Palmer, a nurse and physiotherapist. They and their two daughters and one son enjoyed sailing catamarans and trimarans that Ryle had designed. Ryle died of lung cancer at his home in Cambridge on October 16, 1984.

Knighted in 1966, Ryle was awarded honorary doctorates from the universities of Strathclyde, Oxford, and Toruń (Poland). From 1972 to 1982 he served as Astronomer Royal, a position traditionally reserved for the director of the Royal Greenwich Observatory. He was a member of the Soviet Academy of Sciences, the Danish Academy of Arts and Sciences, the American Academy of Arts and Sciences, and the Royal Society. In addition to the Nobel Prize, he received numerous awards and honors, including the Hughes Medal (1954) and the Royal Medal (1973) of the Royal Society, the Gold Medal of the Royal Astronomical Society (1964), and the Henry Draper Medal of the National Academy of Sciences (1965).

SELECTED WORKS: Search and Research, 1971, with others.

ABOUT: Current Biography September 1973; New York Times October 17, 1984; Physics Today December 1974; Science November 15, 1974.

SAAVEDRA LAMAS, CARLOS
(November 1, 1878–May 5, 1959)
Nobel Prize for Peace, 1936

The Argentine statesman Carlos Saavedra Lamas (sä ä vä' *th*rä läm' äs) was born in Buenos Aires to Mariano Saavedra Zabaleta and the former Luisa Lamas. As a youth, he was privately tutored and then attended a Jesuit school and Lacordaire College. In 1903 he graduated summa cum laude from the University of Buenos Aires with an LL.D.

After traveling abroad and studying in Paris, Saavedra Lamas became a professor of law at the University of La Plata. Later he was a professor at the University of Buenos Aires, where he introduced a course in sociology and taught political economy and constitutional law in the Law School. He edited several treatises on the subject of labor legislation, an area of particular interest to him. His other continuing scholarly interest was international law.

Saavedra Lamas entered government service in 1906 when he was appointed Argentina's director of public credit. He became secretary of the municipality of Buenos Aires the following year and in 1908 began the first of two successive terms as a national deputy. Appointed minister of justice and public education in 1915, he remained in this post only briefly. In the years following, he was an unofficial adviser to both the legislature and the Foreign Ministry in the matter of treaties. In 1927 he was named a delegate to the International Jurists Convention in Rio de Janeiro, and in 1928 he became president of the International Labor Conference in Geneva.

In 1932 General Agustín P. Justo, who had become Argentina's president after two years of revolutionary government, appointed Saavedra Lamas foreign minister. Shortly thereafter, Bolivia and Paraguay went to war over the Chaco, a territory adjoining both nations, whose boundary had been disputed since the end of Spanish rule in Bolivia in 1825. The area, which had been settled by Paraguay and largely ignored by Bolivia, became important when oil was discovered in the Andean foothills in 1924. It then became vital for Bolivia to find a route to the sea in order to ship its oil. Because Bolivia had lost direct access to the Pacific in a war with Chile in 1884, it sought a way to the Atlantic via the Paraguay River,

CARLOS SAAVEDRA LAMAS

which runs through the Chaco. When Paraguay refused to give up the lands it had settled, fighting broke out between the two nations in 1928. A cease-fire was quickly established and protracted negotiations carried out, but ultimately these attempts at settlement failed, and hostilities were resumed in mid-1932. By the end of the bloody struggle in 1935, over 100,000 had been killed.

When the war was renewed, Saavedra Lamas began efforts to end the conflict as well as to enhance his country's influence in the community of nations and promote international goodwill. In 1932 he formulated the Declaration of August 3, in which the nations of the Americas pledged to refuse recognition to boundaries altered by war. He then drafted the South American Antiwar Pact, which he saw as a means for averting war throughout the world.

The pact combined features of the Kellogg-Briand Pact, formulated in 1928 by FRANK KELLOGG and ARISTIDE BRIAND, with features of the Stimson Doctrine, drafted in 1932 by United States Secretary of State Henry Stimson. Like the Kellogg-Briand Pact, Saavedra Lamas's pact called for signatory nations to renounce aggressive war. Like the Stimson Doctrine, it called for nations to refuse to recognize any change of boundaries not created by peaceful means. Saavedra Lamas's pact went further, however, calling for nations not at war to invoke sanctions against aggressor nations and to set up a conciliation mechanism to stop their aggression. By the end of 1933, all the nations of the Americas had signed the pact,

but it failed to halt the war over the Chaco at that time.

While continuing to work on the Bolivia-Paraguay problem, Saavedra Lamas also explored other avenues of international peace. Argentina had broken with the League of Nations in 1920 after other member nations refused to agree to admit all applicants without conditions. Saavedra Lamas persuaded his government to rejoin the league in 1933, and he won acclaim when he presented his Antiwar Pact to the international body the following year. By this time, eleven European nations had also signed the pact.

American President Franklin D. Roosevelt considered Saavedra Lamas a capable statesman and a leading international figure in Latin America. In the mid-1930s, Roosevelt sought his cooperation in implementing the United States Good Neighbor policy toward Latin America. As a result, despite his wariness of the United States because of its military intervention in Latin America earlier in the century, Saavedra Lamas began to play an active role in the Pan-American Union, a Washington-based organization dedicated to furthering cooperation among American nations.

In 1935, after having pursued a number of possible solutions to the ongoing Bolivia-Paraguay problem, Saavedra Lamas attempted to apply the ideas of his Antiwar Pact, which had been signed by both countries but ratified by neither. He arranged for six neutral American nations—Brazil, Chile, Peru, Uruguay, Argentina, and the United States—to form a conciliation commission to mediate between the by then exhausted combatants. The commission brought an end to the hostilities on June 12 of the same year. Saavedra Lamas was elected president of the Assembly of the League of Nations the following year.

For his role as a peacemaker in the Chaco War between Bolivia and Paraguay, Saavedra Lamas received the 1936 Nobel Peace Prize. He was the first South American to receive the prize, and the news was widely hailed throughout the continent. Because he was presiding at the Inter-American Conference for the Maintenance of Peace held in Buenos Aires, Saavedra Lamas was unable to attend the ceremonies, nor did he deliver a Nobel lecture. However, on November 29 he made a brief radio address from Buenos Aires on the significance of the prize.

"The world longs for peace," he stated in his speech. "It needs it as the fertilizing rain is desired by the earth in order that there may again arise a better life for man—the joyous

905

pleasures of the home, the serene march along the paths of labor." He concluded by stating his philosophy of peace. "War of aggression, war which does not imply defense of one's country, is a collective crime," he said. "War implies a lack of comprehension of mutual national interests; it means the undermining and even the end of culture. It is the useless sacrifice of courage erroneously applied, opposed to that other silent courage that signifies the effort to aid others to improve existence by raising all in this fleeting moment of ours to higher levels of existence."

There was some criticism of the selection of Saavedra Lamas for the award because of his close ties to General Justo, a dictator, and because of his acceptance in 1935 of the Iron Cross from Hitler's Germany. Nonetheless, he was internationally respected and had also been awarded honors by ten other nations, including the Grand Cross of the Legion of Honor, given by France.

Saavedra Lamas retired as foreign minister in 1938 and returned to academic pursuits. He served as president of the University of Buenos Aires from 1941 to 1943 and held a professorship there until his retirement in 1946.

His marriage to Rosa Sáenz Peña, daughter of a former president of Argentina, produced one son. Saavedra Lamas died at his home in Buenos Aires from the effects of a brain hemorrhage at the age of eighty.

WORKS IN ENGLISH TRANSLATION: Draft of a Convention for the Maintenance of Peace, 1936.

ABOUT: New York Times June 13, 1935; May 6, 1959; Pratt, J. Cordell Hull (2 vols.) 1964; Time December 7, 1936.

SABATIER, PAUL
(November 5, 1854–August 14, 1941)
Nobel Prize for Chemistry, 1912
(shared with Victor Grignard)

The French chemist Paul Sabatier (sa ba-tyä′) was born in Carcassonne in southern France, one of three sons and the youngest of seven children. His mother was Pauline (Guilham) Sabatier; his father, Alexis Sabatier, was a landlord who opened a hat shop after losing his properties as the result of a defaulted loan. A boy with lively curiosity and keen intelligence, he was educated at the lycée in Carcassone, where his teachers recognized him as a brilliant student who applied himself dili-

PAUL SABATIER

gently to his work. "I study most the subject I like least," he often said. In 1868 Sabatier transferred to the Lycée de Toulouse to prepare for his university entrance examinations. There he also attended public lectures on physics and chemistry that first kindled his desire to teach and to conduct scientific research.

Between 1869 and 1872 Sabatier studied humanities at the Collège Ste.-Marie in Toulouse before going to Paris for two additional years of preparation. He placed first in his entrance examinations in 1874 and was accepted by both the École Normale Supérieure and the École Polytechnique. Choosing the former, he graduated in three years at the head of his class. He spent the following year teaching physics at the lycée in Nîmes, after which he became an assistant to the chemist Marcellin Berthelot at the Collège de France. There Sabatier continued his studies and in 1880 received his doctorate in science for a thesis on the thermochemistry of sulfur and metallic sulfates.

For the next year Sabatier taught physics at the University of Bordeaux. Returning to Toulouse in 1882, within two years he was given the chair in chemistry, a position he retained for the rest of his career. In 1905 he was named dean of the university's Faculty of Science, and although he was invited to succeed HENRI MOISSAN at the University of Paris (the Sorbonne) in 1907, he chose to remain at Toulouse.

Like Berthelot, Sabatier focused his early research on problems in inorganic chemistry. Using the technique of vacuum distillation, he produced pure hydrogen disulfide. He also isolated binary compounds of boron and silicon, discovered several new metallic nitrides, and developed methods for the preparation of nitrosodisulfonic acid and the basic mixed argentocupric salts.

In the 1890s Sabatier turned his attention to organic chemistry. He was especially interested in the catalytic processes involved in hydrogenation, through which unsaturated organic compounds become saturated. (Unsaturated compounds are able to combine chemically, whereas saturated compounds do not tend to combine.) At the time, platinum and palladium were the standard catalytic agents in such reactions, but their high cost precluded large-scale industrial applications. Sabatier was familiar with experiments in which nickel carbonyl was prepared by subjecting pulverized nickel to carbon monoxide. Knowing that a similar reaction occurs when iron is substituted for nickel, Sabatier wondered if other gases could be made to react with nickel or other metals. By 1896 he had effected the chemical union, or fixing, of nitrogen peroxide on copper, cobalt, and nickel.

When he learned that Moissan and Charles Moureu, another French chemist, had failed to produce the same result when using acetylene, Sabatier repeated their experiment with ethylene, a much less reactive substance, passing gaseous ethylene over slivers of nickel. At 300°C, he observed intense incandescence, deposits of pure carbon forming on the nickel, and a buildup of gas. According to Moissan and Moureu, the gas should have been hydrogen. Instead, Sabatier found that it was composed chiefly of ethane, a fully hydrogen-saturated compound. Rather than fixing the ethylene, the reduced nickel had acted as a catalyst to produce a hydrogenated (hydrogen-rich) carbon compound.

Since saturated hydrocarbons are important intermediaries in the production of pharmaceuticals, perfumes, detergents, edible fats, and other commercial products, Sabatier's discovery had immense practical value. Nevertheless, he remained devoted to theoretical research and obtained only a few patents on his discoveries. Working with a student, J. B. Senderens, he went on to demonstrate the capacity of nickel to hydrogenate other hydrocarbons.

Sabatier received the 1912 Nobel Prize for Chemistry in recognition of "his method of hydrogenating organic compounds in the presence of finely disintegrated metals, whereby the progress of organic chemistry has been greatly advanced." He shared the award with the French chemist VICTOR GRIGNARD. "For the past fifteen years," Sabatier remarked in his Nobel lecture, "this idea of mine on the mechanism of catalysis has never left me, and it is to the inferences drawn from it that I owe all my useful results. Theories cannot claim to be indestructible," he added. "They are only the plough which the ploughman uses to draw his furrow and which he has every right to discard for another one, of improved design, after the harvest."

A year after he received the Nobel Prize, Sabatier published findings that contradicted an earlier theory advanced by WILHELM OSTWALD. According to Ostwald, gaseous reactants are absorbed in micropores when they encounter a solid catalyst. Sabatier proposed instead that such reactions take place on the exterior surfaces of the catalysts, forming temporary, unstable, intermediary compounds. These unstable compounds then break down into the observed end product. This general concept remains useful in evaluating the behavior of newly discovered catalysts.

In 1929 Sabatier resigned as dean of the faculty at Toulouse, and he retired the following year.

In 1884 Sabatier married Germaine Hérail, the daughter of a local judge. They had four daughters. Sabatier did not remarry after her death in 1898. Known as a quiet, reserved man, Sabatier continued to lecture at Toulouse until 1939, when his health began to fail. He died in Toulouse on August 14, 1941.

In addition to the Nobel Prize, Sabatier received the Jecker Prize of the Academy of Sciences (1905), the Davy Medal (1915) and the Royal Medal (1918) of the Royal Society of London, and the Franklin Medal of the Franklin Institute (1933). He held honorary degrees from the universities of Pennsylvania and Saragossa. He was a member of the French Academy of Sciences and a foreign member of many professional societies, including the Royal Society of London, the Academy of Sciences of Madrid, the Royal Netherlands Academy of Sciences, the American Chemical Society, the Scientific Society of Brussels, and the British Chemical Society.

SELECTED WORKS: Catalysis in Organic Chemistry, 1923.

ABOUT: Dictionary of Scientific Biography, volume 12, 1975; New York Times August 16, 1941; Nye, M. J. Science in the Provinces, 1986.

SACHS, NELLY
(December 10, 1891–May 12, 1970)
Nobel Prize for Literature, 1966
(shared with S. Y. Agnon)

The German poet Nelly Sachs (zäks) was born in Berlin, the only child of William Sachs, an inventor and industrialist, and Margareta (Karger) Sachs. Raised in a prosperous, upper-middle-class Jewish family that had been thoroughly assimilated into German society, Sachs was tutored by her father and by private teachers before receiving her secondary education at the Berliner Höhere Töchterschule. A shy, quiet girl, she immersed herself in music, literature, and dance, for a while harboring dreams of becoming a professional dancer.

When, at the age of fifteen, she happened to read SELMA LAGERLÖF's novel *Gösta Berlings saga,* Sachs was so impressed that she wrote to the author in Sweden. Lagerlöf's reply initiated a correspondence that lasted some thirty-five years, until Lagerlöf's death. By the time she turned eighteen, Sachs had begun to write poetry. This early work, some of which was published in literary journals, employed traditional rhymes to describe scenes from nature and mythological events. Conventional in style and subject matter, these poems ran counter to the prevailing avant-garde expressionism of the period. Nevertheless, her verse attracted the notice of the Austrian writer Stefan Zweig, who praised its "ecstatic quality" and arranged for the publication of one poem. Later, however, Sachs repudiated her youthful efforts and excluded them from her collected works.

In the same year that she began writing, Sachs fell in love with a man she met while vacationing at a spa with her parents. Although she never disclosed his identity, she learned many years later that he had perished in a Nazi concentration camp, an event that she alluded to in several of her mature poems.

During the 1920s and 1930s Sachs did not regard herself as a full-time writer, although some of her poems appeared in the *Berliner Tageblatt* (Berlin Daily News) and other newspapers. After her father's death in 1930, she lived a reclusive existence with her mother. Three years later Hitler became chancellor of Germany, and as the Nazis set in motion their anti-Jewish measures, many of Sachs's friends and relatives began to disappear. With her own future uncertain, Sachs sought comfort in the Jewish and Christian mystics, the prophets of the Old Testament, the Cabala, and Hasidic

NELLY SACHS

texts. Until 1938 her poems appeared occasionally in Jewish periodicals.

In 1940, as German forces overran Europe, Sachs and her mother fled to Sweden with the aid of Lagerlöf, who had asked the Swedish royal family to issue them visas. By the time they arrived in Stockholm, however, Lagerlöf had died, and the Sachses found themselves isolated in an alien land. Living in poverty, Sachs learned Swedish and managed to support herself and her mother with German translations of Swedish poetry.

Haunted by the fate of her people, Sachs, who had become a Swedish citizen, responded by writing poetry as a "mute outcry" against the Holocaust. This new work represents a radical departure from the romantic vein of her earlier verse. Unrhymed, dense, and filled with startling images, it presents elements of mysticism in a contemporary context. A collection of her poems, *In den Wohnungen des Todes* (In the Habitations of Death), was published in 1946 in East Germany, followed by the collections *Sternverdunkelung* (Blackout of the Stars, 1949), *Und niemand weiss weiter* (And No One Knows How to Go On, 1957), and *Flucht und Verwandlung* (Flight and Transformation, 1959). "Her poems have variety," noted the English poet and critic Stephen Spender, "but they might all be one poem." In these "religious apocalyptic hymns," Spender continued, "the idea of the Jewish people so prevails that the lives and deaths seem aspects of the same consciousness."

During the postwar years Sachs also began writing plays and dramatic fragments, which she called "scenic poetry." Her first play, *Eli: Ein Mysterienspiel vom Leiden Israels* (*Eli: A Mystery Play of the Sufferings of Israel*, 1951), concerns a cobbler's search for the Nazi soldier who murdered a young Polish shepherd. It was performed on West German radio in 1950, staged in Dortmund in 1962, and adapted as an opera by the Swedish composer Moses Pergament. Sachs's other dramatic works include *Abram im Salz* (Abraham in a Landscape of Salt), a symbolic treatment of the biblical story of King Nimrod and young Abraham that was published in the collection *Zeichen im Sand* (Marks in the Sand, 1962).

The appearance in 1959 of *Flucht und Verwandlung* established Sachs as an important voice in German letters. Sachs made her first visit to Germany in twenty years when she accepted the Annette von Droste-Hülshoff Prize in 1960. The following year the city of Dortmund established an annual literary prize in her name and granted her a lifetime pension. In 1965 she was awarded the Peace Award of the West German Association of Book Publishers and Sellers, one of West Germany's most prestigious literary honors.

Sachs was awarded the 1966 Nobel Prize for Literature in recognition of "her outstanding lyrical and dramatic writing, which interprets Israel's destiny with touching strength." She shared the award with S. Y. AGNON. "With moving intensity of feeling she has given voice to the Jewish race's worldwide tragedy," said Anders Österling of the Swedish Academy in his presentation speech. Even though her work does not flinch from "the terrible truth . . . of the extermination camps and the corpse factories," Österling went on, "at the same time [it] rises above all hatred of the persecutors."

"To me," Sachs said in her acceptance speech, "a fairy tale seems to have become a reality." Contrasting herself to her fellow laureate, she added that "Agnon represents the State of Israel. I represent the tragedy of the Jewish people."

After receiving the Nobel Prize, Sachs, who never married, continued to live and work in the same small apartment in Stockholm. After a long illness, she died in St. Görans Hospital in Stockholm at the age of seventy-eight.

Sachs has received wide recognition for her poetic response to the Holocaust. Her poetry, Spender wrote, "teaches one to know what of all things in modern history we ought to know about—the nightmare and the rebirth." "Nelly Sachs offers her readers no easy consolation," remarked the critic Alvin Rosenfeld in the *Times Literary Supplement*. "The slaughter-house is there, constantly present as immediate experience and indelible recollection," and yet these terrible experiences "are transmuted," Rosenfeld wrote, "into fellow-feeling for all that lives."

ADDITIONAL WORKS IN ENGLISH TRANSLATION: Schwebell, G. C. (ed.) Contemporary German Poetry, 1964; O the Chimneys: Selected Poems, 1967; The Seeker and Other Poems, 1970; Spender, S. (ed.) Selected Poems, 1971.

ABOUT: Books Abroad Winter 1967; Current Biography March 1967; Demetz, P. Postwar German Literature, 1970; New York Times May 13, 1970.

SADAT, ANWAR

(December 25, 1918–October 6, 1981)
Nobel Prize for Peace, 1978
(shared with Menachem Begin)

The Egyptian political leader Mohammed Anwar al-Sadat was born in Mît Abu el-Kôm, a Nile Delta village, one of thirteen children of Mohammed al-Sadat, a military hospital clerk, and Sitt el-Barrein. The family was devoutly Muslim, and Sadat attended a local religious primary school, where he studied the Koran. His abiding faith in Islam was manifested by the dark callus on his forehead caused by years of touching his head to the floor during prayer. In 1925 the family moved to the outskirts of Cairo, where Sadat received his secondary education.

Since 1882 the British had controlled Egypt's political and military affairs. Although Egypt achieved legal independence from Britain in 1922, the British continued to play a powerful behind-the-scenes role in Egyptian affairs. As a youth, Sadat longed to become a military officer so that he could help oust the British from his country. In 1936, when the Royal Military Academy was opened to members of the lower and middle classes, Sadat was admitted. There he formed a close friendship with Gamal Abdel Nasser.

After graduating in 1938, Sadat was assigned to a signal corps installation in southern Egypt. There Sadat, Nasser, and ten other officers formed what Sadat later described as a "secret revolutionary society dedicated to the task of liberation"—that is, to armed revolt against the British. This group became the core of the Free Officers Committee that was to overthrow the monarchy in 1952.

Although Egypt remained officially neutral during World War II, Sadat secretly collabo-

ANWAR SADAT

rated with the Germans in his desire to rid Egypt of British rule. At the request of the Germans, he took part in an attempt to smuggle a general who had been dismissed from the Egyptian army into Iraq, to work against the British there. After a series of mishaps, the plot failed and Sadat was arrested. He was subsequently released for lack of evidence and began working with two Nazi spies in Cairo, who implicated him when they were arrested and questioned. In October 1942, following a court-martial, Sadat was dismissed from the Egyptian army and jailed. Two years later, he staged a hunger strike and was transferred to a prison hospital, from which he escaped. He grew a beard and lived as a fugitive for a year, frequently changing disguises, addresses, and jobs.

When the war ended and martial law was lifted, Sadat was able to come out of hiding, but he was jailed again in 1946, accused of conspiring to assassinate a pro-British cabinet minister. He spent almost three years in prison awaiting trial but was ultimately acquitted.

Sadat's army commission was restored in 1950, and he was stationed in the Sinai, where he maintained a liaison between Nasser's Free Officers Committee and civilian terrorist groups. On July 22, 1952, the committee staged a bloodless coup d'état that sent King Farouk I into exile. Sadat supervised the deposed king's departure.

Nasser soon seized power, and he appointed Sadat to a series of prominent, but relatively powerless, posts during the ensuing years. From 1961 to 1968 Sadat was president of the Na-

tional Assembly. He also served as Nasser's representative on ceremonial visits to many countries and as his troubleshooter in Yemen, which was divided by a civil war.

During Nasser's regime, Sadat was regarded as an unambitious, even weak, figure. Dubbed "Nasser's poodle" by his associates and a "black donkey" by Nasser himself, Sadat's abilities were underestimated by many of his colleagues. Sadat knew the value of keeping his ambitions to himself, however. "If you showed ambition with Nasser, that was the end," Sadat recalled. In 1969, after a lengthy illness, Nasser appointed Sadat his vice president, reportedly because he trusted no one else. Nasser died of a heart attack on September 28, 1970, and shortly thereafter Sadat became the uncontroversial and unanimous choice to succeed him.

Since the founding of the state of Israel in 1948, the Arab states, led by Egypt, had opposed its existence with sporadic warfare and invasion. In the Six-Day War of 1967, Israel had gained the Gaza Strip and the Sinai Peninsula. Before the 1970 election in Egypt, Sadat vowed to attack Israel and recover these lost Arab lands. He also agreed to share leadership with his rivals. He received over 90 percent of the popular vote.

Sadat came to power during a precarious cease-fire between Egypt and Israel, to which Nasser had agreed over Sadat's reported opposition. Although Sadat was expected to rekindle the fighting, he did quite the opposite, extending the cease-fire formally through March 1971 and informally for some time thereafter. He soon emerged as a popular leader with a sound instinct for doing what many Egyptian citizens wanted, such as reducing the powers of the secret police and expelling Soviet military experts.

By 1973, however, negotiations with Israel were deadlocked, and Sadat came under fire from domestic critics as an ineffective leader. It was at this time that he decided to carry out his campaign pledge to attack Israel. "The time has come for a shock," he said. "The resumption of the battle is now inevitable." Obtaining Soviet approval for a limited invasion supported by Syria, he carefully concealed his preparations for the attack. On October 6, the Jewish Yom Kippur holy day, Sadat launched the invasion. The Israelis struck back, repulsing the Syrians and forcing Sadat's troops to retreat across the Suez Canal. After eighteen days of fighting, Israeli armored forces were within forty-five miles of Cairo.

Sadat quickly accepted a cease-fire, and the

United States stepped in to ease tensions. Through the offices of Secretary of State HENRY KISSINGER, a disengagement agreement was achieved in which Israel returned part of the Sinai to Egypt. In the months that followed, however, there was little progress toward peace despite repeated efforts by Kissinger and another limited agreement between the two countries.

Meanwhile, Sadat's political position continued to deteriorate. In 1977 his decision to raise food prices led to major riots, his hopes for a Geneva conference on the Mideast were diminishing, and MENACHEM BEGIN became prime minister of an Israel now strong enough to defeat Egypt.

On November 9 Sadat surprised the world and the Egyptian parliament by declaring his readiness to speak personally to Israel's leaders in the cause of peace. He repeated his offer a week later, telling an American journalist that he was prepared to go to Jerusalem if Begin would issue an invitation. Begin quickly responded, and on November 19 Sadat traveled to Jerusalem to attend a meeting of the Israeli parliament. There he submitted his demands, which included restoration of Arab sovereignty in all territory conquered by Israel during the 1967 war and the establishment of a homeland for Palestinians on the West Bank and in the Gaza Strip. In return, he offered recognition of Israel and peace.

The long negotiations sparked by Sadat's initiative produced no results until United States President Jimmy Carter intervened. He invited both men to the United States for a meeting at Camp David, the presidential retreat in the Maryland mountains, in August 1978. Most observers expected this summit meeting to fail. Indeed, its participants doubted it could succeed until almost the end of the thirteen-day conference. On September 17 the former enemies signed "A Framework for Peace in the Middle East" and "A Framework for the Conclusion of a Peace Treaty Between Egypt and Israel." In these documents Israel agreed to return most of the Sinai region to Egypt in exchange for a full peace. The agreements were open-ended on many subjects, including the fate of Israel's controversial settlements on the West Bank of the Jordan and Israel's occupation of the West Bank and the Gaza Strip, but some semblance of peace was achieved after thirty years.

For their contributions to the framework agreements, Sadat and Begin were jointly awarded the 1978 Nobel Prize for Peace. In her presentation speech, Aase Lionæs of the Norwegian Nobel Committee observed, "It is to President Sadat's credit that he realized that the solution to important social and economic problems in his own country demanded too the conclusion of a peace settlement with Israel." Speaking of Sadat's historic visit to Jerusalem, she called it "an act of great courage, both from a personal and from a political point of view. This was a dramatic break with the past and a courageous step forward into a new age."

In his Nobel lecture Sadat also referred to his Jerusalem visit. "I made my trip because I am convinced that we owe it to this generation and the generations to come not to leave a stone unturned in our pursuit of peace," he said. "The ideal is the greatest one in the history of man, and we have accepted the challenge to translate it from a cherished hope into a living reality, and to win, through vision and imagination, the hearts and minds of our peoples and enable them to look beyond the unhappy past."

In awarding the Peace Prize to Begin and Sadat, the Nobel committee wished to do more than honor the two men for previous actions. It acted "to encourage further efforts to work out practical solutions which can give reality to those hopes of a lasting peace as they have been kindled by the framework agreements." The agreements set a December deadline for concluding a peace treaty, but no treaty was made. Most observers blamed Begin for the failure. It was thus ironic that Begin had traveled personally to Oslo for the award ceremonies while Sadat sent a representative.

Three years later, in the midst of a crackdown on domestic religious and political opponents, with peace still only a dream, Sadat was shot and killed as he watched a military parade in Cairo commemorating the 1973 war against Israel. As jet fighters roared overhead, he was assassinated by a group of men in military uniforms who flung hand grenades and fired rifles at the reviewing stand.

Sadat was married twice, first to Ekbel Mady, a woman from his native village, with whom he had three daughters. After divorcing his first wife, he married Jihan Raouf, the half-English daughter of middle-class parents, in 1949. They had a son and three daughters.

In addition to his native language, Sadat spoke English, German, and Persian and was said to be an avid reader of eclectic tastes. An imposing man, tall and impeccably dressed, he usually wore elegant British-style suits but also liked to stroll around his native village in long Arab shirts. According to the *New York*

SAKHAROV

Times, "He could be the high-toned statesman one minute, relishing his associations with other world leaders, and the humdrum homebody the next."

WORKS IN ENGLISH TRANSLATION: Revolt on the Nile, 1957; Programme of National Action, 1971; Speeches by President Anwar al-Sadat, 1971; Speeches and Interviews (2 vols.) 1975–1978; In Search of Identity, 1978; Those I Have Known, 1984.

ABOUT: Aufderheide, P. Anwar Sadat, 1986; Bardenstein, C., and Israeli, R. Man of Defiance, 1985; Blaisse, M., and Muller, K. Anwar Sadat, 1981; Carroll, R. Anwar Sadat, 1982; Eidelberg, P. Sadat's Strategy, 1979; Fernandez-Armesto, F. Sadat and His Statecraft, 1982; Friedlander, M. A. Sadat and Begin, 1983; Haykal, M. H. Autumn of Fury, 1983; Hinnebusch, R. A. Egyptian Politics Under Sadat, 1985; Hirst, D., and Besson, I. Sadat, 1981; Israeli, R. I, Egypt, 1981; Kays, D. Frogs and Scorpions, 1984; Kosman, W. Y. Sadat's Realistic Peace Initiative, 1981; Narrayan, B. K. Anwar al-Sadat, 1977; Sadat, C. My Father and I, 1985; Shukri, G. Egypt, Portrait of a President, 1981; Sullivan, G. Sadat: The Man Who Changed Mid-East History, 1981.

ANDREI SAKHAROV

SAKHAROV, ANDREI
(May 21, 1921–   )
Nobel Prize for Peace, 1975

Andrei Dmitrievich Sakharov, Russian physicist and human rights activist, was born in Moscow. Little is known of his family background except that his father, Dmitri Sakharov, was a respected author and a professor of physics at the Lenin Pedagogical Institute in Moscow. By his own account, Sakharov grew up in a large communal apartment that was "pervaded by a strong, traditional family spirit—a vital enthusiasm for work and professional competence." A shy and soft-spoken young man, he was particularly devoted to his grandmother. She had taught herself English and read to her grandchildren every evening from the works of such writers as Charles Dickens, Christopher Marlowe, and Harriet Beecher Stowe. During Holy Week, she read to them from the gospel.

Sakharov attended Moscow State University, where he was considered perhaps the most brilliant physics student the faculty had ever taught. Graduating with honors in 1942, he was exempted from military service during World War II and assigned to work as an engineer at a munitions factory on the Volga.

Returning to Moscow after the war, Sakharov continued his studies at the Lebedev Institute of the Soviet Academy of Sciences under IGOR TAMM, a specialist in quantum physics.

Two years later, at the age of twenty-six, Sakharov received his doctorate in physical and mathematical sciences, a degree usually granted only to older, more experienced scientists.

In 1948 the young physicist joined a select team of research scientists led by Tamm. Focusing almost exclusively on fusion physics and working under the tightest security, Sakharov, Tamm, and their colleagues developed a hydrogen bomb that was tested in August 1953. Most of the credit for its success was given to Sakharov. In 1953 Sakharov became the youngest person ever elected to full membership in the Soviet Academy of Sciences, the elite ruling body of Soviet science. In this position, he enjoyed an income and standard of living far above the average.

From this time until 1968, Sakharov continued to work on the development and testing of nuclear devices. Describing this period of his life later, he said: "I felt subjectively that I was working for peace, that my work would foster a balance of power and that it would be useful to the Soviet people and even, to some extent, to mankind as a whole." Nevertheless, he came to oppose the testing of nuclear weapons, largely because of the biological hazards of atmospheric testing.

In 1958, when a six-month suspension of Soviet atmospheric testing of nuclear weapons was about to be broken, Sakharov wrote a confidential memorandum that came to the attention of Communist party leader Nikita Khrushchev. In the belief that such testing had become superfluous and might contribute to acceleration of the nuclear arms race, Sakharov proposed that the tests be canceled. What influence he may have wielded is. unknown, but subsequently the Soviet Union joined in an informal moratorium on atmospheric testing that lasted almost three years. When the moratorium ended, Sakharov renewed his efforts to halt further testing but to no avail. "I could not stop something I knew was wrong and unnecessary," he recalled later. "I had an awful sense of powerlessness. After that I was a different man."

Sakharov's protests extended to other issues as well. In 1958 he opposed Khrushchev's plan to curtail secondary education. Five years later, he joined a successful campaign to eradicate from Soviet genetics the influence of the agronomist Trofim Lysenko. Lysenko's unscientific theories (especially his claim that the heredity of plants could be altered by the environment) were blamed for disastrous crop failures during the Stalin years. In 1966 the writers Andrei D. Sinyavsky and Yuli M. Daniel were convicted on charges of having slandered the Soviet Union in books published in the West. Sakharov joined Tamm, PYOTR KAPITZA, and twenty-two other leading intellectuals in signing a letter to Leonid Brezhnev, Khrushchev's successor, declaring that any efforts to reestablish Stalin's policy of intolerance toward dissent would be "a great disaster" for the nation.

Thus far, Sakharov had confined his dissent to official circles. Then in 1968 he wrote "Razmyshlenia o progresse, mirnom sosushchestvovanii i intellektualnoi svobode" (Thoughts on Progress, Peaceful Coexistence, and Intellectual Freedom), a 10,000-word manifesto that the American journalist Harrison E. Salisbury later described as a "high-water mark in the movement for liberalization within the Communist world." Denouncing the nuclear arms race, the document called for cooperation between the Soviet Union and the United States, predicted the eventual convergence of the two systems, and urged a pooling of Soviet and American resources to confront the global threats of hunger, overpopulation, and environmental pollution. Moreover, Sakharov advocated lifting censorship, banning political trials, and outlawing the imprisonment of dissidents in mental hospitals. Circulated widely in the Soviet Union in manuscript form, the manifesto was published in the United States later that year as *Progress, Coexistence, and Intellectual Freedom*.

Official reaction to Sakharov's heterodoxy was swift. He was dismissed from all positions that involved secret military work. A year later, he was assigned to the Lebedev Institute as a senior researcher, the lowest rank at which a member of the Soviet Academy can work. There he continued the highly theoretical research into elementary particles, gravitation, and the structure of the universe that he had begun earlier in the decade.

Around this time, Sakharov's first wife, with whom he had three children, died. In 1970 he and other Soviet physicists founded the Committee for Human Rights, dedicated to promoting the principles of the Universal Declaration of Human Rights. The following year, he married Yelena G. Bonner, a physician he had met during a protest vigil outside a courtroom where political dissidents were on trial.

As he grew progressively alienated from Soviet policies, Sakharov increased his dissident activities with an accelerating campaign of letters, telegrams, appeals, and interviews with Western journalists. In 1973, although he had received a warning from the Soviet deputy prosecutor-general, Sakharov called a press conference with eleven Western journalists and denounced not only that threat of prosecution but the danger of what he called "détente without democratization." Criticism of his statements included a letter published in *Pravda* (The Truth), signed by forty academicians, and another published in *Izvestia* (News), signed by twenty-five physicians, one of whom was Yevgeny Chazov, later a cofounder of INTERNATIONAL PHYSICIANS FOR THE PREVENTION OF NUCLEAR WAR.

Sakharov was awarded the 1975 Nobel Prize for Peace for his "fearless personal commitment in upholding the fundamental principles for peace between men" and for his courageous struggle "against the abuse of power and all forms of violation of human dignity." Aase Lionæs of the Norwegian Nobel Committee noted that "the Nobel committee deeply deplores the fact that Andrei Sakharov has been prevented from being present . . . in person to receive the Peace Prize."

The award was accepted by Yelena Bonner, who informed the audience that her husband was at that moment in Vilnius supporting one of his scientific colleagues who was on trial for participating in a human rights publication. Bonner then read Sakharov's acceptance speech. "To keep one's self-respect," he wrote, "one must . . . act in accordance with the general human longing for peace, for true détente, for genuine disarmament." Calling for "a general political amnesty in all the world" and the "liberation of all prisoners of conscience everywhere," Sakharov asked his listeners to remember that his award was "shared by all prisoners of conscience in the Soviet Union and in other Eastern European countries as well as by all those who fight for their liberation."

The following day, Bonner read her husband's Nobel lecture, "Peace, Progress, Human Rights," in which he argued that the "three goals are insolubly linked to one another." Sakharov reviewed the dangers of nuclear arms, overpopulation, and hunger. He then called progress not only inevitable but indivisible, noting that it requires "freedom of conscience, the existence of an informed public opinion, a system of education of a pluralist nature, freedom of the press, and access to other sources of information." All of these, he said, "are in very short supply in the socialist countries." He went on to outline proposals for achieving détente and disarmament.

Despite Sakharov's outspoken opposition, there was no move to arrest him until 1980, when he condemned the Soviet invasion of Afghanistan. He was stripped of all his awards, including Hero of Socialist Labor, and, without a trial, was placed under virtual house arrest in Gorky, a military-industrial city on the Volga that is closed to non-Soviets. Bonner, who had been allowed to remain in Moscow, was exiled to Gorky four years later when she was accused of anti-Soviet slander; she was also threatened with charges of treason for allegedly planning to seek refuge in the American embassy. In December 1986 Soviet leader Mikhail S. Gorbachev telephoned Sakharov in Gorky, announcing the end of Sakharov's exile. A few days later, he and Bonner returned to Moscow, where Sakharov resumed his scientific research. He has continued to demand the release of Soviet dissidents imprisoned for their political beliefs and to speak out on issues pertaining to human rights. In 1987, on accepting a diploma as a member of the French Academy of Sciences in Moscow, Sakharov chose the occasion to rebuke the Soviet Academy for failing to protest what he termed his "illegal deportation" to Gorky.

Any final assessment of Sakharov's contributions as a physicist must wait until the secrecy that cloaks his most active decades of scientific research has been dispelled. Nevertheless, it is clear that he made critical advances in the development of thermonuclear weapons and the harnessing of nuclear power for peaceful purposes. Likewise, it is difficult to evaluate his other scientific achievements. A highly original paper published in 1969, examining the role of antiquarks as a possible explanation for the symmetry in the balance of matter and antimatter, suggests that his contributions to the understanding of the universe may equal those he made to nuclear technology. Neither may be greater than his efforts in the cause of world peace.

ADDITIONAL WORKS IN ENGLISH TRANSLATION: Sakharov Speaks, 1974; My Country and the World, 1975; Alarm and Hope, 1978; Afghanistan Today, 1981, with others; Collected Scientific Works, 1982; "The Danger of Thermonuclear War," Foreign Affairs Summer 1983; Andrei Sakharov and Peace, 1985; U.S. News and World Report February 24, 1986.

ABOUT: Babyonyshev, A. (ed.) On Sakharov, 1982; Bonner, Y. Alone Together, 1986; Brumberg, A. In Quest of Justice, 1970; Kelley, D. R. The Solzhenitsyn-Sakharov Dialogue, 1982; LeVert, S. The Sakharov File, 1986; New York Times January 23, 1980; Parry, A. The Russian Scientists, 1973; Science September 28, 1973.

SALAM, ABDUS

(January 29, 1926–   )
Nobel Prize for Physics, 1979
(shared with Sheldon L. Glashow and
    Steven Weinberg)

The Pakistani physicist Abdus Salam was born in the rural town of Jhang, the son of Mohammad Hussain, an official in the district Department of Education, and Hajira Hussain. He attended Government College, Punjab University, in Lahore, from which he received an M.A. in 1946. He then entered St. John's College, Cambridge, England, as a Foundation Scholar and in 1949 was awarded a B.A. with highest honors in mathematics and physics. Remaining at Cambridge, he received a Ph.D. in theoretical physics from the Cavendish Laboratory in 1952. His dissertation, on quantum electrodynamics, was published that year and attracted wide attention in the international physics community.

Meanwhile, in 1951, Salam had become a professor of mathematics at Government College. Although he hoped to found a research school in Pakistan, Salam soon realized that he could not pursue a career in theoretical physics at such a great distance from the leading research centers in Europe, and so in 1954 he returned to Cambridge as a lecturer in mathematics. Since 1957 he has held the chair of theoretical physics at Imperial College in London. He is also the director of the International Center for Theoretical Physics in Tri-

ABDUS SALAM

este, Italy, founded in 1964 to encourage the work of scientists from developing nations.

Since the mid-1950s, Salam has sought a unified understanding of all the forces observed in nature, a problem that extends back to the nineteenth century. In the 1870s James Clerk Maxwell, a Scottish mathematician and physicist, completed the unification of electricity and magnetism into a single force that came to be known as electromagnetism. Later researchers sought a theory that would encompass not only electromagnetism but also gravitation, the strong force, and the weak force. The strong force binds together the protons and the neutrons that compose the nucleus of an atom; the weak force repels them. Both the strong force and the weak force differ in an important way from the forces known earlier. Whereas gravitation and electromagnetism have an unlimited range, the strong force is effective only over distances no greater than the size of an atomic nucleus, and the weak force has an even smaller range of action.

The theoretical innovations for which Salam, SHELDON L. GLASHOW, and STEVEN WEINBERG were awarded the Nobel Prize led to a theory that unified electromagnetism and the weak force. This accomplishment, analogous to Maxwell's unification of electricity and magnetism, brought the electromagnetic and weak forces together as different aspects of a single "electroweak" force. In the early 1960s, Salam and Glashow independently attempted a synthesis of electromagnetism and the weak force, basing their theory on a concept called gauge symmetry. Gauge symmetry refers to

physical properties or relationships that remain unchanged when the dimension scale or reference point for a relative measurement is altered. Working at the Brookhaven National Laboratory in 1954, CHEN NING YANG and Robert L. Mills tried unsuccessfully to extend the principle of gauge symmetry to account for the strong force. Their conclusions, however, contributed to the subsequent work of Salam, Glashow, and Weinberg.

In 1960 Glashow devised a unified theory of electromagnetism and the weak force that predicted the existence of four carrier particles: the photon (the carrier of the electromagnetic force) and three particles later named W^+, W^-, and Z^0 (the mediators of weak interactions). One of the chief difficulties in his theory arose from its supposition that all the particles had no mass. According to quantum mechanics, the range of a force is inversely proportional to the mass of the carrier particle; therefore, zero mass means an infinite range for electromagnetism as well as for the weak force, a prediction that was contradicted by experimental evidence.

To correct this failing, Glashow postulated large masses for the W^+, W^-, and Z^0 particles. The strategy was unsuccessful, however, for when the masses were included, the theory yielded impossible results, such as predicting that certain weak interactions would have an infinite strength. Similar problems, encountered two decades earlier in the study of electromagnetism, had been solved by a mathematical procedure called renormalization, but it, too, did not work in this case. The problem of massive W and Z particles was solved some years later when Weinberg, Salam, and others applied new methods.

Using Glashow's gauge symmetry, Salam and Weinberg, working independently in 1968 and 1967, respectively, proposed a unified theory of the weak and electromagnetic forces. They suggested a new mechanism to give mass to the W^+, W^-, and Z^0 particles while leaving the photon massless. Called spontaneous symmetry breaking, the idea for this mechanism had its origins in solid-state physics. Salam has explained the idea by a metaphor in which a group of diners are seated at a round table with a plate directly in front of each chair and napkins placed midway between the plates. The setting is symmetrical (each diner has a napkin to the left and right), but as soon as one diner picks up a napkin, the symmetry is broken. If all the diners pick up napkins, the symmetry may or may not be broken. Although choosing either a left or a right napkin is equally acceptable, symmetry will be retained only if all make the same choice. Otherwise, someone will be left without a nearby napkin, and one napkin will remain on another part of the table, an obvious asymmetry.

Salam proposed that the gauge symmetry relating the electromagnetic and weak forces is spontaneously broken when the energy level is greatly altered. At extremely high energy, the two forces are identical. Under such conditions the masses of the W and Z particles are of little consequence, because massive particles can readily be created out of the available energy (ALBERT EINSTEIN's special theory of relativity in 1905 demonstrated the equivalence of mass and energy). However, W and Z particles—and therefore weak interactions—are scarce at lower energies. Since terrestrial physics is confined to comparatively low energies, investigators have paid attention to the differences between the two forces. In the Weinberg-Salam theory, masses did not have to be artificially supplied for the W^+, W^-, and Z^0 particles; the masses arose naturally from the symmetry-breaking mechanism. Indeed, the masses could be estimated from the theory itself. Each of the two W particles weighs about 80 times as much as a proton, and the Z is even heavier.

Both Weinberg and Salam suspected that through the application of a mathematical procedure called renormalization, finite predictions could be made for all measurable quantities. Partly because they were unable to prove this belief, their theory attracted little attention until 1971. That year, the Dutch physicist Gerhard 't Hooft achieved a breakthrough in the technique of renormalization and, in collaboration with other theorists, completed the proof. Two years later, researchers at the Fermi National Accelerator Laboratory near Chicago and at CERN (the European Organization for Nuclear Research) near Geneva discovered weak neutral currents, thus confirming the theory advanced by Salam, Glashow, and Weinberg. In 1983 the W and Z particles themselves were detected at CERN by CARLO RUBBIA and his colleagues.

Salam, Glashow, and Weinberg received the 1979 Nobel Prize for Physics "for their contributions to the theory of the unified weak and electromagnetic interaction between elementary particles, including, inter alia, the prediction of the weak neutral current." In his Nobel lecture Salam expressed hope for a unified theory of all forces, including the strong force and gravitation. "Just as Einstein comprehended the nature of the gravitational charge in terms of space-time curvature," he asked, "can we comprehend the nature of the other charges—the nature of the entire unified set, *as a set,* in terms of something equally profound? This briefly is the dream, much reinforced by the verification of gauge-theory predictions."

Salam's interests extend well beyond the boundaries of theoretical physics. He served the United Nations in 1955 and 1958 as scientific secretary of the Geneva Conference on Peaceful Uses of Atomic Energy. He was a member of the United Nations Advisory Committee on Science and Technology from 1964 through 1975 and was chairman of the committee in 1971 and 1972. In 1981 he served as chairman of the UNESCO Advisory Panel on Science, Technology, and Society. From 1972 to 1978 he was vice president of the International Union of Pure and Applied Physics. He has also served on many educational and scientific commissions in Pakistan and in 1961 was appointed principal scientific adviser to the office of the president of Pakistan, a post he held until 1974.

In addition to the Nobel Prize, Salam has received the Maxwell Medal of the Physical Society in London (1961), the Hughes Medal (1964) and the Royal Medal (1978) of the Royal Society of London, the Guthrie Medal of the Institute of Physics in London (1976), the Matteucci Gold Medal of the National Academy of Sciences of Italy (1978), the John Torrence Tate Medal of the American Institute of Physics (1978), and the Lomonosov Gold Medal of the Soviet Academy of Sciences (1983), among others. He is a fellow of the Pakistan Academy of Sciences, the Royal Society of London, the Royal Swedish Academy of Sciences, and the Pontifical Academy of Sciences; and he is an honorary or foreign member of the American Academy of Arts and Sciences, the Soviet Academy of Sciences, and the American National Academy of Sciences, as well as other scientific societies. His nearly thirty honorary degrees include awards from Punjab University, the University of Edinburgh, the University of Bristol, Cambridge University, City College of the City University of New York, and the University of Glasgow.

SELECTED WORKS: Symmetry Concepts in Modern Physics, 1966; Ideals and Realities: Selected Essays, 1984.

ABOUT: Ghani, A. Abdus Salam, 1982; New Scientist

October 18, 1979; Science December 14, 1979; The Way of the Scientist, 1962.

SAMUELSON, PAUL
(May 15, 1915–   )
Nobel Memorial Prize in Economic
  Sciences, 1970

The American economist Paul Anthony Samuelson was born in Gary, Indiana, to Frank and Ella (Lipton) Samuelson. In 1935, before his twentieth birthday, he received a B.A. from the University of Chicago, where his instructors included the economists Frank Knight, Jacob Viner, and Henry Simons. Thereafter, his career as a graduate student in economics at Harvard University became legendary. After receiving his M.A. in economics in 1936, Samuelson was appointed a junior fellow of Harvard, one of the highest honors the university can bestow on a student. Upon completion of his oral examinations, his professors are said to have quipped, "Did we pass?" He received his Ph.D. in economics in 1941, together with the university's David A. Wells Prize for his dissertation.

Even before earning his doctorate, Samuelson began to contribute, as few economists had done previously, to elevating the level of methodology used in all the major fields of economic analysis. His precise use of mathematics to analyze fundamental economic theories both revealed the conditions that limit these theories and increased their usefulness in describing real-world problems. His first paper, published in 1938, for example, described the theory of consumers' "revealed preference." According to traditional consumer theory, individuals "maximize utility" (try to obtain the greatest satisfaction) when purchasing goods and services. The theory could not be refuted, since utility, a qualitative factor, could not be measured. Samuelson, however, proved that utility maximization could be tested by comparing consumer choices before and after price changes. Rational consumers will not purchase at new, higher prices those goods or services they could have consumed at the old, lower prices. With this theory, Samuelson paved the way for important advances in the theory of price indexes and in the measurement of national income.

In 1940 Samuelson became an assistant professor of economics at the Massachusetts Institute of Technology (MIT). He rose to full professor in 1947 and since 1966 has been institute professor. In his long career at MIT,

PAUL SAMUELSON

Samuelson has helped transform the economics department into a leading center of research. In addition to teaching economics, Samuelson also served on the staff of MIT's Radiation Laboratory (1945) and taught international economic relations at the Fletcher School of Law and Diplomacy (1945). During World War II he was a consultant at the National Resource Planning Board from 1941 to 1943 and at the War Production Board in 1945.

Samuelson's book *Foundations of Economic Analysis,* published in 1947 and based on his Ph.D. dissertation, proved to be one of the most influential economics books of this century, providing a sound basis for mainstream economic theory. Although the book's style is relentlessly mathematical, Samuelson insists that this is necessary in economic analysis. Otherwise, he has said, one is merely practicing "mental gymnastics of a peculiarly depraved type." Many economists, including SIMON KUZNETS, WASSILY LEONTIEF, and GUNNAR MYRDAL, have argued against the ever-increasing use of advanced mathematics as tending to trivialize the substance of economics: real-world analysis and problem solving. Samuelson maintains that for economic analysis to be clear and unambiguous and for its theorems to have empirical meaning, advanced mathematics is essential. The widespread acceptance of his view in the profession has radically changed the methods and practices of economics.

In *Foundations of Economic Analysis,* advanced mathematics, coupled with analysis, was the starting point of a unified treatment of static and dynamic theory for which Samuelson eventually received the Nobel Prize. In the book, Samuelson asserted that in such diverse fields as consumer and production theory, international trade theory, public finance, and welfare economics, virtually all important results could be derived from the mathematical satisfaction of some function subject to a set of constraints. He also claimed that the static predictions of an economic model and the model's dynamic behavior were connected, a view known as the correspondence principle.

Although Samuelson has shown much originality in the field of neoclassical price theory, his work on stability analysis is his outstanding contribution to the field of economics. Stability analysis concerns general price theory, or the dynamics of how prices are formed in conditions of disequilibrium, when the rate of change of a price is determined by excess demand. This work also provides mathematical precision for theories of the business cycle.

Analytical economics is the common thread that has run through Samuelson's wide-ranging research since the publication of *Foundations of Economic Analysis*. His lucid explanation of the mathematical as well as the basic principles of applied economics has made his book *Economics: An Introductory Analysis* a standard text since its publication in 1948. It has been through many editions and has been translated into Russian, Japanese, Hungarian, Arabic, and many other languages. In its early editions it pointed to the changes brought about by the end of World War II. Subsequently, as the world's economic problems have changed, so has the book's content.

From the outset Samuelson has shown a general interest in the uses of monetary and fiscal policy and has expressed public concern about inflation and unemployment, thus presenting a "neoclassical" synthesis of modern mainstream economics. As a Keynesian, he holds that the achievement of full employment requires policy intervention and that neoclassical theory is valid only when full employment is attained. A noted applicant of general equilibrium analysis, he nevertheless sees its limitations when applied to the real world. At the same time, he has not ignored analysis of the theories of Marx and the New Left.

Samuelson's pathbreaking theoretical research continued throughout the late 1940s and 1950s as his basic assumptions and methods of analysis became more and more accepted. From the mid-1970s on, his articles on "factor-price equalizations" in international trade argued that free trade among nations would tend to reduce the differences between the incomes of labor and capital across countries. These articles have been cited more frequently than any of his others. He also theoretically classified the relevance of gains from trade, suggesting for example, that a rapid flow of Japanese exports could dramatically raise Japanese incomes in relation to those of the rest of the world. This work has been of immense relevance to post–World War II economic events.

Always a prolific writer, Samuelson has published papers and books on a wide variety of topics. *Linear Programming and Economic Analysis* (1958), written with economists Robert Dorfman and Robert M. Solow, emphasized analytical techniques pioneered by the mathematician George Dantzig and the economist LEONID KANTOROVICH that could be applied to the practical problems of allocating resources in business and government. In the same year, Samuelson published "An Exact Consumption Loan Model With or Without the Social Contrivance of Money." This work presented one of his most original contributions to economic theory, a model resembling FRANCO MODIGLIANI's famous "life cycle hypothesis." In Samuelson's model, the middle-aged lend some of their income to the young in return for interest payments to be received when the lenders grow old. The paper posed new questions in demographic and monetary economics in addition to providing a consistent theory of interest-rate determination. Other papers made fundamental contributions to optimal economic growth (such as the "turnpike theorem"), capital theory, general equilibrium economics, and the theory of public goods.

In the 1960s Samuelson's role as a consultant expanded. Already an adviser to many government agencies and private organizations, he gained national recognition as an adviser to President John F. Kennedy. Samuelson characterized himself as a member of the "right wing of the Democratic New Deal economists." Even though he often disagreed publicly with fellow *Newsweek* columnist Milton Friedman, both men display great admiration for each other's work in economics.

Samuelson received the 1970 Nobel Memorial Prize in Economic Sciences "for the scientific work through which he has developed static and dynamic economic theory and actively contributed to raising the level of analysis in economic science." Although his career has been marked by great diversity, his Nobel Prize acceptance speech made it clear that his lifelong work has been to reveal the "role of maximizing principles in analytic economics."

Since receiving the Nobel Prize, Samuelson has continued to publish papers at a rapid pace, addressing such diverse topics as the Marxist theory of exploitation of labor and optimal social security. His view of economics, firmly established as the reigning orthodoxy, was attacked by Marxist economists Marc Linder and Julius Sensat in a 1977 book entitled *Anti-Samuelson*. Few Marxists, however, have examined the problems of left-wing economic theories as deeply as Samuelson.

In 1938 Samuelson married Marion E. Crawford, with whom he had two daughters and four sons. After the death of his first wife, he married Risha Eckaus in 1981.

In addition to the Nobel Prize, Samuelson has received many honors and awards, including the American Economic Association's John Bates Clark Medal (1947) and the Albert Einstein Commemorative Award of Yeshiva University (1971). He has been president of the American Economic Association, the Econometric Society, and the International Economic Association. He has held fellowships from the Guggenheim, Ford, and Carnegie foundations and is a member of the National Academy of Sciences, the American Academy of Arts and Sciences, and the American Philosophical Society and a fellow of the British Academy. He has been awarded honorary degrees from the universities of Chicago, Indiana, Michigan, Keio, Southern California, Pennsylvania, Rochester, East Anglia, Northern Michigan, and Massachusetts and from Harvard University and the Catholic University of Louvain.

ADDITIONAL WORKS: Problems of the American Economy, 1962; Stability and Growth in the American Economy, 1963; Collected Scientific Papers (4 vols.) 1966–1977; Full Employment: Guideposts and Economic Stability, 1967, with Arthur F. Burns.

ABOUT: Breit, W., and Spencer, R. W. (eds.) Lives of the Laureates, 1986; Brown, E. C., and Solow, R. M. (eds.) Paul Samuelson and Modern Economic Theory, 1983; Current Biography May 1965; Feiwel, G. R. (ed.) Samuelson and Neoclassical Economics, 1982; Shackleton, J. R., and Locksley, G. (eds.) Twelve Contemporary Economists, 1981; Wong, S. The Foundations of Paul Samuelson's Revealed Preference Theory, 1978.

SAMUELSSON, BENGT

(May 21, 1934–)
Nobel Prize for Physiology or Medicine, 1982
(shared with Sune Bergström and John R. Vane)

The Swedish biochemist Bengt Ingemar Samuelsson was born in the port city of Halmstad to Kristina and Anders Samuelsson. After attending the local schools, he entered medical school at the University of Lund, where he worked in the research laboratory of SUNE BERGSTRÖM, then professor of physiological chemistry. In 1958, along with Bergström's research group, he moved to the Karolinska Institute in Stockholm. There, Samuelsson studied medicine and biochemistry, submitting his dissertation in 1960 and receiving a doctor of medical sciences degree. The following year he obtained his medical degree and was appointed assistant professor of medical chemistry at the institute. Between 1961 and 1962 Samuelsson was a research fellow in the Department of Chemistry at Harvard University, where he worked in the laboratory of E. J. Corey, studying theoretical and synthetic organic chemistry.

In 1962 Samuelsson returned to the Karolinska Institute and resumed his association with Bergström. At that time Bergström was studying a class of biological compounds called prostaglandins, first described by gynecologists at Columbia University's College of Physicians and Surgeons in 1930. While performing artificial inseminations, the gynecologists noticed that the seminal fluid caused the muscle of the uterus to contract and relax. Later in the 1930s, ULF VON EULER extracted a substance from the seminal fluid of sheep that also stimulated the contraction of uterine muscle. Calling this substance prostaglandin because it was first found in the secretions of the prostate gland, Euler preserved these extracts during World War II, and in 1945 he gave them to Bergström for further study. By the late 1950s Bergström had isolated, purified, and determined the chemical formulas of two of the prostaglandins.

Working with Bergström, Samuelsson studied the production of the prostaglandins in living organisms; within two years he had demonstrated that they are formed from arachidonic acid, an unsaturated fatty acid found in certain meats and vegetables. Over the next several years he traced the steps by which they are produced, finding that arachidonic acid is converted with the help of an

BENGT SAMUELSSON

enzyme into compounds called endoperoxides, one of which is subsequently converted into prostaglandin. Through further research Samuelsson discovered that arachidonic acid and the prostaglandin enzyme systems are present in all nucleated animal cells. Different cells synthesize different prostaglandins, and the various prostaglandins in turn perform various biological functions. The most thoroughly studied prostaglandins—those of the E and F series—may have applications in clinical medicine.

The discoveries of Bergström and Samuelsson gave rise to a series of investigations at the Karolinska Institute into the biological functions of prostaglandins. Prostaglandins of the E series were found to relax the walls of blood vessels and lower blood pressure, to be useful in treating some patients with certain circulatory diseases, and to protect the lining of the stomach from the formation of ulcers and from the toxic effects of aspirin and other drugs. By stimulating the contraction of blood vessels, F-series prostaglandins raise blood pressure. Because they also stimulate contraction of the uterus, they have been used to induce abortions.

From 1967 to 1972 Samuelsson was professor of medical chemistry at the Royal Veterinary College in Stockholm. For the next ten years he served as professor of chemistry and chairman of the Department of Chemistry at the Karolinska Institute, while continuing his study of the biochemistry of the endoperoxides and their derivatives. In the early 1970s he

discovered that in platelets (blood cells involved in the clotting of blood), one of the endoperoxides is converted into compounds he called thromboxanes. Because aspirin interferes with one type of thromboxane, low doses of aspirin have been used to prevent clotting in patients who have a high risk of heart attack from coronary thrombosis.

In the 1970s Samuelsson discovered that in white blood cells, or leukocytes, arachidonic acid is converted by another pathway into compounds he called leukotrienes, which control the symptoms of asthma and anaphylaxis (the shocklike state that follows exposure to certain foreign substances, such as bee-sting toxins). Stimulating the contraction of blood vessels and of bronchioles (the small airways of the lungs), leukotrienes increase the permeability of blood vessels to fluid, causing tissue to swell. One of the leukotrienes causes white blood cells to adhere to injured or inflamed tissue, where they engulf and dispose of tissue debris. Steroid drugs, such as cortisone and cortisone derivatives, interfere with the biosynthesis of leukotrienes.

The work done by Samuelsson on arachidonic acid and prostaglandin systems, his discovery of how one of the endoperoxides is converted into the compound he called thromboxane, and his finding that in white blood cells, arachidonic acid is converted into compounds called leukotrienes are regarded as substantial contributions to various fields of medical knowledge and therapy.

During 1976 Samuelsson was a visiting professor at Harvard University, serving in the same capacity the following year at the Massachusetts Institute of Technology. For the next five years he served as dean of the medical faculty at the Karolinska Institute.

Samuelsson shared the 1982 Nobel Prize for Physiology or Medicine with Bergström and JOHN R. VANE "for their discoveries concerning prostaglandins and related biologically active substances." According to Bengt Pernow of the Karolinska Institute in his presentation speech, whereas Bergström first isolated the prostaglandins and showed that they are part of a whole physiological system, it was Samuelsson who not only "isolated and determined the structure of several of the most significant components within the system" but also "helped us to understand the relationship between its various components."

In 1958 Samuelsson married Inga Karin Bergstein; they have one son and two daughters. The youngest of the three co-winners of the 1982 Nobel Prize for Physiology or Medicine, Samuelsson continues to follow a strict schedule of laboratory research.

The same year that he was awarded the Nobel Prize, Samuelsson was appointed rector of the Karolinska Institute. A member of the Royal Swedish Academy of Sciences and a foreign member of the American Academy of Arts and Sciences, Samuelsson has also been honored with the Anders Jahre Prize in Medicine given by Oslo University (1970), the Louisa Gross Horwitz Prize of Columbia University (1975), the Albert Lasker Basic Medical Research Award (1977), and the Bror Holberg Medal of the Swedish Chemical Society (1982).

ABOUT: New York Times October 12, 1982; Science November 19, 1982.

FREDERICK SANGER

SANGER, FREDERICK
(August 13, 1918–)
Nobel Prize for Chemistry, 1958
Nobel Prize for Chemistry, 1980
(shared with Paul Berg and Walter Gilbert)

The English biochemist Frederick Sanger was born in Rendcombe, Gloucestershire, to a prosperous Quaker family. His mother, the former Cicely Crewsdon, was the daughter of a wealthy cotton manufacturer; his father and namesake was a medical doctor and general practitioner. After attending the Bryanston School in Blandford, Dorset, from 1932 to 1936, he entered St. John's College, Cambridge, in 1936. Although he initially planned to follow his father and take up medicine, he became interested in biochemistry instead. "It seemed to me," he wrote many years later, "that here was a way to really understand living matter and to develop a more scientific basis to many medical problems."

In 1939 Sanger received his B.A. from Cambridge in natural sciences. World War II broke out in September of that year, but Sanger, as a Quaker, was excused from military service and remained at Cambridge for graduate work. After receiving his Ph.D. in 1943, he joined a research group directed by A. C. Chibnall, who had just succeeded FREDERICK GOWLAND HOPKINS as professor of biochemistry at Cambridge. At the time, Chibnall was investigating the chemistry of proteins.

In 1902 EMIL FISCHER had suggested that proteins are made of amino acids linked together by peptide bonds. By the early 1940s Fischer's hypothesis was widely but not universally accepted. When more than two amino acids are linked together, they form a polypeptide chain. Because an amino acid can participate in no more than two peptide bonds, Fischer had predicted that proteins would consist of linear strings of amino acids, with a free nitrogen at the N-terminus and a free carboxyl group (consisting of carbon, hydrogen, and hydrogen) at the other. Chibnall asked Sanger to find a means of attaching a chemical label to one end of a peptide chain. Doing so would establish that proteins are in fact made of linear strings of amino acids; moreover, it would also indicate whether a single protein included more than one kind of peptide chain.

In 1945 Sanger reported that under mildly alkaline conditions a particular reagent (DNP, or dinitrophenol) could unite with an N-terminus amino acid by means of a link that was stronger than a peptide bond. Therefore a protein could be split into its component amino acids by breaking the peptide bonds and the amino acids identified by chromatography. The technique of chromatography, which had only recently been perfected by ARCHER MARTIN and RICHARD SYNGE, separates substances into their components according to the characteristic rates at which they are absorbed by a special filter.

Much of the research in Chibnall's laboratory concerned insulin, one of the few proteins then available in pure form and in large quantities. Sanger's early studies of insulin indicated that it contains two different N-terminus amino acids; therefore, each molecule of insulin is made of two kinds of polypeptide chains. The amino acid cysteine contains a molecule of sulfur; two cysteine molecules can join to form cystine, which in turn can form a disulfide bridge either between two polypeptide chains or between different parts of a single chain. In 1949 Sanger reported that he had discovered a way to break these disulfide bridges and thus had separated the two chains.

Sanger and Hans Tuppy, a visiting Viennese scientist, then worked out a plan for determining the sequence of amino acids in each of insulin's polypeptide chains. By breaking the chain into subsections, the two researchers hoped to identify the sequence of the amino acids in each subsection and from this information to determine the sequence of the complete polypeptide chain. Although Sanger had initially used acid to break up the polypeptide chains, he soon found that enzymes acted with greater precision. In this way Sanger and Tuppy compared fragments obtained using various enzymes to deduce the complete sequence. Determining the sequence for the longer of the two insulin chains was unexpectedly easy and was almost completed when Tuppy left Cambridge in 1950. Because the shorter insulin chain was less chemically tractable, its sequence was not fully determined until 1953. Sanger went on to locate the site of the disulfide bridges between the two chains, and in 1955 he presented the complete structure of the insulin molecule—the first protein molecule to be known in such detail.

Sanger's work had important consequences for biochemistry and for the emerging field of molecular biology. His results proved conclusively that proteins consist of amino acids joined into chains by peptide bonds. In the first part of the twentieth century, many chemists thought of proteins as mixtures of closely related compounds. Sanger, however, established that a protein is a specific chemical substance with a unique structure and that each position in the chain is occupied by a given amino acid. He also proved that enzymes can cut peptide chains at predictable sites. Applying his techniques, other biochemists were able to elucidate the structure of many other proteins.

Sanger was awarded the 1958 Nobel Prize for Chemistry "for his work on the structure of proteins, especially that of insulin." In his Nobel lecture Sanger acknowledged the practical consequence of his work. "The determination of the structure of insulin clearly opens up the way to similar studies on other proteins," he said. "One may also hope that studies on proteins may reveal changes that take place in disease and that our efforts may be of more practical use to humanity."

Even before receiving the Nobel Prize, Sanger had begun to investigate genetics, in part because of his friendship with FRANCIS CRICK. To Sanger, one of the most striking facts about the insulin sequence was the apparent lack of any basic principle determining the unique arrangement of the amino acids, and yet upon this seemingly random order depended important physiological action. He could see no way that the protein could assemble itself into its unique sequence, but it was clear that the order must come from somewhere. In the mid-1950s, Crick (who, with JAMES D. WATSON, had first described the structure of the genetic material deoxyribonucleic acid, or DNA) explained Sanger's discoveries through the "sequence hypothesis," namely that the genes carry the information determining the sequence of amino acids in a protein. It was later established that genes themselves are sequences of units in which each sequence corresponds to a specific amino acid.

The nucleic acids, DNA and ribonucleic acid (RNA), are chains of linked nucleotides. A nucleotide consists of a sugar molecule with a phosphate molecule and any one of four "base" molecules attached to it. The nucleotides link together at the phosphate molecules to form polypeptide chains. In a DNA structure, two parallel chains form the frame of a spiral ladder configuration. A pair of bases form a step of the ladder by joining between the chains in exclusive linkages: adenine (A) with guanine (G), cytosine (C) with thymine (T). The blueprint for an amino acid is carried by a sequence of three bases. The process of building a protein starts as the appropriate section of DNA, including the full directions for assembly, "unzips" along the bond connecting the bases to each other. Free nucleotides (floating randomly in the cell) become attached along the exposed DNA sequence, creating a mirror-image chain called messenger RNA (mRNA). The completed mRNA chain leaves the DNA (which then "rezips" itself) and moves to cellular structures called ribosomes where the protein will be assembled. Shorter chain segments form against the mRNA and then move away to accumulate the appropriate free nucleotides, which they carry back to the mRNA for incorporation into the protein structure. These short chains are called transfer RNAs (tRNAs). At the time Sanger began to study nucleic acids, these processes were poorly understood and the nucleotide sequences not at all.

DNA and RNA sequences are more difficult to study than are protein sequences because they are longer. A typical protein chain may contain as many as fifty amino acids, whereas typical mRNA contains hundreds of nucleotides. The DNA of even the smallest virus is thousands of nucleotides long. Nevertheless, nucleic acid sequences are easier to decode than are protein sequences because of a fundamental difference: whereas each position in a protein chain can be occupied by any one of twenty different amino acids, there are only four choices for each position in a DNA sequence—the nucleotides abbreviated A, T, C, and G (after their bases).

In 1958 ROBERT W. HOLLEY began trying to determine the sequence of a tRNA chain. Even though these short chains are less than 100 nucleotides in length, the complexity of the sequencing delayed completion of the project until 1965. Sanger was impressed with Holley's work but sought a more efficient sequencing method suitable for use on mRNAs, which are often several hundred nucleotides in length. He and his colleagues developed such a procedure in the early 1960s. Using enzymes, they broke the mRNAs into smaller chains and then separated and sequenced them individually. The complete sequence was then assembled by deducing the relationships between the fragments.

The approach was slow and tedious, however, and Sanger set about to devise an analytic technique suited to sequencing DNA, which he achieved in 1973. The procedure involves splitting DNA's double chain into single chains (called strands) and then grouping the resulting material into four samples. Each sample is treated to regenerate the original double-chain sequence from the single-chain template. However, the researchers force the regeneration process to stop at a different nucleotide for each sample, either by limiting the concentration of one or another free nucleotide or by replacing a particular nucleotide in the chain with a chemical that prevents further synthesis. As a result, the reconstructed chains in a sample are of different lengths, but each terminates with the same nucleotide. The four samples are then simultaneously sent through a filtering material called an ultrathin acrylamide gel, which separates the chains by size as the shorter chains move through the gel more rapidly. The nucleotide sequence of the original DNA can then be read directly off the gel by comparing the traces left by the samples.

While Sanger and his colleagues were working on this method (called the dideoxy method,

after the type of limiting chemical used), the Americans WALTER GILBERT and Allan Maxam were developing another procedure for determining nucleotide sequences. In their method, DNA fragments of various lengths are prepared by breaking the chain at specific bases, in a manner that resembles Sanger's protein and RNA sequencing methods. Both the Sanger and the Gilbert techniques became essential tools for genetic engineering, although Sanger's method is somewhat more efficient for work with very long sequences. As early as 1978 Sanger and his colleagues demonstrated the power of the dideoxy method by determining the sequence of the 5,375 bases in the DNA of bacterial virus, the first complete DNA chain ever elucidated in such fine detail.

"For their contributions concerning the determination of base sequences in nucleic acids," Sanger and Gilbert shared half of the 1980 Nobel Prize for Chemistry. The other portion was awarded to PAUL BERG. The three scientists, said Bo G. Malmström of the Royal Swedish Academy of Sciences, "have . . . made it possible to penetrate into further depth in our understanding of the relationship between the chemical structure and biological function of the genetic material."

Sanger retired from the Medical Research Council in 1983. Known as a private and unassuming man, he lives in Cambridge with his wife, Margaret Joan Howe, whom he married in 1940. The couple have two sons and one daughter. Throughout his life Sanger has enjoyed sailing and gardening.

Sanger's many honors include the Corday-Morgan Medal and Prize of the British Chemical Society (1951), the Alfred Benzons Prize of the Alfred Benzons Foundation (1966), the Royal Medal of the Royal Society (1969), the Gairdner Foundation Annual Award (1971, 1979), the Hanbury Memorial Medal of the Pharmaceutical Society of Great Britain (1976), the Copley Medal of the Royal Society (1977), and the Albert Lasker Basic Medical Research Award (1979). He is an honorary member of the American Society of Biological Chemists and the American National Academy of Sciences and holds honorary degrees from the universities of Leicester and Strasbourg and from Cambridge and Oxford universities.

SELECTED WORKS: "Chemistry of Insulin," Science May 12, 1959.

ABOUT: Chemistry and Industry December 13, 1958; Cur-

SARTRE

rent Biography July 1981; New York Times October 15, 1980; April 24, 1983; Science November 21, 1980; Silverstein, A. Frederick Sanger, 1969.

SARTRE, JEAN-PAUL
(June 21, 1905–April 15, 1980)
Nobel Prize for Literature, 1964

Jean-Paul Aymard Sartre (sär' tr'), French philosopher, novelist, and playwright, was born in Paris, the only child of Jean-Baptiste Sartre, a naval officer and marine engineer, and the former Anne-Marie Schweitzer, a member of a prominent family of Alsatian scholars and first cousin of ALBERT SCHWEITZER. When the boy's father died of a tropical fever in 1906, he and his mother went first to Meudon on the outskirts of Paris to live with her parents and then in 1911 to Paris, where Sartre's grandfather, Charles Schweitzer, a professor of German and an author, had founded the Modern Language Institute. Schweitzer, whose authoritarian manner and Calvinist religion had a marked effect on Sartre, considered his grandson a prodigy and had him tutored at home when the boy failed to excel at school. Turning to books in his loneliness, Sartre became even more unhappy when his mother remarried and in 1917 took him to live in the city of La Rochelle in western France.

Returning to Paris in 1920 to attend the Lycée Henri IV, Sartre began to distinguish himself as a student and to write short pieces for literary reviews. In 1924 he was admitted to the elite École Normale Supérieure, where he studied for an *agrégation* in philosophy, the degree required of lycée and university teachers. He failed his examination in 1928, but passed—in first place—in 1929; Simone de Beauvoir, who was to become a noted figure in French literature and his lifelong companion, was second.

After military service in the Meteorological Corps, Sartre taught philosophy at a lycée in Le Havre from 1931 to 1936, except for the academic year 1933–1934, when he accepted a fellowship at the Institut Français in Berlin. There he studied the German philosophers Edmund Husserl and Martin Heidegger, whose work strongly influenced his own theories. Returning to France in 1937, he was appointed to a teaching position in Paris.

During the late 1930s Sartre published his first major works, including four philosophical treatises that examined the nature and operation of consciousness. While teaching in Le Havre, Sartre wrote *La Nausée* (*Nausea*, pub-

JEAN-PAUL SARTRE

UPI/Bettmann Newsphotos

lished in England as *The Diary of Antoine Roquentin*), his first and most successful novel, which was published in 1938. At the same time, Sartre's short story "Le Mur" ("The Wall") appeared in the *Nouvelle Revue Française* (New French Revue). *Nausea* and "The Wall" became the two most widely discussed literary works in France that year.

Nausea is presented as the diary of Antoine Roquentin, who, while working on a biography of an eighteenth-century figure, becomes so conscious of the world around him that he is overwhelmed by the seeming futility of existence. Unable to affirm his faith in any values or to affect the world he inhabits, Roquentin is seized with a debilitating nausea. In the end he concludes that he might make his own existence meaningful by writing a novel.

Exempted from combat duty at the outbreak of World War II because of his poor eyesight, Sartre once again served in the Meteorological Corps. He became a prisoner of war during the German invasion of France and was imprisoned in a stalag in the German city of Trier. Escaping in 1941, he returned to Paris and resumed teaching and writing. During this time politics began to assume a more important role in his life than it had in the 1930s, when, despite his attacks on bourgeois life in *Nausea,* his chief interests were philosophy, psychology, and literature. Although he was not in the forefront of the Resistance movement, he established a Resistance discussion circle with friends and became acquainted with ALBERT CAMUS, who introduced him to the Resistance group known as Combat. Sartre's major publications during this period were the plays *Les Mouches* (*The Flies*, 1943) and *Huis clos* (*No Exit*, 1944), as well as the massive philosophical work *L'Être et le néant* (*Being and Nothingness*, 1943). The success of these writings permitted him to give up teaching at the Lycée Condorcet in 1944.

In *The Flies*, Sartre reworked the Greek legend of Orestes into a discussion of existentialism, the belief that there is no objective morality and that human beings are therefore absolutely free to make their own choices and to determine the course of their own existence through their actions. Orestes refuses to express regret to Zeus for killing his mother, Clytemnestra, and her lover Aegisthus, the murderers of his father, Agamemnon. As a result of his free choice and of his acceptance of responsibility for his act, he liberates his city of a plague of flies, or Furies, taking the plague upon himself. When the German authorities of occupied France realized that Sartre's play was a passionate call for freedom, they suppressed its production.

No Exit consists of a dialogue among three characters in hell, in which Sartre made clear that in existentialist terms, existence precedes essence, that one creates one's character through specific acts—a hero in intention is nevertheless a coward if his one important act before dying is a cowardly one. Most people, Sartre believed, are dependent for their conception of themselves on how others perceive them. In the words of one character, "Hell is other people."

Being and Nothingness, Sartre's most important philosophical work, became a bible to a generation of young French intellectuals. In this work, he argued that there is no reason for the existence of mind or consciousness; consciousness is nothing in itself because there is no such thing as empty or pure consciousness, but only consciousness of things. Human beings are responsible to themselves for their actions, since by every action they create a value, whether or not they are aware of doing so.

By the end of World War II, Sartre was recognized as the leader of the existentialists. His unofficial headquarters, the Café de Flore near the Place St. Germain-des-Prés on the Left Bank of Paris, became a tourist attraction for foreigners as well as for the French. Because of their experience of the German occupation, French intellectuals were attracted by the emphasis existentialism placed on human freedom and by its association with the Resistance. Above all, the euphoria of war-time cooperation among divergent French groups against a common enemy aroused hopes that an activist philosophy such as existentialism could unite intellectuals in forging a new and revolutionary French culture.

The next ten years were extraordinarily productive for Sartre. In addition to reviews and criticism, he wrote six plays, including what is often considered his best, *Les Mains sales* (*Dirty Hands*, 1948), a dramatic study of the painful compromises necessary in political activism. In a three-volume novel, *Les Chemins de la liberté* (*The Roads to Freedom*, 1945–1949), he attempted to show what each person makes of existential freedom, whether accepting or evading responsibility for individual choices of action. Sartre's biographical studies of Charles Baudelaire (1947) and Jean Genet (1952) were efforts to write existentialist biographies by applying the ontological categories of *Being and Nothingness* to the human personality.

Sartre's attraction to Marxism was apparent as early as 1944, when he founded *Les Temps Modernes* (Modern Times), a literary monthly that addressed current issues from a Marxist perspective. In the early 1950s, largely abandoning his previous concerns of fiction, drama, personal ethics, and the individual consciousness, Sartre moved toward a more open espousal of Marxism and a preoccupation with pressing social problems. Breaking with Camus in 1952 over the latter's attack on fanatical ideology and his defense of moderation, liberalism, and democracy, Sartre denounced the ethics of nonviolence and proclaimed that whatever serves to delay revolution is a betrayal of humanism.

In *Les Mots* (*The Words*, 1964), a harsh autobiography of his first ten years, Sartre attacked his grandfather's values as bourgeois, rejected literature that aims primarily at satisfying aesthetic criteria, and proclaimed the necessity of political commitment. His most ambitious product of this period was the philosophical work *Critique de la raison dialectique* (*Critique of Dialectical Reason*, 1960), which attempted to reconcile Marxism and existentialism. Sartre believed he could liberalize Marxism by grounding it in the existential concept of individual freedom, while at the same time broadening existentialism to account not only for the individual but also for society as a whole.

Sartre was awarded the 1964 Nobel Prize for Literature "for his work which, rich in ideas and filled with the spirit of freedom and the quest for truth, has exerted a far-reaching influence on our age." Arguing that he did not wish to be "transformed into an institution" and alarmed that the publicity surrounding the award would inhibit rather than enhance his effectiveness as a radical political figure, Sartre declined the prize.

During the last twenty years of his life, Sartre was noted more for his political pronouncements than for his literary or philosophical activities. With the zeal of a religious reformer, he committed his energies to restoring purity and purpose to socialism. Although never a member of the Communist party, Sartre was strongly pro-Soviet until 1956, when the Soviet Union suppressed the Hungarian uprising. In succeeding years he traveled extensively, speaking out against repression all over the world and using his prestige to defend the rights of ultraleftist groups. An outspoken advocate of Algerian independence, he compared French colonial actions to Nazi war crimes in his 1960 play, *Les Sequestrés d'Altona* (*The Condemned of Altona*). He vigorously opposed American military involvement in Vietnam and in 1967 presided over an ad hoc antiwar commission organized by BERTRAND RUSSELL, which found the United States guilty of war crimes. Originally a fervent supporter of the Chinese and Cuban revolutions, Sartre ultimately became disenchanted with the course both countries took. He hailed the Paris student demonstrations of 1968 but, despairing of revolution in Europe, turned to the support of revolutionary causes in the Third World and demanded that other intellectuals do the same. By the 1970s he had become isolated, a maverick outsider in the politics of the time.

Afflicted with a number of eye problems, chiefly by glaucoma, Sartre was almost totally blind in his last years. He gave up writing and concentrated instead on giving interviews. He discussed politics with friends, was read to by Simone de Beauvoir, and listened to music. He died of uremia on April 15, 1980.

Regarded by philosophers like Heidegger as more of a novelist than a philosopher, and by writers like Vladimir Nabokov as more of a philosopher than a novelist, Sartre's identity and the significance of his accomplishment remain difficult to assess. Many critics are not convinced that he managed to reconcile his earlier individualist ethics with his later passionate concern for social action. Nevertheless, the French structuralist critic Louis Althusser was able to say of Sartre after his death, "He was our Jean Jacques Rousseau." His obituary in *Le Monde* (The World) summed up his importance in these words: "No French intellectual of this century, no Nobel Prize winner, has exerted an influence as profound, as durable, as universal, as Sartre's."

ADDITIONAL WORKS IN ENGLISH TRANSLATION: The Reprieve, 1947; Existentialism, 1947; The Age of Reason, 1947; Anti-Semite and Jew, 1948; The Chips Are Down, 1948; The Emotions, 1948; The Psychology of Imagination, 1948; Intimacy, 1948; What Is Literature? 1949; Black Orpheus, 1949; Baudelaire, 1949; Troubled Sleep, 1950; Existential Psychoanalysis, 1953; Lucifer and the Lord, 1953; In the Mesh, 1954; Kean, 1954; Literary and Philosophical Essays, 1955; Nekrassov, 1956; The Transcendence of the Ego, 1957; Sartre on Cuba, 1961; Imagination, 1962; The Problem of Method, 1963; Essays in Aesthetics, 1963; Saint Genet, Actor and Martyr, 1963; Situations, 1965; The Communists and Peace, 1965; Of Human Freedom, 1967; The Trojan Woman, 1967; On Genocide, 1968; The Ghost of Stalin, 1969; Politics and Literature, 1973; Between Existentialism and Marxism, 1974; Sartre in the Seventies, 1977; Life/Situations: Essays Written and Spoken, 1978; The Family Idiot, Gustave Flaubert, 1981; The War Diaries, 1985; The Freud Scenario, 1986; Thoughtful Passions, 1987.

ABOUT: de Beauvoir, S. Adieux: A Farewell to Sartre, 1984; Brée, G. Camus and Sartre, 1972; Brosman, C. S. Jean-Paul Sartre, 1983; Caws, P. Sartre, 1979; Champigny, R. J. Stages on Sartre's Way, 1959; Cohen-Salal, A. Sartre, A Life, 1987; Cranston, M. Sartre, 1962; Cummings, R. D. The Philosophy of Jean-Paul Sartre, 1972; Desan, W. Tragic Finale, 1954; Greene, N. N. Jean-Paul Sartre: The Existential Ethic, 1960; Halpern, J. Critical Fictions, 1976; Hayman, R. Sartre, 1987; Jameson, F. Sartre: The Origins of a Style, 1961; Jolivet, R. Sartre: The Theology of the Absurd, 1967; Kern, E. G. (ed.) Sartre: A Collection of Critical Essays, 1962; La Farge, R. Jean-Paul Sartre: His Philosophy, 1970; McMahon, J. H. Human Being: The World of Jean-Paul Sartre, 1971; Madsen, A. Hearts and Minds, 1977; Manser, A. Sartre: A Philosophical Study, 1966; Marcel, G. The Philosophy of Existentialism, 1961; Murdock, I. Sartre, Romantic Rationalist, 1953; Peyre, H. Jean-Paul Sartre, 1968; Richter, L. Jean-Paul Sartre, 1968; Salvan, J. To Be and Not to Be, 1962; Schlipp, P. A. (ed.) The Philosophy of Jean-Paul Sartre, 1981; Suhl, B. Jean-Paul Sartre, 1970; Thody, P. Jean-Paul Sartre, 1960; Warnock, M. The Philosophy of Sartre, 1965; Warnock, M. (ed.) Sartre: A Collection of Critical Essays, 1971; Zuidema, S. U. Sartre, 1960.

SATO, EISAKU
(March 27, 1901–June 3, 1975)
Nobel Prize for Peace, 1974
(shared with Sean MacBride)

The Japanese premier Eisaku Sato (sä tō) was born in the village of Tabuse in Yamaguchi Prefecture, the youngest of three sons in a family of ten children. His father, Hidesuke Sato, was a middle-class sake brewer, former prefecture official, and amateur poet. Of his three sons, one, Ichiro, became an admiral and two, Eisaku and Nobusuke, became premiers of Japan—the first brothers to hold that office. Sato's great-grandfather had been

EISAKU SATO

a famous samurai and an imperial governor, and his parents expected him to live up to this heritage. As Sato recalled later, his mother, Moyo Sato, frequently told her sons, "Never forget that we are of samurai lineage, that the Sato family can never suffer a failure."

After attending Kuniki Primary School in Tabuse and high school in Kumamoto, Sato entered Tokyo Imperial University, where he majored in German jurisprudence. Graduating in 1924 with a law degree, he attempted unsuccessfully to enter the Finance Ministry and subsequently joined the Railway Ministry. In 1926 he married his cousin Hiroko Sato, with whom he had two sons. At the Railway Ministry, Sato's efficiency won him several important posts, including director of the Ōsaka Railways Bureau from 1944 to 1946 and vice-minister for transportation from 1947 to 1948.

In March 1948 Sato resigned his transportation post to enter politics. Joining the Democratic Liberals, he was elected president of the party's chapter in Yamaguchi Prefecture. In October, Premier Shigeru Yoshida appointed him chief cabinet secretary. Yoshida had wanted Sato in that post immediately after World War II, but United States occupation authorities had blocked the appointment because Sato's brother Nobusuke had been a member of the wartime cabinet and was suspected of war crimes. Nobusuke, who had changed his surname to Kishi in accordance with Japanese marital custom, was cleared and released without going to trial, and both brothers were free to enter politics.

Sato ran for a seat in the Japanese Diet, or parliament, in 1949, winning a landslide victory for his party. He retained his post as cabinet secretary and also served as chairman of the Policy Research Council, a key party position. Becoming one of Premier Yoshida's closest associates, he served as minister of posts and telecommunications from 1951 to 1952 and minister of construction from 1952 to 1953. He then resigned his cabinet position to become secretary-general of his party.

Sato's career suffered a setback in 1954 when he and several other politicians were accused of accepting a bribe from a shipbuilding association. The charge was eventually dropped, and Sato was tried on the lesser charge of failing to record a political donation. He was acquitted under an amnesty celebrating Japan's admission to the United Nations, but his party was ruined by the scandal. Sato dropped out of public life until 1957, when he became chairman of the executive council of the reconstituted Liberal Democratic party, of which his brother was president.

In 1958 Nobusuke Kishi became premier of Japan and appointed Sato minister of finance. Hiyato Ikeda, a high school classmate of Sato's, succeeded Kishi as premier in 1960 and named Sato minister of international trade and industry in his cabinet. In July 1962 Sato resigned from the cabinet and, in what was seen as a bid for the post of premier, traveled abroad, meeting with leaders of the United States, France, and other major powers. Then, despite his differences with Ikeda, whom he accused of weakness, Sato rejoined Ikeda's cabinet in July 1963, serving in a variety of posts until the fall of 1964. He then announced himself as a candidate opposing Ikeda for the presidency of the party, a post that would lead to the premiership if the party was successful in a general election. Although Ikeda won the party leadership battle and was reelected, he resigned in October 1964 because of ill health. After some internal party politicking, Ikeda chose Sato as his successor, and on November 9, 1964, the Diet elected Sato premier.

At the beginning of his term, Sato declared his intention of strengthening Japan's voice internationally while retaining its postwar pacifist stance. "I think that unarmed nations and nonnuclear nations, such as Japan, should express a more positive voice for the maintenance of peace," he said after his inauguration. He espoused a policy of close relations with the United States and vigorously reaffirmed Japan's postwar constitution, which stated, "War and the threat or use of force are renounced as a means of deciding conflicts with other nations." This reaffirmation was seen as especially significant since Japan, emerging as a major economic power, stood at a crossroads over its national defense policy. Sato made it clear that Japan renounced the use of nuclear weapons and declared his nation's firm resolve "never to produce arms of this nature, never to own them, and never to introduce them into Japan."

Sato also set out to improve Japan's relations with its neighbors. In 1965 he signed a friendship pact and established diplomatic relations with South Korea, a victim of Japanese aggression before and during World War II. Two years later, he made a tour of the Philippines, Australia, New Zealand, South Vietnam, Laos, Thailand, Singapore, Malaysia, Burma, and Indonesia to strengthen cultural and trade relations. As both a staunch ally of the United States and a pacifist, Sato faced difficult choices during the Vietnam War. He attempted several times to mediate in the dispute, but he also upset many Japanese by becoming the only head of a major nation to endorse the United States bombing raids on North Vietnam in 1968.

Sato's close ties to the United States led to his longest-lasting accomplishment: the peaceful return of Okinawa and the Ogasawara Islands to Japanese sovereignty. The United States had occupied the islands since World War II, when it captured them from Japanese forces in a bloody invasion. The territories were returned to Japan in 1972 after five years of negotiations, removing what had been the largest stumbling block in relations between the two countries. Sato also attempted to improve relations with the Soviet Union and the People's Republic of China, although no breakthroughs were made during his administration. In July 1972 his premiership ended when he lost a party leadership contest.

For his role in setting Japan firmly on a course of antimilitarism, Sato was awarded the 1974 Nobel Prize for Peace, which he shared with SEAN MACBRIDE. In her presentation speech, Aase Lionæs of the Norwegian Nobel Committee noted: "By countering the tendency toward a nationalistic policy in Japan after the war, by constantly emphasizing the need for international cooperation and understanding, by playing the role of arbitrator and thus helping to iron out differences, Sato has made a major contribution to peace." Lionæs also pointed out that Sato's leadership was crucial in Japan's emergence as the sole major power to renounce nuclear arms.

In accepting the award, Sato pleaded for nuclear disarmament by the United States and the Soviet Union. He also called for an international agreement on regulations governing the peaceful uses of nuclear energy and suggested that all nations cooperate in the development of nuclear fusion as an energy source.

The selection of Sato as a Peace laureate stirred controversy. Although many Japanese welcomed recognition of their country's antimilitarism, many questioned Sato's pacifism. "Is it a joke?" one television commentator asked. "Are they trying to make fun of Japan?" Chief among objections to Sato's selection for the prize were his endorsement of the bombing of North Vietnam during the Vietnam War and his harsh anti-Communist attitude, which had led his government to vote against admitting the People's Republic of China to the United Nations and to resist establishing normal relations with Peking. Many critics also objected because several prominent Japanese businessmen had lobbied extensively on Sato's behalf among members of the Nobel selection committee.

Sato suffered a cerebral hemorrhage while dining at a Tokyo restaurant on May 19, 1975, and died two weeks later.

ABOUT: Current Biography December 1965; Far Eastern Economic Review November 1, 1974; June 13, 1975; Japan Times Weekly January 2, 1965; Kurzman, D. Kishi and Japan, 1960; New York Times November 9, 1964; Time January 15, 1965; Times (London) June 3, 1975.

SCHALLEY, ANDREW V.

(November 30, 1926–   )
Nobel Prize for Physiology or Medicine, 1977
(shared with Roger Guillemin and Rosalyn S. Yalow)

The American biochemist Andrew Victor Schalley was born in Wilno, Poland (now Vilnius, USSR), the son of Casimir Peter Schalley, a soldier, and the former Maria Lacka. When World War II broke out, Schalley's father joined the Allied forces. "My life and outlook were influenced by the harsh childhood which I spent in Nazi-occupied eastern Europe," Schalley recalled later. He survived the Holocaust in the Polish Jewish community in Romania and in 1945 migrated through Italy and France to Scotland, where he received his diploma from the Bridge Allen School in Scotland the following year. From 1946 until 1950 he studied chemistry at the University of London, and during the next two years he was

ANDREW V. SCHALLEY

base of the brain above the pituitary gland and is connected to the anterior lobe of that gland by a delicate network of blood vessels called the portal vessels. In the 1930s a British physiologist, G. W. Harris, cut the portal vessels and observed that when he did so, secretion from the anterior lobe of the pituitary gland decreased. Harris therefore postulated that the pituitary gland was regulated by blood-borne chemical substances, or hormones, originating in the hypothalamus. No one had yet identified these hypothalamic hormones, and Schalley made this his goal.

In 1955 Schalley demonstrated that extracts of hypothalamic tissue placed in his experimental test system caused the release of ACTH from pituitary cells. This was the first direct experimental evidence for hypothalamic regulation of pituitary function. Schalley called this newly identified hypothalamic hormone corticotropin-releasing factor, or CRF. CRF is now known as corticotropin-releasing hormone, or CRH. With a doctoral dissertation based on these experiments, he received a Ph.D. from McGill University in 1957.

That year Schalley was appointed assistant professor of physiology at the Baylor University School of Medicine in Houston, Texas, where he collaborated with ROGER GUILLEMIN in an effort to isolate and determine the chemical structure of CRF. The chemical structure of CRF (a peptide containing forty-one amino acids) proved to be particularly elusive, however, and was not determined until 1981. When these initial attempts to discover the structure of CRF failed, other investigators in the field viewed the work of Schalley and Guillemin with skepticism. Eventually, working separately and competitively, the two men identified other hypothalamic hormones.

Schalley became an American citizen in 1962 and accepted an offer from Joseph Meyer, chief of research for the Veterans Administration, to be director of the newly established Endocrine and Polypeptide Laboratory at the Veterans Administration Hospital in New Orleans, Louisiana. He was also appointed assistant professor of medicine at Tulane University Medical School, where he achieved the rank of full professor of medicine in 1966.

The organizational problems that confronted both Schalley and Guillemin over the years were considerable. To obtain enough hypothalamic tissue to test for the presence of hormones, it was necessary to process hundreds of thousands of animal hypothalami, which they obtained from slaughterhouses. After the animals were slaughtered, the brains and hypo-

employed as a junior research scientist at the National Institute of Medical Research in London. There he developed skill in laboratory research, experience in experimental methods, and a lasting interest in medical research.

In 1952 Schalley emigrated to Montreal, Canada, and entered McGill University to study endocrinology under D. L. Thomson and to conduct research in the Laboratory of Experimental Therapeutics at the Allen Institute of Psychiatry. Endocrinology is the branch of biology and medicine that deals with the endocrine glands, which include the pituitary, thyroid, and adrenal glands; the pancreas; the ovaries; and the testicles. Hormones, the chemical substances secreted by glands, circulate in the blood and regulate the secretions of other endocrine glands or the functioning of certain tissues. During his first two years in Montreal, Schalley conducted research on the adrenal and pituitary glands. The pituitary gland secretes adrenocorticotropic hormone, or ACTH. In turn, ACTH is transported via the blood to the adrenal gland, where it regulates the secretion and release of cortisol and cortisone, hormones involved in the organism's response to stress. Schalley and his collaborator at McGill developed an experimental test system—known as a biological assay, or bioassay—that enabled them to measure pituitary cell secretion of ACTH.

Schalley soon became interested in a new class of hormones that were thought to be produced by the hypothalamus and to be involved in the regulation of the secretions of the pituitary gland. The hypothalamus lies at the

thalamic tissue had to be removed quickly to prevent the breakdown of the hormones. The hypothalamic tissue was then processed in the laboratory.

In 1966 Schalley's research group isolated the hypothalamic hormone that causes the release of thyrotropin from the pituitary gland. (Thyrotropin in turn causes the release of thyroid hormones from the thyroid gland; it is also called thyroid-stimulating hormone, or TSH.) Schalley called this new hypothalamic hormone thyrotropin-releasing factor, or TRF. It is now called thyrotropin-releasing hormone, or TRH. Initially, Schalley and his collaborators were unable to determine the chemical structure of TRF. However, in 1969 they demonstrated that TRF is a peptide containing three amino acids. That same year, Guillemin's group in Houston also determined the chemical structure of TRF. Schalley and clinical associates in Mexico also proved that TRF causes the release of pituitary thyrotropin in human beings. TRF, or TRH, is now used in the diagnosis and treatment of certain hormone-deficiency diseases.

The hypothalamic hormone that causes the release of gonadotropins from the pituitary gland was isolated by Schalley and his colleagues in the late 1960s. Gonadotropins cause the release of male and female sex hormones from the ovaries and testicles. The hypothalamic hormone is now known as growth-hormone-releasing hormone (GRH); its chemical structure was determined by Schalley's group in 1971. GRH is a peptide containing ten amino acids. Schalley and his associates in Mexico proved that GRH causes the release of pituitary gonadotropins in human subjects. Several chemical analogues of GRH have now been synthesized. (An analogue has a chemical structure similar to that of another compound but differs from it in one component.) Some analogues stimulate the release of GRH from the pituitary; these have been used in treating one type of infertility. Others inhibit the release of the hormone and may prove to be effective birth-control agents. Schalley has been particularly interested in the clinical applications of the GRH analogues.

Schalley and his colleagues had been attempting to isolate growth hormone-releasing factor (GRF). He published the chemical structure of GRF in 1971, only to find that he had identified not the hormone but part of a protein found in red blood cells. In 1976 he correctly identified the structure of a factor in pigs that inhibits the release of growth hormone. Three years earlier Guillemin's group

had isolated this factor in sheep and determined its structure; Guillemin named it somatostatin. Studies by Schalley and other researchers have shown that somatostatin has a variety of effects on the body. Some of its analogues may prove to be useful in the treatment of diabetes, peptic ulcer disease, and acromegaly (a condition caused by an excess of growth hormone).

Half of the 1977 Nobel Prize for Physiology or Medicine was awarded to Schalley and Guillemin "for their discoveries concerning the peptide hormone production of the brain." The other half was awarded to ROSALYN S. YALOW for her work on radioimmunoassays. In his Nobel lecture, Schalley stated that "at the inception of my scientific career, the concept of hypothalamic control of anterior pituitary function was in its formative stage. It was my good fortune to have arrived on the scene at such a crucial time and to have helped place it on the solid foundation on which it now rests."

Schalley's marriage to Margaret Rachel White produced a son and a daughter. After their divorce, he married Ana Maria de Medeiros-Comaru, a Brazilian endocrinologist, in 1974.

Awards and honors received by Schalley include the Charles Mickle Award of the University of Toronto (1974), the Gairdner Foundation International Award (1974), the Borden Award in the Medical Sciences of the Association of American Medical Colleges (1975), and the Albert Lasker Basic Medical Research Award (1975). He is a member of the National Academy of Sciences, the American Society of Biological Chemists, the American Physiology Society, the American Association for the Advancement of Science, and the Endocrine Society. Universities in Canada and other nations have awarded him numerous honorary degrees.

ABOUT: New Scientist October 20, 1977; New York Times October 14, 1977; Science November 11, 1977; Wade, N. The Nobel Duel, 1981.

SCHAWLOW, ARTHUR L.

(May 5, 1921–)
Nobel Prize for Physics, 1981
(shared with Nicolaas Bloembergen and Kai Siegbahn)

The American physicist Arthur Leonard Schawlow (shô′ lō) was born in Mount Vernon, New York. A decade earlier his father, Arthur Schawlow, had immigrated to the United States from Riga, Latvia. Settling in

New York City, he worked as an insurance agent and married a Canadian, Helen Mason. When Arthur was three years old, the family, which also included a daughter, moved to Canada.

Growing up in Toronto, Schawlow attended the Winchester Elementary School; the Normal Model School attached to the teachers' college; and the Vaughan Road Collegiate Institute, a high school from which he graduated in 1937. He had hoped to further his boyhood interest in science by studying radio engineering at the University of Toronto, but his parents could not afford the tuition because of the hardships of the Depression. No engineering scholarships were available, but Schawlow did win a scholarship in mathematics and physics. As he later recalled, "Physics seemed pretty close to radio engineering, and so that is what I pursued."

By the time he received his B.S. in 1941, Canada was at war, and Schawlow taught classes for military personnel at the University of Toronto until 1944, when he went to work on a microwave antenna project at a factory making radar equipment. In 1945 he returned to the University of Toronto, where he did his thesis research on optical spectroscopy under Malcolm F. Crawford, whom he remembered as "highly creative"; he received his Ph.D. in 1949.

A Carbide and Carbon Chemicals postgraduate fellowship brought Schawlow to Columbia University. He spent two years there working with CHARLES H. TOWNES on microwave spectroscopy.

In 1951 Schawlow accepted a research position at Bell Telephone Laboratories in Murray Hill, New Jersey. His chief field of research was superconductivity, the phenomenon discovered in 1911 by the Dutch physicist HEIKE KAMERLINGH ONNES, in which the electrical resistance of certain substances disappears when they are cooled to near absolute zero ($-273°C$). Meanwhile, Schawlow continued his association with Townes, meeting on weekends to complete a book, *Microwave Spectroscopy*, which they had begun while Schawlow was at Columbia. It was published in 1955.

Two years earlier, Townes and two colleagues had succeeded in developing a device he called the maser, for *m*icrowave *a*mplification by *s*timulated *e*mission of *r*adiation. Stimulated emission was a phenomenon predicted by ALBERT EINSTEIN in 1917. Scientists exploring the revolutionary new quantum theory had shown that the atom consisted of electrons surrounding a dense central nucleus (the

ARTHUR L. SCHAWLOW

NIELS BOHR model). The electrons were restricted to motion only in certain discrete orbits, that is, narrowly defined energies. The atom was then said to exist in particular energy states (or levels) by virtue of relationships between the electrons and the nucleus. A lowest level was called the ground state. Electrons could be excited to higher levels by absorption of radiation. Since MAX PLANCK had shown that radiation consisted of separate bits that Einstein named quanta (now called photons), the differences between energy levels corresponded to specific quanta, or photons. Planck also showed that frequency of the radiation was proportional to the energy in a photon. An excited electron soon fell back to a lower energy level, emitting the change in energy as a photon of radiation and giving rise to characteristic radiation spectra that correlated with the differences in energy within each atom's unique set of energy levels.

Excited atoms normally emit photons at random and in a heterogeneous assortment. Einstein theorized that if enough atoms could be excited to a particular energy level, incident radiation whose photons had an energy equal to the difference between the two atomic levels would then trigger a cascade. The excited atoms populating the upper level would be induced to fall to the lower level, simultaneously emitting a large number of photons with the same frequency and in the same phase (same point in the frequency cycle). Townes confirmed this prediction experimentally, using microwaves whose photons had an energy equal to the difference between two energy levels of ammonia, the substance he was working with. (Molecules also have energy levels related to the states and relationships between the atoms they contain.) Since a relatively small microwave signal triggered a relatively large output of photons of the same frequency, the result was amplification. Some of the output was fed back to excite atoms back to the upper energy level so that the amplifier was converted into an oscillator that could sustain more continuous action than a single burst.

Microwaves have lower frequencies (lower photon energies) and therefore longer wavelengths (about 1 to 50 millimeters) than visible light (about 0.0004 to 0.0007 millimeter). During 1957–1958 Townes and Schawlow sought a way to achieve the maser effect with visible light and in December 1958 published a paper in the journal *Physical Review,* "Infrared and Optical Masers," explaining how this might be done. In 1960 Theodore H. Maiman, an American physicist at Hughes Aircraft Company, demonstrated the first laser (*l*ight *a*mplification by *s*timulated *e*mission of *r*adiation). In the same year, Schawlow and others also succeeded in building lasers. During the same period, both the maser and laser were developed independently by NIKOLAI BASOV and ALEKSANDR PROKHOROV.

In 1960 Schawlow returned to Columbia University, this time as a visiting professor. The following year he became professor of physics at Stanford University, where he has remained, serving five years as chairman of the physics department. He has continued to contribute to laser technology to achieve both a highly monochromatic (single-frequency) light output and an adjustable frequency (tunable lasers). In most of his efforts, however, he has used lasers to investigate atoms and molecules; since the early 1960s he has been at the forefront of the rapidly developing field of laser spectroscopy.

Laser spectroscopy uses the fact that atoms and molecules absorb and emit electromagnetic radiation at characteristic frequencies (photon energies) corresponding to the energy differences between their various energy levels. The spectrum of radiation frequencies emitted after excitation to higher energy states, or preferentially absorbed from the incident radiation, helps identify elements, reveal atomic and molecular structure, and test fundamental theories of matter and radiation. The tunable laser was a significant contribution because the laser's light is highly monochromatic (providing an accurate measure of frequency), highly intense (making it possible to record spectra

with relatively few atoms or molecules), and adjustable to the desired frequencies.

In many types of spectroscopy, spectral lines (narrow bands of frequencies) are affected by Doppler broadening. The Doppler effect is a change in the observed frequency due to relative motion between the radiation emitter and the observer. Frequency rises when the emitter is moving toward the observer and falls when the emitter is moving away, the amount of rise or fall depending on how fast the emitter is approaching or retreating. For sound waves, the Doppler effect causes the familiar rise and fall in pitch of a train whistle or automobile horn as the vehicle passes a listener. In spectroscopy, the frequencies emitted by atoms or molecules, forever in motion related to their temperature, are shifted up or down depending on the direction of motion. Since motions are generally in all directions, the result is a widening of the spectral line.

In the case of absorption spectra, the "observer" is the atom or molecule receiving the radiation. The "received" frequency is higher or lower than the frequency of the outside source depending on whether the atom or molecule is moving toward or away from the source. Spectral "lines" are actually peaks with trailing edges. Due to broadening, two closely spaced peaks may overlap, and a small peak may be obscured by a large neighbor and therefore go undetected.

Working with Theodor W. Hänsch at Stanford, Schawlow found several ways to overcome the difficulties of Doppler broadening by isolating the absorption spectra due only to atoms with no component of motion parallel to the laser beam. Since these atoms are not moving toward or away from the light source, the Doppler effect is evaded. In 1972 Schawlow and his co-workers obtained the first Doppler-free optical spectra of atomic hydrogen, allowing them to measure, with unprecedented accuracy, the Rydberg constant, one of the most important numbers of physics.

The spectra of molecules are, in general, enormously more complicated than those of atoms, and Schawlow has used lasers to simplify these spectra by so-called laser labeling. Molecules are "pumped" up to a particular energy state by laser light tuned to provide exactly the right frequency (photon energy), and their return to lower energy levels is then observed. Because the particular state is singled out from its neighbors, it is said to be labeled. Schawlow has also developed laser spectroscopy techniques to detect trace elements in a surrounding material. Since 1978

Schawlow has been J. G. Jackson–C. J. Wood Professor of Physics at Stanford.

Schawlow shared half of the 1981 Nobel Prize for Physics with NICOLAAS BLOEMBERGEN "for their contribution to the development of laser spectroscopy." The other half was awarded to KAI SIEGBAHN for related work on electron spectroscopy. "These methods," said Ingvar Lindgren of the Royal Swedish Academy of Sciences in his presentation speech, "have made it possible to investigate the interior of atoms, molecules, and solids in greater detail than was previously possible."

Schawlow married Charles H. Townes's youngest sister, Aurelia, in 1951. They have a son and two daughters. An amateur clarinetist, Schawlow is fond of traditional jazz and has assembled a large record collection. He is well known as a lecturer and has participated in the production of educational films and television programs on science.

In addition to the Nobel Prize, Schawlow has received the Stuart Ballantine Medal of the Franklin Institute (1962), the Thomas Young Medal and Prize of the Institute of Physics in London (1963), and the Frederick Ives Medal of the Optical Society of America (1976). He is a member of the National Academy of Sciences, the American Association for the Advancement of Science, the American Physical Society, the Optical Society of America, and the Institute of Electrical and Electronics Engineers. His other honors include degrees from the State University of Ghent, the University of Bradford, and the University of Toronto.

ABOUT: New York Times October 20, 1981; Physics Today December 1981; Science November 6, 1981; Science 84 November 1984.

SCHRIEFFER, J. ROBERT
(May 31, 1931–)
Nobel Prize for Physics, 1972
(shared with John Bardeen and Leon N Cooper)

The American physicist John Robert Schrieffer (shrē' fər) was born in Oak Park, Illinois, to John H. Schrieffer and the former Louise Anderson. In 1940 the family moved to Manhasset, New York, and nine years later to Eustis, Florida. After graduating from Eustis High School in 1949, Schrieffer entered the Massachusetts Institute of Technology to study electrical engineering. Two years later he became a physics major and earned his B.S. in

J. ROBERT SCHRIEFFER

1953. He received an M.S. in 1954 from the University of Illinois, where he studied under JOHN BARDEEN, an authority on solid-state physics. His M.S. thesis dealt with the conduction of electrons at the surface of a semiconductor. He then joined Bardeen in studying the phenomenon of superconductivity and the properties of matter at temperatures near absolute zero ($-273°C$).

In 1911 the Dutch physicist HEIKE KAMERLINGH ONNES had discovered that some metals lose all resistance to the flow of electricity when they are cooled to within a few degrees of absolute zero. The discovery, called superconductivity, came as a great surprise, and nearly fifty years elapsed before it was fully understood.

Almost all metals become better conductors as they are cooled because thermal vibrations of the atoms in a metal are a major source of electrical resistance. The vibrations scatter the electrons that carry an electrical current; cooling the metal reduces the amplitude of the vibrations and thus removes an impediment to the flow of electrons. In normal metals the improvement in conductivity is gradual, and the resistance would fall to zero only at a temperature of absolute zero (which cannot be attained in practice). What is surprising about a superconductor is that all electrical resistance disappears abruptly at a certain temperature greater than zero. The atoms of the metal still vibrate, but the current carrying electrons seems to pass unimpeded.

Another odd property of superconductors was discovered in 1933 by the German phys-

933

icist Walther Meissner. Meissner found that superconductors exhibit perfect diamagnetism: a magnetic field is excluded from the interior of the superconducting body, and the body is repelled by both poles of a magnet. As a result, a magnetic material placed above a superconductor hangs suspended, in a state of levitation. If a sufficiently strong magnetic field is applied to a superconducting material, the material loses its superconductivity and becomes a normal conductor. In 1935 the German physicist Fritz London suggested that the diamagnetic aspect of superconductivity is its basic property. He speculated that superconductivity is a quantum phenomenon acting on a macroscopic scale.

In 1950 several American physicists investigated superconductivity in metals that have several isotopes (forms of an element with the same number of electrons and protons—and hence the same chemical properties—but different numbers of neutrons). They discovered that the critical temperature at which an isotope becomes superconductive is inversely proportional to its atomic mass. Knowing that the only way atomic mass changes the properties of a solid is by affecting the propagation of vibrations, Bardeen suggested that superconductivity depends on the interaction of conduction electrons with the vibrational motion of atoms in the metal. The conduction electrons, he reasoned, must be coupled to one another by means of these vibrations.

In 1956 LEON N COOPER, one of Bardeen's postdoctoral research associates at the University of Illinois, showed that the coupling of conduction electrons to the atomic vibrations leads to the formation of bound pairs of electrons. One electron, moving through the metallic crystal, attracts the surrounding, positively charged atoms to itself. This slight deformation of the crystal lattice creates a momentary concentration of positive charge, which in turn attracts the second electron. Thus the two electrons are indirectly bound together through the intermediate action of the crystal lattice; they are said to form a Cooper pair.

Schrieffer and Bardeen sought to extend Cooper's insight about the interaction of pairs of electrons to the behavior of a large fraction of the free electrons in a superconducting solid. Schrieffer was on the verge of giving up when Bardeen left for Sweden to receive the 1956 Nobel Prize for Physics, awarded for his contributions to the invention of the transistor. Bardeen asked Schrieffer to give one more month to the problem, and in that time he worked out the statistical techniques needed to solve it.

When Bardeen returned, he, Cooper, and Schrieffer demonstrated that the interaction between Cooper pairs compels many of the free electrons in a superconducting substance to move in lockstep. As London had guessed, the superconducting electrons form a single quantum state extending throughout the material. Below the critical temperature, the pairing force that holds the electrons in their coordinated motion is stronger than the thermal vibrations of the metal atoms. A disturbance that would deflect a single electron, and therefore give rise to electrical resistance, cannot do so in a superconductor without affecting simultaneously all the electrons participating in the superconducting state. This event is extremely unlikely, and as a result the superconducting electrons drift coherently without loss of energy. For his contributions to the theory of superconductivity, Schrieffer was awarded a Ph.D. by the University of Illinois in 1957.

The Bardeen-Cooper-Schrieffer (BCS) theory has been called one of the most important contributions to theoretical physics since the development of the quantum theory. In 1958, applying the BCS theory, Cooper and his colleagues predicted that very cold liquid helium 3 (an isotope having two protons and one neutron) would exhibit superfluidity, an unusual state of matter characterized by the absence of viscosity and surface tension. Superfluidity had been observed earlier in the more common isotope helium 4 (with two protons and two neutrons), but it had been considered impossible in isotopes with an odd number of nuclear particles. The superfluidity of helium 3 was demonstrated in 1962.

Schrieffer, Cooper, and Bardeen were awarded the 1972 Nobel Prize for Physics "for their jointly developed theory of superconductivity, usually called the BCS theory." "You have in your fundamental work given a complete theoretical explanation of the phenomenon of superconductivity," said Stig Lundqvist of the Royal Swedish Academy of Sciences in his presentation address. "Your theory has also predicted new effects and stimulated an intensive activity in theoretical and experimental research. The further developments in the field of superconductivity have in a striking way confirmed the great range and validity of the concepts and ideas in your fundamental paper from 1957."

The scientific and technological impact of

the BCS theory has been profound. It has led to the creation of superconductors that operate at higher temperatures or in the presence of strong magnetic fields. Such superconductors are crucial for the construction of electromagnets that produce powerful magnetic fields but consume little power. Magnets of this kind have applications in the study of nuclear fusion; in magnetohydrodynamics (generating electricity from a high-temperature ionized gas passed through a magnetic field); in the acceleration of energetic particles for research on elementary particles; in magnetic levitation to permit frictionless motion; in biological and physical research involving the interaction of atoms and electrons with a strong magnetic field; and in the construction of compact, powerful electric generators. The discovery by BRIAN D. JOSEPHSON, a Welsh physicist, of certain behavior at junctions between two superconductors (the Josephson effects) has led to the development of sensors able to reveal magnetic activity within living organisms and to help detect deposits of ore and petroleum based on their magnetic properties.

As a National Science Foundation postdoctoral fellow in 1957–1958, Schrieffer studied superconductivity at the University of Birmingham, England, and at the Niels Bohr Institute in Copenhagen, Denmark. There, in 1960, he met Anne Grete Thomsen; they married a few months later and have two daughters and a son.

Schrieffer has taught physics at the University of Chicago (1957–1960), at the University of Illinois (1959–1960), at the University of Pennsylvania (1962), at Cornell University (1969–1975), and since 1975, at the University of California at Santa Barbara. His research has also encompassed the magnetic properties of materials and properties of alloys and material surfaces. At the University of Pennsylvania, Schrieffer was coauthor of a report that helped establish the university's Afro-American Studies Program. He is a sturdy, unassuming man known for having a ready quip for every occasion.

Schrieffer's awards include the Comstock Prize of the National Academy of Sciences (1968), the Oliver E. Buckley Solid-State Physics Prize of the American Physical Society (1968), and the John Ericsson Medal of the American Society of Swedish Engineers (1976). He holds honorary doctorates from five universities and belongs to the National Academy of Sciences, the American Academy of Arts and Sciences, the American Philosophical Society, and the Royal Danish Academy of Arts and Sciences.

SELECTED WORKS: The Theory of Superconductivity, 1964; Electronic Structure of Impurities in Metals (2 vols.) 1969.

ABOUT: New Scientist October 26, 1972; New York Times October 21, 1972; Parks, R. D. (ed.) Superconductivity, 1969; Science November 3, 1972.

SCHRÖDINGER, ERWIN
(August 12, 1887–January 4, 1961)
Nobel Prize for Physics, 1933
(shared with P. A. M. Dirac)

The Austrian physicist Erwin Schrödinger (shrŭ′ ding ər) was born in Vienna. His father, Rudolph Schrödinger, was the owner of an oilcloth factory and a talented amateur painter with a strong interest in botany. An only child, Erwin received his early education at home from his father, whom he later described as his "friend, teacher, and tireless partner in conversation." In 1898 Schrödinger entered the Akademisches Gymnasium, where he excelled in Greek, Latin, classical literature, mathematics, and physics. He also acquired a love of the theater.

In 1906 Schrödinger entered the University of Vienna, and the following year began attending the physics lectures of Friedrich Hasenöhrl, whose brilliant insights exerted a profound influence on him. After receiving his Ph.D. in 1910, Schrödinger became assistant to the experimental physicist Franz Exner at the University of Vienna's Second Physics Institute, a position he held until the outbreak of World War I. In 1913 Schrödinger and K. W. F. Kohlrausch won the Haitinger Prize of the Imperial Academy of Sciences for their experimental work with radium.

During the war Schrödinger served as an artillery officer and was stationed in remote mountain areas. Making productive use of his free time, he studied ALBERT EINSTEIN's general theory of relativity. After the end of the war, he returned to the Second Physics Institute in Vienna, where he conducted research on general relativity, statistical mechanics (the study of systems with very large numbers of interacting objects, such as the molecules of a gas), and X-ray diffraction. He also conducted extensive experimental and theoretical research on the theory of colors and how they are perceived.

ERWIN SCHRÖDINGER

In 1920 Schrödinger went to Germany as an assistant to Max Wien at the University of Jena but after four months accepted a position as an assistant professor at the technical university in Stuttgart. He left there after one term to become briefly a professor at Breslau (now Wrocław, Poland). He then moved to Switzerland to take a position as a full professor at the University of Zurich, occupying the position held earlier by Einstein and MAX VON LAUE. At Zurich, where he remained from 1921 to 1927, Schrödinger investigated primarily thermodynamics and statistical mechanics and their application to the understanding of the nature of gases and solids. His wide-ranging interests included quantum theory, but he did not concentrate on this field until 1925, when Einstein commented favorably on LOUIS DE BROGLIE's wave representation of matter.

Quantum theory was born in 1900 when MAX PLANCK derived theoretically the relationship between a body's temperature and the radiation it emits, a feat that had eluded many other scientists. Planck assumed, as had others, that atomic oscillators emitted the radiation, but he added that the energy of the oscillators, and therefore of the emitted radiation, existed in small, discontinuous units, which Einstein later called quanta. The energy in a quantum was proportional to the frequency of the radiation. Although Planck's results were admired, his suppositions were startling because they were contrary to classical physics. In 1905 Einstein used quantum theory to explain certain aspects of the photoelectric effect, the

emission of electrons from metal surfaces irradiated by ultraviolet rays. He also pointed out the apparent paradox that light, known to propagate in continuous waves on the basis of centuries of evidence, also behaved like a particle under certain circumstances.

Some eight years later NIELS BOHR extended quantum theory to the atom, to account for the frequencies radiated by atoms excited in a flame or an electric discharge. ERNEST RUTHERFORD had shown that the mass of an atom was concentrated almost entirely in a central nucleus containing the positive electric charge, which was surrounded at relatively large distances by electrons carrying the negative charge that made the whole atom electrically neutral. Bohr proposed that the electrons were restricted to certain discrete orbits, corresponding to different levels of energy, and that the "jump" of an electron from one orbit to another of less energy resulted in emission of a photon whose energy equaled the difference between the two orbital energies. The frequency, in accordance with Planck's theory, was then proportional to the photon energy. Bohr's model of the atom thus established a relationship between different line spectra, which were characteristic of the emitting substance, and atomic structure. Despite initial successes, Bohr's atomic model soon required modification to reconcile discrepancies between theory and experiment. Moreover, the quantum theory at that stage did not provide a systematic procedure for solving many quantum problems.

A new feature was added in 1924 by Broglie's profound proposition that if electromagnetic waves such as light sometimes behaved like particles, as Einstein had demonstrated, then particles such as electrons might sometimes behave like waves. In Broglie's formulation, the frequency associated with a particle also was related to its energy, as in the case of a photon of light, but his mathematical expression was an equivalent relationship between wavelength and the particle's mass and velocity (momentum). Electron waves were experimentally demonstrated in 1927 by CLINTON J. DAVISSON and Lester H. Germer in the United States and by G. P. THOMSON in England. This finding in turn led to the development of the electron microscope in 1933 by ERNST RUSKA.

Stimulated by Einstein's comments on Broglie's ideas, Schrödinger tried to apply the wave description of electrons to a consistent quantum theory that did not depend on Bohr's inadequate atomic model. In a way, he wanted to bring quantum theory closer to classical physics, which contained many examples of mathematical treatments of waves. His first attempt, in 1925, failed. It included electron velocities up to nearly the velocity of light, which required incorporation of Einstein's special theory of relativity and its prediction of a significant increase in electron mass at high speeds. One reason for the failure was the omission of the electron property now called spin (an apparent toplike rotation), about which little was known at the time. His next attempt, in 1926, was restricted to slower electrons for which relativity could be ignored. It resulted in the Schrödinger wave equation, which described matter mathematically in terms of a wave function. Schrödinger called his theory wave mechanics. Solutions of the wave equation agreed with experimental observations and were to have a profound effect on later developments in quantum theory.

Shortly before, WERNER HEISENBERG, MAX BORN, and Pascual Jordan had published a different formulation, called matrix mechanics, which described quantum phenomena in terms of tabulations of observable quantities. The tabulations had the form of a mathematical array called a matrix and could be manipulated according to the rules of an established branch of mathematics. Matrix mechanics also accounted for observed experimental results but, unlike wave mechanics, contained no specific references to spatial coordinates or time. Heisenberg particularly insisted on foregoing any simple pictures or models in favor of dealing only with properties that could be determined by experiment.

Schrödinger went on to prove that wave mechanics and matrix mechanics were mathematically equivalent. Known collectively as quantum mechanics, the two theories provided the long-desired general framework for dealing with quantum phenomena. Many physicists favored wave mechanics because its mathematics was more familiar and the concepts seemed more "physical." Matrix operations are cumbersome.

Shortly after Heisenberg and Schrödinger developed quantum mechanics, P. A. M. DIRAC presented a more general theory that incorporated elements of Einstein's relativity theory with the wave equation. Dirac's equation applied to particles of all velocities. His electron theory intrinsically yielded the spin and magnetic properties of the electron and predicted the existence of antiparticles such as the positron and the antiproton, twins of their counterparts but with reversed electric charges.

"For the discovery of new productive forms of atomic theory," Schrödinger and Dirac shared the 1933 Nobel Prize for Physics. In the same year, Heisenberg was awarded the prize for 1932. In his presentation speech, Hans Pleijel of the Royal Swedish Academy of Sciences hailed Schrödinger for "establishing a new system of mechanics which also holds for motion within the atoms and molecules." Not only does wave mechanics provide a "solution to a number of problems in atomic physics," Pleijel said, "it also provides a simple and convenient method for the study of the properties of atoms and molecules . . . and it has become a great aid to the development of physics."

The physical significance of Schrödinger's wave function was not immediately apparent. For one thing, it could yield mathematically "imaginary" solutions involving the square root of -1. Schrödinger initially described the function as representing the wavelike spreading of the electron's negative electric charge. To avoid the imaginary solutions, he introduced the square of the function (multiped by itself). Born then identified the square of the magnitude of the wave function at a given point as proportional to the probability of finding the particle at that point in an experimental observation. Schrödinger disliked this interpretation because it precluded a definite statement of particle position and velocity. Along with Einstein and Broglie, he opposed the Copenhagen interpretation of quantum mechanics (so named because Bohr, who did extensive work on it, was in Copenhagen) because he was offended by its lack of determinism. The Copenhagen interpretation is based on Heisenberg's uncertainty principle, which states that the position and velocity of a particle cannot both be exactly known at the same time. The closer the position is pinpointed, the more indeterminate is the velocity, and vice versa. A subatomic event can be predicted only as the probabilities of various outcomes of experimental trials. Schrödinger also rejected the Copenhagen view of wave and particle models as "complementary," coexisting pictures of reality, and he continued to search for a description of the behavior of matter in terms of waves alone. He failed, however, and the Copenhagen interpretation became the dominant view.

In 1927 Schrödinger succeeded Planck, at Planck's request, in the chair of theoretical physics at the University of Berlin. He resigned in 1933, when the Nazis came to power, disgusted by Nazi persecutions and specifically in protest against a street attack on one of his assistants who was Jewish. He went to England as a guest professor at Oxford, where word of his being awarded the Nobel Prize arrived shortly after he did. In 1936, despite misgivings about his future, he accepted a position at the University of Graz, in Austria, only to be dismissed in 1938, when Germany annexed Austria. He escaped to Italy. Invited to Ireland, he became a professor in theoretical physics at the Dublin Institute for Advanced Studies, where he remained for seventeen years, conducting research on wave mechanics, statistics, statistical thermodynamics, field theory, and especially general relativity.

After the war, the Austrian government tried to persuade Schrödinger to return to Austria, but he refused as long as Soviet troops occupied the country. In 1956 he accepted a chair in theoretical physics at the University of Vienna, his last position.

In 1920 Schrödinger married Annemarie Bertel; they had no children. All his life he was a lover of nature and an avid hiker. In his career, he was known as a solitary, somewhat unconventional worker who accepted very few research students. Dirac described him as arriving at the prestigious Solvay Physics Conference in Brussels "carrying all his luggage in a rucksack and looking so like a tramp that it needed a great deal of argument at the [hotel] reception desk before he could claim a room."

Schrödinger, who was concerned with not only the scientific aspects but also the philosophical implications of physics, published several thoughtful studies while in Dublin. He was intrigued by the application of physics to biology, proposing a molecular approach to the study of genes in *What Is Life? The Physical Aspects of a Living Cell* (1944), a book that influenced a number of biologists, including FRANCIS CRICK and MAURICE H. F. WILKINS. He also published a volume of poetry. He retired in 1958 at the age of seventy-one and died three years later in Vienna.

In addition to the Nobel Prize, Schrödinger's many honors included the Matteucci Gold Medal of the National Academy of Sciences of Italy, the Max Planck Medal of the German Physical Society, and the German government's Order of Merit. He held honorary degrees from the universities of Ghent, Dublin, and Edinburgh, and he was a member of the Pontifical Academy of Sciences, the Royal Society of London, the Berlin Academy of Sciences, the Soviet Academy of Sciences, the Dublin Academy of Science, and the Academy of Science of Madrid.

SELECTED WORKS: Collected Papers on Wave Mechanics, 1928; Four Lectures on Wave Mechanics, 1928; Science and the Human Temperament, 1935; Statistical Thermodynamics, 1946; Space-Time Structure, 1950; Science and Humanism: Physics in Our Time, 1951; Studies in the Generalized Theory of Gravitation (2 vols.) 1951, with O. Hittmair; Nature and the Greeks, 1954; Expanding Universes, 1956; Mind and Matter, 1958; My View of the World, 1964.

ABOUT: Bernstein, J. A Comprehensive World, 1967; Biographical Memoirs of Fellows of the Royal Society, volume 7, 1961; Dictionary of Scientific Biography, volume 12, 1975; Scott, W. T. Erwin Schrödinger: An Introduction to His Writings, 1967; Thirring, W., and Urban, P. (eds.) The Schrödinger Equation, 1977.

SCHULTZ, THEODORE

(April 30, 1902–   )
Nobel Memorial Prize in Economic
    Sciences, 1979
(shared with W. Arthur Lewis)

The American economist Theodore William Schultz, the son of Anna Elizabeth (Weiss) and Henry Edward Schultz, was born and raised on a farm near Arlington, South Dakota. Owing to the severe shortage of labor during World War I, he worked on the family farm rather than attending high school, but in 1921 he enrolled in a short course in agriculture at South Dakota State College. In the economic depression that began in 1920, farm prices fell abruptly, banks failed, and many farmers suffered foreclosures. Hoping to learn the underlying causes of these economic events, Schultz reentered the college in 1924 and graduated with a B.S. in 1926. Going on to the University of Wisconsin for graduate studies, he received an M.S. in 1928 and a Ph.D. in agricultural economics in 1930.

The University of Wisconsin was at that time distinguished not only by its faculty but by its interdepartmental interest in social problems. Faculty members advised the state government and drafted farm legislation that later became the foundation of the New Deal's agricultural policies during the Great Depression of the 1930s. Schultz has acknowledged his "great intellectual debt" to his professors there.

In 1930 Schultz began teaching agricultural economics at Iowa State College (now Iowa State University) in Ames. Within four years he was named head of an innovative department in economic sociology. Its curriculum included general economics, agricultural economics, and rural sociology, and its faculty collaborated with economic theorists and statisticians in analyzing New Deal farm pro-

Patricia Evans

THEODORE SCHULTZ

grams. At the beginning of World War II, these scholars began a series of studies, the Wartime Food and Farm Policy Series, which, in the Wisconsin tradition, was designed to show how government policy could influence agricultural production in the national interest. In 1943, however, the college administration bowed to political pressure and recalled a report that offended Iowa's dairy industry by recommending the substitution of oleomargarine for butter, which was in short supply. Schultz and several of his colleagues resigned in protest. That year he joined the economics department of the University of Chicago as professor. In 1946 he became Charles L. Hutchinson Distinguished Service Professor there. He was appointed department chairman in 1952 and became professor emeritus in 1972.

During his early years at Chicago, Schultz became interested in worldwide agricultural problems. *Food for the World* (1945), a collection of papers presented at a conference he organized, addressed the factors affecting the supply of food, including the agricultural labor force, technology, the skill of farmers, and the rate of investment in farming. After World War II Schultz became intrigued with broad problems of economic development, an interest stimulated by West Germany's rise to industrial eminence as the result of financial and material aid under the Marshall Plan (named for GEORGE C. MARSHALL).

By the 1950s, when he led Technical Assistance for Latin America (TALA), a project that addressed all the segments of underde-

veloped countries including agriculture and economics, Schultz had already begun to investigate what he called "human capital." According to this concept, the educational level of a population governs its ability to make use of information and technology, for development as well as for redevelopment. Even though the cost of land and machinery had been carefully calculated, little was known about the value of human capital. In an article in the *Journal of Political Economy,* "Capital Formation by Education" (1960), Schultz constructed estimates of the value of human labor, including the cost of education as well as the value of the student's forgone labor. This cost, well known to farmers and working-class families who counted on their children to bolster the family's earning power as early as possible, had been ignored by economists and was considered controversial when it was introduced. Furthermore, Schultz's calculations were not and could not be entirely accurate, and he himself urged his students and colleagues to refine them. Nevertheless, the concept gradually gained acceptance until it was widely recognized that the developed world's investment in education (that is, in human capital) was crucial. Indeed, Schultz has been called the father of the human-investment revolution. For him, it is a broad concept that includes investment in education in the classroom, in the home, and at work as well as in health, education, and research.

In interdisciplinary symposia, papers, and roundtables, Schultz continued to argue for investment in human capital and in agriculture rather than in machinery and factories for undeveloped countries. He exhorted other scholars to discard what he considered the "intellectual mistakes" of traditional economists, especially their emphasis on the value of land instead of on "the quality of human agents." In opposition to the traditional treatment of economic relations, Schultz wanted to take into account the human actors behind the economist's mathematical formulas. His first publication on the subject of human capital was "The Emerging Economic Scene and Its Relation to High School Education," which appeared in the book *The High School in a New Era* in 1958. In the 1960s he launched the Comparative Education Center at the University of Chicago. Its first symposium was a discussion of schooling, investment in education and health, and on-the-job learning.

In his 1964 book *Transforming Traditional Agriculture,* Schultz argued that even primitive farmers behave rationally and use their resources efficiently within the framework of the information available to them. He emphasized the problem of dealing with disequilibrium and the risks and uncertainties inherent in adopting new farming methods, even when they are demonstrably superior. This analysis received impetus from the so-called Green Revolution, an effort to increase agricultural production through the application of genetic engineering and other technology, pioneered in part by NORMAN BORLAUG. Where loans and subsidies had not succeeded, hybrid seeds and new farming techniques were raising levels of crop production, notably in India, Pakistan, and the Philippines.

Later, Schultz became particularly interested in the education of women and in higher education for young people, who would use their knowledge in culturally suitable ways to increase the health, welfare, and economic prosperity of the peoples of the Third World. In short, Schultz is optimistic about the potential for development in poor agricultural nations. "Poor people in low-income countries are not prisoners of an ironclad poverty equilibrium that economics is unable to break," he has said. His strategy is therefore to break down pervasive distortions and focus attention on the choices and information that are available. His chief concern is to find policies that can enlarge opportunities in agriculture and then to exploit them as part of a dynamic growth strategy. In his examination of dynamic development, Schultz pays close attention to equity problems—to structures of earnings and their rising inequality within the context of dynamic development.

Schultz received the 1979 Nobel Memorial Prize in Economic Sciences together with W. ARTHUR LEWIS "for their pioneering research into economic development . . . with particular consideration of the problems of developing countries." In his presentation speech, Erik Lundberg of the Royal Swedish Academy of Sciences pronounced Schultz "the first scholar to systematize the analysis of the influence of investment on agricultural productivity." Schultz and his disciples, Lundberg continued, "have shown that the American economy has long had a higher return on 'human capital' than on physical capital."

Like Lewis, Schultz has combined teaching and research with practical investigation. Wherever he has traveled, to serve on commissions or organize symposia, he has visited farms. "Over the years I have ventured frequently into many low-income countries," he recalled in an autobiographical essay. "To learn what I wanted to know, I went to . . . rural communities and onto actual farms."

Schultz has been married since 1930 to the former Esther Florence Werth, with whom he has two daughters and a son. Described by a colleague at Yale as "a free-swinging, idealistic, and gregarious enthusiast who never tires of teaching," Schultz was still walking to the University of Chicago daily at the age of seventy-seven, when he received the Nobel Prize.

In addition to the Nobel Prize, Schultz has received the American Economic Association's Francis A. Walker Medal (1972) and the International Agricultural Economics Association's Leonard Elmhirst Medal (1976). He is a member of the American Economic Association and the National Academy of Sciences, a founding member of the National Academy of Education, and a fellow of the American Philosophical Society and the American Academy of Arts and Sciences. He has served as a director and vice president of the National Bureau of Economic Research; as governor of the International Development Research Centre, Canada; and as trustee of the Population Council, the Institute of Current World Affairs, and the International Agricultural Development Service. He has been awarded honorary degrees by Grinnell College, Michigan State University, the universities of Illinois and Wisconsin, the Catholic University of Chile, North Carolina State University, Dijon University, and South Dakota State College.

ADDITIONAL WORKS: Redirecting Farm Policy, 1943; Agriculture in an Unstable Economy, 1945; Measures for Economic Development of Underdeveloped Countries, 1951; The Economic Organization of Agriculture, 1953; The Economic Value of Education, 1963; Investment in Human Capital, 1971; Human Resources, Human Capital, 1972; Economic Distortions by the International Donor Community, 1980; Investing in People: The Economics of Population Quality, 1981.

ABOUT: New York Times October 17, 1979; Scandinavian Journal of Economics, number 1, 1980; Science December 21, 1979; Sills, D. L. (ed.) International Encyclopedia of the Social Sciences: Biographical Supplement, 1979.

SCHWEITZER, ALBERT
(January 14, 1875–September 4, 1965)
Nobel Prize for Peace, 1952

Albert Schweitzer, German medical missionary, theologian, and musicologist, was born in Kaysersberg, in Haute Alsace (now Haut-Rhin), the second child and elder son in a

ALBERT SCHWEITZER

family of five children. Shortly after Schweitzer's birth, his parents—Louis Schweitzer, a Lutheran minister, and the former Adele Schillinger—moved to another Alsatian pastorate, in Gunsbach. Because the French province of Alsace had been annexed by Germany at the end of the Franco-Prussian War in 1871, Schweitzer acquired German citizenship at birth. His parents were French, however, and he grew up speaking both French and German fluently. With musical tutoring from his father, he began studying the piano at the age of five, and within four years he was able to substitute occasionally for the organist at the village church.

While attending secondary school in nearby Münster and later in Mülhausen, he studied the organ under Eugene Munch, who first awakened the boy's lifelong passion for the music of Johann Sebastian Bach. Graduating in 1893, Schweitzer enrolled at the University of Strasbourg, where he specialized in theology and philosophy. He passed his first theological examination in 1898 and won a scholarship that enabled him to study philosophy at the University of Paris (Sorbonne) and to take organ instruction from Charles Marie Widor. Requiring only four months to write his dissertation, published as *Die Religionsphilosophie Kants* (*The Essence of Faith: Philosophy of Religion*), Schweitzer earned his Ph.D. in philosophy from Strasbourg in 1899. Two years later, he received his Ph.D. in theology from Strasbourg with a thesis on the significance of the Last Supper.

In 1902 the University of Strasbourg ap-

pointed Schweitzer professor of the Theological College of St. Thomas, and a year later he became its principal. In addition to lecturing and preaching, he played Bach at organ concerts and undertook scholarly research and writing. His major theological work was *Von Reimarus zu Wrede* (1906), translated as *The Quest of the Historical Jesus,* in which he rejected attempts to modernize Jesus or disprove his historical existence. He emphasized instead the eschatological character of Christ's ministry and interpreted his final suffering as a means to the coming of God's kingdom on earth.

Schweitzer became the foremost Bach authority of his time and an outstanding interpreter of his organ music. In *J. S. Bach* (1908), a biography expanded from a thesis he wrote on Bach to qualify for a Ph.D. in music from Strasbourg (1905), he reexamined Bach as a religious mystic whose music united text with "veritable nature poems." Schweitzer's contention that Bach's imagination was fundamentally pictorial remained unchallenged for many years. If the book was instrumental "in overthrowing the pedantic approach that viewed Bach's music as severe and intellectual," as Rosalyn Tureck wrote, "it also broke down . . . the romantic sentimentality with which Bach's performance was infused." Schweitzer also became an expert on the construction of organs. His *Deutsche und französische Orgelbaukunst und Orgelkunst* (German and French Organ Construction and Organ Playing, 1906) saved many old organs from so-called modernization and led to a reconsideration of the baroque organ.

His accomplishments as philosopher, theologian, and musicologist notwithstanding, Schweitzer felt the need to redeem a promise he had made to himself at the age of twenty-one. Wrestling with the question of what he owed the world for the advantages he enjoyed, he had resolved to pursue science and art until the age of thirty and then to devote himself, as he put it, "to the direct service of humanity." An article on the need for doctors in Africa, in a magazine published by the Paris Missionary Society, suggested to Schweitzer how he might act upon his desire. "My new occupation would be not to talk about the gospel of love," he explained later, "but to put it into practice."

Resigning his university position in 1905, Schweitzer enrolled in the University of Strasbourg Medical College, defraying his expenses by giving organ recitals. He passed the state medical examination in 1911, qualifying for a year's internship and course work in the specialty of tropical medicine. The following year he married Hélène Bresslau, a dedicated social worker who had assisted him for the past nine years; their daughter, Rhena, was born in 1919.

On Good Friday, 1913, Schweitzer and his wife set sail for Africa under the auspices of the Paris Missionary Society to establish a hospital at a mission at Lambaréné, French Equatorial Africa (now Gabon). There, in an isolated site on the Ogooué River, Schweitzer began to practice medicine under grueling, primitive conditions, improvising and sometimes constructing rudimentary hospital buildings. The need for his services was acute. Lacking medical care, the Africans suffered from malaria, sleeping sickness, yellow fever, dysentery, and leprosy. Aided by his wife, Schweitzer treated 2,000 cases in the first nine months alone.

In 1917 the Schweitzers, as German citizens in a French colony, were interned in France for the duration of World War I. After their release, Schweitzer spent the next seven years in Europe. Exhausted and ill and needing to pay off debts incurred at Lambaréné, he worked at the municipal hospital in Strasbourg, preached, and resumed organ recitals. At the invitation of Archbishop NATHAN SÖDER-BLOM in 1920, Schweitzer raised money by giving lectures and concerts at the University of Uppsala and elsewhere in Sweden. This trip seemed to renew his sense of purpose.

During these years Schweitzer developed a system of ethical principles that has been termed *Ehrfurcht vor dem Leben* (reverence for life). He expounded these principles in *Kulturphilosophie I: Verfall und Wiederaufbau der Kultur (Cultural Philosophy I: The Decay and the Restoration of Civilization)* and in *Kulturphilosophie II: Kultur und Ethik (Cultural Philosophy II: Civilization and Ethics)*, both published in 1923. "Let me give you a definition of ethics," he explained: "It is good to maintain and further life; it is bad to damage and destroy life. And this ethic, profound, universal, has the significance of a religion. It *is* religion." Reverence for life, he continued, "demands from all that they should sacrifice a portion of their own lives for others."

Setting out once again for Africa in 1924, Schweitzer returned to Lambaréné to find his old hospital in ruins, virtually reclaimed by the jungle. He selected another site nearby on which to rebuild. His new hospital eventually grew into a compound of seventy buildings staffed by unpaid physicians, nurses, and assistants. Schweitzer planned and helped construct this facility, which was modeled after a typical Af-

rican village. Except for the operating rooms, the buildings had no electricity. Animals roamed freely about, and family members were allowed to stay and assist patients during recovery. Schweitzer's aim was to win the trust of the Africans by practicing medicine in the familiar context of their own culture. By the 1960s Lambaréné could accommodate more than 500 patients.

For the remainder of his life, Schweitzer alternated periods of work in Africa with trips to Europe. During his absences from Lambaréné, he lectured, wrote, and gave recitals to raise funds for the hospital. Many honors came to him. In 1928 the city of Frankfurt awarded him the Goethe Prize in recognition of his "Goethe-like spirit" and service to humanity. During the 1930s newspaper publicity, his Bach recordings, and the translation of his works into other languages helped spread Schweitzer's fame. When war again broke out in Europe in 1939, drugs and other supplies came to Lambaréné from as far away as the United States, Australia, and New Zealand. After the war the tributes increased. Schweitzer received the Peace Award of the West German Association of Book Publishers and Sellers in 1951 for his lifetime devotion to building "an ethical world society." That year he was also elected to the French Academy.

Schweitzer was working at Lambaréné in 1953 when news arrived that he had been awarded the 1952 Nobel Peace Prize. In his presentation speech, Gunnar Jahn of the Norwegian Nobel Committee noted that Schweitzer "has shown us that a man's life and his dream can become one. His work has made the concept of brotherhood a living one, and his words have reached and taken root in the minds of countless men." Schweitzer could not leave his duties in Africa to attend the award ceremonies, and the prize was accepted by the French ambassador to Norway. Schweitzer used the prize money, along with other money raised by popular subscription, to establish a leper colony adjacent to the hospital at Lambaréné.

In late 1954 Schweitzer traveled to Oslo and on November 4 delivered his Nobel lecture, "The Problem of Peace." In it he stated his conviction that humanity must reject war for "an ethical reason; namely, that war makes us guilty of the crime of inhumanity." He asserted that "only when an ideal of peace is born in the minds of peoples will the institutions set up to maintain this peace effectively fulfill the function expected of them."

In 1957 Schweitzer issued a Declaration of Conscience, broadcast by radio from Oslo. In it he called on ordinary people worldwide to rise up and demand that their governments agree to ban the testing of atomic weapons. Shortly after this plea, 2,000 American scientists petitioned for an end to atomic testing, and the Campaign for Nuclear Disarmament was launched in Great Britain by BERTRAND RUSSELL and Canon Collins. Moreover, arms control talks began in 1958 and culminated in a formal superpower test-ban treaty five years later.

Assessments of Schweitzer's work have varied widely. Some have considered his decision to practice medicine in the jungle a squandering of talent. Others have accused him of escapism. Gerald McKnight, for example, in *Verdict on Schweitzer,* saw Lambaréné as a place that permitted Schweitzer absolute dominion and control. Many journalists found Schweitzer's paternalistic treatment of his African patients reminiscent of the days of the patronizing missionary. Critics noted that he demonstrated little understanding of Africa's nationalist aspirations. They also noted his egotism and authoritarianism in dealings with his staff. Many visitors questioned the low level of sanitation maintained at the hospital. Yet many, particularly in America, saw Schweitzer as a twentieth-century saint. In his later years, through personal appearances and photographs in the press, his craggy face, shock of hair, waterfall mustache, and rumpled white suit became familiar to people throughout the world. One visitor to Lambaréné noted especially his hands with "huge, responsive fingers equally expert at sewing up incisions, repairing a leak in the roof, resurrecting Bach on the organ, or setting down what Goethe could mean to a decaying civilization."

Schweitzer died at Lambaréné on September 4, 1965, and was buried there next to his wife, who had died in 1957. Control of the hospital passed to their daughter.

ADDITIONAL WORKS IN ENGLISH TRANSLATION: Paul and His Interpreters: A Critical History, 1912; The Mystery of the Kingdom of God, 1914; Christianity and the Religions of the World, 1922; On the Edge of the Primeval Forest, 1922; Memoirs of Childhood and Youth, 1925; The Mysticism of the Apostle Paul, 1931; The Forest Hospital at Lambaréné, 1931; My Life and Thought: An Autobiography, 1933; Indian Thought and Its Development, 1935; From My African Notebook, 1938; The Psychiatric Study of Jesus, 1948; Goethe, 1949; Goethe: Five Studies, 1951; The Problem of Peace in the World of Today, 1955; Peace or Atomic War? 1958; The Light Within Us, 1959; The Teaching of Reverence for Life, 1965; The Essence of Faith: Philosophy of Religion, 1966; The Kingdom of God and Primitive Christianity, 1968.

ABOUT: Anderson, E. The Schweitzer Album, 1965; Ber-

man, E. In Africa With Schweitzer, 1986; Berrill, J. Albert Schweitzer: Man of Mercy, 1956; Brabazon, J. Albert Schweitzer: A Biography, 1975; Cousins, N. Dr. Schweitzer of Lambaréné, 1960; Cremaschi, G. Albert Schweitzer, 1985; Franck, F. Days With Albert Schweitzer, 1959; Gollomb, J. Albert Schweitzer: Genius in the Jungle, 1949; Ice, J. L. Schweitzer: Prophet of Radical Theology, 1971; Jack, H. A. (ed.) To Dr. Albert Schweitzer, 1955; Joy, C. R. Music in the Life of Albert Schweitzer, 1953; Kraus, O., et al. Albert Schweitzer: His Work and His Philosophy, 1944; Langfeld, G. Albert Schweitzer: A Study of His Philosophy of Life, 1960; McKnight, G. Verdict on Schweitzer, 1964; Marshall, G., and Poling, D. Schweitzer: A Biography, 1971; Montague, J. F. The Why of Albert Schweitzer, 1965; Mozley, E. N. The Theology of Albert Schweitzer, 1951; Murry, J. M. The Challenge of Schweitzer, 1951; Payne, R. The Three Worlds of Albert Schweitzer, 1957; Picht, W. Albert Schweitzer: The Man and His Work, 1964; Roback, A. A. (ed.) The Albert Schweitzer Jubilee Book, 1945; Seaver, G. Albert Schweitzer: The Man and His Mind, 1947; Times (London) September 6, 1965.

SCHWINGER, JULIAN S.
(February 12, 1918–   )
Nobel Prize for Physics, 1965
(shared with Richard P. Feynman and
   Sin-itiro Tomonaga)

The American physicist Julian Seymour Schwinger was born in New York City, the second son of Benjamin and Belle (Rosenfeld) Schwinger. His father was a dress designer and manufacturer. A precocious child, the boy read scientific magazines, technical articles in encyclopedias, and most of the physics books in the nearby branches of the public library. He graduated from high school at the age of fourteen and entered the City College of New York, where he began writing original papers on quantum mechanics. One, published in the journal *Physical Review,* attracted the attention of I. I. RABI. Rabi arranged a scholarship for Schwinger at Columbia University that led to a B.S. in physics in 1936. Schwinger then studied at the University of Wisconsin at Madison and at Purdue University as a Tyndall Traveling Fellow, returning to Columbia in 1939 to earn his Ph.D.

After receiving his doctorate, Schwinger remained at Columbia for a year as a National Research Council fellow, followed by another year as a research associate at the University of California at Berkeley. Moving to Purdue in 1941, he served first as an instructor and then as an assistant professor. In 1943 he worked on the development of the atomic bomb at the University of Chicago Metallurgical Laboratory, as part of the Manhattan Project, before going on later that year to the Massachusetts Institute of Technology, where he participated in wartime research to improve radar. After

JULIAN S. SCHWINGER

the war, Schwinger became an associate professor at Harvard University, rising to full professor of physics and receiving an appointment as Higgins Professor in 1966. Since 1973 he has been a professor of physics at the University of California at Los Angeles.

The theoretical advances for which Schwinger received the Nobel Prize grew out of his long-standing interest in the fundamental nature of matter. As a result of his work, he was eventually able to combine two of the most important theories of twentieth-century physics: quantum mechanics and the special theory of relativity. Quantum mechanics was rooted in MAX PLANCK's radical insight, presented in 1900, that radiant energy consists of discrete units (quanta). It was formulated in the early 1920s in an attempt to explain the structure of the atom. In 1905 ALBERT EINSTEIN's special theory of relativity showed, among other things, the equivalence of mass and energy, one being transformable into the other.

In 1927 P. A. M. DIRAC used quantum mechanics and special relativity to express the relationship between electrons, a form of matter, and electromagnetic radiation, a form of energy that includes light, in his theory of quantum electrodynamics. According to Dirac's theory, if a quantum of electromagnetic energy, called a photon, had sufficient energy, it could "materialize" into an electron and a previously unknown particle, the positron. The positron was the electron's antimatter counterpart (same mass but opposite electric charge and other properties). Similarly, if an electron and a positron collided, they could annihilate

each other's mass and create a photon of energy. Dirac's work made it possible to understand more fully interactions between electrically charged particles and between particles and fields. For example, two nearby electrons interact by exchanging a series of photons. The reaction force on each electron (recoil) when it emits a photon and the impact when it absorbs a photon explain the electromagnetic repulsion between particles carrying the same kind of electric charge that tends to drive them apart. Because the exchanged photons are so short-lived and cannot be detected directly, they are said to be virtual particles.

According to the uncertainty principle, proposed in 1927 by WERNER HEISENBERG, the maximum energy of a particle varies inversely with the time available for measuring it. Virtual photons exist so briefly that their energies can be very large; moreover, as the interacting electrons come closer together, the lifetime of the virtual photons becomes still shorter, and the energy limit is raised further. When a single electron emits and then reabsorbs a virtual photon, the lifetime of the photon approaches zero; its allowable energy and its equivalent mass consequently approach infinity.

By the time Schwinger began his career, physicists recognized a logical absurdity in Dirac's theory. It predicted that every electron has both an infinite mass and an infinite electric charge. Since the electron's mass and charge were known to be not only finite but also very small, the prediction was clearly false. Although these infinities were puzzling, they could be (and were) ignored for many purposes, and Dirac's theory accurately predicted the outcomes of many experiments.

In 1947 WILLIS E. LAMB JR. and Robert C. Retherford found experimentally that one energy level of the electron in the hydrogen atom is shifted slightly from the value predicted by Dirac. About the same time, POLYKARP KUSCH and several colleagues at Columbia University discovered that the magnetic moment of the electron also differs slightly from the predicted value. To account for these discrepancies, Schwinger and SIN-ITIRO TOMONAGA, working separately, sought to revise quantum electrodynamics.

Instead of ignoring the apparently infinite mass and charge of the electron, Schwinger and Tomonaga made use of them. They said that the measured mass of the electron must consist of two components: the actual electron mass and the mass associated with the cloud of virtual photons (and other virtual particles) that the electron continually emits and reabsorbs. The infinite mass of the photon cloud and the infinite, but negative, mass of the electron nearly cancel each other, leaving a small, finite residue corresponding to the measured mass. To resolve the puzzle of the electron's infinite charge, Schwinger and Tomonaga postulated an infinitely negative bare charge that attracted a positive cloud of virtual particles, which screened out all but a finite residue of the negative bare charge corresponding to the commonly observed value.

Their procedure, a mathematical technique called renormalization, provided a secure conceptual foundation for quantum electrodynamics. Although it eliminated some infinities, it introduced others, such as infinite, negative masses. However, because an electron cannot be separated from its cloud of virtual particles, the infinite bare mass and charge can never be observed. Therefore, as both Schwinger and Tomonaga pointed out, the only measurable quantities in renormalization are finite, positive masses. No longer a controversial theory, renormalization of quantum electrodynamics has been verified experimentally and its predictions found to be in precise agreement with actual measurements.

Working independently about the same time as Schwinger and Tomonaga, RICHARD P. FEYNMAN approached quantum electrodynamics from a very different, but equally fundamental, point of view. He considered the end points of a path followed by a particle and the relative probabilities of possible interactions it might undergo along the way. These interactions could be expressed as a summation of the various probabilities. Although the resulting series could be exceedingly complex, Feynman described quantum-electrodynamic rules by which the interactions could be elegantly and simply presented in pictorial representations now called Feynman diagrams. Feynman diagrams proved to be a profound and convenient tool for treating quantum-electrodynamic problems.

Schwinger, Feynman, and Tomonaga shared the 1965 Nobel Prize for Physics "for their fundamental work in quantum electrodynamics, with deep-ploughing consequences for the physics of elementary particles." In his Nobel lecture Schwinger cited the extension of his work to other realms of physics. "Experiment reveals an ever-growing number and variety of unstable particles. . . . Surely one must hope that this bewildering complexity is the dynamic manifestation of some conceptually simpler substratum. . . . The relativistic field concept is a specific realization of this

general groping toward a new conception of matter."

In addition to his work on quantum electrodynamics, Schwinger has made significant contributions to nuclear physics and electromagnetic theory (waveguides). For example, in 1957 he proposed that the neutrino, a massless particle predicted and named by ENRICO FERMI, should occur in two forms, one associated with the electron and the other with a heavier particle called the muon. The two neutrino types were first distinguished in the 1960s. Schwinger has since done extensive research in theoretical particle physics, following his own unique approach.

In 1947 Schwinger married Clarice Carrol. They have no children.

In addition to the Nobel Prize, Schwinger has received the University Medal of Columbia University (1951), the Albert Einstein Award of the Lewis and Rosa Strauss Memorial Fund (1951), and the National Medal of Science of the National Science Foundation (1964). He has been awarded honorary degrees from Purdue, Harvard, Brandeis, and Columbia universities. Schwinger is a member of the National Academy of Sciences, the American Physical Society, and the New York Academy of Sciences, as well as a fellow of the American Association for the Advancement of Science and the American Academy of Arts and Sciences.

SELECTED WORKS: Differential Equations of Quantum Field Theory, 1956; The Theory of the Fundamental Interactions, 1957; Lectures on Quantum Field Theory, 1967; Discontinuities in Waveguides, 1968, with David Saxon; Particles and Sources, 1969; Quantum Kinematics and Dynamics, 1970; Particles, Sources, and Fields (2 vols.) 1970–1973; Selected Papers, 1937–1976, 1979; Einstein's Legacy: The Unity of Space and Time, 1985.

ABOUT: Current Biography October 1967; Deser, S. (ed.) Themes in Contemporary Physics, 1979; Science October 29, 1965; Waltz, G. What Makes a Scientist? 1959.

SEABORG, GLENN T.

(April 19, 1912–   )
Nobel Prize for Chemistry, 1951
(shared with Edwin M. McMillan)

The American chemist Glenn Theodore Seaborg was born in Ishpeming, Michigan, to Herman Theodore Seaborg, a machinist, and the former Selma Olive Erickson, both of Swedish descent. Ten years later, the family, which included a sister, moved to a suburb of

Los Angeles, California. As a student in the local public schools, Seaborg showed no particular interest in science until he was inspired by a high school chemistry teacher. He was valedictorian of his high school graduating class in 1929. With tuition money earned from jobs as a stevedore, apricot picker, farm laborer, laboratory assistant for a rubber company, and apprentice linotype operator, Seaborg studied at the University of California at Los Angeles and received a B.A. in chemistry in 1934. He then transferred to the University of California at Berkeley to study nuclear chemistry under the noted chemist Gilbert N. Lewis. For his work on the interactions of fast neutrons with lead, Seaborg was awarded a Ph.D. in 1937. He then became a research associate under Lewis and in 1939 an instructor in chemistry.

Seaborg's early work concerned the effects of isotopic variations on the chemistry of elements. Isotopes are different forms of the same element in which the atoms have the same number of protons but different numbers of neutrons. Working with colleagues, Seaborg discovered many new isotopes of common elements. In 1934 the Italian-born physicist ENRICO FERMI had attempted to create new elements that were heavier than uranium by adding neutrons to the uranium nucleus. Four years later, in Germany, OTTO HAHN, Fritz Strassmann, and Lise Meitner attempted this experiment and produced not the heavier (so-called transuranium) elements they expected but the fission or splitting of the uranium nucleus under neutron bombardment into smaller atoms, accompanied by the release of great amounts of energy. Meitner and Otto R. Frisch reported these findings in 1939. Reading about this work inspired Seaborg to continue the search for the transuranium elements—those with nuclei heavier than that of uranium, which at the time was the heaviest known element.

Using the cyclotron at the Lawrence Radiation Laboratory at Berkeley, one of Seaborg's co-workers, EDWIN M. MCMILLAN, generated neutrons (by directing the proton beam from the cyclotron onto a beryllium target), which then struck a uranium target. McMillan observed that not all uranium nuclei struck by neutrons underwent fission. The nuclei that absorbed neutrons without undergoing fission behaved as Fermi had predicted; they decayed by beta (electron) emission, thereby increasing in atomic number (number of protons) from 92 to 93 and creating a new element. This new element was called neptunium, after the planet Neptune, whose orbit lies beyond that of Uranus, for which uranium was named.

GLENN T. SEABORG

In 1941 Seaborg, McMillan, EMILIO SEGRÈ, Joseph Kennedy, and Arthur Wahl found that through further beta decay, neptunium formed an element with the atomic number 94. They named the new element plutonium, after Pluto, the outermost planet. When bombarded by slow neutrons, the isotope plutonium 239 was found to undergo fission with the release of neutrons and great energy. The researchers realized that this reaction had "the potential for serving as the explosive ingredient for a nuclear bomb," Seaborg said later. The fissionable uranium 233 isotope, which Seaborg and his associates discovered around the same time, offered another source of material for such a weapon.

In 1939, shortly after the outbreak of World War II, ALBERT EINSTEIN and several other scientists had warned the United States government that Germany might attempt to devise an atomic bomb, and in response to this possibility, the Manhattan Project was established in 1942. That year, at the age of thirty, Seaborg took a leave of absence from the University of California to join the Manhattan Project at the Metallurgical Laboratory of the University of Chicago. There he was appointed chief of the division working on chemical techniques that would allow the large-scale separation of plutonium from uranium. The problem was significant because only microgram amounts of material were available (1 microgram is 1 millionth of a gram). Moreover, the close chemical relationship between plutonium and uranium makes these elements extremely difficult to separate. Seaborg and his colleagues developed novel techniques for handling such small amounts of radioactive material, pioneering the experimental methods known as ultramicrochemical analysis. Naturally occurring plutonium was also found in minute quantities in pitchblende and carnotite ores. By 1944 Seaborg's group had achieved large-scale separation of plutonium from uranium and other radioactive fission particles. Enough plutonium had been produced by 1945 to build two nuclear weapons, which destroyed the Japanese cities of Hiroshima and Nagasaki.

Near the end of the war, in 1944, Seaborg resumed his research on the chemistry of the transuranium elements. Because only submicroscopic quantities of material could be produced, it was important to have a basis for predicting the chemical properties of the new elements. The periodic table, devised in 1869 by the Russian chemist Dmitry Mendeleev, lists the chemical elements in order of increasing atomic number. It is arranged in rows and columns, with elements in each column having similar chemical properties. Elements 57 to 71 are a closely related group originally called the rare earth elements, now termed the lanthanide series. Seaborg realized that the radioactive elements 89 through 94—actinium through plutonium—were a new series analogous to the lighter lanthanide series. This enabled him to predict and then discover elements 95 and 96. Separation of these two new elements from each other proved to be so difficult that the staff jokingly referred to them as "pandemonium" and "delirium." When they were completely identified, element 95 was named americium, and element 96 became curium (after PIERRE CURIE and MARIE CURIE).

Returning to Berkeley in 1946 as a full professor (the appointment was made in 1945 while he was still on leave), Seaborg continued his research on transuranium elements at the Lawrence Radiation Laboratory. He and his co-workers discovered additional members of the new actinide series: berkelium (atomic number 97), californium (98), einsteinium (99), fermium (100), mendelevium (101), and nobelium (102). They also discovered element 106, now called unnilhexium. Their work grew increasingly difficult, because the elements become more unstable as the number of protons and neutrons in the nucleus increases. In other words, the elements have shorter half-lives as the atomic mass increases. The half-life of an element is the time required for half of the original material to decay. The half-life of the

longest-lived uranium isotope is 4,510,000,000 years. The half-life of element 106 is less than a second. The short lifetime of the superheavy elements prevents their synthesis by the gradual addition of neutrons. Therefore, researchers synthesize them by colliding atomic nuclei and looking for nuclei that fused together before decaying. Physicists now theorize that the atomic nucleus itself may be composed of shells of protons and shells of neutrons, with possible islands of stability at which shells are said to be "filled" or "closed," just as atomic electrons may be considered to be grouped in shells that are closed for chemically stable elements. The closing of proton or neutron shells means reduced radioactivity and longer half-lives. If the addition of protons and neutrons to the nucleus can reach the condition of closed shells, new series of superheavy elements may possibly be created with long enough half-lives to be conveniently identified and tested for chemical properties.

Seaborg shared the 1951 Nobel Prize for Chemistry with Edwin M. McMillan "for their discoveries in the chemistry of the transuranium elements." In his presentation speech, A. F. Westgren of the Royal Swedish Academy of Sciences declared that Seaborg had "written one of the most brilliant pages in the history of the discovery of chemical elements," producing "not less than four more transuranium elements." Westgren added, "[NIELS] BOHR's prophecy that in the transuranium elements we are dealing with a group of substances of the same sort as the rare earth metals has thus been confirmed."

From 1954 to 1958, Seaborg was associate director of the Lawrence Radiation Laboratory as well as head of its nuclear chemistry research section. In 1958 he gave up research to serve as chancellor of the University of California at Berkeley, a post he held for three years. He was appointed head of the Atomic Energy Commission in 1961. Resigning from the commission in 1971, he returned to Berkeley as university professor of chemistry. His concern with science education led him to become a professor in the university's graduate school of education in 1983.

In 1942 Seaborg married Helen L. Griggs. They have four sons and two daughters. In his leisure time he enjoys playing golf, reading, and gardening.

The recipient of numerous awards, Seaborg has been honored with the Enrico Fermi Award of the United States Atomic Energy Commission (1959), the Franklin Medal of the Franklin Institute (1963), and the Priestley Medal of the American Chemical Society (1979). He is a member of the National Academy of Sciences, the American Chemical Society, the American Physical Society, the American Nuclear Society, and the American Association for the Advancement of Science, as well as a foreign member of ten national academies of science (including that of the Soviet Union). He has been awarded honorary degrees from more than forty universities. A noted administrator and policymaker, Seaborg has served as an officer in many organizations concerned with science, education, and television programming and with their impact upon society.

SELECTED WORKS: Comprehensive Inorganic Chemistry, 1953, with others; The Elements of the Universe, 1958, with Evans Valens; Freedom and the Scientific Society, 1962; Man-Made Transuranium Elements, 1963; The Nuclear Properties of the Heavy Elements (2 vols.) 1964, with others; Education and the Atom, 1964, with Daniel Wilkes; The International Atom: A New Appraisal, 1969; Man and Atom, 1971, with William Corliss; Nuclear Milestones, 1971; Kennedy, Khrushchev, and the Test Ban, 1981, with Benjamin Loeb.

ABOUT: Current Biography December 1961; Madden, C. F. (ed.) Talks With Social Scientists, 1968; National Cyclopedia of American Biography, volume H, 1952; New York Times July 16, 1985; Nova: Adventures in Science, 1983; Waltz, G. What Makes a Scientist? 1959; The Way of the Scientist, 1962.

SEFERIS, GEORGE

(February 29, 1900–September 20, 1971)
Nobel Prize for Literature, 1963

The Greek poet George Seferis (se fe′ ris) was born Georgios Stylianou Sepheriades in Smyrna, Turkey, the eldest of three children. His father was Stelios Sepheriades, a lawyer; his mother was the former Despina Tenekdis, the daughter of a prosperous landowner. Seferis's father ardently embraced the cause of Greek independence and worked closely with nationalist leader Eleutherios Venizelos after he became premier in 1909.

Emulating his father, an amateur poet who wrote in demotic (vernacular) Greek, Seferis began composing verse when he was about thirteen years old. In 1914 the family moved to Athens, since the outbreak of World War I further strained the already tense relations between Greeks and Turks in Asia Minor. In Athens, Seferis attended the First Gymnasium and learned classical Greek. He steeped himself in ancient Greek history, wandering for

GEORGE SEFERIS

hours through the Acropolis and the National Archaeological Museum.

When his father moved to Paris in 1918 to practice international law, Seferis followed, entering the Sorbonne that fall. He studied law while reading the French symbolists, Homer, and the demotic Greek poets in his spare time. Although he often wrote in French during this time, he gravitated toward demotic Greek, which afforded him a more natural voice than the Katharevusa, an artificial form of Greek taught in schools and used for official purposes. Some of his early poems appeared in the short-lived periodical *Vomos* (Altar) in 1921. That year, Seferis also passed his law exams and began graduate studies at the Sorbonne.

The following year, in retaliation for Greek military offensives in Ionia, Turkish troops razed Smyrna. The destruction of his birthplace "was the determining . . . event in Seferis's life," wrote the American scholar Walter Kaiser. "It is this that made him feel permanently and profoundly *heimatlos* [rootless], this that gives all his poetry its sense of irredeemable alienation."

Despite intense loneliness for his family and his native soil, Seferis remained in Paris and completed his doctoral requirements in 1924. After a year of additional study in London, during which time he continued his literary efforts, Seferis returned to Athens on Christmas Eve, 1925, and began preparing for the civil service examinations. He passed them the next year and obtained a post in the Ministry of Foreign Affairs.

Seferis's first volume of poetry, *Strofi,* was published in 1931 in a private edition of 150 copies. Its title, which means both "stanza" and "turning point," was "a prophetic term," according to the critic Anthony Zahareas, "since the collection opened new directions for Greek poetry." Rejecting what he considered to be the rhetorical excesses of his predecessors, Seferis combined a spare, precise diction with sophisticated slant rhymes and imagery that suggest his affinity with the symbolists, especially Paul Valéry.

Shortly after the appearance of *Strofi,* Seferis was posted to London, where he served first as proconsul and later as director of the Greek consulate. While in London, he wrote *I sterna* (The Cistern), which was published in Athens in 1932. During this time Seferis began reading the poems of T. S. ELIOT and translating them into Greek. The founding in 1935 of *Ta Nea Grammata* (New Letters), a literary review edited by George Katsimbalis, provided Seferis with a new outlet for his poems and also allied him with a group of writers who shared his commitment to modernism and the demotic.

With the publication of *Mithistorima* (*Mythical Story*) in 1935, Seferis's poetry displayed "a distinct change in style," according to his translators Edmund Keeley and Philip Sherrard. His new style was "much freer and more natural" than that of his earlier work. *Mithistorima*—which means "novel" but also connotes "myth" and "history"—expresses the poet's sense of past and present, exile and homeland. Its twenty-four sections are narrated by travelers who are at once present-day exiles and the Homeric voyagers of the *Odyssey,* at "one with the plough's blade or the keel of the ship." Through this twin persona, Keeley wrote, "the myth suddenly comes to life, the ancient and modern worlds meet in a metaphor without strain or contrivance."

On vacation in 1936, Seferis met Maria Zannou. They married five years later after her divorce from her first husband. For the next two years, Seferis served as Greek consul in Korçë, Albania. During this time he was also appointed head of the Greek Foreign Press Division.

As German forces overran the Balkan Peninsula in 1941, Seferis accompanied Greek government officials into exile, during which time they stayed in Crete, Egypt, South Africa, and Italy. While in Egypt, Seferis published a collection of his essays and *Imeroloyo katastromatos B'* (*Log Book II,* 1944), a collection of poems written during the years in

exile. The Greek government returned to Athens on October 18, 1944.

Almost at once, civil war broke out, and the government was entrusted to Archbishop Damaskinos, in whose regency Seferis acted as director of the Political Bureau from 1944 to 1945. During the summer of 1946, on his first vacation in nine years, he spent two months on the island of Poros, where a scuttled warship, the *Kihle* (*Thrush*), inspired a long poem of the same name.

Seferis's first publication in English was *The King of Assine and Other Poems,* translated by the English novelist and critic Rex Warner and published in 1948. That year, Seferis began a two-year assignment as counselor to the Greek embassy in Ankara, Turkey. Near the end of this tour, he returned to Smyrna (now known by its Turkish name, İzmir) for the first time since childhood. The visit was at once painful and cathartic. "I shall not have the courage to return," he confided in his journal. "One does not make such trips twice."

Posted to London in 1951, Seferis served for two years as minister-counselor to the Greek embassy, during which time he met T. S. Eliot. Between 1953 and 1956, he was Greek minister to Lebanon, Syria, Jordan, and Iraq and often visited Cyprus, where his sympathies lay with the movement to end British rule. His appointment as ambassador to the United Nations in 1956–1957 enabled him to work actively on behalf of Cypriot independence, which was granted in 1960.

After a year in Athens as head of the Second Political Division at the Ministry of Foreign Affairs, Seferis returned to London, this time as Greek ambassador. There he was awarded a Litt.D. degree from Cambridge University and the Foyle Prize for poetry. Although English translations of his work had begun to appear in magazines and literary journals, it was the publication in 1961 of Edmund Keeley and Philip Sherrard's *Six Poets of Modern Greece* that brought Seferis before a wider public.

Seferis retired from government service in 1962 and settled in Athens. The next year, he was awarded the 1963 Nobel Prize for Literature "for his eminent lyrical writing, inspired by a deep feeling for the Hellenic world of culture." "Seferis's poetic production is not large," said Anders Österling of the Swedish Academy in his presentation address, "but because of the uniqueness of its thought and style and the beauty of its language, it was to become a lasting symbol of all that is indestructible in the Hellenic affirmation of life."

"I find it significant," said Seferis upon accepting the award, "that Sweden wishes to honor not only this poetry, but poetry in general, even when it originates in a small people." In his Nobel lecture, Seferis spoke about the Greek literary revival. Summarizing the divergence between the purist and vernacular currents in the Greek language, he described his own early enthusiasm for the vitality he found in the demotic. Those who have adopted this tradition, he said, "represent to my mind the efforts of a body shackled for centuries which, with its chains finally broken, regains life and gropes and searches for its natural activity."

Seferis spent 1968 as a fellow at the Institute for Advanced Study in Princeton, New Jersey. While in the United States, he gave frequent readings of his work but refused to comment on the political situation in Greece, where a military coup had sent the monarch into exile the preceding year. After his return to Athens in 1969, however, Seferis publicly declared his opposition to the dictatorship, an act that further increased his popularity with the younger generation in Greece.

Seferis died on September 20, 1971, at the Evangelismos Hospital in Athens and was buried at the First Cemetery. Thousands of young people escorted his coffin, Keeley reported, "shouting 'immortal,' 'freedom,' 'elections,' and singing an early Seferis lyric."

"Few countries have had as painful a time in the twentieth century as Greece," the American critic James Goodman has written, and "no poet has expressed Greece's pain better than George Seferis." Yet, if Seferis expressed the abiding concerns of his nation and people, he also possessed what Keeley has called the "capacity to make the personal poetic." Even more important, in Keeley's view, "is his capacity to capture the metaphoric significance of some event that has moved him" and "to transform a personal experience or insight into a metaphor that defines the character of our times." Above all, Seferis sought an authentic poetic voice. "Seferis's tone of voice has a complicated purity about it that depends on his language always being quite genuine," observed the English critic Peter Levi; "everything in the poem . . . rings completely true."

A dedicated career diplomat, Seferis also managed to create a body of work that has been compared in its significance to that of Eliot, WILLIAM BUTLER YEATS, and other major European writers. "I proceed in life, all alone, without help," he once wrote in his journal. "I am fully conscious that we do not live in a time when the poet can believe that fame awaits him, but in a time of oblivion. This doesn't make me less dedicated to my beliefs," he added; "I am more so."

ADDITIONAL WORKS IN ENGLISH TRANSLATION: Six Poems From the Greek, 1946, with Angelos Sikelianos; Poems, 1960; Delphi, 1963; On the Greek Style, 1966; Collected Poems, 1924–1955, 1967; Three Secret Poems, 1969, with others; A Poet's Journal: Days of 1945–1951, 1974.

ABOUT: Books Abroad Spring 1968; Kapre-Karka, K. Love and the Symbolic Journey, 1982; Keeley, E., and Bien, P. (eds.) Modern Greek Writers, 1972; Keeley, E., and Sherrard, P. (eds.) Six Poets of Modern Greece, 1961; Plimpton, G. (ed.) Writers at Work, volume 4, 1976; Saturday Review November 30, 1963; Sherrard, P. The Marble Threshing Floor, 1956; Stanford, W. B. The Ulysses Theme, 1955; Tsatsou, I. My Brother George Seferis, 1982.

SEGRÈ, EMILIO
(February 1, 1905–   )
Nobel Prize for Physics, 1959
(shared with Owen Chamberlain)

The Italian-American physicist Emilio Gino Segrè (sā grā') was born in Tivoli, a small city near Rome, one of three sons of Giuseppe Segrè, a manufacturer, and Amelia (Treves) Segrè. He attended the primary school in Tivoli and then completed his secondary education at the Liceo Mamiani in Rome in 1922. He studied engineering at the University of Rome for five years before switching to physics, an interest since childhood. His transfer was partly influenced by the presence of ENRICO FERMI on the physics faculty. He and Fermi became close friends and colleagues, and his doctorate in physics in 1928 was the first to be awarded under Fermi's sponsorship.

After graduation, Segrè served a year's tour of duty as a second lieutenant of artillery in the Italian army before returning to the University of Rome as an instructor in physics. In 1930 he was promoted to assistant professor and received a Rockefeller Foundation grant that enabled him to study with OTTO STERN in Hamburg and with PIETER ZEEMAN in Amsterdam. Two years later he became an associate professor under Fermi.

Segrè's early research, before his military service, involved atomic spectroscopy, molecular beams, and X rays. He made important findings on the spectroscopy of forbidden lines and on the Zeeman and Stark effects. The Zeeman effect is the splitting of lines into several components by applying a magnetic field; the Stark effect (named for JOHANNES STARK)

EMILIO SEGRÈ

but has been detected spectroscopically in the stars.

Segrè made a second visit to Berkeley in 1938. In collaboration with Dale R. Corson and K. R. MacKenzie, he synthesized an artificial element with atomic number 85 (filling another gap in the periodic table), which was named astatine; and in 1940, with GLENN T. SEABORG and others, he discovered plutonium 239 (atomic number 94).

In the summer of 1938, the Italian government passed anti-Semitic civil service laws, and Segrè, a Jew and longtime opponent of the regime, decided to remain in the United States. As a research associate at the Berkeley radiation laboratory, he conducted further research on artificial radioactivity and nuclear isomerism (the existence of nuclei with the same numbers of protons and neutrons but in different energy states with different nuclear properties). Working with Seaborg, Segrè developed a valuable chemical technique for separating nuclear isomers. In 1944 he became an American citizen.

The discovery of plutonium 239 proved to have unforeseeable significance, for the new element was fissionable. Large quantities were synthesized starting in 1944, and plutonium was the prime source of energy in the atomic bomb dropped on Nagasaki, Japan, in August 1945. After the war, during which he was a group leader in the Los Alamos Laboratory of the Manhattan Project (the vast secret effort to develop the atomic bomb), Segrè returned to Berkeley as a full professor. His subsequent wide-ranging research in particle physics firmly established him as one of the leading theoretical and experimental pioneers of modern physics.

achieves the splitting by means of an electric field.

Later, Segrè's interest turned to nuclear physics. With Fermi and other colleagues, he became a pioneer in the field of neutron physics. The group bombarded many different materials with neutrons. In 1935 they discovered slow neutrons, reduced in speed by collisions with light nuclei, which later became important in the production of nuclear power. Target nuclei capture slow neutrons more readily than fast neutrons and are more likely to undergo nuclear reactions.

In 1936 Segrè was appointed chairman of the physics department of the University of Palermo. That year he also made his first visit to the United States, where he observed the cyclotron at the University of California at Berkeley. For some time he had been seeking an undiscovered element of atomic number 43 (43 protons in the nucleus), a gap in the periodic table of the elements between molybdenum (42) and ruthenium (44). At Berkeley, ERNEST O. LAWRENCE gave him a sample of molybdenum that had been bombarded with deuterons (nuclei of hydrogen with one neutron added to its proton). After returning to Italy, Segrè and a colleague subjected the sample to intense chemical analysis and succeeded in identifying trace amounts of element 43; he named it technetium, from *technētos,* a Greek word meaning "artificial," because it was the first element known to be produced artificially. Technetium, which proved valuable in medicine, does not occur naturally on the earth

In the early 1950s Segrè began a collaboration with OWEN CHAMBERLAIN in an effort to produce and detect a theoretically predicted particle called the antiproton, a negatively charged twin of the positive proton, with certain other opposite properties. More than twenty years earlier, P. A. M. DIRAC had proposed the existence of the positron, a positively charged twin of the familiar negative electron, on the basis of mathematical symmetry in relativistic quantum theory. CARL D. ANDERSON announced the discovery of this particle in 1932 in cosmic rays, high-energy radiation from extraterrestrial sources. This finding stimulated the search for other antiparticles, and, with the use of available particle accelerators, the meson (a particle with a mass between those of the electron and the proton) was found to have an antimeson counterpart. However, accelerator energies were not high enough to produce the antiproton.

Such energy became available with the construction of the bevatron (an acelerator capable of propelling particles to energies reaching billions of electron volts) at Berkeley. The bevatron had been designed partly with the antiproton experiment in mind. Segrè, Chamberlain, and their colleagues used the device to accelerate protons to an energy of 6.2 billion electron volts and direct them at copper atoms. Theory indicated that antiprotons could be produced at this energy. However, the antiprotons were expected to be relatively few, very short-lived (because they almost immediately contact protons, when both are annihilated), and extremely difficult to detect among the large number of other subatomic particles created by the powerful collisions.

The great achievement of Segrè, Chamberlain, and their associates was to devise ingenious techniques for detecting and indisputably identifying the elusive particles. They used an elaborate arrangement of magnets and magnetic focusing devices to sort out particles with the expected antiproton mass, negative charge, and velocity from the others; electronic counters and timers to clock the particles as they traveled a known distance; and a photographic emulsion that recorded proton-antiproton annihilations for final confirmation. Other means were also used to prevent erroneous results. Annihilations in the emulsion gave rise to a starlike spray of tracks showing that the incoming antiprotons on collision with protons vanished and created about five mesons per annihilation.

After accumulating conclusive evidence, the two scientists announced their verification of the existence of antiprotons in 1955. The experiment also established that antiprotons are not produced alone but in proton-antiproton pairs, just as positrons are produced in electron-positron pairs.

"For their discovery of the antiproton," Segrè and Chamberlain shared the 1959 Nobel Prize for Physics. As a result of their work, said Erik Hulthén of the Royal Swedish Academy of Sciences in his presentation speech, "today nothing is better known and [more] clearly elucidated than this process of pair formation and annihilation."

After receiving the Nobel Prize, Segrè continued his work in particle physics at Berkeley until his retirement in 1972. Two years later his career came full circle when he was appointed professor of nuclear physics at the University of Rome, where in 1975 he became professor emeritus.

In 1936 Segrè married Elfriede Spiro, with whom he had one son and two daughters. She died in 1970, and two years later he married Rosa Mines. In addition to his scientific papers, Segrè has shown a talent for popularizing physics in such works as his biography *Enrico Fermi, Physicist* (1970) and other books. He was also an enthusiastic fisherman and mountain climber.

A recipient of the August Wilhelm von Hofmann Medal of the German Chemical Society (1958) and the Stanislao Cannizzaro Prize of the National Academy of Sciences of Italy (1958), among other awards, Segrè is a member of the National Academy of Sciences, the National Academy of Sciences of Italy, the American Philosophical Society, the American Academy of Arts and Sciences, the Indian Academy of Sciences, the Heidelberg Academy of Sciences, the Uruguayan Society of Science, and the National Academy of Science of Peru. He has received honorary degrees from Palermo University, Gustavus Adolphus College, the University of San Marcos in Lima, and Tel Aviv University. He is also a fellow of the American and Italian physical societies.

SELECTED WORKS: Nuclei and Particles: An Introduction to Nuclear and Subnuclear Physics, 1964; From X Rays to Quarks: Modern Physicists and Their Discoveries, 1980; From Falling Bodies to Radio Waves: Classical Physicists and Their Discoveries, 1984.

ABOUT: Current Biography April 1960; Libby, L. M. The Uranium People, 1979; New York Times October 25, 1959; Physics Today December 1959; Stuewer, R. H. (ed.) Nuclear Physics in Retrospect.

SEIFERT, JAROSLAV

(September 23, 1901–January 10, 1986)
Nobel Prize for Literature, 1984

The Czech poet Jaroslav Seifert (sī' fert) was born in Zizkov, a suburb of the Czechoslovakian capital of Prague, then in the Austro-Hungarian Empire. His father, who was at one time a factory worker, became the manager of a small general store selling groceries, clothes, handcrafted objects, and small drawings by local artisans and artists. Young Seifert spent his afternoons delivering these goods on foot to customers throughout Prague, gaining a thorough knowledge of a city that is one of the richest cultural, architectural, and musical centers in Europe. This intimate acquaintance

JAROSLAV SEIFERT

with Prague would eventually exert a profound influence on his poetry.

Although he was not a conscientious student and did not even finish high school, Seifert nonetheless studied literature, music, and foreign languages. His proficiency and enthusiasm enabled him to become, while still in his teens, the editor of several periodicals, a translator of French and Russian literature, and a published poet. Around the end of World War I, when the Czechs finally gained their independence from Austria-Hungary, he began his professional career as a journalist on the Communist party newspaper *Rudé Právo* (Red Rights), and he also worked in the Communist party's publishing house and bookshop. Like many Czechs at the time, Seifert viewed with admiration the Russian Revolution of 1917.

In 1920, under the leadership of the liberal nationalist Tomáš Masaryk, Czechoslovakia officially became a constitutional republic with a democratic parliamentary system of government. That year Seifert helped found an avant-garde literary movement called Devětsil (Group of Nine), influenced by the French writer Guillaume Apollinaire and by the dadaists and dedicated to the concept of "poetism." Using the devices of free association and surreal imagery while experimenting with syntax and logic and emphasizing the visual impact of ordinary objects, Seifert and the Czech Devětsil writers sought to create poetry that would stimulate not just the imagination but life itself.

Most of Seifert's early books, including *Město v slzách* (City in Tears, 1921), *Samá láska* (All Love, 1923), *Svatební cesta* (The Honeymoon,

1925), and *Slavík zpíva špatně* (The Nightingale Sings Badly, 1926), echo the poetist style. His themes, however, vary. What begins as verse full of revolutionary enthusiasm for the proletariat cause ends as poetry that expresses disenchantment with the Communist movement. By 1929 Seifert had rejected the Communists' Stalinist orientation; he signed a manifesto critical of the Communists' new censorship policies, gave up some politically oriented editorial posts, and joined the Social Democratic party. From this point onward, Seifert concentrated mainly on overtly nonpolitical subjects in his creative work, turning to the themes of love, nostalgia for childhood innocence, admiration of women, and the workings of memory.

During this time Seifert also pursued his journalistic career, writing articles for various dailies and periodicals in Prague. He became editor in chief of the theater monthly *Nova Scena* (New Line) in 1930, and he continued to contribute to local daily newspapers throughout the 1930s and 1940s.

During the 1930s Seifert's poetry began to take on the fresh, natural language and heightened lyricism that marked his mature work. This poetry was also the last written during the free democratic state established by Masaryk, who died in 1937. In fact, Masaryk's death and the resulting publication of Seifert's elegy *Osm dní* (*Eight Days*, 1937) effectively ended the period when the poet's political and social themes could be directly enunciated. Pressure from Adolf Hitler caused Eduard Beneš, Masaryk's successor and disciple, to resign; a pro-Nazi government was installed in Prague, and Czechoslovakia fell under German control.

In *Světlem oděná* (Dressed in Light, 1940), *Kamenny most* (The Stone Bridge, 1944), and *Přilba hlíny* (Helmet of Clay, 1945), Seifert dealt with love, beauty, and the Czech heritage, while indirectly condemning war, Nazism, and censorship. With his celebration of the Prague uprising of 1945 in *Přilba hlíny,* he achieved true stature as a Czech national poet.

After the war, as Czechoslovakia came under pro-Soviet Communist domination, Seifert returned to apolitical themes, stressing such common human concerns as the importance of a happy childhood, the influence of parents, the love of simple beauties, and the search for lasting values. In *Píseň o Viktorce* (Song of Viktorka, 1950), which the novelist and critic Josef Škvorecky called Seifert's lyrical masterpiece, the poet attempted to create a symbol of Czech beauty. In his collections *Mozart v Praze* (*Mozart in Prague: Thirteen Rondels,* 1951) and *Praha* (Prague, 1958), he celebrated the rich cultural heritage of his native city. Both the aristocratic and the folk influences of Czechoslovakia blend in these works to form what some critics have called a new mythology powerful enough to unify an entire nation.

After the death of Stalin in 1953, an intellectual thaw in Czechoslovakia revealed that many important writers and artists had become dissatisfied with the official policy of socialist realism. At the 1956 convention of the Czechoslovakian Writers' Union, Seifert became a spokesman for artistic freedom. Condemning the government's persecution of writers and the Communist party's dogmatic attitude toward literature, Seifert proclaimed, "If a writer is silent, he is lying." Despite widespread demand for the relaxation of censorship, the party soon reestablished control over what was published and banned works it labeled as revisionist. Nonetheless, it was during the short-lived thaw that Seifert first came to the attention of the Nobel committee.

The 1960s saw a cautious process of de-Stalinization in Czechoslovakia as a number of social and political reforms were gradually introduced. The reform movement culminated in the "Prague Spring" of 1968, when the new Czech Communist party first secretary, Alexander Dubcek, promised to introduce "socialism with a human face." Censorship was lifted, and Czech writers enjoyed a greater freedom of expression than had ever before been permitted in any Eastern-bloc Communist nation. Czech writers played a leading role in this incipient democracy, issuing the so-called 2,000 Words manifesto denouncing abuses by the previous government. Seifert's role in this movement is uncertain.

In August 1968, alarmed by this open challenge to Communist doctrine, Soviet troops entered the country and put down the reforms of the Dubcek government. In 1969 Seifert was elected president of the Czechoslovakian Writers' Union, but resigned a year later when he was asked to follow new restrictions issued by the Communist party in response to Soviet demands. Seifert's work then began to disappear from bookstores. During the 1970s his work circulated in Czechoslovakia primarily in underground *samizdat* (typewritten and mimeographed) editions. Again eschewing direct political comment in his work, he wrote of the loss of youth, eternal beauty, the love of women, the growing ugliness of the modern technological world, and the vagaries of the poetic life. In 1977 Seifert reentered the political world

when he became one of about 500 Czech writers to sign the Charter on Human Rights condemning the "uncalled-for imprisonment" of fellow writers and urging the government to honor the Czech constitution and the Helsinki Agreement on Human Rights.

That year, after more than fifty years of publishing, Seifert's work first came to the attention of English-speaking readers, appearing in translation in *London Magazine* in England and in the *Hampden-Sydney Poetry Review* in the United States. By 1983 three of his books had become available in English translations: *Odlévání zvonů* (*The Casting of Bells,* 1967), *Morový sloup* (*The Plague Monument,* 1967), and *Deštník z Piccadilly* (*An Umbrella From Piccadilly,* 1979).

Seifert was awarded the 1984 Nobel Prize for Literature for a "poetry which, endowed with freshness, sensuality and rich inventiveness, provides a liberating image of the indominable spirit and versatility of man." Poor health prevented Seifert from attending the presentation ceremony and receiving the award, which was accepted by his daughter, Jana Seifertová. In making the presentation, Lars Gyllensten of the Swedish Academy described the "lightness of touch, sensuality, melody and rhythm, a lively ingenuity and playfulness alternating with feeling," that characterize Seifert's poetry. "[Seifert] is not, however, a naive artist," Gyllensten added, pointing out the poet's mastery of sophisticated poetic form and his affinities with the European modernists and the avant-garde.

In Czechoslovakia little official state recognition was given to the announcement that Seifert had won the Nobel Prize. However, the world attention focused on Seifert forced the Czech government at least to acknowledge the importance of the prize by reporting it in the official press. Although Czech law prohibits the publication of unauthorized speeches in Czechoslovakia, Seifert's Nobel lecture was published in the West. Referring to Czechoslovakia's long struggle for independence, Seifert declared that "our language became our most important means of expressing our national identity." As a result, he said, even in recent times "poetry has occupied a very important position in our cultural life. It is as though poetry, lyrics were predestined not only to speak to people very closely . . . but also to be our deepest and safest refuge, where we seek succor in adversities we sometimes dare not even name."

In 1985, when Seifert became the first Czech writer to receive an honorary degree from an

American college (Hampden-Sydney College in Hampden-Sydney, Virginia), he was allowed to write an uncensored acceptance speech for the occasion. The degree was presented to Seifert in Prague by the American poet Galway Kinnell. "Often . . . my poetry is a spontaneous and unprogrammatic retelling of events I witnessed or participated in, dictated by an impatient heart that always seems restless," wrote Seifert, who also reminded his audience that "poetry should never lose any of its human warmth or its function to remind humans of their earthly existence."

Until his death on January 10, 1986, from a heart ailment, Seifert lived quietly in a small house in the Prague suburbs with his wife Marie. The couple were married in 1928 and had a son and a daughter.

The significance of Seifert's work is the subject of ongoing study by scholars and critics in a number of countries. In Czechoslovakia each of his books has been issued in a limited edition that has sold out quickly and has not been reprinted. His poems continue to be translated into English despite the fact that, as the Czech poet Miroslav Holub has remarked, his "emphasis on musical technique and verbal manipulations make him almost untranslatable into English." Working in structured forms emphasizing rhyme, metrics, and syllabics, Seifert developed a style laden with encoding and double entendre. Yet his Czech readers seem to delight in the art of veiled comment in a poetry that is still clear and direct. In his preface to the translation of *The Plague Monument,* the American critic William E. Harkins wrote, "Seifert has long been the most respected of Czech poets, and he may very likely be regarded as the greatest."

ADDITIONAL WORKS IN ENGLISH TRANSLATION: Otruba, M., and Besat, Z. (eds.) The Linden Tree, 1962; The Plague Column, 1982; Russian Bliny, 1983; The Selected Poetry of Jaroslav Seifert, 1986.

ABOUT: French, A. Czech Writers and Politics, 1982; The Poets of Prague, 1969; Novak, A. Czech Literature, 1976; World Literature Today Autumn 1984.

SEMENOV, NIKOLAY N.

(April 15, 1896–September 25, 1986)
Nobel Prize for Chemistry, 1956
(shared with Cyril N. Hinshelwood)

The Russian physical chemist Nikolay Nikolaevich Semenov (syi myô′ nôf) was born to Nikolai Semenov and Elena Dmitrieva Se-

NIKOLAY N. SEMENOV

menov in Saratov in the southeast European part of Russia. After completing high school in 1913 in Samara (now Kuibyshev), he enrolled in the Physical-Mathematical Department of the University at St. Petersburg (now Leningrad), where he was active in the group of students surrounding the famous Russian physicist Abram F. Joffe.

Upon graduating from the university in 1917, the year of the Russian Revolution, Semenov worked as an assistant in the physics department of Tomsk University in Siberia. At Joffe's invitation Semenov returned to Leningrad in 1920 as deputy director of the Leningrad Physical-Technical Institute and chief of its Electron Physics Laboratory. In collaboration with PYOTR KAPITZA, Semenov proposed the measurement of the magnetic moment of an atom in an inhomogeneous magnetic field and described the experimental procedure in a 1922 publication. The method was later successfully developed by OTTO STERN and Walter Gerlach.

The first scientific problem that seems to have interested Semenov was the ionization of gases. While still a university student, he published his first paper dealing with collisions between electrons and molecules; after returning from Tomsk, he began more extensive investigations into dissociation and recombination, including the ionization potential of metal and salt vapors. The results of these and other studies appeared in the book *Electron Chemistry* (1927), which he wrote in collaboration with two of his students. Semenov was also interested in the molecular aspects of the adsorption and condensation of vapors on hard surfaces. His investigations revealed the relationship between vapor density and the temperature of the condensation surface. In 1925, together with Yakov I. Frenkel, a noted theoretical physicist, he developed a comprehensive theory of these phenomena.

Another of Semenov's interests at this time was the study of electric fields and electric phenomena in gases and solids. In particular, he investigated the passage of electric current through gases, as well as the breakdown of solid dielectrics (electrically inert solids) induced by electric currents. From the latter research Semenov and Vladimir A. Fock, best known for his work in quantum physics, developed a theory that ascribed the breakdown to the effects of heat. This, in turn, stimulated Semenov to work out his first important contribution to the science of combustion, a thermal theory of gaseous explosions. According to this theory, under certain conditions the heat generated in a chemical reaction will not have time to dissipate before it raises the temperature of the reactants, causing the reaction to speed up and produce even more heat. If the evolution of heat increases sufficiently fast, the reaction may result in an explosion.

Shortly after completing this work in 1928, Semenov was appointed professor at the Leningrad Physical-Technical Institute, where he helped organize the Physical-Mechanical Department and also began instruction in physical chemistry. At his urging, and with the help of other colleagues interested in physical chemistry, the Electron Physics Laboratory became the Institute of Chemical Physics of the Soviet Academy of Sciences in 1931. Semenov was its first director. In 1932 he became a full member of the Academy of Sciences, having been elected a corresponding member in 1929.

By this time Semenov was deeply involved in his investigations of chain reactions, which are series of self-propagating steps in a chemical reaction that, once started, continue in domino fashion until stopped by a chain-terminating step. Although the German chemist Max Bodenstein had first suggested the possibility of such reactions in 1913, there was no theory to explain the steps by which a chain reaction proceeds or to predict its rate. The key to a chain reaction is the initial formation of a free radical, an atom or a group of atoms that has a free (unpaired) electron and is thus extremely active chemically. Once formed, a free radical interacts with a molecule in such

a way that the free radical is regenerated as one of the products of the reaction. The newly formed free radical can then interact with another molecule, and the reaction continues until circumstances prevent the free radical from replacing itself.

A particularly important chain reaction is the branched chain, proposed in 1923 by the physicists H. A. Kramers and J. A. Christiansen. In this reaction the free radical not only regenerates itself but actually multiplies, creating new chains and causing the reaction to proceed faster and faster. The actual path of the reaction depends on a number of external constraints, such as the size of the container in which the reaction occurs; if the free radicals increase quickly enough, the reaction can become explosive. In 1926 two of Semenov's students had first observed this phenomenon while studying the oxidation of phosphorus vapor by steam. The reaction did not follow accepted theories of chemical kinetics at that time, and Semenov's explanation—that it was the result of branched-chain reactions—was rejected by Max Bodenstein, then the acknowledged authority on chemical kinetics. Within two years, however, as a result of the extensive research carried out by Semenov and by CYRIL N. HINSHELWOOD, who was working independently in England, it had become clear that Semenov was right.

In 1934 he published *Chemical Kinetics and Chain Reactions,* in which he showed that many chemical reactions, including polymerization, proceed by means of a chain or branched-chain mechanism. During the following decades, Semenov and other researchers who accepted his theories continued to work out the details of chain reaction theory, analyzing abundant experimental data, much of it from his own students and co-workers. A later book, *Some Problems of Chemical Kinetics and Reactivity,* published in 1954, summarizes the experimental findings from the intervening years of work on his theory.

Semenov and Hinshelwood shared the 1956 Nobel Prize for Chemistry "for their researches into the mechanism of chemical reactions." In his Nobel lecture Semenov reviewed his work on chain reactions: "The chain reaction theory makes it possible to come nearer to the solution of a main problem in theoretical chemistry—the connection between reactivity and the structure of the particles entering into the reaction. . . . It is hardly possible to enrich chemical technology to any extent without this knowledge or even to achieve decisive success in biology." He went on to say that "the mutual endeavors of learned men in every country are needed in the resolution of this most important problem, in order to explain the secrets of chemical and biological processes, to the benefit of peaceful development and the well-being of mankind."

After his appointment as a professor at Moscow University in 1944, Semenov continued to publish papers on a variety of topics even into the 1980s, including a 1977 paper on the oxidation of phosphorus vapor, still a fruitful topic after fifty years. The Institute of Chemical Physics was moved to Moscow during World War II, and many of its main areas of research stem directly from Semenov's early interests, although the tools of investigation have become mass spectrometry and quantum mechanics.

Even during his final years, Semenov was characterized by colleagues as infused with scientific enthusiasm, creativity, and intense energy. A tall, thin man, he enjoyed hunting, gardening, and architecture. He and his wife, Natalya Nikolaevna Burtseva, whom he married in 1924, lived in Moscow, where she taught singing. They had one son and one daughter. Semenov died at the age of ninety on September 25, 1986.

For his work in developing chain reaction theory Semenov received the Soviet government's Stalin Prize in 1941. His other awards included seven Orders of Lenin, the Order of the Red Banner of Labor, and the Lomonosov Gold Medal from the Soviet Academy of Sciences. Semenov also received honorary degrees from a number of European universities and was selected as an honorary fellow of the Royal Society of London. In addition to holding numerous offices in the Soviet Academy of Sciences, he was elected to membership in the academies of many other countries, including the United States. A member of the Communist Party of the Soviet Union, he was elected a delegate to the Supreme Soviet (Soviet parliament) in 1947 and was a candidate member of the party's Central Committee from 1961 to 1966.

SELECTED WORKS: On the Fringe of the Unknown, 1967; Science and Community, 1973.

ABOUT: Current Biography March 1957; New York Times September 29, 1986; Science November 23, 1956.

SEPHERIADES, GEORGIOS
See SEFERIS, GEORGE

SHAW, GEORGE BERNARD
(July 26, 1856–November 2, 1950)
Nobel Prize for Literature, 1925

The Irish dramatist George Bernard Shaw was born in Dublin, the youngest of three children of George Carr Shaw and the former Elizabeth Gurley. Shaw's father, a civil servant and later an unsuccessful corn merchant, was an alcoholic. His mother was a talented singer and amateur musician. Although belonging to Dublin's Protestant ascendancy, socially and financially the family had fallen on hard times, a fact of which the young Shaw was painfully conscious. Tutored at home and educated briefly at Catholic and Protestant day schools, Shaw left school before the age of sixteen to work at a Dublin real estate agency. When his mother invited John Vandeleur Lee, a fashionable music teacher, to share the household and expenses for a time, the adults' living arrangement was that of a platonic ménage à trois. Growing up in a musical environment, Shaw developed a love of music and taught himself to play opera scores on the piano.

Leaving her husband, Elizabeth Shaw and her two daughters followed Lee to London in 1873. By the time he joined them three years later, George Bernard Shaw had decided to become a writer, and he began ghostwriting articles about music for Lee. Each morning Shaw wrote five pages of fiction; in the afternoon he studied at the British Museum; and in the evening he attended lectures and debates. Because the five novels he produced between 1879 and 1883 were turned down by every publisher he approached, he depended on his mother's meager earnings as a music teacher.

In 1882 a lecture by Henry George, the American single-tax reformer, attracted Shaw to social issues and socialist ideas. In addition to George's *Progress and Poverty* and other works on economics, Shaw read Karl Marx's *Das Kapital*. In 1884 he and Sidney Webb joined the Fabian Society, formed earlier that year to promote socialist principles and social welfare legislation. Shaw served on the society's executive committee for twenty-seven years, often lecturing three times a week on its behalf.

While reading in the British Museum, Shaw met William Archer, a drama critic, who sug-

GEORGE BERNARD SHAW

gested that he turn his talents to the theater. In 1886 Archer commissioned him as art critic for the *World,* a successful weekly review. From 1885 to 1888 Shaw also reviewed books for the *Pall Mall Gazette.* Under the pseudonym Corno di Bassetto, he also wrote music criticism for the *Star,* a new mass-circulation newspaper. In 1890 he became music critic for the *World.* The poet W. H. Auden later called Shaw "probably the best music critic who ever lived."

In 1895 Shaw became drama critic of the London-based journal *Saturday Review.* He used the position to attack Henry Irving, the leading actor-manager of the day, for neglecting the work of Henrik Ibsen and for rewriting that of William Shakespeare. He also ridiculed the popular plays of Arthur Wing Pinero and the mechanically constructed melodramas of Augustin Scribe and Victorien Sardou ("Sardoodledum," Shaw called them), advocating instead a theater of social reform that portrayed contemporary life realistically. He had already outlined his program in a lecture on Ibsen delivered to the Fabian Society in 1890. Published the following year as *The Quintessence of Ibsenism,* it was the first English study of the Norwegian playwright. The book aroused interest in J. T. Grein's production of Ibsen's *Ghosts,* and Grein subsequently asked Shaw to write a play for his Independent Theater Society. Shaw obliged by rewriting a work he had begun five years earlier in collaboration with William Archer. Calling it *Widowers' Houses,* he delivered it for production in 1892, thus launching his career as a dramatist at the age of thirty-six.

It was an inauspicious beginning: *Widowers' Houses* received uncomplimentary notices and closed after two nights. During the next six years, Shaw wrote nine full-length plays and one short play. No producer was willing to mount his second play, *The Philanderer* (1893), a disenchanted story of a socially approved, but unhappy, marriage. Because his third play, *Mrs. Warren's Profession* (1893), concerned prostitution, it was banned from public performance in England until World War I.

Refusing to bow to censorship, Shaw began publishing his plays privately. He subsidized them with his earnings as an increasingly celebrated journalist and with financial assistance from Charlotte Payne-Townshend, an Irish heiress and socialist whom he married in 1898. (The marriage, in accordance with her wishes, probably remained unconsummated; in any event, the couple had no children. Shaw's affairs with a number of women during his marriage have been documented.) The two-volume collection *Plays: Pleasant and Unpleasant* appeared the year of his wedding. In it Shaw began the practice of writing elaborate descriptions of setting, characters, and action so that the plays could be read almost like novels. The "unpleasant" plays, Shaw explained, used their "dramatic power . . . to force the spectator to face unpleasant facts," such as the discrepancy between middle-class English society's gentility and the unsavory source of its income in *Mrs. Warren's Profession.* The "pleasant" plays—*Arms and the Man* (1894), *Candida* (1897), *The Man of Destiny* (1897), and *You Never Can Tell* (1899)—attempted to show that reality is superior to romantic literary traditions.

Although *Candida* was a major success in New York in 1903, Shaw did not achieve a reputation as a playwright in England until he, his wife, and Harley Granville-Barker leased the Royal Court Theater to demonstrate the possibilities of noncommercial theater. The John Vedrenne–Harley Granville-Barker productions of Shaw's plays that took place between 1904 and 1907 were so popular that out of a total of 988 performances at the Royal Court Theater, Shaw's works were performed 701 times.

Man and Superman (1905), one of Shaw's greatest critical and popular successes, is a philosophical comedy that presents his ideas about religion, women, sex, and marriage. An operatic third act (titled "Don Juan in Hell" and often performed separately) with characters from Mozart's *Don Giovanni* "turns a comedy of manners into a cosmic drama," wrote the critic Margery Morgan. *Major Barbara, a* social satire also written in 1905, offers a taut intellectual debate between religious belief and secular ambition, between hypocrisy and sincerity. In *Pygmalion* (1913), Shaw expounded his theories on phonetics while satirizing the social mannerisms that reinforce class distinctions. *Pygmalion* later became the basis for the musical *My Fair Lady* (1956) by Alan Jay Lerner and Frederick Loewe.

During World War I, Shaw directed his energies toward politics. He published "Common Sense About the War" in the November 1914 issue of the *New Statesman,* a left-wing review he had founded the previous year with Beatrice and Sidney Webb. This eighty-page essay, which blamed both Britain and Germany for the war, advocated negotiations to end the fighting and derided blind patriotism. It cost Shaw his membership in the Dramatist's Club and the friendship of several colleagues. In 1916 he wrote in defense of the Irish Easter Rebellion and offered help to the Anglo-Irish diplomat Sir Roger Casement. Casement was later executed by the British as a traitor for seeking to enlist German support for the Irish independence movement.

After the war, in *Heartbreak House,* Shaw dramatized the self-destructiveness of the generation responsible for the bloodshed. This discursive comedy mingles politics and economics with surrealistic explorations of the characters' fantasy lives. *Back to Methuselah* (1922), Shaw's most ambitious and difficult work, consists of five linked plays that begin in the Garden of Eden and end in A.D. 31,920. In it Shaw elaborated on HENRI BERGSON's notions of creative evolution and his own Fabian conviction that human intelligence can transform society.

After the canonization of Joan of Arc in 1920, Shaw found a new heroine and the subject of his only true tragedy, *Saint Joan* (1924). His Joan exhibits the quick wit, practicality, and energy Shaw admired, as well as the innocence and imagination that threaten the Machiavellian outlook Shaw ascribes to the clergy.

The Nobel Prize for Literature was reserved in 1925 and awarded to Shaw the following year "for his work, which is marked by both idealism and humanity, its stimulating satire often being infused with a singular poetic beauty." His plays, said Per Hallström of the Swedish Academy, "have given him the position of one of the most fascinating dramatic authors of our day, while his prefaces have given him the rank of the Voltaire of our time."

Disapproving of prizes and honors on principle, Shaw did not attend the award ceremony. In his absence, the award was accepted by Arthur Duff, British ambassador to Sweden. With the prize money, Shaw endowed a new Anglo-Swedish Literary Foundation to promote translations, especially those of August Strindberg's work.

In 1928 Shaw published *The Intelligent Woman's Guide to Socialism and Capitalism,* a sensible discussion of political and economic issues addressed to the nonspecialist. In his final plays, Shaw turned away from realism toward greater abstraction, employing some of the conventions of ancient Greek comedy.

After his wife's death in 1943, Shaw moved from London to his country home in Hertfordshire. Shortly after his ninety-fourth birthday, Shaw fell and fractured his thigh while working in the garden; he died on November 2, 1950.

Much critical controversy about Shaw's work stems from the clash between his comic sense and his use of theater for social reform. In his own day he was accused of frivolity, of having, according to Max Beerbohm, "too irresponsible a sense of humor." Yet in Shaw's wit, W. H. Auden recognized the spirit of Rossini, with "all the brio, the humor, the tunes, the clarity, and the virtuosity of that great master of opéra bouffe." To the English poet and critic Stephen Spender, Shaw's political and philosophical concerns made him "a two-dimensional giant moving in his own two-dimensional world." But the scholar John Matthews perceived him as "a resident alien: a clear-sighted, perceptive Irishman at large in a society . . . which had less real meaning for him than the people he knew personally and felt affection for." "He is in the great tradition," wrote American critic Jacques Barzun. "Using everything in the theatrical shop . . . and holding in solution all that was stirring in the wide world of the author's mind, Shaw's plays form a dramatic legacy of the first magnitude."

ADDITIONAL WORKS: Cashel Byron's Profession, 1886; An Unsocial Socialist, 1887; The Perfect Wagnerite, 1898; Love Among the Artists, 1900; Three Plays for Puritans, 1901; Socialism for Millionaires, 1901; Passion, Poison, and Petrification, 1905; The Irrational Knot, 1905; Dramatic Opinions and Essays, 1906; The Sanity of Art, 1908; The Admirable Bashville, 1909; The Glimpse of Reality, 1909; The Fascinating Foundling, 1909; The Doctor's Dilemma, Getting Married, and The Shewing-Up of Blanco Posnet, 1911; Misalliance, The Dark Lady of the Sonnets, and Fanny's First Play, 1914; The Music-Cure, 1914; O'Flaherty, V. C., 1915; The Inca of Perusalem, 1915; Augustus Does His Bit, 1916; Overruled, 1916; Annajanska, the Bolshevik

Empress, 1919; Peace Conference Hints, 1919; The Apple Cart, 1930; Immaturity, 1930; What I Really Wrote About the War, 1931; Our Theatres in the 'Nineties (3 vols.), 1931; Doctor's Delusions, 1931; Pen Portraits and Reviews, 1932; The Adventures of the Black Girl, 1932; Fabian Essays in Socialism, 1932; The Political Madhouse in America, 1933; Prefaces, 1934; Short Stories, Scraps, and Shavings, 1934; Three Plays, 1934; The Simpleton, The Six of Calais, and The Millionairess, 1936; London Music in 1888–89, 1937; In Good King Charles's Golden Days, 1939; Everybody's Political What's What, 1944; Geneva, 1946; The Crime of Punishment, 1946; Sixteen Self-Sketches, 1949; Buoyant Billions, Farfetched Fables, and Shakes Versus Shaw, 1951; Advice to a Young Critic, 1956; An Unfinished Novel, 1958; Religious Speeches, 1963; Collected Letters (4 vols.), 1964–1985; Shaw: An Autobiography (2 vols.), 1969–1970; Shaw's Music (3 vols.), 1981.

ABOUT: Bentley, E. R. Bernard Shaw, 1947; Berst, C. A. Bernard Shaw and the Art of Drama, 1973; Chapplow, A. (ed.) Shaw: The Villager and Human Being, 1961; Chesterson, G. K. George Bernard Shaw, 1909; Crompton, L. Shaw the Dramatist, 1969; Ervine, S. J. Bernard Shaw, His Life, Work, and Friends, 1956; Grene, N. Bernard Shaw, A Critical View, 1984; Harris, F. Bernard Shaw, 1931; Henderson, A. George Bernard Shaw: His Life and Works, 1911; Irvine, W. The Universe of G. B. S., 1949; Joad, C. E. M. Shaw, 1949; Kaufman, R. J. (ed.) G. B. Shaw: A Collection of Critical Essays, 1965; Kronenberger, L. The Thread of Laughter, 1952; Mayne, F. The Wit and Wisdom of Bernard Shaw, 1967; Meisel, M. Shaw and the Nineteenth-Century Theatre, 1963; Morgan, M. M. The Shavian Playground, 1972; Ohmann, R. M. Shaw: The Style and the Man, 1962; Pearson, H. George Bernard Shaw, His Life and Personality, 1942; Rattray, R. F. Bernard Shaw: A Chronicle, 1951; Rosset, B. C. Shaw of Dublin: The Formative Years, 1964; Smith, J. P. The Unrepentant Pilgrim, 1965; Strauss, E. Bernard Shaw: Art and Socialism, 1942; Valency, M. The Cart and the Trumpet, 1973; Weintraub, S. The Unexpected Shaw, 1982; Wilson, C. Bernard Shaw: A Reassessment, 1969.

SHERRINGTON, CHARLES S.

(November 27, 1857–March 4, 1952)
Nobel Prize for Physiology or Medicine, 1932
(shared with Edgar D. Adrian)

The English neurophysiologist Charles Scott Sherrington was born in Islington, a suburb of London, where his mother, Anne (Brookes) Sherrington, was visiting at the time. His father, James Norton Sherrington, a country doctor in Caister, Yarmouth, died when Charles and his two younger brothers were small children. Sherrington's mother later married Caleb Rose, a physician, archaeologist, geologist, and classicist who influenced Sherrington's choice of a medical career and stimulated his wide-ranging interest in art, history, and philosophy.

After attending the Ipswich Grammar School for five years, Sherrington entered St. Thomas's Hospital, London, in 1876 to study medicine. In 1879 he studied as a noncollegiate

CHARLES S. SHERRINGTON

student, under the physiologist Michael Foster, at Cambridge University. An improvement in his family's finances enabled Sherrington to enter Gonville and Caius College, Cambridge University, a year later.

A report issued in 1884 concerning specialized functions of different parts of the brain was the first of 320 scientific papers to be published by Sherrington. His research, performed in collaboration with John Newport Langley (another associate of Foster's), involved the use of animals whose brains had been partially removed surgically by the technique perfected by Friedrich Goltz, a German neurologist. Sherrington went to Strasbourg in late 1884 to learn the technique from Goltz himself. After becoming a licensed physician the next year, he was sent to Spain and Italy to investigate cholera outbreaks. The research eventually led him to Berlin in 1886 to study pathology under Rudolf Virchow and bacteriology under ROBERT KOCH. Returning to London, Sherrington was appointed to a lectureship in systemic physiology at St. Thomas's Hospital in 1887.

Neurophysiology was Sherrington's primary interest, and under the influence of W. H. Gaskell, a lecturer at Cambridge, he began his studies of reflex action and the physiology of the spinal cord. A reflex, such as pulling one's hand back from a fire, is a response to a stimulus from the outside world, but the action requires no conscious thought. Researchers believed that reflex actions might be explained on a mechanical basis, without knowing how the mind itself works. Goltz's research on animals from which the entire brain had been removed conclusively established that many reflexes are controlled solely by the spinal cord, an organ that is much simpler to study than the brain. Sherrington's first papers on the spinal cord appeared in 1891, the same year he was appointed physician-superintendent of the Brown Institute for Pathological Research in London, where studies of animal diseases were made.

At the time, there was little knowledge about the anatomical distribution of the spinal roots, the sensory and motor nerves that emerge from the spinal cord at each vertebra. Sherrington spent many years mapping the areas of the body innervated (supplied by nerves) by each spinal root, either by cutting the root and noting which functions were lost or by observing the results of electrical stimulation.

This painstaking, undramatic research led to several important discoveries. In 1894 Sherrington established that only two-thirds of the nerves in muscles are motor nerves, which bring instructions from the central nervous system to the muscles; the rest are sensory nerves (proprioceptors), which deliver information from the muscles to the central nervous system. He also found that nerves from a given root usually lead to more than one group of muscles, while a given muscle receives nerves from more than one root. The net effect is that muscles do not function as individual units; the nervous system acts to integrate the body as a coherent, coordinated whole.

After he became Holt Professor of Physiology at the University of Liverpool in 1895, Sherrington used these anatomical studies as the foundation for work on spinal reflexes, especially the well-known knee-jerk response. His research was performed on "spinal" monkeys or cats prepared by Goltz's technique, so that isolated reflexes could be observed without interference from the brain.

This detailed examination of the functional relationships of individual nerves was a landmark in neurology. From his findings, Sherrington deduced many of the basic principles by which the nervous system operates. One such concept was the reciprocal innervation and inhibition of antagonistic muscles. For example, if the leg is to move during the knee-jerk reflex, the muscles that straighten the leg must be stimulated, but also those that bend the leg must relax. Sherrington discovered that the nerves that control the two sets of muscles are connected in such a way that stimulation of one inhibits the other. Similar relationships are found throughout the nervous system. As

Sherrington later said, "The whole quantitative grading of the operations of the spinal cord and brain appears to rest upon mutual interaction between the two central processes, *excitation* and *inhibition,* the one no less important than the other."

Sherrington's theories of how nerves react and interact were influenced by the neuroanatomist SANTIAGO RAMÓN Y CAJAL, whom Sherrington had met during his trip to Spain in 1886. Ramón y Cajal proposed that the nervous system is not a continuous network of indistinguishable fibers but is composed of individual nerve cells, or neurons, with discrete interactions. Sherrington realized that his observations on reflexes could be explained as impulses transmitted by contact between nerves, and in 1897 he gave the name *synapse* to the junction where one neuron interacts with the next. This fundamental concept was a bridge between studies of reflex transmission and electrophysiology.

In 1906 Sherrington summarized the basic principles of neurophysiology in *The Integrative Action of the Nervous System,* a book that is still required reading for neurologists. He became Waynflete Professor of Physiology at Oxford University in 1913, where he remained until his retirement twenty-three years later. His neurophysiology studies were interrupted by World War I, when he served as chairman of the Industrial Fatigue Board. Sherrington also investigated such topics as the integration of reflexes into coordinated actions, the importance of inhibitory effects in the nervous system, and the development of new research techniques and apparatus. Among his colleagues at Oxford were the neurophysiologists EDGAR D. ADRIAN and JOHN C. ECCLES.

The 1932 Nobel Prize for Physiology or Medicine was awarded jointly to Adrian and Sherrington "for their discoveries concerning the functions of neurons." Göran Liljestrand of the Karolinska Institute said in his presentation speech, "[Sherrington's] discoveries have ushered in a new epoch in the physiology of the nervous system." Liljestrand added that they had shown themselves "to be of great importance for the understanding of certain disturbances within the nervous system."

Sherrington was not only a dedicated researcher but also an excellent teacher. He was fond of telling his students that "man's analysis of his sensible world seems to have outstripped his analysis of his own mind." Many future neurophysiologists and neurologists were stimulated by his lectures and demonstrations; some of them went on to distinguished careers.

In 1892 Sherrington married Ethel Mary Wright; they had a son. She died in 1933. After his retirement at the age of seventy-nine, Sherrington continued to lecture and write and to serve as adviser to several museums and health services. He died of heart failure in 1952 at Eastbourne, England.

Sherrington, who was knighted in 1922, also received the Royal Medal (1905) and Copley Medal (1927) of the Royal Society. He was a fellow of the Royal Society (serving as president from 1920 to 1925) and held honorary degrees from the universities of Oxford, London, Sheffield, Birmingham, Manchester, Liverpool, Wales, Edinburgh, Glasgow, Paris, Uppsala, and Harvard and from many other institutions.

WILLIAM SHOCKLEY

SELECTED WORKS: Lectures on the Method of Science, 1906; Mammalian Physiology, 1919; The Assaying of Brabantius and Other Verses, 1925; Reflex Activity of the Spinal Cord, 1932; Selected Writings, 1939; Man and His Nature, 1941; Memories, 1957.

ABOUT: Cohen, H. Sherrington, 1958; Dictionary of Scientific Biography, volume 12, 1975; Eccles, J. C., and Gibson, W. C. Sherrington: His Life and Thought, 1979; Granit, R. Charles Scott Sherrington: An Appraisal, 1966; Liddell, E. G. The Discovery of Reflexes, 1960.

SHOCKLEY, WILLIAM
(February 13, 1910–   )
Nobel Prize for Physics, 1956
(shared with John Bardeen and Walter H. Brattain)

The American physicist William Bradford Shockley was born in London, England, where business had taken his parents, William Hillman Shockley, a mining engineer, and the former May Bradford, who had been a federal deputy surveyor of mineral lands. When Shockley was three years old, the family returned to the United States and settled in Palo Alto, California, where he received his early education. His interest in science, stimulated by a neighbor who taught physics at Stanford University, was encouraged by his parents.

After graduating from Hollywood High School in 1927, Shockley attended the University of California at Los Angeles for one year and then transferred to the California Institute of Technology, where he obtained a B.S. in physics in 1932. He did his graduate work at the Massachusetts Institute of Technology (MIT) on a teaching fellowship and received a Ph.D. in physics in 1936 for the thesis "Calculations of Wave Functions for Electrons in Sodium Chloride Crystals." The solid-state physics he learned at MIT and his work on crystals proved to be the foundation of his career research.

Shockley took a job at the Bell Telephone Laboratories in Murray Hill, New Jersey, in 1936, specifically to work with CLINTON J. DAVISSON. Shockley's first project involved the design of an electron multiplier, a special kind of vacuum tube that acted as an amplifier. He then became involved in solid-state physics research and in 1939 proposed a plan for developing solid-state amplifiers as an alternative to vacuum tubes. Although it proved to be unfeasible with the materials available at the time, the concept coincided with the laboratory's goal of developing a telephone exchange that used electronic devices instead of mechanical switches.

During World War II, Shockley turned to military projects, working first on the electronic design of radar equipment at a Bell Labs field station. From 1942 until 1944 he served as research director of the Antisubmarine Warfare Operations Research Group set up by the Navy Department at Columbia University in New York City; from 1944 to 1945 he was an expert consultant to the Office of the Secretary of War. The new field of operations research treated military objectives, such as optimum patterns for dropping depth charges against submarines and the timing and targeting of aerial bombardments, as problems subject to scientific methods of analysis and solution.

Shockley returned to Bell Labs in 1945 as director of the solid-state physics research program. His team included JOHN BARDEEN, a theoretical physicist, and WALTER H. BRATTAIN, an experimental physicist. The group resumed the investigation, begun before the war, of the class of materials called semiconductors. Semiconductors have an electrical conductivity between that of good conductors, such as most metals, and that of insulators. Their conductivity tends to vary greatly with temperature and with the kinds and concentrations of impurities in the material. Semiconductors had already been used as rectifiers, devices that conduct electricity primarily in only one direction and so are able to convert alternating current into direct current. Early crystal radios used the contact between a "cat's whisker" (a curl of wire) and a piece of galena crystal (a semiconductor mineral) to rectify the antenna signals picked up from radio waves.

Crystals were replaced by vacuum tubes, which became the most prevalent electronic devices. Amplifier tubes opened the way for the growth of the electronics industry, but they were relatively short-lived, required power to heat the cathodes, and had bulky, fragile glass enclosures. Shockley and his group hoped to overcome these limitations by making amplifiers out of rectifying semiconductors.

Although the application of quantum theory to solid-state physics had enlarged the knowledge of semiconductor properties, the theory had not been adequately confirmed by quantitative experiments. Shockley planned to simulate the principle of the vacuum tube by applying an electric field across a semiconductor to control the current flow. Although his calculations had indicated that this field effect would produce amplification, he was unable to produce practical results. Bardeen suggested that electrons trapped in a surface layer were preventing the field from penetrating to the interior. This insight led to a series of studies of surface effects that helped three researchers understand the complex behavior of semiconductor devices.

It had been known that conduction in semiconductors involved two kinds of charge carriers: electrons and "holes." The electrons available for conduction were those in excess of the number binding the atoms together into a solid crystal. Holes represented missing electrons. Since an electron carries a negative charge, an unfilled electron state behaves like a positive charge of the same magnitude. Holes

also appear to move, although not at the same rate as electrons and in the opposite direction. When a nearby electron moves "forward" to fill a hole, it leaves a new hole behind so that the hole appears to move backward. Shockley's group found that the contribution of hole flow to the total current had not been sufficiently appreciated. Impurities introduced into the pure crystal in the form of atoms that do not exactly fit into the regular crystal structure selectively produce regions of excess electrons (N type) or excess holes (P type).

In 1947 Bardeen and Brattain made the first successful amplifying semiconductor device, or transistor (transfer plus resistor). Their final version consisted of a block of N-type germanium with two closely spaced point contacts (cat's whiskers) on one face and a broad metal electrode on the opposite face. A small positive voltage was applied to one contact (emitter), relative to the broad electrode (base), and a large negative voltage to the second contact (collector). A signal voltage fed to the emitter, in series with the bias voltage, appeared greatly amplified in the collector circuit. The basic action was the introduction of holes into the germanium by the emitter contact and the flow of the holes directly to the collector contact where they increased the collector current.

Further developments quickly followed. Shockley suggested replacing the point contacts with rectifying junctions between P- and N-type regions in the same crystal. Such a device, called a junction transistor, was made in 1950. It consisted of a thin P region sandwiched between two N regions, all regions having separate external contacts. The junction transistor largely replaced the point-contact transistor because of greater ease of manufacture and superior performance. With improvements in the techniques for growing, purifying, and processing silicon crystals, Shockley's first idea for a field-effect transistor was realized and is the type most widely used in electronic devices. Small silicon chips bearing hundreds of thousands of transistors are now being made, and the number is still rising. The chips have made possible the rapid development of modern computers, hand-held calculators, sophisticated communications equipment, control instruments, hearing aids, medical probes, and other electronic devices.

Shockley, Bardeen, and Brattain shared the 1956 Nobel Prize for Physics "for their researches on semiconductors and their discovery of the transistor effect." In his presentation speech, E. G. Rudberg of the Royal Swedish

Academy of Sciences called their achievement "a supreme effort—of foresight, ingenuity, and perseverance."

Shockley remained at Bell Labs until 1955, serving as director of transistor physics research during his last year. He also held various positions outside the laboratories, including visiting lecturer at Princeton University in 1946, scientific adviser for the Policy Council of the Joint Research and Development Board during 1947–1949, and member of the United States Army Scientific Advisory Panel from 1951 to 1963. In 1954–1955 he was both visiting professor at the California Institute of Technology and director of research for the Weapons Systems Evaluation Group of the United States Department of Defense. From 1958 to 1962 he was also a member of the Air Force Scientific Advisory Board.

After leaving Bell Labs, Shockley formed the Shockley Semiconductor Laboratory (later the Shockley Transistor Corporation, a subsidiary of Beckman Instruments Inc.) in Palo Alto, to develop transistors and other devices. After changing hands twice, the firm was closed in 1968.

In 1962 Shockley became a member of the President's Science Advisory Committee on Scientific and Technical Manpower. He also served on the Scientific and Technical Advisory Committee for the National Aeronautics and Space Administration. In 1963 he was appointed the first Alexander M. Poniatoff Professor of Engineering and Applied Science at Stanford University, where he taught until his retirement in 1975.

Teaching at Stanford stimulated Shockley's interest in the thought process itself and how scientific thinking might be improved. His concerns for the betterment of society gradually led him to expound controversial views on human genetics. He became convinced that the population was threatened with a deterioration in mental capacity because those with low intelligence quotients (IQs) bred far more children than did those with higher IQs. His statements, general at first, concentrated increasingly on race. In 1970, for example, he told the National Academy of Sciences that his research led him "inescapably to the opinion that the principal cause of our American Negro problems is racially genetic." For such views he was severely criticized by many public figures, and by scientists, who pointed out that his contributions to physics did not lend scientific credence to his judgments on genetics.

In addition to his work on semiconductors and transistors, Shockley has made contributions to the use of properties of magnetic materials for computer memory banks and to electromagnetic theory. His other interests have included energy bands in solids, plastic properties of metals, the theory of grain boundaries (interfaces between tiny crystallites that combine to form a multicrystalline body), and order and disorder in alloys. He holds over ninety patents.

Shockley married Jean Alberta Bailey in 1933; they had two sons and a daughter. The marriage ended in divorce in 1955. The same year, he married Emmy Lanning, a psychiatric nurse. When he was younger, Shockley was an eager mountain climber, which his second wife said he approached not as relaxation but as a problem to be solved, and for which he would train vigorously. In later years he enjoyed sailing, swimming, and skin diving.

In addition to the Nobel Prize, Shockley has received the Medal for Merit of the United States government (1946), the Morris E. Liebmann Award of the Institute of Radio Engineers (1952), the Oliver E. Buckley Solid-State Physics Prize of the American Physical Society (1953), the Comstock Prize of the National Academy of Sciences (1954), the Holley Medal of the American Society of Mechanical Engineers (1963), and the Medal of Honor of the Institute of Electrical and Electronics Engineers (1980). Shockley was elected to the Inventors Hall of Fame and the National Academy of Sciences and is a fellow of the American Physical Society, the American Academy of Arts and Sciences, and the Institute of Electrical and Electronics Engineers.

SELECTED WORKS: Electrons and Holes in Semiconductors, 1950; Imperfections of Nearly Perfect Crystals, 1952; Mechanics, 1966, with Walter A. Gong.

ABOUT: Current Biography December 1953; Goodell, R. The Visible Scientists, 1977; National Geographic Society. Those Inventive Americans, 1971; Science 84 November 1984; Thomas, S. Men of Space, volume 4, 1963.

SHOLOKHOV, MIKHAIL
(May 24, 1905–February 2, 1984)
Nobel Prize for Literature, 1965

The Russian novelist Mikhail Aleksandrovich Sholokhov (shô' lu kôf) was born on a farm near the cossack village of Veshenskaya in the Rostov region of southern Russia (now part of the Russian Soviet Federated Socialist Republic). In his books Sholokhov immortalized

MIKHAIL SHOLOKHOV

the Don River, which flows through the southern part of the republic, and the cossacks, the proud peasant-soldier caste of that region who fought fiercely on the side of the czar in prerevolutionary Russia and against the Communists in the civil war that followed the revolution in 1917.

His father, originally a native of the Ryazan region southeast of Moscow, had many occupations, including farming, cattle trading, and milling. His mother, a Ukrainian and the widow of a cossack from the Don region, learned to read and write so that she could correspond with her son when he went away to the public school in the city of Voronezh.

Sholokhov's education was interrupted by the 1917 Russian Revolution and the subsequent civil war. After leaving school in 1918, he joined the Bolshevik (Red) army, even though many from the cossack region sided with the White Russians against the Bolsheviks. At the age of fifteen he became part of a supply detachment and later served as a machine gunner during the bloody fighting in the Don region during the civil war. From the beginning of the revolution, Sholokhov supported the Communists and later worked diligently for the Soviet government. He joined the Communist party in 1932, was elected to the Supreme Soviet (Soviet parliament) in 1937, and was named a member of the Soviet Academy of Sciences two years later. He addressed the Twentieth Communist Party Congress in 1956, and in 1959 he accompanied Soviet Premier Nikita Khrushchev on a trip to Europe and the United States. In 1961 Sholokhov be-

came a member of the party's powerful Central Committee.

In 1922, when Bolshevik control of Russia was complete, Sholokhov went to Moscow to pursue a writing career. There he joined a group of young proletarian writers and supported himself by doing manual labor. His first published work, an essay, appeared in a Communist youth newspaper in 1923, followed the next year by his first story.

In the summer of 1924 Sholokhov returned to Veshenskaya, where he spent the rest of his life. In 1925 a collection of his sketches and short stories about the civil war was published in Moscow under the title *Donskie rasskazy* (*Tales of the Don*). The Soviet critic Vera Alexandrova, in *A History of Soviet Literature,* commented that the tales are impressive for "the vividness of language in the descriptions of the local landscape, the diversity of speech of the various characters, the lively dialogue." However, she added, "Already in these early stories one feels how confining the short story form is to Sholokhov's epic talent."

From 1926 to 1940 Sholokhov worked on *Tikhi Don* (The Silent Don), the novel that established his reputation as a leading Soviet writer. This work was published in serialized form in the Soviet Union: the first and second volumes appeared in 1928 and 1929, the third volume in 1932 and 1933, and the fourth volume from 1937 to 1940. The first two volumes appeared in the West in 1934 as *And Quiet Flows the Don;* the second two volumes appeared in 1940 as *The Don Flows Home to the Sea.*

The best-known and most widely celebrated of Sholokhov's novels, *Tikhi Don* is a panoramic account of world war, revolution, and civil strife and their effects on a cossack village. One of the protagonists, Grigory Melekhov, is a fiery, independent-minded cossack who bravely fights the Germans in World War I but who is torn by conflicting loyalties during the political changes that follow the czar's fall in 1917. Siding first with the Whites, then with the Reds, he finally joins a band of cossack guerrillas (the Greens) in their conflict with the Red Army. After several years of struggle, Grigory, like millions of Russians, is spiritually exhausted and grudgingly accedes to Bolshevism. His dilemma made him the most popular tragic hero in Soviet literature.

Initially, Soviet critics did not share the public's enthusiasm for this work. The first volume displeased them because it dealt with prerevolutionary life and therefore was not pro-Communist in tone, content, or outlook. The second volume drew sharper official criticism because of its supposed anti-Bolshevik bias. In fact, Joseph Stalin wrote to Sholokhov, objecting to his portrayal of the novel's two Communist figures. Despite this initial critical and official umbrage, several prominent Soviets, including Maxim Gorky, the founder of the doctrine of socialist realism in literature, encouraged Sholokhov to complete the cycle.

Sholokhov interrupted his work on *Tikhi Don* in the 1930s to write about the resistance of Russian peasants to the forced collectivization of agriculture during the first Soviet Five-Year Plan (1928–1933). Titled *Podnyataya tselina* (later translated into English in 1960 as *Harvest on the Don*), this work appeared in serial form before Sholokhov completed the first volume in 1931. Like *Tikhi Don,* this novel encountered official criticism. However, members of the Communist party's Central Committee are said to have detected a favorable attitude in the book's supposedly objective treatment of the collectivization process and are believed to have interceded to ensure its publication in 1932. During the 1940s and 1950s, Sholokhov made extensive revisions to the first volume, and in 1960 he completed the second volume, which was included in the English translation that year.

During World War II, Sholokhov wrote about the Soviet war effort for various journals and was inspired by the Battle of Stalingrad to start a third novel, the projected trilogy *Oni srazhalis za rodinu* (*They Fought for Their Country*). Although the first chapters ran in *Pravda* (The Truth) in 1943 and 1944, and others appeared in 1949 and 1954, the first volume was not published until 1958. As far as it is known, Sholokhov never completed the trilogy. Meanwhile, he made extensive revisions to *Tikhi Don,* muting his exuberant style and clearly delineating Communist good from reactionary evil.

Sholokhov's fiftieth birthday was celebrated throughout the Soviet Union, and he was awarded the Order of Lenin—an honor that was also bestowed on him on two later occasions. Serial publication of the second (and final) volume of *Harvest on the Don* began, although its conclusion was delayed until 1960, leading to the speculation that Sholokhov's ideas were not in accord with those of the Communist party. Sholokhov, however, always denied that he wrote anything to suit the censors. After the late 1950s Sholokhov apparently wrote very little.

Sholokhov received the 1965 Nobel Prize for Literature "for the artistic power and integrity with which, in his epic of the Don, [he] has given expression to a historic phase in the life of the Russian people." In his acceptance speech, Sholokhov declared that his aim as a Soviet writer was "to show my great respect for this nation of workers, this nation of builders, this nation of heroes."

In the 1970s ALEKSANDR SOLZHENITSYN, who had been denounced by party members (including Sholokhov) for his criticism of the Communist system, accused Sholokhov of plagiarizing the work of a cossack writer, Fyodor Kryukov, who had died in 1920. In doing so, Solzhenitsyn echoed similar charges that had begun in the 1920s and that again became widespread in the 1970s. However, these accusations remain largely unproven.

Sholokhov married Marie Petrovna in 1924, and they had four children. He died in Veshenskaya in 1984 at the age of seventy-eight.

Sholokhov has remained a folk hero in the Soviet Union. He redeemed himself with his early critics by making postwar alterations in his work, especially *Tikhi Don*. Western critics have usually deplored these changes and have in the main been considerably kinder than their Soviet counterparts in their opinions of the original version. For instance, the Russian-born American literary critic Marc Slonim compared *Tikhi Don* to Tolstoy's *War and Peace,* while conceding that it is not "nearly as magnificent as its model." Nevertheless, he said that "Sholokhov, following in the wake of the master, interwove biography with history, scenes of battles with domestic incidents, movements of masses with the throb of individual emotions; he showed how social upheavals changed personal destinies, how political struggle determined happiness or ruin."

According to the American scholar Ernest J. Simmons, the original *Tikhi Don* is not a political tract: "What political implications it may have are really incidental to the dominant human interest theme of the novel—the narration of a great and moving love story, almost the only great love story in Soviet literature." Noting that the characters in the revised version react to the events of 1917 to 1922 like idealized Communists of the 1950s, Simmons argued, "A pronounced tendentious purpose very much obtrudes in [the revised] edition of [*Tikhi*] *Don* and seriously compromises the artistic integrity of the novel."

Slonim claimed that *Harvest on the Don,* generally considered to be a lesser work of fiction than *Tikhi Don,* "is not an ideological novel . . . it is a lively, old-fashioned narrative that makes no attempt to coerce or educate."

Simmons disagreed, calling the book "subtle Soviet propaganda embodied in the compelling, artistic form of fiction." While acknowledging Sholokhov's role as a "Soviet spokesman and apologist," the American scholar and critic Edward J. Brown reflected most contemporary criticism of Sholokhov when he praised the author's power of expression, particularly in the parts of *Tikhi Don* written in the 1920s. Nevertheless, he believes, with other critics, that Sholokhov cannot be ranked "among the major novelists because he wrote very little, and too little of his production is first-rate."

ADDITIONAL WORKS IN ENGLISH TRANSLATION: Soviet War Stories, 1944; The Fate of a Man, 1957; Short Stories, 1965; Early Stories, 1966; Fierce and Gentle Warriors, 1967; At the Bidding of the Heart, 1973; Collected Works, volume 1, 1984.

ABOUT: Ermolaev, H. Mikhail Sholokhov and His Art, 1982; Iakimenko, L. G. Sholokhov, 1973; Price, R. F. Mikhail Sholokhov in Yugoslavia, 1973; Simmons, E. J. Russian Fiction and Soviet Ideology, 1958; Sofronov, A. V. Meetings With Sholokhov, 1985; Stewart, D. H. Mikhail Sholokhov: A Critical Introduction, 1967.

SIEGBAHN, KAI
(April 20, 1918–   )
Nobel Prize for Physics, 1981
(shared with Nicolaas Bloembergen and
    Arthur L. Schawlow)

The Swedish physicist Kai Manne Börje Siegbahn (sēg′ bän) was born in Lund, the younger of the two sons of Karin (Högbom) and MANNE SIEGBAHN. After graduating from the Uppsala Gymnasium in 1936, he entered the University of Uppsala, where he concentrated on physics, chemistry, and mathematics and received an M.S. in 1942. From 1942 to 1951 he was a research associate at the Nobel Institute for Physics in Stockholm, continuing his postgraduate studies at the University of Stockholm, from which he received a Ph.D. in 1944. His doctoral research concerned beta-ray (electron) emission by radioactive nuclei. In 1951 he was appointed a professor of physics at the Royal Institute of Technology in Stockholm, remaining until his return in 1954 to the University of Uppsala as a professor in the mathematics-physics section of the physics department.

Siegbahn's early work involved electron spectroscopy, the determination of the different energies of electrons emitted by atoms. Some of these electrons are beta rays emitted

KAI SIEGBAHN

directly by the nucleus during some forms of radioactive decay. Since the electron energy is related to the difference in energy between the nuclear states before and after decay, a precise knowledge of electron energies offers a clue to nuclear structure.

Other electrons are due not directly to primary beta decay but to a phenomenon known as internal conversion. Emission of a beta ray leaves the nucleus at an excited energy level from which it then falls to a less excited level, releasing the drop in energy between the two levels in the form of a gamma ray (electromagnetic radiation like light and X rays but higher in energy and therefore in frequency). MAX PLANCK, the founder of quantum theory, had shown that electromagnetic radiation consists of discrete bits of energy (which ALBERT EINSTEIN called quanta and which are now called photons in the case of electromagnetic energy) and that the frequency is proportional to the energy of the photon. Einstein later explained the details of the photoelectric effect (ejection of electrons by incident electromagnetic radiation) in terms of absorption of photons whose energy is high enough to overcome the energy binding electrons to the atom and therefore to dislodge the electrons. In internal conversion, gamma rays from the nucleus do not escape from the atom but instead eject electrons circling the nucleus, which are then mixed with the primary beta rays. To explore nuclear energy levels, knowledge is necessary about the energies of both the primary beta rays and the secondary photoelectrons.

Siegbahn's work was hindered by the limi-

967

tations of existing equipment, which operated according to two methods. In one method, a homogeneous magnetic field like that between the flat pole faces of a large magnet was used. Moving electrons generate a magnetic field. Interaction between this field and the external magnet caused the electrons to travel in planes parallel to the magnet faces in circles whose diameters depended on the electrons' velocities. Since faster electrons travel in wider circles, the system could sort them according to their energies. The other method involved an arrangement of magnets that formed a focusing magnetic lens. The first method provided good resolution but low intensity. The second method focused electron beams into higher intensities but yielded poor resolution. With a collaborator, Nils Svartholm, Siegbahn found a way of focusing in two directions, both in the plane of the circles and at right angles to them, with the use of a mushroom-shaped magnet. This method, known as magnetic double-focusing, achieved good intensity with greatly improved resolution and soon came into wide use.

Around 1950 Siegbahn often had to wait for radioactive samples to be produced by an erratically behaving cyclotron. He sought a way of simulating radioactive radiations by some means he could more easily control. He thought of an arrangement he had found convenient for studying gamma rays, in which he wrapped the gamma-ray source in thin lead foil and recorded in his electron spectrometer the photoelectrons ejected from the lead by the gamma rays. It then occurred to him to substitute an X-ray tube for the gamma-ray source and expel photoelectrons from ordinary materials to learn more about the energies that bound electrons to atoms. In his nuclear physics work, he had needed such information to relate measurements of electrons produced by internal conversion of gamma rays to the nuclear transitions that created the gamma rays. When he studied the scientific literature to see what had been done in this field, he realized that he might be able to make a major contribution by applying to atomic physics his high-resolution instruments and his experience in electron spectrometry for nuclear physics.

Electron spectrometry for atomic physics presented great obstacles. Electron energies are much smaller than those of beta rays, and the energy spectra of electrons ejected by photons do not readily give simple sharp definitions of the electron energy levels, or binding energies, by which atomic structure is described. For example, Einstein had shown that the energy in the absorbed photon equaled the binding energy of the ejected electron only when the electron emerged at zero speed. In general, photon energy is divided between the energy necessary to break the bond and the kinetic energy possessed by the electron after it leaves the atom. Since electrons emerge traveling with a continuous range of speeds, the spectra appear as broad curves rather than as a series of lines.

Atomic electrons had been shown to be grouped into shells. Siegbahn knew that binding energies could be deduced, as he stated, by "measuring . . . the high-energy sides of the extended veils from the various electron distributions" related to the shells. However, the resolutions of electron spectroscopy for atomic physics would have to be 10 to 100 times finer than for radioactivity work.

By the mid-1950s Siegbahn and his co-workers succeeded in producing well-defined lines. In 1957, after overcoming further difficulties and much testing of the equipment, he and two co-workers were able to record their first photoelectron spectrum with extremely sharp lines and with the expected intensities. Among other discoveries, they detected the first evidence of chemical shifts, subtle alterations in binding energies when atoms combine into molecules and their outer electrons mingle together in various ways. The chemical shift revealed details of chemical bonding, including the ionic state of atoms (loss or gain of electrons from the electrically neutral condition).

This form of extremely high-resolution analysis, now known as electron spectroscopy for chemical analysis (ESCA), rapidly became a standard laboratory technique. It proved to be particularly well suited to the study of surfaces and has been used to investigate surface phenomena such as catalysis by plantinum in petroleum refining and metal corrosion. It has also been applied to the analysis of particles in polluted air.

Seigbahn was awarded half of the 1981 Nobel Prize for Physics "for his contribution to the development of high-resolution electron spectroscopy." (His father, Manne Siegbahn, had received the Nobel Prize in 1924 for X-ray spectroscopy.) The other half was shared by NICOLAAS BLOEMBERGEN and ARTHUR L. SCHAWLOW for spectroscopic work using lasers. "With this spectroscopy it became possible to determine the binding energy of atomic electrons with higher accuracy than was previously possible," said Ingvar Lindgren of the Royal Swedish Academy of Sciences on presenting the award. "This was of great importance for testing new atomic models and computation schemes," he noted.

Since receiving the Nobel Prize, Seigbahn has continued his research in nuclear physics at Uppsala. He has also served as president of the International Union of Pure and Applied Physics and as a member of the International Committee of Weights and Measures.

In 1944 Siegbahn married Anna Brita Rhedin. They have three sons, two of whom followed their father and grandfather into the field of physics.

Siegbahn's many awards include the Sixten Heyman Award of the University of Göteborg (1971) and the Charles Frederick Chandler Medal of Columbia University (1976). He is a member of the Swedish Academy of Sciences, the Swedish Academy of Engineering Sciences, the Royal Academy of Arts and Science of Uppsala, the Royal Norwegian Academy of Sciences, and the Norwegian Society of Sciences and Letters, as well as an honorary member of the American Academy of Arts and Sciences. He has received honorary degrees from the universities of Durham, Basel, and Liège, as well as from other institutions.

SELECTED WORKS: ESCA, 1967; ESCA Applied to Free Molecules, 1969.

ABOUT: New York Times October 20, 1981; Physics Today December 1981; Science November 6, 1981.

SIEGBAHN, MANNE

(December 3, 1886–September 25, 1978)
Nobel Prize for Physics, 1924

The Swedish physicist Karl Manne Georg Siegbahn (sēg' bän) was born in Örebro, to Georg Siegbahn, a railway stationmaster, and Emma Sofia Mathilda (Zetterberg) Siegbahn. Entering the University of Lund in 1906, he was immediately attracted to physics. He became clerk of the university's Physics Institute and received a B.S. in 1908 and an M.S. in 1910, after additional study at the universities of Göttingen and Munich. As an assistant to Johannes Rydberg at Lund, he studied electromagnetism and received his doctorate in 1911 with a thesis on magnetic field measurements. He remained at the university as a lecturer in physics after spending the summer of 1911 studying in Berlin and Paris.

Siegbahn had become interested in X rays and, stimulated by visits with scientists in Paris and Heidelberg, he began to study X-ray spec-

MANNE SIEGBAHN

tra in late 1913. He later made major contributions to this field, not only through his discoveries but also through the instruments he developed for making precise measurements.

WILHELM RÖNTGEN gave the name X (for unknown) to rays he discovered in 1895 issuing from the end of a glass vacuum tube opposite the negative electrode (cathode) during an electric discharge. X rays had a surprising ability to pass through opaque objects. After J. J. THOMSON discovered the electron in 1897, it became apparent that the mysterious rays were produced when fast-moving electrons from the cathode collided with other parts of the tube. Scientists suspected that X rays might be electromagnetic radiation such as light and heat, but more penetrating. However, because X-ray frequencies were too high (wavelengths too short), available instruments could not detect the familiar phenomena of refraction, polarization, diffraction, and interference exhibited by visible light. Researchers were at first limited to measuring only the rays' relative ability to penetrate different thicknesses of various materials, a property called hardness. Nevertheless, they were able to discover that different chemical elements used as targets in an X-ray tube emitted characteristic X rays of different hardnesses.

CHARLES G. BARKLA tested a series of elements and showed that the emitted X rays became harder (higher in frequency) with increasing atomic weight until, above a certain atomic weight, a new family of softer X rays appeared. As he tested elements of still higher atomic weight, these softer rays also became harder. He called the two groups K and L radiation. He also found a kind of polarization of X rays, strengthening the belief that X rays were indeed close relatives of light.

The crude methods that revealed K and L radiation could not readily separate X rays according to frequency or wavelength, that is, display them as lines on a spectrum. One way this is done for visible light is with a diffraction grating whose close spacing between parallel grooves is close to the wavelengths of the light. Enough was known about X rays to estimate that their wavelengths were 100 to 1,000 times shorter than those of light. It occurred to MAX VON LAUE that the regular spacings between atoms in a crystal were of an order that might make crystals act like X-ray diffraction gratings. Experiment proved him right and led to the development of X-ray spectroscopy. W. L. BRAGG found a simple formula relating the angle at which the X rays entered and exited from the crystal to the X-ray wavelength and the spacing between imaginary planes through atoms in the crystal lattice. Bragg's father, W. H. BRAGG, designed the first true X-ray spectrometer, using an ionization chamber to measure the X rays emerging from the crystal, and obtained spectral lines at wavelengths that he found were characteristic of the material in the X-ray source.

The young English physicist Henry G. F. Moseley used the spectrometer to make a fundamental discovery. Replacing the ionization chamber with a photographic detector, he found a larger number of characteristic lines in the X-ray spectra than Bragg did and showed that they could be generally classified into two groups. One, of shorter wavelengths, he identified with Barkla's K radiations, and the other, of longer wavelengths, he identified with Barkla's L radiations. Unlike the more heterogeneous optical spectra, X-ray spectra were similar from element to element but rose in frequency as heavier atoms were used as X-ray sources.

Moseley, however, discovered that the key was not the atomic weight but the atomic number. According to the model of the atom first proposed by ERNEST RUTHERFORD in 1911 and elaborated by NIELS BOHR in 1913, all the positive charge and nearly all the mass in an atom are concentrated in a central nucleus. The nucleus is surrounded by electrons, each carrying a unit of negative charge and very little mass, whose number equals the nuclear charge and thus renders the whole atom electrically neutral. The atomic weight primarily

reflects the mass of the nucleus. The atomic number equals the positive charge on the nucleus or, equivalently, the number of electrons in the neutral atom. The relationship between frequency (the position in the X-ray spectrum) and the atomic number is known as Moseley's law and held great significance for atomic physics.

Siegbahn continued in this tradition of X-ray investigations, extending measurements of a line in Barkla's K series to heavier elements. Although hampered by meager funds and facilities at Lund, he and his students did impressive work. A gifted engineer and instrument designer, Siegbahn continually improved his equipment, designing X-ray tubes of greater intensity, making more effective vacuum pumps, and modifying the spectrometers to measure wavelengths with increasing accuracy. When absorption of longer wavelengths by air presented an obstacle, he built a vacuum spectrometer. When more accuracy was needed in measurement, he constructed three different spectrometers adapted to the requirements of three different ranges of wavelength, substantially deviating from Bragg's design. These innovations enabled him and his students to discover many new lines in the K and L series (for example, one K line proved to be two), extend measurements to lighter and heavier elements, investigate X-ray absorption spectra, and find two new series, which he called M and N.

This work produced much new knowledge about virtually all the elements from sodium to uranium and contributed to a better understanding of the atom on the basis of Bohr's model. The simple model (much altered since that time) contained electrons circling in certain "allowed" orbits about the nucleus. When electrons are excited to more energetic orbits (for example, by an electron beam striking the target in an X-ray tube), they then fall back to lower orbits, yielding their acquired energy in the form of discrete quantities (photons) of electromagnetic energy. The energy of a photon equals the energy difference between a higher and a lower orbit. If excitation is relatively mild, transitions occur between outer orbits, and the emitted photons have relatively lower energies. MAX PLANCK, the father of quantum theory, showed that the frequency of the radiation is proportional to the photon energy. Therefore, lower-energy photons appear as lower-frequency (longer-wavelength) radiation, or light. When the excitation is stronger, as in an X-ray tube, inner electrons become involved, the fall from an excited orbit is farther, and the emitted photons have more energy. Therefore, the frequencies are higher and the wavelengths shorter, and the atom emits X rays. Accurate knowledge of X-ray wavelengths allows a deep probe into atomic structure.

In 1922 Siegbahn became professor of physics at the University of Uppsala, where superior resources were available for experimental research. There he and his students continued their investigation of X rays, particularly of long wavelengths. In 1924 they succeeded in demonstrating the refraction of such X rays by a glass prism, which had eluded many researchers before them, including Röntgen himself. This left little doubt that X rays were indeed electromagnetic radiation.

In 1925 Siegbahn received the 1924 Nobel Prize for Physics "for his discoveries and research in the field of X-ray spectroscopy." In his Nobel lecture, "The X-Ray Spectra and the Structure of the Atoms," Siegbahn said that the motivation to conduct research on X rays was not just to achieve medical applications, but that "X rays provide us, in addition, with an insight into the phenomena within the bounds of the atom. All the information on what goes on in this field of physical phenomena is, so to speak, transmitted in the language of the X rays," he went on. "It is a language that we must master if we are to be able to understand and interpret this information properly."

To improve the precision of spectrographic measurements, Siegbahn and his colleagues designed devices to produce diffraction gratings of extreme accuracy. With these gratings, it was possible to investigate wavelength regions hitherto unexplored. They also permitted researchers to compare X-ray wavelengths directly with the wavelengths of visible light, thus providing important confirmations of earlier measurements.

When the Royal Swedish Academy of Sciences established the Nobel Institute of Experimental Physics in 1937, Siegbahn was appointed its first director. In this capacity he continued his spectroscopy research while initiating work on nuclear physics. Within a year, the institute had constructed Sweden's first particle accelerator. During World War II, the institute took in many refugee scientists who contributed to its pure research programs.

After the war, Siegbahn expanded the scope of the institute's research programs and devoted much of his effort to understanding the atomic nucleus. In 1946 and again in 1953, he visited many of his colleagues in the United States at such institutions as the University of California, the Massachusetts Institute of Technology, and the University of Chicago. After retiring in 1964, he remained at the Nobel Institute, where he continued his research.

In 1914 Siegbahn married Karin Högbom; they had two sons, the younger of whom, KAI SIEGBAHN, also became a noted physicist. Siegbahn died at the age of ninety-one on September 25, 1978. He was described by colleagues as a man with a warm and unpretentious nature. "His pioneering work," said GERHARD HERZBERG, "forms an essential experimental basis of atomic theory and will be remembered by generations of physicists."

Siegbahn served on the International Committee of Weights and Measures in 1937 and as president of the International Union of Pure and Applied Physics from 1938 to 1947. In addition to the Nobel Prize, he received the Hughes Medal (1934) and the Rumford Medal (1940) of the Royal Society of London and the Duddell Medal of the Physical Society in London (1948). He was awarded honorary degrees by the University of Freiburg, Oslo University, and the University of Paris, among others, and held membership in the Royal Society of London, the Royal Society of Edinburgh, and the French Academy of Sciences.

SELECTED WORKS: The Spectroscopy of X Rays, 1925; On the Methods of Precision Measurements of X-Ray Wavelengths, 1929.

ABOUT: Lindroth, S. Swedish Men of Science, 1952; Physics Today February 1979.

SIENKIEWICZ, HENRYK
(May 7, 1846–November 15, 1916)
Nobel Prize for Literature, 1905

The Polish novelist Henryk Adam Alexander Pius Sienkiewicz (shen kye' věch) was born in Okrzejska, a town in Russian-ruled Poland (now part of Lithuania), to a Lithuanian-Polish family that had been elevated to the nobility in 1775. His father, Josef Sienkiewicz, who had fought against the Russians in the Polish insurrection of 1831, owned several small estates. His mother, the former Stefania Cieciszowska, came from an aristocratic family that had produced several noted intellectuals. Sienkiewicz spent his early childhood in the country, but by the time he reached school age, a series of economic reverses had forced his family, which included an older

HENRYK SIENKIEWICZ

brother and four sisters, to sell their rural property and move to Warsaw. There the young Sienkiewicz developed an interest in Polish history and literature and began dabbling in prose and verse.

Although only an average student, Sienkiewicz excelled in Polish language and history during his secondary schooling in Warsaw. Particularly impressed by the novels of Sir Walter Scott and Alexandre Dumas, among others, during this time he apparently tried his hand at a novel of his own, *Ofiara* (The Sacrifice), of which no manuscript is known to survive.

After working briefly as a tutor to the children of an aristocratic family on a country estate, Sienkiewicz in 1866 entered Warsaw University, which had been established four years earlier during a brief relaxation of czarist rule. At first he studied law and medicine but soon changed his field of concentration to history and literature.

The 1860s was a decade of political turmoil in Poland. A rebellion against Russian rule in 1863 proved unsuccessful, and the czarist government subsequently undertook a campaign to "Russianize" the Poles by suppressing Polish culture (including ordering that classes at Warsaw University be conducted only in Russian) and making Poland economically dependent on Russia. Polish intellectuals responded by organizing underground nationalist movements to resist this policy. An influential school of Polish nationalist writers advocated a new, progressive program for literature that included dealing realistically with contemporary issues and concerns rather than romantically celebrating Poland's glorious past. Although these events did not immediately affect Sienkiewicz, they had an impact later on his attempts to create a Polish identity.

In 1871 Sienkiewicz found himself penniless and left the university without taking his examinations or receiving a degree. The following year he published *Na marne* (*In Vain*), another novel he had written as a student; despite its flaws, the work was favorably received by Józef Ignacy Kraszewski, a leading Polish writer of the time. Working as a freelance journalist, Sienkiewicz began contributing articles to a number of Polish periodicals and was sent on assignments to Vienna and Paris, as well as Oostende, Belgium. By 1875 his journalistic talents had become widely recognized in Polish intellectual circles. The following year several intellectual acquaintances commissioned him to travel to the United States to help establish a community in California where Polish émigrés could live and work without the fear of repression; the Warsaw newspaper *Gazeta Polska* agreed to pay his way in return for a series of articles about the United States. Sienkiewicz subsequently spent over a year in California; although plans for the colony fell through after an optimistic start, his dispatches, published between 1876 and 1878 and collected in the volume *Listy z podróży do Ameryki* (*Portrait of America: Letters*), were well received.

Returning to Europe in 1878, Sienkiewicz traveled in France and Italy, lecturing, reporting, and writing short stories inspired by his American experiences. These stories, published in several Warsaw periodicals, soon established his reputation in Poland as a writer of penetrating psychological fiction. In Italy in 1879 he met Maria Szetkiewicz, a Polish woman, whom he married two years later. After returning to Warsaw at the end of 1879, he became the editor of a new daily newspaper and also turned his attention to the longer forms of fiction.

In 1884 he published *Ogniem i mieczem* (*With Fire and Sword*), a novel that recounts Poland's struggle for survival in the seventeenth century. Although progressives criticized Sienkiewicz's preoccupation with the distant past, most readers praised the work for its brilliance and verisimilitude and hailed the author as a major literary figure. *Potop* (*The Deluge,* 1886) and *Pan Wołodyjowski* (*Pan Michael,* 1888) completed the trilogy and confirmed Sienkiewicz's mastery of the historical novel. To ensure the accuracy of his work,

Sienkiewicz had thoroughly researched seventeenth-century sources, consulted historians, and traveled to the locations where his fiction would be set. Writing in 1897, the English critic Edmund Gosse offered the following estimation of this massive trilogy: "On the whole, the impression . . . is one of breadth and vigor rather than subtlety. . . . It is all grandiose and magnificent, yet preserved, by an undertone of poignant melancholy and by a constantly supported distinction of sentiment, from the merely melodramatic and tawdry."

In 1882 Maria Sienkiewicz gave birth to a son, Henryk Josef, followed the next year by a daughter, Jadwiga. After the birth of the second child, however, Maria's health deteriorated, and in 1885 she died of consumption.

Throughout this time Sienkiewicz traveled widely, spending time in Egypt in 1891 and joining a safari into the heart of Africa. However, his next published novels, *Bez dogmatu* (*Without Dogma,* 1891) and *Rodzina Połanieckich* (1895, translated as *Children of the Soil*), were set in contemporary Poland and written in the psychological mode of his earlier short stories. Late in 1894 Sienkiewicz entered into a brief, unhappy marriage with Maria Romanowska, a young admirer of his work, which ended in an annulment.

Shortly after this painful episode, Sienkiewicz conceived two historical novels on a vast scale. The first was *Quo Vadis?* (1896, translated under the same title), which dealt with the persecution of the Christians in first-century Rome during the reign of the Emperor Nero. As he had done in preparation for the *With Fire and Sword* trilogy, Sienkiewicz again studied numerous historical sources before undertaking this work. He also visited the sites in Italy that would figure prominently in the story. The result was a novel acclaimed for "the grandeur of the historical vision, its wealth of vivid color of detail, the creative force which gives life to a crowd of Roman and Christian characters," as the critic Roman Dyboski wrote in 1924. By 1916, the year Sienkiewicz died, *Quo Vadis?*, one of the most popular novels of its day, had sold 1.5 million copies in the United States alone. It was one of the first novels to be made into a motion picture; in fact, two versions, one French and one Italian, were filmed in the early 1900s. The book was hailed by critics in Poland, the rest of Europe, and the United States; it also earned Sienkiewicz a special citation from Pope Leo VIII. *Quo Vadis?* was followed in 1900 by *Krzyżacy* (*Knights of the Cross;* published in the United Kingdom as *The Teutonic Knights*), in which the writer described events in early fifteenth-century Poland.

So great was the enthusiasm for Sienkiewicz's writing in his homeland that in 1900, as part of a delayed fiftieth-birthday celebration for the author, a national subscription fund raised enough money to buy Sienkiewicz a small estate, Oblegórek, outside the town of Kielce. Special events in his honor were held throughout Poland, and numerous articles praising his literary accomplishments appeared not only in Poland but also in Russia. Not long afterward, he married Maria Babska, a distant cousin, and in 1905 completed *Na polu chwaly* (*On the Field of Glory*), a sequel to his first historical trilogy.

In 1905 Sienkiewicz was awarded the Nobel Prize for Literature "because of his outstanding merits as an epic writer." In the presentation address, C. D. af Wirsén of the Swedish Academy cited Sienkiewicz as one of the "rare geniuses who concentrate in themselves the spirit of the nation; they represent the national character of the world. If one surveys Sienkiewicz's achievement, it appears gigantic and vast, and at every point noble and controlled. As for his epic style, it is of absolute artistic perfection." In his short acceptance statement, Sienkiewicz noted that "nations are represented by their poets and their writers. . . . Consequently, the award of the prize . . . glorifies not only the author but the people whose son he is." The writer further remarked, "It has been said that Poland is dead, exhausted, enslaved; but here is the proof of her life and triumph."

With the outbreak of World War I, Sienkiewicz fled Oblegórek to neutral Switzerland, where he worked for the Polish Red Cross despite severe sclerosis. He died in Vevey in 1916, and his body was returned to Poland eight years later.

During his lifetime Sienkiewicz was highly regarded by critics in many nations. In *Essays on Modern Novelists* (1910), for example, the American critic William Lyons Phelps called him "one of the greatest living masters of the realistic novel." If, aside from *Quo Vadis?* his works are no longer widely read outside Poland, the author nevertheless remains a major figure in Polish letters. "Sienkiewicz's place in the history of Polish literature is [secure]," wrote the Polish scholar Mieczyslaw Giergielewicz in 1968. "He did not discover any new vehicles of expression, but he combined skillfully the inherited ones and raised them to the level of virtuosity."

SILLANPÄÄ

ADDITIONAL WORKS IN ENGLISH TRANSLATION: Yanko the Musician and Other Stories, 1893; The Light-House Keeper, 1893; The Old Servant, 1897; Charcoal Sketches, 1897; Hania, 1897; For Bread, 1898; Sielanka, 1898; Life and Death, 1904; Whirlpools, 1910; In the Desert and Wilderness, 1912; Tales, 1928; Western Septet, 1973.

ABOUT: Coleman, A. P., and Coleman, M. M. Wanderers Twain, 1964; Dyboski, R. Modern Polish Literature, 1924; Gardner, M. M. The Patriot Novelist of Poland, 1926; Giergielewicz, M. Henryk Sienkiewicz, 1968; Lednicki, W. Henryk Sienkiewicz, 1960; Miłosz, C. The History of Polish Literature, 1969.

SILLANPÄÄ, FRANS
(September 16, 1888–June 3, 1964)
Nobel Prize for Literature, 1939

FRANS SILLANPÄÄ

The Finnish novelist Frans Eemil Sillanpää (sil' län pa) was born into a peasant family in Hämeenkyrö, a rural village in southwest Finland. Following rural custom, his father, Frans Koskinen, had adopted the name of the land he lived on, Sillanpää (bridgehead). Some ten years before his marriage to Louiisa Vilhemiina Iisaksdotter, the elder Sillanpää moved to Hämeenkyrö, where his wife's family had lived for generations. Together, the couple built the small homestead where Sillanpää was born. The youngest of three children, he was the only one to survive into adulthood.

Although poor, Sillanpää's family saved enough money to send him to secondary school in the nearby city of Tampere. A good student, he received money from a benefactor who recognized his abilities. This, together with a few loans, enabled him to enter the University of Helsinki in 1908. There he studied biology with the intention of becoming a physician. At the same time, he was drawn into the social circle of important figures in the capital, particularly that of the Järnefelts, an influential literary and artistic family. Sillanpää never completed his degree, but his schooling imbued him with a deep respect for the biological forces that he believed were fundamentally responsible for human behavior.

While in school, Sillanpää read and was inspired by many authors, including August Strindberg, MAURICE MAETERLINCK, and KNUT HAMSUN. Indeed, he went so far as to refer to Hamsun's Victoria and Pan as "the intoxication of my youth." Sillanpää turned to writing as a way to resolve psychological problems and began to publish his stories in local magazines and newspapers while still a student. This early work was received favorably,

and he soon established a considerable reputation as a writer.

In 1913 Sillanpää withdrew from the university and went home to write. His first novel, Elämä ja aurinko (Life and Sun), was published in 1916. Later, Sillanpää enjoyed recounting how his publisher had to kidnap him and lock him in a hotel room to force him to finish the novel. Life and Sun, which recounts the experiences of three young people, a man and two women, during one summer, received good reviews and was considered, in the words of the Finnish literary critic Lauri Viljanen, "an exceptional first novel."

In 1916 Sillanpää married Sigrid Maria Salomäki, a tenant farmer's daughter from his native parish. They had eight children, one of whom died in infancy.

In 1917, the year Finland became an independent nation, Sillanpää published a collection of short stories, Ihmislapsia elämän saatossa (Children of Mankind in the Procession of Life). The following year saw the tragedy of Finland's civil war, a bloody conflict that pitted the leftist Red Guards against the conservative and ultimately victorious White Guards. The war caused Sillanpää great anguish and inspired him to produce his first important work, the novel Hurskas kurjuus (Meek Heritage, 1919).

In Meek Heritage Sillanpää became the first Finnish writer to come to grips with the horror of the war between the Reds and Whites. He avoided taking sides regarding the political issues but vividly evoked the brutality, pain, and waste inflicted on both sides. Although the novel may seem drab and depressing to a modern reader, it found a receptive and appreciative audience when it appeared. Because Sillanpää described both Reds and Whites with courageous objectivity, his novel was a first step toward healing the wound in the Finnish psyche. In recognition, the Finnish government awarded him a lifetime stipend in 1920.

During the following years, Sillanpää published several short story collections, including *Hiltu ja Ragnar* (Hiltu and Ragnar, 1923), *Enkelten suojatit* (Protected by Angels, 1923), *Maan tasalta* (On Ground Level, 1924), *Töllinmäki* (Cottage Hill, 1925), *Rippi* (The Communion, 1928), and *Kiitos hetkistä, Herra . . .* (Thank You for These Moments, Lord . . . , 1930). These works increased his reputation not only in Finland but throughout Scandinavia. He reached an even larger audience in 1931, when *Nuorena Nukkunut* (translated as *The Maid Silja* in the United States and as *Fallen Asleep While Young* in the United Kingdom) was published. It gained immediate popularity throughout Europe.

The story concerns the quiet life and death of a young girl too decent and sensitive for her environment, the last member of a once-proud family fallen on hard times. The novel expresses Sillanpää's deep love of nature. It has been praised for his portrayal of the girl, who remains good-natured and loving throughout, although she is beset by a multitude of personal disasters that end in her solitary death. In a 1933 review, the American writer and translator Phillips Carleton stated, "The growth of her personality seems as inevitable in its progress, as independent of its surroundings as some planet moving to the appointed stations of its orbit. The result is a queer reversal of values; as the story unfolds, the reality of the outside world grows thinner; the illusions of the girl grow firmer till both blend in death." Carleton continued, "The success of the novel—and it is extraordinarily effective—lies in . . . a carefully devised technique and a beauty of style."

Miehen tie (*The Way of a Man*) was written at the same time as *The Maid Silja* and published in 1932. The literary historian Jaakko Ahokas has called it the one work that truly justifies the many comparisons that have been drawn between Sillanpää and D. H. Lawrence. Sillanpää, noted Ahokas, "stresses the connection between the rhythm of nature expressed in the seasons and the changes in the lives of his characters. In such passages, the novel is not realistic; there is an epic breadth . . . in the description of the work of the farmer, the succession of the seasons, and the actions of the man and woman destined to meet when their time is fulfilled."

Ihmiset suviyössä (*People in the Summer Night,* 1934) is widely considered Sillanpää's most important work. It has been compared to a prose poem in its loosely connected plot and strongly sensory overtones. Ahokas considered it Sillanpää's "most carefully composed and definitely his most complexly structured work," noting that "the author's biological conception of time has a part in the manner in which the events are described; the duration of the action is indicated, but the flow of the duration is experienced differently by the characters." Viljanen, even more generous in his praise of the novel, declared that "rarely has an author been able to evolve from one tiny germ—in this case, a little village community—a life so complex, so boundless in its spiritual dimensions. Sillanpää . . . is a poetic dreamer in whose writings fragrant lyrical moods alternate with keen intellectual analysis in a highly personal way."

In 1939 Sillanpää became severely depressed, a condition that can be ascribed to the death of his wife, the outbreak of World War II, and the Winter War between Finland and the Soviet Union. Later that year, he was married again, this time to Anna Armia von Herzen, but the marriage proved both short and unhappy.

During this period of personal and political turmoil, Sillanpää was awarded the 1939 Nobel Prize for Literature "for his deep understanding of his country's peasantry and the exquisite art with which he has portrayed their way of life and their relationship with nature." Because of the war, no presentation ceremony took place, but Sillanpää received his medal and certificate at a meeting of the Swedish Academy in December 1939. In his remarks, Per Hallström expressed the academy's sympathy for Finland's fate. "In our thanks for what you have given," Hallström said, "our thoughts go still further; they go, with all our admiration and the emotion which grips us, to your people, to your nation."

As far back as 1930 Sillanpää had suffered and recovered from an intellectual and emotional crisis in which he felt that his creativity was failing him. In spite of the honor and recognition bestowed on him by the Nobel Prize, the crisis and depression returned in so severe a form that he was confined to a hospital in 1940 and remained there until 1943. Nevertheless, he continued to write. *Elokuu* (*August,* 1941) and *Ihmiselon ihanuus ja kurjuus*

SIMON

(*The Beauty and Misery of Human Life,* 1945) are pessimistic works with autobiographical overtones about unhappy writers and poets who consider themselves failures.

Three volumes of memoirs were Sillanpää's final works: *Poika eli elämäänsä* (A Boy and His Life, 1953), *Kerron ja kuvailen* (Telling and Describing, 1955), and *Päivä korkeimmillaan* (The High Moment of the Day, 1956). A huge man, bearded and bald, with a great predilection for alcohol, Sillanpää finally became a beloved, if eccentric, elder to the Finnish nation, allowing himself to be called Grandfather by the general public. He gave homespun radio talks and was highly regarded by the Finnish people until the time of his death in Helsinki in 1964.

Lauri Viljanen summed up Sillanpää's literary accomplishments when he wrote, "No other Finnish writer has been able to catch in the same manner the quiet little happenings that take place in village streets, in cabins and hovels, at all times of day and night, on holy days and everydays. Nor do we exaggerate when we say that in all European fiction it is difficult to find anything to equal his peculiar psychological method of seeing." The Finnish critic and essayist Kai Laitinen added, "For Sillanpää, human beings are an essential part of nature, one with it; a vast universal life force works in his characters, the same force which makes the trees grow and the animals continue their species, which does not question its purpose but simply strives to fulfill itself and to find its own channel."

ABOUT: Ahokas, J. A History of Finnish Literature, 1973; American-Scandinavian Review March 1940; Books September 25, 1938; Current Biography January-February 1940; Virginia Quarterly Review Spring 1940.

SIMON, CLAUDE
(October 10, 1913–   )
Nobel Prize for Literature, 1985

CLAUDE SIMON

The French novelist Claude Eugène Henri Simon (sē môn') was born to French parents in Tananarive, on the island of Madagascar off the east coast of Africa. His father, Louis Antoine Simon, a career army officer posted to the French possession where he was in charge of colonial troops, was killed in 1914, at the beginning of World War I. Of peasant stock, his father's family came from the small village of Arbois, in the Franche-Comté region of eastern France; his mother, Suzanne (Denamiel) Simon, traced her origins to minor no-

bility in the Roussillon region of southeastern France. Simon spent his childhood in the city of Perpignan, near the Spanish border, where he was raised by his mother and her family, in particular his maternal uncle. Between the ages of seven and sixteen, he attended the Collège Stanislas in Paris, where he became a keen rugby player and a budding artist.

During the years preceding World War II, Simon studied painting with André Lhôte in Paris and traveled in Europe and the Soviet Union. From 1934 to 1935 he served with the French army's Thirty-first Dragoons. Sympathetic to the Republicans in Spain, he became involved in gunrunning during the Spanish Civil War, but later grew disillusioned with the cause.

With the outbreak of war in 1939, Simon rejoined the Dragoons, and like his father before him, he became a cavalry officer, eventually attaining the rank of brigadier. He took part in the Battle of the Meuse in May 1940; narrowly escaping death, he was taken prisoner by the Germans and sent to Stalag IVB, a prison camp at Mühlberg in Saxony. Transferred to a prisoner-of-war camp in France, he escaped and joined the Resistance movement in Perpignan. After the war he returned to Paris and in 1951 married Yvonne Ducing. Since the war, Simon has divided his time between his Paris apartment in the Latin Quarter and a country estate near the village of Salces, north of Perpignan, in the eastern Pyrenees. He lives with his second wife, Rhea Karavas, a woman of Greek descent, whom he married in 1978.

Simon began writing prior to the outbreak

of World War II and completed his first work, *Le Tricheur* (The Cheater), while he was working for the Resistance in Perpignan. It was published in 1945, after the end of the German occupation, and received mixed reviews. His other early novels include *La Corde raide* (The Tightrope), an autobiographical work published in 1947; *Gulliver* (1952); and *Le Sacre du printemps* (The Rites of Spring, 1954). These early novels indicate that Simon was influenced in part by writers such as WILLIAM FAULKNER, Marcel Proust, Joseph Conrad, and Fedor Dostoevsky. His early efforts show also a thematic preoccupation with time, memory, order, and disorder and a penchant for dislocation of narrative sequence—two techniques that dominate his later work. From the beginning, Simon was much impressed by the advice of the French painter Raoul Dufy, whom he came to know well during the war. In an interview, Simon recalled Dufy's remark: "One must be able to give up the painting one wanted to do for the painting that demands to be painted." Simon has pursued this dictum throughout his career as a novelist, attempting to write the novel that demands to be written. He has continued to use in his writing the collagelike techniques that were first evident in his work in the visual arts and to maintain an ongoing concern with the philosophy of perception.

Le Vent (*The Wind,* 1957) was the first of his works to be translated into English. In 1960 Simon signed the Declaration of the 121, a manifesto by French intellectuals supporting the independence movement in Algeria. *La Route des Flandres* (*The Flanders Road*), which was published in the same year, earned Simon the L'Express Prize in 1961. Through Georges, the main character, Simon relives his own participation in the Battle of the Meuse and reveals the welter of associations and memories that attend it. The American scholar Karen Gould observed the "microscopic" focus of Georges's experiences but also pointed out the mythical dimension of the concerns that Georges shares with all of Simon's narrators. "What they discover," she wrote, "is not the individuality of self, but the archetypal configurations of human behavior." In this work the tension between events and the words used to describe them is pronounced. With the publication of *Histoire* (1967, translated under the same title in 1968), Simon earned the Médicis Prize and reiterated his fundamental formalistic credo: that he writes his books "as one would make a painting. And every painting is first and foremost a composition."

La Bataille de Pharsale (*The Battle of Pharsalus*) was published in 1969. After the Cerisy Colloquy on the New Novel in 1971, French literary criticism began to turn away from its appreciation of the mythical associations of Simon's narrators and to pursue a semiotic analysis of his work. The importance of the power of wordplay in Simon's novels was increasingly stressed, and critics moved toward an understanding of the text as a pattern of signs. The critic Jean Ricardou, who emerged as the foremost exponent of this approach to the New Novel, described *The Battle of Pharsalus* anagrammatically as "La Bataille de la phrase" ("The Battle of the Phrase"), suggesting that the narration may be construed as the adventure of writing itself.

In 1973 Simon was awarded an honorary doctorate by the University of East Anglia, in the United Kingdom. In the same year, the novel *Triptyque* (*Triptych*) was published. It is a "powerfully erotic" novel, according to the English translator and scholar John Fletcher, who noted the quality of tragic eroticism in Simon's work. *Triptych* experiments with representational effects as three inextricably intertwined narratives dealing with love and death are mirrored within one another. *Leçon de choses* (1975, translated as *The World About Us*) takes to the limit the assault on realism waged in *Triptych*. Using a new compositional form, Simon begins the work with a series of images, which, in turn, generates the complexly interwoven pattern of language that forms the text. For the French critic François Jost, the novel constitutes an exercise in textual self-generation: "The fiction seems to organize itself around what the reader is reading."

In *Les Géorgiques* (*Georgics,* 1981), Simon retreats from the extremes of experimentation of his previous novels to echo Virgil's concern for working the earth. In addition to reexploring the fertile terrain of autobiographical concerns that form the basis of all of Simon's novels, it is, as the English critic Alistair Duncan remarked, "also about signs and especially how the forms of the past relate to new forms."

Simon was awarded the 1985 Nobel Prize for Literature. In announcing the award, the Swedish Academy noted in Simon's literary work "the poet's and the painter's creativeness" as well as "a deepened awareness of time in the depiction of the human condition." The academy also expressed the belief that Simon tempers his pessimism and tragic view of history with a sense of "tenderness and loyalty, of devotion to work and duty, to heritage and traditions and solidarity with dead and living kinsmen. Claude Simon's narrative art may appear as a representation of something that lives within us whether we will it or not— something hopeful, in spite of all the cruelty and absurdity which for that seem to characterize our condition and which is so perceptively, penetratingly, and abundantly reproduced in his novels."

In his Nobel lecture, Simon remarked, "One never describes something that happened before the labor of writing, but really what is being produced . . . during this labor, in its very 'present,' and results not from the conflicts between the very vague initial project and the language, but on the contrary from a symbiosis between the two that gives . . . a result infinitely richer than the intent." He continued, "Thus, no longer prove but reveal, no longer reproduce but produce, no longer express but discover. As for painting," he added, "the novel does not propose anymore to extract its pertinence from some association with an important subject, but from the fact that it tries to reflect, as music does, a certain harmony."

The scholar Jean Duffy has argued for an overview of Simon's art as a revolutionary process that tends to dissolve the conventional and familiar elements of the novel's form and language. Duffy has noted the need, recognized by Simon, "for writers to impede or defamiliarize traditional forms and current linguistic usage." Like the image of Valéry's Achilles, motionlessly running, which epigraphically presides over *The Battle of Pharsalus,* Simon's works are remarkable for the manner in which words arrest experience in flight, capturing the essence of that experience in a self-renewing narrative form.

ADDITIONAL WORKS IN ENGLISH TRANSLATION: The Grass, 1960; The Palace, 1963; Conducting Bodies, 1974; Collected Papers, 1985.

ABOUT: Birn, R., and Gould, K. (eds.) Orion Blinded: Essays on Claude Simon, 1981; Carroll, D. The Subject in Question, 1982; Fletcher, J. Claude Simon and Fiction Now, 1975; Gould, K. Claude Simon's Mythic Muse, 1979; Jimenez Fajardo, S. Claude Simon, 1975; Kadish, P. Y. Practices of the New Novel, 1979; LeSage, L. The French New Novel, 1962; Loubère, J. A. E. The Novels of Claude Simon, 1975; Storrs, N. Liquid, 1983; Sturrock, J. The French New Novel, 1969.

SIMON, HERBERT

(June 15, 1916–   )
Nobel Memorial Prize in Economic
Sciences, 1978

The American sociologist and educator Herbert Alexander Simon was born in Milwaukee, Wisconsin, the second son of Arthur Simon and the former Edna Merkel. His father, an electrical engineer, inventor, and patent attorney, had emigrated from Germany in 1905. His mother, a third-generation American of Czech and German descent, was an accomplished pianist. Attending the Milwaukee public schools, Simon obtained what he later recalled to be "an excellent general education." At home, the intellectual environment was stimulating. The dinner table was a place for discussion and debate—often political, sometimes scientific. Admiration for his uncle, Harold Merkel, an economist and writer in economics and psychology, encouraged Simon's interest in the social sciences.

By 1933, when he entered the University of Chicago, Simon had decided to become a mathematical social scientist. His studies included political science, logic, mathematical biophysics, and econometrics. While taking a graduate-level physics course, he developed a lifelong interest in the philosophy of physics and eventually published several articles on this topic.

Earning a B.A. in political science in 1936, Simon became a research assistant in municipal administration in Chicago. His early studies in this field led in 1939 to an appointment as director of a University of California research group engaged in similar work. Three years later, at the end of his research grant, Simon returned to Chicago to continue his graduate studies. During this time he was also an assistant professor of political science at the Illinois Institute of Technology. After receiving his Ph.D. in political science in 1943, Simon remained at the University of Chicago, where he was appointed chairman of the political science department in 1946. Two years later he made a brief venture into public administration, accepting an adjunct position with the United States government to help create the Economic Cooperation Administration. The group administered Marshall Plan aid (named for Secretary of State GEORGE C. MARSHALL) to Western European countries recovering from World War II.

In 1949 Simon left Chicago for Pittsburgh, where he helped establish Carnegie-Mellon University's new Graduate School of Indus-

Carnegie-Mellon University

HERBERT SIMON

trial Administration. There he became professor of administration. Since 1965 he has been Richard King Mellon Professor of Computer Sciences and Psychology. In this capacity he has conducted research in information-processing psychology, computer simulation of cognitive processes, organization theory, artificial intelligence, and decision theory.

Administrative Behavior, one of Simon's several books on theories of organizational decision making, was published in 1947. In it he described the business firm as an adaptive system of physical, personal, and social components, held together by its communications network and by its members' willingness to cooperate to achieve common goals. Simon rejected the classical notion of the firm as an omniscient, rational, profit-maximizing entrepreneur. Instead, he showed that decisions are made collaboratively by organization members whose capacities for rational action are limited both by their inability to know all the consequences of their decisions and by their personal and social perspectives. Because this process can result only in satisfactory—as opposed to best—decisions, Simon observed, firms aim not at maximizing profits but at finding acceptable solutions to complex problems. Often this situation involves pursuing contradictory goals.

In *Models of Man* (1957) and *Organization* (1958), Simon further developed the theories first set forth in *Administrative Behavior.* He expressed his belief that an important ingredient was missing from classical problem-solving theory: the behavioral and cognitive

properties of human beings as information processors and problem solvers. James G. March, a colleague with whom Simon conducted field studies, states that Simon "called attention to human limits on memory and computing power, viewing them as obvious restrictions on full rationality. Thus, he initiated a string of related developments by others that have come collectively to be called a theory of limited, or bounded, rationality. In a proper sense," March adds, "these developments comprise not a theory but a collection of behavioral complications for conventional theory."

Much of Simon's later research has focused on artificial intelligence and the computer sciences. As early as 1952, this interest was whetted by discussions with Allen Newell, then a research scientist at the Rand Corporation. Together they began to study problem solving through computer simulations, and eventually this field became Simon's central research interest. In 1961 Newell joined Simon at Carnegie-Mellon as a university professor. Continuing their collaboration, they published *Human Problem Solving* in 1972. In addition to empirical studies of business decision making and business psychology, Simon has examined the economic growth of firms in relation to their size and made crucial contributions to the central problem of the aggregation of microsystems.

Simon's theories have been criticized, notably by such respected economists as Edward Mason, Fritz Machlup, and MILTON FRIEDMAN. While praising the merits of Simon's descriptive theory of decision making, they question its value for economic analyses. In addition, his realistic account of the decision-making process undermines the assumptions behind general equilibrium analysis and the simple hypotheses of maximization and optimization of profits and utility functions on which it is based. However, these apparently antagonistic approaches are applicable to different sets of problems in economics and are therefore complementary. Simon has opened the field for empirical testing of hypotheses underlying the decision process.

Simon was awarded the 1978 Nobel Memorial Prize in Economic Sciences for his "pioneering research into the decision-making process within economic organizations." In presenting the award, Sune Carlson of the Royal Swedish Academy of Sciences stated that "the study of the structure and the decision making of the firm has become an important task in economic science. It is in this new line of development that Simon's work has been of the utmost importance. . . . Simon's theories and observations on decision making in organizations apply well to the systems and techniques of planning, budgeting, and control that are used in business and public administration. They are, therefore, an excellent foundation of empirical research."

In an autobiographical sketch, Simon noted, "In the 'politics' of science, which these other activities have entailed, I have had two guiding principles—to work for the 'hardening' of the social sciences, so that they will be better equipped with the tools they need for their difficult research tasks; and to work for close relations between natural and social scientists, so that they can jointly contribute their special knowledge and skills to those many complex questions of public policy that call for both kinds of wisdom."

In 1937 Simon married Dorothy Pye. They have a son and two daughters. His personal interests include walking, mountain climbing, sketching, painting, and playing the piano. He speaks several languages fluently.

In addition to the Nobel Prize, Simon has received the Distinguished Scientific Contribution Award of the American Psychological Association (1969). He is a fellow of the American Economic Association, the American Psychological Association, the Econometric Society, and the American Sociological Association and a member of the National Academy of Sciences and the Association of Computational Machines. He has been awarded honorary degrees by the University of Chicago and McGill, Lund, Yale, and Erasmus (Rotterdam) universities.

ADDITIONAL WORKS: Measuring Municipal Activities, 1938, with C. E. Ridley; Public Administration, 1950, with others; The New Science of Management Decision, 1960; The Sciences of the Artificial, 1969; Models of Discovery, 1977; Models of Thought, 1979; Models of Bounded Rationality (2 vols.) 1982; Reason in Human Affairs, 1983; Protocol Analysis: Verbal Reports as Data, 1984, with Karl A. Ericsson.

ABOUT: Hammond, A. (ed.) A Passion to Know, 1984; New York Times November 9, 1978; November 26, 1978; Scandinavian Journal of Economics, number 1, 1979; Science November 24, 1978.

SINGER, ISAAC BASHEVIS
(July 14, 1904–   )
Nobel Prize for Literature, 1978

The Polish-American novelist and short story writer Isaac Bashevis Singer, who writes in

ISAAC BASHEVIS SINGER

Yiddish, was born Icek-Hersz Singer in Leocin, a small village near Warsaw, Poland. Although the official date of his birth is given as July 14, other sources suggest that it may have been October 26. He was the third of four children of Bathsheba (Zylberman) Singer, the daughter of an Orthodox rabbi, and Pinchos-Mendel Singer, a rabbi of the Hasidic school. In his Hasidism, Singer's father embraced a mystical and emotional form of Judaism. His mother, although pious, was a skeptical rationalist. From his father, Singer heard tales about angels and demons; from his mother, he learned family history.

When Singer was four years old, the family moved to Warsaw and settled in the Jewish quarter, where Singer's father became the unofficial rabbi of their street and earned his living by serving as judge in a *Bet Din,* or rabbinic court. At the study house, Singer became acquainted with Jewish law in Hebrew and Aramaic texts. In his spare time he read secular books on modern science, politics, and economics written in Yiddish (the Germanic vernacular spoken by eastern European Jews). His voracious reading also included literary classics, especially the works of the nineteenth-century Russian novelists. Many of these books were provided by Singer's older brother, Israel Joshua, known as I. J., a writer who had forsaken Hasidic beliefs and who advocated the modernization of Judaism by greater participation in mainstream Western culture.

In 1917 Singer accompanied his mother to Bilgoraj, a village in eastern Poland where she had grown up and which had remained virtually unchanged since the Middle Ages. Remaining there for the next four years, he observed shtetl (Jewish village) life and absorbed its traditions. "I had a chance to see our past as it really was," he wrote many years later. "Time seemed to flow backward. I lived Jewish history."

When his father accepted a position as a rabbi in the Polish town of Dzikow in 1920, Singer persuaded his parents to let him return to Warsaw on the condition that he enroll at the Tachkemoni Rabbinical Seminary to pursue his religious studies. However, after spending several months there the following year, and subsequently joining his family briefly in Dzikow, he returned to Bilgoraj, where he supported himself by giving Hebrew lessons.

By 1923 Singer was once again in Warsaw. Remaining there for the next twelve years, he found a job as a proofreader for the *Literarische Bletter* (Literary Pages), a Yiddish literary journal edited by his brother, I. J. Singer. At the same time, he read widely in philosophy, psychology, the natural sciences, and the occult, as well as works of fiction. He also tried his hand at writing. His first published story, "Oyf der Elter" (In Old Age), appeared in *Literarische Bletter* in 1927 under the pseudonym Tse. His second, "Vayber" (Women), was printed the following year under the name Isaac Bashevis (that is, the son of his mother, Bathsheba). For the next five years, Singer continued to write short stories for Yiddish periodicals. Meanwhile, he earned his living as a translator, rendering into Yiddish German thrillers and works by KNUT HAMSUN, THOMAS MANN, and Erich Maria Remarque.

The publication in 1932 of I. J. Singer's novel *Yoshe Kalb* (translated as *The Sinner* in 1933) led to his being invited to join the staff of the *Jewish Daily Forward,* a daily newspaper published in Brooklyn, New York. He accepted the offer and emigrated to the United States. Isaac missed the advice of I. J., who had been his mentor. Isaac continued to write, however, and in 1933 became an associate editor of *Globus,* a literary magazine that published a number of his stories as well as his first novel, *Der Soten in Goray* (*Satan in Goray*), which appeared in installments in 1934 and in book form in 1943. Regarded by many critics as Singer's best novel, *Satan in Goray* was inspired by his experiences in Bilgoraj. Set in a seventeenth-century Jewish village, this gothic tale of demoniac possession recounts a wave of Messianic hysteria that overtakes a small Hasidic community. The episode, wrote the English poet and critic Ted Hughes, "is an accurate metaphor for a cultural landslide that has destroyed all spiritual principles and dumped an entire age into a cynical materialism emptied of meaning."

The mid-1930s were a time of great upheaval for Singer. His mistress, Runia, who was a communist, went to live in the Soviet Union with their son, Israel. At the same time, the Nazi government was taking power in Germany. Fearing Hitler's anti-Semitism, Singer left Warsaw to join his brother in the United States in 1935. He settled in Brooklyn and worked for the *Jewish Daily Forward* on a free-lance basis. For the next ten years, he suffered a writer's block induced by poverty, cultural disorientation, and discouragement at the future of the Yiddish language in the United States. Although he completed a novel, *Messiah the Sinner,* in 1937, which was published serially in New York, Warsaw, and Paris, he considered it a failure.

In 1940 Singer married Alma Wasserman, a German émigré. Two years later, the couple moved from Brooklyn to the Upper West Side of Manhattan. At this time, Singer, writing under the name Isaac Warshofsky, became a full-time staff member of the *Forward.* In 1943 he became an American citizen. Within two years, he was again writing short stories.

In 1944 the death of his brother I. J., whose fame as a novelist had until then overshadowed Isaac's, brought about another crisis of creativity for Singer. He called his brother's death "the greatest misfortune of my entire life." However, the following year he began work on *Di Familye Mushkat* (*The Family Moskat*), the first of three realistic social novels. Published serially between 1945 and 1948 in the *Forward,* it portrays the moral disintegration of Warsaw's Jewish community as Hitler's armies advance. A two-volume Yiddish edition and a one-volume English translation of *The Family Moskat* appeared in 1950.

As a prelude to *The Family Moskat,* Singer produced a work set during the last four decades of the nineteenth century, a time when Polish Jews were emerging from medieval village life into modern industrial society. Appearing in installments in the *Forward* between 1953 and 1955, it was translated into English and published as two separate novels, *The Manor* (1967) and *The Estate* (1969).

The English translation of *The Family Moskat* expanded Singer's audience beyond readers of Yiddish. Critical acclaim followed in 1953 when the *Partisan Review* published SAUL BELLOW's translation of "Gimpel Tam" ("Gimpel the Fool"). The title character of this story is a saintly fool, a good man who believes everything he is told and is easily tricked by his fellow villagers. Gimpel eventually becomes a storyteller. "No doubt the world is entirely an imaginary world," he declares, "but it is only once removed from the true world."

Singer's work came to the attention of Cecil Hemley, the editor of Noonday Press, who helped place the writer's stories in distinguished American literary magazines. In 1955 Noonday brought out an English translation of *Satan in Goray.* Hailed by critics, it established Singer as a writer of note. The first collection of Singer's stories in English, *Gimpel the Fool and Other Stories,* was published two years later to enthusiastic reviews.

The next two decades saw the publication of many of Singer's short stories, several novels, four volumes of autobiography, and a dozen works for children. *Der Kunsmakher fun Lublin (The Magician of Lublin),* written in 1958 and published in English in 1960, is a novel about a charismatic magician who becomes a religious penitent after hurting the women who love him. Singer's second collection of short fiction, *Der Spinozist: Dertseylung (The Spinoza of Market Street,* 1961), includes many previously published stories set in a post–World War II Polish ghetto. The novel *Knekht (The Slave,* 1962), a powerful love story of Jewish life in medieval Poland, quickly became a bestseller. Singer's reputation was further enhanced when he published English translations of two of his works—*A Friend of Kafka and Other Stories* (1970), considered by many critics to be his finest collection, and the novel *Shosha* (1978). In the latter work Singer again explored the themes of innocence, love, and redemption, this time in the context of the Holocaust.

With his election to the National Institute of Arts and Letters in 1964, Singer became its only American member to write in a language other than English. Five years later, he received the National Book Award for children's literature for the autobiographical sketches *A Day of Pleasure: Stories of a Boy Growing Up in Warsaw.* Asked why he wrote for children, Singer once replied that "they still believe in God, the family, angels, devils, witches, goblins, and other such obsolete stuff."

The 1978 Nobel Prize for Literature was awarded to Singer "for his impassioned narrative art which, with roots in a Polish-Jewish cultural tradition, brings universal human conditions to life." In his presentation speech, Lars Gyllensten of the Swedish Academy praised Singer as "a consummate storyteller and stylist," a "master and magician." He particularly singled out the author's medieval tales. "This is where Singer's narrative art celebrates its greatest triumphs," Gyllensten said; here is where "many of his characters step with unquestioned authority into the pantheon of literature . . . people of dream and torment, baseness and grandeur."

In his Nobel lecture, Singer expressed his gratitude for the award as "a recognition of the Yiddish language—a language of exile, without a land, without frontiers . . . a language which possesses no words for weapons, ammunition, military exercises, war tactics." Affirming the survival of the Yiddish tradition, he concluded that "Yiddish is the wise and humble language of us all, the idiom of frightened and hopeful humanity."

Critics have been divided in their assessment of Singer's work. Calling him "a simple writer, both formally and thematically," the American scholar Robert Alter has refused to classify Singer as a modern writer. To Ted Hughes, however, the quintessential theme of modernism is the individual's relation to God. Singer, he said, "raises Jewishness to a symbolic quality, and is no longer writing specifically about Jews but about man in relationship to God." According to the American scholar Richard Burgin, the clarity of Singer's prose, combined with his metaphysical and epistemological interests, makes him a modernist in the same vein as Franz Kafka or Jorge Luis Borges.

Although he was among the first American critics to recognize Singer's talents, the eminent scholar Irving Howe has also commented on the writer's limitations. "Singer seems almost perfect within his stringent limits," said Howe, "but it is a perfection of stasis: he plays the same tune over and over again. . . . Still, can one regard the absence of 'development' as a legitimate critical judgment?" If one American critic, John Simon, has dismissed what he termed Singer's endless repetitiousness, another, John Gross, has applauded him as "a true storyteller" who exhibits "no falling-off in the quality of his writing."

"When I was a boy, they called me a liar . . . for telling stories," Singer recalled in an interview given several years after he received the Nobel Prize. "Now they call me a writer. It's more advanced, but it's the same thing." He added, "Every experience becomes important when it's told, not before."

ADDITIONAL WORKS IN ENGLISH TRANSLATION: Short Friday and Other Stories, 1964; In My Father's Court, 1966; Zlatch the Goat and Other Stories, 1966;

Mazel and Shlimazel, 1967; The Fearsome Inn, 1967; The Séance and Other Stories, 1968; When Schlemiel Went to Warsaw, 1968; Elijah the Slave, 1970; Joseph and Koza, 1970; Alone in the Wild Forest, 1971; The Topsy-Turvy Emperor of China, 1971; The Wicked City, 1972; Enemies: A Love Story, 1972; The Hasidim, 1973; The Fools of Chelm and Their History, 1973; A Crown of Feathers, 1973; Passions, 1975; Yentl, 1977; A Young Man in Search of Love, 1978; Old Love, 1979; Reaches of Heaven, 1980; Lost in America, 1981; The Golem, 1982; The Penitent, 1983; Love and Exile, 1984; Teibele and Her Demon, 1984; Gifts, 1985.

ABOUT: Alexander, E. Isaac Bashevis Singer, 1980; Allentuck, M. (ed.) The Achievement of Isaac Bashevis Singer, 1969; Buchin, I. H. Isaac Bashevis Singer and the Eternal Past, 1968; Burgin, R. Conversations With Isaac Bashevis Singer, 1985; Eastley, C. M. The Singer Saga, 1983; Koppel, G., and Rosenblatt, P. A Certain Bridge, 1971; Koppel, G., and Rosenblatt, P. Isaac Bashevis Singer on Literature and Life, 1979; Kresh, P. Isaac Bashevis Singer: The Magician of West 86th Street, 1979; Malin, I. (ed.) Critical Views of Isaac Bashevis Singer, 1969; Malin, I. Isaac Bashevis Singer, 1972; Miller, D. N. Fear of Fiction, 1985; Plimpton, G. (ed.) Writers at Work, volume 5, 1981; Siegel, B. Isaac Bashevis Singer, 1969; Sinclair, C. The Brothers Singer, 1983.

HAMILTON O. SMITH

SMITH, HAMILTON O.
(August 23, 1931–   )
Nobel Prize for Physiology or Medicine, 1978
(shared with Werner Arber and Daniel Nathans)

The American molecular biologist and geneticist Hamilton Othanel Smith, one of two sons of Bunnie (Othanel) and Tommie Harkey Smith, was born in New York City, where his father took graduate classes in education at Columbia University during the summer months. The rest of the year was spent in Gainesville, Florida, where the boy's father was an assistant professor of education at the University of Florida. In 1937, after receiving his Ph.D., the elder Smith joined the faculty of the University of Illinois and the family moved to Urbana.

While attending the public schools in Urbana, Smith participated in athletics and developed an interest in chemistry and electronics, spending many hours in the basement chemistry laboratory that he and his brother had stocked with supplies bought with their newspaper route earnings. He also studied the piano and became a lifelong admirer of the pianist Arthur Rubinstein. In 1948, after graduating from University High School in only three years, he enrolled in the University of Illinois and began to major in mathematics. In 1950 he transferred to the University of California at Berkeley to study biology and for the first time found courses in cell physiology, biochemistry, and biology that interested him.

Upon receiving his bachelor's degree from Berkeley in 1952, Smith enrolled in the Johns Hopkins School of Medicine, where he pursued a conventional course of study with little opportunity for research. Four years later he received a medical degree, after which he spent a year as a medical intern at the Barnes Hospital of Washington University in St. Louis. That year he also married Elizabeth Anne Bolton, a nursing student; they have four sons and a daughter. Drafted into the United States Navy in 1957, he served for two years as a senior medical officer in San Diego, California. During his leisure time he began reading about genetics.

After his discharge from the navy, Smith spent from 1960 to 1962 as a medical resident at the Henry Ford Hospital in Detroit, Michigan. On his own time he continued to study genetics, specifically bacterial genetics and the biochemistry of the nucleic acids. A postdoctoral fellowship from the National Institutes of Health in 1962 enabled him to study the genetics of the bacteriophage and the mechanism of prophage establishment in the Department of Human Genetics at the University of Michigan. He was particularly interested in the mechanism of bacterial-cell destruction by bacteriophage particles.

Bacteriophages (viruses that infect bacterial cells) are among the simplest forms of life, consisting of an inner core of nucleic acid and an outer coat of protein. When an infective bacteriophage enters a bacterial cell, it may multiply and cause destruction of the cell by releasing new bacteriophage particles. Or it may be incorporated into the genetic structure, or deoxyribonucleic acid (DNA), of the bacterial cell (in which case it is called a prophage) and then be transmitted to daughter cells during bacterial-cell division. A third possibility is that the bacteriophage may be broken down into its constituent parts by bacterial enzyme systems and rendered inactive, a phenomenon known as host-controlled restriction-modification.

Restriction-modification is caused by a pair of bacterial cell enzymes: a restriction endonuclease and a methylase. The restriction endonuclease recognizes a specific nucleotide base sequence on the bacteriophage DNA and cleaves the phage DNA into several parts. The methylase recognizes the identical sequence on the bacterial, or host-cell, DNA, which it treats with methylate and thereby protects against enzymatic cleavage by its own endonuclease enzyme. (The methylation process involves the addition of a methyl group—one carbon atom and three hydrogen atoms—to the DNA molecule.)

Working at the University of Geneva in the 1960s, WERNER ARBER postulated that this two-enzyme system is a general property of bacterial cells. He called it a restriction-modification system because the bacteriophage is restricted while the host is modified. Arber also discovered a restriction endonuclease in the colon bacillus *Escherichia coli* that cut or split phage DNA at random or nonspecific sites and was subsequently called type I. Arber predicted that type II restriction endonucleases, which would cleave or cut at specific sites, would be found in other bacterial species and that these restriction endonucleases would be useful in determining the precise genetic structure of DNA molecules.

After two years at the University of Michigan, Smith was appointed research associate in the microbiology department of Johns Hopkins. There he investigated the enzymology of restriction-modification systems, research that led to a year's work with Arber in Geneva.

Upon his return to Johns Hopkins in 1967, Smith was named assistant professor of microbiology; two years later he became associate professor. At that time Smith and his colleagues performed a series of important experiments on restriction-modification enzymes in the bacteria *Haemophilus influenzae.* Isolating and purifying a type II restriction endonuclease, Smith and his co-workers became the first researchers to identify a site-specific endonuclease enzyme. They also determined the specific DNA nucleotide sequence recognized by the enzyme and its site of cleavage. Since then many type II site-specific enzyme systems have been discovered. As the number of identified restriction-modification systems increased, it became possible to analyze the genetic structure of DNA molecules, just as Arber had predicted. Shortly after Smith purified the restriction endonuclease of *H. influenzae,* one of his associates at Johns Hopkins, DANIEL NATHANS, determined the specific location and function of the genes of the DNA of simian (monkey) virus 40, using Smith's restriction endonuclease and another.

The investigation of the restriction enzymes by Smith, Arber, and Nathans have made it possible to analyze in chemical detail the organization of genetic material. This research has far-reaching results in the study of higher organisms. Because of it, scientists are now in a position to solve the basic problem of cell differentiation. In 1973 Smith was appointed full professor of microbiology at Johns Hopkins. Two years later he spent a year as a Guggenheim Fellow at the Institute for Molecular Biology at the University of Zurich in Switzerland.

Smith shared the 1978 Nobel Prize for Physiology or Medicine with Arber and Nathans for "the discovery of restriction enzymes and their application to problems of molecular genetics." "The discoveries of this year's laureates mark the beginning of a new era of genetics," declared Peter Reichard of the Karolinska Institute in his presentation speech. It was Smith's achievement, he said, to verify Arbor's hypothesis concerning restriction enzymes. "He purified one restriction enzyme and showed that it could cleave foreign DNA. Today maybe 100 such enzymes are known. They all cleave DNA, each at different defined regions. With their aid," Reichard went on, "these giant molecules can be dissected into well-defined segments, which subsequently can be used for structural investigations or in genetic experiments."

Since his appointment as professor of molecular biology and genetics at Johns Hopkins in 1981, Smith has continued to study the enzymology of restriction-modification systems, specifically the steric or three-dimensional chemistry of the molecular interaction between DNA and the endonuclease enzyme.

When not teaching or engaged in research, Smith plays the piano and listens to classical music. He is a member of the National Academy of Sciences, the American Society for Microbiology, the American Society of Biological Chemists, and the American Association for the Advancement of Science; he is also a fellow of the American Academy of Arts and Sciences.

ABOUT: New York Times October 13, 1978; Science December 8, 1978.

SNELL, GEORGE D.
(December 19, 1903–   )
Nobel Prize for Physiology or Medicine, 1980
(shared with Baruj Benacerraf and Jean Dausset)

The American geneticist George Davis Snell was born in Bradford, Massachusetts, the youngest of three children of Katherine (Davis) Snell and Cullen Bryant Snell, a former secretary of a local Young Men's Christian Association and an inventor who devised a method for winding induction coils. When the boy was four years of age, the family moved to Brookline, where he attended the public schools and showed a special interest in mathematics and science. As a youngster he enjoyed reading about astronomy and physics as well as playing football with his friends.

In 1922 Snell entered Dartmouth College. At first his favorite subjects remained mathematics and physics, but, as he recalled later, "a course in genetics taught by Professor John Gerould proved particularly fascinating and it was that course that led me to the choice of a career." After he graduated from Dartmouth with a B.S. in 1926, Snell took Gerould's advice and began graduate studies in genetics at Harvard University. There he worked under William Castle, the first American biologist to apply Mendelian laws of inheritance to genetic studies of mammals. In his graduate research, Snell investigated the association of two or more genes on a chromosome, in which the genes tend to be passed from one generation to another as a unit. This phenomenon, discovered in 1910 by THOMAS HUNT MORGAN and known as linkage, was the subject of Snell's doctoral dissertation, for which he was awarded a Ph.D. in 1930.

After teaching zoology for two years, first at Dartmouth and then at Brown University, Snell received a National Research Council Fellowship that enabled him to work for two years at the University of Texas under HERMANN J. MULLER. While studying the genetic effect of X rays on mice, Snell demonstrated for the first time the induction by X rays of

GEORGE D. SNELL

mutational changes in mammals. In 1933 Snell accepted a position as assistant professor at Washington University in St. Louis, Missouri. Convinced that his future lay in research rather than teaching, however, he joined the staff of the Jackson Laboratory in 1935.

The Jackson Laboratory had been established in 1929 in Bar Harbor, Maine, by Clarence Cook Little, a former student of William Castle's, as a center for studies of mammalian genetics. Although it was a small institution when Snell arrived as a research associate in 1935, the laboratory was already renowned for its program on mouse genetics. Normally, no two mammals have exactly the same genes. However, Little and his colleagues had inbred mice for many generations to produce genetically uniform strains, in which all members were as similar to one another as identical twins.

During his first years at the Jackson Laboratory, Snell continued to investigate radiation-induced mutations. In the late 1930s, while completing his research on mutations, Snell began to consider new projects, among them transplantation genetics. It had long been known that organ transplants between genetically different individuals are rejected. Although Little had shown that this property is controlled by more than one gene, he had been unable to distinguish the effects of the genes involved. Snell called such genetic factors histocompatibility (tissue-compatibility) genes. His early linkage studies led him to map a particular gene, or locus, that is especially important in determining whether a transplant will be accepted or rejected.

In 1937 Peter Gorer of Guy's Hospital, London, found that a blood protein, which he called antigen II, is involved in graft rejection in mice. Gorer came to the Jackson Laboratory in 1946 to collaborate with Snell, and the two scientists discovered that Gorer's antigen and Snell's histocompatibility locus were identical; therefore, they combined their nomenclature to call the gene H-2. However, their studies were complicated by the fact that the lines of mice being compared had many differences in addition to those in the H-2 genes.

It occurred to Snell that he could use the laboratory's inbred mice to isolate the genes responsible for transplant rejection. With this in mind he crossed two inbred lines, A and B, which did not accept grafts from each other. From the hybrid offspring of that cross he chose mice that did not accept A tissue and bred them with A mice. After many generations the proportion of A genes the animals carried gradually increased, although there were always some offspring that rejected A tissue because they still carried histocompatibility genes from the B strain. After some twenty generations Snell obtained a strain of mice identical to the A group except for their ability to accept grafts from the B line and reject them from the A line.

Snell began breeding these "congenic resistant" mice in 1946, but his first lines were destroyed the next year when the Jackson Laboratory burned down, and he was forced to start again. By the mid-1950s, after deriving a number of congenic lines, he began comparing the histocompatibility genes he had isolated. "We identified a group of about ten loci that control graft resistance," he wrote later. "One stood out like a sore thumb in determining whether a graft was accepted." This locus was H-2. The combined research of Snell and Gorer had already shown that H-2 is not a single gene but a set of genes located close together on the same chromosome. The H-2 locus and a few other genes near it were thus renamed the major histocompatibility complex (MHC), which Snell later called a supergene.

In 1957 Snell became a senior staff scientist at the Jackson Laboratory. Research on the MHC—much of it using lines of inbred mice developed by him and his colleagues—increased dramatically in the late 1950s, after JEAN DAUSSET identified the first human histocompatibility protein. In 1965 Dausset hypothesized that many of the human histocompatibility systems described at that time were the products of a single set of human MHC genes (later named human leukocyte locus A, or HLA), similar to the H-2 system

of the mouse. His hypothesis was correct, and the correspondence between the mouse and human systems was demonstrated in detail.

It was pointed out by Snell that "an influence on transplants probably is entirely irrelevant to the true function of [MHC] genes." Important clues to that function were provided by BARUJ BENACERRAF, who discovered in 1969 that genes within the MHC determine whether the body can mount an immunological defense against a particular foreign substance. Working independently in the mid-1970s, a number of scientists, including Benacerraf, found that MHC products—all of which are expressed on cell surfaces—appear to be the cues used by certain white blood cells (T cells) to recognize normal body cells (self-recognition) and distinguish them from abnormal or foreign cells.

The 1980 Nobel Prize for Physiology or Medicine was awarded jointly to Snell, Dausset, and Benacerraf "for their discoveries concerning genetically determined structures on the cell surface that regulate immunological reactions." "The MHC system provides an extraordinarily sensitive surveillance system to detect cells with changed membranes," said Georg Klein of the Karolinska Institute in his presentation address; "it also provides a mechanism to kill cells that are becoming alienated from their community in one way or another. The rejection of foreign grafts is then merely an unavoidable by-product." In concluding his remarks, Klein called the laureates' work "one of the most exciting chapters in the enormous building of modern biology."

In his other research at the Jackson Laboratory, Snell has investigated genes outside the MHC that influence transplant rejection, non-histocompatibility genes within the MHC, and other aspects of transplant rejection and acceptance.

In 1937 Snell married Rhoda Carson, with whom he had three sons. Since retiring from the Jackson Laboratory in 1969, Snell has continued to live and work in Bar Harbor, maintaining correspondence with researchers around the world. An avid gardener throughout his life, Snell devotes much of his time to his vegetable garden.

Snell's many awards include the Osborne and Mendel Award of the American Institute of Nutrition (1951), the Gregor Mendel Medal of the Czechoslovak Academy of Sciences (1967), the Gairdner Foundation International Award (1976), and the Wolf Prize in Medicine of the Wolf Foundation in Israel (1978). He was elected to membership in the

National Academy of Sciences, the Transplantation Society, and the Genetics Society of America.

SELECTED WORKS: Cell Surface Antigens, 1973; Histocompatibility, 1976, with others.

ABOUT: Current Biography May 1986; New Scientist October 16, 1980; New York Times October 11, 1980; Science November 7, 1980.

SODDY, FREDERICK
(September 2, 1877–September 22, 1956)
Nobel Prize for Chemistry, 1921

. FREDERICK SODDY

The English chemist Frederick Soddy was born in Eastbourne, the seventh son of Benjamin Soddy, a London merchant, and the former Hannah Green. Only two years of age when his mother died, Soddy was raised by his half sister. He showed an early interest in science and was encouraged by his science master at Eastbourne College to study chemistry at Oxford. In preparation for this course of study, he attended the University College of Wales, Aberystwyth, for one year before entering Merton College, Oxford, in 1895 with a science scholarship. There he studied chemistry under WILLIAM RAMSAY, earning a degree with first-class honors in 1898. For the next two years, he conducted independent chemical research at Oxford.

In 1900 Soddy accepted a position as demonstrator in chemistry at McGill University in Montreal, Canada. While at McGill, Soddy collaborated with ERNEST RUTHERFORD on the problem of radioactivity. This was a problem related to the foundations of chemical theory, established in 1869 by the Russian chemist Dmitry Mendeleyev. Mendeleyev had arranged the known chemical elements into the periodic table according to the principle that they were stable entities, differing from one another in regular fashion according to their atomic weight. Subsequent investigations, however, had uncovered puzzling irregularities among certain elements, especially the radioactive elements. These were in fact unstable and changed into products that seemingly did not fit into the table. Together, Rutherford and Soddy developed the disintegration theory of radioactive elements. According to this theory, some of the heaviest elements achieve stability by expelling small but measurably discrete units of mass, charge, and energy from their nuclei in the form of alpha, beta, and gamma emissions. In the process of radioactive decay, other elements are formed.

Returning to England in 1903, Soddy worked with Ramsay while continuing his studies at University College, London. Investigating the radioactive decay of radium, he experimentally verified the prediction of his disintegration theory that radium would produce helium. This was the first documented case of the generation of one element from another.

In 1904 Soddy became a lecturer in physical chemistry and radioactivity at the University of Glasgow. His experiments there proved that uranium would gradually decay to produce radium, and he was able to predict that an intermediate element should be produced in this transformation. Soddy's hypothesis was confirmed in 1906 by the American physicist Bertram Boltwood, who named the element ionium.

During his years at Glasgow, Soddy investigated the properties of those radioactive elements that could not be separated from each other by ordinary chemical means. It was Soddy who recognized in 1910 that "elements of different atomic weight may possess identical chemical properties." Within two years he had extended his findings to include nonradioactive elements. In 1913 he proposed the concept of isotopes—atoms of the same element that are nevertheless physically different. Isotopes of an element occupy the same place in the periodic table (the term *isotope* means "equal place") but have different atomic weights.

During this fruitful period in Glasgow, Soddy formulated his displacement law, which states

987

that the emission of an alpha particle transforms an element into an isotope of an element two places lower in the periodic table, while the emission of a beta particle causes the element to move one place higher in the table. With this theory, it was possible to deduce the decay sequences of many radioactive elements, thereby identifying related elements on the basis of the type of emission involved and integrating the elements produced into the periodic table.

Soddy's discoveries were of fundamental importance in chemistry. Traditional chemical theory predicted that the atomic weights of elements should be whole integers, but observation had shown many small variations. Isotopes provided a logical explanation for these variations in atomic weight and reopened the question, first posed by the English chemist William Prout in 1815, of whether all atoms were built of some common constituents. Soddy's colleague FRANCIS W. ASTON furnished the answers and received a Nobel Prize for his work.

Leaving Glasgow in 1914, the year World War I began, Soddy became professor of physical chemistry at the University of Aberdeen. Even though his contributions to the war effort interrupted his research program, he managed to confirm two predictions of the displacement law. By tracing the origins of the element actinium, he showed that common lead is actually a mixture of isotopes.

Appointed professor of inorganic and physical chemistry at Oxford in 1919, Soddy devoted much of his time to improving teaching standards and modernizing the university's laboratory facilities. In 1920 he predicted that because their rates of radioactive decay were known, isotopes could be used to determine the geological age of rocks and fossils. His suggestion eventually led to the development of modern radioactive dating techniques, such as the carbon 14 method devised in the 1940s by the American chemist WILLARD F. LIBBY.

Soddy received the 1921 Nobel Prize for Chemistry "for his important contributions to our knowledge of the chemistry of radioactive substances and his investigations into the origins and nature of isotopes." In his Nobel lecture, "The Origins of the Conception of Isotopes," Soddy described his work as only "a small part of much pioneering work in many lands" over the previous twenty years. He also expressed his gratitude to Rutherford for introducing him to the subject of radioactivity during the early years in Montreal.

After winning the Nobel Prize, Soddy gradually withdrew from active research in chemistry, turning his efforts toward economic, social, and political theory and writing several books on these subjects. He also developed an interest in theoretical mathematical problems. It is for his contributions to atomic theory that Soddy is best known, however. Although he foresaw the potential value of atomic energy for peaceful uses, in his later years he became deeply concerned about atomic weapons and the nuclear arms race and called on his colleagues to assume responsibility for the social consequences of their research.

Soddy married Winifred Beilloy in 1909; they had three children. After his wife's death in 1936, he resigned from Oxford at the age of fifty-nine and retired to Brighton, where he died in 1956.

In addition to the Nobel Prize, Soddy received the Stanislao Cannizzaro Prize of the National Academy of Sciences of Italy (1913), the Albert Medal of the Royal Society of Arts (1951), and an honorary doctorate from Oxford University. He was a fellow of the Chemical Society and the Royal Society. He was also a foreign member of the Italian, Russian, and Swedish academies of science.

SELECTED WORKS: Radioactivity: An Elementary Treatise, 1904; The Interpretation of Radium, 1909; The Chemistry of the Radio-Elements (2 vols.) 1911–1914; Matter and Energy, 1912: The Wrecking of a Scientific Age, 1927; The Interpretation of the Atom, 1932; The Story of Atomic Energy, 1949; Atomic Transmutation: The Greatest Discovery Ever Made, 1953; Radioactivity and Atomic Theory, 1975.

ABOUT: Biographical Memoirs of Fellows of the Royal Society, volume 3, 1957; Dictionary of Scientific Biography, volume 12, 1975; Howorth, M. Pioneer Research on the Atom, 1958; Kaufmann, G. B. Frederick Soddy, 1985; Romer, A. The Restless Atom, 1960; Trenn, T. J. The Self-Splitting Atom: The History of the Rutherford-Soddy Collaboration, 1977; Wise, L. Frederick Soddy: Money Reformer, 1982.

SÖDERBLOM, NATHAN
(January 15, 1866–July 12, 1931)
Nobel Prize for Peace, 1930

Lars Olof Jonathan Söderblom (sûd' ər blüm), Swedish archbishop, was born in Trönö, Hälsingland Province, to Jonas Söderblom, a minister, and the former Sophia Blüme, a descendant of a bishop of Christiania (now Oslo). Raised in a pious home where learning was highly respected, Söderblom began studying Latin with his father at the age of five.

NATHAN SÖDERBLOM

From childhood, he was determined to become a clergyman. An eager student, he received his early education in small-town schools and entered Uppsala University, his father's alma mater, in 1883. There he studied Hebrew, Arabic, and Latin and received his bachelor's degree with honors in Greek. This background prepared him well for the study of theology and the history of religion at the university's School of Theology. He remained there for the next six years, becoming a highly accomplished scholar as well as the president of the student body.

Söderblom's lifelong devotion to ecumenism began during his student years. While attending a Christian student conference in New Haven, Connecticut, in 1890, he heard an address calling for unity among the churches of the world. Inspired, he recorded this prayer in his diary: "Lord, give me humility and wisdom to serve the great cause of the free unity of thy church." Fostering ecumenism—looking beyond sectarian differences to unity among the churches—became his life's work.

Receiving his degree in theology in 1892, Söderblom was ordained in the state-supported Swedish Lutheran church the following year. That year he also published his first book, a study of the theology of German religious reformer Martin Luther. After serving as chaplain to a mental hospital in Uppsala, he was appointed pastor of the Swedish church in Paris. This post gave him enough financial security to marry Anna Forsell, a student at the University of Uppsala, in 1897; they eventually had ten children. During their marriage, his wife collaborated with him on many of his publications.

Söderblom spent seven years in Paris. In his congregation were many prominent Scandinavian artists, diplomats, and business leaders, including Alfred Nobel, a generous contributor to the church. When Nobel died at his villa in San Remo, Italy, on December 10, 1896, Söderblom conducted the memorial service. In his eulogy he recalled Nobel's "immense intellectual power, his remarkable achievements, and his conquests of nature's hidden forces in the service of humanity."

Completing his graduate studies in theology and the history of religions at the University of Paris, Söderblom received his doctorate in theology. His thesis concerned the idea of the afterlife in Zoroastrianism, a Persian religion founded in the sixth century B.C. In 1901 Söderblom returned to Sweden when he was offered a chair in theology at the University of Uppsala. Imbued with an international outlook and influenced by liberal French theology, he plunged energetically into his duties. He held this position at Uppsala until 1914, also teaching the history of religion at Leipzig University from 1912 to 1914.

A gifted teacher and scholar, Söderblom inspired a theological revival in his nation. He stimulated both his colleagues and his students to an interest in comparative religion and in the life and mind of Martin Luther. His warm personality and vigorous intellect made Söderblom popular not only at the university—where crowds of students came to hear him lecture—but also among the clergy. As a renewed interest in religion swept Sweden's universities, students founded a magazine called *Vår Lösen* (Our Watchword) and established a conference center for Christian meetings.

As a founding member of the General World Union of Churches for International Understanding, Söderblom took part in planning its 1914 meeting in Konstanz, Germany, but the outbreak of World War I forced the delegates to return home. He and other church leaders attempted to organize an ecumenical conference in 1917 and again were frustrated when authorities in the belligerent nations refused passports to church leaders; representatives from only five neutral nations attended. The manifesto issued by this conference articulated the two central themes of Söderblom's subsequent work: brotherhood and peace. Appealing to the "deep inner unity which all Christians possess . . . irrespective of national and scriptural differences," the proclamation called upon all churches to work for "the settlement of international differences through mediation and arbitration."

After the war Söderblom continued to work for ecumenism and peace. His energies and growing prestige gave impetus to the Universal Christian Conference on Life and Work, which drew more than 600 delegates from thirty-seven countries to Stockholm in 1925. Although the Roman Catholic church declined to attend, representatives came from the Eastern Orthodox church and from most of the major Protestant denominations. With Söderblom presiding, the delegates discussed such issues as a common ecumenical creed, the reconciliation of differing theological views, and the need to achieve world peace. The group established a continuation committee to arrange future meetings. Its work eventually resulted in the creation of the World Council of Churches in 1948.

In recognition of his commitment to peace through religious unity, Söderblom was awarded the 1930 Nobel Prize for Peace. In his Nobel lecture, he outlined the three tasks he believed the church must pursue to attain peace: to teach Christians that their religion requires nations as well as individuals to adhere to standards of law and justice; to teach the importance of a "supranational judicial system" as a means for settling disputes among nations; and to convert military forces into true guardians of peace by ceasing to glorify combat. Söderblom concluded his address by announcing an ecumenical council to be held in London in 1935. "We must struggle to win peace, struggle against schism, against the mad measures of fear, . . . against hatred and injustice," he said. "The noble and practical measures for world peace will be realized only to the extent to which the supremacy of God conquers the hearts of the people."

A year after receiving the Nobel Prize, Söderblom was invited to deliver the Gifford lectures in Edinburgh. After giving the first ten lectures in May and June, he returned to Sweden. He died of a heart attack at Uppsala on July 12, 1931.

WORKS IN ENGLISH TRANSLATION: Christian Fellowship, 1923; The Church and Peace, 1929; The Living God: Basal Forms of Personal Religion, 1933; The Nature of Revelation, 1933; The Death and Resurrection of Christ, 1967.

ABOUT: Bell, G. K. A. The Stockholm Conference, 1925, 1926; Curtis, C. J. Söderblom: Ecumenical Pioneer, 1967; Katz, P. Nathan Söderblom: A Prophet of Christian Unity, 1949; Rouse, R., and Neill, S. C. (eds.) A History of the Ecumenical Movement, 1954; Sharpe, E. J., and Hultgard, A. Nathan Söderblom and His Contribution to the Study of Religion, 1984.

SOLZHENITSYN, ALEKSANDR
(December 11, 1918–   )
Nobel Prize for Literature, 1970

The Russian novelist, dramatist, and poet Aleksandr Isaevich Solzhenitsyn (sôl-zhä nē' tsin) was born in the resort town of Kislovodsk in the northern Caucasus Mountains between the Black and Caspian seas. Although they were of peasant stock, his parents were well educated. His father, Isai Solzhenitsyn, interrupted his studies at Moscow University to volunteer for service in World War I, during which he was decorated three times. He was killed in a hunting accident six months before Aleksandr was born. To support herself and her son, Solzhenitsyn's mother, the former Taisiya Zakharovna Shcherbak, took a job as a typist; the pair moved to the city of Rostov-na-Donu when the boy was six years old. Solzhenitsyn's early youth coincided with the tumultuous beginning of the Soviet period of Russian history. The year of his birth marked the onset of a brutal civil war between the revolutionary Reds and the counterrevolutionary Whites that ended in the consolidation of Bolshevik power under the leadership of Vladimir Ilyich Lenin and, after 1924, of Joseph Stalin.

An outstanding student, Solzhenitsyn entered Rostov University in 1938. Although primarily interested in literature, he concentrated his studies on physics and mathematics in order to assure himself of a livelihood. In 1940, while still a student, Solzhenitsyn married a fellow student, Natalya Reshetovskaya. In 1941 he earned a degree in mathematics. In the same year, he completed correspondence courses in philosophy, literature, and history given by the Moscow Institute of Philology.

Upon his graduation, he took a job as a mathematics teacher at the Rostov secondary school. With the German invasion in 1941, he was mobilized and served in the Soviet army with distinction as an artillery officer. In February 1945 he was suddenly arrested, stripped of his captain's rank, and transported to Lubyanka Prison in Moscow. Charged with anti-Soviet agitation and convicted by a tribunal of three (one of Stalin's infamous troikas), he was sentenced to eight years in prison, to be followed by permanent internal exile in Siberia. The so-called anti-Soviet agitation for

ALEKSANDR SOLZHENITSYN

which Solzhenitsyn was sentenced consisted of ill-concealed derogatory comments about Stalin that he had made in a letter to a friend and of notes and drafts of stories that had been found in his map case.

Transferred to another prison in Moscow for about a year, Solzhenitsyn worked as a laborer on a building project. He was subsequently sent to Marfino, a specialized prison on the outskirts of Moscow that employed mathematicians and scientists in research. Much later, Solzhenitsyn was to remark that his training as a mathematician saved his life, for conditions at Marfino were less severe than in most Soviet prison camps.

Later in his imprisonment, Solzhenitsyn was transferred to a forced-labor camp for political prisoners in the Kazakh Soviet Socialist Republic, where he developed stomach cancer and was not expected to survive. However, following his release on March 5, 1953 (the day of Stalin's death), he underwent successful radiation therapy at a hospital in Tashkent. Until 1956 Solzhenitsyn lived in internal exile in various parts of Siberia, supporting himself by teaching. Released from exile in June 1956, he settled in the city of Ryazan, southeast of Moscow, where he was employed as a secondary school teacher. His wife, who had remarried during his imprisonment and borne two children to her second husband, obtained a divorce and rejoined Solzhenitsyn.

Beginning in 1956, Soviet Premier Nikita Khrushchev conducted a campaign to discredit the reputation of his predecessor, Stalin, who by conservative estimates had executed or im-

prisoned 10 million Soviet citizens since the early 1930s. As part of this program of de-Stalinization, Khrushchev personally authorized the publication in 1962 of Solzhenitsyn's first novel, *Odin den'Ivana Denisovicha* (*One Day in the Life of Ivan Denisovich*) in the Soviet literary journal *Novy Mir*. Written in a straightforward, understated style, the novel recounts the course of a single day in a Stalinist prison camp from the viewpoint of the principal character, Ivan Denisovich Shukhov. The work met with instant acclaim, and critics favorably compared Solzhenitsyn's tale with Fedor Dostoevsky's celebrated *House of the Dead,* written a century earlier.

The following year, Solzhenitsyn published several short stories in *Novy Mir,* including "Sluchay na stantsii Krechetovka" ("Incident at Krechetovka Station"), "Matrenin dvor" ("Matryona's House"), and "Dlya polzy'dela" ("For the Good of the Cause"), which were collected in English translations in *Stories and Prose Poems by Aleksandr Solzhenitsyn* in 1971. Although he was nominated for the Lenin Prize for Literature in 1964, Solzhenitsyn failed to receive this award, and following Khrushchev's removal from office later the same year, he encountered increasing difficulties in publishing his work. His last published work in the Soviet Union, the short story "Zakhar-Kalita" ("Zakhar the Pouch"), appeared in 1966.

Following a letter he sent to the National Congress of Soviet Writers in 1967, in which he called for an end to censorship and complained that the secret police had confiscated his manuscripts, Solzhenitsyn was repeatedly denounced by the government, and his works were banned. Nevertheless, copies of *V pervom kruge* (*The First Circle,* 1968) and *Rakovyi korpus* (*Cancer Ward,* part I, 1968; part II, 1969) found their way to the West, where they were published in "unauthorized" versions, putting Solzhenitsyn at even greater risk in his homeland. The author denied responsibility for the foreign publications and claimed that the Soviet government had allowed the manuscripts to be smuggled out of the country in order to discredit him and provide a pretext for his arrest.

The First Circle—the title refers to the first circle of hell in Dante's *Inferno*—is a satiric novel set in Mavrino, a specialized institute modeled after Marfino Prison, where Solzhenitsyn had worked as a mathematician. In the West, most critics judged the novel an honest and accurate portrait of life in the Stalinist era, and they praised Solzhenitsyn for his courage in writing it. *Cancer Ward,* based to some extent on Solzhenitsyn's own struggle against the disease that nearly took his life, is set in a provincial hospital in Soviet Central Asia. Although the novel has political overtones, it deals essentially with the human struggle against death. In the world Solzhenitsyn creates, the victims of cancer paradoxically attain a freedom that is denied to the healthy.

Solzhenitsyn was awarded the 1970 Nobel Prize for Literature "for the ethical force with which he has pursued the indispensable traditions of Russian literature." At once, he announced his intention to accept the award "in person on the traditional day," but he was in fact prevented from doing so. As it had done when BORIS PASTERNAK received the Nobel Prize twelve years earlier, the Soviet government denounced the decision as a "politically hostile" act, and Solzhenitsyn, fearing he would be denied reentry to the Soviet Union if he left to attend the ceremony, accepted the award in absentia. In his presentation address, Karl Ragnar Gierow of the Swedish Academy noted that Solzhenitsyn's works testify to "the individual's indestructible dignity." Mindful of the perilous situation in the author's homeland, Gierow continued, "Wherever that dignity is violated, whatever the reason or the means, his message is an accusation but also an assurance: those who commit such a violation are the only ones to be degraded by it." Solzhenitsyn's Nobel lecture, published in 1972, is widely considered to be a powerful and moving statement of his belief that creative artists are the last guardians of truth. Closing his lengthy statement, Solzhenitsyn proclaimed (the capitalizations are his own): "ONE WORD OF TRUTH SHALL OUTWEIGH THE WHOLE WORLD."

The following year, breaking with his previous position, Solzhenitsyn for the first time authorized the publication of his work outside the Soviet Union. Accordingly, his *Avgust chetyrnadtsatogo* (translated as *August 1914*) was brought out in Russian by a London publishing house in 1971 and in an English translation the following year. Conceived as the first book in a multivolume work examining the Russian Revolution, this historical novel has been compared to Leo Tolstoy's *War and Peace.* In it, wrote the American critic Patricia Blake, "Solzhenitsyn has achieved a superb balance in considering the impact of war on the lives of individuals and on the life of the nation."

In 1973, after questioning Solzhenitsyn's typist, the KGB (the Committee for State Se-

curity, or Soviet secret police) confiscated the manuscript of *Arkhipelag Gulag, 1918–1956: Op'bit khudozhestvennopo issledovanija (The Gulag Archipelago,* volume I, 1974; volume II, 1976). Working from memory and from notes he had secretly made during his imprisonment and internal exile, Solzhenitsyn had painstakingly set down a damning account of the Soviet penal system. His purpose was to record a part of Soviet history that does not exist officially and to commemorate the suffering of the millions of Soviet "nonpersons" whose lives have otherwise been erased from history. The term *gulag archipelago* refers to the prisons, labor camps, and towns of internal exile scattered across the Soviet Union. Solzhenitsyn included the stories of more than 200 prisoners he had met during his term in the gulag.

Shortly after the manuscript was seized, Solzhenitsyn sent word to his contacts in Paris, where a copy had been smuggled, giving his permission to publish the book. It appeared in December 1973, and on February 12, 1974, Solzhenitsyn was arrested and charged with treason. The following day he was stripped of his Soviet citizenship and deported to West Germany. His second wife, Natalaya Svetlova (whom he had married in 1973 after divorcing his first wife), and their three sons were permitted to join him later. After two years' residence in Zurich, Switzerland, the Solzhenitsyns moved to the United States, where they live in seclusion in rural Vermont. Solzhenitsyn completed *The Gulag Archipelago* with a third volume published in Russian in 1976 and in an English translation in 1978. He continues to work on the historical series that began with *August 1914* (an expanded edition of this work was published in Russian and French in 1983 and in English in 1986). The full series, now entitled *The Red Wheel,* is intended, in Solzhenitsyn's words, as "the tragic history [of] how Russians themselves in folly destroyed both their past and their future." He noted in 1972 that "the whole work may take as long as twenty years, and probably I will not live to finish it."

Since his move to the West, Solzhenitsyn has been dogged by controversy, and his reputation has fluctuated with his every pronouncement. For instance, his widely publicized 1978 commencement address at Harvard University, in which he condemned the materialism of the capitalist West as vociferously as he excoriated the repression of the communist East, led his detractors to refer to him as a utopian reactionary. The quality of his writing, too, has occasionally been called into question. Yet, as the American critic Joseph Epstein remarked in 1972, for Solzhenitsyn "moral conflict is at the heart of all action." Reviewing *August 1914* in 1972, the Yugoslav writer Milovan Djilas said that "Solzhenitsyn has begun to fill the emptiness superimposed on Russian culture and consciousness. He is returning Russia its soul—the very soul which had been revealed to the world by Pushkin, Gogol, Tolstoy, Dostoevsky, Chekhov, and Gorky." According to the American scholar Joseph Frank, "Solzhenitsyn's fundamental theme is precisely the affirmation of character, the ability to survive in a nightmare world where moral character is the only safeguard of human dignity and the very conception of humanity itself is something precious and valuable."

WOLE SOYINKA

ADDITIONAL WORKS IN ENGLISH TRANSLATION: We Never Make Mistakes, 1963; For the Good of the Cause, 1964; The Love-Girl and the Innocent, 1969; Six Etudes by Aleksandr Solzhenitsyn, 1971; A Lenten Letter to Pimen, Patriarch of All Russia, 1972; Candle in the Wind, 1973; Letter to the Soviet Leaders, 1974; Solzhenitsyn: A Pictorial Autobiography, 1974; From Under the Rubble, 1975, with others; The Calf and the Oak, 1975; Lenin in Zurich, 1976; Warning to the West, 1976; Prussian Nights, 1977; A World Split Apart, 1978; Détente, 1980, with Arthur M. Schlesinger; The Mortal Danger, 1980; East and West, 1980; To Free China, 1982; Victory Celebrations, 1983; Prisoners: A Tragedy, 1983.

ABOUT: Allaback, S. Alexander Solzhenitsyn, 1978; Barker, F. Solzhenitsyn: Politics and Form, 1977; Björkegren, H. Aleksandr Solzhenitsyn: A Biography, 1972; Burg, D., and Feifer, G. Solzhenitsyn, 1972; Carlisle, O. A. Solzhenitsyn and the Secret Circle, 1978; Carter, S. The Politics of Solzhenitsyn, 1977; Curtis, J. M. Solzhenitsyn's Traditional Imagination, 1984; Dunlop, J. B., et al. (eds.) Solzhenitsyn in Exile, 1985; Ericson, E. E. Solzhenitsyn: The Moral Vision, 1980; Fever, K. (ed.) Solzhenitsyn: A Collection of Critical Essays, 1976; Grazzini, G. Solzhenitsyn, 1973; Kelley, D. R. The Solzhenitsyn-Sakharov Dialogue, 1982; Labedz, L. (ed.) Solzhenitsyn: A Documentary Record, 1971; Lukács, G. Solzhenitsyn, 1970; Moody, C. Solzhenitsyn, 1973; Nielson, N. C. Solzhenitsyn's Religion, 1976; Reshetovskaya, N. A. Sanya: My Life With Aleksandr Solzhenitsyn, 1975; Rothberg, A. Aleksandr Solzhenitsyn: The Major Novels, 1971; Rzhevsky, L. D. Solzhenitsyn: Creator and Heroic Deed, 1978; Scammell, M. Solzhenitsyn: A Biography, 1984; Weerakoon, R. Alexander Solzhenitsyn: Soldier, Prisoner, Writer, 1972; Will, G. F., and Novak, M. Solzhenitsyn and American Democracy, 1980.

SOYINKA, WOLE
(July 13, 1934–   )
Nobel Prize for Literature, 1986

The Nigerian dramatist, novelist, and poet Akinwande Oluwole Babatunde Soyinka (shoy ink kä′) was born in Abeokuta, Western Nigeria, then a British dependency. The second of six children of Samuel Ayodele Soyinka, headmaster of St. Peter's (Anglican) Primary School in Abeokuta, and Grace Eniola Soyinka, a shopkeeper and a respected political figure in the community, Soyinka enjoyed a relatively privileged childhood. The Soyinkas were members of the Yoruba tribe, a West African people whose rich and complex traditions are deeply infused with elements of ritual, symbolism, dance, and drama. Yoruba legends and practices made an early impression on the young Soyinka; at the same time, he became familiar with Western (especially British) culture and with Christianity.

After attending St. Peter's Primary School, Soyinka went to Abeokuta Grammar School, where he won several prizes for composition. In 1946 he was accepted by Government College, Ibadan, at the time Nigeria's most elite secondary school, where currents of Nigerian nationalism mingled with British colonial influences. Upon completion of his courses four years later, Soyinka moved to Lagos and found employment as a clerk. During this time he wrote radio plays and short stories that were broadcast on Nigerian radio. In 1952 he entered University College, Ibadan (now the University of Ibadan), another prestigious colonial institution, to study English literature, Greek, and Western history. There he was further exposed to the fledgling Nigerian nationalist movement.

Moving to England in 1954, Soyinka read English literature at the University of Leeds and became acquainted with a number of young, gifted British writers. At Leeds he found a mentor in the noted drama scholar G. Wilson Knight, who stressed the concept of theater as ceremony and as a dialogue with the past. Under Knight's tutelage, Soyinka became deeply conscious of the European dramatic tradition and began seeking ways to fuse this tradition with that of the Yoruba culture. After receiving his B.A. with honors in 1957, Soyinka remained at Leeds, with the intention of earning his M.A., and began a study of the work of EUGENE O'NEILL. At the same time, he wrote his first two important plays, *The Swamp Dwellers* and *The Lion and the Jewel,* in which he examined the uneasy relationship between progress and tradition in modern Africa.

Several members of the Royal Court Theatre in London read *The Lion and the Jewel,* and their enthusiasm for his work encouraged Soyinka to give up his studies. He moved to London in 1958 to work as a play reader for the Royal Court Theatre and became acquainted with the main currents of contemporary British drama. He continued to write and also directed student productions of *The Swamp Dwellers* and *The Invention,* a play that expressed his opposition to racism.

Awarded a Rockefeller Research Fellowship in drama at University College, Ibadan, Soyinka returned to Nigeria in 1960 and established an amateur ensemble acting company, the 1960 Masks. His most elaborate play up to that time, *A Dance of the Forests,* was performed in the capital city of Lagos as part of Nigeria's Independence Day festivities on October 1, 1960. This play, and the satiric *The Trials of Brother Jero,* produced in Ibadan the same year, established Soyinka as Nigeria's foremost dramatist. The following year he devoted himself largely to writing scripts for a weekly series broadcast on Nigerian Radio, and also for television. In 1962 he was appointed a lecturer in English at the University of Ife. During this time, he became embroiled in a number of controversies, notably his attacks on the concept of negritude, a literary movement, often mystic in nature, that celebrated African traditions and subjects and opposed the assimilation of European culture. Soyinka regarded negritude as a nostalgic and indiscriminate glorification of the black African past that ignores the potential benefits of modernization. For Soyinka, negritude was not an adequate solution to African problems. "A tiger does not shout its tigritude," he declared, "it acts."

During this period Soyinka also spoke out against government censorship. In December 1963, in protest to an order from the university administration that all staff members support the government in the Western Region, Soyinka resigned his position. Two years later, following elections in Western Nigeria, a recorded victory speech by the winner was preempted by an unauthorized broadcast in which an unidentified speaker declared that the elections had been rigged and the results were fraudulent. Shortly thereafter, Soyinka was arrested, charged with having made the illegal broadcast, and imprisoned. A host of American and British writers, including Lillian Hellman, Robert Lowell, Lionel Trilling, and Penelope Gilliatt, protested to the Nigerian government. After two months the charges were dropped and Soyinka was released.

Soyinka became a senior lecturer at the University of Lagos in 1965, the same year that his first novel, *The Interpreters,* appeared. The protagonists, five young intellectuals who have recently returned to Nigeria from Europe and the United States, are struggling to interpret not only themselves but a society in transition. Although it is set in Nigeria, writes the scholar Eldred D. Jones, the novel presents the "universal problem" faced by a new generation that is dissatisfied "with what to them is a facade concealing a rotten structure."

In August 1967, on the eve of the Nigerian civil war, Soyinka met secretly at Enugu with the Ibo tribal leader Chukuemeka Odumegwu Ojukwu in an unsuccessful effort to persuade him to reconsider the decision of the Ibo people to secede from Nigeria. Eleven days later, as he arrived at the University of Lagos, Soyinka was arrested on orders from the Nigerian government, led by President Yakubu Gowon, on charges of conspiring with the rebels. For the next twenty-seven months, despite international appeals from leading Western writers, he was held in solitary confinement in a cell that measured four by eight feet. Deprived of human contact, medical care, books, and writing implements, Soyinka feared for his sanity and his life. Nevertheless, he managed to write secretly, producing some poems and notes for plays and for a novel.

Upon his release during the general amnesty in October 1969, following the government victory over the Biafran rebels, Soyinka was allowed to accept the post of director of the School of Drama at the University of Ibadan. He directed a new production of his 1964 play *Kongi's Harvest,* a musical comedy that bitterly satirizes African despotism, a work he subsequently revised for a 1970 film in which he played the title role. Just before the film's release, he went into voluntary exile in Europe. During this time he lectured extensively, held a fellowship at Churchill College, Cambridge, and wrote three important plays: *Jero's Metamorphosis; The Bacchae,* an adaptation of Euripides' play; and *Death and the King's Horseman.* His account of his prison ordeal, *The Man Died,* was published in London and New York in 1972. In 1975 he accepted an offer to become editor of Africa's leading intellectual journal, *Transition,* and moved to Accra, Ghana.

After a coup deposed President Gowon in July 1975, Soyinka returned to Nigeria. Appointed professor of English at the University of Ife the following year, he reasserted his presence by directing a production of *Death and the King's Horseman,* followed in 1977 by the staging of an ambitious new play, *Opera Wonyosi,* an adaptation of Bertolt Brecht's *Threepenny Opera.* In this work and in several playlets designed to be performed in parks and other public places, Soyinka satirized the newfound (and in his view, specious) prosperity brought to Nigeria by the oil boom. Directing and acting in an all-black 1979 production of the Jon Blair and Norman Fenton play *The Biko Inquest,* based on the case of Steve Biko, a black South African social activist who died while in police custody, Soyinka covertly attacked injustice and brutality in black Nigeria as well as white racism in South Africa.

During this period he was also active in the administration of the University of Ife, in the state government (where he took a particular interest in the issue of road safety), and in national party politics. Although considering himself a socialist, he did not join any political party and frequently debated with leftist critics who accused him of being "too European" in his outlook. At the same time, he was an outspoken critic of the corruption fostered by the government of President Shehu Shagari (1979–1983), and often found himself at odds with Shagari's successor, Mohammadu Buhari, who seized power in a New Year's Eve coup at the end of 1983. In 1984 a Nigerian court banned *The Man Died.*

Despite government pressure against him, Soyinka has remained active in the Nigerian theater. His reputation in the West, enhanced by a 1979 Chicago production of *Death and the King's Horseman* (which Soyinka directed) and the 1981 publication of his autobiography, *Aké: The Years of Childhood,* was certified when he was awarded the 1986 Nobel Prize for Literature. Soyinka, the first African to receive the literature prize, was cited by the Swedish Academy as one "who in a wide cultural perspective and with poetic overtones fashions the drama of existence."

Presenting the award, Lars Gyllensten of the Swedish Academy remarked that "[Soyinka's] plays make frequent and skillful use of many elements belonging to stage art and which also have genuine roots in African culture— dance and rites, masques and pantomime, rhythm and music, declamation, theater within the theater." Gyllensten continued, "Soyinka's dramas are deeply rooted in an African world and culture, but he is also a widely read, not to say learned, writer and dramatist. . . . The myths, traditions, and rites are integrated as nourishment for his writing, not a masquerade costume." Soyinka dedicated his Nobel lecture to Nelson Mandela, the imprisoned South African anti-apartheid leader.

In addition to his plays and narrative works, Soyinka has published several books of poetry, of which the best known are *Poems From Prison* (1969) and its expanded version, *A Shuttle in the Crypt* (1972). Although he composes his poems in the Yoruba language, he writes all his other work in English because, as he explains, "Nigeria has several principal languages, and English provides an element of cohesion."

Soyinka's work has been widely acclaimed by both African and Western critics. For Paul Lawley, "Soyinka's best plays contemplate the 'numinous passage' of transition between life and death, the human and the divine, affirming the mediating power of dance . . . and music." In the view of the Nigerian scholar Oyin Ogunba, "What comes across most clearly in all these plays is Soyinka's humanity" and his compassion for "a people who . . . are caught in the ungainly dance of transition." In the words of his American biographer, Henry Louis Gates Jr., "Soyinka's texts are superbly realized, complex mediations between the European dramatic tradition and the equally splendid Yoruba dramatic tradition. This form of verbal expression, uniquely his own, he uses to address the profoundest matters of human moral order and cosmic will."

Soyinka is married and has one son and three daughters.

ADDITIONAL WORKS: The Road, 1965; Idanre and Other Poems, 1967; Madmen and Specialists, 1971; Collected Plays, volume 1, 1973; Season of Anomy, 1973; Collected Plays, volume 2, 1974; Ogun Abibiman, 1976; Myth, Literature, and the African World, 1976; A Play of Giants, 1984; Six Plays, 1984; Requiem for a Futurologist, 1985.

SPEMANN

ABOUT: Gates, H. L., Jr. In the House of Oshugbo, 1984; Gibbs, J. Critical Perspectives on Wole Soyinka, 1980; Gibbs, J. Wole Soyinka, 1986; Jones, E. D. The Writing of Wole Soyinka, 1983; Katrak, K. H. Wole Soyinka and Modern Tragedy, 1986; Moore, G. Wole Soyinka, 1978; Ogunba, O. The Movement of Transition: A Study of the Plays of Wole Soyinka, 1975.

HANS SPEMANN

SPEMANN, HANS
(June 27, 1869–September 12, 1941)
Nobel Prize for Physiology or Medicine, 1935

The German embryologist Hans Spemann (shpä' män) was born in Stuttgart, the eldest of four children, to Johann Wilhelm Spemann, a book publisher, and the former Lisinka Hoffman. Spemann attended the Eberhard Ludwig Gymnasium. Although he was particularly interested in the classics, he decided to pursue a medical career. After spending one year working in his father's business and another fulfilling his military service, Spemann entered the University of Heidelberg in 1891.

Although he had initially planned to become a physician, Spemann became so interested in embryology in the course of his medical studies that he decided to abandon medicine and pursue a research career. Leaving Heidelberg in late 1893, he spent the winter at the University of Munich, and the following spring he began doctoral studies in embryology at the Zoological Institute of the University of Würzburg, where he worked under Theodor Boveri, one of the world's foremost embryologists.

Early in his research career, Spemann addressed a series of issues facing embryologists at the time. As he later framed these questions: "How does that harmonious interlocking of separate processes come about which makes up the complete process of development? Do they go side by side independently of each other, but from the very beginning so in equilibrium that they form the highly complicated end product of the complete organism," he asked, "or is their influence on each other one of mutual stimulation, advancement, or limitation?"

The direction of Spemann's initial study of embryological development was suggested by Gustaf Wolff, a colleague from his Heidelberg days, who had discovered that if the lens is removed from the developing eye of a newt embryo, a new lens will develop from the edge of the retina. Spemann was fascinated by Wolff's experiments but wanted to extend them, for he was less interested in how the lens regenerated than in how it originally came to be formed.

Normally, the lens of the newt's eye develops from a group of cells in the ectoderm (the outer layer of embryonic tissue) when an outgrowth of the brain, the optic cup, reaches the surface. Spemann proved that the lens forms at a signal from the optic cup. When he removed the prelens ectoderm and replaced it with tissue from an entirely different region, he found that the transplanted cells developed into a normal lens. In order to perform this research, Spemann devised techniques and instruments of great sophistication, many of which are still used by embryologists and neurobiologists for extremely fine manipulations of single cells.

Meanwhile, Spemann completed the requirements for his Ph.D. in zoology, botany, and physics, which he received in 1895. He remained at Würzburg and was appointed lecturer in zoology three years later; however, he left in 1908 to accept a position as professor of zoology and comparative anatomy at Rostock. At the beginning of World War I, he became associate director of the Kaiser Wilhelm Institute of Biology (now the Max Planck Institute) in Berlin-Dahlem, where he stayed during the war years. In 1919 he became professor of zoology at the University of Freiburg.

By his early experiments on the lens and the optic cup, Spemann had shown that the development of the prelens ectoderm is determined by an influence from the retina. He studied the timing of determination in the embryo as a whole by squeezing a newt's egg into two sections using a loop made from a single human hair. If this procedure is performed early in embryogenesis (the development of the embryo), each half of the egg may develop into a complete, though abnormally small, larva. If the operation takes place at a later stage, the two egg halves will grow into half embryos. From this phenomenon Spemann was able to deduce that the developmental outcome of the two halves had been determined in the intervening period.

At this point Spemann did not investigate precisely what the determination process involved. Believing that embryonic development was too complicated to be analyzed on the molecular level, he concentrated on the time sequence of determination—that is, which parts of the embryo are determined first and what the relationships among the various parts might be.

To find the answers to these questions, he transplanted tissues between the eggs of two closely related newt species. Since the two species differed in color, he could easily keep track of the implanted cells. He and his colleagues (in particular, Hilde and Otto Mangold) found that—as in Wolff's original lens experiments—the fate of transplanted tissue almost always depends upon its new location, not upon what organ it would have become had it been left in its original position. Spemann noticed one striking exception, however. Part of the embryo near the junction between the three basic cell layers (ectoderm, endoderm, and mesoderm), which had been "transplanted in an indifferent place in another embryo of the same age, did not develop according to its new environment, but rather persisted in the course previously entered upon and constrained its environment to follow it." Experiments reported by Spemann and Hilde Mangold in 1922 extended this work, showing that "there is an area in the embryo whose parts, when transplanted into an indifferent part of another embryo, there organize the primordia [the earliest discernible indications during embryonic development] for a second embryo. These parts were therefore given the name of 'organizers.' "

As he wrote later, Spemann's further experiments on transplants between embryos of different species showed that "the inductive stimulus does not prescribe the specific character [of the induced organ] but releases that already inherent in the reaction system. . . . Most of the complication is based in the structure of the reaction system, and . . . the inductor has only a triggering and in some circumstances directing effect."

The 1935 Nobel Prize for Physiology or Medicine was awarded to Spemann for his "discovery of the organizer effect in embryonic development." As notable as the achievement was, however, it represented only one of Spemann's many contributions. In the techniques he used and the questions he posed, Spemann set the course for embryological research in the first half of the twentieth century. In 1936 he summarized much of his research in *Embryonic Development and Induction,* which remains a classic work of developmental biology.

The importance of Spemann's work lay in his demonstration that interactions between sheets of embryonic cells were responsible for some of the decisions that committed special groups of cells—and their descendants—to develop into the tissues and organs they assumed in the mature embryo. Spemann's precise experiments led him to compose clear, cogent questions concerning the causal sequences of definite and well-defined developmental performances by groups of cells that were identifiable; the aggregate of his work provided the foundations for recent advances in developmental embryology.

Spemann married Clara Binder in 1895; they had two sons. When not involved in research, Spemann sought relaxation in discussions of art, literature, and philosophy; he organized informal evening gatherings of friends and colleagues for this purpose. One of his dicta was: "A scientist in whom the analytic mind is not combined with at least a touch of artistic feeling is, in my opinion, incapable of discerning the ultimate nature of an organism." Spemann died at his country home near Freiburg on September 12, 1941.

ABOUT: Dictionary of Scientific Biography, volume 12, 1975; Needham, J. Biochemistry and Morphogenesis, 1969; Saxén, L., and Toivonen, S. Primary Embryonic Induction, 1962; Science, November 1, 1935.

SPERRY, ROGER W.

(August 20, 1913–)
Nobel Prize for Physiology or Medicine, 1981
(shared with David H. Hubel and Torsten Wiesel)

The American neurologist Roger Wolcott Sperry was born in Hartford, Connecticut, to Francis Bushnell Sperry, a banker, and the

ROGER W. SPERRY

former Florence Kramer. After his father's death, when Sperry was eleven years old, his mother studied business and worked as an assistant to the principal of a local high school. Sperry received his early education in the public schools of Elmwood, a suburb of Hartford, and attended William Hall High School in West Hartford. He entered Oberlin College in Ohio on a scholarship and received a B.A. in English in 1935. Remaining at Oberlin, he earned an M.A. in psychology in 1937.

After another year at Oberlin, during which he pursued his interest in zoology, Sperry entered the University of Chicago for graduate studies in that field under Paul Weiss. While conducting research on the organization of the nervous system, he demonstrated that synapses (nerve-cell connections) develop by a kind of chemical touch process based on differences in the concentration of chemicals in nerve cells. He received his Ph.D. from Chicago in 1941.

For the next five years Sperry was a research fellow at Harvard University and a research associate of Karl Lashley at the Yerkes Laboratory of Primate Biology in Florida, which at that time was under the supervision of Harvard. At the Yerkes Laboratory, Sperry conducted research on split-brain preparations, that is, experimental animals in which the nerves connecting the left and right sides of the brain had been surgically severed. The nerve fibers connecting the two halves of the brain, or cerebral hemispheres, are the anterior commissure and the corpus callosum. The operation that separates the two hemispheres is called a commissurotomy.

Sperry returned to the University of Chicago in 1946, when he was appointed assistant professor of anatomy; later, in 1952, he was named associate professor of psychology. He continued studying the effects of commissurotomy on brain function in animals, work that led to major advances in the understanding of cognition. Sperry's research eventually helped to explain how the brain functions in such areas as memory, language, and the perception of spatial relationships. He and his colleague Ronald Meyers observed that after commissurotomy it appeared that "each disconnected hemisphere behaved as if it were not conscious of the cognitive events in the partner hemisphere." This observation demonstrated that the nerve connections between the hemispheres in the anterior commissure and the corpus callosum are essential to an integrated sense of awareness in the experimental animals. Before Sperry performed these experiments, it was assumed that the commissures were not important to the functioning of the brain.

An appointment as Hixon Professor of Psychobiology at the California Institute of Technology in Pasadena was given to Sperry in 1954. Continuing his research on split-brain functions, in 1961 he collaborated with Joseph Bogen and Phillip Vogel, two neurosurgeons at the White Memorial Medical Center in Los Angeles. Bogen and Vogel were performing commissurotomies on patients with untreatable epilepsy to control the spread of seizure activity from one cerebral hemisphere to the other. Some time after surgery, Sperry and his colleagues performed psychological tests on these patients. The information they gathered contributed greatly to current knowledge of the specialized functions of the left and right cerebral hemispheres of the brain. Sperry's findings also transformed the study of cognition and had significant implications in the diagnosis and treatment of nervous disorders.

A prevalent theory of the brain assumed that the left cerebral hemisphere was dominant and that the left cerebral cortex, or gray matter of the brain, performed higher cognitive functions, such as language, than did the right side of the brain. This traditional view arose from clinical observations of patients who had sustained injuries to areas of the left (and presumably dominant) hemisphere that affected specific cognitive functions. For example, injuries to the speech area of the left cerebral hemisphere produced an impairment in speaking. Since patients with injuries to the left cerebral speech area did not transfer function to the uninjured speech area in the right cerebral hemisphere, it was assumed that the right hemisphere was less developed. Sperry and his colleagues discovered that the right hemisphere was also capable of higher cognitive functions.

New testing procedures that allowed an assessment of the independent cognitive performance of each cerebral hemisphere were developed by Sperry and his associates. These methods involved flashing brief images first in one and then in the other field of vision. Because the optic nerves from each eye are partially crossed in the brain, the left field of vision is processed by the right cerebral cortex and the right field of vision by the left cerebral cortex. During a typical test of a split-brain patient, a picture of an object—for example, an apple—would be flashed in the right field of vision. The image of the apple was processed by the left visual cortex. Sperry or one of his colleagues would then ask the patient to identify the object. When the dominant hemisphere had processed the image, the patient would invariably answer correctly, "An apple." When the same picture was flashed in the left field of vision and was processed by the so-called nondominant hemisphere, the patient would deny seeing an image or would guess. In the second instance, however, the patient could correctly match the image seen by selecting an apple from a set of objects of different shapes. In this experiment, the left cerebral cortex demonstrated its capacity for verbal operations and language production; the right cerebral cortex revealed its capability for nonverbal operations. In other words, the patient knew the object was an apple but could not express this knowledge verbally. Further testing of split-brain individuals demonstrated that the left and right hemispheres of the brain exhibit different cognitive capacities.

The research of Sperry and his colleagues at the California Institute of Technology revealed that the cognitive functions of the left and right cerebral hemispheres differ in the following ways. The left (dominant) cerebral hemisphere processes neural information sequentially, logically, and analytically. It excels at understanding temporal relations as well as performing verbal operations, mathematical calculations, and abstract thinking and interpreting symbolic relationships. It also exhibits a highly developed capacity for language production. By comparison, the right (nondominant) cerebral hemisphere processes neural information intuitively and simultaneously. The

right cerebral hemisphere is superior to the left in interpreting visual and spatial relationships and patterns, such as recognizing faces. The right hemisphere is also better at comprehending complex relationships, interpreting auditory impressions (for example, voices and intonations), and understanding music. Sperry and his colleagues further demonstrated that both hemispheres possess the capacity for self-awareness or self-consciousness, as well as an awareness of social relationships.

As an advocate of the interactionist school of psychology, Sperry accepts the dictum that events of inner experience participate in the causal control of the activities and functions of the brain. He calls these events emergent properties of the brain because they emerge from within consciousness. The interactionist school is opposed to the behaviorist school of psychology, which denies or ignores this aspect of consciousness.

Half of the 1981 Nobel Prize for Physiology or Medicine was awarded to Sperry "for his discoveries concerning the functional specialization of the cerebral hemispheres." The other portion of the prize was awarded jointly to DAVID H. HUBEL and TORSTEN WIESEL. In his Nobel lecture Sperry cited his interactionist view that "cognitive introspective psychology and related cognitive science can no longer be ignored experimentally. . . . The whole world of inner experience (the world of the humanities) long rejected by twentieth-century scientific materialism thus becomes recognized and included within the domain of science."

In 1949 Sperry married Norma Gay Deupree; they have a son and a daughter. Sperry's hobbies include camping in wilderness areas, sculpting, figure drawing, ceramics, folk dancing, and paleontology. He is also involved in what he calls "human problems" and firmly believes that science can no longer remain in conflict with basic human values.

Among other awards bestowed on Sperry are the Howard Crosby Warren Medal of the American Society of Experimental Psychologists (1969), the Distinguished Scientific Contribution Award of the American Psychological Association (1971), the William Thomson Wakeman Award of the National Paraplegia Foundation (1972), the Karl Spencer Lashley Prize of the American Philosophical Society (1976), the Albert Lasker Basic Medical Research Award (1979), and the Ralph W. Gerard Prize for Distinguished Contributions to Neuroscience of the Society for Neurosciences (1979). He has also received honorary doctorates from Cambridge University, Oberlin

College, the University of Chicago, Kenyon College, and the Rockefeller University. The societies and organizations to which Sperry belongs include the American National Academy of Sciences, the American Academy of Arts and Sciences, the American Philosophical Society, the Royal Society of London, and the Pontifical Academy of Science.

SELECTED WORKS: Problems Outstanding in the Evolution of Brain Function, 1964; Science and Moral Priority: Merging Mind, Brain and Human Values, 1983.

ABOUT: Cousins, N. Nobel Prize Conversations, 1985; Current Biography January 1986; New York Times October 10, 1981; Science October 30, 1981; Weintraub, P. (ed.) The Omni Interviews, 1984.

CARL SPITTELER

SPITTELER, CARL
(April 24, 1845–December 28, 1924)
Nobel Prize for Literature, 1919

Carl Friedrich Georg Spitteler (shpit' e lər), Swiss poet, novelist, and essayist, was born to Carl and Anna (Brodbeck) Spitteler in the town of Liestal, near Basel. When his father, a government officeholder, was appointed treasurer of the new Swiss confederation in 1849, the family moved to Bern. The young Spitteler stayed behind, living with an aunt in Basel and attending the local gymnasium. He later moved back to Liestal and commuted daily to the Basel Obergymnasium, which prepared him for specialized studies at the university level.

Showing early artistic and musical talents, Spitteler originally hoped to become a painter. At the Basel Obergymnasium, however, he came under the influence of the philologist Wilhelm Wackernagel and the historian Jakob Burckhardt, both of whom inspired in Spitteler an appreciation for epic poetry, especially the works of the Italian Renaissance poet Ludovico Ariosto. Soon Spitteler began to compose his own verse.

In 1863 Spitteler acceded to his father's wishes and entered the University of Zurich, where he studied law. Between 1865 and 1870 he studied theology in Zurich, Heidelberg, and Basel in preparation for the ministry, but he declined an offer to become a pastor in Arosa, in the canton of Graubünden, in order to pursue a literary career. In 1871 he became a tutor in the home of a Russian general in St. Petersburg (now Leningrad), where he remained, except for occasional excursions to Finland, for the next eight years. During this period Spitteler completed his first major work,

the verse epic *Prometheus und Epimetheus* (*Prometheus and Epimetheus*, 1881), which he had originally conceived while a student in Heidelberg. Written in biblical, hieratic, and rhythmic prose, this modern allegory in a classical setting concerns the struggles of a man of ideals.

After returning to Switzerland in 1879, Spitteler published *Prometheus and Epimetheus* at his own expense under the pseudonym Carl Felix Tandem. The book was ignored by critics and public alike, however, and Spitteler feared that he would be unable to earn a living by writing. In 1881 he took a teaching position in Neuveville, in the canton of Bern, where two years later he married one of his pupils, Marie op der Hoff. He subsequently found work as a newspaperman in Basel (1885–1886) and in Zurich (1890–1892). Despite the demands of his newspaper and teaching work, Spitteler continued to write, publishing *Extramundana* (Of Things Supernatural, 1883), a blank-verse poem; *Schmetterlinge* (Butterflies, 1889), a book of lyrics; *Friedli der Kolderi* (Little Fred of the Kolderi Clan, 1891) and *Gustav* (1892), works of fiction; and *Litterarische Gleichnisse* (Literary Parables, 1892), a collection of satiric verses.

In 1892 Marie Spitteler's parents left her a sizable inheritance that enabled Spitteler to give up teaching and journalism and to concentrate on writing. Moving with his wife and two daughters to Lucerne, he worked in seclusion and produced several more books, including *Balladen* (Ballads, 1896); *Der Gotthard* (St. Gotthard Pass, 1897); the short story *Con-*

rad der Leutnant (Conrad the Lieutenant, 1898); and *Lachende Wahrheiten* (*Laughing Truths*, 1898), a volume of critical essays.

Perhaps because he seemed to be both an idealist and a classicist in an age of realism, Spitteler received little popular recognition at this time. He was, however, noticed and appreciated by a small coterie of writers and critics, among them Joseph Victor Widmann, literary editor of the *Berner Bund* (Federation of Bern), and the German philosopher Friedrich Nietzsche, who recommended him to the editor of the Munich periodical *Kunstwart* (The Arts Observed) in 1887. Ironically, when Spitteler republished *Prometheus and Epimetheus* under his own name ten years after its initial appearance, he was accused of having borrowed themes from Nietzsche's *Thus Spake Zarathustra*. Although Spitteler's work had predated Nietzsche's, his early lack of recognition led to a misapprehension about his originality, and he was compelled to defend himself against charges of plagiarism in *Meine Beziehungen zu Nietzsche* (My Relations With Nietzsche, 1908).

Widespread attention finally came with the verse epic *Olympischer Frühling* (Olympian Spring), the culmination of Spitteler's lifework, which appeared in several installments between 1900 and 1905 and was revised in 1910. A complex combination of mythology, humor, fantasy, religion, and allegory written in iambic hexameter, *Olympischer Frühling* in its final form comprises 600 pages divided into five books. The work was confirmed as a masterpiece in the German-speaking world of the day when the noted conductor Felix Weingartner published a laudatory pamphlet in its honor in 1904.

Spitteler continued to live in seclusion and to avoid addressing political or religious questions. However, in 1914 he publicly supported Swiss neutrality, rejecting proposals, suggested in some circles, that German-speaking Swiss should consider a "racial alliance" with Germany. Consequently, he lost favor with many of those who had encouraged him through his long period of neglect, but he won the approval of the French, who awarded him the medal of the Society of French Men of Letters in 1916.

In 1920, at the age of seventy-five, Spitteler received the 1919 Nobel Prize for Literature "in special appreciation of his epic *Olympischer Frühling*"; the prize had been reserved the previous year. In his presentation address, Harald Hjärne of the Swedish Academy described Spitteler's mythology as "a purely personal form of expression . . . which gives shape to the living turmoil of struggling characters . . . in order to represent on the level of ideal imagination, human sufferings, hopes, and disillusions, the vicissitudes of different human fortunes in the struggle of the free will against imposed necessity." The award was accepted by the Swiss minister of foreign affairs on behalf of Spitteler, who was too ill to travel to Stockholm. Spitteler died four years later in Lucerne on December 28, 1924.

Reflecting the esteem in which Spitteler was held by his contemporaries, particularly the French, ROMAIN ROLLAND, in a tribute delivered after Spitteler's death, proclaimed him "our Homer, the greatest German poet since Goethe, the only master of the epic since Milton died three centuries ago, but a more solitary figure amid the art of his day than either the one or the other of these." In recent years, however, Spitteler's work has again fallen into obscurity.

ADDITIONAL WORKS IN ENGLISH TRANSLATION: The Little Misogynists, 1923; Selected Poems, 1927.

ABOUT: Boyd, E. Studies From Ten Literatures, 1925; Eloesser, A. Modern German Literature, 1933; Robertson, J. G. Essays and Addresses, 1935; Saturday Review of Literature July 31, 1926.

STANLEY, WENDELL M.
(August 16, 1904–June 15, 1971)
Nobel Prize for Chemistry, 1946
(shared with John H. Northrop and
   James B. Sumner)

The American biochemist Wendell Meredith Stanley was born in Ridgeville, Indiana, to Claire (Plessinger) and James G. Stanley, publishers of the local newspaper. While growing up in Ridgeville, Stanley often helped his parents by delivering newspapers and working at the newspaper office. After attending public school, Stanley entered Earlham College in Richmond, Indiana, to study chemistry and mathematics. A popular student and a talented athlete, he was chosen captain of the football team during his senior year and considered a career as a football coach. Shortly before graduating from Earlham in 1926, Stanley visited the University of Illinois with one of his chemistry teachers, who introduced him to Roger Adams, a member of the university's chemistry department. Adams's enthusiasm inspired Stanley's interest in sci-

WENDELL M. STANLEY

entific research and led him to apply for a graduate assistantship at Illinois, where he received an M.S. in 1927 and a Ph.D. in 1929 for work on compounds used to treat leprosy.

After a year of postdoctoral research at Illinois, Stanley was awarded a National Research Council Fellowship in chemistry to work under HEINRICH WIELAND at the University of Munich. Upon his return the following year, Stanley became an assistant at the Rockefeller Institute for Medical Research (now Rockefeller University) in New York City, but transferred in 1932 to the institute's laboratory of animal and plant pathology in Princeton, New Jersey. There he began research into viruses that attack plants.

Viruses were first identified in 1898 by the Dutch botanist Martinus Willem Beijerinck, who reported that tobacco mosaic, a type of plant disease, was caused by an infectious agent much smaller than the smallest bacteria and invisible to the microscope. When Stanley began his work in 1932, it was clear that viruses could reproduce and mutate and must therefore be living organisms. At the same time, however, it seemed doubtful that such minute substances could exhibit respiration, digestion, and other metabolic functions.

Stanley chose the tobacco mosaic virus (TMV) for his initial investigations and subjected the virus to the effects of the enzymes trypsin and pepsin (recently isolated by JOHN H. NORTHROP) and to more than 100 chemical reagents. By 1934 Stanley concluded that TMV consists essentially of protein. Using Northrop's methods, he produced crystals of virus

protein in 1935 and then went on to demonstrate that these crystals could be dissolved, filtered, purified, and recrystallized without destroying their ability to multiply in plants and infect them. Within another year he had isolated nucleic acid from crystalline TMV; and by 1937 it was established by two British scientists, Frederick C. Bawden and Norman W. Pirie, that TMV is a nucleoprotein (a compound of nucleic acids and proteins).

After the United States entered World War II, Stanley was asked to join the Committee for Medical Research of the United States Office of Scientific Research and Development in Washington, D.C. Over the next three years he and his colleagues purified several strains of influenza virus and produced the first influenza vaccine, for which he was awarded the Presidential Certificate of Merit in 1948.

"For their preparation of enzymes and virus proteins in pure form," Stanley and Northrop were awarded half of the 1946 Nobel Prize for Chemistry. The other half of the prize was awarded to JAMES B. SUMNER. In his Nobel lecture Stanley noted that since the discovery of the TMV more than 300 different viruses had been identified, including those that cause smallpox, yellow fever, dengue fever, poliomyelitis, measles, mumps, pneumonia, and the common cold. "The new field of virus research is really in its infancy," he added, "and much remains to be accomplished. Certain basic . . . problems relating to the mode of virus reproduction and mutation have taken definite form. Solution of these problems should yield information of great value to biology, chemistry, genetics, and medicine."

A chance meeting in 1946 with Robert G. Sproul, president of the University of California, led to an invitation to establish and direct a new virus laboratory at the university's Berkeley campus, which Stanley accepted in 1948. Remaining at Berkeley for the rest of his career, Stanley directed research projects that further clarified the nature of viruses. One of his colleagues, Heinz Fraenkel-Conrat, showed that the protein component of a virus is merely its housing and that its genes are carried in ribonucleic acid (RNA), a finding that explained why Stanley had repeatedly failed to produce genetic alterations in the TMV by altering its protein.

During the 1950s the faculty members at the University of California were asked to sign oaths of loyalty to the United States. Although Stanley, who was chairman of the university's committee on academic freedom, willingly signed such an oath, he staunchly defended those who refused to do so, maintaining that requiring them to do so was an infringement of their rights. His opposition to the requirement contributed to a court decision that struck down the measure.

In addition to his research and administrative responsibilities, Stanley lectured extensively and sat on numerous boards and committees. He was a trustee of Mills College from 1951 to 1958 and an adviser to the National Institutes of Health from 1945 until his death. He also served on the Expert Advisory Panel on Virus Diseases of the World Health Organization (1951–1966), the National Advisory Cancer Council of the United States Public Health Service (1952–1956), the National Science Foundation Committee for Medical Research (1955), the Board of Scientific Counselors of the National Cancer Institute (1957–1958), and an advisory committee to the secretary of the United States Department of Health, Education, and Welfare (1967–1968).

In 1929 Stanley married Marian Staples Jay, whom he had met in graduate school; they had three daughters and a son.

Late in his career Stanley became convinced that viruses are responsible for many forms of cancer in humans; he also speculated that viruses could have been the first form of life on earth. While attending the fifth Congress of the Spanish Society of Biochemistry in Salamanca, Spain, where he presented a paper on tumor viruses, Stanley died of a heart attack on June 15, 1971.

Stanley was awarded the Alder Prize of Harvard University (1938), the Nichols Medal of the American Chemical Society (1946), and the Scientific Achievement Award of the American Medical Association (1966). He held honorary degrees from many colleges and universities, including Earlham, Harvard, Yale, Princeton, Illinois, California, and Indiana. He was a member of the American Academy of Arts and Sciences, the American Society of Biological Chemists, the American Association for the Advancement of Science, the American Chemical Society, the American Philosophical Society, and the Society for Experimental Biology, as well as a foreign member of scientific organizations in Japan, Argentina, and France.

SELECTED WORKS: Viruses and the Nature of Life, 1961, with Evan G. Valens.

ABOUT: Current Biography April 1947; National Cyclo-

pedia of American Biography, volume 57, 1977; New York Times June 16, 1971; Sullivan, N. Pioneer Germ Fighters, 1962; Williams, G. Virus Hunters, 1959.

STARK, JOHANNES
(April 15, 1874–June 21, 1957)
Nobel Prize for Physics, 1919

The German physicist Johannes Stark was born in Schickenhof, Bavaria, the son of a landowner. He attended secondary schools in Bayreuth and Regensburg, and in 1894 entered the University of Munich, where he earned his doctorate in 1897 with a dissertation titled "Investigations on Lampblack." That fall he became an assistant to Eugen Lommel at Munich. In 1900 Stark moved to the University of Göttingen to assist Eduard Riecke; he also became a privatdocent (unsalaried lecturer) there. Remaining at Göttingen for the next six years, he proved himself to be a talented experimental physicist, despite an abrasive personality. Stark's chief interest was the behavior of ions in electric fields. In 1904 he founded the periodical *Jahrbuch der Radioaktivität und Elektronik* (Yearbook of Radioactivity and Electronics), which he edited for nine years.

In 1905 Stark observed the Doppler shift in canal rays. Canal rays are positive ions (charged atoms) which are accelerated in a vacuum toward an electrode and which pass through spaces (canals) in the electrode. As WILHELM WIEN had discovered, such ions reach extremely high speeds; their motion alters the apparent frequencies of the light they emit. Frequencies are decreased when the ion moves away from the observer and increased when it moves toward the observer. This change of frequency, or Doppler shift, was well known from the spectra of stars (a spectrum is a series of colored lines produced when light is separated into its component frequencies, or wavelengths), but Stark was the first to observe it in light from a terrestrial source.

Early in his career, Stark was sympathetic toward theories that broke with the ideas of classical physics. When ALBERT EINSTEIN proposed his special theory of relativity in 1905, Stark was among its earliest proponents, and since relativity describes the behavior of moving bodies, he offered his observations of the Doppler shift in its support. In 1907 Stark solicited an article from Einstein on relativity for the *Jahrbuch der Radioaktivität und Elektronik,* and he championed Einstein's idea that light behaves in some respects as if it consisted

JOHANNES STARK

of particles of energy, or quanta. This hypothesis was not fully accepted until the 1920s.

In 1906 Stark left Göttingen to take an untenured professorship at the technical university in Hannover. There his difficult personality led to problems with his superior, who repeatedly tried to have him dismissed. These problems were resolved only in 1909, when with the aid of the theoretical physicist Arnold Sommerfeld, Stark obtained a full professorship at the technical university in Aachen. Soon, however, he was at odds with Sommerfeld over the nature of the X rays emitted by electrons when they are decelerated. Stark maintained that the quantum theory was necessary to explain the distinctive features of this phenomenon, whereas Sommerfeld believed that classical electromagnetism could adequately do so. The debate, which was conducted in print, ended bitterly, and Stark and Sommerfeld never mended their friendship.

In 1896 the Dutch physicist PIETER ZEEMAN had found that a magnetic field applied to a glowing gas splits each of its spectral lines into three or more closely spaced but separate lines (the Zeeman effect). In 1913, Stark, again using canal rays, was able to produce a similar splitting of the spectral lines of hydrogen by means of an electric field. This phenomenon, known as the Stark effect, which other scientists had unsuccessfully sought to produce, could not be explained by classical electromagnetic theory. However, earlier in 1913, NIELS BOHR had proposed a quantum theory of the hydrogen atom, in which electrons occupy only particular orbits, each associated with a specific energy level. According to this theory, the spectral lines of hydrogen are produced as the electrons jump from one orbit to another, each jump producing radiation of a specific wavelength. As Sommerfeld and Paul Epstein demonstrated in 1916, an electric field outside the atom alters the electron orbits, producing different energy levels and thus the multiple spectral lines that Stark observed. Thus, Stark's discovery lent support to the Bohr model of the atom and to quantum theory in general.

"For his discovery of the Doppler effect in canal rays and the splitting of spectral lines in electric fields," Stark was awarded the 1919 Nobel Prize for Physics. "The discovery . . . was instrumental in the proof that canal-ray particles are luminous atoms, or atomic ions," said A. G. Ekstrand of the Royal Swedish Academy of Sciences in his presentation speech. "The further study of the Doppler effect in their spectra, which has been pursued principally by Stark and his pupils, has led to extremely important results," Ekstrand continued, "not only concerning the canal rays themselves . . . but also concerning the nature of the different spectra which one and the same chemical element can emit in different circumstances."

In the years following his discovery of the phenomenon named after him, Stark grew increasingly reactionary in both his scientific and political views. Despite the importance of his own work to the Bohr model of the atom, he never accepted Bohr's conclusions; indeed, in his Nobel lecture he declared that the Bohr model contradicted "the very spirit of physics." His early enthusiasm for Einstein's theories vanished, and as scientific support increased for the quantum theory and relativity, he rejected them both. Stark disliked Einstein's politics as well as his science: Einstein was a pacifist in World War I. In 1917, after being rejected for a position at the University of Göttingen, Stark accepted a post at the University of Greifswald, where the faculty was scientifically and politically conservative.

Mistrusting both the democratic Weimar government of postwar Germany and the Berlin physicists who dominated the German Physical Society, Stark in 1920 helped found an independent physics association that he hoped would advise the government. However, this group received little support and had slight influence. In 1920 Stark accepted a professorship at the University of Würzburg, but a quarrel with his colleagues led to his resignation within two years. While at Würzburg, he had started a porcelain factory, a venture many physicists considered unethical, since much of the capital had come from his Nobel Prize monies.

The porcelain enterprise eventually failed, and Stark attempted to return to academic life. When the presidency of the State Physical-Technical Institute in Berlin became vacant, Stark was passed over for the post, and he spent the next few years in forced retirement on his family estate at Traunstein in Bavaria. Although he was considered for several other academic posts, he was rejected for each of them, presumably because he had made so many enemies. One of Stark's few remaining allies was PHILIPP VON LENARD, an avowed opponent of what Lenard called "Jewish, dogmatic physics." Stark became a leading advocate of what Lenard labeled Aryan physics, by which he meant physics that rejected "highly abstract theory developed by Jewish physicists." The proponents of Aryan physics considered Einstein their principal enemy.

As a native of southern Germany, Stark was familiar with the Nazi party and had supported Adolf Hitler since the early 1920s. When the Nazis came to power in 1933 and the presidency of the State Physical-Technical Institute again became available, Stark's party connections assured him of the post. As president of the institute, Stark had ambitious plans for the reorganization of all German science; he also accepted the presidency of the German Research Association. However, because of the vehemence with which he attacked even non-Jewish advocates of modern physics, including Sommerfeld, MAX VON LAUE, and WERNER HEISENBERG, whom he called "white Jews in science," he was not able to wield influence among German physicists. Moreover, he made enemies in the Reich Education Ministry, under whose authority the Research Association operated. None of his plans were carried out, and eventually he found himself in disfavor with the office of the Nazi ideologist Alfred Rosenberg. Stark was forced to resign the presidency of the Research Association in 1936, after the failure of a gold-mining scheme that he had supported. Nevertheless, he remained president of the Physical-Technical Institute until 1939.

After 1939 Stark lived in retirement on his estate, where he had built a private laboratory. The results of his final research efforts, the supposed discovery of the deflection of light by a nonuniform electric field, have never been confirmed.

Stark was married to the former Luise Uep-ler, with whom he had five children. He was interested in forestry and cultivated fruit trees. He died on June 21, 1957.

In addition to the Nobel Prize, Stark was awarded the Baumgartner Prize of the Vienna Academy of Sciences, the Vahlbruch Prize of the Göttingen Academy, and the Matteucci Gold Medal of the National Academy of Sciences of Italy. He was a member of the scientific academies of Göttingen, Rome, Leiden, Vienna, and Calcutta.

SELECTED WORKS: Electric Spectrum Analysis of the Chemical Atoms, 1914.

ABOUT: Dictionary of Scientific Biography, volume 12, 1975.

STAUDINGER, HERMANN
(March 23, 1881–September 8, 1965)
Nobel Prize for Chemistry, 1953

The German chemist Hermann Staudinger was born in Worms to Franz Staudinger, a professor of philosophy, and Auguste (Wenck) Staudinger. When he decided to be a botanist, his father suggested that chemistry would provide useful training. After graduating from the local gymnasium in 1899, Staudinger began studying chemistry at the University of Halle, Germany. He soon transferred to the technical university at Darmstadt when his father obtained a teaching position there. After a brief period at the University of Munich, he returned to Halle, where, under Daniel Vorlander, he earned his doctorate in organic chemistry in 1903 for work on malonic esters of unsaturated compounds.

Staudinger then became an assistant to Johannes Thiele, a leading figure in the chemistry of unsaturated organic molecules at the University of Strasbourg. During this period Staudinger discovered ketene, a highly reactive unsaturated form of ketone, and carried out extensive research on this new class of compounds. For this work Staudinger received his *habilitation* (teaching qualification) in 1907. He then became an assistant professor at the technical university at Karlsruhe, where he worked with the noted chemical technologist Carl Engler. Engler was also a consultant for the Badische Anilin- und Sodafabrik (BASF), a German chemical company. BASF was interested in the synthesis of rubber, since natural rubber prices were then at an all-time high. Under this impetus, in 1910 Staudinger

HERMANN STAUDINGER

found a new and simpler way to synthesize isoprene, the basic unit of natural rubber. His main line of research, however, remained the study of ketenes, with the assistance of his student LEOPOLD RUŽIČKA.

In 1912 Staudinger succeeded RICHARD WILLSTÄTTER at Zurich's prestigious Federal Institute of Technology. During World War I, Staudinger and Ružička studied the composition of the natural insecticide pyrethrin and developed an artificial pepper. Simultaneously, Staudinger sought a synthetic substitute for the natural drug atropine. With his student TADEUS REICHSTEIN he investigated the chemical basis of the aroma and flavor of coffee and developed a synthetic coffee essence for use in wartime Germany, which was cut off from its usual supplies by a British naval blockade.

After the war Staudinger returned to the study of natural rubber. His brief association with the synthesis of isoprene in 1910 and his interest in botany made him a keen observer of current research on the structure of natural rubber. It is now known that natural rubber is a very large molecule with a molecular weight of about one million. At the time, however, the prevailing view, based on a theory advanced by the German chemist Carl Harries, assumed that rubber was not a single molecule but a loose aggregate of rings, each consisting of two or more isoprene units. The existence of apparently large molecules such as rubber and cellulose was explained by the micellar theory, according to which small molecules were

held together by weak bonds to form aggregates called micelles.

In 1917 Staudinger concluded that the structure for rubber put forward by Harries was incorrect. He argued that the natural rubber molecule was a true, stable molecule composed of a chain of isoprene units held together by primary bonds and containing thousands of atoms. Calling these large molecules macromolecules, Staudinger three years later expanded his ideas into a general macromolecular theory of polymers—long, chain-shaped molecules composed of scores or hundreds of repetitions of a small number of components. Staudinger was then nearly forty years old and a highly respected organic chemist. To expose himself to scathing criticism by rejecting the popular micellar theory was an act of considerable courage, particularly when some of the experimental work published by other scientists during the next four years appeared to confirm the micellar theory.

Staudinger appreciated the strength of the scientific opposition to his ideas and prudently drew up an ambitious research program to confirm his macromolecular theory. Between 1920 and the early 1930s, Staudinger and his associates carried out numerous experiments to verify the existence of giant molecules. They first attacked the structure proposed by Harries. Because the micellar theory held that the aggregate was bound together by the attraction between the double bonds in each ring, the removal of these double bonds by reduction (that is, the addition of hydrogen atoms) should destroy the micelles and produce liquid hydrocarbons. However, in the nineteenth century the French chemist Marcellin Berthelot had reduced rubber and obtained a solid material, results that Staudinger confirmed in 1922. Staudinger also reduced the macromolecules of polystyrene and again did not obtain the liquid hydrocarbons predicted by the micellar theory.

Anxious to sidestep the experimental difficulties surrounding the highly complex natural polymers, Staudinger then decided to study synthetic "model" compounds. He chose polyoxymethylene (paraformaldehyde), the solid form of the preservative formalin, as the model for cellulose. The model for rubber was polystyrene. By 1930 Staudinger had amassed a considerable body of experimental evidence for the existence of the macromolecule and for very long polymer chains. He had also determined that polymers terminate not with a free chemical bond but with ordinary chemical groups taken from the surrounding solution or from within the polymer. This important phase of his research was summarized in his classic monograph *Die hochmolekularen organischen Verbindungen, Kautschuk und Cellulose* (The High-Molecular Organic Compounds Rubber and Cellulose), published in 1932.

Staudinger's views continued to meet with disapproval from many chemists and vigorous opposition from supporters of the micellar theory. Despite this widespread coolness toward his ideas, Staudinger became director of the chemistry laboratory and professor at the University of Freiburg in 1926. That year, at the annual meeting of the Association of German Natural Scientists and Physicians in Düsseldorf, Herman Mark presented Staudinger's carefully assembled experimental evidence and the interpretation of X-ray crystallographic studies. The presentation convinced many chemists, including Willstätter, the meeting's chairman, of the probable existence of extremely large molecules. Staudinger's theories gained support, and when the British Faraday Society held a symposium on polymers nine years later, the speakers could take the existence of macromolecules for granted.

Yet even Staudinger was capable of misunderstanding some aspects of the structure of macromolecules. Because he did not accept the idea that polymers are aggregates of small molecules, Staudinger assumed that macromolecules could not resemble micelles in any way. Maintaining that macromolecules were rigid rods, he attacked the experimental evidence collected by Herman Mark and Frederick Eirich indicating that polymers can exist both as flexible chains and as micellelike bundles. Staudinger's mistakes brought him into conflict with other supporters of the macromolecular theory. This division in the ranks of the new theory's defenders while it was still under intellectual attack was an unfortunate diversion.

Toward the end of the 1920s, Staudinger became acquainted with TEODOR SVEDBERG's use of the ultracentrifuge, a powerful new tool for determining the molecular weight of proteins. Svedberg's discovery that a small macromolecule such as hemoglobin could have a sharply defined molecular weight provided important support for Staudinger's theory, since the micellar theory predicted a variable molecular weight. Staudinger recognized that this method could provide strong evidence for his theory, but his application for an official grant to buy an ultracentrifuge was rejected, an indication of continuing scientific skepticism about macromolecules. Rebuffed, he turned instead

to the study of the viscosity of polymers in solution. Although well established as a method for determining the molecular weight of small molecules, this technique had rarely been applied to polymers. Working with solutions of polystyrene, Staudinger showed that the viscosity of a polymer is directly proportional to its molecular weight—still another contradiction of the micellar theory.

Throughout the 1930s Staudinger maintained his interest in the viscosity of polymer solutions. At the same time he became involved in new research topics, particularly the study of complex biological macromolecules and the direct observation of macromolecules by microscopy.

The Research Institute for Macromolecular Chemistry was established for Staudinger at the University of Freiburg in the 1940s. After World War II, Staudinger studied the relationship between structure and function in biological macromolecules, an area of research now known as molecular biology. In 1947 he founded a journal, *Makromolekulare Chemie,* and published *Makromolekulare Chemie und Biologie* (Macromolecular Chemistry and Biology), in which he gave his view of how molecular biology would develop. His ideas are considered rather simplistic by today's standards, however, and his postwar work made no major contribution to the development of molecular biology.

Staudinger was awarded the 1953 Nobel Prize "for his discoveries in the field of macromolecular chemistry," a quarter of a century after his prizewinning research—perhaps an indication of the controversy his theories had provoked. In his Nobel lecture, "Macromolecular Chemistry," Staudinger commented, "In the light of this new knowledge of macromolecular chemistry, the wonder of life in its chemical aspect is revealed in the astounding abundance and masterly macromolecular architecture of living matter." As it happened, and quite unremarked by Staudinger, JAMES D. WATSON and FRANCIS CRICK had published their account of the double helical structure of the DNA molecule just eight months earlier.

In 1927 Staudinger married Magda Woit, a plant physiologist who became a lifelong collaborator; the couple had no children. A tall man with a whispery voice, Staudinger attracted students from all over the world by his rare combination of sensitivity and intuition about chemistry and combativeness in supporting his theory. He retired from the University of Freiburg in 1951, becoming head of the Research Institute for Macromolecular

Chemistry until 1956. He died in Freiburg of a heart condition on September 8, 1965.

In addition to the Nobel Prize, Staudinger's many prizes and awards included the Emil Fischer Medal of the German Chemical Society (1930), the Leblanc Medal of the French Chemical Society (1931), and the Stanislao Cannizzaro Prize of the National Academy of Sciences of Italy (1933). He received honorary doctorates from the Fridericiana Technical University of Karlsruhe (engineering) and the University of Mainz (natural science).

SELECTED WORKS: Introduction to Qualitative Organic Analysis, 1925; From Organic Chemistry to Macromolecules, 1970.

ABOUT: Current Biography April 1954; Dictionary of Scientific Biography, volume 13, 1976; New York Times November 5, 1953.

WILLIAM H. STEIN

STEIN, WILLIAM H.
(June 25, 1911–February 2, 1980)
Nobel Prize for Chemistry, 1972
(shared with Christian Anfinsen and
  Stanford Moore)

The American biochemist William Howard Stein was born in New York City, the second of three children of Beatrice (Borg) Stein and Freed M. Stein, a businessman. He received his early education at the Lincoln School, a progressive institution affiliated with Teachers College, Columbia University. For his last two years of high school he attended Phillips Exeter Academy in Andover, Massachusetts.

Stein entered Harvard University in 1929 and received his B.S. in chemistry four years later. He continued his study of chemistry at Harvard but did so poorly in his first year that he was on the verge of giving it up. Instead he decided to switch to biochemistry and transferred to Columbia's College of Physicians and Surgeons in New York in 1934. There, finding the intellectual stimulation he sought, he "learned a tremendous amount in a short time," as he recalled later. With a thesis on the amino acid content of the protein elastin, he received his Ph.D. in 1938. Like other proteins, elastin is a large molecule consisting of amino acids linked together into polypeptide chains. Although the structure of elastin had not yet been elucidated, Stein's graduate work marked an important advance in the understanding of its constituents.

After receiving his doctorate, Stein joined the Rockefeller Institute for Medical Research (now Rockefeller University) in New York City to work under Max Bergmann, whom he later described as "one of the very great protein chemists of this century." At Rockefeller, Stein was assigned to work with STANFORD MOORE in an effort to devise a more efficient means for analyzing the amino acids in proteins.

When the United States entered World War II in 1941, Moore was called to Washington while Stein and his colleagues at Rockefeller worked on war-related projects for the United States Office of Scientific Research and Development. Bergmann died in 1944, but after the war ended in 1945, HERBERT S. GASSER, the director of the Rockefeller Institute, asked Stein and Moore to continue their earlier research on quantitative amino acid analysis.

They were now able to take advantage of an important technique for protein separation and purification that had been developed in 1944, when the British chemists ARCHER MARTIN and RICHARD SYNGE pioneered in the application of paper chromatography to biochemical problems. In this method, amino acids that have been split off from the polypeptide chain are separated from one another as they travel through special filter paper at characteristically differing rates.

Although useful, paper chromatography yielded smaller amounts of amino acid than Stein and Moore needed in their investigations. The British chemist FREDERICK SANGER suggested that they use column chromatography, in which the solution to be analyzed is poured into a tube packed with a substance that absorbs the solution's components differentially and separates them into distinct bands on the column. Using potato starch as a filter, Stein and Moore achieved their first success in 1948. The amino acid solution took two weeks to move through the column, however. To speed up the process, they began using ion-exchange resins for packing. These materials, which sort molecules by electrical charge as well as by size, produce results more rapidly and with greater clarity than starch packing.

By the time Stein became a full professor at Rockefeller University in 1954, he had analyzed the amino acids found in a wide variety of proteins. Most of his efforts, however, were focused on the enzyme ribonuclease, one of many thousands of organic catalysts that regulate chemical reactions within living organisms. Although JAMES B. SUMNER and JOHN H. NORTHROP had proved in the 1930s that enzymes are proteinaceous, their molecular structure remained unclear in the mid-1950s. It was assumed that differences in their function reflected differences in their molecular structure.

Stein and Moore set out to determine the amino acid sequence of ribonuclease. Using the ion-exchange technique, they produced highly purified samples of the enzyme. After dissolving its chemical bonds and obtaining a mixture of fifteen peptides, they separated the peptides by chromatography, determined their amino acid sequence, and reported their findings in 1960. From these results other Rockefeller researchers were able to deduce the three-dimensional configuration of ribonuclease in 1967, thus confirming Stein and Moore's predictions about the location of the molecule's active center.

Stein and Moore shared half of the 1972 Nobel Prize for Chemistry "for their contribution to the understanding of the connection between chemical structure and catalytic activity of the active center of the ribonuclease molecule." The other half of the prize was presented to CHRISTIAN ANFINSEN for related research. "From the knowledge of the structure of a large series of enzymes," Stein and Moore said in their joint Nobel lecture, "underlying principles of how nature designs catalysts for given purposes will evolve. And there will be practical dividends from such research on proteins," they predicted, citing recent discoveries about hemoglobin that stemmed from their findings.

In addition to his work on ribonuclease, Stein collaborated with Moore on investigations into the structure and function of pancreatic deoxy-ribonuclease, the enzyme that hydrolyzes (splits) deoxyribonucleic acid. Stein's interest in the dissemination of scientific information led him to devote much of his time to the *Journal of Biological Chemistry*. He served on its editorial committee from 1958 to 1961, on its editorial board in 1962, as its associate editor from 1964 until 1968, and as its editor from then until 1971.

In 1936 Stein married Phoebe Hockstader; the couple had three sons. In 1969 he contracted Guillain-Barré syndrome. Although paralyzed by the disease and confined to a wheelchair, he maintained an active interest in scientific research until his death in New York City on February 2, 1980. He was described by his lifelong colleague Stanford Moore as "a generous and brilliant biochemist."

In addition to the Nobel Prize, Stein and Moore shared the Award in Chromatography and Electrophoresis (1964) and the Theodore Richard Williams Medal (1972) of the American Chemical Society. In 1968–1969 Stein was chairman of the United States National Committee for Biochemistry. He served as a trustee of Montefiore Hospital and on the medical advisory board of the Hebrew University medical school.

SELECTED WORKS: The Composition of Elastin, 1938.

ABOUT: New York Times October 21, 1972; February 3, 1980; Science November 3, 1972.

STEINBECK, JOHN
(February 17, 1902–December 20, 1968)
Nobel Prize for Literature, 1962

The American novelist John Ernst Steinbeck was born in Salinas, California. He was the only son and the third of four children of Olive (Hamilton) Steinbeck, a schoolteacher, and John Ernst Steinbeck, manager and eventually owner of the Sperry Flour Mill, later treasurer of Monterey County. Steinbeck's interest in literature was actively stimulated by both of his parents. The Salinas valley, the rugged hills surrounding it, and the coastal flats bordering Monterey Bay made a lasting impression on the young Steinbeck and later became the backdrop for much of his fiction.

While attending Salinas High School, Steinbeck earned high marks in English, literature, and biology and served as associate editor of the school newspaper. Graduating in 1919, he entered Stanford University as a journalism

JOHN STEINBECK

The Bettmann Archive

major but did poorly in the required subjects and withdrew the following year. For the next two years he worked at a succession of jobs, studied biology at the Hopkins Marine Station in Pacific Grove, and saved enough money to return to Stanford. Several of his poems and short stories appeared in university publications before he again dropped out without receiving a degree.

Shipping out on a freighter, Steinbeck worked his way to New York City. There he briefly held a job on a newspaper, the *New York American,* and tried unsuccessfully to sell his short stories. Discouraged, he returned to California and supported himself as a construction worker, journalist, deckhand, and fruit picker while completing a novel, *Cup of Gold,* which was published in 1929. In this fictional account of the seventeenth-century pirate Henry Morgan, the protagonist's greed and ambition prevent him from finding happiness. Steinbeck later termed this work "an immature experiment" and remarked, "I've outgrown it and it embarrasses me."

The following year Steinbeck married Carol Henning. The couple settled in Pacific Grove in a cottage that was supplied by his father rent-free, with a monthly allowance of twenty-five dollars. It was in Pacific Grove that Steinbeck met Edward F. Ricketts, a marine biologist whose views on the interdependence of all life anticipated later concepts of ecology and profoundly influenced Steinbeck's outlook. In the novel *To a God Unknown* (1933), Steinbeck mingled Ricketts's ideas with Jungian concepts introduced to him by Evelyn Rey-

nolds Ott, a former student of C. G. Jung, and archetypal themes made familiar by his friendship with the mythologist Joseph Campbell. Although important to his development as a novelist, the book was obscure and labored, and it failed both commercially and critically.

His next novel, *Tortilla Flat* (1935), became a best-seller. The first of his works to use a California coastal setting, it portrays a group of colorful characters living in the hills above Monterey. Episodic in form, it was intended to parallel the Arthurian legends Steinbeck loved as a boy and, like *Cup of Gold,* to illustrate the dehumanizing effects of materialism. Turning to contemporary social issues, Steinbeck published the novel *In Dubious Battle* the following year. Taking its title from John Milton's *Paradise Lost,* it tells the story of two men who organize a strike among migrant farm workers in a California apple orchard. It was followed in 1937 by *Of Mice and Men,* an intensely evocative novel about two itinerant farmhands, George and the mentally retarded Lennie, and the accidental violence that shatters their dream of settling down on their own small farm. Its prose "possesses greater sensitivity and naturalness" than that of Steinbeck's earlier work, wrote Paul McCarthy in a 1980 critical biography, and "is generally more realistic and precise." The American scholar Richard Astro called it Steinbeck's version of the pastoral, in which the author "asserts the superiority of the simple human virtues to the mean accumulation of wealth and power." An immensely popular novel that assured Steinbeck's place as a major figure in American literature, *Of Mice and Men* also achieved great success in a stage version written with George S. Kaufman and produced on Broadway in 1937.

The Long Valley, a collection of short stories published in 1938, includes the four pieces that later made up *The Red Pony* (1953). The novel that followed, *The Grapes of Wrath* (1939), is Steinbeck's best known and most ambitious work. It is an account of the Joads, a family of tenant farmers from the Oklahoma dust bowl, in their trouble-plagued journey to California during the Great Depression. Natural forces, social conditions, and the predatory greed of large-scale farmers threaten to destroy the Joads. But they triumph in the end, at least in a philosophical sense, as they finally recognize their place in the "one big soul" to which the entire human family belongs. *The Grapes of Wrath* quickly rose to the top of the best-seller list, reaped critical acclaim, and won the 1940 Pulitzer Prize. It also provoked a storm of controversy in which Steinbeck was branded a Communist propagandist and condemned for distorting his subject matter.

In order to escape the controversy, Steinbeck helped his friend Ricketts organize and conduct a zoological expedition to the Gulf of California, which they described jointly in *Sea of Cortez: A Leisurely Journal of Travel and Research* (1941). This nonfiction work not only records the findings of the expedition but also discusses topics ranging from communications to history to the scientific method. In the same year that it was published, Steinbeck divorced his first wife and moved to New York City with Gwyndolyn Conger, a singer whom he married two years later; they had two sons.

Too old for military service during World War II, Steinbeck served the government as an unpaid consultant on propaganda. Among his contributions to the war effort was an Army Air Corps training book, *Bombs Away* (1942). *The Moon Is Down* (1942), a novel about the invasion and occupation of a small town by totalitarian forces (suggesting the Nazi invasion of Norway), was a popular success, as was the stage version, also written by Steinbeck. During 1943 he covered the war for the *New York Herald Tribune;* his dispatches were published in 1958 as *Once There Was a War*.

Steinbeck's first postwar novel, *Cannery Row* (1945), depicts a group of vagabonds living in Monterey's fish-cannery waterfront district and their efforts to hold a party for their friend Doc, a character patterned after Ricketts. Since it departed from his previous political, social, and philosophical concerns, the book was appraised by some critics as trivial and sentimental. The allegorical novel *The Wayward Bus* and the fable *The Pearl* both appeared in 1947, also to mixed notices. "In these books," said Richard Astro, "Steinbeck's [organic] view of life, his belief that men can work together to fashion a better . . . and more meaningful life, seemed less and less applicable to the world he saw around him." Seeking inspiration, Steinbeck and the photographer Robert Capa toured the Soviet Union on assignment for the *Herald Tribune,* a collaboration that produced *Russian Journal* in 1948. The same year, Ricketts died in an automobile accident and Steinbeck divorced his second wife. The following year he met Elaine Scott, whom he married in 1950.

Steinbeck's play *Burning Bright* closed after thirteen performances in 1950. Nevertheless, his screenplay for *Viva Zapata!,* directed in 1952 by Elia Kazan, "recalls Steinbeck's best work of the 1930s," according to Astro. During this time Steinbeck had been working on his "big novel," as he called it. Published in 1954, *East of Eden* recounts the fictional history of the Hamiltons (a family based largely on his mother's) and the Trasks. It has been described as a modern allegory based on the biblical story of Cain and Abel. Calling it "a strange and original work of art," the American literary critic Mark Schorer praised the novel for its "wide-ranging, imaginative freedom." Other critics were decidedly less enthusiastic.

Released the same year the novel was published, the film version of *East of Eden* was the sixth movie based on Steinbeck's works. Others include *Of Mice and Men, The Grapes of Wrath,* and *Tortilla Flat*. These and other films helped make Steinbeck known to a large popular audience.

His final novel, *The Winter of Our Discontent,* was published in 1961. Steinbeck then concentrated on journalism and travel writing. Perhaps the most successful effort from this period was *Travels With Charley in Search of America* (1962). In this account of a cross-country trip with his dog, Steinbeck rediscovers the nation's natural beauty but laments its increasingly synthetic culture.

Steinbeck was awarded the 1962 Nobel Prize for Literature "for his realistic and imaginative writings, combining as they do sympathetic humor and keen social perception." Praising Steinbeck as one of "the masters of modern American literature," Anders Österling of the Swedish Academy noted that "his sympathies always go out to the oppressed, to the misfits and the distressed; he likes to contrast the simple joy of life with the brutal and cynical craving for money."

In his brief acceptance speech, Steinbeck spoke of "the high duties and the responsibilities of the makers of literature," who are "charged with exposing our many grievous faults and failures" and whose task it is "to declare and to celebrate man's proven capacity for greatness of heart and spirit."

An admirer of President Lyndon B. Johnson, for whom he wrote political speeches, Steinbeck was an outspoken apologist for American military intervention in Vietnam, although he revised his views after traveling there as a journalist. His final work, an unfinished modern version of Sir Thomas Malory's *Morte d'Arthur,* which he had begun in 1957, was published posthumously in 1976 as *The Acts of King Arthur and His Noble Knights*.

Steinbeck suffered strokes in 1961 and 1965

and died in his New York City apartment after a massive heart attack in 1968.

At the time of his death, Steinbeck had fallen out of critical favor and was widely regarded as sentimental, naive, and heavy-handed in his penchant for allegory. "It is impossible to predict the final fate of John Steinbeck's reputation," Richard Astro wrote, "but it seems likely that his lasting fame will rest largely on his great novels of the American Depression." According to his biographer Paul McCarthy, "Steinbeck's strongest convictions and passions appear in his fundamental belief in humanity, in his expectation that man will endure, and that the creative forces of the human spirit will prevail." The American scholar James Gray agreed: "The novels, plays, and short stories of this conscientious artist represent successive efforts to pay his debt to man. Wide in the range of their interest, diverse in mood, passionately concerned in their sympathies, they all celebrate the worth of man." Gray continued, "Much more clearly than in the instance of any other American writer of his time, Steinbeck's consistent effort to establish the dignity of human life offers the measure of the man."

ADDITIONAL WORKS: The Pastures of Heaven, 1932; Nothing So Monstrous, 1936; Saint Katy the Virgin, 1936; Their Blood Is Strong, 1938; The Forgotten Village, 1941; How Edith McGillicuddy Met R. L. S., 1943; The Log From the Sea of Cortez, 1951; Sweet Thursday, 1954; The Crap-shooter, 1957; The Short Reign of Pippin IV, 1957; Letters to Alicia, 1965; America and Americans, 1966; Journal of a Novel, 1969; Collected Poems of Amnesia Glasscock, 1976; Letters to Elisabeth, 1978.

ABOUT: Astro, R., and Hayashi, T. (eds.) Steinbeck: The Man and His Work, 1971; Benson, J. J. The True Adventures of John Steinbeck, Writer, 1984; Davis, R. M. (ed.) Steinbeck: A Collection of Critical Essays, 1972; Fontenrose, J. John Steinbeck, 1963; French, W. John Steinbeck, 1961; Gray, J. John Steinbeck, 1971; Hayashi, T. (ed.) Steinbeck's Literary Dimension, 1973; Kiernan, T. The Intricate Music, 1979; Levant, H. The Novels of John Steinbeck, 1974; Lisca, P. The Wide World of John Steinbeck, 1958; McCarthy, P. John Steinbeck, 1980; Moore, H. T. The Novels of John Steinbeck, 1939; O'Connor, R. John Steinbeck, 1970; Owens, L. John Steinbeck's Re-Visioning of America, 1985; Peterson, C. John Steinbeck, 1972; Plimpton, G. (ed.) Writers at Work, volume 4, 1976; Tedlock, E. W. Steinbeck and His Critics, 1957; Valjean, N. John Steinbeck, The Errant Knight, 1975; Watt, F. W. John Steinbeck, 1962.

STERN, OTTO

(February 17, 1888–August 17, 1969)
Nobel Prize for Physics, 1943

The German-American physicist Otto Stern was born in Sohrau, Germany (now Zory, Po-

OTTO STERN

land). He was the oldest of five children of Eugenie (Rosenthal) and Oscar Stern, who both came from well-to-do families in the flour-milling and grain-selling businesses. When the boy was four years old, the family moved to Breslau (now Wrocław), where Otto attended the Johannes Gymnasium, a public elementary and high school. An avid student, he was encouraged by his parents to read widely. After graduation from the gymnasium, Stern, whose family's wealth made him financially independent, spent several years studying science under a variety of teachers at Freiburg, Munich, and several other German universities. Stern completed his Ph.D. requirements in physical chemistry at the University of Breslau in 1912.

During his undergraduate years, Stern came in contact with some of the leading physicists and chemists of the day. The lectures of Arnold Sommerfeld inspired his interest in theoretical physics, while those of Otto Lummer and Ernst Pringsheim attracted him to experimental physics. However, his private reading of books by Ludwig Boltzman, Rudolf Clausius, and WALTHER NERNST on molecular theory, statistical mechanics, and thermodynamics strongly influenced him, and he chose the field of physical chemistry at Breslau because professors in that department, notably Otto Sackur, were active in the areas of his particular interests.

Through Sackur's connection with FRITZ HABER, a friend of ALBERT EINSTEIN, Stern was accepted by Einstein for postgraduate studies at the University of Prague in 1912.

There he learned much about new developments in physics from Einstein, and they wrote a paper together. When Einstein moved to Zurich the following year, Stern followed. While working with Einstein, he also became a privatdocent (an unsalaried lecturer) at the Federal Institute of Technology. With the outbreak of World War I, Stern was inducted into the German army and sent to Poland in the Meteorological Corps to make weather observations. His undemanding duties allowed him to continue his theoretical studies, particularly on work by Nernst. He applied quantum theory and statistical mechanics to problems in thermodynamics and even published a paper. Late in the war, Stern and other scientists were transferred to Nernst's laboratory at the University of Berlin to do military research for the War Department. At Berlin, Stern worked with MAX BORN, JAMES FRANCK, Max Volmer, and others. His discussions with Franck and Volmer, both skilled experimenters, were influential in shifting Stern's main interest from theoretical to experimental research.

After the war, Born went to the University of Frankfurt to become director of the Institute for Theoretical Physics and invited Stern to become his assistant. Stern published a theoretical paper with Born on the surface energy of solids, but he felt drawn to the problem of finding experimental proof for theories of molecular motions established in the mid-nineteenth century. The noted Scottish physicist James Clerk Maxwell had shown, on theoretical grounds, that gas molecules were perpetually moving in all directions and derived an equation expressing the distribution of velocities. His findings were generally accepted but had not been directly verified by laboratory observation. Stern decided to use the method of molecular beams invented by the French physicist Louis Dunoyer in 1911.

Stern's apparatus consisted of a small oven that evaporated silver atoms from the parent metal (the molecules of silver vapor contain only one atom); a slit through which atoms from the oven traveling in the direction of the slit would emerge into a vacuum chamber; and a more distant slit, in line with the oven slit, that further narrowed the stream of atoms to a thin beam. The alignment of the slits ensured that all the atoms that passed through both slits were moving in the same direction, and the scarcity of gas in the vacuum prevented collisions from diverting the atoms and scattering the beam. The velocities of the atoms emerging from the second slit, and the quantity having each velocity, were then measured

in various ways. One method, although not the most accurate, was to place two toothed wheels in the path of the beam. When the wheels were rotated, atoms passing through gaps between teeth in the first wheel could pass through gaps in the second wheel only if they arrived as a gap rotated into the line of travel. From a knowledge of tooth spacing, speed of rotation, and distance between the wheels, Stern was able to calculate the velocity of the atoms passing through. The measurements, completed in 1920 (refined to greater accuracy in later years), confirmed theoretical predictions.

The method proved to be a powerful tool for observing the behavior of invisible particles with relatively crude laboratory instruments, but the experimental technique was extremely demanding. Stern asked a colleague at Frankfurt, Walther Gerlach, to assist him in using the method to investigate a question concerning the magnetic moments of atoms. Because atoms contain electrically charged particles in motion, which constitute an electric current, they behave like small magnets, just as the current in a coil produces magnetism in an electromagnet. The magnetic moment describes the strength and direction of the magnetism. Classical physics held that the magnetic moment could have any direction. Sommerfeld, on the basis of quantum theory, predicted that the magnetic moment, relative to an external field, could have only two directions, in the same or opposite direction as the field. In the now famous Stern-Gerlach experiment, a molecular beam was passed between the poles of a nonuniform magnet, which caused deflection of the beam. Classical theory predicted that atoms with various moment directions would undergo a continuous range of deflections that would simply broaden the narrow beam. Quantum theory predicted that atoms would only deflect one way or the other, splitting the beam in two. The experiment, performed in 1921, unequivocally showed a split beam.

Stern was appointed professor of physics at the University of Rostock in 1921 and a full professor at the University of Hamburg in 1923. At Hamburg, where a laboratory was built specifically for molecular-beam research, Stern used the method to test a prediction made by LOUIS DE BROGLIE in 1924. Both quantum theory and experiment had shown that electromagnetic radiation such as light also had particle (quantum) as well as wave properties. Although skepticism lingered, Broglie had proposed the even more radical idea that particles might have wave properties, and indicated what their wavelengths should be. CLINTON J. DAVISSON and Lester H. Germer had found experimental proof for electron waves, partly by accident, in 1927, which was followed by reinforcing observations by G. P. THOMSON. Several years later, Stern directed a beam of helium gas through toothed wheels (to establish a known velocity on which the wavelength depended) onto the surface of a lithium fluoride crystal. The result was diffraction, a wave phenomenon, and the known spacing between atoms in the crystal permitted the determination of the wavelength of the helium particles. It agreed with the Broglie formula. The demonstration of the wave properties of large particles such as atoms seemed even more convincing than in the case of electrons, and Stern's experiment was to play an important role in the further development of quantum mechanics. During the ensuing years, Stern, with Immanuel Estermann and O. R. Frisch, measured the magnetic moment of the proton (nucleus of the hydrogen atom) and found, to their surprise and to that of all other physicists, that it was more than twice as large as predicted by P. A. M. DIRAC.

Shortly after Adolf Hitler became chancellor of Germany in 1933, Estermann and other Jewish researchers were dismissed from Frankfurt under the Nazi's anti-Semitic civil service laws. Although Stern also was a Jew, his war service temporarily exempted him from the racial laws. He resigned in protest, however, and with Estermann, he accepted an invitation to join the faculty at the Carnegie Institute of Technology. There, as a research professor, Stern helped construct a molecular-beam laboratory. In 1939 Stern became an American citizen and, when the United States entered World War II, served as a consultant to the United States War Department.

No Nobel Prize for Physics was awarded in 1943, but the following year the 1943 prize was given to Stern "for his contribution to the development of the molecular-ray method and his discovery of the magnetic moment of the proton." Because of the war, regular ceremonies were suspended, and the prize was presented to Stern at a luncheon sponsored by the American Scandinavian Foundation at the Waldorf-Astoria Hotel in New York City. It was not until 1946 that Stern delivered his Nobel lecture, "The Method of Molecular Rays."

After resigning from Carnegie Tech in 1946, Stern moved to Berkeley, California, where two of his sisters had settled. Although he remained in touch with the physics community

and continued to follow developments in particle physics, he lived in relative isolation. He made regular visits to Europe but refused to set foot on German soil or to collect a pension due from the German government.

In his later years Stern, who never married, indulged his taste for fine food and cigars. He enjoyed going to the movies, and it was at a movie theater in Berkeley that he died of a heart attack. According to EMILIO SEGRÈ, "Stern was one of the greatest physicists of [the twentieth] century. He wrote relatively few papers, but of what power were those he did write!"

A member of the National Academy of Sciences and the American Philosophical Society, Stern received honorary degrees from the University of California and from the Swiss Federal Institute of Technology.

ABOUT: Biographical Memoirs of the National Academy of Sciences, volume 43, 1973; Dictionary of Scientific Biography, volume 13, 1976; Estermann, I. (ed.) Recent Research in Molecular Beams, 1959.

STIGLER, GEORGE
(January 17, 1911–   )
Nobel Memorial Prize in Economic
   Sciences, 1982

The American economist George Joseph Stigler was born in Renton, a suburb of Seattle, Washington, the only son of Joseph Stigler, a realtor, and the former Elizabeth Hungler, immigrants from Bavaria and Austria-Hungary, respectively. After attending schools in Seattle, he graduated from the University of Washington with a B.A. in economics in 1931. The following year he received an M.B.A. from Northwestern University and entered the doctoral program in economics at the University of Chicago. As he said later, "It was the middle of the Depression, and it seemed better to go to school than look for work." At Chicago, Stigler was strongly influenced by the economists Frank Knight, Jacob Viner, and Henry Simons, as well as by his fellow students W. Allen Wallis and MILTON FRIEDMAN.

Stigler began his teaching career in 1936 as assistant professor at Iowa State University. In 1938, after receiving his Ph.D. from Chicago with the thesis "Production and Distribution Theories," Stigler joined the faculty at the University of Minnesota, where he remained for eight years, rising to the rank of full professor. During World War II he was a consultant to the Statistical Research Group

GEORGE STIGLER

at Columbia University. In 1946 he moved to Brown University and in 1947 to Columbia University. After eleven years at Columbia, he was appointed Charles R. Walgreen Professor of American Institutions at the University of Chicago, which became his permanent academic home. During his long association with the University of Chicago, he established a highly respected workshop in industrial organization and served as editor of the university's *Journal of Political Economy*.

In the 1940s and 1950s Stigler produced many seminal papers and books in applied microeconomics and industrial organization. "Roofs or Ceilings," an article he wrote with Milton Friedman in 1946, argued that rent controls, used throughout the war and continued afterward in a few cities, led to housing shortages, shoddy construction, and inadequate maintenance. Although sharply criticized at the time, their conclusion is now widely accepted by liberals and conservatives alike. Several of Stigler's monographs for the National Bureau of Economic Research (NBER) were pioneering studies of supply and demand with respect to various types of labor and to the effect on employment of labor legislation, such as the minimum wage. Countless undergraduate and graduate students learned microeconomics from his textbook *The Theory of Price,* first published in 1947.

In 1949 Stigler published an influential critique of "monopolistic competition," a doctrine associated with the economist Edward Chamberlin and the so-called Harvard School of industrial organization. Stigler claimed that

Chamberlin's theory, while admittedly a more realistic description of the industrial structure than had previously been available, predicted little that could not already be derived from the polar models of perfect competition and pure monopoly, both standard tools of price theory. In a 1951 essay, "The Division of Labor Is Limited by the Extent of the Market," he extended Adam Smith's observation that the size of a firm is limited by transport costs and population density.

Another essay, "The Economies of Scale" (1958), introduced the "survivorship principle" into industrial organization theory. Stigler defined the "minimum efficient scale" for survival as the smallest-sized plant (measured in terms of output or labor force) remaining in operation after changes in technology and markets. A new industrial technique, for example, might permit a large steel plant to become profitable, in which case the minimum efficient scale for a factory in the steel industry would rise. Although data are often severely limited, the survivorship principle has been applied increasingly to the analysis of industrial organization.

Stigler's 1961 article "The Economics of Information," which appeared in the *Journal of Political Economy,* asked a deceptively simple question: How long, and how hard, should a consumer search for the lowest price of a commodity? Stigler answered: until the costs of a longer or more intense search exceed the expected benefits of a lower price. Although the answer might appear obvious, Stigler's method provided a model for examining informational issues in economics and implied a new approach to the theory of market behavior. According to Stigler, uncertainty should be treated not as a given but as a degree of ignorance that could be reduced—at a cost—by the acquisition of information. This approach has had a tremendous impact on economic analysis, theoretical as well as empirical, and has been used on a range of subjects, from consumer behavior, price dispersion, and advertising to job searches and inventory behavior.

Throughout the 1960s and 1970s Stigler continued to make contributions to the field of industrial organization. In "A Theory of Oligopoly" (1964), for example, he showed how the difficulty of enforcing collusive agreements limits the success of a cartel. The problems experienced by the Organization of Petroleum Exporting Countries (OPEC) during the 1980s illustrate this idea. *The Behavior of Industrial Prices,* written for the NBER in 1968 in collaboration with the economist James K. Kindhal, demonstrated that the apparent stability of prices in noncompetitive markets is a fiction, because "list" prices are far in excess of, and far more stable than, the real "transaction" prices.

Gradually, Stigler's interests shifted from pure theory and returned to economic regulation. Dissatisfied with the prevailing view that regulatory agencies act in the public interest, he proposed a "capture theory" of regulation. This theory holds that, rather than safeguarding the consumer as intended by state agencies, regulation has tended to shield industries from new competition. For instance, the Interstate Commerce Commission's attempts to limit the spread of interstate trucking actually benefited the railroads, not the public. Stigler's theory of regulation, a pioneering work in interdisciplinary law and economics, shows that the political-economic organization of a state has to be analyzed to understand how and why regulations of industry are imposed.

Although many of Stigler's views on deregulation were put into practice by the administrations of Presidents Jimmy Carter and Ronald Reagan, Stigler maintains his status as an independent scholar. "I'm not a Reaganomics man," he has stated. "I'm not a supply-sider. But reducing unnecessary government burdens on production is a wonderful thing."

An important area of Stigler's work, but one easy to overlook, is in the history of economic ideas. He is an acknowledged world authority on the ideas, works, and personal lives of the early economic theorists. He is also a persuasive popularizer of ideas and is justly famous for his ability to make a telling social point. "Stigler's First Law of Sympathy," for example, analyzes his (fictional) numerical rate of sympathy for his own problems (27 units per minute) compared to his falling off of sympathy for people who are distant from him geographically or socially (numerically unquantifiable rates).

Stigler received the 1982 Nobel Memorial Prize for Economic Sciences for his "seminal studies of industrial structures, functioning of markets, and causes and effects of public regulation." In his Nobel lecture Stigler applied his 1961 "search theory" to what he called the "market for new ideas" in economic science. "Most economists," he said, "are not the suppliers of new ideas but only demanders. Their problem is comparable to that of the automobile buyer: to find a reliable vehicle. Indeed, they usually end up buying a used, and therefore tested, idea."

Unlike KENNETH ARROW, GERARD DEBREU, and PAUL SAMUELSON, Stigler eschews advanced mathematics in his work, preferring a literary approach that has been praised for its clarity, elegance, and erudition. For Stigler, clear and simple economic theory is needed as the basic framework for testing hypotheses by empirical research. Few economists have demonstrated so effectively the usefulness of microeconomic theory for this purpose, as he does, for example, in his penetrating work *Capital and Rates of Return in Manufacturing Industries* (1963).

In 1936 Stigler married Margaret Mack, a fellow student at the University of Chicago. They have three sons.

Although he resigned from the Walgreen Professorship in 1981, Stigler is still associated with the University of Chicago. A former president of the American Economic Association (1964) and the History of Economics Society (1977), he is also a member of the National Academy of Sciences and the American Philosophical Society. He has received honorary degrees from Carnegie-Mellon University, the University of Rochester, the Helsinki School of Economics, and Brown University.

ADDITIONAL WORKS: Production and Distribution Theories, 1941; The Theory of Competitive Price, 1942; The Intellectual and the Marketplace, 1963; Essays in the History of Economic Thought, 1965; The Organization of Industry, 1968; The Citizen and the State: Essays on Regulation, 1975; The Pleasures and Pains of Modern Capitalism, 1982; The Economist as Preacher, 1982.

ABOUT: Breit, W., and Spencer, R. W. (eds.) Lives of the Laureates, 1986; Current Biography July 1983; New York Times October 24, 1982; Scandinavian Journal of Economics, number 1, 1983; Science November 12, 1982.

STONE, RICHARD
(August 30, 1913–)
Nobel Memorial Prize in Economic
  Sciences, 1984

The English economist John Richard Nicholas Stone was born in London, the only child of Elsie and Gilbert Stone. His father, a barrister, encouraged him to pursue a classical education in preparation for a legal career, but Stone showed little interest in the law and was an indifferent student at both the Cliveden Place Preparatory School and the Westminster School. As a boy he preferred building models of trains and boats to academic pursuits. To his father's disappointment, he abandoned his

RICHARD STONE

legal studies two years after entering Gonville and Caius College, Cambridge, in 1931, choosing instead to major in economics. As he put it later, his interest in this field was stimulated by the Great Depression and by the belief, "bred of youthful ignorance and optimism, that if only economics were better understood, the world would be a better place."

Because the college had no economist among its fellows, Stone did his weekly supervisions with Richard Kahn at King's College, Cambridge, then one of the world's centers of economic research. He also studied with the pioneering economic statistician Colin Clark, attended lectures by John Maynard Keynes (who at the time was writing *The General Theory of Employment, Interest, and Money*), and joined the Political Economy Club, which met in Keynes's rooms. The intellectual ferment at King's awakened Stone's mind and initiated his career as a scholar.

Nevertheless, upon his graduation in 1935 Stone did not feel ready to conduct research. Turning down a research studentship from Gonville and Caius College, he wrote an economic newsletter for the insurance firm Lloyd's of London. Despite his disinclination to take up a business career, it offered him a moderate work load that allowed him time for other pursuits. With his wife, the former Winifred Mary Jenkins, a former economics student at Cambridge whom he married in 1936, Stone collaborated on several economic studies, including a 1938 paper on variations in family budget patterns of consumption and saving. In 1937 the Stones began editing *Trends,* an economic

and business monthly which Colin Clark had established and which he turned over to Stone upon his return to Australia. In it the Stones published such economic indicators as employment, output, consumption, retail trade, investment, prices, and foreign trade. Occasionally they included special articles on regional employment or conditions in other countries.

When World War II broke out in 1939, Stone was invited to join the staff of the Ministry of Economic Warfare, where he was responsible for shipping and oil statistics. The following year he was transferred to the Central Economic Information Service of the Offices of the War Cabinet Secretariat to work with Keynes and JAMES MEADE on a general survey of Great Britain's economic and financial situation, work that led to Stone's most important contributions to economic science. The British government needed estimates of the total volume of funds and resources available for the war effort. By December, Stone and Meade had produced these figures, which were published in tabular form as part of the chancellor's budget for 1941. The tables included estimates for 1938 and 1940 of national income and expenditure; personal (or private household) income, expenditure, and savings; and the net amount of funds required by and available from the private sector for government purposes. Stone later described these estimates as a step toward what are now called national income accounts. As he continued working on them throughout the war, he made increasingly elaborate estimates of national income and of its sources and distribution.

Systematic national accounts were first produced in the seventeenth century by William Petty and Gregory King in England and by Pierre Le Pesant Boisguillebert and Marshal Vauban in France. After World War I, pioneering work on national income estimates was done by SIMON KUZNETS and Colin Clark. Stone's work is distinct from these earlier efforts because of his explicit integration of national income into a double-entry bookkeeping framework reflecting income and expenditure data for households, businesses, and government and enabling comparative analysis of the activity of different sectors of the economy and of different countries.

Stone's accounting framework ensures consistency by requiring that income equal expenditures. This is equivalent to requiring, first, that all output be consumed and, second, that all consumption be produced. His double-entry national income accounting system provides an empirical counterpart to the Keynesian revolution in macroeconomic theory. His production, consumption, and accumulation accounts parallel the new Keynesian concepts of aggregate supply, consumption, and investment demand. In fact, Stone's method of national accounting gave impetus to the construction of econometric models, and the accounts provided a framework for organizing the collection of data and testing their consistency.

Stone has always been quick to acknowledge his debt to others, and he was not alone in his work on national income accounting. Before and during World War II, the governments of the United States and Canada, among others, prepared estimates of national income and expenditure. These estimates, however, employed somewhat different concepts and definitions than those used by Stone. In 1944 Stone was sent to America to help establish a common framework.

After leaving government service in 1945, Stone served as director of the newly established Department of Applied Economics at Cambridge where in 1955 he was appointed P. D. Leake Professor of Finance and Accounting. In his continuing research on national accounting, he discovered methods of translating the accounts into real terms and then using the results for constructing consistent price and volume indexes. Not only did he succeed in coordinating the accounts with input-output analysis; he was also a pioneer in including financial transactions in the system and introducing a system of financial balances.

In 1945, while visiting the Institute for Advanced Study in Princeton, New Jersey, Stone prepared a paper for the League of Nations on establishing international guidelines for national income accounting. It was published in 1947 by the United Nations as *Measurement of National Income and the Construction of Social Accounts.* Stone's work on establishing a standard system of national accounts continued, in a variety of contexts, for the next two decades. It led to a series of publications culminating in *A System of National Accounts,* written with Abraham Aidenoff and published by the United Nations in 1968. Stone's system was eventually adopted by many industrialized and developing nations. Subsequently, he developed a system of demographic accounting that reflected such factors as population changes and socioeconomic variables. In 1975 the United Nations published his *Towards a System of Social and Demographic Statistics.*

In addition to his work on national income accounting, Stone has made major contributions to the study of consumer behavior. Using models developed by LAWRENCE KLEIN and Herman Rubin, he predicted patterns of consumer expenditure and saving as a function of levels of income and the relative prices of all goods. He wrote a paper titled "The Analysis of Market Demand" in 1945, and he continued these budget studies at Cambridge, working with Deryck Rowe to produce *The Measurement of Consumers' Expenditure and Behaviour in the United Kingdom,* which appeared in two volumes in 1954 and 1966.

Stone's theory of consumer expenditure systems stemmed in part from his national income account studies, since improved estimates of the determinants of consumer expenditures could lead to improved cost-of-living indices or to better measures of aggregate price inflation, both of which are essential for studying changes in real national income in periods of changing relative prices. Stone's aptitude for devising complex economic models was also evident in the work of his Cambridge Growth Project, a team whose multivolume *A Programme for Growth* elaborated on an econometric growth model of the British economy.

Stone was awarded the 1984 Nobel Memorial Prize in Economic Sciences in recognition of his "pioneering work" and his "vital contribution to the development of economic sciences." In his presentation speech, Erik Lundberg of the Royal Swedish Academy of Sciences called Stone's national accounting systems "indispensable instruments of cyclical and structural analysis." At the same time, said Lundberg, "they yield systematic documentation on which to base forecasts in the form of national budgets."

Since retiring from Cambridge in 1980, Stone has continued his association with the university as a fellow of King's and Gonville and Caius colleges.

In 1941, a year after his first marriage was dissolved, Stone married Feodora Leontinoff, a philosopher, who at the time was secretary of the National Institute of Economic and Social Research. She died in 1956. Four years later, Stone married Giovanna Croft-Murray. Although not trained in economics, she has collaborated with him on much of his subsequent work. Stone, who was knighted in 1978, is a patron of the arts and appreciates fine wines and good cigars. PAUL SAMUELSON once described him as "rather a loner" with "a reserved personality." He and his wife live in Cambridge.

Stone is a member of the Econometric Society (and was its president in 1955) and the International Statistical Institute. He is a foreign member of the American Academy of Arts and Sciences and the American Economic Association. He holds honorary degrees from the universities of Oslo, Brussels, Geneva, Warwick, Paris, and Bristol.

ADDITIONAL WORKS: National Income and Expenditure, 1944, with James Meade; The Role of Measurement in Economics, 1951; Quantity and Price Indexes in National Accounts, 1956; Social Accounting and Economic Models, 1959, with Giovanna Croft-Murray; Input-Output and National Accounts, 1961; Mathematics in the Social Sciences and Other Essays, 1966; Mathematical Models of the Economy and Other Essays, 1970; Demographic Accounting and Model Building, 1971; Aspects of Economic and Social Modelling, 1980.

ABOUT: Deaton, A. (ed.) Essays in the Theory and Measurement of Consumer Behaviour, 1981; New York Times October 19, 1984; Scandinavian Journal of Economics, number 1, 1985; Science January 4, 1985.

STRESEMANN, GUSTAV
(May 10, 1878–October 3, 1929)
Nobel Prize for Peace, 1926
(shared with Aristide Briand)

The German statesman Gustav Stresemann (shtrā' zə män) was born and raised in Berlin, where his father, Ernst Stresemann, was a prosperous tavern owner and bottled-beer distributor. The only member of his family to attend high school, Stresemann maintained an outstanding academic record at the Andreas Realgymnasium. As a young man he also worked in the family business. He studied literature, history, and political economy, first at the University of Berlin and then at the University of Leipzig, where he received his doctorate in 1902. His dissertation concerned the growing pressures that large corporations were placing on the small, independent bottled-beer trade in Berlin.

After completing his graduate studies, Stresemann embarked on a highly successful business career. Starting as assistant manager of the Association of German Chocolate Manufacturers in Dresden, he became business manager of the local branch of the Manufacturers' Alliance the following year. Displaying great organizational skill and a talent for persuasion, Stresemann increased the membership of the alliance from 180 to 1,000 in only two years.

Like most of his contemporaries who had grown up in a middle-class Prussian milieu,

GUSTAV STRESEMANN

Stresemann was politically conservative, certain of Germany's cultural and military superiority, and devoted to the ideals of German nationalism and the monarchy. Keenly aware of the connection between commerce and politics, he won a seat on the Dresden Town Council in 1906, the same year that he married Käthe Kleefeld, the daughter of a Berlin industrialist, with whom he had two sons. The following year he was elected to the Reichstag (parliament) as a deputy of the National Liberal party. While serving in the Reichstag and on the Dresden Town Council, Stresemann was appointed director of the Saxon Industrialists' Union. In this position he also served as editor of the newspaper *Sächsische Industrie* (Saxon Industry).

Rising quickly within the ranks of the National Liberal party, Stresemann argued vigorously for a strong navy, which he believed essential to the protection of Germany's expanding overseas trade. Exempted from military service during World War I because of a heart condition, Stresemann was a considerable force in the Reichstag. He used his debating skills to advocate unlimited submarine warfare and in 1917 helped bring down the government of Chancellor Theobald von Bethmann-Hollweg, whom he regarded as an ineffectual leader. That year Stresemann was chosen head of his party. A loyal supporter of the German war effort, he nevertheless reminded his colleagues in the Reichstag that Germany must be prepared to accept suitable peace terms.

By August 1918 the German front had begun to collapse, and mutinies racked the German fleet. In November 1918, after German government leaders requested an armistice, Kaiser Wilhelm II abdicated and fled into exile. In May 1919 Stresemann and other German politicians met in Weimar to write the constitution for a new German government. The following year Stresemann was elected to the reorganized Reichstag of the Weimar Republic. After three years as opposition leader in the Reichstag, he was elected chancellor of Germany in 1923 at the head of a coalition government. During his brief tenure—less than four months—Stresemann dealt firmly with a Communist revolution in Saxony, restored order after Adolf Hitler's unsuccessful putsch in Bavaria, and imposed strict measures to stabilize the German currency.

Alienated by Stresemann's harsh measures in Saxony, the Social Democrats broke up the coalition and elected William Marx as his successor. Marx appointed Stresemann foreign minister, a position he held until his death. Disillusioned with a foreign policy based on military force, Stresemann recognized that only by improving relations with its neighbors could Germany rebuild its economy and ease the crushing terms of the Treaty of Versailles, which he had voted against accepting in 1919.

At Versailles the Allies had exacted reparations of $35.5 billion. Unable to maintain the burdensome payments, Germany defaulted in 1923. In response, French troops occupied the Ruhr Valley, the heart of the German industrial economy. The following year the Allies met in London to reconsider the reparations issue under an international commission headed by CHARLES DAWES. As German representative, Stresemann negotiated the withdrawal of Allied troops from the Ruhr and the restructuring of his nation's war debt. These measures enabled the German government to obtain loans from the United States and thus speed economic recovery.

In the atmosphere of goodwill brought about by the Dawes Plan, Stresemann sent a note to the French government in 1925 suggesting that England, France, and Germany agree to guarantee the postwar Franco-German border. In October Stresemann met with the French foreign minister, ARISTIDE BRIAND, and the British foreign minister, J. AUSTEN CHAMBERLAIN, in Locarno, Switzerland. Under the terms of the agreement signed there (known as the Locarno Pact), France, Germany, and Belgium pledged not to change their existing borders by force; Britain and Italy guaranteed the demilitarization of the Rhineland; and

Germany was admitted to the League of Nations. At home Stresemann overcame opposition to the pact by arguing that it did not imply final acceptance of Germany's disputed western borders but merely served to protect the nation against armed aggression.

Continuing his peace efforts, Stresemann negotiated a neutrality agreement with the Soviet Union the following year. Signed in Berlin in April 1926, the treaty pledged each nation to refrain from any political alliance or economic boycott against the other. In September Stresemann led the German delegation to its seat in the League of Nations, where he served despite deteriorating health.

Stresemann shared the 1926 Nobel Prize for Peace with Aristide Briand. In his Nobel lecture, titled "The New Germany," Stresemann asked, "Is the recent development of the German people such as to justify the award being given for a policy aimed at peace?" He added that "the question is answered by the very existence of the German policy of reconciliation and peace." This policy he saw reflected in the Locarno Pact and other agreements. " 'We belong to a generation struggling out of the darkness into the light,' " he proclaimed, quoting the words of Goethe. "May his words be true of our own times."

His health failing, Stresemann remained in office against his doctors' advice. He lived long enough to sign the Young Plan, which reduced German reparations payments and established a date for the evacuation of the Rhineland. One year before the agreement took effect, Stresemann suffered a stroke and died in Berlin on October 3, 1929. After his death the German People's party moved sharply to the right, a shift that underscored Germany's growing militarism and foreshadowed the coming of Nazism.

Calling Stresemann "a pragmatic conservative," the American historian Henry Turner remarked that "throughout his career in the republic his goals remained the same as those of most Germans who could be termed, in the broadest sense of the word, conservatives: the restoration of the country's power and prosperity and the preservation of as much of the prerevolutionary social and economic order as was possible." However, Turner added, "In contrast to most of his conservative compatriots, he was, as a pragmatist, willing to be flexible about the political means of achieving these goals."

WORKS IN ENGLISH TRANSLATION: The Locarno

Treaties: Their Importance, Scope, and Possible Consequences, 1926, with others; Essays and Speeches on Various Subjects, 1930; Gustav Stresemann: His Diaries, Letters, and Papers (3 vols.) 1935–1940.

ABOUT: Bretton, H. L. Stresemann and the Revision of Versailles, 1953; Chamberlain, A. Down the Years, 1935; Enssle, M. J. Stresemann's Territorial Revisionism, 1980; Gatzke, H. W. Stresemann and the Rearmament of Europe, 1954; Grathwol, R. P. Stresemann and the DNVP, 1980; Kimmich, C. M. Germany and the League of Nations, 1976; von Rheinbaben, R. Stresemann: The Man and Statesman, 1929; Sontag, R. A Broken World, 1971; Stern-Rubarth, E. Three Men Tried, 1939; Turner, H. A. Stresemann and the Politics of the Weimar Republic, 1963; Vallentin-Luchaire, A. Stresemann, 1931.

J. W. STRUTT

STRUTT, J. W.

(November 12, 1842–June 30, 1919)
Nobel Prize for Physics, 1904

The English physicist John William Strutt, third Baron Rayleigh, was born in Langford Grove, Maldon, Essex, to John James Strutt (second Baron Rayleigh) and Clara Elizabeth (Vicars) Strutt. As a boy, he suffered a series of debilitating illnesses, and his education was frequently interrupted. He briefly attended Eton College when he was ten, spent three years at a private school in Wimbledon, had a short stay at the Harrow School, and received four years of private tutoring. In 1861 Strutt entered Trinity College, Cambridge, where he studied mathematics and the physical sciences with E. J. Routh, a noted mathematician, and graduated in 1865 with highest honors. A year later, Trinity offered him a fellowship, which he held until 1871.

In 1868 Strutt assembled a scientific laboratory at the family seat at Terling Place, Witham, Essex, where he pursued his interest in radiation phenomena. His work resulted in published papers on acoustics and optics, establishing his reputation as an authority on sound. In 1871 he derived the relationship between the scattering of light by very small particles and the light's wavelength, known as Rayleigh scattering, which explained why the sky is blue and sunsets are red. Because shorter (blue) wavelengths are preferentially scattered at large angles by fine particles in the atmosphere, blue predominates in the scattering from light passing overhead. Light from the setting sun, viewed directly, has lost its blue due to side-scattering, and longer (red) wavelengths predominate. Also in 1871, Strutt took a trip up the Nile River to recover from rheumatic

fever, during which he started what was to become a monumental treatise on sound.

When his father died in 1873, Strutt became third Baron Rayleigh and began to manage the family's 7,000-acre estate. Three years later, however, he asked his younger brother to assume this responsibility, and from then on Strutt (known as Lord Rayleigh), devoted himself almost entirely to science, working in his home laboratory. Among his researches were experimental and theoretical studies of optical instruments, which resulted in the first clear definition of the resolving power of a diffraction grating and a fundamental analysis of the optical properties of spectroscopes. Diffraction gratings are plates whose surfaces are marked with fine, closely spaced grooves that separate light into its component colors by virtue of a relationship between light wavelengths and groove spacings. As used in a spectroscope, they produce a series of lines or bands of colors (line spectrum) whose positions correspond to wavelength. The spectroscope was becoming increasingly important in the late 1870s in the study of solar light and emissions from atoms and molecules.

Although Rayleigh would have been content to remain in his own laboratory, in 1879 he reluctantly accepted an offer to become professor of experimental physics (a position established in 1871) and director of the Cavendish Laboratory (opened in 1874) on the death of James Clerk Maxwell, the laboratory's first director. At Cambridge, Rayleigh initiated an ambitious program for the precise redetermination of the electrical units: the volt, the ohm, and the ampere. The program was marked by his habits of meticulous care and patience in the use of fine instruments, and its results, completed in 1884, have required remarkably little correction. He also established the practice, revolutionary in England at that time, of having students do laboratory work in elementary physics, which influenced universities throughout the country.

After five years at Cambridge, Rayleigh resigned his position and returned to Terling Place, where he pursued his researches for the rest of his life. He was always involved in several simultaneous projects, dividing his attention between experiments in his laboratory and theoretical work in his study. He published papers on an exceptionally wide range of subjects, including light and sound waves, electromagnetism, theorems in mechanics, vibrations of elastic media, capillarity, and thermodynamics. His classic, two-volume work, *The Theory of Sound,* was published in 1877–1878 and is still indispensable to modern scientists and engineers.

In 1892 Rayleigh began a series of measurements of gas densities, related to atomic weights, as a continuation of his interest in Prout's law. In 1815 English chemist William Prout had noted that gas densities tended to be whole-number multiples of the density of hydrogen, the lightest of all gases; and he had proposed that all elements were assemblies of hydrogen building blocks. When Rayleigh started his work, the best value for the density of oxygen was 15.96 times that of hydrogen, which was close enough to the whole number 16 to support Prout's hypothesis. Rayleigh made a more accurate determination, correcting the errors of other experimenters, and arrived at 15.88, a figure which cast doubt on the validity of Prout's law. When Rayleigh turned his attention to nitrogen, he discovered, to his surprise, that nitrogen obtained from the decomposition of ammonia was less dense than nitrogen derived from air. After careful measurements to eliminate all doubt, Rayleigh found a clue to the problem in a paper written in 1795 by Henry Cavendish, the English chemist and physicist for whom the laboratory was named. Cavendish had oxidized the nitrogen in air with an electric spark and had found that, regardless of how long he continued the sparking, a small amount of gas remained that he could not oxidize. Rayleigh concluded that air-derived nitrogen was impure and contained a small quantity of other unknown gas or gases. The ammonia-derived nitrogen was purer because ammonia is a compound of hydrogen and nitrogen, and in its formation the hydrogen selectively reacts with nitrogen and not with the impurities.

Repeating the tedious Cavendish process, Rayleigh eliminated the nitrogen by oxidation with electric sparking and, in 1894, slowly accumulated the unknown residual gas. Meanwhile, WILLIAM RAMSAY, a Scottish chemist, learned of Rayleigh's findings and applied more efficient chemical methods to obtain the gas. The two men coordinated their efforts and in 1895 announced that the elusive gas had been discovered. Since it was chemically inert (the reason it, too, was not oxidized with the nitrogen), they named it argon, from the Greek word for "inert." They found that argon composed about 1 percent of the volume of the atmosphere, and its density was over twice that of nitrogen. They also found that the gas they had isolated was not pure argon but contained other inert gases, which Ramsay later identified, including neon, krypton, xenon, and helium. The group is known collectively as the noble gases because of their resistance to chemical reactions.

During his three years of argon research, Rayleigh published a dozen scientific papers on such topics as the interference and scattering of light, the telephone, and sound measurements. In 1900 he published a derivation of the relationship between temperature and wavelength for blackbody radiation, based on existing physical principles. After the English physicist James Jeans made a minor modification to Rayleigh's derivation, it became known as the Rayleigh-Jeans radiation law. However, the law worked only for long wavelengths, and its publication preceded by a few months MAX PLANCK's announcement of his radical solution to the blackbody problem and the birth of quantum theory. Although Rayleigh followed closely the development of modern quantum physics and ALBERT EINSTEIN's theory of relativity, he was too conservative to accept them.

Rayleigh was awarded the 1904 Nobel Prize for Physics "for his investigations of the densities of the most important gases and for his discovery of argon in connection with these studies." (Ramsay received the 1904 prize for chemistry.) In his presentation speech, J. E. Cederblom of the Royal Swedish Academy of Sciences declared that although the methods for isolating the new gas "were known in principle, . . . the problem was . . . to obtain the new gas not only in the purest form possible, but also in a sufficient quantity to allow of a thorough investigation of its essential properties." The discovery of argon, Cederblom said, contributed to Ramsay's discovery of helium and the other noble gases.

An extremely prolific worker, Rayleigh published over 400 papers during the more than fifty years he spent in research. Although he is best known to nonscientists for the discovery of argon, his work encompassed virtually every area of classical physics. He also gave his time to educational, scientific, and government organizations. Although he taught for only a few years, he sat at one time or another on the governing boards of six educational institutions. He was the secretary (1885–1896) and the president (1905–1908) of the Royal Society. His many other activities included serving as president of the Advisory Committee on Aeronautics, as president of the British Association for the Advancement of Science, as chairman of the Explosives Committee of the War Office, and as chief examiner of London's natural gas supply. From 1908 until his death, he was chancellor of Cambridge University.

In 1871 Rayleigh married Evelyn Balfour, sister of Arthur James Balfour, who became prime minister of Great Britain in 1902. They had three sons, the eldest of whom, Robert, became a physicist and his father's biographer. Rayleigh continued working virtually until the day he died at Terling Place, publishing some ninety papers in his last fifteen years and leaving three completed but unpublished. He has been called the last of the great British classical physicists.

In addition to winning the Nobel Prize, Rayleigh was awarded the Royal Medal (1882), the Copley Medal (1899), and the Rumford Medal (1914) of the Royal Society; the Matteuci Gold Medal of the National Academy of Sciences of Italy (1895); the Faraday Medal of the British Chemical Society (1895); the Albert Medal of the Royal Society of Arts (1905); and the Elliott Cresson Medal of the Franklin Institute (1914). He received thirteen honorary degrees and was affiliated with over fifty learned societies.

SELECTED WORKS: Scientific Papers (6 vols.) 1899–1920.

ABOUT: Dictionary of National Biography 1912–1921, 1927; Dictionary of Scientific Biography, volume 13, 1976; Lindsay, R. B. Lord Rayleigh: The Man and His Works, 1970; Rayleigh, R. J. S. John William Strutt, Third Baron Rayleigh, 1924; Thomson, G. The Inspiration of Science, 1961.

SULLY-PRUDHOMME, RENÉ
(March 16, 1839–September 7, 1907)
Nobel Prize for Literature, 1901

The French poet René Sully-Prudhomme (sü lē' prü dôm') was born René François Armand Prudhomme in Paris. His father died when the boy was two, leaving the family destitute. With his widowed mother, Clotilde (Caillat) Prudhomme, and elder sister, he moved into his uncle's house. At the age of eight he was sent to board at the Lycée Bonaparte, where he showed ability in mathematics, classical languages, and French prosody. After graduating at the head of his class in mathematics, he prepared for entrance to the École Polytechnique, hoping to study engineering; but an attack of a serious eye disease forced him to relinquish his plans.

Pressed by his family to choose a career, Prudhomme became a factory correspondence clerk and by 1860 was supporting himself by working in a notary's office. In the evening, he studied philosophy and wrote poetry. His first volume of verse, Stances et poèmes (Stanzas and Poems), appeared in 1865 under the pen name Sully-Prudhomme, which he took from his father's name. This literary debut won high praise from the influential critic Charles Augustin Sainte-Beuve.

The following year the publisher Alphonse Lemerre included some of Sully-Prudhomme's work in a collection entitled Le Parnasse contemporain (Contemporary Parnassus), which heralded the advent of the Parnassians, a group of poets opposed to the lyrical excesses of the romantic school. Lemerre also reissued Stances et poèmes and a collection of Sully-Prudhomme's sonnets, Les Épreuves (Trials). During the next three years, the young poet produced Les Écuries d'Augias (The Augean Stables, 1866), a paraphrased translation of ancient Greek verse; Croquis italiens (Italian Sketches, 1866–1868); and Les Solitudes (Seclusions, 1869). In all these poems the themes of unrequited love and the conflict between science and religion recur. Having been rejected by a cousin he had hoped to marry, Sully-Prudhomme remained a lifelong bachelor.

Early in 1870 Sully-Prudhomme suffered a serious emotional blow when his mother, uncle, and aunt all died within a few days of one another. In July of that year the Franco-Prussian War began, and he enlisted in the militia. Deprivations suffered during the prolonged siege of Paris by Prussian troops further weakened his already fragile health, and by the time

RENÉ SULLY-PRUDHOMME

he was able to leave the city, he had already contracted an illness that paralyzed his lower body. While recuperating, he expressed his patriotism in a book of verse, *Impressions de la guerre* (Impressions of War, 1870).

Sully-Prudhomme's next important lyrical work was *Les Vaines tendresses* (Futile Tendernesses, 1875), which echoes the wistful tone of *Les Solitudes* and contains some of his most frequently anthologized poems. The long philosophical poem *La Justice* (Justice, 1878), a dialogue that shows the formative influence of the Roman poet Lucretius, argues that justice is to be found not in the external universe but in the human heart. A later work, *Le Bonheur* (Happiness, 1888), is a 4,000-line epic that describes humankind's progress toward happiness through curiosity, science, virtue, and sacrifice. Characterizing the impact of Sully-Prudhomme's humanistic ideals on French literature, the French-American scholar Jean-Albert Bédé wrote that "he lifted poetry from some of the gloom into which positivistic pessimism had plunged it for a generation and taught his belief that the road to happiness lies through pain, self-sacrifice, and brotherly love."

In a collection of critical essays published in 1900 as *Le Testament poétique* (Poetic Testament), Sully-Prudhomme registered his objections both to free verse and to the work of the symbolists and the poets of the Decadent school.

In 1901 he was chosen as the first recipient of the Nobel Prize for Literature, in recognition "of his excellent merit as an author, and especially of the high idealism, artistic perfec-

tion, as well as the unusual combination of qualities of the heart and genius to which his work bears witness." The selection disappointed many who had expected Leo Tolstoy to receive the prize.

In his presentation address, C. D. af Wirsén of the Swedish Academy pointed to Sully-Prudhomme's characteristically "inquiring and observing mind, which . . . finds evidence of man's supernatural destiny in the moral realm. . . . From this point of view, Sully-Prudhomme represents better than most writers what [Alfred Nobel] called 'an idealistic tendency' in literature." Too ill to attend the award ceremony, Sully-Prudhomme was represented by the French minister to Sweden.

As his health failed rapidly, Sully-Prudhomme retraced the steps leading to Blaise Pascal's Christian apologetics in *La Vraie Religion selon Pascal* (The True Religion According to Pascal, 1905). In his final work, *La Psychologie du libre arbitre* (The Psychology of Free Will, 1906), he concluded that the concept of free will is objectively grounded in nature and must therefore be true.

Sully-Prudhomme died at his villa in Chatenay-Malabry, a few miles south of Paris, on September 7, 1907.

A highly respected figure in French literary and academic circles in his lifetime, Sully-Prudhomme is today little read either in France or abroad. Some of his shorter verses were translated into English and anthologized early in the twentieth century, but his work in English generally has long been out of print, and he receives virtually no attention from contemporary scholars. The name *Sully-Prudhomme* is perpetuated primarily by a prize in his name that he established for young French poets with his Nobel Prize money.

WORKS IN ENGLISH TRANSLATION: The Problem of God, Freedom, and Immortality, 1891; Carrington, H. (ed.) Anthology of French Poetry, 1900; Boni, A. (ed.) Modern Book of French Verse, 1920.

ABOUT: Baring, M. Punch and Judy and Other Essays, 1924; Dowden, E. Studies in Literature, 1892; France, A. On Life and Letters, 1922; Grierson, F. Parisian Portraits, 1913.

SUMNER, JAMES B.

(November 19, 1887–August 12, 1955)
Nobel Prize for Chemistry, 1946
(shared with John H. Northrop and
  Wendell M. Stanley)

The American biochemist James Batcheller Sumner was born in Canton, Massachusetts,

JAMES B. SUMNER

near Boston, to Elizabeth Rand (Kelly) and Charles Sumner, a prosperous farmer and cotton factory owner whose ancestors had immigrated to Boston in 1636. After receiving his early education at the Eliot Grammar School, Sumner attended Roxbury Latin School, where he quickly became bored by all subjects except chemistry and physics. As a result of a hunting accident at the age of seventeen, he lost his left arm and, although left-handed, taught himself to use his right hand, not only for writing but also for playing tennis and billiards, and for skeet shooting.

Planning a career in electrical engineering, Sumner entered Harvard University in 1906 but soon gravitated to chemistry and received his B.S. in that field in 1910. After graduation he joined the family business, working ten hours a day in his uncle's factory, the Sumner Knitted Padding Company. It was, he recalled later, "dirty work, and uninteresting," and within a year he gladly accepted a temporary position as professor of chemistry at Mt. Allison College in Sackville, New Brunswick, Canada, even though he had no ambition to teach.

To his surprise he found that he enjoyed "the bookish life," and after his temporary post elapsed he taught briefly at the Worcester Polytechnic Institute in Massachusetts before returning to Harvard in 1912 for additional training in chemistry and physiology. At Harvard Medical School he studied biochemistry under Otto Folin, who initially tried to discourage the young chemist in the belief that his physical handicap would hamper a research career. Soon, however, Sumner's remarkable

dexterity in the laboratory impressed not only Folin but other faculty members. In 1913 Sumner received an M.S. and in 1914 a Ph.D. for a dissertation on the formation of urea in the animal body. (Urea is a waste product formed in the body as a result of protein metabolism.)

After graduation from Harvard, Sumner became an assistant professor of chemistry at Cornell University Medical College, then located in Ithaca, New York, where he rose to full professor in 1929. An ambitious researcher, he wanted "to find out what life is, what makes things grow, what makes the whole thing click," as he put it later. Accordingly, he set himself the task of isolating and purifying an enzyme, the first step in identifying the chemical composition of these important, but at the time little-understood, biological compounds.

Enzymes are organic catalysts, substances that are produced by living cells and that regulate many chemical processes in living organisms, such as the ability to digest food. When Sumner began his investigations, the chemistry of enzymes was still a mystery, although it was widely suspected that they consisted of protein. Not even the great German chemist RICHARD WILLSTÄTTER had been able to purify enzymes, which, he concluded, were not proteins but a class of compounds new to science.

In his doctoral research Sumner had already experimented with urease, a plant enzyme involved in the decomposition of urea. In 1916 it was discovered that high concentrations of urease are present in the jack bean, a bushy tropical plant native to South America; and it was from jack bean meal that Sumner tried to isolate the substance. Assuming the enzyme to be proteinaceous, he extracted every possible protein he could detect in large quantities of bean flour, using various solvents, filters, and methods of precipitation.

After nine discouraging years, he produced microscopic crystals that proved to be protein. His findings, published in 1926, were greeted with skepticism and outright ridicule. Willstätter and his students were particularly critical, maintaining that Sumner's crystals were merely a carrier for some small, active, nonprotein substance. For the next four years Sumner defended his work in a series of papers that offered additional supporting data.

Not until 1930, after he had spent a year at the University of Stockholm studying enzymes with HANS VON EULER-CHELPIN, did Sumner's theories receive confirming support from an American biochemist, JOHN H. NORTH-

ROP. Northrop's announcement that he had crystallized the enzyme pepsin, followed five years later by his isolation of trypsin, a pancreatic enzyme, helped persuade biochemists that enzymes are in fact proteins, although some incorporate nonprotein substances as well. By 1946 some thirty enzymes had been isolated and identified.

"For his discovery that enzymes can be crystallized," Sumner shared the 1946 Nobel Prize for Chemistry with Northrop and WENDELL M. STANLEY. In his presentation address ARNE TISELIUS of the Royal Swedish Academy of Sciences declared that "Sumner's results have . . . been accepted as the pioneer work which first convinced research workers that the enzymes are substances which can be purified and isolated in tangible quantities." Through Sumner's efforts, Tiselius said, "the foundation was laid for a more detailed penetration of the chemical nature of these substances, on which an understanding of the reactions taking place in living cells must finally depend."

"A number of persons advised me that my attempt to isolate an enzyme was foolish," Sumner recalled in his Nobel lecture, "but this advice made me feel all the more certain that if successful, the quest would be worthwhile." After summarizing the course of his enzyme research, Sumner pointed to the gains that had been made in this field. "Thanks to relatively recent investigation, practically all of the complicated reactions involved in the breaking down of glycogen to carbon dioxide and water have been made clear," he said. Moreover, "From the work of [CARL F.] CORI and his associates we now have evidence that hormones function through their effect on enzymes."

A year after receiving the Nobel Prize, Sumner was appointed director of Cornell's new Laboratory of Enzyme Chemistry, where he continued his research and maintained a heavy teaching load. Sumner's marriage to Bertha Louise Ricketts in 1915 produced five children but ended in divorce in 1930. The following year he married Agnes Pauline Lundkvist of Sweden; they were divorced in 1943, the same year that Sumner married Mary Morrison Beyer; they had two children.

Known as a demanding, often impatient, teacher, Sumner won his students' respect by his unstinting devotion to teaching. "The most important things I have tried to give my students," he once said, "are a curiosity to discover the world about them and the integrity to look only for the truth." Sumner remained an enthusiastic and highly competitive tennis player throughout most of his life. He also enjoyed photography, cooking, hiking, and the study of foreign languages. Shortly after his retirement from Cornell in 1955, he became ill and died of cancer in Buffalo, New York.

His numerous awards include the Scheele Medal of the Swedish Chemical Society (1937) as well as membership in the National Academy of Sciences, the American Academy of Arts and Sciences, and the Society for Experimental Biology and Medicine.

SELECTED WORKS: Textbook of Biological Chemistry, 1927; Antiurease, 1931, with J. S. Kirk; The Special Effects of Buffers Upon Urease Activity, 1934, with S. F. Howell; Chemistry and Methods of Enzymes, 1943, with G. F. Somers.

ABOUT: Biographical Memoirs of the National Academy of Sciences, volume 31, 1958; Dictionary of American Biography, supplement 5, 1977; Dictionary of Scientific Biography, volume 13, 1976; National Cyclopedia of American Biography, volume 46, 1963.

SUTHERLAND, EARL W., JR.

(November 19, 1915–September 3, 1974)
Nobel Prize for Physiology or Medicine, 1971

The American biochemist Earl Wilbur Sutherland Jr. was born in Burlingame, a small town in eastern Kansas, the fifth of six children. His father and namesake had farmed for ten years in New Mexico and Oklahoma before settling in Burlingame, where he ran a dry-goods business with the help of his wife, the former Edith M. Hartshorn, and their children. Allowed to roam the woods and fields as a child, Sutherland acquired a lifelong love of the natural world. In high school he displayed a keen interest in athletics, especially basketball, football, and tennis. Paul de Kruif's book *Microbe Hunters,* a popular account of the work of Louis Pasteur and other notable medical researchers, awakened the boy's interest in biology and medical science.

Sutherland was accepted at Washburn College in Topeka, Kansas, in 1933, but the Depression had left his parents penniless. A combination of scholarships and earnings from his job as an orderly at a local hospital enabled him to graduate with a B.S. in 1937. That same year he began medical studies at Washington University School of Medicine in St. Louis, where he was a student in CARL F. CORI's pharmacology class. Impressed by Sutherland's work, Cori offered the young man a

EARL W. SUTHERLAND JR.

student laboratory assistantship. While serving in that capacity, Sutherland not only received his first exposure to medical research but also formed a lasting friendship with Cori.

Determined to practice medicine, Sutherland interned at Barnes Hospital in St. Louis after receiving his medical degree in 1942. He was called up for service during the final years of World War II and served first as a battalion surgeon in the Third Army under General George S. Patton and later as a staff physician in a military hospital in Germany.

After receiving his discharge and returning to St. Louis in 1945, he felt torn between a career in medical practice and one in research. "Cori convinced me," he said later, "not so much by anything he said as by his example, that research was the right direction for me to take." For the next eight years Sutherland worked in the biochemistry department at Washington University, first as instructor and later as associate professor. During that time, he concentrated his research on two projects. The first was an investigation of phosphorylase, an enzyme responsible for initiating the breakdown of glycogen in liver and muscle. (Glycogen, the storage form of glucose, is the sugar molecule used by the body for energy.) The second was an effort to determine how the hormones epinephrine (found in the medullary portion of the adrenal glands) and glucagon (a secretion of the pancreas) cause the liver to release glucose.

In 1953 Sutherland joined Western Reserve (now Case Western Reserve) University in Cleveland as director of the pharmacology de-

partment. By that time he had established that in liver extracts, the initial step in glycogen breakdown is stimulated by epinephrine or glucagon and then catalyzed by phosphorylase. Undertaking a detailed examination of phosphorylase, he found that two other enzymes are also present in liver extracts—one that converts active phosphorylase to its inactive form, releasing inorganic phosphate in the process, and another that reactivates the inactive form, incorporating inorganic phosphate back into the molecule. This cycle of phosphorylation-dephosphorylation reaction is one of the body's basic biochemical energy-releasing processes.

At the same time, Erwin G. Krebs and Edmund H. Fischer, two biochemists at the University of Washington, in Seattle, found a similar enzyme in muscle and showed that reactivation of phosphorylase in muscle tissue occurs in the presence of the nucleotide adenosine triphosphate (ATP) and a special enzyme now known as phosphorylase kinase. Aided by this information, Sutherland and his co-worker, Theodore Rall, added hormones to inactive liver phosphorylase preparations in the presence of ATP to see which substances stimulated a reaction. In this way they showed that in cell-free extracts, both glucagon and epinephrine promote the active form of phosphorylase. Since it was previously thought that hormones operated directly on the whole cell, this demonstration cast new light on the action of hormones—particularly by establishing that hormonal action is a molecular process.

Pursuing his investigations, Sutherland found an unknown molecule, cyclic adenosine 3',5'-monophosphate (cyclic AMP), which promotes the conversion of inactive phosphorylase to the active form and carries out the task of glucose release within the cell. The discovery of cyclic AMP led Sutherland to propose the so-called second-messenger hypothesis of hormone action, which showed how hormones instruct their target tissues. He suggested that hormones, such as epinephrine and glucagon, be considered "first messengers," which leave their sites of synthesis and circulate to the target tissues, where they bind to specific receptors on the outer membranes of cells. This hormone-receptor combination then signals the cell to increase the activity of adenyl cyclase, an enzyme found in its membrane. This activity in turn instructs the cell to produce cyclic AMP, which serves as a second messenger to stimulate various enzymes (already present within the cell) to perform their specialized functions. This concept explains how glucagon and epinephrine can produce the same qualitative effect on liver cells.

Although the isolation of cyclic AMP initially aroused little interest, it was later recognized that Sutherland had discovered a new biological principle—a general mechanism for the action of many hormones. Moreover, he found that hormones other than glucagon and epinephrine can activate adenyl cyclase and that cyclic AMP acts on enzyme systems other than that of phosphorylase.

In 1963 Sutherland accepted a position as professor of physiology at Vanderbilt University, in Nashville, Tennessee, where he was able to devote all his time to research. Focusing exclusively on cyclic AMP, he and his colleagues at Vanderbilt demonstrated that more than a dozen mammalian hormones function with this substance as their second messenger. Cyclic AMP was also found to be involved in the activity of nerve cells and to be associated with the expression of genes in bacteria. In certain amoebas, for example, it signals individual cells to come together in reproductive aggregates. Moreover, the presence of cyclic AMP in unicellular as well as in multicellular organisms suggests that its role as a regulator of cellular processes began very early in the scheme of evolution.

The 1971 Nobel Prize for Physiology or Medicine was awarded to Sutherland "for his discoveries concerning the mechanisms of actions of hormones." In presenting the award, Peter Reichard of the Karolinska Institute noted that although the existence of hormones had long been known, their mechanism of action remained a mystery until Sutherland's work. The discovery of cyclic AMP, he added, elucidated "one of the fundamental principles of essentially all life processes."

By the time Sutherland received the Nobel Prize, some 2,000 researchers were studying cyclic AMP. His chain of discoveries opened new areas in specialties ranging from endocrinology to oncology and even psychiatry, since, according to Sutherland, the substance "affects everything from your memory to your toes." After 1971 Sutherland turned his attention to cyclic guanosine 3',5'-monophosphate, or GMP, which like cyclic AMP is widely distributed in mammalian tissues and is present in lower evolutionary species. He moved to the University of Miami in 1973, where he died the next year at the age of fifty-eight after suffering a massive esophageal hemorrhage.

In 1937 Sutherland married Mildred Rice. The marriage ended in divorce, and in 1963 he married Dr. Claudia Sebeste, with whom he had four children. Sutherland was once described as "baldish, gregarious, and easygoing." According to Carl Cori, several characteristics accounted for Sutherland's success as an investigator. "First and perhaps foremost he had the gift of intuition," Cori said. " He could set up the right experiment at the right time without necessarily knowing why. Secondly, his intuition was strong enough to generate a remarkable degree of tenacity. . . . Thirdly, he was an excellent worker in the laboratory who could recall any of the experiments he and his associates had carried out in the past." Added to those traits, Cori went on, were "ambition, a powerful drive, and an intensity and singularity of purpose."

In addition to the Nobel Prize, Sutherland received the Torald Sollman Award in Pharmacology of the American Society for Pharmacology and Experimental Therapeutics (1969), the Dickson Prize in Medicine of the University of Pittsburgh (1970), the Albert Lasker Basic Medical Research Award (1970), and the American Heart Association Research Achievement Award (1971). He was a member of the American Society of Biological Chemists, the American Chemical Society, the American Society for Pharmacology and Experimental Therapeutics, and the American Association for the Advancement of Science. Honorary degrees were awarded to him by Yale University and Washington University.

SELECTED WORKS: Cyclic AMP, 1971, with others.

ABOUT: Biographical Memoirs of the National Academy of Sciences, volume 49, 1978; New York Times March 10, 1974; Science October 22, 1971.

SUTTNER, BERTHA VON
(June 9, 1843–June 21, 1914)
Nobel Prize for Peace, 1905

Bertha von Suttner, Austrian author and pacifist, was born Bertha Sophia Felicita Kinsky in Prague, then part of the Austro-Hungarian Empire. She was the daughter of Austrian field marshall Count Franz Joseph Kinsky von Chinic und Tettau, who died shortly before her birth, and the former Sophia Wilhelmina von Körner, the daughter of an Austrian cavalry officer. Suttner's mother spent much of her time—and money—indulging herself at spas and gambling at casinos throughout Europe. Growing up in Paris, Venice, Baden-Baden, and other European

BERTHA VON SUTTNER

cities, Sutter developed a fluent command of English, French, and Italian and became acquainted with many members of European society. By the time she was thirty years old, her mother had exhausted the family fortune.

After a brief attempt to become a singer, Bertha took a position as governess to the four daughters of the Suttner family in Vienna. There she fell in love with one of the family's three sons, Baron Arthur Gundaccar von Suttner. The Suttners, whose own finances were diminished, hoped that Arthur would marry into wealth. In 1876, faced with the resolute opposition of the Suttners to her relationship with Arthur, Bertha went to Paris to discuss a position as housekeeper and secretary to Alfred Nobel. Within a few days Nobel was called to Sweden on business, and Bertha—homesick and longing to see Arthur—returned to Vienna, where the couple were married secretly.

For the next nine years the Suttners lived in the Caucasus region of Russia, where Bertha had friends. They supported themselves by giving private language and music lessons. At the same time, they began an intensive study of contemporary European culture and politics. Through their reading they adopted progressive views and came to believe that human progress could be achieved through reason and education. When war broke out between Russia and Turkey in 1877, Arthur von Suttner began contributing articles about the Russian front and the Caucasus to Viennese periodicals. The popularity of his articles encouraged Bertha von Suttner to begin writing. She published stories, essays, and articles and, with Arthur, four novels. As novelists, the Suttners belonged to the late-nineteenth-century naturalist movement. As exemplified by Émile Zola, the naturalists sought to base their fiction on scientific observation of social conditions and human behavior.

After the Suttners returned to Vienna in 1885, Bertha continued to express her political and social ideas through fictional characters who represented particular points of view. *Ein schlechter Mensch* (A Bad Lot, 1885) dealt with freethinkers; *Daniela Dormes* (1886) treated Darwinism and anti-Semitism; *High Life* (1886), a book in German with an English title, discussed democracy and progress; and *Vordem Gewitter* (Before the Storm, 1894) examined socialism. She also published her first full-length work of nonfiction, *Inventarium einer Seele* (Inventory of a Soul, 1883), in which she advocated social progress through internationalism and world peace.

In 1886 and 1887 the Suttners lived in Paris, where Bertha again met Alfred Nobel, who introduced her to some of the leading literary and political figures of the day. She and her husband were disturbed by the prowar sentiment of Parisians who were eager to take revenge on Germany for defeating France in the Franco-Prussian War of 1870–1871. The Suttners also learned about the International Arbitration and Peace Association, founded in London to mobilize public support for an international court to replace war as a means of settling conflicts between nations. "This information electrified me," Bertha von Suttner recalled later. She resolved to incorporate the idea into her writing, and in her next book, *Das Maschinenzeitalter* (The Machine Age, 1889), she criticized the nationalistic and militaristic spirit of the era.

In 1889 Suttner also published *Die Waffen nieder* (translated as *Lay Down Your Arms*), a novel about a young woman whose life is ruined by the European wars of the 1860s. It included not only philosophical arguments against war but also "vivid scenes of battlefield horrors." According to the critic Irwin Abrams, writing in the *Journal of Central European Affairs* in 1962, these scenes "rival any to be found in the war-weary literature of later eras."

Lay Down Your Arms had an enormous impact and established Suttner as a major spokeswoman for the peace movement. The book was cited by the Austrian Imperial Council, praised by pacifists such as Leo Tolstoy, reprinted widely in newspapers, and translated into a dozen languages. It became an article of political faith to countless supporters of the peace movement. Modern critics have compared its influence to that of Harriet Beecher Stowe's *Uncle Tom's Cabin.*

The popularity of *Lay Down Your Arms* brought Suttner into closer contact with many European peace groups. In 1891 she attended her first international peace conference, sponsored in Rome by the Interparliamentary Union. That year she founded the Austrian Peace Society, the first peace organization to be established in her nation. In 1892 she became a founding member of the Bern Peace Bureau, an organization designed to coordinate activities and communications among the peace groups that were burgeoning throughout Western Europe. For the next twenty years Suttner served as the bureau's vice president.

During the 1890s, a period of increasing militarism, Suttner attended numerous peace conferences, often as the only female delegate. At The Hague Peace Conference of 1899, she held a salon that was frequented by many prominent delegates from the twenty-six nations represented in the discussions. During these years she also wrote articles, edited a pacifist journal, and lectured extensively.

At a time when women in public life were relatively rare, Suttner won wide support for the peace movement, including that of Alfred Nobel. She corresponded frequently with Nobel, informing him about the activities of various peace organizations and encouraging him to devote his fortune to the cause of peace. In 1893 Nobel wrote to Suttner about his plans to "set aside a portion of my estate for a prize . . . to be awarded to the individual who has advanced furthest in the direction of a peaceful Europe." "Yes, do that—very seriously, I implore you," she replied.

After the death of her husband in 1902, Suttner continued her work, making lecture tours in the United States and Germany in 1904–1905, meeting with American President THEODORE ROOSEVELT, and helping form the Anglo-German Friendship Committee.

By the time she was awarded the 1905 Nobel Peace Prize, Suttner was widely considered the joint leader—with FRÉDÉRIC PASSY—of the European peace movement. In her Nobel lecture she focused on the barbarism of war, the inevitability of moral evolution, and the need for arbitration treaties and an international tribunal to maintain world peace. "This question of whether violence or law shall prevail between states is the most vital of the problems of our eventful era," she declared. "On the solution of this problem depends whether our Europe will become a showpiece of ruins and

failure, or whether we can avoid this danger and so enter sooner the coming era of secure peace and law in which a civilization of unimagined glory will develop."

After receiving the Nobel Prize, Suttner became even more popular as a speaker and writer. She published numerous articles and wrote another novel, *Der Menschheit Hochgedanken* (*When Thoughts Will Soar,* 1911), treating the themes of peace and feminism. In her lectures she warned of the dangers of militarizing China, opposed the development of the airplane for military use, and advocated a united Europe as the only alternative to war. In 1912 Suttner made her second lecture tour of the United States. In August 1913 she addressed the International Peace Congress at The Hague.

During her last years Suttner was both vilified and honored. To the German nationalist press she was known as *Friedensfurie* (Peacefury). She was called a traitor by Austrians who welcomed the approaching war. Irwin Abrams wrote, "In the face of attacks such as none of her colleagues from other countries had to experience, the baroness gave an example of personal courage and dedication." She was appointed honorary president of the INTERNATIONAL PEACE BUREAU at Bern and made an advisory member of the Carnegie Peace Foundation in the United States.

After refusing an operation for suspected cancer, Suttner died on June 21, 1914, less than six weeks before World War I began.

ADDITIONAL WORKS IN ENGLISH TRANSLATION: Memoirs of Bertha von Suttner: The Records of an Eventful Life (2 vols.) 1910.

ABOUT: Journal of Central European Affairs October 1962; Kempf, B. Woman for Peace: The Life of Bertha von Suttner, 1973; Lengyel, E. All Her Paths Were Peace, 1975; Outlook February 1906; Pauli, H. Cry of the Heart, 1957; Playne, C. E. Bertha von Suttner and the Struggle to Avert the World War, 1936.

SVEDBERG, TEODOR

(August 30, 1884–February 25, 1971)
Nobel Prize for Chemistry, 1926

The Swedish chemist Teodor Svedberg (sved' berg) was born at the Fleräng homestead near the city of Gävle, the only child of Elias Svedberg, a civil engineer who managed the local ironworks, and Augusta (Alstermark) Svedberg. The boy's father often took him on long excursions through the country-

TEODOR SVEDBERG

chemistry for Svedberg, a position he retained for thirty-six years. Although he went on to develop other methods for producing colloids, Svedberg is best known for his investigations into the physical properties of colloids. His careful studies of the diffusion and Brownian motion of colloidal particles (the dancing motion of minute particles suspended in a liquid) further supported JEAN PERRIN's 1908 experimental verification of the theoretical work of ALBERT EINSTEIN and Marian Smoluchowski, establishing clearly the existence of molecules in solution. Perrin had shown that the size of large colloidal particles could be determined by measuring their rate of settling. Most colloidal particles, however, sink so slowly in their media that this method seemed impracticable.

Svedberg used the ultramicroscope developed by RICHARD ZSIGMONDY to measure particle sizes of colloids. He was able to show that colloidal solutions obey the classical physical chemical laws for diluted solutions. In most cases, however, this method was incapable of distinguishing the smallest particle sizes and the distribution of particle sizes.

Svedberg believed that the settling of colloidal particles would be hastened in an increased gravitational field produced by a high-speed centrifuge. As a guest professor for eight months at the University of Wisconsin in 1923, he began the construction of an optical centrifuge in which particle sedimentation could be followed photographically. Since the particles moved by convection currents as well as by settling, Svedberg was not able to determine particle size by this method. He knew that the high thermal conductivity of hydrogen would help remove temperature differences, and thus convection currents, from the cell. By designing a wedge-shaped holding cell and by placing the rotor holding the cell in a hydrogen atmosphere, Svedberg, working with his colleague Herman Rinde back in Sweden, obtained convection-free sedimentation in 1924.

Later that year, Svedberg discovered that biological macromolecules (proteins) could also be made to settle out of solution. He demonstrated that the molecules of proteins are of one size only (monodisperse), in contrast to particles of metal colloids that are polydisperse, occurring in many different sizes. Moreover, the rate of sedimentation of proteins gave a direct measure of the size of the molecule. This was the first indication that proteins have well-defined molecular weights and shapes. As a result of these discoveries, the centrifuge became a central tool of biochemical research.

side and encouraged his interest in nature. He also allowed the young Svedberg to experiment in a small laboratory at the ironworks.

As a student at the Karolinska School in Örebro, Svedberg showed a special aptitude for physics, chemistry, and biology. Although he was particularly interested in botany, he decided to pursue chemistry because he thought it would offer greater insight into biological processes. He entered the University of Uppsala in January 1904 and received his B.S. in September 1905, the same year his first paper was published. He remained at Uppsala and received his doctorate in 1907 with a thesis on colloids.

A colloid is a mixture in which minute particles of one substance are dispersed or distributed throughout a second substance. Colloid particles are larger than ordinary crystalloid molecules but not large enough to be observed directly in a microscope or to settle out under the force of gravity. They range in size from about 5 nanometers (5 billionths of a meter) to approximately 200 nanometers. India ink (carbon particles in water), smoke (solid particles in air), and milk fat (fat globules in a water solution) are examples of colloids. In his doctoral thesis Svedberg described a new method using oscillatory electric discharges between metal electrodes placed in a liquid to produce relatively pure colloidal solutions of metals. The conventional method, which employed direct current, produced a high proportion of contaminants.

In 1912 the University of Uppsala created Sweden's first academic chair of physical

The velocity of sedimentation is now given in units called Svedberg units.

The 1926 Nobel Prize for Chemistry was awarded to Svedberg "for his work on disperse systems." In presenting the award, H. G. Söderbaum of the Royal Swedish Academy of Sciences said, "The movement of particles suspended in a liquid . . . provides visual evidence for the real existence of molecules and consequently also for that of atoms, evidence which is all the more remarkable as not so long ago an influential school of scientists declared these particles of matter to be unreal fictions." In his Nobel lecture, delivered the following year, Svedberg reviewed the technical and theoretical issues involved in his work and described the great potential he believed the ultracentrifuge offered for advances in many fields, including medicine, physics, chemistry, and industry.

In a new laboratory for physical chemistry built for him by the Swedish government, Svedberg spent most of the next fifteen years improving the design of the centrifuge. In January 1926 he tested a new oil-turbine model that reached 40,100 revolutions per minute. Five years later, a new oil-turbine centrifuge, capable of 56,000 revolutions per minute, was perfected. A long series of improvements in rotor design led, in 1936, to a centrifuge capable of 120,000 revolutions per minute. At that speed, a centrifugal force of 525,000 G (G represents the force of gravity) was exerted on the sedimenting system.

The initial protein studies had been performed on hemoglobin and hemocyanin. The sedimentation characteristics of 100 respiratory proteins from a wide variety of animals were also analyzed. All the proteins were shown to have round, monodisperse molecules with high molecular weights. Extending his ultracentrifuge studies to other biological macromolecules, Svedberg found that carbohydrates, such as cellulose and starch, form long, thin, polydisperse molecules.

Svedberg also had a lifelong interest in radioactivity. His work with Daniel Strömholm showed that some radioactive elements (previously assumed to be different) are chemically indistinguishable from each other and occupy the same position in the periodic table. This finding anticipated studies by FREDERICK SODDY on isotopes. In the late 1920s Svedberg investigated the effect of alpha particles (produced by radioactive substances) on protein solutions. After the discovery in 1932 of the uncharged neutron particle by JAMES CHADWICK, Svedberg built a small neutron generator to study the effects of neutron irradiation and the production of radioactive isotopes as chemical and biological tracers.

Upon reaching the age of mandatory retirement in 1949, Svedberg resigned his position at Uppsala. However, by special dispensation, he was allowed to continue as director of the university's newly founded Gustaf Werner Institute for Nuclear Chemistry, where a synchrocyclotron was installed mainly through his efforts.

A man of lively intellect and broad interests, Svedberg was an expert amateur photographer and made extensive studies of the photographic process. In the 1920s, using different wavelengths to photograph the "Codex Argenteus," a Gothic Bible from 500 A.D., he found that ultraviolet light made its badly faded writing visible. Through his intense interest in botany, he assembled one of the finest botanical collections in Sweden. Svedberg married four times, to Andrea Andreen (1909), Jane Frodi (1916), Ingrid Blomquist (1938), and Margit Hallén (1948); he had six sons and six daughters.

Svedberg did much to strengthen the connection between academic science and practical technology; for example, during World War II he led a successful effort to develop Swedish production of synthetic rubber. He promoted internationalism in science, especially by welcoming foreign scientists to Uppsala; and his professional work also contributed to the unification of physics, chemistry, and biology. He died in Örebro, Sweden, on February 25, 1971.

Among Svedberg's many awards were the Berzelius Medal of the Royal Swedish Academy of Sciences (1944), the Franklin Medal of the Franklin Institute (1949), and the Gustaf Adolf Medal of the University of Uppsala (1964). He was awarded honorary doctorates by the University of Groningen, the University of Wisconsin, the University of Uppsala, Harvard University, Oxford University, the University of Delaware, and the University of Paris. He was a member of more than thirty professional societies, including the Royal Swedish Academy of Sciences, the Royal Society of London, the American National Academy of Sciences, and the Soviet Academy of Sciences.

SELECTED WORKS: The Formation of Colloids, 1921; Colloid Chemistry, 1924; The Ultracentrifuge, 1940, with K. O. Pederson.

ABOUT: Biographical Memoirs of Fellows of the Royal

Society, volume 18, 1972; Dictionary of Scientific Biography, volume 13, 1976; Lindroth, S. (ed.) Swedish Men of Science, 1952; Tiselius, A. W. K. (ed.) A Collection of Papers Presented to T. Svedberg, 1944.

SYNGE, RICHARD
(October 28, 1914–   )
Nobel Prize for Chemistry, 1952
(shared with Archer Martin)

RICHARD SYNGE

The English biochemist Richard Laurence Millington Synge (sing) was born in Liverpool, the oldest child and only son of Laurence Millington Synge, a stockbroker, and the former Katherine Charlotte Swann. While attending Winchester College, a preparatory school in Hampshire, Synge won a scholarship in classics from Trinity College, Cambridge University. Encouraged by a great-uncle, however, and inspired by a newspaper account of a speech given by FREDERICK GOWLAND HOPKINS, Synge took the honors course in biochemistry after entering Trinity in 1933. Additional scholarships enabled him to continue his studies at the Cambridge Biochemical Laboratory after graduation from Trinity in 1936.

For the next three years, Synge conducted research on glycoproteins, which are complex molecules of carbohydrates and amino acids. During the course of this work, he discovered that acetylated amino acids showed slightly different affinities for water and for chloroform. These differences, however, were not sufficient to allow separation for analysis by any available method. The director of the laboratory, Charles Martin, suggested that Synge collaborate with ARCHER MARTIN, a senior student who was noted for his talents in the separation of complex chemical mixtures. Martin had developed novel countercurrent extraction techniques during his doctoral research on the components of the E vitamins. In 1938 Martin left Cambridge for the Wool Industries Research Association Laboratory at Leeds, and Synge followed him there the next year with financial support from the International Wool Secretariat, a private trade organization. At Leeds, Synge continued his doctoral research on protein analysis.

The industrial process of countercurrent extraction had been used for many years to isolate desired products from mixtures. In this procedure, the mixture to be separated is injected into a stream of two immiscible fluids that are flowing in opposite directions. Slight differences in affinity of the substance for one fluid or the other are magnified by repeated exchanges to allow the separation of the mix-

ture into the two solvents. Martin and Synge built a similar device in which they tried to make chloroform travel in one direction along wool fibers at the same time that water traveled in the other direction along cotton fibers. Because the machine did not have the desired high extraction efficiency, however, they turned to the analytical technique of absorption chromatography.

In 1906 Mikhail Tsvet, a Russian botanist, had developed the method of absorption chromatography for the analysis of complex substances extracted from plants. A long glass tube was filled with a finely divided powder that had differing affinities for the components in the chemical mixture, a sample of which was placed at the beginning of the column. When a solvent was allowed to trickle through the column, substances with a stronger attraction for the surface of the powder traveled down the column more slowly than those with a weaker attraction. Although it was effective, this analytical procedure was limited by the choices of column fillings.

In 1941 Martin and Synge tried an inert filler that would hold a strongly associated solvent motionless while a second solvent phase and dissolved mixture flowed through it. The substances would separate based on their differing affinities for the fixed and flowing solvents. This method allowed a much greater choice of conditions than was possible in absorption chromatography. Since the separation of substances results from their partition between the two solvent phases, the technique was named partition chromatography.

Two years after receiving his Ph.D. in 1943, Synge became a staff biochemist at the Lister Institute of Preventive Medicine in London. While analyzing antibiotic peptides, he also continued to collaborate with Martin on the development of partition chromatographic methods. In 1944, finding that the cellulose in filter paper was an excellent binder for polar solvents such as water, the two scientists developed a paper chromatographic technique. In this method, a drop of the substance to be analyzed is placed near the end of a sheet of filter paper, which is then inserted into a closed vessel containing a saturated solution of water dissolved in the transport solvent. As the transport solvent migrates by capillary action along the paper, the components of the mixture are carried at different rates. The use of two separate solvent systems flowing at right angles, or two-dimensional chromatography, produces an even sharper separation of the components of the mixture being tested. With the aid of two-dimensional paper chromatography, Synge determined the amino acid composition of the antibiotic gramicidin S.

Synge spent the year 1947 at the Institute of Physical Chemistry in Uppsala where he and the Swedish biochemist ARNE TISELIUS studied amino acid and peptide absorption on charcoal. After returning to England in 1948, Synge was named head of the Department of Protein and Carbohydrate Chemistry at the Rowett Research Institute in Aberdeen, Scotland. At the institute, which was directed by JOHN BOYD ORR, Synge investigated animal nutrition and the purification of intermediates in protein metabolism.

Synge and Martin were awarded the 1952 Nobel Prize for Chemistry for their "invention of partition chromatography." In his Nobel lecture Synge discussed the numerous applications of the technique in biochemical studies including amino acid and protein distribution in living organisms; enzyme action; amino acid sequence in peptide chains of proteins; analysis of carbohydrates, lipids, and nucleic acids; and pharmacological products. He also described uses in metallurgical and organic chemistry industries, as well as in food and drug control.

In 1958–1959 Synge was a visiting biochemist at the Ruakura Animal Research Station, Hamilton, New Zealand. From 1967 until his retirement nine years later, he worked at the Agricultural Research Council's Food Research Institute in Norwich, England. He was an honorary professor in the School of Biological Sciences, University of East Anglia,

from 1968 until 1984, and a member of the editorial board of the *Biochemical Journal* from 1949 to 1955.

In 1943 Synge married Ann Stephen, a physician and niece of the writer Virginia Woolf. They have four daughters and three sons. A tall man with blue-gray eyes, Synge enjoys gardening, skiing, foreign languages, travel, and literature.

The recipient of the John Price Wetherill Medal of the Franklin Institute (1959), Synge is a member of the Royal Society, the Royal Irish Academy, the American Society of Biological Chemists, and the Phytochemical Society of Europe.

SELECTED WORKS: Biological Aspects of Proteins in the Light of Recent Chemical Studies, 1952; Science in Society, 1969.

ABOUT: Nature November 15, 1952; New York Times November 7, 1952.

SZENT-GYÖRGYI, ALBERT
(September 16, 1893–October 22, 1986)
Nobel Prize for Physiology or Medicine, 1937

The Hungarian-American biochemist Albert Szent-Györgyi (sänt jôrj) von Nagyrapolt was born in Budapest, Hungary, to Nicholas Szent-Györgyi, a wealthy landowner, and the former Josefine Lenhossek. Szent-Györgyi was raised in a home filled with music and intellectual discussion; he later recalled, "I learned that only intellectual values were worth striving for, artistic or scientific creation being the highest aim." Considered a dull boy, Szent-Györgyi suddenly became a voracious reader in his teens and graduated from high school with top marks.

In 1911 Szent-Györgyi began medical studies at the University of Budapest, where he conducted research in his uncle's laboratory and investigated the microscopic anatomy of the epithelial cells of the anal canal and the vitreous humor of the eye. By his third year in medical school he had published several papers on histology (the study of the structure and function of tissue). With the outbreak of World War I, he was conscripted into the Austro-Hungarian army, served three years on the Russian and Italian fronts, and received the Silver Medal for Valor. Having become "increasingly disgusted with the moral turpitude of military service" and convinced that "we

ALBERT SZENT-GYÖRGYI

were being sacrificed senselessly," he inflicted a gunshot wound to his own arm and was sent home. He resumed his studies and received his medical degree at Budapest in 1917. Szent-Györgyi was assigned to an army bacteriological laboratory, where he protested unethical experiments performed on Italian prisoners of war and was "sent to the north Italian swamps, where tropical malaria made life expectancy very short."

Nevertheless, he survived, and when the war ended he became an assistant in pharmacology at the university in Pozsony (now Bratislava, Czechoslovakia). Within a few months, however, the town was ceded to Czechoslovakia under the terms of the Treaty of Versailles, and Szent-Györgyi returned to Budapest, smuggling his laboratory equipment into the city. After the Communist regime of Béla Kun took power, Szent-Györgyi lost all of his possessions and fled for what proved to be a decade of migratory scientific research throughout northern Europe. He studied electrophysiology in Prague, acid-base chemistry in Berlin, and physical chemistry at the Institute of Tropical Medicine in Hamburg. After two years in the pharmacology department at the University of Leiden in the Netherlands, he became a research associate at the University of Groningen, where he began an investigation into the mechanisms of biological oxidation.

By the 1920s a general model of cellular carbohydrate metabolism, oxidation, and energetics had begun to take form. Biochemists knew that glucose and its storage form, glycogen, are degraded or metabolized by one of two pathways: an anaerobic pathway (in the absence of oxygen), which leads to lactic acid or lactate, and an aerobic pathway (in the presence of oxygen), or glycolysis, in which glucose is converted to pyruvic acid or pyruvate, and then to carbon dioxide and water. OTTO WARBURG argued that the essential reaction in biological oxidation involved the biochemical activation (and addition) of oxygen, whereas HEINRICH WIELAND believed that the activation (and removal) of hydrogen was more significant. Szent-Györgyi demonstrated that activation of both oxygen and hydrogen is necessary in cellular oxidation reactions. He also discovered enzymes of the dicarboxylic acids—succinic and citric acids—that catalyze oxidative reactions intermediate between pyruvate and carbon dioxide and water. This catalytic system is bound to intracellular structures, later shown to be mitochondria (small granules or rod-shaped structures in the cytoplasm of cells), the power centers of the cell. In the 1930s, Szent-Györgyi's discoveries at Groningen furnished the basis for HANS KREBS's clarifications of the biochemical reactions now known as the citric acid cycle, or the Krebs cycle.

When Szent-Györgyi analyzed biological oxidation in plant cells, he discovered a strong reducing substance, or hydrogen donor. Working at Cambridge University in the laboratory of the physiologist FREDERICK GOWLAND HOPKINS, Szent-Györgyi isolated and prepared crystals of the reducing agent from oranges, lemons, and cabbages, as well as from animal adrenal glands. Because the substance contained six carbon atoms and was acidic, he called it hexuronic acid. For this work Cambridge University awarded him a Ph.D. in chemistry in 1927. He remained at Cambridge for the next three years, then spent a year in the United States at the Mayo Clinic in Minnesota, where he isolated large amounts of hexuronic acid from adrenal glands provided by slaughterhouses. He returned to Cambridge with 25 grams of hexuronic acid, which he shared with the chemist WALTER N. HAWORTH, who determined its complete chemical structure.

Upon returning to Hungary, Szent-Györgyi was appointed professor of medical chemistry at the University of Szeged in 1930 and professor of organic chemistry five years later. During the course of his work at Szeged, Szent-Györgyi and his colleagues demonstrated that hexuronic acid, which he and Haworth had renamed ascorbic acid, was identical to vitamin C. Dietary deficiency of ascorbic acid causes scurvy, hence the name *a*scorbic acid. Scurvy, a nutritional disease characterized by weakness, anemia, spongy gums, and a tendency toward hemorrhaging of the skin and mucous membranes, was for centuries common among sailors fed a diet devoid of ascorbic acid or vitamin C. Known today as Barlow's disease, scurvy occurs very rarely.

After using all of his remaining adrenal hexuronic acid for these studies, Szent-Györgyi discovered that paprika, or Hungarian red pepper, contains large quantities of ascorbic acid. "One night we had fresh red pepper for supper," he later recalled. "I did not feel like eating it and thought of a way out. Suddenly it occurred to me that this was practically the only plant that I had never tested. I took it to the laboratory, and about midnight I knew that it was a treasure chest of vitamin C, containing 2 milligrams per gram." Within a few weeks, he had obtained several kilograms of crystalline vitamin C from paprika.

At the University of Szeged, Szent-Györgyi also discovered that flavonoids, plant pigments present in impure preparations of ascorbic acid, reduced the fragility of capillaries, which resulted in the bleeding tendency of patients with Henoch's purpura (a disease characterized by discoloration of the skin, vomiting, diarrhea, abdominal distension, and renal colic). He called these substances vitamin P; their status as a vitamin remains uncertain, however.

Szent-Györgyi was awarded the 1937 Nobel Prize for Physiology or Medicine for "his discoveries in connection with the biological combustion processes, with special reference to vitamin C and the catalysis of fumaric acid." In his presentation speech, Einar Hammarsten of the Karolinska Institute hailed the central role that Szent-Györgyi's findings played in "giving us for the first time a picture of a coherent oxidation process." In his Nobel lecture Szent-Györgyi said that from the pioneering work of Wieland, it became apparent that the human body knows only *one* fuel, hydrogen (rather than carbon and carbon dioxide, as was formerly believed).

A year after receiving the Nobel Prize, Szent-Györgyi was appointed Franchi Professor at the University of Liège in Belgium. Near the end of the decade his interest turned to the biochemistry of muscle cells. He and his colleagues isolated actin, a muscle protein that, together with another protein, myosin, forms the complex actomyosin. When boiled muscle extract was added to actomyosin, the artificial muscle filaments contracted. Szent-Györgyi

went on to identify the energy-rich phosphate bonds of adenosine triphosphate (ATP) as the cause of the actomyosin contraction.

During World War II, Szent-Györgyi remained in Hungary, where he became involved in underground diplomatic activities. Near the end of the war, while pursued by the Nazis, he was made a Swedish citizen overnight by the king of Sweden and smuggled out of Budapest by the Swedish legation only hours before the Gestapo arrived. After the war, disillusioned by the Soviet occupation of Hungary and demoralized by the failure of his own political efforts as a member of the Hungarian Parliament, he emigrated to the United States in 1947 and was naturalized as an American citizen in 1955. He established an Institute for Muscle Research at the Marine Biology Laboratory in Woods Hole, Massachusetts, where he conducted research on the regulation of cancer-cell growth, the electrophysiological properties of biological membranes, and the hormonal function of the thymus glands.

In 1917 Szent-Györgyi married Cornelia Demény, with whom he had a daughter. After his first wife died of cancer, he married Marta Barbiro in 1942. After the end of his second marriage, he married Marcia Houston in 1975. A vocal opponent of the role of the United States in the Vietnam War, Szent-Györgyi also worked on behalf of nuclear disarmament. He died at his home in Woods Hole on October 22, 1986, after suffering kidney failure.

Szent-Györgyi was the recipient of the Cameron Prize and Lectureship of the University of Edinburgh (1946) and the Albert Lasker Award of the American Heart Association (1954). He held memberships in the Budapest Academy of Science, the National Academy of Sciences, the American Academy of Arts and Sciences, and the National Academy of Budapest. He was awarded honorary degrees by the universities of Lausanne, Padua, Paris, and Bordeaux and by Cambridge, Oxford, and Brown universities.

SELECTED WORKS: On Oxidation, Fermentation, Vitamins, Health and Disease, 1939; Chemistry of Muscular Contraction, 1947; Nature of Life, 1948; Bioenergetics, 1957; Introduction to Submolecular Biology, 1960; Science, Ethics, and Politics, 1963; Bioelectronics, 1968; The Crazy Ape, 1970; What Next? 1971; The Living State, 1972; A New Theory of Cancer, 1976.

ABOUT: Current Biography January 1955; The Excitement and Fascination of Science, 1965; Kaminer, B. (ed.) Search and Discovery, 1977; Kasha, M., and Pullman, B. (eds.) Horizons in Biochemistry, 1962; The Way of the Scientist, 1962.

TAGORE, RABINDRANATH
(May 6, 1861–August 7, 1941)
Nobel Prize for Literature, 1913

The Indian poet Rabindranath Tagore (tä′gōr) was born in Calcutta, the youngest of fourteen children in a wealthy and prominent Brahman family. His father, Maharishi Debendranath Tagore, was a respected spiritual teacher who made frequent pilgrimages to India's holy places. His mother, Sarada Devi, died when Tagore was fourteen. As a result, Tagore's early life was plagued by loneliness and isolation. He began writing poetry at the age of eight, receiving his early education first from tutors and then at a variety of private schools. These included the Oriental Seminary in Calcutta, the Normal School, and the Bengal Academy, where he received a thorough schooling in Bengali history and culture. Traveling through northern India with his father in 1873, Tagore was deeply impressed by the beauty of the land and by the wealth of India's long cultural heritage.

In 1878 Tagore's narrative poem *Kabikāhinī* (A Poet's Tale) was published. The same year, he embarked for England to study law at University College, London, but left a year later without obtaining a degree. Returning to India, he settled briefly in Calcutta, where the example of his older brothers encouraged him to study and to write. In 1883 he married Mrinalini Devi, with whom he had two sons and three daughters. Two early collections of his poems—*Sandhyā Sangeet* (Evening Songs, 1882) and *Prabhāt Sangeet* (Morning Songs, 1883)—date from this period.

Tagore's father dispatched him to oversee the family estate at Shelaidaha, East Bengal, in 1890. There Tagore divided his time between the estate headquarters and a houseboat on the Padma River. Finding inspiration in the countryside and in the lives of the peasants, he wrote seven volumes of poetry between 1893 and 1900, including *Sonār Tari* (*The Golden Boat,* 1894) and *Khanikā* (Moments, 1900). It was, he later wrote, "the most productive period of my literary life." The image of the golden boat, a metaphor for life floating on the stream of time, also appears in much of Tagore's subsequent work. In *Khanikā* he moved away from the romantic vein of his earlier work to a more colloquial style that at the time offended many Indian critics by its untraditional, highly personal mode.

In 1901 Tagore moved to Sāntiniketan (Abode of Peace), a plot of land outside Calcutta owned by his family. There his interest

RABINDRANATH TAGORE

in education led him to found a school with five other teachers. To support the fledgling institution, Tagore's wife sold much of her jewelry, and Tagore sold the rights to a collected edition of his works for a pittance. Despite his self-imposed responsibilities, he continued to write prolifically, producing not only poems but novels, stories, a history of India, textbooks, and treatises on pedagogy.

After his wife's death in 1902, Tagore published *Sharan* (Remembrance), a collection of lyric poems that gave voice to his deep sense of loss. In 1903 one of his daughters died of tuberculosis, followed in 1907 by the death of his younger son from cholera.

While accompanying his remaining son, Rathindranath, to the agricultural college at the University of Illinois in 1912, Tagore stopped in London. There he showed some English translations that he had made of his poems to William Rothenstein, a British painter and writer whom he had met the previous year in India. Through Rothenstein's connections, the India Society published the poems that year as *Gitanjali: Song Offerings,* with an introduction by WILLIAM BUTLER YEATS. The book established Tagore's reputation in England and the United States. Ezra Pound, at that time an unofficial secretary to Yeats, praised the poems for "a sort of ultimate common sense, a reminder of one thing and of forty things which we are overlikely to lose sight of in the confusion of our Western life, in the racket of our cities, in the jabber of manufactured literature, in the vortex of advertisement." Many early enthusiasts of Tagore's work, however, misunderstood not only the poetry but the poet. They regarded Tagore as the mystic voice of the Indian people, even though he wrote for a small audience in Bengali, a language that only a fraction of the population could understand.

Tagore was awarded the 1913 Nobel Prize for Literature "because of his profoundly sensitive, fresh, and beautiful verse, by which, with consummate skill, he has made his poetic thought, expressed in his own English words, a part of the literature of the West." In his presentation speech, Harald Hjärne of the Swedish Academy cited *Song Offerings* as "one of [Tagore's] works that more especially arrested the attention" of the Nobel committee of the Swedish Academy. In his address, Hjärne also cited English translations of several other works in both poetry and prose, all of which had been published in 1913. Praising Tagore's poems as "by no means exotic but truly universally human in character," Hjärne went on to characterize the poet as a figure who reconciled the worlds of the East and the West.

Tagore, who was visiting the United States at the time, did not attend the ceremony but sent a telegram expressing his "grateful appreciation of the breadth of understanding which has brought the distant near and has made a stranger a brother." The British ambassador to Sweden accepted the prize in his absence. Tagore donated the prize money to his school, Visva-Bharati, which became a chartered university after World War I.

Knighted in 1915, Tagore renounced his title four years later after British troops at Amritsar killed some 400 Indian demonstrators who were protesting colonial antisedition laws. Over the next three decades, Tagore made a number of visits to Europe, the United States, South America, and the Middle East. His paintings—a pursuit he took up at the age of sixty-eight—were exhibited in Munich, New York, Paris, Moscow, and other cities.

Although best known in the West for his poetry, Tagore also wrote numerous plays: *Visarjan* (*Sacrifice*, 1890) dramatizes a young man's struggle to find religious truth; *Dākghar* (*The Post Office*, 1912) is a wistful story about a young boy; and *Rakta-Karabi* (*Red Oleanders*, 1925) is a drama of social and political protest. Many of Tagore's short stories, which draw heavily on Bengali rural life for their settings and characters, were first published in English in 1913 as *Hungry Stones and Other Stories*.

Tagore received honorary degrees from four Indian universities and an honorary doctorate from Oxford University. He died in Calcutta in 1941 after a long illness.

According to his literary secretary, Amiya Chakravarty, Tagore found comfort in the fact that his works were so well known and so well loved by his own Bengali people that he had become "anonymous" in his lifetime. "People in remote Indian villages sang his songs [of which he wrote more than 3,000], recited his poems, used his thoughts without knowing the authorship," wrote Chakravarty. "Bullock-cart drivers, ferry boatmen, workers in the fields thus accepted his gifts as a part of their perennial inheritance."

Although Tagore remained a well-known and popular author in the West until the end of the 1920s, interest in his work has greatly declined. Mary Lago's critical biography of the poet suggests two possible reasons for this. First, most English translations of his work (other than Tagore's own) fail to convey its true qualities. Second, many of Tagore's early poems and later works have never been translated and remain available only to readers of Bengali. According to the Indian scholar Krishna Kripalāni, in his biography of the poet, "Tagore's main significance lies in the impulse and direction he gave to the course of India's cultural and intellectual development. . . . He gave [his people] faith in their own language and in their cultural and moral heritage."

ADDITIONAL WORKS IN ENGLISH TRANSLATION: Gora, 1908; Chitra, 1913; The Gardener, 1913; The Crescent Moon, 1913; The King of the Dark Chamber, 1914; Sadhana, 1914; Fruit-Gathering, 1916; Stray Birds, 1916; Home and the World, 1916; The Cycle of Spring, 1917; My Reminiscences, 1917; Nationalism, 1917; Personality, 1917; Lover's Gift and Crossing, 1918; Mashi and Other Stories, 1918; A Mother's Prayer, 1919; Autumn Festival, 1919; The Fugitive, 1921; Thought Relics, 1921; The Wreck, 1921; Creative Unity, 1922; Greater India, 1923; The Curse at Farewell, 1924; The Eyesore, 1924; Broken Ties and Other Stories, 1925; Fireflies, 1928; The Religion of Man, 1931; Sheaves, Poems, and Songs, 1932; Man the Artist, 1932; My Boyhood Days, 1940; Last Poems, 1941; Two Sisters, 1944; Crisis in Civilization, 1950; Three Plays, 1951; A Vision of India's History, 1951; Syamali, 1955; A Flight of Swans, 1955; A Tagore Testament, 1955; The Herald of Spring, 1957; Chitrangada, 1957; On the Edges of Time, 1958; The Runaway and Other Stories, 1959; Wings of Death, 1960; A Tagore Reader, 1961; Towards Universal Man, 1961; On Art and Aesthetics, 1961; Devouring Love, 1961; Diary of a Westward Voyage, 1962; Chaturanga, 1963; Boundless Sky, 1964; Binodini, 1965; Lipika, 1969; Patraput, 1969; The Housewarming, 1977.

ABOUT: Ahluwalia, B. K. Tagore and Gandhi, 1981; Aronson, A. Rabindranath Through Western Eyes, 1943; Ayyub, A. S. Tagore's Quest, 1980; Biswas, B. On Tagore, 1984; Chandrasekharan, K. Tagore and Indian Literature, 1972; Chattopadhyaya, S. Art and the Abyss, 1977; Gopal, K.

Social Thought of Rabindranath Tagore, 1974; Hay, S. N. Asian Ideas of East and West, 1970; Khanolkar, G. D. The Lute and the Plough, 1963; Kripalāni, K. Rabindranath Tagore: A Biography, 1962; Lago, M. Rabindranath Tagore, 1976; Mukherjee, S. Passage to America, 1963; Mukherji, D. P. Tagore: A Study, 1972; Mukherji, S. B. The Poetry of Tagore, 1977; Ray, K., and Pulinbihari, S. (eds.) Rabindranath Tagore, 1861–1961, 1961; Ray, N. An Artist in Life, 1967; Rhadakrishnan, S. The Philosophy of Rabindranath Tagore, 1919; Rhys, E. Rabindranath Tagore, 1915; Rothenstein, W. Six Portraits of Rabindranath Tagore, 1915; Sen, S. The Political Thought of Tagore, 1947; Sen Gupta, S. C. Great Sentinel, 1948; Singh, A. Rabindranath Tagore: His Imagery and Ideas, 1984; Thomson, E. J. Tagore, Poet and Dramatist, 1926; Zepp, I. G. Rabindranath Tagore: American Interpretations, 1981.

IGOR TAMM

TAMM, IGOR

(July 8, 1895–April 12, 1971)
Nobel Prize for Physics, 1958
(shared with Pavel Cherenkov and Ilya Frank)

The Russian physicist Igor Evgenievich Tamm was born in the Pacific port city of Vladivostok to Olga (Davydova) and Evgeny Tamm, a civil engineer. He graduated in 1913 from the gymnasium in Elisavetgrad (now Kirovograd) in the Ukraine, where the family had moved in 1901. After a year of study at Edinburgh University (where he acquired a Scottish accent in his English), Tamm returned to Russia and earned a degree in physics from Moscow State University in 1918. While still an undergraduate, he served at the front as a medical volunteer in World War I and was active in the Elisavetgrad municipal government.

In 1919 Tamm began his long career as a teacher of physics, first at the Crimean University and later at the Odessa Polytechnic Institute in Simferopol. After returning to Moscow in 1922, he taught at the J. M. Sverdlov Communist University for three years. Tamm joined the theoretical physics department at the Second Moscow University in 1923, serving as professor from 1927 to 1929. In 1924 he also began lecturing at Moscow State University, where from 1930 to 1937 he was a professor of theoretical physics and head of that department. Tamm received the degree of doctor of physical and mathematical sciences in 1933 and at that time became a corresponding member of the Soviet Academy of Sciences. When the academy moved from Leningrad to Moscow in 1934, Tamm became director of the theoretical section of its P. N. Lebedev Physical Institute, a post he held until his death.

The electrodynamics of anisotropic solids (those having different physical properties in different directions) and crystal optics were Tamm's first areas of scientific research under the direction of Leonid I. Mandelshtam, a professor at the Odessa Polytechnic Institute in the early 1920s and a distinguished Soviet scientist who contributed to many fields of physics, particularly optics and radio physics. Tamm remained closely associated with Mandelshtam until the latter's death in 1944. When Tamm turned to quantum mechanics, he explained acoustic vibration and light scattering in solids. This work introduced the idea of quantized sound waves (later known as "phonons"), a significant concept in many subsequent solid-state theories.

In the late 1920s relativistic quantum mechanics was important to the new physics, and the English physicist P. A. M. Dirac developed the relativistic theory of the electron. Among other things, it predicted negative energy levels for the electron, a concept that many physicists rejected because the existence of the positron (a particle equivalent to the electron, but with positive charge) had not yet been demonstrated experimentally. Tamm, however, proved that the scattering of low-energy light quanta from free electrons takes place by intermediate stages in such a way that the electrons at that time are in negative energy states. As a result, he showed that negative electron energy was essential to Dirac's overall theory of the electron.

Tamm made two significant discoveries in the quantum theory of metals, a popular topic in the early 1930s. Working with a student,

S. P. Shubin, he explained the photoelectric emission of electrons from metals—that is, emission upon exposure to light. His other discovery was that electrons at the surface of a crystal could occupy special bound energy states, subsequently called Tamm surface levels, which later proved important in the study of the surface effects and contact properties of metals and semiconductors.

During this time, Tamm began theorizing about the atomic nucleus. From experimental data, he and S. A. Altshuler predicted that the neutron, despite its lack of charge, possesses a negative magnetic moment (a physical quantity related to, among other things, charge and spin). Although this is now known to be true, at the time many theorists believed Tamm to be wrong. In 1934 Tamm attempted to explain by his so-called beta theory the forces that hold the nucleus together. According to Tamm, the decay of nuclei by emission of beta particles (high-speed electrons) leads to the appearance of forces of a special kind between any two nucleons (protons and neutrons). Using ENRICO FERMI's work on beta decay, Tamm examined what nuclear forces, if any, might arise from the exchange of electron-neutrino pairs between any two nucleons. He found that beta forces, in fact, exist but are too weak to act as the "nuclear glue." One year later, the Japanese physicist HIDEKI YUKAWA correctly postulated the existence of particles called mesons—instead of the electrons and neutrinos that Tamm had suggested—whose exchange processes do, in fact, account for nuclear bonding.

In 1936–1937 Tamm and ILYA FRANK formulated a theory to interpret the radiation observed by PAVEL CHERENKOV from refractive media subjected to gamma radiation. Although Cherenkov had characterized the radiation and demonstrated that it was not luminescence, he was unable to explain its origin. Tamm and Frank considered the case of an electron moving faster than the speed of light in the medium. Although this phenomenon is not possible in a vacuum, it can occur in refractive media because the phase velocity of light in a medium is 3×10^8 meters per second divided by the refractive index of the medium. In the case of water (which has a refractive index of 1.333), the characteristic blue glow occurred when the velocity of the electrons responsible exceeded 2.25×10^8 meters per second (the phase velocity of light in water). Pursuing this model, the two physicists were able to explain Cherenkov radiation (known in the Soviet Union as Vavilov-Cher-

enkov radiation to acknowledge the work done by Cherenkov's and Frank's mentor, the physicist S. I. Vavilov). Tamm, Cherenkov, and Frank also tested other predictions of the theory, which were experimentally confirmed. Their work led eventually to the development of superlight optics, which has practical application to other fields, such as plasma physics. For their discoveries, Tamm, Frank, Cherenkov, and Vavilov received the Soviet government's State Prize in 1946.

Tamm, Frank, and Cherenkov were jointly awarded the 1958 Nobel Prize for Physics "for the discovery and the interpretation of the Cherenkov effect." In his presentation speech, MANNE SIEGBAHN of the Royal Swedish Academy of Sciences pointed out that although Cherenkov's discoveries had "essentially established the general properties of the newly discovered radiation, . . . a mathematical description of the effect was still lacking." The work of Tamm and Frank, he said, provided "an explanation . . . that besides being both simple and clear, also satisfied the requirements for mathematical stringency." Interestingly, Tamm never considered the work for which he was awarded the prize to be among his most important contributions.

After his work on Cherenkov radiation, Tamm returned to nuclear forces and elementary particles. He developed an approximate quantum-mechanical method for describing the interaction of elementary particles at speeds approaching that of light. Developed further by the Russian chemist P. D. Dankov and known as the Tamm-Dankov method, it is widely used in theoretical studies of nucleon-nucleon and nucleon-meson interactions. Tamm also developed a cascade theory of cosmic-ray showers. In 1950 Tamm and ANDREI SAKHAROV suggested confining gaseous discharges with powerful magnetic fields, a principle that still underlies nearly all Soviet efforts to achieve controlled thermonuclear reactions (nuclear fusion). During the 1950s and 1960s, Tamm continued to develop new theories about elementary particles and tried to eliminate some of the fundamental difficulties in existing theories about them.

During his long career, Tamm helped turn Moscow State University's physics laboratory into an important research center and introduced the new topics of quantum mechanics and relativity into the physics curriculum throughout the Soviet Union. Besides being a renowned theoretical physicist, Tamm took part in politics. He spoke out vigorously against government attempts to dictate policy to the

Soviet Academy of Sciences and against bureaucratic control of academy research, with its resultant waste of resources and manpower. Although outspoken and not a member of the Communist party, Tamm was named a Soviet delegate to the 1958 Geneva conference on policing a nuclear test ban and was active in the Pugwash Movement for Science and World Affairs.

Praised for his warmth and humanity, Tamm was described in the *Washington Post* after a 1963 interview on American television as "no word-wielding propagandist, no defensive diplomat, no smug philistine, but a cultured scientist whose stature allows him a breadth of outlook and a candor of expression denied to many of his countrymen." In the interview, Tamm cited the mutual distrust between the United States and the Soviet Union as the main impediment to genuine arms reduction and urged a "drastic change in our political thinking that starts from the point of view that no war at all is possible."

Tamm married Natalia Shuiskaya in 1917; they had a son and a daughter. He died in Moscow on April 12, 1971.

Tamm was elected to full membership in the Soviet Academy of Sciences in 1953. He was also a member of the Polish Academy of Sciences, the American Academy of Arts and Sciences, and the Swedish Physical Society. He was awarded two Orders of Lenin and the Order of the Red Banner of Labor by the Soviet government, and he was named a Hero of Socialist Labor. Tamm wrote the popular textbook *Osnovy teorii elektrichestva* (Principles of the Theory of Electricity) in 1929; it has been reprinted several times.

ABOUT: Current Biography December 1963; Dictionary of Scientific Biography, volume 13, 1976; Science November 14, 1958.

TATUM, EDWARD L.

(December 14, 1909–November 5, 1975)
Nobel Prize for Physiology or Medicine, 1958
(shared with George W. Beadle and Joshua Lederberg)

The American geneticist and biochemist Edward Lawrie Tatum was born in Boulder, Colorado, the first of three children of Arthur Lawrie Tatum, a physician and pharmacologist at the University of Wisconsin, and the former Mabel Webb, one of the first women to graduate from the University of Colorado.

EDWARD L. TATUM

Tatum received his early education in the University of Chicago Experimental School. He attended the University of Chicago for two years before transferring to the University of Wisconsin, where he received a B.A. in chemistry in 1931 and an M.S. in microbiology in 1932. He remained at Wisconsin and received his Ph.D. in biochemistry in 1934 for a dissertation on the nutritional requirements and cellular biochemistry of bacteria. For the next year he worked as a research assistant in biochemistry at Wisconsin, and in 1936 he was awarded a General Education Board Fellowship for a year of postgraduate study at the University of Utrecht in the Netherlands.

After returning to the United States in 1937, Tatum worked as a research associate in the Department of Biological Sciences at Stanford University in Palo Alto, California, where he became an assistant professor four years later. His early research at Stanford focused on the nutritional requirements and cellular biochemistry of microorganisms. He demonstrated that *Neurospora crassa,* the pink mold that grows most commonly on bread, requires biotin, a B-complex vitamin. He also described the nutritional requirements of the fruit fly, *Drosophila,* which is commonly used for genetics research, and identified the biochemical substance kynurenine, which is responsible for its eye color. In the early 1940s Tatum collaborated with the geneticist GEORGE W. BEADLE, a professor at Stanford, to determine the chemical processes involved in the genetic inheritance patterns of *Neurospora.*

The science of genetics had begun in 1866,

when Gregor Mendel, a Dominican monk living in Czechoslovakia, published his theory of the laws of inheritance, based on his studies of pea plants. Mendel postulated that "elements," now called genes, govern the inheritance of physical traits and are expressed in those traits. Mendel's studies demonstrated that some genes are dominant and others recessive. A dominant gene can be expressed when it is carried by only one of a pair of chromosomes; a recessive gene must be carried by both chromosomes in a pair in order to be expressed.

Mendel's laws of inheritance went unrecognized until the beginning of the twentieth century, when they were rediscovered by a new generation of geneticists. It was soon established that genes reside on the chromosomes, strands of genetic material in the nucleus of plant and animal cells. The genes, which are molecules of deoxyribonucleic acid (DNA), carry the genetic code that directs and controls the biochemical processes of the cell. During the first three decades of the twentieth century, geneticists focused on plant breeding (producing, for example, hybrid corn and hybrid wheat) and on the study of normal and abnormal chromosomal behavior.

In 1926 HERMANN J. MULLER showed that X rays produce mutations in the genetic material of the fruit fly and that the mutations result in physical abnormalities and deformities. Twenty-five years earlier Archibald Garrod, an English physician and biochemist, had discovered that certain enzyme deficiencies in his patients were inherited. Garrod's studies raised the question of whether specific genes direct the synthesis of specific enzymes, and it was this question that Tatum and Beadle took up when they began their research in 1941.

The two researchers chose *Neurospora* for their experiments because its rapid growth and prolific reproduction make it possible to study several generations in a short time. Moreover, it reproduces both asexually (by spores produced by a single individual) and sexually (by combination of two individuals). The genetics of *Neurospora* had been partly described by other investigators, and Tatum had already studied its nutritional requirements.

At the outset of their research Tatum and Beadle correctly assumed that, as Beadle said later, "one ought to be able to discover how genes function by making some of them defective." From Muller's work it was known that although genes mutate spontaneously, the mutation rate of genetic material can be increased approximately 100 times by exposing

it to X rays. Therefore, they grew colonies of *Neurospora* on a culture medium that contained only the nutrients essential to its growth and then irradiated the colonies with X rays. After irradiation, some of the colonies reproduced normally and some died; others began to grow but failed to thrive on the minimal culture medium.

It was on this third group of colonies that Tatum and Beadle focused their attention. They replanted its members onto 1,000 different culture media, each containing some added substance that normal *Neurospora* is able to synthesize. On the 199th medium, to which vitamin B_6 had been added, the irradiated organisms grew normally, suggesting that irradiation had produced a mutation in the gene responsible for the synthesis of vitamin B_6. To determine whether it was in fact a genetic defect, the two researchers mated the organisms deficient for vitamin B_6 with normal organisms and found that the defect was inherited as a Mendelian recessive gene, thus proving that specific genes control the synthesis of specific cellular substances.

In 1941 Tatum received an appointment as an assistant professor at Stanford. Penicillin (discovered in 1928 by ALEXANDER FLEMING) is synthesized by a fungus, and the laboratory methods that Tatum developed proved useful in increasing the pharmaceutical production of this antibiotic during World War II, when it was in great demand. During 1944 Tatum served as a civilian staff member of the United States Office of Scientific Research and Development.

At the end of the war he accepted an appointment as professor of botany at Yale University, where he became a professor of microbiology in 1946. At Yale he collaborated with JOSHUA LEDERBERG, a young medical student on leave from Columbia University. Through a series of experiments, Tatum and Lederberg demonstrated that bacterial cells, like fungi and higher organisms, reproduce by sexual means, a process they called genetic or sexual recombination. Genetic recombination of bacteria involves the temporary combining of two separate bacterial cells to form a third cell, called a daughter cell, which in turn acquires traits of each parent cell.

In 1948 Tatum returned to Stanford as professor of biology, rising to professor of biochemistry and head of the biochemistry department in 1956. In this capacity he was instrumental in planning the relocation of the Stanford Medical School from San Francisco to the campus at Palo Alto, California. The following year he became a professor at the Rockefeller Institute (now Rockefeller University) in New York City. He continued to study the genetics of fungi and bacteria, seeking, as he said, "a clear understanding, at the molecular level, of how genes determine the characteristics of living organisms."

Tatum shared half of the 1958 Nobel Prize for Physiology or Medicine with George Beadle "for their discovery that genes act by regulating definite chemical events." Tatum concluded his Nobel lecture by predicting that "with real understanding of the roles of heredity and environment, together with the consequent improvement in man's physical capacities and greater freedom from physical disease, will come an improvement in his approach to, and understanding of, sociological and economic problems." The other half of the Nobel Prize was awarded to Joshua Lederberg, who later paid tribute to Tatum for his decision to study the effects of X-ray-induced mutations, which provided "an effective new methodology" for studying how genes control the biochemical processes of the living cell. This method, Lederberg said, "is so deeply engrained in all experimental biology today . . . that an act of historical will is needed to remind us that it once had to be discovered."

At Rockefeller, Tatum devoted most of his efforts to the development and training of young researchers and to administrative duties. He was a founding member of the *Annual Review of Genetics* and joined the editorial board of the journal *Science* in 1957. He was married in 1934 to June Alton, with whom he had two daughters. They were divorced in 1956, and several months later Tatum married Viola Kantor, a dentist. After her death in 1974, he married Elsie Bergland in the same year. Tall and sturdy in build, Tatum enjoyed swimming and ice skating and was particularly fond of music and photography. He suffered poor health during his final years and died at his home in New York City at the age of sixty-five.

In addition to the Nobel Prize, Tatum received the Remsen Award of the American Chemical Society (1953). He was a member of several professional organizations, among them the American Society of Biological Chemists, the American Association for the Advancement of Science, the American Academy of Arts and Sciences, the Harvey Society, the Botanical Society of America, and the American Philosophical Society. He served on the advisory committees of the National Foundation, the American Committee of the National Research Council on Growth, and the American Cancer Society.

SELECTED WORKS: X-ray-Induced Growth Factor Requirements in Bacteria, 1944, with others.

ABOUT: Current Biography March 1959; The Excitement and Fascination of Science, volume 2, 1978; National Cyclopedia of American Biography, volume J, 1964; New York Times October 31, 1958; November 7, 1975; Time July 14, 1958.

TAUBE, HENRY
(November 30, 1915–   )
Nobel Prize for Chemistry, 1983

The Canadian-American chemist Henry Taube was born in Neudorf, Saskatchewan, Canada, to Albertina (Tiledetzki) and Samuel Taube. After attending local schools, he entered the University of Saskatchewan, where he received a B.S. in 1935 and an M.S. two years later. He then went to the University of California at Berkeley and was awarded a Ph.D. in chemistry in 1940. Remaining at Berkeley as an instructor, he taught undergraduate introductory chemistry for a year. Taube accepted a position as assistant professor at Cornell University in 1941, the same year that he became an American citizen. From 1946 to 1961 he taught at the University of Chicago, where he rose to full professor and served as chairman of the chemistry department from 1956 to 1959. Since 1962 he has been professor of chemistry at Stanford University and in 1978 was appointed chairman of the department.

It was while teaching his first advanced chemistry course at the University of Chicago that Taube became excited by the possibilities of research. Like many other chemists in the years preceding World War II, Taube was interested in the recently discovered radioactive isotopes called radioisotopes. Radioisotopes emit radioactive particles—alpha, beta, or gamma rays—which can be detected by scintillation counters. The use of radioisotopes simplified and extended the range of experimental investigation in the natural sciences. For example, carbon 14, a radioisotope of carbon 12, contains two extra neutrons in its nucleus and emits beta particles (electrons). If carbon 14 is incorporated into a carbon-containing molecule, it can be readily detected and quantified in experimental systems.

At Cornell and Chicago, Taube developed new experimental methods using radioiso-

HENRY TAUBE

topes to quantify and further describe the mechanisms of oxidation-reduction and substitution reactions. Substitution reactions involve the transfer of an atom from one molecule to another. In oxidation-reduction, or redox, reactions, electrons are transferred. Loss of electrons is called oxidation; electron gain is called reduction. By 1940 the qualitative aspects of oxidation-reduction reactions were well understood. The availability of artificially produced radioisotopes meant that rates of redox reactions could now be measured by isotopic tracer methods.

Taube was particularly interested in coordination compounds (first described by ALFRED WERNER), in which a central atom or ion is surrounded by a group of ions called ligands. Coordination chemistry specifically studies the bonding and reactions of metals. Metals differ from nonmetals in that one or more of their outer-shell electrons are only weakly attracted to the nucleus of the molecule and are readily removed, thus transforming the metal into a positively charged ion. In the 1940s Taube proved that metal ions in solution form chemical bonds with water molecules; that is, water molecules act as ligands, a proposition that had been suggested but never shown. Taube also described the relationships that exist between rates of redox reactions, rates of ligand-substitution reactions, and the electron configurations of metals and metal complexes.

Taube demonstrated that there was a strong correlation between the electron structure of certain transition metals (metals with properties intermediate between metals and non-

metals) and ligand-substitution rates. In a 1952 paper he also introduced the concepts of inner-sphere atom transfer and outer-sphere electron transfer. Both mechanisms are now known to be involved in energy-transfer processes in a wide variety of biological systems.

With his colleague Howard Myers, Taube in 1954 published a paper in the *Journal of the American Chemical Society* on the oxidation-reduction reactions of coordination compounds. In it, he described the mechanism of reduction by chromium of a metal ion complex containing cobalt in aqueous solution. He reported that electron transfer from chromium to cobalt is effected by an intermediate compound in which chloride forms a temporary bridge. Prior to Taube's work on the reduction of one metal ion by another, it was known only that electrons were transferred from chromium to cobalt and that chloride was transferred from cobalt to chromium. By introducing the concept of an intermediate bridge, Taube explained how this reaction proceeds.

In 1969 Taube and another co-worker, Carol Creutz, prepared and described a new species of positively charged ion. Called a mixed-valence cation, it consists of two atoms of ruthenium (a metallic element present in platinum ores), each bonded to five molecules of ammonia, with a pyrazine ring forming a bridge between the two ion complexes. This mixed-valence cation, now known as the Creutz-Taube ion, was used in the 1970s by Taube and his colleagues to study rates and mechanisms of intramolecular electron transfer in redox reactions. Their research on the relation between rates of substitution of oxygen atoms and electron structure in transition metals contributed to an understanding, in quantum mechanical terms, of cellular hydroxylation and cytochrome enzyme systems.

In 1976 Taube and his co-workers prepared a technetium complex that is now used as a tracer molecule in clinical nuclear medicine. They also studied the chemistry of osmium and other ruthenium complexes and prepared the first dinitrogen-bridged complex to elucidate further the structural details of chemical bonding between metals and their ligands.

Taube was awarded the 1983 Nobel Prize for Chemistry for "his studies of the mechanisms of electron transfer reactions, particularly of metal complexes." In his presentation speech, Ingvar Lindqvist of the Royal Swedish Academy of Sciences traced the development of chemical theory from SVANTE ARRHENIUS's work on electron-transfer reactions to Taube's contributions in this field. In his acceptance speech Taube pointed to the benefits that chemistry has conferred upon human life. "But the benefits of science are not to be reckoned only in terms of the physical," he went on. "Science as an intellectual exercise enriches our culture and is in itself ennobling. Each new insight into how the atoms in their interactions express themselves in structure and transformations, not only of inanimate matter, but particularly also of living matter, provides a thrill."

In 1952 Taube married Mary Alice Wesche, with whom he has two sons and two daughters. Among his leisure interests are record collecting and gardening.

In addition to the Nobel Prize, Taube has received the Charles Frederick Chandler Medal of Columbia University (1964), the Willard Gibbs Medal of the American Chemical Society (1971), the National Medal of Science of the National Science Foundation (1977), the Bailar Medal of the University of Illinois (1983), the Award in Chemical Sciences of the National Academy of Sciences (1983), and the Priestley Medal of the American Chemical Society (1984). He is a member of the National Academy of Sciences, the American Academy of Arts and Sciences, the American Philosophical Society, and the Royal Physiographical Society of Lund. He holds honorary degrees from the University of Saskatchewan, the Hebrew University of Jerusalem, and the University of Chicago.

SELECTED WORKS: Electron Transfer Reactions of Complex Ions in Solution, 1970.

ABOUT: Lippard, S. (ed.) Progress in Inorganic Chemistry: An Appreciation of Henry Taube, 1983; New York Times October 20, 1983; Science December 2, 1983.

TEMIN, HOWARD M.
(December 10, 1934–   )
Nobel Prize for Physiology or Medicine, 1975
(shared with David Baltimore and Renato Dulbecco)

The American virologist Howard Martin Temin was born in Philadelphia, the second of three sons of Henry Temin, a lawyer, and Annette (Lehman) Temin, who took an active role in community affairs. While attending high school in Philadelphia, Temin spent several summers at the Jackson Laboratory in Bar Harbor, Maine, under a program for gifted

HOWARD M. TEMIN

students. The experience deepened his interest in biological research and gave him practice in conducting laboratory experiments.

In 1951 Temin entered Swarthmore College, where he studied biology in an honors program. During the summer of 1953 he worked at the Institute for Cancer Research in Philadelphia. After receiving his B.S. in biology from Swarthmore in 1955, he returned to the Jackson Laboratory, where he met DAVID BALTIMORE, who was then a high school student. That fall Temin enrolled at the California Institute of Technology (Caltech) in Pasadena for graduate work in experimental embryology, but after a year and a half he switched to animal virology and worked in the laboratory of RENATO DULBECCO. While writing his doctoral dissertation on the Rous sarcoma virus (a filterable virus discovered by PEYTON ROUS in a sarcomalike growth found in Plymouth Rock hens), Temin, in collaboration with Harry Rubin, a postdoctoral fellow, developed a quantitative method for measuring the growth of the virus.

After receiving his Ph.D. in 1959, Temin remained at Caltech and for the next year continued to investigate the Rous sarcoma virus. The work led him to hypothesize that certain viruses alter the genetic information encoded in the cells they attack. The next year Temin was appointed assistant professor of oncology (the study of tumors) at the University of Wisconsin, where he worked in the McArdle Research Laboratory at the medical school.

Using the quantitative assay method he had devised while studying Rous sarcoma at Caltech, Temin began to examine the differences between normal cells and tumor cells and expanded his earlier hypothesis to include other ribonucleic acid (RNA) animal viruses. According to this formulation, called the provirus hypothesis, the protein coat of certain viruses contains an enzyme that catalyzes, or facilitates, the copying of viral genes into the deoxyribonucleic acid (DNA) of the host cell.

Support for the provirus hypothesis, however, depended on proof of the existence of the enzyme. Moreover, it was greeted with some hostility by many other scientists because it appeared to violate the belief, then widely held, that genetic information could be transmitted only from DNA to RNA to proteins, never in the opposite sequence. Realizing that genetic information could in theory be passed from RNA to DNA, Temin accumulated experimental evidence to support his provirus theory. In 1970 he and David Baltimore, who had joined the Massachusetts Institute of Technology, independently isolated the enzyme that copies viral RNA genes into cellular DNA. They called it RNA-directed DNA polymerase and published their findings in the British scientific journal *Nature* in June 1970. The enzyme is now known as reverse transcriptase because, contrary to earlier genetic theories, it transcribes genetic information from RNA to DNA. Viruses that possess reverse transcriptase and exist as a provirus in animal-cell DNA are called retroviruses, which are known to cause a variety of diseases, including acquired immune deficiency syndrome (AIDS), certain cancers, and hepatitis.

Temin has also investigated how genetic information in the provirus is able to transform a normal animal cell into a tumor cell. It has since been determined that a provirus gene may induce the synthesis of certain tumor-producing proteins in the cell if the provirus is activated. The abnormal proteins then interfere with transmission of the cellular growth restriction signals, thus permitting transformed cells to grow unchecked. A year after publishing his findings on viruses, Temin was named Wisconsin Alumni Research Foundation Professor at the University of Wisconsin.

Temin shared the 1975 Nobel Prize for Physiology or Medicine with Baltimore and Dulbecco "for their discoveries concerning the interaction between tumor viruses and the genetic material of the cell." Peter Reichard of the Karolinska Institute said in his presentation address, "This discovery not only marked a new chapter in cancer research, but also had . . . far-reaching biological consequences." For example, other researchers, Reichard said, have found that "many normal cells . . . contain copies of viral RNA, closely related to the RNA of tumor viruses."

In his Nobel lecture Temin called RNA tumor virus replication "not sufficient for cancer formation by RNA tumor viruses," although he indicated his belief "that viruses provide models of the processes involved in the etiology of human cancer." Instead, he attributed human cancers primarily to "other types of carcinogens, for example, the chemicals in cigarette smoke," which "probably act to mutate a special target in the cell DNA to genes for cancer."

Since receiving the Nobel Prize, Temin has continued to work at the McArdle Laboratory for Cancer Research at the University of Wisconsin, where, in 1980, he was appointed Harold Rusch Professor of Cancer Research and, in 1982, Steenbock Professor of the Biological Sciences. He has served on the editorial boards of the *Journal of Virology*, the *Journal of Cellular Physiology*, and the *Proceedings of the National Academy of Sciences* (United States). He is the author and co-author of more than 170 articles and a contributor to several books.

In 1962 Temin married Rayla Greenberg, a population geneticist; the Temins have two daughters.

Among Temin's awards are the United States Steel Foundation Award in Molecular Biology of the National Academy of Sciences (1972), the Award in Enzyme Chemistry of the American Chemical Society (1973), the G. H. A. Clowes Award and Lectureship of the American Association for Cancer Research (1974), the Gairdner Foundation International Award (1974), the Albert Lasker Basic Medical Research Award (1974), and the Lila Gruber Research Award of the American Academy of Dermatology (1981). In addition to membership in the American Academy of Arts and Sciences, Temin is a member of the American Philosophical Society, the American Society of Microbiology, the American Association of Cancer Research, and the American Society of Virology. He holds honorary degrees from Swarthmore College and New York Medical College.

SELECTED WORKS: "RNA-Directed DNA Synthesis," Scientific American January 1972; The Biology of RNA-Tumor Viruses, 1974.

ABOUT: New Scientist October 23, 1975; New York Times October 17, 1975; Science November 14, 1975.

TERESA, MOTHER
(August 26, 1910–)
Nobel Prize for Peace, 1979

Mother Teresa, Albanian nun and missionary, was born Agnes Gonxha Bojaxhiu in Skopje in the Ottoman Empire (now in Yugoslavia). She was the youngest of three children of Nikola Bojaxhiu, a prosperous Albanian building contractor and food importer who was involved in the Albanian nationalist movement and who died under mysterious circumstances the year Agnes was born. Her mother, the former Dranafile Bernai, was a devout Catholic who often took her young daughter with her on visits to the sick and needy in Skopje.

Agnes attended a government school and sang in the choir of Sacred Heart Church. She was greatly influenced in her choice of vocation by her membership in the Sodality of the Blessed Virgin Mary, an organization that promoted service to the poor, especially in foreign countries. Listening to the priest at Sacred Heart Church read letters from missionaries in India, she became deeply interested in the Bengal mission. After prayerful consideration, she decided in 1922 "to go out and give the life of Christ to the people," as she later told the British writer Malcolm Muggeridge in an interview. After graduating from high school in Skopje, she joined the Sisters of Loreto, an Irish order with a mission in India, spent a year studying English at the Loreto Abbey in Dublin, and embarked for Calcutta on January 6, 1929.

Completing her novitiate, Agnes taught geography and history at the Loreto order's St. Mary's High School until 1948, also learning Bengali and Hindi during this time. In 1931 she took her first vows of poverty, chastity, and obedience. She selected Teresa as her religious name after Térèsa de Lisieux, a nineteenth-century French nun who advocated "the little way"—accomplishing good through the joyful performance of the most menial tasks. Six years later, as Mother Teresa, she took her final vows.

Although the Loreto convent offered a cloistered existence, it lay within sight of one of the worst slums in Calcutta. While traveling by train to a retreat in Darjeeling in 1946, Mother Teresa received "a call within a call. The message was clear," she later explained. "I was to leave the convent and help the poor, while living among them." Two years later, she obtained permission from the archbishop of Calcutta to work outside the convent. She

MOTHER TERESA

adopted a new habit, the white sari of India's poor, trimmed in blue and with a crucifix pinned at the shoulder. At the same time, she became an Indian citizen.

After an intensive three-month course in nursing with the American Medical Missionary Sisters at Patna, Mother Teresa founded a school in the slums of Moti Jhil. In 1950 she won Vatican approval for a new congregation, the Missionaries of Charity. Her earliest postulants were former students from the Loreto school. To the three traditional convent vows, she added a fourth—"to give wholehearted, free service to the very poorest."

Appalled by the squalor of Calcutta's teeming slums, Mother Teresa soon extended her efforts to the dying, diseased, and orphaned. For those abandoned and left to die on the streets, she established a Home for the Dying in 1954. By this time, her small group of volunteers numbered twenty-six. Only the most dedicated could meet the rigorous demands that the order imposed: devotions at four o'clock in the morning, no possessions except a single change of clothing, the same diet as that fed to the poor, and sixteen-hour days working among the poor.

Setting high standards for the order, Mother Teresa rescued skeletal bodies infested with maggots, infants tossed onto streetcar tracks, and lepers covered with sores. As word of her accomplishments spread and financial support increased, she was able to found an orphanage for abandoned children, a leper colony, a home for the elderly, and a workshop for the unemployed. Through clinics at railroad stations, her order offered inoculations, dispensed medicine, and provided shelter to women and children. After working for ten years within the Calcutta archdiocese, Mother Teresa received permission to organize missions elsewhere. She has since opened centers in Venezuela (1965), Ceylon (1967), Rome and Tanzania (1968), and Cuba (1986), as well as other locations.

Although she has called her work "a drop in the ocean," Mother Teresa's devotion to the poor has been widely recognized. In 1969 she received the Jawaharlal Nehru Award for International Understanding given by the government of India and two years later was awarded the Vatican's Pope John XXIII Peace Prize. She also received the 1979 Nobel Prize for Peace. The award drew criticism from some who believed that while Mother Teresa had helped needy individuals, she had not contributed to the cause of international peace, for which the prize was meant. However, in his presentation speech, John Sanness of the Norwegian Nobel Committee pointed out that "Mother Teresa has personally succeeded in bridging the gulf that exists between the rich nations and the poor nations. . . . With her message she is able to reach through to something innate in every human kind—if for no other purpose than to create a potential, a seed for good. If this were not the case, the world would be deprived of hope, and work for peace would have little meaning." Sannes concluded his address by quoting Robert MacNamara, president of the World Bank, " 'Mother Teresa deserves Nobel's Peace Prize because she promotes peace in the most fundamental manner, by her confirmation of the inviolability of human dignity.' "

Mother Teresa accepted the award "in the name of the hungry, of the naked, of the homeless, . . . of those who feel unwanted, uncared for." In her Nobel lecture, she spoke of Christian love as the moving force behind her work and emphasized that love and respect for each human life is a prerequisite for world peace. She set aside her prize money to build more homes for the destitute and the poor, especially lepers.

Since receiving the Nobel Prize, Mother Teresa has accepted numerous speaking engagements throughout the world. In 1982 she traveled to Lebanon at the request of Pope John Paul II to serve as an emissary of peace, although she has abstained from overtly political activities. In 1985 she spoke before the General Assembly of the United Nations on the occasion of the organization's fortieth an-

niversary. While in New York City, on Christmas Eve, 1985, she joined John Cardinal Cooke, archbishop of New York, in opening the first church-sponsored hospice for patients with AIDS (acquired immune deficiency syndrome). At her request, three terminally ill inmates were released from the state prison at Ossining to enter the new hospice.

Among Mother Teresa's critics are those who cannot accept her firm opposition to abortion and to all artificial methods of birth control. Her position on this was directly stated in her Nobel lecture: "I feel the greatest destroyer of peace today is abortion, because it is a direct war, a direct killing—direct murder by the mother herself." She has also alienated feminists, especially in India, by urging women to build stable families and to allow "men to do what they are better suited to do." For Mother Teresa, contemporary social stands as such and the mobilization of mass opinion are ultimately irrelevant. Those who have met her have been impressed by her serene spirituality and the sense of love, joy, and reverence for human life that she conveys. "We can do no great things," she has written, "only small things with great love."

WORKS IN ENGLISH TRANSLATION: A Gift for God, 1975; Life in the Spirit: Reflections, Meditations, Prayers, 1983; Mother Teresa, Contemplative in the Heart of the World, 1985; My Life for the Poor, 1985; Jesus, The Word to Be Spoken: Prayers and Meditations for Every Day of the Year, 1986.

ABOUT: America March 22, 1980; D'Cunha, S. Mother of the Motherless, 1975; Doig, D. Mother Teresa: Her People and Her Work, 1975; Egan, E. Such a Vision of the Street, 1985; Leigh, V. Mother Teresa, 1986; Le Joly, E. Mother Teresa of Calcutta: A Biography, 1983; McGovern, J. To Give the Love of Christ, 1978; Muggeridge, M. Something Beautiful for God, 1971; New York Times Magazine December 9, 1979; Srinivasa Murthy, B. Mother Teresa and India, 1983.

THEILER, MAX

(January 30, 1899–August 11, 1972)
Nobel Prize for Physiology or Medicine, 1951

The South African bacteriologist Max Theiler (tīl' ər) was born in Pretoria, the youngest child and one of two sons of Emma (Jegge) and Arnold Theiler, both of whom were Swiss. His father, a prominent veterinarian, was director of the South African government veterinary service. Encouraged by his father to pursue a

MAX THEILER

medical career, Theiler enrolled in a two-year premedical program at the University of Cape Town in 1916. He then went to London, where he studied at St. Thomas's Hospital Medical School and the London School of Hygiene and Tropical Medicine, both of which were branches of the University of London.

After receiving his medical degree in 1922, Theiler accepted a position as an assistant in the Department of Tropical Medicine at the Harvard Medical School. His early work at Harvard concerned amebic dysentery and the controlled use of rat-bite fever as a medical treatment, an approach similar to JULIUS WAGNER VON JAUREGG's use of malarial fever as a cure for syphilis. Soon, however, his interest turned to yellow fever.

Yellow fever is a tropical disease that occurs in the warm areas of Africa and the Americas. Its associated mortality often exceeds 10 percent and even today the disease remains incurable. During the American Panama Canal project, members of the Yellow Fever Commission, which included Walter Reed and William Gorgas, had established that yellow fever is spread by a species of mosquito. Acting on Reed's discoveries, in 1916 the Rockefeller Foundation initiated a program to eradicate yellow fever. The effort seemed particularly urgent because medical experts believed that ships passing through the canal would spread yellow fever from the Caribbean to Asia. The disaster did not occur because immunity to dengue fever produces cross-immunity to yellow fever, but at the time that fact was un-

known, and the Rockefeller program seemed highly advisable.

Based on the findings of the Yellow Fever Commission, scientists concluded that yellow fever affected only humans and could be eradicated either by wiping out the mosquito population or by developing a vaccine. Since the latter course seemed more feasible, basic research into the disease and its causative organism became major goals.

In 1919 the Japanese researcher Hideo Noguchi reported that he had isolated a bacterium responsible for yellow fever. By the mid-1920s other scientists were able to infect laboratory animals with the disease—a significant advance—and in 1926 Theiler and a colleague, Andrew Sellards, found conclusive evidence that yellow fever was caused not by a bacterium but by a filterable virus. The following year, Rockefeller scientists working in West Africa succeeded in infecting a rhesus monkey with blood from a yellow fever patient. Continuing his work at Harvard, Theiler was able to infect mice by injecting the virus into their brains, rather than subcutaneously as other researchers had done. It was an important breakthrough, because the use of mice, which are less expensive and easier to work with than monkeys, accelerated the pace of yellow fever research.

In 1930 Theiler left Harvard to join the International Health Division of the Rockefeller Foundation in New York City. Within a year he perfected the mouse protection test, in which a mixture of yellow fever virus and human serum was injected into a mouse. The survival of the mouse indicated that the serum had neutralized the virus and thus that the serum donor was immune. This test made possible the first accurate survey of the worldwide distribution of yellow fever.

One of the constant hazards of medical research into communicable diseases is that the researcher may become infected. Indeed, between 1928 and 1930 five scientists—including Noguchi—contracted yellow fever and died. Theiler himself caught the disease in 1929 but survived and was subsequently immune to it.

Using a combination of virus and immune serums, Wilbur Sawyer, the director of Theiler's laboratory at Rockefeller, produced the first yellow fever vaccine. Those injected with the mixture did not contract yellow fever and developed an immunity to it. Although too expensive for wide-scale use, it was used to immunize yellow fever researchers.

The yellow fever virus strains that Theiler cultivated in mice eventually became the basis of two vaccines. The first, a weakened mouse strain, was used in 1934 by the French government to protect the residents of French territories in West Africa, where the vaccine proved extremely effective and easy to administer, although not entirely safe (it sometimes caused encephalitis, an inflammation of the brain). Therefore, Theiler and his colleagues developed a second strain. Called 17D, it was produced from the Asibi strain of the virus, which was grown in chicken embryos from which most of the nervous tissue had been removed. Unlike the earlier strain, the new vaccine caused only mild reactions, if any; easier to mass-produce, it came into wide use after 1937. Over the years, these two vaccines have been effective in controlling yellow fever, despite the later discovery that the disease is not confined to humans. In Africa, in particular, it affects monkeys and is periodically reintroduced into the human population through mosquito bites.

"For his discoveries concerning yellow fever and how to combat it," Theiler was awarded the 1951 Nobel Prize for Physiology or Medicine. On presenting the award, Hans Bergstrand of the Karolinska Institute remarked that Theiler's "discovery gives new hope that . . . we shall succeed in mastering other virus diseases, many of which have a devastating effect and against which we are still entirely powerless."

In addition to yellow fever, Theiler investigated a variety of viral diseases. He was especially interested in polio and discovered an apparently identical infection in mice, known as encephalomyelitis or Theiler's disease. In 1964 he became a professor of epidemiology and microbiology at Yale University. He retired in 1967.

In 1928 Theiler married Lillian Graham, with whom he had a daughter. His interests outside of research included reading (especially history and philosophy) and watching baseball games. Although he remained in the United States, Theiler retained his South African citizenship. He died on August 11, 1972.

In addition to the Nobel Prize, Theiler received the Chalmer's Medal of the Royal Society of Tropical Medicine and Hygiene (1939), the Flattery Medal of Harvard University (1945), and the Lasker Award of the American Public Health Association (1949).

SELECTED WORKS: Viral and Rickettsial Infections of Man, 1948, with others; The Arthropod-Borne Viruses of Vertebrates, 1973, with W. G. Downs.

ABOUT: Current Biography January 1952; New York Times October 19, 1951; August 12, 1972; Robinson, D. The Miracle Finders, 1976; Strode, G. K. (ed.) Yellow Fever, 1951; Williams, G. Virus Hunters, 1959.

THEORELL, HUGO
(July 6, 1903–August 15, 1982)
Nobel Prize for Physiology or Medicine, 1955

The Swedish biochemist Axel Hugo Theodor Theorell was born in Linköping, the second of three children, to Thure Theorell, a military surgeon, and Armida (Bill) Theorell. His mother, an accomplished pianist who often accompanied her husband, a talented singer, gave the boy a lasting love of music.

At the age of three Hugo contracted poliomyelitis. Although the disease paralyzed his left leg, a muscle transplant six years later enabled him to walk. During his convalescence he learned to play the violin, and after entering the State Secondary School in Linköping, he became conductor of the student orchestra. He also served as chairman of the school's scientific society. In the summer of 1920 Theorell, who planned to become a civil engineer, was apprenticed to an engineer in the Swedish Railways. After graduating from secondary school the following year, however, he decided to follow in his father's footsteps and take up medicine.

In 1921 Theorell entered the Karolinska Institute in Stockholm; he completed his requirements in three years and received a bachelor of medicine degree in 1924. After a summer at the Pasteur Institute in Paris, where he studied bacteriology, Theorell returned to Stockholm and was appointed an assistant in the Medical Chemistry Institute at Karolinska. One of his first projects there was to investigate the effects of lipids (fats) on a newly devised clinical test, the erythrocyte (red blood cell) sedimentation rate, or ESR. His work showed that lipids tend to reduce the ESR. At the same time, Theorell developed a skill with electrophoresis—a laboratory technique used to separate the plasma proteins albumin and globulin—which he would later use to isolate and purify enzymes and coenzymes (the heat-stable, water-soluble portions of enzymes). After being promoted to associate professor in 1928, Theorell completed his dissertation on plasma lipids (fatty acids) and was awarded a Ph.D. in medicine in 1930.

The following year he married Elin Margit

HUGO THEORELL

Elisabeth Alenius, a pianist and harpsichordist who had studied music with one of Theorell's sisters in Stockholm. The couple eventually had one daughter and three sons. During their honeymoon, Theorell and his wife toured Brittany by bicycle and then went to Paris, where they met the harpsichordist Wanda Landowska. While his wife remained in Paris to study with Landowska for two months, Theorell returned to Sweden and to the Karolinska Institute, where he worked as a physician and lectured on physiological chemistry.

Meanwhile, he continued his research into the physicochemical properties of myoglobin. Myoglobin, a hemoprotein (part iron, part protein) found in muscle cells, was first discovered by investigators at the Karolinska Institute in 1897. Like hemoglobin, the oxygen-carrying molecule in red blood cells, myoglobin has a strong affinity for oxygen.

At the time, it was not clear whether myoglobin and hemoglobin were identical molecules, and Theorell set out to develop an experimental strategy for solving this problem. First, he purified the protein portion of myoglobin by ultracentrifugation (high-speed spinning in a centrifuge) and electrophoresis (the movement of colloidal particles under the influence of an electrical field). He then determined its physical and chemical properties, including sedimentation rate, diffusion rate, affinity for oxygen, and the effects of pH on its oxygen affinity. Finally, he compared the properties of the two molecules and thereby demonstrated that myoglobin and hemoglobin were not identical. However, he incorrectly

concluded that the molecular mass of myoglobin was one-half that of hemoglobin. (It was later shown that the molecular mass of myoglobin is one-quarter that of hemoglobin.) The smaller molecular weight explains why myoglobin is excreted by the kidneys in myoglobinuria, a condition in which myoglobin is found in urine.

In 1932 Theorell was appointed associate professor of medical and physical chemistry at the University of Uppsala, and for the next two years he was a Rockefeller Foundation Fellow at the Institute for Cell Physiology at the Kaiser Wilhelm Institute (now the Max Planck Institute) in Berlin. There, in the laboratory of OTTO WARBURG, he performed experiments aimed at isolating and identifying the enzymes that catalyze cellular respiration or cellular oxidation reactions. By the time Theorell began his research on oxidative enzymes, a biochemical model of biological oxidation and bioenergetics was emerging. In the nineteenth century, the French physiologist Claude Bernard had discovered glycogen in the liver cells of experimental animals, and Louis Pasteur and other researchers had described the metabolic fate of glycogen and glucose in living cells.

Glycogen, a complex carbohydrate, is the form in which glucose, the principal source of cellular energy, is stored in cells. Glycogen and its degradation product, glucose, are metabolized by one of two possible biochemical pathways: aerobic glycolysis, which consumes oxygen, or anaerobic glycolysis, which proceeds in the absence of oxygen. In the latter, glucose is converted to lactic acid, or lactate. The aerobic pathway of glucose metabolism yields considerably more usable cellular energy than does the anaerobic pathway.

ALBERT SZENT-GYÖRGYI had discovered that the oxidation of carbohydrate to carbon dioxide and water is catalyzed by certain carboxylase enzymes, and that the oxidative process involves both the addition of oxygen and the removal of hydrogen and electrons (reduction). By the mid-1930s it was becoming clear that the conversion of pyruvate (a salt or ester of pyruvic acid) to carbon dioxide and water was a cyclic process that generated the energy-rich molecules of adenosine triphosphate (ATP), the principal source of energy for the various biochemical processes of the cell. Theorell was interested in cytochrome c, an enzyme that catalyzes oxidative reactions on the surface of mitochondria, the "power plants" of the cell.

Returning to Stockholm in 1935, Theorell

resumed his research on cytochrome *c*. That year he separated crystalline cytochrome *c* into its two components, a coenzyme (catalyst) and an apoenzyme (pure protein), which work together to produce oxidative reactions. When the Medical Nobel Institute was founded in 1937, Theorell was appointed professor and chairman of the biochemistry department. With another member of the institute, he toured research facilities and laboratories of Europe, with a view to developing a superior research facility within the walls of the yet-unconstructed institute. The outbreak of World War II, however, delayed further work on the project. Although Sweden's neutrality enabled Theorell to continue his research, collaboration with foreign scientists was limited.

In 1939 Theorell spent three months in the United States studying protein biochemistry with LINUS C. PAULING at the California Institute of Technology in Pasadena. When he returned to Stockholm, he again focused his attention on hemoprotein biochemistry, specifically the three-dimensional spatial relationships between the heme (the nonprotein, insoluble, iron protoporphyrin constituent of hemoglobin) and the protein components of cytochrome *c* and the submolecular mechanisms of biologic oxidation-reduction reactions. During the war he also investigated another set of hemoprotein enzymes, those of the peroxidase-catalase system. Peroxidases, which are oxidative enzymes, occur in liver cells and throughout the plant kingdom.

After the war Theorell purified and crystallized myoglobin from the urine and heart muscle of two brothers who had died of paralytic myoglobinuria, a disease characterized by paralysis and excessive myoglobin in the urine. During these years of research he and his colleagues, relying on new techniques of biophysics, developed experimental methods for studying hemoproteins that required relatively small quantities of biologic materials and were a considerable improvement over earlier methods.

The Medical Nobel Institute was opened in Stockholm in 1947, an event made possible in part with support from the Rockefeller Foundation and the United States National Institutes of Health. Because he had little interest in teaching, Theorell organized the work in his laboratories to accommodate his own research interests. Nevertheless, he trained a number of outstanding investigators, including SUNE BERGSTRÖM.

In the late 1940s, in collaboration with Britton Chance of the University of Pennsylvania, Theorell turned his attention to a different set of oxidative enzymes, the alcohol dehydrogenases, of which there are multiple forms. Alcohol dehydrogenase is the enzyme that catalyzes the oxidation of alcohol (ethanol) to aldehyde (acetaldehyde) in liver cells. Because Theorell and Chance clarified the steps in this process, the kinetics of this series of reactions is called the Theorell-Chance mechanism.

The 1955 Nobel Prize for Physiology or Medicine was awarded to Theorell "for his discoveries concerning the nature and mode of action of oxidation enzymes." In his Nobel acceptance speech, Theorell described the final goal of enzyme research as "the filling of the yawning gulf between biochemistry and morphology."

During the 1960s and early 1970s Theorell served as administrator of the Wenner-Gren Society and the Wenner-Gren Center Foundation, which maintains residential and conference facilities in Stockholm designed to accommodate visiting researchers. Upon Theorell's retirement from the Karolinska Institute in 1970, the Wenner-Gren Symposium on Oxidation-Reduction Enzymes was held at the center in his honor.

Known to his colleagues as a kind, friendly man with a quick sense of humor, Theorell served as chairman of the Stockholm Philharmonic Society for many years. After he suffered a stroke in 1974, Theorell's health began to deteriorate, and two years later he relinquished his responsibilities at the Wenner-Gren Center. While visiting the island of Ljusterö off the coast of Sweden during the summer of 1982, he died at the age of seventy-nine.

Theorell's awards included the Paul Karrer Medal in Chemistry of the University of Zurich, the Scheele Medal of the Professional Association of German Pharmacists, the Ciba Medal of the Biochemical Society in London, and the Karolinska Institute 150th Jubilee Medal. He was a member of the Swedish Chemical Association, the Swedish Society of Physicians and Surgeons, the Royal Swedish Academy of Sciences, the International Union of Biochemistry, the Royal Danish, Norwegian, and American Academies of Arts and Sciences, the American Philosophical Society, and the Royal Society of London. He held honorary degrees from the universities of Paris, Pennsylvania, Kentucky, Michigan, and Brussels.

ABOUT: Biographical Memoirs of Fellows of the Royal

Society, volume 29, 1983; Current Biography February 1956; New York Times October 23, 1955.

THO, LE DUC
See LE DUC THO

THOMSON, G. P.
(May 3, 1892–September 10, 1975)
Nobel Prize for Physics, 1937
(shared with Clinton J. Davisson)

G. P. THOMSON

The English physicist George Paget Thomson was born in Cambridge, the only son and elder of two children of J. J. THOMSON, Cavendish Professor of Experimental Physics at Cambridge University and director of the Cavendish Laboratory, and Rose Elisabeth (Paget) Thomson, daughter of George Paget, who was Regius Professor of Medicine at Cambridge. Before their marriage, Rose Paget had been one of J. J. Thomson's students at the Cavendish Laboratory.

G. P., as he was known to his friends and colleagues, received his early education at the Perse School in Cambridge, where he compiled an outstanding academic record. Entering Trinity College, Cambridge, in 1910, he became a major scholar the following year and in 1914 earned first-class honors in the mathematical and natural sciences. Upon graduating with a bachelor's degree that year, he became a fellow and a mathematical lecturer at Corpus Christi College, Cambridge, positions he held until 1922, with an interruption during World War I.

During the war, he served in France from 1914 to 1915 as a second lieutenant and then returned to England to work for four years on problems of aircraft stability and performance. During this time he learned to fly and wrote his first textbook, *Applied Aerodynamics,* which was published in 1919. Later that year, when he returned to Cambridge, Thomson resumed research on the behavior of electrical discharges in gases, work he had begun as a student under his father's direction. In the process, he discovered, simultaneously with FRANCIS W. ASTON, that the element lithium occurs as two isotopes with masses of 6 and 7.

In 1922 Thomson became professor of natural philosophy (physics) at the University of Aberdeen, Scotland, a position he held until 1930 when he was appointed professor of physics at Imperial College in London. In 1952 he returned to Cambridge as master of Corpus Christi College, where he remained until his retirement in 1962.

It was at Aberdeen that Thomson made his most noteworthy contributions to theoretical physics. Between 1919 and 1927, the American physicist CLINTON J. DAVISSON (in collaboration with C. H. Kunsman and Lester H. Germer) studied the interaction of electrons with metal surfaces. Using electron beams and single-crystal metal targets, this team at Bell Telephone Laboratories demonstrated the diffraction of electrons by crystals, a phenomenon predicted by LOUIS DE BROGLIE's hypothesis that electrons are wavelike in nature, the wavelength of each electron being inversely proportional to its velocity. The conclusive piece of evidence in their work, an interference phenomenon resulting from electron diffraction by a single crystal of nickel, was found in January 1927.

Thomson had learned of Davisson's studies in September 1926, while the two scientists were attending a conference at Oxford. Returning to Aberdeen, Thomson began to investigate the interaction of electrons with thin, solid films in a vacuum rather than with the more complex gaseous milieu. He asked one of his students, Alexander Reid, to use a very thin film of celluloid as a target. Many of the energetic electrons that passed through the film were deflected to form diffuse rings on a photographic plate behind the target. As electron energies were increased, the deflection angles decreased, a result that suggested a wavelike behavior of electrons. Because the structure

1053

of celluloid was then unknown, Thomson and Reid changed to metal targets (aluminum, gold, platinum) with a known crystal lattice. In each instance, the deflected electrons formed well-defined rings of a size that was in excellent agreement with predictions from Broglie's formula. Thomson's measurements provided conclusive experimental evidence of the wave-like nature of energetic electrons, complementing Davisson's results obtained with low-energy electrons.

Thomson and Davisson shared the 1937 Nobel Prize for Physics "for their experimental discovery of the diffraction of electrons by crystals." In his presentation speech, Hans Pleijel of the Royal Swedish Academy of Sciences said, "By the aid of electronic beams it has . . . been possible to explain how the structure of the surfaces of metals is changed by various mechanical, thermal, or chemical treatment. It has also been possible to ascertain the properties of thin layers of gases and powder." Illness prevented Thomson from attending the award ceremony, but he traveled to Stockholm the following year to deliver his Nobel lecture.

After 1937 Thomson served at various times as scientific adviser to the British Air Ministry. Under his leadership, the Maud Committee advised the British government in 1941 that it was feasible to produce an atomic bomb, a recommendation that contributed to Great Britain's decision to participate in the Manhattan Project. After World War II, Thomson became deeply involved in efforts to achieve controlled nuclear fusion. He favored maximum international cooperation to develop atomic energy for peaceful purposes. His last contribution to physics was a 1951 study of the cascade production of cosmic-ray stars.

In 1924 Thomson married Kathleen Buchanan, daughter of the principal of the University of Aberdeen. They had two sons and two daughters, all of whom Thomson raised after his wife's death in 1941. From boyhood, Thomson was devoted to sailing and to making miniature ship models. His colleague Michael McCrum once recalled that "[Thomson's] ability to correlate diverse facts, his well-stored practical memory, his wide-ranging, inquisitive mind combined with an insatiable zest for argument to make his table talk fascinating."

Thomson was knighted in 1943. His many awards included the Hughes Medal (1939) and the Royal Medal (1949) of the Royal Society, the Franklin Medal of the Franklin Institute, and the Faraday Medal of the Institution of Electrical Engineers (1960). He was a foreign member of the American Academy of Arts and Sciences and of the Lisbon Academy of Sciences, as well as a corresponding member of the Austrian Academy of Sciences.

SELECTED WORKS: The Atom, 1930; The Wave Mechanics of Free Electrons, 1930; Theory and Practice of Electron Diffraction, 1939, with William Cochrane; The Foreseeable Future, 1955; The Inspiration of Science, 1961; Nuclear Energy in Britain During the Last War, 1962; J. J. Thomson and the Cavendish Laboratory in His Day, 1964; The Electron, 1972.

ABOUT: Biographical Memoirs of Fellows of the Royal Society, volume 23, 1977; Current Biography March 1947; New York Times September 11, 1975.

THOMSON, J. J.
(December 18, 1856–August 30, 1940)
Nobel Prize for Physics, 1906

The English physicist Joseph John Thomson was born in Cheetham Hill, a suburb of Manchester, the son of Joseph James and Emma (Swindells) Thomson. Because his father, a bookseller, wanted the boy to become an engineer, he was sent at the age of fourteen to Owens College (now Manchester University) for preparatory scientific training. Within two years, however, his father died, leaving his son without the means to pay the large apprenticeship fee then required by engineering firms. He nonetheless continued his education with assistance from his mother and a scholarship fund.

Owens College was important for Thomson's career because it had an excellent science faculty and, unlike most colleges of the time, offered experimental physics courses. After earning his engineering degree from Owens in 1876, he entered Trinity College of Cambridge University with a mathematics scholarship. There he studied mathematics and its application to problems of theoretical physics. He received his bachelor's degree in mathematics in 1880. The following year he was elected a fellow of Trinity College and began working in the Cavendish Laboratory at Cambridge.

In 1884 J. W. STRUTT, successor to James Clerk Maxwell as Cavendish Professor of Experimental Physics and director of the Cavendish Laboratory, resigned his position. Thomson applied for the position, even though he was only twenty-seven years old and had not yet achieved any notable success in experimental physics. However, he was highly regarded as a mathematical physicist because

J. J. THOMSON

he had built impressively upon Maxwell's theoretical analyses of electromagnetism, which was sufficient to recommend him for the post.

Upon assuming his new responsibilities at the laboratory, Thomson decided that the main focus of his research would be the conduction of electricity through gases. He was particularly interested in the effects produced when an electric discharge passes between electrodes placed at opposite ends of a glass tube from which most of the air has been evacuated. A number of investigators, among them the English physicist William Crookes, had noted a curious phenomenon in such gas discharge tubes. When the pressure of the gas is sufficiently reduced, the glass walls of the tube opposite the cathode (the negative electrode) begin to glow with a greenish fluorescence, seemingly in response to a beam of radiation emanating from the cathode.

Cathode rays were of great interest to scientists, and their nature was a subject of considerable controversy. British physicists, for the most part, thought them to be charged particles. Many German physicists, on the other hand, considered them to be disturbances—perhaps vibrations or currents—in the ether, a hypothetical, weightless medium through which radiation was believed to propagate. In this view, cathode rays might be a type of high-frequency electromagnetic wave, similar to ultraviolet light. The Germans pointed to experiments by Heinrich Hertz, who had supposedly found that although cathode rays could be deflected by the influence of a magnetic field, they were not deflected by passage through a strong electric field. This observation suggested that cathode rays were not charged particles, since the paths of charged particles are invariably affected by an electric field; even so, the German experimental evidence remained inconclusive.

Research on cathode rays and related phenomena was galvanized by WILHELM RÖNTGEN's discovery of X rays in 1895. For one thing, this previously unsuspected form of radiation was also produced in gas discharge tubes (though from the anode rather than the cathode). Soon Thomson, working with ERNEST RUTHERFORD, found that passing X rays through gases greatly increased their ability to conduct electricity. The X rays ionized the gases—that is, they converted gas atoms into ions, which bear an electrical charge and so are efficient carriers of current. The resulting conduction, Thomson showed, resembled in some ways the conduction by ions during electrolysis of a solution.

Thomson and his students carried out much fruitful research on conduction in gases. Encouraged by these successes, he next turned to the unresolved question that had intrigued him for many years: the composition of cathode rays. Like his British colleagues, Thomson was convinced of the particulate nature of the cathode rays; he believed they might be fast-moving ions or other electrified particles ejected from the cathode. Repeating Hertz's experiments, he demonstrated that cathode rays were in fact deflected by electric fields. (Hertz's negative finding had resulted from the presence of too much residual gas in his evacuated discharge tubes.) Thomson later remarked that "the deflection of the cathode rays by electric forces became quite marked, and its direction indicated that the particles forming the cathode rays were negatively electrified. The result removed the discrepancy between the effects of magnetic and electric forces on the cathode particles; it did much more than this," Thomson added; "it provided a method of measuring v, the velocity of these particles, and also e/m, where m is the mass of the particle and e is its electric charge."

The method Thomson devised was quite straightforward. He deflected a beam of cathode rays by means of an electric field and then used a magnetic field to produce an equal but opposite deflection, so that the beam was again undeviated. With this experimental arrangement it was possible to derive simple equations from which, given the measured strengths of the two fields, both v and e/m could be easily calculated.

The resulting value of e/m for the cathode-ray "corpuscles" (as Thomson called them) proved to be 1,000 times larger than the corresponding value for the hydrogen ion. (It is known today that the correct ratio is closer to 1,800 to 1.) Hydrogen has the largest charge-to-mass ratio of any element. If, as Thomson suspected, the corpuscles carried the same charge as a hydrogen ion (the "unit" electrical charge), then he had discovered a new entity 1,000 times lighter than the simplest atom. This speculation was confirmed when Thomson, using an apparatus designed by C. T. R. WILSON, succeeded in measuring the value of e and showed that it was indeed equal to that of the hydrogen ion. He further found that the charge-to-mass ratio of the cathode-ray corpuscles was the same regardless of what gas was present in his discharge tube or what material its electrodes were made of. Moreover, particles with the same value of e/m could be released from carbon by heating and from metals by the action of ultraviolet light. He concluded that "the atom is not the ultimate limit to the subdivision of matter; we may go further and get to the corpuscle, and at this stage the corpuscle is the same from whatever source it may be derived. . . . [It appears] to form a part of all kinds of matter under the most diverse conditions; it seems natural, therefore, to regard it as one of the bricks of which atoms are built up."

Thomson went on to devise a model of the atom that incorporated his discovery. Early in the twentieth century, he proposed that the atom is a diffuse sphere of positive electrical charge in which negatively charged electrons (as his corpuscles came to be called) are distributed. This model, though soon superseded by Rutherford's nuclear atom, had features that were valuable and suggestive to scientists at that time.

Thomson received the 1906 Nobel Prize for Physics "in recognition of the great merits of his theoretical and experimental investigations on the conduction of electricity by gases." In his presentation speech, J. P. Klason of the Royal Swedish Academy of Sciences congratulated Thomson on "having bestowed upon the world some of the main works that are enabling the natural philosopher of our time to take up new inquiries in new directions." By showing that atoms are not the most fundamental units of matter, as had long been believed, Thomson indeed opened the door to a new era in physical science.

Between 1906 and 1914 Thomson initiated his second and last great period of experimental activity. He studied canal rays, or positive rays, that stream toward the cathode in a discharge tube. Although WILHELM WIEN had already shown that canal rays were positively charged particles, Thomson and his colleagues elucidated their characteristics and separated the different kinds of atoms and atomic groupings present in them. In these experiments Thomson demonstrated an entirely new way of separating atoms, showing that certain atomic groups such as CH, CH_2, and CH_3 could exist even though they have no stable existence under ordinary conditions. Significantly, he found that samples of the inert gas neon contained atoms with two different atomic weights. The discovery of these isotopes proved important in the understanding of the heavy radioactive elements, such as uranium and radium.

During World War I, Thomson worked at the Board of Invention and Research and served as a government adviser. In 1918 he became master of Trinity College. One year later Rutherford succeeded him as Cavendish Professor of Experimental Physics and director of the Cavendish Laboratory.

After 1919 Thomson busied himself with his responsibilities as master of Trinity, with additional research at the Cavendish Laboratory, and with astute financial investments. He delighted in gardening, often taking long hikes in search of unusual plants.

Thomson married Rose Paget in 1890; they had a son and a daughter. His son, G. P. THOMSON, went on to win the 1937 Nobel Prize for Physics. Thomson died on August 30, 1940, and was buried in Westminster Abbey in London.

Thomson influenced physics not only through his brilliant experimental researches but also through his excellent teaching and superlative direction of the Cavendish Laboratory. Attracted by these qualities, hundreds of the world's most talented young physicists chose to study at Cambridge. Of those who worked at the Cavendish under Thomson, seven eventually became Nobel laureates.

In addition to the Nobel Prize, Thomson received many other honors, including the Royal (1894), the Hughes (1902), and the Copley (1914) medals of the Royal Society. He served as president of the Royal Society in 1915 and was knighted in 1908.

SELECTED WORKS: A Treatise on the Motion of Vortex Rings, 1883; Applications of Dynamics to Physics and Chemistry, 1888; Notes on Recent Researches in Electricity and Magnetism, 1893; Elements of the Mathematical Theory of Electricity and Magnetism, 1895; Discharge of Electricity Through Gases, 1897; Conduction of Electricity Through Gases, 1903; Electricity and Matter, 1904; The Structure of Light, 1907; The Corpuscular Theory of Matter, 1907; The Atomic Theory, 1914; The Electron in Chemistry, 1923; Recollections and Reflections, 1936.

ABOUT: Dictionary of Scientific Biography, volume 13, 1976; Fitzpatrick, T. C., et al. A History of the Cavendish Laboratory, 1910; Strutt, J. W. The Life of Sir J. J. Thomson, 1943; Thomson, G. P. J. J. Thomson and the Cavendish Laboratory in His Day, 1965.

TINBERGEN, JAN
(April 12, 1903–)
Nobel Memorial Prize in Economic
   Sciences, 1969
(shared with Ragnar Frisch)

JAN TINBERGEN

The Dutch economist Jan Tinbergen was born in The Hague, the oldest of five children of Dirk Cornelius Tinbergen, a language expert and secondary school teacher, and Jeannette (van Eek) Tinbergen. His parents made their home a fertile learning ground and inculcated in their children an interest in scientific study. One brother, NIKO TINBERGEN, became a professor of animal behavior at Oxford University, and the youngest brother, Luuk, became a professor of zoology.

While attending the University of Leiden from 1922 to 1926, Tinbergen studied physics. One of his teachers, Paul Ehrenfest, for whom he also served as an assistant, greatly influenced Tinbergen's research and problem-solving methods. In 1929 Tinbergen received his doctorate in physics at Leiden with the thesis "Minimum Problems in Physics and Economics." As the title suggests, his interest had shifted from physics to economics, a change that Ehrenfest had helped to stimulate. Retaining his interest in the mathematical basis of physics, Tinbergen began using mathematical formulas to study economies and to create models of how they work. He was one of the few economists at the time to unite the disciplines of mathematics (in the form of statistics and formulas) and economics. The practical goal of this union was to predict the direction of national economies and to give governments useful planning information.

When he was drafted into the Dutch army, Tinbergen refused to serve for reasons of conscience. As an alternative, he served in prison administration in Rotterdam and later in the Dutch government's Central Bureau of Statistics in The Hague. In 1929 he joined a new office at the Central Bureau that was established to investigate business cycles. Soon the guiding spirit of the office, he remained there until 1945, with a leave of absence from 1936 to 1938 to work in Geneva for the League of Nations. He also lectured in statistics at the University of Amsterdam in 1931 and was a professor at the Netherlands School of Economics in Rotterdam in 1933.

During the 1930s Tinbergen, several statisticians, and a few fellow economists (including RAGNAR FRISCH) created the science of econometrics, the marriage of statistics and economic analysis. The econometric methods evolved by Tinbergen and Frisch enabled economists to replace the vague conceptual tools they had been using with concrete statistical instruments. The two economists hoped that greater precision in economic analysis would make it possible to describe economic trends and make economic predictions with increased accuracy.

Using statistical instruments, Tinbergen created a working model of the Dutch economy, a complex system that included twenty-seven behavioral equations with more than fifty variables. Under the auspices of the League of Nations, Tinbergen published what is perhaps his best-known research work, the 1939 book *Business Cycles in the United States, 1919–1932*. In it, using forty-eight equations, he created a model to explain the interplay among different facets of the American economy between World War I and the Great Depression.

Although other economists had discussed the causes of the business cycle, it was Tinbergen who first analyzed the cycle as a complete dynamic model of interrelated variables represented in quantitative form. Instead of the acceleration principle (as in Frisch's contention that changes in investment and income levels can reinforce one another), he saw the level and changes of profits as the main determinants of private investments.

Tinbergen's work at this time, particularly *Business Cycles in the United States,* evoked controversy. John Maynard Keynes, in his reviews of Tinbergen's work, was highly critical of econometric methods, and many other economists failed to appreciate their value. Today, however, this work is widely recognized as having provided the raw material for later development of business cycle theory and for creating a new branch of macroeconomics. "Frisch and I started this work in the 1930s, in the days of the economic depression," Tinbergen later remarked. "We wanted to draw a plan to fight depression causes and keep unemployment under control." Many of their students went on to become leaders in the next generation of economists.

During the German occupation of the Netherlands in World War II, Tinbergen continued his research at the Dutch Central Bureau of Statistics. Although isolated from professional contacts abroad, he continued to publish in international journals. When peace came in 1945, he was named director of the newly formed Netherlands Central Planning Bureau. In this position, which he held for ten years, he focused first on the problems of rebuilding the Netherlands from the ravages of war, then on short-term stabilization policies.

One of Tinbergen's major goals was to develop a basis for government economic policy. In *Economic Policy: Principles and Design* (1956), he employed a quantitative framework for studying policy problems and drew attention to multitarget issues (problems posed by attempting to achieve several economic goals at once). He showed why a policy model of the economy must contain at least as many policy instruments (measures, such as taxes, to achieve those goals) as it has targets. In a series of examples, he analyzed problems that faced the Dutch economy in the early 1950s.

In 1955 Tinbergen resigned as director of the Central Planning Bureau in order to study the problems of developing nations. In this work he applied current growth theory pragmatically, developing planning methods and seeking to define investment needs and savings requirements. Characteristically, it was the application of economics, not theorizing, that interested Tinbergen. He wanted to adapt existing growth analysis to the practical problems in front of him: devising methods for planning long-term development (particularly in Third World countries).

After a year as visiting professor at Harvard University, Tinbergen was elected to a new, full-time position in development planning at the Netherlands School of Economics in 1956. In the 1960s he developed quantitative models for educational planning and for optimal spatial distribution of production and investments among regions throughout an economy.

During this period he served as a consultant to the governments of India, Egypt, Turkey, Suriname, Chile, Indonesia, Syria, Iraq, and Libya. He also advised international organizations such as the World Bank, the European Coal and Steel Community, and various United Nations agencies. In 1966 he became chairman of the United Nations Committee for Development Planning.

Tinbergen made notable contributions to the economic development of Third World countries. His usual method was to start with large investment projects and to integrate them into the macroeconomics of the country by using input-output methods as well as shadow prices and international prices. In this way he attempted to make governments face the long-term limitations of their resources and become competitive in foreign trade.

In 1969 Tinbergen and Ragnar Frisch shared the first Nobel Memorial Prize in Economic Sciences "for having developed and applied dynamic models for the analysis of economic processes." On presenting the award, Erik Lundberg of the Royal Swedish Academy of Sciences said, "The arbitrary 'naming' of causes of cyclical fluctuations . . . and the concentration upon certain simple chains of causal connection [have] given way in the work of Frisch and Tinbergen to mathematical systems that state the mutual relationships between economic variables."

Throughout his life Tinbergen has embraced humanistic ideals. As a young man he developed a strong and lasting interest in public issues, first joining a socialist youth association and later becoming an active member of the Dutch Social Democratic Labor party. His idealism later led him to study the issues of justice and fairness posed by the distribution of power and income among individuals and nations. For him, these issues demand the highest priority in research and policymaking. In the early 1970s he made the theory of personal-income distribution in industrialized countries the topic of his major research. His book *Income Distribution: Analysis and Policies* was published in 1975, the same year that he retired from the University of Leiden.

At the United Nations, Tinbergen greatly influenced the drafting of a proposal for the organization's International Development Strategy for the Second Development Decade (1971–1980). To his deep disappointment, the proposal was accepted only halfheartedly and then only after a rewriting that omitted the commitment to social justice.

In 1929 Tinbergen married Tine De Wit, the daughter of a military officer. They have four daughters. The American economist PAUL SAMUELSON has described Tinbergen as "a gentle soul with an abhorrence for power— truly a 'humanist saint.' . . . By helping to give us the knowledge to make the mixed economy work, [Tinbergen and Frisch] have done more for the preservation of freedom in the world than all the ideologues of laissez-faire."

In addition to the Nobel Prize, Tinbergen has received the Erasmus Prize of the European Cultural Foundation (1967) and more than twenty honorary degrees.

ADDITIONAL WORKS: International Economic Cooperation, 1945; The Dynamics of Business Cycles, 1950; Business Cycles in the United Kingdom 1870–1914, 1951; Econometrics, 1951; On the Theory of Economic Policy, 1952; The Design of Development, 1953; Centralization and Decentralization in Economic Policy, 1954; Mathematical Models of Economic Growth, 1962, with Hendricus Bos; Lessons From the Past, 1963; Central Planning, 1964; Developmental Planning, 1967; Production, Income, and Welfare, 1985.

ABOUT: Bos, H. C. (ed.) Toward Balanced International Growth, 1969; Sills, D. (ed.) International Encyclopedia of the Social Sciences: Biographical Supplement, 1979; Swedish Journal of Economics December 1969.

TINBERGEN, NIKO
(April 15, 1907–   )
Nobel Prize for Physiology or Medicine, 1973
(shared with Karl von Frisch and Konrad Lorenz)

The Dutch-English zoologist and ethologist Nikolaas Tinbergen was born in The Hague, the third of five children, to Dirk Cornelius Tinbergen, a grammar school language and history teacher, and the former Jeannette van Eek. Tinbergen's older brother, JAN TINBERGEN, was a physicist who later turned to economics. Since he lived only an hour's walk from the seashore, Niko Tinbergen developed

NIKO TINBERGEN

an early love of nature and enjoyed collecting seashells, observing birds, and camping—activities he much preferred to school.

After graduation from the local high school ("I only just scraped through," he recalled later), Tinbergen considered university schooling but was discouraged by the prospect of more academic work. Family friends persuaded Tinbergen's father to send the boy to the Vogelwarte Rossitten, a bird observatory where techniques of bird banding were first developed. After working there for several months, Tinbergen felt ready for more schooling and entered the biology program at the State University of Leiden, where he also played on the hockey team. While reading and studying under teachers such as the naturalist Jan Verwey, Tinbergen sharpened his already keen interest in animal behavior. Influenced by KARL VON FRISCH's studies of the bee, he chose as the subject of his doctoral dissertation the homing behavior of bee-killer wasps he had observed at his parents' summer home in Hulshorst near the North Sea.

From his observations, he wrote a "skimpy but interesting little thesis" (the shortest ever accepted by the faculty at Leiden) and received his Ph.D. in 1932, the same year that he married Elisabeth A. Rutten; they eventually had two sons and three daughters. In its methodology, his thesis exemplified the pattern of Tinbergen's subsequent research—to learn all he could through patient observation of an animal's behavior in its natural habitat and then to carry out experiments to confirm his theories. While studying the bee-killer wasp, for example, he removed or altered natural obstacles near the colony's burrows and, by observing the insects' behavior, was able to demonstrate that they find their way home by remembering visual landmarks.

Soon after completing his graduate work, Tinbergen and his wife joined a Dutch meteorological expedition to Greenland, where they spent fourteen months with the Eskimos, studying the behavior of arctic birds and mammals. Returning to Leiden in late 1933, Tinbergen was appointed instructor at the state university. Two years later he was asked to organize an undergraduate course in animal behavior, which he based on the study of selected animals and their environments—the three-spined stickleback (a small fish he had raised and observed as a child) and the insects and birds of Hulshorst, where he set up a permanent research station.

Although by this time Tinbergen had conducted studies of instinctive behavior (especially mating) in a variety of species, his work lacked a firm overall structure. His meeting with KONRAD LORENZ at a seminar in Leiden in 1936 marked the start of pioneering work in the field of ethology (the study of animal behavior in relation to habitat). In writing about the encounter in later years, Tinbergen said, "We 'clicked' at once. . . . Konrad's extraordinary vision and enthusiasm were supplemented and fertilized by my critical sense, my inclination to think his ideas through, and my irrepressible urge to check out 'hunches' by experimentation."

While Tinbergen and his family spent a summer at Lorenz's home near Vienna, the two scientists began to construct a theoretical framework for ethological research. Over the course of a long collaboration, they postulated that instinct is not merely a response to environmental stimuli but arises from impulses, or drives, from within the animal. Instinctive behavior, they said, consists of a stereotyped set of movements—the so-called fixed action pattern (FAP)—which is as distinct as a species' anatomical features. An animal performs an FAP in response to a particular environmental stimulus (the releaser), which may be highly specific. Moreover, they suggested, much animal behavior results from conflicts between drives. The male stickleback, for example, leads a female to his nest in a characteristic zigzag dance. Tinbergen showed that this FAP reflects the conflict between the male's drive to defend his territory and his drive to mate.

Under other circumstances, the conflict between drives may lead to a displacement re-

action, the expression of an altogether different instinct. A typical example occurs when an animal defending its territory faces an attacker that is too strong for direct confrontation. The resulting conflict between the desire to attack and the desire to retreat may produce a third form of behavior, such as eating or grooming.

The outbreak of World War II interrupted the work of Tinbergen and Lorenz. Tinbergen continued to teach at Leiden after the German occupation but was arrested in 1942 for protesting the dismissal of three Jewish faculty members; he spent the rest of the war in a hostage camp. After his release he returned to the university and was appointed professor of experimental biology.

Tinbergen lectured in the United States (which he had visited briefly in 1938) in 1947 and at Oxford University two years later. Remaining at Oxford, he founded the journal *Behavior* and continued his work at the university's newly created animal-behavior division. He became a British subject in 1955, was appointed reader in animal behavior five years later, and was named professor and fellow of Wolfson College in 1966.

During the 1950s and 1960s Tinbergen's extensive studies of gulls firmly established the theories he and Lorenz had sketched out before the war. Through his work as a teacher, he influenced several generations of English-speaking ethologists.

Tinbergen, Lorenz, and Frisch shared the 1973 Nobel Prize for Physiology or Medicine "for their discoveries concerning organization and elicitation of individual and social behavior patterns." If the award to "three animal watchers" (as Tinbergen quipped) was unexpected, it also reflected the value of the laureates' work beyond the field of ethology, mainly "social medicine, psychiatry, and psychosomatic medicine," said Börje Cronholm of the Karolinska Institute in his presentation speech. Tinbergen's Nobel lecture presented his findings on the relationship between ethology and stress diseases, including early-childhood autism, a disorder he has continued to study, in collaboration with his wife, since his retirement from Oxford in 1974.

The Tinbergens divide their time between their home in Oxford and an eighteenth-century farmhouse in northwestern England, near the Irish Sea.

Tinbergen was the recipient of the Jan Swammerdam Medal of the Netherlands Association for the Advancement of Natural, Medical, and Surgical Sciences in 1973. He is a member of many learned societies. In addition to numerous publications, Tinbergen has made a documentary film, *Signals for Survival,* produced with Hugh Falkus for the British Broadcasting Corporation.

SELECTED WORKS: Eskimoland, 1934; An Objectivistic Study of the Innate Behavior of Animals, 1942; Kleew, 1947; The Study of Instinct, 1951; The Herring Gull's World, 1953; Social Behavior in Animals, 1953; Bird Life, 1954; The Tale of John Stickle, 1954; Curious Naturalists, 1958; Animal Behavior, 1965, with others; Tracks, 1967, with Eric Ennion; Signals for Survival, 1970, with others; The Animal in Its World (2 vols.) 1972–1973; Early Childhood Autism, 1972, with Elisabeth Tinbergen; Autistic Children: New Hope for a Cure, 1983, with Elisabeth Tinbergen.

ABOUT: Baerends, G. P., and Beer, C. (eds.) Function and Evolution in Behavior, 1975; Current Biography November 1975; New York Times Magazine April 7, 1974; Psychology Today March 1974; Sills, D. (ed.) International Encyclopedia of the Social Sciences: Biographical Supplement, 1979; Thorpe, W. H. The Origins and Rise of Ethology, 1979.

SAMUEL C. C. TING

TING, SAMUEL C. C.
(January 27, 1936–   )
Nobel Prize for Physics, 1976
(shared with Burton Richter)

The American nuclear physicist Samuel Chao Chung Ting was born in Ann Arbor, Michigan, the eldest of three children of Kuan Hai Ting, an engineering professor who at the time was studying at the University of Michigan, and Tsun-Ying Wang, a psychology professor. Two months after his birth, the family returned to mainland China, where Ting spent his early years. During his teens he lived in Taiwan, where his father taught at the National Taiwan University. Ting returned to the United States in 1956, with only $100 and little knowledge of English, to study at the University of Michigan. Supported by scholarships, he earned bachelor's degrees in mathematics and physics in 1959, an M.S. in physics in 1960, and a Ph.D. in physics in 1962.

Ting spent 1963 at CERN (the European Organization for Nuclear Research) in Geneva, Switzerland, working with the Italian physicist Guiseppe Cocconi on the proton synchrotron, a type of particle accelerator. Two years later he joined the faculty of Columbia University in New York and soon became interested in a recent experiment conducted at Harvard University's Cambridge electron accelerator. The experiment involved "pair production," the simultaneous generation of an electron and its antiparticle, the positron, by a collision between a particle of radiation

(photon) and a nuclear target. (A positron is identical to an electron except that its electric charge is positive rather than negative.) The experimental results seemed to violate certain predictions of quantum electrodynamics, which describes the interaction of matter with electromagnetic radiation.

Taking a leave of absence from Columbia in 1966, Ting went to Hamburg, Germany, to duplicate the Harvard experiment at the DESY facility, named for the Deutsches Elektronen-Synchrotron (German electron synchroton). Ting's Hamburg group built an instrument called a double-arm spectrometer to catch electron-positron pairs. The two arms of the spectrometer allowed the simultaneous measurement of the momenta (mass times velocity) of two particles (by means of their deflection by large magnets) and the angles between their paths and the direction of the incoming beam. A separate measurement of the particle velocities then allowed the calculation of their masses and a determination of their total energies. Particles could then be identified and correlations between them established. The spectrometer could also be tuned to accept only particles with certain momentum values so that different effective masses could be explored. The group's experimental results showed that the quantum electrodynamic description of pair production was correct to distances as small as one hundred-trillionth of a centimeter.

Ting continued to study pair production and to search for new particles whose decay products were electron-positron pairs. Concurrently with his DESY research, he accepted a faculty position in physics at the Massachusetts Institute of Technology (MIT) in 1967; two years later he became a full professor. In 1971 Ting and his group began a particle search with the 30-billion-electron-volt proton accelerator at Brookhaven National Laboratory in Upton, Long Island, New York.

Ting was looking for short-lived, relatively heavy particles. Since a large mass is equivalent to very high energy, in accordance with ALBERT EINSTEIN's relativity theory, only bombardment of a target with sufficiently energetic particles could instigate reactions from which the particles being sought might arise. The primary need for such a search was an extraordinarily capable detector that could identify an event such as the production of an electron-positron pair, at a measurable energy, in a billionth of a second, in the midst of billions of other interactions of no immediate interest, and under the onslaught of 10 trillion protons per second. It was not expected that a particle of the kind contemplated could be captured and observed directly, but that it would reveal its presence by decaying into an electron-positron pair whose energy would equal that of the vanished parent particle. This required high resolution at large masses, that is, the ability to add precisely known small increments of energy to an already large quantity and to measure their effect on pair production. Ting and his colleagues decided to build a highly sophisticated version of the double-arm spectrometer. The extremely complicated apparatus, after careful testing of each component, worked almost the first time it was turned on. This added further luster to the reputation Ting had gained at Hamburg for painstaking experimental skill and insight.

The team directed the proton beam at a beryllium target. In August 1974, after several months of operation, they discovered a sharp, narrow peak of electron-positron–pair production at 3.1 billion electron volts. After several months of double-checking the results in many ways, Ting concluded that he was observing the effects of a new and unpredicted particle. It was twice as heavy as other comparable particles and its mass (in terms of equivalent energy) was a thousand times more narrowly defined, an indication of the narrow range of energy states it could occupy and a possible clue to its nature. Ting wanted to investigate other related problems before publishing his results and did not immediately submit a report. He did inform Giorgio Bel-

lettini, director of the Frascati Laboratory in Italy. Knowing where to look, the Frascati physicists confirmed Ting's discovery in only two days. Papers by Ting and the Frascati group appeared in the same November issue of *Physical Review Letters*.

When Ting was looking for a name for the new particle, someone reminded him that the exciting group of stable particles in modern physics were assigned capital Roman letters, while the more classical group were known by Greek letters. Since his work had involved electromagnetic currents, which bear the symbol *j*, he called his particle J. While attending a routine scheduling meeting at the Stanford Linear Accelerator Center (SLAC) in California, Ting described his findings to SLAC's director, Wolfgang Panofsky. Panofsky informed him that only a few days earlier, a SLAC physicist, BURTON RICHTER, had reported similar findings. After comparing notes, Ting and Richter concluded that they had discovered the same particle, which Richter had called psi. In recognition of their independent and almost simultaneous discoveries, the name *J/psi* was adopted. Many physics laboratories revised their research programs to investigate the new particle, while nuclear theorists attempted to incorporate it into their concepts.

Ting and Richter were awarded the 1976 Nobel Prize for Physics "for their pioneering work in the discovery of a heavy elementary particle of a new kind." According to Gösta Ekspong of the Royal Swedish Academy of Sciences, who presented the award, "Ting discovered the new particle when he investigated how twins of one electron and one positron are born at very high energies. Richter," continued Ekspong, "arranged for electrons and positrons to meet in head-on collisions and the new particle appeared when conditions were exactly right." All elementary particles, Ekspong reminded his listeners, "seem to derive their properties from a deeper level of subdivision where only a few building bricks, called quarks, are required."

Because the J/psi particle survived several thousand times longer than could be explained by the assumption of three fundamental particles called quarks, which combined in various ways, physicists proposed an explanation of J/psi in terms of a fourth quark, called charm. Although charm had been predicted earlier, experimental evidence for its existence was lacking until Ting's and Richter's discovery.

Using accelerators at CERN and DESY, Ting has continued to search for new particles. He also performs his faculty duties at MIT, where he was appointed the first Thomas Dudley Cabot Institute Professor in 1977.

In 1960 Ting married Kay Louise Kuhne, an architect. They have two daughters. He is known as a quiet, intense man and a meticulous scientific experimentalist.

Ting, who is a member of the American Academy of Arts and Sciences and the National Academy of Sciences, as well as the American, European, and Italian physical societies, received the Ernest Orlando Lawrence Memorial Award for Physics of the United States Energy Research and Development Agency (1976). He also holds an honorary degree from the University of Michigan.

ABOUT: New Scientist October 21, 1976; Physics Today December 1976; Science November 19, 1976.

ARNE TISELIUS

TISELIUS, ARNE
(August 10, 1902–October 29, 1971)
Nobel Prize for Chemistry, 1948

The Swedish biochemist Arne Wilhelm Kaurin Tiselius (ti sel′ i us) was born in Stockholm to Hans Abraham J:son Tiselius, who was employed by an insurance company, and the former Rosa Kaurin, daughter of a Norwegian clergyman. When the boy's father died in 1906, his mother moved with her two small children to Göteborg, where she had relatives and close friends. At the gymnasium in Göteborg, Tiselius encountered an inspiring teacher of chemistry and biology who recognized and encouraged his interest in chemistry. Tiselius entered the University of Uppsala in 1921 and earned a master's degree in chemistry, physics, and mathematics in 1925. He remained at Uppsala as a research assistant in physical chemistry to TEODOR SVEDBERG.

One of Svedberg's interests was electrophoresis, or the movement of electrically charged molecules in a solution to which an electric field has been applied. Virtually all large molecules carry an electrical charge when they are in solution. Since molecules usually have different rates of movement, or migration, depending on their size, shape, and electrical charge, electrophoresis in theory makes it possible to separate the molecular constituents of a solution. In practice, however, a variety of factors, especially the presence of convection currents, make it difficult to obtain useful results by this method. Svedberg turned the investigation of this phenomenon over to Tiselius.

Tiselius found that by rigorously controlling temperature and electrical current, he could minimize the convection currents and still obtain migration. Developing sophisticated optical methods of tracing the migration of molecules, he demonstrated that electrophoresis could separate mixtures that appeared to be homogeneous under other types of analysis such as centrifugation. In 1938 he presented these results in his doctoral dissertation, which for many years remained the definitive treatment of electrophoresis.

Despite his success, Tiselius wrote in an article containing his memoirs, "Reflections From Both Sides of the Counter," he felt disappointed. "The method was an improvement, no doubt, but it led me just to the point where I could see indications of very interesting results without being able to prove anything definite. I can still remember this as an almost physical suffering when looking at some of the electrophoresis photographs, especially of serum proteins. I decided to take up an entirely different problem," he said, "but a scar was left in my mind, which some years later would prove significant."

The problem Tiselius took up was measurement of the diffusion of water and other molecules in a mineral called zeolite. Some of this work was conducted at Princeton University's Frick Chemical Laboratory, where he spent the academic year 1934–1935 working with the aid of a Rockefeller Foundation Fellowship. He succeeded in accurately measuring the diffusion of water molecules in zeolite crystals.

Upon returning to Uppsala, Tiselius undertook a systematic investigation, both theoretical and experimental, of the factors controlling electrophoresis. By 1936 he was able to devise a new and more sensitive electrophoretic apparatus. Using it to analyze blood serum, he was able to show that the serum protein known as globulin actually consists of three types, which he called alpha, beta, and gamma globulin. In recognition of this work, Sweden's first professorship in biochemistry was established in 1938 at the University of Uppsala, initially to provide Tiselius with a permanent academic position.

The conviction that methods for the separation of molecular constituents were of central importance to biochemistry had long motivated Tiselius's work on electrophoresis, and in the early 1940s he turned his attention to another method of separation: chromatography. Chromatography utilizes a principle of adsorption, the tendency of various molecules to adhere differentially to the surface of certain substances.

Chromatography was first used in 1906 by the Russian botanist Mikhail Tsvet, who employed it to separate pigments in plant extracts. Tsvet's method consisted of adding a solution containing the material to be studied (the eluate) to a glass tube packed with particles of some adsorbent substance, such as carbon or sugar. The different adsorption rates produced colored bands at different heights in the tube. Since Tiselius extended the technique to the separation of colorless substances, he preferred the term *adsorption analysis* to *chromatography*. Moreover, he separated the substances not by their final positions in the adsorbent column but by the length of time it took the eluate to pass through the column when it was continuously added. Extending his earlier work on electrophoresis and on diffusion in zeolites, he devised optical techniques for detecting the adsorption patterns created by the substances in the eluate.

Tiselius investigated many variations on this technique, including the use of an eluate more strongly adsorbed as a whole than any of the substances being separated, a technique he called displacement analysis. As with his earlier work on electrophoresis, it was his elucidation of the fundamental principles involved in chromatography that allowed him to make great technical strides.

During the 1940s administrative and advisory responsibilities took up an increasing amount of Tiselius's time. He became an influential adviser to the Swedish government in 1944 and served on numerous government committees until his death. In 1946 he accepted the four-year chairmanship of the Swedish Natural Science Research Council, and in 1947 he became vice president of the Nobel Foundation.

The 1948 Nobel Prize for Chemistry was awarded to Tiselius for "his research work on electrophoresis and on analysis by adsorption and, in particular, for his discoveries concerning the heterogeneous nature of the proteins of the serum." On presenting the award, A. F. Westgren of the Royal Swedish Academy of Sciences declared that Tiselius had "made many discoveries of far-reaching effect by applying his method of electrophoresis." For example, by establishing that globulin is not an entirely homogeneous substance, Westgren said, Tiselius laid the foundation for "research work aimed at dividing human blood plasma into fractional parts. . . . Tiselius and his collaborators also carried out experiments of great medical value on the antibodies of a protein nature which are formed in the blood during immunization."

Tiselius always promoted the exchange of ideas between disciplines. He himself applied principles from physics to improve techniques of chemical analysis in order to understand biological systems. Through frequent work as a consultant, he strengthened ties between science and industry as well as those between science and government. He encouraged greater international exchange in science and urged other scientists to take a greater interest in the environmental, ethical, and social implications of scientific and technological advances.

In 1930 Tiselius married Ingrid Margareta Dalén; they had a son and a daughter. A modest, quiet man with a gentle humor, he was an avid bird-watcher and the founder of the Backhammer Academy of Sciences, composed of several friends who shared an interest in ornithology. When in 1960 he became president of the Nobel Foundation, Tiselius established the Nobel Symposia, bringing together leading scientists in each of the prize fields to discuss the latest scientific developments, especially their ethical and social implications. While involved in planning an international meeting of directors of research institutions, he suffered a heart attack and died in Stockholm on October 29, 1971.

In addition to the Nobel Prize, Tiselius's awards included the Franklin Medal of the Franklin Institute (1956) and the Paul Karrer Medal in Chemistry of the University of Zurich (1961). He received honorary degrees from the universities of Stockholm, Paris, Bologna, Glasgow, Madrid, Lyons, St. Peter, California at Berkeley and Prague and from Cambridge and Oxford universities. He was a member of thirty-seven scientific academies, including the American National Academy of Sciences and the Royal Institution of Great Britain. He was also a commander of the Legion of Honor of France.

SELECTED WORKS: Colloid Chemistry, 1928, with T. Svedberg; Purity and Purification of Chemical Substances, 1958.

ABOUT: Biographical Memoirs of Fellows of the Royal Society, volume 20, 1974; Dictionary of Scientific Biography, volume 13, 1976; The Excitement and Fascination of Science, volume 2, 1978; Nature November 13, 1948; New York Times November 5, 1948.

JAMES TOBIN

TOBIN, JAMES
(March 5, 1918–)
Nobel Memorial Prize in Economic
  Sciences, 1981

The American economist James Tobin was born in Champaign, Illinois, the elder of the two sons of Louis Michael Tobin and the former Margaret Edgerton. His father, an avid reader with broad intellectual interests, was the publicity director for athletics at the University of Illinois. His mother resumed a career as a social worker after raising her children and became director of the local family service agency, a position she held for twenty-five years. Tobin credits his father for stimulating his intellectual curiosity, referring to him in later years as his "wise and gentle teacher." After attending public schools in Champaign, Tobin enrolled in the University High School in nearby Urbana, where his extracurricular activities included playing basketball, acting, and editing the school yearbook.

At his father's urging, Tobin entered a nationwide competition inaugurated by Harvard University in 1935 and was awarded a full scholarship to the university. At Harvard he majored in economics. He also participated in the student government, played basketball, and worked on the yearbook. In 1939 he received his B.A. summa cum laude in economics. He continued graduate study at Harvard for the next two years under such professors as Joseph Schumpeter, Alvin Hansen, Seymour Harris, Edward Mason, and WASSILY LEONTIEF. He also became acquainted with younger faculty members and fellow graduate students, including PAUL SAMUELSON, Paul Sweeny, John

Kenneth Galbraith, Abram Bergson, Richard Goodwin, and Lloyd Reynolds.

After receiving an M.S. in economics from Harvard in 1941, Tobin worked first for the Office of Price Administration and then for the Civilian Supply and War Production Board in Washington, D.C. When the United States entered World War II, he joined the United States Navy. Upon completing officers' training at Columbia University, he served four years as gunnery officer, navigator, and executive officer aboard the destroyer USS *Kearny*.

Tobin returned to Harvard in 1946 as a teaching fellow. The following year he was awarded a Ph.D. in economics with the dissertation "Theoretical and Statistical Study of Consumption Function."

Since his undergraduate days, when he first became interested in John Maynard Keynes's revolutionary economic theories, Tobin has embraced Keynesian theory. Keynes's "new economics" rejected the established laissez-faire orthodoxy and advocated government intervention in the economy, through fiscal and monetary policies, to achieve economic growth and full employment. Tobin later made important contributions to the development and expansion of Keynes's work, improving on the Keynesian framework in several strategic respects: by introducing a model of general equilibrium in financial and capital markets, by setting up a new theory of investment determination built on Keynes's supply prices of capital, and by applying a Keynesian approach to issues of stabilization policy.

1065

Elected to the prestigious Society of Fellows at Harvard in 1947, Tobin spent the next three years on study and research. During this time he contributed to *The American Business Creed* (1956) and published articles on macroeconomics, statistical demand analysis, and the theory of rationing.

In 1950 Tobin was appointed associate professor of economics at Yale University, which became his permanent academic home. In addition to teaching, he conducted research into financial markets, developing theories on how changes in financial assets and money markets influence decisions about consumption, production, and investment decisions.

At this time Tobin constructed his "portfolio-selection theory," demonstrating that only rarely do investors seek the highest rates of return to the exclusion of all other factors. He saw that investors tend to balance high-risk investments with less speculative ones in an effort to achieve portfolio balance. From models of asset equilibrium combined with stock-flow relationships, he originated the concept of the q factor, a ratio that measures the relationship of market values of physical assets to their replacement costs. His empirical studies of q demonstrated the important effects of the stock market on private investment. Tobin also extended Keynesian short-term macroeconomic analysis to long-term growth models that became the basis for his engagement in policy problems. Many of Tobin's outstanding contributions have to do with policy implications of macroeconomic theory. Critical of oversimplified monetarist approaches, his sharp attack on MILTON FRIEDMAN's recommendations is especially well known. Tobin's portfolio model of many kinds of financial assets provides a much richer policy model than previous ones. His model has also been used to study the effects of fiscal policy on the economy.

When the Cowles Foundation for Research in Economics, dedicated to relating economic theory to mathematical and statistical studies, moved from the University of Chicago to Yale in 1955, Tobin became its director. Two years later he was appointed Sterling Professor of Economics at Yale, a position he still holds. In 1961, entering the arena of public debate on government economic policy, he published an article in the January issue of *Challenge* that criticized the tight monetary practices of the Federal Reserve Board. Such practices, he argued, would frustrate attempts by President John F. Kennedy's administration to raise levels of employment and production. This became an important theme in a great number of Tobin's contributions during the following decades. Convinced of the tremendous waste involved in unemployment, he was unwilling to accept long and deep recessions as a means of fighting inflation. He often pleaded for more expansive policies and for efforts to reduce unemployment, even below its "natural" level. Far from neglecting the problem of inflation, he often addressed the issue of how the gains from expanding employment should be weighted against the costs of inflation. As one type of solution, he recommended temporary trials of income policies.

In 1970 Tobin was elected president of the American Economic Association. In his acceptance speech he stressed the need for permanent wage and price controls, which he believed were required to bring an end to the recession. With that need in mind, he lent his talents to the presidential campaign of Senator George S. McGovern, collaborating with other economists in devising an income-redistribution plan for raising the incomes of the poor. When McGovern lost the election, Tobin resumed academic research and teaching. He continued to write, publishing *Macroeconomics,* the first of his three-volume *Essays in Economics,* in 1971. The second volume, *Consumption and Econometrics,* was published in 1975, and the third, *Theory and Policy,* appeared in 1982. Given his support for Keynesian economics, it is not surprising that Tobin has been one of the most outspoken critics of President Ronald Reagan's economic policies and of the tight-money stance adopted by the Federal Reserve Board.

Tobin was awarded the 1981 Nobel Memorial Prize in Economic Sciences "for his analysis of financial markets and their relations to expenditure decisions, employment, production, and prices." In his presentation speech, Assar Lindbeck of the Royal Swedish Academy of Sciences noted that Tobin's work is significant "because the effects on the economy of economic policy, monetary as well as fiscal policy, are to a large extent transmitted via the monetary and financial markets." Lindbeck went on to praise Tobin for laying "a solid, and empirically applicable, foundation for studies of the functioning of monetary and financial markets" and for showing "how changes in these markets influence the magnitudes of consumption, investment, production, employment, and economic growth."

Over the years, Tobin has served as a consultant for government and private agencies alike, including the Federal Reserve System, the United States Treasury, the Congressional

Budget Office, and the Ford Foundation. He served as chairman of the New Haven, Connecticut, City Planning Commission from 1967 to 1970 and was a member of the New York City Commission on Inflation and Economic Welfare in 1969 and 1970.

Since 1946 Tobin has been married to the former Elizabeth Fay Ringo, a teacher. They have one daughter and three sons. His recreational activities include bicycling, tennis, skiing, canoeing, fishing, chess, and watching baseball.

Tobin is a member of the National Academy of Sciences, the American Philosophical Society, the American Academy of Arts and Sciences, and the American Statistical Association. He holds honorary degrees from Syracuse University, the University of Illinois, Dartmouth College, Swarthmore College, and the New University of Lisbon.

ADDITIONAL WORKS: National Economic Policy, 1966; The New Economics One Decade Older, 1974; Asset Accumulation and Economic Activity, 1980.

ABOUT: Breit, W., and Spencer, R. W. (eds.) Lives of the Laureates, 1986; Current Biography October 1984; New York Times October 13, 1985; Scandinavian Journal of Economics, number 1, 1982; Science October 30, 1981.

TODD, ALEXANDER
(October 2, 1907–   )
Nobel Prize for Chemistry, 1957

The Scottish chemist Alexander Robertus Todd was born in Glasgow to Alexander Todd, a businessman, and Jean (Lowrie) Todd. Growing up in Glasgow, he attended the Allan Glen School before entering Glasgow University, from which he graduated in 1929 with a B.S. in organic chemistry. After a short period of training in research methods, he enrolled as a graduate student in the University of Frankfurt am Main in Germany. There he studied organic chemistry and received his Ph.D. in 1931 in the natural sciences for a dissertation on the chemistry of bile acids. He then became a postgraduate student at Oxford University under ROBERT ROBINSON.

In Robinson's laboratories, Todd studied anthocyanins (natural pigments that produce the red, blue, and purple coloring in plants), particularly the flower pigments of the rose, mallow, pelargonium, cornflower, and primula. The chemical structure and distribution of chlorophyll and the anthocyanins, as well as the research conducted on them by RICH-

ALEXANDER TODD

ARD WILLSTÄTTER and other investigators, were of considerable interest at the time. In 1933 Todd received a Ph.D. from Oxford for his work on the synthesis of flower pigments. Robinson had taught him that synthesis and degradation of organic compounds were not only complementary methods of analyzing chemical structure but also the means of relating structure to biological function.

Todd returned to Scotland in 1933 and joined the staff of Edinburgh University as an assistant in medical chemistry. In this capacity he collaborated with George Barger in investigating the chemical structure of vitamin B_1, or thiamine, an essential element in the human diet. The absence of thiamine can cause a disease of the nerve cells known as beriberi. Thiamine functions as a coenzyme (the portion of an enzyme needed for digestion or fermentation) in enzyme systems that promote the oxidation of carbohydrates. In Barger's laboratory, Todd synthesized thiamine in crystalline form, a technique that was soon adopted by the British pharmaceutical industry for the large-scale production of vitamin B_1.

In 1936 Todd joined the Lister Institute of Preventive Medicine in London as a lecturer in biochemistry. Continuing his research on vitamins, he concentrated on vitamin E (tocopherol) and vitamin B_{12} (cyanocobalamin). Tocopherol is a fat-soluble vitamin, an antioxidant that tends to stabilize biological membranes, especially those containing polyunsaturated fatty acids. Vitamin B_{12} is a coenzyme required for the normal maturation of red blood cells. A deficiency of vitamin B_{12}

1067

causes pernicious anemia. At the Lister Institute, Todd clarified the chemical structure of vitamin B_{12}. He also studied the active pharmacological principle in *Cannabis sativa,* or marijuana.

In 1938 Todd accepted an appointment as Sir Samuel Hall Professor of Chemistry and director of the chemical laboratories at Manchester University. He was also a visiting professor at the California Institute of Technology at this time. At Manchester, he completed his research on vitamin E and *C. sativa.* In 1942 he was elected a fellow of the Royal Society of London. Two years later, he became professor of organic chemistry and director of the Department of Organic Chemistry at Cambridge, where he was also elected a fellow of Christ's College. He was given complete control of the organization and development of the university chemical laboratory, in keeping with his dictum that responsibility and power are complementary, and that responsibility without power is useless.

In 1942 Todd began to study nucleic acids and nucleotide coenzymes. Employing a variety of techniques, Todd and his associates clarified important details of the chemical structure and reaction mechanisms of the nucleic acids. They also synthesized two important nucleotides, flavin adenine dinucleotide (FAD) and adenosine triphosphate (ATP). FAD is a coenzyme involved in biological oxidation-reduction reactions. ATP contains energy-rich phosphate bonds that are the principal source of energy for the biochemical reactions of living cells. The work of Todd and his associates in the 1940s and 1950s—as well as the research of JAMES D. WATSON and FRANCIS CRICK in the 1950s—eventually elucidated the structure of ribonucleic acid (RNA) and deoxyribonucleic acid (DNA).

Todd was awarded the 1957 Nobel Prize for Chemistry "for his work on nucleotides and nucleotide coenzymes." In his presentation speech, Arne Fredga of the Royal Swedish Academy of Sciences described Todd's fundamental work on the structure of nucleotides as "a solid foundation . . . for future development in this field. Starting from this work, other scientists have advanced very fascinating theories as to the arrangement of the chains [of acids and bases]; it seems that they may be coiled up as a helix with the bases inside."

Todd was elevated to the peerage as Baron Todd of Trumpington in 1962. The following year he was named master of Christ's College and was instrumental in establishing Churchill College, Cambridge.

In 1937 Todd married Alison Sarah Dale, with whom he has one son and two daughters.

Todd's numerous awards include the Lavoisier Medal of the French Chemical Society (1948), the Davy Medal (1949) and Royal Medal (1955) of the Royal Society, the Longstaff Medal of the British Chemical Society (1963), the Copley Medal of the Royal Society (1970), and the Lomonosov Gold Medal of the Soviet Academy of Sciences (1979). From 1950 to 1973 he was managing trustee of the Nuffield Foundation, which funds scientific research in Great Britain. In 1952 he was named chairman of the British government's Advisory Council on Scientific Policy. He served as president of the Royal Society from 1975 to 1980 and holds membership in many other professional societies. He has received honorary degrees from the universities of Durham, London, Glasgow, Warwick, Kiel, Paris, Michigan, and Strasbourg as well as from Harvard, Tufts, Oxford, and Cambridge universities.

SELECTED WORKS: Vitamins, Coenzymes, and Nucleotides, 1949; Problems of the Technological Society, 1973; A Time to Remember: The Autobiography of a Chemist, 1983.

ABOUT: Campbell, W. A., and Greenwood, N. N. Contemporary British Chemists, 1971; Current Biography March 1958; New York Times November 1, 1957; The Way of the Scientist, 1962.

TOMONAGA, SIN-ITIRO
(March 31, 1906–July 8, 1979)
Nobel Prize for Physics, 1965
(shared with Richard P. Feynman and
  Julian S. Schwinger)

The Japanese physicist Sin-itiro Tomonaga (tô mô nä gä') was born in Tokyo, the eldest son of Sanjuro and Hide Tomonaga. In 1913, when his father was appointed professor of philosophy at Kyōto Imperial University, the family moved to Kyōto, where Tomonaga attended the nationally renowned Third High School.

Tomonaga received a bachelor's degree in atomic physics at Kyōto in 1929 and remained there for three more years as a graduate student and as an assistant in the research laboratory of Kajuro Tamaki. One of his colleagues there was HIDEKI YUKAWA, who later predicted the existence of the pion, a particle that transmits the nuclear force between protons

SIN-ITIRO TOMONAGA

and neutrons. In 1932 Tomonaga went to the Institute of Physical and Chemical Research in Tokyo as a research associate in the laboratory of Yoshio Nishina. From 1937 to 1939 he studied at the University of Leipzig with WERNER HEISENBERG. His paper on the physical properties of matter in the nucleus of the atom, published while he was in Germany, was accepted as his doctoral thesis at Tokyo Imperial University in 1939.

In 1941 Tomonaga was appointed professor of physics at Tokyo University of Science and Literature (which was later absorbed into the Tokyo University of Education). During World War II, he worked on radar, a field in which JULIAN S. SCHWINGER, with whom Tomonaga would later share the Nobel Prize, was also active.

Early in his scientific career Tomonaga developed an interest in the field of quantum electrodynamics, and he returned to this interest repeatedly over a period of more than twenty years. His first work in the field was done with Nishina in Tokyo; he pursued it further with Heisenberg in Leipzig and took it up again with his own students in Tokyo during the war. Another major effort began in 1947, and it was this work for which he received the Nobel Prize.

The aim of Tomonaga's research on quantum electrodynamics was to reconcile two of the landmark theories of twentieth-century physics: quantum mechanics and the special theory of relativity. Quantum mechanics, as it was formulated in the mid-1920s, explained the structure of the atom with remarkable success. In one crucial respect, however, this theory was known to be incomplete, for it did not take into account the fact that matter can be converted into energy and vice versa. The possibility of such transformations is a central result of ALBERT EINSTEIN's special theory of relativity.

Starting in 1927, the English physicist P. A. M. DIRAC attempted to bring quantum mechanics and the special theory of relativity into accord. He focused on the relation between electrons and electromagnetic radiation. In the fully developed form of Dirac's theory, a photon, or quantum of electromagnetic energy, could "materialize," giving rise to an electron and a positron (the antimatter counterpart of an electron). Similarly, an electron and a positron could annihilate each other and in the process create a photon. Tomonaga and Nishina investigated these processes in the early 1930s.

Dirac's theory provided a new way of understanding the interactions between electrically charged particles. For example, two nearby electrons could exchange a series of photons, passing them back and forth like medicine balls. The reaction force experienced by each electron as it emits or absorbs a photon would then account for the electromagnetic repulsion that tends to drive electrons apart. The exchanged photons are said to be "virtual" particles because they have only a fleeting existence and can never be detected directly.

The energy of the virtual photons can be calculated from Heisenberg's uncertainty principle, according to which the maximum energy a particle might have depends on the length of time available for measuring the energy. Because the virtual photons exist so briefly, their energies can be large; moreover, as the interacting electrons come closer together, the virtual-photon lifetime becomes still shorter, and the energy limit is raised further. An interesting question is what happens when a single electron emits a virtual photon and then reabsorbs it. In this case, the lifetime of the photon can approach zero, and so its allowable energy is unlimited. The continual emission and reabsorption of such photons would appear to give the electron an infinite mass.

By the early 1940s it was recognized that Dirac's theory predicts that every electron has both an infinite mass and—for similar reasons involving virtual electrons and positrons—an infinite electric charge. These predictions were clearly absurd, since the mass and charge of the electron were known to be finite and indeed rather small. Nevertheless, the theory remained in use because its deficiencies would become apparent only when electrons were examined at extremely close range. For most experiments possible at the time, Dirac's theory gave accurate predictions, and in any case, no better theory was available.

A crisis in quantum electrodynamics arose in 1947 when WILLIS E. LAMB JR. and Robert C. Retherford showed experimentally that one energy level of the electron in the hydrogen atom is shifted slightly from the value predicted by Dirac. At about the same time, POLYKARP KUSCH and his colleagues found that the magnetic moment of the electron also differs slightly from the predicted value. These discrepancies led Tomonaga and Schwinger to reconstruct quantum electrodynamics. Tomonaga, who was isolated in postwar Japan from most Western physicists, heard of Lamb's results not through a scientific journal but from the popular-science column of a weekly American magazine.

There had been earlier attempts to deal with the apparent infinite mass and charge of the electron by simply denying their existence. Tomonaga and Schwinger took another approach: instead of discarding the infinities, they exploited them. They pointed out that the measured mass of the electron must consist of two components: the real, or "bare," mass that an electron would have if it could be observed in isolation, and the mass associated with the cloud of virtual photons (and other virtual particles) that the electron continually emits and reabsorbs. If the photon cloud has an infinite mass, it then follows that the bare mass must also be infinite but negative. When the two contributions to the total mass are added, the infinities cancel each other, leaving only a small, finite residue that corresponds to the measured mass. Using a similar approach with the infinite charge of the electron, Tomonaga and Schwinger postulated an infinitely negative bare charge, which attracted a cloud of positively charged virtual particles. The infinite positive charge of the virtual cloud screened out all but a finite residue of the negative bare charge.

The mathematical procedure Tomonaga and Schwinger devised for canceling infinite masses and charges is called renormalization. Although renormalization gave quantum electrodynamics a secure conceptual foundation, at the outset many physicists considered the cure worse than the disease. Renormalization eliminated some infinities only by introducing others, including masses that are not only infinite but also negative. Tomonaga and Schwinger emphasized, however, that only finite and positive masses are measurable quantities in the theory. An electron can never be separated from its cloud of virtual particles, even in principle, and so the infinite bare mass and charge are forever unobservable. Independently of Tomonaga and Schwinger, and at about the same time, RICHARD P. FEYNMAN discovered a quite different way to express the ideas of quantum electrodynamics. He showed that every interaction between particles (including virtual particles) can be represented by a graph, or diagram, of the particles' trajectories in space and time.

The renormalized theory of quantum electrodynamics has proved to be the most accurate of all physical theories. Certain properties of the electron can be measured to an accuracy of a few parts per billion; the values predicted by the theory are in precise agreement with the experimental results. Furthermore, quantum electrodynamics has served as a model for theories of the other forces of nature, and renormalization is an essential step in making those theories work.

Tomonaga, Feynman, and Schwinger shared the 1965 Nobel Prize for Physics "for their fundamental work in quantum electrodynamics, with deep-ploughing consequences for the physics of elementary particles." In his Nobel lecture Tomonaga discussed the evolution of the ideas that led to his work. The failure of Dirac's theory, he said, "generated in many people a strong distrust of quantum field theory. There were even those with the extreme view that the concept of field reaction itself had nothing to do at all with the true law of nature. . . . Influenced by Heisenberg, I came to believe that the problem of field reactions, far from being meaningless, was one which required a frontal attack."

Tomonaga's work during and immediately after World War II was made known outside Japan primarily through the efforts of Yukawa. As a result, in 1949 Tomonaga was invited to join the Institute for Advanced Study, in Princeton, New Jersey, where he investigated the quantum mechanics of many-body systems, such as solids, and thereby opened a new area of research. When Nishina died in 1951, Tomonaga returned to Japan to direct the Scientific Research Institute. From 1956 to 1962 he was president of the Tokyo University of Education and from 1963 to 1969 served as president of the Science Council of Japan. He also directed the Institute for Optical Research and served on various government committees. He helped establish the Research Institute for Fundamental Physics at

Kyōto University and the Institute for Nuclear Study at Tokyo University.

In 1940 Tomonaga married Ryoko Sekiguchi, the daughter of a director of the Tokyo Metropolitan Observatory. They had two sons and a daughter. Tomonaga died on July 8, 1979.

In addition to the Nobel Prize, Tomonaga received the Japan Academy Prize (1948), the Japanese government's Order of Culture (1952), and the Lomonosov Gold Medal of the Soviet Academy of Sciences (1964). He was a member of the Japan Academy and the Leopoldina German Academy of Researchers in Natural Sciences, a foreign member of the Royal Swedish Academy of Sciences, a corresponding member of the Bavarian Academy of Science, and a foreign associate of the American National Academy of Sciences.

SELECTED WORKS: Quantum Mechanics (2 vols.) 1962–1966; Scientific Papers (2 vols.) 1971–1976.

ABOUT: Physics Today December 1979; Science October 29, 1965.

TOWNES, CHARLES H.
(July 28, 1915–   )
Nobel Prize for Physics, 1964
(shared with Nikolai Basov and Aleksandr Prokhorov)

The American physicist Charles Hard Townes was born in Greenville, South Carolina, the fourth of six children of Henry Keith Townes, a lawyer, and the former Ellen Sumter Hard. Raised on a twenty-acre farm outside Greenville, the boy developed an early curiosity about the natural world. An outstanding student who skipped the seventh grade, he entered Furman University in Greenville at the age of sixteen. With a double major, he earned a B.S. in physics and a B.A. in modern languages in 1935. Although he chose physics for a career, preferring its logic and beauty of structure, he has maintained his ability to read French, German, Spanish, Italian, and Russian. After a year of graduate study at Duke University, Townes received an M.S. in physics in 1936 and then obtained a Ph.D. in 1939 at the California Institute of Technology. His doctoral thesis was "The Separation of Isotopes and the Determination of the Spin of the Nucleus of Carbon 13."

Towne's first job was at Bell Telephone Laboratories, where he stayed from 1939 to

CHARLES H. TOWNES

1947, working principally, and with considerable success, on war-related problems involving airborne radar for use in bombing controls. In one notable instance, his success consisted of predicting failure. Wartime radar used a 3-centimeter wavelength (a frequency of 10,000 megahertz). For postwar use, the Air Force asked Bell Labs to develop a radar system with a 1.25-centimeter wavelength (24,000 megahertz). Not only was the higher-frequency radar expected to be more accurate, but it would weigh less and take up less aircraft space. Townes predicted that the new system would be ineffective because water vapor in the atmosphere characteristically absorbed energy of this frequency. Unconvinced, the Air Force had the radar built, and it failed. However, the experience stimulated Townes's interest in the interaction of high-frequency radio waves (microwaves) with molecules.

In 1948 Townes was appointed associate professor of physics at Columbia University. He became executive director of the university's Radiation Laboratory in 1950, served as chairman of the physics department from 1952 to 1955, and remained as full professor until 1961. During this period, he also studied music and voice in evening classes at the Juilliard School of Music. Pursuing his studies at Columbia, Townes found that the absorption of microwaves formed the basis of a new technique, microwave spectroscopy, for probing molecular structure.

In Townes's work at Bell Labs, radar waves had been generated by electrons oscillating in resonant metal cavities machined to precise dimensions. The dimensions determined the wavelength, and the shortest attainable wavelength was about 1 millimeter (300,000 megahertz). Townes conceived of an alternative using the natural properties of molecules that overcame this limitation.

Physicists in the late nineteenth and early twentieth centuries had learned that atoms and molecules exist in discrete energy states, or levels, the lowest of which is called the ground state. The set of "allowed" levels is unique to a particular atom or molecule. The energy is related to the configurations and motions of the electrons bound to the atoms. Also, electromagnetic radiation such as heat, radio waves, and light consist of discrete packets of energy (photons) whose energy is proportional to the frequency. An atom or molecule can absorb a photon whose energy equals the difference between two levels and thus rise to the higher level. It is then said to be in an excited state. Excited atoms or molecules therefore have excess energy. Shortly after becoming excited, they spontaneously return to the lower energy level, giving up energy in the form of a photon whose energy equals the difference between the two levels. In 1917 ALBERT EINSTEIN had discovered stimulated emission, a third process in the interaction between radiation and matter in addition to absorption and spontaneous emission. In this process, excited atoms or molecules exposed to radiation whose photon energy corresponds to the difference between the excited and ground levels immediately drop back to the ground state, emitting photons indistinguishable from the ones that stimulated the drop.

Townes realized that stimulated emission provided a means of releasing the excess energy of excited molecules, in effect amplifying the radiation that triggered the release. To do so, it was necessary to produce a large population of excited molecules compared with those existing in the ground state. Townes conceived a practical way of accomplishing this through positive feedback in a resonant circuit arrangement, similar in principle to the oscillators that generate radio waves in broadcast transmitters.

NIKOLAI BASOV and ALEKSANDR PROKHOROV independently came to similar conclusions in the Soviet Union. Townes, assisted by graduate students at Columbia University, produced a working device in December 1953 and called it a maser, an acronym for *m*icrowave *a*mplification by *s*timulated *e*mission of *r*adiation. In the first maser, ammonia molecules were passed through specially arranged electric fields that tended to reject molecules in the ground state and focus excited molecules into a resonant cavity. When the cavity contained a sufficient concentration of excited molecules, it was capable of oscillating. A small amount of radiation of the correct frequency (photon energy equal to the difference between the ground state and excited state of the ammonia molecule) could start an avalanche of stimulated emission, excitation of more molecules from the ground state, and more stimulated emission. The result was an intensified output of radiation. The energy difference between the ground state and the excited state of the ammonia molecule determined the energy of the emitted photons and therefore the frequency, which in this case was in the microwave range.

Masers were soon found to possess frequencies so stable that they could serve as highly accurate clocks. Using two masers, Townes and his colleagues checked, and confirmed, Einstein's theory of special relativity in a test that has been called the most precise physical experiment in history.

While Townes was on sabbatical leave at the University of Paris in 1956, he and his colleagues demonstrated that maser action could occur by a three-level process in some solid crystals that contained impurities. Radiation of suitable frequency could excite the atoms of the impurity to the highest of three levels. The atoms would then lose some of their energy and become "trapped" at a relatively stable intermediate energy state. Maser action and emission of excess energy as radiation would then involve a drop from the intermediate to the ground state, amplifying incoming radiation of the same frequency. In such a system, energy must be supplied to the maser medium at a higher frequency (shorter wavelength) than the frequency to be amplifed because it must first excite the atoms to the higher third level. Soon the maser was developed as a sensitive, low-noise amplifier for microwave reception in many different systems. In radio astronomy, for example, it permitted detection of radio sources at great distances from earth.

In 1958 Townes and his brother-in-law, ARTHUR L. SCHAWLOW, described the requirements for building masers to operate at the higher frequencies of infrared, visible, and ultraviolet light. Two years later, the American physicist Theodore H. Maiman built such a device that produced red light, using a rod of synthetic ruby with mirrored ends as a resonant chamber and exciting the atoms of chromium that were an impurity in the ruby. It was called a laser, for *l*ight *a*mplification by *s*timulated *e*mission of *r*adiation. Further development of lasers was explosive, creating the field of quantum electronics. Lasers are now used in communications, metalworking, medicine, instrumentation and measurement, art, and military applications.

Townes shared the 1964 Nobel Prize for Physics with Nikolai Basov and Aleksandr Prokhorov "for [their] fundamental work in the field of quantum electronics, which has led to the construction of oscillators and amplifiers based on the maser-laser principle."

From 1959 to 1961 Townes served as vice president and director of research at the Institute for Defense Analyses (IDA), dealing with problems of defense policy, strategy, and weapons systems. In 1961 he was named provost and professor of physics at the Massachusetts Institute of Technology, and in 1966 he was appointed University Professor of Physics at the University of California at Berkeley, a position he still holds.

Since his days at IDA, Townes has remained active in matters of science policy, serving on numerous corporate and government committees. At the University of California, Townes and colleagues in the fields of infrared and microwave astronomy discovered the first polyatomic molecules in interstellar space, ammonia and water. He also introduced advanced methods of infrared detection, using laser oscillators, for astronomical spectroscopy and interferometry. This work led to the development, in 1987, of a system of mobile infrared telescopes which, according to Townes, will yield as much as 100 times the amount of detail provided by conventional radio telescopes.

Townes served as a trustee of the Salk Institute for Biological Studies from 1963 to 1968 and of the Rand Corporation between 1965 and 1970. He was a member of the scientific advisory board of the United States Air Force from 1958 to 1961 and served as chairman of NASA's Science and Technology Advisory Committee for Manned Space Flight from 1964 to 1969. In 1969 he was a member of the President's Task Force for National Scientific Policy. Between 1971 and 1973 he was a science adviser to the General Motors Corporation.

In 1941 Townes married Frances H. Brown. They have four daughters. An amateur naturalist, Townes enjoys music, languages, skin diving, and travel.

In addition to the Nobel Prize, Townes has received the Comstock Prize of the National Academy of Sciences (1959); the Stuart Bal-

lantine Medal of the Franklin Institute (1959, 1962); the David Sarnoff Award in Electronics of the American Institute of Electrical Engineers (1961); the John A. Carty Medal of the National Academy of Sciences (1962); the Distinguished Public Service Medal of the National Aeronautics and Space Administration (1969); the Niels Bohr International Gold Medal of the Danish Society of Civil, Electrical, and Mechanical Engineers (1979); and the National Medal of Science of the National Science Foundation (1982). He is a member of the National Academy of Sciences, the Institute of Electrical and Electronics Engineers, the American Academy of Arts and Sciences, the American Philosophical Society, and the American Astronomical Society. He is a foreign member of the Royal Society of London. He has received honorary degrees from more than twenty colleges and universities and has served on the editorial boards of the *Review of Scientific Instruments,* the *Physical Review,* and the *Journal of Molecular Spectroscopy.*

SELECTED WORKS: Molecular Microwave Spectra Tables, 1952, with Paul Kisliuk; Microwave Spectroscopy, 1955, with Arthur L. Schawlow.

ABOUT: Berland, T. The Scientific Life, 1962; Current Biography March 1963; National Geographic Society. Those Inventive Americans, 1971; Science November 7, 1964; Thomas, S. Men of Space, volume 5, 1962; The Way of the Scientist, 1962.

TUTU, DESMOND
(October 7, 1931–)
Nobel Prize for Peace, 1984

Desmond Mpilo Tutu, South African archbishop, was born in the gold-mining town of Klerksdorp, Witwatersrand, in the Transvaal region of South Africa. His father, Zachariah Tutu, from the Xhosa Bantu tribe, taught in a Methodist school during Tutu's youth. His mother, Aletta, of Tswana tribal ancestry, worked as a domestic servant. Although baptized a Methodist, Tutu was raised in the Anglican faith after his parents changed denominations. When the family moved to Johannesburg, Tutu took as his mentor and role model Trevor Huddleston, an Anglican cleric and outspoken critic of apartheid.

After graduating from Western High School, Johannesburg, Tutu earned a diploma from the Bantu Normal College in Pretoria and a B.A. from the University of Johannesburg. From 1954 to 1957 he taught high school. In

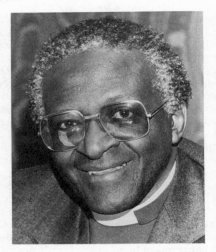

DESMOND TUTU

1955 he married Leah Nomalizo Shenxane. They have three daughters and a son.

In 1957, when the government instituted a state-administered system of inferior Bantu education for black students, Tutu resigned his teaching post in protest and decided to enter the ministry. "I was not moved by very high ideals," he explained many years later. "It just seemed that if the church would accept me, this might be a likely means of service." Following Father Huddleston's example, he entered the Community of the Redemption, a religious order that stressed daily Communion, regular prayer, and meditative retreat. The experience deepened his faith. He received his licentiate in theology from St. Peter's Theological College, Johannesburg, in 1960 and was ordained an Anglican priest the following year.

Tutu's vocational change coincided with significant political developments in South Africa. In 1910 the Union of South Africa had been established as a constitutional monarchy within the British Commonwealth. After World War II the Afrikaner-dominated National party legalized the system of racial segregation known as apartheid. In the 1950s further restrictions on the liberties of the black majority brought about riots at home and criticism from the United Nations abroad. Led by ALBERT LUTHULI, the African National Congress sought a peaceful political solution but was banned in 1960. That October the white minority approved a referendum to withdraw from the commonwealth and establish a republican form of government. On May 31, 1961, the Union of South Africa officially became the Republic of South Africa.

While South Africa was shedding its British ties, Tutu was serving in ministerial assignments at St. Alban's Church, Benoni (1960–1961), and at St. Philip's Church, Alberton (1961–1962). He spent the next four years studying abroad, supporting his family with parish service while he earned a B.A. in divinity and an M.A. in theology from King's College, London. Returning to South Africa, Tutu lectured at the Federal Theological Seminary in Alice from 1967 to 1969 and at the National University of Lesotho from 1970 to 1971.

Tutu later described his experience in England as one that enabled him to cultivate "the proper self-assertion"—that is, the confidence to disagree openly with whites. In 1972 he went again to England as associate director of the Theological Education Fund. In that position he administered scholarship funds for the World Council of Churches and traveled throughout Asia and black Africa. When he returned to South Africa in 1975, it was as Anglican dean of the Johannesburg cathedral. The following year, he was consecrated as the bishop of Lesotho.

For Tutu, religion and politics cannot be compartmentalized. "The God of the Bible is first encountered," he has argued, "not in a religious setting but in an out-and-out political experience, in helping a rabble of slaves to escape from bondage." Thus, in 1976, when angry Soweto youths turned to violence, Tutu worked with the black activist Nhato Motlana in efforts to channel mob anger into peaceful demonstrations. Nonetheless, riots in June of that year left 600 Soweto blacks dead in the streets. Before the crisis exploded, Tutu had sent Prime Minister Balthazar Vorster a warning letter. Thereafter, Tutu's motives were viewed by the government with suspicion and mistrust.

In 1978 Tutu became secretary-general of the South African Council of Churches, an interdenominational, interracial affiliate of the World Council of Churches. Under Tutu's leadership, the organization, which represents 13 million Christians, more than 80 percent of them black, has challenged the government to dismantle apartheid. Much of the council's budget has been used to provide legal assistance for imprisoned blacks and political detainees and to sustain their families. In 1979 Tutu openly criticized the South African government for its so-called homelands policy, which required the forcible relocation of urban blacks to barren tribal reservations. In Denmark that fall, he further antagonized Afrikaner officials by appearing on television and urging the Danish government to cease its purchases of South African coal.

Although his passport was twice confiscated, an action generally regarded as a serious warning, Tutu continued to advocate international economic pressure against South Africa. He also warned government officials that failure to change their policy would lead inexorably to a bloodbath. In response, the government appointed a judicial body, the Eloff Commission, to investigate the financial affairs of the South African Council of Churches. Its report, published in February 1984, criticized the council's financial management, recommended a law that would make it a crime to advocate disinvestment in South Africa, and denounced Tutu's political support of the outlawed African National Congress.

Later that year, while Tutu was on sabbatical at the General Theological Seminary in New York City, the Norwegian Nobel Committee announced that Tutu was its choice to receive the 1984 Nobel Prize for Peace. Egil Aarvik of the Nobel committee stated, "This year's award should be seen as a renewed recognition of the courage and heroism shown by black South Africans in their use of peaceful methods in the struggle against apartheid. . . . It is the committee's wish that the Peace Prize now awarded should be regarded not only as a gesture of support to him and to the South African Council of Churches of which he is leader, but also to all individuals and groups in South Africa who, with their concern for human dignity, fraternity, and democracy, incite the admiration of the world."

In his Nobel lecture, Tutu stated his belief that "there is no peace because there is no justice." Later, he exhorted, "Let us work to be peacemakers, those given a wonderful share in our Lord's ministry of reconciliation. If we want peace, so we have been told, let us work for justice. Let us beat our swords into plowshares."

In November 1984 a synod of Anglican bishops named Tutu the first black Anglican bishop of Johannesburg. He was raised to archbishop two years later. Since becoming bishop, he has chosen to live in the black township of Soweto rather than move to the bishop's traditional residence in a white section of Johannesburg.

Although tension and violence in South Africa have increased since he won the Nobel Prize, Bishop Tutu has continued to hold his moderate position. His advocacy of peaceful change has come under sharp attack from impatient radicals. "We are struggling not to oppress somebody else," he has explained, "but in order to free everybody."

Tutu has traveled and lectured widely to encourage economic sanctions against South Africa. In the United States he has met with business and political leaders. In a speech in Atlanta in January 1986, he promised civil disobedience in South Africa if the South African government did not alter its policies of racial discrimination. In South Africa he has spoken out vigorously for black unity. As confrontation has deepened, his two roles of moderate in the black community and apostle of peace to the whites have become more difficult to sustain.

Called "impish" and "feisty," the diminutive bishop exudes a spirit of joy. Whispers, shouts, sobs, and roars of laughter punctuate his highly emotional speeches, which are delivered in a high-pitched Etonian accent.

During the 1985 enthronement ceremonies at the Cathedral of St. Mary the Virgin, Tutu implored the white minority in South Africa to understand the blacks. "It is that we too are just ordinary human beings. We too love to be with our wives every day, we too want our children to rush out to meet us as we come back from work. These are not extravagant demands," Tutu continued. "They are the expectation of any human being. We want to have a new kind of South Africa where we all, black and white, can walk tall together, black and white, into the glorious future which God is opening up before us."

WORKS BY: The Divine Intention, 1982; Crying in the Wilderness, 1982; Hope and Suffering: Sermons and Speeches, 1983.

ABOUT: Christian Century April 13, 1983; Current Biography January 1985; Greene, C. Bishop Desmond Tutu, 1986; New York Times October 17, 1984; New York Times Magazine March 14, 1982; Thompson, L. M. The Political Mythology of Apartheid, 1985; Tlhagale, B., and Mosala, I. (eds.) Hammering Swords Into Ploughshares: Essays in Honor of Archbishop Mpilo Desmond Tutu, 1987.

UNDSET, SIGRID
(May 20, 1882–June 10, 1949)
Nobel Prize for Literature, 1928

The Norwegian novelist Sigrid Undset (ŏŏn' set) was born in Kalundborg, Denmark, the eldest of three daughters. Her father was the distinguished Norwegian archaeologist

Ingvald Martin Undset. Her mother was the former Anna Charlotte Gyth, a Dane. When Undset was two, the family moved to Christiania (now Oslo), Norway, where her father had been appointed director of the city's Museum of Antiquities. Her earliest memories were of playing with artifacts at the museum. Later, she often assisted her father with his research there.

In the expectation that she would become a scientist, Undset's family sent her to a progressive coeducational school. However, she disliked the school's enthusiastic liberalism and, after her father's death in 1893, enrolled in a commercial school to take business courses. Her family's financial situation deteriorated, and she began working at the age of seventeen. Her job as a clerk in the office of an electrical engineering firm helped finance her sisters' education. In her spare time Undset studied literature, especially the Norse sagas which she had studied with her father and which were to exert an influence profoundly on her work. Increasingly, she turned her attention from botany and painting to writing.

In 1905 a draft of her first novel, a historical work, was turned down by an Oslo publisher who advised her, "Don't try your hand at more historical novels. . . . Try to write something modern." Accepting this advice, she turned to an examination of marriage, parenthood, and human relationships in contemporary Oslo in her first published novel, *Fru Marta Oulie* (Mrs. Marta Oulie, 1907). A collection of short stories, *Den lykkelige alder* (The Happiest Years), appeared the following year. Both the novel and the stories depict the strivings of twentieth-century tradespeople and feature gifted but alienated women as their protagonists. Her second novel, *Fortellingen om Viga-Ljot og Vigdis* (1909, later translated as *Gunnar's Daughter*), is an imitation of an Icelandic saga. While admiring Undset's vivid descriptions of the Norwegian countryside, critics gave these first three books only mild praise.

Shortly after the publication of *Gunnar's Daughter,* a government scholarship enabled Undset to leave the clerical job at which she had labored for ten years. She then traveled to several cities in Germany and Italy, including Rome, where she met and fell in love with the Norwegian painter Anders Castus Svarstad, a married man thirteen years her senior. Their affair provided the background for her next novel, *Jenny: Roman* (*Jenny: A Novel,* 1911). This roman à clef became her first critical success. Set in Norway and Italy, *Jenny* is the story of an artistic young woman who be-

SIGRID UNDSET

comes tragically involved with an older man and his son.

Following Svarstad's divorce, Undset and he were married in Brussels in 1912. They returned to Norway after the birth of their first son, living first in Ski and then on a farm in the small city of Lillehammer, where Undset gave birth to another son and to a mentally retarded daughter. From 1912 to 1920, in spite of frequent ill health, Undset produced two collections of short stories, the novel *Vaaren* (Spring, 1914), and the novellas collected in *Splinten av troldspeilet* (*Images in a Mirror,* 1917). In *Vaaren,* Undset illustrates the idea that compromise in marriage can sometimes create more unhappiness than love outside it. The short stories and novellas typically contain portraits of strong-willed women coping with the problems of modern life.

During World War I, Undset began to question the value of such contemporary Norwegian trends as feminism, socialism, liberalism, and pacifism. After a period of soul-searching, she confirmed her essentially conservative outlook by converting from Lutheranism to Catholicism in 1924. Meanwhile, her marriage had gradually disintegrated. In 1925 it was dissolved on the grounds that the Catholic church did not recognize Svarstad's divorce from his first wife, who was still living. Undset never remarried.

Her ongoing historical studies persuaded Undset that "only the saints seemed to know the true explanation of man's hunger for happiness, peace, justice, and goodness." Her depth of religious conviction became evident in Undset's masterwork, the *Kristin Lavrans-datter* trilogy, consisting of the novels *Kransen* (1920, translated in the United Kingdom as *The Garland* and in the United States as *The Bridal Wreath*), *Husfrue* (1922, translated as *The Mistress of Husaby*), and *Korset* (*The Cross*, 1922). Set in fourteenth-century Norway, the trilogy traces the progress of Kristin, the proud and beautiful daughter of a prosperous land-owner. After marrying a basically unworthy man, Kristin endures much hardship and misfortune, helps victims of the Black Death, and eventually succumbs to the plague herself.

Although *Kristin Lavransdatter* includes no historical figures, Undset accurately recreated medieval life by incorporating details from such primary sources as laws and ballads. In a 1923 review, the critic Edwin Björkman noted that she realistically "give[s] us pictures of the early fourteenth century in Norway so intimate that they make us feel as if we were reading about this morning's happenings in our own particular back alley." Kristin may be a figure "woven out of a poet's fantasy," as Björkman remarked, but the mood of the book is neither sentimental nor romantic. Complementing her impeccable scholarship, Undset blended modern psychological insights with a narrative technique reminiscent of the Norse sagas, in which emphasis is on the tale rather than the teller. The American critic Alrik Gustafson, writing in 1940, was impressed with "the apparent effortlessness of the artistic performance, the seeming lack of any conscious narrative devices or tricks, the complete absence of style in the narrow literary sense of the word."

Undset's next venture into the realm of historical fiction came in the Olav Audunssøn saga, an elaborate revision of the story that had been rejected by the Oslo publishers some twenty years earlier. First published in two volumes, *Olav Audunssøn i Hestviken* (The Master of Hestviken, 1925) and *Olav Audunssøn og hans børn* (Olav Audunssøn and His Children, 1927), the series was subsequently published in English in four parts: *The Axe, The Snake Pit, In the Wilderness,* and *The Son Avenger.* The entire tetralogy is generally known as *The Master of Hestviken.* Like *Kristin Lavransdatter,* it is a lengthy medieval tale in which the characters' many misfortunes frequently result from their excessive pride. Echoing other critics, Gustafson considered the Kristin epic a finer achievement, because "it is less gloomy, less essentially tragic in its final moral implications than is *The Master of Hest-*

viken," in which the author's moralizing tone often interferes with the narrative flow.

Undset was awarded the 1928 Nobel Prize for Literature "principally for her powerful descriptions of Northern life during the Middle Ages." In his presentation speech, Per Hallström of the Swedish Academy traced Undset's work from the early fiction set in contemporary Oslo, in which "she portrayed [modern women] sympathetically but with merciless truthfulness . . . and conveyed the evolution of their destinies with the most implacable logic," through her accomplishments in imaginatively recreating Scandinavian life during the Middle Ages. Hallström particularly noted her perceptive analysis of the demands of honor and faith, as well as her depiction of the complex relations between men and women. He concluded by calling her "a poetic genius whose roots must be in a great and well-ordered spirit." Undset did not deliver a Nobel lecture, saying in her brief acceptance speech that "I write more readily than I speak and I am especially reluctant to talk about myself."

The five novels Undset published between the time she won the Nobel Prize and the outbreak of World War II treat contemporary themes and reflect her profound Catholicism. Indeed, their stress on the efficacy of the Catholic faith overshadows all other elements, and they are not as rich in detail or symbolism as her historical fiction of the previous decade. During this time she also discussed her beliefs in numerous essays, notably those gathered in *Etapper: Ny række* (*Stages on the Road,* 1933).

In 1939 Undset suffered the loss of both her mother and her daughter. When Norway was occupied by the Germans in April 1940, Undset joined the Resistance, but she was soon forced to flee to Sweden. Nazi authorities, angered by her articles denouncing Nazi racial intolerance and by her firm religious faith, banned her books in Norway as well as in Germany. In September 1940, she and her son Hans went to the United States, where they remained for the duration of the war. She resided mainly in Brooklyn, New York, but traveled periodically, lecturing throughout the country. She also carried out assignments for the London-based Norwegian government-in-exile. Her elder son, Anders, was killed during fighting in Norway early in 1940. Upon her return to her homeland at the end of the war, she was decorated by the King of Norway with the Grand Cross of the Order of Saint Olav "for eminent services to literature and the nation." Undset died of a stroke at her home at Lillehammer on June 10, 1949.

Although her early and late works alike are infrequently read, critics continue to praise *Kristin Lavransdatter*. Since its original publication in the 1920s, it has remained almost continuously in print both in Norway and the United States. Writing in 1940, Alrik Gustafson claimed that "among living novelists, one is prone to rank [Undset] next to THOMAS MANN." Gustafson also compared her favorably to George Eliot and Sir Walter Scott. Writing in 1985, the American scholar A. G. Medlicott praised Undset's work from a contemporary perspective, calling *Kristin Lavransdatter* "a genuinely great novel . . . clearly one of the most splendid things written in this century."

ADDITIONAL WORKS IN ENGLISH TRANSLATION: The Wild Orchid, 1931; The Burning Bush, 1932; Ida Elisabeth, 1933; The Longest Years, 1935; The Faithful Wife, 1937; Men, Women, and Places, 1939; Madame Dorothea, 1940; Happy Times in Norway, 1942; Sigurd and His Brave Companions, 1943; Four Stories, 1978.

ABOUT: Bayerschmidt, C. F. Sigrid Undset, 1970; Drake, W. A. Contemporary European Writers, 1928; Gustafson, A. Six Scandinavian Novelists, 1940; Monroe, N. E. The Novel and Society, 1941; Vinde, V. Sigrid Undset: A Nordic Moralist, 1930; Winsnes, A. H. Sigrid Undset: A Study in Christian Realism, 1953.

UNITED NATIONS CHILDREN'S FUND

(founded December 11, 1946)
Nobel Prize for Peace, 1965

The United Nations Children's Fund was established in 1946 as the United Nations International Children's Emergency Fund (UNICEF) by a unanimous resolution of the United Nations General Assembly. Its immediate purpose was to provide aid for the estimated 20 million children living in substandard conditions in the refugee camps and war-ravaged cities of Europe.

Shortly after UNICEF's founding, United Nations Secretary-General Trygve Lie appointed Maurice Pate its first executive director. Pate was an American who had worked with Herbert Hoover in European relief efforts during World War I. Under Pate's leadership, UNICEF spent approximately $112 million in its first three years of operation. It distributed clothing to five million children and mothers in twelve countries, vaccinated eight million children against tuberculosis, rebuilt milk processing and distribution facilities, and provided a daily supplementary meal to millions of children. The distribution of powdered milk donated by the United States and other nations with dairy surpluses was a prominent feature of UNICEF's postwar relief efforts.

With economic recovery in Europe, due largely to the European Recovery Plan (or Marshall Plan, after GEORGE C. MARSHALL), the General Assembly in 1950 directed UNICEF to turn its attention from emergency aid to long-term programs designed to improve the health and nutrition of children in the developing nations. Recognizing that the welfare of the world's children would be an ongoing concern, the General Assembly voted in December 1953 to continue the work of the fund indefinitely and to treat it as a permanent agency of the United Nations, with headquarters in New York City. Although the words *international* and *emergency* were dropped from the fund's title at this time, the acronym UNICEF was retained because it had become so well known throughout the world.

In the 1950s UNICEF spent some $150 million in campaigns against tuberculosis, yaws, leprosy, and malaria. It also worked to improve sanitation and to provide prenatal and child health care education in the developing nations. It increasingly emphasized the importance of nutrition. Working with the United Nations Food and Agriculture Organization (FAO) and World Health Organization (WHO), UNICEF helped develop alternative high-quality protein foods for areas such as Indonesia where dairy products were not widely available. One result of this effort was the development of soybean milk. More than forty countries received UNICEF aid to help increase rural production of poultry, vegetables, and fruit.

UNICEF expanded its efforts to include social services for children and their families in 1958. It instituted informal training in child rearing and home improvement, established day-care centers and youth clubs, and developed family counseling programs.

A 1961 report by UNICEF's thirty-nation executive board announced a significant change in the fund's operating policy. Henceforth, in addition to providing general aid throughout the world, the organization would also coordinate its efforts with individual nations to deal with their specific needs. Subsequently, UNICEF began providing assistance for teacher training, curriculum development, vocational education, and technical assistance.

UNICEF was awarded the 1965 Nobel Prize for Peace in recognition of its role in promoting brotherhood among nations. In presenting the award, Aase Lionæs of the Norwegian Nobel Committee spoke of the disparate conditions in the world's nations and UNICEF's role in promoting peace. "Today the people of the developing countries are fully alive to their own misery; and they are determined to leave it behind," she said. "They contemplate the riches of the West . . . and they compare them with the misery of their own children. This contrast creates a dangerous tension factor that threatens the peace of the world. . . . The aim of UNICEF is to spread a table decked with all the good things that nature provides, for all the children of the world. For this reason the organization is a peace factor of great importance." Lionæs called UNICEF "the breakthrough of the idea of international cooperation."

Maurice Pate died shortly before the award was made; it was accepted by UNICEF's new executive director, the American diplomat Henry Labouisse. He paid tribute to Pate as a "great practical idealist" and "UNICEF's architect and builder." Labouisse went on to discuss briefly the importance of the fund. "The welfare of today's children," he declared, "is inseparably linked with the peace of tomorrow's world." The following day, the chairman of UNICEF's executive board, the Israeli Zena Harman, delivered a Nobel lecture on behalf of UNICEF in which she gave further details of the fund's work. UNICEF used the prize money to establish a prize fund in the name of Maurice Pate. Given yearly, the Maurice Pate Memorial Award is, in the words of a 1986 UNICEF statement, "used to strengthen the training or experience of people serving in child welfare–related fields in countries with which UNICEF [is] cooperating."

Since receiving the Nobel Prize, UNICEF has continued its efforts to improve the quality of life for children in developing countries, enlisting the support of other international, nongovernmental agencies. In 1975 the fund's annual budget for the first time surpassed $100 million.

The only United Nations agency devoted entirely to the welfare of children, UNICEF works only in countries that request its aid. Originally, every country receiving UNICEF assistance was required to bear half the cost of the fund's work in that country. However, since the adoption of the individual-nation approach, sliding scales based on need and ability to pay have been introduced to determine a program's cost to a particular nation. At present, UNICEF provides technical assist-

ance and advice as well as food and material; the host country makes a relatively equal contribution in the form of basic implements, support personnel, lodging, and transportation facilities. Funded solely by voluntary contributions, most of UNICEF's budget is supplied by members of the United Nations. A small amount comes from charitable organizations, the sale of UNICEF holiday greeting cards, and other fund-raising drives.

Although it is an agency of the United Nations, UNICEF is now a semiautonomous organization. It is administered by an executive board of representatives from thirty member countries that meets regularly to set policy, consider requests for assistance, allocate aid, evaluate the progress of projects, and set the operating budget. In addition to its headquarters at the United Nations complex in New York City, UNICEF has some thirty regional offices in Europe, North America, South America, Asia, and Africa, staffed by a total of about 600·workers.

Since its founding, UNICEF has compiled an impressive record of achievement. Through its programs, hundreds of millions of children have been examined and treated for such potentially deadly diseases as trachoma, yaws, tuberculosis, malaria, and leprosy. Several thousand maternity wards and health centers have been established, usually in regions where such facilities were previously unknown. As of 1985, UNICEF had supplied and equipped more than a million schools, nearly 900,000 water systems, and some 700,000 child-nutrition centers. In addition, UNICEF has provided equipment for thousands of family centers, community gardens, and canteens; served millions of supplementary meals and supplied nearly as many articles of clothing; and rendered emergency aid to hundreds of thousands of victims of floods, earthquakes, famine, and other disasters.

The challenges confronting UNICEF in the contemporary world remain enormous. According to the fund's own surveys, there are more than a billion impoverished children in the world today. Progress in preventing infant mortality and early childhood diseases has, in turn, brought new problems of overpopulation and underemployment. As the Indian leader Jawaharlal Nehru remarked, in a world of science and technology, UNICEF has never "lost sight of the fact that, in the last analysis, development depends on the human factor."

SELECTED PUBLICATIONS: Report on Child Nutrition, 1947; For the Children, 1949; UNICEF for All the World's Children, 1952; UNICEF in Asia, 1954; Around the World With UNICEF, 1956; Children of the Developing Countries, 1963; Each and Every Child, 1964; Children's Progress, 1968; UNICEF Study on the Young Child, 1976; UNICEF in Bangladesh, 1982; The Impact of World Recession on Children, 1984.

PERIODICALS: (annual) The State of the World's Children; Report of the Executive Board; The Neglected Years; Annual Progress Report of the Executive Director. (semiannual) Assignment Children. (quarterly) UNICEF News. (periodically) Forum d'Idées.

ABOUT: Gray, V. Love Is Not Enough, 1984; Heilbroner, R. L. Mankind's Children: The Story of UNICEF, 1959; Keeny, S. M. Half the World's Children: A Diary of UNICEF at Work in Asia, 1957; Russell, V. The History of UNICEF, 1974; Yates, E. Rainbow Round the World: A Story of UNICEF, 1954.

HAROLD C. UREY

UNITED NATIONS HIGH COMMISSIONER FOR REFUGEES
See OFFICE OF THE UNITED NATIONS HIGH COMMISSIONER FOR REFUGEES

UREY, HAROLD C.
(April 29, 1893–January 5, 1981)
Nobel Prize for Chemistry, 1934

The American chemist Harold Clayton Urey (ü' ri) was born in Walkerton, Indiana, to Cora Rebecca (Reinoehl) and Samuel Clayton Urey. Urey's father, a schoolteacher and minister of the Brethren church, died when the boy was six years old, and his mother later married another clergyman.

Although his progress in a rural grammar school was marked with difficulty, Urey received his high school diploma in 1911. After three months of teacher training, he taught in country schools for three years, first in Indiana and later in Montana. He entered the University of Montana in 1914, where he majored in zoology with a minor in chemistry. Receiving his B.S. three years later, he took a job as a research chemist with the Barrett Chemical Company in Philadelphia. Industrial chemistry proved to be dissatisfying, however, and he returned to the University of Montana in 1919 as a chemistry instructor. Two years later

he received a fellowship for graduate studies in chemistry at the University of California, Berkeley.

The early 1920s were years of great ferment in the physical sciences. The revolution prompted by MAX PLANCK's quantum theory and ALBERT EINSTEIN's special and general relativity theories, as well as NIELS BOHR's planetary model of the atom, were determinative for theoretical chemistry. Few American scientists realized this better than the physical chemist Gilbert N. Lewis, who taught Urey at Berkeley and encouraged his interest in pursuing the relation between physics and chemistry. After earning his Ph.D. in chemistry in 1923, Urey received an American-Scandinavian Foundation Fellowship to study at Niels Bohr's Institute for Theoretical Physics in Denmark. There he augmented his knowledge of physics, studying under Bohr and other leading scientists.

Returning to the United States in 1924, Urey became an associate in chemistry at the Johns Hopkins University. In this capacity he studied molecular thermodynamics and structure and the light absorption and emission spectra of atoms. The current developments in quantum chemistry were summarized by Urey and Arthur Ruark in Atoms, Molecules, and Quanta, published in 1930.

Urey was appointed associate professor of chemistry at Columbia University in New York City in 1929. At this time scientists had already used spectroscopy to identify isotopes of carbon, nitrogen, and oxygen. (An isotope has as many protons as the parent element but a different number of neutrons.) These discoveries indicated the probable existence of a hydrogen isotope. Urey set out to isolate an isotope that would be twice as massive as ordinary hydrogen.

His first step was to secure a supply of hydrogen containing high concentrations of the suspected isotope. Based on calculations, he devised a distillation process for normal liquid hydrogen in which the lighter isotope would evaporate faster than the heavier one. At Urey's request one of his former students, Ferdinand Brickwedde, a government scientist, produced suitably concentrated samples with this process. Meanwhile, Urey calculated the probable line spectra of the heavier isotope. With an assistant, George Murphy, he analyzed the spectra for hydrogen gas and found faint lines where he had predicted that lines for the isotope would appear. Examining the more concentrated samples, he readily detected the calculated lines and thus confirmed the isotope's existence. In December 1931 he announced his discovery, naming this second-lightest atom deuterium, from the Greek *deuteros* ("second"). He also proposed the name *tritium* for a subsequently discovered isotope with three times the mass of hydrogen.

Deuterium offered a convenient model for physicists and chemists studying nuclear particle interactions, and its discovery accelerated isotope research. It became a valuable tool in other research as well. For example, deuterium can replace hydrogen in water molecules to produce so-called heavy water, used to moderate nuclear fission reactions; its fusion with tritium fuels the thermonuclear reaction in hydrogen bombs. Since deuterium compounds chemically resemble hydrogen compounds, the isotope can also be used to trace biochemical reactions in living tissue.

Urey received the 1934 Nobel Prize for Chemistry "for his discovery of heavy hydrogen." He did not attend the awards ceremonies because of the birth of his third daughter, but he delivered a Nobel lecture in Stockholm three months later. In the lecture he discussed the rationale and experimental conditions involved in his isolation of deuterium. "It is my expectation," he said, "that the next few years will witness the separation of the isotopes of the lighter elements in sufficient quantities for effective research in chemistry, physics, and biology. If this can be effected, the work on deuterium is only the beginning of a very interesting scientific development."

The same year that he received the Nobel Prize, Urey became a professor at Columbia, and between 1939 and 1942 he also served as an executive officer of the chemistry department there. From 1933 to 1940 Urey was the first editor of the *Journal of Chemical Physics*.

With the outbreak of World War II, Urey and other American scientists feared that Nazi Germany would use nuclear fission (discovered by OTTO HAHN, Lise Meitner, and Fritz Strassmann in 1939) to develop an atomic weapon. In 1942 the United States government organized the Manhattan Project in an effort to develop such a bomb. The device would require the fissionable isotope uranium 235. As head of the Substitute Alloy Materials Laboratory at Columbia, Urey directed research into methods of separating this isotope from the more common uranium 238.

In 1945 Urey left Columbia to become distinguished service professor at the Enrico Fermi Institute of Nuclear Studies at the University of Chicago. In 1952 he was named Martin J. Ryerson Distinguished Service Professor. During this time he joined other scientists in warning publicly against the dangers of atomic weapons. Nevertheless, he later supported development of the hydrogen bomb, which is fueled by the deuterium he had discovered.

During his years at the Fermi Institute, Urey applied his knowledge of isotope chemistry to other scientific fields. In paleontology he devised a "thermometer" that calculated past climatic changes by measuring oxygen isotopes in fossils. In cosmology he prepared a study in 1956, with the chemist Hans Suess, that explained the origins and relative natural abundance of elements and isotopes in the universe. In his book *The Planets: Their Origin and Development* (1952), Urey speculated on the chemical processes involved in the formation of the solar system. Interested in the origins of life, he encouraged a student, Stanley Miller, to explore the possibility of producing organic chemicals by passing electric sparks through a mixture of hot gases. These experiments, Urey believed, simulated the early composition of the earth's atmosphere. His application of chemistry to cosmology earned him recognition as "the father of cosmochemistry."

In 1958 Urey joined the University of California at La Jolla as professor at large, serving until 1970, when he became professor emeritus. During the 1960s, he urged the government to incorporate scientific research into the American space program. He was especially curious about the composition, origins, and surface features of the moon and was able to study samples of rocks brought back by the Apollo lunar missions.

In 1926 Urey married Frieda Daum, a bacteriologist. They had four children, three of whom earned doctorates in science. Urey has been described by his colleagues as both overly absorbed in thought and open to new ideas, despite his combative style of speech. He was a warm, helpful friend to his students, and the Ureys' house was well known for its hospitality. His interests included Greek and Hindu sculpture and gardening, especially raising orchids.

In addition to the Nobel Prize, Urey received awards from more than thirty organizations, including the Willard Gibbs Medal of the American Chemical Society (1934), the Davy Medal of the Royal Society of London (1940), the Franklin Medal of the Franklin Institute (1943), the Medal for Merit given by the United States government (1946), the Alexander Hamilton Award of Columbia University (1961), the Gold Medal of the Royal Astronomical Society in London (1966), the Johann Kepler Medal of the American Association for the Advancement of Science (1971), and the Priestley Medal of the American Chemical Society (1973). He was a member of numerous scientific societies, including the American Chemical Society, the American Physical Society, the National Academy of Sciences, and the American Academy of Arts and Sciences. He was awarded honorary degrees by more than twenty-five universities.

SELECTED WORKS: Atomic Energy: Master or Servant? 1946; The Origin of the Earth, 1952; Some Cosmochemical Problems, 1963.

ABOUT: Biographical Memoirs of Fellows of the Royal Society, volume 29, 1983; Craig, H., et al. Isotopic and Cosmic Chemistry, 1964; Libby, L. M. The Uranium People, 1979; National Cyclopedia of American Biography, volume E, 1938; Thomas, S. Men of Space, volume 6, 1963.

VAN DER MEER, SIMON
See MEER, SIMON VAN DER

VAN DER WAALS, JOHANNES
See WAALS, JOHANNES VAN DER

VANE, JOHN R.
(March 29, 1927–   )
Nobel Prize for Physiology or Medicine, 1982
(shared with Sune Bergström and Bengt Samuelsson)

The English pharmacologist John Robert Vane was born in Tardebigge, Worcestershire, the youngest of three children of Maurice Vane, the son of Russian immigrants, and the former Frances Florence Fischer, the daughter of a farming family. After receiving his early education at a state school, he entered King Edward IV High School in a suburb of Birmingham. During the German air raids that began in 1940, the Vane family spent many nights in a bomb shelter in their garden.

At the age of twelve Vane received a chemistry set from his parents, and he soon developed a passion for chemical experimentation. However, shortly after he entered the University of Birmingham in 1944 with the intention of studying chemistry, his interest began to wane. When one of his professors suggested that he train in pharmacology at Oxford with Harold Burn, Vane later recalled that he "grasped the opportunity and immediately went to the library to find out what pharmacology was all about!" He has credited this decision as the event that "reshaped my whole career."

After receiving a B.S. from Birmingham in 1946, he spent two years as a research fellow in Burn's pharmacology laboratory at Oxford, where he learned the essential rules of experimental research and the principles of biological assay. Also known as bioassay, this laboratory procedure enables researchers to determine the biological activity or strength of a substance by measuring its effects on a test system. Burn taught Vane "never to ignore the unusual" in experimental observations and inspired him to make pharmacology his lifework. Vane qualified for his B.S. in pharmacology in 1948.

After a few months as a research assistant in the Department of Pharmacology at Sheffield University, Vane returned to Oxford for doctoral studies at the Nuffield Institute for Medical Research. A Stothert Research Fellowship from the Royal Society of London in 1951 enabled him to complete his graduate studies, and two years later he obtained a Ph.D. In 1953 he moved to New Haven, Connecticut,

JOHN R. VANE

and was first an instructor and then assistant professor of pharmacology at Yale University until his return to England in 1955.

For the next six years Vane was a senior lecturer in pharmacology at the Institute of Basic Medical Sciences of the Royal College of Surgeons. He was a reader in pharmacology between 1961 and 1965 and a professor of experimental pharmacology from 1966 to 1973. During that time, he developed the cascade superfusion bioassay, a technique that allowed him to measure the biological effects of several substances simultaneously in parallel test systems. Using this method, Vane and his colleagues studied a group of hormonelike natural compounds called prostaglandins.

The prostaglandins were first described in 1930 by gynecologists at Columbia University's College of Physicians and Surgeons. While performing artificial inseminations, they noticed that seminal fluid caused uterine muscle to contract and relax. Later in the 1930s ULF VON EULER extracted a substance from the seminal fluid of sheep that produced the same effect on uterine muscle. He called this substance prostaglandin because it was first found in secretions of the prostate gland. Euler preserved these extracts through World War II and in 1945 gave them to SUNE BERGSTRÖM of the Karolinska Institute in Sweden for further study.

In the late 1950s and the early 1960s Bergström and his colleague BENGT SAMUELSSON determined the chemical structure of some of the prostaglandins. In the early 1970s Samuelsson discovered that prostaglandins are produced in the body from arachidonic acid, an unsaturated fatty acid found in certain meats and vegetables. He also learned that arachidonic acid and the systems that convert it to prostaglandin are present in all nucleated animal cells. Different tissues synthesize different prostaglandins, and the various prostaglandins serve various biological functions. Samuelsson also discovered a compound similar to prostaglandin, which he called thromboxane; it differs from prostaglandin in its molecular structure.

In the 1960s Vane and his colleagues at the Royal College of Surgeons used the cascade superfusion bioassay to demonstrate that certain prostaglandins and thromboxanes become biologically inactive after passing through the lungs only once. Vane correctly suggested that these rapidly inactivated compounds are effective only locally, at the site of their release. For this reason, they cannot be considered hormones like cortisol and adrenaline, which circulate in the bloodstream. These rapidly activated compounds, which include prostaglandins of the E and F series and thromboxane A_2, were found to affect the internal diameter of blood vessels. Prostaglandins of the E series are vasodilators; that is, they relax smooth muscle in the walls of blood vessels and thus cause blood pressure to fall. Prostaglandins of the F series are vasoconstrictors; they constrict smooth muscle in the vessel walls and cause blood pressure to rise. Thromboxane A_2 is a potent vasoconstrictor.

While still at the Royal College of Surgeons in 1971, Vane discovered that aspirin inhibits the formation of the prostaglandins and thromboxane A_2. Because thromboxane A_2 causes blood to coagulate, low doses of aspirin can be used to reduce the risk of coronary thrombosis, the blockage of the arteries by blood clots. Vane's research also explained why aspirin is such an effective drug. Although aspirin had been in use since the turn of the century, scientists had not known that it reduces pain and fever by inhibiting the production of prostaglandins.

Appointed director of group research and development at the Wellcome Foundation in London in 1973, Vane formed a prostaglandin research group under the direction of a colleague, Salvador Moncada. Moncada suggested that they study blood vessel tissue, particularly the cells that form the inner lining of blood vessels. They discovered that these cells synthesize an entirely different prostaglandin, which they called prostaglandin X and which is now called prostacyclin, or PGI_2.

Thromboxane A_2 and prostacyclin were found to have opposite effects on blood clotting and vascular smooth muscle. Thromboxane A_2 stimulates clotting and vasoconstriction, whereas prostacyclin inhibits clotting and causes vasodilatation. Prostacyclin is the most potent inhibitor of coagulation now known. Vane and Moncada have postulated that thromboxane A_2 and prostacyclin constitute a kind of homeostatic system, a way of keeping opposing forces in balance. Thromboxane A_2 promotes clotting of blood at sites of injury to vascular tissue; prostacyclin prevents the clot from growing too large and allows the blood to remain fluid enough to continue circulating. Prostacyclin has several clinical uses, including the prevention of clotting in machines used to maintain circulation during open-heart surgery and protection of cardiac tissues from injury in heart attacks.

Vane shared the 1982 Nobel Prize for Physiology or Medicine with Bergström and Samuelsson "for their discoveries concerning prostaglandins and related biologically active substances." In his Nobel lecture, "Adventures and Excursions in Bioassay: The Stepping Stones to Prostacyclin," Vane discussed prostacyclin research and the effects of prostacyclin in the bloodstream.

The discovery of the subtype prostaglandin X (prostacyclin) and Vane's finding that aspirin can block the formation of prostaglandin from arachidonic acid were remarkable advances in the study of prostaglandins. Vane's research opened up a new avenue to the study of the cause and prevention of heart attacks, the leading cause of death in the United States and other technologically advanced countries. "In the next twenty years," Vane has predicted, "we should see a substantial attack on the disease process." He believes that new drugs will be found that will be effective against cardiovascular disease, asthma, and even the ailments associated with old age.

In 1948 Vane married Elizabeth Daphne Page; they have two daughters. According to his wife, Vane thoroughly enjoys his work; for him, "work is life." However, during his rare moments of relaxation, he enjoys waterskiing and snorkeling in tropical waters.

Active in the British Pharmacological Society and the Society for Drug Research, Vane is also a member of the American Academy of Arts and Sciences and the American College of Physicians. In addition to the Nobel Prize, he has received the Baly Medal of the Royal College of Physicians (1977), the Albert Lasker Basic Medical Research Award (1977), the Ciba-Geigy Drew Award of Drew University (1980), and the Dale Medal of the Society for Endocrinology (1981).

SELECTED WORKS: Prostacyclin, 1979, with Sune Bergström.

ABOUT: Current Biography May 1986; New York Times October 12, 1982; Science November 19, 1982.

VAN'T HOFF, JACOBUS
(August 30, 1852–March 1, 1911)
Nobel Prize for Chemistry, 1901

The Dutch chemist Jacobus Henricus van't Hoff was born in Rotterdam, the third of seven children of Alida Jacoba (Kolff) van't Hoff and Jacobus Henricus van't Hoff, a physician and Shakespearean scholar. Van't Hoff was first inspired to experiment with chemistry at home by the instruction at Rotterdam's Hoogere Burgerschool, from which he graduated in 1869. He hoped to pursue a career in chemistry, but his parents believed the prospects for pure research to be poor and persuaded him instead to study engineering at the Polytechnic School at Delft. Van't Hoff completed the three-year program in only two years, receiving the highest score on the final examination. He also developed a lifelong passion for philosophy, poetry (particularly the works of Lord Byron), and mathematics.

After working briefly in a sugar factory, van't Hoff entered the University of Leiden as a mathematics student in 1871. He transferred to the University of Bonn the following year, however, to study chemistry under Friedrich August Kekulé. Two years later he transferred to the University of Paris before returning to Holland to complete work for his doctorate at the University of Utrecht.

The French physicist Jean-Baptiste Biot had noted in the early 1800s that the crystalline forms of some chemical substances could bend polarized light rays passing through them. It had also been observed that certain molecules (called optical isomers) bend light in a direction opposite from most other molecules, even though they have identical types and numbers of atoms. Observing this phenomenon in 1848, Louis Pasteur had hypothesized that such molecules are mirror images of each other and that the atoms of these compounds are arranged in three dimensions.

A few months before receiving his doctorate

JACOBUS VAN'T HOFF

in 1874, van't Hoff published an eleven-page paper titled "An Attempt to Extend to Space the Present Structural Chemical Formulae, With an Observation on the Relation Between Optical Activity and the Chemical Constituents of Organic Compounds." In it he proposed an alternative to the two-dimensional models then used to represent the structures of chemical compounds. He suggested that the optical activity of organic compounds was related to an asymmetrical molecular structure, with a carbon atom at the center of a tetrahedron and with atoms, or groups of atoms, that differed from each other positioned at the four corners. Thus, an interchange of corner atoms or groups could produce molecules identical in chemical composition but mirror images in structure, thereby accounting for different optical effects. Working independently, van't Hoff's former classmate at the University of Paris, Joseph Achille Le Bel, announced similar conclusions two months later in France. Extending the concept of a tetrahedral, asymmetrical carbon molecule to compounds containing carbon-carbon double bonds (sharing edges) and triple bonds (sharing faces), van't Hoff postulated that these geometric isomers share edges and faces of the tetrahedron. Because the van't Hoff–Le Bel theory was extremely controversial, van't Hoff hesitated to offer it as a doctoral dissertation. Instead, he wrote a thesis on cyanoacetic and malonic acids, for which he received a Ph.D. in chemistry in 1874.

Van't Hoff's views on asymmetrical carbon atoms were published in a Dutch journal, where they received little exposure until translated two years later into French and German. Initially, the van't Hoff–Le Bel theory was ridiculed by eminent chemists such as A. W. Hermann Kolbe, who asserted that its "fanciful nonsense carefully avoids any basis of fact and is quite unintelligible to the calm investigator." Eventually, however, it became the foundation of modern stereochemistry (the study of the three-dimensional structure of molecules).

Van't Hoff's academic career began slowly. At first he had to advertise for private students in chemistry and physics, and it was not until 1876 that he obtained a post as a physics lecturer at the Royal Veterinary School in Utrecht. The following year he was appointed lecturer (later professor) of theoretical and physical chemistry at the University of Amsterdam. There, for the next eighteen years, he gave five weekly lectures in organic chemistry and one each in mineralogy, crystallography, geology, and paleontology, in addition to supervising the chemistry laboratory.

Compared with most chemists of his time, van't Hoff had an unusually strong mathematical background, on which he drew as he undertook the complex task of studying reaction velocities and the conditions affecting chemical equilibrium. Through this work he classified chemical reactions as unimolecular, bimolecular, or multimolecular, according to the number of participating molecules, and determined the order of chemical reaction for many compounds.

When a system is in chemical equilibrium, two opposing reversible reactions occur at equal rates with no net change in the system. If such a system is subjected to stress (changes in conditions or in the concentration of its components), the point of equilibrium shifts to relieve the stress. This principle was enunciated in 1884 by the French chemist Henri Louis Le Chatelier. In the same year, van't Hoff applied the principles of thermodynamics to formulate the concept of mobile equilibrium resulting from variations of temperature. He also introduced the now-familiar double-arrow symbol to denote reversible reactions. He discussed his findings in *Études de dynamique chimique* (Studies in Dynamic Chemistry), published in 1884.

The Italian physicist Amedeo Avogadro had stated in 1811 that equal volumes of any gas at the same temperature and pressure contain equal numbers of molecules. Van't Hoff found that this law is also valid for dilute solutions, an important discovery since all chemical and metabolic reactions within living bodies occur in solutions. He also showed that the osmotic pressure of dilute solutions varies with concentration and temperature and thus obeys the thermodynamic laws governing gases. (Osmotic pressure is a measure of the effort of two different solutions to equalize their concentrations when separated by a semipermeable membrane.) Van't Hoff's studies of dilute solutions validated the electrolytic dissociation theory of SVANTE ARRHENIUS. Arrhenius subsequently came to Amsterdam to work with him.

In 1887 van't Hoff helped establish the journal *Zeitschrift für Physikalische Chemie* (Journal of Physical Chemistry) with WILHELM OSTWALD, who had just accepted the chemistry chair at the University of Leipzig. Van't Hoff had also been offered this post but had declined when the University of Amsterdam offered to build him a new chemical laboratory. However, finding his research at Amsterdam hindered by academic obligations, in 1896 van't Hoff accepted a professorship of experimental physics at the University of Berlin, with the condition that he would lecture only once a week and would have a fully equipped laboratory.

At Berlin, van't Hoff applied physical chemistry to geological problems in an analysis of the oceanic salt deposits at Stassfurt. Before World War I, these deposits furnished nearly all the potash used in the manufacture of ceramics, detergents, glass, soaps, and especially fertilizers. He also began examining problems in biochemistry, particularly the enzymes that catalyze chemical changes required in living organisms.

In 1901 the first Nobel Prize for Chemistry was awarded to van't Hoff "in recognition of the extraordinary services he has rendered by the discovery of the laws of chemical dynamics and osmotic pressure in solutions." In his presentation speech, C. T. Odhner of the Royal Swedish Academy of Sciences hailed van't Hoff as the founder of stereochemistry and one of the originators of the study of chemical dynamics. Moreover, Odhner added, "his researches have been a substantial factor in bringing about the magnificent advances in physical chemistry."

In 1878 van't Hoff married Johanna Francina Mees, the daughter of a Rotterdam merchant. They had two daughters and two sons. Throughout his life van't Hoff maintained an active interest in philosophy, nature, and poetry. He died of pulmonary tuberculosis on March 1, 1911, in Steglitz (now part of Berlin), Germany.

In addition to the Nobel Prize, van't Hoff received the Davy Medal of the Royal Society of London (1893) and the Helmholtz Medal of the Prussian Academy of Science (1911). He was a member of the Royal Netherlands Academy of Sciences, the Prussian Academy of Science, the British Chemical Society, the American Chemical Society, the American National Academy of Sciences, and the French Academy of Sciences. He received honorary degrees from the University of Chicago and from Harvard and Yale universities.

SELECTED WORKS: The Foundations of the Theory of Dilute Solutions, 1887, with Svante Arrhenius; Chemistry in Space, 1891; Studies in Chemical Dynamics, 1896; The Arrangement of Atoms in Space, 1898; The Modern Theory of Solution, 1899, with others; Lectures on Theoretical and Physical Chemistry (3 vols.) 1899–1900; The Foundations of Stereochemistry, 1901, with others; Physical Chemistry in the Service of the Sciences, 1903.

ABOUT: Dictionary of Scientific Biography, volume 13, 1976; Farber, E. (ed.) Great Chemists, 1961; Harrow, B. Eminent Chemists, 1927; Ramsay, O. B. (ed.) Van't Hoff–Le Bel Centennial, 1975.

VAN VLECK, JOHN H.

(March 13, 1899–October 27, 1980)
Nobel Prize for Physics, 1977
(shared with Philip W. Anderson and
  Nevill Mott)

The American physicist John Hasbrouck Van Vleck was born in Middletown, Connecticut, the only child of Edward Burr Van Vleck, a professor of mathematics at Wesleyan University, and the former Hester Laurence Raymond. When the boy's father accepted a position at the University of Wisconsin in 1906, the family moved to Madison, where John attended public school before entering the university. He received his B.S. from Wisconsin in 1920, followed by two years of graduate studies at Harvard University under P. W. BRIDGMAN and E. C. Kemble. He received his M.S. in 1921 and his Ph.D. the following year with a thesis in which he calculated the binding energy of a model of the helium atom proposed by both Kemble and NIELS BOHR.

MAX PLANCK had introduced the concept of a quantum of energy in 1900, but it was not until 1913 that Bohr presented the beginnings of a coherent quantum theory of the atom. This "old" quantum theory was superseded in the late 1920s by quantum mechanics, an out-

JOHN H. VAN VLECK

growth of the wave mechanics of ERWIN SCHRÖDINGER and the matrix mechanics of MAX BORN, WERNER HEISENBERG, and P. A. M. DIRAC. In 1926 Van Vleck published *Quantum Principles and Line Spectra,* a treatise on the old quantum theory.

After a postdoctoral year at Harvard, where he served as an instructor in physics, Van Vleck joined the physics department at the University of Minnesota, remaining there from 1923 until 1928. For the next six years he taught at the University of Wisconsin before returning to Harvard in 1934.

After the United States entered World War II in 1941, Van Vleck prepared two reports for the Radiation Laboratory of the Massachusetts Institute of Technology. The following year he was invited by ARTHUR H. COMPTON to join the National Academy Committee on Uranium Fission, in which capacity he spent the summer at the University of California at Berkeley studying the feasibility of nuclear weapons. Returning to Harvard that fall, he divided his time between faculty responsibilities and military research at the university's Radio Research Laboratory. His wartime work included problems associated with signal-to-noise ratio and countermeasures to jam enemy radar using thin strips of aluminum foil.

At the end of the war, Van Vleck succeeded Kemble as chairman of the physics department at Harvard, a position he held until 1949. During this time he recruited to the faculty such notable physicists as NICOLAAS BLOEMBERGEN, EDWARD M. PURCELL, and JULIAN S. SCHWINGER. From 1951 until 1969, when he

became professor emeritus, Van Vleck held the Hollis Chair in Mathematics and Natural Philosophy, the oldest endowed scientific chair in the United States. From 1951 to 1957 he served as dean of engineering and applied physics.

Van Vleck's 1926 work, which showed how quantum mechanics could explain electric and magnetic susceptibilities (the degree to which substances respond to electric and magnetic fields), set the stage for his subsequent preoccupation. His treatise *The Theory of Electric and Magnetic Susceptibilities,* published in 1932, showed clearly and rigorously how quantum mechanics could be applied to a wide range of phenomena that occur in bulk matter, including dielectric constants and ferromagnetism, the type of magnetization shown by ordinary magnets. This work helped establish the new solid-state physics, remained in classroom use for forty-five years, and earned its author the title "father of modern magnetism."

A substance with a slight, but positive, magnetic susceptibility is said to be paramagnetic. Van Vleck explained paramagnetism in certain gases and solids. The term *Van Vleck paramagnetism* is applied to a temperature-independent paramagnetism exhibited by some chemical elements.

Van Vleck's research did much to establish connections between chemistry and physics through the application of quantum mechanics. He helped develop crystal field theory, by which the quantum-mechanical energy levels of an atom or an ion in a crystal can be calculated. Because these energy levels depend, in part, on the immediate atomic environment, they differ from those of the free atom or ion. A precise knowledge of these energy levels is prerequisite to understanding the electric, magnetic, and optical properties of substances; as a result, crystal field theory has found application in the design of lasers and the comprehension of chemical aggregates. In other research, Van Vleck investigated the properties of paramagnetic substances at low temperatures, the optical spectra of paramagnetic ions in solids, and a variety of ferromagnetic phenomena.

After World War II, Van Vleck studied magnetic resonance, a response of electrons, nuclei, or atoms to electromagnetic radiation. Nuclear magnetic resonance spectrometry helps elucidate molecular structure; magnetic resonance imaging became an important diagnostic tool in medicine. Van Vleck also studied the cohesive energies of metals, molecular spectra, and ferrimagnetism (a type of magnetism in which two interpenetrating lattices of magnetic ions are antiparallel and of unequal strength).

Van Vleck, PHILIP W. ANDERSON, and NEVILL MOTT shared the 1977 Nobel Prize for Physics "for their fundamental theoretical investigations of the electronic structure of magnetic and disordered systems." According to Per-Olov Löwdin of the Royal Swedish Academy of Sciences, who presented the award, Van Vleck's work on the electronic structure of magnetic and disordered systems not only constituted a theoretical breakthrough but also held "great importance" for the "chemistry of complex compounds, geology, and later technology."

In 1927 Van Vleck married Abigail June Pearson; the couple had no children. Known as a modest and thoughtful person, Van Vleck enjoyed watching football (especially Harvard-Yale games), playing bridge, and listening to classical music. He was renowned for his vast knowledge of railroad timetables, an interest that began in 1906 while he was traveling with his parents in Europe. In addition to these pastimes, he found great pleasure in walking. While Dirac was in Madison in 1929, he and Van Vleck took long walks together in the surrounding countryside, and in 1931 and 1934 the two scientists took walking trips in the Rocky Mountains. According to Edward Purcell, Van Vleck "helped to promote the union of chemistry and physics," in addition to his fundamental contributions to solid-state physics. "Always, he was teaching us," Purcell wrote, "gently, with inexhaustible patience and good humor, utterly without condescension." Van Vleck died of a heart attack at his home in Cambridge, Massachusetts, on October 27, 1980.

In addition to the Nobel Prize, Van Vleck received the Irving Langmuir Award in Chemical Physics of the General Electric Company (1965), the National Medal of Science of the National Science Foundation (1966), and the Lorentz Medal of the Royal Netherlands Academy of Arts and Sciences (1974). He was awarded honorary degrees by Wesleyan University; the universities of Wisconsin, Maryland, and Chicago; and Oxford University and Harvard University. He was a member of the American Physical Society (and its president in 1952–1953), the American Academy of Arts and Sciences, the National Academy of Sciences, the American Philosophical Society, and the International Union of Pure and Applied Physics. His foreign memberships included the French Academy of Sciences, the Netherlands Physical Society, and the Royal Society of London.

ABOUT: Biographical Memoirs of Fellows of the Royal Society, volume 28, 1982; New York Times October 12, 1977; Price, W. C. Wave Mechanics, 1973; Science November 18, 1977.

VIGNEAUD, VINCENT
See DU VIGNEAUD, VINCENT

VIRTANEN, ARTTURI
(January 15, 1895–November 11, 1973)
Nobel Prize for Chemistry, 1945

The Finnish biochemist Artturi Ilmari Virtanen (vēr' tä nen) was born in Helsinki to Serafina (Isotalo) Virtanen and Kaarlo Virtanen. After graduating from the Classical Lyceum in Viipuri (now the Soviet city of Vyborg), he entered the University of Helsinki, where he studied chemistry, biology, and physics and received an M.S. in 1916. For the next year he worked at the Central Laboratory of Industries in Helsinki before returning to the university and obtaining his doctorate in 1919.

Virtanen pursued postgraduate studies in physical chemistry at Zurich (1920) and in bacteriology at Stockholm (1921). Beginning in 1919, he also worked as a chemist at the Valio Laboratory of the Finnish Cooperative Dairies Association, becoming its director in 1921. By 1923 biochemistry had become his primary interest, and in the academic year 1923–1924 he studied enzymology at Stockholm with HANS VON EULER-CHELPIN.

For some time, the Valio Laboratory had been interested in discovering improved methods of growing fodder, especially nitrogen-fixing plants. Nitrogen compounds are essential to all living organisms. The main source of nitrogen is the atmosphere, but atmospheric nitrogen cannot be utilized by most plants or by any animals until it is incorporated into compounds that the organism can assimilate. Plants that are able to fix nitrogen, or produce these compounds directly from atmospheric nitrogen, include many members of the legume family, such as peas, clover, and soybeans. These plants have the ability, as they decompose, to replenish nitrogen-depleted soil. They also contain high levels of nitrogen-based nutrients, particularly amino acids (the building blocks of proteins), and therefore make excellent fodder for dairy cows and other livestock. Recognizing the value of these plants,

ARTTURI VIRTANEN

Virtanen began investigating their biochemical processes in 1925. Among the questions to be answered were the nature, location, and activities of the bacteria that were believed to play a role in fixing nitrogen.

Virtanen knew that when green fodder, such as clover and grass, was stored as silage, it was subject to rapid and drastic depletion of its nutrients through natural bacterial decay, losses that could decrease the fodder's nutritive value by 25 to 50 percent. The milk of dairy cows using this fodder as winter feed suffered corresponding losses in nutritive value, especially of vitamins A and B_{12}. The inferior quality of winter milk and butter was common knowledge. Reviewing earlier research on the chemical deterioration of silage and on methods of preservation, Virtanen found that it lacked a clear, supportable, theoretical basis. Moreover, no proper nutritional profile had been established for fodder.

Through experimentation, Virtanen discovered that the breakdown of silage could be greatly reduced or even arrested by adding hydrochloric and sulfuric acids to the fodder. Moreover, changing the acidity of the silage enabled him to control the chemical reactions that destroyed its protein and vitamin content. These experiments established the maximum, minimum, and optimal levels of acidity for the treatment of silage. Biopsies of tissues from cows that had been fed treated silage showed that there were no deleterious effects and that the milk was of high quality in both nutrition and taste. The method, called AIV after Virtanen's initials, was first used on dairy farms in Finland in 1929. It was later adopted in many other European countries and, in a modified form, in the United States.

In 1931 Virtanen was appointed director of the Biochemical Research Institute in Helsinki and, concurrently, professor of biochemistry at the Finland Institute of Technology. Continuing his research into nitrogen fixation in plants, he found that leghemoglobin, a red pigment, is similar to the hemoglobin in blood and that it plays an important role in the nitrogen-converting activity of root nodules. During the 1940s his laboratory at the University of Helsinki investigated the biochemistry of more complex plants, work that led to the isolation and chemical elucidation of many amino acids.

It is for his discovery of the AIV method that Virtanen is best remembered. He was awarded the 1945 Nobel Prize for Chemistry "for his research and discoveries in the field of agricultural and nutrition chemistry, and particularly his method of preserving animal fodder." "I consider myself fortunate," Virtanen said in his Nobel lecture, "in having had the opportunity of working in this interesting field and in having advanced development somewhat."

After receiving the Nobel Prize, Virtanen remained actively engaged in research. In addition to his responsibilities as director of the Biochemical Research Institute, in 1948 he became president of the State Academy of Science and Arts in Finland. In 1958 he began investigating the possibility of producing milk from dairy cows that were fed a protein-free diet. From his work with nitrogen-fixing bacteria, he believed that it might be possible for a cow's digestive system to synthesize the amino acids found in milk from the nitrogen compounds present in urea and ammonium salts rather than relying on protein-rich fodder. This hypothesis was confirmed experimentally in 1961.

In 1920 Virtanen married Lilja Moisio, with whom he had two sons. He died in Helsinki at the age of seventy-eight.

As one of Finland's leading scientists, Virtanen represented his nation on the United Nations Commission on Nutrition. In addition to the Nobel Prize, he received many other honors and awards, including honorary degrees from the universities of Lund, Paris, Giessen, and Helsinki.

SELECTED WORKS: Organic Nitrogen Compounds and Higher Plants, 1947; Some Central Nutritional Problems of the Present Time, 1968; Fundamental Studies of Organic Compounds in Plants, 1969.

VON BAEYER

ABOUT: Dictionary of Scientific Biography, volume 14, 1976.

VON BAEYER, ADOLF
See BAEYER, ADOLF VON

VON BEHRING, EMIL
See BEHRING, EMIL VON

VON BÉKÉSY, GEORG
See BÉKÉSY, GEORG VON

VON EULER, ULF
See EULER, ULF VON

VON EULER-CHELPIN, HANS
See EULER-CHELPIN, HANS VON

VON FRISCH, KARL
See FRISCH, KARL VON

VON HAYEK, FRIEDRICH A.
See HAYEK, FRIEDRICH A. VON

VON HEIDENSTAM, VERNER
See HEIDENSTAM, VERNER VON

VON KLITZING, KLAUS
See KLITZING, KLAUS VON

VON LAUE, MAX
See LAUE, MAX VON

VON LENARD, PHILIPP
See LENARD, PHILIPP VON

VON OSSIETZKY, CARL
See OSSIETZKY, CARL VON

VON SUTTNER, BERTHA
See SUTTNER, BERTHA VON

WAALS, JOHANNES VAN DER
(November 23, 1837–March 8, 1923)
Nobel Prize for Physics, 1910

The Dutch physicist Johannes Diderik van der Waals was born in Leiden, the son of Jacobus van der Waals, a carpenter, and the former Elisabeth van den Burg. After attending elementary and secondary schools in Leiden, he became an elementary schoolteacher. From 1862 through 1865 van der Waals attended the University of Leiden as a part-time student. He obtained secondary school teaching certificates in mathematics and physics and taught physics, first in Deventer in 1864, and then, in 1866, as headmaster of a secondary school in The Hague.

Shortly thereafter, he began graduate work in physics and received his Ph.D. from Leiden in 1873. His doctoral dissertation, which concerned the continuity of the gaseous and liquid states, received an enthusiastic review from James Clerk Maxwell, one of the greatest nineteenth-century physicists, who said of van der Waals, "This at once put his name among the foremost in science." The dissertation, which was subsequently translated into German and French, not only established van der Waals's reputation as a brilliant physicist but also provided the subject of his investigations for the rest of his career. Four years after receiving his Ph.D., van der Waals became the first professor of physics at the newly organized University of Amsterdam, where he remained until he retired in 1908 and was succeeded by his son and namesake.

Van der Waals's ideas had been stimulated by an 1857 paper written by Rudolph Julius Emanuel Clausius, a German mathematical physicist who made major contributions to the kinetic theory of gases. According to this theory, the molecules of a gas are in rapid motion in various directions. Their impact on the walls of their container determines the pressure exerted by the gas, and the average velocity of the molecules (their kinetic energy) is directly related to the temperature. Clausius showed how the theory could be used to derive a law found experimentally in 1662 (when molecules were unknown) by Robert Boyle, an Irish physicist and chemist. Boyle's law states that, for a given mass of any gas at a constant temperature, the pressure multiplied by the volume is constant. If the volume is decreased, for example, by advancing a piston into a cylinder, the pressure rises in proportion to keep the product constant. Earlier in the nineteenth century, others, such as the French physicists Jacques Alexandre César Charles and Joseph Louis Gay-Lussac, had shown that, at constant pressure, the gas volume divided by the absolute temperature is constant. This law, too, could be deduced directly from the kinetic theory. The two laws were combined into an equation of state, which applies if the density

JOHANNES VAN DER WAALS

is not too high: $PV = RT$, where P is the pressure, V is the volume, T is the absolute temperature (degrees kelvin, or degrees Celsius above $-273°C$, absolute zero), and R is the same constant for all gases if the volume contains an amount of gas equal to the gram molecular weight.

The equation was known to be inaccurate to various extents for different gases and different conditions. Gases that followed the equation closely were called "ideal." In considering possible sources of the discrepancies, van der Waals noted that the equation was based on two assumptions: that the molecules would act like points with no volume (which is approximately true if they are very far apart) and that the molecules would exert no force on each other (except by collision). He introduced a finite volume for each molecular particle and an attractive force between molecules (without specifying its source) that diminished with increasing distance. (Other researchers later explored the details, but the weak non-chemical attractions between molecules are still often called van der Waals forces.) Van der Waals then developed a modified gas equation: $(P + a/V^2)(V - b) = RT$, where a expresses the mutual attraction between gas molecules (divided by V^2 to account for a weakening of the force at larger volumes, that is, greater average distance between molecules), and b expresses the molecular volume. Both a and b have different values for different gases.

Although van der Waals's equation did not perfectly match all experimental results, it was a significant improvement over the simpler law and had productive consequences. The attraction between molecules gives rise to what van der Waals called an internal pressure, which tends to hold the population of molecules together. As the volume decreases, due to an increase in externally applied pressure, the internal pressure increases much faster. If it equals or exceeds the external pressure, the molecules cling together without the necessity of external pressure from a container. The gas has become a liquid. This illustrated van der Waals's belief, expressed in his dissertation, that the gaseous and liquid states have no essential differences. The same forces and effects of molecular volume act on both. The different properties of gases and liquids arise from differences in the amplitude, not the kind, of forces and volume effects as the molecules are brought closer together or farther apart.

Van der Waals's equation greatly clarified the previously observed existence of a critical temperature, different for different gases, above which a gas cannot be liquefied no matter how much it is compressed. The critical temperature is associated with a critical volume and a critical pressure, which together define the critical point, a set of particular values of temperature, pressure, and volume at which no visible boundary appears between gas and liquid: the two are essentially the same state under those conditions with no abrupt transition. Van der Waals used the critical point to derive an equation in which the variables of temperature, pressure, and volume are expressed in terms of their values at the critical point. This resulted in a universal relationship that applied to all gases, depending in each case only on the critical temperature, pressure, and volume, and not on the nature of the gas. It was the basis for his statement, in 1880, of his most important single finding, the law of corresponding states. According to this law, if the behavior of any one gas and its related liquid is known for all temperatures and pressures, then the state of any other gas or liquid can be calculated for any temperature and pressure if its state at its critical temperature is known. The law did not perfectly describe the exceedingly complex character of gases and liquids, but it was sufficiently accurate to permit a calculation of the approximate conditions needed to liquefy gases on the basis of available experimental data. Using the law as a guide, James Dewar, a Scottish physicist, liquefied hydrogen in 1898, and HEIKE KAMERLINGH ONNES, a Dutch colleague of van der Waals, liquefied helium in 1908.

WAGNER VON JAUREGG

In further research, van der Waals attempted to account for deviations from the gas equation on the basis of variable molecular volume. Molecules were assumed to be capable of forming a cluster, which then behaved as a unit like a molecule of larger size. Since a cluster might contain any number of single molecules, a gas could become a complex mixture. Although van der Waals's original equation was still useful under many conditions, much of its simplicity had to be sacrificed to achieve a more exact representation of gaseous behavior.

Van der Waals received the 1910 Nobel Prize for Physics "for his work on the equation of state for gases and liquids." According to Oscar Montelius of the Royal Swedish Academy of Sciences, who presented the award, "Van der Waals's studies have been of the greatest importance not only for pure research. Modern refrigeration engineering, which is nowadays such a potent factor in our economy and industry, bases its vital methods mainly on van der Waals's theoretical studies."

Van der Waals married Anna Magdalena Smit in 1864. She died when their three daughters and one son were still very young, and he never remarried. A short man who lived simply, van der Waals spent his leisure time playing billiards, reading, and playing solitaire. He died in Amsterdam in 1923.

In addition to receiving an honorary doctorate from Cambridge University, van der Waals was a member of the Royal Netherlands Academy of Arts and Sciences and was elected to foreign membership in the French Academy of Sciences, the Royal Academy of Sciences of Berlin, the Imperial Society of Naturalists of Moscow, the British Chemical Society, and the American National Academy of Sciences.

ABOUT: Dictionary of Scientific Biography, volume 14, 1976; Farber, E. (ed.) Great Chemists, 1961.

WAGNER VON JAUREGG, JULIUS
(March 7, 1857–September 27, 1940)
Nobel Prize for Physiology or Medicine, 1927

The Austrian psychiatrist Julius Wagner von Jauregg (väg' nûr fôn you' reg) was born in Wels, in upper Austria, where his father, Adolf Wagner, was a civil servant. Educated at the Schottengymnasium in Vienna, he entered Vienna University in 1874. As a student, he worked under Salomon Stricker at the Insti-

JULIUS WAGNER VON JAUREGG

tute for General and Experimental Pathology. After receiving his Ph.D. in 1880, he became an assistant in Stricker's laboratory. During that time he established a lifelong friendship with Sigmund Freud, who was also working at the institute. Wagner von Jauregg left the institute in 1882, but he was unable to find a hospital teaching-assistantship. Therefore, when he was invited to work with Max von Leidesdorf at the University of Vienna's psychiatric clinic in 1883, he agreed, although he had never before considered becoming a psychiatrist. Wagner von Jauregg remained at the clinic for six years, qualifying as a teacher of neurology in 1885 and of psychiatry in 1887.

Whereas Freud became interested in the mechanisms by which physical symptoms may be caused by an underlying mental problem, Wagner von Jauregg investigated the physiological causes of mental diseases, especially cretinism and general paresis. Cretinism is a serious form of thyroid deficiency that results from absence of the thyroid gland, a malfunctioning thyroid gland, or a lack of iodine in the diet. It is characterized by retardation of mental and physical development. Cretinism and goiter—a nonmalignant enlargement of the thyroid gland—were once common in central Europe and other areas where the soil is low in iodine.

Wagner von Jauregg studied the distribution of endemic goiter and cretinism in southeast Austria and noticed the beneficial effects of treatment with iodine. In 1898 he proposed that these diseases could be prevented by the use of iodized salt, and in 1923 the Austrian government adopted the suggestion of making iodized salt available, several years after EMIL KOCHER and his associates had persuaded the Swiss government to take similar steps.

General paresis occurs during the tertiary phase of syphilis, when the syphilis spirochete enters the central nervous system, causing progressive insanity, paralysis, and eventually death. Although general paresis is rare today, at the turn of the nineteenth century some 15 percent of all patients in mental institutions suffered from the condition. So swift and fatal was general paresis that most patients survived no more than four years. The rare survivors were of particular interest to Wagner von Jauregg because, as he later wrote, "it must be of the greatest interest for the physician to study healed cases of incurable diseases." His most striking observation was that these rare cures often occurred after the patient had suffered a high fever produced by a disease such as typhus.

In 1887 Wagner von Jauregg proposed that psychoses might be cured by deliberately inducing fevers in mentally ill patients. Initially, he investigated the effects of fever on mental illness in general, but he soon turned to general paresis. Malaria, which produces recurring high fever, was a possible choice, but Wagner von Jauregg feared that it was too dangerous a disease to spread intentionally. After ROBERT KOCH announced his tuberculin treatment for tuberculosis in 1890, Wagner von Jauregg infected some mentally disturbed patients with the tuberculosis-causing bacteria. The results were disappointing, however, because the tubercular fevers were neither high enough nor reliable enough to cure general paresis; moreover, the tuberculin did not cure tuberculosis, and in some cases it could be harmful.

In 1889 Wagner von Jauregg succeeded the neurologist Richard von Krafft-Ebing as professor of psychiatry at the University of Graz. Four years later he returned to Vienna to direct the Psychiatric and Neurological Clinic. By this time he had given up tuberculosis as a method of treatment and was attempting to cure general paresis with various vaccines for febrile diseases. The results were mixed. PAUL EHRLICH's drug Salvarsan (arsphenamine), introduced in 1910, proved dramatically more effective than any previous syphilis treatment, but it could not eliminate the disease in an advanced paretic stage.

A few years later, when it was firmly established that quinine could cure malaria completely, especially the mildest (tertian) variety,

Wagner von Jauregg resumed his work with the disease. "In 1917," he said, "I commenced to put into practice my proposal made in the year 1887, and I injected nine cases of progressive paralysis with tertian malaria. The result was gratifying beyond expectation." He found that when the malaria treatments began early enough, 85 percent of general paretics could be healed—an astounding advance. Over the next few years, Wagner von Jauregg and his colleagues developed useful but relatively noninfectious malaria strains, established appropriate dosages, and determined how long the fevers should be allowed to run before the patient was cured with quinine. Fortunately, tertian malaria induced by injection rather than by mosquito bite proved to be more than normally sensitive to quinine.

Wagner von Jauregg's discovery represented a major advance in the treatment of one of the most feared diseases of the Western world. The reason for its success is still a matter of debate. Malarial infection may stimulate the immune system, or the high temperature of the fever may kill the spirochetes directly. The latter hypothesis is supported by the demonstration that general paresis was sometimes successfully treated by warming the patient more directly, using special electric heaters.

Although unusual by today's standards, malaria treatment was a standard medical practice from the early 1920s to the mid-1940s. ERNST B. CHAIN and HOWARD W. FLOREY's purification of penicillin (discovered in 1928 by ALEXANDER FLEMING) revolutionized the treatment of syphilis, and by the late 1940s, malaria treatment and Salvarsan were both of purely historical interest.

Wagner von Jauregg was awarded the 1927 Nobel Prize for Medicine or Physiology "for his discovery of the therapeutic value of malaria inoculation in the treatment of dementia paralytica." In his presentation speech, Wilhelm Wernstedt of the Karolinska Institute declared, "Wagner von Jauregg has given us a means to a really effective treatment of a terrible disease which was hitherto regarded as resistant to all forms of treatment, and incurable."

A year after receiving the Nobel Prize, Wagner von Jauregg retired from the Psychiatric and Neurological Clinic, where he had served as director since 1893. In addition to his research efforts, until his death he remained active in establishing laws to protect the insane.

Wagner von Jauregg's marriage to Anna Koch in 1899 produced a son and a daughter. Regarded as somewhat aloof and reserved in manner, he was respected for his ability to tolerate a wide range of scientific opinion. He died in Vienna on September 27, 1940.

In addition to the Nobel Prize, Wagner von Jauregg received the Cameron Prize and Lectureship of the University of Edinburgh (1935) and an honorary degree from the University of Vienna.

ABOUT: De Kruif, P. Men Against Death, 1932; Dictionary of Scientific Biography, volume 14, 1976; Eissler, K. R. Freud as an Expert Witness: The Discussion of War Neuroses Between Freud and Wagner-Jauregg, 1986; Haymaker, W., and Schiller, W. The Founders of Neurology, 1970.

WAKSMAN, SELMAN A.
(July 2, 1888–August 16, 1973)
Nobel Prize for Physiology or Medicine, 1952

SELMAN A. WAKSMAN

The American microbiologist Selman Abraham Waksman was born in the small Ukrainian town of Priluki. His mother, Fradia (London) Waksman, was the owner of a dry-goods store, and his father, Jacob Waksman, was a part-time landlord. As a Jew under czarist rule, the boy had little chance of receiving an adequate education, but his mother hired tutors, and he was eventually accepted by a gymnasium in Odessa. He received his diploma in 1910, a year after his mother's death. Seeking better opportunities for a university education, Waksman saved enough money to emigrate to the United States.

After arriving in Philadelphia in 1911, he stayed for a time with two cousins who owned a farm near Metuchen, New Jersey. Waksman had already developed an interest in biology, and, as he recalled later, living on a farm inspired in him "the desire to learn the fundamental principles and the chemical and biological mechanisms that make agriculture. It was to the soil, therefore, that I decided to go for an answer to the many problems that had begun to puzzle me about the cycle of life in nature."

To pursue these interests, Waksman enrolled at the Rutgers College of Agriculture, where he studied soil microbiology and from which he received an M.S. in 1915, the same year he became a United States citizen. Throughout his career, Waksman remained deeply interested in the interactions and ecology of soil microbes. His first scientific paper cataloged different combinations of microbes he had found, including a particularly prominent group, the actinomycetes. Although these microbes are true bacteria, they closely resemble fungi. Even today the role actinomycetes play in soil formation and soil fertility is not well understood; when Waksman began his study of soil microbiology, the organisms were almost completely ignored. His initial investigations convinced Waksman that actinomycetes were important, but he lacked enough biochemistry to pursue this work. After studying enzyme chemistry as a research fellow at the University of California, Berkeley, from 1916 to 1918, he received his Ph.D. in 1918. He returned to Rutgers, where he first lectured and was then appointed associate professor of soil microbiology in 1925, full professor of soil microbiology in 1931, and professor of microbiology in 1943.

At Rutgers, Waksman played a leading role in the development of American soil microbiology, which proceeded from a mere collection of unconnected observations to the stature of a scientific discipline. While teaching and writing extensively for scientific and popular publications, he also conducted pioneering research on soil biochemistry and the interactions between organisms during the formation of soil.

In 1932 Waksman was asked by the American National Association Against Tuberculosis to investigate the process by which the tubercle bacillus is destroyed in the soil. He concluded that antagonistic microbes were responsible. By 1939 Waksman had decided to embark on a research program to apply his work on soil microbiology to the treatment of human diseases. "I felt from my past experience that fungi and actinomycetes would provide far more effective antibacterial agents than the bacteria," he said later. Another motive for this research was World War II, "which was then looming on the horizon," Waksman said, "and which pointed to a need for new agents for the control of various infections and epidemics that would no doubt arise."

Over the next four years, Waksman and his colleagues examined some 10,000 different soil microbes, seeking what he called antibiotic agents that would destroy bacteria without harming human beings. In 1940 the research team isolated actinomycin, a highly toxic antibiotic. Two years later they discovered streptothricin, another antibiotic that was highly effective against the tubercle bacillus. In 1943 Waksman's group found streptomycin in a strain of *Actinomyces* that he had isolated while working on his first scientific paper.

After several years of testing and development, streptomycin became commercially available in 1946. It proved to be a particularly important drug because it is effective against strains of bacteria that are resistant to sulfa drugs and penicillin. Although improved public health measures had reduced the incidence of tuberculosis, the disease was not brought fully under control until the development of streptomycin and the discovery of still more effective antibiotics in the 1950s. The development of streptomycin encouraged other researchers to isolate and modify antibiotics from soil microbes, especially actinomycetes. The phenomenal increase in the number of antibiotics discovered since the early 1950s is largely an outgrowth of programs inspired by Waksman's efforts.

Waksman was awarded the 1952 Nobel Prize for Physiology or Medicine "for his discovery of streptomycin, the first antibiotic effective against tuberculosis." In his presentation speech, Arvid Wallgren of the Karolinska Institute pointed out that "in contrast to the discovery of penicillin by Professor [ALEXANDER] FLEMING, which was largely due to a matter of chance, the isolation of streptomycin has been the result of long-term, systematic, and assiduous research by a large group of workers." Noting that "streptomycin has already saved thousands of human lives," Wallgren hailed Waksman as "one of the greatest benefactors to mankind."

In 1916 Waksman married Bertha Deborah Mitnick, who had also emigrated from his hometown of Priluki; they had one son. Waksman was characterized as a "fatherly, wise lit-

tle man" who inspired his colleagues and students with enthusiasm. After his retirement from Rutgers University in 1958, he remained the dean of American soil microbiologists, writing and lecturing about antibiotics throughout the United States. He died in Hyannis, Massachusetts, on August 16, 1973.

Waksman was named a commander of the Legion of Honor of France in 1950. A recipient of honorary doctorates from the University of Liège and Rutgers University, he was a member of the National Academy of Sciences, the National Research Council, the Society of American Bacteriologists, the Soil Science Society of America, the American Chemical Society, and the Society of Experimental Biology and Medicine.

SELECTED WORKS: Enzymes, 1926, with Wilburt Davison; Principles of Soil Microbiology, 1927; The Soil and the Microbe, 1931, with Robert Starkey; Humus, 1936; Microbial Antagonisms and Antibiotic Substances, 1945; The Literature on Streptomycin, 1952; Sergei N. Winogradsky, His Life and Work, 1953; My Life With Microbes, 1954; The Conquest of Tuberculosis, 1964; The Antibiotic Era, 1975.

ABOUT: Current Biography May 1946; New York Times August 17, 1973; Robinson, D. The Miracle Finders, 1976; Waltz, G. What Makes a Scientist? 1955; Woodruff, H. B. (ed.) Scientific Contributions of Selman A. Waksman, 1968.

WALD, GEORGE

(November 18, 1906–   )
Nobel Prize for Physiology or Medicine, 1967
(shared with Ragnar Granit and H. Keffer Hartline)

The American biologist George Wald was born in New York City to Isaac Wald, a garment-factory tailor from a village in Austrian Poland, and Ernestine (Rosenmann) Wald, an immigrant from Munich, Germany. Wald received his primary and secondary education in the public schools of Brooklyn, New York. After obtaining a B.S. from the Washington Square College of New York University in 1927, he entered Columbia University and received an M.S. in 1928 and a Ph.D. in 1932.

At Columbia, Wald was introduced to the study of vision by Selig Hecht, one of the world's foremost biophysicists. Hecht conducted many studies on the physiology of the eye but was chiefly interested in delineating the biochemistry of vision. In 1877 Franz Boll had discovered that if he dissected a frog's retina (the membrane at the back of the eye) in dim light, it was pink; when the dissected retina was exposed to strong illumination, it turned white. Wilhelm Kühne added to Boll's work by dem-

GEORGE WALD

onstrating that the retina contains a pigment, now known as rhodopsin, that changes from purple to yellow to white when exposed to light and then regenerates in the dark. The bottom layer of the human retina is composed of two differently shaped cells called rods and cones. Kühne found rhodopsin only in the rods, which were known to be the elements of black-and-white night vision; the cones, which discriminate color, are much less sensitive and therefore are active only in the presence of light.

Building on Kühne's research, Hecht hypothesized that the primary event in the process of vision occurs when light separates rhodopsin (one of the pigments involved in color vision) into two products, one of which causes the visual receptor to become electrically excited and thus initiates a nervous impulse. When the two products chemically combine to form the pigment, the process begins again.

"I left Hecht's laboratory," Wald said, "with a great desire to lay hands on the molecules for which these [concepts] were symbols." A National Research Council Fellowship in Biology enabled him to pursue this interest at the Kaiser Wilhelm Institute in Berlin in 1932 under OTTO WARBURG. In Warburg's laboratory, Wald isolated rhodopsin and its separation products, one of which (a protein) he called opsin. The other was a pigment, which proved to be vitamin A. Although, as Wald later admitted, "there were good reasons" to look for vitamin A in the retina—for instance, night blindness was known to be a symptom of vitamin A deficiency—"vitamins were still deeply mysterious, and at that time one hardly expected them to participate directly in physiological processes."

Knowing that the Swiss chemist PAUL KARRER had recently elucidated the structure of vitamin A, Wald went to Karrer's laboratory in Zurich to complete the identification of vitamin A in rhodopsin. He conducted further investigations with OTTO MEYERHOF at the University of Heidelberg in 1933, after which he returned to the United States to spend a year as a fellow at the University of Chicago. He became a biochemistry tutor at Harvard University in 1934 and an instructor in biology the following year. In 1944 he was named an associate professor and in 1948 he became a full professor.

During the late 1930s and the 1940s, Wald investigated the chemical properties of rhodopsin and its products under different lighting conditions and in various species of animals. From his research he concluded that "all the visual pigments we know are built upon a common plan. All of them consist of retinal [vitamin A aldehyde] bound to . . . an opsin."

By 1950 Wald had learned enough about rhodopsin biochemistry to attempt synthesis of the compound. He and one of his graduate students, Ruth Hubbard, first performed the experiment using vitamin A in the form of cod-liver oil. As they expected, the process produced rhodopsin, which was bleached and then reconstituted under various lighting conditions in exactly the same manner as natural rhodopsin. To confirm their results, Wald and Hubbard repeated the experiment using pure crystalline vitamin A. This time, however, no synthesis of rhodopsin occurred.

The experimenters soon realized that, far from having failed, they had stumbled upon the principle of rhodopsin's action. Retinal is a molecule with a long "arm" of carbon atoms, which can be arranged in several different ways; each arrangement is called an isomer. In the most stable form, the carbons are arrayed in a flat plane, which is the "all-*trans*" isomer and represents the type of retinal derived from crystalline vitamin A. Further studies revealed that another pattern of unilluminated retinal (11-*cis*) fits tightly into the opsin protein molecule. "This departure from planarity," Wald explained, "was expected to make the molecule so unstable that one hardly expected to find it. Nevertheless, it has turned out that 11-*cis* retinal, once prepared, is reasonably stable, provided it is kept dark." Because the straighter *trans* isomer no longer fits the opsin binding site, illuminated rhodopsin is dissociated into retinal and opsin components.

Wald explained that "the only action of light in vision is to isomerize the chromophore [atomic grouping upon which the color of a substance depends] of a visual pigment from the 11-*cis* to the all-*trans* configuration. Everything else that happens . . . represents 'dark' consequences of this one light reaction." In an interview in the *New Yorker,* Wald put it much more simply: "The vitamin A in every pigment that we know is bent and twisted . . . . What light does in vision is to straighten out the vitamin A molecule into its natural form. This is all that light does—everything else that happens in the eye could happen in the dark."

During the late 1950s Wald turned his attention to the retinal cones, the receptors of color vision. Ten years earlier RAGNAR GRANIT had shown that the human eye contains three kinds of cones, each of which is sensitive to a different band of the light spectrum. Wald and his associates (especially Paul K. Brown) provided a biochemical basis for Granit's research by determining that each cone contains one of three pigments: blue, green, or red. The pigments all have the same chromophore, 11-*cis* retinal; the differences among them arise from different opsin proteins. Color blindness occurs when a person lacks certain genes that direct the production of one or more of these specialized opsins.

"For their discoveries concerning the primary physiological and chemical visual processes in the eye," Wald, Granit, and H. KEFFER HARTLINE shared the 1967 Nobel Prize for Physiology or Medicine. On presenting the award, Carl Gustaf Bernhard of the Karolinska Institute hailed Wald for his "deep biological insight and great biological skill" in identifying visual pigments and their precursors. "As a by-product, you were able to describe the absorption spectra of different types of cones serving color vision," Bernhard continued. "Your most important discovery of the primary molecular reaction to light in the eye represents a dramatic advance in vision since it plays the role of a trigger in the photoreceptors of all living animals."

Wald, who took as great an interest in teaching as in research, retired from Harvard in 1977. Between 1968 and 1980 he was Higgins Professor of Biology at Harvard. For more than four decades he had followed his own precept that a teacher must be "the most committed student in the room [and must] weave a fabric of relationships and . . . attach this at

so many points to the student's life that it becomes a part of him."

Outside the laboratory and classroom, Wald was involved in a number of political and social issues. He staunchly supported the student activism of the late 1960s and early 1970s and became a familiar figure at rallies against the Vietnam War, nuclear power plants, and arms stockpiling.

In 1931 Wald married Frances Kingsley, with whom he had two sons. The marriage ended in divorce in 1957. A year later, he married Ruth Hubbard; they have a son and daughter.

Among Wald's awards and honors are the Lasker Award of the American Public Health Association (1953), the Rumford Medal of the American Academy of Arts and Sciences (1959), the Frederic Ives Medal of the Optical Society of America (1966), the T. Duckett Jones Memorial Award of the Helen Hay Whitney Foundation (1967), and, jointly with his wife, the Paul Karrer Medal in Chemistry of the University of Zurich (1967). He is a member of the National Academy of Sciences, the American Philosophical Society, the American Academy of Arts and Sciences, and the Optical Society of America.

SELECTED WORKS: Twenty-six Afternoons of Biology, 1962, with others.

ABOUT: Current Biography May 1968; Newsweek June 6, 1977; New Yorker April 16, 1966; Science October 27, 1967; Science News February 19, 1983.

WAŁESA, LECH
(September 29, 1943–   )
Nobel Prize for Peace, 1983

The Polish labor leader Lech Wałesa (vawenz′ a) was born Leszek Michal Wałesa in the village of Popowo, north of Warsaw, during the Nazi occupation of Poland. He was one of eight children born to Bolesław and Feliksa Wałesa. His father, a carpenter, died in 1946 from injuries suffered in a German forced-labor camp.

After receiving his elementary education in the parish grammar school, Wałesa attended the state vocational school at nearby Lipno, where he learned the electrical trade. Although not a good student, Wałesa exhibited strong organizing abilities and a penchant for taking command. "I was always the leader of the class. . . . I was always on top," he once told an interviewer. In 1967, after two years of military service, Wałesa took a job as an electrician in the Lenin Shipyard at Gdańsk on the Baltic Sea.

Gdańsk was the center of protests that broke out in 1970 in response to a government increase in food prices. Striking shipyard workers took to the streets, and during four days of rioting, dozens of demonstrators were killed. As part of a twenty-seven-member action committee at the Lenin yards, Wałesa encouraged the rebellion. In retrospect, he blamed himself for not seizing the moment and attempting to lead the workers to victory. In the wake of the riots, Władysław Gomułka was replaced as Communist party secretary, and the government granted a few concessions to the workers.

Under Edward Gierek, Gomułka's successor, the Polish economy suffered serious setbacks, and in 1976 prices were raised once again to offset the decline. Wałesa, who had become a shop steward, joined the protests that followed and was fired. While supporting himself by doing odd jobs, he joined the Committee for Social Self-Defense, a dissident intellectual group, and established contacts throughout the growing Polish labor movement. Despite harassment by the secret police and frequent arrests, he edited an underground newspaper, *Robotnik wybrzeża* (The Coastal Worker), and in 1979 helped found the illegal Baltic Free Trade Union. Later that year, he joined other labor leaders in signing a charter of workers' rights that demanded, among other items, independent trade unions and the right to strike.

An increase in meat prices in July 1980 touched off a fresh series of riots and work stoppages. A month later, strikers seized the Lenin Shipyard and called for the reinstatement of union activists. Scaling the fence of the shipyard, Wałesa joined his colleagues and became head of a strike committee. The government, faced with widespread rebellion, agreed to negotiate with the strikers. Although Wałesa proved to be a tough bargainer, he carefully avoided any steps that might push the authorities too far. To reduce the chance of violence, he banned the consumption of alcohol among the workers, who turned their energies to decorating the gates of the shipyard with Polish flags, pictures of Pope John Paul II, and flowers—symbols of the nationalism, religious conviction, and hope that the strike embodied.

Negotiations concluded on August 31, when Wałesa and Deputy Prime Minister Mieczys-

LECH WAŁESA

ław Jagielski signed the Gdańsk Agreement. This agreement gave workers the right to form unions and to strike, promised wage increases and other benefits, gave unions and the church access to the broadcast media, and ordered the release of political prisoners. In return, the unions acknowledged the supremacy of the Communist party and the legitimacy of its alliances with other Eastern-bloc nations.

Ten weeks later, Poland's Supreme Court affirmed the right of the union to register as a single national entity known as Solidarity. As chairman of Solidarity's national commission, Wałesa struggled to retain a moderate approach to negotiations even when radicals in the ranks complained that his tactics were high-handed and accused him of being too quick to compromise. The government dragged its feet in fulfilling some of the terms agreed on at Gdańsk. Wildcat strikes, boycotts, and outbreaks of violence became commonplace. On March 27, 1981, virtually all of Poland's 13 million industrial workers staged a four-hour strike to protest the government's harassment of militant unionists. At its first national congress that September, Solidarity delegates called for free elections in Poland. Despite strong opposition from radical challengers, Wałesa managed to retain control and was reelected chairman with 55 percent of the vote.

In December 1981, however, Solidarity radicals in Gdańsk called for a national referendum on the future of the Communist government and demanded a reexamination of Poland's ties to the Soviet Union. "Now you've got what you've been looking for," Wałesa angrily told his fellow union leaders. On December 13 the government proclaimed martial law. General Wojciech Jaruzelski, head of the army, premier, and newly appointed party chairman, had union leaders arrested. Solidarity was outlawed, and the army was dispatched to cities and towns throughout Poland. After being interned for nearly a year, Wałesa emerged from solitary confinement to find his movement crushed.

Wałesa was awarded the 1983 Nobel Peace Prize, an act seen by some as politically motivated. In his presentation speech, Egil Aarvik of the Norwegian Nobel Committee stated, "Lech Wałesa's contribution is more than a domestic Polish concern; the solidarity for which he is spokesman is an expression of precisely the concept of being at one with humanity; therefore he belongs to us all. The world has heard his voice and understood his message," Aarvik went on; "the Nobel Peace Prize is merely a confirmation of this. It is the committee's opinion that he stands as an inspiration and a shining example to all those who, under different conditions, fight for freedom and humanity."

Concerned that he might be denied reentry to Poland if he accepted the prize in person, Wałesa sent his wife Mirosława to the Oslo ceremonies. She bore a message expressing his "most profound gratitude for confirming the vitality and strength of our idea [of human solidarity] by awarding the Nobel Peace Prize to the chairman of Solidarity."

Wałesa's Nobel lecture was read by Bogdan Cywinski, an exiled Solidarity leader living in Brussels. In it, Wałesa stated that "the fundamental necessity in Poland is now understanding and dialogue. I think that the same applies to the whole world: we should go on talking, we must not close any doors or do anything that would block the road to an understanding. And we must remember that only peace built on the foundations of justice and moral order can be a lasting one."

In January 1986 Wałesa was charged by the Polish government with slandering state election officials by charging that they had inflated voter turnout figures for parliamentary elections held the previous year. He would have faced a two-year jail sentence if found guilty; but in February, after Wałesa made a statement just short of apology, the charges were dismissed.

Wałesa lives in Gdańsk with his wife, whom he married in 1969, and their eight children. He is a devout Catholic, attending church daily.

The Catholic church in Poland has played an important part in shaping his nonviolent approach to action, and the church has always supported him. He often wears a medallion of the Virgin Mary as well as a Solidarity button. His speeches are delivered in a simple, sometimes ungrammatical, style that greatly appeals to his audience, and he frequently displays a rich sense of humor. Although the government has allowed him certain amenities—a six-room apartment, a steady job, an adequate income—he believes he is under constant surveillance and always travels with bodyguards. Wałesa has expressed his belief that the Gdańsk Agreement "stands out as a great charter of the rights of working people, which nothing can ever destroy."

ABOUT: Ascherson, N. The Book of Lech Wałesa, 1982; Brolewicz, W. My Brother, Lech Wałesa, 1983; Current Biography April 1981; Dobbs, M., et al. Poland, Solidarity, Wałesa, 1981; Eringer, R. Strike for Freedom: The Story of Lech Wałesa and Polish Solidarity, 1982; New York Times December 14, 1981; October 6, 1983; Playboy February 1982; Time January 4, 1982.

WALLACH, OTTO

(March 27, 1847–February 26, 1931)
Nobel Prize for Chemistry, 1910

The German chemist Otto Wallach (väl' ək) was born in Königsberg (now Kaliningrad in the Soviet Union) to Gerhard Wallach, a Prussian civil servant, and the former Otillie Thoma. Soon after the boy's birth, his father was posted to Stettin and then in 1855 to Potsdam, where Otto received his education at the Potsdam Gymnasium. Although chemistry was only a small part of the curriculum, Wallach pursued the subject at home with a chemistry textbook and some rudimentary laboratory equipment. He also developed a strong interest in art history and literature during his early years.

After graduating from the gymnasium in 1867, Wallach entered the University of Göttingen to study chemistry under Friedrich Wöhler. It was an arduous course of study, beginning at seven in the morning and ending at five in the afternoon, after which the students often continued to work by candlelight. Nevertheless, Wallach completed the requirements in five semesters instead of the usual eight and received his doctorate in 1869 with a dissertation on the position of isomers in the toluene series.

For a brief time Wallach served as an as-

OTTO WALLACH

sistant to August von Hofmann at the University of Berlin. Then in 1870 he became assistant to Friedrich August Kekulé, the noted German chemist, at the University of Bonn. Later that year he was called up for military service during the Franco-Prussian War. After completing his military obligations, he went to work as an industrial chemist for the Berlin firm of Aktien Gesellschaft für Anilin-Fabrikation (later Agfa). He returned to the University of Bonn in 1872, first as an assistant in the organic chemistry laboratory and later as a lecturer. He was named extraordinary professor (associate professor) in 1876 and in 1879 was given the chair in pharmacology, a position that involved him in the study of the essential oils.

Also known as the ethereal oils because of their tendency to change rapidly, the essential oils are fragrant substances produced by plants. Although many chemists had investigated these substances, their chemical composition remained unclear. Wallach began with the terpenes, so named because some are present in turpentine. It was known that all the terpenes had the same percentages of components, often the same atomic weight, and approximately the same boiling point. Their chemical reactions, light-refraction qualities, and other properties, however, suggested that they were distinct substances.

Hundreds of terpenes had been reported, many more than could be formed from the ten carbon and sixteen hydrogen atoms thought to make up a terpene. By 1887 Wallach had demonstrated that in fact they involved only eight substances. Further work enabled him to catalog the reactions that converted one terpene into another as well as the reactions that produced their chemical derivatives. From this data, the structure of the terpene family and the mechanisms of its molecular transitions began to emerge. Wallach classified the terpenes as a special class of alicyclic compounds (open-chain molecules). His results not only commanded theoretical interest but were of great practical benefit to the chemical industries engaged in the production of ethereal oils and artificial perfumes.

In 1889 Wallach accepted the Wöhler Chair at the University of Göttingen, an appointment that also placed him in charge of the university's Chemical Institute. At Göttingen he studied the optical properties of terpenes while also investigating such natural products as the alcohols, ketones, and polyterpenes.

Wallach was awarded the 1910 Nobel Prize for Chemistry "in recognition of his services to organic chemistry and the chemical industry by his pioneer work in the field of alicyclic compounds." The award was presented by Oscar Montelius of the Royal Swedish Academy of Sciences, who stated, "The alicyclic series has, since the middle of the eighties, assumed such size and importance as to make it the equal of the other three main series within organic chemistry. Wallach, contributed more towards this than any other research scientist." In his Nobel lecture Wallach paid tribute to his predecessors in this field—especially Jacob Berzelius and Friedrich Wöhler—reviewed the course of his work, and pointed out some of the problems that remained to be solved, especially "what kind of chemical processes in the plant organism cause the formation of essential oils."

After retiring from the University of Göttingen in 1915, Wallach remained an active figure in chemical research for the next twelve years, publishing papers and participating in professional conferences. On one such occasion, in Göttingen in 1928, LEOPOLD RUŽIČKA first met Wallach. He was struck by the elderly chemist's "clear blue eyes beaming in his exceedingly fine and sage countenance." Ružička later said, "Wallach's highest ideal was not theory, not the formula, but carefully and reliably performed experiment." Wallach, who remained unmarried, died in Göttingen on February 26, 1931.

Among Wallach's many honors were degrees from the universities of Manchester and Leipzig and the Technological Institute of Braunschweig. He also received the German

Imperial Order of the Eagle (1911), the Davy Medal of the Royal Society of London (1912), and the German Royal Order of the Crown (1915). He was a member of numerous scientific societies.

ABOUT: Dictionary of Scientific Biography, volume 14, 1976; Farber, E. (ed.) Great Chemists, 1961.

WALTON, ERNEST
(October 6, 1903–)
Nobel Prize for Physics, 1951
(shared with John Cockcroft)

ERNEST WALTON

The Irish physicist Ernest Thomas Sinton Walton was born in Dungarvan, County Waterford, the son of John Arthur Walton, a Methodist minister, and the former Anna Elizabeth Sinton. The family moved periodically as the elder Walton received new church assignments. Young Walton received his elementary education at day schools in Banbridge and Cookstown. In 1915 he entered Methodist College, Belfast, for his secondary education and graduated in 1922. Walton then entered Trinity College, University of Dublin, where he studied physics and mathematics on scholarship, and received his B.A. in 1926. He remained at Trinity College for a year to do experimental and theoretical work on vortex motion in liquids, earning an M.S. in 1927.

That year, Walton received a government scholarship to study nuclear physics under ERNEST RUTHERFORD at the Cavendish Laboratory, Cambridge University, where he received his Ph.D. in 1931. Rutherford had recently demonstrated that the atomic nucleus could be split by bombarding nitrogen with alpha particles (helium ions) emitted from a radioactive source. In this way he had changed atoms of nitrogen into oxygen, thus becoming the first person to transmute one element into another by external means. To make other atomic transmutations, Rutherford and his assistants sought to build devices that would hurl even more swiftly moving particles at nuclei.

Many other scientists were also keenly interested in developing such devices, using both direct methods, which depend upon a single surge of electricity, and indirect methods, in which the particles are accelerated through lower amounts of electricity several times. In later years, when higher-voltage sources became available, both methods were used as models by others for the development of the betatron and the linear accelerator. Soon after

he arrived at Cambridge in 1927, Walton was asked to determine the feasibility of accelerating electrons in a circular course surrounded by electrical and magnetic forces. Although his first apparatus accelerated electrons as they moved in circular orbits, it was insufficient to penetrate, and thus split, nuclei. His second device accelerated heavier, positively charged particles, moving them forward linearly by varying the electrical forces.

In 1929 Walton joined forces with JOHN COCKCROFT, who had also tried to build particle accelerators. The difficulty in accomplishing this goal arose from the fact that very high energies were needed. Since atomic nuclei are positively charged, they repel positively charged particles directed toward them. Calculations suggested that only particles impelled with an energy exceeding several million electron volts (some ten times the amount that could be achieved in the late 1920s) could overcome this powerful resistance.

By 1929 Cockcroft had decided to use the less favored direct method to induce nuclear transformations in a novel and ingenious way, one that would not require positively charged particles to be accelerated toward nuclei with millions of electron volts of energy. To do so, Cockcroft employed a brilliant insight that had occurred to him after reading a 1928 paper by the Russian-born physicist George Gamow. Gamow suggested that if subatomic particles exhibited wave motion, some could escape from some nuclei, even though according to classical particle theory, they ought not to do so.

It was probable, Gamow believed, that some

alpha particles might escape from the nuclei, if a very large number of nuclei were studied. It occurred to Cockcroft to ask Gamow, who was visiting at the Cavendish at the time, whether the reverse might be true—that is, whether relatively low-energy positively charged particles might penetrate into nuclei. Gamow calculated that they would do so if a large enough number of alpha particles were directed toward the nuclei.

Encouraged by Gamow's theory, Cockcroft and Walton worked for several years to develop a reliable and effective particle accelerator that could direct sufficiently large numbers of positively charged particles toward nuclei. By imparting several hundred thousand electron volts to these particles, Cockcroft and Walton were able to split atoms by early 1932. One of every ten million alpha particles projected toward light atoms, such as lithium and boron, split a nucleus and released energy.

Named a Clerk Maxwell Scholar in 1932, Walton remained at Cambridge for another two years. During this time he continued his work in nuclear transmutations of many other atomic nuclei. In 1934 he returned to Ireland and became a fellow of Trinity College; in 1974 he became a fellow emeritus. From 1946 to 1974 he served as Erasmus Smith's Professor of Natural and Experimental Philosophy at Trinity.

Walton shared the 1951 Nobel Prize for Physics with Cockcroft "for their pioneer work on the transmutation of atomic nuclei by artificially accelerated atomic particles." "The work of Cockcroft and Walton was a bold thrust forward into a new domain of research," declared Ivar Waller of the Royal Swedish Academy of Sciences in his presentation address. "Their discoveries initiated a period of rapid development in nuclear physics. Indeed," Waller continued, "this work may be said to have introduced a totally new epoch in nuclear research."

Through their research, Walton and Cockcroft not only demonstrated the ability to transmute atomic particles entirely under human control and without the use of radioactive material, but also produced atomic reactions that released vast amounts of energy. Moreover, their experiments furnished the first major confirmation of ALBERT EINSTEIN's formula indicating that mass and energy are equivalent. In other research, Walton studied hydrodynamics, microwaves, and other aspects of nuclear physics.

He married Winifred Isabel Wilson, a kin-

dergarten teacher, in 1934; they have two sons and two daughters. Walton, who has been described as a quiet, undemonstrative man, enjoys gardening. He is a member of the Royal Irish Academy and the Royal Dublin Society. He has served on advisory committees for the Dublin Institute for Advanced Studies and the Royal City of Dublin Hospital, among others. He was awarded the Hughes Medal of the Royal Society of London in 1938 and has received honorary degrees from Queen's University, Belfast, and from Gustavus Adolphus College in Minnesota.

ABOUT: Current Biography March 1952; Nature November 24, 1951; New York Times November 16, 1951.

WARBURG, OTTO
(October 8, 1883–August 1, 1970)
Nobel Prize for Physiology or Medicine, 1931

The German biochemist Otto Heinrich Warburg (vär' bŏŏrk) was born in Freiburg, in what is now West Germany, the only son and one of four children of Elizabeth (Gaertner) and Emil Warburg. His father, a physics professor and talented musician, was the descendant of a Jewish banker of the sixteenth century. Generations of distinguished Warburgs were scholars, businessmen, artists, bankers, and philanthropists. His mother was a Christian whose ancestors included accomplished administrators, lawyers, and soldiers. When the boy was twelve years old, the family moved to Berlin, where his father had been appointed professor of physics at the university there. The young Warburg received his early education at the Friedrichs-Werder Gymnasium. The family's home was frequented by musicians, artists, and the elder Warburg's professional colleagues, including MAX PLANCK, ALBERT EINSTEIN, WALTHER NERNST, all physicists; EMIL FISCHER, an organic chemist; and Theodor Engelmann, a physiologist.

Warburg became a chemistry student at the University of Freiburg in 1901, and two years later he transferred to Fischer's department at the University of Berlin. In 1906 he received a Ph.D. in chemistry from the University of Berlin with a dissertation on optically active peptides and their enzymatic hydrolysis. Hoping to make discoveries that would lead to a cure for cancer, he began the study of medi-

OTTO WARBURG

cine at the University of Heidelberg, working in the laboratory of Ludolf von Krehl, an outstanding internist. His collaborators there included the biochemist OTTO MEYERHOF and the biologist Julian Huxley. Warburg's first independent research, published in 1908, showed that the oxygen consumption of sea urchin eggs increases sixfold after fertilization. In 1911 he received his medical degree from the University of Heidelberg.

For the next three years Warburg conducted research at the University of Heidelberg and at the Zoological Station in Naples, Italy, an international center for research in biology. In 1913 he was elected to membership in the Kaiser Wilhelm Society, the foremost scientific society in Germany. He was also appointed head of his own department and laboratory at the Kaiser Wilhelm Institute for Biology in Berlin. These positions gave him complete independence in his choice of research topics, with no teaching or administrative obligations to encumber him.

At the outbreak of World War I in 1914, Warburg volunteered for the military and served four years in the Horse Guards, a cavalry regiment. He became a first lieutenant, was wounded in action on the Russian front, and received the Iron Cross. Warburg enjoyed many aspects of military life and made lasting friendships, but in 1918 Einstein urged him to return to his research, writing in a letter: "You are one of the most promising younger physiologists in Germany. . . . Your life hangs continuously on a thread. . . . Is it not madness? Can your place out there not be taken by any

average man?" Taking Einstein's advice, and persuaded that Germany had already lost the war, Warburg returned to his laboratory in Berlin, with an appointment as professor. He retained his love of horseback riding, however, and rode every morning before work for many years.

Warburg used his laboratory funds mainly for equipment for physical and chemical studies. He had only a few research collaborators, most of whom were skilled technicians that he trained. When asked late in his life why he did not wish to teach more future scientists, Warburg replied, "Meyerhof, [HUGO] THEORELL, and [HANS] KREBS were my pupils. Have I not done enough for the next generation?" Throughout his fifty years of laboratory research, Warburg was concerned with three topics: photosynthesis, cancer, and enzymes of cellular oxidation reactions. The analytic methods he developed include manometry, used to measure changes of gas pressure, as in cell respiration and fermentation; spectrophotometry, or the use of monochromatic light to measure reaction rates and quantities of metabolites; and tissue-slice techniques for testing oxygen consumption without mechanical destruction of cells.

In 1913, while studying oxygen uptake in liver cells, Warburg discovered subcellular particles that he called grana, later shown to be mitochondria. He suggested that oxidative enzymes for the reactions in which the end products of glucose degradation are further oxidized to carbon dioxide and water were physically bound to the grana. In an effort to determine the biochemical changes that occur when normal cells (with controlled growth) become cancer cells (with uncontrolled growth), Warburg measured rates of oxygen consumption, using tissue slices in a manometer. He found that although normal cells and tumor cells consumed equal amounts of oxygen, tumor cells produced abnormally large amounts of lactate in the presence of oxygen. (Glucose is degraded to lactate in most tissue in the absence of oxygen.) He concluded that tumor cells preferentially use the anaerobic pathway to metabolize glucose and that in fact normal cells are transformed into malignant cells because they are deprived of oxygen.

Warburg had observed that normal aerobic respiration is inhibited by compounds such as cyanide. He believed that similar environmental substances were secondary causes of cancer and therefore insisted upon growing his own food without the use of artificial fertilizers or pesticides. To avoid the bleaching additive used by commercial bakers, he had his bread baked at home. Although scientists later concluded that the primary cause of cancer must be determined at the genetic level, as late as 1967 Warburg still maintained that cancer arose from disturbances of energy metabolism.

For his work on tumor metabolism, the Nobel Committee for Physiology or Medicine considered awarding the 1926 Nobel Prize for Physiology or Medicine to Warburg, but they bestowed it instead on the Danish physician and medical researcher JOHANNES FIBIGER.

In the late 1920s Warburg discovered the respiratory enzyme cytochrome oxidase, which catalyzes oxidative reactions on the surface of the grana, or mitochondria (the "power plants" of the cell). Using a technique of radiation physics in which a solution of an enzyme-coenzyme complex is illuminated with monochromatic light and the resulting absorption pattern is analyzed, Warburg deduced that the active coenzyme (an organic cofactor necessary for function) of cytochrome oxidase is a porphyrin molecule, with iron acting as the oxygen-transferring component. This was the first identification of the active group of an enzyme.

Warburg was awarded the 1931 Nobel Prize for Physiology or Medicine "for his discovery of the nature and mode of action of the respiratory enzyme." Praising Warburg for his "bold ideas . . . , keen intelligence, and rare perfection in the art of exact measurement," Erik Hammarsten of the Karolinska Institute noted that Warburg's discovery "was the first demonstration of an effective catalyst, a ferment, in the living organism; . . . this identification is the more important because it throws light on a process of general significance in the maintenance of life."

By the early 1930s Warburg, who in 1931 had been appointed director of the newly established Kaiser Wilhelm (later the Max Planck) Institute for Cellular Physiology, had isolated and crystallized nine enzymes of the anaerobic pathway of glucose metabolism. Spectrophotometric techniques developed by Warburg were indispensable for the enzyme purification. Together with a colleague, Walter Christian, he also isolated two coenzymes: flavin adenine dinucleotide (FAD) and nicotinamide adenine dinucleotide phosphate (NADP), both of which are involved in the transfer of hydrogen and electrons in oxidation reactions catalyzed by yellow enzymes or flavoproteins. The discovery of NADP, which contains the vitamin nicotinic acid, clarified the coenzyme function of vitamins.

Turning his attention to photosynthesis, Warburg sought to determine how efficiently plants convert carbon dioxide and water into sugar and oxygen. Using quantitative methods he had learned in his father's laboratory, as well as innovative techniques of his own, Warburg correlated the amounts of light intensity in the photochemical reaction with rates of photosynthesis. He found that the absorption of four light quanta produced one molecule of oxygen, an efficiency of about 65 percent for the transformation of electromagnetic energy into chemical energy. More recent investigators have obtained values of ten or more light quanta for evolution of each oxygen molecule. Studying nitrate reduction in green plants, Warburg also discovered the electron carrier ferredoxin.

Despite his Jewish ancestry, Warburg remained in Germany during World War II, perhaps because of his research on the causes of cancer, of which Hitler had a morbid fear. He was reclassified as one-quarter Jewish by Hermann Göring of the chancellor's office. Although he was not permitted to teach, Warburg continued to perform research at the Institute for Cellular Physiology until 1943, when Allied bombing forced him to move his office and laboratory to an estate thirty miles north of Berlin. At the end of the war, Warburg's books and laboratory equipment were confiscated by the Russians who occupied the area. He resumed his research four years later in Berlin. The usual retirement regulations were waived for Warburg, and he continued to publish about five papers each year about his studies on photosynthesis and cancer.

Warburg never married; from 1919 until his death he lived with his inseparable companion, Jacob Heiss, who managed Warburg's household and later became an unofficial secretary and manager of the institute. Horseback riding remained a passionate pastime for Warburg until he fell from a ladder at the age of eighty-five and fractured a femur. Two years later he developed a deep vein thrombosis and died from a pulmonary embolus on August 1, 1970.

Known as an aristocratic, highly disciplined man, Warburg read widely in history and literature. In addition to his work, he enjoyed listening to music, especially the compositions of Beethoven and Chopin. Although he had no patience with those who wasted his time—he once told an inquisitive journalist, "Professor Warburg cannot be interviewed: he is dead"—Warburg's friends and colleagues regarded him as a man of considerable charm and thoughtfulness.

Warburg's many honors and awards included membership in the Royal Society of London, an honorary degree from Oxford University, and the Order of Merit of the government of West Germany.

SELECTED WORKS: The Metabolism of Tumours, 1930; Heavy Metals and Enzyme Action, 1949; New Methods of Cell Physiology, 1962; The Prime Cause and Prevention of Cancer, 1969.

ABOUT: Biographical Memoirs of Fellows of the Royal Society, volume 18, 1972; Burk, D. (ed.) Cell Chemistry, 1953; Dictionary of Scientific Biography, volume 14, 1976; The Excitement and Fascination of Science, 1965; Krebs, H. Otto Warburg: Cell Physiologist, Biochemist, and Eccentric, 1981; Nachmanson, D. German-Jewish Pioneers in Science 1900–1933, 1979.

JAMES D. WATSON

WATSON, JAMES D.
(April 6, 1928–   )
Nobel Prize for Physiology or Medicine, 1962
(shared with Francis Crick and Maurice H. F. Wilkins)

The American molecular biologist James Dewey Watson was born in Chicago, Illinois, the only son of James D. Watson, a businessman, and Jean (Mitchell) Watson. Growing up in Chicago, he received his early education at the Horace Mann Grammar School and South Shore High School. It soon became apparent that the boy was a child prodigy, and he appeared on the radio program "The Quiz Kids" in his youth. In 1943, after only two years of high school, Watson received a scholarship to the University of Chicago's experimental four-year college, where he pursued his interest in ornithology. After receiving a B.S. in zoology from the University of Chicago in 1947, he enrolled for graduate work at the University of Indiana in Bloomington, also on scholarship.

By this time, Watson's interest had turned to genetics, and at Indiana he was able to study under the geneticist HERMANN J. MULLER and the bacteriologist SALVADOR LURIA. Watson wrote a dissertation on the effects of X rays on bacteriophage multiplication (bacteriophages are virus particles that infect bacteria) and was awarded a Ph.D. in zoology from the University of Indiana in 1950. A National Research Council grant enabled him to continue his studies of bacteriophage at the University of Copenhagen in Denmark. While there, he conducted research on the biochemistry of deoxyribonucleic acid (DNA) in the bacterio-

phage. However, as he later recalled, he "was becoming frustrated with phage experiments and wanted to learn more about the actual structure of the [DNA] molecules, which geneticists talked about so passionately."

The nucleic acids were first discovered in the nucleus of the human cell by the Swiss researcher Friedrich Miescher in 1869. During the first part of the twentieth century, biologists and biochemists gradually elucidated the composition and nature of the cell. It was shown that one of the nucleic acids, DNA, was an extremely large molecule composed of structural units called nucleotides, each consisting of three molecules. By 1944 the American biologist Oswald Avery, working at the Rockefeller Institute (now Rockefeller University), had produced evidence that genes are made of DNA, a hypothesis that was confirmed in 1952 by ALFRED HERSHEY and Martha Chase. Although it was therefore clear that DNA controlled the biochemical processes governing the cell, neither the structure nor the function of the molecule was understood.

In the spring of 1951, while attending a symposium in Naples, Italy, Watson met MAURICE H. F. WILKINS, an English researcher. Wilkins and Rosalind Franklin—a colleague at King's College, Cambridge—had made X-ray diffraction studies of the DNA molecule and shown that it was a double helix, resembling a ladder twisted into a spiral. Their findings further stimulated Watson's desire to investigate the structural chemistry of the nucleic acids. With a grant from the National Foundation for Infantile Paralysis, Watson went to the

1105

Cavendish Laboratory at Cambridge University in October 1951 to investigate the three-dimensional structure of proteins with JOHN C. KENDREW. There he became acquainted with FRANCIS CRICK, a physicist who had switched to biology and was completing his doctoral studies.

Finding their interests compatible, Watson and Crick set out in 1952 to determine the structure of DNA. The two researchers knew that there were two types of nucleic acid, DNA and ribonucleic acid (RNA), each consisting of five-carbon sugar molecules, phosphate, and four nitrogen-containing bases: adenine, thymine (in RNA, uracil), guanine, and cytosine. During the next eighteen months, Watson and Crick combined existing knowledge with their own research, and they reported their findings on the structure of DNA in February 1953. A month later they completed a three-dimensional model of the molecule made from beads, bits of cardboard, and wire.

According to the Crick-Watson model, DNA is a double helix, consisting of two strands of deoxyribose phosphate, joined by pairs of bases that are analogous to the rungs of a ladder. Through hydrogen bonds, one adenine is paired with each thymine and one guanine is joined with each cytosine. With this model the process by which DNA replicates itself could be visualized. According to Crick and Watson, the two parts of the DNA molecule separate from each other at the points of hydrogen bonding, much like a zipper unzipping. A new molecule is then synthesized opposite each half of the old one. The sequence of bases acts as a template, or mold, for the formation of new molecules. The discovery of the chemical structure of DNA was widely hailed as one of the most important biological developments of the century.

After Crick and Watson published a description of their model in the British journal *Nature* in April 1953, they began working separately. Later that year, Watson was appointed senior research fellow in biology at the California Institute of Technology in Pasadena, California. He worked briefly with Crick again at Cambridge from 1955 until 1956, at which time Watson became an assistant professor of biology at Harvard University in Cambridge, Massachusetts; he was subsequently appointed associate professor in 1958 and full professor in 1961.

Watson, Crick, and Wilkins received the 1962 Nobel Prize for Physiology or Medicine "for their discoveries concerning the molecular structure of nuclear acids and its significance for information transfer in living material." In his presentation speech, A. V. Engström of the Karolinska Institute described DNA as "a high polymer composed of a few types of building blocks. . . . These building blocks are a sugar, a phosphate, and nitrogen-containing chemical bases. The same sugar and the same phosphate are repeated throughout the giant molecule," Engström went on, "but with minor exceptions, there are four types of nitrogenous bases. It is for the discovery of how these building blocks are coupled together in three dimensions" that the three researchers were awarded the Nobel Prize. Engström added that the discovery of the structure of DNA "opens the most spectacular possibilities for the unravelling of the details of the control and transfer of genetic information."

Since 1968 Watson has been director of the Cold Spring Harbor Laboratory of Quantitative Biology in Cold Spring Harbor, Long Island. He relinquished his position at Harvard in 1976 and has since devoted his efforts to directing research programs at the Cold Spring Harbor Laboratory and to increasing the budget and staff. Much of his work has involved neurobiology and the role of viruses and DNA in cancer.

In 1968 Watson married Elizabeth Lewis, a former laboratory assistant. They have two sons and live in a restored nineteenth-century house on the grounds of the laboratory's campus. He is the author of *The Molecular Biology of the Gene* (1965), one of the most widely used and influential textbooks in the field of molecular biology.

Watson's many awards include the Lasker Award of the American Public Health Association (1960), the John J. Carty Gold Medal of the National Academy of Sciences (1971), and the Presidential Medal of Freedom (1977). He is a member of the National Academy of Sciences, the American Society of Biological Chemists, the American Association for Cancer Research, the American Philosophical Society, and the Danish Academy of Arts and Sciences, as well as a senior fellow in the Society of Fellows of Harvard University. He has been awarded honorary degrees by the University of Chicago and by Hofstra, Long Island, Brandeis, Harvard, New York, and Rockefeller universities, as well as by the Albert Einstein College of Medicine.

SELECTED WORKS: The Double Helix, 1968; The DNA Story, 1981, with John Tooze; Molecular Biology of the Cell, 1983; Recombinant DNA, 1983, with others.

ABOUT: Current Biography April 1963; Jevons, F. R. Winner Take All, 1979; New York Times December 26, 1984; Olby, R. The Path to the Double Helix, 1974.

WEINBERG, STEVEN
(May 3, 1933–)
Nobel Prize for Physics, 1979
(shared with Sheldon L. Glashow and
   Abdus Salam)

STEVEN WEINBERG

The American physicist Steven Weinberg was born in New York City, the son of Eva (Israel) Weinberg and Frederick Weinberg, a court stenographer. His early interest in science was encouraged by his father and fostered at the Bronx High School of Science, where SHELDON L. GLASHOW was one of his classmates. By the time Weinberg was sixteen years old, his interest had focused on theoretical physics.

After receiving a B.S. from Cornell University in 1954, Weinberg studied for a year at the Institute for Theoretical Physics in Copenhagen (now the Niels Bohr Institute). Returning to the United States, he earned a Ph.D. at Princeton University in 1957 with a thesis on an application of renormalization, a mathematical technique that was to have an important place in his later work.

Weinberg held a postdoctoral appointment at Columbia from 1957 to 1959 and then taught at the University of California at Berkeley until 1969, when he joined the faculty of the Massachusetts Institute of Technology. In 1973 he moved to Harvard University, succeeding JULIAN S. SCHWINGER as Eugene Higgins Professor of Physics. Concurrently, he served as senior scientist at the Smithsonian Astrophysical Observatory.

By his own account, Weinberg's scientific interests have been broad, including "a wide variety of topics—high-energy behavior of Feynman graphs [devised by RICHARD P. FEYNMAN], second-class weak interaction currents, broken symmetries, scattering theory, muon physics, etc.—topics chosen in many cases because I was trying to teach myself some area of physics." In his most celebrated work, he attempted to unify the fundamental forces of nature.

In the early nineteenth century, physicists reduced the forces at work in the universe to three: gravitation, electricity, and magnetism. In the 1870s the Scottish physicist James Clerk Maxwell established that electricity and magnetism are not independent forces but different aspects of a force now called electromagnetism. Maxwell was able to show that light was an electromagnetic phenomenon and derived its velocity, predicted radio waves, and inspired subsequent theorists to seek an underlying principle that would unify all the forces of nature.

After the discovery of the atomic nucleus in the twentieth century, scientists had to account for two additional forces: the strong force and the weak force. The strong force binds together the protons and the neutrons that compose the atomic nucleus. Instead of binding particles together, the weak force is responsible for breaking them apart, for example, governing the radioactive emission of beta rays (electrons). Unlike gravitation and electromagnetism, which operate over unlimited distances, the strong force does not extend beyond the confines of the nucleus. The weak force has an even smaller range of action. According to Weinberg, Glashow, and ABDUS SALAM, the electromagnetic and weak forces are different aspects of a single "electroweak" force.

Using a concept called gauge symmetry, Glashow first attempted a synthesis of electromagnetism and the weak force in 1960. There are several types of symmetry, including mirror symmetry (exhibited by a pair of gloves) and charge symmetry (the force between two electrically charged particles remains unchanged if the particles' charges are reversed). Gauge symmetry involves mathematical representations whose absolute (as opposed to relative) values do not affect physical interactions, so that the reference point for making a measurement can be changed without altering any observable quantity.

Although the term *gauge symmetry* was introduced in the 1920s, the concept can be traced to earlier work; indeed, Maxwell's theory of electromagnetism can be interpreted as an application of gauge symmetry. The predictions of Maxwell's theory are the same no matter what standard point of reference is chosen for measuring voltages. Such a point of reference is what an electrical engineer would call ground potential. The absolute value of the electric potential plays no part; the voltage is the difference between the potentials at two points, one of which may be chosen as the ground reference. Attempting to apply the principle of gauge symmetry to the more complicated physics of the strong force in 1954, CHEN NING YANG and Robert L. Mills greatly advanced efforts to unify the forces of nature, including the work of Glashow, Weinberg, and Salam.

Another advance occurred in 1960, when Glashow proposed the existence of four particles to serve as carriers of electromagnetism and the weak force. One of them, the photon (or quantum of light), was already known to carry the electromagnetic force. The other three particles (now called W^+, W^-, and Z^0) mediated weak interactions. Because the carrier particles were massless, according to Glashow's theory the weak force would operate over an unlimited range, a view that did not accord with experimental evidence. To account for this difficulty, Glashow postulated large masses for the W^+, W^-, and Z^0 particles, but now the theory predicted that certain weak interactions would have an infinite strength.

Employing gauge theory as Glashow had, Weinberg proposed a unified theory in 1967. His solution, which depended on a mechanism known as spontaneous symmetry breaking, was to leave the photon massless while giving mass to the other three particles. According to this theory, the electromagnetic and weak forces are identical at extremely high energy. The masses of the W and Z particles are of little consequence under these conditions because massive particles can readily be created out of the available energy (ALBERT EINSTEIN's relativity theory had demonstrated the equivalence of mass and energy). Thus the exchange of a W or a Z is just as likely as the exchange of a photon, and the weak force is as strong as electromagnetism. At lower energies, however, W and Z particles are seldom created, so that weak interactions become rarer and shorter in range than electromagnetic interactions. Since the world of terrestrial physics is confined to comparatively low energies, the differences between the two forces are more conspicuous than their similarities.

A year after Weinberg reported his work, Abdus Salam independently proposed a similar theory. Their ideas attracted little attention until 1971, when the Dutch physicist Gerhard 't Hooft applied a mathematical technique called renormalization, developed by Julian S. Schwinger and SIN-ITIRO TOMONAGA, which enabled him and other investigators to complete the proof. The gauge theory developed by Glashow, Weinberg, and Salam was dramatically confirmed in 1973 by the discovery of weak neutral currents in experiments at the Fermi National Accelerator Laboratory near Chicago and at CERN (the European Organization for Nuclear Research) near Geneva. In 1983 the W and Z particles themselves were detected at CERN by CARLO RUBBIA and his colleagues.

Weinberg, Glashow, and Salam were awarded the 1979 Nobel Prize for Physics "for their contributions to the theory of the unified weak and electromagnetic interaction between elementary particles, including, inter alia, the prediction of the weak neutral current." In his Nobel lecture Weinberg spoke on the symmetries, or regularities, apparent in the laws of nature. "We can study matter only at low temperatures, where symmetries are likely to be spontaneously broken, so that nature does not appear very simple or unified. . . . But by looking long and hard," he said, "we can at least make out the shapes of symmetries, which, though broken, are exact principles governing all phenomena."

Since 1982 Weinberg has been Josey Professor of Science at the University of Texas at Austin. He has served as a consultant to the Institute for Defense Analyses (1960–1973) and to the United States Arms Control and Disarmament Agency (1971–1973). In addition to his work in elementary particles and field theory, including quantum theory and general relativity, he is deeply interested in astronomy and astrophysics.

Weinberg and his wife, the former Louise Goldwasser, a law professor, were married in 1954 and have one daughter. In his leisure time he enjoys studying medieval history.

Weinberg has received the J. Robert Oppenheimer Prize of the University of Miami (1973), the Dannie Heineman Prize (1977) of the American Physical Society, and the Elliott Cresson Medal of the Franklin Institute (1979). He is a member of the National Academy of Sciences, the American Academy of Arts and

Sciences, the American Physical Society, the American Astronomical Society, the Royal Society of London, and the American Medieval Academy. He holds honorary degrees from Knox College, the University of Chicago, the University of Rochester, Yale University, the City University of New York, and Clark University.

SELECTED WORKS: The Role of Strong Interactions in Decay Processes, 1957; Advanced Quantum Mechanics Lectures, 1959; Gravitation and Cosmology: Principles and Applications of the General Theory of Relativity, 1972; The First Three Minutes: A Modern View of the Origin of the Universe, 1977; The Discovery of Subatomic Particles, 1983.

ABOUT: New Scientist October 18, 1979; Nova: Adventures in Science, 1982; Science December 14, 1979.

THOMAS H. WELLER

WELLER, THOMAS H.
(June 15, 1915–   )
Nobel Prize for Physiology or Medicine, 1954
(shared with John F. Enders and Frederick C. Robbins)

Thomas Huckle Weller, an American virologist, was born in Ann Arbor, Michigan, to Carl V. Weller, chairman of the pathology department at the University of Michigan Medical School, and Elsie (Huckle) Weller. Growing up in an academic environment, Weller became interested in natural history at an early age. He studied medical zoology at the University of Michigan, from which he received a B.A. in 1936 and an M.S. in 1937 for work on fish parasites.

Entering Harvard Medical School in 1936, Weller continued his studies in parasitology. He was particularly interested in trichinosis and attempted to cultivate the worm responsible for the disease. At the same time, a Harvard professor, JOHN F. ENDERS, was developing new techniques for growing animal cells outside the body, and Weller elected to do his senior research under him. Enders's work on viruses drew Weller into the field of virology and the use of tissue-culture techniques to study infectious diseases. After graduating from medical school in 1940, Weller accepted an appointment at Children's Hospital, Boston, to acquire clinical training with experience in infectious and parasitic diseases.

In 1942, shortly after the United States entered World War II, Weller joined the United States Army Medical Corps. Stationed at the Antilles Medical Laboratory in Puerto Rico, he conducted pioneer research on the tropical liver parasite Schistosoma. He served as head of the bacteriology, virology, and parasitology departments and was discharged with the rank of major.

After the war he returned to Children's Hospital to complete his residency in pediatrics. In 1946 Enders started a new Infectious Diseases Research Laboratory there and asked Weller to join him. Weller suggested another researcher for the team, FREDERICK C. ROBBINS, his roommate from medical school, who joined the laboratory in 1948.

The methods Enders and Weller developed for growing animal cells in tissue culture incorporated several important advances. The researchers were able to keep cells in the same test tube for a relatively long time by changing the medium instead of transferring the cells to different containers. They avoided contamination by using both penicillin and streptomycin to keep bacteria from overgrowing the animal cells.

Once Enders and Weller had demonstrated that their methods worked for mumps virus, Weller returned to his prewar research on varicella, a virus that infects only humans and must be grown in human tissue. Weller prepared cultures of skin and muscle tissue from human embryos to cultivate the varicella virus and stored what was left. At the same time, a frozen specimen of a poliovirus was stored in the laboratory. The virus, known as the Lansing strain, infected mice but was thought to grow only in nerve tissue, which is difficult to cultivate in sufficient quantity for testing a virus. As Weller, Enders, and Robbins later said, "Thereupon it suddenly occurred to us that everything had been prepared almost without conscious effort on our part for a new attempt to cultivate the [poliomyelitis] agent in extraneural tissue."

The three researchers cultivated poliovirus in the cell cultures and, to demonstrate its viability, injected mice with the culture medium. The mice contracted polio. Because this method of testing for the presence of the virus in the cultures was time-consuming and expensive, they sought a better one. Since cells in the cultures were being damaged by the poliovirus, Weller and his associates found that they could track the growth of the virus by looking for evidence of this damage, either by examining cells under a microscope or by observing the change in acidity of the culture fluid produced by the destruction of cells.

Weller, Enders, and Robbins had originally grown cells in suspension, but they knew that cells could be cultivated in a solid layer in bottles that were constantly rolled to keep the cells uniformly nourished. When they infected roller-bottle cultures with poliovirus, they observed the altered cells directly. Instead of waiting two weeks for the cells to degenerate sufficiently to change the acidity of the culture or taking time to isolate cells from suspension and grow them, they could obtain unequivocal results in three to five days.

In many virological studies, tissue culture was now a suitable substitute for the use of expensive laboratory animals. Cultures could also determine whether poliovirus was present in a sample and could test blood for antibodies to polio. The new technique permitted scientists to grow a virus in culture for many generations in an effort to isolate a variant that would multiply without being dangerous—the basic requirement for a live, attenuated vaccine. Although Weller, Enders, and Robbins had no interest in producing polio vaccine themselves, their research paved the way for the vaccines that were eventually produced.

Weller shared the 1954 Nobel Prize for Physiology or Medicine with Enders and Robbins "for their discovery of the ability of poliomyelitis viruses to grow in cultures of various types of tissue." Sven Gard of the Karolinska Institute said on presenting the award, "By giving the virologists a practicable method for the isolation and study of viruses you relieved them of a handicap . . . and placed them for the first time on an even footing with other microbe hunters."

Weller returned to his study of the virus that causes chicken pox and demonstrated that it is the same virus that causes herpes zoster (shingles). Tissue culture proved to be useful in isolating new viruses as well as in studying old ones; Weller used it to isolate cytomegalovirus, which causes cerebral palsy and mental retardation in children. In 1962 he isolated the virus that causes rubella (German measles). His studies of the rubella virus and cytomegalovirus led to the discovery of congenital infection, which occurs when a fetus is infected with certain viruses. Instead of dying or eliminating the virus, the infant can grow up to carry the disease and be a source of virus infection for many years.

Weller worked at Boston Children's Hospital until 1954, when he became chairman of Harvard's Department of Tropical Public Health. He subsequently became director of the Center for Prevention of Infectious Diseases at Harvard School of Public Health. Under his direction Harvard became a center for research on schistosomiasis. Since 1954 he has been Strong Professor of Tropical Public Health at Harvard.

In 1945 Weller married Kathleen Fahey; they have two sons and two daughters.

In addition to the Nobel Prize, Weller shared the Mead Johnson Award of the American Academy of Pediatrics with Robbins in 1953. He has also received the George Ledlie Prize of Harvard University (1963) and the Bristol Award of the Infectious Diseases Society of America (1980). He is a member of the National Academy of Sciences.

ABOUT: Current Biography June 1955; Nature October 30, 1954; New York Times October 22, 1954; Williams, G. Virus Hunters, 1959.

WERNER, ALFRED
(December 12, 1866–November 15, 1919)
Nobel Prize for Chemistry, 1913

The Swiss chemist Alfred Werner (ver' nər) was born in Mulhouse in the province of Alsace, France. He was the last of four children of Jean-Adam Werner, a foreman in an ironworks, and the former Salomé Jeanette Tesché. The family remained in Mulhouse when Alsace became part of the German Empire in 1871, after the Franco-Prussian War, but they continued to identify themselves with France. Werner was sent to the Catholic École Libre des Frères, where his unusual self-confidence

ALFRED WERNER

and stubborn independence were noted. From 1878 to 1885 he studied chemistry at the École Professionelle. While serving his year of required military duty in the German army, he attended classes in organic chemistry at the technical university in Karlsruhe.

After completing his military service, Werner entered the Federal Institute of Technology in Zurich, where he received a diploma in technical chemistry in 1889 and a Ph.D. the following year. Although his school record was weak in mathematics, his chemical talents were remarkable. His doctoral dissertation concerned the spatial arrangement of atoms in nitrogen compounds.

In 1874 Joseph Achille Le Bel and JACOBUS VAN'T HOFF had shown that, when carbon atoms are bonded to other atoms, a tetrahedron (a geometric solid of four faces) centered upon the carbon atom is formed. It was known that nitrogen typically forms three bonds. For example, in the ammonia molecule, the nitrogen atom is at the apex of a triangular pyramid with three hydrogen atoms at the corners of the base. Werner and his thesis adviser, Arthur Hantzsch, showed that the nitrogen atom could also exhibit tetrahedral bonding.

After a year in Paris, where he studied thermochemistry under Marcellin Berthelot, Werner returned to Zurich in 1892 to become a lecturer in organic chemistry at the Federal Institute of Technology. He was appointed associate professor and director of the chemical laboratory the following year. In 1895, he was appointed professor of organic chemistry, a subject on which he began lecturing in 1902.

At this time, it was understood that atoms consist of positively charged nuclei surrounded by negatively charged electrons in orbiting shells. Each shell holds only a certain number of electrons, and the atom is most stable when the outermost shell is full. To achieve this stability, atoms are held together in molecules by chemical bonds. The number of bonds formed by an atom corresponds to its valence, which is the number of electrons in its outer shell. The types of chemical bonds vary. In ionic bonds, electrons are transferred. In covalent bonds, electrons are shared. In hydrogen bonds, a hydrogen atom acts as a bridge between two electronegative atoms. An additional type of bond occurs in crystalline metals, where the valence electrons are shared collectively by all the atoms in the crystal rather than by pairs of atoms as in covalent bonds. The traditional concept of valence explained the binding forces of the atom but did not explain those of the large class composed of inorganic molecular compounds. Some explanation of their structure and the nature of their chemical bonds was needed.

In a paper, "Contribution to the Theory of Affinity and Valence," published in an obscure journal in 1891, Werner defined *affinity* as "a force issuing from the center of the atom, uniformly attractive in all directions, whose geometrical expression is therefore not a given number of guiding lines but a spherical surface." Two years later, in "A Contribution to the Construction of Inorganic Compounds," he proposed his coordination theory, according to which single atoms act as central nuclei in inorganic molecular compounds. Around these central atoms, a definite number of other atoms or molecules are arranged in a simple geometrical octahedron. Werner called the number of atoms grouped around the central nucleus the coordination number. He viewed the coordination bond as the sharing of a pair of electrons contributed by one molecule or atom to another.

Because Werner proposed the existence of compounds that had never been observed or synthesized, his theory was strongly opposed by many noted chemists who thought that it unnecessarily complicated the theoretical understanding of chemical structure and bonding. Therefore, for the next two decades, Werner and his collaborators prepared new molecular compounds whose existence was postulated by his theory. They reported their results in more than 150 publications. Among these compounds were molecules exhibiting optical activity, or the ability to deflect polarized light, but containing no carbon atoms, which were believed necessary for the optical activity of molecules. Werner's synthesis in 1911 of more than forty optically active molecules without carbon atoms convinced the chemical community of the validity of his theories.

The 1913 Nobel Prize for Chemistry was awarded to Werner in "recognition of his work on the linkage of atoms in molecules, by which he has thrown new light on earlier investigations and opened up new fields of research, especially in inorganic chemistry." According to Theodor Nordström of the Royal Swedish Academy of Sciences, who presented the award, Werner's work "set the trend of development in inorganic chemistry" and stimulated fresh interest in the field after a period of neglect.

Werner married Emma Wilhelmine Giesker of Zurich in 1894, the same year he became a Swiss citizen. They had a son and a daughter. Werner was a demanding teacher who served as adviser to more than 200 doctoral students in the course of his career. Known as a sociable man, he enjoyed playing billiards, chess, and the card game jass, and vacationing in the Alps during the fall. Shortly after receiving the Nobel Prize, he was found to have arteriosclerosis of the brain. He resigned his professorship and died a month later, on November 15, 1919, at the age of fifty-two.

In addition to the Nobel Prize, Werner received the Leblanc Medal of the French Chemical Society and an honorary doctorate from the University of Geneva. He was a member of the British Chemical Society, the Göttingen Academy of Sciences, and numerous other scientific societies.

SELECTED WORKS: New Ideas on Inorganic Chemistry, 1911; The Selected Papers of Alfred Werner, 1968.

ABOUT: Dictionary of Scientific Biography, volume 14, 1976; Farber, E. (ed.) Great Chemists, 1961; Kauffman, G. B. Alfred Werner–Founder of Coordination Chemistry, 1966.

WHIPPLE, GEORGE H.

(August 28, 1878–February 1, 1976)
Nobel Prize for Physiology or Medicine, 1934
(shared with George R. Minot and William P. Murphy)

The American physician and pathologist George Hoyt Whipple was born in Ashland,

GEORGE H. WHIPPLE

New Hampshire, the son of Frances (Hoyt) Whipple and Ashley Cooper Whipple, a general practitioner. Growing up in rural surroundings, the boy developed a lifelong love of hunting, fishing, and camping. Even as a student in the local elementary school, Whipple knew that he wanted to become a doctor, and that conviction persisted throughout his high school years in Tilton, New Hampshire, to which he commuted daily by train. At Phillips Andover Academy, he enjoyed courses in biology, chemistry, and physics while preparing for entrance to Yale University.

At Yale, Whipple enrolled in a diversified science curriculum and rowed for his fraternity and class crews. He graduated with a B.A. in 1900. To support his medical studies, he taught mathematics and science for a year at the Holbrook Military Academy in Ossining, New York, while studying Gray's *Anatomy* during his spare time. Two years after entering the Johns Hopkins School of Medicine in 1901, he received a paying instructorship that also helped finance his studies. On receiving his medical degree in 1905, he joined the staff at Johns Hopkins as an assistant in pathology; he went on a leave of absence two years later to study tropical diseases in Panama.

When he returned to Johns Hopkins, Whipple began working with John Sperry, who was attempting to damage the liver of dogs with chloroform to study how liver cells repair themselves. Although similar damage was known to occur in human beings, canine livers exhibited such a rapid repair rate that no sustained injury could be produced. Instead, the dogs developed jaundice, a condition in which the skin and whites of the eyes appear yellow because of excess bile, the substance manufactured in the liver that aids fat digestion. One source of bile is the normal breakdown of hemoglobin, the iron-containing protein of red blood cells.

These experiments led Whipple to focus his research on the interrelationship of liver, bile, and hemoglobin. At that time it was generally believed that bile pigments were derived solely from the hemoglobin of red corpuscles and that the pigmentation process took place only in the liver. Whipple, however, doubted that the liver was the only place where bile transformation could occur. In 1911, while visiting the laboratory of Hans Meyer in Vienna, Whipple learned to perform the Eck fistula technique, by which blood from the intestines is shunted past the liver. By combining the Eck technique with ligation of the hepatic arteries, Whipple and a talented medical student, Charles W. Hooper, were able to exclude all blood from the liver. They observed that within one or two hours hemoglobin injected into the circulation was converted into bile pigments. Even when the circulation of the spleen and intestines was cut off, a conversion of hemoglobin to bile pigments still took place, apparently by the breakdown of hemoglobin in the bloodstream. In this way Whipple and Hooper demonstrated that under experimental conditions, the formation of bile pigments can occur without help from the liver, but that under life conditions, the liver plays a constructive role of some kind in the production of bile pigments.

In 1914 Whipple accepted a position as director of the Hooper Foundation for Medical Research at the University of California, San Francisco. There, as he pursued his work with bile fistulas, Whipple realized that he needed a knowledge of hemoglobin formation to understand its conversion to bile. In 1917–1918 Whipple, Charles Hooper, and Frieda Robbins bled dogs to make them anemic; after feeding them liver, they noticed a marked increase in hemoglobin regeneration.

Whipple was named dean of the University of California Medical School in 1920, and a year later he was named dean of a new medical complex at the University of Rochester in New York. When Whipple arrived in Rochester, however, he found that the buildings were only in the blueprint stage, and he therefore was involved in the earliest aspects of the school's creation. His co-worker Robbins and their group of anemic dogs accompanied Whipple to Rochester, where between 1923 and 1925 Robbins supervised the hemoglobin research while Whipple fulfilled his administrative duties. Their technique for bleeding dogs was refined to the point where they could induce long-term anemia. They bled dogs to a hemoglobin level of one-third of normal and then maintained the anemia by periodic blood lettings. By feeding the dogs a variety of measured foods, they were able to estimate the quantitative rise in hemoglobin levels. Again, liver proved to be the best stimulator of hemoglobin production. After the new medical school opened in 1925, Whipple devoted more time to his experiments. The following year a liver extract was made in cooperation with Eli Lilly and Company for the treatment of human anemias. Although Lilly held the patent, Whipple, who tested and standardized the extract, used the royalties from its sales to fund additional research.

Whipple's work with anemic dogs laid the groundwork for GEORGE R. MINOT's and WILLIAM P. MURPHY's successful utilization in 1926 of liver in the treatment of patients suffering from pernicious anemia, which at the time was a fatal disease. (When Whipple's colleague Hooper had fed liver to three patients with pernicious anemia in 1918, he had observed an improvement; however, he discontinued his line of experimentation when other clinicians derided him.)

"For their discoveries concerning liver therapy in cases of anemia," Whipple, Minot, and Murphy shared the 1934 Nobel Prize for Physiology or Medicine. "This new method," said Israel Holmgren of the Karolinska Institute in his presentation speech, "has already saved thousands of lives, and will in the future save innumerable human beings from death."

In pernicious anemia, unlike any other form of the disease, the building blocks of red blood cells are available but accumulate in the liver. At the time, the mechanism responsible was not known. Whipple suggested in 1934 that this factor probably involved the stroma, or scaffolding, of red blood cells. Fourteen years later, other researchers identified it as vitamin B_{12}; still later, it was determined that vitamin B_{12} is required for the proper arrangement of deoxyribonucleic acid (DNA) that codes for the red blood cell framework.

In other research, Whipple studied how liver affects blood plasma, the yellowish fluid part of blood. In using radioactively tagged amino acids, he found that liver continuously produces plasma proteins that pass from the blood to body tissues. He also used radioactive iron to study hemoglobin metabolism and radioactive cobalt to examine the role of vitamin B_{12} in the formation of red blood cells. Another of his interests was thalassemia, a rare anemia that affects those of Mediterranean ancestry. Whipple was also the first researcher to identify a rare intestinal disease involving impaired fat digestion (Whipple's disease).

After resigning as dean of the medical school at the University of Rochester in 1952, with more than 12,000 graduates in various fields to his credit, Whipple continued to serve in various capacities. In 1963 he established a library fund valued at $750,000, bringing the total university funding for which he was directly responsible to about $1.5 million.

In 1914 Whipple married Katherine Ball Waring, who was a music teacher in New York City. The couple had a son and a daughter. He died in Rochester on February 1, 1976, in the hospital he had helped to build.

Whipple was the recipient of the Kober Medal of the Association of American Physicians (1939), the Jessie Stevenson Kovalenko Medal of the National Academy of Sciences (1962), and the Distinguished Federal Civilian Service Award (1963), which was presented by President John F. Kennedy. He served as a trustee of the Rockefeller Foundation from 1927 to 1943 and as a member of the board of scientific directors of the Rockefeller Institute of Medical Research from 1936 to 1953. Between 1953 and 1960 he served as vice-chairman of the Foundation's Board of Trustees. He was a member of the American Society of Experimental Pathology and the American Association of Pathologists and Bacteriologists. He was awarded honorary degrees from Yale, Colgate, and Tulane universities, and from the University of California, among other institutions.

SELECTED WORKS: Blood Volume Studies, 1912, with others; The Metabolism of Bile Acids, 1919, with M. G. Foster; Hemoglobin, Plasma and Cell Protein, 1948; The Dynamic Equilibrium of Body Proteins, 1956; A Generalized Atomic Energy Program, 1960.

ABOUT: Corner, G. George Hoyt Whipple and His Friends, 1963; Ingle, D. J. (ed.) A Dozen Doctors, 1963; New York Times February 2, 1976; Rowntree, L. G. Amid Masters of Twentieth Century Medicine, 1958.

WHITE, PATRICK
(May 28, 1912–   )
Nobel Prize for Literature, 1973

The Australian novelist Patrick Victor Martindale White was born in England to Ruth (Withycombe) and Victor White, an affluent Australian couple who were traveling abroad at the time of his birth. Six months later, his parents returned to Australia and settled in Sydney, where White received his early education and where his younger sister was born.

At the age of thirteen, White was sent to school in Cheltenham, England. His housemaster there deplored the "morbid kink" that enabled White to appreciate the plays of Henrik Ibsen and August Strindberg. White persuaded his parents to let him return to Australia to see whether he could adapt to "life on the land" before entering Cambridge University. For two years he worked as a *jackeroo*, or cowhand, and began writing fiction. Regarded as an outsider by other Australians because of his English schooling, White was relieved to return to England in 1932. At King's College, Cambridge, he enjoyed French and German literature. During vacations, he visited France and Germany to improve his command of those languages.

His first publication was a volume of verses, undated but written before 1930. After receiving his B.A. from Cambridge in 1935, White went to London to make his living as a writer, supported by a small allowance from his father. That year he published *The Ploughman and Other Poems* and wrote several plays (now lost), sketches for theater revues, and short stories. His first novel, *Happy Valley*, was published in London in 1939. In New York City, where he went to find an American publisher, the book was turned down by a number of publishers before being accepted in 1940 by Viking Press.

During the first months of World War II, White wrote his second novel, *The Living and the Dead* (1941), set in London in the 1930s. He served the next four years in Royal Air Force intelligence, stationed in the Middle East and Greece.

After the war, he wrote two plays, *Return to Abyssinia* and *The Ham Funeral*. The first, now lost, was performed briefly in London. The second was not staged until 1961, in Adelaide, Australia. His third novel, *The Aunt's Story* (1948), received favorable reviews in England and the United States but was generally ignored in Australia. Nevertheless, White felt exhilarated by its reception. *The Aunt's Story*, which marks White's maturity as a writer, presents the world through the eyes of Theodora Goodman, who, having abandoned herself to her inner life, eventually goes mad. She is, wrote the Australian critic R. F. Brissenden, "the first of White's illuminati, . . . those

PATRICK WHITE

Voss (1957), also considered one of White's finest works, was inspired by the life of Ludwig Leichhardt, an explorer who disappeared in 1848 while attempting to cross Australia from east to west. According to Brissenden, *Voss* is "an attempt to investigate the psychological motivations of exploration; and it is a many-leveled allegory, a parable in which Patrick White tries to illuminate, in religious terms, the struggle in man's heart between pride and humility, faith in oneself and faith in God, and in which he tries also . . . to cut through to the spiritual center of Australian society just as Voss, his hero, struggles toward the geographical center of the continent."

Riders in the Chariot (1961) portrays four misfits and contrasts them with the conventional society of Sarsaparilla, a fictitious Australian suburb. White's first collection of short stories, *The Burnt Ones* (1964), contains several fine studies of Sarsaparilla. *Four Plays,* published in 1965, includes *The Season at Sarsaparilla, A Cheery Soul, Night on Bald Mountain,* and, from 1948, *The Ham Funeral.* The first two plays explore Sarsaparilla society, one in a satiric mode. *Night on Bald Mountain,* an eloquent and poetic tragedy, depicts a society on the verge of collapse.

Sarsaparilla is also the setting of *The Solid Mandala* (1966), a novel about the interrelated lives of Waldo and Arthur, twin brothers whose contrasting personalities form a single identity. Arid and intellectual, Waldo lives his life hating his half-witted twin and failing to achieve his literary ambitions or to find love. Although simpleminded, Arthur is a visionary. His four treasured marbles are mandalas, symbols of totality which offer him insight into the mysteries of life and which represent his love for those closest to him. White's psychological and religious preoccupations in *The Solid Mandala* were influenced by his reading of C. G. Jung. In this work, according to the *Times Literary Supplement,* White "[has] seen eternity like a great ring of endless light."

The Vivisectors (1970) shows how the power of vision enables an artist, Hurtle Duffield, to attain the mystic intensity that lies behind everyday life. In *The Eye of the Storm* (1973), the heroine, Elizabeth Hunter, finds pure existence in death, just as she did during a typhoon off the coast of Queensland earlier in life. Its thesis, said Robert Phillips in *Commonweal,* "is simply this: We are all alone in a chaotic world, and only we ourselves can help ourselves during our brief tenure. Others are predators who hinder rather than help."

White received the 1973 Nobel Prize for Lit-

who have been at once blessed and cursed with the ability to see with unusual clarity; and who have as well . . . an intuition that behind . . . the world of ordinary, imperfect experience, there is another world of timeless order and beauty."

Finding London sterile and feeling the need to earn a living through some more reliable means than writing, White returned to Australia in 1946 with a Greek friend, Manoly Lascaris. With the exception of brief trips, they have remained there. White and Lascaris bought an old house in Castle Hill, a suburb of Sydney, and for the next eighteen years they farmed and sold flowers, vegetables, milk, and cream. The failure of *The Aunt's Story* in Australia, his inability to get *The Ham Funeral* produced, and hardships during the first years at Castle Hill made White wonder "whether [he] should ever write another word." In 1951, however, he began *The Tree of Man,* published in the United States in 1955 and subsequently in Great Britain. It immediately established his reputation. According to Brissenden, "Reviewers hailed it as a great novel, and White was acclaimed as a major writer" by critics who compared him to Thomas Hardy, Leo Tolstoy, and D. H. Lawrence.

A long family saga, *The Tree of Man* concerns an ordinary couple who establish a farm in the Australian wilderness, raise their children, have grandchildren, and eventually see their land engulfed by a suburb. In the pioneering life of these simple people, White perceived the significance and grandeur of human life itself.

erature "for an epic and psychological narrative art which has introduced a new continent into literature." In his presentation speech, Artur Lundkvist of the Swedish Academy noted that although White is "constantly assailed by doubts concerning the capacity of thought and art," he "is indefatigable in his high-minded pursuit of both these things." White, who guards his privacy and shuns publicity, did not attend the award ceremonies. The prize was accepted on his behalf by the Australian artist Sidney Nolan.

In 1974 *The Cockatoos,* a collection of six short stories, was published. Two years later, *A Fringe of Leaves* appeared, a novel based on the true story of Mrs. Eliza Fraser, who was shipwrecked off the Great Barrier Reef in 1836. According to the English critic William Walsh, this novel records "the efforts of an ordinary, good, sensitive, but not particularly talented woman, to come closer to what she had missed and to be prepared to suffer in her pursuit of it." *The Oxford History of Australian Literature* asserts that in the 1970s White appeared to have entered "a new phase" in which "the heavily symbolic and allusive language is seen . . . as inventing rather than invoking the vision."

The Twyborn Affair (1979) is a novel about the three incarnations of an Australian whose ambivalent sexual identity highlights the conflict between love and sex. White's recent dramatic works include the play *Big Toys* (1977); a screenplay based on an earlier short story, *The Night The Prowler* (1977); and the plays *Signal Driver* (1982) and *Netherwood* (1983). His acclaimed self-portrait, *Flaws in the Glass,* was published in 1981. The novel *Memoirs of Many in One,* published in 1986, relates the life and erotic adventures of Alex Xenophon Demirjian Gray through a series of fictional diary entries.

Even though White's two short story collections, *The Burnt Ones* and *The Cockatoos,* have been highly praised by reviewers, John Alfred Avant has pointed out that "the short form is not, and probably never will be, the best showcase for his genius." Similarly, John A. Weigel praised White's excellent ear for dialogue in his dramatic works but observed, "No one . . . has seriously suggested that the literary world was significantly changed or even enhanced by White's plays as it has been by his novels."

In the view of the English critic and scholar George Steiner, "The reciprocities of minute material detail and vast time sweeps, the thread of hysteria underneath the dreary crust, the play of European densities against the gross vacancy of the Australian setting, are the constant motifs of White's fiction." Yet if White is "one of the current virtuosos of the grotesque," as Steiner has stated, "the result is strain. White forces his style." Admirers like William Walsh, however, have found in White's work a grandeur and intensity of imagination and "the qualities of largeness, uninhibited confidence, and potent creative energy."

ADDITIONAL WORKS: The God in the Rafters, 1978; Stations, 1978; Seventeen Odes, 1982.

ABOUT: Björksten, I. Patrick White: A General Introduction, 1976; Bliss, C. J. Patrick White's Fiction, 1986; Colmer, J. Patrick White, 1984; Dutton, G. Patrick White, 1978; Kiernan, B. Patrick White, 1980; McCulloch, A. M. A Tragic Vision: The Novels of Patrick White, 1983; Walsh, W. Patrick White's Fiction, 1977; Wolfe, P. Laden Choirs: The Fiction of Patrick White, 1983.

WIELAND, HEINRICH
(June 4, 1877–August 5, 1957)
Nobel Prize for Chemistry, 1927

The German chemist Heinrich Otto Wieland (vē′ länt) was born in Pforzheim to Theodor Wieland, a pharmaceutical chemist, and Elise (Blom) Wieland. After receiving his early education in the local schools, he studied chemistry at the universities of Munich, Berlin, and Stuttgart. He received a Ph.D. in 1901 from the University of Munich, where he then became a lecturer and, in 1909, an associate professor. Four years later he was appointed professor at the Munich Technical University. During World War I, while on leave of absence in 1917–1918, Wieland worked under FRITZ HABER at the Kaiser Wilhelm Institute for Physical Chemistry and Electrochemistry in Berlin on the German effort to develop chemical weapons. After the war, he resumed his position in Munich until 1921, when he moved to the University of Freiburg for three years. He returned to the University of Munich in 1924 as chairman of the organic chemistry department and director of the Baeyer Laboratory (named for ADOLF VON BAEYER), a position he held until his retirement in 1950.

In contrast to the tendency among scientists to concentrate their efforts in increasingly narrow fields, Wieland made significant contri-

HEINRICH WIELAND

butions to a vast range of organic chemistry topics. He also dealt with many problems untouched by previous experimenters.

Wieland first studied the chemistry of organic nitrogen compounds, particularly the mechanism of the addition of nitrogen oxides to carbon-carbon double bonds and the nitration of aromatic hydrocarbons. He went on to demonstrate the sequence of reactions and intermediate compounds in the synthesis of fulminic acid from ethanol, nitric acid, and mercury. His analysis of the color reactions of hydrazines led to the discovery of the first known nitrogen free radicals (highly reactive groups of atoms possessing an odd unpaired electron). Wieland and his colleagues published more than ninety papers about their studies of nitrogen compounds.

Ever since 1774, when the French chemist Antoine Lavoisier had described the role of oxygen in combustion reactions, chemists had believed that the process was caused by "activated" (highly reactive, unstable) oxygen. Drawing on decades of prior research, Wieland developed a dehydrogenation theory based on the activation of hydrogen. He interpreted the oxidation of many organic and inorganic compounds as dehydrogenations (for example, the removal of hydrogen from phosphorous and formic acids, and the formation of sulfuric acid from sulfur dioxide). He unified the disciplines of organic chemistry and biochemistry by demonstrating dehydrogenation in living cells (for example, the conversion of acetates to succinic acid in oxygen-depleted yeast cells).

Another topic of lifelong investigation, begun in 1912, was the chemistry of bile acids, substances stored in the gallbladder that aid in the digestion of lipids. Using classical organic chemistry methods, without the benefit of such modern research tools as spectrometry, chromatography, and X-ray analysis, Wieland undertook what he would later describe as "a long and unspeakably wearisome trek through an arid desert of structure." The demonstration that cholic acid, deoxycholic acid, and lithocholic acid could be converted to cholanic acid indicated that these bile acids have the same carbon skeleton and differ only in the number of attached hydroxyl ($-OH$) groups. At about the same time, ADOLF WINDAUS converted cholesterol into cholanic acid, thus proving a close structural relationship between bile acids and cholesterol. Wieland's group then performed stepwise degradations of the bile acids, which led to inconclusive results about the size of the carbon rings. In 1932 the English chemists Otto Rosenheim and Harold King demonstrated, by means of X-ray crystallography, that all these substances were steroids (organic compounds with a basic four-membered carbon-ring structure). Wieland noted that because bile acids combine with fats and hydrocarbons to form colloidal solutions in water, a physiological function of bile acids is to convert dietary fats into water-soluble compounds.

The 1927 Nobel Prize for Chemistry was awarded to Wieland in 1928 "for his investigations of the constitution of the bile acids and related substances." In his presentation speech, H. G. Söderbaum of the Royal Swedish Academy of Sciences hailed Wieland for his solution to a problem that Söderbaum called "without doubt one of the most difficult which organic chemistry has had to tackle." Noting that "Wieland succeeded in producing from bile a saturated acid which can be regarded as the mother substance or parent acid of the bile acids," Söderbaum compared it to similar discoveries made by Windaus. "When Windaus . . . produced this same parent acid, cholanic acid, from cholesterol, this indicated very clearly the close relationship between cholesterol and the bile acids."

In other work Wieland directed research on the chemistry of naturally occurring substances: morphine and strychnine, the curare and lobelia alkaloids, the poisonous cyclopeptides phalloidine and amanitin from the death cup mushroom, toad poisons, and butterfly-wing pigments (pterins).

Wieland married Josephine Bartmann in

1908. They had three sons (one of whom, Theodor, determined the correct structure of phalloidine) and a daughter, who married FEODOR LYNEN. As evident from his many accomplishments, Wieland had abundant energy and a great capacity for work. He also had a deep interest in painting and music and often took part in musical recitals in his home. He died in Starnberg, West Germany, at the age of eighty.

Known for his encyclopedic knowledge of chemistry, Wieland served for twenty years as editor of *Liebig's Annalen der Chemie* (Liebig's Annals of Chemistry). Among the many learned societies to which he belonged were the Royal Society of London; the American National Academy of Sciences; the American Academy of Arts and Sciences; the chemical societies of London, Romania, Japan, India, and Moscow; and the science academies of Munich, Göttingen, Heidelberg, and Berlin. In 1955 he received the first Otto Hahn Prize for Physics and Chemistry of the German Chemical Society. He held honorary degrees from the universities of Freiburg and Athens.

SELECTED WORKS: On the Mechanism of Oxidation, 1932.

ABOUT: Biographical Memoirs of Fellows of the Royal Society, volume 4, 1958; Dictionary of Scientific Biography, volume 14, 1976; Farber, E. (ed.) Great Chemists, 1961; Journal of the Chemical Society August 1958.

WIEN, WILHELM
(January 13, 1864–August 30, 1928)
Nobel Prize for Physics, 1911

The German physicist Wilhelm Carl Werner Otto Fritz Franz Wien (vēn) was born in Gaffken, then part of East Prussia (now Primorsk in the Soviet Union), the only child of Carl Wien, a farmer, and the former Caroline Gertz. When the boy was two years old, his family moved to a smaller farm in Drachenstein. Introverted like his father, Wilhelm made no friends and was especially close to his mother. As was then the custom, a woman was hired to teach him French, which he spoke before he learned to write German. Wien began his formal education at age eleven at the Rastenburg Gymnasium. He was not an attentive student, preferring to roam in the fields, and received inadequate instruction, especially in

WILHELM WIEN

mathematics. His parents took him out of school in 1879 and brought him home to learn farming, continuing his academic studies with a private tutor. Wien then entered the gymnasium in Königsberg in the fall of 1880 and graduated early in the spring of 1882. Later in the spring, with his mother's encouragement, he enrolled in the University of Göttingen. Dissatisfied with his mathematics courses and disliking the life of the student societies, he left Göttingen after only one semester to tour the Rhineland. He returned home intending to become a farmer, but finding this work unsatisfactory, he resumed his studies in mathematics and physics at the University of Berlin in the fall of 1882.

After two semesters of classes and three years of laboratory work under Hermann von Helmholtz, an eminent physicist, mathematician, and physiologist, with an intervening summer of study at the University of Heidelberg, Wien received his doctorate in 1886. His dissertation was on the diffraction of light at a sharp metallic edge and the effect of absorption by the metal on the colors produced. Diffraction is a phenomenon that results from the wave properties of light. If a screen is placed beyond the metal barrier on the side opposite the light source, a diffraction pattern is formed under appropriate conditions. The pattern consists of alternately bright and dark bands of illumination on the screen, extending below the geometric shadow of the barrier as if the light were bending around the edge. Since the spacing between bright and dark bands is related to the wavelength (corresponding to color), and the pattern produced by each wavelength is displaced from those produced by other wavelengths, diffraction can separate light containing a mixture of colors into colored bands. Wien found that the diffracted light was polarized and that the material of the edge influenced the colors. He believed that the color effect could not be explained on the basis of existing theories because they did not take into account the vibrations of the molecules in the diffracting edge.

In the summer of 1886 Wien went home to help on his parents' farm after a fire had destroyed several buildings. He remained there for the next four years while continuing to study theoretical physics on his own. His future was decided when a drought in 1890 forced his parents to sell their land. Wien then became an assistant to Helmholtz at the new State Physical-Technical Institute in Charlottenburg (now part of West Berlin), doing research on industrial problems.

Wien carried out broad-ranging scientific investigations over a thirty-year period at various academic institutions. In 1892 he became a lecturer at the University of Berlin; in 1896 he was named professor of physics at the technical university in Aachen, succeeding PHILIPP VON LENARD. He spent a brief time as professor of physics at the University of Giessen in 1899 and succeeded WILHELM RÖNTGEN as professor of physics at the University of Würzburg in 1900.

Wien's research encompassed a range of subjects, including hydrodynamics, especially the behavior of sea waves and cyclones. While at the State Physical-Technical Institute, he began his seminal research into thermal radiation, the emissions of bodies due to their temperature. To various degrees, bodies absorb, reflect, or transmit radiation that falls on them; independently, they also radiate energy by virtue of their thermal condition. The filament of a light bulb is a familiar example. In the 1860s Gustav Kirchhoff, in a theoretical study of the relation between emission and absorption, introduced the concept of an ideal blackbody that absorbs all incident radiation and reflects none. An actual body that is black, like carbon soot, is an excellent, but not perfect, absorber and reflects a small fraction of the light that strikes it. It appears black because it returns so little illumination. An ideal blackbody is a perfect absorber, and Kirchhoff showed that it is also the best possible emitter and so provides a standard for describing the relationship between emitted radiation and emitter temperature without concern for the material makeup of the emitter.

Although no ordinary body can be a perfect blackbody, Kirchhoff demonstrated on theoretical grounds that a space completely enclosed by walls at a uniform temperature (a furnace, for example) has the necessary blackbody properties, regardless of the composition of the walls. Evidence of this is presented by the characteristics of a small peephole drilled into one wall. Radiation entering the hole will strike the far wall and be partly absorbed and partly reflected. The reflected portion is highly unlikely to be directed back out through the small hole. Instead, it will undergo a series of internal reflections and absorptions until completely absorbed (slightly warming the walls) and will never reemerge. That is, it will be totally absorbed, as it should be by an ideal blackbody. Kirchhoff deduced that the radiation in such a cavity, composed of rays crisscrossing between the walls, will contain a distribution of wavelengths and intensities that depends only on the temperature and not on the material in the walls.

In 1893 Wien investigated blackbody radiation, using what he called "mental," rather than laboratory, experiments, based on the laws of thermodynamics. The Austrian physicist Ludwig Boltzmann had similarly used thermodynamic theory to confirm a mathematical formula determined empirically by a fellow countryman, Josef Stefan. Stefan had noted that the total energy per second radiated by a blackbody, including all wavelengths, was proportional to the fourth power of the body's absolute temperature (degrees kelvin, or degrees centigrade above $-273°C$, absolute zero). Wien advanced the theoretical exploration by calculating how changes in temperature would affect the energy radiated at each different wavelength, or color (actually narrow bands of wavelength centered about a particular value). It was known from experiments that a heated body emits radiation over a range, or spectrum, of wavelengths, but not uniformly. A graph of radiated energy versus wavelength is a curve that starts at a low value at long wavelengths, rises smoothly to a rounded peak, representing a maximum of intensity at a particular intermediate wavelength, and then falls again to low energy values at shorter wavelengths. Wien found that the curve shifts to shorter or longer wavelengths as the temperature rises or falls, respectively, in accordance with a simple relationship, now known as Wien's displacement law. The wavelength at the peak of radiation multiplied by the absolute temperature remains a constant as both change. Since the curve retains its basic shape as the temperature changes, knowledge of the curve at any one temperature permits a construction of the curve at any other temperature on the basis of Wien's law.

The changes in wavelength are evident in an electric heating element as it rises in temperature. When the element becomes hot enough, it glows a dull red (long wavelength). As it becomes hotter, it glows bright red, then orange, then yellow, and finally white, as the wavelengths become shorter and shorter. White is a mixture of many wavelengths. Short wavelengths are present, in accordance with Wien's law (wavelengths grow shorter as the temperature rises), and all wavelengths, including the less prominent longer ones, have enough energy to contribute to the visible composite in accordance with the Stefan-Boltzmann law (total radiation rises with temperature).

In 1896 Wien extended his calculations to a theoretical explanation of the shape of the energy distribution curve, applying thermodynamic principles and the electromagnetic theory developed by the Scottish physicist James Clerk Maxwell. This explanation became known as Wien's distribution law.

Wien's displacement law was confirmed by measurements of the radiation emerging from a small hole in a blackbody cavity, a study performed by Otto Lummer and Ernst Pringsheim in 1899, using a sensitive device called a bolometer. However, the distribution law was found to agree closely with experiments only at short wavelengths and deviated at long wavelengths. The English physicist J. W. STRUTT (Lord Rayleigh) derived an equation that worked well at long, but not short, wavelengths. It was the effort to reconcile theory with experiment over the full spectrum that led MAX PLANCK to develop his revolutionary quantum theory. As Wien remarked, Planck solved the problem "by introducing the famous hypothesis of elements of energy (quanta), according to which energy is not infinitely divisible, but can only be distributed in rather large quantities that cannot be divided further."

Wien was also involved in other research, primarily on the discharge of electricity through gases at very low pressure in vacuum tubes. The discharges created three types of radiation, then mysterious. One type, called cathode rays, traveled from the cathode (negative electrode) to the anode (positive electrode). A second, called canal rays, traveled in the opposite direction. A third, discovered in 1895 by Wilhelm Röntgen and named X rays, emanated from the region of the anode being struck by cathode rays. Cathode rays, which came to be called electrons, had been discovered by the English physicist J. J. THOMSON in 1897. Wien confirmed that the cathode rays were particles carrying a negative electric charge. He also showed that the canal rays were positively charged atoms (ions) of residual gases in the discharge tubes and made the first estimates of the wavelengths of X rays (much shorter than visible light) by measuring the ratio of their energy to that of the cathode rays that produced them. He continued to make important contributions to radiation physics for the rest of his life, among them refining his calculation of X-ray wavelengths and suggesting the use of crystals to measure them five years before MAX VON LAUE did similar work.

Wien was awarded the 1911 Nobel Prize for Physics "for his discoveries regarding the laws governing the radiation of heat." In his Nobel lecture Wien commented on the value of what he called "thought experiments." "In the application of thermodynamics to the theory of radiation, use is made of those ideal processes that have proved so fruitful in other respects," he said. "They are mental experiments that frequently cannot be carried out in practice, yet lead to reliable results. . . . From these mental experiments we can draw an important conclusion; . . . we can deduce how the spectral composition of the radiation from a blackbody changes with temperature."

During a visit to the United States in 1913, Wien lectured at Columbia University and visited both Harvard and Yale universities. In 1920 he again succeeded Röntgen, this time as professor of physics at the University of Munich, where he supervised the construction of a physics institute. In 1925 and 1926 he served as rector of the university.

In 1898 Wien married Luise Mehler, whom he met in Aachen; they had two sons and two daughters. Wien, who was an avid student of history, literature, and art, died in Munich in 1928. "There are probably only very few physicists who are so equally expert in both the experimental and theoretical sides of their own particular fields as Willy Wien," Max Planck wrote about his colleague.

From 1906 until his death, Wien was coeditor, with Planck, of *Annalen der Physik* (Annals of Physics). He was a member of the American National Academy of Sciences and the scientific academies of Berlin, Göttingen, Vienna, and Stockholm.

ABOUT: Dictionary of Scientific Biography, volume 14, 1976.

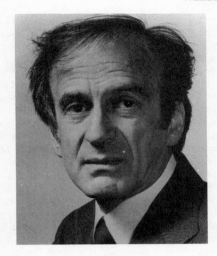

ELIE WIESEL

WIESEL, ELIE
(September 30, 1928–)
Nobel Prize for Peace, 1986

The American writer and educator Eliezer Wiesel (vē zel') was born in Sighet, a small town in the Carpathian Mountains of Transylvania, in Romania. He was the only son of Shlomo and Sarah (Feig) Wiesel, having two older sisters and a younger one. A serious boy, he was imbued by his parents with the Hasidic spirit, a love of study, and the living of a life of devotion to God. His father, who owned a grocery store, was active in the community and participated in the Jewish Community Council. His grandfather, Dodye Feig, a farmer, imparted to the young boy the tales and folklore of Hasidism, the particular strain of middle European Judaism in which Wiesel was nurtured. Hasidism, in part a reaction against overformalization in the Judaism of the time, stressed fervor rather than philosophy and was transmitted through tales rather than tracts.

When word began to filter back to Sighet in the early 1940s that the Nazis were committing atrocities against Jews, the Jewish community, including Wiesel's father, refused to believe the rumors. Even after the German occupation, it was only the increasing restrictions on Jewish activity, leading in 1944 to the forced evacuation of all Sighet's Jews in cattle cars and their arrival at Birkenau, the death camp for Auschwitz, that finally clarified too late what was universal Nazi practice. In his first night in Birkenau, young Elie, who used to sing "I believe in the coming of Messiah, and though he tarry, yet will I wait for him," found the whole fabric of his faith torn apart.

Until the end of the war, Wiesel lived in the midst of the horrors of the death camps, where his father died from starvation and dysentery and his mother and younger sister perished in the gas chambers. In 1945 he was transferred to Buchenwald, from which he was liberated in April of that year. He ended up, virtually by chance, in Paris, where, as an orphaned refugee, he had to construct a new life. This process was eased when he learned that his two older sisters had survived.

From 1948 to 1951 he managed to take some courses at the Sorbonne, where he studied philosophy, hoping that it would help him deal with the monstrous evil he had experienced. He became a journalist and traveled widely for various Jewish, French, and American periodicals, including a year in India seeking to discover what wisdom the East might have to offer about human suffering. In 1956, while in New York covering the activities of the United Nations for *Yedioth Ahronot,* a Tel Aviv daily newspaper, he was nearly killed in an automobile accident; during his recovery, he was almost deported as a stateless person. In 1957, after his recuperation, he joined the staff of the *Jewish Daily Forward,* a Yiddish-language newspaper in New York. He became a United States citizen in 1963.

Not until ten years after his release from Buchenwald did Wiesel feel capable of writing about his experiences in the camps. Then, forced by conscience and a commitment to justice to speak for the dead, he wrote *La Nuit* (*Night,* 1958), his only directly autobiographical work. Written in French, as were most of his subsequent works, it was the first in a succession of novels, essays, plays, and retellings of Hasidic and biblical tales, all intent on forcing readers to remember the events of the Holocaust. He later questioned whether the world could in fact hear his message, and in the novel *Le Serment de Kolvillag* (1973, translated as *The Oath*) he explored (and rejected) the possibility that silence might be more powerful than speech.

Wiesel's earliest novels, *L'Aube* (*Dawn,* 1961), *Le Jour* (1961, translated as *The Accident*), *La Ville de la chance* (1962, translated as *The Town Beyond the Wall*), and *Les Portes de la forêt* (*The Gates of the Forest,* 1964), carry on the story of the struggle of post-Holocaust Jews, begun in *Night,* which had ended with a "survivor" who could see himself only as a corpse. The succeeding novels trace a journey from that living death back toward life; only at the end of *The Town Beyond the Wall* does a redemptive note begin to appear, when the protagonist can for the first time begin to trust another human being. The possibility of human sharing begins to receive communal expression at the conclusion of *The Gates of the Forest.* The next novel, *Le Mendiant de Jérusalem* (*A Beggar in Jerusalem,* 1968), inspired by the Six-Day War of 1967, projects the possibilities of hope on a yet wider scale. In all Wiesel's writings, however, hope must be constantly rewon and can never be taken for granted. There are, at the same time, always tenuous possibilities even in the midst of near-disaster—what Wiesel elsewhere characterizes as "a small measure of victory." His novel *Le Cinquième fils* (*The Fifth Son,* 1983) is about the problem of the children of the Holocaust survivors and the potential legacy of hopelessness that can be laid on them.

In other works, Wiesel has discussed the situation of Jews in the Soviet Union. Concerned about reports of renewed anti-Semitism, he visited the Soviet Union in 1965 and published a series of articles in Hebrew for *Yedioth Ahronot.* They were later translated into English and published in 1966 as *The Jews of Silence,* a work that was expanded and reissued in 1987. His play *Zalmen; ou la folie de Dieu* (*Zalmen; or, the Madness of God*), which also appeared in 1966, concerns the necessity of speaking out against persecution in the Soviet Union. The drama *Le Procès de Shamgorod tel qu'il se déroula le 25 Février 1649,* published in 1979 and translated as *The Trial of God as It Was Held on February 25, 1649, in Shamgorod* the same year, and the novel *Le Testament d'un poète juif assassiné,* published in 1980 and translated as *The Testament* in 1981, also deal with Russian Jewry.

In other work, Wiesel has also drawn on the wisdom of the Jewish past to illumine and empower the present in *Célébration hassidique; portraits et légendes* (1972, translated as *Souls on Fire*). This work, along with *Four Hasidic Masters* (1978) and *Somewhere a Master* (1982), contains vivid retellings of Hasidic tales. In *Célébration biblique; portraits et légendes* (published in 1975 and translated as *Messengers of God; Biblical Portraits and Legends* in 1976), *Images From the Bible* (1980), and *Five Biblical Portraits* (1981), he demonstrates that ancient biblical stories are also contemporary human stories. Viewing his role not so much as a philosopher or historian but simply as a "teller of tales," Wiesel believes that the inherent power of a story can communicate in ways that change lives.

From 1972 to 1976 Wiesel was Distinguished Professor of Judaic Studies at City College, New York, and since 1976 he has been Andrew Mellon Distinguished Professor of the Humanities at Boston University. Widely sought as a lecturer, he has spoken on hundreds of college and university campuses. In 1978 he was named chairman of the President's Commission on the Holocaust, created by President Jimmy Carter and mandated by Congress to propose a suitable Holocaust memorial in the United States. The commission, now called the United States Holocaust Memorial Council, also oversees annual Days of Remembrance of the Holocaust, sponsors research, and plans programs and conferences on issues related to the Holocaust. Wiesel served as its chairman until 1987.

Through the years, Wiesel has traveled to many places of tension and strife, such as Cambodia, South Africa, Bangladesh, and the Soviet Union, to show his identification with victims of oppression and to call public attention to violations of human rights. He has spoken out on behalf of various issues, including an unsuccessful attempt to dissuade President Ronald Reagan from visiting the German army cemetery at Bitburg in 1985, where many Nazi soldiers are buried.

Wiesel's conviction that any infringement of dignity to any human being is a wound to all has enabled him to transmute his own personal suffering into a vehicle for expressing concern for victims of violence everywhere. "Words," he once said to a rabbi who questioned the appropriateness of addressing the problem of human suffering by writing fiction, "could sometimes, in moments of grace, attain the quality of deeds." While recognizing that anger may be a necessary response to injustice, Wiesel realizes that hatred destroys the hater as well as the hated and must be disavowed.

It was for his devotion to and exemplification of these themes that Wiesel was awarded the 1986 Nobel Peace Prize. "Wiesel is a messenger to mankind," said Egil Aarvik of the Norwegian Nobel Committee in announcing the award. "His message is one of peace, atonement, and human dignity. His belief that the forces fighting evil in the world can be victorious is a hard-won belief." Aarvik also noted that "Wiesel's commitment, which originated in the suffering of the Jewish people, has been widened to embrace all oppressed peoples and races." On accepting the award, Wiesel recalled "the kingdom of night" he had encountered—and survived—in the death camps. "I have tried to keep memory alive," he said. "I have tried to fight those who would forget. Because if we forget, we are guilty, we are accomplices." In conclusion he declared, "Our lives no longer belong to us alone; they belong to all those who need us desperately."

Wiesel was married in 1969 to Marion Erster Rose, who also survived the Holocaust and who translates most of his writings into English. The Wiesels, who live in New York City, have a son in addition to a daughter by Mrs. Wiesel's previous marriage. He keeps several projects going at once—always a new novel, always a work drawing on Jewish insights from the past, along with the ongoing essays and commentaries that are written in response to world events.

Wiesel has been the recipient of numerous literary and humanitarian awards, including the Martin Luther King Medallion of the City College of New York (1973), the Jewish Book Council Literary Award (1973), and the Congressional Medal of Achievement (1985). He has been awarded honorary degrees from more than thirty institutions, including the Jewish Theological Seminary, Yeshiva University, Boston University, Yale University, Kenyon College, Wesleyan University, and the University of Notre Dame. He serves on the board of directors of the National Committee on American Foreign Policy and the Hebrew Arts School and is a member of the board of governors of Haifa University, Tel-Aviv University, Bar-Ilan University, and the Oxford Center for Postgraduate Hebrew Studies. During the academic year 1982–1983, he was Henry Luce Visiting Scholar in the Humanities and Social Thought at Yale University.

ADDITIONAL WORKS IN ENGLISH TRANSLATION: Legends of Our Time, 1968; One Generation After, 1970; Ani Maanim, 1973; Dimensions of the Holocaust, 1977; A Jew Today, 1978; The Trial of God, 1979; The Golem, 1983; Against Silence: The Voice and Vision of Elie Wiesel (3 vols.) 1985.

ABOUT: Berenbaum, M. The Vision of the Void, 1979; Brown, R. M. Elie Wiesel: Messenger to All Humanity, 1983; Cargas, H. J. Conversations With Elie Wiesel, 1976; Cargas, H. J. (ed.) Responses to Elie Wiesel, 1978; Estess, T. L. Elie Wiesel, 1980; Fine, E. S. Legacy of Night, 1982; Rosenfeld, A., and Greenberg, I. (eds.) Confronting the Holocaust: The Impact of Elie Wiesel, 1979; Roth, J. R. A Consuming Fire: Encounters With Elie Wiesel and the Holocaust, 1979; Stern, E. N. Elie Wiesel: Witness for Life, 1982.

WIESEL, TORSTEN

(June 3, 1924–   )
Nobel Prize for Physiology or Medicine, 1981
(shared with David H. Hubel and Roger W. Sperry)

The Swedish neurobiologist Torsten Nils Wiesel (vē′ səl) was born in Uppsala to Fritz S. Wiesel, the chief psychiatrist at the Beckomberga Hospital, a mental institution in Stockholm, and Anna-Lisa (Bentzer) Wiesel. As a youth Wiesel lived at the hospital with his family and was educated at Whitlockska Samskolan, a coeducational private school in Stockholm. He has described himself as a "rather lazy, mischievous student, interested mainly in sports." In high school he was president of the school athletic association.

In 1941 Wiesel entered medical school at the Karolinska Institute in Stockholm. There, in the laboratory of Carl Gustaf Bernhard, he became involved in research focusing on the function of the nervous system and also received clinical training in psychiatry. He obtained his medical degree from the Karolinska Institute in 1954, the same year he was appointed instructor in physiology at the institute and assistant in the Department of Child Psychiatry at the Karolinska Hospital.

The following year he accepted an invitation to become a postdoctoral fellow at the Wilmer Institute, Johns Hopkins School of Medicine, where he worked under Stephen Kuffler, an authority on the neurophysiology of vision who was extending important research initiated by H. KEFFER HARTLINE and RAGNAR GRANIT. Two years later Wiesel was appointed assistant professor of ophthalmological physiology at Johns Hopkins.

Kuffler had studied the nervous activity, or microelectrical discharges, of nerve cells in the retina (innermost layer of the eye) of the cat. He had discovered that retinal nerve, or ganglion, cells respond to contrasts of light and not to evenly distributed illumination. He also described the receptive fields of the cells, or the area of the retina which, when stimulated, produces a change in the activity of the nerve cell. Kuffler learned that retinal ganglion cells are either stimulated or inhibited when a circular spot of light is shone on the corresponding receptive field of the retina. If the central spot of light stimulates the retinal cell, light

TORSTEN WIESEL

falling on the doughnut-shaped area of the retina surrounding this central spot inhibits the cell, and vice versa.

When DAVID H. HUBEL joined Kuffler's laboratory in 1958, he and Wiesel decided to study the receptive fields of nerve cells in the visual cortex of the brain. The visual cortex is composed of gray matter and is one of many functional areas of the cerebral cortex, where the cognitive activities of the brain are performed. The visual nervous system begins in the photoreceptor (light-sensitive) cells of the retina, the rods and the cones. The nerve terminals of the rods and cones project to other cells in the retina. From these cells, nerve impulses travel via the optic nerves to the lateral geniculate nuclei, structures in the brain that relay the impulses to the visual cortex. The visual cortex, which consists of many millions of nerve cells arranged in several layers, decodes the neural messages that originate in the retina and provides a view of the world.

One of the first observations made by Wiesel and Hubel clarified the function of the visual nervous system. They had placed a microelectrode (a device used to record the electrical activity of nerve cells) in the visual cortex of a cat and recorded the spontaneous nervous activity, or microelectrical discharges, of a nerve cell. Wiesel and Hubel experimented with different visual stimuli in an attempt to excite some microelectrical activity in the cortical cells. Accidentally, Hubel moved a microscope slide past the receptive field of the nerve cell containing the microelectrode. Suddenly the cell began to discharge. At first the two researchers were puzzled, but they soon realized that the cortical nerve cell was responding to the linear edge of the slide. Whereas Kuffler's retinal cells responded to circular images, the nerve cells in the visual cortex responded to linear images.

When Kuffler was appointed professor of pharmacology at the Harvard Medical School in Boston in 1959, Wiesel, Hubel, and other members of his team joined him there. Wiesel was appointed assistant professor of physiology at Harvard and became professor of physiology in 1964, the same year that Harvard created a Department of Neurobiology with Kuffler as its chairman.

Continuing their research in the new department, Wiesel and Hubel placed a microelectrode in the visual cortex of live cats and monkeys and recorded the spontaneous nervous activity of the cell in which the microelectrode was implanted. Their strategy was to stimulate the retinal fields with linear images of light at various angles until they found the most effective stimuli for a series of nerve cells along the path of the electrode. Sometimes they made vertical penetrations, with the electrode perpendicular to the surface of the brain; at other times they made oblique penetrations. After conducting autopsies on the experimental animals, they compared their findings about the nervous activity of the tissue with its anatomy. They also developed techniques for injecting the eyes with radioactive substances that traveled along the optic nerve fibers from the retina to the visual cortex. These substances further delineated the neuroanatomy of the visual cortex.

The two collaborators discovered that the visual cortex of the brain is organized into periodic vertical subdivisions, which they called ocular dominance columns and orientation columns. These columns of nerve cells perform two essential transformations on information transmitted from the retina to the visual cortex. The ocular dominance columns combine the neural input from the two eyes, while the orientation columns transform the circular receptive fields of retinal and geniculate nerve cells into linear receptive fields. These transformations, they found, are accomplished by a hierarchy of simple, complex, and hypercomplex nerve cells that function according to what Wiesel and Hubel called the principle of increasing or progressive convergence. The principle of progressive convergence explains how the visual cortex is able to generate large images from many small bits of neural information from the retina. It is believed that the other functional areas of the cerebral cortex may be organized in a similar manner.

Wiesel and Hubel's work has had significant implications for the treatment of eye diseases, especially congenital cataracts. They found that such cataracts must be removed early in life if the patient's vision is to be preserved.

In 1968 Wiesel became professor of neurobiology at Harvard University, and in 1974 he was appointed Robert Winthrop Professor of Neurobiology. He succeeded Kuffler as chairman of the Department of Neurobiology in 1973.

Half of the 1981 Nobel Prize for Physiology or Medicine was shared by Wiesel and Hubel "for their discoveries concerning information processing in the visual system"; the other portion of the prize was awarded to ROGER W. SPERRY. In the conclusion of his Nobel lecture, Wiesel stated that "innate mechanisms endow the visual system with highly specific connections, but visual experience early in life is necessary for their maintenance and full development." Wiesel and Hubel's achievement was to disclose one of the most well-guarded secrets of the brain, namely, the method by which the brain cells decode the messages the brain receives from the eyes.

Since 1983 Wiesel has held the Vincent and Brooke Astor Professorship in neuroscience at Rockefeller University.

In 1956 Wiesel married Teeri Stenhammar; they were divorced in 1970. He then married Ann Yee, from whom he was divorced in 1981.

Among the awards and honors bestowed on Wiesel are the Lewis S. Rosenstiel Award for Distinguished Work in Basic Medical Research given by Brandeis University (1972), the Jonas S. Friedenwald Memorial Award of the Association for Research in Vision and Ophthalmology (1975), the Karl Spencer Lashley Prize of the American Philosophical Society (1977), the Louisa Gross Horwitz Prize of Columbia University (1978), the Dickson Prize in Medicine of the University of Pittsburgh (1979), and the George Ledlie Prize of Harvard University (1980). He is a member of the American Physiological Society, the American Philosophical Society, the American Association for the Advancement of Science, the American Academy of Arts and Sciences, the American National Academy of Sciences, the Physiological Society of England, and the Royal Society of London.

SELECTED WORKS: "Brain Mechanism of Vision," Scientific American September 1979, with David Hubel.

ABOUT: Harvard Magazine November–December 1984; New York Times October 10, 1981; Science October 30, 1981.

WIGNER, EUGENE P.
(November 17, 1902–)
Nobel Prize for Physics, 1963
(shared with J. Hans D. Jensen and Maria Goeppert Mayer)

The Hungarian-American physicist Eugene Paul Wigner was born in Budapest to Antal Wigner, a business executive, and the former Elizabeth Einhorn. After graduating from the Lutheran High School in 1920, he attended the Budapest Institute of Technology for a year. He transferred to the technical university in Berlin, where he earned a bachelor's degree in chemical engineering in 1924 and a doctor's degree in engineering in 1925. After a brief stint as a chemical engineer in a tannery, Wigner became a research assistant and then a lecturer in physics at the technical university, spending an intervening year as a research assistant at the University of Göttingen.

In 1930, the year he was made an assistant professor of physics at Göttingen, Wigner immigrated to the United States, where he began an association with Princeton University that lasted his entire career. After a year as a physics lecturer, he served as part-time professor of mathematical physics from 1931 to 1937, except for a leave of absence during 1931, when he worked at the Kaiser Wilhelm Institute in Berlin. In 1937–1938 he was a professor of physics at the University of Wisconsin, but he returned to Princeton in 1938 to become Thomas D. Jones Professor of Mathematical Physics.

A major contribution of Wigner's research was the application of group theory, a mathematical technique, to quantum mechanics, a rapidly developing field in the 1920s and 1930s. His earliest investigations concerned the rates of chemical reactions, and he did important work on the theory of metallic cohesion. He also did pioneering studies of the structure of atoms and nuclei and the characteristics of nuclear reactions. In 1933, the year after the discovery of the neutron by the English physicist JAMES CHADWICK, Wigner demonstrated that the forces binding protons and neutrons together must act only at very close range and must be much stronger than the long-range electric force attracting atomic electrons to the nucleus. With his former high school classmate, the noted mathematician John von Neu-

EUGENE P. WIGNER

mann, he used group theory to relate the energy levels of nuclei to observed nuclear behavior. This work was particularly helpful in attempting to explain the existence of what Wigner called magic numbers. Nuclei containing a magic number of either protons or neutrons were found empirically to be unusually stable and abundant. Wigner's findings aided MARIA GOEPPERT MAYER and J. HANS D. JENSEN in their successful attempts, made independently of each other, to find the underlying source of magic numbers in the quantum-mechanical motions of protons and neutrons in the nucleus.

Wigner was one of the first physicists to appreciate the power of symmetry principles in predicting invariances in physical processes. These principles concern the conservation of certain characteristics, present before a transition, in the end products after the transition. For example, symmetry principles and invariance requirements can help predict which nuclear reactions are favored and which are not.

With the discovery of nuclear fission by OTTO HAHN and Lise Meitner, followed soon by the outbreak of World War II in 1939, physicists in the United States became alarmed that Nazi Germany would attempt to build nuclear weapons. Wigner joined with ALBERT EINSTEIN, ENRICO FERMI, and other scientists in urging the United States government to fund nuclear research, and in 1941 President Franklin D. Roosevelt established the Manhattan Project in an effort to produce an atomic bomb.

In 1941–1942 Wigner served as a consultant to the United States Office of Scientific Research and Development. He then took a leave

of absence from Princeton from 1942 to 1945 to join the Manhattan Project. There, in the Metallurgical Laboratory at the University of Chicago, he performed theoretical calculations and helped in the design of a nuclear reactor to produce fissionable plutonium. He made important advances in neutron theory for predicting the behavior of supercritical nuclear explosives and was present when the first self-sustaining nuclear chain reaction took place on December 2, 1942.

After the war, Wigner spent 1946–1947 as director of research and development at the Atomic Energy Commission's Clinton Laboratories in Oak Ridge, Tennessee, where he was responsible for a team of some 400 scientists and technicians who manufactured the only radioisotopes then available for non-military research. The first such material, carbon 14, was used by the Barnard Free Skin and Cancer Hospital in St. Louis, Missouri.

Returning to Princeton after the war, Wigner remained an active spokesman on nuclear issues. As director of a conference on the future of atomic science, held on the occasion of Princeton's bicentennial in 1946, he urged his fellow scientists to assume social responsibility for the consequences inherent in nuclear technology. Two years later, at a meeting of the American Association for the Advancement of Science in Washington, D.C., he argued that only by finding legitimate civilian applications could atomic energy be harnessed for peaceful purposes. He later expressed his disappointment that the advent of the hydrogen bomb did not force the United Nations to become an effective agency "to neutralize it."

Wigner helped design reactors for producing both electricity and radioisotopes for research, testing, and medical therapy. He feared the development of a nuclear arms race and opposed the view that nuclear technology was inherently military and should be controlled by the military. In his postwar research, Wigner extended his application of group theory to further the understanding of interactions of energetic subatomic particles.

Wigner received the 1963 Nobel Prize for Physics "for his contributions to the theory of the atomic nucleus and the elementary particles, particularly through the discovery and application of fundamental symmetry principles." He shared the prize with Maria Goeppert Mayer and J. Hans D. Jensen. According to Ivar Waller of the Royal Swedish Academy of Sciences, who presented the award, "A very important step in the investigation of these forces [between nucleons] was taken by Wigner in 1933 when he found . . . that the force between two nucleons is very weak except when their distance apart is very small but that the force is then a million times stronger than the electric forces between the electrons in the outer part of the atoms. . . . Wigner has made many other important contributions to nuclear physics." Waller continued, "He has given a general theory of nuclear reactions and has made decisive contributions to the practical use of nuclear energy. He has, often in collaboration with younger scientists, broken new paths in many other domains of physics."

In 1971 Wigner was named emeritus professor at Princeton. He retains an active interest in the philosophical implications of quantum mechanics and in the future of science in relation to society. He served as director of a civil defense project for the National Academy of Sciences in 1963 and as director of a similar project at Oak Ridge in 1964–1965.

Wigner married Amelia Zipora Franck in 1936. She died in 1937. Four years later, he married Mary Annette Wheeler, a professor of physics at Vassar College, with whom he had a son and a daughter. Mary Wigner died in 1977, and Wigner married Eileen C. P. Hamilton in 1979. He has been a United States citizen since 1937.

In addition to the Nobel Prize, Wigner has received the Medal for Merit of the United States government (1946), the Franklin Medal of the Franklin Institute (1950), the Enrico Fermi Prize of the United States Atomic Energy Commission (1958), the Max Planck Medal of the German Physical Society (1961), and the National Medal of Science of the National Science Foundation (1969), among many other honors. He has been awarded honorary degrees from more than twenty colleges and universities in the United States and Europe. He was elected to the National Academy of Sciences in 1945 and is a member of the American Philosophical Society, the American Mathematical Society, the American Academy of Arts and Sciences, and the American Physical Society. He is also a corresponding member of the Academy of Science in Göttingen.

SELECTED WORKS: Nuclear Structure, 1958, with Leonard Eisenbud; The Physical Theory of Neutron Chain Reactors, 1958, with Alvin Weinberg; Group Theory and Its Application to the Quantum Mechanics of Atom Spectra, 1959; The Growth of Science: Its Promise and Its Dangers, 1964; Symmetries and Reflections: Scientific Essays, 1967; Survival and the Bomb, 1969; Science and Society, 1973.

ABOUT: Current Biography April 1953; Libby, L. M. The Uranium People, 1979; National Cyclopedia of American Biography, volume J, 1964; Wagner, F. S. Eugene P. Wigner: An Architect of the Atomic Age, 1981.

WILKINS, MAURICE H. F.
(December 15, 1916–   )
Nobel Prize for Physiology or Medicine, 1962
(shared with Francis Crick and James D. Watson)

The English biophysicist Maurice Hugh Frederick Wilkins was born in Pongaroa, New Zealand. His mother, Eveline (Whittaker) Wilkins, had emigrated from Dublin, Ireland. His father, Edgar Henry Wilkins, a school doctor, had a strong interest in research but little time to pursue it. At the age of six Wilkins was sent to Birmingham, England, to be educated at King Edward's School. In 1934 he enrolled in St. John's College, Cambridge, to study physics. After receiving his B.A. in 1938, he joined the Ministry of Home Security and Aircraft Production. Assigned by the ministry to conduct graduate research on radar at the University of Birmingham, Wilkins received his Ph.D. in 1940 with a dissertation on luminescence and the movement of electrons in crystals. This work contributed to wartime efforts to improve radar screens.

After completing his radar studies, Wilkins was transferred to a team of British researchers who were working on the separation of uranium isotopes for atomic weapons. In 1944 he and other British scientists were sent to the United States, as members of the Manhattan Project. Wilkins was stationed at the University of California at Berkeley. It was during this time that he read ERWIN SCHRÖDINGER'S What Is Life? The Physical Aspects of the Living Cell, which had recently been published. Schrödinger, who was a physicist, proposed that through quantum physics it was possible to understand biological growth and the nature of life itself. Like many young scientists of his generation, Wilkins was deeply impressed by Schrödinger's ideas and as a result he "got interested in going into the biology field," as he recalled later.

An opportunity to do so came after the war in 1945, when J. T. Randall, one of his former professors at the University of Birmingham, invited Wilkins to become a physics lecturer in the newly established biophysics research unit at St. Andrews University in Scotland. The following year the unit moved to King's College, University of London, where Wilkins

MAURICE H. F. WILKINS

joined the Medical Research Council and began investigating deoxyribonucleic acid (DNA), the substance that governs the reproduction of cells in living creatures.

The nucleic acids had been discovered in the 1860s by the Swiss biochemist Friedrich Miescher. During the early decades of the twentieth century biochemists had gradually elucidated the chemical structure of the nucleic acids, and in the 1940s researchers determined that genes consist of DNA, one of the nucleic acids. Moreover, they established that DNA directs the biosynthesis of enzymes and thus controls the biochemical processes of the cell.

At the time Wilkins began his work at King's College, it was known that the nucleic acids occur in two forms: DNA and ribonucleic acid (RNA). Both RNA and DNA are made of five-carbon sugar molecules (ribose or deoxyribose), phosphate, and four nitrogen-containing bases—adenine, thymine (replaced by uracil in RNA), guanine, and cytosine. Erwin Chargaff of Columbia University in New York City showed that DNA contains equal numbers of adenine and thymine and of guanine and cytosine.

Wilkins searched for methods that would further clarify the complex chemical structure of the DNA molecule. Initially he used ultrasonics (techniques using high-frequency sound waves) and ultraviolet microscopes to probe for the structure of DNA. Later, while manipulating cellular material under a microscope with a glass rod, he saw "a thin and almost invisible fiber of DNA . . . drawn out

like a filament of spider's web." With Rosalind Franklin, a colleague at King's College, Wilkins subjected the DNA samples to X-ray diffraction analysis, a technique used to determine the chemical structure of molecules. The diffraction patterns they obtained revealed that the DNA molecule was shaped like a double helix, a figure resembling a ladder twisted into a spiral.

Wilkins and Franklin shared their findings with FRANCIS CRICK and JAMES D. WATSON, two scientists at the Cavendish Laboratory of Cambridge University who were attempting to determine the structure of DNA. In 1953 Crick and Watson proposed a three-dimensional structure for the DNA molecule. According to their model, the double helix of the DNA molecule consists of two strands of deoxyribose phosphate (alternating units of sugar and phosphate) on the outside, joined by pairs of bases within the helix. Adenine is paired with thymine, guanine with cytosine, and the bases to one another by hydrogen bonds. The Crick-Watson model enabled scientists to explain the process by which DNA replicates itself. The two parts of the DNA molecule separate from each other at the points of hydrogen bonding, somewhat like a zipper unzipping. A new molecule is then synthesized opposite each one on the original strand, with the sequence of bases acting as a code for the formation of new DNA molecules.

Wilkins, Crick, and Watson shared the 1962 Nobel Prize for Physiology or Medicine "for their discoveries concerning the molecular structure of nuclear acids and its significance for information transfer in living material." In his presentation speech, A. V. Engström of the Karolinska Institute pointed out that "the discovery of the three-dimensional molecular structure of the deoxyribonucleic acid . . . is of great importance because it outlines the possibilities for an understanding, in its finest details, of the molecular configuration, which dictates the general and individual properties of living matter."

Wilkins served from 1955 to 1970 as deputy director, and from 1970 until 1972, as director, of the Medical Research Council's Biophysics Unit at King's College. He then was appointed director of the council's Neurobiology Unit, where he headed the Cell Biophysics Unit from 1974 to 1980. He was named professor emeritus at King's College in 1981. In addition to his work on the molecular structure of nucleic acids, Wilkins has investigated the structure of nerve membranes.

In 1959 Wilkins married Patricia Chidgey.

They have two sons and two daughters. An avid gardener, Wilkins also enjoys collecting sculpture.

In addition to the Nobel Prize, Wilkins received the Lasker Award of the American Public Health Association (1960). He is a fellow of the Royal Society and an honorary foreign member of the American Society of Biological Chemists and the American Academy of Arts and Sciences. He was president of the British Society for Social Responsibility in Science in 1969 and was a member of the Russell Committee Against Chemical Weapons.

ABOUT: Current Biography June 1963; New York Herald Tribune October 19, 1962; New York Times April 24, 1983; Olby, R. The Path to the Double Helix, 1974; Watson, J. D. The Double Helix, 1968.

GEOFFREY WILKINSON

WILKINSON, GEOFFREY
(July 14, 1921–   )
Nobel Prize for Chemistry, 1973
(shared with Ernst Fischer)

The English chemist Geoffrey Wilkinson was born in Springside, near Manchester. He was the eldest of three children of Ruth and Henry Wilkinson. His father was a master house painter and decorator; his mother was descended from a family of farmers and weavers. Wilkinson developed an early ·interest in chemistry through occasional visits to a small chemical company owned by his maternal uncle. He attended the neighborhood primary school, and in 1932 he won a County scholarship to the private Todmorden Secondary School, where he excelled in chemistry. He graduated in 1939 and received a Royal scholarship to the Imperial College of Science and Technology, University of London.

Following his graduation in 1941, Wilkinson remained at the Imperial College to conduct wartime research. After working briefly with H. V. A. Briscoe, he left England to join the National Research Council of Canada as a junior scientific officer in the Canadian branch of the atomic bomb project. He remained there until 1946. That year he received his doctorate from the Imperial College and, wishing to work with the large cyclotrons constructed during World War II, became a nuclear chemist at the University of California's Lawrence Radiation Laboratory, at Berkeley, then directed by GLENN T. SEABORG.

Wilkinson stayed at Berkeley until 1950. Then, his interest having shifted from nuclear

to inorganic chemistry, he moved to the Massachusetts Institute of Technology in Cambridge, where, as a research associate, he took up the study of transition metals (elements whose inner electron orbit remains incompletely filled and whose properties are intermediate between metals and nonmetals). Becoming an assistant professor at Harvard University the following year, he continued these studies over the next four years.

Wilkinson's most significant research began at Harvard, when he focused his attention on a problem posed by ferrocene, an unusual compound discovered in 1951 by the chemists Thomas J. Kealy and P. L. Pauson. Ferrocene consists of two five-sided rings of hydrogen and carbon atoms united with one atom of iron. Although prevailing theories predicted that molecules of this kind would be highly unstable, ferrocene exhibited remarkable chemical and thermal stability. Seeking to explain these characteristics and to expand the study of transition metals linked with organic molecules, Wilkinson began a detailed investigation of the structure of ferrocene.

Using the newly developed technique of nuclear magnetic resonance spectroscopy, Wilkinson, in collaboration with R. B. WOODWARD, came to an important insight. Kealy and Pauson had believed that the two carbon-hydrogen rings of ferrocene were lying side by side, joined by a single, relatively weak link with the central atom of iron. Wilkinson proposed instead that the two rings form a layered, or sandwich, structure with the iron atom between them. According to his model, the central metal atom is therefore bonded with each of the five carbon atoms in the upper and lower rings. This unusual arrangement explains the molecule's remarkable stability, and with its discovery a new class of compounds was identified.

Wilkinson and his students at Harvard went on to synthesize additional sandwich molecules, including compounds involving carbonyls and nitrosyls. Soon thereafter, he created a sandwich compound featuring direct chemical bonds between rhenium and hydrogen, a matter of considerable interest to chemists at that time. His further studies of the bonding abilities of transition metals helped spark renewed interest in the field of organometallic chemistry.

Following his work with ferrocene and other sandwich compounds, Wilkinson received a Guggenheim Fellowship, which enabled him to work for nine months in the Copenhagen laboratory of the chemist Niels Janniksen Bjerrum. In December 1955 he returned to London to become professor of inorganic chemistry at the Imperial College, which at the time had the only established chair of inorganic chemistry in the United Kingdom. There Wilkinson continued his studies of the transition metals, focusing his attention on the metals ruthenium, rhodium, and rhenium.

Wilkinson and ERNST FISCHER shared the 1973 Nobel Prize for chemistry "for their pioneering work, performed independently, on the chemistry of the organometallic, so-called sandwich compounds." Ingvar Lindqvist of the Royal Swedish Academy of Sciences said in his presentation address, "The facts were available for all the chemists of the world to see, but the right interpretation was lacking" until Wilkinson and Fischer "reached the conclusion that certain compounds could not be understood without the introduction of a new concept, namely that of the sandwich compound." In his Nobel lecture Wilkinson reviewed the long process that led him and his coworkers to the discovery.

The work for which Wilkinson and Fischer received the Nobel Prize stimulated new and highly productive lines of research in the fields of inorganic, organic, and theoretical chemistry. It also laid the foundation for the development of catalysts used in manufacturing new, highly durable plastics, pharmaceuticals (such as L-dopa, for the treatment of Parkinson's disease), and low-lead fuels.

In 1977 Wilkinson was Dwyer Memorial Lecturer at the University of New South Wales, Australia. In 1983 he was the first Chini Lecturer of the Italian Chemical Society and Edward Frankland Lecturer of the Royal Society of Chemistry. He is the author of more than 400 scientific papers.

In 1952 Wilkinson married Lise Sølver Schou, daughter of the former rector of Denmark's Pharmaceutical High School. The Wilkinsons have two daughters. Wilkinson has been described as warm, quick-witted, and optimistic. In his spare time, he enjoys studying organic chemistry.

Wilkinson has received many awards in addition to the Nobel Prize, including the Lavoisier Medal of the French Chemical Society (1959), the Royal Medal of the Royal Society (1981), and the Galileo Medal of the University of Pisa (1983). He is a fellow of the Royal Society and a foreign member of the American Academy of Arts and Sciences and the Royal Danish Academy of Science.

SELECTED WORKS: Some New Radioactive Isotopes, 1949, with H. G. Hicks; Advanced Inorganic Chemistry, 1962, with F. Albert Cotton; Basic Inorganic Chemistry, 1976, with F. Albert Cotton; Comprehensive Organometallic Chemistry, 1982, with others.

ABOUT: New York Times October 24, 1973; Science November 16, 1973.

WILLIAMS, BETTY
(May 22, 1943–   )
Nobel Prize for Peace, 1976
(shared with Mairead Corrigan)

The Irish peace activist Betty Smyth Williams was born in Andersonstown, a poor Catholic section of western Belfast in Northern Ireland, which retains political ties with Great Britain. The elder daughter of a Protestant father who owned a butcher shop and a Roman Catholic mother who worked as a waitress, she was raised a Catholic. Her parents taught her from an early age to resist the bigotry and hatred that have divided Protestants and Catholics in Northern Ireland for hundreds of years. Another formative influence on the young girl was her maternal grandfather, a Polish Jew, much of whose family had perished in World War II.

When Betty was thirteen, her mother was paralyzed by a stroke, leaving the girl to assume the household duties, which included raising her sister, Margaret. She attended St. Teresa's Primary School and St. Dominic's Grammar School and took secretarial classes

BETTY WILLIAMS

at Orange Academy. She then married Ralph Edward Williams, a merchant marine engineer and an English Protestant. Following a period of travel with her husband, Williams worked at a succession of office jobs in Belfast while maintaining a keen interest in world affairs.

Resurgence of the civil war between Protestants and Catholics began in 1968 when Catholic students, influenced by the civil rights movement in the United States, formed the Northern Ireland Civil Rights Association and began demonstrating to protest discrimination against Northern Ireland's Catholic minority. A year later, the eruption of violence and the emergence of a militant arm of the Irish Republican Army (IRA) caused the government of Northern Ireland to request British military assistance. In 1972, amid further violence, the British government suspended the Protestant-dominated parliament of Northern Ireland and instituted direct rule from London.

At first, Williams sympathized with radical elements within the Republican movement. Espousing their goals, she sheltered members of the movement and helped smuggle them over the border into the Republic of Ireland. The IRA's increasing use of terrorism, however, led her to question its methods, especially after two of her cousins became innocent victims of IRA violence. Convinced that violent tactics could lead only to greater violence, she joined Joseph Parker, a Protestant clergyman, in a peace demonstration in front of the mayor's office in 1972. The following year, she was criticized when she attempted to comfort a young British soldier who had been shot

and had fallen on the sidewalk almost at her feet. The experience taught her, she said later, "that people had obviously lost their sense of value of human life."

A similar episode in 1976 moved Williams to take direct action. In August she saw British soldiers kill an escaping IRA member at the wheel of his car, which, careering out of control, struck and killed three children and injured their mother. Outraged at the death of the children, Williams went from door to door collecting signatures for a peace petition. After the children's aunt, MAIREAD CORRIGAN, appeared on television and condemned the IRA, Williams herself went before local television cameras with her petition. She asked all women, regardless of their faith, to join in an effort to halt the IRA's paramilitary actions, she also announced that a peace march would be held in the Catholic district of Andersonstown.

The appeals by Williams and Corrigan brought some 10,000 women into the streets of Andersonstown on August 14. Praying and singing hymns, they marched to the children's graves in defiance of IRA sympathizers who blocked their way. The next day, Williams and Corrigan joined forces with Ciaran McKeown, a reporter for the Dublin-based newspaper the *Irish Press,* and together they founded a movement called the Community of Peace People.

The first phase of the movement called for peace demonstrations to be staged in both the United Kingdom and the Republic of Ireland through the end of 1976. Thousands of demonstrators turned out in Londonderry, Dublin, Glasgow, and London. Simple and direct in their emotional appeal, these events couched a message of peace in nonsectarian religious terms. In Belfast that August, 35,000 Catholic women crossed the army's dividing line into the Protestant Shankill sector where they were welcomed by the women who lived there. In December an international rally with delegations from Canada, Norway, Sweden, West Germany, and the United States was convened in Drogheda, in the Republic of Ireland. The site of the demonstration—the Bridge of Peace over the Boyne River—was symbolic. There, in 1690, the Protestant troops of King William III defeated those of James II, the deposed Catholic monarch, an event still commemorated annually by Northern Irish Protestants.

Of the three founders of the Peace People, Williams was considered the most outspoken and provocative. Critical of the Catholic church, she accused its hierarchy of lacking moral leadership. On one occasion, she was assaulted by two supporters of the IRA whom she had invited to her home. Confessing that it was "damned hard" to love her enemies, Williams nevertheless did not press charges.

When it became known that the work of the two women had begun too late to be considered for the 1976 Nobel Prize for Peace, the Norwegian press, aided by private groups, collected $340,000 as a "People's Peace Prize," which Williams and Corrigan accepted in Oslo that November. That year the Norwegian Nobel Committee evaluated fifty candidates for the Nobel Peace Prize but was unable to decide upon a recipient, and the prize was withheld. The following year, the 1976 Nobel Prize for Peace was awarded to Williams and Corrigan in recognition of their efforts "in the cause of peace and reconciliation." As Egil Aarvik of the Nobel committee said in his presentation address, "They never heeded the difficulty of their task. There was no talk . . . of ingenious theories, or shrewd diplomacy, or pompous declarations." Instead, he continued, the two women offered "a courageous, unselfish act that proved an inspiration to thousands, that lit a light in the darkness, and that gave fresh hope to people who believed that all hope was gone."

"We are deeply, passionately dedicated to the cause of nonviolence," Williams said in her Nobel lecture. "To those who say we are naive, utopian idealists, we say that we are the only realists, and that those who continue to support militarism in our time are supporting the progress toward total self-destruction of the human race."

Despite opposition from both Protestants and Catholics, and heedless of threats against their lives, Williams and Corrigan continued their efforts after receiving the Nobel Prize. In 1977 the estimated number of deaths from violent assault decreased by almost half. In April 1978 Williams, Corrigan, and McKeown resigned their positions to give other members of the movement an opportunity to exercise leadership. Williams eventually broke off her contacts with the Community of Peace People, although she has maintained her interest in political causes. For instance, in 1984 she accompanied a shipment of supplies donated by Norway and Sweden to the government of Nicaragua.

After divorcing her first husband in 1982, Williams married Jim Perkins, an American businessman, and moved to Florida with her son and daughter from her first marriage.

ABOUT: Current Biography March 1979; Deutsch, R.

Mairead Corrigan, Betty Williams, 1977; Family Circle March 27, 1978; Nation April 16, 1977; Newsweek March 27, 1978; New York Times October 11, 1977; October 21, 1984; New York Times Magazine December 19, 1976; O'Donnell, D. The Peace People of Northern Ireland, 1977.

WILLSTÄTTER, RICHARD
(August 13, 1872–August 3, 1942)
Nobel Prize for Chemistry, 1915

The German chemist Richard Martin Willstätter (vil' shtet ər) was born in Karlsruhe to Max Willstätter, a textile merchant, and Sophie (Ulmann) Willstätter. He received his early schooling in Karlsruhe and at the *Realgymnasium* in Nuremberg, where he was such an outstanding student that the rector nominated him for admission to the prestigious Royal Maximilianeum in Munich; the boy was denied admission, however, because he was Jewish. After graduation from the *Realgymnasium* in 1890, he enrolled in the Munich Technical University as a chemistry major. He was dissatisfied with the school, however, and transferred to the University of Munich, where he came under the influence of ADOLF VON BAEYER.

Baeyer recommended Willstätter to a colleague, Alfred Einhorn, and Willstätter began his research career working under Einhorn on the structure of cocaine and related compounds. Willstätter obtained his Ph.D. in chemistry in 1894. Two years later he became a privatdocent (unsalaried lecturer), and in 1902 he was appointed extraordinary professor (associate professor) at Baeyer's own institute. In 1905 he became professor of chemistry at the Federal Institute of Technology in Zurich.

It was in Zurich that Willstätter began his studies on chlorophyll (the green coloring matter found in nearly all flowering plants, mosses, ferns, and algae). Chlorophyll is an important component in photosynthesis, the process by which sugar, starch, and oxygen are produced from carbon dioxide and water through the action of light on green plants. At the time Willstätter began his research, the structure of chlorophyll was not fully understood. In 1906 it had been suggested that any one plant could have many different kinds of chlorophyll and that the plant kingdom was the repository of an unlimited number of chlorophylls. If this theory were true, it would be very difficult to understand the chemistry of photosynthesis because the data obtained from experiments on one species of plant might not be of value to researchers using another plant species.

Willstätter's contributions, many of them

RICHARD WILLSTÄTTER

three anthocyanins and differ only in the number of hydroxyl groups on one ring of the water-solubility structure. Flower colors are the result of mixtures of a few anthocyanins and (for the yellows) carotenoids. Willstätter's anthocyanin research was halted in 1914 by the outbreak of World War I. Injuries he had sustained several years earlier in a mountain-climbing accident disqualified him for military service.

The 1915 Nobel Prize for Chemistry was awarded to Willstätter "for his researches on plant pigments, especially chlorophyll." Because the award ceremonies were cancelled during the war, Willstätter did not receive the prize until 1920. In his Nobel lecture he stated, "The intention behind my work was to establish the constitutional characteristics of the most widely distributed plant pigments of chlorophyll in particular, and to gain some criteria with regard to its chemical function." Willstätter's work with chlorophyll and anthocyanins showed that the diversity of plant pigments is based on only a few chemical compounds. Relating this fact to chlorophyll, Willstätter stated that the biochemical basis of photosynthesis must be universal and therefore subject to scientific analysis.

In 1916 Willstätter had been appointed professor of chemistry at the University of Munich, succeeding Baeyer. After World War I, however, academic life in Germany was hindered by rampant inflation and political instability. Nevertheless, Willstätter began a new research career "to break trails into obscure regions," electing to study enzymes (organic compounds capable of producing changes by catalytic action), a subject about which he and his colleagues knew very little. By 1924, however, anti-Semitism had gained considerable impetus, and a number of Jewish candidates for university positions were being rejected. Aware that a university official appointed by him was responsible for the rejection of the Jewish candidates, Willstätter resigned his position in protest on July 24, 1924. He was succeeded by HEINRICH WIELAND, who provided facilities where Willstätter was able to conduct experiments on leukocytes for the next several years.

When the Nazis came to power in 1933, life became increasingly difficult for Willstätter. Shortly after Adolf Hitler became chancellor, Willstätter visited the United States and Great Britain, where he was offered several research and teaching positions, all of which he declined in order to remain in his homeland. In November 1938 the police arrived to arrest Willstätter, intending to send him to Dachau,

made in collaboration with a student, Arthur Stoll, were technically refined, incontrovertible, and dramatic. Using nettle leaves, a plentiful and cheap source of chlorophyll, he demonstrated that chlorophyll has one basic structure (it is a tetrapyrrole, or compound with four pyrrole rings, that is bound through a central manganese atom). Moreover, he proved that although it has one structure, there are two nearly identical forms of chlorophyll, a and b. He went on to establish the universality of chlorophyll a and b by surveying more than 200 plants. In this way he demonstrated the worldwide presence of one fundamental chlorophyll structure, thus implying that photosynthesis utilizes a universal set of chemical reactions. After making this discovery, Willstätter and Stoll summarized some of the confusing results obtained by previous chlorophyll researchers by stating that these investigators had experimented with materials that "were not impure chlorophyll. They were not chlorophyll at all."

In 1912, at the urging of his friend HANS FISCHER, Willstätter joined the staff of the new Kaiser Wilhelm Institute in Berlin, where he continued his research on the anthocyanins. Most of the red, blue, and purple pigments of plants consist of the anthocyanins, compounds that can be extracted from plants by means of alcohol, ether, or water. For example, the red color resulting from boiling beets in water is caused by anthocyanins. Willstätter learned that the same framework of water-soluble pigments could produce different colors. He found that most flower colors are produced by only

but his housekeeper managed to keep the police out of the garden where he was hiding. Early the following year, he tried to escape to Switzerland (where his former pupil Arthur Stoll offered him sanctuary) but was captured by the Gestapo while rowing across Lake Constance. Later, upon the intervention of the Swiss ambassador, Willstätter was allowed to leave Germany. In Switzerland, Stoll gave him the use of a villa, l'Ermitage, just east of Locarno, where he remained until his death. It was at l'Ermitage that he wrote his autobiography, *From My Life,* published in English in 1965.

In 1903 Willstätter married Sophie Lesen; they had a son and a daughter. His wife died in 1908, and Willstätter never remarried. He died from a heart condition on August 3, 1942, just before his seventieth birthday. According to the British chemist ROBERT ROBINSON, Willstätter "was a great experimentalist and a great deviser of experiments, but his supreme gift as an investigator was his power of organization of a campaign." Deeply devoted to his Jewish heritage, Willstätter was also firmly attached to the music, literature, and intellectual life of Germany.

Willstätter's other awards include the Davy Medal of the Royal Society of London (1932) and the Willard Gibbs Medal of the American Chemical Society (1933). He was a foreign member of the Royal Society of London and an honorary fellow of the British Chemical Society, and he held honorary degrees from Oxford University, Manchester University, and the University of Paris.

SELECTED WORKS: Problems and Methods in Enzyme Research, 1927; Investigations on Chlorophyll, 1928, with Arthur Stoll.

ABOUT: Dictionary of Scientific Biography, volume 14, 1976; Farber, E. (ed.) Great Chemists, 1961; Nachmanson, D. German-Jewish Pioneers in Science 1900–1933, 1979; Obituary Notices of Fellows of the Royal Society, volume 8, 1953.

WILSON, C. T. R.

(February 14, 1869–November 15, 1959)
Nobel Prize for Physics, 1927
(shared with Arthur H. Compton)

The Scottish physicist Charles Thomson Rees Wilson was born on a farm near Glencorse to John Wilson, a sheep farmer, and Annie Clark (Harper) Wilson, of Glasgow. Wilson, known for much of his life as C. T. R., was the young-

C. T. R. WILSON

est of eight children by his father's two marriages. The boy was four years old when his father died, and the family moved to Manchester, England, where they were largely supported by relatives. While attending Greenheyes Collegiate School in Manchester, Wilson showed an interest in natural science and developed skill in preparing specimens for microscopic study. After graduation in 1884, he entered Owens College (now Manchester University), with financial aid from his elder half-brother William. He studied science for three years and received a bachelor's degree in 1887; he then remained an additional year to study philosophy, Latin, and Greek.

In 1888 Wilson entered Sidney Sussex College, Cambridge, on a scholarship. Although he had intended to study medicine when he entered Owens College, he was convinced by this time that physics was his calling. After receiving his degree from Cambridge in 1892, Wilson stayed on to do research, but because his brother William had died earlier that year, the family needed his financial help. Wilson left Cambridge in 1894 to become assistant master at Bradford Grammar School, but after a short time he felt compelled to return and continue his research. While earning a living as a demonstrator for medical students, Wilson conducted experiments at Cambridge's Cavendish Laboratory, which was directed by J. J. THOMSON, whose own research would soon lead to the discovery of the electron.

While vacationing in 1894 on Ben Nevis, a peak in Scotland, Wilson was impressed by optical phenomena, such as coronas, produced by sunlight shining on clouds and mist; the experience gave impetus to his scientific career. Early the next year he set about to reproduce these effects in the laboratory, using a device called an expansion chamber to produce fog and rain. "Almost immediately," he said later, "I came across something which promised to be of more interest than the optical phenomena which I had intended to study." It was known that water vapor in air condenses around dust particles that serve as nuclei for the droplets, and it was assumed that clouds could not form in a dust-free atmosphere. Wilson found, however, that if he removed all dust particles from the chamber through repeated condensation and precipitation, fog and rain could still form if the concentration of water in the air was high enough. This discovery led him to suspect that water droplets can form by condensing around ions (electrically charged atoms or molecules).

Learning of WILHELM RÖNTGEN's discovery of X rays in late 1895, Wilson used a primitive X-ray tube to charge the air in his chamber. The dense fog that was produced supported not only his theory of condensation, but also the existence (still questioned at the time by some physicists) of atoms, molecules, and ions. In the course of this work, Wilson greatly improved the design of the expansion chamber, which came to be known as the cloud chamber.

In the summer of 1895, Wilson had returned to the Scottish mountains, where a "hair-raising" thunderstorm aroused his interest in studying the earth's electrical field. In 1896 he was awarded the Clerk Maxwell Fellowship at the Cavendish Laboratory, and for the next three years he continued to investigate ion condensation and atmospheric electricity. His meticulous experimental work produced important information about the behavior of ions in gases and their effects on the atmosphere.

In 1899 Wilson conducted research for the Meteorological Council; the following year he was elected a fellow of Sidney Sussex College and appointed lecturer and demonstrator. He continued his research at Cavendish, conducting cloud-chamber experiments until 1904; after that he was increasingly absorbed in studies of atmospheric electricity. He invented a new form of electroscope (an instrument used to measure voltages) that was 100 times more sensitive than any in use at the time, and with this device he was able to measure the electric field in the atmosphere.

Wilson returned to his work on condensation in 1910, with the idea of using the cloud chamber to detect the passage of charged sub-atomic particles. Because of their charge, alpha particles (helium atom nuclei) and beta particles (electrons) ionize gas molecules in their paths. Wilson reasoned that water vapor condensing around the ionized molecules should form trails that could be recorded on photographic emulsion. Adapting the cloud chamber to this purpose, he reported in 1911 that he had seen for the first time "the very beautiful sight of the clouds" condensed along the paths of alpha and beta particles. Wilson's photographs of particle tracks made a profound impact on the scientific world. They provided visual evidence of particles whose existence had been deduced only indirectly, distinguishing one from another with enormous clarity and detail.

In 1913 Wilson was appointed observer in meteorological physics at the Solar Physics Observatory in Cambridge, where he stayed until 1918, continuing to conduct cloud-chamber research in addition to studying atmospheric electricity. During World War I, he worked on the problem of protecting airships from fires caused by lightning and other electric discharges.

Wilson's cloud-chamber work, wrote J. J. Thomson, "has rarely been equaled as an example of ingenuity, insight, skill in manipulation, unfailing patience, and dogged determination." This work laid the foundation for further developments by P. M. S. BLACKETT, PYOTR KAPITZA, WALTHER BOTHE, IRÈNE JOLIOT-CURIE, and others. The positron and other elementary particles were discovered by the use of Wilson's cloud chamber, which also became an invaluable tool for the study of cosmic rays. Wilson continued his own cloud-chamber research until 1923, when he published his final two papers on cloud-chamber data. One of these papers provided experimental proof that when an X ray interacts with an atom, it expels an electron, an effect that had been predicted earlier that year by ARTHUR H. COMPTON.

From 1923 onward Wilson concentrated chiefly on atmospheric phenomena, inventing devices that allowed him to measure the total charge transported by a lightning bolt and other electrical characteristics of storms. Wilson's explanations for the origin of electric fields in storms and the atmosphere made pioneering contributions to an understanding of these phenomena. From 1925 to 1934 Wilson was Jacksonian Professor of Natural Philosophy at Cambridge.

Wilson was awarded the 1927 Nobel Prize for Physics "for his method of making the paths of electrically charged particles visible by condensation of vapor." "Although a long time has elapsed since you discovered your elegant expansion method," KAI SIEGBAHN of the Royal Swedish Academy of Sciences declared in his presentation speech, "the high value of your discovery has been greatly augmented both through your own assiduous investigations and through results obtained by others."

After retiring from Cambridge in 1934, Wilson returned to Scotland, settling near his birthplace. Always a lover of natural beauty, he continued climbing mountains and taking long country walks well into his eighties. At the age of eighty-six, he flew for the first time and took great delight in observing thunderstorms from a Royal Air Force plane. He submitted his last article, on thunderstorms, to the Royal Society in 1956, when he was the oldest fellow of the society.

In 1907 Wilson married Jessie Fraser Dick, the daughter of a minister; they had two daughters and a son. Wilson was known as a gentle, serene man, keenly enthusiastic about understanding nature and indifferent to honors and prestige. Thomson described Wilson's work as "proceeding without haste and without rest." After a brief illness, Wilson died at his home in Carlops, near Edinburgh, on November 15, 1959.

In addition to the Nobel Prize, Wilson received the Hughes Medal (1911), the Royal Medal (1922), and the Copley Medal (1935) of the Royal Society; the Hopkins Prize of the Cambridge Philosophical Society (1920); the Gunning Prize of the Royal Society of Edinburgh (1921); and the Howard Potts Medal of the Franklin Institute (1925). He was knighted in 1937. Wilson also held numerous honorary degrees.

KENNETH G. WILSON

SELECTED WORKS: Investigations on Lightning Discharges and on the Electric Field of Thunderstorms, 1920.

ABOUT: Biographical Memoirs of Fellows of the Royal Society, volume 6, 1960; Dictionary of Scientific Biography, volume 14, 1976; Fitzpatrick, T. C., et al. A History of the Cavendish Laboratory, 1910; Oxbury, H. (ed.) Great Britons, 1985; Thomson, G. The Inspiration of Science, 1961.

WILSON, KENNETH G.

(June 8, 1936–   )
Nobel Prize for Physics, 1982

The American physicist Kenneth Geddes Wilson was born in Waltham, Massachusetts, the oldest of six children of Emily Fisher (Buckingham) and Edgar Bright Wilson Jr. His father, an authority on microwave spectroscopy, taught chemistry at Harvard University. Wilson received his early education in private schools in Massachusetts. He was especially gifted in mathematics and remembers passing the time waiting for the school bus by figuring out cube roots of numbers in his head. After a year at Magdalen College School in Oxford, England, Wilson graduated from the George School, a Quaker institution in Pennsylvania, in 1952. Accepted by Harvard at the age of sixteen, he studied mathematics and physics and received his B.A. there in 1956. He then did graduate work in quantum field theory under MURRAY GELL-MANN at the California Institute of Technology (Caltech), receiving his Ph.D. in 1961. His doctoral dissertation was titled "An Investigation of the Low Equation and the Chew-Mandelshtam Equations." He was awarded a postdoctoral fellowship at Harvard, followed by a Ford Foundation Fellowship (1962–1963), to work in Geneva at CERN (the European Organization for Nuclear Research). In 1963 he joined the physics department of Cornell University, where he was appointed a full professor in 1970 and named to the James A. Weeks Chair in 1974.

In his early work, which concerned elementary subatomic particles and their interactions, Wilson came into contact with a mathematical procedure called renormalization group analysis, proposed by Gell-Mann, Francis Low (Gell-Mann's colleague at Caltech), and others to overcome certain difficulties in quantum electrodynamics. Direct application of quantum theory to particle problems encountered such awkward quantities as infinite electric charge. Gell-Mann and Low used renormalization groups to modify the mathematical representation, for example, of a pointlike particle such as the electron, to overcome obstacles to further application of theory. Wilson made contributions to renormalization group analysis in solving a problem in his doctoral thesis dealing with K-mesons (kaons). At Cornell, partly through his colleagues Michael Fisher and Benjamin Widom and their work, he became interested in critical phenomena as a field for further application of renormalization groups.

Critical phenomena are the special behavior of materials near certain environmental conditions (for example, temperature and pressure) at which the materials undergo striking changes. The special conditions are called the critical point. In the case of water, for example, the temperatures at which the liquid becomes solid or vapor depend on pressure. As the pressure is raised, water must be made hotter to boil. At boiling, the liquid and vapor coexist and, if kept in a closed chamber, are said to be in equilibrium; they are normally clearly distinguishable because they differ greatly in density. However, when the boiling point is raised with pressure, the liquid density decreases with rising temperature because the water expands (pressure has only a slight densifying effect on the water), while the vapor (a gas) is much compressed and becomes denser. If heat is added to keep the water boiling as the pressure rises, a point is reached (219 atmospheres pressure, 374°C temperature) when the two densities become equal, and boiling ceases. It is no longer possible to tell liquid from vapor, and the question itself loses its usual meaning. These values of pressure and temperature are the critical point of water. Another example of a critical point is the temperature (Curie point, named for PIERRE CURIE) below which a ferromagnetic material becomes spontaneously magnetized and above which it is nonmagnetic. If a magnet is heated above its Curie point, it loses its magnetism and does not "remember" its initial condition when cooled. Critical phenomena were first studied systematically in the 1860s in carbon dioxide.

Systems with critical points have a special link between very short-range (small-scale) fundamental interactions and gross body characteristics. In the case of water, the small-scale aspects are molecular motions and intermolecular attractions. In the case of magnets, these aspects are the tendency for infinitesimal magnets associated with spins of electrons to influence their neighbors into a common alignment. Near the critical point, these minuscule actions enlarge many orders of magnitude toward a concerted bulk behavior. The quantitative understanding of critical phenomena must contend simultaneously with the complexities of a vast number of independent, short-range actions (degrees of freedom) and longer-range correlations between different regions that come to encompass the entire body of material. Fluctuations in conditions from point to point and region to region reflect many different ranges of interaction, or magnitudes of scale.

Scientists attacked the problem by seeking ways to reduce the complexities to manageable proportions without undermining the validity of underlying theory. In 1937 the Russian physicist LEV LANDAU proposed a method called the mean field theory for the case of magnets, in which he averaged fluctuations in magnetization and assumed that only fluctuations on an atomic scale mattered. In 1944 the Norwegian-American chemist LARS ONSAGER found a quantitative solution for a two-dimensional model that permitted him to calculate magnetic properties and also proved Landau's theory wrong. As a result, a new theory was needed to provide a more general representation. In 1965 Widom suggested that changing the scale of interactions near the critical point would not change the aptness of the mathematical descriptions. In 1966 the American physicist Leo Kadanoff proposed dividing the ferromagnetic system near its critical point into cells, each containing a small number of atomic-level magnets, the size of the cell determining the scale. Other scientists also made contributions to possible solutions of the problem. It was Wilson's application of renormalization group analysis that achieved a successful method for characterizing behavior near the critical point and making quantitative estimates of system properties with the aid of computers.

Wilson, in effect, divided the system into blocks arranged in a latticelike network, similar to that of Kadanoff. Starting at a small scale, with many small blocks, he applied an averaging procedure. Then, gradually enlarging the scale and the size of the blocks, he repeated the procedure over and over until it converged to a conclusive representation that yielded numerical results, which agreed with experimental values. With each step, the smaller-scale fluctuations averaged out, and the larger-scale fluctuations grew closer to including the entire system. He also found that systems near their critical points could be characterized by a few parameters with the quality of universality. That is, similar parameters could be used to calculate the behavior of a surprising number of other systems. He and Fisher later developed some aspects of the method further, increasing its utility.

Other physicists were quick to recognize the importance of Wilson's achievement. Landau had called critical phenomena the most important unsolved problem in theoretical physics, and Wilson himself was later to say that the problems to which the method was being applied were among the most difficult in the physical sciences. "If they were not," he commented, "they would have been solved by easier methods long ago."

Wilson was awarded the 1982 Nobel Prize for Physics "for his theory for critical phenomena in connection with phase transitions." In his presentation speech, Stig Lundqvist of the Royal Swedish Academy of Sciences hailed Wilson for his "elegant and profound" solution to the problem of phase transitions. Wilson's results, he said, "gave a complete theoretical description of the behavior close to the critical point and also gave methods to calculate numerically the crucial quantities. During the decade since he published his first papers," Lundqvist went on, "we have seen a complete breakthrough of his ideas and methods."

Practical applications of renormalization may be expected in such areas as percolation of a fluid through a solid, frost heaving, crack propagation in metals, and oil flow in underground reservoirs, in which complex microscopic physics underlies macroscopic effects. In recent years, Wilson has been trying to apply his technique to the theory of quarks, the particles proposed by Gell-Mann to be the building blocks of protons, neutrons, and other subatomic particles previously considered fundamental in themselves.

Since 1976 Wilson has devoted most of his attention to computer simulations and modeling. Finding his theoretical work limited by the speed and memory of available computers, he has become an advocate of supercomputer centers to provide services to scientists.

In 1982 Wilson married Alison Brown, a computer specialist at Cornell Computer Services. A former amateur oboe player, he enjoys folk dancing and hiking. He has described himself as "a workaholic who takes a lot of breaks—a *lot* of breaks."

Wilson is a member of the National Academy of Sciences and a fellow of the American Academy of Arts and Sciences. His other awards include the Dannie Heineman Prize of the American Physical Society (1973); the Wolf Prize of the Wolf Foundation (1980), which he shared with Fisher and Kadanoff; and the Distinguished Alumni Award of the California Institute of Technology (1981). He holds an honorary doctorate from Harvard University.

ABOUT: Current Biography September 1983; New Scientist October 21, 1982; Physics Today December 1982.

WILSON, ROBERT W.
(January 10, 1936–   )
Nobel Prize for Physics, 1978
(shared with Pyotr Kapitza and Arno A. Penzias)

The American radio astronomer Robert Woodrow Wilson was born in Houston, Texas, the only son and oldest of three children of Ralph Wilson, a chemical engineer who worked for an oil-well service company, and the former Fannie May Willis. As a boy, Wilson often accompanied his father to the oil fields and "puttered around the machine, electronics, and automobile shops." These experiences gave him a keen, lifelong interest in electronics. While in high school, he earned pocket money by repairing radios and television sets.

Wilson entered Rice University, his father's alma mater, in 1953. In his freshman year, finding the electrical engineering curriculum at Rice not "very forward-looking," he switched his major to physics. After graduating with honors in 1957, he worked during the summer for the Exxon Corporation and obtained his first patent, awarded for a high-voltage pulse generator used in a device that charted the progress of drilling.

In the fall of 1957, Wilson began graduate work at the California Institute of Technology (Caltech). During his first year he was introduced to John Bolton, an Australian radio astronomer who had come to Caltech to build an interferometer (two radio telescopes linked electronically to form the equivalent of a much larger telescope) at the institute's Owens Valley Radio Observatory, 200 miles north of Los Angeles. Wilson did his doctoral research under Bolton, making a map of variations in radia-

ROBERT W. WILSON

tion from the Milky Way at a 31-centimeter wavelength. He received his Ph.D. in 1962. He then spent a postdoctoral year at Caltech, before joining the Bell Telephone Laboratories to work at the company's Radio Research Laboratory in Crawford Hill, New Jersey. There he collaborated with ARNO A. PENZIAS.

In 1960 Bell scientists had built a 20-foot horn-reflector antenna at Holmdel, New Jersey, to receive signals from the *Echo* balloon satellite. When the antenna became outdated in 1963, Penzias and Wilson converted it into a telescope for radio astronomy. Its precise calibration and extreme sensitivity were ideal for measuring the intensities of extraterrestrial radio sources. Wilson and Penzias were also able to distinguish and subtract from their measurements radio noise from local sources such as the ground, the earth's atmosphere, and the structure of the antenna itself. This knowledge enabled them to make absolute measurements of the intensity of background radiation from areas of the sky near a source of interest. A reference source built by Penzias was cooled by liquid helium to minimize thermal radiation and so provide a precisely known amount of low-level noise. Wilson devised a switch to connect the telescope amplifier alternately with the antenna and the reference source in order to compare the reference with radio noise received from the sky.

In 1964, operating their system for the first time, Penzias and Wilson measured signals from Cassiopeia A, the brightest radio source in the constellation Cassiopeia. Cas A, as it is familiarly called, is a supernova remnant, an ex-

panding shell of gas cast off by the explosion of a star. The two investigators, to their surprise, found that they were picking up more background noise than they could account for. When the puzzling results persisted during the course of further measurements, Penzias and Wilson thoroughly checked their antenna system and other possible noise sources and made modifications to try to eliminate errors. Nothing they did, however, significantly reduced the anomalous noise.

Radiation is usually expressed in terms of wavelength or its associated frequency. However, since all objects radiate electromagnetic energy at wavelengths that grow shorter as the objects are heated, wavelength can also be related to temperature. White light is a mixture of all colors up to violet, the shortest visible wavelength. Since the radiation also depends on the color and texture of an object's surface, reference is made to a standard blackbody. Although a blackbody emits a spectrum of radiation rather than a single wavelength, each temperature is characterized by a dominant wavelength at which the emission is especially intense. Cold bodies also radiate, but the wavelengths are too long to be visible.

The unexplained background radiation detected by Penzias and Wilson had long (radio) wavelengths corresponding to the emission by a blackbody at 3.5°K (degrees kelvin). Absolute zero, or 0°K, is the theoretical temperature at which all thermal motion stops.

Unknown to Penzias and Wilson, a theoretical group at Princeton University, led by Robert Dicke, was then considering the implications of a cosmological model in which the universe alternately expands and contracts. According to this model, the universe is now expanding, but gravitational forces may eventually reverse the expansion into contraction and collapse to an enormous density, resulting in the recurrence of the so-called big bang, the hypothetical explosion that gave rise to all matter and radiation in the universe. Dicke theorized that radiation from the extremely hot, highly condensed early state of the universe, after some 18 billion years of cooling, might still be observable. Dicke's colleague and former student P. J. E. Peebles calculated a present-day background radiation equivalent to 10°K (later refined to about 3°K), a result he announced in a talk at the Johns Hopkins University. George Gamow, the originator of the big-bang theory, had previously made a similar suggestion.

In 1965 Penzias obtained a copy of Peebles's talk and learned that Peter G. Roll and David

T. Wilkinson, members of Dicke's group, were building an antenna to measure the predicted cosmic background radiation. He met with the Princeton group, and, as a result, the two teams of researchers agreed to collaborate on the simultaneous publication of two papers in the *Astrophysical Journal*—the Princeton group on the cosmological theory and Wilson and Penzias on background radiation they had detected. Within a few years, additional measurements showed that the radiation exhibited the wavelength distribution Dicke's group had predicted for a blackbody at the calculated temperature.

Wilson and Penzias then turned to research of a very different sort, the use of light from a carbon dioxide laser (a device that amplifies light and produces an intense monochromatic beam) to penetrate ground fog. They hoped to achieve applications in communications, but their efforts proved fruitless. Wilson also built a device that measured the sun's brightness at wavelengths of 1 and 2 centimeters, at which the sun's radiation is relatively constant. Transmission of these wavelengths through the earth's atmosphere was of interest because they had been proposed for future satellite communications systems.

Wilson returned to the field of radio astronomy in the late 1960s. Working with Penzias and Bell Labs' atomic physicist Keith Jefferts, he built a receiver that could detect radiation with wavelengths of the order of millimeters. In 1970 they connected their receiver to a newly built 36-foot radio telescope at the National Radio Astronomy Observatory's site at Kitt Peak, Arizona. When the telescope was aimed at the Orion nebula, the spectral line (characteristic emission) of carbon monoxide immediately appeared on the monitor display of the receiver output. Wilson and his colleagues later detected six other interstellar molecules. In 1972 Bell Labs authorized the construction of a millimeter-wavelength facility at Crawford Hill. In addition to directing the design and construction of the antenna, Wilson was responsible for securing the equipment and programming it for radio-astronomical research. In 1976 he was appointed head of the Radio Physics Research Department at Bell Labs. Two years later he became an adjunct professor at the State University of New York.

Wilson and Penzias shared half of the 1978 Nobel Prize for Physics "for their discovery of cosmic microwave background radiation." The other half of the prize was awarded to PYOTR KAPITZA. In his Nobel lecture Wilson said,

"The cosmic microwave background radiation, considered a relic of the explosion at the beginning of the universe some 18 billion years ago, is one of the most powerful aids in determining [the structure and dynamics] of the universe."

Since receiving the Nobel Prize, Wilson has remained at the Holmdel, New Jersey, facility, where he has investigated the dark gas clouds in the Milky Way galaxy. In the course of this work, he determined that "a sizable fraction of the gas in our own galaxy is found in such clouds, and furthermore, [these] are the clouds from which new stars are born."

In 1958 Wilson married Elizabeth Rhoads Sawin, also from Houston; they have two sons and a daughter. Wilson and his family enjoy skiing and ice skating during the winter; he also plays the piano during his leisure time.

In addition to the Nobel Prize, Wilson and Penzias shared the Henry Draper Medal of the National Academy of Sciences (1977) and the Herschel Medal of the Royal Astronomical Society in London (1977). Wilson is a member of the American Astronomical Society, the International Astronomical Union, the American Physical Society, the International Union of Radio Sciences, and the American Academy of Arts and Sciences.

ABOUT: New Yorker August 20, 1984; New York Times October 18, 1978; Physics Today December 1978; Science December 1, 1978.

WILSON, WOODROW
(December 28, 1856–February 3, 1924)
Nobel Prize for Peace, 1919

Thomas Woodrow Wilson, educator and twenty-eighth president of the United States, was born of Scottish stock in Staunton, Virginia. He was the third of four children and the first son born to Joseph Ruggles Wilson, a Presbyterian minister, and Janet (Woodrow) Wilson. Wilson's father, a man of intense piety and rigorous scholarship, actively guided his son's intellectual growth.

In 1875 Wilson entered the College of New Jersey (later renamed Princeton University), where he studied comparative government. After graduating in 1879, he practiced law briefly but returned to graduate school at the Johns Hopkins University in 1883 to study history. Two years later, he married Ellen Louise Axson; they had three daughters. Wilson earned his Ph.D. in 1886 with the publication of

WOODROW WILSON

Congressional Government, an analysis of American legislative practice.

After teaching at Bryn Mawr College and Wesleyan University, Wilson in 1890 joined the faculty of Princeton University as professor of jurisprudence and political economy. Dedicated to "the deep eloquence which awakens purpose," Wilson became popular for his seemingly spontaneous and passionately sincere lectures. In 1902 the Board of Trustees unanimously appointed him president of the university.

During his tenure at Princeton, Wilson exhibited the strengths and weaknesses that were to characterize his later years in politics. He revised the curriculum, changed the student honor system, and raised standards of scholarship. Convinced of a need for greater individual instruction than could be given in the traditional classroom setting, in 1905 he instituted the preceptorial system of small discussion groups under the supervision of a faculty member. Extending his reforms, in 1907 he proposed to divide the student body into colleges; but the plan required the elimination of the university's traditional undergraduate eating clubs, and alumni opposition forced Wilson to abandon the proposal. In a more heated controversy over the disposition of several large bequests, he refused to compromise with the trustees, and in 1910 the board asked for his resignation.

On the verge of dismissal, Wilson accepted an invitation to run for governor of New Jersey on the Democratic ticket. He resigned from Princeton and, to the surprise of professional politicians, won the election with one of the largest majorities in the state's history. Under his vigorous leadership, the state legislature enacted such reforms as a primary election law, a corrupt practices act, an employers' liability act, and a public utilities act. Wilson's meteoric rise thrust him into the national spotlight. At the 1912 Democratic National Convention, he was nominated for president on the forty-sixth ballot. He went on to defeat the badly divided Republicans in the November election.

Although a Southerner, sharing many of the prevailing attitudes toward blacks held by the people of his region, Wilson made a carefully calculated attempt during the election to draw black voters into the Democratic fold. Black leaders, including W. E. B. Du Bois, pressed him for a statement opposing racial disfranchisement. Although such a statement was not forthcoming, Wilson's assurance of "absolute fair dealing" persuaded northern black militants to endorse him. This support was not entirely misplaced, for Wilson appointed and promoted more blacks than either of his Republican predecessors, THEODORE ROOSEVELT or William Howard Taft. After the United States entered World War I, however, he did nothing to alter the segregation of troops in combat and on military posts.

Coming to power at the peak of the Progressive movement, Wilson sought enactment of a legislative program that he called the New Freedom, which promised to restore free enterprise and eliminate special privilege. Under his strong presidential leadership, Congress approved lower tariff rates, a graduated income tax, the Federal Reserve Act, and tighter business regulation through the Federal Trade Commission. As the 1916 presidential election approached, Wilson pushed through the Federal Farm Loan Act, workers' compensation for federal employees, railroad regulation, an inheritance tax, and federal funding for highways. These progressive measures heralded an increasingly active role for the federal government in American life.

In foreign affairs, Wilson took an anti-imperialist position. He attempted to ground United States relations with other nations in justice, respect, and goodwill. "It is a very perilous thing," he announced in 1913, "to determine the foreign policy of a nation in the terms of material interest." At his urging, Congress repealed a clause exempting the United States from paying Panama Canal tolls. Wilson also promised that the United States would not invoke the Monroe Doctrine to intervene in Latin America. It is ironic that during his administration American military forces were used in Nicaragua, Santo Domingo, Haiti, and Mexico. A member of the American Peace Society since 1908, Wilson also sought to make the United States a leading advocate of world peace. Accordingly, he supported international arbitration, extended several treaties negotiated earlier by ELIHU ROOT, and advocated arms reduction.

Upon the outbreak of World War I in 1914, Wilson immediately declared a policy of neutrality and repeatedly tried to bring the belligerents to the peace table. In 1916 Wilson was reelected, and on January 22, 1917, he presented Congress with a plan to establish permanent peace through a League of Nations. Nine days later, however, Germany announced its resumption of unrestricted submarine warfare. After German submarines torpedoed three American ships in March, Wilson convened a special session of Congress and declared that the United States was "but one of the champions of the rights of mankind." Proclaiming that "the right is more precious than peace," he requested and received a declaration of war on April 6, 1917.

Convinced that the United States had entered the war to make "the world safe for democracy," Wilson envisioned a new world order based on reason and mutual cooperation. Accordingly, on January 8, 1918, he outlined a fourteen-point peace program. The first five points included open diplomacy, freedom of the seas, equality in international trade, reduction of armaments, and an adjustment of colonial claims. The next eight points addressed the adjustment of specific territorial borders on the basis of national self-determination. The fourteenth point called for establishment of "a general association of nations . . . affording mutual guarantees of political independence and territorial integrity to great and small states alike."

Germany requested an armistice in November 1918. Wilson and other Allied representatives met in Paris in 1919 to hammer out a treaty. By February a commission had unanimously approved a Covenant for a League of Nations. This became part of the Treaty of Versailles, which was signed in June. Based in Geneva, Switzerland, the newly created League of Nations provided for open diplomacy, the registration of treaties, progressive limitation of armaments, an international court, and the prevention of war through collective action. Wilson was given the honor of issuing the call to the league's first Council meeting, held on January 16, 1920.

Later that year, Wilson was awarded the 1919 Nobel Peace Prize. In remarks made at the session of the Norwegian Parliament at which the award was presented, Anders Johnsen Buen, president of the Parliament, lauded Wilson for "bringing a design for a fundamental law of humanity into present-day international politics." Buen continued, "The basic concept of justice on which it is founded will never die, but will steadily grow in strength, keeping the name of President Wilson fresh in the minds of future generations."

In accepting the award, Albert G. Schmedeman, United States minister to Norway, read a message from Wilson. "Mankind has not yet been rid of the unspeakable horror of war," Wilson wrote. "I am convinced that our generation has, despite its wounds, made notable progress. But it is the better part of wisdom to consider our work as only begun. It will be a continuing labor."

Despite Wilson's efforts, the Treaty of Versailles failed to achieve his hopes for postwar reconciliation. By imposing on Germany ruinous reparations, a forced admission of guilt, and unilateral disarmament, the treaty fostered a new wave of militarism that eventually led to another world war in 1939.

Returning home in 1919, Wilson urged the Senate to ratify the Treaty of Versailles and join the League of Nations. "There can be no question of our ceasing to be a world power," he said. "The only question is whether we can refuse the moral leadership that is offered." The Republican-dominated Senate was split among league supporters, moderates who wished to amend the treaty, and "irreconcilables" who rejected it. "Never! Never!" Wilson retorted when a senator told him there would be no ratification without reservations. Appealing directly to the people, Wilson embarked on a tour to win public support. The speeches, interviews, and travel exhausted him, and he collapsed in Colorado in late September 1919. On October 2 he suffered an incapacitating stroke in the White House. Seven weeks later, he had recovered enough to instruct Democrats to reject an amended treaty. In November both the original treaty and the amended version were defeated in the Senate.

In March 1920 public opinion compelled the Senate to reconsider the issue. Still Wilson would not bend, and the treaty fell seven votes short of the two-thirds majority necessary for approval. Late that year, a Republican landslide in Congress made the league a dead issue in the United States until the end of World War II, when the idea was revived in the form of the United Nations.

His health broken, Wilson left office in 1920. He spent his retirement in Washington, D.C., with his second wife, Edith Bolling Galt, whom he had married on December 18, 1915, six months after the death of his first wife. Although defeated on the issue of the league, Wilson remained quietly convinced that the future would vindicate his position. "The world is run by its ideals," he told a friend. "Only the fool thinks otherwise." In a 1923 radio address celebrating Armistice Day, he urged Americans "to put self-interest away and once more formulate and act upon the highest ideals and purposes of international policy." Three months later, Wilson died in his sleep. On his tomb was carved a crusader's sword, its handle in the shape of a cross.

The success or failure of Wilson's policies has been the subject of considerable debate. At the time, pacifists and internationalists denounced the Treaty of Versailles for its abandonment of Wilson's principles, while Germany felt betrayed by its harsh terms. Isolationists and moderates assailed Wilson for lacking a specific plan in Paris, ignoring his advisers, conducting secret negotiations, and bargaining away national sovereignty by including the league in the treaty.

Historians have offered a variety of explanations for the league's failure in the Senate: Wilson's intolerance, dogmatism, and self-righteousness in dealing with others; a bitter dispute with league opponent Henry Cabot Lodge that sabotaged ratification; and a Senate too bound by tradition to accept Wilson's international ideals.

Nevertheless, Wilson's accomplishments were numerous. He had a clear notion of the president's role and exercised his prerogatives forcefully. Assuming office with an impressive knowledge of government, he secured passage of path-breaking reform legislation. Although he held pacifist views, he steered the nation through a taxing war. As a champion of America's underprivileged, he waged a similar crusade for the poor and the oppressed abroad. Through his persuasive rhetoric, infused with moral earnestness, he awakened the Western nations to a vision of universal peace and brotherhood. At the zenith of his power in 1919, when Europeans cheered him in the streets, he was the symbol of the human yearning for perfection and for a world free of war, injustice, and hatred. Even though the United States rejected the moral leadership Wilson urged upon it, he had the courage to establish the world's first organization designed to maintain international peace.

ADDITIONAL WORKS: The State: Elements of Historical and Practical Politics, 1889; Division and Reunion, 1893; An Old Master and Other Political Essays, 1893; Mere Literature and Other Essays, 1896; George Washington, 1896; A History of the American People (5 vols.) 1902; Constitutional Government in the United States, 1908; Free Life, 1913; The New Freedom, 1913; When a Man Comes to Himself, 1915; On Being Human, 1916; Woodrow Wilson's Case for the League of Nations, 1923; The Public Papers of Woodrow Wilson (6 vols.) 1925–1927; The Papers of Woodrow Wilson (53 vols.) 1966–1986; The Priceless Gift, 1975, with Ellen Louise Axson.

ABOUT: Anderson, D. D. Woodrow Wilson, 1978; Bailey, T. A. Woodrow Wilson and the Peacemakers, 1947; Baker, R. S. Woodrow Wilson: Life and Letters (8 vols.) 1927–1939; Bell, H. C. F. Woodrow Wilson and the People, 1945; Bell, S. Righteous Conquest, 1972; Blum, J. M. Woodrow Wilson and the World Settlement (3 vols.) 1958; Bragdon, H. W. Woodrow Wilson: The Academic Years, 1967; Brooks, E. J. An Historical and Political Assessment of Woodrow Wilson (2 vols.) 1986; Canfield, L. H. The Presidency of Woodrow Wilson, 1966; Cooper, J. M. The Warrior and the Priest, 1983; Creel, G. The War, the World, and Wilson, 1920; Daniels, J. The Wilson Era (2 vols.) 1946; Ferrell, R. H. Woodrow Wilson and World War I, 1985; Greene, T. P. (ed.) Wilson at Versailles, 1957; Hoover, H. The Ordeal of Woodrow Wilson, 1958; House, E. M. The Intimate Papers of Colonel House (4 vols.) 1926; Kerney, J. The Political Education of Woodrow Wilson, 1926; Levin, N. G. Woodrow Wilson and World Politics, 1968; Link, A. S. Wilson (7 vols.) 1947–1982; Low, A. M. Woodrow Wilson: An Interpretation, 1918; Pisney, R. F. Woodrow Wilson: Idealism and Reality, 1977; Robinson, E. E., and West, V. J. The Foreign Policy of Woodrow Wilson, 1917; Seymour, C. American Diplomacy During the World War, 1934; Smith, G. When the Cheering Stopped, 1982; Temperley, H. W. V. (ed.) A History of the Peace Conference of Paris (6 vols.) 1920–1924.

WINDAUS, ADOLF

(December 25, 1876–June 9, 1959)
Nobel Prize for Chemistry, 1928

The German chemist Adolf Otto Reinhold Windaus (vin' dous) was born in Berlin to Adolf Windaus, a descendant of weavers and clothing manufacturers, and Margarete (Elster) Windaus, who came from a family of artisans and craftsmen. The boy received his early education at the French Gymnasium in Berlin, where literature, but very little science, was taught. However, inspired by reading about the bacteriological discoveries of ROBERT KOCH and Louis Pasteur, he set out to become a physician.

Windaus began the study of medicine at the University of Berlin in 1895. During this time he also attended lectures by the chemist EMIL

ADOLF WINDAUS

FISCHER, whose interest in the physiological implications of chemistry had great appeal for Windaus. After passing his preliminary medical examinations in 1897, he continued his studies at the University of Freiburg. Here he learned chemistry under the noted German chemist Heinrich Kiliani, and, deciding to abandon his plans for a medical career, he wrote a dissertation on the cardiac poisons of the digitalis plant, for which he received his Ph.D. in chemistry in 1899.

Following a year of military service in Berlin, Windaus returned to Freiburg, where he became a lecturer in 1903 and assistant professor three years later. In 1913 he was appointed professor of applied medical chemistry at the University of Innsbruck, in Austria. He returned to Germany in 1915 as professor of chemistry and director of the Laboratory for General Chemistry at the University of Göttingen, where he remained for the next twenty-nine years.

Establishing connections between physiologically important chemicals was to be a hallmark of Windaus's research. Kiliani suggested that he study the compound cholesterol. At the time, little was known about the structure or function of this widely distributed substance, and Windaus believed it must be closely associated with other biological compounds known as sterols. Sterols (nitrogen-free complex organic compounds composed of four fused rings with various side chains) are found in different forms in animal, plant, and fungal cells. Cholesterol, the best known, was first discovered in human gallstones. It is often as-

sociated with heart disease and arteriosclerosis and occurs in large quantities in the brain and adrenal cortex. Blood levels of cholesterol rise during pregnancy and fall with infectious diseases.

Earlier in the twentieth century HEINRICH WIELAND, working with bile acids, had isolated a compound called cholanic acid. Windaus prepared the same acid from cholesterol in 1919, proving a close chemical relationship between cholesterol and bile acids. It was not yet clear, however, whether this chemical similarity corresponded to a true biological connection.

At this point in his career, Windaus became interested in vitamin research. Vitamins are organic substances required by human beings and animals for normal growth and maintenance of life. In 1897 the Dutch physician CHRISTIAAN EIJKMAN had described beriberi, a disease resulting from dietary deficiency of a then-unknown substance, later shown to be thiamine, or vitamin B_1. In 1906 FREDERICK GOWLAND HOPKINS had established that unknown "accessory food factors" were essential for health. Together with the Polish chemist Casimir Funk, who coined the term *vitamine* for these substances, Hopkins in 1912 formulated the concept that certain diseases are caused by lack of specific vitamins in the diet.

By the early 1920s vitamin research was being pursued vigorously, although the techniques of chemical analysis were very difficult. Since their structure was unknown, vitamins were often characterized only by their physiological effects. It had long been known that rickets, a skeletal disease that softens the bones of children, occurs in regions with limited sunlight and could be cured by certain fish liver oils containing a substance called vitamin D. Exposure of patients to ultraviolet light also effected a cure for rickets, and the American physiologist Alfred Hess showed in 1924 that some foods irradiated with ultraviolet light also cured rickets. This finding led to the concept of a provitamin, a precursor that, when activated (as by ultraviolet light), is converted into a vitamin. Analysis of the irradiated foods indicated sterols as the active form.

As a leading expert on sterols, Windaus was asked by Hess to come to New York to collaborate in determining the chemical structure of vitamin D and its precursor. Windaus initially believed that cholesterol was the provitamin of vitamin D because a sample of cholesterol had exhibited vitamin D properties after exposure to ultraviolet light. The sample, however, contained a small impurity, identified by Hess and Windaus in 1927 as the fungus sterol ergosterol. A pure vitamin called vitamin D_2, or calciferol, was produced by irradiating ergosterol with ultraviolet light. In 1932 Windaus and his colleagues showed that another compound, 7-dehydrocholesterol, was a provitamin. This substance, called vitamin D_3, was most important since it is a sterol naturally produced in animal and human bodies. The term vitamin D_1 was reserved for the original mixture of calciferol and other sterols. "With no other vitamin did research proceed by such strange and tortuous paths," Windaus later remarked.

Windaus was awarded the 1928 Nobel Prize for Chemistry "for the services rendered through his research into the constitution of the sterols and their connection with the vitamins." H. G. Söderbaum of the Royal Swedish Academy of Sciences said on presenting the award, "As a result of patient and skillful work, Windaus succeeded in producing several of the digitalis glucosides and their components in the pure state. . . . In this way it was shown that these vegetable cardiac poisons are directly related on the one hand to cholesterol and the bile acids, and on the other hand to the animal cardiac poison bufotoxin, which [Heinrich] Wieland studied with great success." Söderbaum went on to point out the importance of Windaus's research on the D vitamins.

In an earlier collaboration with the biochemist Franz Knoop, Windaus had studied the reaction of sugars with ammonia, attempting to convert carbohydrates into amino acids. The resulting products, however, proved to be derivatives of imidazole, compounds containing rings of three carbon and two nitrogen molecules. Analysis of these substances revealed the amino acid histidine and the compound histamine, a dilator of blood vessels now known to play a role in allergies and inflammation. These studies were of interest to the Interessen-Gemeinschaft Farbenindustrie Aktiengesellschaft (I. G. Farben) and other German pharmaceutical companies, which supplied Windaus not only with materials needed for research but also with problems for further investigation.

Two Dutch chemists, B. C. P. Jansen and W. F. Donath, had suggested that vitamin B_1, or thiamine, contained an imidazole ring. Windaus was able to show that sulfur is present in the vitamin, which contains thiazole and pyrimidine rings but no imidazole ring. His later research topics included the structure of colchicine, a drug used in cancer therapy, and

the stereochemistry of ring structures. The determination of sterol ring structure in 1932 enabled Windaus's assistant ADOLF BUTENANDT to elucidate the structure of sex hormones.

Although Windaus was opposed to the Nazi party and to the policies of Adolf Hitler, he was protected by his stature as a scientist and was permitted to continue his work without interference. After 1938 he no longer conducted research, and in 1944 he retired from the university.

In 1915 Windaus married Elisabeth Resau, with whom he had two sons and one daughter. Windaus died in Göttingen in 1959 at the age of eighty-two.

Windaus was the recipient of many awards and honors, including the Louis Pasteur Medal of the French Academy of Sciences (1938), the Goethe Medal of the Goethe Institute (1941), and the Grand Order of Merit with Star given by the German government (1956). He held honorary degrees from the universities of Göttingen, Munich, Freiburg, and Hannover.

ABOUT: Dictionary of Scientific Biography, volume 14, 1976.

WITTIG, GEORG
(June 16, 1897–August 26, 1987)
Nobel Prize for Chemistry, 1979
(shared with Herbert C. Brown)

The German chemist Georg Friedrich Karl Wittig (vit' ik) was born in Berlin to Gustav Wittig, a professor of fine arts at the University of Berlin, and Martha (Dombrowski) Wittig. After attending the Wilhelms-Gymnasium in Kassel, he entered the University of Tübingen in 1916, but his education was interrupted by military service during World War I. In 1920 he entered the University of Marburg and studied chemistry with Karl von Auwers and received his doctoral degree in 1923. After several years of research and teaching at Marburg as assistant and lecturer, Wittig was appointed associate professor at the technical university in Brunswick in 1932. Five years later he joined the faculty at the University of Freiburg as extraordinary professor (associate professor). He was appointed full professor and director of the Chemical Institute at the University of Tübingen in 1944 and made a final transfer to the University of Heidelberg twelve years later. In 1967 he became emeritus professor at Heidelberg.

At the outset of his career, Wittig expressed

GEORG WITTIG

an interest in the detailed mechanisms of certain reactions, particularly the participation of free radicals and carbanions (negatively charged carbon atoms in organic molecules) as reaction intermediates, and in certain kinds of molecular rearrangements. His work on these topics established his reputation as an imaginative organic chemist of great experimental skill.

In the 1940s Wittig took up the challenging task of creating molecules in which five organic groups became covalently bonded to Group V elements in the periodic table, such as nitrogen, phosphorus, and arsenic. Although such molecules were considered theoretically possible, none had been synthesized. Eventually, Wittig and his co-workers succeeded in reaching this goal (except with nitrogen), but during the course of their research they became involved with an interesting family of related products called ylides. In ylides, a Group V quaternary salt (a salt having four organic groups and a halogen attached) loses a proton from one organic group instead of gaining a fifth organic group. In 1953 Wittig found that such ylides react smoothly with carbonyl compounds (molecules possessing a carbon-oxygen double bond, such as aldehydes and ketones), so that the carbanion of the ylide (the deprotonated carbon) is exchanged for the carbonyl oxygen atom. This process results in an olefin with a new carbon-carbon double bond in place of the carbonyl group. Discovered fortuitously and now known as the Wittig reaction, it had incomparably more scientific potential than the successful solution of the initial problem.

Working independently in the 1920s, HERMANN STAUDINGER and Carl S. Marvel had already done much of the background work on this set of reactions. In fact, Staudinger had described the first phosphorus ylide as early as 1919. Because much of their work was unpublished at the time, however, it had little influence on Wittig's research. Ironically, Wittig has noted that it was vital to his success that his knowledge of these predecessors was so limited, since the pathway he would have followed from Marvel's results would have led only to pentavalent phosphorus products, not to the Wittig reaction. The irony is increased by the fact that Staudinger and Wittig were colleagues at Freiburg during the early 1940s; but by then Staudinger had long since ceased work on phosphorus derivatives, and Wittig learned little from this contact.

The Wittig reaction proved to be an enormously useful tool for organic synthesis. With it, chemists could now join two carbon structures easily and reliably by using an appropriate alkyl halide and a carbonyl compound, both of which could easily be prepared from a variety of precursor molecules. Moreover, the reaction proceeded with remarkable ease, high synthetic yields, and no unintentional molecular rearrangements. It is still considered far superior to competing methods of olefin synthesis.

The utility of the reaction was further increased by the studies performed by Wittig and his research group at Tübingen and Heidelberg. Soon other chemists began to explore the reaction. By the early 1960s over a hundred articles concerning specific applications of the Wittig reaction had appeared; by the mid-1980s there were thousands. There have also been numerous technical applications of the Wittig reaction.

Wittig and HERBERT C. BROWN were awarded the 1979 Nobel Prize for Chemistry "for their development of boron- and phosphorus-containing compounds, respectively, into important reagents in organic synthesis." Bengt Lindberg of the Royal Swedish Academy of Sciences said in his presentation address, "Georg Wittig has provided many significant contributions in organic chemistry . . . . [Wittig's] elegant method has found widespread use, for example, in the industrial synthesis of vitamin A."

The Wittig reaction has been invaluable for the preparation of complex pharmaceuticals such as synthetic vitamin A, vitamin D derivatives, steroids, and prostaglandin precursors. It has also been used in the syntheses of insect pheromones for use as natural pest control agents.

In 1930 Wittig married Waltraut Ernst, with whom he had two daughters. Mrs. Wittig died in 1978. With his friend KARL ZIEGLER, Wittig once shared an enthusiasm for mountaineering and other outdoor activities. Wittig's students often noted that his musical talent, which he showed at an early age, could easily have led him to an entirely different career, but chemistry was his consuming passion. Even in retirement, he continued to work and publish with a select group of graduate students. Wittig died in Heidelberg at the age of ninety.

Wittig and his work received extensive international recognition. In addition to the Nobel Prize, his honors included the Adolf von Baeyer Medal (1953) and the Otto Hahn Prize (1967) of the German Chemical Society, the Paul Karrer Medal in Chemistry of the University of Zurich (1972), and the Roger Adams Award of the American Chemical Society (1975). He held honorary degrees from the universities of Paris, Tübingen, and Hamburg.

SELECTED WORKS: Textbook on Stereochemistry, 1930.

ABOUT: Bestmann, H. J., et al., Wittig Chemistry, 1983; New York Times October 16, 1979; Science January 1980.

WOODWARD, R. B.
(April 10, 1917–July 8, 1979)
Nobel Prize for Chemistry, 1965

The American biochemist Robert Burns Woodward was born in Boston, Massachusetts, to Margaret (Burns) and Arthur Chester Woodward. His father died a year after the boy's birth. As a child he spent many hours working in his chemistry laboratory at home. He graduated from Quincy High School at the age of sixteen, with a precocious knowledge of organic chemistry exceeding that of many college science students. Entering the Massachusetts Institute of Technology (MIT) in 1933 on a scholarship, he was allowed to plan his own curriculum and was given laboratory space to conduct private research into hormones. He received a B.S. in 1936 and a Ph.D. in 1937.

After teaching at the University of Illinois during the 1937 summer session, Woodward joined Harvard University as a postdoctoral assistant to Elmer P. Kohler, head of the organic chemistry department. He remained at Harvard for the rest of his career, rising to

R. B. WOODWARD

assistant professor in 1944, associate professor two years later, and full professor in 1950. He was named Morris Loeb Professor of Chemistry in 1953 and Donner Professor of Science in 1960.

Later cited as the "greatest synthetic organic chemist of modern times," Woodward made his first outstanding contribution to chemistry as a consultant to the Polaroid Corporation during World War II. The war had caused a shortage of quinine, a valuable antimalarial drug that is also used in manufacturing lenses. With standard equipment and readily available materials, Woodward and a colleague, William E. Doering, achieved the first synthesis of quinine in 1944 after only fourteen months. Characteristically, Woodward's method was to begin with a simple molecule and, by adding or removing carbon atoms, to form the skeleton of the desired product. He then attached side groups to complete the required molecule. In the case of quinine, this process involved seventeen conversions to construct the carbon structure and many further reactions to replicate natural quinine.

Three years later, in collaboration with the organic chemist C. H. Schramm, Woodward created a protein analogue by joining units of amino acids into a long chain. The resulting polypeptides, which were used in the manufacture of plastics and artificial antibiotics, became a valuable tool for the study of protein metabolism. In 1951 Woodward headed the first team to synthesize a steroid, a highly complex ringed structure of which cholesterol and cortisone are examples. Woodward continued to make "impossible" syntheses, some of which, such as that of strychnine, have never been repeated. Among the compounds he produced were chlorophyll, lanosterol, lysergic acid, reserpine, prostaglandin F_{2a}, colchicine, and vitamin B_{12}.

Some of this work was performed at the Woodward Research Institute in Basel, Switzerland, which was established in 1963 by the Ciba (now Ciba-Geigy) Corporation, with Woodward as its namesake and director, a position he held concurrently with his appointment at Harvard. Under his direction, researchers at the institute synthesized many compounds with commercial applications. One of the most notable was cephalosporin C, a penicillinlike antibiotic used against bacterial infections. At the time of his death, he was working on the synthesis of the antibiotic erythromycin.

Although Woodward is best known for his synthetic work, his contribution to organic chemistry was broader and more fundamental. When he began his career, the principles of organic chemistry were well established. The tetrahedral carbon atom, the nature of the side groups attached to it, and their reactivities were all known. Analysis of unknown substances was based on classical methods that had originated in the nineteenth century. After a compound was broken down and its components identified, its structural arrangement was deduced from the reactions undergone by the substance.

Woodward revolutionized the field by applying the techniques of physical chemistry. He made use of the electronic theory of molecules to analyze reactions and predict their outcome, vital in planning organic syntheses. He popularized the use of spectroscopy to elucidate molecular structure more rapidly and accurately. The rules that relate ultraviolet spectra to the number and type of linkages between carbon atoms and side groups bear his name. In collaboration with ROALD HOFFMANN, he postulated rules based on quantum mechanics for the conservation of orbital symmetry when bonding of atoms occurs in chemical reactions. These techniques permitted Woodward to utilize the natural forces driving the reaction to produce precisely the molecule he wanted.

Woodward received the 1965 Nobel Prize for Chemistry "for his outstanding achievements in the art of organic synthesis." In his presentation speech, Arne Fredga of the Royal Swedish Academy of Sciences jokingly alluded to Woodward's dominance in the field of or-

ganic chemistry: "It is sometimes said that organic synthesis is at the same time an exact science and a fine art. Here nature is the uncontested master, but I dare say that the prizewinner of this year, Dr. Woodward, is a good second."

In 1938 Woodward married Irja Pullman, with whom he had two daughters. His second wife, Eudoxia Muller, whom he married in 1946, was a consultant at Polaroid; they had a son and a daughter. A fluent and stimulating lecturer, Woodward usually spoke without notes or slides. With ROBERT ROBINSON, he founded the journals of organic chemistry *Tetrahedron* and *Tetrahedron Letters* and served on their editorial boards. He was also a member of the board of governors of the Weizmann Institute of Science in Israel. Woodward, who smoked constantly, occasionally played touch football or softball for recreation. He died of a heart attack at the age of sixty-two at his home in Cambridge, Massachusetts.

In addition to the Nobel Prize, Woodward received the George Ledlie Prize of Harvard University (1955), the Davy Medal of the Royal Society of London (1959), the National Medal of Science of the National Science Foundation (1964), the Willard Gibbs Medal of the American Chemical Society (1967), the Lavoisier Medal of the French Chemical Society (1968), and the Arthur C. Cope Award of the American Chemical Society (1973), among others. He was a member of the National Academy of Sciences and the American Academy of Arts and Sciences and held foreign membership in the Royal Society of London as well as professional societies in numerous other countries. He was awarded honorary degrees by Yale University, Harvard University, the University of Southern California, the University of Chicago, Cambridge University, Columbia University, and many others.

SELECTED WORKS: The Conservation of Orbital Symmetry, 1970, with Roald Hoffmann.

ABOUT: Barton, D. (ed.) R. B. Woodward Remembered, 1982; Biographical Memoirs of Fellows of the Royal Society, volume 27, 1981; Current Biography December 1962; New York Times July 10, 1979.

YALOW, ROSALYN S.

(July 19, 1921–   )
Nobel Prize for Medicine or Physiology, 1977
(shared with Roger Guillemin and Andrew V. Schalley)

The American biophysicist Rosalyn Sussman Yalow was born Rosalyn Sussman in New

ROSALYN S. YALOW

York City to Simon Sussman, the owner of a small paper and twine business, and the former Clara Zipper. She obtained her early education in the Bronx public schools and then attended Walton High School. She entered Hunter College (now part of the City University of New York) in 1937, at a time when recent developments in nuclear physics had aroused great interest. In January 1941, when she obtained her B.A. with honors, she became the first woman to graduate from Hunter with a degree in physics. The following month she was accepted as a teaching assistant and graduate student in the College of Engineering at the University of Illinois, where she was the only woman in a class of 400 students.

While engaged in the research leading to her doctoral dissertation, Yalow became highly adept at assembling apparatus for the measurement of radioactive substances, a skill that she put to good use later as a medical physicist. She was awarded a Ph.D. in physics from the University of Illinois College of Engineering in January 1945. That year she returned to New York City, worked briefly in a research laboratory, and then taught physics to preengineering students at Hunter College. In 1947, with the assistance of Dr. Gioacchino Failla, a leading medical physicist, she obtained a position as consultant to the Radiotherapy Service at the Bronx Veterans Administration (VA) Hospital. In that capacity she established and equipped one of the first radioisotope laboratories in the United States. (Radioisotopes are tracer molecules, labeled or tagged with radioactive atoms.) In

1950 she left her teaching position at Hunter College to devote her time to her work at the Bronx VA Hospital.

In 1950 Yalow had begun to work with Solomon A. Berson, who had just completed his residency in internal medicine at the Bronx VA Hospital. Utilizing Berson's training in clinical medicine, physiology, and anatomy and Yalow's background in mathematics and physics, the two researchers began a collaborative effort that lasted twenty-two years. They used radioisotopes to measure blood volume, assess the distribution of serum proteins in bodily tissues, and diagnose thyroid disease. They soon became interested in diabetes, however, and in the course of their investigations of this disease they developed radioimmunoassay (RIA), a method that uses radioactive substances to measure minute substances in blood plasma and other bodily tissues.

At the time, insulin was readily available, and Yalow and Berson knew it could easily be tagged with radioactive iodine. With a radioactive tag, or label, the disappearance rate of insulin from the circulation (plasma) of diabetics could be measured by counting with a radiation counter the radioactivity of samples of plasma obtained at different points in time after the injection of radioactive insulin. It had always been assumed that the supply of insulin from the pancreas was low in diabetic adults, as in diabetic children, and that any available insulin was rapidly utilized by the body. However, Yalow and Berson found the rate of insulin disappearance from the plasma to be unexpectedly low. They postulated that adult diabetics produce antibodies to the foreign insulin molecule, which inactivates the insulin and causes it to be cleared more slowly from the plasma. When they first attempted to publish their observations, their paper was rejected; at the time, scientists believed that the insulin molecule was too small to provoke antibody production. The findings of Yalow and Berson, however, were subsequently accepted.

As an offshoot of their diabetes research, Yalow and Berson published a description of RIA in 1959. Since then it has been used in laboratories around the world to measure concentrations of hormones and other substances in the body that had previously been too small to detect. The technique may be employed to detect drugs in bodily fluids or tissues, in blood banks to screen blood donors for hepatitis virus, for the early detection of cancer, and to measure the levels of neurotransmitters (substances that allow nerve impulses to be transmitted across the gap between nerve cells) or hormones in tissue or plasma.

Yalow has used RIA to measure levels of growth hormone in children of unusually small stature to determine the cause of dwarfism, to track the path of leukemia virus in the stages before actual tumor growth, to identify patients with peptic ulcer disease who are likely to benefit from surgery, and to detect a new class of neurotransmitters in the brain, the cholecystokinins, which may be involved in the perception of satiety (the subjective sensation of fullness in the stomach). Yalow also believes that RIA may have a place in the study of clinical assessment of infectious diseases.

In 1968, when Berson became chairman of the Department of Medicine at Mt. Sinai Medical School in New York City, Yalow was named acting director of the Radioisotope Service at the VA. The following year she was appointed director of the Radioimmunoassay Reference Laboratory there, and in 1970 she was named director of the Nuclear Medicine Service. In 1972 she became a senior medical investigator of the VA. After Berson died unexpectedly in 1972, Yalow became director of the newly created Solomon A. Berson Research Laboratory at the VA Hospital. From 1968 to 1974 she served as research professor in the Department of Medicine at Mt. Sinai, where she was named distinguished service professor in 1974.

Half of the 1977 Nobel Prize for Physiology or Medicine was awarded to Yalow "for the development of radioimmunoassays of peptide hormones." The other portion was shared jointly by ROGER GUILLEMIN and ANDREW V. SCHALLEY for related work on hormones in the brain. Because the prize is not awarded posthumously, Berson did not share this honor. In concluding her Nobel lecture, Yalow pointed out that "the first telescope opened the heavens; the first microscope opened the world of microbes; radioisotopic methodology, as exemplified by RIA, has shown the potential for opening new vistas in science and medicine."

Between 1979 and 1986, Yalow was distinguished professor at large at the Albert Einstein College of Medicine, Yeshiva University; she was concurrently the chairman of the Department of Clinical Science at Montefiore Hospital and Medical Center from 1980 until 1986. Since 1986 she has been Solomon A. Berson Distinguished Professor at Large at Mt. Sinai School of Medicine.

In 1943 Yalow married Aaron Yalow, whom she had met at the University of Illinois; they have a son and a daughter.

Among Yalow's many awards and honors are the Gairdner Foundation International Award (1971), the Scientific Achievement Award of the American Medical Association (1975), the A. Cressy Morrison Prize in Natural Sciences of the New York Academy of Sciences (1975), and the Albert Lasker Basic Medical Research Award (1976). She is a fellow of the New York Academy of Sciences and a member of the Radiation Research Society, the American Association of Physicists in Medicine, the Endocrine Society, and the National Academy of Sciences.

SELECTED WORKS: Methods in Radioimmunoassay of Peptide Hormones, 1976, with others.

ABOUT: Current Biography July 1978; Haber, L. Women Pioneers in Science, 1979; New York Times Magazine April 9, 1978; Nova: Adventures in Science, 1982; Physics Today December 1977.

YANG, CHEN NING

(September 22, 1922–   )
Nobel Prize for Physics, 1957
(shared with Tsung-Dao Lee)

The Chinese-American physicist Chen Ning Yang (yung) was born in Ho-fei, in the province of Anhwei in northern China, the oldest of five children of Ko-Chuan Yang, a professor of mathematics, and the former Meng-Hua Loh. In 1929 the family moved to Peking, where Professor Yang taught at Tsinghua University, and Chen attended Chung Te Middle School. When Japan invaded China in 1937, Tsinghua University was moved to K'un-ming to become consolidated into the National Southwest Associated University. Yang entered the new university, where TSUNG-DAO LEE was later a fellow student, and earned a B.S. in physics in 1942, writing a thesis on group theory and molecular spectra. For his 1944 M.S., he wrote a thesis on contributions to the statistical theory of order-disorder transformations. In 1945, on a fellowship from the National Southwest Associated University, Yang entered the University of Chicago to study under ENRICO FERMI. His Ph.D. thesis in 1948, supervised by Edward Teller, was titled "On the Angular Distribution in Nuclear Reactions and Coincidence Measurements."

Remaining at Chicago for another year, Yang served as an instructor in physics before joining the Institute for Advanced Study in Princeton, New Jersey, in 1949. During the academic

CHEN NING YANG

been universally accepted because it had led to useful theoretical and experimental results, and probably also because it appealed to the desire of physicists to find such symmetries in nature. Most felt intuitively that nature was unlikely to favor right over left or left over right.

The puzzle encountered with regard to parity conservation concerned two apparently different kinds of K-mesons, unstable particles observed among the fragments after high-energy bombardment of atomic nuclei. One, called theta, decayed into two pi-mesons, while the other, called tau, decayed into three pi-mesons. Since a pi-meson has a known parity of -1, two pi-mesons have an overall parity $-1 \times -1 = +1$. Therefore, the parent theta particle should also have a parity of $+1$. The tau particle, parent of three pi-mesons, should have a parity $-1 \times -1 \times -1 = -1$. If the theta and tau mesons have different parities, they must be different particles. On the other hand, experimental evidence, such as the fact that they seemed to have the same mass and lifetime, would ordinarily have suggested that they were the same particle. In considering the seemingly unresolvable dilemma, Yang and Lee boldly decided to investigate the experimental support for parity conservation.

year 1953–1954, he was a senior physicist at Brookhaven National Laboratory on Long Island, New York. He became a professor of physics at the Institute for Advanced Study in 1955 and remained for eleven more years before moving to the State University of New York (SUNY) at Stony Brook, Long Island, as Albert Einstein Professor of Physics and director of the Institute of Theoretical Physics.

It was during this time that Yang began meeting regularly with Lee, who was now at Columbia University, to continue the discussions of physics they had begun while both were in Chicago. In May 1956, they considered a current puzzle concerning the law of conservation of parity. Conservation of parity arises from one of the symmetries of nature recognized by physicists. It means, among other things, that nature is neither right-handed nor left-handed, so that the mirror image of a particle interaction should obey the same laws as the interaction itself, if parity is conserved.

In quantum mechanics, each particle or system of particles is characterized by a mathematical expression called a wave function. Mirror reflection amounts to changing the space coordinates x, y, and z to $-x$, $-y$, and $-z$. If doing so changes the algebraic sign of the function, the parity of the particle or system is -1 (odd). If the function remains unchanged, the parity is $+1$ (even). The law of conservation of parity, first formulated in 1925, stated that the total parity (the product of the parities of all participating particles) is the same before and after an interaction. The law had

Particle interactions involve four forces: the strong force, which binds the protons and neutrons in the nucleus; the electromagnetic force, which acts on charged particles; the weak force, linked to emission of particles during radioactive decay; and gravitation, the force that acts on masses. To their surprise, Yang and Lee found that experimental evidence was abundant for parity conservation in strong and electromagnetic interactions but totally absent for weak interactions. Gravitation is such a comparatively weak force that it is generally negligible in subatomic particle interactions. None of the reports the two scientists examined specifically tested the principle of parity conservation in weak interactions. The decay of theta and tau particles into pi-mesons involved weak interactions. Yang and Lee quickly devised experiments designed to test explicitly and conclusively whether parity was conserved in weak interactions. Since they were theorists, they left experimentation to others.

The first to respond was Chien-Shiung Wu of Columbia University, in collaboration with physicists at the United States National Bureau of Standards. In 1956–1957, after six months of painstaking preparation of the difficult experimental arrangement, Wu placed radioactive cobalt within an electromagnet and cooled it to a temperature near absolute zero to minimize the influence of thermal motions. Cobalt emits beta particles (electrons) and neutrinos (massless, uncharged particles). Since atoms behave like tiny magnets, their directions were aligned with the electromagnet field, establishing a known orientation. If parity were conserved in the radioactive disintegration of cobalt, a weak interaction, equal numbers of emitted electrons would emerge in the directions of the north and south magnet poles. Wu found that more electrons emerged from the south end. Parity was not conserved. Subsequent experiments by others almost immediately confirmed the violation of parity conservation in the decay of pi-mesons into mu-mesons and the decay of the mu-mesons into electrons and neutrinos (or antineutrinos). The mu-mesons and electrons displayed a forward-backward asymmetry.

Without the constraint of the parity law, Yang and Lee could propose that theta and tau were indeed the same particle, capable of two different modes of decay. The failure of the law of conservation of parity stimulated a surge of theoretical and experimental research. New avenues of thought even promised progress toward the goal, especially associated with ALBERT EINSTEIN, of unifying the four known forces into a single theory.

"For their penetrating investigation of the so-called parity laws, which has led to important discoveries regarding the elementary particles," Yang and Lee shared the 1957 Nobel Prize for Physics. In his presentation speech, O. B. Klein of the Royal Swedish Academy of Sciences said, "The result of their investigation was unexpected, namely that the validity of the symmetry assumption even in the best-known process had no experimental support whatsoever, the reason being that all experiments had been so arranged as to give the same result whether the assumption was valid or not." Klein hailed the two laureates for their success in unlocking "a most puzzling deadlock in the field of elementary particle physics where now experimental and theoretical work is pouring forth."

Yang's primary research interests remain in the theory of fields and particles, statistical mechanics (the science of the atomic origin of thermal phenomena), and symmetry principles. A new principle for particle and field interactions, which he proposed in 1954 with Robert L. Mills, who was then at the Brookhaven National Laboratory, became the basis for many developments in the area of fundamental physics known as gauge theory. Gauge theories are considered to underlie all the basic interactions in nature.

Yang has visited the People's Republic of China annually since 1971, helping to promote mutual understanding and friendship between his native country and the United States. He married Chih Li Tu in 1950; they have two sons and a daughter. Before leaving China in 1945 for the United States, Yang decided he would like a first name Americans would find easy to pronounce. He chose Franklin, out of admiration for Benjamin Franklin whose biography he had read, and is called Frank by his American friends. He became a United States citizen in 1964.

Yang has received honorary doctorates from Princeton University, the University of Minnesota, the University of Durham, and several other institutions. He has also received the Albert Einstein Commemorative Award of Yeshiva University in 1957 and the Rumford Medal of the American Academy of Arts and Sciences in 1980. He is a member of the National Academy of Sciences, the American Philosophical Society, the Brazilian Academy of Sciences, and the Venezuelan Academy of Sciences, as well as a fellow of the American Physical Society.

SELECTED WORKS: Special Problems of Statistical Mechanics, 1952; Conservation Laws in Weak Interactions, 1957, with Tsung-Dao Lee; Elementary Particles and Weak Interactions, 1957, with Tsung-Dao Lee; Remarks on Nonvariance Under Time Reversal and Charge Conjugation, 1957, with Tsung-Dao Lee; Elementary Particles: A Short History of Some Discoveries in Atomic Physics, 1961; Theory of Charged Vector Mesons Interacting With the Electromagnetic Field, 1963, with Tsung-Dao Lee; Selected Papers, 1945–1980, 1983.

ABOUT: Crease, R. P., and Mann, C. C. The Second Creation, 1986; New Yorker May 12, 1962.

YEATS, WILLIAM BUTLER
(June 13, 1865–January 28, 1939)
Nobel Prize for Literature, 1923

William Butler Yeats (yāts), Irish poet and dramatist, was born in Dublin, the eldest of four children. His father, John Butler Yeats, the son of an Irish Protestant clergyman, had been trained for the bar but gave up his practice to become a portrait painter. Yeats's mother, the former Susan Pollexfen, a sensitive, withdrawn woman, came from a family of well-to-do merchants and shipowners in Sligo, in the west of Ireland.

Yeats received his early schooling in the

WILLIAM BUTLER YEATS

Hammersmith section of London, where his father had moved the family in order to pursue his painting career. A mediocre student, unhappy in the large and unfamiliar city, Yeats spent the summer months with his mother's relatives in Sligo, "the place that has really influenced my life the most," as he later wrote. His love for Sligo is reflected in many poems and in the largely autobiographical novel *John Sherman* (1891).

In 1880 the Yeatses moved back to Ireland. Between the ages of sixteen and eighteen, Yeats attended high school in Dublin. Then, with painting his primary interest, he continued his education at the Metropolitan School of Art. He began writing poetry in 1882, greatly influenced by Edmund Spenser and Percy Bysshe Shelley, and was first published three years later in the *Dublin University Review*. That same year he helped to form the Dublin Hermetic Society, a group devoted to study of the occult, a subject that preoccupied him throughout his life. After almost two years, having decided that he was a better poet than painter, Yeats left art school and moved back to London with his family in 1887. Two years later, his first book was published, *The Wanderings of Oisin and Other Poems*. Its chief work was a long and startling narrative poem based on Irish mythology.

Yeats attempted early to arrive at a philosophical and aesthetic system that would resolve the conflict between art and nature. He sought also to hammer the contradictions of his own personality into what he called "unity of being." William Blake, Friedrich Nietzsche,

and Emanuel Swedenborg were important influences on his writing, as was his desire to create a new and authentic Irish consciousness. Many of his early compositions were poetic dramas. *The Countess Cathleen* (1892), for example, his earliest significant play, is the story of a noblewoman who sells her soul to save her peasants from starvation. That and his greatest play, *Cathleen ni Houlihan* (1902), were written for Maud Gonne, a celebrated actress, beauty, and agitator for Irish independence, whom Yeats had met in 1889. His long, complex passion for her inspired some of his finest lyric poetry.

Another influential acquaintance was Lady Augusta Gregory, a widow and member of the Protestant landed gentry, to whom he was introduced in 1896. A seminal figure in the Irish literary renaissance, Lady Gregory wrote plays and published Irish folktales. Yeats admired her broad knowledge of the Irish countryside, people, and traditions. After she became his patroness, he spent many summers at Coole, her home in County Galway.

During a stay in Paris in 1896, Yeats met the young Irish dramatist John Millington Synge. Although the destitute Synge had written little at this point, Yeats recognized his lyric and dramatic gifts and urged him to return to Ireland and live among the Irish peasantry. The results of this meeting and of the close friendship that developed between the two writers changed the course of Irish literature. Encouraged by Yeats, Synge produced a series of intensely original Irish plays. Just as importantly, Synge's ear for common speech and his painstaking method of composition profoundly influenced Yeats's work. *In the Seven Woods*, a collection of poems published in 1903, shows a shift from the Celtic romanticism of Yeats's earlier work to a more controlled, colloquial style.

During this period, Yeats, Synge, and Lady Gregory were actively involved in efforts to create a national theater in Ireland, and in 1906 they were named codirectors of the Abbey Theater in Dublin. Yeats devoted much time to managing, fund-raising, and writing plays for the Abbey, while continuing to write poetry. In 1914 he published *Responsibilities,* a collection of poems recognized as a turning point in his development. "I have tried for more self-portraiture," Yeats wrote in 1913 to his father, who had emigrated to New York. "I have tried to make my work convincing with a speech so natural and dramatic that the hearer would feel the presence of a man thinking and feeling."

In both England and Ireland, Yeats associated with important figures in the literary world, among them Oscar Wilde, James Joyce, and Ezra Pound. In the autumn of 1913, Pound worked as Yeats's unofficial secretary. At the time, Pound was also editing translations of the Noh plays of Japan. Impressed with the aristocratic nature of the Japanese drama, Yeats adopted its style in his own *Four Plays for Dancers* (1921).

At the time of the Easter Rebellion against British rule in 1916, Yeats was in England. Although his imagination was stirred by the sacrifice of the rebels, he was horrified by the violence and pettiness of those who claimed to speak for Ireland. In his next collection of poetry, *The Wild Swans at Coole* (1919), Yeats placed the burden of meaning "firmly where it belongs, in people, and in the acts that embody their values," as the Irish literary scholar Denis Donoghue commented. "The poems speak to us directly, to our sense of the human predicament. . . . [Yeats] acknowledges human limitation and tries to live as well as possible under that shadow."

A year after he became a senator of the newly founded Irish Free State, Yeats was awarded the 1923 Nobel Prize for Literature "for his always inspired poetry, which in a highly artistic form gives expression to the spirit of a whole nation." Describing Yeats as "the central point and leader" of the Celtic Revival, Per Hallström of the Swedish Academy declared, "Yeats has achieved what few poets have been able to do: he has succeeded in preserving contact with his people while upholding the most aristocratic artistry."

In his Nobel lecture, "The Irish Dramatic Movement," Yeats recounted the origins of the Abbey Theater and the purpose it served. Hailing the life of the Irish countryside as the source of his inspiration, he declared, "It seemed as if the ancient world lay all about us with its freedom of imagination, its delight in good stories, in man's force and woman's beauty." He paid generous tribute to his compatriots Synge (who had died in 1909) and Lady Gregory as well: "When I received from the hands of your king the great honor your academy has conferred upon me, I felt that a young man's ghost should have stood upon one side of me and at the other a living woman in her vigorous old age."

During his last fifteen years, Yeats reigned as elder statesman of Irish letters. Despite frequent ill health, he produced poetry of increasing passion, technical mastery, and imagination, as demonstrated in the comple-

mentary collections *The Tower* (1928) and *The Winding Stair and Other Poems* (1933). In 1917 Yeats had married a young Englishwoman, Georgiana Hyde-Lees, with whom he had two children. She contributed to the writing of *A Vision* (1925, revised 1937), a mystical explication of history, human psychology, and the soul. Travel to the United States, France, Italy, and Majorca provided new material for Yeats's poetry and further enhanced his reputation.

After a brief illness, Yeats died at Cap-Martin on the French Riviera, where he had gone to escape the rigors of the Irish winter. He was interred in nearby Roquebrune. In 1948, in accordance with a wish expressed in one of his last poems, "Under Ben Bulben," his remains were returned to Ireland and buried at Drumcliff, near Sligo.

In addition to the Nobel Prize, Yeats received honorary degrees from Queens College, Belfast; Trinity College, Dublin; Oxford University; and Cambridge University. The annual Yeats International Summer School in Sligo, founded in 1960, is devoted to the study of his work.

In the opinion of most critics, Yeats remains the most important of all Irish poets. T. S. ELIOT called him "the greatest poet of our time—certainly the greatest in this language, and so far as I am able to judge, in any language." His biographer, the American scholar Richard Ellmann, wrote, "By his devotion to his craft and his refusal to accept the placidity to which his years entitled him, he lived several lifetimes in one and made his development inseparable from that of modern verse and, to some extent, of modern man." The Irish poet Seamus Heaney concluded in a 1978 lecture, "Above all, [Yeats] reminds you that art is intended, that it is part of the creative push of civilization itself."

ADDITIONAL WORKS: Mosada, 1886; Irish Fairy Tales, 1892; The Celtic Twilight, 1893; The Land of Heart's Desire, 1894; Poems, 1895; The Secret Rose, 1897; The Tables of the Law, The Adoration of the Magi, 1897; The Wind Among the Reeds, 1899; The Shadowy Waters, 1900; When There Is Nothing, 1902; Ideas of Good and Evil, 1903; The Hour Glass, 1903; The Pot of Broth, 1904; The King's Threshold and On Baile's Strand, 1904; Stories of Red Hanrahan, 1905; Dierdre, 1907; Discoveries, 1907; The Unicorn From the Stars, 1908; The Green Helmet, 1910; Synge and the Ireland of His Time, 1911; Plays for an Irish Theatre, 1912; Poems Written in Discouragement, 1913; Per Amica Silentia Lunae, 1918; The Cutting of an Agate, 1919; Two Plays for Dancers, 1919; Michael Robartes, 1921; Trembling of the Veil, 1922; The Player Queen, 1922; Plays and Controversies, 1923; The Cat and the Moon, 1924; The

Bounty of Sweden, 1925; October Blast, 1927; The Death of Synge, 1928; Fighting the Waves, 1929; A Packet for Ezra Pound, 1929; St. Patrick's Breastplate, 1929; Words for Music, Perhaps, 1932; The Words Upon the Window Pane, 1934; Wheels and Butterflies, 1934; Letters to the New Island, 1934; The King of the Great Clock Tower, 1934; Dramatis Personae, 1935; A Full Moon in March, 1935; A Vision, 1937; The Herne's Egg, 1938; Autobiographies, 1938; On the Boiler, 1939; If I Were Four and Twenty, 1940; Pages From a Diary, 1944; The Collected Poems of W. B. Yeats, 1950; The Collected Plays of W. B. Yeats, 1952; Letters, 1954; The Variorum Edition of the Poems of W. B. Yeats, 1957; Senate Speeches, 1960; Essays and Introductions, 1961; Explorations, 1962; Mythologies, 1962; The Death of Cuchulain, 1982; The Poems of W. B. Yeats, 1983; Purgatory, 1986; Collected Letters of W. B. Yeats, 1986.

ABOUT: Bloom, H. Yeats, 1970; Cross, K. G. W., et al. (eds.) Centenary Tribute (4 vols.) 1965; Donoghue, D. Yeats, 1971; Dorn, K. Player and Painted Stage: The Theatre of W. B. Yeats, 1984; Ellmann, R. Yeats: The Man and the Masks, 1948; Ellmann, R. The Identity of Yeats, 1954; Flannery, M. C. Yeats and Magic, 1977; Gibbons, M. The Masterpiece and the Man, 1959; Hall, J., and Steinmann, M. (eds.) The Permanence of Yeats, 1950; Henn, T. R. The Lonely Tower, 1950; Hone, J. M. W. B. Yeats, 1865–1939, 1942; Jeffares, A. N. W. B. Yeats, Man and Poet, 1949; Kermode, F. Romantic Image, 1957; Koch, V. Yeats: The Tragic Phase, 1951; Krans, H. S. William Butler Yeats and the Irish Literary Revival, 1904; MacLiammóir, M., and Boland, E. W. B. Yeats and His World, 1971; MacNeice, L. The Poetry of W. B. Yeats, 1941; Menon, V. K. N. The Development of William Butler Yeats, 1942; Moore, V. The Unicorn, 1954; Nathan, L. E. The Tragic Drama of William Butler Yeats, 1965; Parkinson, T. W. B. Yeats, Self-Critic, 1951; Peterson, R. F. William Butler Yeats, 1982; Sherman, J. W. B. Yeats: A Critical Study, 1915; Stallworthy, J. Between the Lines, 1963; Tuohy, F. Yeats, 1976; Unterecker, J. (ed.) Yeats: A Collection of Critical Essays, 1963; Ure, P. William Butler Yeats, 1964; Whitaker, T. R. Swan and Shadow, 1964; Wilson, F. A. C. W. B. Yeats and Tradition, 1958.

YUKAWA, HIDEKI
(January 23, 1907–September 8, 1981)
Nobel Prize for Physics, 1949

The Japanese physicist Hideki Yukawa (yŏŏ kä wä) was born Hideki Ogawa in Tokyo, the fifth of seven children of Takuji and Koyuki Ogawa. A year after his birth, the family moved to Kyōto, where his father had been appointed professor of geology at Kyōto Imperial University. He assumed his wife's family name of Yukawa when he was adopted into her family after their marriage.

Yukawa was raised in an atmosphere of wide-ranging intellectual inquiry. His father had an active interest in the archaeology, history, and literature of ancient China and Japan. As a young child, Yukawa learned the Chinese classics from his paternal grandfather, a classical scholar. At Third High School in Kyōto, from

HIDEKI YUKAWA

which he graduated in 1926, Yukawa enjoyed literature, philosophy, and mathematics, but he was most attracted to modern physics after coming across writings on relativity and quantum mechanics in Japanese in the school library. He taught himself some German and read MAX PLANCK's Introduction to Theoretical Physics, which he found while browsing in a bookstore.

Upon graduation from high school, Yukawa entered Kyōto Imperial University, where he took an accelerated program in physics and excelled in advanced work in the laboratory of Kajuro Tamaki. After writing a senior thesis on the properties of P. A. M. DIRAC's equation, which applies the theory of relativity to quantum mechanics in describing the motion of atomic particles, he received his M.S. in 1929. He remained in Tamaki's laboratory as an unpaid assistant, but grew more interested in theoretical physics than in experimental physics. Exciting work was being done in Europe in the field of quantum theory, and Yukawa was intrigued by its many unresolved problems. He learned little quantum theory in his university courses but between 1929 and 1932 taught himself through systematic reading. He spoke with WERNER HEISENBERG and Dirac when they visited Kyōto and also became acquainted with Yoshio Nishina, who had worked with NIELS BOHR in Copenhagen. Yukawa later cited both Tamaki and Nishina as the major influences in his decision to pursue theoretical physics, also noting that experimental ambitions would have been hampered by his inability "to master the art

1155

of making simple glass laboratory equipment." In 1932 he was appointed lecturer in physics at Kyōto Imperial University and one year later at Ōsaka University. He became an assistant professor at Ōsaka in 1936.

At Ōsaka, Yukawa began to think seriously about a problem that had puzzled physicists for over two decades: Why doesn't the nucleus of an atom split apart? The nucleus had been known for some time to contain closely packed, positively charged particles (protons). Since like electric charges repel each other, and the force increases rapidly as the charges come closer, the cohesion between protons was a mystery. In 1932 JAMES CHADWICK's discovery of the neutron, an uncharged particle with a mass almost identical to that of the proton, further complicated matters. The neutron, soon recognized as another occupant of the nucleus, explained the existence of isotopes, elements with the same number of protons but different numbers of neutrons. The proton cohesion problem remained, however, compounded by the need to explain the cohesion of neutrons to each other and to the protons. Gravitation, a mutual attraction between all masses, is too weak to have a significant effect in nuclear binding.

Several eminent physicists, including Heisenberg, proposed nuclear theories, but none survived critical analysis. It was natural to imagine the existence of a previously unknown nuclear force, but it had to be immensely strong and short-range. Moreover, quantum physicists had come to regard the known forces as acting through the exchange of particles containing units of energy, or quanta, of the force field. For the electromagnetic field, the particle is the photon, the quantum of electromagnetic energy. The photon has no rest mass. Light either moves or does not exist.

In 1935 Yukawa proposed that a strong nuclear binding force was associated with an exchange particle that had a relatively large mass. He published a complex, but consistent, theory that enabled him to calculate the mass (about 200 times that of the electron) and other characteristics of the hypothetical particle. He also showed that it could not be detected in ordinary nuclear reactions, because its large mass was equivalent to a very high energy, but might be found in the violent collisions between cosmic rays and atomic nuclei. Yukawa's paper appeared in a Japanese physics periodical. Although it was written in English, it went unnoticed for two years.

The American physicist CARL D. ANDERSON had discovered the positron in 1932 by examining photographs of condensation trails formed by the passage of cosmic radiation in cloud chambers. (Particles like those in cosmic rays are invisible but electrify water vapor in the chamber and cause it to condense into visible droplets.) In 1937, apparently unaware of Yukawa's hypothesis, Anderson observed cloud-chamber tracks of a previously unknown particle with a mass similar to that of Yukawa's hypothetical particle. It was first called the mesotron, then the meson (from *meso*, which is Greek for "middle," since the particle's mass was between those of the electron and the proton). This discovery brought Yukawa's prediction into prominence, and Western physicists explored possible connections. After several years, however, they realized that Anderson's and Yukawa's particles were not the same. In particular, the observed meson interacted weakly with the nucleus (Yukawa postulated a strong interaction), and its lifetime was over 100 times longer than the predicted one hundred-millionth of a second. Some physicists began to suspect that Yukawa was on the wrong track.

Yukawa returned to Kyōto Imperial University as a professor in 1939. Because he was by then a well-known theorist, his presence helped give the Kyōto physics department international standing. World War II interrupted communications between Japanese and Western physicists, but Yukawa continued his particle research. In 1942 two of his co-workers, Yasutaka Tanikawa and Shoichi Sakata, proposed that two kinds of mesons existed, heavier and lighter, and that Anderson had discovered the lighter kind as a component of cosmic rays at sea level. Yukawa's heavier particle was likely to be found only in the earth's upper atmosphere where primary cosmic rays collided with nuclei for the first time. It would then rapidly decay into the lighter kind of meson whose longer life enabled it to survive at lower altitudes.

In 1947 CECIL F. POWELL discovered Yukawa's predicted particle with the use of a cloud chamber lofted to high altitudes. He almost certainly did not know of the work of Tanikawa and Sakata, but he was likely to have been familiar with the two-meson hypothesis independently proposed by Robert E. Marshak and HANS A. BETHE in 1947. In 1948 mesons were created artificially in a laboratory of the University of California at Berkeley.

With these discoveries, Yukawa was vindicated and received the 1949 Nobel Prize for Physics "for his prediction of the existence of mesons on the basis of theoretical work on nuclear forces." Yukawa's particle became known as the pi-meson, then simply pion. Anderson's lighter particle became the mu-meson, then muon. Pions are actually triplets; one type is electrically neutral, a second carries a positive charge, and a third is negatively charged. Muons appear to be almost identical to electrons except for their heavy mass. Many other kinds of mesons have been observed subsequently.

When he received word of the award, Yukawa was in the United States, having taken a leave of absence from Kyōto University a year earlier to do research at the Institute for Advanced Study in Princeton, New Jersey. After spending a year at the institute, he accepted an invitation from Columbia University to serve as a visiting professor. The Columbia faculty granted Yukawa tenure in 1951 and designated him professor of physics. In 1953 Yukawa returned to Kyōto University to become director of the Research Institute for Fundamental Physics. There he continued his study of quantum physics and his research into elementary particles. Most significantly, he directed the training of a generation of Japan's young physicists until his retirement in 1970.

Starting in 1954, when a nuclear test conducted by the United States demolished Bikini Atoll in the Pacific Ocean, Yukawa began to speak publicly against nuclear weapons "as a scientist, a Japanese, and a member of the human race." He was one of the signers of the Russell Statement (after its author, BERTRAND RUSSELL), which called upon governments to settle their differences by peaceful means. Yukawa also participated in international conferences at which scientists discussed disarmament.

Yukawa (then Ogawa) married Sumi Yukawa in 1932. They had two sons. In his later years he was again drawn to his early interests in history, literature, and philosophy, and he wrote poems in Japanese. Besides his scientific writings, he also published his reflections on philosophy. In his book *Creativity and Intuition: A Physicist Looks at East and West* (1973), Yukawa acknowledged the influence of Oriental philosophers, particularly the Taoist philosophers Lao-tsu and Chuang-tsu, on his own thinking.

In addition to the Nobel Prize, Yukawa received the Imperial Prize of the Japan Academy (1940), the Lomonosov Gold Medal of the Soviet Academy of Sciences (1964), the Order of Merit of the Federal Republic of Germany (1967), and the Japanese government's Order of the Rising Sun (1977). He was a member of ten prestigious national scientific societies, including the American National Academy of Sciences, the Physical Society of Japan, the Royal Society of London, and the Soviet Academy of Sciences.

SELECTED WORKS: Quantum Theory and Nonlocal Fields, 1952; Scientific Works, 1979; Tabibito, the Traveler, 1982.

ABOUT: Biographical Memoirs of Fellows of the Royal Society, volume 29, 1983; Current Biography January 1950; Podell, J. (ed.) Annual Obituary 1981, 1982.

ZEEMAN, PIETER

(May 25, 1865–October 9, 1943)
Nobel Prize for Physics, 1902
(shared with Hendrik Lorentz)

The Dutch physicist Pieter Zeeman (zā' män) was born in the village of Zonnemaire to Catharinus Forandinus Zeeman, a Lutheran clergyman, and the former Wilhelmina Worst. After his elementary education in Zonnemaire, he attended secondary school in Zierikzee, a town five miles away, and then studied Latin and Greek for two years in Delft to satisfy a university entrance requirement. Indications of his scientific ability were already apparent. He published an account of the aurora borealis, readily visible in Zonnemaire, and impressed the Dutch physicist HEIKE KAMERLINGH ONNES, whom he met in Delft, with his understanding of the treatise on heat by the Scottish physicist James Clerk Maxwell.

In 1885 Zeeman entered the University of Leiden where he studied under Kamerlingh Onnes and the theoretical physicist HENDRIK LORENTZ. Five years later he became Lorentz's assistant. His experimental skill in investigating the Kerr effect for his doctoral dissertation won him a gold medal from the Netherlands Scientific Society of Haarlem in 1892 and his Ph.D. the following year. The effect, discovered by the Scottish physicist John Kerr in 1875, involved the influence of magnetism on polarized light. Ordinary light consists of electric and magnetic fields oscillating in directions perpendicular to the line of travel (the two fields are interdependent and perpendicular to each other). The frequency of oscillation corresponds to the color perceived by the eye. If one of the fields oscillates mostly in one of the many possible directions, the light is said to be polarized in the plane defined by the favored field direction and the direction

PIETER ZEEMAN

of the light path. Kerr found that reflection of plane-polarized light from the polished pole face of a magnet rotated the plane of polarization. (Another "Kerr effect," also discovered in 1875, was the creation of birefringence, or double refraction, in a transparent substance by an electric field. In birefringence, the velocity of light is different along different directions in the substance, so that an incoming ray is bent into two separate outgoing rays.)

After a semester at the Kohlrausch Institute in Strasbourg, France, Zeeman returned to the University of Leiden in 1894 as a privatdocent (unsalaried lecturer). He devoted his research once more to the interaction between magnetism and light. Only two magneto-optic effects had previously been observed: the one by Kerr and one by the English physicist and chemist Michael Faraday, who discovered in 1845 that the plane of polarization was rotated when light passed through certain bodies placed in a strong magnetic field. Zeeman's new research concentrated not on the light itself but on the light source, beginning with a sodium flame positioned between the pole faces of a strong electromagnet. The light from such a flame does not contain a continuous rainbow of colors (frequencies), like light from the sun, but is composed of discrete frequencies characteristic of the source material. If the light is passed through a narrow slit and viewed (or photographed) with an optical spectroscope, the frequencies are separated and displayed as a series of colored lines called a spectrum. The positions of the spectral lines indicate their frequencies. The sodium spectrum contains two

prominent yellow-orange lines, on which Zeeman focused.

Zeeman's aims were based on the electromagnetic theory conceived by Maxwell in the 1860s and developed further by Lorentz. Maxwell was the first to demonstrate theoretically that light was made up of electromagnetic fields. Moreover, he showed that his theory predicted the velocity of light already known from many laboratory measurements and indicated that oscillating electric currents should emit electromagnetic radiation. His theory was confirmed by the German physicist Heinrich Hertz, who produced electromagnetic (radio) waves with an electric circuit and showed that they had the anticipated characteristics, such as the same velocity as light. Lorentz grounded the theory in concrete images of electrically charged particles (later referred to as electrons) in atoms or molecules vibrating at frequencies that corresponded to the colors of emitted light. Since moving charged particles constitute an electric current, their motions should be affected by a magnetic field, just as the current in an electric motor interacts with the magnetism of the pole pieces to make a shaft turn. Zeeman hoped his magnet would alter the vibrations of the hypothetical particles in the sodium flame and that the frequency changes would be observable as a broadening of the spectral lines. Although Maxwell's convincing theory had stimulated others to work along related lines, none had been successful. Zeeman's first attempts were also disappointing.

Zeeman then learned that Faraday had performed a similar experiment in 1862 and failed. Having enormous respect for Faraday, Zeeman decided that the experiment warranted further effort. He returned to the task, using equipment capable of greater resolution and, in August 1896, observed the broadening he had sought in the sodium spectral lines. Since the effect was small, Zeeman wondered whether "we really succeeded in altering the period of vibration, which Maxwell . . . held to be impossible." Even J. W. STRUTT (Lord Rayleigh) was not able to find it, although he did not question Zeeman's accomplishment. To eliminate doubt, Zeeman repeated the experiment many times, both at Leiden and at the University of Amsterdam, to which he moved in 1897 as a lecturer in physics.

The experiment was especially difficult because of the use of a device called a concave mirror diffraction grating, developed in 1882 by the American physicist J. H. Rowland. With a 10-foot arm between the mirror and the photographic plate, this device was extremely sensitive to vibrations caused by movements in the laboratory and by nearby street traffic. Zeeman often traveled to the more rural University of Groningen where conditions permitted more precise measurements.

Lorentz had predicted that a magnetic field would cause the electrically charged particles in matter to oscillate in different modes, with slightly different frequencies, from that of the undisturbed particles. Thus, he expected the single spectral line not merely to broaden but to split into three distinct lines. He also predicted that the emitted light would be polarized in certain ways in correspondence to the varied particle motions. Zeeman was able to detect the predicted polarization and, after a painstaking search with flames from other substances, such as cadmium, resolved broadened lines into their separate components.

Zeeman's precise measurements indicated that the vibrating particle could not be as heavy as an atom, the candidate proposed by the English mathematician Joseph Larmor. The splitting of the lines permitted an estimation of the ratio of the electric charge to the mass of the vibrating particle, a ratio that proved to be surprisingly large, and a determination that the charge was negative. These findings not only agreed with Lorentz's description of his electron, but also suggested that Lorentz's electron was identical to the electron discovered in 1897 by J. J. THOMSON in his investigation of electric discharges in glass vacuum tubes. "That which vibrates in the light source," Zeeman concluded, "is the same as that which travels in cathode rays." The name *cathode rays* was given to the particles flowing from the negative electrode (cathode) to the positive electrode (anode) in the discharge tube. The difference was that Lorentz's electrons were somehow part of and bound to atoms, whereas Thomson's electrons were free-moving particles in the vacuum of the discharge tube.

Zeeman's assertion was both a brilliant insight and a fundamental contribution to the effort to understand the structure of matter. The magnetic splitting of spectral lines, which became known as the Zeeman effect, is an essential tool in the exploration of the nature of the atom and is useful in determining the magnetic fields of stars. The discovery that spectral lines may split into many more components than the triplets envisioned by Lorentz revealed weaknesses in the theory of the time, but it also provided significant clues for the quantum theory, particularly in regard to the energy states of atoms.

In 1900 Zeeman accepted a post as professor at the University of Amsterdam. There he spent much of the remainder of his scientific career refining his spectral studies.

The 1902 Nobel Prize for Physics was awarded to Zeeman and Lorentz "in recognition of the extraordinary services they rendered by their researches into the influence of magnetism upon radiation phenomena." In his presentation speech, Hjalmar Théel of the Royal Swedish Academy of Sciences declared that the Zeeman effect "represents one of the most important experimental advances that recent decades have to show." He added that "the consequences of Zeeman's discovery promise to yield the most interesting contributions to our knowledge of the constitution of spectra and of the molecular structure of matter."

In 1908 Zeeman was appointed director of the University of Amsterdam's Physical Institute. When the university established its new Physics Laboratory (later named the Zeeman Laboratory) in 1923, Zeeman was appointed its director. His later work included extremely difficult and precise measurements of the velocity of light in moving solid transparent media such as glass and quartz (others had made such measurements in moving water). He found that changes depended not only on the speed and index of refraction of the moving medium, but also on the frequency of the light. His results agreed with the then new theory of relativity proposed by ALBERT EINSTEIN. He also developed a technique combining magnetic and electric deflections of electrically charged atoms to separate them according to their mass and discovered several new isotopes (chemical elements whose atoms have different masses but the same nuclear charge).

Zeeman married Johanna Elisabeth Lebret in 1895. They had three daughters and a son. A dignified but kindly man, with a pleasant manner, he enjoyed the affection and respect of colleagues and staff. His informal discussions of problems with students encouraged them in their laboratory research. His proficiency with languages helped him establish cordial relationships with many other European physicists. He was required by the prevailing custom to retire at the age of seventy, in 1935, from the University of Amsterdam; he died eight years later.

In addition to the Nobel Prize, Zeeman received many awards and honors, including honorary doctorates from Oxford University and from the universities of Göttingen, Strasbourg, Glasgow, Brussels, and Paris. He was awarded the Rumford Medal of the Royal Society of London, the Wilde Prize of the French Academy of Sciences, the Baumgartner Prize of the Austrian Academy of Sciences, and the Henry Draper Medal of the American National Academy of Sciences.

SELECTED WORKS: The Effects of a Magnetic Field on Radiation, 1900, with others; Miscellaneous Papers, 1911; Researches in Magneto-Optics, 1913.

ABOUT: Dictionary of Scientific Biography, volume 14, 1976; Obituary Notices of Fellows of the Royal Society, volume 4, 1944.

ZERNIKE, FRITS
(July 16, 1888–March 10, 1966)
Nobel Prize for Physics, 1953

FRITS ZERNIKE

The Dutch physicist Frits Zernike was born in Amsterdam, the second of six children of Carl Frederick August Zernike, headmaster of an elementary school, mathematics teacher, and author of several mathematics textbooks, and Antje (Dieperink) Zernike, also a mathematics teacher. As a boy, Zernike loved to conduct experiments in his homemade laboratory and enjoyed solving difficult mathematics problems. In secondary school he showed little interest in other subjects but excelled in the physical sciences.

In 1905 Zernike entered the University of Amsterdam, where he majored in chemistry and minored in physics and mathematics. Three years later he entered an essay competition sponsored by the University of Groningen and won a gold medal for an essay on mathematical probabilities. He received a similar award from the Dutch Society for Sciences in 1912 for his solution to a problem on the scattering of light by pure substances and by mixtures. An extended version of this work served as his dissertation when he received his doctoral degree from Amsterdam in 1915.

The same year, Zernike, who was already regarded as a leading figure in his field, succeeded L. S. Örnstein as lecturer in theoretical physics at the University of Groningen where, two years earlier, the noted astronomer J. C. Kapteyn had made Zernike his assistant. By 1920, when he was appointed a full professor of theoretical physics, Zernike and Örnstein had conducted joint research on statistical mechanics widely recognized for its significant contributions to the field. Zernike had also used his mathematical abilities and skill as an instrument maker to improve such scientific

tools as the galvanometer, but after 1930 he devoted most of his efforts to optics research.

Zernike had previously become interested in the effect of flaws in diffraction gratings. A diffraction grating is a clear glass or mirror whose surface is scored by a large number of fine, closely spaced, equidistant grooves. The grooves divide the transmitted or reflected light into many individual slitlike sources. When light rays from the multitude of sources (usually brought to a focus by a lens) strike a point on a screen, the resulting brightness is the summation of all the rays. Since light is an electromagnetic wave consisting of electric and magnetic fields undergoing repeated cycles, the rays add or subtract depending on whether they arrive at the viewing point with their fields in the same or opposing (reversed) phases of their cycle. A particular point in a cycle is called a phase. A ray completes a full cycle (returns to the same phase) for each wavelength it travels along the light path. Because the rays from different parts of a given slitlike source, as well as those from different slits, travel different path lengths to any point on the screen, they arrive at various phases of a cycle. If the light is monochromatic (single wavelength), the result is a pattern of narrow bands, or lines, alternately bright (when rays arrive in phase) and dark (when rays arrive out of phase with each other). If the light is a mixture of wavelengths (colors for visible light), each wavelength produces its own diffraction pattern on the screen displaced from the others. The result is then a continuous spectrum of separate colors like a rainbow.

Many scientists had observed that a grating containing repetitive errors in groove spacings, due to imperfections in the ruling machine, produces extra lines, called ghosts, on either side of a prominent bright line. They dismissed their importance, giving various explanations that Zernike never accepted. Believing that the ghosts represented phase shifts caused by the imperfections, he performed a series of experiments that not only confirmed his expectations but led to his invention of what he called the phase-contrast microscope.

Optical microscopes had already been developed to an impressive degree by German optical companies. However, the visibility of magnified details depended on their ability to transmit or reflect an amount of light significantly different from that coming from their surroundings. In the case of relatively transparent specimens, such as those encountered in biology and medicine, conventional microscopes presented serious shortcomings. Zernike reasoned that light passing through transparent details in specimens differed from light passing outside them and therefore contained the desired information. The difference was not in amplitude, which the eye could detect, but in phase, which the eye could not detect. The phases differ because light travels at different speeds in different substances. If a substance is transparent, it does not change the quantity of light transmitted; but it does alter the number of wavelengths, or fractions of wavelengths, in the optical path because it reduces the speed of light and therefore the distance traveled during a cycle. It is said to retard the phase. Zernike, in his experiments with ghosts in diffraction patterns, found a way to convert the phase change into an amplitude change, which would then make the transparent detail visible to the eye.

The principle was to superimpose the light passing through the transparent object on a uniform background illumination representing a small portion of the direct light (light that bypasses the object) deliberately advanced in phase by a quarter of a wavelength. The effect of combining the light through the transparent object, which was retarded in phase relative to the direct light, with the background illumination, which was advanced in phase, was destructive interference, that is, a reduction in brightness. To the viewer's eye, it appeared as if the transparent object had absorbed light. Zernike created the desired background illumination by introducing what he called a phase plate (a glass plate with an etched groove in

it) into the light path in the focal plane of the microscope objective lens.

Zernike's phase-contrast microscope made it possible to view colorless organisms, such as cells or bacteria, without the use of dyes, which often killed the specimens. It enabled more accurate observations than could be obtained with dark field illumination, another method that often caused misinterpretation of minute details. The phase-contrast technique also proved to be useful in assessing imperfections in optical surfaces such as telescope mirrors and in the diffraction gratings from which the idea was born.

When Zernike had first proved the soundness of his invention and realized its value, he discussed his design with officials at the Zeiss Optical Works in Jena, Germany, the foremost microscope manufacturers of the time. They showed no interest. "They said if it were practical, they would already have developed it," Zernike recalled.

In 1940, after the outbreak of World War II, German troops overran the Netherlands. In a survey of inventions that might prove useful in the war effort, German military officials came across a description of Zernike's work on the phase-contrast microscope, and in 1941 the first instruments were manufactured. It was not until after the war, however, that this technology was fully exploited.

The phase-contrast microscope became a tool of great importance, especially in medical research. As a visiting professor of physics at the Johns Hopkins University in Baltimore in 1948–1949, Zernike continued to perfect his design and was able to achieve colored images.

Zernike received the 1953 Nobel Prize for Physics "for his demonstration of the phase-contrast method, especially for his invention of the phase-contrast microscope." "When . . . a Nobel Prize is awarded for contributions in classical physics," said Erik Hulthén of the Royal Swedish Academy of Sciences in his presentation address, "the fact is so remarkable that we must go back to the very earliest Nobel Prizes to find a counterpart," since with few exceptions, subsequent awards had been made "for discoveries in atomic and nuclear physics."

In 1930 Zernike married Theodora Willemina van Bommel van Vloten, who had a daughter by a previous marriage; they had one son. Zernike's first wife died in 1945, and in 1954 he married Lena Baanders. They had no children. In 1958, after more than forty years of teaching and research, Zernike retired from the University of Groningen and settled in the town of Naarden, near Amsterdam. Before his death, he was increasingly affected by Parkinson's disease.

Although recognition of Zernike's work came to him late in life, he received many honors in addition to the Nobel Prize, including the Rumford Medal of the Royal Society of London (1952) and honorary degrees from the universities of Amsterdam, London, Poitiers, and Modena. He was elected to membership in the Royal Netherlands Academy of Sciences in 1946.

ABOUT: Biographical Memoirs of Fellows of the Royal Society, volume 13, 1967; Current Biography February 1955; Dictionary of Scientific Biography, volume 14, 1976.

ZIEGLER, KARL
(November 26, 1898–August 11, 1973)
Nobel Prize for Chemistry, 1963
(shared with Giulio Natta)

KARL ZIEGLER

The German organic chemist Karl Ziegler (tsēg′ lər) was born in Helsa, the son of Luise (Rall) and Karl Ziegler, a Lutheran minister. He matriculated at the University of Marburg in 1916, studying chemistry under the noted organic chemist Karl von Auwers and receiving his Ph.D. in 1920. Three years later he attained the habilitation (academic certification) and continued at Marburg as a lecturer. After spending 1925 as visiting lecturer at the University of Frankfurt, he moved to Heidelberg, becoming professor of chemistry there in 1927. He was appointed professor of chemistry and director of the Chemical Institute at the University of Halle nine years later. In 1943 he became director of the Kaiser Wilhelm Institute for Coal Research in Mülheim, where he spent the rest of his career.

At Heidelberg, Ziegler initiated research into free radicals (chemical compounds containing unpaired electrons), large ring compounds, and the synthesis of organometallic compounds. But not until moving to the Kaiser Wilhelm Institute (later called the Max Planck Institute) did he develop the methods of polymerization that later brought him worldwide recognition. Ziegler and his colleagues had been studying the mechanisms of polymerization reactions of unsaturated hydrocarbons such as ethylene and propylene. Since the turn of the century it had been known that such light substances were capable of forming giant molecules by linking together thousands of identical molecules in long chains. In fact, these high polymers form the basis of many modern ma-

terials such as plastics and synthetic fabrics. When Ziegler began his work on this topic, however, chemists were unable to control the orientation of molecules within the chains. Ziegler's research team found that certain organometallic substances, such as aluminum triethyl, catalyzed the self-condensation of ethylene to form not polyethylene but rather organometallic and unsaturated molecules of intermediate sizes.

In 1952, after four years of exploring this scientifically interesting reaction, Ziegler discovered that traces of nickel prevented polymerization by strongly catalyzing competing reactions. Ziegler's team then began a systematic survey of the periodic table to find other inorganic compounds that would exert a similar effect; their goal was, as Ziegler put it later, "asepsis"—the ability to exclude all traces of catalysts that would inhibit polymerization. Ironically, when they tested a certain zirconium compound they found that, rather than inhibiting polymerization, it acted in conjunction with the aluminum triethyl to strongly catalyze the true ethylene polymerization reaction. Polyethylene was produced smoothly and rapidly.

Ethylene had always been considered extremely difficult to polymerize. Imperial Chemical Industries' "polythene," first developed in 1936, required very high temperatures and pressures (200°C and at least a thousand atmospheres), and the properties of the resulting plastic were somewhat disappointing. Ziegler's new mixed catalyst not only produced polymerization at much lower temperatures and pressures; it also yielded a material with vastly improved properties—higher density, greater rigidity, and better resistance to high temperatures. The discovery of the new reaction in November 1953 was followed by several weeks of feverish activity, in which a number of other inorganics—compounds of such metals as titanium, thorium, and iron—were found to have similar properties. Titanium tetrachloride, for example, permitted polymerization at room temperature and normal atmospheric pressure.

Even before publication of the scientific paper describing this work, Ziegler licensed the process, and many workers began to develop both the scientific and the technological aspects of the reaction. The Italian chemist GIULIO NATTA, an early licensee, discovered analogous reactions with propylene, resulting in polypropylenes. Natta also explored the remarkable structural properties and stereospecificity of the reactions promoted by the Ziegler-Natta catalysts. That is, it was found that these catalysts afforded chemists unequaled control over the precise structure and spatial orientation of the new polymers. Chemists had long known that extremely subtle differences of molecular architecture could result in radical differences in properties—as, for example, with the low-density "polythene" versus high-density Ziegler polyethylene. Using Ziegler-Natta catalysts, it became possible to synthesize a material that was absolutely identical to natural rubber. These discoveries revolutionized the plastics industry, as well as other polymer technologies. As early as 1955, 200 metric tons of the new polyethylene had been produced; by 1958 output had grown to 17,000 tons, and by 1962 to 120,000 tons—all made by various processes derived directly or indirectly from Ziegler's work.

Ziegler shared the 1963 Nobel Prize for Chemistry with Natta "for their discoveries in the field of chemistry and technology of high polymers." In his presentation speech, Arne Fredga of the Royal Swedish Academy of Sciences hailed Ziegler's "excellent work on organometallic compounds [which] has unexpectedly led to new polymerization reactions, and thus paved the way for new and highly useful industrial processes." Ziegler, in his Nobel lecture, traced the development of his method, comparing the recent "precipitous expansion of macromolecular chemistry and its industrial applications . . . to an explosion."

Despite the enormous technological implications of his work, Ziegler always maintained that he was fundamentally a pure scientist. The research carried out over his entire career was directed not at invention but at scientific discovery, and this research program exhibits a remarkable overall unity. For instance, the studies of the polymerization of ethylene were based on earlier research into reactions involving organometallics, and this work developed from Ziegler's initial fascination during his doctoral studies with free radicals, which at the time had only recently been discovered.

When he was negotiating with the Kaiser Wilhelm Institute for Coal Research in 1943, Ziegler insisted as a condition of his employment that no restrictions be imposed on the subject of his research. As he put it later, such limits "would have completely dried up the springs of my creative activity." The character of this activity he described in his Nobel lecture: "I have never started with anything like a formally presented problem. The whole effort developed quite spontaneously, from a beginning which was actually irrational in nature. . . . My method resembled a meandering through a new land, during which interesting prospects kept opening up . . . but such that one never quite knew where this trip was actually leading." Although careful always to disclaim the title of technological chemist, Ziegler nevertheless protected his financial interests in his discoveries. He collected large royalties from the Ziegler processes, and shortly before his retirement in 1969 he created the Ziegler Fund with an endowment of 40 million marks.

Known as a highly modest and friendly man, Ziegler was regarded as an inspiring and dedicated teacher who served as a doctoral adviser for some 150 students. He married Maria Kurtz in 1922; they had two children, Marianne and Erhart, and ten grandchildren. Maria survived her husband upon his death in Mülheim in 1973, after fifty-one years of marriage.

In addition to the Nobel Prize, Ziegler's international honors included the Carl Duisberg Award of the German Chemical Society (1953), the Lavoisier Medal of the French Chemical Society (1955), and the Swinburne Medal of the Plastics and Rubber Institute in London (1964). He held honorary doctorates from the technical universities of Hannover and Darmstadt and the universities of Heidelberg and Giessen.

ABOUT: Biographical Memoirs of Fellows of the Royal Society, volume 21, 1975; New York Times November 6, 1963.

ZSIGMONDY, RICHARD
(April 1, 1865–September 23, 1929)
Nobel Prize for Chemistry, 1925

The German chemist Richard Adolf Zsigmondy (zhig' môn dē) was one of four children born in Vienna, Austria, to Irma (von Szakmáry) and Adolf Zsigmondy. His father, a prosperous physician who published several medical papers, encouraged the boy's interest in science. From his mother, he acquired an appreciation of nature and the arts. In addition to swimming and mountain climbing, he enjoyed reading chemistry books and performing experiments in his small laboratory at home.

After studying chemistry at the University of Vienna and the technical university in Vienna, Zsigmondy entered the University of Munich in 1887. Three years later he received his Ph.D. in organic chemistry. In 1893, after three more years as an assistant at the university, he accepted a position as lecturer in chemical technology at the technical university in Graz, Austria. There he became interested in the coloring of glass and china, an interest that led him to study colloidal chemistry. While working as an industrial chemist for the Schott Glass Manufacturing Company in Jena, Germany, from 1897 to 1900, he developed Jena milk glass. In 1900 Zsigmondy resigned from the glassworks and for the next seven years, supported by his family's wealth, pursued pure research into colloids. He continued this research after he joined the faculty at the University of Göttingen in 1907 as a professor and later as director of the university's Institute of Inorganic Chemistry.

Colloids are substances in which extremely fine particles are stably dispersed in a fluid medium. A common example is egg white. The particles in a colloid can impart to it unique characteristics, such as the coloring effects of powdered gold that Zsigmondy had studied in glass. At the turn of the century, the nature of colloids had not been fully clarified. Zsigmondy believed that the action of glass dyes was caused by finely distributed, chemically inert particles so small that they were beyond the reach of contemporary microscopes. Not only was there no visible evidence for such particles, but the solution was stable and did not settle, as would be expected with a mixture of particles in a fluid medium.

Zsigmondy devised a number of hybrid techniques to determine the nature of colloids. In one such technique he added agents to the fluid medium in an effort to make the colloid coagulate, thereby learning much about this

RICHARD ZSIGMONDY

transition of states. His chief objective, however, was to observe the particles themselves. To accomplish this goal, he developed the ultramicroscope in 1903, working with H. F. W. Siedentopf, a physicist with the Zeiss Optical Works in Jena.

Instead of illuminating a sample along the optical axis, as in a standard microscope, the ultramicroscope employs perpendicular illumination. The system is analogous to the everyday phenomenon in which fine, airborne dust particles can be seen in a shaft of sunlight when the light beam is viewed from the side. By improving the technology of what is called dark-field illumination, Zsigmondy and the technicians at Zeiss were able to resolve particles as small as 10 millimicrons (10 millionths of a millimeter). Further refinements produced the so-called immersion ultramicroscope. With this tool, which reveals particles of 4 millimicrons, Zsigmondy observed the behavior of glass dyes and established that certain changes in color resulted from the coagulation of colloidal particles.

In the course of his investigations, Zsigmondy studied the dynamics of colloids. Knowing that particles of gold in a colloid are electrically negative, he deduced that the resulting mutual repulsion between these like-charged particles accounts for their stability. The addition of salts to the colloid provides centers of electrical attraction around which the gold begins to aggregate until the particles precipitate out of colloidal suspension. Assisted by the theoretical physicist Marian Smoluchowski, Zsigmondy then computed how close the gold colloid particles must be in order for aggregation to occur.

The 1925 Nobel Prize for Chemistry was awarded to Zsigmondy in 1926 "for his demonstration of the heterogeneous nature of colloid solutions and for the methods he used, which have since become fundamental in modern colloid chemistry." In his presentation speech H. G. Söderbaum of the Royal Swedish Academy of Sciences pointed out "that all manifestations of organic life are finally bound to the colloidal media of the protoplasm."

In subsequent research at Göttingen, Zsigmondy supervised investigations into ultrafiltration, a technique that proved useful in examining many substances, including gel structures. He retired from the university in 1919.

In 1903 Zsigmondy married Laura Luise Müller, the daughter of a lecturer in physiology at the University of Jena. The couple had two daughters. Zsigmondy and his wife enjoyed vacations at his estate in the Tirol, where he could indulge his love of nature and mountain climbing. He died in Göttingen on September 23, 1929.

SELECTED WORKS: Colloids and the Ultramicroscope, 1908; The Chemistry of Colloids, 1917, with others.

ABOUT: Dictionary of Scientific Biography, volume 14, 1976.